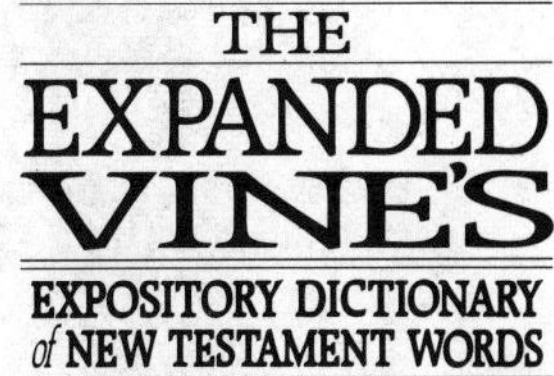

Originally published in England by Oliphants, Marshall Pickering, 1940, under the title *An Expository Dictionary of New Testament Words*

Published by Bethany House Publishers
A Division of Bethany Fellowship, Inc.
6820 Auto Club Road, Minneapolis, MN 55438

Printed in the United States of America

Library of Congress Cataloging in Publication Data

Vine, W. E. (William Edwy), 1873-1949.
The expanded Vine's expository dictionary of New Testament words.

Rev. ed. of: An expository dictionary of New Testament words. 1940.
Includes index.
1. Greek language, Biblical—Dictionaries. 2. Bible. N.T.—Dictionaries.
I. Kohlenberger, John R. II. Title. III. Title: Vine, W. E. (William Edwy), 1873-1949.
Expository dictionary of New Testament words.
PA881.V5 1984 487'.4 84-21591
ISBN 0-87123-619-2

THE EXPANDED VINE'S

EXPOSITORY DICTIONARY *of* NEW TESTAMENT WORDS

W. E. VINE

John R. Kohlenberger III, Editor

with James A. Swanson

BETHANY HOUSE PUBLISHERS

MINNEAPOLIS, MINNESOTA 55438

A Division of Bethany Fellowship, Inc.

INTRODUCTION TO THE EXPANDED VINE'S

For the Bible student, the greatest treasures discovered along the Nile are not those of precious stone and metal found in the tombs of the ancient Pharaohs, but those of papyrus found in the trash heaps of ancient cities. For these simple scraps of centuries-old paper contain the writings of kings and commoners, a literary and non-literary witness to the thoughts, words and grammar of the ancient world. And those in Greek give valuable insight into the literary, linguistic and cultural background of the New Testament.

The explosion in discoveries of the Greek papyri of Egypt began a century ago, and this contribution to biblical studies continues to the present day. Among the many reference works bringing these fascinating materials to the student and the general reader, standards were established that remain in print to this day. Notable among these are the pioneering *Light from the Ancient East* by Adolf Deissman (Grand Rapids: Baker, 4th edition 1922 [Reprint, 1965]) and Moulton and Milligan's authoritative *Vocabulary of the Greek New Testament* (Grand Rapids: Eerdmans, one-volume edition 1930 [Reprint, 1974]).

But the volume that captured popular attention and critical acclaim for its completeness and simplicity was William Edwy Vine's *Expository Dictionary of New Testament Words,* originally published in 1940 by Oliphants Ltd., and currently offered by several different Houses. In his Foreword to the one-volume edition, F. F. Bruce summarized the reasons for the popularity of his work: "Mr. Vine's Greek scholarship was wide, accurate and up-to-date, and withal unobtrusive."

While that assessment was true of Vine's Dictionary in 1952, the continuing explosion of biblical reference works, critical and popular, has weakened that assessment for the present. In order to keep Vine's scholarship "wide, accurate and up-to-date," it would be necessary to revise the entire Dictionary in many minor and some major points. However, as the bulk of the material remains useful and as the Dictionary in its original and familiar form has found such a wide audience, Bethany House Publishers decided to supplement and expand Vine's original work while leaving that original work intact. The result is *The Expanded Vine's Expository Dictionary of New Testament Words* (hereafter referred to as *The Expanded Vine's*).

This expansion was undertaken by John R. Kohlenberger III with the invaluable assistance of James A. Swanson and Sandra Swanson, who combined computer technology and personal research to index Vine's original work to the current standards of biblical Greek scholarship.

Each Greek word of Vine's Index was first keyed to the numbering system developed by James Strong for his *Exhaustive Concordance to the Bible*. This allows those not familiar with the Greek alphabet to access the resources of many other reference works discussed below.

Further, each word was indexed to the outstanding *A Greek-English Lexicon of the New Testament and Other Early Christian Literature* of Walter Bauer, as translated and revised by Arndt, Gingrich and Danker (Univ. of Chicago/Zondervan, 1979). This work provides the most accurate and up-to-date definitions for the vocabulary of the Greek NT.

Finally, each word was indexed to the valuable *New International Dictionary of New Testament Theology,* edited by Colin Brown (Grand Rapids: Zondervan, 1975-1979). This three-volume set, like Vine's Dictionary, provides historical, linguistic and biblical insights into NT vocabulary, but from a deeper and broader base than was available to Vine.

HOW TO USE *THE EXPANDED VINE'S*

The English Organization

Vine assembled his dictionary to provide English readers easy access to insights into the vocabulary of the Greek NT. Vine was not the first to do this, however, for in 1877 E.W. Bullinger had published his *Critical Lexicon and Concordance to the English and Greek New Testament* (Grand Rapids: Zondervan, Reprint 1975). This volume arranged its contents in English alphabetical order, but provided a complete Greek index, allowing the reader to find information from either the English or Greek NT.

Vine adopted this organization (whether deliberately or not) and supplemented the skeletal lexical and concordance information with expository comments drawn from the rich discoveries of papyri from NT times and from other historical and grammatical resources (which he duly cites). *The Expanded Vine's* maintains and improves on this organization.

Therefore, the first method of access to *The Expanded Vine's* is simply to *look up the English word you wish to study*. This works well for major theological terms such as BAPTISM, GRACE and SALVATION. However, because Vine based his vocabulary on that of the British Revised Version of 1881 (practically identical to the American Standard Version of 1901), many words common to modern versions of the NT are missing.

The Expanded Vine's offers a partial solution to this problem by inserting many of these terms into the margin and cross-referencing them to an original entry. In assembling this vocabulary, the *New International Version* received primary attention as the best-selling modern version, though the major vocabulary of all modern versions was considered. Thus, though the original Vine's did not contain references to such words as CONCEITED, COUNSELOR, ORPHAN, PARALYTIC or PROSTITUTE, *The Expanded Vine's* directs you to the articles under which the relevant Greek words are discussed.

In the event that you do not find the word you wish to study in Vine's headings or in the marginal additions, look up your word in the King James Version, Revised Standard Version or American Standard. If you still cannot find the word, you must approach the information through the Greek Index, discussed below.

Assuming you do find your word, you have only begun your search. For most English articles are subdivided into the various Greek nouns, verbs, adjectives and adverbs they translate. Thus, you need to locate the *biblical reference* in which the word you are studying is located. For example, if you wanted to study the word "eye-witness" (see page 395) in 2 Peter 1:16, you would not read article 1 on AUTOPTES, for it deals only with Luke 1:2. Rather, you would read article 2 on EPOPTES, which refers to the 2 Peter passage.

This example was simple, for it involved only two rather brief articles. Much more complex is the entry on GO (page 486), which lists 30 numbered articles and another 30 notes, but with relatively few biblical references. In order to be certain you locate the correct Greek word—and locate it quickly and efficiently—you will want to use the new Greek Index, discussed below.

The Greek Index

Approaching the information in *The Expanded Vine's* through the Greek Index has three advantages. First, all of the information relating to that word is there—every appearance of the Greek word within Vine's and the indexing to the resources outside Vine's. Actually, *both* of these features, not just the latter, are unique to *The Expanded Vine's*. For while the original included a Greek Index, that Index was missing more than 625 *references* which were discovered in the computer analysis of the book! The Index of *The Expanded Vine's* is the only complete Index and is the most accurate Index of any edition.

The second advantage is that you will know immediately where the word is discussed because the Greek Index is not limited to a certain English version of the NT. Third, you will be able to locate *every* heading under which the word is discussed. And you will want to look under every heading for some, obviously, will contain more material and insights than others.

Note: When an English word is followed by *"Note,"* this indicates that the Greek word is discussed in a Note rather than in a numbered article. When followed by an asterisk (*), this indicates that though this English word is indeed a translation of the Greek word, there is no discussion of the Greek word under that English heading. (For an example of both, see ABUSSOS in the first column of page 1273.)

Of course, you need to know the Greek word you wish to study. Some have become part of our ecclesiastical vocabulary, such as AGAPE, EKKLESIA and KOINONIA. Most have to be discovered. The easiest route is via the Concordance. The well-known Concordances of Strong and Young provide information based on the KJV. *An Analytical Concordance to the Revised Standard Version of the New Testament* (Philadelphia: Westminster, 1979) and the *New American Standard Exhaustive Concordance of the Bible* (Nashville: Holman, 1981) provide information based on those versions.

To use these Concordances, begin by locating your word in their alphabetic arrangements. *(Be sure you are using the right version with the right Concordance!)* Young's and the RSV give you the Greek word in Greek and in English characters on the spot. Strong's and the NAS give you a number which identifies the word (again in Greek and English) in a Dictionary in the back of the book. Once you have the word, you can look it up in the Index and proceed to study it through.

Note: The transliteration systems of these books differ slightly. A complete table of their systems follows this introduction. Also, Vine's Index is in *English* alphabetical order, not Greek. Thus Strong's numbers are not always in sequence, if you attempt to use them to locate your word (see ABUSSOS [12] and ACHARISTOS [884] in the first column of page 1273).

The Exposition

Once you have located your word by the English organization or by the Greek Index, you only have to read to get your information. But this reading involves a bit of discernment. In his Foreword to the first edition, W. Graham Scroggie rightly noted that Vine's Dictionary was "at once a concordance, a dictionary, and a commentary." As such, you need to *use* Vine's as you would use these tools.

A concordance is a rather concrete tool; it is simply an index to occurences of words. When Vine tells you this word is located in a particular book, chapter and verse, you can take his word for it. Certainly, there might be a mistake or typo here and there, but by and large this is good information.

Vine often refers to words found in "some texts" and in "the best texts" (see articles 2 and 3 under TITHE). By "some texts" he means the so-called "Received Text" of 1633, which is the basis of most reference works done before this century and is similar to that which was used to translate the NT of the KJV. By "the best texts" he means the critical texts which underlie the Revised Version and most modern versions. In this way, Vine's materials can be used in studying any version of the NT and its corresponding Greek texts.

Because a dictionary deals with *meaning,* it is a more abstract tool than a concordance. The definition, or at least its nuance, is often based on the perspective of the definer. Further, in the case of ancient literature, new discoveries and continuing research are constantly adding depth and dimension to our understanding. Thus, as a dictionary, Vine's needs a bit of discernment.

The majority of Vine's definitions can be accepted without question—but it is always in order to check further. That is why each word is indexed to Bauer's Lexicon, discussed below. But a word of caution concerning Vine's overuse of etymology. In brief, etymology is the study of the formation and history of a word. Whenever Vine discusses a compound word, he always breaks it into its components and often tells you that its meaning is the sum of the parts. However, this is no more true in Greek than in English!

For example, we use the word "prevent" to mean "stop" or "impede." Etymologically, however, "prevent" means "to go before" or "precede." If you read 1 Thessalonians 4:15 in the KJV, which uses the *etymological* (and at that time *proper*) definition of "prevent," you would *not* read it eytmologically, but according to current, standard use.

In the article on READ, Vine defines the word ANAGINOSKO as meaning "to know certainly, to know again, recognize." However, to "read" something does *not* mean you know *certainly,* nor *again,* nor that you *recognize* anything, nor that you know *upward* (another definition of ANA). It simply means you *read* it.

Unfortunately, Vine—and far too many pastors, teachers and writers—use etymology to define NT vocabulary in a way they would never define contemporary English. Etymology works with *spatial* concepts (see the entries under GO), but rarely outside such concepts. So you will do better to attend to functional and contextual definitions than to etymology.

A commentary presents the interpretations of a commentator and is usually subject to his or her presuppositions and interpretive framework. You may not think of Vine's Dictionary as a commentary, but most of his longer expositions are just that. His article on SALVATION, for example, shows that he was Dispensational and believed in the pretribulation Rapture. His article on TONGUE(-S) states that the gift ceased in Apostolic times. His article on SEED shows that he did believe in eternal security and did not believe in sinless perfection.

Obviously, there is nothing wrong with Vine giving commentary on specific texts and theological concepts. What would be wrong, however, would be for you to believe that the definition of a word *demands* the implication or application which Vine (or any other commentator) makes of it. Theology is made up of much more than single words.

INDEXING TO ADDITIONAL RESOURCES

The comments thus far have related to using *The Expanded Vine's* as a self-contained reference work. But valuable as it is, it is limited by date, scope, depth and theological distinctives. (This is not intended as a criticism, but simply a statement which could be made about any reference work!) Thus in order to bring the reader more up-to-date, to add scope and depth, and broaden theological perspectives, each word in the text and the Greek Index has been keyed to other reference works. But before these are discussed, a few words concerning this indexing.

Everywhere a numbered entry occurs in *The Expanded Vine's,* a list of three numbers parallels it in the margin. The first is Strong's numeric designation, the second (abbreviated AG) is the page and "quadrant" of Bauer's *Greek-English Lexicon* as translated and revised by Arndt, Gingrich and Danker, and the third (abbreviated CB:) is the page and column of the third volume of Brown's *New International Dictionary*. (A "quadrant" is a quarter of a page. "A" is the first half of the left-hand column, "B" the lower half; "C" is the first half of the right-hand column, "D" the lower half.)

When the spelling of the word differs from that of Vine, the alternate spelling follows the page designation. Under ABHOR on page 1, (-OMAI) following AG:138A indicates the *Lexicon* spells the word BDELUSSOMAI instead of BDELUSSO. If this spelling occurs *before* the indexing, all three reference works differ from Vine (see ANDRIZO, page 731).

When any of these works have no information on a particular word, a dash (—) appears in place of a page number. (See under ABHOR, page 1.) In the Greek Index, the "CB:" entries sometimes refer to related words with the abbreviation "Cf." (See ANALOGIZOMAI.) Some insights into the basic meanings of these words may be gleaned from studying its "relatives."

When discussing the word which heads a particular article, Vine often refers to synonymous or antynomous words. When there is space, these words and their three-fold indexing are set in the margin. (See under SPIRIT, pages 1067-1068.)

When words in the original Vine's are closely clustered on a page or in a paragraph, and it would be unclear to which words the marginal indexing referred, the words are reproduced in the margin. If necessary in the interest of space, the reference to Brown's *Dictionary* is eliminated when this reference simply indicates the *Dictionary* has no information ("CB:—"). (See page 1034 for examples of both.)

We cannot discuss here the full use of each of these tools. Indispensable to basic or beginning biblical language study is E.W. Goodrick's *Do It Yourself Hebrew and Greek* (Multnomah Press/Zondervan, 1976.) This workbook will acquaint you with the basics of Greek and Hebrew and will take you step-by-step through the function of all the major reference works. Another valuable self-study guide to NT Greek is *Basic Greek in 30 Minutes a Day,* by James Found (Minneapolis: Bethany House, 1984).

Strong's Numbering System

The first reference in the indexing is to the numbering system developed by James Strong for his *Exhaustive Concordance to the Bible* (in print from dozens of publishers). This was chosen not because of the excellence of this system, but because of its pervasive popularity.

Because Strong's work is based on the so-called "Received Text," he has no reference to dozens of words found in Vine's and in the critical editions of the Greek NT. Further, he chose to index some inflected words and not to index some compound words. For example, the word UPEREKPERISSOU is not numbered, but appears after word number

5240. Thus it is referred to in the indexing as "After 5240."

Though each word is indexed to Strong's system, his dictionary and definitions will add little to Vine's and, because of their datedness and speculation, are not particularly recommended for today's Bible student. Rather, his numbering system may be used to gain access into other, more thorough concordances, lexicons and even an interlinear. Publishers have reprinted older, public-domain works, simply adding Strong's numbers, though they are not revised or edited in any other way. A partial list of this growing corpus, old and "new," which employs Strong's system follows:

The New Englishman's Greek Concordance, Wigram (Baker)
(This volume is based on the KJV and the "Received Text.")

The Word Study New Testament and Concordance, Winter (Tyndale)
(Essentially the same Concordance. The NT is a KJV with Strong's numbers typed between the lines.)

Concordance to the Greek Testament, Moulton and Geden (T&T Clark)
(Long a standard—but *all* in Greek; the latest edition has Strong's numbers typed in.)

Interlinear Greek-English New Testament: With Greek-English Lexicon and New Testament Synonyms, Berry and Strong (Baker)
(Each word of the Greek ["Received"] text is matched to an English word and to Strong's number.)

A Greek-English Lexicon of the New Testament, Thayer (Baker)
(This volume is a century old and was essentially replaced by Bauer's *Lexicon*.)

Theological Dictionary of the New Testament, Kittel and Friedrich (Eerdmans)
(The tenth volume of this massive set employs Strong's numbers in the Greek Index. This set is not recommended for the average reader because of its enormous size, technical and Greek vocabulary, occasionally questionable methodology and radical theology. But it does contain more material on NT words than any other set. Brown's *Dictionary*, however, gleans most of what would be valuable for most students.)

Bauer's *Greek-English Lexicon*

A Greek-English Lexicon of the New Testament and Other Early Christian Literature of Walter Bauer, as translated and revised by Arndt, Gingrich and Danker (Univ. of Chicago/Zondervan, 1979) is the most up-to-date and accurate resource for defining NT vocabulary. (Its abbreviation "AG:" reflects the initials of its primary translators, Arndt and Gingrich, by whose names the lexicon is usually known among Greek students.)

Though all of the entries are headed by Greek words written in Greek characters, the majority of the articles are in English. Chapter 11 of Goodrick's *Do It Yourself Hebrew and Greek* is devoted to a detailed discussion of the use of this superb tool.

In brief, the Greek word is usually followed by a basic definition in *italics*. Specific definitions relating to specific contexts follow in separate, numbered sections and paragraphs. Sometimes, in the case of prepositions, conjunctions and inflected forms, the indexing of *The Expanded Vine's* refers to one of these subsections. For example, SPOUDAIOTERóS is found in the article on SPOUDAIóS, paragraph 2.

The New International Dictionary of New Testament Theology

The three-volume *New International Dictionary of New Testament Theology,* edited by Colin Brown (Grand Rapids: Zondervan, 1975-1979) is, like Vine's, a Greek reference work for English readers. It is arranged in English alphabetical order with the relevant Greek words listed and exposited. Each volume is individually indexed. The indexing of *The Expanded Vine's* refers to the third volume, which contains the master index to all three volumes.

In 1986, Brown's *Dictionary* was released in a four-volume set, with all the index materials in the fourth volume. Though the Greek index in the four-volume set is identical to that in the original, the pagination differs by 894. To find the proper page reference in the four-volume set, subtract 894 from the reference given in this book or consult the table on page 1349.

Unlike Vine's, the material in Brown's work was contributed by dozens of German and British scholars of diverse but basically evangelical backgrounds. Thus, there is no one theological perspective represented. Often, a note by the English translators and editors interacts with the German original. The article on BAPTISM, for example, contains a separate treatment arguing in favor of Infant Baptism, as opposed to the main article which denies its validity. You will want to be sensitive to the tensions you may find in this and in other reference works, remembering to test and think through the information.

Among the valuable features of Brown's *Dictionary* are the extensive bibliographies which follow many articles. These will direct you to thousands of other pages of information on biblical words and themes and theological concepts.

SUMMARY

1. To Study an English Word or Concept:
   a. Look it up in alphabetical order.
   b. If not referred to in the Heading or "See" References:
      1) Look it up in the King James, Revised or American Standard Version, or
      2) Find the underlying Greek word in a concordance and locate the proper English article through the Greek Index.
2. To Study a Greek Word:
   a. Locate it in the Greek Index (which is in English alphabetical order).
   b. Read under all English headings:
      1) *Note* indicates the information on that Greek word is found in a Note, not in a numbered article.
      2) An asterisk indicates there is no discussion of that Greek word under that English heading.
3. For further or more up-to-date information, use the indexing in the margins or Greek Index:
   a. The first number refers to Strong's numbering system, employed by many new and reprinted reference works.
   b. The "AG:" reference refers to the authoritative *Lexicon* of Bauer, as translated and revised by Arndt, Gingrich and Danker.
   c. The "CB:" reference refers to the index in the third volume of *New International Dictionary of New Testament Theology*.

The editors and publisher hope this new edition of an established classic will make its valuable information—and that of the other indexed works—more easily available to you in your study of God's Word.

GREEK TRANSLITERATION TABLE

LETTER	BAUER	VINE	STRONG	BROWN	YOUNG	MORRISON	THOMAS
Alpha	Α, α	A, a	A, a	A, a	A, a	A	A, a
Beta	Β, β	B, b	B, b	B, b	B, b	B	B, b
Gamma	Γ, γ	G, g	G, g	G, g	G, g	G	G, g
Double Gamma	γγ	NG, ng	gg	ng	GG, gg	GG	g̃g
Gamma Kappa	γκ	NK, nk	gk	nk	GK, gk	GK	g̃k
Gamma Xi	γξ	NX, nx	gx	nx	GX, gx	GX	g̃x
Gamma Chi	γχ	NCH, nch	gch	nch	GCH, gch	GCH	g̃ch
Delta	Δ, δ	D, d	D, d	D, d	D, d	D	D, d
Epsilon	Ε, ϵ	E, e	Ĕ, ĕ	E, e	E, e	E	E, e
Zeta	Ζ, ζ	Z, z	Z, z	Z, z	Z, z	Z	Z, z
Eta	Η, η	Ē, ē	Ē, ē	Ē, ē	Ē, ē	Ē	Ē, ē
Theta	Θ, θ	TH, th	TH, th	TH, th	TH, th	TH	TH, th
Iota	Ι, ι	I, i	I, i	I, i	I, i	I	I, i
Kappa	Κ, κ	K, k	K, k	K, k	K, k	K	K, k
Lambda	Λ, λ	L, l	L, l	L, l	L, l	L	L, l
Mu	Μ, μ	M, m	M, m	M, m	M, m	M	M, m
Nu	Ν, ν	N, n	N, n	N, n	N, n	N	N, n
Xi	Ξ, ξ	X, x	X, x	X, x	X, x	X	X, x
Omicron	Ο, ο	O, o	Ŏ, ŏ	O, o	O, o	O	O, o
Pi	Π, π	P, p	P, p	P, p	P, p	P	P, p
Rho	Ρ, ρ	R, r	R, r	R, r	R, r	R	R, r
Rho with breathing	Ῥ, ῥ	Rh, rh	Rh, rh	Rh, rh	Rh, rh	RH	Rh, rh
Sigma	Σ, σ, ς	S, s	S, s	S, s	S, s	S	S, s
Tau	Τ, τ	T, t	T, t	T, t	T, t	T	T, t
Upsilon	Υ, υ	U, u	U, u	Y, y	U, u	Y	U, u
Phi	Φ, φ	PH, ph	Ph, ph	Ph, ph	PH, ph	PH	Ph, ph
Chi	Χ, χ	CH, ch	Ch, ch	Ch, ch	CH, ch	CH	Ch, ch
Psi	Ψ, ψ	PS, ps	Ps, ps	Ps, ps	PS, ps	PS	Ps, ps
Omega	Ω, ω	Ō, ō	Ō, ō	Ō, ō	Ō, ō	Ō	Ō, ō
Rough breathing	ʽ	H, h	H, h	H, h	H, h	H	H, h
Alpha Upsilon	ΑΥ, αυ	AU, au	au	au	AU, au	AU	au
Epsilon Upsilon	ΕΥ, ϵυ	EU, eu	Eu, eu	Eu, eu	EU, eu	EU	EU, eu
Omicron Upsilon	ΟΥ, ου	OU, ou	Ou, ou	Ou, ou	OU, ou	OU	Ou, ou
Upsilon Iota	ΥΙ, υι	UI, ui	ui	yi	UI, ui	UI	ui

Bauer—*A Greek-English Lexicon of the New Testament and Other Early Christian Literature* as translated and revised by Arndt, Gingrich and Danker (Univ. of Chicago/Zondervan, 1979)

Vine—*The Expanded Vine's Expository Dictionary of New Testament Words* (Minneapolis: Bethany House, 1984)

Strong—*The Exhaustive Concordance to the Bible* (Nashville: Abingdon; and many others)

Brown—*New International Dictionary of New Testament Theology* (Grand Rapids: Zondervan, 1975-1979)

Young—*Analytical Concordance to the Bible* (Grand Rapids: Eerdmans; and many others)

Morrison—*Analytical Concordance to the Revised Standard Version of the New Testament* (Philadelphia: Westminster, 1979)

Thomas—*New American Standard Exhaustive Concordance of the Bible* (Nashville: Holman, 1981)

ABASE

TAPEINOŌ (ταπεινόω) signifies to make low, bring low, (*a*) of bringing 5013
to the ground, making level, reducing to a plain, as in Luke 3 : 5 ; AG:804C CB:1271A
(*b*) metaphorically in the Active Voice, to bring to a humble condition, to abase, 2 Cor. 11 : 7, and in the Passive, to be abased, Phil. 4 : 12 ; in Matt. 23 : 12 ; Luke 14 : 11 ; 18 : 14, the A.V. has "shall be abased," the R.V. "shall be humbled." It is translated "humble yourselves" in the Middle Voice sense in Jas. 4 : 10 ; 1 Pet. 5 : 6 ; "humble," in Matt. 18 : 4 ; 2 Cor. 12 : 21 and Phil. 2 : 8. See HUMBLE, LOW.¶ Cp., *tapeinos*, lowly, *tapeinōsis*, humiliation, and *tapeinophrosunē*, humility.

ABANDON See LEAVE

ABBA

ABBA ('Aββᾶ) is an Aramaic word, found in Mark 14 : 36 ; Rom. 8 : 15 5
and Gal. 4 : 6. In the Gemara (a Rabbinical commentary on the Mishna, AG:1B CB:1233A
the traditional teaching of the Jews) it is stated that slaves were forbidden to address the head of the family by this title. It approximates to a personal name, in contrast to "Father," with which it is always joined in the N.T. This is probably due to the fact that, "Abba" having practically become a proper name, Greek-speaking Jews added the Greek word *patēr*, father, from the language they used. "Abba" is the word framed by the lips of infants, and betokens unreasoning trust ; "father" expresses an intelligent apprehension of the relationship. The two together express the love and intelligent confidence of the child.

ABHOR

1. APOSTUGEŌ (ἀποστυγέω) denotes to shudder (*apo*, from, here used 655
intensively, *stugeō*, to hate) ; hence, to abhor, Rom. 12 : 9.¶ AG:100C CB:—
2. BDELUSSŌ (βδελύσσω), to render foul (from *bdeō*, to stink), to cause 948
to be abhorred (in the Sept. in Ex. 5 : 21 ; Lev. 11 : 43 ; 20 : 25 etc.), is AG:138A (-OMAI)
used in the Middle Voice, signifying to turn oneself away from (as if CB:—
from a stench) ; hence, to detest, Rom. 2 : 22. In Rev. 21 : 8 it denotes "to be abominable." See ABOMINABLE.¶

In the following pages † indicates that the word referred to (preposition, conjunction, or particle) is not dealt with in this volume.

¶ indicates that all the N.T. occurrences of the Greek word under consideration are mentioned under the heading or sub-heading.

ABIDE, ABODE

A. Verbs.

3306 AG:503C CB:1258B 1. MENŌ (μένω), used (*a*) of place, e.g., Matt. 10 : 11, metaphorically 1 John 2 : 19, is said of God, 1 John 4 : 15 ; Christ, John 6 : 56 ; 15 : 4, etc. ; the Holy Spirit, John 1 : 32, 33 ; 14 : 17 ; believers, John 6 : 56 ; 15 : 4 ; 1 John 4 : 15, etc. ; the Word of God, 1 John 2 : 14 ; the truth, 2 John 2, etc. ; (*b*) of time ; it is said of believers, John 21 : 22, 23 ; Phil. 1 : 25 ; 1 John 2 : 17 ; Christ, John 12 : 34 ; Heb. 7 : 24 ; the Word of God, 1 Pet. 1 : 23 ; sin, John 9 : 41 ; cities, Matt. 11 : 23 ; Heb. 13 : 14 ; bonds and afflictions, Acts 20 : 23 ; (*c*) of qualities ; faith, hope, love, 1 Cor. 13 : 13 ; Christ's love, John 15 : 10 ; afflictions, Acts 20 : 23 ; brotherly love, Heb. 13 : 1 ; the love of God, 1 John 3 : 17 ; the truth, 2 John 2.

The R.V. usually translates it by " abide," but " continue " in 1 Tim. 2 : 15 ; in the following, the R.V. substitutes to abide for the A.V., to continue, John 2 : 12 ; 8 : 31 ; 15 : 9 ; 2 Tim. 3 : 14 ; Heb. 7 : 24 ; 13 : 14 ; 1 John 2 : 24. Cp. the noun *monē*, below. See CONTINUE, DWELL, ENDURE, REMAIN, STAND, TARRY.

1961 AG:296B CB:1246A 2. EPIMENŌ (ἐπιμένω), to abide in, continue in, tarry, is a strengthened form of *menō* (*epi*, intensive), sometimes indicating perseverance in continuing, whether in evil, Rom. 6 : 1 ; 11 : 23, or good, Rom. 11 : 22 ; 1 Tim. 4 : 16. See CONTINUE, TARRY.

2650 AG:414D CB:— 3. KATAMENŌ (καταμένω), *kata*, down (intensive), and No. 1, is used in Acts 1 : 13. The word may signify constant residence, but more probably indicates frequent resort. In 1 Cor. 16 : 6, it denotes to wait.¶

3887 AG:620C CB:1262A 4. PARAMENŌ (παραμένω), to remain beside (*para*, beside), to continue near, came to signify simply to continue, e.g., negatively, of the Levitical priests, Heb. 7 : 23. In Phil. 1 : 25, the Apostle uses both the simple verb *menō* and the compound *paramenō* (some mss. have *sumparamenō*), to express his confidence that he will " abide," and " continue to abide," with the saints. In 1 Cor. 16 : 6 some mss. have this word. In Jas. 1 : 25, of stedfast continuance in the law of liberty. See CONTINUE.¶

5278 AG:845D CB:1252B 5. HUPOMENŌ (ὑπομένω), lit., to abide under (*hupo*, under), signifies to remain in a place instead of leaving it, to stay behind, e.g., Luke 2 : 43 ; Acts 17 : 14 ; or to persevere, Matt. 10 : 22 ; 24 : 13 ; Mark 13 : 13 ; in each of which latter it is used with the phrase " unto the end ; " or to endure bravely and trustfully, e.g., Heb. 12 : 2, 3, 7, suggesting endurance under what would be burdensome. See also Jas. 1 : 12 ; 5 : 11 ; 1 Pet. 2 : 20. Cp., *makrothumeō*, to be longsuffering. See ENDURE, SUFFER, TAKE, Notes (12), TARRY.

4357 AG:717C CB:1267B 6. PROSMENŌ (προσμένω), to abide still longer, continue with (*pros*, with) is used (*a*) of place, Matt. 15 : 32 ; Mark 8 : 2 ; Acts 18 : 18 ; 1 Tim. 1 : 3 ; (*b*) metaphorically, of cleaving unto a person, Acts 11 : 23, indicating persistent loyalty ; of continuing in a thing, Acts 13 : 43 ;

1 Tim. 5 : 5. See CLEAVE, CONTINUE, TARRY.¶ In the Sept., Judg. 3 : 25.¶

7. DIATRIBŌ (διατρίβω), lit., to wear through by rubbing, to wear 1304
away (*dia*, through, *tribō*, to rub), when used of time, to spend or pass AG:190A CB:—
time, to stay, is found twice in John's Gospel, 3 : 22 and 11 : 54, R.V., "tarried," instead of "continued;" elsewhere only in the Acts, eight times, 12 : 19; 14 : 3, 28; 15 : 35; 16 : 12; 20 : 6; 25 : 6, 14. See CONTINUE, TARRY.¶

8. ANASTREPHŌ (ἀναστρέφω), used once in the sense of abiding, 390
Matt. 17 : 22, frequently denotes to behave oneself, to live a certain AG:61B CB:1235B
manner of life; here the most reliable mss. have *sustrephomai*, to travel about. See BEHAVE, CONVERSATION, LIVE, OVERTHROW, PASS, RETURN.

9. AULIZOMAI (αὐλίζομαι), to lodge, originally to lodge in the *aulē*, or 835
courtyard, is said of shepherds and flocks; hence, to pass the night in the AG:121C CB:—
open air, as did the Lord, Luke 21 : 37; to lodge in a house, as of His visit to Bethany, Matt. 21 : 17.¶

10. AGRAULEŌ (ἀγραυλέω), to lodge in a fold in a field (*agros*, a 63
field, *aulē*, a fold), is used in Luke 2 : 8.¶ See LODGE. AG:13B CB:—

11. HISTĒMI (ἵστημι), to stand, to make to stand, is rendered "abode" 2476
in John 8 : 44, A.V.; "continue," in Acts 26 : 22. In these places the AG:381D CB:1250C
R.V. corrects to "stood" and "stand." This word is suggestive of fidelity and stability. It is rendered "lay . . . to the charge" in Acts 7 : 60. See APPOINT, CHARGE, ESTABLISH, HOLDEN, PRESENT, SET, STANCH, STAND.

12. POIEŌ (ποιέω), to do, make, is used of spending a time or tarrying, 4160
in a place, Acts 15 : 33; 20 : 3; in 2 Cor. 11 : 25 it is rendered "I have AG:680D CB:1265C
been (a night and a day);" a preferable translation is 'I have spent,' as in Jas. 4 : 13, "spend a year" (R.V.). So in Matt. 20 : 12. Cp., the English idiom "did one hour;" in Rev. 13 : 5 "continue" is perhaps the best rendering. See DO.

B. Noun.

MONĒ (μονή), an abode (akin to No. 1), is found in John 14 : 2, 3438
"mansions" (R.V. marg., "abiding places"), and 14 : 23, "abode."¶ AG:527A CB:1259B

ABILITY, ABLE

A. Nouns.

1. DUNAMIS (δύναμις) is (*a*) power, ability, physical or moral, as 1411
residing in a person or thing; (*b*) power in action, as, e.g., when put forth in AG:207B CB:1242B
performing miracles. It occurs 118 times in the N.T. It is sometimes used of the miracle or sign itself, the effect being put for the cause, e.g., Mark 6 : 5, frequently in the Gospels and Acts. In 1 Cor. 14 : 11 it is rendered "meaning"; "force" would be more accurate. Cp., the corresponding verbs, B. 1, 2, 3 and the adjective C. 1, below. See ABUNDANCE, DEED, MIGHT, POWER, STRENGTH, VIOLENCE, VIRTUE, WORK.

2479 AG:383C CB:1253A 2. ISCHUS (ἰσχύς), connected with *ischō* and *echō*, to have, to hold (from the root *ech*—, signifying holding), denotes ability, force, strength; "ability" in 1 Pet. 4 : 11, A.V. (R.V., "strength"). In Eph. 1 : 19 and 6 : 10, it is said of the strength of God bestowed upon believers, the phrase "the power of His might" indicating strength afforded by power. In 2 Thess. 1 : 9, "the glory of His might" signifies the visible expression of the inherent Personal power of the Lord Jesus. It is said of angels in 2 Pet. 2 : 11 (cp., Rev. 18 : 2, A.V., "mightily"). It is ascribed to God in Rev. 5 : 12 and 7 : 12. In Mark 12 : 30, 33, and Luke 10 : 27 it describes the full extent of the power wherewith we are to love God. See MIGHT, POWER, STRENGTH.¶

B. Verbs.

1410 AG:207A CB:1242B 1. DUNAMAI (δύναμαι), to be able, to have power, whether by virtue of one's own ability and resources, e.g., Rom. 15 : 14; or through a state of mind, or through favourable circumstances, e.g., 1 Thess. 2 : 6; or by permission of law or custom, e.g., Acts 24 : 8, 11; or simply to be able, powerful, Matt. 3 : 9; 2 Tim. 3 : 15, etc. See CAN, MAY, POSSIBLE, POWER.

1412 AG:208C CB:1242B 2. DUNAMOŌ (δυναμόω), to make strong, confirm, occurs in Col. 1 : 11 (some authorities have the 1st aorist or momentary tense, in Heb. 11 : 34 also). Cp. *endunamoō*, to enable, strengthen.¶

1414 AG:208C CB:1242B 3. DUNATEŌ (δυνατέω) signifies to be mighty, to show oneself powerful, Rom. 4 : 14; 2 Cor. 9 : 8; 13 : 3. See A, No. 1.¶

2480 AG:383D CB:1253A 4. ISCHUŌ (ἰσχύω), akin to A, No. 2, to be strong, to prevail, indicates a more forceful strength or ability than ***dunamai***, e.g., Jas. 5 : 16, where it is rendered "availeth much" (i.e., "prevails greatly"). See AVAIL, CAN, DO, MAY, PREVAIL, STRENGTH, WORK.

EXISCHUŌ 1840 AG:276C CB:— KATISCHUŌ 2729 AG:424A CB:1254C *Note:* Still stronger forms are *exischuō*, to be thoroughly strong, Eph. 3 : 18, "may be strong" (not simply "may be able," A.V.).¶; *katischuō*, Matt. 16 : 18, and Luke 23 : 23, in the former, of the powerlessness of the gates of Hades to prevail against the Church; in the latter, of the power of a fierce mob to prevail over a weak ruler (see Notes on Galatians, by Hogg and Vine, p. 251); also Luke 21 : 36. The prefixed prepositions are intensive in each case.¶

2192 AG:331D CB:1242C 5. ECHŌ (ἔχω), to have, is translated "your ability" in 2 Cor. 8 : 11, and "ye may be able" in 2 Pet. 1 : 15, and is equivalent to the phrase 'to have the means of.' See CAN, HAVE.

2141 AG:324B CB:— 6. EUPOREŌ (εὐπορέω), lit., to journey well (*eu*, well, *poreō*, to journey), hence, to prosper, is translated "according to (his) ability," in Acts 11 : 29.¶

2427 AG:374D CB:1250C *Note: Hikanoō*, corresponding to the adjective ***hikanos*** (see below) signifies to make competent, qualify, make sufficient; in 2 Cor. 3 : 6, A.V., "hath made (us) able;" R.V., "hath made us sufficient;" in Col. 1 : 12, "hath made (us) meet." See ENOUGH, SUFFICIENT.¶

C. Adjectives.

1. DUNATOS (δυνατός), corresponding to A, No. 1, signifies powerful. 1415
See, e.g., Rom. 4 : 21 ; 9 : 22 ; 11 : 23 ; 12 : 18 ; 15 : 1 ; 1 Cor. 1 : 26 ; AG:208C CB:1242B
2 Cor. 9 : 8. See MIGHTY, POSSIBLE, POWER, STRONG.

2. HIKANOS (ἱκανός), translated " able," is to be distinguished 2425
from *dunatos*. While *dunatos* means possessing power, *hikanos*, primarily, AG:374B CB:1250C
reaching to, has accordingly the meaning " sufficient." When said of things it signifies enough, e.g., Luke 22 : 38 ; when said of persons, it means " competent," " worthy," e.g., 2 Cor. 2 : 6, 16 ; 3 : 5 ; 2 Tim. 2 : 2. See CONTENT, ENOUGH, GOOD, GREAT, LARGE, LONG, MANY, MEET, MUCH, SECURITY, SUFFICIENT, WORTHY.

Note : *Ischuros* denotes strong, mighty ; in an Active sense, mighty, 2478
in having inherent and moral power, e.g., Matt. 12 : 29 ; 1 Cor. 4 : 10 ; AG:383A CB:1253A
Heb. 6 : 18.

ABLUTION See WASH

ABOARD

EPIBAINŌ (ἐπιβαινω), to go upon (*epi*, upon, *bainō*, to go), is once 1910
translated " we went aboard," Acts 21 : 2, the single verb being short AG:289D CB:—
for going aboard ship. In ver. 6 it is rendered " we went on board ; " in 27 : 2 " embarking ; " in Matt. 21 : 5, " riding upon." See COME, No. 16.

ABOLISH

KATARGEŌ (καταργέω), lit., to reduce to inactivity (*kata*, down, 2673
argos, inactive), is translated " abolish " in Eph. 2 : 15 and 2 Tim. 1 : 10, AG:417B CB:1254B
in the R.V. only in 1 Cor. 15 : 24, 26. It is rendered " is abolished " in the A.V. of 2 Cor. 3 : 13 ; the R.V. corrects to " was passing away " (marg., " was being done away "). In this and similar words not loss of being is implied, but loss of well being.

The barren tree was cumbering the ground, making it useless for the purpose of its existence, Luke 13 : 7 ; the unbelief of the Jews could not " make of none effect " the faithfulness of God, Rom. 3 : 3 ; the preaching of the Gospel could not make of none effect the moral enactments of the Law, 3 : 31 ; the Law could not make the promise of none effect, 4 : 14 ; Gal. 3 : 17 ; the effect of the identification of the believer with Christ in His death is to render inactive his body in regard to sin, Rom. 6 : 6 ; the death of a woman's first husband discharges her from the law of the husband, that is, it makes void her status as his wife in the eyes of the law, 7 : 2 ; in that sense the believer has been discharged from the Law, 7 : 6 ; God has chosen things that are not " to bring to nought things that are," i.e., to render them useless for practical purposes, 1 Cor. 1 : 28 ; the princes of this world are brought to nought, i.e., their wisdom becomes ineffective, 2 : 6 ; the use for which the human stomach exists ceases with man's death, 6 : 13 ; knowledge, prophesyings, and that which was in part were to be "done away," 1 Cor. 13 : 8, 10, i.e., they were to be rendered of no effect after their temporary use was fulfilled; when the Apostle became a man he did away with the ways of a child, verse 11; God is going to abolish all rule and authority and power, i.e., He is going to render them inactive, 1 Cor. 15 : 24; the last enemy that shall be abolished, or reduced to inactivity, is death, ver. 26; the glory shining in the face of Moses, "was passing away," 2 Cor. 3 : 7, the transitoriness of its character being of a special significance; so in verses 11, 13; the veil upon the heart of Israel is "done away" in Christ, ver. 14; those who seek justification by the Law are "severed" from Christ, they are rendered inactive in relation to Him, Gal. 5 : 4; the essential effect of the preaching of the Cross would become inoperative by the preaching of circumcision, 5 : 11; by the death of Christ the barrier between Jew and Gentile is rendered inoperative as such, Eph. 2 : 15; the Man of Sin is to be reduced to inactivity by the manifestation of the Lord's Parousia with His people, 2 Thess. 2 : 8; Christ has rendered death inactive for the believer, 2 Tim. 1 : 10, death becoming the means of a more glorious life, with Christ; the Devil is to be reduced to inactivity through the death of Christ, Heb. 2 : 14. See CEASE, CUMBER, DESTROY, DO, *Note* (7), OF NONE EFFECT, NOUGHT, PUT, No. 19, VOID.¶

ABOMINABLE, ABOMINATION

A. Adjectives.

111 AG:20D CB:— 1. ATHEMITOS (ἀθέμιτος) occurs in Acts 10 : 28, "unlawful," and 1 Pet. 4 : 3, "abominable" (*a*, negative, *themitos*, an adjective from *themis*, "law"), hence, unlawful. See UNLAWFUL.¶

947 AG:138A CB:— 2. BDELUKTOS (βδελυκτός), Tit. 1 : 16, is said of deceivers who profess to know God, but deny Him by their works.¶

B. Verb.

BDELUSSŌ (βδελύσσω): See ABHOR, No. 2.

C. Noun.

946 AG:137D CB:1239A BDELUGMA (βδέλυγμα), akin to A, No. 2 and B, denotes an object of disgust, an abomination. This is said of the image to be set up by Antichrist, Matt. 24 : 15; Mark 13 : 14; of that which is highly esteemed amongst men, in contrast to its real character in the sight of God, Luke 16 : 15. The constant association with idolatry suggests that what is highly esteemed among men constitutes an idol in the human heart. In Rev. 21 : 27, entrance is forbidden into the Holy City on the part of the unclean, or one who "maketh an abomination and a lie." It is also used of the contents of the golden cup in the hand of the evil woman described in Rev. 17 : 4, and of the name ascribed to her in the following verse.¶

For ABOUND see ABUNDANCE

ABOUT

A. Adverbs, etc.

Besides prepositions, the following signify " about " :—

1. KUKLOTHEN (κυκλόθεν), round about, or all round (from *kuklos*, 2943
a circle ; Eng., cycle), is found in the Apocalypse only, 4 : 3, 4, 8.¶ AG:456D

2. KUKLŌ (κύκλῳ), the dative case of *kuklos* (see above), means CB:—
round about, lit., in a circle. It is used in the same way as No. 1, 2944 AG:456D
Mark 3 : 34 ; 6 : 6, 36 ; Luke 9 : 12 ; Rom. 15 : 19 ; Rev. 4 : 6 ; 5 : 11 ; CB:1256B (-LOS)
7 : 11.¶

3. POU (πού), an indefinite particle, signifying " somewhere," some- 4225
where about, nearly, has a limiting force, with numerals, e.g., Rom. 4 : 19. AG:696B
In referring to a passage in the O.T., it is translated " somewhere," in the CB:1266B
R.V. of Heb. 2 : 6 and 4 : 4 (A.V., " in a certain place ") ; by not mentioning the actual passage referred to, the writer acknowledged the familiar acquaintance of his readers with the O.T. See PLACE.

4. HŌS (ὡς) usually means " as." Used with numerals it signifies 5613
" about," e.g. Mark 5 : 13 ; 8 : 9 ; John 1 : 40 ; 6 : 19 ; 11 : 18 ; Acts AG:897A
1 : 15 ; Rev. 8 : 1. CB:1251B

5. HŌSEI (ὡσεί), " as if," before numerals, denotes about, nearly, 5616
something like, with perhaps an indication of greater indefiniteness than AG:899B
No. 4 ; e.g., Matt. 14 : 21 ; Luke 3 : 23 ; 9 : 14, 28 ; Acts 2 : 41 ; with CB:—
a measure of space, Luke 22 : 41, "about a stone's cast." See LIKE.

B. Verb.

MELLŌ (μέλλω) signifies (*a*) of intention, to be about to do something, 3195
e.g., Acts 3 : 3 ; 18 : 14 ; 20 : 3 ; Heb. 8 : 5 ; (*b*) of certainty, compulsion AG:500D
or necessity, to be certain to act, e.g., John 6 : 71. See ALMOST, BEGIN, CB:1258A
COME, INTEND, MEAN, MIND, POINT OF (at), READY, SHALL, SHOULD, TARRY.

Note : *Zēteō*, to seek, is translated " were about " in the A.V. of
Acts 27 : 30 ; R.V., correctly, " were seeking to." 2212 AG:338D CB:1273C

ABOVE

The following adverbs have this meaning (prepositions are omitted here) :—

1. ANŌ (ἄνω) denotes above, in a higher place, Acts 2 : 19 (the opposite 507
to *katō*, below). With the article it means that which is above, Gal. 4 : 26 ; AG:76D
Phil. 3 : 14, " the high calling " (R.V. marg., " upward ") ; with the CB:—
plural article, the things above, John 8 : 23, lit., ' from the things above ; ' Col. 3 : 1, 2. With *heōs*, as far as, it is translated " up to the brim," in John 2 : 7. It has the meaning " upwards " in John 11 : 41 and Heb. 12 : 15. See BRIM, HIGH, UP.¶

2. ANŌTERON (ἀνώτερον), the comparative degree of No. 1, is the 511 (-OS)
neuter of the adjective *anōteros*. It is used (*a*) of motion to a higher place, AG:77C
" higher," Luke 14 : 10 ; (*b*) of location in a higher place, i.e., in the (-OS)
preceding part of a passage, " above," Heb. 10 : 8. See HIGHER.¶ CB:—

1883 3. EPANŌ (ἐπάνω), *epi*, over, *anō*, above, is used frequently as a
AG:283B preposition with a noun; adverbially, of number, e.g., Mark 14:5,
CB:— R.V.; 1 Cor. 15:6.

4119 *Note:* In Acts 4:22, A.V., the adjective *pleion*, more, is translated
AG:687C (POLUS II.) "above," the R.V. corrects to "more than (forty years)."

CB:1265B 509 4. ANŌTHEN (ἄνωθεν), from above, is used of place, (*a*) with the
AG:77A meaning "from the top," Matt. 27:51; Mark 15:38, of the temple veil;
CB:1236A in John 19:23, of the garment of Christ, lit., 'from the upper parts' (plural); (*b*) of things which come from heaven, or from God in Heaven, John 3:31; 19:11; Jas. 1:17; 3:15, 17. It is also used in the sense of "again." See AGAIN.

For ABROAD, see the verbs with which it is used, DISPERSE, NOISE, SCATTER, SHED, SPREAD.

ABSENCE, ABSENT

A. Noun.

666 APOUSIA (ἀπουσία), lit., a being away from, is used in Phil. 2:12,
AG:101D
CB:— of the Apostle's absence from Philippi, in contrast to his *parousia*, his presence with the saints there (*parousia* does not signify merely a coming, it includes or suggests the presence which follows the arrival).¶

B. Verbs.

548 1. APEIMI (ἄπειμι), to be absent (*apo*, from, *eimi*, to be), is found in
AG:83A I.
CB:— 1 Cor. 5:3; 2 Cor. 10:1, 11; 13:2, 10; Phil. 1:27; Col. 2:5. See GO.¶

1553 2. EKDĒMEŌ (ἐκδημέω), lit., to be away from people (*ek*, from, or
AG:238B
CB:1243C out of, *dēmos*, people), hence came to mean either (*a*) to go abroad, depart; the Apostle Paul uses it to speak of departing from the body as the earthly abode of the spirit, 2 Cor. 5:8; or (*b*) to be away; in the same passage, of being here in the body and absent from the Lord (ver. 6), or being absent from the body and present with the Lord (ver. 8). Its other occurrence is in ver. 9.¶

C. Preposition.

817 ATER (ἄτερ) means without, Luke 22:35, "without purse;" in ver. 6,
AG:120A
CB:— "in the absence (of the multitude)," marg., "without tumult." See WITHOUT.¶

ABSTAIN, ABSTINENCE

568 APECHŌ (ἀπέχω), to hold oneself from (*apo*, from, *echomai*, the
AG:84D
CB:1236B Middle Voice of *echō*, to have, i.e., to keep oneself from), in the N.T., invariably refers to evil practices, moral and ceremonial, Acts 15:20, 29; 1 Thess. 4:3; 5:22; 1 Tim. 4:3; 1 Pet. 2:11; so in the Sept. in Job 1:1; 2:3. See ENOUGH, RECEIVE.¶

776 *Note:* The noun "abstinence" in Acts 27:21, A.V., translates *asitia*,
AG:116B
CB:— "without food", R.V. (*a*, negative, *sitos*, food). Cp. *asitos*, fasting, ver. 33.¶

ABUNDANCE, ABUNDANT, ABUNDANTLY, ABOUND

A. Nouns.

1. HADROTĒS (ἁδρότης), which, in 2 Cor. 8 : 20, in reference to the 100
gifts from the church at Corinth for poor saints in Judæa, the R.V. renders AG:18D
"bounty" (A.V., "abundance"), is derived from *hadros*, thick, fat, CB:—
full-grown, rich (in the Sept. it is used chiefly of rich and great men, e.g., Jer. 5 : 5). In regard, therefore, to the offering in 2 Cor. 8 : 20 the thought is that of bountiful giving, a fat offering, not mere abundance.¶

2. PERISSEIA (περισσεία), an exceeding measure, something above 4050
the ordinary, is used four times ; Rom. 5 : 17, of abundance of grace ; AG:650C
2 Cor. 8 : 2, of abundance of joy ; 2 Cor. 10 : 15, of the extension of the CB:1263C
Apostle's sphere of service through the practical fellowship of the saints at Corinth ; in Jas. 1 : 21 it is rendered, metaphorically, "overflowing," A.V. "superfluity", with reference to wickedness. Some would render it "residuum," or what remains. See No. 3.¶

3. PERISSEUMA (περίσσευμα) denotes abundance in a slightly more 4051
concrete form, 2 Cor. 8 : 13, 14, where it stands for the gifts in kind AG:650C CB:1263C
supplied by the saints. In Matt. 12 : 34 and Luke 6 : 45 it is used of the abundance of the heart ; in Mark 8 : 8, of the broken pieces left after feeding the multitude "that remained over" (A.V. "that was left"). See REMAIN.¶ In the Sept., Eccl. 2 : 15.¶

4. HUPERBOLĒ (ὑπερβολή), lit., a throwing beyond (*huper*, over, 5236
ballō, to throw), denotes excellence, exceeding greatness, of the power AG:840B CB:—
of God in His servants, 2 Cor. 4 : 7 ; of the revelations given to Paul, 12 : 7 ; with the preposition *kata*, the phrase signifies "exceeding," Rom. 7 : 13 ; "still more excellent," 1 Cor. 12 : 31 ; "exceedingly," 2 Cor. 1 : 8 ; "beyond measure," Gal. 1 : 13 ; and, in a more extended phrase, "more and more exceedingly," 2 Cor. 4 : 17. See EXCELLENCY, EXCELLENT, MEASURE.¶

B. Verbs.

1. PERISSEUŌ (περισσεύω), akin to A, Nos. 2 and 3, is used in- 4052
transitively (*a*) of exceeding a certain number, or measure, to be over, to AG:650C
remain, of the fragments after feeding the multitude (cp. *perisseuma*), CB:1263C
Luke 9 : 17 ; John 6 : 12, 13 ; to exist in abundance ; as of wealth, Luke 12 : 15 ; 21 : 4 ; of food, 15 : 17. In this sense it is used also of consolation, 2 Cor. 1 : 5 ; of the effect of a gift sent to meet the need of saints, 2 Cor. 9 : 12 ; of rejoicing, Phil. 1 : 26 ; of what comes or falls to the lot of a person in large measure, as of the grace of God and the gift by the grace of Christ, Rom. 5 : 15 ; of the sufferings of Christ, 2 Cor. 1 : 5. In Mark 12 : 44 and Luke 21 : 4, the R.V. has "superfluity."

(*b*) to redound to, or to turn out abundantly for something, as of the liberal effects of poverty, 2 Cor. 8 : 2 ; in Rom. 3 : 7, argumentatively, of the effects of the truth of God, as to whether God's truthfulness becomes more conspicuous and His glory is increased through man's untruthfulness ; of numerical increase, Acts 16 : 5.

(*c*) to be abundantly furnished, to abound in a thing, as of material benefits, Luke 12 : 15 ; Phil. 4 : 18 of spiritual gifts, 1 Cor. 14 : 12, or to be pre-eminent, to excel, to be morally better off, as regards partaking of certain meats, 1 Cor. 8 : 8, " are we the better " ; to abound in hope, Rom. 15 : 13 ; the work of the Lord, 1 Cor. 15 : 58 ; faith and grace, 2 Cor. 8 : 7 ; thanksgiving, Col. 2 : 7 ; walking so as to please God, Phil. 1 : 9 ; 1 Thess. 4 : 1, 10 ; of righteousness, Matt. 5 : 20 ; of the Gospel, as the ministration of righteousness, 2 Cor. 3 : 9, " exceed."

It is used transitively, in the sense of to make to abound, e.g., to provide a person richly so that he has abundance, as of spiritual truth, Matt. 13 : 12 ; the right use of what God has entrusted to us, 25 : 29 ; the power of God in conferring grace, 2 Cor. 9 : 8 ; Eph. 1 : 8 ; to make abundant or to cause to excel, as of the effect of grace in regard to thanksgiving, 2 Cor. 4 : 15 ; His power to make us to abound in love, 1 Thess. 3 : 12. See BETTER, ENOUGH, EXCEED, EXCEL, INCREASE, REDOUND, REMAIN.¶

5248
AG:841D 2. HUPERPERISSEUŌ (ὑπερπερισσεύω), a strengthened form of
CB:1252A No. 1, signifies to abound exceedingly, Rom. 5 : 20, of the operation of
grace ; 2 Cor. 7 : 4, in the Middle Voice, of the Apostle's joy in the saints. See JOYFUL.¶

4121
AG:667B 3 PLEONAZŌ (πλεονάζω), from *pleion*, or *pleon*, " more " (greater in
CB:1265B quantity), akin to *pleō*, to fill, signifies, (*a*) intransitively, to superabound, of a trespass or sin, Rom. 5 : 20 ; of grace, Rom. 6 : 1 ; 2 Cor. 4 : 15 ; of spiritual fruit, Phil. 4 : 17 ; of love, 2 Thess. 1 : 3 ; of various fruits, 2 Pet. 1 : 8 ; of the gathering of the manna, 2 Cor. 8 : 15, " had . . . over " ; (*b*) transitively, to make to increase, 1 Thess. 3 : 12. See INCREASE, OVER.¶

5250
AG:842A 4. HUPERPLEONAZŌ (ὑπερπλεονάζω), a strengthened form of No. 3,
CB:1252A signifying to abound exceedingly, is used in 1 Tim. 1 : 14, of the grace of God.¶

4129
AG:669A 5. PLĒTHUNŌ (πληθύνω), a lengthened form of *plēthō*, to fill, akin to
CB:1265B No. 3, and to *plēthos*, a multitude, signifies to increase, to multiply, and, in the Passive Voice, to be multiplied, e.g., of iniquity, Matt. 24 : 12, R.V. See MULTIPLY.

5235
AG:840B *Note : Huperballō*, akin to A, No. 4, to exceed, excel, is translated
CB:— " passeth " in Eph. 3 : 19. See also 2 Cor. 3 : 10 (R.V., " surpasseth ; " A.V., " excelleth ") ; 9 : 14, " exceeding ; " Eph. 1 : 19 ; 2 : 7. See EXCEED, EXCEL.¶

C. Adjectives.

4053
AG:651B 1. PERISSOS (περισσός), akin to B, No. 1, " abundant," is translated
CB:1263C " advantage " in Rom. 3 : 1, " superfluous " in 2 Cor. 9 : 1. See ADVANTAGE, MORE, B, No. 2, SUPERFLUOUS.

4054
AG:651C 2. PERISSOTEROS (περισσότερος), the comparative degree of No. 1,
CB:1263C is translated as follows : in Matt. 11 : 9, and Luke 7 : 26, R.V., " much

more" (A.V., "more"); in Mark 12 : 40, "greater;" in Luke 12 : 4, 48, "more;" in 1 Cor. 12 : 23, 24, "more abundant;" in 2 Cor. 2 : 7, "overmuch;" in 2 Cor. 10 : 8, R.V., "abundantly," A.V., "more." See GREATER, MORE, OVERMUCH.

D. Adverbs.

1. PERISSŌS (περισσῶς), corresponding to Adjective No. 1 above, 4057
is found in Matt. 27 : 23, R.V., "exceedingly," A.V., "the more;" Mark AG:651D
10 : 26, R.V., "exceedingly," A.V., "out of measure;" 15 : 14; Acts. CB:1263C
26 : 11, "exceedingly." See EXCEEDINGLY, B, No. 4, MEASURE, B,
No. 2, MORE.¶

2. PERISSOTEROS (περισσοτέρως), the adverbial form of No. 2, 4056
above, means 'more abundantly;' in Heb. 2 : 1, lit., 'we ought to give heed AG:651D
more abundantly.' It is most frequent in 2 Cor. In 11 : 23, see the R.V. CB:1263C
See EARNEST, EXCEEDINGLY, RATHER.

3. HUPERPERISSŌS (ὑπερπερισσῶς), a strengthened form of No. 1, 5249 AG:842A
signifies "exceeding abundantly," Mark 7 : 37.¶ CB:1252A

4. HUPEREKPERISSOU (ὑπερεκπερισσοῦ), a still further strengthened After 5240 AG:840C
form, is translated "exceeding abundantly" in Eph. 3 : 20; "ex- CB:1252A
ceedingly" in 1 Thess. 3 : 10; 5 : 13. See EXCEEDINGLY.¶

Note: *Huperballontōs*, akin to A, No. 4, denotes "above measure," 5234
2 Cor. 11 : 23.¶ AG:840A CB:—

5. PLOUSIŌS (πλουσίως), connected with *ploutos*, riches, is rendered 4146
"abundantly," Tit. 3 : 6 and 2 Pet. 1 : 11; "richly," Col. 3 : 16 and 1 Tim. AG:673D
6 : 17. It is used of (*a*) the gift of the Holy Spirit; (*b*) entrance into the CB:1265B
coming Kingdom; (*c*) the indwelling of the Word of Christ; (*d*) material
benefits. See RICHLY.¶

Notes: (1) *Dunamis*, power, is translated "abundance" in the 1411
A.V. of Rev. 18 : 3 (R.V. and A.V. marg., "power"). AG:207B CB:1242B

(2) *Polus*, much, many, is rendered "abundant" in 1 Pet. 1 : 3, A.V. 4183
(marg., "much"), R.V., "great." AG:687C CB:1266A

(3) For the verbs *plouteō* and *ploutizō*, see RICH and ENRICH.

(4) For *ploutos*, wealth, riches, and *plousios*, rich, see RICH.

ABUSE, ABUSERS

A. Verb.

KATACHRAOMAI (καταχράομαι), lit., to use overmuch (*kata*, down, 2710
intensive, *chraomai*, to use), is found in 1 Cor. 7 : 31, with reference to the AG:420D CB:—
believer's use of the world (marg., "use to the full"), and 1 Cor. 9 : 18,
A.V., "abuse," R.V., "use to the full." See USE.¶

B. Noun.

For the noun *arsenokoitēs*, see 1 Cor. 6 : 9, and 1 Tim. 1 : 10.¶ 733 AG:109D CB:1237C

For ABYSS see BOTTOM.

ACCEPT, ACCEPTED, ACCEPTABLE

A. Verbs.

1209 AG:177B CB:1240B 1. DECHOMAI (δέχομαι) signifies to accept, by a deliberate and ready reception of what is offered (cp. No. 4), e.g., 1 Thess. 2 : 13, R.V., "accepted;" 2 Cor. 8 : 17; 11 : 4. See RECEIVE, TAKE.

588 AG:90A CB:1236C 2. APODECHOMAI (ἀποδέχομαι), consisting of *apo*, from, intensive, and No. 1, expresses *dechomai* more strongly, signifying to receive heartily, to welcome, Luke 8 : 40 (R.V., "welcomed," A.V., "gladly received"); Acts 2 : 41; 18 : 27; 24 : 3; 28 : 30. See RECEIVE, WELCOME.

4327 AG:712B CB:1267A 3. PROSDECHOMAI (προσδέχομαι), *pros*, to, and No. 1, to accept favourably, or receive to oneself, is used of things future, in the sense of expecting; with the meaning of accepting, it is used negatively in Heb. 11 : 35, "not accepting their deliverance;" of receiving, e.g., Luke 15 : 2; Rom. 16 : 2; Phil. 2 : 29. See ALLOW, LOOK (for), RECEIVE, TAKE, WAIT.

2983 AG:464A CB:1256C 4. LAMBANŌ (λαμβάνω), almost synonymous with *dechomai*, is distinct from it, in that it sometimes means to receive as merely a self-prompted action, without necessarily signifying a favourable reception, Gal. 2 : 6. See ATTAIN, CALL, CATCH, HAVE, HOLD, OBTAIN, RECEIVE, TAKE.

5487 AG:879A CB:1239C *Note:* The verb *charitoō*, to make acceptable, is translated "made accepted," in Eph. 1 : 6, A.V.; R.V., "freely bestowed."

B. Adjectives.

The following adjectives are translated "acceptable," or in some cases "accepted." The R.V. more frequently adopts the former rendering.

1184 AG:174B CB:1240C 1. DEKTOS (δεκτός), akin to No. 1, denotes a person or thing who has been regarded favourably, Luke 4 : 19, 24; Acts 10 : 35; 2 Cor. 6 : 2 (in this verse No. 3 is used in the second place); Phil. 4 : 18.¶

587 AG:90A CB:1236C 2. APODEKTOS (ἀποδεκτός), a strengthened form of No. 1 (*apo*, from, used intensively), signifies acceptable, in the sense of what is pleasing and welcome, 1 Tim. 2 : 3; 5 : 4.¶

2144 AG:324C CB:1247B 3. EUPROSDEKTOS (εὐπρόσδεκτος), a still stronger form of No. 1, signifies a very favourable acceptance (*eu*, well, *pros*, towards, No. 1), Rom. 15 : 16, 31; 2 Cor. 6 : 2; 8 : 12; 1 Pet. 2 : 5.¶

2101 AG:318D CB:1247A 4. EUARESTOS (εὐάρεστος), *eu*, well, *arestos*, pleasing, is rendered "acceptable," in the A.V. of Rom. 12 : 1, 2; 14 : 18; in 2 Cor. 5 : 9, "accepted"; Eph. 5 : 10. The R.V. usually has "well-pleasing;" so A.V. and R.V. in Phil. 4 : 18; Col. 3 : 20; in Tit. 2 : 9, "please well," A.V.; Heb. 13 : 21. See PLEASING.¶

C. Adverb.

2102 AG:318D CB:— EUARESTŌS (εὐαρέστως), corresponding to B, No. 4, is used in Heb. 12 : 28, "so as to please." See PLEASE.¶

D. Nouns.

1. APODOCHĒ (ἀποδοχή), akin to B, No. 2, signifies worthy to be 594
received with approbation, acceptation, 1 Tim. 1 : 15 ; 4 : 9. The phrase AG:91A
in 1 : 15 is found in a writing in the 1st century expressing appreciation CB:1236C
of a gift from a princess.¶

2. CHARIS (χάρις), grace, indicating favour on the part of the giver, 5485
thanks on the part of the receiver, is rendered " acceptable " in 1 Pet. AG:877B
2 : 19, 20. See margin. See BENEFIT, FAVOUR, GRACE, LIBERALITY, CB:1239C
PLEASURE, THANK.

ACCESS

PROSAGŌGĒ (προσαγωγή), lit., a leading or bringing into the presence 4318
of (*pros*, to, *agō*, to lead), denotes access, with which is associated the AG:711C
thought of freedom to enter through the assistance or favour of another. CB:1267A
It is used three times, (*a*) Rom. 5 : 2, of the access which we have by faith, through our Lord Jesus Christ, into grace ; (*b*) Eph. 2 : 18, of our access in one Spirit through Christ, unto the Father ; (*c*) Eph. 3 : 12, of the same access, there said to be " in Christ," and which we have " in confidence through our faith in Him." This access involves the acceptance which we have in Christ with God, and the privilege of His favour towards us. Some advocate the meaning " introduction."¶

ACCOMPANY

A. Verbs.

1. SUNEPOMAI (συνέπομαι), lit., to follow with (*sun*, with, *hepomai*, 4902
to follow), hence came to mean simply to accompany, Acts 20 : 4.¶ AG:787C CB:—

2. SUNERCHOMAI (συνέρχομαι), chiefly used of assembling together, 4905
signifies to accompany, in Luke 23 : 55 ; John 11 : 33 ; Acts 9 : 39 ; AG:788A
10 : 45 ; 11 : 12 ; 15 : 38 ; 21 : 16. In Acts 1 : 21 it is said of men who CB:1270C
had " companied with " the Apostles all the time the Lord Jesus was with them. See ASSEMBLE, COME, COMPANY, GO, RESORT.

3. ECHŌ (ἔχω), to have, is rendered " accompany," in Heb. 6 : 9, 2192
" things that accompany salvation." The margin gives perhaps the AG:331D
better sense, " things that are near to salvation." CB:1242C

4. PROPEMPŌ (προπέμπω), translated " accompanied," in Acts 4311
20 : 38, A.V., lit. means " to send forward ; " hence, of assisting a person AG:709B
on a journey either (*a*) in the sense of fitting him out with the requisites CB:—
for it, or (*b*) actually accompanying him for part of the way. The former seems to be indicated in Rom. 15 : 24 and 1 Cor. 16 : 6, and ver. 11, where the R.V. has " set him forward." So in 2 Cor. 1 : 16 and Tit. 3 : 13, and of John's exhortation to Gaius concerning travelling evangelists, " whom thou wilt do well to set forward on their journey worthily of God," 3 John 6, R.V. While personal accompaniment is not excluded, practical assistance seems to be generally in view, as indicated by Paul's word to Titus to set forward Zenas and Apollos on their journey and to see " that nothing

be wanting unto them." In regard to the parting of Paul from the elders of Ephesus at Miletus, personal accompaniment is especially in view, perhaps not without the suggestion of assistance, Acts 20 : 38, R.V., " brought him on his way ; " accompaniment is also indicated in 21 : 5 ; " they all with wives and children brought us on our way, till we were out of the city." In Acts 15 : 3, both ideas perhaps are suggested. See BRING, CONDUCT.¶

ACCOMPLISH, ACCOMPLISHMENT

A. Verbs.

1822 1. EXARTIZŌ (ἐξαρτίζω), to fit out, (from *ek*, out, and a verb derived
AG:273C CB:1247C from *artos*, a joint), hence means to furnish completely, 2 Tim. 3 : 17, or
to accomplish, Acts 21 : 5, there said of a number of days, as if to render the days complete by what was appointed for them. See FURNISH.¶ In the Sept., Ex. 28 : 7.¶

4137 2. PLĒROŌ (πληρόω), to fulfil, to complete, carry out to the full
AG:670C CB:1265B (as well as to fill), is translated " perfect " in Rev. 3 : 2, A.V. ; R.V.,
" I have found no works of thine fulfilled before My God ; " " accomplish " in Luke 9 : 31. See COMPLETE, END, EXPIRE, FILL, FULFIL, FULL, PREACH.

1603 *Note :* Its strengthened form, *ekplēroō*, to fulfil, lit., fill out, is used
AG:244A CB:1243C in Acts 13 : 33, of the fulfilment of a Divine promise of the resurrection
of Christ.

5055 3. TELEŌ (τελέω), to finish, to bring to an end (*telos*, an end), fre-
AG:810D CB:1271B quently signifies, not merely to terminate a thing, but to carry out a
thing to the full. It is used especially in the Apocalypse, where it occurs eight times, and is rendered " finish " in 10 : 7 ; 11 : 7, and in the R.V. of 15 : 1, which rightly translates it " (in them) is finished (the wrath of God)." So in ver. 8 ; in 17 : 17, R.V., " accomplish," and " finish " in 20 : 3, 5, 7 ; in Luke 2 : 39, R.V., " accomplish," for A.V., " performed." See END, EXPIRE, FILL, FINISH, FULFIL, GO, No. 5, PAY, PERFORM.

2005 4. EPITELEŌ (ἐπιτελέω), *epi*, up, intensive, and No. 3, is a
AG:302B strengthened form of that verb, in the sense of " accomplishing."
CB:1246A (-EISTHAI) The fuller meaning is to accomplish perfectly ; in Rom. 15 : 28, R.V.,
" accomplish ; " " perfecting " in 2 Cor. 7 : 1 ; " complete " in 8 : 6 and 11 ; " completion " in the latter part of this 11th verse, which is better than " performance ; " " perfected " in Gal. 3 : 3 ; " perfect " in Phil. 1 : 6. In Heb. 8 : 5 the margin rightly has " complete " instead of " make," with regard to the Tabernacle. In Heb. 9 : 6 it is translated " accomplish " and in 1 Pet. 5 : 9. See COMPLETE, DO, FINISH, MAKE, PERFECT, PERFORM.¶

5048 5. TELEIOŌ (τελειόω), though distinct grammatically from *teleō*,
AG:809D CB:1271B has much the same meaning. The main distinction is that *teleō* more
frequently signifies to fulfil, *teleioō*, more frequently, to make perfect, one of the chief features of the Epistle to the Hebrews, where it occurs

nine times. It is rendered "accomplish" in the R.V. of John 4 : 34; 5 : 36; 17 : 4, and Acts 20 : 24. See CONSECRATE, FINISH, FULFIL, PERFECT.

6. PLĒTHŌ (πλήθω), to fulfil, is translated "accomplished" in the 4130
A.V. of Luke 1 : 23; 2 : 6, 21, 22 (R.V., "fulfilled"). See FILL, AG:658A
No. 5, FURNISH, *Note*. CB:1265A

B. Noun.

EKPLĒRŌSIS (ἐκπλήρωσις), see A, No. 2, Note, means an entire 1604
fulfilment (*ek*, out, *plērosis*, a filling), Acts 21 : 26, of the fulfilment of AG:244B
days of purification.¶ CB:—

ACCORD

A. Adverb.

HOMOTHUMADON (ὁμοθυμαδόν), of one accord (from *homos*, same, 3661
thumos, mind), occurs eleven times, ten in the Acts, 1 : 14; 2 : 46; AG:566C
4 : 24; 5 : 12; 7 : 57; 8 : 6; 12 : 20; 15 : 25; 18 : 12; 19 : 29, and CB:1251A
the other in Rom. 15 : 6, where, for A.V., "with one mind," the R.V.
has "with one accord," as throughout the Acts. See MIND.¶

Note: In Acts 2 : 1, the adverb *homou*, "together," is so rendered in 3674
the R.V., for A.V., "of one accord." AG:569B CB:1251A (-OIOS)

B. Adjectives.

"Of one's own accord."

1. AUTHAIRETOS (αὐθαίρετος), from *autos*, self, and *haireomai*, 830
to choose, self-chosen, voluntary, of one's own accord, occurs in 2 Cor. 8 : 3, AG:121A
and 17, of the churches of Macedonia as to their gifts for the poor saints in CB:—
Judæa, and of Titus in his willingness to go and exhort the church in
Corinth concerning the matter. In 8 : 3 the R.V. translates it "(gave)
of their own accord," consistently with the rendering in ver. 17. See
WILLING.¶

2. AUTOMATOS (αὐτομάτος), from *autos*, self, and a root *ma*—, 844
signifying desire, denotes of oneself, moved by one's own impulse. It AG:122C
occurs in Mark 4 : 28, of the power of the earth to produce plants and CB:1238B
fruits of itself; Acts 12 : 10, of the door which opened of its own accord.
See SELF.¶ In the Sept., Lev. 25 : 5, "spontaneous produce;" ver. 11,
"produce that comes of itself;" Josh. 6 : 5; 2 Kings 19 : 29, "(that which
groweth) of itself;" Job 24 : 24, of an ear of corn "(falling off) of itself
(from the stalk)."¶

3. SUMPSUCHOS (σύμψυχος), lit., fellow-souled or minded (*sun*, with, 4861
psuchē, the soul), occurs in Phil. 2 : 2, "of one accord."¶ AG:781B CB:1270B

ACCORDING AS

1. KATHOTI (καθότι), from *kata*, according to, and *hoti*, that, lit., 2530
because that, Luke 1 : 7; 19 : 9; Acts 2 : 24, is translated "according AG:391B
as" in Acts 2 : 45, R.V. (A.V., "as") and in 4 : 35; "inasmuch as" B:—
17 : 31.¶

2531 AG:391B 2. KATHŌS (καθώς), from *kata*, according to, and *hōs*, as, signifies
CB:1254C "according as" or "even as," e.g., 1 Cor. 1 : 31 ; 2 Cor. 9 : 7.

5613 AG:897A 3. HŌS (ὡς) is sometimes rendered "according as," e.g., Rev. 22 : 12 ;
CB:1251B in 2 Pet. 1 : 3, the R.V. has "seeing that," for the A.V. "according as."

4. KATHO (καθό) : see INASMUCH AS.

ACCORDING TO : See Note † p. 1

ACCOUNT (-ED) (Verbs and Noun)

A. Verbs.

1380 AG:201D
CB:1242A 1. DOKEŌ (δοκέω), primarily, to be of opinion, think, suppose, also signifies to seem, be accounted, reputed, translated "accounted" in Mark 10 : 42 ; Luke 22 : 24. It is not used ironically here, nor in Gal. 2 : 2, 6, 9, "those who were of repute." See REPUTE, SEEM, SUPPOSE, THINK.

1677 AG:252B
CB:1244B 2. ELLOGEŌ (or-AŌ) (ἐλλογέω), to put to a person's account, Philm. 18, is used of sin in Rom. 5 : 13, "reckon" (A.V., "impute"). See IMPUTE, No. 2.¶

2233 AG:343C
CB:1249C 3. HĒGEOMAI (ἡγέομαι) primarily signifies to lead ; then, to consider ; it is translated "accounting" in Heb. 11 : 26, R.V. (A.V., "esteeming") ; 2 Pet. 3 : 15, "account." See CHIEF, COUNT, ESTEEM, GOVERNOR, JUDGE, RULE, SUPPOSE, THINK.

3049 AG:475D
CB:1257A 4. LOGIZOMAI (λογίζομαι) primarily signifies to reckon, whether by calculation or imputation, e.g., Gal. 3 : 6 (R.V., "reckoned") ; then, to deliberate, and so to suppose, account, Rom. 8 : 36 ; 14 : 14 (A.V., "esteemeth") ; 1 Cor. 4 : 1 ; Heb. 11 : 19 ; John 11 : 50 (A.V., "consider") ; Acts 19 : 27 ("made of no account" ; A.V., "despised") ; 1 Pet. 5 : 12 (A.V., "suppose"). It is used of love in 1 Cor. 13 : 5, as not taking account of evil, R.V. (A.V., "thinketh"). In 2 Cor. 3 : 5 the Apostle uses it in repudiation of the idea that he and fellow-servants of God are so self-sufficient as to "account anything" (R.V.) as from themselves (A.V., "think"), i.e., as to attribute anything to themselves. Cp. 12 : 6. In 2 Tim. 4 : 16 it is used of laying to a person's "account" (R.V.) as a charge against him (A.V., "charge").

Note : In Phil. 4 : 8 it signifies to think upon a matter by way of taking account of its character (R.V. margin). See CONCLUDE, COUNT, CHARGE, ESTEEM, IMPUTE, NUMBER, REASON, RECKON, THINK, SUPPOSE.

2661 AG:415C
CB:1254B 5. KATAXIOŌ (καταξιόω) denotes to account worthy (*kata*, intensive, *axios*, worthy), to judge worthy, Luke 20 : 35 ; some mss. have it in 21 : 36 (so the A.V.) ; the most authentic mss. have the verb *katischuō*, to prevail ; Acts 5 : 41, "were counted worthy ;" so 2 Thess. 1 : 5.¶

1848 AG:277C
CB:1247C 6. EXOUTHENEŌ (ἐξουθενέω), to make of no account, frequently signifies to despise. In 1 Cor. 6 : 4, it is used, not in a contemptuous sense, but of Gentile judges, before whom the saints are not to go to law with one another, such magistrates having no place, and therefore being

" of no account " (R.V.), in the church. The Apostle is not speaking of any believers as " least esteemed " (A.V.). In 2 Cor. 10 : 10, for A.V., " contemptible," the R.V. suitably has " of no account." See DESPISE.

B. Noun.

LOGOS (λόγος), a word or saying, also means an account which one 3056
gives by word of mouth (cp. No. 4), Matt. 12 : 36 ; Matt. 18 : 23, R.V., AG:477A
" reckoning ; " 16 : 2 ; Acts 19 : 40 ; 20 : 24 (A.V., " count ") ; Rom. CB:1257A
14 : 12 ; Phil. 4 : 17 ; Heb. 13 : 17 ; 1 Pet. 4 : 5. See CAUSE, COMMUNICATION, DO, DOCTRINE, FAME, INTENT, MATTER, MOUTH, PREACHING, QUESTION, REASON, RECKONING, RUMOUR, SAYING, SHEW, SPEECH, TALK, THING, TIDINGS, TREATISE, UTTERANCE, WORD, WORK.

ACCURATELY

AKRIBŌS (ἀκριβῶς) is correctly translated in the R.V. of Luke 1 : 3, 199
" having traced the course of all things accurately " (A.V., " having had AG:33B
perfect understanding "). It is used in Matt. 2 : 8, of Herod's command CB:—
to the wise men as to searching for the young Child (R.V., " carefully," A.V., " diligently ") ; in Acts 18 : 25, of Apollos' teaching of " the things concerning Jesus " (R.V., " carefully," A.V., " diligently ") ; in Eph. 5 : 15, of the way in which believers are to walk (R.V., " carefully ; " A.V., " circumspectly ") ; in 1 Thess. 5 : 2, of the knowledge gained by the saints through the Apostle's teaching concerning the Day of the Lord (R.V. and A.V., " perfectly "). The word expresses that accuracy which is the outcome of carefulness. It is connected with *akros*, pointed.

This word and its other grammatical forms, *akribeia*, *akribēs*, *akribesteron* and *akriboō*, are used especially by Luke, who employs them eight times out of the thirteen in the N.T. ; Matthew uses them three times, Paul twice. See CAREFUL, DILIGENT, EXACTLY, PERFECT.¶

For ACCURSED see CURSE, A, No. 3

ACCUSATION, ACCUSE

A. Nouns.

1. AITIA (αἰτία) probably has the primary meaning of a cause, 156
especially an occasion of something evil, hence a charge, an accusation. AG:26B
It is used in a forensic sense, of (*a*) an accusation, Acts 25 : 18 (R.V., CB:1234A
" charge "), 27 ; (*b*) a crime, Matt. 27 : 37 ; Mark 15 : 26 ; John 18 : 38 ; 19 : 4, 6 ; Acts 13 : 28 ; 23 : 28 ; 28 : 18. See CASE, CAUSE, CHARGE, CRIME, FAULT.

2. AITIŌMA (αἰτιώμα), an accusation, expressing No. 1 more con- 157 (-AMA)
cretely, is found in Acts 25 : 7, R.V., " charges," for A.V., " complaints." AG:26D
See COMPLAINT.¶ CB:1234A

3. ENKLĒMA (ἔγκλημα) is an accusation made in public, but not 1462
necessarily before a tribunal. That is the case in Acts 23 : 29, " laid to AG:216B CB:1245A

his charge." In 25 : 16 it signifies a matter of complaint ; hence the R.V. has " the matter laid against him " (A.V., " crime "). See CHARGE, CRIME.¶

2724 AG:423C CB:1254B 4. KATĒGORIA (κατηγορία), an accusation, is found in John 18 : 29 ; 1 Tim. 5 : 19 and Tit. 1 : 6, lit., 'not under accusation.' This and the verb *katēgoreō*, to accuse, and the noun *katēgoros*, an accuser (see below), all have chiefly to do with judicial procedure, as distinct from *diaballō*, to slander. It is derived from *agora*, a place of public speaking, prefixed by *kata*, against ; hence it signifies a speaking against a person before a public tribunal. It is the opposite to *apologia*, a defence.¶

2920 AG:452C CB:1256A *Note : Krisis*, which has been translated " accusation," in the A.V. of 2 Pet. 2 : 11 and Jude 9 (R.V., " judgement "), does not come under this category. It signifies a judgment, a decision given concerning anything.

B. Verbs.

1225 AG:181D CB:1241A 1. DIABALLŌ (διαβάλλω), used in Luke 16 : 1, in the Passive Voice, lit. signifies to hurl across (*dia*, through, *ballō*, to throw), and hence suggests a verbal assault. It stresses the act rather than the author, as in the case of *aitia* and *katēgoria*. *Diabolos* is connected.¶

1458 AG:215C CB:1245A 2. ENKALEŌ (ἐγκαλέω), — see A, No. 3, to bring a charge against, or to come forward as an accuser against, lit. denotes to call in (*en*, in, *kaleō*, to call), i.e., to call (something) in or against (someone) ; hence, to call to account, to accuse, Acts 19 : 38, R.V. (A.V., " implead ") ; in ver. 40, " accused " (A.V., " call in question "). It is used in four other places in the Acts, 23 : 28, 29 ; 26 : 2, 7, and elsewhere in Rom. 8 : 33, " shall lay to the charge." See CALL, IMPLEAD.¶

1908 AG:285D CB:— 3. EPĒREAZŌ (ἐπηρεάζω), besides its more ordinary meaning, to insult, treat abusively, despitefully, Luke 6 : 28, has the forensic significance to accuse falsely, and is used with this meaning in 1 Pet. 3 : 16, R.V., " revile." See DESPITEFULLY, REVILE.¶

2723 AG:423A CB:1254B 4. KATĒGOREŌ (κατηγορέω), to speak against, accuse (cp. A, No. 4), is used (*a*) in a general way, to accuse, e.g., Luke 6 : 7, R.V., " how to accuse ; " Rom. 2 : 15 ; Rev. 12 : 10 ; (*b*) before a judge, e.g., Matt. 12 : 10 ; Mark 15 : 4 (R.V., " witness against ") ; Acts 22 : 30 ; 25 : 16. In Acts 24 : 19, R.V. renders it " make accusation," for the A.V., " object." See OBJECT, WITNESS.

4811 AG:776C CB:— 5. SUKOPHANTEŌ (συκοφαντέω), Eng., sycophant, means (*a*) to accuse wrongfully, Luke 3 : 14 (A.V. and R.V., margin) ; R.V., " exact wrongfully ; " (*b*) to exact money wrongfully, to take anything by false accusation, Luke 19 : 8, and the R.V. text of 3 : 14. It is more frequently found in the Sept. ; see Gen. 43 : 18, to inform against ; Lev. 19 : 11, " neither shall each falsely accuse his neighbour ; " Job. 35 : 9, " they that are oppressed by false accusation ; " Psalm 119 : 122, " let not the proud accuse me falsely ; " Prov. 14 : 31 and 22 : 16, " he that oppresses the needy by false accusation."

The word is derived from *sukon*, a fig, and *phainō*, to show. At Athens a man whose business it was to give information against anyone who might be detected exporting figs out of the province, is said to have been called a *sukophantēs* (see Note (2) below). Probably, however, the word was used to denote one who brings figs to light by shaking the tree, and then in a metaphorical sense one who makes rich men yield up their fruit by false accusation. Hence in general parlance it was used to designate a malignant informer, one who accused from love of gain. See EXACT.¶

Note: *Proaitiaomai* denotes to bring a previous charge against, 4256
Rom. 3 : 9, R.V. See CHARGE.¶ AG:702C
CB:—

ACCUSER

1. DIABOLOS (διάβολος), an accuser (cp. Accuse, B, No. 1), is used 1228
34 times as a title of Satan, " the Devil " (the English word is derived AG:182A
from the Greek); once of Judas, John 6 : 70, who, in his opposition to CB:1241A
God, acted the part of the Devil. Apart from John 6 : 70, men are never spoken of as devils. It is always to be distinguished from *daimōn*, a demon. It is found three times, 1 Tim. 3 : 11; 2 Tim. 3 : 3; Tit. 2 : 3, of false accusers, slanderers.

2. KATĒGOROS (κατήγορος), an accuser (see p. 26), is used in John 2725
8 : 10; Acts 23 : 30, 35; 24 : 8; 25 : 16, 18. In Rev. 12 : 10, it is used AG:423C
of Satan.¶ In the Sept., Prov. 18 : 17.¶ CB:1254B

Notes: (1) *Sukophantia*, a false accusation or oppression, is used in Eccl. 5 : 7; 7 : 8; Psa. 119 : 134 and Amos 2 : 8 (not in the N.T.). See No. 5, above.

(2) *Sukophantēs*, a false accuser, or oppressor, occurs in Psa. 72 : 4; Prov. 28 : 16 (not in the N.T.).

ACCUSTOMED See CUSTOM

ACHIEVE See ATTAIN

ACKNOWLEDGE (-MENT)

A. Verb.

EPIGINŌSKŌ (ἐπιγινώσκω) signifies (*a*) to know thoroughly (*epi*, 1921
intensive, *ginōskō*, to know); (*b*) to recognize a thing to be what it really AG:291A
is, to acknowledge, 1 Cor. 14 : 37 (R.V., " take knowledge of "); 16 : 18; CB:1245C
2 Cor. 1 : 13, 14. See KNOW, KNOWLEDGE, PERCEIVE.

Note: In 1 John 2 : 23, " acknowledgeth " translates the verb *homo-* 3670
logeō, to confess, R.V., " confesseth." AG:568A
CB:1251A

B. Noun.

EPIGNŌSIS (ἐπίγνωσις), akin to A, full, or thorough knowledge, 1922
discernment, recognition, is translated " acknowledging " in the A.V. AG:291B
of 2 Tim. 2 : 25; Tit. 1 : 1 and Philm. 6 (in all three, R.V., " knowledge, " CB:1245C
properly, " thorough knowledge "). In Col. 2 : 2, A.V., " acknowledgement," R.V., " that they may know " (i.e., ' unto the full knowledge '). See KNOWLEDGE.

ACQUAINTANCE

1110 AG:164B CB:1248B 1. GNŌSTOS (γνωστός), from *ginōskō*, to know, signifies known, or knowable; hence, one's acquaintance; it is used in this sense, in the plural, in Luke 2 : 44 and 23 : 49. See KNOWN, NOTABLE.

2398 AG:369C CB:1252C 2. IDIOS (ἴδιος), one's own, is translated "acquaintance" in the A.V. of Acts 24 : 23, "friends" (R.V.). See COMPANY.

AQUIRE See POSSESS

For ACROSS (Acts 27 : 5, R.V.), see Note † p. 9.

ACQUIT See JUSTIFY

ACT

1888 AG:125A (AUTOPHōROS) CB:— 1. EPAUTOPHŌRŌ (ἐπαυτοφώρῳ) primarily signifies caught in the act of theft (*epi*, upon, intensive, *autos*, self, *phōr*, a thief); then, caught in the act of any other crime, John 8 : 4. In some texts the preposition *epi* is detached from the remainder of the adjective, and appears as *ep' autophōrō*.¶

1345 AG:198A CB:1241C 2. DIKAIŌMA (δικαίωμα) signifies an act of righteousness, a concrete expression of righteousness, as in the R.V. of Rom. 5 : 18, in reference to the Death of Christ; the A.V. wrongly renders it "the righteousness of One." The contrast is between the one trespass by Adam and the one act of Christ in His atoning Death. In Rev. 15 : 4 and 19 : 8, the word is used in the plural to signify, as in the R.V., "righteous acts," respectively, of God, and of the saints. See JUDGMENT, JUSTIFICATION, ORDINANCE, RIGHTEOUSNESS.

4238 AG:698B CB:1266B 3. PRASSŌ (πράσσω), to do, to practise, is translated "act" in the R.V. of Acts 17 : 7 (A.V., "do"). See COMMIT, DO, EXACT, KEEP, REQUIRE, USE.

ACTIVE

1756 AG:265D CB:1245A ENERGĒS (ἐνεργής), lit., 'in work' (cp. Eng., energetic), is used (*a*) of the Word of God, Heb. 4 : 12 (R.V., "active," A.V., "powerful"); (*b*) of a door for the Gospel, 1 Cor. 16 : 9, "effectual;" (*c*) of faith, Philm. 6, "effectual." See EFFECTUAL, POWERFUL. Cp. the synonymous words *dunatos* and *ischuros* (see ABLE).¶

ACTUALLY

3654 AG:565B CB:1251A HOLŌS (ὅλως), from *holos*, all, whole, is translated "actually" in 1 Cor. 5 : 1, R.V. ("it is actually reported"); the A.V. "commonly" does not convey the meaning. In 6 : 7 it is translated "altogether" (A.V. "utterly"); in 15 : 29, "at all," as in Matt. 5 : 34. See ALL, ALTOGETHER ¶

ADD

2007 AG:302D CB:1246B 1. EPITITHĒMI (ἐπιτίθημι), lit., to put upon (*epi*, upon, *tithēmi*, to put), has a secondary and somewhat infrequent meaning, to add to, and is found in this sense in Mark 3 : 16, 17, lit., 'He added the name

Peter to Simon,' 'He added to them the name Boanerges,' and Rev. 22 : 18, where the word is set in contrast to "take away from" (ver. 19). See LADE, LAY, PUT, SET.

2. PROSTITHĒMI (προστίθημι), to put to (*pros*, to, *tithēmi*, to put), 4369
to add, or to place beside (the primary meaning), in Luke 17 : 5 is trans- AG:718D
lated "increase," in the request "increase our faith;" in Luke 20 : 11, 12, CB:1267B
"he sent yet" (A.V. "again he sent"), lit., 'he added and sent,' as in 19 : 11, "He added and spake." In Acts 12 : 3, R.V., "proceeded," A.V., "proceeded further" (of repeating or continuing the action mentioned by the following verb); in Acts 13 : 36, "was laid unto"; in Heb. 12 : 19, "more . . . be spoken," (lit., 'that no word should be added'). In Gal. 3 : 19, "What then is the law? It was added because of transgressions," there is no contradiction of what is said in verse 15, where the word is *epidiatassō* (see No. 4), for there the latter word conveys the idea of supplementing an agreement already made; here in ver. 19 the meaning is not that something had been added to the promise with a view to complete it, which the Apostle denies, but that something had been given in addition to the promise, as in Rom. 5 : 20, "The law came in beside." See GIVE, INCREASE, LAY, PROCEED, SPEAK.

3. PROSANATITHĒMI (προσανατίθημι), lit., to lay upon in addition, 4323
came to be used in the sense of putting oneself before another, for the AG:711D
purpose of consulting him; hence simply to consult, to take one into CB:—
counsel, to confer. With this meaning it is used only in Gal. 1 : 16. In Gal. 2 : 2, a shorter form, *anatithēmi*, is used, which means to lay before (A.V., "communicated unto"). This less intensive word may have been purposely used there by the Apostle to suggest that he described to his fellow-apostles the character of his teaching, not to obtain their approval or their advice concerning it, but simply that they might have the facts of the case before them on which they were shortly to adjudicate.

It was also used to signify to communicate, to impart. With this meaning it is used only in Gal. 2 : 6, in the Middle Voice, the suggestion being to add from one's store of things. In regard to his visit to Jerusalem the Apostle says "those who were of repute imparted nothing to me" (A.V., "in conference added"), that is to say, they neither modified his teaching nor added to his authority. See CONFER.¶

4. EPIDIATASSŌ (ἐπιδιατάσσω), lit., to arrange in addition (*epi*, 1928
upon, *dia*, through, *tassō*, to arrange), is used in Gal. 3 : 15 ("addeth," (-OMAI) AG:292B
or rather, 'ordains something in addition'). If no one does such a (-OMAI)
thing in the matter of a human covenant, how much more is a covenant CB:—
made by God inviolable! The Judaizers by their addition violated this principle, and, by proclaiming the Divine authority for what they did, they virtually charged God with a breach of promise. He gave the Law, indeed, but neither in place of the promise nor to supplement it.¶

5. PAREISPHERŌ (παρεισφέρω), to bring in besides (*para*, besides, 3923 AG:625A
eis, in, *pherō*, to bring), means "to add," 2 Pet. 1 : 5, "adding on your CB:—

part" (R.V.); the words "on your part" represent the intensive force of the verb; the A.V., "giving" does not provide an adequate meaning.¶

2023 AG:305A CB:— 6. EPICHORĒGEŌ (ἐπιχορηγέω) is translated "add" in the A.V. of 2 Pet. 1:5. Its meaning is to supply, to minister (*epi*, to, *chorēgeō*, to minister); R.V., "supply." See MINISTER.

1325 AG:192C CB:1241C 7. DIDŌMI (δίδωμι), to give, is translated "add," in Rev. 8:3, R.V., for A.V., "offer" (marg., "add"). See GIVE.

Note: In Phil. 1::17, R.V., *egeirō*, to raise, is translated "add" in the A.V. (R.V., "raise up"). See BRING, A, No. 6.

ADDRESS See PREACH

For ADDICTED (A.V. of 1 Cor. 16:15) see SET, No. 10.

ADJURE

3726 AG:581B CB:1251B 1. HORKIZŌ (ὁρκίζω), to cause to swear, to lay under the obligation of an oath (*horkos*, Mark 5:7; Acts 19:13), is connected with the Heb. word for a thigh, cp. Gen. 24:2, 9; 47:29. Some mss. have this word in 1 Thess. 5:27. The most authentic have No. 3 (below). See CHARGE.¶

1844 AG:277B CB:1247C (EXHO-) 2. EXORKIZŌ (ἐξορκίζω), an intensive form of No. 1, signifies to appeal by an oath, to adjure, Matt. 26:63.¶ In the Sept., Gen. 24:3; Judg. 17:2; 1 Kings 22:16.¶

— AG:267C CB:— 3. ENORKIZŌ (ἐνορκίζω), to put under (or bind by) an oath, is translated "adjure" in the R.V. of 1 Thess. 5:27 (A.V., "charge").¶ In the Sept., Neh. 13:25.¶

3660 AG:565D CB:1260C *Note:* The synonymous verb *omnumi* signifies to make an oath, to declare or promise with an oath. See, e.g., Mark 6:23, in contrast to 5:7 (*horkizō*). See OATH and SWEAR.

For the A.V. ADMINISTER and ADMINISTRATION see MINISTER and MINISTRATION, SERVE and SERVICE.

For the A.V. ADMIRATION and ADMIRE see WONDER and MARVEL.

ADMONITION, ADMONISH

A. Noun.

3559 AG:544A CB:1260A NOUTHESIA (νουθεσία), lit., a putting in mind (*nous*, mind, *tithēmi*, to put), is used in 1 Cor. 10:11, of the purpose of the Scriptures; in Eph. 6:4, of that which is ministered by the Lord: and in Tit. 3:10, of that which is to be administered for the correction of one who creates trouble in the church. *Nouthesia* is "the training by word," whether of encouragement, or, if necessary, by reproof or remonstrance. In contrast to this, the synonymous word *paideia* stresses training by act, though both words are used in each respect.¶

B. Verbs.

3560 AG:544B CB:1260A 1. NOUTHETEŌ (νουθετέω), cp. the noun above, means to put in mind, admonish, Acts 20:31 (A.V., "warn"); Rom. 15:14; 1 Cor. 4:14

(A.V., "warn"); Col. 1 : 28 (A.V., "warning"); Col. 3 : 16; 1 Thess. 5 : 12, 14 (A.V., "warn"); 2 Thess. 3 : 15.

It is used, (*a*) of instruction, (*b*) of warning. It is thus distinguished from *paideuō*, to correct by discipline, to train by act, Heb. 12 : 6; cp. Eph. 6 : 4.

"The difference between 'admonish' and 'teach' seems to be that, whereas the former has mainly in view the things that are wrong and call for warning, the latter has to do chiefly with the impartation of positive truth, cp. Col. 3 : 16; they were to let the word of Christ dwell richly in them, so that they might be able (1) to teach and admonish one another, and (2) to abound in the praises of God.

"Admonition differs from remonstrance, in that the former is warning based on instruction; the latter may be little more than expostulation. For example, though Eli remonstrated with his sons, 1 Sam. 2 : 24, he failed to admonish them, 3 : 13, LXX. Pastors and teachers in the churches are thus themselves admonished, i.e., instructed and warned, by the Scriptures, 1 Cor. 10 : 11, so to minister the Word of God to the saints, that, naming the Name of the Lord, they shall depart from unrighteousness, 2 Tim. 2 : 19."* See WARN.¶

2. PARAINEŌ (παραινέω), to admonish by way of exhorting or 3867
advising, is found in Acts 27 : 9 ("Paul admonished them") and ver. 22 AG:616B
("and now I exhort you"). See EXHORT.¶ CB:1262A

3. CHRĒMATIZŌ (χρηματίζω), primarily, to transact business, then, 5537
to give advice to enquirers (especially of official pronouncements of AG:885C
magistrates), or a response to those consulting an oracle, came to signify CB:1240A
the giving of a Divine admonition or instruction or warning, in a general way; "admonished" in Heb. 8 : 5, A.V. (R.V., "warned"). Elsewhere it is translated by the verb to warn.

The word is derived from *chrēma*, an affair, business. Names were given to men from the nature of their business (see the same word in Acts 11 : 26; Rom. 7 : 3); hence the idea of dealing with a person and receiving instruction. In the case of oracular responses, the word is derived from *chrēsmos*, an oracle. See CALL, REVEAL, SPEAK, WARN.

ADO

THORUBEŌ (θορυβέω), to make an uproar, to throw into confusion, 2350
or to wail tumultuously, is rendered "make . . . ado," in Mark 5 : 39; AG:362D
elsewhere in Matt. 9 : 23; Acts 17 : 5; 20 : 10. See NOISE, TROUBLE, CB:1272B
UPROAR.¶

Note: For the corresponding noun, *thorubos*, see TUMULT, UPROAR.

ADOPTION

HUIOTHESIA (υἱοθεσία), from *huios*, a son, and *thesis*, a placing, 5206 AG:833B CB:1251C

* From Notes on Thessalonians by Hogg and Vine, pp. 179, 180.

akin to *tithēmi*, to place, signifies the place and condition of a son given to one to whom it does not naturally belong. The word is used by the Apostle Paul only.

In Rom. 8 : 15, believers are said to have received "the Spirit of adoption," that is, the Holy Spirit who, given as the Firstfruits of all that is to be theirs, produces in them the realisation of sonship and the attitude belonging to sons. In Gal. 4 : 5 they are said to receive "the adoption of sons," i.e., sonship bestowed in distinction from a relationship consequent merely upon birth; here two contrasts are presented, (1) between the sonship of the believer and the unoriginated Sonship of Christ, (2) between the freedom enjoyed by the believer and bondage, whether of Gentile natural condition, or of Israel under the Law. In Eph. 1 : 5 they are said to have been foreordained unto "adoption as sons" through Jesus Christ, R.V.: the A.V., "adoption of children" is a mistranslation and misleading. God does not adopt believers as children; they are begotten as such by His Holy Spirit through faith. Adoption is a term involving the dignity of the relationship of believers as sons; it is not a putting into the family by spiritual birth, but a putting into the position of sons. In Rom. 8 : 23 the adoption of the believer is set forth as still future, as it there includes the redemption of the body, when the living will be changed and those who have fallen asleep will be raised. In Rom. 9 : 4 adoption is spoken of as belonging to Israel, in accordance with the statement in Ex. 4 : 12, "Israel is My Son." Cp. Hos. 11 : 1. Israel was brought into a special relation with God, a collective relationship, not enjoyed by other nations, Deut. 14 : 1; Jer. 31 : 9, etc.¶

ADORN, ADORNING

A. Verb.

2885 AG:445A CB:1255C KOSMEŌ (κοσμέω), primarily to arrange, to put in order (Eng., cosmetic), is used of furnishing a room, Matt. 12 : 44; Luke 11 : 25, and of trimming lamps, Matt. 25 : 7. Hence, to adorn, to ornament, as of garnishing tombs, Matt. 23 : 29; buildings, Luke 21 : 5; Rev. 21 : 19; one's person, 1 Tim. 2 : 9; 1 Pet. 3 : 5; Rev. 21 : 2; metaphorically, of adorning a doctrine, Tit. 2 : 10. See GARNISH, TRIM.¶

B. Noun.

2889 AG:445D CB:1255C KOSMOS (κόσμος), a harmonious arrangement or order, then, adornment, decoration, hence came to denote the world, or the universe, as that which is Divinely arranged. The meaning "adorning" is found in 1 Pet. 3 : 3. Elsewhere it signifies the world. Cp. *kosmios*, decent, modest, 1 Tim. 2 : 9; 3 : 2. See WORLD.

ADULT See MAN 5.

ADULTERER (-ESS), ADULTEROUS, ADULTERY

A. Nouns.

3432 AG:526C CB:1259A 1. MOICHOS (μοιχός) denotes one who has unlawful intercourse with the spouse of another, Luke 18 : 11 ; 1 Cor. 6 : 9 ; Heb. 13 : 4. As to Jas. 4 : 4, see below.¶

2. MOICHALIS (μοιχαλίς), an adulteress, is used (*a*) in the natural 3428
sense, 2 Pet. 2 : 14 ; Rom. 7 : 3 ; (*b*) in the spiritual sense, Jas. 4 : 4 ; AG:526A
here the R.V. rightly omits the word " adulterers." It was added by a CB:1259A
copyist. As in Israel the breach of their relationship with God through their idolatry, was described as adultery or harlotry (e.g., Ezek. 16 : 15, etc. ; 23 : 43), so believers who cultivate friendship with the world, thus breaking their spiritual union with Christ, are spiritual adulteresses, having been spiritually united to Him as wife to husband, Rom. 7 : 4. It is used adjectivally to describe the Jewish people in transferring their affections from God, Matt. 12 : 39 ; 16 : 4 ; Mark 8 : 38. In 2 Pet. 2 : 14, the lit. translation is " full of an adulteress " (R.V. marg.).¶

3. MOICHEIA (μοιχεία), adultery, is found in Matt. 15 : 19 ; Mark 3430
7 : 21 ; John 8 : 3 (A.V. only).¶ AG:526B CB:1259A

B. Verbs.

1. MOICHAŌ (μοιχάω), used in the Middle Voice in the N.T, is said 3429
of men in Matt. 5 : 32 ; 19 : 9 ; Mark 10 : 11 ; of women in Mark 10 : 12.¶ AG:526A
2. MOICHEUŌ (μοιχεύω) is used in Matt. 5 : 27, 28, 32 (in ver. 32 CB:1259A 3431
some texts have No. 1) ; 19 : 18 ; Mark 10 : 19 ; Luke 16 : 18 ; 18 : 20 ; AG:526B
John 8 : 4 ; Rom. 2 : 22 ; 13 : 9 ; Jas. 2 : 11 ; in Rev. 2 : 22, metaphori- CB:1259A
cally, of those who are by a Jezebel's solicitations drawn away to idolatry.¶

ADVANCE

PROKOPTŌ (προκόπτω), lit., to strike forward, cut forward a way, 4298
i.e., to make progress, is translated " advanced " in Luke 2 : 52, R.V., of AG:707D
the Lord Jesus (A.V., " increased ") ; in Gal. 1 : 14 " advanced," of Paul's CB:1266C
former progress in the Jews' religion (A.V., " profited ") ; in Rom. 13 : 12, " is far spent," of the advanced state of the " night " of the world's spiritual darkness ; in 2 Tim. 2 : 16, " will proceed further," of profane babblings ; in 3 : 9 " shall proceed no further," of the limit Divinely to be put to the doings of evil men ; in ver. 13, of the progress of evil men and impostors, " shall wax," lit., ' shall advance to the worse.' See INCREASE, PROCEED, PROFIT, SPENT, WAX.¶

Note : The corresponding noun *prokopē* is found in Phil. 1 : 12 and 25, 4297
" progress " (A.V., " furtherance ") ; 1 Tim. 4 : 15, " progress " (A.V., AG:707D
" profiting," an inadequate meaning).¶ CB:1266C

ADVANTAGE

A. Nouns.

1. PERISSOS (περισσός), primarily, what is above and over, super- 4053
added, hence came to denote what is superior and advantageous, AG:651B
Rom. 3 : 1, in a comparison between Jew and Gentile ; only here with CB:1263C
this meaning. See ABUNDANT, C, No. 1.

3786 2. OPHELOS (ὄφελος), akin to *ophellō*, to increase, comes from a
AG:599B root signifying to increase; hence, advantage, profit; it is rendered as a
CB:— verb in its three occurrences, 1 Cor. 15 : 32 (A.V., "advantageth;" R.V., "doth it profit"); Jas. 2 : 14, 16, lit., 'What (is) the profit?' See PROFIT.¶ In the Sept., Job 15 : 3.¶

5622 3. ŌPHELEIA (ὠφέλεια), an alternative form to No. 2, akin to C,
AG:900B No. 1, is found in Rom. 3 : 1, "profit," and Jude 16, "advantage."
CB:1261A (i.e., they shew respect of persons for the sake of what they may gain from them). See PROFIT.¶

5624 *Note:* *Ōphelimos*, profitable, is used only in the Pastoral Epistles,
AG:900D 1 Tim. 4 : 8; 2 Tim. 3 : 16; Tit. 3 : 8. See PROFIT.¶
CB:—

B. Verbs.

5623 1. ŌPHELEŌ (ὠφελέω) signifies to be useful, do good, profit, Rom.
AG:900C 2 : 25; with a negative, to be of no use, to effect nothing, Matt. 27 : 24;
CB:1261A John 6 : 63, "profiteth;" 12 : 19, "prevail;" in Luke 9 : 25, A.V., "(what is a man) advantaged?" R.V., "profited." See BETTERED (to be), PREVAIL, PROFIT.

4122 2. PLEONEKTEŌ (πλεονεκτέω), lit., to seek to get more (*pleon*,
AG:667C more, *echō*, to have); hence to get an advantage of, to take advantage of.
CB:1265B In 2 Cor. 7 : 2 the A.V. has "defrauded," the R.V., "took advantage of;" in 1 Thess. 4 : 6, A.V., "defraud," R.V., "wrong." In the other three places the R.V. consistently translates it by the verb to take advantage of, 2 Cor. 2 : 11, of Satan's effort to gain an advantage over the church, through their neglect to restore the backslider; in 2 Cor. 12 : 17, 18, A.V., "make a gain of." See DEFRAUD, GAIN, WRONG.¶

Note: Cp. *pleonektēs*, a covetous person, *pleonexia*, covetousness.

ADVENTURE

1325 DIDŌMI (δίδωμι), to give, is once used of giving oneself to go into a
AG:192C place, to adventure into, Acts 19 : 31, of Paul's thought of going into the
CB:1241C midst of the mob in the theatre at Ephesus. See BESTOW, COMMIT, DELIVER, GIVE.

ADVERSARY

A. Noun.

476 ANTIDIKOS (ἀντίδικος), firstly, an opponent in a lawsuit, Matt. 5 : 25
AG:74A (twice); Luke 12 : 58; 18 : 3, is also used to denote an adversary or an
CB:1236A enemy, without reference to legal affairs, and this is perhaps its meaning in 1 Pet. 5 : 8, where it is used of the Devil. Some would regard the word as there used in a legal sense, since the Devil accuses men before God.¶

B. Verb.

480 ANTIKEIMAI (ἀντικείμαι) is, lit., to lie opposite to, to be set over
AG:74B against. In addition to its legal sense it signifies to withstand; the
CB:— present participle of the verb with the article, which is equivalent to a noun, signifies an adversary, e.g., Luke 13 : 17; 21 : 15; 1 Cor. 16 : 9;

Phil. 1 : 28 ; 1 Tim. 5 : 14. This construction is used of the Man of Sin, in 2 Thess. 2 : 4, and is translated " He that opposeth," where, adopting the noun form, we might render by ' the opponent and self-exalter against . . .' In Gal. 5 : 17 it is use of the antagonism between the Holy Spirit and the flesh in the believer ; in 1 Tim. 1 : 10, of anything, in addition to persons, that is opposed to the doctrine of Christ. In these two places the word is rendered " contrary to."¶ In the Sept. it is used of Satan, Zech. 3 : 1, and of men, Job 13 : 24 ; Isa. 66 : 6. See CONTRARY, OPPOSE.¶

C. Adjective.

HUPENANTIOS (ὑπεναντίος), contrary, opposed, is a strengthened 5227
form of *enantios* (*en*, in, and *antios*, set against). The intensive force AG:838B CB:1252A
is due to the preposition *hupo*. It is translated " contrary to, " in Col. (-ION)
2 : 14, of ordinances ; in Heb. 10 : 27, " adversaries." In each place a more violent form of opposition is suggested than in the case of *enantios*. See CONTRARY.¶

For ADVERSITY, in Heb. 13 : 3, where the verb *kakoucheomai* is translated in the A.V., " suffer adversity," see SUFFER, (*b*), No. 6.

ADVICE, ADVISE

1. GNŌMĒ (γνώμη), connected with *ginōskō*, to know, perceive, firstly 1106
means the faculty of knowledge, reason ; then, that which is thought or AG:163A CB:1248B
known, one's mind. Under this heading there are various meanings : (1) a view, judgment, opinion, 1 Cor. 1 : 10 ; Philm. 14 ; Rev. 17 : 13, 17 ; (2) an opinion as to what ought to be done, either (*a*) by oneself, and so a resolve, or purpose, Acts 20 : 3 ; or (*b*) by others, and so, judgment. advice, 1 Cor. 7 : 25, 40 ; 2 Cor. 8 : 10. See AGREE, JUDGMENT, MIND, PURPOSE, WILL.¶

2. BOULĒ (βουλή), from a root meaning a will, hence a counsel, a 1012
piece of advice, is to be distinguished from *gnōmē* ; *boulē* is the result of AG:145D CB:1239B
determination, *gnōmē* is the result of knowledge. *Boulē* is everywhere rendered by " counsel " in the R.V. except in Acts 27 : 12, " advised," lit., 'gave counsel.' In Acts 13 : 36 the A.V. wrongly has " by the will of God fell on sleep ; " the R.V., " after he had served the counsel of God, fell on sleep." The word is used of the counsel of God, in Luke 7 : 30 ; Acts 2 : 23 ; 4 : 28 ; 13 : 36 ; 20 : 27 ; Eph. 1 : 11 ; Heb. 6 : 17 ; in other passages, of the counsel of men, Luke 23 : 51 ; Acts 27 : 12, 42 ; 1 Cor. 4 : 5. See COUNSEL, WILL.¶

For ADVOCATE see COMFORTER.

AFAR

1. MAKRAN (μακράν), from *makros*, far, Matt. 8 : 30 (A.V., " a good 3112
way ; " R.V., " afar "), a long way off, is used with *eis*, unto, in Acts 2 : 39, AG:487C CB:1257C

" afar off." With the article, in Eph. 2 : 13, 17, it signifies " the (ones) far off." See Far and Way.

3113 AG:487D CB:1257C 2. MAKROTHEN (μακρόθεν), also from *makros*, signifies afar off, from far, Matt. 26 : 58 ; 27 : 55, etc. It is used with *apo*, from, in Mark 5 : 6 ; 14 : 54 ; 15 : 40, etc. ; outside the Synoptists, three times, Rev. 18 : 10, 15, 17.

4207 AG:693D CB:— 3. PORRŌTHEN (πόρρωθεν), afar off, from *porrō*, at a distance, a great way off, is found in Luke 17 : 12 and Heb. 11 : 13.¶

Note : In 2 Pet. 1 : 9, *muōpazō*, to be shortsighted, is translated
3467 AG:531A CB:— " cannot see afar off " (A.V.) ; R.V., " seeing only what is near."

AFFAIR (-S)

4230 AG:697B CB:1266B PRAGMATIA, or PRAGMATEIA (πραγματία), from *pragma*, a deed, denotes a business, occupation, the prosecution of any affair ; in the plural, pursuits, affairs (of life), 2 Tim. 2 : 4.¶

2596 AG:405C CB:1253C *Notes :* (1) *Ta kata*, lit., the (things), with, or respecting a (person), is translated " affairs " in Eph. 6 : 21 and Col. 4 : 7, R.V.

4012 AG:644B CB:1263B (2) *Ta peri*, lit., the (things) concerning (a person), is translated " affairs " in the A.V. of Eph. 6 : 22 and Phil. 1 : 27 (R.V., " state," in each place).

AFFECT

2559 AG:398B CB:1253B KAKOŌ (κακόω), from *kakos*, evil, to treat badly, to hurt, also means to make evil affected, to embitter, Acts 14 : 2. See Evil, Harm, Hurt.

2206 AG:338A CB:1273B *Note :* *Zēloō*, akin to *zeō*, to boil (Eng., zeal), means (*a*) to be jealous, Acts 7 : 9 ; 17 : 5 ; to envy, 1 Cor. 13 : 4 ; to covet, Jas. 4 : 2 ; in a good sense (" jealous over "), in 2 Cor. 11 : 2 ; (*b*) to desire earnestly, 1 Cor. 12 : 31 ; 14 : 1, 39 ; to take a warm interest in, to seek zealously, Gal. 4 : 17, 18, A.V., " zealously affect," " to be zealously affected." The R.V. corrects this to " zealously seek," etc. See Covet, Desire, Envy, Jealous, Zealous.¶

AFFECTION (-S), AFFECTED

A. Nouns.

3806 AG:602D CB:1262C 1. PATHOS (πάθος), from *paschō*, to suffer, primarily denotes whatever one suffers or experiences in any way ; hence, an affection of the mind, a passionate desire. Used by the Greeks of either good or bad desires, it is always used in the N.T. of the latter, Rom. 1 : 26 (A.V., " affections," R.V., " passions ") ; Col. 3 : 5 (A.V., " inordinate affection," R.V., " passion ") ; 1 Thess. 4 : 5 (A.V., " lust," R.V., " passion "). See Lust.¶

4698 AG:763A CB:1269C 2. SPLANCHNA (σπλάγχνα), lit., the bowels, which were regarded by the Greeks as the seat of the more violent passions, by the Hebrews as the seat of the tender affections ; hence the word denotes " tender mercies " and is rendered " affections " in 2 Cor. 6 : 12 (A.V., " bowels ") ; " inward affection," 2 Cor. 7 : 15. See Bowels, Compassion, Heart, Mercy. Cp. *epithumia*, desire.

3. PATHĒMA (πάθημα), akin to No. 1, translated " affections " in 3804
Gal. 5 : 24, A.V., is corrected to " passions " in the R.V. See Affliction, AG:602B CB:1262C
B, No. 3.

B. Adjectives.

1. ASTORGOS (ἄστοργος) signifies without natural affection (*a*, 794
negative, and *storgē*, love of kindred, especially of parents for children AG:118A CB:1238A
and children for parents ; a fanciful etymology associates with this the " stork "), Rom. 1 : 31 ; 2 Tim. 3 : 3.¶

2. PHILOSTORGOS (φιλόστοργος), tenderly loving (from *philos*, 5387
friendly, *storgē*, see No. 1), is used in Rom. 12 : 10, R.V., " tenderly AG:861C CB:1264B
affectioned " (A.V., " kindly affectioned ").¶

Notes: (1) *Phroneō*, to think, to set the mind on, implying moral 5426
interest and reflexion, is translated " set your affection on " in Col. 3 : 2, AG:866A CB:1264C
A.V. (R.V., " set your mind on "). See Careful, Mind, Regard, Savour, Think, Understand.

(2) For *homeiromai* (or *himeiromai*), to be affectionately desirous of, 2442
1 Thess. 2 : 8, see Desire.¶ AG:565B CB:—

AFFIRM

1. DIABEBAIOOMAI (διαβεβαιόομαι), *dia*, intensive, and *bebaioō*, 1226
to confirm, make sure, denotes to assert strongly, " affirm confidently," AG:181D CB:—
1 Tim. 1 : 7 ; Tit. 3 : 8 (A.V., " affirm constantly ").¶

2. DIISCHURIZOMAI (διισχυρίζομαι), as in No. 1, and *ischurizomai*, 1340
to corroborate (*ischuros* " strong ; " see Ability, A, No. 2 and C, No. 2, AG:195B CB:—
Note), primarily signifies to lean upon, then, to affirm stoutly, assert vehemently, Luke 22 : 59 ; Acts 12 : 15.¶

3. PHASKŌ (φάσκω), a frequentative form of the verb *phēmi* (No. 4), 5335
denotes to allege, to affirm by way of alleging or professing, Acts 24 : 9 AG:854B CB:—
(R.V., " affirming," A.V., " saying ") ; 25 : 19 ; Rom. 1 : 22, " professing." Some mss. have it in Rev. 2 : 2, instead of the verb *legō*, to say. See Profess, Say.¶

4. PHĒMI (φημί), to say (primarily by way of enlightening, explaining), 5346
is rendered " affirm " in Rom. 3 : 8. See Say. AG:856B CB:1264A

AFFLICT (-ED), AFFLICTION

A. Verbs.

1. KAKOŌ (κακόω) is translated " afflict," in Acts 12 : 1, R.V. 2559
(A.V., " vex "). See Affect. AG:398B CB:1253B

2. KAKOUCHEŌ (κακουχέω), from *kakos*, evil, and *echō*, to have, 2558
signifies, in the Passive Voice, to suffer ill, to be maltreated, tormented, AG:398B CB:—
Heb. 11 : 37 (A.V., " tormented," R.V., " afflicted ") ; 13 : 3, A.V.,

" suffer adversity," R.V., " evil entreated." See ENTREAT, TORMENT.¶ In the Sept., 1 Kings, 2 : 26 ; 11 : 39.¶

4778 (-Eo) AG:773B CB:— *Note : Sunkakoucheō* (*sun*, with, and No. 1), to be evil entreated with, is used in Heb. 11 : 25.¶

2553 AG:397C CB:1253B 3. KAKOPATHEŌ (κακοπαθέω), from *kakos*, evil, *pathos*, suffering, signifies to suffer hardship. So the R.V. in 2 Tim. 2 : 9 ; and 4 : 5 ; in Jas. 5 : 13, " suffer " (A.V., " afflicted "). See ENDURE, SUFFER.¶

Note : For *sunkakopatheō*, 2 Tim. 1 : 8, see HARDSHIP.

2346 AG:362A CB:1272B 4. THLIBŌ (θλίβω), to suffer affliction, to be troubled, has reference to sufferings due to the pressure of circumstances, or the antagonism of persons, 1 Thess. 3 : 4 ; 2 Thess. 1 : 6, 7 ; " straitened," in Matt. 7 : 14 (R.V.) ; " throng," Mark 3 : 9 ; " afflicted," 2 Cor. 1 : 6 ; 7 : 5 (R.V.) ; 1 Tim. 5 : 10 ; Heb. 11 : 37 ; " pressed," 2 Cor. 4 : 8. Both the verb and the noun (see B, No. 4), when used of the present experience of believers, refer almost invariably to that which comes upon them from without. See NARROW, PRESS, STRAITENED, THRONG, TRIBULATION, TROUBLE.¶

5003 AG:803A CB:1271A 5. TALAIPŌREŌ (ταλαιπωρέω), to be afflicted, is used in Jas. 4 : 9, in the Middle Voice (' afflict yourselves '). It is derived from *tlaō*, to bear, undergo, and *pōros*, a hard substance, a callus, which metaphorically came to signify that which is miserable.¶

-PŌRIA 5004 AG:803B CB:1271A *Note : Talaipōria* (akin to No. 5) denotes misery, hardship, Rom. 3 : 16; Jas. 5 : 1.¶ The corresponding adjective is *talaipōros*, " wretched," Rom. 7 : 24 ; Rev. 3 : 17.¶

-PŌROS 5005 AG:803B CB:1271A

B. Nouns.

2552 AG:397B CB:1253B 1. KAKOPATHEIA (κακοπάθεια), from *kakos*, evil, and *paschō*, to suffer, is rendered " suffering " in Jas. 5 : 10, R.V. (A.V., " suffering affliction ").¶ In Sept., Mal. 1 : 13.¶

2561 AG:398C CB:1253B 2. KAKŌSIS (κάκωσις), affliction, ill treatment, is used in Acts 7 : 34.¶

3804 AG:602B CB:1262C 3. PATHĒMA (πάθημα), from *pathos*, suffering, signifies affliction. The word is frequent in Paul's Epistles and is found three times in Hebrews, four in 1 Peter ; it is used (*a*) of afflictions, Rom. 8 : 18 etc. ; of Christ's sufferings, 1 Pet. 1 : 11 ; 5 : 1 ; Heb. 2 : 9 ; of those as shared by believers, 2 Cor. 1 : 5 ; Phil. 3 : 10 ; 1 Pet. 4 : 13 ; 5 : 1 ; (*b*) of an evil emotion, passion, Rom. 7 : 5 ; Gal. 5 : 24. The connection between the two meanings is that the emotions, whether good or evil, were regarded as consequent upon external influences exerted on the mind (cp. the two meanings of the English " passion "). It is more concrete than No. 1, and expresses in sense (*b*) the uncontrolled nature of evil desires, in contrast to *epithumia*, the general and comprehensive term, lit., what you set your heart upon (Trench, Syn. § lxxxvii). Its concrete character is seen in Heb. 2 : 9. See AFFECTION, MOTION, PASSION, SUFFERING.

3805 AG:602D CB:1262C *Note :* The corresponding verbal form *pathētos*, used in Acts 26 : 23 of the sufferings of Christ, signifies destined to suffer.¶

2347 AG:362B CB:1272B 4. THLIPSIS (θλῖψις) primarily means a pressing, pressure (see A,

No. 4), anything which burdens the spirit. In two passages in Paul's Epistles it is used of future retribution, in the way of affliction, Rom. 2 : 9; 2 Thess. 1 : 6. In Matt. 24 : 9, the A.V. renders it as a verb, "to be afflicted," (R.V., "unto tribulation.") It is coupled with *stenochōria*, anguish, in Rom. 2 : 9; 8 : 35; with *ananke*, distress, 1 Thess. 3 : 7; with *diōgmos*, persecution, Matt. 13 : 21; Mark 4 : 17; 2 Thess. 1 : 4. It is used of the calamities of war, Matt. 24 : 21, 29; Mark 13 : 19, 24; of want, 2 Cor. 8 : 13, lit., 'distress for you;' Phil. 4 : 14 (cp. 1 : 16); Jas. 1 : 27; of the distress of woman in child-birth, John 16 : 21; of persecution, Acts 11 : 19; 14 : 22; 20 : 23; 1 Thess. 3 : 3, 7; Heb. 10 : 33; Rev. 2 : 10; 7 : 14; of the afflictions of Christ, from which (His vicarious sufferings apart) his followers must not shrink, whether sufferings of body or mind, Col. 1 : 24; of sufferings in general, 1 Cor. 7 : 28; 1 Thess. 1 : 6 etc. See ANGUISH, BURDENED, DISTRESS, PERSECUTION, TRIBULATION, TROUBLE.

AFFORD
See
ABILITY

AFFRIGHTED

A. Adjective.

EMPHOBOS (ἔμφοβος), lit., in fear (*en*, in, *phobos*, fear), means 1719
"affrighted," Luke 24 : 5, R.V. (A.V., "afraid"); 24 : 37; Acts 10 : 4, AG:257D CB:—
R.V. (A.V., "afraid"); Rev. 11 : 13. The R.V. omits it in Acts 22 : 9.
See TREMBLE.

B. Verbs.

1. PTURŌ (πτύρω), to frighten, scare, is used in the Passive Voice 4426
in Phil. 1 : 28, "be affrighted," R.V., "be terrified," A.V. See AG:727D CB:—
TERRIFY.¶

2. EKTHAMBEŌ (ἐκθαμβέω), to throw into terror, is used in the 1568
Passive sense, to be amazed, "affrighted," Mark 16 : 5, 6, A.V. (R.V., AG:240B CB:1244A
"amazed"); Mark 9 : 15, "were greatly amazed;" 14 : 33, "to be
greatly amazed" (R.V.), "to be sore amazed" (A.V.). See AMAZE,
B, No. 4.¶

AFLAME
See BURN

For AFOOT see FOOT, B, No. 2

AFORE, AFOREHAND

The Greek words with these meanings consist of prefixes to verbs, signifying to come, prepare, promise, write afore, etc. See under these words.

AFOREPROMISED

PROEPANGELLOMAI (προεπαγγέλλομαι), to promise before (*pro*, 4279
before, *epangellomai*, to promise), is translated by the one word "afore- AG:705B CB:1266C
promised," in the R.V. of 2 Cor. 9 : 5; in Rom. 1 : 2, "promised afore."¶

AFORETIME

4218 AG:695A CB:1266B 1. POTE (ποτέ) signifies once, at some time, John 9 : 13 (cp. *proteron*, in ver. 8) ; Eph. 2 : 2, 11 ; Col. 3 : 7 ; Tit. 3 : 3 ; Philm. 11 ; 1 Pet. 3 : 5, 20. In all these the R.V. translates it "aforetime." The A.V. varies it with "in time past," "some time," "sometimes," "in the old time."

4386 AG:721D CB:1267B 2. PROTERON (πρότερον), the comparative of *pro*, before, aforetime, as being definitely antecedent to something else, is more emphatic than *pote* in this respect. See, e.g., John 6 : 62 ; 7 : 50 ; 9 : 8 ; 2 Cor. 1 : 13 ; Gal. 4 : 13 ; 1 Tim. 1 : 13 ; Heb. 4 : 6 ; 7 : 27 ; 10 : 32 ; 1 Pet. 1 : 14. See BEFORE, FIRST, FORMER.¶

For AFRAID see AFFRIGHTED, A, FEAR, A, No. 2, B, No. 3, D, SORE

For AFRESH see under CROSS, CRUCIFY, B

AFTER, AFTERWARD (-S)

The following are adverbs only. For prepositions and conjunctions see Note † p. 9.

1564 AG:239B CB:— 1. EKEITHEN (ἐκεῖθεν), thence, is once used to signify "afterwards," in the sense of "then," from that time, Acts 13 : 21. See THENCE.

1836 AG:276A CB:— 2 HEXĒS (ἑξῆς) denotes "after" with the significance of a succession of events, an event following next in order after another, Luke 7 : 11 ; 9 : 37 ; Acts 21 : 1 ; 25 : 17 ; 27 : 18.¶

2517 AG:388D CB:— 3. KATHEXĒS (καθεξῆς), a strengthened form of No. 2, denotes "afterward," or "in order" (*kata*, according to, and No. 2), Luke 1 : 3 ; 8 : 1 ; Acts 3 : 24 ; 11 : 4 ; 18 : 23.¶

3347 AG:514A CB:— 4. METEPEITA (μετέπειτα), afterwards, without necessarily indicating an order of events, as in Nos. 1 and 2, is found in Heb. 12 : 17.¶

5305 AG:849C CB:1252B 5. HUSTERON (ὕστερον), afterwards, with the suggestion of at length, is found in Matt. 4 : 2 ; 21 : 29, 32, 37 (A.V., "last of all") ; 22 : 27 ; 25 : 11 ; 26 : 60 (A.V., "at the last") ; Mark 16 : 14 ; Luke 4 : 2 ; 20 : 32 (A.V., "last") ; John 13 : 36 ; Heb. 12 : 11. See LAST.¶

EITA 1534 AG:233D CB:1243B EPEITA 1899 AG:284C CB:— *Note : Eita* and *epeita*, then, afterwards, or thereupon, are translated "afterward" or "afterwards" in the A.V. of Mark 4 : 17 (*eita*) and Gal. 1 : 21 ; 1 Cor. 15 : 23, 46 (*epeita*) ; always "then" in the R.V. See THEN.

AGAIN

1364 AG:199D CB:— 1. DIS (δίς), the ordinary numeral adverb signifying twice, is rendered "again" in Phil. 4 : 16, "ye sent once and again unto my need," and in 1 Thess. 2 : 18, where Paul states that he would have come to the Thessalonians "once and again," that is, twice at least he had attempted to do so. See TWICE.

3825 AG:606C CB:1261C 2. PALIN (πάλιν), the regular word for "again," is used chiefly in two senses, (*a*) with reference to repeated action ; (*b*) rhetorically, in the sense of " moreover " or " further," indicating a statement to be added in the course of an argument, e.g., Matt. 5 : 33 ; or with the meaning ' on the other hand,' ' in turn,' Luke 6 : 43 ; 1 Cor. 12 : 21 ; 2 Cor. 10 : 7 ; 1 John 2 : 8. In the first chapter of Hebrews, ver. 5, *palin* simply introduces an additional quotation ; in ver. 6 this is not so. There the R.V. rightly puts the word " again " in connection with " He bringeth in the firstborn into the world," " When He again bringeth etc." That is to say, *palin* is here set in contrast to the time when God *first* brought His Son into the world. This statement, then, refers to the future Second Advent of Christ. The word is used far more frequently in the Gospel of John than in any other book in the New Testament.

Note : Other words are rendered " again " in the A.V., which the **DEUTEROS**
R.V. corrects, namely, *deuteros* and *anōthen*. *Deuteros* signifies " a second **1208 AG:177A**
time," John 9 : 24 ; Acts 11 : 9. *Anōthen* signifies from above, or anew. **CB:1241A**
See the R.V. of John 3 : 3, 7, and the A.V. and R.V. of ver. 31. Nicodemus **ANŌTHEN**
was not puzzled about birth from Heaven ; what perplexed him was that **509 AG:77A**
a person must be born a second time. This the context makes clear. **CB:1236A**
This is really the meaning in Gal. 4 : 9, where it is associated with *palin*, " over again." The idea is " anew," for, though the bondage would be the same in essence and effect, it would be new in not being in bondage to idols but to the Law. See also Matt. 27 : 51 ; Mark 15 : 38 ; John 19 : 23, " from the top." *Anōthen* may mean " from the first," in Luke 1 : 3 and Acts 26 : 5. For the meaning " from above," see Jas. 1 : 17; 3 : 15, 17.¶

AGAINST : see Note, † p. 1

AGE

A. Nouns.

1. AIŌN (αἰών), an age, era (to be connected with *aei*, ever, rather **165**
than with *aō*, to breathe), signifies a period of indefinite duration, or time **AG:27B CB:1234A**
viewed in relation to what takes place in the period.

The force attaching to the word is not so much that of the actual length of a period, but that of a period marked by spiritual or moral characteristics. This is illustrated in the use of the adjective [see Note (1) below] in the phrase " life eternal," in John 17 : 3, in respect of the increasing knowledge of God.

The phrases containing this word should not be rendered literally, but consistently with its sense of indefinite duration. Thus *eis ton aiōna* does not mean " unto the age " but " for ever " (see, e.g., Heb. 5 : 6). The Greeks contrasted that which came to an end with that which was expressed by this phrase, which shows that they conceived of it as expressing interminable duration.

The word occurs most frequently in the Gospel of John, the Hebrews and Revelation. It is sometimes wrongly rendered " world." See COURSE, ETERNAL, WORLD. It is a characteristic word of John's Gospel.

166 AG:28B CB:1234A *Notes*: (1) *Aiōnios*, the adjective corresponding, denoting eternal, is set in contrast with *proskairos*, lit., 'for a season,' 2 Cor. 4 : 18. It is used of that which in nature is endless, as, e.g., of God, Rom. 16 : 26, His power, 1 Tim. 6 : 16, His glory, 1 Pet. 5 : 10, the Holy Spirit, Heb. 9 : 14, redemption, Heb. 9 : 12, salvation, 5 : 9, life in Christ, John 3 : 16, the resurrection body, 2 Cor. 5 : 1, the future rule of Christ, 2 Pet. 1 : 11, which is declared to be without end, Luke 1 : 33, of sin that never has forgiveness, Mark 3 : 29, the judgment of God, Heb. 6 : 2, and of fire, one of its instruments, Matt. 18 : 8 ; 25 : 41 ; Jude 7. See ETERNAL, EVERLASTING.

(2) In Rev. 15 : 3, the R.V. has "King of the ages," according to the texts which have *aiōnōn* ; the A.V. has "of saints" (*hagiōn*, in inferior mss.). There is good ms. evidence for *ethnōn*, "nations," (A.V., marg.), probably a quotation from Jer. 10 : 7.

1074 AG:153D CB:1248A 2. GENEA (γενεά), connected with *ginomai*, to become, primarily signifies a begetting, or birth ; then that which has been begotten, a family ; or successive members of a genealogy, Matt. 1 : 17, or of a race of people, possessed of similar characteristics, pursuits, etc., (of a bad character) Matt. 17 : 17 ; Mark 9 : 19 ; Luke 9 : 41 ; 16 : 8 ; Acts 2 : 40 ; or of the whole multitude of men living at the same time, Matt. 24 : 34 ; Mark 13 : 30 ; Luke 1 : 48 ; 21 : 32 ; Phil. 2 : 15, and especially of those of the Jewish race living at the same period, Matt. 11 : 16, etc. Transferred from people to the time in which they lived, the word came to mean an age, i.e., a period ordinarily occupied by each successive generation, say, of thirty or forty years, Acts 14 : 16 ; 15 : 21 ; Eph. 3 : 5 ; Col. 1 : 26 ; see also, e.g., Gen. 15 : 16. In Eph. 3 : 21 *genea* is combined with *aiōn* in a remarkable phrase in a doxology : "Unto Him be the glory in the church and in Christ Jesus, unto all generations for ever and ever (wrongly in A.V. 'all ages, world without end')." The word *genea* is to be distinguished from *aiōn*, as not denoting a period of unlimited duration. See GENERATION, NATION, TIME.

2244 AG:345A CB:1249C 3. HĒLIKIA (ἡλικία), primarily an age, as a certain length of life, came to mean (*a*) a particular time of life, as when a person is said to be "of age," John 9 : 21, 23, or beyond a certain stage of life, Heb. 11 : 11 ; (*b*) elsewhere only of stature, e.g., Matt. 6 : 27 ; Luke 2 : 52 ; 12 : 25 ; 19 : 3 ; Eph. 4 : 13. Some regard Matt. 6 : 27 and Luke 12 : 25 as coming under (*a*). It is to be distinguished from *aiōn* and *genea*, since it has to do simply with matters relating to an individual, either his time of life or his height. See STATURE.¶

2250 AG:345D CB:1249C 4. HĒMERA (ἡμέρα), a day, is rendered "age" in Luke 2 : 36, "of a great age" (lit., 'advanced in many days'). In Luke 3 : 23 there is no word in the original corresponding to age. The phrase is simply "about thirty years." See DAY, JUDGMENT, TIME, YEAR.

B. Adjectives.

5230 AG:839D CB:1252A 1. HUPERAKMOS (ὑπέρακμος) in 1 Cor. 7 : 36 is rendered "past the flower of her age ; " more lit., ' beyond the bloom or flower (*acme*) of life.'¶

2. TELEIOS (τέλειος), complete, perfect, from *telos*, an end, is trans- 5046
lated " of full age " in Heb. 5 : 14, A.V. (R.V., " fullgrown man "). AG:809A CB:1271B

Note: In Mark 5 : 42, R.V., " old," A.V., " of the age of," is, lit., ' of twelve years.' For " of great age," Luke 2 : 36, see STRICKEN. For " of mine own age," Gal. 1 : 14, R.V., see EQUAL, B, No. 2.

AGED

A. Nouns.

1. PRESBUTĒS (πρεσβύτης), an elderly man, is a longer form of 4246
presbus, the comparative degree of which is *presbuteros*, a senior, elder, AG:700D CB:1266B
both of which, as also the verb *presbeuō*, to be elder, to be an ambassador, are derived from *proeisbainō*, to be far advanced. The noun is found in Luke 1 : 18, " an old man ; " Tit. 2 : 2, " aged men," and Philm. 9, where the R.V. marg., " Paul an ambassador," is to be accepted, the original almost certainly being *presbeutēs* (not *presbutēs*), an ambassador. So he describes himself in Eph. 6 : 20. As Lightfoot points out, he is hardly likely to have made his age a ground of appeal to Philemon, who, if he was the father of Archippus, cannot have been much younger than Paul himself. See OLD.

2. PRESBUTIS (πρεσβῦτις), the feminine of No. 1, an aged woman, 4247
is found in Tit. 2 : 3.¶ AG:700D CB:1266B

B. Verb.

GĒRASKŌ (γηράσκω), from *gēras*, old age, signifies to grow old, 1095
John 21 : 18 (" when thou shalt be old ") and Heb. 8 : 13 (R.V., " that AG:158A CB:1248B
which . . . waxeth aged," A.V., " old "). See OLD.¶

AGENT See SERVANT

For AGO see LONG, A, No. 5, and in combination with other words.

AGITATE See STIR

AGONY

AGŌNIA (ἀγωνία), Eng., agony, was used among the Greeks as an 74
alternative to *agōn*, a place of assembly ; then for the contests or games AG:15A CB:1233C
which took place there, and then to denote intense emotion. It was more frequently used eventually in this last respect, to denote severe emotional strain and anguish. So in Luke 22 : 44, of the Lord's agony in Gethsemane.¶

AGREE, AGREEMENT

A. Verbs.

1. SUMPHŌNEŌ (συμφωνέω), lit., to sound together (*sun*, together, 4856
phōnē, a sound), i.e., to be in accord, primarily of musical instruments, AG:780D CB:—
is used in the N.T. of the agreement (*a*) of persons concerning a matter, Matt. 18 : 19 ; 20 : 2, 13 ; Acts 5 : 9 ; (*b*) of the writers of Scripture, Acts 15 : 15 ; (*c*) of things that are said to be congruous in their nature, Luke 5 : 36.¶

Note: Cp. *sumphōnēsis*, concord, 2 Cor. 6 : 15,¶, and *sumphōnia*, music, Luke 15 : 25.¶

4934 2. SUNTITHĒMI (συντίθημι), lit., to put together (*sun*, with, *tithēmi*,
(-EMAI) AG:790C to put), in the Middle Voice, means to make an agreement, or to assent to;
CB:— translated "covenanted" in Luke 22 : 5, "agreed" in John 9 : 22, and
Acts 23 : 20; "assented" in Acts 24 : 9.¶

Note: For the synonym *sunkatatithēmi*, a strengthened form of No. 2, see CONSENT, No. 4.

2132 AG:323B 3. EUNOEŌ (εὐνοέω), lit., to be well-minded, well-disposed (*eu*, well,
CB:— *nous*, the mind), is found in Matt. 5 : 25, "agree with,"¶
3982 4. PEITHŌ (πείθω), to persuade, is rendered "agreed" in Acts 5 : 40,
AG:639A CB:1263A where the meaning is "they yielded to him." See ASSURE, BELIEVE,
CONFIDENT, FRIEND, OBEY, PERSUADE, TRUST, YIELD.

B. Nouns.

1106 1. GNŌMĒ (γνώμη), mind, will, is used with *poieō*, to make, in the
AG:163A CB:1248B sense of to agree, Rev. 17 : 17 (twice), lit., 'to do His mind, and to make
one mind;' R.V., "to come to one mind," A.V., "to agree." See
ADVICE, JUDGMENT, MIND, PURPOSE, WILL.
4783 2. SUNKATATHESIS (συγκατάθεσις), akin to A, No. 3, occurs in
AG:773C CB:— 2 Cor. 6 : 16.¶

C. Adjectives.

800 1. ASUMPHŌNOS (ἀσύμφωνος), inharmonious (*a*, negative,
AG:118C CB:— *sumphōnos*, harmonious), is used in Acts 28 : 25, "they agreed not."¶
2470 2. ISOS (ἴσος), equal, is used with the verb to be, signifying to agree,
AG:381A CB:1253A Mark 14 : 56, 59, lit., 'their thought was not equal one with the other.'
See EQUAL, LIKE, MUCH.
SUMPHŌNOS *Note:* *Sumphōnos*, harmonious, agreeing, is used only with the
4859 AG:781B preposition *ek* in the phrase *ek sumphōnou*, by consent, lit., out of agree-
CB:— ment, 1 Cor. 7 : 5. In Mark 14 : 70 some texts have the verb *homoiazō*,
HOMOIAZŌ 3662 "agreeth," A.V.
AG:566C CB:—

For AGROUND see RUN, No. 11

AH!

3758 1. OUA (οὐά), an interjection of derision and insult, is translated
AG:591A CB:— Ha! in Mark 15 : 29, R.V.¶
1436 2. EA (ἔα), an interjection of surprise, fear and anger, was the
AG:211A CB:— ejaculation of the man with the spirit of an unclean demon, Luke 4 : 34,
AID See HELP R.V.; the A.V. renders it "Let us alone" (see R.V. marg.).¶

AIL(MENT) See SICK(NESS)

AIM

PHILOTIMEOMAI (φιλοτιμέομαι), lit., to be fond of honour (*phileō*, to
5389 love, *timē*, honour), and so, actuated by this motive, to strive to bring
AG:861C CB:1264B something to pass; hence, to be ambitious, to make it one's aim, Rom.

15 : 20, of Paul's aim in Gospel pioneering, R.V. (A.V., "strive"); 2 Cor. 5 : 9, of the aim of believers "to be well-pleasing" unto the Lord, R.V. (A.V., "labour"); in 1 Thess. 4 : 11, of the aim of believers to be quiet, do their own business and work with their own hands; both Versions translate it "study." Some would render it, 'strive restlessly;' perhaps 'strive earnestly' is nearer the mark, but 'make it one's aim' is a good translation in all three places. See LABOUR, STRIVE, STUDY.¶

AIR

1. AĒR (ἀήρ), (Eng., air), signifies the atmosphere, certainly in five of 109
the seven occurrences, Acts 22 : 23; 1 Cor. 9 : 26; 14 : 9; Rev. 9 : 2; AG:20B CB:1233A
16 : 17, and almost certainly in the other two, Eph. 2 : 2 and 1 Thess. 4 : 17.¶

2. OURANOS (οὐρανός) denotes the heaven. The R.V. always renders 3772
it "heaven." The A.V. translates it "air" in Matt. 8 : 20. In the AG:593D CB:1261B
phrase "the fowls (or birds) of the heaven" the A.V. always has "air;" "sky" in Matt. 16 : 2, 3; Luke 12 : 56; in all other instances "heaven." The word is probably derived from a root meaning to cover or encompass. See HEAVEN, SKY.

For ALABASTER see CRUSE

ALARM(ED) See AMAZE(D), FEAR

For ALAS! see WOE

ALBEIT

HINA (ἵνα), a conjunction, meaning "that," and so rendered in 2443
Philm. 19, R.V., for A.V., "albeit." AG:376D CB:1250C

ALERT See AWAKE, WATCHFUL

ALIEN

ALLOTRIOS (ἀλλότριος), primarily, belonging to another (the opposite 245
to *idios*, one's own), hence came to mean foreign, strange, not of one's AG:40C CB:1234C
own family, alien, an enemy; "aliens" in Heb. 11 : 34, elsewhere "strange," etc. See MAN'S, *Note* (1), STRANGE, STRANGER.

ALIENATE

APALLOTRIOŌ (ἀπαλλοτριόω) consists of *apo*, from, and the above; 526
it signifies to be rendered an alien, to be alienated. In Eph. 2 : 12 the AG:80B CB:1236B
R.V. corrects to the verbal form "alienated," for the noun "aliens;" elsewhere in Eph. 4 : 18 and Col. 1 : 21; the condition of the unbeliever is presented in a threefold state of alienation, (*a*) from the commonwealth of Israel, (*b*) from the life of God, (*c*) from God Himself.¶ The word is used of Israelites in the Sept. of Ezek. 14 : 5 ("estranged") and of the wicked in general, Psa. 58 : 3.

ALIKE

Note: In Rom. 14 : 5, this word is in italics. This addition is not needed in the translation.

For ALIVE see LIFE, C, LIVE, No. 6

ALL

A. Adjectives.

3956 AG:631A CB:1262C 1. PAS (πᾶς) radically means "all." Used without the article it means "every," every kind or variety. So the R.V. marg. in Eph. 2 : 21, "every building," and the text in 3 : 15, "every family," and the R.V. marg. of Acts 2 : 36, "every house;" or it may signify the highest degree, the maximum of what is referred to, as, "with all boldness" Acts 4 : 29. Before proper names of countries, cities and nations, and before collective terms, like "Israel," it signifies either "all" or "the whole," e.g., Matt. 2 : 3; Acts 2 : 36. Used with the article, it means the whole of one object. In the plural it signifies the totality of the persons or things referred to. Used without a noun it virtually becomes a pronoun, meaning "everyone" or "anyone." In the plural with a noun it means "all." The neuter singular denotes "everything" or "anything whatsoever." One form of the neuter plural (*panta*) signifies wholly, together, in all ways, in all things, Acts 20 : 35; 1 Cor. 9 : 25. The neuter plural without the article signifies all things severally, e.g., John 1 : 3; 1 Cor. 2 : 10; preceded by the article it denotes all things, as constituting a whole, e.g., Rom. 11 : 36; 1 Cor. 8 : 6; Eph. 3 : 9. See EVERY, *Note* (1), WHOLE.

537 AG:81D CB:1249B 2. HAPAS (ἅπας), a strengthened form of *pas*, signifies quite all, the whole, and, in the plural, all, all things. Preceded by an article and followed by a noun it means the whole of. In 1 Tim. 1 : 16 the significance is 'the whole of His longsuffering,' or 'the fulness of His longsuffering.' See EVERY, WHOLE.

3650 AG:564D CB:1251A 3. HOLOS (ὅλος), the whole, all, is most frequently used with the article followed by a noun, e.g., Matt. 4 : 23. It is used with the article alone, in John 7 : 23, "every whit;" Acts 11 : 26; 21 : 31; 28 : 30; Tit. 1 : 11; Luke 5 : 5, in the best texts. See ALTOGETHER.

3648 AG:564C CB:— *Note:* The adjective *holoklēros*, lit., whole-lot, entire, stresses the separate parts which constitute the whole, no part being incomplete. See ENTIRE.

B. Adverbs.

3654 AG:565B CB:1251A 1. HOLŌS (ὅλως) signifies "at all," Matt. 5 : 34; 1 Cor. 15 : 29; "actually," 1 Cor. 5 : 1, R.V. (A.V., wrongly, "commonly"); "altogether," 1 Cor. 6 : 7 (A.V., "utterly").¶

3651 AG:565A CB:— *Notes:* (1) *Holotelēs*, from A, No. 3, and *telos*, complete, signifies wholly, through and through, 1 Thess. 5 : 23, lit., 'whole complete'; there, not an increasing degree of sanctification is intended, but the sanctification of the believer in every part of his being.¶

(2) The synonym *katholou*, a strengthened form of *holou* signifies 2527 AG:391A
"at all," Acts 4 : 18.¶ CB:—

2. PANTŌS (πάντως), when used without a negative, signifies wholly, 3843 AG:609B CB:—
entirely, by all means, Acts 18 : 21 (A.V.) ; 1 Cor. 9 : 22 ; altogether, 1 Cor. 9 : 10 ; no doubt, doubtless, Luke 4 : 23, R.V. (A.V., "surely") ; Acts 28 : 4. In 21 : 22 it is translated "certainly," R.V., for A.V., "needs" (lit., 'by all means'). With a negative it signifies in no wise, Rom. 3 : 9 ; 1 Cor. 5 : 10 ; 16 : 12 ("at all"). See ALTOGETHER, DOUBT (NO), MEANS, SURELY, WISE.¶

C. Pronoun.

HOSA (ὅσα), the neuter plural of *hosos*, as much as, chiefly used in the 3745 AG:586B CB:1251B
plural, is sometimes rendered "all that," e.g., Acts 4 : 23 ; 14 : 27. It really means "whatsoever things." See Luke 9 : 10, R.V., "what things."

ALLEGE

PARATITHĒMI (παρατίθημι), to place beside or to set before (*para*, 3908 AG:622D CB:—
beside, *tithēmi*, to put), while often used in its literal sense of material things, as well as in its more common significance, to commit, entrust, twice means to set before one in teaching, as in putting forth a parable, Matt. 13 : 24, 31, R.V. Once it is used of setting subjects before one's hearers by way of argument and proof, of Paul, in "opening and alleging" facts concerning Christ, Acts 17 : 3. See COMMEND, COMMIT, PUT, SET.

Note : Legō is rendered "put forth" in the A.V. of Luke 14 : 7 ; 3004 AG:468A CB:1256C
but *legō* signifies to speak ; hence the R.V., "spake." The A.V. seems to be an imitation of *paratithēmi* in Matt. 13 : 24, 31. See SAY.

ALLEGORY

ALLĒGOREŌ (ἀλληγορέω), translated in Gal. 4 : 24 "contain an 238 AG:39B CB:1234C
allegory" (A.V., "are an allegory"), formed from *allos*, other, and *agoreuō*, to speak in a place of assembly (*agora*, the market-place), came to signify to speak, not according to the primary sense of the word, but so that the facts stated are applied to illustrate principles. The allegorical meaning does not do away with the literal meaning of the narrative. There may be more than one allegorical meaning though, of course, only one literal meaning. Scripture histories represent or embody spiritual principles, and these are ascertained, not by the play of the imagination, but by the rightful application of the doctrines of Scripture.¶

ALLEY See LANE

For ALLELUIA (which has been robbed of its initial aspirate) see HALLELUJAH.

ALLOT See DISTRIBUTE, DIVIDE

For ALLOTTED see CHARGE, A (*b*), No. 4

ALLOW

1381 1. DOKIMAZŌ (δοκιμάζω), to prove with a view to approving, is
AG:202C CB:1242A twice translated by the verb to allow in the A.V.; the R.V. corrects to
"approveth" in Rom. 14:22, and "have been approved," 1 Thess. 2:4,
of being qualified to be entrusted with the Gospel; in Rom. 1:28, with
the negative, the R.V. has "refused," for A.V., "did not like." See
APPROVE.

1097 2. GINŌSKŌ (γινώσκω), to know, is rendered "allow" in Rom. 7:15
AG:160D CB:1248B (A.V.); the R.V. has "that which I do I know not;" i.e., 'I do not
recognize, as a thing for which I am responsible.' See AWARE, CAN,
FEEL, KNOW, PERCEIVE, RESOLVE, SPEAK, SURE, UNDERSTAND.

4909 3. SUNEUDOKEŌ (συνευδοκέω), to consent or fully approve (*sun*,
AG:788D CB:— with, *eu*, well, *dokeō*, to think), is translated "allow" in Luke 11:48;
"was consenting" in Acts 8:1; 22:20. See CONSENT.

4327 4. PROSDECHOMAI (προσδέχομαι), mistranslated "allow" in Acts
AG:712B CB:1267A 24:15, A.V., means to wait for, in contrast to rejection, there said of
entertaining a hope; hence the R.V., "look for." See ACCEPT, A, No. 3.

ALLOWANCE See PORTION

For ALLURE see BEGUILE, No. 4, ENTICE

ALMIGHTY

3841 PANTOKRATŌR (παντοκράτωρ), almighty, or ruler of all (*pas*, all,
AG:608D CB:1261C *krateō*, to hold, or to have strength), is used of God only, and is found,
in the Epistles, only in 2 Cor. 6:18, where the title is suggestive in connection with the context; elsewhere only in the Apocalypse, nine times. In one place, 19:6, the A.V. has "omnipotent," R.V., "(the Lord our God,) the Almighty."¶ The word is introduced in the Sept. as a translation of "Lord (or God) of hosts," e.g., Jer. 5:14 and Amos 4:13.

ALMOST

A. Adverb.

4975 SCHEDON (σχεδόν) is used either (*a*) of locality, Acts 19:26, or
AG:797A CB:— (*b*) of degree, Acts 13:44; Heb. 9:22.¶

B. Verb.

3195 MELLŌ (μέλλω), to be about to do anything, or to delay, is used in
AG:500D CB:1258A connection with a following verb in the sense of "almost," in Acts 21:27,
lit., 'And when the seven days were about to be completed.' In Acts 26:28 the A.V., "Almost thou persuadest me to be a Christian" obscures the sense; the R.V. rightly has "with but little persuasion;" lit., 'in a little.' See ABOUT, B.

ALMS, ALMSDEEDS

1654 ELEĒMOSUNĒ (ἐλεημοσύνη), connected with *eleēmōn*, merciful,
AG:249D CB:1244A signifies (*a*) mercy, pity, particularly in giving alms, Matt. 6:1 (see
below), 2, 3, 4; Acts 10:2; 24:17; (*b*) the benefaction itself, the

alms (the effect for the cause), Luke 11 : 41 ; 12 : 33 ; Acts 3 : 2, 3, 10 ; 9 : 36, " alms-deeds " ; 10 : 2, 4, 31.¶

Note : In Matt. 6 : 1, the R.V., translating *dikaiosunē*, according to the most authentic texts, has " righteousness," for A.V., " alms."

ALOES

ALOĒ (ἀλόη), an aromatic tree, the soft, bitter wood of which was 250
used by Orientals for the purposes of fumigation and embalming, John AG:41B CB:—
19 : 39 (see also Num. 24 : 6 ; Psa. 45 : 8 ; Prov. 7 : 17).¶ In the Sept.,
S. of Sol. 4 : 14.¶

ALONE (LET ALONE)

A. Adjective.

MONOS (μόνος) denotes single, alone, solitary, Matt. 4 : 4 etc. See ONLY, SELF.

B. Adverbs.

1. MONON (μόνον), the neuter of A., meaning only, exclusively, 3440
e.g., Rom. 4 : 23 ; Acts 19 : 26, is translated " alone " in the A.V. of AG:527C CB:1259B
John 17 : 20 ; R.V., " only." See ONLY.

2. KATA MONAS (κατὰ μόνας) signifies apart, in private, alone, 2651 AG:527C
Mark 4 : 10 ; Luke 9 : 18. Some texts have the phrase as one word.¶ (MONOS 3.)

C. Verb. CB:1253C

APHIĒMI (ἀφίημι) signifies to send away, set free ; also to let alone, 863
Matt. 15 : 14 ; Mark 14 : 6 ; Luke 13 : 8 ; John 11 : 48 ; 12 : 7 (R.V., AG:125C CB:1236B
" suffer her ") ; in Acts 5 : 38 some texts have *easate* from *eaō*, to permit.
See CRY, FORGIVE, FORSAKE, LAY, *Note* (2), LEAVE, LET, OMIT, PUT,
No. 16, *Note*, REMIT, SEND, SUFFER, YIELD.

Notes : (1) The phrase *kath' heautēn* means " by (or in) itself," Jas. HEAUTOU 1438
2 : 17, R.V., for A.V., " being alone " (see A.V., margin). AG:211D
(2) The phrase *kat' idian*, Mark 4 : 34, signifies in private, " privately," CB:1249B
R.V. (A.V., " when they were alone "). IDIOS 2398
(3) For " let us alone " see AH ! AG:369C CB:1252C

For ALONG see the R.V. of Acts 17 : 23 and 27 : 13.

For ALOUD see CRY, B, No. 2

ALREADY

ĒDĒ (ἤδη) is always used of time in the N.T. and means now, at (or by) 2235
this time, sometimes in the sense of " already," i.e. without mentioning AG:344A CB:1242C
or insisting upon anything further, e.g., 1 Tim. 5 : 15. In 1 Cor. 4 : 8
and 1 John 2 : 8 the R.V. corrects the A.V. " now," and, in 2 Tim. 4 : 6,
the A.V. " now ready to be," by the rendering " already."

See also John 9 : 27 (A.V., " already," R.V., " even now ") and 1 Cor. 6 : 7 (A.V., " now," R.V., " already ").

5348 AG:856D CB:1264C *Notes:* (1) *Phthanō*, to anticipate, be beforehand with, signifies to attain already, in Phil. 3 : 16. See ATTAIN, COME, PRECEDE.

4258 AG:702C CB:— (2) *Proamartanō*, to sin before, or heretofore, is translated "have sinned already" in 2 Cor. 12 : 21, A.V.; both Versions have "heretofore" in 13 : 2.

ALSO

2532 AG:391D CB:1253A 1. KAI (*καί*) has three chief meanings, "and," "also," "even." When *kai* means "also" it precedes the word which it stresses. In English the order should be reversed. In John 9 : 40, e.g., the R.V. rightly has "are we also blind?" instead of "are we blind also?" In Acts 2 : 26 the R.V. has "moreover My flesh also," instead of "moreover also . . ." See EVEN.

2089 AG:315C CB:1247A 2. ETI (*ἔτι*), "yet" or "further," is used (*a*) of time, (*b*) of degree, and in this sense is once translated "also," Luke 14 : 26, "his own life also." Here the meaning probably is 'and, further, even his own life' (the force of the *kai* being "even"). No other particles mean "also." See EVEN, FURTHER, LONGER, MORE, MOREOVER, STILL, THENCEFORTH, YET.

5037 AG:807B CB:— *Note:* The particle *te* means "both" or "and."

ALTAR

2379 AG:366D CB:1272C 1. THUSIASTĒRION (*θυσιαστήριον*), probably the neuter of the adjective *thusiastērios*, is derived from *thusiazō*, to sacrifice. Accordingly it denotes an altar for the sacrifice of victims, though it was also used for the altar of incense, e.g., Luke 1 : 11. In the N.T. this word is reserved for the altar of the true God, Matt. 5 : 23, 24; 23 : 18–20, 35; Luke 11 : 51; 1 Cor. 9 : 13; 10 : 18, in contrast to *bōmos*, No. 2, below. In the Sept. *thusiastērion* is mostly, but not entirely, used for the Divinely appointed altar; it is used for idol altars, e.g., in Judg. 2 : 2; 6 : 25; 2 Kings 16 : 10.

1041 AG:148D CB:1239B 2. BŌMOS (*βωμός*), properly, an elevated place, always denotes either a pagan altar or an altar reared without Divine appointment. In the N.T. the only place where this is found is Acts 17 : 23, as this is the only mention of such. Three times in the Sept., but only in the Apocrypha, *bōmos* is used for the Divine altar. In Josh. 22 the Sept. translators have carefully observed the distinction, using *bōmos* for the altar which the two and a half tribes erected, verses 10, 11, 16, 19, 23, 26, 34, no Divine injunction being given for this; in verses 19, 28, 29, where the altar ordained of God is mentioned, *thusiastērion* is used.¶

ALTER See CHANGE

For ALTERED see OTHER, No. 2

ALTHOUGH: see Note †, p. 1

ALTOGETHER

A. Adjective.

HOLOS (ὅλος), whole, is rendered " altogether " in John 9 : 34. It 3650
is sometimes subjoined to an adjective or a verb, as in this case, to show AG:564D CB:1251A
that the idea conveyed by the adjective or verb belongs to the whole person or thing referred to. So here, lit., ' thou wast altogether (i.e., completely) born in sins.' Cp. Matt. 13 : 33, R.V. ; Luke 11 : 36 ; 13 : 21 ; John 13 : 10, R.V. (rendered " every whit "). See ALL, and EVERY WHIT.

B. Adverbs.

1. PANTŌS (πάντως), from *pas*, " all," is translated in various ways. 3843
The rendering " altogether " is found only in 1 Cor. 5 : 10 (where the AG:609B CB:—
R.V. margin gives the alternative meaning, " not at all meaning the fornicators of this world ") and 9 : 10 (marg., " doubtless "). The other renderings are, in Luke 4 : 23, " doubtless " (A.V., " surely ") ; in Acts 18 : 21, " by all means," (A.V., only) ; so in 1 Cor. 9 : 22, both R.V. and A.V. ; in Acts 21 : 22, " certainly " (A.V., " needs," which does not give an accurate meaning) ; in Acts 28 : 4, " no doubt ; " in Rom. 3 : 9, " in no wise " (lit., ' not at all '), so in 1 Cor. 16 : 12. In Acts 26 : 29 the A.V. has given a misleading rendering in the phrase " both almost and altogether ; " there is no Greek word here which means " altogether ; " the R.V. corrects to " whether with little or with much." See ALL.¶

2. HOLŌS denotes altogether or actually, or assuredly. See 3654
ACTUALLY, and ALL, B, No. 1. AG:565B CB:1251A

ALWAY, ALWAYS

1. AEI (ἀεί) has two meanings : (*a*) perpetually, incessantly, Acts 104
7 : 51 ; 2 Cor. 4 : 11 ; 6 : 10 ; Tit. 1 : 12 ; Heb. 3 : 10 ; (*b*) invariably, at AG:19C CB:1233A
any and every time, of successive occurrences, when some thing is to be repeated, according to the circumstances, 1 Pet. 3 : 15 ; 2 Pet. 1 : 12. See EVER.¶

2. HEKASTOTE (ἑκάστοτε), from *hekastos*, each, is used in 2 Pet. 1539
1 : 15, R.V., " at every time " (A.V., " always "). See TIME.¶ AG:236D CB:—

3. DIAPANTOS (διαπαντός) is, lit., ' through all,' i.e., ' through all 1275
time,' (*dia*, through, *pas*, all). In the best texts the words are separated. AG:179B (A.II.1a.)
The phrase, which is used of the time throughout which a thing is done, is CB:—
sometimes rendered " continually," sometimes " always ; " " always " or " alway " in Mk. 5 : 5 ; Acts 10 : 2 ; 24 : 16 ; Rom. 11 : 10 ; " continually " in Luke 24 : 53 ; Heb. 9 : 6 ; 13 : 15, the idea being that of a
continuous practice carried on without being abandoned. See CON- PANTĒ
TINUALLY.¶ 3839

4 and 5. PANTĒ (πάντῃ) and PANTOTE (πάντοτε) are derived from AG:608D CB:—
pas, all. The former is found in Acts 24 : 3.¶ The latter is the usual PANTOTE
word for " always." See EVER, EVERMORE. 3842 AG:609B

Note : Two phrases, rendered " always " or " alway " in the A.V., CB:1261C

KAIROS 2540 AG:394D CB:1253A are *en panti kairō* (lit., ' in every season '), Luke 21 : 36, R.V., " at every season," Eph. 6 : 18, R.V., " at all seasons," and *pasas tas hēmeras*, (lit., ' all the days '), Matt. 28 : 20, A.V. and R.V., " alway."

HĒMERA 2250 AG:345D CB:1249C

AMAZE, AMAZEMENT

A. Nouns.

1611 AG:245A CB:1244A 1. EKSTASIS (ἔκστασις) is, lit., 'a standing out (*ek*, out of, *stasis*, a standing).' Eng. " ecstasy " is a transliteration. It is translated " amazement " in Acts 3 : 10. It was said of any displacement, and hence, especially, with reference to the mind, of that alteration of the normal condition by which the person is thrown into a state of surprise or fear, or both ; or again, in which a person is so transported out of his natural state that he falls into a trance, Acts 10 : 10 ; 11 : 5 ; 22 : 17. As to the other meaning, the R.V. has " amazement " in Mark 5 : 42 and Luke 5 : 26, but " astonishment " in Mark 16 : 8. See TRANCE.¶

2285 AG:350C CB:1271C 2. THAMBOS (θάμβος), amazement, wonder, is probably connected with a root signifying to render immovable ; it is frequently associated with terror as well as astonishment, as with the verb (No. 3, below) in Acts 9 : 6. It occurs in Luke 4 : 36 ; 5 : 9 ; Acts 3 : 10. See WONDER.¶

4423 AG:727C CB:— *Note : Ptoēsis* signifies " terror," not " amazement," 1 Pet. 3 : 6, R.V.¶

B. Verbs.

1839 AG:276B CB:1247C (EXHI-) 1. EXISTĒMI (ἐξίστημι), akin to A, No. 1, lit. means to stand out from. Like the noun, this is used with two distinct meanings : (*a*) in the sense of amazement, the word should be invariably rendered " amazed," as in the R.V., e.g., in the case of Simon Magus (for A.V., " bewitched "), Acts 8 : 9 and 11. It is used, in the Passive Voice, of Simon himself in the 13th ver., R.V., " he was amazed," for A.V., " wondered." " Amaze " is preferable to " astonish " throughout ; (*b*) in Mark 3 : 21 and 2 Cor. 5 : 13 it is used with its other meaning of being beside oneself. See BESIDE ONESELF (to be), BEWITCH, WONDER.

1605 AG:244B CB:1243C 2. EKPLĒSSŌ (ἐκπλήσσω), from *ek*, out of, *plēssō*, to strike, lit., to strike out, signifies to be exceedingly struck in mind, to be astonished (*ek*, intensive). The English " astonish " should be used for this verb, and " amaze " for *existēmi*, as in the R.V. ; see Matt. 19 : 25 ; Luke 2 : 48 ; 9 : 43.

2284 AG:350C CB:1271C 3. THAMBEŌ (θαμβέω), akin to A, No. 2, is used in Mark 1 : 27 ; 10 : 24, 32 (and Acts 9 : 6, A.V.). The R.V. has " amazed " in each place ; A.V., " astonished," in Mark 10 : 24.¶

1568 AG:240B CB:1244A 4. EKTHAMBEŌ (ἐκθαμβέω), an intensive form of No. 3, is found in Mark's Gospel only ; in 9 : 15, " were greatly amazed ; " in 14 : 33, A.V., " were sore amazed ; " in 16 : 5, R.V., " were amazed," A.V., " were affrighted ; " in ver. 6, R.V., " be not amazed," A.V., " be not affrighted." See AFFRIGHTED.¶

1569 AG:240B CB:1244A

C. Adjective.

EKTHAMBOS (ἔκθαμβος), a strengthened form of A, No. 2, is found in

Acts 3 : 11. The intensive force of the word is brought out by the rendering " greatly wondering." See WONDER.¶

AMBASSADOR, AMBASSAGE

A. Verb.

PRESBEUŌ (πρεσβεύω) denotes (*a*) to be elder or eldest, prior in 4243
birth or age ; (*b*) to be an ambassador, 2 Cor. 5 : 20, and Eph. 6 : 20 ; for AG:699C CB:1266B
Philm. 9 see under AGED. There is a suggestion that to be an ambassador for Christ involves the experience suggested by the word " elder." Elder men were chosen as ambassadors.

B. Noun.

PRESBEIA (πρεσβεία), primarily, age, eldership, rank, hence, an 4242
embassy or ambassage, is used in Luke 14 : 32 ; in 19 : 14, R.V., AG:699B CB:1266B
" ambassage," for A.V., " message."¶ AMBITION See DESIRE

AMEN

AMBUSH See LIE IN WAIT

AMĒN (ἀμήν) is transliterated from Hebrew into both Greek and
English. "Its meanings may be seen in such passages as Deut. 7 : 9,
' the faithful (the Amen) God,' Isa. 49 : 7, ' Jehovah that is faithful,' 281
65 : 16, ' the God of truth,' marg., ' the God of Amen.' And if God is faith- AG:45C CB:1234C
ful His testimonies and precepts are ' sure (*amen*),' Psa. 19 : 7 ; 111 : 7, as are also His warnings, Hos. 5 : 9, and promises, Isa. 33 : 16 ; 55 : 3. ' Amen ' is used of men also, e.g., Prov. 25 : 13.

" There are cases where the people used it to express their assent to a law and their willingness to submit to the penalty attached to the breach of it, Deut. 27 : 15, cp. Neh. 5 : 13. It is also used to express acquiescence in another's prayer, 1 Kings 1 : 36, where it is defined as ' (let) God say so too,' or in another's thanksgiving, 1 Chron. 16 : 36, whether by an individual, Jer. 11 : 5, or by the congregation, Psa. 106 : 48.

" Thus ' Amen ' said by God = ' it is and shall be so,' and by men, ' so let it be.'

" Once in the N.T. ' Amen ' is a title of Christ, Rev. 3 : 14, because through Him the purposes of God are established, 2 Cor. 1 : 20.

" The early Christian churches followed the example of Israel in associating themselves audibly with the prayers and thanksgivings offered on their behalf, 1 Cor. 14 : 16, where the article ' the ' points to a common practice. Moreover this custom conforms to the pattern of things in the Heavens, see Rev. 5 : 14, etc.

" The individual also said ' Amen ' to express his ' let it be so ' in response to the Divine ' thus it shall be,' Rev. 22 : 20. Frequently the speaker adds ' Amen ' to his own prayers and doxologies, as is the case at Eph. 3 : 21, e.g.

" The Lord Jesus often used ' Amen,' translated ' verily,' to introduce new revelations of the mind of God. In John's Gospel it is always repeated, ' Amen, Amen,' but not elsewhere. Luke does not use it at all, but where Matthew, 16 : 28, and Mark, 9 : 1, have 'Amen,' Luke has 'of a truth;' thus by varying the translation of what the Lord said, Luke throws light on His meaning."* See VERILY.

AMEND

2866 AG:443A CB:— ECHŌ KOMPSOTERON, lit., to have more finely, i.e., to be better, is used in John 4 : 52, "to amend." The latter word in the phrase is the comparative of *kompsos*, elegant, nice, fine. Cp. Eng., "he's doing nicely."¶

AMETHYST

271 AG:44C CB:1234C AMETHUSTOS (ἀμέθυστος), primarily meaning "not drunken" (*a*, negative, and *methu*, wine), became used as a noun, being regarded as possessing a remedial virtue against drunkenness. Pliny, however, says that the reason for its name lay in the fact that in colour it nearly approached that of wine, but did not actually do so, Rev. 21 : 20.¶

For AMIDST see MIDST

AMISS

A. Adjective.

824 AG:120C CB:— ATOPOS (ἄτοπος), lit., out of place (*a*, negative, *topos*, a place), hence denotes unbecoming, not befitting. It is used four times in the N.T., and is rendered "amiss" three times in the R.V.; in the malefactor's testimony of Christ, Luke 23 : 41; in Festus's words concerning Paul, Acts 25 : 5, "if there is anything amiss in the man" (A.V., "wickedness"); in Acts 28 : 6, of the expected effect of the viper's attack upon Paul (A.V., "harm"); in 2 Thess. 3 : 2, of men capable of outrageous conduct, "unreasonable." See HARM, UNREASONABLE.

B. Adverb.

2560 AG:398C CB:1253B KAKŌS (κακῶς), akin to *kakos*, evil, is translated "amiss" in Jas. 4 : 3; elsewhere in various ways. See EVIL, GRIEVOUS, MISERABLE, SORE.

AMOUNT See MEASURE, PORTION

AMONG: See Note †, p. 1

ANCESTOR See FAMILY, FATHER

For ANATHEMA see under CURSE

ANCHOR

45 AG:10C CB:— ANKURA (ἄγκυρα), Eng., anchor, was so called because of its curved form (*ankos*, a curve), Acts 27 : 29, 30, 40; Heb. 6 : 19. In Acts 27 : 13 the verb *airō*, to lift, signifies to lift anchor (the noun being understood), R.V., "they weighed anchor" (A.V., "loosing thence").¶

ANCIENT See OLD

* From Notes on Galatians by Hogg and Vine, pp. 26, 27.

ANEW

ANŌTHEN (ἄνωθεν), lit., 'from above,' in the phrase rendered 509
"anew" in the R.V. (A.V., "again") of John 3 : 3, 7. See AGAIN. AG:77A CB:1236A
Note : In Phil. 3 : 21 "fashion anew" translates the verb *metaschēma-* 3345
tizō, which signifies to change the form of. AG:513B CB:1258C

ANGEL

ANGELOS (ἄγγελος), a messenger (from *angellō*, to deliver a message), 32
sent whether by God or by man or by Satan, "is also used of a guardian AG:7A CB:1235C
or representative in Rev. 1 : 20, cp. Matt. 18 : 10; Acts 12 : 15 (where it is better understood as = 'ghost'), but most frequently of an order of created beings, superior to man, Heb. 2 : 7; Psa. 8 : 5, belonging to Heaven, Matt. 24 : 36; Mark 12 : 25, and to God, Luke 12 : 8, and engaged in His service, Psa. 103 : 20. Angels are spirits, Heb. 1 : 14, i.e., they have not material bodies as men have; they are either human in form, or can assume the human form when necessary, cp. Luke 24 : 4, with ver. 23, Acts 10 : 3 with ver. 30.

"They are called 'holy' in Mark 8 : 38, and 'elect,' 1 Tim. 5 : 21, in contrast with some of their original number, Matt. 25 : 41, who 'sinned,' 2 Pet. 2 : 4, 'left their proper habitation,' Jude 6, *oikētērion*, a word which occurs again, in the N.T., only in 2 Cor. 5 : 2. Angels are always spoken of in the masculine gender, the feminine form of the word does not occur."*

Note : Isangelos, "equal to the angels," occurs in Luke 20 : 36.¶ 2465 AG:380D CB:1253A

ANGER, ANGRY (to be)

A. Noun.

ORGĒ (ὀργή), originally any natural impulse, or desire, or disposition, 3709
came to signify anger, as the strongest of all passions. It is used of the AG:578D CB:1261A
wrath of man, Eph. 4 : 31; Col. 3 : 8; 1 Tim. 2 : 8; Jas. 1 : 19, 20; the displeasure of human governments, Rom. 13 : 4, 5; the sufferings of the Jews at the hands of the Gentiles, Luke 21 : 23; the terrors of the Law, Rom. 4 : 15; the anger of the Lord Jesus, Mark 3 : 5; God's anger with Israel in the wilderness, in a quotation from the O.T., Heb. 3 : 11; 4 : 3; God's present anger with the Jews nationally, Rom. 9 : 22; 1 Thess. 2 : 16; His present anger with those who disobey the Lord Jesus in His Gospel, John 3 : 36; God's purposes in judgment, Matt. 3 : 7; Luke 3 : 7; Rom. 1 : 18; 2 : 5, 8; 3 : 5; 5 : 9; 12 : 19; Eph. 2 : 3; 5 : 6; Col. 3 : 6; 1 Thess. 1 : 10; 5 : 9. See INDIGNATION, VENGEANCE, WRATH.¶

Notes : (1) *Thumos*, wrath (not translated "anger"), is to be dis- 2372
tinguished from *orgē*, in this respect, that *thumos* indicates a more agitated AG:365B CB:1272C
condition of the feelings, an outburst of wrath from inward indignation, while *orgē* suggests a more settled or abiding condition of mind, frequently with a view to taking revenge. *Orgē* is less sudden in its rise than *thumos*,

---

* From Notes on Thessalonians by Hogg and Vine, p. 229.

but more lasting in its nature. *Thumos* expresses more the inward feeling, *orgē* the more active emotion. *Thumos* may issue in revenge, though it does not necessarily include it. It is characteristic that it quickly blazes up and quickly subsides, though that is not necessarily implied in each case.

3950 AG:629D CB:1262C (2) *Parorgismos*, a strengthened form of *orgē*, and used in Eph. 4 : 26, R.V. margin, " provocation," points especially to that which provokes the wrath, and suggests a less continued state than No. (1). " The first keenness of the sense of provocation must not be cherished, though righteous resentment may remain " (Westcott). The preceding verb, *orgizō*, in this verse implies a just occasion for the feeling. This is confirmed by the fact that it is a quotation from Psa. 4 : 4 (Sept.), where the Hebrew word signifies to quiver with strong emotion.

Thumos is found eighteen times in the N.T., ten of which are in the Apocalypse, in seven of which the reference is to the wrath of God ; so in Rom. 2 : 8, R.V., " wrath (*thumos*) and indignation " (*orgē*) ; the order in the A.V. is inaccurate. Everywhere else the word *thumos* is used in a bad sense. In Gal. 5 : 20, it follows the word jealousies, which when smouldering in the heart break out in wrath. *Thumos* and *orgē* are coupled in two places in the Apocalypse, 16 : 19, " the fierceness (*thumos*) of His wrath " (*orgē*) ; and 19 : 15, " the fierceness of the wrath of Almighty God." See WROTH (be).

24 AG:4B CB:— (3) *Aganaktēsis* originally signified physical pain or irritation (probably from *agan*, very much, and *achomai*, to grieve), hence, annoyance, vexation, and is used in 2 Cor. 7 : 11, " indignation."¶

B. Verbs.

3710 AG:579C CB:1261A 1. ORGIZŌ (ὀργίζω), to provoke, to arouse to anger, is used in the Middle Voice in the eight places where it is found, and signifies to be angry, wroth. It is said of individuals, in Matt. 5 : 22 ; 18 : 34 ; 22 : 7 ; Luke 14 : 21 ; 15 : 28, and Eph. 4 : 26 (where a possible meaning is " be ye angry with yourselves ") ; of nations, Rev. 11 : 18 ; of Satan as the Dragon, 12 : 17. See WRATH.¶

3949 AG:629D CB:1262C 2. PARORGIZŌ (παροργίζω) is to arouse to wrath, provoke (*para*, used intensively, and No. 1) ; Rom. 10 : 19, " will I anger ; " Eph. 6 : 4, " provoke to wrath." See PROVOKE.¶

5520 AG:883B CB:— 3. CHOLAŌ (χολάω), connected with *cholē*, gall, bile, which became used metaphorically to signify bitter anger, means to be enraged, John 7 : 23, " wroth," R.V., in the Lord's remonstrance with the Jews on account of their indignation at His having made a man whole on the Sabbath Day.¶

2371 AG:365B CB:— *Notes :* (1) *Thumomacheō* (from *thumos*, wrath, *machomai*, to fight) originally denoted to fight with great animosity, and hence came to mean to be very angry, to be exasperated, Acts 12 : 20, of the anger of Herod, " was highly displeased."¶

2373 AG:365C CB:1272C (2) *Thumoō*, the corresponding verb, signifies to provoke to anger, but in the Passive Voice to be wroth, as in Matt. 2 : 16, of the wrath of Herod, " was exceeding wroth."¶

(3) *Aganakteō*, see A, Note (3), is rendered in various ways in 23 AG:4B CB:—
the seven places where it is used ; " moved with indignation," Matt. 20 : 24 and 21 : 15, R.V. (A.V., " sore displeased ") ; " had indignation," Matt. 26 : 8 ; Mark 14 : 4. In Mark 10 : 14 the R.V. has " was moved with indignation " (A.V., " was much displeased "), said of the Lord Jesus. The same renderings are given in ver. 41. In Luke 13 : 14 (A.V., " with indignation "), the R.V. rightly puts " being moved with indignation." These words more particularly point to the cause of the vexation. See DISPLEASE, INDIGNATION.¶

(4) In Col. 3 : 21 *erethizō* signifies to provoke. The R.V. correctly 2042 AG:308D CB:—
omits " to anger."

C. Adjective.

ORGILOS (ὀργίλος), angry, prone to anger, irascible (see B, Nos. 1, 2), 3711 AG:579D CB:1261A
is rendered " soon angry " in Tit. 1 : 7.¶

ANGUISH

A. Nouns.

2347 AG:362B CB:1272B
1. THLIPSIS (θλῖψις) ; see AFFLICTION (No. 4).

2. STENOCHŌRIA (στενοχωρία), lit., narrowness of place (*stenos*, 4730 AG:766C CB:1270A
narrow, *chōra*, a place), metaphorically came to mean the distress arising from that condition, anguish. It is used in the plural, of various forms of distress, 2 Cor. 6 : 4 and 12 : 10, and of anguish or distress in general, Rom. 2 : 9 ; 8 : 35, R.V., " anguish " for A.V., " distress." The opposite state, of being in a large place, and so metaphorically in a state of joy, is represented by the word *platusmos* in certain Psalms as, e.g., Psa. 118 : 5 ; see also 2 Sam. 22 : 20. See DISTRESS.¶

3. SUNOCHĒ (συνοχή), lit., a holding together, or compressing (*sun*, 4928 AG:791D CB:—
together, *echō*, to hold), was used of the narrowing of a way. It is found only in its metaphorical sense, of straits, distress, anguish, Luke 21 : 25, " distress of nations," and 2 Cor. 2 : 4, " anguish of heart." See DISTRESS.¶

Note : Anankē is associated with *thlipsis*, and signifies a condition of 318 AG:52B CB:1235B
necessity arising from some form of compulsion. It is therefore used not only of necessity but of distress, Luke 21 : 23 ; 1 Thess. 3 : 7, and in the plural in 2 Cor. 6 : 4 ; 12 : 10.

B. Verbs.

1. STENOCHŌREŌ (στενοχωρέω), akin to A, No. 2, lit., to crowd into 4729 AG:766C CB:1270A
a narrow space, or, in the Passive Voice to be pressed for room, hence, metaphorically, to be straitened, 2 Cor. 4 : 8 and 6 : 12 (twice), is found in its literal sense in two places in the Sept., in Josh. 17 : 15 and Isa. 49 : 19, and in two places in its metaphorical sense, in Judg. 16 : 16, where Delilah is said to have pressed Samson sore with her words continually, and to have " straitened him," and in Isa. 28 : 20. See DISTRESS, STRAITENED.

4912 AG:789A CB:1270C 2. SUNECHŌ (συνέχω), akin to A, No. 3, lit., to hold together, is used physically of being held, or thronged, Luke 8 : 45; 19 : 43; 22 : 63; of being taken with a malady, Matt. 4 : 24; Luke 4 : 38; Acts 28 : 8; with fear, Luke 8 : 37; of being straitened or pressed in spirit, with desire, Luke 12 : 50; Acts 18 : 5; Phil. 1 : 23; with the love of Christ, 2 Cor. 5 : 14. In one place it is used of the stopping of their ears by those who killed Stephen. See CONSTRAIN, HOLD, KEEP, PRESS, SICK (lie), STOP, STRAIT (be in a), STRAITENED, TAKE, THRONG.

3600 AG:555A CB:— 3. ODUNAŌ (ὀδυνάω), in the Middle and Passive Voices, signifies to suffer pain, be in anguish, be greatly distressed (akin to *odunē*, pain, distress); it is rendered "sorrowing" in Luke 2 : 48; in 16 : 24, 25, R.V., "in anguish," for A.V., "tormented;" in Acts 20 : 38, "sorrowing." See SORROW, TORMENT.¶

ANIMAL See **BEAST**

For ANIMALS (2 Pet. 2 : 12, R.V.), see NATURAL.

ANISE

432 AG:66A CB:1235C ANĒTHON (ἄνηθον), dill, anise, was used for food and for pickling, Matt. 23 : 23.¶

ANKLE-BONES

4974 AG:797A CB:— SPHURON (σφυρόν) or SPHUDRON (σφυδρόν) denotes the ankle, or ankle-bone (from *sphura*, a hammer, owing to a resemblance in the shape), Acts 3 : 7.¶

ANNOUNCE

312 AG:51B CB:1235B ANANGELLŌ (ἀναγγέλλω), to declare, announce (*ana*, up, *angellō*, to report), is used especially of heavenly messages, and is translated "announced" in the R.V. of 1 Pet. 1 : 12, for A.V., "reported," and in 1 John 1 : 5, R.V., "announce," for A.V., "declare." See DECLARE, REHEARSE, REPORT, SHOW, SPEAK, TELL.

ANNUAL See **YEAR**

ANOINT, ANOINTING

A. Verbs.

218 AG:35B CB:1234B 1. ALEIPHŌ (ἀλείφω) is a general term used for an anointing of any kind, whether of physical refreshment after washing, e.g., in the Sept. of Ruth 3 : 3; 2 Sam. 12 : 20; Dan. 10 : 3; Micah 6 : 15; in the N.T., Matt. 6 : 17; Luke 7 : 38, 46; John 11 : 2; 12 : 3; or of the sick. Mark 6 : 13; Jas. 5 : 14; or a dead body, Mark 16 : 1. The material used was either oil, or ointment, as in Luke 7 : 38, 46.¶ In the Sept. it is also used of anointing a pillar, Gen. 31 : 13, or captives, 2 Chron. 28 : 15, or of daubing a wall with mortar, Ezek. 13 : 10, 11, 12, 14, 15; and, in the sacred sense, of anointing priests, in Ex. 40 : 15 (twice), and Numb. 3 : 3.

5548 AG:887C CB:1240A 2. CHRIŌ (χρίω) is more limited in its use than No. 1; it is confined to sacred and symbolical anointings; of Christ as the Anointed of God, Luke 4 : 18; Acts 4 : 27; 10 : 38, and Heb. 1 : 9, where it is used metaphorically in connection with "the oil of gladness." The title Christ signifies "The Anointed One." The word (*Christos*) is rendered "(His) Anointed" in Acts 4 : 26, R.V. Once it is said of believers, 2 Cor. 1 : 21. *Chriō* is very frequent in the Sept., and is used of kings, 1 Sam. 10 : 1, and priests, Ex. 28 : 41, and prophets, 1 Kings 19 : 16. Among the Greeks it was used in other senses than the ceremonial, but in the Scriptures it is not found in connection with secular matters.¶

Note : The distinction referred to by Trench (Syn. § xxxviii), that *aleiphō* is the mundane and profane, *chriō*, the sacred and religious word, is not borne out by evidence. In a papyrus document *chrisis* is used of "a lotion for a sick horse" (Moulton and Milligan, Vocab. of Greek Test).

3. ENCHRIŌ (ἐγχρίω), primarily, to rub in, hence, to besmear, to (EGCH-)
anoint, is used metaphorically in the command to the church in Laodicea 1472
to anoint their eyes with eyesalve, Rev. 3 : 18.¶ In the Sept., Jer. 4 : 30, AG:217A CB:—
it is used of the anointing of the eyes with a view to beautifying them.

4. EPICHRIŌ (ἐπιχρίω), primarily, to rub on (*epi*, upon), is used of the 2025
blind man whose eyes Christ anointed, and indicates the manner in which AG:305B CB:—
the anointing was done, John 9 : 6, 11.¶

5. MURIZŌ (μυρίζω) is used of anointing the body for burial, in 3462
Mark 14 : 8.¶ AG:529D CB:—

B. Noun.

CHRISMA (χρίσμα), the corresponding noun to No. 2, above, signifies 5545
an unguent, or an anointing. It was prepared from oil and aromatic herbs. AG:886C CB:1240A
It is used only metaphorically in the N.T. ; by metonymy, of the Holy Spirit, 1 John 2 : 20, 27, twice. The R.V. translates it "anointing" in all three places, instead of the A.V. "unction" and "anointing."

That believers have "an anointing from the Holy One" indicates that this anointing renders them holy, separating them to God. The passage teaches that the gift of the Holy Spirit is the all-efficient means of enabling believers to possess a knowledge of the truth. In the Sept., it is used of the oil for anointing the high priest, e.g., Ex. 29 : 7, lit., 'Thou shalt take of the oil of the anointing.' In Ex. 30 : 25, etc., it is spoken of as "a holy anointing oil." In Dan. 9 : 26 *chrisma* stands for the anointed one, "Christ," the noun standing by metonymy for the Person Himself, as for the Holy Spirit in 1 John 2. See UNCTION.¶

Notes : (1) *Aleimma*, akin to A, No. 1 (not in the N.T.), occurs three times in the Sept., Ex. 30 : 31, of the anointing of the priests ; Isa. 61 : 3, metaphorically, of the oil of joy ; Dan. 10 : 3, of physical refreshment.

(2) *Muron*, a word akin to A, No. 5, denotes ointment. The MURON 3464
distinction between this and *elaion*, oil, is observable in Christ's reproof of AG:529D
the Pharisee who, while desiring Him to eat with him, failed in the CB:1259B
ordinary marks of courtesy ; "My head with oil (*elaion*) thou didst not ELAION 1637
anoint, but she hath anointed My feet with ointment" (*muron*), Luke AG:247D
7 : 46. CB:1244A

ANON

2117 *Note:* This is the A.V. rendering of *euthus*, in Matt. 13 : 20 and Mark
AG:321A CB:1247B 1 : 30, R.V., "straightway."

ANOTHER

ALLOS 243 ALLOS (ἄλλος) and HETEROS (ἕτερος) have a difference in meaning,
AG:39D which despite a tendency to be lost, is to be observed in numerous passages.
2087 *Allos* expresses a numerical difference and denotes another of the same
HETEROS 2087 sort; *heteros* expresses a qualitative difference and denotes another of a
AG:315A different sort. Christ promised to send "another Comforter" (*allos*,
CB:1250A another like Himself, not *heteros*), John 14 : 16. Paul says "I see a different (A.V., 'another') law," *heteros*, a law different from that of the spirit of life (not *allos*, a law of the same sort), Rom. 7 : 23. After Joseph's death "another king arose," *heteros*, one of quite a different character, Acts 7 : 18. Paul speaks of "a different gospel (*heteros*), which is not another" (*allos*, another like the one he preached), Gal. 1 : 6, 7. See *heteros* (not *allos*) in Matt. 11 : 3, and Acts 27 : 1; in Luke 23 : 32 *heteroi* is used of the two malefactors crucified with Christ. The two words are only apparently interchanged in 1 Cor. 1 : 16 and 6 : 1; 12 : 8–10; 14 : 17 and 19, e.g., the difference being present, though not so readily discernible.

They are not interchangeable in 1 Cor. 15 : 39–41; here *heteros* is used to distinguish the heavenly glory from the earthly, for these differ in genus, and *allos* to distinguish the flesh of men, birds, and fishes, which in each case is flesh differing not in genus but in species. *Allos* is used again to distinguish between the glories of the heavenly bodies, for these also differ not in kind but in degree only. For *allos*, see MORE, OTHER, etc. For *heteros*, see OTHER, STRANGE.

Note: The distinction comes out in the compounds of *heteros*, viz., *heteroglōssos*, "strange tongues," 1 Cor. 14 : 21; ¶; *heterodidaskaleō*, "to teach a different doctrine," 1 Tim. 1 : 3; 6 : 3; ¶; *heterozugō*, "to be unequally yoked" (i.e., with those of a different character), 2 Cor. 6 : 14.¶

ANSWER

A. Nouns.

612 1. APOKRISIS (ἀπόκρισις), lit., a separation or distinction, is the
AG:93D CB:— regular word for "answer," Luke 2 : 47; 20 : 26; John 1 : 22 and 19 : 9.¶
610 2. APOKRIMA (ἀπόκριμα), akin to No. 1, denotes a judicial
AG:93B CB:— "sentence," 2 Cor. 1 : 9, A.V., and R.V., margin, or an "answer" (R.V., text), an answer of God to the Apostle's appeal, giving him strong confidence. In an ancient inscription it is used of an official decision. In a papyrus document it is used of a reply to a deputation. See SENTENCE.¶
5538 3. CHRĒMATISMOS (χρηματισμός), a Divine response, an oracle, is
AG:885D CB:1240A used in Rom. 11 : 4, of the answer given by God to Elijah's complaint against Israel.¶ See the verb under CALL.

4. APOLOGIA (ἀπολογία), a verbal defence, a speech in defence, is 627
sometimes translated "answer," in the A.V., Acts 25 : 16; 1 Cor. 9 : 3; AG:96A
2 Tim. 4 : 16, all which the R.V. corrects to "defence." See Acts CB:1237A
22 : 1; Phil. 1 : 7, 16; 2 Cor. 7 : 11, "clearing." Once it signifies an "answer," 1 Pet. 3 : 15. Cp. B, No. 4. See CLEARING, DEFENCE.¶

Note: *Eperōtēma*, 1 Pet. 3 : 21, is not, as in the A.V., an "answer." 1906
It was used by the Greeks in a legal sense, as a demand or appeal. AG:285C
Baptism is therefore the ground of an appeal by a good conscience against CB:1245C
wrong doing.¶

B. Verbs.

1. APOKRINOMAI (ἀποκρίνομαι), akin to A, No. 1, above, signifies 611
either to give an answer to a question (its more frequent use) or to begin AG:93B
to speak, but always where something has preceded, either statement or CB:—
act to which the remarks refer, e.g., Matt. 11 : 25; Luke 14 : 3; John 2 : 18. The R.V. translates by "answered," e.g., Matt. 28 : 5; Mark 12 : 35; Luke 3 : 16, where some have suggested 'began to say' or 'uttered solemnly,' whereas the speaker is replying to the unuttered thought or feeling of those addressed by him.

2. ANTAPOKRINOMAI (ἀνταποκρίνομαι), *anti*, against, and No. 1, 470
a strengthened form, to answer by contradiction, to reply against, is AG:73B
found in Luke 14 : 6 and Rom. 9 : 20.¶ CB:—

3. HUPOLAMBANŌ (ὑπολαμβάνω) signifies (*a*) to take or bear up 5274
from beneath, Acts 1 : 9; (*b*) to receive, 3 John 8; (*c*) to suppose, Luke AG:845B
7 : 43; Acts 2 : 15; (*d*) to catch up (in speech), to answer, Luke 10 : 30; CB:1252B
in sense (*d*) it indicates that a person follows what another has said, either by controverting or supplementing it. See RECEIVE, SUPPOSE.¶

4. APOLOGEOMAI (ἀπολογέομαι), cp. A, No. 4, lit., to talk oneself 626
off from (*apo*, from, *legō*, to speak), to answer by way of making a defence AG:95D
for oneself (besides its meaning to excuse, Rom. 2 : 15; 2 Cor. 12 : 19), CB:1237A
is translated "answer" in Luke 12 : 11; 21 : 14; in Acts 19 : 33, A.V. and R.V. both have "made defence;" in Acts 24 : 10; 25 : 8; 26 : 1, 2, the R.V. has the verb to make a defence, for the A.V., to answer, and in 26 : 24 for the A.V., "spake for himself." See DEFENCE, EXCUSE, SPEAK.¶

5. ANTILEGŌ (ἀντιλέγω), to speak against, is rendered "answering 483
again" in the A.V. of Tit. 2 : 9 (R.V., "gainsaying"). See CONTRADICT, AG:74D
DENY, GAINSAY, SPEAK. CB:—

6. SUSTOICHEŌ (συστοιχέω), lit., to be in the same line or row with 4960
(*sun*, with, *stoichos*, a row), is translated "answereth to" in Gal. 4 : 25.¶ AG:795B
Note: Cp. *stoicheō*, to walk (in line), 5 : 25; 6 : 16. For *hupakouō*, CB:1271A
rendered to answer in Acts 12 : 13, R.V., see HEARKEN, No. 1, *Note*.

ANTICHRIST

ANTICHRISTOS (ἀντίχριστος) can mean either against Christ or 500
instead of Christ, or perhaps, combining the two, "one who, assuming AG:76B CB:1236A

the guise of Christ, opposes Christ" (Westcott). The word is found only in John's Epistles, (*a*) of the many antichrists who are forerunners of the Antichrist himself, 1 John 2 : 18, 22 ; 2 John 7 ; (*b*) of the evil power which already operates anticipatively of the Antichrist, 1 John 4 : 3.¶

What the Apostle says of him so closely resembles what he says of the first beast in Rev. 13, and what the Apostle Paul says of the Man of Sin in 2 Thess. 2, that the same person seems to be in view in all these passages, rather than the second beast in Rev. 13, the false prophet ; for the latter supports the former in all his Antichristian assumptions.

5580 AG:892B *Note :* The term *pseudochristos*, a false Christ, is to be distinguished
CB:1267C from the above ; it is found in Matt. 24 : 24 and Mark 13 : 22. The false Christ does not deny the existence of Christ, he trades upon the expectation of His appearance, affirming that he is the Christ. The Antichrist denies the existence of the true God (Trench, Syn. §, xxx).¶

For ANXIETY and ANXIOUS see CARE, A, No. 1, B, No. 1

ANY : see Note †, p. 1

ANYTHING

Note : See the R.V. of Mark 15 : 5 ; John 16 : 23 ; 1 Tim. 6 : 7 ; in Luke 24 : 41, the R.V. suitably has "anything to eat," for, A.V., "any meat."

APART

5565 AG:890C 1. CHŌRIS (χωρίς) is used both as an adverb and as a preposition.
CB:1240A As an adverb it signifies separately, by itself, John 20 : 7, of the napkin which had been around the Lord's head in the tomb ; as a preposition (its more frequent use), apart from, without, separate from. It is rendered "apart from" in the R.V. of John 15 : 5 ; Rom. 3 : 21, 28 ; 4 : 6 ; 2 Cor. 12 : 3 ; Heb. 9 : 22, 28 ; 11 : 40 ; Jas. 2 : 18, 20, 26. See BESIDE, WITHOUT.

Note : The opposite of *chōris* is *sun*, with. A synonymous preposition,
ANEU 427 *aneu*, denotes without, Matt. 10 : 29 ; 1 Pet. 3 : 1 and 4 : 9.¶
AG:65C 2. KAT' IDIAN (κατ' ἰδίαν), lit., according to one's own, i.e., privately,
CB:— alone, is translated "apart" in Matt. 14 : 13, 23 ; 17 : 1, 19 ; 20 : 17 ;
IDIOS 2398 Mark 6 : 31, 32 (A.V., "privately") ; 9 : 2.
AG:369C CB:1252C 3. KATA MONAS (κατὰ μόνας) : see ALONE.

APIECE

303 AG:49D ANA (ἀνά), used with numerals or measures of quantity with a dis-
CB:1235A tributive force, is translated "apiece" in Luke 9 : 3, "two coats apiece," A.V. ; in John 2 : 6, "two or three firkins apiece." In Matt. 20 : 9, 10, "every man a penny," is a free rendering for "a penny apiece ;" in

Luke 9 : 14, the R.V. adds "each" to translate the *ana* ; in 10 : 1, *ana duo* is "two by two." See Rev. 4 : 8, "each." See EACH, EVERY.

APOSTLE, APOSTLESHIP

1. APOSTOLOS (ἀπόστολος) is, lit., one sent forth (*apo*, from, *stellō*, 652
to send). "The word is used of the Lord Jesus to describe His relation AG:99C
to God, Heb. 3 : 1 ; see John 17 : 3. The twelve disciples chosen by the CB:1237A
Lord for special training were so called, Luke 6 : 13 ; 9 : 10. Paul, though he had seen the Lord Jesus, 1 Cor. 9 : 1 ; 15 : 8, had not 'companied with' the Twelve 'all the time' of His earthly ministry, and hence was not eligible for a place among them, according to Peter's description of the necessary qualifications, Acts 1 : 22. Paul was commissioned directly, by the Lord Himself, after His Ascension, to carry the Gospel to the Gentiles.

"The word has also a wider reference. In Acts 14 : 4, 14, it is used of Barnabas as well as of Paul ; in Rom. 16 : 7 of Andronicus and Junias. In 2 Cor. 8 : 23 (R.V., margin) two unnamed brethren are called 'apostles of the churches ;' in Phil. 2 : 25 (R.V., margin) Epaphroditus is referred to as 'your apostle.' It is used in 1 Thess. 2 : 6 of Paul, Silas and Timothy, to define their relation to Christ."*

2. APOSTOLĒ (ἀποστολή), a sending, a mission, signifies an apostle- 651
ship, Acts 1 : 25 ; Rom. 1 : 5 ; 1 Cor. 9 : 2 ; Gal. 2 : 8.¶ AG:99B CB:1237A

Note : *Pseudapostoloi*, "false apostles," occurs in 2 Cor. 11 : 13.¶ 5570 AG:891B CB:1267C

APPAREL, APPARELLED

1. ESTHĒS (ἐσθής) and ESTHĒSIS (ἔσθησις), connected with *hennumi*, 2066 (2067)
to clothe, mean clothing, raiment, usually suggesting the ornate, the AG:312B CB:1246C
goodly. The former is found in Luke 23 : 11, R.V., "apparel" (A.V., "robe") ; 24 : 4 (A.V., "garments") ; Acts 10 : 30 (A.V., "clothing") ; 12 : 21 ; Jas. 2 : 2 (R.V., "clothing," twice ; A.V., "apparel" and "raiment") ; 2 : 3 ("clothing"). *Esthēsis* is used in Acts 1 : 10, "apparel." See CLOTHING.¶

2. HIMATION (ἱμάτιον), a diminutive of *heima*, a robe, was used 2440
especially of an outer cloak or mantle, and in general of raiment, AG:376B CB:1250C
"apparel" in 1 Pet. 3 : 3. The word is not in the original in the next verse, but is supplied in English to complete the sentence. See CLOTHING, No. 2, GARMENT, RAIMENT, ROBE.

3. HIMATISMOS (ἱματισμός), a collective word, is translated 2441
"apparelled" in Luke 7 : 25, and preceded by *en*, "in," lit., 'in apparel.' AG:376D CB:—
See CLOTHING, No. 4, RAIMENT, VESTURE.

4. KATASTOLĒ (καταστολή), connected with *katastellō*, to send or let 2689
down, to lower (*kata*, down, *stellō*, to send), was primarily a garment let AG:419A CB:—
down ; hence, dress, attire, in general (cp. *stolē*, a loose outer garment worn by kings and persons of rank,—Eng., stole) ; 1 Tim. 2 : 9, "apparel." See CLOTHING.¶

• From Notes on Thessalonians by Hogg and Vine, pp. 59, 60.

APPARITION

5326 AG:853C CB:1263C PHANTASMA (φάντασμα), a phantasm or phantom (from *phainō*, to appear), is translated "apparition" in the R.V. of Matt. 14 : 26 and Mark 6 : 49 (A.V., "spirit").¶ In the Sept., Job 20 : 8; Is. 28 : 7.¶

APPEAL

1941 (-OMAI) AG:294A CB:1245C (-OMAI) EPIKALEŌ (ἐπικαλέω), to call upon, has the meaning appeal in the Middle Voice, which carries with it the suggestion of a special interest on the part of the doer of an action in that in which he is engaged. Stephen died "calling upon the Lord," Acts 7 : 59. In the more strictly legal sense the word is used only of Paul's appeal to Cæsar, Acts 25 : 11, 12, 21, 25; 26 : 32; 28 : 19. See CALL (upon), SURNAME. See also *eperotēma*, under ANSWER.

APPEAR, APPEARING

A. Verbs.

5316 AG:851B CB:1263C 1. PHAINŌ (φαίνω) signifies, in the Active Voice, to shine; in the Passive, to be brought forth into light, to become evident, to appear. In Rom. 7 : 13, concerning sin, the R.V. has "might be shewn to be," for A.V., "appear."

It is used of the appearance of Christ to the disciples, Mark 16 : 9; of His future appearing in glory as the Son of Man, spoken of as a sign to the world, Matt. 24 : 30; there the genitive is subjective, the sign being the appearing of Christ Himself; of Christ as the light, John 1 : 5; of John the Baptist, 5 : 35; of the appearing of an angel of the Lord, either visibly, Matt. 1 : 20, or in a dream, 2 : 13; of a star, 2 : 7; of men who make an outward show, Matt. 6 : 5; 6 : 18 (see the R.V.); 23 : 27, 28; 2 Cor. 13 : 7; of tares, Matt. 13 : 26; of a vapour, Jas. 4 : 14; of things physical in general, Heb. 11 : 3; used impersonally in Matt. 9 : 33, "it was never so seen;" also of what appears to the mind, and so in the sense of to think, Mark 14 : 64, or to seem, Luke 24 : 11 (R.V., "appeared"). See SEE, SEEM, SHINE, THINK.

2014 AG:304A CB:1246A 2. EPIPHAINŌ (ἐπιφαίνω), a strengthened form of No. 1 but differing in meaning, *epi* signifying upon, is used in the Active Voice with the meaning to give light, Luke 1 : 79; in the Passive Voice, to appear, become visible. It is said of heavenly bodies, e.g., the stars, Acts 27 : 20 (R.V., "shone"); metaphorically, of things spiritual, the grace of God, Tit. 2 : 11; the kindness and the love of God, 3 : 4. See LIGHT.¶ Cp. *epiphaneia*, B, No. 2.

398 AG:63A CB:— 3. ANAPHAINŌ (ἀναφαίνω), *ana*, forth, or up, perhaps originally a nautical term, to come up into view, hence, in general, to appear suddenly, is used in the Passive Voice, in Luke 19 : 11, of the Kingdom of God; Active Voice, in Acts 21 : 3, to come in sight of, R.V.; "having sighted" would be a suitable rendering (A.V., "having discovered").¶

5319 AG:852D CB:1263C 4. PHANEROŌ (φανερόω), akin to No. 1, signifies, in the Active

Voice, to manifest; in the Passive Voice, to be manifested; so, regularly, in the R.V., instead of to appear. See 2 Cor. 7 : 12; Col. 3 : 4; Heb. 9 : 26; 1 Pet 5 : 4; 1 John 2 : 28; 3 : 2; Rev. 3 : 18. To be manifested, in the Scriptural sense of the word, is more than to appear. A person may appear in a false guise or without a disclosure of what he truly is; to be manifested is to be revealed in one's true character; this is especially the meaning of *phaneroō*, see, e.g., John 3 : 21; 1 Cor. 4 : 5; 2 Cor. 5 : 10, 11; Eph. 5 : 13.

5 EMPHANIZŌ (ἐμφανίζω), from *en*, in, intensive, and *phainō*, to **1718**
shine, is used, either of physical manifestation, Matt. 27 : 53; Heb. 9 : 24; **AG:257D**
cp. John 14 : 22, or, metaphorically, of the manifestation of Christ by the **CB:1244B**
Holy Spirit in the spiritual experience of believers who abide in His love, John 14 : 21. It has another, secondary meaning, to make known, signify, inform. This is confined to the Acts, where it is used five times, 23 : 15, 22; 24 : 1; 25 : 2, 15. There is perhaps a combination of the two meanings in Heb. 11 : 14, i.e., to declare by oral testimony and to manifest by the witness of the life. See INFORM, MANIFEST, SHEW, SIGNIFY.¶

6. OPTOMAI (ὄπτομαι), to see (from *ōps*, the eye; cp. Eng. optical, **(HORAō)**
etc.), in the Passive sense, to be seen, to appear, is used (*a*) objectively, **3708 AG:577D**
with reference to the person or thing seen, e.g., 1 Cor. 15 : 5, 6, 7, 8, R.V. **CB:1251A**
"appeared," for A.V., "was seen;" (*b*) subjectively, with reference to an inward impression or a spiritual experience, John 3 : 36, or a mental occupation, Acts 18 : 15, "look to it;" cp. Matt. 27 : 4, 24, "see (thou) to it," "see (ye) to it," throwing responsibility on others. *Optomai* is to be found in dictionaries under the word *horaō*, to see; it supplies some forms that are lacking in that verb.

These last three words, *emphanizō*, *phaneroō* and *optomai* are used with reference to the appearances of Christ in the closing verses of Heb. 9; *emphanizō* in ver. 24, of His presence before the face of God for us; *phaneroō* in ver. 26, of His past manifestation for "the sacrifice of Himself;" *optomai* in ver. 28, of His future appearance for His saints.

7. OPTANŌ (ὀπτάνω), in the Middle Voice signifies to allow oneself **(-OMAI)**
to be seen. It is rendered "appearing" in Acts 1 : 3, R.V., for A.V., **3700 AG:576C**
"being seen," of the Lord's appearances after His resurrection; the **CB:1261A**
Middle Voice expresses the Personal interest the Lord took in this.¶

Note: In Acts 22 : 30 *sunerchomai* (in its aorist form), to come **4905**
together, is translated "appear," A.V.; R.V., "come together." **AG:788A CB:1270C**

B. Nouns.

1. APOKALUPSIS (ἀποκάλυψις), lit., an uncovering, unveiling (*apō*, **602**
from, *kaluptō*, to hide, cover), denotes a revelation, or appearing (Eng., **AG:92B CB:1236C**
apocalypse). It is translated "the appearing" in 1 Pet. 1 : 7, A.V. (R.V., "revelation"). See COMING, MANIFESTATION, REVELATION. **2015**

2. EPIPHANEIA (ἐπιφάνεια), Eng., epiphany, lit., 'a shining forth **AG:304A CB:1246A**
was used of the appearance of a god to men, and of an enemy to an army

in the field, etc. In the N.T. it occurs of (*a*) the advent of the Saviour when the Word became flesh, 2 Tim. 1 : 10 ; (*b*) the coming of the Lord Jesus into the air to the meeting with His saints, 1 Tim. 6 : 14 ; 2 Tim. 4 : 1, 8 ; (*c*) the shining forth of the glory of the Lord Jesus "as the lightning cometh forth from the east, and is seen even unto the west," Matt. 24 : 27, immediately consequent on the unveiling, *apokalupsis*, of His *Parousia* in the air with His saints, 2 Thess. 2 : 8 ; Tit. 2 : 13.¶*

5321 *Notes :* (1) *Phanerōsis*, akin to A, No. 4, a manifestation, is used in
AG:853B CB:1263C 1 Cor. 12 : 7 and 2 Cor. 4 : 2.¶

5318 AG:852B (2) For *phaneros*, wrongly translated "may appear," in 1 Tim. 4 : 15,
CB:1263C A.V. (R.V., "may be manifest," not mere appearance), see MANIFEST.

1717 AG:257C (3) *Emphanēs*, akin to A, No. 5, manifest, is used in Acts 10 : 40 and
CB:1244B Rom. 10 : 20. See MANIFEST, OPENLY.¶

82 (4) For *adēlos*, "which appear not," Luke 11 : 44, see UNCERTAIN.

AG:16C CB:—

APPEARANCE

A. Nouns.

1491 AG:221B CB:1243A 1. EIDOS (εἶδος), properly that which strikes the eye, that which is exposed to view, signifies the external appearance, form, or shape, and in this sense is used of the Holy Spirit in taking bodily form, as a dove, Luke 3 : 22 ; of Christ, 9 : 29, "the fashion of His countenance." Christ used it, negatively, of God the Father, when He said "Ye have neither heard His voice at any time, nor seen His form," John 5 : 37. Thus it is used with reference to each Person of the Trinity. Probably the same meaning attaches to the word in the Apostle's statement, "We walk by faith, not by sight (*eidos*)," 2 Cor. 5 : 7, where *eidos* can scarcely mean the act of beholding, but the visible appearance of things which are set in contrast to that which directs faith. The believer is guided, then, not only by what he beholds but by what he knows to be true though it is invisible.

It has a somewhat different significance in 1 Thess. 5 : 22, in the exhortation "Abstain from every form of evil," i.e., every sort or kind of evil (not "appearance," A.V.). This meaning was common in the papyri, the Greek writings of the closing centuries, B.C., and the New Testament era. See FASHION, SHAPE, SIGHT.¶ Cp. No. 4.

4383 AG:720D CB:1267B 2. PROSŌPON (πρόσωπον), *pros*, towards, *ōps*, an eye, lit. the part round the eye, the face, in a secondary sense the look, the countenance, as being the index of the inward thoughts and feelings (cp. 1 Pet. 3 : 12, there used of the face of the Lord), came to signify the presentation of the whole person (translated "person," e.g., in Matt. 22 : 16). Cp. the expression in O.T. passages, as Gen. 19 : 21 (A.V. marg., "thy face"), where it is said by God of Lot, and 33 : 10, where it is said by Jacob of Esau ; see also Deut. 10 : 17 ("persons"), Lev. 19 : 15 ("person"). It also signifies the presence of a person, Acts 3 : 13 ; 1 Thess. 2 : 17 ; or the

* From Notes on Thessalonians by Hogg and Vine, p. 263.

presence of a company, Acts 5 : 41. In this sense it is sometimes rendered " appearance," 2 Cor. 5 : 12. In 2 Cor. 10 : 7, A.V., " appearance," the R.V. corrects to " face." See COUNTENANCE, FACE, FASHION, PERSON, PRESENCE.

3. OPSIS (ὄψις), from *ōps*, the eye, connected with *horaō*, to see 3799
(cp. No. 2), primarily denotes seeing, sight ; hence, the face, the coun- AG:601D CB:1261A
tenance, John 11 : 44 (" face ") ; Rev. 1 : 16 (" countenance ") ; the outward " appearance," the look, John 7 : 24, only here, of the outward aspect of a person. See COUNTENANCE, FACE.

4. EIDEA (εἰδέα), an aspect, appearance, is used in Matt. 28 : 3, 2397
R.V., " appearance ; " A.V., " countenance."¶ AG:369C CB:—

B. Verb.

PHANTAZŌ (φαντάζω), to make visible, is used in its participial form 5324
(Middle Voice), with the neuter article, as equivalent to a noun, and is AG:853B CB:1263C
translated " appearance," R.V., for A.V., " sight," Heb. 12 : 21.¶

APPEASE

KATASTELLŌ (καταστέλλω), to quiet (lit., to send down, *kata*, down, 2687
stellō, to send), in the Passive Voice, to be quiet, or to be quieted, is used AG:419A CB:—
in Acts 19 : 35 and 36, in the former verse in the Active Voice, A.V., " appeased ; " R.V., " quieted ; " in the latter, the Passive, " to be quiet "
(lit., ' to be quieted '). See QUIET.¶ APPETITE See DESIRE

APPOINT, APPOINTED

1. HISTĒMI (ἵστημι), to make to stand, means to appoint, in Acts 2476
17 : 31, of the day in which God will judge the world by Christ. In AG:381D CB:1250C
Acts 1 : 23, with reference to Joseph and Barnabas, the R.V. has " put forward ; " for these were not both appointed in the accepted sense of the term, but simply singled out, in order that it might be made known which of them the Lord had chosen. See ABIDE, No. 10.

2. KATHISTĒMI (καθίστημι), a strengthened form of No. 1, usually 2525
signifies to appoint a person to a position. In this sense the verb is often AG:390B CB:1254C
translated to make or to set, in appointing a person to a place of authority, e.g., a servant over a household, Matt. 24 : 45, 47 ; 25 : 21, 23 ; Luke 12 : 42, 44 ; a judge, Luke 12 : 14 ; Acts 7 : 27, 35 ; a governor, Acts 7 : 10 ; man by God over the work of His hands, Heb. 2 : 7. It is rendered " appoint," with reference to the so-called seven deacons in Acts 6 : 3. The R.V. translates it by " appoint " in Tit. 1 : 5, instead of " ordain," of the elders whom Titus was to appoint in every city in Crete. Not a formal ecclesiastical ordination is in view, but the appointment, for the recognition of the churches, of those who had already been raised up and qualified by the Holy Spirit, and had given evidence of this in their life and service (see No. 11). It is used of the priests of old, Heb. 5 : 1 ; 7 : 28 ; 8 : 3 (R.V., " appointed "). See CONDUCT, MAKE, ORDAIN, SET.

5087 AG:815D 3. TITHĒMI (τίθημι), to put, is used of appointment to any form of
CB:1272C service. Christ used it of His followers, John 15 : 16 (R.V., "appointed" for A.V., "ordained"). "I set you" would be more in keeping with the metaphor of grafting. The verb is used by Paul of his service in the ministry of the Gospel, 1 Tim. 1 : 12 (R.V., "appointing" for "putting"); 2 : 7 (R.V., "appointed" for "ordained"); and 2 Tim. 1 : 11 (R.V., "appointing" for "putting"); of the overseers, or bishops, in the local church at Ephesus, as those appointed by the Holy Ghost, to tend the church of God, Acts 20 : 28 ("hath made"); of the Son of God, as appointed Heir of all things, Heb. 1 : 2. It is also used of appointment to punishment, as of the unfaithful servant, Matt. 24 : 51; Luke 12 : 46; of unbelieving Israel, 1 Pet. 2 : 8. Cp. 2 Pet. 2 : 6. See Bow, Commit, Conceive, Lay, Make, Ordain, Purpose, Put, Set, Sink.

4287 AG:706B *Note:* Akin to *tithēmi* is the latter part of the noun ***prothesmia***, Gal.
(-MIA) 4 : 2, of a term or period appointed.¶

CB:— 4. DIATITHĒMI (διατίθημι), a strengthened form of No. 3 (*dia*,
1303 through, intensive), is used in the Middle Voice only. The Lord used it
(-EMAI) AG:189D of His disciples with reference to the Kingdom which is to be theirs
CB:1241B hereafter, and of Himself in the same respect, as that which has been appointed for Him by His Father, Luke 22 : 29. For its use in connection with a covenant, see Make and Testator.

5021 AG:805D 5. TASSŌ (τάσσω), to place in order, arrange, signifies to appoint,
CB:1271A e.g., of the place where Christ had appointed a meeting with His disciples after His resurrection, Matt. 28 : 16; of positions of military and civil authority over others, whether appointed by men, Luke 7 : 8, or by God, Rom. 13 : 1, "ordained." It is said of those who, having believed the Gospel, "were ordained to eternal life," Acts 13 : 48. The house of Stephanas at Corinth had "set themselves" to the ministry of the saints (A.V., "addicted"), 1 Cor. 16 : 15. Other instances of the arranging of special details occur in Acts 15 : 2; 22 : 10; 28 : 23. See Determine, Ordain, Set.¶

1299 AG:189C 6. DIATASSŌ (διατάσσω), a strengthened form of No. 5 (*dia*, through,
CB:1241B intensive), frequently denotes to arrange, appoint, prescribe, e.g., of what was appointed for tax collectors to collect, Luke 3 : 13; of the tabernacle, as appointed by God for Moses to make, Acts 7 : 44; of the arrangements appointed by Paul with regard to himself and his travelling companions, Acts 20 : 13; of what the Apostle "ordained" in all the churches in regard to marital conditions, 1 Cor. 7 : 17; of what the Lord "ordained" in regard to the support of those who proclaimed the Gospel, 1 Cor. 9 : 14; of the Law as Divinely "ordained," or administered, through angels, by Moses, Gal. 3 : 19.

In Tit. 1 : 5, A.V., "had appointed thee," the sense is rather that of commanding, R.V., "gave thee charge." See Command, No. 1, Ordain,
4929 Order.

AG:791D CB:— 7. SUNTASSŌ (συντάσσω), ***sun***, with, and No. 5, lit., to arrange together with, hence to appoint, prescribe, is used twice, in Matt. 26 : 19 of what the Lord appointed for His disciples, and in 27 : 10, in a quotation concerning the price of the potter's field.¶

8. PROTASSŌ (προτάσσω), *pro*, before, and No. 5, to appoint before, 4384
is used in Acts 17 : 26 (R.V., " appointed "), of the seasons arranged by AG:721D CB:1267B
God for nations, and the bounds of their habitation.¶

9. KEIMAI (κεῖμαι), to lie, is used in 1 Thess. 3 : 3 of the appointment 2749
of affliction for faithful believers. It is rendered " set " in Luke 2 : 34 AG:426C CB:1254C
and Phil. 1 : 16, R.V., where the sense is the same. The verb is a perfect tense, used for the perfect Passive of *tithēmi*, to place, 'I have been placed,' i.e., 'I lie.' See LAY, LIE, MADE (be), SET.

10. APOKEIMAI (ἀποκεῖμαι), *apo*, from, and No. 9, signifies to be laid, 606
reserved, Luke 19 : 20 ; Col. 1 : 5 ; 2 Tim. 4 : 8 ; " appointed," in AG:92D CB:—
Heb. 9 : 27, where it is said of death and the judgment following (R.V., marg., " laid up "). See LAY.¶

11. CHEIROTONEŌ (χειροτονέω), primarily used of voting in the 5500
Athenian legislative assembly and meaning to stretch forth the hands AG:881A CB:1239C
(*cheir*, the hand, *teinō*, to stretch), is not to be taken in its literal sense ; it could not be so taken in its compound *procheirotoneō*, to choose before, since it is said of God, Acts 10 : 41. *Cheirotoneō* is said of the appointment of elders by apostolic missionaries in the various churches which they revisited, Acts 14 : 23, R.V., " had appointed," i.e., by the recognition of those who had been manifesting themselves as gifted of God to discharge the functions of elders (see No. 2). It is also said of those who were appointed (not by voting, but with general approbation) by the churches in Greece to accompany the Apostle in conveying their gifts to the poor saints in Judæa, 2 Cor. 8 : 19. See CHOOSE, ORDAIN.¶

12. PROCHEIRIZŌ (προχειρίζω), from *procheiros*, at hand, signifies 4400
(*a*) to deliver up, appoint, Acts 3 : 20 (R.V., " appointed ") ; (*b*) in the (-OMAI) AG:724C
Middle Voice, to take into one's hand, to determine, appoint beforehand, CB:1266C
translated " appointed " in Acts 22 : 14, R.V. (for A.V., " hath chosen "), and " to appoint " in 26 : 16 (for A.V., " to make ").¶

13. HORIZŌ (ὁρίζω) (Eng., horizon), lit., to mark by a limit, hence, to 3724
determine, ordain, is used of Christ as ordained of God to be a Judge of AG:580D CB:1251B
the living and the dead, Acts 17 : 31 ; of His being 'marked out' as the Son of God, Rom. 1 : 4 ; of Divinely appointed seasons, Acts 17 : 26, " having determined." See DEFINE.

14. ANADEIKNUMI (ἀναδείκνυμι), lit., to show up, to show clearly, 322
also signifies to appoint to a position or a service ; it is used in this sense AG:53B CB:1235A
of the 70 disciples, Luke 10 : 1 ; for the meaning " show," see Acts 1 : 24.¶

15. POIEŌ (ποιέω), to do, to make, is rendered " appointed " in 4160
Heb. 3 : 2, of Christ. For Mark 3 : 14, R.V., see ORDAIN, *Note* (2). AG:680D CB:1265C

Note : Epithanatios, " appointed to death," doomed to it by con- 1935
demnation, 1 Cor. 4 : 9, A.V., is corrected to " doomed to death " in the AG:292D
R.V. (*epi*, for, *thanatos*, death). CB:—

For APPORTIONED (R.V. in 2 Cor. 10 : 13) see DISTRIBUTE

APPREHEND

2638 AG:412D CB:1254A (-OMAI) 1. KATALAMBANŌ (καταλαμβάνω) properly signifies to lay hold of; then, to lay hold of so as to possess as one's own, to appropriate. Hence it has the same twofold meaning as the Eng. "apprehend;" (*a*), to seize upon, take possession of, (1) with a beneficial effect, as of laying hold of the righteousness which is of faith, Rom. 9 : 30 (not there a matter of attainment, as in the Eng. Versions, but of appropriation); of the obtaining of a prize, 1 Cor. 9 : 24 (R.V., "attain"); of the Apostle's desire to apprehend, or lay hold of, that for which he was apprehended by Christ, Phil. 3 : 12, 13; (2) with a detrimental effect, e.g., of demon power, Mark 9 : 18; of human action in seizing upon a person, John 8 : 3, 4; metaphorically, with the added idea of overtaking, of spiritual darkness in coming upon people, John 12 : 35; of the day of the Lord, in suddenly coming upon unbelievers as a thief, 1 Thess. 5 : 4; (*b*), to lay hold of with the mind, to understand, perceive, e.g., metaphorically, of darkness with regard to light, John 1 : 5, though possibly here the sense is that of (*a*) as in 12 : 35; of mental perception, Acts 4 : 13; 10 : 34; 25 : 25; Eph. 3 : 18. See ATTAIN, No. 2, COME, *Note* (8), FIND, OBTAIN, OVERTAKE, PERCEIVE, TAKE.¶

Note: Cp. *epilambanō*, to take hold of, always in the Middle Voice in the N.T. See HOLD.

4084 AG:657A CB:— 2. PIAZŌ (πιάζω), to lay hold of, with the suggestion of firm pressure or force, is used in the Gospels only in John, six times of efforts to seize Christ. and is always rendered "take" in the R.V., 7 : 30, 32, 44; 8 : 20; 10 : 39; 11 : 57. The A.V. has "laid hands on" in 8 : 20. In Acts 12 : 4 and 2 Cor. 11 : 32 (A.V.), it is translated respectively "apprehended" and "apprehend" (R.V., "had taken," and "take"). In Rev. 19 : 20 it is used of the seizure of the Beast and the False Prophet. In John 21 : 3, 10 it is used of catching fish. Elsewhere in Acts 3 : 7. See CATCH, LAY HANDS ON, TAKE.¶ In the Sept., S. of Sol. 2 : 15.¶

APPREHENSIVE See FEAR

APPROACH

A. Verb.

1448 AG:213C CB:1245A ENGIZŌ (ἐγγίζω), to draw near, to approach, from *engus*, near, is used (*a*) of place and position, literally and physically, Matt. 21 : 1; Mark 11 : 1; Luke 12 : 33; 15 : 25; figuratively, of drawing near to God, Matt. 15 : 8; Heb. 7 : 19; Jas. 4 : 8; (*b*) of time, with reference to things that are imminent, as the Kingdom of Heaven, Matt. 3 : 2; 4 : 17; 10 : 7; the Kingdom of God, Mark 1 : 15; Luke 10 : 9, 11; the time of fruit, Matt. 21 : 34; the desolation of Jerusalem, Luke 21 : 8; redemption, 21 : 28; the fulfilment of a promise, Acts 7 : 17; the Day of Christ in contrast to the present night of the world's spiritual darkness, Rom.

13 : 12 ; Heb. 10 : 25 ; the coming of the Lord, Jas. 5 : 8 ; the end of all things, 1 Pet. 4 : 7. It is also said of one who was drawing near to death, Phil. 2 : 30. See COME, *Note* (16), DRAW, *B*, No. 1, HAND (at), NIGH.

B. Adjective.

APROSITOS (ἀπρόσιτος), unapproachable, inaccessible (*a*, negative, and an adjective formed from *proseimi*, to go to), is used, in 1 Tim. 6 : 16, of the light in which God dwells (A.V., " which no man can approach unto ; " R.V., " unapproachable ").¶ 676 AG:102C CB:—

APPROPRIATE See BECOME

APPROVE, APPROVED

A. Verbs.

1. DOKIMAZŌ (δοκιμάζω), primarily, of metals (e.g., the Sept. of Prov. 8 : 10 ; 17 : 3), signifies to prove, e.g., 1 John 4 : 1, more frequently to prove with a view to approval, e.g., Rom. 1 : 28, A.V., " they did not like to retain God in their knowledge ; " R.V., " they refused ; " marg., " did not approve," the true meaning. Their refusal was not the outcome of ignorance ; they had the power to make a deliberate choice ; they wilfully disapproved of having God in their knowledge. 1381 AG:202C CB:1242A

In the next chapter, the Apostle speaks of the Jew as " approving things that are excellent," 2 : 18. The Jew knew God's will, and mentally approved of the things in which God had instructed him out of the Law.

In Rom. 14 : 22, he is said to be happy who " judgeth not himself in that which he approveth ; " that is to say, in that which he approves of after having put the matter to the test. The A.V. " alloweth " has not now this meaning.

As to the gifts from the church at Corinth for poor saints in Judæa, those who were " approved " by the church to travel with the offering would be men whose trustworthiness and stability had been proved, 1 Cor. 16 : 3 (the R.V. margin seems right, " whomsoever ye shall approve, them will I send with letters ") ; cp. 2 Cor. 8 : 22.

In Phil. 1 : 10 the Apostle prays that the saints may " approve the things that are excellent " or ' things that differ,' i.e., approve after distinguishing and discerning.

In 1 Thess. 2 : 4, the Apostle and his fellow-missionaries were " approved of God to be entrusted with the Gospel " (not " allowed," A.V.). Not permission to preach, but Divine approval after Divine testing is intended. See ALLOW, DISCERN, EXAMINE, LIKE, PROVE, REFUSE, TRY.

Note : Cp. *dokimē*, proof, experience ; see also B.

2. SUNISTĒMI (συνίστημι), lit., to set together (*sun*, with, *histēmi*, to stand), hence signifies to set one person or thing with another by way of presenting and commending. This meaning is confined to Romans and 2 Corinthians. The saints at Corinth had ' approved themselves in everything to be pure,' in the matter referred to, 2 Cor. 7 : 11. The word often denotes to commend, so as to meet with approval, Rom. 3 : 5 ; 4921 AG:790C CB:1270C

5 : 8 ; 16 : 1 ; 2 Cor. 4 : 2 ; 6 : 4 (R.V.) ; 10 : 18 ; 12 : 11, etc. See COMMEND, COMPACTED, CONSIST (No. 2), STAND.

584 AG:89C CB:1236C 3. APODEIKNUMI (ἀποδείκνυμι), lit., to point out, to exhibit (*apo*, forth, *deiknumi*, to show), is used once in the sense of proving by demonstration, and so bringing about an approval. The Lord Jesus was " a Man approved of God by mighty works and wonders and signs," Acts 2 : 22. See PROVE, SET, No. 17, SHEW.

B. Adjective.

1384 AG:203A CB:1242A DOKIMOS (δόκιμος), akin to *dechomai*, to receive, always signifies " approved ; " so the R.V. everywhere, e.g., in Jas. 1 : 12 for A.V., " when he is tried." The word is used of coins and metals in the Sept. ; in Gen. 23 : 16, " four hundred didrachms of silver approved with merchants ; " in Zech. 11 : 13, in regard to the 30 pieces of silver, " Cast them into a furnace and I will see if it is good (approved) metal."

APRON

4612 AG:751A CB:— SIMIKINTHION (σιμικίνθιον), a thing girded round half the body (Latin, *semicinctium*), was a narrow apron, or linen covering, worn by workmen and servants, Acts 19 : 12.¶

ARAMAIC See TONGUE C.

For APT see TEACH, B

ARCHANGEL

743 AG:111A CB:1237B ARCHANGELOS (ἀρχάγγελος) " is not found in the O.T., and in the N.T. only in 1 Thess. 4 : 16 and Jude 9, where it is used of Michael, who in Daniel is called ' one of the chief princes,' and ' the great prince ' (Sept., ' the great angel '), 10 : 13, 21 ; 12 : 1. Cp. also Rev. 12 : 7. . . . Whether there are other beings of this exalted rank in the heavenly hosts, Scripture does not say, though the description ' one of the chief princes ' suggests that this may be the case ; cp. also Rom. 8 : 38 ; Eph. 1 : 21 ; Col. 1 : 16, where the word translated ' principalities ' is *archē*, the prefix in archangel."* In 1 Thess. 4 : 16 the meaning seems to be that the voice of the Lord Jesus will be of the character of an archangelic shout.¶

ARCHITECT See BUILDER

AREA See REGION

ARGUE See DISPUTE

For ARIGHT (R.V. of 2 Tim. 2 : 15) see HANDLE, No. 5

ARISE, AROSE, AROUSE, RAISE, RISE, ROUSE

450 AG:70A CB:1235C (ANHI-) 1. ANISTĒMI (ἀνίστημι), to stand up or to make to stand up, according as its use is intransitive or transitive (*ana*, up, *histēmi*, to stand), is used (*a*) of a physical change of position, e.g., of rising from sleep, Mark 1 : 35 ; from a meeting in a synagogue, Luke 4 : 29 ; of the illegal rising of the high priest in the tribunal in Matt. 26 : 62 ; of an invalid rising from his couch, Luke 5 : 25 ; the rising up of a disciple from his

---

* From Notes on Thessalonians by Hogg and Vine, p. 142.

vocation to follow Christ, Luke 5 : 28 ; cp. John 11 : 31 ; rising up from prayer, Luke 22 : 45 ; of a whole company, Acts 26 : 30 ; 1 Cor. 10 : 7 ; (*b*) metaphorically, of rising up antagonistically against persons, e.g., of officials against people, Acts 5 : 17 ; of a seditious leader, 5 : 36 ; of the rising up of Satan, Mark 3 : 26 ; of false teachers, Acts 20 : 30 ; (*c*) of rising to a position of pre-eminence or power ; e.g., of Christ as a Prophet, Acts 3 : 22 ; 7 : 37 ; as God's servant in the midst of the nation of Israel, Acts 3 : 26 ; as the Son of God in the midst of the nation, 13 : 33 (not here of Resurrection, but with reference to the Incarnation : the A.V. " again " has nothing corresponding to it in the original, it was added as a misinterpretation : the mention of His Resurrection is in the next verse, in which it is stressed by way of contrast and by the addition, " from the dead ") ; as a Priest, Heb. 7 : 11, 15 ; as King over the nations, Rom. 15 : 12 ; (*d*) of a spiritual awakening from lethargy, Eph. 5 : 14 ; (*e*) of resurrection from the dead : (1) of the Resurrection of Christ, Matt. 17 : 9 ; 20 : 19 ; Mark 8 : 31 ; 9 : 9, 10, 31 ; 10 : 34 ; Luke 18 : 33 ; 24 : 7, 46 ; John 20 : 9 ; Acts 2 : 24, 32 ; 10 : 41 ; 13 : 34 ; 17 : 3, 31 ; 1 Thess. 4 : 14 ; (2) of believers, John 6 : 39, 40, 44, 54 ; 11 : 24 ; 1 Thess. 4 : 16 ; of unbelievers, Matt. 12 : 41. See LIFT, RAISE (up), STAND.

2. EXANISTĒMI (ἐξανίστημι), a strengthened form of No. 1 (*ex*, 1817
i.e., *ek*, intensive), signifies to raise up, Mark 12 : 19 ; Luke 20 : 28 ; AG:272D CB:1247C
intransitively, to rise up, Acts 15 : 5.¶

3. EGEIRŌ (ἐγείρω) is frequently used in the N.T. in the sense of 1453
raising (Active Voice), or rising (Middle and Passive Voices) : (*a*) from AG:214C CB:1242C
sitting, lying, sickness, e.g., Matt. 2 : 14 ; 9 : 5, 7, 19 ; Jas. 5 : 15 ; Rev. 11 : 1 ; (*b*) of causing to appear, or, in the Passive, appearing, or raising up so as to occupy a place in the midst of people, Matt. 3 : 9 ; 11 : 11 ; Mark 13 : 22 ; Acts 13 : 22. It is thus said of Christ in Acts 13 : 23 ; cp. No. 1, (*c*) ; (*c*) of rousing, stirring up, or rising against, Matt. 24 : 7 ; Mark 13 : 8 ; (*d*) of raising buildings, John 2 : 19, 20 ; (*e*) of raising or rising from the dead ; (1) of Christ, Matt. 16 : 21 ; and frequently elsewhere (but not in Phil., 2 Thess., 1 Tim., Tit., Jas., 2 Pet., Epp. of John and Jude) ; (2) of Christ's raising the dead, Matt. 11 : 5 ; Mark 5 : 41 ; Luke 7 : 14 ; John 12 : 1, 9, 17 ; (3) of the act of the disciples, Matt. 10 : 8 ; (4) of the resurrection of believers, Matt. 27 : 52 ; John 5 : 21 ; 1 Cor. 15 : 15, 16, 29, 32, 35, 42, 43, 44, 52 ; 2 Cor. 1 : 9 ; 4 : 14 ; of unbelievers, Matt. 12 : 42 (cp. ver. 41, No. 1).

Egeirō stands in contrast to *anistēmi* (when used with reference to resurrection) in this respect, that *egeirō* is frequently used both in the transitive sense of raising up and the intransitive of rising, whereas *anistēmi* is comparatively infrequent in the transitive use. See AWAKE.

4. DIEGEIRŌ (διεγείρω), a strengthened form of No. 3 (*dia*, through, 1326
intensive), signifies to rouse, to awaken from sleep. The Active Voice AG:193D CB:—
is not used intransitively. In Matt. 1 : 24, R.V., " Joseph arose from his sleep," the Passive Participle is, lit., ' being aroused.' In Mark

4 : 39 (A.V., "he arose," R.V., "he awoke"), the lit. rendering is 'he being awakened.' In John 6 : 18 the imperfect tense of the Passive Voice is used, and the rendering should be, 'the sea was being aroused.' See AWAKE, No. 2.

1096 AG:158A CB:1248B 5. GINOMAI (γίνομαι), to become, to take place, is sometimes suitably translated "arise;" e.g., Matt. 8 : 24; Mark 4 : 37, "there arose a great tempest." So of the arising of persecution, Matt. 13 : 21; Mark 4 : 17; this might be translated 'taketh place;' of a tumult, Matt. 27 : 24, R.V., "arising," for A.V., "made;" of a flood, Luke 6 : 48; a famine, 15 : 14; a questioning, John 3 : 25; a murmuring, Acts 6 : 1; a tribulation, 11 : 19 (R.V.); a stir in the city, 19 : 23; a dissension, 23 : 7; a great clamour, ver. 9. See BECOME.

305 AG:50A CB:1235A 6. ANABAINŌ (ἀναβαίνω), to go up, to ascend, is once rendered "arise" in the R.V., Luke 24 : 38, of reasonings in the heart; in Rev. 13 : 1, R.V., "coming up," for A.V., "rise up," with reference to the beast; in 17 : 8, A.V., "ascend," for R.V., "to come up;" in 19 : 3, R.V., "goeth up," for A.V., "rose up." See CLIMB UP, COME, ENTER, GO, GROW, RISE, SPRING.

4911 AG:789A CB:— 7. SUNEPHISTĒMI (συνεφίστημι), to rise up together (*sun*, together, *epi*, up, *histēmi*, to stand), is used in Acts 16 : 22, of the rising up of a multitude against Paul and Silas.¶

1525 AG:232C CB:1243B 8. EISERCHOMAI (εἰσέρχομαι), lit., to go in (*eis*, in, *erchomai*, to go), to enter, is once rendered "arose," metaphorically, with reference to a reasoning among the disciples which of them should be the greatest, Luke 9 : 46. See COME, ENTER, GO.

393 AG:62A CB:1235B 9. ANATELLŌ (ἀνατέλλω), to arise, is used especially of things in the natural creation, e.g., the rising of the sun, moon and stars; metaphorically, of light, in Matt. 4 : 16, "did spring up;" of the sun, Matt. 5 : 45; 13 : 6 (R.V.); Mark 4 : 6; James 1 : 11; in Mark 16 : 2 the R.V. has "when the sun was risen," keeping to the verb form, for the A.V., "at the rising of;" of a cloud, Luke 12 : 54; of the day-star, 2 Pet. 1 : 19; in Heb. 7 : 14 metaphorically, of the Incarnation of Christ: "Our Lord hath sprung out of Judah," more lit., 'Our Lord hath arisen out of Judah,' as of the rising of the light of the sun. See RISE, SPRING, UP.¶

395 AG:62B CB:— *Notes:* (1) A corresponding noun, *anatolē*, signifies the east, i.e., the place of the sunrising.

906 AG:130D CB:1238B (2) In Acts 27 : 14, the verb *ballō*, to beat (intransitive), is translated "arose" in the A.V.; R.V., "beat."

ARK

2787 AG:431D CB:1255A KIBŌTOS (κιβωτός), a wooden box, a chest, is used of (*a*) Noah's vessel, Matt. 24 : 38; Luke 17 : 27; Heb. 11 : 7; 1 Pet. 3 : 20; (*b*) the ark of the Covenant in the Tabernacle, Heb. 9 : 4; (*c*) the ark seen in vision in the Heavenly Temple, Rev. 11 : 19.¶

ARM (physical)

1. ANKALĒ (ἀγκάλη), used in the plural, in Luke 2 : 28, originally 43
denoted the curve, or the inner angle, of the arm. The word is derived AG:10C
from a term signifying to bend, to curve ; the Eng. " angle " is connected.¶ CB:1235C

Note : Enankalizomai (*en*, in, and a verb akin to No. 1), to take 1723
into the arms, to embrace, is used in Mark 9 : 36 and 10 : 16, of the AG:261D
tenderness of Christ towards little children.¶ CB:1244C

2. BRACHIŌN (βραχίων), the shorter part of the arm, from the 1023
shoulder to the elbow, is used metaphorically to denote strength, power, AG:147B
and always in the N.T. of the power of God, Luke 1 : 51 ; John 12 : 38 ; CB:—
Acts 13 : 17 ; frequently so in the O.T., especially in Deuteronomy, the Psalms and Isaiah ; see, e.g., Deut. 4 : 34 ; 5 : 15 ; Psa. 44 : 3 ; 71 : 18, where " strength " is, lit., 'arm ;' 77 : 15 ; Isa. 26 : 11, where " hand " is, lit., 'arm ;' 30 : 30 ; 40 : 10, 11, etc.¶

ARMS (weapons), ARMOUR, TO ARM

A. Nouns.

1. HOPLON (ὅπλον), originally any tool or implement for preparing 3696
a thing, became used in the plural for weapons of warfare. Once in the AG:575C
N.T. it is used of actual weapons, John 18 : 3 ; elsewhere, metaphorically, CB:1251A
of (*a*) the members of the body as instruments of unrighteousness and as instruments of righteousness, Rom. 6 : 13 ; (*b*) the armour of light, Rom. 13 : 12 ; the armour of righteousness, 2 Cor. 6 : 7 ; the weapons of the Christian's warfare, 2 Cor. 10 : 4.¶

2. PANOPLIA (πανοπλία), Eng., panoply, lit., all armour, full armour, 3833
(*pas*, all, *hoplon*, a weapon), is used (*a*) of literal armour, Luke 11 : 22 ; AG:607D
(*b*) of the spiritual helps supplied by God for overcoming the temptations CB:1261C
of the Devil, Eph. 6 : 11, 13. Among the Greeks the *panoplia* was the complete equipment used by heavily armed infantry.¶

B. Verbs.

1. HOPLIZŌ (ὁπλίζω), to arm oneself, is used in 1 Pet. 4 : 1, in an 3695
exhortation to arm ourselves with the same mind as that of Christ in AG:575C
regard to His sufferings.¶ CB:1251A

2. KATHOPLIZŌ (καθοπλίζω) is an intensive form, to furnish fully 2528
with arms, *kata*, down, intensive, *hoplon*, a weapon, Luke 11 : 21, lit., AG:391A
'a strong man fully armed.'¶ In the Sept., Jer. 46 : 9.¶ CB:—

ARMY

1. STRATEUMA (στράτευμα) denotes (*a*) an army of any size, large 4753
or small, Matt. 22 : 7 ; Rev. 9 : 16 ; 19 : 14, 19 (twice) ; (*b*) a company of AG:770B
soldiers, such as Herod's bodyguard, Luke 23 : 11 (R.V., " soldiers "), CB:1270A
or the soldiers of a garrison, Acts 23 : 10, 27 (R.V., " the soldiers," for A.V., " an army "). See SOLDIER, WAR.¶

2. STRATOPEDON (στρατόπεδον), from *stratos*, a military host, 4760 AG:771A
pedon, a plain, strictly denotes an army encamped, a camp ; in Luke CB:1270B

21 : 20, of the soldiers which were to be encamped about Jerusalem in fulfilment of the Lord's prophecy concerning the destruction of the city; the phrase might be translated 'by camps' (or encampments).¶

3925 AG:625B CB:1262B 3. PAREMBOLĒ (παρεμβολή), lit., a casting in among, an insertion (*para*, among, *ballō*, to throw), in the Macedonian dialect, was a military term. In the N.T. it denotes the distribution of troops in army formation, "armies," Heb. 11 : 34; a camp, as of the Israelites, Ex. 19 : 17; 29 : 14; 32 : 17; hence, in Heb. 13 : 11, 13, of Jerusalem, since the city was to the Jews what the camp in the wilderness had been to the Israelites; in Rev. 20 : 9, the armies or camp of the saints, at the close of the Millennium.

AROMA See **SAVOUR**

AROUSE See **STIR**

It also denoted a castle or barracks, Acts 21 : 34, 37; 22 : 24; 23 : 10, 16, 32.¶

ARRANGE See **ORDER**

AROUND: see Note †, p. 9.

ARREST See **SEIZE, GUARD**

For ARRAY, see CLOTHE, No. 6, PUT

ARRIVE

2658 AG:415B CB:1254A 1. KATANTAŌ (καταντάω), to come to, arrive at, is used (*a*) literally, of locality, Acts 16 : 1, "came to;" so 18 : 19, 24; 20 : 15 ("came"); 21 : 7; 25 : 13; 27 : 12 (A.V., "attain to," R.V., "reach"); 28 : 13; (*b*) metaphorically, of attainment, Acts 26 : 7, "attain;" so Eph. 4 : 13; Phil. 3 : 11. In 1 Cor. 10 : 11 ("upon whom the ends of the ages are come," R.V.), the metaphor is apparently that of an inheritance as coming down or descending to an heir, the "ends" (*telē*) being the spiritual revenues (cp. Matt. 17 : 25, revenues derived from taxes, and Rom. 13 : 7, where the singular, *telos*, "custom," is used); the inheritance metaphor is again seen in 1 Cor. 14 : 36, of the coming (or descending) of the word of God to the Corinthians. See ATTAIN.

2668 AG:416D CB:— 2. KATAPLEŌ (καταπλέω) denotes to sail down (*kata*, down, *pleō*, to sail), i.e., from the high sea to the shore, Luke 8 : 26.¶

3854 AG:613C CB:— 3. PARAGINOMAI (παραγίνομαι), lit., to become near, hence, to come on the scene, Matt. 3 : 1, of John the Baptist, is translated, "arrive" in the R.V. of 1 Cor. 16 : 3, for A.V., "come." See COME, GO, PRESENT.

3846 AG:611D CB:1262A 4. PARABALLŌ (παραβάλλω), *para*, alongside, *ballō*, to throw, signifies, nautically, "touched at;" so the R.V. of Acts 20 : 15 (A.V., "arrived"); or, perhaps, to strike across, from one place to another. In Mark 4 : 30, some mss. have this verb (A.V., "compare"); the most authentic have *tithēmi*, to set forth (with the word "parable"). See COMPARE.

5348 AG:856D CB:1264C 5. PHTHANŌ (φθάνω), to anticipate, reach to, is translated "did arrive at," Rom. 9 : 31, R.V., of Israel's failure to attain to the Law (A.V., "hath attained to"). See ATTAIN, COME, PRECEDE.

ARROGANCE See **PRIDE**

ART, ARTS

5078 AG:814B CB:1271A 1. TECHNĒ (τέχνη), an art, handicraft, trade, is used in Acts 17 : 29, of the plastic art; in Acts 18 : 3, of a trade or craft (A.V., "occupation,"

R.V., "trade"); in Rev. 18 : 22, "craft" (cp. *technitēs*, a craftsman, Eng., technical). See CRAFT, OCCUPATION, TRADE.¶

2. PERIERGOS (περίεργος), lit., a work about (*peri*, about, *ergon*, a work), hence, 'busy about trifles,' is used, in the plural, of things superfluous, "curious (or magical) arts," Acts 19 : 19; in 1 Tim. 5 : 13, "busybodies." See BUSYBODY.¶ 4021 AG:646D CB:—

AS (and connected phrases): see Note †, p. 1

For ASCEND see ARISE, No. 6

ASCERTAIN See FIND

ASHAMED (to be), SHAME

A. Verbs.

1. AISCHUNŌ (αἰσχύνω), from *aischos*, shame, always used in the Passive Voice, signifies (*a*) to have a feeling of fear or shame which prevents a person from doing a thing, e.g., Luke 16 : 3; (*b*) the feeling of shame arising from something that has been done, e.g., 2 Cor. 10 : 8; Phil. 1 : 20; 1 John 2 : 28, of the possibility of being ashamed before the Lord Jesus at His Judgment Seat in His Parousia with His saints; in 1 Pet. 4 : 16, of being ashamed of suffering as a Christian.¶ 153 (-OMAI) AG:25C CB:1234A (-OMAI)

2. EPAISCHUNOMAI (ἐπαισχύνομαι), a strengthened form of No. 1 (*epi*, upon, intensive), is used only in the sense (*b*) in the preceding paragraph. It is said of being ashamed of persons, Mark 8 : 38; Luke 9 : 26; the Gospel, Rom. 1 : 16; former evil doing, Rom. 6 : 21; "the testimony of our Lord," 2 Tim. 1 : 8; suffering for the Gospel, ver. 12; rendering assistance and comfort to one who is suffering for the Gospel's sake, ver. 16. It is used in Heb., of Christ in calling those who are sanctified His brethren, 2 : 11, and of God in His not being ashamed to be called the God of believers, 11 : 16.¶ In the Sept., in Job 34 : 19; Ps. 119 : 6; Is. 1 : 29.¶ 1870 AG:282A CB:1245B

3. KATAISCHUNŌ (καταισχύνω), another strengthened form (*kata*, down, intensive), is used (*a*) in the Active Voice, to put to shame, e.g., Rom. 5 : 5; 1 Cor. 1 : 27 (A.V., "confound"); 11 : 4, 5 ("dishonoureth"), and ver. 22; (*b*) in the Passive Voice, Rom. 9 : 33; 10 : 11; 2 Cor. 7 : 14; 1 Pet. 2 : 6; 3 : 16. See CONFOUND, DISHONOUR, SHAME. 2617 AG:410D CB:1254A

4. ENTREPŌ (ἐντρέπω), to put to shame, in the Passive Voice, to be ashamed, lit. means to turn in (*en*, in, *trepō*, to turn), that is, to turn one upon himself and so produce a feeling of shame, a wholesome shame which involves a change of conduct, 1 Cor. 4 : 14; 2 Thess. 3 : 14; Titus 2 : 8, the only places where it has this meaning. See also REGARD, REVERENCE. 1788 AG:269D CB:—

B. Nouns.

1. AISCHUNĒ (αἰσχύνη), shame, akin to A, No. 1, signifies (*a*) subjectively, the confusion of one who is ashamed of anything, a sense of shame, Luke 14 : 9; those things which shame conceals, 2 Cor. 4 : 2; 152 AG:25B CB:1234A

(*b*) objectively, ignominy, that which is visited on a person by the wicked, Heb. 12 : 2 ; that which should arise from guilt, Phil. 3 : 19 ; (*c*) concretely, a thing to be ashamed of, Rev. 3 : 18 ; Jude 13, where the word is in the plural, lit., 'basenesses,' 'disgraces.' See DISHONESTY.¶

1791 AG:269D CB:— 2. ENTROPĒ (ἐντροπή), akin to A, No. 4, lit., a turning in upon oneself, producing a recoil from what is unseemly or vile, is used in 1 Cor. 6 : 5 ; 15 : 34. It is associated with *aischunē* in the Psalms, in the Sept., e.g., 35 : 26, where it follows *aischunē*, "let them be clothed with shame (*aischunē*) and confusion (*entropē*) ;" 44 : 15, "all the day my shame is before me and the confusion of my face has covered me ;" 69 : 19, "Thou knowest my reproach and my shame and my confusion ;" so in 71 : 13. In 109 : 29 the words are in the opposite order.¶

127 AG:22B CB:1233C *Note : Aidōs*, used in 1 Tim. 2 : 9, denotes modesty, shamefastness (the right spelling for the A.V., "shamefacedness"). In comparison with *aischunē*, *aidōs* is "the nobler word, and implies the nobler motive : in it is involved an innate moral repugnance to the doing of the dishonourable act, which moral repugnance scarcely or not at all exists in *aischunē*" (Trench, Syn. § xix). See SHAMEFASTNESS.¶

C. Adjectives.

150 AG:25B CB:1234A 1. AISCHROS (αἰσχρός), base (akin to No. 1), is used in 1 Cor. 11 : 6 ; 14 : 35 ; Eph. 5 : 12. See FILTHY, B, No. 1. ¶Cp. *aischrotēs*, filthiness, Eph. 5 : 4.¶

422 AG:65A CB:— 2. ANEPAISCHUNTOS (ἀνεπαίσχυντος), an intensive adjective (*a*, negative, *n* euphonic, *epi*, upon, intensive, *aischunē*, shame), not ashamed, having no cause for shame, is used in 2 Tim. 2 : 15.¶

ASHES

A. Noun.

4700 AG:763B CB:— SPODOS (σποδός), ashes, is found three times, twice in association with sackcloth, Matt. 11 : 21 and Luke 10 : 13, as tokens of grief (cp. Esth. 4 : 1, 3 ; Isa. 58 : 5 ; 61 : 3 ; Jer. 6 : 26 ; Jonah 3 : 6) ; of the ashes resulting from animal sacrifices, Heb. 9 : 13 ; in the O.T., metaphorically, of one who describes himself as dust and ashes, Gen. 18 : 27, etc.¶

B. Verb.

5077 AG:814B CB:— TEPHROŌ (τεφρόω), to turn to ashes, is found in 2 Pet. 2 : 6, with reference to the destruction of Sodom and Gomorrah.¶

Notes : (1) *Tephra*, frequently used of the ashes of a funeral pile, is not found in the N.T.

(2) The Hebrew verb, rendered "accept" in Psa. 20 : 3, "accept thy burnt sacrifice," signifies to turn to ashes (i.e., by sending fire from heaven). See also Ex. 27 : 3, and Num. 4 : 13, "shall take away the ashes."

ASIARCH See CHIEF 9.

For ASHORE (Acts 27 : 29), see CAST, A, No. 3

For ASIDE see LAY, No. 8, TAKE, No. 3, TURN, Nos. 3, 17, *Note* (1)

ASK

A. Verbs.

1. AITEŌ (αἰτέω), to ask, is to be distinguished from No. 2. *Aiteō* 154
more frequently suggests the attitude of a suppliant, the petition of one AG:25D CB:1234A
who is lesser in position than he to whom the petition is made ; e.g., in the case of men in asking something from God, Matt. 7 : 7 ; a child from a parent, Matt. 7 : 9, 10 ; a subject from a king, Acts 12 : 20 ; priests and people from Pilate, Luke 23 : 23 (R.V., "asking" for A.V., "requiring") ; a beggar from a passer by, Acts 3 : 2. With reference to petitioning God, this verb is found in Paul's Epistles in Eph. 3 : 20 and Col. 1 : 9 ; in James four times, 1 : 5, 6 ; 4 : 2, 3 ; in 1 John, five times, 3 : 22 ; 5 : 14, 15 (twice), 16. See Beg, Call for, Crave, Desire, Require.

2. ERŌTAŌ (ἐρωτάω) more frequently suggests that the petitioner 2065
is on a footing of equality or familiarity with the person whom he requests. AG:311D CB:1246C
It is used of a king in making request from another king, Luke 14 : 32 ; of the Pharisee who "desired" Christ that He would eat with him, an indication of the inferior conception he had of Christ, Luke 7 : 36 ; cp. 11 : 37 ; John 9 : 15 ; 18 : 19.

In this respect it is significant that the Lord Jesus never used *aiteō* in the matter of making request to the Father. "The consciousness of His equal dignity, of His potent and prevailing intercession, speaks out in this, that as often as He asks, or declares that He will ask anything of the Father, it is always *erōtaō*, an asking, that is, upon equal terms, John 14 : 16 ; 16 : 26 ; 17 : 9, 15, 20, never *aiteō*, that He uses. Martha, on the contrary, plainly reveals her poor unworthy conception of His person, that . . . she ascribes that *aiteō* to Him which He never ascribes to Himself, John 11 : 22" (Trench, Syn. § xl).

In passages where both words are used, the distinction should be noticed, even if it cannot be adequately represented in English. In John 16 : 23, "in that day ye shall ask Me nothing," the verb is *erōtaō*, whereas in the latter part of the verse, in the sentence, "If ye shall ask anything of the Father," the verb is *aiteō*. The distinction is brought out in the R.V. margin, which renders the former clause "Ye shall ask Me no question," and this meaning is confirmed by the fact that the disciples had been desirous of asking Him a question (*erōtaō*, ver. 19). If the Holy Spirit had been given, the time for asking questions from the Lord would have ceased. In John 14 : 14, where, not a question, but a request is made by the disciples, *aiteō* is used.

Both verbs are found in 1 John 5 : 16 : in the sentence "he shall ask, and God will give him life for them that sin not unto death," the verb is *aiteō*, but with regard to the sin unto death, in the sentence "not concerning this do I say that he shall make request," the verb is *erōtaō*.

Later, the tendency was for *erotaō* to approximate to *aiteō*. See Beseech, Desire, Intreat, Pray, Request.

Note : In Matt. 19 : 17, the R.V., following the most authentic mss., has "Why askest (*erotaō*) thou Me concerning that which is good?"

1905 AG:285B CB:1245C 3. EPERŌTAŌ (ἐπερωτάω), a strengthened form of No. 2 (*epi*, in addition), is frequently used in the Synoptic Gospels, but only twice in the Gospel of John, 18 : 7, 21. In Rom. 10 : 20 it is rendered "asked of" (A.V., "asked after"). The more intensive character of the asking may be observed in Luke 2 : 46; 3 : 14; 6 : 9; 17 : 20; 20 : 21, 27, 40; 22 : 64; 23 : 3, 6, 9. In Matt. 16 : 1, it virtually signifies to demand (its meaning in later Greek). See DEMAND, DESIRE, QUESTION.

Note: For the corresponding noun *eperōtēma*, see ANSWER.

4441 AG:729C CB:— 4. PUNTHANOMAI (πυνθάνομαι), to ask by way of enquiry, not by way of making a request for something, is found in the Gospels and the Acts, five times in the former, seven in the latter; in Matt. 2 : 4, A.V., "demanded," R.V., "enquired," so Acts 21 : 33. See DEMAND, INQUIRE, UNDERSTAND.

1833 AG:275C CB:— 5. EXETAZŌ (ἐξετάζω), to search out (*ek*, out, intensive, *etazō*, to examine), is translated "ask," in John 21 : 12, A.V. (R.V., "inquire"); in Matt. 2 : 8, A.V., "search;" R.V., "search out," expressing the intensive force of the verb, so Matt. 10 : 11 (A.V., "inquire"). See INQUIRE, SEARCH.¶

3004 AG:468A CB:1256C 6. LEGŌ (λέγω), to say, occasionally signifies to ask, as of an enquiry, the reason being that *legō* is used for every variety of speaking, e.g., Acts 25 : 20, "I asked whether he would come to Jerusalem." See BID, BOAST, CALL, DESCRIBE, GIVE, NAME, PUT, *Note* (2), SAY, SPEAK, TELL, UTTER.

350 AG:56B CB:1235A 7. ANAKRINŌ (ἀνακρίνω), to judge, sometimes has the meaning to ask a question; e.g., 1 Cor. 10 : 25, 27. See DISCERN, EXAMINE, JUDGE, SEARCH.

1809 AG:272A CB:1247B *Notes*: (1) For *apaiteō*, Luke 6 : 30, see REQUIRE, No. 3. (2) In Luke 22 : 31, R.V., *exaiteomai* is rendered "hath asked to have."¶

B. Noun.

155 AG:26B CB:1234A AITĒMA (αἴτημα), akin to No. 1, lit., that which has been asked for, is used in Luke 23 : 24, R.V., "what they asked for" (A.V., "required"); Phil. 4 : 6, "requests;" 1 John 5 : 15, "petitions." See PETITION, REQUEST, REQUIRE.¶

ASLEEP, SLEEP

A. Verbs.

2518 AG:388D CB:1254C 1. KATHEUDŌ (καθεύδω); to go to sleep, is chiefly used of natural sleep, and is found most frequently in the Gospels, especially Matthew and Luke. With reference to death it is found in the Lord's remark concerning Jairus' daughter, Matt. 9 : 24; Mark 5 : 39; Luke 8 : 52. In the Epistles of Paul it is used as follows: (*a*) of natural sleep, e.g., 1 Thess. 5 : 7; (*b*) of carnal indifference to spiritual things on the part of believers, Eph. 5 : 14; 1 Thess. 5 : 6, 10 (as in Mark 13 : 36), a condition of insensibility to Divine things involving conformity to the world (cp. ***hupnos*** below).

2. KOIMAOMAI (*κοιμάομαι*) is used of natural sleep, Matt. 28 : 13 ; 2837
Luke 22 : 45 ; John 11 : 12 ; Acts 12 : 6 ; of the death of the body, but AG:437C
only of such as are Christ's ; yet never of Christ Himself, though He is CB:1255B
"the firstfruits of them that have fallen asleep," 1 Cor. 15 : 20 ; of saints who departed before Christ came, Matt. 27 : 52 ; Acts 13 : 36 ; of Lazarus, while Christ was yet upon the earth, John 11 : 11 ; of believers since the Ascension, 1 Thess. 4 : 13, 14, 15, and Acts 7 : 60 ; 1 Cor. 7 : 39 ; 11 : 30 ; 15 : 6, 18, 51 ; 2 Pet. 3 : 4.¶

Note : " This metaphorical use of the word sleep is appropriate, because of the similarity in appearance between a sleeping body and a dead body ; restfulness and peace normally characterise both. The object of the metaphor is to suggest that, as the sleeper does not cease to exist while his body sleeps, so the dead person continues to exist despite his absence from the region in which those who remain can communicate with him, and that, as sleep is known to be temporary, so the death of the body will be found to be. . . .

" That the body alone is in view in this metaphor is evident, (*a*) from the derivation of the word *koimaomai*, from *keimai*, to lie down (cp. *anastasis*, resurrection, from *ana*, ' up,' and *histēmi*, to cause to stand) ; cp. Is. 14 : 8, where for ' laid down,' the Sept. has ' fallen asleep ; ' (*b*) from the fact that in the N.T. the word resurrection is used of the body alone ; (*c*) from Dan. 12 : 2, where the physically dead are described as ' them that sleep (Sept. *katheudō*, as at 1 Thess. 5 : 6) in the dust of the earth,' language inapplicable to the spiritual part of man ; moreover, when the body returns whence it came, Gen. 3 : 19, the spirit returns to God who gave it, Eccles. 12 : 7.

" When the physical frame of the Christian (the earthly house of our tabernacle, 2 Cor. 5 : 1) is dissolved and returns to the dust, the spiritual part of his highly complex being, the seat of personality, departs to be with Christ, Phil. 1 : 23. And since that state in which the believer, absent from the body, is at home with the Lord, 2 Cor. 5 : 6–9, is described as ' very far better ' than the present state of joy in communion with God and of happy activity in His service, everywhere reflected in Paul's writings, it is evident the word ' sleep,' where applied to the departed Christians, is not intended to convey the idea that the spirit is unconscious. . . .

" The early Christians adopted the word *koimētērion* (which was used by the Greeks of a rest-house for strangers) for the place of interment of the bodies of their departed ; thence the English word ' cemetery,' ' the sleeping place,' is derived."*

3. EXUPNIZO (*ἐξυπνίζω*), to awake (*ek*, out, *hupnos*, sleep), to awake 1852
out of sleep, is used in John 11 : 11.¶ In the Sept., Judg. 16 : 14, 20 ; AG:279B
1 Kings 3 : 15 ; Job. 14 : 12.¶ CB:—

4. APHUPNOŌ (*ἀφυπνόω*), to fall asleep (*apo*, away), is used of natural 879 AG:127D CB:—

* From Notes on Thessalonians by Hogg and Vine, p. 172.

sleep, Luke 8 : 23, of the Lord's falling asleep in the boat on the lake of Galilee.¶

B. Adjective.

1853 AG:279B CB:— EXUPNOS (ἔξυπνος), Acts 16 : 27, signifies "out of sleep."¶

C. Noun.

5258 AG:843A CB:1252A HUPNOS (ὕπνος) is never used of death. In five places in the N.T. it is used of physical sleep; in Rom. 13 : 11, metaphorically, of a slumbering state of soul, i.e., of spiritual conformity to the world, out of which believers are warned to awake.

ASP

785 AG:117B CB:1238A ASPIS (ἀσπίς), a small and very venomous serpent, the bite of which is fatal, unless the part affected is at once cut away, in Rom. 3 : 13 is said, metaphorically, of the conversation of the ungodly.¶

ASS

ONOS 3688 AG:574A CB:1261A 1. ONOS (ὄνος) is the usual word. *Onarion*, the diminutive of *onos*, a young ass, or ass's colt, is used in John 12 : 14, together with *onos*.¶

ONARION 3678 AG:570A CB:1260C
5268 AG:844C CB:— 2. HUPOZUGION (ὑποζύγιον), lit., under a yoke (*hupo*, under, *zugos*, a yoke), is used as an alternative description of the same animal, in Matt. 21 : 5, where both words are found together, "Behold, thy king cometh unto thee, meek and riding upon an ass (*onos*), and upon a colt the foal of an ass (*hupozugion*)." It was upon the colt that the Lord sat, John 12 : 14. In 2 Pet. 2 : 16, it is used of Balaam's ass.¶

ASSASSIN

4607 AG:750B CB:— SIKARIOS (σικάριος) is a Latin word (*sicarius*, from *sica*, a dagger) denoting one who carries a dagger or short sword under his clothing, an assassin, Acts 21 : 38, R.V. Here it is used as a proper name (see the R.V.) of the Sicarii, Assassins, the fanatical Jewish faction which arose in Judæa after Felix had rid the country of the robbers referred to by Josephus (Ant., XX). They mingled with the crowds at Festivals and stabbed their political opponents unobserved (A.V., "murderers").¶

ASSAULT

A. Verb.

2186 AG:330D CB:— EPHISTĒMI (ἐφίστημι), lit., to stand over (*epi*, over, *histēmi*, to stand), signifies to assault; said in Acts 17 : 5, of those who attacked the house of Jason. For its usual meanings see Come (in, to, upon), Hand (at), Instant, Present, Stand.

B. Noun.

3730 AG:581D CB:1251B HORMĒ (ὁρμή), rendered "assault" in Acts 14 : 5, A.V.; R.V., "onset," corresponds to *hormaō*, to rush. See Impulse, Onset.¶

For ASSAY see TRY, No. 2

ASSEMBLE

1. SUNAGŌ (συνάγω), to assemble (*sun*, together, *agō*, to bring), 4863
is used of the gathering together of people or things; in Luke 12:17, 18, AG:782A
"bestow," with reference to the act of gathering one's goods; so in CB:1270B
Luke 15:13, suggesting that the Prodigal, having gathered all his goods together, sold them off; in John 6:12, of gathering up fragments; in John 18:2, "resorted," with reference to the assembling of Christ with His disciples in the garden of Gethsemane, there in the Passive Voice (unsuitable, however, in an English translation). In Acts 11:26, the R.V. has "were gathered together (with the church)," for A.V., "assembled themselves" (possibly 'they were hospitably entertained by'). The verb is not found in the most authentic mss. in Rev. 13:10. See BESTOW, GATHER, LEAD, TAKE, No. 29.

Note: *Episunagō*, to gather together, is found only in the Synoptic 1996
Gospels; twice of the gathering together of people, Mark 1:33; Luke AG:301D
12:1; twice of the desire of the Lord to gather together the inhabitants CB:1246A
of Jerusalem, Matt. 23:37; Luke 13:34; twice of His future act in gathering together His elect through the instrumentality of the angels, Matt. 24:31; Mark 13:27. See GATHER.¶

2. SUNALIZŌ (συναλίζω), to gather together, to assemble, with the 4871
suggestion of a crowded meeting (*sun*, with, *halizō*, to crowd, or mass: AG:783D
the corresponding adjective is *halēs*, thronged), is used in Acts 1:4. The CB:1270B
meaning to eat with, suggested by some, as if the word were derived from *hals*, "salt," is not to be accepted.¶

3. SUNERCHOMAI (συνέρχομαι), to come together (*sun*, together, 4905
erchomai, to come), is once rendered "assemble," Mark 14:53, A.V. AG:788A
It is frequently used of "coming together," especially of the gathering of CB:1270C
a local church, 1 Cor. 11:17, 18, 20, 33, 34; 14:23, 26; it is rendered "resorted" in Acts 16:13, A.V., where the R.V. adheres to the lit. rendering, "came together." See ACCOMPANY.

Notes: (1) In Acts 15:25, *ginomai*, to become, is translated "having 1096
come to (one accord)," correcting the A.V., "being assembled with AG:158A
(one accord)." CB:1248B

(2) *Sunagōgē*, akin to A, No. 1, is, lit., a place where people assemble. 4864
In Acts 13:43 the R.V. suitably has "synagogue," for the A.V. "con- AG:782D
gregation," the building standing by metonymy for the people therein CB:1270B
(cp. Matt. 10:17, etc.). In Jas. 2:2 (A.V., "assembly") the word is "synagogue" (R.V.). See SYNAGOGUE.

(3) *Episunagōgē*, akin to No. 1, *Note*, an assembling together, is used 1997
in 2 Thess. 2:1, of the Rapture of the saints into the air to meet the AG:301D
Lord, "our gathering together;" in Heb. 10:25, of the gatherings of CB:1246A
believers on earth during the present period. See GATHERING.

ASSEMBLY 1577

AG:240D

1. EKKLESIA (ἐκκλησία), from *ek*, out of, and *klēsis*, a calling (*kaleō*, CB:1243C

to call), was used among the Greeks of a body of citizens gathered to discuss the affairs of State, Acts 19 : 39. In the Sept. it is used to designate the gathering of Israel, summoned for any definite purpose, or a gathering regarded as representative of the whole nation. In Acts 7 : 38 it is used of Israel ; in 19 : 32, 41, of a riotous mob. It has two applications to companies of Christians, (*a*) to the whole company of the redeemed throughout the present era, the company of which Christ said, " I will build My Church," Matt. 16 : 18, and which is further described as " the Church which is His Body," Eph. 1 : 22 ; 5 : 23, (*b*) in the singular number (e.g., Matt. 18 : 17, R.V. marg., " congregation "), to a company consisting of professed believers, e.g., Acts 20 : 28 ; 1 Cor. 1 : 2 ; Gal. 1 : 13 ; 1 Thess. 1 : 1 ; 2 Thess. 1 : 1 ; 1 Tim. 3 : 5, and in the plural, with reference to churches in a district.

There is a apparent exception in the R.V. of Acts 9 : 31, where, while the A.V. has " churches," the singular seems to point to a district ; but the reference is clearly to the church as it was in Jerusalem, from which it had just been scattered, 8 : 1. Again, in Rom. 16 : 23, that Gaius was the host of " the whole church," simply suggests that the assembly in Corinth had been accustomed to meet in his house, where also Paul was entertained. See CHURCH.

3831 AG:607D CB:1261C 2. PANĒGURIS (πανήγυρις), from *pan*, all, and *agora*, any kind of assembly, denoted, among the Greeks, an assembly of the people in contrast to the Council of National Leaders, or a gathering of the people in honour of a god, or for some public festival, such as the Olympic games. The word is used in Heb. 12 : 23, coupled with the word Church, as applied to all believers who form the Body of Christ.¶

4128 AG:668B CB:1265B 3. PLĒTHOS (πλῆθος), a multitude, the whole number, is translated " assembly " in Acts 23 : 7, R.V. See BUNDLE, COMPANY, MULTITUDE.

Note : For *sunagōgē*, see ASSEMBLE, Note (2).

ASSIGN See APPOINT

ASSOCIATE See DEAL (WITH), FELLOWSHIP

ASSUME See SUPPOSE

For ASSENT see AGREE, No. 2

For ASSIST see HELP, B, *Note*

ASSURANCE, ASSURE, ASSUREDLY

A. Nouns.

4102 AG:662B CB:1265A 1. PISTIS (πίστις), faith, has the secondary meaning of an assurance or guarantee, e.g., Acts 17 : 31 ; by raising Christ from the dead, God has given " assurance " that the world will be judged by Him (the A.V. margin, " offered faith " does not express the meaning). Cp. 1 Tim. 5 : 12, where " faith " means " pledge." See BELIEF, FAITH, FIDELITY.

4136 AG:670C CB:1265B 2. PLĒROPHORIA (πληροφορία), a fulness, abundance, also means full assurance, entire confidence ; lit., a ' full-carrying ' (*plēros*, full, *pherō*, to carry). Some explain it as full fruitfulness (cp. R.V., " fulness " in Heb. 6 : 11). In 1 Thess. 1 : 5 it describes the willingness and freedom of spirit enjoyed by those who brought the Gospel to Thessalonica; in Col. 2:2, the freedom of mind and confidence resulting from an understanding in Christ; in Heb. 6:11 (A.V., "full assurance," R.V., "fulness"), the engrossing effect of the expectation of the fulfilment of God's promises; in Heb. 10:22, the character of the faith by which we are to draw near to God. See FULNESS.¶

3. HUPOSTASIS (ὑπόστασις), lit., a standing under, support (*hupo*, 5287
under, *histēmi*, to stand), hence, an "assurance," is so rendered in Heb. AG:847A
11:1, R.V., for A.V., "substance." It here may signify a title-deed, CB:1252B
as giving a guarantee, or reality. See CONFIDENCE, PERSON, SUBSTANCE.

Note: In Acts 16:10, for the A.V. (of *sumbibazomai*), "assuredly 4822
gathering," see CONCLUDE. AG:777D
CB:—

B. Verbs.

1. PISTOŌ (πιστόω), to trust or give assurance to (cp. A, No. 1), has 4104
a secondary meaning, in the Passive Voice, to be assured of, 2 Tim. 3:14.¶ AG:665B
CB:1265A

2. PLĒROPHOREŌ (πληροφορέω), akin to A, No. 2, to bring in full 4135
measure, to fulfil, also signifies to be fully assured, Rom. 4:21, R.V., of AG:670B
Abraham's faith. In 14:5 it is said of the apprehension of the will of CB:1265B
God. So in Col. 4:12 in the best mss. In these three places it is used subjectively, with reference to an effect upon the mind. For its other and objective use, referring to things external, see FULFIL; see also BELIEVE, KNOW, PERSUADE, PROOF.¶ In the Sept., Eccl. 8:11.¶

3. PEITHŌ (πείθω), to persuade, is rendered "assure" in 1 John 3982
3:19 (marg., "persuade"), where the meaning is that of confidence AG:639A
toward God consequent upon loving in deed and in truth. See BELIEVE, CB:1263A
CONFIDENCE, FRIEND, OBEY, PERSUADE, TRUST, YIELD.

C. Adverb.

ASPHALŌS (ἀσφαλῶς) means (*a*) safely, Mark 14:44; Acts 16:23; 806
(*b*) assuredly, Acts 2:36; the knowledge there enjoined involves freedom AG:119A
from fear of contradiction, with an intimation of the impossibility of CB:1238A
escape from the effects. See SAFELY.

For ASTONISH and ASTONISHMENT see AMAZE and AMAZEMENT

ASTOUND See AMAZE

For ASTRAY see ERR

For ASUNDER see BREAK, BURST, CUT, PART, PUT, REND and SAW

AT: see Note †, p. 1

ATHLETE See CONTEND 1.

For ATHIRST see THIRST

ATONEMENT

2643 AG:414A CB:1254A

KATALLAGĒ (καταλλαγή), translated "atonement" in the A.V.

of Rom. 5 : 11, signifies, not "atonement," but "reconciliation," as in the R.V. See also Rom. 11 : 15; 2 Cor. 5 : 18, 19.¶ So with the corresponding verb *katallassō*, see under RECONCILE. "Atonement" (the explanation of this English word as being at-one-ment is entirely fanciful) is frequently found in the O.T. See, for instance, Leviticus, chapters 16 and 17. The corresponding N.T. words are *hilasmos*, propitiation, 1 Jno. 2 : 2; 4 : 10, and *hilastērion*, Rom. 3 : 25; Heb. 9 : 5, "mercy-seat," the covering of the ark of the Covenant. These describe the means (in and through the Person and work of the Lord Jesus Christ,
ATTACH in His death on the Cross by the shedding of His blood in His vicarious
See JOIN sacrifice for sin) by which God shows mercy to sinners. See PROPITIATION.

ATTACK See WAR

ATTAIN

2658 AG:415B CB:1254A 1. KATANTAŌ (καταντάω), a strengthened form of *antaō*, to come opposite to, signifies to reach, to arrive at. It is used in its local significance several times in the Acts, e.g., 27 : 12, R.V., "could reach."

In its metaphorical sense of attaining to something it is used in three places: Acts 26 : 7, of the fulfilment of the promise of God made to the ancestors of Israel, to which promise the twelve tribes "hope to attain" (R.V.); in Eph. 4 : 13, of attaining to the unity of the faith and of the knowledge of the Son of God; in Phil. 3 : 11, of the paramount aims of the Apostle's life, "if by any means," he says, "I might attain unto the resurrection from the dead," not the physical resurrection, which is assured to all believers hereafter, but to the present life of identification with Christ in His Resurrection. For the metaphorical sense in 1 Cor. 10 : 11 and 14 : 36, see ARRIVE, A, No. 1. See also COME, No. 28.

2638 AG:412D CB:1254A (-OMAI) 2. KATALAMBANŌ (καταλαμβάνω), to seize, to apprehend, whether physically or mentally, is rendered "attain" in the sense of making something one's own, appropriating a thing, Rom. 9 : 30, said of the Gentiles, who through the Gospel have attained to, or laid hold of, the righteousness which is of faith, in contrast to the present condition of Israel; in 1 Cor. 9 : 24, of securing a prize, R.V., "attain," for A.V., "obtain." See APPREHEND.

5348 AG:856D CB:1264C 3. PHTHANŌ (φθάνω), to anticipate, also means to reach, attain to a thing; negatively of Israel (see ARRIVE, No. 5). The only other passage where it has this significance is Phil. 3 : 16, "we have attained." See COME, PREVENT.

5177 AG:829B CB:— 4. TUNCHANŌ (τυγχάνω), to reach, meet with, signifies to attain to, in Luke 20 : 35, R.V. (for A.V., "obtain"). See CHANCE, ENJOY, OBTAIN.

3877 AG:618D CB:1262A *Notes:* (1) *Parakoloutheō*, rendered "attained" in 1 Tim. 4 : 6, A.V. (R.V., "hast followed"), does not signify attainment, but following fully. It is an intensive form of *akoloutheō*, to follow. So in 2 Tim. 3 : 10, R.V., "didst follow" (A.V., "fully known"); 'follow fully' would be suitable. In Mark 16 : 17 it is translated "follow;" in Luke 1 : 3, "having traced" (R.V.). See FOLLOW, KNOW, *Notes* (1), UNDERSTAND.¶

(2) *Lambanō*, incorrectly translated "attained" in the A.V. of 2983
Phil. 3 : 12, means "obtained" (R.V.). AG:464A CB:1256C

ATTEND, ATTENDANCE, ATTENDANT

A. Verbs.

1. PROSECHŌ (προσέχω), to take heed, give heed, is said of the 4337
priests who "gave attendance at the altar," Heb. 7 : 13. It suggests AG:714B
devotion of thought and effort to a thing. In 1 Tim. 4 : 13 (in the CB:—
exhortation regarding the public reading of the Scriptures), the R.V. translates it "give heed," for the A.V., "give attendance." In Acts 16 : 14, "to give heed" (for A.V., "attended"). See BEWARE, GIVE, No. 17, REGARD.

2. PROSKARTEREŌ (προσκαρτερέω), to be stedfast, a strengthened 4342
form of *kartereō* (*pros*, towards, intensive, *karteros*, strong), denotes to AG:715C
continue stedfastly in a thing and give unremitting care to it, e.g., Rom. CB:1267A
13 : 6, of rulers in the discharge of their functions. See CONTINUE, WAIT. In the Sept., Numb. 13 : 21.¶

B. Adjective.

EUPAREDROS (εὐπάρεδρος), lit., sitting well beside (*eu*, well, —
para, beside, *hedra*, a seat), i.e., sitting constantly by, and so applying AG:324A CB:—
oneself diligently to, anything, is used in 1 Cor. 7 : 35, with *pros*, upon, 2145
"that ye may attend upon." Some mss. have *euprosedron*.¶ AG:324D CB:—

C. Noun.

HUPĒRETĒS (ὑπηρέτης), lit., an under-rower; hence, a servant, is 5257
rendered "attendant" in Luke 4 : 20 and Acts 13 : 5, R.V. See MINISTER, AG:842C
OFFICER, SERVANT. CB:1252A

For ATTENTIVE, in the A.V. of Luke 19 : 48, see HANG, No. 2 ATTENTION See HEAR

For AUDIENCE see HEARING, A, No. 1, B, No. 1 ATTITUDE See MIND

AUGHT

AUGHT: See † page 9 (footnote). It is wrongly spelt "ought" in the A.V. in some places, e.g., in John 4 : 33, "ought to eat" (there is no word in the original there for "aught").

AUSTERE

AUSTĒROS (αὐστηρός), akin to *auō*, to dry up (Eng., austere), 840
primarily denotes stringent to the taste, like new wine not matured by AG:122B
age, unripe fruit, etc.; hence, harsh, severe, Luke 19 : 21, 22.¶ CB:—

Note: Synonymous with *austēros*, but to be distinguished from it, is
sklēros (from *skellō*, to be dry). It was applied to that which lacks 4642
moisture, and so is rough and disagreeable to the touch, and hence came to AG:756A CB:1269A
denote harsh, stern, hard. It is used by Matthew to describe the unprofitable servant's remark concerning his master, in the parable corresponding to that in Luke 19 (see *austēros*, above). *Austēros* is derived from

a word having to do with the taste, *sklēros*, with the touch. *Austēros* is not necessarily a term of reproach, whereas *sklēros* is always so, and indicates a harsh, even inhuman, character. *Austēros* is "rather the exaggeration of a virtue pushed too far, than an absolute vice" (Trench, Syn. § xiv). *Sklēros* is used of the character of a man, Matt. 25 : 24; of a saying, John 6 : 60; of the difficulty and pain of kicking against the ox-goads, Acts 9 : 5; 26 : 14; of rough winds, Jas. 3 : 4 and of harsh speeches, Jude 15. See FIERCE, HARD.¶ Cp. *sklērotēs*, hardness, *sklērunō*, to harden, *sklērokardia*, hardness of heart, and *sklērotrachēlos*, stiff-necked.

AUTHOR

159 AG:26D CB:1234A 1. AITIOS (αἴτιος), an adjective (cp. *aitia*, a cause), denotes that which causes something. This and No. 2 are both translated "author" in Hebrews. *Aitios*, in Heb. 5 : 9, describes Christ as the "Author of eternal salvation unto all them that obey Him," signifying that Christ, exalted and glorified as our High Priest, on the ground of His finished work on earth, has become the Personal mediating cause (R.V., margin) of eternal salvation. It is difficult to find an adequate English equivalent to express the meaning here. Christ is not the merely formal cause of our salvation. He is the concrete and active cause of it. He has not merely caused or effected it, He is, as His Name, "Jesus," implies, our salvation itself, Luke 2 : 30; 3 : 6.

747 AG:112C CB:1237B 2. ARCHĒGOS (ἀρχηγός), translated "Prince" in Acts 3 : 15 (marg., "Author") and 5 : 31, but "Author" in Heb. 2 : 10, R.V., "Captain," R.V. marg., and A.V., and "Author" in 12 : 2, primarily signifies one who takes a lead in, or provides the first occasion of, anything. In the Sept. it is used of the chief of a tribe or family, Num. 13 : 2 (R.V., prince); of the "heads" of the children of Israel, ver. 3; a captain of the whole people, 14 : 4; in Micah 1 : 13, of Lachish as the leader of the sin of the daughter of Sion: there, as in Heb. 2 : 10, the word suggests a combination of the meaning of leader with that of the source from whence a thing proceeds. That Christ is the Prince of life signifies, as Chrysostom says, that "the life He had was not from another; the Prince or Author of life must be He who has life from Himself." But the word does not necessarily combine the idea of the source or originating cause with that of leader. In Heb. 12 : 2 where Christ is called the "Author and Perfecter of faith," He is represented as the One who takes precedence in faith and is thus the perfect Exemplar of it. The pronoun "our" does not correspond to anything in the original, and may well be omitted. Christ in the days of His flesh trod undeviatingly the path of faith, and as the Perfecter has brought it to a perfect end in His own Person. Thus He is the leader of all others who tread that path. See PRINCE.¶

Note: In 1 Cor. 14 : 33, the A.V., "the author," represents no word in the original; R.V. "a God of."

AUTHORITY

A. Nouns.

1. EXOUSIA (ἐξουσία) denotes authority (from the impersonal verb 1849
exesti, " it is lawful "). From the meaning of leave or permission, or AG:277D
liberty of doing as one pleases, it passed to that of the ability or strength CB:1247C
with which one is endued, then to that of the power of authority, the right to exercise power, e.g., Matt. 9 : 6 ; 21 : 23 ; 2 Cor. 10 : 8 ; or the power of rule or government, the power of one whose will and commands must be obeyed by others, e.g., Matt. 28 : 18 ; John 17 : 2 ; Jude 25 ; Rev. 12 : 10 ; 17 : 13 ; more specifically of apostolic authority, 2 Cor. 10 : 8 ; 13 : 10 ; the power of judicial decision, John 19 : 10 ; of managing domestic affairs, Mark 13 : 34. By metonymy, or name-change (the substitution of a suggestive word for the name of the thing meant), it stands for that which is subject to authority or rule, Luke 4 : 6 (R.V. " authority," for the A.V. " power ") ; or, as with the English " authority," one who possesses authority, a ruler, magistrate, Rom. 13 : 1–3 ; Luke 12 : 11 ; Tit. 3 : 1 ; or a spiritual potentate, e.g., Eph. 3 : 10 ; 6 : 12 ; Col. 1 : 16 ; 2 : 10, 15 ; 1 Pet. 3 : 22. The R.V. usually translates it " authority."

In 1 Cor. 11 : 10 it is used of the veil with which a woman is required to cover herself in an assembly or church, as a sign of the Lord's authority over the Church. See JURISDICTION, LIBERTY, POWER, RIGHT, STRENGTH.

2. EPITAGĒ (ἐπιταγή), an injunction (from *epi,* upon, *tassō,* to order), 2003
is once rendered " authority," Tit. 2 : 15 (R.V., marg., " commandment "). AG:302A
See COMMANDMENT. CB:—

Note : The corresponding verb is *epitassō,* to command. See COMMAND.

3. HUPEROCHĒ (ὑπεροχή), primarily, a projection, eminence, as a 5247
mountain peak, hence, metaphorically, pre-eminence, superiority, AG:841D
excellency, is once rendered " authority," 1 Tim. 2 : 2, A.V. (marg., CB:—
" eminent place "), R.V., " high place," of the position of magistrates ; in 1 Cor. 2 : 1, " excellency " (of speech). Cp. *huperechō,* to surpass. See EXCELLENCY.¶

4. DUNASTĒS (δυνάστης), akin to *dunamis,* power, Eng., dynasty, 1413
signifies a potentate, a high officer ; in Acts 8 : 27, of a high officer, it is AG:208C
rendered " of great authority ; " in Luke 1 : 52, R.V., " princes," (A.V., CB:1242B
" the mighty ") ; in 1 Tim. 6 : 15 it is said of God (" Potentate "). See
MIGHTY, POTENTATE. ¶ 1850

B. Verbs. AG:279A CB:1247C

1. EXOUSIAZŌ (ἐξουσιάζω), akin to A, No. 1, signifies to exercise 2715
power, Luke 22 : 25 ; 1 Cor. 6 : 12 ; 7 : 4 (twice). See POWER.¶ AG:421C CB:1254B

2. KATEXOUSIAZŌ (κατεξουσιάζω), *kata,* down, intensive, and No. 1, 831
to exercise authority upon, is used in Matt. 20 : 25, and Mark 10 : 42.¶ AG:121A CB:1238B

3. AUTHENTEŌ (αὐθεντέω), from *autos,* self, and a lost noun *hentēs,* (-TEIN)

probably signifying working (Eng., authentic), to exercise authority on one's own account, to domineer over, is used in 1 Tim. 2 : 12, A.V., " to usurp authority," R.V., " to have dominion." In the earlier usage of the word it signified one who with his own hand killed either others or himself. Later it came to denote one who acts on his own authority; hence, to exercise authority, dominion. See DOMINION, *Note*.¶

AUTUMN

5352 AG:857C PHTHINOPŌRINOS (φθινοπωρινός), an adjective signifying autumnal
CB:— (from *phthinopōron*, late autumn, from *phthinō*, to waste away, or wane, and *opōra*, autumn), is used in Jude 12, where unfruitful and worthless men are figuratively described as trees such as they are at the close of autumn, fruitless and leafless (A.V., " trees whose fruit withereth ").¶

AVAIL

2480 AG:383D ISCHUŌ (ἰσχύω) signifies (*a*) to be strong in body, to be robust, in
CB:1253A sound health, Matt. 9 : 12 ; Mark 2 : 17 ; (*b*) to have power, as of the Gospel, Acts 19 : 20 ; to prevail against, said of spiritual enemies, Rev. 12 : 8 ; of an evil spirit against exorcists, Acts 19 : 16 ; (*c*) to be of force, to be effective, capable of producing results, Matt. 5 : 13 (" it is good for nothing ; " lit., ' it availeth nothing ') ; Gal. 5 : 6 ; in Heb. 9 : 17 it apparently has the meaning to be valid (R.V., " for doth it ever avail . . .? ", for A.V., " it is of no strength "). It is translated " avail " with reference to prayer, in Jas. 5 : 16 ; cp. the strengthened form *exischuō* in Eph. 3 : 18. See ABLE, CAN, GOOD, MAY, PREVAIL, STRENGTH, WHOLE, WORK.

AVENGE, AVENGER

A. Verb.

1556 AG:238C EKDIKEŌ (ἐκδικέω), *ek*, from, *dikē*, justice, i.e., that which proceeds
CB:1243C from justice, means (*a*) to vindicate a person's right, (*b*) to avenge a thing. With the meaning (*a*), it is used in the parable of the unjust judge, Luke 18 : 3, 5, of the vindication of the rights of the widow ; with the meaning (*b*) it is used in Rev. 6 : 10 and 19 : 2, of the act of God in avenging the blood of the saints ; in 2 Cor. 10 : 6, of the Apostle's readiness to use his apostolic authority in punishing disobedience on the part of his readers ; here the R.V. substitutes " avenge " for the A.V., " revenge ; " in Rom. 12 : 19 of avenging oneself, against which the believer is warned.¶

Note : In Rev. 18 : 20, the A.V. mistranslates *krinō* and *krima* " hath avenged you ; " R.V., " hath judged your judgement."

B. Nouns.

1558 AG:238D 1. EKDIKOS (ἔκδικος), primarily, without law, then, one who exacts a
CB:1243C penalty from a person, an avenger, a punisher, is used in Rom. 13 : 4 of a civil authority in the discharge of his function of executing wrath on the evildoer (A.V., wrongly, " revenger ") ; in 1 Thess. 4 : 6, of God as the Avenger of the one who wrongs his brother, here particularly in the matter of adultery.¶

2. EKDIKĒSIS (ἐκδίκησις), vengeance, is used with the verb *poieō*, to make, i.e., to avenge, in Luke 18 : 7, 8 ; Acts 7 : 24 ; twice it is used in statements that " vengeance " belongs to God, Rom. 12 : 19 ; Heb. 10 : 30. In 2 Thess. 1 : 8 it is said of the act of Divine justice which will be meted out to those who know not God and obey not the Gospel, when the Lord comes in flaming fire at His Second Advent. In the Divine exercise of judgment there is no element of vindictiveness, nothing by way of taking revenge. In Luke 21 : 22, it is used of the days of vengeance upon the Jewish people ; in 1 Pet. 2 : 14, of civil governors as those who are sent of God " for vengeance on evildoers " (A.V. " punishment ") ; in 2 Cor. 7 : 11, of the self-avenging of believers, in their godly sorrow for wrong doing, R.V., " avenging," for A.V., " revenge." See PUNISHMENT, VENGEANCE.¶ 1557 AG:238D CB:1243C

AVOID

1. EKKLINŌ (ἐκκλίνω), to turn away from, to turn aside, lit., to bend out of (*ek*, out, *klinō*, to bend), is used in Rom. 3 : 12, of the sinful condition of mankind, A.V., " gone out of the way," R.V., " turned aside ; " in Rom. 16 : 17, of turning away from those who cause offences and occasions of stumbling (A.V., " avoid ") ; in 1 Pet. 3 : 11 of turning away from evil (A.V., " eschew "). See ESCHEW, WAY.¶ 1578 AG:241C CB:—

2. EKTREPŌ (ἐκτρέπω), lit., to turn or twist out, is used in the Passive Voice in Heb. 12 : 13, " that which is lame be not turned out of the way " (or rather, ' put out of joint ') ; in the sense of the Middle Voice (though Passive in form) of turning aside, or turning away from, 2 Tim. 4 : 4 (A.V., " shall be turned unto fables," R.V., " shall turn aside ") ; in 1 Tim. 1 : 6, of those who, having swerved from the faith, have turned aside unto vain talking ; in 5 : 15, of those who have turned aside after Satan ; in 6 : 20, R.V., of " turning away from (A.V., " avoiding ") profane babblings and oppositions of the knowledge which is falsely so called." See TURN. In the Sept., Amos 5 : 8.¶ 1624 AG:246B CB:1244A

3. PARAITEOMAI (παραιτέομαι), lit., to ask aside (*para*, aside, *aiteō*, to ask), signifies (*a*) to beg of (or from) another, Mark 15 : 6, in the most authentic mss. ; (*b*) to deprecate, (1) to entreat (that) not, Heb. 12 : 19 ; (2) to refuse, decline, avoid, 1 Tim. 4 : 7 ; 5 : 11 ; 2 Tim. 2 : 23 ; Tit. 3 : 10 (see No. 4 for ver. 9) ; Heb. 12 : 25 ; (*c*) to beg off, ask to be excused, Luke 14 : 18, 19 (some would put Heb. 12 : 25 here). See EXCUSE, INTREAT, REFUSE, REJECT.¶ 3868 AG:616C CB:1262A

4. PERIISTĒMI (περιΐστημι), in the Active Voice, means to stand around (*peri*, around, *histēmi*, to stand), John 11 : 42 ; Acts 25 : 7 ; in the Middle Voice, to turn oneself about, for the purpose of avoiding something, to avoid, shun, said of profane babblings, 2 Tim. 2 : 16 ; of foolish questions, genealogies, strife, etc., Tit. 3 : 9 (A.V., " avoid "). See SHUN, STAND.¶ 4026 AG:647C CB:—

4724 AG:766A CB:1270A
5. STELLŌ (στέλλω), to place, sometimes signifies, in the Middle

Voice, to take care against a thing, to avoid, 2 Cor. 8 : 20 ; in 2 Thess. 3 : 6, of withdrawing from a person. See WITHDRAW.¶

AWAIT See HOPE

For AWAIT (A.V. of Acts 9 : 24 ; 20 : 3, 19 ; 23 : 30) see PLOT

AWAKE

1453 AG:214C CB:1242C 1. EGEIRŌ (ἐγείρω) is used, (*a*) in the Active Voice, of arousing a person from sleep ; in Matt. 8 : 25 of the act of the disciples in awaking the Lord ; in Acts 12 : 7, of the awaking of Peter R.V., " awake him " ; (*b*) in the Passive Voice, with a Middle significance, of the virgins, in arousing themselves from their slumber, Matt. 25 : 7 ; in Rom. 13 : 11, and Eph. 5 : 14, metaphorically, of awaking from a state of moral sloth. See ARISE, LIFT, RAISE, REAR, RISE, STAND, TAKE.

1326 AG:193D CB:— 2. DIEGEIRŌ (διεγείρω) is used of awaking from natural sleep, Matt. 1 : 24 ; Mark 4 : 38 ; of the act of the disciples in awaking the Lord, Luke 8 : 24 (cp. *egeirō*, in Matt. 8 : 25) ; metaphorically, of arousing the mind, 2 Pet. 1 : 13 ; 3 : 1. See ARISE, RAISE, STIR UP.

1594 AG:243B CB:1243C 3. EKNĒPHŌ (ἐκνήφω), primarily, to return to one's sense from drunkenness, to become sober, is so used in the Sept., e.g., Gen. 9 : 24 ; metaphorically, in Joel 1 : 5 ; Hab. 2 : 7 ; lit., in 2 : 19, of the words of an idolater to an image ; in the N.T. in 1 Cor. 15 : 34, " Awake up righteously and sin not " (R.V.), suggesting a return to soberness of mind from the stupor consequent upon the influence of evil doctrine.¶

1852 AG:279B CB:— 4. EXUPNIZŌ (ἐξυπνίζω), from *ek*, out of, and *hupnos*, sleep, to rouse a person out of sleep, is used metaphorically, in John 11 : 11.¶

1235 AG:182C CB:— 5. DIAGRĒGOREŌ (διαγρηγορέω), *dia*, intensive, *grēgoreō*, to watch, is used in Luke 9 : 32, R.V., " were fully awake." A.V. " were awake."¶

For AWARE see KNOW, A, No. 1, end of 1st par.

AWAY

142 AG:24B CB:1234A *Note :* This word is to be taken in connection with various verbs. The verb *airō*, to seize, to lift up, take away, is translated " away with," in Luke 23 : 18 ; John 19 : 15 ; Acts 21 : 36 ; 22 : 22, implying a forcible removal for the purpose of putting to death. See BEAR, No. 9.

AWE See AMAZE, FEAR

AWE

127 (AIDōS) AG:175B CB:— DEOS (δέος), awe, is so rendered in Heb. 12 : 28, R.V. ; the previous word " reverence " represents the inferior reading *aidōs* (see SHAMEFASTNESS).

AXE

513 AG:77D CB:— AXINĒ (ἀξίνη), an axe, akin to *agnumi*, to break, is found in Matt. 3 : 10, and Luke 3 : 9.¶

B

BABBLER, BABBLINGS

1. SPERMOLOGOS (σπερμολόγος), a babbler, is used in Acts 17 : 18. 4691
Primarily an adjective, it came to be used as a noun signifying a crow, AG:762B
or some other bird, picking up seeds (*sperma*, a seed, *legō*, to collect). CB:1269C
Then it seems to have been used of a man accustomed to hang about the streets and markets, picking up scraps which fall from loads; hence a parasite, who lives at the expense of others, a hanger on.

Metaphorically it became used of a man who picks up scraps of information and retails them secondhand, a plagiarist, or of those who make a show, in unscientific style, of knowledge obtained from misunderstanding lectures. Prof. Ramsay points out that there does not seem to be any instance of the classical use of the word as a babbler or a mere talker. He finds in the word a piece of Athenian slang, applied to one who was outside any literary circle, an ignorant plagiarist. Other suggestions have been made, but without satisfactory evidence.¶

2. KENOPHŌNIA (κενοφωνία), babbling (from *kenos*, empty, and 2757
phonē, a sound), signifies empty discussion, discussion on useless subjects, AG:428A
1 Tim. 6 : 20 and 2 Tim. 2 : 16.¶ CB:—

BABE

1. BREPHOS (βρέφος) denotes (*a*) an unborn child, as in Luke 1 : 41, 1025
44; (*b*) a newborn child, or an infant still older, Luke 2 : 12, 16; 18 : 15; AG:147B
Acts 7 : 19; 2 Tim. 3 : 15; 1 Pet. 2 : 2. See CHILD, INFANT.¶ CB:1239B

2. NĒPIOS (νήπιος), lit., 'without the power of speech,' denotes a little 3516
child, the literal meaning having been lost in the general use of the word. AG:357C
It is used (*a*) of infants, Matt. 21 : 16; (*b*) metaphorically, of the unsophisticated in mind and trustful in disposition, Matt. 11 : 25 and Luke 10 : 21, where it stands in contrast to the wise; of those who are possessed merely of natural knowledge, Rom. 2 : 20; of those who are carnal, and have not grown, as they should have done, in spiritual understanding and power, the spiritually immature, 1 Cor. 3 : 1, those who are so to speak partakers of milk, and "without experience of the word of righteousness," Heb. 5 : 13; of the Jews, who, while the Law was in force, were in a state corresponding to that of childhood, or minority, just as the word "infant" is used of a minor, in English law, Gal. 4 : 3, "children;" of believers in an immature condition, impressionable and CB:1259C

liable to be imposed upon instead of being in a state of spiritual maturity, Eph. 4 : 14, "children." Immaturity is always associated with this word. See CHILD, No. 7¶

Note: The corresponding verb, *nēpiazō*, is found in 1 Cor. 14 : 20, where believers are exhorted to be as "babes" (R.V.) in malice, unable to think or speak maliciously.¶

BACK (Noun)

3577 NŌTOS (νῶτος), the back, is derived from a root *nō—*, signifying to
AG:547C CB:— bend, curve. It is used in Rom. 11 : 10.¶

BACK (Adverb), BACKSIDE, BACKWARD

3694 1. OPISŌ (ὀπίσω), connected with *hepomai*, to follow, is used
AG:575A CB:1261A adverbially, of place, with the meaning "back," "backward," in the
phrase *eis ta opisō*, lit., unto the things behind, in Mark 13 : 16; Luke 9 : 62;
17 : 31; John 6 : 66; 18 : 6; 20 : 14. Cp. Phil. 3 : 13, "the things which
are behind." See BEHIND.

3693 2. OPISTHEN (ὄπισθεν), of place, behind, after, is rendered "back-
AG:574D CB:1261A side" in Rev. 5 : 1, A.V. (R.V., "back"). See BEHIND.

BACKBITER, BACKBITING

2637 KATALALOS (κατάλαλος), a backbiter, and KATALALIA (καταλαλία),
AG:412D CB:1254A backbiting, are formed from *kata*, against, and *laleō*, to speak. *Katalalos*
2636 is used in Rom. 1 : 30.¶ *Katalalia* is translated "evil speaking" in
AG:412D 1 Pet. 2 : 1, "backbiting" in 2 Cor. 12 : 20.¶
CB:1254A 2635 *Note:* The corresponding verb *katalaleō* the R.V. translates "speak
AG:412C against," in its five occurrences, Jas. 4 : 11 (three times); 1 Pet. 2 : 12,
CB:1254A and 3 : 16; A.V., "speak evil," in all the passages except 1 Pet. 2 : 12.¶

For BADE see BID

BAD

2556 1. KAKOS (κακός) indicates the lack in a person or thing of those
AG:397D CB:1253B qualities which should be possessed; it means bad in character (*a*) morally,
by way of thinking, feeling or acting, e.g., Mark 7 : 21, "thoughts;"
1 Cor. 15 : 33, "company;" Col. 3 : 5, "desire;" 1 Tim. 6 : 10, "all
kinds of evil;" 1 Pet. 3 : 9, "evil for evil;" (*b*) in the sense of what is
injurious or baneful, e.g., the tongue as "a restless evil," Jas. 3 : 8;
"evil beasts," Tit. 1 : 12; "harm," Acts 16 : 28; once it is translated
"bad," 2 Cor. 5 : 10. It is the opposite of *agathos*, good. See EVIL,
HARM, ILL, NOISOME, WICKED.

4190 2. PONĒROS (πονηρός), connected with *ponos*, labour, expresses
AG:690D CB:1266A especially the active form of evil, and is practically the same in meaning
as (*b*), under No. 1. It is used, e.g., of thoughts, Matt. 15 : 19 (cp. *kakos*,
in Mark 7 : 21); of speech, Matt. 5 : 11 (cp. *kakos*, in 1 Pet. 3 : 10); of

acts, 2 Tim. 4 : 18. Where *kakos* and *ponēros* are put together, *kakos* is always put first and signifies bad in character, base, *ponēros*, bad in effect, malignant : see 1 Cor. 5 : 8, and Rev. 16 : 2. *Kakos* has a wider meaning, *ponēros* a stronger meaning. *Ponēros* alone is used of Satan and might well be translated 'the malignant one,' e.g., Matt. 5 : 37 and five times in 1 John (2 : 13, 14 ; 3 : 12 ; 5 : 18, 19, R.V.) ; of demons, e.g., Luke 7 : 21. Once it is translated "bad," Matt. 22 : 10. See EVIL, GRIEVOUS, HARM, LEWD, MALICIOUS, WICKED.

3. SAPROS (σαπρός), corrupt, rotten (akin to *sēpō*, to rot), primarily, 4550
of vegetable and animal substances, expresses what is of poor quality, AG:742B CB:1268B
unfit for use, putrid. It is said of a tree and its fruit, Matt. 7 : 17, 18 ; 12 : 33 ; Luke 6 : 43 ; of certain fish, Matt. 13 : 48 (here translated "bad") ; of defiling speech, Eph. 4 : 29. See CORRUPT.¶

BAG

1. GLŌSSOKOMON (γλωσσόκομον), from *glōssa*, a tongue, and *komeō*, 1101
to tend, was, firstly, a case in which to keep the mouthpiece of wind AG:162D CB:1248B
instruments ; secondly, a small box for any purpose, but especially a casket or purse, to keep money in. It is used of the bag which Judas carried, John 12 : 6 ; 13 : 29 ; in the Sept. of 2 Chron. 24 : 8, 10, used of the box appointed by King Joash for offerings for the repair of the Temple.¶

2. BALLANTION (βαλλάντιον), from *ballō*, to cast, a money-box or 905
purse, is found in Luke's Gospel, four times, 10 : 4 ; 12 : 33 (A.V., "bag") ; AG:130D CB:1238B
22 : 35, 36. See PURSE.¶

Note : *Zōnē*, a girdle or belt, also served as a purse for money, Matt. 2223
10 : 9 ; Mark 6 : 8. See GIRDLE. AG:341B CB:1273C

BAGGAGE

EPISKEUAZŌ (ἐπισκευάζω), to furnish with things necessary ; —
in the Middle Voice, to furnish for oneself ; it was used of equipping AG:298C (-OMAI)
baggage animals for a journey ; in Acts 21 : 15, R.V., it is translated CB:—
"we took up our baggage" (A.V., "we took up our carriages"). The form is the 1st aorist participle, and lit. means 'having made ready (the things that were necessary for the journey).'¶

Note : Some mss. have the verb *aposkeuazō*, which has the same 643
meaning. AG:98A CB:—

BALANCE

ZUGOS (ζυγός), a yoke, also has the meaning of a pair of scales, 2218
Rev. 6 : 5. So the Sept. of Lev. 19 : 36 ; Isa. 40, 12. See YOKE.¶ AG:339D CB:1273C

BAND

1. SPEIRA (σπεῖρα), primarily anything round, and so whatever 4686
might be wrapped round a thing, a twisted rope, came to mean a body AG:761A CB:—

of men at arms, and was the equivalent of the Roman *manipulus*. It was also used for a larger body of men, a cohort, about 600 infantry, commanded by a tribune. It is confined to its military sense. See, e.g., Matt. 27 : 27, and corresponding passages.

1199 AG:176A CB:1240C 2. DESMOS (δεσμός), a band, fetter, anything for tying (from *deō*, to bind, fasten with chains etc.), is sometimes translated "band," sometimes "bond;" "bands," in Luke 8 : 29; Acts 16 : 26; 22 : 30, A.V. only. In the case of the deaf man who had an impediment in his speech, whom the Lord took aside, Mark 7 : 35, the A.V. says "the string of his tongue was loosed;" the R.V., more literally, "the bond of his tongue." See BOND, CHAIN, STRING.

4886 AG:785B CB:1270C 3. SUNDESMOS (σύνδεσμος), an intensive form of No. 2, denoting that which binds firmly together, is used metaphorically of the joints and bands of the mystic Body of Christ, Col. 2 : 19; otherwise in the following phrases, "the bond of iniquity," Acts 8 : 23; "the bond of peace," Eph. 4 : 3; "the bond of perfectness," Col. 3 : 14. See BOND.¶

2202 AG:337B CB:— 4. ZEUKTĒRIA (ζευκτηρία), a bond (connected with *zugos*, a yoke), is found once, of the rudder band of a ship, Acts 27 : 40.¶

BANDED

4963 AG:795C CB:— POIEŌ SUSTROPHĒN (ποιέω συστροφήν), Acts 23 : 12, of the Jews who "banded together" with the intention of killing Paul, consists of the verb *poieō*, to make, and the noun *sustrophē*, primarily a twisting up together, a binding together; then, a secret combination, a conspiracy. Accordingly it might be translated 'made a conspiracy.' The noun is used elsewhere in 19 : 40. See CONCOURSE.¶

BANDIT See ROBBER

BANK, BANKERS

5132 AG:824B CB:1273A 1. TRAPEZA (τράπεζα), primarily a table, denotes (*a*) an eating-table, e.g., Matt. 15 : 27; (*b*) food etc. placed on a table, Acts 6 : 2; 16 : 34; (*c*) a feast, a banquet, 1 Cor. 10 : 21; (*d*) the table or stand of a money-changer, where he exchanged money for a fee, or dealt with loans and deposits, Matt. 21 : 12; Mark 11 : 15; Luke 19 : 23; John 2 : 15. See MEAT, TABLE.

5133 AG:824D CB:— 2. TRAPEZITĒS (τραπεζίτης), a money-changer, broker, banker; translated "bankers" in Matt. 25 : 27, R.V. (A.V., "exchangers").¶

Note: For *charax*, Luke 19 : 43, see TRENCH.

For BANQUETING see CAROUSINGS

BAPTISM, BAPTIST, BAPTIZE

A. Nouns.

908 AG:132C CB:1238B 1. BAPTISMA (βάπτισμα), baptism, consisting of the processes of immersion, submersion and emergence (from *baptō*, to dip), is used

(*a*) of John's baptism, (*b*) of Christian baptism, see B. below ; (*c*) of the overwhelming afflictions and judgments to which the Lord voluntarily submitted on the Cross, e.g., Luke 12 : 50 ; (*d*) of the sufferings His followers would experience, not of a vicarious character, but in fellowship with the sufferings of their Master. Some mss. have the word in Matt. 20 : 22, 23 ; it is used in Mark 10 : 38, 39, with this meaning.

2. BAPTISMOS (βαπτισμός), as distinct from *baptisma* (the ordinance), 909
is used of the ceremonial washing of articles, Mark 7 : 4, 8, in some texts ; AG:132D
Heb. 9 : 10 ; once in a general sense, Heb. 6 : 2.¶ See WASHING. CB:1238C

3. BAPTISTĒS (βαπτιστής), a baptist, is used only of John the 910
Baptist, and only in the Synoptists, 14 times. AG:132D CB:1238C

B. Verb.

BAPTIZŌ (βαπτίζω), to baptize, primarily a frequentative form of 907
baptō, to dip, was used among the Greeks to signify the dyeing of a garment, AG:131C CB:1238C
or the drawing of water by dipping a vessel into another, etc. Plutarchus uses it of the drawing of wine by dipping the cup into the bowl (*Alexis*, 67) and Plato, metaphorically, of being overwhelmed with questions (*Euthydemus*, 277 D).

It is used in the N.T. in Luke 11 : 38 of washing oneself (as in 2 Kings 5 : 14, " dipped himself," Sept.) ; see also Isa. 21 : 4, lit., 'lawlessness overwhelms me.' In the early chapters of the four Gospels and in Acts 1 : 5 ; 11 : 16 ; 19 : 4, it is used of the rite performed by John the Baptist who called upon the people to repent that they might receive remission of sins. Those who obeyed came " confessing their sins," thus acknowledging their unfitness to be in the Messiah's coming Kingdom. Distinct from this is the baptism enjoined by Christ, Matt. 28 : 19, a baptism to be undergone by believers, thus witnessing to their identification with Him in death, burial and resurrection, e.g., Acts 19 : 5 ; Rom. 6 : 3, 4 ; 1 Cor. 1 : 13–17 ; 12 : 13 ; Gal. 3 : 27 ; Col. 2 : 12. The phrase in Matt. 28 : 19, " baptizing them into the Name " (R.V. ; cp. Acts 8 : 16, R.V.), would indicate that the baptized person was closely bound to, or became the property of, the one into whose Name he was baptized.

In Acts 22 : 16 it is used in the Middle Voice, in the command given to Saul of Tarsus, " arise and be baptized," the significance of the Middle Voice form being 'get thyself baptized.' The experience of those who were in the ark at the time of the Flood was a figure or type of the facts of spiritual death, burial and resurrection, Christian baptism being an ***antitupon***, " a corresponding type," a " like figure," 1 Pet. 3 : 21. Likewise the nation of Israel was figuratively baptized when made to pass through the Red Sea under the cloud, 1 Cor. 10 : 2. The verb is used metaphorically also in two distinct senses : firstly, of baptism by the Holy Spirit, which took place on the day of Pentecost ; secondly, of the calamity which would come upon the nation of the Jews, a baptism of the fire of Divine judgment for rejection of the will and word of God, Matt. 3 : 11 ; Luke 3 : 16.

BARBARIAN, BARBAROUS

915 BARBAROS (*βάρβαρος*) properly meant one whose speech is rude, or
AG:133B CB:1238C harsh; the word is onomatopœic, indicating in the sound the uncouth
character represented by the repeated syllable "bar-bar." Hence it signified one who speaks a strange or foreign language. See 1 Cor. 14:11. It then came to denote any foreigner ignorant of the Greek language and culture. After the Persian war it acquired the sense of rudeness and brutality. In Acts 28:2, 4, it is used unreproachfully of the inhabitants of Malta, who were of Phœnician origin. So in Rom. 1:14, where it stands in distinction from Greeks, and in implied contrast to both Greeks and Jews. Cp. the contrasts in Col. 3:11, where all such distinctions are shown to be null and void in Christ. "Berber" stood similarly in the language of the Egyptians for all non-Egyptian peoples.¶

BARE (Adjective)

1131 GUMNOS (*γυμνός*), naked, is once translated "bare," 1 Cor. 15:37,
AG:167D where, used of grain, the meaning is made clearer by translating the
CB:1248C phrase by "a bare grain," R.V. See NAKED.

For BARE (Verb) see BEAR

BARLEY

A. Noun.

2915 AG:450C CB:— KRITHĒ (*κριθή*), barley, is used in the plural in Rev. 6:6.¶

B. Adjective.

2916 AG:450C CB:— KRITHINOS (*κρίθινος*) signifies made of barley, John 6:9, 13.¶

BARN

596 APOTHĒKĒ (*ἀποθήκη*), lit., a place where anything is stored (Eng.,
AG:91A apothecary), hence denoted a garner, granary, barn, Matt. 3:12; 6:26;
CB:— 13:30; Luke 3:17; 12:18, 24. See also under GARNER.¶

5009 *Note:* For *tameion*, a storehouse, store-chamber, more especially an
AG:803C CB:— inner chamber or secret room, Matt. 6:6; 24:26; Luke 12:3, 24, see CHAMBER.¶

BARRACKS See ARMY 3.

BARREN

4723 1. STEIROS (*στεῖρος*), from a root *ster*— meaning hard, firm (hence
AG:766A (-RA) Eng., sterile), signifies barren, not bearing children, and is used with
CB:— the natural significance three times in the Gospel of Luke, 1:7, 36; 23:29; and with a spiritual significance in Gal. 4:27, in a quotation from Is. 54:1. The circumstances of Sarah and Hagar, which Isaiah no doubt had in mind, are applied by the Apostle to the contrast between the works of the Law and the promise by grace.¶

692 2. ARGOS (*ἀργός*), denoting idle, barren, yielding no return, because
AG:104C CB:1237C of inactivity, is found in the best mss. in Jas. 2:20 (R.V., "barren");

it is rendered "barren" in 2 Pet. 1 : 8, A.V., (R.V., "idle"). In Matt. 12 : 36, the "idle word" means the word that is thoughtless or profitless. See IDLE, SLOW; cp. *katargeō*, under ABOLISH.

BASE, BASER

1. AGENĒS (ἀγενής), of low birth (*a*, negative, *genos*, family, race), 36
hence denoted that which is of no reputation, of no account, 1 Cor. 1 : 28, AG:8C CB:—
"the base things of the world," i.e., those which are of no account or fame in the world's esteem. That the neuter plural of the adjective bears reference to persons is clear from verse 26.¶

2. TAPEINOS (ταπεινός), primarily that which is low, and does not 5011
rise far from the ground, as in the Sept. of Ezek. 17 : 24, hence, meta- AG:804A CB:1271A
phorically, signifies lowly, of no degree. So the R.V. in 2 Cor. 10 : 1. Cp. Luke 1 : 52 and Jas. 1 : 9, "of low degree." Cp. *tapeinophrosunē*, lowliness of mind, and *tapeinoō*, to humble. See CAST, *Note* (7), HUMBLE, LOW, LOWLY.

3. AGORAIOS (ἀγοραῖος), translated in the A.V. of Acts 17 : 5 "of 60
the baser sort," R.V., "of the rabble," signifies, lit., relating to the market AG:13A CB:1233C
place; hence, frequenting markets, and so sauntering about idly. It is also used of affairs usually transacted in the market-place, and hence of judicial assemblies, Acts 19 : 38, R.V., "courts" (A.V., "law"); the margin in both R.V. and A.V. has "court days are kept." See COURT.¶

BASKET, BASKETFUL

1. KOPHINOS (κόφινος) was a wicker basket, originally containing 2894
a certain measure of capacity, Matt. 14 : 20; 16 : 9; Mark 6 : 43 (R.V., AG:447C CB:—
"basketfuls"); 8 : 19; Luke 9 : 17; 13 : 8 in some mss.; John 6 : 13.¶

2. SPURIS (σπυρίς), or *sphuris*, signifies something round, twisted or 4711
folded together (connected with *speira*, anything rolled into a circle; AG:764A CB:—
Eng., sphere); hence a reed basket, plaited, a capacious kind of hamper, sometimes large enough to hold a man, Matt. 15 : 37; 16 : 10; Mark 8 : 8, 20 (R.V., "basketfuls"); Acts 9 : 25.¶

3. SARGANĒ (σαργάνη) denotes (*a*) a braided rope or band, (*b*) a 4553
large basket made of ropes, or a wicker basket made of entwined twigs, AG:742C CB:—
2 Cor. 11 : 33. That the basket in which Paul was let down from a window in Damascus is spoken of by Luke as a *spuris*, and by Paul himself as a *sarganē*, is quite consistent, the two terms being used for the same article.¶

BASIC (PRINCIPLES) See ELEMENTS

BASON

NIPTĒR (νιπτήρ), the vessel into which the Lord poured water to 3537
wash the disciples' feet, was a large ewer, John 13 : 5. The word is AG:540A CB:—
connected with the verb *niptō*, to wash.¶

BASTARD

3541 AG:540D CB:1260A NOTHOS (νόθος) denotes an illegitimate child, one born out of lawful wedlock, Heb. 12 : 8.¶

BATHED

3068 AG:480D CB:1257B LOUŌ (λούω) signifies to bathe or to wash. In John 13 : 10 the R.V. "bathed" is necessary to distinguish the act from the washing of feet. See WASH.

BATTALION See ARMY, BAND

BATTLE

4171 AG:685A CB:1265C POLEMOS (πόλεμος), a war, is incorrectly rendered "battle" in the A.V. of 1 Cor. 14 : 8; Rev. 9 : 7, 9; 16 : 14; 20 : 8; R.V., invariably, "war."

BAY

2859 AG:442B CB:1255C KOLPOS (κόλπος), translated "bay" in the R.V. of Acts 27 : 39, is wider than a "creek" (A.V.). Eng., gulf, is connected. See BOSOM.

For BE see BEING

BEACH

123 AG:21D CB:— AIGIALOS (αἰγιαλός), translated "shore" in the A.V. in each place where it is used, Matt. 13 : 2, 48; John 21 : 4; Acts 21 : 5; 27 : 39, 40, is always in the R.V. translated "beach." It is derived from a root signifying to press, drive; *aigis* denotes a wind-storm.¶

BEACON See LAMP

BEAM

1385 AG:203A CB:— DOKOS (δοκός), a beam, is perhaps etymologically connected with the root *dek—*, seen in the word *dechomai*, to receive, beams being received at their ends into walls or pieces of timber. The Lord used it metaphorically, in contrast to a mote, of a great fault, or vice, Matt. 7 : 3, 4, 5; Luke 6 : 41, 42.¶

BEAR (*in the sense of carrying, supporting*)

For the verb to bear in the sense of begetting, see BEGET.

941 AG:137B CB:1238C 1. BASTAZŌ (βαστάζω) signifies to support as a burden. It is used with the meaning (*a*) to take up, as in picking up anything, stones, John 10 : 31; (*b*) to carry something, Matt. 3 : 11; Mark 14 : 13; Luke 7 : 14; 22 : 10; Acts 3 : 2; 21 : 35; Rev. 17 : 7; to carry on one's person, Luke 10 : 4; Gal. 6 : 17; in one's body, Luke 11 : 27; to bear a name in testimony, Acts 9 : 15; metaphorically, of a root bearing branches, Rom. 11 : 18; (*c*) to bear a burden, whether physically, as of the Cross, John 19 : 17, or metaphorically in respect of sufferings endured in the cause of Christ, Luke 14 : 27; Rev. 2 : 3; it is said of physical endurance, Matt. 20 : 12; of sufferings borne on behalf of others, Matt. 8 : 17;

Rom. 15 : 1 ; Gal. 6 : 2 ; of spiritual truths not able to be borne, John 16 : 12 ; of the refusal to endure evil men, Rev. 2 : 2 ; of religious regulations imposed on others, Acts 15 : 10 ; of the burden of the sentence of God to be executed in due time, Gal. 5 : 10 ; of the effect at the Judgment Seat of Christ, to be borne by the believer for failure in the matter of discharging the obligations of discipleship, Gal. 6 : 5 ; (*d*) to bear by way of carrying off, John 12 : 6 ; 20 : 15. See Carry, Take.¶

2. PHERŌ (φέρω), to bring or bear, is translated in the R.V. by the 5342
latter verb in Luke 23 : 26 ; John 2 : 8 (twice) ; 12 : 24 ; 15 : 2 (twice) ; AG:854D
Heb. 13 : 13. See Bring, No. 1 and words there. CB:1264A

3. ANAPHERŌ (ἀναφέρω), No. 2, with *ana*, up, is used of leading 399
persons up to a higher place, and, in this respect, of the Lord's Ascension, AG:63A
Luke 24 : 51. It is used twice of the Lord's propitiatory sacrifice, in His CB:1235B
bearing sins on the Cross, Heb. 9 : 28 and 1 Pet. 2 : 24 ; the A.V. margin, "to the tree," is to be rejected. The A.V. text, "on," and the R.V. "upon" express the phrase rightly. See Bring, Carry, Lead, Offer.

4. EKPHERŌ (ἐκφέρω), No. 2, with *ek*, out, is used, literally, of 1627
carrying something forth, or out, e.g., a garment, Luke 15 : 22 ; sick folk, AG:246D
Acts 5 : 15 ; a corpse, Acts 5 : 6, 9, 10 ; of the impossibility of carrying CB:—
anything out from this world at death, 1 Tim. 6 : 7. The most authentic mss. have this word in Mark 8 : 23, of the blind man, whom the Lord brought out of the village (R.V.). It is also used of the earth, in bringing forth produce, Heb. 6 : 8. See Bring, Carry.¶

5. PERIPHERŌ (περιφέρω), No. 2, with *peri*, about, signifies to carry 4064
about, or bear about, and is used literally, of carrying the sick, Mark 6 : 55, AG:653B
or of physical sufferings endured in fellowship with Christ, 2 Cor. 4 : 10 ; CB:1263B
metaphorically, of being carried about by different evil doctrines, Eph. 4 : 14 ; Heb. 13 : 9 ; Jude 12. See Carry.

6. HUPOPHERŌ (ὑποφέρω), lit., to bear up under, is best rendered 5297
by "endure," as 1 Cor. 10 : 13, R.V., of enduring temptations ; of AG:848C
enduring persecutions, 2 Tim. 3 : 11 ; grief, 1 Pet. 2 : 19. See Endure.¶ CB:—

7. PHOREŌ (φορέω), a frequentative form of *pherō*, is to be distin- 5409
guished from it as denoting, not a simple act of bearing, but a continuous AG:864D
or habitual condition, e.g., of the civil authority in bearing the sword as CB:—
symbolic of execution, Rom. 13 : 4 ; of a natural state of bodily existence in this life, spoken of as "the image of the earthy," and the spiritual body of the believer hereafter, "the image of the heavenly," 1 Cor. 15 : 49, the word "image" denoting the actual form and not a mere similitude. See Wear.

8. TROPOPHOREŌ (τροποφορέω), from *tropos*, a manner, and 5159
phoreō, to endure, is found in Acts 13 : 18, where some ancient authorities AG:827C
have the verb *trophophoreō*, "He bare them as a nursing father," (from CB:—
trophos, a feeder, a nurse, and *phoreō* to carry).¶

9. AIRŌ (αἴρω) signifies (*a*) to raise up, to lift, to take upon oneself 142
and carry what has been raised, physically (its most frequent use), or as AG:24B CB:1234A

applied to the mind, to suspend, to keep in suspense, as in John 10 : 24, lit., 'How long doth thou suspend our souls ? ;' (*b*) to take away what is attached to anything, to remove, as of Christ, in taking (or bearing, marg.) away the sin of the world, John 1 : 29 ; Christ "was manifested to take away sins," 1 John 3 : 5, where, not the nature of the Atonement is in view, but its effect in the believer's life. See CARRY, DOUBT, No. 6, LIFT, LOOSE, PUT, No. 17, REMOVE, SUSPENSE, TAKE.

4160 10. POIEŌ (ποιέω), to do, sometimes means to produce, bear,
AG:680D CB:1265C Luke 8 : 8 ; 13 : 9 ; Jas. 3 : 12 (A.V., "bear," R.V., "yield") ; Rev. 22 : 2. See COMMIT, DO.

4722 11. STEGŌ (στέγω), primarily to protect, or preserve by covering,
AG:765D CB:1270A hence means to keep off something which threatens, to bear up against, to hold out against, and so to endure, bear, forbear, 1 Cor. 9 : 12. The idea of supporting what is placed upon a thing is prominent in 1 Thess. 3 : 1, 5 ("forbear"), and 1 Cor. 13 : 7. See FORBEAR and SUFFER.¶

430 12. ANECHOMAI (ἀνέχομαι) signifies to hold up against a thing and
AG:65D CB:– so to bear with (*ana*, up, and *echomai*, the Middle Voice of *echō*, to have, to hold), e.g., Matt. 17 : 7 ; 1 Cor. 4 : 12 ; 2 Cor. 11 : 1, 4, 19, 20 ; Heb. 13 : 22, etc. See ENDURE, FORBEAR, SUFFER.

3356 13. METRIOPATHEŌ (μετριοπαθέω), to treat with mildness, or
AG:514D CB:– moderation, to bear gently with (*metrios*, moderate, and *paschō*, to suffer), is used in Heb. 5 : 2 (R.V. and A.V. marg.). The idea is that of not being unduly disturbed by the faults and ignorance of others ; or rather perhaps of feeling in some measure, in contrast to the full feeling with expressed in the verb *sumpatheō* in 4 : 15, with reference to Christ as the High Priest. See COMPASSION, No. 5.¶

3114 14. MAKROTHUMEŌ (μακροθυμέω), to be long-tempered (*makros*,
AG:488A CB:1257C long, *thumos*, temper), is translated "is longsuffering over" in Luke 18 : 7, R.V. (A.V., "bear long with"). See PATIENT, SUFFER.

Notes : (1) For "bear (or give) witness," see WITNESS.

(2) For "bear up into," in Acts 27 : 15, see FACE.

(3) In 1 Cor. 10 : 13 the adjective *anthrōpinos*, human (from *anthrōpos*, man) is translated "is common to man," A.V. (R.V., "man can bear").

2592 (4) For *karpophoreō*, to bear fruit, e.g., Mark 4 : 20, (*karpos*, fruit,
AG:405A CB:1253B and No. 7), A.V., "bring forth," see FRUIT.

2702 (5) In Acts 20 : 9, R.V., *katapherō* is rendered "borne down." See
AG:419D CB:– GIVE. No. 12.

BEAR (animal)

715 AG:107B CB:– ARK(T)OS (ἄρκος), a bear, occurs in Rev. 13 : 2.¶

BEARING See **BEHAVIOUR**

BEAST

2226 1. ZŌON (ζῷον) primarily denotes a living being (*zōē*, life). The Eng.,
AG:341C "animal," is the equivalent, stressing the fact of life as the characteristic
CB:1273C feature. In Heb. 13 : 11 the A.V. and the R.V. translate it "beasts"

(" animals " would be quite suitable). In 2 Pet. 2 : 12 and Jude 10, the A.V. has " beasts," the R.V. " creatures." In the Apocalypse, where the word is found some 20 times, and always of those beings which stand before the Throne of God, who give glory and honour and thanks to Him, 4 : 6, and act in perfect harmony with His counsels, 5 : 14 ; 6 : 1–7, e.g., the word " beasts " is most unsuitable ; the R.V., " living creatures," should always be used ; it gives to *zōon* its appropriate significance. See CREATURE.

2. THĒRION (θηρίον), to be distinguished from *zōon*, almost invariably denotes a wild beast. In Acts 28 : 4, " venomous beast " is used of the viper which fastened on Paul's hand. *Zōon* stresses the vital element, *thērion* the bestial. The idea of a beast of prey is not always present. Once, in Heb. 12 : 20, it is used of the animals in the camp of Israel, such, e.g., as were appointed for sacrifice. But in the Sept. *thērion* is never used of sacrificial animals ; the word *ktēnos* (see below) is reserved for these. 2342 AG:361A CB:1272B

Thērion, in the sense of wild beast, is used in the Apocalypse for the two Antichristian potentates who are destined to control the affairs of the nations with Satanic power in the closing period of the present era, 11 : 7 ; 13 : 1–18 ; 14 : 9, 11 ; 15 : 2 ; 16 : 2, 10, 13 ; 17 : 3–17 ; 19 : 19, 20 ; 20 : 4, 10.

3. KTĒNOS (κτῆνος) primarily denotes property (the connected verb *ktaomai* means to possess) ; then, property in flocks and herds. In Scripture it signifies, (*a*) a beast of burden, Luke 10 : 34 ; Acts 23 : 24, (*b*) beasts of any sort, apart from those signified by *thērion* (see above), 1 Cor. 15 : 39 ; Rev. 18 : 13, (*c*) animals for slaughter ; this meaning is not found in the N.T., but is very frequent in the Sept.¶ 2934 AG:455B CB:1256A

4. TETRAPOUS (τετράπους), a four-footed beast (*tetra*, four, and *pous*, a foot) is found in Acts 10 : 12 ; 11 : 6 ; Rom. 1 : 23.¶ 5074 AG:814A CB:—

5. SPHAGION (σφάγιον), from *sphazō*, to slay, denotes a victim, slaughtered for sacrifice, a slain beast, Acts 7 : 42, in a quotation from Amos 5 : 25.¶ 4968 AG:796A CB:—

BEAT

1. DERŌ (δέρω), from a root *der*—, skin (*derma*, a skin, cp. Eng., dermatology), primarily to flay, then to beat, thrash or smite, is used of the treatment of the servants of the owner of the vineyard by the husbandmen, in the parable in Matt. 21 : 35 ; Mark 12 : 3, 5 ; Luke 20 : 10, 11 ; of the treatment of Christ, Luke 22 : 63, R.V., " beat," for A.V., " smote ; " John 18 : 23 ; of the followers of Christ, in the synagogues, Mark 13 : 9 ; Acts 22 : 19 ; of the punishment of unfaithful servants, Luke 12 : 47, 48 ; of the beating of apostles by the High Priest and the Council of the Sanhedrin, Acts 5 : 40 ; by magistrates, 16 : 37. The significance of flogging does not always attach to the word ; it is used of the infliction of a single blow, John 18 : 23 ; 2 Cor. 11 : 20, and of beating the air, 1194 AG:175D CB:1240C

1 Cor. 9 : 26. The usual meaning is that of thrashing or cudgelling, and when used of a blow it indicates one of great violence. See SMITE.¶

5180 AG:830B CB:1273B 2. TUPTŌ (τύπτω), from a root *tup*—, meaning a blow, (*tupos*, a figure or print: Eng., type) denotes to smite, strike, or beat, usually not with the idea of giving a thrashing as with *derō*. It frequently signifies a blow of violence, and, when used in a continuous tense, indicates a series of blows. In Matt. 27 : 30 the imperfect tense signifies that the soldiers kept on striking Christ on the head. So Mark 15 : 19. The most authentic mss. omit it in Luke 22 : 64. In that verse the word *paiō*, to smite, is used of the treatment given to Christ (*derō* in the preceding verse). The imperfect tense of the verb is again used in Acts 18 : 17, of the beating given to Sosthenes. Cp. Acts 21 : 32, which has the present participle. It is used in the metaphorical sense of wounding, in 1 Cor. 8 : 12. See SMITE, STRIKE, WOUND.

4463 AG:733B CB:1268A 3. RHABDIZŌ (ῥαβδίζω), to beat with a rod, or stick, to cudgel, is the verbal form of *rhabdos*, a rod, or staff, Acts 16 : 22 ; 2 Cor. 11 : 25.¶

906 AG:130D CB:1238B 4. BALLŌ (βάλλω), to throw or cast, is once rendered "beat," Acts 27 : 14 R.V., of the tempestuous wind that beat down upon the ship. So the A.V. margin. See CAST.

1911 AG:289D CB:— 5. EPIBALLŌ (ἐπιβάλλω), No. 4, with *epi*, upon, to cast upon, or lay hands upon, signifies to beat into, in Mark 4 : 37, of the action of the waves. See CAST, No. 7, FALL, No. 11, LAY, PUT, No. 8, STRETCH, THINK, No. 15.

4350 AG:716B CB:1267B 6. PROSKOPTŌ (προσκόπτω), to stumble, to strike against (*pros*, to or against, *koptō*, to strike), is once used of a storm beating upon a house, Matt. 7 : 27. See DASH, STUMBLE, and cp. *proskomma* and *proskopē*, a stumbling-block, offence.

4363 AG:718A CB:— 7. PROSPIPTŌ (προσπίπτω), to fall upon (*pros*, to, *piptō*, to fall), is translated "beat" in Matt. 7 : 25 ; elsewhere, to fall down at or before. See FALL.

4366 AG:718B (-ēSSō) CB:— 8. PROSRĒGNUMI (προσρήγνυμι), to break upon, is translated "beat vehemently upon," or against (*pros*, upon, *rhēgnumi*, to break), in Luke 6 : 48, 49, of the violent action of a flood (R.V., "brake").¶

Note: In Luke 10 : 30, the phrase lit. rendered 'inflicting blows,' is translated "wounded" (A.V.), R.V., correctly, "beat."

BEAUTIFUL

5611 AG:896D CB:1251A 1. HŌRAIOS (ὡραῖος) describes that which is seasonable, produced at the right time, as of the prime of life, or the time when anything is at its loveliest and best (from *hōra*, a season, a period fixed by natural laws and revolutions, and so the best season of the year). It is used of the outward appearance of whited sepulchres in contrast to the corruption within, Matt. 23 : 27 ; of the Jerusalem gate called "Beautiful," Acts 3 : 2, 10 ; of the feet of those that bring glad tidings, Rom. 10 : 15.¶

In the Sept. it is very frequent, and especially in Genesis and the

Song of Solomon. In Genesis it is said of all the trees in the garden of Eden, 2 : 9, especially of the tree of the knowledge of good and evil, 3 : 6 ; of the countenances of Rebekah, 26 : 7, Rachel, 29 : 17 and Joseph, 39 : 6. It is used five times in the Song of Solomon, 1 : 16 ; 2 : 14 ; 4 : 3 and 6 : 3, 5.

2. ASTEIOS (ἀστεῖος), connected with *astu*, a city, was used primarily 791
of that which befitted the town, town-bred (corresponding Eng. words AG:117C
are " polite," " polished," connected with *polis*, a town ; cp. " urbane," CB:—
from Lat., *urbs*, a city). Among Greek writers it is set in contrast to *agroikos*, rustic, and *aischros*, base, and was used, e.g., of clothing. It is found in the N.T. only of Moses, Acts 7 : 20, " (exceeding) fair," lit., ' fair (to God),' and Heb. 11 : 23, " goodly " (A.V., " proper "). See FAIR, GOODLY, *Note*, PROPER.¶

Notes : (1) In the Sept. it is far less frequent than *hōraios*. It is said of Moses in Ex. 2 : 2 ; negatively, of Balaam's procedure in the sight of God, Num. 22 : 32 ; of Eglon in Judg. 3 : 17.

(2) *Asteios* belongs to the realm of art, *hōraios*, to that of nature. *Asteios* is used of that which is beautiful because it is elegant ; *hōraios* describes that which is beautiful because it is, in its season, of natural excellence.

(3) *Kalos*, good, describes that which is beautiful as being well pro- 2570
portioned in all its parts, or intrinsically excellent. See BETTER, FAIR, AG:400B CB:1253B
GOOD, etc.

For BECAME see BECOME

BECAUSE : see Note † p 1

BECKON

1. NEUŌ (νεύω), lit., to give a nod, to signify by a nod, is used in 3506
John 13 : 24, of Peter's beckoning to John to ask the Lord of whom He AG:536D CB:—
had been speaking ; in Acts 24 : 10, of the intimation given by Felix to Paul to speak.¶

2. DIANEUŌ (διανεύω), to express one's meaning by a sign (No. 1, 1269
with *dia*, through, used intensively), is said of the act of Zacharias, Luke AG:187A CB:—
1 : 22 (R.V., " continued making signs," for A.V., " beckoned "). In Sept., Psa. 35 : 19, " wink."¶

3. KATANEUŌ (κατανεύω), No. 1, with *kata*, down, intensive, is 2656
used of the fishermen-partners in Luke 5 : 7, " beckoned."¶ AG:415A CB:—

4. KATASEIŌ (κατασείω), lit., to shake down (*kata*, down, *seiō*, to 2678
shake), of shaking the hand, or waving, expresses a little more vigorously AG:418A CB:1254B
the act of beckoning, Acts 12 : 17 ; 13 : 16 ; 19 : 33 ; 21 : 40. *Neuō* and its compounds have primary reference to a movement of the head ; *kataseiō*, to that of the hand.¶

BECOME (to be fitting)

A. Verb.

4241 AG:699B CB:1266B PREPŌ (πρέπω) means to be conspicuous among a number, to be eminent, distinguished by a thing, hence, to be becoming, seemly, fit. The adornment of good works "becometh women professing godliness," 1 Tim. 2 : 10. Those who minister the truth are to speak "the things which befit the sound doctrine," Tit. 2 : 1. Christ, as a High Priest "became us," Heb. 7 : 26. In the impersonal sense, it signifies it is fitting, it becometh, Matt. 3 : 15 ; 1 Cor. 11 : 13 ; Eph. 5 : 3 ; Heb. 2 : 10. See BEFIT, COMELY.¶

B. Adjective.

2412 AG:372D CB:1250B HIEROPREPĒS (ἱεροπρεπής), from *hieros*, sacred, with the adjectival form of *prepō*, denotes suited to a sacred character, that which is befitting in persons, actions or things consecrated to God, Tit. 2 : 3, R.V., "reverent," A.V., "as becometh holiness," (marg., "holy women"). Trench (Syn. §xcii) distinguishes this word from *kosmios*, modest, and *semnos*, grave, honourable.¶

516 AG:78D CB:1238B *Notes :* (1) The A.V. translates the adverb *axiōs*, "as becometh," in Rom. 16 : 2 ; Phil. 1 : 27 (R.V. corrects to "worthily" and "worthy").

1096 AG:158A CB:1248B (2) *Ginomai*, to become, is mentioned under various other headings.

(3) For "become of no effect," Gal. 5 : 4, A.V., R.V., "severed from," see ABOLISH.

BED

2825 AG:436B CB:— 1. KLINĒ (κλίνη), akin to *klinō*, to lean (Eng., recline, incline etc.), a bed, e.g., Mark 7 : 30, also denotes a couch for reclining at meals, Mark 4 : 21, or a couch for carrying the sick, Matt. 9 : 2, 6. The metaphorical phrase 'to cast into a bed,' Rev. 2 : 22, signifies to afflict with disease (or possibly, to lay on a bier). In Mark 7 : 4 the A.V. curiously translates the word "tables" (marg., "beds"), R.V., marg. only, "couches." See COUCH.

— AG:436B CB:— 2. KLINARION (κλινάριον), a diminutive of No. 1, a small bed, is used in Acts 5 : 15. Some mss. have *klinōn*. See also No. 4. See COUCH.¶

2845 AG:440A CB:1255B 3. KOITĒ (κοίτη), primarily a place for lying down (connected with *keimai*, to lie), denotes a bed, Luke 11 : 7 ; the marriage bed, Heb. 13 : 4 ; in Rom. 13 : 13, it is used of sexual intercourse. By metonymy, the cause standing for the effect, it denotes conception, Rom. 9 : 10.¶

2895 AG:447C CB:— 4. KRABBATOS (κράββατος), a Macedonian word (Lat. *grabatus*), is a somewhat mean bed, pallet, or mattress for the poor, Mark 2 : 4, 9, 11, 12 ; 6 : 55 ; John 5 : 8–11 ; Acts 5 : 15 ; 9 : 33. See also No. 2. See COUCH.¶

4766 AG:771C CB:— *Note :* The verb *strōnnuō* or *strōnnumi*, to spread, signifies, in Acts 9 : 34, to make a bed ; elsewhere it has its usual meaning. See FURNISH, SPREAD.

BEFALL

1. GINOMAI (γίνομαι), to become, is rendered " befell " in Mark 5 : 16 ; 1096
" hath befallen " in Rom. 11 : 25, R.V., for A.V., " is happened to ; " AG:158A CB:1248B
so the R.V. in 2 Cor. 1 : 8 ; 2 Tim. 3 : 11.

2. SUMBAINŌ (συμβαίνω), lit., to walk, or go together (*sun*, with, 4819
bainō, to go), is used of things which happen at the same time ; hence, AG:777B CB:—
to come to pass, " befall," Acts 20 : 19. In 21 : 35, it is translated " so
it was." See HAPPEN.

3. SUNANTAŌ (συναντάω), to meet with (*sun*, with, *antaō*, to meet), 4876
is used much in the same way as *sumbainō*, of events which come to pass ; AG:784C
" befall," Acts 20 : 22. See MEET. CB:1270C

Note : The phrase in Matt. 8 : 33, " what was befallen to them that were possessed with demons," is, lit., ' the things of the demonized.'

BEFIT, BEFITTING

1. PREPŌ (πρέπω) is translated " befit " in Tit. 2 : 1, R.V. (A.V., 4241
" become "). See BECOME. AG:699B CB:1266B

2. ANĒKŌ (ἀνήκω), primarily, to have arrived at, reached to, pertained 433
to, came to denote what is due to a person, one's duty, what is befitting. AG:66B
It is used ethically in the N.T. ; Eph. 5 : 4, R.V., " are (not) befitting," CB:1235C
for A.V., " are (not) convenient " ; Col. 3 : 18, concerning the duty of wives towards husbands, R.V., " as is fitting," for A.V., " as it is fit." In Philm. 8, the participle is used with the article, signifying " that which is befitting," R.V. (A.V., " that which is convenient "). See CONVENIENT. For synonymous words see BECOME.¶

BEFORE, BEFORETIME

A. Adverbs.

1. PRŌTON (πρῶτον), the neuter of the adjective *prōtos* (the super- 4412
lative degree of *pro*, before), signifies first, or at the first, (*a*) in order of AG:725 (-OS)
time, e.g., Luke 10 : 5 ; John 18 : 13 ; 1 Cor. 15 : 46 ; 1 Thess. 4 : 16 ; CB:1267B
1 Tim. 3 : 10 ; (*b*) in enumerating various particulars, e.g., Rom. 3 : 2 ; 1 Cor. 11 : 18 ; 12 : 28 ; Heb. 7 : 2 ; Jas. 3 : 17. It is translated " before " in John 15 : 18. See CHIEFLY, FIRST.

2. PROTERON (πρότερον), the neuter of *proteros*, the comparative 4386
degree of *pro*, is always used of time, and signifies aforetime, " before," AG:721D CB:1267B
e.g., John 6 : 62 ; 9 : 8 ; 2 Cor. 1 : 15 ; Heb. 7 : 27 ; in Gal. 4 : 13, " the first time " (R.V.), lit., ' the former time,' i.e., the former of two previous visits ; in Heb. 10 : 32 it is placed between the article and the noun, " the former days ; " so in 1 Pet. 1 : 14, " the former lusts," i.e., the lusts formerly indulged. See FIRST, FORMER.

3. PRIN (πρίν), before, formerly (etymologically akin to *pro*, before), 4250
has the force of a conjunction, e.g., Matt. 1 : 18 ; 26 : 34, 75 ; John 14 : 29 ; AG:701A CB:—
Acts 7 : 2.

1715 4. EMPROSTHEN (ἔμπροσθεν) is used of place or position only;
AG:257A CB:1244B adverbially, signifying in front, Luke 19 : 28; Phil. 3 : 13; Rev. 4 : 6;
as a preposition, e.g., Matt. 5 : 24; John 10 : 4; with the meaning 'in the sight of a person,' e.g., Matt. 5 : 16; 6 : 1; 17 : 2; Luke 19 : 27; John 12 : 37; 1 Thess. 2 : 19, R.V., "before;" A.V., "in the presence of;" Rev. 19 : 10, R.V., "before," especially in phrases signifying in the sight of God, as God wills, Matt. 11 : 26; 18 : 14 (lit., 'a thing willed before your Father,' R.V., marg.); Luke 10 : 21; in the sense of priority of rank or position or dignity, John 1 : 15, 30 (in some texts, ver. 27); in an antagonistic sense, "against," Matt. 23 : 13 (R.V., marg., "before").

1726 5. ENANTION (ἐναντίον), from *en*, in, and *anti*, over against, the
AG:261D neuter of the adjective *enantios*, and virtually an adverb, is also used as a
CB:1244C preposition signifying in the presence of, in the sight of, Luke 20 : 26; Acts 7 : 10: 8 : 32; in the judgment of, Luke 24 : 19.¶

1725 6. ENANTI (ἔναντι), an adverb, used as a preposition, has meanings
AG:261D CB:1244C like those of No. 5, "before," Luke 1 : 8; in the judgment of, Acts 8 : 21. Some texts have the word in Acts 7 : 10.¶

561 7. APENANTI (ἀπέναντι), *apo*, from, with No. 6, denotes (*a*) opposite,
AG:84A CB:— Matt. 27 : 61; (*b*) in the sight of, before, Matt. 27 : 24; Acts 3 : 16; Rom. 3 : 18; (*c*) against, Acts 17 : 7. See CONTRARY, PRESENCE.¶

2713 8. KATENANTI (κατέναντι), *kata*, down, with No. 6, lit., down over
AG:421B against, is used (*a*) of locality, e.g., Mark 11 : 2; 13 : 3; Luke 19 : 30;
CB:— (*b*) as 'in the sight of,' Rom. 4 : 17; in most mss. in 2 Cor. 2 : 17; 12 : 19.

1799 9. ENŌPION (ἐνώπιον), from *en*, in, and *ōps*, the eye, is the neuter of
AG:270C CB:1245B the adjective *enōpios*, and is used prepositionally, (*a*) of place, that which is before or opposite a person, towards which he turns his eyes, e.g. Luke 1 : 19; Acts 4 : 10; 6 : 6; Rev. 1 : 4; 4 : 10; 7 : 15; (*b*) in metaphorical phrases after verbs of motion, Luke 1 : 17; 12 : 9; Acts 9 : 15, etc.; signifying in the mind or soul of persons, Luke 12 : 6; Acts 10 : 31; Rev. 16 : 19; (*c*) in one's sight or hearing, Luke 24 : 43; John 20 : 30; 1 Tim. 6 : 12; metaphorically, Rom. 14 : 22; especially in Gal. 1 : 20; 1 Tim. 5 : 21; 6 : 13; 2 Tim. 2 : 14; 4 : 1; before, as having a person present to the mind, Acts 2 : 25; Jas. 4 : 10; in the judgment of a person, Luke 16 : 15; 24 : 11, R.V., "in their sight," for A.V., "to;" Acts 4 : 19; Rom. 3 : 20; 12 : 17; 2 Cor. 8 : 21; 1 Tim. 2 : 3; in the approving sight of God, Luke 1 : 75; Acts 7 : 46; 10 : 33; 2 Cor. 4 : 2; 7 : 12. See PRESENCE, SIGHT OF (in the).

2714 AG:421B 10. KATENŌPION (κατενώπιον), *kata*, against, with No. 9, signifies
CB:1254B right over against, opposite; (*a*) of place, Jude 24; (*b*) before God as Judge, Eph. 1 : 4; Col. 1 : 22. See No. 8 (*b*).¶

B. Verb.

4391 PROUPARCHŌ (προυπάρχω), to exist before, or be beforehand, is
AG:722C CB:— found in Luke 23 : 12, and Acts 8 : 9, "beforetime."¶ In the Sept., Job 42 : 18.¶

BEG, BEGGAR, BEGGARLY

A. Verb. 1871

1. EPAITEŌ (ἐπαιτέω), a strengthened form of *aiteō*, is used in Luke AG:282B
16 : 3.¶ CB:—

2. PROSAITEŌ (προσαιτέω), lit., to ask besides (*pros*, towards, used 4319
intensively, and *aiteō*), to ask earnestly, to importune, continue asking, AG:711C
is said of the blind beggar in John 9 : 8. In Mark 10 : 46 and Luke 18 : 35 CB:—
certain mss. have this verb ; the most authentic have *prosaitēs*, a beggar, a word used in John 9 : 8, as well as the verb (see the R.V.).¶

Note : "Begged" in Matt. 27 : 58 and Luke 23 : 52, R.V., "asked 154
for," translates the verb *aiteō* ; see Ask. AG:25D

B. Adjective. CB:1234A

PTŌCHOS (πτωχός), an adjective describing one who crouches and 4434
cowers, is used as a noun, a beggar (from *ptōssō*, to cower down or hide AG:728B CB:1268A
oneself for fear), Luke 14 : 13, 21 ("poor") ; 16 : 20, 22 ; as an adjective, "beggarly" in Gal. 4 : 9, i.e., poverty-stricken, powerless to enrich, metaphorically descriptive of the religion of the Jews.

While *prosaitēs* is descriptive of a beggar, and stresses his begging, *ptōchos* stresses his poverty-stricken condition. See Poor.

For BEGAN see BEGIN

BEGET, BEAR (of begetting), BORN

A. Verbs.

1. GENNAŌ (γεννάω), to beget, in the Passive Voice, to be born, is 1080
chiefly used of men begetting children, Matt. 1 : 2–16 ; more rarely of AG:155B
women begetting children, Luke 1 : 13, 57, "brought forth" (for CB:1248A
"delivered," in this ver., see No. 4) ; 23 : 29 ; John 16 : 21, "is delivered of," and of the child, "is born" (for "is in travail" see No. 4). In Gal. 4 : 24, it is used allegorically, to contrast Jews under bondage to the Law, and spiritual Israel, A.V., "gendereth," R.V., "bearing children," to contrast the natural birth of Ishmael and the supernatural birth of Isaac. In Matt. 1 : 20 it is used of conception, "that which is conceived in her." It is used of the act of God in the Birth of Christ, Acts 13 : 33 ; Heb. 1 : 5 ; 5 : 5, quoted from Psalm 2 : 7, none of which indicate that Christ became the Son of God at His Birth.

It is used metaphorically (*a*) in the writings of the Apostle John, of the gracious act of God in conferring upon those who believe the nature and disposition of "children," imparting to them spiritual life, John 3 : 3, 5, 7 ; 1 John 2 : 29 ; 3 : 9 ; 4 : 7 ; 5 : 1, 4, 18 ; (*b*) of one who by means of preaching the Gospel becomes the human instrument in the impartation of spiritual life, 1 Cor. 4 : 15 ; Philm. 10 ; (*c*) in 2 Pet. 2 : 12, with reference to the evil men whom the Apostle is describing, the R.V. rightly has "born mere animals" (A.V., "natural brute beasts") ; (*d*) in the sense of gendering strife, 2 Tim. 2 : 23. See A, No. 3, BRING, CONCEIVE, DELIVER, GENDER, SPRING.

313 AG:51C CB:1235A 2. ANAGENNAŌ (ἀναγεννάω), *ana*, again, or from above, with No. 1, is found in 1 Pet. 1 : 3, 23.¶

Note: In John 3 : 3, 5, 7, the adverb *anōthen*, anew, or from above, accompanies the simple verb *gennaō*. See ABOVE.

616 AG:94A CB:1237A 3. APOKUEŌ (ἀποκυέω), to give birth to, to bring forth (from *kueō*, to be pregnant), is used metaphorically of spiritual birth by means of the Word of God, Jas. 1 : 18, and of death as the offspring of sin (ver. 15; so in the best texts). See BRING, A, No. 30.¶

5088 AG:816D CB:1272C 4. TIKTŌ (τίκτω), to bring forth, Luke 1 : 57; John 16 : 21; Heb. 11 : 11; Rev. 12 : 2, 4, or, to be born, said of the Child, Matt. 2 : 2; Luke 2 : 11, is used metaphorically in Jas. 1 : 15, of lust as bringing forth sin. See *apokueō*, above, used in the same verse. See BRING, DELIVER, TRAVAIL (be in).

B. Nouns.

1085 AG:156A CB:1248B 1. GENOS (γένος), a generation, kind, stock, is used in the dative case, with the article, to signify "by race," in Acts 18 : 2 and 24, R.V., for the A.V., "born." See COUNTRYMEN, DIVERSITY, GENERATION, KIND, KINDRED, NATION, OFFSPRING, STOCK.

1626 AG:246C CB:1244A 2. EKTRŌMA (ἔκτρωμα) denotes an abortion, an untimely birth; from *ektitrōskō*, to miscarry. In 1 Cor. 15 : 8 the Apostle likens himself to "one born out of due time;" i.e., in point of time, inferior to the rest of the Apostles, as an immature birth comes short of a mature one.¶

C. Adjectives.

1084 AG:156A CB:— 1. GENNĒTOS (γεννητός), born (related to *gennaō*, verb No. 1), is used in Matt. 11 : 11 and Luke 7 : 28 in the phrase "born of women," a periphrasis for "men," and suggestive of frailty.¶

738 AG:110C CB:— 2. ARTIGENNĒTOS (ἀρτιγέννητος), newborn (*arti*, newly, recently, and No. 1), is used in 1 Pet. 2 : 2.¶

Notes: (1) For *prōtotokos* see FIRSTBORN.

(2) For *monogenēs*, see ONLY BEGOTTEN.

For BEGGAR see BEG

BEGIN, BEGINNING, BEGINNER

A. Verbs.

756 AG:113C CB:1237B 1. ARCHOMAI (ἄρχομαι) denotes to begin. In Luke 3 : 23 the present participle is used in a condensed expression, lit., 'And Jesus Himself was beginning about thirty years.' Some verb is to be supplied in English. The R.V. has "when He began to teach, was about thirty years of age." The meaning seems to be that He was about thirty years when He began His public career (cp. Acts 1 : 1). The A.V. has "began to be about thirty years of age." In Acts 11 : 4 the R.V. suitably has "began,

and expounded," instead of "from the beginning." See B, No. 1, below, and REIGN, RULE.

2. ENARCHOMAI (ἐνάρχομαι), lit., to begin in (*en*, in, with No. 1), is 1728
used in Gal. 3 : 3 ("having begun in the Spirit"), to refer to the time of AG:262B
conversion; similarly in Phil. 1 : 6, "He which began a good work in CB:—
you." The *en* may be taken in its literal sense in these places.¶

3. PROENARCHOMAI (προενάρχομαι), lit., to begin in before (*pro*, 4278
with No. 2), is used in 2 Cor. 8 : 6, "he had made a beginning before;" AG:705A
and in ver. 10, "were the first to make a beginning" (R.V.).¶ CB:—

4. MELLŌ (μέλλω), to be about to, is rendered "begin" in the A.V. 3195
of Rev. 10 : 7; R.V. suitably, "when he is about to sound." See COME, AG:500D
INTEND, MEAN, MIND, READY, SHALL, SHOULD, TARRY, WILL, WOULD. CB:1258A

Note: For "began to wax" in 1 Tim. 5 : 11, see WANTON, B, No. 2.

B. Noun.

ARCHĒ (ἀρχή) means a beginning. The root *arch*— primarily 746
indicated what was of worth. Hence the verb *archō* meant 'to be first,' AG:111D
and *archōn* denoted a ruler. So also arose the idea of a beginning, the CB:1237B
origin, the active cause, whether a person or thing, e.g., Col. 1 : 18.

In Heb. 2 : 3 the phrase "having at the first been spoken" is, lit., 'having received a beginning to be spoken.' In 2 Thess. 2 : 13 ("God chose you from the beginning"), there is a well supported alternative reading, "chose you as first-fruits" (i.e., *aparchēn*, instead of *ap' archēs*). In Heb. 6 : 1, where the word is rendered "first principles," the original has 'let us leave the word of the beginning of Christ,' i.e., the doctrine of the elementary principles relating to Christ.

In John 8 : 25, Christ's reply to the question "Who art Thou?," "Even that which I have spoken unto you from the beginning," does not mean that He had told them before; He declares that He is consistently the unchanging expression of His own teaching and testimony from the first, the immutable embodiment of His doctrine. See CORNER, FIRST, MAGISTRATE, POWER, PRINCIPALITY, RULE.

Note: In the following passages the A.V. faulty translations, "since the world began" etc. are rightly rendered in the R.V. by "before times eternal" and similar phrases, Rom. 16 : 25; Eph. 3 : 9; 2 Tim. 1 : 9; Tit. 1 : 2. The alteration has not been made, however, in Luke 1 : 70; John 9 : 32; Acts 3 : 21; 15 : 18.

C. Adverb.

PRŌTON (πρῶτον), the neuter of *prōtos* (the superlative degree of 4412
proteros), first, at the first, is rendered "at the beginning" in John 2 : 10, AG:725 (-OS)
A.V., R.V., "setteth on first." See BEFORE. CB:1267B

For BEGOTTEN see BEGET

BEGUILE

1. APATAŌ (ἀπατάω), to deceive, is rendered "beguiled" in the R.V. 538 AG:81D
of 1 Tim. 2 : 14. See No. 2. CB:—

1818 2. EXAPATAŌ (ἐξαπατάω), a strengthened form of No. 1, is rendered
AG:273A "beguile," 2 Cor. 11 : 3; the more adequate rendering would be 'as the
CB:1247C serpent thoroughly beguiled Eve.' So in 1 Tim. 2 : 14, in the best mss., this stronger form is used of Satan's deception of Eve, lit., 'thoroughly beguiled;' the simpler verb, No. 1, is used of Adam. In each of these passages the strengthened form is used. So of the influence of sin, Rom. 7 : 11 (R.V., "beguile"); of self-deception, 1 Cor. 3 : 18 (R.V., "deceive"); of evil men, who cause divisions, Rom. 16 : 18 (R.V., "beguile"); of deceitful teachers, 2 Thess. 2 : 3 (R.V., "beguile"). See DECEIVE.¶ In the Sept., Ex. 8 : 29.¶

3884 3. PARALOGIZOMAI (παραλογίζομαι), lit. and primarily, to reckon
AG:620B wrong, hence means to reason falsely (*para*, from, amiss, *logizomai*, to
CB:1262A reason) or to deceive by false reasoning; translated "delude" in Col. 2 : 4, R.V. (A.V., "beguile") and Jas. 1 : 22 (A.V., "deceive"). See DECEIVE, DELUDE.¶

1185 4. DELEAZŌ (δελεάζω) originally meant to catch by a bait (from
AG:174B *delear*, a bait); hence to beguile, entice by blandishments: in Jas. 1 : 14,
CB:— "entice;" in 2 Pet. 2 : 14, A.V., "beguile;" in ver. 18, A.V., "allure;" R.V., "entice" in both. See ENTICE.¶

2603 *Note*: In Col. 2 : 18, the verb *katabrabeuō*, to give judgment against,
AG:409B
CB:1254A condemn, is translated "beguile . . . of your reward," A.V.; R.V., "rob . . . of your prize." The verb was used of an umpire's decision against a racer; hence the translations (or paraphrases) in the Eng. Versions. See ROB.

BEHALF

3313 1. MEROS (μέρος), a part, is translated "behalf" in the A.V. of
AG:505D
CB:1258B 2 Cor. 9 : 3 (R.V., "respect") and 1 Pet. 4 : 16; here the most authentic texts have *onoma*, a name; hence R.V., "in this name." See COAST, CRAFT, PART, PIECE, PORTION, RESPECT, SORT.

5228 2. HUPER (ὑπέρ), on behalf of, is to be distinguished from *anti*,
AG:838B
CB:1252A instead of. See Note †, p. 1.

BEHAVE, BEHAVIOUR

A. Verbs.

390 1. ANASTREPHŌ (ἀναστρέφω), to turn back, return (*ana*, back,
AG:61B
CB:1235B *strephō*, to turn), hence, to move about in a place, to sojourn, and, in the Middle and Passive Voices, to conduct oneself, indicating one's manner of life and character, is accordingly rendered "behave" in 1 Tim. 3 : 15, lit., 'how it is necessary to behave,' not referring merely to Timothy himself, but to all the members of the local church (see the whole Epistle); in Eph. 2 : 3, A.V., "we had our conversation," R.V., "we lived;" in 2 Cor. 1 : 12 "behaved ourselves," for A.V. "have had our conversation." See ABIDE, etc.

2. GINOMAI (γίνομαι), to become, is rendered " behave " in 1 Thess. 1096 AG:158A CB:1248B
2 : 10 ; lit., ' we became among you ' (cp. 1 : 5).

3. ATAKTEŌ (ἀτακτέω), lit., to be disorderly (*a*, negative, and *taxis*, 812 AG:119C CB:—
order), to lead a disorderly life, is rendered " behave disorderly " in 2 Thess. 3 : 7.¶ Cp. *ataktos*, disorderly, unruly, and *ataktōs*, disorderly.

4. ASCHĒMONEŌ (ἀσχημονέω), to be unseemly (*a*, negative, and 807 AG:119B CB:—
schēma, a form), is used in 1 Cor. 7 : 36, " behave (himself) unseemly," i.e., so as to run the risk of bringing the virgin daughter into danger or disgrace, and in 13 : 5, " doth (not) behave itself unseemly."¶

B. Nouns.

1. ANASTROPHĒ (ἀναστροφή), lit., a turning back (cp. No. 1, above), 391 AG:61C CB:1235B
is translated " manner of life," " living," etc. in the R.V., for A.V., " conversation," Gal. 1 : 13 ; Eph. 4 : 22 ; 1 Tim. 4 : 12 ; Heb. 13 : 7 ; Jas. 3 : 13 ; 1 Pet. 1 : 15, 18 ; 2 : 12 (" behaviour ") ; 3 : 1, 2, 16 (ditto) ; 2 Pet. 2 : 7 ; 3 : 11. See CONVERSATION, LIFE.¶

2. KATASTĒMA (κατάστημα), akin to *kathistēmi* (see APPOINT, No. 2), 2688 AG:419A CB:—
denotes a condition, or constitution of anything, or deportment, Tit. 2 : 3, " demeanour," R.V., for A.V., " behaviour." See DEMEANOUR.¶

C. Adjective.

KOSMIOS (κόσμιος), orderly, modest, is translated " orderly " in 2887 AG:445C CB:1255C
1 Tim. 3 : 2, R.V., for A.V., " of good behaviour." Both have " modest " in 1 Tim. 2 : 9. Cp. *kosmeō*, to adorn, *kosmos*, adornment.¶

BEHEAD

1. APOKEPHALIZŌ (ἀποκεφαλίζω), *apo*, from, off, *kephalē*, a head, 607 AG:93A CB:—
is found in Matt. 14 : 10 ; Mark 6 : 16, 27 ; Luke 9 : 9.¶

2. PELEKIZŌ (πελεκίζω) denotes, to cut with an axe (from *pelekus*, 3990 AG:641C CB:—
an axe), Rev. 20 : 4.¶

BEHIND, COME BEHIND

A. Adverbs.

1. OPISTHEN (ὄπισθεν), behind, is used only of place, e.g., Matt. 3693 AG:574D CB:1261A
9 : 20 ; Mark 5 : 27 ; Luke 8 : 44 ; Rev. 4 : 6 ; as a preposition, Matt. 15 : 23 (" after "), and Luke 23 : 26 ; in Rev. 5 : 1, R.V., " on the back ; " A.V., " backside." See BACK.¶

2. OPISŌ (ὀπίσω), after (see BACK, adverb). 3694 AG:575A CB:1261A

B. Verbs.

1. HUSTEREŌ (ὑστερέω), to come late, be behind, is translated 5302 AG:849A CB:1252B
" come behind," in 1 Cor. 1 : 7 ; " to be behind," 2 Cor. 11 : 5 and 12 : 11. See COME, No. 39, DESTITUTE, FAIL, LACK, NEED, B, *Note*, WANT, WORSE.

2. HUPOMENŌ (ὑπομένω), to abide, endure, is once rendered " tarry 5278 AG:845D CB:1252B
behind," Luke 2 : 43. See ABIDE.

Note : In 1 Thess. 3 : 1, the R.V. " left behind " adequately expresses 2641 AG:413C CB:1254A
the verb *kataleipō*.

C. Noun.

5303 AG:849B HUSTERĒMA (ὑστέρημα), akin to B.1, denotes that which is lacking,
CB:1252B 1 Cor. 16 : 17 ; Phil. 2 : 30 ; Col. 1 : 24 (A.V., " that which is behind of
the afflictions of Christ "), R.V., " that which is lacking ; " 1 Thess.
3 : 10. For the other meaning, " want," see LACK, PENURY, WANT.

BEHOLD, BEHELD

3708 1. HORAŌ (ὁράω), with its aorist form *eidon*, to see (in a few places
AG:577D CB:1251A the A.V. uses the verb to behold), is said (*a*) of bodily vision, e.g., Mark
6 : 38 ; John 1 : 18, 46 ; (*b*) of mental perception, e.g., Rom. 15 : 21 ;
Col. 2 : 18 ; (*c*) of taking heed, e.g., Matt. 8 : 4 ; 1 Thess. 5 : 15 ; (*d*) of
experience, as of death, Luke 2 : 26 ; Heb. 11 : 5 ; life, John 3 : 36 ;
corruption, Acts 2 : 27 ; (*e*) of caring for, Matt. 27 : 4 ; Acts 18 : 15 (here
the form *opsomai* is used). See APPEAR, HEED, LOOK, PERCEIVE, SEE,
SHEW.

991 2. BLEPŌ (βλέπω) is also used of (*a*) bodily and (*b*) mental vision,
AG:143B CB:1239A (*a*) to perceive, e.g., Matt. 13 : 13 ; (*b*) to take heed, e.g., Mark 13 : 23, 33 ;
it indicates greater vividness than *horaō*, expressing a more intent, earnest
contemplation ; in Luke 6 : 41, of beholding the mote in a brother's eye ;
Luke 24 : 12, of beholding the linen clothes in the empty tomb ; Acts 1 : 9,
of the gaze of the disciples when the Lord ascended. The greater earnestness is sometimes brought out by the rendering " regardest," Matt. 22 : 16.
See BEWARE, HEED, LIE, LOOK, PERCEIVE, REGARD, SEE, SIGHT.

1689 AG:254C 3. EMBLEPŌ (ἐμβλέπω), from *en*, in (intensive), and No. 2, (not to be
CB:1244B rendered literally), expresses earnest looking, e.g., in the Lord's command
to behold the birds of the heaven, with the object of learning lessons of
faith from them, Matt. 6 : 26. See also 19 : 26 ; Mark 8 : 25 ; 10 : 21, 27 ;
14 : 67 ; Luke 20 : 17 ; 22 : 61 ; John 1 : 36 ; of the Lord's looking
upon Peter, John 1 : 42 ; Acts 1 : 11 ; 22 : 11. See GAZE, LOOK, SEE.¶

2396; 2400 AG:369B; 4. IDE and IDOU (ἴδε and ἰδού) are Imperative Moods, Active and
370D Middle Voices, respectively, of *eidon*, to see, calling attention to what may
CB:1252C be seen or heard or mentally apprehended in any way. These are regularly
rendered " behold." See especially the Gospels, Acts and the Apocalypse.
See LO, SEE.

(EPEIDON) 1896 5. EPIDE (ἔπιδε), a strengthened form of No. 4 (with *epi*, upon,
AG:284B prefixed), is used in Acts 4 : 29 of the entreaty made to the Lord to behold
CB:— the threatenings of persecutors.¶

2334 6. THEŌREŌ (θεωρέω), from *theōros*, a spectator, is used of one who
AG:360A CB:1272A looks at a thing with interest and for a purpose, usually indicating the
careful observation of details ; this marks the distinction from No. 2 ;
see, e.g., Mark 15 : 47 ; Luke 10 : 18 ; 23 : 35 ; John 20 : 6 (R.V.,
" beholdeth," for A.V., " seeth ; ") ; so in verses 12 and 14 ; " consider,"
in Heb. 7 : 4. It is used of experience, in the sense of partaking of, in
John 8 : 51 ; 17 : 24. See CONSIDER, LOOK, PERCEIVE, SEE. Cp. *theōria*,
sight, Luke 23 : 48, only.

7. ANATHEŌREŌ (ἀναθεωρέω), *ana*, up (intensive), and No. 6, to 333 AG:54C
view with interest, consider contemplatively, is translated "beheld," in CB:—
Acts 17 : 23, R.V., "observed;" "considering" in Heb. 13 : 7. See CONSIDER.¶

8. THEAOMAI (θεάομαι), to behold, view attentively, contemplate, 2300 AG:353A
had, in earlier Greek usage, the sense of a wondering regard. This idea was CB:1271C
gradually lost. It signifies a more earnest contemplation than the ordinary verbs for to see, "a careful and deliberate vision which interprets . . . its object," and is more frequently rendered "behold" in the R.V. than the A.V. Both translate it by "behold" in Luke 23 : 55 (of the sepulchre); "we beheld," in John 1 : 14, of the glory of the Son of God; "beheld," R.V., in John 1 : 32; Acts 1 : 11; 1 John 1 : 1 (more than merely seeing); 4 : 12, 14. See LOOK, SEE.

9. EPOPTEUŌ (ἐποπτεύω), from *epi*, upon, and a form of *horaō*, to 2029
see, is used of witnessing as a spectator, or overseer, 1 Pet. 2 : 12; 3 : 2.¶ AG:305C CB:1246B

Note: The corresponding noun *epoptēs*, an eye-witness, found in 2 Pet. 2030
1 : 16, was used by the Greeks of those who had attained to the highest AG:305D
grade of certain mysteries, and the word is perhaps purposely used here of CB:1246B
those who were at the transfiguration of Christ. See EYE-WITNESS.¶

10. ATENIZŌ (ἀτενίζω) from *atenēs*, strained, intent, denotes to gaze 816 AG:119D
upon, "beholding earnestly," or "stedfastly" in Acts 14 : 9; 23 : 1. CB:1238A
See FASTEN, LOOK, SET, B, *Note* (5).

11. KATANOEŌ (κατανοέω), a strengthened form of *noeō*, to perceive, 2657
(*kata*, intensive), denotes the action of the mind in apprehending certain AG:415A
facts about a thing; hence, to consider; "behold," Acts 7 : 31, 32; CB:1254A
Jas. 1 : 23, 24. See CONSIDER, DISCOVER, PERCEIVE.

12. KATOPTRIZŌ (κατοπτρίζω), from *katoptron*, a mirror (*kata*, 2734
down, *ōps*, an eye or sight), in the Active Voice, signifies to make to (-OMAI)
reflect, to mirror; in the Middle Voice, to reflect as a mirror; so the R.V. AG:424D CB:—
in 2 Cor. 3 : 18, for A.V., "beholding as in a glass." The whole context in the 3rd chapter and the first part of the 4th bears out the R.V.¶

Note: For *epeidon* (from *ephoraō*), Acts 4 : 29, see LOOK, No. 9. For *prooraō*, Acts 2 : 25, R.V., "behold," see FORESEE.

BEHOVE

1. OPHEILŌ (ὀφείλω), to owe, is once rendered "behove," Heb. 2 : 17; 3784
it indicates a necessity, owing to the nature of the matter under con- AG:598D
sideration; in this instance, the fulfilment of the justice and love of God, CB:1261A
voluntarily exhibited in what Christ accomplished, that He might be a merciful and faithful High Priest. See BOUND, DEBT, DUE, DUTY, GUILTY, INDEBTED, MUST, NEED, OUGHT, OWE.

2. DEI (δεῖ), "it is necessary," is rendered "behoved," in Luke 24 : 46; 1163
R.V., (that the Christ) "should" (suffer). *Dei* expresses a logical AG:172A
necessity, *opheilō*, a moral obligation; cp. *chrē*, Jas. 3 : 10, "ought," CB:1240B

which expresses a need resulting from the fitness of things (Trench, § cvii). See MEET, MUST, NEED, OUGHT.

BEING

When not part of another verb (usually the participle), or part of a phrase, this word translates one of the following :—
EIMI (*a*) the present participle of *eimi*, to be, the verb of ordinary existence ;
1510 AG:222D (*b*) the participle of *ginomai*, to become, signifying origin or result ;
CB:1243A (*c*) the present participle of *huparchō*, to exist, which always involves a
GINOMAI pre-existent state, prior to the fact referred to, and a continuance of the
1096 AG:158A state after the fact. Thus in Phil. 2 : 6, the phrase " who being (*huparchōn*)
CB:1248B in the form of God," implies His pre-existent Deity, previous to His Birth,
HUPARCHŌ 5225 and His continued Deity afterwards.
AG:838A In Acts 17 : 28 the phrase " we have our being " represents the present
CB:— tense of the verb to be, " we are."

BELIAL

955 BELIAL (βελίαλ, or βελίαρ) is a word frequently used in the Old
AG:139A CB:1239A Testament, with various meanings, especially in the books of Samuel, where it is found nine times. See also Deut. 13 : 13 ; Judg. 19 : 22 ; 20 : 13 ; 1 Kings 21 : 10, 13 ; 2 Chron. 13 : 7. Its original meaning was either worthlessness or hopeless ruin (see the R.V., margin). It also had the meanings of extreme wickedness and destruction, the latter indicating the destiny of the former. In the period between the O.T. and the N.T. it came to be a proper name for Satan. There may be an indication of this in Nahum 1 : 15, where the word translated " the wicked one " is Belial.

The oldest form of the word is Beliar, possibly from a phrase signifying " Lord of the forest," or perhaps simply a corruption of the form Belial, due to harsh Syriac pronunciation. In the N.T., in 2 Cor. 6 : 15, it is set in contrast to Christ, and represents a personification of the system of impure worship connected especially with the cult of Aphrodite.¶

BELIEF, BELIEVE, BELIEVERS

A. Verbs.

4100 1. PISTEUŌ (πιστεύω), to believe, also to be persuaded of, and hence,
AG:660B CB:1265A to place confidence in, to trust, signifies, in this sense of the word, reliance upon, not mere credence. It is most frequent in the writings of the Apostle John, especially the Gospel. He does not use the noun (see below). For the Lord's first use of the verb, see 1 : 50. Of the writers of the Gospels, Matthew uses the verb ten times, Mark ten, Luke nine, John ninety-nine. In Acts 5 : 14 the present participle of the verb is translated " believers."
3982 AG:639A See COMMIT, INTRUST, TRUST.
CB:1263A 2. PEITHŌ (πείθω), to persuade, in the Middle and Passive Voices

signifies to suffer oneself to be persuaded, e.g., Luke 16 : 31 ; Heb. 13 : 18 ; it is sometimes translated " believe " in the R.V., but not in Acts 17 : 4, R.V., " were persuaded," and 27 : 11, " gave (more) heed ; " in Acts 28 : 24, " believed." See AGREE, ASSURE, OBEY, PERSUADE, TRUST, YIELD.

Note : For *apisteō*, the negative of No. 1, and *apeitheō*, the negative of No. 2, see DISBELIEVE, DISOBEDIENT.

B. Noun.

PISTIS (πίστις), faith, is translated " belief " in Rom. 10 : 17 ; 4102
2 Thess. 2 : 13. Its chief significance is a conviction respecting God and AG:662B
His Word and the believer's relationship to Him. See ASSURANCE, CB:1265A
FAITH, FIDELITY.

Note : In 1 Cor. 9 : 5 the word translated " believer " (R.V.), is 79
adelphē, a sister, so 7 : 15 ; Rom. 16 : 1 ; Jas. 2 : 15, used, in the spiritual AG:15D
sense, of one connected by the tie of the Christian faith. CB:1233A

C. Adjective.

PISTOS (πιστός), (*a*) in the Active sense means believing, trusting ; 4103
(*b*) in the Passive sense, trusty, faithful, trustworthy. It is translated AG:664C
" believer " in 2 Cor. 6 : 15 ; " them that believe " in 1 Tim. 4 : 12, R.V. CB:1265A
(A.V., " believers ") ; in 1 Tim. 5 : 16, " if any woman that believeth," lit., 'if any believing woman.' So in 6 : 2, " believing masters." In 1 Pet. 1 : 21 the R.V., following the most authentic mss., gives the noun form, " are believers in God " (A.V., " do believe in God "). In John 20 : 27 it is translated " believing." It is best understood with significance (*a*), above, e.g., in Gal. 3 : 9 ; Acts 16 : 1 ; 2 Cor. 6 : 15 ; Tit. 1 : 6 ; it has significance (*b*), e.g., in 1 Thess. 5 : 24 ; 2 Thess. 3 : 3 (see Notes on Thess. p. 211, and Gal. p. 126, by Hogg and Vine). See FAITHFUL, SURE.

Notes : (1) The corresponding negative verb is *apisteō*, 2 Tim. 2 : 13, 569
A.V., " believe not " R.V., " are faithless," in contrast to the statement AG:85B
" He abideth faithful." CB:1236C

(2) The negative noun *apistia*, " unbelief," is used twice in Matthew 570
(13 : 58 ; 17 : 20), three times in Mark (6 : 6 ; 9 : 24 ; 16 : 14), four times AG:85C
in Romans (3 : 3 ; 4 : 20 ; 11 : 20, 23) ; elsewhere in 1 Tim. 1 : 13 and CB:1236C
Heb. 3 : 12, 19.¶

(3) The adjective *apistos* is translated " unbelievers " in 1 Cor. 6 : 6, 571
and 2 Cor. 6 : 14 ; in ver. 15, R.V., " unbeliever " (A.V., " infidel ") ; so AG:85D
in 1 Tim. 5 : 8 ; " unbelieving " in 1 Cor. 7 : 12, 13, 14, 15 ; 14 : 22, 23, 24 ; CB:1236C
2 Cor. 4 : 4 ; Tit. 1 : 15 ; Rev. 21 : 8 ; " that believe not " in 1 Cor. 10 : 27. In the Gospels it is translated " faithless " in Matt. 17 : 17 ; Mark 9 : 19 ; Luke 9 : 41 ; John 20 : 27, but in Luke 12 : 46, R.V., " unfaithful," A.V., " unbelievers." Once it is translated " incredible," Acts 26 : 8. See FAITHLESS, INCREDIBLE, UNBELIEVER.¶

(4) *Plērophoreō*, in Luke 1 : 1 (A.V., " are most surely believed," lit., 4135
have had full course), the R.V. renders " have been fulfilled." See AG:670B
FULFIL, KNOW, PERSUADE, PROOF. CB:1265B

BELLY

2836 1. KOILIA (κοιλία), from *koilos*, hollow (Lat., *coelum*, heaven, is
AG:437B connected), denotes the entire physical cavity, but most frequently was
CB:1255B used to denote the womb. In John 7 : 38 it stands metaphorically for
the innermost part of man, the soul, the heart. See WOMB.

1064 2. GASTĒR (γαστήρ), (cp. Eng., gastritis), is used much as No. 1,
AG:152C but in Tit. 1 : 12, by synecdoche (a figure of speech in which the part is
CB:— put for the whole, or vice versa), it is used to denote " gluttons," R.V.,
for A.V., " bellies." See GLUTTON, WOMB.

BELONG

1510 *Note :* This word represents (*a*) a phrase consisting of *eimi*, to be,
AG:222D with or without a preposition and a noun, and usually best rendered, as
CB:1243A in the R.V., by the verb to be, Mark 9 : 41, lit., 'ye are of Christ ;'
Luke 23 : 7 and Heb. 5 : 14 ; cp. Rom. 12 : 19, " belongeth unto Me,"
R.V. ; (*b*) a phrase consisting of the neuter plural of the definite article,
4314 either with the preposition *pros*, unto, as in Luke 19 : 42, where the phrase
AG:709C " the things which belong unto peace " (R.V.) is, lit., 'the (things) unto
CB:1267A peace,' or with the genitive case of the noun, as in 1 Cor. 7 : 32, A.V.,
" the things that belong to the Lord," R.V., suitably, " the things of the
3348 Lord ; " (*c*) a distinct verb, e.g., *metechō*, to partake of, share in, Heb.
AG:514A 7 : 13 R.V., " belongeth to (another tribe)," A.V., " pertaineth to."
CB:1258C

BELOVED

A. Adjective.

27 AGAPĒTOS (ἀγαπητός), from *agapaō*, to love, is used of Christ as loved
AG:6B by God, e.g., Matt. 3 : 17 ; of believers (ditto), e.g., Rom. 1 : 7 ; of
CB:1233B believers, one of another, 1 Cor. 4 : 14 ; often, as a form of address, e.g.,
1 Cor. 10 : 14. Wherever the A.V. has " dearly beloved," the R.V. has
" beloved ; " so, " well beloved " in 3 John 1 ; in 1 John 2 : 7, A.V.,
" brethren " (*adelphos*), the R.V. has " beloved," according to the mss.
which have *agapētos*. See DEAR.

B. Verb.

25 AGAPAŌ (ἀγαπάω), in its perfect participle Passive form, is translated
AG:4B " beloved " in Rom. 9 : 25 ; Eph. 1 : 6 ; Col. 3 : 12 ; 1 Thess. 1 : 4 ;
CB:1233B 2 Thess. 2 : 13. In Jude 1 the best texts have this verb (R.V.) ; the A.V.,
BELT See " sanctified " follows those which have *hagiazō*. See LOVE.
GIRDLE *Note :* In Luke 9 : 35, the R.V., translating from the most authentic
BENCH See SEAT mss., has " My chosen " (*eklegō*), for A.V., " beloved " (*agapētos*) ; so in
BEND See BOW, Philm. 2, " sister " (*adelphē*).
KNEEL,
STOOP

BENEATH

2736 KATŌ (κάτω) signifies (*a*) down, downwards, Matt. 4 : 6 ; Luke 4 : 9 ;
AG:425A John 8 : 6, 8 ; Acts 20 : 9 ; (*b*) below, beneath, of place, Mark 14 : 66 ;
CB:1254C the realms that lie below in contrast to heaven, John 8 : 23 ; the earth,

as contrasted with the heavens, Acts 2 : 19; with *heōs*, unto, Matt. 27 : 51; Mark 15 : 38. The comparative degree, *katōterō*, under, is used in Matt. 2 : 16. See BOTTOM, UNDER.¶

BENEFIT, BENEFACTOR

1. EUERGESIA (εὐεργεσία), lit., 'good work (*eu*, well, *ergon*, work),' 2108
is found in Acts 4 : 9, "good deed," and 1 Tim. 6 : 2, "benefit."¶ AG:319D CB:1247A
2. EUERGETĒS (εὐεργέτης), a benefactor, expresses the agent, Luke 2110
22 : 25.¶ AG:320A CB:1247A

Note: Cp. *euergeteō*, to do good.

3. CHARIS (χάρις), grace, is once rendered "benefit," 2 Cor. 1 : 15; 5485
it stresses the character of the benefit, as the effect of the gracious dis- AG:877B CB:1239C
position of the benefactor. See ACCEPTABLE, FAVOUR, GRACE, LIBERALITY, PLEASURE, THANK.

4. AGATHON (ἀγαθόν), the neuter of *agathos*, used as a noun in Philm. 18
14, is translated "benefit," A.V.; R.V., "goodness." See GOOD. AG:2D CB:1233B

BENEVOLENCE

EUNOIA (εὔνοια), good will (*eu*, well, *nous*, the mind), is rendered 2133
"benevolence" in 1 Cor. 7 : 3, A.V. The R.V., following the texts AG:323B CB:—
which have *opheilēn* ("due"), has "her due," a more comprehensive expression; in Eph. 6 : 7, "good will."¶

BEREAVED, BEREFT

1. APORPHANIZOMAI (ἀπορφανίζομαι), lit., to be rendered an 642 (-Zō)
orphan (*apo*, from, with the thought of separation, and *orphanos*, an AG:98A (-Zō) CB:—
orphan), is used metaphorically in 1 Thess. 2 : 17 (A.V., "taken from;" R.V., "bereaved"), in the sense of being bereft of the company of the saints through being compelled to leave them (cp. the similes in 7 and 11). The word has a wider meaning than that of being an orphan.¶

Note: The corresponding adjective, *orphanos*, is translated "desolate" 3737
in John 14 : 18 (A.V., "comfortless"); "fatherless" in Jas. 1 : 27; AG:583A CB:1261B
see DESOLATE, FATHERLESS.¶

2. APOSTEREŌ, to rob, defraud, deprive, is used in 1 Tim. 6 : 5, 650
in the Passive Voice, of being deprived or "bereft" (of the truth), with AG:99A CB:1237A
reference to false teachers (A.V., "destitute"). See DEFRAUD, DESTITUTE, FRAUD.

BERYL

BĒRULLOS (βήρυλλος), beryl, is a precious stone of a sea-green colour, 969
Rev. 21 : 20 (cp. Ex. 28 : 20).¶ AG:140B CB:1239A

BESEECH

1. PARAKALEŌ (παρακαλέω), the most frequent word with this 3870
meaning, lit. denotes to call to one's side, hence, to call to one's aid. It AG:617A CB:1262A

is used for every kind of calling to a person which is meant to produce a particular effect, hence, with various meanings, such as comfort, exhort, desire, call for, in addition to its significance to beseech, which has a stronger force than *aiteō* (see ASK). See, e.g., the R.V. " besought " in Mark 5 : 18 ; Acts 8 : 31 ; 19 : 31 ; 1 Cor. 16 : 12. See CALL, No. 6, Note (2), COMFORT, DESIRE, EXHORT, INTREAT, PRAY.

2065 AG:311D CB:1246C 2. ERŌTAŌ (ἐρωτάω), often translated by the verb to beseech, in the Gospels, is elsewhere rendered " beseech " in 1 Thess. 4 : 1 ; 5 : 12 ; 2 Thess. 2 : 1 ; 2 John 5. See under ASK, No. 2.

1189 AG:175A CB:1240C 3. DEOMAI (δέομαι), to desire, to long for, usually representing the word " need," is sometimes translated " beseech," e.g., Luke 5 : 12 ; Acts 21 : 39 ; 2 Cor. 10 : 2 ; Gal. 4 : 12. It is used of prayer to God, in Matt. 9 : 38 ; Luke 10 : 2 ; 21 : 36 ; 22 : 32 ; Acts 4 : 31 ; 8 : 22, 24 ; 10 : 2 ; Rom. 1 : 10 ; 1 Thess. 3 : 10. See PRAY, REQUEST.

4352 AG:716C CB:1267B *Note : Proskuneō* is wrongly rendered " besought " in the A.V. marg. of Matt. 18 : 26. The word signifies " to worship."

BESET

2139 AG:324A CB:— EUPERISTATOS (εὐπερίστατος), used in Heb. 12 : 1, and translated " which doth so easily beset," lit. signifies ' standing well (i.e., easily) around ' (*eu*, well, *peri*, around, *statos*, standing, i.e., easily encompassing). It describes sin as having advantage in favour of its prevailing.¶

BESIDE, BESIDES

5565 AG:890C CB:1240A 1. CHŌRIS (χωρίς), separately, apart from, besides, is translated " beside " in Matt. 14 : 21 ; 15 : 38 ; 2 Cor. 11 : 28. See APART, SEPARATE, WITHOUT.

3063 AG:479D (LOIPOS 3.b.) CB:1257B 2. LOIPON (λοιπόν) is rendered " besides " in 1 Cor. 1 : 16. See FINALLY.

3922 AG:624D CB:1262B *Notes :* (1) *Pareiserchomai*, in Rom. 5 : 20, signifies to come in beside, i.e., of the Law, as coming in addition to sin committed previously apart from law, the prefix *par-* (i.e., *para*) denoting " beside " (the A.V., " entered " is inadequate) ; in Gal. 2 : 4 (" came in privily "). See COME.¶

4359 AG:717D CB:— (2) In Philm. 19, *prosopheilō* signifies to owe in addition (*pros*, besides, and *opheilō*, to owe) : " thou owest (to me even thine own self) besides."¶

(3) In 2 Pet. 1 : 5, the phrase, wrongly translated in the A.V., " beside this," means " for this very cause " (R.V.).

BESIDE ONESELF (to be)

1839 AG:276B CB:1247C (EXHI-) 1. EXISTĒMI (ἐξίστημι), primarily and lit. means to put out of position, displace ; hence, (*a*) to amaze, Luke 24 : 22 (for A.V., " make . . . astonished ") ; Acts 8 : 9, 11 (A.V., " bewitched ") ; or to be amazed, astounded, Matt. 12 : 23 ; Mark 6 : 51 ; (*b*) to be out of one's mind, to be beside oneself, Mark 3 : 21 ; 2 Cor. 5 : 13, in the latter of which it is contrasted with *sōphroneō*, to be of a sound mind, sober. See AMAZE.

3105 AG:486B CB:1257B 2. MAINOMAI (μαίνομαι), to be mad, to rave, is said of one who so speaks that he appears to be out of his mind, Acts 26 : 24, translated " thou art beside thyself," A.V. ; R.V., " thou art mad." In ver. 25 ; John 10 : 20 ; Acts 12 : 15 ; 1 Cor. 14 : 23, both Versions use the verb to be mad. See MAD.¶

Note : For *paraphroneō*, 2 Cor. 11 : 23, R.V., see FOOL, B, No. 2. 3912 AG:623C CB:—

BEST

1. PRŌTOS (πρῶτος) is one of two words translated " best " in the 4413
A.V., but the only one so rendered in the R.V. In Luke 15 : 22 " the best AG:725B CB:1267B
(robe) " is, lit., 'the first (robe),' i.e., chief, principal, first in rank or
quality. See BEFORE, BEGINNING, CHIEF, FIRST, FORMER.

2. MEIZŌN (μείζων), greater, is translated " best " in 1 Cor. 12 : 31, 3187
" the best gifts," greater, not in quality, but in importance and value. AG:497C
It is the comparative degree of *megas*, great ; the superlative, *megistos*, (MEGAS)
is used only in 2 Pet. 1 : 4. See ELDER, GREATER and MORE. CB:1258A

BESTOW

1. DIDŌMI (δίδωμι), to give, is rendered " bestow " in 1 John 3 : 1, 1325
the implied idea being that of giving freely. The A.V. has it in 2 Cor. 8 : 1 ; AG:192C
the R.V. adheres to the lit. rendering, " the grace of God which hath been CB:1241C
given in the churches of Macedonia." See ADVENTURE and especially
GIVE.

2. SUNAGŌ (συνάγω), to bring together (*sun*, together, *agō*, to bring), 4863
is used in the sense of bestowing, or stowing, by the rich man who laid up AG:782A
his goods for himself, Luke 12 : 17, 18. See ASSEMBLE, COME, GATHER, CB:1270B
LEAD, RESORT, TAKE.

3. KOPIAŌ (κοπιάω), (*a*) to grow tired with toil, Matt. 11 : 28 ; John 2872
4 : 6 ; Rev. 2 : 3, also means (*b*) to bestow labour, work with toil, AG:443C
Rom. 16 : 6 ; Gal. 4 : 11 ; in John 4 : 38, A.V., " bestowed (no) labour," CB:1255C
R.V., " have (not) laboured," and, in the same verse, A.V. and R.V.,
" laboured." See LABOUR, TOIL, WEARY.

4. PSŌMIZŌ (ψωμίζω), primarily to feed by putting little bits into the 5595
mouths of infants or animals, came to denote simply to give out food, AG:894D
to feed, and is rendered by the phrase " bestow . . . to feed " in 1 Cor. CB:—
13 : 3 ; " feed," Rom. 12 : 20 ; there the person to be fed is mentioned ; in 1 Cor. 13 : 3 the material to be given is specified, and the rendering " bestow . . . to feed " is necessary. See FEED.¶

5. PERITITHĒMI (περιτίθημι), to put around or on (*peri*, around, 4060
tithēmi, to put), is translated in 1 Cor. 12 : 23 (metaphorically) " bestow " AG:652C
(marg., " put on "). See PUT, SET, No. 5. CB:—

6. CHARIZOMAI (χαρίζομαι), to show favour, grant, bestow, is 5483
rendered " bestowed " in Luke 7 : 21, R.V., for A.V., " gave." Here and AG:876C
in Gal. 3 : 18, the verb might be translated " graciously conferred." See CB:1239C
DELIVER, FORGIVE, GIVE, GRANT.

Note : For " freely bestowed " see ACCEPT, A, *Note*.

BETRAY, BETRAYER

A. Verb.

3860 PARADIDŌMI (παραδίδωμι), to betray (*para*, up, *didōmi*, to give),
AG:614B CB:1262A lit., to give over, is used either (*a*) in the sense of delivering a person or
thing to be kept by another, to commend, e.g., Acts 28 : 16 ; (*b*) to deliver to prison or judgment, e.g., Matt. 4 : 12 ; 1 Tim. 1 : 20 ; (*c*) to deliver over treacherously by way of betrayal, Matt. 17 : 22 (R.V., " delivered ") ; 26 : 16 ; John 6 : 64 etc. ; (*d*) to hand on, deliver, e.g., 1 Cor. 11 : 23 : (*e*) to allow of something being done, said of the ripening of fruit, Mark 4 : 29, R.V., " is ripe " (marg., " alloweth "). See BRING, p. 153, *Note* (4), CAST, COMMIT, DELIVER, GIVE, HAZARD, PUT (in prison), RECOMMEND.

B. Noun.

4273 PRODOTĒS (προδότης), a betrayer (akin to A), is translated " be-
AG:704C CB:– trayers " in Acts 7 : 52 ; " traitor," " traitors," in Luke 6 : 16 and 2 Tim.
3 : 4. See TRAITOR.¶

BETROTH

3423 MNĒSTEUŌ (μνηστεύω), in the Active Voice, signifies to woo a woman
AG:525C CB:– and ask for her in marriage ; in the N.T., only in the Passive Voice, to
be promised in marriage, to be betrothed, Matt. 1 : 18 ; Luke 1 : 27 ; 2 : 5, R.V., " betrothed," (A.V., " espoused "). See ESPOUSED.¶

BETTER

2908 1. KREISSŌN (κρείσσων), from *kratos*, strong (which denotes power
AG:449D CB:1256A in activity and effect), serves as the comparative degree of *agathos*, good
(good or fair, intrinsically). *Kreissōn* is especially characteristic of the Epistle to the Hebrews, where it is used 12 times ; it indicates what is (*a*) advantageous or useful, 1 Cor. 7 : 9, 38 ; 11 : 17 ; Heb. 11 : 40 ; 12 : 24 ; 2 Pet. 2 : 21 ; Phil. 1 : 23, where it is coupled with *mallon*, more, and *pollō*, much, by far, " very far better " (R.V.) ; (*b*) excellent, Heb. 1 : 4 ; 6 : 9 ; 7 : 7, 19, 22 ; 8 : 6 ; 9 : 23 ; 10 : 34 ; 11 : 16, 35.¶

2570 2. KALON . . . MALLON (καλὸν . . . μᾶλλον), the neuter of *kalos*,
AG:400B CB:1253B with *mallon*, more, is used in Mark 9 : 42, "it were better (lit., much
better) for him if a great millstone were hanged about his neck." In verses 43, 45, 47, *kalos* is used alone (R.V., " good," for A.V., " better ").

5543 *Note :* In Luke 5 : 39 the most authentic texts have *chrēstos*, good,
AG:886A CB:1240A instead of the comparative, *chrēstoteros*, better.

BETTER (be)

1308 1. DIAPHERŌ (διαφέρω), used (*a*) transitively, means to carry through
AG:190B CB:– or about (*dia*, through, *pherō*, to carry), Mark 11 : 16 (" carry . . .
through ") ; Acts 13 : 49 ; 27 : 27 (" driven to and fro ") ; (*b*) intransitively, (1) to differ, Rom. 2 : 18 ; Gal. 2 : 6 ; Phil. 1 : 10 ; (2) to excel, be better, e.g., Matt. 6 : 26 ; 10 : 31 (" of more value ") ; 12 : 12 ; Luke

12 : 7, 24 ; 1 Cor. 15 : 41 ; Gal. 4 : 1 ; some would put Rom. 2 : 18 and Phil. 1 : 10 here (see marg.). See CARRY, DIFFER, DRIVE, EXCELLENT, MATTER (make), PUBLISH.¶

2. PERISSEUŌ (περισσεύω), to be over or above (a number), to be 4052
more than enough, to be pre-eminent, superior, Matt. 5 : 20, is translated AG:650C CB:1263C
" are we the better," in 1 Cor. 8 : 8 (cp. 15 : 58 ; Rom. 15 : 13 ; 2 Cor. 3 : 9 ; 8 : 7 ; Phil. 1 : 9 ; Col. 2 : 7 ; 1 Thess. 4 : 1, 10). See ABOUND.

3. LUSITELEŌ (λυσιτελέω) signifies to indemnify, pay expenses, pay 3081 (-LEI)
taxes (from *luō*, to loose, *telos*, toll, custom) ; hence, to be useful, advan- AG:482B CB:—
tageous, to be better, Luke 17 : 2.¶

4. HUPERECHŌ (ὑπερέχω) lit. means to hold or have above (*huper*, 5242
above, *echō*, to hold) ; hence, metaphorically, to be superior to, to be AG:840D CB:1252A
better than, Phil. 2 : 3 ; 1 Pet. 2 : 13, " supreme," in reference to kings ; in Rom. 13 : 1, " higher;" Phil. 3 : 8, " excellency," more strictly ' the surpassing thing, (namely, the knowledge of Christ) ' ; in 4 : 7 " passeth." See EXCELLENCY, HIGHER, PASS, SUPREME.¶

Notes : (1) In Rom. 3 : 9 the R.V. rightly translates *proechō* (which 4284
there is used in the Passive Voice, not the Middle) " are we in worse case (-OMAI) AG:705D
than . . . ? , " i.e., ' are we surpassed ? ' ' are we at a disadvantage ? ' CB:—
The question is, are the Jews, so far from being better off than the Gentiles, in such a position that their very privileges bring them into a greater disadvantage or condemnation than the Gentiles ? The A.V. " are we better " does not convey the meaning.

(2) *Sumpherō*, in Matt. 18 : 6, A.V., is translated " it were better for 4851
him," R.V., " profitable." See Matt. 5 : 29, 30 etc. See BRING, Ex- AG:780B CB:—
PEDIENT, GOOD, D, *Note* (2), PROFITABLE.

BETTERED (to be)

ŌPHELEŌ (ὠφελέω) in the Active Voice signifies to help, to succour, 5623
to be of service ; in the Passive to receive help, to derive profit or AG:900C CB:1261A
advantage ; in Mark 5 : 26, " was (nothing) bettered," of the woman who had an issue of blood. See under ADVANTAGE, C, No. 1, and cp. A, Nos. 2, 3 and B.

BETWEEN

In addition to the prepositions *en* and *pros* (see Note † p. 9), the following have this meaning :

1. ANA MESON (ἀνὰ μέσον), lit., up to the middle of, i.e., among, or 3319
in the midst of, hence, between, is used in 1 Cor. 6 : 5, of those in the AG:507B CB:1258B
church able to decide between brother and brother, instead of their going to law with one another in the world's courts.

2. METAXU (μεταξύ), in the midst, or between (from *meta*, and *xun*, 3342
i.e., *sun*, with), is used as a preposition, (*a*) of mutual relation, Matt. AG:512D
18 : 15 ; Acts 15 : 9 ; Rom. 2 : 15, R.V., " one with another," lit., CB:—
' between one another,' for A.V., " the meanwhile ; " (*b*) of place, Matt.

23 : 35 ; Luke 11 : 51 ; 16 : 26 ; Acts 12 : 6 ; (*c*) of time, " meanwhile," John 4 : 31. In Acts 13 : 42, the A.V. marg. has " in the week between," the literal rendering. See WHILE.¶

Note : The phrase ***ek meta*** (***ek***, out of, ***meta***, with) is translated " between . . . and " in the A.V. of John 3 : 25 (R.V., " on the part of . . . with ").

BEWAIL

2799 AG:433A CB:1255A 1. KLAIŌ (κλαίω), to wail, whether with tears or any external expression of grief, is regularly translated " weep " in the R.V. ; once in the A.V. it is rendered " bewail," Rev. 18 : 9. See WEEP.

Note : The associated noun is ***klauthmos***, weeping. Cp. ***dakruō***, to weep, John 11 : 35.¶

2875 AG:444A CB:1255C 2. KOPTŌ (κόπτω), primarily, to beat, smite ; then, to cut off, Matt. 21 : 8 ; Mark 11 : 8, is used in the Middle Voice, of beating oneself, beating the breast, as a token of grief ; hence, to bewail, Matt. 11 : 17 (R.V., " mourn," for A.V., " lament ") ; 24 : 30, " mourn ; " Rev. 1 : 7 (R.V., " mourn ; " A.V., " wail ") ; in Luke 8 : 52 ; 23 : 27, " bewail ; " in Rev. 18 : 9, " wail " (for A.V., " lament "). See CUT, MOURN.¶ Cp. *koptos*, lamentation, Acts 8 : 2.¶

3996 AG:642C CB:— 3. PENTHEŌ (πενθέω) denotes to lament, mourn, especially for the dead ; in 2 Cor. 12 : 21, R.V., " mourn " (A.V., " bewail "). See also Rev. 18 : 11, 15, 19. Cp. *penthos*, mourning. See MOURN.

2354 AG:363B CB:1272B *Notes :* (1) *Thrēneō*, to sing a dirge, to lament, is rendered " wail " in Matt. 11 : 17, R.V. ; " mourned " in Luke 7 : 32 ; to lament in Luke 23 : 27 and John 16 : 20.¶ *Thrēnos*, lamentation, occurs in Matt. 2 : 18.¶

3602 AG:555B CB:1260B (2) *Odurmos* from *oduromai*, to wail (a verb not found in the N.T.), denotes " mourning," Matt. 2 : 18 and 2 Cor. 7 : 7.¶

(3) Cp. *lupeomai*, to grieve, and see Trench, Syn. § lxv.

BEWARE

991 AG:143B CB:1239A 1. BLEPŌ (βλέπω), to see, is applied to mental vision, and is sometimes used by way of warning to take heed against an object, Mark 8 : 15 ; 12 : 38 ; Acts 13 : 40 ; Phil. 3 : 2 (three times) ; in Col. 2 : 8, R.V., " take heed," marg., " see whether." See BEHOLD.

4337 AG:714B CB:— 2. PROSECHŌ (προσέχω), lit., to hold to (*pros*, to, *echō*, to have, to hold), hence, to turn one's mind or attention to a thing by being on one's guard against it, is translated " beware " in Matt. 7 : 15 ; 10 : 17 ; 16 : 6, 11, 12 ; Luke 12 : 1 ; 20 : 46. See ATTEND, HEED, REGARD.

5442 AG:868B CB:1264C 3. PHULASSŌ (φυλάσσω), to guard, watch, keep, is used, in the Middle Voice, of being on one's guard against (the Middle V. stressing personal interest in the action), Luke 12 : 15, " beware of," R.V., " keep yourselves from," as in Acts 21 : 25 ; in 2 Tim. 4 : 15, " be thou ware ; " in 2 Pet. 3 : 17, " beware." See GUARD, KEEP, OBSERVE, SAVE.

BEWILDER See CONFOUND

BEWITCH

1. BASKAINŌ (βασκαίνω), primarily, to slander, to prate about 940
anyone; then to bring evil on a person by feigned praise, or mislead by AG:137A CB:1238C
an evil eye, and so to charm, bewitch (Eng., fascinate is connected), is used figuratively in Gal. 3 : 1, of leading into evil doctrine.¶

2. EXISTEMI (ἐξίστημι) is rendered "bewitch" in Acts 8 : 9, 11, 1839
A.V., concerning Simon the sorcerer; it does not mean to bewitch, as AG:276B CB:1247C
in the case of the preceding verb, but to confuse, amaze (R.V.). See (EXHI-)
AMAZE, B. No. 1.

BEWRAY

Note: The word "bewrayeth", Matt. 26 : 73, is a translation of 1212
poieō, to make, with *dēlos*, manifest, evident; lit., 'maketh thee manifest.' AG:178B CB:1240C

BEYOND

In addition to the preposition *huper*, over, rendered "beyond" in 5228
2 Cor. 8 : 3, the following adverbs have this meaning: AG:838B CB:1252A

1. EPEKEINA (ἐπέκεινα), *epi*, upon, and *ekeina*, those, the word 1900
"parts" being understood, is used in Acts 7 : 43.¶ AG:284D CB:—

2. PERAN (πέραν), on the other side, across, is used with the definite 4008
article, signifying the regions beyond, the opposite shore, Matt. 8 : 18 AG:643D CB:—
etc. With verbs of going it denotes direction towards and beyond a place, e.g., John 10 : 40. It frequently indicates "beyond," of locality, without a verb of direction, Matt. 16 : 5; Mark 10 : 1, R.V.; John 1 : 28; 3 : 26. See FARTHER, SIDE.

Note: In 2 Cor. 10 : 14, the verb *huperekteinō*, to stretch overmuch, HUPEREKTEINŌ 5239
is so rendered in the R.V., for A.V., ". . . beyond our measure."¶ In AG:840D CB:—
2 Cor. 10 : 16 the adverb *huperekeina*, beyond, is used as a preposition. HUPEREKTEINA 5238 AG:840C CB:—

BID, BIDDEN, BADE, BID AGAIN

1. KALEŌ (καλέω), to call, often means to bid, in the sense of invite, 2564
e.g., Matt. 22 : 3, 4, 8, 9; Luke 14 : 7, 8, 9, 10, 13, R.V.; Rev. 19 : 9, AG:398D CB:1253B
R.V. See CALL, NAME, SURNAME.

2. KELEUŌ (κελεύω), to command, is translated "bid" in Matt. 2753
14 : 28, only. See COMMAND, No. 5. Compare the synonym *entellō*, to AG:427B CB:1254C
command.

3. EIPON (εἶπον), used as the aorist tense of *legō*, to speak, to say, 3004
sometimes has the meaning of commanding, or bidding, and is translated (LEGō)
"bid," or "bade," e.g., in Matt. 16 : 12; 23 : 3; Luke 10 : 40; 9 : 54, AG:226A CB:1243A
A.V., "command," R.V., "bid;" Acts 11 : 12; "bidding," Acts 22 : 24,
R.V. See SAY, SPEAK.

4. ANTIKALEŌ (ἀντικαλέω), to bid again, invite in turn, is found in 479 AG:74B CB:—
Luke 14 : 12.¶

Notes: (1) *Legō*, to say, is translated "bid" and "biddeth" in 3004 AG:468A CB:1256C the A.V. of 2 John 10, 11; R.V., "give (him no greeting)," "giveth (him greeting"). See GREETING.

4367 AG:718C CB:1267B (2) In Matt. 1 : 24, *prostassō*, to command, is translated "had bidden," A.V.; R.V., "commanded." See COMMAND.

BID FAREWELL

657 AG:100D CB:— 1. APOTASSŌ (ἀποτάσσω) is used in the Middle Voice to signify to bid adieu to a person. It primarily means to set apart, separate (*apo*, from, *tassō*, to set, arrange); then, to take leave of, to bid farewell to, Mark 6 : 46 (R.V.); Luke 9 : 61; to give parting instructions to, Acts 18 : 18, 21; 2 Cor. 2 : 13; to forsake, renounce, Luke 14 : 33. See FORSAKE, RENOUNCE, SEND, *Note* (2) at end.¶

Cf. 782 AG:81D CB:1238A 2. APASPAZOMAI (ἀπασπάζομαι), to bid farewell (*apo*, from, *aspazomai*, to greet), is used in Acts 21 : 6, A.V., "had taken our leave of;" R.V., "bade . . . farewell."¶

BIER

4673 AG:759B CB:— SOROS (σορός) originally denoted a receptacle for containing the bones of the dead, a cinerary urn; then a coffin, Gen. 50 : 26; Job. 21 : 32; then, the funeral couch or bier on which the Jews bore their dead to burial, Luke 7 : 14.¶

BIG See GREAT

BILL

975 AG:141B CB:1239A 1. BIBLION (βιβλίον), primarily a small book, a scroll, or any sheet on which something has been written; hence, in connection with *apostasion*, divorce, signifies a bill of divorcement, Matt. 19 : 7 (A.V., "writing"); Mark 10 : 4. See BOOK, SCROLL, WRITING.

1121 AG:165B CB:1248C 2. GRAMMA (γράμμα), from *graphō*, to write (Eng., graph, graphic etc.), in Luke 16 : 6, A.V., is translated "bill." It lit. signifies that which is drawn, a picture; hence, a written document; hence, a bill, or bond, or note of hand, showing the amount of indebtedness. In the passage referred to the word is in the plural, indicating perhaps, but not necessarily, various bills. The bonds mentioned in Rabbinical writings, were formal, signed by witnesses and the Sanhedrin of three, or informal, when only the debtor signed. The latter were usually written on wax, and easily altered. See LEARNING, LETTER, SCRIPTURE, WRITING.

For BILLOWS, Luke 21 : 25, R.V., see WAVE

BIND, BINDING (see also BOUND)

1210 AG:177D CB:1240C 1. DEŌ (δέω), to bind, is used (*a*) literally, of any sort of binding, e.g., Acts 22 : 5; 24 : 27, (*b*) figuratively, of the Word of God, as not being bound, 2 Tim. 2 : 9, i.e., its ministry, course and efficacy were not hindered by the bonds and imprisonment suffered by the Apostle. A woman who was bent together, had been "bound" by Satan through the work of a demon, Luke 13 : 16. Paul speaks of himself, in Acts 20 : 22, as being "bound in the spirit," i.e. compelled by his convictions, under the constraining power of the Spirit of God, to go to Jerusalem. A wife is said to be "bound" to her husband, Rom. 7 : 2 ; 1 Cor. 7 : 39 ; and the husband to the wife, 1 Cor. 7 : 27. The Lord's words to the Apostle Peter in Matt. 16 : 19, as to binding, and to all the disciples in 18 : 18, signify, in the former case, that the Apostle, by his ministry of the Word of Life, would keep unbelievers outside the kingdom of God, and admit those who believed. So with regard to 18 : 18, including the exercise of disciplinary measures in the sphere of the local church ; the application of the Rabbinical sense of forbidding is questionable. See BOND, KNIT, *Note*, TIE.

2. PERIDEŌ (περιδέω), *peri*, around, with No. 1, to bind around, is 4019
used in John 11 : 44 of the napkin around the face of Lazarus.¶ Cp. AG:646C
Job 12 : 18, Sept. CB:—

3. HUPODEŌ (ὑποδέω), *hupō*, under, with No. 1, to bind underneath, 5265
is used of binding of sandals, Acts 12 : 8 ; rendered "shod" in Mark 6 : 9 AG:844B
and Eph. 6 : 15. See SHOD.¶ CB:—

4. KATADEŌ (καταδέω), *kata*, down, with No. 1, to bind or tie down, 2611
or bind up, is used in Luke 10 : 34 of the act of the good Samaritan.¶ AG:410B CB:—

5. SUNDEŌ (συνδέω), *sun*, together, and No. 1, to bind together, 4887
implying association, is used in Heb. 13 : 3 of those bound together in AG:785C
confinement.¶ CB:—

6. DESMEUŌ or DESMEŌ (δεσμεύω) signifies to put in fetters or any 1195
kind of bond, Luke 8 : 29 ; Acts 22 : 4, or to bind a burden upon a person, AG:175D CB:1240C
Matt. 23 : 4. The verb is connected with No. 1.¶ DESMOS

Notes : (1) Cp. *desmos*, a band, bond, fetter, e.g., Luke 13 : 16, and 1199
desmios, "bound," Acts 25 : 14, A.V. (R.V., "a prisoner") ; in Heb. AG:176A
13 : 3, "them that are in bonds." See BOND, CHAIN, PRISONER, STRING. CB:1240C DESMIOS

(2) *Sundesmos* (see No. 5, above), that which binds together, is 1198
translated "bands," in Col. 2 : 19. See BONDS. AG:176A CB:1240C

7. PROTEINŌ (προτείνω), lit., to stretch forth (*pro*, forth, *teinō*, to 4886
stretch), is used in Acts 22 : 25, A.V., "they bound ;" R.V., "they had AG:785B CB:1270C
tied (him) up," in reference to the preparations made for scourging, pro- 4385
bably, to stretch the body forward, to make it tense for severer punish- AG:721D CB:—
ment. See TIE.¶

BIRD (Fowl) 3732

1. ORNEON (ὄρνεον) is probably connected with a word signifying AG:581D
to perceive, to hear ; Rev. 18 : 2 ; 19 : 17, 21. See FOWL. Cp. *ornis*, CB:—
a hen.¶ 4071

2. PETEINON (πετεινόν) signifies that which is able to fly, winged. AG:654A CB:1263C
It is connected with *ptenon* signifying "feathered, winged," which is PTēNON
used in 1 Cor. 15 : 39. Cp. *petomai* and *petaomai*, to fly. In the Gospels 4421 AG:727C
the R.V. always translates it "birds," e.g., Matt. 6 : 26 ; but "fowls" CB:—

in Acts 10 : 12 ; 11 : 6. The A.V. unsuitably has " fowls," in the Gospels, except Matt. 8 : 20 ; 13 : 32 ; Luke 9 : 58.

BIRTH

1083 AG:156A CB:— 1. GENNĒSIS (γέννησις), a birth, begetting, producing (related to *gennaō*, to beget), is used in Matt. 1 : 18 and Luke 1 : 14. Some mss. have *genesis*, lineage, birth (from *ginomai*, to become).¶

1079 AG:155A CB:— 2. GENETĒ (γενετή), a being born, or the hour of birth (related to *genea*, race, generation), is connected with *ginomai*, to become, to be born, and is used in John 9 : 1.¶

Notes (1) For *genesis* and *gennēma* see FRUIT, GENERATION, NATURE.

5605 AG:895D CB:1260B (2) In Gal. 4 : 19, *ōdinō*, to have birth pangs, is rendered " travail in birth," A.V. ; R.V., " am in travail." See Rev. 12 : 2.

BIRTHDAY

1077 AG:154C CB:— GENESIA (γενέσια), a neuter plural (akin to *genesis*, lineage, from *ginomai*), primarily denoted the festivities of a birthday, a birthday feast, though among the Greeks it was also used of a festival in commemoration of a deceased friend. It is found in Matt. 14 : 6 and Mark 6 : 21. Some have regarded it as the day of the king's accession, but this meaning is not confirmed in Greek writings.¶

BIRTHRIGHT

4415 AG:726C CB:— PRŌTOTOKIA (πρωτοτόκια), a birthright (from *prōtos*, first, *tiktō*, to beget), is found in Heb. 12 : 16, with reference to Esau (cp. *prōtotokos*, firstborn). The birthright involved pre-eminence and authority, Gen. 27 : 29 ; 49 : 3. Another right was that of the double portion, Deut. 21 : 17 ; 1 Chron. 5 : 1, 2. Connected with the birthright was the progenitorship of the Messiah. Esau transferred his birthright to Jacob for a paltry mess of pottage, profanely despising this last spiritual privilege, Gen. 25 and 27. In the history of the nation God occasionally set aside the birthright, to show that the objects of His choice depended not on the will of the flesh, but on His own authority. Thus Isaac was preferred to Ishmael, Jacob to Esau, Joseph to Reuben, David to his elder brethren, Solomon to Adonijah. See FIRSTBORN.¶

BISHOP (Overseer)

1985 AG:299B CB:1246A 1. EPISKOPOS (ἐπίσκοπος), lit., an overseer (*epi*, over, *skopeō*, to look or watch), whence Eng. " bishop," which has precisely the same meaning, is found in Acts 20 : 28 ; Phil. 1 : 1 ; 1 Tim. 3 : 2 ; Tit. 1 : 7 ; 1 Pet. 2 : 25. See OVERSEER.¶

4245 AG:699D CB:1266B *Note : Presbuteros*, an elder, is another term for the same person as bishop or overseer. See Acts 20 : 17 with verse 28. The term " elder " indicates the mature spiritual experience and understanding of those so described ; the term " bishop," or " overseer," indicates the character of the work undertaken. According to the Divine will and appointment, as in the N.T., there were to be bishops in every local church, Acts 14 : 23 ; 20 : 17 ; Phil. 1 : 1 ; Tit. 1 : 5 ; Jas. 5 : 14. Where the singular is used, the passage is describing what a bishop should be, 1 Tim. 3 : 2 ; Tit. 1 : 7. Christ Himself is spoken of as "the . . . Bishop of our souls," 1 Pet. 2 : 25. See ELDER.

2. EPISKOPĒ (ἐπισκοπή), besides its meaning, visitation, e.g., 1 Pet. 1984
2 : 12 (cp. the Sept. of Ex. 3 : 16 ; Is. 10 : 3 ; Jer. 10 : 15), is rendered AG:299A
"office," in Acts 1 : 20, R.V. (A.V., "bishoprick") ; in 1 Tim. 3 : 1, "the CB:1246A
office of a bishop," lit., '(if any one seeketh) overseership,' there is no word representing office.

Note : The corresponding verb is *episkopeō*, which, in reference to the 1983
work of an overseer, is found in 1 Pet. 5 : 2, R.V., "exercising the over- AG:298D
sight," for A.V. "taking the oversight." See OVERSIGHT. CB:1246A

For BIT see BRIDLE

BITE

DAKNŌ (δάκνω), to bite, in Gal. 5 : 15, "if ye bite and devour one 1143
another," is used metaphorically of wounding the soul, or rending with AG:169D
reproaches.¶ CB:—

BITTER, BITTERLY, BITTERNESS

A. Adjective.

PIKROS (πικρός), from a root *pik*—, meaning to cut, to prick, hence, 4089
lit., pointed, sharp, keen, pungent to the sense of taste, smell, etc., is AG:657C
found in Jas. 3 : 11, 14. In ver. 11 it has its natural sense, with reference CB:1265A
to water ; in ver. 14 it is used metaphorically of jealousy, R.V.¶

B. Verb.

PIKRAINŌ (πικραίνω), related to A, signifies, in the Active Voice, 4087
to be bitter, Col. 3 : 19, or to embitter, irritate, or to make bitter, Rev. AG:657B
10 : 9 ; the Passive Voice, to be made bitter, is used in Rev. 8 : 11 ; CB:1265A
10 : 10.¶

C. Noun.

PIKRIA (πικρία) denotes bitterness. It is used in Acts 8 : 23, meta- 4088
phorically, of a condition of extreme wickedness, "gall of bitterness" or AG:657C
"bitter gall ;" in Rom. 3 : 14, of evil speaking ; in Eph. 4 : 31, of bitter CB:1265A
hatred ; in Heb. 12 : 15, in the same sense, metaphorically, of a root of bitterness, producing bitter fruit.¶

D. Adverb.

PIKRŌS (πικρῶς), bitterly, is used of the poignant grief of Peter's 4090
weeping for his denial of Christ, Matt. 26 : 75 ; Luke 22 : 62.¶ AG:657D
Note : In the Sept., *pikris* (not in the N.T.), a bitter herb, is used in CB:1265A
Ex. 12 : 8 ; Num. 9 : 11.¶

BLACK, BLACKNESS

A. Adjective.

3189 AG:499D MELAS (μέλας), black, Matt. 5 : 36 ; Rev. 6 : 5, 12, is derived from a
CB:1258A root *mal*—, meaning to be dirty ; hence Latin, *malus*, bad. See INK.

B. Nouns.

1105 AG:163A 1. GNOPHOS (γνόφος), Heb. 12 : 18, blackness, gloom, seems to have
CB:— been associated with the idea of a tempest. It is related to *skotos*, darkness, in that passage, and in the Sept. of Ex. 10 : 22 ; Deut. 4 : 11 ; Zeph. 1 : 15.¶

2217 AG:339D 2. ZOPHOS (ζόφος), akin to No. 1, especially the gloom of the regions
CB:— of the lost, is used four times ; 2 Pet. 2 : 4, " darkness " (R.V.) ; 2 : 17, R.V., " blackness," for A.V., " mist ;" Jude 6, " darkness ; " ver. 13, " blackness," suggesting a kind of emanation. See DARKNESS, MIST.¶

For BLADE see GRASS

BLAME, BLAMELESS

A. Verb.

3469 AG:531A MŌMAOMAI (μωμάομαι), to find fault with, to blame, or calumniate,
CB:— is used in 2 Cor. 6 : 3, of the ministry of the Gospel ; in 8 : 20, of the ministration of financial help.¶

3201 AG:502B *Notes :* (1) Cp. the synonymous verb, *memphomai*, to find fault, Mark
CB:1258B 7 : 2 ; Rom. 9 : 19 ; Heb. 8 : 8. See FAULT.¶

2607 AG:409D (2) In Gal. 2 : 11, *kataginōskō* is rightly rendered " stood condemned,"
CB:1254A R.V., for A.V., " was to be blamed." See CONDEMN.

B. Adjectives.

299 1. AMŌMOS (ἄμωμος) : See BLEMISH, B.

AG:47D CB:1234C 2. AMŌMĒTOS (ἀμώμητος), translated in Phil. 2 : 15 " without
298 AG:47D blemish " (A.V., " without rebuke "), is rendered " blameless " in 2 Pet.
CB:1234C 3 : 14 (A.V. and R.V.).¶

273 3. AMEMPTOS (ἄμεμπτος), related to *memphomai* (A., Note), is trans-
AG:45A lated " unblameable " in 1 Thess. 3 : 13 ; " blameless," in Luke 1 : 6 ;
CB:1234C Phil. 2 : 15 ; 3 : 6 ; " faultless " in Heb. 8 : 7. See FAULTLESS, UNBLAMEABLE.¶

" If *amōmos* is the ' unblemished,' *amemptos* is the ' unblamed.' . . . Christ was *amōmos* in that there was in Him no spot or blemish, and He could say, ' Which of you convinceth (convicteth) Me of sin ? ' but in strictness of speech He was not *amemptos* (unblamed), nor is this epithet ever given to Him in the N.T., seeing that He endured the contradiction of sinners against Himself, who slandered His footsteps and laid to His charge ' things that He knew not ' (i.e., of which He was guiltless)." Trench, Syn. §103.

338 AG:55B 4. ANAITIOS (ἀναίτιος), guiltless (*a*, negative, *n*, euphonic, and
CB:1235A *aitia*, a charge), is translated, " blameless " in the A.V. of Matt. 12 : 5,

" guiltless " in 12 : 7. The R.V. has " guiltless " in both places.¶ In the Sept., in Deut. 19 : 10, 13, and 21 : 8, 9.¶ See GUILTLESS.

5. ANEPILĒPTOS (ἀνεπίληπτος), lit., that cannot be laid hold of, 423
hence, not open to censure, irreproachable (from *a*, negative, *n*, euphonic, AG:65B (-ēMP-)
and *epilambanō*, to lay hold of), is used in 1 Tim. 3 : 2; 5 : 7; 6 : 14 CB:1235C
(in all three places the R.V. has " without reproach ; " in the first two, A.V., " blameless," in the last, " unrebukeable ; " an alternative rendering would be ' irreprehensible '). See REPROACH, UNREBUKEABLE.¶

6. ANENKLĒTOS (ἀνέγκλητος) signifies that which cannot be called 410
to account (from *a*, negative, *n*, euphonic, and *enkaleō*, to call in), AG:64B
i.e., with nothing laid to one's charge (as the result of public investigation) ; CB:1235C
in 1 Cor. 1 : 8, R.V., " unreproveable," A.V., " blameless ; " in Col. 1 : 22, A.V. and R.V., " unreproveable ; " in 1 Tim. 3 : 10 and Tit. 1 : 6, 7, A.V. and R.V., " blameless." It implies not merely acquittal, but the absence of even a charge or accusation against a person. This is to be the case with elders.¶

C. Adverb.

AMEMPTŌS (ἀμέμπτως), in 1 Thess. 2 : 10, " unblameably ; " in 274
5 : 23, " without blame," A.V., " blameless," is said of believers at the AG:45A
Judgment-Seat of Christ in His Parousia (His presence after His coming), CB:1234C
as the outcome of present witness and stedfastness. See B, No. 3, above.¶

BLASPHEME, BLASPHEMY, BLASPHEMER, BLASPHEMOUS

A. Noun.

BLASPHĒMIA (βλασφημία), either from *blax*, sluggish, stupid, or, 988
probably, from *blaptō*, to injure, and *phēmē*, speech, Eng. " blasphemy," AG:143A
is so translated thirteen times in the R.V., but " railing " in Matt. 15 : 19 ; CB:1239A
Mark 7 : 22 ; Eph. 4 : 31 ; Col. 3 : 8 ; 1 Tim. 6 : 4 ; Jude 9. The word " blasphemy " is practically confined to speech defamatory of the Divine Majesty. See Note, below. See EVIL SPEAKING, RAILING.

B. Verb.

BLASPHĒMEŌ (βλασφημέω), to blaspheme, rail at or revile, is used 987
(*a*) in a general way, of any contumelious speech, reviling, calumniating, AG:142C
railing at etc., as of those who railed at Christ, e.g., Matt. 27 : 39 ; Mark CB:1239A
15 : 29 ; Luke 22 : 65 (R.V., " reviling ") ; 23 : 39 ; (*b*) of those who speak contemptuously of God or of sacred things, e.g., Matt. 9 : 3 ; Mark 3 : 28 ; Rom. 2 : 24 ; 1 Tim. 1 : 20 ; 6 : 1 ; Rev. 13 : 6 ; 16 : 9, 11, 21 ; " hath spoken blasphemy," Matt. 26 : 65 ; " rail at," 2 Pet. 2 : 10 ; Jude 8, 10 ; " railing," 2 Pet. 2 : 12 ; " slanderously reported," Rom. 3 : 8 ; " be evil spoken of," Rom. 14 : 16 ; 1 Cor. 10 : 30 ; 2 Pet. 2 : 2 ; " speak evil of," Tit. 3 : 2 ; 1 Pet. 4 : 4 ; " being defamed," 1 Cor. 4 : 13. The verb (in the present participial form) is translated " blasphemers " in Acts 19 : 37 ; in Mark 2 : 7, " blasphemeth," R.V., for A.V., " speaketh blasphemies."

There is no noun in the original representing the English " blasphemer."

This is expressed either by the verb, or by the adjective *blasphemos*. See DEFAME, RAIL, REPORT, REVILE.

C. Adjective.

989 AG:143A CB:1239A BLASPHĒMOS (βλάσφημος), abusive, speaking evil, is translated "blasphemous," in Acts 6 : 11, 13; "a blasphemer," 1 Tim. 1 : 13; "railers," 2 Tim. 3 : 2, R.V.; "railing," 2 Pet. 2 : 11. See RAIL.¶

Note: As to Christ's teaching concerning blasphemy against the Holy Spirit, e.g., Matt. 12 : 32, that anyone, with the evidence of the Lord's power before His eyes, should declare it to be Satanic, exhibited a condition of heart beyond Divine illumination and therefore hopeless. Divine forgiveness would be inconsistent with the moral nature of God. As to the Son of Man, in his state of humiliation, there might be misunderstanding, but not so with the Holy Spirit's power demonstrated.

BLAZE See BURN

BLAZE ABROAD

1310 AG:190C CB:— DIAPHĒMIZŌ (διαφημίζω), to spread abroad (*dia*, throughout, *phēmizō*, to speak), is so translated in the R.V. in Matt. 9 : 31; 28 : 15 (A.V., "commonly reported"); Mark 1 : 45 (A.V., "blaze abroad").¶

BLEMISH

A. Noun.

3470 AG:531A CB:— MŌMOS (μῶμος), akin to *mōmaomai* (see BLAME, A), signifies (*a*) a blemish (Sept. only); (*b*) a shame, a moral disgrace, metaphorical of the licentious, 2 Pet. 2 : 13.¶

B. Adjective.

299 AG:47D CB:1234C AMŌMOS (ἄμωμος), without blemish, is always so rendered in the R.V., Eph. 1 : 4; 5 : 27; Phil. 2 : 15; Col. 1 : 22; Heb. 9 : 14; 1 Pet. 1 : 19; Jude 24; Rev. 14 : 5. This meaning is to be preferred to the various A.V. renderings, "without blame," Eph. 1 : 4, "unblameable," Col. 1 : 22, "faultless," Jude 24, "without fault," Rev. 14 : 5. The most authentic mss. have *amōmos*, "without blemish," in Phil. 2 : 15, for *amōmētos*, "without rebuke."¶ In the Sept., in reference to sacrifices, especially in Lev. and Num., the Psalms and Ezek., of blamelessness in character and conduct. See BLAME, FAULT.

BLESS, BLESSED, BLESSEDNESS, BLESSING

A. Verbs.

2127 AG:322B CB:1247B 1. EULOGEŌ (εὐλογέω), lit., to speak well of (*eu*, well, *logos*, a word), signifies, (*a*) to praise, to celebrate with praises, of that which is addressed to God, acknowledging His goodness, with desire for His glory, Luke 1 : 64; 2 : 28; 24 : 51, 53; Jas. 3 : 9; (*b*) to invoke blessings upon a person, e.g., Luke 6 : 28; Rom. 12 : 14. The present participle Passive, blessed, praised, is especially used of Christ in Matt. 21 : 9; 23 : 39, and the parallel passages; also in John 12 : 13; (*c*) to consecrate a thing with solemn prayers, to ask God's blessing on a thing, e.g., Luke 9 : 16; 1 Cor.

10 : 16 ; (*d*) to cause to prosper, to make happy, to bestow blessings on, said of God, e.g., in Acts 3 : 26 ; Gal. 3 : 9 ; Eph. 1 : 3. Cp. the synonym *aineō*, to praise. See PRAISE.

2. ENEULOGEOMAI (ἐνευλογέομαι), to bless, is used in the Passive Voice, Acts 3 : 25, and Gal. 3 : 8. The prefix *en* apparently indicates the person on whom the blessing is conferred.¶ 1757 (-Eō) AG:265D (-Eō) CB:1245A

3. MAKARIZŌ (μακαρίζω), from a root *mak*—, meaning large, lengthy, found also in *makros*, long, *mēkos*, length, hence denotes to pronounce happy, blessed, Luke 1 : 48 and Jas. 5 : 11. See HAPPY.¶ 3106 AG:486C CB:1257C

B. Adjectives.

1. EULOGĒTOS (εὐλογητός), akin to A, 1, means blessed, praised ; it is applied only to God, Mark 14 : 61 ; Luke 1 : 68 ; Rom. 1 : 25 ; 9 : 5 ; 2 Cor. 1 : 3 ; 11 : 31 ; Eph. 1 : 3 ; 1 Pet. 1 : 3.¶ In the Sept. it is also applied to man, e.g., in Gen. 24 : 31 ; 26 : 29 ; Deut. 7 : 14 ; Judg. 17 : 2 ; Ruth 2 : 20 ; 1 Sam. 15 : 13. 2128 AG:322C CB:1247B

2. MAKARIOS (μακάριος), akin to A, No. 3, is used in the beatitudes in Matt. 5 and Luke 6, is especially frequent in the Gospel of Luke, and is found seven times in Revelation, 1 : 3 ; 14 : 13 ; 16 : 15 ; 19 : 9 ; 20 : 6 ; 22 : 7, 14. It is said of God twice, 1 Tim. 1 : 11 ; 6 : 15. In the beatitudes the Lord indicates not only the characters that are blessed, but the nature of that which is the highest good. 3107 AG:486C CB:1257C

C. Nouns.

1. EULOGIA (εὐλογία), akin to A, 1, lit., good speaking, praise, is used of (*a*) God and Christ, Rev. 5 : 12, 13 ; 7 : 12 ; (*b*) the invocation of blessings, benediction, Heb. 12 : 17 ; Jas. 3 : 10 ; (*c*) the giving of thanks, 1 Cor. 10 : 16 ; (*d*) a blessing, a benefit bestowed, Rom. 15 : 29 ; Gal. 3 : 14 ; Eph. 1 : 3 ; Heb. 6 : 7 ; of a monetary gift sent to needy believers, 2 Cor. 9 : 5, 6 ; (*e*) in a bad sense, of fair speech, Rom. 16 : 18, R.V., where it is joined with *chrēstologia*, smooth speech, the latter relating to the substance, *eulogia* to the expression. See BOUNTY.¶ 2129 AG:322D CB:1247B

2. MAKARISMOS (μακαρισμός), akin to A, 3, blessedness, indicates an ascription of blessing rather than a state ; hence in Rom. 4 : 6, where the A.V. renders it as a noun, " (describeth) the blessedness ; " the R.V. rightly puts " (pronounceth) blessing." So ver. 9. In Gal. 4 : 15 the A.V. has " blessedness," R.V., " gratulation." The Galatian believers had counted themselves happy when they heard and received the Gospel. Had they lost that opinion ? See GRATULATION.¶ 3108 AG:487A CB:1257C

Note : In Acts 13 : 34, *hosia*, lit., 'holy things,' is translated " mercies " (A.V.), " blessings " (R.V.). 3741 AG:585C CB:1251B

For BLEW see BLOW

BLIND, BLINDNESS

A. Verbs.

1. TUPHLOŌ (τυφλόω), to blind (from a root *tuph*—, to burn, smoke ; 5186 AG:831A CB:—

cp. *tuphos*, smoke), is used metaphorically, of the dulling of the intellect, John 12 : 40 ; 2 Cor. 4 : 4 ; 1 John 2 : 11.¶

4456 AG:732A
CB:1266A 2. PŌROŌ (πωρόω) signifies to harden (from *pōros*, a thick skin, a hardening) ; rendered " blinded," A.V., in Rom. 11 : 7 and 2 Cor. 3 : 14 (R.V., " hardened ") ; cp. 4 : 4. See HARDEN.

B. Adjective.

5185
AG:830D
CB:1273A TUPHLOS (τυφλός), blind, is used both physically and metaphorically, chiefly in the Gospels ; elsewhere four times ; physically, Acts 13 : 11 ; metaphorically, Rom. 2 : 19 ; 2 Pet. 1 : 9 ; Rev. 3 : 17. The word is frequently used as a noun, signifying a blind man.

C. Noun.

4457
AG:732A
CB:1266A PŌRŌSIS (πώρωσις), akin to A. No. 2, primarily means a covering with a callus, a " hardening," Rom. 11 : 25 and Eph. 4 : 18, R.V., for A.V., " blindness ; " Mark 3 : 5, R.V., for A.V., " hardness." It is metaphorical of a dulled spiritual perception. See HARDNESS.¶

Note : In John 9 : 8, the most authentic mss. have *prosaitēs*, a beggar, R.V., instead of *tuphlos*, blind.

BLINDFOLD

4028
AG:647D
CB:— PERIKALUPTŌ (περικαλύπτω) signifies to blindfold (*peri*, around, *kaluptō*, to hide), Luke 22 : 64. See COVER, OVERLAY.

(STUMBLING) BLOCK See OFFENSE

BLOOD

A. Nouns.

129
AG:22C
CB:1249A 1. HAIMA (αἷμα), (hence Eng., prefix *hæm*—), besides its natural meaning, stands, (*a*) in conjunction with *sarx*, flesh, " flesh and blood," Matt. 16 : 17 ; 1 Cor. 15 : 50 ; Gal. 1 : 16 ; the original has the opposite order, blood and flesh, in Eph. 6 : 12 and Heb. 2 : 14 ; this phrase signifies, by *synecdoche*, man, human beings. It stresses the limitations of humanity ; the two are essential elements in man's physical being ; " the life of the flesh is in the blood," Lev. 17 : 11 ; (*b*) for human generation, John 1 : 13 ; (*c*) for blood shed by violence, e.g., Matt. 23 : 35 ; Rev. 17 : 6 ; (*d*) for the blood of sacrificial victims, e.g., Heb. 9 : 7 ; of the blood of Christ, which betokens His death by the shedding of His blood in expiatory sacrifice ; to drink His blood is to appropriate the saving effects of His expiatory death, John 6 : 53. As " the life of the flesh is in the blood," Lev. 17 : 11, and was forfeited by sin, life eternal can be imparted only by the expiation made, in the giving up of the life by the sinless Saviour.

130
AG:23B
CB:1249A 2. HAIMATEKCHUSIA (αἱματεκχυσία) denotes shedding of blood, Heb. 9 : 22 (*haima*, blood, *ekchunō*, to pour out, shed).¶

B. Verb.

131
AG:23C
CB:— HAIMORRHOEŌ (αἱμορροέω), from *haima*, blood, *rheō*, to flow (Eng., hæmorrhage), signifies to suffer from a flow of blood, Matt. 9 : 20.¶

Notes : (1) In Mark 5 : 25 and Luke 8 : 43, different constructions are used, the translations respectively being " having a flowing of blood " and " being in (i.e., with) a flowing of blood."

(2) In Acts 17 : 26 (R.V., " of one ; " A.V., " of one blood "), the most authentic mss. do not contain the noun *haima*, blood. So with the phrase " through His blood," in Col. 1 : 14.

(3) For " bloody flux " in Acts 28 : 8, A.V., see DYSENTERY (R.V.).

BLOT OUT

EXALEIPHŌ (ἐξαλείφω), from *ek*, out, used intensively, and *aleiphō*, 1813
to wipe, signifies to wash, or to smear completely. Hence, metaphorically, AG:272C CB:1247B
in the sense of removal, to wipe away, wipe off, obliterate ; Acts 3 : 19, of sins ; Col. 2 : 14, of writing ; Rev. 3 : 5, of a name in a book ; Rev. 7 : 17 ; 21 : 4, of tears.¶

BLOW (Noun)

RHAPISMA (ῥάπισμα), (*a*) a blow with a rod or staff, (*b*) a blow with 4475
the hand, a slap or cuff, is found in three places, of the maltreatment of AG:734C CB:1268A
Christ by the officials or attendants of the high priest, Mark 14 : 65, R.V., " received (according to the most authentic mss.) Him with blows of their hands," (A.V., " did strike Him with the palms of their hands ") ; that they received, or took, Him would indicate their rough handling of Him ; John 18 : 22 and 19 : 3 ; in all three places the R.V. marg. gives the meaning (*a*), as to the use of a rod.¶

So with the corresponding verb *rhapizō*, in Matt. 26 : 67. The soldiers subsequently beat Him with a reed, 27 : 30, where *tuptō*, to beat, is used ; *rhapizō* occurs elsewhere in Matt. 5 : 39. See SMITE.¶

BLOW (Verb)

1. PNEŌ (πνέω) signifies (*a*) to blow, e.g., Matt. 7 : 25 ; John 3 : 8 ; 4154
in Acts 27 : 40 the present participle is used as a noun, lit., ' to the AG:679C CB:1265B
blowing ' (i.e., to the wind) ; (*b*) to breathe. See BREATHE.

2. HUPOPNEŌ (ὑποπνέω), *hupo*, under (indicating repression), and 5285
No. 1, denotes to blow softly, Acts 27 : 13.¶ AG:846D CB:—

Note : In Acts 28 : 13, *epiginomai*, to come on, is used of the springing 1920
up of a wind, A.V., " blew ; " R.V., " sprang up." AG:290D CB:—

BOARD

SANIS (σανίς) denotes a plank, or board, Acts 27 : 44.¶ 4548 AG:742A CB:—

BOAST, BOASTER, BOASTFUL

A. Verbs.

1. KAUCHAOMAI (καυχάομαι), and its related words *katakauchaomai*, to glory or boast and the nouns *kauchēsis* and *kauchēma*, translated " boast," and " boasting," in the A.V., are always translated " glory,"

and "glorying" in the R.V., e.g., 2 Cor. 10 : 15 ; 11 : 10, 17 ; Eph. 2 : 9. See GLORY.

3166 AG:496D CB:— 2. MEGALAUCHEŌ (μεγαλαυχέω), from *megala*, great things, and *aucheō*, to lift up the neck, hence, to boast, is found in some texts of Jas. 3 : 5. The most authentic mss. have the two words separated. It indicates any kind of haughty speech which stirs up strife or provokes others.¶

3004 AG:468A CB:1256C *Note :* In Acts 5 : 36, the verb *legō*, to say, is rendered "boasting" in the A.V. ; "giving out" (R.V.).

B. Nouns.

213 AG:34D CB:1234B 1. ALAZŌN (ἀλαζών), a boaster, Rom. 1 : 30 and 2 Tim. 3 : 2, A.V., "boasters," R.V., "boastful," primarily signifies a wanderer about the country (from *alē*, wandering), a vagabond ; hence, an impostor.¶

212 AG:34C CB:1234B 2. ALAZONEIA (ἀλαζονεία), the practice of an *alazōn*, denotes quackery ; hence, arrogant display, or boastings, Jas. 4 : 16, R.V., "vauntings ;" in 1 John 2 : 16, R.V., "vainglory ;" A.V., "pride." See PRIDE, VAUNT.¶

5287 AG:847A CB:1252B *Note :* In 2 Cor. 9 : 4, *hupostasis*, a support, substance, means "confidence" (R.V.) ; A.V., "confident boasting."

BOAT

4142 AG:673B CB:— 1. PLOIARION (πλοιάριον), a skiff or small boat, is a diminutive of *ploion* (No. 2), Mark 3 : 9 ; 4 : 36 ; John 6 : 22 (but No. 2 in the 2nd part of the verse), 23 (here some texts have No. 2), 24 ; 21 : 8.¶

4143 AG:673B CB:— 2. PLOION (πλοῖον), A.V., "ship," is preferably translated "boat" (R.V.) in the Gospels, where it is of frequent use ; it is found 18 times in Acts, where, as in Jas. 3 : 4 ; Rev. 8 : 9 ; 18 : 19, it signifies a ship. See SHIP.

4627 AG:753C CB:— 3. SKAPHĒ (σκάφη) is, lit., anything dug or scooped out (from *skaptō*, to dig), as a trough, a tub, and hence a light boat, or skiff, a boat belonging to a larger vessel, Acts 27 : 16, 30, 32.¶

BODY, BODILY

A. Nouns.

4983 AG:799A CB:1269B 1. SŌMA (σῶμα) is the body as a whole, the instrument of life, whether of man living, e.g., Matt. 6 : 22, or dead, Matt. 27 : 52 ; or in resurrection, 1 Cor. 15 : 44 ; or of beasts, Heb. 13 : 11 ; of grain, 1 Cor. 15 : 37, 38 ; of the heavenly hosts, 1 Cor. 15 : 40. In Rev. 18 : 13 it is translated "slaves." In its figurative uses the essential idea is preserved.

Sometimes the word stands, by *synecdoche*, for the complete man, Matt. 5 : 29 ; 6 : 22 ; Rom. 12 : 1 ; Jas. 3 : 6 ; Rev. 18 : 13. Sometimes the person is identified with his or her body, Acts 9 : 37 ; 13 : 36, and this is so even of the Lord Jesus, John 19 : 40 with 42. The body is not the man, for he himself can exist apart from his body, 2 Cor. 12 : 2, 3. The body is an essential part of the man and therefore the redeemed are not perfected till the resurrection, Heb. 11 : 40 ; no man in his final state will be without his body, John 5 : 28, 29 ; Rev. 20 : 13.

The word is also used for physical nature, as distinct from *pneuma*, the spiritual nature, e.g., 1 Cor. 5 : 3, and from *psuchē*, the soul, e.g., 1 Thess. 5 : 23. "*Sōma*, body, and *pneuma*, spirit, may be separated; *pneuma* and *psuchē*, soul, can only be distinguished" (Cremer).

It is also used metaphorically, of the mystic Body of Christ, with reference to the whole Church, e.g., Eph. 1 : 23 ; Col. 1 : 18, 22, 24 ; also of a local church, 1 Cor. 12 : 27.

2. CHRŌS (χρώς) signifies the surface of a body, especially of the 5559
human body, Acts 19 : 12, with reference to the handkerchiefs carried AG:889A CB:—
from Paul's body to the sick.¶

3. PTŌMA (πτῶμα) denotes, lit., a fall (akin to *piptō*, to fall) ; hence, 4430
that which is fallen, a corpse, Matt. 14 : 12 ; 24 : 28, "carcase ;" Mark AG:727D CB:1268A
6 : 29 ; 15 : 45, "corpse ;" Rev. 11 : 8, 9, "dead bodies" (Gk., "carcase," but plural in the 2nd part of ver. 9). See Carcase, Corpse.¶

B. Adjectives.

1. SUSSŌMOS (σύσσωμος), *sun*, with, and A, No. 1., means united in 4954
the same body, Eph. 3 : 6, of the Church.¶ AG:794D CB:—

2. SŌMATIKOS (σωματικός), bodily, is used in Luke 3 : 22, of the 4984
Holy Spirit in taking a bodily shape ; in 1 Tim. 4 : 8 of bodily exercise.¶ AG:800B CB:1269B

C. Adverb.

SŌMATIKŌS (σωματικῶς), bodily, corporeally, is used in Col. 2 : 9.¶ 4985 AG:800B CB:1269B

BOISTEROUS

Note : The A.V. "boisterous" in Matt. 14 : 30 is a rendering of the 2478
word *ischuros*, "strong" (see margin) ; it is not in the most authentic AG:383A CB:1253A
mss.

BOLD, BOLDNESS, BOLDLY

A. Verbs.

1. THARREŌ (θαῤῥέω), a later form of *tharseō* (see Cheer, 2292
Comfort), is connected with *therō*, to be warm (warmth of tempera- AG:352A CB:1271C
ment being associated with confidence) ; hence, to be confident, bold, courageous ; R.V., invariably, to be of good courage ; 2 Cor. 5 : 6, 8 (A.V., to be confident) ; 7 : 16 (A.V., to have confidence) ; 10 : 1, 2 (A.V., to be bold) ; Heb. 13 : 6, A.V., "boldly ;" R.V., "with good courage" (lit., 'being courageous'). See Courage.

2. PARRHĒSIAZOMAI (παῤῥησιάζομαι), to speak boldly, or freely, 3955
primarily had reference to speech (see B, below), but acquired the meaning AG:631A CB:1262C
of being bold, or waxing bold, 1 Thess. 2 : 2 ; in Acts 13 : 46, R.V., "spake out boldly" (the aorist participle here signifies 'waxing bold') ; Acts 9 : 27, 29, "preached boldly" (see also 18 : 26 ; 19 : 8) ; in 26 : 26, "speak freely." See Freely.

3. TOLMAŌ (τολμάω) signifies to dare to do, or to bear, something 5111 AG:821D CB:1272C

terrible or difficult; hence, to be bold, to bear oneself boldly, deal boldly; it is translated "be bold" in 2 Cor. 10 : 2, as contrasted with *tharreō* in verse 1, and the first line of verse 2, "shew courage" (see No. 1, above); in 10 : 12, R.V., "are not bold to," for A.V., "dare not make ourselves of." *Tharreō* denotes confidence in one's own powers, and has reference to character; *tolmaō* denotes boldness in undertaking and has reference to manifestation (Thayer). See COURAGE, DARE.

662 4. APOTOLMAŌ (ἀποτολμάω), *apo* (intensive), with No. 3, means to
AG:101B CB:— be very bold, to speak out boldly, and is used in Rom. 10 : 20.¶

B. Noun.

3954 PARRHĒSIA (παῤῥησία), from *pas*, all, *rhēsis*, speech (see A, No. 2),
AG:630C CB:1262C denotes (*a*), primarily, freedom of speech, unreservedness of utterance,
Acts 4 : 29, 31; 2 Cor. 3 : 12; 7 : 4; Philm. 8; or to speak without ambiguity, plainly, John 10 : 24; or without figures of speech, John 16 : 25; (*b*) the absence of fear in speaking boldly; hence, confidence, cheerful courage, boldness, without any connection necessarily with speech; the R.V. has "boldness" in the following; Acts 4 : 13; Eph. 3 : 12; 1 Tim. 3 : 13; Heb. 3 : 6; 4 : 16; 10 : 19, 35; 1 John 2 : 28; 3 : 21; 4 : 17; 5 : 14; (*c*) the deportment by which one becomes conspicuous, John 7 : 4; 11 : 54, acts openly, or secures publicity, Col. 2 : 15. See CONFIDENCE, OPENLY, PLAINNESS.

C. Adverb.

5112 TOLMĒROTERŌS (τολμηροτέρως), the comparative degree of *tolmērōs*,
AG:822A (-MēROS) means the more boldly, Rom. 15 : 15; in some texts, *tolmēroteron*. Cp. A,
CB:1272C (-TORON) No. 3.¶ Cp. *tolmētēs*, presumptuous; R.V., "daring," 2 Pet. 2 : 10.¶

BOND

1199 1. DESMOS (δεσμός), from *deō*, to bind (see BAND), is usually found
AG:176A CB:1240C in the plural, either masculine or neuter; (*a*) it stands thus for the actual
bonds which bind a prisoner, as in Luke 8 : 29; Acts 16 : 26; 20 : 23 (the only three places where the neuter plural is used); 22 : 30; (*b*) the masculine plural stands frequently in a figurative sense for a condition of imprisonment, Phil. 1 : 7, 13, i.e., 'so that my captivity became manifest as appointed for the cause of Christ'; verses 14, 16; Col. 4 : 18; 2 Tim. 2 : 9; Philm. 10, 13; Heb. 10 : 34.

In Mark 7 : 35 "the bond (A.V., string)" stands metaphorically for the infirmity which caused an impediment in his speech. So in Luke 13 : 16, of the infirmity of the woman who was bowed together. See BAND, CHAIN, STRING.

1198 2. DESMIOS (δέσμιος), a binding, denotes "a prisoner," e.g., Acts
AG:176A CB:1240C 25 : 14, R.V., for the A.V., "in bonds;" Heb. 13 : 3, "them that are in
bonds." Paul speaks of himself as a prisoner of Christ, Eph. 3 : 1; 2 Tim. 1 : 8; Philm. 1, 9; "in the Lord," Eph. 4 : 1. See PRISONER.

4886 3. SUNDESMOS (σύνδεσμος), that which binds together (*sun*, with,
AG:785B CB:1270C and No. 1), is said of "the bond of iniquity," Acts 8 : 23; "the bond of

peace," Eph. 4 : 3 ; " the bond of perfectness," Col. 3 : 14 (figurative of the ligaments of the body) ; elsewhere, Col. 2 : 19, " bands," figuratively of the bands which unite the Church, the Body of Christ. See BAND.¶

4. HALUSIS (ἅλυσις) denotes a chain ; so the R.V. in Eph. 6 : 20, **254**
for A.V., " bonds." See CHAIN. **AG:41C CB:—**

5. GRAMMA (γράμμα), in Luke 16 : 6, R.V., means a bill or note of **1121**
hand. See BILL, No. 2. **AG:165B**

6. CHEIROGRAPHOS (χειρόγραφος), a handwriting, is rendered **CB:1248C 5498**
" bond " in Col. 2 : 14, R.V. **AG:880C (-ON) CB:1239C (-ON)**

BONDAGE

A. Noun.

DOULEIA (δουλεία), akin to *deō*, to bind, primarily the condition of **1397**
being a slave, came to denote any kind of bondage, as, e.g., of the condition **AG:205A CB:1242B**
of creation, Rom. 8 : 21 ; of that fallen condition of man himself which makes him dread God, ver. 15, and fear death, Heb. 2 : 15 ; of the condition imposed by the Mosaic Law, Gal. 4 : 24. See SERVE.

B. Verbs.

1. DOULEUŌ (δουλεύω), to serve as a slave, to be a slave, to be in **1398**
bondage, is frequently used without any association of slavery, e.g., **AG:205A CB:1242B**
Acts 20 : 19 ; Rom. 6 : 6 ; 7 : 6 ; 12 : 11 ; Gal. 5 : 13. See SERVE.

2. DOULOŌ (δουλόω), different from No. 1, in being transitive instead **1402**
of intransitive, signifies to make a slave of, to bring into bondage, Acts **AG:206A CB:—**
7 : 6 ; 1 Cor. 9 : 19, R.V. ; in the Passive Voice, to be brought under bondage, 2 Pet. 2 : 19 ; to be held in bondage, Gal. 4 : 3 (lit., ' were reduced to bondage ') ; Tit. 2 : 3, of being enslaved to wine ; Rom. 6 : 18, of service to righteousness (lit., ' were made bondservants '). As with the purchased slave there were no limitations either in the kind or the time of service, so the life of the believer is to be lived in continuous obedience to God. See ENSLAVED, GIVE, SERVANT.

3. DOULAGŌGEŌ (δουλαγωγέω), to bring into bondage (from A, **1396**
above, and *agō*, to bring), is used in 1 Cor. 9 : 27, concerning the body, **AG:205A**
R.V., " bondage," for A.V., " subjection."¶ **CB:1242A (-ōGō)**

4. KATADOULOŌ (καταδουλόω), to bring into bondage, occurs in **2615**
2 Cor. 11 : 20 ; Gal. 2 : 4.¶ **AG:410C CB:—**

BONDMAN, BONDMAID

DOULOS (δοῦλος), from *deō*, to bind, a slave, originally the lowest **1401**
term in the scale of servitude, came also to mean one who gives himself **AG:205C CB:1242B**
up to the will of another, e.g., 1 Cor. 7 : 23 ; Rom. 6 : 17, 20, and became the most common and general word for " servant," as in Matt. 8 : 9, without any idea of bondage. In calling himself, however, a ' bondslave of Jesus Christ,' e.g., Rom. 1 : 1, the Apostle Paul intimates (1) that he had been formerly a bondslave of Satan, and (2) that, having been bought by Christ, he was now a willing slave, bound to his new Master. See SERVANT.

The feminine, *doulē*, signifies a handmaid, Luke 1 : 38, 48 ; Acts 2 : 18.¶

3814 AG:604B CB:1261C PAIDISKĒ (παιδίσκη), a young girl, maiden, also denoted a young female slave, bondwoman, or handmaid. For the A.V., "bondmaid" or "bondwoman," in Gal. 4 : 22, 23, 30, 31, the R.V. has "handmaid." See DAMSEL, HANDMAID, MAID.

For BONDSERVANT see SERVANT

BONE

3747 AG:586C CB:1261B OSTEON (ὀστέον), probably from a word signifying strength, or firmness, sometimes denotes hard substances other than bones, e.g., the stone or kernel of fruit. In the N.T. it always denotes bones, Matt. 23 : 27 ; Luke 24 : 39 ; John 19 : 36 ; Heb. 11 : 22.¶

Note : As to Eph. 5 : 30, R.V., " We are members of His body " (in contrast to the A.V.), " the words that follow in the common text are an unintelligent gloss, in which unsuccessful endeavour is made to give greater distinctness to the Apostle's statement " (Westcott).

BOOK

976 AG:141C CB:1239A 1. BIBLOS (βίβλος), Eng. " Bible," was the inner part, or rather the cellular substance, of the stem of the papyrus (Eng. " paper "). It came to denote the paper made from this bark in Egypt, and then a written book, roll, or volume. It is used in referring to books of Scripture, the book, or scroll, of Matthew's Gospel, Matt. 1 : 1 ; the Pentateuch, as the book of Moses, Mark 12 : 26 ; Isaiah, as " the book of the words of Isaiah," Luke 3 : 4 ; the Psalms, Luke 20 : 42 and Acts 1 : 20 ; " the prophets," Acts 7 : 42 ; to " the Book of Life," Phil. 4 : 3 ; Rev. 3 : 5 ; 20 : 15. Once only it is used of secular writings, Acts 19 : 19.¶

975 AG:141B CB:1239A 2. BIBLION (βιβλίον), a diminutive of No. 1, had in Hellenistic Greek almost lost its diminutive force and was ousting *biblos* in ordinary use ; it denotes a scroll or a small book. It is used in Luke 4 : 17, 20, of the book of Isaiah ; in John 20 : 30, of the Gospel of John ; in Gal. 3 : 10 and Heb. 10 : 7, of the whole of the O.T. ; in Heb. 9 : 19, of the book of Exodus ; in Rev. 1 : 11 ; 22 : 7, 9, 10, 18 (twice), 19, of the Apocalypse ; in John 21 : 25 and 2 Tim. 4 : 13, of books in general ; in Rev. 13 : 8 ; 17 : 8 ; 20 : 12 ; 21 : 27, of the Book of Life (see Note, below) ; in Rev. 20 : 12, of other books to be opened in the Day of Judgment, containing, it would seem, the record of human deeds. In Rev. 5 : 1–9 the Book represents the revelation of God's purposes and counsels concerning the world. So with the " little book " in Rev. 10 : 8. In 6 : 14 it is used of a scroll, the rolling up of which illustrates the removal of the heaven.

In Matt. 19 : 7 and Mark 10 : 4 the word is used of a bill of divorcement. See BILL.¶

Note : In Rev. 22 : 19, the most authentic mss. have ***xulon***, tree (of life), instead of " ***biblion***."

3. BIBLARIDION (βιβλαρίδιον), another diminutive of No. 1, is 974
always rendered " little book," in Rev. 10 : 2, 9, 10. Some texts have it AG:141A
also in verse 8, instead of *biblion* (but see beginning of No. 2).¶ CB:—

BOON

DŌRĒMA (δώρημα), translated " boon " in Jas. 1 : 17, R.V., is 1434
thus distinguished, as the thing given, from the preceding word in AG:210D
the verse, *dosis*, the act of giving (A.V., " gift " in each case) ; elsewhere CB:1242A
in Rom. 5 : 16. It is to be distinguished also from *dōron*, the usual word
for a gift. See GIFT.¶

BOOTH See CUSTOM (TOLL) 2., TABERNACLE

BORDER

1. KRASPEDON (κράσπεδον) was primarily the extremity or pro- 2899
minent part of a thing, an edge ; hence the fringe of a garment, or a little AG:448B
fringe, hanging down from the edge of the mantle or cloak. The Jews CB:—
had these attached to their mantles to remind them of the Law, according to Num. 15 : 38, 39 ; Deut. 22 : 12 ; Zech. 8 : 23.¶. This is the meaning in Matt. 23 : 5. In Matt. 9 : 20 ; 14 : 36 ; Mark 6 : 56 ; Luke 8 : 44, it is used of the border of Christ's garment (A.V. " hem," in the first two places). See HEM.¶

2. HORION (ὅριον), the border of a country or district (cp. Eng., 3725
horizon), is always used in the plural. The A.V. has " coasts," but AG:581B
" borders " in Matt. 4 : 13 ; the R.V. always " borders," Matt. 2 : 16 ; CB:1251B
4 : 13 ; 8 : 34 ; 15 : 22, 39 ; 19 : 1 ; Mark 5 : 17 ; 7 : 31 (twice) ; 10 : 1 ; Acts 13 : 50. In some of these it signifies territory. See COAST.¶

3. METHORION (μεθόριον), *meta*, with, and No. 2, similar in meaning, 3181 (-OS)
is found, in some mss., in Mark 7 : 24.¶ Cp. *horothesia*, under BOUND. AG:499B
CB:—

For BORN see BEGET

For BORNE see BEAR

BORROW

DANEIZŌ (δανείζω), in the Active Voice, signifies to lend money, 1155
as in Luke 6 : 34, 35 ; in the Middle Voice, to have money lent to one- AG:170D
self, to borrow, Matt. 5 : 42.¶ Cp. *dan(e)ion*, a debt, Matt. 18 : 27,¶ CB:—
and *dan(e)istēs*, a creditor, Luke 7 : 41.¶ See LEND.

BOSOM

KOLPOS (κόλπος) signifies (*a*) the front of the body between the arms ; 2859
hence, to recline in the bosom was said of one who so reclined at table AG:442B
that his head covered, as it were, the bosom of the one next to him, CB:1255C
John 13 : 23. Hence, figuratively, it is used of a place of blessedness with another, as with Abraham in Paradise, Luke 16 : 22, 23 (plural in ver. 23), from the custom of reclining at table in the bosom, a place of honour ;

of the Lord's eternal and essential relation with the Father, in all its blessedness and affection as intimated in the phrase, " The Only-begotten Son, which is in the bosom of the Father " (John 1 : 18) ; (*b*) of the bosom of a garment, the hollow formed by the upper forepart of a loose garment, bound by a girdle and used for carrying or keeping things ; thus figuratively of repaying one liberally, Luke 6 : 38 ; cp. Isa. 65 : 6 ; Jer. 39 : 18 ; (*c*) of an inlet of the sea, because of its shape, like a bosom, Acts 27 : 39. See BAY, CREEK.¶

BOTH : see Note †, p. 1 .

For BOTTLE see SKIN

BOTTOM, BOTTOMLESS

A. Adverb.

KATŌ (κάτω) ; for this see BENEATH.

B. Adjective.

12 ABUSSOS (ἄβυσσος), bottomless (from *a*, intensive, and *bussos*, a
AG:2B CB:1233A depth ; akin to *bathus*, deep ; Eng., bath), is used as a noun denoting the abyss (A.V., " bottomless pit "). It describes an immeasurable depth, the underworld, the lower regions, the abyss of Sheol. In Rom. 10 : 7, quoted from Deut. 30 : 13, the abyss (the abode of the lost dead) is substituted for the sea (the change in the quotation is due to the facts of the Death and Resurrection of Christ); the A.V. has "deep" here and in Luke 8 : 31 ; the reference is to the lower regions as the abode of demons, out of which they can be let loose, Rev. 11 : 7 ; 17 : 8 ; it is found seven times in the Apocalypse, 9 : 1, 2, 11 ; 11 : 7 ; 17 : 8 ; 20 : 1, 3 ; in 9 : 1, 2 the R.V. has " the pit of the abyss." See DEEP.¶

For BOUGHT see BUY

BOUND (Noun)

3734 HOROTHESIA (ὁροθεσία), the fixing of a boundary, rather than the
AG:582A boundary itself (from *horos*, a boundary, and *tithēmi*, to place), is used
CB:— in Acts 17 : 26, " bounds."¶

BOUND (to be)

(*a*) *of obligation :*

3784 OPHEILŌ (ὀφείλω), to owe, whether of a debt or any obligation, is
AG:598D CB:1261A translated " we are bound," in 2 Thess. 1 : 3 and 2 : 13 (the Apostle expressing his obligation to give thanks for his readers). See BEHOVE.

1163 *Note : Dei*, it is necessary (for which see MUST), expresses, not the
AG:172A CB:1240B obligation (as does *opheilō*) but the certainty or inevitableness of what is bound to happen, e.g., John 3 : 15, " must be lifted up " (i.e., inevitably), and Acts 4 : 12, " wherein we must be saved " (i.e., there is a certainty of salvation).

(*b*) *of binding :*

PERIKEIMAI (περίκειμαι), lit., to lie around (*peri*, around, *keimai*, 4029
to lie), to be compassed, is used of binding fetters around a person, Acts AG:647D CB:—
28 : 20 ; in Mark 9 : 42, and Luke 17 : 2, to hang about a person's neck ; in Heb. 5 : 2, to compass about, metaphorically of infirmities ; in 12 : 1, of those who have witness borne to their faith. See COMPASS, HANG.¶

Note : For " bound " in Acts 22 : 5 ; 24 : 27, see BIND, No. 1 ; for Acts 22 : 25, A.V., see BIND, No. 7 ; for Luke 8 : 29, see BIND, No. 6.

BOUNTY, BOUNTIFULLY

1. EULOGIA (εὐλογία), a blessing, has the meaning of bounty in 2129
2 Cor. 9 : 5, of the offering sent by the church at Corinth to their needy AG:322D CB:1247B
brethren in Judæa.

Note : In the next verse the adverb " bountifully " is a translation of the phrase *ep' eulogiais*, lit., 'with blessings' (R.V. marg.), that is, that blessings may accrue. See BLESSING.

2. HAPLOTĒS (ἁπλότης), from *haplous*, simple, single, is translated 572
" bountifulness " in 2 Cor. 9 : 11, A.V. ; R.V., " liberality " (marg., AG:85D CB:1249B
" singleness ") ; cp. 8 : 2 ; 9 : 13 ; from sincerity of mind springs " liberality." The thought of sincerity is present in Rom. 12 : 8 ; 2 Cor. 11 : 3 ; Eph. 6 : 5 ; Col. 3 : 22. See LIBERAL, SIMPLICITY, SINGLENESS.¶

3. CHARIS (χάρις), grace, is rendered, " bounty " in 1 Cor. 16 : 3, 5485
R.V., (A.V., " liberality "), by metonymy for a material gift. See AG:877B CB:1239C
BENEFIT, No. 3.

4. HADROTĒS (ἁδρότης), lit., fatness (from *hadros*, thick, well-grown), 100
is used of a monetary gift, in 2 Cor. 8 : 20, A.V., " abundance," R.V., AG:18D CB:—
" bounty."¶

BOW, BOWED (Verb)

1. KAMPTŌ (κάμπτω), to bend, is used especially of bending the 2578
knees in religious veneration, Rom. 11 : 4 ; 14 : 11 ; Eph. 3 : 14 ; Phil. AG:402B CB:1253B
2 : 10.¶

2. SUNKAMPTŌ (συγκάμπτω) signifies to bend completely together, 4781
to bend down by compulsory force, Rom. 11 : 10.¶ AG:773B CB:—

3. SUNKUPTŌ (συγκύπτω), to bow together (*sun*, together with, 4794
kuptō, to bow), is said, in Luke 13 : 11, of the woman crippled with a AG:775A CB:—
physical infirmity.¶

4. KLINŌ (κλίνω), to incline, to bow down, is used of the women 2827
who in their fright bowed their faces to the earth at the Lord's empty AG:436C CB:—
tomb, Luke 24 : 5 ; of the act of the Lord on the Cross immediately before giving up His Spirit. What is indicated in the statement " He bowed His head," is not the helpless dropping of the head after death, but the deliberate putting of His head into a position of rest, John 19 : 30. The

verb is deeply significant here. The Lord reversed the natural order. The same verb is used in His statement in Matt. 8 : 20 and Luke 9 : 58, " the Son of Man hath not where to lay His head." It is used, too, of the decline of day, Luke 9 : 12 ; 24 : 29 ; of turning enemies to flight, Heb. 11 : 34. See LAY, SPENT, No. 7, TURN, WEAR.¶

5087 5. TITHĒMI (τίθημι), to put, or place, is said of the soldiers who
AG:815D CB:1272C mockingly bowed their knees to Christ, Mark 15 : 19. See **APPOINT.**
1120 *Note :* For *gonupeteō*, to bow the knee, Matt. 27 : 29, see **KNEEL.**
AG:165B
CB:1248C

BOW (Noun)

5115 TOXON (τόξον), a bow, is used in Rev. 6 : 2. Cp. Hab. 3 : 8, 9. The
AG:822B CB:1273A instrument is frequently mentioned in the Sept., especially in the Psalms.¶

BOWELS

4698 SPLANCHNON (σπλάγχνον), always in the plural, properly denotes
AG:763A CB:1269C the physical organs of the intestines, and is once used in this respect, Acts 1 : 18 (for the use by Greeks and Hebrews, see AFFECTION, No. 2). The R.V. substitutes the following for the word " bowels : " " affections," 2 Cor. 6 : 12 ; " affection," 2 Cor. 7 : 15 ; " tender mercies," Phil. 1 : 8 ; 2 : 1 ; " a heart (of compassion)," Col. 3 : 12 ; " heart," Philm. 12, 20 ; " hearts," Philm. 7 ; " compassion," 1 John 3 : 17. The word is rendered " tender " in the A.V. and R.V. of Luke 1 : 78, in connection with the word " mercy." See AFFECTION, No. 2, COMPASSION, **A, No. 2 and B, No. 2.**¶

BOWL

5357 PHIALĒ (φιάλη), Eng., phial, denotes a bowl ; so the R.V., for A.V.,
AG:858B CB:— " vial," in Rev. 5 : 8 ; 15 : 7 ; 16 : 1, 2, 3, 4, 8, 10, 12, 17 ; 17 : 1 ; 21 : 9 ; the word is suggestive of rapidity in the emptying of the contents. While the seals (ch. 6) give a general view of the events of the last " week " or " hebdomad," in the vision given to Daniel, Dan. 9 : 23–27, the " trumpets " refer to the judgments which, in a more or less extended period, are destined to fall especially, though not only, upon apostate Christendom and apostate Jews. The emptying of the bowls betokens the final series of judgments in which this exercise of the wrath of God is " finished " (Rev. 15 : 1, R.V.). These are introduced by the 7th trumpet. See Rev. 11 : 15 and the successive order in ver. 18, " the nations were wroth, and Thy wrath came . . . ;" see also 6 : 17 ; 14 : 19, 20 ; 19 : 11–21.¶

BOX

211 ALABASTRON (ἀλάβαστρον), an alabaster vessel, is translated, in
AG:34C CB:— the A.V. of Matt. 26 : 7 ; Mark 14 : 3 ; Luke 7 : 37, " box," R.V., " cruse." The breaking refers to the seal, not to the box or cruse. See **CRUSE.**¶

BOY

PAIS (παῖς) denotes a boy (in contrast to *paidion*, a diminutive of *pais*, 3816
and to *teknon*, a child). With reference to Christ, instead of the A.V. AG:604C CB:1261C
" child," the R.V. suitably translates otherwise as follows: Luke 2 : 43,
" the boy Jesus;" Acts 4 : 27, 30, " Thy Holy Servant, Jesus." So in
the case of others, Matt. 17 : 18 and Luke 9 : 42 (" boy "). See CHILD,
MAID, MANSERVANT, SERVANT, SON, YOUNG MAN. **BRAG See BOAST**

BRAIDED (A.V., BROIDED)

PLEGMA (πλέγμα) signifies what is woven (from *plekō*, to weave, plait), 4117
whether a net or basket (Josephus uses it of the ark of bulrushes in which AG:667A CB:—
the infant Moses was laid), or of a web, plait, braid. It is used in 1 Tim. 2 : 9, of " braided hair," which the Vulgate signifies as ringlets, curls.¶

Notes: (1) Cp. *emplokē*, 1 Pet. 3 : 3, " plaiting," i.e., intertwining the 1708
hair in ornament.¶ AG:256C CB:—

(2) " Broided " is to be distinguished from " broidered," which means to adorn with needlework (not to plait).

For BRAMBLE BUSH see BUSH

For BRAKE see BREAK

BRANCH

1. KLADOS (κλάδος), from *klaō*, to break (cp. *klasma*, a broken piece), 2798
properly a young tender shoot, broken off for grafting, is used for any kind AG:433A
of branch, Matt. 13 : 32; 21 : 8; 24 : 32; Mark 4 : 32; 13 : 28; Luke CB:1255A
13 : 19; the descendants of Israel, Rom. 11 : 16–19, 21.¶

2. KLĒMA (κλῆμα), akin to *klaō*, to break, denotes a tender, flexible 2814
branch, especially the shoot of a vine, a vine sprout, John 15 : 2, 4, 5, 6.¶ AG:434C CB:1255B

3. STOIBAS or STIBAS (στοιβάς), from *steibō*, to tread on, primarily 4746
denoted a layer of leaves, reeds, twigs or straw, serving for a bed; then AG:768B
a branch full of leaves, soft foliage, which might be used in making a bed, (-BOS)
or for treading upon, Mark 11 : 8.¶ CB:—

4. BAION (βαῖον), of Egyptian origin, frequent in the papyri writings, 902
denotes a branch of the palm tree, John 12 : 13.¶ AG:130C CB:—

Note: Matthew, Mark and John each use a different word for ' branch ' in narrating Christ's entry into Jerusalem.

BRANDED

KAUSTĒRIAZO (καυστηριάζω), to burn in with a branding iron 2743
(cp. Eng., caustic), is found, in the best mss., in 1 Tim. 4 : 2, R.V. AG:425C CB:1254C
" branded." Others have *kautēriazō* (from *kautērion*, a branding-iron, Eng., cauterize), to mark by branding, an act not quite so severe as that indicated by the former. The reference is to apostates whose consciences are branded with the effects of their sin. See SEARED.¶

Note: In the R.V. of Gal. 6 : 17, " branded " does not represent a
4742 word in the original; it serves to bring out the force of the Apostle's meta-
AG:768C phor of bearing in his body the *stigmata*, the marks, of the Lord Jesus.
CB:1270A The reference is not to the branding of slaves, soldiers and criminals, but rather to the religious devotee, who branded himself with the mark of the god whom he specially worshipped. So Paul describes the physical marks due to the lictor's rods at Philippi and to the stones at Lystra, marks which, while not self-inflicted, betokened his devotion to Christ and his rejoicing therein.

BRASS, BRAZEN

5475 1. CHALKOS (χαλκός), primarily, copper, became used for metals in
AG:875A CB:1239B general, later was applied to bronze, a mixture of copper and tin, then, by metonymy, to any article made of these metals, e.g., money, Matt. 10 : 9; Mark 6 : 8; 12 : 41, or a sounding instrument, 1 Cor. 13 : 1, figurative of a person destitute of love. See Rev. 18 : 12. See MONEY.¶

5470 2. CHALKEOS (χάλκεος), made of brass or bronze, is used of idols,
AG:875B (-KOUS) Rev. 9 : 20.¶

CB:— 3. CHALKION (χαλκίον) is used in Mark 7 : 4 of brazen vessels.¶

5473 AG:874D 4. CHALKOLIBANON (χαλκολίβανον) is used of white or shining
CB:1239B copper or bronze, and describes the feet of the Lord, in Rev. 1 : 15 and
5474 2 : 18.¶

AG:875A CB:1239B 5. CHALKEUS (χαλκεύς) denotes a coppersmith, 2 Tim. 4 : 14.¶

5471 AG:874D CB:1239B

BRAWLER

BRAVE 1. PAROINOS (πάροινος), an adjective, lit., tarrying at wine (*para*,
See BOLD at, *oinos*, wine), " given to wine," 1 Tim. 3 : 3 and Tit. 1 : 7, A.V., probably
3943 AG:629B has the secondary sense, of the effects of wine-bibbing, viz., abusive
CB:1262C brawling. Hence R.V., " brawler." See WINE.¶

269 2. AMACHOS (ἄμαχος), an adjective, lit., not fighting (*a*, negative,
AG:44C CB:1234C *machē*, a fight), came to denote, metaphorically, not contentious, 1 Tim. 3 : 3, and Tit. 3 : 2, R.V., for A.V., " not a brawler," " not brawlers." See CONTENTIOUS.¶

BREAD (Loaf)

740 1. ARTOS (ἄρτος), bread (perhaps derived from *arō*, to fit together,
AG:110C CB:1237C or from a root *ar*—, the earth), signifies (*a*) a small loaf or cake, composed of flour and water, and baked, in shape either oblong or round, and about as thick as the thumb; these were not cut, but broken and were consecrated to the Lord every Sabbath and called the shewbread (loaves of presentation), Matt. 12 : 4; when the shewbread was reinstituted by Nehemiah (Neh. 10 : 32) a poll-tax of ⅓ shekel was laid on the Jews, Matt. 17 : 24; (*b*) the loaf at the Lord's Supper, e.g., Matt. 26 : 26 (" Jesus took a loaf," R.V., marg.); the breaking of bread became the name for this institution, Acts 2 : 42; 20 : 7; 1 Cor. 10 : 16; 11 : 23; (*c*) bread of

any kind, Matt. 16 : 11 ; (*d*) metaphorically, of Christ as the Bread of God, and of Life, John 6 : 33, 35 ; (*e*) food in general, the necessities for the sustenance of life, Matt. 6 : 11 ; 2 Cor. 9 : 10, etc.

2. AZUMOS (ἄζυμος) denotes unleavened bread, i.e., without any 106
process of fermentation ; hence, metaphorically, of a holy, spiritual AG:19D
condition, 1 Cor 5 : 7, and of sincerity and truth (ver. 8). With the CB:1238B
article it signifies the feast of unleavened bread, Matt. 26 : 17 ; Mark 14 : 1, 12 ; Luke 22 : 1, 7 ; Acts 12 : 3 ; 20 : 6.¶

For BREADTH see BROAD

BREAK, BREAKER, BREAKING, BRAKE

A. Verbs.

1. KLAŌ or KLAZŌ (κλάω), to break, to break off pieces, is used of 2806
breaking bread, (*a*) of the Lord's act in providing for people, Matt. 14 : 19 ; AG:433D
15 : 36 ; Mark 8 : 6, 19 ; (*b*) of the breaking of bread in the Lord's Supper, CB:1255A
Matt. 26 : 26 ; Mark 14 : 22 ; Luke 22 : 19 ; Acts 20 : 7 ; 1 Cor. 10 : 16 ; 11 : 24 ; (*c*) of an ordinary meal, Acts 2 : 46 ; 20 : 11 ; 27 : 35 ; (*d*) of the Lord's act in giving evidence of His resurrection, Luke 24 : 30.¶

2. EKKLAŌ (ἐκκλάω), *ek*, off, and No. 1, to break off, is used meta- 1575
phorically of branches, Rom. 11 : 17, 19, 20.¶ AG:240C CB:1243C

3. KATAKLAŌ (κατακλάω), *kata*, down, and No. 1, is used in Mark 2622
6 : 41 and Luke 9 : 16, of Christ's breaking loaves for the multitudes.¶ AG:411C CB:—

4. LUŌ (λύω), to loosen, especially by way of deliverance, sometimes
has the meaning of breaking, destructively, e.g., of breaking command- 3089
ments, not only infringing them, but loosing the force of them, rendering AG:483C CB:1257B
them not binding, Matt. 5 : 19 ; John 5 : 18 ; of breaking the Law of Moses, John 7 : 23 ; Scripture, John 10 : 35 ; of the breaking up of a ship, Acts 27 : 41 ; of the breaking down of the middle wall of partition, Eph. 2 : 14 ; of the marriage tie, 1 Cor. 7 : 27. See DESTROY, DISSOLVE, LOOSE, MELT, PUT, *Note* (5), UNLOOSE.

5. SUNTRIBŌ (συντρίβω), lit., to rub together, and so to shatter, 4937
shiver, break in pieces by crushing, is said of the bruising of a reed, AG:793B CB:—
Matt. 12 : 20 (No. 9 is used in the next clause) ; the breaking of fetters in pieces, Mark 5 : 4 ; the breaking of an alabaster cruse, Mark 14 : 3 ; an earthenware vessel, Rev. 2 : 27 ; of the physical bruising of a person possessed by a demon, Luke 9 : 39 ; concerning Christ, " a bone of Him shall not be broken," John 19 : 36 ; metaphorically of the crushed condition of a " broken-hearted " person, Luke 4 : 18 (A.V. only) ; of the eventual crushing of Satan, Rom. 16 : 20. See BRUISE.¶ This verb is frequent in the Sept. in the Passive Voice, e.g., Ps. 51 : 17 ; Is. 57 : 15, of a contrite heart, perhaps a figure of stones made smooth by being rubbed together in streams. Cp. *suntrimma*, destruction.

6. RHĒGNUMI (ῥήγνυμι), to tear, rend, as of garments etc., is trans- 4486 AG:735A
lated " break " in the A.V. of Matt. 9 : 17, of wine-skins (R.V., " burst ") ; CB:—

as in Mark 2 : 22 and Luke 5 : 37 ; " break forth " in Gal. 4 : 27. See BURST, REND, TEAR.

1284 AG:188A CB:1241B 7. DIARRHĒGNUMI (διαῤῥήγνυμι), *dia*, through (intensive), and No. 6, to burst asunder, to rend, cleave, is said of the rending of garments, Matt. 26 : 65 ; Mark 14 : 63 ; Acts 14 : 14 ; of the breaking of a net, Luke 5 : 6 ; of fetters, 8 : 29. See REND.¶

4366 AG:718B (-ēSSō) CB:— 8. PROSRHĒGNUMI (προσρήγνυμι) : see BEAT, No. 8.

2608 AG:409D CB:— 9. KATAGNUMI (κατάγνυμι), *kata*, down (intensive), and No. 6, is used of the breaking of a bruised reed, Matt. 12 : 20, and of the breaking of the legs of those who were crucified, John 19 : 31, 32, 33.¶

4917 AG:790A CB:— 10. SUNTHLAŌ (συνθλάω), *sun*, together (intensive), and *thlaō*, to break or crush, to break in pieces, to shatter, is used in Matt. 21 : 44 and Luke 20 : 18 of the physical effect of falling on a stone.¶

4919 AG:790A CB:— 11. SUNTHRUPTŌ (συνθρύπτω), *sun*, and *thruptō*, to crush, to break small, weaken, is used metaphorically of breaking one's heart, Acts 21 : 13.¶

4977 AG:797B CB:1268C 12. SCHIZŌ (σχίζω), to split, to rend open, is said of the veil of the temple, Matt. 27 : 51 ; the rending of rocks, Matt. 27 : 51 ; the rending of the heavens, Mark 1 : 10 ; a garment, Luke 5 : 36 ; John 19 : 24 ; a net, John 21 : 11 ; in the Passive Voice, metaphorically, of being divided into factions, Acts 14 : 4 ; 23 : 7. See DIVIDE, *Note*, OPEN, REND, RENT.

Note : Cp. *schisma* (Eng., schism), said of the rent in a garment, Matt. 9 : 16. See DIVISION, RENT, SCHISM.

1358 AG:199B CB:1242A 13. DIORUSSŌ (διορύσσω), lit., to dig through (*dia*, through, *orussō*, to dig), is used of the act of thieves in breaking into a house, Matt. 6 : 19, 20 ; 24 : 43 ; Luke 12 : 39.¶

1846 AG:277C CB:— 14. EXORUSSŌ (ἐξορύσσω), lit., to dig out (cp. No. 13), is used of the breaking up of part of a roof, Mark 2 : 4, and, in a vivid expression, of plucking out the eyes, Gal. 4 : 15. See PLUCK.¶

Note : For *aristaō*, to break one's fast, see DINE.

B. Nouns.

2800 AG:433B CB:1255A 1. KLASIS (κλάσις), a breaking (akin to A, No. 1), is used in Luke 24 : 35 and Acts 2 : 42, of the breaking of bread.¶

2801 AG:433B CB:1255B 2. KLASMA (κλάσμα), a broken piece, fragment, is always used of remnants of food, Matt. 14 : 20 ; 15 : 37 and corresponding passages. See PIECE.

3847 AG:611D CB:1262A 3. PARABASIS (παράβασις), a transgression (*para*, across, *bainō*, to go), is translated " breaking " in Rom. 2 : 23, A.V. ; R.V., " transgression ; " A.V. and R.V. ditto in 4 : 15 ; 5 : 14 ; Gal. 3 : 19 ; 1 Tim. 2 : 14 ; Heb. 2 : 2 ; 9 : 15. See TRANSGRESSION.

3848 AG:612A CB:1262A 4. PARABATĒS (παραβάτης), a transgressor (cp. No. 3), is translated " breaker," Rom. 2 : 25, A.V. ; R.V., " transgressor." In ver. 27 the A.V. turns it into a verb, " dost transgress." See Gal. 2 : 18 ; Jas. 2 : 9, 11.¶

BREAST

1. STĒTHOS (στῆθος), connected with *histēmi*, to stand, i.e., that which 4738
stands out, is used of mourners in smiting the breast, Luke 18 : 13 ; AG:767D
23 : 48 ; of John in reclining on the breast of Christ, John 13 : 25 ; 21 : 20 ; CB:—
of the breasts of the angels in Rev. 15 : 6.¶

2. MASTOS (μαστός), used in the plural, "paps," Luke 11 : 27 ; 3149
23 : 29 ; Rev. 1 : 13, A.V., is preferably rendered "breasts," in the AG:495B
R.V.¶ CB:1258A

BREASTPLATE

THŌRAX (θώραξ), primarily, the breast, denotes a breastplate or 2382
corselet, consisting of two parts and protecting the body on both sides, AG:367C
from the neck to the middle. It is used metaphorically of righteousness, CB:1272B
Eph. 6 : 14 ; of faith and love, 1 Thess. 5 : 8, with perhaps a suggestion of the two parts, front and back, which formed the coat of mail (an alternative term for the word in the N.T. sense) ; elsewhere in Rev. 9 : 9, 17.¶

BREATH, BREATHE

A. Nouns.

1. PNOĒ (πνοή), akin to *pneō*, to blow, lit., a blowing, signifies (*a*) 4157
breath, the breath of life, Acts 17 : 25 ; (*b*) wind, Acts 2 : 2. See WIND.¶ AG:680B CB:1265C

2. PNEUMA (πνεῦμα), spirit, also denotes breath, Rev. 11 : 11 and 4151
13 : 15, R.V. In 2 Thess. 2 : 8, the A.V. has "spirit" for R.V., "breath." AG:674C
See GHOST, LIFE, SPIRIT, WIND. CB:1265B

B. Verbs.

1. EMPNEŌ (ἐμπνέω), lit., to breathe in, or on, is used in Acts 9 : 1, 1709
indicating that threatening and slaughter were, so to speak, the elements AG:256C
from which Saul drew and expelled his breath.¶ CB:1244B

2. EMPHUSAŌ (ἐμφυσάω), to breathe upon, is used of the symbolic 1720
act of the Lord Jesus in breathing upon His Apostles the communication AG:258A
of the Holy Spirit, John 20 : 22.¶ CB:1244B

BRETHREN See BROTHER

BRIDE, BRIDE-CHAMBER, BRIDEGROOM

BRIDE, BRIDECHAMBER, BRIDEGROOM

NUMPHĒ (νύμφη), Eng. nymph, a bride, or young wife, John 3 : 29 ; 3565
Rev. 18 : 23 ; 21 : 2, 9 ; 22 : 17, is probably connected with the Latin AG:545B
nubō, to veil ; the bride was often adorned with embroidery and jewels CB:1260A
(see Rev. 21 : 2), and was led veiled from her home to the bridegroom. Hence the secondary meaning of daughter-in-law, Matt. 10 : 35 ; Luke 12 : 53. See DAUGHTER-IN-LAW.¶ For the relationship between Christ and a local church, under this figure, see 2 Cor. 11 : 2 ; regarding the
whole Church, Eph. 5 : 23–32 ; Rev. 22 : 17. 3566 AG:545B
NUMPHIOS (νυμφίος), a bridegroom, occurs fourteen times in the CB:1260A

Gospels, and in Rev. 18 : 23. "The friend of the bridegroom," John 3 : 29, is distinct from "the sons of the bride-chamber" who were numerous. When John the Baptist speaks of "the friend of the Bride-groom," he uses language according to the customs of the Jews.

3567 NUMPHŌN (νυμφών) signifies (*a*) the room or dining hall in
AG:545B CB:1260A which the marriage ceremonies were held, Matt. 22 : 10; some mss.
have *gamos*, a wedding, here; (*b*) the chamber containing the bridal bed, "the sons of the bride-chamber" being the friends of the bridegroom, who had the charge of providing what was necessary for the nuptials, Matt. 9 : 15; Mark 2 : 19; Luke 5 : 34.¶

BRIDLE

A. Noun.

5469 CHALINOS (χαλινός), a bridle, is used in Jas. 3 : 3 (A.V., "bits"),
AG:874C and Rev. 14 : 20. "The primitive bridle was simply a loop on the
CB:— halter-cord passed round the lower jaw of the horse. Hence in Ps. 32 : 9
the meaning is bridle and halter" (Hastings, Bib. Dic.).¶

B. Verb.

5468 CHALINAGŌGEŌ (χαλιναγωγέω), from *chalinos* and *agō*, to lead,
AG:874C CB:— signifies to lead by a bridle, to bridle, to hold in check, restrain; it is
used metaphorically of the tongue and of the body in Jas. 1 : 26 and 3 : 2.¶

BRIEFLY

(OLIGOS) DI' OLIGŌN (δι' ὀλίγων) lit. means 'by few.' In 1 Pet. 5 : 12 it
3641 signifies by means of few words, "briefly." The R.V. of Rom. 13 : 9
AG:563C CB:1260C omits "briefly," the meaning being "it is summed up."¶

For BRIER see THISTLE

BRIGAND See ROBBER

BRIGHT, BRIGHTNESS

A. Adjectives.

5460 1. PHŌTEINOS (φωτεινός), bright (from *phōs*, light), is said of a cloud,
AG:872D CB:1264B Matt. 17 : 5; metaphorically of the body, Matt. 6 : 22, "full of light;"
Luke 11 : 34, 36. See LIGHT.¶

2986 2. LAMPROS (λαμπρός), shining, brilliant, bright, is used of the
AG:465D CB:1256C clothing of an angel, Acts 10 : 30 and Rev. 15 : 6; symbolically, of
the clothing of the saints in glory, Rev. 19 : 8, R.V., in the best texts (A.V., "white"); of Christ as the Morning Star, 22 : 16; of the water of
2988 life, 22 : 1, A.V., "clear." See CLEAR, GAY, GOODLY, GORGEOUS, WHITE.
AG:466A CB:1256C *Note:* Cp. *lamprōs*, sumptuously, Luke 16 : 19.¶

B. Nouns.

2987 AG:466A 1. LAMPROTĒS (λαμπρότης), brightness, akin to A, No. 2, above,
CB:1256C is found in Acts 26 : 13.¶
541 AG:82B 2. APAUGASMA (ἀπαύγασμα), a shining forth (*apo*, from, *augē*, bright-
CB:1236B

ness), of a light coming from a luminous body, is said of Christ in Heb. 1 : 3, A.V., " brightness," R.V., " effulgence," i.e., shining forth (a more probable meaning than reflected brightness).¶

Note : Epiphaneia (ἐπιφάνεια), lit., shining forth or upon, is rendered 2015
" brightness " in the A.V. of 2 Thess. 2 : 8 ; R.V., " manifestation." AG:304A
See APPEARING. CB:1246A

BRIM

ANŌ (ἄνω), above, on high, in a higher place, in John 2 : 7 is used to 507
denote the brim of a waterpot, lit., up to above, i.e., up to the higher AG:76D
parts, i.e., the brim. See ABOVE, HIGH, UP. CB:1235C

BRIMSTONE

1. THEION (θεῖον) originally denoted fire from heaven. It is con- 2303
nected with sulphur. Places touched by lightning were called *theia*, AG:353D
and, as lightning leaves a sulphurous smell, and sulphur was used in pagan CB:1271C
purifications, it received the name of *theion*, Luke 17 : 29 ; Rev. 9 : 17, 18 ; 14 : 10 ; 19 : 20 ; 20 : 10 ; 21 : 8.¶

2. THEIŌDĒS (θειώδης), akin to No. 1, signifies brimstone-like, or 2306
consisting of brimstone, Rev. 9 : 17.¶ AG:354A
CB:—

BRING, BRINGING, BROUGHT

A. Verbs.

1. PHERŌ (φέρω), to bear, or carry, is used also of bearing or bringing 5342
forth fruit, Mark 4 : 8 ; John 15 : 5, etc. To bring is the most frequent AG:854D
meaning. See BEAR, CARRY, DRIVE, ENDURE, GO, LEAD, MOVE, REACH, CB:1264A
RUSHING, UPHOLD.

Compounds of No. 1, translated by the verb to bring, are as follows :

2. ANAPHERŌ (ἀναφέρω) denotes to bring up, Matt. 17 : 1. See 399
BEAR, No. 3. AG:63A
CB:1235B

3. APOPHERŌ (ἀποφέρω), to carry forth, is rendered " bring," in the 667
A.V. of 1 Cor. 16 : 3 ; Acts 19 : 12 (R.V., " carried away ") ; some mss. AG:101D
have *epipherō* here. See CARRY. CB:—

4. EISPHERŌ (εἰσφέρω), denotes to bring to, Acts 17 : 20 ; to bring 1533 AG:233D
into, Luke 5 : 18, 19 ; 1 Tim. 6 : 7 ; Heb. 13 : 11. See LEAD, No. 11. CB:1243B

5. EKPHERŌ (ἐκφέρω), to bring forth. See BEAR, No. 4. 1627 AG:246D

6. EPIPHERŌ (ἐπιφέρω), signifies (*a*) to bring upon, or to bring CB:—
against, Jude 9 ; (*b*) to impose, inflict, visit upon, Rom. 3 : 5. Some mss. 2018
have it in Acts 25 : 18 (for No. 1) ; some in Phil. 1 : 16 (R.V., ver. 17, AG:304C
" raise up," translating *egeirō*).¶ CB:1246A

7. PROPHERŌ (προφέρω) denotes to bring forth, Luke 6 : 45, twice.¶ 4393 AG:722D

8. PROSPHERŌ (προσφέρω) means (*a*) to bring (in addition), Matt. CB:—
25 : 20 ; to bring unto, Matt. 5 : 23 (R.V., " art offering ") ; Mark 10 : 13 ; 4374 AG:719C
(*b*) to offer, Matt. 5 : 24. See DEAL WITH, DO, OFFER, PRESENT, PUT. CB:1267B

4851 AG:780B 9. SUMPHERŌ (συμφέρω), to bring together, has this meaning in
CB:— Acts 19 : 19. See BETTER (be), EXPEDIENT, GOOD, PROFIT.
71 10. AGŌ (ἄγω), to lead, to lead along, to bring, has the meaning to
AG:14B CB:1233C bring (besides its occurrences in the Gospels and Acts) in 1 Thess. 4 : 14,
2 Tim. 4 : 11, and Heb. 2 : 10. See CARRY, GO, KEEP, LEAD.

Compounds of this verb are :

321 11. ANAGŌ (ἀνάγω), to lead or bring up to, Luke 2 : 22 ; Acts 9 : 39
AG:53A CB:— etc. ; to bring forth, Acts 12 : 4 ; to bring again, Heb. 13 : 20 ; to bring up
again, Rom. 10 : 7. See DEPART, LAUNCH, LEAD, LOOSE, OFFER, TAKE
UP, SAIL.
520 12. APAGŌ (ἀπάγω), to lead away, bring forth, bring unto, Acts
AG:79C 23 : 17. See CARRY, DEATH, LEAD, TAKE.
1521 13. EISAGŌ (εἰσάγω), to bring in, into, Luke 2 : 27 etc. See LEAD.
AG:232B 1806 14. EXAGŌ (ἐξάγω), to lead out, bring forth, Acts 5 : 19 ; 7 : 36, 40
AG:271C etc. See FETCH, LEAD.
1863 15. EPAGŌ (ἐπάγω), to bring upon, Acts 5 : 28 ; 2 Pet. 2 : 1, 5.¶
AG:281B 2609 16. KATAGŌ (κατάγω), to bring down, Acts 9 : 30 ; 22 : 30 ; 23 : 15,
AG:410A 20 ; Rom. 10 : 6 ; to bring forth, Acts 23 : 28 ; of boats, to bring to land,
CB:— Luke 5 : 11. See LAND, TOUCH.
3919 17. PAREISAGŌ (παρεισάγω), to bring in privily (lit., to bring in
AG:624C beside), to introduce secretly, 2 Pet. 2 : 1.¶
4254 18. PROAGŌ (προάγω), to bring or lead forth, e.g., Acts 12 : 6 ; 16 :
AG:702A 30 ; 25 : 26. See GO, No. 10.
4317 19. PROSAGŌ (προσάγω), to bring to, or unto, Acts 16 : 20 ; 1 Pet.
AG:711B CB:— 3 : 18. For Acts 27 : 27 see DRAW, (*B*), No. 3.¶

Other verbs are :

2865 20. KOMIZŌ (κομίζω), usually, to receive, to bring in, Luke 7 : 37.
AG:442D CB:1255C See RECEIVE.
(-OMAI) 21. PARECHŌ (παρέχω), usually, to offer, furnish, supply (lit., to have
3930 AG:626B near), to bring, in the sense of supplying, Acts 16 : 16 ; 19 : 24. See
DO, GIVE, KEEP, MINISTER, OFFER, SHEW, TROUBLE.
654 22. APOSTREPHŌ (ἀποστρέφω), to turn, or put, back, is translated
AG:100B CB:1237A " brought back " in Matt. 27 : 3. See PERVERT, PUT, TURN.
2601 23. KATABIBAZŌ (καταβιβάζω), in the Active Voice, to cause to go
AG:409A CB:— down, is used in the Passive in the sense of being brought down, Luke
10 : 15 (A.V., " thrust down ") ; " go down " in Matt. 11 : 23 (marg.,
" be brought down ").¶
4822 24. SUMBIBAZŌ (συμβιβάζω), rendered " brought " in Acts 19 : 33.
AG:777D 4311 25. PROPEMPŌ (προπέμπω), to send forth, to bring on one's way,
AG:709B Acts 15 : 3 ; 20 : 38, R.V. ; 21 : 5 ; Rom. 15 : 24 ; 1 Cor. 16 : 6, 11 ;
2 Cor. 1 : 16 ; Tit. 3 : 13 ; 3 John 6. See ACCOMPANY, CONDUCT.¶
985 AG:142B 26. BLASTANŌ (βλαστάνω), to bud, spring up, translated " brought
CB:1239A forth " (i.e., caused to produce), in Jas. 5 : 18. See BUD, SPRING.
4160 AG:680D 27. POIEŌ (ποιέω), to make, to do, used of the bringing forth of fruit,
CB:1265C Matt. 3 : 8, 10 ; 7 : 17, 18. See DO.

28. EKBALLŌ (ἐκβάλλω), to cast out, used of bringing forth good and 1544
evil things from the heart, Matt. 12 : 35. See CAST, No. 5. AG:237B CB:1243B
29. TIKTŌ (τίκτω), to beget, "bring forth," Matt. 1 : 21, 23, 25 ; 5088
Jas. 1 : 15 (first part of verse, according to the best mss.) ; Rev. 12 : 5 AG:816D CB:1272C
(R.V., "was delivered of"). See BEGET, BORN, DELIVER.
30. APOKUEŌ (ἀποκύεω), to bear young, "bringeth forth" in Jas. 616
1 : 15 (end of verse) and "brought forth," ver. 18 (A.V., "begat"). See AG:94A CB:1237A
BEGET.¶
31. GENNAŌ (γεννάω), to beget, translated "brought forth" in 1080
Luke 1 : 57. See BEGET, A, No. 1. AG:155B CB:1248A
32. EUPHOREŌ (εὐφορέω), to bear well, be productive, "brought 2164
forth plentifully", Luke 12 : 16.¶ Cp. *karpophoreō*, Mark 4 : 20, R.V. AG:327C
"bear;" so, Col. 1 : 6. CB:—
33. TREPHŌ (τρέφω), to rear, bring up, Luke 4 : 16. See FEED, 5142 AG:825C
NOURISH. CB:—
34. ANATREPHŌ (ἀνατρέφω), to nourish, Acts 7 : 20, 21; "brought 397
up," Acts 22 : 3.¶ AG:62D CB:—
35. EKTREPHŌ (ἐκτρέφω), to nourish, Eph. 5 : 29; "bring up," 1625
6 : 4, A.V.; R.V., "nurture." See NURTURE.¶ AG:246C CB:1244A
36. APANGELLŌ (ἀπαγγέλλω), to announce, is translated "bring 518
word" in Matt. 2 : 8, R.V. (the A.V. unnecessarily adds "again") ; AG:79B
28 : 8. See DECLARE, REPORT, SHEW, TELL. CB:1236B

B. Noun.

EPEISAGŌGĒ (ἐπεισαγωγή), lit., 'a bringing in besides,' is trans- 1898
lated "a bringing in thereupon" in Heb. 7 : 19.¶ AG:284C CB:—
Notes: (1) In Mark 4 : 21, *erchomai*, to come, is translated "is brought," 2064
lit., '(does a lamp) come.' AG:310B CB:1246B
(2) In Mark 13 : 9, the verb translated "be brought," A.V., is *histēmi*, 2476
to stand (R.V.) ; in Acts 27 : 24, *paristēmi*, to stand before (A.V., "be AG:381D CB:1250C
brought before"). PARISTēMI
(3) In Acts 5 : 36, *ginomai*, to become, is rendered "came (to nought)," 3936
R.V., for A.V., "were brought." So in 1 Cor. 15 : 54, "come to pass," AG:627C CB:1262B
for "shall be brought to pass." GINOMAI
(4) In Mark 4 : 29, *paradidōmi* is rendered "is ripe," R.V. and A.V. 1096 AG:158A
marg., for A.V., "brought forth." CB:1248B
(5) In Matt. 1 : 11, 12, 17, *metoikesia* signifies a removal, or carrying PARADIDōMI 3860
away (not "they were brought," ver. 12, A.V.). AG:614B
(6) In Acts 13 : 1, *suntrophos* denotes a foster-brother, R.V. (A.V., CB:1262A METOIKESIA
marg.).¶ 3350
(7) In 1 Cor. 4 : 17, for "bring you into remembrance" (R.V., AG:514B
"put . . ."), see REMEMBRANCE. CB:1258C SUNTROPHOS
(8) In Luke 1 : 19, for R.V., "bring you good tidings," and Acts 4939
13 : 32, and Rom. 10 : 15 (end), see PREACH. AG:793C
(9) In 1 Cor. 1 : 19, *atheteō*, to reject (R.V.), is rendered "bring to 114 AG:21A
nothing" (A.V.). See DESPISE, Note (1). CB:1238A

(10) For *katargeō*, "bring to nought," R.V., "destroy," 1 Cor. 6 : 13 etc., see ABOLISH, DESTROY.

(11) For *eipon* in Matt. 2 : 13, A.V., "bring . . . word," see TELL.

(12) See also DESOLATION, No. 1, PERFECTION, B.

(13) For "bring into bondage" see BONDAGE, B.

2983 (14) In Matt. 16 : 8 some mss. have *lambanō* (A.V., "ye have
AG:464A CB:1256C brought").

BROAD, BREADTH

A. Adjective.

2149 EURUCHŌROS (εὐρύχωρος), from *eurus*, broad, and *chōra*, a place,
AG:326A CB:— signifies, lit., (with) a broad place, i.e., broad, spacious, Matt. 7 : 13.¶

B. Verb.

4115 PLATUNŌ (πλατύνω), connected with *plak*, a flat, broad surface,
AG:667A CB:1265A signifies to make broad; said of phylacteries, Matt. 23 : 5; used figuratively
in 2 Cor. 6 : 11, 13, "to be enlarged," in the ethical sense, of the heart.¶

C. Noun.

4114 PLATOS (πλάτος) denotes breadth, Eph. 3 : 18; Rev. 20 : 9; 21 : 16
AG:666D CB:1265A (twice).¶

For BROIDED see BRAIDED

For BROKENHEARTED, see BREAK, A, No. 5.

BROILED

3702 OPTOS (ὀπτός), broiled (from *optaō*, to cook, roast), is said of food
AG:576C CB:— prepared by fire, Luke 24 : 42.¶

For BROKEN see BREAK

BROOD

NOSSIA 3555 NOSSIA (νοσσιά), primarily, a nest, denotes a brood, Luke 13 : 34.
AG:543D CB:1260A Some texts have *nossion* in the plural, as Matt. 23 : 37, "chicken."¶

NOSSION 3556 AG:543D CB:—

BROOK

CHEIMARRHOS (χείμαρρος), lit., winter-flowing (from *cheima*,
5493 winter, and *rheō*, to flow), a stream which runs only in winter or when
AG:879C CB:— swollen with rains, a brook, John 18 : 1.¶

BROTHER, BRETHREN, BROTHERHOOD, BROTHERLY

80 ADELPHOS (ἀδελφός) denotes a brother, or near kinsman; in the
AG:15D CB:1233A plural, a community based on identity of origin or life. It is used of :—

(1) male children of the same parents, Matt. 1 : 2; 14 : 3; (2) male descendants of the same parents, Acts 7 : 23, 26; Heb. 7 : 5; (3) male children of the same mother, Matt. 13 : 55; 1 Cor. 9 : 5; Gal. 1 : 19; (4) people of the same nationality, Acts 3 : 17, 22; Rom. 9 : 3. With

" men " (*anēr*, male), prefixed, it is used in addresses only, Acts 2 : 29, 37, etc. ; (5) any man, a neighbour, Luke 10 : 29 ; Matt. 5 : 22 ; 7 : 3 ; (6) persons united by a common interest, Matt. 5 : 47 ; (7) persons united by a common calling, Rev. 22 : 9 ; (8) mankind, Matt. 25 : 40 ; Heb. 2 : 17 ; (9) the disciples, and so, by implication, all believers, Matt. 28 : 10 ; John 20 : 17 ; (10) believers, apart from sex, Matt. 23 : 8 ; Acts 1 : 15 ; Rom. 1 : 13 ; 1 Thess. 1 : 4 ; Rev. 19 : 10 (the word " sisters " is used of believers, only in 1 Tim. 5 : 2) ; (11) believers, with *anēr*, male, prefixed, and with " or sister " added, 1 Cor. 7 : 14 (R.V.), 15 ; Jas. 2 : 15, male as distinct from female, Acts 1 : 16 ; 15 : 7, 13, but not 6 : 3.*

Notes : (1) Associated words are *adelphotēs*, primarily, a brotherly 81
relation, and so, the community possessed of this relation, a brotherhood, AG:16C CB:1233A
1 Pet. 2 : 17 (see 5 : 9, marg.)¶ ; *philadelphos*, (*philēo*, to love, and 5361
adelphos), fond of one's brethren, 1 Pet. 3 : 8 ; " loving as brethren," AG:858C
R.V.¶ ; *philadelphia*, " brotherly love," Rom. 12 : 10 ; 1 Thess, 4 : 9 ; CB:1264A
Heb. 13 : 1 ; " love of the brethren," 1 Pet. 1 : 22 and 2 Pet. 1 : 7, R.V.¶ ; 5360 AG:858C
pseudadelphos, " false brethren," 2 Cor. 11 : 26 ; Gal. 2 : 4.¶ CB:1264A

(2) In Luke 6 : 16 and Acts 1 : 13, the R.V. has " son," for A.V., 5569 AG:891B
" brother." CB:1267C

(3) In Acts 13 : 1, for *suntrophos*, see BRING, B, Note (6).

For BROUGHT see BRING

BROW

OPHRUS (ὀφρύς), an eyebrow, stands for the brow of a hill, Luke 3790
4 : 29, from the resemblance to an eyebrow, i.e., a ridge with an AG:600B CB:—
overhanging bank.¶

BRUISE

4937

1. SUNTRIBŌ (συντρίβω) : see BREAK, A, No. 5. AG:793B CB:—

2. THRAUŌ (θραύω), to smite through, shatter, is used in Luke 2352
4 : 18, " them that are bruised," i.e., broken by calamity.¶ AG:363B CB:—

BRUTE

ALOGOS (ἄλογος), translated " brute " in the A.V. of 2 Pet. 2 : 12 249
and Jude 10, signifies " without reason," R.V., though, as J. Hastings AG:41A CB:1234C
points out, " brute beasts " is not at all unsuitable, as " brute " is from Latin *brutus*, which means dull, irrational ; in Acts 25 : 27 it is rendered " unreasonable."¶

BUD

BLASTANŌ (βλαστάνω), to bud, is said of Aaron's rod, Heb. 9 : 14 ; 985
" spring up," Matt. 13 : 26, and Mark 4 : 27 ; elsewhere, in Jas. 5 : 18. AG:142B CB:1239A
See BRING, No. 26, SPRING, No. 6.¶

---

* From Notes on Thessalonians by Hogg and Vine, p. 32.

BUFFET

2852 AG:441A CB:1255B 1. KOLAPHIZŌ (κολαφίζω) signifies to strike with clenched hands, to buffet with the fist (*kolaphos*, a fist), Matt. 26:67; Mark 14:65; 1 Cor. 4:11; 2 Cor. 12:7; 1 Pet. 2:20.¶

5299 AG:848D CB:1252B 2. HUPŌPIAZŌ (ὑπωπιάζω), lit., to strike under the eye (from *hupōpion*, the part of the face below the eye; *hupo*, under, *ōps*, an eye), hence, to beat the face black and blue (to give a black eye), is used metaphorically, and translated "buffet" in 1 Cor. 9:27 (A.V., "keep under"), of Paul's suppressive treatment of his body, in order to keep himself spiritually fit (R.V. marg., "bruise"); so R.V. marg. in Luke 18:5, of the persistent widow, text, "wear out" (A.V., "weary"). See KEEP, WEAR, WEARY.¶

BUILD, BUILDER, BUILDING

A. Verbs.

3618 AG:558A CB:1260B 1. OIKODOMEŌ (οἰκοδομέω), lit., to build a house (*oikos*, a house, *domeō*, to build), hence, to build anything, e.g., Matt. 7:24; Luke 4:29; 6:48, R.V., "well builded" (last clause of verse); John 2:20; is frequently used figuratively, e.g., Acts 20:32 (some mss. have No. 3 here); Gal. 2:18; especially of edifying, Acts 9:31; Rom. 15:20; 1 Cor. 10:23; 14:4; 1 Thess. 5:11 (R.V.). In 1 Cor. 8:10 it is translated "emboldened" (marg., "builded up"). The participle with the article (equivalent to a noun) is rendered "builder," Matt. 21:42; Acts 4:11; 1 Pet. 2:7. See EDIFY, EMBOLDEN.

456 AG:71C CB:— 2. ANOIKODOMEŌ (ἀνοικοδομέω) signifies to build again (*ana*, again), Acts 15:16.¶

2026 AG:305B CB:1246B 3. EPOIKODOMEŌ (ἐποικοδομέω) signifies to build upon (*epi*, upon), 1 Cor. 3:10, 12, 14: Eph. 2:20; Jude 20; or up, Acts 20:32; Col. 2:7.¶

4925 AG:791C CB:1270C 4. SUNOIKODOMEŌ (συνοικοδομέω), to build together (*sun*, with), is used in Eph. 2:22, metaphorically, of the Church, as a spiritual dwelling-place for God.¶

2680 AG:418B CB:1254B 5. KATASKEUAZŌ (κατασκευάζω), to prepare, establish, furnish, is rendered "builded" and "built" in Heb. 3:3, 4. See MAKE, ORDAIN, PREPARE.

B. Nouns.

3619 AG:558D CB:1260B 1. OIKODOMĒ (οἰκοδομή), a building, or edification (see A, No. 1), is used (*a*) literally, e.g., Matt. 24:1; Mark 13:1, 2; (*b*) figuratively, e.g., Rom. 14:19 (lit., 'the things of building up'); 15:2; of a local church as a spiritual building, 1 Cor. 3:9, or the whole Church, the Body of Christ, Eph. 2:21. It expresses the strengthening effect of teaching, 1 Cor. 14:3, 5, 12, 26; 2 Cor. 10:8; 12:19; 13:10, or other ministry, Eph. 4:12, 16, 29 (the idea conveyed is progress resulting from patient effort). It is also used of the believer's resurrection body, 2 Cor. 5:1. See EDIFICATION, EDIFY.¶

2. ENDŌMĒSIS (ἐνδώμησις), a thing built, structure (*en*, in, *dōmaō*, 1739
to build), is used of the wall of the heavenly city, Rev. 21 : 18 (some AG:264B
suggest that the word means a fabric; others, a roofing or coping; these CB:—
interpretations are questionable; the probable significance is a building).¶

3. KTISIS (κτίσις), a creation, is so translated in the R.V. of 2937
Heb. 9 : 11 (A.V. "building,"). See CREATION, B, No. 1, CREATURE, AG:455D
ORDINANCE. CB:1256A

4. TECHNITĒS (τεχνίτης), an artificer, one who does a thing by 5079
rules of art, is rendered "builder" in Heb. 11 : 10, marg., "architect," AG:814B
which gives the necessary contrast between this and the next noun in the CB:1271B
verse. See CRAFTSMAN, No. 2.

For BULL see OX BUNCH (of GRAPES) See CLUSTER

BUNDLE

1. DESMĒ (δέσμη), from *deō*, to bind (similarly, Eng. "bundle" is 1197
akin to "bind"), is used in Matt. 13 : 30.¶ AG:176A CB:1240C

2. PLĒTHOS (πλῆθος), a great number (akin to *pleō*, to fill), is the 4128
word for the bundle of sticks which Paul put on the fire, Acts 28 : 3. See AG:668B
COMPANY, MULTITUDE. CB:1265B

BURDEN, BURDENED, BURDENSOME

A. Nouns.

1. BAROS (βάρος) denotes a weight, anything pressing on one 922
physically, Matt. 20 : 12, or that makes a demand on one's resources, AG:133D
whether material, 1 Thess. 2 : 6 (to be burdensome), or spiritual, Gal. 6 : 2; CB:1238C
Rev. 2 : 24, or religious, Acts 15 : 28. In one place it metaphorically
describes the future state of believers as "an eternal weight of glory,"
2 Cor. 4 : 17. See WEIGHT.¶

2. PHORTION (φορτίον), lit., something carried (from *pherō*, to bear), 5413
is always used metaphorically (except in Acts 27 : 10, of the lading of a AG:865A
ship); of that which, though "light," is involved in discipleship of CB:1264B
Christ, Matt. 11 : 30; of tasks imposed by the Scribes, Pharisees and
lawyers, Matt. 23 : 4; Luke 11 : 46; of that which will be the result, at
the Judgment-Seat of Christ, of each believer's work, Gal. 6 : 5.¶

Note: The difference between *phortion* and *baros* is, that *phortion* is simply something to be borne, without reference to its weight, but *baros* always suggests what is heavy or burdensome. Thus Christ speaks of His burden (*phortion*) as "light;" here *baros* would be inappropriate; but the burden of a transgressor is *baros*, "heavy." Contrast *baros* in Gal. 6 : 2, with *phortion* in ver. 5.

3. GOMOS (γόμος), from a root *gem-*, signifying full, or heavy, seen 1117
in *gemō*, to be full, *gemizō*, to fill, Lat. *gemo*, to groan, denotes the AG:164D
lading of freight of a ship, Acts 21 : 3, or merchandise conveyed in a CB:—
ship, and so merchandise in general, Rev. 18 : 11, 12. See MERCHANDISE.¶

B. Verbs.

916 AG:133C CB:1238C 1. BAREŌ (βαρέω), akin to A, No. 1, is used of the effect of drowsiness, "were heavy," Matt. 26 : 43; Mark 14 : 40; Luke 9 : 32; of the effects of gluttony, Luke 21 : 34 ("overcharged"); of the believer's present physical state in the body, 2 Cor. 5 : 4; of persecution, 2 Cor. 1 : 8; of a charge upon material resources, 1 Tim. 5 : 16 (R.V.). See CHARGE, HEAVY, PRESS.¶

1912 AG:290B CB:1245C 2. EPIBAREŌ (ἐπιβαρέω), *epi*, upon (intensive), to burden heavily, is said of material resources, 1 Thess. 2 : 9 (R.V.); 2 Thess. 3 : 8, R.V., "burden," A.V., "be chargeable to;" of the effect of spiritual admonition and discipline, 2 Cor. 2 : 5, R.V., "press heavily," A.V., "overcharge." See CHARGEABLE, PRESS.¶

2599 AG:408D CB:1254A 3. KATABAREŌ (καταβαρέω), to weigh down (*kata*, down), overload, is used of material charges, in 2 Cor. 12 : 16.¶

2655 AG:414D CB:— 4. KATANARKAŌ (καταναρκάω), to be a burden, to be burdensome, primarily signifies to be numbed or torpid, to grow stiff (*narkē* is the torpedo or cramp fish, which benumbs anyone who touches it); hence to be idle to the detriment of another person (like a useless limb), 2 Cor. 11 : 9; 12 : 13, 14. See CHARGEABLE.¶

2347 AG:362B CB:1272B *Note:* For *thlipsis*, distress, affliction, "burdened" (A.V. of 2 Cor. 8 : 13), see AFFLICTION, B. No. 4.

C. Adjective.

4 AG:1B CB:— ABARĒS (ἀβαρής), without weight (*a*, negative, and *baros*, see A, No. 1), is used in 2 Cor. 11 : 9, lit. 'I kept myself burdensomeless.'¶

BURGLAR See ROBBER

BURIAL, BURY, BURYING

A. Nouns.

1780 AG:268B CB:1245B 1. ENTAPHIASMOS (ἐνταφιασμός), lit., an entombing (from *en*, in, *taphos*, a tomb), "burying," occurs in Mark 14 : 8; John 12 : 7. Cp. B.1.¶

5027 AG:806B CB:1271A 2. TAPHĒ (ταφή), a burial (cp. No. 1, and Eng., epitaph), is found in Matt. 27 : 7, with *eis*, unto, lit. 'with a view to a burial (place) for strangers.'¶

B. Verbs.

1779 AG:268B CB:1245B 1. ENTAPHIAZŌ (ἐνταφιάζω), see A, No. 1, to prepare a body for burial, is used of any provision for this purpose, Matt. 26 : 12; John 19 : 40.¶

2290 AG:351D CB:1271C 2. THAPTŌ (θάπτω) occurs in Matt. 8 : 21, 22, and parallels in Luke; Matt. 14 : 12; Luke 16 : 22; Acts 2 : 29; 5 : 6, 9, 10; of Christ's burial, 1 Cor. 15 : 4.¶

4916 AG:789D CB:1271A 3. SUNTHAPTŌ (συνθάπτω), akin to A. 2, to bury with, or together (*sun*), is used in the metaphorical sense only, of the believer's identification with Christ in His burial, as set forth in baptism, Rom. 6 : 4; Col. 2 : 12.¶

BURN, BURNING

A. Verbs.

1. KAIŌ (καίω), to set fire to, to light; in the Passive Voice, to be 2545
lighted, to burn, Matt. 5:15; John 15:6; Heb. 12:18; Rev. 4:5; AG:396B CB:1253A
8:8, 10; 19:20; 21:8; 1 Cor. 13:3, is used metaphorically of the
heart, Luke 24:32; of spiritual light, Luke 12:35; John 5:35. See
LIGHT.¶

2. KATAKAIŌ (κατακαίω), from *kata*, down (intensive), and No. 1, 2618
signifies to burn up, burn utterly, as of chaff, Matt. 3:12; Luke 3:17; AG:411A CB:—
tares, Matt. 13:30, 40; the earth and its works, 2 Pet. 3:10; trees and
grass, Rev. 8:7. This form should be noted in Acts 19:19; 1 Cor.
3:15; Heb. 13:11; Rev. 17:16. In each place the full rendering
'burn utterly' might be used, as in Rev. 18:8.¶

3. EKKAIŌ (ἐκκαίω), from *ek*, out (intensive), and No. 1, lit., to 1572
burn out, in the Passive Voice, to be kindled, burn up, is used of the AG:240C CB:—
lustful passions of men, Rom. 1:27.¶

4. PUROOMAI (πυρόομαι), from *pur*, fire, to glow with heat, is said 4448
of the feet of the Lord, in the vision in Rev. 1:15; it is translated AG:731A CB:1268A
"fiery" in Eph. 6:16 (of the darts of the evil one); used metaphorically
of the emotions, in 1 Cor. 7:9; 2 Cor. 11:29; elsewhere literally, of the
heavens, 2 Pet. 3:12; of gold, Rev. 3:18 (R.V., "refined"). See
FIERY, FIRE, TRY.¶

5. EMPIPRĒMI (ἐμπίπρημι), or EMPRĒTHŌ, to burn up, occurs in 1714
Matt. 2:7.¶ AG:256B CB:—

B. Nouns.

1. KAUSIS (καῦσις), akin to A, No. 1 (Eng., caustic), is found in 2740
Heb. 6:8, lit., 'whose end is unto burning.'¶ Cp. BRANDED. AG:425B CB:—

2. KAUSŌN (καύσων) is rendered "burning heat" in Jas. 1:11, 2742
A.V. (R.V., "scorching"). See HEAT. AG:425C CB:—

3. PURŌSIS (πύρωσις), akin to A. No. 4, is used literally in Rev. 4451
18:9, 18; metaphorically in 1 Pet. 4:12, "fiery trial." See TRIAL.¶ AG:731C CB:1268A

BURNISHED

CHALKOLIBANON (χαλκολίβανον): see BRASS.

BURNT (offering)

HOLOKAUTŌMA (ὁλοκαύτωμα) denotes a whole burnt offering (*holos*, 3646
whole, *kautos*, for *kaustos*, a verbal adjective from *kaiō*, to burn), i.e., a AG:564B CB:1251A
victim, the whole of which is burned, as in Ex. 30:20; Lev. 5:12;
23:8, 25, 27. It is used in Mark 12:33, by the scribe who questioned
the Lord as to the first commandment in the Law, and in Heb. 10:6, 8,
R.V., "whole burnt offerings." See OFFERING.¶

BURST (asunder) 4486

1. RHĒGNUMI (ῥήγνυμι); see BREAK, A. No. 6. AG:735A CB:—

2997 2. LAKEŌ or LASKŌ (λάσκω), primarily, to crack, or crash, denotes
AG:463A CB:1256C to burst asunder with a crack, crack open (always of making a noise), is
used in Acts 1 : 18.¶

For BURY see BURIAL

BUSH

942 BATOS (βάτος) denotes a bramble bush, as in Luke 6 : 44. In Mark
AG:137C CB:— 12 : 26 and Luke 20 : 37 the phrase " in the place concerning the Bush "
signifies in that part of the book of Exodus concerning it. See also Acts 7 : 30, 35.¶

BUSHEL

3426 MODIOS (μόδιος) was a dry measure containing about a peck, Matt.
AG:525D CB:— 5 : 15 ; Mark 4 : 21 ; Luke 11 : 33.¶

BUSINESS

A. Nouns.

5532 1. CHREIA (χρεία), translated " business " in Acts 6 : 3, of the
AG:884D distribution of funds, signifies a necessity, a need, and is used in this
CB:1240A place concerning duty or business. See LACK, NECESSITY, NEED, USE, WANT.

2039 2. ERGASIA (ἐργασία) denotes a business, Acts 19 : 24, 25, R.V.,
AG:307C CB:1246B A.V., " gain " and " craft " (from *ergon*, work). See DILIGENCE.

B. Adjective.

2398 IDIOS (ἴδιος) expresses what is one's own (hence, Eng. " idiot," in
AG:369C CB:1252C a changed sense, lit., a person with his own opinions) ; the neuter plural
with the article (*ta idia*) signifies one's own things. In 1 Thess. 4 : 11, the noun is not expressed in the original but is supplied in the English Versions by " business," " your own business." For the same phrase, otherwise expressed, see John 1 : 11, " His own (things) ; " 16 : 32 and 19 : 27, " his own (home) ; " Acts 21 : 6, " home." In Luke 2 : 49, the phrase " in My Father's house " (R.V.), " about My Father's business " (A.V.), is, lit., ' in the (things, the neuter plural of the article) of my Father.' See ACQUAINTANCE, COMPANY, No. 8, DUE, HOME, OWN, PRIVATE, PROPER, SEVERAL.

4229 *Notes :* (1) In the A.V. of Rom. 16 : 2 *pragma* is translated " business,"
AG:697A CB:1266B R.V., " matter." See MATTER, THING, WORK.

4710 (2) In Rom. 12 : 11 *spoudē*, translated " business " (A.V.), signifies
AG:763D CB:1269C " diligence " (R.V.). See DILIGENCE.

BUSYBODY

A. Verb.

4020 PERIERGAZOMAI (περιεργάζομαι), lit., to be working round about,
AG:646D CB:1263B instead of at one's own business (*peri*, around, *ergon*, work), signifies to

take more pains than enough about a thing, to waste one's labour, to be meddling with, or bustling about, other people's matters. This is found in 2 Thess. 3 : 11, where, following the verb *ergazomai*, to work, it forms a paronomasia. This may be produced in a free rendering : 'some who are not busied in their own business, but are overbusied in that of others.'¶

B. Adjective.

PERIERGOS (περίεργος), akin to A, denoting taken up with trifles, is 4021
used of magic arts in Acts 19 : 19 ; " busybodies " in 1 Tim. 5 : 13, AG:646D CB:1263B
i.e., meddling in other persons' affairs. See CURIOUS.¶

C. Noun.

ALLOTRIOEPISKOPOS (ἀλλοτριοεπίσκοπος), from *allotrios*, belonging 244
to another person, and *episkopos*, an overseer, translated " busybody " AG:40C CB:1234C
in the A.V. of 1 Pet. 4 : 15, " meddler," R.V., was a legal term for a charge brought against Christians as being hostile to civilized society, their purpose being to make Gentiles conform to Christian standards. Some explain it as a pryer into others' affairs. See MEDDLER.¶

BUY, BOUGHT

1. AGORAZŌ (ἀγοράζω), primarily, to frequent the market-place, 59
the *agora*, hence to do business there, to buy or sell, is used lit., e.g., in AG:12D CB:1233C
Matt. 14 : 15. Figuratively Christ is spoken of as having bought His redeemed, making them His property at the price of His blood (i.e., His death through the shedding of His blood in expiation for their sins), 1 Cor. 6 : 20 ; 7 : 23 ; 2 Pet. 2 : 1 ; see also Rev. 5 : 9 ; 14 : 3, 4 (not as A.V., " redeemed "). *Agorazō* does not mean to redeem. See REDEEM.

2. ŌNEOMAI (ὠνέομαι), to buy, in contradistinction to selling, is used 5608
in Acts 7 : 16, of the purchase by Abraham of a burying place.¶ AG:895D CB:1260C

Note : In Jas. 4 : 13 (A.V.) the verb *emporeuomai* (Eng., emporium) 1710
is rendered " buy and sell." Its meaning is to trade, traffic, R.V. It AG:256D
primarily denotes to travel, to go on a journey, then, to do so for traffic CB:1244B
purposes ; hence to trade ; in 2 Pet. 2 : 3, " make merchandise of." See MERCHANDISE.¶

BY. See Note †, p. 1.

Note : The phrase " by and by " in the A.V. is in several places misleading. The three words *exautēs*, Mark 6 : 25, *euthus*, Matt. 13 : 21, and *eutheōs*, Luke 17 : 7 ; 21 : 9, mean " straightway," " immediately." See under these words.

BYSTANDER See STAND

C

CAGE

PHULAKĒ (φυλακή), from *phulassō*, to guard, denotes (*a*) a watching, 5438
keeping watch, Luke 2 : 8 ; (*b*) persons keeping watch, a guard, Acts AG:867D CB:1264C
12 : 10 ; (*c*) a period during which watch is kept, e.g., Matt. 24 : 43 ; (*d*) a prison, a hold. In Rev. 18 : 2, A.V., Babylon is described figuratively, first as a " hold " and then as a " cage " of every unclean and hateful bird (R.V., " hold " in both clauses ; marg., " prison "). The word is almost invariably translated " prison." See HOLD, IMPRISONMENT, PRISON, WARD, WATCH.

CALCULATE See COUNT

CALF

MOSCHOS (μόσχος) primarily denotes anything young, whether 3448
plants or the offspring of men or animals, the idea being that which is AG:528C CB:1259B
tender and delicate ; hence a calf, young bull, heifer, Luke 15 : 23, 27, 30 ; Heb. 9 : 12, 19 ; Rev. 4 : 7.¶

MOSCHOPOIEŌ (μοσχοποιέω) signifies to make a calf (*moschos*, and 3447
poieō, to make), Acts 7 : 41.¶ AG:528C CB:—

CALL, CALLED, CALLING

A. Verbs.

1. KALEŌ (καλέω), derived from the root *kal*—, whence Eng. " call " 2564
and " clamour " (see B. and C., below), is used (*a*) with a personal object, AG:398D CB:1253B
to call anyone, invite, summon, e.g., Matt. 20 : 8 ; 25 : 14 ; it is used particularly of the Divine call to partake of the blessings of redemption, e.g., Rom. 8 : 30 ; 1 Cor. 1 : 9 ; 1 Thess. 2 : 12 ; Heb. 9 : 15 ; cp. B. and C., below ; (*b*) of nomenclature or vocation, to call by a name, to name ; in the Passive Voice, to be called by a name, to bear a name. Thus it suggests either vocation or destination ; the context determines which, e.g., Rom. 9 : 25, 26 ; " surname," in Acts 15 : 37, A.V., is incorrect (R.V., " was called "). See BID, NAME.

2. EISKALEŌ (εἰσκαλέω), lit., to call in, hence, to invite (*eis*, in, 1528
and No. 1), is found in Acts 10 : 23.¶ AG:233B (-OMAI) CB:1243B

3. EPIKALEŌ (ἐπικαλέω), *epi*, upon, and No. 1., denotes (*a*) to
surname ; (*b*) to be called by a person's name ; hence it is used of being 1941 (-OMAI) AG:294A CB:1245C
declared to be dedicated to a person, as to the Lord, Acts 15 : 17 (from Amos 9 : 12) ; Jas. 2 : 7 ; (*c*) to call a person by a name by charging him with an offence, as the Pharisees charged Christ with doing His works

by the help of Beelzebub, Matt. 10 : 25 (the most authentic reading has *epikaleō*, for *kaleō*) ; (*d*) to call upon, invoke ; in the Middle Voice, to call upon for oneself (i.e., on one's behalf), Acts 7 : 59, or to call upon a person as a witness, 2 Cor. 1 : 23, or to appeal to an authority, Acts 25 : 11, etc. ; (*e*) to call upon by way of adoration, making use of the Name of the Lord, Acts 2 : 21 ; Rom. 10 : 12, 13, 14 ; 2 Tim. 2 : 22. See APPEAL, SURNAME.

3333 4. METAKALEŌ (μετακαλέω), *meta*, implying change, and No. 1,
AG:511A CB:1258B to call from one place to another, to summon (cp. the Sept. of Hos. 11 : 1),
(-OMAI) is used in the Middle Voice only, to call for oneself, to send for, call
hither, Acts 7 : 14 ; 10 : 32 ; 20 : 17 ; 24 : 25.¶

4341 5. PROSKALEŌ (προσκαλέω), *pros*, to, and No. 1, signifies (*a*) to call
(-OMAI) AG:715C to oneself, to bid to come ; it is used only in the Middle Voice, e.g.,
CB:1267A Matt. 10 : 1 ; Acts 5 : 40 ; Jas. 5 : 14 ; (*b*) God's call to Gentiles through
the Gospel, Acts 2 : 39 ; (*c*) the Divine call in entrusting men with the
preaching of the Gospel, Acts 13 : 2 ; 16 : 10.¶

4779 AG:773B 6. SUNKALEŌ (συγκαλέω) signifies to call together, Mark 15 : 16 ;
CB:— Luke 9 : 1 ; 15 : 6, 9 ; 23 : 13 ; Acts 5 : 21 ; 10 : 24 ; 28 : 17.¶

1458 *Notes :* (1) *Enkaleō*, Acts 19 : 40, A.V., " called in question," signifies
AG:215C CB:1245A to accuse, as always in the R.V. See ACCUSE, IMPLEAD.

3870 (2) *Parakaleō*, to beseech, intreat, is rendered " have called for " in
AG:617A Acts 28 : 20, A.V. ; R.V., " did intreat " (marg., " call for "). It is used
CB:1262A only here with this meaning. See BESEECH.

154 7. AITEŌ (αἰτέω), to ask, is translated " called for " in Acts 16 : 29
AG:25D CB:1234A (" he called for lights "). See ASK, A. No. 1.

Note : For the R.V. of Matt. 19 : 17 (A.V., " callest "), see ASK (A, No. 2, *Note*).

5455 8. PHŌNEŌ (φωνέω), to sound (Eng., 'phone), is used of the crowing
AG:870B CB:1264B of a cock, e.g., Matt. 26 : 34 ; John 13 : 38 ; of calling out with a clear
or loud voice, to cry out, e.g., Mark 1 : 26 (some mss. have *krazō* here) ; Acts 16 : 28 ; of calling to come to oneself, e.g., Matt. 20 : 32 ; Luke 19 : 15 ; of calling forth, as of Christ's call to Lazarus to come forth from the tomb, John 12 : 17 ; of inviting, e.g., Luke 14 : 12 ; of calling by name, with the implication of the pleasure taken in the possession of those called, e.g., John 10 : 3 ; 13 : 13. See CROW, CRY.

3004 9. LEGŌ (λέγω), to speak, is used of all kinds of oral communication,
AG:468A CB:1256C e.g., to call, to call by name, to surname, Matt. 1 : 16 ; 26 : 36 ; John
4 : 5 ; 11 : 54 ; 15 : 15 ; Rev. 2 : 2, R.V., " call themselves," etc. See ASK.

1951 10. EPILEGŌ (ἐπιλέγω), *epi*, upon, and No. 9, signifies to call in
(-OMAI) AG:295C addition, i.e., by another name besides that already intimated, John
CB:1246A 5 : 2 ; for its other meaning in Acts 15 : 40, see CHOOSE.¶

5537 11. CHRĒMATIZŌ (χρηματίζω) occasionally means to be called or
AG:885C CB:1240A named, Acts 11 : 26 (of the name " Christians ") and Rom. 7 : 3, the only
places where it has this meaning. Its primary significance, to have

business dealings with, led to this. They "were (publicly) called" 3004 (LEGō)
Christians, because this was their chief business. See ADMONISH, REVEAL, AG:226A
SPEAK, WARN. CB:1243A

12. EIPON (εἶπον), to say, speak, means to call by a certain appella- KRINō 2919
tion, John 10 : 35. See BID, No. 3. AG:451B

13. KRINŌ (κρίνω), to judge, is translated to call in question, in CB:1256A ONOMA
Acts 23 : 6 ; 24 : 21. 3686

Notes : (1) For *onoma*, a name, translated "called," A.V., in Luke AG:570D CB:1260C
24 : 13, Acts 10 : 1, *onomazō*, to name, translated "called," A.V., 1 Cor. ONOMAZō
5 : 11, and *eponomazō*, to surname, translated "art called," Rom. 2 : 17, 3687 AG:573D
see NAME and SURNAME. CB:1261A

(2) *Legō*, to say, is rendered "calleth" in 1 Cor. 12 : 3, A.V., which EPONOMAZō 2028
the R.V. corrects to "saith ;" what is meant is not calling Christ AG:305C
"Anathema," but making use of the phrase "Anathema Jesus," i.e., CB:1246B
'Jesus is accursed.' PROSAGOREUō 4316

(3) *Prosagoreuō*, Heb. 5 : 10, means "to be named." See NAME.¶ AG:711B

(4) *Metapempō*, rendered "call for," in Acts 10 : 5, A.V., and 11 : 13, CB:— METAPEMPō
signifies to fetch, R.V. See FETCH, SEND, No. 9. 3343

(5) *Sunathroizō*, to assemble, is translated "he called together," in AG:513B CB:—
the A.V. of Acts 19 : 25 ; R.V., "he gathered together." SUNATHROIZō

(6) *Lambanō*, to take or receive, is found with the noun *hupomnēsis*, 4867 AG:783B
remembrance, in 2 Tim. 1 : 5 ; R.V., "having been reminded" (lit., CB:1270C
'having received remembrance'), for A.V., "when I call to remembrance." LAMBANō 2983

(7) In Acts 10 : 15 and 11 : 9, *koinoō*, to make common (R.V.) is AG:464A
translated "call common" in the A.V. CB:1256C

(8) For *prosphōneō*, to call unto, see SPEAK, No. 12. KOINOō 2840

B. Noun. AG:438B

KLĒSIS (κλῆσις), a calling (akin to A, No. 1), is always used in the CB:1255B
N.T. of that calling the origin, nature and destiny of which are heavenly PROSPHōNEō 4377
(the idea of invitation being implied) ; it is used especially of God's invita- AG:720C
tion to man to accept the benefits of salvation, Rom. 11 : 29 ; 1 Cor. 1 : 26 ; CB:— KLeSIS
7 : 20 (said there of the condition in which the calling finds one) ; Eph. 2821
1 : 18, "His calling ;" Phil. 3 : 14, the "high calling ;" 2 Thess. 1 : 11 AG:435D CB:1255B
and 2 Pet. 1 : 10, "your calling ;" 2 Tim. 1 : 9, a "holy calling ;" Heb.
3 : 1, a "heavenly calling ;" Eph. 4 : 1, "the calling wherewith ye were
called ;" 4 : 4, "in one hope of your calling." See VOCATION.¶

C. Adjective.

KLĒTOS (κλητός), called, invited, is used, (*a*) of the call of the Gospel, 2822
Matt. 20 : 16 ; 22 : 14, not there an effectual call, as in the Epistles, AG:436A CB:1255B
Rom. 1 : 1, 6, 7 ; 8 : 28 ; 1 Cor. 1 : 2, 24 ; Jude 1 ; Rev. 17 : 14 ; in
Rom. 1 : 7 and 1 Cor. 1 : 2 the meaning is 'saints by calling ;' (*b*) of an
appointment to apostleship, Rom. 1 : 1 ; 1 Cor. 1 : 1.¶ CALLOUS

See HARD

CALM

GALĒNĒ (γαλήνη) primarily signifies calmness, cheerfulness (from a 1055 AG:150B CB:1248A root *gal*—, from which *gelaō*, to smile, is also derived; hence the calm of the sea, the smiling ocean being a favourite metaphor of the poets), Matt. 8 : 26; Mark 4 : 39; Luke 8 : 24.¶

CALVARY

2898 KRANION (κρανίον), *kara*, a head (Eng., cranium), a diminutive of
AG:448A *kranon*, denotes a skull (Latin *calvaria*), Matt. 27 : 33; Mark 15 : 22;
CB:— Luke 23 : 33; John 19 : 17. The corresponding Aramaic word is Golgotha
(Heb. *gulgōleth*; see Judg. 9 : 53; 2 Kings 9 : 35).¶

For CAME see COME

CAMEL

2574 KAMĒLOS (κάμηλος), from a Hebrew word signifying a bearer,
AG:401C CB:1253B carrier, is used in proverbs to indicate (*a*) something almost or altogether
impossible, Matt. 19 : 24, and parallel passages, (*b*) the acts of a person
who is careful not to sin in trivial details, but pays no heed to more
important matters, Matt. 23 : 24.

For CAMP see ARMY

CAN (CANST, COULD, CANNOT)

1410 AG:207A 1. DUNAMAI (δύναμαι); see ABILITY, B, No. 1.
CB:1242B 2. ISCHUŌ (ἰσχύω) is translated "I can do" in Phil. 4 : 13; see
2480 AG:383D ABLE, B, No. 4.
CB:1253A 3. ECHŌ (ἔχω), to have, is translated "could" in Mark 14 : 8, lit.,
2192 'she hath done what she had;' in Luke 14 : 14, for the A.V., "cannot,"
AG:331D CB:1242C the R.V. has "they have not wherewith;" in Acts 4 : 14, "could say
nothing against" is, lit., 'had nothing to say against;' in Heb. 6 : 13,
"he could swear" is, lit., 'He had (by none greater) to swear.' See ABLE,
HAVE.

1097 AG:160D 4. GINŌSKŌ (γινώσκω), to know, is so rendered in the R.V. of
CB:1248B Matt. 16 : 3, "ye know how to," for A.V., "ye can" (*dunamai* is used in
the next sentence). This verb represents knowledge as the effect of
experience. In Acts 21 : 37, for "canst thou speak Greek?" the R.V.
has "dost . . ." See ALLOW, KNOW.

1492 5. OIDA (οἶδα), to know by perception, is the word in Pilate's remark
(EIDō) AG:555D "make it as sure as ye can" (marg. "sure, as ye know"), Matt. 27 : 65.
CB:1260B The phrases "cannot tell," "canst not tell," etc., are in the R.V. rendered
"know not" etc., Matt. 21 : 27; Mark 11 : 33; Luke 20 : 7; John 3 : 8;
(EIMI) 8 : 14; 16 : 18; 2 Cor. 12 : 2, 3. See KNOW.

1510 AG:222D 6. ESTI (ἐστί), meaning "it is," is translated "we cannot," in Heb.
CB:1243A 9 : 5, lit., 'it is not possible (now to speak);' so in 1 Cor. 11 : 20; see
1735 margin.

(-ETAI) AG:262D 7. ENDECHOMAI (ἐνδέχομαι), to accept, admit, allow of, is used
CB:— impersonally in Luke 13 : 33, "it can (not) be," i.e., it is not admissible.¶

For CANDLE and CANDLESTICK see LAMP and LAMPSTAND CANCEL See FORGIVE

For CANKER see GANGRENE and RUST CAPABLE See ABILITY

CAPTAIN

CAPSTONE See CORNERSTONE

1. CHILIARCHOS (χιλίαρχος), denoting a commander of 1000 soldiers
(from *chilios*, a thousand, and *archō*, to rule), was the Greek word for the
Persian vizier, and for the Roman military tribune, the commander of a 5506
Roman cohort, e.g., John 18:12; Acts 21:31–33, 37. One such AG:881D CB:1239C
commander was constantly in charge of the Roman garrison in Jerusalem. The word became used also for any military commander, e.g., a captain or chief captain, Mark 6:21; Rev. 6:15; 19:18.

2. STRATĒGOS (στρατηγός), originally the commander of an army 4755
(from *stratos*, an army, and *agō*, to lead), came to denote a civil commander, AG:770C CB:1270A
a governor (Latin, *duumvir*), the highest magistrate, or any civil officer in chief command, Acts 16:20, 22, 35, 36, 38; also the chief captain of the Temple, himself a Levite, having command of the Levites who kept guard in and around the Temple, Luke 22:4, 52; Acts 4:1; 5:24, 26. Cp. Jer. 20:1.¶

3. ARCHĒGOS (ἀρχηγός): see AUTHOR (No. 2). 747 AG:112C

Note: In Acts 28:16 some mss. have the word *stratopedarchēs* (lit., CB:1237B
camp-commander), which some take to denote a prætorian prefect, or 4759 AG:771A
commander of the prætorian cohorts, the Emperor's bodyguard, "the CB:1270B
captain of the prætorian guard." There were two prætorian prefects, to whose custody prisoners sent bound to the Emperor were consigned. But the word probably means the commander of a detached corps connected with the commissariat and the general custody of prisoners.

CAPTIVE, CAPTIVITY

A. Nouns.

1. AICHMALŌTOS (αἰχμάλωτος), lit., one taken by the spear (from 164
aichmē, a spear, and *halōtos*, a verbal adjective, from *halōnai*, to be AG:27A CB:1233C
captured), hence denotes a captive, Luke 4:18.¶

2. AICHMALŌSIA (αἰχμαλωσία), captivity, the abstract noun in 161
contrast to No. 1, the concrete, is found in Rev. 13:10 and Eph. 4:8, AG:26D CB:1233C
where "He led captivity captive" (marg., "a multitude of captives") seems to be an allusion to the triumphal procession by which a victory was celebrated, the captives taken forming part of the procession. See Judg. 5:12. The quotation is from Psa. 68:18, and probably is a forceful expression for Christ's victory, through His Death, over the hostile powers of darkness. An alternative suggestion is that at His Ascension Christ transferred the redeemed Old Testament saints from Sheol to His own presence in glory.¶

B. Verbs.

162

1. AICHMALŌTEUŌ (αἰχμαλωτεύω) signifies (*a*) to be a prisoner of AG:26D CB:1233C

war, (*b*) to make a prisoner of war. The latter meaning is the only one used in the N.T., Eph. 4 : 8.¶

163 2. AICHMALŌTIZŌ (αἰχμαλωτίζω), practically synonymous with
AG:27A
CB:1233C No. 1, denotes either to lead away captive, Luke 21 : 24, or to subjugate, to bring under control, said of the effect of the Law in one's members in bringing the person into captivity under the law of sin, Rom. 7 : 23; or of subjugating the thoughts to the obedience of Christ, 2 Cor. 10 : 5; or of those who took captive " silly women laden with sins," 2 Tim. 3 : 6.¶

2221 3. ZŌGREŌ (ζωγρέω) lit. signifies to take men alive (from *zōos*, alive,
AG:340A
CB:— and *agreuō*, to hunt or catch), Luke 5 : 10 (marg. " take alive "), there of the effects of the work of the Gospel; in 2 Tim. 2 : 26 it is said of the power of Satan to lead men astray. The verse should read ' and that they may recover themselves out of the snare of the Devil (having been taken captive by him), unto the will of God.' This is the probable meaning rather than to take alive or for life. See CATCH.¶

CARCASE

2966 1. KŌLON (κῶλον) primarily denotes a member of a body, especially
AG:461B
CB:— the external and prominent members, particularly the feet, and so, a dead body (see, e.g., the Sept., in Lev. 26 : 30; Num. 14 : 29, 32; Is. 66 : 24, etc.). The word is used in Heb. 3 : 17, from Num. 14 : 29, 32.¶

4430 2. PTŌMA (πτῶμα): see BODY, No. 3.
AG:727D
CB:1268A

CARE (noun and verb), CAREFUL, CAREFULLY, CAREFULNESS

A. Nouns.

3308 1. MERIMNA (μέριμνα), probably connected with *merizō*, to draw in
AG:504D
CB:1258B different directions, distract, hence signifies that which causes this, a care, especially an anxious care, Matt. 13 : 22; Mark 4 : 19; Luke 8 : 14; 21 : 34; 2 Cor. 11 : 28 (R.V., " anxiety for "); 1 Pet. 5 : 7 (R.V., " anxiety "). See ANXIETY.¶

275 *Note:* The negative adjective *amerimnos* (*a*, negative) signifies free
AG:45B
CB:1234C from care, Matt. 28 : 14, R.V., " we will . . . rid you of care," A.V., " we will . . . secure you " (" secure " lit. means ' free from care '); 1 Cor. 7 : 32, A.V., " without carefulness."¶

4710 2. SPOUDĒ (σπουδή), primarily haste, zeal, diligence, hence means
AG:763D
CB:1269C earnest care, carefulness, 2 Cor. 7 : 11, 12; 8 : 16 (R.V., " earnest care," in each place). *Merimna* conveys the thought of anxiety, *spoudē*, of watchful interest and earnestness. See BUSINESS, DILIGENCE (A, No. 2), EARNESTNESS, FORWARDNESS, HASTE.

B. Verbs.

3309 1. MERIMNAŌ (μεριμνάω), akin to A, No. 1, signifies to be anxious
AG:505A
CB:1258B about, to have a distracting care, e.g., Matt. 6 : 25, 28, R.V., " be anxious," for A.V., " take thought; " 10 : 19; Luke 10 : 41 (R.V., " anxious," for A.V., " careful "); 12 : 11 (R.V., " anxious "); to be careful for, 1 Cor.

7 : 32, 33, 34 ; to have a care for, 1 Cor. 12 : 25 ; to care for, Phil. 2 : 20 ; " be anxious," Phil. 4 : 6, R.V. See THOUGHT (to take).

2. MELEI (μέλει), the third person sing. of *melō*, used impersonally, 3190
signifies that something is an object of care, especially the care of fore- AG:500A
thought and interest, rather than anxiety, Matt. 22 : 16 ; Mark 4 : 38 ; CB:—
12 : 14 ; Luke 10 : 40 ; John 10 : 13 ; 12 : 6 ; Acts 18 : 17 ; 1 Cor. 9 : 9 (R.V., " Is it for the oxen that God careth ? " The A.V. seriously misses the point. God does care for oxen, but there was a Divinely designed significance in the O.T. passage, relating to the service of preachers of the Gospel) ; 7 : 21 ; 1 Pet. 5 : 7.¶

3. EPIMELEOMAI (ἐπιμελέομαι) signifies to take care of, involving 1959
forethought and provision (*epi* indicating the direction of the mind AG:296A
toward the object cared for), Luke 10 : 34, 35, of the Good Samaritan's CB:—
care for the wounded man, and in 1 Tim. 3 : 5, of a bishop's (or overseer's) care of a church—a significant association of ideas.¶

4. PHRONTIZŌ (φροντίζω), to think, consider, be thoughtful (from 5431
phrēn, the mind), is translated " be careful " in Tit. 3 : 8.¶ AG:866D CB:1264C

5. PHRONEŌ (φρονέω), translated " be careful," in Phil. 4 : 10, A.V. 5426
[R.V., " (ye did) take thought "], has a much wider range of meaning AG:866A
than No. 5, and denotes to be minded, in whatever way. See AFFECTION, CB:1264C
B, *Note* (1), MIND, REGARD, SAVOUR, THINK, UNDERSTAND.

Note : *Episkopeō*, to oversee, is rendered " looking carefully," in 1983
Heb. 12 : 15, R.V. See OVERSIGHT.¶ AG:298D CB:1246A

C. Adverbs.

1. AKRIBŌS (ἀκριβῶς), carefully ; see ACCURATELY. AKRIBōS 199
Note : For *akribesteron*, more carefully, see EXACTLY. AG:33B
2. SPOUDAIOTERŌS, the comparative adverb corresponding to A, CB:— AKRIBESTERON
No. 2, signifies " the more diligently," Phil. 2 : 28, R.V. (A.V., " care- 197
fully ").¶ The adverb *spoudaiōs* denotes " diligently," 2 Tim. 1 : 17 AG:33B (-BoS)
(some mss. have the comparative here) ; Tit. 3 : 13 ; or " earnestly," CB:— SPOUDAIOTERōS
Luke 7 : 4 (A.V., " instantly "). See also *spoudaios* and its comparative, 4708
in 2 Cor. 8 : 17, 22, R.V., " earnest," " more earnest."¶ AG:763D (-IōS 2.)

CB:1269C

CARNAL, CARNALLY

(-IōS) SPOUDAIōS

1. SARKIKOS (σαρκικός), from *sarx*, flesh, signifies (*a*) having the 4709
nature of flesh, i.e., sensual, controlled by animal appetites, governed by AG:763D CB:1268B
human nature, instead of by the Spirit of God, 1 Cor. 3 : 3 (for ver. 1, see SPOUDAIOS
below ; some mss. have it in ver. 4) ; having its seat in the animal nature, 4559
or excited by it, 1 Pet. 2 : 11, " fleshly ; " or as the equivalent of " human," AG:742D CB:1268B
with the added idea of weakness, figuratively of the weapons of spiritual warfare, " of the flesh " (A.V., " carnal "), 2 Cor. 10 : 4 ; or with the idea of unspirituality, of human wisdom, " fleshly," 2 Cor. 1 : 12 ; (*b*) pertaining to the flesh (i.e., the body), Rom. 15 : 27 ; 1 Cor. 9 : 11.¶ 4560 AG:743A

2. SARKINOS (σάρκινος), (*a*) consisting of flesh, 2 Cor. 3 : 3, " tables CB:1268C

that are hearts of flesh" (A.V., "fleshy tables of the heart"); (*b*) pertaining to the natural, transient life of the body, Heb. 7 : 16, "a carnal commandment;" (*c*) given up to the flesh, i.e., with almost the same significance as *sarkikos*, above, Rom. 7 : 14, "I am carnal, sold under sin;" 1 Cor. 3 : 1 (some texts have *sarkikos*, in both these places, and in those in (*a*) and (*b*), but textual evidence is against it). It is difficult to discriminate between *sarkikos* and *sarkinos* in some passages. In regard to 1 Pet. 2 : 11, Trench (Syn §§ lxxi, lxxii) says that *sarkikos* describes the lusts which have their source in man's corrupt and fallen nature, and the man is *sarkikos* who allows to the flesh a place which does not belong to it of right; in 1 Cor. 3 : 1 *sarkinos* is an accusation far less grave than *sarkikos* would have been. The Corinthian saints were making no progress, but they were not anti-spiritual in respect of the particular point with which the Apostle was there dealing. In vv. 3, 4, they are charged with being *sarkikos*. See FLESHLY, FLESHY.¶

CAROUSINGS

4224 POTOS (πότος), lit., a drinking, signifies not simply a banquet but a
AG:696A CB:1266B drinking bout, a carousal, 1 Pet. 4 : 3 (R.V., "carousings," A.V., "ban-
quetings").¶ Synonymous is *kraipalē*, "surfeiting," Luke 21 : 34.¶

CARPENTER

5045 TEKTŌN (τέκτων) denotes any craftsman, but especially a worker in
AG:809A CB:1271B wood, a carpenter, Matt. 13 : 55; Mark 6 : 3.¶

For CARRIAGE see BAGGAGE

CARRY

4792 1. SUNKOMIZŌ (συγκομίζω), to carry together, to help in carrying
AG:774C CB:— (*sun*, with, *komizō*, to carry), is used in Acts 8 : 2, R.V., "buried," for
A.V., "carried to his burial." The verb has also the meaning of re-
1580 covering or getting back a body.¶
AG:241D 2. EKKOMIZŌ (ἐκκομίζω), to carry out, is found in Luke 7 : 12.¶
CB:— 3. PHERŌ (φέρω), to bear, to bring, is translated "carry" only
5342 AG:854D in John 21 : 18. See Note below.
CB:1264A 4. DIAPHERŌ (διαφέρω) has the meaning "to carry through" in
1308 AG:190B Mark 11 : 16. See BETTER, DIFFER, DRIVE, EXCELLENT, MATTER,
CB:— PUBLISH, VALUE.
3346 5. METATITHĒMI (μετατίθημι), to place among, put in another place
AG:513C CB:1258C (*meta*, implying change, and *tithēmi*, to put), has this latter meaning in
520 Acts 7 : 16, "carried over." See CHANGE, REMOVE, TRANSLATE, TURN.
AG:79C 6. APAGŌ (ἀπάγω), to lead away (*apo*, from, *agō*, to lead), is rendered
CB:— "carried" in 1 Cor. 12 : 2, A.V. (R.V., "were led"). See BRING.
4879 AG:784D 7. SUNAPAGŌ (συναπάγω), to carry away with (*sun*, with, and No.
CB:— 6), is used in a bad sense, in Gal. 2 : 13 and 2 Pet. 3 : 17, "being carried

away with " (R.V.) ; in a good sense in Rom. 12 : 16 ; the R.V. marg. " be carried away with " is preferable to the text " condescend " (R.V., and A.V.), and to the A.V. marg., " be contented (with mean things)." A suitable rendering would be ' be led along with.'¶

Notes : (1) For *pherō*, to carry, or bring, *apopherō*, to carry away, *peripherō*, to carry about, *ekpherō*, to carry forth, *anapherō*, to carry up, *airō*, to lift and carry away, to take away, *bastazō*, to support, carry about, *agō*, to lead or carry, *apagō*, to carry away, see BEAR and BRING.

(2) For *elaunō*, rendered " carry " in 2 Pet. 2 : 17, see DRIVE.

CARRYING AWAY

A. Noun.

METOIKESIA (μετοικεσία), a change of abode, or a carrying away by 3350
force (*meta*, implying change, *oikia*, a dwelling), is used only of the AG:514B CB:1258C
carrying away to Babylon, Matt. 1 : 11, 12, 17.¶

B. Verb.

METOIKIZŌ (μετοικίζω), akin to A, is used of the removal of Abraham 3351
into Canaan, Acts 7 : 4, and of the carrying into Babylon, 7 : 43.¶ AG:514B CB:—

CASE

1. AITIA (αἰτία) : see under ACCUSATION, A, No. 1. 156
2. ECHŌ (ἔχω), to have, is idiomatically used in the sense of being AG:26B CB:1234A
in a case or condition, as with the infirm man at the pool of Bethesda, 2192
John 5 : 6, lit., ' that he had already much time (in that case).' AG:331D CB:1242C

Note : In Acts 25 : 14 the phrase in the original is ' the things concerning Paul,' A.V., " cause " (as if translating *aitia*) ; R.V., " Festus laid Paul's case before the king."

3. PROECHŌ (προέχω), lit., to have before, in the Middle Voice, Rom. 4284
3 : 9, is rightly translated " are we in worse case ? " (R.V.), as is borne (-OMAI) AG:705D
out by the context. See BETTER (be), Note (1).¶ CB:—

4. The preposition *en*, followed by the dative of the pronoun, lit., 1722
' in me,' is translated in the R.V.," in my case," in 1 Cor. 9 : 15 ; " unto AG:258B CB:1244B
me," in 1 Cor. 14 : 11 (marg. " in my case"). Similarly, in the plural, in 1 John 4 : 16, R.V. " in us " (marg., " in our case ") ; A.V., incorrectly, " to us."

Note : In Matt. 5 : 20 the strong double negative *ou mē* is translated " in no case " (A.V.) : R.V., " in no wise."

CAST

A. Verbs.

1. BALLŌ (βάλλω), to throw, hurl, in contrast to striking, is frequent 906
in the four Gospels and Revelation ; elsewhere it is used only in Acts. AG:130D CB:1238B
In Matt. 5 : 30 some mss. have this verb (A.V., " should be cast ") ; the most authentic have *aperchomai*, to go away, R.V., " go." See ARISE, BEAT, DUNG, LAY, POUR, PUT, SEND, STRIKE, THROW, THRUST.

4496 2. RHIPTO (ῥίπτω) denotes to throw with a sudden motion, to jerk,
(-TEō 4495) AG:736C cast forth; "cast down," Matt. 15:30 and 27:5; "thrown down,"
CB:— Luke 4:35; "thrown," 17:2 (A.V., "cast"); [*rhipteō* in Acts 22:23
(A.V., "cast off"), of the casting off of clothes (in the next sentence
ballō, No. 1, is used of casting dust into the air)]; in 27:19 "cast out,"
of the tackling of a ship; in ver. 29 "let go" (A.V., "cast"), of anchors;
in Matt. 9:36, "scattered," said of sheep. See THROW, SCATTER.¶

1601 3. EKPIPTŌ (ἐκπίπτω), lit., to fall out, is translated "be cast ashore,"
AG:243D CB:1243C in Acts 27:29, R.V., A.V., "have fallen upon" See EFFECT, FAIL,
FALL, NOUGHT.

A number of compound verbs consisting of *ballō* or *rhiptō*, with prepositions prefixed, denote to cast, with a corresponding English preposition. Compounds of *ballō* are:

577 AG:88D 4. APOBALLŌ (ἀποβάλλω), to throw off from, to lay aside, to cast
CB:— away, Mark 10:50; Heb. 10:35.¶

580 AG:89A *Note:* *Apobolē*, "casting away" (akin to No. 4), is used of Israel
CB:— in Rom. 11:15; elsewhere, Acts 27:22, "loss" (of life).¶

1544 5. EKBALLŌ (ἐκβάλλω), to cast out of, from, forth, is very frequent
AG:237B CB:1243B in the Gospels and Acts; elsewhere, in Gal. 4:30; 3 John 10; in Jas.
2:25, "sent out;" in Rev. 11:2, "leave out" (marg., "cast without").
See BRING, No. 28, DRIVE, EXPEL, LEAVE, PLUCK, PULL, PUT, SEND,
1685 TAKE, THRUST.

AG:254A 6. EMBALLŌ (ἐμβάλλω), to cast into, is used in Luke 12:5.¶
CB:1244B

1911 7. EPIBALLŌ (ἐπιβάλλω), to cast on, or upon, is used in this sense in
AG:289D Mark 11:7 and 1 Cor. 7:35. See BEAT (No. 5), FALL, No. 11, LAY,
CB:— PUT, No. 8, STRETCH.

2598 8. KATABALLŌ (καταβάλλω) signifies to cast down, 2 Cor. 4:9,
AG:408D CB:1253C A.V., "cast down," R.V., "smitten down;" Heb. 6:1, "laying"
— See LAY.¶ Some mss. have this verb in Rev. 12:10 (for *ballō*).

AG:47B 9. AMPHIBALLŌ (ἀμφιβάλλω), to cast around, occurs Mark 1:16.¶
CB:1234C

4016 10. PERIBALLŌ (περιβάλλω), to cast about, or around, is used in
AG:646A 23 of its 24 occurrences, of putting on garments, clothing, etc.; it
CB:— is translated "cast about" in Mark 14:51; Acts 12:8; in Luke 19:43,
used of casting up a bank or palisade against a city (see R.V. and marg.),
A.V., "shall cast a trench about thee." See CLOTHE, No. 6, PUT.

641 Compounds of *rhiptō* are:

(-RR-) AG:97D 11. APORIPTŌ (ἀπορίπτω), to cast off, Acts 27:43, of shipwrecked
CB:— people in throwing themselves into the water.¶

1977 AG:298B 12. EPIRIPTŌ (ἐπιρίπτω), to cast upon, (*a*) lit., of casting garments on
CB:— a colt, Luke 19:35; (*b*) figuratively, of casting care upon God, 1 Pet.
5:7.¶

683 Other verbs are:

(-OMAI) AG:103B 13. APŌTHEŌ (ἀπωθέω), to thrust away (*apo*, away, *ōtheō*, to thrust),
CB:— in the N.T. used in the Middle Voice, signifying to thrust from oneself,

to cast off, by way of rejection, Acts 7 : 27, 39 ; 13 : 46 ; Rom. 11 : 1, 2 ; 1 Tim. 1 : 19. See PUT and THRUST.¶

14. KATHAIREŌ (καθαιρέω), *kata*, down, *haireō*, to take, to cast down, 2507
demolish, in 2 Cor. 10 : 5, of strongholds and imaginations. See DESTROY, AG:386C CB:—
PULL, PUT, TAKE.

Note : The corresponding noun *kathairesis*, a casting down, is so 2506
rendered in 2 Cor. 10 : 4 (A.V., " pulling down ") and 13 : 10 (A.V., AG:386B CB:—
" destruction ").

15. DIALOGIZOMAI (διαλογίζομαι), to reason (*dia*, through, *logizomai*, 1260
to reason), is translated " cast in (her) mind," Luke 1 : 29. See DISPUTE, AG:186A CB:1241B
MUSING, REASON, THINK.

16. APOTITHĒMI (ἀποτίθημι), to put off, lay aside, denotes, in the 659
Middle Voice, to put off from oneself, cast off, used figuratively of works AG:101A CB:1237B
of darkness, Rom. 13 : 12, " let us cast off," (aorist tense, denoting a definite act). See LAY, No. 8, PUT, No. 5.

17. EKTITHĒMI (ἐκτίθημι), to expose, cast out (*ek*, out, *tithēmi*, 1620
to put), is said of a new-born child in Acts 7 : 21. In ver. 19 " cast out " AG:245D CB:—
translates the phrase *poieō*, to make, with *ekthetos*, exposed, a verbal form EKTHETOS
of *ektithēmi*. See EXPOUND. 1570 AG:240B

18. PERIAIREŌ (περιαιρέω), to take away, is used in Acts 27 : 40, CB:—
as a nautical term, R.V., " casting off," A.V., " taken up." See TAKE. 4014

Notes : (1) For *zēmioō*, " cast away," Luke 9 : 25, see FORFEIT. AG:645D CB:—
(2) For *katakrēmnizō*, Luke 4 : 29 (A.V., " cast down headlong "), see THROW.¶ (3) For *oneidizō*, Matt. 27 : 44 (A.V., " cast in one's teeth "), see REPROACH. (4) For *paradidōmi*, Matt. 4 : 12 (A.V., " cast into prison "), see DELIVER. (5) For *atheteō*, 1 Tim. 5 : 12 (A.V., " cast off "), see REJECT. (6) For *ekteinō*, Acts 27 : 30 (A.V., " cast out "), see LAY No. 13. (7) For *tapeinos*, 2 Cor. 7 : 6 (A.V., " cast down "), see LOWLY

B. Noun.

BOLE (βολή) denotes a throw (akin to *ballō*, to throw), and is used in 1000
Luke 22 : 21 in the phrase " a stone's cast," of the distance from which AG:144D CB:—
the Lord was parted from the disciples in the garden of Gethsemane.¶

Note : In Jas. 1 : 17, *aposkiasma* (from *aposkiazō*, to cast a shadow), 644
is rendered " shadow that is cast," R.V.¶ AG:98A CB:1237A

C. Adjective.

ADOKIMOS (ἀδόκιμος) signifies not standing the test, rejected, (*a*, neg- 96
ative, and *dokimos*, tested, approved) ; it is said of things, e.g., the land, AG:18C CB:1233A
Heb. 6 : 8, " rejected," and of persons, Rom. 1 : 28, " reprobate ; " 1 Cor. 9 : 27, A.V., " castaway," R.V. " rejected " (i.e., disapproved, and so rejected from present testimony, with loss of future reward) ; 2 Cor. 13 : 5, 6, 7, " reprobate " (sing. in R.V. in each verse), i.e., that will not stand the test ; 2 Tim. 3 : 8, " reprobate (concerning the faith)," Tit. 1 : 16, " reprobate." See REJECT, REPROBATE.¶

For CASTLE see ARMY (No. 3)

CATCH

726 AG:109A CB:1249B 1. HARPAZŌ (ἁρπάζω), to snatch or catch away, is said of the act of the Spirit of the Lord in regard to Philip in Acts 8 : 39 ; of Paul in being caught up to Paradise, 2 Cor. 12 : 2, 4 ; of the Rapture of the saints at the return of the Lord, 1 Thess. 4 : 17 ; of the rapture of the man child in the vision of Rev. 12 : 5. This verb conveys the idea of force suddenly exercised, as in Matt. 11 : 12, " take (it) by force ; " 12 : 29, " spoil " (some mss. have *diarpazō* here) ; in 13 : 19, R.V., " snatcheth ; " for forceful seizure, see also John 6 : 15 ; 10 : 12, 28, 29 ; Acts 23 : 10 ; in Jude 23, R.V., " snatching ". See PLUCK, PULL, SNATCH, TAKE (by force).¶

2983 AG:464A CB:1256C 2. LAMBANŌ (λαμβάνω), to receive, is once used of catching by fraud, circumventing, 2 Cor. 12 : 16. In Matt. 21 : 39 and Mark 12 : 3, R.V. " took," for A.V. " caught." See ACCEPT, No. 4.

64 AG:13B CB:— 3. AGREUŌ (ἀγρεύω), to take by hunting (from *agra*, a hunt, a catch), is used metaphorically, of the Pharisees and Herodians in seeking to catch Christ in His talk, Mark 12 : 13.¶

2340 AG:360D CB:— 4. THĒREUŌ (θηρεύω), to hunt or catch wild beasts (*thērion*, a wild beast), is used by Luke of the same event as in No. 3, Luke 11 : 54.¶

2221 AG:340A 5. ZŌGREŌ (ζωγρέω), to take alive: see CAPTIVE, B, No. 3.

4084 AG:657A 6. PIAZŌ (πιάζω), to capture: see APPREHEND, No. 2.

4884 AG:785B CB:— 7. SUNARPAZŌ (συναρπάζω), *sun*, used intensively, and No. 1, to snatch, to seize, to keep a firm grip of, is used only by Luke, and translated " caught " in the A.V. of Luke 8 : 29, of demon-possession ; in Acts 6 : 12, of the act of the elders and scribes in seizing Stephen, R.V., more suitably, " seized." So in Acts 19 : 29. In 27 : 15, it is used of the effects of wind upon a ship. See SEIZE.¶

4815 AG:776D CB:1270B 8. SULLAMBANŌ (συλλαμβάνω), *sun*, and No. 2, to seize, is used, similarly to No. 7, in Acts 26 : 21, of the act of the Jews in seizing Paul in the temple. See CONCEIVE, HELP, SEIZE, TAKE.

1949 (-OMAI) AG:295A (-OMAI) CB:1246A 9. EPILAMBANŌ (ἐπιλαμβάνω), to lay hold (*epi*, intensive, and No. 2), is translated " caught " in Acts 16 : 19, A.V. ; R.V., " laid hold." See HOLD, TAKE.

CATTLE

2353 AG:363B CB:1272B 1. THREMMA (θρέμμα), whatever is fed or nourished (from *trephō*, to nourish, nurture, feed), is found in John 4 : 12.¶

2934 AG:455B CB:1256A 2. KTĒNOS (κτῆνος), cattle as property: see BEAST, No. 3.

4165 AG:683D CB:1265C *Note:* The verb *poimainō*, to act as a shepherd (*poimēn*), to keep sheep, is translated " keeping sheep " in Luke 17 : 7, R.V., for A.V., " feeding cattle."

CAUSE (Noun and Verb)

A. Nouns.

156 AG:26B CB:1234A 1. AITIA (αἰτία), a cause: see ACCUSATION, A, No. 1.

2. AITION (*αἴτιον*), a fault (synonymous with No. 1, but more limited 158
in scope), is translated " cause (of death) " in Luke 23 : 22 ; " cause " AG:26D (-OS)
in Acts 19 : 40 (of a riot); " fault " in Luke 23 : 4, 14. See FAULT.¶ CB:1234A

3. LOGOS (*λόγος*), a word spoken for any purpose, denotes, in one 3056
place, a cause or reason assigned, Matt. 5 : 32. AG:477A CB:1257A

The following phrases are rendered by an English phrase containing the word " cause " (see WHEREFORE) :

" For this cause "

1. ANTI TOUTOU (*ἀντὶ τούτου*), lit., instead of this, i.e., for this ANTI 473
cause, signifying the principle or motive, Eph. 5 : 31. AG:73C 3.

2. DIA TOUTO (*διὰ τοῦτο*), lit., on account of this, for this cause, CB:1236A
signifying the ground or reason, e.g., R.V. in Mark 12 : 24 ; John 1 : 31 ; DIA 1223
5 : 16, 18 ; 6 : 65 ; 7 : 22 ; 8 : 47 ; 12 : 18, 27, 39 ; Rom. 1 : 26 ; 4 : 16 ; AG:179B II.2.
13 : 6 ; 1 Cor. 4 : 17 ; 11 : 10, 30 ; Eph. 1 : 15 ; Col. 1 : 9 ; 1 Thess. CB:1241A
2 : 13 ; 3 : 5, 7 ; 2 Thess. 2 : 11 ; 1 Tim. 1 : 16 ; Heb. 9 : 15 ; 1 John 3 : 1.

3. HENEKEN TOUTOU (*ἕνεκεν τούτου*), lit., for the sake of this, HENEKA
therefore, as a reason for, Matt. 19 : 5 ; Mark 10 : 7 ; *heneka toutōn*, ' for 1752 AG:264D
the sake of these things,' Acts 26 : 21 ; and *heneken tou*, for the cause of CB:1250A
the (one) etc., 2 Cor. 7 : 12 (twice).

4. CHARIN TOUTOU, or TOUTOU CHARIN (*τούτου χάριν*), for this CHARIN
cause, not simply as a reason, as in the preceding phrase, but in favour of, 5484 AG:877A
Eph. 3 : 1, 14 ; Tit. 1 : 5. CB:1239C (CHARIS)

" For this very cause "

AUTO TOUTO (*αὐτὸ τοῦτο*), lit., (as to) this very thing, 2 Pet. 1 : 5. AUTOS
Notes : (1) This phrase often represents one containing *aitia* (see 846 AG:122C 1.h.
above). CB:1238B

(2) In John 18 : 37, *eis touto*, unto this, denotes " unto this end," R.V. EIS 1519
(A.V., " for this cause "). AG:228A 4.f.

(3) For the phrase " for which cause " (*dio*), Rom. 15 : 22 ; 2 Cor. CB:1243A
4 : 16, see WHEREFORE, *Note* (2) (R.V.).

(4) In Phil. 2 : 18, *to auto*, is rendered " for the same cause," A.V. ; R.V., " in the same manner."

" without a cause "

DŌREAN (*δωρεάν*), lit., as a gift, gratis, (connected with *dōron*, a gift), 1432
is rendered " without a cause," John 15 : 25 ; " for nought," 2 Cor. 11 : 7 ; AG:210C CB:1242A
Gal. 2 : 21 ; 2 Thess. 3 : 8 ; " freely," Matt. 10 : 8 ; Rom. 3 : 24 ; Rev.
21 : 6 ; 22 : 17.¶

Notes : (1) *Eikē*, " in vain," " without a cause," Matt. 5 : 22 (A.V.), 1500
is absent from the most authentic mss. AG:221D CB:1243A

(2) For " cause," in Acts 25 : 14, A.V., see CASE.

(3) In 2 Cor. 5 : 13 (R.V., " unto you "), the A.V. has " for your cause."

B. Verbs.

1. POIEŌ (*ποιέω*), to do, is translated by the verb to cause in John 4160 AG:680D
11 : 37 ; Acts 15 : 3 ; Rom. 16 : 17 ; Col. 4 : 16 ; Rev. 13 : 15, 16. See DO. CB:1265C

1325 AG:192C CB:1241C 2. DIDŌMI (δίδωμι), to give, is translated " cause " in 1 Cor. 9 : 12, R.V., for A.V., " (lest we) should."

Notes : (1) In Matt. 5 : 32 the R.V. translates *poieō* " maketh (her an adulteress) : " in Rev. 13 : 12, R.V., " maketh," for A.V., " causeth."

2716 AG:421C CB:— (2) In 2 Cor. 9 : 11, *katergazomai,* to work, is translated " causeth " in the A.V. ; R.V., " worketh."

2358 AG:363D CB:1272B (3) In 2 Cor. 2 : 14, *thriambeuō* is rendered " causeth us to triumph," A.V. ; R.V., " leadeth us in triumph," the metaphor being taken from the circumstances of the procession of a Roman " triumph."

CAUTION See CHARGE

CAVALRY See HORSEMEN

CAVE

3692 AG:574D CB:— 1. OPĒ (ὀπή), perhaps from *ōps,* sight, denotes a hole, an opening, such as a fissure in a rock, Heb. 11 : 38. In Jas. 3 : 11, the R.V. has " opening," of the orifice of a fountain (A.V., " place "). See PLACE.¶

4693 AG:762C CB:1269C 2. SPĒLAION (σπήλαιον), a grotto, cavern, den (Lat., *spelunca*), " cave," John 11 : 38, is said of the grave of Lazarus ; in the R.V. in Heb. 11 : 38 and Rev. 6 : 15 (A.V., " dens ") ; in the Lord's rebuke concerning the defilement of the Temple, Matt. 21 : 13 ; Mark 11 : 17 ; Luke 19 : 46, " den " is used.¶

CEASE

A. Verbs.

3973 AG:638A CB:— 1. PAUŌ (παύω), to stop, to make an end, is used chiefly in the Middle Voice in the N.T., signifying to come to an end, to take one's rest, a willing cessation (in contrast to the Passive Voice which denotes a forced cessation), Luke 5 : 4, of a discourse ; 8 : 24, of a storm ; 11 : 1, of Christ's prayer ; Acts 5 : 42, of teaching and preaching ; 6 : 13, of speaking against ; 13 : 10, of evil doing ; 20 : 1, of an uproar ; 20 : 31, of admonition ; 21 : 32, of a scourging ; 1 Cor. 13 : 8, of tongues ; Eph. 1 : 16, of giving thanks ; Col. 1 : 9, of prayer ; Heb. 10 : 2, of sacrifices ; 1 Pet. 4 : 1, of ceasing from sin. It is used in the Active Voice in 1 Pet. 3 : 10, ' let him cause his tongue to cease from evil.' See LEAVE, REFRAIN.¶

1257 AG:185D CB:1241A 2. DIALEIPŌ (διαλείπω), lit., to leave between, i.e., to leave an interval, whether of space or time (*dia,* between, *leipō,* to leave) ; hence, to intermit, desist, cease, in Luke 7 : 45 is used of the kissing of the Lord's feet.¶

2270 AG:349A CB:1250A 3. HĒSUCHAZŌ (ἡσυχάζω), to be quiet, still, at rest, is said of Paul's friends in Cæsarea, in ceasing to persuade him not to go to Jerusalem, Acts 21 : 14 ; it is used of silence (save in Luke 23 : 56 and 1 Thess. 4 : 11) in Luke 14 : 4 and Acts 11 : 18. See PEACE (hold one's), QUIET, REST.¶

2869 AG:443B CB:— 4. KOPAZŌ (κοπάζω), to cease through being spent with toil, to cease raging (from *kopos,* labour, toil, *kopiaō,* to labour), is said of the wind only, Matt. 14 : 32 ; Mark 4 : 39 ; 6 : 51.¶

863 AG:125C CB:1236B 5. APHIĒMI (ἀφίημι), to let go, is translated " let us cease to " in

Heb. 6 : 1, R.V. (marg., " leave ") for A.V., " leaving." See FORGIVE, LEAVE.

6. KATAPAUŌ (καταπαύω), to rest (*kata*, down, intensive, and No. 1), 2664
is so translated in Heb. 4 : 10, for the A.V. " hath ceased." See REST, AG:415D CB:1254A
RESTRAIN.

Notes : (1) *Katargeō*, to render inactive, to bring to naught, to do 2673
away, is so rendered in Gal. 5 : 11, R.V., for the A.V. " ceased." See AG:417B CB:1254B
ABOLISH.

(2) *Akatapaustos*, incessant, not to be set at rest (from *a*, negative, 180
kata, down, *pauō*, to cease), is used in 2 Pet. 2 : 14, of those who " cannot AG:30A CB:—
cease " from sin, i.e., who cannot be restrained from sinning.¶

B. Adjective.

ADIALEIPTOS (ἀδιάλειπτος), unceasing (from *a*, negative, *dia*, 88
through, *leipō*, to leave), is used of incessant heart pain, Rom. 9 : 2, A.V., AG:17B CB:1233A
" continual," R.V., " unceasing," and in 2 Tim. 1 : 3, of remembrance in prayer ; the meaning in each place is not that of unbroken continuity, but without the omission of any occasion. Cp. A, No. 2. See CONTINUAL.¶

C. Adverb.

ADIALEIPTŌS (ἀδιαλείπτως), unceasingly, without ceasing, is used 89
with the same significance as the adjective, not of what is not interrupted, AG:17B CB:1233A
but of that which is constantly recurring ; in Rom. 1 : 9 and 1 Thess. 5 : 17, of prayer ; in 1 Thess. 1 : 3, of the remembrance of the work, labour and patience of saints ; in 1 Thess. 2 : 13, of thanksgiving.¶

Note : Ektenēs, lit., stretched out, signifies earnest, fervent ; Acts 12 : 5, 1618 AG:245C
R.V., for A.V., " without ceasing." See 1 Pet. 4 : 8, " fervent."¶ CB:—

For CELESTIAL see HEAVEN, HEAVENLY, B, No. 2

CELEBATE See VIRGIN

CELEBRATE See FEAST, REJOICE

CELL

OIKĒMA (οἴκημα), lit., a habitation (akin to *oikeō*, to dwell), is 3612
euphemistically put for a prison, in Acts 12 : 7, R.V., " cell." See AG:557A CB:—
PRISON.¶

CELLAR

KRUPTĒ (κρυπτή),—Eng., crypt—a covered way or vault (akin to 2926
kruptos, hidden, secret), is used in Luke 11 : 33, of lighting a lamp and AG:454A CB:1256A
putting it " in a cellar," R.V. See PLACE, *Note* (8).¶

CEMETARY See TOMB

CENSER

1. THUMIATĒRION (θυμιατήριον), a vessel for burning incense 2369
(2 Chron. 26 : 19 ; Ezek. 8 : 11), is found in Heb. 9 : 4.¶ AG:365B CB:1272C

2. LIBANŌTOS (λιβανωτός) denotes frankincense, the gum of the 3031
libanos, the frankincense tree ; in a secondary sense, a vessel in which AG:473D CB:1257A
to burn incense, Rev. 8 : 3, 5.¶

Note : No. 1 derives its significance from the act of burning (*thumiaō*) ;
No. 2 from that which was burned in the vessel.

CENSUS See ENROLLMENT

CENTURION

1543 1. HEKATONTARCHOS (ἑκατόνταρχος), a centurion, denotes a
AG:237A CB:1249C military officer commanding from 50 to 100 men, according to the size
of the legion of which it was a part (*hekaton*, a hundred, *archō*, to rule), e.g., Matt. 8 : 5, 8.

1543 2. HEKATONTARCHĒS (ἑκατοντάρχης) has the same meaning as
AG:237A CB:1249C No. 1, e.g., Acts 10 : 1, 22. The Sept. has this word frequently, to denote
captains of hundreds.

2760 3. KENTURIŌN (κεντυρίων) is a Greek transliteration of the Latin
AG:428C CB:1255A *centurio*, signifying practically the same as No. 1, Mark 15 : 39, 44, 45.
There were ten centurions to a cohort when the numbers were complete. There were several at Jerusalem under the chief captain mentioned in
CEREMONIALLY See CLEAN, UNCLEAN Acts 21 : 31.¶

CERTAIN, CERTAINTY, CERTAINLY, CERTIFY

A. Noun.

803 ASPHALEIA (ἀσφάλεια), primarily, not liable to fall, stedfast, firm,
AG:118D CB:1238A hence denoting safety, Acts 5 : 23, and 1 Thess. 5 : 3, has the further
meaning, "certainty," Luke 1 : 4. See SAFETY.¶

B. Adjective.

804 ASPHALĒS (ἀσφαλής), safe, is translated "certainty," Acts 21 : 34;
AG:119A CB:1238A 22 : 30; "certain," Acts 25 : 26; "safe," Phil. 3 : 1; "sure," Heb. 6 : 19.
See SAFE, SURE.¶

1212 *Notes*: (1) *Dēlos*, evident, visible, is translated "certain" in 1 Tim.
AG:178B CB:1240C 6 : 7, A.V. The most authentic mss. omit it.

(2) The rendering "certain," is frequently changed in the R.V., or
5100 omitted, e.g., Luke 5 : 12; 8 : 22; Acts 23 : 17; Heb. 2 : 6; 4 : 4.

AG:819D (3) The indefinite pronoun *tis* signifies anyone, some one, a certain
CB:1272C one; the neuter, *ti*, a certain thing, e.g., Matt. 20 : 20; Mark 14 : 51.

1107 (4) In the A.V. of Gal. 1 : 11, *gnōrizō* is rendered "certify," R.V.,
AG:163B CB:1248B "to make known."

(5) For "a certain island," Acts 27 : 16, see the R.V., "small island."

790 (6) In 1 Cor. 4 : 11, the verb *astateō*, to be unsettled, to lead a
AG:117B CB:— homeless life, is rendered "we . . . have no certain dwelling place."
The unsettlement conveyed by the word has suggested the meaning "we
CERTIFICATE See BILL are vagabonds" or "we lead a vagabond life," a probable significance.¶

C. Adverbs.

3689 1. ONTŌS (ὄντως), really, actually, verily (from *eimi*, to be), is
AG:574A CB:— translated "certainly" in Luke 23 : 47. See CLEAN, INDEED, TRUTH,
VERILY.

3843 AG:609B CB:— 2. PANTŌS (πάντως): see ALTOGETHER, B.

---

892 AG:129A

CHAFF

CB:— ACHURON (ἄχυρον), chaff, the stalk of the grain from which the kernels have been beaten out, or the straw broken up by a threshing machine, is found in Matt. 3 : 12 and Luke 3 : 17.¶

CHAIN

HALUSIS (ἅλυσις) denotes a chain or bond for binding the body, or 254
any part of it (the hands or feet). Some derive the word from *a*, negative, AG:41C CB:—
and *luō*, to loose, i.e., not to be loosed ; others from a root connected with
a word signifying to restrain. It is used in Mark 5 : 3, 4 ; Luke 8 : 29 ;
Acts 12 : 6, 7 ; 21 : 33 ; 28 : 20 ; Eph. 6 : 20 ; 2 Tim. 1 : 16 ; Rev. 20 : 1.
See Bond.¶

Notes : (1) Some ancient authorities have *seira*, a cord, rope, band, 4577
chain, in 2 Pet. 2 : 4, instead of *seiros*, a cavern, R.V., " pits." AG:746B CB:—
(2) In Jude 6 the R.V. renders *desmos* by " bonds " (for the A.V. 1199
" chains "). See Bond.¶ AG:176A CB:1240C

CHALCEDONY

CHALKĒDŌN (χαλκηδών), the name of a gem, including several 5472
varieties, one of which resembles a cornelian, is " supposed to denote a AG:874D CB:1239B
green silicate of copper found in the mines near Chalcedon " (*Swete, on
the Apocalypse*), Rev. 21 : 19.¶ CHALLENGE See PROVOKE

CHAMBER (Store-chamber)

1. TAMEION (ταμεῖον) denotes, firstly, a store-chamber, then, any 5009
private room, secret chamber, Matt. 6 : 6 ; R.V., " inner chamber " AG:803C CB:—
(A.V., " closet ") ; 24 : 26, " inner (A.V., secret) chambers ; " Luke 12 : 3,
R.V., ditto, for A.V., " closets ; " it is used in Luke 12 : 24 (" store-
chamber ") of birds.¶

2. HUPERŌON (ὑπερῷον), the neuter of *huperōos*, " above," denotes 5253
an upper room, upper chamber (*huper*, above), Acts 1 : 13 ; 9 : 37, 39 ; AG:842B CB:—
20 : 8. See Room.¶

CHAMBERING

KOITĒ (κοίτη), primarily a place in which to lie down, hence, a bed, 2845
especially the marriage bed, denotes, in Rom. 13 : 13, illicit intercourse. AG:440A CB:1255B
See Bed, Conceive.

CHAMBERLAIN

HO EPI TOU KOITŌNOS, lit., the (one) over the bedchamber (*epi*, KOITŌN 2846
over, *koitōn*, a bedchamber), denotes a chamberlain, an officer who had AG:440B
various duties in the houses of kings and nobles. The importance of the CB:—
position is indicated by the fact that the people of Tyre and Sidon sought
the favour of Herod Agrippa through the mediation of Blastus, Acts 12 : 20.

Note : In Rom. 16 : 23, *oikonomos*, a person who manages the domestic 3623
affairs of a family, in general, a manager, a steward, is translated AG:560A CB:1260B
" chamberlain " in the A.V., which the R.V. corrects to " treasurer."

CHANCE

4795 AG:775A 1. SUNKURIA (συγκυρία), lit., a meeting together with, a coincidence
CB:— of circumstances, a happening, is translated " chance " in Luke 10 : 31.
TUNCHANŌ But concurrence of events is what the word signifies, rather than chance.¶
5177 *Note :* Some texts have *tucha* here (from *tunchanō*, to happen).
AG:829B CB:— 2. EI TUCHOI (εἰ τύχοι), lit., ' if it may happen ' (*ei*, if, *tunchanō*,
to happen), signifies " it may chance," 1 Cor. 15 : 37.¶

CHANGE (Noun and Verb)

A. Noun.

3331 AG:511A METATHESIS (μετάθεσις), a transposition, or a transference from
CB:1258C one place to another (from *meta*, implying change, and *tithēmi*, to put), has the meaning of change in Heb. 7 : 12, in connection with the necessity of a change of the Law (or, as margin, law), if the priesthood is changed (see B, No. 3). It is rendered " translation " in 11 : 5, " removing " in 12 : 27. See REMOVING, TRANSLATION.¶

B. Verbs.

236 1. ALLASSŌ (ἀλλάσσω), to make other than it is (from *allos*, another),
AG:39A CB:1234C to transform, change, is used (*a*) of the effect of the Gospel upon the precepts of the Law, Acts 6 : 14 ; (*b*) of the effect, on the body of a believer, of Christ's Return, 1 Cor. 15 : 51, 52 ; (*c*) of the final renewal of the material creation, Heb. 1 : 12 ; (*d*) of a change in the Apostle's mode of speaking (or dealing), Gal. 4 : 20. In Rom. 1 : 23 it has its other meaning, to exchange.¶

3337 AG:511C 2. METALLASSŌ (μεταλλάσσω), from *meta*, implying change, and
CB:1258C No. 1, to change one thing for another, or into another, Rom. 1 : 25, 26, is translated " exchange " in ver. 25. See EXCHANGE.¶

3346 AG:513C 3. METATITHĒMI (μετατίθημι), to place differently, to change,
CB:1258C (akin to A, above), is said of priesthood, Heb. 7 : 12. See CARRY, No. 5.

3328 4. METABALLŌ (μεταβάλλω), *meta*, as in No. 2, and *ballō*, to throw,
AG:510D CB:— signifies to turn quickly, or, in the Middle Voice, to change one's mind,
METASCHĒMATIZŌ and is found in Acts 28 : 6.¶

3345 AG:513B *Notes :* (1) In Phil. 3 : 21, for the A.V. rendering of *metaschēmatizō*,
CB:1258C " change," the R.V. has " fashion anew ; " in 2 Cor. 3 : 18 *metamorphoō*
METAMORPHOŌ is rendered " change," in the A.V. (R.V., " transform ").

3339 AG:511D CB:1258C (2) For *metanoia*, a change of mind, see REPENTANCE.

CHANGER (Money-changer)

2855 AG:442A 1. KOLLUBISTĒS (κολλυβιστής), from *kollubos* (lit., clipped), a small
CB:— coin or rate of change (*koloboō* signifies to cut off, to clip, shorten, Matt. 24 : 22), denotes a money-changer, lit., money-clipper, Matt. 21 : 12 ; Mark 11 : 15 ; John 2 : 15.¶

2773 AG:429D 2. KERMATISTĒS (κερματιστής), from *kermatizō* (not found in the
CB:— N.T.), to cut into small pieces, to make small change (*kerma* signifies a small coin, John 2 : 15 ; akin to *keirō*, to cut short). In the court of the

Gentiles, in the Temple precincts, were the seats of those who sold
selected and approved animals for sacrifice, and other things. The
magnitude of this traffic had introduced the bankers' or brokers' business,
John 2 : 14.¶ CHANT See SING

CHARGE (Nouns, Adjective and Verbs), CHARGEABLE

A. Nouns.

(*a*) *With the meaning of an accusation.*

1. AITIA (αἰτία), a cause, accusation, is rendered " charges " in 156
Acts 25 : 27 (A.V., " crimes ") ; cp. ver. 18. See ACCUSATION, CAUSE. AG:26B CB:1234A

2. AITIŌMA (αἰτίωμα), in some texts *aitiama*, denotes a charge, 157 (-AMA)
Acts 25 : 7. See ACCUSATION, A, No. 2. AG:26D CB:1234A

3. ENKLĒMA (ἔγκλημα) : see ACCUSATION, A, No. 3. 1462

(*b*) *With the meaning of something committed or bestowed.* AG:216B

4. KLĒROS (κλῆρος), a lot, allotment, heritage (whence Eng. CB:1245A 2819
" clergy "), is translated in 1 Pet. 5 : 3, R.V., " the charge allotted to AG:435B
you ; " here the word is in the plural, lit., ' charges.' See INHERITANCE, CB:1255B
LOT, PART.

5. OPSŌNION (ὀψώνιον), from *opson*, meat, and *ōneomai*, to buy, 3800
primarily signified whatever is brought to be eaten with bread, provisions, AG:602A CB:1261A
supplies for an army, soldier's pay, " charges," 1 Cor. 9 : 7, of the service
of a soldier. It is rendered " wages " in Luke 3 : 14 ; Rom. 6 : 23 ;
2 Cor. 11 : 8. See WAGES.¶

6. PARANGELIA (παραγγελία), a proclamation, a command or 3852
commandment, is strictly used of commands received from a superior AG:613A CB:1262B
and transmitted to others. It is rendered " charge " in Acts. 16 : 24 ;
1 Thess. 4 : 2, R.V. (where the word is in the plural) ; 1 Tim. 1 : 5 (R.V.)
and ver. 18. In Acts 5 : 28 the lit. meaning is ' Did we not charge you
with a charge ? ' See also COMMANDMENT, STRAITLY. Cp. C, No. 8,
below.¶

B. Adjective.

ADAPANOS (ἀδάπανος), lit., ' without expense ' (*a*, negative, and 77
dapanē, expense, cost), is used in 1 Cor. 9 : 18, " without charge " (of AG:15C CB:—
service in the Gospel).¶

C. Verbs.

1. DIAMARTUROMAI (διαμαρτύρομαι), a strengthened form of 1263
marturomai (*dia*, through, intensive), is used in the Middle Voice ; AG:186C CB:1241B
primarily it signifies to testify through and through, bear a solemn
witness ; hence, to charge earnestly, 1 Tim. 5 : 21 ; 2 Tim. 2 : 14 ; 4 : 1.
See TESTIFY, WITNESS.

2. DIASTELLOMAI (διαστέλλομαι), lit., to draw asunder (*dia*, asunder, 1291
stellō, to draw), signifies to admonish, order, charge, Matt. 16 : 20 ; Mark AG:188D CB:1241B
5 : 43 ; 7 : 36 (twice) ; 8 : 15 ; 9 : 9. In Acts 15 : 24 it is translated
" gave commandment ; " in Heb. 12 : 20, A.V., " commanded," R.V.,
" enjoined." See COMMAND, *Note* (2).¶

3. DIATASSŌ (διατάσσω): see APPOINT, No. 6.
1690 AG:254D 4. EMBRIMAOMAI (ἐμβριμάομαι), from *en*, in, intensive, and *brimē*,
CB:1244B strength, primarily signifies to snort with anger, as of horses. Used of
men it signifies to fret, to be painfully moved; then, to express indignation
against; hence, to rebuke sternly, to charge strictly, Matt. 9:30; Mark
1:43; it is rendered "murmured against" in Mark 14:5; "groaned"
in John 11:33; "groaning" in ver. 38. See GROAN, MURMUR.¶
5. ENKALEŌ (ἐγκαλέω): see ACCUSE, B, No. 2.
1781 AG:268B 6. ENTELLOMAI (ἐντέλλομαι), to order, command, enjoin (from *en*,
CB:1245B in, used intensively, and *teleō*, to fulfil), is translated by the verb to give
charge, Matt. 4:6; 17:9 (A.V.); Luke 4:10. See COMMAND, ENJOIN.
2008 AG:303B 7. EPITIMAŌ (ἐπιτιμάω) signifies (*a*) to put honour upon (*epi*, upon,
CB:1246B *timē*, honour); (*b*) to adjudge, to find fault with, rebuke; hence to charge,
or rather, to charge strictly (*epi*, intensive), e.g., Matt. 12:16; Mark
3:12, "charged much;" Mark 8:30; in 10:48, R.V., "rebuked."
See REBUKE.
3853 AG:613B 8. PARANGELLŌ (παραγγέλλω), lit., to announce beside (*para*,
CB:1262B beside, *angellō*, to announce), to hand on an announcement from one to
another, usually denotes to command, to charge, Luke 5:14; 8:56;
1 Cor. 7:10 (A.V., "command"), "give charge," R.V.; 11:17, "in
giving you this charge," R.V.; 1 Tim. 1:3; 6:13, R.V., and 6:17.
It is rendered by the verb to charge in the R.V. of Acts 1:4; 4:18;
5:28; 15:5; 1 Thess. 4:11. See Acts 5:28 under A, No. 6. See
4256 COMMAND, DECLARE.
AG:702C 9. PROAITIAOMAI (προαιτιάομαι), to accuse beforehand, to have
CB:— already brought a charge (*pro*, before, *aitia*, an accusation), is used in
5083 AG:814D Rom. 3:9, "we before laid to the charge."¶
CB:1271B MARTUREō 10. TĒREŌ (τηρέω), to keep, to guard, is translated "to be kept in
AG:492C charge," in Acts 24:23; 25:4, R.V. (A.V., "kept"). See HOLD, KEEP,
CB:1257C ENORKIZō OBSERVE, PRESERVE, WATCH.
Cf. 3726 AG:267C *Notes:* (1) *Martureō*, to testify, translated "charged" in 1 Thess.
CB:— 2:11, A.V., is found there in the most authentic mss. and translated
HORKIZō "testifying" in the R.V. (2) *Enorkizō*, to adjure (*en*, in, used inten-
3726 AG:581B sively, *horkos*, an oath), is translated "I adjure," in 1 Thess. 5:27, R.V.,
CB:1251B EPITASSō for A.V., "I charge." Some mss. have *horkizō* here. (3) The following
2004 are translated by the verb to charge or to be chargeable in the A.V., but
AG:302B CB:1246A differently in the R.V., and will be found under the word BURDEN:
DAPANAō *bareō*, B, No. 1; *epibareō*, B, No. 2; *katanarkaō*, B, No. 5. (4) *Epitassō*,
1159 AG:171A to command, is so translated in Mark 9:25, R.V., for the A.V., "charge."
CB:— LOGIZOMAI (5) *Dapanaō*, to be at the expense of anything (cp. B, above), is translated
3049 "be at charges," in Acts 21:24. See CONSUME, SPEND. (6) In 2 Tim.
AG:475D CB:1257A 4:16, *logizomai* is rendered "laid to (their) charge," A.V.; R.V., ". . .
HISTēMI account." (7) In Acts 8:27, the R.V. translates the verb *eimi*, to be,
2476 AG:381D with *epi*, over, "was over," A.V., "had the charge of." (8) In Acts 7:
CB:1250C 60 *histēmi*, to cause to stand, is rendered "lay . . . to the charge."

CHARGER

PINAX (πίναξ), primarily a board or plank, came to denote various 4094
articles of wood; hence, a wooden trencher, charger, Matt. 14:8, 11; AG:658C
Mark 6:25, 28; Luke 11:39. See PLATTER.¶ CB:—

CHARIOT

1. HARMA (ἅρμα), akin to *ararisko*, to join, denotes a war chariot 716
with two wheels, Acts 8:28, 29, 38; Rev. 9:9.¶ AG:107B
CB:1249B
2. RHEDĒ (ῥέδη), a waggon with four wheels, was chiefly used for 4480 (-DA)
travelling purposes, Rev. 18:13.¶ AG:734D
CB:—

For CHARITY see LOVE

CHARISMA
See GIFT

CHASTE

HAGNOS (ἁγνός) signifies (*a*) pure from every fault, immaculate,
2 Cor. 7:11 (A.V., "clear"); Phil. 4:8; 1 Tim. 5:22; Jas. 3:17;
1 John 3:3 (in all which the R.V. rendering is "pure"), and 1 Pet. 3:2,
"chaste;" (*b*) pure from carnality, modest, 2 Cor. 11:2, R.V., "pure;" 53 AG:11D
Tit. 2:5, "chaste." See CLEAR, HOLY, PURE.¶ CB:1249A

Note: Cp. *hagios*, holy, as being free from admixture of evil; *hosios*, holy, as being free from defilement; *eilikrinēs*, pure, as being tested, lit., judged by the sunlight; *katharos*, pure, as being cleansed.

CHASTEN, CHASTENING, CHASTISE, CHASTISEMENT

A. Verb.

PAIDEUŌ (παιδεύω) primarily denotes to train children, suggesting 3811
the broad idea of education (*pais*, a child), Acts 7:22; 22:3; see also AG:603D
Tit. 2:12, "instructing" (R.V.), here of a training gracious and firm; CB:1261C
grace, which brings salvation, employs means to give us full possession of it; hence, to chastise, this being part of the training, whether (*a*) by correcting with words, reproving, and admonishing, 1 Tim. 1:20 (R.V., "be taught"); 2 Tim. 2:25, or (*b*) by chastening by the infliction of evils and calamities, 1 Cor. 11:32; 2 Cor. 6:9; Heb. 12:6, 7, 10; Rev. 3:19. The verb also has the meaning to chastise with blows, to scourge, said of the command of a judge, Luke 23:16, 22. See CORRECTION, B, INSTRUCT, LEARN, TEACH, and cp. CHILD (Nos. 4 to 6).¶

CHATTER
See
TALK(ING)
CHEAT
See
WRONG

B. Noun.

PAIDEIA (παιδεία) denotes the training of a child, including 3809
instruction; hence, discipline, correction, "chastening," Eph. 6:4, AG:603B
R.V. (A.V., "nurture"), suggesting the Christian discipline that regulates CB:1261B
character; so in Heb. 12:5, 7, 8 (in ver. 8, A.V., "chastisement," the R.V. corrects to "chastening"); in 2 Tim. 3:16, "instruction." See INSTRUCTION, NURTURE.¶

CHEEK

4600 AG:749C SIAGŌN (σιαγών) primarily denotes the jaw, the jaw-bone ; hence
CB:— " cheek," Matt. 5 : 39 ; Luke 6 : 29.¶

CHEER, CHEERFUL, CHEERFULLY, CHEERFULNESS

A. Verbs.

2114 AG:320D 1. EUTHUMEŌ (εὐθυμέω) signifies, in the Active Voice, to put in
CB:— good spirits, to make cheerful (*eu*, well, *thumos*, mind or passion) ; or, intransitively, to be cheerful, Acts 27 : 22, 25 ; Jas. 5 : 13 (R.V., " cheerful," for A.V., " merry "). See MERRY.¶

2293 AG:352A 2. THARSEŌ (θαρσέω), to be of good courage, of good cheer (*tharsos*,
CB:1271C courage, confidence), is used only in the Imperative Mood, in the N.T. ; " be of good cheer," Matt. 9 : 2, 22 ; 14 : 27 ; Mark 6 : 50 ; 10 : 49 ; Luke 8 : 48 ; John 16 : 33 ; Acts 23 : 11. See BOLD, A, No. 1, COMFORT, COURAGE.¶

B. Adjectives.

2115 AG:320D 1. EUTHUMOS (εὔθυμος) means of good cheer (see A, No. 1), Acts
CB:— 27 : 36.¶

2431 AG:375B 2. HILAROS (ἱλαρός), from *hileōs*, propitious, signifies that readiness
CB:1250C of mind, that joyousness, which is prompt to do anything ; hence, cheerful (Eng., hilarious), 2 Cor. 9 : 7, " God loveth a cheerful (hilarious) giver."¶

Note : In the Sept. the verb *hilarunō* translates a Hebrew word meaning " to cause to shine," in Ps. 104 : 15.¶

C. Adverb.

2115 (-MOS) EUTHUMŌS (εὐθύμως), cheerfully (see A, No. 1), is found in the
AG:320D most authentic mss., in Acts 24 : 10, instead of the comparative degree,
CB:— *euthumoteron*.¶

D. Noun.

2432 AG:375B HILAROTĒS (ἱλαρότης), cheerfulness (akin to B, No. 2), is used in
CB:— Rom. 12 : 8, in connection with shewing mercy.¶

CHERISH

2282 AG:350B THALPŌ (θάλπω) primarily means to heat, to soften by heat ; then,
CB:— to keep warm, as of birds covering their young with their feathers, Deut. 22 : 6, Sept. ; metaphorically, to cherish with tender love, to foster with tender care, in Eph. 5 : 29 of Christ and the Church ; in 1 Thess. 2 : 7 of the care of the saints at Thessalonica by the Apostle and his associates, as of a nurse for her children.¶

CHERUBIM

5502 AG:881B CHEROUBIM (χερουβίμ) are regarded by some as the ideal
(-OUB) representatives of redeemed animate creation. In the Tabernacle and
CB:1239C Temple they were represented by the two golden figures of two-winged living-creatures. They were all of one piece with the golden lid of the Ark of the Covenant in the Holy of Holies, signifying that the prospect

of redeemed and glorified creatures was bound up with the sacrifice of Christ.

This in itself would indicate that they represent redeemed human beings in union with Christ, a union seen, figuratively, proceeding out of the Mercy Seat. Their faces were towards this Mercy Seat, suggesting a consciousness of the means whereby union with Christ has been produced.

The first reference to the cherubim is in Gen. 3 : 24, which should read '. . . at the East of the Garden of Eden He caused to dwell in a tabernacle the cherubim, and the flaming sword which turned itself to keep the way of the Tree of Life.' This was not simply to keep fallen human beings out; the presence of the cherubim suggests that redeemed men, restored to God on God's conditions, would have access to the Tree of Life. (See Rev. 22 : 14).

Certain other references in the O.T. give clear indication that angelic beings are upon occasion in view, e.g., Psalm 18 : 10; Ezek. 28 : 4. So with the Vision of the Cherubim in Ezek. 10 : 1–20; 11 : 22. In the N.T. the word is found in Heb. 9 : 5, where the reference is to the Ark in the Tabernacle, and the thought is suggested of those who minister to the manifestation of the glory of God.

We may perhaps conclude, therefore, that, inasmuch as in the past and in the present angelic beings have functioned and do function administratively in the service of God, and that redeemed man in the future is to act administratively in fellowship with Him, the Cherubim in Scripture represent one or other of these two groups of created beings according to what is set forth in the various passages relating to them.¶

For CHICKEN see BROOD

CHIEF, CHIEFEST, CHIEFLY

A. Adjective.

PRŌTOS (πρῶτος) denotes the first, whether in time or place. It is translated "chief" in Mark 6 : 21, R.V., of men of Galilee; in Acts 13 : 50, of men in a city; in 28 : 7, of the chief man in the island of Melita; in 17 : 4, of chief women in a city; in 28 : 17, of Jews; in 1 Tim. 1 : 15, 16, of a sinner. In the following, where the A.V. has "chief," or "chiefest," the R.V. renderings are different: Matt. 20 : 27 and Mark 10 : 44, "first;" Luke 19 : 47 and Acts 25 : 2, "principal men;" Acts 16 : 12, said of Philippi, "the first (city) of the district," R.V., for incorrect A.V., "the chief city of that part of Macedonia." Amphipolis was the chief city of that part. *Prōtos* here must mean the first in the direction in which the Apostle came. See BEGINNING, BEFORE, BEST, FIRST, FORMER. **4413 AG:725B CB:1267B**

B. Nouns.

1. KEPHALAION (κεφάλαιον), akin to the adjective *kephalaios*, **2774 AG:429D CB:1255A**

belonging to the head, and *kephalē*, the head, denotes the chief point or principal thing in a subject, Heb. 8 : 1, " the chief point is this " (A.V., " the sum ") ; elsewhere in Acts 22 : 28 (of principal, as to money), " (a great) sum." See SUM.¶

Certain compound nouns involving the significance of chief, are as follows :

749 AG:112D CB:1237B 2. ARCHIEREUS (ἀρχιερεύς), a chief priest, high priest (*archē*, first, *hiereus*, a priest), is frequent in the Gospels, Acts and Hebrews, but there only in the N.T. It is used of Christ, e.g., in Heb. 2 : 17 ; 3 : 1 ; of chief priests, including ex-high-priests and members of their families, e.g., Matt. 2 : 4 ; Mark 8 : 31.

750 AG:113A CB:1237B 3. ARCHIPOIMĒN (ἀρχιποίμην), a chief shepherd (*archē*, chief, *poimēn*, a shepherd), is said of Christ only, 1 Pet. 5 : 4. Modern Greeks use it of tribal chiefs.¶

754 AG:113B CB:1237B 4. ARCHITELŌNĒS (ἀρχιτελώνης) denotes a chief tax-collector, or publican, Luke 19 : 2.¶

204 AG:33D CB:1234B 5. AKROGŌNIAIOS (ἀκρογωνιαῖος) denotes a chief corner-stone (from *akros*, highest, extreme, *gōnia*, a corner, angle), Eph. 2 : 20 and 1 Pet. 2 : 6.¶ In the Sept., Is. 28 : 16.¶

4410 AG:725B CB:1267B 6. PRŌTOKATHEDRIA (πρωτοκαθεδρία), a sitting in the first or chief seat (*prōtos*, first, *kathedra*, a seat), is found in Matt. 23 : 6 ; Mark 12 : 39 ; Luke 11 : 43 ; 20 : 46.¶

4411 AG:725B CB:1267B 7. PRŌTOKLISIA (πρωτοκλισία), the first reclining place, the chief place at table (from *prōtos*, and *klisia*, a company reclining at a meal ; cp. *klinō*, to incline), is found in Matt. 23 : 6 ; Mark 12 : 39 (as with No. 6) ; Luke 14 : 7, 8 ; 20 : 46.¶

8. CHILIARCHOS (χιλίαρχος) denotes a chief captain : see CAPTAIN, No. 1.

775 AG:116A CB:— 9. ASIARCHĒS (Ἀσιαρχής), an Asiarch, was one of certain officers elected by various cities in the province of Asia, whose function consisted in celebrating, partly at their own expense, the public games and festivals ; in Acts 19 : 31, R.V., the word is translated " chief officers of Asia " (A.V., " chief of Asia ").

It seems probable, according to Prof. Ramsay, that they were " the high priests of the temples of the Imperial worship in various cities of Asia ; " further, that " the Council of the Asiarchs sat at stated periods in the great cities alternately . . . and were probably assembled at Ephesus for such a purpose when they sent advice to St. Paul to consult his safety." A festival would have brought great crowds to the city.¶

758 AG:113D CB:1237B 10. ARCHŌN (ἄρχων), a ruler, is rendered " chief " in the A.V. of Luke 14 : 1 (R.V., " ruler ") ; " chief rulers," in John 12 : 42, R.V., " rulers (of the people)," i.e., of members of the Sanhedrin ; " chief," in Luke 11 : 15 (R.V., " prince "), in reference to Beelzebub, the prince of demons. See MAGISTRATE, PRINCE, RULER.

752 AG:113B CB:— 11. ARCHISUNAGŌGOS (ἀρχισυνάγωγος), a ruler of a synagogue,

translated " chief ruler of the synagogue," in Acts 18 : 8, 17, A.V., was the administrative officer supervising the worship.

C. Verb.

HĒGEOMAI (ἡγέομαι), to lead the way, to preside, rule, be the chief, **2233**
is used of the ambition to be chief among the disciples of Christ, Luke **AG:343C**
22 : 26 ; of Paul as the chief speaker in Gospel testimony at Lystra, **CB:1249C**
Acts 14 : 12 ; of Judas and Silas, as chief (or rather, 'leading') men among the brethren at Jerusalem, Acts 15 : 22. See ACCOUNT, COUNT, ESTEEM, GOVERNOR, JUDGE, SUPPOSE, THINK.

D. Adverbs.

1. HUPERLIAN (ὑπερλίαν), chiefest (*huper*, over, *lian*, exceedingly, **After 5244**
pre-eminently, very much), is used in 2 Cor. 11 : 5 ; 12 : 11, of Paul's **AG:841B**
place among the Apostles.¶ **CB:—**

2. MALISTA (μάλιστα), the superlative of *mala*, very, very much, is **3122**
rendered " chiefly " in 2 Pet. 2 : 10 and in the A.V. of Phil. 4 : 22 (R.V., **AG:488D**
" especially "). See ESPECIALLY, MOST. **CB:—**

Note: In Rom. 3 : 2, R.V., the adverb *prōton* is translated " first of **4412**
all " (A.V., " chiefly "). **AG:725**
(-OS)
CB:1267B

CHILD, CHILDREN, CHILD-BEARING, CHILDISH, CHILDLESS

1. TEKNON (τέκνον), a child (akin to *tiktō*, to beget, bear), is used in **5043**
both the natural and the figurative senses. In contrast to *huios*, son **AG:808B**
(see below), it gives prominence to the fact of birth, whereas *huios* stresses **CB:1271B**
the dignity and character of the relationship. Figuratively, *teknon* is used of children of (*a*) God, John 1 : 12 ; (*b*) light, Eph. 5 : 8 ; (*c*) obedience, 1 Pet. 1 : 14 ; (*d*) a promise, Rom. 9 : 8 ; Gal. 4 : 28 ; (*e*) the Devil, 1 John 3 : 10 ; (*f*) wrath, Eph. 2 : 3 ; (*g*) cursing, 2 Pet. 2 : 14 ; (*h*) spiritual relationship, 2 Tim. 2 : 1 ; Philm. 10. See DAUGHTER, SON.

2. TEKNION (τεκνίον), a little child, a diminutive of No. 1, is used **5040**
only figuratively in the N.T., and always in the plural. It is found **AG:808A**
frequently in 1 John, see 2 : 1, 12, 28 ; 3 : 7, 18 ; 4 : 4 ; 5 : 21 ; elsewhere, **CB:1271B**
once in John's Gospel, 13 : 33, once in Paul's Epistles, Gal. 4 : 19. It is a term of affection by a teacher to his disciples under circumstances requiring a tender appeal, e.g., of Christ to the Twelve just before His death ; the Apostle John used it in warning believers against spiritual dangers ; Paul, because of the deadly errors of Judaism assailing the Galatian churches. Cp. his use of *teknon* in Gal. 4 : 28.¶

3. HUIOS (υἱός), a son, is always so translated in the R.V., except **5207**
in the phrase " children of Israel," e.g., Matt. 27 : 9 ; and with reference **AG:833C**
to a foal, Matt. 21 : 5. The A.V. does not discriminate between *teknon* **CB:1251C**
and *huios*. In the 1st Ep. of John, the Apostle reserves the word for the Son of God. See *teknia*, " little children " (above), and *tekna*, " children," in John 1 : 12 ; 11 : 52. See *paidion* (below). For the other use of
huios, indicating the quality of that with which it is connected, see SON. **3816** **AG:604C**

4. PAIS (παῖς) signifies (*a*) a child in relation to descent, (*b*) a boy or **CB:1261C**

girl in relation to age, (*c*) a servant, attendant, maid, in relation to condition. As an instance of (*a*) see Matt. 21 : 15, " children," and Acts 20 : 12 (R.V., " lad "). In regard to (*b*) the R.V. has " boy " in Matt. 17 : 18 and Luke 9 : 42. In Luke 2 : 43 it is used of the Lord Jesus. In regard to (*c*), see Matt. 8 : 6, 8, 13, etc. As to (*a*) note Matt. 2 : 16, R.V., " male children." See MAID, MANSERVANT, SERVANT, SON, YOUNG MAN.

3813 5. PAIDION (παιδίον), a diminutive of *pais*, signifies a little or young
AG:604A CB:1261C child ; it is used of an infant just born, John 16 : 21 ; of a male child recently born, e.g., Matt. 2 : 8 ; Heb. 11 : 23 ; of a more advanced child, Mark 9 : 24 ; of a son, John 4 : 49 ; of a girl, Mark 5 : 39, 40, 41 ; in the plural, of children, e.g., Matt. 14 : 21. It is used metaphorically of believers who are deficient in spiritual understanding, 1 Cor. 14 : 20, and in affectionate and familiar address by the Lord to His disciples, almost like the Eng., " lads," John 21 : 5 ; by the Apostle John to the youngest believers in the family of God, 1 John 2 : 13, 18 ; there it is to be distinguished from *teknia*, which term he uses in addressing all his readers (vv. 1, 12, 28 : see *teknia*, above). See DAMSEL.

3812 AG:604A *Note :* The adverb *paidiothen*, " from (or of) a child," is found in
CB:— Mark 9 : 21.¶

3808 6. PAIDARION (παιδάριον), another diminutive of *pais*, is used of
AG:603B CB:1261B boys and girls, in Matt. 11 : 16 (the best texts have *paidiois* here), and a lad, John 6 : 9 ; the tendency in colloquial Greek was to lose the diminutive character of the word.¶

3516 AG:357C 7. NĒPIOS (νήπιος), lit., not-speaking (from *nē*, a negative, and *epos*,
CB:1259C a word is rendered " childish " in 1 Cor. 13 : 11 : see BABE.

3439 8. MONOGENĒS (μονογενής), lit., only-begotten, is translated " only
AG:527B CB:1259B child " in Luke 9 : 38. See ONLY, ONLY-BEGOTTEN.

5042 9. TEKNOGONIA (τεκνογονία), *teknon* and a root *gen*—, whence *gennaō*,
AG:808B CB:1271B to beget, denotes bearing children, implying the duties of motherhood, 1 Tim. 2 : 15.¶

B. Verbs.

3515 AG:537C 1. NĒPIAZŌ (νηπιάζω), to be a babe, is used in 1 Cor. 14 : 20, " (in
CB:— malice) be ye babes " (akin to No 7, above).¶

5044 2. TEKNOTROPHEŌ (τεκνοτροφέω), to rear young, *teknon*, and
AG:808D CB:1271B *trephō*, to rear, signifies to bring up children, 1 Tim. 5 : 10.¶

5041 3. TEKNOGONEŌ (τεκνογονέω), to bear children (*teknon*, and
AG:808A CB:1271B *gennaō*, to beget), see No. 9 above, is found in 1 Tim. 5 : 14.¶

C. Adjectives.

1471 AG:216D 1. ENKUOS (ἔγκυος) denotes " great with child " (*en*, in, and *kuō*,
CB:— to conceive), Luke 2 : 5.¶

5388 2. PHILOTEKNOS (φιλότεκνος), from *phileō*, to love, and *teknon*,
AG:861C CB:1264B signifies loving one's children, Tit. 2 : 4.¶

815 3. ATEKNOS (ἄτεκνος), from *a*, negative, and *teknon*, signifies " child-
AG:119D CB:— less," Luke 20 : 28, 29, 30.¶

Notes : (1) For *brephos*, a new born babe, always rendered " babe "

or " babes " in the R.V. (A.V., " young children ", Acts 7 : 19 ; " child," 1025
2 Tim. 3 : 15), see under Babe. AG:147B CB:1239B
(2) *Huiothesia*, " adoption of children," in the A.V. of Eph. 1 : 5, is 5206
corrected to " adoption as sons " in the R.V. See on Adoption. AG:833B CB:1251C

CHOKE

1. PNIGŌ (πνίγω) is used, in the Passive Voice, of perishing by 4155
drowning, Mark 5 : 13 ; in the Active, to seize a person's throat, to throttle, AG:679D CB:1265C
Matt. 18 : 28. See Throat.¶
2. APOPNIGŌ (ἀποπνίγω), a strengthened form of No. 1 (*apo*, from, 638
intensive ; cp. Eng., to choke off), is used metaphorically, of thorns AG:97C CB:1237A
crowding out seed sown and preventing its growth, Matt. 13 : 7 ; Luke
8 : 7. It is Luke's word for suffocation by drowning, Luke 8 : 33 (cp.
Mark 5 : 13, above).¶
3. SUMPNIGŌ (συμπνίγω) gives the suggestion of choking together 4846
(*sun*, with), i.e., by crowding, Matt. 13 : 22 ; Mark 4 : 7, 19 ; Luke 8 : 14. AG:779D CB:1270B
It is used in Luke 8 : 42, of the crowd that thronged the Lord, almost,
so to speak, to suffocation.¶

CHOICE, CHOOSE, CHOSEN

A. Verbs.

1. EKLEGŌ (ἐκλέγω), to pick out, select, means, in the Middle Voice, (-OMAI)
to choose for oneself, not necessarily implying the rejection of what is 1586 AG:242B
not chosen, but choosing with the subsidiary ideas of kindness or favour CB:1243C
or love, Mark 13 : 20 ; Luke 6 : 13 ; 9 : 35 (R.V.) ; 10 : 42 ; 14 : 7 ;
John 6 : 70 ; 13 : 18 ; 15 : 16, 19 ; Acts 1 : 2, 24 ; 6 : 5 ; 13 : 17 ; 15 : 22,
25 ; in 15 : 7 it is rendered " made choice ; " 1 Cor. 1 : 27, 28 ; Eph. 1 : 4 ;
Jas. 2 : 5.¶
2. EPILEGŌ (ἐπιλέγω), in the Middle Voice, signifies to choose, 1951
either in addition or in succession to another. It has this meaning in (-OMAI)
Acts 15 : 40, of Paul's choice of Silas. For its other meaning, to call or AG:295C CB:1246A
name, John 5 : 2, see Call.¶
3. HAIREŌ (αἱρέω), to take, is used in the Middle Voice only, in the 138
sense of taking for oneself, choosing, 2 Thess. 2 : 13, of a choice made by (-OMAI)
God (as in Deut. 7 : 6, 7 ; 26 : 18, Sept.) ; in Phil. 1 : 22 and Heb. 11 : 25, AG:24A CB:1249A
of human choice. Its special significance is to select rather by the act of
taking, than by shewing preference or favour.¶
4. HAIRETIZŌ (αἱρετίζω), akin to the verbal adjective *hairetos*, 140
that which may be taken (see No. 3), signifies to take, with the implication AG:24A CB:1249A
that what is taken is eligible or suitable ; hence, to choose, by reason of
this suitability, Matt. 12 : 18, of God's delight in Christ as His " chosen."¶
It is frequent in the Sept., e.g., Gen. 30 : 20 ; Num. 14 : 8 ; Psa. 25 : 12 ;
119 : 30, 173 ; 132 : 13, 14 ; Hos. 4 : 18 ; Hag. 2 : 23 (" he hath chosen the
Canaanites ") ; Zech. 1 : 17 ; 2 : 12 ; Mal. 3 : 17. 5500
5. CHEIROTONEŌ (χειροτονέω) : see Appoint, No. 11. AG:881A CB:1239C

4401 AG:724C CB:1266C 6. PROCHEIROTONEŌ (προχειροτονέω) signifies to choose before, Acts 10 : 41, where it is used of a choice made before by God.¶

Notes : (1) For *procheirizō* see APPOINT, No. 12.

4758 AG:770D CB:1270A (2) *Stratologeō*, in 2 Tim. 2 : 4 (A.V., "chosen to be a soldier"), signifies to enrol as a soldier (R.V.). See SOLDIER.

B. Adjective.

1588 AG:242D CB:1243C EKLEKTOS (ἐκλεκτός), akin to A, No. 1, signifies chosen out, select, e.g., Matt. 22 : 14 ; Luke 23 : 35 ; Rom 16 : 13 (perhaps in the sense of eminent) ; Rev. 17 : 14. In 1 Pet. 2 : 4, 9, the R.V. translates it "elect." See ELECT.

C. Noun.

1589 AG:243A CB:1243C EKLOGĒ (ἐκλογή), akin to A, No. 1 and B, a picking out, choosing (Eng., eclogue), is translated "chosen" in Acts 9 : 15, lit., 'he is a vessel of choice unto Me.' In the six other places where this word is found it is translated "election." See ELECTION.

CHRIST

5547 AG:886D CB:1240A CHRISTOS (χριστός), anointed, translates, in the Sept., the word Messiah, a term applied to the priests who were anointed with the holy oil, particularly the High Priest, e.g., Lev. 4 : 3, 5, 16. The prophets are called *hoi christoi Theou*, "the anointed of God," Psa. 105 : 15. A king of Israel was described upon occasion as *christos tou Kuriou*, "the anointed of the Lord," 1 Sam. 2 : 10, 35 ; 2 Sam. 1 : 14 ; Ps. 2 : 2 ; 18 : 50 ; Hab. 3 : 13 ; the term is used even of Cyrus, Is. 45 : 1.

The title *ho Christos*, "the Christ," is not used of Christ in the Sept. Version of the Inspired Books of the O.T. In the N.T. the word is frequently used with the article, of the Lord Jesus, as an appellative rather than a title, e.g., Matt. 2 : 4 ; Acts 2 : 31 ; without the article, Luke 2 : 11 ; 23 : 2 ; John 1 : 41. Three times the title was expressly accepted by the Lord Himself, Matt. 16 : 17 ; Mark 14 : 61, 62 ; John 4 : 26.

It is added as an appellative to the proper name "Jesus," e.g., John 17 : 3, the only time when the Lord so spoke of Himself ; Acts 9 : 34 ; 1 Cor. 3 : 11 ; 1 John 5 : 6. It is distinctly a proper name in many passages, whether with the article, e.g., Matt. 1 : 17 ; 11 : 2 ; Rom. 7 : 4 ; 9 : 5 ; 15 : 19 ; 1 Cor. 1 : 6, or without the article, Mark 9 : 41 ; Rom. 6 : 4 ; 8 : 9, 17 ; 1 Cor. 1 : 12 ; Gal. 2 : 16. The single title *Christos* is sometimes used without the article to signify the One who by His Holy Spirit and power indwells believers and moulds their character in conformity to His likeness, Rom. 8 : 10 ; Gal. 2 : 20 ; 4 : 19 ; Eph. 3 : 17. As to the use or absence of the article, the title with the article specifies the Lord Jesus as "the Christ ;" the title without the article stresses His character and His relationship with believers. Again, speaking generally, when the title is the subject of a sentence it has the article ; when it forms part of the predicate the article is absent. See also JESUS.

FALSE CHRISTS

PSEUDOCHRISTOS (ψευδόχριστος) denotes one who falsely lays 5580
claim to the Name and office of the Messiah, Matt. 24 : 24 ; Mark 13 : 22.¶ AG:892B
See Note under ANTICHRIST. CB:1267C

CHRISTIAN

CHRISTIANOS (χριστιανός), Christian, a word formed after the 5546
Roman style, signifying an adherent of Jesus, was first applied to such by AG:886C
the Gentiles and is found in Acts 11 : 26 ; 26 : 28 ; 1 Pet. 4 : 16. CB:1240A

Though the word rendered " were called " in Acts 11 : 26 (see under CALL) might be used of a name adopted by oneself or given by others, the Christians do not seem to have adopted it for themselves in the times of the Apostles. In 1 Pet. 4 : 16, the Apostle is speaking from the point of view of the persecutor ; cp. " as a thief," " as a murderer." Nor is it likely that the appellation was given by Jews. As applied by Gentiles there was no doubt an implication of scorn, as in Agrippa's statement in Acts 26 : 28. Tacitus, writing near the end of the first century, says, " The vulgar call them Christians. The author or origin of this denomination, Christus, had, in the reign of Tiberius, been executed by the Procurator, Pontius Pilate " (Annals xv. 44). From the second century onward the term was accepted by believers as a title of honour.¶

CHRYSOLITE

CHRUSOLITHOS (χρυσόλιθος), lit., a gold stone (*chrusos*, gold, 5555
lithos, a stone), is the name of a precious stone of a gold colour, now called AG:888C
a topaz, Rev. 21 : 20 (see also Ex. 28 : 20 and Ezek. 28 : 13).¶ CB:1240B

CHRYSOPRASUS

CHRUSOPRASOS (χρυσόπρασος), from *chrusos*, gold, and *prasos*, 5556
a leek), is a precious stone like a leek in colour, a translucent, golden AG:888D
green. Pliny reckons it among the beryls. The word occurs in Rev. CB:1240B
21 : 20.¶

For CHURCH see ASSEMBLY and CONGREGATION

CINNAMON

KINNAMŌMON (κιννάμωμον) is derived from an Arabic word 2792
signifying to emit a smell ; the substance was an ingredient in the holy AG:432D
oil for anointing, Ex. 30 : 23. See also Prov. 7 : 17 and S. of S. 4 : 14. CB:—
In the N.T. it is found in Rev. 18 : 13. The cinnamon of the present day is the inner bark of an aromatic tree called *canella zeylanica*.¶

CIRCUIT

PERIERCHOMAI (περιέρχομαι), to go about (*peri*, about, *erchomai*, 4022
to go), is said of navigating a ship under difficulty owing to contrary AG:646D
CB:1263B

winds, Acts 28 : 13, R.V., "we made a circuit," for A.V., "we fetched a compass." See COMPASS, STROLLING, WANDER.

CIRCUMCISION, UNCIRCUMCISION, CIRCUMCISE

A. Nouns.

4061 AG:652D CB:1263C 1. PERITOMĒ (περιτομή), lit., a cutting round, circumcision (the verb is *peritemnō*), was a rite enjoined by God upon Abraham and his male descendants and dependents, as a sign of the covenant made with him, Gen. 17 ; Acts 7 : 8 ; Rom. 4 : 11. Hence Israelites termed Gentiles "the uncircumcised," Judg. 15 : 18 ; 2 Sam. 1 : 20. So in the N.T., but without the suggestion of contempt, e.g., Rom. 2 : 26 ; Eph. 2 : 11.

The rite had a moral significance, Ex. 6 : 12, 30, where it is metaphorically applied to the lips ; so to the ear, Jer. 6 : 10, and the heart, Deut. 30 : 6 ; Jer. 4 : 4. Cp. Jer. 9 : 25, 26. It refers to the state of circumcision, in Rom. 2 : 25–28 ; 3 : 1 ; 4 : 10 ; 1 Cor. 7 : 19 ; Gal. 5 : 6 ; 6 : 15 ; Col. 3 : 11.

"In the economy of grace no account is taken of any ordinance performed on the flesh ; the old racial distinction is ignored in the preaching of the Gospel, and faith is the sole condition upon which the favour of God in salvation is to be obtained, Rom. 10 : 11–13; 1 Cor. 7 : 19. See also Rom. 4 : 9–12."*

Upon the preaching of the Gospel to, and the conversion of, Gentiles, a sect of Jewish believers arose who argued that the Gospel, without the fulfilment of circumcision, would make void the Law and make salvation impossible, Acts 15 : 1. Hence this party was known as "the circumcision," Acts 10 : 45 ; 11 : 2 ; Gal. 2 : 12 ; Col. 4 : 11 ; Tit. 1 : 10 (the term being used by metonymy, the abstract being put for the concrete, as with the application of the word to Jews generally, Rom. 3 : 30 ; 4 : 9, 12 ; 15 : 8 ; Gal. 2 : 7–9 ; Eph. 2 : 11). It is used metaphorically and spiritually of believers with reference to the act, Col. 2 : 11 and Rom. 2 : 29 ; to the condition, Phil. 3 : 3.

The Apostle Paul's defence of the truth, and his contention against this propaganda, form the main subject of the Galatian Epistle. Cp. *katatomē*, "concision," Phil. 3 : 2. See CONCISION.

203 AG:33D CB:1234B 2. AKROBUSTIA (ἀκροβυστια), uncircumcision, is used (*a*) of the physical state, in contrast to the act of circumcision, Acts 11 : 3 (lit., 'having uncircumcision') ; Rom. 2 : 25, 26 ; 4 : 10, 11 ("though they be in uncircumcision," R.V.), 12 ; 1 Cor. 7 : 18, 19 ; Gal. 5 : 6 ; 6 : 15 ; Col. 3 : 11 ; (*b*) by metonymy, for Gentiles, e.g., Rom. 2 : 26, 27 ; 3 : 30 ; 4 : 9 ; Gal. 2 : 7 ; Eph. 2 : 11 ; (*d*) in a metaphorical or transferred sense, of the moral condition in which the corrupt desires of the flesh still operate, Col. 2 : 13.¶

Note : In Rom. 4 : 11, the phrase "though they be in uncircum-

* From Notes on Galatians by Hogg and Vine, p. 69.

cision " translates the Greek phrase *di' akrobustias*, lit., ' through uncircumcision ; ' here *dia* has the local sense of proceeding from and passing out.

B. Adjective.

APERITMĒTOS (ἀπερίτμητος), uncircumcised (*a*, negative, *peri*, 564
around, *temnō*, to cut), is used in Acts 7 : 51, metaphorically, of " heart AG:84B CB:1236B
and ears."¶

C. Verbs.

1. PERITEMNŌ (περιτέμνω), to circumcise, is used (*a*) lit., e.g., Luke 4059
1 : 59 ; 2 : 21 ; of receiving circumcision, Gal. 5 : 2, 3 ; 6 : 13, R.V. ; AG:652B CB:1263C
(*b*) metaphorically, of spiritual circumcision, Col. 2 : 11.

2. EPISPAOMAI (ἐπισπάομαι), lit., to draw over, to become uncircum- 1986
cised, as if to efface Judaism, appears in 1 Cor. 7 : 18.¶ AG:299D CB:—

For CIRCUMSPECTLY see ACCURATELY

CIRCUMSTANCE See ESTATE

CITIZEN, CITIZENSHIP

1. POLITĒS (πολίτης), a member of a city or state, or the inhabitant 4177
of a country or district, Luke 15 : 15, is used elsewhere in Luke 19 : 14 ; AG:686D CB:1265C
Acts 21 : 39, and, in the most authentic mss., in Heb. 8 : 11 (where some texts have *plēsion*, a neighbour). Apart from Heb. 8 : 11, the word occurs only in the writings of Luke (himself a Greek).¶

2. SUMPOLITĒS (συμπολίτης), *sun*, with, and No. 1, denotes a fellow- 4847
citizen, i.e., possessing the same citizenship, Eph. 2 : 19, used metaphori- AG:780A CB:1270B
cally in a spiritual sense.¶

3. POLITEIA (πολιτεία) signifies (*a*) the relation in which a citizen 4174
stands to the state, the condition of a citizen, citizenship, Acts 22 : 28, AG:686A CB:1265C
" with a great sum obtained I this citizenship " (A.V., " freedom "). While Paul's citizenship of Tarsus was not of advantage outside that city, yet his Roman citizenship availed throughout the Roman Empire and, besides private rights, included (1) exemption from all degrading punishments ; (2) a right of appeal to the Emperor after a sentence ; (3) a right to be sent to Rome for trial before the Emperor if charged with a capital offence. Paul's father might have obtained citizenship (1) by manumission ; (2) as a reward of merit ; (3) by purchase ; the contrast implied in Acts 22 : 28 is perhaps against the last mentioned ; (*b*) a civil polity, the condition of a state, a commonwealth, said of Israel, Eph. 2 : 12. See COMMONWEALTH.¶

4. POLITEUMA (πολίτευμα) signifies the condition, or life, of a citizen, 4175
citizenship ; it is said of the heavenly status of believers, Phil. 3 : 20, AG:686B CB:1265C
" our citizenship (A.V., " conversation ") is in Heaven." The R.V. marg. gives the alternative meaning, " commonwealth," i.e., community. See COMMONWEALTH, FREEDOM.¶ (-OMAI)

Note : *Politeuō*, Phil. 1 : 27, signifies to be a *politēs* (see No. 1), and is 4176
used in the Middle Voice, signifying, metaphorically, conduct characteristic AG:686C CB:1266A

of heavenly citizenship, R.V., " let your manner of life (A.V., " conversation ") be worthy (marg., ' behave as citizens worthily ') of the Gospel of Christ." In Acts 23 : 1 it is translated " I have lived." See CONVERSATION, LIVE.¶

CITY

4172 POLIS (πόλις), primarily a town enclosed with a wall (perhaps from a
AG:685B
CB:1265C root *plē*—, signifying fulness, whence also the Latin *plēo*, to fill, Eng., polite, polish, politic etc.), is used also of the heavenly Jerusalem, the abode and community of the redeemed, Heb. 11 : 10, 16 ; 12 : 22 ; 13 : 14. In the Apocalypse it signifies the visible capital of the Heavenly Kingdom, as destined to descend to earth in a coming age, e.g., Rev. 3 : 12 ; 21 : 2, 14, 19. By metonymy the word stands for the inhabitants, as in the English use, e.g., Matt. 8 : 34 ; 12 : 25 ; 21 : 10 ; Mark 1 : 33 ; Acts 13 : 44.

4439 *Note :* In Acts 16 : 13, the most authentic mss. have *pulē*, gate, R.V.,
AG:729B
CB:1268A " without the gate."

CLAMOUR

2906 KRAUGĒ (κραυγή), an onomatopœic word, imitating the raven's
AG:449C cry, akin to *krazō* and *kraugazō*, to cry, denotes an outcry, " clamour,"
CB:— Acts 23 : 9, R.V. ; Eph. 4 : 31, where it signifies the tumult of controversy. See CRY.

CLANGING

214 ALALAZŌ (ἀλαλάζω), an onomatopœic word, from the battle-cry,
AG:34D *alala*, is used of raising the shout of battle, Josh. 6 : 20 ; hence, to make a
CB:— loud cry or shout, e.g., Psa. 47 : 1 ; to wail, Jer. 29 : 2 ; in the N.T., in Mark 5 : 38, of wailing mourners ; in 1 Cor. 13 : 1, of the " clanging " of cymbals (A.V., " tinkling ").¶

CLAY

4081 PĒLOS (πηλός), clay, especially such as was used by a mason or potter,
AG:656B
CB:1263A is used of moist clay, in John 9 : 6, 11, 14, 15, in connection with Christ's healing the blind man ; in Rom. 9 : 21, of potter's clay, as to the potter's right over it as an illustration of the prerogatives of God in His dealings with men.¶

CLEAN, CLEANNESS, CLEANSE, CLEANSING

A. Adjective.

2513 KATHAROS (καθαρός), free from impure admixture, without blemish,
AG:388A
CB:1254B spotless, is used (*a*) physically, e.g., Matt. 23 : 26 ; 27 : 59 ; John 13 : 10 (where the Lord, speaking figuratively, teaches that one who has been entirely cleansed, needs not radical renewal, but only to be cleansed from every sin into which he may fall) ; 15 : 3 ; Heb. 10 : 22 ;

Rev. 15 : 6 ; 19 : 8, 14 ; 21 : 18, 21 ; (*b*) in a Levitical sense, Rom. 14 : 20 ; Tit. 1 : 15, " pure ; " (*c*) ethically, with the significance free from corrupt desire, from guilt, Matt. 5 : 8 ; John 13 : 10, 11 ; Acts 20 : 26 ; 1 Tim. 1 : 5 ; 3 : 9 ; 2 Tim. 1 : 3 ; 2 : 22 ; Tit. 1 : 15 ; Jas. 1 : 27 ; blameless, innocent (a rare meaning for this word), Acts 18 : 6 ; (*d*) in a combined Levitical and ethical sense ceremonially, Luke 11 : 41, " all things are clean unto you." See CLEAR, C, Note (2), PURE.¶

B. Verbs.

1. KATHARIZŌ (καθαρίζω), akin to A, signifies (1) to make clean, to 2511
cleanse (*a*) from physical stains and dirt, as in the case of utensils, Matt. AG:387B
23 : 25 (figuratively in verse 26) ; from disease, as of leprosy, Matt. 8 : 2 ; CB:1254B
(*b*) in a moral sense, from the defilement of sin, Acts 15 : 9 ; 2 Cor. 7 : 1 ; Heb. 9 : 14 ; Jas. 4 : 8, " cleanse " from the guilt of sin, Eph. 5 : 26 ; 1 John 1 : 7 ; (2) to pronounce clean in a Levitical sense, Mark 7 : 19, R.V. ; Acts 10 : 15 ; 11 : 9 ; to consecrate by cleansings, Heb. 9 : 22, 23 ; 10 : 2. See PURGE, PURIFY.

2. DIAKATHARIZŌ (διακαθαρίζω), to cleanse thoroughly, is used in 1245
Matt. 3 : 12, R.V.¶ AG:183D
CB:—

Note : For *kathairō*, John 15 : 2, R.V., see PURGE, No. 1. For *diakathairō*, Luke 3 : 17, R.V., see PURGE, No. 3.

C. Nouns.

1. KATHARISMOS (καθαρισμός), akin to A, denotes cleansing, (*a*) 2512
both the action and its results, in the Levitical sense, Mark 1 : 44 ; Luke AG:387D
2 : 22, " purification ; " 5 : 14, " cleansing ; " John 2 : 6 ; 3 : 25, CB:—
" purifying ; " (*b*) in the moral sense, from sins, Heb. 1 : 3 ; 2 Pet. 1 : 9, R.V., " cleansing." See PURGE, PURIFICATION, PURIFYING.¶

2. KATHAROTĒS (καθαρότης), akin to B, cleanness, purity, is used 2514
in the Levitical sense in Heb. 9 : 13, R.V., " cleanness." See PURIFY.¶ AG:388B CB:1254B
Note : In 2 Pet. 2 : 18, some inferior mss. have *ontōs*, " certainly " 3689
(A.V., " clean "), for *oligōs*, " scarcely " (R.V., " just "). AG:574A CB:—

CLEAR, CLEARING, CLEARLY

A. Verb.

KRUSTALLIZŌ (κρυσταλλίζω), to shine like crystal, to be of 2929
crystalline brightness, or transparency, is found in Rev. 21 : 11, " clear AG:454D
as crystal." The verb may, however, have a transitive force, signifying CB:1256A
to crystallize or cause to become like crystal. In that case it would speak of Christ (since He is the " Lightgiver," see the preceding part of the verse), as the One who causes the saints to shine in His own likeness.¶

B. Adjective.

LAMPROS (λαμπρός) is said of crystal, Rev. 22 : 1, A.V., " clear," 2986
R.V., " bright." See BRIGHT, GAY, GOODLY, GORGEOUS, WHITE. AG:465D
Note : The corresponding adverb *lamprōs* signifies " sumptuously." CB:1256C 2988

C. Adverb. AG:466A

TĒLAUGŌS (τηλαυγῶς), from *tēle*, afar, and *augē*, radiance, signifies CB:1256C

DēLAUGōS — conspicuously, or clearly, Mark 8 : 25, of the sight imparted by Christ
AG:178B to one who had been blind.¶ Some mss. have *dēlaugōs*, clearly (*dēlos*,
HAGNOS 53 clear).

AG:11D *Notes:* (1) In 2 Cor. 7 : 11, A.V., *hagnos* is rendered "clear." See
CB:1249A PURE. (2) In Rev. 21 : 18, *katharos*, ("pure," R.V.) is rendered "clear,"
KATHAROS 2513 in the A.V. See CLEAN. (3) *Apologia* (Eng., apology), a defence against
AG:388A an accusation, signifies, in 2 Cor. 7 : 11, a clearing of oneself. (4) For
CB:1254B APOLOGIA *diablepō*, to see clearly, Matt. 7 : 5; Luke 6 : 42, and *kathoraō*, ditto,
627 Rom. 1 : 20, see SEE.

AG:96A CB:1237A

DIABLEPō

CLEAVE, CLAVE

1227 AG:181D 1. KOLLAŌ (κολλάω), to join fast together, to glue, cement, is
KATHORAō primarily said of metals and other materials (from *kolla*, glue). In the
2529 N.T. it is used only in the Passive Voice, with reflexive force, in the
AG:391A CB:1254C sense of cleaving unto, as of cleaving to one's wife, Matt. 19 : 5; some
KOLLAō mss. have the intensive Verb No. 2, here; 1 Cor. 6 : 16, 17, "joined." In
2853 the corresponding passage in Mark 10 : 7, the most authentic mss. omit
AG:441C CB:1255C the sentence. In Luke 10 : 11 it is used of the cleaving of dust to the feet; in Acts 5 : 13; 8 : 29; 9 : 26; 10 : 28; 17 : 34, in the sense of becoming associated with a person so as to company with him, or be on his side, said, in the last passage, of those in Athens who believed: in Rom. 12 : 9, ethically, of cleaving to that which is good. For its use in Rev. 18 : 5 see REACH (R.V.,marg. "clave together"). See COMPANY, JOIN.¶

4347 AG:716A CB:1267A 2. PROSKOLLAŌ (προσκολλάω), in the Passive Voice, used reflexively, to cleave unto, is found in Eph. 5 : 31 (A.V. "joined to").

4357 AG:717C CB:1267B 3. PROSMENŌ (προσμένω), lit., to abide with (*pros*. toward or with, and *menō*, to abide), is used of cleaving unto the Lord, Acts 11 : 23. See ABIDE.

CLEMENCY

1932 AG:292C CB:1245C EPIEIKEIA (ἐπιείκεια), mildness, gentleness, kindness (what Matthew Arnold has called "sweet reasonableness"), is translated "clemency" in Acts 24 : 4; elsewhere, in 2 Cor. 10 : 1, of the gentleness of Christ. See GENTLENESS.¶ Cp. *epieikēs* (see FORBEARANCE).

For CLERK, see under TOWNCLERK

CLIMB UP

305 AG:50A CB:1235A ANABAINŌ (ἀναβαίνω), to ascend, is used of climbing up, in Luke 19 : 4 and John 10 : 1. See ARISE.

CLING See HOLD

CLOKE (Pretence)

1942 AG:294B CB:— 1. EPIKALUMMA (ἐπικάλυμμα) is a covering, a means of hiding (*epi*, upon, *kaluptō*, to cover); hence, a pretext, a cloke, for wickedness,

1 Pet. 2 : 16.¶ In the Sept. it is used in Ex. 26 : 14 ; 39 : 21," coverings ; " 2 Sam. 17 : 19 ; Job 19 : 29, " deceit." ¶

2. PROPHASIS (πρόφασις), either from *pro*, before, and *phainō*, to cause to appear, shine, or, more probably, from *pro*, and *phēmi*, to say, is rendered " cloke " (of covetousness) in 1 Thess. 2 : 5 ; " excuse " in John 15 : 22 (A.V. " cloke ") ; " pretence " in Matt. 23 : 14 ; Mark 12 : 40 ; Luke 20 : 47 (A.V. " shew ") ; Phil. 1 : 18 ; " colour " in Acts 27 : 30. It signifies the assuming of something so as to disguise one's real motives. See PRETENCE, SHEW.¶ 4392 AG:722C CB:—

CLOKE (Garment)

For the various words for garments, see CLOTHING.

CLOSE (Verb)

1. KAMMUŌ (καμμύω), derived by syncope (i.e., shortening and assimilation of *t* to *m*) from *katamuō*, i.e., *kata*, down, and *muō*, from a root *mu*—, pronounced by closing the lips, denotes to close down ; hence, to shut the eyes, Matt. 13 : 15 and Acts 28 : 27, in each place of the obstinacy of Jews in their opposition to the Gospel.¶ 2576 AG:402A CB:—

2. PTUSSŌ (πτύσσω), to fold, double up, is used of a scroll of parchment, Luke 4 : 20.¶ Cp. *anaptussō*, to open up, ver. 17.¶ 4428 AG:727D CB:—

Notes : (1) For " close-sealed," Rev. 5 : 1, see SEAL. ANAPTUSSŌ

(2) In Luke 9 : 36, *sigaō*, to be silent, is translated " they kept it close," A.V. (R.V., " they held their peace "). 380 AG:60A CB:— 4601 AG:749C CB:—

CLOSE (Adverb)

ASSON (ἆσσον), the comparative degree of *anchi*, near, is found in Acts 27 : 13, of sailing close by a place.¶ 788 AG:117B CB:—

For the word CLOSET see CHAMBER

CLOTH

RHAKOS (ῥάκος) denotes a ragged garment, or a piece of cloth torn off, a rag ; hence, a piece of undressed cloth, Matt. 9 : 16 ; Mark 2 : 21. 4470 AG:734A CB:—

Note : For other words, *othonion*, *sindon*, see LINEN, Nos. 1 and 3.¶

CLOTHE

1. AMPHIENNUMI (ἀμφιέννυμι), to put clothes round (*amphi*, around, *hennumi*, to clothe), to invest, signifies, in the Middle Voice, to put clothing on oneself, e.g., Matt. 6 : 30 ; 11 : 8 ; Luke 7 : 25 ; 12 : 28.¶ 294 AG:47C CB:—

2. ENDUŌ (ἐνδύω), Eng., endue), signifies to enter into, get into, as into clothes, to put on, e.g., Mark 1 : 6 ; Luke 8 : 27 (in the best mss.) ; 24 : 49 (A.V., " endued ") ; 2 Cor. 5 : 3 ; Rev. 1 : 13 ; 19 : 14. See ARRAY, ENDUE, PUT ON. 1746 AG:264A CB:1245A

1737 AG:263A 3. ENDIDUSKŌ (ἐνδιδύσκω) has the same meaning as No. 2; the
CB:— termination, —*skō* suggests the beginning or progress of the action.
The verb is used in the Middle Voice in Luke 16 : 19 (of a rich man).
Some mss. have it in 8 : 27, for No. 2 (of a demoniac). In Mark 15 : 17
the best texts have this verb (some have No. 2). See WEAR.¶

(-OMAI) 1902 4. EPENDUŌ (ἐπενδύω), a strengthened form of No. 2, used in the
AG:284D Middle Voice, to cause to be put on over, to be clothed upon, is found in
CB:1245C 2 Cor. 5 : 2, 4, of the future spiritual body of the redeemed.¶

2439 AG:376B 5. HIMATIZŌ (ἱματίζω) means to put on raiment (see *himation*,
CB:— below), Mark 5 : 15; Luke 8 : 35.¶

4016 6. PERIBALLŌ, to cast around or about, to put on, array, or, in the
AG:646A CB:— Middle and Passive Voices, to clothe oneself, e.g., Matt. 25 : 36, 38,
43, is most frequent in the Apocalypse, where it is found some 12 times
1463 (see *peribolaion*, below). See CAST, No. 10, PUT, No. 9).
AG:216B *Note:* The verb *enkomboomai*, to gird oneself with a thing, in 1 Pet.
CB:— 5 : 5, is rendered in the A.V., "be clothed with."

CLOTHING, CLOTHS, CLOTHES, CLOKE, COAT

5341 1. PHELONĒS, or *phailonēs* (φαιλόνης), probably by metathesis from
AG:851A (PHAIL-) *phainolēs* (Latin *paenula*), a mantle, denotes a travelling cloak for protec-
CB:— tion against stormy weather, 2 Tim. 4 : 13. Some, however, regard it as a Cretan word for *chitōn*, a tunic. It certainly was not an ecclesiastical vestment. The Syriac renders it a case for writings (some regard it as a book-cover), an explanation noted by Chrysostom, but improbable. It may have been "a light mantle like a cashmere dust-cloak, in which the books and parchments were wrapped" (Mackie in Hastings' Dic. of the Bible).¶

2440 2. HIMATION (ἱμάτιον), an outer garment, a mantle, thrown over the
AG:376B CB:1250C *chitōn*. In the plural, clothes (the cloak and the tunic), e.g., Matt. 17 :
2; 26 : 65; 27 : 31, 35. See APPAREL, No. 2.

5509 3. CHITŌN (χιτών) denotes the inner vest or under garment, and is to be
AG:882B CB:— distinguished, as such, from the *himation*. The distinction is made, for instance, in the Lord's command in Matt. 5 : 40: "If any man would go to law with thee, and take away thy coat (*chitōn*), let him have thy cloke (*himation*) also." The order is reversed in Luke 6 : 29, and the difference lies in this, that in Matt. 5 : 40 the Lord is referring to a legal process, so the claimant is supposed to claim the inner garment, the less costly. The defendant is to be willing to let him have the more valuable one too. In the passage in Luke an act of violence is in view, and there is no mention of going to law. So the outer garment is the first one which would be seized.

When the soldiers had crucified Jesus they took His garments (*himation*, in the plural), His outer garments, and the coat, the *chitōn*, the inner garment, which was without seam, woven from the top throughout,

John 19 : 23. The outer garments were easily divisible among the four soldiers, but they could not divide the *chitōn* without splitting it, so they cast lots for it.

Dorcas was accustomed to make coats (*chitōn*) and garments (*himation*), Acts 9 : 39, that is, the close fitting under garments and the long, flowing outer robes.

A person was said to be " naked " (*gumnos*), whether he was without clothing, or had thrown off his outer garment, e.g., his *ependutēs*, (No. 6, below), and was clad in a light undergarment, as was the case with Peter, in John 21 : 7. The High Priest, in rending his clothes after the reply the Lord gave him in answer to his challenge, rent his under garments (*chitōn*), the more forcibly to express his assumed horror and indignation, Mark 14 : 63. In Jude 23, " the garment spotted by the flesh " is the *chitōn*, the metaphor of the under garment being appropriate ; for it would be that which was brought into touch with the pollution of the flesh.

4. HIMATISMOS (ἱματισμός), in form a collective word, denoting **2441**
vesture, garments, is used generally of costly or stately raiment, the **AG:376D**
apparel of kings, of officials, etc. See Luke 7 : 25, where " gorgeously **CB:—**
apparelled " is, lit., 'in gorgeous vesture.' See also Acts 20 : 33 and 1 Tim. 2 : 9, " costly raiment." This is the word used of the Lord's white and dazzling raiment on the Mount of Transfiguration, Luke 9 : 29. It is also used of His *chitōn*, His under-garment (see note above), for which the soldiers cast lots, John 19 : 23, 24, " vesture ; " in Matt. 27 : 35 it is also translated " vesture." See APPAREL, RAIMENT, VESTURE.¶

5. ENDUMA (ἔνδυμα), akin to *enduō* (see CLOTHE, No. 2), denotes **1742**
anything put on, a garment of any kind. It was used of the clothing of **AG:263C**
ancient prophets, in token of their contempt of earthly splendour, 1 Kings **CB:1245A**
19 : 13 ; 2 Kings 1 : 8, R.V. ; Zech. 13 : 4. In the N.T. it is similarly used of John the Baptist's raiment, Matt. 3 : 4 ; of raiment in general, Matt. 6 : 25, 28 ; Luke 12 : 23 ; metaphorically, of sheep's clothing, Matt. 7 : 15 ; of a wedding garment, 22 : 11, 12 ; of the raiment of the angel at the tomb of the Lord after His resurrection, 28 : 3. See GARMENT, RAIMENT.¶

6. EPENDUTĒS (ἐπενδύτης) denotes an upper garment (*epi*, upon, **1903**
enduō, to clothe). The word is found in John 21 : 7, where it apparently **AG:285A**
denotes a kind of linen frock, which fishermen wore when at their work. **CB:—**
See No. 3.¶

7. ESTHĒS (ἐσθής), " clothing," Acts 10 : 30 ; see APPAREL, No. 1. **2066 AG:312B**

8. STOLĒ (στολή), (Eng., stole), denotes any stately robe, a long **CB:1246C 4749**
garment reaching to the feet or with a train behind. It is used of the **AG:769C**
long clothing in which the scribes walked, making themselves conspicuous **CB:1270A**
in the eyes of men, Mark 12 : 38 ; Luke 20 : 46 ; of the robe worn by the young man in the Lord's tomb, Mark 16 : 5 ; of the best or, rather, the chief robe, which was brought out for the returned prodigal, Luke 15 : 22 ; five times in the Apocalypse, as to glorified saints, 6 : 11 ; 7 : 9, 13, 14 ;

22 : 14.¶ In the Sept. it is used of the holy garments of the priests, e.g., Ex. 28 : 2 ; 29 : 21 ; 31 : 10.

4018 AG:646C CB:1263B *Notes :* (1) *Peribolaion*, from *periballō*, to throw around, lit., that which is thrown around, was a wrap or mantle. It is used in 1 Cor. 11 : 15, of the hair of a woman which is given to her as a veil ; in Heb. 1 : 12, of the earth and the heavens, which the Lord will roll up "as a mantle," R.V., for A.V., "vesture." The other word in that verse rendered "garment," R.V., is *himation*.¶

1745 AG:263D CB:— (2) *Endusis*, is "a putting on (of apparel)," 1 Pet. 3 : 3. Cp. No. 5.¶

(3) *Esthēsis*. See APPAREL, No. 1.

5511 AG:882B CB:— (4) The *chlamus* was a short cloak or robe, worn over the *chitōn* (No. 3), by emperors, kings, magistrates, military officers, etc. It is used of the scarlet robe with which Christ was arrayed in mockery by the soldiers in Pilate's Judgment Hall, Matt. 27 : 28, 31.

What was known as purple was a somewhat indefinite colour. There is nothing contradictory about its being described by Mark and John as "purple," though Matthew speaks of it as "scarlet." The soldiers put it on the Lord in mockery of His Kingship.¶

4158 AG:680B CB:— (5) The *podērēs* was another sort of outer garment, reaching to the feet (from *pous*, the foot, and *arō*, to fasten). It was one of the garments of the high priests, a robe (Hebrew, *chetoneth*), mentioned after the ephod in Ex. 28 : 4, etc. It is used in Ezek. 9 : 2, where instead of "linen" the Sept. reads "a long robe ;" and in Zech. 3 : 4, "clothe ye him with a long robe ;" in the N.T. in Rev. 1 : 13, of the long garment in which the Lord is seen in vision amongst the seven golden lampstands. There, *podērēs* is described as "a garment down to the feet," indicative of His High Priestly character and acts.¶

(6) For *katastolē*, see APPAREL, No. 4.

CLOUD

3509 AG:537A CB:1259C 1. NEPHOS (νέφος) denotes a cloudy, shapeless mass covering the heavens. Hence, metaphorically, of a dense multitude, a throng, Heb. 12 : 1.¶

3507 AG:536D CB:1259C 2. NEPHELĒ (νεφέλη), a definitely shaped cloud, or masses of clouds possessing definite form, is used, besides the physical element, (*a*) of the cloud on the mount of transfiguration, Matt. 17 : 5 ; (*b*) of the cloud which covered Israel in the Red Sea, 1 Cor. 10 : 1, 2 ; (*c*), of clouds seen in the Apocalyptic visions, Rev. 1 : 7 ; 10 : 1 ; 11 : 12 ; 14 : 14, 15, 16 ; (*d*), metaphorically in 2 Pet. 2 : 17, of the evil workers there mentioned ; but R.V., "and mists" (*homichlē*), according to the most authentic mss.

In 1 Thess. 4 : 17, the clouds referred to in connection with the Rapture of the saints are probably the natural ones, as also in the case of those in connection with Christ's Second Advent to the earth. See Matt. 24 : 30 ; 26 : 64, and parallel passages. So at the Ascension, Acts 1 : 9.

CLOVEN

DIAMERIZŌ (διαμερίζω), to part asunder (*dia*, asunder, *meros*, a part), 1266
is translated " cloven " in the A.V. of Acts 2 : 3, R.V., " parting asunder." AG:186D CB:—
See DIVIDE, PART.

CLUB See STAFF

CLUSTER

BOTRUS (βότρυς), a cluster, or bunch, bunch of grapes, is found 1009
in Rev. 14 : 18.¶ AG:145C CB:—

Note: Cp. *staphulē*, a bunch of grapes, the ripe cluster, stressing the 4718
grapes themselves, Matt. 7 : 16 ; Luke 6 : 44 ; Rev. 14 : 18.¶ AG:765C CB:—

COALS

1. ANTHRAX (ἄνθραξ), a burning coal (cp. Eng., *anthracite*), is used 440
in the plural in Rom. 12 : 20, metaphorically in a proverbial expression, AG:67C CB:1236A
" thou shalt heap coals of fire on his head " (from Prov. 25 : 22), signifying retribution by kindness, i.e., that, by conferring a favour on your enemy, you recall the wrong he has done to you, so that he repents, with pain of heart.¶

2. ANTHRAKIA (ἀνθρακιά), akin to No. 1, is a heap of burning coals, 439
or a charcoal fire, John 18 : 18 ; 21 : 9.¶ AG:67C CB:—

COAST, COASTING

A. Noun.

HORION (ὅριον), a bound, boundary, limit, frontier (akin to *horizō*, to 3725
bound, limit), is rendered " coasts " ten times in the A.V., but " borders " AG:581B CB:1251B
in Matt. 4 : 13, and is always translated " borders " in the R.V. See BORDER.

B. Adjective.

PARALIOS (παράλιος), by the sea (*para*, by, *hals*, salt), hence denotes 3882 AG:620A
a sea coast, Luke 6 : 17.¶ In the Sept., Gen. 49 : 13 ; Deut. 1 : 7 ; 33 : 19; PARALEGŌ
Josh. 9 : 1 ; 11 : 3 (twice) ; Job 6 : 3 ; Is. 9 : 1. (-OMAI)

C. Verb.

3881
PARALEGŌ (παραλέγω) is used, in the Middle Voice, as a nautical AG:619D METHORION
term, to sail past, Acts 27 : 8, " coasting along ; " ver. 13, " sailed by."¶ 3181 (-OS)

Notes: (1) *Methorion* (*meta*, with, and A), in Mark 7 : 24, is trans- AG:499B PARATHALASSIOS
lated " borders." (2) The phrase " upon the sea coast," Matt. 4 : 13, 3864
A.V., translates *parathalassios* (*para*, by, *thalassa*, the sea), R.V. " by AG:616A MEROS
the sea."¶ (3) *Meros*, a part, is translated " coasts " in Matt. 15 : 21 ; 3313
16 : 13, A.V. (R.V., " parts,") ; " country," R.V., in Acts 19 : 1, A.V. AG:505D CB:1258B
" coasts ; " this refers to the high land in the interior of Asia Minor. See CHŌRA
BEHALF, CRAFT, PART, PARTICULAR, PIECE, PORTION, RESPECT, SOME- 5561
WHAT, SORT. (4) *Chōra*, a country, rendered " coasts " in Acts 26 : 20, AG:889B CB:1240A
A.V., is corrected in the R.V. to " country." See COUNTRY, FIELD, KATA
GROUND, LAND, REGION. (5) In Acts 27 : 2 the phrase in the R.V., " on 2596 AG:405C
the coast of," translates the preposition *kata*, along, and the complete CB:1253C)

clause, "unto the places on the coast of Asia," R.V., is curiously condensed in the A.V. to "by the coasts of Asia."

For COAT (*ependeutēs*) see CLOKE, CLOTHING

COCK, COCK-CROWING

220 1. ALEKTŌR (ἀλέκτωρ), a cock, perhaps connected with a Hebrew
AG:35C phrase for the on-coming of the light, is found in the passages concerning
CB:— Peter's denial of the Lord, Matt. 26 : 34, 74, 75 ; Mark 14 : 30, 68, 72 ;
Luke 22 : 34, 60, 61 ; John 13 : 38 ; 18 : 27.¶

219 2. ALEKTOROPHŌNIA (ἀλεκτοροφωνία) denotes cock-crowing
AG:35B (*alektōr*, and *phōnē*, a sound), Mark 13 : 35. There were two cock-
CB:1234B crowings, one after midnight, the other before dawn. In these watches the Jews followed the Roman method of dividing the night. The first cock-crowing was at the third watch of the night. That is the one mentioned in Mark 13 : 35. Mark mentions both ; see 14 : 30. The latter, the second, is that referred to in the other Gospels and is mentioned especially as "the cock-crowing."¶

CODE See LETTER
COHORT See BAND
COIN See PIECE

COLD

A. Noun.

5593 PSUCHOS (ψύχος), coldness, cold, appears in John 18 : 18 ; Acts
AG:894C 28 : 2 ; 2 Cor. 11 : 27.¶
CB:1267C

B. Adjective.

5592 PSUCHROS (ψυχρός), cool, fresh, cold, chilly (fuller in expression
AG:894C than *psuchos*), is used in the natural sense in Matt. 10 : 42, "cold water ;"
CB:1267C metaphorically in Rev. 3 : 15, 16.¶

C. Verb.

5594 PSUCHŌ (ψύχω), to breathe, blow, cool by blowing, Passive Voice,
AG:894D grow cool, is used metaphorically in Matt. 24 : 12, in the sense of waning
CB:1267C zeal or love.¶

COLLAPSE See FAINT, FALL

COLLECTION

3048 AG:475D (LOGEIA) LOGIA (λογία), akin to *legō*, to collect, is used in 1 Cor. 16 : 1, 2 ; in
CB:1257A (LOGEIA) the latter verse, A.V. "gatherings," R.V., "collections," as in ver. 1. See GATHERING.¶

(TAX) COLLECTOR See PUBLICAN
COLONADE See PORCH

COLONY

2862 KOLŌNIA (κολωνία) transliterates the Latin *colonia*. Roman colonies belonged to three periods and classes, (*a*) those of the earlier republic before 100 B.C., which were simply centres of Roman influence in conquered territory ; (*b*) agrarian colonies, planted as places for the
AG:442C overflowing population of Rome ; (*c*) military colonies during the time
CB:— of the Civil wars and the Empire, for the settlement of disbanded soldiers. This third class was established by the *imperator*, who appointed a legate

to exercise his authority. To this class Philippi belonged as mentioned in Acts 16 : 12, R.V., " a Roman colony." They were watch-towers of the Roman State and formed on the model of Rome itself. The full organization of Philippi as such was the work of Augustus, who, after the battle of Actium, 31 B.C., gave his soldiers lands in Italy and transferred most of the inhabitants there to other quarters including Philippi. These communities possessed the right of Roman freedom, and of holding the soil under Roman law, as well as exemption from poll-tax and tribute. Most Roman colonies were established on the coast.¶

For the word COLOUR (Acts 27 : 30) see CLOKE

COLT

PŌLOS (πῶλος), a foal, whether colt or filly, had the general 4454
significance of a young creature ; in Matt. 21 : 2, and parallel passages, AG:731D CB:1266A
an ass's colt.

COME, CAME (see also COMING)

1. ERCHOMAI (ἔρχομαι), the most frequent verb, denoting either to 2064
come, or to go, signifies the act, in contrast with *hēkō* (see No. 22, below), AG:310B CB:1246B
which stresses the arrival, as, e.g., ' I am come and am here,' John 8 : 42
and Heb. 10 : 9. See BRING, B, *Note* (1), FALL, GO, GROW, LIGHT, PASS,
RESORT.

Compounds of this with prepositions are as follows (2 to 11) :

2. EISERCHOMAI (εἰσέρχομαι), to come into, or to go into (*eis*, into), 1525
e.g., Luke 17 : 7. See ENTER. AG:232C CB:1243B

3. EXERCHOMAI (ἐξέρχομαι), to come out, or go out or forth 1831
(*ek*, out), e.g., Matt. 2 : 6. See DEPART, ESCAPE, GET, (*b*), No. 3, GO, AG:274B CB:1247C
Note (1), PROCEED, SPREAD.

4. EPANERCHOMAI (ἐπανέρχομαι), to come back again, return (*epi*, 1880
on, *ana*, again), Luke 10 : 35 ; 19 : 15.¶ AG:283A CB:—

5. DIERCHOMAI (διέρχομαι), to come or go through (*dia*, through), 1330
e.g., Acts 9 : 38. See DEPART, GO, PASS, PIERCE, TRAVEL, WALK. AG:194C CB:1241C

6. EPERCHOMAI (ἐπέρχομαι), to come or go upon (*epi*, upon), e.g., 1904
Luke 1 : 35 ; in Luke 21 : 26, used of coming events, suggesting their AG:285A
certainty ; in Eph. 2 : 7, said of the on-coming of the ages ; in Acts 14 : 19, CB:1245C
of Jews coming to (lit., upon) a place.

7. KATERCHOMAI (κατέρχομαι), to come down (*kata*, down), e.g., 2718
Luke 9 : 37. See DEPART, DESCEND, GO, *Note* (1), LAND. AG:422A CB:—

8. PAREISERCHOMAI (παρεισέρχομαι), lit., to come in (*eis*) beside 3922
or from the side (*para*) so as to be present with, is used (*a*) in the literal AG:624D
sense, of the coming in of the Law in addition to sin, Rom. 5 : 20 ; (*b*) in CB:1262B
Gal. 2 : 4, of false brethren, suggesting their coming in by stealth. See
ENTER.¶ 3928 AG:625D

9. PARERCHOMAI (παρέρχομαι), (*para*, by or away), signifies (*a*) to CB:1262B

come or go forth, or arrive, e.g., Luke 12 : 37 ; 17 : 7 (last part) ; Acts 24 : 7 ; (*b*) to pass by, e.g., Luke 18 : 37 ; (*c*) to neglect, e.g., Luke 11 : 42. See Go, Pass, Transgress.

4334 AG:713A CB:1267A 10. PROSERCHOMAI (προσέρχομαι) denotes to come or go near to (*pros*, near to), e.g., Matt. 4 : 3 ; Heb. 10 : 1, A.V., " comers," R.V., " them that draw nigh." See Consent, Draw, Go, *Note* (1).

4905 AG:788A CB:1270C 11. SUNERCHOMAI (συνέρχομαι), to come together (*sun* with), e.g., John 18 : 20, is often translated by the verb to assemble ; see the R.V. of 1 Cor. 11 : 20 ; 14 : 23. See Accompany, Assemble, Company, Go with, Resort.

565 AG:84C CB:1236B *Note : Aperchomai*, to come away or from, is differently translated in the R.V. ; see, e.g., Mark 3 : 13 where it signifies that they went from the company or place where they were to Him ; it usually denotes to go away.

1096 AG:158A CB:1248B 12. GINOMAI (γίνομαι) to become, signifies a change of condition, state or place, e.g., Mark 4 : 35. In Acts 27 : 33, the verb is used with *mellō*, to be about to, to signify the coming on of day.

3854 AG:613C CB:— 13. PARAGINOMAI (παραγίνομαι), *para*, near or by, denotes to arrive, to be present, e.g., Matt. 2 : 1. See Go, Present.

4836 AG:779A CB:— 14. SUMPARAGINOMAI (συμπαραγίνομαι), (*sun*, with, *para*, near), to come together, is used in Luke 23 : 48 ; 2 Tim. 4 : 16, lit., ' stood at my side with me.' See Stand.¶

Note : For " come by " in Acts 27 : 16, A.V., the R.V. suitably has " secure."

Compounds of the verb bainō, to go, are as follows (15 to 21) :

305 AG:50A CB:1235A 15. ANABAINŌ (ἀναβαίνω), to come upon, to arrive in a place (*ana*, up or upon), is translated " come into " in Acts 25 : 1. See Arise, Ascend, Enter, Go, Climb, Grow, Rise, Spring.

1910 AG:289D CB:— 16. EPIBAINŌ (ἐπιβαίνω), to come to or into, or go upon, is rendered, in Acts 20 : 18, R.V., " set foot in." See Enter, Go, Take, *Note* (16).

— AG:237B 17. EKBAINŌ (ἐκβαίνω), to come or go out, appears in the best mss. in Heb. 11 : 15 ; A.V., " came out," R.V., " went out."¶

1224 AG:181C CB:— 18. DIABAINŌ (διαβαίνω), to pass through, is translated " come over " in Acts 16 : 9 ; " pass " in Luke 16 : 26 ; " pass through " in Heb. 11 : 29. See Pass.¶

2597 AG:408B CB:1253C 19. KATABAINŌ (καταβαίνω) signifies to come down, e.g., Matt. 8 : 1. See Descend, Fall, Get, Go, Step (down).

4872 AG:784B 20. SUNANABAINŌ (συναναβαίνω), to come up with (*sun*, with, *ana*, up), is used in Mark 15 : 41 ; Acts 13 : 31.¶

1684 AG:254A 21. EMBAINŌ (ἐμβαίνω), to go into, is rendered, in Mark 5 : 18, A.V., " was come into," R.V., " was entering." See Enter, Get, Go, Step.

576 AG:88C *Note : Apobainō*, to go away, is rendered, in the A.V. of John 21 : 9, " were come to ; " R.V., " got out upon."

2240 AG:344C CB:1249C 22. HĒKŌ (ἥκω) means (*a*) to come, to be present (see above, on No. 1); (*b*) to come upon, of time and events, Matt. 24 : 14 ; John 2 : 4 ; 2 Pet.

3 : 10 ; Rev. 18 : 8 ; (*c*) metaphorically, to come upon one, of calamitous
times, and evils, Matt. 23 : 36 ; Luke 19 : 43.

23. APHIKNEOMAI (ἀφικνέομαι), to arrive at a place, is used in 864
Rom. 16 : 19, " come abroad " (of the obedience of the saints).¶ AG:126C CB:—

24. CHŌREŌ (χωρέω), lit., to make room (*chōra*, a place) for another, 5562
and so to have place, receive, is rendered " come " (followed by " to AG:889C
repentance ") in 2 Pet. 3 : 9 ; the meaning strictly is ' have room (i.e., CB:1240A
space of time) for repentance.' See CONTAIN, GO, PLACE, ROOM,
RECEIVE.

25. EIMI (εἰμί), to be, is, in the Infinitive Mood, rendered " come," 1510
in John 1 : 46 and in the future Indicative " will come," in 2 Tim. 4 : 3. AG:222D CB:1243A

26. ENISTĒMI (ἐνίστημι), lit., to stand in, or set in (*en*, in, *histēmi*, 1764
to stand), hence to be present or to be imminent, is rendered " shall AG:266D
come " in 2 Tim. 3 : 1 ; it here expresses permanence, ' shall settle in CB:—
(upon you).' See AT HAND, PRESENT.

27. EPHISTĒMI (ἐφίστημι) signifies to stand by or over (*epi*, upon), 2186
Luke 2 : 9, R.V. ; Acts 12 : 7 ; " before," Acts 11 : 11 ; to come upon, AG:330D
Luke 20 : 1 (here with the idea of suddenness) ; Acts 4 : 1 ; 6 : 12 ; CB:—
23 : 27 ; 1 Thess. 5 : 3 ; " coming up," of the arrival of Anna at the
Temple, Luke 2 : 38 ; " came up to (Him)," of Martha, Luke 10 : 40 ;
" is come," 2 Tim. 4 : 6 (probably with the same idea as in Luke 20 : 1).
The R.V. is significant in all these places. See ASSAULT, AT HAND,
PRESENT, STAND.

28. KATANTAŌ (καταντάω) denotes (*a*) to come to, or over against, 2658
a place, arrive, Acts 16 : 1 ; 18 : 19, 24 ; 20 : 15 (in 21 : 7 and 25 : 13, AG:415B
R.V., " arrived ; " in 27 : 12 , " reach," for A.V., " attain to) ; 28 : 13 ; CB:1254A
(*b*) of things or events, to arrive at a certain time, or come upon certain
persons in the period of their lifetime, 1 Cor. 10 : 11 ; or to come to
persons so that they partake of, as of the Gospel, 1 Cor. 14 : 36. For
the remaining instances, Acts 26 : 7 ; Eph. 4 : 13 ; Phil. 3 : 11, see
ATTAIN.¶

29. MELLŌ (μέλλω), to be about (to do something), often implying 3195
the necessity and therefore the certainty of what is to take place, is AG:500D
frequently rendered " to come," e.g., Matt. 3 : 7 ; 11 : 14 ; Eph. 1 : 21 ; CB:1258A
1 Tim. 4 : 8 ; 6 : 19 ; Heb. 2 : 5. See ALMOST, BEGIN, MEAN, MIND,
SHALL, TARRY, WILL.

30. PARISTĒMI (παρίστημι), to stand by or near, to be at hand 3936
(*para*, near), is translated " is come," of the arrival of harvest, Mark 4 : 29. AG:627C
See BRING, COMMEND, GIVE, PRESENT, PROVE, PROVIDE, SHEW, STAND, CB:1262B
YIELD.

31. PHERŌ (φέρω), to bear, carry, is rendered " came," in the sense 5342
of being borne from a place, in 2 Pet. 1 : 17, 18, 21. See BEAR, CARRY. AG:854D CB:1264A

32. PHTHANŌ (φθάνω) denotes to anticipate, to come sooner than 5348
expected, 1 Thess. 2 : 16, " is come upon," of Divine wrath ; cp. Rom. AG:856D
9 : 31, " did not arrive at ; " or to come in a different manner from what CB:1264C

EKPOREUŌ was expected, Matt. 12 : 28, " come upon ; " Luke 11 : 20, of the Kingdom
(-OMAI) 1607 of God ; so of coming to a place, 2 Cor. 10 : 14. See ATTAIN, PRECEDE,
AG:244B PREVENT.¶

CB:1244A PROSPOREUOMAI *Two of the compounds of the verb poreuomai, to go, proceed, are trans-*
4365 AG:718B *lated " come," with a preposition or adverb :*

CB:— 33. EKPOREUŌ (ἐκπορεύω), in the Middle Voice, to come forth (*ek*, out
PROSENGIZŌ 4331 of), Mark 7 : 15, 20 ; John 5 : 29. See DEPART, GO, ISSUE, PROCEED.

AG:712D 34. PROSPOREUOMAI (προσπορεύομαι), in Mark 10 : 35, is translated
CB:— SUMPLĒROŌ " come near unto."¶

4845 AG:779C *Notes :* (1) No. 33 is rendered " proceed " in the R.V. of Mark
CB:1270B 7 : 15, 20, 23 (A.V., " come "). (2) For *epiporeuomai*, in Luke 8 : 4,
SUNTUNCHANŌ 4940 see RESORT.¶

AG:793C 35. PROSENGIZŌ (προσεγγίζω) denotes to come near (*pros*, to,
CB:— KUKLOŌ *engizō*, to be near, to approach), Mark 2 : 4, used of those who tried
2944 AG:456D to bring a palsied man to Christ.¶

CB:— 36. SUMPLĒROŌ (συμπληρόω), to fill completely (*sun*, with, intensive),
HUSTEREŌ 5302 is used, in the Passive Voice, of time to be fulfilled or completed, Luke
AG:849A 9 : 51, " the days were well-nigh come ; " Acts 2 : 1, " the day . . . was
CB:1252B DEURO now come " (A.V. " was fully come "). In Luke 8 : 23, it is used in the
1204 AG:176C Active Voice, of the filling of a boat in a storm. See FILL.¶

CB:1241A DEUTE 37. SUNTUNCHANŌ (συντυγχάνω), to meet with (*sun*, with, and
1205 *tunchanō*, to reach), is rendered " to come at " in Luke 8 : 19, (of the
AG:176D CB:1241A efforts of Christ's mother and brethren to get at Him through a crowd).¶

PROLAMBANŌ 38. KUKLOŌ (κυκλόω), to compass (Eng., cycle), is translated " came
4301 AG:708B round about," in John 10 : 24. See COMPASS, ROUND, STAND.

CB:1266C DIADECHOMAI 39. HUSTEREŌ (ὑστερέω), to be behind, is translated " to have
1237 come short," in Heb. 4 : 1. See BEHIND, B, No. 1.

AG:182C CB:— *Notes :* (1) *Deuro*, hither, here, is used (sometimes with verbs of motion)
EPISTREPHŌ 1994 in the singular number, in calling a person to come, Matt. 19 : 21 ; Mark
AG:301A 10 : 21 ; Luke 18 : 22 ; John 11 : 43 ; Acts 7 : 3, 34 ; Rev. 17 : 1 ; 21 : 9.
CB:1246A EPISUNTRECHŌ For its other meaning, " hitherto," Rom. 1 : 13, see HITHERTO.¶ It
1998 has a plural, *deute*, frequent in the Gospels ; elsewhere in Rev. 19 : 17. *In*
AG:301D CB:— *the following the R.V. has a different rendering* :—(2) In Mark 14 : 8,
KATALUŌ *prolambanō*, to anticipate, to be beforehand, A.V., " hath come aforehand
2647 AG:414B to anoint My body," R.V., " hath anointed My body aforehand." (3)
CB:1254A In Acts 7 : 45, *diadechomai*, to succeed one, to take the place of, A.V.,
KATALAMBANŌ 2638 " who came after," R.V., " in their turn."¶ (4) In Luke 8 : 55, *epistrephō*,
AG:412D to return to, A.V., " came again," R.V., " returned." (5) In Acts 24 : 27,
CB:1254A (-OMAI) EPISTASIS *lambanō*, with *diadochos*, a successor, A.V., " came into the room of,"
— R.V., " was succeeded by." (6) In Mark 9 : 23, for *episuntrechō*, to come
AG:300B CB:— running together, see under RUN.¶ (7) In Acts 5 : 38, *kataluō*, to destroy,
EPISUSTASIS 1999 A.V., " will come to nought," R.V., " will be overthrown." (8) In
AG:301D John 12 : 35, *katalambanō*, to seize, A.V., " come upon," R.V., " overtake."
CB:1246A (9) In 2 Cor. 11 : 28, *epistasis* (in some mss. *episustasis*), lit., a standing

together upon, hence, a pressing upon, as of cares, A.V., " cometh upon," PAREIMI 3918
R.V., " presseth upon." (10) In Acts 19 : 27, *erchomai*, with *eis apelegmon*, AG:624A CB:1262B
R.V., " come into disrepute," A.V., " be set at nought." (11) For *pareimi*, SUNAGō
John 7 : 6, see PRESENT, No. 1. (12) *Sunagō*, to gather together, is always 4863
so rendered in R.V., e.g., Matt. 27 : 62 ; Mark 7 : 1 ; Luke 22 : 66 ; Acts AG:782A CB:1270B
13 : 44 ; 15 : 6 ; 20 : 7. See GATHER, No. 1. (13) For come to nought EISPOREUOMAI
see NOUGHT. (14) For *eisporeuomai* see ENTER, No. 4. (15) For " was 1531 AG:233C
come again," Acts 22 : 17, A.V., see RETURN, No. 4. (16) For *engizō*, to CB:—
come near, see APPROACH, NIGH. ENGIZō 1448
AG:213C CB:1245A

For COME BEHIND, see BEHIND

COMELINESS, COMELY

A. Noun.

EUSCHĒMOSUNĒ (εὐσχημοσύνη), elegance of figure, gracefulness, 2157
comeliness (*eu*, well, *schēma*, a form), is found in this sense in 1 Cor. 12 : 23. AG:327A CB:1247B

B. Adjective.

EUSCHĒMŌN (εὐσχήμων), akin to A, elegant in figure, well formed, 2158
graceful, is used in 1 Cor. 12 : 24, of parts of the body (see above) ; in AG:327A
1 Cor. 7 : 35, R.V., " (that which is) seemly," A.V., " comely ; " " honour- CB:—
able," Mark 15 : 43 ; Acts 13 : 50 ; 17 : 12. See HONOURABLE.¶

Note : In 1 Cor. 11 : 13, *prepō*, to be becoming, is rendered in the 4241
A.V., " is it comely ? " R.V., " is it seemly ? " See BECOME, SEEMLY. AG:699B CB:1266B

COMFORT, COMFORTER, COMFORTLESS

A. Nouns.

1. PARAKLĒSIS (παράκλησις), means a calling to one's side (*para*, 3874
beside, *kaleō*, to call) ; hence, either an exhortation, or consolation, AG:618A CB:1262A
comfort, e.g., Luke 2 : 25 (here " looking for the consolation of Israel " is equivalent to waiting for the coming of the Messiah) ; 6 : 24 ; Acts 9 : 31 ; Rom. 15 : 4, 5 ; 1 Cor. 14 : 3, " exhortation ; " 2 Cor. 1 : 3, 4, 5, 6, 7 ; 7 : 4, 7, 13 ; 2 Thess. 2 : 16 ; Philm. 7. In 2 Thess. 2 : 16 it combines encouragement with alleviation of grief. The R.V. changes " consolation " into " comfort," except in Luke 2 : 25 ; 6 : 24 ; Acts 15 : 31 ; in Heb. 6 : 18, " encouragement ; " in Acts 4 : 36, " exhortation." R.V. (A.V., " consolation "). See CONSOLATION, ENCOURAGEMENT, EXHORTATION, INTREATY.

2. PARAMUTHIA (παραμυθία), primarily a speaking closely to anyone 3889
(*para*, near, *muthos*, speech), hence denotes consolation, comfort, with a AG:620D CB:1262B
greater degree of tenderness than No. 1, 1 Cor. 14 : 3.¶

3. PARAMUTHION (παραμύθιον) has the same meaning as No. 2, 3890 AG:620D
the difference being that *paramuthia* stresses the process or progress of the CB:1262B
act, *paramuthion* the instrument as used by the agent, Phil. 2 : 1.¶ 3931 AG:626D

4. PARĒGORIA (παρηγορία), primarily an addressing, address, hence CB:—

denotes a soothing, solace, Col. 4 : 11.¶ A verbal form of the word signifies medicines which allay irritation (Eng., paregoric).

3875 AG:618B CB:1262A 5. PARAKLĒTOS (παράκλητος), lit., called to one's side, i.e., to one's aid, is primarily a verbal adjective, and suggests the capability or adaptability for giving aid. It was used in a court of justice to denote a legal assistant, counsel for the defence, an advocate; then, generally, one who pleads another's cause, an intercessor, advocate, as in 1 John 2 : 1, of the Lord Jesus. In the widest sense, it signifies a succourer, comforter. Christ was this to His disciples, by the implication of His word "another (*allos*, another of the same sort, not *heteros*, different) Comforter," when speaking of the Holy Spirit, John 14 : 16. In 14 : 26; 15 : 26; 16 : 7 He calls Him "the Comforter.¶ ''" Comforter" or "Consoler" corresponds to the name "*Menahem*," given by the Hebrews to the Messiah.

B. Verbs.

3870 AG:617A CB:1262A 1. PARAKALEŌ (παρακαλέω) has the same variety of meanings as Noun, No. 1, above, e.g., Matt. 2 : 18; 1 Thess. 3 : 2, 7; 4 : 18. In 2 Cor. 13 : 11, it signifies to be comforted (so the R.V.). See BESEECH.

4837 AG:779A CB:— 2. SUMPARAKALEŌ (συμπαρακαλέω), *sun*, with, and No. 1, signifies to comfort together, Rom. 1 : 12.¶

3888 AG:620D CB:1262B 3. PARAMUTHEOMAI (παραμυθέομαι), akin to Noun No. 2, to soothe, console, encourage, is translated, in John 11 : 31, "comforted;" in ver. 19, R.V., "console." In 1 Thess. 2 : 11 and 5 : 14, R.V., "encourage," as the sense there is that of stimulating to the earnest discharge of duties. See CONSOLE, ENCOURAGE.¶

2174 AG:329D CB:— 4. EUPSUCHEŌ (εὐψυχέω) signifies to be of good comfort (*eu*, well, *psuchē*, the soul), Phil. 2 : 19.¶

2293 AG:352A CB:1271C *Notes:* (1) For the verb *tharseō*, "be of good comfort," see CHEER, No. 2.

3737 AG:583A CB:1261B (2) *Orphanos* is rendered "comfortless" in John 14 : 18, A.V.; R.V., "desolate." See DESOLATE, FATHERLESS.

COMING (Noun)

1529 AG:233B CB:1243B 1. EISODOS (εἴσοδος), an entrance (*eis*, in, *hodos*, a way), an entering in, is once translated "coming," Acts 13 : 24, of the coming of Christ into the nation of Israel. For its meaning "entrance" see 1 Thess. 1 : 9; 2 : 1; Heb. 10 : 19; 2 Pet. 1 : 11. See ENTER, ENTRANCE.¶

1660 AG:251A CB:1244B 2. ELEUSIS (ἔλευσις), a coming (from *erchomai*, to come), is found in Acts 7 : 52.¶

3952 AG:629D CB:1262C 3. PAROUSIA (παρουσία), lit., a presence, *para*, with, and *ousia*, being (from *eimi*, to be), denotes both an arrival and a consequent presence with. For instance, in a papyrus letter a lady speaks of the necessity of her *parousia* in a place in order to attend to matters relating to her property there. Paul speaks of his *parousia* in Philippi, Phil. 2 : 12 (in contrast to his *apousia*, his absence; see ABSENCE). Other words denote the arrival (see *eisodos* and *eleusis*, above). *Parousia* is used to describe the presence of Christ with His disciples on the Mount of Transfiguration, 2 Pet. 1 : 16. When used of the return of Christ, at the Rapture of the Church, it signifies, not merely His momentary coming for His saints, but His presence with them from that moment until His revelation and manifestation to the world. In some passages the word gives prominence to the beginning of that period, the course of the period being implied, 1 Cor. 15 : 23 ; 1 Thess. 4 : 15 ; 5 : 23 ; 2 Thess. 2 : 1 ; Jas. 5 : 7, 8 ; 2 Pet. 3 : 4. In some, the course is prominent, Matt. 24 : 3, 37 ; 1 Thess. 3 : 13 ; 1 John 2 : 28 ; in others the conclusion of the period, Matt. 24 : 27 ; 2 Thess. 2 : 8.

The word is also used of the Lawless One, the Man of Sin, his access to power and his doings in the world during his *parousia*, 2 Thess. 2 : 9. In addition to Phil. 2 : 12 (above), it is used in the same way of the Apostle, or his companions, in 1 Cor. 16 : 17 ; 2 Cor. 7 : 6, 7 ; 10 : 10 ; Phil. 1 : 26 ; of the Day of God, 2 Pet. 3 : 12. See PRESENCE.

Note : The word *apokalupsis*, rendered " coming " in 1 Cor. 1 : 7, 602
A.V., denotes a " revelation " (R.V.). For a fuller treatment of *Parousia*, AG:92B CB:1236C
see *Notes on Thessalonians*, by Hogg and Vine, pp. 87, 88.

COMMAND (Verbs)

1. DIATASSŌ (διατάσσω) signifies to set in order, appoint, command, 1299
Matt. 11 : 1 ; Luke 8 : 55 ; 17 : 9, 10 ; Acts 18 : 2 ; 23 : 31 ; " gave AG:189C CB:1241B
order," 1 Cor. 16 : 1, R.V. So in Acts 24 : 23, where it is in the Middle Voice. See APPOINT, No. 6.

2. EPŌ (ἔπω) denotes to speak (connected with *eipon*, to say) ; hence, 3004 (LEGo)
among various renderings, to bid, command, Matt. 4 : 3 ; Mark 5 : 43 ; AG:226A CB:1243A
8 : 7 ; Luke 4 : 3 ; 19 : 15. See BID.

Note : In 2 Cor. 4 : 6, the R.V. rightly has " said," followed by the quotation " Light shall shine out of darkness."

3. ENTELLŌ (ἐντέλλω) signifies to enjoin upon, to charge with ; 1781
it is used in the Middle Voice in the sense of commanding, Matt. 19 : 7 ; AG:268B CB:1245B
28 : 20 ; Mark 10 : 3 ; 13 : 34 ; John 8 : 5 ; 15 : 14, 17 ; Acts 13 : 47 ; Heb. 9 : 20 ; 11 : 22, " gave commandment." See CHARGE, ENJOIN.

4. EPITASSŌ (ἐπιτάσσω) signifies to appoint over, put in charge 2004
(*epi*, over, *tassō*, to appoint) ; then, to put upon one as a duty, to enjoin, AG:302B CB:1246A
Mark 1 : 27 ; 6 : 27, 39 ; 9 : 25 ; Luke 4 : 36 ; 8 : 25, 31 ; 14 : 22 ; Acts 23 : 2 ; Philm. 8. See CHARGE, ENJOIN.¶

5. KELEUŌ (κελεύω), to urge, incite, order, suggests a stronger 2753
injunction than No. 6, Matt. 14 : 9, 19 ; 15 : 35 ; 18 : 25 ; 27 : 58, 64 ; AG:427B CB:1254C
Luke 18 : 40 ; Acts 4 : 15 (frequently in Acts, not subsequently in the N.T.). See BID.

6. PARANGELLŌ (παραγγέλλω), to announce beside (*para*, beside, 3853
angellō, to announce), to pass on an announcement, hence denotes to AG:613B CB:1262B
give the word, order, give a charge, command, e.g., Mark 6 : 8 ; Luke

8 : 29 ; 9 : 21 ; Acts 5 : 28 ; 2 Thess. 3 : 4, 6, 10, 12. See CHARGE, B,
No. 8.
4367 7. PROSTASSŌ (προστάσσω) denotes to arrange or set in order
AG:718C CB:1267B towards (*pros*, towards, *tassō*, to arrange); hence to prescribe, give
RHEō command, Matt. 1 : 24 ; 8 : 4 ; Mark 1 : 44 ; Luke 5 : 14 ; Acts 10 : 33, 48.
4483 For Matt. 21 : 6 see Note (3) below. See BID.¶
AG:226A (EIPON 3.c.) *Notes :* (1) In Rev. 9 : 4, *rheō*, to speak, is translated "said" in the
CB:1268A R.V. (A.V., "commanded"). (2) in Heb. 12 : 20 *diastellomai*, to charge,
DIASTELLOMAI 1291 enjoin (so in the R.V.), is rendered "commanded" in the A.V. (3) in
AG:188D Matt. 21 : 6, the R.V., translating *suntassō*, as in the best mss., has
CB:1241B "appointed," A.V., "commanded."
SUNTASSō 4929 AG:791D CB:—

COMMANDMENT

1297 1. DIATAGMA (διάταγμα) signifies that which is imposed by decree
AG:189B CB:1241B or law, Heb. 11 : 23. It stresses the concrete character of the commandment more than *epitagē* (No. 4). Cp. COMMAND, No. 1. For the verb in ver. 22 see No. 3 under COMMAND.¶

1785 AG:269A 2. ENTOLĒ (ἐντολή), akin to No. 3, above, denotes, in general, an
CB:1245B injunction, charge, precept, commandment. It is the most frequent term, and is used of moral and religious precepts, e.g., Matt. 5 : 19 ; it is frequent in the Gospels, especially that of John, and in his Epistles. See also, e.g., Acts 17 : 15 ; Rom. 7 : 8–13 ; 13 : 9 ; 1 Cor. 7 : 19 ; Eph. 2 : 15 ; Col. 4 : 10. See PRECEPT.

1778 AG:268B 3. ENTALMA (ἔνταλμα), akin to No. 2, marks more especially the
CB:— thing commanded, a commission ; in Matt. 15 : 9 ; Mark 7 : 7 ; Col. 2 : 22, R.V., "precepts," A.V., "commandments." See PRECEPT.¶

2003 AG:302A 4. EPITAGĒ (ἐπιταγή), akin to No. 4, above, stresses the authorita-
CB:— tiveness of the command ; it is used in Rom. 16 : 26 ; 1 Cor. 7 : 6, 25 ; 2 Cor. 8 : 8 ; 1 Tim. 1 : 1 ; Tit. 1 : 3 ; 2 : 15. See AUTHORITY.¶

3852 AG:613A *Notes :* (1) For *parangelia* (cp. *parangellō*, above), a proclamation, see
CB:1262B CHARGE. (2) In Rev. 22 : 14 the R.V., "wash their robes" (for A.V., "do His commandments") follows the most authentic mss.

COMMEND, COMMENDATION

A. Verbs.

1867 AG:281C 1. EPAINEŌ (ἐπαινέω), to praise, is an intensive form of *aineō*, Luke
CB:1245B 16 : 8. It is elsewhere translated by the verb to praise, in the R.V., Rom. 15 : 11 ; 1 Cor. 11 : 2, 17, 22. See LAUD, PRAISE.¶

3860 AG:614B 2. PARADIDŌMI (παραδίδωμι), lit., to give or deliver over (*para*,
CB:1262A over, *didōmi*, to give), is said of commending, or committing, servants of God to Him (A.V., "recommend"), Acts 14 : 26 ; 15 : 40. See BETRAY, BRING, B, *Note* (4), CAST, COMMIT, DELIVER, GIVE, HAZARD, PUT (in
3908 prison), RECOMMEND.

AG:622D CB:— 3. PARATITHĒMI (παρατίθημι), lit., to put near (*para*, near), in the

Middle Voice, denotes to place with someone, entrust, commit. In the sense of commending, it is said (*a*) of the Lord Jesus in commending His spirit into the Father's hands, Luke 23 : 46 ; (*b*) of commending disciples to God, Acts 14 : 23 ; (*c*) of commending elders to God, Acts 20 : 32. See ALLEGE, COMMIT, PUT, No. 3, SET, No. 4. Cp. No. 2.

4. PARISTĒMI (παρίστημι), lit., to place near, set before, (*para*, near, 3936
histēmi, to set), is used of self-commendation, 1 Cor. 8 : 8. See ASSIST, AG:627C CB:1262B
BRING, COME, GIVE, PRESENT, PROVE, PROVIDE, SHEW, STAND, YIELD.

5. SUNISTĒMI (συνίστημι), or SUNISTANŌ (συνιστάνω), lit., to place 4921
together, denotes to introduce one person to another, represent as worthy, AG:790C CB:1270C
e.g., Rom. 3 : 5 ; 5 : 8 ; 16 : 1 ; 2 Cor. 4 : 2 ; 6 : 4 ; 10 : 18 ; 12 : 11. In 2 Cor. 3 : 1 ; 5 : 12 and 10 : 12, the verb *sunistanō* is used. See APPROVE, CONSIST, MAKE, STAND.

B. Adjective.

SUSTATIKOS (συστατικός), akin to A, No. 5, lit., placing together, 4956
hence, commendatory, is used of letters of commendation, 2 Cor. 3 : 1, AG:795A CB:—
lit., 'commendatory letters.'¶

COMMIT, COMMISSION

A. Verbs.

(I) *In the sense of doing or practising.*

1. ERGAZOMAI (ἐργάζομαι), to work, is translated by the verb to 2038
commit (of committing sin), in Jas. 2 : 9. This is a stronger expression AG:306D CB:1246C
than *poieō*, to do, or *prassō*, to practise (Nos. 2 and 3). See DO, LABOUR, MINISTER, TRADE, WORK.

2. POIEŌ (ποιέω), to do, cause etc., sometimes signifies to commit, 4160
of any act, as of murder, Mark 15 : 7 ; sin, John 8 : 34 ; 2 Cor. 11 : 7 ; AG:680D CB:1265C
Jas. 5 : 15. See DO.

Note : In 1 John 3 : 4, 8, 9, the A.V. wrongly has "commit" (an impossible meaning in ver. 8) ; the R.V. rightly has "doeth," i.e., of a continuous habit, equivalent to *prassō*, to practise. The committal of an act is not in view in that passage.

3. PRASSŌ (πράσσω), to do, work, practise, is said of continuous 4238
action, or action not yet completed, Acts 25 : 11, 25 ; it is rendered AG:698B CB:1266B
"practise" in the R.V., for the incorrect A.V. "commit," in Rom. 1 : 32 ; 2 : 2. See DO, EXACT, KEEP, REQUIRE, USE.

(II) *In the sense of delivering or entrusting something to a person.*

1. PARADIDŌMI (παραδίδωμι), to give over, is often rendered by 3860
the verb to commit, e.g., to prison, Acts 8 : 3 ; to the grace of God, Acts AG:614B CB:1262A
14 : 26 ; to God, 1 Pet. 2 : 23 ; by God to pits of darkness, 2 Pet. 2 : 4. See COMMEND, No. 2.

2. PISTEUŌ (πιστεύω) signifies to entrust, commit to, Luke 16 : 11 ; 4100 AG:660B
1 Tim. 1 : 11, "committed to (my) trust." See BELIEVE. CB:1265A

3. TITHĒMI (τίθημι), to put, place, signifies, in the Middle Voice, 5087 AG:815D CB:1272C

to put for oneself, assign, place in, 2 Cor. 5 : 19, " having committed (unto us)."

3908 4. PARATITHĒMI (παρατίθημι), see COMMEND, No. 3, signifies to
AG:622D CB:— entrust, commit to one's charge, e.g., in Luke 12 : 48 ; 1 Tim. 1 : 18 ;
DIDōMI 2 Tim. 2 : 2 ; 1 Pet. 4 : 19 (A.V., " commit the keeping ").

1325 *Notes :* (1) *Didōmi*, to give, is rendered " committed " in the A.V.
AG:192C CB:1241C of John 5 : 22 (R.V., " given "). (2) For *porneuō* (to commit fornication)
HIEROSULEō see FORNICATION. (3) In Rom. 2 : 22, *hierosuleō*, to rob temples, is so
2416 rendered in the R.V., for A.V., " commit sacrilege." (4) In Acts 27 : 40,
AG:373C CB:1250B *eaō*, to let, leave, is rendered in the R.V., " left (the anchors) in ",
EAō 1439 for A.V., " committed themselves to."

AG:212C

B. Nouns.

CB:— 1. PARATHĒKĒ (παραθήκη), a putting with, a deposit (*para*, with,
3866 AG:616B *tithēmi*, to put), and its longer form, *parakatathēkē*, are found, the former
CB:1262B in 2 Tim. 1 : 12, " that which He hath committed unto me," R.V., marg.,
PARAKATATHĒKĒ lit., ' my deposit ' (perhaps, ' my deposit with Him '), the latter in 1 Tim.
3872 6 : 20, where " guard that which is committed unto thee " is, lit., ' guard
AG:617D CB:— the deposit,' and 2 Tim. 1 : 14, " that good thing which was committed unto thee," i.e., the good deposit ; R.V., marg., " the good deposit."¶

2011 2. EPITROPĒ (ἐπιτροπή) denotes a turning over (to another), a
AG:303D CB:— referring of a thing to another (*epi*, over, *trepō*, to turn), and so a committal of full powers, a commission, Acts 26 : 12.¶

COMMODIOUS (not)

428 ANEUTHETOS (ἀνεύθετος), not commodious, lit., ' not-well-placed '
AG:65C CB:— (from *a*, not, *n*, euphonic, *eu*, well, *thetos*, from *tithēmi*, to put, place), is found in Acts 27 : 12, where it is said of the haven at the place called Fair Havens.¶

COMMON, COMMONLY

A. Adjective.

2839 KOINOS (κοινός) denotes (*a*) common, belonging to several (Lat.,
AG:438A CB:1255B *communis*), said of things had in common, Acts 2 : 44 ; 4 : 32 ; of faith, Tit. 1 : 4 ; of salvation, Jude 3 ; it stands in contrast to *idios*, one's own ; (*b*) ordinary, belonging to the generality, as distinct from what is peculiar to the few ; hence the application to religious practices of Gentiles in contrast with those of Jews ; or of the ordinary people in contrast with those of the Pharisees ; hence the meaning unhallowed, profane, Levitically unclean (Lat., *profanus*), said of hands, Mark 7 : 2 (A.V., " defiled,") R.V. marg., " common ; " of animals, ceremonially unclean, Acts 10 : 14 ; 11 : 8 ; of a man, 10 : 28 ; of meats, Rom. 14 : 14, " unclean ; " of the blood of the covenant, as viewed by an apostate, Heb. 10 : 29, " unholy " (R.V., marg., " common ") ; of everything unfit for the holy city, Rev.

21 : 27, R.V., " unclean " (marg., " common "). Some mss. have the verb here. See Defiled, Unclean, Unholy.¶

B. Verb.

KOINOŌ (*κοινόω*), to make, or count, common, has this meaning in 2840
Acts 10 : 15 ; 11 : 9. See Defile, Pollute, Unclean. AG:438B CB:1255B

Notes : (1) *Polus*, used of number, signifies many, numerous ; used 4183
of space, it signifies wide, far reaching ; hence, with the article it is said AG:687C
of a multitude as being numerous ; it is translated " common " (people) CB:1266A
in Mark 12 : 37 (see the R.V., marg.). It does not, however, mean the ordinary folk, but the many folk. See Abundant, Great, Long, Many, Much, Plenty.

(2) *Ochlos* denotes a crowd, a great multitude ; with the article it is 3793
translated " the common people," in John 12 : 9, 12 (R.V., marg.). See AG:600C CB:1260B
Company, Crowd, Multitude, Number, People, Press.

(3) *Tunchanō*, to happen, is used as an adjective in Acts 28 : 2, of the 5177
kindness shown by the people of Melita to the shipwrecked company ; AG:829B CB:—
A.V., " (no) little ; " R.V., " (no) common ; " the idea suggested by the verb is that which might happen anywhere or at all times ; hence, little, ordinary, or casual. See Chance, Enjoy, Obtain.

(4) In Matt. 27 : 27, what the A.V. describes as " the common hall," is the prætorium, R.V., " palace," the official residence of the Governor of a Province (marg., " prætorium ").

(5) In Acts 5 : 18, *dēmosios* (A.V., " common," with reference to the 1219
prison) signifies " public," belonging to the people, *dēmos*, (R.V., AG:179B CB:1240C
" public ").

(6) In 1 Cor. 5 : 1, *holōs*, altogether (A.V., " commonly ") means 3654
" actually " (R.V.). AG:565B CB:1251A

(7) In Matt. 28 : 15, *diaphēmizō*, to spread abroad (as in the R.V.), 1310
is rendered in the A.V., " is commonly reported." See Spread, *Note* (5). AG:190C CB:—

COMMONWEALTH

1. POLITEIA (*πολιτεία*) : see Citizenship, No. 3.
2. POLITEUMA (*πολίτευμα*) : see Citizenship, No. 4.

For COMMOTION see CONFUSION, TUMULT

COMMUNE

1. DIALALEŌ (*διαλαλέω*) signifies to speak with anyone (*dia*, by 1255
turns, *laleō*, to speak), Luke 6 : 11 ; in 1 : 65, to talk over, to noise AG:185C CB:—
abroad. The idea that *laleō* and its compounds bear no reference to the word spoken or the sentiment, is unfounded. See Noise.¶

2. HOMILEŌ (*ὁμιλέω*), from *homos*, together, signifies to be in 3656 AG:565C
company, to associate with any one ; hence, to have intercourse with, CB:—

Luke 24 : 14 (R.V., " communed ; " A.V., " talked "), 15 ; Acts 24 : 26 ; in 20 : 11, " talked with." See TALK.¶

4814 AG:776C CB:— 3. SULLALEŌ (συλλαλέω), to talk together, is translated " communed " in Luke 22 : 4, of the conspiracy of Judas with the chief priests. See CONFER, SPEAK, TALK.

2980 AG:463A CB:1256B *Note : Laleō* and its compounds, and the noun *lalia*, speech, have a more dignified meaning in the Hellenistic Greek than to chatter, its frequent meaning in earlier times.

COMMUNICATE, COMMUNICATION

A. Verbs.

2841 AG:438C CB:1255B 1. KOINŌNEŌ (κοινωνέω) is used in two senses, (*a*) to have a share in, Rom. 15 : 27 ; 1 Tim. 5 : 22 ; Heb. 2 : 14 ; 1 Pet. 4 : 13 ; 2 John 11 ; (*b*) to give a share to, go shares with, Rom. 12 : 13, R.V., " communicating," for A.V., " distributing ; " Gal. 6 : 6, " communicate ; " Phil. 4 : 15, A.V., " did communicate," R.V., " had fellowship with." See DISTRIBUTE, FELLOWSHIP, PARTAKE.¶

4790 AG:774B CB:1270C 2. SUNKOINŌNEŌ (συγκοινωνέω), to share together with (*sun* and No. 1), is translated " communicated with " in Phil. 4 : 14 ; " have fellowship with," Eph. 5 : 11 ; " be . . . partakers of," Rev. 18 : 4 (R.V., " have fellowship "). The thought is that of sharing with others what one has, in order to meet their needs. See FELLOWSHIP, B, No. 2, PARTAKE, B, No. 2.¶

394 (-EMAI) AG:62B CB:— *Note : Anatithēmi*, to set forth, is rendered " laid before " in Gal. 2 : 2, R.V., for A.V., " communicated unto ; " in Acts 25 : 14, R.V., " laid before," for A.V., " declared."¶

B. Nouns.

2842 AG:438D CB:1255B 1. KOINŌNIA (κοινωνία), akin to A (which see), is translated in Heb. 13 : 16 " to communicate," lit., ' be not forgetful of good deed and of fellowship ; ' " fellowship " (A.V., " communication ") in Philm. 6, R.V. See COMMUNION.

3056 AG:477A CB:1257A 2. LOGOS (λόγος), a word, that which is spoken (*legō*, to speak), is used in the plural with reference to a conversation ; " communication," Luke 24 : 17. Elsewhere with this significance the R.V. renders it " speech," Matt. 5 : 37 ; Eph. 4 : 29. See ACCOUNT.

148 AG:25B CB:1234A *Note :* In Col. 3 : 8, where the A.V. translates *aischrologia* by " filthy communication," the R.V. renders it " shameful speaking " (*aischros*, base, *legō*, to speak).

C. Adjective.

2843 AG:439C CB:1255B KOINŌNIKOS (κοινωνικός), akin to A, No. 1 and B, No. 1, means apt, or ready, to communicate, 1 Tim. 6 : 18.¶

3657 AG:565C CB:— *Note : Homilia*, a company, association, or intercourse with (see COMMUNE, No. 2), is translated " company " in 1 Cor. 15 : 33, R.V. (A.V., " communications ") ; the word is in the plural, " evil companies," i.e., associations. See COMPANY, No. 6.¶

COMMUNION

A. Noun.

KOINŌNIA (κοινωνία), a having in common (*koinos*), partnership, 2842
fellowship (see COMMUNICATE), denotes (*a*) the share which one has in AG:438D
anything, a participation, fellowship recognized and enjoyed; thus it CB:1255B
is used of the common experiences and interests of Christian men, Acts 2:42; Gal. 2:9; of participation in the knowledge of the Son of God, 1 Cor. 1:9; of sharing in the realization of the effects of the Blood (i.e., the Death) of Christ and the Body of Christ, as set forth by the emblems in the Lord's Supper, 1 Cor. 10:16; of participation in what is derived from the Holy Spirit, 2 Cor. 13:14 (R.V., "communion"); Phil. 2:1; of participation in the sufferings of Christ, Phil. 3:10; of sharing in the resurrection life possessed in Christ, and so of fellowship with the Father and the Son, 1 John 1:3, 6, 7; negatively, of the impossibility of communion between light and darkness, 2 Cor. 6:14; (*b*) fellowship manifested in acts, the practical effects of fellowship with God, wrought by the Holy Spirit in the lives of believers as the outcome of faith, Philm. 6, and finding expression in joint ministration to the needy, Rom. 15:26; 2 Cor. 8:4; 9:13; Heb. 13:16, and in the furtherance of the Gospel by gifts, Phil. 1:5. See COMMUNICATION, CONTRIBUTION, DISTRIBUTION, FELLOWSHIP.¶

B. Adjective.

KOINŌNOS (κοινωνός), having in common, is rendered "have com- 2844
munion with (the altar),"—the altar standing by metonymy for that AG:439C
which is associated with it—in 1 Cor. 10:18, R.V. (for A.V., "are partakers CB:1255B
of"), and in ver. 20, for A.V., "have fellowship with (demons)." See COMPANION.

COMPACTED

1. SUNISTĒMI (συνίστημι), and transitively *sunistaō*, to stand together 4921
(*sun*, with, *histēmi*, to stand), is rendered "compacted," in 2 Pet. 3:5, of AG:790C
the earth as formerly arranged by God in relation to the waters. See CB:1270C
APPROVE, COMMEND, CONSIST, MAKE, STAND.

2. SUMBIBAZŌ (συμβιβάζω), to unite, to knit, is translated "com- 4822
pacted" in the A.V. of Eph. 4:16 (R.V., "knit together"), concerning AG:777D
the Church as the Body of Christ. See CONCLUDE, GATHER, INSTRUCT, CB:—
KNIT, PROVE.

COMPANION

1. SUNEKDĒMOS (συνέκδημος), a fellow-traveller (*sun*, with, *ek*, 4898
from, *dēmos*, people; i.e., away from one's people), is used in Acts 19:29, AG:787A
of Paul's companions in travel; in 2 Cor. 8:19, "travel with;" a closer CB:—
rendering would be '(as) our fellow-traveller.' See TRAVEL.¶ KOINŌNOS 2844

2. KOINŌNOS (κοινωνός) is rendered "companions" in the A.V. of AG:439C
Heb. 10:33 (R.V. "partakers"). So *sunkoinōnos* in Rev. 1:9, A.V., CB:1255B SUNKOINŌNOS
"companion;" R.V., "partaker with you." See B, above, PARTAKER, 4791 AG:774B
PARTNER. Cp. COMMUNICATE. CB:1270C

4904 3. SUNERGOS (συνεργός), a fellow-worker (*sun*, with, *ergon*, work),
AG:787D is translated in Phil. 2 : 25 " companion in labour," A.V. (R.V., " fellow-
CB:1270C worker "). See HELPER, LABOURER, WORKER.

COMPANY (Noun and Verb)

A. Nouns and Phrases.

3793 1. OCHLOS (ὄχλος), a throng of people, an irregular crowd, most
AG:600C usually a disorganised throng ; in Acts 6 : 7, however, it is said of a
CB:1260B company of the priests who believed ; the word here indicates that they
had not combined to bring this about. The R.V. usually translates this
word " company " or " multitude." Cp. B, *Note* 3. See COMMON,
CROWD, MULTITUDE, and Trench, Syn. §xcviii.

4923 2. SUNODIA (συνοδία), lit., a way or journey together (*sun*, with,
AG:791A *hodos*, a way), denotes, by metonymy, a company of travellers ; in Luke
CB:— 2 : 44, of the company from which Christ was missed by Joseph and
Mary. (Eng., synod).¶

4849 3. SUMPOSION (συμπόσιον), lit. denotes a drinking together (*sun*,
AG:780A with, *pinō*, to drink), a drinking-party ; hence, by metonymy, any table
CB:— party or any company arranged as a party. In Mark 6 : 39 the noun is
repeated, in the plural, by way of an adverbial and distributive phrase,
sumposia sumposia, lit., 'companies-companies' (i.e., by companies).¶

2828 4. KLISIA (κλισία), akin to *klinō*, to recline, primarily means a place
AG:436D for lying down in, and hence a reclining company, for the same purpose
CB:— as No. 3. It is found in the plural in Luke 9 : 14, corresponding to
Mark's word *sumposia* (No. 3, above), signifying companies reclining
at a meal.¶

4128 5. PLĒTHOS (πλῆθος), lit., a fulness, hence denotes a multitude, a
AG:668B large or full company, Luke 23 : 1 ; " a multitude," ver. 27 (A.V., " a
CB:1265B great company "). See BUNDLE, MULTITUDE.

3657 6. HOMILIA (ὁμιλία), an association of people, those who are of the
AG:565C same company (*homos*, same), is used in 1 Cor. 15 : 33, A.V., " (evil)
CB:— communications ; " R.V., " (evil) company."¶

3658 7. HOMILOS (ὅμιλος), akin to No. 6, a throng or crowd, is found, in
AG:565D some mss., in Rev. 18 : 17, " all the company in ships," A.V. *Homilos*
CB:— denotes the concrete ; *homilia* is chiefly an abstract noun.¶

2398 8. IDIOS (ἴδιος) one's own, is used in the plural with the article in
AG:369C Acts 4 : 23, to signify " their own (company)." See BUSINESS, B.
CB:1252C

Notes : (1) The preposition *ex* (i.e., *ek*), of, with the first personal
AUTOS 846 pronoun in the genitive plural (*hēmōn*, us), signifies " of our company,"
AG:122C lit., ' of us,' in Luke 24 : 22 ; so *ex autōn*, in Acts 15 : 22, " men out of
CB:1238B their company," lit., ' men out of them.' (2) The phrase in Acts 13 : 13,
HĒMEIS 2249 *hoi peri Paulon*, lit., ' the (ones) about Paul,' signifies " Paul and his
AG:217A (EGō) company." (3) *Murias*, a noun connected with the adjective *murios*
MURIAS 3461 (numberless, infinite), signifies a myriad (whence the English word), and
AG:529C is used hyperbolically, of vast numbers, e.g., Heb. 12 : 22, A.V., an

innumerable company; R.V., "innumerable hosts." (Contrast ***murioi***, 10,000, Matt. 18:24). (4) In Acts 21:8, the phrase translated "that were of Paul's company" is absent from the best texts.

B. Verbs.

1. SUNANAMIGNUMI (συναναμίγνυμι), lit., to mix up with (***sun***, 4874
with, ***ana***, up, ***mignumi***, to mix, mingle), signifies to have, or keep, AG:784B CB:—
company with, 1 Cor. 5:9, 11; 2 Thess. 3:14.¶

2. SUNERCHOMAI (συνέρχομαι), to come, or go, with, is rendered 4905 AG:788A
"have companied" in Acts 1:21. See COME, No. 11. CB:1270C

Notes: (1) *Aphorizō*, to separate, is translated "separate (you) from 873
(their) company," in Luke 6:22, the latter part being added in italics AG:127B
to supply the meaning of excommunication. See DIVIDE. CB:1236C

(2) *Kollaō*, to join, is rendered "keep company," in Acts 10:28, A.V.; 2853 AG:441C
R.V., "join himself." See CLEAVE, JOIN. CB:1255C

(3) *Ochlopoieō*, lit., to make a crowd (*ochlos*, a crowd, *poieō*, to 3792
make), is translated "gathered a company," in Acts 17:5, A.V.; the R.V. AG:600C
corrects this to "gathering a crowd." See CROWD.¶ CB:—

COMPARE, COMPARISON

1. SUNKRINŌ (συγκρίνω) denotes (*a*) to join fitly, to combine, 1 Cor. 4793 AG:774D
2:13, either in the sense of combining spiritual things with spiritual, CB:1270C
adapting the discourse to the subject, under the guidance of the Holy Spirit, or communicating spiritual things by spiritual things or words, or in the sense of interpreting spiritual things to spiritual men, R.V. and A.V., "comparing" (cp. the Sept. use, of interpreting dreams, etc. Gen. 40:8, 16, 22; 41:12, 15; Dan. 5:12); (*b*) to place together; hence, judge or discriminate by comparison, compare, with or among,
2 Cor. 10:12 (thrice).¶ PARABALLō 3846

2. PARABALLŌ (παραβάλλω), to place side by side, to set forth, AG:611D
and the noun *parabolē* (Eng., parable), occur in Mark 4:30, R.V., "In CB:1262A PARABOLē
what parable shall we set it forth?", A.V., "with what comparison 3850
shall we compare it?" See ARRIVE. AG:612B CB:1262A

Note: The preposition *pros*, towards, is sometimes used of mental 4314
direction, in the way of estimation, or comparison, as in the phrase AG:709C
"(worthy) to be compared," or '(worthy) in comparison with,' Rom. CB:1267A
8:18.

COMPASS

1. KUKLEUŌ (κυκλεύω) denotes to encircle, surround, and is found —
in the best texts in John 10:24, "came round about," and Rev. 20:9, AG:456D CB:—
of a camp surrounded by foes; some mss. have No. 2 in each place.¶

2. KUKLOŌ (κυκλόω), (cp. Eng., cycle), signifies to move in a circle, 2944
to compass about, as of a city encompassed by armies, Luke 21:20; AG:456D
Heb. 11:30; in Acts 14:20, "stood round about." See COME, No. 38, CB:—
STAND.¶

4033 AG:648B CB:— 3. PERIKUKLOŌ (περικυκλόω), *peri*, about, with No. 2, is used in Luke 19 : 43, "shall compass . . . round."¶

4013 AG:645C CB:— 4. PERIAGŌ (περιάγω), to lead about, 1 Cor. 9 : 5, or, intransitively, to go about, to go up and down, is so used in Matt. 4 : 23; 9 : 35; Mark 6 : 6; Acts 13 : 11; to compass regions, Matt. 23 : 15. See GO, LEAD.¶

4029 AG:647D CB:— 5. PERIKEIMAI (περίκειμαι), to be encompassed: see BOUND (*b*), HANG.

4022 AG:646D CB:1263B 6. PERIERCHOMAI (περιέρχομαι), lit., to go, or come, about (*peri*, about, *erchomai*, to come), is translated in Acts 28 : 13, A.V., "fetched a compass." See CIRCUIT.

COMPASSION, COMPASSIONATE

A. Verbs.

3627 AG:561D CB:— 1. OIKTEIRŌ (οἰκτείρω), to have pity, a feeling of distress through the ills of others, is used of God's compassion, Rom. 9 : 15.¶

4697 AG:762D CB:1269C 2. SPLANCHNIZOMAI (σπλαγχνίζομαι), to be moved as to one's inwards (*splanchna*), to be moved with compassion, to yearn with compassion, is frequently recorded of Christ towards the multitude and towards individual sufferers, Matt. 9 : 36; 14 : 14; 15 : 32; 18 : 27; 20 : 34; Mark 1 : 41; 6 : 34; 8 : 2; 9 : 22 (of the appeal of a father for a demon-possessed son); Luke 7 : 13; 10 : 33; of the father in the parable of the prodigal son, 15 : 20. (Moulton and Milligan consider the verb to have been coined in the Jewish Dispersion).¶

4834 AG:778D CB:1270B 3. SUMPATHEŌ (συμπαθέω), to suffer with another (*sun*, with, *paschō*, to suffer), to be affected similarly (Eng., sympathy), to have compassion upon, Heb. 10 : 34, of compassionating those in prison, is translated "be touched with" in Heb. 4 : 15, of Christ as the High Priest. See TOUCH.¶

1653 AG:249C CB:1244A 4. ELEEŌ (ἐλεέω), to have mercy (*eleos*, mercy), to show kindness, by beneficence, or assistance, is translated "have compassion" in Matt. 18 : 33 (A.V.); Mark 5 : 19 and Jude 22. See MERCY.

3356 AG:514D CB:— 5. METRIOPATHEŌ (μετριοπαθέω) is rendered "have compassion," in Heb. 5 : 2, A.V. See BEAR, No. 13.¶

B. Nouns.

3628 AG:561D CB:1260C 1. OIKTIRMOS (οἰκτιρμός), akin to A, No. 1, is used with *splanchna* (see below), the viscera, the inward parts, as the seat of emotion, the "heart," Phil. 2 : 1; Col. 3 : 12, "a heart of compassion" (A.V., "bowels of mercies"). In Heb. 10 : 28 it is used with *chōris*, "without," (lit., 'without compassions'). It is translated "mercies" in Rom. 12 : 1 and 2 Cor. 1 : 3. See MERCY.¶

4698 AG:763A CB:1269C 2. SPLANCHNON (σπλάγχνον), always used in the plural, is suitably rendered "compassion" in the R.V. of Col. 3 : 12 and 1 John 3 : 17; "compassions" in Phil. 2 : 1. Cp. A, No. 2. See BOWELS.

C. Adjective.

SUMPATHĒS (συμπαθής) denotes suffering with, "compassionate," 4835
1 Pet. 3 : 8, R.V. (A.V., "having compassion"). See A, No. 3.¶ AG:779A CB:—

COMPEL

1. ANANKAZŌ (ἀναγκάζω) denotes to put constraint upon (from 315 AG:52A
anankē, necessity), to constrain, whether by threat, entreaty, force or CB:1235B
persuasion; Christ "constrained" the disciples to get into a boat, Matt. 14 : 22; Mark 6 : 45; the servants of the man who made a great supper were to constrain people to come in, Luke 14 : 23 (R.V., "constrain"); Saul of Tarsus "strove" to make saints blaspheme, Acts 26 : 11, R.V. (A.V., "compelled"); Titus, though a Greek, was not "compelled" to be circumcised, Gal. 2 : 3, as Galatian converts were, 6 : 12, R.V.; Peter was "compelling" Gentiles to live as Jews, Gal. 2 : 14; Paul was "constrained" to appeal to Cæsar, Acts 28 : 19, and was "compelled" by the church at Corinth to become foolish in speaking of himself, 2 Cor. 12 : 11. See CONSTRAIN.¶

2. ANGAREUŌ (ἀγγαρεύω), to despatch as an *angaros* (a Persian 29
courier kept at regular stages with power of impressing men into service), AG:6D CB:—
and hence, in general, to impress into service, is used of compelling a person to go a mile, Matt. 5 : 41; of the impressing of Simon to bear Christ's Cross, Matt. 27 : 32; Mark 15 : 21.¶

COMPETE See CONTEND

COMPETENT See ABLE

COMPLAINER, COMPLAINT

1. MEMPSIMOIROS (μεμψίμοιρος) denotes one who complains, lit., 3202
complaining of one's lot (*memphomai*, to blame, *moira*, a fate, lot); hence, AG:502C CB:1258B
discontented, querulous, repining; it is rendered "complainers" in Jude 16.¶

2. MOMPHĒ (μομφή) denotes blame (akin to *memphomai*, see No. 1), 3437
an occasion of complaint, Col. 3 : 13 (A.V., "quarrel"). See QUARREL.¶ AG:527A CB:—

3. AITIŌMA (αἰτίωμα), a charge, is translated "complaints" in 157 (-AMA)
Acts 25 : 7, A.V. See CHARGE.¶ AG:26D CB:1234A

COMPLETE, COMPLETION, COMPLETELY

A. Verbs.

1. EPITELEŌ (ἐπιτελέω), to complete: see ACCOMPLISH, No. 4. 2005 AG:302B CB:—

2. EXARTIZŌ (ἐξαρτίζω), to fit out (*ek*, out, intensive, *artos*, a joint; 1822
or from *artios*, perfect, lit., exactly right), is said of the equipment of AG:273C CB:1247C
the man of God, 2 Tim. 3 : 17, "furnished completely" (A.V., "throughly furnished"); elsewhere in Acts 21 : 5, "accomplished." Cp. B. See FURNISH.¶

3. SUNTELEŌ (συντελέω), to end together, bring quite to an end 4931
(*sun*, together, intensive, *telos*, an end), is said (*a*) of the completion of a AG:792A CB:1271A
period of days, Luke 4 : 2; Acts 21 : 27; (*b*) of completing something; some mss. have it in Matt. 7 : 28, of the Lord, in ending His discourse

(the best mss. have *teleō* to finish) ; of God, in finishing a work, Rom. 9 : 28, in making a new covenant, Heb. 8 : 8, marg., "accomplish ;" of the fulfilment of things foretold, Mark 13 : 4 ; of the Devil's temptation of the Lord, Luke 4 : 13. See END, FINISH, FULFIL, MAKE.¶

4137 4. PLĒROŌ (πληρόω), to fill (in the Passive Voice, to be made full),
AG:670C CB:1265B is translated " complete " in the A.V. of Col. 2 : 10 (R.V., " made full ; "
cp. v. 9). See ACCOMPLISH.

4135 AG:670B 5. PLEROPHOREŌ (πληροφορέω), to be fully assured, is translated
CB:1265B " complete " in Col. 4 : 12. See ASSURED, B, No. 2.

B. Adjective.

739 AG:110C ARTIOS (ἄρτιος), fitted, complete (from *artos*, a limb, joint), is used
CB:1237C in 2 Tim. 3 : 17, R.V., " complete," A.V., " perfect." See PERFECT.¶

C. Noun.

535 AG:81B APARTISMOS (ἀπαρτισμός) is rendered "complete" in Luke 14 : 28,
CB:— R.V.¶

For COMPREHEND see APPREHEND, John 1 : 5, A.V., and SUM UP

CONCEAL

3871 PARAKALUPTŌ (παρακαλύπτω), to conceal thoroughly (*para*, beside,
AG:617D CB:— intensive, *kaluptō*, to hide), is found in Luke 9 : 45, of concealing from the
disciples the fact of the delivering up of Christ.

CONCEITED See PUFF (UP)

CONCEITS

HEAUTOU 1438 1. EN HEAUTOIS (ἐν ἑαυτοῖς), lit., 'in yourselves,' is used with
AG:211D *phronimos*, " wise," in Rom. 11 : 25, " (wise) in your own conceits (i.e.,
CB:1249B (-OS) opinions)."

2. PAR' HEAUTOIS (παρ' ἑαυτοῖς), (*para*, with, in the estimation of), in Rom. 12 : 16 has the same rendering as No. 1.

CONCEIVE

1080 1. GENNAŌ (γεννάω), to conceive, beget : see BEGET, A, No. 1.
AG:155B CB:1248A 2. SULLAMBANŌ (συλλαμβάνω), lit., to take together (*sun*, with,
4815 *lambanō*, to take or receive), is used (*a*) of a woman, to conceive, Luke
AG:776D CB:1270B 1 : 24, 31, 36 ; in the Passive Voice, Luke 2 : 21 ; (*b*) metaphorically,
of the impulse of lust in the human heart, enticing to sin, Jas. 1 : 15.
For its other meanings see CATCH, No. 8.

5087 AG:815D 3. TITHĒMI (τίθημι), to put, set, is used in Acts 5 : 4, of the sin of
CB:1272C Ananias, in conceiving a lie in his heart.

2845 AG:440A *Notes :* (1) The phrase *echō*, to have, with *koitē*, a lying down, a bed,
CB:1255B especially the marriage bed, denotes to conceive, Rom. 9 : 10.¶

2602 AG:409A (2) The phrase *eis katabolēn*, lit., for a casting down, or in, is used of
CB:1254A conception in Heb. 11 : 11.¶

CONCERN (-ETH)

1. The neuter plural of the article (' the things '), with the genitive HO (1)
case of a noun, is used in 2 Cor. 11 : 30 of Paul's infirmity, " the things 3588 AG:549B
that concern my infirmity," lit., ' the (things) of my infirmity.' CB:—

2. The neuter singular of the article, with the preposition *peri*, con- PERI
cerning, is used by the Lord in Luke 22 : 37, " that which concerneth," 4012 AG:644B
lit., ' the (thing) concerning (Me).' The same construction is found in CB:1263B
Luke 24 : 27 ; Acts 19 : 8 ; 28 : 31.

CONCERN See CARE

CONCERNING : see Note †, p. 1

CONCISION

KATATOMĒ (κατατομή), lit., a cutting off (*kata*, down, *temnō*, to cut), 2699
a mutilation, is a term found in Phil. 3 : 2, there used by the Apostle, AG:419D CB:1254B
by a paranomasia, contemptuously, for the Jewish circumcision with its Judaistic influence, in contrast to the true spiritual circumcision.¶

CONCLUDE

SUMBIBAZŌ (συμβιβάζω), lit., to make to come together, is translated 4822
" concluding " in Acts 16 : 10, R.V., for the A.V., " assuredly gathering." AG:777D CB:—
See COMPACTED, INSTRUCT, KNIT, PROVE.

Notes : (1) For *krinō*, to judge, give judgment, rendered " concluded " 2919
in the A.V. of Acts 21 : 25, R.V., " giving judgment," see JUDGMENT. AG:451B CB:1256A

(2) For *logizomai*, to reckon, translated " conclude " in Rom. 3 : 28, 3049
A.V., R.V., " reckon," see RECKON. AG:475D CB:1257A

(3) For *sunkleiō*, to shut up with, translated " concluded " in Rom. 4788
11 : 32 ; Gal. 3 : 22, A.V., R.V., " shut up," see INCLOSE, SHUT. AG:774A CB:1270C

CONCORD

SUMPHŌNĒSIS (συμφώνησις), lit., a sounding together (*sun*, with, 4857
phōnē, a sound ; Eng., symphony), is found in 2 Cor. 6 : 15, in the AG:781A CB:—
rhetorical question " what concord hath Christ with Belial ? " See AGREE, A, No. 1.¶

CONCOURSE

SUNTROPHĒ (συντροφή), a turning together (*sun*, with, *trepō*, to 4963
turn), signifies (*a*) that which is rolled together ; hence (*b*) a dense mass AG:795C CB:—
of people, concourse, Acts 19 : 40.¶ See BANDED.

For CONCUPISCENCE (A.V. of Rom. 7 : 8 ; Col. 3 : 5 ; 1 Thess. 4 : 5), see COVET, DESIRE, LUST.

CONDEMN, CONDEMNATION

A. Verbs.

2607

1. KATAGINŌSKŌ (καταγινώσκω), to know something against (*kata*, AG:409D CB:1254A

against, *ginōskō*, to know by experience), hence, to think ill of, to condemn, is said, in Gal. 2 : 11, of Peter's conduct (R.V., "stood condemned"), he being self-condemned as the result of an exercised and enlightened conscience, and condemned in the sight of others ; so of self-condemnation due to an exercise of heart, 1 John 3 : 20, 21. See BLAME.¶

2613 AG:410B CB:1254A 2. KATADIKAZŌ (*καταδικάζω*) signifies to exercise right or law against anyone ; hence, to pronounce judgment, to condemn (*kata*, down, or against, *dikē*, justice), Matt. 12 : 7, 37 ; Luke 6 : 37 ; Jas. 5 : 6.¶

2919 AG:451B CB:1256A 3. KRINŌ (*κρίνω*), to distinguish, choose, give an opinion upon, judge, sometimes denotes to condemn, e.g., Acts 13 : 27 ; Rom. 2 : 27 ; Jas. 5 : 9 (in the best mss.). Cp. No. 1, below. See CALL (No. 13), CONCLUDE, DECREE, DETERMINE, ESTEEM, JUDGE, LAW (go to), ORDAIN, SUE, THINK.

2632 AG:412A CB:1254A 4. KATAKRINŌ (*κατακρίνω*), a strengthened form of No. 3, signifies to give judgment against, pass sentence upon ; hence, to condemn, implying (*a*) the fact of a crime, e.g., Rom. 2 : 1 ; 14 : 23 ; 2 Pet. 2 : 6 ; some mss. have it in Jas. 5 : 9 ; (*b*) the imputation of a crime, as in the condemnation of Christ by the Jews, Matt. 20 : 18 ; Mark 14 : 64. It is used metaphorically of condemning by a good example, Matt. 12 : 41, 42 ; Luke 11 : 31, 32 ; Heb. 11 : 7.

In Rom. 8 : 3, God's condemnation of sin is set forth in that Christ, His own Son, sent by Him to partake of human nature (sin apart) and to become an offering for sin, died under the judgment due to our sin.

B. Nouns.

2917 AG:450C CB:1256A 1. KRIMA (*κρίμα*) denotes (*a*) the sentence pronounced, a verdict, a condemnation, the decision resulting from an investigation, e.g., Mark 12 : 40 ; Luke 23 : 40 ; 1 Tim. 3 : 6 ; Jude 4 ; (*b*) the process of judgment leading to a decision, 1 Pet. 4 : 17 ("judgment"), where *krisis* (see No. 3, below) might be expected. In Luke 24 : 20, "to be condemned" translates the phrase *eis krima*, "unto condemnation" (i.e., unto the pronouncement of the sentence of condemnation). For the rendering "judgment," see, e.g., Rom. 11 : 33 ; 1 Cor. 11 : 34 ; Gal. 5 : 10 ; Jas. 3 : 1. In these (*a*) the process leading to a decision and (*b*) the pronouncement of the decision, the verdict, are to be distinguished. In 1 Cor. 6 : 7 the word means a matter for judgment, a lawsuit. See JUDGMENT.

2631 AG:412A CB:1254A 2. KATAKRIMA (*κατάκριμα*), cp. No. 4, above, is the sentence pronounced, the condemnation with a suggestion of the punishment following ; it is found in Rom. 5 : 16, 18 ; 8 : 1.¶

2920 AG:452C CB:1256A 3. KRISIS (*κρίσις*) (*a*) denotes the process of investigation, the act of distinguishing and separating (as distinct from *krima*, see No. 1 above) ; hence a judging, a passing of judgment upon a person or thing ; it has a variety of meanings, such as judicial authority, John 5 : 22, 27 ; justice, Acts 8 : 33 ; Jas. 2 : 13 ; a tribunal, Matt. 5 : 21, 22 ; a trial, John 5 : 24 ; 2 Pet. 2 : 4 ; a judgment, 2 Pet. 2 : 11 ; Jude 9 ; by metonymy, the standard of judgment, just dealing, Matt. 12 : 18, 20 ; 23 : 23 ; Luke 11 : 42 ; Divine judgment executed, 2 Thess. 1 : 5 ; Rev. 16 : 7 ; (*b*) sometimes it has the meaning " condemnation," and is virtually equivalent to *krima* (*a*) ; see Matt. 23 : 33 ; John 3 : 19 ; Jas. 5 : 12, *hupo krisin*, " under judgment." See ACCUSATION, A (Note), DAMNATION, JUDGMENT.

Note : In John 9 : 39, " For judgment (*krima*) came I into this world," the meaning would appear to be, ' for being judged ' (as a touchstone for proving men's thoughts and characters), in contrast to 5 : 22, ' hath given all judging (*krisis*) to the Son ; ' in Luke 24 : 20, " delivered Him up to be condemned to death," the latter phrase is, lit., ' to a verdict (*krima*) of death ' (which they themselves could not carry out) ; in Mark 12 : 40, " these shall receive greater condemnation " (*krima*), the phrase signifies a heavier verdict (against themselves).

4. KATAKRISIS (κατάκρισις), a strengthened form of No. 3, denotes 2633
a judgment against, condemnation, with the suggestion of the process AG:412B
leading to it, as of " the ministration of condemnation," 2 Cor. 3 : 9 ; CB:1254A
in 7 : 3, " to condemn," more lit., ' with a view to condemnation.'¶

C. Adjectives.

1. AUTOKATAKRITOS (αὐτοκατάκριτος), self-condemned (*auto*, self, 843
katakrinō, to condemn), i.e., on account of doing himself what he condemns AG:122C
in others, is used in Tit. 3 : 11.¶ CB:1238B

2. AKATAGNŌSTOS (ἀκατάγνωστος), akin to A, No. 1, with negative 176
prefix, *a*, " not to be condemned," is said of sound speech, in Tit. 2 : 8.¶ AG:29D
CB:—

CONDESCEND

SUNAPAGŌ (συναπάγω) : see CARRY, No. 7.

CONDITIONS

Note : This translates the phrase *ta pros* in Luke 14 : 32, lit., ' the PROS 4314
(things) towards,' i.e., the things relating to, or conditions of, (peace). AG:709C
CB:1267A

CONDUCT

A. Noun.

AGŌGĒ (ἀγωγή), from *agō*, to lead, properly denotes a teaching ; 72
then, figuratively, a training, discipline, and so, the life led, a way or AG:14D
course of life, conduct, 2 Tim. 3 : 10, R.V., " conduct ; " A.V., " manner CB:1233C
of life." See LIFE.¶

B. Verbs.

1. KATHISTĒMI (καθίστημι), lit., to stand down or set down (*kata*, 2525
down, *histēmi*, to stand), has, among its various meanings, the significance AG:390B
of bringing to a certain place, conducting, Acts 17 : 15 (so the Sept. in CB:1254C
Josh. 6 : 23 ; 1 Sam. 5 : 3 ; 2 Chron. 28 : 15). See APPOINT.

2. PROPEMPŌ (προπέμπω) signifies to set forward, conduct : see 4311 AG:709B
ACCOMPANY, No. 4. CB:—

CONFER, CONFERENCE

4323 AG:711D CB:— 1. PROSANATITHĒMI (προσανατίθημι), lit., to put before (*pros*, towards, *ana*, up, and *tithēmi*, to put), i.e., to lay a matter before others so as to obtain counsel or instruction, is used of Paul's refraining from consulting human beings, Gal. 1 : 16 (translated "imparted" in 2 : 6; A.V., "added . . . in conference"). Cp. the shorter form *anatithēmi*, in 2 : 2, "laid before," the less intensive word being used there simply to signify the imparting of information, rather than conferring with others to seek advice. See ADD, IMPART.¶

4814 AG:776C CB:— 2. SULLALEŌ (συλλαλέω), to speak together with (*sun*, with, *laleō*, to speak), is translated "conferred" in Acts 25 : 12; elsewhere of talking with Matt. 17 : 3; Mark 9 : 4; Luke 4 : 36; 9 : 30; "communed" in Luke 22 : 4. See COMMUNE, SPEAK, TALK.¶

4820 AG:777B CB:— 3. SUMBALLŌ (συμβάλλω), lit., to throw together (*sun*, with, *ballō*, to throw), is used of conversation, to discourse or consult together, confer, Acts 4 : 15. See ENCOUNTER, HELP, MEET WITH, PONDER.

Note: For the A.V., "conference" in Gal. 2 : 6, see No. 1, above.

CONFESS, CONFESSION

A. Verbs.

3670 AG:568A CB:1251A 1. HOMOLOGEŌ (ὁμολογέω), lit., to speak the same thing (*homos*, same, *legō*, to speak), to assent, accord, agree with, denotes, either (*a*) to confess, declare, admit, John 1 : 20; e.g., Acts 24 : 14; Heb. 11 : 13; (*b*) to confess by way of admitting oneself guilty of what one is accused of, the result of inward conviction, 1 John 1 : 9; (*c*) to declare openly by way of speaking out freely, such confession being the effect of deep conviction of facts, Matt. 7 : 23; 10 : 32 (twice) and Luke 12 : 8 (see next par.); John 9 : 22; 12 : 42; Acts 23 : 8; Rom. 10 : 9, 10 ("confession is made"); 1 Tim. 6 : 12 (R.V.); Tit. 1 : 16; 1 John 2 : 23; 4 : 2,15; 2 John 7 (in John's Epp. it is the necessary antithesis to Gnostic doceticism); Rev. 3 : 5, in the best mss. (some have No. 2 here); (*d*) to confess by way of celebrating with praise, Heb. 13 : 15; (*e*) to promise, Matt. 14 : 7.

In Matt. 10 : 32 and Luke 12 : 8 the construction of this verb with *en*, in, followed by the dative case of the personal pronoun, has a special significance, namely, to confess in a person's name, the nature of the confession being determined by the context, the suggestion being to make a public confession. Thus the statement, "every one . . . who shall confess Me (lit., in Me, i.e., in My case) before men, him (lit., in him, i.e., in his case) will I also confess before My Father . . .," conveys the thought of confessing allegiance to Christ as one's Master and Lord, and, on the other hand, of acknowledgment, on His part, of the faithful one as being His worshipper and servant, His loyal follower; this is appropriate to the original idea in *homologeō* of being identified in thought or language. See PROFESS, PROMISE, THANK.¶

2. EXOMOLOGEŌ (ἐξομολογέω), *ek*, out, intensive, and No. 1, and 1843
accordingly stronger than No. 1, to confess forth, i.e., freely, openly, is AG:277A CB:1247C
used (*a*) of a public acknowledgment or confession of sins, Matt. 3 : 6 ; (EXHO-)
Mark 1 : 5 ; Acts 19 : 18 ; Jas. 5 : 16 ; (*b*) to profess or acknowledge openly, Matt. 11 : 25 (translated " thank," but indicating the fuller idea) ; Phil. 2 : 11 (some mss. have it in Rev. 3 : 5 : see No. 1) ; (*c*) to confess by way of celebrating, giving praise, Rom. 14 : 11 ; 15 : 9. In Luke 10 : 21, it is translated " I thank," the true meaning being ' I gladly acknowledge.' In Luke 22 : 6 it signifies to consent (R.V.), for A.V., " promised." See Consent, Promise, Thank.¶

B. Noun.

HOMOLOGIA (ὁμολογία), akin to A, No. 1, denotes confession, by 3671
acknowledgment of the truth, 2 Cor. 9 : 13 ; 1 Tim. 6 : 12, 13 ; Heb. 3 : 1 ; AG:568D CB:1251A
4 : 14 ; 10 : 23 (A.V., incorrectly, " profession," except in 1 Tim. 6 : 13).¶

Note : For the adverb *homologoumenōs*, confessedly, see Controversy.

CONFIDENCE (Noun, or Verb with " have "), CONFIDENT (-LY)

A. Nouns.

1. PEPOITHĒSIS (πεποίθησις), akin to *peithō*, B, No. 1 below, denotes 4006
persuasion, assurance, confidence, 2 Cor. 1 : 15 ; 3 : 4, A.V., " trust ; " AG:643B CB:1263B
8 : 22 ; 10 : 2 ; Eph. 3 : 12 ; Phil. 3 : 4. See Trust.¶

2. HUPOSTASIS (ὑπόστασις), lit., a standing under (*hupo*, under, 5287
stasis, a standing), that which stands, or is set, under, a foundation, AG:847A CB:1252B
beginning ; hence, the quality of confidence which leads one to stand under, endure, or undertake anything, 2 Cor. 9 : 4 ; 11 : 17 ; Heb. 3 : 14. Twice in Heb. it signifies substance, 1 : 3 (A.V., " Person ") and 11 : 1. See Substance.¶

3. PARRHĒSIA (παῤῥησία), often rendered " confidence " in the 3954
A.V., is in all such instances rendered " boldness " in the R.V., Acts AG:630C CB:1262C
28 : 31 ; Heb. 3 : 6 ; 1 John 2 : 28 ; 3 : 21 ; 5 : 14. See Boldness, Openly, Plainness.

B. Verbs.

1. PEITHŌ (πείθω), to persuade, or, intransitively, to have confidence, 3982
to be confident (cp. A, No. 1), has this meaning in the following, Rom. AG:639A CB:1263A
2 : 19 ; 2 Cor. 2 : 3 ; Gal. 5 : 10 ; Phil. 1 : 6, 14 (R.V., " being confident," for A.V., " waxing confident "), 25 ; 3 : 3, 4 ; 2 Thess. 3 : 4 ; Philm. 21. See Agree, Assure, Believe, Obey, Persuade, Trust, Yield.

2. THARREŌ (θαρρέω), to be of good courage, is so translated in the 2292
R.V. of 2 Cor. 5 : 6 ; 7 : 16 (A.V., to have confidence, or be confident). AG:352A CB:1271C
See Courage.

Note : The adverb " confidently " is combined with the verb " affirm " DIISCHURIZOMAI
to represent the verbs *diïschurizomai*, Luke 22 : 59 and Acts 12 : 15, R.V. 1340 AG:195B
(A.V., " constantly affirmed "),¶, and *diabebaioomai*, 1 Tim. 1 : 7, A.V., DIABEBAIOOMAI
" affirm," and Tit. 3 : 8, A.V., " affirm constantly." See Affirm.¶ 1226 AG:181D

CONFIRM, CONFIRMATION

A. Verbs.

950 AG:138C CB:1239A 1. BEBAIOŌ (βεβαιόω), to make firm, establish, make secure (the connected adjective *bebaios* signifies stable, fast, firm), is used of confirming a word, Mark 16 : 20 ; promises, Rom. 15 : 8 ; the testimony of Christ, 1 Cor. 1 : 6 ; the saints by the Lord Jesus Christ, 1 Cor. 1 : 8 ; the saints by God, 2 Cor. 1 : 21 (" stablisheth ") ; in faith, Col. 2 : 7 ; the salvation spoken through the Lord and confirmed by the Apostles, Heb. 2 : 3 ; the heart by grace, Heb. 13 : 9 (" stablished ").¶

1991 AG:300D CB:1246A 2. EPISTĒRIZŌ (ἐπιστηρίζω), to make to lean upon, strengthen (*epi*, upon, *stērix*, a prop, support), is used of confirming souls, Acts 14 : 22 ; brethren, 15 : 32 ; churches, 15 : 41 ; disciples, 18 : 23, in some mss. (" stablishing," R.V., " strengthening," A.V.) ; the most authentic mss. have *stērizō* in 18 : 23. See STRENGTHEN.¶

2964 AG:461A CB:1256B 3. KUROŌ (κυρόω), to make valid, ratify, impart authority or influence (from *kuros*, might, *kurios*, mighty, a head, as supreme in authority), is used of spiritual love, 2 Cor. 2 : 8 ; a human covenant, Gal. 3 : 15.¶. In the Sept., see Gen. 23 : 20, e.g.

4300 AG:708B CB:1266C 4. PROKUROŌ (προκυρόω), *pro*, before, and No. 3, to confirm or ratify before, is said of the Divine confirmation of a promise given originally to Abraham, Gen. 12, and confirmed by the vision of the furnace and torch, Gen. 15, by the birth of Isaac, Gen. 21, and by the oath of God, Gen. 22, all before the giving of the Law, Gal. 3 : 17.¶

3315 AG:506D CB:1258B 5. MESITEUŌ (μεσιτεύω), to act as a mediator, to interpose, is rendered " confirmed," in the A.V. of Heb. 6 : 17 (marg., and R.V., " interposed "). See INTERPOSED.¶

B. Noun.

951 AG:138D CB:1239A BEBAIŌSIS (βεβαίωσις), akin to A, No. 1, is used in two senses (*a*) of firmness, establishment, said of the confirmation of the Gospel, Phil. 1 : 7 ; (*b*) of authoritative validity imparted, said of the settlement of a dispute by an oath to produce confidence, Heb. 6 : 16. The word is found frequently in the Papyri of the settlement of a business transaction.¶

CONFLICT (Noun)

73 AG:15A CB:1233C 1. AGŌN (ἀγών), from *agō*, to lead, signifies (*a*) a place of assembly, especially the place where the Greeks assembled for the Olympic and Pythian games ; (*b*) a contest of athletes, metaphorically, 1 Tim. 6 : 12 ; 2 Tim. 4 : 7, "fight ;" Heb. 12 : 1, "race ;" hence, (*c*) the inward conflict of the soul ; inward conflict is often the result, or the accompaniment, of outward conflict, Phil. 1 : 30 ; 1 Thess. 2 : 2, implying a contest against spiritual foes, as well as human adversaries ; so Col. 2 : 1, " conflict," A.V. ; R.V., " (how greatly) I strive," lit., 'how great a conflict I have.' See CONTENTION, FIGHT, RACE.¶. Cp. *agōnizomai* (Eng., agonize), 1 Cor. 9 : 25 etc.

119 AG:21C CB:1238A 2. ATHLĒSIS (ἄθλησις) denotes a combat, contest of athletes ; hence,

a struggle, fight, Heb. 10 : 32, with reference to affliction. See FIGHT.¶ Cp. *athleō*, to strive, 2 Tim. 2 : 5 (twice).¶

CONFORMED, CONFORMABLE

A. Verb.

SUMMORPHIZŌ (συμμορφίζω), to make of like form with another — AG:778D
person or thing, to render like (*sun*, with, *morphē*, a form), is found in CB:1270B
Phil. 3 : 10 (in the Passive Participle of the verb), " becoming conformed " (-OMAI)
(or ' growing into conformity ') to the death of Christ, indicating the -PHOō 4833
practical apprehension of the death of the carnal self, and fulfilling his AG:778D
share of the sufferings following upon the sufferings of Christ. Some CB:1270B (-OMAI)
texts have the alternative verb *summorphoō*, which has practically the
same meaning.

B. Adjectives.

1. SUMMORPHOS (σύμμορφος), akin to A, signifies having the same 4832 AG:778D
form as another, conformed to ; (*a*) of the conformity of children of God CB:1270B
"to the image of His Son," Rom. 8 : 29 ; (*b*), of their future physical
conformity to His body of glory, Phil. 3 : 21. See FASHION.¶

2. SUSCHĒMATIZŌ (συσχηματίζω), to fashion or shape one thing 4964 AG:795C
like another, is translated " conformed " in Rom. 12 : 2, A.V. ; R.V., CB:1271A
" fashioned ; " " fashioning " in 1 Pet. 1 : 14. This verb has more especial
reference to that which is transitory, changeable, unstable ; *summorphizō*,
to that which is essential in character and thus complete or durable, not
merely a form or outline. *Suschēmatizō* could not be used of inward
transformation. See FASHION (*schēma*) and FORM (*morphē*).¶

CONFOUND, CONFUSE, CONFUSION

A. Nouns.

1. AKATASTASIA (ἀκαταστασία), instability, (*a*, negative, *kata*, down, 181 AG:30A
stasis, a standing), denotes a state of disorder, disturbance, confusion, CB:1234B
tumult, 1 Cor. 14 : 33 ; Jas. 3 : 16, revolution or anarchy ; translated
" tumults " in Luke 21 : 9 (A.V., " commotions ") ; 2 Cor. 6 : 5 ; 12 : 20.
See TUMULT.¶

2. SUNCHUSIS (σύγχυσις), a pouring or mixing together (*sun*, with, 4799 AG:775C
cheō, to pour) ; hence a disturbance, confusion, a tumultuous disorder, CB:—
as of riotous persons, is found in Acts 19 : 29.¶

B. Verbs.

1. SUNCHEŌ (συγχέω), or SUNCHUNNŌ or SUNCHUNŌ (the verb 4797 AG:775A
form of A. 2), lit., to pour together, commingle, hence (said of persons), CB:—
means to trouble or confuse, to stir up, Acts 19 : 32 (said of the mind) ;
to be in confusion, 21 : 31, R.V. (A.V., " was in an uproar ") ; 21 : 27,
" stirred up ; " Acts 2 : 6 ; 9 : 22, " confounded." See STIR, UPROAR.¶

2. KATAISCHUNŌ (καταισχύνω), to put to shame, is translated 2617 AG:410D
" confound " in 1 Cor. 1 : 27, and 1 Pet. 2 : 6, A.V. (R.V., " put to shame "). CB:1254A
See ASHAMED, DISHONOUR, SHAME.

CONFUTE

1246 AG:184A CB:— DIAKATELENCHOMAI (διακατελέγχομαι), to confute powerfully, is an intensive form of *elenchō*, to convict (*dia*, through, *kata*, down, both intensive), Acts 18 : 28, implying that he met the opposing arguments in turn (*dia*), and brought them down to the ground (*kata*). It carries also the thought that he brought home moral blame to them.

CONGREGATION

1577 AG:240D CB:1243C 1. EKKLĒSIA (ἐκκλησία) is translated " congregation " in Heb. 2 : 12, R.V., instead of the usual rendering " church." See ASSEMBLY.

4864 AG:782D CB:1270B 2. SUNAGŌGĒ (συναγωγή) is translated " congregation " in Acts 13 : 43, A.V. (R.V., " synagogue "). See SYNAGOGUE.

CONQUER, CONQUEROR

3528 AG:539A CB:1259C 1. NIKAŌ (νικάω), to overcome (its usual meaning), is translated " conquering " and " to conquer " in Rev. 6 : 2. See OVERCOME, PREVAIL, VICTORY.

5245 AG:841C CB:1252A 2. HUPERNIKAŌ (ὑπερνικάω), to be more than conqueror (*huper*, over, and No. 1), to gain a surpassing victory, is found in Rom. 8 : 37, lit., ' we are hyper-conquerors,' i.e., we are pre-eminently victorious.¶

CONSCIENCE

4893 AG:786C CB:1270C SUNEIDĒSIS (συνείδησις), lit., a knowing with (*sun*, with, *oida*, to know), i.e., a co-knowledge (with oneself), the witness borne to one's conduct by conscience, that faculty by which we apprehend the will of God, as that which is designed to govern our lives ; hence (*a*) the sense of guiltiness before God; Heb. 10 : 2 ; (*b*) that process of thought which distinguishes what it considers morally good or bad, commending the good, condemning the bad, and so prompting to do the former, and avoid the latter ; Rom. 2 : 15 (bearing witness with God's Law) ; 9 : 1 ; 2 Cor. 1 : 12 ; acting in a certain way because conscience requires it, Rom. 13 : 5 ; so as not to cause scruples of conscience in another, 1 Cor. 10 : 28, 29 ; not calling a thing in question unnecessarily, as if conscience demanded it, 1 Cor. 10 : 25, 27 ; ' commending oneself to every man's conscience,' 2 Cor. 4 : 2 ; cp. 5 : 11. There may be a conscience not strong enough to distinguish clearly between the lawful and the unlawful, 1 Cor. 8 : 7, 10, 12 (some regard consciousness as the meaning here). The phrase " conscience toward God," in 1 Pet. 2 : 19, signifies a conscience (or perhaps here, a consciousness) so controlled by the apprehension of God's presence, that the person realizes that griefs are to be borne in accordance with His will. Heb. 9 : 9 teaches that sacrifices under the Law could not so perfect a person that he could regard himself as free from guilt.

For various descriptions of conscience see Acts 23 : 1 ; 24 : 16 ;

1 Cor. 8 : 7 ; 1 Tim. 1 : 5, 19 ; 3 : 9 ; 4 : 2 ; 2 Tim. 1 : 3 ; Tit. 1 : 15 ;
Heb. 9 : 14 ; 10 : 22 ; 13 : 18 ; 1 Pet. 3 : 16, 21.¶

CONSECRATE TELEIOŌ 5048 AG:809D

Note : In Heb. 7 : 28 the verb *teleioō* is translated " perfected " in the CB:1271B ENKAINIZŌ
R.V., for A.V., " consecrated ; " so in 9 : 18 and 10 : 20, *enkainizō*, R.V., 1457 AG:215B
" dedicated." See DEDICATE, PERFECT. CB:1245A

CONSENT

A. Verbs.

1. EXOMOLOGEŌ (ἐξομολογέω), to agree openly, to acknowledge 1843
outwardly, or fully (*ex*, for *ek*, out, intensive), is translated " consented " AG:277A CB:1247C
in the R.V. of Luke 22 : 6 (A.V., " promised "). See CONFESS, THANK. (EXHO-)

2. EPINEUŌ (ἐπινεύω), lit. signifies to nod to (*epi*, upon or to, *neuō*, 1962 AG:296C
to nod) ; hence, to nod assent, to express approval, consent, Acts 18 : 20. CB:—

3. PROSERCHOMAI (προσέρχομαι), to come to, signifies to consent, 4334 AG:713A
implying a coming to agreement with, in 1 Tim. 6 : 3. See COME, No. 10. CB:1267A

4. SUNKATATITHĒMI (συγκατατίθημι), lit., to put or lay down 4784 (-EMAI)
together with (*sun*, with, *kata*, down, *tithēmi*, to put), was used of AG:773C CB:—
depositing one's vote in an urn ; hence, to vote for, agree with, consent to. It is said negatively of Joseph of Arimathæa, who had not " consented " to the counsel and deed of the Jews, Luke 23 : 51 (Middle Voice).¶

5. SUMPHĒMI (συμφήμι), lit., to speak with (*sun*, with, *phēmi*, to 4852 AG:780C
speak), hence, to express agreement with, is used of consenting to the CB:—
Law, agreeing that it is good, Rom. 7 : 16.¶

6. SUNEUDOKEŌ (συνευδοκέω), lit., to think well with (*sun*, with, 4909 AG:788D
eu, well, *dokeō*, to think), to take pleasure with others in anything, to CB:—
approve of, to assent, is used in Luke 11 : 48, of consenting to the evil deeds of predecessors (A.V., " allow ") ; in Rom. 1 : 32, of consenting in doing evil ; in Acts 8 : 1 ; 22 : 20, of consenting to the death of another. All these are cases of consenting to evil things. In 1 Cor. 7 : 12, 13, it is used of an unbelieving wife's consent to dwell with her converted husband, and of an unbelieving husband's consent to dwell with a believing wife (A.V., " be pleased ; " R.V., " be content "). See ALLOW, CONTENT, PLEASE.¶

B. Phrases. APO 575

1. APO MIAS, lit., ' from one,' is found in Luke 14 : 18, some word AG:86C VI.
like " consent " being implied ; e.g., " with one consent."¶ CB:1236C

2. EK SUMPHŌNOU, lit., ' from (or by) agreement ' (*sun*, with, SUMPHŌNOS 4859
phōnē, a sound), i.e., by consent, is found in 1 Cor. 7 : 5. Cp. AGREE.¶ AG:781B CB:—

CONSIDER

1. EIDON (εἶδον), used as the aorist tense of *horaō*, to see, is translated 3708 AG:577D
" to consider " in Acts 15 : 6, of the gathering of the Apostles and elders CB:1251A
regarding the question of circumcision in relation to the Gospel.

4894 (-Dō) 2. SUNEIDON (συνεῖδον), *sun*, with, and No. 1, used as the aorist
AG:791B tense of *sunoraō*, to see with one view, to be aware, conscious, as the
CB:1270C result of mental perception, is translated "considered" in Acts 12 : 12,
of Peter's consideration of the circumstances of his deliverance from
See KNOW, PRIVY.

2648 3. KATAMANTHANŌ (καταμανθάνω), lit., to learn thoroughly (*kata*,
AG:414C down, intensive, *manthanō*, to learn), hence, to note accurately, consider
CB:— well, is used in the Lord's exhortation to consider the lilies, Matt. 6 : 28.¶

3539 (NOIEō) 4. NOEŌ (νοέω), to perceive with the mind (*nous*), think about,
AG:540B ponder, is translated "consider," only in Paul's exhortation to Timothy
CB:1259C in 2 Tim. 2 : 7. See PERCEIVE, THINK, UNDERSTAND.

2657 5. KATANOEŌ (κατανοέω), to perceive clearly (*kata*, intensive, and
AG:415A No. 4), to understand fully, consider closely, is used of not considering
CB:1254A thoroughly the beam in one's own eye, Matt. 7 : 3 and Luke 6 : 41 (A.V., "perceivest"); of carefully considering the ravens, Luke 12 : 24; the lilies, ver. 27; of Peter's full consideration of his vision, Acts 11 : 6; of Abraham's careful consideration of his own body, and Sarah's womb, as dead, and yet accepting by faith God's promise, Rom. 4 : 19 (R.V.); of considering fully the Apostle and High Priest of our confession, Heb. 3 : 1; of thoughtfully considering one another to provoke unto love and good works, Heb. 10 : 24. It is translated by the verbs behold, Acts 7 : 31, 32; Jas. 1 : 23, 24; perceive, Luke 20 : 23; discover, Acts 27 : 39. See BEHOLD, DISCOVER, PERCEIVE.¶

3049 6. LOGIZOMAI (λογίζομαι) signifies to take account of, 2 Cor. 10 : 7
AG:475D (R.V., "consider," A.V., "think"), the only place where the R.V.
CB:1257A translates it "consider." See ACCOUNT.

7. THEŌREŌ (θεωρέω): see BEHOLD, No. 6.

333 8. ANATHEŌREŌ (ἀναθεωρέω), to consider carefully: see BEHOLD,
AG:54C
CB:— No. 7.

357 9. ANALOGIZOMAI (ἀναλογίζομαι), to consider, occurs in Heb. 12:3.¶
AG:57B
CB:— *Notes:* (1) *Skopeō*, to look, is translated "looking to" in Gal. 6 : 1, R.V. (A.V., "considering"). See HEED, LOOK, MARK. (2) *Suniēmi*, to understand, is translated "considered" in Mark 6 : 52 (A.V.), R.V., "understood." (3) In John 11 : 50 (A.V., *dialogizomai*) the best texts have No. 6.

CONSIST

1510
AG:222D 1. EIMI (εἰμί), to be, is rendered "consist" (lit., 'is') in Luke 12 : 15.
CB:1243A
4921 2. SUNISTĒMI (συνίστημι), *sun*, with, *histēmi*, to stand, denotes,
AG:790C in its intransitive sense, to stand with or fall together, to be constituted,
CB:1270C to be compact; it is said of the universe as upheld by the Lord, Col. 1 : 17, lit., 'by Him all things stand together,' i.e., "consist" (the Latin *consisto*, to stand together, is the exact equivalent of *sunistēmi*). See APPROVE, COMMEND, MAKE, STAND.

CONSOLATION, CONSOLE

A. Nouns.

1. PARAKLĒSIS (παράκλησις) is translated "consolation," in both 3874
A.V. and R.V., in Luke 2 : 25 ; 6 : 24 ; Acts 15 : 31 ; in 1 Cor. 14 : 3, AG:618A CB:1262A
A.V., "exhortation," R.V., "comfort ;" in the following the A.V. has "consolation," the R.V., "comfort," Rom. 15 : 5 ; 2 Cor. 1 : 6, 7 ; 7 : 7 ; Phil. 2 : 1 ; 2 Thess. 2 : 16 ; Philm. 7 ; in Acts 4 : 36, R.V., "exhortation ;" in Heb. 6 : 18, R.V., "encouragement." See COMFORT.

2. PARAMUTHIA (παραμυθία), a comfort, consolation : see COMFORT, 3889
A, No. 2. AG:620D CB:1262B

3. PARAMUTHION (παραμύθιον), an encouragement, "consolation," 3890
Phil. 2 : 1, R.V., in the phrase "consolation of love." See COMFORT, AG:620D CB:1262B
A, No. 3.

B. Verb.

PARAMUTHEOMAI (παραμυθέομαι), to speak soothingly to, is 3888
translated "console," John 11 : 19, R.V. ; in ver. 31 "were comforting ;" AG:620D CB:1262B
in 1 Thess. 2 : 11 and 5 : 14, A.V., "comforted" and "comfort," R.V., "encouraged" and "encourage."

CONSORT (with)

PROSKLĒROŌ (προσκληρόω), lit., to assign by lot (*pros*, to, *klēros*, 4345
a lot), to allot, is found in Acts 17 : 4, "consorted with," imparting to AG:716A CB:1267A
the Passive Voice (the form of the verb there) a Middle Voice significance, i.e., 'they joined themselves to,' or 'threw in their lot with.' The Passive Voice significance can be retained by translating (in the stricter sense of the word), "they were allotted" (i.e., by God) to Paul and Silas, as followers or disciples.¶

CONSPIRACY

SUNŌMOSIA (συνωμοσία) denotes, lit., a swearing together (*sun*, with, 4945
omnumi, to swear), a being leagued by oath, and so a conspiracy, Acts AG:793D CB:—
23 : 13.¶

For CONSTANTLY see AFFIRM

CONSTRAIN, CONSTRAINT

A. Verbs.

1. ANANKAZŌ (ἀναγκάζω) : see COMPEL, No. 1. 315 AG:52A CB:1235B

2. PARABIAZOMAI (παραβιάζομαι) primarily denotes to employ 3849
force contrary to nature and right, to compel by using force (*para*, AG:612B CB:—
alongside, intensive, *biazō*, to force), and is used only of constraining by intreaty, as the two going to Emmaus did to Christ, Luke 24 : 29 ; as Lydia did to Paul and his companions, Acts 16 : 15.¶

3. SUNECHŌ (συνέχω), to hold together, confine, secure, to hold fast 4912
(*echō*, to have or hold), to constrain, is said (*a*) of the effect of the word AG:789A CB:1270C
of the Lord upon Paul, Acts 18 : 5 (A.V., "was pressed in spirit," R.V.,

" was constrained by the word ") ; of the effect of the love of Christ, 2 Cor. 5 : 14 ; (*b*) of being taken with a disease, Matt. 4 : 24 ; Luke 4 : 38 ; Acts 28 : 8 ; with fear, Luke 8 : 37 ; (*c*) of thronging or holding in a person, Luke 8 : 45 ; being straitened, Luke 12 : 50 ; being in a strait betwixt two, Phil. 1 : 23 ; keeping a city in on every side, Luke 19 : 43 ; keeping a tight hold on a person, as the men who seized the Lord Jesus did, after bringing Him into the High Priest's house, Luke 22 : 63 ; (*d*) of stopping the ears in refusal to listen, Acts 7 : 57. Luke uses the word nine times out of its twelve occurrences in the N.T. See HOLD, KEEP, No. (1), PRESS, SICK (lie), STOP, STRAIT (be in a), TAKEN (be), THRONG.¶

ANANKē 318 *Note :* The verb *echō*, to have, with *anankē*, a necessity, is translated
AG:52B " I was constrained," in Jude 3, R.V. (A.V., " it was needful ").

CB:1235B **B. Adverb.**

317 AG:52B ANANKASTŌS (ἀναγκαστῶς), akin to A, No. 1, by force, unwillingly,
CB:1235B by constraint, is used in 1 Pet. 5 : 2.¶

CONSULT, CONSULTATION

A. Verbs.

1011 AG:145C 1. BOULEUŌ (βουλεύω), used in the Middle Voice, means (*a*) to
CB:1239B consult, Luke 14 : 31 ; (*b*) to resolve, John 12 : 10, A.V., " consulted ; "
(-OMAI) R.V., " took counsel." See COUNSEL.

4823 AG:777D 2. SUMBOULEUŌ (συμβουλεύω), to take counsel together, is translated
CB:1270B " consulted together," in Matt. 26 : 4, A.V. (R.V., " took counsel.") See
COUNSEL.

B. Noun.

4824 AG:778A SUMBOULION (συμβούλιον), a word of the Græco-Roman period
CB:1270B (akin to A, No. 2), counsel, advice, is translated " consultation " in
Mark 15 : 1 (with *poieō*, to make), to hold a consultation ; elsewhere " counsel " in the R.V., except in Acts 25 : 12, where, by metonymy, it means a " council." See COUNCIL.

CONSUME

355 AG:57A 1. ANALISKŌ (ἀναλίσκω), to use up, spend up, especially in a bad
CB:— sense, to destroy, is said of the destruction of persons, (*a*) literally, Luke
9 : 54 and the R.V. marg. of 2 Thess. 2 : 8 (text, " shall slay ") ; (*b*) metaphorically, Gal. 5 : 15, " (that) ye be not consumed (one of another)."¶

2654 AG:414D 2. KATANALISKŌ (καταναλίσκω), to consume utterly, wholly (*kata*,
CB:— intensive), is said, in Heb. 12 : 29, of God as " a consuming fire."¶

853 AG:124C 3. APHANIZŌ (ἀφανίζω), lit., to cause to disappear, put out of sight,
CB:1236B came to mean to do away with (*a*, negative, *phainō*, to cause to appear),
said of the destructive work of moth and rust, Matt. 6 : 19, 20 (R.V., " consume," A.V., " corrupt "). See CORRUPT, DISFIGURE, PERISH, VANISH.

1159 AG:171A *Note : Dapanaō*, to expend, be at an expense, is translated " consume "
CB:— in the A.V. of James 4 : 3 (R.V., " spend "). See SPEND.

CONTAIN

1. CHŌREŌ (χωρέω) signifies (*a*), lit., to give space, make room 5562
(*chōra*, a place); hence, transitively, to have space or room for a thing, AG:889C CB:1240A
to contain, said of the waterpots as containing a certain quantity, John 2 : 6; of a space large enough to hold a number of people, Mark 2 : 2; of the world as not possible of containing certain books, John 21 : 25; (*b*) to go, Matt. 15 : 17; to have place, John 8 : 37; to come, 2 Pet. 3 : 9; (*c*) metaphorically, of receiving with the mind, Matt. 19 : 11, 12; or into the heart, 2 Cor. 7 : 2. See COME (No. 24), GO, PLACE, RECEIVE, ROOM.¶

2. PERIECHŌ (περιέχω), lit., to have round (*peri*, around, *echō*, to 4023
have), means to encompass, enclose, contain, as a writing contains details, AG:647A CB:1263B
1 Pet. 2 : 6. Some mss. have it in Acts 23 : 25, lit., 'having this form' (the most authentic have *echō*, to have). For the secondary meaning, amazed (A.V., "astonished"), Luke 5 : 9 (lit., amazement encompassed, i.e., seized, him).¶

Notes: (1) The verb *allēgoreō* in Gal. 4 : 24, R.V., is translated "contain 238
an allegory" (A.V., "are an allegory"), i.e., they apply the facts of the AG:39B CB:1234C
narrative to illustrate principles. (2) In Eph. 2 : 15 "the law of commandments contained in ordinances" is, lit., the law of commandments in ordinances. (3) In Rom. 2 : 14, the R.V., translating literally, has "the things of the Law;" the A.V. inserts the words "contained in." (4) In 1 Cor. 7 : 9, for the A.V., "if they cannot contain," see CONTINENCY. CONTAINER See VESSEL

CONTAMINATE See DEFILE

For CONTEMPTIBLE, see ACCOUNT, No. 6

CONTEMPT See DESPISE

CONTEND (-ING)

1. ATHLEŌ (ἀθλέω), to engage in a contest (cp. Eng., athlete), to 118
contend in public games, is used in 2 Tim. 2 : 5, R.V., "contend in the AG:21B CB:1238A
games," for the A.V., "strive for the masteries." See STRIVE.¶

Note: In 1 Cor. 9 : 25, the verb *agōnizomai*, to strive, is used in the 75 AG:15B
same connection, R.V., "striveth in the games." Cp. No. 3. CB:1233C

2. DIAKRINŌ (διακρίνω), lit., to separate throughout or wholly 1252
(*dia*, asunder, *krinō*, to judge, from a root *kri*, meaning separation), then, AG:185A CB:1241A
to distinguish, decide, signifies, in the Middle Voice, to separate oneself from, or to contend with, as did the circumcisionists with Peter, Acts 11 : 2; as did Michael with Satan, Jude 9. See R.V. marg. of ver. 22, where the thought may be that of differing in opinion. See DIFFER, DISCERN, DOUBT, JUDGE, PARTIAL, STAGGER, WAVER.

3. EPAGŌNIZOMAI (ἐπαγωνίζομαι) signifies to contend about a 1864
thing, as a combatant (*epi*, upon or about, intensive, *agōn*, a contest), to AG:281B CB:1245B
contend earnestly, Jude 3. The word "earnestly" is added to convey the intensive force of the preposition.¶

CONTENT (to be), CONTENTMENT

A. Verb.

714 1. ARKEŌ (ἀρκέω) primarily signifies to be sufficient, to be possessed
AG:107A of sufficient strength, to be strong, to be enough for a thing; hence, to
CB:1237C defend, ward off; in the Middle Voice, to be satisfied, contented with, Luke 3 : 14, with wages; 1 Tim. 6 : 8, with food and raiment; Heb. 13 : 5, with "such things as ye have;" negatively of Diotrephes, in 3 John 10, "not content therewith." See ENOUGH, SUFFICE, SUFFICIENT.

4909 2. SUNEUDOKEŌ (συνευδοκέω), in 1 Cor. 7 : 12, 13, R.V., signifies
AG:788D to be content: see CONSENT, No. 6.
CB:—

B. Adjectives.

842 1. AUTARKĒS (αὐτάρκης), as found in the papyri writings, means
AG:122B sufficient in oneself (*autos*, self, *arkeō*, see A), self-sufficient, adequate,
CB:1238B needing no assistance; hence, content, Phil. 4 : 11.¶

2425 2. HIKANOS (ἱκανός), sufficient, used with *poieō*, to do, in Mark 15 : 15,
AG:374B is translated "to content (the multitude)," i.e., to do sufficient to satisfy
CB:1250C them. See ABLE.

C. Noun.

841 AUTARKEIA (αὐτάρκεια), contentment, satisfaction with what one
AG:122B has, is found in 1 Tim. 6 : 6. For its other meaning "sufficiency," in
CB:1238B 2 Cor. 9 : 8, see SUFFICIENCY.¶

CONTENTION, CONTENTIOUS

A. Nouns.

2054 1. ERIS (ἔρις), strife, quarrel, especially rivalry, contention, wrangling,
AG:309C as in the church in Corinth, 1 Cor. 1 : 11, is translated "contentions" in
CB:1246C Tit. 3 : 9, A.V. See DEBATE, STRIFE, VARIANCE.

3948 2. PAROXUSMOS (παροξυσμός), Eng., paroxysm, lit., a sharpening,
AG:629C hence a sharpening of the feeling, or action (*para*, beside, intensive, *oxus*,
CB:1262C sharp), denotes an incitement, a sharp contention, Acts 15 : 39, the effect of irritation; elsewhere in Heb. 10 : 24, "provoke," unto love. See PROVOKE.¶

5379 3. PHILONEIKIA (φιλονεικία), lit., love of strife (*phileō*, to love,
AG:860D *neikos*, strife), signifies eagerness to contend; hence, a contention, said
CB:1264A of the disciples, Luke 22 : 24. Cp. B, 2.¶

B. Adjectives.

269 1. AMACHOS (ἄμαχος), lit., not fighting (*a*, negative, *machē*, a fight,
AG:44C combat, quarrel), primarily signifying invincible, came to mean not
CB:1234C contentious, 1 Tim. 3 : 3, R.V.; Tit. 3 : 2 (A.V., "not a brawler," "no brawlers").¶

5380 2. PHILONEIKOS (φιλόνεικος), akin to A, No. 3, is used in 1 Cor.
AG:860D 11 : 16.¶ In the Sept., Ezek. 3 : 7, "stubborn."¶
CB:1264A

2052 *Notes*: (1) *Eritheia*, "contention," A.V., in Phil. 1 : 17, is translated
AG:309B "faction," in the R.V. The phrase *hoi ex eritheias*, Rom. 2 : 8, lit., 'those
CB:1246C

of strife,' is rendered "contentious," in the A.V.; R.V., "factious."
See Factious, Strife.

(2) For *agōn,* a contest, "contention," 1 Thess. 2 : 2, A.V.; 73 AG:15A
"conflict," R.V., see Conflict. CB:1233C

CONTINENCY

ENKRATEUOMAI (ἐγκρατεύομαι), *en,* in, *kratos,* power, strength, 1467
lit., to have power over oneself, is rendered "(if) they have (not) AG:216C CB:1245A
continency" (i.e., are lacking in self-control), in 1 Cor. 7 : 9, R.V.; A.V.,
"can (not) contain;" in 9 : 25, "is temperate." See Temperate.¶

CONTINUAL, CONTINUALLY (see also CONTINUE)

A. Adverbial Phrases.

1. EIS TELOS (εἰς τέλος), lit., 'unto (the) end,' signifies "continual," TELOS 5056
in Luke 18 : 5, of the importunate widow's applications to the unrighteous AG:811B
judge; see also Matt. 10 : 22; 24 : 13; Mark 13 : 13; John 13 : 1; CB:1271B
1 Thess. 2 : 16. Cp. *heōs telous,* lit., 'until the end,' 1 Cor. 1 : 8; 2 Cor.
1 : 13; ¶ *mechri telous,* ditto, Heb. 3 : 6, 14; ¶ *achri telous,* Heb.
6 : 11; Rev. 2 : 26.¶

2. DIA PANTOS (διὰ παντός) is used of a period throughout or during 1275 AG:179B
which anything is done; it is said of the disciples' continuance in the A.II.1a.
Temple after the Ascension of Christ, Luke 24 : 53; of the regular entrance CB:—
of the priests into the first tabernacle, Heb. 9 : 6, R.V. (A.V. "always");
of the constant sacrifice of praise enjoined upon believers, Heb. 13 : 15.
See also Matt. 18 : 10; Mark 5 : 5; Acts 10 : 2; 24 : 16; Rom. 11 : 10;
2 Thess. 3 : 16, "at all times." See Always, No. 3, and Note under
No. 3 below).¶

3. EIS TO DIĒNEKES (εἰς τὸ διηνεκές), lit., unto the carried-through DIĒNEKĒS 1336 (-KES)
(*dia,* through, *enenka,* to carry), i.e., unto (the) unbroken continuance, is AG:195A
used of the continuous Priesthood of Christ, Heb. 7 : 3, and of the continual CB:—
offering of sacrifices under the Law, Heb. 10 : 1. It is translated "for
ever," in Heb. 10 : 12, of the everlasting session of Christ at the right
hand of God; and in 10 : 14, of the everlasting effects of His sacrifice
upon "them that are sanctified," See Ever.¶

Note: No. 2 indicates that a certain thing is done frequently throughout a period; No. 3 stresses the unbroken continuity of what is mentioned.

B. Adjective.

ADIALEIPTOS (ἀδιάλειπτος), continual, unceasing: see Cease, B. 88 AG:17B CB:1233A

CONTINUE, CONTINUANCE

1. GINOMAI (γίνομαι) signifies (*a*) to begin to be (suggesting origin); 1096 AG:158A
(*b*) to become (suggesting entrance on a new state); (*c*) to come to pass CB:1248B
(suggesting effect); hence with the meaning (*c*) it is translated
"continued" in Acts 19 : 10. See Arise. 1300 AG:189C

2. DIATELEŌ (διατελέω), to bring through to an end (*dia,* through, CB:—

telos, an end), to finish fully or, when used of time, continue right through,
is said of continuing fasting up to the time mentioned, Acts 27 : 33.¶
3306 AG:503C 3. MENŌ (μένω) : see ABIDE.
CB:1258B *Compounds of menō with this meaning, are as follows :*
1265 AG:186C 4. DIAMENŌ (διαμένω), to continue throughout, i.e., without inter-
CB:— ruption (No. 3 with *dia*, through), is said of the dumbness of Zacharias,
Luke 1 : 22, A.V., " remained ; " of the continuance of the disciples with
Christ, Luke 22 : 28 ; of the permanency of the truth of the Gospel with
churches, Gal. 2 : 5 ; of the unchanged course of things, 2 Pet. 3 : 4 ;
of the eternal permanency of Christ, Heb. 1 : 11. See REMAIN.¶
1696 AG:255B 5. EMMENŌ (ἐμμένω), to remain in (*en*, in), is used of abiding in a
CB:1244B house, Acts 28 : 30 (in the best mss.) ; of continuing in the faith, Acts
14 : 22 ; in the Law, Gal. 3 : 10 ; in God's Covenant, Heb. 8 : 9.¶
1961 AG:296B 6. EPIMENŌ (ἐπιμένω), lit., to remain on, i.e., in addition to (*epi*,
CB:1246A upon, and No. 3), to continue long, still to abide, is used of continuing to
ask, John 8 : 7 ; to knock, Acts 12 : 16 ; in the grace of God, 13 : 43 ;
in sin, Rom. 6 : 1 ; in God's goodness, 11 : 22 ; in unbelief, 11 : 23 (A.V.,
" abide ") ; in the flesh, Phil. 1 : 24 ; in the faith, Col. 1 : 23 ; in doctrine,
1 Tim. 4 : 16 ; elsewhere of abiding in a place. See ABIDE, TARRY.
3887 AG:620C 7. PARAMENŌ (παραμένω), to remain by or near (*para*, beside, and
CB:1262A No. 3), hence, to continue or persevere in anything, is used of the inability
of Levitical priests to continue, Heb. 7 : 23 ; of persevering in the law of
liberty, Jas. 1 : 25 ; it is translated " abide " in Phil. 1 : 25 (2nd clause,
in the best mss.), R.V. [see Note (1)], and in 1 Cor. 16 : 6. See ABIDE.¶
4357 AG:717C 8. PROSMENŌ (προσμένω), to remain with (*pros*, with, and No. 3),
CB:1267B to continue with a person, is said of the people with Christ, Matt. 15 : 32 ;
Mark 8 : 2 (A.V., " been with ") ; of continuing in supplications and
prayers, 1 Tim. 5 : 5. See ABIDE, CLEAVE (unto), TARRY.
4342 AG:715C 9. PROSKARTEREŌ (προσκαρτερέω), lit., to be strong towards
CB:1267A (*pros*, towards, used intensively, and *kartereō*, to be strong), to endure in,
or persevere in, to be continually stedfast with a person or thing, is used
of continuing in prayer with others, Acts 1 : 14 ; Rom. 12 : 12 ; Col. 4 : 2 ;
in the Apostles' teaching, Acts 2 : 42 ; in the Temple, 2 : 46 (" continuing
stedfastly," R.V.), the adverb representing the intensive preposition ;
DIANUKTEREUō in prayer and the ministry, 6 : 4 (R.V., " will continue stedfastly ") ; of
1273 AG:187B Simon Magus with Philip, 8 : 13. In Mark 3 : 9 and Acts 10 : 7, it
CB:1241B signifies to wait on ; in Rom. 13 : 6, to attend continually upon. See
DIATRIBō ATTEND, INSTANT, WAIT.¶
1304 AG:190A 10. DIANUKTEREUŌ (διανυκτερεύω), to pass the night through
HISTēMI (*dia*, through, *nux*, a night), to continue all night, is found in Luke 6 : 12,
2476 AG:381D of the Lord in spending all night in prayer.¶
CB:1250C *Notes :* (1) The following are translated by the verb to continue, in
KATHIZō the A.V., in the places mentioned : *diatribō*, to tarry, (according to
2523 AG:389D inferior mss.) John 11 : 54 ; Acts 15 : 35 (R.V., " tarried ") ; *histēmi*, to
CB:1254C stand, Acts 26 : 22 (R.V., " stand ") : *kathizō*, to sit down, Acts 18 : 11

(R.V., “ dwelt ”) : *parateinō*, to extend, stretch, Acts 20 : 7 (R.V., PARATEINŌ
“ prolonged ”) ; *paramenō*, to abide together with, Phil. 1 : 25, R.V., 3905 AG:622C
“ abide with ; ” the A.V., “ continue,” translating *sumparamenō* (in some SUMPARAMENŌ
mss.), marks the difference from the preceding *menō*. See ABIDE, No. 4. 4839 AG:779A
(2) In Rom. 2 : 7, for A.V., “ patient continuance,” the R.V. has POIEo
“ patience ” (lit., ‘ according to patience ’). 4160 AG:680D
(3) In Rev. 13 : 5 *poieō*, to do, is rendered “ to continue.” CB:1265C

CONTRADICT, CONTRADICTION

A. Verb.

ANTILEGŌ (ἀντιλέγω), lit., to speak against (*anti*, against, *legō*, to 483
speak), is translated “ contradict ” in Acts 13 : 45. See ANSWER, AG:74D CB:—
GAINSAY, SPEAK (against).

B. Noun.

ANTILOGIA (ἀντιλογία), akin to A, is translated “ contradiction ” 485
in the A.V. of Heb. 7 : 7 ; 12 : 3, “ dispute,” and “ gainsaying.” See AG:75A CB:—
DISPUTE, GAINSAY, STRIFE.

CONTRARIWISE.

T'OUNANTION (τοὐναντίον), for *to enantion*, the contrary, on the 5121
contrary or contrariwise, is used in 2 Cor. 2 : 7 ; Gal. 2 : 7 ; 1 Pet. 3 : 9.¶ AG:261D (ENANTION) CB:1244C (ENANTION)

CONTRARY

A. Verb.

ANTIKEIMAI (ἀντίκειμαι), to be contrary (*anti*, against, *keimai*, to 480
lie), Gal. 5 : 17 ; 1 Tim. 1 : 10. See ADVERSARY. AG:74B CB:—

B. Prepositions.

1. PARA (παρά), beside, has the meaning “ contrary to ” in Acts 3844
18 : 13 ; Rom. 11 : 24 ; 16 : 17 ; “ other than ” in Gal. 1 : 8. AG:609C CB:1261C

2. APENANTI (ἀπέναντι), lit., from over against, opposite to (*apo*, 561
from, *enantios*, against), is translated “ contrary to ” in Acts 17 : 7 ; AG:84A CB:—
“ before ” in Matt. 27 : 24 ; Rom. 3 : 18 ; “ over against,” in Matt. 27 : 61 ;
“ in the presence of,” in Acts 3 : 16.¶

Note : The most authentic mss. have *katenanti*, “ over against,” in 2713
Matt. 21 : 2. AG:421B CB:—

C. Adjectives.

1. ENANTIOS (ἐναντίος), over against (*en*, in, *antios*, against), is used 1727
primarily of place, Mark 15 : 39 ; of an opposing wind, Matt. 14 : 24 ; AG:262A CB:1244C
Mark 6 : 48 ; Acts 27 : 4 ; metaphorically, opposed as an adversary, (-ON)
antagonistic, Acts 26 : 9 ; 1 Thess. 2 : 15 ; Tit. 2 : 8 ; Acts 28 : 17,
“ against.”¶

2. HUPENANTIOS (ὑπεναντίος), *hupo*, under, and No. 1, opposite to, 5227
is used of that which is contrary to persons, Col. 2 : 14, and as a noun, AG:838B CB:1252A
“ adversaries,” Heb. 10 : 27. See ADVERSARY.¶ (-ON)

CONTRIBUTION

2842 AG:438D KOINŌNIA (κοινωνία) is twice rendered " contribution," Rom. 15 : 26,
CB:1255B and 2 Cor. 9 : 13, R.V., (A.V., " distribution "). See COMMUNION.

CONTROVERSY (without)

3672 AG:569A HOMOLOGOUMENŌS (ὁμολογουμένως), confessedly, by common
CB:— consent, akin to *homologeō*, to confess (*homos*, same, *legō*, to speak), is
CONTROL rendered in 1 Tim. 3 : 16 " without controversy ; " some translate it
See " confessedly." See CONFESS, A, No. 1, and B.¶

CONTINENCY, POWER

EUKAIROS

CONVENIENT, CONVENIENTLY

2121

A. Adjective.

AG:321C CB:1247B EUKAIROS (εὔκαιρος), lit., well-timed (*eu*, well, *kairos*, a time, season),
EUKAIRIA hence signifies timely, opportune, convenient ; it is said of a certain day,
2120 Mark 6 : 21 ; elsewhere, Heb. 4 : 16, " in time of need." See NEED.¶
AG:321B CB:1247B Cp. *eukairia*, opportunity, Matt. 26 : 16 ; Luke 22 : 6 ;¶ *eukaireō*, to have
EUKAIREŌ opportunity, Mark 6 : 31 ; Acts 17 : 21 (" they spent their time," marg.
2119 AG:321B " had leisure for nothing else ") ; 1 Cor. 16 : 12. See OPPORTUNITY,
CB:1247B NEED, C, *Note*.¶

B. Adverb.

2122 AG:321C EUKAIRŌS (εὐκαίρως), conveniently, Mark 14 : 11, is used elsewhere
CB:1247B in 2 Tim. 4 : 2, " in season."¶ See SEASON, C.

C. Verbs.

433 AG:66B 1. ANĒKŌ (ἀνήκω) is rendered " befitting " in Eph. 5 : 4, for A.V.,
CB:— " convenient ; " so in Philm. 8. See BEFIT.

2520 2. KATHĒKŌ (καθήκω), to be fitting, is so translated in Rom. 1 : 28,
AG:389A CB:1254C R.V. ; A.V., " (not) convenient ; " in Acts 22 : 22, " it is (not) fit." See
FIT.¶

ANASTROPHĒ

CONVERSATION

391

AG:61C *This word is not used in the R.V., as it does not now express the meaning*
CB:1235B *of the words so translated in the A.V. These are as follows :*

TROPOS 5158

A. Nouns.

AG:827B 1. ANASTROPHĒ (ἀναστροφή) : see BEHAVIOUR, B. No. 1.

CB:1273A POLITEUMA 2. TROPOS (τρόπος), a turning, a manner, is translated simply " be
4175 ye," R.V. in Heb. 13 : 5, instead of " let your conversation be." See
AG:686B MANNER, MEANS, WAY.

CB:1265C ANASTREPHŌ 3. POLITEUMA (πολίτευμα) : see CITIZENSHIP, No. 4.

390

B. Verbs.

AG:61B CB:1235B 1. ANASTREPHŌ (ἀναστρέφω) : see BEHAVE, A, No. 1.

POLITEUŌ (-OMAI) 2. POLITEUŌ (πολιτεύω) : see CITIZENSHIP, No. 4, Note.

4176 AG:686C CB:1266A

CONVERT, CONVERSION

STREPHŌ

A. Verbs.

4762 AG:771A 1. STREPHŌ (στρέφω), to turn, is translated " be converted " in
CB:1270B Matt. 18 : 3, A.V. See TURN.

2. EPISTREPHŌ (ἐπιστρέφω), to turn about, turn towards (*epi*, 1994
towards and No. 1), is used transitively, and so rendered "convert" AG:301A
(of causing a person to turn) in Jas. 5 : 19, 20. Elsewhere, where the A.V. CB:1246A
translates this verb, either in the Middle Voice and intransitive use, or the Passive, the R.V. adheres to the Middle Voice significance, and translates by "turn again," Matt. 13 : 15; Mark 4 : 12; Luke 22 : 32; Acts 3 : 19; 28 : 27. See COME (again), Note (4), GO (again), RETURN, TURN.

B. Noun.

EPISTROPHĒ (ἐπιστροφή), akin to A, No. 2, a turning about, or round, 1995
conversion, is found in Acts 15 : 3. The word implies a turning from and AG:301C
a turning to; corresponding to these are repentance and faith; cp. CB:1246A
"turned to God from idols" (1 Thess. 1 : 9). Divine grace is the efficient cause, human agency the responding effect.¶

CONVERT See PROSELYTE

CONVEY

EKNEUŌ (ἐκνεύω), primarily, to bend to one side, to turn aside; 1593
then to take oneself away, withdraw, is found in John 5 : 13, of Christ's AG:243B
conveying Himself away from one place to another. Some have regarded CB:—
the verb as having the same meaning as *ekneō*, to escape, as from peril, slip away secretly; but the Lord did not leave the place where He had healed the paralytic in order to escape danger, but to avoid the applause of the throng.¶

CONVICT (*including the A.V.*, "*convince*")

1. ELENCHŌ (ἐλέγχω) signifies (*a*) to convict, confute, refute, usually 1651
with the suggestion of putting the convicted person to shame; see Matt. AG:249B
18 : 15, where more than telling the offender his fault is in view; it is CB:1244A
used of convicting of sin, John 8 : 46; 16 : 8; gainsayers in regard to the faith, Tit. 1 : 9; transgressors of the Law, Jas. 2 : 9; some texts have the verb in John 8 : 9; (*b*) to reprove, 1 Cor. 14 : 24, R.V. (for A.V., "convince"), for the unbeliever is there viewed as being reproved for, or convicted of, his sinful state; so in Luke 3 : 19; it is used of reproving works, John 3 : 20; Eph. 5 : 11, 13; 1 Tim. 5 : 20; 2 Tim. 4 : 2; Tit. 1 : 13; 2 : 15; all these speak of reproof by word of mouth. In Heb.
12 : 5 and Rev. 3 : 19, the word is used of reproving by action. See FAULT, 1827
REBUKE, REPROVE.¶ AG:274A CB:—

2. EXELENCHŌ (ἐξελέγχω), an intensive form of No. 1, to convict 1246
thoroughly, is used of the Lord's future conviction of the ungodly, Jude AG:184A
15.¶ CB:—

Note: For *diakatelenchō*, to confute powerfully in disputation, Acts 18 : 28 (A.V., "convinced"), see CONFUTE.¶

CONVINCED See CONFIDENT, PERSUADED

CONVULSION See TEAR

COOL

KATAPSUCHŌ (καταψύχω), Luke 16 : 24, denotes to cool off, make 2711
cool (*kata*, down, *psuchō*, to cool).¶ In the Sept., Gen. 18 : 4.¶ AG:421A CB:—

For COPPERSMITH see under BRASS

COPY

5262 HUPODEIGMA (ὑπόδειγμα), from *hupŏ*, under, *deiknumi*, to show,
AG:844A CB:1252B properly denotes what is shown below or privately; it is translated "example," Heb. 8:5, A.V. (R.V., "copy"). It signifies (*a*) a sign suggestive of anything, the delineation or representation of a thing, and so, a figure, copy; in Heb. 9:23 the R.V. has "copies," for the A.V., "patterns;" (*b*) an example for imitation, John 13:15; Jas. 5:10; for warning, Heb. 4:11; 2 Pet. 2:6 (A.V. "ensample"). See EXAMPLE, PATTERN.¶

5261 AG:843D *Note:* Cp. *hupogrammos* (*hupo*, under, *graphō*, to write), an under-
CB:1252B writing, a writing copy, an example, is used in 1 Pet. 2:21.

CORBAN

2878 KORBAN (κορβᾶν) signifies (*a*) an offering, and was a Hebrew term for
AG:444B CB:1255C any sacrifice, whether by the shedding of blood or otherwise; (*b*) a gift offered to God, Mark 7:11.¶ Jews were much addicted to rash vows; a saying of the Rabbis was, "It is hard for the parents, but the law is clear, vows must be kept." The Sept. translates the word by *dōron*, a gift. See *korbanas*, under TREASURY, Matt. 27:6.¶

CORD

4979 SCHOINION (σχοινίον), a cord or rope, a diminutive of *schoinos*, a
AG:797D CB:— rush, bulrush, meant a cord made of rushes; it denotes (*a*) a small cord, John 2:15 (plural), (*b*) a rope, Acts 27:32. See ROPE.¶

CORN, CORNFIELD

4621 1. SITOS (σῖτος), wheat, corn; in the plural, grain, is translated
AG:752B CB:1269A "corn" in Mark 4:28; "wheat," Matt. 3:12; 13:25, 29, 30; Luke 3:17; 12:18 (some mss. have *genēmata*, "fruits," here); 16:7; 22:31; John 12:24; Acts 27:38; 1 Cor. 15:37; Rev. 6:6; 18:13.
4621 (SITOS) See WHEAT.¶

AG:752A CB:1269A (SITOS) 2. SITION (σίτιον), corn, grain, a diminutive of No. 1, is found in Acts 7:12.¶

4702 AG:763B 3. SPORIMOS (σπόριμος), lit., sown, or fit for sowing (*speirō* to sow,
CB:— scatter seed), denotes, in the plural, sown fields, fields of grain, cornfields, Matt. 12:1, R.V.; Mark 2:23; Luke 6:1 (cp. *spora*, 1 Pet. 1:23,¶ and *sporos*, seed).¶

4719 AG:765D 4. STACHUS (στάχυς) means an ear of grain, Matt. 12:1; Mark
CB:1269C 2:23; 4:28; Luke 6:1. Cp. the name *Stachys* in Rom. 16:9.¶

248 *Notes:* (1) *Aloaō*, to thresh, from *alōn*, a threshing-floor, is translated
AG:41A CB:— "treadeth out (the) corn," in 1 Cor. 9:9, 10 and 1 Tim. 5:18. Cp. THRESH, TREAD.¶

(2) *Kokkos*, a grain (its regular meaning), is translated " corn " in the 2848
A.V. of John 12 : 24 (R.V., " grain "). See GRAIN. AG:440C CB:—

CORNER, CORNERSTONE

1. GŌNIA (γωνία), an angle (Eng., *coign*), signifies (*a*) an external 1137
angle, as of the corner of a street, Matt. 6 : 5 ; or of a building, 21 : 42 ; AG:168D CB:1248C
Mark 12 : 10 ; Luke 20 : 17 ; Acts 4 : 11 ; 1 Pet. 2 : 7, the corner stone or head-stone of the corner (see below) ; or the four extreme limits of the earth, Rev. 7 : 1 ; 20 : 8 ; (*b*) an internal corner, a secret place, Acts 26 : 26. See QUARTER.¶

2. ARCHĒ (ἀρχή), a beginning (its usual meaning), first in time, order, 746
or place, is used to denote the extremities or corners of a sheet, Acts 10 : AG:111D CB:1237B
11 ; 11 : 5. See BEGINNING.

Note : For the adjective *akrogōniaios* (from *akros*, extreme, highest, 204
and No. 1), a chief corner stone, see CHIEF. They were laid so as to give AG:33D CB:1234B
strength to the two walls with which they were connected. So Christ unites Jew and Gentile, Eph. 2 : 20 ; again, as one may carelessly stumble over the corner stone, when turning the corner, so Christ proved a stumbling stone to Jews, 1 Pet. 2 : 6.

CORPSE 4430

PTŌMA (πτῶμα) : see BODY, No. 3. AG:727D CB:1268A

CORRECT, CORRECTION, CORRECTOR, CORRECTING

A. Nouns.

1. DIORTHŌMA (διόρθωμα) signifies a reform, amendment, correc- —
tion, lit., a making straight (*dia*, through, *orthoō*, to make straight). AG:199A CB:—
In Acts 24 : 2, lit., 'reformations come about (or take place, lit., KATORTHŌMA
'become '),' the R.V. has " evils are corrected," A.V., " worthy deeds 2735
are done ; " there is no word for " worthy " or for " deeds " in the original. AG:424D CB:—
Some texts have *katorthōma*, which has the same meaning.¶ See *diorthōsis*, " reformation," Heb. 9 : 10.¶

2. EPANORTHŌSIS (ἐπανόρθωσις), lit., a restoration to an upright or 1882
right state (*epi*, to, *ana*, up, or again, and *orthoō*, see No. 1), hence, " correc- AG:283A CB:1245C
tion," is used of the Scripture in 2 Tim. 3 : 16, referring to improvement of life and character.¶

3. PAIDEUTĒS (παιδευτής) has two meanings, corresponding to the 3810
two meanings of the verb *paideuō* (see below) from which it is derived, AG:603D CB:1261C
(*a*) a teacher, preceptor, corrector, Rom. 2 : 20 (A.V., " instructor "), (*b*) a chastiser, Heb. 12 : 9, rendered " to chasten " (A.V., " which corrected ; " lit., ' chastisers '). See INSTRUCTOR.¶

B. Verb.

PAIDEUŌ (παιδεύω), to train up a child (*pais*), is rendered " correct- 3811
ing " in 2 Tim. 2 : 25, R.V., A.V., " instructing." See CHASTEN. AG:603D CB:1261C

CORROSION
See RUST

CORRUPT, verb and adjective.
CORRUPTION, CORRUPTIBLE, INCORRUPTION, INCORRUPTIBLE

A. Verbs.

2585 AG:403A 1. KAPĒLEUŌ (καπηλεύω) primarily signifies to be a retailer, to
CB:1253B peddle, to huckesterize (from *kapēlos*, an inn-keeper, a petty retailer, especially of wine, a huckster, pedlar, in contrast to *emporos*, a merchant); hence, to get base gain by dealing in anything, and so, more generally, to do anything for sordid personal advantage. It is found in 2 Cor. 2:17, with reference to the ministry of the Gospel. The significance can be best ascertained by comparison and contrast with the verb *doloō* (δολόω) in 4:2 (likewise there only in the N.T.), to handle deceitfully. The meanings are not identical. While both involve the deceitful dealing of adulterating the word of truth, *kapēleuō* has the broader significance of doing so in order to make dishonest gain. Those to whom the Apostle refers in 2:17 are such as make merchandise of souls through covetousness (cp. Tit. 1:11; 2 Pet. 2:3, 14, 15; Jude 11, 16; Ezek. 13:19); accordingly "hucksterizing" would be the most appropriate rendering in this passage, while "handling deceitfully" is the right meaning in 4:2. See Trench, Syn. § lxii.¶ In Is. 1:22, the Sept. has "thy wine-merchants" (*kapēloi*, hucksterizers).¶

5351 AG:857B 2. PHTHEIRŌ (φθείρω) signifies to destroy by means of corrupting,
CB:1264C and so bringing into a worse state; (*a*) with this significance it is used of the effect of evil company upon the manners of believers, and so of the effect of association with those who deny the truth and hold false doctrine, 1 Cor. 15:33 (this was a saying of the pagan poet Menander, which became a well known proverb); in 2 Cor. 7:2, of the effects of dishonourable dealing by bringing people to want (a charge made against the Apostle); in 11:3, of the effects upon the minds (or thoughts) of believers by corrupting them "from the simplicity and the purity that is toward Christ;" in Eph. 4:22, intransitively, of the old nature in waxing corrupt, "morally decaying, on the way to final ruin" (Moule), "after the lusts of deceit;" in Rev. 19:2, metaphorically, of the Babylonish harlot, in corrupting the inhabitants of the earth by her false religion.

(*b*) With the significance of destroying, it is used of marring a local church by leading it away from that condition of holiness of life and purity of doctrine in which it should abide, 1 Cor. 3:17 (A.V., "defile"), and of God's retributive destruction of the offender who is guilty of this sin (id.); of the effects of the work of false and abominable teachers upon themselves, 2 Pet. 2:12 (some texts have *kataphtheirō*; A.V., "shall utterly perish"), and Jude 10 (A.V., "corrupt themselves." R.V., marg., "are corrupted"). See DEFILE AND DESTROY.¶

1311 AG:190C 3. DIAPHTHEIRŌ (διαφθείρω), *dia*, through, intensive, and No. 2,
CB:1241B to corrupt utterly, through and through, is said of men "corrupted in mind," whose wranglings result from the doctrines of false teachers,

1 Tim. 6 : 5 (the A.V. wrongly renders it as an adjective, " corrupt "). It is translated " destroyeth " instead of " corrupteth," in the R.V. of Luke 12 : 33, of the work of a moth ; in Rev. 8 : 9, of the effect of Divine judgments hereafter upon navigation ; in 11 : 18, of the Divine retribution of destruction upon those who have destroyed the earth ; in 2 Cor. 4 : 16 it is translated " is decaying," said of the human body. See DESTROY, PERISH.¶

4. KATAPHTHEIRŌ (καταφθείρω), *kata*, down, intensive, and No. 2, 2704
is said of men who are reprobate concerning the faith, " corrupted in AG:420A
mind " (A.V., " corrupt "), 2 Tim. 3 : 8. For 2 Pet. 2 : 12, R.V., " shall CB:—
be destroyed," see No. 2.¶

5. SĒPŌ (σήπω) signifies to make corrupt, to destroy ; in the Passive 4595
Voice with Middle sense, to become corrupt or rotten, to perish, said AG:749B
of riches, Jas. 5 : 2, of the gold and silver of the luxurious rich who have CB:—
ground down their labourers. The verb is derived from a root signifying to rot off, drop to pieces.¶

6. APHANIZŌ (ἀφανίζω) : see CONSUME, No. 3. 853 AG:124C CB:1236B

B. Nouns.

1. PHTHORA (φθορά), connected with *phtheirō*, No. 2, above, signifies 5356
a bringing or being brought into an inferior or worse condition, a destruc- AG:858A
tion or corruption. It is used (*a*) physically, (1), of the condition of CB:1264C
creation, as under bondage, Rom. 8 : 21 ; (2) of the effect of the withdrawal of life, and so of the condition of the human body in burial, 1 Cor. 15 : 42 ; (3) by metonymy, of anything which is liable to corruption, 1 Cor. 15 : 50 ; (4) of the physical effects of merely gratifying the natural desires and ministering to one's own needs or lusts, Gal. 6 : 8, to the flesh in contrast to the Spirit, " corruption " being antithetic to " eternal life ; " (5) of that which is naturally short-lived and transient, Col. 2 : 22, " perish ; " (*b*) of the death and decay of beasts, 2 Pet. 2 : 12, R.V., " destroyed " (first part of verse ; lit., ' unto . . . destruction ') ; (*c*) ethically, with a moral significance, (1) of the effect of lusts, 2 Pet. 1 : 4 ; (2) of the effect upon themselves of the work of false and immoral teachers, 2 Pet. 2 : 12, R.V., " destroying ; " A.V., " corruption," and verse 19. See DESTROY, PERISH.¶

Note : There is nothing in any of these words suggesting or involving annihilation.

2. DIAPHTHORA (διαφθορά), an intensified form of No. 1, utter or 1312
thorough corruption, referring in the N.T. to physical decomposition AG:190D
and decay, is used six times, five of which refer, negatively, to the body CB:1241B
of God's " Holy One," after His death, which body, by reason of His absolute holiness, could not see corruption, Acts 2 : 27, 31 ; 13 : 34, 35, 37 ; once it is used of a human body, that of David, which, by contrast, saw corruption, Acts 13 : 36.¶

3. APHTHARSIA (ἀφθαρσία), incorruption, *a*, negative, with A, 861 AG:125B
No. 2, is used (*a*) of the resurrection body, 1 Cor. 15 : 42, 50, 53, 54 ; CB:1236C

(*b*) of a condition associated with glory and honour and life, including perhaps a moral significance, Rom. 2 : 7 ; 2 Tim. 1 : 10 ; this is wrongly translated " immortality " in the A.V. ; (*c*) of love to Christ, that which is sincere and undiminishing, Eph. 6 : 24 (translated " uncorruptness "). See IMMORTALITY, SINCERITY.¶

Note : For Tit. 2 : 7 (where some texts have *aphtharsia*), see No. 4.

— AG:125C 4. APHTHORIA (ἀφθορία), similar to No. 3, uncorruptness, free from
CB:— (moral) taint, is said of doctrine, Tit. 2 : 7 (some texts have *adiaphthoria*,
the negative form of No. 2, above).¶

C. Adjectives.

5349 1. PHTHARTOS (φθαρτός), corruptible, akin to A, No. 2, is used (*a*)
AG:857A CB:1264C of man as being mortal, liable to decay (in contrast to God), Rom. 1 : 23 ;
(*b*) of man's body as death-doomed, 1 Cor. 15 : 53, 54 ; (*c*) of a crown of reward at the Greek games, 1 Cor. 9 : 25 ; (*d*) of silver and gold, as specimens of corruptible things, 1 Pet. 1 : 18 ; (*e*) of natural seed, 1 Pet. 1 : 23.¶

862 2. APHTHARTOS (ἄφθαρτος), not liable to corruption or decay,
AG:125B CB:1236C incorruptible (*a*, negative, and A, No. 2), is used of (*a*) God, Rom. 1 : 23 ;
1 Tim 1 : 17 (A.V., " immortal ") ; (*b*) the raised dead, 1 Cor. 15 : 52 ; (*c*) rewards given to the saints hereafter, metaphorically described as a " crown," 1 Cor. 9 : 25 ; (*d*) the eternal inheritance of the saints, 1 Pet. 1 : 4 ; (*e*) the Word of God, as incorruptible seed, 1 Pet. 1 : 23 ; (*f*) a meek and quiet spirit, metaphorically spoken of as incorruptible apparel, 1 Pet. 3 : 4. See IMMORTAL.¶

4550 3. SAPROS (σαπρός), corrupt, akin to *sēpō*, A, No. 5 ; see BAD, No. 3.
AG:742B CB:1268B *Note :* (1) Trench, Syn. § lxviii, contrasts this with *amarantos*, and
AMARANTOS *amarantinos*, unwithering, not fading away, 1 Pet. 1 : 4 ; 5 : 4. These
263 AG:42C are, however, distinct terms (see FADE) and are not strictly synonymous,
CB:— though used in the same description of the heavenly inheritance.

AMARANTINOS 262 AG:42B CB:—

COST, COSTLINESS, COSTLY

A. Nouns.

1160 1. DAPANĒ (δαπάνη), expense, cost (from *daptō*, to tear ; from a
AG:171A CB:— root *dap*— meaning to divide), is found in Luke 14 : 28, in the Lord's illustration of counting the cost of becoming His disciple. Cp. *dapanaō*, to spend, and its compounds, under CHARGE, SPEND.¶

5094 2. TIMIOTĒS (τιμιότης), costliness (from *timios*, valued at great price,
AG:818B CB:— precious ; see No. 3, below), is connected with *timē*, honour, price, and used in Rev. 18 : 19, in reference to Babylon.¶

B. Adjectives.

5093 1. TIMIOS (τίμιος), akin to A, No. 2, is translated " costly " in
AG:818A CB:1272C 1 Cor. 3 : 12, of costly stones, in a metaphorical sense (A.V., " precious ").
Cp. Rev. 17 : 4 ; 18 : 12, 16 ; 21 : 19. See DEAR, HONOURABLE, PRECIOUS,
4185 AG:690A REPUTATION.
CB:1266A 2. POLUTELĒS (πολυτελής), primarily, the very end or limit (from

polus, much, *telos*, revenue), with reference to price, of highest cost, very expensive, is said of spikenard, Mark 14 : 3 ; raiment, 1 Tim. 2 : 9 ; metaphorically, of a meek and quiet spirit, 1 Pet. 3 : 4, " of great price ; " cp. No. 1 and A, No. 2, above. See PRECIOUS, PRICE.¶

3. POLUTIMOS (πολύτιμος), lit., of great value (see A, No. 2 and B, 4186
No. 1), is used of a pearl, Matt. 13 : 46 ; of spikenard, John 12 : 3 (R.V., AG:690A
" very precious," A.V. " very costly "). See PRICE.¶ The comparative CB:—
polutimo(v.l.iō)teros, " much more precious," is used in 1 Pet. 1 : 7.¶

COUCH

1. KLINIDION (κλινίδιον), a small bed, a diminutive form of *klinē*, 2826
a bed (from *klinō*, to incline, recline), is used in Luke 5 : 19, 24 of the bed AG:436C CB:—
(*klinē*, in ver. 18) on which the palsied man was brought. See BED.¶ 2895
2. KRABBATOS (κράββατος) : see BED, No. 4. AG:447C CB:—

COULD

1. ECHŌ (ἔχω), to have, is rendered " could " in Mark 14 : 8, " she 2192
hath done what she could," lit., ' she hath done what she had.' See HAVE. AG:331D CB:1242C
2. ISCHUŌ (ἰσχύω), to have strength, is translated in Mark 14 : 37 2480
" couldest thou not." See ABLE. AG:383D CB:1253A

Notes: (1) *Emblepō* in Acts 22 : 11, lit., ' I was not seeing,' is translated " I could not see." See BEHOLD.

(2) See CAN, when not used as part of another verb.

COUNCIL, COUNCILLOR

1. SUMBOULION (συμβούλιον), a uniting in counsel (*sun*, together, 4824
boulē, counsel, advice), denotes (*a*) counsel which is given, taken and AG:778A CB:1270B
acted upon, e.g., Matt. 12 : 14, R.V., " took counsel," for A.V., " held a council ; " 22 : 15 ; hence (*b*) a council, an assembly of counsellors or persons in consultation, Acts 25 : 12, of the council with which Festus conferred concerning Paul. The governors and procurators of provinces had a board of advisers or assessors, with whom they took counsel, before pronouncing judgment. See CONSULTATION.

2. SUNEDRION (συνέδριον), properly, a settling together (*sun*, 4892
together, *hedra*, a seat), hence, (*a*) any assembly or session of persons AG:786A CB:1270C
deliberating or adjusting, as in the Sept. of Psa. 26 : 4 (lit., ' with a council of vanity ') ; Prov. 22 : 10 ; Jer. 15 : 17, etc. ; in the N.T., e.g., Matt. 10 : 17 ; Mark 13 : 9 ; John 11 : 47, in particular, it denoted (*b*) the Sanhedrin, the Great Council at Jerusalem, consisting of 71 members, namely, prominent members of the families of the high priest, elders and scribes. The Jews trace the origin of this to Num. 11 : 16. The more important causes came up before this tribunal. The Roman rulers of Judæa permitted the Sanhedrin to try such cases, and even to pronounce sentence of death, with the condition that such a sentence should be valid only if confirmed by the Roman Procurator. In John 11 : 47, it is used

of a meeting of the Sanhedrin ; in Acts 4 : 15, of the place of meeting.
1010 AG:145C 3. BOULEUTĒS (βουλευτής) : Joseph of Arimathaea is described as
CB:— " a councillor of honourable estate," Mark 15 : 43, R.V. ; cp. Luke 23 : 50
(not as A.V., " counsellor ").¶

COUNSEL. For COUNSELLOR see above.

1012

A. Nouns.

AG:145D 1. BOULĒ (βουλή) : see under ADVICE.
CB:1239B 2. SUMBOULOS (σύμβουλος), a councillor with, occurs in Rom.
4825 AG:778B 11 : 34.¶

CB:1270B

B. Verbs.

1011 1. BOULEUŌ (βουλεύω), to take counsel, to resolve, is used in the
AG:145C Middle Voice in the N.T., " took counsel " in Acts 5 : 33, A.V. (R.V.
CB:1239B (-OMAI) translates *boulomai*) ; both in 27 : 39 ; in Luke 14 : 31, R.V. " take
" counsel " (A.V., " consulteth ") ; in John 11 : 53, A.V and R.V. (so
the best mss.) ; 12 : 10, R.V., " took counsel," for A.V., " consulted ; "
in 2 Cor. 1 : 17 (twice), " purpose." See CONSULT, MINDED, PURPOSE.¶

4823 2. SUMBOULEUŌ (συμβουλεύω), in the Active Voice, to advise, to
AG:777D CB:1270B counsel, John 18 : 14, " gave counsel ; " in Rev. 3 : 18, " I counsel ; " in
the Middle Voice, to take counsel, consult, Matt. 26 : 4, R.V., " took
counsel together," for A.V., " consulted ; " Acts 9 : 23, " took counsel "
(R.V. adds " together ") ; in some mss. John 11 : 53. See CONSULT.¶

COUNT

2192 1. ECHŌ (ἔχω), to have, to hold ; then, to hold in the mind, to regard,
AG:331D CB:1242C to count, has this significance in Matt. 14 : 5, " they counted Him as a
prophet ; " Philm. 17, " If then thou countest me a partner ; " Mark
11 : 32, A.V., (R.V., " hold ") ; Acts 20 : 24, A.V. See ABLE.

2233 AG:343C 2. HĒGEOMAI (ἡγέομαι), primarily, to lead the way ; hence, to lead
CB:1249C before the mind, account, is found with this meaning in Phil. 2 : 3, R.V.
(A.V., " esteem ") ; 2 : 6, R.V. (A.V., " thought ") ; 2 : 25 (A.V.,
" supposed ") ; Phil. 3 : 7, 8 ; 2 Thess. 3 : 15 ; 1 Tim. 1 : 12 ; 6 : 1 ;
Heb. 10 : 29 ; Jas. 1 : 2 ; Heb. 11 : 11 (A.V., " judged ") ; 2 Pet. 2 : 13 ;
3 : 9. See ACCOUNT.

3049 3. LOGIZOMAI (λογίζομαι), to reckon, is rendered " count " in 2 Cor.
AG:475D 10 : 2, R.V. (A.V., " think ") ; " counted " in the A.V. of Rom. 2 : 26 ;
CB:1257A 4 : 3, 5 ; 9 : 8 (R.V., " reckoned ").

5585 AG:892D 4. PSĒPHIZŌ (ψηφίζω), akin to *psēphos*, a stone, used in voting,
CB:— occurs in Luke 14 : 28 ; Rev. 13 : 18.¶

4860 AG:781B 5. SUMPSĒPHIZŌ (συμψηφίζω), to count up, occurs in Acts 19 : 19.¶
CB:— *Note :* In Jas. 5 : 11, *makarizō*, to pronounce blessed, is rendered
3106 AG:486C " count . . . happy," A.V. (R.V., " call . . . "). For *kataxioō* see ACCOUNT,
CB:1257C No. 5. For " descent is counted " see GENEALOGY.

COUNTENANCE

3799 1. OPSIS (ὄψις) : only Rev. 1 : 16 has " countenance." See APPEAR
AG:601D CB:1261A ANCE.

2. PROSŌPON (πρόσωπον) is translated "countenance" in Luke 4383
9 : 29; Acts 2 : 28, and in the A.V. of 2 Cor. 3 : 7 (R.V., "face"). See AG:720D CB:1267B
APPEARANCE.

3. EIDEA (εἰδέα), akin to *eidon*, to see: see APPEARANCE. 2397
Notes: (1) In Acts 13 : 24 *prosōpon* is translated "before" (lit., AG:369C CB:—
'before the presence of His coming').

(2) *Skuthrōpos,* "of a sad countenance" (*skuthros*, gloomy, sad, 4659
ōps, an eye), is used in Matt. 6 : 16 and Luke 24 : 17, "sad." AG:758B CB:—

(3) *Stugnazō,* to be or become hateful, gloomy, in aspect, is translated 4768
"his countenance fell," Mark 10 : 22, R.V. (A.V., "he was sad"). It AG:771D CB:—
is used of the heaven or sky in Matt. 16 : 3, "lowring." See LOWRING.¶

COUNTERFEIT See LIE

COUNTRY

A. Nouns.

1. AGROS (ἀγρός) denotes a field, especially a cultivated field; 68
hence, the country in contrast to the town (Eng., agrarian, agriculture), AG:13D CB:1233C
e.g., Mark 5 : 14; 6 : 36; 15 : 21; 16 : 12; Luke 8 : 34; 9 : 12 (plural,
lit., 'fields'); 23 : 26; a piece of ground, e.g., Mark 10 : 29; Acts
4 : 37. See FARM.

2. PATRIS (πατρίς) primarily signifies one's fatherland, native 3968
country, of one's own town, Matt. 13 : 54, 57; Mark 6 : 1, 4; Luke 4 : AG:636D CB:1263A
23, 24; John 4 : 44; Heb. 11 : 14.¶

3. CHŌRA (χώρα) properly denotes the space lying between two 5561
limits or places; accordingly it has a variety of meanings: "country," AG:889B CB:1240A
Matt. 2 : 12; 8 : 28; Mark 1 : 5, R.V. (A.V., "land"); 5 : 1, 10; Luke
2 : 8; 8 : 26; 15 : 13, 14, R.V. (A.V., "land"), 15; 19 : 12; 21 : 21;
Acts 10 : 39, R.V. (A.V., "land"); 12 : 20; 26 : 20, R.V. (A.V.,
"coasts"); 27 : 27; in Mark 6 : 55 (in the best mss.) and Acts 18 :
23, R.V., "region." See COAST, FIELD, GROUND, LAND, REGION.

4. PERICHŌROS (περίχωρος), *peri*, around, and No. 3, signifies 4066
"country round about," Luke 8 : 37; "country about," Luke 3 : 3, AG:653C CB:—
A.V. (R.V., "region round about"); in Matt. 14 : 35 and Luke 4 : 37,
A.V., "country round about" (R.V., "region round about"); Matt.
3 : 5; Mark 1 : 28; Luke 4 : 14; 7 : 17; Acts 14 : 6. See REGION.¶

5. MEROS (μέρος), a part, is rendered "country" in Acts 19 : 1, R.V. 3313
Note: Some inferior mss. have No. 4 in Mark 6 : 55, for No. 3. AG:505D CB:1258B

B. Adjectives.

1. ANŌTERIKOS (ἀνωτερικός), upper, is used in the plural in Acts 510
19 : 1, to denote upper regions, with A.V., "coast," R.V., "country," i.e., AG:77C CB:—
the high central plateau, in contrast to the roundabout way by the river
through the valley. See COAST.¶

2. OREINOS (ὀρεινός), hilly (from *oros*, a hill, mountain), is translated 3714
"hill country" in Luke 1 : 39, 65.¶ AG:580A CB:1261A

C. Verb.

APODĒMEŌ (ἀποδημέω) signifies to go or travel into a far country, 589 AG:90A CB:1236C lit., 'to be away from one's people' (*apo*, from, *dēmos*, a people), Matt. 21 : 33 ; 25 : 14 ; in ver. 15 the verb is translated in the R.V., " went on his journey " (A.V., " took his journey ") ; Mark 12 : 1 ; Luke 20 : 9, " went into another country," R.V. In Luke 15 : 13 both Versions translate by " took his journey " (" into a far country " being separately expressed) ; see JOURNEY.¶

590 AG:90B CB:— Cp. *apodēmos*, lit., away from one's own people, gone abroad, Mark 13 : 34.¶

1093 AG:157C CB:1248A *Notes :* (1) *Gē*, earth, land, is translated " country " in the A.V. of Matt. 9 : 31 and Acts 7 : 3 ; R.V., " land." See LAND.

1085 AG:156A CB:1248B (2) *Genos*, a race, is mistranslated " country " in the A.V. of Acts 4 : 36 (R.V., " by race "). See below.

COUNTRYMEN

1085 AG:156A CB:1248B 1. GENOS (γένος) properly denotes an offspring ; then, a family ; then, a race, nation ; otherwise, a kind or species ; it is translated " countrymen," in 2 Cor. 11 : 26, in Paul's reference to his fellow-nationals ; so in Gal. 1 : 14, R.V., for A.V., " nation." See BEGET.

4853 AG:780C CB:— 2. SUMPHULETĒS (συμφυλέτης), lit., a fellow-tribesman (*sun*, with, *phulē*, a tribe, race, nation, people), hence, one who is of the same people, a fellow-countryman, is found in 1 Thess. 2 : 14.¶

COUPLED

Note : The word " coupled " is inserted in italics in 1 Pet. 3 : 2, the more adequately to express the original, which is, lit., 'your chaste behaviour in fear.'

COURAGE

A. Noun.

2294 AG:352A CB:— THARSOS (θάρσος), akin to *tharseō*, to be of good cheer, is found in Acts 28 : 15.¶

B. Verb.

2292 AG:352A CB:1271C THARREŌ (θαρρέω) is translated by some form of the verb to be of good courage, in the R.V. in five of the six places where it is used : 2 Cor. 5 : 6, " being of good courage " (A.V., " we are . . . confident ") ; 5 : 8, " we are of good courage " (A.V., " we are confident ") ; 7 : 16, " I am of good courage " (A.V., " I have confidence ") ; 10 : 1, " I am of good courage " (A.V., " I am bold ") ; 10 : 2, " show courage " (A.V., " be bold ") ; Heb. 13 : 6, " with good courage," lit., 'being of good courage' (A.V., " boldly "). See BOLD, CONFIDENCE.¶

Note : *Tharreō* is a later form of *tharseō*. Cp. *tolmaō*, to be bold.

COURSE

A. Nouns.

165 AG:27B CB:1234A 1. AIŌN (αἰών), an **age** (see AGE), is sometimes wrongly spoken of as

a "dispensation," which does not mean a period of time, but a mode of dealing. It is translated "course" in Eph. 2 : 2, "the course of this world," i.e., the cycle or present round of things. See AGE, ETERNAL, EVER, WORLD.

2. DROMOS (δρόμος), properly, a running, a race (from *edramon*, to 1408
run), hence, metaphorically, denotes a career, course of occupation, or AG:206D CB:1242B
of life, viewed in a special aspect, Acts 13 : 25 ; 20 : 24 ; 2 Tim. 4 : 7.¶

3. EPHĒMERIA (ἐφημερία), primarily, daily service, as, e.g., in the 2183
Sept. of 2 Chron. 13 : 11 (from *epi*, upon, or by, *hēmera*, a day, Eng., AG:330C CB:—
ephemeral), hence denoted a class, or course, into which the priests were
divided for the daily service in the Temple, each class serving for seven EPHĒMEROS
days (see 1 Chron. 9 : 25). In the N.T. it is used in Luke 1 : 5, 8.¶ 2184

Note: Cp. *ephēmeros*, "daily (food)," Jas. 2 : 15.¶ AG:330C CB:—

4. TROCHOS (τροχός), a wheel, is translated "wheel" in Jas. 3 : 6, 5164
R.V., with metaphorical reference to the round of human activity (A.V., AG:828A CB:1273A
"course"), as a glowing axle would set on fire the whole wooden wheel.¶

B. Verb.

CHŌREŌ (χωρέω), to make room for, to go forward, is rendered "hath 5562
not free course," in John 8 : 37, R.V. (A.V., "hath no place"). See AG:889C CB:1240A
COME, No. 24. EUTHUDROMEŌ

Notes: (1) Connected with *dromos*, A, No. 2, is *euthudromeō*, to make 2113 AG:320D
(or run) a straight course (*euthus*, straight), Acts 16 : 11 and 21 : 1.¶ TRECHŌ
(2) In 2 Thess. 3 : 1, *trechō*, to run (R.V.), is translated "have free course" 5143
(A.V.).¶ (3) In 1 Cor. 14 : 27, *ana meros*, "by turn," "in turn" (R.V.), AG:825D CB:1273A
is rendered "by course" (A.V.). (4) For *ploos*, a sailing or voyage, MEROS
"course," Acts 21 : 7, A.V. (R.V., "voyage"), see VOYAGE. 3313 AG:505D CB:1258B

COURT

PLOOS

1. AGORAIOS (ἀγοραῖος) is an adjective, signifying pertaining to the 4144 AG:673C
agora, any place of public meeting, and especially where trials were held, 60
Acts 19 : 38 ; the R.V. translates the sentence "the courts are open ;" AG:13A CB:1233C
a more literal rendering is 'court days are kept.' In Acts 17 : 5 it is translated in the R.V., "rabble ;" A.V., "baser sort," lit., frequenters of the markets. See BASER.¶

2. AULĒ (αὐλή), primarily, an uncovered space around a house, 833
enclosed by a wall, where the stables were, hence was used to describe AG:121B CB:1238B
(*a*) the courtyard of a house ; in the O.T. it is used of the courts of the Tabernacle and Temple ; in this sense it is found in the N.T. in Rev. 11 : 2 ; (*b*) the courts in the dwellings of well-to-do folk, which usually had two, one exterior, between the door and the street (called the *proaulion*, or porch, Mark 14 : 68.¶), the other, interior, surrounded by the buildings of the dwellings, as in Matt. 26 : 69 (in contrast to the room where the judges were sitting); Mark 14 : 66 ; Luke 22 : 55 ; A.V., "hall ;" R.V. "court" gives the proper significance, Matt. 26 : 3, 58 ; Mark 14 : 54 ; 15 : 16 (R.V., "Prætorium") ; Luke 11 : 21 ; John 18 : 15. It is here

to be distinguished from the Prætorium, translated " palace." See HALL, PALACE. For the other meaning " sheepfold," John 10 : 1, 16, see FOLD.¶

933 3. BASILEION (*βασίλειον*), an adjective meaning " royal," signifies,
AG:136A (-IOS) in the neuter plural, a royal palace, translated " kings' courts " in Luke
CB:1238C 7 : 25 ; in the singular, 1 Pet. 2 : 9, " royal." See ROYAL.¶

COURTEOUS, COURTEOUSLY

A. Adjective.

— TAPEINOPHRŌN (*ταπεινόφρων*), lowly-minded, is used in 1 Pet. 3 : 8,
AG:804C CB:1271A " be courteous," A.V. (R.V., " humble-minded ").¶

B. Adverbs.

5390 1. PHILOPHRONŌS (*φιλοφρόνως*), lit., friendly, or, more fully, ' with
AG:861D CB:1264A friendly thoughtfulness ' (*philos*, friend, *phrēn*, the mind), is found in Acts 28 : 7, of the hospitality showed by Publius to Paul and his fellow-shipwrecked travellers.¶

5391 AG:861D CB:1264A *Note :* Some mss. have the corresponding adjective *philophrōn*, " courteous," in 1 Pet. 3 : 8 ; the most authentic mss. have *tapeinophrōn*, " humble-minded."

5364 AG:858D CB:1264A 2. PHILANTHRŌPŌS (*φιλανθρωπῶς*) is translated " courteously " in Acts 27 : 3, A.V. ; R.V., " kindly " (Eng., philanthropically). See KINDLY.¶

COUSIN

431 1. ANEPSIOS (*ἀνεψιός*), in Col. 4 : 10 denotes a cousin rather than a
AG:66A CB:— nephew (A.V., " sister's son "). " Cousin " is its meaning in various periods of Greek writers.¶ In this sense it is used in the Sept., in Numb. 36 : 11.¶ In later writings it denotes a nephew ; hence the A.V. rendering. As Lightfoot says, there is no reason to suppose that the Apostle would have used it in any other than its proper sense. We are to understand, therefore, that Mark was the cousin of Barnabas. See SISTER.

SUNGENIS — 2. SUNGENIS (*συγγενίς*) in Luke 1 : 36 (so in the most authentic mss.)
AG:772D CB:— and *sungenēs* in ver. 58 (plural), A.V., " cousin " and " cousins,"
SUNGENēS respectively signify " kinswoman " and " kinsfolk," (R.V.) ; so the R.V.
4773 and A.V. in 2 : 44 and 21 : 16. The word lit. signifies ' born with,'
AG:772C CB:1270C i.e., of the same stock, or descent ; hence kinsman, kindred. See KIN, KINSFOLK, KINSWOMAN.

COVENANT (Noun and Verb)

A. Noun.

1242 DIATHĒKĒ (*διαθήκη*) primarily signifies a disposition of property
AG:183A CB:1241B by will or otherwise. In its use in the Sept., it is the rendering of a Hebrew word meaning a covenant or agreement (from a verb signifying to cut or divide, in allusion to a sacrificial custom in connection with covenant-making, e.g., Gen. 15 : 10, " divided . " Jer. 34 : 18, 19). In contradistinction to the English word " covenant " (lit., a coming together), which signifies a mutual undertaking between two parties or more, each

binding himself to fulfil obligations, it does not in itself contain the idea of joint obligation, it mostly signifies an obligation undertaken by a single person. For instance, in Gal. 3 : 17 it is used as an alternative to a " promise " (vv. 16, 17 and 18). God enjoined upon Abraham the rite of circumcision, but His promise to Abraham, here called a covenant, was not conditional upon the observance of circumcision, though a penalty attached to its non-observance.

" The N.T. uses of the word may be analysed as follows : (*a*) a promise or undertaking, human or divine, Gal. 3 : 15 ; (*b*) a promise or undertaking on the part of God, Luke 1 : 72 ; Acts 3 : 25 ; Rom. 9 : 4 ; 11 : 27 ; Gal. 3 : 17 ; Eph. 2 : 12; Heb. 7 : 22 ; 8 : 6, 8, 10 ; 10 : 16 ; (*c*) an agreement, a mutual undertaking, between God and Israel, see Deut. 29 and 30 (described as a 'commandment,' Heb. 7 : 18, cp. ver. 22) ; Heb. 8 : 9 ; 9 : 20 ; (*d*) by metonymy, the token of the covenant, or promise, made to Abraham, Acts 7 : 8 ; (*e*) by metonymy, the record of the covenant, 2 Cor. 3 : 14 ; Heb. 9 : 4 ; cp. Rev. 11 : 19 ; (*f*) the basis, established by the death of Christ, on which the salvation of men is secured, Matt. 26 : 28 ; Mark 14 : 24 ; Luke 22 : 20 ; 1 Cor. 11 : 25 ; 2 Cor. 3 : 6 ; Heb. 10 : 29 ; 12 : 24 ; 13 : 20.

" This covenant is called the 'new,' Heb. 9 : 15, the 'second,' 8 : 7, the 'better,' 7 : 22. In Heb. 9 : 16, 17, the translation is much disputed. There does not seem to be any sufficient reason for departing in these verses from the word used everywhere else. The English word 'Testament' is taken from the titles prefixed to the Latin Versions."*¶ See TESTAMENT.

B. Verb.

SUNTITHĒMI (συντίθημι), lit., to put together, is used only in the 4934 (-EMAI)
Middle Voice in the N.T., and, means to determine, agree, John 9 : 22 and AG:790C
Acts 23 : 20 ; to assent, Acts 24 : 9 ; to covenant, Luke 22 : 5. See CB:—
AGREE, ASSENT.¶

Note : In Matt. 26 : 15 the A.V. translates *histēmi*, to place (in the 2476
balances), i.e., to weigh, " they covenanted with ; " R.V., " they weighed AG:381D
unto." CB:1250C

COVENANT-BREAKERS

ASUNTHETOS (ἀσύνθετος), from *suntithēmi* (see above), with the 802
negative prefix *a*, hence signifies " not covenant-keeping," i.e., refusing AG:118D
to abide by covenants made, covenant-breaking, faithless, Rom. 1 : 31.¶ CB:—
In the Sept. it is found in Jer. 3 : 8–11.¶ Cp. the corresponding verb, *asuntithēmi*, in the Sept. of Ps. 73 : 15, to deal treacherously (R.V.), and the noun *asunthesia*, transgression, or covenant-breaking, e.g., Ezra 9 : 2, 4 ; 10 : 6.

Note : Trench, Syn. § lii, notes the distinction between *asunthetos* ASPONDOS
and *aspondos*, " implacable," the latter, in 2 Tim. 3 : 3 only, being derived 786
AG:117B
CB:—

* From Notes on Galatians by Hogg and Vine, p. 144.

from *spondē*, a sacrificial libation, which accompanied treaty-making; hence, with the negative prefix *a*, "without a treaty or covenant," thus denoting a person who cannot be persuaded to enter into a covenant. He points out that *asunthetos* presumes a state of peace interrupted by the unrighteous, *aspondos* a state of war, which the implacable refuse to terminate equitably. The words are clearly not synonymous.

COVER, COVERING

A. Verbs.

2572 1. KALUPTŌ (καλύπτω) signifies to cover, Matt. 8 : 24 ; 10 : 26 ;
AG:401A CB:1253B Luke 8 : 16 ; 23 : 30 ; Jas. 5 : 20 (R.V.) ; 1 Pet. 4 : 8 ; to veil, in 2 Cor. 4 : 3 (R.V. ; A.V., "hid"). See HIDE.¶

Note : Cp. the corresponding noun *kalumma*, a veil, 2 Cor. 3 : 13, 14, 15, 16. See VEIL.¶

1943 2. EPIKALUPTŌ (ἐπικαλύπτω), to cover up or over (*epi*, over), is
AG:294C CB:— used in Rom. 4 : 7, lit., 'whose sins are covered over.'¶ Cp. *epikalumma*, a cloke, 1 Pet. 2 : 16.¶

4028 AG:647D 3. PERIKALUPTŌ (περικαλύπτω), to cover around (*peri*, around),
CB:— e.g., the face, and so, to blindfold, is translated "cover" in Mark 14 : 65, "blindfold" in Luke 22 : 64. In Heb. 9 : 4, it signifies to overlay. See BLINDFOLD, OVERLAY.¶

4780 4. SUNKALUPTŌ (συγκαλύπτω), lit., to cover together ; the *sun-*,
AG:773B CB:1270C however, is intensive, and the verb signifies to cover wholly, to cover up, Luke 12 : 2.¶

2619 AG:411A 5. KATAKALUPTŌ (κατακαλύπτω), to cover up (*kata*, intensive), in
CB:1254A the Middle Voice, to cover oneself, is used in 1 Cor. 11 : 6, 7 (R.V.,
(-OMAI) "veiled").¶

Note : In 1 Cor. 11 : 4, "having his head covered" is, lit., 'having (something) down the head.'

B. Nouns.

4018 AG:646C 1. PERIBOLAION (περιβόλαιον) lit. denotes something thrown around
CB:1263B (*peri*, around, *ballō*, to throw) ; hence, a veil, covering, 1 Cor. 11 : 15 (marg.), or a mantle around the body, a vesture, Heb. 1 : 12. See CLOTHING, Note (1), VESTURE.¶

4629 AG:753D 2. SKEPASMA (σκέπασμα), a covering (*skepazō*, to cover), strictly,
CB:— a roofing, then, any kind of shelter or covering, is used in the plural in 1 Tim. 6 : 8 (A.V., "raiment ;" R.V., "covering").¶

COVET, COVETOUS, COVETOUSNESS

A. Verbs.

1937 1. EPITHUMEŌ (ἐπιθυμέω), to fix the desire upon (*epi*, upon, used
AG:293A CB:1246B intensively, *thumos*, passion), whether things good or bad ; hence, to long for, lust after, covet, is used with the meaning to covet evilly in Acts 20 : 33, of coveting money and apparel ; so in Rom. 7 : 7 ; 13 : 9. See DESIRE, FAIN, LUST.

2. ZĒLOŌ (ζηλόω) is rendered " covet earnestly," in 1 Cor. 12 : 31, **2206**
A.V.; R.V., " desire earnestly," as in 14 : 39 (A.V., " covet "). See **AG:338A CB:1273B**
AFFECT, DESIRE, ENVY, JEALOUS, ZEALOUS.

3. OREGŌ (ὀρέγω), to stretch after, is rendered " covet after " in **3713 (-OMAI)**
1 Tim. 6 : 10, A.V.; R.V., " reaching after." See DESIRE, REACH. **AG:579D CB:1261A (-OMAI)**

B. Nouns.

1. EPITHUMĒTĒS (ἐπιθυμητής), a luster after (akin to A, No. 1), **1938**
is translated in 1 Cor. 10 : 6, in verbal form, " should not lust after." **AG:293B CB:—**
See LUST.¶

2. EPITHUMIA (ἐπιθυμία) denotes " coveting," Rom. 7 : 7, 8, R.V.; **1939**
A.V., " lust " and " concupiscence ; " the commandment here referred to **AG:293B CB:1246B**
convicted him of sinfulness in his desires for unlawful objects besides that of gain. See DESIRE, LUST.

3. PLEONEXIA (πλεονεξία), covetousness, lit., a desire to have more **4124**
(*pleon*, more, *echō*, to have), always in a bad sense, is used in a general **AG:667D CB:1265B**
way in Mark 7 : 22 (plural, lit., ' covetings,' i.e., various ways in which covetousness shows itself); Rom. 1 : 29; Eph. 5 : 3; 1 Thess. 2 : 5. Elsewhere it is used, (*a*) of material possessions, Luke 12 : 15; 2 Pet. 2 : 3; 2 Cor. 9 : 5 (R.V., " extortion "), lit., ' as (a matter of) extortion,' i.e., a gift which betrays the giver's unwillingness to bestow what is due; (*b*) of sensuality, Eph. 4 : 19, " greediness ; " Col. 3 . 5 (where it is called idolatry); 2 Pet. 2 : 14 (A.V., " covetous practices "). See EXTORTION.¶

Note : Cp. the corresponding verb *pleonekteō*, to gain, take advantage of, wrong. See ADVANTAGE, DEFRAUD, GAIN, B, *Note* (2), WRONG

C. Adjectives.

1. PLEONEKTĒS (πλεονέκτης), lit., (eager) to have more (see B, **4123**
No. 3), i.e., to have what belongs to others; hence, greedy of gain, **AG:667C CB:1265B**
covetous, 1 Cor. 5 : 10, 11; 6 : 10; Eph. 5 : 5 (" covetous man ").¶

2. PHILARGUROS (φιλάργυρος), lit., money-loving, is rendered **5366**
" covetous " in the A.V. of Luke 16 : 14 and 2 Tim. 3 : 2; R.V., " lovers **AG:859A CB:1264A**
of money," the wider and due significance.¶

3. APHILARGUROS (ἀφιλάργυρος), No. 2, with negative prefix, is **866**
translated " without covetousness " in Heb. 13 : 5, A.V.; R.V., " free **AG:126C CB:—**
from the love of money." In 1 Tim. 3 : 3, the A.V. has " not covetous," the R.V., " no lover of money."

Note : Trench, Syn. § 24, points out the main distinction between *pleonexia* and *philarguria* as being that between covetousness and avarice, the former having a much wider and deeper sense, being " the genus of which *philarguria* is the species." The covetous man is often cruel as well as grasping, while the avaricious man is simply miserly and stinting.

CRAFT, CRAFTSMAN

1. TECHNĒ (τέχνη), craft, Rev. 18 : 22 : see ART. **5078 AG:814B CB:1271A**

2. TECHNITĒS (τεχνίτης), akin to No. 1, an artificer, artisan, **5079 AG:814B**
craftsman, is translated " craftsman " in Acts 19 : 24, 38 and Rev. 18 : 22. **CB:1271B**

It is found elsewhere in Heb. 11 : 10, " builder ; " but this is practically the same as " maker " (*demiourgos*, the next noun in the verse ; see No. 5, Note). Trench, Syn. § cv, suggests that *technitēs* brings out the artistic side of creation, viewing God as " moulding and fashioning . . . the materials which He called into existence." This agrees with the usage
2039 of the word in the Sept. See BUILDER.¶
AG:307C 3. ERGASIA (ἐργασία) : see DILIGENCE.
CB:1246B 4. HOMOTECHNOS (ὁμότεχνος), one of the same trade (from *homos*,
3673 AG:569B same, and *technē*, see No. 1), is used in Acts 18 : 3 (R.V., " trade ").¶
CB:— Cp. *architektōn*, " master-builder," 1 Cor. 3 : 10.¶
3313 5. MEROS (μέρος), a part, portion, is translated " craft " in Acts
AG:505D 19 : 27, A.V. ; " trade," R.V. (cp. *ergasia* in ver. 25). See BEHALF,
CB:1258B COAST, PART, PIECE, PORTION, RESPECT, SORT.
1217 AG:178D *Note : Dēmiourgos*, a maker, properly signifies one who works for the
CB:1240C people, or whose work stands forth to the public gaze (*dēmos*, people, *ergon*, work), but this idea has been lost in the use of the word, which came to signify a maker, Heb. 11 : 10. This has reference to the structure, No. 2 to the design. Cp. *ktistēs*, a creator.¶

CRAFTINESS, CRAFTY

A. Noun.

3834 AG:608A PANOURGIA (πανουργία), lit., ' all-working,' i.e., doing everything
CB:1261C (*pan*, all, *ergon*, work), hence, unscrupulous conduct, craftiness, is always used in a bad sense in the N.T.. Luke 20 : 23 ; 1 Cor. 3 : 19 ; 2 Cor. 4 : 2 ; 11 : 3 ; Eph. 4 : 14, A.V., " cunning craftiness." See SUBTILTY.¶ In the Sept. it is used in a good sense, Prov. 1 : 4 ; 8 : 5 ; indifferently in Numb. 24 : 22 and Josh. 9 : 4.¶

B. Adjective.

3835 AG:608A PANOURGOS (πανοῦργος), cunning, crafty, is found in 2 Cor. 12 : 16,
CB:1261C where the Apostle is really quoting an accusation made against him by his detractors.¶ In the Sept. it is used in a good sense in Prov. 13 : 1 ; 28 : 2.¶

C. Noun.

1388 AG:203B DOLOS (δόλος), primarily, a bait, hence, fraud, guile, deceit, is rendered
CB:— " craft " in the A.V. of Mark 14 : 1 (R.V. " subtilty "). See DECEIT, GUILE, SUBTILTY.

CRAVE

154 AG:25D *Note :* The word " crave," found in the A.V. of Mark 15 : 43, translates
CB:1234A the verb *aiteō*, to ask (R.V., " asked for "). See ASK.

CREATE, CREATION, CREATOR, CREATURE

A. Verb.

2936 AG:455C KTIZŌ (κτίζω), used among the Greeks to mean the founding of a
CB:1256B place, a city or colony, signifies, in Scripture, to create, always of the

act of God, whether (*a*) in the natural creation, Mark 13 : 19 ; Rom. 1 : 25 (where the title " The Creator " translates the article with the aorist participle of the verb) ; 1 Cor. 11 : 9 ; Eph. 3 : 9 ; Col. 1 : 16 ; 1 Tim. 4 : 3 ; Rev. 4 : 11 ; 10 : 6, or (*b*) in the spiritual creation, Eph. 2 : 10, 15 ; 4 : 24 ; Col. 3 : 10. See MAKE.¶

B. Nouns.

1. KTISIS (κτίσις), primarily the act of creating, or the creative act 2937 AG:455D CB:1256A
in process, has this meaning in Rom. 1 : 20 and Gal. 6 : 15. Like the English word " creation," it also signifies the product of the creative act, the creature, as in Mark 16 : 15, R.V. ; Rom. 1 : 25 ; 8 : 19 ; Col. 1 : 15 etc. ; in Heb. 9 : 11, A.V., " building." In Mark 16 : 15 and Col. 1 : 23 its significance has special reference to mankind in general. As to its use in Gal. 6 : 15 and 2 Cor. 5 : 17, in the former, apparently, " the reference is to the creative act of God, whereby a man is introduced into the blessing of salvation, in contrast to circumcision done by human hands, which the Judaizers claimed was necessary to that end. In 2 Cor. 5 : 17 the reference is to what the believer is in Christ ; in consequence of the creative act he has become a new creature."*

Ktisis is once used of human actions, 1 Pet. 2 : 13, " ordinance " (marg., " creation "). See BUILDING, ORDINANCE.

2. KTISMA (κτίσμα) has the concrete sense, the created thing, the 2938 AG:456B CB:1256A
creature, the product of the creative act, 1 Tim. 4 : 4 ; Jas. 1 : 18 ; Rev. 5 : 13 ; 8 : 9.¶

3. KTISTĒS (κτίστης), among the Greeks, the founder of a city etc., 2939 AG:456B CB:1256B
denotes in Scripture the Creator, 1 Pet. 4 : 19 (cp. Rom. 1 : 20, under B, No. 1, above).¶

Note : It is a significant confirmation of Rom. 1 : 20, 21, that in all non-Christian Greek literature these words are never used by Greeks to convey the idea of a Creator or of a creative act by any of their gods. The words are confined by them to the acts of human beings.

4. ZŌON (ζῷον), a living creature : see BEAST. 2226 AG:341C CB:1273C

For CREDITOR see LEND, LENDER

CREDIT See RECKON, THANK

For CREEK see BAY

CREEP, CREEPING, CREPT

A. Verbs.

1. ENDUNŌ (ἐνδύνω), properly, to envelop in (*en*, in, *dunō*, to enter), 1744 AG:263D CB:—
to put on, as of a garment, has the secondary and intransitive significance of creeping into, insinuating oneself into, and is found with this meaning in 2 Tim. 3 : 6. Cp. *enduō*, to clothe.¶

2. PAREISDUNŌ (παρεισδύνω), to enter in by the side (*para*, beside, 3921 AG:624D CB:—

---

* From Notes on Galatians by Hogg and Vine, p. 339.

eis, in), to insinuate oneself into, by stealth, to creep in stealthily, is used in Jude 4.¶

B. Noun.

2062 AG:310B CB:— HERPETON (ἑρπετόν) signifies a creeping thing (*herpō*, to creep; Eng., "serpent" is from the same root), Jas. 3:7 (R.V., "creeping things," for A.V., "serpents," which form only one of this genus); it is set in contrast to quadrupeds and birds, Acts 10:12; 11:6; Rom. 1:23. See SERPENT.¶

For CRIME see CHARGE

For CRIPPLE see HALT

CROOKED

4646 AG:756B CB:— SKOLIOS (σκολιός), curved, crooked, was especially used (*a*) of a way, Luke 3:5, with spiritual import (see Prov. 28:18, Sept.); it is set in contrast to *orthos* and *euthus*, straight; (*b*) metaphorically, of what is morally crooked, perverse, froward, of people belonging to a particular generation, Acts 2:40 (A.V., "untoward"); Phil. 2:15; of tyrannical or unjust masters, 1 Pet. 2:18, "froward;" in this sense it is set in contrast to *agathos*, good.¶

CROP See FRUIT

CROSS, CRUCIFY

A. Noun.

4716 AG:764D CB:1270A STAUROS (σταυρός) denotes, primarily, an upright pale or stake. On such malefactors were nailed for execution. Both the noun and the verb *stauroō*, to fasten to a stake or pale, are originally to be distinguished from the ecclesiastical form of a two beamed cross. The shape of the latter had its origin in ancient Chaldea, and was used as the symbol of the god Tammuz (being in the shape of the mystic Tau, the initial of his name) in that country and in adjacent lands, including Egypt. By the middle of the 3rd cent. A.D. the churches had either departed from, or had travestied, certain doctrines of the Christian faith. In order to increase the prestige of the apostate ecclesiastical system pagans were received into the churches apart from regeneration by faith, and were permitted largely to retain their pagan signs and symbols. Hence the Tau or T, in its most frequent form, with the cross-piece lowered, was adopted to stand for the cross of Christ.

As for the Chi, or X, which Constantine declared he had seen in a vision leading him to champion the Christian faith, that letter was the initial of the word "Christ" and had nothing to do with "the Cross" (for *xulon*, a timber beam, a tree, as used for the *stauros*, see under TREE).

The method of execution was borrowed by the Greeks and Romans from the Phoenicians. The *stauros* denotes (*a*) the cross, or stake itself, e.g., Matt. 27:32; (*b*) the crucifixion suffered, e.g., 1 Cor. 1:17, 18, where "the word of the cross," R.V., stands for the Gospel; Gal. 5 : 11, where crucifixion is metaphorically used of the renunciation of the world, that characterizes the true Christian life; 6 : 12, 14; Eph. 2 : 16; Phil. 3 : 18.

The judicial custom by which the condemned person carried his stake to the place of execution, was applied by the Lord to those sufferings by which His faithful followers were to express their fellowship with Him, e.g., Matt. 10 : 38.

B. Verbs.

1. STAUROŌ (*σταυρόω*) signifies (*a*) the act of crucifixion, e.g., Matt. 4717
20 : 19; (*b*) metaphorically, the putting off of the flesh with its passions AG:765B CB:1270A
and lusts, a condition fulfilled in the case of those who are "of Christ Jesus," Gal. 5 : 24, R.V.; so of the relationship between the believer and the world, 6 : 14.

2. SUSTAUROŌ (*συσταυρόω*), to crucify with (*su-*, for, *sun*, with), is 4957
used (*a*) of actual crucifixion in company with another, Matt. 27 : 44; AG:795A CB:1271A
Mark 15 : 32; John 19 : 32; (*b*) metaphorically, of spiritual identification with Christ in His death, Rom. 6 : 6, and Gal. 2 : 20.¶

3. ANASTAUROŌ (*ἀνασταυρόω*) (*ana*, again) is used in Heb. 6 : 6 of 388
Hebrew apostates, who as merely nominal Christians, in turning back to AG:61A CB:1235B
Judaism, were thereby virtually guilty of crucifying Christ again.¶

4. PROSPĒGNUMI (*προσπήγνυμι*), to fix or fasten to anything (*pros*, 4362
to, *pēgnumi*, to fix), is used of the crucifixion of Christ, Acts 2 : 23.¶ AG:718A CB:—

CROSS (Verb)

DIAPERAŌ (*διαπεράω*), to pass over, to cross over (*dia*, through, 1276
peraō, to pass: akin to this are *peran*, across, *peras*, a boundary, Latin, AG:187C CB:—
porta, a gate, Eng., portal, port, etc.), is translated by the verb to cross in the R.V., but differently in the A.V.; in Matt. 9 : 1; Mark 5 : 21; 6 : 53 (A.V., "passed"); Matt. 14 : 34 (A.V., "were gone"); Luke 16 : 26 (A.V., "neither can they pass"); Acts 21 : 2 (A.V., "sailing"). See GO, PASS, SAIL.¶ In the Sept., Deut. 30 : 13; Is. 23 : 2.¶

For the verb CROW (CREW) see CALL, A, No. 8

CROWD

A. Noun.

OCHLOS (*ὄχλος*), a confused throng, is usually translated "multitude." 3793
The R.V. translates it "crowd" (A.V., "press" in some) in Matt. AG:600C CB:1260B
9 : 23, 25; Mark 2 : 4; 3 : 9; 5 : 27, 30; Luke 8 : 19; 19 : 3; Acts 21 : 34, 35; 24 : 12, 18. See COMPANY, MULTITUDE, NUMBER, PEOPLE.

B. Verb.

OCHLOPOIEŌ (*ὀχλοποιέω*), to make a crowd (A, with *poieō*, to make), 3792
is translated "gathered a crowd" in Acts 17 : 5, R.V. (A.V., "company"). AG:600C CB:—

CROWN (Noun and Verb)

A. Nouns.

4735 AG:767A CB:1270A 1. STEPHANOS (*στέφανος*), primarily, that which surrounds, as a wall or crowd (from *stephō*, to encircle), denotes (*a*) the victor's crown, the symbol of triumph in the games or some such contest; hence, by metonymy, a reward or prize; (*b*) a token of public honour for distinguished service, military prowess etc., or of nuptial joy, or festal gladness, especially at the parousia of kings. It was woven as a garland of oak, ivy, parsley, myrtle or olive, or in imitation of these in gold. In some passages the reference to the games is clear, 1 Cor. 9 : 25; 2 Tim. 4 : 8 ("crown of righteousness"); it may be so in 1 Pet. 5 : 4, where the fadeless character of "the crown of glory" is set in contrast to the garlands of earth. In other passages it stands as an emblem of life, joy, reward and glory, Phil. 4 : 1; 1 Thess. 2 : 19; Jas. 1 : 12 ("crown of life"); Rev. 2 : 10 (ditto); 3 : 11; 4 : 4, 10: of triumph, 6 : 2; 9 : 7; 12 : 1; 14 : 14.

It is used of the crown of thorns which the soldiers plaited and put on Christ's head, Matt. 27 : 29; Mark 15 : 17; John 19 : 2, 5. At first sight this might be taken as an alternative for *diadēma*, a kingly crown (see below), but considering the blasphemous character of that masquerade, and the materials used, obviously *diadēma* would be quite unfitting and the only alternative was *stephanos* (see Trench § xxxii).¶

1238 AG:182D CB:1241A 2. DIADĒMA (*διάδημα*) is never used as *stephanos* is; it is always the symbol of kingly or imperial dignity, and is translated "diadem" instead of "crown" in the R.V., of the claims of the Dragon, Rev. 12 : 3; 13 : 1; 19 : 12. See DIADEM.¶

B. Verb.

4737 AG:767C CB:1270A STEPHANOŌ (*στεφανόω*), to crown, conforms in meaning to *stephanos*; it is used of the reward of victory in the games, in 2 Tim. 2 : 5; of the glory and honour bestowed by God upon man in regard to his position in creation, Heb. 2 : 7; of the glory and honour bestowed upon the Lord Jesus in His exaltation, ver. 9.¶

For CRUCIFY see CROSS

CRUMB

5589 AG:893A CB:— PSICHION (*ψιχίον*), a small morsel, a diminutive of *psix*, a bit, or crumb; of bread or meat, it is used in Matt. 15 : 27 and Mark 7 : 28; some mss. have it in Luke 16 : 21.¶

CRUSE

211 AG:34C CB:— ALABASTRON (*ἀλάβαστρον*) was a vessel for holding ointment or perfume; it derived its name from the alabaster stone, of which it was usually made. "Cruse," R.V., is a more suitable rendering than "box;" Matt. 26 : 7; Mark 14 : 3; Luke 7 : 37.¶

CRUSH

APOTHLIBŌ (ἀποθλίβω), a strengthened form of *thlibō*, to throng 598
(*apo*, intensive), is used in Luke 8 : 45, R.V., " crush," for A.V., " press," AG:91B
of the multitude who were pressing around Christ (cp. the preceding word CB:—
sunechō, to press).¶ In the Sept., Numb. 22 : 25.¶

CRY (Noun and Verb), CRYING

A. Nouns.

1. KRAUGĒ (κραυγή), an onomatopœic word, is used in Matt. 25 : 6 ; 2906
Luke 1 : 42 (some mss. have *phōnē*) ; Acts 23 : 9, R.V., " clamour ; " AG:449C
Eph. 4 : 31, " clamour ; " Heb. 5 : 7 ; Rev. 21 : 4, " crying." Some mss. CB:—
have it in Rev. 14 : 18 (the most authentic have *phōnē*). See CLAMOUR.¶

2. BOĒ (βοή), especially a cry for help, an onomatopœic word (cp. 995
Eng., boo), connected with *boaō* (see B, No. 1), is found in Jas. 5 : 4.¶ AG:144C CB:1239B

B. Verbs.

1. BOAŌ (βοάω), akin to A, No. 2, signifies (*a*) to raise a cry, whether 994
of joy, Gal. 4 : 27, or vexation, Acts 8 : 7 ; (*b*) to speak with a strong AG:144B CB:1239B
voice, Matt. 3 : 3 ; Mark 1 : 3 ; 15 : 34 ; Luke 3 : 4 ; 9 : 38 (some mss.
have *anaboaō* here : see No. 2) ; John 1 : 23 ; Acts 17 : 6 ; 25 : 24 (some
mss. have *epiboaō*, No. 3, here) ; (*c*) to cry out for help, Luke 18 : 7, 38.¶
For Acts 21 : 34, see No. 8.

2. ANABOAŌ (ἀναβοάω), *ana*, up, intensive, and No. 1, to lift up the 310
voice, cry out, is said of Christ at the moment of His Death, a testimony AG:51A CB:1235A
to His supernatural power in giving up His life, Matt. 27 : 46 ; in some
mss. in Mark 15 : 8, of the shouting of a multitude ; in some mss. in
Luke 9 : 38, of the crying out of a man in a company (see No. 1).¶

3. EPIBOAŌ (ἐπιβοάω), *epi*, upon, intensive, and No. 1, to cry out, 1916
exclaim vehemently, is used in some mss. in Acts 25 : 24 (see No. 1.¶) AG:290C CB:—

4. KRAZŌ (κράζω), akin to A, No. 1, to cry out, an onomatopœic word, 2896
used especially of the cry of the raven ; then, of any inarticulate cries, AG:447C
from fear, pain etc. ; of the cry of a Canaanitish woman, Matt. 15 : 22 CB:1256A
(so the best mss., instead of *kraugazō*) ; of the shouts of the children in
the Temple, Matt. 21 : 15 ; of the people who shouted for Christ to be
crucified, 27 : 23 ; Mark 15 : 13, 14 ; of the cry of Christ on the Cross at
the close of His sufferings, Matt. 27 : 50 ; Mark 15 : 39 (see No. 2, above).

In John's Gospel it is used three times, out of the six, of Christ's utterances, 7 : 28, 37 ; 12 : 44. In the Acts it is not used of cries of distress, but chiefly of the shouts of opponents ; in the Apocalypse, chiefly of the utterances of heavenly beings concerning earthly matters ; in Rom. 8 : 15 and Gal. 4 : 6, of the appeal of believers to God the Father ; in Rom. 9 : 27, of a prophecy concerning Israel ; in Jas. 5 : 4, metaphorically, of hire kept back by fraud.

Note : A recent translator renders this verb in Matt. 27 : 50 " uttered a scream," an utterly deplorable mistranslation, and a misrepresentation of the nature of the Lord's cry.

249 5. ANAKRAZŌ (ἀνακράζω), *ana*, up, intensive, and No. 4, signifies
AG:56B CB:— to cry out loudly, Mark 1 : 23 ; 6 : 49 ; Luke 4 : 33 ; 8 : 28 ; 23 : 18.¶

2905 6. KRAUGAZŌ (κραυγάζω), a stronger form of No. 4, to make a
AG:449B clamour or outcry (A, No. 1), is used in Matt. 12 : 19, in a prophecy from
CB:1256A Isaiah of Christ ; in Luke 4 : 41 (in the best mss., instead of *krazō*) ; John 11 : 43 ; 12 : 13 (in the best mss.) ; 18 : 40 ; 19 : 6, 12, 15 ; Acts 22 : 23.¶

5455 7. PHŌNEŌ (φωνέω), to utter a loud sound or cry, whether of
AG:870B CB:1264B animals, e.g., Matt. 26 : 34 ; or persons, Luke 8 : 8 ; 16 : 24 ; this is the word which Luke uses to describe the cry of the Lord at the close of His sufferings on the Cross, Luke 23 : 46 (see under *anaboaō* and *krazō*, above) ; also, e.g., Acts 16 : 28 ; Rev. 14 : 18. See CALL, A, No. 8, CROW.

2019 8. EPIPHŌNEŌ (ἐπιφωνέω), No. 7, with *epi*, upon, or against,
AG:304D CB:1246A signifies to shout, either against, Luke 23 : 21 ; Acts 21 : 34 (in the best mss., No. 1) ; 22 : 24, or in acclamation, Acts 12 : 22. See SHOUT.¶

863 *Note :* For *aphiēmi*, Mark 15 : 37, see UTTER.

AG:125C CB:1236B Comparing the various verbs, *kaleō*, denotes to call out for any purpose, *boaō*, to cry out as an expression of feeling, *krazō*, to cry out loudly. *Kaleō* suggests intelligence, *boaō*, sensibilities, *krazō*, instincts.

CRYSTAL

A. Noun.

2930 KRUSTALLOS (κρύσταλλος), from *kruos*, ice, and hence properly
AG:454D CB:1256A anything congealed and transparent, denotes crystal, a kind of precious stone, Rev. 4 : 6 ; 22 : 1. Rock-crystal is pure quartz ; it crystallizes in hexagonal prisms, each with a pyramidical apex.¶

B. Verb.

2929 KRUSTALLIZŌ (κρυσταλλίζω), to be of crystalline brightness and
AG:454D CB:1256A transparency, to shine like crystal, is found in Rev. 21 : 11, where it is said of Christ as the " Light-giver " (*phōstēr*) of the Heavenly City (not *phōs*, light, R.V. and A.V.). Possibly there the verb has a transitive force, to transform into crystal splendour, as of the effect of Christ upon His saints.¶

CUBIT

4083 PĒCHUS (πῆχυς) denotes the fore-arm, i.e., the part between the
AG:656D CB:— hand and the elbow-joint ; hence, a measure of length, not from the wrist to the elbow, but from the tip of the middle finger to the elbow joint, i.e., about a foot and a half, or a little less than two feet, Matt. 6 : 27 ; Luke 12 : 25 ; John 21 : 8 ; Rev. 21 : 17.¶

CUMBER

2673 1. KATARGEŌ (καταργέω), lit., to reduce to idleness or inactivity
AG:417B CB:1254B (*kata*, down, and *argos*, idle), is once rendered " cumber," Luke 13 : 7. See ABOLISH.

2. PERISPAŌ (περισπάω), lit., to draw around (*peri*), draw away, 4049
distract, is used in the Passive Voice in the sense of being over-occupied AG:650B
about a thing, to be cumbered, Luke 10 : 40.¶ CB:—

CUMMIN

KUMINON (κύμινον) is an umbelliferous plant with aromatic seeds, 2951
used as a condiment, Matt. 23 : 23. AG:457C CB:1256B

For the A.V. CUNNING see CRAFTINESS. For CUNNINGLY see DEVISED

CUP

POTĒRION (ποτήριον), a diminutive of *potēr*, denotes, primarily, a 4221
drinking vessel; hence, a cup (*a*) literal, as, e.g., in Matt. 10 : 42. The AG:695B CB:1266B
cup of blessing, 1 Cor. 10 : 16, is so named from the third (the fourth according to Edersheim) cup in the Jewish Passover Feast, over which thanks and praise were given to God. This connection is not to be rejected on the ground that the church at Corinth was unfamiliar with Jewish customs. That the contrary was the case, see 5 : 7; (*b*) figurative, of one's lot or experience, joyous or sorrowful (frequent in the Psalms; cp. Ps. 116 : 18, "cup of salvation"); in the N.T. it is used most frequently of the sufferings of Christ, Matt. 20 : 22, 23; 26 : 39; Mark 10 : 38, 39; 14 : 36; Luke 22 : 42; John 18 : 11; also of the evil deeds of Babylon, Rev. 17 : 4; 18 : 6; of Divine punishments to be inflicted, Rev. 14 : 10; 16 : 19. Cp. Ps. 11 : 6; 75 : 8; Is. 51 : 17; Jer. 25 : 15; Ezek. 23 : 32–34; Zech. 12 : 2.

CURE (Noun and Verb)

A. Noun.

IASIS (ἴασις), a healing, a cure (akin to *iaomai*, to heal, and *iatros*, 2392
a physician), is used in the plural in Luke 13 : 32; in Acts 4 : 22, AG:368C
"healing;" in 4 : 30 with the preposition *eis*, unto, lit., 'unto healing,' CB:1252C
translated "heal." See HEALING.¶

B. Verb.

THERAPEUŌ (θεραπεύω), Eng., therapeutics, etc., denotes (*a*) 2323
primarily, to serve (cp. *therapeia* and *therapōn*), Acts 17 : 25 (A.V., AG:359A CB:1272B
"worshipped"); then, (*b*) to heal, restore to health, to cure; it is usually translated "to heal," but "cure" in Matt. 17 : 16, 18; Luke 7 : 21; 9 : 1; John 5 : 10, Acts 28 : 9, R.V. See HEAL, WORSHIP.

CURIOUS

Note: For the adjective *periergos*, busy about trifles, see BUSYBODY: 4021
it is used of magic arts in Acts 19 : 19 (lit., 'things that are around work,' AG:646D CB:1263B
and thus superfluous), i.e., the arts of those who pry into forbidden things, with the aid of evil spirits. See also 1 Tim. 5 : 13, where the meaning is "inquisitive," prying into other people's affairs.¶

CURSE, CURSING (Noun and Verb), CURSED, ACCURSED

A. Nouns.

685 1. ARA (ἀρά), in its most usual meaning, a malediction, cursing
AG:103D (its other meaning is "a prayer"), is used in Rom. 3 : 14 (often in the
CB:1237B Sept.).¶

2671 2. KATARA (κατάρα), *kata*, down, intensive, and No. 1, denotes an
AG:417A execration, imprecation, curse, uttered out of malevolence, Jas. 3 : 10 ;
CB:1254B 2 Pet. 2 : 14 ; or pronounced by God in His righteous judgment, as upon a land doomed to barrenness, Heb. 6 : 8 ; upon those who seek for justification by obedience, in part or completely, to the Law, Gal. 3 : 10, 13 ; in this 13th verse it is used concretely of Christ, as having "become a curse" for us, i.e., by voluntarily undergoing on the Cross the appointed penalty of the curse. He thus was identified, on our behalf, with the doom of sin. Here, not the verb in the Sept. of Deut. 21 : 23 is used (see B, No. 3), but the concrete noun.¶

331 3. ANATHEMA (ἀνάθεμα), transliterated from the Greek, is frequently
AG:54A used in the Sept., where it translates the Heb. *cherem*, a thing devoted
CB:1235B to God, whether (*a*) for His service, as the sacrifices, Lev. 27 : 28 (cp. *anathēma*, a votive offering, gift), or (*b*) for its destruction, as an idol, Deut. 7 : 26, or a city, Josh. 6 : 17. Later it acquired the more general meaning of the disfavour of Jehovah, e.g., Zech. 14 : 11. This is the meaning in the N.T. It is used of (*a*) the sentence pronounced, Acts 23 : 14 (lit., 'cursed themselves with a curse ;' see *anathematizō* below) ; (*b*) of the object on which the curse is laid, "accursed ;" in the following, the R.V. keeps to the word "anathema," Rom. 9 : 3 ; 1 Cor. 12 : 3 ; 16 : 22 ; Gal. 1 : 8, 9, all of which the A.V. renders by "accursed" except 1 Cor. 16 : 22, where it has "Anathema." In Gal. 1 : 8, 9, the Apostle declares in the strongest manner that the Gospel he preached was the one and only way of salvation, and that to preach another was to nullify the Death of Christ.¶

2652 4. KATATHEMA (κατάθεμα), or, as in some mss., the longer form
AG:414D *katanathema*, is stronger than No. 3 (*kata*, intensive), and denotes, by
CB:1254B metonymy, an accursed thing (the object cursed being put for the curse pronounced), Rev. 22 : 3.¶

B. Verbs.

332 1. ANATHEMATIZŌ (ἀναθεματίζω), akin to No. 3, signifies to declare
AG:54C anathema, i.e., devoted to destruction, accursed, to curse, Mark 14 : 71,
CB:1235B or to bind by a curse, Acts 23 : 12, 14, 21.¶

2653 2. KATANATHEMATIZŌ (καταναθεματίζω), a strengthened form
AG:414D of No. 1, denotes to utter curses against, Matt. 26 : 74 ; cp. Mark's word
CB:1254B concerning the same occasion (No. 1).¶

2672 3. KATARAOMAI (καταράομαι), akin to A, No. 2, primarily signifies
AG:417A to pray against, to wish evil against a person or thing ; hence to curse,
CB:1254B Matt. 25 : 41 ; Mark 11 : 21 ; Luke 6 : 28 ; Rom. 12 : 14 ; Jas. 3 : 9. Some mss. have it in Matt. 5 : 44.¶

4. KAKOLOGEŌ (κακολογέω), to speak evil (*kakos*, evil, *legō*, to 2551 AG:397B
speak), is translated by the verb to curse in Matt. 15 : 4, and Mark 7 : 10, CB:1253B
to speak evil of father and mother, not necessarily to curse, is what the Lord intended (R.V.). A.V. and R.V. have the verb to speak evil in Mark 9 : 39 and Acts 19 : 9. See EVIL.

C. Adjectives.

1. EPIKATARATOS (ἐπικατάρατος), cursed, accursed (*epi*, upon, and 1944 AG:294C
A, No. 2), is used in Gal. 3 : 10, 13.¶ CB:1245C

2. EPARATOS (ἐπάρατος), accursed, is found, in the best mss., in — AG:283C
John 7 : 49, R.V., " accursed," instead of No. 1. CB:1245C

For CUSHION see PILLOW CURTAIN See VEIL

CUSTOM (Usage), ACCUSTOM (Verb)

A. Nouns.

1. ETHOS (ἔθος) denotes (*a*) a custom, usage, prescribed by law, 1485 AG:218D
Acts 6 : 14 ; 15 : 1 ; 25 : 16 ; a rite or ceremony, Luke 2 : 42 ; (*b*) a CB:1247A
custom, habit, manner, Luke 22 : 39 ; John 19 : 40 ; Heb. 10 : 25 (A.V., " manner "). See MANNER, WONT.

2. SUNĒTHEIA (συνήθεια), *sun*, with, *ethos* (see No. 1), denotes (*a*) 4914 AG:789C
an intercourse, intimacy, a meaning not found in the N.T. ; (*b*) a custom, CB:—
customary usage, John 18 : 39 ; 1 Cor. 11 : 16 ; or force of habit, 1 Cor. 8 : 7, R.V., " being used to " (some mss. here have *suneidēsis*, conscience ; whence A.V., " with conscience of ").¶

B. Verbs.

1. ETHIZŌ (ἐθίζω), akin to A, No. 1, signifies to accustom, or in the 1480 AG:218B
Passive Voice, to be accustomed. In the participial form it is equivalent CB:—
to a noun, " custom," Luke 2 : 27.¶

2. ETHŌ (ἔθω), to be accustomed, as in the case of No. 1, 1486
is used in the Passive participle as a noun, signifying a custom, Luke AG:234A (EIōTHA)
4 : 16 ; Acts 17 : 2 (A.V., " manner ; " R.V., " custom ") ; in Matt. CB:1243A
17 : 15 and Mark 10 : 1, " was wont." See MANNER, WONT.¶ (EIōTHOS)

CUSTOM (Toll)

1. TELOS (τέλος), an end, termination, whether of time or purpose, 5056 AG:811B
denotes, in its secondary significance, what is paid for public ends, a toll, CB:1271B
tax, custom, Matt. 17 : 25 (R.V., " toll ") ; Rom. 13 : 7 (R.V. and A.V., " custom "). In Palestine the Herods of Galilee and Peræa received the custom ; in Judæa it was paid to the Procurator for the Roman Government. See END, FINALLY, UTTERMOST.

2. TELŌNION (τελώνιον) denotes a custom-house, for the collection 5058 AG:812C
of the taxes, Matt. 9 : 9 ; Mark 2 : 14 ; Luke 5 : 27 (R.V., " place of toll "). CB:1271B

CUT

1. KOPTŌ (κόπτω) denotes to cut by a blow, e.g., branches, Matt. 2875 AG:444A
21 : 8 ; Mark 11 : 8. See BEWAIL, LAMENT, MOURN, WAIL. CB:1255C

609 AG:93A CB:1237A 2. APOKOPTŌ (ἀποκόπτω), to cut off, or cut away (*apo*, from, and No. 1), is used (*a*) literally, of members of the body, Mark 9 : 43, 45 ; John 18 : 10, 26 ; of ropes, Acts 27 : 32 ; (*b*) metaphorically, in the Middle Voice, of cutting off oneself, to excommunicate, Gal. 5 : 12, of the Judaizing teachers, with a reference, no doubt, to circumcision.¶

1581 AG:241D CB:1243C 3. EKKOPTŌ (ἐκκόπτω), lit., to cut or strike out (*ek*,out or off, and No. 1), to cut down, is used (*a*) literally, Matt. 5 : 30 (in 3 : 10 and 7 : 19 and Luke 3 : 9, " hewn down ") ; 18 : 8 ; Luke 13 : 7, 9 ; (*b*) metaphorically, of cutting off from spiritual blessing, Rom. 11 : 22, 24 ; of depriving persons of an occasion for something, 2 Cor. 11 : 12. See HEW.¶

1465 AG:216C CB:1245A *Note :* In 1 Pet. 3 : 7 the best mss. have *enkoptō*, to hinder ; some have *ekkoptō*.

2629 AG:412A CB:— 4. KATAKOPTŌ (κατακόπτω), lit., to cut down, cut in pieces (*kata*, down, intensive), Mark 5 : 5, of the demoniac.¶

1282 AG:187D CB:— 5. DIAPRIŌ (διαπρίω) signifies to saw asunder (*dia*, asunder, *priō*, to saw), to divide by a saw (as in 1 Chron. 20 : 3, Sept.), hence, metaphorically, to be sawn through mentally, to be rent with vexation, to be cut to the heart, is used in Acts 5 : 33 ; 7 : 54.¶

1371 AG:200C CB:— 6. DICHOTOMEŌ (διχοτομέω), lit., to cut into two parts (*dicha*, apart, *temnō*, to cut, *tomē*, a cutting), Matt. 24 : 51, to cut asunder, is used in Luke 12 : 46. Some take the reference to be to the mode of punishment by which criminals and captives were cut in two ; others, on account of the fact that in these passages the delinquent is still surviving after the treatment, take the verb to denote to cut up by scourging, to scourge severely, the word being used figuratively.

As to Matt. 24 : 51, it has been remarked that the cutting asunder was an appropriate punishment for one who had lived a double life. In both passages the latter part of the sentence applies to retribution beyond this life.¶ In the Sept. the verb is used in Ex. 29 : 17 of the dividing of the ram as a whole burnt offering at the consecration of the priests.¶ The corresponding noun is found in Gen. 15 : 11, 17 ; Ex. 29 : 17 ; Lev. 1 : 8 ; Ezek. 24 : 4.¶

4932 AG:792B CB:— 7. SUNTEMNŌ (συντέμνω), lit., to cut together (*sun*, with, *temnō*, to cut ; the simple verb *temnō* is not found in the N.T.), signifies to contract by cutting, to cut short ; thus, to bring to an end or accomplish speedily ; it is said of a prophecy or decree, Rom. 9 : 28 (twice), from the Sept. of Is. 10 : 23. See SHORT.¶

851 AG:124B CB:1236B 8. APHAIREŌ (ἀφαιρέω), to take away, remove, is translated " cut off " in Mark 14 : 47, A.V., and Luke 22 : 50, and " smote off " in Matt. 26 : 51 ; R.V., " struck off " in each place. See SMITE, TAKE.

CYMBAL

2950 AG:457C CB:— KUMBALON (κύμβαλον), a cymbal, was so called from its shape (akin to *kumbos*, a hollow basin, *kumbē*, a cup), and was made of bronze, two being struck together, 1 Cor. 13 : 1.¶

DAILY (Adjective)

1. EPIOUSIOS (ἐπιούσιος) is found in Matt. 6 : 11 and Luke 11 : 3. 1967
Some would derive the word from *epi*, upon, and *eimi*, to be, as if to AG:296D
signify " (bread) present," i.e., sufficient bread, but this formation is CB:1246A
questionable. The same objection applies to the conjecture, that it is derived from *epi*, and *ousia*, and signifies " (bread) for sustenance." The more probable derivation is from *epi*, and *eimi*, to go, (bread) for going on, i.e., for the morrow and after, or (bread) coming (for us). See the R.V. marg. This suits the added *sēmeron*, " to-day," i.e., the prayer is to be for bread that suffices for this day and next, so that the mind may conform to Christ's warning against anxiety for the morrow. Confirmation of this derivation is also to be found in the word *epiousē*, in the phrase " the next day," Acts 7 : 26 ; 16 : 11.¶

2. EPHĒMEROS (ἐφήμερος) signifies " for the day " (*epi*, upon, 2184 AG:330C
or for, *hēmera*, a day, Eng., ephemeral), Jas. 2 : 15.¶ CB:—

3. KATHĒMERINOS (καθημερινός) means, lit., according to (*kata*) 2522
the day (*hēmera*), day by day, daily, Acts 6 : 1.¶ AG:389D CB:—

Notes : The following phrases contain the word *hēmera*, day, and are 2250
translated " daily " or otherwise : (*a*) *kath' hēmeran*, lit., according to, or AG:345D
for, (the) day, or throughout the day, " day by day," e.g., Luke 11 : 3 ; CB:1249C
Acts 3 : 2 ; 16 : 5 ; 1 Cor. 15 : 31 ; Heb. 7 : 27 ; (*b*) *hēmera kai hēmera*, lit., day and day, " day by day," 2 Cor. 4 : 16 ; (*c*) *hēmeran ex hēmeras*,
lit., day from day, " from day to day," 2 Pet. 2 : 8 ; (*d*) *sēmeron*, " this SĒMERON
day," or " to-day," used outside the Synoptists and the Acts, in 2 Cor. 4594 AG:749A
3 : 14, 15, eight times in Hebrews, and in Jas. 4 : 13 ; (*e*) *tēs sēmeron* CB:1268A
hēmeras, " (unto) this very day," Rom. 11 : 8 (R.V.) ; (*f*) *tas hēmeras*, Luke 21 : 37, R.V., " every day," for A.V., " in the daytime ; " (*g*) *pasan hēmeran*, Acts 5 : 42, R.V., " every day ; " preceded by *kata* in Acts 17 : 17, R.V., " every day ; " (*h*) *kath' hekastēn hēmeran*, lit., ' according to each day,' Heb. 3 : 13, " day by day," R.V.

DAINTY

LIPAROS (λιπαρός) properly signifies oily, or anointed with oil (from 3045 AG:475C
lipos, grease, connected with *aleiphō*, to anoint) ; it is said of things which CB:—

pertain to delicate and sumptuous living ; hence, " dainty," Rev. 18 : 14.¶ In the Sept., Judg. 3 : 29 ; Neh. 9 : 35 ; Is. 30 : 23.¶

For DAMAGE see LOSS

For DAMNABLE, DAMNATION and DAMNED, see CONDEMNATION, DESTRUCTION, JUDGE, JUDGMENT

DAMSEL

2877 1. KORASION (κοράσιον), a diminutive of *korē*, a girl, denotes a little
AG:444B CB:1255C girl (properly a colloquial word, often used disparagingly, but not so in later writers) ; in the N.T. it is used only in familiar conversation, Matt. 9 : 24, 25 (A.V., " maid ") ; 14 : 11 ; Mark 5 : 41, 42 ; 6 : 22, 28.¶

3813 2. PAIDION (παιδίον), a diminutive of *pais*, denotes a young child
AG:604A CB:1261C (male or female) in the A.V. of Mark 5 : 39, 40, 41 (1st line) ; the R.V. corrects " damsel " to " child," so as to distinguish between the narrative of facts, and the homely address to the little girl herself, in which, and in the following sentence, *korasion* is used. (See No. 1). See CHILD.

3814 3. PAIDISKĒ (παιδίσκη) denotes a young girl, or a female slave ;
AG:604B CB:1261C " damsel," A.V., in John 18 : 17 ; Acts 12 : 13 ; 16 : 16 ; R.V. " maid " in each case. See BONDMAID, BONDWOMAN, MAID, MAIDEN.

DANCE

(-OMAI) ORCHEŌ (ὀρχέω), cp. Eng., orchestra, probably originally signified
3738 AG:583B to lift up, as of the feet ; hence, to leap with regularity of motion. It
CB:1261A is always used in the Middle Voice, Matt. 11 : 17 ; 14 : 6 ; Mark 6 : 22 ; Luke 7 : 32. The performance by the daughter of Herodias is the only clear instance of artistic dancing, a form introduced from Greek customs.¶

DANCING

5525 CHOROS (χορός), Eng., chorus, primarily denoted an enclosure for
AG:883D CB:— dancing ; hence, a company of dancers and singers. The supposition that the word is connected with *orcheō* by metathesis (i.e., change of place, of the letters *ch* and *o*) seems to be without foundation. The word is used in Luke 15 : 25.¶

DANGER, DANGEROUS

A. Verb.

2793 KINDUNEUŌ (κινδυνεύω) properly signifies to run a risk, face danger,
AG:432B CB:1255A but is used in the N.T. in the sense of being in danger, jeopardy, Acts 19 : 27, 40. It is translated " were in jeopardy " in Luke 8 : 23, and " stand we in jeopardy," 1 Cor. 15 : 30.¶

2794 AG:432B *Note : Kindunos*, akin to A, peril, danger, is always rendered " peril,"
CB:1255A Rom. 8 : 35 and 2 Cor. 11 : 26 (eight times).¶

B. Adjectives.

1. ENOCHOS (ἔνοχος), lit., held in, contained in (*en*, in, *echō*, to have, 1777
hold), hence, bound under obligation to, liable to, subject to, is used in AG:267D CB:1245B
the sense of being in danger of the penal effect of a misdeed, i.e., in a forensic sense, signifying the connection of a person with (*a*) his crime, " guilty of an eternal sin," Mark 3 : 29, R.V. ; (*b*) the trial or tribunal, as a result of which sentence is passed, Matt. 5 : 21, 22, " the judgment," " the council ; " *enochos* here has the obsolete sense of control (J. Hastings) ; (*c*) the penalty itself, 5 : 22, " the hell of fire," and, with the translation " worthy " (A.V., " guilty "), of the punishment determined to be inflicted on Christ, Matt. 26 : 66 and Mark 14 : 64, " death ; " (*d*) the person or thing against whom or which the offence is committed, 1 Cor. 11 : 27, " guilty," the crime being against " the body and blood of the Lord ; " Jas. 2 : 10, " guilty " of an offence against all the Law, because of a breach of one commandment.

Apart from the forensic sense, this adjective is used of the thing by which one is bound, " subject to " (bondage), in Heb. 2 : 15. See GUILTY, SUBJECT, WORTHY.¶

2. EPISPHALĒS (ἐπισφαλής), lit., prone to fall (*epi*, upon, i.e., near 2000
upon, *sphallō*, to fall), hence, insecure, dangerous, is used in Acts 27 : 9.¶ AG:302A CB:—

DARE, DARING, DURST

A. Verb.

TOLMAŌ (τολμάω) signifies to dare, (*a*) in the sense of not dreading 5111
or shunning through fear, Matt. 22 : 46 ; Mark 12 : 34 ; Mark 15 : 43, AG:821D CB:1272C
" boldly," lit., ' having dared, went in ; ' Luke 20 : 40 ; John 21 : 12 ; Acts 5 : 13 ; 7 : 32 ; Rom. 15 : 18 ; 2 Cor. 10 : 2, R.V., " shew courage," (A.V., " be bold ") ; 10 : 12, R.V., " are (not) bold ; " 11 : 21 ; Phil. 1 : 14, " are bold ; " Jude 9 ; (*b*) in the sense of bearing, enduring, bringing oneself to do a thing, Rom. 5 : 7 ; 1 Cor. 6 : 1.¶ Cp. *apotolmaō*, to be very bold, Rom. 10 : 20.¶ See BOLD.

B. Adjective.

TOLMĒTĒS (τολμητής), akin to A, daring, is used in 2 Pet. 2 : 10, 5113
R.V., " daring " (A.V., " presumptuous "), shameless and irreverent AG:822A CB:1272C
daring.¶

DARK, DARKEN, DARKLY, DARKNESS

A. Adjectives.

1. SKOTEINOS (σκοτεινός), full of darkness, or covered with darkness, 4652
is translated " dark " in Luke 11 : 36 ; " full of darkness," in Matt. 6 : 23 AG:757B CB:1269B
and Luke 11 : 34, where the physical condition is figurative of the moral. The group of *skot*-words is derived from a root *ska*—, meaning to cover. The same root is to be found in *skēnē*, a tent.¶

Note : Contrast *phōteinos*, full of light, e.g., Matt. 6 : 22. 850 AG:124B

2. AUCHMĒROS (αὐχμηρός), from *auchmos*, drought produced by CB:—

excessive heat, hence signifies dry, murky, dark, 2 Pet. 1 : 19 (R.V. marg., " squalid "). No. 1 signifies darkness produced by covering; No. 2, darkness produced by being squalid or murky.¶

B. Nouns.

4653 1. SKOTIA (*σκοτία*) is used (*a*) of physical darkness, " dark," John
AG:757B
CB:1269B 6 : 17, lit., ' darkness had come on,' and 20 : 1, lit., ' darkness still being ; ' (*b*) of secrecy, in general, whether what is done therein is good or evil, Matt. 10 : 27 ; Luke 12 : 3 ; (*c*) of spiritual or moral darkness, emblematic of sin, as a condition of moral or spiritual depravity, Matt. 4 : 16 ; John 1 : 5 ; 8 : 12 ; 12 : 35, 46 ; 1 John 1 : 5 ; 2 : 8, 9, 11.¶

4655 2. SKOTOS (*σκότος*), an older form than No. 1, grammatically
AG:757C
CB:1269B masculine, is found in some mss. in Heb. 12 : 18.¶

3. SKOTOS (*σκότος*), a neuter noun, frequent in the Sept., is used in the N.T. as the equivalent of No. 1 ; (*a*) of physical darkness, Matt. 27 : 45 ; 2 Cor. 4 : 6 ; (*b*) of intellectual darkness, Rom. 2 : 19 (cp. C, No. 1) ; (*c*) of blindness, Acts 13 : 11 ; (*d*) by metonymy, of the place of punishment, e.g., Matt. 8 : 12 ; 2 Pet. 2 : 17 ; Jude 13 ; (*e*) metaphorically, of moral and spiritual darkness, e.g., Matt. 6 : 23 ; Luke 1 : 79 ; 11 : 35 ; John 3 : 19 ; Acts 26 : 18 ; 2 Cor. 6 : 14 ; Eph. 6 : 12 ; Col. 1 : 13 ; 1 Thess. 5 : 4, 5 ; 1 Pet. 2 : 9 ; 1 John 1 : 6 ; (*f*) by metonymy, of those who are in moral or spiritual darkness, Eph. 5 : 8 ; (*g*) of evil works, Rom. 13 : 12 ; Eph. 5 : 11 ; (*h*) of the evil powers that dominate the world, Luke 22 : 53 ; (*i*) of secrecy [as in No. 1, (*b*)]. While *skotos* is used more than twice as many times as *skotia* in the N.T., the Apostle John uses *skotos* only once, 1 John 1 : 6, but *skotia* 15 times out of the 18.

" With the exception of the significance of secrecy [No. 1, (*b*) and No. 3 (*i*)], darkness is always used in a bad sense. Moreover the different forms of darkness are so closely allied, being either cause and effect, or else concurrent effects of the same cause, that they cannot always be distinguished ; 1 John 1 : 5 ; 2 : 8, e.g., are passages in which both spiritual and moral darkness are intended."*

2217
AG:339D 4. ZOPHOS (*ζόφος*) denotes the gloom of the nether world ; hence,
CB:— thick darkness, darkness that may be felt ; it is rendered " darkness " in Heb. 12 : 18 ; 2 Pet. 2 : 4 and Jude 6 ; in 2 Pet. 2 : 17, R.V., " blackness," A.V., " mists ; " in Jude 13, R.V. and A.V., " blackness." See BLACKNESS, B, Nos. 1 and 2, MIST.¶

C. Verbs.

4654 1. SKOTIZŌ (*σκοτίζω*), to deprive of light, to make dark, is used
AG:757C
CB:1269B in the N.T. in the Passive Voice only, (*a*) of the heavenly bodies, Matt. 24 : 29 ; Mark 13 : 24 ; Rev. 8 : 12 ; (*b*) metaphorically, of the mind, Rom. 1 : 21 ; 11 : 10 ; (some mss. have it in Luke 23 : 45).¶

4656 2. SKOTOŌ (*σκοτόω*), to darken, is used (*a*) of the heavenly bodies,
AG:758A
CB:1269B Rev. 9 : 2 ; 16 : 10 ; (*b*) metaphorically, of the mind, Eph. 4 : 18.¶

* From Notes on Thessalonians by Hogg and Vine, pp. 157, 158.

Note: The phrase *en ainigmati*, lit., 'in an enigma,' is rendered 135
" darkly " in 1 Cor. 13 : 12. *Ainigma* is akin to the verb *ainissomai*, to AG:23C CB:1234A
hint obscurely. The allusion is to Numb. 12 : 8 (Sept.), " not in (*dia*,
by means of) dark speeches " (lit., enigmas) ; God's communications to
Moses were not such as in the case of dreams, etc. After the same analogy,
what we see and know now is seen " darkly " compared with the direct
vision in the presence of God hereafter. The riddles of seeming obscurity BELOS
in life will all be made clear. 956

AG:139B CB:1239A

DART

BOLē 1000

BELOS (βέλος), akin to *ballō*, to throw, denotes a missile, an arrow, AG:144D
javelin, dart, etc., Eph. 6 : 16 (see FIERY).¶ Cp. *bolē*, a stone's throw or CB:—
cast, Luke 22 : 41,¶ ; *bolizō*, to sound (to fathom the depth of water), BOLIZō 1001
Acts 27 : 28.¶ AG:144D

Note: The noun *bolis*, a dart, is found in some texts in Heb. 12 : 20 CB:— BOLIS
(see A.V.).¶ 1002

AG:144D CB:—

DASH

1. PROSKOPTŌ (προσκόπτω) denotes to beat upon or against, to 4350
strike against, dash against (*pros*, to or against, *koptō*, to strike, beat) ; AG:716B CB:1267B
hence, of the foot, to stumble, " dash " (A.V. and R.V.), Matt. 4 : 6;
Luke 4 : 11. See BEAT, STUMBLE.

2. RHĒGNUMI (ῥήγνυμι), to tear, rend, break, is used of the action of 4486
a demon upon a human victim, Mark 9 : 18, " dasheth . . . down," R.V. ; AG:735A CB:—
(A.V., marg. ; A.V., text, " teareth ") ; Luke 9 : 42, R.V., " dashed
. . . down " (A.V., " threw . . . down "). See BREAK, No. 6.

3. EDAPHIZŌ (ἐδαφίζω), to beat level with the earth, e.g., as a 1474
threshing floor (cp. *edaphos*, the ground), Luke 19 : 44 ; R.V., " shall AG:217C CB:—
dash (thee) to the ground ; " (A.V., " shall lay (thee) even with the
ground "). See GROUND.¶ DATE See SEASON

DAUGHTER, DAUGHTER-IN-LAW

1. THUGATĒR (θυγάτηρ), a daughter, (etymologically, Eng., daughter 2364
is connected), is used of (*a*) the natural relationship (frequent in the AG:364D CB:1272C
Gospels) ; (*b*) spiritual relationship to God, 2 Cor. 6 : 18, in the sense of the
practical realization of acceptance with, and the approval of, God (cp.
Isa. 43 : 6), the only place in the N.T. where it applies to spiritual
relationship ; (*c*) the inhabitants of a city or region, Matt. 21 : 5 ; John
12 : 15 (" of Zion ") ; cp. Is. 37 : 22 ; Zeph. 3 : 14 (Sept.) ; (*d*) the
women who followed Christ to Calvary, Luke 23 : 28 ; (*e*) women of
Aaron's posterity, Luke 1 : 5 ; (*f*) a female descendant of Abraham, 2365
Luke 13 : 16. AG:365A

2. THUGATRION (θυγάτριον), a diminutive of No. 1, denotes a little CB:—
daughter, Mark 5 : 23 ; 7 : 25.¶ 3933 AG:627A

3. PARTHENOS (παρθένος), a maiden, virgin, e.g., Matt. 1 : 23, CB:1262C

signifies a virgin-daughter in 1 Cor. 7 : 36, 37, 38 (R.V.) ; in Rev. 14 : 4, it is used of chaste persons. See VIRGIN.

3565 4. NUMPHĒ (νύμφη), Eng., nymph, denotes a bride, John 3 : 29;
AG:545B CB:1260A also a daughter-in-law, Matt. 10 : 35 ; Luke 12 : 53. See BRIDE.

5043 *Note:* In 1 Pet. 3 : 6, *teknon*, a child, is translated " daughters "
AG:808B CB:1271B (A.V.), " children " (R.V.).

AUGAZō 826

DAWN

A. Verbs.

AG:120C CB:1238B 1. AUGAZŌ (αὐγάζω), to shine, is used metaphorically of the light of
AUGē dawn, in 2 Cor. 4 : 4 (some texts have *kataugazō*). Cp. *augē*, brightness or
827 AG:120D break of day, Acts 20 : 11. The word formerly meant to see clearly, and
CB:1238B it is possible that this meaning was continued in general usage.¶

DIAUGAZō 2. DIAUGAZŌ (διαυγάζω) signifies to shine through (*dia*, through,
1306 AG:190A *augē*, brightness) ; it describes the breaking of daylight upon the darkness
CB:1241B of night, metaphorically in 2 Pet. 1 : 19, of the shining of spiritual light into
DIAUGēS — the heart. A probable reference is to the Day to be ushered in at the
AG:190B Second Coming of Christ : ' until the Day gleam through the present
CB:— DIAPHANēS darkness, and the Light-bringer dawn in your hearts.'¶

1307 *Note:* Cp. *diaugēs*, translucent, transparent, Rev. 21 : 21 (some texts
AG:190B have *diaphanēs*, " transparent ").¶

CB:— EPIPHōSKō 3. EPIPHŌSKŌ (ἐπιφώσκω), to grow light (*epi*, upon, *phōs*, light),
2020 AG:304D in the sense of shining upon, is used in Matt. 28 : 1; in Luke 23 : 54,
CB:— " drew on " (of the Sabbath-day) ; R.V., marg., " began to dawn."
ORTHROS See DRAW.¶

3722 AG:580C

B. Noun.

CB:— ORTHROS (ὄρθρος), daybreak, denotes " at early dawn," Luke
ORTHRINOS 3720 24 : 1 (R.V.), " early in the morning " (A.V.), and John 8 : 2 (A.V. and
AG:580C R.V.) ; in Acts 5 : 21, R.V., " about daybreak," for A.V., " early in the
CB:— morning."¶

ORTHRIOS 3721 *Note:* Cp. *orthrios*, " early," in some texts in Luke 24 : 22 ;¶
AG:580C CB:— *orthrinos*, a later form of *orthros*, in some mss. in Rev. 22 : 16 ;¶ *orthrizō*,
ORTHRIZō to do anything early in the morning, in Luke 21 : 38.¶

3719 AG:580C CB:—

DAY

A. Nouns.

2250 AG:345D 1. HĒMERA (ἡμέρα), a day, is used of (*a*) the period of natural light,
CB:1249C Gen. 1 : 5 ; Prov. 4 : 18 ; Mark 4 : 35 ; (*b*) the same, but figuratively, for a period of opportunity for service, John 9 : 4 ; Rom. 13 : 13 ; (*c*) one period of alternate light and darkness, Gen. 1 : 5 ; Mark 1 : 13 ; (*d*) a period of undefined length marked by certain characteristics, such as " the day of small things," Zech. 4 : 10 ; of perplexity and distress, Isa. 17 : 11 ; Obad. 12–14 ; of prosperity and of adversity, Ecc. 7 : 14 ; of trial or testing, Psa. 95 : 8 ; of salvation, Isa. 49 : 8 ; 2 Cor. 6 : 2 ; cp. Luke 19 : 42 ; of evil, Eph. 6 : 13 ; of wrath and revelation of the judg-

ments of God, Rom. 2 : 5 ; (*e*) an appointed time, Ecc. 8 : 6 ; Eph. 4 : 30 ; (*f*) a notable defeat in battle, etc. Isa. 9 : 4 ; Psa. 137 : 7 ; Ezek. 30 : 9 ; Hos. 1 : 11 ; (*g*) by metonymy = 'when,' 'at the time when ;' (1), of the past, Gen. 2 : 4 ; Numb. 3 : 13 ; Deut. 4 : 10, (2), of the future, Gen. 2 : 17 ; Ruth 4 : 5 ; Matt. 24 : 50 ; Luke 1 : 20 ; (*h*) a judgment or doom, Job. 18 : 20.* (i) of a time of life, Luke 1 : 17, 18 (" years ").

As the day throws light upon things that have been in darkness, the word is often associated with the passing of judgment upon circumstances. In 1 Cor. 4 : 3, "man's day," A.V., "man's judgement," R.V., denotes mere human judgment upon matters ("man's" translates the adjective *anthrōpinos*, human), a judgment exercised in the present period of human rebellion against " God ; " probably therefore " the Lord's Day," Rev. 1 : 10, or 'the Day of the Lord' (where an adjective, *kuriakos*, is similarly used), is the Day of His manifested judgment on the world.

The phrases " the day of Christ, " Phil. 1 : 10 ; 2 : 16 ; " the day of Jesus Christ," 1 : 6 ; " the day of the Lord Jesus," 1 Cor. 5 : 5 ; 2 Cor. 1 : 14 ; " the day of our Lord Jesus Christ," 1 Cor. 1 : 8, denote the time of the Parousia of Christ with His saints, subsequent to the Rapture, 1 Thess. 4 : 16, 17. In 2 Pet. 1 : 19 this is spoken of simply as " the day," (see DAY-STAR).

From these the phrase " the day of the Lord " is to be distinguished ; in the O.T. it had reference to a time of the victorious interposition by God for the overthrow of the foes of Israel, e.g., Is. 2 : 12 ; Amos 5 : 18 ; if Israel transgressed in the pride of their hearts, the Day of the Lord would be a time of darkness and judgment. For their foes, however, there would come 'a great and terrible day of the Lord,' Joel 2 : 31 ; Mal. 4 : 5. That period, still future, will see the complete overthrow of Gentile power and the establishment of Messiah's Kingdom, Isa. 13 : 9–11 ; 34 : 8 ; Dan. 2 : 34, 44 ; Obad. 15 ; cp. Isa. 61 : 2 ; John 8 : 56.

In the N.T. " the day of the Lord " is mentioned in 1 Thess. 5 : 2 and 2 Thess. 2 : 2, R.V., where the Apostle's warning is that the church at Thessalonica should not be deceived by thinking that " the Day of the Lord is now present." This period will not begin till the circumstances mentioned in verses 3 and 4 take place.

For the eventual development of the Divine purposes in relation to the human race see 2 Pet. 3 : 12, " the Day of God."

2. AUGĒ (αὐγή), brightness, bright, shining, as of the sun ; hence, the beginning of daylight, is translated " break of day " in Acts 20 : 11.¶ 827 AG:120D CB:1238B

B. Adverb.

ENNUCHA (ἔννυχα), the neuter plural of *ennuchos*, used adverbially, lit., in night (*en*, in, *nux*, night, with *lian*, " very "), signifies very early, yet in the night, " a great while before day," Mark 1 : 35.¶ 1773 (-ON) AG:267B (-OS) CB:—

Notes : (1) For phrases, see DAILY. (2) In Mark 6 : 35, the clause " the day was far spent " is, lit., 'a much hour (i.e., a late hour) having

* From Notes on Thessalonians by Hogg and Vine, pp. 150, 151.

become,' or, perhaps, 'many an hour having become,' i.e. many hours having passed. In the end of the ver., R.V., "day," for A.V., "time." (3) In Mark 2 : 26, A.V., "in the days of," there is no word for "days" in the original; R.V. (from best mss.), "when;" in Acts 11 : 28, "in the days
4405 (-IA) of". (4) In John 21 : 4, the adjective *prōios*, at early morn, is translated
AG:724D (-IA) "day" (R.V., for A.V., "the morning"); see Matt. 27 : 1.¶ (5) In
CB:— 2 Thess. 2 : 3, "that day shall not come" (A.V.) translates nothing in the original; it is inserted to supply the sense (see the R.V.); cp. Luke 7 : 11 (R.V., "soon afterwards"); 1 Cor. 4 : 13 (R.V., "even until now").

(6) For "day following" see MORROW.

For DAYBREAK (R.V., in Acts 5 : 21), see DAWN, B

DAYSPRING

395 ANATOLĒ (ἀνατολή), lit., a rising up (cp. *anatellō*, to cause to rise), is
AG:62B used of the rising of the sun and stars; it chiefly means the east, as in
CB:— Matt. 2 : 1, etc.; rendered "dayspring" in Luke 1 : 78. Its other meaning, "a shoot," is found in the Sept. in Jer. 23 : 5; Zech. 6 : 12. See also the margin of Luke 1 : 78, "branch." See EAST.

DAY-STAR

5459 PHŌSPHOROS (φωσφόρος), Eng., phosphorus, lit., light-bearing (*phōs*,
AG:872D light, *phĕro*, to bear), is used of the morning star, as the light-
CB:1264B bringer, 2 Pet. 1 : 19, where it indicates the arising of the light of Christ as the Personal fulfilment, in the hearts of believers, of the prophetic Scriptures concerning His Coming to receive them to Himself.¶

DAZZLING

797 1. ASTRAPTŌ (ἀστράπτω), to flash forth, lighten, is said of lightning,
AG:118B Luke 17 : 24, and of the apparel of the two men by the Lord's sepulchre,
CB:— 24 : 4, A.V., "shining." See LIGHTEN, SHINE.¶

1823 2. EXASTRAPTŌ (ἐξαστράπτω), a strengthened form of No. 1 (*ek*,
AG:273D out of), signifies to flash like lightning, gleam, be radiant, in Luke
CB:— 9 : 29 of the Lord's raiment at His transfiguration, R.V., "dazzling;" A.V., "glistering."¶ In the Sept., Ezek. 1 : 4, 7; Nahum 3 : 3.¶

DEACON

1249 DIAKONOS (διάκονος), whence Eng. deacon, primarily denotes a
AG:184C servant, whether as doing servile work, or as an attendant rendering free
CB:1241A service, without particular reference to its character. The word is probably connected with the verb *diōkō*, to hasten after, pursue (perhaps originally said of a runner). "It occurs in the N.T. of domestic servants, John 2 : 5, 9; the civil ruler, Rom. 13 : 4; Christ, Rom. 15 : 8; Gal. 2 : 17; the followers of Christ in relation to their Lord, John 12 : 26; Eph. 6 : 21; Col. 1 : 7; 4 : 7; the followers of Christ in relation to one another,

Matt. 20 : 26 ; 23 : 11 ; Mark 9 : 35 ; 10 : 43 ; the servants of Christ in DOULOS
the work of preaching and teaching, 1 Cor. 3 : 5 ; 2 Cor. 3 : 6 ; 6 : 4 ; 1401 AG:205C
11 : 23 ; Eph. 3 : 7 ; Col. 1 : 23, 25 ; 1 Thess. 3 : 2 ; 1 Tim. 4 : 6 ; those CB:1242B
who serve in the churches, Rom. 16 : 1 (used of a woman here only in LEITOURGOS 3011
N.T.) ; Phil. 1 : 1 ; 1 Tim. 3 : 8, 12 ; false apostles, servants of Satan, AG:471B
2 Cor. 11 : 15. Once *diakonos* is used where, apparently, angels are CB:1256C MISTHIOS
intended, Matt. 22 : 13 ; in ver. 3, where men are intended, *doulos* is 3407
used."* AG:523A

Diakonos is, generally speaking, to be distinguished from *doulos*, a CB:1259A MISTHŌTOS
bondservant, slave ; *diakonos* views a servant in relationship to his work ; 3411
doulos views him in relationship to his master. See, e.g., Matt. 22 : 2–14 ; AG:523D CB:1259A
those who bring in the guests (vv. 3, 4, 6, 8, 10) are *douloi ;* those who OIKETĒS
carry out the king's sentence (v. 13) are *diakonoi.*¶ 3610 AG:557A

Note : As to synonymous terms, *leitourgos* denotes one who performs CB:1260B
public duties ; *misthios* and *misthōtos*, a hired servant ; *oiketēs*, a household HUPĒRETĒS 5257
servant ; *hupēretēs*, a subordinate official waiting on his superior (originally AG:842C
an under-rower in a war-galley) ; *therapōn*, one whose service is that of CB:1252A THERAPŌN
freedom and dignity. See MINISTER, SERVANT. 2324

The so-called Seven Deacons in Acts 6 are not there mentioned by that AG:359B CB:1272B
name, though the kind of service in which they were engaged was of the
character of that committed to such.

DEAD

A. Noun and Adjective.

NEKROS (νεκρός) is used of (*a*) the death of the body, cp. Jas. 2 : 26, 3498 AG:534D
its most frequent sense : (*b*) the actual spiritual condition of unsaved CB:1259C
men, Matt. 8 : 22 ; John 5 : 25 ; Eph. 2 : 1, 5 ; 5 : 14 ; Phil. 3 : 11 ; Col. 2 : 13 ; cp. Luke 15 : 24 : (*c*) the ideal spiritual condition of believers in regard to sin, Rom. 6 : 11 : (*d*) a church in declension, inasmuch as in that state it is inactive and barren, Rev. 3 : 1 : (*e*) sin, which apart from law cannot produce a sense of guilt, Rom. 7 : 8 : (*f*) the body of the believer in contrast to his spirit, Rom. 8 : 10 : (*g*) the works of the Law, inasmuch as, however good in themselves, Rom. 7 : 13, they cannot produce life, Heb. 6 : 1 ; 9 : 14 : (*h*) the faith that does not produce works, Jas. 2 : 17, 26 ; cp. ver. 20.†

B. Verbs.

1. NEKROŌ (νεκρόω), to put to death, is used in the Active Voice 3499 AG:535C
in the sense of destroying the strength of, depriving of power, with CB:1259C
reference to the evil desires which work in the body, Col. 3 : 5. In the
Passive Voice it is used of Abraham's body as being "as good as dead," 2289
Rom. 4 : 19 with Heb. 11 : 12.¶ AG:351C

2. THANATOŌ (θανατόω), to put to death : see DEATH, C. No. 1. CB:1271C

---

* From Notes on Thessalonians by Hogg and Vine, p. 91.

† From Notes on Thessalonians by Hogg and Vine, p. 143.

DEADLY

2287 AG:350D 1. THANATĒPHOROS (θανατηφόρος), lit., death-bearing, deadly
CB:— (*thanatos*, death, *pherō*, to bear), is used in Jas. 3 : 8.¶ In the Sept.,
Numb. 18 : 22 ; Job 33 : 23.¶

2286 AG:350D 2. THANASIMOS (θανάσιμος), from *thanatos* (see No. 1), belonging to
CB:— death, or partaking of the nature of death, is used in Mark 16 : 18.¶

HALF DEAD

2253 AG:348A HĒMITHANĒS (ἡμιθανής), from *hēmi*, half, and *thnēskō*, to die, is
CB:— used in Luke 10 : 30.¶

DEADNESS

3500 AG:535C NEKRŌSIS (νέκρωσις), a putting to death (cp. DEAD, A and B), is
CB:1259C rendered "dying" in 2 Cor. 4 : 10 ; "deadness" in Rom. 4 : 19, i.e.,
the state of being virtually dead.¶

DEAF

2974 AG:462A KŌPHOS (κωφός), akin to *koptō*, to beat, and *kopiaō*, to be tired
CB:1255C (from a root *kop*—, to cut), signifies blunted, dull, as of a weapon ; hence,
blunted in tongue, dumb, Matt. 9 : 32 etc. ; in hearing, deaf, Matt. 11 : 5 ;
Mark 7 : 32, 37 ; 9 : 25 ; Luke 7 : 22. See DUMB.

For a GREAT DEAL see GREAT

DEAL

3307 AG:504C MERIZŌ (μερίζω) signifies to divide into parts (*meros*, a portion,
CB:1258B part) ; hence, to distribute, divide out, deal out to, translated "hath
dealt" in Rom. 12 : 3. See DIFFERENCE, DISTRIBUTE, DIVIDE.

DEAL WITH, HAVE DEALINGS WITH

4160 AG:680D 1. POIEŌ (ποιέω), to do, used to describe almost any act, whether
CB:1265C complete or repeated, like the Eng. "do," is translated to deal with, in
Luke 2 : 48. In Luke 1 : 25, A.V., "hath dealt with (me)," the R.V.,
adhering to the ordinary meaning, translates by "hath done unto (me)".

4374 AG:719C 2. PROSPHERŌ (προσφέρω), to bring or bear to (*pros*, to, *pherō*, to
CB:1267B bear), signifies, in the Middle Voice, to bear oneself towards any one, to
deal with anyone in a certain manner, Heb. 12 : 7, "God dealeth with you."
See BRING, OFFER, PRESENT.

4798 AG:775B 3. SUNCHRAOMAI (συγχράομαι), lit., to use with (*sun*, with, *chraomai*,
CB:— to use), to have in joint use, and hence to have dealings with, is said, in
John 4 : 9, of Jews and Samaritans.¶

1793 *Notes* : (1) In Acts 25 : 24, *entunchanō*, to fall in with, meet and talk
AG:270A CB:1245B with, and hence to make suit to a person by way of pleading with him,
is translated "have dealt with" in the A.V. ; correctly in the R.V., "have

made suit to," of the Jews in appealing to Festus against Paul. See INTERCESSION.

(2) *Katasophizomai*, to circumvent by fraud, conquer by subtle devices 2686
(*kata*, down, intensive, and *sophizō*, to devise cleverly or cunningly; AG:418D CB:—
cp. Eng., sophist, sophistry), is translated "dealt subtilly," in Acts 7 : 19, of Pharaoh's dealings with the Israelites.¶ This is the word in the Sept. of Ex. 1 : 10. See SUBTILLY.¶

(3) In 1 Thess. 2 : 11 the italicised phrase "we dealt with" (R.V.), has no corresponding word in the original, but is inserted in order to bring out the participial forms of the verbs "exhorting," "encouraging," "testifying," as showing the constant practice of the apostles at Thessalonica. The incompleteness of the sentence in the original illustrates the informal homeliness of the Epistle.

(4) In 2 Cor. 13 : 10, the verb *chraomai*, to use, is rendered, in the 5530
R.V., "deal (sharply)," A.V., "use (sharpness)." AG:884B CB:1240A

DEAR

1. TIMIOS (τίμιος), from *timē*, honour, price, signifies (*a*), primarily, 5093
accounted as of great price, precious, costly, 1 Cor. 3 : 12; Rev. 17 : 4; AG:818A CB:1272C
18 : 12, 16; 21 : 19, and in the superlative degree, 18 : 12; 21 : 11; the comparative degree is found in 1 Pet. 1 : 7 (*polutimoteros*, in the most POLUTIMOS
authentic mss., "much more precious"); (*b*) in the metaphorical sense, 4186
held in honour, esteemed, very dear, Acts 5 : 34, "had in honour," R.V. AG:690A CB:—
(A.V., "had in reputation"); so in Heb. 13 : 4, R.V., "let marriage be had in honour;" A.V., "is honourable;" Acts 20 : 24, "dear," negatively of Paul's estimate of his life; Jas. 5 : 7, "precious" (of fruit); 1 Pet. 1 : 19, "precious" (of the blood of Christ); 2 Pet. 1 : 4 (of God's promises). See COSTLY, HONOURABLE, REPUTATION, PRECIOUS.¶ Cp. *timiōtes*, preciousness, Rev. 18 : 19.¶

2. ENTIMOS (ἔντιμος), held in honour (*timē*, see above), precious, 1784
dear, is found in Luke 7 : 2, of the centurion's servant; 14 : 8, "more AG:268D CB:1245B
honourable;" Phil. 2 : 29, "honour" (A.V., "reputation"), of devoted servants of Christ; in 1 Pet. 2 : 4, 6, "precious," of stones, metaphorically. See HONOURABLE, REPUTATION, PRECIOUS.¶

3. AGAPĒTOS (ἀγαπητός), from *agapē*, love, signifies beloved; it is 27
rendered "very dear" in 1 Thess. 2 : 8 (A.V., "dear"), of the affection of AG:6B CB:1233B
Paul and his fellow-workers for the saints at Thessalonica; in Eph. 5 : 1 and Col. 1 : 7, A.V., "dear;" R.V., "beloved." See BELOVED.

Note: In Col. 1 : 13, *agapē* is translated "dear" in the A.V.; the 26
R.V., adhering to the noun, has "the Son of His love." AG:5B CB:1233B

For DEARLY see BELOVED

For DEARTH see FAMINE

DEATH, DEATH-STROKE

(*See also DIE*)

A. Nouns.

2288 AG:350D CB:1271C 1. THANATOS (θάνατος), death, is used in Scripture of:

(*a*) the separation of the soul (the spiritual part of man) from the body (the material part), the latter ceasing to function and turning to dust, e.g., John 11 : 13; Heb. 2 : 15; 5 : 7; 7 : 23. In Heb. 9 : 15, the A.V., " by means of death " is inadequate; the R.V., " a death having taken place " is in keeping with the subject. In Rev. 13 : 3, 12, the R.V., " death-stroke " (A.V., " deadly wound ") is, lit., the stroke of death:

(*b*) the separation of man from God; Adam died on the day he disobeyed God, Gen. 2 : 17, and hence all mankind are born in the same spiritual condition, Rom. 5 : 12, 14, 17, 21, from which, however, those who believe in Christ are delivered, John 5 : 24; 1 John 3 : 14. Death is the opposite of life; it never denotes non-existence. As spiritual life is " conscious existence in communion with God," so spiritual death is " conscious existence in separation from God."

" Death, in whichever of the above-mentioned senses it is used, is always, in Scripture, viewed as the penal consequence of sin, and since sinners alone are subject to death, Rom. 5 : 12, it was as the Bearer of sin that the Lord Jesus submitted thereto on the Cross, 1 Pet. 2 : 24. And while the physical death of the Lord Jesus was of the essence of His sacrifice, it was not the whole. The darkness symbolised, and His cry expressed, the fact that He was left alone in the Universe, He was ' forsaken; ' cp. Matt. 27 : 45, 46."*

336 AG:54D CB:— 2. ANAIRESIS (ἀναίρεσις), another word for death, lit. signifies a taking up or off (*ana*, up, *airō*, to take), as of the taking of a life, or putting to death; it is found in Acts 8 : 1, of the murder of Stephen. Some mss. have it in 22 : 20. See *anaireō*, under KILL.¶ In the Sept., Numb. 11 : 15; Judg. 15 : 17, " the lifting of the jawbone."¶

5054 AG:810C CB:1271B 3. TELEUTĒ (τελευτή), an end, limit (cp. *telos*, see END), hence, the end of life, death, is used of the death of Herod, Matt. 2 : 15.¶

B. Adjective.

1935 AG:292D CB:— EPITHANATIOS (ἐπιθανάτιος), doomed to death (*epi*, upon, *thanatos*, A, No. 1), is said of the apostles, in 1 Cor. 4 : 9.¶

C. Verbs.

2289 AG:351C CB:1271C 1. THANATOŌ (θανατόω), to put to death (akin to A, No. 1), in Matt. 10 : 21; Mark 13 : 12; Luke 21 : 16, is translated " shall . . . cause (them) to be put to death," lit., ' shall put (them) to death ' (R.V. marg.). It is used of the Death of Christ in Matt. 26 : 59; 27 : 1; Mark 14 : 55 and 1 Pet. 3 : 18. In Rom. 7 : 4 (Passive Voice) it is translated " ye . . . were made dead," R.V. (for A.V., " are become "), with reference to the change from bondage to the Law to union with Christ;

* From Notes on Thessalonians by Hogg and Vine, p. 134.

in 8 : 13, " mortify " (marg., " make to die "), of the act of the believer in regard to the deeds of the body ; in 8 : 36, " are killed ; " so in 2 Cor. 6 : 9. See KILL, MORTIFY.¶

2. ANAIREŌ (ἀναιρέω), lit., to take or lift up or away (see A, No. 2), **337**
hence, to put to death, is usually translated to kill or slay ; in two places **AG:54D CB:—**
" put to death," Luke 23 : 32 ; Acts 26 : 10. It is used 17 times, with this meaning, in Acts. See KILL, SLAY, TAKE.

3. APAGŌ (ἀπάγω), lit., to lead away (*apo*, away, *agō*, to lead), is used **520**
especially in a judicial sense, to put to death, e.g., Acts 12 : 19. See **AG:79C CB:—**
BRING, CARRY, LEAD, TAKE.

4. APOKTEINŌ (ἀποκτείνω), to kill, is so translated in the R.V., **615**
for the A.V., " put to death," in Mark 14 : 1 ; Luke 18 : 33 ; in John **AG:93D CB:1237A**
11 : 53 ; 12 : 10 and 18 : 31, R.V., " put to death." See KILL, SLAY.

ESCHATōS

Note : The phrase *eschatōs echō*, lit., to have extremely, i.e., to be in **2079**
extremity, *in extremis*, at the last (gasp), to be at the point of death, is **AG:314B**
used in Mark 5 : 23.¶ **CB:1246C**

DEBATE See DISPUTE

For the A.V., DEBATE (Rom. 1 : 29 and 2 Cor. 12 : 20), see STRIFE.

DEBAUCHERY See LASCIVIOUS

DEBT

1. OPHEILĒ (ὀφειλή), that which is owed (see Note, below), is **3782**
translated " debt " in Matt. 18 : 32 ; in the plural, " dues," Rom. 13 : 7 ; **AG:598C CB:1261A**
" (her) due," 1 Cor. 7 : 3, of conjugal duty : some texts here have *opheilomenēn* (*eunoian*) " due (benevolence)," A.V. ; the context confirms the R.V. See DUE.¶

2. OPHEILĒMA (ὀφείλημα), a longer form of No. 1, expressing a debt **3783 AG:598C**
more concretely, is used (*a*) literally, of that which is legally due, **CB:1261A**
Rom. 4 : 4 ; (*b*) metaphorically, of sin as a debt, because it demands expiation, and thus payment by way of punishment, Matt. 6 : 12.¶

3. DANEION (δάνειον), a loan (akin to *danos*, a gift), is translated **1156**
" debt " in Matt. 18 : 27 (R.V., marg., " loan "), of the ten thousand **AG:170D CB:—**
talents debtor.¶ Cp. *daneizō*, to lend, and *daneistēs*, a money-lender, a creditor.

Note : In Matt. 18 : 30, *opheilō*, to owe, is translated " debt " in the **3784**
A.V. (R.V., " that which was due."). See DUE. **AG:598D CB:1261A**

DEBTOR

1. OPHEILETĒS (ὀφειλέτης), one who owes anything to another, **3781**
primarily in regard to money ; in Matt. 18 : 24, " who owed " (lit., **AG:598B CB:1261A**
'one was brought, a debtor to him of ten thousand talents '). The slave could own property, and so become a debtor to his master, who might seize him for payment.

It is used metaphorically,

(*a*) of a person who is under an obligation, Rom. 1 : 14, of Paul, in the matter of preaching the Gospel ; in Rom. 8 : 12, of believers, to mortify the deeds of the body; in Rom. 15 : 27, of Gentile believers, to assist afflicted Jewish believers; in Gal. 5 : 3, of those who would be justified by circumcision, to do the whole Law: (*b*) of those who have not yet made amends to those whom they have injured, Matt. 6 : 12, "our debtors;" of some whose disaster was liable to be regarded as a due punishment, Luke 13 : 4 (R.V., "offenders;" A.V., "sinners;" marg., "debtors").¶

5533 AG:885B CB:— 2. CHREŌPHEILETĒS (χρεωφειλέτης), lit., a debt-ower (*chreōs*, a loan, a debt, and No. 1), is found in Luke 7 : 41, of the two debtors mentioned in the Lord's parable addressed to Simon the Pharisee, and in 16 : 5, of the debtors in the parable of the unrighteous steward. This parable indicates a system of credit in the matter of agriculture.¶ In the Sept., Job 31 : 37, "having taken nothing from the debtor;" Prov. 29 : 13, "when the creditor and the debtor meet together."¶ The word is more expressive than No. 1.

3784 AG:598D CB:1261A *Note:* In Matt. 23 : 16 *opheilō*, to owe (see DEBT), is translated "he is a debtor." The R.V. marg., keeping the verbal form, has "bound by his oath" (A.V., marg., "bound"). In the 18th verse the A.V., "he is guilty," means that he is under obligation to make amends for his misdeeds.

DECAY

3822 AG:606A CB:1261C 1. PALAIOŌ (παλαιόω), to make old (*palaios*), is translated in Heb. 8 : 13, firstly, "hath made . . . old," secondly (Passive Voice), R.V. "is becoming old" (A.V., "decayeth"); "wax old," Luke 12 : 33 and Heb. 1 : 11. See OLD.¶

1311 AG:190C CB:1241B 2. DIAPHTHEIRŌ (διαφθείρω), to destroy utterly, as used in 2 Cor. 4 : 16 (here in the Passive Voice, lit., 'is being destroyed'), is rendered "is decaying" (R.V., for A.V., "perish"). See CORRUPT, DESTROY.

DECEASE

A. Noun.

1841 AG:276D CB:1247C EXODOS (ἔξοδος), Eng., exodus, lit. signifies a way out (*ex*, out, *hodos*, a way); hence, a departure, especially from life, a decease; in Luke 9 : 31, of the Lord's Death, "which He was about to accomplish;" in 2 Pet. 1 : 15, of Peter's death (marg., "departure" in each case); "departure" in Heb. 11 : 22, R.V. See DEPARTURE.¶

B. Verb.

5053 AG:810C CB:1271B TELEUTAŌ (τελευτάω), lit., to end, is used intransitively and translated "deceased" in Matt. 22 : 25. See DEATH, A, No. 3, DIE.

DECEIT, DECEITFUL, DECEITFULLY, DECEITFULNESS, DECEIVE, DECEIVABLENESS

539 AG:82A

A. Nouns.

CB:1236B 1. APATĒ (ἀπάτη), deceit or deceitfulness (akin to *apataō*, to cheat, deceive, beguile), that which gives a false impression, whether by appearance, statement or influence, is said of riches, Matt. 13 : 22 ; Mark 4 : 19 ; of sin, Heb. 3 : 13. The phrase in Eph. 4 : 22, " deceitful lusts," A.V., " lusts of deceit," R.V., signifies lusts excited by deceit, of which deceit is the source of strength, not lusts deceitful in themselves. In 2 Thess. 2 : 10, " all deceit of unrighteousness," R.V., signifies all manner of unscrupulous words and deeds designed to deceive (see Rev. 13 : 13–15). In Col. 2 : 8, " vain deceit " suggests that deceit is void of anything profitable.¶

Note : In 2 Pet. 2 : 13, the most authentic texts have " revelling in their love-feasts," R.V. (*agapais*), for A.V., " deceivings " (*apatais*). 26 AG:5B CB:1233B

2. DOLOS (δόλος), primarily a bait, snare ; hence, craft, deceit, guile, is translated " deceit " in Mark 7 : 22 ; Rom. 1 : 29. See CRAFT, GUILE, SUBTILTY. 1388 AG:203B CB:—

Notes : (1) *Planē*, rendered " deceit " in 1 Thess. 2 : 3, A.V., signifies wandering (cp. Eng., " planet "), hence, " error " (R.V.), i.e., a wandering from the right path ; in Eph. 4 : 14, " wiles of error," A.V., " to deceive." See DELUDE, ERROR. 4106 AG:665D CB:1265A

(2) For *dolioō*, to use deceit, see C, No. 4.

B. Adjective.

DOLIOS (δόλιος), deceitful, is used in 2 Cor. 11 : 13, of false apostles as " deceitful workers ; " cp. A, No. 2 and Note (2).¶ 1386 AG:203B CB:—

C. Verbs.

1. APATAŌ (ἀπατάω), to beguile, deceive (see A, No. 1), is used (*a*) of those who deceive " with empty words," belittling the true character of the sins mentioned, Eph. 5 : 6 ; (*b*) of the fact that Adam was " not beguiled," 1 Tim. 2 : 14, R.V. (cp. what is said of Eve ; see No. 2 below) ; (*c*) of the self-deceit of him who thinks himself religious, but bridles not his tongue, Jas. 1 : 26.¶ 538 AG:81D CB:1236B

2. EXAPATAŌ (ἐξαπατάω), *ek* (*ex*), intensive, and No. 1, signifies to beguile thoroughly, to deceive wholly, 1 Tim. 2 : 14, R.V. See BEGUILE. 1818 AG:273A CB:1247C

3. PHRENAPATAŌ (φρεναπατάω), lit., to deceive in one's mind (*phrēn*, the mind, and No. 1), " to deceive by fancies " (Lightfoot), is used in Gal. 6 : 3, with reference to self-conceit, which is self-deceit, a sin against common sense. Cp. Jas. 1 : 26 (above).¶ 5422 AG:865D CB:—

Note : Cp. *phrenapatēs*, No. 2, under DECEIVER.

4. DOLIOŌ (δολιόω), to lure, as by a bait (see A, No. 2), is translated " have used deceit " in Rom. 3 : 13.¶ 1387 AG:203B CB:—

5. DOLOŌ (δολόω), a short form of No. 4, primarily signifies to ensnare ; hence, to corrupt, especially by mingling the truths of the Word of God with false doctrines or notions, and so handling it deceitfully, 2 Cor. 4 : 2.¶ Cp. *kapēleuō*, to corrupt by way of hucksterizing, 2 : 17.¶ For the difference between the words see CORRUPT, A, No. 1. 1389 AG:203B CB:1242A

6. PLANAŌ (πλανάω), akin to *planē*, A, Note (1) (Eng., planet), in the Passive form sometimes means to go astray, wander, Matt. 18 : 12 ; 4105 AG:665B CB:1265A

1 Pet. 2 : 25 ; Heb. 11 : 38 ; frequently Active, to deceive, by leading into error, to seduce, e.g., Matt. 24 : 4, 5, 11, 24 ; John 7 : 12, " leadeth astray," R.V. (cp. 1 John 3 : 7). In Rev. 12 : 9 the present participle is used with the definite article, as a title of the Devil, " the Deceiver," lit., ' the deceiving one.' Often it has the sense of deceiving oneself, e.g., 1 Cor. 6 : 9 ; 15 : 33 ; Gal. 6 : 7 ; Jas. 1 : 16, " be not deceived," R.V., " do not err," A.V. See ERR, LEAD (astray), SEDUCE, WANDER, WAY (be out of the).

3884 AG:620B CB:1262A 7. PARALOGIZOMAI (παραλογίζομαι) ; see BEGUILE, No. 3.

DECEIVER

4108 AG:666A CB:1265A 1. PLANOS (πλάνος) is, properly, an adjective, signifying wandering, or leading astray, seducing, 1 Tim. 4 : 1, " seducing (spirits) ; " used as a noun, it denotes an impostor of the vagabond type, and so any kind of deceiver or corrupter, Matt. 27 : 63 ; 2 Cor. 6 : 8 ; 2 John 7 (twice), in the last of which the accompanying definite article necessitates the translation " the deceiver," R.V. See SEDUCE.¶

5423 AG:865D CB:— 2. PHRENAPATĒS (φρεναπάτης), akin to C, No. 3, under DECEIVE, lit., a mind-deceiver, is used in Tit. 1 : 10.¶

Note : For " the deceiver," in Rev. 12 : 9, see DECEIVE, C, No. 6.

DECENTLY

2156 AG:327A CB:— EUSCHĒMONŌS (εὐσχημόνως) denotes gracefully, becomingly, in a seemly manner (*eu*, well, *schēma*, a form, figure) ; " honestly," in Rom. 13 : 13 (marg., " decently "), in contrast to the shamefulness of Gentile social life ; in 1 Thess. 4 : 12, the contrast is to idleness and its concomitant evils and the resulting bad testimony to unbelievers ; in 1 Cor. 14 : 40, " decently," where the contrast is to disorder in oral testimony in the churches. See HONESTLY.¶

Note : Cp. *euschēmosunē*, comeliness, 1 Cor. 12 : 23.¶, and *euschēmōn*, comely, honourable. See COMELY.

DECIDE, DECISION

A. Verb.

1252 AG:185A CB:1241A DIAKRINŌ (διακρίνω) primarily signifies to make a distinction, hence, to decide, especially judicially, to decide a dispute, to give judgment, 1 Cor. 6 : 5, A.V., " judge ; " R.V., " decide," where church members are warned against procuring decisions by litigation in the world's law courts. See CONTEND.

B. Nouns.

1233 AG:182C CB:— 1. DIAGNŌSIS (διάγνωσις), transliterated in English, primarily
denotes a discrimination (*dia*, apart, *ginōskō*, to know), hence, a judicial
decision, which is its meaning in Acts 25 : 21, R.V., " for the decision of
1231 AG:182B CB:— the Emperor " (A.V., " hearing ").¶

Note : Cp. *diaginōskō*, to distinguish, Acts 23 : 15, to judge (A.V.,

" enquire "), or " determine," 24 : 22, R.V. (A.V., " know the uttermost of ").¶

2. DIAKRISIS (διάκρισις), a distinguishing, and so a decision (see A), 1253
signifies " discerning " in 1 Cor. 12 : 10 ; Heb. 5 : 14, lit., ' unto a dis- AG:185B CB:1241A
cerning of good and evil ' (translated " to discern ") ; in Rom. 14 : 1, " not to (doubtful) disputations " is more literally rendered in the margin " not for decisions (of doubts)." See DISCERN. Cp. JUDGE.¶ In the Sept., Job. 37 : 16.¶

DECK (Verb)

CHRUSOŌ (χρυσόω), lit., to gild with gold (*chrusos*, gold), is used in 5558 AG:889A
Rev. 17 : 4 ; 18 : 16.¶ CB:1240B

DECLARE, DECLARATION

A. Verbs.

1. ANANGELLŌ (ἀναγγέλλω) signifies to announce, report, bring 312
back tidings (*ana*, back, *angellō*, to announce). Possibly the *ana* carries AG:51B CB:1235B
the significance of upward, i.e., heavenly, as characteristic of the nature of the tidings. In the following, either the A.V. or the R.V. translates the word by the verb to declare ; in John 4 : 25, R.V., " declare," A.V., " tell ; " in 16 : 13, 14, 15, R.V., " declare," A.V., " shew ; " in Acts 15 : 4, R.V., " rehearsed," A.V., " declared ; " in 19 : 18, R.V., " declaring," A.V., " shewed " (a reference, perhaps, to the destruction of their idols, in consequence of their new faith) ; in 20 : 20, R.V., " declaring," A.V., " have shewed ; " in 1 John 1 : 5, R.V., " announce," A.V., " declare." See REHEARSE, REPORT, SHEW, SPEAK, TELL.

2. APANGELLŌ (ἀπαγγέλλω) signifies to announce or report from a 518
person or place (*apo*, from) ; hence, to declare, publish ; it is rendered AG:79B
" declare " in Luke 8 : 47 ; Heb. 2 : 12 ; 1 John 1 : 3. It is very frequent CB:1236B
in the Gospels and Acts ; elsewhere, other than the last two places mentioned, only in 1 Thess. 1 : 9 and 1 John 1 : 2. See BRING, A, No. 36.

3. DIANGELLŌ (διαγγέλλω), lit., to announce through, hence, to 1229
declare fully, or far and wide (*dia*, through), is translated " declaring " AG:182B CB:1241B
in Acts 21 : 26, R.V. (A.V., " to signify ") ; in Luke 9 : 60, R.V., " publish abroad " (for A.V. " preach "), giving the verb its fuller significance ; so in Rom. 9 : 17, for A.V., " declared." See PREACH, SIGNIFY.¶

4. KATANGELLŌ (καταγγέλλω), lit., to report down (*kata*, intensive), 2605
is ordinarily translated to preach ; " declare " in Acts 17 : 23, A.V. AG:409B CB:1254A
(R.V., " set forth ") ; in 1 Cor. 2 : 1, R.V., " proclaiming," for A.V., " declaring." It is nowhere translated by " declare " in the R.V. See
PREACH, SHEW, SPEAK, TEACH. 3853

5. PARANGELLŌ (παραγγέλλω) : see CHARGE, B, No. 8. AG:613B

6. DIĒGEOMAI (διηγέομαι), to conduct a narration through to the CB:1262B 1334
end (*dia*, through, intensive, *hegēomai*, to lead), hence denotes to recount, AG:195A
to relate in full, Mark 5 : 16 ; Luke 8 : 39 ; 9 : 10 ; Acts 8 : 33 ; 9 : 27 ; CB:1241C
12 : 17 ; in Mark 9 : 9 and Heb. 11 : 32, " tell." See SHEW, TELL.¶

1555 AG:238C CB:1243C 7. EKDIĒGEOMAI (ἐκδιηγέομαι), properly, to narrate in full, came to denote, to tell, declare ; it is used in Acts 13 : 41 ; 15 : 3.¶

1834 AG:275D CB:1247C 8. EXĒGEOMAI (ἐξηγέομαι), lit., to lead out, signifies to make known, rehearse, declare, Luke 24 : 35 (A.V., " told ; " R.V., rehearsed "); Acts 10 : 8 ; 15 : 12, 14 ; 21 : 19. In John 1 : 18, in the sentence " He hath declared Him," the other meaning of the verb is in view, to unfold in teaching, to declare by making known. See TELL.¶

3724 AG:580D CB:1251B 9. HORIZŌ (ὁρίζω), to mark off by boundaries, signifies to determine, usually of time ; in Rom. 1 : 4, Christ is said to have been marked out as the Son of God, by the fact of His resurrection ; " declared " (R.V., marg., " determined "). See DEFINE.

1213 AG:178C CB:1240C 10. DĒLOŌ (δηλόω), to make plain, is rendered to declare in 1 Cor. 1 : 11, A.V. ; 3 : 13 ; Col. 1 : 8. See SIGNIFY.

5419 AG:865C CB:— 11. PHRAZŌ (φράζω), to declare, occurs in Matt. 15 : 15 and (in some texts) in 13 : 36 (as A.V.).

Note : For *gnōrizō*, to make known, rendered to declare in John 17 : 26 ; 1 Cor. 15 : 1 and Col. 4 : 7, see KNOW, A, No. 8. For *emphanizō*, to declare plainly, Heb. 11 : 14, A.V., see MANIFEST, B, No. 2. For *phaneroō*, see MANIFEST, B, No. 1. For *anatithēmi*, Acts 25 : 14, A.V., see COMMUNICATE. For " declare glad tidings " see TIDINGS.

B. Noun.

1732 AG:262D CB:1244C ENDEIXIS (ἔνδειξις), a showing, pointing out (*en*, in, *deiknumi*, to show), is said of the showing forth of God's righteousness, in Rom. 3 : 25, 26, A.V., " to declare ; " R.V., " to shew," and " (for) the shewing." In 2 Cor. 8 : 24, " proof ; " Phil. 1 : 28, " an evident token." See SHEW, TOKEN.¶

1335 AG:195A CB:1241C *Notes :* (1) In Luke 1 : 1, *diēgēsis* is a " narrative " (R.V.), not a " declaration " (A.V.).

(2) In 2 Cor. 8 : 19, " declaration " does not represent any word in the original.

DECREASE (Verb)

1642 AG:248B CB:— ELATTOŌ (ἐλαττόω) signifies to make less or inferior, in quality, position or dignity ; " madest . . . lower " and " hast made . . . lower," in Heb. 2 : 7, 9. In John 3 : 30, it is used in the Middle Voice, in John the Baptist's " I must decrease," indicating the special interest he had in his own decrease, i.e., in authority and popularity. See LOWER.¶

DECREE (Noun and Verb)

1378 AG:201C CB:1242A DOGMA (δόγμα), transliterated in English, primarily denoted an opinion or judgment (from *dokeō*, to be of opinion), hence, an opinion expressed with authority, a doctrine, ordinance, decree ; " decree," Luke 2 : 1 ; Acts 16 : 4 ; 17 : 7 ; in the sense of ordinances, Eph. 2 : 15 ; Col. 2 : 14. See ORDINANCE.¶

2919 AG:451B CB:1256A *Note :* *Krinō*, to determine, is translated " hath decreed " in 1 Cor. 7 : 37, A.V. ; R.V., " hath determined."

DEDICATE, DEDICATION

A. Verb.

ENKAINIZŌ (ἐγκαινίζω) primarily means to make new, to renew 1457
(*en*, in, *kainos*, new), as in the Sept. of 2 Chron. 15 : 8 ; then, to initiate AG:215B CB:1245A
or dedicate, Heb. 9 : 18, with reference to the first Covenant, as not dedicated without blood ; in 10 : 20, of Christ's dedication of the new and living way (A.V., " consecrated ; " R.V., " dedicated "). See CONSECRATE.¶ In the Sept. it has this meaning in Deut. 20 : 5 ; 2 Chron. 7 : 5 ; Isa. 16 : 11 ; 41 : 1 ; 45 : 16, " keep a feast (to Me)."

B. Noun.

ENKAINIA (ἐγκαίνια), akin to A, frequent in the Sept., in the sense of 1456
dedication, became used particularly for the annual eight days' feast AG:215B CB:—
beginning on the 25th of Chisleu (mid. of Dec.), instituted by Judas Maccabæus, 164, B.C., to commemorate the cleansing of the Temple from the pollutions of Antiochus Epiphanes ; hence it was called the Feast of the Dedication, John 10 : 22. This Feast could be celebrated anywhere. The lighting of lamps was a prominent feature ; hence the description " Feast of Lights." Westcott suggests that John 9 : 5 refers to this.¶

DEED, DEEDS

1. ERGON (ἔργον) denotes a work (Eng., " work " is etymologically 2041
akin), deed, act. When used in the sense of a deed or act, the idea of AG:307D CB:1246C
working is stressed, e.g., Rom. 15 : 18 ; it frequently occurs in an ethical sense of human actions, good or bad, e.g., Matt. 23 : 3 ; 26 : 10 ; John 3 : 20, 21 ; Rom. 2 : 7, 15 ; 1 Thess. 1 : 3 ; 2 Thess. 1 : 11, etc. ; sometimes in a less concrete sense, e.g., Tit. 1 : 16 ; Jas. 1 : 25 (R.V., " that worketh," lit., ' of work '). See LABOUR, WORK.

2. PRAXIS (πρᾶξις) denotes a doing, transaction, a deed the action of 4234
which is looked upon as incomplete and in progress (cp. *prassō*, to AG:697D CB:1266B
practise) ; in Matt. 16 : 27, R.V., " deeds," for A.V., " works ; " in Luke 23 : 51, " deed " ; in ver. 41, the verb is used [see Note (2) below] ; Acts 19 : 18 ; Rom. 8 : 13 ; Col. 3 : 9. In Rom. 12 : 4 it denotes an action, business, or function, translated " office." See OFFICE, WORK.¶

Note : Contrast *pragma*, that which has been done, an accomplished 4229 AG:697A
act, e.g., Jas. 3 : 16, R.V., " deed," A.V., " work." CB:1266B

3. POIĒSIS (ποίησις), a doing (akin to *poieō*, to do), is translated 4162
" deed " in Jas. 1 : 25, A.V. (R.V., " doing ").¶ AG:683B CB:1265C

Note : Cp. *poiēma*, a work done, Rom. 1 : 20 ; Eph. 2 : 10.¶ 4161

4. EUERGESIA (εὐεργεσία) : see BENEFIT, No. 1. AG:683B CB:1265C

Notes : (1) *Katergazomai*, to work out, bring about something, to 2716
perpetrate a deed, is used with the neuter demonstrative pronoun *touto*, AG:421C
this, in 1 Cor. 5 : 3, " hath (so) done this deed," A.V. ; R.V., " hath (so) CB:—
wrought this thing." 4238

(2) *Prassō* (see No. 2), is used in Luke 23 : 41, with the neuter plural AG:698B CB:1266B

of the relative pronoun, "of our deeds;" lit., '(the things) which we practised.'

1411 AG:207B CB:1242B (3) In 2 Cor. 12 : 12 the phrase "mighty deeds" (R.V., "mighty works") translates *dunameis*, "powers" (marg.). See WORK.

— AG:199A CB:— (4) In Acts 24 : 2, *diorthōma*, a straightening, with *ginomai*, to become, is translated in the A.V., "very worthy deeds are done," R.V., "evils are corrected;" more lit., 'reforms take place.'¶ For the variant reading *katorthōma* see CORRECTION, No. 1.

DEEM

5282 AG:846D CB:— HUPONOEŌ (ὑπονοέω), to suppose, conjecture, surmise, is translated "deemed" in Acts 27 : 27, A.V. (R.V., "surmised"); in 13 : 25, "think ye" (A.V.); R.V., "suppose ye;" in 25 : 18, "supposed." See SUPPOSE, THINK.¶

DEEP (Noun and Adjective), DEEPNESS, DEEPLY, DEPTH

A. Nouns.

899 AG:130A CB:1238C 1. BATHOS (βάθος) is used (*a*) naturally, in Matt. 13 : 5, "deepness;" Mark 4 : 5, A.V., "depth," R.V., "deepness;" Luke 5 : 4, of deep water; Rom. 8 : 39 (contrasted with *hupsōma*, height); (*b*) metaphorically, in Rom. 11 : 33, of God's wisdom and knowledge; in 1 Cor. 2 : 10, of God's counsels; in Eph. 3 : 18, of the dimensions of the sphere of the activities of God's counsels, and of the love of Christ which occupies that sphere; in 2 Cor. 8 : 2, of deep poverty; some mss. have it in Rev. 2 : 24.¶

1037 AG:148C CB:— 2. BUTHOS (βυθός), a depth, is used in the N.T. only in the natural sense, of the sea, 2 Cor. 11 : 25.¶

1036 AG:148C CB:— *Notes:* (1) Cp. *buthizō*, to sink (intransitive), Middle Voice, Luke 5 : 7; (transitive) to drown, 1 Tim. 6 : 9.¶

12 AG:2B CB:1233A (2) *Abussos*, Eng., abyss, is translated "the deep" in Luke 8 : 31 and Rom. 10 : 7, A.V. See ABYSS, BOTTOM.

B. Adjective and Adverb.

901 AG:130B CB:1238C BATHUS (βαθύς), akin to A, No. 1, deep, is said in John 4 : 11, of a well; in Acts 20 : 9, of sleep; in Rev. 2 : 24 the plural is used, of the deep things, the evil designs and workings, of Satan.

Notes: (1) In Luke 24 : 1, some mss. have *batheos*, the genitive case, with *orthros*, dawn; the most authentic mss. have *batheōs*, deeply, i.e., very early.

389 AG:61B CB:— (2) In Mark 8 : 12, "He sighed deeply" represents *anastenazō*, to fetch a deep-drawn sigh (*ana*, up, *stenazō*, to sigh or groan). See SIGH.¶

C. Verb.

900 AG:130B CB:— BATHUNŌ (βαθύνω), to deepen, make deep, is used in Luke 6 : 48 (A.V., "digged deep"). The original has two separate verbs, *skaptō*, to dig, and *bathunō*; the R.V. therefore has "digged and went deep."¶

DEFAME

DUSPHĒMEŌ (δυσφημέω), lit., to speak injuriously (from *dus*—, an inseparable prefix signifying opposition, injury etc., and *phēmi*, to speak), is translated "defamed," 1 Cor. 4 : 13. Some mss. have *blasphēmeō*. See BLASPHEME.¶ — AG:209D CB:—

DEFECT

HĒTTĒMA (ἥττημα), primarily a lessening, a decrease, diminution, denotes a loss. It is used of the loss sustained by the Jewish nation in that they had rejected God's testimonies and His Son and the Gospel, Rom. 11 : 12, the reference being not only to national diminution but to spiritual loss; R.V., "loss," for A.V., "diminishing." Here the contrasting word is *plērōma*, fulness. In 1 Cor. 6 : 7 the reference is to the spiritual loss sustained by the church at Corinth because of their discord and their litigious ways in appealing to the world's judges. Here the R.V. has "defect" (marg. "loss"), for A.V., "fault." The preceding adverb "altogether" shows the comprehensiveness of the defect; the loss affected the whole church, and was "an utter detriment." 2275 AG:349C CB:1250B

In the Sept. of Isa. 31 : 8 the word signifies the loss of a defeat, with reference to the overthrow of the Assyrians; lit. 'his young men shall be for loss' (i.e., "tributary"). See DIMINISHING, FAULT, LOSS.¶

Note: Cp. *hēttaō*, to make inferior, used in the Passive Voice, to be overcome (of spiritual defeat, 2 Pet. 2 : 20), and the adjective *hēttōn* or *hēssōn*, less, worse. HēTTAō 2274 (-Oō) AG:349C CB:— HēTTōN 2276 AG:349A (HeSSōN) CB:—

DEFENCE

A. Noun.

APOLOGIA (ἀπολογία), a speech made in defence. See ANSWER. 627 AG:96A CB:1237A

B. Verb.

APOLOGEOMAI (ἀπολογέομαι): see ANSWER, B, No. 4. 626 AG:95D CB:1237A

DEFEND

AMUNŌ (ἀμύνω), to ward off, is used in the Middle Voice in Acts 7 : 24, of the assistance given by Moses to his fellow-Israelite against an Egyptian (translated "defended"). The Middle Voice indicates the special personal interest Moses had in the act.¶ (-OMAI) 292 AG:47A CB:—

DEFER

ANABALLŌ (ἀναβάλλω), lit., to throw up (*ana*, up, *ballō*, to throw), hence to postpone, is used in the Middle Voice in Acts 24 : 22, in the forensic sense of deferring the hearing of a case.¶ 306 (-OMAI) AG:50C CB:—

Note: Cp. *anabolē*, a putting off, delay, Acts 25 : 17.¶ 311 AG:51A CB:—

DEFILE, DEFILEMENT

A. Verbs.

1. KOINOŌ (κοινόω) denotes (*a*) to make common; hence, in a 2840 AG:438B CB:1255B

ceremonial sense, to render unholy, unclean, to defile, Matt. 15 : 11, 18, 20 ; Mark 7 : 15, 18, 20, 23 ; Acts 21 : 28 (R.V., " defiled ; " A.V., " polluted ") ; Heb. 9 : 13 (R.V., " them that have been defiled," A.V., " the unclean ") ; (*b*) to count unclean, Acts 10 : 15 ; 11 : 9. In Rev. 21 : 27, some mss. have this verb, " defileth ; " the most authentic have the adjective, *koinos*, " unclean." See CALL, COMMON.¶

3392 AG:520D CB:1258C 2. MIAINŌ (μιαίνω), primarily, to stain, to tinge or dye with another colour, as in the staining of a glass, hence, to pollute, contaminate, soil, defile, is used (*a*) of ceremonial defilement, John 18 : 28 ; so in the Sept., in Lev. 22 : 5, 8 ; Num. 19 : 13, 20 etc. ; (*b*) of moral defilement, Tit. 1 : 15 (twice) ; Heb. 12 : 15 ; of moral and physical defilement, Jude 8. See B, Nos. 1 and 2.¶

3435 AG:526D CB:1259A 3. MOLUNŌ (μολύνω) properly denotes to besmear, as with mud or filth, to befoul. It is used in the figurative sense, of a conscience defiled by sin, 1 Cor. 8 : 7 ; of believers who have kept themselves (their " garments ") from defilement, Rev. 3 : 4, and of those who have not soiled themselves by adultery or fornication, Rev. 14 : 4.¶

Note : The difference between *miainō* and *molunō* is that the latter is not used in a ritual or ceremonial sense, as *miainō* is (Trench, Syn. xxxi).

4695 AG:762D CB:— 4. SPILOŌ (σπιλόω), to make a stain or spot, and so to defile, is used in Jas. 3 : 6 of the defiling effects of an evil use of the tongue ; in Jude 23, " spotted," with reference to moral defilement. See SPOT.¶

Note : (1) Cp. *spilos*, a spot, a moral blemish, Eph. 5 : 27 ; 2 Pet. 2 : 13 ;¶ *aspilos*, without spot, spotless, 1 Tim. 6 : 14 ; Jas. 1 : 27 ; 1 Pet. 1 : 19 ; 2 Pet. 3 : 14 ;¶ *spilas*, Jude 12, " hidden rocks," R.V. (A.V. " spots," a late meaning, equivalent to *spilos*).¶

5351 AG:857B CB:1264C 5. PHTHEIRŌ (φθείρω) : see CORRUPT, A, No. 2.

B. Nouns.

3393 AG:521A CB:1258C 1. MIASMA (μίασμα), whence the Eng. word, denotes defilement (akin to A, No. 2), and is found in 2 Pet. 2 : 20, A.V., " pollutions," R.V., " defilements," the vices of the ungodly which contaminate a person in his intercourse with the world.¶

3394 AG:521A CB:1258C 2. MIASMOS (μιασμός), also akin to A, No. 2, primarily denotes the act of defiling, the process, in contrast to the defiling thing (No. 1). It is found in 2 Pet. 2 : 10 (A.V., " uncleanness," R.V., " defilement.")¶

3436 AG:527A CB:1259A 3. MOLUSMOS (μολυσμός), akin to A, No. 3, denotes defilement, in the sense of an action by which anything is defiled, 2 Cor. 7 : 1.¶ Cp. the synonymous word *spilos*, A, No. 4, Note.

C. Adjective.

2839 AG:438A CB:1255B KOINOS (κοινός), akin to A, No. 1, common, and, from the idea of coming into contact with everything, " defiled," is used in the ceremonial sense in Mark 7 : 2 ; in ver. 5, R.V., " defiled," for A.V., " unwashen " (the verb is used in 7 : 15). See COMMON, UNCLEAN.

DEFINE

HORIZŌ (ὁρίζω), Eng., horizon, primarily means to mark out the 3724
boundaries of a place (as in the Sept. of Numb. 34 : 6 ; Josh. 13 : 27) ; AG:580D
hence to determine, appoint. In Heb. 4 : 7, where the reference is to the CB:1251B
time of God's invitation to enter into His rest, in contrast to Israel's failure to do so, the word may mean either the appointing of the day (i.e., the period), or the defining of the day, i.e., marking its limits. So the R.V. (A.V., " limiteth "). See DECLARE, DETERMINE, LIMIT, ORDAIN.

DEFRAUD

1. APOSTEREŌ (ἀποστερέω) signifies to rob, despoil, defraud, Mark 650
10 : 19 ; 1 Cor. 6 : 8 ; 7 : 5 (of that which is due to the condition of natural AG:99A
relationship of husband and wife) ; in the Middle Voice, to allow one- CB:1237A
self to be defrauded, 1 Cor. 6 : 7 ; in the Passive Voice, " bereft," 1 Tim. 6 : 5, R.V., with reference to the truth, with the suggestion of being retributively robbed of the truth, through the corrupt condition of the mind. Some mss. have this verb in Jas. 5 : 4 for *aphustereō*, to keep back by fraud. See BEREFT, DESTITUTE, FRAUD.¶ In the Sept., Ex. 21 : 10 ; in some mss., Deut. 24 : 14.¶

2. PLEONEKTEŌ (πλεονεκτέω), translated " defraud " in 1 Thess. 4122
4 : 6, A.V. (R.V. " wrong "), the reference being to the latter part of AG:667C
the Tenth Commandment. See ADVANTAGE, C, No. 2. CB:1265B

DEGREE

BATHMOS (βαθμός) denotes a step, primarily of a threshold or stair, 898
and is akin to *bainō*, to go ; figuratively, a standing, a stage in a career, AG:130A
position, degree, 1 Tim. 3 : 13, of faithful deacons.¶ CB:—

Note : *Tapeinos*, low, humble, whether in condition or mind, is 5011
translated " of low degree " in Luke 1 : 52 and Jas. 1 : 9.¶ AG:804A CB:1271A

DELAY

A. Verbs.

1. OKNEŌ (ὀκνέω), akin to *oknos*, a shrinking, to be loath or slow to 3635
do a thing, to hesitate, delay, is used in Acts 9 : 38.¶ In the Sept. in AG:563A
Numb. 22 : 16, " do not delay " ; Judg. 18 : 9.¶ CB:—

2. CHRONIZŌ (χρονίζω), from *chronos*, time, lit. means to while away 5549
time, i.e., by way of lingering, tarrying, delaying ; " delayeth," Matt. AG:887D
24 : 48 ; Luke 12 : 45 ; " tarried," Matt. 25 : 5 ; " tarried so long," CB:1240B
Luke 1 : 21 ; " will (not) tarry," Heb. 10 : 37. See TARRY.¶

B. Noun.

ANABOLĒ (ἀναβολή) lit. signifies that which is thrown up (*ana*, up, 311 AG:51A
ballō, to throw) ; hence a delay, Acts 25 : 17. See DEFER.¶ CB:—

Note : In Rev. 10 : 6, *chronos* is translated " delay " in R.V. marg., 5550
and is to be taken as the true meaning. AG:887D CB:1240B

DELICACIES

4764 *Note:* For *strēnos,* rendered "delicacies" in Rev. 18 : 3, A.V.,
AG:771C CB:— denoting "wantonness" (R.V.), i.e., arrogant luxury, see WANTON.¶
Cp. the verb *strēniaō,* below, under DELICATELY.

DELICATELY (live)

A. Verbs.

5171 TRUPHAŌ (τρυφάω), from *thruptō,* to enervate, signifies to lead a
AG:828C CB:— voluptuous life, to give oneself up to pleasure, Jas. 5 : 5, R.V., "ye have
lived delicately;" A.V., "ye have lived in pleasure."¶

4684 *Notes:* (1) Cp. *spatalaō,* from *spatalē,* wantonness, to live riotously,
AG:761A CB:— used with A in Jas. 5 : 5, "ye have lived in pleasure" (R.V., "have
taken your . . ."); cp. 1 Tim. 5 : 6, of carnal women in the church, A.V.,
"liveth in pleasure," R.V., "giveth herself to pleasure." See PLEASURE.¶

4763 AG:771C (2) Cp. also *strēniaō,* to run riot, translated "lived deliciously," in
CB:— Rev. 18 : 7, 9, A.V. (R.V., "waxed wanton" and "lived wantonly").
KATASTRēNIAō Cp. DELICACIES (above). See WANTON.¶ Cp. the intensive form *kata-*
2691 AG:419B *strēniaō,* to wax utterly wanton, 1 Tim. 5 : 11.¶
CB:— (3) *Spatalaō* "might properly be laid to the charge of the prodigal,
scattering his substance in riotous living, Luke 15 : 13; . . . *truphaō* to
the charge of the rich man, faring sumptuously every day, Luke 16 : 19;
strēniaō to Jeshurun, when, waxing fat, he kicked, Deut. 32 : 15" (Trench,
Syn. § liv).

B. Noun.

5172 TRUPHĒ (τρυφή), akin to A, is used with *en,* in the phrase *en*
AG:828D CB:— *truphē,* luxuriously, "delicately," Luke 7 : 25, and denotes effeminacy,
softness; "to revel" in 2 Pet. 2 : 13 (A.V., "riot"), lit., 'counting
revelling in the day time a pleasure.' See REVEL, RIOT.¶

1792 *Note: Entruphaō,* to revel luxuriously, is used in 2 Pet. 2 : 13, R.V.,
AG:270A CB:— "revelling" (A.V., "sporting themselves").¶

For DELICIOUSLY, Rev. 18 : 7, 9, A.V., see Note (1) above.

DELIGHT IN

4913 SUNĒDOMAI (συνήδομαι), lit., to rejoice with (anyone), to delight in
AG:789C CB:— (a thing) with (others), signifies to delight with oneself inwardly in a
thing, in Rom. 7 : 22.¶

Note: Cp. *hēdonē,* desire, pleasure.

DELIVER, DELIVERANCE, DELIVERER

A. Verbs.

1325 AG:192C 1. DIDŌMI (δίδωμι), to give, is translated "delivered" in Luke
CB:1241C 7 : 15; R.V., "gave;" so 19 : 13. See GIVE.

325 2. ANADIDŌMI (ἀναδίδωμι), *ana,* up, and No. 1, to deliver over,
AG:53C CB:— give up, is used of delivering the letter mentioned in Acts 23 : 33.¶

Note: For the different verb in Acts 15 : 30, see No. 4.

3. APODIDŌMI (ἀποδίδωμι), *apo*, from, and No. 1, lit., to give away, 591
hence, to give back or up, is used in Pilate's command for the Lord's body AG:90B CB:1236C
to be given up, Matt. 27 : 58 ; in the sense of giving back, of the Lord's act in giving a healed boy back to his father, Luke 9 : 42. See GIVE, PAY, PAYMENT, PERFORM, RECOMPENSE, RENDER, REPAY, REQUITE, RESTORE, REWARD, SELL, YIELD.

4. EPIDIDŌMI (ἐπιδίδωμι), lit., to give upon or in addition, as from 1929
oneself to another, hence, to deliver over, is used of the delivering of the AG:292B CB:—
roll of Isaiah to Christ in the synagogue, Luke 4 : 17 ; of the delivering of the epistle from the elders at Jerusalem to the church at Antioch, Acts 15 : 30. See DRIVE (let), GIVE, OFFER.

5. PARADIDŌMI (παραδίδωμι), to deliver over, in Rom. 6 : 17, R.V. 3860
" that form of teaching whereunto ye were delivered," the figure being AG:614B CB:1262A
that of a mould which gives its shape to what is cast in it (not as the A.V.). In Rom. 8 : 32 it is used of God in delivering His Son to expiatory Death ; so 4 : 25 ; see Mark 9 : 31 ; of Christ in delivering Himself up, Gal. 2 : 20 ; Eph. 5 : 2, 25. See BETRAY, A. In Mark 1 : 14, R.V., it is used of delivering John the Baptist to prison. See PUT, No. 12.

6. APALLASSŌ (ἀπαλλάσσω), lit., to change from (*apo*, from, *allassō*, 525
to change), to free from, release, is translated " might deliver " in Heb. AG:80A CB:1236B
2 : 15 ; in Luke 12 : 58, it is used in a legal sense of being quit of a person, i.e., the opponent being appeased and withdrawing his suit. For its other meaning, to depart, in Acts 19 : 12, see DEPART.¶

7. ELEUTHEROŌ (ἐλευθερόω), to set free, is translated " deliver " in 1659
Rom. 8 : 21. In six other places it is translated " make free," John 8 : 32, AG:250D CB:1244B
36 ; Rom. 6 : 18, 22 ; 8 : 2 ; Gal. 5 : 1, R.V., " set free." See FREE.¶

8. EXAIREŌ (ἐξαιρέω), lit., to take out, denotes, in the Middle Voice, 1807
to take out for oneself, hence, to deliver, to rescue, the person who does AG:271D CB:—
so having a special interest in the result of his act. Thus it is used, in Gal. 1 : 4, of the act of God in delivering believers " out of this present evil world," the Middle Voice indicating His pleasure in the issue of their deliverance. It signifies to deliver by rescuing from danger, in Acts 12 : 11 ; 23 : 27 ; 26 : 17 ; from bondage, Acts 7 : 10, 34. For its other meaning, to pluck out of, Matt. 5 : 29 ; 18 : 9, see PLUCK.¶

9. KATARGEŌ (καταργέω) : see ABOLISH.

10. RHUOMAI (ῥύομαι), to rescue from, to preserve from, and so, to 4506
deliver, the word by which it is regularly translated, is largely synonymous AG:737C CB:1268B
with *sōzō*, to save, though the idea of rescue from is predominant in *rhuomai* (see Matt. 27 : 43), that of preservation from, in *sōzō*. In Rom. 11 : 26 the present participle is used with the article, as a noun, " the Deliverer." This is the construction in 1 Thess. 1 : 10, where Christ is similarly spoken of. Here the A.V. wrongly has " which delivered " (the tense is not past) ; R.V., " which delivereth ; " the translation might well be (as in Rom. 11 : 26), ' our Deliverer,' that is, from the retributive

calamities with which God will visit men at the end of the present age. From that wrath believers are to be delivered. The verb is used with *apo*, away from, in Matt. 6 : 13 ; Luke 11 : 4 (in some mss.) ; so also in 11 : 4 ; Rom. 15 : 31 ; 2 Thess. 3 : 2 ; 2 Tim. 4 : 18 ; and with *ek*, from, out of, in Luke 1 : 74 ; Rom. 7 : 24 ; 2 Cor. 1 : 10 ; Col. 1 : 13, from bondage ; in 2 Pet. 2 : 9, from temptation ; in 2 Tim. 3 : 11, from persecution ; but *ek* is used of ills impending, in 2 Cor. 1 : 10 ; in 2 Tim. 4 : 17, *ek* indicates that the danger was more imminent than in ver. 18, where *apo* is used. Accordingly the meaning 'out of the midst of' cannot be pressed in 1 Thess. 1 : 10.¶

5483 11. CHARIZOMAI (χαρίζομαι), to gratify, to do what is pleasing to
AG:876C anyone, is translated " deliver " in the A.V. of Acts 25 : 11, 16 ; R.V.,
CB:1239C " give up " (marg., " grant by favour," i.e., to give over to the Jews so
as to gratify their wishes). See FORGIVE, GIVE, GRANT.

Note : For *gennaō* and *tiktō*, to bear, to be delivered (said of women at childbirth), see BEGET.

B. Nouns.

629 1. APOLUTRŌSIS (ἀπολύτρωσις) denotes redemption (*apo*, from,
AG:96B *lutron*, a price of release). In Heb. 11 : 35 it is translated " deliverance ; "
CB:1237A usually the release is effected by the payment of a ransom, or the required
price, the *lutron* (ransom). See REDEMPTION.

859 2. APHESIS (ἄφεσις) denotes a release, from bondage, imprisonment
AG:125A etc. (the corresponding verb is *aphiēmi*, to send away, let go) ; in Luke
CB:1236B 4 : 18 it is used of liberation from captivity (A.V., " deliverance," R.V.,
" release "). See FORGIVENESS, REMISSION.

3086 3. LUTRŌTĒS (λυτρωτής), a redeemer, one who releases (see No. 1),
AG:483A is translated " deliverer " in Acts 7 : 35 (R.V. marg., " redeemer ").¶
CB:1257B *Note :* See also DELIVER, A, No. 10.

C. Verbal Adjective.

1560 EKDOTOS (ἔκδοτος), lit., given up (*ek*, out of, *didōmi*, to give),
AG:239A delivered up (to enemies, or to the power or will of someone), is used of
CB:1243C Christ in Acts 2 : 23.¶

DELUDE, DELUSION

A. Verb.

3884
AG:620B PARALOGIZOMAI (παραλογίζομαι) : see BEGUILE.
CB:1262A

B. Noun.

4106 PLANĒ (πλάνη), lit., a wandering, whereby those who are led astray
AG:665D roam hither and thither, is always used in the N.T., of mental straying,
CB:1265A wrong opinion, error in morals or religion. In 2 Thess. 2 : 11, A.V., it
is translated " delusion," R.V., " error." See DECEIT, ERROR.

DEMAND

Note : For DEMAND (Matt. 2 : 4 and Acts 21 : 33), see INQUIRE ; for its use in Luke 3 : 14 and 17 : 20, see under ASK.

DEMEANOUR

KATASTĒMA (κατάστημα) : see BEHAVIOUR, B, No. 2. 2688 AG:419A CB:—

DEMON, DEMONIAC

A. Nouns.

1. DAIMŌN (δαίμων), a demon, signified, among pagan Greeks, an 1142 AG:169D CB:1240B
inferior deity, whether good or bad. In the N.T. it denotes an evil spirit. It is used in Matt. 8 : 31, mistranslated " devils."

Some would derive the word from a root *da*—, meaning to distribute. More probably it is from a similar root *da*—, meaning to know, and hence means a knowing one.¶

2. DAIMONION (δαιμόνιον), not a diminutive of *daimōn*, No. 1, but 1140 AG:169A CB:1240B
the neuter of the adjective *daimonios*, pertaining to a demon, is also mistranslated " devil," " devils." In Acts 17 : 18, it denotes an inferior pagan deity. Demons are the spiritual agents acting in all idolatry. The idol itself is nothing, but every idol has a demon associated with it who induces idolatry, with its worship and sacrifices, 1 Cor. 10 : 20, 21 ; Rev. 9 : 20 ; cp. Deut. 32 : 17 ; Isa. 13 : 21 ; 34 : 14 ; 65 : 3, 11. They disseminate errors among men, and seek to seduce believers, 1 Tim. 4 : 1. As seducing spirits they deceive men into the supposition that through mediums (those who have " familiar spirits," Lev. 20 : 6, 27, e.g.) they can converse with deceased human beings. Hence the destructive deception of Spiritism, forbidden in Scripture, Lev. 19 : 31 ; Deut. 18 : 11 ; Isa. 8 : 19. Demons tremble before God, Jas. 2 : 19 ; they recognized Christ as Lord and as their future Judge, Matt. 8 : 29 ; Luke 4 : 41. Christ cast them out of human beings by His own power. His disciples did so in His Name, and by exercising faith, e.g., Matt. 17 : 20.

Acting under Satan (cp. Rev. 16 : 13, 14), demons are permitted to afflict with bodily disease, Luke 13 : 16. Being unclean they tempt human beings with unclean thoughts, Matt. 10 : 1 ; Mark 5 : 2 ; 7 : 25 ; Luke 8 : 27–29 ; Rev. 16 : 13 ; 18 : 2, e.g. They differ in degrees of wickedness, Matt. 12 : 45. They will instigate the rulers of the nations at the end of this age to make war against God and His Christ, Rev. 16 : 14. See DEVIL.

B. Verb.

DAIMONIZOMAI (δαιμονίζομαι) signifies to be possessed of a demon, 1139 AG:169A CB:1240B
to act under the control of a demon. Those who were thus afflicted expressed the mind and consciousness of the demon or demons indwelling them, e.g., Luke 8 : 28. The verb is found chiefly in Matt. and Mark ; Matt. 4 : 24 ; 8 : 16, 28, 33 ; 9 : 32 ; 12 : 22 ; 15 : 22 ; Mark 1 : 32 ; 5 : 15, 16, 18 ; elsewhere in Luke 8 : 36 and John 10 : 21, " him that hath a devil (demon)."¶

C. Adjective.

DAIMONIŌDĒS (δαιμονιώδης) signifies proceeding from, or resembling, 1141 AG:169D CB:—

a demon, "demoniacal;" see marg. of Jas. 3:15, R.V. (text, "devilish").¶

DEMONSTRATE See DECLARE

DEMONSTRATION

585 AG:89D CB:1236C APODEIXIS (ἀπόδειξις), lit., a pointing out (*apo*, forth, *deiknumi*, to show), a showing or demonstrating by argument, is found in 1 Cor. 2:4, where the Apostle speaks of a proof, a showing forth or display, by the operation of the Spirit of God in him, as affecting the hearts and lives of his hearers, in contrast to the attempted methods of proof by rhetorical arts and philosophic arguments.¶

DEN

4693 AG:762C CB:1269C SPĒLAION (σπήλαιον): see CAVE.

DENY

720 AG:107D CB:1237C 1. ARNEOMAI (ἀρνέομαι) signifies (*a*) to say . . . not, to contradict, e.g., Mark 14:70; John 1:20; 18:25, 27; 1 John 2:22; (*b*) to deny by way of disowning a person, as, e.g., the Lord Jesus as Master, e.g., Matt. 10:33; Luke 12:9; John 13:38 (in the best mss.); 2 Tim. 2:12; or, on the other hand, of Christ Himself, denying that a person is His follower, Matt. 10:33; 2 Tim. 2:12; or to deny the Father and the Son, by apostatizing and by disseminating pernicious teachings, to deny Jesus Christ as Master and Lord by immorality under a cloak of religion, 2 Pet. 2:1; Jude 4; (*c*) to deny oneself, either in a good sense, by disregarding one's own interests, Luke 9:23, or in a bad sense, to prove false to oneself, to act quite unlike oneself, 2 Tim. 2:13; (*d*) to abrogate, forsake, or renounce a thing, whether evil, Tit. 2:12, or good, 1 Tim. 5:8; 2 Tim. 3:5; Rev. 2:13; 3:8; (*e*) not to accept, to reject something offered, Acts 3:14; 7:35, "refused;" Heb. 11:24, "refused." See REFUSE.

533 AG:81A CB:1236B 2. APARNEOMAI (ἀπαρνέομαι), a strengthened form of No. 1, with *apo*, from, prefixed (Lat., *abnego*), means (*a*) to deny utterly, to abjure, to affirm that one has no connection with a person, as in Peter's denial of Christ, Matt. 26:34, 35, 75; Mark 14:30, 31, 72; Luke 22:34, 61 (some mss. have it in John 13:38). This stronger form is used in the Lord's statements foretelling Peter's denial, and in Peter's assurance of fidelity; the simple verb (No. 1) is used in all the records of his actual denial. The strengthened form is the verb used in the Lord's warning as to being "denied" in the presence of the angels, Luke 12:9; in the preceding clause, "he that denieth Me," the simple verb *arneomai* is used; the rendering therefore should be 'he that denieth Me in the presence of men, shall be utterly denied in the presence of the angels of God;' (*b*) to deny oneself as a follower of Christ, Matt. 16:24; Mark 8:34; Luke 9:23.¶

483 AG:74D CB:— 3. ANTILEGŌ (ἀντιλέγω) means to speak against, contradict.

In Luke 20 : 27, the R.V., " they which say that there is no resurrection," follows the texts which have the simple verb *legō;* for the A.V., which translates the verb *antilegō*, " which deny that there is any resurrection." See ANSWER, CONTRADICT, GAINSAY, SPEAK, No. 6.

DEPART

(*a*) *Compounds of agō.*

1. ANAGŌ (ἀνάγω), lit., to lead up (*ana*, up, *agō*, to lead), is used, 321
in the Middle Voice, as a nautical term, signifying to set sail, put to sea ; AG:53A
" to depart," Acts 27 : 12, A.V. (R.V., " put to sea ") ; 28 : 10 (R.V., CB:—
" sailed ") ; ver. 11 (R.V., " set sail "). Cp. *epanagō*, in Luke 5 : 3, to put out. See BRING, No. 11.

2. PARAGŌ (παράγω), used intransitively, means to pass by (*para*, 3855
by, beside), and is so translated everywhere in the Gospels, except in the AG:613D
A.V. of Matt. 9 : 27, " departed ; " R.V., " passed by." Outside the CB:—
Gospels it is used in its other meaning, to pass away, 1 Cor. 7 : 31 ; 1 John 2 : 8 (R.V.), 17. See PASS.

3. HUPAGŌ (ὑπάγω), to go, translated " depart " in Jas. 2 : 16, A.V., 5217
primarily and lit. meant to lead under (*hupo*, under) ; in its later use, it AG:836C
implied a going, without noise or notice, or by stealth. In this passage CB:—
the idea is perhaps that of a polite dismissal, ' Go your ways.' See GET, Go.

(*b*) *Compounds of erchomai.*

4. APERCHOMAI (ἀπέρχομαι), lit., to come or go away (*apo*), hence, 565
to set off, depart, e.g., Matt. 8 : 18, is frequent in the Gospels and Acts ; AG:84C
Rev. 18 : 14, R.V., " are gone." See COME, No. 11 (Note), Go, PASS. CB:1236B

5. DIERCHOMAI (διέρχομαι), to come or go through, to pass through 1330
to a place, is translated " departed " in Acts 13 : 14, A.V. ; R.V., " passing AG:194C
through ; " elsewhere it is usually translated " pass through " or " go CB:1241C
through." See COME, No. 5.

6. EXERCHOMAI (ἐξέρχομαι) denotes to come out, or go out of, to 1831
go forth. It is frequently translated by the verb to depart, e.g., Matt. AG:274B
9 : 31 ; in Luke 4 : 42, for the A.V., " He departed and went (No. 8)," CB:1247C
the R.V. has " He came out and went ; " in 9 : 6 the A.V. and R.V. agree. See COME, No. 3.

7. KATERCHOMAI (κατέρχομαι), to come down (its usual meaning), 2718
is translated " departed " in Acts 13 : 4, A.V. (R.V., " went down "). AG:422A
See COME, No. 7. CB:—

(*c*) *Poreuō and a compound.*

8. POREUŌ (πορεύω), akin to *poros*, a passage, in the Middle Voice 4198
signifies to go on one's way, to depart from one place to another. In some AG:692B
places, where the A.V. has the verb to depart, the R.V. translates by to CB:1266A
go one's way, e.g., Matt. 2 : 9, " went their way ; " 11 : 7 ; 24 : 1, " was going on His way." In the following the R.V. has the verb to go, for the A.V. depart, Luke 4 : 42 (latter part of verse) ; 13 : 31 ; John 16 : 7 ;

2 Tim. 4 : 10. In Luke 21 : 8, "go (after)," is said of disciples or partisans. In some places both A.V. and R.V. translate by the verb to depart, e.g., Matt. 19 : 15; 25 : 41; Acts 5 : 41; Acts 22 : 21. This verb is to be distinguished from others signifying to go. It is best rendered, as often as possible, to go on one's way. See GO, JOURNEY, WALK.

(-OMAI) 1607 9. EKPOREUŌ (ἐκπορεύω), *ek*, from, in the Middle and Passive, to
AG:244B proceed from or forth, more expressive of a definite course than simply
CB:1244A to go forth, is translated "go forth," in Mark 6 : 11; "went out" in Matt. 20 : 29, R.V. (A.V., "departed"); both have "depart" in Acts 25 : 4. It is frequently translated by the verb to proceed, and is often best so rendered, e.g., in Rev. 9 : 17, 18, R.V., for A.V., "issued." See COME, No. 33.

(*d*) *Compounds of chōreō.*

402 AG:63C 10. ANACHŌREŌ (ἀναχωρέω), to go back, recede, retire (*ana*, back
CB:1235A or up, *chōreō*, to make room for, betake oneself, *chōros*, a place), is translated "departed" in Matt. 2 : 12, 13, 14; 4 : 12 (R.V., "withdrew"); so in 14 : 13 and 15 : 21, but "departed" in 27 : 5; "withdrew" in John 6 : 15. In Matt. 2 : 22 the R.V. has "withdrew," which is preferable to the A.V., "turned aside." The most suitable translation wherever possible, is by the verb to withdraw. See PLACE, B, No. 1, GO, No. 15, TURN, *Note* (1), WITHDRAW.

672 AG:102A 11. APOCHŌREŌ (ἀποχωρέω), to depart from (*apo*), is so translated
CB:— in Matt. 7 : 23; Luke 9 : 39; Acts 13 : 13 (both A.V. and R.V.). Some mss. have it in Luke 20 : 20.¶

1633 AG:247C 12. EKCHŌREŌ (ἐκχωρέω) signifies to depart out (*ek*), to leave a
CB:— place, Luke 21 : 21.¶

(*e*) *Chōrizō and compounds.*

5563 AG:890A 13. CHŌRIZŌ (χωρίζω), to put apart, separate, means, in the Middle
CB:1240A Voice, to separate oneself, to depart from, Acts 1 : 4; 18 : 1, 2; in marital affairs, 1 Cor. 7 : 10, 11, 15; "departed" (R.V. corrects to "was parted"), Phlm. 15. The verb is also used in Matt. 19 : 6; Mark 10 : 9; Rom. 8 : 35, 39; Heb. 7 : 26. See PUT, No. 14, SEPARATE.¶

673 AG:102B 14. APOCHŌRIZŌ (ἀποχωρίζω) signifies to separate off (*apo*); in
CB:— the Middle Voice, to depart from, Acts 15 : 39, A.V., "departed asunder;" R.V., "parted asunder;" Rev. 6 : 14, R.V., "was removed." See PART, REMOVE.¶

1316 (-OMAI) 15. DIACHŌRIZŌ (διαχωρίζω), lit., to separate throughout (*dia*),
AG:191A i.e., completely, in the Middle Voice, to separate oneself definitely from,
CB:1241A (-ESTHAI) is used in Luke 9 : 33, R.V., "were parting from."¶

(*f*) *Various other verbs.*

360 AG:57C 16. ANALUŌ (ἀναλύω), lit., to unloose, undo (*ana*, up, or again),
CB:1235A signifies to depart, in the sense of departing from life, Phil. 1 : 23, a metaphor drawn from loosing moorings preparatory to setting sail, or, according to some, from breaking up an encampment, or from the

unyoking of baggage animals. See DEPARTING, No. 1. In Luke 12 : 36, it has its other meaning, to return. See RETURN.¶

17. APOLUŌ (ἀπολύω), to loose from (*apo*), in the Middle Voice, 630
signifies to depart, Luke 2 : 29 ; Acts 23 : 22, R.V., " let go ; " 28 : 25. AG:96C CB:1237A
See DISMISS.

18. EXEIMI (ἔξειμι), to go out (*ex*, out, *eimi*, to go), is rendered " went 1826
out " in Acts 13 : 42 ; in 27 : 43, " got," of mariners getting to shore ; AG:275B (EXESTI)
in 17 : 15, " departed ; " in 20 : 7, " to depart." See GET, GO.¶ CB:1247C

19. METAIRŌ (μεταίρω), to make a distinction, to remove, to lift 3332
away (in its transitive sense), is used intransitively in the N.T., signifying AG:511A CB:—
to depart, and is said of Christ, in Matt. 13 : 53 ; 19 : 1. It could be well translated " removed."¶

20. APHISTĒMI (ἀφίστημι), in the Active Voice, used transitively, 868
signifies to cause to depart, to cause to revolt, Acts 5 : 37 ; used AG:126D CB:1236B
intransitively, to stand off, or aloof, or to depart from anyone, Luke 4 : 13 ; 13 : 27 ; Acts 5 : 38 (" refrain from ") ; 12 : 10 ; 15 : 38 ; 19 : 9 ; 22 : 29 ; 2 Cor. 12 : 8 ; metaphorically, to fall away, 2 Tim. 2 : 19 ; in the Middle Voice, to withdraw or absent oneself from, Luke 2 : 37 ; to apostatize, Luke 8 : 13 ; 1 Tim. 4 : 1 ; Heb. 3 : 12, R.V., " falling away." See DRAW (away), FALL, No. 14, REFRAIN, WITHDRAW.¶

21. APALLASSŌ (ἀπαλλάσσω), lit., to change from (*apo*, from, *allassō*, 525
to change), is used once of departing, said of the removal of diseases, Acts AG:80A CB:1236B
19 : 12. In Heb. 2 : 15 it signifies to deliver, release. In Luke 12 : 58, it is used in a legal sense, to be quit of. See DELIVER.¶

22. METABAINŌ (μεταβαίνω) is rendered to depart in Matt. 8 : 34 ; 3327
11 : 1 ; 12 : 9 ; 15 : 29 ; John 7 : 3 ; 13 : 1 ; Acts 18 : 7. AG:510C CB:1258B

DEPARTING, DEPARTURE

1. ANALUSIS (ἀνάλυσις), an unloosing (as of things woven), a dis- 359
solving into separate parts (Eng., analysis), is once used of departure from AG:57B CB:—
life, 2 Tim. 4 : 6, where the metaphor is either nautical, from loosing from moorings (thus used in Greek poetry), or military, from breaking up an encampment ; cp. *kataluō* in 2 Cor. 5 : 1 (cp. DEPART, No. 16).¶

2. APHIXIS (ἄφιξις), most frequently an arrival (akin to *aphikneomai*, 867
see COME), also signifies a departure (*apo*, from, *hikneomai*, to come : AG:126D CB:—
etymologically, to come far enough, reach ; cp. *hikanos*, sufficient), the departure being regarded in relation to the end in view. Thus Paul speaks of his " departing," Acts 20 : 29.¶

3. EXODOS (ἔξοδος) : see DECEASE. 1841 AG:276D CB:1247C

DEPOSE

KATHAIREŌ (καθαιρέω) lit. signifies to take down (*kata*, down, 2507
haireō, to take), the technical term for removing a body after crucifixion, AG:386C CB:—
e.g., Mark 15 : 36 ; hence, to pull down, demolish ; in Acts 19 : 27, according to the most authentic mss., the translation is (as the R.V.) " that she

(Diana) should even be deposed from her magnificence" (possibly, in the partitive sense of the genitive, 'destroyed from, or diminished in, somewhat of her magnificence'). See CAST, DESTROY, PULL, PUT, TAKE (down).

For DEPOSIT see COMMIT, B, No. 1

899 AG:130A

DEPTH

CB:1238C 1. BATHOS (*βάθος*): see DEEP.

3989 AG:641B CB:— 2. PELAGOS (*πέλαγος*), the sea, Acts 27:5, denotes also "the depth" (of the sea), Matt. 18:6. The word is most probably connected with a form of *plēssō*, to strike, and *plēgē*, a blow, suggestive of the tossing of the waves. Some would connect it with *plax*, a level board, but this is improbable, and less applicable to the general usage of the word, which commonly denotes the sea in its restless character. See SEA.¶

DEPRAVED See REPROBATE

For DEPUTY see PROCONSUL

DERIDE

1592 AG:243B CB:1243C *Note:* For *ekmuktērizō*, lit., to turn up the nose at, to deride out and out, Luke 16:14; 23:35, see SCOFF.¶

DESCEND

2597 AG:408B CB:1253C 1. KATABAINŌ (*καταβαίνω*), to go down (*kata*, down, *bainō*, to go), used for various kinds of motion on the ground (e.g., going, walking, stepping), is usually translated to descend. The R.V. uses the verb to come down, for A.V., descend, in Mark 15:32; Acts 24:1; Rev. 21:10. See COME, No. 19.

2718 AG:422A CB:— 2. KATERCHOMAI (*κατέρχομαι*), to come or go down, is translated "descendeth," in Jas. 3:15, A.V.; R.V., "cometh down." See COME, No. 7.

DESCENT

2600 AG:409A CB:— KATABASIS (*κατάβασις*) denotes a going down, akin to No. 1 under DESCEND, a way down, Luke 19:37.¶

Note: For "descent" (A.V. in Heb. 7:3, 6), see GENEALOGY (the R.V. rendering).

DESCRIBE

1125 AG:166C CB:1248C 1. GRAPHŌ (*γράφω*), to write, is rendered "describeth" in Rom. 10:5, A.V., "For Moses describeth the righteousness which is of the Law . . . ;" this the R.V. corrects to "For Moses writeth that the man that doeth the righteousness which is of the Law . . ." See WRITE.

3004 AG:468A CB:1256C 2. LEGŌ (*λέγω*), to say, is rendered "describeth" in Rom. 4:6, A.V., "David describeth the blessedness . . . ;" this the R.V. corrects to,

" David pronounceth blessing upon . . ." This might be regarded as the meaning, if David is considered as the human agent acting for God as the real pronouncer of blessing. Otherwise the verb *legō* is to be taken in its ordinary sense of telling or relating; especially as the blessedness (*makarismos*) is not an act, but a state of felicity resulting from God's act of justification.

DESECRATE See DEFILE

DESERT See FORSAKE

DESERT (Noun and Adjective)

A. Noun.

EREMIA (ἐρημία), primarily a solitude, an uninhabited place, in 2047 AG:308D CB:1246B
contrast to a town or village, is translated " deserts " in Heb. 11 : 38; " the wilderness " in Matt. 15 : 33, A.V., " a desert place," R.V.; so in Mark 8 : 4; " wilderness " in 2 Cor. 11 : 26. It does not always denote a barren region, void of vegetation; it is often used of a place uncultivated, but fit for pasturage. See WILDERNESS.¶

B. Adjective.

ERĒMOS (ἔρημος), used as a noun, has the same meaning as *erēmia*; 2048 AG:309A CB:1246B
in Luke 5 : 16 and 8 : 29, R.V., " deserts," for A.V., " wilderness; " in Matt. 24 : 26 and John 6 : 31, R.V., " wilderness," for A.V., " desert." As an adjective, it denotes (*a*), with reference to persons, " deserted," desolate, deprived of the friends and kindred, e.g., of a woman deserted by a husband, Gal. 4 : 27; (*b*) so of a city, as Jerusalem, Matt. 23 : 38; or uninhabited places, " desert," e.g., Matt. 14 : 13, 15; Acts 8 : 26; in Mark 1 : 35, R.V., " desert," for A.V., " solitary." See DESOLATE, WILDERNESS.

DESERVING See WORTHY

DESIGNATE See APPOINT

DESIRE (Noun and Verb), DESIROUS

A. Nouns.

1. EPITHUMIA (ἐπιθυμία), a desire, craving, longing, mostly of evil 1939 AG:293B CB:1246B
desires, frequently translated " lust," is used in the following, of good desires: of the Lord's wish concerning the last Passover, Luke 22 : 15; of Paul's desire to be with Christ, Phil. 1 : 23; of his desire to see the saints at Thessalonica again, 1 Thess. 2 : 17.

With regard to evil desires, in Col. 3 : 5 the R.V. has " desire," for the A.V., " concupiscence; " in 1 Thess 4 : 5, R.V., " lust," for A.V., " concupiscence; " there the preceding word *pathos* is translated " passion," R.V., for A.V., " lust " (see AFFECTION); also in Col. 3 : 5 *pathos* and *epithumia* are associated, R.V., " passion," for A.V., " inordinate affection." *Epithumia* is combined with *pathēma*, in Gal. 5 : 24; for the A.V., " affections and lusts," the R.V. has " passions, and the lusts thereof." *Epithumia* is the more comprehensive term, including all manner of lusts and desires; *pathēma* denotes suffering; in the passage in Gal. (l.c.) the sufferings are those produced by yielding to the flesh; *pathos* points more to the evil state from which lusts spring. Cp. *orexis*, lust, Rom. 1 : 27. See CONCUPISCENCE, LUST, and Trench, Syn. lxxxvii.

2107 AG:319C CB:1247A 2. EUDOKIA (*εὐδοκία*), lit., good pleasure (*eu*, well, *dokeō*, to seem), implies a gracious purpose, a good object being in view, with the idea of a resolve, shewing the willingness with which the resolve is made. It is often translated "good pleasure," e.g., Eph. 1 : 5, 9 ; Phil. 2 : 13 ; in Phil. 1 : 15, "good will ;" in Rom. 10 : 1, "desire," (marg., "good pleasure") ; in 2 Thess. 1 : 11, R.V., "desire," A.V. and R.V., marg., "good pleasure."

It is used of God in Matt. 11 : 26 ("well pleasing," R.V., for A.V., "seemed good") ; Luke 2 : 14, R.V., "men in whom He is well pleased," lit., 'men of good pleasure' (the construction is objective) ; 10 : 21 ; Eph. 1 : 5, 9 ; Phil. 2 : 13. See PLEASURE, SEEM, WILL.¶

1972 AG:298A CB:1246A 3. EPIPOTHĒSIS (*ἐπιπόθησις*), an earnest desire, a longing for (*epi*, upon, intensive, *potheō*, to desire), is found in 2 Cor. 7 : 7, 11, A.V., "earnest desire," and "vehement desire ;" R.V., "longing" in both places. See LONGING.¶

1974 AG:298A CB:1246A 4. EPIPOTHIA (*ἐπιποθία*), with the same meaning as No. 3, is used in Rom. 15 : 23, R.V., "longing," A.V., "great desire."¶ Cp. *epipothētos*, Phil. 4 : 1, "longed for"¶, and *epipotheō*, to long for [see B, Note (4)]. See LONGING.

2307 AG:354B CB:1271C 5. THELĒMA (*θέλημα*) denotes a will, that which is willed (akin to B, No. 6). It is rendered "desires," in Eph. 2 : 3. See PLEASURE, WILL.

1013 AG:145D CB:1239B *Note :* In 1 Pet. 4 : 3, R.V., *boulēma* is rendered "desire." See WILL.

B. Verbs.

515 AG:78C CB:1238B 1. AXIOŌ (*ἀξιόω*), to deem worthy, is translated "desire" in Acts 28 : 22, where a suitable rendering would be 'We think it meet (or good) to hear of thee ;' so in 15 : 38. See THINK.

1937 AG:293A CB:1246B 2. EPITHUMEŌ (*ἐπιθυμέω*), to desire earnestly (as with A, No. 1), stresses the inward impulse rather than the object desired. It is translated to desire in Luke 16 : 21 ; 17 : 22 ; 22 : 15 ; 1 Tim. 3 : 1 ; Heb. 6 : 11 ; 1 Pet. 1 : 12 ; Rev. 9 : 6. See COVET.

2065 AG:311D CB:1246C 3. ERŌTAŌ (*ἐρωτάω*), in Luke 7 : 36 is translated "desired ;" in 14 : 32, R.V., "asketh," for A.V., "desireth ;" so in John 12 : 21 ; Acts 16 : 39 ; 18 : 20 ; 23 : 20 ; in ver. 18 "asked," for A.V., "prayed." See ASK.

2442 AG:565B CB:— 4. HOMEIROMAI, or HIMEIROMAI (*ὁμείρομαι*), to have a strong affection for, a yearning after, is found in 1 Thess. 2 : 8, "being affectionately desirous of you." It is probably derived from a root indicating remembrance.¶

3713 (-OMAI) AG:579D CB:1261A (-OMAI) 5. OREGŌ (*ὀρέγω*), to reach or stretch out, is used only in the Middle Voice, signifying the mental effort of stretching oneself out for a thing, of longing after it, with stress upon the object desired (cp. No. 2) ; it is translated "desire" in Heb. 11 : 16 ; in 1 Tim. 3 : 1, R.V., "seeketh," for A.V., "desireth ;" in 1 Tim. 6 : 10, R.V., "reached after," for A.V., "coveted after." In Heb. 11 : 16, a suitable rendering would be 'reach after.' See COVET, SEEK.¶ Cp. *orexis*, lust, Rom. 1 : 27.¶

6. THELŌ (θέλω), to will, to wish, implying volition and purpose, 2309
frequently a determination, is most usually rendered to will. It is trans- AG:354D CB:1271C
lated to desire in the R.V. of the following: Matt. 9:13; 12:7; Mark
6:19; Luke 10:29; 14:28; 23:20; Acts 24:27; 25:9; Gal.
4:17; 1 Tim. 5:11; Heb. 12:17; 13:18. See Disposed, Forward,
Intend, List, Love, Mean, Pleased, Rather, Voluntary, Will.

7. BOULOMAI (βούλομαι), to wish, to will deliberately, expresses 1014
more strongly than *thelō* (No. 6) the deliberate exercise of the will; it is AG:146A CB:1239B
translated to desire in the R.V. of the following: Acts 22:30; 23:38;
27:43; 28:18; 1 Tim. 2:8; 5:14; 6:9 and Jude 5. See
Disposed, Intend, List, Minded, Willing, Wish, Would.

8. ZĒLOŌ (ζηλόω), to have a zeal for, to be zealous towards, whether 2206
in a good or evil sense, the former in 1 Cor. 14:1, concerning spiritual AG:338A CB:1273B
gifts R.V., "desire earnestly," A.V., "desire;" in an evil sense, in Jas.
4:2, R.V., "covet," for A.V., "desire to have."

9. AITEŌ (αἰτέω), to ask, is rendered to desire in A.V., e.g., in 154
Matt. 20:20; Luke 23:25 [R.V., always 'to ask (for)']. AG:25D CB:1234A

10. SPEUDŌ (σπεύδω) is translated "earnestly desiring" in 2 Pet. 4692
3:12, R.V. See Haste. AG:762B CB:1269C

Note: The following are translated by the verb to desire in the A.V. EPERŌTAŌ
(1) *Eperōtaō*, No. 3, with *epi*, intensive, to ask, interrogate, inquire 1905
of, consult, or to demand of a person; in Matt. 16:1, R.V., "asked." AG:285B CB:1245C
See Ask. (2) *Zēteō*, to seek; in Matt. 12:46, 47, R.V., "seeking;" in ZĒTEŌ
Luke 9:9, R.V., "sought." See Endeavour, Go, *Note* (2), (*a*), Inquire, 2212 AG:338D
Require, Seek. (3) *Epizēteō*, to seek earnestly (No. 2, with *epi*, inten- CB:1273C
sive), in Acts 13:7, R.V., "sought;" in Phil. 4:17, R.V., "seek for" EPIZĒTEŌ 1934
(twice). See Inquire, Seek. (4) *Epipotheō*, to long after, to lust; in AG:292D
2 Cor. 5:2, R.V., "longing;" in 1 Thess. 3:6 and 2 Tim. 1:4, R.V., CB:1246B EPIPOTHEŌ
"longing;" in 1 Pet. 2:2, R.V., "long for." See A, Nos. 3, 4. See 1971
Long, Lust. (5) *Exaiteomai*, intensive of No. 9, occurs in Luke 22:31.¶ AG:297D
(6) For *parakaleō*, see Beseech, Exhort, Intreat. (7) For "desirous CB:1246A EXAITEOMAI
of vain glory," see Vainglory. 1809 AG:272A CB:1247B

DESOLATE (Verb and Adjective), DESOLATION PARAKALEŌ 3870

A. Verbs. AG:617A CB:1262A

1. ERĒMOŌ (ἐρημόω) signifies to make desolate, lay waste. From 2049
the primary sense of making quiet comes that of making lonely. It is AG:309B CB:1246B
used only in the Passive Voice in the N.T.; in Rev. 17:16, "shall make
desolate" is, lit., 'shall make her desolated;' in 18:17, 19, "is made
desolate;" in Matt. 12:25 and Luke 11:17, "is brought to desolation."
See Nought (come to).¶ Cp. Desert.

2. MONOŌ (μονόω), to leave alone (akin to *monos*, alone), is used in 3443
1 Tim. 5:5, in the Passive Voice, but translated "desolate," lit., 'was AG:528B CB:—
made desolate' or 'left desolate.'¶

B. Adjectives.

2048 AG:309A CB:1246B 1. ERĒMOS (ἔρημος) is translated "desolate" in the Lord's words against Jerusalem, Matt. 23:38; some mss. have it in Luke 13:35; in reference to the habitation of Judas, Acts 1:20, and to Sarah, from whom, being barren, her husband had turned, Gal. 4:27. See DESERT.

3737 AG:583A CB:1261B 2. ORPHANOS (ὀρφανός) (Eng., orphan; Lat., *orbus*), signifies bereft of parents or of a father. In Jas. 1:27 it is translated "fatherless." It was also used in the general sense of being friendless or desolate. In John 14:18 the Lord uses it of the relationship between Himself and His disciples, He having been their Guide, Teacher and Protector; R.V., "desolate," A.V., "comfortless." Some mss. have the word in Mark 12:40. See FATHERLESS.¶

C. Noun.

2050 AG:309B CB:1246B ERĒMŌSIS (ἐρήμωσις), akin to A, No. 1, denotes desolation, (*a*) in the sense of making desolate, e.g., in the phrase "the abomination of desolation," Matt. 24:15; Mark 13:14; the genitive is objective, 'the abomination that makes desolate;' (*b*) with stress upon the effect of the process, Luke 21:20, with reference to the desolation of Jerusalem.¶

DESPAIR

1820 (-OMAI) AG:273A CB:— 1. EXAPOREŌ (ἐξαπορέω) is used in the N.T. in the Passive Voice, with Middle sense, to be utterly without a way (*ek*, out of, intensive, *a*, negative, *poros*, a way through; cp. *poreuō*, to go through; Eng., 'ferry' is connected), to be quite at a loss, without resource, in despair. It is used in 2 Cor. 1:8, with reference to life; in 4:8, in the sentence "perplexed, yet not unto (A.V. 'in') despair," the word "perplexed" translates the verb *aporeō*, and the phrase "unto despair" translates the intensive form *exaporeō*, a play on the words.¶ In the Sept., Ps. 88:15, where the translation is "having been lifted up, I was brought low and into despair."¶

560 AG:83D CB:1236B 2. APELPIZŌ (ἀπελπίζω), lit., to hope away (*apo*, away from, *elpizō*, to hope), i.e., to give up in despair, to despair, is used in Luke 6:35, R.V., "nothing despairing," i.e., without anxiety as to the result, or not despairing of the recompense from God; this is probably the true meaning; A.V., "hoping for nothing again." The marg., "of no man," is to be rejected.¶

DESPISE, DESPISER

A. Verbs.

1848 AG:277C CB:1247C 1. EXOUTHENEŌ (ἐξουθενέω), to make of no account (*ex*, out, *oudeis*, nobody, alternatively written, *outheis*), to regard as nothing, to despise utterly, to treat with contempt. This is usually translated to set at nought, Luke 18:9, R.V., A.V., "despised." So in Rom. 14:3. Both have "set at nought" in Luke 23:11; Acts 4:11; Rom. 14:10. Both have "despise" in 1 Cor. 16:11; Gal. 4:14, and 1 Thess. 5:20;

in 2 Cor. 10 : 10, R.V., " of no account," for A.V., " contemptible ; " in 1 Cor. 1 : 28, A.V. and R.V., " despised." For the important rendering in 1 Cor. 6 : 4, R.V., see ACCOUNT.¶

Note : In Mark 9 : 12 some mss. have this verb ; the most authentic have the alternative spelling *exoudeneō*, " set at nought."

2. KATAPHRONEŌ (καταφρονέω), lit., to think down upon or against 2706
anyone (*kata*, down, *phrēn*, the mind), hence signifies to think slightly of, AG:420B CB:1254B
to despise, Matt. 6 : 24 ; 18 : 10 ; Luke 16 : 13 ; Rom. 2 : 4 ; 1 Cor. 11 : 22 ; 1 Tim. 4 : 12 ; 6 : 2 ; Heb. 12 : 2 ; 2 Pet. 2 : 10.¶

3. PERIPHRONEŌ (περιφρονέω) lit. denotes to think round a thing, 4065
to turn over in the mind ; hence, to have thoughts beyond, to despise, AG:653B CB:1263B
Tit. 2 : 15.¶

Notes : The following verbs, translated to despise etc. in the A.V., are given suitable meanings in the R.V. : ATHETEŌ
(1) *Atheteō*, lit., to displace, to set aside, R.V., to reject, Luke 10 : 16 ; 114
1 Thess. 4 : 8 ; in 1 Tim. 5 : 12, " rejected," for A.V., " cast off ; " in AG:21A
Heb. 10 : 28, " hath set at nought ; " so Jude 8. See DISANNUL, REJECT, CB:1238A ATIMAZŌ
VOID, No. 2. (2) *Atimazō*, to dishonour (*a*, negative, *timē*, honour) ; 818
in Jas. 2 : 6, R.V., " have dishonoured." See DISHONOUR, ENTREAT, AG:120A CB:1238A
SHAME, C, No. 1, SHAMEFULLY. (3) *Oligōreō*, to care little for, regard OLIGŌREŌ
lightly (*oligos*, little) ; in Heb. 12 : 5, R.V., " regard lightly." See 3643 AG:564A
REGARD.¶ (4) The phrase *logizomai eis ouden* signifies to reckon as CB:1260C
nothing ; in the Passive Voice, to be counted as nothing ; in Acts 19 : 27, LOGIZOMAI 3049
R.V., " be made of no account." AG:475D

B. Adjective.

CB:1257A

ATIMOS (ἄτιμος), without honour, see Note (2), above, is translated 820
as a verb in 1 Cor. 4 : 10, A.V., " are despised ; " R.V., " have dishonour," AG:120B CB:1238B
lit., ' (we are) without honour ; ' " without honour " in Matt. 13 : 57 ; Mark 6 : 4. The comparative degree *atimoteros*, " less honourable," is used in 1 Cor. 12 : 23.¶

Note : *Aphilagathos*, not loving the good (*a*, negative, *phileō*, to love, 865
agathos, good), is used in 2 Tim. 3 : 3, A.V., " despisers of those that are AG:126C CB:—
good," R.V., " no lovers of good."See LOVER.¶

C. Noun.

KATAPHRONĒTĒS (καταφρονητής), lit., one who thinks down against, 2707 (-NTēS)
hence, a despiser (see A, No. 2), is found in Acts 13 : 41.¶ In the Sept., AG:420C CB:1254B
Hab. 1 : 5 ; 2 : 5 and Zeph. 3 : 4.¶

DESPITE, DESPITEFUL, DESPITEFULLY (use)

1. ENUBRIZŌ (ἐνυβρίζω), to treat insultingly, with contumely 1796
(*en*, intensive, *hubrizō*, to insult ; some connect it with *huper*, above, AG:270B CB:—
over, Lat. *super*, which suggests the insulting disdain of one who considers himself superior), is translated " hath done despite " in Heb.
10 : 29.¶ 5195

Notes : (1) *Hubrizō*, to insult, act with insolence, is translated " to AG:831D CB:1251C use despitefully" in Acts 14 : 5, A.V.; R.V., "to entreat . . . shamefully." See (ENTREAT) SHAMEFULLY, (ENTREAT) SPITEFULLY, REPROACH, B, No. 2.

5197 AG:832A CB:1251C (2) The noun *hubristēs*, a violent man, is translated "despiteful" in Rom. 1 : 30, A.V.; R.V., "insolent;" in 1 Tim. 1 : 13, "injurious."¶

1908 AG:285D CB:— 2. EPĒREAZŌ (ἐπηρεάζω), for which see ACCUSE, B, No. 3, is found in some mss. in Matt. 5 : 44, and translated "despitefully use," A.V. (the R.V. follows the mss. which omit the sentence). In the corresponding passage in Luke 6 : 28, the A.V. and R.V. have "despitefully use;" in 1 Pet. 3 : 16, A.V., "falsely accuse," R.V., "revile." See ACCUSE, REVILE.¶

DESTINE See APPOINT

DESTITUTE (be, etc.)

650 AG:99A CB:1237A 1. APOSTEREŌ (ἀποστερέω): see DEFRAUD.

5302 AG:849A CB:1252B 2. HUSTEREŌ (ὑστερέω), primarily, to be behind, to be last, hence, to lack, fail of, come short of, is translated "being destitute" in Heb. 11 : 37. See BEHIND, B, No. 1.

3007 AG:470B CB:1256C 3. LEIPŌ (λείπω) signifies to leave, forsake; in the Passive Voice, to be left, forsaken, destitute; in Jas. 2 : 15, A.V., "destitute," R.V., "be in lack." See LACK, WANT.

DESTROY, DESTROYER, DESTRUCTION, DESTRUCTIVE

A. Verbs.

622 AG:95A CB:1237A 1. APOLLUMI (ἀπόλλυμι), a strengthened form of *ollumi*, signifies to destroy utterly; in Middle Voice, to perish. The idea is not extinction but ruin, loss, not of being, but of well-being. This is clear from its use, as, e.g., of the marring of wine skins, Luke 5 : 37; of lost sheep, i.e., lost to the shepherd, metaphorical of spiritual destitution, Luke 15 : 4, 6, etc.; the lost son, 15 : 24; of the perishing of food, John 6 : 27; of gold, 1 Pet. 1 : 7. So of persons, Matt. 2 : 13, "destroy;" 8 : 25, "perish;" 22 : 7; 27 : 20; of the loss of well-being in the case of the unsaved hereafter, Matt. 10 : 28; Luke 13 : 3, 5; John 3 : 16 (ver. 15 in some mss.); 10 : 28; 17 : 12; Rom. 2 : 12; 1 Cor. 15 : 18; 2 Cor. 2 : 15, "are perishing;" 4 : 3; 2 Thess. 2 : 10; Jas. 4 : 12; 2 Pet. 3 : 9. Cp. B, II, No. 1. See DIE, LOSE, MARRED, PERISH.

2673 AG:417B CB:1254B 2. KATARGEŌ (καταργέω): see ABOLISH.

2507 AG:386C CB:— 3. KATHAIREŌ (καθαιρέω), to cast down, pull down by force, etc., is translated to destroy in Acts 13 : 19. In Acts 19 : 27, A.V., "should be destroyed," the R.V. suitably has "should be deposed." See CAST, No. 13, PULL, PUT, TAKE.

3089 AG:483C CB:1257B 4. LUŌ (λύω), to loose, dissolve, sever, break, demolish, is translated "destroy," in 1 John 3 : 8, of the works of the Devil. See BREAK, A, No. 4.

2647 AG:414B CB:1254A 5. KATALUŌ (καταλύω), *kata*, down, intensive, and No. 4, to destroy utterly, to overthrow completely, is rendered "destroy," in Matt. 5 ; 17, twice, of the Law; Matt. 24 : 2; 26 : 61; 27 : 40; Mark 13 : 2; 14 : 58; 15 : 29; Luke 21 : 6, of the Temple; in Acts 6 : 14, of Jerusalem; in Gal. 2 : 18, of the Law as a means of justification; in Rom. 14 : 20 (A.V., "destroy," R.V., "overthrow"), of the marring of a person's spiritual well-being (in ver. 15 *apollumi*, No. 1, is used in the same sense); in Acts 5 : 38 and 39 (R.V., "overthrow") of the failure of purposes; in 2 Cor. 5 : 1, of the death of the body ("dissolved"). See DISSOLVE, NOUGHT (come to), OVERTHROW, THROW.

For its other meaning, to lodge, see Luke 9 : 12 and 19 : 7. See GUEST, LODGE.¶

6. OLOTHREUŌ (ὀλοθρεύω), to destroy, especially in the sense of 3645
slaying, is found in Heb. 11 : 28, where the R.V. translates the present AG:564B CB:1260C
participle with the article by the noun "destroyer."¶ See B, below. The verb occurs frequently in the Sept., e.g., Ex. 12 : 23; Josh. 3 : 10; 7 : 25; Jer. 2 : 30; 5 : 6; 22 : 7.

7. EXOLOTHREUŌ (ἐξολοθρεύω), *ek*, out of (intensive), and No. 6, 1842
to destroy utterly, to slay wholly, is found in Acts 3 : 23, R.V., "utterly AG:276D (EXOLE-)
destroyed," referring to the destruction of one who would refuse to CB:1247C
hearken to the voice of God through Christ.¶ This verb is far more abun- (EXOLE-)
dantly used in the Sept. than No. 6; it occurs 35 times in Deut.; 34 in
Josh.; 68 in the Psalms. 5351 AG:857B

8. PHTHEIRŌ (φθείρω): see CORRUPT, A, No. 2. CB:1264C

9. DIAPHTHEIRŌ (διαφθείρω); see CORRUPT, A, No. 3. 1311 AG:190C

Note: *Portheō*, to ruin by laying waste, to make havock of, is translated CB:1241B
"destroyed" in Acts 9 : 21, of the attacks upon the church in Jerusalem 4199
by Saul of Tarsus; "wasted," in Gal. 1 : 13, with reference to the same; AG:693A CB:—
"destroyed" in Gal. 1 : 23, where "the faith" is put by metonymy (one thing being put for another associated with it), for those who held the faith. In each of these places the R.V. consistently translates by "made havock of." See HAVOCK, WASTE.¶

B. Nouns.

(I) (*Personal*: *DESTROYER*)

OLOTHREUTĒS (ὀλοθρευτής), akin to A, No. 6, a destroyer, is found 3644 AG:564B
in 1 Cor. 10 : 10.¶ CB:1260C

Note: For the construction in Heb. 11 : 28, "the destroyer," see A, No. 6. Cp. *apolluōn*, in Rev. 9 : 11, the present participle of *apollumi*, A, No. 1, used as a proper noun.¶

(II) (*Abstract*: *DESTRUCTION*)

1. APŌLEIA (ἀπώλεια), akin to A, No. 1, and likewise indicating loss 684
of well-being, not of being, is used (*a*) of things, signifying their waste, AG:103B CB:1237A
or ruin; of ointment, Matt. 26 : 8; Mark 14 : 4; of money, Acts 8 : 20 ("perish"); (*b*) of persons, signifying their spiritual and eternal perdition, Matt. 7 : 13; John 17 : 12; 2 Thess. 2 : 3, where "son of perdition" signifies the proper destiny of the person mentioned; metaphorically of men persistent in evil, Rom. 9 : 22, where "fitted" is in the Middle Voice,

indicating that the vessels of wrath fitted themselves for destruction; of the adversaries of the Lord's people, Phil. 1:28 ("perdition"); of professing Christians, really enemies of the Cross of Christ, Phil. 3:19 (R.V., "perdition"); of those who are subjects of foolish and hurtful lusts, 1 Tim. 6:9 (for the preceding word "destruction" see No. 3, below); of professing Hebrew adherents who shrink back into unbelief, Heb. 10:39; of false teachers, 2 Pet. 2:1, 3; of ungodly men, 3:7; of those who wrest the Scriptures, 3:16; of the Beast, the final head of the revived Roman Empire, Rev. 17:8, 11; (*c*) of impersonal subjects, as heresies, 2 Pet. 2:1, where "destructive heresies" (R.V.; A.V., "damnable") is, lit., 'heresies of destruction' (marg., "sects of perdition"); in ver. 2 the most authentic mss. have *aselgeiais*, "lascivious," instead of *apōleiais*. See PERDITION, PERNICIOUS, WASTE.¶

2506
AG:386B 2. KATHAIRESIS (καθαίρεσις), akin to A, No. 3, a taking down, a
CB:— pulling down, is used three times in 2 Cor., "casting down" in the R.V. in each place; in 10:4 (A.V., "pulling down"); in 10:8 and 13:10 (A.V., "destruction"). See PULL.¶

3639
AG:563B 3. OLETHROS (ὄλεθρος), ruin, destruction, akin to A, No. 6, always
CB:1260C translated "destruction," is used in 1 Cor. 5:5, of the effect upon the physical condition of an erring believer for the purpose of his spiritual profit; in 1 Thess. 5:3 and 2 Thess. 1:9, of the effect of the Divine judgments upon men at the ushering in of the Day of the Lord and the revelation of the Lord Jesus; in 1 Tim. 6:9, of the consequences of the indulgence of the flesh, referring to physical ruin and possibly that of the whole being, the following word *apōleia* (see No. 1) stressing the final, eternal and irrevocable character of the ruin.¶

5356
AG:858A 4. PHTHORA (φθορά), akin to A, No. 8, denotes the destruction that
CB:1264C comes with corruption. In 2 Pet. 2:12 it is used twice; for the A.V., "made to be taken and destroyed . . . shall utterly perish (*phtheirō*) in their own corruption," the R.V. has "to be taken and destroyed (lit., unto capture and destruction, *phthora*) . . . shall in their destroying (*phthora*) surely be destroyed," taking the noun in the last clause in the sense of their act of destroying others. See CORRUPT, CORRUPTION.

4938
AG:793C 5. SUNTRIMMA (σύντριμμα), a breaking in pieces, shattering (the
CB:— corresponding verb is *suntribō*; see under BREAK, BRUISE), hence, ruin, destruction, is compounded of *sun*, together, and *trimma*, a rubbing or wearing away. The latter, and *tribō*, to beat, are derived from a root, signifying to rub, wear away; hence Eng., tribulation and trouble. It is used, metaphorically, of destruction, in Rom. 3:16 (from Isa. 59:7), which, in a passage setting forth the sinful state of mankind in general,
DETACHMENT suggests the wearing process of the effects of cruelty.¶ The word is
See BAND frequent in the Sept., especially in Isaiah and Jeremiah.

2919
AG:451B
DETERMINE, DETERMINATE

CB:1256A 1. KRINŌ (κρίνω), primarily, to separate, hence, to be of opinion, approve, esteem, Rom. 14 : 5, also to determine, resolve, decree, is used in this sense in Acts 3 : 13 ; 20 : 16 ; 25 : 25 ; 27 : 1 ; 1 Cor. 2 : 2 ; 2 Cor. 2 : 1 ; Tit. 3 : 12. See CONDEMN, JUDGE, JUDGMENT, LAW, B, No. 2.

2. HORIZŌ (ὁρίζω) denotes to bound, to set a boundary (Eng., 3724
horizon) ; hence, to mark out definitely, determine ; it is translated AG:580D
to determine in Luke 22 : 22, of the fore-ordained pathway of Christ ; CB:1251B
Acts 11 : 29, of a determination to send relief ; 17 : 26, where it is used of fixing the bounds of seasons. In Acts 2 : 23 the verb is translated "determinate," with reference to counsel. Here the verbal form might have been adhered to by the translation 'determined ;' that is to say, in the sense of 'settled.'

In Rom. 1 : 4 it is translated "declared," where the meaning is that Christ was marked out as the Son of God by His resurrection and that of others (see under DECLARE). In Acts 10 : 42 and 17 : 31 it has its other meaning of ordain, that is, to appoint by determined counsel. In Heb. 4 : 7, it is translated "limiteth," but preferably in the R.V., "defineth," with reference to a certain period ; here again it approaches its primary meaning of marking out the bounds of. See DECLARE, No. 9, LIMIT, ORDAIN.¶

3. PROORIZŌ (προορίζω), *pro*, beforehand, and No. 2, denotes to 4309
mark out beforehand, to determine before, foreordain ; in Acts 4 : 28, AG:709B
A.V., "determined before," R.V., "foreordained ;" so the R.V. in CB:—
1 Cor. 2 : 7, A.V., "ordained ;" in Rom. 8 : 29, 30 and Eph. 1 : 5, 11, A.V., "predestinate," R.V., "foreordain." See ORDAIN, *Note* (1), PREDESTINATE.¶

4. EPILUŌ (ἐπιλύω), lit., to loosen upon, denotes to solve, expound, 1956
Mark 4 : 34 ; to settle, as of a controversy, Acts 19 : 39, A.V., "it shall be AG:295D
determined," R.V., "it shall be settled." See EXPOUND, SETTLE.¶ CB:1246A

5. DIAGINŌSKŌ (διαγινώσκω), besides its meaning to ascertain 1231 AG:182B
exactly, Acts 23 : 15, was an Athenian law term signifying to determine, CB:— 5021
so used in 24 : 22, R.V., "determine ;" A.V., "know the uttermost of."¶ AG:805D

6. TASSŌ (τάσσω) : see APPOINT, No. 5. CB:1271A

Note : Boulomai, to be minded, to purpose, is translated "determined" 1014 AG:146A
in Acts 15 : 37 ; R.V., "was minded." See MINDED, No. 2. CB:1239B

DETESTABLE See ABOMINABLE

DEVICE

1. ENTHUMĒSIS (ἐνθύμησις), a cogitation, an inward reasoning 1761
(generally, evil surmising or supposition), is formed from *en*, in, and AG:266B
thumos, strong feeling, passion (cp. *thumoō*, in the Middle Voice, to be CB:1245B
wroth, furious) ; Eng., fume is akin ; the root, *thu*, signifies to rush, rage. The word is translated "device" in Acts 17 : 29, of man's production of images ; elsewhere, "thoughts," Matt. 9 : 4 ; 12 : 25 ; Heb. 4 : 12, where the accompanying word *ennoia* denotes inward intentions. See THOUGHT.¶

3540 2. NOĒMA (νόημα) denotes thought, that which is thought out (cp.
AG:540D CB:1259C *noeō*, to understand); hence, a purpose, device; translated "devices" in 2 Cor. 2:11; "minds" in 2 Cor. 3:14; 4:4; 11:3; in 2 Cor. 10:5, "thought;" in Phil. 4:7, A.V., "minds," R.V., "thoughts." See MIND, THOUGHT.¶

DEVIL, DEVILISH

DIABOLOS 1228 DIABOLOS (διάβολος), an accuser, a slanderer (from *diaballō*, to
AG:182A accuse, to malign), is one of the names of Satan. From it the English
CB:1241A word "Devil" is derived, and should be applied only to Satan, as a
DAIMōN proper name. *Daimōn*, a demon, is frequently, but wrongly, translated
1142 AG:169D "devil;" it should always be translated "demon," as in the R.V. margin.
CB:1240B There is one Devil, there are many demons. Being the malignant enemy of God and man, he accuses man to God, Job 1:6–11; 2:1–5; Rev. 12:9, 10, and God to man, Gen. 3. He afflicts men with physical sufferings, Acts 10:38. Being himself sinful, 1 John 3:8, he instigated man to sin, Gen. 3, and tempts man to do evil, Eph. 4:27; 6:11, encouraging him thereto by deception, Eph. 2:2. Death having been brought into the world by sin, the Devil had the power of death, but Christ through His own Death, has triumphed over him, and will bring him to nought, Heb. 2:14; his power over death is intimated in his struggle with Michael over the body of Moses, Jude 9. Judas, who gave himself over to the Devil, was so identified with him, that the Lord described him as such, John 6:70 (see 13:2). As the Devil raised himself in pride against God and fell under condemnation, so believers are warned against similar sin, 1 Tim. 3:6; for them he lays snares, ver. 7, seeking to devour them as a roaring lion, 1 Pet. 5:8; those who fall into his snare may be recovered therefrom unto the will of God, 2 Tim. 2:26, "having been taken captive by him (i.e., by the Devil);" "by the Lord's servant" is an alternative, which some regard as confirmed by the use of *zōgreō* (to catch alive) in Luke 5:10; but the general use is that of taking captive in the usual way. If believers resist he will flee from them, Jas. 4:7. His fury and malignity will be especially exercised at the end of the present age, Rev. 12:12. His doom is the lake of fire, Matt. 25:41; Rev. 20:10. The noun is applied to slanderers, false accusers, 1 Tim. 3:11; 2 Tim. 3:3; Tit. 2:3.

Note: For "devilish," Jas. 3:17, see DEMON, C.

DEVISED (cunningly)

4679 SOPHIZŌ (σοφίζω), from *sophos*, wise (connected etymologically with
AG:760B CB:1269B *sophēs*, tasty), in the Active Voice signifies to make wise, 2 Tim. 3:15 (so in the Sept. of Ps. 19:7, e.g., "making babes wise;" in 119:98, "Thou hast made me wiser than mine enemies"). In the Middle Voice it means (*a*) to become wise; it is not used thus in the N.T., but is so found in the Sept., e.g., in Eccles. 2:15, 19; 7:17; (*b*) to play the

sophist, to devise cleverly; it is used with this meaning in the Passive Voice in 2 Pet. 1 : 16, "cunningly devised fables." See WISE.¶

Note: Cp. *katasophizomai*, to deal subtilly. See DEAL WITH, *Note* (2). 2686 AG:418D CB:—

DEVOTION

Note: For this word, in Acts 17 : 23, A.V., which translates ***sebasma***, 4574 AG:745D CB:1268C
"devotions," marg., "gods that ye worship," R.V., "objects of your worship," in 2 Thess. 2 : 4, "that is worshipped," see WORSHIP.¶ Cp. Acts 14 : 15, where, in translating ***mataia***, the A.V. has "vanities," the abstract for the concrete (R.V., "vain things").

DEVOUR

1. ESTHIŌ (ἐσθίω) is a strengthened form of an old verb *edō*, from 2068 AG:312B CB:1246C
the root *ed*—, whence Lat., *edo*, Eng., eat. The form *ephagon*, used as the 2nd Aorist Tense of this verb, is from the root *phag*—, to eat up. It is translated "devour" in Heb. 10 : 27; elsewhere, by the verb to eat. See EAT.

2. KATESTHIŌ and KATAPHAGŌ (κατεσθίω and καταφάγω), ***kata***, 2719 AG:422A CB:—
down, intensive, and No. 1, signifies (*a*) to consume by eating, to devour, said of birds, Matt. 13 : 4; Mark 4 : 4; Luke 8 : 5; of the Dragon, Rev. 12 : 4; of a prophet, eating up a book, suggestive of spiritually eating and digesting its contents, Rev. 10 : 9 (cp. Ezek. 2 : 8; 3 : 1–3; Jer. 15 : 16); (*b*) metaphorically, to squander, to waste, Luke 15 : 30; to consume one's physical powers by emotion, John 2 : 17; to devour by forcible appropriation, as of widows' property, Matt. 23 : 14 (A.V. only); Mark 12 : 40; to demand maintenance, as false apostles did to the church at Corinth, 2 Cor. 11 : 20; to exploit or prey on one another, Gal. 5 : 15, where "bite . . . devour . . . consume" form a climax, the first two describing a process, the last the act of swallowing down; to destroy by fire, Rev. 11 : 5; 20 : 9. See EAT.¶

3. KATAPINŌ (καταπίνω), from *kata*, down, intensive, *pinō*, to drink, 2666 AG:416B CB:1254B
in 1 Pet. 5 : 8 is translated "devour," of Satan's activities against believers. The meaning to swallow is found in Matt. 23 : 24; 1 Cor. 15 : 54; 2 Cor. 2 : 7; 5 : 4; Heb. 11 : 29, R.V. (for A.V., "drowned"); Rev. 12 : 16. See SWALLOW.¶

DEVOUT

1. EULABĒS (εὐλαβής), lit., taking hold well (*eu*, well, *lambanō*, to 2126 AG:322A CB:1247B
take hold), primarily, cautious, signifies in the N.T., careful as to the realization of the presence and claims of God, reverencing God, pious, devout; in Luke 2 : 25 it is said of Simeon; in Acts 2 : 5, of certain Jews; in 8 : 2, of those who bore Stephen's body to burial; of Ananias, 22 : 12 (see No. 2). "In that mingled fear and love which, combined, constitute the piety of man toward God, the Old Testament placed its emphasis on the fear, the New places it on the love (though there was

love in the fear of God's saints then, as there must be fear in their love now)," Trench, Syn., § xlviii.¶

EULABEIA 2124 *Note:* Cp. the noun ***eulabeia***, reverence, and the verb ***eulabeomai***, to
AG:321D reverence.

CB:1247B 2. EUSEBĒS (εὐσεβής), from ***eu***, well, *sebomai*, to reverence, the
EULABEOMAI 2125 root *seb-* signifying sacred awe, describes reverence exhibited especially
AG:321D in actions, reverence or awe well directed. Among the Greeks it was
CB:1247B EUSEBēS used, e.g., of practical piety towards parents. In the N.T. it is used of
2152 a pious attitude towards God, Acts 10 : 2, 7; (in some mss. in 22 : 12);
AG:326B "godly," in 2 Pet. 2 : 9. See GODLY.¶ In the Sept., Prov. 12 : 12;
CB:1247B Is. 24 : 16; 26 : 7; 32 : 8; Mic. 7 : 2.¶

Notes: (1) While *eulabēs* especially suggests the piety which characterizes the inner being, the soul, in its attitude towards God, *eusebēs*
THEOSEBEIA directs us rather to the energy which, directed by holy awe of God, finds
2317 expression in devoted activity.¶

AG:358B CB:1272A (2) Cp. *theosebeia*, and *theosebēs*, which, by their very formation
THEOSEBēS (*theos*, God, and *sebomai*), express reverence towards God. See Trench
2318 AG:358B (§ xlviii).

CB:1272B 3. SEBOMAI (σέβομαι), to feel awe, whether before God or man,
SEBOMAI 4576 to worship, is translated "devout," in Acts 13 : 43, R.V. (A.V.,
AG:746A "religious"); 13 : 50; 17 : 4, 17. See WORSHIP.
CB:1268C

DIADEM

1238 DIADĒMA (διάδημα) is derived from *diadeō*, to bind round. It was
AG:182D CB:1241A the kingly ornament for the head, and especially the blue band marked with white, used to bind on the turban or tiara of Persian kings. It was adopted by Alexander the Great and his successors. Among the Greeks and Romans it was the distinctive badge of royalty. Diocletian was the first Roman Emperor to wear it constantly. The word is found in Rev. 12 : 3; 13 : 1; 19 : 12, in which passages it symbolises the rule respectively of the Dragon, the Beast, and Christ.¶ In the Sept., Esth. 1 : 11; 2 : 17; in some mss. in 6 : 8 and 8 : 15; also in Is. 62 : 3.¶ For the distinction between this and *stephanos*, see CROWN.

DIE, DEAD (to be, become), DYING

2348 1. THNĒSKŌ (θνήσκω), to die (in the perf. tense, to be dead), in the
AG:362C CB:1272B N.T. is always used of physical death, except in 1 Tim. 5 : 6, where it is metaphorically used of the loss of spiritual life. The noun *thanatos*, and the verb *thanatoō* (below) are connected. The root of this group of words probably had the significance of the breathing out of the last breath. Cp. words under DEATH.

599 2. APOTHNĒSKŌ (ἀποθνήσκω), lit., to die off or out, is used (*a*) of
AG:91B CB:1237B the separation of the soul from the body, i.e., the natural death of human beings, e.g., Matt. 9 : 24; Rom. 7 : 2; by reason of descent from Adam, 1 Cor. 15 : 22; or of violent death, whether of men or animals; with

regard to the latter it is once translated "perished," Matt. 8 : 32; of vegetation, Jude 12; of seeds, John 12 : 24; 1 Cor. 15 : 36; it is used of death as a punishment in Israel under the Law, in Heb. 10 : 28; (*b*) of the separation of man from God; all who are descended from Adam not only die physically, owing to sin, see (*a*) above, but are naturally in the state of separation from God, 2 Cor. 5 : 14. From this believers are freed both now and eternally, John 6 : 50; 11 : 26, through the Death of Christ, Rom. 5 : 8, e.g.; unbelievers, who die physically as such, remain in eternal separation from God, John 8 : 24. Believers have spiritually died to the Law as a means of life, Gal. 2 : 19; Col. 2 : 20; to sin, Rom. 6 : 2, and in general to all spiritual association with the world and with that which pertained to their unregenerate state, Col. 3 : 3, because of their identification with the Death of Christ, Rom. 6 : 8 (see No. 3, below). As life never means mere existence, so death, the opposite of life, never means non-existence. See PERISH.

3. SUNAPOTHNĒSKŌ (συναποθνήσκω), to die with, to die together, 4880
is used of association in physical death, Mark 14 : 31; in 2 Cor. 7 : 3, AG:784D CB:1270C
the Apostle declares that his love to the saints makes separation impossible, whether in life or in death. It is used once of association spiritually with Christ in His death, 2 Tim. 2 : 11. See No. 2 (*b*).¶

4. TELEUTAŌ (τελευτάω), to end (from *telos*, an end), hence, to end 5053
one's life, is used (*a*) of the death of the body, Matt. 2 : 19; 9 : 18; 15 : 4, AG:810C CB:1271B
where "die the death" means "surely die," R.V., marg., lit., 'let him end by death;' Mark 7 : 10; Matt. 22 : 25, "deceased;" Luke 7 : 2; John 11 : 39, some mss. have verb No. 1 here; Acts 2 : 29; 7 : 15; Heb. 11 : 22 (R.V., "his end was nigh"); (*b*) of the gnawings of conscience in self reproach, under the symbol of a worm, Mark 9 : 48 (vv. 44 and 46, A.V.). See DECEASE.¶

5. KOIMAŌ (κοιμάω), in the Middle and Passive Voices, its only use 2837
in the N.T., signifies to fall asleep. It is connected etymologically with AG:437C CB:1255B
keimai, to lie down, the root *ki*— signifying to lie. Hence it is used metaphorically of death, Matt. 27 : 52, etc. It is translated "be dead" in 1 Cor. 7 : 39. See ASLEEP.

6. APOGINOMAI (ἀπογίνομαι), lit., to be away from (*apo*, from, 581 (-MENOS)
ginomai, to be, become; *apo* here signifies separation), is used in 1 Pet. AG:89B CB:1236C
2 : 24 of the believer's attitude towards sin as the result of Christ's having borne our sins in His body on the Tree; R.V., "having died unto sins," the aorist or momentary tense, expressing an event in the past.¶

Note: *Apollumi*, to destroy, is found in the Middle Voice in some mss. 622
in John 18 : 14, and translated "die." The most authentic mss. have AG:95A CB:1237A
apothnēskō (No. 2, above).

DIFFER, DIFFERING, DIFFERENT, DIFFERENCE 1308

A. Verbs. AG:190B

1. DIAPHERŌ (διαφέρω), lit., to bear through, carry different ways, CB:—

hence, to be different from, is said of the stars, 1 Cor. 15 : 41 ; of a child under age in comparison with a servant, Gal. 4 : 1 ; in Phil. 1 : 10, marg., " things that differ," for " things that are excellent." See BETTER (be)

3307 2. MERIZŌ (μερίζω) denotes to divide (from *meros*, a part : the root
AG:504C *mer*— indicates distribution, or measuring out, and is seen in *meris*, a
CB:1258B district). In 1 Cor. 7 : 34 the perfect tense of the Passive Voice is translated " there is a difference." Some take the verb with what precedes, with reference to the married brother, and translate " he has been divided." See DEAL, DISTRIBUTE, DIVIDE, GIVE, PART.

1252 3. DIAKRINŌ (διακρίνω), lit., to separate throughout, to make a
AG:185A distinction, Acts 15 : 9, R.V., is translated to make to differ, in 1 Cor.
CB:1241A 4 : 7. In Jude 22, where the Middle Voice is used, the A.V. has " making a difference ; " the R.V., adopting the alternative reading, the accusative case, has " who are in doubt," a meaning found in Matt. 21 : 21 ; Mark 11 : 23 ; Acts 10 : 20 ; Rom. 14 : 23 ; Jas. 1 : 6 ; 2 : 4. See CONTEND.

B. Nouns.

1243 1. DIAIRESIS (διαίρεσις) lit. signifies to take asunder, from *dia*,
AG:183C apart, and *haireō*, to take (Eng., diæresis, i.e., distinguishing two successive
CB:1241A vowels as separate sounds) ; it is rendered in the A.V., " diversities " in 1 Cor. 12 : 4 and 6 ; " differences " in ver. 5 ; R.V., " diversities," in each place.¶

1293 2. DIASTOLĒ (διαστολή) signifies a setting asunder (*dia*, asunder,
AG:188D *stellō*, to set, place, arrange), hence, a distinction ; in Rom. 3 : 22 and
CB:— 10 : 12, A.V., " difference ; " R.V., " distinction ; " in 1 Cor. 14 : 7 it is used of the distinction in musical sounds.¶

C. Adjectives.

1313 1. DIAPHOROS (διάφορος), akin to A, No. 1, signifies varying in
AG:190D kind, different, diverse. It is used of spiritual gifts, Rom. 12 : 6 ; of
CB:— ceremonial washings, Heb. 9 : 10 (" divers "). See DIVERS, and for its other meaning, in Heb. 1 : 4 ; 8 : 6, see EXCELLENT.¶

2087 2. HETEROS (ἕτερος), R.V., " different," for A.V., " another," in
AG:315A Rom. 7 : 23 ; 2 Cor. 11 : 4 ; Gal. 1 : 6 ; cp. 1 Tim. 1 : 3 ; 6 : 3. See
CB:1250A ANOTHER.

DIFFICULTY

3433 MOLIS (μόλις) signifies with difficulty, hardly (from *molos*, toil).
AG:526D In Luke 9 : 39, it is rendered " hardly," of the difficulty in the departure
CB:— of a demon. In Acts 27 : 7, 8, 16, where the A.V. has three different renderings, " scarce," " hardly," and " much work," respectively, the R.V. has " with difficulty " in each place. For its other meanings, scarce, scarcely, see Acts 14 : 18 ; Rom. 5 : 7 ; 1 Pet. 4 : 18. See HARDLY, No. 3.¶

3736
AG:582D
DIG, DIG DOWN

CB:— 1. ORUSSŌ (ὀρύσσω), to dig, dig up soil, dig a pit, is said of a place

for a winepress, Matt. 21 : 33 ; Mark 12 : 1 ; of digging a pit for hiding
something, Matt. 25 : 18.¶

Notes : (1) *Diorussō*, lit., to dig through (*dia*, through), is translated 1358
to break through (or up) in Matt. 6 : 19, 20 ; 24 : 43 ; Luke 12 : 39. See AG:199B CB:1242A
BREAK.¶

(2) *Exorussō*, lit., to dig out, is translated to break up in Mark 2 : 4 ; 1846
to pluck out (the eyes) in Gal. 4 : 15. See BREAK, PLUCK.¶ AG:277C CB:—

2. SKAPTŌ (σκάπτω), primarily, to dig, by way of hollowing out, 4626
hence, denotes to dig. The root *skap* is seen in *skapanē*, a spade, *skapetos*, AG:753B CB:—
a ditch, *skaphē*, a boat, and in Eng., scoop, skiff, and ship (i.e., something KATASKAPTŌ
hollowed out). The verb is found in Luke 6 : 48 ; 13 : 8 ; 16 : 3.¶ 2679

3. KATASKAPTŌ (κατασκάπτω), to dig down (*kata*, down, and No. 2), AG:418B CB:—
is found in Rom. 11 : 3, of altars, and in some mss. in Acts 15 : 16, " ruins," KATASTREPHŌ
lit., ' the things dug down.' Here the best texts have *katastrephō*, to 2690 AG:419A
overthrow, overturn.¶ CB:—

DIGNITY, DIGNITIES

DOXA (δόξα) primarily denotes an opinion, estimation, repute ; in 1391
the N.T., always good opinion, praise, honour, glory, an appearance AG:203C CB:1242B
commanding respect, magnificence, excellence, manifestation of glory ; hence, of angelic powers, in respect of their state as commanding recognition, " dignities," 2 Pet. 2 : 10 ; Jude 8. See GLORY, HONOUR, PRAISE, WORSHIP.

DILIGENCE, DILIGENT, DILIGENTLY

A. Nouns.

1. ERGASIA (ἐργασία), (*a*) lit., a working (akin to *ergon*, work), is 2039
indicative of a process, in contrast to the concrete, *ergon*, e.g., Eph. 4 : 19, AG:307C CB:1246B
lit., ' unto a working ' (R.V. marg., ' to make a trade of ') ; contrast *ergon* in ver. 12 ; (*b*) " business," Acts 19 : 25, R.V. (for A.V., " craft ") ; or gain got by work, Acts 16 : 16, 19 ; 19 : 24 ; (*c*) endeavour, pains, " diligence," Luke 12 : 58. See CRAFT, GAIN, WORK.¶

2. SPOUDĒ (σπουδή), earnestness, zeal, or sometimes the haste 4710
accompanying this, Mark 6 : 25 ; Luke 1 : 39, is translated " diligence " AG:763D CB:1269C
in Rom. 12 : 8 ; in ver. 11, A.V., " business " (R.V., " diligence ") ; in 2 Cor. 8 : 7, A.V., " diligence," R.V., " earnestness ; " both have " diligence " in Heb. 6 : 11 ; 2 Pet. 1 : 5 ; Jude 3 ; in 2 Cor. 7 : 11, 12, R.V., " earnest care," A.V., " carefulness," and " care." See CARE.¶

B. Verbs.

1. SPOUDAZŌ (σπουδάζω) has meanings corresponding to A, No. 2 ; 4704
it signifies to hasten to do a thing, to exert oneself, endeavour, give AG:763C CB:1269C
diligence ; in Gal. 2 : 10, of remembering the poor, A.V., " was forward," R.V., " was zealous ; " in Eph. 4 : 3, of keeping the unity of the Spirit, A.V. " endeavouring," R.V., " giving diligence ; " in 1 Thess. 2 : 17, of going to see friends, " endeavoured ; " in 2 Tim. 4 : 9 ; 4 : 21, " do thy diligence ; " in the following the R.V. uses the verb to give diligence :

2 Tim. 2 : 15, A.V., " study ; " Tit. 3 : 12, A.V., " be diligent ; " Heb. 4 : 11, of keeping continuous Sabbath rest, A.V., " let us labour ; " in 2 Pet. 1 : 10, of making our calling and election sure ; in 2 Pet. 1 : 15, of enabling believers to call Scripture truth to remembrance, A.V., " endeavour ; " in 2 Pet. 3 : 14, of being found in peace without fault and blameless, when the Lord comes, A.V., " be diligent." See ENDEAVOUR, FORWARD, LABOUR, STUDY, ZEALOUS.¶

3191 2. MELETAŌ (μελετάω), signifies to care for, attend carefully (from
AG:500B CB:— *meletē*, care) ; in 1 Tim. 4 : 15, A.V., " meditate," R.V., " be diligent in ; "
in Acts 4 : 25, " imagine " (marg., " meditate ") ; in Mark 13 : 11, the
most authentic mss. have *promerimnaō*. See IMAGINE, MEDITATE.¶

C. Adjectives.

4705 1. SPOUDAIOS (σπουδαῖος), akin to A, No. 2 and B, No. 1, primarily
AG:763C CB:1269C signifies in haste ; hence, diligent, earnest, zealous, 2 Cor. 8 : 22, A.V.,
" diligent," R.V., " earnest." See EARNEST, FORWARD.¶ In the Sept.,
Ezek. 41 : 25, " stout (planks)."¶

4706 2. SPOUDAIOTEROS (σπουδαιότερος), the comparative degree of
AG:763D (-IOS) No. 1, 2 Cor. 8 : 22, A.V., " more diligent," R.V., " more earnest ; " in
CB:1269C ver. 17, A.V., " more forward," R.V., " very earnest." See EARNEST ;
(-IOS) cp. FORWARD.¶

D. Adverbs.

1960 1. EPIMELŌS (ἐπιμελῶς), from *epi*, intensive, and an adverbial form
AG:296A CB:— of the impersonal verb *melei*, it is a care (cp. B, No. 2), signifies carefully,
diligently, Luke 15 : 8.¶

4435 2. PUGMĒ (πυγμῇ), the dative case of *pugmē*, a fist, lit. means ' with
AG:728C CB:1268A the fist ' (one hand being rubbed with the clenched fist of the other), a
metaphorical expression for thoroughly, in contrast to what is superficial ;
Mark 7 : 3, R.V. and A.V. marg., " diligently " (A.V., text, " oft ").
It also signified boxing (not in the N.T.) ; cp. *puktēs* and *pugmachos*, a
boxer (Lat., *pugnus* and *pugno* ; Eng., pugilist).¶ In the Sept., Ex.
21 : 18 ; Is. 58 : 4.¶

4709 3. SPOUDAIŌS (σπουδαίως), speedily, earnestly, diligently (cp. the
AG:763D CB:— corresponding noun, verb and adjective above), is translated " earnestly "
in the R.V. of Luke 7 : 4 (A.V., " instantly ") ; " diligently " in Tit. 3 : 13.
See INSTANTLY.

4708 4. SPOUDAIOTERŌS (σπουδαιοτέρως), the comparative degree of
AG:763D (-IoS 2.) No. 3, " more diligently," is used in Phil. 2 : 28, R.V., " the more
CB:— diligently " (A.V., " the more carefully "). See CAREFULLY.¶

Notes : (1) Some mss. have the neuter of the comparative adjective *spoudaioteron* in 2 Tim. 1 : 17. The most authentic texts have the adverb, No. 4.

199 (2) *Akribōs* (ἀκριβῶς) means accurately, exactly. The A.V. translates
AG:33B CB:— it " diligently " in Matt. 2 : 8 and Acts 18 : 25 ; " perfectly " in 1 Thess.
5 : 2 (cp. Luke 1 : 3). See ACCURATELY, CAREFUL, CIRCUMSPECTLY,
PERFECTLY.

DIMINISHING

HĒTTĒMA (ἥττημα): see Defect. 2275
AG:349C
CB:1250B

DINE, DINNER

A. Verb.

ARISTAŌ (ἀριστάω), primarily, to breakfast (see B), was later used 709
also with the meaning to dine, e.g., Luke 11 : 37 ; in John 21 : 12, 15, AG:106C
R.V., " break your fast," and " had broken their fast," for A.V., " dine ; " CB:—
obviously there it was the first meal in the day.¶ In the Sept., Gen.
43 : 25 ; 1 Sam. 14 : 24 ; 1 Chron. 13 : 7.¶

B. Noun.

ARISTON (ἄριστον), primarily, the first food, taken early in the 712
morning before work ; the meal in the Pharisee's house, in Luke 11 : 37, AG:106D
was a breakfast or early meal (see R.V., marg.) ; the dinner was called CB:—
deipnon. Later the breakfast was called *akratisma* (not in N.T.), and
dinner, *ariston*, as in Matt. 22 : 4 ; Luke 11 : 38 ; 14 : 12.¶

DIP, DIPPED, DIPPETH

1. BAPTŌ (βάπτω), to immerse, dip (derived from a root signifying 911
deep), also signified to dye, which is suggested in Rev. 19 : 13, of the AG:132D
Lord's garment " dipped (i.e., dyed) in blood " (R.V., " sprinkled " trans- CB:1238C
lates the verb *rhantizō* : see Sprinkled. It is elsewhere translated to
dip, Luke 16 : 24 ; John 13 : 26. Cp. the longer form *baptizō* (primarily
a frequentative form). See Baptize.¶

2. EMBAPTŌ (ἐμβάπτω), *en*, in, and No. 1, to dip into, is used of the 1686
act of Judas in dipping his hand with that of Christ in the dish, Matt. AG:254B
26 : 23 ; Mark 14 : 20.¶ CB:—

DIRECT

KATEUTHUNŌ (κατευθύνω), to make straight (*kata*, down, intensive, 2720
euthus, straight, *euthunō*, to straighten), is translated " guide " in Luke AG:422B
1 : 79, of the Lord's guidance of the feet of His people ; " direct," in CB:—
1 Thess. 3 : 11, of His directing the way of His servants ; in 2 Thess.
3 : 5, of His directing the hearts of His saints into the love of God.
See Guide.¶ DISABLED See HALT

DISALLOW

APODOKIMAZŌ (ἀποδοκιμάζω), to reject as the result of disapproval 593
(*apo*, away from, *dokimazō*, to approve), is always translated to reject, AG:90D
except in the A.V. of 1 Pet. 2 : 4 and 7. See Reject. CB:1236C

DISANNUL, DISANNULLING

A. Verbs.

1. ATHETEŌ (ἀθετέω) signifies to put as of no value (*a*, negative, 114 AG:21A
theton, what is placed, from *tithēmi*, to put, place) ; hence, (*a*) to act CB:1238A

towards anything as though it were annulled ; e.g., to deprive a law of its force by opinions or acts contrary to it, Gal. 3 : 15, A.V., " disannulleth," R.V., " maketh void ; " (*b*) to thwart the efficacy of anything, to nullify, to frustrate it, Luke 7 : 30, " rejected ; " 1 Cor. 1 : 19, " will I reject ; " to make void, Gal. 2 : 21 ; to set at nought, Jude 8, R.V. (A.V., " despised ") ; the parallel passage, in 2 Pet. 2 : 10, has *kataphroneō*. In Mark 6 : 26, the thought is that of breaking faith with. See DESPISE, A, Note (1).

208 AG:34B CB:— 2. AKUROŌ (ἀκυρόω), to deprive of authority (*a*, negative, *kuros*, force, authority ; cp. *kurios*, a lord, *kuroō*, to strengthen), hence, to make of none effect, Matt. 15 : 6 ; Mark 7 : 13, with reference to the commandment or word of God, R.V., to make void, is translated " disannul " in Gal. 3 : 17, of the inability of the Law to deprive of force God's covenant with Abraham. This verb stresses the effect of the act, while No. 1 stresses the attitude of the rejector. See VOID.¶

B. Noun.

115 AG:21B CB:1238A ATHETĒSIS (ἀθέτησις), akin to A, No. 1, a setting aside, abolition, is translated " disannulling " in Heb. 7 : 18, with reference to a commandment ; in 9 : 26 " to put away," with reference to sin, lit., ' for a putting away.' See PUTTING, *Note*.¶

DISAPPEAR See PASS

DISBELIEVE

569 AG:85B CB:1236C APISTEŌ (ἀπιστέω), to be unbelieving (*a*, negative, *pistis*, faith ; cp. *apistos*, unbelieving), is translated " believed not," etc. in the A.V. (except in 1 Pet. 2 : 7, " be disobedient ") ; " disbelieve " (or " disbelieved ") in the R.V., in Mark 16 : 11, 16 ; Luke 24 : 11, 41 ; Acts 28 : 24 ; " disbelieve " is the best rendering, implying that the unbeliever has had a full opportunity of believing and has rejected it ; some mss. have *apeitheō*, to be disobedient, in 1 Pet. 2 : 7 ; Rom. 3 : 3, R.V., " were without faith ; " 2 Tim. 2 : 13, R.V., " are faithless." Cp. DISOBEDIENT, C. See BELIEVE.¶

DISCERN, DISCERNER, DISCERNMENT

A. Verbs.

350 AG:56B CB:1235A 1. ANAKRINŌ (ἀνακρίνω), to distinguish, or separate out so as to investigate (*krinō*) by looking throughout (*ana*, intensive) objects or particulars, hence signifies to examine, scrutinize, question, to hold a preliminary judicial examination preceding the trial proper (this first examination, implying more to follow, is often present in the non-legal uses of the word), e.g., Luke 23 : 14 ; figuratively, in 1 Cor. 4 : 3 ; it is said of searching the Scriptures in Acts 17 : 11 ; of discerning or determining the excellence or defects of a person or thing, e.g., 1 Cor. 2 : 14, A.V., " discerned ; " R.V., " judged ; " in 1 Cor. 10 : 27, " asking (no) question " (i.e., not raising the question as to whether the meat is the residue from an idolatrous sacrifice). Except in Luke 23 : 14, this word is found only in Acts and 1 Cor. See EXAMINE, JUDGE.

2. DIAKRINŌ (διακρίνω) signifies to separate, discriminate; then, 1252
to learn by discriminating, to determine, decide. It is translated "dis- AG:185A
cern" in Matt. 16 : 3, of discriminating between the varying conditions of CB:1241A
the sky (see *dokimazō*, No. 3, below, in Luke 12 : 56), and in 1 Cor. 11 : 29, with reference to partaking of the bread and the cup of the Lord's Supper unworthily, by not discerning or discriminating what they represent; in ver. 31, the R.V. has "discerned," for the A.V., "would judge," of trying oneself, discerning one's condition, and so judging any evil before the Lord; in 14 : 29, regarding oral testimony in a gathering of believers, it is used of discerning what is of the Holy Spirit, R.V., "discern" (A.V., "judge"). See CONTEND, DECIDE, DIFFER, etc.

3. DOKIMAZŌ (δοκιμάζω) signifies to test, prove, scrutinize, so as 1381
to decide. It is translated "discern" in the A.V. of Luke 12 : 56; R.V., AG:202C
"interpret" (marg., "prove"). See APPROVE. CB:1242A

B. Noun.

DIAKRISIS (διάκρισις), cp. A, No. 2, a distinguishing, a clear 1253
discrimination, discerning, judging, is translated "discernings" in AG:185B
1 Cor. 12 : 10, of discerning spirits, judging by evidence whether they CB:1241A
are evil or of God. In Heb. 5 : 14 the phrase consisting of *pros*, with this noun, lit., 'towards a discerning,' is translated "to discern," said of those who are capable of discriminating between good and evil. In Rom. 14 : 1 the word has its other sense of decision or judgment, and the phrase "doubtful disputations" is, lit., 'judgments of reasonings' (marg., "not for decisions of doubts," i.e., not to act as a judge of the weak brother's scruples). See DECISION, B, No. 2.¶

Note: For "discernment," Phil. 1 : 19, see JUDGMENT, *Note* (4).

C. Adjective.

KRITIKOS (κριτικός) signifies that which relates to judging (*krinō*, 2924
to judge), fit for, or skilled in, judging (Eng., critical), found in Heb. AG:453D
4 : 12, of the Word of God as "quick to discern the thoughts and intents CB:1256A
of the heart," (lit., 'critical of etc.'), i.e., discriminating and passing judgment on the thoughts and feelings.¶

DISCHARGED

KATARGEŌ (καταργέω) means to reduce to inactivity. "Discharged" 2673
is the R.V. translation of the word in Rom. 7 : 2 and 6 (A.V., "is loosed," AG:417B
and "are delivered"). In ver. 2 the meaning is that the death of a CB:1254B
woman's first husband makes void her status as a wife in the eyes of the Law; she is therefore discharged from the prohibition against remarrying; the prohibition is rendered ineffective in her case. So, in ver. 6, with the believer in relation to the Law, he has been made dead to the Law as a means of justification and life. It is not the Law that has died (A.V.), but the believer (see the R.V.), who has been discharged, through being put to death, as to the old nature, in identification with the Death of Christ, that he might have life in Christ. See ABOLISH.

DISCIPLE

A. Nouns.

3101 AG:485C 1. MATHĒTĒS (μαθητής), lit., a learner (from *manthanō*, to learn,
CB:1258A from a root *math*—, indicating thought accompanied by endeavour), in contrast to *didaskalos*, a teacher; hence it denotes one who follows one's teaching, as the disciples of John, Matt. 9:14; of the Pharisees, Matt. 22:16; of Moses, John 9:28; it is used of the disciples of Jesus (*a*) in a wide sense, of Jews who became His adherents, John 6:66; Luke 6:17, some being secretly so, John 19:38; (*b*) especially of the twelve Apostles, Matt. 10:1; Luke 22:11, e.g.; (*c*) of all who manifest that they are His disciples by abiding in His Word, John 8:31; cp. 13:35; 15:8; (*d*) in the Acts, of those who believed upon Him and confessed Him, 6:1, 2, 7; 14:20, 22, 28; 15:10; 19:1 etc.

A disciple was not only a pupil, but an adherent; hence they are
3102 spoken of as imitators of their teacher; cp. John 8:31; 15:8.
AG:486A 2. MATHĒTRIA (μαθήτρια), a female disciple, is said of Tabitha,
CB:— Acts. 9:36.¶

4827 AG:778B 3. SUMMATHĒTĒS (συμμαθητής) means a fellow-disciple (*sun*, with,
CB:— and No. 1), John 11:16.¶

80 *Note:* In Acts 1:15, the R.V. translates the mss. which have *adelphōn*,
AG:15D CB:1233A "brethren;" in 20:7, R.V., "we," for A.V., "disciples."

B. Verb.

3100 MATHĒTEUŌ (μαθητεύω) is used in the Active Voice, intransitively,
AG:485C CB:1258A in some mss., in Matt. 27:57, in the sense of being the disciple of a person; here, however, the best mss. have the Passive Voice, lit., 'had been made a disciple,' as in Matt. 13:52, R.V., "who hath been made a disciple." It is used in this transitive sense in the Active Voice in 28:19 and Acts 14:21.¶

DISCIPLINE

4995 SŌPHRONISMOS (σωφρονισμός), from *sōphrōn*, lit., saving the mind,
AG:802B CB:— from *saos*, contracted to *sōs*, safe (cp. *sōzō*, to save), *phrēn*, the mind, primarily, an admonishing or calling to soundness of mind, or to self-control, is used in 2 Tim. 1:7, A.V., "a sound mind;" R.V., "discipline." Cp. *sōphroneō* (to be of sound mind), *sōphronizō* (to admonish), *sōphronōs*
DISCLOSE See REVEAL (soberly), and *sōphrōn*, of sound mind. See MIND.¶ Cp. CHASTISEMENT.

DISCOURAGE (-D)

120 ATHUMEŌ (ἀθυμέω), to be disheartened, dispirited, discouraged
AG:21C CB:— (*a*, negative, *thumos*, spirit, courage, from the root *thu*, found in *thuō*, to rush, denoting feeling, passion; hence Eng., fume), is found in Col. 3:21.¶

DISCOURSE

1256 DIALEGOMAI (διαλέγομαι) primarily denotes to ponder, resolve
AG:185C CB:1241A in one's mind (*dia*, through, *legō*, to say); then, to converse, dispute,

discuss, discourse with; most frequently, to reason or dispute with In Heb. 12 : 5 the R.V., "reasoneth with" is to be preferred to the A.V., "speaketh unto." The A.V. translates it "preached," in Acts 20 : 7 and 9; this the R.V. corrects to "discoursed," lit., 'dialogued,' i.e., not by way of a sermon, but by a discourse of a more conversational character. See DISPUTE, PREACH, REASON, SPEAK. In the Sept., Ex. 6 : 27; Judg. 8 : 1; Is. 63 : 1.

DISCOVER

Two verbs are translated by the verb to discover, in the A.V. The R.V. translates differently in each case. 398 AG:63A

1. ANAPHAINŌ (ἀναφαίνω): see APPEAR, A, No. 3. CB:—

2. KATANOEŌ (κατανοέω), to perceive distinctly, discern clearly, 2657
descry, is translated "discovered" in Acts 27 : 39, A.V., of finding a AG:415A CB:1254A
bay with a creek (R.V., "perceived"). See BEHOLD.

DISCREET, DISCREETLY

A. Adjective.

SŌPHRŌN (σώφρων), of sound mind, self-controlled (for the 4998
derivation, see DISCIPLINE), is translated "sober-minded," in its four AG:802C CB:1269B
occurrences in the R.V., 1 Tim. 3 : 2 (A.V., "sober"); Tit. 1 : 8 (A.V., ditto); 2 : 2 (A.V., "temperate"); 2 : 5 (A.V., "discreet"). See SOBER, TEMPERATE.¶

B. Adverb.

NOUNECHŌS (νουνεχῶς), lit., mind-possessing (*nous*, mind, under- 3562
standing, *echō*, to have), hence denotes discreetly, sensibly, prudently. AG:544B CB:—
Mark 12 : 34.¶

DISCUSS See REASON

DISEASE, DISEASED (BE)

A. Nouns.

1. ASTHENEIA (ἀσθένεια), lit., lacking strength (*a*, negative, *sthenos*, 769
strength), weakness, infirmity, is translated "diseases" in Matt. 8 : 17, AG:115A CB:1238A
R.V., for A.V., "sicknesses," and in Acts 28 : 9. Its usual rendering is "infirmity" or "infirmities;" "sickness," in John 11 : 4. Cp. B, No. 1. See INFIRMITY, SICKNESS, WEAKNESS.

2. MALAKIA (μαλακία) primarily denotes softness (cp. *malakos*, soft, 3119
Matt. 11 : 8 etc.); hence, debility, disease. It is found in Matthew only, AG:488C CB:1257C
4 : 23; 9 : 35; 10 : 1.¶ It is frequent in the Sept., e.g., Gen. 42 : 4; 44 : 29; Deut. 7 : 15; 28 : 61; Is. 38 : 9; 53 : 3.

3. NOSOS (νόσος), akin to Lat. *nocere*, to injure (Eng., nosology), is 3554
the regular word for disease, sickness, Matt. 4 : 23; 8 : 17; 9 : 35; AG:543C CB:1260A
10 : 1, R.V., "disease," A.V., "sickness;" in Matt. 4 : 24; Mark 1 : 34; Luke 4 : 40; 6 : 17; 9 : 1; Acts 19 : 12, A.V. and R.V. render it "diseases." In Luke 7 : 21, A.V. has "infirmities." The most authentic mss. omit the word in Mark 3 : 15. See SICKNESS.¶

3553 4. NOSĒMA (νόσημα), an alternative form of No. 3, is found in some
AG:543C mss. in John 5 : 4.¶ Cp. *noseō*, to dote about, have a diseased craving
CB:1260A for, 1 Tim. 6 : 4.¶

B. Verbs.

770 1. ASTHENEŌ (ἀσθενέω), akin to A, No. 1, to lack strength, to be
AG:115B weak, sick, is translated " were diseased " in John 6 : 2, A.V. (R.V.,
CB:1238A " were sick "). See IMPOTENT, SICK, WEAK.

KAKōS 2. ECHŌ KAKŌS (ἔχω κακῶς), lit., to have badly, i.e., to be ill or in
2560 an evil case, is used in Matt. 14 : 35 (A.V., " were diseased," R.V., " were
AG:398C sick ") ; so in Mark 1 : 32 ; Luke 7 : 2. See SICK.¶
CB:1253B

DISFIGURE

853 APHANIZŌ (ἀφανίζω) primarily means to cause to disappear, hence
AG:124C (*a*) to make unsightly, to disfigure, as of the face, Matt. 6 : 16 ; (*b*) to
CB:1236B cause to vanish away, consume, Matt. 6 : 19, 20 ; (*c*) in the Passive Voice,
to perish, Acts 13 : 41, or to vanish away, Jas. 4 : 14. See CONSUME.¶

DISGRACE See REPROACH

DISH

5165 TRUBLION (τρύβλιον) denotes a bowl, somewhat deep, Matt. 26 : 23 ;
AG:828B Mark 14 : 20 ; among the Greeks it was a measure in medical prescrip-
CB:— tions.¶

DISH See PLATTER

DISHONESTY

152 AISCHUNĒ (αἰσχύνη), shame, so the R.V. in 2 Cor. 4 : 2 (for A.V.,
AG:25B " dishonesty "), is elsewhere rendered " shame," Luke 14 : 9 ; Phil. 3 : 19 ;
CB:1234A Heb. 12 : 2 ; Jude 13 ; Rev. 3 : 18. See SHAME.¶

DISHONOUR

A. Noun.

819 ATIMIA (ἀτιμία), from *a*, negative, *timē*, honour, denotes dishonour,
AG:120A ignominy, disgrace, in Rom. 1 : 26, " vile passions " (R.V.), lit., ' passions
CB:1238B of dishonour ; ' in Rom. 9 : 21, " dishonour," of vessels designed for meaner household purposes (in contrast to *timē*, honour, as in 2 Tim. 2 : 20) ; in 1 Cor. 11 : 14, said of long hair, if worn by men, R.V., " dishonour," for A.V., " shame," in contrast to *doxa*, glory, ver. 15 ; so in 1 Cor. 15 : 43, of the " sowing " of the natural body, and in 2 Cor. 6 : 8, of the Apostle Paul's ministry. In 2 Cor. 11 : 21 he uses it in self-disparagement, A.V., " reproach," R.V., " disparagement." See DISPARAGEMENT, REPROACH, SHAME, VILE.¶

B. Adjective.

820 ATIMOS (ἄτιμος), akin to A : see DESPISE, B.
AG:120B
CB:1238B

C. Verbs.

818 1. ATIMAZŌ (ἀτιμάζω) akin to A, signifies to dishonour, treat shame-
AG:120A fully, insult, whether in word, John 8 : 49, or deed, Mark 12 : 4 ; Luke
CB:1238A 20 : 11, R.V., " handled (him) shamefully," (A.V. " entreated . . .

shamefully "); Rom. 1 : 24; 2 : 23, "dishonourest;" Jas. 2 : 6, R.V., "ye have dishonoured (the poor)," (A.V., "despised"); in the Passive Voice, to suffer dishonour, Acts 5 : 41 (A.V., "suffer shame"). See DESPISE, A, Note (2).¶

Note: *Atimaō* is found in some mss. in Mark 12 : 4.

2. KATAISCHUNŌ (καταισχύνω): see ASHAMED, No. 3. 2617 AG:410D CB:1254A

DISMISS (-ED)

APOLUŌ (ἀπολύω), lit., to loose from (*apo*, from, *luō*, to loose), is translated "dismiss" in Acts 15 : 30, 33, R.V. (A.V., "let go") and 19 : 41. See DEPART, DIVORCE, FORGIVE, GO, LIBERTY, LOOSE, PUT, No. 16, RELEASE, SEND. 630 AG:96C CB:1237A

DISOBEDIENCE, DISOBEDIENT

A. Nouns.

1. APEITHEIA (ἀπείθεια), lit., the condition of being unpersuadable (*a*, negative, *peithō*, to persuade), denotes obstinacy, obstinate rejection of the will of God; hence, "disobedience;" Eph. 2 : 2; 5 : 6; Col. 3 : 6, and in the R.V. of Rom. 11 : 30, 32 and Heb. 4 : 6, 11 (for A.V., "unbelief"), speaking of Israel, past and present. See UNBELIEF.¶ 543 AG:82C CB:1236B

2. PARAKOĒ (παρακοή), primarily, hearing amiss (*para*, aside, *akouō*, to hear), hence signifies a refusal to hear; hence, an act of disobedience, Rom. 5 : 19; 2 Cor. 10 : 6; Heb. 2 : 2. It is broadly to be distinguished from No. 1, as an act from a condition, though *parakoē* itself is the effect, in transgression, of the condition of failing or refusing to hear. Carelessness in attitude is the precursor of actual disobedience. In the O.T. disobedience is frequently described as a refusing to hear, e.g., Jer. 11 : 10; 35 : 17; cp. Acts 7 : 57. See Trench, Syn. § lxvi.¶ 3876 AG:618D CB:1262A

B. Adjective.

APEITHĒS (ἀπειθής), akin to A, No. 1, signifies unwilling to be persuaded, spurning belief, disobedient, Luke 1 : 17; Acts 26 : 19; Rom. 1 : 30; 2 Tim. 3 : 2; Tit. 1 : 16; 3 : 3.¶ 545 AG:82D CB:1236B

Note: In 1 Tim. 1 : 9 *anupotaktos*, insubordinate, unsubjected (*a*, negative, *n*, euphonic, *hupo*, under, *tassō*, to order), is translated "disobedient" in the A.V.; the R.V. has "unruly," as in Tit. 1 : 6, 10; in Heb. 2 : 8, "not subject" (R.V.), "not put under" (A.V.). See PUT, UNRULY.¶ 506 AG:76D CB:—

C. Verb.

APEITHEŌ (ἀπειθέω), akin to A, No. 1, and B, to refuse to be persuaded, to refuse belief, to be disobedient, is translated "disobedient," or by the verb to be disobedient, in the R.V. of Acts 14 : 2 (A.V., "unbelieving"), and 19 : 9 (A.V., "believed not"); it is absent from the most authentic mss. in Acts 17 : 5; in John 3 : 36 "obeyeth not," R.V. (A.V., "believeth not"); in Rom. 2 : 8 "obey not;" in 10 : 21, "disobedient;" in 11 : 30, 31, "were disobedient" (A.V., "have not 544 AG:82C CB:1236B believed "); so in 15 : 31; Heb. 3 : 18; 11 : 31; in 1 Pet. 2 : 8, " disobedient; " so in 3 : 20; in 3 : 1 and 4 : 17, " obey not." In 2 : 7 the best mss. have *apisteō*, to disbelieve. See OBEY, B, No. 4, UNBELIEVING.¶

DISORDERLY

A. Adjective.

813 AG:119C CB:— ATAKTOS (ἄτακτος) signifies not keeping order (*a*, negative, *tassō*, to put in order, arrange); it was especially a military term, denoting not keeping rank, insubordinate; it is used in 1 Thess. 5 : 14, describing certain church members who manifested an insubordinate spirit, whether by excitability or officiousness or idleness. See UNRULY.¶

B. Adverb.

814 AG:119D CB:— ATAKTŌS (ἀτάκτως) signifies disorderly, with slackness (like soldiers not keeping rank), 2 Thess. 3 : 6; in ver. 11 it is said of those in the church who refused to work, and became busybodies (cp. 1 Tim. 5 : 13).¶

C. Verb.

812 AG:119C CB:— ATAKTEŌ (ἀτακτέω) signifies to be out of rank, out of one's place, undisciplined, to behave disorderly: in the military sense, to break rank; negatively in 2 Thess. 3 : 7, of the example set by the Apostle and his fellow-missionaries, in working for their bread while they were at Thessalonica so as not to burden the saints. See BEHAVE.¶

DISOWN See DENY

DISPARAGEMENT

819 AG:120A CB:1238B For this R.V. translation of *atimia* in 2 Cor. 11 : 21, see DISHONOUR, A.

DISPENSATION

3622 AG:559C CB:1260B OIKONOMIA (οἰκονομία) primarily signifies the management of a household or of household affairs (*oikos*, a house, *nomos*, a law); then the management or administration of the property of others, and so a stewardship, Luke 16 : 2, 3, 4; elsewhere only in the Epistles of Paul, who applies it (*a*) to the responsibility entrusted to him of preaching the Gospel, 1 Cor. 9 : 17 (R.V., " stewardship," A.V., " dispensation "); (*b*) to the stewardship committed to him " to fulfil the Word of God," the fulfilment being the unfolding of the completion of the Divinely arranged and imparted cycle of truths which are consummated in the truth relating to the Church as the Body of Christ, Col. 1 : 25 (R.V. and A.V., " dispensation "); so in Eph. 3 : 2, of the grace of God given him as a stewardship (" dispensation ") in regard to the same " mystery "; (*c*) in Eph. 1 : 10 and 3 : 9, it is used of the arrangement or administration by God, by which in " the fulness of the times " (or seasons) God will sum up all things in the heavens and on earth in Christ. In Eph. 3 : 9 some mss. have *koinōnia*, " fellowship," for *oikonomia*, " dispensation." In 1 Tim. 1 : 4 *oikonomia* may mean either a stewardship in the sense of (*a*) above, or a dispensation in the sense of (*c*). The reading *oikodomia*,

" edifying," in some mss., is not to be accepted. See STEWARDSHIP.¶

Note: A dispensation is not a period or epoch (a common, but erroneous, use of the word), but a mode of dealing, an arrangement or administration of affairs. Cp. *oikonomos*, a steward, and *oikonomeō*, to be a steward.

DISPERSE, DISPERSION

A. Verbs.

1. DIALUŌ (διαλύω), to dissolve, is used in Acts 5 : 36 of the breaking 1262
up and dispersion of a company of men, R.V., " dispersed," A.V., AG:186B CB:1241B
" scattered." See SCATTER.¶

2. SKORPIZŌ (σκορπίζω), to scatter (probably from a root, *skarp–*, 4650
signifying to cut asunder, akin to *skorpios*, a scorpion), is used in Matt. AG:757A CB:1269B
12 : 30 ; Luke 11 : 23 ; John 10 : 12 ; 16 : 32 ; in the R.V. of 2 Cor. 9 : 9, " scattered abroad " (A.V., " he hath dispersed abroad "), of one who liberally dispenses benefits. See SCATTER.¶

3. DIASKORPIZŌ (διασκορπίζω), *dia*, through, and No. 2, signifies 1287
to scatter abroad, in Matt. 26 : 31 ; Mark 14 : 27, metaphorically of AG:188B CB:1241B
sheep ; in Luke 1 : 51, of the proud ; in John 11 : 52, of the scattering of the children of God ; in Acts 5 : 37, of the followers of Judas of Galilee (A.V., " were dispersed ") ; cp. No. 1, re ver. 36 ; of scattering grain by winnowing, Matt. 25 : 24, 26 ; in Luke 15 : 13 and 16 : 1, it signifies to waste. See SCATTER, STRAWED, WASTE.¶

4. DIASPEIRŌ (διασπείρω), to scatter abroad (*dia*, through, *speirō*, 1289
to sow), is used in Acts 8 : 1, 4 ; 11 : 19.¶ AG:188C CB:1241B

B. Noun.

DIASPORA (διασπορά), akin to A, No. 4, a scattering, a dispersion, 1290
was used of the Jews who from time to time had been scattered among AG:188C CB:1241B
the Gentiles, John 7 : 35 ; later with reference to Jews, so scattered, who had professed, or actually embraced, the Christian faith, " the Dispersion," Jas. 1 : 1, R.V. ; especially of believers who were converts from Judaism and scattered throughout certain districts, " sojourners of the Dispersion," 1 Pet. 1 : 1, R.V.¶ In the Sept., of Israelites, scattered and exiled, e.g., Deut. 28 : 25 ; 30 : 4 ; Neh. 1 : 9.

DISPLAY See SHEW

DISPLEASED

1. AGANAKTEŌ (ἀγανακτέω), from *agan*, much, and *achomai*, to 23
grieve, primarily meant to feel a violent irritation, physically ; it was AG:4B CB:—
used, too, of the fermenting of wine ; hence, metaphorically, to show signs of grief, to be displeased, to be grieved, vexed ; it is translated " sore displeased " in Matt. 21 : 15, A.V. ; " much displeased," in Mark 10 : 14, 41 ; the R.V. always renders it to be moved with, or to have, indignation, as the A.V. elsewhere, Matt. 20 : 24 ; 26 : 8 ; Mark 14 : 4 ; Luke 13 : 14. See INDIGNATION.¶

2. PROSOCHTHIZŌ (προσοχθίζω), to be wroth or displeased with 4360 AG:717D CB:—

(*pros*, toward, or with, *ochtheō*, to be sorely vexed), is used in Heb. 3 : 10, 17 (A.V., "grieved;" R.V., "displeased"). "Grieved" does not adequately express the righteous anger of God intimated in the passage. See GRIEVE.¶

2371 3. THUMOMACHEŌ (θυμομαχέω), lit., to fight with great animosity
AG365B (*thumos*, passion, *machomai*, to fight), hence, to be very angry, to be
CB:— highly displeased, is said of Herod's displeasure with the Tyrians and
Sidonians, Acts 12 : 20.¶

DISPOSED (to be)

1014 1. BOULOMAI (βούλομαι), to wish, to purpose, to will deliberately,
AG:146A indicating a predisposition acting through the deliberate will, is trans-
CB:1239B lated "was disposed" in Acts 18 : 27, A.V. (R.V., "was minded").
It expresses more strongly than *thelō* (No. 2) the deliberate exercise of the will. See DESIRE, B, No. 7.

2309 2. THELŌ (θέλω) means to will; it signifies more especially the
AG:354D natural impulse or volition, and indicates a less formal or deliberate
CB:1271C purpose than No. 1. It is translated "are disposed" in 1 Cor. 10 : 27.
See DESIRE, B, No. 6.

DISPOSITION

1296 DIATAGĒ (διαταγή), an ordinance, e.g., Rom. 13 : 2 (cp. *diatassō*,
AG:189B to appoint, ordain), is rendered "disposition" in Acts 7 : 53; R.V.,
CB:— "as it (the law) was ordained by angels" (marg., "as the ordinance of
angels;" lit., 'unto ordinances of angels'). Angels are mentioned in connection with the giving of the Law of Moses in Deut. 33 : 2. In Gal. 3 : 19 and Heb. 2 : 2 the purpose of the reference to them is to show the superiority of the Gospel to the Law. In Acts 7 : 53 Stephen mentions the angels to stress the majesty of the Law. See ORDAIN, ORDINANCE.¶

DISPUTATION

ZēTēSIS
2214 1. ZĒTĒSIS (ζήτησις) denotes, firstly, a seeking (*zēteō*, to seek),
AG:339B then, a debate, dispute, questioning, Acts 15 : 2, 7 (some texts have
CB:1273C
SUZēTēSIS *suzētēsis*, reasoning, in both verses), R.V., "questioning," for A.V.,
4803 "disputation" and "disputing;" for John 3 : 25; Acts 25 : 20; 1 Tim.
AG:775D
CB:— 1 : 4; 6 : 4; 2 Tim. 2 : 23; Tit. 3 : 9, see QUESTION, QUESTIONING.¶

1261 2. DIALOGISMOS (διαλογισμός) is translated "disputations" in
AG:186A Rom. 14 : 1. See below.
CB:1241B

DISPUTE, DISPUTER, DISPUTING

A. Nouns.

1261 1. DIALOGISMOS (διαλογισμός) denotes, primarily, an inward
AG:186A reasoning, an opinion (*dia*, through, suggesting separation, *logismos*, a
CB:1241B reasoning), e.g., Luke 2 : 35; 5 : 22; 6 : 8; then, a deliberating, questioning, Luke 24 : 38; (more strongly) a disputing, Phil. 2 : 14; 1 Tim. 2 : 8 (A.V., "doubtings"); in Rom. 14 : 1, "disputations;" marg., "(not

for decisions) of doubts" (lit., 'not unto discussions of doubts,' which is perhaps a suitable rendering). Cp. *dialogizomai*, to reason. See DOUBTING, IMAGINATION, REASONING, THOUGHT.

2. LOGOMACHIA (λογομαχία) denotes a dispute about words (*logos*, 3055
a word, *machē*, a fight), or about trivial things, 1 Tim. 6 : 4, R.V., " dis- AG:477A CB:1257A
putes," A.V., " strifes." See STRIFE.¶

3. DIAPARATRIBĒ (διαπαρατριβή) denotes a constant or incessant DIAPARATRIBE
wrangling (*dia*, through, *para*, beside, *tribō*, to wear out, suggesting the —
attrition or wearing effect of contention), 1 Tim. 6 : 5, R.V., " wranglings," AG:187C PARADIATRIBE
A.V., " perverse disputings." Some mss. have the word *paradiatribē*, 3859
in the opposite order of the prefixed prepositions. See WRANGLING.¶ AG:614B

4. ANTILOGIA (ἀντιλογία) denotes a gainsaying, contradiction (*anti*, 485
against, *legō*, to speak), Heb. 6 : 16 (A.V., "strife," R.V., " dispute,"); AG:75A CB:—
7 : 7, a gainsaying (R.V., " dispute ;" A.V., " contradiction "); 12 : 3 (R.V., " gainsaying ;" A.V., " contradiction "); Jude 11 (" gainsaying "). See CONTRADICTION, B.¶

5. SUZĒTĒTĒS (συζητητής), from *sun*, with, *zēteō*, to seek, denotes 4804
a disputer, 1 Cor. 1 : 20, where the reference is especially to a learned AG:775D CB:—
disputant, a sophist.¶

B. Verbs.

1. DIALEGOMAI (διαλέγομαι), akin to A, No. 1, primarily signifies 1256
to think different things with oneself, to ponder ; then, with other AG:185C CB:1241A
persons, to converse, argue, dispute ; it is translated to dispute in Mark 9 : 34 (for ver. 33 see No. 2), the R.V. and A.V. " had disputed " is somewhat unsuitable here, for the delinquency was not that they had wrangled, but that they had reasoned upon the subject at all ; in Acts 17 : 17, A.V. (R.V., " reasoned," as in the A.V. of 18 : 4, 19) ; in 19 : 8, 9 (R.V., " reasoning ") ; in 24 : 12, " disputing ; " in Jude 9, " disputed." See DISCOURSE.

2. DIALOGIZOMAI (διαλογίζομαι), akin to A, No. 1, to bring together 1260
different reasons, to reckon them up, to reason, discuss, in Mark 9 : 33 AG:186A CB:1241B
is translated " ye disputed among yourselves," A.V. ; R.V., " were reasoning." See CAST, No. 15, REASON.

3. SUZĒTEŌ (συζητέω), akin to A, No. 5, lit., to seek or examine 4802
together, signifies to discuss, but is translated to dispute in Acts 6 : 9, AG:775D CB:—
and 9 : 29 ; elsewhere only in Mark and Luke. See INQUIRE, QUESTION, REASON.

DISREPUTE

APELEGMOS (ἀπελεγμός), from *apo*, from, and *elenchō*, to refute, 557
denotes censure, repudiation (of something shown to be worthless), hence, AG:83D CB:—
contempt, " disrepute," Acts 19 : 27, R.V., " (come into) disrepute," for A.V., " (to be) set at nought." It is akin to *apelenchō*, to convict, refute (not in the N.T.), *elenchō*, to convict, *elenxis*, rebuke, and *elegmos*, reproof. See NOUGHT.¶

For DISSEMBLE see DISSIMULATION

DISSENSION

4714 STASIS (στάσις), akin to *histēmi*, to stand, denotes (*a*) a standing,
AG:764C CB:1270A stability, Heb. 9 : 8, " (while as the first tabernacle) is yet standing ; " (*b*) an insurrection, uproar, Mark 15 : 7 ; Luke 23 : 19, 25 ; Acts 19 : 40 ; 24 : 5 ; (*c*) a dissension, Acts 15 : 2 ; 23 : 7, 10. See INSURRECTION, SEDITION, STANDING, UPROAR.¶

DISSIMULATION, DISSEMBLE

A. Noun.

5272 HUPOKRISIS (ὑπόκρισις), primarily, a reply, came to mean the acting
AG:845A CB:1252B of a stage-player, because such answered one another in dialogue ; hence the meaning dissembling or pretence. It is translated " dissimulation " in Gal. 2 : 13 (see B). See HYPOCRISY.

B. Verb.

4942 SUNUPOKRINOMAI (συνυποκρίνομαι), *sun*, with, *hupokrinomai*, akin
AG:793D CB:— to A, to join in acting the hypocrite, in pretending to act from one motive, whereas another motive really inspires the act. So in Gal. 2 : 13, Peter with other believing Jews, in separating from believing Gentiles at Antioch, pretended that the motive was loyalty to the Law of Moses, whereas really it was fear of the Judaizers.¶

C. Adjective.

505 ANUPOKRITOS (ἀνυπόκριτος), from *a*, negative, *n*, euphonic, and an
AG:76D CB:— adjectival form corresponding to A, signifies unfeigned ; it is said of love, 2 Cor. 6 : 6 ; 1 Pet. 1 : 22 ; Rom. 12 : 9, A.V., " without dissimulation," R.V., " without hypocrisy ; " of faith, 1 Tim. 1 : 5 ; 2 Tim. 1 : 5, " unfeigned ; " of the wisdom that is from above, Jas. 3 : 17, " without hypocrisy." See HYPOCRISY.¶

DISSOLVE

3089 1. LUŌ (λύω), to loose, is used of the future demolition of the elements
AG:483C CB:1257B or heavenly bodies, 2 Pet. 3 : 10, 11, 12 ; in ver. 10, A.V., " shall melt," R.V., " shall be dissolved ; " in verses 11, 12, A.V. and R.V., " dissolved." See BREAK.

2647 AG:414B CB:1254A 2. KATALUŌ (καταλύω) : see DESTROY, A, No. 5.

DISTORT See PERVERT

For DISTINCTION (*diastolē*) see DIFFERENCE

DISTRACTION (without)

563 APERISPASTŌS (ἀπερισπάστως), from *a*, negative, *perispaō*, to draw
AG:84B CB:— around, draw away, distract (for which see CUMBER), is found in 1 Cor. 7 : 35.¶

DISTRESS, DISTRESSED

A. Nouns.

1. ANANKĒ (ἀνάγκη) denotes (*a*) a necessity, imposed whether by ANANKē
external circumstances, e.g., Luke 23 : 17, or inward pressure, e.g., 318 AG:52B
1 Cor. 9 : 16 ; (*b*) straits, distress, Luke 21 : 23 (in ver. 25, " distress " CB:1235B
translates No. 3) ; 1 Cor. 7 : 26 ; 1 Thess. 3 : 7 ; the last two refer to the STENOCHōRIA 4730
lack of material things. See NECESSARY, NECESSITY, NEEDS. AG:766C

2. STENOCHŌRIA (στενοχωρία) : see ANGUISH. CB:1270A SUNOCHē

3. SUNOCHĒ (συνοχή) : see ANGUISH. 4928

4. THLIPSIS (θλῖψις) : see AFFLICTION, B, No. 5. AG:791D THLIPSIS

B. Verbs. 2347

1. BASANIZŌ (βασανίζω), properly signifies to test by rubbing on AG:362B CB:1272B
the touchstone (*basanos*, a touchstone), then, to question by applying 928
torture ; hence to vex, torment ; in the Passive Voice, to be harassed, AG:134C
distressed ; it is said of men struggling in a boat against wind and waves, CB:1238C
Matt. 14 : 24, R.V., " distressed " (A.V., " tossed ") ; Mark 6 : 48, R.V.,
" distressed " (A.V., " toiling "). See PAIN, TOIL, TORMENT, VEX.

2. SKULLŌ (σκύλλω) primarily signifies to skin, to flay ; then to rend, 4660
mangle ; hence, to vex, trouble, annoy ; it is found in the most authentic AG:758B
mss. in Matt. 9 : 36, R.V., " distressed " (of the multitudes who applied CB:—
to the Lord for healing) ; A.V., " fainted," translating the alternative
reading, *ekluō*, lit., to loosen out. It is also used in Mark 5 : 35 ; Luke
7 : 6 ; 8 : 49. See TROUBLE.¶ 4729

3. STENOCHŌREŌ (στενοχωρέω) : see ANGUISH. AG:766C CB:1270A

4. KATAPONEŌ (καταπονέω), primarily, to tire down with toil, 2669
exhaust with labour (*kata*, down, *ponos*, labour), hence signifies to afflict, AG:416D
oppress ; in the Passive Voice, to be oppressed, much distressed ; it is CB:—
translated " oppressed " in Acts 7 : 24, and " sore distressed " in 2 Pet. 2 : 7, R.V., (A.V., " vexed "). See OPPRESS, VEX.¶

DISTRIBUTE, DISTRIBUTION

A. Verbs.

1. DIADIDŌMI (διαδίδωμι), lit., to give through, (*dia*, through, 1239
didōmi, to give), as from one to another, to deal out, is said of distributing AG:182D CB:—
to the poor, Luke 18 : 22 ; Acts 4 : 35, " distribution was made," or to a company of people, John 6 : 11. It is translated " divideth " in Luke 11 : 22. In Rev. 17 : 13 the most authentic mss. have the verb *didōmi*, to give, instead of the longer form.¶

2. MERIZŌ (μερίζω) is translated " hath distributed " in 1 Cor. 7 : 17, 3307
and in the A.V. of 2 Cor. 10 : 13, where, however, this rendering is un- AG:504C CB:1258B
suitable, as it is not a case of distributing among a number, but apportioning a measure to the Apostle and his co-workers ; hence the R.V., " apportioned." See DIFFER, A, No. 2.

Note : Koinōneō, to share in common with, is translated " distributing " 2841 AG:438C
in Rom. 12 : 13, A.V. The verb does not mean to distribute ; hence CB:1255B

2842 AG:438D R.V., "communicating." Similarly *koinōnia*, fellowship, communion,
CB:1255B is translated "distribution" in 2 Cor. 9 : 13, A.V.; R.V., "contribution."

B. Adjective.

2130 AG:323A EUMETADOTOS (εὐμετάδοτος), ready to impart (*eu*, well, *meta*,
CB:— with, *didōmi*, to give: see A, No. 1), is used in 1 Tim. 6 : 18, "ready to
distribute."¶

DISTRICT

3310 MERIS (μερίς) denotes a part (akin to *merizō*, DISTRIBUTE, A., No. 2),
AG:505A CB:1258B Luke 10 : 42; Acts 8 : 21; 2 Cor. 6 : 15; Col. 1 : 12 (lit., 'unto the
part,' or share, of the inheritance). In Acts 16 : 12 the R.V. translates it
DISTURB See TROUBLE "district," with reference to Macedonia. See PART.¶

DITCH

999 BOTHUNOS (βόθυνος), any kind of deep hole or pit (probably con-
AG:144D CB:— nected with *bathos*, deep), is translated "ditch" in the A.V. of Matt. 15 : 14
and Luke 6 : 39, R.V., "pit" in each place, as in both Versions of Matt.
12 : 11. See PIT.¶

DIVERS

A. Adjectives.

1313 AG:190D 1. DIAPHOROS (διάφορος) is rendered "divers" in Heb. 9 : 10.
CB:— See DIFFER, C.

4164 AG:683C 2. POIKILOS (ποικίλος) denotes parti-coloured, variegated (*poikillō*
CB:— means to make gay: the root of the first syllable is *pik*—, found in
Eng., picture), hence "divers," Matt. 4 : 24; Mark 1 : 34; Luke 4 : 40;
2 Tim. 3 : 6; Tit. 3 : 3; Heb. 2 : 4 (R.V., "manifold"); 13 : 9; Jas. 1 : 2
(R.V., "manifold"); in 1 Pet. 1 : 6 and 4 : 10, "manifold," both A.V.
4182 and R.V. See MANIFOLD.¶

AG:687B *Notes:* (1) Cp. *polupoikilos*, Eph. 3 : 10, "manifold" (lit., 'much
CB:— varied').

5100 AG:819D (2) The pronoun *tines*, "some" (the plural of *tis*, someone), is trans-
CB:1272C lated "divers" in the A.V. of Mark 8 : 3 and Acts 19 : 9; R.V., "some."

(3) In 1 Cor. 12 : 28, *genos*, in the plural, is rendered "divers kinds."
See DIVERSITIES.

B. Adverb.

4187 AG:690A POLUTROPŌS (πολυτρόπως) means in many ways (*polus*, much,
CB:— *tropos*, a manner, way; Eng., trope), "in divers manners," Heb. 1 : 1.¶

KATA *Note:* The phrase *kata topous*, lit., throughout places (*kata*, down,
2596 AG:405C or throughout, in a distributive sense, *topos*, a place), is translated "in
CB:1253C divers places," in Matt. 24 : 7; Mark 13 : 8 and Luke 21 : 11.

DIVERSITY, DIVERSITIES

1243 AG:183C DIAIRESIS (διαίρεσις): See DIFFER, B, No. 1.

CB:1241A *Note: Genos*, a kind, class, sort (Eng., genus), is translated "diver-
1085 AG:156A sities" in the A.V. of 1 Cor. 12 : 28 (marg., "kinds"); R.V., "divers
CB:1248B kinds."

DIVIDE, DIVIDER, DIVIDING

A. Verbs.

1. APHORIZŌ (ἀφορίζω), lit., to mark off by boundaries or limits 873
(*apo*, from, *horizō*, to determine, mark out), denotes to separate ; " divi- AG:127B CB:1236C
deth," Matt. 25 : 32, A.V. ; R.V., " separateth," as in the preceding part
of the verse. See SEPARATE, SEVER.

2. DIAIREŌ (διαιρέω), lit., to take asunder (see DIFFER, B, No. 1), 1244
to divide into parts, to distribute, is found in Luke 15 : 12 and 1 Cor. AG:183D CB:—
12 : 11.¶ 1239

3. DIADIDŌMI (διαδίδωμι) : see DISTRIBUTE, A, No. 1. AG:182D

4. DIAKRINŌ (διακρίνω), to separate, discriminate, hence, to be at 1252
variance with oneself, to be divided in one's mind, is rendered " divided " AG:185A CB:1241A
in Jas. 2 : 4, R.V. ; A.V., " partial." See DISCERN.

5. GINOMAI (γίνομαι), to become, is translated " was divided " in 1096 AG:158A
Rev. 16 : 19 (of " the great city "), lit., ' became into three parts.' CB:1248B

6. MERIZŌ (μερίζω), akin to *meros*, a part, to part, divide into, in 3307
the Middle Voice means to divide anything with another, to share with. AG:504C CB:1258B
The usual meaning is to divide, Matt. 12 : 25, 26 ; Mark 3 : 24, 25, 26 ;
6 : 41 ; Luke 12 : 13 (Middle Voice) ; Rom. 12 : 3, " hath dealt ; "
1 Cor. 1 : 13 ; Heb. 7 : 2, R.V. (A.V., " gave a part "). Elsewhere with
other meanings, 1 Cor. 7 : 17, 34 ; 2 Cor. 10 : 13. See DEAL, DIFFER,
A, No. 2, DISTRIBUTE, A, No. 2, GIVE.¶

7. DIAMERIZŌ (διαμερίζω), *dia*, through, and No. 6, to divide 1266
through, i.e., completely, to divide up, is translated to divide in Luke AG:186D CB:—
11 : 17, 18 ; 12 : 52, 53 ; 22 : 17 ; " parted " in Matt. 27 : 35 ; Mark
15 : 24 ; Luke 23 : 34 ; John 19 : 24 ; Acts 2 : 45 ; in Acts 2 : 3, A.V.,
" cloven," R.V., " parting asunder." See CLOVEN.¶

8. ORTHOTOMEŌ (ὀρθοτομέω), lit., to cut straight (*orthos*, straight, 3718
temnō, to cut), is found in 2 Tim. 2 : 15, A.V., " rightly dividing," R.V., AG:580B CB:1261B
" handling aright " (the word of truth) ; the meaning passed from the
idea of cutting or dividing, to the more general sense of rightly dealing
with a thing. What is intended here is not dividing Scripture from
Scripture, but teaching Scripture accurately.¶ In the Sept., of directing
one's paths, Prov. 3 : 6 and 11 : 5 (" righteousness traces out blameless
paths ").¶

Note : In Acts 13 : 19, the A.V., " He divided their land . . . by KATAKLĒRODOTEŌ 2624
lot," represents the verb *kataklērodoteō*, from *kata*, suggesting distribution, AG:411D
klēros, a lot, *didōmi*, to give. The most authentic mss. have *kataklēro-* CB:—
nomeō, to distribute, as an inheritance, from *klēronomia*, an inheritance ; SCHIZŌ 4977
hence R.V., " He gave them their land for an inheritance."¶ For *schizō*, AG:797B
Acts 14 : 4 ; 23 : 7, see BREAK, No. 12. CB:1268C

B. Nouns.

3312 AG:505D

1. MERISTĒS (μεριστής), a divider, is found in Luke 12 : 14.¶ CB:—

2. MERISMOS (μερισμός), akin to No. 1, primarily denotes a division, 3311 AG:505C
partition (*meros*, a part) ; hence, (*a*) a distribution, Heb. 2 : 4, " gifts " CB:—

(marg. of R.V., "distributions"); (*b*) a dividing or separation, Heb. 4 : 12, "dividing" (A.V., "dividing asunder"). Some take this in the Active sense, "as far as the cleaving asunder or separation of soul and spirit;" others in the Passive sense, "as far as the division (i.e., the dividing line) between soul and spirit," i.e., where one differs from the other. The former seems more in keeping with the meaning of the word. See GIFT.¶

DIVINATION

4436 PUTHŌN (πύθων), Eng., python, in Greek mythology was the name
AG:728D CB:1268A of the Pythian serpent or dragon, dwelling in Pytho, at the foot of mount
Parnassus, guarding the oracle of Delphi, and slain by Apollo. Thence the name was transferred to Apollo himself. Later the word was applied to diviners or soothsayers, regarded as inspired by Apollo. Since demons are the agents inspiring idolatry, 1 Cor. 10 : 20, the young woman in Acts 16 : 16 was possessed by a demon instigating the cult of Apollo, and thus had "a spirit of divination."¶

DIVINE

A. Adjective.

2304 THEIOS (θεῖος), divine (from *theos*, God), is used of the power of God,
AG:353D CB:1271C 2 Pet. 1 : 3, and of His nature, ver. 4, in each place, as that which proceeds
from Himself. In Acts 17 : 29 it is used as a noun with the definite article, to denote "the Godhead," the Deity (i.e., the one true God). This word, instead of *theos*, was purposely used by the Apostle in speaking to Greeks on Mars Hill, as in accordance with Greek usage. Cp. DIVINITY.¶ In the Sept., Ex. 31 : 3; 35 : 31; Job 27 : 3; 33 : 4; Prov. 2 : 17.¶

B. Noun.

2999 LATREIA (λατρεία), akin to *latreuō*, to serve, primarily, any service
AG:467B CB:1256C for hire, denotes in Scripture the service of God according to the require-
ments of the Levitical Law, Rom. 9 : 4; Heb. 9 : 1, 6, "Divine service." It is used in the more general sense of service to God, in John 16 : 2; Rom. 12 : 1. See SERVICE.¶

DIVINITY

THEIOTēS THEIOTĒS (θειότης), divinity, the R.V. rendering in Rom. 1 : 20
2305 AG:354A (A.V., "Godhead"), is derived from *theios* (see DIVINE, A), and is to
CB:1271C be distinguished from *theotēs*, in Col. 2 : 9, "Godhead." In Rom. 1 : 20
THEOTēS 2320 the Apostle "is declaring how much of God may be known from the
AG:358C revelation of Himself which He has made in nature, from those vestiges
CB:1272B of Himself which men may everywhere trace in the world around them.
Yet it is not the personal God whom any man may learn to know by these aids; He can be known only by the revelation of Himself in His Son; . . . But in the second passage (Col. 2 : 9), Paul is declaring that in the Son there dwells all the fulness of absolute Godhead; they were

no mere rays of Divine glory which gilded Him, lighting up His Person for a season and with a splendour not His own; but He was, and is, absolute and perfect God; and the Apostle uses *theotēs* to express this essential and personal Godhead of the Son" (Trench, Syn. § ii). *Theotēs* indicates the Divine essence of Godhood, the Personality of God; *theiotēs*, the attributes of God, His Divine nature and properties. See GODHEAD.¶

DIVISION

1. DIAMERISMOS (διαμερισμός), primarily, a parting, distribution, 1267
denotes a discussion, dissension, division or discord, breaking up as of AG:186D CB:1241B
family ties (*dia*, asunder, *meros*, a part), it is found in Luke 12:51, where it is contrasted with *eirēnē*, peace. Cp. DIVIDE, A, No. 7.

2. DICHOSTASIA (διχοστασία), lit., a standing apart (*dichē*, asunder, 1370
apart, *stasis*, a standing; the root *di*— indicating division, is found in AG:200B CB:1241B
many words in various languages), is used in Rom. 16:17, where believers are enjoined to mark those who cause division and to turn away from them; and in Gal. 5:20, R.V. (A.V., "seditions"), where divisions are spoken of as "works of the flesh." Some mss. have this noun in 1 Cor. 3:3.¶

3. SCHISMA (σχίσμα), Eng., schism, denotes a cleft, a rent, Matt. 4978
9:16; Mark 2:21; then, metaphorically, a division, dissension, John AG:797C CB:1268C
7:43; 9:16; 10:19; 1 Cor. 1:10; 11:18; in 1 Cor. 12:25 it is translated "schism" (marg., "division"). The root is *skid*—, seen in the corresponding verb *schizō*, to cleave (Lat. *scindo*). See SCHISM. Cp. *hairesis*, a sect.¶

DIVORCE, DIVORCEMENT

A. Verb.

APOLUŌ (ἀπολύω), to let loose from, let go free (*apo*, from, *luō*, to 630
loose), is translated "is divorced" in the A.V. of Matt. 5:32 (R.V., AG:96C CB:1237A
"is put away"); it is further used of divorce in Matt. 1:19; 19:3, 7–9; Mark 10:2, 4, 11; Luke 16:18. The Lord also used it of the case of a wife putting away her husband, Mark 10:12, a usage among Greeks and Romans, not among Jews. See DISMISS.

B. Noun.

APOSTASION (ἀποστάσιον), primarily, a defection, lit., a standing off 647
(*apo*, from, *stasis*, a standing; cp. *aphistēmi*, to cause to withdraw), AG:98B CB:1237A
denotes, in the N.T., a writing or bill of divorcement, Matt. 5:31; 19:7; Mark 10:4.¶ In Sept., Deut. 24:3; Isa. 50:1; Jer. 3:8.¶

DO, DONE

In English the verb to do serves the purpose of a large number of verbs, and has a large variety of meanings. It therefore translates a considerable number of Greek verbs. These, with their specific meanings, are as follows:

4160 AG:680D CB:1265C 1. POIEŌ (ποιέω) signifies (*a*) to make, (*b*) to do, i.e., to adopt a way of expressing by act the thoughts and feelings. It stands for a number of such acts, chiefly to make, produce, create, cause, e.g., Matt. 17 : 4. See ABIDE, APPOINT, BEAR, BRING, CAUSE, COMMIT, CONTINUE, DEAL, EXECUTE, EXERCISE, FULFIL, GAIN, GIVE, HOLD, KEEP, MAKE, MEAN, OBSERVE, ORDAIN, PERFORM, PROVIDE, PURPOSE, PUT, SHEW, SHOOT FORTH, SPEND, TAKE, TARRY, WORK, YIELD.

4238 AG:698B CB:1266B 2. PRASSŌ (πράσσω) signifies to practise, though this is not always to be pressed. The Apostle John, in his Epistles, uses the continuous tenses of *poieō*, to indicate a practice, the habit of doing something, e.g., 1 John 3 : 4 (the A.V., " committeth " and " commit " in 1 John 3 : 8 and 9, e.g., is wrong ; " doeth," R.V., in the sense of practising, is the meaning). He uses *prassō* twice in the Gospel, 3 : 20 and 5 : 29. The Apostle Paul uses *prassō* in the sense of practising, and the R.V. so renders the word in Rom. 1 : 32 ; 2 : 2, instead of A.V., " commit," though, strangely enough, the R.V. translates it " committed," instead of " practised," in 2 Cor. 12 : 21.

Generally speaking, in Paul's Epistles *poieō* denotes an action complete in itself, while *prassō* denotes a habit. The difference is seen in Rom. 1 : 32, R.V. Again, *poieō* stresses the accomplishment, e.g., " perform," in Rom. 4 : 21 ; *prassō* stresses the process leading to the accomplishment, e.g., " doer," in 2 : 25. In Rom. 2 : 3 he who does, *poieō*, the things mentioned, is warned against judging those who practise them, *prassō*.

The distinction in John 3 : 20, 21 is noticeable : " Every one that doeth (*prassō*, practiseth) ill . . . he that doeth (*poieō*) the truth." While we cannot draw the regular distinction, that *prassō* speaks of doing evil things, and *poieō* of doing good things, yet very often " where the words assume an ethical tinge, there is a tendency to use the verbs with this distinction " (Trench, Syn., § xcvi). See COMMIT, EXACT, KEEP, REQUIRE, USE.

1096 AG:158A CB:1248B 3. GINOMAI (γίνομαι), to become, is sometimes translated " do " or " done," e.g., Luke 4 : 23, " done (at Capernaum)," followed by *poieō* in the next clause. In Matt. 21 : 42 and Mark 12 : 11, this verb is translated, in the A.V., " (the Lord's) doing ; " R.V., " this was from the Lord." See BECOME.

2038 AG:306D CB:1246C 4. ERGAZOMAI (ἐργάζομαι) denotes to work (*ergon*, work). In Gal. 6 : 10 the R.V. renders it " let us work," for A.V., " let us do ; " in 3 John 5, " thou doest." See COMMIT, LABOUR, MINISTER, TRADE, WORK.

2716 AG:421C CB:— 5. KATERGAZOMAI (κατεργάζομαι), *kata* (intensive), is a more emphatic verb than No. 4. In Rom. 2 : 9 the R.V. has " worketh " for A.V., " doeth." In Rom. 7 : 15, 17, both translate it " I do " (R.V. marg., " work ") ; so in ver. 20, " I that do." In 1 Cor. 5 : 3 the R.V. has " wrought," for A.V., " done." In Eph. 6 : 13 both render it " having done (all) ; " more suitably, ' having wrought (all) ; ' the A.V. marg.

" having overcome " does not give the correct meaning. See CAUSE, B, Note (2), PERFORM, WORK, WROUGHT.

6. ISCHUŌ (ἰσχύω) signifies to be strong, to prevail. It is translated 2480
" I can do," in Phil. 4 : 13. See ABLE, etc. AG:383D CB:1253A

7. PARECHŌ (παρέχω) lit. means to hold near (*para*, beside, and 3930
echō, to have), i.e., to present, offer, supply. It is translated " do for " in AG:626B
Luke 7 : 4. See BRING, No. 21. CB:—

Notes: (1) In Phil. 2 : 13 *energeō*, to work, is translated " to do," A.V.; ENERGEō
R.V., " to work." (2) In Luke 13 : 32 *apoteleō*, to complete, perform, is 1754 AG:265B
translated " I . . . do," A.V.; R.V., " I perform " (some mss. have CB:1245A
epiteleō here). (3) In Acts 15 : 36, *echō*, to have, to hold, sometimes used APOTELEō 658
to express the condition in which a person is, how he is faring, is translated AG:100D
" (how) they do," A.V.; R.V., " how they fare." It is often used of a EPITELEō 2005
physical condition, e.g., Matt. 4 : 24 (see SICK). (4) In Acts 25 : 9 AG:302B
katatithēmi, to deposit, or lay up, for future use, to lay up favour for one- CB:1246A (-ESTHAI)
self with a person, is translated " to do (the Jews a pleasure)," A.V.; ECHō
R.V., " to gain (favour with the Jews)." (5) In John 16 : 2 *prospherō*, 2192
to bring near, offer, present, is translated " doeth (service)," A.V.; AG:331D CB:1242C
R.V., " offereth (service)." (6) In Heb. 4 : 13 the phrase *hēmin ho logos*, KATATITHēMI
rendered " (with whom) we have to do," is, lit., ' (with whom is) the 2698 AG:419C
account to us.' (7) In 1 Cor. 13 : 10, *katargeō*, to render inactive, abolish, PROSPHERō
so is translated " shall be done away ;" 2 Cor, 3 : 7, A.V., " was to be 4374 AG:719C
done away," R.V., " was passing away ;" ver. 11. See ABOLISH, DE- CB:1267B
STROY. (8) For " done aforetime," Rom. 3 : 25, R.V., see PAST. For LOGOS 3056
" did," 2 Tim. 4 : 14, A.V., see SHEW, No. 3. For " do good " see GOOD. AG:477A

CB:1257A KATARGEō 2673

For DOING see DEED, No. 3, DO, No. 3 AG:417B CB:1254B

DOCTOR

1. DIDASKALOS (διδάσκαλος), a teacher (from *didaskō*, to teach), 1320
cp. *didaskalia*, teaching, doctrine, instruction, is translated " doctors," AG:191C CB:1241B
with reference to the teachers of the Jewish religion, Luke 2 : 46. Cp. *paideutēs*, a teacher. See MASTER, TEACHER.

2. NOMODIDASKALOS (νομοδιδάσκαλος), a teacher of the Law 3547
(*nomos*, a law, and No. 1), with reference to the teachers of the Mosaic AG:541D CB:1260A
Law, is used in the same sense as No. 1, Luke 5 : 17; Acts 5 : 34; also of those who went about among Christians, professing to be instructors of the Law, 1 Tim. 1 : 7. See TEACHER.¶ See under LAW.

DOCTRINE

1. DIDACHĒ (διδαχή), akin to No. 1, under DOCTOR, denotes teaching, 1322
either (*a*) that which is taught, e.g., Matt. 7 : 28, A.V., " doctrine," R.V., AG:192B CB:1241B
" teaching ; " Tit. 1 : 9, R.V.; Rev. 2 : 14, 15, 24, or (*b*) the act of teaching, instruction, e.g., Mark 4 : 2, A.V., " doctrine," R.V.,

" teaching ; " the R.V. has " the doctrine " in Rom. 16 : 17. See Note (1) below.

1319 AG:191C CB:1241B 2. DIDASKALIA (διδασκαλία) denotes, as No. 1 (from which, however, it is to be distinguished), (*a*) that which is taught, doctrine, Matt. 15 : 9 ; Mark 7 : 7 ; Eph. 4 : 14 ; Col. 2 : 22 ; 1 Tim. 1 : 10 ; 4 : 1, 6 ; 6 : 1, 3 ; 2 Tim. 4 : 3 ; Tit. 1 : 9 (" doctrine," in last part of verse : see also No. 1) ; 2 : 1, 10 ; (*b*) teaching, instruction, Rom. 12 : 7, " teaching ; " 15 : 4, " learning ; " 1 Tim. 4 : 13, A.V., " doctrine," R.V., " teaching ; " ver. 16, A.V., " the doctrine," R.V., (correctly) " thy teaching ; " 5 : 17, A.V., " doctrine," R.V. " teaching ; " 2 Tim. 3 : 10, 16 (ditto) ; Tit. 2 : 7, " thy doctrine." Cp. No. 1, under DOCTOR. See LEARNING.¶

Notes : (1) Whereas *didachē* is used only twice in the Pastoral Epistles, 2 Tim. 4 : 2, and Tit. 1 : 9, *didaskalia* occurs fifteen times. Both are used in the active and passive senses (i.e., the act of teaching and what is taught), the passive is predominant in *didachē*, the active in *didaskalia ;* the former stresses the authority, the latter the act (Cremer). Apart from the Apostle Paul, other writers make use of *didachē* only, save in Matt. 15 : 9 and Mark 7 : 7 (*didaskalia*).

3056 AG:477A CB:1257A (2) In Heb. 6 : 1, *logos*, a word, is translated " doctrine," A.V. ; the R.V. margin gives the lit. rendering, " the word (of the beginning of Christ)," and, in the text, " the (first) principles (of Christ)."

DOER

4163 AG:683B CB:1265C POIĒTĒS (ποιητής), akin to *poieō*, see DO, No. 1, signifies a doer, Rom. 2 : 13 ; Jas. 1 : 22, 23, 25 ; 4 : 11. Its meaning " poet " is found in Acts 17 : 28.¶

Notes : (1) For *prassō*, rendered " doer " in Rom. 2 : 25, see DO, No. 2.

2557 AG:398B CB:1253B (2) In 2 Tim. 2 : 9, *kakourgos* is rendered " evil doer " (R.V., " malefactor ").

DOG

2965 AG:461B CB:1256B 1. KUŌN (κύων) is used in two senses, (*a*) natural, Matt. 7 : 6 ; Luke 16 : 21 ; 2 Pet. 2 : 22, (*b*) metaphorical, Phil. 3 : 2 ; Rev. 22 : 15, of those whose moral impurity will exclude them from the New Jerusalem. The Jews used the term of Gentiles, under the idea of ceremonial impurity. Among the Greeks it was an epithet of impudence. Lat., *canis*, and Eng., hound are etymologically akin to it.¶

2952 AG:457D CB:1256B 2. KUNARION (κυνάριον), a diminutive of No. 1, a little dog, a puppy, is used in Matt. 15 : 26, 27 ; Mark 7 : 27, 28.¶

DOMINION (have . . . over)

A. Nouns.

2904 AG:449A CB:1256A 1. KRATOS (κράτος), force, strength, might, more especially manifested power, is derived from a root *kra*—, to perfect, to complete : " creator " is probably connected. It also signifies dominion, and is so rendered frequently in doxologies, 1 Pet. 4 : 11 ; 5 : 11 ; Jude 25 ; Rev. 1 : 6 ; 5 : 13 (R.V.) ; in 1 Tim. 6 : 16, and Heb. 2 : 14 it is translated "power." See MIGHT, POWER, STRENGTH.

Note : Synonymous words are ***bia***, force, often oppressive, ***dunamis***, BIA 970
power, especially inherent power ; ***energeia***, power especially in exercise, AG:140C
operative power ; ***exousia***, primarily liberty of action, then authority CB:1239A DUNAMIS
either delegated or arbitrary ; ***ischus***, strength, especially physical, power 1411
as an endowment. AG:207B CB:1242B

2. KURIOTĒS (κυριότης) denotes lordship (*kurios*, a lord), power, ENERGEIA
dominion, whether angelic or human, Eph. 1 : 21 ; Col. 1 : 16 ; 2 Pet. 1753 AG:265A
2 : 10 (R.V., for A.V., "government") ; Jude 8. In Eph. and Col. CB:1245A
it indicates a grade in the angelic orders, in which it stands second.¶ EXOUSIA 1849

B. Verbs. AG:277D

1. KURIEUŌ (κυριεύω), to be lord over, rule over, have dominion CB:1247C ISCHUS
over (akin to A, No. 2), is used of (*a*) Divine authority over men, Rom. 2479
14 : 9, "might be Lord ;" (*b*) human authority over men, Luke 22 : 25, AG:383C CB:1253A
"lordship," 1 Tim. 6 : 15, "lords" (R.V., marg., "them that rule as KURIOTĒS
lords") ; (*c*) the permanent immunity of Christ from the dominion of 2963
death, Rom. 6 : 9 ; (*d*) the deliverance of the believer from the dominion AG:460D CB:1256B
of sin, Rom. 6 : 14 ; (*e*) the dominion of law over men, Rom. 7 : 1 ; (*f*) KURIEUŌ
the dominion of a person over the faith of other believers, 2 Cor. 1 : 24 2961 AG:458D
(R.V., "lordship"). See LORD.¶ CB:1256B

2. KATAKURIEUŌ (κατακυριεύω), *kata*, down (intensive), and No. 1, 2634
to exercise, or gain, dominion over, to lord it over, is used of (*a*) the AG:412C CB:1254A
lordship of Gentile rulers, Matt. 20 : 25, A.V., "exercise dominion," R.V., "lord it ;" Mark 10 : 42, A.V., "exercise lordship," R.V., "lord it ;" (*b*) the power of demons over men, Acts 19 : 16, A.V., "overcame," R.V., "mastered ;" (*c*) of the evil of elders in lording it over the saints under their spiritual care, 1 Pet. 5 : 3. See LORDSHIP, OVERCOME.

Note : For ***authenteō***, to have dominion, 1 Tim. 2 : 12, R.V., see 831
AUTHORITY, No. 3. AG:121A CB:1238B (-TEIN)

DOOMED

For R.V. in 1 Cor. 4 : 9, see APPOINT (Note at end), DEATH, B. DONKEY See ASS

DOOR

THURA (θύρα), a door, gate (Eng., door is connected), is used (*a*) 2374
literally, e.g., Matt. 6 : 6 ; 27 : 60 ; (*b*) metaphorically, of Christ, John AG:365D CB:1272C
10 : 7, 9 ; of faith, by acceptance of the Gospel, Acts 14 : 27 ; of openings for preaching and teaching the Word of God, 1 Cor. 16 : 9 ; 2 Cor. 2 : 12 ; Col. 4 : 3 ; Rev. 3 : 8 ; of entrance into the Kingdom of God, Matt. 25 : 10 ; Luke 13 : 24, 25 ; of Christ's entrance into a repentant believer's heart, Rev. 3 : 20 ; of the nearness of Christ's Second Advent, Matt. 24 : 33 ; Mark 13 : 29 ; cp. Jas. 5 : 9 ; of access to behold visions relative to the purposes of God, Rev. 4 : 1.

2377 AG:366A CB:— *Note :* For the phrase " that kept the door," *thurōros*, John 18 : 16, 17 (" porter " in Mark 13 : 34 ; John 10 : 3), see PORTER.¶

DOTE

3552 AG:543C CB:1260A NOSEŌ (νοσέω) signifies to be ill, to be ailing, whether in body or mind ; hence, to be taken with such a morbid interest in a thing as is tantamount to a disease, to dote, 1 Tim. 6 : 4 (marg., " sick "). The primary meaning of dote is to be foolish (cp. Jer. 50 : 36), the evident meaning of *noseō*, in this respect, is to be unsound.¶

DOUBLE

A. Adjective.

1362 AG:199C CB:1242A DIPLOUS (διπλοῦς) denotes twofold, double, 1 Tim. 5 : 17 ; Rev. 18 : 6 (twice).¶ The comparative degree *diploteron* (neuter) is used adverbially in Matt. 23 : 15, " twofold more."¶

B. Verb.

1363 AG:199D CB:— DIPLOŌ (διπλόω) signifies to double, to repay or render twofold, Rev. 18 : 6.¶

DOUBLE-EDGED See TWO-EDGED

DOUBLE-MINDED

1374 AG:201A CB:1242A DIPSUCHOS (δίψυχος) lit. means two-souled (*dis*, twice, *psuchē*, a soul), hence, double-minded, Jas. 1 : 8 ; 4 : 8.¶

DOUBLE-TONGUED

1351 AG:198D CB:— DILOGOS (δίλογος) primarily means saying the same thing twice, or given to repetition (*dis*, twice, *logos*, a word, or speech) ; hence, saying a thing to one person and giving a different view of it to another, double-tongued, 1 Tim. 3 : 8.¶

DOUBT (be in, make to), DOUBTFUL, DOUBTING

A. Verbs.

639 AG:97C CB:— 1. APOREŌ (ἀπορέω), always used in the Middle Voice, lit. means to be without a way (*a*, negative, *poros*, a way, transit), to be without resources, embarrassed, in doubt, perplexity, at a loss, as was Herod regarding John the Baptist, Mark 6 : 20 (R.V., following the most authentic mss., " was much perplexed ") ; as the disciples were, regarding the Lord's betrayal, John 13 : 22, " doubting ; " and regarding the absence of His body from the tomb, Luke 24 : 4, " were perplexed ; " as was Festus, about the nature of the accusations brought against Paul, Acts 25 : 20, A.V. " doubted," R.V., " being perplexed ; " as Paul was, in his experiences of trial, 2 Cor. 4 : 8, " perplexed," and, as to the attitude of the believers of the churches in Galatia towards Judaistic errors, Gal. 4 : 20, A.V., " I stand in doubt," R.V., " I am perplexed." Perplexity is the main idea. See PERPLEX.¶ Cp. the noun *aporia*, " distress," Luke 21 : 25.¶

2. DIAPOREŌ (διαπορέω), *dia*, asunder (intensive), and No. 1, signi- 1280
fies to be thoroughly perplexed, with a perplexity amounting to despair, AG:187D CB:—
Acts 2 : 12 ; 5 : 24 and 10 : 17, A.V., "were in doubt," "doubted," R.V., "were (was) perplexed." See also Luke 9 : 7 (some mss. have it in Luke 24 : 4, where the most authentic have No. 1). See PERPLEX.¶

3. DIAKRINŌ (διακρίνω) : see CONTEND and DIFFER, A, No. 2 ; 1252
in Acts 11 : 12, A.V., "nothing doubting," R.V., "making no distinc- AG:185A CB:1241A
tion ;" in Jude 22, R.V., "who are in doubt" (A.V., "making a difference," R.V., marg., "while they dispute") ; in Jas. 1 : 6, A.V., "wavereth," R.V., "doubteth." This verb suggests, not so much weakness of faith, as lack of it (contrast, Nos. 4 and 5).

4. DISTAZŌ (διστάζω), to stand in two ways (*dis*, double, *stasis*, a 1365
standing), implying uncertainty which way to take, is used in Matt. AG:200A CB:1242A
14 : 31 and 28 : 17 ; said of believers whose faith is small. Cp. No. 5.¶

5. METEŌRIZŌ (μετεωρίζω), from *meteōros* (Eng., meteor), signifying 3349
in mid air, raised on high, was primarily used of putting a ship out to sea, AG:514A (-OMAI)
or of raising fortifications, or of the rising of the wind. In the Sept., CB:—
it is used, e.g., in Micah 4 : 1, of the exaltation of the Lord's house ; in Ezek. 10 : 16, of the lifting up of the wings of the cherubim ; in Obad. 4, of the mounting up of the eagle ; in the N.T. metaphorically, of being anxious, through a distracted state of mind, of wavering between hope and fear, Luke 12 : 29, "neither be ye of doubtful mind" (A.V., marg., "live not in careful suspense"), addressed to those who have little faith. Cp. No. 4. The interpretation "do not exalt yourselves" is not in keeping with the context.¶

6. PSUCHĒN AIRŌ (ψυχὴν αἴρω), lit., to raise the breath, or to lift PSUCHē
the soul, signifies to hold in suspense, R.V. of John 10 : 24 (A.V., "make 5590 AG:893B
us to doubt"), suggestive of "an objective suspense due to lack of light" CB:1267C
(Warfield), through a failure of their expectations, rather than, subjectively, AIRō 142
through unbelief. The meaning may thus be, 'How long dost Thou raise AG:24B
our expectations without satisfying them ?' CB:1234A

B. Noun.

DIALOGISMOS (διαλογισμός) expresses reasoning or questioning 1261
hesitation, 1 Tim. 2 : 8. See DISPUTE, A, No. 1. AG:186A CB:1241B

Note : For A.V., "doubtful" in Rom. 14 : 1 see DECISION, B, No. 2. DOUGH See LUMP

DOUBT (No), DOUBTLESS

PANTOS 3843

PANTŌS (πάντως) : see ALTOGETHER, B. AG:609B CB:—

Notes : (1) In 2 Cor. 12 : 1 the best texts have no word representing ARA
"doubtless." (2) In Luke 11 : 20, the particle *ara*, A.V., "no doubt," 686
means "then" (R.V.). (3) In 1 Cor. 9 : 10 the conjunction *gar*, A.V., AG:103D CB:1237B
"no doubt," here means "assuredly," or "yea" (R.V.). (4) In Phil. GAR 1063
3 : 8, the opening phrase means "yea, verily," as R.V. (5) In 1 Cor. 9 : 2, AG:151C
the R.V., "at least," gives the right sense (not "doubtless," A.V.) CB:1248A

DOVE, TURTLE-DOVE

4058 AG:651D CB:1263C 1. PERISTERA (περιστερά) denotes a dove or pigeon, Matt. 3 : 16; 10 : 16 (indicating its proverbial harmlessness); 21 : 12; Mark 1 : 10; 11 : 15; Luke 2 : 24 ("pigeons"); 3 : 22; John 1 : 32; 2 : 14, 16.¶

5167 AG:828B CB:— 2. TRUGŌN (τρυγών) denotes a turtle-dove (from *truzō*, to murmur, to coo), Luke 2 : 24.¶

DOWN : see Note †, p. 1

DRAG

4951 AG:794C CB:— 1. SURŌ (σύρω), to draw, drag, haul, is used of a net, John 21 : 8; of violently dragging persons along, Acts 8 : 3, "haling;" 14 : 19, R.V., "dragged," A.V., "drew;" 17 : 6 (ditto); Rev. 12 : 4, A.V., "drew," R.V., "draweth." See DRAW, HALE.¶

2694 AG:419B CB:— *Note:* Cp. the strengthened form *katasurō*, to hale, used in Luke 12 : 58.¶

1670 AG:251C CB:— 2. HELKUŌ (or HELKŌ) (ἑλκύω or ἕλκω), to draw, differs from *surō*, as drawing does from violent dragging. It is used of drawing a net, John 21 : 6, 11 (cp. No. 1, in ver. 8); Trench remarks, "At vv. 6 and 11 *helkō* (or *helkuō*) is used; for there a *drawing* of the net to a certain point is intended; by the disciples to themselves in the ship, by Peter to himself upon the shore. But at ver. 8 *helkō* gives place to *surō:* for nothing is there intended but the *dragging* of the net, which had been fastened to the ship, after it through the water" (Syn., § xxi).

This less violent significance, usually present in *helkō*, but always absent from *surō*, is seen in the metaphorical use of *helkō*, to signify drawing by inward power, by Divine impulse, John 6 : 44; 12 : 32. So in the Sept., e.g., S. of S., 1 : 4, and Jer. 31 : 3, "with lovingkindness have I drawn thee." It is used of a more vigorous action, in John 18 : 10, of drawing a sword; in Acts 16 : 19; 21 : 30, of forcibly drawing men to or from a place; so in Jas. 2 : 6, A.V., "draw," R.V., "drag." See DRAW.¶

DRAGON

1404 AG:206B CB:1242B DRAKŌN (δράκων) denoted a mythical monster, a dragon; also a large serpent, so called because of its keen power of sight (from a root *derk*—, signifying to see). Twelve times in the Apocalypse it is used of the Devil, 12 : 3, 4, 7, 9, 13, 16, 17; 13 : 2, 4, 11; 16 : 13; 20 : 2.¶

For DRANK see DRINK

DRAUGHT

61 AG:13A CB:— 1. AGRA (ἄγρα), a hunting, catching (from *agō*, to lead), is used only in connection with fishing. In Luke 5 : 4 it signifies the act of catching fish; in ver. 9 it stands for the catch itself.¶

2. APHEDRŌN (ἀφεδρών), a latrine, a sink, drain, is found in Matt. 856 AG:124D
15 : 17 and Mark 7 : 19.¶ CB:—

For DRAVE and DROVE see DRIVE

DRAW (Away, Back, Nigh, On, Out, Up)

(*A*) *In the sense of dragging, pulling, or attracting :*

1. ANABIBAZŌ (ἀναβιβάζω), a causal form of *anabainō*, to go up, 307
denotes, lit., to make go up, cause to ascend (*ana*, up, *bibazō*, to cause to AG:50D
mount), hence, to draw a boat up on land, Matt. 13 : 48.¶ CB:—

2. HELKŌ (ἕλκω) is translated to draw in the A.V., of Acts 21 : 30 1670 AG:251C
and Jas. 2 : 6 ; see DRAG, No. 2. CB:—

3. SURŌ (σύρω) : see DRAG, No. 1.

4. SPAŌ (σπάω), to draw or pull, is used, in the Middle Voice, of 4685 AG:761A
drawing a sword from its sheath, Mark 14 : 47 ; Acts 16 : 27.¶ CB:—

5. ANASPAŌ (ἀνασπάω), *ana*, up, and No. 4, to draw up, is used of 385 AG:60B
drawing up an animal out of a pit, Luke 14 : 5 (R.V., " draw up ; " A.V., CB:—
" pull out "), and of the drawing up of the sheet into heaven, in the vision
in Acts 11 : 10.¶

6. APOSPAŌ (ἀποσπάω), *apo*, from, and No. 4, to draw away, lit., 645 AG:98A
to wrench away from, is used of a sword, Matt. 26 : 51 ; of drawing away CB:—
disciples into error, Acts 20 : 30 ; of Christ's withdrawal from the disciples,
in Gethsemane, Luke 22 : 41, A.V., " was withdrawn," R.V., " was parted "
(or ' was reft away from them ') ; of parting from a company, Acts 21 : 1
(A.V., " were gotten," R.V., " were parted "). See GET, PART.¶

7. ANTLEŌ (ἀντλέω) signified, primarily, to draw out a ship's bilge- 501 AG:76C
water, to bale or pump out (from *antlos*, bilge-water), hence, to draw CB:—
water in any way (*ana*, up, and a root, *tel*—, to lift, bear), John 2 : 8, 9 ;
4 : 7, 15.¶

Note : In John 4 : 11, " to draw with " translates the corresponding 502 AG:76C
noun *antlēma*, a bucket for drawing water by a rope.¶ CB:—

8. EXELKŌ (ἐξέλκω), *ek*, out of, and No. 2, to draw away, or lure 1828 AG:274A
forth, is used metaphorically in Jas. 1 : 14, of being drawn away by lust. CB:—
As in hunting or fishing the game is lured from its haunt, so man's lust
allures him from the safety of his self-restraint.¶

9. ANATASSOMAI (ἀνατάσσομαι), to arrange in order, is used in 392
Luke 1 : 1 ; R.V., " to draw up " (some interpret the word to mean to AG:61D CB:1235B
bring together from memory assisted by the Holy Spirit).¶

(*B*) *In the sense of approaching or withdrawing :*

1. ENGIZŌ (ἐγγίζω), to come near, draw nigh (akin to *engus*, near), 1448
is translated by the verb draw near or nigh, in the R.V., Luke 12 : 33, AG:213C CB:1245A
A.V., " approacheth ; " Heb. 10 : 25, A.V., " approaching ; " Luke
18 : 35 ; 19 : 29, 37 ; Acts 22 : 6, A.V., " was come nigh ; " Luke 7 : 12, 4334
" came nigh ; " Acts 9 : 3, " came near " See APPROACH. AG:713A

2. PROSERCHOMAI (προσέρχομαι) is translated " draw near " in CB:1267A

Heb. 4 : 16 ; 7 : 25, R.V., and 10 : 22, A.V. and R.V. ; in Acts 7 : 31,
' drew near." See COME, GO.

4317 AG:711B 3. PROSAGŌ (προσάγω), used transitively, to bring to ; intransitively,
CB:— to draw near, is so rendered in Acts 27 : 27. See BRING.

5288 AG:847B 4. HUPOSTELLŌ (ὑποστέλλω), to draw back, withdraw, perhaps a
CB:— metaphor from lowering a sail and so slackening the course, and
HUPOSTOLē hence of being remiss in holding the truth ; in the Active Voice,
5289 AG:847C rendered " drew back " in Gal. 2 : 12, R.V. (A.V., " withdrew ") ; in the
CB:1252B Middle, in Heb. 10 : 38, " shrink back " R.V. (A.V., " draw back ") ; the
prefix *hupo*, underneath, is here suggestive of stealth. In verse 39 the
corresponding noun, *hupostolē*, is translated " of them that shrink back,"
R.V. ; A.V., " draw back " (lit., ' of shrinking back '). In Acts 20 : 20, 27,
" shrank," R.V. See KEEP, *Note* (6), SHRINK, SHUN, WITHDRAW.¶

5. APHISTĒMI (ἀφίστημι) : see DEPART, A, No. 20.

1096 AG:158A 6. GINOMAI (γίνομαι), to become, begin to be, is translated " drawing
CB:1248B nigh," in John 6 : 19. See BECOME.

2020 AG:304D 7. EPIPHŌSKŌ (ἐπιφώσκω), to dawn (lit., to make to shine upon),
CB:— is said of the approach of the Sabbath, Luke 23 : 54 (marg., " began to
dawn ") ; cp. Matt. 28 : 1.¶ See DAWN, A, No. 3.

4358 AG:717D *Notes :* (1) In Mark 6 : 53, *prosormizō*, to bring a ship (or boat) to
CB:— anchor, cast anchor, land at a place (*pros*, to, *hormizō*, to moor, bring to
anchorage), is translated " moored to the shore," in the R.V., for A.V.,
" drew."¶

4264 AG:703C (2) In Acts 19 : 33, where the most authentic mss. have *sumbibazō*,
CB:— the R.V. translates it " brought " (marg., " instructed "), A.V., " draw
out." Some mss. have *probibazō*, to bring or drag forward. See BRING,
No. 24.

DREAM (noun and verb), DREAMER

A. Nouns.

3677 AG:569D 1. ONAR (ὄναρ) is a vision in sleep, in distinction from a waking
CB:1260C vision, Matt. 1 : 20 ; 2 : 12, 13, 19, 22 ; 27 : 19.¶

1798 AG:270C 2. ENUPNION (ἐνύπνιον), is, lit., what appears in sleep (*en*, in, *hupnos*,
CB:1245B sleep), an ordinary dream, Acts 2 : 17. For synonymous nouns see
VISION.¶

B. Verb.

(-OMAI) ENUPNIAZŌ (ἐνυπνιάζω), akin to A, No. 2, is used in Acts 2 : 17,
1797 AG:270B in the Passive Voice, in a phrase (according to the most authentic mss.)
CB:1245B which means ' shall be given up to dream by dreams,' translated " shall
dream dreams ; " metaphorically in Jude 8, of being given over to sensuous
" dreamings," R.V., A.V., " dreamers," and so defiling the flesh.¶

DRESSED

1090 AG:157B *Note :* This is the A.V. translation of the Passive of *geōrgeō*, Heb. 6 : 7,
CB:— to till the ground, to practise as a farmer ; R.V., " is tilled." See TILL.¶

DRESSER

Note: For *ampelourgos,* "dresser," Luke 13 : 7, A.V. (R.V., "vine- 289 AG:47A
dresser"), see VINEDRESSER. CB:1234C

---

for DRIED see DRY, B

DRIFT

PARARHEŌ (παραρέω), lit., to flow past, glide by (*para,* by, *rheō,* to 3901 (-RRHUEō)
flow), is used in Heb. 2 : 1, where the significance is to find oneself AG:621D
flowing or passing by, without giving due heed to a thing, here "the CB:1262B
things that were heard," or perhaps the salvation of which they spoke ; hence the R.V., "lest haply we drift away from them," for A.V., "let them slip." The A.V. marg. "run out as leaking vessels," does not give the meaning.¶ In the Sept., Prov. 3 : 21 ; Isa. 44 : 4.¶

DRINK (-ETH, -ER, -ING), DRANK

A. Nouns.

1. POMA (πόμα), akin to B, No. 1, denotes the thing drunk (from a 4188
root *po—,* found in the Eng., potion ; it is connected with the root AG:690B CB:1266A
pi—; see B, No. 3), 1 Cor. 10 : 4 ; Heb. 9 : 10.¶

2. POSIS (πόσις), akin to B, No. 1, suggests the act of drinking, John 4213
6 : 55 (where it is practically equivalent to No. 1) ; Rom. 14 : 17, AG:694B CB:1266A
"drinking," R.V. ; Col. 2 : 16.¶

3. SIKERA (σίκερα) is a strong, intoxicating drink, made from any 4608
sweet ingredients, whether grain, vegetables, or the juice of fruits, or a AG:750B
decoction of honey ; "strong drink," Luke 1 : 15.¶ In the Sept., CB:—
Lev. 10 : 9 ; Num. 6 : 3 ; 28 : 7 ; Deut 14 : 26 ; 29 : 6 ; Isa 5 : 11, 22 ; 24 : 9 ; 28 : 7 ; 29 : 9.

B. Verbs.

1. PINŌ (πίνω), to drink, is used chiefly in the Gospels and in 1 Cor., 4095
whether literally (most frequently), or figuratively, (*a*) of drinking of the AG:658C CB:1265A
Blood of Christ, in the sense of receiving eternal life, through His Death, John 6 : 53, 54, 56 ; (*b*) of receiving spiritually that which refreshes, strengthens and nourishes the soul, John 7 : 37 ; (*c*) of deriving spiritual life from Christ, John 4 : 14, as Israel did typically, 1 Cor. 10 : 4 ; (*d*) of sharing in the sufferings of Christ humanly inflicted, Matt. 20 : 22, 23 ; Mark 10 : 38, 39 ; (*e*) of participating in the abominations imparted by the corrupt religious and commercial systems emanating from Babylon, Rev. 18 : 3 ; (*f*) of receiving Divine judgment, through partaking unworthily of the Lord's Supper, 1 Cor. 11 : 29 ; (*g*) of experiencing the wrath of God, Rev. 14 : 10 ; 16 : 6 ; (*h*) of the earth's receiving the benefits of rain, Heb. 6 : 7.

2. METHUŌ (μεθύω), from *methu,* wine, to be drunk, is used in John 3184
2 : 10 in the Passive Voice, and is translated in the P.V., "have drunk AG:499C CB:1258C
freely ;" A.V., "have well drunk." See DRUNK.

4222 AG:695D CB:1266B 3. POTIZŌ (ποτίζω), to give to drink, to make to drink, is used (*a*) in the material sense, in Matt. 10 : 42 ; 25 : 35, 37, 42 (here of ministering to those who belong to Christ and thus doing so virtually to Him) ; 27 : 48 ; Mark 9 . 41 ; 15 : 36 ; Luke 13 : 15 ("to watering") ; Rom. 12 : 20 ; 1 Cor. 3 : 7, 8 ; (*b*) figuratively, with reference to teaching of an elementary character, 1 Cor. 3 : 2, "I fed (you with milk) ;" of spiritual watering by teaching the word of God, 3 : 6 ; of being provided and satisfied by the power and blessing of the Spirit of God, 1 Cor. 12 : 13 ; of the effect upon the nations of partaking of the abominable mixture, provided by Babylon, of paganism with details of the Christian faith, Rev. 14 : 8. See FEED, WATER.¶

4844 AG:779C CB:— 4. SUMPINŌ (συμπίνω), to drink together (*sun*, with, and B, No. 1), is found in Acts 10 : 41.¶

5202 AG:832D CB:— 5. HUDROPOTEŌ (ὑδροποτέω), to drink water (*hudōr*, water, *poteō*, to drink), is found in 1 Tim. 5 : 23, R.V., "be (no longer) a drinker of water."¶

DRIVE, DRIVEN, DRAVE, DROVE

1544 AG:237B CB:1243B 1. EKBALLŌ (ἐκβάλλω) denotes, lit., to cast forth, with the suggestion of force (*ek*, out, *ballō*, to cast) ; hence to drive out or forth. It is translated "driveth" in Mark 1 : 12, R.V., "driveth forth." In John 2 : 15 for the A.V., "drove," the R.V. has "cast," the more usual translation. See CAST, No. 5.

1559 AG:239A CB:1243C 2. EKDIŌKŌ (ἐκδιώκω), to chase away, drive out (*ek*, out, *diōkō*, to pursue), is used in 1 Thess. 2 : 15, R.V., "drave out," A.V., "have persecuted." Some mss. have this verb for *diōkō*, in Luke 11 : 49.¶

1643 AG:248C CB:— 3. ELAUNŌ (ἐλαύνω) signifies to drive, impel, urge on. It is used of rowing, Mark 6 : 48 and John 6 : 19 ; of the act of a demon upon a man, Luke 8 : 29 ; of the power of winds upon ships, Jas. 3 : 4 ; and of storms upon mists, 2 Pet. 2 : 17, A.V., "carried," R.V., "driven." See also CARRY, Note (2), ROW.

556 AG:83C CB:— 4. APELAUNŌ (ἀπελαύνω), *apo*, from, and No. 3, to drive from, is used in Acts 18 : 16.¶

1856 AG:280A CB:— 5. EXŌTHEŌ (ἐξωθέω), to thrust out (*ek*, out, *ōtheō*, to push, thrust), is translated "thrust" in Acts 7 : 45, R.V. (A.V., "drave") ; in 27 : 39, of driving a storm-tossed ship ashore (R.V., "drive," A.V., "thrust"). Cp. No. 6. See THRUST.¶

5342 AG:854D CB:1264A 6. PHERŌ (φέρω), to bear, is translated "driven" in Acts 27 : 15, 17, of being borne in a storm-tossed ship. See BEAR, etc.

1308 AG:190B CB:— 7. DIAPHERŌ (διαφέρω), lit., to bear through (*dia*, through, and No. 6), in Acts 27 : 27 signifies to be borne hither and thither (R.V., "were driven to and fro ;" A.V., "up and down"). See BETTER (be), No. 1.

416 AG:64C CB:— 8. ANEMIZŌ (ἀνεμίζω), to drive by the wind (*anemos*, wind), is used in Jas. 1 : 6.¶

Note : For "let . . . drive," Acts 27 : 15, see GIVE, No. 3.

DROP (Noun)

THROMBOS (θρόμβος), a large, thick drop of clotted blood (etymo- 2361
logically akin to *trephō*, to curdle), is used in Luke 22 : 44, in the plural, AG:364B
in the narrative of the Lord's agony in Gethsemane.¶ CB:—

DROPSY

HUDRŌPIKOS (ὑδρωπικός), dropsical, suffering from dropsy (*hudrops*, 5203
dropsy), is found in Luke 14 : 2, the only instance recorded of the healing AG:832D
of this disease by the Lord.¶ CB:—

DROWN

1. BUTHIZŌ (βυθίζω), to plunge into the deep, to sink (*buthos*, bottom, 1036
the deep, the sea), akin to *bathos*, depth, and *abussos*, bottomless, and Eng., AG:148C
bath, is used in Luke 5 : 7 of the sinking of a boat ; metaphorically in CB:—
1 Tim. 6 : 9, of the effect of foolish and hurtful lusts, which " drown men in destruction and perdition." See SINK.¶

2. KATAPINŌ (καταπίνω), lit., to drink down (*pinō*, to drink, prefixed 2666
by *kata*, down), signifies to swallow up (R.V., in Heb. 11 : 29, for A.V., AG:416B
" were drowned "). It is elsewhere translated by the verb to swallow, CB:1254B
or swallow up, except in 1 Pet. 5 : 8, " devour." See DEVOUR, No. 3, SWALLOW.

3. KATAPONTIZŌ (καταποντίζω), to throw into the sea (*kata*, down, 2670
pontos, the open sea), in the Passive Voice, to be sunk in, to be drowned, AG:417A
is translated " were drowned," in Matt. 18 : 6, A.V. (R.V., " should be CB:—
sunk ") ; elsewhere in 14 : 30, " (beginning) to sink." See SINK.¶

DRUNK (-EN, be), DRUNKARD, DRUNKENNESS

A. Verbs.

1. METHUŌ (μεθύω) signifies to be drunk with wine (from *methu*, 3184
mulled wine ; hence Eng., mead, honey-wine ; originally it denoted simply AG:499C
a pleasant drink). For John 2 : 10 see under DRINK. The verb is used CB:1258C
of being intoxicated in Matt. 24 : 49 ; Acts 2 : 15 ; 1 Cor. 11 : 21 ; 1 Thess. 5 : 7*b* ; metaphorically, of the effect upon men of partaking of the abominations of the Babylonish system, Rev. 17 : 2 ; of being in a state of mental intoxication, through the shedding of men's blood profusely, ver. 6.¶

2. METHUSKŌ (μεθύσκω) signifies to make drunk, or to grow drunk 3182
(an inceptive verb, marking the process of the state expressed in No. 1), AG:499B
to become intoxicated, Luke 12 : 45 ; Eph. 5 : 18 ; 1 Thess. 5 : 7*a*.¶ CB:1258C

B. Adjective.

METHUSOS (μέθυσος), drunken (cp. No. 2), is used as noun, in the 3183
singular, in 1 Cor. 5 : 11, and in the plural, in 6 : 10, " drunkard," AG:499B
" drunkards."¶ CB:1258C

3178

C. Noun. AG:498D

METHĒ (μέθη), strong drink (akin to *methu*, wine, see under A. 1, CB:1258C above), denotes drunkenness, habitual intoxication, Luke 21 : 34 ; Rom. 13 : 13 ; Gal. 5 : 21.¶

DRY

A. Adjectives.

3584 AG:548C CB:1273B 1. XĒROS (ξηρός) is used (*a*) naturally, of dry land, Heb. 11 : 29 ; or of land in general, Matt. 23 : 15, " land ; " or of physical infirmity, " withered," Matt. 12 : 10 ; Mark 3 : 3 ; Luke 6 : 6, 8 ; John 5 : 3 ; (*b*) figuratively, in Luke 23 : 31, with reference to the spiritual barrenness of the Jews, in contrast to the character of the Lord. Cp. Ps. 1 : 3 ; Isa. 56 : 3 ; Ezek. 17 : 24 ; 20 : 47. See LAND, WITHERED.¶

504 AG:76C CB:— 2. ANUDROS (ἄνυδρος), waterless (*a*, negative, *n*, euphonic, ***hudōr***, water), is rendered " dry " in Matt. 12 : 43, A.V., and Luke 11 : 24 (R.V., " waterless ") ; " without water " in 2 Pet. 2 : 17 and Jude 12. See WATER.¶

B. Verb.

3583 AG:548C CB:1273B XĒRAINŌ (ξηραίνω), akin to A. 1, to dry, dry up, make dry, wither, is translated " dried " (of physical infirmity), in Mark 5 : 29 ; of a tree, in the A.V. of Mark 11 : 20 (R.V., " withered away ") ; of water, in Rev. 16 : 12. It is translated " ripe " (R.V., " over-ripe ") in Rev. 14 : 15, of a harvest (used figuratively of the gathered nations against Jerusalem at the end of this age) ; " pineth away," in Mark 9 : 18. See OVER-RIPE, PINE AWAY, RIPE, WITHER.

DUE

A. Adjective.

2398 AG:369C CB:1252C IDIOS (ἴδιος), one's own, is applied to *kairos*, a season, in Gal. 6 : 9, " in due season," i.e., in the season Divinely appointed for the reaping. So in 1 Tim. 2 : 6, " the testimony to be borne in its own (A.V., ' due ') times (seasons) ; " 6 : 15, " in its own (*idios*) times (seasons) ; " similarly in Tit. 1 : 3. See BUSINESS, B.

514 AG:78A CB:1238B *Note :* For *axios*, " the due reward," see REWARD, *Note* (1).

B. Verbs.

3784 AG:598D CB:1261A 1. OPHEILŌ (ὀφείλω) signifies to owe, to be indebted, especially financially, Matt. 18 : 30, R.V., " that which was due ; " 18 : 34, " all that was due." See BEHOVE, BOUND (to be).

1163 AG:172A CB:1240B 2. DEI (δεῖ), an impersonal verb signifying " it is necessary," is translated " was due " in Rom. 1 : 27, R.V. (A.V., " was meet "). See BEHOVE.

C. Noun.

3782 AG:598C CB:1261A OPHEILĒ (ὀφειλή), akin to B, No. 1, is rendered " dues " in Rom. 13 : 7. In 1 Cor. 7 : 3, R.V., it is translated " her due " (the A.V. " due benevolence " follows another reading)..

Notes : (1) In the phrases " in due season " in Matt. 24 : 45 ; Luke 12 : 42 ; Rom. 5 : 6 (lit., ' according to time '), and " in due time,"

1 Pet. 5 : 6, there is no word representing “ due ” in the original, and the phrases are, lit., “ in season,” “ in time.”

(2) For the phrase “ born out of due time,” in 1 Cor. 15 : 8, see Beget, B, No. 2.

DULL

A. Adjective.

NŌTHROS (νωθρός), slow, sluggish, indolent, dull (the etymology 3576
is uncertain), is translated “ dull ” in Heb. 5 : 11 (in connection with AG:547C
akoē, hearing ; lit., ‘ in hearings ’) ; “ sluggish,” in 6 : 12. See Sloth- CB:—
ful, Sluggish.¶ In the Sept., Prov. 22 : 29.¶ Cp. *nōthrokardios*,
“ slow of heart ” (*kardia*, the heart), Prov. 12 : 8.¶

Note : In Luke 24 : 25 “ slow (of heart) ” translates the synonymous
word *bradus*. Of these Trench says (Syn. § civ), “ *Bradus* differs from the 1021
words with which it is here brought into comparison, in that no moral AG:147A
fault or blame is necessarily involved in it ; so far indeed is it from this, CB:—
that of the three occasions on which it is used in the N.T. two are in honour ; for to be ‘ slow ’ to evil things, to rash speaking, or to anger (Jas. 1 : 19, twice), is a grace, and not the contrary. . . . There is a deeper, more inborn sluggishness implied in *nōthros*, and this bound up as it were in the very life, more than in either of the other words of this group.” Trench compares and contrasts *argos*, idle, but this word is not strictly synonymous with the other two.¶

B. Adverb.

BAREŌS (βαρέως), heavily, with difficulty (*barus*, heavy), is used with 917
akouō, to hear, in Matt. 13 : 15 , and Acts 28 : 27 (from Isa. 6 : 10), lit., AG:133C
to hear heavily, to be dull of hearing.¶ In the Sept., Gen. 31 : 35 (lit., CB:1238C
‘ bear it not heavily ’) ; Isa. 6 : 10.¶

DUMB

A. Adjectives.

1. ALALOS (ἄλαλος), lit., speechless (*a*, negative, and *laleō*, to speak), 216 AG:34D
is found in Mark 7 : 37 ; 9 : 17, 25.¶ In the Sept., Ps. 38 : 13.¶ CB:1234B

2. APHŌNOS (ἄφωνος), lit., voiceless, or soundless (*a*, negative, and 880
phōnē, a sound), has reference to voice, Acts 8 : 32 ; 1 Cor. 12 : 2 ; 2 Pet. AG:128A CB:—
2 : 16, while *alalos* has reference to words. In 1 Cor. 14 : 10 it is used metaphorically of the significance of voices or sounds, “ without signification.”¶ In the Sept. Isa. 53 : 7.¶

3. KŌPHOS (κωφός) denotes blunted or dulled ; see Deaf. 2974 AG:462A

B. Verb. CB:1255C

SIŌPAŌ (σιωπάω), from *siōpē*, silence, to be silent, is used of Zacharias' 4623
dumbness, Luke 1 : 20. See Peace (hold one's). AG:752C CB:—

DUNG 4657 AG:758A

1. SKUBALON (σκύβαλον) denotes refuse, whether (*a*) excrement, that CB:1269B

which is cast out from the body, or (*b*) the leavings of a feast, that which is thrown away from the table. Some have derived it from ***kusibalon*** (with *metathesis* of k and s), "thrown to dogs;" others connect it with a root meaning "shred." Judaizers counted Gentile Christians as dogs, while they themselves were seated at God's banquet. The Apostle, reversing the image, counts the Judaistic ordinances as refuse upon which their advocates feed, Phil. 3 : 8.¶

— AG:443D CB:1255C 2. KOPRION (κόπριον), manure, Luke 13 : 8, used in the plural with *ballō*, to throw, is translated by the verb to dung. Some mss. have the accusative case of the noun *kopria*, a dunghill. See below.¶

DUNGHILL

2874 AG:443D CB:1255C KOPRIA (κοπρία), a dunghill, is found in Luke 14 : 35.¶

For DURE see under WHILE, *Note* 1

DURING: see Note †, p. 1

For DURST see DARE

DUST

A. Nouns.

5522 AG:884B CB:1240A 1. CHOUS, or CHOOS (χοῦς or χόος), from *cheō*, to pour, primarily, earth dug out, an earth heap, then, loose earth or dust, is used in Mark 6 : 11 and Rev. 18 : 19.¶

2868 AG:443B CB:— 2. KONIORTOS (κονιορτός), raised or flying dust (*konia*, dust, ***ornumi***, to stir up), is found in Matt. 10 : 14; Luke 9 : 5; 10 : 11; Acts 13 : 51; 22 : 23.¶

B. Verb.

3039 AG:474D CB:— LIKMAŌ (λικμάω), primarily, to winnow (from *likmos*, a winnowing-fan), hence, to scatter as chaff or dust, is used in Matt. 21 : 44 and Luke 20 : 18, R.V., "scatter as dust," A.V., "grind to powder." There are indications in the papyri writings that the word came to denote to ruin, to destroy.¶

DUTY

3784 AG:598D CB:1261A OPHEILŌ (ὀφείλω), to owe, to be indebted, is translated "it was our duty," in Luke 17 : 10, lit., 'we owe (ought) to do;' so in Rom. 15 : 27, A.V., "their duty is;" R.V., "they owe it." See BEHOVE, BOUND.

DWELL, DWELLERS, DWELLING (place)

A. Verbs.

3611 AG:557A CB:1260B 1. OIKEŌ (οἰκέω), to dwell (from *oikos*, a house), to inhabit as one's abode, is derived from the Sanskrit, *vic*, a dwelling place (the Eng. termination —wick is connected). It is used (*a*) of God as dwelling in light, 1 Tim. 6 : 16 ; (*b*) of the indwelling of the Spirit of God in the believer, Rom. 8 : 9, 11, or in a church, 1 Cor. 3 : 16 ; (*c*) of the indwelling of sin, Rom. 7 : 20 ; (*d*) of the absence of any good thing in the flesh of the believer, Rom. 7 : 18 ; (*e*) of the dwelling together of those who are married, 1 Cor. 7 : 12, 13.¶

2. KATOIKEŌ (κατοικέω), *kata*, down, and No. 1, the most frequent 2730
verb with this meaning, properly signifies to settle down in a dwelling, AG:424A CB:1254C
to dwell fixedly in a place. Besides its literal sense, it is used of (*a*) the indwelling of the totality of the attributes and powers of the Godhead in Christ, Col. 1 : 19 ; 2 : 9 ; (*b*) the indwelling of Christ in the hearts of believers (' may make a home in your hearts '), Eph. 3 : 17 ; (*c*) the dwelling of Satan in a locality, Rev. 2 : 13 ; (*d*) the future indwelling of righteousness in the new heavens and earth, 2 Pet. 3 : 13. It is translated " dwellers " in Acts 1 : 19 ; 2 : 9 ; " inhabitants " in Rev. 17 : 2, A.V. (R.V., " they that dwell "), " inhabiters " in Rev. 8 : 13 and 12 : 12, A.V. (R.V., " them that dwell ").

Cp. the nouns *katoikēsis* (below), *katoikia*, habitation, Acts 17 : 26¶ ; *katoikētērion*, a habitation, Eph. 2 : 22 ; Rev. 18 : 2.¶ Contrast *paroikeō*, to sojourn, the latter being temporary, the former permanent. See HABITATION, INHABITANT.

3. KATOIKIZŌ (κατοικίζω), to cause to dwell, is said of the act of —
God concerning the Holy Spirit in Jas. 4 : 5, R.V. (some mss. have No. 2).¶ AG:424C CB:1254C

4. ENOIKEŌ (ἐνοικέω), lit., to dwell in (*en*, in, and No. 1), is used, 1774
with a spiritual significance only, of (*a*) the indwelling of God in believers, AG:267B CB:1245B
2 Cor. 6 : 16 ; (*b*) the indwelling of the Holy Spirit, Rom. 8 : 11 ; 2 Tim. 1 : 14 ; (*c*) the indwelling of the word of Christ, Col. 3 : 16 ; (*d*) the indwelling of faith, 2 Tim. 1 : 5 ; (*e*) the indwelling of sin in the believer, Rom. 7 : 17.¶

5. PERIOIKEŌ (περιοικέω), *peri*, around, and No. 1, to dwell around, 4039
be a neighbour, is used in Luke 1 : 65.¶ Cp. *perioikos*, a neighbour, AG:648D CB:—
Luke 1 : 58.¶

4924
6. SUNOIKEŌ (συνοικέω), *sun*, with, and No. 1, to dwell with, is used AG:791C
in 1 Pet. 3 : 7.¶ CB:—

7. ENKATOIKEŌ (ἐγκατοικέω), *en*, in, and No. 2, to dwell among, 1460
is used in 2 Pet. 2 : 8.¶ AG:216A CB:—

8. MENŌ (μένω), to abide, remain, is translated to dwell, in the A.V. 3306
of John 1 : 38, 39 ; 6 : 56 ; 14 : 10, 17 ; Acts 28 : 16. The R.V. adheres AG:503C CB:1258B
throughout to the verb to abide. See ABIDE.

9. SKĒNOŌ (σκηνόω), to pitch a tent (*skēnē*), to tabernacle, is trans- 4637
lated " dwelt," in John 1 : 14, A.V., R.V. marg., " tabernacled ; " in AG:755C CB:1269A
Rev. 7 : 15, A.V., " shall dwell," R.V., " shall spread (His) tabernacle ; " in Rev. 12 : 12 ; 13 : 6 ; 21 : 3, " dwell." See TABERNACLE.

10. KATASKĒNOŌ (κατασκηνόω), to pitch one's tent (*kata*, down, 2681
skēnē, a tent), is translated " lodge " in Matt. 13 : 32 ; Mark 4 : 32 ; AG:418C CB:1254B
Luke 13 : 19 ; in Acts 2 : 26, R.V., " dwell," A.V., " rest."¶

1687 11. EMBATEUŌ (ἐμβατεύω), primarily, to step in, or on (from *embainō*,
AG:254B CB:— to enter), hence (*a*) to frequent, dwell in, is used metaphorically in Col. 2 : 18, R.V., " dwelling in " (marg., " taking his stand upon ") ; (*b*) with reference to the same passage, alternatively, to invade, to enter on ; perhaps used in this passage as a technical term of the mystery religions, denoting the entrance of the initiated into the new life (A.V., " intruding into "). A suggested alternative reading involves the rendering " treading on air," i.e., indulging in vain speculations, but evidences in the papyri writings make the emendation unnecessary.¶

2521 AG:389B 12. KATHĒMAI (κάθημαι), to sit down, is translated " dwell," in
CB:1254C Luke 21 : 35. See Set, Sit.

2523 AG:389D 13. KATHIZŌ (καθίζω), to sit down, denotes to dwell, in Acts 18 : 11
CB:1254C (R.V., " dwelt," for A.V., " continued ").

790 14. ASTATEŌ (ἀστατέω), to wander about (*a*, negative, *histēmi*, to
AG:117B CB:— stand), to have no fixed dwelling-place, is used in 1 Cor. 4 : 11.¶ Cp. *akatastatos*, unstable, Jas. 1 : 8 ; 3 : 8.¶ ; *akatastasia*, revolution, confusion, e.g., 1 Cor. 14 : 33.

B. Nouns.

3940 1. PAROIKIA (παροικία) denotes a sojourning, Acts 13 : 17, lit.,
AG:629A CB:1262B 'in the sojourning,' translated " when they sojourned," R.V. (A.V., " dwelt as strangers ") ; in 1 Pet. 1 : 17, " sojourning."¶

2731 2. KATOIKĒSIS (κατοίκησις), akin to A, No. 2, a dwelling, a habita-
AG:424C CB:— tion, is used in Mark 5 : 3.¶

Note : Cp. *oikia*, and *oikos*, a house, *oikēma*, a prison, *katoikia*, a habitation (see A, No. 2).

3410 3. MISTHŌMA (μίσθωμα), primarily, a price, a hire (akin to *misthos*,
AG:523D CB:1259A wages, hire, and *misthoō*, to let out for hire), is used in Acts 28 : 30 to denote a hired dwelling.¶

For DYING see DEADNESS

DYSENTERY

1420 (-RIA) DUSENTERION (δυσεντέριον), whence Eng., dysentery, is so trans-
AG:209C CB:— lated in Acts 28 : 8, R.V., for A.V. " bloody flux " (*enteron* denotes an intestine).¶

EACH, EACH MAN, EACH ONE

1. HEKASTOS (ἕκαστος), each or every, is used of any number separately, either (*a*) as an adjective qualifying a noun, e.g., Luke 6 : 44 ; John 19 : 23 ; Heb. 3 : 13, where " day by day," is, lit., ' according to each day ; ' or, more emphatically with *heis*, one, in Matt. 26 : 22 ; Luke 4 : 40 ; 16 : 5 ; Acts 2 : 3, 6 ; 20 : 31 ; 1 Cor. 12 : 18 ; Eph. 4 : 7, 16, R.V., " each (several)," for A.V., " every ; " Col. 4 : 6 ; 1 Thess. 2 : 11 ; 2 Thess. 1 : 3 ; (*b*) as a distributive pronoun, e.g., Acts 4 : 35 ; Rom. 2 : 6 ; Gal. 6 : 4 ; in Phil. 2 : 4, it is used in the plural ; some mss. have it thus in Rev. 6 : 11. The repetition in Heb. 8 : 11 is noticeable, " every man " (i.e., everyone). Prefixed by the preposition *ana*, apiece (a colloquialism), it is used, with stress on the individuality, in Rev. 21 : 21, of the gates of the heavenly city, " each one of the several," R.V. ; in Eph. 5 : 33, preceded by *kath' hena*, ' by one,' it signifies " each (one) his own." 1538 AG:236C CB:1249C ANA 303 AG:49D CB:1235A

2. The phrase *hen kath' hen*, lit., ' one by one,' is used in Rev. 4 : 8, " each one of them." HEIS 1520 AG:230D CB:1249C

EACH OTHER

ALLĒLŌN (ἀλλήλων), a reciprocal pronoun, preceded by the preposition *meta*, with, signifies " with each other," Luke 23 : 12, R.V., for A.V., " together." Similarly in 24 : 14 *pros allēlous*, where *pros* suggests greater intimacy. See ONE ANOTHER. 240 AG:39C CB:1234C

EAGER See READY, ZEALOUS

EAGLE

AETOS (ἀετός), an eagle (also a vulture), is perhaps connected with *aēmi*, to blow, as of the wind, on account of its windlike flight. In Matt. 24 : 28 and Luke 17 : 37 the vultures are probably intended. The meaning seems to be that, as these birds of prey gather where the carcase is, so the judgments of God will descend upon the corrupt state of humanity. The figure of the eagle is used in Ezek. 17 to represent the great powers of Egypt and Babylon, as being employed to punish corrupt and faithless Israel. Cp. Job 39 : 30 ; Prov. 30 : 17. The eagle is mentioned elsewhere in the N.T. in Rev. 4 : 7 ; 8 : 13 (R.V.) ; 12 : 14. There are eight species in Palestine.¶ 105 AG:19D CB:1233B

In the following pages † indicates that the word referred to (preposition, conjunction, or particle) is not dealt with in this volume.

¶ indicates that all the N.T. occurrences of the Greek word under consideration are mentioned under the heading or sub-heading.

EAR (of the body)

3775 AG:595C CB:1261B 1. OUS (οὖς), Latin *auris*, is used (*a*) of the physical organ, e.g., Luke 4 : 21 ; Acts 7 : 57 ; in Acts 11 : 22, in the plural with *akouō*, to hear, lit., ' was heard into the ears of someone,' i.e., came to the knowledge of ; similarly, in the singular, Matt. 10 : 27, in familiar private conversation ; in Jas. 5 : 4 the phrase is used with *eiserchomai*, to enter into ; in Luke 1 : 44, with *ginomai*, to become, to come ; in Luke 12 : 3, with *lalein*, to speak and *pros*, to ; (*b*) metaphorically, of the faculty of perceiving with the mind, understanding and knowing, Matt. 13 : 16 ; frequently with *akouō*, to hear, e.g., Matt. 11 : 15 ; 13 : 9, 43 ; Rev. 2 and 3, at the close of each of the messages to the churches ; in Matt. 13 : 15 and Acts 28 : 27, with *bareōs*, heavily, of being slow to understand and obey ; with a negative in Mark 8 : 18 ; Rom. 11 : 8 ; in Luke 9 : 44 the lit. meaning is ' put those words into your ears,' i.e., take them into your mind and keep them there ; in Acts 7 : 51 it is used with *aperitmētos*, uncircumcised. As seeing is metaphorically associated with conviction, so hearing is with obedience (*hupakoē*, lit., hearing under ; the Eng., " obedience " is etymologically ' hearing over against,' i.e., with response in the hearer).

5621 AG:900B CB:— 2. ŌTION (ὠτίον), a diminutive of No. 1, but without the diminutive force, it being a common tendency in everyday speech to apply a diminutive form to most parts of the body, is used in Matt. 26 : 51 ; Mark 14 : 47 (in some mss.) ; Luke 22 : 51 ; John 18 : 10 (in some mss.) and ver. 26, all with reference to the ear of Malchus.¶

— AG:900B CB:— *Note :* The most authentic mss. have the alternative diminutive *ōtarion*, in Mark 14 : 47 and John 18 : 10.¶

189 AG:30D CB:1234B 3. AKOĒ (ἀκοή), hearing, akin to *akouō*, to hear, denotes (*a*) the sense of hearing, e.g., 1 Cor. 12 : 17 ; 2 Pet. 2 : 8 ; (*b*) that which is heard, a report, e.g., Matt. 4 : 24 ; (*c*) the physical organ, Mark 7 : 35, standing for the sense of hearing ; so in Luke 7 : 1, R.V., for A.V., " audience ; " Acts 17 : 20 ; 2 Tim. 4 : 3, 4 (in ver. 3, lit., ' being tickled as to the ears ') ; (*d*) a message or teaching, John 12 : 38 ; Rom. 10 : 16, 17 ; Gal. 3 : 2, 5 ; 1 Thess. 2 : 13 ; Heb. 4 : 2, R.V., " (the word) of hearing," for A.V., " (the word) preached." See FAME, HEARING, PREACH, REPORT, RUMOUR.

191 AG:31D CB:1234B *Note :* In Matt. 28 : 14, the verb *akouō* is used with the preposition *epi*, upon or before (or *hupo*, by, in some mss.), lit., ' if this come to a hearing before the governor.'

EAR (of corn)

4719 AG:765D CB:1269C STACHUS (στάχυς) is found in Matt. 12 : 1 ; Mark 2 : 23 ; 4 : 28 (" ear," twice) ; Luke 6 : 1. The first part of the word is derived from the root *sta*— found in parts of the verb *histēmi*, to cause to stand. It is used as a proper name in Rom. 16 : 9.¶

EARLY

A. Noun.

ORTHROS (ὄρθρος) denotes daybreak, dawn (cp. Lat. *orior*, to rise). 3722
Used with the adverb *batheōs*, deeply, in Luke 24 : 1, it means "at AG:580C CB:—
early dawn" (R.V.). In John 8 : 2 it is used in the genitive case, *orthrou*, (BATHUS)
at dawn, i.e., "early in the morning." In Acts 5 : 21, it is used with 901
the article and preceded by the preposition *hupo*, under, or about, lit., AG:130 CB:1238
'about the dawn,' "about daybreak," R.V. (for A.V., "early in the morning.").¶

B. Adjectives.

1. ORTHRINOS (ὀρθρινός) early, akin to A., is a later form of *orthrios*. 3720
It is found, in the most authentic mss., in Luke 24 : 22, of the women AG:580C ORTHRIOS
at the sepulchre, lit., 'early ones' (some texts have the form *orthrios*, 3721
at daybreak).¶ AG:580C

2. PRŌIMOS (πρώϊμος) or *proimos*, a longer and later form of *proios*, 4406
pertaining to the morning, is formed from *prō*, before (cp. *prōtos*, first), AG:706D CB:1266C
and used in Jas. 5 : 7, of the early rain.¶ PRōIOS

C. Adverb. 4405 (-IA) AG:724D (-IA)

PRŌI (πρωΐ), early in the day, at morn, is derived from *prō*, before 4404
(see B, No. 2, above). In Mark 16 : 2, A.V., it is translated "early in AG:724D CB:1266C
the morning;" in Mark 16 : 9 and John 18 : 28; 20 : 1, "early;" in Matt. 16 : 3; 20 : 1; 21 : 18; Mark 1 : 35; 11 : 20; 13 : 35; 15 : 1, "in the morning;" in Acts 28 : 23, "(from) morning." See MORNING.¶

Note: In Matt. 20 : 1, *hama*, at once, is rendered "early." 260 AG:42A CB:1249A

EARNEST (Noun)

ARRABŌN (ἀρραβών), originally, earnest-money deposited by the 728
purchaser and forfeited if the purchase was not completed, was probably AG:109B CB:1237C
a Phœnician word, introduced into Greece. In general usage it came to denote a pledge or earnest of any sort; in the N.T. it is used only of that which is assured by God to believers; it is said of the Holy Spirit as the Divine pledge of all their future blessedness, 2 Cor. 1 : 22; 5 : 5; in Eph. 1 : 14, particularly of their eternal inheritance.¶ In the Sept., Gen. 38 : 17, 18, 20.¶ In modern Greek *arrabōna* is an engagement ring.

EARNEST, EARNESTNESS, EARNESTLY EARN See GAIN

A. Noun.

SPOUDĒ (σπουδή), akin to *speudō*, to hasten, denotes haste, Mark 4710
6 : 25; Luke 1 : 39; hence, "earnestness," 2 Cor. 8 : 7, R.V., for A.V., AG:763D CB:1269C
"diligence," and ver. 8, for A.V., "forwardness;" in 7 : 12, "earnest care," for A.V., "care;" in 8 : 16, "earnest care." See BUSINESS, CARE, CAREFULNESS, DILIGENCE, FORWARDNESS, HASTE.

B. Adjective. 4705

SPOUDAIOS (σπουδαῖος), akin to A, denotes active, diligent, earnest, AG:763C CB:1269C

2 Cor. 8 : 22, R.V., "earnest," for A.V., "diligent;" in the latter part
4706 AG:763D (-IOS) of the verse the comparative degree, *spoudaioteros*, is used, R.V., "more
earnest," for A.V., "more diligent;" in ver. 17, R.V., in the superlative
CB:1269C (-IOS) sense, "very earnest," for A.V., "more forward." See DILIGENT,
FORWARD.¶

C. Adverbs.

1619 AG:245D 1. EKTENŌS (ἐκτενῶς), earnestly (*ek*, out, *teinō*, to stretch; Eng.,
CB:1244A tension, etc.), is used in Acts 12 : 5, "earnestly," R.V., for A.V., "without
ceasing" (some mss. have the adjective *ektenēs*, earnest); in 1 Pet. 1 : 22,
"fervently." The idea suggested is that of not relaxing in effort, or
acting in a right spirit. See FERVENTLY.¶

1617 AG:245 2. EKTENESTERON (ἐκτενέστερον), the comparative degree of
(EKTENēS) No. 1, used as an adverb in this neuter form, denotes more earnestly,
CB:— fervently, Luke 22 : 44.¶

4709 3. SPOUDAIŌS (σπουδαίως), akin to B, signifies with haste, or with
AG:763D CB:— zeal, earnestly, Luke 7 : 4, R.V., "earnestly," for A.V., "instantly;"
in 2 Tim. 1 : 17, R.V., and Tit. 3 : 13, "diligently;"¶ in Phil. 2 : 28,
the comparative *spoudaioterōs*, R.V., "the more diligently," A.V., "the
more carefully." See CAREFULLY, DILIGENTLY, INSTANTLY.¶

D. Adverbial Phrase.

EKTENEIA 1616 EN EKTENEIA (ἐν ἐκτενείᾳ), lit., 'in earnestness,' cp. C, No. 1, is
AG:245C translated "earnestly" in Acts 26 : 7, R.V., for A.V., "instantly." See
ZēLOō 2206 INSTANTLY.¶

AG:338A *Notes:* (1) For the phrase "earnest expectation," Rom. 8 : 19 and
CB:1273B Phil. 1 : 20, see EXPECTATION. (2) In 1 Cor. 12 : 31; 14 : 1, 39, *zēloō*,
SPEUDō 4692 to be zealous about, is translated "desire earnestly." See DESIRE.
AG:762B (3) In 2 Pet. 3 : 12, *speudō* is translated "earnestly desiring," for A.V.,
CB:1269C EPAGōNIZOMAI "hasting unto." See HASTEN. (4) In Jude 3, *epagōnizō*, to contend
1864 earnestly, is so translated.¶ (5) In Jas. 5 : 17 the dative case of the
AG:281B noun *proseuchē* is translated "earnestly" (A.V.), in connection with
CB:1245B PROSEUCHē the corresponding verb, lit., 'he prayed with prayer' (R.V., "fervently"),
4335 implying persevering continuance in prayer with fervour. Cp., e.g.,
AG:713B CB:1267A Ps. 40 : 1, lit., 'in waiting I waited.' See FERVENT. (6) *Atenizō*, akin
ATENIZō to C, No. 1, to fix the eyes upon, gaze upon, is translated "earnestly
816 AG:119D looked" in Luke 22 : 56, A.V. (R.V., "looking stedfastly"); in Acts
CB:1238A 3 : 12, A.V., "look ye earnestly," R.V., "fasten ye your eyes on;"
PERISSOTERōS 4056 in Acts 23 : 1, A.V., "earnestly beholding," R.V., "looking stedfastly
AG:651D on." (7) In Heb. 2 : 1, *prosechō*, to give heed, is used with the adverb
CB:1263C *perissoterōs*, more abundantly, to signify "to give the more earnest heed;"
lit., 'to give heed more exceedingly.' For the verb see ATTEND, GIVE,
No. 16, HEED, REGARD.

EARTH

1093 AG:157C 1. GĒ (γῆ) denotes (*a*) earth as arable land, e.g., Matt. 13 : 5, 8, 23;
CB:1248A in 1 Cor. 15 : 47 it is said of the earthly material of which "the first man"

was made, suggestive of frailty; (*b*) the earth as a whole, the world, in contrast, whether to the heavens, e.g., Matt. 5 : 18, 35, or to Heaven, the abode of God, e.g., Matt. 6 : 19, where the context suggests the earth as a place characterized by mutability and weakness; in Col. 3 : 2 the same contrast is presented by the word " above;" in John 3 : 31 (R.V., " of the earth," for A.V., " earthly ") it describes one whose origin and nature are earthly and whose speech is characterized thereby, in contrast with Christ as the One from Heaven; in Col. 3 : 5 the physical members are said to be " upon the earth," as a sphere where, as potential instruments of moral evils, they are, by metonymy, spoken of as the evils themselves; (*c*) the inhabited earth, e.g., Luke 21 : 35; Acts 1 : 8; 8 : 33; 10 : 12; 11 : 6; 17 : 26; 22 : 22; Heb. 11 : 13; Rev. 13 : 8. In the following the phrase " on the earth " signifies 'among men,' Luke 12 : 49; 18 : 8; John 17 : 4; (*d*) a country, territory, e.g., Luke 4 : 25; John 3 : 22; (*e*) the ground, e.g., Matt. 10 : 29; Mark 4 : 26, R.V., " (upon the) earth," for A.V., " (into the) ground;" (*f*) land, e.g., Mark 4 : 1; John 21 : 8, 9, 11. Cp. Eng. words beginning with *ge*—, e.g., geodetic, geodesy, geology, geometry, geography. See COUNTRY, GROUND, LAND, WORLD.

2. OIKOUMENĒ (οἰκουμένη), the present participle, Passive Voice, 3625
of *oikeō*, to dwell, inhabit, denotes the inhabited earth. It is translated AG:561B
" world " in every place where it has this significance, save in Luke 21 : 26, CB:1260C
A.V., where it is translated " earth." See WORLD.

Note: For *epigeios*, translated " on earth " in Phil. 2 : 10, *ostrakinos*, " of earth," 2 Tim. 2 : 20, and *katachthonios*, " under the earth," Phil. 2 : 10,¶ see EARTHEN.

EARTHEN, EARTHLY, EARTHY

1. OSTRAKINOS (ὀστράκινος) signifies made of earthenware or clay 3749
(from *ostrakon*, baked clay, potsherd, shell; akin to *osteon*, a bone), AG:587C CB:1261B
2 Tim. 2 : 20, " of earth;" 2 Cor. 4 : 7, " earthen."¶

2. EPIGEIOS (ἐπίγειος), on earth (*epi*, on, *gē*, the earth), is rendered 1919
" earthly " in John 3 : 12; 2 Cor. 5 : 1; Phil 3 : 19; Jas. 3 : 15; in AG:290C CB:1245C
Phil. 2 : 10, " on earth," R.V.; " terrestrial " in 1 Cor. 15 : 40 (twice).
See TERRESTRIAL.¶

3. CHOÏKOS (χοϊκός) denotes " earthy," made of earth, from *chous*, 5517
soil, earth thrown down or heaped up, 1 Cor. 15 : 47, 48, 49.¶ AG:883A CB:1240A

4. KATACHTHONIOS (καταχθόνιος), under the earth, subterranean 2709
(*kata*, down, *chthōn*, the ground, from a root signifying that which is deep), AG:420D CB:1254A
is used in Phil. 2 : 10.¶

EARTHQUAKE

SEISMOS (σεισμός), a shaking, a shock, from *seiō*, to move to and fro, 4578
to shake, chiefly with the idea of concussion (Eng., seismic, seismology, AG:746B CB:1268C
seismometry), is used (*a*) of a tempest in the sea, Matt. 8 : 24; (*b*) of
earthquakes, Matt. 24 : 7; 27 : 54; 28 : 2; Mark 13 : 8; Luke 21 : 11;

Acts 16 : 26 ; Rev. 6 : 12 ; 8 : 5 ; 11 : 13 (twice), 19 ; 16 : 18 (twice). See TEMPEST.¶

EASE, EASED

A. Verb.

373 AG:58D CB:1235B ANAPAUŌ (ἀναπαύω) signifies to cause or permit one to cease from any labour or movement so as to recover strength. It implies previous toil and care. Its chief significance is that of taking, or causing to take, rest ; it is used in the Middle Voice in Luke 12 : 19, " take (thine) ease," indicative of unnecessary, self-indulgent relaxation. In the papyri it is used technically, as an agricultural term. Cp. *anapausis*, rest. See REFRESH, REST.

B. Noun.

425 AG:65B CB:— ANESIS (ἄνεσις) denotes a letting loose, relaxation, easing, it is connected with *aniēmi*, to loosen, relax (*ana*, back, and *hiēmi*, to send). It signifies rest, not from toil, but from endurance and suffering. Thus it is said (*a*) of a less vigorous condition in imprisonment, Acts 24 : 23, " indulgence," A.V., " liberty ; " (*b*) relief from anxiety, 2 Cor. 2 : 13 ; 7 : 5, " relief " (A.V., " rest ") ; (*c*) relief from persecutions, 2 Thess. 1 : 7, " rest ; " (*d*) of relief from the sufferings of poverty, 2 Cor. 8 : 13, " be eased," lit., ' (that there should be) easing for others (trouble to you).' Cp. the synonymous word *anapausis*, cessation or rest (akin to A). See INDULGENCE, LIBERTY, RELIEF, REST.¶ In the Sept., 2 Chron. 23 : 15.¶

For EASILY see EASY

EAST

395 AG:62B CB:1235B ANATOLE (ἀνατολή), primarily a rising, as of the sun and stars, corresponds to *anatellō*, to make to rise, or, intransitively, to arise, which is also used of the sunlight, as well as of other objects in nature. In Luke 1 : 78 it is used metaphorically of Christ as " the Dayspring," the One through Whom light came into the world, shining immediately into Israel, to dispel the darkness which was upon all nations. Cp. Mal. 4 : 2. Elsewhere it denotes the east, as the quarter of the sun's rising, Matt. 2 : 1, 2, 9 ; 8 : 11 ; 24 : 27 ; Luke 13 : 29 ; Rev. 7 : 2 ; 16 : 12 ; 21 : 13. The east in general stands for that side of things upon which the rising of the sun gives light. In the heavenly city itself, Rev. 21 : 13, the reference to the east gate points to the outgoing of the influence of the city eastward. See DAYSPRING.¶

EASTER

3957 AG:633B CB:1262C PASCHA (πάσχα), mistranslated " Easter " in Acts 12 : 4, A.V., denotes the Passover (R.V.). The phrase " after the Passover " signifies after the whole festival was at an end. The term Easter is not of Christian origin. It is another form of *Astarte*, one of the titles of the Chaldean goddess, the queen of heaven. The festival of Pasch held by Christians in post-apostolic times was a continuation of the Jewish feast, but was not instituted by Christ, nor was it connected with Lent. From this Pasch the Pagan festival of Easter was quite distinct and was introduced into the apostate Western religion, as part of the attempt to adapt Pagan festivals to Christianity. See PASSOVER.

EASY, EASIER, EASILY

1. CHRĒSTOS (χρηστός) primarily signifies fit for use, able to be 5543
used (akin to *chraomai*, to use), hence, good, virtuous, mild, pleasant AG:886A
(in contrast to what is hard, harsh, sharp, bitter). It is said (*a*) of the CB:1240A
character of God as kind, gracious, Luke 6 : 35 ; 1 Pet. 2 : 3 ; good, Rom. 2 : 4, where the neuter of the adjective is used as a noun, " the goodness " (cp. the corresponding noun *chrēstotēs*, " goodness," in the same verse) ; of the yoke of Christ, Matt. 11 : 30, " easy " (a suitable rendering would be ' kindly ') ; (*c*) of believers, Eph. 4 : 32 ; (*d*) of things, as wine, Luke 5 : 39, R.V., " good," for A.V., " better " (cp. Jer. 24 : 3, 5, of figs) ; (*e*) ethically, of manners, 1 Cor. 15 : 33. See GOOD, GRACIOUS, KIND.¶

2. EUKOPŌTEROS (εὐκοπώτερος), the comparative degree of *eukopos*, 2123
easy, with easy labour (*eu*, well, *kopos*, labour), hence, of that which is easier AG:321D (-POS)
to do, is found in the Synoptists only, Matt. 9 : 5 ; 19 : 24 ; Mark 2 : 9 ; CB:—
10 : 25 ; Luke 5 : 23 ; 16 : 17 ; 18 : 25.¶

Notes : (1) The adverb " easily " is included in the translation of
euperistatos in Heb. 12 :1, " easily beset," lit., ' the easily besetting sin,' 2139
probably a figure from a garment, ' easily surrounding,' and therefore AG:324A
easily entangling. See BESET. (2) In 1 Cor. 13 : 5, A.V., " is not easily CB:—
provoked," there is no word in the original representing " easily ; " R.V., " is not provoked." (3) For " easy to be entreated " see INTREAT. For " easy to be understood " see UNDERSTAND.

EAT, EAT WITH, EATING

A. Verbs.

1. ESTHIŌ (ἐσθίω) signifies to eat (as distinct from *pinō*, to drink) ; 2068
it is a lengthened form from *edō* (Lat., *edō* ; cp. Eng., edible) ; in Heb. AG:312B
10 : 27, metaphorically, " devour ; " it is said of the ordinary use of food CB:1246C
and drink, 1 Cor. 9 : 7 ; 11 : 22 ; of partaking of food at table, e.g., Mark 2 : 16 ; of revelling, Matt. 24 : 49 ; Luke 12 : 45. Cp. the strengthened form *katesthiō*, and the verb *sunesthiō*, below. See DEVOUR.

2. PHAGŌ (φάγω), to eat, devour, consume, is obsolete in the present 5315
and other tenses, but supplies certain tenses which are wanting in No. 1, AG:312B (ESTHIŌ)
above. In Luke 8 : 55 the A.V. has " (to give her) meat," the R.V. CB:—
" (that something be given her) to eat." The idea that this verb combines both eating and drinking, while No. 1 differentiates the one from the other, is not borne out in the N.T. The word is very frequent in the Gospels and is used eleven times in 1 Cor. See also No. 3. See MEAT.

5176 3. TRŌGŌ (τρώγω), primarily, to gnaw, to chew, stresses the slow
AG:829B process; it is used metaphorically of the habit of spiritually feeding upon
CB:1273A Christ, John 6 : 54, 56, 57, 58 (the aorists here do not indicate a definite act, but view a series of acts seen in perspective); of the constant custom of eating in certain company, John 13 : 18; of a practice unduly engrossing the world, Matt. 24 : 38.

In John 6, the change in the Lord's use from the verb *esthiō* (*phagō*) to the stronger verb *trōgō*, is noticeable. The more persistent the unbelief of His hearers, the more difficult His language and statements became. In vv. 49 to 53 the verb *phagō* is used; in 54, 58, *trōgō* (in ver. 58 it is put into immediate contrast with *phagō*). The use of *trōgō* in Matt. 24 : 38 and John 13 : 18 is a witness against pressing into the meaning of the word the sense of munching or gnawing; it had largely lost this sense in its common usage.¶

1089 4. GEUŌ (γεύω), primarily, to cause to taste, to give one a taste of,
AG:157A is used in the Middle Voice and denotes (*a*) to taste, its usual meaning;
CB:1248B (*b*) to take food, to eat, Acts 10 : 10; 20 : 11; 23 : 14; the meaning to taste must not be pressed in these passages, the verb having acquired the more general meaning. As to whether Acts 20 : 11 refers to the Lord's Supper or to an ordinary meal, the addition of the words "and eaten" is perhaps a sufficient indication that the latter is referred to here, whereas ver. 7, where the single phrase "to break bread" is used, refers to the Lord's Supper. A parallel instance is found in Acts 2 : 43, 46. In the former verse the phrase "the breaking of bread," unaccompanied by any word about taking food, clearly stands for the Lord's Supper; whereas in ver. 46 the phrase "breaking bread at home" is immediately explained by "they did take their food," indicating their ordinary meals. See TASTE.

977 5. BIBRŌSKŌ (βιβρώσκω), to eat, is derived from a root, *bor—*, to
AG:141C devour (likewise seen in the noun *brōma*, food, meat; cp. Eng., car-
CB:— nivorous, voracious, from Lat. *vorax*). This verb is found in John 6 : 13. The difference between this and *phagō*, No. 2, above, may be seen perhaps in the fact that whereas in the Lord's question to Philip in ver. 5, *phagō* intimates nothing about a full supply, the verb *bibrōskō*, in ver. 13, indicates that the people had been provided with a big meal, of which they had partaken eagerly.¶

2719 6. KATAPHAGŌ (καταφάγω) signifies to eat up (*kata*, used intensively,
AG:422A and No. 2), John 2 : 17; Rev. 10 : 9, 10; elsewhere it is translated
CB:— "devour," as also is *katesthiō* (see No. 1). See DEVOUR.

2880 7. KORENNUMI (κορέννυμι), to satiate, to satisfy, as with food, is
AG:444C used in the Middle Voice in Acts 27 : 38, "had eaten enough;" in 1 Cor.
CB:— 4 : 8, "ye are filled." See FILL.¶

4906 8. SUNESTHIŌ (συνεσθίω), to eat with (*sun*, with, and No. 1), is found
AG:788B
CB:— in Luke 15 : 2; Acts 10 : 41; 11 : 3; 1 Cor. 5 : 11; Gal. 2 : 12.¶

9. NOMĒN ECHŌ (νομὴν ἔχω) is a phrase consisting of the noun *nomē*, denoting (*a*) pasturage, (*b*) growth, increase, and *echō*, to have. In John 10 : 9 the phrase signifies to find pasture (*a*). In 2 Tim. 2 : 17, with the meaning (*b*), the phrase is, lit., 'will have growth,' translated "will eat," i.e., 'will spread like a gangrene.' It is used in Greek writings, other than the N.T., of the spread of a fire, and of ulcers. See PASTURE.¶ NOMē 3542 AG:541A CB:1260A

Note: The verb *metalambanō*, to take a part or share of anything with others, to partake of, share, is translated "did eat," in Acts 2 : 46, corrected in the R.V. to "did take;" a still more suitable rendering would be 'shared,' the sharing of food being suggested; cp. *metadidōmi*, to share, e.g., Luke 3 : 11. 3335 AG:511B CB:1258B

B. Nouns.

1. BRŌSIS (βρῶσις), akin to A, No. 5, denotes (*a*) the act of eating, e.g., Rom. 14 : 17; said of rust, Matt. 6 : 19, 20; or, more usually, (*b*) that which is eaten, food (like *brōma*, food), meat, John 4 : 32; 6 : 27, 55; Col. 2 : 16; Heb. 12 : 16 ("morsel of meat"); "food," 2 Cor. 9 : 10; "eating," 1 Cor. 8 : 4. See FOOD, MEAT, RUST.¶ 1035 AG:148B CB:1239B

2. PROSPHAGION (προσφάγιον), primarily a dainty or relish (especially cooked fish), to be eaten with bread (*pros*, to, and A, No. 2), then, fish in general, is used in John 21 : 5, "Have ye aught to eat?" (A.V., "have ye any meat?"). Moulton remarks that the evidences of the papyri are to the effect that *prosphagion*, "is not so broad a word as 'something to eat.' The apostles had left even loaves behind them once, Mark 8 : 14; they might well have left the 'relish' on this occasion. It would normally be fish; cp. Mark 6 : 38" (Gram. of N.T. Greek, Vol. 1, p. 170).¶ 4371 AG:719C CB:—

C. Adjective.

BRŌSIMOS (βρώσιμος), akin to A, No. 5, and B., signifying eatable, is found in Luke 24 : 41, R.V., appropriately, "to eat," for the A.V., "meat."¶ In the Sept., Lev. 19 : 23; Neh. 9 : 25; Ezek. 47 : 12.¶ 1034 AG:148B CB:1239B

EDGE, EDGED

A. Noun.

STOMA (στόμα), the mouth (cp. Eng., stomach, from *stomachos*, 1 Tim. 5 : 23), has a secondary and figurative meaning in reference to the edge of a sharp instrument, as of a sword, Luke 21 : 24; Heb. 11 : 34 (cp. the Sept., e.g., Gen. 34 : 26; Jud. 18 : 27). See FACE, MOUTH. 4750 AG:769D CB:1270A

B. Adjective.

DISTOMOS (δίστομος), lit., double-mouthed (*dis*, twice, and A.), two-edged, is used of a sword with two edges, Heb. 4 : 12; Rev. 1 : 16; 2 : 12.¶ In the Sept., Judg. 3 : 16; Psa. 149 : 6; Prov. 5 : 4.¶ 1366 AG:200A CB:1242A

EDIFICATION, EDIFY, EDIFYING

A. Noun.

OIKODOMĒ (οἰκοδομή) denotes (*a*) the act of building (*oikos*, a home, 3619 AG:558D CB:1260B and *demō*, to build); this is used only figuratively in the N.T., in the sense of edification, the promotion of spiritual growth (lit., the things of building up), Rom. 14 : 19; 15 : 2; 1 Cor. 14 : 3, 5, 12, 26, e.g.; (*b*) a building, edifice, whether material, Matt. 24 : 1, e.g., or figurative, of the future body of the believer, 2 Cor. 5 : 1, or of a local church, 1 Cor. 3 : 9, or the whole Church, "the body of Christ," Eph. 2 : 21. See BUILDING.

B. Verb.

3618 OIKODOMEŌ (οἰκοδομέω), lit., to build a house (see above), (*a*) usually
AG:558A CB:1260B signifies to build, whether literally, or figuratively; the present participle,
lit., 'the (ones) building,' is used as a noun, "the builders," in Matt. 21 : 42; Mark 12 : 10; Luke 20 : 17; Acts 4 : 11 (in some mss.; the most authentic have the noun *oikodomos*); 1 Pet. 2 : 7; (*b*) is used metaphorically, in the sense of edifying, promoting the spiritual growth and development of character of believers, by teaching or by example, suggesting such spiritual progress as the result of patient labour. It is said (1) of the effect of this upon local churches, Acts 9 : 31; 1 Cor. 14 : 4; (2) of the individual action of believers towards each other, 1 Cor. 8 : 1; 10 : 23; 14 : 17; 1 Thess. 5 : 11; (3) of an individual in regard to himself, 1 Cor. 14 : 4. In 1 Cor. 8 : 10, where it is translated "emboldened," the Apostle uses it with pathetic irony, of the action of a brother in "building up" his brother who had a weak conscience, causing him to compromise his scruples; 'strengthened,' or 'confirmed,' would be suitable renderings. See BUILD, EMBOLDEN.

EFFECT (of none)

208 1. AKUROŌ (ἀκυρόω) signifies to render void, deprive of force and
AG:34B CB:— authority (from *a*, negative, and *kuros*, might, authority; *kurios*, a
lord, is from the same root), the opposite to *kuroō*, to confirm (see CONFIRM). It is used of making void the Word of God, Matt. 15 : 6; Mark 7 : 13 (A.V., "making of none effect"), and of the promise of God to Abraham as not being deprived of authority by the Law 430 years after, Gal. 3 : 17, "disannul." *Kuroō* is used in verse 15. See DISANNUL, VOID.¶

2673 2. KATARGEŌ (καταργέω), to reduce to inactivity, to render useless,
AG:417B CB:1254B is translated to make of none effect, in Rom. 3 : 3, 31; 4 : 14; Gal. 3 : 17
(cp. *akuroō*, No. 1, in the same verse), and in the A.V. of Gal. 5 : 4, R.V., "ye are severed" (from Christ). For the meaning and use of the word see ABOLISH and DESTROY.

2758 3. KENOŌ (κενόω), to make empty, to empty, is translated "should
AG:428A CB:1255A be made of none effect" in 1 Cor. 1 : 17, A.V. (R.V. "made void");
it is used (*a*) of the Cross of Christ, there; (*b*) of Christ, in emptying Himself, Phil. 2 : 7; (*c*) of faith, Rom. 4 : 14; (*d*) of the Apostle Paul's glorying in the Gospel ministry, 1 Cor. 9 : 15; (*e*) of his glorying on behalf
of the church at Corinth, 2 Cor. 9 : 3. See EMPTY, VAIN, VOID.¶

1601 AG:243D CB:1243C *Note:* In Rom. 9 : 6 the verb *ekpiptō*, lit., to fall out of, as of a ship falling out of its course (cp. the same word in Acts 27 : 17, " were driven "), is translated " hath taken none effect," A.V. (R.V., " hath come to nought "). See NOUGHT.

EFFECTUAL

A. Adjective.

ENERGĒS (ἐνεργής) denotes active, powerful in action (*en*, in, 1756
ergon, work ; Eng. " energy ; " the word " work " is derived from the AG:265D CB:1245A
same root). It is translated "effectual" in 1 Cor. 16 : 9, of the door opened for the Gospel in Ephesus, and made effectual in the results of entering it ; and in Philm. 6, of the fellowship of Philemon's faith " in the knowledge of every good thing " (R.V.). In Heb. 4 : 12 it describes the Word of God as " active," R.V. (A.V., " powerful "), i.e., full of power to achieve results. See ACTIVE, POWERFUL.¶

B. Verb.

ENERGEŌ (ἐνεργέω), to put forth power, be operative, to work 1754
(its usual meaning), is rendered by the verb to work effectually, or to be AG:265B CB:1245A
effectual, in the A.V. of 2 Cor. 1 : 6 ; Gal. 2 : 8 and 1 Thess. 2 : 13 ; in each case the R.V. translates it by the simple verb to work (past tense, " wrought "). In Jas. 5 : 16 the R.V. omits the superfluous word " effectual," and translates the sentence " the supplication of a righteous man availeth much in its working," the verb being in the present participial form. Here the meaning may be 'in its inworking,' i.e., in the effect produced in the praying man, bringing him into line with the will of God, as in the case of Elijah. For a fuller treatment of the word see WORK. See also DO, MIGHTY, SHEW, *Note* (11).

Note : The noun *energeia*, working, is translated " effectual working," 1753
in the A.V. of Eph. 3 : 7, and 4 : 16. AG:265A CB:1245A

EFFEMINATE

MALAKOS (μαλακός), soft, soft to the touch (Lat., *mollis*, Eng., mollify, 3120
emollient, etc., are from the same root), is used (*a*) of raiment, Matt. 11 : 8 AG:488D CB:—
(twice) ; Luke 7 : 25 ; (*b*) metaphorically, in a bad sense, 1 Cor. 6 : 9, " effeminate," not simply of a male who practises forms of lewdness, but persons in general, who are guilty of addiction to sins of the flesh, voluptuous.¶

EFFORT See DILIGENCE

EFFULGENCE

APAUGASMA (ἀπαύγασμα), radiance, effulgence, is used of light 541
shining from a luminous body (*apo*, from, and *augē*, brightness). The word AG:82B CB:1236B
is found in Heb. 1 : 3, where it is used of the Son of God as " being the effulgence of His glory." The word " effulgence " exactly corresponds (in its Latin form) to *apaugasma*. The glory of God expresses all that He is in His nature and His actings and their manifestation. The Son, being one with the Father in Godhood, is in Himself, and ever was, the

shining forth of the glory, manifesting in Himself all that God is and does, all, for instance, that is involved in His being " the very image of His substance," and in His creative acts, His sustaining power, and in His making purification of sins, with all that pertains thereto and issues from it.¶

EGG

5609 AG:896A CB:— ŌON (ὠόν) denotes an egg (Lat., *ovum*), Luke 11 : 12.¶

EIGHT, EIGHTEEN, EIGHTH

3638 AG:563A CB:1260C OKTŌ (ὀκτώ), eight (Lat., *octo, octavus ;* cp. Eng., octagon, octave, octavo, October, etc.), is used in Luke 2 : 21 ; 9 : 28 ; John 20 : 26 ; Acts 9 : 33 ; 25 : 6 ; 1 Pet. 3 : 20 ; in composition with other numerals, *oktō kai deka,* lit., eight and ten, eighteen, Luke 13 : 4, 11, 16 ; *triakonta kai oktō,* thirty and eight, John 5 : 5.¶

3590 AG:552D CB:1260B OGDOOS (ὄγδοος), eighth (connected with the preceding), is used in Luke 1 : 59 ; Acts 7 : 8 ; 2 Pet. 2 : 5 ; Rev. 17 : 11 ; 21 : 20.¶

3637 AG:563A CB:— OKTAĒMEROS (ὀκταήμερος), an adjective, signifying an eighth-day person or thing, eight days old (*oktō,* and *hēmera,* a day), is used in Phil. 3 : 5. This, and similar numerical adjectives not found in the N.T., indicate duration rather than intervals. The Apostle shows by his being an ' eighth-day ' person as to circumcision, that his parents were neither Ishmaelites (circumcised in their thirteenth year) nor other Gentiles, converted to Judaism (circumcised on becoming Jews).¶

EITHER

2228 AG:342A 1.b. CB:— Ē (ἤ) is a disjunctive particle. One of its uses is to distinguish things which exclude each other, or one of which can take the place of another. It is translated " either " in Matt. 6 : 24 ; 12 : 33 ; Luke 16 : 13 ; Acts 17 : 21 ; 1 Cor. 14 : 6. The R.V. rightly omits it in Luke 6 : 42, and translates it by " or " in Luke 15 : 8 ; Phil. 3 : 12 and Jas. 3 : 12.

1782 AG:268C CB:— *Note :* The adverb *enteuthen,* denoting " hence," is repeated in the phrase rendered " on either side," (lit., ' hence and hence ') in John 19 : 18. The R.V. of Rev. 22 : 2 translates it " on this side," distinguishing it from *ekeithen,* " on that side ; " the A.V., following another reading for the latter adverb, has " on either side." See HENCE.

ELDER, ELDEST

A. Adjectives.

4245 AG:699D CB:1266B 1. PRESBUTEROS (πρεσβύτερος), an adjective, the comparative degree of *presbus,* an old man, an elder, is used (*a*) of age, whether of the elder of two persons, Luke 15 : 25, or more, John 8 : 9, " the eldest ; " or of a person advanced in life, a senior, Acts 2 : 17 ; in Heb. 11 : 2, the " elders " are the forefathers in Israel ; so in Matt. 15 : 2 ; Mark 7 : 3, 5 ; the feminine of the adjective is used of elder women in the churches, 1 Tim.

5 : 2, not in respect of position but in seniority of age ; (*b*) of rank or positions of responsibility, (1) among Gentiles, as in the Sept. of Gen. 50 : 7 ; Num. 22 : 7 ; (2) in the Jewish nation, firstly, those who were the heads or leaders of the tribes and families, as of the seventy who assisted Moses, Num. 11 : 16 ; Deut. 27 : 1, and those assembled by Solomon ; secondly, members of the Sanhedrin, consisting of the chief priests, elders and scribes, learned in Jewish Law, e.g., Matt. 16 : 21 ; 26 : 47 ; thirdly, those who managed public affairs in the various cities, Luke 7 : 3 ; (3) in the Christian churches, those who, being raised up and qualified by the work of the Holy Spirit, were appointed to have the spiritual care of, and to exercise oversight over, the churches. To these the term bishops, *episkopoi*, or overseers, is applied (see Acts 20, ver. 17 with ver. 28, and Tit. 1 : 5 and 7), the latter term indicating the nature of their work, *presbuteroi* their maturity of spiritual experience. The Divine arrangement seen throughout the N.T. was for a plurality of these to be appointed in each church, Acts 14 : 23 ; 20 : 17 ; Phil. 1 : 1 ; 1 Tim. 5 : 17 ; Tit. 1 : 5. The duty of elders is described by the verb *episkopeō*. They were appointed according as they had given evidence of fulfilling the Divine qualifications, Tit. 1 : 6 to 9 ; cp. 1 Tim. 3 : 1–7 and 1 Pet. 5 : 2 ; (4) the twenty-four elders enthroned in Heaven around the throne of God, Rev. 4 : 4, 10 ; 5 : 5–14 ; 7 : 11, 13 ; 11 : 16 ; 14 : 3 ; 19 : 4. The number twenty-four is representative of earthly conditions. The word " elder " is nowhere applied to angels. See OLD.

2. SUMPRESBUTEROS (συμπρεσβύτερος), a fellow-elder (*sun*, with), 4850 AG:780A
is used in 1 Pet. 5 : 1.¶ CB:—

3. MEIZŌN (μείζων), greater, the comparative degree of *megas*, great, 3187
is used of age, and translated " elder " in Rom. 9 : 12, with reference to AG:497C (MEGAS)
Esau and Jacob. See GREATER, GREATEST, MORE. CB:1258A

B. Noun.

PRESBUTERION (πρεσβυτέριον), an assembly of aged men, denotes 4244
(*a*) the Council or Senate among the Jews, Luke 22 : 66 ; Acts 22 : 5 ; AG:699C CB:1266B
(*b*) the elders or bishops in a local church, 1 Tim. 4 : 14, " the presbytery." For their functions see A, No. 1, (3).

ELECT, ELECTED, ELECTION

A. Adjectives.

1. EKLEKTOS (ἐκλεκτός) lit. signifies picked out, chosen (*ek*, from, 1588
legō, to gather, pick out), and is used of (*a*) Christ, the chosen of God, AG:242D CB:1243C
as the Messiah, Luke 23 : 35 (for the verb in 9 : 35 see Note below), and metaphorically as a " living Stone," " a chief corner Stone," 1 Pet. 2 : 4, 6 ; some mss. have it in John 1 : 34, instead of *huios*, Son ; (*b*) angels, 1 Tim. 5 : 21, as chosen to be of especially high rank in administrative association with God, or as His messengers to human beings, doubtless in contrast to fallen angels (see 2 Pet. 2 : 4 and Jude 6) ; (*c*) believers (Jews or Gentiles), Matt. 24 : 22, 24, 31 ; Mark 13 : 20, 22, 27 ; Luke 18 : 7 ;

Rom. 8 : 33 ; Col. 3 : 12 ; 2 Tim. 2 : 10 ; Tit. 1 : 1 ; 1 Pet. 1 : 1 ; 2 : 9 (as a spiritual race) ; Matt. 20 : 16 ; 22 : 14 and Rev. 17 : 14, " chosen ; " individual believers are so mentioned in Rom. 16 : 13 ; 2 John 1, 13.¶

Believers were chosen " before the foundation of the world " (cp. " before times eternal," 2 Tim. 1 : 9), in Christ, Eph. 1 : 4, to adoption, Eph. 1 : 5 ; good works, 2 : 10 ; conformity to Christ, Rom. 8 : 29 ; salvation from the delusions of the Antichrist and the doom of the deluded, 2 Thess. 2 : 13 ; eternal glory, Rom. 9 : 23.

The source of their election is God's grace, not human will, Eph. 1 : 4, 5 ; Rom. 9 : 11 ; 11 : 5. They are given by God the Father to Christ as the fruit of His Death, all being foreknown and foreseen by God, John 17 : 6 and Rom. 8 : 29. While Christ's Death was sufficient for all men, and is effective in the case of the elect, yet men are treated as responsible, being capable of the will and power to choose. For the rendering ' being chosen as firstfruits,' an alternative reading in 2 Thess. 2 : 13, see FIRSTFRUITS. See CHOICE, B.

4899 AG:787B CB:— 2. SUNEKLEKTOS (συνεκλεκτός) means " elect together with," 1 Pet. 5 : 13.¶

B. Noun.

1589 AG:243A CB:1243C EKLOGĒ (ἐκλογή) denotes a picking out, selection (Eng., eclogue), then, that which is chosen ; in Acts 9 : 15, said of the choice of God of Saul of Tarsus, the phrase is, lit., ' a vessel of choice.' It is used four times in Romans ; in 9 : 11, of Esau and Jacob, where the phrase " the purpose . . . according to election " is virtually equivalent to ' the electing purpose ; ' in 11 : 5, the " remnant according to the election of grace " refers to believing Jews, saved from among the unbelieving nation ; so in ver. 7 ; in ver. 28, " the election " may mean either the act of choosing or the chosen ones ; the context, speaking of the fathers, points to the former, the choice of the nation according to the covenant of promise. In 1 Thess. 1 : 4, " your election " refers not to the church collectively, but to the individuals constituting it ; the Apostle's assurance of their election gives the reason for his thanksgiving. Believers are to give ' the more diligence to make their calling and election sure,' by the exercise of the qualities and graces which make them fruitful in the knowledge of God, 2 Pet. 1 : 10.¶ For the corresponding verb *eklegomai*, see CHOOSE.

ELEMENTS

4747 AG:768D CB:1270A STOICHEION (στοιχεῖον), used in the plural, primarily signifies any first things from which others in a series, or a composite whole, take their rise ; the word denotes an element, first principle (from *stoichos*, a row, rank, series ; cp. the verb *stoicheō*, to walk or march in rank ; see WALK) ; it was used of the letters of the alphabet, as elements of speech. In the N.T. it is used of (*a*) the substance of the material world, 2 Pet. 3 : 10, 12 ; (*b*) the delusive speculations of Gentile cults and of Jewish theories, treated as elementary principles, " the rudiments of the world," Col. 2 : 8, spoken of as " philosophy and vain deceit ; " these were presented as superior to faith in Christ ; at Colossæ the worship of angels, mentioned in ver. 18, is explicable by the supposition, held by both Jews and Gentiles in that district, that the constellations were either themselves animated heavenly beings, or were governed by them ; (*c*) the rudimentary principles of religion, Jewish or Gentile, also described as " the rudiments of the world," Col. 2 : 20, and as " weak and beggarly rudiments," Gal. 4 : 3, 9, R.V., constituting a yoke of bondage ; (*d*) the elementary principles (the A.B.C.) of the O.T., as a revelation from God, Heb. 5 : 12, R.V., " rudiments," lit., ' the rudiments of the beginning of the oracles of God,' such as are taught to spiritual babes. See PRINCIPLES, RUDIMENTS.¶

ELEVEN, ELEVENTH

HENDEKA (ἕνδεκα), lit., one ten (Lat., *undecim*), is used only of the 1733
eleven Apostles remaining after the death of Judas Iscariot, Matt. 28 : 16 ; AG:262D
Mark 16 : 14 ; Luke 24 : 9, 33 ; Acts 1 : 26 ; 2 : 14.¶ CB:—

HENDEKATOS (ἑνδέκατος), an adjective derived from the above, is 1734
found in Matt. 20 : 6, 9 ; Rev. 21 : 20.¶ AG:262D CB:—

ELOQUENT

LOGIOS (λόγιος), an adjective, from *logos*, a word, primarily meant 3052
learned, a man skilled in literature and the arts. In the A.V. of Acts AG:476D CB:1257A
18 : 24, it is translated " eloquent," said of Apollos ; the R.V. is almost certainly right in translating it " learned." It was much more frequently used among the Greeks of one who was erudite than of one who was skilled in words. He had stores of learning and could use it convincingly.¶

ELSE

EPEI (ἐπεί), a conjunction, when used of cause, meaning " since," 1893
" otherwise," " for then," " because ; " in an ellipsis, " else," as in AG:284A CB:—
1 Cor. 7 : 14, where the ellipsis would be ' if the unbelieving husband were not sanctified in the wife, your children would be unclean ; ' cp. Rom. 11 : 6, 22 ; 1 Cor. 5 : 10 ; Heb. 9 : 26. Sometimes it introduces a question, as in Rom. 3 : 6 ; 1 Cor. 14 : 16 ; 15 : 29 ; Heb. 10 : 2. It is translated " else " in 1 Cor. 14 : 16 and in the R.V. in Heb. 9 : 26 and 10 : 2, for A.V., " for then."

ELSEWHERE

ALLACHOU (ἀλλαχοῦ), connected with *allos*, another, is used in —
Mark 1 : 38 (R.V. only).¶ AG:39B CB:—

For EMBARK (R.V., in Acts 27 : 2) see ABOARD

EMBOLDEN

3618 OIKODOMEŌ (οἰκοδομέω) is rendered " embolden " in 1 Cor. 8 : 10,
AG:558A in reference to blameworthy actions (see marg.), the delinquent being
CB:1260B built up, so to speak, to do what is contrary to his conscience. See BUILD, EDIFICATION.

EMBRACE

782 1. ASPAZOMAI (ἀσπάζομαι) lit. signifies to draw to oneself; hence,
AG:116C to greet, salute, welcome, the ordinary meaning, e.g., in Rom. 16, where
CB:1238A it is used 21 times. It also signifies to bid farewell, e.g., Acts 20 : 1, R.V., " took leave of " (A.V., " embraced "). A salutation or farewell was generally made by embracing and kissing (see Luke 10 : 4, which indicates the possibility of delay on the journey by frequent salutation). In Heb. 11 : 13 it is said of those who greeted the promises from afar, R.V., " greeted," for A.V., " embraced." Cp. *aspasmos*, a salutation. See GREET, LEAVE (take), SALUTE.

Note: In Acts 21 : 6 the most authentic texts have *apaspazomai* (*apo*, and No. 1), to bid farewell.

4843 2. SUMPERILAMBANŌ (συμπεριλαμβάνω), lit., to take around with,
AG:779C (*sun*, with, *peri*, around, *lambanō*, to take), to embrace, is used in Acts
CB:— 20 : 10, in connection with Paul's recovery of Eutychus.¶ In the Sept., Ezra 5 : 3, " to enclose."¶

EMPEROR

4575 SEBASTOS (σεβαστός), august, reverent, the masculine gender of an
AG:745D adjective (from *sebas*, reverential awe), became used as the title of the
CB:1268C Roman Emperor, Acts 25 : 21, 25, R.V., for A.V., " Augustus ; " then, taking its name from the Emperor, it became a title of honour applied to certain legions or cohorts or battalions, marked for their valour, Acts 27 : 1.¶ Cp. *sebazomai*, to worship, Rom. 1 : 25 ;¶ *sebasma*, an object of worship, Acts 17 : 23 ; 2 Thess. 2 : 4.¶

EMERALD

A. Noun.

4665 SMARAGDOS (σμάραγδος) is a transparent stone of a light green
AG:758C colour, occupying the first place in the second row on the high priest's
CB:1269B breastplate, Ex. 28 : 18. Tyre imported it from Syria, Ezek. 27 : 16. It is one of the foundations of the Heavenly Jerusalem, Rev. 21 : 19. The name was applied to other stones of a similar character, such as the carbuncle.¶

B. Adjective.

4664 SMARAGDINOS (σμαράγδινος), emerald in character, descriptive of
AG:758C the rainbow round about the Throne in Rev. 4 : 3, is used in the papyri
CB:1269B to denote emerald green.¶

EMPTY

A. Verbs.

1. KENOŌ (κενόω), to empty, is so translated in Phil. 2 : 7, R.V., 2758
for A.V., "made . . . of no reputation." The clauses which follow AG:428A
the verb are exegetical of its meaning, especially the phrases "the form CB:1255A
of a servant," and "the likeness of men." Christ did not empty Himself of Godhood. He did not cease to be what He essentially and eternally was. The A.V., while not an exact translation, goes far to express the act of the Lord (see GIFFORD on the Incarnation). For other occurrences of the word see Rom. 4 : 14; 1 Cor. 1 : 17; 9 : 15; 2 Cor. 9 : 3.¶ In the Sept., Jer. 14 : 2; 15 : 9.¶

2. SCHOLAZŌ (σχολάζω), from *scholē*, leisure, that for which leisure 4980
is employed, such as a lecture (hence, the place where lectures are given; AG:797D
Eng., school), is used of persons, to have time for anything and so to be CB:—
occupied in, 1 Cor. 7 : 5; of things, to be unoccupied, empty, Matt. 12 : 44 (some mss. have it in Luke 11 : 25). See GIVE (oneself to).¶

B. Adjective.

KENOS (κενός) expresses the hollowness of anything, the absence 2756
of that which otherwise might be possessed. It is used (*a*) literally, AG:427D
Mark 12 : 3; Luke 1 : 53; 20 : 10, 11; (*b*) metaphorically, of imagina- CB:1255A
tions, Acts 4 : 25; of words which convey erroneous teachings, Eph. 5 : 6; of deceit, Col. 2 : 8; of a person whose professed faith is not accompanied by works, Jas. 2 : 20; negatively, concerning the grace of God, 1 Cor. 15 : 10; of refusal to receive it, 2 Cor. 6 : 1; of faith, 1 Cor. 15 : 14; of preaching (id.); and other forms of Christian activity and labour, 1 Cor. 15 : 58; Gal. 2 : 2; Phil. 2 : 16; 1 Thess. 2 : 1; 3 : 5.¶ The
synonymous word *mataios*, vain, signifies void of result, it marks the MATAIOS
aimlessness of anything. The vain (*kenos*) man in Jas. 2 : 20 is one who 3152
is empty of Divinely imparted wisdom; in 1 : 26 the vain (*mataios*) AG:495C CB:1258A
religion is one that produces nothing profitable. *Kenos* stresses the absence of quality, *mataios*, the absence of useful aim or effect. Cp. the corresponding adverb *kenōs*, "in vain," in Jas. 4 : 5,¶ the noun *kenodoxia*, vainglory, Phil. 2 : 3,¶ the adjective *kenodoxos*, vainglorious, Gal. 5 : 26,¶ and the noun *kenophōnia*, vain, or empty, babblings, 1 Tim. 6 : 20; 2 Tim. 2 : 16.¶

For EMULATION, A.V. (Rom. 11 : 14; Gal. 5 : 20) see JEALOUSY

ENABLE

ENDUNAMOŌ (ἐνδυναμόω), to render strong (*en*, in, *dunamis*, power), 1743
is translated "enabled" in 1 Tim. 1 : 12, more lit., 'in-strengthened,' AG:263D
'inwardly strengthened,' suggesting strength in soul and purpose (cp. CB:1245A
Phil. 4 : 13). See STRENGTH, STRONG. (In the Sept., Judg. 6 : 34; 1 Chron. 12 : 18; Psa. 52 : 7.¶)

ENACT

3549 AG:541D CB:1260A NOMOTHETEŌ (νομοθετέω), to ordain by law, to enact (*nomos*, a law, *tithēmi*, to put), is used in the Passive Voice, and rendered " enacted " in Heb. 8 : 6, R.V., for A.V., " established ; " in 7 : 11, used intransitively, it is rendered " received the Law." See ESTABLISH, LAW.¶

ENCIRCLE See ROUND

For ENCLOSE see INCLOSE

ENCOUNTER

4820 AG:777B CB:– SUMBALLŌ (συμβάλλω), lit., to throw together (*sun*, with, *ballō*, to throw), is used of encountering in war, Luke 14 : 31, R.V., " to encounter . . . (in war)," for A.V., " to make war against ; " of meeting in order to discuss, in Acts 17 : 18, " encountered," of the philosophers in Athens and the Apostle. See CONFER, HELP, MAKE, MEET, PONDER.

ENCOURAGE, ENCOURAGEMENT

A. Verbs.

4389 AG:722B CB:– 1. PROTREPŌ (προτρέπω), to urge forward, persuade, is used in Acts 18 : 27 in the Middle Voice, R.V., " encouraged," indicating their particular interest in giving Apollos the encouragement mentioned ; the A.V., " exhorting," wrongly connects the verb.¶

3888 AG:620D CB:1262B 2. PARAMUTHEOMAI (παραμυθέομαι), from *para*, with, and *muthos*, counsel, advice, is translated " encouraging " in 1 Thess. 2 : 11, R.V., and " encourage " in 5 : 14, R.V., there signifying to stimulate to the discharge of the ordinary duties of life. In John 11 : 19, 31, it means to comfort. See COMFORT.¶

Cp. the nouns *paramuthia*, 1 Cor. 14 : 3, ¶ and *paramuthion*, Phil 2 : 1, comfort.¶

B. Noun.

3874 AG:618A CB:1262A PARAKLĒSIS (παράκλησις), a calling to one's aid (*para*, by the side, *kaleō*, to call), then, an exhortation, encouragement, is translated " encouragement " in Heb. 6 : 18, R.V., for A.V., " consolation ; " it is akin to *parakaleō*, to beseech or exhort, encourage, comfort, and *paraklētos*, a paraclete or advocate. See COMFORT, CONSOLATION, EXHORTATION, INTREATY.

END, ENDING

A. Nouns.

5056 AG:811B CB:1271B 1. TELOS (τέλος) signifies (*a*) the limit, either at which a person or thing ceases to be what he or it was up to that point, or at which previous activities were ceased, 2 Cor. 3 : 13 ; 1 Pet. 4 : 7 ; (*b*) the final issue or result of a state or process, e.g., Luke 1 : 33 ; in Rom. 10 : 4, Christ is described as " the end of the Law unto righteousness to everyone that believeth ; " this is best explained by Gal. 3 : 23–26 ; cp. Jas. 5 : 11 ; the following more especially point to the issue or fate of a thing, Matt.

26 : 58 ; Rom. 6 : 21 ; 2 Cor. 11 : 15 ; Phil. 3 : 19 ; Heb. 6 : 8 ; 1 Pet. 1 : 9 ; (*c*) a fulfilment, Luke 22 : 37, A.V. " (have) an end ; " (*d*) the utmost degree of an act, as of the love of Christ towards His disciples, John 13 : 1 ; (*e*) the aim or purpose of a thing, 1 Tim. 1 : 5 ; (*f*) the last in a succession or series Rev. 1 : 8 (A.V., only, " ending ") ; 21 : 6 ; 22 : 13. See CONTINUAL, CUSTOM (Toll), FINALLY, UTTERMOST.

Note : The following phrases contain *telos* (the word itself coming under one or other of the above) : *eis telos,* " unto the end," e.g., Matt. 10 : 22 ; 24 : 13 ; Luke 18 : 5, " continual ; " John 13 : 1 (see above) ; 2 Cor. : 13, " on the end " (R.V.) ; *heōs telous,* " unto the end," 1 Cor. 1 : 8 ; 2 Cor. 1 : 13 ;¶ *achri telous,* " even to the end " (a stronger expression than the preceding), Heb. 6 : 11 ; Rev. 2 : 26 (where ' even ' might well have been added) ;¶ *mechri telous,* with much the same meaning as *achri telous,* Heb. 3 : 6, 14.¶ See other expressions in the Notes after C.

2. SUNTELEIA (συντέλεια) signifies a bringing to completion together 4930
(*sun* with, *teleō,* to complete, akin to No. 1), marking the completion or AG:792A CB:1271A
consummation of the various parts of a scheme. In Matt. 13 : 39, 40, 49 ; 24 : 3 ; 28 : 20, the rendering " the end of the world " (A.V. and R.V., text) is misleading ; the R.V. marg., " the consummation of the age," is correct. The word does not denote a termination, but the heading up of events to the appointed climax. *Aiōn* is not the world, but a period or epoch or era in which events take place. In Heb. 9 : 26, the word translated " world " (A.V.) is in the plural, and the phrase is ' the consummation of the ages.' It was at the heading up of all the various epochs appointed by Divine counsels that Christ was manifested (i.e., in His Incarnation) " to put away sin by the sacrifice of Himself."¶

3. PERAS (πέρας), a limit, boundary (from *pera,* beyond), is used 4009
(*a*) of space, chiefly in the plural, Matt. 12 : 42, R.V., " ends," for A.V., AG:644A CB:1263B
" uttermost parts ; " so Luke 11 : 31 (A.V., " utmost ") ; Rom. 10 : 18 (A.V. and R.V., " ends ") ; (*b*) of the termination of something occurring in a period, Heb. 6 : 16, R.V., " final," for A.V., " an end," said of strife. See UTTERMOST.¶

4. EKBASIS (ἔκβασις) denotes a way out (*ek,* out, *bainō,* to go), 1 Cor. 1545
10 : 13, " way of escape ; " or an issue, Heb. 13 : 7 (A.V., " end," R.V., AG:237D CB:—
" issue "). See ISSUE.¶

B. Verbs.

1. TELEŌ (τελέω), to complete, finish, bring to an end, is translated 5055
" had made an end," in Matt. 11 : 1. See ACCOMPLISH. AG:810D CB:1271B

2. SUNTELEŌ (συντελέω), cp. A, No. 2, signifies (*a*) to bring to an end, 4931
finish completely (*sun,* together, imparting a perfective significance to AG:792A CB:1271A
teleō), Matt. 7 : 28 (in some mss.) ; Luke 4 : 2, 13 ; Acts 21 : 27, R.V., " completed ; " (*b*) to bring to fulfilment, Mark 13 : 4 ; Rom. 9 : 28 ;
(*c*) to effect, make, Heb. 8 : 8. See FINISH, FULFIL, MAKE.¶ 4137

3. PLĒROŌ (πληρόω), (*a*) to fill, (*b*) to fulfil, complete, end, is trans- AG:670C CB:1265B

lated "had ended" in Luke 7:1; "were ended" (Passive) in Acts 19:21. See ACCOMPLISH.

1096 *Note:* In John 13:2, the verb *ginomai*, there signifying to be in
AG:158A CB:1248B progress, and used in the present participle, is translated "during
supper" (R.V.). A less authentic reading, is *genomenou*, "being ended"
(A.V.).

C. Adjective.

2078 ESCHATOS (ἔσχατος), last, utmost, extreme, is used as a noun (*a*) of
AG:313D CB:1246C time, rendered "end" in Heb. 1:2, R.V., "at the end of these days,"
i.e., at the end of the period under the Law, for A.V., "in these last days;" so in 1 Pet. 1:20, "at the end of the times." In 2 Pet. 2:20, the plural, *ta eschata*, lit., 'the last things,' is rendered "the latter end," A.V., (R.V., "the last state"); the same phrase is used in Matt. 12:45; Luke 11:26; (*b*) of place, Acts 13:47, A.V., "ends (of the earth)," R.V., "uttermost part." See LAST, LOWEST, UTTERMOST.

OPSE *Notes:* (1) In Matt. 28:1, *opse*, late (in the evening), is rendered
3796 AG:601B "in the end (of)," A.V., R.V., "late (on)." (2) In 1 Pet. 1:13, *teleiōs*,
CB:1261A "perfectly," R.V., is rendered "to the end," in A.V. (3) The phrase
TELEIōS 5049 *eis touto*, lit., 'unto this,' signifies "to this end," John 18:37, R.V.
AG:810B (twice; A.V., "for this cause," in the second clause); so Mark 1:38;
CB:1271B EIS Acts 26:16; Rom. 14:9; 2 Cor. 2:9; 1 Tim. 4:10 (A.V., "therefore");
1519 1 Pet. 4:6; 1 John 3:8 (A.V., "for this purpose"). (4) *Eis*, unto,
AG:228A followed by the article and the infinitive mood of a verb, signifies "to
CB:1243A PROS the end that . . ," marking the aim of an action, Acts 7:19; Rom.
4314 1:11; 4:16, 18; Eph. 1:12; 1 Thess. 3:13; 2 Thess. 1:5; 2:2, 6;
AG:709C CB:1267A 1 Pet. 3:7. In Luke 18:1, *pros*, to, has the same construction and
HINA meaning. (5) The conjunction *hina*, in order that, is sometimes rendered
2443 AG:376D "to the end that," Eph. 3:17; 2 Thess. 3:14; Tit. 3:8. (6) In Matt.
CB:1250C 24:31, the prepositions *apo*, from, and *heōs*, unto, are used with the
AKRON 206 plural of *akros*, highest, extreme, signifying "from one end . . . to the
AG:34A CB:— other," lit., 'from extremities . . . to extremities.'

ENDEAVOUR

4704 1. SPOUDAZŌ (σπουδάζω), to make haste, to be zealous, and hence,
AG:763C CB:1269C to be diligent, is rendered "endeavouring" in Eph. 4:3, A.V.; R.V.,
"giving diligence." In 2 Pet. 1:15, A.V., "endeavour," R.V., "give diligence." Both have "endeavoured" in 1 Thess. 2:17. See DILIGENCE.

2212 2. ZĒTEŌ (ζητέω), to seek after, is translated "endeavour" in Acts
AG:338D CB:1273C 16:10, A.V., R.V., "sought." See ABOUT (to be), DESIRE, INQUIRE, SEEK.

ENDLESS

179 AG:30A 1. AKATALUTOS (ἀκατάλυτος) denotes indissoluble (from *a*, negative,
CB:1234A *kata*, down, *luō*, to loose), Heb. 7:16, "endless;" see the R.V., marg.,

i.e., a life which makes its Possessor the holder of His priestly office for
evermore.¶

2. APERANTOS (ἀπέραντος), from *a*, negative and *perainō*, to 562
complete, finish, signifies interminable, endless; it is said of genealogies, AG:84A CB:—
1 Tim. 1:4.¶ In the Sept., Job 36:26.¶

ENDUE

ENDUŌ (ἐνδύω), in the Middle Voice, to put on oneself, be clothed 1746
with, is used metaphorically of power, Luke 24:49, R.V., "clothed." AG:264A CB:1245A
See CLOTHE.

Note: In Jas. 3:13 the adjective *epistēmōn*, knowing, skilled, is 1990
translated "endued with knowledge," A.V., R.V., "understanding."¶ AG:300C CB:—

ENDURE, ENDURING

A. Verbs.

1. MENŌ (μένω), to abide, is rendered to endure in the A.V. of John 3306
6:27 and 1 Pet. 1:25 (R.V., "abideth"); Heb. 10:34, A.V., "enduring AG:503C CB:1258B
(substance)," R.V., "abiding." See ABIDE.

2. HUPOMENŌ (ὑπομένω), a strengthened form of No. 1, denotes 5278
to abide under, to bear up courageously (under suffering), Matt. 10:22; AG:845D CB:1252B
24:13; Mark 13:13; Rom. 12:12, translated "patient;" 1 Cor.
13:7; 2 Tim. 2:10, 12 (A.V., "suffer"); Heb. 10:32; 12:2, 3, 7;
Jas. 1:12; 5:11; 1 Pet. 2:20, "ye shall take it patiently." It has its
other significance, to tarry, wait for, await, in Luke 2:43; Acts 17:14
(in some mss., Rom. 8:24).¶ Cp. B. See ABIDE, PATIENT, SUFFER,
TARRY. Cp. *makrothumeō*, to be longsuffering (see No. 7).

3. PHERŌ (φέρω), to bear, is translated "endured" in Rom. 9:22 5342 AG:854D
and Heb. 12:20. See BEAR. CB:1264A

4. HUPOPHERŌ (ὑποφέρω), a strengthened form of No. 3, to bear 5297
or carry, by being under, is said metaphorically of enduring temptation, AG:848C CB:—
1 Cor. 10:13, A.V., "bear;" persecutions, 2 Tim. 3:11; griefs, 1 Pet.
2:19. See BEAR.¶

5. ANECHŌ (ἀνέχω), to hold up (*ana*, up, *echō*, to hold or have), 430
always in the Middle Voice in the N.T., is rendered "endure" in 2 Thess. AG:65D CB:1235B
1:4, of persecutions and tribulations; in 2 Tim. 4:3, of sound doctrine.
See BEAR.

6. KARTEREŌ (καρτερέω), to be stedfast, patient, is used in Heb. 2594
11:27, "endured," of Moses in relation to Egypt.¶ In the Sept., Job AG:405B CB:1253C
2:9; Isa. 42:14.¶

7. MAKROTHUMEŌ (μακροθυμέω), to be long-tempered (*makros*, 3114
long, *thumos*, mind), is rendered "patiently endured" in Heb. 6:15, AG:488A CB:1257C
said of Abraham. See B. below. See BEAR, LONGSUFFERING, PATIENCE,
SUFFER. 2553

Note: In 2 Tim. 2:9, *kakopatheō*, to suffer evil (*kakos*, evil, *paschō*, AG:397C CB:1253B to suffer), is translated "endure hardness," A.V.; R.V., "suffer hardship;" so in 4 : 5, A.V., "endure afflictions;" elsewhere in Jas. 5 : 13.¶ In 2 Tim. 2 : 3 the most authentic mss. have *sunkakopatheō*, to suffer hardship with, as in 1 : 8.¶ See HARDSHIP, SUFFER.

B. Noun.

5281 AG:846B CB:1252B HUPOMONĒ (ὑπομονή), patience, lit., a remaining under (akin to A, No. 2), is translated "patient enduring" in 2 Cor. 1 : 6, R.V., for A.V., "enduring." Cp. *makrothumia*, longsuffering (akin to A, No. 7). See PATIENCE.

ENEMY

2190 AG:331B CB:1242C ECHTHROS (ἐχθρός), an adjective, primarily denoting hated or hateful (akin to *echthos*, hate; perhaps associated with *ektos*, outside), hence, in the Active sense, denotes hating, hostile; it is used as a noun signifying an enemy, adversary, and is said (*a*) of the Devil, Matt. 13 : 39; Luke 10 : 19; (*b*) of death, 1 Cor. 15 : 26; (*c*) of the professing believer who would be a friend of the world, thus making Himself an enemy of God, Jas. 4 : 4; (*d*) of men who are opposed to Christ, Matt. 13 : 25, 28; 22 : 44; Mark 12 : 36; Luke 19 : 27; 20 : 43; Acts 2 : 35; Rom. 11 : 28; Phil. 3 : 18; Heb. 1 : 13; 10 : 13; or to His servants, Rev. 11 : 5, 12; to the nation of Israel, Luke 1 : 71, 74; 19 : 43; (*e*) of one who is opposed to righteousness, Acts 13 : 10; (*f*) of Israel in its alienation from God, Rom. 11 : 28; (*g*) of the unregenerate in their attitude toward God, Rom. 5 : 10; Col. 1 : 21; (*h*) of believers in their former state, 2 Thess. 3 : 15; (*i*) of foes, Matt. 5 : 43, 44; 10 : 36; Luke 6 : 27, 35; Rom. 12 : 20; 1 Cor. 15 : 25; of the Apostle Paul because he told converts "the truth," Gal. 4 : 16. See FOE. Cp. *echthra*, enmity.¶

ENGRAFTED

1721 AG:258A CB:1244B *Note:* This is the A.V. rendering of *emphutos*, Jas. 1 : 21, an adjective derived from *emphuō*, to implant; the R.V. has "implanted."¶ The metaphor is that of a seed rooting itself in the heart; cp. Matt. 13 : 21; 15 : 13: 1 Cor. 3 : 6, and the kindred word *sumphutos*, Rom. 6 : 5, "planted together" (*sun*, with).¶ The A.V. "engrafted" would translate the word *emphuteuton* (from *emphuteuō*, to graft), which is not found in the N.T.; it uses *enkentrizō* in Rom. 11. Cp. *ekphuō*, to cause to grow out, put forth (leaves), Matt. 24 : 32; Mark 13 : 28.

ENGRAVE

1795 AG:270B CB:— ENTUPOŌ (ἐντυπόω), to imprint, engrave (*en*, in, *tupos*, a mark, impression, form, type), is used of the engraving of the Law on the two stones, or tablets, 2 Cor. 3 : 7.¶ In the Sept., Ex. 36 : 39 (some texts have *ektupoō*).¶ See also GRAVEN.

ENJOIN

1. ENTELLOMAI (ἐντέλλομαι) is translated "hath enjoined" in 1781 AG:268B
the A.V. of Heb. 9 : 20. See COMMAND (R.V.). CB:1245B

2. EPITASSŌ (ἐπιτάσσω), lit., to set or arrange over, to charge, 2004 AG:302B
command, is rendered "enjoin" in Philm. 8. See COMMAND. Cp. *keleuō*, CB:1246A
to order.

ENJOY

A. Verb.

TUNCHANŌ (τυγχάνω), used transitively, denotes to hit upon, meet 5177 AG:829B
with; then, to reach, get, obtain; it is translated "enjoy" (i.e., obtain CB:—
to our satisfaction) in Acts 24 : 2. See CHANCE, COMMON, *Note* (3), OBTAIN.

B. Noun.

APOLAUSIS (ἀπόλαυσις), enjoyment (from *apolauō*, to take hold of, 619 AG:94D
enjoy a thing), suggests the advantage or pleasure to be obtained from CB:—
a thing (from a root, *lab*— seen in *lambanō*, to obtain); it is used with the preposition *eis*, in 1 Tim. 6 : 17, lit., 'unto enjoyment,' rendered "to enjoy;" with *echō*, to have, in Heb. 11 : 25, lit., 'to have pleasure (of sin),' translated "to enjoy the pleasures."¶ See PLEASURE.

ENLARGE

1. MEGALUNŌ (μεγαλύνω) denotes to make great (from *megas*, 3170 AG:497A
great), Matt. 23 : 5, "enlarge;" 2 Cor. 10 : 15, A.V., "enlarged," R.V., CB:1258A
"magnified;" elsewhere in the A.V. it is rendered by the verb to magnify, except in Luke 1 : 58, A.V., "had shewed great (mercy)," R.V., "had magnified (His mercy); see Luke 1 : 46; Acts 5 : 13; 10 : 46; 19 : 17; Phil. 1 : 20. See MAGNIFY.¶

2. PLATUNŌ (πλατύνω), to make broad, from *platus*, broad, is 4115 AG:667A
translated "enlarged" in 2 Cor. 6 : 11, 13 (metaphorically), "make CB:1265A
broad," Matt. 23 : 5 (literally). From the primary sense of freedom comes that of the joy that results from it. See BROAD.¶ Cp. *platos*, breadth, and *plateia*, a street.

ENLIGHTEN

PHŌTIZŌ (φωτίζω), from *phōs*, light, (*a*), used intransitively, signifies 5461 AG:872D
to give light, shine, Rev. 22 : 5; (*b*), used transitively, to enlighten, CB:1264B
illumine, is rendered "enlighten" in Eph. 1 : 18, metaphorically of spiritual enlightenment; so John 1 : 9, i.e., "lighting every man" (by reason of His coming); Eph. 3 : 9, "to make (all men) see" (R.V. marg., "to bring to light"); Heb. 6 : 4, "were enlightened;" 10 : 32, R.V., "enlightened," A.V., "illuminated." See ILLUMINATED, LIGHT. Cp. *phōtismos*, light, and *phōteinos*, full of light.

ENMITY 2189 AG:331B

ECHTHRA (ἔχθρα), from the adjective *echthros* (see ENEMY) is CB:1242C rendered "enmity" in Luke 23:12; Rom. 8:7; Eph. 2:15, 16; Jas. 4:4; "enmities," Gal. 5:20, R.V., for A.V., "hatred." It is the opposite of *agapē*, love.¶

ENOUGH

A. Adjectives.

713 AG:107A CB:1237C 1. ARKETOS (ἀρκετός), sufficient, akin to *arkeō* (see B, No. 1), is rendered "enough" in Matt. 10:25; "sufficient" in Matt. 6:34; "suffice" in 1 Pet. 4:3, lit., "(is) sufficient." See SUFFICE, SUFFICIENT.¶

2425 AG:374B CB:1250C 2. HIKANOS (ἱκανός), sufficient, competent, fit (akin to *hikanō* and *hikō*, to reach, attain and *hikanoō*, to make sufficient), is translated "enough" in Luke 22:38, of the Lord's reply to Peter concerning the swords. See ABLE.

PERISSEUŌ 4052 AG:650C CB:1263C KORENNUMI 2880 AG:444C CB:— *Note:* In Luke 15:17 the verb *perisseuō*, to have abundance, is translated "have enough and to spare." In Acts 27:38 the verb *korennumi*, to satisfy, is translated "had eaten enough."

B. Verbs.

714 AG:107A CB:1237C 1. ARKEŌ (ἀρκέω), to ward off; hence, to aid, assist; then, to be strong enough, i.e., to suffice, to be enough (cp. A, No. 1), is translated "be enough" in Matt. 25:9. See CONTENT.

568 AG:84D CB:1236B 2. APECHŌ (ἀπέχω), lit., to hold off from, to have off or out (*apō*, from, *echō*, to have), i.e., to have in full, to have received, is used impersonally in Mark 14:41, "it is enough," in the Lord's words to His slumbering disciples in Gethsemane. It is difficult, however, to find examples of this meaning in Greek usage of the word, and *apechō* may here refer, in its commercial significance, to Judas (who is mentioned immediately afterwards), with the meaning 'he hath received' (his payment); cp. the same use in Matt. 6:2, 5, 16 (see Deissmann, *Light from the Ancient East*, pp. 110 ff.). See ABSTAIN, HAVE, RECEIVE.

ENRAGE See ANGER

For ENQUIRE see INQUIRE

ENRICH

4148 AG:674A CB:1265B PLOUTIZŌ (πλουτίζω), to make rich (from *ploutos*, wealth, riches), is used metaphorically, of spiritual riches, in 1 Cor. 1:5, "ye were enriched;" 2 Cor. 6:10, "making rich;" 2 Cor. 9:11, "being enriched." See RICH.¶

ENROL, ENROLMENT

A. Verb.

583 AG:89B CB:1236C APOGRAPHŌ (ἀπογράφω) primarily signifies to write out, to copy; then, to enrol, to inscribe, as in a register. It is used of a census, Luke 2:1, R.V., "be enrolled," for A.V., "be taxed;" in the Middle Voice, vv. 3, 5, to enrol oneself, A.V., "be taxed." Confirmation that this census (not taxation) was taken in the dominions of the Roman Empire

is given by the historians Tacitus and Suetonius. Augustus himself drew up a sort of Roman Doomsday Book, a Rationarium, afterwards
epitomized into a Breviarium, to include the allied kingdoms, appointing KATALEGŌ
twenty commissioners to draw up the lists. In Heb. 12 : 23 the members 2639
of the Church of the firstborn are said to be "enrolled," R.V.¶ AG:413B CB:—

Note: For R.V., 1 Tim. 5 : 9, *katalegō*, see TAKE, *Note* (18); for R.V., STRATOLOGEŌ
2 Tim. 2 : 4, *stratologeō*, see SOLDIER, B, *Note* (2). 4758 AG:770D

B. Noun. CB:1270A

APOGRAPHĒ (ἀπογραφή) primarily denotes a written copy, or, as 582
a law term, a deposition; then, a register, census, enrolment, Luke 2 : 2; AG:89B CB:—
Acts 5 : 37, R.V., for A.V., "taxing." Luke's accuracy has been vindicated, as against the supposed inconsistency that as Quirinius was Governor of Syria in A.D. 6, ten years after the birth of Christ, the census, as "the first" (R.V.), could not have taken place. At the time mentioned by Luke, Cilicia, of which Quirinius was Governor, was separated from Cyprus and joined to Syria. His later direct governorship of Syria itself accounts for the specific inclusion of, and reference to, his earlier connection with that Province. Justin Martyr, a native of Palestine, writing in the Middle of the 2nd century, asserts thrice that Quirinius was present in Syria at the time mentioned by Luke (see Apol., 1 : 34, 46; Trypho 78). Noticeable, too, are the care and accuracy taken by Luke in his historical details, 1 : 3, R.V.

As to charges made against Luke's accuracy, Moulton and Milligan say as follows:—"The deduction so long made . . . about the census apparently survives the demonstration that the blunder lay only in our lack of information: the microbe is not yet completely expelled. Possibly the salutary process may be completed by our latest inscriptional evidence that Quirinius was a legate in Syria for census purposes in 8–6 B.C."¶

ENSAMPLE

1. TUPOS (τύπος) primarily denoted a blow (from a root *tup*—, seen 5179
also in *tuptō*, to strike), hence, (*a*) an impression, the mark of a blow, John AG:829D CB:1273B
20 : 25; (*b*) the impress of a seal, the stamp made by a die, a figure, image, Acts 7 : 43; (*c*) a form or mould, Rom. 6 : 17 (see R.V.); (*d*) the sense or substance of a letter, Acts 23 : 25; (*e*) an ensample, pattern, Acts 7 : 44; Heb. 8 : 5, "pattern;" in an ethical sense, 1 Cor. 10 : 6; Phil. 3 : 17; 1 Thess. 1 : 7; 2 Thess. 3 : 9; 1 Tim. 4 : 12, R.V., "ensample;" Tit. 2 : 7, R.V., "ensample," for A.V., "pattern;" 1 Pet. 5 : 3; in a doctrinal sense, a type, Rom. 5 : 14. See EXAMPLE, FASHION, FIGURE, FORM, MANNER, PATTERN, PRINT.¶

2. HUPOTUPŌSIS (ὑποτύπωσις), an outline, sketch, akin to *hupotupoō*, 5296
to delineate, is used metaphorically to denote a pattern, an ensample, AG:848C CB:1252B
1 Tim. 1 : 16, R.V., "ensample," for A.V., "pattern;" 2 Tim. 1 : 13, R.V., "pattern," for A.V., "form." See FORM, PATTERN.¶

5262 AG:844A CB:1252B
3. HUPODEIGMA (ὑπόδειγμα), lit., that which is shown (from *hupo*, under, and *deiknumi*, to show), hence, (*a*) a figure, copy, Heb. 8 : 5, R.V., " copy," for A.V., " example ; " 9 : 23 ; (*b*) an example, whether for imitation, John 13 : 15 ; Jas. 5 : 10, or for warning, Heb. 4 : 11 ; 2 Pet. 2 : 6, R.V., " example." See EXAMPLE, PATTERN.¶

ENSLAVED

1402 AG:206A CB:—
DOULOŌ (δουλόω), to make a slave of, is rendered " enslaved " (to much wine) in Tit. 2 : 3, R.V., for A.V., " given to." See BONDAGE.

ENSNARE

3802 AG:602A CB:—
PAGIDEUŌ (παγιδεύω), to entrap, lay snares for (from *pagis*, anything which fixes or grips, hence, a snare), is used in Matt. 22 : 15, of the efforts of the Pharisees to entrap the Lord in His speech, A.V., " entangle." See ENTANGLE.¶

For ENSUE see PURSUE

ENTANGLE

1. PAGIDEUŌ : see ENSNARE.

1707 AG:256C CB:—
2. EMPLEKŌ (ἐμπλέκω), to weave in (*en*, in, *plekō*, to weave), hence, metaphorically, to be involved, entangled in, is used in the Passive Voice in 2 Tim. 2 : 4, " entangleth himself ; " 2 Pet. 2 : 20, " are entangled."¶ In the Sept., Prov. 28 : 18.¶

1758 AG:265D CB:1245A
3. ENECHŌ (ἐνέχω), to hold in, is said (*a*) of being entangled in a yoke of bondage, such as Judaism, Gal. 5 : 1. Some mss. have the word in 2 Thess. 1 : 4, the most authentic have *anechō*, to endure ; (*b*) with the meaning to set oneself against, be urgent against, said of the plotting of Herodias against John the Baptist, Mark 6 : 19, R.V., " set herself against," A.V., " had a quarrel against ; " of the effort of the Scribes and Pharisees to provoke the Lord to say something which would provide them with a ground of accusation against Him, Luke 11 : 53, R.V., " to press upon," marg., " to set themselves vehemently against," A.V., " to urge."¶

ENTER, ENTERING, ENTRANCE

A. Verbs.

1525 AG:232C CB:1243B
1. EISERCHOMAI (εἰσέρχομαι), to come into (*eis*, in, *erchomai*, to come), is frequently rendered " entered " in the R.V. for A.V., " went into," e.g., Matt. 9 : 25 ; 21 : 12 ; or " go in," e.g., Matt. 7 : 13 ; Luke 8 : 51 ; " go," Luke 18 : 25 ; " was coming in," Acts 10 : 25. See COME, No. 2, GO (Notes).

4897 AG:787A CB:1270C
2. SUNEISERCHOMAI (συνεισέρχομαι), to enter together, is used in John 6 : 22 (in the best mss. ; see No. 6) and 18 : 15.¶

3. PAREISERCHOMAI (παρεισέρχομαι), (*a*) to come in beside (*para*, 3922
beside, and No. 1), is rendered "entered" in Rom. 5 : 20, A.V., for R.V., AG:624D
"came in beside," the meaning being that the Law entered in addition CB:1262B
to sin ; (*b*) to enter secretly, by stealth, Gal. 2 : 4, "came in privily," to
accomplish the purposes of the circumcision party. See Come, No. 8.¶
Cp. *pareisduō* (or —*dunō*), Jude 4, "crept in privily."¶

4. EISPOREUOMAI (εἰσπορεύομαι), to go into, found only in the 1531
Synoptists and Acts, is translated to enter, in the R.V. of Mark 1 : 21 ; AG:233C
6 : 56 ; 11 : 2 ; Luke 8 : 16 ; 11 : 33 (A.V., "come in") ; 19 : 30 (A.V., CB:—
"at your entering") ; 22 : 10 ; in the following the R.V. has the verb to
go, for the A.V., to enter, Matt. 15 : 17 ; Mark 5 : 40 ; 7 : 15, 18, 19 ;
in Acts 28 : 30, "went," A.V., "came ;" in 9 : 28, R.V., "going," A.V.,
"coming ;" in the following both A.V. and R.V. have the verb to enter,
Mark 4 : 19 ; Luke 18 : 24 (in the best mss.) ; Acts 3 : 2 ; 8 : 3. See
Go, No. 5.¶

5. ANABAINŌ (ἀναβαίνω), to go up (*ana*, up, *bainō*, to go), is trans- 305
lated "entered" in 1 Cor. 2 : 9, metaphorically, of coming into the mind. AG:50A
In John 21 : 3, the best mss. have No. 6. See Arise, No. 6. CB:1235A

6. EMBAINŌ (ἐμβαίνω), to go in (*en*, in), is used only in the Gospels, 1684
of entering a boat, Matt. 8 : 23 ; 9 : 1 ; 13 : 2 ; 14 : 22, 32 ; 15 : 39 ; AG:254A
Mark 4 : 1 ; 5 : 18 ; 6 : 45 ; 8 : 10, 13 ; Luke 5 : 3 ; 8 : 22, 37 ; John 6 : 17, CB:—
(in some mss., in ver. 22), 24, R.V., "got into the boats," for A.V., "took
shipping ;" 21 : 3 (some mss. have No. 5 here) ; Acts 21 : 6 (in the
best mss.) ; of stepping into water, John 5 : 4 (R.V. omits the verb).
See Come, No. 21, Get, No. 5, Go, *Note* (2), *m*, Step, Take, *Note* (3).¶

7. EPIBAINŌ (ἐπιβαίνω), to go upon (*epi*, upon), is used of going on 1910
board ship, Acts 21 : 2 ; 27 : 2, A.V., "entering into," R.V., "embarking AG:289D
in." See Aboard, Come, No. 16, Sit, *Note*. CB:—

8. EISEIMI (εἴσειμι), to go into (*eis*, into, *eimi*, to go), Acts 3 : 3 ; 1524
21 : 18, 26, A.V., "entered ;" Heb. 9 : 6, R.V., "go in," for A.V., "went AG:232C
into." See Go, No. 12.¶ CB:—

Notes : (1) *Erchomai*, to come, is never translated to enter, in the ERCHOMAI
R.V. ; in the A.V., Mark 1 : 29 ; Acts 18 : 7. (2) In 2 John 7, the most 2064 AG:310B
authentic mss. have the verb *exerchomai*, "gone forth," R.V., for A.V. CB:1246B
(No. 1), "entered." (3) In Luke 16 : 16, *biazō*, to force, to enter in BIAZō 971
violently, is so rendered in the R.V., for A.V., "presseth." AG:140C

B. Noun. CB:1239A

EISODOS (εἴσοδος), lit., a way in (*eis*, in, *hodos*, a way), an entrance, is 1529
used (*a*) of the coming of Christ into the midst of the Jewish nation, AG:233B
Acts 13 : 24, R.V. marg., "entering in ;" (*b*) of entrance upon Gospel CB:1243B
work in a locality, 1 Thess. 1 : 9 ; 2 : 1 ; (*c*) of the present access of
believers into God's presence, Heb. 10 : 19, lit., 'for entrance into ;'
(*d*) of their entrance into Christ's eternal Kingdom, 2 Pet. 1 : 11. See
Coming.¶

ENTERTAIN

3579 AG:547D CB:1273B XENIZŌ (ξενίζω) signifies (*a*) to receive as a guest (*xenos*, a guest), rendered " entertained " in Acts 28 : 7, R.V., for A.V., " lodged ; " in Heb. 13 : 2, " have entertained ; " (*b*) to be astonished by the strangeness of a thing, Acts 17 : 20 ; 1 Pet. 4 : 4, 12. See LODGE, STRANGE (think).

5381 AG:860D CB:1264B *Note :* In Heb. 13 : 2 (first part), *philoxenia*, lit., love of strangers (*phileō*, to love, and *xenos*, a stranger or guest), is translated to show love to, R.V., for A.V., " entertain." See HOSPITALITY.

ENTICE, ENTICING

A. Verb.

1185 AG:174B CB:— DELEAZŌ (δελεάζω), primarily, to lure by a bait (from *delear*, a bait), is used metaphorically in Jas. 1 : 14, of the enticement of lust ; in 2 Pet. 2 : 14, of seducers, R.V., " enticing," for A.V., " beguiling ; " in ver. 18, R.V., " entice (in)," for A.V., " allure (through)."¶

B. Adjective.

3981 AG:639A CB:1263A PEITHOS (πειθός), apt to persuade (from *peithō*, to persuade), is used in 1 Cor. 2 : 4, A.V., " enticing," R.V., " persuasive."¶

4086 AG:657B CB:1265A *Note :* In Col. 2 : 4, *pithanologia*, persuasive speech (from *pithanos*, persuasive, plausible, akin to the above, and *logos*, speech), is rendered " enticing " in the A.V. (R.V., " persuasiveness of.") It signifies the employment of plausible arguments, in contrast to demonstration.¶ Cp. *eulogia*, " fair speech," Rom. 16 : 18, i.e., ' nice style.'¶

ENTIRE

3648 AG:564C CB:— HOLOKLĒROS (ὁλόκληρος), complete, sound in every part (*holos*, whole, *klēros*, a lot, i.e., with all that has fallen by lot), is used ethically in 1 Thess. 5 : 23, indicating that every grace present in Christ should be manifested in the believer ; so Jas. 1 : 4.¶ In the Sept. the word is used, e.g., of a full week, Lev. 23 : 15 ; of altar stones unhewn, Deut. 27 : 6 and Josh. 8 : 31 ; of a full-grown vine tree, useless for work, Ezek. 15 : 5 ; of the sound condition of a sheep, Zech. 11 : 16.

HOLOKLĒRIA 3647 AG:564C CB:— The corresponding noun *holoklēria* is used in Acts 3 : 16, " perfect soundness."¶ The synonymous word *teleios*, used also in Jas. 1 : 4,
TELEIOS 5046 AG:809A CB:1271B " perfect," indicates the development of every grace into maturity.

The Heb. *shalom*, peace, is derived from a root meaning " wholeness." See, e.g., Is. 42 : 19, marg., " made perfect," for text, " at peace ; " cp. 26 : 3. Cp. also Col. 1 : 28 with 2 Pet. 3 : 14.

For ENTREAT, to request, see INTREAT ;
for ENTREATY see INTREATY

ENTREAT (to deal with, to treat)

Note : The distinction between this and the preceding word is maintained in the R.V., which confines the initial " e " to the sense of dealing with, or uses the Verb to treat.

CHRAOMAI (χράομαι) denotes (*a*) to use (of things) ; (*b*) to use well or 5530
ill, to treat, deal with (of persons) ; " treated (kindly)," Acts 27 : 3, R.V., AG:884B CB:1240A
A.V., " (courteously) entreated." The remaining ten instances come under (*a*). See USE.

Note : In Luke 20 : 11, *atimazō*, to dishonour (*a*, negative, *timē*, 818
honour), is translated " entreated shamefully," A.V. (R.V., " handled AG:120A CB:1238A
shamefully "). For *kakoucheō*, Heb. 11 : 37, R.V., and *sunkakoucheomai*,
Heb. 11 : 25, R.V., see SUFFER, Nos. 6 and 7. ENTRUST See GIVE, INTRUST

ENVY, ENVYING

ENVELOPE See OVERSHADOW

A. Noun.

PHTHONOS (φθόνος), envy, is the feeling of displeasure produced
by witnessing or hearing of the advantage or prosperity of others ; this 5355
evil sense always attaches to this word, Matt. 27 : 18 ; Mark 15 : 10 ; AG:857D CB:1264C
Rom. 1 : 29 ; Gal. 5 : 21 ; Phil. 1 : 15 ; 1 Tim. 6 : 4 ; Tit. 3 : 3 ; 1 Pet. 2 : 1 ; so in Jas. 4 : 5, where the question is rhetorical and strongly remonstrative, signifying that the Spirit (or spirit) which God made to dwell in us was certainly not so bestowed that we should be guilty of envy.¶

Note : *Zēlos*, zeal or jealousy, translated " envy " in the A.V., in Acts 2205
13 : 45 ; Rom. 13 : 13 ; 1 Cor. 3 : 3 ; 2 Cor. 12 : 20 ; Jas. 3 : 14, 16, is to AG:337D CB:1273B
be distinguished from *phthonos*, and, apart from the meanings " zeal " and " indignation," is always translated " jealousy " in the R.V. The distinction lies in this, that envy desires to deprive another of what he has, jealousy desires to have the same or the same sort of thing for itself. See FERVENT, INDIGNATION, JEALOUSY, ZEAL.

B. Verbs.

1. PHTHONEŌ (φθονέω), to envy (akin to A.), is used in Gal. 5 : 26.¶ 5354 AG:857C CB:1264C
2. ZĒLOŌ (ζηλόω) denotes to be zealous, moved with jealousy, Acts 2206
7 : 9 and 17 : 5, R.V., " moved with jealousy " (A.V., " moved with AG:338A CB:1273B
envy ") ; both have " envieth " in 1 Cor. 13 : 4. See the Note under A. See AFFECT, COVET, DESIRE, JEALOUS, ZEALOUS.

EPHPHATHA

Note : *Ephphatha* is an Aramaic word signifying to open, used in 2188
the Imperative Mood, " be opened," Mark 7 : 34 ; while the application AG:331B CB:1245C
in this case was to the ears, the tongue was remedially affected.

EPILEPTIC

SELĒNIAZŌ (σεληνιάζω), lit., to be moon struck (from *selēnē*, the (-OMAI) 4583
moon), is used in the Passive Voice with Active significance, R.V., " epi- AG:746D
leptic," for A.V., " lunatick," Matt. 4 : 24 ; 17 : 15 ; the corresponding CB:1268C
English word is lunatic. Epilepsy was supposed to be influenced by the moon.¶

EPISTLE

1992 AG:300D CB:1246A EPISTOLĒ (ἐπιστολή), primarily a message (from *epistellō*, to send to), hence, a letter, an epistle, is used in the singular, e.g., Acts 15 : 30 ; in the plural, e.g., Acts 9 : 2 ; 2 Cor. 10 : 10. " Epistle is a less common word for a letter. A letter affords a writer more freedom, both in subject and expression, than does a formal treatise. A letter is usually occasional, that is, it is written in consequence of some circumstance which requires to be dealt with promptly. The style of a letter depends largely on the occasion that calls it forth."* " A broad line is to be drawn between the letter and the epistle. The one is essentially a spontaneous product dominated throughout by the image of the reader, his sympathies and interests, instinct also with the writer's own soul : it is virtually one half of an imaginary dialogue, the suppressed responses of the other party shaping the course of what is actually written . . . ; the other has a general aim, addressing all and sundry whom it may concern : it is like a public speech and looks towards publication " (J. V. Bartlet, in *Hastings' Bib. Dic.*).

In 2 Pet. 3 : 16 the Apostle includes the Epistles of Paul as part of the God-breathed Scriptures.

EQUAL, EQUALITY

A. Adjective.

2470 AG:381A CB:1253A ISOS (ἴσος), the same in size, number, quality, etc., is translated " equal " in John 5 : 18 ; Phil. 2 : 6 ; in the latter the word is in the neuter plural, lit., ' equalities ; ' " in the R.V. the words are translated ' on an equality with God,' instead of ' equal with God,' as in the A.V. The change is of great importance to the right interpretation of the whole passage. The rendering ' equal with God,' is evidently derived from the Latin Version. . . . It was apparently due at first to the fact that the Latin language had no adequate mode of representing the exact form and meaning of the Greek. The neuter plural denotes the various modes or states in which it was possible for the nature of Deity to exist and manifest itself as Divine."†

ISOTIMOS 2472 AG:381B CB:1253A ISOPSUCHOS 2473 AG:381B CB:1253A *Note :* Cp. *isotimos*, equally precious, 2 Pet. 1 : 1 ;¶ *isopsuchos* of equal soul, like-minded, Phil. 2 : 20 ;¶ also Eng. words beginning with the prefix *iso*—.

B. Nouns.

2471 AG:381B CB:1253A 1. ISOTĒS (ἰσοτής), equality (akin to A.), is translated " equality " in 2 Cor. 8 : 14, twice ; in Col. 4 : 1, with the article, " that which is . . . equal," (lit., ' the equality,' as marg.), i.e., equity, fairness, what is equitable.¶ In the Sept., Job 36 : 29 ; Zech. 4 : 7.¶

4915 AG:789D CB:— 2. SUNĒLIKIŌTĒS (συνηλικιώτης) denotes one of the same age, an equal in age (*sun*, with, *hēlikia*, an age), a contemporary, Gal. 1 : 14,

* From Notes on Thessalonians by Hogg and Vine, p. 5.
† Gifford, The Incarnation, p. 20.

R.V., " of mine own age," for A.V. " mine equals," the reference being to the Apostle's good standing among his fellow-students in the Rabbinical Schools ; cp. Acts 22 : 3.¶

EQUIP See FURNISH

ERE : see Note † p. 1

ERR

1. PLANAŌ (πλανάω), in the Active Voice, signifies to cause to 4105
wander, lead astray, deceive (*planē*, a wandering ; cp. Eng., planet) ; AG:665B CB:1265A
in the Passive Voice, to be led astray, to err. It is translated " err," in Matt. 22 : 29 ; Mark 12 : 24, 27 ; Heb. 3 : 10 ; Jas. 1 : 16 (A.V., " do not err," R.V., " be not deceived ") ; 5 : 19. See DECEIVE, SEDUCE, WANDER, WAY, *Note* (5).

2. APOPLANAŌ (ἀποπλανάω), to cause to wander away from, to lead 635 AG:97B
astray from (*apō*, from, and No. 1), is used metaphorically of leading into CB:1237A
error, Mark 13 : 22, A.V., " seduce," R.V., " lead astray ; " 1 Tim. 6 : 10, in the Passive Voice, A.V., " have erred," R.V., " have been led astray." See SEDUCE.¶

3. ASTOCHEŌ (ἀστοχέω), to miss the mark, fail (*a*, negative, *stochos*, 795
a mark), is used only in the Pastoral Epistles, 1 Tim. 1 : 6, " having AG:118A CB:1238A
swerved ; " 6 : 21 and 2 Tim. 2 : 18, " have erred." See SWERVE.¶

ERROR

1. PLANĒ (πλάνη), akin to *planaō* (see ERR, No. 1), " a wandering, a 4106
forsaking of the right path, see Jas. 5 : 20, whether in doctrine, 2 Pet. 3 : 17 ; AG:665D CB:1265A
1 John 4 : 6, or in morals, Rom. 1 : 27 ; 2 Pet. 2 : 18 ; Jude 11, though, in Scripture, doctrine and morals are never divided by any sharp line. See also Matt. 27 : 64, where it is equivalent to ' fraud.' "*

Errors in doctrine are not infrequently the effect of relaxed morality, and vice versa.

In Eph. 4 : 14 the R.V. has " wiles of error," for A.V., " they lie in wait to deceive ; " in 1 Thess. 2 : 3, R.V., " error," for A.V., " deceit ; " in 2 Thess. 2 : 11, R.V., " a working of error," for A.V., " strong delusion." See DECEIT.¶ Cp. *planētēs*, a wandering, Jude 13,¶ and the adjective *planos*, leading astray, deceiving, a deceiver.

2. AGNOĒMA (ἀγνόημα), a sin of ignorance (cp. *agnoia*, ignorance, 51
and *agnoeō*, to be ignorant), is used in the plural in Heb. 9 : 7.¶ AG:11C CB:1233B

ESCAPE

A. Verbs.

1. PHEUGŌ (φεύγω), to flee (Lat., *fuga*, flight, etc. ; cp. Eng., fugitive, 5343
subterfuge), is rendered " escape " in Matt. 23 : 33 ; Heb. 11 : 34. See AG:855D CB:1264A
FLEE.

* From Notes on Thessalonians by Hogg and Vine, p. 53.

668
AG:101D
CB:1237A 2. APOPHEUGŌ (ἀποφεύγω), to flee away from (*apo*, from, and No. 1), is used in 2 Pet. 1 : 4; 2 : 18, 20.¶

1309
AG:190C
CB:— 3. DIAPHEUGŌ (διαφεύγω), lit., to flee through, is used of the escaping of prisoners from a ship, Acts 27 : 42. For the word in verse 44 see No. 5.¶

1628
AG:246D
CB:1243C 4. EKPHEUGŌ (ἐκφεύγω), to flee out of a place (*ek*, out of, and No. 1), is said of the escape of prisoners, Acts 16 : 27; of Sceva's sons, fleeing from the demoniac, 19 : 16; of Paul's escape from Damascus, 2 Cor. 11 : 33; elsewhere with reference to the judgments of God, Luke 21 : 36; Rom. 2 : 3; Heb. 2 : 3; 12 : 25; 1 Thess. 5 : 3. See FLEE.¶

1295
AG:189A
CB:1241B 5. DIASŌZŌ (διασώζω), in the Active Voice, to bring safely through a danger (*dia*, through, intensive, *sōzō*, to save), to make completely whole, to heal, Luke 7 : 3; to bring safe, Acts 23 : 24; to save, 27 : 43; in the Passive Voice, Matt. 14 : 36, "were made whole;" 1 Pet. 3 : 20; It is also used in the Passive Voice, signifying to escape, said of shipwrecked mariners, Acts 27 : 44; 28 : 1, 4. See HEAL, SAFE, SAVE.¶

1831
AG:274B
CB:1247C *Note*: *Exerchomai*, to come or go out of a place, is rendered "He escaped," in John 10 : 39, A.V., an unsuitable translation, both in meaning and in regard to the circumstances of the Lord's departure from His would-be captors. The R.V. "went forth" is both accurate and appropriate to the dignity of the Lord's actions.

B. Noun.

1545
AG:237D
CB:— EKBASIS (ἔκβασις), a way out (*ek*, out, *bainō*, to go), denotes (*a*) an escape, 1 Cor. 10 : 13, used with the definite article and translated "the way of escape," as afforded by God in case of temptation; (*b*) an issue or result, Heb. 13 : 7. See END, ISSUE.¶ Cp. *ekbainō*, to go out, Heb. 11 : 15 (some mss. have *exerchomai*).¶

ESCHEW

1578
AG:241C
CB:— EKKLINŌ (ἐκκλίνω), to turn aside (*ek*, from, *klinō*, to turn, bend), is used metaphorically (*a*) of leaving the right path, Rom. 3 : 12, R.V., "turned aside," for A.V., "gone out of the way;" (*b*) of turning away from division-makers, and errorists, 16 : 17, R.V., "turn away from;" (*c*) of turning away from evil, 1 Pet. 3 : 11, R.V., "turn away from," A.V., "eschew." See AVOID, TURN.¶ In the Sept. the verb is frequently used of declining or swerving from God's ways, e.g., Job 23 : 11; Psa. 44 : 18; 119 : 51, 157.

ESPECIALLY

3122
AG:488D
CB:— MALISTA (μάλιστα), most, most of all, above all, is the superlative of *mala*, very much; translated "especially" in Acts 26 : 3; Gal. 6 : 10; 1 Tim. 5 : 17; 2 Tim. 4 : 13; Phil. 4 : 22, R.V. (for A.V., "chiefly"); "specially," Acts 25 : 26; 1 Tim. 4 : 10; 5 : 8; Tit. 1 : 10; Philm. 16; in Acts 20 : 38, "most of all." See CHIEFLY, MOST.

ESPOUSED

1. HARMOZŌ (ἁρμόζω), to fit, join (from *harmos*, a joint, joining ; 718
the root *ar*—, signifying to fit, is in evidence in various languages ; cp. AG:107C
arthron, a joint, *arithmos*, a number, etc.), is used in the Middle Voice, CB:1249B
of marrying or giving in marriage ; in 2 Cor. 11 : 2 it is rendered "espoused," metaphorically of the relationship established between Christ and the local church, through the Apostle's instrumentality. The thought may be that of fitting or joining to one Husband, the Middle Voice expressing the Apostle's interest or desire in doing so.¶

2. MNĒSTEUŌ (μνηστεύω), to woo and win, to espouse or promise in 3423
marriage, is used in the Passive Voice in Matt. 1 : 18 ; Luke 1 : 27 ; 2 : 5, AG:525C CB:—
all with reference to the Virgin Mary, R.V., "betrothed," for A.V., "espoused," in each case. See BETROTH.¶

ESTABLISH

1. STĒRIZŌ (στηρίζω), to fix, make fast, to set (from *stērix*, a prop), 4741
is used of establishing or stablishing (i.e., the confirmation) of persons ; AG:768A
the Apostle Peter was called by the Lord to establish his brethren, CB:1270A
Luke 22 : 32, translated "strengthen ;" Paul desired to visit Rome that the saints might be "established," Rom. 1 : 11 ; cp. Acts 8 : 23 ; so with Timothy at Thessalonica, 1 Thess. 3 : 2 ; the confirmation of the saints is the work of God, Rom. 16 : 25, "to stablish (you) ;" 1 Thess. 3 : 13, "stablish (your hearts) ;" 2 Thess. 2 : 17, "stablish them (in every good work and word) ;" 1 Pet. 5 : 10, "stablish ;" the means used to effect the confirmation is the ministry of the Word of God, 2 Pet. 1 : 12, "are established (in the truth which is with you) ;" James exhorts Christians to "stablish" their hearts, Jas. 5 : 8 ; cp. Rev. 3 : 2, R.V.

The character of this confirmation may be learned from its use in Luke 9 : 51, "stedfastly set ;" 16 : 26, "fixed," and in the Sept. in Ex. 17 : 12, "stayed up" (also from its strengthened form *epistērizō*, to confirm, in Acts 14 : 22 ; 15 : 32, 41 ; in some mss. to strengthen, in 18 : 23 ; see CONFIRM ¶). Neither the laying on of hands nor the impartation of the Holy Spirit is mentioned in the N.T. in connection with either of these words, or with the synonymous verb *bebaioō* (see 1 Cor. 1 : 8 ; 2 Cor. 1 : 21, etc.). See FIX, SET, STRENGTHEN.¶

2. STEREOŌ (στερεόω), to make firm, or solid (akin to *stereos*, hard, 4732
firm, solid ; cp. Eng., stereotype), is used only in Acts, (*a*) physically, AG:766D CB:—
3 : 7, "received strength ;" 3 : 16, "hath made strong ;" (*b*) metaphorically, of establishment in the faith, 16 : 5, R.V., "strengthened," 2476
for A.V., "established."¶ AG:381D

3. HISTĒMI (ἵστημι), to cause to stand, is translated "establish" CB:1250C
in Rom. 3 : 31 ; 10 : 3 ; Heb. 10 : 9. See ABIDE, APPOINT, STAND, etc. 950 AG:138C

4. BEBAIOŌ (βεβαιόω), to confirm, is rendered "stablish," 2 Cor. CB:1239A

1 : 21 ; "stablished," Col. 2 : 7 ; "be established," Heb. 13 : 9 : see CONFIRM.

3549 5. NOMOTHETEŌ (νομοθετέω) : see ENACT.
AG:541D
CB:1260A

ESTATE, STATE

2158 1. EUSCHĒMŌN (εὐσχήμων), signifying elegant, graceful, comely
AG:327A (*eu*, well, *schēma*, figure, fashion), is used (*a*) in a moral sense, seemly,
CB:— becoming, 1 Cor. 7 : 35 ; (*b*) in a physical sense, comely, 1 Cor. 12 : 24 ; (*c*) with reference to social degree, influential, a meaning developed in later Greek, and rendered of "honourable estate" in the R.V. of Mark 15 : 43 ; Acts 13 : 50 ; 17 : 12 (for A.V., "honourable"). See COMELY, HONOURABLE.¶

5014 2. TAPEINŌSIS (ταπείνωσις) denotes abasement, humiliation, low
AG:805A estate (from *tapeinos*, lowly), Luke 1 : 48, "low estate ;" Acts 8 : 33,
CB:1271A "humiliation ;" Phil. 3 : 21, R.V., "of humiliation," for A.V., "vile ;" Jas. 1 : 10, "is made low," lit., 'in his low estate.' See HUMILIATION, LOW, VILE.¶

5311 3. HUPSOS (ὕψος), signifying height, is rendered "(in his) high
AG:850C estate," Jas. 1 : 9, R.V., for A.V., "in that he is exalted ;" "on high,"
CB:1252B Luke 1 : 78 ; 24 : 49 ; Eph. 4 : 8 ; "height," Eph. 3 : 18 ; Rev. 21 : 16. See EXALT HEIGHT, HIGH.¶

PRESBUTERION *Notes :* (1) In Acts 22 : 5, *presbuterion*, presbytery, a body of elders,
4244 AG:699C is translated "estate of the elders," lit., 'the presbytery,' i.e., the
CB:1266B Sanhedrin. (2) In Col. 4 : 7 the plural of the definite article with the
PRŌTOS preposition *kata*, and the singular personal pronoun with *panta*, all, is
4413 AG:725B rendered "all my state," A.V., R.V., "all my affairs ;" in ver. 8 the
CB:1267B preposition *peri*, with the personal pronoun, lit., 'the things concerning
TAPEINOS 5011 us,' is translated "our estate," i.e., 'how we fare ;' so in Phil. 2 : 19, 20,
AG:804A "your state," i.e., 'your condition.' (3) In Mark 6 : 21 *prōtos*, lit., first,
CB:1271A is rendered "chief estates," A.V., R.V., "the chief men," i.e., the men
ARCHē 746 to whom belongs the dignity. (4) In Rom. 12 : 16 *tapeinos*, in the plural
AG:111D with the article, lit., the lowly, is translated "men of low estate," A.V.,
CB:1237B R.V., "things that are lowly." (5) In Jude 6 *archē*, "principality," R.V., A.V. has "first estate," (6) For "last state" see LAST, p. 311, ll. 4–6.

ESTEEM

1. HĒGEOMAI (ἡγέομαι) signifies to lead ; then, to lead before the mind, to suppose, consider, esteem ; translated "esteem" in Phil. 2 : 3, A.V., R.V., "counting ;" in 1 Thess. 5 : 13, "esteem ;" in Heb. 11 : 26, A.V., "esteeming," R.V., "accounting."

2. KRINŌ (κρίνω) signifies to separate, choose ; then, to approve, esteem ; translated "esteemeth" in Rom. 14 : 5 (twice), said of days ; here the word "alike" (A.V.) is rightly omitted in the R.V., the meaning being that every day is especially regarded as sacred. See DETERMINE.

3. LOGIZOMAI (λογίζομαι), to reckon, is translated " esteemeth " in 3049 AG:475D
Rom. 14 : 14 (R.V., " accounteth "). See ACCOUNT. CB:1257A
Notes : (1) In 1 Cor. 6 : 4, A.V., *exoutheneō*, to set at nought, is rendered EXOUTHENEŌ
" are least esteemed ; " the meaning is that judges in the world's tribunals 1848 AG:277C
have no place (are not of account) in the church. See ACCOUNT. (2) In CB:1247C
the A.V. marg. of 1 Pet. 2 : 17, *timaō*, to honour, is rendered " esteem." TIMAŌ 5091
(3) For " highly esteemed," Luke 16 : 15, A.V., see EXALT, B. AG:817A CB:1272C

ETERNAL

1. AIŌN (αἰών), an age, is translated " eternal " in Eph. 3 : 11, lit., 165
' (purpose) of the ages ' (marg.), and 1 Tim. 1 : 17, lit. ' (king) of the ages ' AG:27B CB:1234A
(marg.). See AGE.

2. AIŌNIOS (αἰώνιος) " describes duration, either undefined but not 166
endless, as in Rom. 16 : 25 ; 2 Tim. 1 : 9 ; Tit. 1 : 2 ; or undefined because AG:28B CB:1234A
endless as in Rom. 16 : 26, and the other sixty-six places in the N.T.

" The predominant meaning of *aiōnios*, that in which it is used every- 126
where in the N.T., save the places noted above, may be seen in 2 Cor. 4 : 18, AG:22a CB:1233C
where it is set in contrast with *proskairos*, lit., ' for a season,' and in Philm. 15, where only in the N.T. it is used without a noun. Moreover it is used of persons and things which are in their nature endless, as, e.g., of God, Rom. 16 : 26 ; of His power, 1 Tim. 6 : 16, and of His glory, 1 Pet. 5 : 10 ; of the Holy Spirit, Heb. 9 : 14 ; of the redemption effected by Christ, Heb. 9 : 12, and of the consequent salvation of men, 5 : 9, as well as of His future rule, 2 Pet. 1 : 11, which is elsewhere declared to be without end, Luke 1 : 33 ; of the life received by those who believe in Christ, John 3 : 16, concerning whom He said, ' they shall never perish,' 10 : 28, and of the resurrection body, 2 Cor. 5 : 1, elsewhere said to be ' immortal,' 1 Cor. 15 : 53, in which that life will be finally realized, Matt. 25 : 46 ; Tit. 1 : 2.

" *Aiōnios* is also used of the sin that ' hath never forgiveness,' Mark 3 : 29, and of the judgment of God, from which there is no appeal, Heb. 6 : 2, and of the fire, which is one of its instruments, Matt. 18 : 8 ; 25 : 41 ; Jude 7, and which is elsewhere said to be ' unquenchable,' Mark 9 : 43.

" The use of *aiōnios* here shows that the punishment referred to in 2 Thess. 1 : 9, is not temporary, but final, and accordingly, the phraseology shows that its purpose is not remedial but retributive."*

3. AIDIOS (ἀΐδιος) ; see EVERLASTING.

ESTRANGE See ALIENATE

ETHNARCH See GOVERNOR

EUNUCH

A. Noun.

EUNOUCHOS (εὐνοῦχος) denotes (*a*) an emasculated man, a eunuch, 2135 AG:323C
Matt. 19 : 12 ; (*b*) in the 3rd instance in that verse, one naturally incapaci- CB:1247B

* From Notes on Thessalonians by Hogg and Vine, pp. 232, 233.

tated for, or voluntarily abstaining from, wedlock ; (*c*) one such, in a position of high authority in a court, a chamberlain, Acts 8 : 27–39.¶

B. Verb.

2134 AG:323C EUNOUCHIZŌ (εὐνουχίζω), to make a eunuch (from A.), is used in Matt.
CB:1247B 19 : 12, as under (*b*) in A. ; and in the Passive Voice, " were made eunuchs," probably an allusion by the Lord to the fact that there were eunuchs in the courts of the Herods, as would be well known to His hearers.¶

EVANGELIST

2099 AG:318C EUANGELISTĒS (εὐαγγελιστής), lit., a messenger of good (*eu*, well,
CB:1247A *angelos*, a messenger), denotes a preacher of the Gospel, Acts 21 : 8 ; Eph. 4 : 11, which makes clear the distinctiveness of the function in the
EUANGELIZŌ churches ; 2 Tim. 4 : 5.¶ Cp. *euangelizō*, to proclaim glad tidings, and
2097 *euangelion*, good news, gospel. Missionaries are evangelists, as being
AG:317B essentially preachers of the Gospel.

CB:1247A EUANGELION 2098 AG:317D CB:1247A

EVEN (Noun), EVENING, EVENTIDE

A. Nouns.

2073 1. HESPERA (ἑσπέρα), properly, the feminine of the adjective *hesperos*,
AG:313C of, or at, evening, western (Lat., *vesper*, Eng., vespers), is used as a noun
CB:— in Luke 24 : 29 ; Acts 4 : 3, " eventide ; " 28 : 23. Some mss. have the word in 20 : 15, ' in the evening (we touched),' instead of *hetera*, " next (day)."

3798 (-IOS) 2. OPSIA (ὀψία), the feminine of the adjective *opsios*, late, used as a
AG:601C noun, denoting evening, with *hora*, understood (see No. 1), is found
CB:— seven times in Matthew, five in Mark, two in John, and in these places only in the N.T. (some mss. have it in Mark 11 : 11, see B.). The word really signifies the late evening, the latter of the two evenings as reckoned by the Jews, the first from 3 p.m. to sunset, the latter after sunset ; this is the usual meaning. It is used, however, of both, e.g., Mark 1 : 32 (cp. *opsimos*, latter, said of rain, Jas. 5 : 7).

B. Adverb.

3796 AG:601B OPSE (ὀψέ), long after, late, late in the day, at evening (in contrast
CB:1261A to *prōi*, early, e.g., Matt. 20 : 1), is used practically as a noun in Mark 11 : 11, lit., ' the hour being at eventide ; ' 11 : 19 ; 13 : 35 ; in Matt. 28 : 1 it is rendered " late on," R.V., for A.V., " in the end of." Here, however, the meaning seems to be " after," a sense in which the word was used by late Greek writers. See LATE.¶ In the Sept., Gen. 24 : 11 ; Ex. 30 : 8 ; Jer. 2 : 23 ; Isa. 5 : 11.¶

— AG:313C *Note :* In Luke 12 : 38 some mss. have the adjective *hesperinos*, of the
CB:— evening (see A, No. 1), lit., ' in the evening watch.'

EVEN (Adjective)

1474 AG:217C *Notes :* (1) In Luke 19 : 44 (A.V., " shall lay thee even with the
CB:— ground "), there is no word representing " even ; " the verb *edaphizō*

signifies to beat level (like a threshing floor); hence, to dash to the ground. See DASH.¶

(2) In Heb. 12 : 13 the adjective *orthos*, straight, is rendered "even" 3717
in the A.V., marg. AG:580B
CB:1261B

EVEN (Adverb, etc.), EVEN AS, EVEN SO

1. KAI (*καί*), a conjunction, is usually a mere connective, meaning 2532
"and;" it frequently, however, has an ascensive or climactic use, AG:391D
signifying "even," the thing that is added being out of the ordinary, CB:1253A
and producing a climax. The determination of this meaning depends on the context. Examples are Matt. 5 : 46, 47; Mark 1 : 27; Luke 6 : 33 (R.V.); 10 : 17; John 12 : 42; Gal. 2 : 13, 17, where "also" should be "even;" Eph. 5 : 12. Examples where the R.V. corrects the A.V. "and" or "also," by substituting "even," are Luke 7 : 49; Acts 17 : 28; Heb. 11 : 11; in 1 John 4 : 3 the R.V. rightly omits "even."

When followed by "if" or "though," *kai* often signifies "even," e.g., Matt. 26 : 35; John 8 : 14. So sometimes when preceded by "if," e.g., 1 Cor. 7 : 11, where "but and if" should be "but even if."

The epexegetic or explanatory use of *kai* followed by a noun in apposition, and meaning "namely," or "even" is comparatively rare. Winer's cautionary word needs heeding, that "this meaning has been introduced into too many passages" (Gram. of the N.T., p. 546.). Some think it has this sense in John 3 : 5, "water, even the Spirit," and Gal. 6 : 16, "even the Israel of God."

2. DE (*δέ*), usually signifying "but," is sometimes used for emphasis, 1161 AG:171C
signifying "even," e.g., Rom. 3 : 22; 9 : 30, "even the righteousness;" CB:—
Phil. 2 : 8 (R.V., "yea"). This is to be distinguished from No. 1. 2089

3. ETI (*ἔτι*), an adverb, as yet, still, is rendered "even" in Luke 1 : 15. AG:315C CB:1247A

4. HŌS (*ὡς*), "as," in comparative sentences, is sometimes translated 5613
"even as," Matt. 15 : 28; Mark 4 : 36; Eph. 5 : 33; 1 Pet. 3 : 6 (A.V. AG:897A
only); Jude 7. CB:1251B

5. HOUTŌS (*οὕτως*), or *houtō*, so, thus, is frequently rendered "even 3779
so," e.g., Matt. 7 : 17; 12 : 45; 18 : 14; 23 : 28; "so" in 1 Cor. 11 : 12 AG:597C
and 1 Thess. 2 : 4, R.V. CB:—

6. KATHŌS (*καθώς*), according as (*kata*, according to, and No. 4), 2531
is frequently translated "even as," e.g., Mark 11 : 6; Luke 1 : 2; AG:391B
1 Thess. 5 : 11. CB:1254C

7. HŌSPER (*ὥσπερ*), No. 4, strengthened by *per*, is translated "even 5618 AG:899C
as" in Matt. 20 : 28. CB:1251B

8. KATHAPER (*καθάπερ*), just as, even as, is rendered "even as" 2509
in Rom. 4 : 6; 9 : 13; 10 : 15; 12 : 4 (R.V.); 2 Cor. 3 : 18; 1 Thess. 3 : 6, AG:387A
12; 4 : 5; Heb. 4 : 2; "according as," Rom. 11 : 8; elsewhere simply CB:—
"as."

3483 AG:532D
9. NAI (*ναί*), a particle of strong affirmation, yea, verily, even so, is CB:—

rendered " even so " in the A.V., " yea " in the R.V., in Matt. 11 : 26 ; Luke 10 : 21 ; Rev. 16 : 7 ; both A.V. and R.V. have it in Rev. 1 : 7 ; the most authentic mss. omit it in 22 : 20. See SURELY, TRUTH, VERILY, YEA, YES.

3676 AG:569C CB:— 10. HOMŌS (ὅμως), yet, nevertheless, is translated " even " in 1 Cor. 14 : 7 (A.V., " and even ") ; elsewhere John 12 : 42, " nevertheless ; " Gal. 3 : 15, " yet " (i.e., 'nevertheless,' an example of hyperbaton, by which a word is placed out of its true position).¶

Notes : (1) In Rom. 1 : 26, there is no word representing " even " in
TE 5037 AG:807B CB:— the original. The A.V. seems to have put it for the particle *te*, which simply annexes the statement to the preceding and does not require translation. (2) In 1 Thess. 2 : 18 the A.V. renders the particle *men*
MEN 3303 AG:502C CB:1258B by " even ; " if translated, it signifies " indeed." (3) In 1 Cor. 12 : 2, *hōs* (see No. 4, above), followed by the particle *an*, means " howsoever " (R.V., for A.V., " even as "). (4) In Matt. 23 : 37, " even as " translates
TROPOS 5158 AG:827B CB:1273A the phrase *hon tropon*, lit., '(in) what manner.' (5) In 1 Tim. 3 : 11, *hōsautōs*, a strengthened form of No. 4, likewise, in like manner, is rendered
HōSAUTōS 5615 AG:899B CB:— " even so," A.V. (R.V., " in like manner "). (6) *Kàgō*, for *kai egō*, means either " even I " or " even so I " or " I also." In John 10 : 15, the R.V. has " and I " for the A.V., " even so . . . I ; " in 17 : 18 and 20 : 21, A.V. and R.V., " even so I ; " in the following, *kàgō* is preceded by *hōs*, or *kathōs*, " even as I," 1 Cor. 7 : 8 ; 10 : 33 ; " even as I also," 11 : 1 ; " as I also," Rev. 2 : 27. (7) In Luke 12 : 7 the R.V. renders *kai* by " very " (for A.V., " even the very "). (8) In John 6 : 57 *kàkeinos* (for *kai ekeinos*, " also he "), is translated " he also," R.V., for A.V., " even he." (9) In Eph. 1 : 10 there is no word in the original for " even." The R.V. expresses the stress on the pronoun by " in Him, I say."

EVER, FOR EVER, EVERMORE

A. Adverbs.

3842 AG:609B CB:1261C 1. PANTOTE (πάντοτε), at all times, always (akin to *pas*, all), is translated " ever " in Luke 15 : 31 ; John 18 : 20 ; 1 Thess. 4 : 17 ; 5 : 15 ; 2 Tim. 3 : 7 ; Heb. 7 : 25 ; " evermore " in John 6 : 34 ; in 1 Thess. 5 : 16, R.V., " alway," for A.V., " evermore." It there means 'on all occasions,' as, e.g., in 1 Thess. 1 : 2 ; 3 : 6 ; 5 : 15 ; 2 Thess. 1 : 3, 11 ; 2 : 13. See ALWAYS.

104 AG:19C CB:1233A 2. AEI (ἀεί), ever, is used (*a*) of continuous time, signifying unceasingly, perpetually, Acts 7 : 51 ; 2 Cor. 4 : 11 ; 6 : 10 ; Tit. 1 : 12 ; Heb. 3 : 10 ; (*b*) of successive occurrences, signifying 'on every occasion,' 1 Pet. 3 : 15 ; 2 Pet. 1 : 12. Some texts have the word in Mark 15 : 8. See ALWAYS.¶

1336 (-KES) AG:195A CB:— *Note :* The adjective *diēnekēs*, unbroken, continuous, is used in a phrase with *eis*, unto, and the article, signifying perpetually, for ever, Heb. 7 : 3 ; 10 : 1, 12, 14.¶

B. Phrases.

The following phrases are formed in connection with *aiōn*, an age : 165
they are idiomatic expressions betokening undefined periods and are AG:27B
not to be translated literally : (*a*) *eis aiōna*, lit., ' unto an age,' Jude 13, CB:1234A
" for ever ; " (*b*) *eis ton aiōna*, lit., ' unto the age,' " for ever " (or, with a negative, " never "), Matt. 21 : 19 ; Mark 3 : 29 ; 11 : 14 ; Luke 1 : 55 ; John 4 : 14 ; 6 : 51, 58 ; 8 : 35 (twice), 51, 52 ; 10 : 28 ; 11 : 26 ; 12 : 34 ; 13 : 8 ; 14 : 16 ; 1 Cor. 8 : 13 ; 2 Cor. 9 : 9 ; Heb. 5 : 6 ; 6 : 20 ; 7 : 17, 21, 24, 28 ; 1 Pet. 1 : 25 ; 1 John 2 : 17 ; 2 John 2 ; (*c*) *eis tous aiōnas*, lit., ' unto the ages,' " for ever," Matt. 6 : 13 (A.V. only) ; Luke 1 : 33 ; Rom. 1 : 25 ; 9 : 5 ; 11 : 36 ; 16 : 27 (some mss. have the next phrase here) ; 2 Cor. 11 : 31 ; Heb. 13 : 8 ; (*d*) *eis tous aiōnas tōn aiōnōn*, lit. ' unto the ages of the ages,' " for ever and ever," or " for evermore," Gal. 1 : 5 ; Phil. 4 : 20 ; 1 Tim. 1 : 17 ; 2 Tim. 4 : 18 ; Heb. 13 : 21 ; 1 Pet. 4 : 11 ; 5 : 11 [(*c*) in some mss.] ; Rev. 1 : 6 [(*c*) in some mss.] ; 1 : 18, " for evermore ; " 4 : 9, 10 ; 5 : 13 ; 7 : 12 ; 10 : 6 ; 11 : 15 ; 15 : 7 ; 19 : 3 ; 20 : 10 ; 22 : 5 ; (*e*) *eis aiōnas aiōnōn*, lit., ' unto ages of ages,' " for ever and ever," Rev. 14 : 11 ; (*f*) *eis ton aiōna tou aiōnos*, lit., ' unto the age of the age,' " for ever and ever," Heb. 1 : 8 ; (*g*) *tou aiōnos tōn aiōnōn*, lit., ' of the age of the ages,' " for ever and ever," Eph. 3 : 21 ;
(*h*) *eis pantas tous aiōnas*, lit., ' unto all the ages,' Jude 25 (" for evermore," HēMERA
R.V. ; " ever," A.V.) ; (*i*) *eis hēmeran aiōnos*, lit., ' unto a day of an age,' 2250 AG:345D
" for ever," 2 Pet. 3 : 18. CB:1249C

EVERLASTING 166

1. AIŌNIOS (αἰώνιος) : see Eternal. AG:28B CB:1234A

2. AIDIOS (ἀΐδιος) denotes everlasting (from *aei*, ever), Rom. 1 : 20, 126
R.V., " everlasting," for A.V., " eternal ; " Jude 6, A.V. and R.V., AG:22A
" everlasting." *Aiōnios*, should always be translated " eternal " and CB:1233C
aidios, " everlasting." " While *aiōnios* . . . negatives the end either of a space of time or of unmeasured time, and is used chiefly where something future is spoken of, *aidios* excludes interruption and lays stress upon permanence and unchangeableness " (Cremer).¶

EVERY, EVERYONE (MAN), EVERYTHING

1. PAS (πᾶς) signifies (1) with nouns without the article, (*a*) every 3956
one of the class denoted by the noun connected with *pas*, e.g., Matt. 3 : 10, AG:631A
" every tree ; " Mark 9 : 49, " every sacrifice ; " see also John 2 : 10 ; CB:1262C
Acts 2 : 43 ; Rom. 2 : 9 ; Eph. 1 : 21 ; 3 : 15 ; 2 Thess. 2 : 4 ; 2 Tim. 3 : 16, R.V. ; (*b*) any and every, of every kind, " all manner of," e.g., Matt. 4 : 23 ; " especially with nouns denoting virtues or vices, emotions, condition, indicating every mode in which a quality manifests itself ; or any object to which the idea conveyed by the noun belongs " (Grimm-Thayer). This is often translated " all," e.g., Acts 27 : 20 ; Rom. 15 : 14 ; 2 Cor. 10 : 6 ; Eph. 4 : 19, 31 ; Col. 4 : 12, " all the will of God," i.e.,

everything God wills; (2) without a noun, every one, everything, every man (i.e., person), e.g., Luke 16 : 16; or with a negative, not everyone, e.g., Mark 9 : 49; with a participle and the article, equivalent to a relative clause, everyone who, e.g., 1 Cor. 9 : 25; Gal. 3 : 10, 13; 1 John 2 : 29; 3 : 3, 4, 6, 10, 15, rendered "whosoever." So in the neuter, 1 John 2 : 16; 5 : 4, often rendered "whatsoever;" governed by the preposition *en*, in, without a noun following, it signifies in every matter, or condition, Phil. 4 : 6; 1 Thess. 5 : 18; in every way or particular, 2 Cor. 4 : 8, translated "on every side;" so 2 Cor. 7 : 5; "in everything," Eph. 5 : 24; Phil. 4 : 12, lit., 'in everything and (perhaps "even") in all things.' See THOROUGHLY, WHOLE.

537 AG:81D CB:1249B 2. HAPAS (ἅπας), a strengthened form of No. 1, signifies all, the whole, altogether; it is translated "every one" in Acts 5 : 16, where it occurs in the plural. In Mark 8 : 25, the A.V., "every man" translates the text with the masculine plural; the best mss. have the neuter plural, R.V., "all things." See ALL, WHOLE.

1538 AG:236C CB:1249C 3. HEKASTOS (ἕκαστος): see EACH, No. 1. It is used with *heis*, one, in Acts 2 : 6, "every man," and in Eph. 4 : 16, "each several (part)," for A.V., "every (part)." In Rev. 22 : 2 the most authentic mss. omit the numeral in the phrase "every month." It is preceded by *kath hena* (*kata*, according to, *hena*, one), a strengthened phrase, in Eph. 5 : 33, A.V., "everyone . . . in particular," R.V., "severally, each one." The same kind of phrase with *ana*, each, before the numeral, is used in Rev. 21 : 21, R.V., "each one of the several (gates)," for A.V., "every several (gate)." See EACH, PARTICULAR, SEVERAL.

2596 AG:405C CB:1253C *Notes*: (1) The preposition *kata*, down, is sometimes found governing a noun, in the sense of "every," e.g., Luke 2 : 41, "every year;" 16 : 19, "every day;" Heb. 9 : 25, "every year" (R.V., "year by year"); so 10 : 3. This construction sometimes signifies "in every . . .," e.g., Acts 14 : 23, "in every church;" 15 : 21, "in every city;" so 20 : 23; Tit. 1 : 5; Acts 22 : 19, "in every synagogue" (plural); Acts 8 : 3 "(into) every house." In Luke 8 : 1 the phrase means "throughout every city," as in the A.V.; in ver. 4 "of every city," R.V. In Acts 5 : 42 the R.V. renders *kat' oikon* "at home," for A.V., "in every house;" in 2 : 46, for A.V., "from house to house" (marg., "at home"). In Acts 15 : 21 (last part) the adjective *pas* (all) is placed between the preposition and the noun for the sake of emphasis. In Acts 26 : 11, *kata*, followed by the plural of *pas* and the article before the noun, is rendered "in all the synagogues," R.V., for A.V., "in every synagogue." The presence of the article confirms the R.V. See SEVERALLY.

303 AG:49D CB:1235A (2) In Matt. 20 : 9, 10, the preposition *ana*, upward (used distributively), governing the noun *dēnarion*, is translated "every man (a penny)." There is no word for "every man," and an appropriate rendering would be 'a penny apiece;' cp. Luke 9 : 14, "fifty each," R.V.; 10 : 1, "two

and two;" John 2:6, "two or three . . . apiece;" Rev. 4:8, "each . . . six wings."

(3) The pronoun *tis*, anyone, is rendered "any" in Acts 2:45, R.V., 5100
for the incorrect A.V., "every." In Mark 15:24, the interrogative form AG:819D
is rendered "what each (should take)" (A.V., "every man"), lit., 'who CB:1272C
(should take) what.'

EVERYWHERE, EVERY QUARTER, EVERY SIDE

1. PANTACHĒ (πανταχῇ), everywhere, is used in Acts 21:28.¶ AG:608B CB:—

2. PANTACHOU (πανταχοῦ), a variation of No. 1, is translated 3837
"everywhere" in Mark 1:28, R.V., of the report throughout Galilee AG:608B
concerning Christ; in Mark 16:20, of preaching; Luke 9:6, of healing; CB:—
Acts 17:30, of a Divine command for repentance; 28:22, of disparagement of Christians; 1 Cor. 4:17, of apostolic teaching; in Acts 24:3,
it is rendered "in all places."¶ In the Sept., Isa. 42:22.¶ See PLACE. 3840

3. PANTOTHEN (παντόθεν) or *pantachothen*, from all sides, is AG:608D
translated "from every quarter," Mark 1:45; in Luke 19:43, "on CB:—
every side;" in Heb. 9:4, "round about."¶ PANTACHOTHEN 3836

Notes: (1) In Phil. 4:12, the phrase *en panti*, A.V., "everywhere," AG:608B
is corrected to "in everything," in the R.V.; in 2 Cor. 4:8, "on every CB:— PAS
side." 3956

(2) In 1 Tim. 2:8, *en panti topō*, "in every place," R.V., is translated AG:631A CB:1262C
"everywhere" in the A.V. TOPOS 5117

EVERY WHIT AG:822B CB:1273A

HOLOS (ὅλος), all, whole, complete, is rendered "every whit" in 3650
John 7:23; 13:10. See ALL. AG:564D CB:1251A

For EVIDENCE (Heb. 11:1) see REPROOF, A

EVIDENT, EVIDENTLY

A. Adjectives.

1. DĒLOS (δῆλος), properly signifying visible, clear to the mind, 1212
evident, is translated "evident" in Gal. 3:11 and 1 Cor. 15:27, R.V. AG:178B CB:1240C
(A.V., "manifest"); "bewrayeth," Matt. 26:73; "certain," 1 Tim. 6:7, A.V. Cp. *dēloō*, to declare, signify. See BEWRAY, CERTAIN, MANIFEST.¶

2. KATADĒLOS (κατάδηλος), a strengthened form of No. 1, quite 2612
manifest, evident, is used in Heb. 7:15 (A.V., "more evident").¶ For AG:410B CB:—
the preceding verse see No. 3.

3. PRODĒLOS (πρόδηλος), manifest beforehand (*pro*, before, and 4271
No. 1), is used in Heb. 7:14 in the sense of 'clearly evident.' So in AG:704B CB:—
1 Tim. 5:24, 25, R.V., "evident," for A.V., "open beforehand," and
"manifest beforehand." The *pro* is somewhat intensive.¶ 5318

Note: *Phaneros*, visible, manifest (akin to *phainomai*, to appear), is AG:852B CB:1263C synonymous with the above, but is not translated " evident " in the N.T. For " evident token " see TOKEN.

B. Adverb.

5320 AG:853A CB:1263C PHANERŌS (φανερῶς), manifestly (see note above), is rendered " openly " in Mark 1 : 45 ; " publicly " in John 7 : 10, R.V. (opposite to " in secret ") ; in Acts 10 : 3, R.V., " openly," for A.V., " evidently." See OPENLY, PUBLICLY.¶

Note : For the A.V. " evidently " in Gal. 3 : 1, see OPENLY.

EVIL, EVIL-DOER

A. Adjectives.

2556 AG:397D CB:1253B 1. KAKOS (κακός) stands for whatever is evil in character, base, in distinction (wherever the distinction is observable) from *ponēros* (see No. 2), which indicates what is evil in influence and effect, malignant. *Kakos* is the wider term and often covers the meaning of *ponēros*. *Kakos* is antithetic to *kalos*, fair, advisable, good in character, and to *agathos*, beneficial, useful, good in act ; hence it denotes what is useless, incapable, bad ; *ponēros* is essentially antithetic to *chrēstos*, kind, gracious, serviceable ; hence it denotes what is destructive, injurious, evil. As evidence that *ponēros* and *kakos* have much in common, though still not interchangeable, each is used of thoughts, cp. Matt. 15 : 19 with Mark 7 : 21 ; of speech, Matt. 5 : 11 with 1 Pet. 3 : 10 ; of actions, 2 Tim. 4 : 18 with 1 Thess. 5 : 15 ; of man, Matt. 18 : 32 with 24 : 48.

The use of *kakos* may be broadly divided as follows : (*a*) of what is morally or ethically evil, whether of persons, e.g., Matt. 21 : 41 ; 24 : 48 ; Phil. 3 : 2 ; Rev. 2 : 2, or qualities, emotions, passions, deeds, e.g., Mark 7 : 21 ; John 18 : 23, 30 ; Rom. 1 : 30 ; 3 : 8 ; 7 : 19, 21 ; 13 : 4 ; 14 : 20 ; 16 : 19 ; 1 Cor. 13 : 5 ; 2 Cor. 13 : 7 ; 1 Thess. 5 : 15 ; 1 Tim. 6 : 10 ; 2 Tim. 4 : 14 ; 1 Pet. 3 : 9, 12 ; (*b*) of what is injurious, destructive, baneful, pernicious, e.g., Luke 16 : 25 ; Acts 16 : 28 ; 28 : 5 ; Tit. 1 : 12 ; Jas. 3 : 8 ; Rev. 16 : 2, where *kakos* and *ponēros* come in that order, " noisome and grievous." See B, No. 3. For compounds of *kakos*, see below.

4190 AG:690D CB:1266A 2. PONĒROS (πονηρός), akin to *ponos*, labour, toil, denotes evil that causes labour, pain, sorrow, malignant evil (see No. 1) ; it is used (*a*) with the meaning bad, worthless, in the physical sense, Matt. 7 : 17, 18 ; in the moral or ethical sense, evil, wicked ; of persons, e.g., Matt. 7 : 11 ; Luke 6 : 45 ; Acts 17 : 5 ; 2 Thess. 3 : 2 ; 2 Tim. 3 : 13 ; of evil spirits, e.g., Matt. 12 : 45 ; Luke 7 : 21 ; Acts 19 : 12, 13, 15, 16 ; of a generation, Matt. 12 : 39, 45 ; 16 : 4 ; Luke 11 : 29 ; of things, e.g., Matt. 5 : 11 ; 6 : 23 ; 20 : 15 ; Mark 7 : 22 ; Luke 11 : 34 ; John 3 : 19 ; 7 : 7 ; Acts 18 : 14 ; Gal. 1 : 4 ; Col. 1 : 21 ; 1 Tim. 6 : 4 ; 2 Tim. 4 : 18 ; Heb. 3 : 12 ; 10 : 22 ; Jas. 2 : 4 ; 4 : 16 ; 1 John 3 : 12 ; 2 John 11 ; 3 John 10 ; (*b*) with the meaning toilsome, painful, Eph. 5 : 16 ; 6 : 13 ; Rev. 16 : 2. Cp. *ponēria*, iniquity, wickedness. For its use as a noun see B, No. 2.

3. PHAULOS (φαῦλος) primarily denotes slight, trivial, blown about 5337
by every wind; then, mean, common, bad, in the sense of being worthless, AG:854C CB:1264A
paltry or contemptible, belonging to a low order of things; in John 5 : 29, those who have practised evil things, R.V., "ill" (*phaula*), are set in contrast to those who have done good things (*agatha*); the same contrast is presented in Rom. 9 : 11 and 2 Cor. 5 : 10, in each of which the most authentic mss. have *phaulos* for *kakos*; he who practises evil things (R.V., "ill") hates the light, John 3 : 20; jealousy and strife are accompanied by "every vile deed," Jas. 3 : 16. It is used as a noun in Tit. 2 : 8 (see B, No. 4). See BAD, ILL, VILE.¶

B. Nouns.

1. KAKIA (κακία), primarily, badness in quality (akin to A, No. 1), 2549
denotes (*a*) wickedness, depravity, malignity, e.g., Acts 8 : 22, "wicked- AG:397A CB:1253A
ness;" Rom. 1 : 29, "maliciousness;" in Jas. 1 : 21, A.V., "naughtiness;" (*b*) the evil of trouble, affliction, Matt. 6 : 34, only, and here alone translated "evil." See MALICE, MALICIOUSNESS, NAUGHTINESS, WICKEDNESS.

2. PONĒROS (πονηρός), the adjective (A, No. 2), is used as a noun, 4190
(*a*) of Satan as the evil one, Matt. 5 : 37; 6 : 13; 13 : 19, 38; Luke 11 : 4 AG:690D CB:1266A
(in some texts); John 17 : 15; Eph. 6 : 16; 2 Thess. 3 : 3; 1 John 2 : 13, 14; 3 : 12; 5 : 18, 19; (*b*) of human beings, Matt. 5 : 45; (probably ver. 39); 13 : 49; 22 : 10; Luke 6 : 35; 1 Cor. 5 : 13; (*c*) neuter, "evil (things)," Matt. 9 : 4; 12 : 35; Mark 7 : 23; Luke 3 : 19; "that which is evil," Luke 6 : 45; Rom. 12 : 9; Acts 28 : 21, "harm."

3. KAKON (κακόν), the neuter of A, No. 1, is used with the article, as 2556
a noun, e.g., Acts 23 : 9; Rom. 7 : 21; Heb. 5 : 14; in the plural, "evil AG:397D CB:1253B
things," e.g., 1 Cor. 10 : 6; 1 Tim. 6 : 10, "all kinds of evil," R.V.

4. PHAULON (φαῦλον), the neuter of A, No. 3, is used as a noun in 5337
Tit. 2 : 8. AG:854C CB:1264A

5. KAKOPOIOS (κακοποιός), properly the masculine gender of 2555
the adjective, denotes an evil-doer (*kakon*, evil, *poieō*, to do), 1 Pet. 2 : 12, AG:397C CB:1253B
14; 4 : 15; in some mss. in 3 : 16 and John 18 : 30 (so the A.V.).¶ For a synonymous word see Note (1). Cp. the verb below. In the Sept., Prov. 12 : 4; 24 : 19. See MALEFACTOR.¶

Notes: (1) *Kakourgos*, an evil-worker (*kakon*, evil, *ergon*, a work), is 2557
translated "evil-doer" in 2 Tim. 2 : 9, A.V. (R.V., "malefactor"). AG:398B CB:1253B
Cp. Luke 23 : 32, 33, 39.¶

(2) *Adikēma*, an injustice (*a*, negative, *dikaios*, just), is translated 92
"evil-doing," in Acts 24 : 20, A.V., R.V., "wrong-doing." See INIQUITY, AG:17D CB:1233A
WRONG.

C. Verbs.

1. KAKOŌ (κακόω), to ill-treat (akin to A, No. 1), is rendered to 2559
entreat evil in Acts 7 : 6, 19; "made (them) evil affected," 14 : 2. AG:398B CB:1253B
See AFFECT, AFFLICT, HARM, HURT, VEX.

2554 AG:397C CB:1253B 2. KAKOPOIEŌ (κακοποιέω) signifies to do evil (cp. B, No. 5), Mark 3 : 4 (R.V., " to do harm ") ; so, Luke 6 : 9 ; in 3 John 11, " doeth evil ; " in 1 Pet. 3 : 17, " evil doing." See HARM.¶

Note : Cp. *kakologeō*, to speak evil (see CURSE, SPEAK) ; *kakopatheō*, to endure evil (see ENDURE, SUFFER) ; *kakopatheia*, suffering affliction (see SUFFER) ; *kakoucheō*, to suffer adversity (see SUFFER).

D. Adverb.

2560 AG:398C CB:1253B KAKŌS (κακῶς), badly, evilly, akin to A, No. 1, is used in the physical sense, to be sick, e.g., Matt. 4 : 24 ; Mark 1 : 32, 34 ; Luke 5 : 31 (see DISEASE). In Matt. 21 : 41 this adverb is used with the adjective, " He will miserably destroy those miserable men," more lit., ' He will evilly destroy those men (evil as they are),' with stress on the adjective ; (*b*) in the moral sense, to speak evilly, John 18 : 23 ; Acts 23 : 5 ; to ask evilly, Jas. 4 : 3. See AMISS, GRIEVOUSLY, SICK, SORE.

EVIL SPEAKING

988 AG:143A CB:1239A 1. BLASPHĒMIA (βλασφημία) is translated " evil speaking " in Eph. 4 : 31, A.V. (R.V., " railing "). See BLASPHEMY.

2636 AG:412D CB:1254A 2. KATALALIA (καταλαλία), " evil speaking," 1 Pet. 2 : 1 : see BACKBITING.

EXACT (Verb)

4238 AG:698B CB:1266B 1. PRASSŌ (πράσσω), to do, to practise, also has the meaning of transacting, or managing in the matter of payment, to exact, to get money from a person, Luke 3 : 13 (R.V., " extort "). Cp. the English idiom ' to do a person.' This verb is rendered " required," in 19 : 23.

4811 AG:776C CB:— 2. SUKOPHANTEŌ (συκοφαντέω), to accuse falsely, Luke 3 : 14, has its other meaning, to exact wrongfully, in 19 : 8. See ACCUSE.¶

EXACT, EXACTLY

197 AG:33B (-BōS) CB:— AKRIBESTERON (ἀκριβέστερον), the comparative degree of *akribōs*, accurately, carefully, is used in Acts 18 : 26, A.V., " more perfectly," R.V., " more carefully ; " 23 : 15, A.V., " more perfectly," R.V., " more exactly ; " so ver. 20 ; 24 : 22, A.V., " more perfect," R.V., " more exact " (lit., ' knowing more exactly '). See CAREFULLY, PERFECTLY.¶

AKRIBEIA 195 AG:33A AKRIBOō 198 AG:33B Cp. *akribeia*, precision, exactness, Acts 22 : 3,¶ and *akriboō*, to learn carefully, to enquire with exactness, Matt. 2 : 7, 16.¶

EXALT, EXALTED

A. Verbs.

5312 AG:850 CB:1252B 1. HUPSOŌ (ὑψόω), to lift up (akin to *hupsos*, height), is used (*a*) literally of the lifting up of Christ in His crucifixion, John 3 : 14 ; 8 : 28 ; 12 : 32, 34 ; illustratively, of the serpent of brass, John 3 : 14 ;

(*b*) figuratively, of spiritual privileges bestowed on a city, Matt. 11 : 23 ; Luke 10 : 15 ; of raising to dignity and happiness, Luke 1 : 52 ; Acts 13 : 17 ; of haughty self-exaltation, and, contrastingly, of being raised to honour, as a result of self-humbling, Matt. 23 : 12 ; Luke 14 : 11 ; 18 : 14 ; of spiritual uplifting and revival, Jas. 4 : 10 ; 1 Pet. 5 : 6 ; of bringing into the blessings of salvation through the Gospel, 2 Cor. 11 : 7 ; (*c*) with a combination of the literal and metaphorical, of the exaltation of Christ by God the Father, Acts 2 : 33 ; 5 : 31. See LIFT.¶

2. HUPERUPSOŌ (ὑπερυψόω), to exalt highly (*huper*, over, and No. 1), is used of Christ, as in No. 1, (*c*), in Phil. 2 : 9.¶ 5251 AG:842A CB:1252A

3. EPAIRŌ (ἐπαίρω), to lift up (*epi*, up, *airō*, to raise), is said (*a*) literally, of a sail, Acts 27 : 40 ; hands, Luke 24 : 50 ; 1 Tim. 2 : 8 ; heads, Luke 21 : 28 ; eyes, Matt. 17 : 8, etc. ; (*b*) metaphorically, of exalting oneself, being lifted up with pride, 2 Cor. 10 : 5 ; 11 : 20. See LIFT. 1869 AG:281D CB:—

4. HUPERAIRŌ (ὑπεραίρω), to raise over (*huper*, above, and *airō*, see No. 3), is used in the Middle Voice, of exalting oneself exceedingly, 2 Cor. 12 : 7 ; 2 Thess. 2 : 4.¶ 5229 (-OMAI) AG:839D CB:—

B. Adjective.

HUPSĒLOS (ὑψηλός), high, lofty, is used metaphorically in Luke 16 : 15, as a noun with the article, R.V., " that which is exalted," A.V., " that which is highly esteemed." See ESTEEM, HIGH. 5308 AG:849B CB:1252B

Note : For Jas. 1 : 9, R.V., " in his high estate," see ESTATE, No. 3.

EXAMINATION, EXAMINE

A. Noun.

ANAKRISIS (ἀνάκρισις), from *ana*, up or through, and *krinō*, to distinguish, was a legal term among the Greeks, denoting the preliminary investigation for gathering evidence for the information of the judges, Acts 25 : 26.¶ 351 AG:56C CB:—

B. Verbs.

1. ANAKRINŌ (ἀνακρίνω), to examine, investigate, is used (*a*) of searching or enquiry, Acts 17 : 11 ; 1 Cor. 9 : 3 ; 10 : 25, 27 ; (*b*) of reaching a result of the enquiry, judging, 1 Cor. 2 : 14, 15 ; 4 : 3, 4 ; 14 : 24 ; (*c*) forensically, of examining by torture, Luke 23 : 14 ; Acts 4 : 9 ; 12 : 19 ; 24 : 8 ; 28 : 18. See ASK, DISCERN, JUDGE, SEARCH.¶ 350 AG:56B CB:1235A

2. ANETAZŌ (ἀνετάζω), to examine judicially (*ana*, up, *etazō*, to test), is used in Acts 22 : 24, 29.¶ Cp. the synonymous verb *exetazō*, to search or enquire carefully, Matt. 2 : 8 ; 10 : 11 ; John 21 : 12.¶ 426 AG:65C CB:—

3. DOKIMAZŌ (δοκιμάζω), to prove, test, approve, is rendered " examine " in 1 Cor. 11 : 28, A.V. (R.V., " prove "). See APPROVE. 1381 AG:202C CB:1242A

4. PEIRAZŌ (πειράζω), to tempt, try, is rendered " examine " in 2 Cor. 13 : 5, A.V. (R.V., " try "). See GO, PROVE, TEMPT, TRY. 3985 AG:640B CB:1263A

EXAMPLE

A. Nouns.

1164 AG:172C 1. DEIGMA (δεῖγμα), primarily a thing shown, a specimen (akin to
CB:1240B *deiknumi*, to show), denotes an example given as a warning, Jude 7.¶

Note : The corresponding word in 2 Pet. 2 : 6 is No. 2.

2. HUPODEIGMA (ὑπόδειγμα) : see ENSAMPLE, No. 3.

3. TUPOS (τύπος) : see ENSAMPLE, No. 1.

5261 AG:843D 4. HUPOGRAMMOS (ὑπογραμμός), lit., an under-writing (from
CB:1252B *hupographō*, to write under, to trace letters for copying by scholars) ; hence, a writing-copy, an example, 1 Pet. 2 : 21, said of what Christ left for believers, by His sufferings (not expiatory, but exemplary), that they might " follow His steps."

1165 AG:172C
B. Verbs.

CB:1240C 1. DEIGMATIZŌ (δειγματίζω), to make a show of, to expose (akin
PARADEIGMATIZŌ 3856 to A, No. 1), is translated " to make a public example," in Matt. 1 : 19
AG:614A (some mss. have the strengthened form *paradeigmatizō* here ; " put . . .
CB:1262A to an open shame," Heb. 6 : 6,¶) ; in Col. 2 : 15, " made a show of."¶

5263 AG:844B 2. HUPODEIKNUMI (ὑποδείκνυμι), primarily, to show secretly
CB:— (*hupo*, under, *deiknumi*, to show), to show by tracing out (akin to A, No. 2) ; hence, to teach, to show by example, Acts 20 : 35, R.V., " I gave you an example," for A.V., " I shewed you." Elsewhere, to warn, Matt. 3 : 7 ; Luke 3 : 7 ; 12 : 5, R.V., for A.V., " forewarn ; " to show, Luke 6 : 47 ;
EXASPERATE See ANGER, PROVOKE Acts 9 : 16. See FOREWARN, SHEW, WARN.¶

EXCEED, EXCEEDING, EXCEEDINGLY

A. Verbs.

5235 AG:840B 1. HUPERBALLŌ (ὑπερβάλλω), to throw over or beyond (*huper*, over,
CB:— *ballō*, to throw), is translated " exceeding " in 2 Cor. 9 : 14 ; Eph. 1 : 19 ; 2 : 7 ; " excelleth " (R.V., " surpasseth ") in 2 Cor. 3 : 10 ; " passeth " in Eph. 3 : 19 (" surpasseth " might be the meaning here). See EXCEL, SURPASS.¶ Cp. *huperbolē*, under EXCEL, B, No. 1.

4052 AG:650C 2. PERISSEUŌ (περισσεύω), to be over and above, over a certain
CB:1263C number or measure, to abound, exceed, is translated " exceed " in Matt. 5 : 20 ; 2 Cor. 3 : 9. See ABUNDANCE, B, No. 1.

B. Adverbs and Adverbial Phrases.

3029 AG:473B 1. LIAN (λίαν), very, exceedingly, is translated " exceeding " in
CB:1257A Matt. 2 : 16 (for ver. 10, see No. 2) ; 4 : 8 ; 8 : 28 ; Mark 9 : 3 ; Luke 23 : 8. See GREATLY (GREAT), SORE, VERY.

4970 AG:796A 2. SPHODRA (σφόδρα), properly the neuter plural of *sphodros*,
CB:1269C excessive, violent (from a root indicating restlessness), signifies very, very much, exceedingly, Matt. 2 : 10 ; 17 : 6, " sore ; " 17 : 23 ; 18 : 31, R.V., " exceeding," for A.V., " very ; " 19 : 25 ; 26 : 22 ; 27 : 54, R.V., " exceedingly " for A.V., " greatly ; " Mark 16 : 4, " very ; " Luke 18 : 23 (ditto) ; Acts 6 : 7, R.V., " exceedingly," for A.V., " greatly ; " Rev. 16 : 21. See GREATLY, SORE, VERY.¶

3. SPHODRŌS (σφοδρῶς), exceedingly (see No. 2), is used in Acts 4971 AG:796B
27 : 18.¶ CB:—

4. PERISSŌS (περισσῶς) is used in Matt. 27 : 23, R.V., " exceedingly," 4057
for A.V., " the more ; " Mark 10 : 26, R.V., " exceedingly," for A.V., AG:651D CB:1263C
" out of measure ; " in Acts 26 : 11, " exceedingly." In Mark 15 : 14,
the most authentic mss. have this word (R.V., " exceedingly ") for
No. 5 (A.V., " the more exceedingly "). See MORE.¶

5. PERISSOTERŌS (περισσοτέρως), the comparative degree of No. 4, 4056
abundantly, exceedingly (akin to A, No. 2), Gal. 1 : 14, " more ex- AG:651D CB:1263C
ceedingly ; " 1 Thess. 2 : 17, R.V., " the more exceedingly," for A.V.,
" the more abundantly ; " see ABUNDANCE, D, No. 2.

6. HUPEREKPERISSOU (ὑπερεκπερισσοῦ) denotes superabundantly After 5240
(*huper*, over, *ek*, from, *perissos*, abundant) ; in 1 Thess. 3 : 10, " ex- AG:840C CB:1252A
ceedingly ; " Eph. 3 : 20, " exceeding abundantly."¶ Another form,
huperekperissōs (*huper*, and *ek* and No. 4), is used in 1 Thess. 5 : 13 (in the
best mss.), " exceeding highly."¶ Cp. the verb *huperperisseuō*, to abound
more exceedingly, Rom. 5 : 21 ; in 2 Cor. 7 : 4, " I overflow (with joy),"
R.V., for A.V., " I am exceeding (joyful). See ABUNDANT, D, No. 2.

Notes : (1) In Acts 7 : 20, the phrase " exceeding fair " (*asteios*) is, ASTEIOS
lit., ' fair to God ' (see marg.). (2) In Matt. 26 : 7, *barutimos* (*barus*, 791 AG:117C
weighty, *timē* value), is rendered " exceeding precious," R.V., for A.V., CB:—
" very precious." (3) In Mark 4 : 41, " they feared exceedingly " is, BARUTIMOS
lit., ' they feared a great fear.' See FEAR. (4) For other combinations 927 AG:134B
of the adverb, see GLAD, GREAT, JOYFUL, SORROWFUL, SORRY. CB:1238C

EXCEL, EXCELLENCY, EXCELLENT

A. Verbs.

1. HUPERBALLŌ (ὑπερβάλλω), lit., to throw over : see EXCEED, 5235 AG:840B
No. 1. CB:—

2. PERISSEUŌ (περισσεύω), to be over and above, is rendered 4052
" abound in 1 Cor. 14 : 12, R.V., for A.V., " excel." See ABUNDANCE, AG:650C CB:1263C
B, No. 1,and EXCEED, A, No. 2.

3. HUPERECHŌ (ὑπερέχω), lit., to have over (*huper*, over, *echō*, to 5242
have), is translated " excellency " in Phil. 3 : 8, ' the surpassingness ' AG:840D CB:1252A
(Moule) ; the phrase could be translated ' the surpassing thing, which
consists in the knowledge of Christ Jesus,' and this is the probable meaning.
This verb is used three times in Philippians, here and in 2 : 3 ; 4 : 7.
See also Rom. 13 : 1 ; 1 Pet. 2 : 13. See BETTER, No. 4.¶

4. DIAPHERŌ (διαφέρω), to differ, is used in the neuter plural of 1308
the present participle with the article, in Phil. 1 : 10, " the things that AG:190B CB:—
are excellent " (marg., " the things that differ "), lit., ' the excellent things.'
See DIFFER.

B. Nouns.

1. HUPERBOLĒ (ὑπερβολή), lit., a throwing beyond, hence, a sur- 5236 AG:840B
passing, an excellence, is translated " excellency " in 2 Cor. 4 : 7, A.V. ; CB:—

R.V., "exceeding greatness." It always betokens pre-eminence. It is used with *kata*, according to, in the phrase *kath' huperbolēn*, signifying beyond measure, exceedingly, Rom. 7 : 13, "exceeding sinful ;" in 2 Cor. 1 : 8, R.V., "exceedingly," for A.V., "out of measure ;" in Gal. 1 : 13, "beyond measure ;" in 1 Cor. 12 : 31, "more excellent." In 2 Cor. 4 : 17, there is an expanded phrase *kath' huperbolēn eis huperbolēn*, lit., 'according to a surpassing unto a surpassing,' R.V., "more and more exceedingly," which corrects the A.V., "a far more exceeding ;" the phrase refers to "worketh," showing the surpassing degree of its operation, and not to the noun "weight" (nor does it qualify "eternal"). In 2 Cor. 12 : 7, the R.V. has "exceeding greatness," the A.V., "abundance." See ABUNDANCE.¶

5247 2. HUPEROCHĒ (ὑπεροχή), akin to A, No. 3, strictly speaking, the
AG:841D act of overhanging (*huper*, and *echō*, to hold) or the thing which overhangs,
CB:— hence, superiority, pre-eminence, is translated "excellency (of speech)" in 1 Cor. 2 : 1 ; elsewhere, in 1 Tim. 2 : 2, R.V., "high place," for A.V., "authority." See AUTHORITY, PLACE.¶

703 *Note :* In 1 Pet. 2 : 9 R.V. renders *aretē* (virtue) "excellencies."
AG:105D
CB:1237C

C. Adjectives.

3169 1. MEGALOPREPĒS (μεγαλοπρεπής) signifies magnificent, majestic,
AG:497A that which is becoming to a great man (from *megas*, great, and *prepō*,
CB:— to be fitting or becoming), in 2 Pet. 1 : 17, "excellent."¶

1313 (-OROS) 2. DIAPHORŌTEROS (διαφορώτερος), comparative degree of *diaphoros*,
AG:190D (-OROS 2.) excellent, akin to A, No. 4, is used twice, in Heb. 1 : 4, "more excellent
CB:— (name)," and 8 : 6, "more excellent (ministry)."¶ For the positive degree see Rom. 12 : 6 ; Heb. 9 : 10. See under DIFFER.¶

4119 3. PLEIŌN (πλείων), more, greater, the comparative degree of *polus*,
AG:687C (POLUS II.) much, is translated "more excellent" in Heb. 11 : 4, of Abel's sacrifice ;
CB:1265B *pleiōn* is used sometimes of that which is superior by reason of inward worth, cp. 3 : 3, "more (honour) ;" in Matt. 6 : 25, of the life in comparison with meat.

2903 4. KRATISTOS (κράτιστος), mightiest, noblest, best, the superlative
AG:449A degree of *kratus*, strong (cp. *kratos*, strength), is used as a title of honour
CB:1256A and respect, "most excellent," Luke 1 : 3 (Theophilus was quite possibly a man of high rank) ; Acts 23 : 26 ; 24 : 3 and 26 : 25, R.V., for A.V., "most noble."¶

Note : The phrase *kath' huperbolēn* (for which see B, No. 1) is translated "more excellent" in 1 Cor. 12 : 31.

EXCEPT, EXCEPTED

Note : For the negative conjunctions *ean mē* and *ei mē*, see † p. 1

1622 1. EKTOS (ἐκτός), an adverb, lit., outside, is used with *ei mē*, as an
AG:246A extended conjunction signifying "except ;" so in 1 Cor. 14 : 5 ; in
CB:— 15 : 2, R.V., for A.V., "unless ;" in 1 Tim. 5 : 19, R.V., for A.V., "but."

It has the force of a preposition in the sense of (*a*) outside of, in 1 Cor. 6 : 18, " without ; " in 2 Cor. 12 : 2, " out of ; " (*b*) besides, except, in Acts 26 : 22, R.V., " but," for A.V., " other than ; " in 1 Cor. 15 : 27 " excepted." For its use as a noun see Matt. 23 : 26, " (the) outside." See OTHER, OUT OF, OUTSIDE, UNLESS, WITHOUT.¶

2. PAREKTOS (παρεκτός), a strengthened form of No. 1 (*para*, beside), is used (*a*) as an adverb, signifying " without," 2 Cor. 11 : 28 ; lit., ' the things without,' i.e., the things happening without ; (*b*) as a preposition signifying " except ; " in Matt. 5 : 32, " saving ; " in Acts 26 : 29, " except."¶ 3924 AG:625A CB:1262B

Note : In Matt. 19 : 9, the A.V. and R.V., translating the mss. which have the negative *mē*, followed by *epi*, render it " except for." The authorities mentioned in the R.V. marg. have *parektos*, followed by *logou*, i.e., ' saving for the cause of.'

3. PLĒN (πλήν), an adverb, most frequently signifying yet, howbeit, or only, sometimes has the meaning " except (that)," " save (that)," Acts 20 : 23 ; Phil. 1 : 18, R.V., " only that," for A.V., " notwithstanding." It is also used as a preposition, signifying except, save, Mark 12 : 32, " but ; " John 8 : 10, " but " (A.V. only) ; Acts 8 : 1, " except ; " Acts 15 : 28, " than ; " 27 : 22, " but (only)." 4133 AG:669B CB:1265B

EXCESS

1. AKRASIA (ἀκρασία) lit. denotes want of strength (*a*, negative, *kratos*, strength), hence, want of self-control, incontinence, Matt. 23 : 25, " excess ; " 1 Cor. 7 : 5, " incontinency."¶ Cp. *akratēs*, powerless, incontinent, 2 Tim. 3 : 3, R.V., " without self-control."¶ 192 AG:33A CB:1234B

2. ANACHUSIS (ἀνάχυσις), lit., a pouring out, overflowing (akin to *anacheō*, to pour out), is used metaphorically in 1 Pet. 4 : 4, " excess," said of the riotous conduct described in ver. 3.¶ 401 AG:63C CB:—

Notes : (1) *Asōtia* denotes prodigality, profligacy, riot (from *a*, negative, and *sōzō*, to save) ; it is translated " riot " in Eph. 5 : 18, R.V., for A.V., " excess ; " in Tit. 1 : 6 and 1 Pet. 4 : 4, " riot " in A.V. and R.V. See RIOT.¶ Cp. the adverb *asōtōs*, wastefully, " in riotous living," Luke 15 : 13.¶ A synonymous noun is *aselgeia*, lasciviousness, outrageous conduct, wanton violence. 810 AG:119C CB:—

(2) In 1 Pet. 4 : 3, *oinophlugia*, drunkenness, debauchery (*oinos*, wine, *phluō*, to bubble up, overflow), is rendered " excess of wine," A.V. (R.V., " winebibbings ") ¶ 3632 AG:562C CB:1260C

EXCHANGE

A. Noun.

ANTALLAGMA (ἀντάλλαγμα), the price received as an equivalent of, or in exchange for, an article, an exchange (*anti*, instead of, *allassō*, to change, akin to *allos*, another), hence denotes the price at which the 465 AG:72D CB:1236A exchange is effected, Matt. 16 : 26 ; Mark 8 : 37.¶ Connected with this is the conception of atonement, as in the word *lutron*, a ransom. Cp. *allagma* in the Sept., e.g., in Isa. 43 : 3.

B. Verb.

3337 AG:511C CB:1258C METALLASSŌ (μεταλλάσσω) denotes (*a*) to exchange, *meta*, with, implying change, and *allassō* (see A.), Rom. 1 : 25, of exchanging the truth for a lie, R.V., for A.V., "changed ;" (*b*) to change, ver. 26, a different meaning from that in the preceding verse. See CHANGE.¶ In the Sept., Esth. 2 : 7, 20.¶

474 AG:74A CB:— *Note :* In Luke 24 : 17, "what communications are these that ye have one with another ?" the verb *antiballō*, to throw in turn, to exchange, is used of conversation, lit., 'what words are these that ye exchange one with another ?'

EXCHANGE See CHANGE

For EXCHANGERS see BANKERS

EXCLAIM See CRY

EXCLUDE

1576 AG:240C CB:— EKKLEIŌ (ἐκκλείω), to shut out (*ek*, from, *kleiō*, to shut), is said of glorying in works as a means of justification, Rom. 3 : 27 ; of Gentiles, who by Judaism would be excluded from salvation and Christian fellowship, Gal. 4 : 17.¶

EXCUSE

A. Noun.

4392 AG:722C CB:— PROPHASIS (πρόφασις), a pretence, pretext (from *pro*, before, and *phēmi*, to say), is translated "excuse" in John 15 : 22, R.V., for A.V., "cloke ;" "cloke" in 1 Thess. 2 : 5, A.V. and R.V. See CLOKE, PRETENCE, SHOW (Noun).

B. Adjective (*negative*).

379 AG:60A CB:1235B ANAPOLOGĒTOS (ἀναπολόγητος), without excuse, inexcusable (*a*, negative, *n*, euphonic, and *apologeomai*, see C, No. 1, below), is used, Rom. 1 : 20, "without excuse," of those who reject the revelation of God in creation ; 2 : 1, R.V., for A.V., "inexcusable," of the Jew who judges the Gentile.¶

C. Verbs.

626 AG:95D CB:1237A 1. APOLOGEOMAI (ἀπολογέομαι), lit., to speak oneself off, hence to plead for oneself, and so, in general, (*a*) to defend, as before a tribunal ; in Rom. 2 : 15, R.V., "excusing them," means one excusing others (not themselves) ; the preceding phrase "one with another" signifies one person with another, not one thought with another ; it may be paraphrased, 'their thoughts with one another, condemning or else excusing one another ;' conscience provides a moral standard by which men judge one another ; (*b*) to excuse oneself, 2 Cor. 12 : 19 ; cp. B. See ANSWER.

3868 AG:616C CB:1262A 2. PARAITEOMAI (παραιτέομαι) is used in the sense of begging off, asking to be excused or making an excuse, in Luke 14 : 18 (twice) and ver. 19. In the first part of ver. 18 the verb is used in the Middle Voice, " to make excuse " (acting in imagined self-interest) ; in the latter part and in ver. 19 it is in the Passive Voice, " have me excused."

EXECUTE

1. POIEŌ (ποιέω), to do, to make, is thrice rendered " execute," of 4160
the Lord's authority and acts in executing judgment, (*a*) of His authority AG:680D CB:1265C
as the One to whom judgment is committed, John 5 : 27 ; (*b*) of the judgment which He will mete out to all transgressors at His Second Advent, Jude 15 ; (*c*) of the carrying out of His word (not " work," as in the A.V.) in the earth, especially regarding the nation of Israel, the mass being rejected, the remnant saved, Rom. 9 : 28. That He will " execute His word finishing and cutting it short," is expressive of the summary and decisive character of His action. See Do.

2. HIERATEUŌ (ἱερατεύω), to be a priest, to officiate as such, is 2407
translated " executed the priest's office," in Luke 1 : 8.¶ It occurs AG:371D CB:1250B
frequently in the Sept., and in Inscriptions. Cp. *hierateuma*, priesthood, 1 Pet. 2 : 5, 9,¶ *hierateia*, a priest's office, Luke 1 : 9 ; Heb. 7 : 5,¶ *hiereus*, a priest, and *hieros*, sacred.

For EXECUTIONER, Mark 6 : 27, see GUARD, A, No. 2

EXERCISE

A. Verbs.

1. GUMNAZŌ (γυμνάζω) primarily signifies to exercise naked (from GUMNAZō
gumnos, naked) ; then, generally, to exercise, to train the body or mind 1128 AG:167C
(Eng., gymnastic), 1 Tim. 4 : 7, with a view to godliness ; Heb. 5 : 14, of CB:1248C
the senses, so as to discern good and evil ; 12 : 11, of the effect of chasten- ASKEō 778
ing, the spiritual exercise producing the fruit of righteousness ; 2 Pet. AG:116B
2 : 14, of certain evil teachers with hearts " exercised in covetousness," CB:1238A
R.V.¶ POIEō 4160
2. ASKEŌ (ἀσκέω) signifies to form by art, to adorn, to work up raw AG:680D
material with skill ; hence, in general, to take pains, endeavour, exercise CB:1265C EXOUSIAZō
by training or discipline, with a view to a conscience void of offence, Acts 1850 AG:279A
24 : 16.¶ CB:1247C
3. POIEŌ (ποιέω), to do, is translated " exerciseth " in Rev. 13 : 12, KURIEUō 2961
said of the authority of the second " Beast." Cp. EXECUTE. See Do. AG:458D
Notes : The following verbs contain in translation the word " exercise " CB:1256B KATEXOUSIAZō
but belong to other headings : *exousiazō*, to exercise authority over, 2715
Luke 22 : 25 (*exousia*, authority) ; in the first part of this verse, the AG:421C
verb *kurieuō*, to be lord, is translated " exercise lordship," A.V. (R.V., CB:1254B KATAKURIEUō
" have lordship ") ; *katexousiazō*, a strengthened form of the preceding 2634 AG:412C
(*kata*, down, intensive), Matt. 20 : 25 ; Mark 10 : 42, " exercise authority " CB:1254A
(in the first part of these verses the synonymous verb *katakurieuō*, is

1983 AG:298D CB:1246A rendered " lord it," R.V., for A.V., " exercise dominion," and " exercise lordship," respectively) ; *episkopeō*, to look over or upon (*epi*, over, *skopeō*, to look), to care for, 1 Pet. 5 : 2 (absent in some mss.), R.V., " exercising the oversight," for A.V. " taking etc."

B. Noun.

1129 AG:167D CB:1248C GUMNASIA (γυμνασία) primarily denotes gymnastic exercise (akin to A, No. 1), 1 Tim. 4 : 8, where the immediate reference is probably not to mere physical training for games but to discipline of the body such as that to which the Apostle refers in 1 Cor. 9 : 27, though there may be an allusion to the practices of asceticism.

EXHORT, EXHORTATION

A. Verbs.

3870 AG:617A CB:1262A 1. PARAKALEŌ (παρακαλέω), primarily, to call to a person (*para*, to the side, *kaleō*, to call), denotes (*a*) to call on, entreat ; see BESEECH ; (*b*) to admonish, exhort, to urge one to pursue some course of conduct (always prospective, looking to the future, in contrast to the meaning to comfort, which is retrospective, having to do with trial experienced), translated " exhort " in the R.V. of Phil. 4 : 2 ; 1 Thess. 4 : 10 ; Heb. 13 : 19, 22, for A.V., " beseech ; " in 1 Tim. 5 : 1, for A.V., " intreat ; " in 1 Thess. 5 : 11, for A.V., " comfort ; " " exhorted " in 2 Cor. 8 : 6 and 12 : 18, for A.V., " desired ; " in 1 Tim. 1 : 3, for A.V., " besought." See BESEECH.

3867 AG:616B CB:1262A 2. PARAINEŌ (παραινέω), primarily, to speak of near (*para*, near, and *aineō*, to tell of, speak of, then, to recommend), hence, to advise, exhort, warn, is used in Acts 27 : 9, " admonished," and ver. 22, " I exhort." See ADMONISH.¶

4389 AG:722B CB:— 3. PROTREPŌ (προτρέπω), lit., to turn forward, propel (*pro*, before, *trepō*, to turn) ; hence, to impel morally, to urge forward, encourage, is used in Acts 18 : 27, R.V., " encouraged him " (Apollos), with reference to his going into Achaia ; A.V., " exhorting the disciples ; " while the encouragement was given to Apollos, a letter was written to the disciples in Achaia to receive him.¶

B. Noun.

3874 AG:618A CB:1262A PARAKLĒSIS (παράκλησις), akin to A, No. 1, primarily a calling to one's side, and so to one's aid, hence denotes (*a*) an appeal, " entreaty," 2 Cor. 8 : 4 ; (*b*) encouragement, exhortation, e.g., Rom. 12 : 8 ; in Acts 4 : 36, R.V., " exhortation," for A.V., " consolation ; " (*c*) consolation and comfort, e.g., Rom. 15 : 4. See COMFORT. Cp. *paraklētos*, an advocate, comforter.

EXILE See CARRYING AWAY

EXIST

5225 AG:838A CB:— HUPARCHŌ (ὑπάρχω), primarily, to make a beginning (*hupo*, under, *archē*, a beginning), denotes to be, to be in existence, involving an existence or condition both previous to the circumstances mentioned and continuing after it. This is important in Phil. 2 : 6, concerning the Deity of Christ. The phrase " being (existing) in the form (*morphē*, the essential and specific form and character) of God," carries with it the two facts of the antecedent Godhood of Christ, previous to His Incarnation, and the continuance of His Godhood at and after the event of His Birth (see Gifford, on the Incarnation, pp. 11, sqq.). It is translated " exist " in 1 Cor. 11 : 18, R.V., for A.V., " there be." Cp. Luke 16 : 14 ; 23 : 50 ; Acts 2 : 30 ; 3 : 2 ; 17 : 24 ; 22 : 3 etc. See BEING, GOODS, LIVE, POSSESS, SUBSTANCE.

EXODUS See DEPARTURE

EXORCIST

EXORKISTĒS (ἐξορκιστής) denotes (*a*) one who administers an oath ; 1845
(*b*) an exorcist (akin to *exorkizō*, to adjure, from *orkos*, an oath), one who AG:277B CB:1247C
employs a formula of conjuration for the expulsion of demons, Acts 19 :13. (EXHO-)
The practice of exorcism was carried on by strolling Jews, who used their power in the recitation of particular names.¶

EXPECT, EXPECTATION

A. Verbs.

1. EKDECHOMAI (ἐκδέχομαι), lit. and primarily, to take or receive 1551
from (*ek*, from, *dechomai*, to receive), hence denotes to await, expect, AG:238B CB:1243C
the only sense of the word in the N.T. ; it suggests a reaching out in readiness to receive something ; " expecting," Heb. 10 : 13 ; " expect," 1 Cor. 16 : 11, R.V. (A.V., " look for ") ; to wait for, John 5 : 3 (A.V. only) ; Acts 17 : 16 ; 1 Cor. 11 : 33, R.V. (A.V., " tarry for ") ; Jas. 5 : 7 ; to wait, 1 Pet. 3 : 20 in some mss. ; " looked for," Heb. 11 : 10. Cp. B, No. 1. See LOOK, TARRY, WAIT.¶

2. PROSDOKAŌ (προσδοκάω), to watch toward, to look for, expect 4328
(*pros*, toward, *dokeō*, to think : *dokaō* does not exist), is translated AG:712C CB:1267A
" expecting " in Matt. 24 : 50 and Luke 12 : 46, R.V. (A.V., " looketh for ") ; Luke 3 : 15, " were in expectation ; " Acts 3 : 5, " expecting " (A.V. and R.V.) ; 28 : 6 (twice), " expected that," R.V. (A.V., " looked when ") and " when they were long in expectation " (A.V., " after they had looked a great while "). See LOOK, TARRY, WAIT.

B. Nouns.

1. APOKARADOKIA (ἀποκαραδοκία), primarily a watching with 603
outstretched head (*apo*, from, *kara*, the head, and *dokeō*, to look, to watch), AG:92C CB:1236C
signifies strained expectancy, eager longing, the stretching forth of the head indicating an expectation of something from a certain place, Rom. 8 : 19 and Phil. 1 : 20. The prefix *apo* suggests " abstraction and absorption " (Lightfoot), i.e., abstraction from anything else that might engage the attention, and absorption in the object expected " till the fulfilment is realized " (Alford). The intensive character of the noun, in comparison

with No. 2 (below), is clear from the contexts; in Rom. 8 : 19 it is said figuratively of the creation as waiting for the revealing of the sons of God ("waiting" translates the verb *apekdechomai*, a strengthened form of A, No. 1; see WAIT FOR). In Phil. 1 : 20 the Apostle states it as his "earnest expectation" and hope, that, instead of being put to shame, Christ shall be magnified in his body, "whether by life, or by death," suggesting absorption in the Person of Christ, abstraction from aught that hinders.¶

4329 AG:712C 2. PROSDOKIA (προσδοκία), a watching for, expectation (akin to A,
CB:— No. 2, which see), is used in the N.T. only of the expectation of evil, Luke 21 : 26, R.V., "expectation," A.V., "looking for," regarding impending calamities; Acts 12 : 11, "the expectation," of the execution of Peter.¶

1561 AG:239A 3. EKDOCHĒ (ἐκδοχή), primarily a receiving from, hence, expecta-
CB:1243C tion (akin to A, No. 1), is used in Heb. 10 : 27 (R.V., "expectation;" A.V., "looking for"), of judgment.¶

EXPEDIENT

4851 AG:780B SUMPHERŌ (συμφέρω) signifies (*a*), transitively, lit., to bring together,
CB:— (*sun*, with, *pherō*, to bring), Acts 19 : 19; (*b*) intransitively, to be an advantage, profitable, expedient (not merely 'convenient'); it is used mostly impersonally, "it is (it was) expedient;" so in Matt. 19 : 10, R.V. (negatively), A.V., "it is (not) good;" John 11 : 50; 16 : 7; 18 : 14; 1 Cor. 6 : 12; 10 : 23; 2 Cor. 8 : 10; 12 : 1; "it is profitable," Matt. 5 : 29, 30; 18 : 6, R.V.; "was profitable," Acts 20 : 20; "to profit withal," 1 Cor. 12 : 7; in Heb. 12 : 10, used in the neuter of the present participle with the article as a noun, "for (our) profit." See PROFIT.¶ Cp. the adjective *sumphoros* (or *sumpheron*), profitable, used with the article as a noun, 1 Cor. 7 : 35; 10 : 33.¶

EXPENSIVE See PRECIOUS

For EXPELLED, Acts 13 : 50, A.V., see CAST, No. 5

EXPERIENCE (without), EXPERIMENT

552 AG:83B I. 1. APEIROS (ἄπειρος), without experience (*a*, negative, *peira*, a trial,
CB:1236B experiment), is used in Heb. 5 : 13, R.V., "without experience," A.V., "unskilful," with reference to "the word of righteousness."¶ In the Sept., Numb. 14 : 23, of youths; Jer. 2 : 6, of a land, "untried;" Zech. 11 : 15, of a shepherd.¶

1382 AG:202D 2. DOKIMĒ (δοκιμή) means (*a*) the process of proving; it is rendered
CB:1242A "experiment" in 2 Cor. 9 : 13, A.V., R.V., "the proving (of you);" in 8 : 2, A.V., "trial," R.V., "proof;" (*b*) the effect of proving, approval, approvedness, R.V., "probation," Rom. 5 : 4 (twice), for A.V., "experience;" A.V. and R.V., "proof" in 2 Cor. 2 : 9; 13 : 3 and Phil. 2 : 22. See EXPERIENCE, PROOF.¶ Cp. *dokimos*, approved, *dokimazō*, to prove, approve; see APPROVE.

EXPERT 1109

GNŌSTĒS (γνώστης), one who knows (akin to *ginōskō*, to know), AG:164A
denotes an expert, a connoisseur, Acts 26 : 3.¶ Cp. *gnōstos*, known. EXPERT (IN THE LAW) See LAWYER

EXPIRE

Note : In Acts 7 : 30, the A.V. " were expired " translates the verb PLĒROŌ 4137
plēroō, to fulfil (R.V.). See FULFIL. In Rev. 20 : 7, the A.V. " are AG:670C CB:1265B
expired " translates the verb *teleō*, to finish (R.V.). See FINISH. TELEŌ 5055 AG:810D CB:1271B

EXPLAIN

DIASAPHEŌ (διασαφέω), to make clear, explain fully (*dia*, through, 1285
intensive, and *saphēs*, clear), is translated " explain " in Matt. 13 : 36 AG:188B PHRAZŌ
R.V. (A.V., " declare ") translates *phrazō* ; in 18 : 31, told," of the 5419
account of the unforgiving debtor's doings, given by his fellow-servants. AG:865C
The preferable rendering would be ' they made clear ' or ' they explained,' EXPLOIT See
suggesting a detailed explanation of the circumstances.¶ CORRUPT

EXPOUND

EXPOSE See MANIFEST, GAZINGSTOCK, SHAME

1. EKTITHĒMI (ἐκτίθημι), to set out, expose (*ek*, out, *tithēmi*, to
place), is used (*a*) literally, Acts 7 : 21 ; (*b*) metaphorically, in the Middle 1620
Voice, to set forth, expound, of circumstances, Acts 11 : 4 ; of the way of AG:245D
God, 18 : 26 ; of the Kingdom of God, 28 : 23.¶ CB:—

2. EPILUŌ (ἐπιλύω), primarily, to loose, release, a strengthened form 1956
of *luō*, to loose, signifies to solve, explain, expound, Mark 4 : 34, " ex- AG:295D CB:1246A
pounded ; " in Acts 19 : 39, of settling a controversy, R.V., " it shall be settled," for A.V., " it shall be determined." See DETERMINE.¶ Cp. *epilusis*, an interpretation, 2 Pet. 1 : 20.¶

3. DIERMĒNEUŌ (διερμηνεύω), to interpret fully (*dia*, through, 1329
intensive, *hermēneuō*, to interpret ; Eng., hermeneutics), is translated " He AG:194B CB:1241C
expounded " in Luke 24 : 27, A.V., R.V., " interpreted ; " in Acts 9 : 36, " by interpretation," lit., ' being interpreted ; ' see also 1 Cor. 12 : 30 ; 14 : 5, 13, 27. See INTERPRET.¶

For EXPRESS, Heb. 1 : 3, A.V., see IMAGE, No. 2 EXPRESS See UTTER

EXPRESSLY

RHĒTŌS (ῥητῶς), meaning ' in stated terms ' (from *rhētos*, stated, 4490
specified ; from *rheō*, or *erō*, to say ; cp. *rhēma*, a word), is used in 1 Tim. AG:736A CB:—
4 : 1, " expressly."¶

EXTORT, EXTORTION, EXTORTIONER

A. Verb.

PRASSŌ (πράσσω), to practise, has the special meaning " extort " in 4238 AG:698B
Luke 3 : 13, R.V. (A.V., " exact "). In Luke 19 : 23 it is translated CB:1266B

"required;" it may be that the master, in addressing the slothful servant, uses the word 'extort' or 'exact' (as in 3 : 13), in accordance with the character attributed to him by the servant.

B. Nouns.

724
AG:108B
CB:1249B
1. HARPAGĒ (ἁρπαγή) denotes pillage, plundering, robbery, extortion [akin to *harpazō*, to seize, carry off by force, and *harpagmos*, a thing seized, or the act of seizing; from the root *arp* (sic), seen in Eng., rapacious; an associated noun, with the same spelling, denoted a rake, or hook for drawing up a bucket]; it is translated "extortion" in Matt. 23 : 25; Luke 11 : 39, R.V., A.V., "ravening;" Heb. 10 : 34, "spoiling." See RAVENING, SPOILING.¶ Cp. C. below.

4124
AG:667D
CB:1265B
2. PLEONEXIA (πλεονεξία), covetousness, desire for advantage, is rendered "extortion" in 2 Cor. 9 : 5, R.V. (A.V. and R.V. marg., "covetousness"). See COVET.

C. Adjective.

727
AG:109B
CB:1249B
HARPAX (ἅρπαξ), rapacious (akin to No. 1), is translated as a noun, "extortioners," in Luke 18 : 11; 1 Cor. 5 : 10, 11; 6 : 10; in Matt. 7 : 15 "ravening" (of wolves).¶ In the Sept., Gen. 49 : 27.¶

EXTRA
See TWO

EYE

3788
AG:599B
CB:1261A
1. OPHTHALMOS (ὀφθαλμός), akin to *opsis*, sight, probably from a root signifying penetration, sharpness (Curtius, Gk. Etym.) (cp. Eng., ophthalmia, etc.), is used (*a*) of the physical organ, e.g., Matt. 5 : 38; of restoring sight, e.g., Matt. 20 : 33; of God's power of vision, Heb. 4 : 13; 1 Pet. 3 : 12; of Christ in vision, Rev. 1 : 14; 2 : 18; 19 : 12; of the Holy Spirit in the unity of Godhood with Christ, Rev. 5 : 6; (*b*) metaphorically, of ethical qualities, evil, Matt. 6 : 23; Mark 7 : 22 (by metonymy, for envy); singleness of motive, Matt. 6 : 22; Luke 11 : 34; as the instrument of evil desire, "the principal avenue of temptation," 1 John 2 : 16; of adultery, 2 Pet. 2 : 14; (*c*) metaphorically, of mental vision, Matt. 13 : 15; John 12 : 40; Rom. 11 : 8; Gal. 3 : 1, where the metaphor of the "evil eye" is altered to a different sense from that of bewitching (the posting up or placarding of an eye was used as a charm, to prevent mischief); by Gospel-preaching Christ had been, so to speak, placarded before their eyes; the question may be paraphrased, 'What evil teachers have been malignly fascinating you?;' Eph. 1 : 18, of the "eyes of the heart," as a means of knowledge.

3659
AG:565D
CB:1260C
2. OMMA (ὄμμα), sight, is used in the plural in Matt. 20 : 34 (No. 1 is used in ver. 33); Mark 8 : 23 (No. 1 is used in ver. 25). The word is more poetical in usage than No. 1, and the writers may have changed the word with a view to distinguishing the simple desire of the blind man from the tender act of the Lord Himself.¶

5168
AG:828B
CB:—
3. TRUMALIA (τρυμαλιά) is used of the eye of a needle, Mark 10 : 25 (from *trumē*, a hole, *truō*, to wear away).¶ Cp. *trēma*, a hole, perforation,

Matt. 19 : 24 (some texts have *trupēma*, a hole, from *trupaō*, to bore a hole) **TRēMA —**
and Luke 18 : 25, as in the most authentic mss. (some texts have ***trumalia*** **AG:826A**
here).¶ **CB:— TRUPēMA 5169 AG:828C**

EYE (with one)

MONOPHTHALMOS (*μονόφθαλμος*), one-eyed, deprived of one eye **3442**
(*monos*, only, and No. 1, above), is used in the Lord's warning in Matt. **AG:528B CB:—**
18 : 9; Mark 9 : 47.¶

EYE-SALVE

KOLLOURION (*κολλούριον*), primarily a diminutive of ***kollura***, and **2854**
denoting a coarse bread roll (as in the Sept. of 1 Kings 12 : after ver. 24, **AG:441D CB:1255C**
lines 30, 32, 39; Eng. Version, 14 : 3 ¶), hence an eye-salve, shaped like a roll, Rev. 3 : 18, of the true knowledge of one's condition and of the claims of Christ. The word is doubtless an allusion to the Phrygian powder used by oculists in the famous medical school at Laodicea (Ramsay, *Cities and Bishoprics of Phrygia*, Vol. I, p. 52).

EYE-SERVICE

OPHTHALMODOULIA (*ὀφθαλμοδουλία*) denotes service performed **3787**
only under the master's eye (*ophthalmos*, an eye, *doulos*, a slave), diligently **AG:599B CB:—**
performed when he is looking, but neglected in his absence, Eph. 6 : 6 and Col. 3 : 22.¶

EYE-WITNESS

1. AUTOPTĒS (*αὐτόπτης*) signifies seeing with one's own eyes (*autos*, **845 AG:122C**
self, and a form, *optanō*, to see), Luke 1 : 2.¶ **CB:—**

2. EPOPTĒS (*ἐπόπτης*), primarily an overseer (*epi*, over), then, a **2030**
spectator, an eye-witness of anything, is used in 2 Pet. 1 : 16 of those who **AG:305D CB:1246B**
were present at the Transfiguration of Christ. Among the Greeks the word was used of those who had attained to the third grade, the highest, of the Eleusinian mysteries, a religious cult at Eleusis, with its worship, rites, festival and pilgrimages; this brotherhood was open to all Greeks.¶ In the Sept., Esth. 5 : 1, where it is used of God as the Overseer and Preserver of all things.¶ Cp. *epopteuō*, to behold, 1 Pet. 2 : 12 and 3 : 2.¶

FABLE

MUTHOS (μῦθος) primarily signifies speech, conversation. The first 3454
syllable comes from a root *mu*—, signifying to close, keep secret, be AG:529A CB:1259B
dumb; whence, *muō*, to close (eyes, mouth) and *mustērion*, a secret, a
mystery; hence, a story, narrative, fable, fiction (Eng., myth). The
word is used of Gnostic errors and of Jewish and profane fables and
genealogies, in 1 Tim. 1:4; 4:7; 2 Tim. 4:4; Tit. 1:14; of fiction,
in 2 Pet. 1:16.¶ ALēTHEIA

Muthos is to be contrasted with *alētheia*, truth, and with *logos*, a story, 225
a narrative purporting to set forth facts, e.g., Matt. 28:15, a "saying" AG:35 CB:1234B
(i.e., an account, story, in which actually there is a falsification of facts); LOGOS
Luke 5:15, R.V., "report." 3056 AG:477A CB:1257A

FACE

1. PROSŌPON (πρόσωπον) denotes the countenance, lit., the part 4383
towards the eyes (from *pros*, towards, *ōps*, the eye), and is used (*a*) of the AG:720D CB:1267B
face, Matt. 6:16, 17; 2 Cor. 3:7, 2nd part (A.V., "countenance"); in 2 Cor. 10:7, in the R.V., "things that are before your face" (A.V., "outward appearance"), the phrase is figurative of superficial judgment; (*b*) of the look, i.e., the face, which by its various movements affords an index of inward thoughts and feelings, e.g., Luke 9:51, 53; 1 Pet. 3:12; (*c*) the presence of a person, the face being the noblest part, e.g., Acts 3:13, R.V., "before the face of," A.V., "in the presence of;" 5:41, "presence;" 2 Cor. 2:10, "person;" 1 Thess. 2:17 (first part), "presence;" 2 Thess. 1:9, R.V., "face," A.V., "presence;" Rev. 12:14, "face;" (*d*) the person himself, e.g., Gal. 1:22; 1 Thess. 2:17 (second part); (*e*) the appearance one presents by his wealth or poverty, his position or state, Matt. 22:16; Mark 12:14; Gal. 2:6; Jude 16; (*f*) the outward appearance of inanimate things, Matt. 16:3; Luke 12:56; 21:35; Acts 17:26.

To spit in a person's face was an expression of the utmost scorn and aversion, e.g., Matt. 26:67 (cp. 27:30; Mark 10:34; Luke 18:32). See APPEARANCE.

2. OPSIS (ὄψις) is primarily the act of seeing; then, (*a*) the face; 3799
of the body of Lazarus, John 11:44; of the countenance of Christ in a AG:601D CB:1261A
vision, Rev. 1:16; (*b*) the outward appearance of a person or thing, John 7:24. See APPEARANCE.¶

STOMA *Note:* The phrase " face to face " translates two phrases in Greek:
4750 AG:769D (1) *kata prosōpon* (*kata*, over against, and No. 1), Acts 25 : 16; (2) *stoma*
CB:1270A *pros stoma*, lit., ' mouth to mouth ' (*stoma*, a mouth), 2 John 12; 3 John
ANTOPHTHALMEŌ 503 14. See MOUTH. (3) For *antophthalmeō*, Acts 27 : 15, R.V. has ' to face.'

AG:76C CB:—

FACTION, FACTIOUS

2052 AG:309B ERITHIA (or —*eia*) (ἐριθία) denotes ambition, self-seeking, rivalry,
CB:1246C self-will being an underlying idea in the word; hence it denotes party-making. It is derived, not from *eris*, strife, but from *erithos*, a hireling; hence the meaning of seeking to win followers, " factions," so rendered in the R.V. of 2 Cor. 12 : 20, A.V., " strifes; " not improbably the meaning here is rivalries, or base ambitions (all the other words in the list express abstract ideas rather than factions); Gal. 5 : 20 (ditto); Phil. 1 : 17 (R.V.; A.V., ver. 16, " contention "); 2 : 3 (A.V., " strife "); Jas. 3 : 14, 16 (ditto); in Rom. 2 : 8 it is translated as an adjective, " factious " (A.V., " contentious "). The order strife, jealousy, wrath, faction, is the same in 2 Cor. 12 : 20 and Gal. 5 : 20. Faction is the fruit of jealousy.¶
HAIRETIKOS Cp. the synonymous adjective *hairetikos*, Tit. 3 : 10, causing division
141 AG:24A (marg., " factious "), not necessarily " heretical," in the sense of holding
CB:1249A false doctrine.¶

FADE (away)

A. Verb.

3133 MARAINŌ (μαραίνω) was used (*a*) to signify to quench a fire, and in
AG:491B CB:— the Passive Voice, of the dying out of a fire; hence (*b*) in various relations, in the Active Voice, to quench, waste, wear out; in the Passive, to waste away, Jas. 1 : 11, of the fading away of a rich man, as illustrated by the flower of the field.¶ In the Sept., Job 15 : 30; 24 : 24.¶

B. Adjectives (negative).

263 AG:42C 1. AMARANTOS (ἀμάραντος), unfading (*a*, negative, and A., above),
CB:— whence the " amaranth," an unfading flower, a symbol of perpetuity (see *Paradise Lost*, iii. 353), is used in 1 Pet. 1 : 4 of the believer's inheritance, " that fadeth not away." It is found in various writings in the language of the *Koinē*, e.g., on a gladiator's tomb; and as a proper name (Moulton and Milligan, Vocab.).¶

262 AG:42B 2. AMARANTINOS (ἀμαράντινος) primarily signifies composed of
CB:— amaranth (see No. 1); hence, unfading, 1 Pet. 5 : 4, of the crown of glory promised to faithful elders.¶ Cp. *rhodinos*, made of roses (*rhodon*, a rose).

FAIL

A. Verbs.

1587 1. EKLEIPŌ (ἐκλείπω), to leave out (*ek*, out, *leipō*, to leave), used
AG:242C CB:1243C intransitively, means to leave off, cease, fail; it is said of the cessation of earthly life, Luke 16 : 9; of faith, 22 : 32; of the light of the sun, 23 : 45 (in the best mss.); of the years of Christ, Heb. 1 : 12.¶

2. EPILEIPŌ (ἐπιλείπω), not to suffice for a purpose (*epi*, over), is said 1952
of insufficient time, in Heb. 11 : 32.¶ AG:295C CB:—

3. PIPTŌ (πίπτω), to fall, is used of the Law of God in its smallest 4098
detail, in the sense of losing its authority or ceasing to have force, Luke AG:659B CB:1265A
16 : 17. In 1 Cor. 13 : 8 it is used of love (some mss. have *ekpiptō*, to
fall off). See FALL. EKPIPTŌ

Notes : (1) In 1 Cor. 13 : 8, *katargeō*, to reduce to inactivity (see 1601
ABOLISH), in the Passive Voice, to be reduced to this condition, to be done AG:243D CB:1243C
away, is translated " shall fail," A.V. This, however, misses the dis- KATARGEŌ
tinction between what has been previously said of love and what is here 2673 AG:417B
said of prophecies (see No. 3) ; the R.V. has " shall be done away ; " so CB:1254B
also as regards knowledge (same verse). (2) In Heb. 12 : 15, *hustereō*, HUSTEREŌ 5302
to come behind, fall short, miss, is rendered " fail " in the A.V., R.V., AG:849A
" falleth short." (3) In Luke 21 : 26, *apopsuchō*, lit., to breathe out life, CB:1252B
hence, to faint, is translated " hearts failing," in the A.V., R.V., APOPSUCHŌ 674
" fainting." See FAINT.¶ AG:102B CB:—

B. Adjective.

ANEKLEIPTOS (ἀνέκλειπτος), unfailing (*a*, negative, and A, No. 1), 413
is rendered " that faileth not," in Luke 12 : 33.¶ In a Greek document AG:64B CB:—
dated A.D. 42, some contractors undertake to provide unfailing heat for
a bath during the current year (Moulton and Milligan, Vocab.).¶

FAIN

1. BOULOMAI (βούλομαι), to will deliberately, wish, desire, be 1014
minded, implying the deliberate exercise of volition (contrast No. 3), is AG:146A CB:1239B
translated " would fain " in Philm. 13 (in the best mss.). See DISPOSED.

2. EPITHUMEŌ (ἐπιθυμέω), to set one's heart upon, desire, is trans- 1937 AG:293A
lated " would fain " in Luke 15 : 16, of the prodigal son. See DESIRE. CB:1246B

3. THELŌ (θέλω), to wish, to design to do anything, expresses the 2309
impulse of the will rather than the intention (see No. 1) ; the R.V. AG:354D CB:1271C
translates it " would fain " in Luke 13 : 31, of Herod's desire to kill Christ, A.V., " will (kill) ; " in 1 Thess. 2 : 18, of the desire of the missionaries to return to the church in Thessalonica. See DISPOSED.

Note : In Acts 26 : 28, in Agrippa's statement to Paul, the R.V. rendering is " with but little persuasion thou wouldest fain make me a Christian." The lit. rendering is ' with (or in) little (labour or time) thou art persuading me so as to make (me) a Christian.' There is no verb for " wouldest " in the original, but it brings out the sense.

FAINT

1. EKLUŌ (ἐκλύω) denotes (*a*) to loose, release (*ek*, out, *luō*, to loose) ; 1590
(*b*) to unloose, as a bow-string, to relax, and so, to enfeeble, and is used AG:243A CB:1243C
in the Passive Voice with the significance to be faint, grow weary, (1) of the body, Matt. 15 : 32 ; (some mss. have it in 9 : 36) ; Mark 8 : 3 ;

(2) of the soul, Gal. 6 : 9 (last clause), in discharging responsibilities in obedience to the Lord; in Heb. 12 : 3, of becoming weary in the strife against sin; in ver. 5, under the chastening hand of God.¶ It expresses the opposite of ***anazōnnumi***, to gird up, 1 Pet. 1 : 13.¶

1573 2. ENKAKEŌ or EKKAKEŌ (ἐνκακέω), to lack courage, lose heart,
AG:215C CB:1245A be fainthearted (*en*, in, *kakos*, base), is said of prayer, Luke 18 : 1; of
Gospel ministry, 2 Cor. 4 : 1, 16; of the effect of tribulation, Eph. 3 : 13;
as to well doing, 2 Thess. 3 : 13, "be not weary" (A.V. marg., "faint
not"). Some mss. have this word in Gal. 6 : 9 (No. 1).¶

2577 3. KAMNŌ (κάμνω) primarily signified to work; then, as the effect
AG:402A CB:— of continued labour, to be weary; it is used in Heb. 12 : 3, of becoming
weary (see also No. 1), R.V., "wax not weary;" in Jas. 5 : 15, of
sickness; some mss. have it in Rev. 2 : 3, A.V., "hast (not) fainted,"
R.V., "grown weary." See SICK, WEARY.¶

Note: For *apopsuchō*, Luke 21 : 26, R.V., see FAIL, *Note* (3).¶

FAINTHEARTED

3642 OLIGOPSUCHOS (ὀλιγόψυχος), lit., small-souled (*oligos*, small,
AG:564A CB:1260C *psuchē*, the soul), denotes despondent; then, "fainthearted," 1 Thess.
5 : 14, R.V., for the incorrect A.V., "feeble-minded." ¶ In the Sept., similarly, in a good sense, Isa. 57 : 15, 'who giveth endurance to the fainthearted,' for R.V. "to revive the spirit of the humble;" in a bad sense, Prov. 18 : 14, 'who can endure a fainthearted man?'

FAIR

791 1. ASTEIOS (ἀστεῖος), lit., of the city (from *astu*, a city; like Lat.
AG:117C CB:— *urbanus*, from *urbs*, a city; Eng., urbane; similarly, polite, from *polis*,
a town), hence, fair, elegant (used in the papyri writings of clothing), is said of the external form of a child, Acts 7 : 20, of Moses "(exceeding) fair," lit., 'fair to God;' Heb. 11 : 23 (R.V., "goodly," A.V., "proper"). See BEAUTIFUL, GOODLY, *Note*.¶

2105 2. EUDIA (εὐδία) denotes fair weather, Matt. 16 : 2, from *eudios*,
AG:319A CB:1247A calm; from *eu*, good, and *dios*, divine, among the pagan Greeks, akin to
the name for the god Zeus, or Jupiter. Some would derive *Dios* and the Latin *deus* (god) and *dies* (day) from a root meaning bright. Cp. the Latin *sub divo*, 'under a bright, open sky.'¶

2570 AG:400B 3. KALOS (καλός), beautiful, fair, in appearance, is used as part of the
CB:1253B proper name, Fair Havens, Acts 27 : 8. See BETTER, GOOD.

2129 *Notes:* (1) In Rom. 16 : 18 *eulogia*, which generally signifies blessing,
AG:322D CB:1247B is used in its more literal sense, "fair speech," i.e., a fine style of utterance,
giving the appearance of reasonableness.

2146 (2) In Gal. 6 : 12 the verb *euprosōpeō*, to look well, lit., to be fair of
AG:324D CB:— face (*eu*, well, and *prosōpon*, a face), signifies to make a fair or plausible
show, used there metaphorically of making a display of religious zeal.¶

FAITH

PISTIS (πίστις), primarily, firm persuasion, a conviction based upon 4102
hearing (akin to *peithō*, to persuade), is used in the N.T. always of faith AG:662B
in God or Christ, or things spiritual. CB:1265A

The word is used of (*a*) trust, e.g., Rom. 3 : 25 [see Note (4) below]; 1 Cor. 2 : 5; 15 : 14, 17; 2 Cor. 1 : 24; Gal. 3 : 23 [see Note (5) below]; Phil. 1 : 25; 2 : 17; 1 Thess. 3 : 2; 2 Thess. 1 : 3; 3 : 2; (*b*) trustworthiness, e.g., Matt. 23 : 23; Rom. 3 : 3, R.V., "the faithfulness of God;" Gal. 5 : 22 (R.V., "faithfulness"); Tit. 2 : 10, "fidelity;" (*c*) by metonymy, what is believed, the contents of belief, the faith, Acts 6 : 7; 14 : 22; Gal. 1 : 23; 3 : 25 [contrast 3 : 23, under (*a*)]; 6 : 10; Phil. 1 : 27; 1 Thess. 3 : 10; Jude 3, 20 (and perhaps 2 Thess. 3 : 2); (*d*) a ground for faith, an assurance, Acts 17 : 31 (not as in A.V., marg., "offered faith"); (*e*) a pledge of fidelity, plighted faith, 1 Tim. 5 : 12.

The main elements in faith in its relation to the invisible God, as distinct from faith in man, are especially brought out in the use of this noun and the corresponding verb, *pisteuō*; they are (1) a firm conviction, producing a full acknowledgement of God's revelation or truth, e.g., 2 Thess. 2 : 11, 12; (2) a personal surrender to Him, John 1 : 12; (3) a conduct inspired by such surrender, 2 Cor. 5 : 7. Prominence is given to one or other of these elements according to the context. All this stands in contrast to belief in its purely natural exercise, which consists of an opinion held in good faith without necessary reference to its proof. The object of Abraham's faith was not God's promise (that was the occasion of its exercise); his faith rested on God Himself, Rom. 4 : 17, 20, 21. See ASSURANCE, BELIEF, FAITHFULNESS, FIDELITY.

Notes: (1) In Heb. 10 : 23, *elpis*, hope, is mistranslated "faith" in ELPIS
the A.V. (R.V., "hope"). (2) In Acts 6 : 8 the most authentic mss. 1680
have *charis*, grace, R.V., for *pistis*, faith. (3) In Rom. 3 : 3, R.V., *apistia*, AG:252D CB:1244B
is rendered "want of faith," for A.V., "unbelief" (so translated else- APISTIA
where). See UNBELIEF. The verb *apisteō* in that verse is rendered 570 AG:85C
"were without faith," R.V., for A.V., "did not believe." (4) In Rom. CB:1236C
3 : 25, the A.V. wrongly links "faith" with "in His blood," as if faith APISTEō 569
is reposed in the blood (i.e., the Death) of Christ; the *en* is instrumental; AG:85B
faith rests in the living Person; hence the R.V. rightly puts a comma CB:1236C
after "through faith," and renders the next phrase "by His blood," which is to be connected with "a propitiation." Christ became a propitiation through His blood (i.e., His death in expiatory sacrifice for sin). (5) In Gal. 3 : 23, though the article stands before "faith" in the original, faith is here to be taken as under (*a*) above, and as in ver. 22, and not as under (*c*), the faith; the article is simply that of renewed mention. (6) For the difference between the teaching of Paul and that of James, on faith and works, see Notes on Galatians, by Hogg and Vine, pp. 117–119.

FAITH (of little)

3640 OLIGOPISTOS (ὀλιγόπιστος), lit., little of faith (*oligos*, little, ***pistis***,
AG:563B faith), is used only by the Lord, and as a tender rebuke, for anxiety,
CB:— Matt. 6 : 30 and Luke 12 : 28 ; for fear, Matt. 8 : 26 ; 14 : 31 ; 16 : 8.¶

FAITHFUL, FAITHFULLY, FAITHLESS

4103 1. PISTOS (πιστός), a verbal adjective, akin to ***peithō*** (see **FAITH**),
AG:664C is used in two senses, (*a*) Passive, faithful, to be trusted, reliable, said of
CB:1265A God, e.g., 1 Cor. 1 : 9 ; 10 : 13 ; 2 Cor. 1 : 18 (A.V., " true ") ; 2 Tim. 2 : 13 ; Heb. 10 : 23 ; 11 : 11 ; 1 Pet. 4 : 19 ; 1 John 1 : 9 ; of Christ, e.g., 2 Thess. 3 : 3 ; Heb. 2 : 17 ; 3 : 2 ; Rev. 1 : 5 ; 3 : 14 ; 19 : 11 ; of the words of God, e.g., Acts 13 : 34, " sure ; " 1 Tim. 1 : 15 ; 3 : 1 (A.V., " true ") ; 4 : 9 ; 2 Tim. 2 : 11 ; Tit. 1 : 9 ; 3 : 8 ; Rev. 21 : 5 ; 22 : 6 ; of servants of the Lord, Matt. 24 : 45 ; 25 : 21, 23 ; Acts 16 : 15 ; 1 Cor. 4 : 2, 17 ; 7 : 25 ; Eph. 6 : 21 ; Col. 1 : 7 ; 4 : 7, 9 ; 1 Tim. 1 : 12 ; 3 : 11 ; 2 Tim. 2 : 2 ; Heb. 3 : 5 ; 1 Pet. 5 : 12 ; 3 John 5 ; Rev. 2 : 13 ; 17 : 14 ; of believers, Eph. 1 : 1 ; Col. 1 : 2 ; (*b*) Active, signifying believing, trusting, relying, e.g., Acts 16 : 1 (feminine) ; 2 Cor. 6 : 15 ; Gal. 3 : 9 seems best taken in this respect, as the context lays stress upon Abraham's faith in God, rather than upon his faithfulness. In John 20 : 27 the context requires the Active sense, as the Lord is reproaching Thomas for his want of faith. See No. 2.

With regard to believers, they are spoken of sometimes in the Active sense, sometimes in the Passive, i.e., sometimes as believers, sometimes as faithful. See Lightfoot on Galatians, p. 155.

Note : In 3 John 5 the R.V. has " thou doest a faithful work," for A.V., " thou doest faithfully." The lit. rendering is ' thou doest (*poieō*)
2038 a faithful thing, whatsoever thou workest (*ergazō*).' That would not do
AG:306D as a translation. To do a faithful work is to do what is worthy of a
CB:1246C faithful man. The A.V. gives a meaning but is not exact as a translation. Westcott suggests ' thou makest sure (*piston*) whatsoever thou workest ' (i.e., it will not lose its reward). The change between ***poieō***, to do, and *ergazō*, to work, must be maintained. Cp. Matt. 26 : 10 (***ergazō*** and ***ergon***).

571 2. APISTOS (ἄπιστος) is used with meanings somewhat parallel to
AG:85D No. 1 ; (*a*) untrustworthy (*a*, negative, and No. 1), not worthy of con-
CB:1236C fidence or belief, is said of things " incredible," Acts 26 : 8 ; (*b*) unbelieving, distrustful, used as a noun, " unbeliever," Luke 12 : 46 ; 1 Tim. 5 : 8 (R.V., for A.V., " infidel ") ; in Tit. 1 : 15 and Rev. 21 : 8, " unbelieving ; " " faithless " in Matt. 17 : 17 ; Mark 9 : 19 ; Luke 9 : 41 ; John 20 : 27. The word is most frequent in 1 and 2 Corinthians. See BELIEVE, INCREDIBLE, INFIDEL, UNBELIEVER, UNFAITHFUL. (In the Sept., Prov. 17 : 6 ; 28 : 25 ; Is. 17 : 10.¶).

FAITHFULNESS

Note: This is not found in the A.V. The R.V. corrects the A.V. "faith" to "faithfulness" in Rom. 3 : 3; Gal. 5 : 22. See FAITH.

FALL, FALLEN, FALLING, FELL

A. Nouns.

1. PTŌSIS (πτῶσις), a fall (akin to B, No. 1), is used (*a*) literally, 4431
of the overthrow of a building, Matt. 7 : 27; (*b*) metaphorically, Luke AG:728A
2 : 34, of the spiritual fall of those in Israel who would reject Christ; CB:1268A
the word "again" in the A.V. of the next clause is misleading; the "rising up" (R.V.) refers to those who would acknowledge and receive Him, a distinct class from those to whom the "fall" applies. The fall would be irretrievable, cp. (*a*); such a lapse as Peter's is not in view.¶

2. PARAPTŌMA (παράπτωμα), primarily a false step, a blunder 3900
(*para*, aside, *piptō*, to fall), then a lapse from uprightness, a sin, a moral AG:621D
trespass, misdeed, is translated "fall" in Rom. 11 : 11, 12, of the sin CB:1262B
and downfall of Israel in their refusal to acknowledge God's claims and His Christ; by reason of this the offer of salvation was made to Gentiles; cp. *ptaiō*, to stumble, in ver. 11. See FAULT, OFFENCE, SIN, TRESPASS.

3. APOSTASIA (ἀποστασία), a defection, revolt, apostasy, is used in 646
the N.T. of religious apostasy; in Acts 21 : 21, it is translated "to AG:98B
forsake," lit., 'thou teachest apostasy from Moses.' In 2 Thess. 2 : 3 CB:1237A
"the falling away" signifies apostasy from the faith. In papyri documents it is used politically of rebels.¶ *Note:* For "mighty fall," Rev. 18 : 21, R.V., see VIOLENCE.

B. Verbs.

1. PIPTŌ (πίπτω), to fall, is used (*a*) of descent, to fall down from, e.g., 4098
Matt. 10 : 29; 13 : 4; (*b*) of a lot, Acts 1 : 26; (*c*) of falling under judg- AG:659B
ment, Jas. 5 : 12 (cp. Rev. 18 : 2, R.V.); (*d*) of persons in the act of prostra- CB:1265A
tion, to prostrate oneself, e.g., Matt. 17 : 6; John 18 : 6; Rev. 1 : 17; in homage and worship, e.g., Matt. 2 : 11; Mark 5 : 22; Rev. 5 : 14; 19 : 4; (*e*) of things, falling into ruin, or failing, e.g., Matt. 7 : 25; Luke 16 : 17, R.V., "fall," for A.V., "fail;" Heb. 11 : 30; (*f*) of falling in judgment upon persons, as of the sun's heat, Rev. 7 : 16, R.V., "strike," A.V., "light;" of a mist and darkness, Acts 13 : 11 (some mss. have *epipiptō*); (*g*) of persons, in falling morally or spiritually, Rom. 14 : 4; 1 Cor. 10 : 8, 12; Rev. 2 : 5 (some mss. have No. 3 here). See FAIL, LIGHT (upon), STRIKE.

2. APOPIPTO (ἀποπίπτω), to fall from (*apo*, from), is used in Acts 634
9 : 18, of the scales which fell from the eyes of Saul of Tarsus.¶ AG:97B CB:—

3. EKPIPTŌ (ἐκπίπτω), to fall out of (*ek*, out, and No. 1)," is used 1601
in the N.T., literally, of flowers that wither in the course of nature, AG:243D
Jas. 1 : 11; 1 Pet. 1 : 24; of a ship not under control, Acts 27 : 17, 26, CB:1243C
29, 32; of shackles loosed from a prisoner's wrist, 12 : 7; figuratively, of the Word of God (the expression of His purpose), which cannot fall away from the end to which it is set, Rom. 9 : 6; of the believer who is warned

lest he fall away from the course in which he has been confirmed by the Word of God, 2 Pet. 3 : 17."* So of those who seek to be justified by law, Gal. 5 : 4, " ye are fallen away from grace." Some mss. have this verb in Mark 13 : 25, for No. 1 ; so in Rev. 2 : 5. See CAST, EFFECT.¶

1706 4. EMPIPTŌ (ἐμπίπτω), to fall into, or among (*en*, in, and No. 1),
AG:256B is used (*a*) literally, Matt. 12 : 11 ; Luke 6 : 39 (some mss. have No. 1
CB:— here) ; 10 : 36 ; some mss. have it in 14 : 5 ; (*b*) metaphorically, into condemnation, 1 Tim. 3 : 6 ; reproach, 3 : 7 ; temptation and snare, 6 : 9 ; the hands of God in judgment, Heb. 10 : 31.¶

1968 5. EPIPIPTŌ (ἐπιπίπτω), to fall upon (*epi*, upon, and No. 1), is used
AG:297C (*a*) literally, Mark 3 : 10, " pressed upon ; " Acts 20 : 10, 37 ; (*b*) meta-
CB:— phorically, of fear, Luke 1 : 12 ; Acts 19 : 17 ; Rev. 11 : 11 (No. 1, in some mss.) ; reproaches, Rom. 15 : 3 ; of the Holy Spirit, Acts 8 : 16 ; 10 : 44 ; 11 : 15.

Note : Some mss. have this verb in John 13 : 25 ; Acts 10 : 10 ; 13 : 11. See PRESS.¶

2667
AG:416C 6. KATAPIPTŌ (καταπίπτω), to fall down (*kata*, down, and No. 1),
CB:1254B is used in Luke 8 : 6 (in the best mss.) ; Acts 26 : 14 ; 28 : 6.¶

3895 7. PARAPIPTŌ (παραπίπτω), akin to A, No. 2, properly, to fall in
AG:621B
CB:1262B one's way (*para*, by), signifies to fall away (from adherence to the realities and facts of the faith), Heb. 6 : 6.¶

4045 8. PERIPIPTŌ (περιπίπτω), to fall around (*peri*, around), hence
AG:649D
CB:1263B signifies to fall in with, or among, to light upon, come across, Luke 10 : 30, " among (robbers) ; " Acts 27 : 41, A.V., " falling into," R.V., " lighting upon," a part of a shore ; Jas. 1 : 2, into temptation (i.e., trials). See LIGHT (to l. upon).¶ In the Sept., Ruth 2 : 3 ; 2 Sam. 1 : 6 ; Prov. 11 : 5.¶

4363 9. PROSPIPTŌ (προσπίπτω), to fall towards anything (*pros*, towards),
AG:718A
CB:— to strike against, is said of " wind," Matt. 7 : 25 ; it also signifies to fall down at one's feet, fall prostrate before, Mark 3 : 11 ; 5 : 33 ; 7 : 25 ; Luke 5 : 8 ; 8 : 28, 47 ; Acts 16 : 29.¶

5302 10. HUSTEREŌ (ὑστερέω), to come late, to be last, behind, inferior,
AG:849A
CB:1252B is translated " falleth short " in Heb. 12 : 15, R.V., for A.V., " fail," and " fall short " in Rom. 3 : 23, for A.V., " come short," which, in view of the preceding " have," is ambiguous, and might be taken as a past tense. See BEHIND.

1911 11. EPIBALLŌ (ἐπιβάλλω), to cast upon (*epi*, on, *ballō*, to throw),
AG:289D
CB:— also signifies to fall to one's share, Luke 15 : 12, " that falleth." The phrase is frequently found in the papyri documents as a technical formula. See CAST, A, No. 7.

2064 12. ERCHOMAI (ἔρχομαι), to come, is translated " have fallen out,"
AG:310B
CB:1246B in Phil. 1 : 12, of the issue of circumstances. See COME.

1096 13. GINOMAI (γίνομαι), to become, is translated " falling " (headlong)
AG:158A
CB:1248B in Acts 1 : 18. See Note (1) below. See BECOME.

* From Notes on Galatians by Hogg and Vine, p. 242.

14. APHISTĒMI (ἀφίστημι), when used intransitively, signifies to 868
stand off (*apo*, from, *histēmi*, to stand), to withdraw from; hence, to AG:126D CB:1236B
fall away, to apostatize, 1 Tim. 4 : 1, R.V., " shall fall away," for A.V.,
" shall depart ; " Heb. 3 : 12, R.V., " falling away." See DEPART, No. 20.

15. PARABAINŌ (παραβαίνω), to transgress, fall (*para*, away, across, 3845
bainō, to go), is translated " fell away " in Acts 1 : 25, R.V., for A.V., AG:611C CB:1262A
" by transgression fell." See TRANSGRESS.

16. KATABAINŌ (καταβαίνω) denotes to come (or fall) down, Luke 2597
22 : 44 ; in Rev. 16 : 21, " cometh down," R.V. See COME, DESCEND. AG:408B CB:1253C

Notes : (1) In Rev. 16 : 2, *ginomai*, to become, is translated " it
became," R.V., for A.V., " there fell." (2) In 2 Pet. 1 : 10, *ptaiō*, to
stumble, is translated " stumble," R.V., for A.V., " fall." (3) In Rom. PTAIŌ 4417
14 : 13, *skandalon*, a snare, a means of doing wrong, is rendered " an AG:727A
occasion of falling," R.V., for A.V. " an occasion to fall." (4) *Koimaō*, CB:1267C SKANDALON
in the Middle Voice, signifies to fall asleep, Matt. 27 : 52, R.V., " had fallen 4625
asleep," for A.V., " slept." See ASLEEP. (5) In Acts 27 : 34, *apollumi*, AG:753A
to perish, is translated " shall . . . perish," R.V., for A.V., " shall . . . CB:1269A KOIMAŌ(-OMAI)
fall." (6) In Jude 24 the adjective *aptaistos*, without stumbling, sure 2837
footed (*a*, negative, and *ptaiō*, to stumble), is translated " from stumbling," AG:437C
R.V., for A.V., " from falling." (7) In Acts 1 : 18 the phrase *prēnēs*, CB:1255B APOLLUMI
headlong, with the aorist participle of *ginomai*, to become, " falling 622 AG:95A
headlong." lit., ' having become headlong,' is used of the suicide of Judas CB:1237A
Iscariot. Some would render the word (it is a medical term) " swollen," APTAISTOS 679
(as connected with a form of the verb *pimprēmi*, to burn), indicating the AG:102C
condition of the body of certain suicides. (8) In Acts 20 : 9, A.V., *kata-* CB:— PRĒNĒS
pherō, to bear down, is translated " being fallen into " (R.V., " borne 4248
down "), and then " he sunk down " (R.V., ditto), the first of gradual AG:700D CB:1266B
oppression, the second (the aorist tense) of momentary effect. (9) In KATAPHERŌ
Acts 19 : 35 *diopetēs*, from *dios*, heaven, *piptō*, to fall, i.e., fallen from the 2702
sky, is rendered " image which fell down from Jupiter " (R.V. marg., AG:419D CB:—
" heaven "). DIOPETĒS 1356 AG:199A CB:—

FALSE, FALSEHOOD, FALSELY

A. Adjectives.

1. PSEUDĒS (ψευδής), is used of false witnesses, Acts 6 : 13 ; false 5571
apostles, Rev. 2 : 2, R.V., " false," A.V., " liars ; " Rev. 21 : 8, " liars."¶ AG:891C CB:1267C

Note : For compound words with this adjective, see APOSTLE, BRETHREN, CHRIST, PROPHET, WITNESS.

2. PSEUDŌNUMOS (ψευδώνυμος), under a false name (No. 1, and 5581
onoma, a name ; Eng., pseudonym), is said of the knowledge professed AG:892C CB:1267C
by the propagandists of various heretical cults, 1 Tim. 6 : 20.¶

B. Noun.

PSEUDOS (ψεῦδος), a falsehood (akin to A, No. 1), is so translated 5579
in Eph. 4 : 25, R.V. (A.V., " lying ") ; in 2 Thess. 2 : 9, " lying wonders " AG:892B CB:1267C
is lit. ' wonders of falsehood,' i.e., wonders calculated to deceive ; it is

elsewhere rendered "lie," John 8 : 44 ; Rom. 1 : 25 ; 2 Thess. 2 : 11 ; 1 John 2 : 21, 27 ; Rev. 14 : 5, R.V. ; 21 : 27 ; 22 : 15. See GUILE, LIE.¶

C. Verb.

(-OMAI) 5574 PSEUDŌ (ψεύδω), to deceive by lies, is used in the Middle Voice,
AG:891 translated "to say . . . falsely," in Matt. 5 : 11 ; it is elsewhere rendered
CB:1267C to lie, Acts 5 : 3, 4 ; Rom. 9 : 1 ; 2 Cor. 11 : 31 ; Gal. 1 : 20 ; Col. 3 : 9 ;
1 Tim. 2 : 7. See LIE.

FAME

A. Noun.

PHēMē PHĒMĒ (φήμη) originally denoted a Divine voice, an oracle ; hence,
5345 AG:856B a saying or report (akin to *phēmi*, to say, from a root meaning to shine,
CB:— to be clear ; hence, Lat., *fama*, Eng., fame), is rendered "fame" in
LOGOS 3056 Matt. 9 : 26 and Luke 4 : 14.¶
AG:477A *Notes :* (1) In Luke 5 : 15, R.V., *logos*, a word, report, account, is
CB:1257A AKOē translated "report," for A.V., "fame." See REPORT. (2) *Akoē*, a
189 hearing, is translated "report" in the R.V. of Matt. 4 : 24 ; 14 : 1 ;
AG:30D CB:1234B Mark 1 : 28, for A.V., "fame." See EAR, No. 3, HEARING. (3) *Ēchos*, a
ēCHOS noise, report, sound, is translated "rumour," in the R.V. of Luke 4 : 37,
2279 AG:349D for A.V., "fame ;" "sound" in Acts 2 : 2 ; Heb. 12 : 19. See RUMOUR,
CB:1242C SOUND.¶

B. Verb.

1310 DIAPHĒMIZŌ (διαφημίζω) signifies to spread abroad a matter,
AG:190C CB:— Matt. 28 : 15, R.V. ; Mark 1 : 45, R.V. (from *dia*, throughout, and *phēmi*,
to say) ; hence, to spread abroad one's fame, Matt. 9 : 31. All the passages under this heading relate to the testimony concerning Christ in the days of His flesh.¶

FAMILY

3624 1. OIKOS (οἶκος) signifies (*a*) a dwelling, a house (akin to *oikeō*, to
AG:560B dwell) ; (*b*) a household, family, translated "family" in 1 Tim. 5 : 4,
CB:1260B R.V., for A.V., "at home." See HOME, HOUSE, HOUSEHOLD, TEMPLE.

3965 2. PATRIA (πατριά), primarily an ancestry, lineage, signifies in the
AG:636D CB:1263A N.T. a family or tribe (in the Sept. it is used of related people, in a sense
wider than No. 1, but narrower than *phulē*, a tribe, e.g., Ex. 12 : 3 ; Numb. 32 : 28) ; it is used of the family of David, Luke 2 : 4, R.V., for A.V., "lineage ;" in the wider sense of nationalities, races, Acts 3 : 25, R.V., "families," for A.V., "kindreds ;" in Eph. 3 : 15, R.V., "every family," for A.V., "the whole family," the reference being to all those who are spiritually related to God the Father, He being the Author of their spiritual relationship to Him as His children, they being united to one another in family fellowship (*patria* is akin to *patēr*, a father) ; Luther's translation, "all who bear the name of children," is advocated by Cremer, p. 474. The phrase, however, is lit., 'every family.'¶ See KINDRED.¶

FAMINE

LIMOS (λιμός) is translated "hunger" in Luke 15 : 17; 2 Cor. 11 : 27; 3042
elsewhere it signifies a famine, and is so translated in each place in the AG:475A
R.V.; the A.V. has the word "dearth" in Acts 7 : 11 and 11 : 28, and CB:1257A
"hunger" in Rev. 6 : 8; the R.V. "famine" is preferable there; see
Matt. 24 : 7; Mark 13 : 8; Luke 4 : 25; 15 : 14; 21 : 11; Rom. 8 : 35;
Rev. 18 : 8. See HUNGER.¶

FAN

PTUON (πτύον) denotes a winnowing shovel or fan, with which 4425
grain is thrown up against the wind, in order to separate the chaff, AG:727C
Matt. 3 : 12; Luke 3 : 17.¶ CB:1268A

FAR

A. Adjective.

MAKROS (μακρός) is used (*a*) of space and time, long, said of prayers 3117
(in some mss., Matt. 23 : 14), Mark 12 : 40; Luke 20 : 47; (*b*) of distance, AG:488C
far, far distant, Luke 15 : 13; 19 : 12. See LONG.¶ CB:—

B. Adverbs.

1. MAKRAN (μακράν), properly a feminine form of the adjective 3112
above, denotes a long way, far, (*a*) literally, Matt. 8 : 30, R.V., "afar off." AG:487C
Luke 7 : 6; 15 : 20, R.V., "afar off;" John 21 : 8; Acts 17 : 27; 22 : 21; CB:1257C
(*b*) metaphorically, "far (from the kingdom of God)," Mark 12 : 34; in
spiritual darkness, Acts 2 : 39; Eph. 2 : 13, 17. See AFAR.¶

2. MAKROTHEN (μακρόθεν), from far (akin to No. 1), Mark 8 : 3: 3113
see AFAR. AG:487D CB:1257C

3. PORRŌ (πόρρω) is used (*a*) literally, Luke 14 : 32, "a great way 4206
off;" the comparative degree *porrōteron*, "further," is used in 24 : 28; AG:693D
(*b*) metaphorically, of the heart in separation from God, Matt. 15 : 8; CB:1266A
Mark 7 : 6. See FURTHER, WAY.¶ Cp. *porrōthen*, afar off; see AFAR.

Notes: (1) In Matt. 16 : 22, Peter's word to the Lord "be it far from
Thee" translates the phrase *hileōs soi*, lit., '(God be) propitious to Thee,' HILEōS
R.V., marg., "God have mercy on Thee." Some would translate it 2436
"God avert this from Thee!" Others render it "God forbid!" Luther's AG:376A CB:1250C
translation is 'spare Thyself.' Lightfoot suggests 'Nay, verily!' or HEōS
'Away with the thought!' It was the vehement and impulsive utterance 2193 AG:334B
of Peter's horrified state of mind. *Hileōs* signifies propitious, "merciful," CB:1250A
Heb. 8 : 12. See MERCY, C.¶ (2) In Luke 22 : 51, "thus far" translates GINOMAI 1096
the phrase *heōs toutou*, lit., 'unto this.' (3) In Gal. 6 : 14 the R.V. "far AG:158A
be it" translates the phrase *mē genoito*, lit., 'let it not be,' elsewhere CB:1248B
translated idiomatically "God forbid," e.g., Luke 20 : 16. See FORBID. PERISSOTERON
(4) In Heb. 7 : 15 the A.V. "far more" translates *perissoteron*, R.V., 4054 AG:651C
"more abundantly;" see ABUNDANT. (5) In the following the verb CB:1263C APODēMEō
apodēmeō, to go abroad, is rendered, in the A.V., to go into a far country, 589
R.V., to go into another country, Matt. 21 : 33; 25 : 14; Mark 12 : 1; AG:90A CB:1236C

in Matt. 25 : 15, R.V., " he went on his journey " (A.V., " took etc.").
In Luke 15 : 13 the A.V. and R.V. have " took (his) journey into a
far country ;" in Luke 20 : 9, R.V., " another country," for A.V.,
APODēMOS " a far country."¶ The adjective *apodēmos* in Mark 13 : 34 is rendered in
590 AG:90B the A.V., " taking a far journey," R.V., " sojourning in another country."
CB:— See JOURNEY.¶ (6) In 2 Cor. 4 : 17 the phrase ***kath' huperbolēn*** is translated
HUPERBOLē 5236 " more and more," R.V., for A.V., " a far more." (7) In the following,
AG:840B *heōs*, used as a preposition, is translated " as far as " in the R.V., for
CB:— different words in the A.V. ; Acts 17 : 14, in the best mss., instead of
APO 575 *hōs*, which the A.V. renders " as it were ;" 17 : 15, " unto ;" 23 : 23,
AG:86C " to." Both Versions have " as far as " in 11 : 19, 22 ; in Luke 24 : 50,
CB:1236C the R.V. has " until they were over against," for A.V., " as far as to."
(8) In Rev. 14 : 20, the preposition *apo*, from, is translated " as far as "
in the R.V., for A.V., " by the space of."

FARE, FAREWELL

2165 AG:327C CB:1247B 1. EUPHRAINŌ (εὐφραίνω), in the Active Voice, signifies to cheer, gladden, 2 Cor. 2 : 2 ; in the Passive, to rejoice, make merry ; translated " faring sumptuously " in Luke 16 : 19, especially of food (R.V., marg., " living in mirth and splendour"). See GLAD, MERRY, REJOICE.

4517 AG:738D CB:— 2. RHŌNNUMI (ῥώννυμι), to strengthen, to be strong, is used in the Imperative Mood as a formula at the end of letters, signifying " Farewell," Acts 15 : 29 ; some mss. have it in 23 ; 30 (the R.V. omits it, as do most Versions).¶

2192 AG:331D CB:1242C 3. ECHŌ (ἔχω), to have, is used idiomatically in Acts 15 : 36, R.V., " (how) they fare," A.V., " how they do."

5463 AG:873B CB:1239B 4. CHAIRŌ (χαίρω), to joy, rejoice, be glad, is used in the Imperative Mood in salutations, (*a*) on meeting, " Hail," e.g., Matt. 26 : 49 ; or with *legō*, to say, to give a greeting, 2 John 11 ; in letters, " greeting," e.g., Acts 15 : 23 ; (*b*) at parting, the underlying thought being joy, 2 Cor. 13 : 11 (R.V., marg., " rejoice ") ; (*c*) on other occasions, see the R.V. marg. in Phil. 3 : 1 ; 4 : 4. See GLAD, GREETING, NO. 2, HAIL, JOY, JOYFULLY.

Note : As " farewell " is inadequate to express *chairō*, which always conveys the thought of joy or cheer. (*b*) properly comes under (*c*).

657 AG:100D CB:— 5. APOTASSŌ (ἀποτάσσω) primarily denotes to set apart ; then, in the Middle Voice, (*a*) to take leave of, bid farewell to, Mark 6 : 46, " had taken leave of ;" cp. Acts 18 : 18, 21 ; 2 Cor. 2 : 13 (in these three verses, the verb may signify to give final instructions to) ; Luke 9 : 61, " to bid farewell ; " (*b*) to forsake, Luke 14 : 33. In the papyri, besides saying goodbye, the stronger meaning is found of getting rid of a person (Moulton
782 AG:116C and Milligan). See FORSAKE, LEAVE (take), RENOUNCE, SEND (away).¶
CB:1238A *Note :* For *aspazomai*, to bid farewell, see LEAVE (*c*), No. 2.

FARM

AGROS (ἀγρός) denotes (*a*) a field (cp. Eng., agriculture), e.g., Matt. 68
6 : 28 ; (*b*) the country, e.g., Mark 15 : 21, or, in the plural, country AG:13D CB:1233C
places, farms, Mark 5 : 14 ; 6 : 36, 56 ; Luke 8 : 34 ; 9 : 12 ; (*c*) a piece of
ground, e.g., Mark 10 : 29 ; Acts 4 : 37 ; a farm, Matt. 22 : 5. See
COUNTRY, FIELD, GROUND, LAND.

Note : For the synonymous word *chōra*, a country, land, see COUNTRY. 5561
Moulton and Milligan point out that *agros* is frequent in the Sept., and AG:889B CB:1240A
in the Synoptic Gospels, but that Luke uses *chōra* especially, and that
possibly *agros* was a favourite word with translators from Hebrew and FARMER See HUSBANDMAN
Aramaic.

For FARTHER SIDE, Mark 10 : 1, see BEYOND, No. 2

FARTHING

1. ASSARION (ἀσσάριον), a diminutive of the Latin *as*, was one-tenth 787
of a drachma, or one-sixteenth of a Roman *denarius*, i.e., about three AG:117B CB:—
farthings, Matt. 10 : 29 ; Luke 12 : 6.¶

2. KODRANTĒS (κοδράντης) was the Latin *quadrans*, the fourth 2835
part of an *as* (see No. 1), about two thirds of a farthing, Matt. 5 : 26 ; AG:437A CB:—
Mark 12 : 42.¶

FASHION

A. Nouns.

1. EIDOS (εἶδος), that which is seen, an appearance, is translated 1491
"fashion" in Luke 9 : 29, of the Lord's countenance at the Transfigura- AG:221B CB:1243A
tion. See APPEARANCE, and Note under IMAGE, No. 1.

2. PROSŌPON (πρόσωπον), the face, countenance, is translated 4383
"fashion" in Jas. 1 : 11, of the flower of grass. See COUNTENANCE. AG:720D CB:1267B
Cp. ver. 24, "what manner of man," which translates *hopoios*, of what sort.

3. SCHĒMA (σχῆμα), a figure, fashion (akin to *echō*, to have), is trans- 4976
lated "fashion" in 1 Cor. 7 : 31, of the world, signifying that which AG:797B CB:1268C
comprises the manner of life, actions, etc. of humanity in general ; in Phil. 2 : 8 it is used of the Lord in His being found "in fashion" as a man, and signifies what He was in the eyes of men, "the entire outwardly perceptible mode and shape of His existence, just as the preceding words *morphē*, form, and *homoiōma*, likeness, describe what He was in Himself as Man" (Gifford on the Incarnation, p. 44). "Men saw in Christ a human form, bearing, language, action, mode of life . . . in general the state and relations of a human being, so that in the entire mode of His appearance He made Himself known and was recognized as a man" (Meyer).

4. TUPOS (τύπος), a type, figure, example, is translated "fashion" 5179
in the A.V. of Acts 7 : 44, R.V., "figure," said of the Tabernacle. See AG:829D CB:1273B
ENSAMPLE.

B. Adverb.

3779 AG:597C CB:— HOUTŌS (οὕτως), thus, so, in this way, is rendered " on this fashion " in Mark 2 : 12. See EVEN, No. 5, LIKEWISE, MANNER, SO, THUS, WHAT.

C. Verbs.

3345 AG:513B CB:1258C 1. METASCHĒMATIZŌ (μετασχηματίζω), to change in fashion or appearance (*meta*, after, here implying change, *schēma*, see A, No. 3), is rendered " shall fashion anew " in Phil. 3 : 21, R.V. ; A.V., " shall change," of the bodies of believers as changed or raised at the Lord's Return ; in 2 Cor. 11 : 13, 14, 15, the R.V. uses the verb to fashion oneself, for A.V., to transform, of Satan and his human ministers, false apostles ; in 1 Cor. 4 : 6 it is used by way of a rhetorical device, with the significance of transferring by a figure. See CHANGE, TRANSFORM.¶

4964 AG:795C CB:1271A 2. SUSCHĒMATIZŌ (συσχηματίζω), to give the same figure or appearance as, to conform to (*sun*, with, *schēma*, cp. No. 1), used in the Passive Voice, signifies to fashion oneself, to be fashioned, Rom. 12 : 2, R.V., " be not fashioned according to," for A.V., " be not conformed to ; " 1 Pet. 1 : 14, " (not) fashioning yourselves." See CONFORMED.¶

Note : In Rom. 12 : 2 being outwardly conformed to the things of this age is contrasted with being transformed (or transfigured) inwardly by the renewal of the thoughts through the Holy Spirit's power. A similar distinction holds good in Phil. 3 : 21 ; the Lord will " fashion anew," or change outwardly, the body of our humiliation, and conform it in its nature (*summorphos*) to the body of His glory.

D. Adjective.

4832 AG:778D CB:1270B SUMMORPHOS (σύμμορφος), having like form with (*sun*, with, *morphē*, form), is used in Rom. 8 : 29 and Phil. 3 : 21 (A.V., " fashioned," R.V., " conformed "). See CONFORM.¶

FAST, FASTING

A. Nouns.

3521 AG:538A CB:1259C 1. NĒSTEIA (νηστεία), a fasting, fast (from *nē*, a negative prefix, and *esthiō*, to eat), is used (*a*) of voluntary abstinence from food, Luke 2 : 37 ; Acts 14 : 23 (some mss. have it in Matt. 17 : 21 and Mark 9 : 29) ; fasting had become a common practice among Jews, and was continued among Christians ; in Acts 27 : 9, " the Fast " refers to the Day of Atonement, Lev. 16 : 29 ; that time of the year would be one of dangerous sailing ; (*b*) of involuntary abstinence (perhaps voluntary is included), consequent upon trying circumstances, 2 Cor. 6 : 5 ; 11 : 27.¶

3523 AG:538C CB:1259C 2. NĒSTIS (νῆστις), not eating (see No. 1), fasting, is used of lack of food, Matt. 15 : 32 ; Mark 8 : 3.¶

776 AG:116B CB:— *Note : Asitia*, Acts 27 : 21, means " without food " (not through lack of supplies), i.e., abstinence from food. See ABSTINENCE, and cp. C, below.

B. Verb.

3522 AG:538B CB:1259C NĒSTEUŌ (νηστεύω), to fast, to abstain from eating (akin to A, Nos.

1 and 2), is used of voluntary fasting, Matt. 4 : 2 ; 6 : 16, 17, 18 ; 9 : 14, 15 ; Mark 2 : 18, 19, 20 ; Luke 5 : 33, 34, 35 ; 18 : 12 ; Acts 13 : 2, 3. Some of these passages show that teachers to whom scholars or disciples were attached, gave them special instructions as to fasting. Christ taught the need of purity and simplicity of motive.

The answers of Christ to the questions of the disciples of John and of the Pharisees reveal His whole purpose and method. No doubt He and His followers observed such a Fast as that on the Day of Atonement, but He imposed no frequent fasts in addition. What He taught was suitable to the change of character and purpose which He designed for His disciples. His claim to be the Bridegroom, Matt. 9 : 15, and the reference there to the absence of fasting, virtually involved a claim to be the Messiah (cp. Zech. 8 : 19).¶ Some mss. have the verb in Acts 10 : 30.

C. Adjective.

ASITOS (ἄσιτος), without food (*a*, negative, *sitos*, corn, food), is used 777 AG:116B
in Acts 27 : 33, " fasting." Cp. *asitia*, Note under A, No. 2.¶ CB:—

FAST (to make)

ASPHALIZŌ (ἀσφαλίζω), to make secure, safe, firm (akin to *asphalēs*, 805 AG:119A
safe), (*a*, negative, and *sphallō*, to trip up), is translated " make . . . CB:1238A
fast," in Acts 16 : 24, of prisoners' feet in the stocks. In Matt. 27 : 64, 65, 66, it is rendered 'to make sure.' See SURE.¶

Note : For HOLD (fast) and STAND (fast), see HOLD and STAND, No. 7

FASTEN

1. ATENIZŌ (ἀτενίζω), from *atenēs*, strained, intent, and *teinō*, to 816 AG:119D
stretch, strain (from a root *ten*—, seen in Eng., tension, tense etc.), signifies CB:1238A
to look fixedly, gaze, fasten one's eyes upon, and is found twelve times in the writings of Luke (ten in the Acts), out of its fourteen occurrences. It always has a strongly intensive meaning, and is translated to fasten the eyes upon in the A.V. and R.V. in Luke 4 : 20 ; Acts 3 : 4 ; 11 : 6 ; so in the R.V., where the A.V. has different renderings, in Acts 6 : 15 (for A.V., " looking stedfastly ") ; 10 : 4 (" looked ") ; 13 : 9 (" set his eyes ") ; 14 : 9 (" stedfastly beholding "). In Acts 7 : 55, both have " looked up stedfastly." In the following the R.V. also varies the translation, Luke 22 : 56 ; Acts 1 : 10 ; 3 : 12 ; 23 : 1 ; 2 Cor. 3 : 7, 13. See BEHOLD, LOOK.¶

2. KATHAPTŌ (καθάπτω), to fasten on, lay hold of, attack, is used 2510 AG:387A
of the serpent which fastened on Paul's hand, Acts 28 : 3.¶ CB:—

FATHER

A. Noun.

PATĒR (πατήρ), from a root signifying a nourisher, protector, up- 3962 AG:635A
holder (Lat., *pater*, Eng., father, are akin), is used (*a*) of the nearest CB:1262C
ancestor, e.g., Matt. 2 : 22 ; (*b*) of a more remote ancestor, the progenitor of the people, a forefather, e.g., Matt. 3 : 9 ; 23 : 30 ; 1 Cor. 10 : 1 ;

the patriarchs, 2 Pet. 3 : 4 ; (*c*) one advanced in the knowledge of Christ, 1 John 2 : 13 ; (*d*) metaphorically, of the originator of a family or company of persons animated by the same spirit as himself, as of Abraham, Rom. 4 : 11, 12, 16, 17, 18, or of Satan, John 8 : 38, 41, 44 ; (*e*) of one who, as a preacher of the Gospel and a teacher, stands in a father's place, caring for his spiritual children, 1 Cor. 4 : 15 (not the same as a mere title of honour, which the Lord prohibited, Matt. 23 : 9) ; (*f*) of the members of the Sanhedrin, as of those who exercised religious authority over others, Acts 7 : 2 ; 22 : 1 ; (*g*) of God in relation to those who have been born anew (John 1 : 12, 13), and so are believers, Eph. 2 : 18 ; 4 : 6 (cp. 2 Cor. 6 : 18), and imitators of their Father, Matt. 5 : 45, 48 ; 6 : 1, 4, 6, 8, 9, etc. Christ never associated Himself with them by using the personal pronoun "our ;" He always used the singular, "My Father," His relationship being unoriginated and essential, whereas theirs is by grace and regeneration, e.g., Matt. 11 : 27 ; 25 : 34 ; John 20 : 17 ; Rev. 2 : 27 ; 3 : 5, 21 ; so the Apostles spoke of God as the Father of the Lord Jesus Christ, e.g., Rom. 15 : 6 ; 2 Cor. 1 : 3 ; 11 : 31 ; Eph. 1 : 3 ; Heb. 1 : 5 ; 1 Pet. 1 : 3 ; Rev. 1 : 6 ; (*h*) of God, as the Father of lights, i.e., the Source or Giver of whatsoever provides illumination, physical and spiritual, Jas. 1 : 17 ; of mercies, 2 Cor. 1 : 3 ; of glory, Eph. 1 : 17 ; (*i*) of God, as Creator, Heb. 12 : 9 (cp. Zech. 12 : 1).

Note : Whereas the everlasting power and Divinity of God are manifest in creation, His Fatherhood in spiritual relationship through faith is the subject of N.T. revelation, and waited for the presence on earth of the Son, Matt. 11 : 27 ; John 17 : 25. The spiritual relationship is not universal, John 8 : 42, 44 (cp. John 1 : 12 and Gal. 3 : 26).

B. Adjectives.

3971 AG:637B CB:— 1. PATRŌOS (πατρῷος) signifies of one's fathers, or received from one's fathers (akin to A), Acts 22 : 3 ; 24 : 14 ; 28 : 17.¶ In the Sept., Prov. 27 : 10.¶

3967 AG:636D CB:1263A 2. PATRIKOS (πατρικός), from one's fathers, or ancestors, is said of that which is handed down from one's forefathers, Gal. 1 : 14.¶

540 AG:82B CB:1236B 3. APATŌR (ἀπάτωρ), without father (*a*, negative, and *patēr*), signifies, in Heb. 7 : 3, with no recorded genealogy.¶

3970 AG:637A CB:— 4. PATROPARADOTOS (πατροπαράδοτος), handed down from one's fathers (*patēr*, and *paradidomi*, to hand down), is used in 1 Pet. 1 : 18.¶

FATHER-IN-LAW

3995 AG:642C CB:— PENTHEROS (πενθερός), a wife's father (from a root signifying a bond, union), is found in John 18 : 13.¶

FATHERLESS

3737 AG:583A CB:1261B ORPHANOS (ὀρφανός), properly, an orphan, is rendered "fatherless" in Jas. 1 : 27 ; "desolate" in John 14 : 18, for A.V., "comfortless." See COMFORTLESS.¶

FATHOM

ORGUIA (ὀργυιά), akin to *oregō*, to stretch, is the length of the 3712
outstretched arms, about six feet, Acts 27 : 28 (twice).¶ AG:579D CB:—

FATLING, FATTED

1. SITISTOS (σιτιστός), fattened, lit., ' fed with grain ' (from *siteuō*, 4619
to feed, to fatten), is used as a neuter plural noun, " fatlings," in Matt. AG:752A CB:—
22 : 4.¶ Cp. *asitos*, under FASTING.

2. SITEUTOS (σιτευτός), fed (with grain), denotes " fatted," Luke 4618
15 : 23, 27, 30.¶ AG:752A CB:1269A

FATNESS

PIOTĒS (πιότης), from *piōn*, fat, from a root, *pi*—, signifying swelling, 4096
is used metaphorically in Rom. 11 : 17. The Gentile believer had AG:659A CB:1265A
become a sharer in the spiritual life and blessing bestowed by Divine
covenant upon Abraham and his descendants as set forth under the
figure of " the root of (not ' and ') the fatness of the olive tree."¶

FAULT, FAULTLESS

A. Noun. AITION 158

AITION (αἴτιον), properly the neuter of *aitios*, causative of, responsible AG:26D (-OS)
for, is used as a noun, a crime, a legal ground for punishment, translated CB:1234A
" fault " in Luke 23 : 4, 14 ; in ver. 22, " cause." See AUTHOR, CAUSE. AITIA 156

Notes: (1) For *aitia*, rendered " fault " in John 18 : 38 : 19 : 4, 6, AG:26B
A.V. (like *aition*, denoting a ground for punishment), see ACCUSATION, CB:1234A HēTTēMA
CAUSE, CHARGE. (2) For *hēttēma*, a loss, translated " fault " in 1 Cor. 2275
6 : 7, A.V., see DEFECT (R.V.). (3) For *paraptōma*, a false step, a trespass, AG:349C CB:1250B
translated " fault " in Gal. 6 : 1, A.V., and " faults " in Jas. 5 : 16, A.V., PARAPTōMA
see SIN, A, No. 2, *Note* (1), TRESPASS. 3900 AG:621D

B. Adjective. CB:1262B

AMEMPTOS (ἄμεμπτος), without blame, is rendered " faultless," 273
in Heb. 8 : 7. See BLAMELESS. AG:45A CB:1234C

Note: For *amōmos*, without blemish, rendered " faultless," i.e., 299
without any shortcoming, in Jude 24, and " without fault " in Rev. 14 : 5, AG:47D CB:1234C
A.V., see BLEMISH.

C. Verbs.

1. MEMPHOMAI (μέμφομαι), to blame, is translated " to find fault " 3201
in Rom. 9 : 19 and Heb. 8 : 8. Some mss. have the verb in Mark 7 : 2. AG:502B CB:1258B
See BLAME.

2. ELENCHŌ (ἐλέγχω), to convict, reprove, rebuke, is translated 1651
" shew (him) his fault " in Matt. 18 : 15. See CONVICT. AG:249B CB:1244A

Note: In 1 Pet. 2 : 20, A.V., the verb *hamartanō*, to sin (strictly, to 264
miss the mark) is rendered " for your faults." The R.V. corrects to AG:42B CB:1249A
" when ye sin (and are buffeted for it)."

FAVOUR, FAVOURED

A. Noun.

5485 AG:877B CB:1239C CHARIS (*χάρις*) denotes (*a*) objectively, grace in a person, graciousness, (*b*) subjectively, (1) grace on the part of a giver, favour, kindness, (2) a sense of favour received, thanks. It is rendered " favour " in Luke 1 : 30 ; 2 : 52 ; Acts 2 : 47 ; 7 : 10, 46 ; 24 : 27 and 25 : 9, R.V. (for A.V., " pleasure ") ; 25 : 3 ; see more fully under GRACE.

B. Verb.

5487 AG:879A CB:1239C CHARITOŌ (*χαριτόω*), akin to A., to endow with *charis*, primarily signified to make graceful or gracious, and came to denote, in Hellenistic Greek, to cause to find favour, Luke 1 : 28, " highly favoured " (marg., " endued with grace ") ; in Eph. 1 : 6, it is translated " made . . . accepted," A.V., " freely bestowed," R.V. (lit., ' graced ') ; it does not here mean to endue with grace. Grace implies more than favour ; grace is a free gift, favour may be deserved or gained.¶

FEAR, FEARFUL, FEARFULNESS

A. Nouns.

5401 AG:863C CB:1264B 1. PHOBOS (*φόβος*) first had the meaning of flight, that which is caused by being scared ; then, that which may cause flight, (*a*) fear, dread, terror, always with this significance in the four Gospels ; also e.g., in Acts 2 : 43 ; 19 : 17 ; 1 Cor. 2 : 3 ; 1 Tim. 5 : 20 (lit., ' may have fear ') ; Heb. 2 : 15 ; 1 John 4 : 18 ; Rev. 11 : 11 ; 18 : 10, 15 ; by metonymy, that which causes fear, Rom. 13 : 3 ; 1 Pet. 3 : 14, R.V., " (their) fear," A.V. " (their) terror," an adaptation of the Sept. of Isa. 8 : 12, " fear not their fear ; " hence some take it to mean, as there, ' what they fear,' but in view of Matt. 10 : 28, e.g., it seems best to understand it as that which is caused by the intimidation of adversaries ; (*b*) reverential fear, (1) of God, as a controlling motive of the life, in matters spiritual and moral, not a mere fear of His power and righteous retribution, but a wholesome dread of displeasing Him, a fear which banishes the terror that shrinks from His presence, Rom. 8 : 15, and which influences the disposition and attitude of one whose circumstances are guided by trust in God, through the indwelling Spirit of God, Acts 9 : 31 ; Rom. 3 : 18 ; 2 Cor. 7 : 1 ; Eph. 5 : 21 (R.V., " the fear of Christ ") ; Phil. 2 : 12 ; 1 Pet. 1 : 17 (a comprehensive phrase : the reverential fear of God will inspire a constant carefulness in dealing with others in His fear) ; 3 : 2, 15 ; the association of " fear and trembling," as, e.g., in Phil. 2 : 12, has in the Sept. a much sterner import, e.g., Gen. 9 : 2 ; Ex. 15 : 16 ; Deut. 2 : 25 ; 11 : 25 ; Ps. 55 : 5 ; Is. 19 : 16 ; (2) of superiors, e.g., Rom. 13 : 7 ; 1 Pet. 2 : 18. See TERROR.

1167 AG:173A CB:1240C 2. DEILIA (*δειλία*), fearfulness (from *deos*, fright), is rightly rendered " fearfulness " in 2 Tim. 1 : 7, R.V. (for A.V., " fear "). That spirit is not given us of God. The word denotes cowardice and timidity and is

DEILIAō
never used in a good sense, as No. 1 is.¶ Cp. *deilos*, B, No. 2, below, and 1168 AG:173A
deiliaō, to be fearful (A.V., "afraid"), John 14 : 27.¶ CB:1240C

3. EULABEIA (εὐλάβεια) signifies, firstly, caution; then, reverence, 2124
godly fear, Heb. 5 : 7; 12 : 28, in best mss., "reverence"; in general, AG:321D CB:1247B
apprehension, but especially holy fear, "that mingled fear and love which, combined, constitute the piety of man toward God; the O.T. places its emphasis on the fear, the N.T. . . . on the love, though there was love in the fear of God's saints then, as there must be fear in their love now" (Trench, Syn. § xlviii).¶ In the Sept., Josh. 22 : 24; Prov. 28 : 14.¶

Note: In Luke 21 : 11, *phobētron* (akin to No. 1) denotes a terror, R.V., 5400
"terrors," for A.V., "fearful sights," i.e., 'objects or instruments of AG:863C CB:1264B
terror.'¶

B. Adjectives.

1. PHOBEROS (φοβερός), fearful (akin to A, No. 1), is used only in 5398
the Active sense in the N.T., i.e., causing fear, terrible, Heb. 10 : 27, 31; AG:862B CB:1264B
12 : 21, R.V., "fearful," for A.V., "terrible."¶

2. DEILOS (δειλός), cowardly (see A, No. 2), timid, is used in Matt. 1169
8 : 26; Mark 4 : 40; Rev. 21 : 8 (here "the fearful" are first in the list AG:173A CB:—
of the transgressors).¶

3. EKPHOBOS (ἔκφοβος) signifies frightened outright (*ek*, out, inten- 1630
sive, and A, No. 1), Heb. 12 : 21 (with *eimi*, I am), "I exceedingly fear" AG:247A CB:—
(see No. 4); Mark 9 : 6, "sore afraid."¶

4. ENTROMOS (ἔντρομος), trembling with fear (*en*, in, intensive, 1790
and *tremō*, to tremble, quake; Eng., tremor, etc.), is used with *ginomai*, AG:269D CB:—
to become, in Acts 7 : 32, "trembled;" 16 : 29, R.V., "trembling for fear;" with *eimi*, to be, in Heb. 12 : 21, "quake" (some mss. have
ektromos here). See QUAKE, TREMBLE.¶ The distinction between No. EKTROMOS
3 and No. 4, as in Heb. 12 : 21, would seem to be that *ekphobos* stresses —
the intensity of the fear, *entromos* the inward effect, 'I inwardly tremble AG:246C CB:—
(or quake).'

C. Adverb.

APHOBŌS (ἀφόβως) denotes "without fear" (*a*, negative, and A, 870
No. 1), and is said of serving the Lord, Luke 1 : 74; of being among the AG:127A CB:1236B
Lord's people as His servant, 1 Cor. 16 : 10; of ministering the Word of God, Phil. 1 : 14; of the evil of false spiritual shepherds, Jude 12.¶ In the Sept., Prov. 1 : 33.¶

D. Verbs.

1. PHOBEŌ (φοβέω), in earlier Greek, to put to flight (see A, No. 1), 5399
in the N.T. is always in the Passive Voice, with the meanings either AG:862B CB:1264B
(*a*) to fear, be afraid, its most frequent use, e.g., Acts 23 : 10, according to the best mss. (see No. 2); or (*b*) to show reverential fear [see A, No. 1, (*b*)], (1) of men, Mark 6 : 20; Eph. 5 : 33, R.V., "fear," for A.V., "reverence;" (2) of God, e.g., Acts 10 : 2, 22; 13 : 16, 26; Col. 3 : 22 (R.V., "the Lord"); 1 Pet. 2 : 17; Rev. 14 : 7; 15 : 4; 19 : 5; (*a*) and

(*b*) are combined in Luke 12 : 4, 5, where Christ warns His followers not to be afraid of men, but to fear God. See MARVEL, B, No. 1, *Note*.

2125 2. EULABEOMAI (εὐλαβέομαι), to be cautious, to beware (see A,
AG:321D No. 3), signifies to act with the reverence produced by holy fear,
CB:1247B Heb. 11 : 7, "moved with godly fear."

Notes : (1) In Acts 23 : 10 some mss. have this verb with the meaning (*a*) under No. 1.

1286 (2) In Luke 3 : 14, *diaseiō*, to shake violently, to intimidate, to extort
AG:188B by violence, blackmail, is rendered "put no man in fear" in A.V. marg.
CB:1241B See VIOLENCE.

FEAST

A. Nouns.

1859 1. HEORTĒ (ἑορτή), a feast or festival, is used (*a*) especially of those
AG:280B of the Jews, and particularly of the Passover ; the word is found mostly
CB:1250A in John's Gospel (seventeen times) ; apart from the Gospels it is used in this way only in Acts 18 : 21 ; (*b*) in a more general way, in Col. 2 : 16, A.V., "holy day," R.V., "a feast day."

1173 2. DEIPNON (δεῖπνον) denotes (*a*) the chief meal of the day, dinner
AG:173B or supper, taken at or towards evening ; in the plural "feasts," Matt.
CB:1240C 23 : 6 ; Mark 6 : 21 ; 12 : 39 ; Luke 20 : 46 ; otherwise translated "supper," Luke 14 : 12, 16, 17, 24 ; John 12 : 2 ; 13 : 2, 4 ; 21 : 20 ; 1 Cor. 11 : 21 (of a social meal) ; (*b*) the Lord's Supper, 1 Cor. 11 : 20 ; (*c*) the supper or feast which will celebrate the marriage of Christ with His spiritual Bride, at the inauguration of His Kingdom, Rev. 19 : 9 ; (*d*) figuratively, of that to which the birds of prey will be summoned after the overthrow of the enemies of the Lord at the termination of the war of Armageddon, 19 : 17 (cp. Ezek. 39 : 4, 17–20). See SUPPER.¶

1403 3. DOCHĒ (δοχή), a reception feast, a banquet (from *dechomai*, to
AG:206B
CB:1242A receive), Luke 5 : 29 ; 14 : 13 (not the same as No. 2 ; see ver. 12).¶

1062 4. GAMOS (γάμος), a wedding, especially a wedding feast (akin to
AG:151B
CB:1248A *gameō*, to marry) ; it is used in the plural in the following passages (the R.V. rightly has "marriage feast" for the A.V., "marriage," or "wedding"), Matt. 22 : 2, 3, 4, 9 (in verses 11, 12, it is used in the singular, in connection with the wedding garment) ; 25 : 10 ; Luke 12 : 36 ; 14 : 8 ; in the following it signifies a wedding itself, John 2 : 1, 2 ; Heb. 13 : 4 ; and figuratively in Rev. 19 : 7, of the marriage of the Lamb ; in ver. 9 it is used in connection with the supper, the wedding supper (or what in English is termed breakfast), not the wedding itself, as in ver. 7.

26 5. AGAPĒ (ἀγάπη), love, is used in the plural in Jude 12, signifying
AG:5B "love feasts," R.V. (A.V., "feasts of charity") ; in the corresponding
CB:1233B passage, 2 Pet. 2 : 13, the most authentic mss. have the word ***apatē***, in the plural, "deceivings."

Notes : (1) In 1 Cor. 10 : 27 the verb *kaleō*, to call, in the sense of inviting to one's house, is translated "biddeth you (to a feast) ;" in the most authentic texts there is no separate phrase representing "to a feast," as in some mss., *eis deipnon* (No. 2). (2) In Mark 14 : 2 and John 2 : 23 the A.V. translates *heortē* (see No. 1) by "feast day" (R.V., "feast"). (3) For the Feast of the Dedication, John 10 : 22, see DEDICATION.

B. Verbs.

1. HEORTAZŌ (ἑορτάζω), to keep festival (akin to A, No. 1) is trans- 1858
lated "let us keep the feast," in 1 Cor. 5 : 8. This is not the Lord's AG:280A CB:1250A
Supper, nor the Passover, but has reference to the continuous life of the believer as a festival or holy-day (see A.V., margin), in freedom from "the leaven of malice and wickedness, but with the unleavened bread of sincerity and truth."¶

2. SUNEUŌCHEŌ (συνευωχέω), to entertain sumptuously with, is 4910
used in the Passive Voice, denoting to feast sumptuously with (*sun*, AG:789A (-OMAI)
together, and *euōchia*, good cheer), to revel with, translated "feast with" CB:—
in 2 Pet. 2 : 13 and Jude 12.¶

FEEBLE

ASTHENĒS (ἀσθενής), without strength (*a*, negative, and *sthenos*, 772
strength), is translated feeble in 1 Cor. 12 : 22, of members of the body. AG:115C CB:1238A
See IMPOTENT, SICK, STRENGTH, B, *Note* (5), WEAK.

Notes: (1) In Heb. 12 : 12 *paraluō*, to weaken, enfeeble, in the Passive 3886
Voice, to be enfeebled, as by a paralytic stroke, is translated "feeble" AG:620B CB:1262A
in the A.V. (R.V., "palsied"). (2) For "feeble-minded" in 1 Thess. 5 : 14, A.V., see FAINTHEARTED.

FEED, FED

1. BOSKŌ (βόσκω), to feed, is primarily used of a herdsman (from 1006
boō, to nourish, the special function being to provide food; the root is AG:145B CB:1239B
bo, found in *botēr*, a herdsman or herd, and *botanē*, fodder, pasture); its uses are (*a*) literal, Matt. 8 : 30; in ver. 33, the R.V. corrects the A.V., "they that kept," to "they that fed," as in Mark. 5 : 14 (A.V. and R.V.) and Luke 8 : 34; in Mark 5 : 11 and Luke 8 : 32, "feeding;" Luke 15 : 15; (*b*) metaphorical, of spiritual ministry, John 21 : 15, 17 (see note on No. 2). See KEEP.¶

2. POIMAINŌ (ποιμαίνω), to act as a shepherd (from *poimēn*, a shep- 4165
herd), is used (*a*) literally, Luke 17 : 7, R.V., "keeping sheep," for AG:683D CB:1265C
A.V., "feeding cattle;" 1 Cor. 9 : 7; (*b*) metaphorically, to tend, to shepherd; said of Christ, Matt. 2 : 6, R.V., "shall be Shepherd of" (for A.V., "shall rule"); of those who act as spiritual shepherds under Him, John 21 : 16, R.V., "tend" (for A.V. "feed"); so 1 Pet. 5 : 2; Acts 20 : 28, "to feed" ('to tend' would have been a consistent rendering; a shepherd does not only feed his flock); of base shepherds, Jude 12. See RULE.

Note: In John 21 : 15, 16, 17, the Lord, addressing Peter, first uses No. 1, *boskō* (ver. 15), then No. 2, *poimainō* (ver. 16), and then returns to *boskō* (ver. 17). These are not simply interchangeable (nor are other variations in His remarks); a study of the above notes will show this. Nor, again, is there a progression of ideas. The lesson to be learnt, as Trench points out (Syn. § xxv), is that, in the spiritual care of God's children, the feeding of the flock from the Word of God is the constant and regular necessity; it is to have the foremost place. The tending (which includes this) consists of other acts, of discipline, authority, restoration, material assistance of individuals, but they are incidental in comparison with the feeding.

5142 AG:825C 3. TREPHŌ (τρέφω) signifies (*a*) to make to grow, bring up, rear, Luke
CB:— 4 : 16, "brought up;" (*b*) to nourish, feed, Matt. 6 : 26; 25 : 37;
Luke 12 : 24; Acts 12 : 20; Rev. 12 : 6, 14; of a mother, to give suck, Luke 23 : 29 (some mss. here have *thēlazō*, to suckle); to fatten, as of fattening animals, Jas. 5 : 5, "ye have nourished (your hearts)." See BRING, A, No. 33.¶

5526 AG:883D 4. CHORTAZŌ (χορτάζω), to feed, to fatten, is used (*a*) primarily of
CB:1240A animals, Rev. 19 : 21; (*b*) of persons, to fill or satisfy with food. It is usually translated by the verb "to fill," but is once rendered "to be fed," in Luke 16 : 21, of Lazarus, in his desire for the crumbs (he could be well supplied with them) that fell from the rich man's table, a fact which throws light upon the utter waste that went on at the table of the latter. The crumbs that fell would provide no small meal. See FILL, SATISFY.

5595 AG:894D 5. PSŌMIZŌ (ψωμίζω) primarily denotes to feed with morsels, as
CB:— nurses do children; then, to dole out or supply with food, Rom. 12 : 20; 1 Cor. 13 : 3.¶ Cp. *psōmion*, a fragment, morsel, John 13 : 26, 27, 30 ("sop").¶

4222 AG:695D 6. POTIZŌ (ποτίζω), to give to drink, is translated "I fed (you with
CB:1266B milk)" in 1 Cor. 3 : 2. See DRINK, WATER.

FEEL, FEELING, FELT

1097 AG:160D 1. GINŌSKŌ (γινώσκω), to know, perceive, is translated "she felt
CB:1248B (in her body)," of the woman with the issue of blood, Mark 5 : 29, i.e., she became aware of the fact. See KNOW.

5426 AG:866A 2. PHRONEŌ (φρονέω), to think, to be minded, is translated "I felt"
CB:1264C in the R.V. of 1 Cor. 13 : 11 (for A.V., "I understood"). See CAREFUL.

5584 AG:892C 3. PSĒLAPHAŌ (ψηλαφάω), to feel or grope about (from *psaō*, to
CB:— touch), expressing the motion of the hands over a surface, so as to feel it, is used (*a*) metaphorically, of seeking after God, Acts 17 : 27; (*b*) literally, of physical handling or touching, Luke 24 : 39 with 1 John 1 : 1; Heb. 12 : 18. See HANDLE, TOUCH.¶

4834 AG:778D 4. SUMPATHEŌ (συμπαθέω), to have a fellow-feeling for or with, is
CB:1270B rendered "touched with the feeling of" in Heb. 4 : 15; "have com-
524 AG:80A passion" in 10 : 34. See COMPASSION.¶

CB:— 5. APALGEŌ (ἀπαλγέω) signifies to cease to feel pain for (*apo*, from, *algeō*, to feel pain ; cp. Eng., neuralgia) ; hence, to be callous, " past feeling," insensible to honour and shame, Eph. 4 : 19.¶

Note : In Acts 28 : 5 *paschō*, to suffer, is rendered " felt (no harm)," 3958
R.V., " took," lit., ' suffered no ill (effect).' AG:633D CB:1262C

For FEET see FOOT

FEIGN, FEIGNED

A. Verb.

HUPOKRINOMAI (ὑποκρίνομαι) primarily denotes to answer ; 5271 AG:845A
then, to answer on the stage, play a part, and so, metaphorically, to CB:1252B
feign, pretend, Luke 20 : 20.¶ Cp. *hupokritēs*, a hypocrite, and *hupokrisis*, hypocrisy.

B. Adjective.

PLASTOS (πλαστός) primarily denotes formed, moulded (from *plassō*, 4112
to mould ; Eng., plastic) ; then, metaphorically, made up, fabricated, AG:666C CB:–
feigned, 2 Pet. 2 : 3.¶ Cp. *plasma*, that which is moulded, Rom. 9 : 20.¶

For FELL see FALL

FELLOW

1. ANĒR (ἀνήρ) denotes a man, in relation to his sex or age ; in 435
Acts 17 : 5 (plural) it is rendered " fellows," as more appropriate to the AG:66C CB:1235C
accompanying description of them. See HUSBAND, MAN, SIR.

2. HETAIROS (ἑταῖρος), a companion, comrade, is translated 2083
" fellows " in Matt. 11 : 16 [where, however, the most authentic mss. have AG:314C CB:1250A
heterois, " (the) others "]. The word is used only by Matthew and is translated " friend " in 20 : 13 ; 22 : 12 ; 26 : 50. See FRIEND.¶

3. METOCHOS (μέτοχος), properly an adjective, signifying sharing 3353
in, partaking of, is translated " partners " in Luke 5 : 7 ; " partakers " AG:514C CB:1258C
in Heb. 3 : 1, 14 ; 6 : 4 ; 12 : 8 ; " fellows " in Heb. 1 : 9, of those who share in a heavenly calling, or have held, or will hold, a regal position in relation to the earthly, Messianic Kingdom. (Cp. *summetochos*, " fellow-partakers," in Eph. 3 : 6, R.V.). See PARTAKER, PARTNER.

Notes : (1) In Acts 24 : 5 *loimos*, a plague, a pest, is rendered " a LOIMOS
pestilent fellow." This is a sample of the strongest use of the epithet 3061 AG:479D
" fellow." (2) *Toioutos*, an adjective, " such a one," is often used as CB:–
a noun, e.g., Acts 22 : 22, where it is translated " such a fellow." TOIOUTOS 5108
(3) *Houtos*, this, is translated " this fellow " in the A.V. of Luke 23 : 2 AG:821B
(R.V., " this man "). So in John 9 : 29. Both Versions have " this CB:1272C HOUTOS
man," e.g., in Mark 2 : 7 ; John 6 : 52, in the same contemptuous sense. 3778
(4) For the word in combination with various nouns see CITIZEN, DISCIPLE, AG:596B CB:1251B
ELDER, HEIR, HELPER, LABOURER, MEMBER, PARTNER, PRISONER, SERVANT, SOLDIER, WORK, WORKER.

FELLOWSHIP

A. Nouns.

2842 AG:438D CB:1255B 1. KOINŌNIA (κοινωνία), (*a*) communion, fellowship, **sharing in** common (from *koinos*, common), is translated " communion " in 1 Cor. 10 : 16 ; Philm. 6, R.V., " fellowship," for A.V., " communication ; " it is most frequently translated " fellowship ; " (*b*) that which is the outcome of fellowship, a contribution, e.g., Rom. 15 : 26 ; 2 Cor. 8 : 4. See COMMUNION, CONTRIBUTION, etc.

Note : In Eph. 3 : 9, some mss. have ***koinōnia***, instead of ***oikonomia***, dispensation, R.V.

3352 AG:514C CB:1258C 2. METOCHĒ (μετοχή), partnership (akin to No. 3, under FELLOW), is translated " fellowship " in 2 Cor. 6 : 14.¶ In the Sept., Ps. 122 : 3, " Jerusalem is built as a city whose fellowship is complete."¶ The word seems to have a more restricted sense than ***koinōnia***. Cp. **the** verb form in Heb. 2 : 14.

2844 AG:439C CB:1255B 3. KOINŌNOS (κοινωνός) denotes a partaker or partner (akin to No. 1) ; in 1 Cor. 10 : 20 it is used with *ginomai*, to become, " that ye should have communion with," R.V. (A.V., " fellowship with "). See COMPANION, PARTAKER, PARTNER.

B. Verbs.

2841 AG:438C CB:1255B 1. KOINŌNEŌ (κοινωνέω), to have fellowship, is so translated in Phil. 4 : 15, R.V., for A.V., " did communicate." See COMMUNICATE.

4790 AG:774B CB:1270C 2. SUNKOINŌNEŌ (συγκοινωνέω), to have fellowship with or in (*sun*, with, and No. 1), is used in Eph. 5 : 11 ; Phil. 4 : 14, R.V., " ye had fellowship," for A.V., " ye did communicate ; " Rev. 18 : 4, R.V., " have (no) fellowship with," for A.V., " be (not) partakers of." See COMMUNICATE, PARTAKER.¶

For FELT see FEEL

FEMALE

2338 AG:360C CB:1271C THĒLUS (θῆλυς), an adjective (from *thēlē*, a breast), is used in the form *thēlu* (grammatically neuter) as a noun, " female," in Matt. 19 : 4 ; Mark 10 : 6 ; Gal. 3 : 28 ; in the feminine form ***thēleia***, in Rom. 1 : 26, " women ; " ver. 27 " woman." See WOMAN.¶

FERMENTED See STRONG

FERVENT, FERVENTLY

A. Adjective.

1618 AG:245C CB:— EKTENĒS (ἐκτενής) denotes strained, stretched (*ek*, out, ***teinō***, to stretch) ; hence, metaphorically, " fervent," 1 Pet. 4 : 8. Some mss. have it in Acts 12 : 5, for the adverb (see B).¶ Cp. *ekteneia* (with *en*), intently, strenuously, in Acts 26 : 7, A.V., " instantly," R.V., " earnestly." Cp. EARNEST.

B. Adverb.

1619 AG:245D CB:1244A EKTENŌS (ἐκτενῶς), fervently (akin to A.), is said of love, in 1 Pet.

1 : 22 ; of prayer, in some mss., Acts 12 : 5 (see under A.) ; for the comparative degree in Luke 22 : 44, see EARNESTLY.¶

C. Verb.

ZEŌ (ζέω), to be hot, to boil (Eng. " zeal " is akin), is metaphorically 2204
used of fervency of spirit, Acts 18 : 25 ; Rom. 12 : 11.¶ AG:337C CB:1273C

Notes : (1) In Col. 4 : 12, the verb *agōnizomai*, to strive, is translated AGŌNIZOMAI
" labouring fervently," A.V. (R.V., " striving "). (2) In 2 Cor. 7 : 7, the 75 AG:15B
noun *zēlos*, zeal (akin to C.), is translated " fervent mind," A.V. (R.V., CB:1233C
" zeal "). (3) In Jas. 5 : 17, " he prayed fervently " (A.V., " earnestly ") ZĒLOS 2205
translates the noun *proseuchē*, followed by the corresponding verb, lit., AG:337D
' he prayed with prayer.' In ver. 16 *deēsis*, supplication, is so translated CB:1273B PROSEUCHĒ
in the R.V., for the A.V., " effectual fervent prayer." There is nothing 4335
in the original corresponding to the word " effectual." The phrase, AG:713B CB:1267A
including the verb *energeomai*, to work in, is, lit., ' the inworking supplication,' suggesting a supplication consistent with inward conformity to the mind of God. (4) For "fervent heat " see HEAT, B.

FETCH

METAPEMPŌ (μεταπέμπω), to send after or for (*meta*, after, *pempō*, 3343
to send), in the Middle Voice, is translated " fetch " in the R.V. of Acts AG:513B CB:—
10 : 5 and 11 : 13. See CALL.

Notes : (1) In Acts 16 : 37, the R.V. gives to *exagō*, to bring out, the 1806
adequate meaning " let them . . . bring us out," for the A.V., " let them AG:271C CB:—
fetch us out." " Fetch " is not sufficiently dignified for the just demand made. (2) For Acts 28 : 13, A.V., " fetched a compass," see CIRCUIT.

FETTER

PEDĒ (πέδη), a fetter (akin to *peza*, the instep, and *pous*, a foot ; cp. 3976
Eng. prefix *ped*—), occurs in Mark 5 : 4 and Luke 8 : 29. Cp. FOOT,¶ AG:638C CB:—

FEVER (to be sick of)

A. Noun.

PURETOS (πυρετός), feverish heat (from *pur*, fire), hence, a fever, 4446
occurs in Matt. 8 : 15 ; Mark 1 : 31 ; John 4 : 52 ; Acts 28 : 8 ; in AG:730D CB:1268A
Luke 4 : 38, with *megas*, great, a high fever ; ver. 39. Luke, as a physician, uses the medical distinction by which the ancients classified fevers into great and little.¶ In the Sept., Deut. 28 : 22.¶

B. Verb.

PURESSŌ (πυρέσσω) signifies to be ill of a fever (akin to A.), 4445
Matt. 8 : 14 ; Mark 1 : 30.¶ AG:730D CB:1268A

FEW

A. Adjectives.

1. OLIGOS (ὀλίγος), used of number, quantity, and size, denotes few, 3641 AG:563C
little, small, slight, e.g., Matt. 7 : 14 ; 9 : 37 ; 15 : 34 ; 20 : 16 ; neuter CB:1260C

plural, " a few things," Matt. 25 : 21, 23 ; Rev. 2 : 14 (20 in some mss.) ; in Eph. 3 : 3, the phrase *en oligō*, in brief, is translated " in a few words."

1024 AG:147B CB:1239B 2. BRACHUS (βραχύς) denotes (*a*) short, in regard to time, e.g., Heb. 2 : 7 ; or distance, Acts 27 : 28 ; (*b*) few, in regard to quantity, Heb. 13 : 22, in the phrase *dia bracheōn*, lit., ' by means of few,' i.e., " in few words." See LITTLE.

Note : In Luke 10 : 42, in the Lord's words to Martha, many ancient authorities provide the rendering, ' but there is need of few things (neuter plural) or one.'

B. Adverb.

4935 AG:793A CB:— SUNTOMŌS (συντόμως), concisely, briefly, cut short (from *suntemnō*, to cut in pieces, *sun*, used intensively, *temnō*, to cut), occurs in the speech of Tertullus, Acts 24 : 4.¶

FICKLENESS

1644 AG:248C CB:— ELAPHRIA (ἐλαφρία) denotes lightness, levity, " fickleness," 2 Cor. 1 : 17, R.V. (for A.V., " lightness ").¶ The corresponding adjective is *elaphros*, light, Matt. 11 : 30 ; 2 Cor. 4 : 17.¶

FIDELITY

4102 AG:662B CB:1265A PISTIS (πίστις), faith, faithfulness, is translated " fidelity " in Tit. 2 : 10. See FAITH (*b*).

FIELD, CORNFIELD

68 AG:13D CB:1233C 1. AGROS (ἀγρός), a cultivated field, or fields in the aggregate, e.g., Matt. 6 : 28 ; Mark 11 : 8 (some mss. here have *dendrōn*, trees) ; Luke 15 : 15. See FARM.

5561 AG:889B CB:1240A 2. CHŌRA (χώρα), (*a*) a space, place, then, (*b*) land, country, region, is translated " fields " in John 4 : 35 ; Jas. 5 : 4. See COUNTRY.

5564 AG:890B CB:1240A 3. CHŌRION (χωρίον), a diminutive of No. 2, denotes (*a*) a place, region, (*b*) a piece of land, property, rendered " field " in Acts 1 : 18, 19. See LAND, PARCEL, PLACE, POSSESSION.

4702 AG:763B CB:— 4. SPORIMOS (σπόριμος) signifies fit for sowing (from *speirō*, to sow), and denotes a cornfield, Matt. 12 : 1 ; Mark 2 : 23 ; Luke 6 : 1.¶ In the Sept., Gen. 1 : 29 ; Lev. 11 : 37.¶

FIERCE, FIERCENESS

A. Adjectives.

434 AG:66C CB:— 1. ANĒMEROS (ἀνήμερος) signifies ' not tame,' savage (from *a*, negative, and *hēmeros*, gentle), 2 Tim. 3 : 3. Epictetus describes those who forget God as their Creator, as resembling lions, ' wild, savage and fierce (*anēmeroi*) ' (Moulton and Milligan, Greek Test. Vocab.).¶

5467 AG:874C CB:1239B 2. CHALEPOS (χαλεπός), hard, (*a*) hard to do or deal with, difficult, fierce, is said of the Gadarene demoniacs, Matt. 8 : 28 ; (*b*) hard to bear, painful, grievous, said of the last times, 2 Tim. 3 : 1, R.V., "grievous," for A.V., "perilous." See GRIEVOUS.¶

Notes : (1) In Jas. 3 : 4, *sklēros*, hard, rough, violent, is said of winds, SKLēROS
R.V., "rough," for A.V., "fierce." (2) In Luke 23 : 5, the verb *epischuō*, 4642 AG:756A
to make or grow stronger (from *epi*, over, intensive, and *ischus*, strength), CB:1269A
is used metaphorically, "they were the more urgent," R.V., for A.V., EPISCHUō 2001
"the more fierce."¶ AG:302A

B. Nouns. CB:—

1. THUMOS (θυμός), hot anger, wrath, is rendered "fierceness" in 2372
Rev. 16 : 19; 19 : 15, of the wrath of God. See ANGER (A, Notes), AG:365B CB:1272C
INDIGNATION, WRATH.

2. ZĒLOS (ζῆλος), zeal, jealousy, is rendered "fierceness" in Heb. 2205
10 : 27, R.V. (of fire). AG:337D CB:1273B

FIERY

PUROŌ (πυρόω), to set on fire, burn up (from *pur*, fire), always used 4448
in the Passive Voice in the N.T., is translated "fiery" in Eph. 6 : 16, AG:731A CB:1268A
metaphorically of the darts of the evil one; 'fire-tipped' would perhaps bring out the verbal force of the word. The most ancient mss. have the article repeated, lit., 'the darts of the evil one, the fiery (darts),' marking them as particularly destructive. Some mss. omit the repeated article. In ancient times, darts were often covered with burning material. See BURN, FIRE, TRY, *Note* (1).

Notes : (1) For Heb. 10 : 27, R.V., see FIRE (cp. FIERCE, B, No. 2).
(2) For *purōsis*, a fiery trial, 1 Pet. 4 : 12, (lit., a burning, as in Rev. 4451
18 : 9, 18), a refining, or trial by fire, see TRIAL. AG:731C CB:1268A

FIFTEEN, FIFTEENTH

DEKAPENTE (δεκαπέντε), lit., ten-five, occurs in John 11 : 18; 1178
Acts 27 : 28; Gal. 1 : 18.¶ AG:173D (DEKA)

Notes : (1) In Acts 7 : 14, "threescore and fifteen" translates a CB:—
different numeral, lit., 'seventy-five.' This refers to all Joseph's kindred whom he sent for. There is no discrepancy between this and Gen. 46 : 26. The Sept. translations give the number as 75 in Gen. 46 : 27 and in Ex. 1 : 5, and this Stephen follows, being a Grecian Jew. (2) The corresponding ordinal numeral *pentekaidekatos*, fifteenth (lit., five and tenth) is found 4003
in Luke 3 : 1, where Luke dates the reign of Tiberias from the period of his AG:643A CB:—
joint rule with Augustus.

FIFTH

PEMPTOS (πέμπτος), akin to *pente*, five, is found only in the 3991
Apocalypse, 6 : 9; 9 : 1; 16 : 10; 21 : 20.¶ AG:641C CB:—

FIFTY

PENTĒKONTA (πεντήκοντα) is found in Luke 7 : 41; 16 : 6; 4004 AG:643A
John 8 : 57; 21 : 11; Acts 13 : 20; in Mark 6 : 40 with *kata* (in the most CB:—

authentic mss.), according to, "by fifties;" in Luke 9 : 14, with *ana*, up, used distributively, "fifty each," R.V. (Luke adds *hōsei*, "about").¶

FIG

4810 AG:776B 1. SUKON (σῦκον) denotes the ripe fruit of a *sukē*, a fig-tree (see
CB:— below; cp. No. 2), Matt. 7 : 16; Mark 11 : 13; Luke 6 : 44; Jas. 3 : 12.¶
3653 AG:565A 2. OLUNTHOS (ὄλυνθος) denotes an unripe fig, which grows in winter
CB:— and usually falls off in the Spring, Rev. 6 : 13.¶ In the Sept., S. of Sol.,
2 : 13.¶

FIG-TREE

4808 AG:776B SUKĒ, or SUKEA (συκῆ), a fig tree, is found in Matt. 21 : 19, 20, 21;
CB:1270B 24 : 32; Mark 11 : 13, 20, 21; 13 : 28; Luke 13 : 6, 7; 21 : 29; John
1 : 48, 50; Jas. 3 : 12; Rev. 6 : 13 (see *sukon*, above).¶

Note: A fig tree with leaves must have young fruits already, or it will be barren for the season. The first figs ripen in late May or early June. The tree in Mark 11 : 13 should have had fruit, unripe indeed, but existing. In some lands fig-trees bear the early fruit under the leaves and the later fruit above the leaves. In that case the leaves were a sign that there should have been fruit, unseen from a distance, underneath the leaves. The condemnation of this fig-tree lay in the absence of any sign of fruit.

FIGHT

A. Nouns.

73 AG:15A 1. AGŌN (ἀγών), akin to *agō*, to lead, primarily a gathering, then,
CB:1233C a place of assembly, and hence, a contest, conflict, is translated "fight"
in 1 Tim. 6 : 12; 2 Tim. 4 : 7. See CONFLICT.
119 AG:21C 2. ATHLĒSIS (ἄθλησις) is translated "fight" in Heb. 10 : 32, A.V.
CB:1238A See CONFLICT.¶
4171 AG:685A *Note:* In Heb. 11 : 34, *polemos*, war, is translated "fight," A.V.
CB:1265C (R.V., "war"); it is misrendered "battle" in the A.V. of 1 Cor. 14 : 8;
Rev. 9 : 7, 9; 16 : 14; 20 : 8.

B. Verbs.

75 AG:15B 1. AGŌNIZOMAI (ἀγωνίζομαι), from A, No. 1, denotes (*a*) to contend
CB:1233C in the public games, 1 Cor. 9 : 25 ("striveth in the games," R.V.); (*b*) to fight, engage in conflict, John 18 : 36; (*c*) metaphorically, to contend perseveringly against opposition and temptation, 1 Tim. 6 : 12; 2 Tim. 4 : 7 (cp. A, No. 1; in regard to the meaning there, the evidence of *Koinē* inscriptions is against the idea of games-contests); to strive as in a contest for a prize, straining every nerve to attain to the object, Luke 13 : 24; to put forth every effort, involving toil, Col. 1 : 29; 1 Tim. 4 : 10 (some mss. have *oneidizomai* here, to suffer reproach); to wrestle earnestly in prayer, Col. 4 : 12 (cp. *sunagōnizomai*, Rom. 15 : 30). See LABOUR, STRIVE.¶

2. PUKTEUŌ (πυκτεύω), to box (from *puktēs*, a pugilist), one of the 4438 (PUKTEō)
events in the Olympic games, is translated " fight " in 1 Cor. 9 : 26.¶ AG:729A CB:—

3. MACHOMAI (μάχομαι), to fight, is so rendered in Jas. 4 : 2 (cp. 3164
" fightings," ver. 1, see below), and translated " strive " in 2 Tim. 2 : 24 ; AG:496C CB:1257B
" strove " in John 6 : 52 ; Acts 7 : 26. See STRIVE.¶

4. THĒRIOMACHEŌ (θηριομαχέω) signifies to fight with wild beasts 2341
(*thērion*, a beast, and No. 3), 1 Cor. 15 : 32. Some think that the Apostle AG:360D CB:—
was condemned to fight with wild beasts ; if so, he would scarcely have omitted it from 2 Cor. 11 : 23–end. Moreover, he would have lost his status as a Roman citizen. Probably he uses the word figuratively of contending with ferocious men. Ignatius so uses it in his Ep. to the Romans.¶

Notes : (1) In Rev. 2 : 16 and 12 : 7, A.V., *polemeō*, to war, is translated POLEMEō
" to fight," R.V., " will make war," " *going forth* to war," and " warred." 4170 AG:685A
(2) In Acts 23 : 9 some mss. have the verb *theomacheō*, to fight against CB:1265C
God. Cp. the corresponding adjective, below, under FIGHTING. THEOMACHEō 2313 AG:356C CB:—

FIGHTING

A. Noun.

MACHĒ (μάχη), a fight, strife (akin to B, No. 3, under FIGHT), is 3163
always used in the plural in the N.T., and translated " fightings " in AG:496C CB:1257B
2 Cor. 7 : 5 ; Jas. 4 : 1 ; and Tit. 3 : 9, R.V. (for A.V., " strivings ") ; " strifes " in 2 Tim. 2 : 23. See STRIFE.¶

B. Adjective.

THEOMACHOS (θεομάχος), fighting against God (*theos*, God, and A, 2314
occurs in Acts 5 : 39 (A.V., " to fight "), lit., ' God-fighters.'¶ AG:356C CB:1272A

FIGURE

1. TUPOS (τύπος), a type, figure, pattern, is translated " figures " 5179
(i.e., representations of gods) in Acts 7 : 43 ; in the R.V. of ver. 44 AG:829D CB:1273B
(for A.V., " fashion ") and in Rom. 5 : 14, of Adam as a " figure " of Christ. See ENSAMPLE.

2. ANTITUPOS (ἀντίτυπος) an adjective, used as a noun, denotes, 499
lit., a striking back ; metaphorically, resisting, adverse ; then, in a AG:76A CB:1236A
Passive sense, struck back ; in the N.T. metaphorically, ' corresponding to,' (*a*) a copy of an archetype (*anti*, corresponding to, and No. 1), i.e., the event or person or circumstance corresponding to the type, Heb. 9 : 24, R.V., " like in pattern " (A.V., " the figure of "), of the Tabernacle, which, with its structure and appurtenances, was a pattern of that " holy place," " Heaven itself," " the true," into which Christ entered, " to appear before the face of God for us." The earthly Tabernacle anticipatively represented what is now made good in Christ ; it was a " figure " or " parable " (9 : 9), " for the time now present," R.V., i.e., pointing to the present time, not " then present," A.V. (see below) ;

(*b*) a corresponding type, 1 Pet. 3 : 21, said of baptism ; the circumstances of the flood, the ark and its occupants, formed a type, and baptism forms 'a corresponding type' (not an antitype), each setting forth the spiritual realities of the death, burial, and resurrection of believers in their identification with Christ. It is not a case of type and antitype, but of two types, that in Genesis, the type, and baptism, the corresponding type.¶

3850 AG:612B 3. PARABOLĒ (παραβολή), a casting or placing side by side (*para*,
CB:1262A beside, *ballō*, to throw) with a view to comparison or resemblance, a parable, is translated " figure " in the A.V. of Heb. 9 : 9 (R.V., " a parable for the time now present ") and 11 : 19, where the return of Isaac was (parabolically, in the lit. sense of the term) figurative of resurrection (R.V., " parable "). See No. 2 (*a*). See PARABLE

5296 AG:848C *Notes :* (1) The synonymous noun *hupotupōsis*, an example, pattern,
CB:1252B 1 Tim. 1 : 16 ; 2 Tim. 1 : 13, denotes simply a delineation or outline.¶
3345 (2) For *metaschēmatizō*, rendered " I have in a figure transferred " in
AG:513B 1 Cor. 4 : 6, where the fact stated is designed to change its application,
CB:1258C i.e., from Paul and Apollos to circumstances in Corinth, see FASHION.

FILL, FILL UP

A. Verbs.

4137 AG:670C 1. PLĒROŌ (πληρόω) denotes (I) to make full, to fill to the full ;
CB:1265B in the Passive Voice, to be filled, made full ; it is used (1) of things : a net, Matt. 13 : 48 ; a building, John 12 : 3 ; Acts 2 : 2 ; a city, Acts 5 : 28 ; needs, Phil. 4 : 19, A.V., " supply," R.V., " fulfil ; " metaphorically, of valleys, Luke 3 : 5 ; figuratively, of a measure of iniquity, Matt. 23 : 32 ; (2) of persons : (*a*) of the members of the Church, the Body of Christ, as filled by Him, Eph. 1 : 23 ('all things in all the members') ; 4 : 10 ; in 3 : 19, of their being filled 'into' (*eis*), R.V., " unto," A.V., " with " (all the fulness of God) ; of their being " made full " in Him, Col. 2 : 10 (R.V., for A.V., " complete ") ; (*b*) of Christ Himself : with wisdom, in the days of His flesh, Luke 2 : 40 ; with joy, in His return to the Father, Acts 2 : 28 ; (*c*) of believers : with the Spirit, Eph. 5 : 18 ; with joy, Acts 13 : 52 ; 2 Tim. 1 : 4 ; with joy and peace, Rom. 15 : 13 ; [from these are to be distinguished those passages which speak of joy as being fulfilled or completed, which come under FULFIL, John 3 : 29 ; 15 : 11 (R.V.) ; 16 : 24 (R.V.) ; Phil. 2 : 2 ; 1 John 1 : 4 (R.V.) ; 2 John 12 (R.V.)] ; with knowledge, Rom. 15 : 14 ; with comfort, 2 Cor. 7 : 4 ; with the fruits of righteousness, Phil. 1 : 11 (Gk. 'fruit') ; with the knowledge of God's will, Col. 1 : 9 ; with abundance through material supplies by fellow-believers, Phil. 4 : 18 ; (*d*) of the hearts of believers as the seat of emotion and volition, John 16 : 6 (sorrow) ; Acts 5 : 3 (deceitfulness) ;
378 (*e*) of the unregenerate who refuse recognition of God, Rom. 1 : 29 ;
AG:59C (II) to accomplish, complete, fulfil. See ACCOMPLISH, FULFIL.
CB:1235B 2. ANAPLĒROŌ (ἀναπληρόω), to fill up adequately, completely (*ana*,

up, and No. 1), is twice translated by the verbs to fill, to fill up, in 1 Cor. 14 : 16, R.V. (for A.V., " occupieth "), of a believer as a member of an assembly, who fills the position or condition (not one who fills it by assuming it) of being unable to understand the language of him who had the gift of tongues ; in 1 Thess. 2 : 16, " to fill up their sins," of the Jews who persisted in their course of antagonism and unbelief. See FULFIL.

3. ANTANAPLĒROŌ (ἀνταναπληρόω), to fill up in turn (or on one's **466**
part ; *anti*, corresponding to, and No. 2), is used in Col. 1 : 24, of the **AG:72D**
Apostle's responsive devotion to Christ in filling up, or undertaking on **CB:1236A**
his part a full share of, the sufferings which follow after the sufferings of Christ, and are experienced by the members of His Body, the Church. " The point of the Apostle's boast is that Christ, the sinless Master, should have left something for Paul, the unworthy servant, to suffer " (Lightfoot, on Col., p. 165).¶

4. SUMPLĒROŌ (συμπληρόω), to fill completely (*sun*, with, and **4845**
No. 1), is used in the Passive Voice (*a*) of a boat filling with water, and, **AG:779C**
by metonymy, of the occupants themselves, Luke 8 : 23 (R.V., " were **CB:1270B**
filling ") ; (*b*) of fulfilling, with regard to time, " when the days were well-nigh come," R.V., for A.V., " when the time was come " (R.V., marg., " were being fulfilled "), Luke 9 : 51 ; Acts 2 : 1, see R.V., marg. See COME.¶ In the Sept. Jer. 25 : 12.¶

5. PIMPLĒMI (πίμπλημι) and PLĒTHŌ (πλήθω), lengthened forms **4130**
of *pleō*, to fill (*plēthō* supplies certain tenses of *pimplēmi*), is used (1) of **AG:658A**
things ; boats, with fish, Luke 5 : 7 ; a sponge, with vinegar, Matt. 27 : 48 **CB:1265A**
(some mss. have this verb in John 19 : 29) ; a city, with confusion, Acts 19 : 29 ; a wedding, with guests, Matt. 22 : 10 ; (2) of persons (only in Luke's writings) : (*a*) with the Holy Spirit, Luke 1 : 15, 41, 67 ; Acts 2 : 4 ; 4 : 8, 31 ; 9 : 17 ; 13 : 9 ; (*b*) with emotions : wrath, Luke 4 : 28 ; fear, 5 : 26 ; madness, 6 : 11 ; wonder, amazement, Acts 3 : 10 ; jealousy, 5 : 17, R.V., for A.V., " indignation," and 13 : 45 (A.V., " envy "). For its other significance, to complete, see ACCOMPLISH.

6. EMPIPLĒMI (ἐμπίπλημι) or EMPLĒTHŌ (as in No. 5), to fill **1705**
full, to satisfy, is used (*a*) of filling the hungry, Luke 1 : 53 ; John 6 : 12 ; **AG:256A**
of the abundance of the rich, Luke 6 : 25 ; (*b*) metaphorically, of a company **CB:1244B**
of friends, Rom. 15 : 24, R.V., " satisfied," for A.V., " filled."¶

7. EMPIPLAŌ (ἐμπιπλάω), an alternative form of No. 6, is found in Acts 14 : 17, " filling (your hearts)," of God's provision for mankind.¶

8. CHORTAZŌ (χορτάζω), to fill or satisfy with food, e.g., Matt. **5526**
15 : 33 ; Phil. 4 : 12, is used metaphorically in Matt. 5 : 6 ; Luke 6 : 21. **AG:883D**
See FEED. **CB:1240A**

9. GEMIZŌ (γεμίζω), to fill or load full, is used of a boat, Mark 4 : 37 **1072**
(R.V., " was filling ") ; a sponge, Mark 15 : 36 (cp. No. 5, Matt. 27 : 48) ; **AG:153C**
a house, Luke 14 : 23 ; the belly, Luke 15 : 16 ; waterpots, John 2 : 7 ; **CB:1248A**

baskets, 6 : 13 ; bowls, with fire, Rev. 8 : 5 ; the Temple, with smoke,
15 : 8.¶ Cp. *gemō*, to be full. See FULL.

2880 10. KORENNUMI (κορέννυμι), to satisfy (akin to *koros*, a surfeit), is
AG:444C CB:— used metaphorically of spiritual things, in 1 Cor. 4 : 8, R.V., " ye are
filled ; " in Acts 27 : 38, " had eaten enough," lit., ' having being satisfied
with food ' See EAT, ENOUGH.¶

3325 11. MESTOŌ (μεστόω), to fill full, from *mestos*, full, is used of being
AG:508C CB:— filled with wine, Acts 2 : 13, R.V., " are filled with."¶

B. Noun.

4138 AG:672A PLĒRŌMA (πλήρωμα), fulness, has two meanings, (*a*) in the active
CB:1265B sense, that which fills up, a piece of undressed cloth on an old garment,
Matt. 9 : 16 ; Mark 2 : 21, lit., ' the filling ' (R.V., " that which should
fill it up "), i.e., the patch, which is probably the significance ; (*b*) that
which has been completed, the fulness, e.g., Mark 8 : 20. See FULNESS.

KERANNUMI *Notes :* (1) In Rev. 18 : 6, A.V., *kerannumi*, to mix, is incorrectly
2767 AG:429A rendered to fill full (R.V., to mingle). (2) In Rev. 15 : 1, A.V., *teleō*, to
CB:1255A finish, complete, is incorrectly rendered " filled up " (R.V., " finished ") ;
TELEō 5055 the contents of the seven bowls are not the sum total of the Divine
AG:810D judgments ; they form the termination of them ; there are many which
CB:1271B precede (see previous chapters), which are likewise comprised under
" the wrath of God," to be executed at the closing period of the present
age, e.g., 6 : 17 ; 11 : 18 ; 14 : 10, 19.

FILTH

4027 AG:647D 1. PERIKATHARMA (περικάθαρμα) denotes offscouring, refuse (lit.,
CB:1263B cleanings, i.e., that which is thrown away in cleansing ; from *perikathairō*,
to purify all around, i.e., completely, as in the Sept. of Deut. 18 : 10 ;
Josh. 5 : 4.¶) It is once used in the Sept. (Prov. 21 : 18) as the price of
expiation ; among the Greeks the term was applied to victims sacrificed
to make expiation ; they also used it of criminals kept at the public
expense, to be thrown into the sea, or otherwise killed, at the outbreak of
a pestilence, etc. It is used in 1 Cor. 4 : 13 much in this sense (not of
sacrificial victims), " the filth of the world," representing " the most
abject and despicable men " (Grimm-Thayer), the scum or rubbish of
humanity.¶

4509 AG:738A 2. RHUPOS (ῥύπος) denotes dirt, filth, 1 Pet. 3 : 21.¶ Cp. *rhuparia*,
CB:1268B filthiness (see A, No. 2, below) ; *rhuparos*, vile, Jas. 2 : 2 ; Rev. 22 : 11,
in the best mss. (see B, No. 3, below) ;¶ *rhupoō*, to make filthy,
Rev. 22 : 11 ;¶ *rhupainō* (see D. below).

FILTHINESS, FILTHY (to make)

A. Nouns.

151 AG:25B 1. AISCHROTĒS (αἰσχρότης), baseness (from *aischos*, shame,
CB:1234A disgrace), is used in Eph. 5 : 4, of obscenity, all that is contrary to purity.¶

2. RHUPARIA (ῥυπαρία) denotes dirt, filth (cp. No. 2, under FILTH), 4507 AG:738A
and is used metaphorically of moral defilement in Jas. 1 : 21.¶ CB:1268B

3. MOLUSMOS (μολυσμός), a soiling, defilement, is used in 2 Cor. 7 : 1. 3436 AG:527A
See DEFILEMENT.¶ CB:1259A

4. ASELGEIA (ἀσέλγεια), wantonness, licentiousness, lasciviousness, 766
is translated "filthy (conversation)," in 2 Pet. 2 : 7, A.V.; R.V., AG:114D CB:1238A
"lascivious (life)." See LASCIVIOUSNESS, WANTONNESS.

Notes: (1) Broadly speaking, *aischrotēs* signifies whatever is disgraceful; *rhuparia*, that which is characterized by moral impurity; *molusmos*, that which is defiling by soiling the clean; *aselgeia*, that which
is an insolent disregard of decency. (2) In Col. 3 : 8 *aischrologia*, which 148
denotes any kind of base utterance, the utterance of an uncontrolled AG:25B CB:1234A
tongue, is rendered "filthy communication" in the A.V.; but this is only part of what is included in the more comprehensive R.V. rendering, "shameful speaking." In the papyri writings the word is used of abuse. In general it seems to have been associated more frequently with foul or filthy, rather than abusive, speaking (Moulton and Milligan).¶

B. Adjectives.

1. AISCHROS (αἰσχρός), base, shameful (akin to A, No. 1), is used 150
of base gain, "filthy (lucre)," Tit. 1 : 11, and translated "shame" in AG:25B CB:1234A
1 Cor. 11 : 6, with reference to a woman with shorn hair; in 14 : 35, of oral utterances of women in a church gathering (R.V., "shameful"); in Eph. 5 : 12, of mentioning the base and bestial practices of those who live lascivious lives. See SHAME.¶

2. AISCHROKERDĒS (αἰσχροκερδής), greedy of base gain (No. 1, 146
and *kerdos*, gain), is used in 1 Tim. 3 : 8 and Tit. 1 : 7, "greedy of filthy AG:25A CB:1234A
lucre;" some mss. have it also in 1 Tim. 3 : 3.¶

3. RHUPAROS (ῥυπαρός), akin to A, No. 2 (see also FILTH, No. 2), 4508
dirty, is said of shabby clothing, Jas. 2 : 2: metaphorically, of moral AG:738A CB:1268B
defilement, Rev. 22 : 11 (in the best mss.).¶

Note: For *akathartos* see UNCLEAN, No. 1. 169 AG:29A

C. Adverb.

CB:1234B

AISCHROKERDŌS (αἰσχροκερδῶς), eagerness for base gain (akin to 147
B, No. 2), is used in 1 Pet. 5 : 2, "for filthy lucre."¶ AG:25B CB:—

D. Verb.

RHUPAINŌ

RHUPAINŌ (ῥυπαίνω), to make filthy, defile (from A, No. 2), is —
used in the Passive Voice, in an ethical sense, in Rev. 22 : 11 (cp. B, AG:737D CB:1268B
No. 3, in the same verse), "let him be made filthy," R.V. The tense RHUPAREUOMAI
(the aorist) marks the decisiveness of that which is decreed. Some texts — AG:738A (-EUŌ)
have *rhupareuomai*, here, with the same meaning; some have *rhupoō*, CB:1268B (-EUŌ)
in the Middle Voice, to make oneself filthy.¶ RHUPOŌ 4510

AG:738B

FINAL, FINALLY

CB:1268B (-EŌ)

A. Nouns.

4009 AG:644A

1. PERAS (πέρας), a limit, end, is translated "final" in Heb. 6 : 16, CB:1263B

R.V., " an oath is final for confirmation " (the A.V. connects the clauses differently). See END.

5056 AG:811B 2. TELOS (τέλος), an end, most frequently of the termination of
CB:1271B something, is used with the article adverbially, meaning " finally " or
'as to the end,' i.e., as to the last detail, 1 Pet. 3 : 8. See END.

B. Adverb.

3063 AG:479D LOIPON (λοιπόν) is the neuter of the adjective *loipos*, remaining (which
(LOIPOS 3.b.) is used in its different genders as a noun, ' the rest '), and is used either
CB:1257B with the article or without, to signify " finally," lit., ' for the rest.' The Apostle Paul uses it frequently in the concluding portion of his Epistles, introducing practical exhortations, not necessarily implying that the letter is drawing to a close, but marking a transition in the subject-matter, as in Phil. 3 : 1, where the actual conclusion is for the time postponed and the farewell injunctions are resumed in 4 : 8. See also 1 Thess. 4 : 1 (A.V., " furthermore "); 2 Thess. 3 : 1.

FIND, FOUND

2147 AG:324D 1. HEURISKŌ (εὑρίσκω) denotes (*a*) to find, either with previous
CB:1250B search, e.g., Matt. 7 : 7, 8, or without, e.g., Matt. 27 : 32; in the Passive Voice, of Enoch's disappearance, Heb. 11 : 5; of mountains, Rev. 16 : 20; of Babylon and its occupants, 18 : 21, 22; (*b*) metaphorically, to find out by enquiry, or to learn, discover, e.g., Luke 19 : 48; John 18 : 38; 19 : 4, 6; Acts 4 : 21; 13 : 28; Rom. 7 : 10; Gal. 2 : 17, which indicates " the surprise of the Jew " who learned for the first time that before God he had no moral superiority over the Gentiles whom he superciliously dubbed " sinners," while he esteemed himself to be ' righteous;' 1 Pet. 1 : 7; Rev. 5 : 4; (*c*) in the Middle Voice, to find for oneself, gain, procure, obtain, e.g., Matt. 10 : 39; 11 : 29, " ye shall find (rest);" Luke 1 : 30; Acts 7 : 46; 2 Tim. 1 : 18. See GET, OBTAIN.

429 AG:65D 2. ANEURISKŌ (ἀνευρίσκω), to find out (by search), discover
CB:— (*ana*, up, and No. 1), implying diligent searching, is used in Luke 2 : 16, of the shepherds in searching for and finding Mary and Joseph and the Child; in Acts 21 : 4, of Paul and his companions, in searching for and finding " the disciples " at Tyre (in ver. 2, No. 1, is used).¶

2983 AG:464A 3. LAMBANŌ (λαμβάνω), to take, receive, is translated " finding
CB:1256C (occasion) " in Rom. 7 : 11, R.V. (A.V., " taking "). See ACCEPT.

2638 AG:412D 4. KATALAMBANŌ (καταλαμβάνω), to lay hold of, said of mental
CB:1254A action, to comprehend by laying hold of or finding facts, is translated
(-OMAI) " I found," of Festus regarding charges made against Paul, Acts 25 : 25. See APPREHEND.

SUNANPAUOMAI 4875 *Notes:* (1) For *sunanapauomai*, to be refreshed in spirit, in Rom.
AG:784B 15 : 32, R.V., " find rest with," see FIND, REFRESH. (2) In Rom. 7 : 18,
ANEXICHNIASTOS 421 there is no word in the original for " find." Hence the R.V. has " is not."
AG:65A (3) In Rom. 11 : 33, *anexichniastos*, untraceable, is rendered " past

finding out," A.V., R.V., " past tracing out " (*ichniazō*, to track out) ; in Eph. 3 : 8, " unsearchable." See TRACE, UNSEARCHABLE.¶

For FINE see BRASS, No. 4, FLOUR, GOODLY, Note, LINEN

FINGER

DAKTULOS (δάκτυλος), Matt. 23 : 4 ; Mark 7 : 33 ; Luke 11 : 46 ; 1147
16 : 24 ; John 8 : 6 ; 20 : 25, 27, is used metaphorically in Luke 11 : 20, AG:170A
for the power of God, the effects of which are made visible to men (cp. CB:1240B
Matt. 12 : 28, " by the Spirit of God ; " cp. also Ex. 8 : 19).¶

FINISH

1. TELEŌ (τελέω), to bring to an end (*telos*, an end), in the Passive 5048
Voice, to be finished, is translated by the verb to finish in Matt. 13 : 53 ; AG:809D
19 : 1 ; 26 : 1 ; John 19 : 28, where the R.V. " are . . . finished " brings CB:1271B
out the force of the perfect tense (the same word as in ver. 30, " It is finished "), which is missed in the A.V. ; as Stier says, " the word was in His heart before He uttered it ; " 2 Tim. 4 : 7 ; Rev. 10 : 7 ; 11 : 7 ; 20 : 3, R.V., " should be finished " (A.V., " fulfilled "), 5, 7, R.V., " finished " (A.V., " expired "). In Rev. 15 : 1 the verb is rightly translated " is finished," R.V., see FILL, Note (2). In 15 : 8 the R.V., " should be finished " corrects the A.V., " were fulfilled." See ACCOMPLISH.

2. TELEIOŌ (τελειόω), akin to the adjective *teleios*, complete, perfect, 5055
and to No. 1, denotes to bring to an end in the sense of completing or AG:810D
perfecting, and is translated by the verb to finish in John 4 : 34 ; 5 : 36 ; CB:1271B
17 : 4 ; Acts 20 : 24. See CONSECRATE, FULFIL, PERFECT. 1615

3. EKTELEŌ (ἐκτελέω), lit., to finish out, i.e., completely (*ek*, out, AG:245C CB:—
intensive, and No. 1), is used in Luke 14 : 29, 30.¶ 2005

4. EPITELEŌ (ἐπιτελέω), to bring through to an end, is rendered AG:302B
" finish " in 2 Cor. 8 : 6, A.V. (R.V., " complete "). See ACCOMPLISH. CB:1246A (-EISTHAI)

5. SUNTELEŌ (συντελέω), to bring to fulfilment, to effect, is translated 4931
" finishing " (A.V., " will finish ") in Rom. 9 : 28. See COMPLETE. AG:792A CB:1271A

6. DIANUŌ (διανύω) is translated " had finished," in Acts 21 : 7, 1274
of the voyage from Tyre to Ptolemais. As this is so short a journey, and AG:187B CB:—
this verb is intensive in meaning, some have suggested the rendering ' but we having (thereby) completed our voyage (i.e., from Macedonia, 20 : 6), came from Tyre to Ptolemais.' In late Greek writers, however, the verb is used with the meaning to continue, and this is the probable sense here.¶

7. GINOMAI (γίνομαι), to become, to come into existence, is translated 1096 AG:158A
" were finished " in Heb. 4 : 3, i.e., were brought to their predestined end. CB:1248B

Notes : (1) In Luke 14 : 28, *apartismos* denotes a completion, and the APARTISMOS
phrase is, lit., ' unto a completion.' The A.V. has " to finish " (R.V., 535 AG:81B
" to complete "). See COMPLETE.¶ (2) In Jas. 1 : 15, *apoteleō*, to perfect, APOTELEŌ
to bring to maturity, to become " fullgrown," R.V. (A.V., " is finished "), 658 AG:100D

5051 AG:810C CB:1271B is said of the full development of sin. (3) In Heb. 12 : 2, the R.V. suitably translates *teleiōtēs* " perfecter," for A.V., " finisher."

FIRE

A. Nouns.

4442 AG:729D CB:1268A 1. PUR (πῦρ) (akin to which are No. 2, *pura*, and *puretos*, a fever, Eng., fire, etc.) is used (besides its ordinary natural significance):

(*a*) of the holiness of God, which consumes all that is inconsistent therewith, Heb. 10 : 27 ; 12 : 29 ; cp. Rev. 1 : 14 ; 2 : 18 ; 10 : 1 ; 15 : 2 ; 19 : 12 ; similarly of the holy angels as His ministers, Heb. 1 : 7 ; in Rev. 3 : 18 it is symbolic of that which tries the faith of saints, producing what will glorify the Lord :

(*b*) of the Divine judgment, testing the deeds of believers, at the Judgment-Seat of Christ, 1 Cor. 3 : 13 and 15 :

(*c*) of the fire of Divine judgment upon the rejectors of Christ, Matt. 3 : 11 (where a distinction is to be made between the baptism of the Holy Spirit at Pentecost and the fire of Divine retribution ; Acts 2 : 3 could not refer to baptism); Luke 3 : 16 :

(*d*) of the judgments of God at the close of the present age previous to the establishment of the Kingdom of Christ in the world, 2 Thess. 1 : 8 ; Rev. 18 : 8 :

(*e*) of the fire of Hell, to be endured by the ungodly hereafter, Matt. 5 : 22 ; 13 : 42, 50 ; 18 : 8, 9 ; 25 : 41 ; Mark 9 : 43, 48 ; Luke 3 : 17 :

(*f*) of human hostility both to the Jews and to Christ's followers, Luke 12 : 49 :

(*g*) as illustrative of retributive judgment upon the luxurious and tyrannical rich, Jas. 5 : 3 :

(*h*) of the future overthrow of the Babylonish religious system at the hands of the Beast and the nations under him, Rev. 17 : 16 :

(*i*) of turning the heart of an enemy to repentance by repaying his unkindness by kindness, Rom. 12 : 20 :

(*j*) of the tongue, as governed by a fiery disposition and as exercising a destructive influence over others, Jas. 3 : 6 :

(*k*) as symbolic of the danger of destruction, Jude 23.

Note : See also under FLAME.

4443 AG:730C CB:1268A 2. PURA (πυρά), from No. 1, denotes a heap of fuel collected to be set on fire (hence Eng., pyre), Acts 28 : 2, 3.¶

Note : In Mark 14 : 54, the italicised phrase " of the fire " is added in the Eng. Versions to indicate the light as coming from the fire.

B. Adjective.

4447 AG:731A CB:1268A PURINOS (πύρινος), " fiery " (akin to A, No. 1), is translated " of fire " in Rev. 9 : 17.¶ In the Sept., Ezek. 28 : 14, 16.¶

C. Verbs.

4448 AG:731A CB:1268A 1. PUROŌ (πυρόω) is translated " being on fire " (Middle Voice) in 2 Pet. 3 : 12. See FIERY.

2. PHLOGIZŌ (φλογίζω), to set on fire, burn up, is used figuratively, 5394
in both Active and Passive Voices, in Jas. 3 : 6, of the tongue, firstly, of AG:862A CB:—
its disastrous effects upon the whole round of the circumstances of life ;
secondly, of Satanic agency in using the tongue for this purpose.¶

FIRKIN

METRĒTĒS (μετρητής) is a liquid measure (akin to *metreō*, to measure), 3355
equivalent to one and a half Roman *amphoræ*, or about nine gallons, AG:514D CB:1258C
John 2 : 6.¶

FIRM

1. BEBAIOS (βέβαιος), firm, stedfast, secure (from *bainō*, to go), 949
is translated " firm " in Heb. 3 : 6, of the maintenance of the boldness AG:138B CB:1239A
of the believer's hope, and in 3 : 14, R.V., of " the beginning of our
confidence " (A.V., " stedfast "). See STEDFAST, SURE.

2. STEREOS (στερεός), solid, hard, stiff, is translated " firm " in 4731
2 Tim. 2 : 19, R.V., " the firm (foundation of God)," A.V., " (standeth) AG:766D CB:1270A
sure ; " *stereos* is not part of the predicate ; " solid (food) " in Heb. 5 : 12,
14, R.V. ; " stedfast " in 1 Pet. 5 : 9. See SOLID, STEDFAST, STRONG.¶

Note : Cp. *stereoō*, to make strong, establish, Acts 3 : 7, 16 ; 16 : 5, and *stereōma*, stedfastness, Col. 2 : 5.¶

FIRST

A. Adjective.

PRŌTOS (πρῶτος), the superlative degree of *pro*, before, is used 4413
(I) of time or place, (*a*) as a noun, e.g., Luke 14 : 18 ; Rev. 1 : 17 ; opposite AG:725B CB:1267B
to ' the last,' in the neuter plural, Matt. 12 : 45 ; Luke 11 : 26 ; 2 Pet. 2 : 20 ; in the neuter singular, opposite to ' the second,' Heb. 10 : 9 ; in 1 Cor. 15 : 3, *en prōtois*, lit., ' in the first (things, or matters) ' denotes " first of all ; " (*b*) as an adjective, e.g., Mark 16 : 9, used with " day " understood, lit., ' the first (day) of (i.e., after) the Sabbath,' in which phrase the " of " is objective, not including the Sabbath, but following it (cp. B, No. 3) ; in John 20 : 4, 8 ; Rom. 10 : 19, e.g., equivalent to an English adverb ; in John 1 : 15, lit., ' first of me,' i.e., " before me " (of superiority) ; (II) of rank or dignity, see CHIEF. Cp. B, Nos. 3 and 4.

B. Adverbs.

1. PROTERON (πρότερον), the comparative degree of *pro* (see No. 1), 4386
former, before, denotes " first " in Heb. 7 : 27 ; in 4 : 6, R.V., " before " AG:721D CB:1267B
(A.V., " first "), speaking of Israel as having heard God's good tidings previously to the ministry of the Gospel ; in Gal. 4 : 13, " I preached . . . unto you the first time " means on the former of his two previous
visits. 509

2. ANŌTHEN (ἄνωθεν), from above, is rendered " from the first " AG:77A
in Luke 1 : 3, R.V. ; it may mean ' from their beginning, or source.' CB:1236A

3. PRŌTŌS (πρώτως), firstly, is used in Acts 11 : 26, " first " (some — AG:727A
mss. have No. 4 here).¶ CB:—

4412 AG:725 (-OS) CB:1267B 4. PRŌTON (πρῶτον), the neuter of the adjective *prōtos*, is used as an adverb, signifying first, firstly, e.g., of time, Matt. 8 : 21 ; of order, Rom. 3 : 2 (A.V., " chiefly ") ; in John 7 : 51, R.V., " except it first hear from himself " (the A.V., " before it hear him," follows the mss. which have No. 1).

C. Numeral.

3391 AG:230D (HEIS) CB:1258C HEIS 1520 AG:230D CB:1249C MIA (μία), a grammatically feminine form of *heis*, one, is translated " first " in certain occurrences of the phrase " on the first day of the week," e.g., Luke 24 : 1 ; 1 Cor. 16 : 2 ; cp. A. and see DAY ; also in Tit. 3 : 10, of a first admonition to a heretical man. See ONE.

D. Noun.

746 AG:111D CB:1237B ARCHĒ (ἀρχή), a beginning, is translated " first " in Heb. 5 : 12, " of the first (principles of the oracles of God)," lit., ' (the principles) of the beginning (of the oracles of God) ; ' in 6 : 1 " the first (principles) of Christ," lit., ' (the account) of the beginning of Christ,' i.e., the elementary teaching concerning Christ. In Acts 26 : 4, where the word is preceded by *apo*, from, the A.V. has " at the first," the R.V., " from the beginning."

Notes : (1) In Jude 6 *archē* has the meaning " principality," as in the R.V. and the A.V. margin.

4295 AG:707C CB:1266C (2) In 2 Cor. 8 : 12 *prokeimai*, to be present, lit., to lie beforehand (*pro*, before, *keimai*, to lie), R.V. renders " (if the readiness) is there," for A.V., " if there be first (a willing mind)." See SET, A, No. 23.

FIRST-BEGOTTEN, FIRSTBORN

4416 AG:726C CB:1267B PRŌTOTOKOS (πρωτότοκος), firstborn (from *prōtos*, first, and *tiktō*, to beget), is used of Christ as born of the Virgin Mary, Luke 2 : 7 ; further, in His relationship to the Father, expressing His priority to, and preeminence over, creation, not in the sense of being the first to be born. It is used occasionally of superiority of position in the O.T. ; see Ex. 4 : 22 ; Deut. 21 : 16, 17, the prohibition being against the evil of assigning the privileged position of the firstborn to one born subsequently to the first child.

The five passages in the N.T. relating to Christ may be set forth chronologically thus : (*a*) Col. 1 : 15, where His eternal relationship with the Father is in view, and the clause means both that He was the Firstborn before all creation and that He Himself produced creation (the genitive case being objective, as ver. 16 makes clear) ; (*b*) Col. 1 : 18 and Rev. 1 : 5, in reference to His resurrection ; (*c*) Rom. 8 : 29, His position in relationship to the Church ; (*d*) Heb. 1 : 6, R.V., His Second Advent (the R.V. " when He again bringeth in," puts " again " in the right place, the contrast to His First Advent, at His Birth, being implied) ; cp. Psa. 89 : 27. The word is used in the plural, in Heb. 11 : 28, of the firstborn sons in the families of the Egyptians, and in 12 : 23, of the members of the Church.¶

Note : With (*a*) cp. John 1 : 30, " He was before me," lit., ' He was first (*prōtos*) of me,' i.e., 'in regard to me,' expressing all that is involved in His pre-existence and priority.

FIRSTFRUIT(S)

APARCHĒ (ἀπαρχή) denotes, primarily, an offering of firstfruits 536
(akin to *aparchomai*, to make a beginning; in sacrifices, to offer firstfruits). AG:81B CB:1236B
" Though the English word is plural in each of its occurrences save Rom. 11 : 16, the Greek word is always singular. Two Hebrew words are thus translated, one meaning the chief or principal part, e.g., Num. 18 : 12; Prov. 3 : 9; the other, the earliest ripe of the crop or of the tree, e.g., Ex. 23 : 16; Neh. 10 : 35; they are found together, e.g., in Ex. 23 : 19, " the first of the firstfruits."

" The term is applied in things spiritual, (*a*) to the presence of the Holy Spirit with the believer as the firstfruits of the full harvest of the Cross, Rom. 8 : 23; (*b*) to Christ Himself in resurrection in relation to all believers who have fallen asleep, 1 Cor. 15 : 20, 23; (*c*) to the earliest believers in a country in relation to those of their countrymen subsequently converted, Rom. 16 : 5; 1 Cor. 16 : 15; (*d*) to the believers of this age in relation to the whole of the redeemed, 2 Thess. 2 : 13 (see Note below) and Jas. 1 : 18. Cp. Rev. 14 : 4."¶*

Notes: (1) In Jas. 1 : 15 the qualifying phrase, " a kind of," may suggest a certain falling short, on the part of those mentioned, of what they might be. (2) In 2 Thess. 2 : 13, instead of *ap' archēs*, " from the beginning," there is an alternative reading, well supported, viz., *aparchēn*, ' (God chose you) as firstfruits.'

FISH

1. ICHTHUS (ἰχθύς) denotes a fish, Matt. 7 : 10; Mark 6 : 38, etc.; 2486 AG:384B
apart from the Gospels, only in 1 Cor. 15 : 39. CB:1252C

2. ICHTHUDION (ἰχθύδιον) is a diminutive of No. 1, a little fish, 2485 AG:384B
Matt. 15 : 34; Mark 8 : 7.¶ CB:1252C

3. OPSARION (ὀψάριον) is a diminutive of *opson*, cooked meat, or a 3795
relish, a dainty dish, especially of fish; it denotes a little fish, John 6 : 9, AG:601B CB:1261A
11; 21 : 9, 10, 13.¶

FISH (Verb), FISHER, FISHERMAN

A. Noun.

HALIEUS (ἁλιεύς), a fisherman, fisher (from *hals*, the sea), occurs 231 AG:37C
in Matt. 4 : 18, 19; Mark 1 : 16, 17; Luke 5 : 2.¶ CB:—

B. Verb.

HALIEUŌ (ἁλιεύω), to fish (akin to A.), occurs in John 21 : 3.¶ In 232 AG:37D
the Sept., Jer. 16 : 16.¶ CB:—

---

* From Notes on Thessalonians by Hogg and Vine, p. 271.

FIT (Adjective and Verb), FITLY, FITTING

A. Adjectives.

2111 1. EUTHETOS (εὔθετος), ready for use, fit, well adapted, lit., well
AG:320B CB:— placed (*eu*, well, *tithēmi*, to place), is used (*a*) of persons, Luke 9 : 62,
negatively, of one who is not fit for the Kingdom of God; (*b*) of things,
Luke 14 : 35, of salt that has lost its savour; rendered "meet" in
Heb. 6 : 7, of herbs. See MEET.¶

701 2. ARESTOS (ἀρεστός), pleasing (akin to *areskō*, to please), is translated
AG:105D CB:1237C "(it is not) fit," R.V. (A.V., "reason"), in Acts 6 : 2. See PLEASE,
REASON.

B. Verbs.

433 1. ANĒKŌ (ἀνήκω), properly, to have come up to (*ana*, up, and
AG:66B CB:— *hēkō*, to arrive), is translated "is fitting," in Col. 3 : 18, R.V. See
BEFITTING.

2520 2. KATHĒKŌ (καθήκω), to come or reach down to (*kata*, down),
AG:389A CB:1254C hence, to befit, be proper, is translated "is (not fit)," in Acts 22 : 22;
in Rom. 1 : 28, R.V., "fitting" (A.V., "convenient"). See CONVENIENT.¶

2675 3. KATARTIZŌ (καταρτίζω), to make fit, to equip, prepare (*kata*,
AG:417D CB:1254B down, *artos*, a joint), is rendered "fitted" in Rom. 9 : 22, of vessels of
wrath; here the Middle Voice signifies that those referred to fitted themselves for destruction (as illustrated in the case of Pharaoh, the self-hardening of whose heart is accurately presented in the R.V. in the first part of the series of incidents in the Exodus narrative, which records Pharaoh's doings; only after repeated and persistent obstinacy on his part is it recorded that God hardened his heart.) See FRAME, JOIN, PERFECT, PREPARE, RESTORE.

4883 4. SUNARMOLOGEŌ (συναρμολογέω), to fit or frame together
AG:785B CB:— (*sun*, with, *harmos*, a joint, in building, and *legō*, to choose), is used
FIST metaphorically of the various parts of the Church as a building, Eph. 2 : 21,
See PALM "fitly framed together;" also of the members of the Church as the Body
FIX See LOOK of Christ, 4 : 16, R.V., "fitly framed . . . together."¶

PENTE 4002

FIVE, FIVE TIMES

AG:643A CB:1263A PENTE (πέντε) is derived by some from words suggesting the fingers
PENTAKIS 3999 of a hand, or a fist. The word is frequent in the Gospels. *Pentakis*,
AG:643A five times, is found in 2 Cor. 11 : 24;¶ *pentakosioi*, five hundred, in
PENTAKOSIOI Luke 7 : 41; 1 Cor. 15 : 6;¶ *pentakischilioi*, five thousand (*chilios*,
4001 AG:643A a thousand), in Matt. 14 : 21; 16 : 9 and corresponding passages. See
PENTAKISCHILIOI FIFTEENTH, FIFTH, FIFTY.

4000 AG:643A CB:1263A

FIX

4741 STĒRIZŌ (στηρίζω), to set forth, make fast, fix, is translated "fixed"
AG:768A in Luke 16 : 26, of the great gulf separating Hades or Sheol from the
CB:1270A region called "Abraham's bosom." See ESTABLISH.

FLAME, FLAMING

PHLOX (φλόξ), akin to Lat. *fulgeō*, to shine, is used apart from *pur*, 5395
fire, in Luke 16 : 24 ; with *pur*, it signifies a fiery flame, lit., a flame of AG:862A CB:—
fire, Acts 7 : 30 ; 2 Thess. 1 : 8, where the fire is to be understood as the instrument of Divine judgment ; Heb. 1 : 7, where the meaning probably is that God makes His angels as active and powerful as a flame of fire ; in Rev. 1 : 14 ; 2 : 18 ; 19 : 12, of the eyes of the Lord Jesus as emblematic of penetrating judgment, searching out evil.¶

FLASH See **MOMENT, SHINE**

FLATTERY (-ING)

KOLAKIA (or -EIA) (κολακία), akin to *kolakeuō*, to flatter, is used in 2850
1 Thess. 2 : 5 of "words of flattery" (R.V.), adopted as "a cloke of AG:440D CB:—
covetousness," i.e., words which flattery uses, not simply as an effort to give pleasure, but with motives of self-interest.¶

FLAX

LINON (λίνον) primarily denotes flax (Eng., linen) ; then, that which 3043
is made of it, a wick of a lamp, Matt. 12 : 20 ; several ancient mss. have AG:475B CB:—
the word in Rev. 15 : 6 (A.V. only, "linen"). See LINEN.¶

FLEE, FLED

1. PHEUGŌ (φεύγω), to flee from or away (Lat., *fugio ;* Eng., fugitive, 5343
etc.), besides its literal significance, is used metaphorically, (*a*) transitively, AG:855D CB:1264A
of fleeing fornication, 1 Cor. 6 : 18 ; idolatry, 10 : 14 ; evil doctrine, questionings, disputes of words, envy, strife, railings, evil surmisings, wranglings, and the love of money, 1 Tim. 6 : 11 ; youthful lusts, 2 Tim. 2 : 22 ; (*b*) intransitively, of the flight of physical matter, Rev. 16 : 20 ; 20 : 11 ; of death, 9 : 6. See ESCAPE.

2. EKPHEUGŌ (ἐκφεύγω), to flee away, escape (*ek*, from, and No. 1), 1628
is translated "fled" in Acts 16 : 27 (A.V. only) ; 19 : 16. In Heb. 12 : 25 AG:246D CB:1243C
the best mss. have this verb instead of No. 1. See ESCAPE.

3. KATAPHEUGŌ (καταφεύγω), to flee for refuge (*kata*, used intensively, and No. 1), is used (*a*) literally in Acts 14 : 6 ; (*b*) metaphorically in Heb. 6 : 18, of fleeing for refuge to lay hold upon hope.¶ 2703 AG:420A CB:1254B

Note : For *apopheugō* and *diapheugō*, see ESCAPE.

FLESH

1. SARX (σάρξ) has a wider range of meaning in the N.T. than in 4561
the O.T. Its uses in the N.T. may be analysed as follows : AG:743B CB:1268C

"(*a*) the substance of the body, whether of beasts or of men, 1 Cor. 15 : 39 ; (*b*) the human body, 2 Cor. 10 : 3a ; Gal. 2 : 20 ; Phil. 1 : 22 ; (*c*) by synecdoche, of mankind, in the totality of all that is essential to manhood, i.e., spirit, soul, and body, Matt. 24 : 22 ; John 1 : 13 ; Rom. 3 : 20 ; (*d*) by synecdoche, of the holy humanity of the Lord Jesus, in the totality of all that is essential to manhood, i.e., spirit, soul, and body, John 1 : 14 ; 1 Tim. 3 : 16 ; 1 John 4 : 2 ; 2 John 7 ; in Heb. 5 : 7, ' the days of His flesh,' i.e., His past life on earth in distinction from His present life in resurrection ; (*e*) by synecdoche, for the complete person, John 6 : 51-57 ; 2 Cor. 7 : 5 ; Jas. 5 : 3 ; (*f*) the weaker element in human nature, Matt. 26 : 41 ; Rom. 6 : 19 ; 8 : 3a ; (*g*) the unregenerate state of men, Rom. 7 : 5 ; 8 : 8, 9 ; (*h*) the seat of sin in man (but this is not the same thing as in the body), 2 Pet. 2 : 18 ; 1 John 2 : 16 ; (*i*) the lower and temporary element in the Christian, Gal. 3 : 3 ; 6 : 8, and in religious ordinances, Heb. 9 : 10 ; (*j*) the natural attainments of men, 1 Cor. 1 : 26 ; 2 Cor. 10 : 2, 3b ; (*k*) circumstances, 1 Cor. 7 : 28 ; the externals of life, 2 Cor. 7 : 1 ; Eph. 6 : 5 ; Heb. 9 : 13 ; (*l*) by metonymy, the outward and seeming, as contrasted with the spirit, the inward and real, John 6 : 63 ; 2 Cor. 5 : 16 ; (*m*) natural relationship, consanguine, 1 Cor. 10 : 18 ; Gal. 4 : 23, or marital, Matt. 19 : 5."*

In Matt. 26 : 41 ; Rom. 8 : 4, 13 ; 1 Cor. 5 : 5 ; Gal. 6 : 8 (not the Holy Spirit, here), flesh is contrasted with spirit ; in Rom. 2 : 28, 29, with heart and spirit ; in Rom. 7 : 25, with the mind ; cp. Col. 2 : 1, 5. It is coupled with the mind in Eph. 2 : 3, and with the spirit in 2 Cor. 7 : 1.

Note : In Col. 2 : 18 the noun *sarx* is used in the phrase " (by his) fleshly mind," lit., ' by the mind of his flesh' [see (*h*) above], whereas the mind ought to be dominated by the Spirit.

2907 AG:449C CB:1256A 2. KREAS (κρέας) denotes flesh in the sense of meat. It is used in the plural in Rom. 14 : 21 ; 1 Cor. 8 : 13.¶

FLESHLY, FLESHY

4559 AG:742D CB:1268B 1. SARKIKOS (σαρκικός), akin to No. 1, under FLESH, signifies (*a*) associated with or pertaining to, the flesh, carnal, Rom. 15 : 27 ; 1 Cor. 9 : 11 ; (*b*) of the nature of the flesh, sensual, translated " fleshly " in 2 Cor. 1 : 12, of wisdom ; in 1 Pet. 2 : 11, of lusts ; in 2 Cor. 10 : 4, negatively, of the weapons of the Christian's warfare, R.V., " of the flesh " (A.V., " carnal "). See CARNAL.

4560 AG:743A CB:1268C 2. SARKINOS (σάρκινος) denotes ' of the flesh,' fleshly (the termination —*inos* signifying the substance or material of a thing) ; in 2 Cor. 3 : 3, R.V., " (tables that are hearts) of flesh," A.V., " fleshy (tables)," etc. See CARNAL.

Note : The adjectives " fleshly," " carnal " are contrasted with spiritual qualities in Rom. 7 : 14 ; 1 Cor. 3 : 1, 3, 4 ; 2 Cor. 1 : 12 ; Col. 2 : 18 (lit., ' mind of flesh '). Speaking broadly, the carnal denotes the sinful element in man's nature, by reason of descent from Adam ; the spiritual is that which comes by the regenerating operation of the Holy Spirit.

---

* **From Notes on Galatians by Hogg and Vine, pp. 111, 112.**

FLIGHT

A. Noun.

PHUGĒ (φυγή), akin to *pheugō* (see FLEE), is found in Matt. 24 : 20. 5437
Some inferior mss. have it in Mark 13 : 18.¶ AG:867C CB:1264C

B. Verb.

KLINŌ (κλίνω), to make to bend, is translated " turned to flight " in 2827
Heb. 11 : 34. See Bow. AG:436C CB:—

FLOCK

1. POIMNĒ (ποίμνη), akin to *poimēn*, a shepherd, denotes a flock 4167
(properly, of sheep), Matt. 26 : 31; Luke 2 : 8; 1 Cor. 9 : 7; meta- AG:684C CB:1265C
phorically, of Christ's followers, John 10 : 16, R.V., for the erroneous A.V., " fold." What characterizes Christ's sheep is listening to His voice, and the flock must be one as He is one.¶

2. POIMNION (ποίμνιον), possibly a diminutive of No. 1, is used 4168
in the N.T. only metaphorically, of a group of Christ's disciples, Luke AG:684C CB:1265C
12 : 32; of local churches cared for by elders, Acts 20 : 28, 29; 1 Pet. 5 : 2, 3.¶

FLOG See SCOURGE

FLOOD

A. Nouns.

1. KATAKLUSMOS (κατακλυσμός), a deluge (Eng., cataclysm), 2627
akin to *katakluzō*, to inundate, 2 Pet. 3 : 6, is used of the flood in Noah's AG:411D CB:1254A
time, Matt. 24 : 38, 39; Luke 17 : 27; 2 Pet. 2 : 5.¶

2. PLĒMMURA (πλήμμυρα), akin to *plēthō* and *pimplēmi*, to fill, a 4132
flood of sea or river, the latter in Luke 6 : 48.¶ In the Sept., Job 40 : 18 AG:669B CB:—
(ver. 23 in the E.V.).¶

3. POTAMOS (ποταμός), a river, stream, torrent, is translated " flood " 4215
in Matt. 7 : 25, 27; in Rev. 12 : 15, 16, A.V., " flood," R.V., " river." AG:694D CB:1266B
See RIVER, WATER.

B. Adjective.

POTAMOPHORĒTOS (ποταμοφόρητος) signifies carried away by a 4216
stream or river (A, No. 3, and *pherō*, to carry), Rev. 12 : 15, R.V., AG:694D CB:1266A
" carried away by the stream " (A.V., " of the flood ").¶

For FLOOR see THRESHING-FLOOR

FLOUR

SEMIDALIS (σεμίδαλις) denotes the finest wheaten flour, Rev. 18 : 13.¶ 4585 AG:746D CB:—

For FLOURISH in Phil. 4 : 10, see REVIVE

FLOW

RHEŌ (ῥέω), to flow, is used figuratively in John 7 : 38 of the Holy 4482 AG:735A
Spirit, acting in and through the believer.¶ CB:1268A

FLOWER

A. Noun.

438 AG:67C CB:1236A ANTHOS (ἄνθος), a blossom, flower (used in certain names of flowers), occurs in Jas. 1 : 10, 11 ; 1 Pet. 1 : 24 (twice).¶

B. Adjective.

5230 AG:839D CB:1252A HUPERAKMOS (ὑπέρακμος), past the bloom of youth (from *huper*, beyond, and *akmē*, the highest point of anything, the full bloom of a flower : Eng., acme), is used in 1 Cor. 7 : 36, " past the flower of her age ; " Lightfoot prefers the rendering " of full age."

For FLUX see DYSENTERY

FLUTE-PLAYERS

834 AG:121B CB:— AULĒTĒS (αὐλητής), a flute-player (from *auleō*, to play the flute), occurs in Matt. 9 : 23 (A.V., " minstrel "), and Rev. 18 : 22 (A.V., " pipers "). In the papyri writings of the time the word is chiefly associated with religious matters (Moulton and Milligan, Vocab.). Cp. MINSTREL.¶

FLY

4072 AG:654A CB:— PETOMAI (πέτομαι), to fly (the root of which is seen in *pteron* and *pterux*, a wing, *ptilon*, a feather, etc.), is confined to the Apocalypse, 4 : 7 ; 8 : 13 ; 12 : 14 ; 14 : 6 ; 19 : 17. Some mss. have the verb *petaomai*, a frequentative form.¶

FOAL

5207 AG:833C CB:1251C HUIOS (υἱός), a son, primarily signifying the relation of offspring to parent, is used of the foal of an ass in Matt. 21 : 5. See SON.

FOAM

A. Verbs.

875 AG:127C CB:— 1. APHRIZŌ (ἀφρίζω) denotes to foam at the mouth (akin to *aphros*, foam ; see B.), Mark 9 : 18, 20.¶

1890 AG:283D CB:— 2. EPAPHRIZŌ (ἐπαφρίζω), to foam out, or up (*epi*, up, and No. 1), is used metaphorically in Jude 13, of the impious libertines, who had crept in among the saints, and foamed out their own shame with swelling words. The metaphor is drawn from the refuse borne on the crest of waves and cast up on the beach.¶

B. Noun.

876 AG:127D CB:— APHROS (ἀφρός), foam, occurs in Luke 9 : 39, where it is used with the preposition *meta*, with, lit., ' (teareth him) with (accompanied by) foam.'¶

2190 AG:331B CB:1242C

FOE

ECHTHROS (ἐχθρός), an adjective signifying hated, hateful, or hostile, is used also as a noun denoting an enemy, translated " foes " in Matt. 10 : 36 and the A.V. of Acts 2 : 35. See ENEMY.

FOLD

AULĒ (αὐλή) first signifies an open courtyard before a house; then, an enclosure in the open, a sheepfold, John 10 : 1, 16. In the papyri " the word is extremely common, denoting the court attached to a house " (Moulton and Milligan, Vocab.). The sheepfold was usually surrounded by a stone wall, Numb. 32 : 16, preferably near a well, Ex. 2 : 16; Psa. 23 : 2, and often protected by a tower, 2 Chron. 26 : 10; Mic. 4 : 8. See COURT, HALL, PALACE. **833 AG:121B CB:1238B**

Note: For the erroneous A.V. rendering, " fold," of *poimnē*, a flock, in John 10 : 16, see FLOCK. **4167 AG:684C CB:1265C**

For FOLD UP see ROLL, A, No. 4

For FOLK see IMPOTENT, B, SICK, B, No. 2

FOLLOW, FOLLOW AFTER

1. AKOLOUTHEŌ (ἀκολουθέω), to be an *akolouthos*, a follower, or companion (from the prefix *a*, here expressing union, likeness, and *keleuthos*, a way; hence, one going in the same way), is used (*a*) frequently in the literal sense, e.g., Matt. 4 : 25; (*b*) metaphorically, of discipleship, e.g., Mark 8 : 34; 9 : 38; 10 : 21. It is used 77 times in the Gospels, of following Christ, and only once otherwise, Mark 14 : 13. **190 AG:31A CB:1234B**

2. EXAKOLOUTHEŌ (ἐξακολουθέω), to follow up, or out to the end (*ek*, out, used intensively, and No. 1), is used metaphorically, and only by the Apostle Peter in his Second Epistle: in 1 : 16, of cunningly devised fables; 2 : 2, of lascivious doings; 2 : 15, of the way of Balaam.¶ In the Sept., Job 31 : 9; Is. 56 : 11; Jer. 2 : 2; Amos 2 : 4.¶ **1811 AG:272B CB:1247B**

3. EPAKOLOUTHEŌ (ἐπακολουθέω), to follow after, close upon (*epi*, upon, and No. 1), is used of signs following the preaching of the Gospel. Mark 16 : 20; of following good works, 1 Tim 5 : 10; of sins following after those who are guilty of them, 5 : 24; of following the steps of Christ, 1 Pet. 2 : 21.¶ **1872 AG:282B CB:1245B**

4. KATAKOLOUTHEŌ (κατακολουθέω), to follow behind or intently after (*kata*, after, used intensively, and No. 1), is used of the women on their way to Christ's tomb, Luke 23 : 55; of the demon-possessed maid in Philippi in following the missionaries, Acts 16 : 17.¶ **2628 AG:412A CB:—**

5. PARAKOLOUTHEŌ (παρακολουθέω) lit. signifying to follow close up, or side by side, hence, to accompany, to conform to (*para*, beside, and No. 1), is used of signs accompanying " them that believe," Mark 16 : 17; of tracing the course of facts, Luke 1 : 3, R.V.; of following the good doctrine, 1 Tim. 4 : 6, R.V. (A.V., " attained "); similarly of **3877 AG:618D CB:1262A**

following teaching so as to practise it, 2 Tim. 3 : 10, R.V., " didst follow " (A.V., " hast fully known "). See ATTAIN, KNOW, TRACE, UNDERSTAND.¶

4870 AG:783D 6. SUNAKOLOUTHEŌ (συνακολουθέω), to follow along with, to
CB:1270B accompany a leader (*sun*, with, and No. 1), is given its true rendering in the R.V. of Mark 5 : 37, " He suffered no man to follow with Him ; " in 14 : 51, of the young man who " followed with " Christ (inferior mss. have No. 1 here) ; Luke 23 : 49, of the women who " followed with " Christ from Galilee.¶

1377 7. DIŌKŌ (διώκω) denotes (*a*) to drive away, Matt. 23 : 34 ; (*b*) to
AG:201B CB:1242A pursue without hostility, to follow, follow after, said of righteousness, Rom. 9 : 30 ; the Law, 9 : 31 ; 12 : 13, hospitality (" given to ") lit., ' pursuing ' (as one would a calling) ; the things which make for peace, 14 : 19 ; love, 1 Cor. 14 : 1 ; that which is good, 1 Thess. 5 : 15 ; righteousness, godliness, faith, love, patience, meekness, 1 Tim. 6 : 11 ; righteousness, faith, love, peace, 2 Tim. 2 : 22 ; peace and sanctification, Heb. 12 : 14 ; peace, 1 Pet. 3 : 11 ; (*c*) to follow on (used intransitively), Phil. 3 : 12, 14, R.V., " I press on ; " ' follow after,' is an inadequate meaning. See
2614 AG:410C GIVE, PERSECUTE, PRESS, PURSUE.

CB:1254A 8. KATADIŌKŌ (καταδιώκω), to follow up or closely, with the
GINOMAI 1096 determination to find (*kata*, down, intensive, giving the idea of a hard,
AG:158A persistent search, and No. 7), Mark 1 : 36, " followed after (Him)," is said
CB:1248B EPEIMI of the disciples in going to find the Lord who had gone into a desert place
1966 to pray.¶ The verb is found, e.g., in 1 Sam. 30 : 22 ; Psa. 23 : 6, and
(EPIOUSA) with hostile intent in Gen. 31 : 36.

AG:284C CB:1245C 9. GINOMAI (γίνομαι), to become, to come into existence, is used in
ECHō 2192 Rev. 8 : 17 ; 11 : 15, 19, in the sense of taking place after, translated
AG:331D " there followed." See BECOME.

CB:1242C EPAURION 10. EPEIMI (ἔπειμι), to come upon, or, of time, to come on or after
1887 (*epi*, upon, and *eimi*, to go), is used in the present participle as an adjective,
AG:283D in reference to a day, in Acts 7 : 26 ; 16 : 11 ; 20 : 15 ; 21 : 18 ; a night,
CB:— HEXēS 23 : 11, R.V., " following," in each place (A.V., " next ").¶

1836 AG:276A *Notes :* (1) In Luke 13 : 33, the present participle, Middle Voice, of
CB:— the verb *echō*, to have, to be next, is used with the article, the word
MIMEOMAI 3401 *hēmera*, a day, being understood, signifying " the day following." (2) In
AG:521D John 1 : 43 and 6 : 22 the adverb *epaurion* with the article, " on the
CB:1259A MIMēTēS morrow," is translated " the day following " in the A.V. See MORROW.
3402 (3) In Acts 21 : 1 the adverb *hexēs*, in order, next, is translated " the
AG:522A CB:1259A day following " (A.V.). (4) *Mimeomai*, to imitate, be an imitator, is so
SUMMIMēTēS translated always in the R.V., where the A.V. uses the verb to follow ;
4831 AG:778C it is always used in a good sense, 2 Thess. 3 : 7, 9 ; Heb. 13 : 7 ; 3 John 11.
CB:1270B So with the nouns *mimētēs*, an imitator, and *summimētēs*, an imitator
DEUTE together. See IMITATE, IMITATOR. (5) In Matt. 4 : 19, *deute*, come
1205 AG:176D hither, with *opisō*, after, is translated " come ye after," R.V. (A.V.,
CB:1241A " follow "). (6) In Matt. 27 : 62, R.V., the phrase *eimi meta*, to be after,

is translated " (which) is (the day) after " (A.V., " that followed "). (7) In 1 Pet. 1 : 11, the phrase *meta tauta*, lit., ' after these things,' is translated " that should follow," said of glories after the sufferings of Christ. (8) In Luke 22 : 49, the phrase *to esomenon*, lit. ' the (thing) about to be ' (from *eimi*, to be), is translated " what would follow." (9) In Acts 3 : 24,
the adverb *kathexēs*, successively, in order, is translated " (them) that **2517**
followed after," i.e., those who succeeded (him), lit., ' the (ones) success- **AG:388D**
ively (to him).' Cp. Note (3) above. See AFTERWARD. **CB:—**

FOLLY

ANOIA (ἄνοια) lit. signifies ' without understanding ' (*a*, negative, **454**
nous, mind) ; hence, folly, or, rather, senselessness, 2 Tim. 3 : 9 ; in Luke **AG:70D**
6 : 11 it denotes violent or mad rage, " madness." See MADNESS.¶ **CB:1235C**
Cp. *anoētos*, foolish.

Note : For *aphrosunē*, rendered " folly " in 2 Cor. 11 : 1, A.V., see **877**
FOOLISHNESS (R.V.). **AG:127D**
CB:1236C

FOOD

1. TROPHĒ (τροφή) denotes nourishment, food (akin to *trephō*, to **5160**
rear, nourish, feed) ; it is used literally, in the Gospels, Acts and Jas. **AG:87D**
2 : 15 ; metaphorically, in Heb. 5 : 12, 14, R.V., " (solid) food," A.V., **CB:—**
" (strong) meat," i.e., deeper subjects of the faith than that of elementary instruction. The word is always rendered " food " in the R.V., where the A.V. has " meat ; " e.g., Matt. 3 : 4 ; 6 : 25 ; 10 : 10 ; 24 : 45 ; Luke 12 : 23 ; John 4 : 8 ; Acts 2 : 46, " did take their food," R.V. (A.V., " did eat their meat ") ; 9 : 19, " took food ; " 27 : 33, 34, 36. The A.V. also has " food " in Acts 14 : 17 and Jas. 2 : 15.¶

2. DIATROPHĒ (διατροφή), sustenance, food, a strengthened form of **1305** **AG:190A**
No. 1 (*dia*, through, suggesting a sufficient supply), is used in 1 Tim. 6 : 8.¶ **CB:—**

3. BRŌSIS (βρῶσις), eating, the act of eating (akin to *bibrōskō*, to **1035**
eat) is translated " food " in 2 Cor. 9 : 10. See EATING, MEAT, RUST. **AG:148B** **CB:1239B**

4. SITOMETRION (σιτομέτριον), a measured " portion of food "(*sitos*, **4620**
corn, *metreō*, to measure), is used in Luke 12 : 42, R.V.¶ **AG:752A** **CB:—**

5. BRŌMA (βρῶμα), akin to No. 3, frequently translated " meat," **1033**
and always so in the A.V. except in Matt. 14 : 15, " victuals," is rendered **AG:148A**
" food " in the R.V. in Matt. 14 : 15 ; Luke 3 : 11 ; 9 : 13. **CB:1239B**

Note : For *asitia*, without food, see ABSTINENCE. **776**
AG:116B
CB:—

FOOL, FOOLISH, FOOLISHLY, FOOLISHNESS

A. Adjectives.

1. APHRŌN (ἄφρων) signifies ' without reason ' (*a*, negative, *phrēn*, **878**
the mind), " want of mental sanity and sobriety, a reckless and incon- **AG:127D**
siderate habit of mind " (Hort), or " the lack of commonsense perception **CB:1236C**
of the reality of things natural and spiritual . . . or the imprudent ordering of one's life in regard to salvation " (G. Vos, in Hastings' Bible

Dic.); it is mostly translated "foolish" or "foolish ones" in the R.V.; Luke 11 : 40; 12 : 20; Rom. 2 : 20; 1 Cor. 15 : 36; 2 Cor. 11 : 16 (twice), 19 (contrasted with *phronimos*, prudent); 12 : 6, 11; Eph. 5 : 17; 1 Pet. 2 : 15.¶

453 2. ANOĒTOS (ἀνόητος) signifies not understanding (*a*, negative,
AG:70D *noeō*, to perceive, understand), not applying *nous*, the mind, Luke 24 : 25;
CB:— in Rom. 1 : 14 and Gal. 3 : 1, 3 it signifies senseless, an unworthy lack of understanding; sometimes it carries a moral reproach (in contrast with *sōphrōn*, sober-minded, self-controlled) and describes one who does not govern his lusts, Tit. 3 : 3; in 1 Tim. 6 : 9 it is associated with evil desires, lusts. See UNWISE.¶

3474 3. MŌROS (μωρός) primarily denotes dull, sluggish (from a root
AG:531C *muh*, to be silly); hence, stupid, foolish; it is used (*a*) of persons,
CB:1259B Matt. 5 : 22, "Thou fool;" here the word means morally worthless, a scoundrel, a more serious reproach than "Raca;" the latter scorns a man's mind and calls him stupid; *mōros* scorns his heart and character; hence the Lord's more severe condemnation; in 7 : 26, "a foolish man;" 23 : 17, 19, "fools;" 25 : 2, 3, 8, "foolish;" in 1 Cor. 3 : 18, "a fool;" the Apostle Paul uses it of himself and his fellow-workers, in 4 : 10, "fools" (i.e., in the eyes of opponents); (*b*) of things, 2 Tim. 2 : 23, "foolish and ignorant questionings;" so Tit. 3 : 9; in 1 Cor. 1 : 25, "the foolishness of God," not *mōria*, foolishness as a personal quality (see C, No. 1), but adjectivally, that which is considered by the ignorant as a foolish policy or mode of dealing, lit., 'the foolish (thing);' so in ver. 27, "the foolish (things) of the world."¶

801 4. ASUNETOS (ἀσύνετος) denotes without discernment, or under-
AG:118C standing (*a*, negative, *suniēmi*, to understand); hence "senseless,"
CB:1238A as in the R.V. of Rom. 1 : 21 (A.V., "foolish"), of the heart; in 10 : 19, A.V., "foolish," R.V., "void of understanding." See UNDERSTANDING.

Note: For "fools," Eph. 5 : 15, see UNWISE, No. 3.

B. Verbs.

3471 1. MŌRAINŌ (μωραίνω) is used (*a*) in the causal sense, to make
AG:531B
CB:1259B foolish, 1 Cor. 1 : 20; (*b*) in the passive sense, to become foolish, Rom. 1 : 22; in Matt. 5 : 13 and Luke 14 : 34 it is said of salt that has lost its flavour, becoming tasteless. See SAVOUR.¶

3912 2. PARAPHRONEŌ (παραφρονέω), to be beside oneself (from *para*,
AG:623C
CB:— contrary to, and *phrēn*, the mind), to be deranged, 2 Cor. 11 : 23, R.V., "as one beside himself," for A.V., "as a fool."¶

3472 **C. Nouns.**

AG:531B
CB:1259B 1. MŌRIA (μωρία) denotes foolishness (akin to A, No. 3 and B, No. 1),
877 and is used in 1 Cor. 1 : 18, 21, 23; 2 : 14; 3 : 19.¶

AG:127D 2. APHROSUNĒ (ἀφροσύνη), senselessness, is translated "foolishness"
CB:1236C
3473 in Mark 7 : 22; 2 Cor. 11 : 1, 17, 21, "foolishness," R.V. (A.V., "folly"
AG:531B and "foolishly"). See FOLLY.¶

CB:1259B *Note:* *Mōrologia* denotes foolish talking, Eph. 5 : 4. See TALKING.¶

FOOT, FEET

A. Nouns.

1. POUS (πούς), besides its literal meaning, is used, by metonymy, 4228
of a person in motion, Luke 1 : 79 ; Acts 5 : 9 ; Rom. 3 : 15 ; 10 : 15 ; AG:696C CB:1266B
Heb. 12 : 13. It is used in phrases expressing subjection, 1 Cor. 15 : 27, R.V. ; of the humility and receptivity of discipleship, Luke 10 : 39 ; Acts 22 : 3 ; of obeisance and worship, e.g., Matt. 28 : 9 ; of scornful rejection, Matt. 10 : 14 ; Acts 13 : 51. Washing the feet of another betokened the humility of the service and the comfort of the guest, and was a feature of hospitality, Luke 7 : 38 ; John 13 : 5 ; 1 Tim. 5 : 10 (here figuratively).

Note : In Acts 7 : 5 *bēma*, a step, is used with *podos*, the genitive case of *pous*, lit., ' the step of a foot,' i.e., a foot breadth, what the foot can stand on, " (not so much as) to set his foot on."

2. BASIS (βάσις), lit., a step (*akin* to *bainō*, to go), hence denotes 939
that with which one steps, a foot, and is used in the plural in Acts 3 : 7.¶ AG:137A CB:1238C

B. Adjectives.

1. PODĒRĒS (ποδήρης) signifies reaching to the feet, from *pous*, and 4158
arō, to fit (akin to A, No. 1), and is said of a garment, Rev. 1 : 13.¶ In AG:680B CB:—
the Sept. it is used of the high priest's garment, e.g., Ex. 28 : 4.

2. PEZOS (πεζός), an adjective, " on foot," is used in one of its forms 3979 (PEZē)
as an adverb in Matt. 14 : 13, and Mark 6 : 33, in each place signifying AG:638D CB:—
' by land,' in contrast to ' by sea.'¶

Cp. *pezeuō*, to go on foot, Acts 20 : 13, R.V., " to go by land " (marg., 3978
" on foot "). AG:638D CB:—

Notes : (1) In Acts 20 : 18, the R.V. " set foot in " expresses more EPIBAINō
literally the verb *epibainō* (lit., to go upon) than the A.V. " came into." 1910 AG:289D
So again in 21 : 4 (some mss. have *anabainō* here). (2) In Luke 8 : 5, CB:—
katapateō, to tread down (*kata*, down, *pateō*, to tread, trample), is trans- KATAPATEō 2662
lated " was trodden under foot," R.V. (A.V., " was trodden down "). AG:415D CB:1254A

FOOTSTOOL

HUPOPODION (ὑποπόδιον), from *hupo*, under, and *pous*, a foot, is 5286
used (*a*) literally in Jas. 2 : 3, (*b*) metaphorically, of the earth as God's AG:846D CB:—
footstool, Matt. 5 : 35 ; of the foes of the Lord, Matt. 22 : 44 (in some mss.) ; Mark 12 : 36, " underneath " (in some mss.) ; Luke 20 : 43 ; Acts 2 : 35 ; 7 : 49 ; Heb. 1 : 13 ; 10 : 13. The R.V., adhering to the literal rendering, translates the phrase " the footstool of My (Thy, His) feet," for the A.V., " My (etc.) footstool," but in Matt. 22 : 44, " (till I put Thine enemies) underneath thy feet."¶

FOR and FORASMUCH : see Note †, p. 1

For FORBADE see FORBID

FORBEAR, FORBEARANCE

A. Verbs.

430 1. ANECHŌ (ἀνέχω), to hold up (*ana*, up, *echō*, to have or hold), is
AG:65D CB:1235B used in the Middle Voice in the N.T., signifying to bear with, endure; it is rendered "forbearing (one another)" in Eph. 4:2 and Col. 3:13. See BEAR. Cp. B, No. 1, below.

447 2. ANIĒMI (ἀνίημι), lit., to send up or back (*ana*, up, *hiēmi*, to send),
AG:69D CB:— hence, to relax, loosen, or, metaphorically, to desist from, is translated "forbearing" (threatening) in Eph. 6:9 ('giving up your threatening,' T. K. Abbott). SEE LEAVE, LOOSE.

5339 AG:854D 3. PHEIDOMAI (φείδομαι), to spare (its usual meaning), to refrain
CB:— from doing something, is rendered "I forbear" in 2 Cor. 12:6. See SPARE.

4722 AG:765D 4. STEGŌ (στέγω) properly denotes to protect by covering; then,
CB:1270A to conceal; then, by covering, to bear up under; it is translated "forbear" in 1 Thess. 3:1, 5. See BEAR.

2038 AG:306D *Note:* In 1 Cor. 9:6, the verb *ergazomai*, to work, is used in the
CB:1246C present infinitive, with a negative, and translated "to forbear working" (lit., 'not working').

B. Noun.

463 AG:72C ANOCHĒ (ἀνοχή), a holding back (akin to A, No. 1), denotes for-
CB:— bearance, a delay of punishment, Rom. 2:4; 3:25, in both places of God's forbearance with men; in the latter passage His forbearance is the ground, not of His forgiveness, but of His prætermission of sins, His withholding punishment. In 2:4 it represents a suspense of wrath which must eventually be exercised unless the sinner accepts God's conditions; in 3:25 it is connected with the passing over of sins in times past, previous to the atoning work of Christ.¶

Note: Cp. the noun *epieikeia*, Acts 24:4, "clemency;" 2 Cor. 10:1,
MAKROTHUMIA 3115 "gentleness." Synonymous with this are ***makrothumia***, longsuffering,
AG:488B and ***hupomonē***, patience (see Col. 1:11). *Anochē* and ***makrothumia*** are
CB:1257C used together in Rom 2:4. See also Eph. 4:2 (where A, No. 1, is used in this combination). Trench (Syn.) and Abbott-Smith (Lex.) state that
HUPOMONĒ 5281 *hupomonē* expresses patience with regard to adverse things, ***makrothumia***
AG:846B patience with regard to antagonistic persons. It must be observed,
CB:1252B however, that in Heb. 6:15 the verb ***makrothumeō*** is used of Abraham's patience under the pressure of trying circumstances (cp. also Jas. 5:7, 8). *Makrothumia* and *hupomonē* are often found together, e.g., 2 Cor. 6:4 and 6; 2 Tim. 3:10.

"Longsuffering is that quality of self-restraint in the face of provocation which does not hastily retaliate or promptly punish; it is the opposite of anger and is associated with mercy, and is used of God, Ex. 34:6, Sept.; Rom. 2:4; 1 Pet. 3:20. Patience is the quality that does not surrender to circumstances or succumb under trial; it is the opposite of despondency and is associated with hope, in 1 Thess. 1 : 3 ; it is not used of God."*

C. Adjectives.

1. ANEXIKAKOS (ἀνεξίκακος) denotes patiently forbearing evil, 420
lit., 'patient of wrong,' (from *anechō*, A, No. 1 and *kakos*, evil), enduring ; AG:65A CB:—
it is rendered " forbearing " in 2 Tim. 2 : 24.¶

2. EPIEIKĒS (ἐπιεικής), an adjective (from *epi*, used intensively, and 1933
eikos, reasonable), is used as a noun with the article in Phil. 4 : 5, and AG:292C CB:1245C
translated " forbearance " in the R.V. ; A.V., " moderation," R.V., marg., " gentleness," ' sweet reasonableness ' (Matthew Arnold). See GENTLE.

FORBID, FORBADE

A. Verb.

KŌLUŌ (κωλύω), to hinder, restrain, withhold, forbid (akin to 2967
kolos, docked, lopped, clipped), is most usually translated to forbid, often AG:461B CB:1255C
an inferior rendering to that of hindering or restraining, e.g., 1 Thess. 2 : 16 ; Luke 23 : 2 ; 2 Pet. 2 : 16, where the R.V. has " stayed ; " in Acts 10 : 47 " forbid." In Luke 6 : 29, the R.V. has " withhold not (thy coat also)." See HINDER, KEEP, *Note* (7), STAY, SUFFER, A, *Note* (3), WITHHOLD, WITHSTAND, No. 1.

Notes : (1) The strengthened form *diakōluō* (*dia*, through, used 1254
intensively) is used in Matt. 3 : 14, where, for the A.V., " forbad " the R.V. AG:185C CB:—
has " would have hindered him " [" forbad " is unsuitable with reference to the natural and persistent (*dia*) effort to prevent Christ from being baptized.]¶

(2) The phrase *mē genoito*, lit., ' let it not be ' (*mē*, negative, and
ginomai, to become), is idiomatically translated " God forbid " in Luke 1096
20 : 16 ; Rom. 3 : 4, 6, 31 ; 6 : 2, 15 ; 7 : 7, 13 ; 9 : 14 ; 11 : 1, 11 ; AG:158A CB:1248B
1 Cor. 6 : 15 ; Gal. 2 : 17 ; 3 : 21, and in the A.V. of 6 : 14 ; here the R.V. has " far be it from me (to glory)," which the American R.V. uses in the O.T. In Paul's Epistles it is almost entirely used to express the Apostle's repudiation of an inference which he apprehends may be drawn from his argument.

B. Adverb.

AKŌLUTŌS (ἀκωλύτως), without hindrance (*a*, negative, and A, 209
No. 1), is translated " none forbidding him," in Acts 28 : 31. From the AG:34B CB:—
2nd century A.D. onwards the word is found constantly in legal documents (Moulton and Milligan, Vocab., who draw attention to the triumphant note on which the word brings the Acts to a close).¶

FORCE

A. Adjective.

949
BEBAIOS (βέβαιος), firm, secure, is translated " of force " (present AG:138B CB:1239A

---

* From Notes on Thessalonians by Hogg and Vine, pp. 183, 184.

usage would translate it 'in force') in Heb. 9 : 17, of a testament, or covenant, in relation to a death. See FIRM.

B. Verb.

726 AG:109A CB:1249B 1. HARPAZŌ (ἁρπάζω), to snatch away, carry off by force, is used in the next sentence in Matt. 11 : 12, to that referred to under No. 1, "men of violence (A.V. 'the violent') take it by force," the meaning being, as determined by the preceding clause, that those who are possessed of eagerness and zeal, instead of yielding to the opposition of religious foes, such as the Scribes and Pharisees, press their way into the Kingdom, so as to possess themselves of it. It is elsewhere similarly rendered in John 6 : 15, of those who attempted to seize the Lord, and in Acts 23 : 10, of the chief captain's command to the soldiers to rescue Paul. See CATCH, PLUCK, PULL. Cp. *diarpazō*, to plunder, e.g., Matt. 12 : 29, and ***sunarpazō***, to seize and carry away, e.g., Acts 6 : 12, and ***harpax***, rapacious, ravening, e.g., Matt. 7 : 15.

971 AG:140C CB:1239A *Notes :* (1) *Biazō*, to force (from *bia*, force), is used in the Passive Voice in Matt. 11 : 12, of the Kingdom of Heaven as 'suffering violence ;' so in Luke 16 : 16, "entereth violently into it," here in the Middle Voice, expressive of the special interest which the doer of the act has in what he is doing. This meaning is abundantly confirmed by the similar use in the papyri. Moulton and Milligan (Vocab.) remark that Luke's statement can be naturally rendered 'everyone is entering it violently.' See VIOLENCE.

973 AG:141A CB:1239A (2) In Matt. 11 : 12, the corresponding noun, *biastēs*, violence, is rendered "men of violence," R.V. (see No. 2). See VIOLENCE.

FOREFATHER

4269 AG:704A CB:– 1. PROGONOS (πρόγονος), an adjective, primarily denoting born before (*pro*, before, and ***ginomai***, to become), is used as a noun in the plural, 2 Tim. 1 : 3, "forefathers" (in 1 Tim. 5 : 4, "parents"). See PARENTS.¶

— AG:709B CB:1266C 2. PROPATŌR (προπάτωρ), a forefather (***pro***, before, ***patēr***, a father), is used of Abraham in Rom. 4 : 1.¶

FOREGOING

4254 AG:702A CB:– PROAGŌ (προάγω), when used intransitively, signifies either to lead the way, or to go before, precede ; in Heb. 7 : 18, it is used of the commandment of the Law (ver. 16), as preceding the bringing in of "a better hope" (R.V., "foregoing"). See BRING, GO.

FOREHEAD

3359 AG:515B CB:– METŌPON (μέτωπον), from ***meta***, with, and *ōps*, an eye, occurs only in the Apocalypse, 7 : 3 ; 9 : 4 ; 13 : 16 ; 14 : 1, 9 ; 17 : 5 ; 20 : 4 ; 22 : 4.¶

FOREIGN, FOREIGNER

EXŌ (ἔξω), an adverb, signifying outside, without, is used in Acts 1854
26 : 11, R.V., " foreign," for A.V. " strange," of cities beyond the limits AG:279B
of Palestine, lit., ' unto (the) cities without,' including Damascus. See CB:1247C PAROIKOS
FORTH, OUTWARD, STRANGE, WITHOUT. 3941

Note: In Eph. 2 : 19, *paroikos*, lit., dwelling near (*para*, near, *oikos*, a AG:629A CB:1262B
dwelling), denotes an alien, a sojourner, in contrast to fellow-citizens, ALLOTRIOS
R.V., " sojourners " (A.V., " foreigners ") ; in 1 Pet. 2 : 11, A.V., 245 AG:40C
" strangers ; " see also Acts 7 : 6, 29. See SOJOURNER, STRANGER. CB:1234C
Cp. *allotrios*, e.g., Acts 7 : 6 ; Heb. 11 : 9, 34 ; *allophulos*, Acts 10 : 28 ;¶. ALLOPHULOS 246
xenos, Matt. 25 : 35, 38, 43 ; 27 : 7 ; Acts 17 : 21, etc. AG:41A CB:1234C XENOS

FOREKNOW, FOREKNOWLEDGE 3581

A. Verb. AG:548A CB:1273B

PROGINŌSKŌ (προγινώσκω), to know before (*pro*, before, *ginoskō*, 4267
to know), is used (*a*) of Divine knowledge, concerning (1) Christ, 1 Pet. AG:703D CB:1266C
1 : 20, R.V., " foreknown " (A.V., " foreordained ") ; (2) Israel as God's earthly people, Rom. 11 : 2 ; (3) believers, Rom. 8 : 29 ; the foreknowledge of God is the basis of His foreordaining counsels ; (*b*) of human knowledge, (1) of persons, Acts 26 : 5 ; (2) of facts, 2 Pet. 3 : 17.¶

B. Noun.

PROGNŌSIS (πρόγνωσις), a foreknowledge (akin to A.), is used only 4268
of Divine foreknowledge, Acts 2 : 23 ; 1 Pet. 1 : 2.¶ Foreknowledge is AG:703D CB:1266C
one aspect of omniscience ; it is implied in God's warnings, promises and predictions. See Acts 15 : 18. God's foreknowledge involves His electing grace, but this does not preclude human will. He foreknows the exercise of faith which brings salvation. The Apostle Paul stresses especially the actual purposes of God rather than the ground of the purposes, see, e.g., Gal. 1 : 16 ; Eph. 1 : 5, 11. The Divine counsels will ever be unthwartable. Cp. FORESHEW.

For FOREORDAIN see DETERMINE, No, 3, FOREKNOW, A FOREMAN See STEWARD

For FOREPART see FORESHIP

FORERUNNER

PRODROMOS (πρόδρομος), an adjective signifying running forward, 4274
going in advance, is used as a noun, of those who were sent before to take AG:704C CB:1266C
observations, acting as scouts, especially in military matters ; or of one sent before a king to see that the way was prepared, Isa. 40 : 3 ; (cp. Luke 9 : 52 ; and, of John the Baptist, Matt. 11 : 10, etc). In the N.T. it is said of Christ in Heb. 6 : 20, as going in advance of His followers who are to be where He is, when He comes to receive them to Himself.¶ In the Sept., Numb. 13 : 21, " forerunners (of the grape) ; " Is. 28 : 4, " an early (fig)."¶

FORESAIL

736 AG:110A CB:— ARTEMŌN (ἀρτέμων), from *artaō*, to fasten to, is rendered " mainsail " in Acts 27 : 40, A.V. ; R.V., " foresail." As to the particular kind of sail there mentioned, Sir William Ramsay, quoting from Juvenal concerning the entrance of a disabled ship into harbour by means of a prow-sail, indicates that the *artemōn* would be a sail set on the bow.¶

FORESEE, FORESEEN

4308 AG:709A CB:— 1. PROORAŌ (προοράω), with the aorist form *proeidon* (used to supply tenses lacking in *prooraō*), to see before (*pro*, before, *horaō*, to see), is used with reference (*a*) to the past, of seeing a person before, Acts 21 : 29 ; (*b*) to the future, in the sense of foreseeing a person or thing, Acts 2 : 25, with reference to Christ and the Father, R.V., " beheld " (here the Middle Voice is used).¶

(PROORAŌ) 4308 AG:709A CB:— 2. PROEIDON (προεῖδον), an aorist tense form without a present, to foresee, is used of David, as foreseeing Christ, in Acts 2 : 31, R.V., " foreseeing " (A.V., " seeing before ") ; in Gal. 3 : 8, it is said of the Scripture, personified, personal activity being attributed to it by reason of its Divine source (cp. ver. 22). " What saith the Scripture ? " was a common formula among the Rabbis.¶ In the Sept., Gen. 37 : 18 ; Ps. 16 : 8 (*prooraō*) ; 139 : 3.¶

4265 AG:703C CB:— 3. PROBLEPŌ (προβλέπω), from *pro*, before, and *blepō*, to see, perceive, is translated " having provided " in Heb. 11 : 40 (Middle Voice), marg., " foreseen," which is the lit. meaning of the verb, as with Eng. ' provide.'¶ In the Sept., Psa. 37 : 13.¶

FORESHEW

4293 AG:707B CB:1266C PROKATANGELLŌ (προκαταγγέλλω), to announce beforehand (*pro*, before, *katangellō*, to proclaim), is translated " foreshewed " in Acts 3 : 18, R.V. (A.V., " before had shewed ") ; in 7 : 52, A.V. and R.V., " shewed before."¶

FORESHIP

4408 AG:725A CB:— PRŌRA (πρῶρα) denotes the forward part of a ship, the prow, Acts 27 : 30 ; in ver. 41 (A.V., " forepart ") in contrast to *prumna*, the stern.¶

FORETELL

4302 AG:708B CB:1266C PROLEGŌ (προλέγω), with the aorist form *proeipon*, and a perfect form *proeirēka* (from *proereō*), signifies (1) to declare openly or plainly, or to say or tell beforehand (*pro*, before, *legō*, to say), translated in 2 Cor. 13 : 2 (in the first sentence), R.V., " I have said beforehand," A.V., " I told . . . before ; " in the next sentence, A.V., " I foretell," R.V., " I do say beforehand " (marg., " plainly ") ; not prophecy is here in view, but a warning given before and repeated (see under FOREWARN) ; (2) to speak before, of prophecy, as foretelling the future, Mark 13 : 23,

A.V., “ have foretold,” R.V., “ have told . . . beforehand ; ” Acts 1 : 16 PROKATANGELLŌ 4293
(of the prophecy concerning Judas) ; Rom. 9 : 29 ; 2 Pet. 3 : 2 ; Jude 17 ; AG:707B
some inferior mss. have it in Heb. 10 : 15. See FOREWARN, SPEAK, TELL. CB:1266C KATANGELLŌ

Note : In Acts 3 : 24 some mss. have *prokatangellō* (see FORESHEW) ; 2605
the most authentic have *katangellō*, R.V., “ told.” AG:409B CB:1254A

FOREVER See EVER

FOREWARN

PROLEGŌ (προλέγω), with verbal forms as mentioned above, is 4302
translated “ I forewarn ” and “ I did forewarn,” in the R.V. of Gal. 5 : 21, AG:708B CB:1266C
A.V., “ I tell (you) before ” and “ I have told (you) in time past ; ” here, however, as in 2 Cor. 13 : 2 and 1 Thess. 3 : 4 (see below), the R.V. marg., “ plainly ” is to be preferred to “ beforehand ” or “ before ” (see under FORETELL) ; the meaning in Gal. 5 : 21 is not so much that Paul prophesied the result of the practice of the evils mentioned, but that he had told them before of the consequence and was now repeating his warning, as leaving no possible room for doubt or misunderstanding ; in 1 Thess. 3 : 4, the subject told before was the affliction consequent upon the preaching of the Gospel ; in 1 Thess. 4 : 6, “ we forewarned,” the warning was as to the consequences of whatsoever violates chastity.

Note : In Luke 12 : 5 the verb *hupodeiknumi*, to shew, teach, make 5263
known, is translated “ will warn ” in the R.V. (A.V., “ forewarn ”). See AG:844B CB:—
EXAMPLE (B, No. 2), SHEW, WARN.

FORFEIT

ZĒMIOŌ (ζημιόω), in the Active Voice, signifies to damage ; in the 2210
Passive, to suffer loss, forfeit, Matt. 16 : 26 and Mark 8 : 36, of the “ life,” AG:338C CB:1273C
R.V. ; A.V., and R.V. marg., “ soul ;” in each place the R.V. has “ forfeit,” (-OMAI)
for A.V., “ lose ; ” Luke 9 : 25, “ his own self ” (R.V., “ forfeit,” A.V., “ be cast away ; ” here the preceding word “ lose ” translates *apollumi*, to destroy). What is in view here is the act of forfeiting what is of the greatest value, not the casting away by Divine judgment, though that is involved, but losing or penalising one's own self, with spiritual and eternal loss. The word is also used in 1 Cor. 3 : 15 ; 2 Cor. 7 : 9 ; Phil. 3 : 8. See CAST, LOSE, LOSS (suffer).¶

FORGET, FORGETFUL

A. Verbs.

1. LANTHANŌ (λανθάνω), to escape notice, is translated “ they 2990
(wilfully) forget ” in 2 Pet. 3 : 5, R.V., lit., ‘ this escapes them (i.e., their AG:466B CB:1256C
notice, wilfully on their part),’ A.V., “ they willingly are ignorant of ; ” in ver. 8, R.V., “ forget not,” lit., ‘ let not this one thing escape you ’ (your notice), A.V., “ be not ignorant of.” See HIDE, IGNORANT, UNAWARES.

2. EPILANTHANOMAI (ἐπιλανθάνομαι), to forget, or neglect (*epi*, 1950 AG:295B
upon, used intensively, and No. 1), is said (*a*) negatively of God, indicating CB:—

His remembrance of sparrows, Luke 12 : 6, and of the work and labour of love of His saints, Heb. 6 : 10 ; (*b*) of the disciples regarding taking bread, Matt. 16 : 5 ; Mark 8 : 14 ; (*c*) of Paul regarding "the things which are behind," Phil. 3 : 13 ; (*d*) of believers, as to shewing love to strangers, Heb. 13 : 2, R.V., and as to doing good and communicating, ver. 16 ; (*d*) of a person who, after looking at himself in a mirror, forgets what kind of person he is, Jas. 1 : 24.¶

1585 3. EKLANTHANOMAI (ἐκλανθάνομαι), to forget utterly (*ek*, out,
AG:242B **CB:—** intensive), is used in the Middle Voice in Heb. 12 : 5, of forgetting an
exhortation.¶

B. Nouns.

3024 1. LĒTHĒ (λήθη), forgetfulness (from *lēthō*, to forget, an old form of
AG:472D **CB:1256C** *lanthanō*, see A, No. 1 ; cp. Eng. lethal, lethargy, and the mythical river
Lethe, which was supposed to cause forgetfulness of the past to those who drank of it), is used with *lambanō*, to take, in 2 Pet. 1 : 9, "having forgotten," lit., 'having taken forgetfulness' (cp. 2 Tim. 1 : 5, lit., 'having taken reminder'), a periphrastic expression for a single verb.¶

1953 2. EPILĒSMONĒ (ἐπιλησμονή), forgetfulness (akin to A, No. 2), is used
AG:295D **CB:—** in Jas. 1 : 25, "a forgetful hearer," R.V., "a hearer that forgetteth," lit.,
'a hearer of forgetfulness,' i.e., a hearer characterized by forgetfulness.¶

FORGIVE, FORGAVE, FORGIVENESS

A. Verbs.

863 1. APHIĒMI (ἀφίημι), primarily, to send forth, send away (*apo*, from,
AG:125C **CB:1236B** *hiēmi*, to send), denotes, besides its other meanings, to remit or forgive
(*a*) debts, Matt. 6 : 12 ; 18 : 27, 32, these being completely cancelled ; (*b*) sins, e.g., Matt. 9 : 2, 5, 6 ; 12 : 31, 32 ; Acts 8 : 22 ("the thought of thine heart") ; Rom. 4 : 7 ; Jas. 5 : 15 ; 1 John 1 : 9 ; 2 : 12. In this latter respect the verb, like its corresponding noun (below), firstly signifies the remission of the punishment due to sinful conduct, the deliverance of the sinner from the penalty Divinely, and therefore righteously, imposed ; secondly, it involves the complete removal of the cause of offence ; such remission is based upon the vicarious and propitiatory sacrifice of Christ. In the O.T. atoning sacrifice and forgiveness are often associated, e.g., Lev. 4 : 20, 26. The verb is used in the N.T. with reference to trespasses (*paraptōma*), e.g., Matt. 6 : 14, 15 ; sins (*hamartia*), e.g., Luke 5 : 20 ; debts (see above) (*opheilēma*), Matt. 6 : 12 ; (*opheilē*), 18 : 32 ; (*daneion*), 18 : 27 ; the thought (*dianoia*) of the heart,
KALUPTō Acts 8 : 22. Cp. *kaluptō*, to cover, 1 Pet. 4 : 8 ; Jas. 5 : 20 ; and
2572 **AG:401A** *epikaluptō*, to cover over, Rom. 4 : 7, representing the Hebrew words for
CB:1253B atonement.

EPI- Human forgiveness is to be strictly analogous to Divine forgiveness,
1943 **AG:294C** e.g., Matt. 6 : 12. If certain conditions are fulfilled, there is no limitation
CB:— to Christ's law of forgiveness, Matt. 18 : 21, 22. The conditions are
repentance and confession, Matt. 18 : 15-17 ; Luke 17 : 3.

As to limits to the possibility of Divine forgiveness, see Matt. 12 : 32, 2nd part (see BLASPHEMY) and 1 John 5 : 16 (see DEATH). See FORSAKE, LAY, *Note* (2) at end, LEAVE, LET, OMIT, PUT, No. 16, *Note*, REMIT, SEND, *Note* (1), SUFFER, YIELD.

2. CHARIZOMAI (χαρίζομαι), to bestow a favour unconditionally, **5483**
is used of the act of forgiveness, whether Divine, Eph. 4 : 32 ; Col. 2 : 13 ; **AG:876C CB:1239C**
3 : 13 ; or human, Luke 7 : 42, 43 (debt) ; 2 Cor. 2 : 7, 10 ; 12 : 13 ; Eph. 4 : 32 (1st mention). Paul uses this word frequently, but No. 1 only, in Rom. 4 : 7, in this sense of the word. See DELIVER.

Note : Apoluō, to let loose from (*apo*, from, *luō*, to loose), to release, **630**
is translated " forgive," " ye shall be forgiven," Luke 6 : 37, A.V. (R.V., **AG:96C CB:1237A**
" release," " ye shall be released "), the reference being to setting a person free as a quasi-judicial act. The verb does not mean to forgive. See DISMISS, RELEASE.

B. Noun.

APHESIS (ἄφεσις) denotes a dismissal, release (akin to A, No. 1) ; **859**
it is used of the remission of sins, and translated " forgiveness " in Mark **AG:125A CB:1236B**
3 : 29 ; Eph. 1 : 7 ; Col. 1 : 14, and in the A.V. of Acts 5 : 31 ; 13 : 38 ; 26 : 18, in each of which the R.V. has " remission." Eleven times it is followed by " of sins," and once by " of trespasses." It is never used of the remission of sins in the Sept., but is especially connected with the year of Jubilee (Lev. 25 : 10, etc.). Cp. the R.V. of Luke 4 : 18, " release " (A.V., " liberty "). For the significance in connection with remission of sins and the propitiatory sacrifice of Christ, see A, No. 1. See DELIVERANCE, LIBERTY, RELEASE, REMISSION. Cp. the different word *paresis*, a passing over, a remission, of sins committed under the old Covenant, Rom. 3 : 25. The R.V. should be used here. This passing over, or by, was neither forgetting nor forgiving ; it was rather a suspension of the just penalty ; cp. Acts 17 : 30, " the times of ignorance God overlooked," R.V. ; see also, e.g., Ps. 78 : 38.

FORK (WINNOWING) See FAN

FORM (Noun)

1. MORPHĒ (μορφή) denotes the special or characteristic form or **3444**
feature of a person or thing ; it is used with particular significance in the **AG:528B CB:1259B**
N.T., only of Christ, in Phil. 2 : 6, 7, in the phrases " being in the form of God," and " taking the form of a servant." An excellent definition of the word is that of Gifford : " *morphē* is therefore properly the nature or essence, not in the abstract, but as actually subsisting in the individual, and retained as long as the individual itself exists. . . . Thus in the passage before us *morphē Theou* is the Divine nature actually and inseparably subsisting in the Person of Christ. . . . For the interpretation of ' the form of God ' it is sufficient to say that (1) it includes the whole nature and essence of Deity, and is inseparable from them, since they could have no actual existence without it ; and (2) that it does not include in itself anything ' accidental ' or separable, such as particular

modes of manifestation, or conditions of glory and majesty, which may at one time be attached to the 'form,' at another separated from it. . . .

The true meaning of *morphē* in the expression 'form of God' is confirmed by its recurrence in the corresponding phrase, 'form of a servant.' It is universally admitted that the two phrases are directly antithetical, and that 'form' must therefore have the same sense in both."*

The definition above mentioned applies to its use in Mark 16 : 12, as to the particular ways in which the Lord manifested Himself.¶

Note : For the synonymous word *schēma*, see FASHION. For the verb *morphoō*, see FORMED, No. 1, below.

3446 AG:528C CB:1259B 2. MORPHŌSIS (μόρφωσις), a form or outline, denotes in the N.T., an image or impress, an outward semblance, Rom. 2 : 20, of knowledge of the truth ; 2 Tim. 3 : 5, of godliness. It is thus to be distinguished from *morphē* (No. 1) ; it is used in almost the same sense as *schēma*, fashion (which see), but is not so purely the outward form as *schēma* is.¶

5179 AG:829D CB:1273B 3. TUPOS (τύπος), the representation or pattern of anything (for which see ENSAMPLE), is rendered " form " in Rom. 6 : 17, " that form (or mould) of teaching whereunto ye were delivered," R.V. The metaphor is that of a cast or frame into which molten material is poured so as to take its shape. The Gospel is the mould ; those who are obedient to its teachings become conformed to Christ, whom it presents. In Acts 23 : 25, it is used of a letter, R.V., " form " (A.V., " manner "), with reference to the nature of the contents.

1491 AG:221B CB:1243A 4. EIDOS (εἶδος), lit., that which is seen (*eidon*, to see), an appearance or external form, is rendered " form " in the R.V. of Luke 3 : 22, of the Holy Spirit's appearance at the baptism of Christ ; in John 5 : 37, in the Lord's testimony concerning the Father ; in Luke 9 : 29 it is said of Christ Himself ; it is translated " sight " in 2 Cor. 5 : 7, the Christian being guided by what he knows to be true, though unseen ; in 1 Thess. 5 : 22 Christians are exhorted to abstain from " every form of evil," R.V. (the A.V., " appearance " is inadequate), i.e., from every kind of evil. See FASHION, SHAPE, SIGHT.¶

5296 AG:848C CB:1252B 5. HUPOTUPŌSIS (ὑποτύπωσις), an outline, sketch (akin to *hupotupoō*, to delineate, *hupo*, under, and No. 3), is used metaphorically to denote a pattern, example, " form," in 2 Tim. 1 : 13, " of sound words " (R.V., " pattern ") ; in 1 Tim. 1 : 16, " pattern " and " ensample." See ENSAMPLE.¶

FORMED

A. Verbs.

3445 AG:528C CB:1259B 1. MORPHOŌ (μορφόω), like the noun (A, No. 1), refers, not to the external and transient, but to the inward and real ; it is used in Gal. 4 : 19, expressing the necessity of a change in character and conduct to correspond

* From Gifford, " The Incarnation," pp. 16, 19, 39.

with inward spiritual condition, so that there may be moral conformity to Christ.¶

Cp. *metamorphoō*, to transform, transfigure, *summorphizō* and *suschematizō*, to conform to.

2. PLASSŌ (πλάσσω), to mould, to shape, was used of the artist who 4111
wrought in clay or wax (Eng., plastic, plasticity), and occurs in AG:666C CB:1265A
Rom. 9 : 20 ; 1 Tim. 2 : 13.¶

B. Noun.

PLASMA (πλάσμα) denotes anything moulded or shaped into a form 4110
(akin to A, No. 2), Rom. 9 : 20, " the thing formed."¶ Cp. the adjective AG:666B CB:—
plastos, made up, fabricated, feigned, 2 Pet. 2 : 3.¶

FORMER

1. PRŌTOS (πρῶτος), first, is translated " former " in Acts 1 : 1, 4413
of Luke's first treatise ; in Rev. 21 : 4, R.V., " first " (A.V., " former "). AG:725B CB:1267B
See Before, First.

2. PROTEROS (πρότερος), before, former, is translated " former " in 4386
Eph. 4 : 22 ; Heb. 10 : 32 ; 1 Pet. 1 : 14. See Before. AG:721D CB:1267B

FORNICATION, FORNICATOR

A. Nouns.

1. PORNEIA (πορνεία) is used (*a*) of illicit sexual intercourse, in 4202
John 8 : 41 ; Acts 15 : 20, 29 ; 21 : 25 ; 1 Cor. 5 : 1 ; 6 : 13, 18 ; 2 Cor. AG:693B CB:1266A
12 : 21 ; Gal. 5 : 19 ; Eph. 5 : 3 ; Col. 3 : 5 ; 1 Thess. 4 : 3 ; Rev. 2 : 21 ; 9 : 21 ; in the plural in 1 Cor. 7 : 2 ; in Matt. 5 : 32 and 19 : 9 it stands for, or includes, adultery ; it is distinguished from it in 15 : 19 and Mark 7 : 21 ; (*b*) metaphorically, of the association of pagan idolatry with doctrines of, and professed adherence to, the Christian faith, Rev. 14 : 8 ; 17 : 2, 4 ; 18 : 3 ; 19 : 2 ; some suggest this as the sense in 2 : 21.¶

2. PORNOS (πόρνος) denotes a man who indulges in fornication, a 4205
fornicator, 1 Cor. 5 : 9, 10, 11 ; 6 : 9 ; Eph. 5 : 5, R.V. ; 1 Tim. 1 : 10, AG:693D CB:1266A
R.V. ; Heb. 12 : 16 ; 13 : 4, R.V. ; Rev. 21 : 8 and 22 : 15, R.V. (A.V., " whoremonger ").¶

B. Verbs.

1. PORNEUŌ (πορνεύω), to commit fornication, is used (*a*) literally, 4203
Mark 10 : 19 ; 1 Cor. 6 : 18 ; 10 : 8 ; Rev. 2 : 14, 20, see (*a*) and (*b*) AG:693C CB:1266A
above ; (*b*) metaphorically, Rev. 17 : 2 ; 18 : 3, 9.¶

2. EKPORNEUŌ (ἐκπορνεύω), a strengthened form of No. 1, (*ek*, used 1608
intensively), to give oneself up to fornication, implying excessive indul- AG:244D CB:—
gence, Jude 7.¶

FORSAKE

A. Verbs.

1. KATALEIPŌ (καταλείπω), a strengthened form of *leipō*, to leave, 2641 AG:413C
signifies (*a*) to leave, to leave behind, e.g., Matt. 4 : 13 ; (*b*) to leave CB:1254A

remaining, reserve, e.g., Luke 10 : 40 ; (*c*) to forsake, in the sense of abandoning, translated to forsake in the R.V. of Luke 5 : 28 and Acts 6 : 2 ; in Heb. 11 : 27 and 2 Pet. 2 : 15, A.V. and R.V. In this sense it is translated to leave, in Mark 10 : 7 ; 14 : 52 ; Luke 15 : 4 ; Eph. 5 : 31. See Leave, Reserve.

1459 AG:215D CB:— 2. ENKATALEIPŌ (ἐγκαταλείπω), from *en*, in, and No. 1, denotes (*a*) to leave behind, among, leave surviving, Rom. 9 : 29 ; (*b*) to forsake, abandon, leave in straits, or helpless, said by, or of, Christ, Matt. 27 : 46 ; Mark 15 : 34 ; Acts 2 : 27, 31 (No. 1 in some mss.) ; of men, 2 Cor. 4 : 9 ; 2 Tim. 4 : 10, 16 ; by God, Heb. 13 : 5 ; of things, by Christians (negatively), Heb. 10 : 25. See Leave.¶

863 AG:125C CB:1236B 3. APHIĒMI (ἀφίημι) sometimes has the significance of forsaking, Mark 1 : 18 ; 14 : 50 (R.V., " left ") ; so Luke 5 : 11. See Forgive.

657 AG:100D CB:— 4. APOTASSŌ (ἀποτάσσω), primarily, to set apart (*apo*, off, from, *tassō*, to arrange), is used in the Middle Voice, meaning (*a*) to take leave of, e.g., Mark 6 : 46, (*b*) to renounce, forsake, Luke 14 : 33, A.V., " forsaketh," R.V., " renounceth " (" all that he hath "). See Bid farewell, Renounce, Send, *Note* (2) at end, Take, *Note* (14).

B. Noun.

646 AG:98B CB:1237A APOSTASIA (ἀποστασία), an apostasy, defection, revolt, always in N.T. of religious defection, is translated " to forsake " in Acts 21 : 21, lit., ' (thou teachest) apostasy (from Moses) ; ' in 2 Thess. 2 : 3, " falling away." See Fall.¶

FORSOMUCH : see † p.1

FORSWEAR

1964 AG:296D CB:— EPIORKEŌ (ἐπιορκέω) signifies to swear falsely, to undo one's swearing, forswear oneself (*epi*, against, *orkos*, an oath), Matt. 5 : 33.¶ Cp. *epiorkos*, a perjured person, a perjurer, 1 Tim. 1 : 10, " false swearers."¶

FORTH

1854 AG:279B CB:1247C EXŌ (ἔξω), outside, without (from, *ek*, out of, from), frequently signifies " forth," especially after verbs of motion, e.g., John 11 : 43 ; 19 : 4, 13. See Outward, Strange, Without.

Notes : (1) For the word " forth " in combination with various verbs, see, e.g., Break, Bring, Come, Put. (2) In Matt. 26 : 16, the R.V. omits " forth," as the phrase *apo tote*, 'from then,' simply means " from that time ; " in the similar phrase " from that day forth," Matt. 22 : 46 ; John 11 : 53, there is no word in the original representing " forth." (3) In John 2 : 11 the R.V. rightly omits " forth."

FORTHWITH

1824 AG:273D CB:— 1. EXAUTĒS (ἐξαυτῆς), at once (from, *ek*, out of, and *autēs*, the genitive case of *autos*, self or very, agreeing with " hour " understood, i.e., 'from that very hour'), is translated "forthwith" in the R.V. in Mark 6 : 25 (A.V., "by and by"); Acts 10 : 33 (A.V., "immediately"); 11 : 11 (ditto); 21 : 32 (ditto); 23 : 30 (A.V., "straightway"); Phil. 2 : 23 (A.V., "presently"). The word is frequent in the period of the *koinē* Greek (see Preface). See IMMEDIATELY, PRESENTLY, STRAIGHTWAY.¶

2. EUTHEŌS (εὐθέως), at once, straightway (from the adjective, 2112
euthus, straight), is translated "forthwith," in the A.V. of Matt. 13 : 5; AG:320B CB:1247B
26 : 49; (it occurs in some mss. in Mark 5 : 13; the R.V. omits it); Acts 12 : 10; 21 : 30 (R.V., "straightway," in each place). See IMMEDIATELY, SHORTLY, STRAIGHTWAY.

3. EUTHUS (εὐθύς), an alternative adverb to No. 2, is translated 2117
"forthwith" in the A.V. of Mark 1 : 29; 1 : 43 (in the best mss.), and AG:321A CB:1247B
John 19 : 34 (R.V., "straightway"). See ANON, IMMEDIATELY, STRAIGHTWAY.¶

Note: *Parachrēma*, a synonymous word denoting instantly, on the 3916
spot, is not translated "forthwith" in A.V. or R.V. See IMMEDIATELY. AG:623D CB:—

FORTY

TESSARAKONTA (τεσσαράκοντα) is used in circumstances in Scripture 5062
which indicate the number as suggesting probation, separation or judgment, e.g., Matt. 4 : 2; Acts 1 : 3; Heb. 3 : 9, 17. AG:813A CB:1271B

Note: *Tessarakontaetēs*, forty years (*etos*, a year), is found in Acts 5063
7 : 23; 13 : 18.¶ AG:813B CB:—

FORWARD (be), FORWARDNESS

THELō 2309

Notes: (1) The verb *thelō*, to will, wish, is translated "to be forward," AG:354D CB:1271C
in the A.V. of 2 Cor. 8 : 10, which the R.V. corrects to "to will." (2) In SPOUDAZō
Gal. 2 : 10, *spoudazō*, to be zealous, is so rendered in the R.V. (A.V., "I was 4704
forward"). (3) In 2 Cor. 8 : 17, the corresponding adjective *spoudaios*, AG:763C CB:1269C
earnest, is so rendered in the R.V. (A.V., "forward"). So in ver. 8, SPOUDAIOS
the noun *spoudē*, earnestness, is thus rendered in the R.V. (A.V., "forwardness"). (4) In 9 : 2, R.V., the noun *prothumia*, "readiness" 4705 AG:763C CB:1269C
(*pro*, before, *thumos*, impulse), is so rendered (A.V., "forwardness of SPOUDē 4710
mind"). (5) For the combination of this word with verbs see GO, PUT, AG:763D
SET, STRETCH. CB:1269C PROTHUMIA 4288 AG:706C CB:1267B

FOSTER-BROTHER

SUNTROPHOS (σύντροφος) primarily denotes one nourished or 4939
brought up with another (*sun*, with, *trephō*, to rear); it is rendered AG:793C CB:—
"foster-brother" in Acts 13 : 1, R.V. It has, however, been found in Hellenistic usage as a court term, signifying an intimate friend of a king (Deissmann), and this would seem to be the meaning regarding Manaen and Herod the Tetrarch.

FOUL

169 AG:29A CB:1234B AKATHARTOS (ἀκάθαρτος) denotes unclean, impure (*a*, negative, and *kathairō*, to purify), (*a*) ceremonially, e.g., Acts 10 : 14, 28 ; (*b*) morally, always, in the Gospels, of unclean spirits ; it is translated " foul " in the A.V. of Mark 9 : 25 and Rev. 18 : 2, but always " unclean " in the R.V. Since the word primarily had a ceremonial significance, the moral significance is less prominent as applied to a spirit, than when *ponēros*, wicked, is so applied. Cp. *akatharsia*, uncleanness. See UNCLEAN.

168 AG:29A CB:— *Note :* In Rev. 17 : 4 the best mss. have this word in the plural, R.V., " the unclean things " (*akathartēs*, filthiness, in some mss.).

FOUNDATION (to lay), FOUNDED

A. Nouns.

2310 AG:355D CB:1272A 1. THEMELIOS, or THEMELION (θεμέλιος) is properly an adjective denoting belonging to a foundation (connected with *tithēmi*, to place). It is used (1) as a noun, with *lithos*, a stone, understood, in Luke 6 : 48, 49 ; 14 : 29 ; Heb. 11 : 10 ; Rev. 21 : 14, 19 ; (2) as a neuter noun in Acts 16 : 26, and metaphorically, (*a*) of the ministry of the gospel and the doctrines of the faith, Rom. 15 : 20 ; 1 Cor. 3 : 10, 11, 12 ; Eph. 2 : 20, where the " of " is not subjective (i.e., consisting of the apostles and prophets), but objective, (i.e., laid by the apostles, etc.) ; so in 2 Tim. 2 : 19, where " the foundation of God " is ' the foundation laid by God,'—not the Church (which is not a foundation), but Christ Himself, upon whom the saints are built ; Heb. 6 : 1 ; (*b*) of good works, 1 Tim. 6 : 19.¶

2602 AG:409A CB:1254A 2. KATABOLĒ (καταβολή), lit., a casting down, is used (*a*) of conceiving seed, Heb. 11 : 11 ; (*b*) of a foundation, as that which is laid down, or in the sense of founding ; metaphorically, of the foundation of the world ; in this respect two phrases are used, (1) " from the foundation of the world," Matt. 25 : 34 (in the most authentic mss. in 13 : 35 there is no phrase representing " of the world ") ; Luke 11 : 50 ; Heb. 4 : 3 ; 9 : 26 ; Rev. 13 : 8 ; 17 : 8 ; (2) " before the foundation of the world," John 17 : 24 ; Eph. 1 : 4 ; 1 Pet. 1 : 20. The latter phrase looks back to the past eternity.¶

B. Verb.

2311 AG:356A CB:1272A THEMELIOŌ (θεμελιόω), to lay a foundation, to found (akin to A, No. 1), is used (*a*) literally, Matt. 7 : 25 ; Luke 6 : 48 ; Heb. 1 : 10 ; (*b*) metaphorically, Eph. 3 : 17, " grounded (in love) ; " Col. 1 : 23 (ditto, " in the faith ") ; 1 Pet. 5 : 10, A.V., " settle." See GROUND, SETTLE.¶

FOUNTAIN

4077 AG:655D CB:1263A PĒGĒ (πηγή), a spring or fountain, is used of (*a*) an artificial well, fed by a spring, John 4 : 6 ; (*b*) metaphorically (in contrast to such a well), the indwelling Spirit of God, 4 : 14 ; (*c*) springs, metaphorically in 2 Pet. 2 : 17, R.V., for A.V., " wells ; " (*d*) natural fountains or springs, Jas. 3 : 11, 12 ; Rev. 8 : 10 ; 14 : 7 ; 16 : 4 ; (*e*) metaphorically, eternal life and the future blessings accruing from it, Rev. 7 : 17 ; 21 : 6 ; (*f*) a flow of blood, Mark 5 : 29.¶

FOUR (-TH), FOURTEEN (-TH), FOUR HUNDRED

TESSARES (τέσσαρες), four, is not found in the N.T. outside the Gospels, the Acts and Apocalypse ; in the last it is very frequent. *Tetartos*, fourth, is found in Matt. 14 : 25 ; Mark 6 : 48 and seven times in the Apocalypse ; also in Acts 10 : 30, " four days ago," lit., ' from a fourth day.' *Dekatessares*, fourteen (lit., ten-four), is found in Matt. 1 : 17 ; 2 Cor. 12 : 2 ; Gal. 2 : 1 ;¶ *tessareskaidekatos*, fourteenth (lit., four-and-tenth), Acts 27 : 27, 33 ;¶ *tetrakosia*, four hundred, Acts 5 : 36 ; 7 : 6 ; 13 : 20 ; Gal. 3 : 17.¶ In Acts 7 : 6 the 400 years refers to Abraham's descendants and to the sojourning and the bondage. This agrees with Gen. 15 : 13. In Ex. 12 : 40 the 430 years dates from the call of Abraham himself. Likewise the giving of the Law was 430 years from the promise in Gen. 12 : 3, which agrees with Gal. 3 : 17. In John 11 : 39 *tetartaios*, lit., ' a fourth day (one),' is rendered " four days." **TESSARES 5064 AG:813B CB:1271B TETARTOS 5067 AG:813C DEKATESSARES 1180 AG:173D (DEKA) TESSARES-KAIDEKATOS 5065 AG:813B TETRAKOSIA 5071 AG:813D (-SIOI) TETARTAIOS 5066 AG:813C**

FOURFOLD

TETRAPLOOS (τετραπλόος), an adjective, is found in Luke 19 : 8.¶ **5073 AG:813D (-OUS) CB:—**

FOURFOOTED

TETRAPOUS (τετράπους), from *tetra*, four (used in compound words), and *pous*, a foot, is used of beasts, Acts 10 : 12 ; 11 : 6 ; Rom. 1 : 23.¶ **5074 AG:814A CB:—**

FOURSCORE

OGDOĒKONTA (ὀγδοήκοντα), from *ogdoos*, eighth, is found in Luke 2 : 37 ; 16 : 7.¶ **3589 AG:552D CB:—**

FOURSQUARE

TETRAGŌNOS (τετράγωνος), four-cornered (from *tetra*, see above, and *gōnia*, a corner, or angle), is found in Rev. 21 : 16.¶ **5068 AG:813C CB:—**

For FOWL see BIRD

FOX

ALŌPĒX (ἀλώπηξ) is found in Matt. 8 : 20 ; Luke 9 : 58 ; metaphorically, of Herod, in Luke 13 : 32.¶ **258 AG:41D CB:1234C**

FRAGRANT See SAVOUR

For FRAGMENTS see PIECE, No. 4

FRAME (Verb)

1. KATARTIZŌ (καταρτίζω), to fit, to render complete, is translated "have been framed" in Heb. 11 : 3, of the worlds or ages. See FIT. **2675 AG:417D CB:1254B**

2. SUNARMOLOGEŌ (συναρμολογέω), to fit or frame together (*sun*, with, *harmos*, a joint, *legō*, to choose), is used metaphorically of the Church **4883 AG:785B CB:—**

as a spiritual temple, the parts being "fitly framed together," Eph. 2 : 21; as a body, 4 : 16, R.V., "fitly framed," (for A.V., "fitly joined").¶

FRANKINCENSE

3030 LIBANOS (λίβανος), from a Semitic verb signifying to be white, is a
AG:473C CB:1257A vegetable resin, bitter and glittering, obtained by incisions in the bark
of the *arbor thuris*, the incense tree, and especially imported through
Arabia; it was used for fumigation at sacrifices, Ex. 30 : 7 etc., or for
perfume, S. of Sol., 3 : 6. The Indian variety is called *looban*. It was
among the offerings brought by the wise men, Matt. 2 : 11. In Rev.
18 : 13 it is listed among the commodities of Babylon. The "incense"
of Rev. 8 : 3 should be "frankincense." Cp. INCENSE.¶

FRANKLY

5483 *Note:* In Luke 7 : 42, the verb *charizomai*, to forgive (as a matter of
AG:876C CB:1239C grace), is rendered "frankly forgave," so as to bring out the force of the
grace in the action. Older versions had "forgave," and to this the
R.V. returns.

FRAUD

— AG:128A APHUSTEREŌ (ἀφυστερέω), to keep back, deprive (*apo*, from,
CB:— *hustereō*, to be lacking), is used in Jas. 5 : 4, "is kept back by fraud" (some
APOS- mss. have *apostereō*, to defraud). The word is found in a papyrus writing
650 AG:99A of A.D. 42, of a bath insufficiently warmed (Moulton and Milligan, Vocab.).
CB:1237A The Law required the prompt payment of the labourer, Deut. 24 : 15.¶

FREE, FREEDOM, FREELY, FREEMAN, FREEDMAN, FREEWOMAN

A. Adjective.

1658 ELEÚTHEROS (ἐλεύθερος), primarily of freedom to go wherever one
AG:250D CB:1244B likes, is used (*a*) of freedom from restraint and obligation in general, Matt. 17 : 26; Rom. 7 : 3; 1 Cor. 7 : 39, R.V., "free," of the second marriage of a woman; 9 : 1, 19; 1 Pet. 2 : 16; from the Law, Gal. 4 : 26; from sin, John 8 : 36; with regard to righteousness, Rom. 6 : 20 (i.e., righteousness laid no sort of bond upon them, they had no relation to it); (*b*) in a civil sense, free from bondage or slavery, John 8 : 33; 1 Cor. 7 : 21, 22, 2nd part (for ver. 22, 1st part, see C, No. 2); 12 : 13; Gal. 3 : 28; Eph. 6 : 8; Rev. 13 : 16; 19 : 18; as a noun, "freeman," Col. 3 : 11, R.V.; Rev. 6 : 15; "freewoman," Gal. 4 : 22, 23, 30, and ver. 31. R.V.¶

Notes: (1) ¶In Matt. 15 : 6 and Mark 7 : 11, the words "he shall be
free," A.V., have nothing to represent them in the Greek. (2) In Heb.
13 : 5, R.V., "be ye free from the love of money," is an abbreviated
866 AG:126C rendering of the adjective *aphilarguros* (not loving money) with the
CB:— noun *tropos*, turn (of mind); hence the marg., "let your turn of mind be
free etc.," for A.V., "let your conversation be without covetousness."

B. Verb.

ELEUTHEROŌ (ἐλευθερόω), to make free (akin to A.), is used of deliverance from (*a*) sin, John 8 : 32, 36 ; Rom. 6 : 18, 22 ; (*b*) the Law, Rom. 8 : 2 ; Gal. 5 : 1 (see, however, under C.) ; (*c*) the bondage of corruption, Rom. 8 : 21. See DELIVER.¶ 1659 AG:250D CB:1244B

Note : In Rom. 6 : 7, the verb *dikaioō*, translated " is freed," signifies to justify, as in the R.V., " is justified," i.e., in the legal sense ; death annuls all obligations. The death penalty which Christ endured holds good for the believer, through his identification with Christ in His death ; having been crucified as to his unregenerate nature, and justified from sin, he walks in newness of life in Christ. 1344 AG:197C CB:1241C

C. Nouns.

1. ELEUTHERIA (ἐλευθερία), liberty (akin to A. and B.), is rendered " freedom " in Gal. 5 : 1, " with freedom did Christ set us free." The combination of the noun with the verb stresses the completeness of the act, the aorist (or point) tense indicating both its momentary and comprehensive character ; it was done once for all. The R.V. margin " for freedom " gives perhaps the preferable meaning, i.e., ' not to bring us into another form of bondage did Christ liberate us from that in which we were born, but in order to make us free from bondage.' 1657 AG:250C CB:1244B

The word is twice rendered " freedom " in the R.V. of Gal. 5 : 13 (A.V., " liberty "). The phraseology is that of manumission from slavery, which among the Greeks was effected by a legal fiction, according to which the manumitted slave was purchased by a god ; as the slave could not provide the money, the master paid it into the temple Treasury in the presence of the slave, a document being drawn up containing the words " for freedom." No one could enslave him again, as he was the property of the god. Hence the word *apeleutheros*, No. 2. The word is also translated " freedom " in 1 Pet. 2 : 16, R.V. In 2 Cor. 3 : 17 the word denotes freedom of access to the presence of God. See LIBERTY.

2. APELEUTHEROS (ἀπελεύθερος), a freed man (*apo*, from, and A.), is used in 1 Cor. 7 : 22, " the Lord's freedman." See the illustration above under No. 1. Here the fuller word brings out the spiritual emancipation in contrast to the natural freedman. 558 AG:83D CB:1236B

Note : (1) In Acts 22 : 28, the word *politeia*, rendered " freedom " (A.V.), denotes citizenship, as in the R.V. (see CITIZENSHIP) ; in the next sentence the Greek is, lit., ' But I was even born ; ' the necessary word to be supplied is " Roman," from the previous verse ; hence the R.V., " But I am a Roman born." (2) For " free gift " (*charisma*), Rom. 5 : 15, 16 ; 6 : 23, see GIFT. POLITEIA 4174 AG:686A CB:1265C CHARISMA 5486 AG:878D CB:1239C

D. Adverb.

DŌREAN (δωρεάν), from *dōrea*, a gift, is used as an adverb in the sense " freely," in Matt. 10 : 8 ; Rom. 3 : 24 ; 2 Cor. 11 : 7 (R.V., " for 1432 AG:210C CB:1242A

PARRHĒSIAZOMAI nought ") ; Rev. 21 : 6 ; 22 : 17. Here the prominent thought is the
3955 grace of the Giver. See CAUSE.
AG:631A CB:1262C *Notes :* (1) In Acts 26 : 26 *parrhēsiazomai*, to be bold in speech, is
PARRHĒSIA translated, to speak freely. (2) In Acts 2 : 29 the noun *parrhēsia* with the
3954 AG:630C preposition *meta*, with, is rendered " freely," lit., ' with free-spokenness.'
CB:1262C (3) For *charizomai*, to give freely, Rom. 8 : 32 ; 1 Cor. 2 : 12, see GIVE.
CHARIZOMAI 5483 (4) In 2 Thess. 3 : 1, A.V., the verb *trechō*, to run, is rendered " may have
AG:876C free course ; " this the R.V. corrects to " may run." (5) For *charitoō*, to
CB:1239C CHARITOŌ bestow freely, Eph. 1 : 6, see ACCEPT, *Note*. (6) For " have drunk freely,"
5487 John 2 : 10, R.V., see DRINK, B, No. 2.
AG:879A
CB:1239C

FREIGHT

1546 AG:238A CB:— EKBOLĒ (ἐκβολή), lit., a throwing out (from *ekballō*, to throw out), denotes a jettison, a throwing out of cargo, Acts 27 : 18, lit., ' they made a throwing out,' R.V., " they began to throw the freight overboard," A.V., " they lightened the ship."¶ In the Sept., Ex. 11 : 1 ; Jonah 1 : 5.¶

For FREQUENT, 2 Cor. 11 : 23, see ABUNDANT, D

FRESH

3501 AG:535D CB:1259C NEOS (νέος), new (in respect of time, as distinct from *kainos*, new, in respect of quality), is translated " fresh " in the R.V. of Matt. 9 : 17 ; Mark 2 : 22 ; Luke 5 : 38, with reference to wineskins. See NEW.

1099 AG:162A CB:1248B *Note : Glukus*, sweet, is used in Jas. 3 : 11, 12 (in this verse, A.V., " fresh," R.V., " sweet," as in both elsewhere) ; Rev. 10 : 9, 10. See SWEET.¶

FRIEND (make one's)

A. Nouns.

5384 AG:861A CB:1264A 1. PHILOS (φίλος), primarily an adjective, denoting loved, dear, or friendly, became used as a noun, (*a*) masculine, Matt. 11 : 19 ; fourteen times in Luke (once feminine, 15 : 9) ; six in John ; three in Acts ; two in James, 2 : 23, " the friend of God ; " 4 : 4, " a friend of the world ; " 3 John 14 (twice) ; (*b*) feminine, Luke 15 : 9, " her friends."

2083 AG:314C CB:1250A 2. HETAIROS (ἑταῖρος), a comrade, companion, partner, is used as a term of kindly address in Matt. 20 : 13 ; 22 : 12 ; 26 : 50. This, as expressing comradeship, is to be distinguished from No. 1, which is a term of endearment. Some mss. have the word in Matt. 11 : 16 ; the best have *heterois*, others, A.V. and R.V., " fellows." See FELLOW.

Notes : (1) The phrase *hoi para autou*, in Mark 3 : 21, " his friends," lit. means ' the (ones) beside Him,' i.e., those belonging to him. (2) In Mark 5 : 19, " thy friends " represents the phrase *hoi soi*, lit., ' the (ones) to thee,' i.e., ' thine own.'

B. Verb.

3982 AG:639A CB:1263A PEITHŌ (πείθω), to persuade, influence, is rendered " having made

. . . their friend" in Acts 12 : 20, of the folks of Tyre and Sidon in winning the good will of Blastus, Herod's chamberlain, possibly with bribes. See ASSURE, B, No. 3.

FRIENDSHIP

PHILIA (φιλία), akin to *philos*, a friend (see above), is rendered in 5373
Jas. 4 : 4, " the friendship (of the world)." It involves " the idea of loving AG:859D CB:1264A
as well as being loved" (Mayor); cp. the verb in John 15 : 19.¶

FRO and FROM; see † p. 1.

FROG

BATRACHOS (βάτραχος) is mentioned in Rev. 16 : 13. Quacks 944
were represented as frogs and were associated metaphorically with AG:137D CB:–
serpents.¶

For FROWARD see CROOKED

FRUIT (bear), FRUITFUL, UNFRUITFUL

A. Nouns.

1. KARPOS (καρπός), fruit, is used (I) of the fruit of trees, fields, the 2590
earth, that which is produced by the inherent energy of a living organism, AG:404C CB:1253B
e.g., Matt. 7 : 17; Jas. 5 : 7, 18; plural, e.g., in Luke 12 : 17 [for the next verse, see Note (1) below] and 2 Tim. 2 : 6; of the human body, Luke 1 : 42; Acts 2 : 30; (II) metaphorically, (*a*) of works or deeds, fruit being the visible expression of power working inwardly and invisibly, the character of the fruit being evidence of the character of the power producing it, Matt. 7 : 16. As the visible expressions of hidden lusts are the works of the flesh, so the invisible power of the Holy Spirit in those who are brought into living union with Christ (John 15 : 2-8, 16) produces " the fruit of the Spirit," Gal. 5 : 22, the singular form suggesting the unity of the character of the Lord as reproduced in them, namely, " love, joy, peace, longsuffering, kindness, goodness, faithfulness, meekness, temperance," all in contrast with the confused and often mutually antagonistic " works of the flesh." So in Phil. 1 : 11, marg., " fruit of righteousness." In Heb. 12 : 11, the fruit of righteousness is described as " peaceable fruit," the outward effect of Divine chastening; "the fruit of righteousness is sown in peace," Jas. 3 : 18, i.e., the seed contains the fruit; those who make peace, produce a harvest of righteousness; in Eph. 5 : 9, " the fruit of the light" (R.V., and see context) is seen in " goodness and righteousness and truth," as the expression of the union of the Christian with God (Father, Son and Holy Spirit); for God is good, Mark 10 : 18, the Son is " the righteous One," Acts 7 : 52, the Spirit is " the Spirit of truth," John 16 : 13; (*b*) of advantage, profit, consisting

(1) of converts as the result of evangelistic ministry, John 4 : 36 ; Rom. 1 : 13 ; Phil. 1 : 22 ; (2) of sanctification, through deliverance from a life of sin and through service to God, Rom. 6 : 22, in contrast to (3) the absence of anything regarded as advantageous as the result of former sins, ver. 21 ; (4) of the reward for ministration to servants of God, Phil. 4 : 17 ; (5) of the effect of making confession to God's Name by the sacrifice of praise, Heb. 13 : 15.

1081 (GENN-) AG:155A CB:1248A (GENN-) 2. GENĒMA (γένημα), from *ginomai*, to come into being, denotes fruit (*a*) as the produce of the earth, e.g., the vine ; in the following the best mss. have this noun, Matt. 26 : 29 ; Mark 14 : 25 ; Luke 22 : 18 ; [12 : 18 in some mss. ; see Note (1)] ; (*b*) metaphorically, as " the fruits of . . . righteousness " (i.e., of material ministrations to the needy), 2 Cor. 9 : 10.¶

Notes : (1) In Luke 12 : 18 some mss. have *gennēmata*, a mistake for *genēmata* ; the best have *sitos*, corn. (2) *Genēma* is to be distinguished
1081 AG:155D CB:1248A from *gennēma*, offspring (from *gennaō*, to beget), Matt. 3 : 7 ; 12 : 34 ; 23 : 33 ; Luke 3 : 7.¶

3703 AG:576D CB:— 3. OPŌRA (ὀπώρα) primarily denotes late summer or early autumn, i.e., late July, all August and early September. Since that is the time of fruit-bearing, the word was used, by metonymy, for the fruits themselves, Rev. 18 : 14.¶

5352 AG:857C CB:— *Note :* Cp. *phthinopōrinos*, autumnal, in Jude 12, " autumn trees," bearing no fruit when fruit should be expected.¶

B. Adjectives.

2593 AG:405B CB:— 1. KARPOPHOROS (καρποφόρος) denotes fruitful (A, No. 1, and *pherō*, to bear), Acts 14 : 17.¶ Cp. C. below.

175 AG:29D CB:1234A 2. AKARPOS (ἄκαρπος), unfruitful (*a*, negative, and A, No. 1), is used figuratively (*a*) of " the word of the Kingdom," rendered unfruitful in the case of those influenced by the cares of the world and the deceitfulness of riches, Matt. 13 : 22 ; Mark 4 : 19 ; (*b*) of the understanding of one praying with a " tongue," which effected no profit to the church without an interpretation of it, 1 Cor. 14 : 14 ; (*c*) of the works of darkness, Eph. 5 : 11 ; (*d*) of believers who fail " to maintain good works," indicating the earning of one's living so as to do good works to others, Tit. 3 : 14 ; of the effects of failing to supply in one's faith the qualities of virtue, knowledge, temperance, patience, godliness, love of the brethren, and love, 2 Pet. 1 : 8. In Jude 12 it is rendered " without fruit," of ungodly men, who oppose the Gospel while pretending to uphold it, depicted as " autumn trees " (see Note under A, No. 3).¶ In the Sept., Jer. 2 : 6.¶

C. Verb.

2592 AG:405A CB:1253B KARPOPHOREŌ (καρποφορέω), to bear or bring forth fruit (see B, No. 1), is used (*a*) in the natural sense, of the fruit of the earth, Mark 4 : 28 ; (*b*) metaphorically, of conduct, or that which takes effect in conduct, Matt. 13 : 23 ; Mark 4 : 20 ; Luke 8 : 15 ; Rom. 7 : 4, 5 (the latter, of evil fruit, borne " unto death," of activities resulting from a state of

alienation from God) ; Col. 1 : 6, in the Middle Voice ; Col. 1 : 10.¶
Note : For " bring forth fruit to perfection," Luke 8 : 14, see PERFECTION, B.

For FRUSTRATE, Gal. 2 : 21, see VOID

FULFIL, FULFILLING, FULFILMENT

A. Verbs.

1. PLĒROŌ (*πληρόω*) signifies (1) to fill (see FILL) ; (2) to fulfil, 4137
complete, (*a*) of time, e.g., Mark 1 : 15 ; Luke 21 : 24 ; John 7 : 8 (A.V., AG:670C CB:1265B
" full come ") ; Acts 7 : 23, R.V., " he was well-nigh forty years old " (A.V., " was full " etc.), lit., ' the time of forty years was fulfilled to him ; ' ver. 30, A.V., " were expired ; " 9 : 23 ; 24 : 27 (A.V.," after two years ; " R.V., " when two years were fulfilled ") ; (*b*) of number, Rev. 6 : 11 ; (*c*) of good pleasure, 2 Thess. 1 : 11 ; (*d*) of joy, Phil. 2 : 2 ; in the Passive Voice, ' to be fulfilled,' John 3 : 29 and 17 : 13 ; in the following the verb is rendered " fulfilled " in the R.V., for the A.V., " full," John 15 : 11 ; 16 : 24 ; 1 John 1 : 4 ; 2 John 12 ; (*e*) of obedience, 2 Cor. 10 : 6 ; (*f*) of works, Rev. 3 : 2 ; (*g*) of the future Passover, Luke 22 : 16 ; (*h*) of sayings, prophecies, etc., e.g., Matt. 1 : 22 (twelve times in Matt., two in Mark, four in Luke, eight in John, two in Acts) ; Jas. 2 : 23 ; in Col. 1 : 25 the word signifies to preach fully, to complete the ministry of the Gospel appointed. See FILL.

2. ANAPLĒROŌ (*ἀναπληρόω*), to fill up, fill completely (*ana*, up, 378
up to, and No. 1), is used (*a*) of Isaiah's prophecy of Israel's rejection of AG:59C CB:1235B
God, fulfilled in the rejection of His Son, Matt. 13 : 14 ; (*b*) of the status of a person in a church, R.V., " filleth the place," for A.V., " occupieth the room," 1 Cor. 14 : 16 ; (*c*) of an adequate supply of service, 1 Cor. 16 : 17, " supplied ; " Phil. 2 : 30, " to supply ; " (*d*) of sins, 1 Thess. 2 : 16 ; (*e*) of the law of Christ, Gal. 6 : 2. See FILL, OCCUPY, SUPPLY.¶

3. TELEŌ (*τελέω*), to end (akin to *telos*, an end), signifies, among its 5055
various meanings, to give effect to, and is translated " fulfil," of the Law, AG:810D CB:1271B
intentionally, Jas. 2 : 8, or unconsciously, Rom. 2 : 27 ; of the prophetic Scriptures concerning the Death of Christ, Acts 13 : 29 ; prohibitively, of the lust of the flesh, Gal. 5 : 16. See ACCOMPLISH, FINISH.

Notes : (1) In regard to this word in Rev. 15 : 1 and 8, the R.V., " finished," corrects the A.V., " filled up," and " fulfilled," as the judgments there indicated finish the whole series of those consisting of the wrath of God ; so in 20 : 3, of the thousand years of the Millennium (cp. vv. 5, 7). (2) In 17 : 17, the R.V. has " should be accomplished," for A.V., " shall be fulfilled." (3) In Luke 22 : 37 the A.V. has " be accomplished " (R.V., " be fulfilled ").

4. SUNTELEŌ (*συντελέω*), to complete, is translated " fulfilled " in 4931 AG:792A
the A.V. of Mark 13 : 4 (R.V., " accomplished "). See COMPLETE. CB:1271A

5048 AG:809D 5. TELEIOŌ (τελειόω), to bring to an end, fulfil, is rendered to fulfil,
CB:1271B of days. Luke 2 : 43 ; of the Scripture, John 19 : 28 See FINISH.

4135 6. PLĒROPHOREŌ (πληροφορέω), to bring in full measure, from
AG:670B CB:1265B *plēroō* (see No. 1), and *phoreō*, to bring; hence, to fulfil, of circumstances relating to Christ, Luke 1 : 1, R.V., "have been fulfilled" (A.V. "are most surely believed"); of evangelical ministry, 2 Tim. 4 : 5, "fulfil" (A.V., "make full proof"); so in ver. 17, R.V., "fully proclaimed" (A.V., "fully known"). See ASSURE, PERSUADE.

1603 7. EKPLĒROŌ (ἐκπληρόω), a strengthened form of No. 1, occurs in
AG:244A
CB:1243C Acts 13 : 33.¶

POIEō *Notes:* (1) *Poieō*, to do, is so rendered in the R.V., for A.V. "fulfil,"
4160 AG:680D in Acts 13 : 22; Eph. 2 : 3; Rev. 17 : 17 [for the end of this verse see
CB:1265C Note (2) under *teleō*, above]. (2) *Ginomai*, to become, to take place, is
GINOMAI 1096 rendered "fulfilled" in the A.V. of Matt. 5 : 18; 24 : 34; Luke 21 : 32,
AG:158A R.V., "accomplished," in each place.

CB:1248B

B. Nouns.

4138 AG:672A 1. PLĒRŌMA (πλήρωμα) stands for the result of the action expressed
CB:1265B in *pleroō*, to fill. It is used to signify (*a*) that which has been completed, the complement, fulness, e.g., John 1 : 16; Eph. 1 : 23; some suggest that the "fulness" here points to the Body as the filled receptacle of the power of Christ (words terminating in —*ma* are frequently concrete in character; cp. *dikaiōma* in Rom. 5 : 18, act of righteousness); in Mark 8 : 20 the rendering "basketfuls" (R.V.) represents the plural of this word, lit., 'the fulnesses of (how many baskets);' (*b*) that which fills up, Matt. 9 : 16; Mark 2 : 21 (see FILL); (*c*) a filling up, fulfilment, Rom. 13 : 10, of the fulfilling of the Law. See FULNESS (below).

5050 2. TELEIŌSIS (τελείωσις), a fulfilment, is so rendered in Luke 1 : 45,
AG:810B CB:1271B R.V. (A.V., "performance"). See PERFECTION.

FULL

A. Adjectives.

4134 1. PLĒRĒS (πλήρης) denotes full, (*a*) in the sense of being filled,
AG:669D CB:1265B materially, Matt. 14 : 20; 15 : 37; Mark 8 : 19 (said of baskets full of bread crumbs); of leprosy, Luke 5 : 12; spiritually, of the Holy Spirit, Luke 4 : 1; Acts 6 : 3; 7 : 55; 11 : 24; grace and truth, John 1 : 14; faith, Acts 6 : 5; grace and power, 6 : 8; of the effects of spiritual life and qualities, seen in good works, Acts 9 : 36; in an evil sense, of guile and villany, Acts 13 : 10; wrath, 19 : 28; (*b*) in the sense of being complete, "full corn in the ear," Mark 4 : 28; of a reward hereafter, 2 John 8.¶

3324 2. MESTOS (μεστός), probably akin to a root signifying to measure,
AG:508B CB:1258B hence conveys the sense of having full measure, (*a*) of material things, a vessel, John 19 : 29; a net, 21 : 11; (*b*) metaphorically, of thoughts and feelings, exercised (1) in evil things, hypocrisy, Matt. 23 : 28; envy,

murder, strife, deceit, malignity, Rom. 1 : 29; the utterances of the tongue, Jas. 3 : 8; adultery, 2 Pet. 2 : 14; (2) in virtues, goodness, Rom. 15 : 14; mercy, etc., Jas. 3 : 17.¶

B. Verb.

GEMŌ (γέμω), to be full, to be heavily laden with, was primarily 1073
used of a ship; it is chiefly used in the N.T. of evil contents, such as AG:153D CB:1248A
extortion and excess, Matt. 23 : 25; dead men's bones, ver. 27; extortion and wickedness, Luke 11 : 39; cursing, Rom. 3 : 14; blasphemy, Rev. 17 : 3; abominations, ver. 4; of Divine judgments, 15 : 17; 21 : 9; (R.V., "laden," A.V., "full"); of good things, 4 : 6, 8; 5 : 8.¶

Notes: (1) *Gemizō* (see FILL, A, No. 9) is always rendered to fill in 1072
R.V. (2) For Acts 2 : 13, A.V., see FILL, No. 11. (3) For "fullgrown," AG:153C CB:1248A
Heb. 5 : 14, R.V., see AGE, No. 2; for Jas. 1 : 15, R.V., see FINISH, *Note* (2).

FULLER

GNAPHEUS (γναφεύς), akin to *knaptō*, to card wool, denotes a cloth- 1102
carder, or dresser (*gnaphos*, the prickly teasel-cloth; hence, a carding AG:162D CB:—
comb); it is used of the raiment of the Lord in Mark 9 : 3.¶

FULLGROWN: see AGE, B, No. 2, FINISH, *Note* (2)

FULLY: see ASSURED, COME, KNOW, PERSUADE, PREACH, RIPE

FULNESS

PLERŌMA (πλήρωμα) denotes fulness, that of which a thing is full; 4138
it is thus used of the grace and truth manifested in Christ, John 1 : 16; AG:672A CB:1265B
of all His virtues and excellencies, Eph. 4 : 13; "the blessing of Christ," Rom. 15 : 29, R.V. (not as A.V.); the conversion and restoration of Israel, Rom. 11 : 12; the completion of the number of Gentiles who receive blessing through the Gospel, ver. 25; the complete products of the earth, 1 Cor. 10 : 26; the end of an appointed period, Gal 4 : 4; Eph. 1 : 10; God, in the completeness of His Being, Eph. 3 : 19; Col. 1 : 19; 2 : 9; the Church as the complement of Christ, Eph. 1 : 23. In Mark 6 : 43, "basketfuls," R.V., is, lit., 'fulnesses of baskets.' For Matt. 9 : 16; Mark 2 : 21 see FILL, (B); for 8 : 20 see FULFIL, B.

Note: For *plērophoria*, "fulness," Heb. 6 : 11, R.V., see ASSURANCE. 4136 AG:670C CB:1265B

FURLONG

STADION (στάδιον) denotes (*a*) a stadium, i.e., a measure of length, 4712
600 Greek feet, or one-eighth of a Roman mile, Matt. 14 : 24 (in the best AG:764A CB:—
mss.); Luke 24 : 13; John 6 : 19; 11 : 18; Rev. 14 : 20; 21 : 16; (*b*) a race course, the length of the Olympic course, 1 Cor. 9 : 24.¶

FURNACE

2575 AG:401D

KAMINOS (κάμινος), an oven, furnace, kiln (whence Lat. *caminus*, CB:—

Eng., chimney), used for smelting, or for burning earthenware, occurs in Matt. 13 : 42, 50 ; Rev. 1 : 15 ; 9 : 2.¶

FURNISH

4766 AG:771C CB:— 1. STRŌNNUMI (στρώννυμι), or *strōnnuō*, to spread, is used of furnishing a room, Mark 14 : 15 ; Luke 22 : 12 ; of making a bed, Acts 9 : 34 ; in Matt. 21 : 8 ; Mark 11 : 8, "spread" (A.V., "strawed," twice). See SPREAD.¶

1822 AG:273C CB:1247C 2. EXARTIZŌ (ἐξαρτίζω), to fit out, to prepare perfectly, to complete for a special purpose (*ex*, out, used intensively, and *artios*, joined, *artos*, a joint), is used of accomplishing days, Acts 21 : 5, i.e., of terminating a space of time ; of being "completely furnished," by means of the Scriptures, for spiritual service, 2 Tim. 3 : 17. See ACCOMPLISH.

4130 AG:658A CB:1265A 3. PLĒTHŌ (πλήθω), Matt. 21 : 10, "furnished" R.V., "filled." See FILL, No. 5.

FURTHER

2089 AG:315C CB:1247A 1. ETI (ἔτι), yet, still, further, is used (*a*) of time, most usually translated "yet," e.g., Matt. 12 : 46 ; or negatively, "any more," "no more," e.g., Heb. 8 : 12 ; (*b*) of degree, translated "further," or "any further," Matt. 26 : 65 ; Mark 5 : 35 ; 14 : 63 ; Luke 22 : 71 ; Heb. 7 : 11 ; in Acts 21 : 28, R.V., "moreover" (A.V., "further"). See LONGER,
(PORRō) MORE, MOREOVER, STILL, THENCEFORTH, YET.

4206 AG:693D CB:— 2. PORRŌTERON (πορρώτερον), the comparative degree of *porrō*, far off, signifies "further," Luke 24 : 28. See FAR.

1024 AG:147B CB:1239B *Note :* In Acts 27 : 28, *brachu*, a little, is rendered "a little further," A.V. (R.V., "after a little space").

FURTHERANCE

4297 AG:707D CB:1266C *Notes :* (1) In Phil. 1 : 12, 25, A.V., *prokopē*, a striking forward (*pro*, forward, *koptō*, to cut), is translated "furtherance ;" "progress" in R.V., as in 1 Tim. 4 : 15. Originally the word was used of a pioneer cutting his way through brushwood. See PROGRESS.¶ (2) In Phil. 1 : 5 the R.V. "(for your fellowship) in furtherance of the Gospel," and in 2 : 22, "in furtherance of the Gospel," are, lit., 'unto the Gospel.'

FURTHERMORE

1534 AG:233D CB:1243B EITA (εἶτα), which is chiefly used of time or enumerations, signifying 'then' or 'next,' is once used in argument, signifying 'furthermore,' Heb. 12 : 9. See AFTERWARD, THEN.

3063 AG:479D (LOIPOS 3.b.) CB:1257B *Note :* In 1 Thess. 4 : 1 the A.V. "furthermore" translates the phrase *to loipon*, lit., 'for the rest,' R.V., "finally." See FINALLY.

FURY See FIERCE, WRATH

FUTILE See VAIN; FUTURE See HENCEFORTH

GAIN (Noun and verb)

A. Nouns.

1. ERGASIA (ἐργασία) signifies (*a*) work, working, performance (from 2039
ergon, work), Eph. 4 : 19 ; in Luke 12 : 58, "diligence ;" (*b*) business or AG:307C
gain got by work, Acts 16 : 16, 19 ; in 19 : 24, 25, the R.V. adheres to the CB:1246B
meaning "business" (A.V., "gain" and "craft"). See CRAFT,
DILIGENCE.¶

2. PORISMOS (πορισμός) primarily denotes a providing (akin to 4200
porizō, to procure), then, a means of gain, 1 Tim. 6 : 5 (R.V., "a way of AG:693A
gain") ; 6 : 6.¶ CB:—

3. KERDOS (κέρδος), gain (akin to *kerdainō*, see below), occurs in 2771
Phil. 1 : 21 ; 3 : 7 ; Tit. 1 : 11. See LUCRE.¶ AG:429C CB:1255A

B. Verbs.

1. KERDAINŌ (κερδαίνω), akin to A, No. 3, signifies (I), literally, 2770
(*a*) to gain something, Matt. 16 : 26 ; 25 : 16 (in the best mss.), 17, 20, 22 ; AG:429C
Mark 8 : 36 ; Luke 9 : 25 ; (*b*) to get gain, make a profit, Jas. 4 : 13 ; CB:1255A
(II), metaphorically, (*a*) to win persons, said (1) of gaining an offending
brother who by being told privately of his offence, and by accepting the
representations, is won from alienation and from the consequences of his DIAPRAGMATEUOMAI
fault, Matt. 18 : 15 ; (2) of winning souls into the Kingdom of God by the 1281 AG:187D
Gospel, 1 Cor. 9 : 19, 20 (twice), 21, 22, or by godly conduct, 1 Pet. 3 : 1 CB:1241B PERIPOIEō
(R.V., "gained") ; (3) of so practically appropriating Christ to oneself (-OMAI)
that He becomes the dominating power in and over one's whole being 4046 AG:650A
and circumstances, Phil. 3 : 8 (R.V., "gain") ; (*b*) to gain things, said CB:1263B
of getting injury and loss, Acts 27 : 21, R.V. "gotten." See GET.¶ PROSERGAZOMAI 4333

2. DIAPRAGMATEUOMAI (διαπραγματεύομαι) signifies to gain by AG:713A
trading, Luke 19 : 15 (from *dia*, through, used intensively, and CB:— POIEō
pragmateuomai, to busy oneself, to be engaged in business).¶ 4160

3. PERIPOIEŌ (περιποιέω), to save for oneself, gain, is in the Middle AG:680D
Voice in the best mss. in Luke 17 : 33, R.V., "gain." See PURCHASE. CB:1265C PLEONEKTEō

Notes : (1) In Luke 19 : 16, A.V., *prosergazomai*, to work out in 4122
addition, or to earn in addition, is translated "gained" (R.V., "made") ; AG:667C CB:1265B
in ver. 18 the verb *poieō*, to make, is translated in the same way, the ERGAZOMAI
English verb "make" standing both for earning and for producing. 2038 AG:306D
(2) In 2 Cor. 12 : 17, 18, *pleonekteō*, to claim unduly, to overreach, is CB:1246C
translated "make a gain of," A.V. (R.V., "take advantage of"). (3) KATATITHēMI
For *ergazomai*, Rev. 18 : 17, R.V., see TRADE. (4) In Acts 25 : 9, R.V., 2698 AG:419C
katatithēmi, Middle Voice, to lay up for oneself, is rendered "to gain." CB:—

GAINSAY, GAINSAYER, GAINSAYING

A. Verbs.

483 AG:74D CB:— 1. ANTILEGŌ (*ἀντιλέγω*), to contradict, oppose, lit., say against, is translated "gainsaying" in Rom. 10 : 21 and Tit. 2 : 9, R.V. (A.V., "answering again"), of servants in regard to masters; in Tit. 1 : 9 "gainsayers." Moulton and Milligan (Vocab.) illustrate from the papyri "the strong sense of *antilegō* in Rom. 10 : 21, 'contradict,' 'oppose'." See ANSWER, CONTRADICT.

471 (-EPō) AG:73B CB:— 2. ANTEIPON (*ἀντεῖπον*), which serves as an aorist tense of No. 1, is rendered "gainsay" in Luke 21 : 15; "say against" in Acts 4 : 14. See SAY.¶

B. Noun.

485 AG:75A CB:— ANTILOGIA (*ἀντιλογία*), akin to A, No. 1, is rendered "gainsaying," in Heb. 12 : 3, R.V., and Jude 11. Opposition in act seems to be implied in these two places; though this sense has been questioned by some, it is confirmed by instances from the papyri (Moulton and Milligan, Vocab.). See CONTRADICTION, DISPUTE, STRIFE.

C. Adjective.

368 AG:58C CB:— ANANTIRRHĒTOS (*ἀναντίρρητος*), lit., not to be spoken against (*a*, negative, *n*, euphonic, *anti*, against, *rhētos*, spoken), is rendered "cannot be gainsaid" in Acts 19 : 36, R.V.¶

D. Adverb.

369 AG:58C CB:— ANANTIRRHĒTŌS (*ἀναντιρρήτως*), corresponding to C, is translated "without gainsaying" in Acts 10 : 29; it might be rendered 'unquestioningly.'¶

GALL

5521 AG:883B CB:1240A CHOLĒ (*χολή*), a word probably connected with *chloē*, yellow, denotes gall, (*a*) literal, Matt. 27 : 34 (cp. Ps. 69 : 21); some regard the word here as referring to myrrh, on account of Mark 15 : 23; (*b*) metaphorical, Acts 8 : 23, where "gall of bitterness" stands for extreme wickedness, productive of evil fruit.¶ In the O.T. it is used (*a*) of a plant characterized by bitterness (probably wormwood), Deut. 29 : 18; Hos. 10 : 4; Amos 6 : 12; (*b*) as the translation of the word *mererah*, bitterness, Job. 13 : 26, e.g.; (*c*) as the translation of *rôsh*, venom; in Deut. 32 : 32 "(grapes) of gall." In Job 20 : 25, the gall bladder is referred to (the receptacle of bile). The ancients supposed that the poison of serpents lay in the gall (see Job 20 : 14).

GALLON See **FIRKIN**

GAMES, see CONTEND

GANGRENE

1044 AG:149A CB:— GANGRAINA (*γάγγραινα*), an eating sore, spreading corruption and producing mortification, is used, in 2 Tim. 2 : 17, of errorists in the church, who, pretending to give true spiritual food, produce spiritual gangrene (A.V., "canker," R.V., "gangrene").¶

GARDEN

KĒPOS (κῆπος), a garden, occurs in Luke 13 : 19, in one of the Lord's parables; in John 18 : 1, 26, of the garden of Gethsemane; in 19 : 41, of the garden near the place of the Lord's crucifixion.¶ KēPOS 2779 AG:430D KēPOUROS 2780 AG:430D

GARDENER

KĒPOUROS (κηπουρός), lit., a garden-keeper (from *kēpos*, see above, and *ouros*, a watcher), occurs in John 20 : 15.¶ STEMMA 4725 AG:766A CB:1270A HIMATION 2440

GARLAND

STEMMA (στέμμα) denotes a wreath (from *stephō*, to put around, enwreath), as used in sacrifices, Acts 14 : 13.¶ AG:376B CB:1250C ESTHēSIS 2067 AG:312B (ESTHēS)

GARMENT

Note: For *himation*, the usual word for "garment," see CLOTHING, where see also *esthēsis* (translated "garments" in the A.V. of Luke 24 : 4, R.V., "apparel"), *enduma*, *chitōn*, and *stolē* (R.V., "robe" in Mark 16 : 5). The fact of the wedding garment, *enduma* in Matt. 22, vv. 11, 12, indicates that persons of high rank showed their magnificence by providing the guests with festal garments. See APPAREL. ENDUMA 1742 AG:263C CB:1245 CHITōN 5509 AG:882B STOLē 4749 AG:769C CB:1270A

GARNER

APOTHĒKĒ (ἀποθήκη), a storehouse, granary (from *apo*, away, and *tithēmi*, to put), is translated "garner" in Matt. 3 : 12 and Luke 3 : 17. See BARN. 596 AG:91A CB:—

GARNISH

KOSMEŌ (κοσμέω) is translated by the verb to garnish in Matt. 12 : 44; 23 : 29; Luke 11 : 25; and in the A.V. of Rev. 21 : 19. See ADORN. 2885 AG:445A CB:1255C

For GARRISON see GUARD, B, No. 3

GATE

1. PULĒ (πύλη) is used (*a*) literally, for a larger sort of gate, in the wall either of a city or palace or temple, Luke 7 : 12, of Nain (burying places were outside the gates of cities); Acts 3 : 10; 9 : 24; 12 : 10; Heb. 13 : 12; (*b*) metaphorically, of the gates at the entrances of the ways leading to life and to destruction, Matt. 7 : 13, 14; some mss. have *pulē*, for *thura*, a door, in Luke 13 : 24 (see the R.V.); of the gates of Hades, Matt. 16 : 18, than which nothing was regarded as stronger. The importance and strength of gates made them viewed as synonymous with power. By metonymy, the gates stood for those who held government and administered justice there.¶ 4439 AG:729B CB:1268A

2. PULŌN (πυλών), akin to No. 1, primarily signifies a porch or 4440 AG:729C CB:1268A

vestibule, e.g., Matt. 26 : 71 ; Luke 16 : 20 ; Acts 10 : 17 ; 12 : 13, 14 ; then, the gateway or gate tower of a walled town, Acts 14 : 13 ; Rev. 21 : 12, 13, 15, 21, 25 ; 22 : 14.¶

THURA 2374 AG:365D CB:1272C PROBATIKOS 4262 AG:703A CB:— *Notes :* (1) In Acts 3 : 2 *thura* denotes, not a gate, but a door, R.V. See DOOR. (2) *Probatikos*, signifying of, or belonging to, sheep, denotes a sheep gate in John 5 : 2, R.V., and A.V. marg. (3) The conjectural emendation which suggests the idea of "floods" for "gates" in Matt. 16 : 18 is not sufficiently substantiated to be accepted.

GATHER, GATHERING

A. Verbs.

4863 AG:782A CB:1270B 1. SUNAGŌ (συνάγω), to gather or bring together, is said of (*a*) persons, e.g., Matt. 2 : 4 ; (*b*) things, e.g., Matt. 13 : 30 ; in Luke 15 : 13 the idea is that of gathering his goods together for sale, i.e., 'having sold off all.' See ASSEMBLE, BESTOW, COME, RESORT.

1996 AG:301D CB:1246A 2. EPISUNAGŌ (ἐπισυνάγω), to gather together, suggesting stress upon the place at which the gathering is made (*epi*, to), is said of a hen and her chickens, Matt. 23 : 37 ; and so of the Lord's would-be protecting care of the people of Jerusalem, *id.*, and Luke 13 : 34 ; of the gathering together of the elect, Matt. 24 : 31 ; Mark 13 : 27 ; of the gathering together of a crowd, Mark 1 : 33 ; Luke 12 : 1.¶

4816 AG:777A CB:1270B 3. SULLEGŌ (συλλέγω), to collect, gather up or out (*sun*, with *legō*, to pick out), is said of gathering grapes and figs, Matt. 7 : 16 ; Luke 6 : 44 (cp. No. 5) ; tares, Matt. 13 : 28, 29, 30, 40 ; good fish, 13 : 48 ; "all things that cause stumbling, and them that do iniquity," 13 : 41.¶

4962 AG:795C CB:1271A 4. SUSTREPHŌ (συστρέφω) signifies (*a*) to twist together or roll into a mass (*sun*, together, *strephō*, to turn), said of the bundle of sticks gathered by Paul, Acts 28 : 3 ; (*b*) to assemble or gather together (possibly, to journey about together), of persons, Matt. 17 : 22 (in the best mss.), R.V., marg.¶

5166 AG:828B CB:1273A 5. TRUGAŌ (τρυγάω) signifies to gather in, of harvest, vintage, ripe fruits (*trugē* denotes fruit, etc., gathered in autumn), Luke 6 : 44, of grapes (last part of ver. ; for the previous clause, as to figs, see No. 3) ; metaphorically, of the clusters of "the vine of the earth," Rev. 14 : 18 ; of that from which they are gathered, ver. 19.¶

— AG:21C CB:1238B 6. ATHROIZŌ (ἀθροίζω) denotes to assemble, gather together, Luke 24 : 33 (according to the best mss.) ; the word is akin to *athroos*, assembled in crowds (not found in the N.T.).¶

4867 AG:783B CB:1270C 7. SUNATHROIZŌ (συναθροίζω), *sun*, together, and No. 6, signifies (*a*) to gather together, Acts 19 : 25, R.V. (A.V., "called together") ; in the Passive Voice, 12 : 12.¶

1865 AG:281B CB:— 8. EPATHROIZŌ (ἐπαθροίζω), to assemble besides (*epi*), said of multitudes, Luke 11 : 29, is rendered "were gathering together" (Middle Voice), R.V. (A.V., "were gathered thick together").¶

Notes : (1) In Eph. 1 : 10, A.V., the verb *anakephalaioō*, to sum up,

head up, is rendered " might gather together in one " (R.V., " sum up "). ANAKEPHALAIOō
(2) In Luke 8 : 4, A.V. (*suneimi*, to come together) as " were gathered (-IOMAI) 346
together " (see R.V.). (4) For " assuredly gathering " see CONCLUDE. AG:55D CB:1235A

B. Noun. SUNEIMI

EPISUNAGŌGĒ (ἐπισυναγωγή), a gathering together, is used in 4895
2 Thess. 2 : 1, of the 'rapture' of the saints; for Heb. 10 : 25, see AG:787A CB:—
ASSEMBLE. EPISUNAGōGē 1997

Note: For *logia*, 1 Cor. 16 : 2, A.V., see COLLECTION. AG:301D CB:1246A

For GAY see GOODLY, A, *Note*. LOGIA 3048 AG:475D

For GAZE see BEHOLD, No. 3. (LOGEIA) CB:1257A (LOGEIA)

GAZINGSTOCK

THEATRIZŌ (θεατρίζω) signifies to make a spectacle (from *theatron*, 2301
a theatre, spectacle, show); it is used in the Passive Voice in Heb. AG:353C CB:1271C
10 : 33, " being made a gazingstock."¶ (-OMAI)

GEAR

SKEUOS (σκεῦος), an implement, vessel, utensil, is used of the tackling 4632
or gear of a ship, Acts 27 : 17, R.V. (A.V., " sail "). AG:754A CB:1269A

For GENDER see BEGET, No. 1

GENEALOGY

A. Noun.

GENEALOGIA (γενεαλογία) is used in 1 Tim. 1 : 4 and Tit. 3 : 9, 1076
with reference to such genealogies as are found in Philo, Josephus and AG:154B CB:1248A
the book of Jubilees, by which Jews traced their descent from the patriarchs and their families, and perhaps also to Gnostic genealogies and orders of æons and spirits. Amongst the Greeks, as well as other nations, mythological stories gathered round the birth and genealogy of their heroes. Probably Jewish genealogical tales crept into Christian communities. Hence the warnings to Timothy and Titus.¶

B. Verb.

GENEALOGEŌ (γενεαλογέω), to reckon or trace a genealogy (from 1075
genea, a race, and *legō*, to choose, pick out), is used, in the Passive Voice, AG:154B CB:1248A
of Melchizedek in Heb. 7 : 6, R.V., " whose genealogy (A.V., 'descent') is not counted."¶

C. Adjective (*negative*).

AGENEALOGĒTOS (ἀγενεαλόγητος), denoting without recorded 35
pedigree (*a*, negative, and an adjectival form from B.), is rendered AG:8C CB:1233B
" without genealogy " in Heb. 7 : 3. The narrative in Gen. 14 is so framed in facts and omissions as to foreshadow the Person of Christ.¶

GENERAL See CAPTAIN For GENERAL (Assembly) see ASSEMBLY, No. 2

1074 AG:153D
GENERATION

CB:1248A 1. GENEA (γενεά) : see AGE, No. 2.
1078 2. GENESIS (γένεσις) denotes an origin, a lineage, or birth, translated
AG:154D CB:1248A " generation " in Matt. 1 : 1. See NATURAL, NATURE.
GENNĒMA *Notes :* (1) For *gennēma*, translated " generation " in the A.V. of Matt.
1081 3 : 7 ; 12 : 34 ; 23 : 33 ; Luke 3 : 7, see OFFSPRING¶ (2) For *genos*,
AG:155D CB:1248A translated " generation " in 1 Pet. 2 : 9, A.V., see KIND.

GENOS 1085 AG:156A CB:1248B
GENTILES

A. Nouns.

1484 1. ETHNOS (ἔθνος), whence Eng., " heathen," denotes, firstly, a
AG:218B CB:1246C multitude or company ; then, a multitude of people of the same nature
GENEROUS See GOOD, LIBERAL or genus, a nation, people ; it is used in the singular, of the Jews, e.g., Luke 7 : 5 ; 23 : 2 ; John 11 : 48, 50–52 ; in the plural, of nations (Heb., *goïim*) other than Israel, e.g., Matt. 4 : 15 ; Rom. 3 : 29 ; 11 : 11 ; 15 : 10 ; Gal. 2 : 8 ; occasionally it is used of Gentile converts in distinction from Jews, e.g., Rom. 11 : 13 ; 16 : 4 ; Gal. 2 : 12, 14 ; Eph. 3 : 1.
1672 AG:251D 2. HELLĒN (ἕλλην) originally denoted the early descendants of
CB:1249C Thessalian Hellas ; then, Greeks as opposed to barbarians, Rom. 1 : 14. It became applied to such Gentiles as spoke the Greek language, e.g., Gal. 2 : 3 ; 3 : 28. Since that was the common medium of intercourse in the Roman Empire, Greek and Gentile became more or less interchangeable terms. For this term the R.V. always adheres to the word " Greeks," e.g., John 7 : 35 ; Rom. 2 : 9, 10 ; 3 : 9 ; 1 Cor. 10 : 32, where the local church is distinguished from Jews and Gentiles ; 12 : 13.

B. Adjective.

1482 AG:218B ETHNIKOS (ἐθνικός) is used as noun, and translated " Gentiles "
CB:1246C in the R.V. of Matt. 5 : 47 ; 6 : 7 ; " the Gentile " in 18 : 17 (A.V., " an heathen man ") ; " the Gentiles " in 3 John 7, A.V. and R.V.¶

C. Adverb.

1483 AG:218B ETHNIKŌS (ἐθνικῶς), in Gentile fashion, in the manner of Gentiles,
CB:1246C is used in Gal. 2 : 14, " as do the Gentiles," R.V.¶
2992 AG:466C *Notes :* (1) For the synonymous word *laos*, a people, see PEOPLE.
CB:1256C (2) When, under the new order of things introduced by the Gospel the mystery of the Church was made known, the word *ethnos* was often used in contrast to the local church, 1 Cor. 5 : 1 ; 10 : 20 ; 12 : 2 ; 1 Thess. 4 : 5 ; 1 Pet. 2 : 12.

GENTLE, GENTLENESS, GENTLY

A. Adjectives.

1933 AG:292C 1. EPIEIKĒS (ἐπιεικής), from *epi*, unto, and *eikos*, likely, denotes
CB:1245C seemly, fitting ; hence, equitable, fair, moderate, forbearing, not insisting on the letter of the law ; it expresses that considerateness that

looks " humanely and reasonably at the facts of a case " ; it is rendered " gentle " in 1 Tim. 3 : 3, R.V. (A.V., " patient "), in contrast to contentiousness ; in Tit. 3 : 2, " gentle," in association with meekness ; in Jas. 3 : 17, as a quality of the wisdom from above ; in 1 Pet. 2 : 18, in association with the good ; for the R.V. rendering " forbearance " in Phil. 4 : 5, R.V., see FORBEARANCE. Cp. B. See PATIENT.¶ In the Sept., Esth. 8 : 13 ; Ps. 86 : 5.¶

2. ĒPIOS (ἤπιος), mild, gentle, was frequently used by Greek writers 2261
as characterizing a nurse with trying children or a teacher with refractory AG:348B CB:1246A
scholars, or of parents toward their children. In 1 Thess. 2 : 7, the Apostle uses it of the conduct of himself and his fellow-missionaries towards the converts at Thessalonica (cp. 2 Cor. 11 : 13, 20) ; in 2 Tim. 2 : 24, of the conduct requisite for a servant of the Lord.¶

B. Noun.

EPIEIKEIA (ἐπιείκεια), or *epieikia*, denotes fairness, moderation, 1932
gentleness, " sweet reasonableness " (Matthew Arnold) ; it is said of Christ, AG:292C CB:1245C
2 Cor. 10 : 1, where it is coupled with *praütēs*, " meekness " ; for its
meaning in Acts 24 : 4, see CLEMENCY.¶. Trench (Syn. § xlviii) considers PRAUTēS (-OTēS)
that the ideas of equity and justice, which are essential to the meaning, 4240
do not adequately express it in English. In contrast with *praütēs* AG:699A
(meekness), which is more especially a temperament or habit of mind, CB:1266B CHRēSTOTēS
epieikeia expresses an active dealing with others. 5544

Notes : (1) For *chrēstotēs*, kindness, goodness of heart, rendered AG:886B CB:1240A
" gentleness " in Gal. 5 : 22, A.V., see KINDNESS. The corresponding METRIOPATHEō
adjective *chrēstos* is translated " good," " kind," " easy," " gracious." 3356 AG:514D
(2) For *metriopatheō*, to bear gently with, Heb. 5 : 2, see BEAR, No. 13. CB:—

GET, GOT, GOTTEN

(*a*) *In the sense of acquiring :* HEURISKō 2147
1. HEURISKŌ (εὑρίσκω), to find, is translated " get " in Luke AG:324D
9 : 12, of victuals. See FIND. CB:1250B KTAOMAI

2. KTAOMAI (κτάομαι), to acquire, procure for oneself, gain, is 2932
rendered " get " in the R.V. of Matt. 10 : 9 and A.V. marg. (A.V., text, AG:455A CB:1256A
" provide ") ; in Luke 18 : 12 (for A.V., " possess "). See OBTAIN, KERDAINō
POSSESS, PROVIDE, PURCHASE. 2770 AG:429C

3. KERDAINŌ (κερδαίνω), to gain, is rendered " have gotten " CB:1255A
in Acts 27 : 21, R.V. (of injury and loss) ; the word is there used meta- PLEONEKTEō 4122
phorically, however, of avoiding, or saving oneself from. For the meaning, AG:667C
to get gain, Jas. 4 : 13, see GAIN. CB:1265B NIKAō

Notes : (1) For *pleonekteō*, to get an advantage of (A.V., in 2 Cor. 3528
2 : 11 ; R.V., " an advantage may be gained over,"), see ADVANTAGE. AG:539A CB:1259C
(2) In Rev. 15 : 2, A.V., *nikaō*, to conquer, prevail over, is translated PLOUTEō
" had gotten the victory " (R.V., " come victorious "). (3) In Rev. 4147 AG:673D
3 : 17, R.V., *plouteō*, to become rich, is rendered " I have gotten riches." CB:1265B

1826 (*b*) *In the sense of going :*
AG:275B (EXESTI) 1. EXEIMI (ἔξειμι), to go or come out, is used in Acts 27 : 43 of getting
CB:1247C to land. See DEPART, GO, No. 23.
5217 2. HUPAGŌ (ὑπάγω), to go away, withdraw, is rendered "get,"
AG:836C CB:— "get . . . hence," in Matt. 4 : 10 ; 16 : 23 ; Mark 8 : 33 ; some mss.
have it in Luke 4 : 8. See DEPART, GO, No. 8.
1831 3. EXERCHOMAI (ἐξέρχομαι), to come or go out, is translated
AG:274B CB:1247C "get . . . out" in Luke 13 : 31 ; Acts 7 : 3 ; 22 : 18. See COME, No. 3,
GO (Notes).
2597 4. KATABAINŌ (καταβαίνω), to descend, is translated "get . . .
AG:408B CB:1253C down," in Acts 10 : 20. See COME, No. 19.
1684 5. EMBAINŌ (ἐμβαίνω), to enter, is translated "they got into" in
AG:254A CB:— John 6 : 24 (of boats), R.V. [A.V., "took (shipping)."]. See COME,
No. 21.
576 6. APOBAINŌ (ἀποβαίνω), to go from, is translated "they got out"
AG:88C CB:— in John 21 : 9, R.V. (A.V., "were come to"). See COME, 21 (Note).
645 *Note :* In Acts 21 : 1, A.V., *apospaō*, to withdraw or part from, is
AG:98A CB:— rendered "we had gotten (from)," R.V., "had parted (from)." After
the scene described at the end of ch. 20, it may well have the force of
being reft away (or tearing themselves away) from them. Cp. the same
verb in Luke 22 : 41 (' He was reft away from them '). See DRAW, PART,
WITHDRAW.

For GHOST see SPIRIT

GHOST (give up the)

1606 1. EKPNEŌ (ἐκπνέω), lit., to breathe out (*ek*, out, *pneō*, to breathe),
AG:244B CB:1243C to expire, is used in the N.T., without an object, "soul" or "life" being
understood, Mark 15 : 37, 39, and Luke 23 : 46, of the Death of Christ.
In Matt. 27 : 50 and John 19 : 30, where different verbs are used, the
act is expressed in a way which stresses it as of His own volition : in the
former, "Jesus . . . yielded up His spirit (*pneuma*) ; in the latter, "He
gave up His spirit."¶
1634 2. EKPSUCHŌ (ἐκψύχω), to expire, lit., to breathe out the soul (or
AG:247C CB:— life), to give up the ghost (*ek*, out, *psuchē*, the soul), is used in Acts 5 : 5, 10 ;
12 : 23.¶

GIFT, GIVING

1435 1. DŌRON (δῶρον), akin to *didōmi*, to give, is used (*a*) of gifts presented
AG:210D CB:1242A as an expression of honour, Matt. 2 : 11 ; (*b*) of gifts for the support of
the temple and the needs of the poor, Matt. 15 : 5 ; Mark 7 : 11 ; Luke
21 : 1, 4 ; (*c*) of gifts offered to God, Matt. 5 : 23, 24 ; 8 : 4 ; 23 : 18, 19 ;
Heb. 5 : 1 ; 8 : 3, 4 ; 9 : 9 ; 11 : 4 ; (*d*) of salvation by grace, as the gift
1431 of God, Eph. 2 : 8 ; (*e*) of presents for mutual celebration of an occasion,
AG:210B Rev. 11 : 10. See OFFERING.¶
CB:1242A 2. DŌREA (δωρεά) denotes a free gift, stressing its gratuitous

character; it is always used in the N.T. of a spiritual or supernatural gift, John 4 : 10; Acts 8 : 20; 11 : 17; Rom. 5 : 15; 2 Cor. 9 : 15; Eph. 3 : 7; Heb. 6 : 4; in Eph. 4 : 7, "according to the measure of the gift of Christ," the gift is that given by Christ; in Acts 2 : 28, "the gift of the Holy Ghost," the clause is epexegetical, the gift being the Holy Ghost Himself; cp. 10 : 45; 11 : 17, and the phrase, "the gift of righteousness," Rom. 5 : 17.¶

Note: For *dōrean*, a form of this noun, used adverbially, see FREELY.

3. DŌRĒMA (δώρημα): see BOON. 1434 AG:210D CB:1242A

4. DOMA (δόμα) lends greater stress to the concrete character of the gift, than to its beneficent nature, Matt. 7 : 11; Luke 11 : 13; Eph. 4 : 8; Phil. 4 : 17.¶ 1390 AG:203C CB:—

5. DOSIS (δόσις) denotes, properly, the act of giving, Phil. 4 : 15, euphemistically referring to gifts as a matter of debt and credit accounts; then, objectively, a gift, Jas. 1 : 17 (1st mention; see BOON).¶ 1394 AG:204D CB:1242A

6. CHARISMA (χάρισμα), a gift of grace, a gift involving grace (*charis*) on the part of God as the Donor, is used (*a*) of His free bestowments upon sinners, Rom. 5 : 15, 16; 6 : 23; 11 : 29; (*b*) of His endowments upon believers by the operation of the Holy Spirit in the churches, Rom. 12 : 6; 1 Cor. 1 : 7; 12 : 4, 9, 28, 30, 31; 1 Tim. 4 : 14; 2 Tim. 1 : 6; 1 Pet. 4 : 10; (*c*) of that which is imparted through human instruction, Rom. 1 : 11; (*d*) of the natural gift of continence, consequent upon the grace of God as Creator, 1 Cor. 7 : 7; (*e*) of gracious deliverances granted in answer to the prayers of fellow-believers, 2 Cor. 1 : 11.¶ 5486 AG:878D CB:1239C

Note: In the A.V. of 2 Cor. 8 : 4 *charis*, grace, is translated "gift." The R.V., "in regard of this grace," adheres to the true meaning, as in ver. 6. 5485 AG:877B CB:1239C

7. MERISMOS (μερισμός), a dividing (from *meros*, a part), is translated "gifts" in Heb. 2 : 4, "gifts of the Holy Ghost" (marg., "distributions"); in 4 : 12, "dividing". See DIVIDING.¶ 3311 AG:505C CB:—

Note: In the A.V. of Luke 21 : 5 *anathēma*, a votive offering, is translated "gifts" (R.V., "offerings").¶ 334 AG:54C CB:1235B

GIRD, GIRDED, GIRT (about, up)

1. ZŌNNUMI (ζώννυμι), or ZŌNNUŌ, to gird, in the Middle Voice, to gird oneself, is used of the long garments worn in the east, John 21 : 18: Acts 12 : 8 (*perizōnnumi* in some mss.).¶ 2224 AG:341C CB:1273C

2. ANAZŌNNUMI (ἀναζώννυμι), to gird up (*ana*, up, and No. 1), is used metaphorically of the loins of the mind, 1 Pet. 1 : 13; cp. Luke 12 : 35 (see No. 4). The figure is taken from the circumstances of the Israelites as they ate the passover in readiness for their journey, Ex. 12 : 11; the Christian is to have his mental powers alert in expectation of Christ's Coming. The verb is in the Middle Voice, indicating the special interest the believer is to take in so doing.¶ 328 AG:53D CB:—

1241 AG:182D 3. DIAZŌNNUMI (διαζώννυμι), to gird round, i.e., firmly (*dia*, through-
CB:1241B out, used intensively), is used of the Lord's act in girding Himself with a
towel, John 13 : 4, 5, and of Peter's girding himself with his coat, 21 : 7.¶

4024 AG:647B 4. PERIZŌNNUMI (περιζώννυμι), to gird around or about, is used
CB:1263C (*a*) literally, of girding oneself for service, Luke 12 : 37 ; 17 : 8 ; for
rapidity of movement, Acts 12 : 8 ; (*b*) figuratively, of the condition for service on the part of the followers of Christ, Luke 12 : 35 ; Eph. 6 : 14 ; (*c*) emblematically, of Christ's Priesthood, Rev. 1 : 13, indicative of majesty of attitude and action, the Middle Voice suggesting the particular interest taken by Christ in girding Himself thus ; so of the action of the angels mentioned in 15 : 6.¶

GIRDLE

2223 AG:341B ZŌNĒ (ζώνη), Eng., zone, denotes a belt or girdle, Matt. 3 : 4 ; Mark
CB:1273C 1 : 6 ; Acts 21 : 11 ; Rev. 1 : 13 ; 15 : 6 ; it was often hollow, and hence
served as a purse, Matt. 10 : 9 ; Mark 6 : 8.¶

GIVE

1325 AG:192C 1. DIDŌMI (δίδωμι), to give, is used with various meanings according
CB:1241C to the context ; it is said, e.g., of seed yielding fruit, Mark 4 : 7, 8 ; of
giving (i.e., exercising) diligence, Luke 12 : 58 ; of giving lots, Acts 1 : 26, R.V. (A.V., "gave forth") ; of rendering vengeance, 2 Thess. 1 : 8 ; of striking or smiting Christ, John 18 : 22 (lit., 'gave a blow') and 19 : 3 (lit., 'they gave Him blows') ; of putting a ring on the hand, Luke 15 : 22 ; of Paul's adventuring himself into a place, Acts 19 : 31. (In Rev. 17 : 13
DIADIDŌMI 1239 some mss. have *diadidōmi*, to divide). See ADVENTURE, BESTOW, No. 1,
AG:182D COMMIT, *Note* (1), DELIVER, GRANT, MAKE, MINISTER, OFFER, PUT, SET,
CB:— SHEW, SUFFER, TAKE, UTTER, YIELD.

Note: In the following the R.V. gives the correct rendering : Acts 7 : 25, "was giving them deliverance" (A.V., "would deliver them") ; Acts 10 : 40, "gave Him to be made manifest" (A.V., "shewed Him openly") ; Rev. 13 : 14, 15, "it was given him" (A.V., "he had power").

591 AG:90B 2. APODIDŌMI (ἀποδίδωμι) signifies to give up or back, to restore,
CB:1236C return, render what is due, to pay, give an account (*apo*, back, and No. 1),
e.g., of an account. Matt. 5 : 26 ; 12 : 36 ; Luke 16 : 2 ; Acts. 19 : 40 ; Heb. 13 : 17 ; 1 Pet. 4 : 5 ; of wages, etc., e.g., Matt. 18 : 25–34 ; 20 : 8 ; of conjugal duty, 1 Cor. 7 : 3 ; of a witness, Acts 4 : 33 ; frequently of recompensing or rewarding, 1 Tim. 5 : 4 ; 2 Tim. 4 : 8, 14 ; 1 Pet. 3 : 9 ; Rev. 18 : 6 ; 22 : 12. In the Middle Voice it is used of giving up what is one's own ; hence, to sell, Acts 5 : 8 ; 7 : 9 ; Heb. 12 : 16. See DELIVER.

1929 AG:292B 3. EPIDIDŌMI (ἐπιδίδωμι) signifies (*a*) to give by handing, to hand
CB:— (*epi*, over), e.g., Matt. 7 : 9, 10 ; Luke 4 : 17 ; 24 : 30, here of the Lord's
act in handing the broken loaf to the two at Emmaus, an act which was the means of the revelation of Himself as the crucified and risen Lord ; the simple verb, No. 1, is used of His handing the bread at the institution

of the Lord's Supper, Matt. 26 : 26 ; Mark 14 : 22 ; Luke 22 : 19 ; this meaning of the verb *epididōmi* is found also in Acts 15 : 30, " they delivered ; " (*b*) to give in, give way, Acts 27 : 15, R.V., " we gave way to it." See DELIVER.

4. METADIDŌMI (μεταδίδωμι), to give a share of, impart (*meta*, with), 3330 AG:510D
as distinct from giving. The Apostle Paul speaks of sharing some CB:1258B
spiritual gift with Christians at Rome, Rom. 1 : 11, " that I may impart," and exhorts those who minister in things temporal, to do so as sharing, and that generously, 12 : 8, " he that giveth ; " so in Eph. 4 : 28 ; Luke 3 : 11 ; in 1 Thess. 2 : 8 he speaks of himself and his fellow-missionaries as having been well pleased to impart to the converts both God's Gospel and their own souls (i.e., so sharing those with them as to spend themselves and spend out their lives for them). See IMPART.¶

5. PARADIDŌMI (παραδίδωμι), to give or hand over, is said of giving 3860 AG:614B
up the ghost, John 19 : 30 ; of giving persons up to evil, Acts 7 : 42 ; CB:1262A
Rom. 1 : 24, 26 ; of giving one's body to be burned, 1 Cor. 13 : 3 ; of Christ's giving Himself up to death, Gal. 2 : 20 ; Eph. 5 : 2, 25. See BETRAY, COMMIT, DELIVER.

6. PRODIDŌMI (προδίδωμι), to give before, or first (*pro*, before), 4272 AG:704C
is found in Rom. 11 : 35.¶ CB:—

7. CHARIZOMAI (χαρίζομαι) primarily denotes to show favour or 5483 AG:876C
kindness, as in Gal. 3 : 18, R.V., " hath granted " (A.V., " gave ") ; CB:1239C
then, to give freely, bestow graciously ; in this sense it is used almost entirely of that which is given by God, Acts 27 : 24, " God hath granted thee all them that sail with thee " (R.V.) ; in Rom. 8 : 32, " shall . . . freely give ; " 1 Cor. 2 : 12, " are freely given ; " Phil. 1 : 29, " it hath been granted " (said of believing on Christ and suffering for Him) ; 2 : 9, " hath given " (said of the Name of Jesus as given by God) ; Philm. 22, " I shall be granted unto you " (R.V.). In Luke 7 : 21, it is said in regard to the blind, upon whom Christ " bestowed " sight (R.V.). The only exceptions, in this sense of the word, as to Divinely imparted gifts, are Acts 3 : 14, of the granting of Barabbas by Pilate to the Jews, and Acts 25 : 11, 16, of the giving up of a prisoner to his accusers or to execution. See DELIVER, FORGIVE, GRANT.

8. PARECHŌ (παρέχω), in the Active Voice, signifies to afford, furnish, 3930
provide, supply (lit., to hold out or towards ; *para*, near, *echō*, to hold) ; AG:626B CB:—
it is translated " hath given " in Acts 17 : 31 ; " giveth " in 1 Tim. 6 : 17 (in the sense of affording) ; in Col. 4 : 1, R.V., " render " (A.V., " give "). See BRING, DO, KEEP, MINISTER, OFFER, RENDER, SHEW, TROUBLE.

9. DŌREŌ (δωρέω), akin to No. 1, and used in the Middle Voice, (-OMAI)
to bestow, make a gift of, is translated in the R.V. by the verb to grant, 1433 AG:210C
instead of the A.V., to give, Mark 15 : 45 ; 2 Pet. 1 : 3, 4. See GRANT.¶ CB:1242A

10. APONEMŌ (ἀπονέμω), to assign, apportion (*apo*, away, *nemō*, 632 AG:97A
to distribute), is rendered " giving " in 1 Pet. 3 : 7, of giving honour CB:—

to the wife. In the papyri writings it is said of a prefect who gives to all their dues.¶ In the Sept., Deut. 4 : 19.¶

POIEō 4160 AG:680D CB:1265C

11. POIEŌ (ποιέω), to do, is used in Jude 3 of giving diligence (the Middle Voice indicating Jude's especial interest in his task).

KATAPHERō 2702 AG:419D

12. KATAPHERŌ (καταφέρω), to bring down or against (*kata*, down), said of an accusation in Acts 25 : 7 (in the best mss.), and of being " borne down " with sleep, 20 : 9, R.V., is used of casting a ballot or giving a vote in 26 : 10. See FALL, Note (8), SINK.¶

PROSTITHēMI 4369 AG:718D CB:1267B

13. PROSTITHĒMI (προστίθημι), lit., to put in addition (*pros*, to, *tithēmi*, to put), to give more, is translated " shall more be given," in Mark 4 : 24 (Passive Voice). See ADD.

SCHOLAZō 4980 AG:797D

14. SCHOLAZŌ (σχολάζω), to be at leisure, hence, to have time or opportunity for, to be occupied in, is said of ' giving oneself ' to prayer, 1 Cor. 7 : 5 ; of an " empty " house, ' lying vacant,' Matt. 12 : 44.¶

LEGō 3004 AG:468A CB:1256C

15. LEGŌ (λέγω), to say, is rendered " giving out," of the self-advertisement of Simon Magus, Acts 8 : 9. See SAY.

PROSECHō 4337 AG:714B CB:1267A

16. PROSECHŌ (προσέχω), to turn one's mind to, attend to, is used of giving oneself up to, 1 Tim. 3 : 8 (to wine) ; of giving heed to, Acts 8 : 6, 10, 11 (R.V.) ; 16 : 14 (R.V.) ; 1 Tim. 1 : 4 ; 4 : 1, 13 (R.V.) ; Tit. 1 : 14 ; Heb. 2 : 1. See ATTEND.

DIōKō 1377 AG:201B CB:1242A

17. DIŌKŌ (διώκω), to pursue, is translated " given to " in Rom. 12 : 13, lit., ' pursuing hospitality.' See FOLLOW.

TITHēMI 5087 AG:815D CB:1272C PAREISPHERō 3923 AG:625A MARTUREō 3140 AG:492C CB:1257C CHORēGEō 5524 AG:883D MERIZō 3307 AG:504C CB:1258B PARISTēMI 3936 AG:627C CB:1262B DOULOō 1402 AG:206A EIMI 1510 AG:222D CB:1243A EPIKRINō 1948 AG:295A PROSKARTEREō 4342 AG:715C CB:1267A

Notes : (1) In John 10 : 11, R.V., *tithēmi*, to put, lay down etc., is rendered " layeth down," for the A.V., " giveth." (2) For *pareispherō*, to add, rendered " giving " in 2 Pet. 1 : 5, A.V., see ADD. (3) For *martureō*, to bear witness, A.V., " gave (record) " in 1 John 5 : 10, R.V., " hath borne (witness)," see WITNESS. (4) For *chorēgeō*, to supply, minister, rendered " giveth " (R.V., " supplieth ") in 1 Pet. 4 : 11, see MINISTER. (5) For *merizō*, to divide into parts, rendered " gave a part " (R.V., " divided ") in Heb. 7 : 2, see DIVIDE. (6) For *paristēmi*, to place by, rendered " give " in Matt. 26 : 53, A.V. (R.V., " send "), see SEND. (7) For *douloō*, in the Passive Voice, to be enslaved, rendered " given to " in Tit. 2 : 3, A.V., see ENSLAVE. (8) In 1 Tim. 4 : 15, the Imperative Mood of *eimi*, to be, with *en*, in, lit., ' be in,' is translated " give thyself wholly to." (9) In Luke 10 : 7, the phrase, lit., ' the (things) by them,' is rendered " such things as they give." (10) For *epikrinō*, see SENTENCE. (11) For *proskartereō*, to give oneself continually, Acts 6 : 4, see CONTINUE. (12) See CHARGE, COMMANDMENT, DRINK, HOSPITALITY, LAW, LIGHT, MARRIAGE, PLACE, PLEASURE, SUCK, THANKS.

GIVER

DOTēS 1395 AG:205A CB:1242A

DOTĒS (δότης), akin to *didōmi*, to give, is used in 2 Cor. 9 : 7 of him who gives cheerfully (hilariously) and is thereby loved of God.¶

GLAD (be, make), GLADLY

A. Verbs.

1. CHAIRŌ (χαίρω) is the usual word for rejoicing, being glad ; 5463
it is rendered by the verb to be glad in Mark 14 : 11 ; Luke 15 : 32 ; AG:873B CB:1239B
22 : 5 ; 23 : 8 ; John 8 : 56 ; 11 : 15 ; 20 : 20 ; Acts 11 : 23 ; 13 : 48 ; in the following the R.V. has 'to rejoice' for A.V., 'to be glad,' Rom. 16 : 19 ; 1 Cor. 16 : 17 ; 2 Cor. 13 : 9 ; 1 Pet. 4 : 13 ; Rev. 19 : 7. See Farewell, No. 4, Greeting, Hail, Joy, Rejoice.

2. AGALLIAŌ (ἀγαλλιάω), to exult, rejoice greatly, is chiefly used 21
in the Middle Voice (Active in Luke 1 : 47 ; some mss. have the Passive AG:3D CB:1233B
in John 5 : 35, 'to be made glad'). In the O.T., it is found abundantly in the Psalms, from 2 : 11 onward to 149 : 2, 5 (Sept.). It conveys the idea of jubilant exultation, spiritual gladness, Matt. 5 : 12, "be exceeding glad," the Lord's command to His disciples ; Luke 1 : 47, in Mary's song ; 10 : 21, of Christ's exultation ("rejoiced") ; cp. Acts 2 : 26, "(My tongue) was glad," A.V. (R.V., "rejoiced") ; John 8 : 56, of Abraham ; Acts 16 : 34, R.V., "rejoiced greatly" (of the Philippian jailor) ; 1 Pet. 1 : 6, 8 ; 4 : 13 ("with exceeding joy"), of believers in general ; in Rev. 19 : 7, R.V., "be exceeding glad" (A.V., "rejoice"). See Rejoice.¶

3. EUPHRAINŌ (εὐφραίνω), to cheer, gladden, is rendered "maketh 2165
. . . glad" in 2 Cor. 2 : 2. See Fare, Merry, Rejoice. AG:327C CB:1247B

B. Adverbs.

1. HĒDEŌS (ἡδέως), gladly (from *hēdus*, sweet), is used in Mark 2234 AG:343D
6 : 20 ; 12 : 37 ; 2 Cor. 11 : 19.¶ CB:1249C

2. HĒDISTA (ἥδιστα), the superlative degree of No. 1, most gladly, 2236
most delightedly, with great relish, is rendered "most gladly" in AG:343D (HēDEōS)
2 Cor. 12 : 9, and in ver. 15 (R.V. ; A.V., "very gladly").¶ CB:—

3. ASMENŌS (ἀσμένως), with delight, delightedly, gladly, is found in 780
Acts 21 : 17. It is absent from the best texts in 2 : 41 (see the R.V.).¶ AG:116C CB:—

GLADNESS

1. CHARA (χαρά), joy, delight (akin to A, No. 1 above), is rendered 5479
"gladness" in the A.V. of Mark 4 : 16 ; Acts 12 : 14 and Phil. 2 : 29 AG:875C CB:1239B
(R.V. "joy", as elsewhere in both Versions). See Joy.

2. AGALLIASIS (ἀγαλλίασις), exultation, exuberant joy (akin to 20
A, No. 2), is translated "gladness" in Luke 1 : 14 ; Acts 2 : 6 ; AG:3D CB:1233B
Heb. 1 : 9 ; "joy" in Luke 1 : 44 ; "exceeding joy" in Jude 24. It indicates a more exultant joy than No. 1. In the Sept. this word is found chiefly in the Psalms, where it denotes joy in God's redemptive work, e.g., 30 : 5 ; 42 : 4 ; 45 : 7, 15. See Joy.

3. EUPHROSUNĒ (εὐφροσύνη), good cheer, joy, mirth, gladness of 2167
heart (akin to A, No. 3), from *eu*, well, and *phrēn*, the mind, is rendered AG:328A CB:1247B
"gladness" in Acts 2 : 28, R.V. (A.V., "joy") and 14 : 17. See Joy.¶

GLASS, GLASSY

A. Nouns.

5194 1. HUALOS (ὕαλος) primarily denoted anything transparent, e.g.,
AG:831D CB:— a transparent stone or gem, hence, a lens of crystal, a glass, Rev. 21 : 18, 21.¶

2072 2. ESOPTRON (ἔσοπτρον), a mirror, is rendered "glass" in the
AG:313B CB:1246C A.V. of 1 Cor. 13 : 12 and Jas. 1 : 23. See MIRROR.¶

Note: For the corresponding verb *katoptrizō* in 2 Cor. 3 : 18 (Middle Voice), see BEHOLD, No. 12.

B. Adjective.

5193 HUALINOS (ὑάλινος) signifies glassy, made of glass (akin to A, No. 1),
AG:831D CB:1251B Rev. 4 : 6; 15 : 2 (twice), R.V., "glassy."¶

GLOOM See HEAVINESS, DARKNESS

For GLISTERING see DAZZLING and SHINE, No. 4

GLORIFY

1392 1. DOXAZŌ (δοξάζω) primarily denotes "to suppose" (from *doxa*,
AG:204C CB:1242B an opinion); in the N.T. (*a*) to magnify, extol, praise (see DOXA below), especially of glorifying God, i.e., ascribing honour to Him, acknowledging Him as to His being, attributes and acts, i.e., His glory (see GLORY), e.g., Matt. 5 : 16; 9 : 8; 15 : 31; Rom. 15 : 6, 9; Gal. 1 : 24; 1 Pet. 4 : 16; the word of the Lord, Acts 13 : 48; the Name of the Lord, Rev. 15 : 4; also of glorifying oneself, John 8 : 54; Rev. 18 : 7;. (*b*) to do honour to, to make glorious, e.g., Rom. 8 : 30; 2 Cor. 3 : 10; 1 Pet. 1 : 8, "full of glory," Passive Voice (lit., 'glorified'); said of Christ, e.g., John 7 : 39; 8 : 54, R.V., "glorifieth," for A.V., "honour" and "honoureth" (which would translate *timaō*, to honour); of the Father, e.g., John 13 : 31, 32; 21 : 19; 1 Pet. 4 : 11; of glorifying one's ministry, Rom. 11 : 13, R.V., "glorify" (A.V., "magnify"); of a member of the body, 1 Cor. 12 : 26, "be honoured" (R.V. marg., "be glorified").

"As the glory of God is the revelation and manifestation of all that He has and is . . . , it is said of a Self-revelation in which God manifests all the goodness that is His, John 12 : 28. So far as it is Christ through whom this is made manifest, He is said to glorify the Father, John 17 : 1, 4; or the Father is glorified in Him, 13 : 31; 14 : 13; and Christ's meaning is analogous when He says to His disciples, 'Herein is My Father glorified, that ye bear much fruit; and so shall ye be My disciples,' John 15 : 8. When *doxazō* is predicated of Christ . . . , it means simply that His innate glory is brought to light, is made manifest; cp. 11 : 4. So 7 : 39; 12 : 16, 23; 13 : 31; 17 : 1, 5. It is an act of God the Father in Him. . . . As the revelation of the Holy Spirit is connected with the glorification of
1740 Christ, Christ says regarding Him, 'He shall glorify Me,' 16 : 14"
AG:263 (-OMAI) (Cremer).

CB:1245A 2. ENDOXAZŌ (ἐνδοξάζω), No. 1 prefixed by *en*, "in," signifies, in the Passive Voice, to be glorified, i.e., to exhibit one's glory ; it is said of God, regarding His saints in the future, 2 Thess. 1 : 10, and of the Name of the Lord Jesus as glorified in them in the present, ver. 12.¶

3. SUNDOXAZŌ (συνδοξάζω), to glorify together (*sun*, with), is used 4888 AG:785D
in Rom. 8 : 17.¶ CB:1270C

GLORY, GLORIOUS

A. Nouns.

1. DOXA (δόξα), glory (from *dokeō*, to seem), primarily signifies an 1391 AG:203C
opinion, estimate, and hence, the honour resulting from a good opinion. CB:1242B
It is used (I) (*a*) of the nature and acts of God in self-manifestation, i.e., what He essentially is and does, as exhibited in whatever way he reveals Himself in these respects, and particularly in the Person of Christ, in whom essentially His glory has ever shone forth and ever will do, John 17 : 5, 24 ; Heb. 1 : 3 ; it was exhibited in the character and acts of Christ in the days of His flesh, John 1 : 14 ; John 2 : 11 ; at Cana both His grace and His power were manifested, and these constituted His glory ; so also in the resurrection of Lazarus, 11 : 4, 40 ; the glory of God was exhibited in the resurrection of Christ, Rom. 6 : 4, and in His ascension and exaltation, 1 Pet. 1 : 21, likewise on the Mount of Transfiguration, 2 Pet. 1 : 17. In Rom. 1 : 23 His " everlasting power and Divinity " are spoken of as His glory, i.e., His attributes and power as revealed through creation ; in Rom. 3 : 23 the word denotes the manifested perfection of His character, especially His righteousness, of which all men fall short ; in Col. 1 : 11 " the might of His glory " signifies the might which is characteristic of His glory ; in Eph. 1 : 6, 12, 14, " the praise of the glory of His grace " and " the praise of His glory " signify the due acknowledgement of the exhibition of His attributes and ways ; in Eph. 1 : 17, " the Father of glory " describes Him as the source from whom all Divine splendour and perfection proceed in their manifestation, and to whom they belong ; (*b*) of the character and ways of God as exhibited through Christ to and through believers, 2 Cor. 3 : 18 and 4 : 6 ; (*c*) of the state of blessedness into which believers are to enter hereafter through being brought into the likeness of Christ, e.g., Rom. 8 : 18, 21 ; Phil. 3 : 21 (R.V., " the body of His glory ") ; 1 Pet. 5 : 1, 10 ; Rev. 21 : 11 ; (*d*) brightness or splendour, (1) supernatural, emanating from God (as in the Shekinah glory, in the pillar of cloud and in the Holy of Holies, e.g., Ex. 16 : 10 ; 25 : 22), Luke 2 : 9 ; Acts 22 : 11 ; Rom. 9 : 4 ; 2 Cor. 3 : 7 ; Jas. 2 : 1 ; in Tit. 2 : 13 it is used of Christ's return, " the appearing of the glory of our great God and Saviour Jesus Christ " (R.V.) ; cp. Phil. 3 : 21, above ; (2) natural, as of the heavenly bodies, 1 Cor. 15 : 40, 41 ; (II) of good reputation, praise, honour, Luke 14 : 10 (R.V., " glory," for A.V., " worship ") ; John 5 : 41 (R.V., " glory," for A.V., " honour ") ; 7 : 18 ; 8 : 50 ; 12 : 43 (R.V., " glory," for A.V., " praise ") ; 2 Cor. 6 : 8 (R.V., " glory," for A.V. " honour ") ; Phil. 3 : 19 ; Heb. 3 : 3 ; in 1 Cor.

11 : 7, of man as representing the authority of God, and of woman as rendering conspicuous the authority of man ; in 1 Thess. 2 : 6, " glory " probably stands, by metonymy, for material gifts, an honorarium, since in human estimation glory is usually expressed in things material.

The word is used in ascriptions of praise to God, e.g., Luke 17 : 18 ; John 9 : 24, R.V., " glory " (A.V., " praise ") ; Acts 12 : 23 ; as in doxologies (lit., glory-words), e.g., Luke 2 : 14 ; Rom. 11 : 36 ; 16 : 27 ; Gal. 1 : 5 ; Rev. 1 : 6. See DIGNITY, HONOUR, PRAISE, WORSHIP.

2811 AG:434B 2. KLEOS (κλέος), good report, fame, renown, is used in 1 Pet. 2 : 20.¶
CB:1255B The word is derived from a root signifying hearing ; hence, the meaning 'reputation.'

Note : In 2 Cor. 3 : 11 the phrase *dia doxēs*, through (i.e., by means of) glory, is rendered " with glory " in the R.V. (A.V., " glorious ") ; in the same verse *en doxę̄*, " in glory " (R.V.), i.e., accompanied by glory, is rendered " glorious " in the A.V. The first is said of the ministration of the Law, the second of that of the Gospel.

B. Adjective.

1741 AG:263B ENDOXOS (ἔνδοξος) signifies (*a*) held in honour (*en*, in, *doxa*, honour),
CB:1245A of high repute, 1 Cor. 4 : 10, R.V., " have glory " (A.V., " are honourable "); (*b*) splendid, glorious, said of apparel, Luke 7 : 25, " gorgeously ; " of the works of Christ, 13 : 17 ; of the Church, Eph. 5 : 27. See GORGEOUSLY, HONOURABLE.¶

GLORY (to boast), GLORYING

A. Verbs.

2744 AG:425C 1. KAUCHAOMAI (καυχάομαι), to boast or glory, is always translated
CB:1254C in the R.V. by the verb to glory, where the A.V. uses the verb to boast (see, e.g., Rom. 2 : 17, 23 ; 2 Cor. 7 : 14 ; 9 : 2 ; 10 : 8, 13, 15, 16) ; it is used (*a*) of vainglorying, e.g., 1 Cor. 1 : 29 ; 3 : 21 ; 4 : 7 ; 2 Cor. 5 : 12 ; 11 : 12, 18 ; Eph. 2 : 9 ; (*b*) of valid glorying, e.g., Rom. 5 : 2, " rejoice ; " 5 : 3, 11 (R.V., " rejoice ") ; 1 Cor. 1 : 31 ; 2 Cor. 9 : 2 ; 10 : 8 ; 12 : 9 ; Gal. 6 : 14 ; Phil. 3 : 3 and Jas. 1 : 9, R.V., " glory " (A.V., " rejoice "). See BOAST, JOY, REJOICE.

2620 AG:411B 2. KATAKAUCHAOMAI (κατακαυχάομαι), a strengthened form of
CB:1254A No. 1 (*kata*, intensive), signifies to boast against, exult over, Rom. 11 : 18, R.V., " glory " (A.V., " boast ") ; Jas. 2 : 13, R.V., " glorieth " (A.V., " rejoiceth ") ; 3 : 14, " glory (not)." See BOAST, REJOICE.¶

— AG:216A 3. ENKAUCHAOMAI (ἐνκαυχάομαι), *en*, in, and No. 1, to glory in,
CB:1245A is found, in the most authentic mss., in 2 Thess. 1 : 4.¶

4068 AG:653D *Note :* Cp. *perpereuomai*, to vaunt oneself, to be *perperos*, vainglorious,
CB:— 1 Cor. 13 : 4.¶

B. Nouns.

2745 AG:426A 1. KAUCHĒMA (καύχημα), akin to A, No. 1, denotes (*a*) that in which
CB:1254C one glories, a matter or ground of glorying, Rom. 4 : 2 and Phil. 2 : 16, R.V., " whereof to glory " (for Rom. 3 : 27, see No. 2) ; in the following

the meaning is likewise a ground of glorying: 1 Cor. 5 : 6; 9 : 15, "glorying," 16, "to glory of;" 2 Cor. 1 : 14, R.V.; 9 : 3, R.V.; Gal. 6 : 4, R.V. (A.V., "rejoicing"); Phil. 1 : 26 (ditto); Heb. 3 : 6 (ditto). In 2 Cor. 5 : 12 and 9 : 3 the word denotes the boast itself, yet as distinct from the act (see No. 2).¶

2. KAUCHĒSIS (καύχησις) denotes the act of boasting, Rom. 3 : 27; **2746**
15 : 17, R.V., "(my) glorying" (A.V., "whereof I may glory"); 1 Cor. **AG:426B**
15 : 31, R.V., "glorying;" 2 Cor. 1 : 12 (ditto); 7 : 4, 14 (A.V., **CB:1254C**
"boasting"); 8 : 24; 11 : 10, and 17 (ditto); 1 Thess. 2 : 19 (A.V., "rejoicing"); Jas. 4 : 16 (ditto). The distinction between this and No. 1 is to be observed in 2 Cor. 8 : 24, speaking of the Apostle's act of glorying in the liberality of the Corinthians, while in 9 : 3 he exhorts them not to rob him of the ground of his glorying (No. 1). Some take the word in 2 Cor. 1 : 12 (see above) as identical with No. 1, a boast, but there seems to be no reason for regarding it as different from its usual sense, No. 2.¶

Note: Cp. *alazoneia* (or *-ia*), vainglory, ostentatious (or arrogant) **ALAZON(E)IA 212**
display, Jas. 4 : 16 and 1 John 2 : 16,¶ and *alazōn*, a boaster, Rom. 1 : 30 **AG:34C CB:1234B**
and 2 Tim. 3 : 2.¶ **ALAZŌN 213 AG:34D CB:1234B**

GLUTTON

GASTĒR (γαστήρ) denotes a belly; it is used in Tit. 1 : 12, with the **1064**
adjective *argos*, idle, metaphorically, to signify a glutton, R.V., "(idle) **AG:152C CB:—**
gluttons" [A.V. "(slow) bellies"]; elsewhere, Luke 1 : 31. See WOMB.¶

GLUTTONOUS

PHAGOS (φάγος), akin to *phagō*, to eat, a form used for the aorist **5314**
or past tense of *esthiō*, denotes a glutton, Matt. 11 : 19; Luke 7 : 34.¶ **AG:851A CB:—**

GNASH, GNASHING

A. Verbs.

1. BRUCHŌ (βρύχω), primarily, to bite or eat greedily (akin to **1031 AG:148A**
brukō, to chew), denotes to grind or gnash with the teeth, Acts 7 : 54.¶ **CB:1239B**

2. TRIZŌ (τρίζω), primarily used of the sounds of animals, to chirp, **5149**
cry, squeak, came to signify to grind or gnash with the teeth, Mark 9 : 18.¶ **AG:826B CB:—**

B. Noun.

BRUGMOS (βρυγμός), akin to A, No. 1, denotes "gnashing" ("of **1030**
teeth" being added), Matt. 8 : 12; 13 : 42, 50; 22 : 13; 24 : 51; 25 : 30; **AG:147D CB:1239B**
Luke 13 : 28.¶

GNAT

KŌNŌPS (κώνωψ) denotes the wine-gnat or midge, which breeds in **2971**
fermenting or evaporating wine, Matt. 23 : 24, where the A.V., "strain **AG:462A CB:1255C**
at" is corrected to "strain out," in the R.V.¶

GNAW

3145 MASAOMAI or MASSAOMAI (μασάομαι) denotes to bite or chew,
AG:495A CB:— Rev. 16 : 10.¶ In the Sept., Job. 30 : 4.¶

GO (WENT), GO ONWARD, etc.

4198 1. POREUOMAI (πορεύομαι), to go on one's way, to proceed from one
AG:692B
CB:1266A place to another (from *poros*, a passage, a ford, Eng., pore), is always used
in the Middle Voice in the N.T. and the Sept., and is the most frequent
verb signifying to go; it is more distinctly used to indicate procedure
or course than the verb *eimi*, to go (not found in the N.T.). It is often
rendered "go thy (your) way," in Oriental usage the customary dismissal,
marking the close of a case in court. Hence, in ordinary parlance, marking
the end of a conversation, etc., e.g., Luke 7 : 22; 17 : 19; John 4 : 50;
Acts 9 : 15; 24 : 25; cp. Dan. 12 : 9; in Rom. 15 : 24 (1st part), R.V.,
"go" (A.V., "take my journey"); in Acts 9 : 3 and 26 : 13, "journeyed"
(A.V. and R.V.). See DEPART, JOURNEY, WALK.

3899 2. PARAPOREUOMAI (παραπορεύομαι) denotes to go past, to pass
AG:621D CB:— by (*para*, by, and No. 1), Mark 2 : 23, A.V., "went (through)," R.V.,
"was going (through);" some mss. have No. 4 here. See PASS.

4313 3. PROPOREUOMAI (προπορεύομαι), to go before (*pro*, and No. 1),
AG:709C CB:— is used in Luke 1 : 76 and Acts 7 : 40.¶

1279 4. DIAPOREUOMAI (διαπορεύομαι), to go through (*dia*, through,
AG:187D CB:— and No. 1), to pass across, is translated to go through, in Luke 6 : 1;
13 : 22, "went on His way through," R.V.; Acts 16 : 4; "going by"
in Luke 18 : 36, R.V. (A.V., "pass by"); "in my journey" in Rom.
15 : 24 (2nd part). For Mark 2 : 23 see No. 2. See JOURNEY.

1531 5. EISPOREUOMAI (εἰσπορεύομαι), to go in, enter, is never rendered
AG:233C CB:— by the verb to come in, in the R.V. See, e.g., Luke 11 : 33, "enter;"
Acts 9 : 28, "going in;" 28 : 30, "went in." See ENTER.

4848 6. SUMPOREUOMAI (συμπορεύομαι), to go together with (*sun*, with),
AG:780A CB:— is used in Mark 10 : 1, R.V., "come together" (A.V., "resort"); Luke
7 : 11; 14 : 25; 24 : 15. See RESORT.¶

71 7. AGŌ (ἄγω), to bring, lead, is used intransitively, signifying "let
AG:14B CB:1233C us go" (as if to say, 'let us be leading on,' with the point of departure
especially in view), Matt. 26 : 46; Mark 1 : 38; 14 : 42; John 11 : 7,
15, 16; 14 : 31. See BRING.

5217 8. HUPAGŌ (ὑπάγω), to go away or to go slowly away, to depart,
AG:836C CB:— withdraw oneself, often with the idea of going without noise or notice
(*hupo*, under, and No. 7), is very frequent in the Gospels; elsewhere it is
used in Jas. 2 : 16; 1 John 2 : 11; Rev. 10 : 8; 13 : 10; 14 : 4; 16 : 1;
17 : 8, 11. It is frequently rendered "go your (thy) way," See DEPART.

4013 9. PERIAGŌ (περιάγω), to lead about (*peri*, about, and No. 7), as
AG:645C CB:— in 1 Cor. 9 : 5, is used intransitively with the meaning to go about;
"went about," Matt. 4 : 23; 9 : 35; Mark 6 : 6; Acts 13 : 11; in Matt.
23 : 15, "ye compass." See COMPASS, LEAD.¶

10. PROAGŌ (προάγω), to lead forth, used intransitively signifies 4254
to go before, usually of locality, e.g., Matt. 2 : 9; figuratively, in AG:702A CB:—
1 Tim. 1 : 18, " went before " (R.V., marg., " led the way to "), of the
exercise of the gifts of prophecy which pointed to Timothy as one chosen
by God for the service to be committed to him ; in 5 : 24, of sins " going
before unto judgment." In 2 John 9, where the best mss. have this
verb (instead of *parabainō*, to transgress, A.V.), the R.V. renders it
" goeth onward " (marg., " taketh the lead "), of not abiding in the
doctrine of Christ. Cp. Mal. 4 : 4. See BRING.

11. APEIMI (ἄπειμι), to go away, is found in Acts 17 : 10.¶ 549 AG:83A II.

12. EISEIMI (εἴσειμι), to go into, enter, is used in Acts 3 : 3; 1524
21 : 18, 26 ; Heb. 9 : 6, R.V., " go in " (A.V., " went . . . into "). See AG:232C CB:—
ENTER.¶

13. METABAINŌ (μεταβαίνω), to go or pass over from one place to 3327
another, is translated " go " in Luke 10 : 7. See DEPART. AG:510C CB:1258B

14. APERCHOMAI (ἀπέρχομαι), to go away (*apo*, from), is chiefly 565
used in the Gospels ; it signifies to go aside in Acts 4 : 15. See DEPART. AG:84C CB:1236B

15. ANACHŌREŌ (ἀναχωρέω) signifies to withdraw, often in the 402
sense of avoiding danger, e.g., Acts 23 : 19, R.V., " going aside " (A.V., AG:63C CB:1235A
" went . . . aside "). See DEPART.

16. HUPOCHŌREŌ (ὑποχωρέω), to go back, retire (*hupo*, under, 5298
suggesting privacy), Luke 5 : 16 ; 9 : 10, A.V., " went aside " (R.V., AG:848C CB:—
" withdrew apart "). See WITHDRAW.¶

17. PROERCHOMAI (προέρχομαι), to go before, precede, go forward 4281
or farther (*pro*, before), is used of (*a*) place, e.g., Matt. 26 : 39 ; Acts 12 : 10, AG:705B CB:1266C
" passed on through ; " (*b*) time, Luke 1 : 17 ; Acts 20 : 5, 13 ; 2 Cor. 9 : 5.
See OUTGO, PASS.

18. EPIDUŌ (ἐπιδύω) signifies to go down, and is said of the sun in 1931
Eph. 4 : 26 ; i.e., put wrath away before sunset (see ANGER, A, *Note* (2). AG:292C CB:—
In the Sept., Deut. 24 : 15 ; Josh. 8 : 29 ; Jer. 15 : 9.¶

19. SUNKATABAINŌ (συνκαταβαίνω), to go down with, is used in 4782
Acts 25 : 5.¶ In the Sept., Psa. 49 : 17.¶ AG:773C CB:—

20. PROBAINŌ (προβαίνω), to go on, forwards, advance, is used of 4260
locality, Matt. 4 : 21 ; Mark 1 : 19 ; for the metaphorical use with reference AG:702D CB:1266C
to age, Luke 1 : 7, 18 ; 2 : 36, see AGE, STRICKEN.¶

21. APOBAINŌ (ἀποβαίνω), to go away or from, is translated " had 576
gone out," in Luke 5 : 2, i.e., disembarked. See COME, 21, Note, TURN. AG:88C CB:—

22. PROSANABAINŌ (προσαναβαίνω), to go up higher (*pros*, towards), 4320
is used of moving to a couch of greater honour at a feast, Luke 14 : 10.¶ AG:711C CB:—

23. EXEIMI (ἔξειμι), to go out, is so rendered in Acts 13 : 42. See 1826
DEPART, GET. AG:275B (EXESTI) CB:1247C

24. SBENNUMI (σβέννυμι), to quench, is used in the Passive Voice, 4570
of the going out of the light of a torch or lamp, Matt. 25 : 8, " are going AG:745B CB:1268C
out " (R.V.). See QUENCH.

5055 25. TELEŌ (τελέω), to finish, is rendered to go through or over in
AG:810D Matt. 10 : 23, of going through the cities of Israel (A.V., marg., " end,"
CB:1271B or " finish "). See END, FINISH.

1353 26. DIODEUŌ (διοδεύω), to travel throughout or along (*dia*, through,
AG:198D CB:— *hodos*, a way), is used in Luke 8 : 1, of going throughout (A.V.) or about
through (R.V.) cities and villages ; of passing through towns, Acts 17 : 1.
See PASS.

589 27. APODĒMEŌ (ἀποδημέω), to be abroad, is translated " going into
AG:90A CB:1236C another country," in Matt. 25 : 14 (A.V., " travelling etc."). See JOURNEY.

424 28. ANERCHOMAI (ἀνέρχομαι), to go up (*ana*), occurs in John 6 : 3 ;
AG:65B Gal. 1 : 17, 18.¶

4022 29. PERIERCHOMAI (περιέρχομαι), to go around, or about, is
AG:646D CB:1263B translated " going about " in 1 Tim. 5 : 13, R.V. (A.V., " wandering
about ") ; " went about " in Heb. 11 : 37, R.V. (A.V., " wandered
about "). See CIRCUIT.

2021 30. EPICHEIREŌ (ἐπιχειρέω), lit., to put the hand to (*epi*, to,
AG:304D CB:— *cheir*, the hand), to take in hand, undertake, occurs in Luke 1 : 1, " have
taken in hand ; " in Acts 9 : 29, " they went about ; " in 19 : 13, " took
upon them." See TAKE.¶

Notes : (1) The following verbs signify both to come and to go,
ZēTEō with prefixed prepositions accordingly, and are mentioned under the
2212 word COME : *erchomai* (No. 1) ; *eiserchomai* (No. 2) ; *exerchomai* (No. 3) ;
AG:338D CB:1273C *dierchomai* (No. 5) ; *katerchomai* (No. 7) ; Luke 17 : 7, *parerchomai*
PEIRAZō (No. 9) ; *proserchomai*, " go near," Acts 8 : 29 (No. 10) ; *sunerchomai*,
3985 AG:640B " went with," Acts 9 : 39 ; 15 : 38 ; 21 : 16 (No. 11) ; *anabainō*, (No. 15) ;
CB:1263A *katabainō* (No. 19) ; *paraginomai*, Acts 23 : 16, A.V., " went," R.V.
PEIRAō " entered " (No. 13) ; *ekporeuō* (No. 33) ; *chōreō*, Matt. 15 : 17, A.V.,
3987 AG:641A " goeth," R.V.," passeth " (No. 24) ; *anabainō*, Luke 19 : 28, R.V., " going
CB:1263A up " ; *ekbainō* (No. 17).

EPISTREPHō 1994 (2) In the following, the verbs mentioned, translated in the A.V.
AG:301A by some form of the verb to go, are rendered in the R.V. more precisely
CB:1246A HUPERBAINō in accordance with their true meaning : (*a*) *zēteō*, to seek, so the R.V. in
5233 John 7 : 19, 20 ; Acts 21 : 31 ; Rom. 10 : 3 (A.V., to go about) ; (*b*)
AG:840A CB:1252A *peirazō*, to make an attempt, Acts 24 : 6, R.V., " assayed " (A.V., " have
DIISTēMI gone about ") ; (*c*) *peiraō*, to attempt, Acts 26 : 21, R.V., " assayed "
1339 AG:195B A.V., " went about ") ; (*d*) *epistrephō*, to return, Acts 15 : 16, R.V.,
SUNEISERCHOMAI " let us return " (A.V., " let us go again ") ; (*e*) *huperbainō*, to overstep,
4897 AG:787A 1 Thess. 4 : 6, R.V., " transgress " (A.V., " go beyond ") ; (*f*) *diistēmi*,
CB:1270C to set apart, make an interval, Acts 27 : 28, R.V., " (after) a space "
PHERō 5342 (A.V., " had gone further ") ; (*g*) *suneiserchomai*, to go in with, John
AG:854D 6 : 22 and 18 : 15, R.V., " entered (in) with " (A.V., " went . . . with ") ;
CB:1264A (*h*) *pherō*, in the Middle Voice, lit., to bear oneself along, Heb. 6 : 1, R.V.,
EKKLINō 1578 " let us press on " (A.V., " let us go on ") ; (*i*) *ekklinō*, to bend or turn
AG:241C away, Rom. 3 : 12, R.V., " have turned aside " (A.V., " have gone out of

the way ") ; (*j*) *diaperaō*, to pass through, or across, Matt. 14 : 34, R.V., DIAPERAŌ
" had crossed over " (A.V., " were gone over ") ; (*k*) *strateuomai*, to serve 1276 AG:187C
in war, 1 Cor. 9 : 7, R.V., " (what) soldier . . . serveth " (A.V., " goeth STRATEUŌ
a warfare ") ; (*l*) *hodoiporeō*, to be on a journey, Acts 10 : 9, R.V., " as 4754 (-OMAI)
they were on their journey " (A.V., " as they went etc.") ; (*m*) *embainō*, AG:770B
to enter, Matt. 13 : 2 and Luke 8 : 22, R.V., " entered " (A.V., " went CB:1270A
into ") ; in ver. 37 (A.V., " went up into ") ; (*n*) *apoluō*, to set free, Luke HODOIPOREŌ 3596
23 : 22 and John 19 : 12, R.V., " release " (A.V., " let . . . go ") ; Acts AG:553D
15 : 33, R.V., " dismissed " (A.V., ditto) ; Acts 28 : 18, R.V., " set at CB:1251A EMBAINŌ
liberty " (A.V., ditto) ; (*o*) *epibainō*, to go upon, Acts 21 : 4, R.V., " set 1684
foot " (A.V., " go ") ; some mss. have *anabainō* ; (*p*) *apangellō*, to an- AG:254A APOLUŌ
nounce, Acts 12 : 17, R.V., " tell " (A.V., " go shew ") ; (*q*) *aperchomai*, 630
to go away, Matt. 5 : 30, R.V., " go " (A.V., " be cast ") ; some mss. AG:96C CB:1237A
have *ballō*, to cast ; (*r*) *peripateō*, to walk, Mark 12 : 38, R.V., " walk " EPIBAINŌ
(A.V. " go ") ; (*s*) *For* " gone by," Acts 14 : 16, R.V., see PASS, No. 17. 1910 AG:289D

GOAD

APANGELLŌ 518

KENTRON (κέντρον), from *kenteō*, to prick, denotes (*a*) a sting, Rev. AG:79B CB:1236B
9 : 10 ; metaphorically, of sin as the sting of death, 1 Cor. 15 : 55, 56 ; PERIPATEŌ
(*b*) a goad, Acts 26 : 14, R.V., " goad " (marg., " goads "), for A.V., 4043 AG:649A
" pricks " (in some mss. also in 9 : 5), said of the promptings and mis- CB:1263B
givings which Saul of Tarsus had resisted before conversion.¶ KENTRON 2759

AG:428B CB:1255A

GOAL

SKOPOS (σκοπός), primarily, a watcher (from *skopeō*, to look at ; 4649
Eng., scope), denotes a mark on which to fix the eye, and is used meta- AG:756D CB:1269B
phorically of an aim or object in Phil. 3 : 14, R.V., " goal " (A.V.,
" mark "), See MARK. GOAL See AIM, END

GOAT

1. ERIPHOS (ἔριφος) denotes a kid or goat, Matt. 25 : 32 (R.V., 2056
marg., " kids ") ; Luke 15 : 29, " a kid ; " some mss. have No. 2 here, AG:309D CB:1246C
indicating a sneer on the part of the elder son, that his father had never
given him even a tiny kid.¶

2. ERIPHION (ἐρίφιον), a diminutive of No. 1, is used in Matt. 25 : 33. 2055
In ver. 32 *eriphos* is purely figurative ; in ver 33, where the application AG:309D CB:1246C
is made, though metaphorically, the change to the diminutive is suggestive
of the contempt which those so described bring upon themselves by their
refusal to assist the needy.¶ 5131

3. TRAGOS (τράγος) denotes a he-goat, Heb. 9 : 12, 13, 19 ; 10 : 4, AG:824B CB:1273A
the male prefiguring the strength by which Christ laid down His own life AIGEIOS
in expiatory sacrifice. 122

AG:21D

GOATSKIN

DERMA

Note : The adjective *aigeios* signifies belonging to a goat (from *aix*, 1192 AG:175C
a goat) ; it is used with *derma*, a skin, in Heb. 11 : 37. CB:1240C

GOD

2316
AG:356D
CB:1272A THEOS (θέος), (A) in the polytheism of the Greeks, denoted a god or deity, e.g., Acts 14 : 11 ; 19 : 26 ; 28 : 6 ; 1 Cor. 8 : 5 ; Gal. 4 : 8.

(B) (*a*) Hence the word was appropriated by Jews and retained by Christians to denote the one true God. In the Sept. *theos* translates (with few exceptions) the Hebrew words Elohim and Jehovah, the former indicating His power and pre-eminence, the latter His unoriginated, immutable, eternal and self-sustained existence.

In the N.T., these and all the other Divine attributes are predicated of Him. To Him are ascribed, e.g., His unity, or monism, e.g., Mark 12 : 29 ; 1 Tim. 2 : 5 ; self-existence, John 5 : 26 ; immutability, Jas. 1 : 17 ; eternity, Rom. 1 : 20 ; universality, Matt. 10 : 29 ; Acts 17 : 26–28 ; almighty power, Matt. 19 : 26 ; infinite knowledge, Acts 2 : 23 ; 15 : 18 ; Rom. 11 : 33 ; creative power, Rom. 11 : 36 ; 1 Cor. 8 : 6 ; Eph. 3 : 9 ; Rev. 4 : 11 ; 10 : 6 ; absolute holiness, 1 Pet. 1 : 15 ; 1 John 1 : 5 ; righteousness, John 17 : 25 ; faithfulness, 1 Cor. 1 : 9 ; 10 : 13 ; 1 Thess. 5 : 24 ; 2 Thess. 3 : 3 ; 1 John 1 : 9 ; love, 1 John 4 : 8, 16 ; mercy, Rom. 9 : 15, 18 ; truthfulness, Tit. 1 : 2 ; Heb. 6 : 18. See GOOD, No. 1 (*b*).

(*b*) The Divine attributes are likewise indicated or definitely predicated of Christ, e.g., Matt. 20 : 18–19 ; John 1 : 1–3 ; 1 : 18, R.V., marg. ; 5 : 22–29 ; 8 : 58 ; 14 : 6 ; 17 : 22–24 ; 20 : 28 ; Rom. 1 : 4 ; 9 : 5 ; Phil. 3 : 21 ; Col. 1 : 15 ; 2 : 3 ; Tit. 2 : 13, R.V. ; Heb. 1 : 3 ; 13 : 8 ; 1 John 5 : 20 ; Rev. 22 : 12, 13.

(*c*) Also of the Holy Spirit, e.g., Matt. 28 : 19 ; Luke 1 : 35 ; John 14 : 16 ; 15 : 26 ; 16 : 7–14 ; Rom. 8 : 9, 26 ; 1 Cor. 12 : 11 ; 2 Cor. 13 : 14.

(*d*) *Theos* is used (1) with the definite article, (2) without (i.e., as an anarthrous noun). " The English may or may not have need of the article in translation. But that point cuts no figure in the Greek idiom. Thus in Acts 27 : 23 (' the God whose I am,' R.V.) the article points out the special God whose Paul is, and is to be preserved in English. In the very next verse (*ho theos*) we in English do not need the article " (A. T. Robertson, Gram. of Greek, N.T., p. 758).

As to this latter it is usual to employ the article with a proper name, when mentioned a second time. There are, of course, exceptions to this, as when the absence of the article serves to lay stress upon, or give precision to, the character or nature of what is expressed in the noun. A notable instance of this is in John 1 : 1, " and the Word was God ; " here a double stress is on *theos*, by the absence of the article and by the emphatic position. To translate it literally, ' a god was the Word,' is entirely misleading. Moreover, that " the Word " is the subject of the sentence, exemplifies the rule that the subject is to be determined by its having the article when the predicate is anarthrous (without the article). In Rom. 7 : 22, in the phrase " the law of God," both nouns have the article ; in ver. 25, neither has the article. This is in accordance with a general rule that if two nouns are united by the genitive case (the " of " case), either both have the article, or both are without. Here, in the first instance, both nouns, " God " and " the law " are definite, whereas in ver. 25 the word " God " is not simply titular, the absence of the article stresses His character as Lawgiver.

Where two or more epithets are applied to the same person or thing, one article usually serves for both (the exceptions being when a second article lays stress upon different aspects of the same person or subject, e.g., Rev. 1 : 17). In Tit. 2 : 13 the R.V. correctly has " our great God and Saviour Jesus Christ." Moulton (Prol., p. 84) shows, from papyri writings of the early Christian era, that among Greek-speaking Christians this was " a current formula " as applied to Christ. So in 2 Pet. 1 : 1 (cp. 1 : 11 ; 3 : 18).

In the following titles God is described by certain of His attributes ; the God of glory, Acts 7 : 2 ; of peace, Rom. 15 : 33 ; 16 : 20 ; Phil. 4 : 9 ; 1 Thess. 5 : 23 ; Heb. 13 : 20 ; of love and peace, 2 Cor. 13 : 11 ; of patience and comfort, Rom. 15 : 5 ; of all comfort, 2 Cor. 1 : 3 ; of hope, Rom. 15 : 13 ; of all grace, 1 Pet. 5 : 10. These describe Him, not as in distinction from other persons, but as the Source of all these blessings ; hence the employment of the definite article. In such phrases as ' the God of a person,' e.g., Matt. 22 : 32, the expression marks the relationship in which the person stands to God and God to him.

(*e*) In the following the nominative case is used for the vocative, and always with the article ; Mark 15 : 34 ; Luke 18 : 11, 13 ; John 20 : 28 ; (Acts 4 : 24 in some mss.) ; Heb. 1 : 8 ; 10 : 7.

(*f*) The phrase " the things of God " (translated literally or otherwise) stands for (1) His interests, Matt. 16 : 23 ; Mark 8 : 33 ; (2) His counsels, 1 Cor. 2 : 11 ; (3) things which are due to Him, Matt. 22 : 21 ; Mark 12 : 17 ; Luke 20 : 25. The phrase " things pertaining to God," Rom. 15 : 17 ; Heb. 2 : 17 ; 5 : 1, describes, in the Heb. passages, the sacrificial service of the priest ; in the Rom. passage the Gospel ministry as an offering to God.

(C) The word is used of Divinely appointed judges in Israel, as representing God in His authority, John 10 : 34, quoted from Psa. 82 : 6, which indicates that God Himself sits in judgment on those whom He has appointed. The application of the term to the Devil, 2 Cor. 4 : 4, and the belly, Phil. 3 : 19, virtually places these instances under (A).

GOD-BREATHED See INSPIRED

For GOD-SPEED see GREETING

GOD (without)

ATHEOS (ἄθεος), cp. Eng., atheist, primarily signifies godless (*a*, negative), i.e., destitute of God ; in Eph. 2 : 12 the phrase indicates, not only that the Gentiles were void of any true recognition of God, and hence 112 AG:20D CB:1238A became morally godless (Rom. 1 : 19–32), but that, being given up by God, they were excluded from communion with God and from the privileges granted to Israel (see the context and cp. Gal. 4 : 8). As to pagan ideas, the popular cry against the early Christians was " away with the atheists " (see the account of the martyrdom of Polycarp, in Eusebius, Eccles. Hist. iv. 15, 19).¶

GODDESS

2299 AG:353A CB:1271C THEA (θεά) is found in Acts 19 : 27 (in some mss. in vv. 35, 37).¶

GODLESS See PROFANE

For GODHEAD see DIVINE, DIVINITY

GODLINESS, GODLY

A. Nouns.

2150 AG:326A CB:1247B 1. EUSEBEIA (εὐσέβεια), from *eu*, well, and *sebomai*, to be devout, denotes that piety which, characterized by a Godward attitude, does that which is well-pleasing to Him. This and the corresponding verb and adverb (see below) are frequent in the Pastoral Epistles, but do not occur in previous Epistles of Paul. The Apostle Peter has the noun four times in his 2nd Epistle, 1 : 3, 6, 7 ; 3 : 11. Elsewhere it occurs in Acts 3 : 12 ; 1 Tim. 2 : 2 ; 3 : 16 ; 4 : 7, 8 ; 6 : 3, 5, 6, 11 ; 2 Tim. 3 : 5 ; Tit. 1 : 1. In 1 Tim. 6 : 3 " the doctrine which is according to godliness " signifies that which is consistent with godliness, in contrast to false teachings ; in Tit. 1 : 1, " the truth which is according to godliness " is that which is productive of godliness ; in 1 Tim. 3 : 16, " the mystery of godliness " is godliness as embodied in, and communicated through, the truths of the faith concerning Christ ; in 2 Pet. 3 : 11, the word is in the plural, signifying acts of godliness.¶

THEOSEBEIA 2317 AG:358B CB:1272A 2. THEOSEBEIA (θεοσέβεια) denotes the fear or reverence of God, from *theos*, god, and *sebomai* (see No. 1), 1 Tim. 2 : 10.¶ Cp. the adjective *theosebēs*, God-fearing, John 9 : 31.¶ In the Sept., Gen. 20 : 11 and Job 28 : 28.¶

EULABEIA 2124 AG:321D CB:1247B EULABEOMAI 2125 AG:321D CB:1247B EUSEBEŌ 2151 AG:326B CB:1247B *Note :* For *eulabeia*, godly fear, Heb. 5 : 7 ; 12 : 28, see FEAR, A, No. 3 ; for *eulabeomai*, to reverence, Heb. 11 : 7 (" for His godly fear "), see FEAR, D, No. 2 ; for the verb *eusebeō*, to show piety, 1 Tim. 5 : 4 ; to worship, Acts 17 : 23, see PIETY and WORSHIP.¶

B. Adjective.

2152 AG:326B CB:1247B EUSEBĒS (εὐσεβής), akin to A, No. 1, denotes pious, devout, godly, indicating reverence manifested in actions ; it is rendered " godly " in 2 Pet. 2 : 9. See DEVOUT.

C. Adverb.

2153 AG:326C CB:1247B EUSEBŌS (εὐσεβῶς) denotes piously, godly ; it is used with the verb to live (of manner of life) in 2 Tim. 3 : 12 ; Tit. 2 : 12.¶

2316 AG:356D CB:1272A *Notes :* (1) In the following the word " godly " translates the genitive case of the noun *theos*, lit., ' of God,' 2 Cor. 1 : 12, A.V., " godly (sincerity)," R.V., " (sincerity) of God ; " 2 Cor. 11 : 2, " a godly jealousy," lit., ' a

jealousy of God' (R.V., marg.); 1 Tim. 1 : 4, R.V., "a dispensation of God" (*oikonomia*, in the best mss.), A.V., "godly edifying" (*oikodomē*, lit., 'an edifying of, i.e., by, God'). (2) In 2 Cor. 7 : 10, "godly (sorrow)," and in vv. 9 and 11, "after a godly sort," are in all three places, lit., 'according to God.' (3) In 3 John 6, where the A.V. translates the adverb
axiōs, with the noun *theos*, "after a godly sort," the R.V. rightly AXIŌS
substitutes "worthily of God." 516 AG:78D CB:1238B

GODWARD

Note: This translates the phrase *pros ton theon*, lit., 'toward God,' in 2 Cor. 3 : 4, and 1 Thess. 1 : 8.

GOLD, GOLDEN

A. Nouns.

1. CHRUSOS (χρυσός) is used (*a*) of coin, Matt. 10 : 9; Jas. 5 : 3; 5557
(*b*) of ornaments, Matt. 23 : 16, 17; Jas. 5 : 3 (perhaps both coin and AG:888D
ornaments); Rev. 18 : 12; some mss. have it instead of No. 2 in 1 Cor. CB:1240B
3 : 12; (*c*) of images, Acts 17 : 29; (*d*) of the metal in general, Matt. 2 : 11; Rev. 9 : 7 (some mss. have it in Rev. 18 : 16).¶

2. CHRUSION (χρυσίον), a diminutive of No. 1, is used (*a*) of coin, 5553
primarily smaller than those in No. 1 (*a*), Acts 3 : 6; 20 : 33; 1 Pet. 1 : 18; AG:888C CB:1240B
(*b*) of ornaments, 1 Pet. 3 : 3, and the following (in which some mss. have No. 1), 1 Tim. 2 : 9; Rev. 17 : 4; 18 : 16; (*c*) of the metal in general, Heb. 9 : 4; 1 Pet. 1 : 7; Rev. 21 : 18, 21; metaphorically, (*d*) of sound doctrine and its effects, 1 Cor. 3 : 12; (*e*) of righteousness of life and conduct, Rev. 3 : 18.¶

B. Adjective.

CHRUSEOS (χρυσέος) denotes golden, i.e., made of, or overlaid with, 5552
gold, 2 Tim. 2 : 20; Heb. 9 : 4, and fifteen times in the Apocalypse. AG:888D (-SOUS) CB:1240B (-SOUS)

GOLD RING

CHRUSODAKTULIOS (χρυσοδακτύλιος), an adjective denoting 'with 5554
a gold ring' (*daktulos*, a finger), occurs in Jas. 2 : 2.¶ AG:888C CB:—

GOOD, GOODLY, GOODNESS

A. Adjectives.

1. AGATHOS (ἀγαθός) describes that which, being good in its character 18
or constitution, is beneficial in its effect; it is used (*a*) of things physical, AG:2D CB:1233B
e.g., a tree, Matt. 7 : 17; ground, Luke 8 : 8; (*b*) in a moral sense, frequently of persons and things. God is essentially, absolutely and consummately good, Matt. 19 : 17; Mark 10 : 18; Luke 18 : 19. To certain persons the word is applied in Matt. 20 : 15; 25 : 21, 23; Luke 19 : 17; 23 : 50; John 7 : 12; Acts 11 : 24; Tit. 2 : 5; in a general application, Matt. 5 : 45; 12 : 35; Luke 6 : 45; Rom. 5 : 7; 1 Pet. 2 : 18.

The neuter of the adjective with the definite article signifies that which is good, lit., 'the good,' as being morally honourable, pleasing to God, and therefore beneficial. Christians are to prove it, Rom. 12 : 2; to cleave to it, 12 : 9; to do it, 13 : 3; Gal. 6 : 10; 1 Pet. 3 : 11 (here, and here only, the article is absent); John 5 : 29 (here, the neuter plural is used, 'the good things'); to work it, Rom. 2 : 10; Eph. 4 : 28; 6 : 8; to follow after it, 1 Thess. 5 : 15; to be zealous of it, 1 Pet. 3 : 13; to imitate it, 3 John 11; to overcome evil with it, Rom. 12 : 21. Governmental authorities are ministers of good, i.e., that which is salutary, suited to the course of human affairs, Rom. 13 : 4. In Philm. 14, "thy goodness," R.V. (lit., 'thy good'), means 'thy benefit.' As to Matt. 19 : 17, "why askest thou Me concerning that which is good?" the R.V. follows the most ancient mss.

The neuter plural is also used of material goods, riches, etc., Luke 1 : 53; 12 : 18, 19; 16 : 25; Gal. 6 : 6 (of temporal supplies); in Rom. 10 : 15; Heb. 9 : 11; 10 : 1, the good things are the benefits provided through the sacrifice of Christ, in regard both to those conferred through the Gospel and to those of the coming Messianic Kingdom. See further under No. 2. See BENEFIT, GOODS.

2570 AG:400B CB:1253B 2. KALOS (καλός) denotes that which is intrinsically good, and so, goodly, fair, beautiful, as (*a*) of that which is well adapted to its circumstances or ends, e.g., fruit, Matt. 3 : 10; a tree, 12 : 33; ground, 13 : 8, 23; fish, 13 : 48; the Law, Rom. 7 : 16; 1 Tim. 1 : 8; every creature of God, 1 Tim. 4 : 4; a faithful minister of Christ and the doctrine he teaches, 4 : 6; (*b*) of that which is ethically good, right, noble, honourable, e.g., Gal. 4 : 18; 1 Tim. 5 : 10, 25; 6 : 18; Tit. 2 : 7, 14; 3 : 8, 14. The word does not occur in the Apocalypse, nor indeed after 1 Peter.

Christians are to "take thought for things honourable" (*kalos*), 2 Cor. 8 : 21, R.V.; to do that which is honourable, 13 : 7; not to be weary in well doing, Gal. 6 : 9; to hold fast "that which is good," 1 Thess. 5 : 21; to be zealous of good works, Tit. 2 : 14; to maintain them, 3 : 8; to provoke to them, Heb. 10 : 24; to bear testimony by them, 1 Pet. 2 : 12.

Kalos and *agathos* occur together in Luke 8 : 15, an "honest" (*kalos*) heart, i.e., the attitude of which is right towards God; a "good" (*agathos*) heart, i.e., one that, instead of working ill to a neighbour, acts beneficially towards him. In Rom. 7 : 18, "in me . . . dwelleth no good thing" (*agathos*) signifies that in him is nothing capable of doing good, and hence he lacks the power "to do that which is good" (*kalos*). In 1 Thess. 5 : 15, "follow after that which is good" (*agathos*), the good is that which is beneficial; in ver. 21, "hold fast that which is good (*kalos*)," the good describes the intrinsic value of the teaching. See BETTER, FAIR, HONEST, MEET, WORTHY.

5543 AG:886A CB:1240A 3. CHRĒSTOS (χρηστός), said of things, that which is pleasant, said of persons, kindly, gracious, is rendered "good" in 1 Cor. 15 : 33; "goodness" in Rom. 2 : 4. See EASY.

Note : *Lampros* denotes gay, bright, " goodly " in Jas. 2 : 2, A.V., LAMPROS
(R.V., " fine ") ; in 2 : 3, A.V., " gay ; " in Rev. 18 : 14 (R.V., " sump- 2986 AG:465D
tuous "). See GORGEOUS, SUMPTUOUS. For *asteios*, " goodly," Heb. CB:1256C
11 : 23, R.V., see BEAUTIFUL. For *hikanos*, Acts 18 : 18, A.V., " a good ASTEIOS 791
while " see WHILE, *Note* (16). AG:117C

B. Nouns.

HIKANOS

1. CHRĒSTOTĒS (χρηστότης), akin to A, No. 3, denotes goodness 2425 AG:374B
(*a*) in the sense of what is upright, righteous, Rom. 3 : 12 (translated CB:1250C
" good ") ; (*b*) in the sense of kindness of heart or act, said of God, Rom. CHRĒSTOTĒS
2 : 4 ; 11 : 22 (thrice) ; Eph. 2 : 7 (" kindness ") ; Tit. 3 : 4 (" kindness ") ; 5544 AG:886B
said of believers and rendered " kindness," 2 Cor. 6 : 6 ; Col. 3 : 12 ; CB:1240A
Gal. 5 : 22 (R.V. ; A.V., " gentleness "). It signifies " not merely goodness as a quality, rather it is goodness in action, goodness expressing itself in deeds ; yet not goodness expressing itself in indignation against sin, for it is contrasted with severity in Rom. 11 : 22, but in grace and tenderness and compassion."* See GENTLENESS, KINDNESS.¶

2. AGATHŌSUNĒ (ἀγαθωσύνη), goodness, signifies that moral 19
quality which is described by the adjective *agathos* (see A, No. 1). It AG:3D CB:1233B
is used, in the N.T., of regenerate persons, Rom. 15 : 14 ; Gal. 5 : 22 ; Eph. 5 : 9 ; 2 Thess. 1 : 11 ; in the last, the phrase " every desire of goodness " (R.V. ; the addition of " His " in the A.V. is an interpolation ; there is no pronoun in the original) may be either subjective, i.e., desire characterised by goodness, good desire, or objective, i.e., desire after goodness, to be and do good.¶

Trench, following Jerome, distinguishes between *chrēstotēs* and *agathōsunē* in that the former describes the kindlier aspects of goodness, the latter includes also the sterner qualities by which doing good to others is not necessarily by gentle means. He illustrates the latter by the act of Christ in cleansing the temple, Matt. 21 : 12, 13, and in denouncing the Scribes and Pharisees, 23 : 13–29 ; but *chrēstotēs* by His dealings with the penitent woman, Luke 7 : 37–50. Lightfoot regards *chrēstotēs* as a kindly disposition towards others ; *agathōsunē* as a kindly activity on their behalf.

J. A. Robertson (on Eph. 5 : 9) remarks that *agathōsunē* is " the kindlier, as *dikaiosunē* (righteousness) the sterner, element in the ideal character."

3. EUPOIIA (εὐποιία), beneficence, doing good (*eu*, well, *poieō*, to do), 2140
is translated as a verb in Heb. 13 : 16, " to do good."¶ AG:324A CB:—

C. Adverbs.

1. KALŌS (καλῶς), well, finely, is used in some mss. in Matt. 5 : 44, 2573
with *poieō*, to do, and translated " do good." In Jas. 2 : 3 it is rendered AG:401B CB:1253B
" in a good place " (A.V. marg., " well " or " seemly "). See WELL.

2. EU (εὖ), well, used with *poieō*, is translated " do . . . good " in 2095
Mark 14 : 7. See WELL. AG:317B CB:1247A

* From Notes on Galatians, by Hogg and Vine, p. 292.

D. Verbs (to do, or be, good).

15 AG:2C 1. AGATHOPOIEŌ (ἀγαθοποιέω), from A, No. 1, and *poieō*, to do, is
CB:1233B used (*a*) in a general way, to do well, 1 Pet. 2 : 15, 20 ; 3 : 6, 17 ; 3 John
11 ; (*b*) with pointed reference to the benefit of another, Luke 6 : 9, 33, 35 ;
in Mark 3 : 4 the parts of the word are separated in some mss. Some
mss. have it in Acts 14 : 17, for No. 2.¶ Cp. the noun *agathopoiia*, well-
doing, 1 Pet. 4 : 19, and the adjective *agathopoios*, doing well, 1 Pet. 2 : 14.

(-OERGEŌ) 2. AGATHOURGEŌ (ἀγαθουργέω), for *agathoergeō*, to do good (from A,
14 AG:2B No. 1, and *ergon*, a work), is used in Acts 14 : 17 (in the best mss. ; see
CB:1233B No. 1), where it is said of God's beneficence towards man, and 1 Tim. 6 : 18,
where it is enjoined upon the rich.¶

2109 AG:320A 3. EUERGETEŌ (εὐεργετέω), to bestow a benefit, to do good (*eu*, well,
CB:1247A and a verbal form akin to *ergon*), is used in Acts 10 : 38.¶

ISCHUŌ *Notes :* (1) The verb *ischuō*, to be strong (*ischus*, strength), to have
2480 AG:383D efficacy, force or value, is said of salt in Matt. 5 : 13, negatively, " it is
CB:1253A good for nothing." (2) In Matt. 19 : 10, A.V., *sumpherō*, to be profitable,
SUMPHERŌ expedient (*sun*, together, *pherō*, to bring), is rendered with a negative
4851 AG:780B " it is not good " (R.V., " it is not expedient "). (3) In Mark 14 : 7, the
CB:— two words *eu*, well, and *poieō*, to do, are in some mss. treated as one verb
eupoieō, to do good.

GOOD-BY See BID FAREWELL

GOODMAN

3617 AG:558A OIKODESPOTĒS (οἰκοδεσπότης) denotes the master of a house
CB:1260B (*oikos*, a house, *despotēs*, a master), a householder. It occurs only in the
Synoptists, and there 12 times. It is rendered " goodman " in Luke
22 : 11, where " of the house " is put separately ; in Matt. 20 : 11, where
the A.V. has " the goodman of the house " for the one word, the R.V.
renders it by " householder," as in ver. 1 ; in 24 : 43, " master ; " so
in Luke 12 : 39 ; in Mark 14 : 14, both have " the goodman of the house."
See HOUSEHOLDER, MASTER.

GOODS

18 AG:2D 1. For the neuter plural of *agathos*, used as a noun, " goods," see
CB:1233B Luke 12 : 18, 19, where alone this word is so rendered.

5223 2. HUPARXIS (ὕπαρξις), primarily, subsistence, then, substance,
AG:837D CB:1252A property, goods (akin to *huparchō*, to exist, be, belong to), is translated
" goods " in Acts 2 : 45 ; " possession," R.V. (A.V., " substance ") in
Heb. 10 : 34.¶

979 3. BIOS (βίος), which denotes (*a*) life, lifetime, (*b*) livelihood, living,
AG:141D CB:1239A means of living, is translated " goods " in 1 John 3 : 17, R.V. (A.V.,
" good "). See LIFE, No. 2.

4632 AG:754A 4. SKEUOS (σκεῦος), a vessel, denotes " goods " in Matt. 12 : 29 ;
CB:1269A Mark 3 : 27 ; Luke 17 : 31, R.V. (A.V., " stuff "). See VESSEL.

5225 *Notes :* (1) The neuter plural of the present participle of *huparchō*,
AG:838A is used as a noun denoting goods, in Matt. 24 : 47, A.V. " his goods,"

R.V., " that he hath ; " " goods " in Matt. 25 : 14 ; Luke 11 : 21 ; 16 : 1 ; 19 : 8 ; 1 Cor. 13 : 3 ; in Heb. 10 : 34 (1st part). (2) In Luke 6 : 30 " thy goods " translates the neuter plural of the possessive pronoun with the article, lit., ' thy things,' or possessions. (3) In Rev. 3 : 17, the A.V. " I am . . . increased with goods " translates the perfect tense of the verb *plouteō*, to be rich; R.V., " I have gotten riches." (4) See SUBSTANCE. **PLOUTEō 4147 AG:673D CB:1265B**

GORGEOUS, GORGEOUSLY

LAMPROS (λαμπρός), bright, splendid, is rendered " gorgeous " in **2986**
Luke 23 : 11, of the apparel in which Herod and his soldiers arrayed **AG:465D CB:1256C**
Christ. See BRIGHT.

Note : For the A.V., " gorgeously apparelled " in Luke 7 : 25, see GLORIOUS, B.

GOSPEL (Noun and Verb : to preach)

A. Noun.

EUANGELION (εὐαγγέλιον) originally denoted a reward for good **2098**
tidings ; later, the idea of reward dropped, and the word stood for the good **AG:317D CB:1247A**
news itself. The Eng. word gospel, i.e. good message, is the equivalent of *euangelion* (Eng., evangel). In the N.T. it denotes the good tidings of the Kingdom of God and of salvation through Christ, to be received by faith, on the basis of His expiatory death, His burial, resurrection, and ascension, e.g., Acts 15 : 7 ; 20 : 24 ; 1 Pet. 4 : 17. Apart from those references and those in the Gospels of Matthew and Mark, and Rev. 14 : 6, the noun is confined to Paul's Epistles. The Apostle uses it of two associated yet distinct things, (*a*) of the basic facts of the death, burial and resurrection of Christ, e.g., 1 Cor. 15 : 1–3 ; (*b*) of the interpretation of these facts, e.g., Rom. 2 : 16 ; Gal. 1 : 7, 11 ; 2 : 2 ; in (*a*) the Gospel is viewed historically, in (*b*) doctrinally, with reference to the interpretation of the facts, as is sometimes indicated by the context.

The following phrases describe the subjects or nature or purport of the message ; it is the gospel of God, Mark 1 : 14 ; Rom. 1 : 1 ; 15 : 16 ; 2 Cor. 11 : 7 ; 1 Thess. 2 : 2, 9 ; 1 Pet. 4 : 17 ; God, concerning His Son, Rom. 1 : 1–3 ; His Son, Rom. 1 : 9 ; Jesus Christ, the Son of God, Mark 1 : 1 ; our Lord Jesus, 2 Thess. 1 : 8 ; Christ, Rom. 15 : 19, etc. ; the glory of Christ, 2 Cor. 4 : 4 ; the grace of God, Acts 20 : 24 ; the glory of the blessed God, 1 Tim. 1 : 11 ; your salvation, Eph. 1 : 13 ; peace, Eph. 6 : 15. Cp. also " the gospel of the Kingdom," Matt. 4 : 23 ; 9 : 35 ; 24 : 14 ; " an eternal gospel," Rev. 14 : 6.

In Gal. 2 : 14, " the truth of the gospel " denotes, not the true gospel, but the true teaching of it, in contrast to perversions of it.

The following expressions are used in connection with the Gospel : (*a*) with regard to its testimony ; (1) *kērussō*, to preach it as a herald, e.g., Matt. 4 : 23 ; Gal. 2 : 2 (see PREACH) ; (2) *laleō*, to speak, 1 Thess. 2 : 2 ; (3) *diamarturomai*, to testify (thoroughly), Acts 20 : 24 ; (4) *euangelizō*, to preach, e.g., 1 Cor. 15 : 1 ; 2 Cor. 11 : 7 ; Gal. 1 : 11 (see B, No. 1 below) ; (5) *katangellō*, to proclaim, 1 Cor. 9 : 14 ; (6) *douleuō eis*, to serve unto (" in furtherance of "), Phil. 2 : 22 ; (7) *sunathleō en*, to labour with in, Phil. 4 : 3 ; (8) *hierourgeō*, to minister, Rom. 15 : 16 ; (8) *plēroō*, to preach fully, Rom. 15 : 19 ; (10) *sunkakopatheō*, to suffer hardship with, 2 Tim. 1 : 8 ; (*b*) with regard to its reception or otherwise : (1) *dechomai*, to receive, 2 Cor. 11 : 4 ; *hupakouō*, to hearken to, or obey, Rom. 10 : 16 ; 2 Thess. 1 : 8 ; *pisteuō en*, to believe in, Mark 1 : 15 ; *metastrephō*, to pervert, Gal. 1 : 7.

Note : In connection with (*a*), the Apostle's statement in 1 Cor. 9 : 23 is noticeable, " I do all things for the Gospel's sake, that I may be a joint partaker thereof," R.V., for the incorrect A.V., " that I might be partaker thereof with you."

B. Verbs.

2097 AG:317B CB:1247A

1. EUANGELIZŌ (εὐαγγελίζω), to bring or announce glad tidings (Eng., evangelize), is used (*a*) in the Active Voice in Rev. 10 : 7 (" declared ") and 14 : 6 (" to proclaim," R.V., A.V., " to preach ") ; (*b*) in the Passive Voice, of matters to be proclaimed as glad tidings, Luke 16 : 16 ; Gal. 1 : 11 ; 1 Pet. 1 : 25 ; of persons to whom the proclamation is made, Matt. 11 : 5 ; Luke 7 : 22 ; Heb. 4 : 2, 6 ; 1 Pet. 4 : 6 ; (*c*) in the Middle Voice, especially of the message of salvation, with a personal object, either of the Person preached, e.g., Acts 5 : 42 ; 11 : 20 ; Gal. 1 : 16, or, with a preposition, of the persons evangelized, e.g., Acts 13 : 32, " declare glad tidings ; " Rom. 1 : 15 ; Gal. 1 : 8 ; with an impersonal object, e.g., " the word," Acts 8 : 4 ; " good tidings," 8 : 12 ; " the word of the Lord," 15 : 35 ; " the gospel," 1 Cor. 15 : 1 ; 2 Cor. 11 : 7 ; " the faith," Gal. 1 : 23 ; " peace," Eph. 2 : 17 ; " the unsearchable riches of Christ," 3 : 8. See PREACH, SHEW, TIDINGS.

4283 AG:705D CB:1266C

2. PROEUANGELIZOMAI (προευαγγελίζομαι), to announce glad tidings beforehand, is used in Gal. 3 : 8.¶

Note : For other verbs see above.

GOUGE See PLUCK

For GOT and GOTTEN see GET

GOVERNMENT

KUBERNĒSIS 2941 AG:456C CB:1256B KUBERNĒTĒS 2942 AG:456C CB:1256B KURIOTĒS 2963 AG:460D CB:1256B

KUBERNĒSIS (κυβέρνησις), from *kubernaō*, to guide (whence Eng., govern), denotes (*a*) steering, pilotage ; (*b*) metaphorically, governments or governings, said of those who act as guides in a local church, 1 Cor. 12 : 28.¶ Cp. *kubernētēs*, a pilot, Acts 27 : 11 ; Rev. 18 : 17.¶

Note : For *kuriotēs*, lordship, dominion, rendered " government " in 2 Pet. 2 : 10, A.V., see DOMINION.

GOVERNOR

A. Nouns.

2232 AG:343B CB:1249C

1. HĒGEMŌN (ἡγεμών) is a term used (*a*) for rulers generally, Mark

13 : 9; 1 Pet. 2 : 14; translated "princes" (i.e., leaders) in Matt. 2 : 6; (*b*) for the Roman Procurators, referring, in the Gospels to Pontius Pilate, e.g., Matt. 27 : 2; Luke 20 : 20 (so designated by Tacitus, Annals, xv. 44); to Felix, Acts 23 : 26. Technically the Procurator was a financial official under a proconsul or proprætor, for collecting the Imperial revenues, but entrusted also with magisterial powers for decisions of questions relative to the revenues. In certain provinces, of which Judæa was one (the Procurator of which was dependent on the Legate of Syria), he was the general administrator and supreme judge, with sole power of life and death. Such a governor was a person of high social standing. Felix, however, was an ex-slave, a freedman, and his appointment to Judæa could not but be regarded by the Jews as an insult to the nation. The headquarters of the governor of Judæa was Cæsarea, which was made a garrison town. See PRINCE, RULER. For *anthupatos*, a proconsul, see PROCONSUL.

2. ETHNARCHĒS (ἐθνάρχης), an ethnarch, lit. a ruler of a nation **1481**
(*ethnos*, a people, *archē*, rule), is translated "governor" in 2 Cor. 11 : 32; **AG:218B**
it describes normally the ruler of a nation possessed of separate laws and **CB:—**
customs among those of a different race. Eventually it denoted a ruler
of a Province, superior to a tetrarch, but inferior to a king (e.g., Aretas).¶

3. OIKONOMOS (οἰκονόμος), lit., one who rules a house (*oikos*, a house, **3623**
nomos, a law), Gal. 4 : 2, denotes a superior servant responsible for the **AG:560A**
family housekeeping, the direction of other servants, and the care of the **CB:1260B**
children under age. See CHAMBERLAIN, STEWARD.

4. ARCHITRIKLINOS (ἀρχιτρίκλινος), from *archē*, rule, and *triklinos*, **755**
a room with three couches, denotes the ruler of a feast, John 2 : 8, R.V. **AG:113B**
(A.V., "the governor of the feast"), a man appointed to see that the **CB:—**
table and couches were duly placed and the courses arranged, and to
taste the food and wine.¶

B. Verbs.

1. HĒGEOMAI (ἡγέομαι), akin to A, No. 1, is used in the present **2233**
participle to denote a governor, lit., '(one) governing,' Matt. 2 : 6; **AG:343C**
Acts 7 : 10. **CB:1249C**

2. HĒGEMONEUŌ (ἡγεμονεύω), to be a *hēgemōn*, to lead the way, **2230**
came to signify to be a governor of a Province; it is used of Quirinius, **AG:343A**
governor of Syria, Luke 2 : 2, R.V. (for the circumstances see under **CB:—**
ENROLMENT); of Pontius Pilate, governor of Judæa, 3 : 1.¶ In the first
clause of this verse the noun *hēgemonia*, a rule or sovereignty, is translated
"reign;" Eng., hegemony.¶

Note. In Jas. 3 : 4, the verb *euthunō*, to make or guide straight, is **2116**
used in the present participle, as a noun, denoting the "steersman" **AG:320D**
(R.V.) or pilot of a vessel, A.V., "governor." **CB:—**

GRACE **5485**

1. CHARIS (χάρις) has various uses, (*a*) objective, that which bestows **AG:877B** **CB:1239C**

or occasions pleasure, delight, or causes favourable regard; it is applied, e.g., to beauty, or gracefulness of person, Luke 2 : 40; act, 2 Cor. 8 : 6, or speech, Luke 4 : 22, R.V., " words of grace " (A.V., " gracious words "); Col. 4 : 6; (*b*) subjective, (1) on the part of the bestower, the friendly disposition from which the kindly act proceeds, graciousness, loving-kindness, goodwill generally, e.g., Acts 7 : 10; especially with reference to the Divine favour or grace, e.g., Acts 14 : 26; in this respect there is stress on its freeness and universality, its spontaneous character, as in the case of God's redemptive mercy, and the pleasure or joy He designs for the recipient; thus it is set in contrast with debt, Rom. 4 : 4, 16, with works, 11 : 6, and with law, John 1 : 17; see also, e.g., Rom. 6 : 14, 15; Gal. 5 : 4; (2) on the part of the receiver, a sense of the favour bestowed, a feeling of gratitude, e.g., Rom. 6 : 17 (" thanks "); in this respect it sometimes signifies to be thankful, e.g., Luke 17 : 9 (" doth he thank the servant ? " lit., ' hath he thanks to '); 1 Tim. 1 : 12; (*c*) in another objective sense, the effect of grace, the spiritual state of those who have experienced its exercise, whether (1) a state of grace, e.g., Rom. 5 : 2; 1 Pet. 5 : 12; 2 Pet. 3 : 18, or (2) a proof thereof in practical effects, deeds of grace, e.g., 1 Cor. 16 : 3, R.V., " bounty " (A.V., " liberality "); 2 Cor. 8 : 6, 19 (in 2 Cor. 9 : 8 it means the sum of earthly blessings); the power and equipment for ministry, e.g., Rom. 1 : 5; 12 : 6; 15 : 15; 1 Cor. 3 : 10; Gal. 2 : 9; Eph. 3 : 2, 7.

To be in favour with is to find grace with, e.g., Acts 2 : 47; hence it appears in this sense at the beginning and the end of several Epistles, where the writer desires grace from God for the readers, e.g., Rom. 1 : 7; 1 Cor. 1 : 3; in this respect it is connected with the imperative mood of the word *chairō*, to rejoice, a mode of greeting among Greeks, e.g., Acts 15 : 23; Jas. 1 : 1 (marg.); 2 John 10, 11, R.V., " greeting " (A.V., " God speed ").

The fact that grace is received both from God the Father, 2 Cor. 1 : 12, and from Christ, Gal. 1 : 6; Rom. 5 : 15 (where both are mentioned), is a testimony to the Deity of Christ. See also 2 Thess. 1 : 12, where the phrase " according to the grace of our God and the Lord Jesus Christ " is to be taken with each of the preceding clauses, " in you," " and ye in Him."

In Jas. 4 : 6, " But He giveth more grace " (Greek, ' a greater grace,' R.V., marg.), the statement is to be taken in connection with the preceding verse, which contains two remonstrating, rhetorical questions, " Think ye that the Scripture speaketh in vain ? " and " Doth the Spirit (the Holy Spirit) which He made to dwell in us long unto envying ? " (see the R.V.). The implied answer to each is ' it cannot be so.' Accordingly, if those who are acting so flagrantly, as if it were so, will listen to the Scripture instead of letting it speak in vain, and will act so that the Holy Spirit may have His way within, God will give even ' a greater grace,' namely, all that follows from humbleness and from turning away from the world. See BENEFIT, BOUNTY, LIBERALITY, THANK.

Note: The corresponding verb *charitoō*, to endue with Divine favour 5487
or grace, is used in Luke 1 : 28, " highly favoured " (marg., " endued AG:879A CB:1239C
with grace ") and Eph. 1 : 6, A.V., " hath made . . . accepted ; " R.V., " freely bestowed " (marg., " endued.").¶

2. EUPREPEIA (εὐπρέπεια), comeliness, goodly appearance, is said of 2143
the outward appearance of the flower of the grass, Jas. 1 : 11.¶ AG:324B CB:—

GRACIOUS

CHRĒSTOS (χρηστός) is rendered " gracious " in 1 Pet. 2 : 3, as an 5543 AG:886A
attribute of the Lord. See EASY, GOOD, KIND. CB:1240A

Note: *Euphēmos*, fair-sounding (*eu*, well, *phēmē*, a saying, or report), 2163
" of good report," Phil. 4 : 8, is rendered " gracious " in the R.V. marg. AG:327C CB:—

GRAFF, GRAFT (R.V.)

ENKENTRIZŌ (ἐνκεντρίζω) denotes to graft in (*en*, in, *kentrizō*, to 1461
graft), to insert a slip of a cultivated tree into a wild one. In Rom. AG:216A CB:1245A
11 : 17, 19, 23, 24, however, the metaphor is used " contrary to nature " (ver. 24), of grafting a wild olive branch (the Gentile) into the good olive tree (the Jews) ; that unbelieving Jews (branches of the good tree) were broken off that Gentiles might be grafted in, afforded no occasion for glorying on the part of the latter. Jew and Gentile alike must enjoy the Divine blessings by faith alone. So Jews who abide not in unbelief shall, as " the natural branches, be grafted into their own olive tree."¶

GRAIN

KOKKOS (κόκκος) denotes a grain, Matt. 13 : 31 ; 17 : 20 ; Mark 2848
4 : 31 ; Luke 13 : 19 ; 17 : 6 ; John 12 : 24 (A.V., " corn ") ; 1 Cor. 15 : 37 AG:440C CB:—
(where the R.V. has " a . . . grain," to distinguish it from grain in general). See CORN.¶

GRANDCHILDREN

EKGONOS (ἔκγονος), an adjective, denoting born of (*ek*, from, *ginomai*, 1549
to become or be born), was used as a noun, signifying a child ; in the (-NON) AG:238A
plural, descendants, " grand-children," 1 Tim. 5 : 4, R.V. (A.V., CB:—
" nephews ").¶

GRANDMOTHER

MAMMĒ (μάμμη), an onomatopœic word, was primarily a child's 3125
name for its mother ; later it denoted a grandmother, 2 Tim. 1 : 5.¶ AG:490A CB:—

GRANT

1. DIDŌMI (διδώμι), to give, is rendered " grant " in Mark 10 : 37 ; 1325 AG:192C
Luke 1 : 74 ; Acts 4 : 29 ; 11 : 18 ; 14 : 3. See GIVE. CB:1241C

(-OMAI) 1433 AG:210C CB:1242A 2. DŌREŌ (δωρέω), to present, bestow (akin to No. 1), is rendered "granted" in Mark 15 : 45, R.V. (A.V., "gave"); in 2 Pet. 1 : 3, 4, "hath granted," "He hath granted," R.V. (A.V., "hath given" and "are given"); in each place Middle Voice. See GIVE.¶

5483 AG:876C CB:1239C 3. CHARIZOMAI (χαρίζομαι) primarily signifies to show favour or kindness (akin to *charis*, see GRACE), Gal. 3 : 18, R.V., "hath granted" (A.V., "gave"; it signifies more than to give); then, to give freely, bestow, rendered to grant in Acts 3 : 14; 27 : 24, R.V. (A.V., "given"); Phil. 1 : 29, R.V.; Philm. 22, R.V. See DELIVER.

GRAPE

4718 AG:765C CB:— STAPHULĒ (σταφυλή) denotes a bunch of grapes, or a grape, Matt. 7 : 16; Luke 6 : 44; Rev. 14 : 18. It is to be distinguished from *omphax*, an unripe grape (not in N.T.), e.g., in the Sept. of Job 15 : 33, and from *botrus*, a cluster, used together with *staphulē* in Rev. 14 : 18.¶

GRASP See APPREHEND, UNDERSTAND, TAKE

GRASS

5528 AG:884A CB:1240A CHORTOS (χόρτος) primarily denoted a feeding enclosure (whence Latin *hortus*, a garden; Eng., yard, and garden); then, food, especially grass for feeding cattle; it is translated "grass" in Matt. 6 : 30; 14 : 19; Mark 6 : 39 (where "the green grass" is the first evidence of early spring); Luke 12 : 28; John 6 : 10; Jas. 1 : 10, 11; 1 Pet. 1 : 24; Rev. 8 : 7; 9 : 4; "blade" in Matt. 13 : 26; Mark 4 : 28; "hay" in 1 Cor. 3 : 12, used figuratively. In Palestine or Syria there are 90 genera and 243 species of grass.¶

GRATULATION

3108 AG:487A CB:1257C MAKARISMOS (μακαρισμός) denotes a declaration of blessedness, a felicitation; it is translated "gratulation" in Gal. 4 : 15, R.V. (A.V., "blessedness"); the Galatian converts had counted themselves happy when they heard and received the Gospel from Paul; he asks them rhetorically what had become of that spirit which had animated them; the word is rendered "blessing" in Rom. 4 : 6, 9. See BLESSING, C, No. 2.¶

GRAVE (Noun)

3419 AG:524C CB:1259A 1. MNĒMEION (μνημεῖον) primarily denotes a memorial (akin to *mnaomai*, to remember), then, a monument (the significance of the word rendered "tombs," A.V., "sepulchres," in Luke 11 : 47), anything done to preserve the memory of things and persons; it usually denotes a tomb, and is translated either "tomb" or "sepulchre" or "grave." Apart from the Gospels, it is found only in Acts 13 : 29. Among the Hebrews it was generally a cavern, closed by a door or stone, often decorated. Cp. Matt. 23 : 29. See TOMB.

2. MNĒMA (μνῆμα), akin to No. 1, like which it signified a memorial 3418 AG:524C CB:1259A
or record of a thing or a dead person, then a sepulchral monument, and hence a tomb; it is rendered "graves" in the A.V. of Rev. 11 : 9 (R.V., "a tomb"); "tomb" or "tombs," Mark 5 : 3, 5 (some mss. have No. 1, as in 15 : 46, A.V., "sepulchre") and 16 : 2 (A.V., "sepulchre"); Luke 8 : 27; Acts 2 : 29 and 7 : 16 (A.V., "sepulchre"). See TOMB.

Note: In 1 Cor. 15 : 55, where some texts have "Hades," A.V., 2288 AG:350D CB:1271C
"grave," the most authentic have *thanatos*, death.

GRAVE (Adjective)

SEMNOS (σεμνός) first denoted reverend, august, venerable (akin 4586 AG:746D CB:1269A
to *sebomai*, to reverence); then, serious, grave, whether of persons, 1 Tim. 3 : 8, 11 (deacons and their wives); Tit. 2 : 2 (aged men); or things, Phil. 4 : 8, R.V., "honourable" (marg., "reverend"), A.V., "honest." Trench (Syn.,§ xcii) points out that "grave" and "gravity" fail to cover the full meaning of their original; "the word we want is one in which the sense of gravity and dignity is combined." Cremer describes it as denoting what inspires reverence and awe, and says that *semnos* and *hosios*, holy, consecrated, are only secondary designations of the conception of holiness. "The word points to seriousness of purpose and to self-respect in conduct" (Moule).¶ Cp. *semnotēs*, gravity (see below).

GRAVE-CLOTHES

KEIRIA (κειρία) denotes, firstly, a band either for a bed girth, or bed 2750 AG:427A CB:—
sheets themselves (Sept. of Prov. 7 : 16.¶); then, the swathings wrapped round a corpse; it is used in the plural in John 11 : 44.¶

GRAVEN

CHARAGMA (χάραγμα), from *charassō*, to engrave (akin to *charaktēr*, 5480 AG:876A CB:1239B
an impress, R.V., marg., of Heb. 1 : 3), denotes (*a*) a mark or stamp, e.g., Rev. 13 : 16, 17; 14 : 9, 11; 16 : 2; 19 : 20; 20 : 4; 15 : 2 in some mss.; (*b*) a thing graven, Acts 17 : 29.¶

GRAVITY

SEMNOTĒS (σεμνότης) denotes venerableness, dignity; it is a 4587 AG:747A CB:1269A
necessary characteristic of the life and conduct of Christians, 1 Tim. 2 : 2, R.V., "gravity" (A.V., "honesty"), a qualification of a bishop or overseer in a church, in regard to his children, 1 Tim. 3 : 4; a necessary characteristic of the teaching imparted by a servant of God, Tit. 2 : 7.¶ Cp. the adjective *semnos*, under GRAVE.

GREAT

1. MEGAS (μέγας) is used (*a*) of external form, size, measure, e.g., 3173 AG:497C CB:1258A
of a stone, Matt. 27 : 60; fish, John 21 : 11; (*b*) of degree and intensity, e.g., of fear, Mark 4 : 41; wind, John 6 : 18; Rev. 6 : 13, R.V., "great"

(A.V., "mighty"); of a circumstance, 1 Cor. 9:11; 2 Cor. 11:15; in Rev. 5:2, 12, the R.V. has "great" (A.V., "loud"), of a voice; (*c*) of rank, whether of persons, e.g., God, Tit. 2:13; Christ as a "great Priest," Heb. 10:21, R.V.; Diana, Acts 19:27; Simon Magus, Acts 8:9 "(some) great one;" in the plural, "great ones," Matt. 20:25; Mark 10:42, those who hold positions of authority in Gentile nations; or of things, e.g., a mystery, Eph. 5:32. Some mss. have it in Acts 8:8, of joy (see No. 2). See also Note (2) below. See GREATEST, HIGH, LOUD, MIGHTY, STRONG.

4183 AG:687C CB:1266A 2. POLUS (πολύς), much, many, great, is used of number, e.g., Luke 5:6; Acts 11:21; degree, e.g., of harvest, Matt. 9:37 [See Note (8)]; mercy, 1 Pet. 1:3, R.V., "great" (A.V., "abundant"); glory, Matt. 24:30; joy, Philm. 7, R.V., "much" (A.V., "great"); peace, Acts 24:2. The best mss. have it in Acts 8:8 (R.V., "much"), of joy. See ABUNDANT, COMMON, *Note* (1), LONG, MANY, MUCH, OFT, SORE, STRAITLY.

2425 AG:374B CB:1250C 3. HIKANOS (ἱκανός), lit., reaching to (from *hikanō*, to reach), denotes sufficient, competent, fit, and is sometimes rendered "great," e.g., of number (of people), Mark 10:46; of degree (of light), Acts 22:6. See ABLE, ENOUGH, GOOD, LARGE, LONG, MANY, MEET, MUCH, SECURITY, SUFFICIENT, WORTHY.

2245 AG:345C CB:— 4. HĒLIKOS (ἡλίκος) primarily denotes as big as, as old as (akin to *hēlikia*, an age); then, as an indirect interrogation, what, what size, how great, how small (the context determines the meaning), said of a spiritual conflict, Col. 2:1, A.V., "what great (conflict) I have;" R.V., "how greatly (I strive);" of much wood as kindled by a little fire, Jas. 3:5 (twice in the best mss.), "how much (wood is kindled by) how small (a fire)," R.V., said metaphorically of the use of the tongue. Some mss. have No. 4 in Gal 6:11; the most authentic have No. 5.¶

4080 AG:656B CB:— 5. PĒLIKOS (πηλίκος), primarily a direct interrogative, how large? how great? is used in exclamations, indicating magnitude, like No. 4 (No. 6 indicates quantity), in Gal. 6:11, of letter characters (see No. 4, Note); in Heb. 7:4, metaphorically, of the distinguished character of Melchizedek.¶

4214 AG:694B CB:— 6. POSOS (πόσος), an adjective of number, magnitude, degree etc., is rendered "how great" in Matt. 6:23. See MANY, MUCH.

3745 AG:586B CB:1251B 7. HOSOS (ὅσος), how much, how many, is used in the neuter plural to signify how great things, Mark 5:19, 20; Luke 8:39 (twice); Acts 9:16, A.V. (R.V., "how many things"); in Rev. 21:16 (in the best mss.), "as great as," R.V. (A.V., "as large as," said of length). See ALL, MANY, No. 5, WHATSOEVER.

5118 AG:823B CB:— 8. TOSOUTOS (τοσοῦτος), so great, so many, so much, of quantity, size, etc., is rendered "so great," in Matt. 8:10, and Luke 7:9, of faith; Matt. 15:33, of a multitude; Heb. 12:1, of a cloud of witnesses; Rev. 18:17, of riches. See LARGE, LONG, MANY, MUCH.

9. TĒLIKOUTOS (τηλικοῦτος), so great, is used in the N.T. of things 5082
only, a death, 2 Cor. 1 : 10 ; salvation, Heb. 2 : 3 ; ships, Jas. 3 : 4 ; AG:814C
an earthquake, Rev. 16 : 18, A.V., " so mighty," corrected in the R.V. CB:—
to " so great." See MIGHTY.¶

Notes : (1) In Mark 7 : 36, " so much the more a great deal " translates MEGISTAN
a phrase lit. signifying 'more abundantly ;' in 10 : 48, " the more a (-NES)
great deal " translates a phrase lit. signifying 'more by much.' (2) 3175 AG:498C
For the noun *megistan*, in the plural, rendered " Lords " in the A.V. of CB:1258A
Mark 6 : 21, see LORD ; in Rev. 6 : 15 and 18 . 23, see PRINCE. (3) In MEGALUNŌ 3170
Luke 1 : 58, the verb *megalunō*, to magnify, make great (akin to No. 1), AG:497A
is rendered " had magnified (His mercy)," R.V. [A.V., " had shewed great CB:1258A PALAI
(mercy) "]. (4) In Luke 10 : 13, the adverb *palai*, of old, long ago, is so 3819
rendered in the R.V. (A.V., " a great while ago "). (5) In 2 Pet. 1 : 4, AG:605C CB:1261C
megistos, the superlative of *megas* (No. 1), said of the promises of God, MEGISTOS
is rendered " exceeding great."¶ (6) In Matt. 21 : 8, *pleistos*, the superlative 3176
of *polus* (No. 2), said of a multitude, is rendered " very great " in the AG:497C (MEGAS 2b.)
A.V. (R.V., " the most part "). (7) In Rev. 21 : 10, the most authentic CB:1258A PLEISTOS
mss. omit " that great " [R.V., " the holy (city) "]. (8) In Luke 10 : 2, 4118
the R.V. renders *polus* by " plenteous " (A.V., " great "). (9) In Mark AG:687C
1 : 35, the adverb *lian*, exceedingly (see GREATLY), is rendered " a great (POLUS III.) LIAN
while." See DAY, B. (10) In Luke 1 : 49 some texts have *megaleia*, 3029
" great things ; " the best have No. 1. AG:473B CB:1257A

MEGALEIOS 3167 AG:496D CB:1258A

GREATER

1. MEIZŌN (μείζων) is the comparative degree of *megas* (see GREAT, 3187
No. 1), e.g., Matt. 11 : 11 ; in Matt. 13 : 32, the R.V. rightly has " greater AG:497C (MEGAS)
than " (A.V., " the greatest among ") ; 23 : 17 ; in Luke 22 : 26, R.V., CB:1258A
" the greater (among you) " (A.V., " greatest ") ; in Jas. 3 : 1, R.V.,
" the heavier (marg., greater) judgment " (A.V., " the greater condemnation ") ; it is used in the neuter plural in John 1 : 50, " greater things ; " in 14 : 12, " greater works " (lit., 'greater things') ; in 1 Cor. 12 : 31, R.V., " the greater," A.V., " the best ". See GREATEST, No. 2.

Note : In Matt. 20 : 31, the neuter of *meizōn*, used as an adverb, is translated " the more." See MORE.

3186
2. MEIZOTEROS (μειζότερος), a double comparative of *megas* (cp. No. AG:497C
1, above), is used in 3 John 4, of joy.¶ (MEGAS) CB:—

3. PLEIŌN (πλείων), the comparative of *polus* (see GREAT, No. 2), 4119
is used (*a*) as an adjective, greater, more, e.g., Acts 15 : 28 ; (*b*) as a noun, AG:687C (POLUS II.)
e.g., Matt. 12 : 41, " a greater (than Jonah) ; " ver. 42, " a greater (than CB:1265B
Solomon) ; " in these instances the neuter *pleion*, 'something greater,' is " a fixed or stereotyped form " of the word ; in 1 Cor. 15 : 6, " the greater part " (masculine plural) ; (*c*) as an adverb, e.g., Matt. 5 : 20, lit., '(except your righteousness abound) more greatly (than of scribes

and Pharisees); ' so 26 : 53, "more"; Luke 9 : 13. See ABOVE, LONGER, MANY, MORE, MOST, YET.

4054 AG:651C CB:1263C 4. PERISSOTEROS (περισσότερος), the comparative of *perissos*, over and above, abundant, signifies more abundant, greater, e.g., of condemnation, Mark 12 : 40; Luke 20 : 47. See ABUNDANT, C, No. 2.

GREATEST

3173 AG:497C CB:1258A 1. MEGAS (μέγας), for which see GREAT, No. 1, is translated "the greatest," in Acts 8 : 10 and Heb. 8 : 11. The whole phrase, lit., 'from small to great,' is equivalent to the Eng. idiom "one and all." It is used in the Sept., e.g., in 1 Sam. 5 : 9 ('God smote the people of Gath from the least to the greatest,' "both small and great") So 1 Sam. 30 : 19; 2 Chron. 34 : 30, etc. See GREAT.

3187 AG:497C (MEGAS) CB:1258A 2. MEIZŌN (μείζων), the comparative of No. 1, is sometimes translated "greatest;" besides the two cases given under GREATER, No. 1, where the R.V. corrects the A.V., "greatest" to "greater" (Matt. 13 : 32 and Luke 22 : 26), the R.V. itself has "greatest" for this comparative in the following, and relegates "greater" to the margin, Matt. 18 : 1, 4; 23 : 11; Mark 9 : 34; Luke 9 : 46; 22 : 24. See GREATER, MORE.

GREATLY

3029 AG:473B CB:1257A 1. LIAN (λίαν), very, exceedingly, is rendered "greatly" in Matt. 27 : 14, of wonder; 2 Tim. 4 : 15, of opposition; 2 John 4 and 3 John 3, of joy. See EXCEEDING, SORE, VERY.

4183 AG:687C CB:1266A 2. POLUS (πολύς) is used in the neuter singular (*polu*) or the plural (*polla*), as an adverb; in the sing., e.g., Mark 12 : 27; in the plur., e.g., Mark 1 : 45, "much;" 5 : 23, "greatly" (R.V., "much"); ver. 38, A.V. and R.V., "greatly;" 1 Cor. 16 : 12 (R.V., "much"). See LONG, MUCH.

Note: In Acts 28 : 6, A.V., *polu* is rendered "a great while" (R.V., "long").

3171 AG:497B CB:— 3. MEGALŌS (μεγάλως), from *megas* (GREAT, No. 1), is used of rejoicing, Phil. 4 : 10.¶

5479 AG:875C CB:1239B 4. CHARA (χαρά), joy, is used in the dative case adverbially with the verb *chairō*, to rejoice, in John 3 : 29, "rejoiceth greatly," lit., 'rejoiceth with joy.'

4970 AG:796A CB:1269C *Notes:* (1) For *sphodra*, R.V., "exceedingly," in Matt. 27 : 54 and Acts 6 : 7, see EXCEED, B, No. 2. (2) In the following the R.V. omits "greatly," as the verbs are adequately translated without, Phil. 1 : 8; 1 Thess. 3 : 6; 2 Tim. 1 : 4. In the following the R.V. adds "greatly" to express the fuller force of the verb, Luke 1 : 29; Acts 16 : 34; 1 Pet. 1 : 8. (3) In 1 Pet. 1 : 6, "ye greatly rejoice," the adverb is not separately expressed, but is incorporated in the rendering of the verb *agalliaō*, to rejoice much, to exult.

GREATNESS

1. MEGETHOS (μέγεθος), akin to *megas* (see GREAT, No. 1), is said 3174
of the power of God, in Eph. 1 : 19.¶ AG:498C CB:--

2. HUPERBOLĒ (ὑπερβολή) denotes "exceeding greatness," 2 Cor. 5236
4 : 7 ; 12 : 7. see EXCEL, B, No. 1. AG:840B CB:—

For GREEDILY see RUN, No. 9

For GREEDINESS see COVETOUSNESS, B, No. 3

For GREEDY see LUCRE

GREEN

1. CHLŌROS (χλωρός), akin to *chloē*, tender foliage (cp. the name 5515
Chloe, 1 Cor. 1 : 11, and Eng., chlorine), denotes (*a*) pale green, the AG:882D CB:1240A
colour of young grass, Mark 6 : 39 ; Rev. 8 : 7 ; 9 : 4, "green thing ;" hence, (*b*) pale, Rev. 6 : 8, the colour of the horse whose rider's name is Death. See PALE.¶

2. HUGROS (ὑγρός) denotes wet, moist (the opposite of *xēros*, dry) ; 5200
said of wood, sappy, "green," Luke 23 : 31, i.e., if they thus by the fire AG:832C CB:1251C
of their wrath treated Christ, the guiltless, holy, the fruitful, what would be the fate of the perpetrators, who were like the dry wood, exposed to the fire of Divine wrath.¶

GREET, GREETING

A. Verbs.

1. ASPAZOMAI (ἀσπάζομαι) signifies to greet, welcome, or salute. 782
In the A.V. it is chiefly rendered by either of the verbs to greet or to salute. AG:116C CB:1238A
"There is little doubt that the Revisers have done wisely in giving 'salute' . . . in the passages where A.V. has 'greet.' For the cursory reader is sure to imagine a difference of Greek and of meaning when he finds, e.g., in Phil. 4 : 21, 'Salute every saint in Christ Jesus. The brethren which are with me greet you,' or in 3 John 14, 'Our friends salute thee. Greet the friends by name'" (Hastings, Bible Dic.). In Acts 25 : 13 the meaning virtually is 'to pay his respects to.'

In two passages the renderings vary otherwise ; in Acts 20 : 1, of bidding farewell, A.V., "embraced them," R.V., "took leave of them," or, as Ramsay translates it, 'bade them farewell' ; in Heb. 11 : 13, of welcoming promises, A.V., "embraced," R.V., "greeted."

The verb is used as a technical term for conveying greetings at the close of a letter, often by an amanuensis, e.g., Rom. 16 : 22, the only instance of the use of the first person in this respect in the N.T. ; see also 1 Cor. 16 : 19, 20 ; 2 Cor. 13 : 13 ; Phil. 4 : 22 ; Col. 4 : 10-15 ; 1 Thess. 5 : 26 ; 2 Tim. 4 : 21 ; Tit. 3 : 15 ; Philm. 23 ; Heb. 13 : 24 ; 1 Pet. 5 : 13, 14 ; 2 John 13. This special use is largely illustrated in the papyri, one example of this showing how keenly the absence of the greeting was felt. The papyri also illustrate the use of the addition "by name," when several persons are included in the greeting, as in 3 John 14 (Moulton and Milligan, Vocab). See EMBRACE, LEAVE, SALUTE.

5463 2. CHAIRŌ (χαίρω), to rejoice, is thrice used as a formula of salutation
AG:873B CB:1239B in Acts 15 : 23, A.V., "send greeting," R.V., "greeting;" so 23 : 26; Jas. 1 : 1. In 2 John 10, 11, the R.V. substitutes the phrase (to give) greeting, for the A.V. (to bid) God speed. See FAREWELL, GLAD, HAIL, JOY, REJOICE.

B. Noun.

783 ASPASMOS (ἀσπασμός), a salutation, is always so rendered in the R.V.;
AG:117A CB:1238A A.V., "greetings" in Matt. 23 : 7; Luke 11 : 43; 20 : 46; it is used (*a*) orally in those instances and in Mark 12 : 38; Luke 1 : 29, 41, 44; (*b*) in written salutations, 1 Cor. 16 : 21 (cp. A, No. 1, in ver. 20); Col. 4 : 18; 2 Thess. 3 : 17.¶

GRIEF, GRIEVE

A. Noun.

3077 LUPĒ (λύπη) signifies pain, of body or mind; it is used in the plural
AG:482A CB:1257B in 1 Pet. 2 : 19 only, R.V., "griefs" (A.V., "grief"); here, however, it stands, by metonymy, for 'things that cause sorrow,' grievances; hence Tyndale's rendering, "grief," for Wycliffe's "sorews;" everywhere else it is rendered "sorrow," except in Heb. 12 : 11, where it is translated "grievous" (lit., 'of grief'). See HEAVINESS, SORROW.

B. Verbs.

3076 1. LUPEŌ (λυπέω), akin to A, denotes (*a*), in the Active Voice, to cause
AG:481C CB:1257B pain, or grief, to distress, grieve, e.g., 2 Cor. 2 : 2 (twice, Active and Passive Voices); ver. 5 (twice), R.V., "hath caused sorrow" (A.V., "have caused grief," and "grieved"); 7 : 8, "made (you) sorry"; Eph. 4 : 30, of grieving the Holy Spirit of God (as indwelling the believer); (*b*) in the Passive Voice, to be grieved, to be made sorry, to be sorry, sorrowful, e.g., Matt. 14 : 9, R.V., "(the king) was grieved" (A.V., "was sorry"); Mark 10 : 22, R.V., "(went away) sorrowful" (A.V., "grieved"); John 21 : 17, "(Peter) was grieved;" Rom. 14 : 15, "(if . . . thy brother) is grieved;" 2 Cor. 2 : 4, "(not that) ye should be made sorry," R.V., A.V., "ye should be grieved." See HEAVINESS, SORROW, SORROWFUL, SORRY.

4818 2. SUNLUPEŌ (συνλυπέω), or *sullupeō*, is used in the Passive Voice
AG:777A CB:— in Mark 3 : 5, to be grieved or afflicted together with a person, said of Christ's grief at the hardness of heart of those who criticised His healing on the Sabbath Day; it here seems to suggest the sympathetic nature of His grief because of their self-injury. Some suggest that the ***sun*** indicates the mingling of grief with His anger.¶

4727 AG:766B 3. STENAZŌ (στενάζω), to groan (of an inward, unexpressed feeling
CB:1270A of sorrow), is translated "with grief" in Heb. 13 : 17 (marg. "groaning").

It is rendered "sighed" in Mark 7 : 34; "groan," in Rom. 8 : 23; 2 Cor. 5 : 2, 4; "murmur," in Jas. 5 : 9, R.V. (A.V., "grudge"). See GROAN, MURMUR, SIGH.¶

Notes: (1) *Diaponeō*, to work out with labour, in the Passive Voice, DIAPONEō
to be sore troubled, is rendered "being grieved" in Acts 4 : 2 and 16 : 18, 1278 AG:187C
A.V. (R.V., "sore troubled"). See TROUBLE.¶ In some mss., Mark (-OMAI) CB:—
14 : 4. (2) *Prosochthizō*, to be angry with, is rendered "was grieved" PROSOCHTHIZō
in Heb. 3 : 10, 17, A.V. (R.V., "was displeased"). See DISPLEASE.¶ 4360 AG:717D CB:—

GRIEVOUS, GRIEVOUSLY

A. Adjectives.

1. BARUS (βαρύς) denotes heavy, burdensome; it is always used 926
metaphorically in the N.T., and is translated "heavy" in Matt. 23 : 4, AG:134B CB:1238C
of Pharisaical ordinances; in the comparative degree "weightier," 23 : 23, of details of the Law of God; "grievous," metaphorically of wolves, in Acts 20 : 29; of charges, 25 : 7; negatively of God's commandments, 1 John 5 : 3 (causing a burden on him who fulfils them); in 2 Cor. 10 : 10, "weighty," of Paul's letters. See HEAVY, WEIGHTY.¶

2. PONĒROS (πονηρός), painful, bad, is translated "grievous" in 4190 AG:690D
Rev. 16 : 2, of a sore inflicted retributively. See BAD. CB:1266A

3. DUSBASTAKTOS (δυσβάστακτος), hard to be borne (from *dus*, 1419
an inseparable prefix, like Eng. mis-, and un-, indicating difficulty, AG:209B CB:—
injuriousness, opposition, etc., and *bastazō*, to bear), is used in Luke 11 : 46 and, in some mss., in Matt. 23 : 4, "grievous to be borne;" in the latter the R.V. marg. has "many ancient authorities omit."¶

4. CHALEPOS (χαλεπός), hard, signifies (*a*) hard to deal with, Matt. 5467
8 : 28 (see FIERCE); (*b*) hard to bear, grievous, 2 Tim. 3 : 1, R.V., AG:874C CB:1239B
"grievous" (A.V., "perilous"), said of a characteristic of the last days of this age. See FIERCE.¶

Notes: (1) For the noun *lupē*, "grievous," in Heb. 12 : 11, see GRIEF. LUPē
(2) In Phil. 3 : 1, the adjective *oknēros*, shrinking, or causing shrinking, 3077 AG:482A
hence, tedious (akin to *okneō*, to shrink), is rendered "irksome" in the CB:1257B
R.V. (A.V., "grievous"); the Apostle intimates that, not finding his OKNēROS
message tedious, he has no hesitation in giving it. In Matt. 25 : 26 and 3636 AG:563A
Rom. 12 : 11, "slothful."¶ CB:—

B. Adverbs.

1. DEINŌS (δεινῶς), akin to *deos*, fear, signifies (*a*) terribly, Matt. 1171
8 : 6, "grievously (tormented);" (*b*) vehemently, Luke 11 : 53. See AG:173B CB:—
VEHEMENTLY.¶

2. KAKŌS (κακῶς), badly, ill, is translated "grievously (vexed)," 2560
in Matt. 15 : 22. See AMISS, EVIL, MISERABLY, SORE. AG:398C CB:1253B

Notes: (1) In Mark 9 : 20 and Luke 9 : 42, the R.V. renders the verb
susparassō "tare (him) grievously," the adverb bringing out the intensive 4952
force of the prefix *su*—(i.e., *sun*); the meaning may be 'threw violently AG:794C CB:—
to the ground.' (2) In Matt. 17 : 15, the idiomatic phrase, consisting of

No. 2 (above) with *echō*, to have, (lit., 'hath badly'), is rendered "suffereth grievously," R.V. (A.V., "is . . . sore vexed").

GRIND

229 AG:37B 1. ALĒTHŌ (ἀλήθω) signifies to grind at the mill, Matt. 24 : 41 ; Luke
CB:— 17 : 35.¶ The Sept. has both the earlier form *aleō*, Is. 47 : 2,¶, and the later one *alēthō*, used in the *Koinē* period, Numb. 11 : 8 ; Judg. 16 : 21 ; Eccles. 12 : 3, 4.¶

5149 AG:826B 2. TRIZŌ (τρίζω), primarily of animal sounds, to chirp, cry, etc., is
CB:— used of grinding the teeth, Mark 9 : 18, R.V. "grindeth" (A.V., "gnasheth with"). See GNASH.¶

3039 AG:474D *Note :* In Matt. 21 : 44 and Luke 20 : 18, *likmaō*, to winnow, as of
CB:— grain, by throwing it up against the wind, to scatter the chaff and straw, hence has the meaning to scatter, as chaff or dust, and is translated "will scatter . . . as dust," R.V. (A.V., "will grind . . . to powder"). In the Sept. it is used of being scattered by the wind or of sifting (cp. Amos 9 : 9). The use of the verb in the papyri writings suggests the meaning, to ruin, destroy (Deissmann).¶

GROAN, GROANING

A. Verbs.

1690 AG:254D 1. EMBRIMAOMAI (ἐμβριμάομαι), from *en*, in, and *brimē*, strength,
CB:1244B is rendered "groaned" in John 11 : 33 (preferable to the R.V. marg., "He had indignation"); so in ver. 38. The Lord was deeply moved doubtless with the combination of circumstances, present and in the immediate future. Indignation does not here seem to express His
4727 AG:766B feelings. See CHARGE.
CB:1270A 2. STENAZŌ (στενάζω) : see GRIEVE, B, No. 3.
4959 AG:795B 3. SUSTENAZŌ (συστενάζω), to groan together (*sun*, with, and No. 2),
CB:— is used of the creation in Rom. 8 : 22. In ver. 23, No. 2 is used.¶.

B. Noun.

4726 AG:766B STENAGMOS (στεναγμός), akin to A, No. 2, is used in Acts 7 : 34,
CB:1270A in a quotation from Ex. 3 : 7, but not from the Sept., which there has *kraugē*, a cry ; the word is used, however, in Ex. 2 : 24 ; in Rom. 8 : 26, in the plural, of the intercessory groanings of the Holy Spirit.¶

GROSS (to wax)

3975 AG:638B PACHUNŌ (παχύνω), from *pachus*, thick, signifies to thicken, fatten ;
CB:1261B in the Passive Voice, to grow fat ; metaphorically said of the heart, to wax gross or dull, Matt. 13 : 15 ; Acts 28 : 27.¶

GROUND, GROUNDED

A. Nouns.

1093 AG:157C 1. GĒ (γῆ), the earth, land, etc., often denotes the ground, e.g., Matt.
CB:1248A 10 : 29 ; Mark 8 : 6. See EARTH.

2. EDAPHOS (ἔδαφος), a bottom, base, is used of the ground in Acts 1475
22 : 7, suggestive of that which is level and hard.¶ Cp. B, No. 1, below. AG:217D CB:—
3. CHŌRA (χώρα), land, country, is used of property, ground, in 5561
Luke 12 : 16, "the ground (of a certain rich man)." See COUNTRY. AG:889B CB:1240A
4. CHŌRION (χωρίον), a diminutive of No. 3, a piece of land, a place, 5564
estate, is translated "parcel of ground" in John 4 : 5. See FIELD. AG:890B CB:1240A
5. HEDRAIŌMA (ἑδραίωμα), a support, bulwark, stay (from *hedraios*, 1477
stedfast, firm; from *hedra*, a seat), is translated "ground" in 1 Tim. 3 : 15 AG:218A CB:1249C
(said of a local church); the R.V. marg., "stay" is preferable.¶ PETRŌDĒS
Notes: (1) In Mark 4 : 16 the R.V. rightly has "rocky places" 4075
(*petrōdēs*) for A.V., "stony ground." (2) In Acts 27 : 29, for the A.V., AG:655C
"rocks" the R.V. has "rocky ground," lit., 'rough places,' i.e., a rocky CB:1263C AGROS
shore. (3) In Luke 14 : 18, *agros*, a field, is translated "a piece of ground," 68
A.V., R.V., "a field." See FIELD. AG:13D CB:1233C

B. Verbs. 1474

1. EDAPHIZŌ (ἐδαφίζω), akin to A, No. 2: see DASH. AG:217C CB:—
2. THEMELIOŌ (θεμελιόω) signifies to lay the foundation of, to 2311
found (akin to *themelios*, a foundation; from *tithēmi*, to put), and is AG:356A CB:1272A
rendered "grounded" in Eph. 3 : 17, said of the condition of believers with reference to the love of Christ; in Col. 1 : 23, of their continuance in the faith. See FOUND.

C. Adverb. 5476

CHAMAI (χαμαί) (akin to Lat., *humi*, on the ground, and *homo*, man), AG:875B CB:—
signifies "on the ground," John 9 : 6, of the act of Christ in spitting on GROUP
the ground before anointing the eyes of a blind man; in 18 : 6, "to the See COMPANIES
ground," of the fall of the rabble that had come to seize Christ in GROVE
Gethsemane.¶ See GARDEN

GROW

1. AUXANŌ (αὐξάνω), to grow or increase, of the growth of that which 837
lives, naturally or spiritually, is used (*a*) transitively, signifying to make AG:121C CB:1238B
to increase, said of giving the increase, 1 Cor. 3 : 6, 7; 2 Cor. 9 : 10, the effect of the work of God, according to the analogy of His operations in nature; to grow, become greater, e.g. of plants and fruit, Matt. 6 : 28; used in the Passive Voice in 13 : 32 and Mark 4 : 8, "increase;" in the Active in Luke 12 : 27; 13 : 19; of the body, Luke 1 : 80; 2 : 40; of Christ, John 3 : 30, "increase;" of the work of the Gospel of God, Acts 6 : 7, "increased;" 12 : 24; 19 : 20; of people, Acts 7 : 17; of faith, 2 Cor. 10 : 15 (Passive Voice), R.V., "groweth" (A.V., "is increased");
of believers individually, Eph. 4 : 15; Col. 1 : 6, R.V., 10 (Passive Voice), 838
"increasing;" 1 Pet. 2 : 2; 2 Pet. 3 : 18; of the Church, Col. 2 : 19; AG:122A
of churches, Eph. 2 : 21. See INCREASE.¶ CB:1238B
Note: Cp. *auxēsis*, increase, Eph. 4 : 16; Col. 2 : 19.¶ 1096 AG:158A
2. GINOMAI (γίνομαι), to become or come to be, is translated "grow" CB:1248B

in Acts 5 : 24, of the development of apostolic work. See ARISE, No. 5.

Notes : (1) In Matt. 21 : 19, for A.V., " let (no fruit) grow," the R.V., more strictly, has " let there be (no fruit)." (2) In Heb. 11 : 24, *ginomai* is used with *megas*, great, of Moses, lit., ' had become great,' R.V., " had grown up " (A.V., " had come to years ").

2064 AG:310B 3. ERCHOMAI (ἔρχομαι), to come or go, is translated " grew
CB:1246B (worse)," in Mark 5 : 26. See COME, No. 1.

305 AG:50A 4. ANABAINŌ (ἀναβαίνω), to ascend, when used of plants, signifies
CB:1235A to grow up, Mark 4 : 7, 32 ; in 4 : 8, of seed, " growing up," R.V., A.V., " that sprang up," (for the next word, " increasing," see No. 1). See ARISE, No. 6.

3373 (-Nō) AG:518D 5. MĒKUNOMAI (μηκύνομαι), to grow long, lengthen, extend (from
CB:— *mēkos*, length), is used of the growth of plants, in Mark 4 : 27.¶

Note : Three different words are used in Mark 4 of the growth of plants or seed, Nos. 1, 4, 5.

5232 AG:840A 6. HUPERAUXANŌ (ὑπεραυξάνω), to increase beyond measure
CB:1252A (*huper*, over, and No. 1), is used of faith and love, in their living and practical effects, 2 Thess. 1 : 3. Lightfoot compares this verb and the next in the verse (*pleonazō*, to abound) in that the former implies " an internal, organic growth, as of a tree," the latter " a diffusive or expansive character, as of a flood irrigating the land."¶

4885 AG:785B 7. SUNAUXANŌ (συναυξάνω), to grow together, is in Matt. 13 : 30.¶

5453 AG:870B 8. PHUŌ (φύω), to produce, is rendered " grew " (Passive V.) in Luke
CB:1264C 8 : 6. See SPRING.

4855 AG:780D 9. SUMPHUŌ (συμφύω) is used in Luke 8 : 7, R.V., " grow with."¶
CB:—

For GRUDGE (Jas. 5 : 9), GRIEVE, B, No. 3, GRUDGING (1 Pet. 4 : 9) see MURMUR

GRUDGINGLY

3077 AG:482A *Note :* In 2 Cor. 9 : 7, the phrase *ek lupēs*, lit., ' out of sorrow ' (*ek*,
CB:1257B out of, or from, *lupē*, sorrow, grief), is translated " grudgingly " (R.V. marg., " of sorrow ") ; the grudging regret is set in contrast to cheerfulness enjoined in giving, as is the reluctance expressed in " of necessity.'

GUARANTEE See EARNEST

GUARD (Noun and Verb)

A. Nouns.

2892 AG:447B 1. KOUSTŌDIA (κουστωδία), a guard, (Latin, *custodia* ; Eng.,
CB:— custodian), is used of the soldiers who guarded Christ's sepulchre, Matt. 27 : 65, 66 and 28 : 11, and is translated " (ye have) a guard," " the guard (being with them)," and " (some of) the guard," R.V., A.V., " . . . a watch," " (setting a) watch," and " . . . the watch." This was the Temple Guard, stationed under a Roman officer in the Tower of Antonia, and having charge of the high priestly vestments. Hence the significance of Pilate's words " Ye have a guard." See WATCH.¶

2. SPEKOULATŌR (σπεκουλάτωρ), Latin, *speculator*, primarily denotes 4688
a lookout officer, or scout, but, under the Emperors, a member of the AG:761C
bodyguard; these were employed as messengers, watchers and CB:—
executioners; ten such officers were attached to each legion; such a guard was employed by Herod Antipas, Mark 6 : 27, R.V., "a soldier of his guard" (A.V., "executioner").¶

3. PHULAX (φύλαξ), a guard, keeper (akin to *phulassō*, to guard, keep), 5441
is translated "keepers" in Acts 5 : 23; in 12 : 6, 19, R.V., "guards" AG:868B
(A.V., "keepers"). See KEEPER.¶ CB:1264C STRATOPEDARCHĒS

Notes: (1) In Acts 28 : 16, some mss. have the sentence containing 4759
the word *stratopedarchēs*, a captain of the guard. See CAPTAIN. (2) In AG:771A CB:1270B
Phil. 1 : 13, the noun *praitōrion*, the "Prætorian Guard," is so rendered PRAITŌRION
in the R.V. (A.V., "palace"). 4232 AG:697C

B. Verbs.

CB:—

1. PHULASSŌ (φυλάσσω), to guard, watch, keep (akin to A, No. 3), 5442
is rendered by the verb to guard in the R.V. (A.V., to keep) of Luke 11 : 21; AG:868B
John 17 : 12; Acts 12 : 4; 28 : 16; 2 Thess. 3 : 3; 1 Tim. 6 : 20; 2 Tim. CB:1264C
1 : 12, 14; 1 John 5 : 21; Jude 24. In Luke 8 : 29, "was kept under guard," R.V. (A.V., "kept"). See BEWARE, KEEP, OBSERVE, PRESERVE, SAVE, WARE OF, WATCH.

2. DIAPHULASSŌ (διαφυλάσσω), a strengthened form of No. 1 1314
(*dia*, through, used intensively), to guard carefully, defend, is found in AG:191A
Luke 4 : 10 (from the Sept. of Psa. 91 : 11), R.V., "to guard" (A.V., CB:—
"to keep").¶

3. PHROUREŌ (φρουρέω), a military term, to keep by guarding, to 5432
keep under guard, as with a garrison (*phrouros*, a guard, or garrison), AG:867B
is used, (*a*) of blocking up every way of escape, as in a siege; (*b*) of CB:1264C
providing protection against the enemy, as a garrison does; see 2 Cor. 11 . 32, "guarded," A.V., "kept," i.e., kept the city, "with a garrison." It is used of the security of the Christian until the end, 1 Pet. 1 : 5, R.V., "are guarded," and of the sense of that security that is his when he puts all his matters into the hand of God, Phil. 4 : 7, R.V., "shall guard." In these passages the idea is not merely that of protection, but of inward garrisoning as by the Holy Spirit; in Gal. 3 : 23 ("were kept in ward"), it means rather a benevolent custody and watchful guardianship in view of worldwide idolatry (cp. Is. 5 : 2). See KEEP.¶

GUARDIAN

EPITROPOS (ἐπίτροπος), lit., one to whose care something is com- 2012
mitted (*epi*, upon, *trepō*, to turn or direct), is rendered "guardians" AG:303D
in Gal. 4 : 2, R.V., A.V., "tutors" (in Matt. 20 : 8 and Luke 8 : 3, CB:1246B
"steward").¶

"The corresponding verb, *epitrepō*, is translated 'permit,' 'give leave,' 'suffer;' see 1 Cor. 14 : 34; 16 : 7; 1 Tim. 2 : 12, e.g., . . . An allied noun, *epitropē*, is translated 'commission' in Acts 26 : 12 (¶) and refers to delegated authority over persons. This usage of cognate words suggests that the *epitropos* was a superior servant responsible for the persons composing the household, whether children or slaves."*

GUEST

345
AG:55D
CB:1235A
ANAKEIMAI (ἀνάκειμαι), to recline at table, frequently rendered to sit at meat, is used in its present participial form (lit., 'reclining ones') as a noun denoting "guests," in Matt. 22 : 10, 11. See LEAN, LIE, SIT.

2647
AG:414B
CB:1254A
Note : For *kataluō*, to unloose, rendered to be a guest in Luke 19 : 7, A.V., (R.V., to lodge), see LODGE.

GUEST-CHAMBER

2646
AG:414B
CB:1254A
KATALUMA (κατάλυμα), akin to *kataluō* (see Note above), signifies (*a*) an inn, lodging-place, Luke 2 : 7 ; (*b*) a guest-room, Mark 14 : 14 ; Luke 22 : 11. The word lit. signifies a loosening down (*kata*, down, *luō*, to loose), used of the place where travellers and their beasts untied their packages, girdles and sandals. "In the East, no figure is more invested with chivalry than the guest. In his own right he cannot cross the threshold, but when once he is invited in, all do him honour and unite in rendering service ; cp. Gen. 18 : 19 ; Judg. 19 : 9, 15." These two passages in the N.T. "concern a room in a private house, which the owner readily placed at the disposal of Jesus and His disciples for the celebration of the Passover . . . At the festivals of Passover, Pentecost and Tabernacles the people were commanded to repair to Jerusalem ; and it was a boast of the Rabbis that, notwithstanding the enormous crowds, no man could truthfully say to his fellow, 'I have not found a fire where to roast my paschal lamb in Jerusalem,' or 'I have not found a bed in Jerusalem to lie in,' or 'My lodging is too strait in Jerusalem' " (Hastings, Bib. Dic., GUEST-CHAMBER and INN). See INN.¶

GUIDE (Noun and Verb)

A. Noun.

3595
AG:553C
CB:1251A
HODĒGOS (ὁδηγός), a leader on the way (*hodos*, a way, *hēgeomai*, to lead), a guide, is used (*a*) literally, in Acts 1 : 16 ; (*b*) figuratively, Matt. 15 : 14, R.V., "guides" (A.V., "leaders") ; Matt. 23 : 16, 24, "guides ;" Rom. 2 : 19, "a guide." Cp. B, No. 1.¶

B. Verbs.

3594
AG:553B
CB:1251A
1. HODĒGEŌ (ὁδηγέω), to lead the way (akin to A), is used (*a*) literally, R.V., "guide" (A.V., "lead"), of guiding the blind, in Matt. 15 : 14 ; Luke 6 : 39 ; of guiding unto fountains of waters of life, Rev. 7 : 17 ; (*b*) figuratively, in John 16 : 13, of guidance into the truth by the Holy Spirit ; in Acts 8 : 31, of the interpretation of Scripture. See LEAD.¶

* From Notes on Galatians, by Hogg and Vine, p. 180.

2. KATEUTHUNŌ (κατευθύνω), to make straight, is said of guiding 2720
the feet into the way of peace, Luke 1 : 79. See DIRECT. AG:422B CB:—

Notes: (1) In 1 Tim. 5 : 14, the R.V. rightly translates the verb
oikodespoteō by "rule the household" (A.V., "guide the house"), the OIKODESPOTEŌ
meaning being that of the management and direction of household affairs. 3616
See RULE.¶ (2) *Hēgeomai*, to lead, in Heb. 13 : 7, 24, is rendered "that AG:558A CB:1260B
had the rule over" and "that have etc.," more lit., 'them that were HĒGEOMAI 2233
(are) your leaders,' or guides. AG:343C CB:1249C

GUILE

DOLOS (δόλος), a bait, snare, deceit, is rendered "guile" in John 1388
1 : 47, negatively of Nathanael; Acts 13 : 10, R.V., A.V., "subtlety" AG:203B CB:—
(of Bar-Jesus); 2 Cor. 12 : 16, in a charge made against Paul by his detractors, of catching the Corinthian converts by guile (the Apostle is apparently quoting the language of his critics); 1 Thess. 2 : 3, negatively, of the teaching of the Apostle and his fellow-missionaries; 1 Pet. 2 : 1, of that from which Christians are to be free; 2 : 22, of the guileless speech of Christ (cp. GUILELESS, No. 2); 3 : 10, of the necessity that the speech of Christians should be guileless. See also Matt. 26 : 4; Mark 7 : 22; 14 : 1. See CRAFT, DECEIT, SUBTILTY.¶

Note: In Rev. 14 : 5, some mss. have *dolos*; the most authentic 5579
have *pseudos*, a "lie." AG:892B CB:1267C

GUILELESS (WITHOUT GUILE)

1. ADOLOS (ἄδολος), without guile (*a*, negative, and *dolos*, see GUILE), 97
pure, unadulterated, is used metaphorically of the teaching of the Word AG:18D CB:1233A
of God, 1 Pet. 2 : 2, R.V. It is used in the papyri writings of seed, corn, wheat, oil, wine, etc.¶

2. AKAKOS (ἄκακος), lit., without evil (*a*, negative, *kakos*, evil), 172
signifies simple, guileless, Rom. 16 : 18, "simple," of believers (perhaps= AG:29B CB:1234A
unsuspecting, or, rather, innocent, free from admixture of evil); in Heb. 7 : 26, R.V., "guileless" (A.V., "harmless"), the character of Christ (more lit., 'free from evil').¶ Cp. Sept., Job 2 : 3; 8 : 20; Prov. 1 : 4; 14 : 15. See HARMLESS.

GUILTLESS

ANAITIOS (ἀναίτιος), innocent, guiltless (*a*, negative, *n*, euphonic, 338
aitia, a charge of crime), is translated "blameless" in Matt. 12 : 5, A.V., AG:55B CB:1235A
"guiltless" in ver. 7; R.V., "guiltless" in each place. See BLAMELESS.¶

GUILTY (Adjective) 1777 AG:267D

ENOCHOS (ἔνοχος), lit., held in, bound by, liable to a charge or action CB:1245B
at law: see DANGER. 5267 AG:844C

Notes: (1) In Rom. 3 : 19, A.V., *hupodikos*, brought to trial, lit., CB:—

'under judgment' (*hupo*, under, *dikē*, justice), is incorrectly rendered "guilty;" R.V., "under the judgement of." See JUDGMENT. (2) In
3784 AG:598D CB:1261A Matt. 23 : 18, *opheilō*, to owe, to be indebted, to fail in duty, be a delinquent, is misrendered "guilty" in the A.V.; R.V., "a debtor."

GULF

5490 AG:879B CB:— CHASMA (χάσμα), akin to *chaskō*, to yawn (Eng., chasm), is found in Luke 16 : 26.¶ In the Sept., 2 Sam. 18 : 17, two words are used with reference to Absalom's body, *bothunos* which signifies a great pit, and *chasma*, a yawning abyss, or precipice, with a deep pit at the bottom, into which the body was cast.¶

GUSH OUT

1632 AG:247B (EKCHEō) CB:1243B EKCHUNŌ, or EKCHUNNŌ (ἐκχύνω), a Hellenistic form of *ekcheō*, to pour forth, is translated "gushed out" in Acts 1 : 18, of the bowels of Judas Iscariot. See POUR, RUN, SHED, SPILL.

H

For HA (Mark 15 : 29, R.V.) see AH

HABITATION

1. OIKĒTĒRION (*οἰκητήριον*), a habitation (from *oikētēr*, an inhabi- 3613
tant, and *oikos*, a dwelling), is used in Jude 6, of the heavenly region AG:557B
appointed by God as the dwelling place of angels ; in 2 Cor. 5 : 2, R.V., CB:1260B
"habitation," A.V., "house," figuratively of the spiritual bodies of believers when raised or changed at the return of the Lord. See HOUSE.¶

2. KATOIKĒTĒRION (*κατοικητήριον*), (*kata*, down, used intensively, 2732
and No. 1), implying more permanency than No. 1, is used in Eph. 2 : 22 AG:424C
of the Church as the dwelling-place of the Holy Spirit ; in Rev. 18 : 2 of CB:1254C
Babylon, figuratively, as the dwelling-place of demons.¶

3. KATOIKIA (*κατοικία*), a settlement, colony, dwelling (*kata*, and 2733
oikos, see above), is used in Acts 17 : 26, of the localities Divinely appointed AG:424C CB:—
as the dwelling-places of the nations.¶

4. EPAULIS (*ἔπαυλις*), a farm, a dwelling (*epi*, upon, *aulis*, a place 1886
in which to pass the night, a country-house, cottage or cabin, a fold), is AG:283D
used in Acts 1 : 20 of the habitation of Judas.¶ CB:—

5. SKĒNĒ (*σκηνή*), akin to *skēnoō*, to dwell in a tent or tabernacle, is 4633
rendered "habitations" in Luke 16 : 9, A.V. (R.V., "tabernacles"), of the AG:754C CB:1269A
eternal dwelling-places of the redeemed. See TABERNACLE.

6. SKĒNŌMA (*σκήνωμα*), a booth, or tent pitched (akin to No. 5), 4638
is used of the Temple as God's dwelling, as that which David desired to AG:755C CB:1269A
build, Acts 7 : 46 (R.V., "habitation," A.V., "tabernacle") ; metaphorically of the body as a temporary tabernacle, 2 Pet. 1 : 13, 14.¶ See TABERNACLE.

HADES

HADĒS (*ᾅδης*), the region of departed spirits of the lost (but including 86
the blessed dead in periods preceding the Ascension of Christ). It has AG:16D CB:1248C
been thought by some that the word etymologically meant the unseen (from *a*, negative, and *eidō*, to see), but this derivation is questionable ; a more probable derivation is from *hadō*, signifying all-receiving. It corresponds to "Sheol" in the O.T. In the A.V. of the O.T. and N.T., it has been unhappily rendered "Hell," e.g., Psa. 16 : 10 ; or "the grave," e.g., Gen. 37 : 35 ; or "the pit," Num. 16 : 30, 33 ; in the N.T. the Revisers have always used the rendering "Hades ;" in the O.T.

they have not been uniform in the translation, e.g., in Isa. 14 : 15, " hell " (marg., " Sheol ") ; usually they have " Sheol " in the text and " the grave " in the margin. It never denotes the grave, nor is it the permanent region of the lost ; in point of time it is, for such, intermediate between decease and the doom of Gehenna. For the condition, see Luke 16 : 23-31.

The word is used four times in the Gospels, and always by the Lord, Matt. 11 : 23 ; 16 : 18 ; Luke 10 : 15 ; 16 : 23 ; it is used with reference to the soul of Christ, Acts 2 : 27, 31 ; Christ declares that He has the keys of it, Rev. 1 : 18 ; in Rev. 6 : 8 it is personified, with the signification of the temporary destiny of the doomed ; it is to give up those who are therein, 20 : 13, and is to be cast into the lake of fire, ver. 14.¶

2288 AG:350D CB:1271C *Note :* In 1 Cor. 15 : 55 the most authentic mss. have *thanatos*, death, in the 2nd part of the verse, instead of *Hades*, which the A.V. wrongly renders " grave " (" hell," in the marg.).

HAIL (Noun)

5464 AG:874B CB:1239B CHALAZA (χάλαζα), akin to *chalaō*, to let loose, let fall, is always used as an instrument of Divine judgment, and is found in the N.T. in Rev. 8 : 7 ; 11 : 19 ; 16 : 21.¶

HAIL (Verb)

5463 AG:873B CB:1239B CHAIRŌ (χαίρω), to rejoice, is used in the imperative mood, (*a*) as a salutation, only in the Gospels ; in this respect it is rendered simply " hail," in mockery of Christ, Matt. 26 : 49 ; 27 : 29 ; Mark 15 : 18 ; John 19 : 3 ; (*b*) as a greeting, by the angel Gabriel to Mary, Luke 1 : 28, and, in the plural, by the Lord to the disciples after His resurrection, Matt. 28 : 9.

HAIR

A. Nouns.

2359 AG:363D CB:1272B 1. THRIX (θρίξ) denotes the hair, whether of beast, as of the camel's hair which formed the raiment of John the Baptist, Matt. 3 : 4 ; Mark 1 : 6 ; or of man. Regarding the latter (*a*) it is used to signify the minutest detail, as that which illustrates the exceeding care and protection bestowed by God upon His children, Matt. 10 : 30 ; Luke 12 : 7 ; 21 : 18 ; Acts 27 : 34 ; (*b*) as the Jews swore by the hair, the Lord used the natural inability to make one hair white or black, as one of the reasons for abstinence from oaths, Matt. 5 : 36 ; (*c*) while long hair is a glory to a woman (see B), and to wear it loose or dishevelled is a dishonour, yet the woman who wiped Christ's feet with her hair (in place of the towel which Simon the Pharisee omitted to provide), despised the shame in her penitent devotion to the Lord (slaves were accustomed to wipe their masters' feet), Luke 7 : 38, 44 (R.V., " hair ") ; see also John 11 : 2 ; 12 : 3 ; (*d*) the dazzling whiteness of the head and hair of the Son of Man in the vision of Rev. 1 (ver. 14) is suggestive of the holiness and wisdom of "the Ancient of Days;" (*e*) the long hair of the spirit-beings described as locusts in Rev. 9 : 8 is perhaps indicative of their subjection to their Satanic master (cp. 1 Cor. 11 : 10, R.V.); (*f*) Christian women are exhorted to refrain from adorning their hair for outward show, 1 Pet. 3 : 3.¶

Note: Goat's hair was used in tent-making, as, e.g., in the case of Paul's occupation, Acts 18 : 3; the haircloth of Cilicia, his native province was noted, being known in commerce as *cilicium*.

2. KOMĒ (κόμη) is used only of human hair, but not in the N.T. of 2864
the ornamental. The word is found in 1 Cor. 11 : 15, where the context AG:442D
shows that the "covering" provided in the long hair of the woman is as CB:—
a veil, a sign of subjection to authority, as indicated in the headships spoken of in vers. 1–10.¶

B. Verb.

KOMAŌ (κομάω) signifies to let the hair grow long, to wear long hair, 2863
a glory to a woman, a dishonour to a man (as taught by nature), 1 Cor. AG:442D
11 : 14, 15.¶ CB:—

C. Adjective.

TRICHINOS (τρίχινος), akin to A, No. 1, signifies hairy, made of hair, 5155
Rev. 6 : 12, lit., 'hairy sackcloth.' Cp. SACKCLOTH.¶ AG:827A
CB:—

HALE (Verb)

1. SURŌ (σύρω) to drag, haul, is rendered "haling" in Acts 8 : 3, 4951
of taking to trial or punishment. See DRAG. AG:794C
CB:—

2. KATASURŌ (κατασύρω), an intensive form of No. 1, lit., to pull 2694
down (*kata*), hence, to drag away, is used in Luke 12 : 58, of haling a person AG:419B
before a judge.¶ CB:—

HALF

HĒMISUS (ἥμισυς), an adjective, is used (*a*) as such in the neuter 2255 (-SU)
plural, in Luke 19 : 8, lit., 'the halves (of my goods);' (*b*) as a noun, AG:348A
in the neuter sing., "the half," Mark 6 : 23; "half (a time)," Rev. 12 : 14; CB:—
"a half," 11 : 9, 11, R.V.¶

For HALF-SHEKEL see SHEKEL

HALL

1. AULĒ (αὐλή), a court, most frequently the place where a governor 833
dispensed justice, is rendered "hall" in Mark 15 : 16 and Luke 22 : 55, AG:121B
A.V. (R.V., "court"). See COURT, FOLD, PALACE. CB:1238B

2. PRAITŌRION (πραιτώριον) is translated "common hall" in 4232
Matt. 27 : 27, A.V. (R.V., "palace"); "Prætorium" in Mark 15 : 16; AG:697C
"hall of judgment" or "judgment hall" in John 18 : 28, 33; 19 : 9; CB:—
Acts 23 : 35 (R.V., "palace," in each place); "prætorian guard," Phil. 1 : 13 (A.V., "palace"). See PALACE.¶

HALLELUJAH

239 HALLĒLOUIA (Ἀλληλουιά) signifies "Praise ye Jah." It occurs as a
AG:39C CB:1249A short doxology in the Psalms, usually at the beginning, e.g., 111, 112, or the end, e.g., 104, 105, or both, e.g., 106, 135 (where it is also used in ver. 3), 146-150. In the N.T. it is found in Rev. 19 : 1, 3, 4, 6, as the key-note in the song of the great multitude in Heaven. Alleluia, without the initial H, is a misspelling.¶

HALLOW

37 HAGIAZŌ (ἁγιάζω), to make holy (from *hagios*, holy), signifies (*a*)
AG:8C CB:1249A to set apart for God, to sanctify, to make a person or thing the opposite of *koinos*, common ; it is translated "Hallowed," with reference to the Name of God the Father in the Lord's Prayer, Matt. 6 : 9 ; Luke 11 : 2. See SANCTIFY.

HALT

5560 CHŌLOS (χωλός), lame, is translated "halt" in Matt. 18 : 8 ; Mark
AG:889A CB:1240A 9 : 45 ; John 5 : 3 ; in Acts 14 : 8, "cripple ;" in Luke 14 : 21, A.V.,
"halt," R.V., "lame ;" elsewhere, "lame," Matt. 11 : 5 ; 15 : 30, 31 ;
AUTOS 21 : 14 ; Luke 7 : 22 ; 14 : 13 ; Acts 3 : 2 ; 8 : 7 ; Heb. 12 : 13 ; some
846 AG:122C mss. have it in Acts 3 : 11 (A.V., "the lame man"), R.V., "he,"
CB:1238B translating *autou*, as in the best texts.¶

2948 *Note :* For *kullos*, Matt. 18 : 8, R.V., "halt," see MAIMED, No. 2.
AG:457B CB:1256B

HAND

5495 CHEIR (χείρ), the hand (cp. Eng., chiropody), is used, besides its
AG:879D CB:1239C ordinary significance, (*a*) in the idiomatic phrases, by the hand of, at the hand of, etc., to signify by the agency of, Acts 5 : 12 ; 7 : 35 ; 17 : 25 ; 14 : 3 ; Gal. 3 : 19 (cp. Lev. 26 : 46) ; Rev. 19 : 2 ; (*b*) metaphorically, for the power of God, e.g., Luke 1 : 66 ; 23 : 46 ; John 10 : 28, 29 ; Acts 11 : 21 ; 13 : 11 ; Heb. 1 : 10 ; 2 : 7 ; 10 : 31 ; (*c*) by metonymy, for power, e.g., Matt. 17 : 22 ; Luke 24 : 7 ; John 10 : 39 ; Acts 12 : 11.

AT HAND

A. Adverb.

1451 ENGUS (ἐγγύς), near, nigh, frequently rendered "at hand," is used
AG:214A CB:1245A (*a*) of place, e.g., of the Lord's sepulchre, John 19 : 42, "nigh at hand ;" (*b*) of time, e.g., Matt. 26 : 18 ; Luke 21 : 30, 31, R.V., "nigh," A.V., "nigh at hand ;" in Phil. 4 : 5, "the Lord is at hand," it is possible to regard the meaning as that either of (*a*) or (*b*) ; the following reasons may point to (*b*) : (1) the subject of the preceding context has been the return of Christ, 3 : 20, 21 ; (2) the phrase is a translation of the Aramaic Maran-atha, 1 Cor. 16 : 22, a Christian watchword, and the use of the title "the Lord" is appropriate ; (3) the similar use of the adverb in Rev. 1 : 3 and 22 : 10 ; (4) the similar use of the corresponding verb (see B) in Rom.

13 : 12 ; Heb. 10 : 25, " drawing nigh," R.V. ; Jas. 5 : 8 ; cp. 1 Pet. 4 : 7. See NEAR, NIGH, READY.

B. Verb. 1448

ENGIZŌ (ἐγγίζω) : See APPROACH, A. AG:213C CB:1245A

Notes : (1) In 2 Thess. 2 : 2, A.V., the verb *enistēmi*, to be present 1764
(*en*, in, *histēmi*, to cause to stand), is wrongly translated " is at hand ; " AG:266D CB:—
the R.V. correctly renders it, " is (now) present ; " the Apostle is counteracting the error of the supposition that " the Day of the Lord " (R.V.), a period of Divine and retributive judgments upon the world, had already begun.

(2) In 2 Tim. 4 : 6, A.V., the verb *ephistēmi*, to stand by, to come to 2186
or upon (*epi*, upon, *histēmi*, to make to stand), is rendered " is at hand," AG:330D CB:—
of the Apostle's departure from this life ; the R.V. " is come " represents the vivid force of the statement, expressing suddenness or imminence.

HAND (lead by the)

A. Adjective.

CHEIRAGŌGOS (χειραγωγός), lit., a hand-leader (*cheir*, the hand, 5497
agō, to lead), is used as a noun (plural) in Acts 13 : 11, " some to lead him AG:880D CB:—
by the hand."¶

B. Verb.

CHEIRAGŌGEŌ (χειραγωγέω), to lead by the hand, is used in 5496
Acts 9 : 8 ; 22 : 11.¶ AG:880D CB:—

HANDED DOWN

PATROPARADOTOS (πατροπαράδοτος), an adjective, denoting handed 3970
down from one's fathers, is used in 1 Pet. 1 : 18, R.V., for A.V., " *received* AG:637A CB:—
by tradition from your fathers " (from *patēr*, a father, and *paradidōmi*, to hand down).¶

HAND (with one's own)

AUTOCHEIR (αὐτόχειρ), a noun (*autos*, self, *cheir*, the hand), is used 849
in the plural in Acts 27 : 19, " with their own hands."¶ AG:124A CB:—

HAND (take in)

EPICHEIREŌ (ἐπιχειρέω), to put the hand to (*epi*, to, *cheir*, the hand), 2021
is rendered " have taken in hand " in Luke 1 : 1. See TAKE. AG:304D CB:—

KRATEō 2902 AG:448C CB:1256A
For LAY HANDS ON (*krateō* in Matt. 18 : 28 ; 21 : 46 ; *piazō* in John 8 : 20), see HOLD and APPREHEND. PIAZō 4084 AG:657A CB:—

HANDS (made by, not made with)

1. CHEIROPOIĒTOS (χειροποίητος), made by hand, of human 5499
handiwork (*cheir*, and *poieō*, to make), is said of the temple in Jerusalem, AG:880D
Mark 14 : 58 ; temples in general, Acts 7 : 48 (R.V., " houses ") ; 17 : 24 ; CB:1239C

negatively, of the heavenly and spiritual tabernacle, Heb. 9 : 11 ; of the holy place in the earthly tabernacle, ver. 24 ; of circumcision, Eph. 2 : 11.¶ In the Sept., of idols, Lev. 26 : 1, 30 ; Isa. 2 : 18 ; 10 : 11 ; 16 : 12 ; 19 : 1 ; 21 : 9 ; 31 : 7 ; 46 : 6.¶

886 AG:128B 2. ACHEIROPOIĒTOS (ἀχειροποίητος), not made by hands (*a*,
CB:1233A negative, and No. 1), is said of an earthly temple, Mark 14 : 58 ; of the
resurrection body of believers, metaphorically as a house, 2 Cor. 5 : 1 ;
metaphorically, of spiritual circumcision, Col. 2 : 11.¶ This word is not
found in the Sept.

HANDKERCHIEF

4676 SOUDARION (σουδάριον), a Latin word, *sudarium* (from *sudor*, sweat),
AG:759C CB:— denotes (*a*) a cloth for wiping the face, etc., Luke 19 : 20 ; Acts 19 : 12 ;
(*b*) a head-covering for the dead, John 11 : 44 ; 20 : 7. See NAPKIN.¶

HANDLE

5584 1. PSĒLAPHAŌ (ψηλαφάω), to feel, touch, handle, is rendered by the
AG:892C CB:— latter verb in Luke 24 : 39, in the Lord's invitation to the disciples to
accept the evidence of His resurrection in His being bodily in their midst ;
in 1 John 1 : 1, in the Apostle's testimony (against the Gnostic error that
Christ had been merely a phantom) that he and his fellow-apostles had
handled Him. See FEEL.

2345 AG:361D 2. THINGANŌ (θιγγάνω) signifies (*a*) to touch, to handle (though to
CB:— handle is rather stronger than the actual significance compared with No 1).
HAPTŌ In Col. 2 : 21 the R.V. renders it " touch," and the first verb (*haptō*, to
681 lay hold of) " handle," i.e., ' handle not, nor taste, nor touch ; ' " touch "
AG:102D CB:1249B is the appropriate rendering ; in Heb. 12 : 20 it is said of a beast's touching
Mount Sinai ; (*b*) to touch by way of injuring, Heb. 11 : 28. See TOUCH.¶
In the Sept., Ex. 19 : 12.¶

Note : The shortened form found in the passages mentioned is an aorist (or point) tense of the verb.

1389 3. DOLOŌ (δολόω), to corrupt, is used in 2 Cor. 4 : 2, " handling
AG:203B CB:1242A (the Word of God) deceitfully," in the sense of using guile (*dolos*) ; the
meaning approximates to that of adulterating (cp. *kapēleuō*, in 2 : 17).¶

ATIMAZŌ 4. ATIMAZŌ (ἀτιμάζω), to dishonour, insult, is rendered " handled
818 AG:120A shamefully " in Mark 12 : 4. Some mss. have the alternative verb
CB:1238A *atimaō*. See DESPISE, DISHONOUR.

ATIMAŌ 821 (-MOŌ) 5. ORTHOTOMEŌ (ὀρθοτομέω), to cut straight, as in road-making
AG:120A (*orthos*, straight, *temnō*, to cut), is used metaphorically in 2 Tim. 2 : 15,
CB:— of ' handling aright (the word of truth),' R.V. (A.V., " rightly dividing ").
ORTHOTOMEŌ 3718 The stress is on *orthos ;* the Word of God is to be handled strictly along
AG:580B the lines of its teaching. If the metaphor is taken from ploughing, cutting
CB:1261B a straight furrow, the word would express a careful cultivation, the Word
of God viewed as ground designed to give the best results from its ministry
and in the life. See DIVIDE.¶

In the Sept., in Prov. 3 : 6 and 11 : 5, the knowledge of God's wisdom and the just dealing of the upright are enjoined as producing a straight walk in the life.¶

For HANDMAID and HANDMAIDEN see under BONDMAN

For HANDWRITING see BOND

HANG

1. KREMANNUMI (*κρεμάννυμι*) is used (*a*) transitively in Acts 5 : 30 ; 2910
10 : 39 ; in the Passive Voice, in Matt. 18 : 6, of a millstone about a neck, AG:450A CB:1256A
and in Luke 23 : 39, of the malefactors ; (*b*) intransitively, in the Middle Voice, in Matt. 22 : 40, of the dependence of " the Law and the prophets " (i.e., that which they enjoin) upon the one great principle of love to God and one's neighbour (as a door hangs on a hinge, or as articles hang on a nail) ; in Acts 28 : 4, of the serpent hanging from Paul's hand ; in Gal. 3 : 13 the word is used in a quotation from the Sept. of Deut. 21 : 23.¶

2. EKKREMANNUMI (*ἐκκρεμάννυμι*), to hang from, or upon (*ek*, 1582
and No. 1), is used in the Middle Voice (*ekkremamai*) metaphorically in (-MAMAI) AG:242A
Luke 19 : 48, R.V., " (the people all) hung upon (Him, listening)," A.V., CB:—
" were very attentive."¶ In the Sept., Gen. 44 : 30.¶

3. PARIĒMI (*παρίημι*) signifies (*a*) to disregard, leave alone, leave 3935
undone, Luke 11 : 42 (some mss. have *aphiēmi*, here) ; (*b*) to relax, loosen, AG:627C CB:1262B
and, in the Passive Voice, to be relaxed, exhausted, said of hands that hang down in weakness, Heb. 12 : 12.¶

4. PERIKEIMAI (*περίκειμαι*) signifies to lie round (*peri*, around, 4029
keimai, to lie) ; then, to be hanged round, said of " a great millstone " AG:647D CB:—
(lit., ' a millstone turned by an ass '), Mark 9 : 42, R.V., and marg., to be hung round the neck of him who causes one of Christ's " little ones " to stumble ; in Luke 17 : 2, " a millstone." See BOUND (to be).

5. APANCHŌ (*ἀπάγχω*) signifies to strangle ; in the Middle Voice, to 519 (-OMAI)
hang oneself, Matt. 27 : 5.¶ In the Sept. it is said of Ahithophel (2 Sam. AG:79C CB:—
17 : 23).¶

HAPLY (if, lest) ARA 686

1. EI ARA (*εἰ ἄρα*) denotes if therefore, if accordingly (i.e., if in AG:103D
these circumstances), e.g., Mark 11 : 13, of Christ and the fig tree (not ' if CB:1237B ARAGE
perchance,' but marking a correspondence in point of fact). After 688

2. EI ARAGE (*εἰ ἄραγε*) denotes if in consequence, e.g., Acts 17 : 27, AG:104A (ARA)
" if haply " they might feel after God, in consequence of seeking Him. CB:— MēPOTE

3. MĒ POTE (*μή ποτε*), lit., lest ever, " lest haply," e.g., Luke 14 : 29, 3379
of laying a foundation, with the possibility of being unable to finish the AG:519B CB:1258B
building ; Acts 5 : 39, of the possibility of being found fighting against POTE
God ; Heb. 3 : 12, R.V., " lest haply," of the possibility of having an evil 4218 AG:695A
heart of unbelief. The R.V. usually has " lest haply " (A.V. " lest at CB:1266B

MēPōS 3381 any time "), e.g., Matt. 4 : 6 ; 5 : 25 ; 13 : 15 ; Mark 4 : 12 ; Luke 4 : 11 ;
AG:519C 21 : 34 ; Heb. 2 : 1 ; in Matt. 25 : 9, the R.V. has " peradventure ; " in
PōS 2 Tim. 2 : 25, A.V. and R.V., have " if peradventure ; " in John 7 : 26
4458 AG:732B the R.V. has " Can it be that," for the word " Do " in the A.V.
MēPOU 4. MĒ PŌS (μή πως) denotes lest in any way, by any means, e.g.,
— AG:519C 2 Cor. 9 : 4, A.V., " lest haply," R.V., " lest by any means."
POU 5. MĒ POU (μή που) denotes lest somehow ; the R.V. has " lest
4225 AG:696B haply " in Acts 27 : 29 (some mss. have No. 4, here).
CB:1266B

HAPPEN

4819 1. SUMBAINŌ (συμβαίνω), lit., to go or come together (*sun*, with,
AG:777B CB:— *bainō*, to go), signifies to happen together, of things or events, Mark 10 : 32 ;
Luke 24 : 14 ; Acts 3 : 10 ; 1 Cor. 10 : 11 ; 1 Pet. 4 : 12 ; 2 Pet. 2 : 22 ;
" befell " in Acts 20 : 19 ; in Acts 21 : 35, " so it was." See BEFALL.¶
KATA *Notes :* (1) In Phil. 1 : 12, the phrase *ta kat'* (i.e., *kata*) *eme*, lit., ' the
2596 AG:405C things relating to me,' is rendered " the things *which happened* unto me."
CB:1253C (2) In Luke 24 : 35, the phrase " the things *that happened* in the way,"
R.V. (A.V., " what things were done in the way "), is, lit., ' the things in
the way.'

HAPPY, HAPPIER

A. Adjective.

3107 MAKARIOS (μακάριος), blessed, happy, is rendered " happy " in the
AG:486C CB:1257C R.V., in two places only, as in the A.V., Acts 26 : 2 and Rom. 14 : 22
(where " blessed " would have done) ; also the comparative " happier "
in 1 Cor. 7 : 40. Elsewhere the R.V. uses " blessed " for A.V. " happy,"
e.g., John 13 : 17 ; 1 Pet. 3 : 14 ; 4 : 14. See BLESSED.

B. Verb.

3106 AG:486C MAKARIZŌ (μακαρίζω), to call blessed, Luke 1 : 48, is rendered " we
CB:1257C count . . . happy " in Jas. 5 : 11. See BLESSED.¶

HARASSED See AFFLICTED, DISTRESSED

HARD, HARDEN, HARDENING, HARDNESS

A. Adjectives.

4642 AG:756A 1. SKLĒROS (σκληρός), from *skellō*, to dry, signifies trying, exacting :
CB:1269A see AUSTERE.
1422 2. DUSKOLOS (δύσκολος) primarily means hard to satisfy with food
AG:209C CB:— (*dus*, a prefix like Eng., *un*— or *mis*—, indicating difficulty, opposition,
injuriousness, etc., the opposite of, *eu*, well, and *kolon*, food) ; hence,
difficult, Mark 10 : 24, of the difficulty, for those who trust in riches, to
enter into the Kingdom of God.¶

B. Nouns.

4643 AG:756B 1. SKLĒROTĒS (σκληρότης), akin to A, No. 1, is rendered " hardness "
CB:1269A in Rom 2 : 5.¶
4457 AG:732A 2. PŌRŌSIS (πώρωσις) denotes a hardening, a covering with a *pōros*,
CB:1266A a kind of stone, indicating a process (from *pōroō*, C, No. 1), and is used

metaphorically of dulled spiritual perception, Mark 3 : 5, R.V., " at the hardening of their hearts ; " Rom. 11 : 25, R.V., " a hardening " (A.V., " blindness "), said of the state of Israel ; Eph. 4 : 18, R.V., " hardening," of the heart of Gentiles. See BLINDNESS.¶

Note : See also under HARDSHIP and HEART (hardness of).

C. Verbs.

1. PŌROŌ (πωρόω), to make hard, callous, to petrify (akin to B, 4456
No. 2), is used metaphorically, of the heart, Mark 6 : 52 ; 8 : 17 ; John AG:732A
12 : 40 ; of the mind (or thoughts), 2 Cor. 3 : 14, of those in Israel who CB:1266A
refused the revealed will and ways of God in the Gospel, as also in Rom. 11 : 7, R.V., " hardened " (A.V., " blinded "), in both places. See BLINDNESS.¶

2. SKLĒRUNŌ (σκληρύνω), to make dry or hard (akin to A, No. 1 4645
and B, No. 1), is used in Acts 19 : 9 ; in Rom. 9 : 18, illustrated by the AG:756B
case of Pharaoh, who first persistently hardened his heart (see the R.V. CB:1269A
marg. of Ex. 7 : 13, 22 ; 8 : 19 ; text of ver. 32 and 9 : 7), all producing the retributive hardening by God, after His much long-suffering, 9 : 12, etc. ; in Heb. 3 : 8, 13, 15 ; 4 : 7, warnings against the hardening of the heart.¶

HARDLY

1. DUSKOLŌS (δυσκόλως), the adverbial form of HARD, A, No. 2, 1423
is used in Matt. 19 : 23 ; Mark 10 : 23 ; Luke 18 : 24 of the danger of AG:209D
riches.¶ CB:—

2. MOGIS (μόγις), with labour, pain, trouble (akin to *mogos*, toil), is 3425
found in some mss. in Luke 9 : 39, instead of No. 3.¶ AG:525D CB:—

3. MOLIS (μόλις), with difficulty, scarcely, hardly (akin to *molos*, 3433
toil), is used as an alternative for No. 2, and occurs in the most authentic AG:526D
mss. in Luke 9 : 39 ; it is rendered " hardly " in Acts 27 : 8, A.V. See CB:—
DIFFICULTY.

HARDSHIP (to suffer)

1. KAKOPATHEŌ (κακοπαθέω), to suffer evil, is translated " suffer 2553
hardship " in three places in the R.V., 2 Tim. 2 : 3 (in some mss. ; see AG:397C
No. 2), A.V., " endure hardness ; " 2 : 9, A.V., " suffer trouble ; " 4 : 5, CB:1253B
A.V., " endure affliction ; " in Jas. 5 : 13, R.V., " suffering " (A.V., " afflicted "). See AFFLICT, ENDURE, SUFFER.¶ In the Sept., Jonah 4 : 10.¶

2. SUNKAKOPATHEŌ (συγκακοπαθέω), to suffer hardship with, 4777
is so rendered in 2 Tim. 1 : 8, R.V., A.V., " be thou partaker of the AG:773B
afflictions " (of the Gospel), and, in the best mss., in 2 : 3, " suffer hardship CB:1270C
with me." See AFFLICTION, No. 3, *Note*.¶

HARLOT

PORNĒ (πόρνη), a prostitute, harlot (from *pernēmi*, to sell), is used 4204
(*a*) literally, in Matt. 21 : 31, 32, of those who were the objects of the AG:693C
mercy shown by Christ ; in Luke 15 : 30, of the life of the prodigal ; in CB:1266A

1 Cor. 6 : 15, 16, in a warning to the Corinthian church against the prevailing licentiousness which had made Corinth a byword; in Heb. 11 : 31 and Jas. 2 : 25, of Rahab; (*b*) metaphorically, of mystic Babylon, Rev. 17 : 1, 5 (A.V., "harlots"), 15, 16; 19 : 2, R.V., for A.V., "whore."¶

HARM

2556 **A. Nouns.**

AG:397D 1. KAKOS (κακός), evil, is rendered "harm" in Acts 16 : 28; 28 : 5.
CB:1253B See EVIL.

4190 AG:690D 2. PONĒROS (πονηρός), evil, generally of a more malignant sort than
CB:1266A No. 1, is translated "harm" in Acts 28 : 21. See EVIL.

824 AG:120C 3. ATOPOS (ἄτοπος): see AMISS.

5196 4. HUBRIS (ὕβρις) primarily denotes wantonness, insolence; then,
AG:832A an act of wanton violence, an outrage, injury, 2 Cor. 12 : 10, R.V.,
CB:1251B "injuries," A.V., "reproaches" (more than reproach is conveyed by the term); metaphorically of a loss by sea, Acts 27 : 10, R.V., "injury," A.V., "hurt," and ver. 21, R.V., "injury," A.V., "harm." See HURT, INJURY, REPROACH.¶

B. Verb.

2559 1. KAKOŌ (κακόω), to do evil to a person (akin to A, No. 1), is rendered
AG:398B CB:1253B "harm" in 1 Pet. 3 : 13, and in the R.V. of Acts 18 : 10 (A.V., "hurt"). See AFFECT, EVIL.

2554 2. KAKOPOIEŌ (κακοποιέω), to do harm (A, No. 1, and *poieō*, to do),
AG:397C CB:1253B is so rendered in the R.V. of Mark 3 : 4 and Luke 6 : 9 (A.V., "to do evil"), with reference to the moral character of what is done; in 1 Pet. 3 : 17, "evil doing;" 3 John 11, "doeth evil."¶

HARMLESS

185 1. AKERAIOS (ἀκέραιος), lit., unmixed, with absence of foreign mixture
AG:30B CB:— (from *a*, negative, and *kerannumi*, to mix), pure, is used metaphorically in the N.T. of what is guileless, sincere, Matt. 10 : 16, "harmless" (marg., "simple"), i.e., with the simplicity of a single eye, discerning what is evil, and choosing only what glorifies God; Rom. 16 : 19, "simple (unto that which is evil)," A.V. marg., "harmless;" Phil. 2 : 15, "harmless," A.V. marg., "sincere." The Greeks used it of wine unmixed with water, of unalloyed metal; in the papyri writings it is used of a loan the interest of which is guaranteed (Moulton and Milligan, Vocab.). Trench compares it and synonymous words as follows: "as the *akakos* (see No. 2, below) has no harmfulness in him, and the *adolos* no guile, so the *akeraios* no foreign mixture, and the *haplous* no folds" (Syn., § lvi). *Haplous* is
172 AG:29B said of the single eye, Matt. 6 : 22; Luke 11 : 34.¶

CB:1234A 2. AKAKOS (ἄκακος), the negative of *kakos* (see HARM, A, No. 1),
HARMONY See LIKEMINDED, MIND void of evil, is rendered "harmless" in Heb. 7 : 26 (R.V., "guileless"), of the character of Christ as a High Priest; in Rom. 16 : 18, R.V., "innocent," A.V., "simple."¶

HARP

A. Noun.

KITHARA (κιθάρα), whence Eng., guitar, denotes a lyre or harp; it 2788
is described by Josephus as an instrument of ten strings, played by a AG:432A
plectrum (a smaller instrument was played by the hand); it is mentioned CB:—
in 1 Cor. 14:7; Rev. 5:8; 14:2; 15:2.¶

B. Verb.

KITHARIZŌ (κιθαρίζω) signifies to play on the harp, 1 Cor. 14:7; 2789
Rev. 14:2.¶ In the Sept., Isa. 23:16.¶ AG:432A
CB:—

HARPER

KITHARŌDOS (κιθαρῳδός) denotes one who plays and sings to the 2790
lyre (from *kithara*, a lyre, and *aoidos*, a singer), Rev. 14:2; 18:22.¶ AG:432A
CB:—

HARVEST

THERISMOS (θερισμός), akin to *therizō*, to reap, is used (*a*) of the act 2326
of harvesting, John 4:35; (*b*) the time of harvest, figuratively, Matt. AG:359C
13:30, 39; Mark 4:29; (*c*) the crop, figuratively, Matt. 9:37, 38; CB:1272B
Luke 10:2; Rev. 14:15. The beginning of harvest varied according to natural conditions, but took place on the average about the middle of April in the eastern lowlands of Palestine, in the latter part of the month in the coast plains and a little later in high districts. Barley harvest usually came first and then wheat. Harvesting lasted about seven weeks, and was the occasion of festivities.¶

HARSH See **BITTER, SHARP, SEVERITY**

HASTE, WITH HASTE, HASTILY

A. Noun.

SPOUDĒ (σπουδή) denotes (*a*) haste, speed, accompanied by "with," 4710
Mark 6:25; Luke 1:39; (*b*) zeal, diligence, earnestness: see BUSINESS, AG:763D
CARE, CAREFULNESS, DILIGENCE, FORWARDNESS. CB:1269C

B. Verb.

SPEUDŌ (σπεύδω) denotes (*a*) intransitively, to hasten, Luke 2:16, 4692
"with haste," lit., '(they came) hastening;' Luke 19:5, 6; Acts 20:16; AG:762B
22:18; (*b*) transitively, to desire earnestly, 2 Pet. 3:12, R.V., "earnestly CB:1269C
desiring" (marg., "hastening"), A.V., "hasting" (the day of God), i.e., in our practical fellowship with God as those who are appointed by Him as instruments through prayer and service for the accomplishment of His purposes, purposes which will be unthwartably fulfilled both in time and manner of accomplishment. In this way the earnest desire will find its fulfilment.¶

C. Adverb.

TACHEŌS (ταχέως), quickly, is used in a warning to lay hands 5030
"hastily" on no man (with a suggestion of rashness), 1 Tim. 5:22, R.V. AG:806D
(A.V., "suddenly"); in John 11:31, R.V., "(she rose up) quickly" CB:—
(A.V., "hastily"). See QUICKLY, SHORTLY, SUDDENLY.

HATE, HATEFUL, HATER, HATRED

A. Verb.

3404 AG:522C CB:1259A MISEŌ (μισέω), to hate, is used especially (*a*) of malicious and unjustifiable feelings towards others, whether towards the innocent or by mutual animosity, e.g., Matt. 10 : 22 ; 24 : 10 ; Luke 6 : 22, 27 ; 19 : 14 ; John 3 : 20, of hating the light (metaphorically) ; 7 : 7 ; 15 : 18, 19, 23–25 ; Tit. 3 : 3 ; 1 John 2 : 9, 11 ; 3 : 13, 15 ; 4 : 20 ; Rev. 18 : 2, where " hateful " translates the perfect participle Passive Voice of the verb, lit., ' hated,' or ' having been hated ; ' (*b*) of a right feeling of aversion from what is evil ; said of wrong doing, Rom. 7 : 15 ; iniquity, Heb. 1 : 9 ; " the garment (figurative) spotted by the flesh," Jude 23 ; " the works of the Nicolaitans," Rev. 2 : 6 (and ver. 15, in some mss. ; see the A.V.) ; (*c*) of relative preference for one thing over another, by way of expressing either aversion from, or disregard for, the claims of one person or thing relatively to those of another, Matt. 6 : 24, and Luke 16 : 13, as to the impossibility of serving two " masters ; " Luke 14 : 26, as to the claims of parents relatively to those of Christ ; John 12 : 25, of disregard for one's life relatively to the claims of Christ ; Eph. 5 : 29, negatively, of one's flesh, i.e. of one's own, and therefore a man's wife as one with him.

Note : In 1 John 3 : 15, he who hates his brother is called a murderer ; for the sin lies in the inward disposition, of which the act is only the outward expression.

B. Adjective.

4767 AG:771D CB:— STUGĒTOS (στυγητός), hateful (from *stugeō*, to hate, not found in the N.T.), is used in Tit. 3 : 3.¶

C. Nouns.

2189 AG:331B CB:1242C 1. ECHTHRA (ἔχθρα), hatred : see ENMITY.

2319 AG:358C CB:1272B 2. THEOSTUGĒS (θεοστυγής), from *theos*, God, and *stugeō* (see B), is used in Rom. 1 : 30, A.V., and R.V. marg., " haters of God," R.V., " hateful to God ; " the former rendering is appropriate to what is expressed by the next words, " insolent," " haughty," but the R.V. text seems to give the true meaning. Lightfoot quotes from the Epistle of Clement of Rome, in confirmation of this, " those who practise these things are hateful to God."¶

HAUGHTY

5244 AG:841B CB:1252A HUPERĒPHANOS (ὑπερήφανος), showing oneself above others (*huper*, over, *phainomai*, to appear), though often denoting pre-eminent, is always used in the N.T. in the evil sense of arrogant, disdainful, haughty ; it is rendered " haughty " in Rom. 1 : 30 and 2 Tim. 3 : 2, R.V., A.V., " proud," but " proud " in both Versions in Luke 1 : 51 ; Jas. 4 : 6, and 1 Pet. 5 : 5 ; in the last two it is set in opposition to *tapeinos*, humble, lowly. Cp. the noun *huperēphania*, Mark 7 : 22, pride.¶

HAVE

(*Note :* The following are distinct from the word when it is auxiliary to the tenses of other verbs.)

1. ECHŌ (ἔχω), the usual verb for to have, is used with the following 2192
meanings : (*a*) to hold, in the hand, etc., e.g., Rev. 1 : 16 ; 5 : 8 ; (*b*) to AG:331D CB:1242C
hold fast, keep, Luke 19 : 20 ; metaphorically, of the mind and conduct, e.g., Mark 16 : 8 ; John 14 : 21 ; Rom. 1 : 28 ; 1 Tim. 3 : 9 ; 2 Tim. 1 : 13 ; (*c*) to hold on, cling to, be next to, e.g., of accompaniment, Heb. 6 : 9. " things that accompany (salvation)," lit., ' the things holding themselves of salvation ' (R.V., marg., " are near to ") ; of place, Mark 1 : 38, " next (towns)," lit., ' towns holding nigh ; ' of time, e.g., Luke 13 : 33, " (the day) following," lit., ' the holding (day) ; ' Acts 13 : 44 ; 20 : 15 ; 21 : 26 ; (*d*) to hold, to count, consider, regard, e.g., Matt. 14 : 5 ; 21 : 46 ; Mark 11 : 32 ; Luke 14 : 18 ; Philm. 17 ; (*e*) to involve, Heb. 10 : 35 ; Jas. 1 : 4 ; 1 John 4 : 18 ; (*f*) to wear, of clothing, arms, etc., e.g., Matt. 3 : 4 ; 22 : 12 ; John 18 : 10 ; (*g*) to be (with child), of a woman, Mark 13 : 17 ; Rom. 9 : 10 (lit., ' having conception ') ; (*h*) to possess, the most frequent use, e.g., Matt. 8 : 20 ; 19 : 22 ; Acts 9 : 14 ; 1 Thess. 3 : 6 ; (*i*) of complaints, disputes, Matt. 5 : 23 ; Mark 11 : 25 ; Acts 24 : 19 ; Rev. 2 : 4, 20 ; (*j*) of ability, power, e.g., Luke 12 : 4 ; Acts 4 : 14 (lit., ' had nothing to say ') ; (*k*) of necessity, e.g., Luke 12 : 50 ; Acts 23 : 17–19 ; (*l*) to be in a certain condition, as, of readiness, Acts 21 : 13 (lit., ' I have readily ') ; of illness, Matt. 4 : 24, " all that were sick " (lit., ' that had themselves sickly ') ; Mark 5 : 23, " lieth (lit., ' hath herself ') at the point of death ; " Mark 16 : 18, " they shall recover " (lit., ' shall have themselves well ') ; John 4 : 52, " he began to amend " (lit., ' he had himself better ') ; of evil works, 1 Tim. 5 : 25, " they that are otherwise," (lit., ' the things having otherwise ') ; to be so, e.g., Acts 7 : 1, " are these things so ? " (lit., ' have these things thus ? ') ; of time, Acts 24 : 25, " for this time " (lit., ' the thing having now ').

2. APECHŌ (ἀπέχω) denotes to have in full, to have received (*apo*, 568
from, and No. 1), Matt. 6 : 2, 5, 16, R.V., " have received," for A.V., AG:84D
" have ; " Luke 6 : 24, A.V. and R.V., " have received," but Phil. 4 : 18, CB:1236B
" I have ; " Philm. 15, " (that) thou shouldest have (him) " (A.V., " receive "). Deissmann, in *Light from the Ancient East*, and Moulton and Milligan (Vocab. of Gk. Test.) show that the verb was constantly used " as a technical expression in drawing up a receipt. Consequently in the Sermon on the Mount we are led to understand ' they have received their reward ' as ' they have signed the receipt of their reward : their right to receive their reward is realised, precisely as if they had already given a receipt for it.' "

Is there not a hint of this in Paul's word to Philemon concerning receiving Onesimus (ver. 17) ? Philemon would give the Apostle a receipt for his payment in sending him. This is in keeping with the metaphorical terms of finance in vv. 18, 19. See ABSTAIN.

1096 AG:158A CB:1248B 3. GINOMAI (*γίνομαι*), to begin to be, come to pass, happen, is rendered "have" in Matt. 18 : 12; "had" in Acts 15 : 2; "shall have" in 1 Cor. 4 : 5, lit., 'praise shall be,' or come to pass. See BECOME.

3335 AG:511B CB:1258B 4. METALAMBANŌ (*μεταλαμβάνω*), to have, or get a share of, is rendered "I have (a convenient season)," in Acts 24 : 25. See EAT, PARTAKE, RECEIVE, TAKE.

5225 AG:838A CB:— 5. HUPARCHŌ (*ὑπάρχω*), to be in existence, to be ready, at hand, is translated by the verb to have in Acts 3 : 6, lit., 'silver and gold is not to me' (in the next clause, "such as I have," *echō* is used); 4 : 37, "having (land)," lit., '(land) being (to him);' Matt. 19 : 21, "that (thou) hast," lit., '(things that) are (thine),' i.e., 'thy belongings;' similarly Luke 12 : 33, 44; 14 : 33. See BEING.

474 AG:74A CB:— 6. ANTIBALLŌ (*ἀντιβάλλω*), lit., to throw in turn, exchange (*anti*, corresponding to, *ballō*, to throw), hence, metaphorically, to exchange thoughts, is used in Luke 24 : 27, "ye have," i.e., 'ye exchange.'¶

1510 AG:222D CB:1243A 7. EIMI (*εἰμί*), to be, is often used in its various forms with some case of the personal pronoun, to signify to be to, or of, a person, e.g., Matt. 19 : 27, "(what then) shall we have," lit., 'what then shall be to us?;' Acts 21 : 23, "we have four men," lit., 'there are to us, etc.'

1746 AG:264A CB:1245A 8. ENDUŌ (*ἐνδύω*), to put on, is rendered "having on" in Eph. 6 : 14. See CLOTHE.

Notes: (1) In John 5 : 4 (in those mss. which contain the passage), *katechō*, to hold fast, is used in the Passive Voice, in the phrase "whatsoever disease he had," lit., '(by whatsoever disease) he was held.' (2) In Mark 12 : 22, in some mss., *lambanō*, to take or receive, is translated "had," in the statement "the seven had her;" in Acts 25 : 16, R.V., "have had" (A.V., "have"); in Heb. 11 : 36, "had." (3) In Matt. 27 : 19, "Have thou nothing to do with that righteous man" translates what is lit. 'nothing to thee and that righteous man,' the verb being omitted. Similarly with the phrase, "What have I to do with thee?" lit., 'what (is) to me and thee?' Mark 5 : 7; Luke 8 : 28; John 2 : 4, where Westcott translates it 'What is there to Me and to thee?;' Ellicott, 'What is that to Me and to thee," i.e., 'What is My concern and thine in the matter?' There is certainly nothing disparaging in the question. On the contrary,
KATECHō it answers what must have been the thought in Mary's heart, and suggests
2722 that while there is no obligation either on Him or her, yet the need is a
AG:422C CB:1254B case for rendering help. For the construction with the plural pronoun
LAMBANō see Matt. 8 : 29; Mark 1 : 24; Luke 4 : 34. (4) In Heb. 4 : 13, "with
2983 whom we have to do" is, lit., 'with whom (is) the account (*logos*) to us.'
AG:464A CB:1256C (5) In Heb. 13 : 5, "such things as ye have" is, lit., 'the (things) present'
ENEIMI 1751 (6) In Mark 5 : 26, "all that she had" is, lit., 'all the (things) with her.'
AG:264C (7) For Luke 15 : 31, A.V., "all that I have," lit., 'all my (things),' see
CB:— R.V. (8) For *eneimi*, Luke 11 : 41, "ye have," see WITHIN, *Note* (*h*).

HAVEN

LIMĒN (*λιμήν*) is mentioned in Acts 27 : 8, "Fair Havens," and 3040
ver. 12 ; for the first of these see FAIR. The first mention in the Bible AG:475A CB:—
is in Gen. 49 : 13 (see R.V. marg.).¶

HAVOCK

1. PORTHEŌ (*πορθέω*), to destroy, ravage, lay waste, is used of the 4199
persecution inflicted by Saul of Tarsus on the church in Jerusalem, AG:693A CB:—
Acts 9 : 21, and Gal. 1 : 23, R.V., "made havock," for A.V., "destroyed;"
Gal. 1 : 13, ditto, for A.V., "wasted." See DESTROY, *Note.*¶

2. LUMAINOMAI (*λυμαίνομαι*), to maltreat, outrage (*lumē*, an out- 3075
rage), is translated "made havock" in Acts 8 : 3, A.V. (R.V., "laid AG:481C CB:—
waste.")¶

For HAY see GRASS

HAZARD

1. PARADIDŌMI (*παραδίδωμι*), to give over, deliver, signifies to risk, 3860
to hazard, in Acts 15 : 26, of Barnabas and Paul, who hazarded their AG:614B CB:1262A
lives for the Name of the Lord Jesus. See BETRAY.

2. PARABOLEUOMAI (*παραβολεύομαι*), lit., to throw aside (*para*, 3851
aside, *ballō*, to throw), hence, to expose oneself to danger, to hazard one's AG:612B CB:—
life, is said of Epaphroditus in Phil. 2 : 30, R.V., "hazarding." Some
mss. have *parabouleuomai* here, to consult amiss, A.V., "not regarding."¶

HE

Note : This pronoun is generally part of the translation of a verb. Frequently it translates the article before nouns, adjectives, numerals, adverbs, prepositional phrases and the participial form of verbs. Apart from these it translates one of the following :

1. AUTOS (*αὐτός*), he himself and no other, emphatic, e.g., Matt. 1 : 21, 846
where the R.V. brings out the emphasis by the rendering "it is He ;" AG:122C CB:1238B
3 : 11 (last clause), where the repeated "He" brings out the emphasis ; in some cases it can be marked only by a circumlocution which would not constitute a translation, e.g., 8 : 24 ; this use is very frequent, especially in the Gospels, the Epistles of John and the Apocalypse ; see also, e.g., Eph. 2 : 14 ; 4 : 11 ; 5 : 23, 27. See SAME, SELF, THIS, VERY.

2. HOUTOS (*οὗτος*), this, this person here, is always emphatic ; it is 3778
used with this meaning, sometimes to refer to what precedes, e.g., Matt. AG:596B CB:1251B
5 : 19, "he (shall be called great) ;" John 6 : 46, "he (hath seen) ;" often rendered "this," e.g., Rom. 9 : 9, or "this man," e.g., Matt. 27 : 58, R.V. ; Jas. 1 : 25 ; "the same," e.g., Luke 9 : 48. See THAT, THIS, THESE.

3. EKEINOS (*ἐκεῖνος*) denotes that one, that person (in contrast to 1565
No. 2) ; its use marks special distinction, favourable or unfavourable ; AG:239B CB:1243C
this form of emphasis should always be noted ; e.g., John 2 : 21 "(But)

He (spake);" 5 : 19, "(what things soever) He (doeth);" 7 : 11; 2 Cor. 10 : 18, lit., 'for not he that commendeth himself, he (*ekeinos*) is approved;' 2 Tim. 2 : 13, "He (in contrast to "we") abideth faithful;" 1 John 3 : 3, "(even as) He (is pure);" ver. 5, "He (was manifested);" ver. 7, "He (is righteous);" ver. 16, "He laid down;" 4 : 17, "(as) He (is)." See OTHER, THAT, THIS.

5100 AG:819D CB:1272C *Note:* The indefinite pronoun *tis*, anyone, any man, is rendered "he" in Acts 4 : 35, A.V. (R.V., rightly, "any one"); in Heb. 10 : 28, R.V., "a man."

HE HIMSELF

846 AG:122C CB:1238B 1. AUTOS (αὐτός): see No. 1, above.

1438 AG:211D CB:1249B (-OS) 2. HEAUTON (ἑαυτόν), oneself, himself, a reflexive of No. 1, is rendered "he himself" in Luke 23 : 2 and Acts 25 : 4.

HE THAT

3739 AG:583B CB:— 1. HOS (ὅς), the relative pronoun who, is sometimes rendered "he that," e.g., Matt. 10 : 38; with the particle *an*, expressing possibility, uncertainty or a condition, signifying whosoever, Mark 3 : 29, A.V. (R.V., "whosoever"); 4 : 25 and 9 : 40 (with *an*, in the best mss.). See WHATSOEVER, WHICH, WHO, WHOSOEVER.

— AG:583B (HOS I.10b.) CB:- 2. HOSGE (ὅσγε), who even (No. 1, and the particle *ge*), indicates a greater in regard to a less, Rom. 8 : 32, "He that (spared not)."

5100 AG:819D CB:1272C *Notes:* (1) In Rev. 13 : 10, *ei tis*, if anyone, is rendered "if any man" in the R.V., for A.V., "he that."

3748 AG:586D CB:— (2) In Matt. 23 : 12, *hostis*, No. 1, combined with the indefinite pronoun *tis* (see preceding note), is properly rendered "whosoever," R.V., for A.V., "he that."

HEAD

2776 AG:430A CB:1255A KEPHALĒ (κεφαλή), besides its natural significance, is used (*a*) figuratively in Rom. 12 : 20, of heaping coals of fire on a head (see COALS); in Acts 18 : 6, "Your blood be upon your own heads," i.e., 'your blood-guiltiness rest upon your own persons,' a mode of expression frequent in the O.T., and perhaps here directly connected with Ezek. 3 : 18, 20; 33 : 6, 8; see also Lev. 20 : 16; 2 Sam. 1 : 16; 1 Kings 2 : 37; (*b*) metaphorically, of the authority or direction of God in relation to Christ, of Christ in relation to believing men, of the husband in relation to the wife, 1 Cor. 11 : 3; of Christ in relation to the Church, Eph. 1 : 22; 4 : 15; 5 : 23; Col. 1 : 18; 2 : 19; of Christ in relation to principalities and powers, Col. 2 : 10. As to 1 Cor. 11 : 10, taken in connection with the context, the word "authority" probably stands, by metonymy, for a sign of authority (R.V.), the angels being witnesses of the pre-eminent relationship as established by God in the creation of man as just mentioned, with the spiritual significance regarding the position of Christ in relation to the Church ; cp. Eph. 3 : 10 ; it is used of Christ as the foundation of the spiritual building set forth by the Temple, with its " corner stone," Matt. 21 : 42 ; symbolically also of the Imperial rulers of the Roman power, as seen in the Apocalyptic visions, Rev. 13 : 1, 3 ; 17 : 3, 7, 9.

HEAD (to wound in the)

KEPHALIOŌ, or KEPHALAIOŌ (κεφαλιόω), from *kephalion,* a 2775
diminutive of *kephalē,* usually meant to sum up, to bring under heads ; AG:430A
in Mark 12 : 4 it is used for wounding on the head, the only place where CB:1255A
it has this meaning.¶

HEADLONG (to cast, to fall)

1. KATAKRĒMNIZŌ (κατακρημνίζω) signifies to throw over a 2630
precipice (*kata,* down, *krēmnos,* a steep bank, etc.), said of the purpose AG:412A
of the people of Nazareth to destroy Christ, Luke 4 : 29.¶ CB:—

2. PRĒNĒS (πρηνής), an adjective denoting headlong, prone, is used 4248
with the verb *ginomai,* to become, in Acts 1 : 18, of the death of Judas, AG:700D
" falling headlong ; " various suggestions have been made as to the CB:1266B
actual details ; some ascribe to the word the meaning " swelling up."¶

HEADSTRONG (R.V.), HEADY (A.V.)

PROPETĒS (προπετής) lit. means falling forwards (from *pro,* forwards, 4312
and *piptō,* to fall) ; it is used metaphorically to signify precipitate, rash, AG:709C
reckless, and is said (*a*) of persons, 2 Tim. 3 : 4 ; " headstrong " is the CB:—
appropriate rendering ; (*b*) of things, Acts 19 : 36, R.V., " (nothing) rash " (A.V., " rashly ").¶

HEAL, HEALING

A. Verbs.

1. THERAPEUŌ (θεραπεύω) primarily signifies to serve as a *therapōn,* 2323
an attendant ; then, to care for the sick, to treat, cure, heal (Eng., thera- AG:359A
peutics). It is chiefly used in Matthew and Luke, once in John (5 : 10), CB:1272B
and, after the Acts, only Rev. 13 : 3 and 12. See CURE.

2. IAOMAI (ἰάομαι), to heal, is used (*a*) of physical treatment 22 times ; 2390
in Matt. 15 : 28, A.V., " made whole," R.V., " healed ; " so in Acts AG:368B
9 : 34 ; (*b*) figuratively, of spiritual healing, Matt. 13 : 15 ; John 12 : 40 ; CB:1252C
Acts 28 : 27 ; Heb. 12 : 13 ; 1 Pet. 2 : 24 ; possibly, Jas. 5 : 16 includes both (*a*) and (*b*) ; some mss. have the word, with sense (*b*), in Luke 4 : 18. Apart from this last, Luke, the physician, uses the word fifteen times. See WHOLE.

3. SŌZŌ (σώζω), to save, is translated by the verb to heal in the A.V. 4982
of Mark 5 : 23 and Luke 8 : 36 (R.V., to make whole ; so A.V. frequently) ; AG:798A
the idea is that of saving from disease and its effects. See SAVE. CB:1269C

4. DIASŌZŌ (διασώζω), to save thoroughly (*dia,* through, and No. 3), 1295 AG:189A
is translated " heal " in Luke 7 : 3, A.V. (R.V., " save "). See ESCAPE. CB:1241B

B. Nouns.

2322 AG:358D CB:1272B 1. THERAPEIA (θεραπεία), akin to A, No. 1, primarily denotes care, attention, Luke 12 : 42 (see HOUSEHOLD) ; then, medical service, healing (Eng., therapy), Luke 9 : 11 ; Rev. 22 : 2, of the effects of the leaves of the tree of life, perhaps here with the meaning " health."¶

2386 AG:368A CB:1252C 2. IAMA (ἴαμα), akin to A, No. 2, formerly signified a means of healing ; in the N.T., a healing (the result of the act), used in the plural, in 1 Cor. 12 : 9, 28, 30, R.V., " healings ; " of Divinely imparted gifts in the churches in Apostolic times.¶

2392 AG:368C CB:1252C 3. IASIS (ἴασις), akin to A, No. 2, stresses the process as reaching completion, Luke 13 : 32, " cures," of the acts of Christ in the days of His flesh ; Acts 4 : 22, 30, " to heal," lit. ' unto healing.'¶

HEALTH (to be in)

5198 AG:832B CB:1251C HUGIAINŌ (ὑγιαίνω) denotes to be healthy, sound, in good health (Eng., hygiene), rendered " mayest be in health," in 3 John 2 ; rendered " safe and sound " in Luke 15 : 27. See SAFE, D, No. 2, SOUND, WHOLE, B, No. 1.

4991 AG:801B CB:1269C *Note :* In Acts 27 : 34, *sōtēria*, salvation, safety, is translated " health " in the A.V. ; the R.V., gives the right meaning, " safety."

HEAP (to)

4987 AG:800C CB:— 1. SŌREUŌ (σωρεύω), to heap one thing on another, is said of heaping coals of fire on the head, Rom. 12 : 20 (for the meaning see COALS) ; in 2 Tim. 3 : 6 it is used metaphorically of women " laden " (or overwhelmed) with sins. See LADEN.¶ In the Sept., Prov. 25 : 22.¶

2002 AG:302A CB:— 2. EPISŌREUŌ (ἐπισωρεύω), to heap upon or together (*epi*, upon, and No. 1), is used metaphorically in 2 Tim. 4 : 3 of appropriating a number of teachers to suit the liking of those who do so. The reference may be to those who, like the Athenians, run about to hear and follow those who proclaim new ideas of their own invention.¶

HEAR, HEARING

A. Verbs.

191 AG:31D CB:1234B 1. AKOUŌ (ἀκούω), the usual word denoting to hear, is used (*a*) intransitively, e.g., Matt. 11 : 15 ; Mark 4 : 23 ; (*b*) transitively when the object is expressed, sometimes in the accusative case, sometimes in the genitive. Thus in Acts 9 : 7, " hearing the voice," the noun " voice " is in the partitive genitive case [i.e., hearing (something) of], whereas in 22 : 9, " they heard not the voice," the construction is with the accusative. This removes the idea of any contradiction. The former indicates a hearing of the sound, the latter indicates the meaning or message of the voice (this they did not hear). " The formeı denotes the sensational perception, the latter (the accusative case) the thing perceived " (Cremer). In John 5 : 25, 28, the genitive case is used, indicating a " sensational

perception " that the Lord's voice is sounding ; in 3 : 8, of hearing the wind, the accusative is used, stressing " the thing perceived."

That God hears prayer signifies that He answers prayer, e.g., John 9 : 31 ; 1 John 5 : 14, 15. Sometimes the verb is used with *para* (from beside), e.g., John 1 : 40, " one of the two which heard John speak," lit., ' heard from beside John,' suggesting that he stood beside him ; in John 8 : 26, 40, indicating the intimate fellowship of the Son with the Father ; the same construction is used in Acts 10 : 22 and 2 Tim. 2 : 2, in the latter case, of the intimacy between Paul and Timothy. See HEARKEN.

2. EISAKOUŌ (εἰσακούω), to listen to (*eis*, to, and No. 1), has two 1522
meanings, (*a*) to hear and to obey, 1 Cor. 14 : 21, " they will not hear ; " AG:232B
(*b*) to hear so as to answer, of God's answer to prayer, Matt. 6 : 7 ; Luke CB:1243B
1 : 13 ; Acts 10 : 31 ; Heb. 5 : 7.¶

3. DIAKOUŌ (διακούω), to hear through, hear fully (*dia*, through, 1251 (-OMAI)
and No. 1), is used technically, of hearing judicially, in Acts 23 : 35, of AG:185A
Felix in regard to the charges against Paul.¶ In the Sept., Deut. 1 : 16 ; CB:—
Job 9 : 33.¶

4. EPAKOUŌ (ἐπακούω), to listen to, hear with favour, at or upon 1873
an occasion (*epi*, upon, and No. 1), is used in 2 Cor. 6 : 2 (R.V., AG:282C CB:1245B
" hearken ").¶

5. EPAKROAOMAI (ἐπακροάομαι), to listen attentively to (*epi*, used 1874
intensively, and a verb akin to No. 1), is used in Acts 16 : 25, " (the AG:282C CB:1245B
prisoners) were listening to (them)," R.V., expressive of rapt attention.¶

6. PROAKOUŌ (προακούω) signifies to hear before (*pro*), Col. 1 : 5, 4257
where Lightfoot suggests that the preposition contrasts what they heard AG:702C
before, the true Gospel, with the false gospel of their recent teachers.¶ CB:—

7. PARAKOUŌ (παρακούω) primarily signifies to overhear, hear 3878
amiss or imperfectly (*para*, beside, amiss, and No. 1) ; then (in the N.T.) AG:619A
to hear without taking heed, to neglect to hear, Matt. 18 : 17 (twice) ; in CB:1262A
Mark 5 : 36 the best mss. have this verb, which the R.V. renders " not heeding " (marg., " overhearing ") ; some mss. have No. 1, A.V., " hearing." It seems obvious that the Lord paid no attention to those from the ruler's house and their message that his daughter was dead.¶ Cp. the noun *parakoē*, disobedience.

B. Nouns.

1. AKOĒ (ἀκοή), akin to A, No. 1, denotes (*a*) the sense of hearing, 189
1 Cor. 12 : 17 ; 2 Pet. 2 : 8 ; a combination of verb and noun is used in AG:30D
phrases which have been termed Hebraic as they express somewhat CB:1234B
literally an O.T. phraseology, e.g., " By hearing ye shall hear," Matt. 13 : 14 ; Acts 28 : 26, R.V., a mode of expression conveying emphasis ; (*b*) the organ of hearing, Mark 7 : 35, " ears ; " Luke 7 : 1, R.V., " ears," for A.V., " audience ; " Acts 17 : 20 ; 2 Tim. 4 : 3, 4 ; Heb. 5 : 11, " dull of hearing," lit., ' dull as to ears ; ' (*c*) a thing heard, a message or teaching,

John 12 : 38, " report ; " Rom. 10 : 16 ; 1 Thess. 2 : 13, " the word of the message," lit. 'the word of hearing' (A.V., " which ye heard") ; Heb. 4 : 2, " the word of hearing," R.V., for A.V., " the word preached ; " in a somewhat similar sense, a rumour, report, Matt. 4 : 24 ; 14 : 1 ; Mark 1 : 28, A.V., " fame," R.V., " report ; " Matt. 24 : 6 ; Mark 13 : 7, " rumours (of wars) ; " (*d*) the receiving of a message, Rom. 10 : 17, something more than the mere sense of hearing [see (*a*)] ; so with the phrase " the hearing of faith," Gal. 3 : 2, 5, which it seems better to understand so than under (*c*). See EAR, FAME, PREACH, REPORT, RUMOUR.¶

DIAGNŌSIS 1233 *Notes :* (1) For *diagnōsis* (investigation, followed by decision), rendered
AG:182C " hearing " in Acts 25 : 21, A.V., see DECISION. (2) For the phrase to be
CB:— dull of hearing, lit., 'to hear heavily,' Matt. 13 : 15 ; Acts 28 : 27, see
AKROATĒRION 201 DULL. (3) For *akroatērion*, a place of hearing, Acts 25 : 23, see PLACE.¶
AG:33C
CB:—

HEARER

202 AKROATĒS (ἀκροατής), from *akroaomai*, to listen, is used in Rom.
AG:33C
CB:1234B 2 : 13, " of a law ; " Jas. 1 : 22, 23, " of the word ; " ver. 25, " a (forgetful) hearer."¶

191 *Note :* In Eph. 4 : 29 and 2 Tim. 2 : 14, the verb *akouō*, to hear, is
AG:31D
CB:1234B rendered " hearers " in the A.V. (R.V., " them that hear ").

HEARKEN

191 1. AKOUŌ (ἀκούω), to hear, is rendered " hearken " in the A.V.
AG:31D
CB:1234B and R.V., in Mark 4 : 3 ; Acts 4 : 19 ; 7 : 2 ; 15 : 13 ; Jas. 2 : 5 ; in the R.V. only, in Acts 3 : 22, 23 ; 13 : 16 (A.V., " give audience ") ; 15 : 12, " hearkened " (A.V. " gave audience "). See HEAR, No. 1.

5219 *Note :* In Acts 12 : 13, *hupakouō*, lit., to hearken, with the idea of still-
AG:837B
CB:1251C ness, or attention (*hupo*, under, *akouō*, to hear), signifies to answer a knock at a door, R.V., " to answer " (A.V., " to hearken "). See OBEY.

1873 2. EPAKOUŌ (ἐπακούω) denotes to hearken to, 2 Cor. 6 : 2, R.V.
AG:282C
CB:1245B (see HEAR, A, No. 4).¶

1801 3. ENŌTIZOMAI (ἐνωτίζομαι), to give ear to, to hearken (from *en*,
AG:271A
CB:1245B in, and *ous*, an ear), is used in Acts 2 : 14, in Peter's address to the men of Israel.¶

3980 4. PEITHARCHEŌ (πειθαρχέω), to obey one in authority, be obedient
AG:638D
CB:1263A (*peithomai*, to be persuaded, *archē*, rule), is translated to hearken unto in Acts 27 : 21, in Paul's reminder to the shipwrecked mariners that they should have given heed to his counsel. See OBEY.

HEART, HEARTILY

2588 KARDIA (καρδία), the heart (Eng., cardiac, etc.), the chief organ of
AG:403B
CB:1253B physical life (" for the life of the flesh is in the blood," Lev. 17 : 11), occupies the most important place in the human system. By an easy transition the word came to stand for man's entire mental and moral

activity, both the rational and the emotional elements. In other words, the heart is used figuratively for the hidden springs of the personal life. " The Bible describes human depravity as in the ' heart,' because sin is a principle which has its seat in the centre of man's inward life, and then ' defiles ' the whole circuit of his action, Matt. 15 : 19, 20. On the other hand, Scripture regards the heart as the sphere of Divine influence, Rom. 2 : 15 ; Acts 15 : 9. . . . The heart, as lying deep within, contains ' the hidden man,' 1 Pet. 3 : 4, the real man. It represents the true character but conceals it " (J. Laidlaw, in Hastings' Bible Dic.).

As to its usage in the N.T. it denotes (*a*) the seat of physical life, Acts 14 : 17 ; Jas. 5 : 5 ; (*b*) the seat of moral nature and spiritual life, the seat of grief, John 14 : 1 ; Rom. 9 : 2 ; 2 Cor. 2 : 4 ; joy, John 16 : 22 ; Eph. 5 : 19 ; the desires, Matt. 5 : 28 ; 2 Pet. 2 : 14 ; the affections, Luke 24 : 32 ; Acts 21 : 13 ; the perceptions, John 12 : 40 ; Eph. 4 : 18 ; the thoughts, Matt. 9 : 4 ; Heb. 4 : 12 ; the understanding, Matt. 13 : 15 ; Rom. 1 : 21 ; the reasoning powers, Mark 2 : 6 ; Luke 24 : 38 ; the imagination, Luke 1 : 51 ; conscience, Acts 2 : 37 ; 1 John 3 : 20 ; the intentions, Heb. 4 : 12, cp. 1 Pet. 4 : 1 ; purpose, Acts 11 : 23 ; 2 Cor. 9 : 7 ; the will, Rom. 6 : 17 ; Col. 3 : 15 ; faith, Mark 11 : 23 ; Rom. 10 : 10 ; Heb. 3 : 12.

The heart, in its moral significance in the O.T., includes the emotions, the reason and the will.

2. PSUCHĒ (ψυχή), the soul, or life, is rendered " heart " in Eph. 6 : 6 5590
(marg., " soul "), " doing the will of God from the heart." In Col. 3 : 23, AG:893B CB:1267C
a form of the word *psuchē* preceded by *ek*, from, lit., ' from (the) soul,' is rendered " heartily."

Notes : (1) The R.V., " heart " is substituted for A.V., " bowels," in Col. 3 : 12 ; Philm. 7, 12, 20. (2) In 2 Cor. 3 : 3, the R.V. has " tables that are hearts of flesh," for A.V., " fleshy tables of the heart." (3) In Eph. 1 : 18, the best mss. have *kardia*, " (the eyes of your) heart ; "
some have *dianoia*, " understanding " (A.V.). (4) In Heb. 8 : 10 and DIANOIA
10 : 16, the A.V. has " in their hearts " and " into their hearts ; " R.V., 1271 AG:187A
" on their heart." (5) In Luke 21 : 26, where there is no word for CB:1241B
" hearts " in the original, the R.V. has " men fainting (for fear)." (6) In CHōREō 5562
2 Cor. 7 : 2, the verb *chōreō*, to make room for, " receive " (A.V.), is trans- AG:889C
lated, or rather, interpreted, " open your hearts," R.V., marg., " make CB:1240A
room for (us)."

HEART (hardness of)

SKLĒROKARDIA (σκληροκαρδία), hardness of heart (*sklēros*, hard, 4641
and *kardia*), is used in Matt. 19 : 8 ; Mark 10 : 5 ; 16 : 14.¶ In the Sept., AG:756A CB:1269A
Deut. 10 : 16 ; Jer. 4 : 4.¶

HEART (knowing the)

KARDIOGNŌSTĒS (καρδιογνώστης), a knower of hearts (*kardia* 2589 AG:404C
and *ginōskō*, to know), is used in Acts 1 : 24 ; 15 : 8.¶ CB:1253B

HEAT

A. Nouns.

2742 AG:425C CB:— 1. KAUSŌN (καύσων) denotes a burning heat (from *kaiō*, to burn; cp. Eng., caustic, cauterize), Matt. 20 : 12; Luke 12 : 55 (A.V., "heat"), R.V., in each place, "scorching heat" (marg., "hot wind"); in Jas. 1 : 11, "a burning heat," A.V., R.V., "the scorching wind," like the Sirocco. Cp. Amos 4 : 9, where the Sept. has *purōsis*, burning (*pur*, fire). See BURNING.

2738 AG:425B CB:1254C 2. KAUMA (καῦμα), heat (akin to No. 1), signifies the result of burning, or the heat produced, Rev. 7 : 16; 16 : 9;¶ cp. *kaumatizō*, to scorch, *kausis*, burning, *kautēriazomai*, to brand, sear.

2329 AG:359C CB:1272B 3. THERMĒ (θέρμη) denotes warmth, heat, Acts 28 : 3 (Eng., thermal, etc.).¶

B. Verb.

2741 AG:425B CB:— KAUSOŌ (καυσόω) was used as a medical term, of a fever; in the N.T., to burn with great heat (akin to A, No. 1), said of the future destruction of the natural elements, 2 Pet. 3 : 10, 12, "with fervent heat," Passive Voice, lit., 'being burned.'¶

For HEATHEN see GENTILES

HEAVEN, HEAVENLY (-IES)

A. Nouns.

3772 AG:593D CB:1261B 1. OURANOS (οὐρανός), probably akin to *ornumi*, to lift, to heave, is used in the N.T. (*a*) of the aërial heavens, e.g., Matt. 6 : 26; 8 : 20; Acts 10 : 12; 11 : 6 (R.V., "heaven," in each place, A.V., "air"); Jas. 5 : 18; (*b*) the sidereal, e.g., Matt. 24 : 29, 35; Mark 13 : 25, 31; Heb. 11 : 12, R.V., "heaven," A.V., "sky;" Rev. 6 : 14; 20 : 11; they, (*a*) and (*b*), were created by the Son of God, Heb. 1 : 10, as also by God the Father, Rev. 10 : 6; (*c*) the eternal dwelling place of God, Matt. 5 : 16; 12 : 50; Rev. 3 : 12; 11 : 13; 16 : 11; 20 : 9. From thence the Son of God descended to become Incarnate, John 3 : 13, 31; 6 : 38, 42. In His ascension Christ "passed through the heavens," Heb. 4 : 14, R.V.; He "ascended far above all the heavens," Eph. 4 : 10, and was "made higher than the heavens," Heb. 7 : 26; He "sat down on the right hand of the throne of the Majesty in the heavens," Heb. 8 : 1; He is "on the right hand of God," having gone into Heaven, 1 Pet. 3 : 22. Since His Ascension it is the scene of His present life and activity, e.g., Rom. 8 : 34; Heb. 9 : 24. From thence the Holy Spirit descended at Pentecost, 1 Pet. 1 : 12. It is the abode of the angels, e.g., Matt. 18 : 10; 22 : 30; cp. Rev. 3 : 5. Thither Paul was "caught up," whether in the body or out of the body, he knew not, 2 Cor. 12 : 2. It is to be the eternal dwelling-place of the saints in resurrection glory, 2 Cor. 5 : 1. From thence Christ will descend to the air to receive His saints at the Rapture, 1 Thess. 4 : 16; Phil. 3 : 20, 21, and will subsequently come with His saints and with His holy angels at His Second Advent, Matt. 24 : 30 ; 2 Thess. 1 : 7. In the present life heaven is the region of the spiritual citizenship of believers, Phil. 3 : 20. The present heavens, with the earth, are to pass away, 2 Pet. 3 : 10, " being on fire," ver. 12 (see ver. 7) ; Rev. 20 : 11, and new heavens and earth are to be created, 2 Pet. 3 : 13 ; Rev. 21 : 1, with Is. 65 : 17, e.g.

In Luke 15 : 18, 21, heaven is used, by metonymy, for God. See AIR.

Notes : (1) For the phrase in Luke 11 : 13, see Note on B, No. 2. (2) In Luke 11 : 2, the A.V., " as in heaven," translates a phrase found in some mss.

2. MESOURANĒMA (*μεσουράνημα*) denotes mid-heaven, or the midst 3321
of the heavens (*mesos*, middle, and No. 1), Rev. 8 : 13 ; 14 : 6 ; 19 : 17.¶ AG:508A CB:—

B. Adjectives.

1. OURANIOS (*οὐράνιος*), signifying of heaven, heavenly, corres- 3770
ponding to A, No. 1, is used (*a*) as an appellation of God the Father, AG:593C CB:1261B
Matt. 6 : 14, 26, 32, " your heavenly Father ; " 15 : 13, " My heavenly Father ; " (*b*) as descriptive of the holy angels, Luke 2 : 13 ; (*c*) of the vision seen by Paul, Acts 26 : 19.¶

2. EPOURANIOS (*ἐπουράνιος*), heavenly, what pertains to, or is in, 2032
heaven (*epi*, in the sense of ' pertaining to,' not here, ' above '), has meanings AG:305D CB:1246B
corresponding to some of the meanings of *ouranos*, A, No. 1. It is used (*a*) of God the Father, Matt. 18 : 35 ; (*b*) of the place where Christ " sitteth at the right hand of God " (i.e., in a position of Divine authority), Eph. 1 : 20; and of the present position of believers in relationship to Christ, 2 : 6; where they possess ' every spiritual blessing,' 1 : 3 ; (*c*) of Christ as " the Second Man," and all those who are related to Him spiritually, 1 Cor. 15 : 48 ; (*d*) of those whose sphere of activity or existence is above, or in contrast to that of earth, of " principalities and powers," Eph. 3 : 10 ; of " spiritual hosts of wickedness," 6 : 12, R.V., " in heavenly places," for A.V., " in high places ; " (*e*) of the Holy Spirit, Heb. 6 : 4 ; (*f*) of " heavenly things," as the subjects of the teaching of Christ, John 3 : 12, and as consisting of the spiritual and heavenly Sanctuary and " true tabernacle " and all that appertains thereto in relation to Christ and His sacrifice as antitypical of the earthly tabernacle and sacrifices under the Law, Heb. 8 : 5 ; 9 : 23 ; (*g*) of the " calling " of believers, Heb. 3 : 1 ; (*h*) of Heaven as the abode of the saints, " a better country " than that of earth, Heb. 11 : 16, and of the spiritual Jerusalem, 12 : 22 ; (*i*) of the Kingdom of Christ in its future manifestation, 2 Tim. 4 : 18 ; (*j*) of all beings and things, animate and inanimate, that are " above the earth," Phil. 2 : 10 ; (*k*) of the resurrection and glorified bodies of believers, 1 Cor. 15 : 49 ; (*l*) of the heavenly orbs, 1 Cor. 15 : 40 (" celestial," twice, and so rendered here only).¶

Note : In connection with (*a*), the word " heavenly," used of God the Father in Luke 11 : 13, represents the phrase *ex ouranou*, ' from heaven.'

C. Adverb.

3771 AG:593D CB:1261B OURANOTHEN (οὐρανόθεν), formed from A, No. 1, and denoting 'from heaven,' is used of (*a*) the aërial heaven, Acts 14 : 17; (*b*) heaven, as the uncreated sphere of God's abode, 26 : 13.¶

HEAVY, HEAVINESS

A. Nouns.

3077 AG:482A CB:1257B 1. LUPĒ (λύπη), grief, sorrow, is rendered " heaviness " in the A.V. of Rom. 9 : 2; 2 Cor. 2 : 1 (R.V., " sorrow," in both places). See GRIEF, SORROW.

2726 AG:423C CB:— 2. KATĒPHEIA (κατήφεια) probably denotes a downcast look, expressive of sorrow; hence, dejection, heaviness; it is used in Jas. 4 : 9.¶

B. Verbs.

85 AG:16D CB:— 1. ADĒMONEŌ (ἀδημονέω), to be troubled, much distressed, is used of the Lord's sorrow in Gethsemane, Matt. 26 : 37; Mark 14 : 33, A.V., " to be very heavy," R.V., " to be sore troubled;" of Epaphroditus, because the saints at Philippi had received news of his sickness, Phil. 2 : 26, A.V., " was full of heaviness," R.V., " was sore troubled." See TROUBLE, B, No. 12.¶

3076 AG:481C CB:1257B 2. LUPEŌ (λυπέω), to distress, grieve (akin to A, No. 1), is rendered " are in heaviness " in 1 Pet. 1 : 6, A.V. (R.V., " have been put to grief "); here, as frequently, it is in the Passive Voice. See GRIEF, SORROWFUL.

916 AG:133C CB:1238C 3. BAREŌ (βαρέω), always in the Passive Voice in the N.T., is rendered " were heavy " in Matt. 26 : 43; Mark 14 : 40; Luke 9 : 32. See BURDEN.

Note: For " heavy laden," Matt. 11 : 28, see LADE, No. 3.

C. Adjective.

926 AG:134B CB:1238C BARUS (βαρύς), heavy (akin to B, No. 3), is so rendered in Matt. 23 : 4. See GRIEVOUS.

HEDGE

5418 AG:865C CB:1264B PHRAGMOS (φραγμός) denotes any sort of fence, hedge, palings or wall (akin to *phrassō*, to fence in, stop). It is used (*a*) in its literal sense, in Matt. 21 : 33, lit. '(he put) a hedge (around);' Mark 12 : 1; Luke 14 : 23; (*b*) metaphorically, of the " partition " which separated Gentile from Jew, which was broken down by Christ through the efficacy of His expiatory sacrifice, Eph. 2 : 14.¶

HEED (to give, to take)

991 AG:143B CB:1239A 1. BLEPŌ (βλέπω), to look, see, usually implying more especially an intent, earnest contemplation, is rendered " take heed " in Matt. 24 : 4; Mark 4 : 24; 13 : 5, 9, 23, 33; Luke 8 : 18; 21 : 8; 1 Cor. 3 : 10; 8 : 9; 10 : 12; Gal. 5 : 15; Col. 2 : 8 (A.V., " beware "); 4 : 17; Heb. 3 : 12. See BEHOLD, BEWARE, LIE, LOOK, PERCEIVE, REGARD, SEE.

3708 AG:577D CB:1251A 2. HORAŌ (ὁράω), to see, usually expressing the sense of vision, is rendered "take heed" in Matt. 16 : 6 ; 18 : 10, A.V. (R.V., "see") ; Mark 8 : 15 ; Luke 12 : 15 ; Acts 22 : 26 (A.V. only). See Behold, See.

3. PROSECHŌ (προσέχω), lit., to hold to, signifies to turn to, turn 4337
one's attention to ; hence, to give heed ; it is rendered "take heed" in AG:714B CB:1267A
Matt. 6 : 1 ; Luke 17 : 3 ; 21 : 34 ; Acts 5 : 35 ; 20 : 28 ; 2 Pet. 1 : 19 ; to give heed to, in Acts 8 : 6, 10 ; in ver. 11 (A.V., "had regard to") ; 16 : 14 (A.V., "attended unto") ; 1 Tim. 1 : 4 ; 4 : 1, 13 (A.V., "give attendance to") ; Tit. 1 : 14 ; Heb. 2 : 1, lit., 'to give heed more earnestly.' See Attend, Beware, Give, Regard.

4. EPECHŌ (ἐπέχω), lit., to hold upon, then, to direct towards, to 1907
give attention to, is rendered "gave heed," in Acts 3 : 5 ; "take heed," AG:285C CB:—
in 1 Tim. 4 : 16. See Hold (forth), Mark, Stay.

Notes : (1) In Luke 11 : 35, A.V., *skopeō*, to look, is translated "take 4648
heed (that)," R.V., "look (whether)." (2) Nos. 2 and 3 are used together AG:756D CB:1269B
in Matt. 16 : 6 ; Nos. 2 and 1, in that order, in Mark 8 : 15 ; but in Luke 12 : 15 the R.V. rightly follows No. 2 by "keep yourselves from" (*phulassō*, to guard). (3) For the R.V. of Mark 5 : 36, "not heeding," see under Hear, No. 7. (4) In Rom. 11 : 21 the A.V. adds "take heed," because of a variant reading which introduces the clause by a conjunctive phrase signifying "lest."

HEEL

PTERNA (πτέρνα) is found in John 13 : 18, where the Lord quotes 4418
from Ps. 41 : 9 ; the metaphor is that of tripping up an antagonist in AG:727B CB:1267C
wrestling.¶ Cp. the verb in Gen. 27 : 36 ; Jer. 9 : 4 ; Hos. 12 : 3.

HEIFER

DAMALIS (δάμαλις), etymologically one of fit age to be tamed to the 1151
yoke (*damaō*, to tame), occurs in Heb. 9 : 13, with reference to the "red AG:170D CB:1240B
heifer" of Numb. 19.¶

HEIGHT

1. HUPSOS (ὕψος), a summit, top, is translated "height" in Eph. 5311
3 : 18, where it may refer either to "the love of Christ" or to "the fulness AG:850C CB:1252B
of God ;" the two are really inseparable, for they who are filled into the fulness of God thereby enter appreciatively into the love of Christ, which 'surpasseth knowledge ;' in Rev. 21 : 16, of the measurement of the Heavenly Jerusalem. See Estate, High.

2. HUPSŌMA (ὕψωμα), more concrete than No. 1, is used (*a*) of a 5313
height, as a mountain or anything definitely termed a height, Rom. 8 : 39 AG:851C CB:1252B
(metaphorically) ; (*b*) of a high thing lifted up as a barrier or in antagonistic exaltation, 2 Cor. 10 : 5. See High.¶ Cp. *hupsoō*, to exalt.

HEIR

A. Noun.

2818 AG:435B
1. KLĒRONOMOS (κληρονόμος) lit. denotes one who obtains a lot or CB:1255B

portion (*klēros*, a lot, *nemomai*, to possess), especially of an inheritance. The N.T. usage may be analysed as under : " (*a*) the person to whom property is to pass on the death of the owner, Matt. 21 : 38 ; Mark 12 : 7 ; Luke 20 : 14 ; Gal. 4 : 1 ; (*b*) one to whom something has been assigned by God, on possession of which, however, he has not yet entered, as Abraham, Rom. 4 : 13, 14 ; Heb. 6 : 17 ; Christ, Heb. 1 : 2 ; the poor saints, Jas. 2 : 5 ; (*c*) believers, inasmuch as they share in the new order of things to be ushered in at the return of Christ, Rom. 8 : 17 ; Gal. 3 : 29 ; 4 : 7 ; Tit. 3 : 7 ; (*d*) one who receives something other than by merit, as Noah, Heb. 11 : 7."*¶

In the Sept., Judg. 18 : 7 ; 2 Sam. 14 : 7 ; Jer. 8 : 10 ; Mic. 1 : 15.¶

4789 2. SUNKLĒRONOMOS (συγκληρονόμος), a joint-heir, co-inheritor
AG:774A (*sun*, with, and No. 1), " is used of Isaac and Jacob as participants with
CB:1270C Abraham in the promises of God, Heb. 11 : 9 ; of husband and wife who are also united in Christ, 1 Pet. 3 : 7 ; of Gentiles who believe, as participants in the gospel with Jews who believe, Eph. 3 : 6 ; and of all believers as prospective participants with Christ in His glory, as recompense for their participation in His sufferings, Rom. 8 : 17."*¶

B. Verb.

2816 KLĒRONOMEŌ (κληρονομέω), to be an heir to, to inherit (see A, No. 1),
AG:434D is rendered " shall (not) inherit with " in Gal. 4 : 30, R.V., A.V., " shall
CB:1255B (not) be heir with ; " in Heb. 1 : 14, R.V., " shall inherit," A.V., " shall be heirs of." See INHERIT. Cp. *klēroomai*, to be taken as an inheritance, *klēronomia*, an inheritance, *klēros*, a lot, an inheritance.

HELL

1067 1. GEENNA (γεέννα) represents the Hebrew Gê-Hinnom (the valley
AG:153B of Tophet) and a corresponding Aramaic word ; it is found twelve times in
CB:1248A the N.T.,eleven of which are in the Synoptists, in every instance as uttered
(GEH-) by the Lord Himself. He who says to his brother, Thou fool (see under FOOL), will be in danger of " the hell of fire," Matt. 5 : 22 ; it is better to pluck out (a metaphorical description of irrevocable law) an eye that causes its possessor to stumble, than that his " whole body be cast into hell," ver. 29 ; similarly with the hand, ver. 30 ; in Matt. 18 : 8, 9, the admonitions are repeated, with an additional mention of the foot ; here, too, the warning concerns the person himself (for which obviously the " body " stands in chapt. 5) ; in ver. 8, " the eternal fire " is mentioned as the doom, the character of the region standing for the region itself, the two being combined in the phrase " the hell of fire," ver. 9. To the passage in Matt. 18, that in Mark 9 : 43-47, is parallel ; here to the word " hell " are applied the extended descriptions " the unquenchable fire " and " where their worm dieth not and the fire is not quenched."

---

* From Notes on Galatians, by Hogg and Vine, pp. 177, 178.
* ditto, p. 178.

That God, "after He hath killed, hath power to cast into hell," is assigned as a reason why He should be feared with the fear that keeps from evil doing, Luke 12 : 5 ; the parallel passage to this in Matt. 10 : 28 declares, not the casting in, but the doom which follows, namely, the destruction (not the loss of being, but of well-being) of "both soul and body."

In Matt. 23 the Lord denounces the Scribes and Pharisees, who in proselytizing a person "make him two-fold more a son of hell" than themselves (ver. 15), the phrase here being expressive of moral characteristics, and declares the impossibility of their escaping "the judgment of hell," ver. 33. In Jas. 3 : 6 hell is described as the source of the evil done by misuse of the tongue ; here the word stands for the powers of darkness, whose characteristics and destiny are those of hell.¶

For terms descriptive of hell, see e.g., Matt. 13 : 42 ; 25 : 46 ; Phil. 3 : 19 ; 2 Thess. 1 : 9 ; Heb. 10 : 39 ; 2 Pet. 2 : 17 ; Jude 13 ; Rev. 2 : 11 ; 19 : 20 ; 20 : 6, 10, 14 ; 21 : 8.

Notes : (1) For the rendering "hell" as a translation of Hades, HADēS
corresponding to Sheol, wrongly rendered "the grave" and "hell," see 86 AG:16D
HADES. (2) The verb *tartaroō*, translated "cast down to hell" in 2 Pet. CB:1248C
2 : 4, signifies to consign to Tartarus, which is neither Sheol nor Hades TARTAROō 5020
nor Hell, but the place where those angels whose special sin is referred to AG:805D
in that passage are confined "to be reserved unto judgment ;" the CB:—
region is described as "pits of darkness," RV.¶

For HELM (Jas. 3 : 4) see RUDDER

HELMET

PERIKEPHALAIA (περικεφαλαία), from *peri*, around, and *kephalē*, 4030
a head, is used figuratively in Eph. 6 : 17, with reference to salvation, AG:648A
and 1 Thess. 5 : 8, where it is described as "the hope of salvation." The CB:1263B
head is not to be regarded here as standing for the seat of the intellect ; the word is not so used elsewhere in Scripture. In Eph. 6 : 17 salvation is a present experience of the Lord's deliverance of believers as those who are engaged in spiritual conflict ; in 1 Thess. 5 : 8, the hope is that of the Lord's Return, which encourages the believer to resist the spirit of the age in which he lives.¶

HELP, HOLPEN

A. Nouns.

1. ANTILĒPSIS or ANTILĒMPSIS (ἀντίληψις) properly signifies a 484
laying hold of, an exchange (*anti*, in exchange, or, in its local sense, in AG:75A
front, and *lambanō*, to take, lay hold of, so as to support) ; then, a help CB:—
(akin to B, No. 1) ; it is mentioned in 1 Cor. 12 : 28, as one of the ministrations in the local church, by way of rendering assistance, perhaps especially of help ministered to the weak and needy. So Theophylact defines the

injunction in 1 Thess. 5 : 14, " support the weak ; " cp. Acts 20 : 35 ; not official functionaries are in view in the term " helps," but rather the functioning of those who, like the household of Stephanas, devote themselves to minister to the saints. Hort defines the ministration as " anything that would be done for poor or weak or outcast brethren."¶

996 2. BOĒTHEIA (βοήθεια), from *boē*, a shout, and *theō*, to run, denotes
AG:144C CB:— help, succour, Heb. 4 : 16, lit., ' (grace) unto (timely) help ; ' in Acts 27 : 17, where the plural is used, the term is nautical, ' frapping.'¶

1947 3. EPIKOURIA (ἐπικουρία) strictly denotes such aid as is rendered
AG:294D CB:— by an *epikouros*, an ally, an auxiliary ; Paul uses it in his testimony to Agrippa, " having therefore obtained the help that is from God," Acts 26 : 22, R.V.¶

B. Verbs.

482 1. ANTILAMBANŌ (ἀντιλαμβάνω), lit., to take instead of, or in turn
AG:74C CB:— (akin to A, No. 1), is used in the Middle Voice, and rendered " He hath holpen " in Luke 1 : 54 ; " to help," R.V., " to support," A.V., in Acts 20 : 35 ; its other meaning, to partake of, is used of partaking of things, 1 Tim. 6 : 2, " that partake of," for A.V., " partakers of." See PARTAKE, SUPPORT.¶

4815 2. SULLAMBANŌ (συλλαμβάνω), to assist, take part with (*sun*, with,
AG:776D CB:1270B and *lambanō*), is used, in the Middle Voice, of rendering help in what others are doing, Luke 5 : 7, of bringing in a catch of fish ; in Phil. 4 : 3, in an appeal to Synzygus (" yokefellow ") to help Euōdia and Syntychē (ver. 2). See CATCH, CONCEIVE.

(-OMAI) 3. SUNANTILAMBANŌ (συναντιλαμβάνω) signifies to take hold with
4878 AG:784C at the side for assistance (*sun*, with, and No. 1) ; hence, to take a share in,
CB:— help in bearing, to help in general. It is used, in the Middle Voice, in Martha's request to the Lord to bid her sister help her, Luke 10 : 40 ; and of the ministry of the Holy Spirit in helping our infirmities, Rom. 8 : 26.¶ In the Sept., Ex. 18 : 22 ; Num. 11 : 17 ; Ps. 89 : 21.

997 4. BOĒTHEŌ (βοηθέω), to come to the aid of anyone, to succour
AG:144C CB:— (akin to A, No. 2), is used in Matt. 15 : 25 ; Mark 9 : 22, 24 ; Acts 16 : 9 ; 21 : 28 ; 2 Cor. 6 : 2, " did I succour ; " Heb. 2 : 18, " to succour ; " Rev. 12 : 16.¶

4820 5. SUMBALLŌ (συμβάλλω), lit., to throw together (*sun*, with, *ballō*, to
AG:777B CB:— throw), is used in the Middle Voice in Acts 18 : 27, of helping or benefiting believers by discussion or ministry of the Word of God. See CONFER, ENCOUNTER, MAKE (war), MEET, PONDER.

4943 6. SUNUPOURGEŌ (συνυπουργέω) denotes to help together, join in
AG:793D CB:— helping, to serve with anyone as an underworker (*sun*, with, *hupourgeō*, to serve ; *hupo*, under, *ergon*, work) ; it is used in 2 Cor. 1 : 11.¶

4903 7. SUNERGEŌ (συνεργέω), to help in work, to co-operate, be a co-
AG:787C CB:1270C worker, is rendered " that helpeth with " in 1 Cor. 16 : 16. See WORK.

Note : Paristēmi, to place beside (*para*, by, *histēmi*, to cause to stand),

to stand by, be at hand, is used of standing up for help, in Rom. 16 : 2, PARISTēMI
" that ye assist," and 2 Tim. 4 : 17, " stood with." See BRING, COME, 3936 AG:627C
COMMEND, GIVE, PRESENT, PROVE, PROVIDE, SHEW, STAND, YIELD. CB:1262B

HELPER, FELLOW-HELPER

1. BOĒTHOS (βοηθός), an adjective, akin to A, No. 2, and B, No. 4, 998
under HELP, signifying helping, is used as a noun in Heb. 13 : 6, of God AG:144B CB:1239B
as the Helper of His saints.¶

2. SUNERGOS (συνεργός), an adjective, akin to B, No. 7, under 4904
HELP, a fellow-worker, is translated " helper " in the A.V. of Rom. 16 : 3, 9, AG:787D CB:1270C
R.V., " fellow-worker ; " in 2 Cor. 1 : 24, A.V. and R.V., " helpers ; " in
2 Cor. 8 : 23, A.V., " fellow-helper," R.V., " fellow-worker ; " so the
plural in 3 John 8: See COMPANION, LABOURER, etc.

For HEM see BORDER

HEN

ORNIS (ὄρνις), a bird, is used, in the N.T., only of a hen, Matt. 23 : 37 ; 3733
Luke 13 : 34.¶ AG:582A CB:1261B

HENCE

1. ENTHEN (ἔνθεν) is found in the best mss. in Matt. 17 : 20 ; Luke — AG:266A
16 : 26.¶ 1782

2. ENTEUTHEN (ἐντεῦθεν), akin to No. 1, is used (*a*) of place, AG:268C
" hence," or " from hence," Luke 4 : 9 ; 13 : 31 ; John 2 : 16 ; 7 : 3 ; MAKRAN 3112
14 : 31 ; 18 : 36 ; in John 19 : 18, " on either side (one)," lit., ' hence and AG:487C
hence ; ' in Rev. 22 : 2, it is contrasted with ***ekeithen***, thence, R.V., " on CB:1257C META
this side . . . on that " (A.V., " on either side "), lit. ' hence . . . 3326
thence ; ' (*b*) causal, Jas. 4 : 1, " (come they not) hence," i.e., ' owing to.'¶ AG:508C CB:1258B

Notes : (1) For ***makran***, " far hence," in Acts 22 : 21, see FAR. (2) In APARTI
Acts 1 : 5, the phrase " not many days hence " is, lit., ' not after (***meta***) 534
many days.' AG:110B 3. ARTI
737

HENCEFORTH (from, and negatives), HENCEFORWARD. AG:110B CB:1237C

Notes : (1) Positively, " henceforth " stands for the following : LOIPON
(*a*) *ap' arti* (i.e., *apo arti*), lit., ' from now,' e.g., Matt. 26 : 64 ; Luke 22 : 69; 3063
John 13 : 19, R.V., and A.V. marg., " from henceforth " ; Rev. 14 : 13 AG:479D (LOIPOS 3.b.)
(where ***aparti*** is found as one word in the best mss.) ; (*b*) *to loipon*, lit., CB:1257B
(for) the remaining (time), Heb. 10 : 13 ; *tou loipou*, Gal. 6 : 17 ; (*c*) *apo* NUN 3568
tou nun, lit., ' from the now,' e.g., Luke 1 : 48 ; 5 : 10 ; 12 : 52 ; Acts AG:545C
18 : 6 ; 2 Cor. 5 : 16 (1st part) ; (2) negatively, " henceforth . . . not " CB:1260A OUKETI
(or " no more ") translates one or other of the negative adverbs *ouketi* 3765
and ***mēketi***, no longer, e.g., Acts 4 : 17, A.V., and R.V., " henceforth AG:592C MēKETI
(to no man) ; " in the following the R.V. has " no longer " for the A.V., 3371
" henceforth " (with a negative), John 15 : 15 ; Rom. 6 : 6 ; 2 Cor. 5 : 15 ; AG:518C

Eph. 4 : 17; in 2 Cor. 5 : 16 (last part), R.V., "no more;" in Matt. 21 : 19 and Mark 11 : 14, "no (fruit . . .) henceforward;" A.V. in the latter, "hereafter." See HEREAFTER.

For HER and HERSELF see the forms under HE

HERB

3001 1. LACHANON (λάχανον) denotes a garden herb, a vegetable (from
AG:467D CB:1256B *lachainō*, to dig), in contrast to wild plants, Matt. 13 : 32; Mark 4 : 32;
Luke 11 : 42; Rom. 14 : 2.¶

1008 AG:145B 2. BOTANĒ (βοτάνη) denotes grass, fodder, herbs (from *boskō*, to feed :
CB:1239B Eng., botany), Heb. 6 : 7.¶

HERD

34 AG:8B AGELĒ (ἀγέλη), from *agō*, to lead, is used, in the N.T., only of swine,
CB:— Matt. 8 : 30, 31, 32; Mark 5 : 11, 13; Luke 8 : 32, 33.¶

HERE

5602 AG:895B 1. HŌDE (ὧδε), an adverb signifying (*a*) here (of place), e.g., Matt.
CB:— 12 : 6; Mark 9 : 1; used with the neuter plural of the article, Col. 4 : 9, "(all) things (that are done) here," lit., '(all) the (things) here;' in Matt. 24 : 23, *hōde* is used in both parts, hence the R.V., "Lo, here (is the Christ, or) Here;" in Mark 13 : 21 *hōde* is followed by *ekei*, "there." The word is used metaphorically in the sense of in this circumstance, or connection, in 1 Cor. 4 : 2; Rev. 13 : 10, 18; 14 : 12; 17 : 9. See HITHER.

1759 AG:266A 2. ENTHADE (ἐνθάδε) has the same meanings as No. 1; "here"
CB:— in Luke 24 : 41; Acts 16 : 28; 25 : 24. See HITHER (John 4 : 15, 16;
Acts 25 : 17).¶

847 AG:124A 3. AUTOU (αὐτοῦ), the genitive case of *autos*, self, signifies 'just here'
CB:— in Matt. 26 : 36. See THERE, No. 5.

HERE (to be, be present)

3918 AG:624A PAREIMI (πάρειμι), to be by or beside or here (*para*, by, and *eimi*,
CB:1262B to be), is rendered "to have been here" in Acts 24 : 19. See COME, PRESENT.

Note : For *sumpareimi*, to be here present, see PRESENT.

META 3326

HEREAFTER

AG:508C CB:1258B *Notes :* (1) This adverb translates the phrase *meta tauta*, lit., 'after
OUKETI these things,' John 13 : 7; Rev. 1 : 19, and frequently in the Apocalypse,
3765 AG:592C see 4 : 1 (twice); 7 : 9; 9 : 12; 15 : 5; 18 : 1; 19 : 1; 20 : 3. (2) For
CB:— Matt. 26 : 64 and Luke 22 : 69 (A.V., "hereafter") see HENCEFORTH;
MELLō for Mark 11 : 14 see HENCEFORWARD. (3) In John 14 : 30, *ouk eti* is
3195 AG:500D rendered "no more" in the R.V. (A.V., "Hereafter . . . not"). (4) In
CB:1258A 1 Tim. 1 : 16, "hereafter" translates the verb *mellō*, to be about to.

HEREBY

Notes: (1) This translates the phrase *en toutō*, lit., 'in this,' 1 Cor. EN
4:4; 1 John 2:3, 5; 3:16, 19, 24; 4:2, 13; 5:2 (R.V., "hereby," 1722 AG:258B 3.a.
A.V., "by this"). (2) In 1 John 4:6, A.V., *ek toutou*, lit., 'out of this,' CB:1244B
i.e., in consequence of this, is rendered "hereby" (R.V., "by this").¶ HOUTOS 3778
AG:596B 1.b.

HEREIN CB:1251B EK

Note: This translates the phrase *en toutō*, 'in this,' in John 4:37; 1537
9:30; 15:8; Acts 24:16; 2 Cor. 8:10; 1 John 4:9 (A.V., "in this"), AG:234A 3.f. CB:1243B
10, 17.¶ EN 1722

HEREOF AG:258B 3.a. CB:1244B

Notes: (1) This translates the word ***hautē***, this, the feminine of *houtos*, HOUTOS
this, in Matt. 9:26, lit., 'this (fame),' A.V., and R.V. marg. (2) In 3778
Heb. 5:3, A.V., *dia tautēn*, lit., 'by reason of (*dia*) this' (i.e., this infir- AG:596B 1.b. CB:1251B
mity), is rendered "hereof;" the best texts have ***autēn***, R.V., "thereof." DIA 1223
AG:179B B.II.2.

HERESY CB:1241A

HAIRESIS (αἵρεσις) denotes (*a*) a choosing, choice (from ***haireomai***, 139
to choose); then, that which is chosen, and hence, an opinion, especially a AG:23D CB:1249A
self-willed opinion, which is substituted for submission to the power of truth, and leads to division and the formation of sects, Gal. 5:20 (marg., "parties"); such erroneous opinions are frequently the outcome of personal preference or the prospect of advantage; see 2 Pet. 2:1, where "destructive" (R.V.) signifies leading to ruin; some assign even this to (*b*); in the papyri the prevalent meaning is "choice" (Moulton and Milligan, Vocab.); (*b*) a sect; this secondary meaning, resulting from (*a*), is the dominating significance in the N.T., Acts 5:17; 15:5; 24:5, 14; 26:5; 28:22; "heresies" in 1 Cor. 11:19 (see marg.). See SECT.¶

HERETICAL

HAIRETIKOS (αἱρετικός), akin to the above, primarily denotes capable 141
of choosing (***haireomai***); hence, causing division by a party spirit, factious, AG:24A CB:1249A
Tit. 3:10, R.V., "heretical".¶

For HERETOFORE see SIN, C, No. 2

HEREUNTO EIS 1519

Note: This translates the phrase *eis touto*, lit., 'unto this,' in 1 Pet. AG:228A CB:1243A
2:21. HOUTOS 3778

For *HEREWITH* see TRADE, A, No. 2 AG:596B CB:1251B

HERITAGE 2820 AG:435D

KLĒROŌ (κληρόω), primarily, to cast lots or to choose by lot, then, CB:1255B to assign a portion, is used in the Passive Voice in Eph. 1 : 11, "we were made a heritage," R.V. (A.V., "we have obtained an inheritance"). The R.V. is in agreement with such O.T. passages as Deut. 4 : 20, "a people of inheritance;" 9 : 29; 32 : 9; Psa. 16 : 6. The meaning 'were chosen by lot,' as in the Vulgate, and in 1 Sam. 14 : 41, indicating the freedom of election without human will (so Chrysostom and Augustine), is not suited to this passage.¶

HEW, HEW DOWN, HEWN

A. Verbs.

1581 AG:241D CB:1243C 1. EKKOPTŌ (ἐκκόπτω), to cut out or down (*ek*, out of, *koptō*, to cut), is rendered to hew down, of trees, Matt. 3 : 10; 7 : 19 (a similar testimony by John the Baptist and Christ); Luke 3 : 9. See CUT, HINDER.

2998 AG:467B CB:— 2. LATOMEŌ (λατομέω) signifies to hew out stones (from *latomos*, a stone-cutter; *las*, a stone, *temnō*, to cut), and is used of the sepulchre which Joseph of Arimathæa had hewn out of a rock for himself, where the body of the Lord was buried, Matt. 27 : 60; Mark 15 : 46.¶

B. Adjective.

2991 AG:466C CB:— LAXEUTOS (λαξευτός) denotes hewn in stone (*las*, a stone, *xeō*, to scrape; cp. A, No. 2), is used of Christ's tomb, in Luke 23 : 53.¶

HIDE, HID, HIDDEN

A. Verbs.

2928 AG:454B CB:1256A 1. KRUPTŌ (κρύπτω), to cover, conceal, keep secret (Eng., crypt, cryptic, etc.), is used (*a*) in its physical significance, e.g., Matt. 5 : 14; 13 : 44; 25 : 18 (some mss. have No. 2); (*b*) metaphorically, e.g., Matt. 11 : 25 (some mss. have No. 2 here); 13 : 35, R.V., "(things) hidden;" A.V., "(things) which have been kept secret;" Luke 18 : 34; 19 : 42; John 19 : 38, "secretly." See SECRET.

613 AG:93D CB:1237A 2. APOKRUPTŌ (ἀποκρύπτω), to conceal from, to keep secret (*apo*, from, and No. 1), is used metaphorically, in Luke 10 : 21, of truths hidden from the wise and prudent and revealed to babes; 1 Cor. 2 : 7, of God's wisdom; Eph. 3 : 9, of the mystery of the unsearchable riches of Christ, revealed through the gospel; Col. 1 : 26, of the mystery associated with the preceding.¶

1470 AG:216D CB:1245B 3. ENKRUPTŌ (ἐγκρύπτω), to hide in anything (*en*, in, and No. 1), is used in Matt. 13 : 33, of leaven hidden in meal.¶

4032 AG:648B (-UBō) CB:— 4. PERIKRUPTŌ (περικρύπτω) signifies to hide by placing something around, to conceal entirely, to keep hidden (*peri*, around, used intensively, and No. 1), Luke 1 : 24.¶

2572 AG:401A CB:1253B 5. KALUPTŌ (καλύπτω) signifies to cover, conceal, so that no trace of it can be seen (hence somewhat distinct from No. 1); it is not translated to hide in the R.V.; in 2 Cor. 4 : 3 it is rendered "veiled," suitably continuing the subject of 3 : 13–18; in Jas. 5 : 20, "shall hide," A.V. (R.V., "shall cover"). See COVER.

6. PARAKALUPTŌ (παρακαλύπτω), lit., to cover with a veil, A.V., 3871 AG:617D
"hid," in Luke 9 : 45, 'it was veiled from them;' see CONCEAL.¶ CB:—

7. LANTHANŌ (λανθάνω), to escape notice, to be hidden from, is 2990
rendered "(could not) be hid" in Mark 7 : 24, of Christ; "was (not) hid," AG:466B CB:1256C
Luke 8 : 47, of the woman with the issue of blood; "is hidden," Acts 26 : 26, of the facts concerning Christ; the sentence might be rendered 'none of these things has escaped the king's notice.' See FORGET, UNAWARES.

B. Adjectives.

1. KRUPTOS (κρυπτός), akin to A, No. 1, hidden, secret, is translated 2927
"hid" in Matt. 10 : 26; Mark 4 : 22; Luke 8 : 17, R.V., for A.V., AG:454A CB:1256A
"secret;" 12 : 2 (last part); in 1 Cor. 4 : 5, "hidden (things of darkness);" 2 Cor. 4 : 2, "hidden (things of shame);" 1 Pet. 3 : 4, "hidden (man of the heart)." See INWARDLY, SECRET.

2. APOKRUPHOS (ἀπόκρυφος), hidden away from (corresponding to 614
A, No. 2; cp. Eng., apocryphal), is translated, "made (A.V., kept) secret," AG:93D CB:1237A
in Mark 4 : 22; in Luke 8 : 17, R.V., "secret," for A.V., "hid;" in Col. 2 : 3, R.V., "hidden," A.V., "hid." See SECRET.¶

HIGH (from on, most), HIGHLY

A. Adjectives.

1. HUPSĒLOS (ὑψηλός), high, lofty, is used (*a*) naturally, of moun- 5308
tains, Matt. 4 : 8; 17 : 1; Mark 9 : 2; Rev. 21 : 10; of a wall, Rev. AG:849B CB:1252B
21 : 12; (*b*) figuratively, of the arm of God, Acts 13 : 17; of heaven, "on high," plural, lit., 'in high (places),' Heb. 1 : 3; (*c*) metaphorically, Luke 16 : 15, R.V., "exalted" (A.V., "highly esteemed"); Rom. 11 : 20, in the best texts, "high-minded" [lit., 'mind (not) high things']; 12 : 16.¶

2. HUPSISTOS (ὕψιστος), most high, is a superlative degree, the 5310
positive not being in use; it is used of God in Luke 1 : 32, 35, 76; 6 : 35, AG:850B CB:1252B
in each of which the R.V. has "the most High," for A.V., "the highest;" A.V. and R.V. in Mark 5 : 7; Luke 8 : 28; Acts 7 : 48; 16 : 17; Heb. 7 : 1. See HIGHEST (below).

3. MEGAS (μέγας), great, is translated "high" in John 19 : 31, of 3173
the Sabbath Day at the Passover season; here the meaning is virtually AG:497C CB:1258A
equivalent to 'holy.' See GREAT.

Note: In Heb. 10 : 21, the R.V. rightly has "a great (priest)," A.V., "high." For "high places," Eph. 6 : 12, A.V., see HEAVENLY, B, No. 2.

B. Nouns.

1. HUPSOS (ὕψος), height, is used with *ex* (*ek*) from, in the phrase 5311
"on high," Luke 1 : 78; 24 : 49; with *eis*, in or into, Eph. 4 : 8. See AG:850C CB:1252B
ESTATE, HEIGHT, No. 1.

2. HUPSŌMA (ὕψωμα), high thing, 2 Cor. 10 : 5; in Rom. 8 : 39, 5313 AG:851C
"height." See HEIGHT, No. 2.¶ CB:1252B

C. Adverb.

507 ANŌ (ἄνω), above, upward, is used in Phil. 3 : 14, of the " high calling
AG:76D CB:1235C of God in Christ Jesus," the prize of which is set before believers as their
goal, lit., ' calling upward ' (R.V., marg.), a preferable rendering to
' heavenly calling.' See Above.

HIGHER

A. Adverb.

(-ROS) 511 1. ANŌTERON (ἀνώτερον), the neuter of *anōteros*, higher, the com-
AG:77C parative of *anō* (see C, under High), is used as an adverb of place in
CB:— Luke 14 : 10 ; for the meaning " above," in Heb. 10 : 8, see Above.¶

B. Verb.

5242 HUPERECHŌ (ὑπερέχω), lit., to hold over anything, as being superior,
AG:840D CB:1252A is used metaphorically in Rom. 13 : 1, of rulers, as the " higher " powers ;
cp. 1 Pet. 2 : 13, " supreme." See Better, Excellency, Pass, Supreme.

HIGHEST

5310 HUPSISTOS (ὕψιστος) is used in the plural in the phrase " in the
AG:850B CB:1252B highest," i.e., in the highest regions, the abode of God, Matt. 21 : 9 ;
Mark 11 : 10 ; Luke omits the article, Luke 2 : 14 ; 19 : 38 ; for its
use as a title of God, see High, A, No. 2.

For HIGHLY see DISPLEASE, EXALT, EXCEEDING, FAVOUR, THINK

HIGH-MINDED

5187 1. TUPHOŌ (τυφόω) properly means to wrap in smoke (from *tuphos*,
AG:831A CB:— smoke ; metaphorically, for conceit) ; it is used in the Passive Voice,
metaphorically in 1 Tim. 3 : 6, " puffed up," R.V. (A.V., " lifted up with
pride ") ; so 6 : 4, A.V., " proud," and 2 Tim. 3 : 4, A.V., " high-minded."
See Proud, Puff (up).¶ Cp. *tuphomai*, to smoke, Matt. 12 : 20,¶ and
tuphōnikos, tempestuous (with *anemos*, wind, understood), Acts 27 : 14.¶

5309 AG:850A 2. HUPSĒLOPHRONEŌ (ὑψηλοφρονέω), to be highminded, is used
CB:1252B in 1 Tim. 6 : 17.¶

HIGHWAY, HIGHWAYSIDE

3598 HODOS (ὁδός), a way, path, road, is rendered " highways " in
AG:553D CB:1251A Matt. 22 : 10 ; Luke 14 : 23 ; in Mark 10 : 46, R.V., " way side," A.V.,
DIEXODOS " highway side ; " in Matt. 22 : 9, the word is used with *diexodoi* (ways
1327 AG:194A out through), and the phrase is rightly rendered in the R.V., " the
CB:1241C partings of the highways " (i.e., the crossroads), A.V., " the highways."
See Way.

HILL

1. OROS (ὄρος), a hill or mountain, is translated "hill" in Matt. **3735**
5 : 14; Luke 4 : 29; "mountain" in Luke 9 : 37, R.V., A.V., "hill" **AG:582B CB:1261B**
(of the mount of transfiguration) as in ver. 28. See MOUNTAIN.

2. OREINOS (ὀρεινός), an adjective meaning mountainous, hilly, is **3714**
used in the feminine, *oreinē*, as a noun, and rendered "hill country" in **AG:580A CB:1261A**
Luke 1 : 39, 65. See COUNTRY.¶

3. BOUNOS (βουνός), a mound, heap, height, is translated "hill" **1015 AG:146C**
in Luke 3 : 5; "hills" in 23 : 30.¶ **CB:—**

Note: In Acts 17 : 22, A.V., *pagos* is translated "hill." "The **697**
Areopagus," R.V., stands for the Council (not hill) held near by. **AG:105B CB:1261B**

For HIM and HIMSELF see HE

HINDER, HINDRANCE

A. Verbs.

1. ENKOPTŌ (ἐγκόπτω), lit., to cut into (*en*, in, *koptō*, to cut), was **ENKOPTŌ**
used of impeding persons by breaking up the road, or by placing an **1465 AG:216C**
obstacle sharply in the path; hence, metaphorically, of detaining a **CB:1245A**
person unnecessarily, Acts 24 : 4; of hindrances in the way of reaching **ANAKOPTŌ 348**
others, Rom. 15 : 22; or returning to them, 1 Thess. 2 : 18; of hindering **AG:56B**
progress in the Christian life, Gal. 5 : 7 (*anakoptō* in some mss.), where the **CB:— EKKOPTŌ**
significance virtually is 'who broke up the road along which you were **1581**
travelling so well?'; of hindrances to the prayers of husband and wife, **AG:241D CB:1243C**
through low standards of marital conduct, 1 Pet. 3 : 7 (*ekkoptō*, to cut
out, repulse, in some mss.).¶

2. KŌLUŌ (κωλύω), to hinder, forbid, restrain, is translated to **2967**
hinder in Luke 11 : 52; Acts 8 : 36; Rom. 1 : 13, R.V. (A.V., "was let"); **AG:461B CB:1255C**
Heb. 7 : 23, R.V. (A.V., "were not suffered"). See FORBID.

3. DIAKŌLUŌ (διακωλύω), a strengthened form of No. 2, to hinder **1254**
thoroughly, is used in Matt. 3 : 14, of John the Baptist's endeavour to **AG:185C CB:—**
hinder Christ from being baptized, A.V., "forbad," R.V., "would have
hindered," lit., 'was hindering.'¶

B. Noun.

ENKOPĒ (ἐγκοπή), a hindrance, lit., a cutting in, akin to A, No. 1, **1464**
with corresponding significance, is used in 1 Cor. 9 : 12, with *didōmi*, to **AG:216B CB:1245A**
give, R.V., "(that) we may cause (no) hindrance," A.V., "(lest) we should
hinder."¶

For HINDER (part) see STERN

HIRE, HIRED

A. Noun.

MISTHOS (μισθός) denotes (*a*) wages, hire, Matt. 20 : 8; Luke 10 : 7; **3408 AG:523B**
Jas. 5 : 4; in 1 Tim. 5 : 18; 2 Pet. 2 : 13; Jude 11, R.V., "hire" (A.V., **CB:1259A**

"reward"); in 2 Pet. 2:15, R.V., "hire" (A.V., "wages"). See REWARD.

B. Verb.

3409 AG:523D MISTHOŌ (μισθόω), to let out for hire, is used in the Middle Voice,
CB:1259A signifying to hire, to engage the services of anyone by contract, Matt.
20:1, 7.¶

Note: In ver. 9 there is no word for "hired" in the original.

HIRED HOUSE

3410 MISTHŌMA (μίσθωμα), akin to A and B, above, primarily denotes a
AG:523D CB:1259A hire, as in the Sept. of Deut. 23:18; Prov. 19:13; Ezek. 16:31, 34, 41,
etc.; in the N.T., it is used of a hired dwelling, Acts 28:30.¶

HIRED SERVANT, HIRELING

3411 1. MISTHŌTOS (μισθωτός), an adjective denoting hired, is used as a
AG:523D CB:1259A noun, signifying one who is hired, "hired servants," Mark 1:20; "hireling," John 10:12, 13; here, it expresses, not only one who has no real interest in his duty (that may or may not be present in its use in Mark 1:20, and in *misthios*, No. 2), but one who is unfaithful in the discharge of it; that sense attaches always to the word rendered "hireling."¶

3407 2. MISTHIOS (μίσθιος), an adjective, akin to No. 1, and similarly
AG:523A CB:1259A signifying a hired servant, is used in Luke 15:17, 19 (in some texts, ver. 21).¶

HIS, HIS OWN

AUTOS *Note:* These translate (*a*) forms of pronouns under HE, No. 1 (a fre-
846 AG:122C quent use: in 1 Pet. 2:24, "His own self"); the form *autou*, "his,"
CB:1238B becomes emphatic when placed between the article and the noun, e.g.,
HEAUTOU 1 Thess. 2:19; Tit. 3:5; Heb. 2:4; also under HE, No. 3 (in which
1438 AG:211D "his" is emphasized), e.g., John 5:47; 9:28; 1 Cor. 10:28; 2 Cor.
CB:1249B 8:9; 2 Tim. 2:26; Tit. 3:7; 2 Pet. 1:16; (*b*) *heautou*, of himself,
(-OS) his own; the R.V. rightly puts "his own," for the A.V., "his," in Luke
IDIOS 2398 11:21; 14:26; Rom. 4:19; 5:8, "His own (love);" 1 Cor. 7:37;
AG:369C Gal. 6:8; Eph. 5:28, 33; 1 Thess. 2:11, 12; 4:4; in Rev. 10:7
CB:1252C the change has not been made; it should read 'his own servants;'
HIT See (*c*) *idios*, one's own, "his own," in the R.V., in Matt. 22:5; John 5:18;
SMITE 2 Pet. 2:16; in Matt. 25:15, it is rendered "his several;" in John 19:27, "his own home," lit., 'his own things;' in 1 Tim. 6:15, R.V., "its own (times)," referring to the future appearing of Christ; in Heb. 4:10 (end of verse), both A.V. and R.V. have "his," where it should be 'his own;' so in Acts 24:23, for A.V. and R.V., "his;" in 1 Cor. 7:7, R.V., "his own," A.V., "his proper;" (*d*) in Acts 17:28, the genitive case of the definite article, "His (offspring)," lit., 'of the' (i.e., the one referred to, namely, God).

HITHER

1. HŌDE (ὧδε), primarily an adverb of manner, then, of place, (*a*) of HōDE
motion or direction towards a place, e.g., Matt. 8 : 29 ; Mark 11 : 3 ; 5602 AG:895B
Luke 9 : 41 ; John 6 : 25 ; (*b*) of position ; see HERE, PLACE. ENTHADE
2. ENTHADE (ἐνθάδε) has the same meaning as No. 1 ; "hither," 1759 AG:266A
John 4 : 15, 16 ; Acts 17 : 6 ; 25 : 17. See HERE. HEōS
Note : For *deuro,* "come hither," see COME, and HITHERTO, *Note* (2). 2193 AG:334B CB:1250A

HITHERTO

ARTI
Notes : (1) The phrase *heōs arti,* until now, is rendered "hitherto" in 737 AG:110B
John 16 : 24, A.V., and R.V. ; in 5 : 17, R.V., "even until now," which CB:1237C
more definitely expresses the meaning than the A.V., "hitherto ;" the ACHRI(S) 891
rest of the Father and the Son having been broken by man's sin, they AG:128D
were engaged in the accomplishment of their counsels of grace with a CB:1233A DEURO
view to redemption. (2) The phrase *achri tou deuro,* lit., ' until the hither,' 1204
or ' the present,' is used of time in Rom. 1 : 13, "hitherto." (3) In 1 Cor. AG:176C
3 : 2, A.V., *oupō,* not yet, is translated "hitherto . . . not," R.V., "not CB:1241A OUPō
yet." 3768 AG:593C CB:1261B

HOISE UP, HOIST UP

1. AIRŌ (αἴρω), to raise, is used of hoisting up a skiff, or little boat, 142
before undergirding the ship, Acts 27 : 17, R.V., "had hoisted up," for AG:24B CB:1234A
A.V., "had taken up." See AWAY, TAKE.
2. EPAIRŌ (ἐπαίρω), to raise up (*epi,* up, and No. 1), is used of hoisting 1869
up the foresail of a vessel, Acts 27 : 40, R.V., "hoisting up." See EXALT, AG:281D CB:—
LIFT.

HOLD (Noun)

1. TĒRĒSIS (τήρησις), translated "hold" in Acts 4 : 3, A.V., 5084
"prison" in 5 : 18 (R.V., "ward"), signifies (*a*) a watching, guarding ; AG:815C CB:1271B
hence, imprisonment, ward (from *tēreō,* to watch, keep) ; the R.V., has "ward" in both places ; (*b*) a keeping, as of commandments, 1 Cor. 7 : 19. See KEEPING, WARD.¶
2. PHULAKĒ (φυλακή), a guarding or guard (akin to *phulassō,* to 5438
guard or watch), also denotes a prison, a hold, Rev. 18 : 2 (twice), R.V., AG:867D CB:1264C
"hold" in both places, A.V., "cage," in the second (R.V., marg., "prison," in both). See CAGE, IMPRISONMENT, PRISON.

HOLD (down, fast, forth, on, to, up), HELD, HOLDEN, (take) HOLD

1. ECHŌ (ἔχω), to have or hold, is used of mental conception, to 2192
consider, account, e.g., Matt. 21 : 26 ; of stedfast adherence to faith, or AG:331D CB:1242C
the faith, e.g., 1 Tim. 1 : 19 ; 3 : 9 ; 2 Tim. 1 : 13. See HAVE.
2. KATECHŌ (κατέχω), to hold firmly, hold fast (*kata,* down, and 2722
No. 1), is rendered "hold fast" in 1 Cor. 11 : 2, R.V. (A.V., "keep") ; AG:422C CB:1254B
1 Thess. 5 : 21 ; Heb. 3 : 6, 14 (R.V.) ; 10 : 23 ; "hold down," Rom.

1 : 18, R.V., of unrighteous men who restrain the spread of truth by their unrighteousness, or, as R.V. marg., " who hold the truth in (or with) unrighteousness," contradicting their profession by their conduct (cp. 2 : 15, R.V.) ; in Rom. 7 : 6, R.V., " holden," A.V., " held," of the Law as that which had held in bondage those who through faith in Christ were made dead to it as a means of life. See KEEP, MAKE (toward), POSSESS, RESTRAIN, RETAIN, SEIZE, STAY, TAKE.

472 AG:73B 3. ANTECHŌ (ἀντέχω), *anti*, against, or to, and No. 1, signifies in the
CB:— Middle Voice, (*a*) to hold firmly to, cleave to, of holding or cleaving to a person, Matt. 6 : 24 ; Luke 16 : 13 ; of holding to the faithful word, Tit. 1 : 9, R.V., A.V., " holding fast ; " (*b*) to support, 1 Thess. 5 : 14 (the weak). See SUPPORT.¶

4912 AG:789A 4. SUNECHŌ (συνέχω), *sun*, with, intensive, and No. 1, is used of
CB:1270C holding a prisoner, in Luke 22 : 63. See CONSTRAIN, KEEP, PRESS, STOP, STRAIT, STRAITENED, TAKE.

1907 AG:285C 5. EPECHŌ (ἐπέχω) is used in Phil. 2 : 16, of holding forth the word
CB:— of life (*epi*, forth, and No. 1). See (give) HEED, (take) HEED, MARK, STAY.

2902 AG:448C 6. KRATEŌ (κρατέω), to be strong, mighty, to prevail, (1) is most
CB:1256A frequently rendered to lay or take hold on (*a*) literally, e.g., Matt. 12 : 11 ; 14 : 3 ; 18 : 28 and 21 : 46, R.V. (A.V., " laid hands on ") ; 22 : 6, R.V. (A.V., " took ") ; 26 : 55, A.V. (R.V., " took ") ; 28 : 9, R.V., " took hold of " (A.V., " held by ") ; Mark 3 : 21 ; 6 : 17 ; 12 : 12 ; 14 : 51 ; Acts 24 : 6, R.V. (A.V., " took ") ; Rev. 20 : 2 ; (*b*) metaphorically, of laying hold of the hope of the Lord's return, Heb. 6 : 18 ; (2) also signifies to hold or hold fast, i.e., firmly, (*a*), literally, Matt. 26 : 48, A.V. (R.V., " take ") ; Acts 3 : 11 ; Rev. 2 : 1 ; (*b*) metaphorically, of holding fast a tradition or teaching, in an evil sense, Mark 7 : 3, 4, 8 ; Rev. 2 : 14, 15 ; in a good sense, 2 Thess. 2 : 15 ; Rev. 2 : 25 ; 3 : 11 ; of holding Christ, i.e., practically apprehending Him, as the Head of His Church, Col. 2 : 19 ; a confession, Heb. 4 : 14 ; the Name of Christ, i.e., abiding by all that His Name implies, Rev. 2 : 13 ; of restraint, Luke 24 : 16, " (their eyes) were holden ; " of the winds, Rev. 7 : 1 ; of the impossibility of Christ's being holden of death, Acts 2 : 24. See KEEP, RETAIN (of sins), TAKE.

1949 (-OMAI) 7. EPILAMBANŌ (ἐπιλαμβάνω), to lay hold of, to take hold of (*epi*,
AG:295A upon, *lambanō*, to take), with a special purpose, always in the Middle
(-OMAI) CB:1246A Voice, is so translated in Luke 20 : 20, 26, of taking hold of Christ's words ; in 23 : 26 and Acts 21 : 33, R.V., of laying hold of persons ; in 1 Tim. 6 : 12, 19, of laying hold on eternal life, i.e., practically appropriating all the benefits, privileges and responsibilities involved in the possession of it ; in Heb. 2 : 16, R.V. " He taketh hold " (A.V., " took on "), perhaps to be viewed in connection with " deliver " (v. 15) and " succour " (v. 18). See APPREHEND, CATCH, TAKE.

5083 AG:814D CB:1271B 8. TĒREŌ (τηρέω), akin to A, No. 1, under HOLD (Noun), to watch

over, keep, give heed to, observe, is rendered " hold fast " in Rev. 3 : 3 EIMI
A.V. (R.V., " keep "). See KEEP, OBSERVE, RESERVE, WATCH. 1510
9. EIMI (εἰμί), to be, is used in the imperfect tense, with the prepo- AG:222D CB:1243A
sition, *sun*, with, in the idiomatic phrase " held with," in Acts 14 : 4, lit., HISTēMI
' were with.' 2476 AG:381D

Notes : (1) In Rom. 14 : 4, ***histēmi***, to cause to stand, in the Passive CB:1250C
Voice, to be made to stand, is used in both forms, the latter in the first LAMBANō 2983
part, R.V., " he shall be made to stand " (A.V., " he shall be holden AG:464A
up "), the Active Voice in the second part, A.V., and R.V., " to make CB:1256C POIEō
stand." (2) In Matt. 12 : 14, R.V., *lambanō*, to take, is translated " took 4160
(counsel)," A.V., " held (a council)." (3) In Mark 15 : 1, some mss. have AG:680D
the verb *poieō*, to make, rendered " held (a consultation) ; " the most CB:1265C HETOIMAZō
authentic have *hetoimazō*, to prepare, also translated " held." 2090 AG:316A CB:1250B

HOLE

1. PHŌLEOS (φωλεός), a lair, burrow, den or hole, is used of foxes 5454 AG:870B
in Matt. 8 : 20 and Luke 9 : 58.¶ CB:—

2. OPĒ (ὀπή) is translated " holes " in Heb. 11 : 38, R.V., A.V. 3692 AG:574D
" caves." See CAVE, OPENING. CB:—

HOLINESS, HOLY, HOLILY

A. Nouns.

1. HAGIASMOS (ἁγιασμός), translated " holiness " in the A.V. 38 AG:9A CB:1249A
of Rom. 6 : 19, 22 ; 1 Thess. 4 : 7 ; 1 Tim. 2 : 15 ; Heb. 12 : 14, is always rendered " sanctification " in the R.V. It signifies (*a*) separation to God, 1 Cor. 1 : 30 ; 2 Thess. 2 : 13 ; 1 Pet. 1 : 2 ; (*b*) the resultant state, the conduct befitting those so separated, 1 Thess. 4 : 3, 4, 7, and the four other places mentioned above. Sanctification is thus the state predetermined by God for believers, into which in grace He calls them, and in which they begin their Christian course and so pursue it. Hence they are called " saints " (*hagioi*). See SANCTIFICATION.¶

Note : The corresponding verb ***hagiazō*** denotes to set apart to God. 37 AG:8C
See HALLOW, SANCTIFY. CB:1249A

2. HAGIŌSUNĒ (ἁγιωσύνη) denotes the manifestation of the quality 42 AG:10B CB:1249A
of holiness in personal conduct ; (*a*) it is used in Rom. 1 : 4, of the absolute holiness of Christ in the days of His flesh, which distinguished Him from all merely human beings ; this (which is indicated in the phrase " the spirit of holiness ") and (in vindication of it) His resurrection from the dead, marked Him out as (He was " declared to be ") the Son of God ; (*b*) believers are to be " perfecting holiness in the fear of God," 2 Cor. 7 : 1, i.e., bringing holiness to its predestined end, whereby (*c*) they may be found " unblameable in holiness " in the Parousia of Christ, 1 Thess. 3 : 13.¶

" In each place character is in view, perfect in the case of the Lord Jesus, growing toward perfection in the case of the Christian. Here the exercise of love is declared to be the means God uses to develop likeness to Christ in His children. The sentence may be paraphrased thus :—' The Lord enable you more and more to spend your lives in the interests of others, in order that He may so establish you in Christian character now, that you may be vindicated from every charge that might possibly be brought against you at the Judgment-seat of Christ ; ' cp. 1 John 4 : 16, 17."*

41 AG:10B CB:1249A 3. HAGIOTĒS (ἁγιότης), sanctity, the abstract quality of holiness, is used (*a*) of God, Heb. 12 : 10 ; (*b*) of the manifestation of it in the conduct of the Apostle Paul and his fellow-labourers, 2 Cor. 1 : 12 (in the best mss., for *haplotēs*).¶

3742 AG:585D CB:1251B 4. HOSIOTĒS (ὁσιότης) is to be distinguished from No. 3, as denoting that quality of holiness which is manifested in those who have regard equally to grace and truth ; it involves a right relation to God ; it is used in Luke 1 : 75 and Eph. 4 : 24, and in each place is associated with righteousness.¶

EUSEBEIA 2150 AG:326A CB:1247B HIEROPREPeS 2412 AG:372D CB:1250B *Notes :* (1) In Acts 3 : 12, the A.V. translates *eusebeia*, by " holiness," R.V., " godliness," as everywhere, the true meaning of the word. See GODLINESS. (2) In Tit. 2 : 3, A.V., *hieroprepēs*, which denotes suited to a sacred character, reverent, is rendered " as becometh holiness," R.V., " reverent." See REVERENT.¶

B. Adjectives.

40 AG:9B CB:1249A 1. HAGIOS (ἅγιος), akin to A, Nos. 1 and 2, which are from the same root as *hagnos* (found in *hazō*, to venerate), fundamentally signifies separated (among the Greeks, dedicated to the gods), and hence, in Scripture in its moral and spiritual significance, separated from sin and therefore consecrated to God, sacred.

(*a*) It is predicated of God (as the absolutely Holy One, in His purity, majesty and glory) : of the Father, e.g., Luke 1 : 49 ; John 17 : 11 ; 1 Pet. 1 : 15, 16 ; Rev. 4 : 8 ; 6 : 10 ; of the Son, e.g., Luke 1 : 35 ; Acts 3 : 14 ; 4 : 27, 30 ; 1 John 2 : 20 ; of the Spirit, e.g., Matt. 1 : 18 and frequently in all the Gospels, Acts, Romans, 1 and 2 Cor., Eph., 1 Thess. ; also in 2 Tim. 1 : 14 ; Tit. 3 : 5 ; 1 Pet. 1 : 12 ; 2 Pet. 1 : 21 ; Jude 20.

(*b*) It is used of men and things (see below) in so far as they are devoted to God. Indeed the quality, as attributed to God, is often presented in a way which involves Divine demands upon the conduct of believers. These are called *hagioi*, saints, i.e., ' sanctified ' or ' holy ones.'

This sainthood is not an attainment, it is a state into which God in grace calls men ; yet believers are called to sanctify themselves (consistently with their calling, 2 Tim. 1 : 9), cleansing themselves from all defilement, forsaking sin, living a holy manner of life, 1 Pet. 1 : 15 ; 2 Pet. 3 : 11, and experiencing fellowship with God in His holiness. The saints are thus figuratively spoken of as " a holy temple," 1 Cor. 3 : 17 (a local

* From Notes on Thessalonians by Hogg and Vine, pp. 108, 115.

church); Eph. 2 : 21 (the whole Church), cp. 5 : 27; "a holy priesthood," 1 Pet. 2 : 5; "a holy nation," 2 : 9.

"It is evident that *hagios* and its kindred words . . . express something more and higher than *hieros*, sacred, outwardly associated with God; . . . something more than *semnos*, worthy, honourable; something more than *hagnos*, pure, free from defilement. *Hagios* is . . . more comprehensive. . . . It is characteristically godlikeness" (G. B. Stevens, in Hastings' Bib. Dic.).

The adjective is also used of the outer part of the Tabernacle, Heb. 9 : 2 (R.V., "the Holy place"); of the inner sanctuary, 9 : 3, R.V., "the Holy of Holies;" 9 : 24, "a holy place," R.V.; ver. 25 (plural), of the Presence of God in Heaven, where there are not two compartments as in the Tabernacle, all being "the holy place;" 9 : 8, 12 (neuter plural); 10 : 19, "the holy place," R.V. (A.V., "the holiest," neut. plural), see SANCTUARY; of the city of Jerusalem, Rev. 11 : 2; its temple, Acts 6 : 13; of the faith, Jude 20; of the greetings of saints, 1 Cor. 16 : 20; of angels, e.g., Mark 8 : 38; of apostles and prophets, Eph. 3 : 5; of the future heavenly Jerusalem, Rev. 21 : 2, 10; 22 : 19.

2. HOSIOS (ὅσιος), akin to A, No. 4, signifies religiously right, holy, 3741
as opposed to what is unrighteous or polluted. It is commonly associated AG:585C
with righteousness (see A, No. 4). It is used "of God, Rev. 15 : 4; 16 : 5; CB:1251B
and of the body of the Lord Jesus, Acts 2 : 27; 13 : 35, citations from Ps. 16 : 10, Sept.; Heb. 7 : 26; and of certain promises made to David, which could be fulfilled only in the resurrection of the Lord Jesus, Acts 13 : 34. In 1 Tim. 2 : 8 and Tit. 1 : 8, it is used of the character of Christians. . . . In the Sept., *hosios* frequently represents the Hebrew word *chasid*, which varies in meaning between 'holy' and 'gracious,' or 'merciful;' cp. Ps. 16 : 10 with 145 : 17."*

Notes: (1) For Acts 13 : 34, see the R.V. and the A.V. marg.; the R.V. in Rev. 16 : 5, "Thou Holy One," translates the most authentic
mss. (A.V., "and shalt be"). (2) For *hieros* (see No. 1), subserving a 2413
sacred purpose, translated "holy" in 2 Tim. 3 : 15, A.V. (of the Scrip- AG:372D
tures), see SACRED. CB:1250B

C. Adverb.

HOSIŌS (ὁσίως), akin to A, No. 4, and B No. 2, "holily," i.e., pure 3743
from evil conduct, and observant of God's will, is used in 1 Thess. 2 : 10, AG:585D
of the conduct of the Apostle and his fellow-missionaries.¶ CB:—

D. Verb.

HAGIAZŌ (ἁγιάζω), to hallow, sanctify, in the Passive Voice, to be 37
made holy, be sanctified, is translated "let him be made holy" in Rev. AG:8C
22 : 11, the aorist or point tense expressing the definiteness and com- CB:1249A
pleteness of the Divine act; elsewhere it is rendered by the verb to sanctify. See HALLOW, SANCTIFY.

HOLLOW
See VAIN

* From Notes on Thessalonians by Hogg and Vine, p. 64.

For HOLY GHOST see under SPIRIT and HOLY, B, No. 1 (a)

HOLYDAY

1859 AG:280B CB:1250A HEORTĒ (ἑορτή) denotes a feast, festival; it is translated "a holy-day" in the A.V. of Col. 2:16; R.V., "a feast day." See FEAST.

HOME, AT HOME (to be; workers)

A. Noun and Phrases.

3624 AG:560B CB:1260B 1. OIKOS (οἶκος), a house, dwelling, is used (*a*) with the preposition *eis*, unto, with the meaning 'to home,' lit., to a house, in Mark 8:3, R.V., "to (their) home," A.V., "to (their own) houses;" so 8:26, "to (his) home;" Luke 15:6, "home," lit., 'into the house;' (*b*) with the preposition *en*, in, 1 Cor. 11:34, "(let him eat) at home;" 14:35, "(let them ask . . .) at home;" (*c*) with the preposition *kata*, down, Acts 2:46, "(breaking bread) at home," R.V. (A.V., "from house to house"); so in 5:42 (A.V., "in every house").

Notes: (1) In Mark 3:19, the A.V. and R.V. marg., have "home," for the text "to a house;" the latter seems the more probable. See HOUSE. (2) In 1 Tim. 5:4, the phrase *ton idion oikon*, is rendered "at home," of the necessity that children should show piety there; R.V., "towards their own family," the house being put by metonymy for the family.

2398 AG:369C CB:1252C 2. The neuter plural of *idios*, one's own, with the article, preceded by *eis*, unto, lit., 'unto one's own (things),' is translated "home" in Acts 21:6; in John 19:27, "unto his own home" ("home" being italicised).

Note: In John 16:32, this phrase is rendered "to his own" (of the predicted scattering of the disciples), A.V. marg., "his own home;" cp. John 1:11, "His own things," R.V., marg. (i.e., 'His possessions').

3614 AG:557B CB:1260B For *oikia* in Matt. 8:6, A.V., "at home," see HOUSE.

3. In Luke 24:12 the reflexive pronoun ***hauton*** (in some mss. ***heauton***), preceded by *pros*, to, is rendered "to his home," R.V. (lit., 'to himself'), of the departure of Peter from the Lord's tomb; in John 20:10, the same construction is used, in the plural, of Peter and John on the same occasion, and rendered "unto their own home."

B. Adjective.

3626 AG:561C CB:— OIKOURGOS (οἰκουργός), working at home (*oikos*, and a root of *ergon*, work), is used in Tit. 2:5, "workers at home," R.V., in the injunction given to elder women regarding the training of the young women. Some mss. have *oikouros*, watching or keeping the home (*oikos*, and *ouros*, a keeper), A.V., "keepers at home."¶

C. Verb.

1736 AG:263A CB:1244C ENDĒMEŌ (ἐνδημέω), lit., to be among one's people (*en*, in, ***dēmos***, people; *endēmos*, one who is in his own place or land), is used metaphorically of the life on earth of believers, 2 Cor. 5:6, "at home (in the body);" in ver. 8 of the life in Heaven of the spirits of believers, after their decease,

" at home (with the Lord)," R.V. (A.V., " present ") ; in ver. 9, " at
home " (A.V., " present ") refers again to the life on earth. In each
verse the verb is contrasted with *ekdēmeō*, to be away from home, to be
absent ; in ver. 6, " we are absent," i.e., away from home (from the
Lord) ; in ver. 8, " to be absent " (i.e., away from the home of the body) ;
so in ver. 9, " absent." The implication in being " at home with the
Lord " after death is a testimony against the doctrine of the unconscious-
ness of the spirit, when freed from the natural body.¶ **HOMOSEXUAL See ABUSER**

HONEST, HONESTLY, HONESTY

A. Adjectives.

1. KALOS (καλός), good, admirable, becoming, has also the ethical **2570**
meaning of what is fair, right, honourable, of such conduct as deserves **AG:400B CB:1253B**
esteem ; it is translated " honest " [cp. Latin *honestus* (from *honos*,
honour)], which has the same double meaning as " honest " in the A.V.,
namely, regarded with honour, honourable, and bringing honour, becoming ; in Luke 8 : 15 (A.V., and R.V.), " an honest and good (*agathos*)
heart ;" Rom. 12 : 17 ; 2 Cor. 8 : 21 and 13 : 7, R.V., " honourable "
(A.V., " honest "), of things which are regarded with esteem ; in 1 Pet.
2 : 12, of behaviour, R.V., " seemly," A.V., " honest " (i.e., becoming).
See Good.

Note : In Tit. 3 : 14, the R.V. and A.V. margins give what is probably
the accurate meaning, " (to profess) honest occupations " (A.V., " trades ") ;
in the texts " (to maintain) good works."

2. SEMNOS (σεμνός), august, venerable, is rendered " honest " in **4586**
Phil. 4 : 8, A.V. (marg., " venerable "), R.V., " honourable " (marg., **AG:746D CB:1269A**
" reverent "). Matthew Arnold suggests 'nobly serious.' See Grave.

Note : In Acts 6 : 3, " men of honest (R.V., good) report " translates
the Passive Voice of *martureō*, lit., 'having had witness borne.' **3140 AG:492C CB:1257C**

B. Adverbs.

1. KALŌS (καλῶς), corresponding to A, No. 1, is used in Heb. 13 : 18, **2573**
" honestly," i.e., honourably. See Place, C, *Note* (4), Well. **AG:401B CB:1253B**

2. EUSCHĒMONŌS (εὐσχημόνως), becomingly, decently, is rendered **2156**
" honestly " in Rom. 13 : 13, where it is set in contrast with the confusion **AG:327A CB:—**
of Gentile social life, and in 1 Thess. 4 : 12, of the manner of life of
believers as a witness to " them that are without ;" in 1 Cor. 14 : 40,
" decently," in contrast with confusion in the churches. See Decently.¶

C. Noun.

SEMNOTĒS (σεμνότης) denotes gravity, dignified seriousness ; it is **4587**
rendered " honesty " in the A.V. of 1 Tim. 2 : 2, R.V., " gravity." See **AG:747A CB:1269A**
Gravity.

HONEY

MELI (μέλι) occurs with the adjective *agrios*, wild, in Matt. 3 : 4 ; **3192 AG:500C**
Mark 1 : 6 ; in Rev. 10 : 9, 10, as an example of sweetness.¶ As honey **CB:—**

is liable to ferment, it was precluded from offerings to God, Lev. 2 : 11. The liquid honey mentioned in Psa. 19 : 10 and Prov. 16 : 24 is regarded as the best ; a cruse of it was part of the present brought to Ahijah by Jeroboam's wife, 1 Kings 14 : 3.

3193
HONEY-COMB

AG:500D MELISSIOS (μελίσσιος), signifying made by bees from *melissa*, a bee,
CB:— is found, with *kerion*, a comb, in some mss. in Luke 24 : 42.¶

KēRION
2781
AG:430D
HONOUR (Noun and Verb)

CB:—
A. Nouns.

5092
AG:817B 1. TIMĒ (τιμή), primarily a valuing, hence, objectively, (*a*) a price
CB:1272C paid or received, e.g., Matt. 27 : 6, 9 ; Acts 4 : 34 ; 5 : 2, 3 ; 7 : 16, R.V., " price " (A.V., " sum ") ; 19 : 19 ; 1 Cor. 6 : 20 ; 7 : 23 ; (*b*) of the preciousness of Christ unto believers, 1 Pet. 2 : 7, R.V., i.e., the honour and inestimable value of Christ as appropriated by believers, who are joined, as living stones, to Him the Corner-Stone ; (*c*) in the sense of value, of human ordinances, valueless against the indulgence of the flesh, or, perhaps of no value in attempts at asceticism, Col. 2 : 23 (see extended note under INDULGENCE, No. 2) ; (*d*) honour, esteem, (1) used in ascriptions of worship to God, 1 Tim. 1 : 17 ; 6 : 16 ; Rev. 4 : 10 11 ; 5 : 13 ; 7 : 12 ; to Christ, 5 : 12, 13 ; (2) bestowed upon Christ by the Father, Heb. 2 : 9 ; 2 Pet. 1 : 17 ; (3) bestowed upon man, Heb. 2 : 7 ; (4) bestowed upon Aaronic priests, Heb. 5 : 4 ; (5) to be the reward hereafter of " the proof of faith " on the part of tried saints, 1 Pet. 1 : 7, R.V. ; (6) used of the believer who as a vessel is " meet for the Master's use," 2 Tim. 2 : 21 ; (7) to be the reward of patience in well-doing, Rom. 2 : 7, and of working good (a perfect life to which man cannot attain, so as to be justified before God thereby), 2 : 10 ; (8) to be given to all to whom it is due, Rom. 13 : 7 (see 1 Pet. 2 : 17, under B, No. 1) ; (9) as an advantage to be given by believers one to another instead of claiming it for self, Rom. 12 : 10 ; (10) to be given to elders that rule well (" double honour "), 1 Tim. 5 : 17 (here the meaning may be an honorarium) ; (11) to be given by servants to their master, 1 Tim. 6 : 1 ; (12) to be given to wives by husbands, 1 Pet. 3 : 7 ; (13) said of the husband's use of the wife, in contrast to the exercise of the passion of lust, 1 Thess. 4 : 4 (some regard the " vessel " here as the believer's body) ; (14) of that bestowed upon parts of the body, 1 Cor. 12 : 23, 24 ; (15) of that which belongs to the builder of a house in contrast to the house itself, Heb. 3 : 3 ; (16) of that which is not enjoyed by a prophet in his own country, John 4 : 44 ; (17) of that bestowed by the inhabitants of Melita upon Paul and his fellow-passengers, in gratitude for his benefits of healing, Acts 28 : 10 ; (18) of the festive honour to be possessed by nations, and brought into the Holy City, the Heavenly Jerusalem, Rev. 21 : 26 (in some mss., ver. 24) ; (19) of honour bestowed upon things inanimate, a potters' vessel, Rom.

9 : 21 ; 2 Tim. 2 : 20. See PRECIOUSNESS, PRICE, SUM, VALUE.¶

Note: For *entimos*, 'in honour,' see HONOURABLE, No. 2.

2. DOXA (δοξά), glory, is translated " honour " in the A.V. of John 1391
5 : 41, 44 (twice) ; 8 : 54 ; 2 Cor. 6 : 8, and Rev. 19 : 7 ; the R.V. keeps AG:203C CB:1242B
to the word " glory," as the A.V. everywhere else. See GLORY.

B. Verbs.

1. TIMAŌ (τιμάω), to honour (akin to A, No. 1), is used of (*a*) valuing 5091
Christ at a price, Matt. 27 : 9, cp. A, No. 1, (*a*) ; (*b*) honouring a person : AG:817A CB:1272C
(1) the honour done by Christ to the Father, John 8 : 49 ; (2) honour bestowed by the Father upon him who serves Christ, John 12 : 26 ; (3) the duty of all to honour the Son equally with the Father, 5 : 23 ; (4) the duty of children to honour their parents, Matt. 15 : 4 ; 19 : 19 ; Mark 7 : 10 ; 10 : 19 ; Luke 18 : 20 ; Eph. 6 : 2 ; (5) the duty of Christians to honour the king, and all men, 1 Pet. 2 : 17 ; (6) the respect and material assistance to be given to widows " that are widows indeed," 1 Tim. 5 : 3 ; (7) the honour done to Paul and his companions by the inhabitants of Melita, Acts 28 : 10 ; (8) mere lip profession of honour to God, Matt. 15 : 8 ; Mark 7 : 6.¶

2. DOXAZŌ (δοξάζω), to glorify (from *doxa*, A, No. 2), is rendered 1392
" honour " and " honoureth " in the A.V. of John 8 : 54 ; in 1 Cor. AG:204C CB:1242B
12 : 26, however, in reference to the members of the body, both A.V. and R.V. have " honoured " (R.V. marg., " glorified "). Everywhere else it is translated by some form of the verb to glorify, have glory, or be made glorious, except in Rom. 11 : 13, " magnify," A.V. See GLORIFY.

HONOURABLE, WITHOUT HONOUR

1. ENDOXOS (ἔνδοξος) denotes (*a*) held in honour (*en*, in, *doxa*, 1741
honour ; cp. HONOUR, A, No. 2), of high repute, 1 Cor. 4 : 10, A.V. " (are) AG:263B CB:1245A
honourable," R.V., " (have) glory," in contrast to *atimos*, without honour (see No. 6 below). See GLORIOUS, GORGEOUSLY.

2. ENTIMOS (ἔντιμος), lit., in honour (*en*, in, *timē*, honour : see 1784
HONOUR, A, No. 1), is used of the centurion's servant in Luke 7 : 2, AG:268D CB:1245B
" dear " (R.V. marg., " precious . . . or honourable ") ; of self-sacrificing servants of the Lord, said of Epaphroditus, Phil. 2 : 29, R.V. " (hold such) in honour " (A.V., " in reputation ; " marg., " honour such ") ; of Christ, as a precious stone, 1 Pet. 2 : 4, 6 (R.V. marg., " honourable "). Cp. *timios* in 1 : 7, 19 ; see No. 4.¶ ENTIMOTEROS
The comparative degree, *entimoteros*, is used (in the best mss.) of degrees (-MOS)
of honour attached to persons invited to a feast, a marriage feast, Luke 1784
14 : 8, " a more honourable man." See PRECIOUS.¶ AG:268D CB:1245B

3. EUSCHĒMŌN (εὐσχήμων) signifies elegant, comely, of honourable 2158
position, A.V., " honourable," R.V., " of honourable estate," Mark AG:327A CB:—
15 : 43 ; Acts 13 : 50 ; 17 : 12 ; for other renderings in 1 Cor. 7 : 35 and 12 : 24 see COMELY, B.

5093 AG:818A 4. TIMIOS (τίμιος), precious, valuable, honourable (akin to *timē*,
CB:1272C honour ; see No. 2), is used of marriage in Heb. 13 : 4, A.V , as a statement, " (marriage) is honourable (in all)," R.V., as an exhortation, " let (marriage) be had in honour (among all)." See DEAR, PRECIOUS, REPUTATION.

2570 AG:400B 5. KALOS (καλός), good, fair, is translated " honourable " in Rom.
CB:1253B 12 : 17 ; 2 Cor. 8 : 21 ; 13 : 7, R.V. (A.V., " honest "). See GOOD, HONEST.

820 AG:120B 6. ATIMOS (ἄτιμος), without honour (*a*, negative, or privative,
CB:1238B *timē*, honour), despised, is translated " without honour " in Matt. 13 : 57 ;
ATIMOTEROS (-MOS) Mark 6 : 4 ; " dishonour " in 1 Cor. 4 : 10, R.V. (A.V., " despised ").
See DESPISE.¶

820 AG:120B The comparative degree *atimoteros* is used in the best mss. in 1 Cor.
CB:1238B 12 : 23, " less honourable."¶

SEMNOS 4586 AG:746D CB:1269A *Note* : For *semnos*, honourable, Phil. 4 : 8, R.V., see GRAVE.

HOOK

44 AG:10C ANKISTRON (ἄγκιστρον), a fish-hook (from *ankos*, a bend ; Lat.
CB:— *angulus* ; Eng., anchor and angle are akin), is used in Matt. 17 : 27.¶ In the Sept., 2 Kings 19 : 28 ; Job 40 : 20 ; Is. 19 : 8 ; Ezek. 32 : 3 ; Hab. 1 : 15.¶

HOPE (Noun and Verb), HOPE (for)

A. Noun.

1680 AG:252D ELPIS (ἐλπίς), in the N.T., favourable and confident expectation
CB:1244B (contrast the Sept. in Isa. 28 : 19, " an evil hope "). It has to do with the unseen and the future, Rom. 8 : 24, 25. Hope describes (*a*) the happy anticipation of good (the most frequent significance), e.g., Tit. 1 : 2 ; 1 Pet. 1 : 21 ; (*b*) the ground upon which hope is based, Acts 16 : 19 ; Col. 1 : 27, " Christ in you the hope of glory ; " (*c*) the object upon which the hope is fixed, e.g., 1 Tim. 1 : 1.

Various phrases are used with the word hope, in Paul's Epistles and speeches : (1) Acts 23 : 6, " the hope and resurrection of the dead ; " this has been regarded as a hendiadys (one by means of two), i.e., the hope of the resurrection ; but the *kai*, " and," is epexegetic, defining the hope, namely, the resurrection ; (2) Acts 26 : 6, 7, " the hope of the promise (i.e., the fulfilment of the promise) made unto the fathers ; " (3) Gal. 5 : 5, " the hope of righteousness ; " i.e., the believer's complete conformity to God's will, at the Coming of Christ ; (4) Col. 1 : 23, " the hope of the Gospel," i.e., the hope of the fulfilment of all the promises presented in the Gospel ; cp. 1 : 5 ; (5) Rom. 5 : 2, " (the) hope of the glory of God," i.e., as in Tit. 2 : 13, " the blessed hope and appearing of the glory of our great God and Saviour Jesus Christ ; " cp. Col. 1 : 27 ; (6) 1 Thess. 5 : 8, " the hope of salvation," i.e., of the Rapture of believers, to take place at the opening of the Parousia of Christ ; (7) Eph. 1 : 18,

" the hope of His (God's) calling," i.e., the prospect before those who respond to His call in the Gospel; (8) Eph. 4 : 4, " the hope of your calling," the same as (7), but regarded from the point of view of the called; (9) Tit. 1 : 2, and 3 : 7, " the hope of eternal life," i.e., the full manifestation and realization of that life which is already the believer's possession; (10) Acts 28 : 20, " the hope of Israel," i.e., the expectation of the coming of the Messiah. See Notes on Galatians by Hogg and Vine, pp. 248, 249.

In Eph. 1 : 18; 2 : 12 and 4 : 4, the hope is objective. The objective and subjective use of the word need to be distinguished; in Rom. 15 : 4, e.g., the use is subjective.

In the N.T. three adjectives are descriptive of hope: " good," 2 Thess. 2 : 16; " blessed," Tit. 2 : 13; " living," 1 Pet. 1 : 3. To these may be added Heb. 7 : 19, " a better hope," i.e., additional to the commandment, which became disannulled (v. 18), a hope centred in a new Priesthood.

In Rom. 15 : 13 God is spoken of as " the God of hope," i.e., He is the Author, not the Subject, of it. Hope is a factor in salvation, Rom. 8 : 24; it finds its expression in endurance under trial, which is the effect of waiting for the Coming of Christ, 1 Thess. 1 : 3; it is " an anchor of the soul," staying it amidst the storms of this life, Heb. 6 : 18, 19; it is a purifying power, " every one that hath this hope set on Him (Christ) purifieth himself, even as He is pure," 1 John 3 : 3, R.V. (the Apostle John's one mention of hope).

The phrase " fulness of hope," Heb. 6 : 11, R.V., expresses the completeness of its activity in the soul; cp. " fulness of faith," 10 : 22, and " of understanding," Col. 2 : 2 (R.V., marg.).

B. Verbs.

1. ELPIZŌ (ἐλπίζω), to hope, is not infrequently translated in the **1679**
A.V., by the verb to trust; the R.V. adheres to some form of the verb **AG:252C CB:1244B**
to hope, e.g., John 5 : 45, " Moses, on whom ye have set your hope;" 2 Cor. 1 : 10, " on whom we have set our hope;" so in 1 Tim. 4 : 10; 5 : 5; 6 : 17; see also, e.g., Matt. 12 : 21; Luke 24 : 21; Rom. 15 : 12, 24.

The verb is followed by three prepositions: (1) *eis*, rendered " on " in John 5 : 45 (as above); the meaning is really " in " as in 1 Pet. 3 : 5, " who hoped in God;" the hope is thus said to be directed to, and to centre in, a Person; (2) *epi*, " on," Rom. 15 : 12, " On Him shall the Gentiles hope," R.V.; so 1 Tim. 4 : 10; 5 : 5 (in the best mss.); 6 : 17, R.V.; this expresses the ground upon which hope rests; (3) *en*, " in," 1 Cor. 15 : 19, " we have hoped in Christ," R.V., more lit., ' we are (men) that have hoped in Christ,' the preposition expresses that Christ is not simply the ground upon whom, but the sphere and element in whom, the hope is placed. The form of the verb (the perfect participle with the verb to be, lit., ' are having hoped ') stresses the character of those who hope, more than the action ; hope characterizes them, showing what sort of persons they are. See TRUST.

4276 AG:705A CB:1266C 2. PROELPIZŌ (προελπίζω), to hope before (*pro*, before, and No. 1), is found in Eph. 1 : 12.¶

560 AG:83D CB:1236B 3. APELPIZŌ (ἀπελπίζω), lit., to hope from (*apo*, and No. 1) : see DESPAIR.

HORN

2768 AG:429B CB:1255A KERAS (κέρας), a horn, is used in the plural, as the symbol of strength, (*a*) in the Apocalyptic visions ; (1) on the head of the Lamb as symbolic of Christ, Rev. 5 : 6 ; (2) on the heads of beasts as symbolic of national potentates, Rev. 12 : 3 ; 13 : 1, 11 ; 17 : 3, 7, 12, 16 (cp. Dan. 7 : 8 ; 8 : 9 ; Zech. 1 : 18, etc.) ; (3) at the corners of the golden altar, Rev. 9 : 13 (cp. Ex. 30 : 2 ; the horns were of one piece with the altar, as in the case of the brazen altar, 27 : 2, and were emblematic of the efficacy of the ministry connected with it) ; (*b*) metaphorically, in the singular, " a horn of salvation," Luke 1 : 69 (a frequent metaphor in the O.T., e.g., Psa. 18 : 2 ; cp. 1 Sam. 2 : 10 ; Lam. 2 : 3).¶

HORSE

2462 AG:380C CB:1250C HIPPOS (ἵππος), apart from the fifteen occurrences in the Apocalypse, occurs only in Jas. 3 : 3 ; in the Apocalypse horses are seen in visions in 6 : 2, 4, 5, 8 ; 9 : 7, 9, 17 (twice) ; 14 : 20 ; 19 : 11, 14, 19, 21 ; otherwise in 18 : 13 ; 19 : 18.¶

HORSEMEN

2460 AG:380C CB:— 1. HIPPEUS (ἱππεύς), a horseman, is used in the plural in Acts 23 : 23, 32.¶

2461 (-ON) AG:380C CB:1250C 2. HIPPIKOS (ἱππικός), an adjective signifying ' of a horse ' or ' of horsemen,' equestrian, is used as a noun denoting cavalry, in Rev. 9 : 16, " horsemen," numbering " twice ten thousand times ten thousand," R.V.¶

HOSANNA

5614 AG:899A CB:1251B HŌSANNA (ὡσαννά), in the Hebrew, means " save, we pray." The word seems to have become an utterance of praise rather than of prayer, though originally, probably, a cry for help. The people's cry at the Lord's triumphal entry into Jerusalem (Matt. 21 : 9, 15 ; Mark 11 : 9, 10 ; John 12 : 13) was taken from Psa. 118, which was recited at the Feast of Tabernacles (see FEAST) in the great Hallel (Psalms 113 to 118) in responses with the priest, accompanied by the waving of palm and willow branches. " The last day of the feast " was called " the great Hosanna ; " the boughs also were called hosannas.¶

HOSPITALITY

A. Noun.

PHILOXENIA (φιλοξενία), love of strangers (*philos*, loving, *xenos*, a stranger), is used in Rom. 12 : 13 ; Heb. 13 : 2, lit. ' (be not forgetful of) hospitality.' See ENTERTAIN, Note.¶ 5381 AG:860D CB:1264B

B. Adjective.

PHILOXENOS (φιλόξενος), hospitable, occurs in 1 Tim. 3 : 2; Tit. 1 : 8; 1 Pet. 4 : 9.¶ 5382 AG:860D CB:1264B

Note : For *xenodocheō*, 1 Tim. 5 : 10, see STRANGER, B.¶ 3580 AG:548A CB:1273B

HOST (of guests)

1. XENOS (ξένος), in addition to the meaning stranger, mentioned above under A, denotes one or other of the parties bound by ties of hospitality, (*a*) the guest (not in the N.T.), (*b*) the host, Rom. 16 : 23.¶ 3581 AG:548A CB:1273B

2. PANDOCHEUS (πανδοχεύς), lit., one who receives all (*pas*, all, *dechomai*, to receive), denotes an innkeeper, host, Luke 10 : 35.¶ 3830 AG:607D CB:—

HOST (of angels, etc.)

STRATIA (στρατιά), an army, is used of angels, Luke 2 : 13 ; of stars, Acts 7 : 42 ; some mss. have it instead of *strateia*, in 2 Cor. 10 : 4 (" warfare ").¶ Cp. *strateuma*, an army. 4756 AG:770D CB:1270A

HOSTILE See CONTRARY, ENMITY

HOT

ZESTOS (ζεστός), boiling hot (from *zeō*, to boil, be hot, fervent ; Eng., zest), is used, metaphorically, in Rev. 3 : 15, 16.¶ 2200 AG:337B CB:1273C

HOUR

HŌRA (ὥρα), whence Lat., *hora*, Eng., hour, primarily denoted any time or period, expecially a season. In the N.T. it is used to denote (*a*) a part of the day, especially a twelfth part of day or night, an hour, e.g., Matt. 8 : 13 ; Acts 10 : 3, 9 ; 23 : 23 ; Rev. 9 : 15 ; in 1 Cor. 15 : 30, " every hour " stands for ' all the time ;' in some passages it expresses duration, e.g., Matt. 20 : 12 ; 26 : 40 ; Luke 22 : 59 ; inexactly, in such phrases as " for a season," John 5 : 35 ; 2 Cor. 7 : 8 ; " for an hour," Gal. 2 : 5 ; " for a short season," 1 Thess. 2 : 17, R.V. (A.V., " for a short time," lit., ' for the time of an hour ') ; (*b*) a period more or less extended, e.g., 1 John 2 : 18, " it is the last hour," R.V. ; (*c*) a definite point of time, e.g., Matt. 26 : 45, " the hour is at hand ; " Luke 1 : 10 ; 10 : 21 ; 14 : 17, lit., ' at the hour of supper ;' Acts 16 : 18 ; 22 : 13 ; Rev. 3 : 3 ; 11 : 13 ; 14 : 7 ; a point of time when an appointed action is to begin, Rev. 14 : 15 ; in Rom. 13 : 11, " it is high time," lit., ' it is already an hour,' indicating that a point of time has come later than would have been the case had responsibility been realised. In 1 Cor. 4 : 11, it indicates a point of time previous to which certain circumstances have existed. 5610 AG:896A CB:1251A

Notes : (1) In 1 Cor. 8 : 7, A.V., " unto this hour," the phrase in the

2256 AG:348A CB:— original is simply, "until now," as R.V. (2) In Rev. 8 : 1, *hēmiōron*, half an hour (*hēmi*, half, and *hōra*), is used with *hōs*, "about," of a period of silence in Heaven after the opening of the 7th seal, a period corresponding to the time customarily spent in silent worship in the Temple during the burning of incense.¶

HOUSE

A. Nouns.

3624 AG:560B CB:1260B 1. OIKOS (οἶκος) denotes (*a*) a house, a dwelling, e.g., Matt. 9 : 6, 7 ; 11 : 8 ; it is used of the Tabernacle, as the House of God, Matt. 12 : 4, and the Temple similarly, e.g., Matt. 21 : 13 ; Luke 11 : 51, A.V., "temple," R.V., "sanctuary ;" John 2 : 16, 17 ; called by the Lord "your house" in Matt. 23 : 38 and Luke 13 : 35 (some take this as the city of Jerusalem) ; metaphorically of Israel as God's house, Heb. 3 : 2, 5, where "his house" is not Moses', but God's ; of believers, similarly, ver. 6, where Christ is spoken of as "over God's House" (the word "own" is rightly omitted in the R.V.) ; Heb. 10 : 21 ; 1 Pet. 2 : 5 ; 4 : 17 ; of the body, Matt. 12 : 44 ; Luke 11 : 24 ; (*b*) by metonymy, of the members of a household or family, e.g., Luke 10 : 5 ; Acts 7 : 10 ; 11 : 14 ; 1 Tim. 3 : 4, 5, 12 ; 2 Tim. 1 : 16 ; 4 : 19, R.V. (A.V., "household") ; Tit. 1 : 11 (plural) ; of a local church, 1 Tim. 3 : 15 ; of the descendants of Jacob (Israel) and David, e.g., Matt. 10 : 6 ; Luke 1 : 27, 33 ; Acts 2 : 36 ; 7 : 42. See HOME, A, No. 1, *Note* (1), HOUSEHOLD.

3614 AG:557B CB:1260B 2. OIKIA (οἰκία) is akin to No. 1, and used much in the same way ; in Attic law *oikos* denoted the whole estate, *oikia* stood for the dwelling only ; this distinction was largely lost in later Greek. In the N.T. it denotes (*a*) a house, a dwelling, e.g., Matt. 2 : 11 ; 5 : 15 ; 7 : 24–27 ; 2 Tim. 2 : 20 ; 2 John 10 ; it is not used of the Tabernacle or the Temple, as in the case of No. 1 ; (*b*) metaphorically, the heavenly abode, spoken of by the Lord as "My Father's house," John 14 : 2, the eternal dwelling place of believers ; the body as the dwelling place of the soul, 2 Cor. 5 : 1 ; similarly the resurrection body of believers (*id.*) ; property, e.g., Mark 12 : 40 ; by metonymy, the inhabitants of a house, a household, e.g., Matt. 12 : 25 ; John 4 : 53 ; 1 Cor. 16 : 15. See HOUSEHOLD.

B. Adverb.

3832 AG:607D CB:— PANOIKEI (πανοικεί) denotes 'with all the house,' Acts 16 : 34, i.e., the household.¶

3613 AG:557B CB:1260B *Notes :* (1) In 2 Cor. 5 : 2, *oikētērion*, a habitation (see R.V.) is translated "house" in the A.V., of the resurrection body (cp. *oikia* in the preceding verse ; see above). (2) In 1 Tim. 5 : 13, "from house to house" is, lit., 'the houses.' (3) For "in every house," Acts 5 : 42 (cp. 2 : 46), see HOME. (4) For "them which are of the house," 1 Cor. 1 : 11, A.V., see HOUSEHOLD.

For GOODMAN of the HOUSE see HOUSEHOLDER

For MASTER of the HOUSE see HOUSEHOLDER

HOUSEHOLD

A. Nouns.

1. OIKOS (οἶκος) is translated " household " in Acts 16 : 15 ; 1 Cor. 3624
1 : 16 ; in the A.V. of 2 Tim. 4 : 19 (R.V., " house "). See House, No. 1. AG:560B CB:1260B

2. OIKIA (οἰκία) is translated " household " in Phil. 4 : 22. See 3614
House, No. 2. AG:557B CB:1260B

3. OIKETEIA (οἰκετεία) denotes a household of servants, Matt. —
24 : 45 (some mss. have No. 4 here).¶ AG:556D CB:—

4. THERAPEIA (θεραπεία), service, care, attention, is also used in 2322
the collective sense of a household, in Luke 12 : 42 (see No. 3). See AG:358D CB:1272B
Healing.

Notes : (1) In Rom. 16 : 10, 11, the phrase " those of the household " translates a curtailed phrase in the original, lit., ' the (persons) of (*ek*, consisting of) the (members of the household of).' (2) In 1 Cor. 1 : 11, " they which are of the household (A.V., house) of Chloe " is, lit., ' the . . . of Chloe,' the Eng. translation being necessary to express the idiom.

B. Adjectives.

1. OIKEIOS (οἰκεῖος), akin to A, No. 1, primarily signifies of, or 3609
belonging to, a house, hence, of persons, one's household, or kindred, as in AG:556D CB:1260B
1 Tim. 5 : 8, R.V., " household," A.V. " house," marg., " kindred ; " in Eph. 2 : 19, " the household of God " denotes the company of the redeemed ; in Gal. 6 : 10, it is called " the household of the faith," R.V. In these two cases *oikeios* is used in the same sense as those mentioned under *oikos* (A, No. 1).¶

2. OIKIAKOS (οἰκιακός), from A, No. 2, denotes belonging to one's 3615
household, one's own ; it is used in Matt. 10 : 25, 36.¶ AG:557D CB:—

HOUSEHOLDER

A. Noun.

OIKODESPOTĒS (οἰκοδεσπότης), a master of a house (*oikos*, a house, 3617
despotēs, a master), is rendered " master of the house " in Matt. 10 : 25 ; AG:558A CB:1260B
Luke 13 : 25, and 14 : 21, where the context shows that the authority of the householder is stressed ; in Matt. 24 : 43 and Luke 12 : 39, the R.V. " master of the house " (A.V., " goodman of the house ", does not give the exact meaning) ; " householder " is the rendering in both Versions in Matt. 13 : 27, 52 ; 20 : 1 ; 21 : 33 ; so the R.V. in 20 : 11 (for A.V., " goodman of the house ") ; both have " goodman of the house " in Mark 14 : 14 ; in Luke 22 : 11, " goodman." See Goodman.¶

B. Verb.

OIKODESPOTEŌ (οἰκοδεσποτέω), corresponding to A, to rule a house, 3616
is used in 1 Tim. 5 : 14, R.V., " rule the household " (A.V., " guide the AG:558A CB:1260B
house ").¶

HOUSEHOLD-SERVANT

3610 OIKETĒS (οἰκέτης), a house-servant, is translated "household-
AG:557A CB:1260B servants" in Acts 10 : 7; elsewhere, "servant" or "servants," Luke 16 : 13; Rom. 14 : 4; 1 Pet. 2 : 18. See SERVANT.¶

HOUSETOP

1430 DŌMA (δῶμα), akin to *demō*, to build, denotes a housetop. The
AG:210B CB:1242A housetop was flat, and guarded by a low parapet wall (see Deut. 22 : 8). It was much frequented and used for various purposes, e.g., for proclamations, Matt. 10 : 27; Luke 12 : 3; for prayer, Acts 10 : 9. The house was often built round a court, across the top of which cords were fixed from the parapet walls for supporting a covering from the heat. The housetop could be reached by stairs outside the building; the paralytic in Luke 5 : 19 could be let down into the court or area by rolling back the covering. External flight from the housetop in time of danger is enjoined in Matt. 24 : 17; Mark 13 : 15; Luke 17 : 31.¶

HOW and HOWBEIT, see † p. 1

For HOW GREAT see GREAT, Nos. 4, 5, 6

HOWL

3649 OLOLUZŌ (ὀλολύζω), an onomatopœic verb (expressing its significance
AG:564C CB:— in its sound), to cry aloud (the Sept. uses it to translate the Heb. *yālal*,
HUGE e.g., Is. 13 : 6; 15 : 3; Jer. 4 : 8; Ezek. 21 : 12; Lat., *ululare*, and
See GREAT Eng., howl are akin), was primarily used of crying aloud to the gods; it is
HUMAN See FLESH, MAN, SEED found in Jas. 5 : 1 in an exhortation to the godless rich.¶

HUMBLE (Adjective and Verb)

A. Adjectives.

5011 1. TAPEINOS (ταπεινός) primarily signifies low-lying. It is used
AG:804A CB:1271A always in a good sense in the N.T., metaphorically, to denote (*a*) of low degree, brought low, Luke 1 : 52; Rom. 12 : 16, A.V., "(men) of low estate," R.V., "(things that are) lowly" (i.e., of low degree); 2 Cor. 7 : 6, A.V., "cast down," R.V., "lowly;" the preceding context shows that this occurrence belongs to (*a*); Jas. 1 : 9, "of low degree;" (*b*) humble in spirit, Matt. 11 : 29; 2 Cor. 10 : 1, R.V., "lowly," A.V. "base;" Jas. 4 : 6; 1 Pet. 5 : 5. See BASE, CAST, *Note* (7), DEGREE (Note), LOWLY.¶

— AG:804C 2. TAPEINOPHRŌN (ταπεινόφρων), "humble-minded" (*phrēn*, the
CB:1271A mind), 1 Pet. 3 : 8; see COURTEOUS.¶

B. Verb.

5013 TAPEINOŌ (ταπεινόω), akin to A, signifies to make low, (*a*) literally,
AG:804C CB:1271A of mountains and hills, Luke 3 : 5 (Passive Voice); (*b*) metaphorically, in the Active Voice, Matt. 18 : 4; 23 : 12 (2nd part); Luke 14 : 11 (2nd

part); 18:14 (2nd part); 2 Cor. 11:7 ("abasing"); 12:21; Phil. 2:8; in the Passive Voice, Matt. 23:12 (1st part), R.V., "shall be humbled," A.V., "shall be abased;" Luke 14:11 (ditto); 18:14 (ditto); Phil. 4:12, "to be abased;" in the Passive, with Middle Voice sense, Jas. 4:10, "humble yourselves;" 1 Pet. 5:6 (ditto). See ABASE, LOW (to bring).¶

HUMBLENESS OF MIND, HUMILITY

TAPEINOPHROSUNĒ (ταπεινοφροσύνη), lowliness of mind (*tapeinos*, 5012
see A, above, under HUMBLE, and *phrēn*, the mind), is rendered "humility AG:804C CB:1271A
of mind" in Acts 20:19, A.V. (R.V., "lowliness of mind"); in Eph. 4:2, "lowliness;" in Phil. 2:3, "lowliness of mind;" in Col. 2:18, 23, of a false humility; in Col. 3:12, A.V., "humbleness of mind," R.V., "humility;" 1 Pet. 5:5, "humility." See LOWLINESS.¶

HUMILIATION

TAPEINŌSIS (ταπείνωσις), akin to *tapeinos* (see above), is rendered 5014
"low estate" in Luke 1:48; "humiliation," Acts 8:33; Phil. 3:21, AG:805A CB:1271A
R.V. "(the body of our) humiliation," A.V., "(our) vile (body);" Jas. 1:10, where "in that he is made low," is, lit., 'in his humiliation.' See ESTATE, LOW.¶

HUNDRED, HUNDREDFOLD

1. HEKATON (ἑκατόν), an indeclinable numeral, denotes a hundred, 1540
e.g., Matt. 18:12, 28; it also signifies a hundredfold, Matt. 13:8, 23, AG:236D CB:—
and the R.V. in the corresponding passage, Mark 4:8, 20 (for A.V., "hundred"), signifying the complete productiveness of sown seed. In the passage in Mark the phrase is, lit., 'in thirty and in sixty and in a hundred.' In Mark 6:40 it is used with the preposition *kata*, in the phrase "by hundreds." It is followed by other numerals in John 21:11; Acts 1:15; Rev. 7:4; 14:1, 3; 21:17.

2. HEKATONTAPLASIŌN (ἑκατονταπλασίων), an adjective, denotes 1542
a hundredfold, Mark 10:30; Luke 8:8; the best mss. have it in Matt. AG:237A CB:—
19:29 for *pollaplasiōn*, many times more. See the R.V. margin.¶

For multiples of a hundred, see under the numerals TWO, THREE, etc. For "a hundred years," see YEARS.

HUNGER (Noun and Verb), HUNGERED, HUNGRY

A. Noun.

LIMOS (λιμός) has the meanings famine and hunger; hunger in 3042
Luke 15:17; 2 Cor. 11:27; in Rev. 6:8, R.V. "famine" (A.V., AG:475A
"hunger"). See FAMINE. CB:1257A 3983

B. Verb. AG:640A

PEINAŌ (πεινάω), to hunger, be hungry, hungered, is used (*a*) literally, CB:1263A

HURL See CAST, RAIL
HURRY See QUICKLY

e.g., Matt. 4 : 2 ; 12 : 1 ; 21 : 18 ; Rom. 12 : 20 ; 1 Cor. 11 : 21, 34 ; Phil. 4 : 12 ; Rev. 7 : 16 ; Christ identifies Himself with His saints in speaking of Himself as suffering in their sufferings in this and other respects, Matt. 25 : 35, 42 ; (*b*) metaphorically, Matt. 5 : 6 ; Luke 6 : 21, 25 ; John 6 : 35.

C. Adjective.

4316 AG:718A CB:— PROSPEINOS (πρόσπεινος) signifies hungry (*pros*, intensive, *peina*, hunger), Acts 10 : 10, A.V., " very hungry," R.V., " hungry."¶

HURT (Noun and Verb), HURTFUL

A. Noun.

5196 AG:832A CB:1251B HUBRIS (ὕβρις) is rendered " hurt " in Acts 27 : 10, A.V. only. See HARM.

B. Verbs.

91 AG:17C CB:1233A 1. ADIKEŌ (ἀδικέω) signifies, intransitively, to do wrong, do hurt, act unjustly (*a*, negative, and *dikē*, justice), transitively, to wrong, hurt or injure a person. It is translated to hurt in the following : (*a*), intransitively, Rev. 9 : 19 ; (*b*) transitively, Luke 10 : 19 ; Rev. 2 : 11 (Passive) ; 6 : 6 ; 7 : 2, 3 ; 9 : 4, 10 ; 11 : 5. See INJURE, OFFENDER, UNJUST, UNRIGHTEOUSNESS, WRONG, WRONG-DOER.

984 AG:142B CB:1239A 2. BLAPTŌ (βλάπτω) signifies to injure, mar, do damage to, Mark 16 : 18, " shall (in no wise) hurt (them)" ; Luke 4 : 35, " having done (him no) hurt," R.V. *Adikeō* stresses the unrighteousness of the act, *blaptō* stresses the injury done.¶

2559 AG:398B CB:1253B 3. KAKOŌ (κακόω), to do evil to anyone : see HARM.

C. Adjective.

983 AG:142B CB:— BLABEROS (βλαβερός), akin to B, No. 2, signifies hurtful, 1 Tim. 6 : 9, said of lusts.¶ In the Sept., Prov. 10 : 26.¶

HUSBAND

A. Noun.

435 AG:66C CB:1235C ANĒR (ἀνήρ) denotes, in general, a man, an adult male (in contrast to *anthrōpos*, which generically denotes a human being, male or female) ; it is used of man in various relations, the context deciding the meaning ; it signifies a husband, e.g., Matt. 1 : 16, 19 ; Mark 10 : 12 ; Luke 2 : 36 ; 16 : 18 ; John 4 : 16, 17, 18 ; Rom. 7 : 23. See MAN.

B. Adjectives.

5362 AG:858C CB:1264A 1. PHILANDROS (φίλανδρος), primarily, loving man, signifies ' loving a husband,' Tit. 2 : 4, in instruction to young wives to love their husbands, lit., ' (to be) lovers of their husbands.'¶ The word occurs frequently in epitaphs.

5220 AG:837C CB:— 2. HUPANDROS (ὕπανδρος), lit., ' under (i.e. subject to) a man,' married, and therefore, according to Roman law under the legal authority of the husband, occurs in Rom. 7 : 2, " that hath a husband."¶

HUSBANDMAN

GEŌRGOS (*γεωργός*), from *gē*, land, ground, and ***ergō*** (or ***erdō***), to do 1092
(Eng., George), denotes (*a*) a husbandman, a tiller of the ground, 2 Tim. AG:157B
2 : 6 ; Jas. 5 : 7 ; (*b*) a vine-dresser, Matt. 21 : 33–35, 38, 40, 41 ; Mark CB:—
12 : 1, 2, 7, 9 ; Luke 20 : 9, 10, 14, 16 ; John 15 : 1, where Christ speaks
of the Father as the Husbandman, Himself as the Vine, His disciples as
the branches, the object being to bear much fruit, life in Christ producing
the fruit of the Spirit, i.e., character and ways in conformity to Christ.¶

HUSBANDRY

GEŌRGION (*γεώργιον*), akin to the above, denotes tillage, cultivation, 1091
husbandry, 1 Cor. 3 : 9, where the local church is described under this AG:157B
metaphor (A.V., marg., " tillage," R.V., marg., " tilled land "), suggestive CB:—
of the diligent toil of the Apostle and his fellow-missionaries, both in the
ministry of the gospel, and the care of the church at Corinth ; suggestive,
too, of the effects in spiritual fruitfulness.¶ Cp. ***geōrgeomai***, to till the
ground, Heb. 6 : 7.¶

HUSKS

KERATION (*κεράτιον*), a little horn (a diminutive of ***keras***, a horn ; 2769
see HORN), is used in the plural in Luke 15 : 16, of carob-pods, given to AG:429B
swine, and translated " husks."¶ CB:—

HYMN (Noun and Verb)

A. Noun.

HUMNOS (*ὕμνος*) denotes a song of praise addressed to God (Eng., 5215
hymn), Eph. 5 : 19 ; Col. 3 : 16, in each of which the punctuation should AG:836B
probably be changed ; in the former " speaking to one another " goes CB:1251C
with the end of ver. 18, and should be followed by a semi-colon ; similarly
in Col. 3 : 16, the first part of the verse should end with the words " ad- PSALMOS
monishing one another," where a semi-colon should be placed.¶ 5568

Note : The *psalmos* denoted that which had a musical accompaniment ; AG:891B
the *ōdē* (Eng., ode) was the generic term for a song ; hence the accom- CB:1267C ŌDE
panying adjective " spiritual." 5603 AG:895C

B. Verb.

CB:1260B

HUMNEŌ (*ὑμνέω*), akin to A, is used (*a*) transitively, Matt. 26 : 30 ; 5214
Mark 14 : 26, where the hymn was that part of the Hallel consisting of AG:836B
Psalms 113–118 ; (*b*) intransitively, where the verb itself is rendered to CB:1251C
sing praises or praise, Acts 16 : 25 ; Heb. 2 : 12. The Psalms are called,
in general, " hymns," by Philo ; Josephus calls them " songs and hymns."¶

HYPOCRISY

HUPOKRISIS (*ὑπόκρισις*) primarily denotes a reply, an answer 5272
(akin to ***hupokrinomai***, to answer) ; then, play-acting, as the actors spoke AG:845A
in dialogue ; hence, pretence, hypocrisy ; it is translated " hypocrisy " CB:1252B

in Matt. 23 : 28 ; Mark 12 : 15 ; Luke 12 : 1 ; 1 Tim. 4 : 2 ; the plural in
505 1 Pet. 2 : 1. For Gal. 2 : 13 and *anupokritos*, "without hypocrisy," in
AG:76D CB:— Jas. 3 : 17, see DISSIMULATION.¶

HYPOCRITE

5273 AG:845B HUPOKRITĒS (ὑποκριτής), corresponding to the above, primarily
CB:1252B denotes one who answers ; then, a stage-actor ; it was a custom for Greek and Roman actors to speak in large masks with mechanical devices for augmenting the force of the voice ; hence the word became used metaphorically of a dissembler, a hypocrite. It is found only in the Synoptists, and always used by the Lord, fifteen times in Matthew ; elsewhere, Mark 7 : 6 ; Luke 6 : 42 ; 11 : 44 (in some mss.) ; 12 : 56 ; 13 : 15.

HYSSOP

5301 AG:849A HUSSŌPOS (ὕσσωπος), a bunch of which was used in ritual sprinklings,
CB:— is found in Heb. 9 : 19 ; in John 19 : 29 the reference is apparently to a branch or rod of hyssop, upon which a sponge was put and offered to the Lord on the Cross. The suggestion has been made that the word in the original may have been *hussos*, a javelin ; there seems to be no valid reason for the supposition.¶

I

I

EGŌ (ἐγώ) is the nominative case of the first personal pronoun. The 1473
pronoun, "I," however, generally forms a part of the verb itself in Greek; AG:217A CB:1242C
thus *luō* itself means "I loose," the pronoun being incorporated in the
verb form. Where the pronoun *egō* is added to the verb, it is almost invariably, if not entirely, emphatic. The emphasis may not be so apparent in some instances, as e.g., Matt. 10 : 16, but even here it may be taken that something more of stress is present than if the pronoun were omitted. By far the greater number of instances are found in the Gospel of John, and there in the utterances of the Lord concerning Himself, e.g., 4 : 14, 26, 32, 38; 5 : 34, 36, 43, 45; 6 : 35, 40, 41, 48, 51 (twice), 63, 70; instances in the Epistles are Rom. 7 : 9, 14, 17, 20 (twice), 24, 25; there are more in that chapter than in any other outside the Gospel of John.

In other cases of the pronoun than the nominative, the pronoun is usually more necessary to the meaning, apart from any stress.

For *k'agō* (i.e., *kai egō*), see EVEN, *Note* (6).

IDLE

ARGOS (ἀργός) denotes inactive, idle, unfruitful, barren (*a*, negative, 692
and *ergon*, work; cp. the verb *katargeō*, to reduce to inactivity: see AG:104C CB:1237C
ABOLISH); it is used (*a*) literally, Matt. 20 : 3, 6; 1 Tim. 5 : 13 (twice); KATARGEŌ
Tit. 1 : 12, R.V., "idle (gluttons);" 2 Pet. 1 : 8, R.V., "idle," A.V., 2673
"barren;" (*b*) metaphorically in the sense of ineffective, worthless, as of AG:417B CB:1254B
a word, Matt. 12 : 36; of faith unaccompanied by works, Jas. 2 : 20 (some mss. have *nekra*, dead).¶

For IDLE TALES (Luke 24 : 11, R.V., "idle talk") see TALK

IDOL

EIDŌLON (εἴδωλον), primarily a phantom or likeness (from *eidos*, an 1497
appearance, lit., that which is seen), or an idea, fancy, denotes in the AG:221C CB:1243A
N.T. (*a*) an idol, an image to represent a false god, Acts 7 : 41; 1 Cor. 12 : 2; Rev. 9 : 20; (*b*) the false god worshipped in an image, Acts 15 : 20; Rom. 2 : 22; 1 Cor. 8 : 4, 7; 10 : 19; 2 Cor. 6 : 16; 1 Thess. 1 : 9; 1 John 5 : 21.¶

"The corresponding Heb. word denotes 'vanity,' Jer. 14 : 22; 18 : 15; 'thing of nought,' Lev. 19 : 4, marg., cp. Eph. 4 : 17. Hence what represented a deity to the Gentiles, was to Paul a 'vain thing,' Acts 14 : 15 ; 'nothing in the world,' 1 Cor. 8 : 4 ; 10 : 19. Jeremiah calls the idol a 'scarecrow' (' pillar in a garden,' 10 : 5, marg.), and Isaiah, 44 : 9–20, etc., and Habakkuk, 2 : 18, 19 and the Psalmist, 115 : 4–8, etc., are all equally scathing. It is important to notice, however, that in each case the people of God are addressed. When he speaks to idolaters, Paul, knowing that no man is won by ridicule, adopts a different line, Acts 14 : 15–18 ; 17 : 16, 21–31."*

IDOLS (full of)

2712 AG:421A CB:1254B KATEIDŌLOS (*κατείδωλος*), an adjective denoting "full of idols" (*kata*, throughout, and *eidōlon*), is said of Athens in Acts 17 : 16, R.V., and A.V., marg. (A.V., "wholly given to idolatry").¶

IDOLS (offered to, sacrificed to)

1494 AG:221B (-OS) CB:1243A 1. EIDŌLOTHUTOS (*εἰδωλόθυτος*) is an adjective signifying sacrificed to idols (*eidōlon*, as above, and *thuō*, to sacrifice), Acts 15 : 29 ; 21 : 25 ; 1 Cor. 8 : 1, 4, 7, 10 ; 10 : 19 (in all these the R.V. substitutes "sacrificed" for the A.V.) ; Rev. 2 : 14, 20 (in these the R.V. and A.V. both have "sacrificed"). Some inferior mss. have this adjective in 1 Cor. 10 : 28 ; see No. 2. The flesh of the victims, after sacrifice, was eaten or sold.¶

— AG:372B CB:1250C 2. HIEROTHUTOS (*ἱερόθυτος*), "offered in sacrifice" (*hieros*, sacred, and *thuō*, to sacrifice), is found in the best mss. in 1 Cor. 10 : 28 (see No. 1).¶

IDOL'S TEMPLE

1493 (-LEION) AG:221B (-LEION) CB:1243A EIDŌLION (or *eidōleion*) (*εἰδώλιον*), an idol's temple, is mentioned in 1 Cor. 8 : 10 ; feasting in the temple usually followed the sacrifice.¶

IDOLATER

1496 AG:221C CB:1243A EIDŌLOLATRĒS (*εἰδωλολάτρης*), an idolater (from *eidōlon*, and *latris*, a hireling), is found in 1 Cor. 5 : 10, 11 ; 6 : 9 ; 10 : 7 ; the warning is to believers against turning away from God to idolatry, whether "openly or secretly, consciously or unconsciously" (Cremer) ; Eph. 5 : 5 ; Rev. 21 : 8 ; 22 : 15.¶

IDOLATRY

1495 AG:221C CB:1243A EIDŌLOLATRIA (or -EIA) (*εἰδωλολατρία*), whence Eng., idolatry, (from *eidōlon*, and *latreia*, service), is found in 1 Cor. 10 : 14 ; Gal. 5 : 20 ; Col. 3 : 5 ; and, in the plural, in 1 Pet. 4 : 3.¶

Heathen sacrifices were sacrificed to demons, 1 Cor. 10 : 19 ; there was a dire reality in the cup and table of demons and in the involved communion with demons. In Rom. 1 : 22–25, idolatry, the sin of the mind against God (Eph. 2 : 3), and immorality, sins of the flesh, are associated,

---

* From Notes on Thessalonians, pp. 44, 45, by Hogg and Vine.

and are traced to lack of the acknowledgment of God and of gratitude to Him. An idolater is a slave to the depraved ideas his idols represent, Gal. 4 : 8, 9 ; and thereby, to divers lusts, Tit. 3 : 3 (see Notes on Thess. by Hogg and Vine, p. 44).

For IDOLATRY (wholly given to) see IDOLS (full of)

IF : See † p. 1

IGNORANCE, IGNORANT, IGNORANTLY

A. Nouns.

1. AGNOIA (ἄγνοια), lit., want of knowledge or perception (akin to 52
agnoeō, to be ignorant), denotes ignorance on the part of the Jews regarding AG:11D CB:1233B
Christ, Acts 3 : 17 ; of Gentiles in regard to God, 17 : 30 ; Eph. 4 : 18 (here including the idea of wilful blindness : see Rom. 1 : 28, not the ignorance which mitigates guilt) ; 1 Pet. 1 : 14, of the former unregenerate condition of those who became believers (R.V., " in *the time of* your ignorance ").¶

2. AGNŌSIA (ἀγνωσία) denotes ignorance as directly opposed to 56
gnōsis, which signifies knowledge as a result of observation and experience AG:12B CB:1233C
(*a*, negative, *ginōskō*, to know ; cp. Eng., agnostic) ; 1 Cor. 15 : 34 (" no knowledge ") ; 1 Pet. 2 : 15. In both these passages reprehensible ignorance is suggested. See KNOWLEDGE.¶

3. AGNOĒMA (ἀγνόημα), a sin of ignorance, occurs in Heb. 9 : 7, 51
" errors " (R.V. marg., " ignorances ").¶ For the corresponding verb in AG:11C CB:1233B
Heb. 5 : 2 see B, No. 1. What is especially in view in these passages is unwitting error. For Israel a sacrifice was appointed, greater in proportion to the culpability of the guilty, greater, for instance, for a priest or ruler than for a private person. Sins of ignorance, being sins, must be expiated. A believer guilty of a sin of ignorance needs the efficacy of the expiatory sacrifice of Christ, and finds " grace to help." Yet, as the conscience of the believer receives enlightenment, what formerly may have been done in ignorance becomes a sin against the light and demands a special confession, to receive forgiveness, 1 John 1 : 8, 9.¶

4. IDIŌTĒS (ἰδιώτης), primarily a private person in contrast to a State 2399
official, hence, a person without professional knowledge, unskilled, AG:370C CB:1252C
uneducated, unlearned, is translated " unlearned " in 1 Cor. 14 : 16, 23, 24, of those who have no knowledge of the facts relating to the testimony borne in and by a local church ; " rude " in 2 Cor. 11 : 6, of the Apostle's mode of speech in the estimation of the Corinthians ; " ignorant men," in Acts 4 : 13, of the speech of the Apostle Peter and John in the estimation of the rulers, elders and scribes in Jerusalem.

While *agrammatoi* (" unlearned ") may refer to their being AGRAMMATOS 62
unacquainted with Rabbinical learning, *idiōtai* would signify ' laymen,' AG:13B
in contrast with the religious officials. See RUDE, UNLEARNED.¶ CB:1233C

B. Verbs.

50 AG:11B CB:1233B 1. AGNOEŌ (ἀγνοέω), signifies (*a*) to be ignorant, not to know, either intransitively, 1 Cor. 14 : 38 (in the 2nd occurrence in this verse, the R.V. text translates the Active Voice, the margin the Passive) ; 1 Tim. 1 : 13, lit., 'being ignorant (I did it) ;' Heb. 5 : 2, "ignorant ;" or transitively, 2 Pet. 2 : 12, A.V., "understand not," R.V., "are ignorant (of) ;" Acts 13 : 27, "knew (Him) not ;" 17 : 23, R.V., "(what ye worship) in ignorance," for A.V., "(whom ye) ignorantly (worship)," lit., '(what) not knowing (ye worship) ;' also rendered by the verb to be ignorant that, or to be ignorant of, Rom. 1 : 13 ; 10 : 3 ; 11 : 25 ; 1 Cor. 10 : 1 ; 12 : 1 ; 2 Cor. 1 : 8 ; 2 : 11 ; 1 Thess 4 : 13 ; to know not, Rom. 2 : 4 ; 6 : 3 ; 7 : 1 ; to be unknown (Passive Voice), 2 Cor. 6 : 9 ; Gal. 1 : 22 ; (*b*) not to understand, Mark 9 : 32 ; Luke 9 : 45. See KNOW, UNDERSTAND.¶

2990 AG:466B CB:1256C 2. LANTHANŌ (λανθάνω) ; for 2 Pet. 3 : 5, 8, A.V., see FORGET.

Note : For adjectives see UNLEARNED.

ILL

2556 AG:397D CB:1253B KAKOS (κακός), bad, is used in the neuter as a noun in Rom. 13 : 10, and translated "ill." See BAD.

5337 AG:854C CB:1264A *Note :* For *phaulos*, John 5 : 29, R.V., see EVIL, A, No. 3.

For ILLUMINATED (Heb. 10 : 32) see ENLIGHTEN

IMAGE

1504 AG:222B CB:1243A 1. EIKŌN (εἰκών) denotes an image ; the word involves the two ideas of representation and manifestation. "The idea of perfection does not lie in the word itself, but must be sought from the context" (Lightfoot) ; the following instances clearly show any distinction between the imperfect and the perfect likeness.

ILLEGITIMATE See BASTARD, FORNICATION

The word is used (1) of an image or a coin (not a mere likeness), Matt. 22 : 20 ; Mark 12 : 16 ; Luke 20 : 24 ; so of a statue or similar representation (more than a resemblance), Rom. 1 : 23 ; Rev. 13 : 14, 15 (thrice) ; 14 : 9, 11 ; 15 : 2 ; 16 : 2 ; 19 : 20 ; 20 : 4 ; of the descendants of Adam as bearing his image, 1 Cor. 15 : 49, each a representation derived from the prototype ; (2) of subjects relative to things spiritual, Heb. 10 : 1, negatively of the Law as having "a shadow of the good things to come, not the very image of the things," i.e., not the essential and substantial form of them ; the contrast has been likened to the difference between a statue and the shadow cast by it ; (3) of the relations between God the Father, Christ, and man, (*a*) of man as he was created as being a visible representation of God, 1 Cor. 11 : 7, a being corresponding to the Original ; the condition of man as a fallen creature has not entirely effaced the image ; he is still suitable to bear responsibility, he still has Godlike qualities, such as love of goodness and beauty, none of which are found in a mere animal ; in the Fall man ceased to be a perfect vehicle for the

representation of God; God's grace in Christ will yet accomplish more than what Adam lost; (*b*) of regenerate persons, in being moral representations of what God is, Col. 3:10; cp. Eph. 4:24; (c) of believers, in their glorified state, not merely as resembling Christ but representing Him, Rom. 8:29; 1 Cor. 15:49; here the perfection is the work of Divine grace; believers are yet to represent, not something like Him, but what He is in Himself, both in His spiritual body and in His moral character; (*d*) of Christ in relation to God, 2 Cor. 4:4, "the image of God," i.e., essentially and absolutely the perfect expression and representation of the Archetype, God the Father; in Col. 1:15, "the image of the invisible God" gives the additional thought suggested by the word "invisible," that Christ is the visible representation and manifestation of God to created beings; the likeness expressed in this manifestation is involved in the essential relations in the Godhead, and is therefore unique and perfect;
"he that hath seen Me hath seen the Father," John 14:9. "The **HOMOIōMA**
epithet 'invisible' . . . must not be confined to the apprehension of the **3667 AG:567C**
bodily senses, but will include the cognisance of the inward eye also" **CB:1251A**
(Lightfoot).¶ **EIDOS 1491**

As to synonymous words, *homoiōma*, likeness, stresses the resemblance **AG:221B**
to an archetype, though the resemblance may not be derived, whereas **CB:1243A SKIA**
eikōn is a derived likeness (see LIKENESS); *eidos*, a shape, form, is an **4639**
appearance, "not necessarily based on reality" (see FORM); *skia*, is **AG:755D CB:1269A**
"a shadowed resemblance" (see SHADOW); *morphē* is "the form, as indi- **MORPHē**
cative of the inner being" (Abbott-Smith); see FORM. For *charaktēr*, **3444 AG:528B**
see No. 2. **CB:1259B**

2. CHARAKTĒR (χαρακτήρ) denotes, firstly, a tool for graving (from **5481**
charassō, to cut into, to engross; cp. Eng., character, characteristic); **AG:876B CB:1239C**
then, a stamp or impress, as on a coin or a seal, in which case the seal or die which makes an impression bears the image produced by it, and, *vice versa*, all the features of the image correspond respectively with those of the instrument producing it. In the N.T. it is used metaphorically in Heb. 1:3, of the Son of God as "the very image (marg., 'the impress') of His substance," R.V. The phrase expresses the fact that the Son "is both personally distinct from, and yet literally equal to, Him of whose essence He is the adequate imprint" (Liddon). The Son of God is not merely his image (His *charaktēr*), He is the image or impress of His substance, or essence. It is the fact of complete similarity which this word stresses in comparison with those mentioned at the end of No. 1.¶ In the Sept., Lev. 13:28, 'the mark (of the inflammation).'¶

"In John 1:1–3, Col. 1:15–17, and Heb. 1:2, 3, the special function of creating and upholding the universe is ascribed to Christ under His titles of Word, Image, and Son, respectively. The kind of Creatorship so predicated of Him is not that of a mere instrument or artificer in the formation of the world, but that of One 'by whom, in whom, and for whom ' all things are made, and through whom they subsist. This implies the assertion of His true and absolute Godhood" (Laidlaw, in Hastings' Bib. Dic.).

5480
AG:876A
CB:1239B
Note : The similar word *charagma*, a mark (see GRAVEN and MARK), has the narrower meaning of the thing impressed, without denoting the special characteristic of that which produces it, e.g., Rev. 13 : 16, 17. In Acts 17 : 29 the meaning is not " graven (*charagma*) by art," but 'an engraved work of art.'

IMAGINATION

3053
AG:476D
CB:1257A
1. LOGISMOS (λογισμός), a reasoning, a thought (akin to *logizomai*, to count, reckon), is translated " thoughts " in Rom. 2 : 15, suggestive of evil intent, not of mere reasonings ; " imaginations " in 2 Cor. 10 : 5 (R.V., marg., " reasonings," in each place). The word suggests the contemplation of actions as a result of the verdict of conscience. See THOUGHT.¶

1261
AG:186A
CB:1241B
2. DIALOGISMOS (διαλογισμός), *dia*, and No. 1, is rendered " imaginations " in Rom. 1 : 21, carrying with it the idea of evil purposes, R.V., " reasonings " ; it is most frequently translated " thoughts." See DISPUTE.

1271
AG:187A
CB:1241B
3. DIANOIA (διάνοια), strictly, a thinking over, denotes the faculty of thinking ; then, of knowing ; hence, the understanding, and in general, the mind, and so, the faculty of moral reflection ; it is rendered " imagination " in Luke 1 : 51, " the imagination of their heart " signifying their thoughts and ideas. See MIND, UNDERSTANDING.

IMAGINE

3191
AG:500B
CB:—
MELETAŌ (μελετάω) signifies to care for (*meletē*, care) ; then, to attend to, " be diligent in," 1 Tim. 4 : 15, R.V., i.e., to practise as the result of devising or planning ; thirdly, to ponder, " imagine," Acts 4 : 25, R.V., marg., " meditate." Some inferior mss. have it in Mark 13 : 11. See DILIGENT, MEDITATE.¶

IMITATE, IMITATOR

A. Verb.

3401
AG:521D
CB:1259A
MIMEOMAI (μιμέομαι), a mimic, an actor (Eng., mime, etc.), is always translated to imitate in the R.V., for A.V., to follow, (*a*) of imitating the conduct of missionaries, 2 Thess. 3 : 7, 9 ; the faith of spiritual guides, Heb. 13 : 7 ; (*b*) that which is good, 3 John 11. The verb is always used in exhortations, and always in the continuous tense, suggesting a constant habit or practice. See FOLLOW.

B. Nouns.

3402
AG:522A
CB:1259A
1 MIMĒTĒS (μιμητής), akin to A, an imitator, so the R.V. for A.V., " follower," is always used in a good sense in the N.T. In 1 Cor. 4 : 16 ; 11 : 1 ; Eph. 5 : 1 ; Heb. 6 : 12, it is used in exhortations, accompanied

by the verb *ginomai*, to be, become, and in the continuous tense (see A) except in Heb. 6 : 12, where the aorist or momentary tense indicates a decisive act with permanent results ; in 1 Thess. 1 : 6 ; 2 : 14, the accompanying verb is in the aorist tense, referring to the definite act of conversion in the past. These instances, coupled with the continuous tenses referred to, teach that what we became at conversion we must diligently continue to be thereafter. See FOLLOW, *Note* (4).¶

2. SUMMIMĒTĒS (συμμιμητής) denotes a fellow-imitator (*sun*, with, **4831**
and No. 1), Phil. 3 : 17, R.V., " imitators together " (A.V., " followers to- **AG:778C CB:1270B**
gether "). See FOLLOW, *Note* (4).¶

IMMEDIATELY

1. PARACHRĒMA (παραχρῆμα), lit., with the matter (or business) **3916**
itself (*para*, with, *chrēma*, a business, or event), and so, immediately, **AG:623D CB:—**
Matt. 21 : 19 (A.V., " presently "), 20 ; Luke 1 : 64 ; 4 : 39 ; 5 : 25 ;
8 : 44, 47, 55 ; 13 : 13 ; 18 : 43 ; 19 : 11 ; 22 : 60 ; Acts 3 : 7 ; 5 : 10 ; **EUTHUS**
12 : 23 ; 13 : 11 ; 16 : 26, 33 ; it is thus used by Luke only, save for the **2117**
two instances in Matthew. See FORTHWITH. It is also rendered " pre- **AG:321A CB:1247B**
sently," " soon," " straightway."¶ **EUTHEōS**

2. EUTHUS (εὐθύς) : see FORTHWITH. **2112**

3. EUTHEŌS (εὐθέως) : ditto. **AG:320B CB:1247B**

4. EXAUTĒS (ἐξαυτῆς) : ditto. **EXAUTēS 1824 AG:273D CB:—**

IMMORTAL, IMMORTALITY

ATHANASIA (ἀθανασία), lit., deathlessness (*a*, negative, *thanatos*, **110**
death), is rendered " immortality " in 1 Cor. 15 : 53, 54, of the glorified **AG:20C CB:1238A**
body of the believer ; 1 Tim. 6 : 16, of the nature of God. Moulton and Milligan (Vocab.) show that in early times the word had the wide connotation of freedom from death ; they also quote Ramsay (*Luke the Physician*, p. 273), with reference to the use of the word in sepulchral epitaphs. In a papyrus writing of the sixth century, " a petitioner says that he will send up ' unceasing (*athanatous*) ' hymns to the Lord Christ for the life of the man with whom he is pleading." In the N.T., however, *athanasia* expresses more than deathlessness, it suggests the quality of the life enjoyed, as is clear from 2 Cor. 5 : 4 ; for the believer what is mortal is to be " swallowed up of life."¶

Note : The adjective *aphthartos*, translated " immortal " in 1 Tim. **APHTHARTOS 862**
1 : 17, A.V., does not bear that significance, it means ' incorruptible.' **AG:125B**
So with the noun *aphtharsia*, incorruption, translated " immortality," **CB:1236C**
in the A.V. of Rom. 2 : 7 and 2 Tim. 1 : 10. See CORRUPT, B, No. 3, and **APHTHARSIA 861**
C, No. 2. **AG:125B CB:1236C**

IMMUTABLE, IMMUTABILITY

AMETATHETOS (ἀμετάθετος), an adjective signifying immutable **276**
(*a*, negative, *metatithēmi*, to change), Heb. 6 : 18, where the " two im- **AG:45B CB:1234C**
mutable things " are the promise and the oath. In ver. 17 the word is **(-TON)**

used in the neuter with the article, as a noun, denoting "the immutability," with reference to God's counsel. Examples from the papyri show that the word was used as a technical term in connection with wills, "The connotation adds considerably to the force of Heb. 6 : 17 (and foll.)" (Moulton and Milligan).¶

IMPART

4323 AG:711D CB:— 1. PROSANATITHĒMI (προσανατίθημι) is used in the Middle Voice in the N.T., in Gal. 1 : 16, "conferred," or 'had recourse to,' and 2 : 6, R.V., "imparted." See CONFER.¶

3330 AG:510D CB:1258B 2. METADIDŌMI (μεταδίδωμι) : see GIVE, No. 4.

IMPEDIMENT

3424 AG:525D CB:1259A MOGILALOS (μογιλάλος) denotes speaking with difficulty (*mogis*, hardly, *laleō*, to talk), stammering, Mark 7 : 32 ; some mss. have *moggilalos*, thick-voiced (from *moggos*, with a hoarse, hollow voice).¶ In the Sept., Isa. 35 : 6 "(the tongue) of stammerers."¶

IMPENITENT

279 AG:45C CB:1234C AMETANOĒTOS (ἀμετανόητος), lit., without change of mind (*a*, negative, *metanoeō*, to change one's mind, *meta*, signifying change, *nous*, the mind), is used in Rom. 2 : 5, "impenitent" (or 'unrepentant').¶ Moulton and Milligan show from the papyri writings that the word is also used "in a passive sense, 'not affected by change of mind,' like *ametamelētos* in Rom. 11 : 29," "without repentance."

IMPERISHABLE See CORRUPT

IMPLACABLE

786 AG:117B CB:— ASPONDOS (ἄσπονδος) lit. denotes without a libation (*a*, negative, *spondē*, a libation), i.e., without a truce, as a libation accompanied the making of treaties and compacts ; then, one who cannot be persuaded to enter into a covenant, "implacable," 2 Tim. 3 : 3 (A.V., "truce-breakers"). Some mss. have this word in Rom. 1 : 31.¶

Note : Trench (Syn., § lii) contrasts *aspondos* with *asunthetos ;* see Note under COVENANT-BREAKERS. *Aspondos* may signify untrue to one's promise, *asunthetos* not abiding by one's covenant, treacherous.

For IMPLEAD see ACCUSE, B, No. 2

IMPLANTED

1721 AG:258A CB:1244B EMPHUTOS (ἔμφυτος), implanted, or rooted (from *emphuō*, to implant), is used in Jas. 1 : 21, R.V., "implanted," for A.V., "engrafted," of the word of God, "as the 'rooted word,' i.e., a word whose property it is to root itself like a seed in the heart. "The A.V. seems to identify it with *emphuteuton*, which however would be out of place here, since the word is sown, not grafted, in the heart" (Mayor).¶

IMPORTUNITY

ANAIDIA (or ANAIDEIA) (ἀναιδία) denotes shamelessness, impor- 335
tunity (*a*, negative, *n*, euphonic, and *aidōs*, shame, modesty), and is used AG:54C CB:—
in the Lord's illustration concerning the need of earnestness and perseverance in prayer, Luke 11 : 8. If shameless persistence can obtain a boon from a neighbour, then certainly earnest prayer will receive our Father's answer.¶

IMPORTANT See CHIEF, GREAT, WEIGHTIER

IMPOSED

EPIKEIMAI (ἐπίκειμαι) denotes to be placed on, to lie on, (*a*) literally, 1945
as of the stone on the sepulchre of Lazarus, John 11 : 38 ; of the fish on AG:294C CB:—
the fire of coals, 21 : 9 ; (*b*) figuratively, of a tempest (to press upon), Acts 27 : 20 ; of a necessity laid upon the Apostle Paul, 1 Cor. 9 : 16 ; of the pressure of the multitude upon Christ to hear Him, Luke 5 : 1, " pressed upon ; " of the insistence of the chief priests, rulers and people that Christ should be crucified, Luke 23 : 23, " were instant ; " of carnal ordinances " imposed " under the Law until a time of reformation, brought in through the High-Priesthood of Christ, Heb. 9 : 10. See INSTANT, LIE, PRESS.¶

IMPOSSIBLE

A. Adjectives.

1. ADUNATOS (ἀδύνατος), from *a*, negative, and *dunatos*, able, 102
strong, is used (*a*) of persons, Acts 14 : 8, " impotent ; " figuratively, AG:19A CB:1233A
Rom. 15 : 1, " weak ; " (*b*) of things, " impossible," Matt. 19 : 26 ; Mark 10 : 27 ; Luke 18 : 27 ; Heb. 6 : 4, 18 ; 10 : 4 ; 11 : 6 ; in Rom. 8 : 3, " for what the Law could not do," is, more lit., ' the inability of the law ; ' the meaning may be either ' the weakness of the Law,' or ' that which was impossible for the Law ; ' the latter is perhaps preferable ; literalism is ruled out here, but the sense is that the Law could neither justify nor impart life.¶

2. ANENDEKTOS (ἀνένδεκτος) signifies inadmissible (*a*, negative, 418
n, euphonic, and *endechomai*, to admit, allow), Luke 17 : 1, of occasions AG:65A CB:—
of stumbling, where the meaning is ' it cannot be but that they will come.'¶

B. Verb.

ADUNATEŌ (ἀδυνατέω) signifies to be impossible (corresponding to 101
A, No. 1), unable ; in the N.T. it is used only of things, Matt. 17 : 20, AG:19A CB:—
" (nothing) shall be impossible (unto you) ; " Luke 1 : 37, A.V. " (with God nothing) shall be impossible ; " R.V., " (no word from God—a different construction in the best mss.) shall be void of power ; " *rhēma* may mean either " word " or " thing " (i.e., fact).¶ In the Sept. the verb is always used of things and signifies either to be impossible or to be impotent, e.g., Gen. 18 : 14 ; Lev. 25 : 35, " he fail ; " Deut. 17 : 8 ; Job 4 : 4, " feeble ; " 42 : 2 ; Dan. 4 : 6 ; Zech. 8 : 6.

IMPOSTORS

1114 GOĒS (γόης) primarily denotes a wailer (*goaō*, to wail); hence, from
AG:164D the howl in which spells were chanted, a wizard, sorcerer, enchanter,
CB:1248C and hence, a juggler, cheat, impostor, rendered "impostors" in 2 Tim. 3:13, R.V. (A.V., "seducers"); possibly the false teachers referred to practised magical arts; cp. ver. 8.

IMPOTENT

A. Adjectives.

102
AG:19A
CB:1233A 1. ADUNATOS (ἀδύνατος): see IMPOSSIBLE, A, No. 1.
772 2. ASTHENĒS (ἀσθενής), without strength (*a*, negative, *sthenos*,
AG:115C
CB:1238A strength), is translated "impotent" in Acts 4:9. See FEEBLE, SICK, WEAK.

B. Verb.

770 ASTHENEŌ (ἀσθενέω), to be without strength (akin to A, No. 2),
AG:115B
CB:1238A is translated "impotent folk" in John 5:3, A.V.; cp. ver. 7 (the present participle, lit., 'being impotent'). See DISEASED, SICK, WEAK.

IMPRISON, IMPRISONMENT

A. Verb.

5439
AG:868A PHULAKIZŌ (φυλακίζω), to imprison, akin to *phulax*, a guard, a
CB:1264C keeper, and *phulassō*, to guard, and B, below, is used in Acts 22:19.¶

B. Noun.

5438
AG:867D PHULAKĒ (φυλακή), besides its other meanings, denotes imprison-
CB:1264C ment, in 2 Cor. 6:5 (plural) and Heb. 11:36. See CAGE.

IMPULSE

3730 HORMĒ (ὁρμή) denotes (*a*) an impulse or violent motion, as of the
AG:581D
CB:1251B steersman of a vessel, Jas. 3:4, R.V., "impulse" (A.V. omits); (*b*) an
IMPURE assault, onset, Acts 14:5. See ASSAULT.¶

IMPURE See COMMON, UNCLEAN

IMPUTE

3049 1. LOGIZOMAI (λογίζομαι), to reckon, take into account, or, meta-
AG:475D
CB:1257A phorically, to put down to a person's account, is never rendered in the R.V. by the verb to impute. In the following, where the A.V. has that rendering, the R.V. uses the verb to reckon, which is far more suitable; Rom. 4:6, 8, 11, 22, 23, 24; 2 Cor. 5:19; Jas. 2:23. See ACCOUNT, and especially, in the above respect, RECKON.

1677
AG:252B 2. ELLOGAŌ, or -EŌ (ἐλλογάω) (the *-ao* termination is the one
CB:1244B found in the *Koinē*, the language covering the N.T. period), denotes to charge to one's account, to lay to one's charge, and is translated "imputed" in Rom. 5:13, of sin as not being "imputed when there is no law." This principle is there applied to the fact that between Adam's transgression and the giving of the Law at Sinai, sin, though it was in the world, did not partake of the character of transgression; for there was no law.

The law of conscience existed, but that is not in view in the passage, which deals with the fact of external commandments given by God. In Philm. 18 the verb is rendered " put (that) to (mine) account." See ACCOUNT.¶

IN: See † p. 1

INASMUCH AS

1. KATHO (καθό), lit., according to what (*kata*, according to, and *ho*, KATHO
the neuter of the relative pronoun), is translated " inasmuch as " in 1 Pet. 2526 AG:390D
4:13, A.V. (R.V., " insomuch as "); in Rom. 8:26, " as (we ought);" CB:—
in 2 Cor. 8:12, R.V., " according as " (A.V., " according to that "). See EPI 1909
INSOMUCH.¶ AG:285D

2. EPH'HOSON (ἐφ'ὅσον), lit., upon how much (*epi*, upon, *hosos*, CB:1245C HOSOS
how much), is translated " inasmuch as " in Matt. 25:40, 45; Rom. 3745
11:13.¶ AG:586B CB:1251B

3. KATHOTI (καθότι): see ACCORDING AS, No. 1. KATHOTI

4. KATH' HOSON (καθ' ὅσον), *kata*, according to, and *hosos*, how 2530
much, is translated " inasmuch as " in Heb. 3:3, A.V. (R.V., " by so AG:391B CB:—
much as "); 7:20; 9:27, R.V. (A.V., " as "). KATA

Note: In Phil. 1:7, the phrase " inasmuch as " translates the present 2596 AG:405C
participle of the verb *eimi*, to be, lit., '(ye) being (all partakers).' CB:1253C

INCENSE (burn)

A. Noun.

THUMIAMA (θυμίαμα) denotes fragrant stuff for burning, incense 2368
(from *thuō*, to offer in sacrifice), Luke 1:10, 11; in the plural, Rev. 5:8 AG:365A CB:1272C
and 18:13, R.V. (A.V., " odours "); 8:3, 4, signifying frankincense here. In connection with the Tabernacle, the incense was to be prepared from stacte, onycha, and galbanum, with pure frankincense, an equal weight of each; imitation for private use was forbidden, Ex. 30:34–38. See ODOUR.¶ Cp. *thumiatērion*, a censer, Heb. 9:4, and *libanos*, frankincense, Rev. 18:13; see FRANKINCENSE.¶

B. Verb.

THUMIAŌ (θυμιάω), to burn incense (see A), is found in Luke 1:9.¶ 2370 AG:365B CB:1272C

INCLOSE

SUNKLEIŌ (συγκλείω), to shut together, shut in on all sides (*sun*, 4788
with, *kleiō*, to shut), is used of a catch of fish, Luke 5:6; metaphorically AG:774A CB:1270C
in Rom. 11:32, of God's dealings with Jew and Gentile, in that He has " shut up (A.V., concluded) all unto disobedience, that He might have mercy upon all." There is no intimation in this of universal salvation. The meaning, from the context, is that God has ordered that all should be convicted of disobedience without escape by human merit, that He might display His mercy, and has offered the Gospel without national distinction, and that when Israel is restored, He will, in the resulting Millennium, show

His mercy to all nations. The word "all" with reference to Israel, is to be viewed in the light of ver. 26, and, in reference to the Gentiles, in the light of verses 12–25; in Gal. 3 : 22, 23 ("the Scripture hath shut up all things under sin"), the Apostle shows that, by the impossibility of being justified by keeping the Law, all, Jew and Gentile, are under sin, so that righteousness might be reckoned to all who believe. See CONCLUDE, SHUT.¶

INCONTINENCY, INCONTINENT

A. Noun.

192
AG:33A
CB:1234B
AKRASIA (ἀκρασία) denotes want of power (*a*, negative, *kratos*, power); hence, want of self-control, incontinency, 1 Cor. 7 : 5; in Matt. 23 : 25, "excess." See EXCESS.¶

B. Adjective.

193
AG:33A
CB:1234B
AKRATĒS (ἀκρατής) denotes powerless, impotent; in a moral sense, unrestrained, "without self-control," 2 Tim. 3 : 3, R.V. (A.V., "incontinent"). See SELF-CONTROL.¶

For INCORRUPTIBLE and INCORRUPTION, see under CORRUPT

For the noun INCREASE, see GROW, No. 1, Note

837
AG:121C
CB:1238B

INCREASE (Verb)

1. AUXANŌ (αὐξάνω): see GROW, No. 1.

4052
AG:650C
CB:1263C
2. PERISSEUŌ (περισσεύω), to be over and above, to abound, is translated "increased" in Acts 16 : 5, of churches; "increase" in the A.V. of 1 Thess. 4 : 10 (R.V., "abound"). See ABOUND, under ABUNDANCE, B, No. 1.

4121
AG:667B
CB:1265B
3. PLEONAZŌ (πλεονάζω), to make to abound, is translated "make (you) to increase" in 1 Thess. 3 : 12, with No. 2. See ABUNDANCE, B, No. 3.

4298
AG:707D
CB:1266C
4. PROKOPTŌ (προκόπτω) is translated by the verb to increase in Luke 2 : 52 and in the A.V. of 2 Tim. 2 : 16 (R.V., "will proceed further"). See ADVANCE, PROCEED.

4369
AG:718D
CB:1267B
5. PROSTITHĒMI (προστίθημι), to put to, add to, is translated "increase" in Luke 17 : 5. See ADD, No. 2.

Note: For "increased in strength" see STRENGTH.

INCREDIBLE

571
AG:85D
CB:1236C
APISTOS (ἄπιστος) is once rendered "incredible," Acts 26 : 8, of the doctrine of resurrection; elsewhere it is used of persons, with the meaning unbelieving. See BELIEF, C, *Note* (3).

INDEBTED (to be)

3784
AG:598D
CB:1261A
OPHEILŌ (ὀφείλω), to owe, to be a debtor, is translated "is indebted" in Luke 11 : 4. Luke does not draw a parallel between our forgiving and God's; he speaks of God's forgiving sins, of our forgiving debts, moral

debts, probably not excluding material debts. Matthew speaks of our sins as *opheilēmata*, debts, and uses parallel terms. Ellicott and others suggest that Luke used a term more adapted to the minds of Gentile readers. The inspired language provides us with both, as intended by the Lord.

INDEED

1. MEN (μέν), a conjunctive particle (originally a form of *mēn*, verily, **3303**
truly, found in Heb. 6 : 14.¶), usually related to an adversative con- **AG:502C CB:1258B**
junction or particle, like *de*, in the following clause, which is placed in
opposition to it. Frequently it is untranslateable; sometimes it is rendered **MēN 3375**
"indeed," e.g., Matt. 3 : 11; 13 : 32; 17 : 11, R.V. (A.V., "truly"); **AG:518D**
20 : 23; 26 : 41; (some mss. have it in Mark 1 : 8); Mark 9 : 12, R.V. **CB:1258B**
(A.V., "verily").

2. ALĒTHĒS (ἀληθής), true, is rendered "indeed" in John 6 : 55 **227 AG:36D**
(twice), see R.V. marg.; some mss. have No. 3 here. **CB:1234B**

3. ALĒTHŌS (ἀληθῶς), truly (from No. 2), is translated "indeed" **230 AG:37B**
in John 1 : 47; 4 : 42; 8 : 31. **CB:1234B**

4. ONTŌS (ὄντως), an adverb from *ōn*, the present participle of *eimi*, **3689**
to be, denotes really, actually; it is translated "indeed" in Mark 11 : 32 **AG:574A CB:—**
(R.V., "verily"); Luke 24 : 34; John 8 : 36; 1 Cor. 14 : 25, R.V.
(A.V., "of a truth"); 1 Tim. 5 : 3, 5, 16; 6 : 19, R.V., where some mss.
have *aiōnios*, "eternal" (A.V.); in Gal. 3 : 21, "verily."

5. KAI GAR (καὶ γάρ) signifies 'and in fact,' 'for also' (*kai*, and, or **KAI**
even, or also; *gar*, for; *gar*, always comes after the first word in the **2532 AG:391D**
sentence); it is translated "For indeed" in the R.V. of Acts 19 : 40; **CB:1253A**
2 Cor. 5 : 4; 1 Thess. 4 : 10 (A.V., "And indeed"); A.V. and R.V. in **GAR 1063**
Phil. 2 : 27. This phrase has a confirmatory sense, rather than a modi- **AG:151C**
fying effect, e.g., Matt. 15 : 27, R.V., "for even," instead of the A.V. **CB:1248A**
"yet;" the woman confirms that her own position as a Gentile 'dog' **OUDE 3761**
brings privilege, 'for indeed the dogs, etc.' **AG:591C**

6. OUDE GAR (οὐδὲ γάρ), for neither, is rendered "neither indeed" **CB:— ALLA**
in Rom. 8 : 7. **235**

7. ALLA KAI (ἀλλὰ καί), but even, or but also, is rendered "nay **AG:38A**
indeed" in 2 Cor. 11 : 1, R.V. (A.V., "and indeed;" R.V. marg., "but **CB:— KAI**
indeed"). **2532**

8. KAI (καί), preceded by the particle *ge*, 'at least,' 'ever,' is rendered **AG:391D CB:1253A**
"indeed" in Gal. 3 : 4, R.V. (A.V., "yet"). *Kai* alone is rendered **EI**
"indeed" in Phil. 4 : 10, R.V. (A.V., "also"). **1487 AG:219A**

9. EI MĒTI (εἰ μήτι), if not indeed, is rendered "unless indeed" in **CB:1242C**
2 Cor. 13 : 5, R.V. (A.V., "except"). **MēTI 3385 AG:520B CB:—**

INDIGNATION

A. Noun.

AGANAKTĒSIS (ἀγανάκτησις) is rendered "indignation" in 2 Cor. **24 AG:4B CB:—**
7 : 11. See ANGER, A, Note (3).¶

ORGĒ 3709 *Notes :* (1) *Orgē*, wrath, is translated " indignation " in Rev. 14 : 10,
AG:578D A.V. ; R.V., " anger." See ANGER, A, No. 1. (2) For *thumos*, see
CB:1261A ANGER, A, Notes (1) and (2). (3) In Acts 5 : 17, the A.V. translates
THUMOS 2372 *zēlos* by " indignation " (R.V. " jealousy ") ; in Heb. 10 : 27, A.V.,
AG:365B CB:1272C " indignation " (R.V., " fierceness ; " marg., " jealousy "). See
ZĒLOS 2205 JEALOUSY.

B. Verb.

AG:337D CB:1273B AGANAKTEŌ (ἀγανακτέω), to be indignant, to be moved with
indignation (from *agan*, much, *achomai*, to grieve), is translated " were
23 moved with indignation " of the ten disciples against James and John,
AG:4B CB:— Matt. 20 : 24 ; in Mark 10 : 41, R.V. (A.V., " they began to be much
displeased ") ; in Matt. 21 : 15, of the chief priests and scribes, against Christ and the children, R.V., " they were moved with indignation " (A.V., " they were sore displeased ") ; in 26 : 8, of the disciples against the woman who anointed Christ's feet, " they had indignation ; " so Mark 14 : 4 ; in Mark 10 : 14, of Christ, against the disciples, for rebuking the children, " He was moved with indignation," R.V. (A.V., " he was much displeased ") ; in Luke 13 : 14, of the ruler of the synagogue against Christ for healing on the Sabbath, " being moved with indignation," R.V., A.V., " (answered) with indignation." See ANGER, B, Note (3).¶

INDULGENCE

425 AG:65B 1. ANESIS (ἄνεσις), a loosening, relaxation of strain (akin to *aniēmi*,
CB:— to relax, loosen), is translated " indulgence " in Acts 24 : 23, R.V. (A.V., " liberty "), in the command of Felix to the centurion, to moderate restrictions upon Paul. The papyri and inscriptions illustrate the use of the word as denoting relief (Moulton and Milligan, Vocab.) In the N.T. it always carries the thought of relief from tribulation or persecution ; so 2 Thess. 1 : 7, " rest " ; in 2 Cor. 2 : 13 and 7 : 5 it is rendered " relief," R.V. (A.V., " rest ") ; in 8 : 13, " eased." Josephus speaks of the rest or relief (*anesis*) from ploughing and tillage, given to the land in the year of Jubilee. See EASE, LIBERTY, RELIEF, REST.¶

4140 2. PLĒSMONĒ (πλησμονή), a filling up, satiety (akin to *pimplēmi*,
AG:673A CB:— to fill), is translated " indulgence (of the flesh) " in Col. 2 : 23, R.V. (A.V., " satisfying "). Lightfoot translates the passage " yet not really of any value to remedy indulgence of the flesh." A possible meaning is, ' of no value in attempts at asceticism.' Some regard it as indicating that the ascetic treatment of the body is not of any honour to the satisfaction of the flesh (the reasonable demands of the body) : this interpretation is unlikely. The following paraphrase well presents the contrast between the asceticism which " practically treats the body as an enemy, and the Pauline view which treats it as a potential instrument of a righteous life : " ordinances, ' which in fact have a specious look of wisdom (where there is no true wisdom), by the employment of self-chosen acts of religion and humility (and) by treating the body with brutality instead of treating it

with due respect, with a view to meeting and providing against over-indulgence of the flesh' (Parry, in the Camb. Greek Test.).¶

For INEXCUSABLE see EXCUSE

For INFALLIBLE see PROOF

For INFANT see BABE

INFERIOR

HĒTTAOMAI, or HĒSSAOMAI (ἡττάομαι), to be less or inferior, is 2274 (-OŌ)
used in the Passive Voice, and translated "ye were made inferior," AG:349C CB:—
in 2 Cor. 12 : 13, R.V., for A.V., "ye were inferior," i.e., were treated with less consideration than other churches, through his independence in
not receiving gifts from them. In 2 Pet. 2 : 19, 20 it signifies to be over- HēTTōN
come, in the sense of being subdued and enslaved. See OVERCOME.¶ 2276 AG:349A
Cp. *hēssōn*, less, 2 Cor. 12 : 15; in 1 Cor. 11 : 17, "worse;"¶ *hēttēma*, a (HēSSōN)
loss, a spiritual defect, Rom. 11 : 12; 1 Cor. 6 : 7.¶ Also *elattoō*, to CB:— HēTTēMA
decrease, make lower, John 3 : 30; Heb. 2 : 7, 9.¶ 2275 AG:349C CB:1250B

For INFIDEL (R.V., UNBELIEVER), see BELIEF, C. Note (3) ELATTOō 1642 AG:248B CB:—

INFIRMITY

1. ASTHENEIA (ἀσθένεια), lit., want of strength (*a*, negative, *sthenos*, 769
strength), weakness, indicating inability to produce results, is most AG:115A CB:1238A
frequently translated "infirmity," or "infirmities;" in Rom. 8 : 26, the R.V. has "infirmity" (A.V., "infirmities"); in 2 Cor. 12 : 5, 9, 10, "weaknesses" and in 11 : 30, "weakness" (A.V., "infirmities"); in Luke 13 : 11 the phrase "a spirit of infirmity" attributes her curvature directly to Satanic agency. The connected phraseology is indicative of trained medical knowledge on the part of the writer.

2. ASTHENĒMA (ἀσθένημα), akin to No. 1, is found in the plural in 771
Rom. 15 : 1, "infirmities," i.e., those scruples which arise through weak- AG:115C CB:—
ness of faith. The strong must support the infirmities of the weak (*adunatos*) by submitting to self-restraint.¶

Note: In Luke 7 : 21, A.V., *nosos*, a disease, is translated "infirmities" 3554
(R.V., "diseases"). AG:543C CB:1260A

INFLICTED

Note: This is inserted in 2 Cor. 2 : 6 to complete the sentence; there is no corresponding word in the original, which lit. reads 'this punishment, the (one) by the majority.'

INFORM

1718 AG:257D
1. EMPHANIZŌ (ἐμφανίζω), to manifest, exhibit, in the Middle and CB:1244B

Passive Voices, to appear, also signifies to declare, make known, and is translated " informed " in Acts 24 : 1 ; 25 : 2, 15. For all the occurrences of the word see APPEAR, A, No. 5.

2727 AG:423D CB:1254B 2. KATĒCHEŌ (κατηχέω) primarily denotes to resound (*kata*, down, *ēchos*, a sound) ; then, to sound down the ears, to teach by word of mouth, instruct, inform (Eng., catechize, catechumen) ; it is rendered, in the Passive Voice, by the verb to inform, in Acts 21 : 21, 24. Here it is used of the large numbers of Jewish believers at Jerusalem whose zeal for the Law had been stirred by information of accusations made against the Apostle Paul, as to certain anti-Mosaic teaching he was supposed to have given the Jews. See INSTRUCT, TEACH.

For INHABITANTS, INHABITERS, see DWELL, A, No. 2

INHERIT, INHERITANCE

A. Verbs.

2816 AG:434D CB:1255B 1. KLĒRONOMEŌ (κληρονομέω) strictly means to receive by lot (*klēros*, a lot, *nemomai*, to possess) ; then, in a more general sense, to possess oneself of, to receive as one's own, to obtain. The following list shows how in the N.T. the idea of inheriting broadens out to include all spiritual good provided through and in Christ, and particularly all that is contained in the hope grounded on the promises of God.

The verb is used of the following objects :

" (*a*) birthright, that into the possession of which one enters in virtue of sonship, not because of a price paid or of a task accomplished, Gal. 4 : 30 ; Heb. 1 : 4 ; 12 : 17 :

(*b*) that which is received as a gift, in contrast with that which is received as the reward of law-keeping, Heb. 1 : 14 ; 6 : 12 (' through,' i.e., ' through experiences that called for the exercise of faith and patience,' but not ' on the ground of the exercise of faith and patience.') :

(*c*) that which is received on condition of obedience to certain precepts, 1 Pet. 3 : 9, and of faithfulness to God amidst opposition Rev. 21 : 7 :

(*d*) the reward of that condition of soul which forbears retaliation and self-vindication, and expresses itself in gentleness of behaviour . . ., Matt. 5 : 5. The phrase " inherit the earth," or " land," occurs several times in O.T. See especially Psa. 37 : 11, 22 :

(*e*) the reward (in the coming age, Mark 10 : 30) of the acknowledgment of the paramountcy of the claims of Christ, Matt. 19 : 29. In the three accounts given of this incident, see Mark 10 : 17–31, Luke 18 : 18–30, the words of the question put to the Lord are, in Matthew, ' that I may have,' in Mark and Luke, ' that I may inherit.' In the report of the Lord's word to Peter in reply to his subsequent question, Matthew has ' inherit eternal life,' while Mark and Luke have ' receive eternal life.' It seems to follow that the meaning of the word ' inherit ' is here ruled by the words ' receive ' and ' have,' with which it is interchanged in each of the three Gospels, i.e., the less common word ' inherit ' is to be regarded as equivalent to the more common words ' receive ' and ' have.' Cp. Luke 10 : 25 :

(*f*) the reward of those who have shown kindness to the ' brethren ' of the Lord in their distress, Matt. 25 : 34 :

(*g*) the Kingdom of God, which the morally corrupt cannot inherit, 1 Cor. 6 : 9, 10, the inheritance of which is likewise impossible to the present physical constitution of man, 1 Cor. 15 : 50 :

(*h*) incorruption, impossible of inheritance by corruption, 1 Cor. 15 : 50."*

See HEIR.¶

Note: In regard to (*e*), the word clearly signifies entrance into eternal life without any previous title ; it will not bear the implication that a child of God may be divested of his inheritance by the loss of his right of succession.

2. KLĒROŌ (*κληρόω*) is used in the Passive Voice in Eph. 1 : 11, A.V., " we have obtained an inheritance ; " R.V., " we were made a heritage." See HERITAGE.¶ **2820 AG:435D CB:1255B**

B. Nouns.

1 KLĒRONOMIA (*κληρονομία*), a lot (see A), properly an inherited property, an inheritance. " It is always rendered inheritance in N.T., but only in a few cases in the Gospels has it the meaning ordinarily attached to that word in English, i.e., that into possession of which the heir enters only on the death of an ancestor. The N.T. usage may be set out as follows: (*a*) that property in real estate which in ordinary course passes from father to son on the death of the former, Matt. 21 : 38 ; Mark 12 : 7 ; Luke 12 : 13 ; 20 : 14 ; (*b*) a portion of an estate made the substance of a gift, Acts 7 . 5 ; Gal. 3 : 18, which also is to be included under (*c*) ; (*c*) the prospective condition and possessions of the believer in the new order of things to be ushered in at the return of Christ, Acts 20 : 32 ; Eph. 1 : 14 ; 5 : 5 ; Col. 3 : 24 ; Heb. 9 : 15 ; 1 Pet. 1 : 4 ; (*d*) what the believer will be to God in that age, Eph. 1 : 18."† **2817 AG:435A CB:1255B**

Note: In Gal. 3 : 18, " if the inheritance is of the Law," the word " inheritance " stands for ' the title to the inheritance.'

2. KLĒROS (*κλῆρος*), (whence Eng., clergy), denotes (*a*) a lot, given or cast (the latter as a means of obtaining Divine direction), Matt. 27 : 35 ; Mark 15 : 24 ; Luke 23 : 24 ; John 19 : 24 ; Acts 1 : 26 ; (*b*) a person's share in anything, Acts 1 : 17, R.V., " portion " (A.V., " part ") ; 8 : 21, " lot ; " (*c*) a charge (lit., ' charges ') " allotted," to elders, 1 Pet. 5 : 3, R.V. [A.V., " (God's) heritage "] ; the figure is from portions of lands allotted to be cultivated ; (*d*) an inheritance, as in No. 1 (*c*) ; Acts 26 : 18 ; Col. 1 : 12. See CHARGE, A, No. 4, LOT(S), PART, PORTION.¶ **2819 AG:435B CB:1255B**

---

* From Notes on Galatians, by Hogg and Vine, pp. 286–289.
† From Notes on Galatians, by Hogg and Vine, pp. 146, 147.

INIQUITY

458
AG:71D 1. ANOMIA (ἀνομία), lit., lawlessness (*a*, negative, *nomos*, law), is used
CB:1235C in a way which indicates the meaning as being lawlessness or
wickedness. Its usual rendering in the N.T. is "iniquity," which lit. means unrighteousness. It occurs very frequently in the Sept., especially in the Psalms, where it is found about 70 times. It is used (*a*) of iniquity in general, Matt. 7 : 23 ; 13 : 41 ; 23 : 28 ; 24 : 12 ; Rom. 6 : 19 (twice) ; 2 Cor. 6 : 14, R.V., "iniquity" (A.V., "unrighteousness") ; 2 Thess. 2 : 3, in some mss. ; the A.V. and R.V. follow those which have *hamartia*, "(man of) sin ;" 2 : 7, R.V., "lawlessness" (A.V., "iniquity") ; Tit. 2 : 14; Heb. 1 : 9; 1 John 3 : 4 (twice), R.V., "(doeth) . . . lawlessness" and "lawlessness" (A.V., "transgresseth the law" and "transgression of the law") ; (*b*) in the plural, of acts or manifestations of lawlessness, Rom. 4 : 7 ; Heb. 10 : 17 (some inferior mss. have it in 8 : 12, for the word *hamartia*). See LAWLESSNESS, TRANSGRESSION, UNRIGHTEOUSNESS.¶

Note : In the phrase "man of sin," 2 Thess. 2 : 3, the word suggests the idea of contempt of Divine law, since the Antichrist will deny the existence of God.

93 2. ADIKIA (ἀδικία) denotes unrighteousness, lit., 'unrightness'
AG:17D
CB:1233A (*a*, negative, *dikē*, right), a condition of not being right, whether with God,
according to the standard of His holiness and righteousness, or with man, according to the standard of what man knows to be right by his conscience. In Luke 16 : 8 and 18 : 6, the phrases lit. are, 'the steward of unrighteousness' and 'the judge of injustice,' the subjective genitive describing their character ; in 18 : 6 the meaning is 'injustice' and so perhaps in Rom. 9 : 14. The word is usually translated "unrighteousness," but is rendered "iniquity" in Luke 13 : 27 ; Acts 1 : 18 ; 8 : 23 ; 1 Cor. 13 : 6, A.V. (R.V., "unrighteousness") ; so in 2 Tim. 2 : 19 ; Jas. 3 : 6.

92 3. ADIKĒMA (ἀδίκημα) denotes a wrong, injury, misdeed (akin to
AG:17D
CB:1233A No. 2 ; from *adikeō*, to do wrong), the concrete act, in contrast to the
general meaning of No. 2, and translated "a matter of wrong," in Acts 18 : 14 ; "wrong-doing," 24 : 20 (A.V., "evil-doing") ; "iniquities," Rev. 18 : 5. See EVIL, WRONG.¶

4189
AG:690C 4. PONĒRIA (πονηρία), akin to *poneō*, to toil (cp. *ponēros*, bad, worth-
CB:1266A less ; see BAD), denotes wickedness, and is so translated in Matt. 22 : 18 ;
Mark 7 : 22 (plural) ; Luke 11 : 39 ; Rom. 1 : 29 ; 1 Cor. 5 : 8 ; Eph. 6 : 12 ; in Acts 3 : 26, "iniquities." See WICKEDNESS.¶ Cp. *kakia*, evil.

3892
AG:621A 5. PARANOMIA (παρανομία), law-breaking (*para*, against, *nomos*,
CB:— law), denotes transgression, so rendered in 2 Pet. 2 : 16, for A.V.,
"iniquity."¶

INJURE, INJURIOUS, INJURY

91
AG:17C **A. Verb.**
CB:1233A ADIKEŌ (ἀδικέω), akin to Nos. 2 and 3, under INIQUITY, is usually

translated either to hurt, or by some form of the verb to do wrong. In the A.V. of Gal. 4 : 12, it is rendered " ye have (not) injured me," which the R.V. corrects, both in tense and meaning, to " ye did (me no) wrong." See HURT.

B. Adjective.

HUBRISTĒS (ὑβριστής), a violent, insolent man (akin to C), is trans- 5197
lated " insolent " in Rom. 1 : 30, R.V., for A.V., " despiteful ; " in 1 Tim. AG:832A CB:1251C
1 : 13, " injurious." See DESPITEFUL, INSOLENT.¶

C. Noun.

HUBRIS (ὕβρις) : see HARM, A, No. 4. 5196 AG:832A CB:1251B

INK

MELAN (μέλαν), the neuter of the adjective *melas*, black (see Matt. 3188
5 : 36 ; Rev. 6 : 5, 12), denotes ink, 2 Cor. 3 : 3 ; 2 John 12 ; 3 John 13.¶ AG:499D CB:1258A

INN

2646 AG:414B CB:1254A
1. KATALUMA (κατάλυμα) : see GUEST-CHAMBER.

2. PANDOCHEION (πανδοχεῖον), lit., a place where all are received 3829
(*pas*, all, *dechomai*, to receive), denotes a house for the reception of AG:607C CB:—
strangers, a *caravanserai*, translated " inn," in Luke 10 : 34, in the parable of the Good Samaritan. Cattle and beasts of burden could be sheltered there, and this word must thereby be distinguished from No. 1.¶ Cp. *pandocheus* in the next verse, " (the) host."¶

INNER

1. ESŌ (ἔσω), an adverb connected with *eis*, into, is translated " inner " 2080
in the A.V. of Eph. 3 : 16 (R.V., " inward ") ; after verbs of motion, it AG:214B CB:1246C
denotes 'into,' Mark 15 : 16 ; after verbs of rest, " within." See WITHIN.

2. ESŌTEROS (ἐσώτερος), the comparative degree of No. 1, denotes 2082
" inner," Acts 16 : 24 (of a prison) ; Heb. 6 : 19, with the article, and AG:314C CB:1246C
practically as a noun, " that which is within (the veil)," lit., 'the inner (of the veil).'¶ Cp. Eng., esoteric.

Note : For " inner chamber(s) " see CHAMBER, No. 1.

INNOCENT

1. ATHŌOS (ἀθῷος) primarily denotes unpunished (*a*, negative, 121
thōē, a penalty) ; then, innocent, Matt. 27 : 4, " innocent blood," i.e., AG:21D CB:—
the blood of an innocent person, the word " blood " being used both by synecdoche (a part standing for the whole), and by metonymy (one thing standing for another), i.e., for death by execution (some mss. have *dikaion*, righteous) ; ver. 24, where Pilate speaks of himself as " innocent."¶

2. AKAKOS (ἄκακος), lit., not bad (*a*, negative, *kakos*, bad), denotes 172
guileless, innocent, Rom. 16 : 18, R.V., " innocent " (A.V., " simple ") ; AG:29B CB:1234A
" harmless " in Heb. 7 : 26. See HARMLESS.¶

INNUMERABLE

382 AG:60A 1. ANARITHMĒTOS (ἀναρίθμητος), *a*, negative, *n*, euphonic, *arithmeō*
CB:— to number, is used in Heb. 11 : 12.¶
3461 2. MURIAS (μυριάς) denotes either ten thousand, or, indefinitely, a
AG:529C myriad, a numberless host, in the plural, Acts 19 : 19; lit. 'five ten-
CB:— thousands,' Rev. 5 : 11; 9 : 16; in the following, used of vast numbers,
Luke 12 : 1, A.V., "an innumerable multitude," R.V., "the many
thousands" (R.V. marg., "the myriads"); Acts 21 : 20, "thousands;"
Heb. 12 : 22, "innumerable hosts;" Jude 14, "ten thousands" (R.V.,
marg., in each place, "myriads"). See COMPANY, THOUSANDS.¶ Cp.
MURIOI the adjective *murios*, ten thousand, Matt. 18 : 24; 1 Cor. 4 : 15; 14 : 19.¶
3463 AG:529D
CB:— For INORDINATE see AFFECTION, No. 1

INQUIRE, INQUIRY (make)

A. Verbs.

4441 1. PUNTHANOMAI (πυνθάνομαι), to inquire, is translated "inquired"
AG:729C CB:— in Matt. 2 : 4, and Acts 21 : 33, R.V. (A.V., "demanded"); in Luke
15 : 26; 18 : 36 and Acts 4 : 7 (A.V., "asked"); "inquired" (A.V.,
"enquired") in John 4 : 52; "inquire" (A.V., "enquire") in Acts
23 : 20; in Acts 23 : 34 it denotes to learn by enquiry, A.V., and R.V.,
"when (he) understood;" elsewhere it is rendered by the verb to ask,
Acts 10 : 18, 29; 23 : 19. See ASK, UNDERSTAND.¶
2212 AG:338D 2. ZĒTEŌ (ζητέω), to seek, is rendered "inquire" in John 16 : 19;
CB:1273C "inquire . . . for" in Acts 9 : 11. See ABOUT, B, Note, DESIRE,
ENDEAVOUR, GO, *Note* (2), *a*, REQUIRE, SEEK.
1331 AG:194D 3. DIERŌTAŌ (διερωτάω), to find by inquiry, to inquire through to
CB:— the end (*dia*, intensive, *erōtaō*, to ask), is used in Acts 10 : 17.¶
1833 AG:275C 4. EXETAZŌ (ἐξετάζω), to examine, seek out, inquire thoroughly, is
CB:— translated "enquire" in Matt. 10 : 11, A.V. (R.V., "search out"); in
EPIZĒTEŌ John 21 : 12, "durst) inquire," R.V. [A.V., "(durst) ask"]; in Matt. 2 : 8,
1934 AG:292D R.V., "search out" (A.V., "search"). See ASK, SEARCH.¶
CB:1246B *Notes:* (1) *Epizēteō*, to seek after or for (*epi*, after, *zēteō*, to seek), is
SU(N)ZĒTEŌ 4802 rendered "enquire" in Acts 19 : 39, A.V. (R.V., "seek"). (2) *Sunzēteō*,
AG:775D to search or examine together, is rendered "to enquire" in Luke 22 : 23,
CB:— EKZĒTEŌ A.V. (R.V., "to question"). (3) *Ekzēteō*, to seek out, search after, is
1567 rendered "have inquired" in 1 Pet. 1 : 10, A.V. (R.V., "sought").
AG:240A CB:1244A (4) *Diaginōskō*, to ascertain exactly, or to determine, is rendered "enquire"
DIAGINŌSKŌ in Acts 23 : 15, A.V. (R.V., "judge"). (5) *Akriboō*, to learn by diligent or
1231 AG:182B exact inquiry, is rendered "enquired diligently" and "had diligently
CB:— enquired" respectively, in Matt. 2 : 7, 16, A.V. (R.V., "learned care-
AKRIBOŌ fully," and "had carefully learned"). (6) In 2 Cor. 8 : 23, the words "any
198 AG:33B inquire" are inserted to complete the meaning, lit., 'whether about
CB:— Titus.'

B. Noun.

ZĒTĒSIS (ζήτησις) primarily denotes a search; then, an inquiry, 2214
a questioning, debate; it forms part of a phrase translated by the verb AG:339B CB:1273C
to inquire, in Acts 25 : 20, R.V., " how to inquire," lit. ' (being perplexed as to) the inquiry.' See QUESTION.

INSCRIPTION

EPIGRAPHŌ (ἐπιγράφω), to write upon, inscribe (*epi*, upon, *graphō*, 1924
to write), is usually rendered by the verb to write upon, over, or in, Mark AG:291C CB:1245C
15 : 26; Heb. 8 : 10; 10 : 16; Rev. 21 : 12; it is translated by a noun phrase in Acts 17 : 23, " (with this) inscription," lit., ' (on which) had been inscribed.'¶ Cp. the noun *epigraphē*, a superscription.

INSIDE

1. ENTOS (ἐντός), an adverb denoting within, or among, is once used 1787
with the article, as a noun, of " the inside (of the cup and of the platter)," AG:269B CB:1245B
Matt. 23 : 26, R.V. (A.V., " that which is within etc."); elsewhere, Luke 17 : 21. See WITHIN.¶

2. ESŌTHEN (ἔσωθεν), an adverb denoting from within, or within, is 2081
used with the article, as a noun, of the inner being, the secret intents of the AG:314B CB:—
heart, which, the Lord declared, God made, as well as the visible physical frame, Luke 11 : 40. In ver. 39, it is rendered " inward part." See INWARD, WITHIN.

INSIGHT See DISCERNMENT, UNDERSTANDING

INSOLENT

HUBRISTĒS (ὑβριστής), violent, injurious, insolent, is rendered 5197
" insolent " in Rom. 1 : 30, R.V. (A.V., " despiteful "). See DESPITEFUL, AG:832A CB:1251C
INJURIOUS.

INSOMUCH THAT, or AS

1. HŌSTE (ὥστε), a consecutive particle, is used with the meaning 5620
" insomuch that," or " so that," or " that," to express the effect or result AG:899D CB:—
of anything, e.g., Matt. 8 : 24; 13 : 54; 15 : 31; 27 : 14; Acts 1 : 19 (A.V., " insomuch as "); 5 : 15; 19 : 12 (A.V., " so that "); 2 Cor. 1 : 8; Gal. 2 : 13. See WHEREFORE.

2. EIS TO (εἰς τό), lit., unto the, followed by the infinitive mood, is EIS 1519
sometimes used of result, and is rendered " insomuch that " in 2 Cor. 8 : 6. AG:228A CB:1243A

3. KATHO (καθό) is translated " insomuch as " in 1 Pet. 4 : 13, R.V. 2526
(A.V., " inasmuch as "). See INASMUCH. AG:390D CB:—

INSPIRATION OF GOD, INSPIRED OF GOD

THEOPNEUSTOS (θεόπνευστος), inspired by God (*Theos*, God, *pneō*, 2315
to breathe), is used in 2 Tim. 3 : 16, of the Scriptures as distinct from non- AG:356C CB:1272A
inspired writings. Wycliffe, Tyndale, Coverdale and the Great Bible have the rendering " inspired of God."¶

INSTANT, BE INSTANT, INSTANTLY

A. Verbs.

1945 AG:294C CB:— 1. EPIKEIMAI (ἐπίκειμαι), to lie or press upon, is rendered "they were instant" in Luke 23 : 23 (Amer. R.V., "they were urgent"). See IMPOSE.

2186 AG:330D CB:— 2. EPHISTĒMI (ἐφίστημι), to set upon or by, is used in the N.T. intransitively, either in the Middle Voice, or in certain tenses of the Active, signifying to stand by, be present, be at hand, come on or upon, and is translated "be instant" in 2 Tim. 4 : 2. See ASSAULT, COME, etc.

4342 AG:715C CB:1267A *Note:* For *proskartereō*, in Rom. 12 : 12, A.V., rendered "continuing instant," R.V., "stedfastly," see CONTINUE, No. 9.

B. Noun.

5610 AG:896A CB:1251A *Note:* The word *hōra*, an hour, is translated "instant" in Luke 2 : 38, A.V.; the R.V. renders it "hour." See HOUR.

C. Adverb.

4709 AG:763D CB:— SPOUDAIŌS (σπουδαίως), earnestly, diligently, is rendered "instantly" in Luke 7 : 4, A.V. (R.V., "earnestly"). See EARNEST.

EKTENEIA 1616 AG:245C CB:— *Note:* For the phrase *en ekteneią*, rendered "instantly" in Acts 26 : 7, A.V., see EARNEST, D.

INSTRUCT, INSTRUCTION, INSTRUCTOR

A. Verbs.

2727 AG:423D CB:1254B 1. KATĒCHEŌ (κατηχέω), to teach orally, inform, instruct, is translated by the verb to instruct in Luke 1 : 4; Acts 18 : 25 (R.V. marg., "taught by word of mouth"); Rom. 2 : 18; 1 Cor. 14 : 19, R.V. (A.V., "teach"). See INFORM, TEACH.

3811 AG:603D CB:1261C 2. PAIDEUŌ (παιδεύω), to train children, teach, is rendered "was instructed," in Acts 7 : 22, R.V. (A.V., "learned"); "instructing" in 2 Tim. 2 : 25, A.V. (R.V., "correcting"); Tit. 2 : 12, R.V., "instructing" (A.V., "teaching"). The verb is used of the family discipline, as in Heb. 12 : 6, 7, 10; cp. 1 Cor. 11 : 32; 2 Cor. 6 : 9; Rev. 3 : 19. In 1 Tim. 1 : 20 (Passive Voice) it is translated "might be taught," R.V. (A.V., "may learn"), but, "however the passage is to be understood, it is clear that not the impartation of knowledge but severe discipline is intended. In Luke 23 : 16, 22, Pilate, since he had declared the Lord guiltless of the charge brought against Him, and hence could not punish Him, weakly offered, as a concession to the Jews, to 'chastise, *paideuō*, Him, and let Him go.'"*

This sense of *paideuō* is confirmed by Heb. 12 : 6, where it is joined (in a quotation from the Sept. of Prov. 3 : 12) with to lash or scourge. Cp. the scene in the *Pilgrim's Progress* where a shining one with a whip of small cords "chastised sore" the pilgrims foolishly caught in the net of the flatterer and said to them, "As many as I love I rebuke and chasten" (*paideuō*). See CORRECT, TEACH.¶

INSULT See RAIL, REPROACH

* From Notes on Galatians, by Hogg and Vine, p. 165.

3. MATHĒTEUŌ (μαθητεύω), used transitively, to make a disciple, 3100
is translated " which is instructed " in Matt. 13 : 52, A.V. (R.V., " who AG:485C CB:1258A
hath been made a disciple "). See DISCIPLE.

4. MUEŌ (μυέω), to initiate into the mysteries, is used in the Passive 3453
Voice, in Phil. 4 : 12, A.V., " I am instructed," R.V., " have I learned the AG:529A CB:1259B
secret." See LEARN.¶

5. PROBIBAZŌ (προβιβάζω), to lead forward, lead on (the causal of 4264
probainō, to go forward ; *pro*, forward, *bibazō*, to lift up), is used in the AG:703C CB:—
Passive Voice in Matt. 14 : 8, and translated, A.V., " being before instructed," R.V., " being put forward." Some mss. have it in Acts 19 : 33, instead of No. 6.¶

6. SUMBIBAZŌ (συμβιβάζω), to join, knit, unite (*sun*, with), then, to 4822
compare, and so, to prove, hence, to teach, instruct, is so rendered in AG:777D CB:—
1 Cor. 2 : 16 ; it is found in the best mss. in Acts 19 : 33 (R.V. marg., " instructed "). See COMPACTED, CONCLUDE, KNIT TOGETHER, PROVE.

B. Nouns.

(INSTRUCTION)

PAIDEIA (παιδεία), training, instruction, is translated " instruction " 3809
in 2 Tim. 3 : 16. See CHASTEN. AG:603B CB:1261B

(INSTRUCTOR)

1. PAIDAGŌGOS (παιδαγωγός), a guide, or guardian or trainer of boys, 3807
lit., a child-leader (*pais*, a boy, or child, *agō*, to lead), a tutor, is translated AG:603A CB:1261B
" instructors " in 1 Cor. 4 : 15, A.V. (R.V., " tutors ") ; here the thought is that of pastors rather than teachers ; in Gal. 3 : 24, 25, A.V., " schoolmaster " (R.V., " tutor,"), but here the idea of instruction is absent. " In this and allied words the idea is that of training, discipline, not of impartation of knowledge. The *paidagōgos* was not the instructor of the child ; he exercised a general supervision over him and was responsible for his moral and physical well-being. Thus understood, *paidagōgos* is appropriately used with ' kept in ward ' and ' shut up,' whereas to
understand it as equivalent to ' teacher ' introduces an idea entirely foreign EPITROPOS
to the passage, and throws the Apostle's argument into confusion."*¶ 2012
Cp. *epitropos*, a steward, guardian, tutor. AG:303D CB:1246B

2. PAIDEUTĒS (παιδευτής), akin to A, No. 2, denotes (*a*) an instructor, 3810
a teacher, Rom. 2 : 20, A.V., " an instructor " (R.V., " a corrector ") ; AG:603D CB:1261C
(*b*) one who disciplines, corrects, chastens, Heb. 12 : 9, R.V., " to chasten " [A.V., " which corrected " (lit., ' correctors ')]. In (*a*) the discipline of the school is in view ; in (*b*) that of the family. See CORRECTOR.¶. Cp. *epitropos*, a steward, guardian, tutor.

INSTRUMENTS

HOPLON (ὅπλον), a tool, instrument, weapon, is used metaphorically 3696
in Rom. 6 : 13 of the members of the body as " instruments " (marg., AG:575C CB:1251A

* From Notes on Galatians, by Hogg and Vine, pp. 163, 164.

" weapons "), negatively, of unrighteousness, positively, of righteousness. The metaphor is probably military (cp. ver. 23, " wages," i.e., soldiers' pay); Moule renders it ' implements;' ' weapons' seems to be the meaning. See ARMOUR, WEAPONS.

INSURRECTION

A. Nouns.

4714 1. STASIS (στάσις), akin to *histēmi*, to make to stand, denotes
AG:764C CB:1270A (*a*) primarily, a standing or place, Heb. 9 : 8; (*b*) an insurrection, sedition,
translated " insurrection " in Mark 15 : 7; " insurrections " in Acts
24 : 5, R.V. (A.V., " sedition "); in Luke 23 : 19, 25 (A.V. " sedition ");
" riot," Acts 19 : 40, R.V. (A.V., " uproar "); (*c*) a dissension, Acts
— 15 : 2; in Acts 23 : 7, 10, " dissension." See DISSENSION.¶
AG:764B 2. STASIASTĒS (στασιαστής) denotes a rebel, revolutionist, one who
CB:— stirs up sedition (from *stasiazō*, to stir up sedition), Mark 15 : 7, " had made
4955 insurrection." Some mss. have *sustasiastēs*, a fellow-rioter, a fellow-mover
AG:794D CB:— of sedition, A.V., " had made insurrection with (him)."¶

B. Verb.

2721 AG:422C KATEPHISTĒMI (κατεφίστημι) signifies to rise up against (lit., to
(-AMAI) cause to stand forth against, *kata*, against, *epi*, forth, *histēmi*, to cause to
CB:— stand), Acts 18 : 12, A.V., " made insurrection " (R.V., " rose up against)."¶

INTEGRITY See TRUE

INTEND

1014 1. BOULOMAI (βούλομαι), to will, wish, desire, purpose (expressing
AG:146A CB:1239B a fixed resolve, the deliberate exercise of volition), is translated " intend "
in Acts 5 : 28, and " intending " in 12 : 4. See DESIRE.
2309 AG:354D 2. THELŌ (θέλω), to will, be willing, desire (less strong, and more
CB:1271C frequent than No. 1), is translated " intending " in Luke 14 : 28, A.V.
(R.V., " desiring "). See DESIRE.
3195 AG:500D 3. MELLŌ (μέλλω), to be about to do a thing, indicating simply the
CB:1258A formation of a design, is translated " intend " in Acts 5 : 35, A.V. (R.V.,
" are about "); " intending," in Acts 20 : 7, R.V. (A.V., " ready ");
20 : 13 (1st part); in the 2nd part of the ver., R.V., " intending " (A.V.,
" minding ").

INTENT

1771 AG:267A 1. ENNOIA (ἔννοια), primarily a thinking, idea, consideration,
CB:1245B denotes purpose, intention, design (*en*, in, *nous*, mind); it is rendered
" intents " in Heb. 4 : 12; " mind," in 1 Pet. 4 : 1 (R.V., marg.,
" thought "). See MIND.¶ Cp. *Enthumēsis*, thought (see DEVICE).
3056 AG:477A 2. LOGOS (λόγος), a word, account, etc., sometimes denotes a reason,
CB:1257A cause, intent, e.g., Matt. 5 : 32, " cause; " it is rendered " intent " in
EIS Acts 10 : 29. See CAUSE.
1519 AG:228A *Notes:* (1) The phrase *eis touto*, lit., ' unto this,' i.e., for this pur-
CB:1243A pose, is rendered " for this (A.V., ' that ') intent " in Acts 9 : 21, R.V.

(2) The phrase *eis to*, ' unto the,' followed by a verb in the infinitive mood, **PROS**
is translated " to the intent " in 1 Cor. 10 : 6. (3) The phrase *pros ti*, **4314**
lit., ' in reference to what,' is rendered " for what intent " in John 13 : 28. **AG:709C CB:1267A**
(4) In John 11 : 15 the conjunction *hina*, to the end that, is translated **2443**
" to the intent," and in Eph. 3 : 10, " to the intent that." **AG:376D CB:1250C**

INTERCESSIONS

A. Noun.

ENTEUXIS (ἔντευξις) primarily denotes a lighting upon, meeting with **1783**
(akin to B) ; then, a conversation ; hence, a petition, a meaning frequent **AG:268D CB:1245B**
in the papyri ; it is a technical term for approaching a king, and so for approaching God in intercession ; it is rendered " prayer " in 1 Tim. 4 : 5 ; in the plural in 2 : 1 (i.e., seeking the presence and hearing of God on behalf of others).¶ For the synonymous words, *proseuchē*, *deēsis*, see Prayer.

B. Verbs.

1. ENTUNCHANŌ (ἐντυγχάνω), primarily to fall in with, meet with in **1793**
order to converse ; then, to make petition, especially to make intercession, **AG:270A CB:1245B**
plead with a person, either for or against others ; (*a*) against, Acts 25 : 24, " made suit to (me)," R.V. [A.V., " have dealt with (me) "], i.e., against Paul ; in Rom. 11 : 2, of Elijah in ' pleading ' with God, R.V. (A.V., " maketh intercession to "), against Israel ; (*b*) " for," in Rom. 8 : 27, of the intercessory work of the Holy Spirit for the saints ; ver. 34, of the similar intercessory work of Christ ; so Heb. 7 : 25. See Deal with, Plead, Suit.¶

2. HUPERENTUNCHANŌ (ὑπερεντυγχάνω), to make a petition or **5241**
intercede on behalf of another (*huper*, on behalf of, and No. 1), is used in **AG:840D CB:1252A**
Rom. 8 : 26 of the work of the Holy Spirit in making intercession (see No. 1, ver. 27).¶

INTEREST

TOKOS (τόκος), primarily a bringing forth, birth (from *tiktō*, to beget), **5110**
then, an offspring, is used metaphorically of the produce of money lent out, **AG:821D CB:1272C**
interest, usury, Matt. 25 : 27 ; Luke 19 : 23. See Usury.¶

INTERPOSED

MESITEUŌ (μεσιτεύω), to mediate, give surety (akin to *mesitēs*, a **3315**
mediator), is translated " interposed " in Heb. 6 : 17, R.V. See Confirm, **AG:506D CB:1258B**
No. 5.¶

INTERPRET, INTERPRETATION, INTERPRETER

A. Verbs.

1. HERMĒNEUŌ (ἑρμηνεύω), (cp. *Hermēs*, the Greek name of the **2059**
pagan god Mercury, who was regarded as the messenger of the gods), **AG:310A CB:1250A**
denotes to explain, interpret (Eng., hermeneutics), and is used of explaining the meaning of words in a different language, John 1 : 38 (in some mss.),

see No. 3; 9:7 ("Siloam," interpreted as "sent"); Heb. 7:2 (Melchizedec, "by interpretation," lit., 'being interpreted,' King of righteousness).¶

1329 AG:194B CB:1241C
2. DIERMĒNEUŌ (διερμηνεύω), a strengthened form of No. 1 (*dia*, through, used intensively), signifies to interpret fully, to explain. In Luke 24:27, it is used of Christ in interpreting to the two on the way to Emmaus "in all the Scriptures the things concerning Himself," R.V., "interpreted" (A.V., "expounded"); in Acts 9:36, it is rendered "is by interpretation," lit., 'being interpreted' (of Tabitha, as meaning Dorcas); in 1 Cor. 12:30 and 14:5, 13, 27, it is used with reference to the temporary gift of tongues in the churches; this gift was inferior in character to that of prophesying, unless he who spoke in a "tongue" interpreted his words, 14:5; he was, indeed, to pray that he might interpret, ver. 13; only two, or at the most three, were to use the gift in a gathering, and that "in turn" (R.V.); one was to interpret; in the absence of an interpreter, the gift was not to be exercised, ver. 27. See Expound.¶

3177 AG:498D CB:1258C
3. METHERMĒNEUŌ (μεθερμηνεύω), to change or translate from one language to another (*meta*, implying change, and No. 1), to interpret, is always used in the Passive Voice in the N.T., "being interpreted," of interpreting the names, Immanuel, Matt. 1:23; Golgotha, Mark 15:22; Barnabas, Acts 4:36; in Acts 13:8, of Elymas, the verb is rendered "is . . . by interpretation," lit., 'is interpreted;' it is used of interpreting or translating sentences in Mark 5:41; 15:34; in the best mss., John 1:38 (Rabbi, interpreted as "Master"); ver. 41 (Messiah, interpreted as "Christ"); see No. 1.¶

B. Nouns.

(Interpretation)

2058 AG:310A CB:1250A
1. HERMĒNIA (or *-ia*) (ἑρμηνία), akin to A, No. 1, is used in 1 Cor. 12:10; 14:26 (see A, No. 2).¶

1955 AG:295D CB:1246A
2. EPILUSIS (ἐπίλυσις), from *epiluō*, to loose, solve, explain, denotes a solution, explanation, lit., a release (*epi*, up, *luō*, to loose), 2 Pet. 1:20, "(of private) interpretation;" i.e., the writers of Scripture did not put their own construction upon the 'God-breathed' words they wrote.¶

Note: For "hard of interpretation," Heb. 5:11, R.V., see Utter, *Note* (1).

(Interpreter)

1328 AG:194B CB:1241C
DIERMĒNEUTĒS (διερμηνευτής), lit., a thorough interpreter (cp. A, No. 2), is used in 1 Cor. 14:28 (some mss. have *hermēneutēs*).¶

INTERROGATION

1906 AG:285C CB:1245C
EPERŌTĒMA (ἐπερώτημα), primarily a question or enquiry, denotes a demand or appeal; it is found in 1 Pet. 3:21, R.V., "interrogation" (A.V., "answer"). See Answer, Note. Some take the word to indicate that baptism affords a good conscience, an appeal against the accuser.¶

INTO: see † p. 1.

INTREAT, INTREATY

A. Verbs.

1. ERŌTAŌ (ἐρωτάω), to ask, beseech, is rendered "intreat," e.g., 2065 AG:311D
in Phil. 4 : 3, A.V. (R.V., "beseech"). See Ask. CB:1246C

2. PARAKALEŌ (παρακαλέω), to beseech, comfort, exhort, is rendered 3870
by the verb to intreat in Luke 8 : 31, R.V., "intreated" (A.V., "be- AG:617A CB:1262A
sought"); 15 : 28; Acts 9 : 38, R.V., "intreating" (A.V., "desiring"); 28 : 20, R.V. (A.V., "called for"); 1 Cor. 4 : 13; 2 Cor. 9 : 5, R.V. (A.V., "exhort"); 10 : 1, R.V. (A.V., "beseech"); 1 Tim. 5 : 1, A.V. (R.V., "exhort"). See Beseech.

3. PARAITEOMAI (παραιτέομαι), to ask to be excused, to beg, etc., 3868
is rendered "intreated" in Heb. 12 : 19. See Avoid. AG:616C CB:1262A

B. Adjective.

EUPEITHĒS (εὐπειθής), ready to obey (*eu*, well, *peithomai*, to obey, 2138
to be persuaded), compliant, is translated "easy to be intreated" in AG:324A CB:—
Jas. 3 : 17, said of the wisdom that is from above.¶

C. Noun.

PARAKLĒSIS (παράκλησις), an appeal, a comfort, exhortation, etc., 3874
is translated "intreaty" in 2 Cor. 8 : 4. AG:618A CB:1262A

For INTRUDE (Col. 2 : 18) see DWELL, A, No. 11

INTRUST

PISTEUŌ (πιστεύω), to believe, also means to entrust, and in the 4100
Active Voice is translated to commit, in Luke 16 : 11; John 2 : 24; in AG:660B CB:1265A
the Passive Voice, to be intrusted with, Rom. 3 : 2, R.V., "they were intrusted with" (A.V., "unto them were committed"), of Israel and the oracles of God; 1 Cor. 9 : 17, R.V., "I have . . . intrusted to me" (A.V., "is committed unto me"), of Paul and the stewardship of the Gospel; so Gal. 2 : 7; Tit. 1 : 3; in 1 Thess. 2 : 4, where he associates with himself his fellow-missionaries, R.V., "to be intrusted with" (A.V., "to be put in trust with"). See Believe, Commit.

INVENTORS

EPHEURETĒS (ἐφευρετής), an inventor, contriver (akin to *epheuriskō*, 2182
to find out; *epi*, on, used intensively, *heuriskō*, to find), occurs in the AG:330B CB:—
plural in Rom. 1 : 30.¶

INVISIBLE

AORATOS (ἀόρατος), lit., unseen (*a*, negative, *horaō*, to see), is 517
translated "invisible" in Rom. 1 : 20, of the power and Divinity of God; AG:79A CB:1236A
of God Himself, Col. 1 : 15; 1 Tim. 1 : 17; Heb. 11 : 27; of things INVITE
unseen, Col. 1 : 16.¶ In the Sept., Gen. 1 : 2; Is. 45 : 3, "unseen See ASK,
(treasures)."¶ BID, CALL

INWARD (man, part), INWARDLY

2080 1. ESŌ (ἔσω), within, inward, is used adjectivally in Rom. 7 : 22,
AG:214B CB:1246C " (the) inward (man) ;" 2 Cor. 4 : 16, with "man" expressed in the
preceding clause, but not repeated in the original, " (our) inward (man) "
(some mss. have *esōthen*, from within) ; Eph. 3 : 16, R.V., " (the) inward
(man) " (A.V., " inner "). See INNER, WITHIN.

2081 2. ESŌTHEN (ἔσωθεν) is used in Luke 11 : 39, as a noun with the
AG:314B CB:— article, " part " being understood, " (your) inward part ; " in Matt. 7 : 15
it has its normal use as an adverb, " inwardly." See WITHIN.

2927 *Note :* In Rom. 2 : 29 the phrase *en tō kruptō*, lit., in (the) secret, or
AG:454A CB:1256A hidden (' part ' being understood), is rendered " inwardly," said of a
spiritual Jew, in contrast to the one who is merely naturally circumcised
and so is one outwardly. See HIDE, SECRET.

IRKSOME

3636 OKNĒROS (ὀκνηρός), shrinking, timid (from *okneō*, to shrink, delay),
AG:563A CB:— is used negatively in Phil. 3 : 1, R.V., " irksome " (A.V., " grievous "),
i.e., ' I do not hesitate ' ; in Matt. 25 : 26, and Rom. 12 : 11, " slothful."
See GRIEVOUS, SLOTHFUL.¶

IRON

A. Noun.

4604 AG:750A SIDĒROS (σίδηρος), iron, occurs in Rev. 18 : 12.¶
CB:1269A

B. Adjective.

4603 SIDĒREOS (σιδήρεος), of iron, occurs in Acts 12 : 10, of an iron gate ;
AG:750A (-ROUS) " of iron," Rev. 2 : 27 ; 9 : 9 ; 12 : 5 ; 19 : 15.¶
CB:1269A (-ROUS)

ISLAND, ISLE

3520 AG:538A 1. NĒSOS (νῆσος), an island, occurs in Acts 13 : 6 ; 27 : 26 ; 28 : 1,
CB:— 7, 9, 11 ; Rev. 1 : 9 ; 6 : 14 ; 16 : 20.¶

3519 2. NĒSION (νησίον), a diminutive of No. 1, a small island, occurs in
AG:538A CB:— Acts 27 : 16, Cauda, R.V.¶

ISSUE

A. Nouns.

1545 AG:237D 1. EKBASIS (ἔκβασις), a way out, " way of escape," 1 Cor. 10 : 13
RHUSIS (*ek*, out, *bainō*, to go), is rendered " issue " in Heb. 13 : 7, R.V., for A.V.,
4511 AG:738B " end," regarding the manner of life of deceased spiritual guides. See
CB:1268B END.¶

SPERMA 4690 2. RHUSIS (ῥύσις), a flowing (akin to *rheō*, to flow), an issue, is used
AG:761D in Mark 5 : 25 ; Luke 8 : 43, 44.¶

CB:1269C *Note :* In Matt. 22 : 25, A.V., *sperma*, seed, is translated " issue "
(-OMAI) (R.V., " seed ").

1607 AG:244B

B. Verb.

CB:1244A EKPOREUŌ (ἐκπορεύω), to cause to go forth (*ek*, out, *poreuō*, to cause to go), is used in the Middle Voice in Rev. 9 : 17, 18, of the coming forth of fire, smoke and brimstone from the mouths of the symbolic horses in a vision, A.V., "issued" (the R.V. renders it by the verb to proceed). See COME, DEPART, GO, PROCEED.

IT

Note : The pronouns used are the same, in their neuter forms, as Nos. 1, 2, 3 under HE.

ITCHING

KNĒTHŌ (κνήθω), to scratch, tickle, is used in the Passive Voice, 2833
metaphorically, of an eagerness to hear, in 2 Tim. 4 : 3, lit., 'itched (as to AG:437A CB:—
the hearing),' of those who, not enduring sound doctrine, heap to themselves teachers.¶

ITSELF

Note : The pronouns used are the same in their neuter forms, as those under HIMSELF.

IVORY

ELEPHANTINOS (ἐλεφάντινος), an adjective from *elephas* (whence 1661
Eng., elephant), signifies 'of ivory,' Rev. 18 : 12.¶ AG:251A CB:—

J

JACINTH

A. Noun.

HUAKINTHOS (ὑάκινθος) primarily denoted a hyacinth, probably the 5192
dark blue iris; then, a precious stone, most likely the sapphire, Rev. AG:831B CB:1251B
21 : 20.¶

B. Adjective.

HUAKINTHINOS (ὑακίνθινος) signifies hyacinthine, perhaps primarily 5191
having the colour of the hyacinth. Some regard its colour as that of the AG:831B CB:—
martagon lily, a dusky red. According to Swete, the word in Rev. 9 : 17 is "doubtless meant to describe the blue smoke of a sulphurous flame."¶

JAIL See WARD

JAILOR

DESMOPHULAX (δεσμοφύλαξ), a prison-keeper, gaoler (*desmos*, a 1200
band, *phulax*, a guard, keeper), occurs in Acts 16 : 23, 27, 36.¶ AG:176B CB:1240C

JAR See CRUSE, VESSEL, WATERPOT

For JANGLING (1 Tim. 1 : 6, A.V.) see TALKING (vain)

JASPER

IASPIS (ἴασπις), a Phœnician word (cp. Heb. *yāsh'pheh*, e.g., 2393
Ex. 28 : 20; 39 : 16), seems to have denoted a translucent stone of various AG:368D CB:1252C
colours, especially that of fire, Rev. 4 : 3; 21 : 11, 18, 19. The sardius and the jasper, of similar colour, were the first and last stones on the breastplate of the High Priest, Ex. 28 : 17, 20.¶

JEALOUS, JEALOUSY

A. Noun.

ZĒLOS (ζῆλος), zeal, jealousy, is rendered "jealousy" in the R.V. 2205
(A.V., "envying") in Rom. 13 : 13; 1 Cor. 3 : 3; Jas. 3 : 14, 16; in AG:337D CB:1273B
2 Cor. 12 : 20 (A.V., "envyings"); in Gal. 5 : 20, R.V. "jealousies" (A.V., "emulations"); in Acts 5 : 17 (A.V., "indignation"); in 13 : 45 (A.V., "envy"); in 2 Cor. 11 : 2 it is used in the phrase "with a godly jealousy," lit., 'with a jealousy of God' (R.V., marg.). See ENVY.

B. Verbs.

1. ZĒLOŌ (ζηλόω), akin to A, to be jealous, to burn with jealousy 2206
(otherwise, to seek or desire eagerly), is rendered "moved with jealousy," AG:338A CB:1273B
in Acts 7 : 9 and 17 : 5, R.V. (A.V., "moved with envy"); in 1 Cor. 13 : 4, "envieth (not)," A.V. and R.V.; in Jas. 4 : 2, R.V. marg., "are jealous" (text "covet;" A.V., "desire to have"). See AFFECT, *Note*, DESIRE.

3863 AG:616A CB:— 2. PARAZĒLOŌ (παραζηλόω), to provoke to jealousy (*para*, beside, used intensively, and No. 1), is found in Rom. 10 : 19 and 11 : 11, of God's dealings with Israel through his merciful dealings with Gentiles; in 11 : 14, R.V., " I may provoke to jealousy " (A.V., " . . . emulation "), of the Apostle's evangelical ministry to Gentiles with a view to stirring his fellow-nationals to a sense of their need and responsibilities regarding the Gospel; in 1 Cor. 10 : 22, of the provocation of God on the part of believers who compromise their Divine relationship by partaking of the table of demons; in Gal 5 : 20, of the works of the flesh.¶

For JEOPARDY see DANGER

JESTING

2160 AG:327C CB:— EUTRAPELIA (εὐτραπελία) properly denotes wit, facetiousness, versatility (lit., easily turning, from *eu*, well, *trepō*, to turn). It was used in the literal sense to describe the quick movements of apes and persons. Pericles speaks of the Athenians of his day (430 B.C.) as distinguished by a happy and gracious ' flexibility.' In the next century Aristotle uses it of ' versatility ' in the give and take of social intercourse, quick repartee. In the sixth century, B.C., the poet Pindar speaks of one Jason as never using a word of ' vain lightness,' a meaning approaching to its latest use. Its meaning certainly deteriorated, and it came to denote coarse jesting, ribaldry, as in Eph. 5 : 4, where it follows *mōrologia*, foolish talking.¶

JESUS

2424 AG:373D CB:1252C IĒSOUS (Ἰησοῦς) is a transliteration of the Heb. " Joshua," meaning ' Jehovah is salvation,' i.e., ' is the Saviour,' " a common name among the Jews, e.g., Ex. 17 : 9; Luke 3 : 29 (R.V.); Col. 4 : 11. It was given to the Son of God in Incarnation as His personal name, in obedience to the command of an angel to Joseph, the husband of His Mother, Mary, shortly before He was born, Matt. 1 : 21. By it He is spoken of throughout the Gospel narratives generally, but not without exception, as in Mark 16 : 19, 20; Luke 7 : 13, and a dozen other places in that Gospel, and a few in John.

" ' Jesus Christ ' occurs only in Matt. 1 : 1, 18; 16 : 21, marg.; Mark 1 : 1; John 1 : 17; 17 : 3. In Acts the name ' Jesus ' is found frequently. ' Lord Jesus ' is the normal usage, as in Acts 8 : 16; 19 : 5, 17; see also the reports of the words of Stephen, 7 : 59, of Ananias, 9 : 17, and of Paul, 16 : 31; though both Peter, 10 : 36, and Paul, 16 : 18, also used ' Jesus Christ.'

" In the Epp. of James, Peter, John and Jude, the personal name is not once found alone, but in Rev. eight times (R.V.), 1 : 9; 12 : 17; 14 : 12; 17 : 6; 19 : 10 (twice); 20 : 4; 22 : 16.

" In the Epp. of Paul ' Jesus ' appears alone just thirteen times, and in the Hebrews eight times; in the latter the title ' Lord ' is added once only, at 13 : 20. In the Epp. of James, Peter, John, and Jude, men who had companied with the Lord in the days of His flesh, ' Jesus Christ ' is the invariable order (in the R.V.) of the Name and Title, for this was the order of their experience ; as ' Jesus ' they knew Him first, that He was Messiah they learnt finally in His resurrection. But Paul came to know Him first in the glory of heaven, Acts 9 : 1–6, and his experience being thus the reverse of theirs, the reverse order, ' Christ Jesus,' is of frequent occurrence in his letters, but, with the exception of Acts 24 : 24, does not occur elsewhere in the R.V.

" In Paul's letters the order is always in harmony with the context. Thus ' Christ Jesus ' describes the Exalted One who emptied Himself, Phil. 2 : 5, and testifies to His pre-existence ; ' Jesus Christ ' describes the despised and rejected One Who was afterwards glorified, Phil. 2 : 11, and testifies to His resurrection. ' Christ Jesus ' suggests His grace, ' Jesus Christ ' suggests His glory."*

JEW(-S) (live as do the), JEWESS, JEWISH, JEWRY, JEWS' RELIGION

A. Adjectives.

1. IOUDAIOS (Ἰουδαῖος) is used (*a*) adjectivally, with the lit. meaning, **2453 AG:379B CB:1252C**
' Jewish,' sometimes with the addition of *anēr*, a man, Acts 10 : 28 ; 22 : 3 ; in 21 : 39 with *anthrōpos*, in some mss. (a man in the generic sense) ; the best mss. omit the phrase here ; in 13 : 6, lit., ' a Jewish false-prophet ; ' in John 3 : 22, with the word *chōra*, land or country, signifying ' Judæan,' lit., ' Judæan country ; ' used by metonymy for the people of the country ; (*b*) as a noun, a Jew, Jews, e.g., Matt. 2 : 2 ; Mark 7 : 3. The name ' Jew ' is primarily " tribal " (from ' Judah '). It is first found in 2 Kings 16 : 6, as distinct from Israel, of the Northern Kingdom. After the Captivity it was chiefly used to distinguish the race from Gentiles, e.g., John 2 : 6 ; Acts 14 : 1 ; Gal. 2 : 15, where it denotes Christians of Jewish race ; it distinguishes Jews from Samaritans, in John 4 : 9 ; from proselytes, in Acts 2 : 10. The word is most frequent in John's Gospel and the Acts ; in the former " it especially denotes the typical representatives of Jewish thought contrasted with believers in Christ . . . or with other Jews of less pronounced opinions, e.g., John 3 : 25 ; 5 : 10 ; 7 : 13 ; 9 : 22 " (Lukyn Williams, in Hastings' Bib. Dic.) ; such representatives were found, generally, in opposition to Christ ; in the Acts they are chiefly those who opposed the apostles and the Gospel. In Rom. 2 : 28, 29 the word is used of ideal Jews, i.e., Jews in spiritual reality, believers, whether Jews or Gentiles by natural birth. The feminine, " Jewess," is found in Acts 16 : 1 ; 24 : 24.

It also denotes Judæa, e.g., Matt. 2 : 1 ; Luke 1 : 5 ; John 4 : 3, the word ' country ' being understood [cp. (*a*) above]. In Luke 23 : 5 and

---

* From Notes on Thessalonians, by Hogg and Vine, pp. 26, 29.

John 7 : 1, where the A.V. has " Jewry," the R.V. translates it as usual, " Judæa."

2451 AG:379B CB:1252C 2. IOUDAIKOS (Ἰουδαϊκός) denotes " Jewish," Tit. 1 : 14.¶

B. Noun.

2454 AG:379D CB:1252C IOUDAISMOS (Ἰουδαϊσμός), Judaism, denotes " the Jews' religion," Gal. 1 : 13, 14, and stands, not for their religious beliefs, but for their religious practices, not as instituted by God, but as developed and extended from these by the traditions of the Pharisees and scribes. In the Apocrypha it denotes comprehensively " the Government, laws, institutions and religion of the Jews."¶

C. Verb.

2450 AG:379B CB:1252C IOUDAIZŌ (Ἰουδαΐζω), lit., to Judaize, i.e., to conform to Jewish religious practices and manners, is translated " to live as do the Jews," in Gal. 2 : 14.¶

D. Adverb.

2452 AG:379B CB:1252C IOUDAIKŌS (Ἰουδαϊκῶς), in Jewish fashion, is translated " as do the Jews," in Gal. 2 : 14.¶

JEWELS

5553 AG:888C CB:1240B CHRUSION (χρυσίον), gold, is used of ornaments in 1 Pet. 3 : 3, R.V., " jewels." See GOLD, No. 2.

JOIN

2853 AG:441C CB:1255C 1. KOLLAŌ (κολλάω), primarily, to glue or cement together, then, generally, to unite, to join firmly, is used in the Passive Voice signifying to join oneself to, to be joined to, Luke 15 : 15 ; Acts 5 : 13 ; 8 : 29 ; 9 : 26 ; 10 : 28, R.V. (A.V., " to keep company with ") ; 1 Cor. 6 : 16, 17 ; elsewhere, to cleave to, Luke 10 : 11 ; Acts 17 : 34 ; Rom. 12 : 9. See CLEAVE.¶

4347 AG:716A CB:1267A 2. PROSKOLLAŌ (προσκολλάω), to stick to, a strengthened form of No. 1, with *pros*, to, intensive, is used in the Passive Voice, reflexively, in a metaphorical sense, with the meanings (*a*) to join oneself to, in Acts 5 : 36 ; (*b*) to cleave to, of the husband with regard to the wife, Matt. 19 : 5 ; Mark 10 : 7 ; in Eph. 5 : 31, R.V., " shall cleave to " (A.V., " shall be joined to "). See CLEAVE.¶

— AG:775C CB:1271A 3. SU(N)ZEUGNUMI (συνζεύγνυμι), to yoke together (*sun*, with, *zugos*, a yoke), is used metaphorically of union in wedlock, in Matt. 19 : 6 ; Mark 10 : 9.¶

4927 AG:791C CB:— 4. SUNOMOREŌ (συνομορέω), to border on, is used of a house as being contiguous with a synagogue, in Acts 18 : 7, " joined hard to."¶

KATARTIZŌ 2675 AG:417D CB:1254B SUNARMOLOGEŌ 4883 AG:785B CB:— *Notes :* (1) In 1 Cor. 1 : 10, *katartizō*, to render complete, to perfect (*kata*, down, intensive, and *artios*, complete, jointed), to restore, is translated " be perfectly joined together," A.V. (R.V., " be perfected together ") ; see FIT. (2) In Eph. 4 : 16, *sunarmologeō*, to fit or frame together, is translated " fitly joined together," A.V. (R.V., " fitly framed . . . together ") ; cp. 2 : 21.¶

JOINT

1. HARMOS (ἁρμός), a joining, joint (akin to ***harmozō***, to fit, join), is 719
found in Heb. 4 : 12, figuratively (with the word " marrow ") of the AG:107D
inward moral and spiritual being of man, as just previously expressed CB:1249B
literally in the phrase " soul and spirit."¶

2. HAPHĒ (ἁφή), a ligature, joint (akin to ***haptō***, to fit, to fasten), 860
occurs in Eph. 4 : 16 and Col. 2 : 19.¶ AG:125A
CB:1249B

For JOINT-HEIR see HEIR

JOKING
See
JESTING

JOT

IŌTA (ἰῶτα), from the Heb. *yod*, the smallest Hebrew letter, is 2503
mentioned by the Lord in Matt. 5 : 18 (together with *keraia*, a little horn, AG:386A
a tittle, the point or extremity which distinguishes certain Hebrew letters CB:1252C
from others), to express the fact that not a single item of the Law will
pass away or remain unfulfilled.¶

JOURNEY (Noun and Verb), JOURNEYINGS

A. Nouns.

1. HODOS (ὁδός), a way, path, road, used of a traveller's way, a 3598
journey, is rendered "journey" in Matt. 10 : 13; Mark 6 : 8; Luke AG:553D
2 : 44, " a day's journey " (probably to Beeroth, six miles north of CB:1251A
Jerusalem); 9 : 3; 11 : 6; Acts 1 : 12, " a Sabbath day's journey," i.e., the journey which a Jew was allowed to take on the Sabbath, viz., about 2,000 yards or cubits (estimates vary). The regulation was not a Mosaic enactment, but a Rabbinical tradition, based upon an exposition of Ex. 16 : 29, and a comparison of the width of the suburb of a Levitical city as enjoined in Num. 35 : 4, 5, and the distance between the Ark and the people at the crossing of the Jordan, Josh. 3 : 4. In regard to Acts 1 : 12, there is no discrepancy between this and Luke 24 : 50, where the R.V. rightly translates by " over against Bethany," which does not fix the exact spot of the Ascension. See HIGHWAY, WAY.

2. HODOIPORIA (ὁδοιπορία), a way-faring, journeying (No. 1, and 3597
poros, a way, a passage), is used of the Lord's journey to Samaria, John AG:553D
4 : 6, and of Paul's " journeyings," 2 Cor. 11 : 26. Cp. B, No. 3. CB:—

Note: In Luke 13 : 22 the noun *poreia*, a journey, a going (cp. *poros*, 4197
No. 2, above), is used with the verb *poieō*, to make, with the meaning ' to AG:692A
journey,' lit., ' making (for Himself, Middle Voice) a way ', " journeying." CB:—
In Jas. 1 : 11, " ways." See WAY.¶

B. Verbs.

1. POREUOMAI (πορεύομαι) is used in the Middle Voice in the N.T., 4198
signifying to go, proceed, go on one's way; it is translated by the verb AG:692B
to journey in Acts 9 : 3; 22 : 6, " as I made (my) journey;" 26 : 13; CB:1266A
Rom. 15 : 24 (1st part), A.V., " I take my journey," R.V., " I go " (for the 2nd part, " in my journey," see No. 2). See GO, No. 1.

1279 AG:187D CB:— 2. DIAPOREUŌ (διαπορεύω), to carry over, used in the Passive Voice with the meaning to pass by, to journey through, is translated "in my journey," in Rom. 15 : 24, lit., 'journeying through;' in Luke 18 : 36, R.V., "going by" (A.V. "pass by"). See Go, No. 4.

3596 AG:553D CB:1251A 3. HODOIPOREŌ (ὁδοιπορέω), to travel, journey (akin to A, No. 2), is found in Acts 10 : 9.¶

3593 AG:553B CB:— 4. HODEUŌ (ὁδεύω), to be on the way, journey (from *hodos*, a way), the simplest form of the verbs denoting to journey, is used in the parable of the Good Samaritan, Luke 10 : 33.¶

4922 AG:791A CB:— 5. SUNODEUŌ (συνοδεύω), *sun*, with, and No. 4, to journey with, occurs in Acts 9 : 7.¶ In the Sept., Zech. 8 : 21.¶

2137 AG:323D CB:— 6. EUODOŌ (εὐοδόω), to help on one's way (*eu*, well, and *hodos*), is used in the Passive Voice with the meaning 'to have a prosperous journey;' so the A.V. of Rom. 1 : 10; the R.V., "I may be prospered" rightly expresses the metaphorical use which the verb acquired, without reference to a journey; see 1 Cor. 16 : 2; 3 John 2.¶

4311 AG:709B CB:— 7. PROPEMPŌ (προπέμπω), to send before or forth (*pro*, before, *pempō*, to send), also means to set forward on a journey, to escort; in 1 Cor. 16 : 6, "may set (me) forward on my journey," R.V. [A.V., "may bring (me) etc."]; so Tit. 3 : 13, and 3 John 6. See ACCOMPANY, CONDUCT, WAY.

589 AG:90A CB:1236C 8. APODĒMEŌ (ἀποδημέω) denotes to go on a journey to another country, go abroad, Matt. 21 : 33; 25 : 14, 15; Mark 12 : 1; Luke 15 :13; 20 : 9. See COUNTRY.¶

590 AG:90B CB:— *Note:* For the adjective *apodēmos*, Mark 13 : 34, A.V., "taking a far journey," R.V., "sojourning in another country," see COUNTRY.

JOY (Noun and Verb), JOYFULNESS, JOYFULLY, JOYOUS

A. Nouns.

5479 AG:875C CB:1239B 1. CHARA (χαρά), joy, delight (akin to *chairō*, to rejoice), is found frequently in Matthew and Luke, and especially in John, once in Mark (4 : 16, R.V., "joy," A.V., "gladness"); it is absent from 1 Cor. (though the verb is used three times), but is frequent in 2 Cor., where the noun is used five times (for 7 : 4, R.V., see Note below), and the verb eight times, suggestive of the Apostle's relief in comparison with the circumstances of the 1st Epistle; in Col. 1 : 11, A.V., "joyfulness," R.V., "joy." The word is sometimes used, by metonymy, of the occasion or cause of joy, Luke 2 : 10 (lit., 'I announce to you a great joy'); in 2 Cor. 1 : 15, in some mss., for *charis*, "benefit"; Phil. 4 : 1, where the readers are called the Apostle's joy; so 1 Thess. 2 : 19, 20; Heb. 12 : 2, of the object of Christ's joy; Jas. 1 : 2, where it is connected with falling into trials; perhaps also in Matt. 25 : 21, 23, where some regard it as signifying, concretely, the circumstances attending co-operation in the authority of the Lord. See also the Note following No. 3.

Note: In Heb. 12 : 11, "joyous" represents the phrase *meta*, with,
followed by *chara*, lit., 'with joy.' So in 10 : 34, "joyfully;" in 2 Cor.
7 : 4 the noun is used with the Middle Voice of *huperperisseuō*, to abound HUPERPERISSEUŌ 5248
more exceedingly, and translated "(I overflow) with joy," R.V. (A.V., "I AG:841D
am exceeding joyful"). CB:1252A
2. AGALLIASIS (ἀγαλλίασις), exultation, exuberant joy. Cp. B, 20 AG:3D
No. 3, below. See GLADNESS. CB:1233B
3. EUPHROSUNĒ (εὐφροσύνη) is rendered "joy" in the A.V. of Acts 2167
2 : 28, R.V., "gladness," as in 14 : 17. See GLADNESS.¶ AG:328A CB:1247B

Note: Joy is associated with life, e.g., 1 Thess. 3 : 8, 9. Experiences of sorrow prepare for, and enlarge, the capacity for joy, e.g., John 16 : 20; Rom. 5 : 3, 4; 2 Cor. 7 : 4; 8 : 2; Heb. 10 : 34; Jas. 1 : 2. Persecution for Christ's sake enhances joy, e.g., Matt. 5 : 11, 12; Acts 5 : 41. Other sources of joy are faith, Rom. 15 : 13; Phil. 1 : 25; hope, Rom. 5 : 2 (*kauchaomai*, see B, No. 2); 12 : 12 (*chairō*, see B, No. 1); the joy of others, 12 : 15, which is distinctive of Christian sympathy. Cp. 1 Thess. 3 : 9. In the O.T. and the N.T. God Himself is the ground and object of the believer's joy, e.g., Ps. 35 : 9; 43 : 4; Is. 61 : 10; Luke 1 : 47; Rom. 5 : 11; Phil. 3 : 1; 4 : 4.

B. Verbs.

1. CHAIRŌ (χαίρω), to rejoice, be glad, is translated "joyfully" in 5463
Luke 19 : 6, lit., 'rejoicing;' "we joyed," 2 Cor. 7 : 13; "I joy," AG:873B CB:1239B
Phil. 2 : 17; "do ye joy," 2 : 18; "joying," Col. 2 : 5; "we joy," 1 Thess. 3 : 9. It is contrasted with weeping and sorrow, e.g., in John 16 : 20, 22; Rom. 12 : 15; 1 Cor. 7 : 30 (cp. Ps. 30 : 5). See FAREWELL, GLAD, GREETING, HAIL, REJOICE.

2. KAUCHAOMAI (καυχάομαι), to boast, glory, exult, is rendered "we 2744
joy," in Rom. 5 : 11, A.V. (R.V., "we rejoice"). It would have been an AG:425C CB:1254C
advantage to translate this word distinctively by the verbs to glory or to exult.

3. AGALLIAŌ (ἀγαλλιάω), to exult, rejoice greatly, is translated 21
"with exceeding joy" in 1 Pet. 4 : 13 (Middle Voice), lit., '(ye rejoice, AG:3D CB:1233B
chairō) exulting.' Cp. A, No. 2. See GLAD, REJOICE.

4. ONINĒMI (ὀνίνημι), to benefit, profit, in the Middle Voice, to have 3685
profit, derive benefit, is translated "let me have joy" in Philm. 20 (R.V. AG:570D CB:1260C
marg., "help"); the Apostle is doubtless continuing his credit and debit metaphors and using the verb in the sense of 'profit.'¶

JUDGE (Noun and Verb)

A. Nouns.

1. KRITĒS (κριτής), a judge (from *krino*, see B, No. 1), is used (*a*) of 2923
God, Heb. 12 : 23, where the order in the original is 'to a Judge who is AG:453C CB:1256A
God of all;' this is really the significance; it suggests that He who is the Judge of His people is at the same time their God; that is the order in 10 : 30; the word is also used of God in Jas. 4 : 12, R.V.; (*b*) of Christ,

Acts 10 : 42 ; 2 Tim. 4 : 8 ; Jas. 5 : 9 ; (*c*) of a ruler in Israel in the times of the Judges, Acts 13 : 20 ; (*d*) of a Roman procurator, Acts 24 : 10 ; (*e*) of those whose conduct provides a standard of judging, Matt. 12 : 27 ; Luke 11 : 19 ; (*f*) in the forensic sense, of one who tries and decides a case, Matt. 5 : 25 (twice) ; Luke 12 : 14 (some mss. have No. 2 here) ; 12 : 58 (twice) ; 18 : 2 ; 18 : 6 (lit., 'the judge of unrighteousness,' expressing subjectively his character) ; Acts 18 : 15 ; (*g*) of one who passes, or arrogates to himself, judgment on anything, Jas. 2 : 4 (see the R.V.) ; 4 : 11.

1348 AG:198B CB:— 2. DIKASTĒS (δικαστής) denotes a judge (from *dikē*, right, a judicial hearing, justice ; akin to *dikazō*, to judge), Acts 7 : 27, 35 ; some mss. have it in Luke 12 : 14 (see No. 1) ; while *dikastēs* is a forensic term, *kritēs* " gives prominence to the mental process " (Thayer). At Athens the *dikastēs* acted as a juryman, the *kritēs* being the presiding judge.¶

B. Verbs.

2919 AG:451B CB:1256A 1. KRINŌ (κρίνω) primarily denotes to separate, select, choose ; hence, to determine, and so to judge, pronounce judgment. " The uses of this verb in the N.T. may be analysed as follows : (*a*) to assume the office of a judge, Matt. 7 : 1 ; John 3 : 17 ; (*b*) to undergo process of trial, John 3 : 18 ; 16 : 11 ; 18 : 31 ; Jas. 2 : 12 ; (*c*) to give sentence, Acts 15 : 19 ; 16 : 4 ; 21 : 25 ; (*d*) to condemn, John 12 : 48 ; Acts 13 : 27 ; Rom. 2 : 27 ; (*e*) to execute judgment upon, 2 Thess. 2 : 12 ; Acts 7 : 7 ; (*f*) to be involved in a lawsuit, whether as plaintiff, Matt. 5 : 40 ; 1 Cor. 6 : 1 ; or as defendant, Acts 23 : 6 ; (*g*) to administer affairs, to govern, Matt. 19 : 28 ; cp. Judg. 3 : 10 ; (*h*) to form an opinion, Luke 7 : 43 ; John 7 : 24 ; Acts 4 : 19 ; Rom. 14 : 5 ; (*i*) to make a resolve, Acts 3 : 13 ; 20 : 16 ; 1 Cor. 2 : 2 "*

See CALL, No. 13, CONCLUDE, CONDEMN, DECREE, DETERMINE, ESTEEM, LAW (go to), ORDAIN, SENTENCE, THINK.

Note : In Acts 21 : 25, the R.V. has " giving judgement " (A.V., " concluded ") ; see JUDGMENT, *Note* (5).

350 AG:56B CB:1235A 2. ANAKRINŌ (ἀνακρίνω), to examine, investigate, question (*ana*, up, and No. 1), is rendered " judged " in 1 Cor. 2 : 14, R.V. (A.V., " are . . . discerned ; " R.V. marg., " examined "), said of the things of the Spirit of God ; in ver. 15, " judgeth " (R.V. marg., " examineth "), said of the exercise of a discerning judgment of all things as to their true value, by one who is spiritual ; in the same verse, " is judged (of no man)," R.V. marg., " examined ", i.e., the merely natural mind cannot estimate the motives of the spiritual ; in 4 : 3, " I should be judged," i.e., as to examining and passing sentence on the fulfilment or non-fulfilment of the Apostle's stewardship ; so in the same verse, " I judge (not mine own self)," and in ver. 4 " (he that) judgeth (me is the Lord) ; " in 14 : 24, " he is judged (of all)," i.e., the light of the heart-searching testimony of the

* From Notes on Thessalonians by Hogg and Vine, p. 267.

assembly probes the conscience of the unregenerate, sifting him judicially. See ASK, No. 7, DISCERN, A, No. 1.

3. DIAKRINŌ (διακρίνω) denotes to separate throughout (*dia*, and 1252
No. 1), discriminate, discern, and hence, to decide, to judge (also to AG:185A CB:1241A
contend, to hesitate, to doubt); it is rendered "to judge" in 1 Cor. 6 : 5,
in the sense of arbitrating; in 11 : 31 (1st part), the R.V. has "(if we)
discerned (ourselves)," A.V. "(if we would) judge" (*krinō*, No. 1, is used
in the 2nd part); so in 14 : 29, R.V., "discern" (A.V., "judge"). See
DECIDE, A, DISCERN, A. No. 2.

Notes: (1) In 1 Cor. 6 : 2 (last clause) "to judge" represents the noun
kritērion, which denotes a tribunal, a law court, and the meaning thus KRITēRION
is 'are ye unworthy of sitting upon tribunals of least importance?' 2922 AG:453B
(see R.V. marg.), i.e., to judge matters of smallest importance. Some CB:—
would render it 'cases,' but there is no clear instance elsewhere of this HēGEOMAI 2233
meaning. See JUDGMENT-SEAT. (2) In Heb. 11 : 11, the verb *hēgeomai*, AG:343C
to consider, think, account, is rendered "she judged (Him faithful)," CB:1249C
A.V. (R.V., "she counted"). See COUNT, No. 2.

JUDGMENT

1. KRISIS (κρίσις) primarily denotes a separating, then, a decision, 2920
judgment, most frequently in a forensic sense, and especially of Divine AG:452C CB:1256A
judgment. For the variety of its meanings, with references, see CONDEMNATION, B, No. 3.

Notes: (1) The Holy Spirit, the Lord said, would convict the world of
(*peri*, in respect of), i.e., of the actuality of, God's judgment, John 16 : 8, 11.
Cp. 2 Thess. 1 : 5. (2) In Rom. 2 : 5 the word *dikaiokrisia*, "righteous 1341
judgment," combines the adjective *dikaios*, righteous, with *krisis*, the two AG:195C CB:1241C
words which are used separately in 2 Thess. 1 : 5.¶

2. KRIMA (κρίμα) denotes the result of the action signified by the 2917
verb *krinō*, to judge; for its general significance see CONDEMNATION, AG:450C CB:1256A
B, No. 1: it is used (*a*) of a decision passed on the faults of others, Matt. 7 : 2; (*b*) of judgment by man upon Christ, Luke 24 : 20; (*c*) of God's judgment upon men, e.g., Rom. 2 : 2, 3; 3 : 8; 5 : 16; 11 : 33; 13 : 2; 1 Cor. 11 : 29; Gal. 5 : 10; Heb. 6 : 2; Jas. 3 : 1; through Christ, e.g., John 9 : 39; (*d*) of the right of judgment, Rev. 20 : 4; (*e*) of a law-suit, 1 Cor. 6 : 7.

3. HĒMERA (ἡμέρα), a day, is translated "judgment" in 1 Cor. 4 : 3, 2250
where "man's judgment" (lit., 'man's day,' marg.) is used of the present AG:345D CB:1249C
period in which man's mere judgment is exercised, a period of human rebellion against God. The adjective *anthrōpinos*, human, belonging to man (*anthrōpos*), is doubtless set in contrast here to *kuriakos*, belonging to the Lord (*kurios*, a lord), which is used in the phrase "the Day of the Lord," in Rev. 1 : 10, "The Lord's Day," a period of Divine judgments. See DAY.

1106 AG:163A 4. GNŌMĒ (γνώμη), primarily a means of knowing (akin to *ginōskō*,
CB:1248B to know), came to denote a mind, understanding; hence (*a*) a purpose,
Acts 20:3, lit., '(it was his) purpose;' (*b*) a royal purpose, a decree,
Rev. 17:17, R.V., "mind" (A.V., "will"); (*c*) judgment, opinion,
1 Cor. 1:10, "(in the same) judgment;" Rev. 17:13, "mind;" (*d*)
counsel, advice, 1 Cor. 7:25, "(I give my) judgment;" 7:40, "(after
my) judgment;" Philm. 14, "mind." See MIND, PURPOSE, WILL.¶

Notes: (1) In 1 Cor. 6:4, A.V., *kritērion*, a tribunal, is rendered
"judgments" (R.V., "to judge," marg., "tribunals"). See JUDGE, B,
DIKAIŌMA 1345 No. 3, Note (1). (2) In Rom. 1:32, A.V., *dikaiōma*, an ordinance,
AG:198A righteous act, is translated "judgment" (R.V. "ordinance"); in Rev.
CB:1241C KATADIKĒ 15:4, "judgments" (R.V., "righteous acts"). (3) In Acts 25:15,
— A.V., *katadikē*, a sentence, condemnation, is translated "judgment"
AG:410B (R.V., "sentence"). Some mss. have *dikē*. See SENTENCE. (4) In
CB:1254A DIKĒ Phil. 1:9, A.V., *aisthēsis*, perception, discernment, is translated "judg-
1349 ment" (R.V., "discernment"). (5) In Acts 21:25, in the record of the
AG:198C CB:1242A decree from the Apostles and elders at Jerusalem to the churches of the
AISTHĒSIS Gentiles, the verb *krinō* (see JUDGE, B, No. 1), is translated "giving
144 AG:25A judgement," R.V. (A.V., "concluded").

CB:1234A
B. Adjective.

5267 HUPODIKOS (ὑπόδικος), brought to trial, answerable to (*hupo*, under,
AG:844C CB:— *dikē*, justice), Rom. 3:19, is translated "under the judgement," R.V.
(A.V., "guilty").¶

For HALL OF JUDGMENT, JUDGMENT HALL, see HALL

JUDGMENT-SEAT

968 AG:140B 1. BĒMA (βῆμα), primarily, a step, a pace (akin to *bainō*, to go), as
CB:1239A in Acts 7:5, translated "to set (his foot) on," lit., 'foot-room,' was used
to denote a raised place or platform, reached by steps, originally that at Athens in the Pnyx Hill, where was the place of assembly; from the platform orations were made. The word became used for a tribune, two of which were provided in the law-courts of Greece, one for the accuser and one for the defendant; it was applied to the tribunal of a Roman magistrate or ruler, Matt. 27:19; John 19:13; Acts 12:21, translated "throne;" 18:12, 16, 17; 25:6, 10, 17.

In two passages the word is used of the Divine tribunal before which all believers are hereafter to stand. In Rom. 14:10 it is called "The judgement-seat of God," R.V. (A.V., "of Christ"), according to the most authentic mss. The same tribunal is called "the judgment-seat of Christ," 2 Cor. 5:10, to whom the Father has given all judgment, John 5: 22, 27. At this *bēma* believers are to be made manifest, that each may 'receive the things done in (or through) the body,' according to what he has done, 'whether it be good or bad.' There they will receive rewards for their faithfulness to the Lord. For all that has been contrary in their lives to His will they will suffer loss, 1 Cor. 3 : 15. This judgment-seat is to be distinguished from the pre-millennial, earthly Throne of Christ, Matt. 25 : 31, and the post-millennial "Great White Throne," Rev. 20 : 11, at which only "the dead" will appear. The judgment-seat of Christ will be a tribunal held 'in His Parousia,' i.e., His presence with His saints after His return to receive them to Himself.¶

2. KRITĒRION (κριτήριον) primarily a means of judging (akin to 2922
krinō, to judge : Eng., criterion), then, a tribunal, law-court, or lawsuit, AG:453B CB:—
1 Cor. 6 : 2 (last clause), for which see JUDGE, B, No. 3, Note (1) ; 6 : 4, for
which see JUDGMENT, Note (1) at end ; Jas. 2 : 6.¶

JUMP See CAST, LEAP, SPRING

JURISDICTION

EXOUSIA (ἐξουσία), power, authority, is used, by metonymy, to denote 1849
jurisdiction, in Luke 23 : 7. For the different meanings of the word and AG:277D CB:1247C
other instances of its use by metonymy, see AUTHORITY, A, No. 1.

JUST, JUSTLY

A. Adjectives.

1. DIKAIOS (δίκαιος) was first used of persons observant of *dikē*, 1342
custom, rule, right, especially in the fulfilment of duties towards gods and AG:195C CB:1241C
men, and of things that were in accordance with right. The Eng. word "righteous" was formerly spelt 'rightwise', i.e., (in a) straight way. In the N.T. it denotes righteous, a state of being right, or right conduct, judged whether by the Divine standard, or according to human standards, of what is right. Said of God, it designates the perfect agreement between His nature and His acts (in which He is the standard for all men). See RIGHTEOUSNESS. It is used (1) in the broad sense, of persons : (*a*) of God, e.g., John 17 : 25 ; Rom. 3 : 26 ; 1 John 1 : 9 ; 2 : 29 ; 3 : 7 ; (*b*) of Christ, e.g., Acts 3 : 14 ; 7 : 52 ; 22 : 14 ; 2 Tim. 4 : 8 ; 1 Pet. 3 : 18 ; 1 John 2 : 1 ; (*c*) of men, Matt. 1 : 19 ; Luke 1 : 6 ; Rom. 1 : 17 ; 2 : 13 ; 5 : 7. (2) of things ; blood (metaphorical), Matt. 23 : 35 ; Christ's judgment, John 5 : 30 ; any circumstance, fact or deed, Matt. 20 : 4 (v. 7, in some mss.) ; Luke 12 : 57 ; Acts 4 : 19 ; Eph. 6 : 1 ; Phil. 1 : 7 ; 4 : 8 ; Col. 4 : 1 ; 2 Thess. 1 : 6 ; "the commandment" (the Law), Rom. 7 : 12 ; works, 1 John 3 : 12 ; the ways of God, Rev. 15 : 3. See RIGHTEOUS.

2. ENDIKOS (ἔνδικος), just, righteous (*en*, in, *dikē*, right), is said of 1738
the condemnation of those who say "Let us do evil, that good may come," AG:263B CB:—
Rom. 3 : 8 ; of the recompense of reward of transgressions under the Law, Heb. 2 : 2.¶

Note : As to the distinction between No. 1 and No. 2, "*dikaios* characterizes the subject so far as he or it is (so to speak) one with *dikē*, right ; *endikos*, so far as he occupies a due relation to *dikē* ; . . . in Rom. 3 : 8 *endikos* presupposes that which has been decided righteously, which leads to the just sentence" (Cremer).

B. Adverb.

1346 AG:198B CB:1241C DIKAIŌS (δικαίως), justly, righteously, in accordance with what is right, is said (*a*) of God's judgment, 1 Pet. 2 : 23 ; (*b*) of men, Luke 23 : 41, " justly ; " 1 Cor. 15 : 34, R.V., " righteously " (A.V., " to righteousness ") ; 1 Thess. 2 : 10, R.V., " righteously ; " Tit. 2 : 12.¶

JUSTICE

1349 AG:198C CB:1242A DIKĒ (δίκη), primarily custom, usage, came to denote what is right ; then, a judicial hearing ; hence, the execution of a sentence, " punishment," 2 Thess. 1 : 9, R.V. ; Jude 7, " punishment," R.V. (A.V., " vengeance "). In Acts 28 : 4 (A.V., " vengeance ") it is personified and denotes the goddess Justice or Nemesis (Lat., *Justitia*), who the Melita folk supposed was about to inflict the punishment of death upon Paul by means of the viper. See PUNISHMENT, VENGEANCE.¶

JUSTIFICATION, JUSTIFIER, JUSTIFY

A. Nouns.

1347 AG:198B CB:1241C 1. DIKAIŌSIS (δικαίωσις) denotes the act of pronouncing righteous, justification, acquittal ; its precise meaning is determined by that of the verb *dikaioō*, to justify (see B) ; it is used twice in the Ep. to the Romans, and there alone in the N.T., signifying the establishment of a person as just by acquittal from guilt. In Rom. 4 : 25 the phrase " for our justification," is, lit., ' because of our justification ' (parallel to the preceding clause " for our trespasses," i.e., because of trespasses committed), and means, not with a view to our justification, but because all that was necessary on God's part for our justification had been effected in the Death of Christ. On this account He was raised from the dead. The propitiation being perfect and complete, His resurrection was the confirmatory counterpart. In 5 : 18, " justification of life " means ' justification which results in life ' (cp. ver. 21). That God justifies the believing sinner on the ground of Christ's Death, involves His free gift of life. On the distinction between *dikaiōsis* and *dikaiōma*, see below.¶ In the Sept., Lev. 24 : 22.¶

1345 AG:198A CB:1241C 2. DIKAIŌMA (δικαίωμα) has three distinct meanings, and seems best described comprehensively as " a concrete expression of righteousness ; " it is a declaration that a person or thing is righteous, and hence, broadly speaking, it represents the expression and effect of *dikaiōsis* (No. 1). It signifies (*a*) an ordinance, Luke 1 : 6 ; Rom. 1 : 32, R.V., " ordinance," i.e., what God has declared to be right, referring to His decree of retribution (A.V., " judgment ") ; Rom. 2 : 26, R.V., " ordinances of the Law " (i.e., righteous requirements enjoined by the Law) ; so 8 : 4, " ordinance of the Law," i.e., collectively, the precepts of the Law, all that it demands as right ; in Heb. 9 : 1, 10, ordinances connected with the Tabernacle ritual ; (*b*) a sentence of acquittal, by which God acquits men of their guilt, on the conditions (1) of His grace in Christ, through His expiatory sacrifice, (2) the acceptance of Christ by faith, Rom. 5 : 16 ; (*c*) a righteous act,

Rom. 5 : 18, " (through one) act of righteousness," R.V., not the act of justification, nor the righteous character of Christ (as suggested by the A.V. : *dikaiōma* does not signify character, as does *dikaiosunē*, righteous- 1343
ness), but the Death of Christ, as an act accomplished consistently with AG:196B CB:1241C
God's character and counsels ; this is clear as being in antithesis to the " one trespass " in the preceding statement. Some take the word here as meaning a decree of righteousness, as in ver. 16 ; the Death of Christ could indeed be regarded as fulfilling such a decree, but as the Apostle's argument proceeds, the word, as is frequently the case, passes from one shade of meaning to another, and here stands not for a decree, but an act ; so in Rev. 15 : 4, R.V., " righteous acts " (A.V., " judgments "), and 19 : 8, " righteous acts (of the saints) " (A.V., " righteousness ").¶

Note : For *dikaiosunē*, always translated " righteousness," see RIGHTEOUSNESS.

B. Verb.

DIKAIOŌ (δικαιόω) primarily, to deem to be right, signifies, in the 1344
N.T., (*a*) to show to be right or righteous ; in the Passive Voice, to be justi- AG:197C CB:1241C
fied, Matt. 11 : 19 ; Luke 7 : 35 ; Rom. 3 : 4 ; 1 Tim. 3 : 16 ; (*b*) to declare to be righteous, to pronounce righteous, (1) by man, concerning God, Luke 7 : 29 (see Rom. 3 : 4, above) ; concerning himself, Luke 10 : 29 ; 16 : 15 ; (2) by God concerning men, who are declared to be righteous before Him on certain conditions laid down by Him.

Ideally the complete fulfilment of the Law of God would provide a basis of justification in His sight, Rom. 2 : 13. But no such case has occurred in mere human experience, and therefore no one can be justified on this ground, Rom. 3 : 9–20 ; Gal. 2 : 16 ; 3 : 10, 11 ; 5 : 4. From this negative presentation in Rom. 3, the Apostle proceeds to show that, consistently with God's own righteous character, and with a view to its manifestation, He is, through Christ, as " a propitiation . . . by (*en*, instrumental) His blood," 3 : 25, R.V., " the Justifier of him that hath faith in Jesus " (ver. 26), justification being the legal and formal acquittal from guilt by God as Judge, the pronouncement of the sinner as righteous, who believes on the Lord Jesus Christ. In ver. 24, " being justified " is in the present continuous tense, indicating the constant process of justification in the succession of those who believe and are justified. In 5 : 1, " being justified " is in the aorist, or point, tense, indicating the definite time at which each person, upon the exercise of faith, was justified. In 8 : 1, justification is presented as " no condemnation." That justification is in view here is confirmed by the preceding chapters and by verse 34. In 3 : 26, the word rendered " Justifier " is the present participle of the verb, lit., 'justifying ;' similarly in 8 : 33 (where the article is used), " God that justifieth," is, more lit., 'God is the (One) justifying,' with stress upon the word " God."

Justification is primarily and gratuitously by faith, subsequently and evidentially by works. In regard to justification by works, the so-called contradiction between James and the Apostle Paul is only apparent. There is harmony in the different views of the subject. Paul has in mind Abraham's attitude toward God, his acceptance of God's word. This was a matter known only to God. The Romans Epistle is occupied with the effect of this Godward attitude, not upon Abraham's character or actions, but upon the contrast between faith and the lack of it, namely, unbelief, cp. Rom. 11 : 20. James (2 : 21–26) is occupied with the contrast between faith that is real and faith that is false, a faith barren and dead, which is not faith at all.

Again, the two writers have before them different epochs in Abraham's life—Paul, the event recorded in Gen. 15, James, that in Gen. 22. Contrast the words ' believed ' in Gen. 15 : 6 and ' obeyed ' in 22 : 18.

Further, the two writers use the words ' faith ' and ' works ' in somewhat different senses. With Paul, faith is acceptance of God's word; with James, it is acceptance of the truth of certain statements about God, (ver. 19), which may fail to affect one's conduct. Faith, as dealt with by Paul, results in acceptance with God., i.e., justification, and is bound to manifest itself. If not, as James says ' Can that faith save him ? ' (ver. 14). With Paul, works are dead works; with James they are life works. The works of which Paul speaks could be quite independent of faith : those referred to by James can be wrought only where faith is real, and they will attest its reality.

So with righteousness, or justification : Paul is occupied with a right relationship with God, James, with right conduct. Paul testifies that the ungodly can be justified by faith, James that only the right-doer is justified. See also under RIGHTEOUS, RIGHTEOUSNESS.

KEEP, KEEPING (Noun)

A. Verbs.

1. TĒREŌ (τηρέω) denotes (*a*) to watch over, preserve, keep, watch, e.g., Acts 12 : 5, 6 ; 16 : 23 ; in 25 : 21, R.V. (1st part), " kept " (A.V., " reserved ") ; the present participle is translated " keepers " in Matt. 28 : 4, lit. ' the keeping (ones) ; ' it is used of the keeping power of God the Father and Christ, exercised over His people, John 17 : 11, 12, 15 ; 1 Thess. 5 : 23, " preserved ; " 1 John 5 : 18, where " He that was begotten of God," R.V., is said of Christ as the Keeper (" keepeth him," R.V., for A.V., " keepeth himself ") ; Jude 1, R.V., " kept for Jesus Christ " (A.V., " preserved in Jesus Christ ") ; Rev. 3 : 10 ; of their inheritance, 1 Pet. 1 : 4 (" reserved ") ; of judicial reservation by God in view of future doom, 2 Pet. 2 : 4, 9, 17 ; 3 : 7 ; Jude 6, 13 ; of keeping the faith, 2 Tim. 4 : 7 ; the unity of the Spirit, Eph. 4 : 3 ; oneself, 2 Cor. 11 : 9 ; 1 Tim. 5 : 22 ; Jas. 1 : 27 ; figuratively, one's garments, Rev. 16 : 15 ; (*b*) to observe, to give heed to, as of keeping commandments, etc., e.g., Matt. 19 : 17 ; John 14 : 15 ; 15 : 10 ; 17 : 6 ; Jas. 2 : 10 ; 1 John 2 : 3, 4, 5 ; 3 : 22, 24 ; 5 : 2 (in some mss.), 3 ; Rev. 1 : 3 ; 2 : 26 ; 3 : 8, 10 ; 12 : 17 ; 14 : 12 ; 22 : 7, 9. See RESERVE. **5083 AG:814D CB:1271B**

2. DIATĒREŌ (διατηρέω), to keep carefully (*dia*, intensive, and No. 1), is said of " the Mother of Jesus," in keeping His sayings in her heart, Luke 2 : 51, and of the command of the Apostles and elders in Jerusalem to Gentile converts in the churches to keep themselves from the evils mentioned in Acts 15 : 29.¶ **1301 AG:189D CB:1241B**

3. SUNTĒREŌ (συντηρέω) denotes to preserve, keep safe, keep close (*sun*, together with, used intensively, and No. 1), in Luke 2 : 19, as in ver. 51 (see No. 2, above), of the Mother of Jesus in regard to the words of the shepherds ; in Mark 6 : 20 it is used of Herod's preservation of John the Baptist from Herodias, R.V., " kept (him) safe," A.V., " observed (him) " (marg., " kept ") ; in Matt. 9 : 17 (in some mss., Luke 5 : 38), of the preservation of wine-skins. See OBSERVE, PRESERVE.¶ **4933 AG:792C CB:—**

4. PHULASSŌ (φυλάσσω) denotes (*a*) to guard, watch, keep watch, e.g., Luke 2 : 8 ; in the Passive Voice, 8 : 29 ; (*b*) to keep by way of protection, e.g., Luke 11 : 21 ; John 12 : 25 ; 17 : 12 (2nd part ; No. 1 in 1st part and in ver. 11) ; (*c*) metaphorically, to keep a law, precept, etc., e.g., Matt. 19 : 20 and Luke 18 : 21, " have observed ; " Luke 11 : 28 ; John 12 : 47 (in the best mss.) ; Acts 7 : 53 ; 16 : 4 ; 21 : 24 ; Rom. 2 : 26 ; Gal. 6 : 13 ; 1 Tim. 5 : 21 (" observe ") ; in the Middle Voice, Mark 10 : 20 (" have observed ") ; (*d*) in the Middle Voice, to keep oneself **5442 AG:868B CB:1264C**

from, Acts 21 : 25; elsewhere translated by the verb to beware. See
Beware, No. 3, Guard, B, No. 1.

1314 AG:191A 5. DIAPHULASSŌ (διαφυλάσσω), an intensive form of No. 4, to guard
CB:— thoroughly; see Guard.

5432 AG:867B 6. PHROUREŌ (φρουρέω), to keep with a military guard, e.g., Gal.
CB:1264C 3 : 23, R.V., "kept in ward;" see Guard, B, No. 3.

4160 AG:680D 7. POIEŌ (ποιέω), to do, make, signifies to keep, in Matt. 26 : 18, in
CB:1265C the Lord's statement, "I will keep the passover;" so in Acts 18 : 21,
in some mss.; in John 7 : 19, where the A.V. has "keepeth (the law),"
the R.V. adheres to the usual meaning "doeth."

2192 AG:331D 8. ECHŌ (ἔχω), to have, to hold, is rendered "I kept" in Luke 19 : 20,
CB:1242C R.V. (A.V., "I have kept"), of keeping a pound laid up in a napkin.
See Have.

2902 AG:448C 9. KRATEŌ (κρατέω), to be strong, get possession of, hold fast, is used
CB:1256A in Mark 9 : 10, "(and) they kept (the saying)," i.e., they held fast to the
Lord's command to refrain from telling what they had seen in the mount
of Transfiguration. See Hold.

3557 (-OMAI) 10. NOSPHIZŌ (νοσφίζω), to set apart, remove, signifies, in the Middle
AG:543D Voice, to set apart for oneself, to purloin, and is rendered "purloining"
CB:— in Tit. 2 : 10; "kept back" (and "keep") in Acts 5 : 2, 3, of the act of
Ananias and his wife in retaining part of the price of the land.¶

4912 AG:789A 11. SUNECHŌ (συνέχω), to hold together, is translated "shall . . .
CB:1270C keep (thee) in," in Luke 19 : 43. See also Note (8), below. See Constrain.

PARECHŌ 3930 *Notes:* (1) In Acts 22 : 2, A.V., *parechō*, to afford, give, cause, is ren-
AG:626B dered "kept (the more silence)," R.V., "were (the more quiet)." (2) In
AGŌ 71 Matt. 14 : 6 some mss. have the verb *agō*, to lead, hold (of a feast), of
AG:14B keeping Herod's birthday; the most authentic have *ginomai*, to become,
CB:1233C GINOMAI take place; hence the R.V., "when Herod's birthday came." The verb
1096 *agō* is used in Acts 19 : 38 of keeping certain occasions, as of the holding
AG:158A of law courts, R.V. "(the courts) are open," A.V. marg., "court days
CB:1248B BOSKŌ are kept;" Moulton and Milligan illustrate from the papyri the use
1006 of the adjective *agoraios*, in the plural with *hēmerai*, days, understood,
AG:145B CB:1239B in regard to certain market days; certain court days are what are indicated
KATAKEIMAI here. The conjecture that the meaning is 'courts are now being held'
2621 AG:411C (*sunodoi* being understood as meetings of the court instead of 'days')
PRASSŌ is scarcely so appropriate to the circumstances. (3) In Matt. 8 : 33,
4238 AG:698B *boskō*, to feed (swine etc.), is translated "(they that) fed," R.V. for A.V.
CB:1266B "(they that) kept." (4) In Acts 9 : 33, *katakeimai*, to lie down, is used
HUPOSTELLŌ 5288 with *epi*, upon, with the meaning to keep one's bed (see Lie, No. 2).
AG:847B (5) In Rom. 2 : 25, *prassō*, to do (continuously), to practise, is rendered
KŌLUŌ "be a doer of," R.V. (A.V., "keep"). (6) In Acts 20 : 20, *hupostellō*, to
2967 AG:461B shrink, draw back from, is translated "I shrank (not)" (Middle Voice),
CB:1255C R.V., A.V., "I kept back (nothing)." (7) In Acts 27 : 43, *kōluō*, to

hinder, is translated " stayed (them from)," R.V., A.V., " kept (them KATECHŌ
from)." (8) In Luke 8 : 15 and 1 Cor. 11 : 2, *katechō*, to hold fast (a 2722 AG:422C
strengthened form of *echō*, No. 8), is translated " hold fast," R.V., A.V., CB:1254B
" keep ; " in 15 : 2, R.V., " hold fast," A.V., " keep in memory." (9) For PARATITHĒMI 3908
keep secret, see SECRET. (10) For keep under, see BUFFET. (11) *Para-* AG:622D
tithēmi is rendered " commit the keeping " in 1 Pet. 4 : 19, A.V.. (12) For CB:—
" keep the feast " see FEAST, B, No. 2

B. Noun.

TĒRĒSIS (τήρησις), akin to A, No. 1, denotes (*a*) a watching, and hence, 5084
imprisonment, prison, Acts 4 : 3 and 5 : 18, " ward," R.V. (A.V., " hold " AG:815C CB:1271B
and " prison ") ; (*b*) " keeping," 1 Cor. 7 : 19. See HOLD, PRISON.¶

KEEPER

PHULAX (φύλαξ), akin to A, No. 4, above, a guard : see GUARD. 5441
Note : For *tēreō*, in Matt. 28 : 4, see A, No. 1, above. AG:868B CB:1264C

KEY

KLEIS (κλείς), a key, is used metaphorically (*a*) of " the keys of the 2807
kingdom of heaven," which the Lord committed to Peter, Matt. 16 : 19, AG:433D CB:1255B
by which he would open the door of faith, as he did to Jews at Pentecost, and to Gentiles in the person of Cornelius, acting as one commissioned by Christ, through the power of the Holy Spirit ; he had precedence over his fellow-disciples, not in authority, but in the matter of time, on the ground of his confession of Christ (ver. 16) ; equal authority was committed to them (18 : 18) ; (*b*) of " the key of knowledge," Luke 11 : 52, i.e., knowledge of the revealed will of God, by which men entered into the life that pleases God ; this the religious leaders of the Jews had presumptuously ' taken away,' so that they neither entered in themselves, nor permitted their hearers to do so ; (*c*) of " the keys of death and of Hades," Rev. 1 : 18, R.V. (see HADES), indicative of the authority of the Lord over the bodies and souls of men ; (*d*) of " the key of David," Rev. 3 : 7, a reference to Is. 22 : 22, speaking of the deposition of Shebna and the investiture of Eliakim, in terms evidently Messianic, the metaphor being that of the right of entrance upon administrative authority ; the mention of David is symbolic of complete sovereignty ; (*e*) of " the key of the pit of the abyss," Rev. 9 : 1 ; here the symbolism is that of competent authority ; the pit represents a shaft or deep entrance into the region (see ABYSS), from whence issued smoke, symbolic of blinding delusion ; (*f*) of " the key of the abyss," Rev. 20 : 1 ; this is to be distinguished from (*e*) : the symbolism is that of the complete supremacy of God over the region of the lost, in which, by angelic agency, Satan is destined to be confined for a thousand years.¶

KICK

LAKTIZŌ (λακτίζω), to kick (from *lax*, an adverb signifying ' with the 2979
foot '), is used in Acts 26 : 14 (some mss. have it in 9 : 5). AG:463A CB:—

For KID see GOAT

KILL

615 1. APOKTEINŌ (ἀποκτείνω), to kill, is used (*a*) physically, e.g., Matt.
AG:93D 10 : 28 ; 14 : 5, " put . . . to death," similarly rendered in John 18 : 31 ;
CB:1237A often of Christ's Death ; in Rev. 2 : 13, R.V., " was killed " (A.V., " was slain ") ; 9 : 15, R.V., " kill " (A.V., " slay ") ; 11 : 13, R.V., " were killed " (A.V., " were slain ") ; so in 19 : 21 ; (*b*) metaphorically, Rom. 7 : 11, of the power of sin, which is personified, as " finding occasion, through the commandment," and inflicting deception and spiritual death, i.e., separation from God, realized through the presentation of the commandment to conscience, breaking in upon the fancied state of freedom ; the argument shows the power of the Law, not to deliver from sin, but to enhance its sinfulness ; in 2 Cor. 3 : 6, " the letter killeth," signifies not the literal meaning of Scripture as contrasted with the spiritual, but the power of the Law to bring home the knowledge of guilt and its punishment ; in Eph. 2 : 16 " having slain the enmity " describes the work of Christ through His death in annulling the enmity, " the Law " (ver. 15), between Jew and Gentile, reconciling regenerate Jew and Gentile to God in spiritual unity " in one body." See DEATH, C, No. 4, SLAY.

337 2. ANAIREŌ (ἀναιρέω) denotes (*a*) to take up (*ana*, up, *haireō*, to take),
AG:54D
CB:— said of Pharaoh's daughter, in taking up Moses, Acts 7 : 21 ; (*b*) to take away in the sense of removing, Heb. 10 : 9, of the legal appointment of sacrifices, to bring in the will of God in the sacrificial offering of the Death of Christ ; (*c*) to kill, used physically only (not metaphorically as in No. 1), e.g., Luke 22 : 2 ; in 2 Thess. 2 : 8, instead of the future tense of this verb, some texts (followed by R.V. marg.) read the future of *analiskō*, to consume. See DEATH, C, No. 2, SLAY.

2380 3. THUŌ (θύω) primarily denotes to offer firstfruits to a god ; then (*a*)
AG:367A
CB:1272C to sacrifice by slaying a victim, Acts 14 : 13, 18, to do sacrifice ; 1 Cor. 10 : 20, to sacrifice ; 1 Cor. 5 : 7, " hath been sacrificed," of the Death of Christ as our Passover ; (*b*) to slay, kill, Matt. 22 : 4 ; Mark 14 : 12 ; Luke 15 : 23, 27, 30 ; 22 : 7 ; John 10 : 10 ; Acts 10 : 13 ; 11 : 7.¶

5407 4. PHONEUŌ (φονεύω), to murder, akin to *phoneus*, a murderer, is
AG:864C
CB:— always rendered by the verb to kill (except in Matt. 19 : 18, A.V., " do . . . murder," and in Matt. 23 : 35, A.V. and R.V., " ye slew ") ; Matt. 5 : 21 (twice) ; 23 : 31 ; Mark 10 : 19 ; Luke 18 : 20 ; Rom. 13 : 9 ; Jas. 2 : 11 (twice) ; 4 : 2 ; 5 : 6.¶

2289 5. THANATOŌ (θανατόω), to put to death (from *thanatos*, death), is
AG:351C
CB:1271C translated " are killed " in Rom. 8 : 36 ; " killed " in 2 Cor. 6 : 9. See DEATH, C, No. 1.

1315 6. DIACHEIRIZŌ (διαχειρίζω), primarily, to have in hand, manage
(-OMAI) (*cheir*, the hand), is used in the Middle Voice, in the sense of laying hands
AG:191A
CB:— on with a view to kill, or of actually killing, Acts 5 : 30, " ye slew ;" 26 : 21, " to kill." See SLAY.¶

7. SPHAZŌ, or SPHATTŌ (σφάζω), to slay, to slaughter, especially 4969
victims for sacrifice, is most frequently translated by the verb to slay; AG:796A CB:1269C
so the R.V. in Rev. 6:4 (A.V., "should kill"); in 13:3, R.V., "smitten
unto death" (A.V., "wounded"). See SLAY, WOUND. Cp. *katasphazō*, KATASPHAZŌ
to kill off, Luke 19:27;¶ *sphagē*, slaughter, e.g., Acts 8:32, and *sphagion*, — AG:419C
a victim for slaughter, Acts 7:42.¶ SPHAGē 4967

AG:795D

KIN, KINSFOLK, KINSMAN, KINSWOMAN

SPHAGION 4968

A. Adjective.

AG:796A

SUNGENĒS (συγγενής), primarily denoting congenital, natural, innate 4773
(*sun*, with, *genos*, a family, race, offspring), then, 'akin to,' is used as a AG:772C CB:1270C
noun, denoting (*a*) of family relationship, kin, a kinsman, kinsfolk(s),
Luke 1:58, R.V., "kinsfolk" (A.V., "cousins"); 14:12; 21:16;
John 18:26; Acts 10:24; (*b*) of tribal or racial kinship, fellow-nationals,
Rom. 9:3; 16:7, 11, 21.¶

B. Nouns.

1. SUNGENIS (συγγενίς), a late feminine form of A (some mss. have —
sungenēs), denotes a kinswoman, Luke 1:36, R.V., "kinswoman" AG:772D CB:—
(A.V., "cousin"). Cp. *sungeneia* (see KINDRED).¶

2. SUNGENEUS (συγγενεύς), an alternative form of A, is used in (-NēS) 4773
Mark 6:4, "kin," and Luke 2:44, "kinsfolk."¶ AG:772C

CB:1270C

KIND (Noun)

1. GENOS (γένος), akin to *ginomai*, to become, denotes (*a*) a family, 1085
Acts 4:6, "kindred;" 7:13, R.V., "race" (A.V., "kindred"); 13:26, AG:156A CB:1248B
"stock"; (*b*) an offspring, Acts 17:28; Rev. 22:16; (*c*) a nation, a race, Mark 7:26, R.V., "race" (A.V., "nation"); Acts 4:36, R.V. "(a man of Cyprus) by race," A.V., "of the country (of Cyprus);" *genos* does not mean a country, the word here signifies parentage (Jews had settled in Cyprus from, or even before, the reign of Alexander the Great); 7:19, R.V., "race" (A.V., "kindred"); 18:2, 24, R.V., "by race" (A.V., "born"); 2 Cor. 11:26, "countrymen;" Gal. 1:14, R.V., "countrymen" (A.V., "nation"); Phil. 3:5, "stock;" 1 Pet. 2:9, R.V., "race" (A.V., "generation"); (*d*) a kind, sort, class, Matt. 13:47, "kind;" in some mss. in 17:21, A.V., "kind;" Mark 9:29, "kind;" 1 Cor. 12:10, 28, "kinds" (A.V., "diversities"); 14:10
(ditto).¶ See BEGET, B. 5449

2. PHUSIS (φύσις) among its various meanings denotes the nature, the AG:869B
natural constitution or power of a person or thing, and is translated "kind" CB:1264C
in Jas. 3:7 (twice), "kind" (of beasts etc.), and "(man)kind," lit., TIS 5100
'human kind.' See NATURE, NATURAL. AG:819D

Notes: (1) The indefinite pronoun *tis*, some, a certain, one, is used CB:1272C LOIPON
adjectively with the noun *aparchē*, firstfruits, in Jas. 1:18, "a kind of." 3063
(2) In 1 Cor. 15:37, R.V., "some other kind" (A.V., "some other grain") AG:479D (LOIPOS 3.b.)
translates a phrase which, lit. rendered, is 'some (one) of the rest (*loipos*).' CB:1257B

(3) In 2 Cor. 6 : 13, " (for a recompense) in like kind," R.V. (A.V., " in the same "), is, lit., ' (as to) the same (recompense).'

KIND (Adjective), KIND (be), KINDLY, KINDNESS

A. Adjectives.

5543 AG:886A CB:1240A 1. CHRĒSTOS (χρηστός), serviceable, good, pleasant (of things), good, gracious, kind (of persons), is translated " kind " in Luke 6 : 35, of God ; in Eph. 4 : 32, enjoined upon believers. See BETTER, EASY, GOOD, GOODNESS, GRACIOUS.

18 AG:2D CB:1233B 2. AGATHOS (ἀγαθός), good, is translated " kind " in Tit. 2 : 5, R.V. See GOOD.

B. Verb.

5541 AG:886A CB:1240A CHRĒSTEUOMAI (χρηστεύομαι), akin to A, No. 1, to be kind, is said of love, 1 Cor. 13 : 4.¶

C. Nouns.

5544 AG:886B CB:1240A 1. CHRĒSTOTĒS (χρηστότης), akin to A, No. 1, and B, used of goodness of heart, kindness, is translated " kindness " in 2 Cor. 6 : 6 ; Gal. 5 : 22, R.V. (A.V., " gentleness ") ; Eph. 2 : 7 ; Col. 3 : 12 ; Tit. 3 : 4. See GOODNESS.

5363 AG:858D CB:1264A 2. PHILANTHRŌPIA (φιλανθρωπία), from *philos*, loving, *anthrōpos*, man (Eng., philanthropy), denotes kindness, and is so translated in Acts 28 : 2, of that which was shown by the inhabitants of Melita to the shipwrecked voyagers ; in Tit. 3 : 4, of the kindness of God, translated " (His) love toward man." See LOVE.¶

D. Adverb.

5364 AG:858D CB:1264A PHILANTHRŌPŌS (φιλανθρώπως), akin to C, No. 2, humanely, kindly, is translated " kindly " in Acts 27 : 3 (A.V., " courteously "). See COURTEOUSLY.¶

KINDLE

681 AG:102D CB:1249B 1. HAPTŌ (ἅπτω), properly, to fasten to, is used in Acts 28 : 2 (in the most authentic mss., some mss. have No. 3), of kindling a fire. See No. 2.

Note : Haptō is used of lighting a lamp, in Luke 8 : 16 ; 11 : 33 ; 15 : 8. For the Middle Voice see TOUCH.

— AG:645D CB:— 2. PERIAPTŌ (περιάπτω), properly, to tie about, attach (*peri*, around, and No. 1), is used of lighting a fire in the midst of a court in Luke 22 : 55 (some mss. have No. 1).¶

381 AG:60A CB:— 3. ANAPTŌ (ἀνάπτω), to light up (*ana*, up, and No. 1), is used (*a*) literally, in Jas. 3 : 5, " kindleth ; " (*b*) metaphorically, in the Passive Voice, in Luke 12 : 49, of the kindling of the fire of hostility ; see FIRE, A (*f*). For Acts 28 : 2, see No. 1, above.¶

KINDRED

4772 AG:772C CB:1270C 1. SUNGENEIA (συγγένεια) primarily denotes kinship ; then, kinsfolk, kindred (cp. *sungenēs*, a kinsman ; see KIN), Luke 1 : 61 ; Acts. 7 : 3, 14.¶

2. GENOS (γένος); see KIND (Noun), No. 1. 1085 AG:156A
Notes: (1) *Phulē*, a tribe, rendered "kindreds" in the A.V. of CB:1248B
Rev. 1:7; 7:9; 11:9; 13:7, "kindred" in 5:9; 14:6, and elsewhere, PHULē 5443
"tribe," "tribes," is always translated by the latter in the R.V. See AG:868D
TRIBE. (2) For *patria*, rendered "kindreds" in Acts 3:25, A.V., see CB:1264C PATRIA
FAMILY. 3965 AG:636D

KING CB:1263A

A. Noun.

BASILEUS (βασιλεύς), a king (cp. Eng., Basil), e.g., Matt. 1:6, 935 AG:136A CB:1238C
is used of the Roman Emperor in 1 Pet. 2:13, 17 (a command of general application); this reference to the Emperor is illustrated frequently in the *koinē* (for which see Preface to Vol. I); of Herod the Tetrarch (used by courtesy), Matt. 14:9; of Christ, as the King of the Jews, e.g., Matt. 2:2; 27:11, 29, 37; as the King of Israel, Mark 15:32; John 1:49; 12:13; as King of kings, Rev. 17:14; 19:16; as "the King" in judging nations and men at the establishment of the Millennial Kingdom, Matt. 25:34, 40; of God, "the great King," Matt. 5:35; "the King eternal, incorruptible, invisible," 1 Tim. 1:17; "King of kings," 1 Tim. 6:15, see Note (2) below; "King of the ages," Rev. 15:3, R.V. (A.V., "saints"). Christ's Kingship was predicted in the O.T., e.g., Psa. 2:6, and in the N.T., e.g., Luke 1:32, 33; He came as such, e.g., Matt. 2:2; John 18:37; was rejected and died as such, Luke 19:14; Matt. 27:37; is now a King Priest, after the order of Melchizedek, Heb. 5:6; 7:1, 17; and will reign for ever and ever, Rev. 11:15.

Notes: (1) In Rev. 1:6 and 5:10, the most authentic mss. have the
word *basileia*, kingdom, instead of the plural of *basileus*, A.V., "kings;" BASILEIA 932
R.V., "a kingdom (to be priests)," and "a kingdom (and priests)." The AG:134D
kingdom was conditionally offered by God to Israel, that they should be CB:1238C
to Him "a kingdom of priests," Ex. 19:6, the entire nation fulfilling priestly worship and service. Their failure to fulfil His covenant resulted in the selection of the Aaronic priesthood. The bringing in of the new and better covenant of grace has constituted all believers a spiritual Kingdom, a holy and royal priesthood, 1 Pet. 2:5, 9. (2) In 1 Tim. 6:15,
the word "kings" translates the present participle of the verb *basileuō*, BASILEUō
to be king, to have kingship, lit., 'of (those) who are kings.' See REIGN. 936 AG:136C
(3) Deissmann has shown that the title "king of kings" was "in very CB:1238C
early eastern history a decoration of great monarchs and also a divine title" (*Light from the Ancient East*, pp. 367, f.). Moulton and Milligan illustrate the use of the title among the Persians, from documents discovered in Media.

B. Adjectives.

1. BASILEIOS (βασίλειος), denoting royal, as in 1 Pet. 2:9, is used 934
in the plural, of the courts or palaces of kings, Luke 7:25, "kings' AG:136A CB:1238C
courts;" a possible meaning is 'among royal courtiers or persons.'¶

937 2. BASILIKOS (βασιλικός), royal, belonging to a king, is used in Acts
AG:136D 12 : 20 with 'country' understood, "their country was fed from the
CB:1238C king's," lit., 'the royal (country).' See NOBLEMAN, ROYAL.

KINGDOM

932 BASILEIA (βασιλεία) is primarily an abstract noun, denoting
AG:134D sovereignty, royal power, dominion, e.g., Rev. 17 : 18, translated "(which)
CB:1238C reigneth," lit., 'hath a kingdom' (R.V. marg.); then, by metonymy, a concrete noun, denoting the territory or people over whom a king rules, e.g., Matt. 4 : 8; Mark 3 : 24. It is used especially of the Kingdom of God and of Christ.

"The Kingdom of God is (*a*) the sphere of God's rule, Ps. 22 : 28; 145 : 13; Dan. 4 : 25; Luke 1 : 52; Rom. 13 : 1, 2. Since, however, this earth is the scene of universal rebellion against God, e.g., Luke 4 : 5, 6; 1 John 5 : 19; Rev. 11 : 15-18, the Kingdom of God is (*b*) the sphere in which, at any given time, His rule is acknowledged. God has not relinquished His sovereignty in the face of rebellion, demoniac and human, but has declared His purpose to establish it, Dan. 2 : 44; 7 : 14; 1 Cor. 15 : 24, 25. Meantime, seeking willing obedience, He gave His law to a nation and appointed kings to administer His Kingdom over it, 1 Chron. 28 : 5. Israel, however, though declaring still a nominal allegiance shared in the common rebellion, Isa. 1 : 2-4, and, after they had rejected the Son of God, John 1 : 11 (cp. Matt. 21 : 33-43), were "cast away," Rom. 11 : 15, 20, 25. Henceforth God calls upon men everywhere, without distinction of race or nationality, to submit voluntarily to His rule. Thus the Kingdom is said to be 'in mystery' now, Mark 4 : 11, that is, it does not come within the range of the natural powers of observation, Luke 17 : 20, but is spiritually discerned, John 3 : 3 (cp. 1 Cor. 2 : 14). When, hereafter, God asserts His rule universally, then the Kingdom will be in glory, that is, it will be manifest to all; cp. Matt. 25 : 31-34; Phil. 2 : 9-11; 2 Tim. 4 : 1, 18.

"Thus, speaking generally, references to the Kingdom fall into two classes, the first, in which it is viewed as present and involving suffering for those who enter it, 2 Thess. 1 : 5; the second, in which it is viewed as future and is associated with reward, Matt. 25 : 34, and glory, 13 : 43. See also Acts 14 : 22.

"The fundamental principle of the Kingdom is declared in the words of the Lord spoken in the midst of a company of Pharisees, "the Kingdom of God is in the midst of you," Luke 17 : 21, marg., that is, where the King is, there is the Kingdom. Thus at the present time and so far as this earth is concerned, where the King is and where His rule is acknowledged, is, first, in the heart of the individual believer, Acts 4 : 19; Eph. 3 : 17; 1 Pet. 3 : 15; and then in the churches of God, 1 Cor. 12 : 3, 5, 11; 14 : 37; cp. Col. 1 : 27, where for "in" read 'among.'

"Now, the King and His rule being refused, those who enter the Kingdom of God are brought into conflict with all who disown its allegiance, as well as with the desire for ease, and the dislike of suffering and unpopularity, natural to all. On the other hand, subjects of the Kingdom are the objects of the care of God, Matt. 6 : 33, and of the rejected King, Heb. 13 : 5.

"Entrance into the Kingdom of God is by the new birth, Matt. 18 : 3; John 3 : 5, for nothing that a man may be by nature, or can attain to by any form of self-culture, avails in the spiritual realm. And as the new nature, received in the new birth, is made evident by obedience, it is further said that only such as do the will of God shall enter into His Kingdom, Matt. 7 : 21, where, however, the context shows that the reference is to the future, as in 2 Pet. 1 : 10, 11. Cp. also 1 Cor. 6 : 9, 10; Gal. 5 : 21; Eph. 5 : 5.

"The expression 'Kingdom of God' occurs four times in Matthew, 'Kingdom of the Heavens' usually taking its place. The latter (cp. Dan. 4 : 26) does not occur elsewhere in N.T., but see 2 Tim. 4 : 18, "His heavenly Kingdom." . . . This Kingdom is identical with the Kingdom of the Father (cp. Matt. 26 : 29 with Mark 14 : 25), and with the Kingdom of the Son (cp. Luke 22 : 30). Thus there is but one Kingdom, variously described: of the Son of Man, Matt. 13 : 41; of Jesus, Rev. 1 : 9; of Christ Jesus, 2 Tim. 4 : 1; "of Christ and God," Eph. 5 : 5; "of our Lord, and of His Christ," Rev. 11 : 15; "of our God, and the authority of His Christ," 12 : 10; "of the Son of His love," Col. 1 : 13.

"Concerning the future, the Lord taught His disciples to pray, "Thy Kingdom come," Matt. 6 : 10, where the verb is in the point tense, precluding the notion of gradual progress and development, and implying a sudden catastrophe as declared in 2 Thess. 2 : 8.

"Concerning the present, that a man is of the Kingdom of God is not shown in the punctilious observance of ordinances, which are external and material, but in the deeper matters of the heart, which are spiritual and essential, viz., 'righteousness, and peace, and joy in the Holy Spirit,' Rom. 14 : 17."*

"With regard to the expressions 'the Kingdom of God' and the 'Kingdom of the Heavens,' while they are often used interchangeably, it does not follow that in every case they mean exactly the same and are quite identical.

"The Apostle Paul often speaks of the Kingdom of God, not dispensationally but morally, e.g., in Rom. 14 : 17; 1 Cor. 4 : 20, but never so of the Kingdom of Heaven. 'God' is not the equivalent of 'the heavens.' He is everywhere and above all dispensations, whereas 'the heavens' are distinguished from the earth, until the Kingdom comes in judgment

* From Notes on Thessalonians by Hogg and Vine, pp. 68–70.

and power and glory (Rev. 11 : 15, R.V.) when rule in heaven and on earth will be one.

" While, then, the sphere of the Kingdom of God and the Kingdom of Heaven are at times identical, yet the one term cannot be used indiscriminately for the other. In the ' Kingdom of Heaven ' (32 times in Matt.), heaven is in antithesis to earth, and the phrase is limited to the Kingdom in its earthly aspect for the time being, and is used only dispensationally and in connection with Israel. In the ' Kingdom of God ', in its broader aspect, God is in antithesis to ' man ' or ' the world,' and the term signifies the entire sphere of God's rule and action in relation to the world. It has a moral and spiritual force and is a general term for the Kingdom at any time. The Kingdom of Heaven is always the Kingdom of God, but the Kingdom of God is not limited to the Kingdom of Heaven, until in their final form, they become identical ; e.g., Rev. 11 : 15, R.V. ; John 3 : 5 ; Rev. 12 : 10." (*An Extract*).

For KINSFOLK and KINSMAN see KIN

KISS (Noun and Verb)

A. Noun.

5370 AG:859C
CB:1264A
PHILĒMA (φίλημα), a kiss (akin to B), Luke 7 : 45 ; 22 : 48, was a token of Christian brotherhood, whether by way of welcome or farewell, " a holy kiss," Rom. 16 : 16 ; 1 Cor. 16 : 20 ; 2 Cor. 13 : 12 ; 1 Thess. 5 : 26, " holy " (*hagios*), as free from anything inconsistent with their calling as saints (*hagioi*) ; " a kiss of love," 1 Pet. 5 : 14. There was to be an absence of formality and hypocrisy, a freedom from prejudice arising from social distinctions, from discrimination against the poor, from partiality towards the well-to-do. In the churches masters and servants would thus salute one another without any attitude of condescension on the one part or disrespect on the other. The kiss took place thus between persons of the same sex. In the " Apostolic Constitutions," a writing compiled in the 4th century, A.D., there is a reference to the custom whereby men sat on one side of the room where a meeting was held, and women on the other side of the room (as is frequently the case still in parts of Europe and Asia), and the men are bidden to salute the men, and the women the women, with " the kiss of the Lord."¶

B. Verbs.

5368 AG:859B
CB:1264A
1. PHILEŌ (φιλέω), to love, signifies to kiss, in Matt. 26 : 48 ; Mark 14 : 44 ; Luke 22 : 47.

2705 AG:420B
CB:1254B
2. KATAPHILEŌ (καταφιλέω) denotes to kiss fervently (*kata*, intensive, and No. 1) ; the stronger force of this verb has been called in question, but the change from *phileō* to *kataphileō* in Matt. 26 : 49 and Mark 14 : 45 can scarcely be without significance, and the act of the traitor was almost certainly more demonstrative than the simple kiss of salu-

tation. So with the kiss of genuine devotion, Luke 7 : 38, 45 ; 15 : 20 ; Acts 20 : 37, in each of which this verb is used.¶

KNEE

GONU (γόνυ), a knee (Latin, *genu*), is used (*a*) metaphorically in 1119
Heb. 12 : 12, where the duty enjoined is that of " courageous self-recovery AG:165A CB:1248C
in God's strength ; " (*b*) literally, of the attitude of a suppliant, Luke 5 : 8 ; Eph. 3 : 14 ; of veneration, Rom. 11 : 4 ; 14 : 11 ; Phil. 2 : 10 ; in mockery, Mark 15 : 19. See KNEEL.

KNEEL

1. GONUPETEŌ (γονυπετέω) denotes to bow the knees, kneel, from 1120
gonu (see above) and *piptō*, to fall prostrate, the act of one imploring AG:165B CB:—
aid, Matt. 17 : 14 ; Mark 1 : 40 ; of one expressing reverence and honour, Mark 10 : 17 ; in mockery, Matt. 27 : 29.¶

2. A phrase consisting of *tithēmi*, to put, with *gonata*, the plural of TITHĒMI 5087
gonu, the knee (see above), signifies to kneel, and is always used of an AG:815D
attitude of prayer, Luke 22 : 41 (lit., ' placing the knees ') ; Acts 7 : 60 ; CB:1272C GONU
9 : 40 ; 20 : 36 ; 21 : 5.¶ 1119 AG:165A CB:1248C

KNIT TOGETHER

SUMBIBAZŌ (συμβιβάζω) signifies to cause to coalesce, to join or knit 4822
together, Eph. 4 : 16, R.V., " knit together " (A.V., " compacted)" ; AG:777D CB:—
Col. 2 : 2, where some would assign the alternative meaning, to instruct, as, e.g., in 1 Cor. 2 : 16 ; in Col. 2 : 19, " knit together," it is said of the Church, as the Body of which Christ is the Head. See COMPACTED.

Note : In Acts 10 : 11 some mss. have the verb *deō*, to bind, translated 1210
" knit," of the four corners of the sheet in Peter's vision. The R.V. AG:177D CB:1240C
" let down " translates the verb *kathiēmi*, found in the best texts.

KNOCK

KROUŌ (κρούω), to strike, knock, is used in the N.T. of knocking 2925
at a door, (*a*) literally, Luke 12 : 36 ; Acts 12 : 13, 16 ; (*b*) figuratively, AG:453D CB:1256A
Matt. 7 : 7, 8 ; Luke 11 : 9, 10 (of importunity in dealing with God) ; 13 : 25 ; Rev. 3 : 20.¶

KNOW, KNOWN, KNOWLEDGE, UNKNOWN

A. Verbs.

1. GINŌSKŌ (γινώσκω) signifies to be taking in knowledge, to come 1097
to know, recognize, understand, or to understand completely, e.g., AG:160D CB:1248B
Mark 13 : 28, 29 ; John 13 : 12 ; 15 : 18 ; 21 : 17 ; 2 Cor. 8 : 9 ; Heb. 10 : 34 ; 1 John 2 : 5 ; 4 : 2, 6 (twice), 7, 13 ; 5 : 2, 20 ; in its past tenses it frequently means to know in the sense of realising, the aorist or point tense usually indicating definiteness, Matt. 13 : 11 ; Mark 7 : 24 ; John 7 : 26 ; in 10 : 38 " that ye may know (aorist tense) and understand, (present tense) ; " 19 : 4 ; Acts 1 : 7 ; 17 : 19 ; Rom. 1 : 21 ; 1 Cor. 2 : 11 (2nd

part), 14; 2 Cor. 2 : 4; Eph. 3 : 19; 6 : 22; Phil. 2 : 19; 3 : 10; 1 Thess. 3 : 5; 2 Tim. 2 : 19; Jas. 2 : 20; 1 John 2 : 13 (twice), 14; 3 : 6; 4 : 8; 2 John 1; Rev. 2 : 24; 3 : 3, 9. In the Passive Voice, it often signifies to become known, e.g., Matt. 10 : 26; Phil. 4 : 5. In the sense of complete and absolute understanding on God's part, it is used, e.g., in Luke 16 : 15; John 10 : 15 (of the Son as well as the Father); 1 Cor. 3 : 20. In Luke 12 : 46, A.V., it is rendered "he is . . . aware."

In the N.T. *ginōskō* frequently indicates a relation between the person knowing and the object known; in this respect, what is known is of value or importance to the one who knows, and hence the establishment of the relationship, e.g., especially of God's knowledge, 1 Cor. 8 : 3, "if any man love God, the same is known of Him;" Gal. 4 : 9, "to be known of God;" here the knowing suggests approval and bears the meaning 'to be approved;' so in 2 Tim. 2 : 19; cp. John 10 : 14, 27; Gen. 18 : 19; Nahum 1 : 7; the relationship implied may involve remedial chastisement, Amos 3 : 2. The same idea of appreciation as well as knowledge underlies several statements concerning the knowledge of God and His truth on the part of believers, e.g., John 8 : 32; 14 : 20, 31; 17 : 3; Gal. 4 : 9 (1st part); 1 John 2 : 3, 13, 14; 4 : 6, 8, 16; 5 : 20; such knowledge is obtained, not by mere intellectual activity, but by operation of the Holy Spirit consequent upon acceptance of Christ. Nor is such knowledge marked by finality; see, e.g., 2 Pet. 3 : 18; Hos. 6 : 3, R.V.

The verb is also used to convey the thought of connection or union, as between man and woman, Matt. 1 : 25; Luke 1 : 34.

AG:555D̄ CB:1260B 2. OIDA (οἶδα), from the same root as *eidon*, to see, is a perfect tense with a present meaning, signifying, primarily, to have seen or perceived; hence, to know, to have knowledge of, whether absolutely, as in Divine knowledge, e.g., Matt. 6 : 8, 32; John 6 : 6, 64; 8 : 14; 11 : 42; 13 : 11; 18 : 4; 2 Cor. 11 : 31; 2 Pet. 2 : 9; Rev. 2 : 2, 9, 13, 19; 3 : 1, 8, 15; or in the case of human knowledge, to know from observation, e.g., 1 Thess. 1 : 4, 5; 2 : 1; 2 Thess. 3 : 7.

The differences between *ginōskō* (No. 1) and *oida* demand consideration: (*a*) *ginōskō*, frequently suggests inception or progress in knowledge, while *oida* suggests fulness of knowledge, e.g., John 8 : 55, "ye have not known Him" (*ginōskō*), i.e., begun to know, "but I know Him" (*oida*), i.e., 'know Him perfectly;' 13 : 7, "What I do thou knowest not now," i.e. Peter did not yet perceive (*oida*) its significance, "but thou shalt understand," i.e., 'get to know (*ginōskō*), hereafter;' 14 : 7, "If ye had known Me" (*ginōskō*), i.e., 'had definitely come to know Me,' "ye would have known My Father also" (*oida*), i.e., 'would have had perception of:' "from henceforth ye know Him" (*ginōskō*), i.e., having unconsciously been coming to the Father, as the One who was in Him, they would now consciously be in the constant and progressive experience of knowing Him; in Mark 4 : 13, "Know ye not (*oida*) this parable ? and how shall ye know (*ginōskō*) all the parables ? " (R.V.), i.e., ' Do ye not understand this parable ? How shall ye come to perceive all . . .' the intimation being that the first parable is a leading and testing one ; (*b*) while *ginōskō* frequently implies an active relation between the one who knows and the person or thing known (see No. 1, above), *oida* expresses the fact that the object has simply come within the scope of the knower's perception ; thus in Matt. 7 : 23 " I never knew you " (*ginōskō*) suggests ' I have never been in approving connection with you,' whereas in 25 : 12, " I know you not " (*oida*) suggests ' you stand in no relation to Me.'

3. EPIGINŌSKŌ (ἐπιγινώσκω) denotes (*a*) to observe, fully perceive, notice attentively, discern, recognize (*epi*, upon, and No. 1) ; it suggests generally a directive, a more special, recognition of the object known than does No. 1 ; it also may suggest advanced knowledge or special appreciation ; thus, in Rom. 1 : 32, " knowing the ordinance of God " (*epiginōskō*) means ' knowing full well,' whereas in verse 21 " knowing God " (*ginōskō*) simply suggests that they could not avoid the perception. Sometimes *epiginōskō* implies a special participation in the object known, and gives greater weight to what is stated ; thus in John 8 : 32, " ye shall know the truth," *ginōskō* is used, whereas in 1 Tim. 4 : 3, " them that believe and know the truth," *epiginōskō* lays stress on participation in the truth. Cp. the stronger statement in Col. 1 : 6 (*epiginōskō*) with that in 2 Cor. 8 : 9 (*ginōskō*), and the two verbs in 1 Cor. 13 : 12, " now I know in part (*ginōskō*) ; but then shall I know (*piginōskō*) even as also I have been known (*epiginōskō*)," a knowledge " which perfectly unites the subject with the object ; " (*b*) to discover, ascertain, determine, e.g., Luke 7 : 37 ; 23 : 7 ; Acts 9 : 30 ; 19 : 34 ; 22 : 29 ; 28 : 1 ; in 24 : 11 the best mss. have this verb instead of No. 1 ; hence the R.V., " take knowledge." J. Armitage Robinson (on Ephesians) points out that *epignōsis* is " knowledge directed towards a particular object, perceiving, discerning," whereas *gnōsis* is knowledge in the abstract. See ACKNOWLEDGE. **1921 AG:291A CB:1245C**

4. PROGINŌSKŌ (προγινώσκω), to know beforehand, is used (*a*) of the Divine foreknowledge concerning believers, Rom. 8 : 29 ; Israel, 11 : 2 ; Christ as the Lamb of God, 1 Pet. 1 : 20, R.V., " foreknown " (A.V., " foreordained ") ; (*b*) of human previous knowledge, of a person, Acts 26 : 5, R.V., " having knowledge of " (A.V., " which knew ") ; of facts, 2 Pet. 3 : 17. See FOREKNOW.¶ **4267 AG:703D CB:1266C**

5. EPISTAMAI (ἐπίσταμαι), to know, know of, understand (probably an old Middle Voice form of *ephistēmi*, to set over), is used in Mark 14 : 68, " understand," which follows *oida* "I (neither) know ; " most frequently in the Acts, 10 : 28 ; 15 : 7 ; 18 : 25 ; 19 : 15, 25 ; 20 : 18 ; 22 : 19 ; 24 : 10 ; 26 : 26 ; elsewhere, 1 Tim. 6 : 4 ; Heb. 11 : 8 ; Jas. 4 : 14 ; Jude 10. See UNDERSTAND.¶ **1987 AG:300A CB:1246A**

— AG:791B 6. SUNOIDA (σύνοιδα), *sun*, with,and No. 2, a perfect tense with a
CB:1270C present meaning, denotes (*a*) to share the knowledge of, be privy to, Acts
5 : 2 ; (*b*) to be conscious of, especially of guilty consciousness, 1 Cor.
SUNEIDON 4894 (-DŌ) 4 : 4, " I know nothing against (A.V., by) myself." The verb is connected
AG:791B with *suneidon*, found in Acts 12 : 12 ; 14 : 6 (in the best texts). See
50 CONSIDER, PRIVY, WARE.¶
AG:11B CB:1233B 7. AGNOEŌ (ἀγνοέω), not to know, to be ignorant : see IGNORANT.
1107 AG:163B 8. GNŌRIZŌ (γνωρίζω) signifies (*a*) to come to know, discover, know,
CB:1248B Phil. 1 : 22, " I wot (not)," i.e., ' I know not,' ' I have not come to know '
(the R.V., marg. renders it, as under (*b*), " I do not make known ") ;
(*b*) to make known, whether (I) communicating things before unknown,
DIAGNŌRIZŌ 1232 Luke 2 : 15, 17 ; in the latter some mss. have the verb *diagnōrizō* (hence
AG:182B the A.V., " made known abroad) ; " John 15 : 15, " I have made
CB:— known ; " 17 : 26 ; Acts 2 : 28 ; 7 : 13 (1st part), see Note (3) below ;
Rom. 9 : 22, 23 ; 16 : 26 (Passive Voice) ; 2 Cor. 8 : 1, " we make known
(to you)," R.V., A.V., " we do (you) to wit ; " Eph. 1 : 9 ; 3 : 3, 5, 10
(all three in the Passive Voice) ; 6 : 19, 21 ; Col. 1 : 27 ; 4 : 7, 9, " shall
make known " (A.V., " shall declare ") ; 2 Pet. 1 : 16 ; or (II) reasserting
things already known, 1 Cor. 12 : 3, " I give (you) to understand " (the
Apostle reaffirms what they knew) ; 15 : 1, of the Gospel ; Gal. 1 : 11
(he reminds them of what they well knew, the ground of his claim to
PARAKOLOUTHEŌ Apostleship) ; Phil. 4 : 6 (Passive Voice), of requests to God. See CERTIFY,
3877 DECLARE (Note), UNDERSTAND, WIT, WOT.¶
AG:618D CB:1262A *Notes :* (1) In 2 Tim. 3 : 10, A.V., *parakoloutheō*, to follow closely,
PLĒROPHOREŌ follow as a standard of conduct, is translated " hast fully known " (R.V.,
4135 AG:670B " didst follow "). See FOLLOW. (2) In 2 Tim. 4 : 17, A.V., *plērophoreō*,
CB:1265B to fulfil, accomplish, is translated " might be fully known " (R.V., " might
ANAGNŌRIZŌ 319 (-OMAI) be fully proclaimed "). See FULFIL. (3) In Acts 7 : 13, some mss.
AG:52D have the verb *anagnōrizō*, to make oneself known, " was made known,"
CB:— PHANEROS instead of No. 8 (which see).¶ (4) In Acts 7 : 13 (2nd part) the A.V.,
5318 " was made known " translates the phrase *phaneros ginomai*, to become
AG:852B CB:1263C manifest (R.V., " became manifest "). See MANIFEST. (5) For
DIAGINŌSKŌ *diagnōrizō*, to make known, in Luke 2 : 17, see No. 8. (6) For *diaginōskō*,
1231 AG:182B in Acts 24 : 22, " I will know the uttermost of," see DETERMINE, No. 5.
CB:—

B. Adjectives.

1110 AG:164B 1. GNŌSTOS (γνωστός), a later form of *gnōtos* (from No. 1), most
CB:1248B frequently denotes " known ; " it is used ten times in the Acts, always
with that meaning (save in 4 : 16, where it means " notable ") ; twice
in the Gospel of John, 18 : 15, 16 ; in Luke 2 : 44 and 23 : 49 it denotes
" acquaintance ; " elsewhere only in Rom. 1 : 19, " (that which) may be
known (of God)," lit., ' the knowable of God,' referring to the physical
universe, in the creation of which God has made Himself knowable, that
is, by the exercise of man's natural faculties, without such supernatural
revelations as those given to Israel. See ACQUAINTANCE.

2. PHANEROS (φανερός), visible, manifest, is translated " known " **5318**
in Matt. 12 : 16 and Mark 3 : 12. See APPEAR, MANIFEST, OPENLY, **AG:852B CB:1263C**
OUTWARDLY.

3. EPISTĒMŌN (ἐπιστήμων), akin to A, No. 5, knowing, skilled, is **1990**
used in Jas. 3 : 13, A.V., " endued with knowledge " (R.V. " under- **AG:300C CB:—**
standing ").¶

4. AGNŌSTOS (ἄγνωστος), the negative of No. 1, " unknown," is **57**
found in Acts 17 : 23.¶ **AG:12B CB:1233C**

C. Nouns.

1. GNŌSIS (γνῶσις), primarily a seeking to know, an enquiry, **1108**
investigation (akin to A, No. 1), denotes, in the N.T., knowledge, especially **AG:163D CB:1248B**
of spiritual truth ; it is used (*a*) absolutely, in Luke 11 : 52 ; Rom. 2 : 20 ; 15 : 14 ; 1 Cor. 1 : 5 ; 8 : 1 (twice), 7, 10, 11 ; 13 : 2, 8 ; 14 : 6 ; 2 Cor. 6 : 6 ; 8 : 7 ; 11 : 6 ; Eph. 3 : 19 ; Col. 2 : 3 ; 1 Pet. 3 : 7 ; 2 Pet. 1 : 5, 6 ; (*b*) with an object : in respect of (1) God, 2 Cor. 2 : 14 ; 10 : 5 ; (2) the glory of God, 2 Cor. 4 : 6 ; (3) Christ Jesus, Phil. 3 : 8 ; 2 Pet. 3 : 18 ; (4) salvation, Luke 1 : 77 ; (*c*) subjectively, of God's knowledge, Rom. 11 : 33 ; the word of knowledge, 1 Cor. 12 : 8 ; knowledge falsely so called, 1 Tim. 6 : 20.¶

2. EPIGNŌSIS (ἐπίγνωσις), akin to A, No. 3, denotes exact or full **1922**
knowledge, discernment, recognition, and is a strengthened form of **AG:291B CB:1245C**
No. 1, expressing a fuller or a full knowledge, a greater participation by the knower in the object known, thus more powerfully influencing him. It is not found in the Gospels and Acts. Paul uses it 15 times (16 if Heb. 10 : 26 is included) out of the 20 occurrences ; Peter 4 times, all in his 2nd Epistle. Contrast Rom. 1 : 28 (*epignōsis*) with the simple verb in ver. 21. " In all the four Epistles of the first Roman captivity it is an element in the Apostle's opening prayer for his correspondents' well-being, Phil. 1 : 9 ; Eph. 1 : 17 ; Col. 1 : 9 ; Philm. 6 " (Lightfoot).

It is used with reference to God in Rom. 1 : 28 ; 10 : 2 ; Eph. 1 : 17 ; Col. 1 : 10 ; 2 Pet. 1 : 3 ; God and Christ, 2 Pet. 1 : 2 ; Christ, Eph. 4 : 13 ; 2 Pet. 1 : 8 ; 2 : 20 ; the will of the Lord, Col. 1 : 9 ; every good thing, Philm. 6, R.V. (A.V., " acknowledging ") ; the truth, 1 Tim. 2 : 4 ; 2 Tim. 2 : 25, R.V. ; 3 : 7 ; Tit. 1 : 1, R.V. ; the mystery of God, Col.
2 : 2, R.V., " (that they) may know " (A.V., " to the acknowledgment **AGNōSIA**
of "), lit., 'into a full knowledge.' It is used without the mention of an **56**
object in Phil. 1 : 9 ; Col. 3 : 10, R.V., " (renewed) unto knowledge." **AG:12B CB:1233C**
See ACKNOWLEDGE.¶ **SUNESIS**

3. AGNŌSIA (ἀγνωσία), the negative of No. 1, ignorance, is rendered **4907**
" no knowledge " in 1 Cor. 15 : 34, R.V. (A.V., " not the knowledge ") ; **AG:788C CB:1270C**
in 1 Pet. 2 : 15, " ignorance." See IGNORANCE.¶ **KARDIOGNōSTeS**

Note : In Eph. 3 : 4, A.V., *sunesis*, understanding, is translated **2589 AG:404C**
knowledge ; ' R.V., " understanding." For *kardiognōstēs* see p. 207. **CB:1253B**

L

LABOUR (Noun and Verb)

A. Nouns.

1. KOPOS (κόπος) primarily denotes a striking, beating (akin to 2873
koptō, to strike, cut); then, toil resulting in weariness, laborious toil, AG:443C
trouble; it is translated "labour" or "labours" in John 4:38; CB:1255C
1 Cor. 3:8; 15:58; 2 Cor. 6:5; 10:15; 11:23, 27, R.V., "labour" (A.V., "weariness"); 1 Thess. 1:3; 2:9; 3:5; 2 Thess. 3:8; (in some mss., Heb. 6:10); Rev. 2:2 (R.V. "toil"); 14:13. In the following the noun is used as the object of the verb *parechō*, to afford, give, cause, the phrase being rendered to trouble, lit., to cause toil or trouble, to embarrass a person by giving occasion for anxiety, as some disciples did to the woman with the ointment, perturbing her spirit by their criticisms, Matt. 26:10; Mark 14:6; or by distracting attention or disturbing a person's rest, as the importunate friend did, Luke 11:7; 18:5; in Gal. 6:17, "let no man trouble me," the Apostle refuses, in the form of a peremptory prohibition, to allow himself to be distracted further by the Judaizers, through their proclamation of a false gospel and by their malicious attacks upon himself.¶

2. PONOS (πόνος) denotes (*a*) labours, toil, Col. 4:13, in the best mss. 4192
(some have *zēlos*, zeal, A.V.); (*b*) the consequence of toil, viz., distress, AG:691C
suffering, pain, Rev. 16:10, 11; 21:4. See PAIN.¶ CB:1266A

Notes: (1) In Phil. 1:22, A.V., *ergon*, work, is translated "labour" ERGON
(R.V., "work"); work refers to what is done, and may be easy and 2041
pleasant; *kopos* suggests the doing, and the pains taken therein. (2) A AG:307D CB:1246C
synonymous word is *mochthos*, toil, hardship, distress, 2 Cor. 11:27; MOCHTHOS
1 Thess. 2:9; 2 Thess. 3:8.¶ 3449 AG:528D CB:1259A

B. Verbs.

1. KOPIAŌ (κοπιάω), akin to A, No. 1, has the two different meanings 2872
(*a*) growing weary, (*b*) toiling; it is sometimes translated to bestow AG:443C
labour (see under BESTOW, No. 3). It is translated by the verb to labour CB:1255C
in Matt. 11:28; John 4:38 (2nd part); Acts 20:35; Rom. 16:12 (twice); 1 Cor. 15:10; 16:16; Eph. 4:28; Phil. 2:16; Col. 1:29; 1 Thess. 5:12; 1 Tim. 4:10; 5:17; 2 Tim. 2:6; Rev. 2:3; 1 Cor. 4:12, R.V., "toil" (A.V., "labour"). See TOIL.

2. CHEIMAZŌ (χειμάζω), from *cheima*, winter-cold, primarily, to 5492
expose to winter cold, signifies to drive with a storm; in the Passive AG:879C
Voice, to be driven with storm, to be tempest-tossed, Acts 27:18, R.V., CB:—
"as (we) laboured with the storm" (A.V., "being . . . tossed with a tempest").¶

4866 AG:783B 3. SUNATHLEŌ (συναθλέω), to contend along with a person (*sun*,
CB:1270C with, *athleō*, to contend), is said in Phil. 4 : 3 of two women who " laboured
with " the Apostle in the Gospel ; in 1 : 27, R.V., " striving (for)," marg.,
" with," A.V., " striving together (for)." See STRIVE.¶

ERGAZOMAI 2038 *Notes :* (1) In John 6 : 27 and 1 Thess. 2 : 9, A.V., *ergazomai*, to work,
AG:306D is translated respectively " labour " and " labouring " (R.V., " working ").
CB:1246C SPOUDAZŌ It is used of manual work here and in 4 : 11 and Eph. 4 : 28 ; of work
4704 for Christ in general, in 1 Cor. 16 : 10. See COMMIT. (2) In Heb. 4 : 11,
AG:763C CB:1269C A.V., *spoudazō*, to be diligent, is translated " let us labour " (R.V., " let
AGŌNIZOMAI us give diligence "). (3) In Col. 4 : 12, A.V., *agōnizomai*, to strive, wrestle,
75 AG:15B is translated " labouring fervently " (R.V., and A.V., marg., " striving ").
CB:1233C (4) In 2 Cor. 5 : 9, A.V., *philotimeomai*, to seek after honour, and hence,
PHILOTIMEOMAI 5389 to be ambitious, is translated " we labour," marg., " endeavour " (R.V.,
AG:861C " we make it our aim," marg., " are ambitious ") ; cp. Rom. 15 : 20 ;
CB:1264B 1 Thess. 4 : 11, R.V., marg.¶

LABOURER, FELLOW-LABOURER

2040 AG:307C ERGATĒS (ἐργάτης), akin to *ergazomai*, to work, and *ergon*, work,
CB:1246B denotes (*a*) a field-labourer, a husbandman, Matt. 9 : 37, 38 ; 20 : 1, 2, 8 ;
Luke 10 : 2 (twice) ; Jas. 5 : 4 ; (*b*) a workman, labourer, in a general sense, Matt. 10 : 10 ; Luke 10 : 7 ; Acts 19 : 25 ; 1 Tim. 5 : 18 ; it is used (*c*) of false apostles and evil teachers, 2 Cor. 11 : 13 ; Phil. 3 : 2 ; (*d*) of a servant of Christ, 2 Tim. 2 : 15 ; (*e*) of evildoers, Luke 13 : 27.¶

4904 AG:787D *Note :* In the A.V. of Philm. 1 and 24, *sunergos*, a fellow-worker, is
CB:1270C translated " fellow-labourer," R.V., " fellow-worker " ; in Phil. 4 : 3,
the plural, R.V., " fellow-workers ; " in Phil. 2 : 25, A.V., " companion in labour," R.V., " fellow-worker ;" in 1 Cor. 3 : 9, A.V., " labourers together (with God)," R.V., " God's fellow-workers," i.e., fellow-workers belonging to and serving God ; in 3 John 8, A.V., " fellow-helpers " (to the truth), R.V., " fellow-workers (with the truth)," i.e., acting together with the truth as an operating power ; in 1 Thess. 3 : 2, some ancient authorities have the clause " fellow-worker (with God)," R.V., marg. ; it is absent from the most authentic mss. See HELPER.

LACK, LACKING

A. Noun.

5303 AG:849B HUSTERĒMA (ὑστέρημα) denotes (*a*) that which is lacking,
CB:1252B deficiency, shortcoming (akin to *hustereō*, to be behind, in want), 1 Cor.
16 : 17 ; Phil. 2 : 30 ; Col. 1 : 24, R.V., " that which is lacking " [A.V., " that which is behind " (of the afflictions of Christ)], where the reference is not to the vicarious sufferings of Christ, but to those which He endured previously, and those which must be endured by His faithful servants ; 1 Thess. 3 : 10, where " that which is lacking " means that which Paul had not been able to impart to them, owing to the interruption of his spiritual instruction among them ; (*b*) need, want, poverty, Luke 21 : 4,

R.V., "want" (A.V., "penury"); 2 Cor. 8:14 (twice), "want;" 9:12, "wants" (A.V., "want"); 11:9, R.V., "(the measure of my) want" [A.V., "that which was lacking (to me)"]. See BEHIND, PENURY, WANT.¶

Note: In 1 Thess. 4:12, A.V., *chreia*, need, is translated "lack" 5532
(R.V., "need"). See NEED. AG:884D CB:1240A

B. Adjective.

ENDEĒS (ἐνδεής), from *endeō*, to lack, signifies needy, in want, trans- 1729
lated "that lacked" in Acts 4:34.¶ AG:262C CB:—

C. Verbs.

1. HUSTEREŌ (ὑστερέω), akin to A, to come or be behind, is used in 5302
the sense of lacking certain things, Matt. 19:20; Mark 10:21 ("one AG:849A CB:1252B
thing;" cp. No. 3 in Luke 18:22); Luke 22:35; in the sense of being inferior, 1 Cor. 12:24 (Middle Voice). Elsewhere it is translated in various ways; see BEHIND, B, No. 1, COME, No. 39, DESTITUTE, FAIL, *Note* (2), NEED, WANT, WORSE.

2. ELATTONEŌ (ἐλαττονέω), to be less (from *elattōn*, less), is trans- 1641
lated "had no lack," 2 Cor. 8:15 (quoted from the Sept. of Ex. 16:18), AG:248B CB:—
the circumstance of the gathering of the manna being applied to the equalising nature of cause and effect in the matter of supplying the wants of the needy.¶

3. LEIPŌ (λείπω), to leave, denotes (*a*) transitively, in the Passive 3007
Voice, to be left behind, to lack, Jas. 1:4, "ye may be lacking in AG:470B CB:1256C
(nothing)," R.V. (A.V., "wanting"); ver. 5, "lacketh" (A.V., "lack"); 2:15, R.V., "be . . . in lack" (A.V., "be . . . destitute"); (*b*) intransitively, Active Voice, Luke 18:22, "(one thing thou) lackest," is, lit., '(one thing) is lacking (to thee);' Tit. 1:5, "(the things) that were wanting;" 3:13, "(that nothing) be wanting." See DESTITUTE, WANTING.¶

Note: In 2 Pet. 1:9, "he that lacketh" translates a phrase the lit.
rendering of which is '(he to whom these things) are not present' (*pareimi*, 3918
to be present). AG:624A CB:1262B

For LAD, in John 6:9, see CHILD, A, No. 6

LADE, LADEN

1. SŌREUŌ (σωρεύω) signifies (*a*) to heap on (from *sōros*, a heap, 4987
not in the N.T.; in the Sept., e.g., Josh. 7:26; 8:29; 2 Sam. 18:17; AG:800C CB:—
2 Chron. 31:6–9), Rom. 12:20, of coals of fire; 2 Tim. 3:6, said of silly women ('womanlings') laden with sins. See HEAP.¶ In the Sept., Prov. 25:22.¶ 1073

2. GEMŌ (γέμω), to be full, is translated "laden" in Rev. 21:9, AG:153D
R.V. See FULL. CB:1248A

3. PHORTIZŌ (φορτίζω), to load (akin to *pherō*, to bear), is used in 5412 AG:865A
the Active Voice in Luke 11:46, "ye lade;" in the Passive Voice, CB:1264B

metaphorically, in Matt. 11 : 28, "heavy laden." See BURDEN.¶ In the Sept., Ezek. 16 : 33.¶

2007 AG:302D CB:1246B *Note:* In Acts 28 : 10, A.V., *epitithēmi*, to put on (*epi*, on, *tithēmi*, to put), is translated "they laded (us) with," R.V., "they put on (board)."

LADING

5413 AG:865A CB:1264B PHORTOS 5414 AG:865B CB:1264B PHORTION (φορτίον), a burden, load (a diminutive of *phortos*, a load, from *pherō*, to bear), is used of the cargo of a ship, Acts 27 : 10, "lading," (some mss. have *phortos*). See BURDEN, A, No. 2.

LADY

2959 AG:458B CB:1256B KURIA (κυρία) is the person addressed in 2 John 1 and 5. Not improbably it is a proper name (Eng., Cyria), in spite of the fact that the full form of address in ver. 1 is not quite in accord, in the original, with those in ver. 13 and in 3 John 1. The suggestion that the Church is addressed is most unlikely. Possibly the person is one who had a special relation with the local church.¶

For LAID see LAY

LAKE

3041 AG:475A CB:1257A LIMNĒ (λίμνη), a lake, is used (*a*) in the Gospels, only by Luke, of the Sea of Galilee, Luke 5 : 2 ; 8 : 22, 23, 33, called Gennesaret in 5 : 1 (Matthew and Mark use *thalassa*, a sea) ; (*b*) of the lake of fire, Rev. 19 : 20 ; 20 : 10, 14, 15 ; 21 : 8.¶

LAKE See SEA

LAMA

2982 AG:464A CB:1224B LAMA (λαμά) is the Hebrew word for "Why ?" (the variant *lema* is the Aramaic form), Matt. 27 : 46 ; Mark 15 : 34.¶

LAMB

704 AG:106A CB:1237C 1. ARĒN (ἀρήν), a noun the nominative case of which is found only in early times, occurs in Luke 10 : 3. In normal usage it was replaced by *arnion* (No. 2), of which it is the equivalent.¶

721 AG:108B CB:1237C 2. ARNION (ἀρνίον) is a diminutive in form, but the diminutive force is not to be pressed (see Note under No. 3). The general tendency in the vernacular was to use nouns in *-ion* freely, apart from their diminutive significance. It is used only by the Apostle John, (*a*) in the plural, in the Lord's command to Peter, John 21 : 15, with symbolic reference to young converts ; (*b*) elsewhere, in the singular, in the Apocalypse, some 28 times, of Christ as the Lamb of God, the symbolism having reference to His character and His vicarious Sacrifice, as the basis both of redemption and of Divine vengeance. He is seen in the position of sovereign glory and honour, e.g., 7 : 17, which He shares equally with the Father, 22 : 1, 3, the centre of angelic beings and of the redeemed and the object of their

veneration, e.g. 5 : 6, 8, 12, 13 ; 15 : 3, the Leader and Shepherd of His saints, e.g., 7 : 17 ; 14 : 4, the Head of His spiritual Bride, e.g., 21 : 9, the luminary of the heavenly and eternal city, 21 : 23, the One to whom all judgment is committed, e.g., 6 : 1, 16 ; 13 : 8, the Conqueror of the foes of God and His people, 17 : 14 ; the song that celebrates the triumph of those who ' gain the victory over the Beast,' is the song of Moses . . . and the song of the Lamb, 15 : 3. His sacrifice, the efficacy of which avails for those who accept the salvation thereby provided, forms the ground of the execution of Divine wrath for the rejector, and the defier of God, 14 : 10 ; (*c*) in the description of the second " Beast," Rev. 13 : 11, seen in the vision " like a lamb," suggestive of his acting in the capacity of a false Messiah, a travesty of the true. For the use in the Sept. see Note under No. 3.

3. AMNOS (ἀμνός), a lamb, is used figuratively of Christ, in John 1 : 29, 286
36, with the article, pointing Him out as the expected One, the One to be AG:46C CB:1234C
well known as the Personal fulfilment and embodiment of all that had been indicated in the O.T., the One by whose sacrifice deliverance from Divine judgment was to be obtained ; in Acts 8 : 32 (from the Sept. of Is. 53 : 7) and 1 Pet. 1 : 19, the absence of the article stresses the nature and character of His sacrifice as set forth in the symbolism. The reference in each case is to the lamb of God's providing, Gen. 22 : 8, and the Paschal lamb of God's appointment for sacrifice in Israel, e.g., Ex. 12 : 5, 14, 27 (cp. 1 Cor. 5 : 7).¶

Note : The contrast between ***arnion*** and ***amnos*** does not lie in the diminutive character of the former as compared with the latter. As has been pointed out under No. 2, ***arnion*** lost its diminutive force. The contrast lies in the manner in which Christ is presented in the two respects. The use of *amnos* points directly to the fact, the nature and character of His sacrifice ; *arnion* (only in the Apocalypse) presents Him, on the ground, indeed, of His Sacrifice, but in His acquired majesty, dignity, honour, authority and power.

In the Sept. *arnion* is used in Ps. 114 : 4, 6 ; in Jer. 11 : 19, with the adjective *akakos*, innocent ; in Jer. 27 : 45, " lambs." There is nothing in these passages to suggest a contrast between a lamb in the general sense of the term and the diminutive ; the contrast is between lambs and sheep. Elsewhere in the Sept. *amnos* is in general used some 100 times in connection with lambs for sacrifice.

For LAME see HALT

For LAMENT and LAMENTATION see BEWAIL

LAMP

1. LAMPAS (λαμπάς) denotes a torch (akin to *lampō*, to shine), fre- 2985 AG:465C
quently fed, like a lamp, with oil from a little vessel used for the purpose CB:1256C

(the *angeion* of Matt. 25 : 4) ; they held little oil and would frequently need replenishing. Rutherford (*The New Phrynichus*) points out that it became used as the equivalent of *luchnos* (No. 2), as in the parable of the Ten Virgins, Matt. 25 : 1, 3, 4, 7, 8 ; John 18 : 3, " torches ; " Acts 20 : 8, " lights ; " Rev. 4 : 5 ; 8 : 10 (R.V., " torch," A.V., " lamp "). See Note below.¶ Cp. *phanos*, a torch, John 18 : 3 (translated " lanterns ").¶

3088 AG:483B CB:1257B 2. LUCHNOS (λύχνος), frequently mistranslated " candle," is a portable lamp usually set on a stand (see LAMPSTAND) ; the word is used (*a*) literally, Matt. 5 : 15 ; Mark 4 : 21 ; Luke 8 : 16 ; 11 : 33, 36 ; 15 : 8 ; Rev. 18 : 23 ; 22 : 5 ; (*b*) metaphorically, of Christ as the Lamb, Rev. 21 : 23, R.V., " lamp " (A.V., " light ") ; of John the Baptist, John 5 : 35, R.V., " the lamp " (A.V., " a . . . light ") ; of the eye, Matt. 6 : 22, and Luke 11 : 34, R.V., " lamp ; " of spiritual readiness, Luke 12 : 35, R.V., " lamps ; " of " the word of prophecy," 2 Pet. 1 : 19, R.V., " lamp." See LIGHT.¶

" In rendering *luchnos* and *lampas* our Translators have scarcely made the most of the words at their command. Had they rendered *lampas* by ' torch ' not once only (John 18 : 3), but always, this would have left ' lamp,' now wrongly appropriated by *lampas*, disengaged. Altogether dismissing ' candle,' they might then have rendered *luchnos* by ' lamp ' wherever it occurs. At present there are so many occasions where ' candle ' would manifestly be inappropriate, and where, therefore, they
PHŌS are obliged to fall back on ' light,' that the distinction between *phōs* and
5457 *luchnos* nearly, if not quite, disappears in our Version. The advantages
AG:871D CB:1264B of such a re-distribution of the words would be many. In the first place, it would be more accurate. *Luchnos* is not a ' candle ' (' candela,' from ' candeo,' the white wax light, and then any kind of taper), but a hand-lamp, fed with oil. Neither is *lampas* a ' lamp,' but a ' torch ' " (Trench Syn., § xlvi).

Note : There is no mention of a candle in the original either in the O.T. or in the N.T. The figure of that which feeds upon its own substance to provide its light would be utterly inappropriate. A lamp is supplied by oil, which in its symbolism is figurative of the Holy Spirit.

LAMPSTAND

3087 AG:483A CB:1257B LUCHNIA (λυχνία) is mistranslated " candlestick " in every occurrence in the A.V. and in certain places in the R.V. ; the R.V. has " stand " in Matt. 5 : 15 ; Mark 4 : 21 ; Luke 8 : 16 ; 11 : 33 ; " candlestick " in Heb. 9 : 2 ; Rev. 1 : 12, 13, 20 (twice) ; 2 : 1, 5 ; 11 : 4 ; the R.V. marg., gives " lampstands " in the passages in Rev., but not in Heb. 9 : 2.¶

LAND

A. Nouns.

1093 AG:157C CB:1248A 1. GĒ (γῆ), in one of its usages, denotes (*a*) land as distinct from sea or other water, e.g., Mark 4 : 1 ; 6 : 47 ; Luke 5 : 3 ; John 6 : 21 ; (*b*) land as subject to cultivation, e.g., Luke 14 : 35 (see GROUND) ; (*c*) land as describing a country or region, e.g., Matt. 2 : 20, 21 ; 4 : 15 ; Luke 4 : 25 ; in 23 : 44, R.V., " (the whole) land," A.V., " (all the) earth ; " Acts 7 : 29 ; Heb. 11 : 9, R.V., " a land (not his own)," A.V. " a (strange) country ; " Jude 5. In Acts 7 : 11 the A.V. follows a reading of the noun with the definite article which necessitates the insertion of " land." See EARTH.

2. CHŌRA (χώρα) is used with the meaning land, (*a*) of a country, 5561
region, e.g., Mark 1 : 5 ; Luke 15 : 14 ; sometimes translated " region," AG:889B CB:1240A
e.g., Matt. 4 : 16 ; Luke 3 : 1 ; Acts 8 : 1 ; 13 : 49 ; 16 : 6 ; (*b*) of property, Luke 12 : 16, " ground." See COUNTRY, A, No. 3.

3. CHŌRION (χωρίον), a diminutive of No. 2, in form, but not in 5564
meaning, is translated " land " in the sense of property, in Acts 4 : 34 ; AG:890B CB:1240A
5 : 3, 8 ; 28 : 7, R.V., " lands " (A.V., " possessions "). See FIELD, GROUND, A, No. 4, PLACE, POSSESSION.

4. AGROS (ἀγρός), a field, or piece of ground, or the country as distinct 68
from the town, is translated " lands " in Matt. 19 : 29 ; Mark 10 : 29, 30 ; AG:13D CB:1233C
Acts 4 : 37 (cp. No. 3 in ver. 34). See COUNTRY, A, No. 1, FARM, FIELD, GROUND.

B. Adjective.

XĒROS (ξηρός), dry, " dry land," Matt. 23 : 15 (*gē*, land, being 3584
understood) ; Heb. 11 : 29 : see DRY. AG:548C CB:1273B

Note : In Luke 4 : 26, the R.V., " in the land (of) " and A.V., " a city (of)," represent no word in the original, but give the sense of the phrase.

C. Verb.

KATERCHOMAI (κατέρχομαι), to come down, or go down, descend, 2718
is used of coming to port by ship, in Acts 18 : 22, " landed ; " 21 : 3 AG:422A CB:—
(ditto) ; 27 : 5, " came to." See COME, No. 7, GO, Note (1).

Notes : (1) In Acts 28 : 12, R.V., *katagō*, to bring down, used as a KATAGō
nautical term in the Passive Voice, is translated " touching " (A.V., 2609 AG:410A
" landing "). (2) In Acts 21 : 3, some mss. have the verb *katagō*, with CB:—
reference to Cyprus. (3) In Acts 20 : 13, *pezeuō*, to travel by land or on PEZEUō 3978
foot (*pezos*, on foot ; *pous*, a foot), is translated " to go by land," R.V., AG:638D
A.V., " to go afoot," and R.V. marg., " to go on foot."¶ CB:—

LANE

RHUMĒ (ῥύμη) in earlier Greek meant the force or rush or swing of a 4505
moving body ; in later times, a narrow road, lane or street ; it is translated AG:737C CB:—
" lanes " in Luke 14 : 21 ; " streets " in Matt. 6 : 2 ; " street " in Acts 9 : 11 ; 12 : 10. See STREET.¶ In the Sept., Is. 15 : 3.¶

LANGUAGE

DIALEKTOS (διάλεκτος), primarily a conversation, discourse (akin to 1258
dialegomai, to discourse or discuss), came to denote the language or dialect AG:185D CB:1241A
of a country or district ; in the A.V. and R.V. of Acts 2 : 6 it is translated " language ; " in the following the R.V. retains " language," for A.V.,

"tongue," Acts 1 : 19; 2 : 8; 21 : 40; 22 : 2; 26 : 14. See TONGUE.¶ In the Sept., Esth. 9 : 26.¶

LANTERN

5322 AG:853B CB:— PHANOS (φανός) denotes either a torch or a lantern (from *phainō*, to cause to shine, to give light), John 18 : 3, where it is distinguished from *lampas* (see LAMP, No. 1); it was "a link or torch consisting of strips of resinous wood tied together" (Rutherford). "Torch" would seem to be the meaning.¶

LARGE

3173 AG:497C CB:1258A 1. MEGAS (μέγας), great, large, of physical magnitude, is translated "large" in Mark 14 : 15 and Luke 22 : 12, of the upper room. See GREAT, No. 1.

2425 AG:374B CB:1250C 2. HIKANOS (ἱκανός), of persons, denotes sufficient, competent, fit; of things, sufficient, enough, much, many (so of time); it is translated "large" in Matt. 28 : 12, of money. See ABLE, C, No. 2.

4080 AG:656B CB:— 3. PĒLIKOS (πηλίκος), how large, is used of letters of the alphabet, characters in writing, Gal. 6 : 11, "with how large (letters);" it is said of personal greatness in Heb. 7 : 4. See GREAT, No. 5.¶

LASCIVIOUS, LASCIVIOUSNESS

766 AG:114D CB:1238A ASELGEIA (ἀσέλγεια) denotes excess, licentiousness, absence of restraint, indecency, wantonness; "lasciviousness" in Mark 7 : 22, one of the evils that proceed from the heart; in 2 Cor. 12 : 21, one of the evils of which some in the church at Corinth had been guilty; in Gal. 5 : 19, classed among the works of the flesh; in Eph. 4 : 19, among the sins of the unregenerate who are "past feeling;" so in 1 Pet. 4 : 3; in Jude 4, of that into which the grace of God had been turned by ungodly men; it is translated "wantonness" in Rom. 13 : 13, one of the sins against which believers are warned; in 2 Pet. 2 : 2, according to the best mss., "lascivious (doings)," R.V. (the A.V. "pernicious ways" follows those texts which have *apōleiais*); in ver. 7, R.V., "lascivious (life)," A.V., "filthy (conversation)," of the people of Sodom and Gomorrah; in 2 : 18, R.V., "lasciviousness" (A.V., "wantonness"), practised by the same persons as mentioned in Jude. The prominent idea is shameless conduct. Some have derived the word from *a*, negative, and *selgē*, a city in Pisidia. Others, with similar improbability, trace it to *a*, negative, and *selgō*, or *thelgō*, to charm. See WANTONNESS.¶

LAST

A. Adjective.

2078 AG:313D CB:1246C ESCHATOS (ἔσχατος), last, utmost, extreme, is used (*a*) of place, e.g., Luke 14 : 9, 10, "lowest;" Acts 1 : 8 and 13 : 47, "uttermost part;" (*b*) of rank, e.g., Mark 9 : 35; (*c*) of time, relating either to persons or things, e.g., Matt. 5 : 26, " the last (farthing)," R.V. (A.V., " uttermost ") ; Matt. 20 : 8, 12, 14 ; Mark 12 : 6, 22 ; 1 Cor. 4 : 9, of apostles as last in the programme of a spectacular display ; 1 Cor. 15 : 45, " the last Adam ; " Rev. 2 : 19 ; of the last state of persons, Matt. 12 : 45, neuter plural, lit., ' the last (things) ; ' so Luke 11 : 26 ; 2 Pet. 2 : 20, R.V., " the last state " (A.V., " the latter end ") ; of Christ as the Eternal One, Rev. 1 : 17 (in some mss. ver. 11) ; 2 : 8 ; 22 : 13 ; in eschatological phrases as follows : (*a*) " the last day," a comprehensive term including both the time of the resurrection of the redeemed, John 6 : 39, 40, 44, 54 and 11 : 24, and the ulterior time of the judgment of the unregenerate, at the Great White Throne, John 12 : 48 ; (*b*) " the last days," Acts 2 : 17, a period relative to the supernatural manifestation of the Holy Spirit at Pentecost and the resumption of the Divine interpositions in the affairs of the world at the end of the present age, before " the great and notable Day of the Lord," which will usher in the Messianic Kingdom ; (*c*) in 2 Tim. 3 : 1, " the last days " refers to the close of the present age of world conditions ; (*d*) in Jas. 5 : 3, the phrase " in the last days " (R.V.) refers both to the period preceding the Roman overthrow of the city and the land in A.D. 70, and to the closing part of the age in consummating acts of Gentile persecution including " the time of Jacob's trouble " (cp. verses 7, 8) ; (*e*) in 1 Pet. 1 : 5, " the last time " refers to the time of the Lord's Second Advent ; (*f*) in 1 John 2 : 18, " the last hour " (R.V.) and, in Jude 18, " the last time " signify the present age previous to the Second Advent.

Notes : (1) In Heb. 1 : 2, R.V., " at the end of these days " (A.V., " in these last days "), the reference is to the close of the period of the testimony of the prophets under the Law, terminating with the presence of Christ and His redemptive sacrifice and its effects, the perfect tense " hath spoken " indicating the continued effects of the message embodied in the risen Christ ; so in 1 Pet. 1 : 20, R.V., " at the end of the times " (A.V., " in these last times ").

B. Adverb.

HUSTERON (ὕστερον), the neuter of the adjective *husteros*, is used as 5305
an adverb signifying ' afterwards,' ' later,' see AFTER, No. 5. Cp. the AG:849C CB:1252B
adjective, under LATER.

Note : In Phil. 4 : 10 the particle *pote*, sometime, used after *ēdē*, now, POTE
already, to signify " now at length," is so rendered in the R.V., A.V., 4218 AG:695A
" (now) at the last." CB:1266B

LATCHET

HIMAS (ἱμάς) denotes a thong, strap, whether for binding prisoners, 2438
Acts 22 : 25, " (the) thongs " (for scourging ; see BIND, No. 7), or for AG:376B CB:—
fastening sandals, Mark 1 : 7 ; Luke 3 : 16 ; John 1 : 27. " Among the Orientals everything connected with the feet and shoes is defiled and debasing, and the stooping to unfasten the dusty latchet is the most insignificant in such service " (Mackie, in Hastings' Bib. Dic.).¶

LATE

3796 AG:601B CB:1261A OPSE (ὀψέ), an adverb of time, besides its meaning at evening or at eventide, denotes late in, or on, Matt. 28 : 1, R.V., "late on (the Sabbath day)" (A.V., "in the end of"); it came also to denote 'late after,' which seems to be the meaning here. See EVENING.

3568 AG:545C CB:1260A *Note:* In John 11 : 8, A.V., *nun*, now, is translated "of late" (R.V., "but now").

LATELY

4373 AG:719C CB:— PROSPHATŌS (προσφάτως) denotes recently, lately, from the adjective *prosphatos*, new, fresh, recent; primarily, newly slain, Heb. 10 : 20 (*phatos*, slain), is also found in Acts 18 : 2.¶ In the Sept., Deut. 24 : 5; Ezek. 11 : 3.¶

LATER

5306 AG:849C CB:1252B HUSTEROS (ὕστερος) denotes later or latter and is used in 1 Tim. 4 : 1, R.V., "in later (times)," A.V., "in (the) latter (times)." Several mss. have it in Matt. 21 : 31, 'the former,' for *prōtos*, "the first."¶

LATIN

4515 AG:738C CB:— RHŌMAISTI (ῥωμαϊστί), an adverb, "in Latin," occurs in John 19 : 20, lit., 'in Roman.'¶

4513 AG:738C CB:— *Note:* In Luke 23 : 38, some mss. have the adjective *Rhōmaikos*, 'of Latin,' agreeing with "letters."

LATTER

3797 AG:601C CB:1261A OPSIMOS (ὄψιμος), akin to *opse* and *opsios* (see LATE), denotes late, or latter, and is used of "the latter rain" in Jas. 5 : 7 (the most authentic mss. omit *huetos*, rain; some have *karpos*, fruit); this rain falls in March and April, just before the harvest, in contrast to the early rain, in October.¶ In the Sept., Deut. 11 : 14; Prov. 16 : 15; Jer. 5 : 24; Hos. 6 : 3; Joel 2 : 23; Zech. 10 : 1.¶

Note: For "latter" (*husteros*) in the A.V. of 1 Tim. 4 : 1 see LATER, and for 2 Pet. 2 : 20 see LAST.

For LAUD (Rom. 15 : 11, A.V.) see PRAISE, B, No. 1

LAUGH, LAUGH TO SCORN

1070 AG:153C CB:1248A 1. GELAŌ (γελάω), to laugh, is found in Luke 6 : 21, 25. This signifies loud laughter in contrast to demonstrative weeping.¶

2606 AG:409C CB:1254A 2. KATAGELAŌ (καταγελάω) denotes to laugh scornfully at, more emphatic than No. 1 (*kata*, down, used intensively, and No. 1), and signifies derisive laughter, Matt. 9 : 24; Mark 5 : 40; Luke 8 : 53.¶

EKMUKTĒRIZŌ 1592 (-TERIZō) AG:243B CB:1243C Cp. *ekmuktērizō*, to deride.

Note: The laughter of incredulity, as in Gen. 17 : 17 and 18 : 12, is not mentioned in the N.T.

LAUGHTER

GELŌS (γέλως) denotes laughter, Jas. 4 : 9.¶ This corresponds to the 1071 AG:153C
kind of laughter mentioned above (see LAUGH, No. 1). CB:1248A

LAUNCH

1. ANAGŌ (ἀνάγω), to bring up (*ana*, up, *agō*, to lead), is used in the 321 AG:53A
Middle Voice as a nautical term signifying to put to sea; it is translated CB:–
"launch forth" in Luke 8 : 22; "set sail" in Acts 13 : 13, R.V. (A.V., "loosed"); similarly in 16 : 11; in 18 : 21, for A.V., "sailed;" similarly in 20 : 3, 13; in 21 : 1, R.V., "set sail," (A.V., "launched"), and in ver. 2, for A.V., "set forth;" in 27 : 2 and 4 the R.V. has the verb to put to sea, for A.V. to launch; in ver. 12 for A.V., "depart;" in ver. 21, R.V., "set sail" (A.V., "loosed"); in 28 : 10, 11, "sailed" and "set sail" (A.V., "departed"). See BRING, DEPART, LEAD, LOOSE, OFFER, PUT, SAIL, SET.

2. EPANAGŌ (ἐπανάγω), to lead up upon (*epi*, upon, and No. 1), is 1877 AG:282D
used as a nautical term with *ploion*, a ship, understood, denoting to put CB:–
out to sea, translated in Luke 5 : 3, "put out," R.V. (A.V., "thrust out"); in ver. 4, for A.V., "launch." For the non-nautical significance to return, see Matt. 21 : 18. See PUT, RETURN, THRUST.¶ In the Sept., Zech. 4 : 12, "that communicate with (the golden oil vessels)."

LAVISH See ABUNDANCE, BESTOW

LAW

A. Nouns.

1. NOMOS (νόμος), akin to *nemō*, to divide out, distribute, primarily 3551 AG:542A
meant that which is assigned; hence, usage, custom, and then, law, law CB:1260A
as prescribed by custom, or by statute; the word *ēthos*, custom, was ETHOS
retained for unwritten law, while *nomos* became the established name for 1485 AG:218D
law as decreed by a state and set up as the standard for the administration CB:1247A
of justice.

In the N.T. it is used (*a*) of law in general, e.g., Rom. 2 : 12, 13, "a law" (R.V.), expressing a general principle relating to law; ver. 14, last part; 3 : 27, "By what manner of law?" i.e., 'by what sort of principle (has the glorying been excluded)?'; 4 : 15 (last part); 5 : 13, referring to the period between Adam's trespass and the giving of the Law; 7 : 1 (1st part, R.V. marg., "law"); against those graces which constitute the fruit of the Spirit "there is no law," Gal. 5 : 23; "the ostensible aim of the law is to restrain the evil tendencies natural to man in his fallen estate; yet in experience law finds itself not merely ineffective, it actually provokes those tendencies to greater activity. The intention of the gift of the Spirit is to constrain the believer to a life in which the natural tendencies shall have no place, and to produce in him their direct contraries. Law, therefore, has nothing to say against the fruit of the Spirit; hence the believer is not only not under law, ver. 18, the law finds no scope in his life, inasmuch as, and in so far as, he is led by the Spirit;"*

* From Notes on Galatians by Hogg and Vine, p. 298.

(*b*) of a force or influence impelling to action, Rom. 7 : 21, 23 (1st part), "a different law," R.V. ; (*c*) of the Mosaic Law, the Law of Sinai, (1) with the definite article, e.g., Matt. 5 : 18 ; John 1 : 17 ; Rom. 2 : 15, 18, 20, 26, 27 ; 3 : 19 ; 4 : 15 ; 7 : 4, 7, 14, 16, 22 ; 8 : 3, 4, 7 ; Gal. 3 : 10, 12, 19, 21, 24 ; 5 : 3 ; Eph. 2 : 15 ; Phil. 3 : 6 ; 1 Tim. 1 : 8 ; Heb. 7 : 19 ; Jas. 2 : 9 ; (2) without the article, thus stressing the Mosaic Law in its quality as law, e.g., Rom. 2 : 14 (1st part) ; 5 : 20 ; 7 : 9, where the stress on the quality lies in this, that "the commandment which was unto (i.e., which he thought would be a means of) life," he found to be "unto (i.e., to have the effect of revealing his actual state of) death ;" 10 : 4 ; 1 Cor. 9 : 20 ; Gal. 2 : 16, 19, 21 ; 3 : 2, 5, 10 (1st part), 11, 18, 23 ; 4 : 4, 5, 21 (1st part) ; 5 : 4, 18 ; 6 : 13 ; Phil. 3 : 5, 9 ; Heb. 7 : 16 ; 9 : 19 ; Jas. 2 : 11 ; 4 : 11 ; (in regard to the statement in Gal. 2 : 16, that "a man is not justified by the works of the Law," the absence of the article before *nomos* indicates the assertion of a principle, 'by obedience to law,' but evidently the Mosaic law is in view. Here the Apostle is maintaining that submission to circumcision entails the obligation to do the whole Law. Circumcision belongs to the ceremonial part of the Law, but, while the Mosaic Law is actually divisible into the ceremonial and the moral, no such distinction is made or even assumed in Scripture. The statement maintains the freedom of the believer from the law of Moses in its totality as a means of justification) ;

(*d*) by metonymy, of the books which contain the law, (1) of the Pentateuch, e.g., Matt. 5 : 17 ; 12 : 5 ; Luke 16 : 16 ; 24 : 44 ; John 1 : 45 ; Rom. 3 : 21 ; Gal. 3 : 10 ; (2) of the Psalms, John 10 : 34 ; 15 : 25 ; of the Psalms, Isaiah, Ezekiel and Daniel, 12 : 34 ; the Psalms and Isaiah, Rom. 3 : 19 (with vv. 10–18) ; Isaiah, 1 Cor. 14 : 21 ; from all this it may be inferred that "the law" in the most comprehensive sense was an alternative title to "The Scriptures."

The following phrases specify laws of various kinds ; (*a*) "the law of Christ," Gal. 6 : 2, i.e., either given by Him (as in the Sermon on the Mount and in John 13 : 14, 15 ; 15 : 4), or the law or principle by which Christ Himself lived (Matt. 20 : 28 ; John 13 : 1) ; these are not actual alternatives, for the law imposed by Christ was always that by which He Himself lived in the "days of His flesh." He confirmed the Law as being of Divine authority (cp. Matt. 5 : 18) ; yet He presented a higher standard of life than perfunctory obedience to the current legal rendering of the Law, a standard which, without annulling the Law, He embodied in His own character and life (see, e.g., Matt. 5 : 21–48 ; this breach with legalism is especially seen in regard to the ritual or ceremonial part of the Law in its wide scope) ; He showed Himself superior to all human interpretations of it ; (*b*) "a law of faith," Rom. 3 : 27, i.e., a principle which demands only faith on man's part ; (*c*) "the law of my mind," Rom. 7 : 23, that principle which governs the new nature in virtue of the new birth ; (*d*) "the law of sin," Rom. 7 : 23, the principle by which sin exerts its influence and power despite the desire to do what is right ; "of sin and death," 8 : 2, death being the effect ; (*e*) "the law of liberty," Jas. 1 : 25 ; 2 : 12, a term comprehensive of all the Scriptures, not a law of compulsion enforced from without, but meeting with ready obedience through the desire and delight of the renewed being who is subject to it ; into it he looks, and in its teaching he delights ; he is "under law (*ennomos*, 'in law,' implying union and subjection) to Christ," 1 Cor. 9 : 21 ; cp., e.g., Ps. 119 : 32, 45, 97; 2 Cor. 3 : 17 ; (*f*) "the royal law," Jas. 2 : 8, i.e., the law of love, royal in the majesty of its power, the law upon which all others hang, Matt. 22 : 34-40 ; Rom. 13 : 8 ; Gal. 5 : 14 ; (*g*) "the law of the Spirit of life," Rom. 8 : 2, i.e., the animating principle by which the Holy Spirit acts as the Imparter of life (cp. John 6 : 63) ; (*h*) "a law of righteousness," Rom. 9 : 31, i.e., a general principle presenting righteousness as the object and outcome of keeping a law, particularly the Law of Moses (cp. Gal. 3 : 21) ; (*i*) "the law of a carnal commandment," Heb. 7 : 16, i.e., the law respecting the Aaronic priesthood, which appointed men conditioned by the circumstances and limitations of the flesh. In the Epistle to the Hebrews the Law is treated of especially in regard to the contrast between the Priesthood of Christ and that established under the Law of Moses, and in regard to access to God and to worship. In these respects the Law "made nothing perfect," 7 : 19. There was "a disannulling of a foregoing commandment . . . and a bringing in of a better hope." This is established under the "new Covenant," a covenant instituted on the basis of "better promises," 8 : 6.

Notes : (1) In Gal. 5 : 3, the statement that to receive circumcision constitutes a man a debtor to do "the whole Law," views the Law as made up of separate commands, each essential to the whole, and predicates the unity of the Law ; in ver. 14, the statement that "the whole law" is fulfilled in the one commandment concerning love, views the separate commandments as combined to make a complete law. (2) In Rom. 8 : 3, "what the law could not do," is lit., 'the inability (*adunaton*, the neuter of the adjective *adunatos*, unable, used as a noun) of the Law ;' this may mean either 'the weakness of the Law' or 'that which was impossible for the Law ;' the latter is preferable ; the significance is the same in effect ; the Law could neither give freedom from condemnation nor impart life. (3) For the difference between the teaching of Paul and that of James in regard to the Law, see under JUSTIFICATION. (4) For Acts 19 : 38, A.V., "the law is open" (R.V., "courts" etc.) see COURT, No. 1. (5) For *nomodidaskaloi*, "doctors of the law," Luke 5 : 17, singular in Acts 5 : 34, "teachers of the law," 1 Tim. 1 : 7, see DOCTOR.

2. NOMOTHESIA (νομοθεσία) denotes legislation, lawgiving (No. 1, **3548**
and *tithēmi*, to place, to put), Rom. 9 : 4, "(the) giving of the law." **AG:541D** **CB:1260A**
Cp. B, No. 1.¶

B. Verbs.

3549 AG:541D CB:1260A 1. NOMOTHETEŌ (νομοθετέω), (*a*) used intransitively, signifies to make laws (cp. A, No. 2, above); in the Passive Voice, to be furnished with laws, Heb. 7:11, "received the law," lit., 'was furnished with (the) law;' (*b*) used transitively, it signifies to ordain by law, to enact; in the Passive Voice, Heb. 8:6. See ENACT.¶

2919 AG:451B CB:1256A 2. KRINŌ (κρίνω), to esteem, judge, etc., signifies to go to law, and is so used in the Middle Voice in Matt. 5:40, R.V., "go to law" (A.V., "sue . . . at the law"); 1 Cor. 6:1, 6. See ESTEEM.

Note: In 1 Cor. 6:7, the A.V., "go to law," is a rendering of the phrase *echō krimata*, to have lawsuits, as in the R.V.

3891 AG:621A CB:1262B 3. PARANOMEŌ (παρανομέω), to transgress law (*para*, contrary to, and *nomos*), is used in the present participle in Acts 23:3, and translated "contrary to the law," lit., 'transgressing the law.'¶

C. Adjectives.

3544 AG:541B CB:1260A 1. NOMIKOS (νομικός) denotes relating to law; in Tit. 3:9 it is translated "about the law," describing "fightings" (A.V., "strivings"); see LAWYER.

1772 AG:267B CB:1245B 2. ENNOMOS (ἔννομος), (*a*) lawful, legal, lit., in law (*en*, in, and *nomos*), or, strictly, what is within the range of law, is translated "lawful" in Acts 19:39, A.V. (R.V., "regular"), of the legal tribunals in Ephesus; (*b*) "under law" (R.V.), in relation to Christ, 1 Cor. 9:21, where it is contrasted with *anomos* (see No. 3 below); the word as used by the Apostle suggests not merely the condition of being under law, but the intimacy of a relation established in the loyalty of a will devoted to his Master. See LAWFUL.

459 AG:72A CB:1235C 3. ANOMOS (ἄνομος) signifies "without law" (*a*, negative) and has this meaning in 1 Cor. 9:21 (four times). See LAWLESS, TRANSGRESSOR, UNLAWFUL, WICKED.

D. Adverb.

460 AG:72B CB:1235C ANOMŌS (ἀνόμως), without law (the adverbial form of C, No. 3), is used in Rom. 2:12 (twice), where "(have sinned) without law" means in the absence of some specifically revealed law, like the law of Sinai; "(shall perish) without law" predicates that the absence of such a law will not prevent their doom; the law of conscience is not in view here. The succeeding phrase "under law" is lit., 'in law,' not the same as the adjective *ennomos* (C, No. 2), but two distinct words.¶

LAWFUL, LAWFULLY

A. Verb.

1832 AG:275B CB:1247C EXESTI (ἔξεστι), an impersonal verb, signifying it is permitted, it is lawful (or interrogatively, is it lawful?), occurs most frequently in the Synoptic Gospels and the Acts; elsewhere in John 5:10; 18:31; 1 Cor. 6:12; 10:23; 2 Cor. 12:4; in Acts 2:29, it is rendered "let me (speak)," lit., 'it being permitted;' in the A.V. of 8:37, "thou mayest," lit., ' it is permitted ; ' 16 : 21 ; in 21 : 37, " may I," lit., ' is it permitted ? ' See LET, MAY.

Note : For *ennomos*, see C, No. 2, (under LAW).

B. Adverb.

NOMIMŌS (νομίμως), lawfully, is used in 1 Tim. 1 : 8, " the Law is 3545
good, if a man use it lawfully," i.e., agreeably to its design ; the meaning AG:541C CB:1260A
here is that, while no one can be justified or obtain eternal life through its instrumentality, the believer is to have it in his heart and to fulfil its requirements ; walking " not after the flesh but after the spirit," Rom. 8 : 4, he will " use it lawfully." In 2 Tim. 2 : 5 it is used of contending in the games and adhering to the rules.¶

LAWGIVER

NOMOTHETĒS (νομοθέτης), a lawgiver (see LAW, A, No. 2, and B, 3550 AG:542A
No. 1), occurs in Jas. 4 : 12, of God, as the sole Lawgiver ; therefore, to CB:1260A
criticize the Law is to presume to take His place, with the presumption of enacting a better law.¶

LAWLESS, LAWLESSNESS

A. Adjective.

ANOMOS (ἄνομος), without law, also denotes lawless, and is so rendered 459 AG:72A
in the R.V. of Acts 2 : 23, " lawless (men)," marg., " (men) without the CB:1235C
law," A.V., " wicked (hands) ; " 2 Thess. 2 : 8, " the lawless one " (A.V., " that wicked "), of the man of sin (ver. 4) ; in 2 Pet. 2 : 8, of deeds (A.V., " unlawful "), where the thought is not simply that of doing what is unlawful, but of flagrant defiance of the known will of God. See LAW, C, No. 3.

B. Noun.

ANOMIA (ἀνομία), lawlessness, akin to A, is most frequently translated 458 AG:71D
" iniquity ; " in 2 Thess. 2 : 7, R.V., " lawlessness " (A.V., " iniquity ") ; CB:1235C
" the mystery of lawlessness " is not recognized by the world, for it does not consist merely in confusion and disorder (see A) ; the display of lawlessness by the lawless one (ver. 8) will be the effect of the attempt by the powers of darkness to overthrow the Divine government. In 1 John 3 : 4, the R.V. adheres to the real meaning of the word, " every one that doeth sin (a practice, not the committal of an act) doeth also lawlessness : and sin is lawlessness." This definition of sin sets forth its essential character as the rejection of the law, or will, of God and the substitution of the will of self. See INIQUITY and synonymous words.

LAWYER

NOMIKOS (νομικός), an adjective, learned in the law (see Tit. 3 : 9, 3544
under LAW, C, No. 1), is used as a noun, a lawyer, Matt. 22 : 35 ; Luke AG:541B CB:1260A
7 : 30 ; 10 : 25 ; 11 : 45, 46, 52 (ver. 53 in some mss.) ; 14 : 3 ; Tit. 3 : 13, where Zenas is so named. As there is no evidence that he was one skilled

in Roman jurisprudence, the term may be regarded in the usual N.T. sense as applying to one skilled in the Mosaic Law.¶

GRAMMATEUS The usual name for a scribe is *grammateus*, a man of letters; for a doctor
1122 of the law, *nomodidaskalos* (see DOCTOR). " A comparison of Luke 5 : 17
AG:165D CB:1248C with ver. 21 and Mark 2 : 6 and Matt. 9 : 3 shows that the three terms were
NOMODIDASKALOS used synonymously, and did not denote three distinct classes. The
3547 scribes were originally simply men of letters, students of Scripture, and
AG:541D CB:1260A the name first given to them contains in itself no reference to the law; in course of time, however, they devoted themselves mainly, though by no means exclusively, to the study of the law. They became jurists rather than theologians, and received names which of themselves called attention to that fact. Some would doubtless devote themselves more to one branch of activity than to another; but a ' lawyer ' might also be a ' doctor,' and the case of Gamaliel shows that a ' doctor ' might also be a member of the Sanhedrin, Acts 5 : 34 " (Eaton, in Hastings' Bib. Dic.).

LAY

5087 AG:815D CB:1272C 1. TITHĒMI (τίθημι), to put, place, set, frequently signifies to lay, and is used of (*a*) laying a corpse in a tomb, Matt. 27 : 60; Mark 6 : 29; 15 : 47; 16 : 6; Luke 23 : 53, 55; John 11 : 34; 19 : 41, 42; 20 : 2, 13, 15; Acts 7 : 16; 13 : 29; Rev. 11 : 9, R.V., " to be laid " (A.V., " to be put "); in an upper chamber, Acts 9 : 37; (*b*) laying the sick in a place, Mark 6 : 56; Luke 5 : 18; Acts 3 : 2; 5 : 15; (*c*) laying money at the Apostles' feet, Acts 4 : 35, 37; 5 : 2; (*d*) Christ's laying His hands upon children, Mark 10 : 16, R.V., " laying " (A.V., " put "); upon John, Rev. 1 : 17 (in the best mss.); (*e*) laying down one's life, (1) of Christ, John 10 : 11, R.V., " layeth down " (A.V., " giveth "); vers. 17, 18 (twice); 1 John 3 : 16; (2) of Peter for Christ's sake, John 13 : 37, 38; (3) of Christ's followers, on behalf of others, 1 John 3 : 16; (4) of anyone, for his friends, John 15 : 13; (*f*) laying up sayings in one's heart, Luke 1 : 66 (Middle Voice, in the sense of ' for themselves '); in 9 : 44, of letting Christ's words " sink " (Middle Voice, in the sense of ' for oneself; ' A.V., " sink down ") into the ears; (*g*) laying a foundation (1) literally, Luke 6 : 48; 14 : 29; (2) metaphorically, of Christ in relation to an assembly, 1 Cor. 3 : 10, 11; (*h*) God in laying Christ as a " stone of stumbling " for Israel, Rom. 9 : 33; (*i*) Christ's laying aside His garments, John 13 : 4; (*j*) Christians, in laying money in store for the help of the needy, 1 Cor. 16 : 2 (lit., ' let him put '); (*k*) depositing money, Luke 19 : 21, 22. See APPOINT.

2698 AG:419C CB:— 2. KATATITHĒMI (κατατίθημι), to lay down (*kata*), is used in Mark 15 : 46 of the act of Joseph of Arimathæa in laying Christ's body in the tomb (some mss. have No. 1 here). See DO, Note (4), SHEW.

906 AG:130D CB:1238B 3. BALLŌ (βάλλω), to cast, throw, place, put, is used in the Passive Voice signifying to be laid, e.g., Mark 7 : 30; Luke 16 : 20; for Matt. 8 : 14, R.V., " lying " (A.V., " laid ") and 9 : 2, see LIE, No. (3). See CAST.

4. EPIBALLŌ (ἐπιβάλλω), to lay upon, is used of seizing men, to 1911
imprison them, Acts 4 : 3. See CAST. AG:289D CB:—

5. KATABALLŌ (καταβάλλω), to cast down (*kata*), is used meta- 2598
phorically in Heb. 6 : 1, in the Middle Voice, negatively, of laying a AG:408D CB:1253C
foundation of certain doctrines. See CAST.

6. KLINŌ (κλίνω), to make to bend, to bow, or to make to lean, to 2827
rest, is used in Matt. 8 : 20 and Luke 9 : 58, in the Lord's statement, " the AG:436C CB:—
Son of man hath not where to lay His head ; " it is significant that this verb is used in John 19 : 30 of the Lord's act at the moment of His Death in placing His head into a position of rest, not a helpless drooping of the head as in all other cases of crucifixion. He reversed the natural order, by first reclining His head (indicative of His submission to His Father's will), and then ' giving up His spirit.' The rest He found not on earth in contrast to His creatures the foxes and birds, He found in this consummating act on the Cross. See BOW.

7. ANAKLINŌ (ἀνακλίνω), to lay down, make to recline (in the 347
Passive Voice, to lie back, recline), is used in Luke 2 : 7, of the act of the AG:56A CB:1235A
Virgin Mary in laying her Child in a manger. See SIT. (-OMAI)

8. APOTITHĒMI (ἀποτίθημι), to put off from oneself (*apo*, from, and 659
No. 1), always in the Middle Voice in the N.T., is used metaphorically in AG:101A CB:1237B
Heb. 12 : 1, " laying aside (every weight) ; " in Jas. 1 : 21, A.V., " lay apart," R.V., " putting away ; " in Acts 7 : 58 of laying down garments, after taking them off, for the purpose of stoning Stephen. See CAST, PUT.

9. HUPOTITHĒMI (ὑποτίθημι), to place under, lay down (*hupo*, 5294
under, and No. 1), is used metaphorically in Rom. 16 : 4, of risking one's AG:848B CB:—
life, " laid down " (their own necks). In the Middle Voice in 1 Tim. 4 : 6 it is used of putting persons in mind, R.V., (A.V., " in remembrance "). See REMEMBRANCE.¶

10. EPITITHĒMI (ἐπιτίθημι), to add to, lay upon, etc., is used 2007
of laying hands on the sick, for healing, Matt. 9 : 18 ; 19 : 13, R.V., AG:302D CB:1246B
" lay " (A.V., " put ") ; 19 : 15 ; Mark 5 : 23 ; 6 : 5 ; 7 : 32 ; 8 : 23, R.V., " laid " (A.V., " put ") ; so in ver. 25 ; 16 : 18 ; Luke 4 : 40 ; 13 : 13 ; Acts 6 : 6 ; 8 : 17, 19 ; 9 : 12 and 17, R.V., " laying " (A.V., " putting ") ; 13 : 3 ; 19 : 6 ; 28 : 8 ; in some mss. in Rev. 1 : 17, see No. 1, (*d*) ; of laying hands on a person by way of public recognition, 1 Tim. 5 : 22 ; of a shepherd's laying a sheep on his shoulders, Luke 15 : 5 ; of laying the Cross on Christ's shoulders, Luke 23 : 26 ; of laying on stripes, Acts 16 : 23 ; wood on a fire, 28 : 3 ; metaphorically, of laying burden's on men's shoulders, Matt. 23 : 4 ; similarly of giving injunctions, Acts 15 : 28 (cp. " put . . . upon " in ver. 10). See LADE, PUT, SET, SURNAME, WOUND.

11. ANATITHĒMI (ἀνατίθημι), to put up or before (*ana*), is used 394
in the Middle Voice of laying a case before an authority, Acts 25 : 14, R.V., (-EMAI) AG:62B
" laid before," for A.V., " declared unto ; " of setting forth a matter for CB:—

consideration, Gal. 2 : 2, R.V., "laid before (them the gospel)," for A.V., "communicated unto." See COMMUNICATE, DECLARE.¶

4369 AG:718D CB:1267B 12. PROSTITHĒMI (προστίθημι), to put to, add, is used in the Passive Voice in Acts 13 : 36, "was laid" (unto his fathers), of the burial of David. See ADD, No. 2.

1614 AG:245B CB:1244A 13. EKTEINŌ (ἐκτείνω), to stretch out or forth, especially of the hand, is used of laying out anchors from a vessel, in Acts 27 : 30, R.V., "lay out" (A.V., "cast . . . out"). See CAST, Notes, STRETCH.

2749 AG:426C CB:1254C 14. KEIMAI (κεῖμαι), to be laid, to lie, is used as the Passive Voice of *tithēmi*, to put, and is translated by some part of the verb to be laid in Matt. 3 : 10 and Luke 3 : 9, of an axe; Luke 12 : 19, of goods; John 21 : 9, where the verb has been omitted from the translation, after the words "a fire of coals" (for *epikeimai*, of the fish, see No. 15); 1 Cor. 3 : 11, of Christ, as a foundation. See APPOINT, LIE, MADE (be), SET.

Notes: (1) In Luke 23 : 53, the R.V. has "had lain" (intransitive: see LIE), for A.V., "was laid." (2) In Luke 24 : 12, some mss. have the verb, with reference to the linen cloths (the clause is absent in the best mss.); the translation should be "lying," not as A.V., "laid." (3) In John 11 : 41, the verb is not found in the best mss.

1945 AG:294C CB:— 15. EPIKEIMAI (ἐπίκειμαι), to be placed, to lie on (*epi*, upon,and No. 14), is translated by the verb to be laid upon, in John 21 : 9, of a fish; in 1 Cor. 9 : 16, of necessity. See IMPOSED, INSTANT, LIE, PRESS.

606 AG:92D CB:— 16. APOKEIMAI (ἀπόκειμαι), to be laid away, or up, is used of money in a napkin, Luke 19 : 20; metaphorically, of a hope, Col. 1 : 5; the crown of righteousness, 2 Tim. 4 : 8. In Heb. 9 : 27, said of physical death, it is translated "it is appointed" (R.V. marg., "laid up"). See APPOINT.¶

2343 AG:361B CB:1272B 17. THĒSAURIZŌ (θησαυρίζω), to lay up, store up (akin to *thēsauros*, a treasury, a storehouse, a treasure), is used of laying up treasures, on earth, Matt. 6 : 19; in Heaven, ver. 20; in the last days, Jas. 5 : 3, R.V., "ye have laid up your treasure" (A.V., "ye have heaped treasure together"); in Luke 12 : 21, "that layeth up treasure (for himself);" in 1 Cor. 16 : 2, of money for needy ones (here the present participle is translated "in store," lit. 'treasuring' or 'storing,' the 'laying by' translating the preceding verb *tithēmi*, see No. 1); in 2 Cor. 12 : 14, negatively, of children for parents; metaphorically, of laying up wrath, Rom. 2 : 5, "treasurest up." In 2 Pet. 3 : 7 the Passive Voice is used of the heavens and earth as "stored up" for fire, R.V. (marg., "stored" with fire), A.V., "kept in store." See STORE, TREASURE.¶

5136 AG:824D CB:— 18. TRACHĒLIZŌ (τραχηλίζω), to seize and twist the neck (from *trachēlos*, the throat), was used of wrestlers, in the sense of taking by the throat. The word is found in Heb. 4 : 13, "laid open," R.V. (A.V., "opened"). The literal sense of the word seems to be 'with the head thrown back and the throat exposed.' Various suggestions have been made as to the precise significance of the word in this passage. Some

have considered that the metaphor is from the manner of treating victims PHERŌ
about to be sacrificed. Little help, however, can be derived from these 5342 AG:854D
considerations. The context serves to explain the meaning and the CB:1264A APHIĒMI
R.V. rendering is satisfactory.¶ 863

Notes: (1) In Acts 25:7, A.V., *pherō*, to bear, bring, is rendered AG:125C
"laid . . . (complaints)," R.V., "bringing . . . (charges)." (2) In Mark CB:1236B EPILAMBANŌ
7:8, A.V., ***aphiēmi***, to leave, is translated "laying aside" (R.V., "ye 1949
leave"). (3) For ***epilambanō***, to lay hold, see HOLD, No. 7. (-OMAI) AG:295A

For LAY WAIT see LIE IN WAIT (-OMAI) CB:1246A

For LAYING (Acts 9:24) see PLOT

LAY WASTE

LUMAINOMAI (λυμαίνομαι), to maltreat, to outrage (from *lumē*, a 3075
brutal outrage), is translated "laid waste" (the church), in Acts 8:3, AG:481C CB:—
R.V. (A.V., "made havock of").¶

LAYING ON

EPITHESIS (ἐπίθεσις), a laying on (*epi*, on, *tithēmi*, to put), is used 1936
in the N.T. (*a*) of the laying on of hands by the Apostles, accompanied by AG:293A CB:1246B
the impartation of the Holy Spirit in outward demonstration, in the cases of those in Samaria who had believed, Acts 8:18; such supernatural manifestations were signs especially intended to give witness to Jews as to the facts of Christ and the faith; they were thus temporary; there is no record of their continuance after the time and circumstances narrated in Acts 19 (in ver. 6 of which the corresponding verb *epitithēmi* is used; see below), nor was the gift delegated by the Apostles to others (see LAY, Nos. 1 and 10); (*b*) of the similar act by the elders of a church on occasions when a member of a church was set apart for a particular work, having given evidence of qualifications necessary for it, as in the case of Timothy, 1 Tim. 4:14; of the impartation of a spiritual gift through the laying on of the hands of the Apostle Paul, 2 Tim. 1:6, R.V., "laying" (A.V., "putting"); cp. the verb *epitithēmi* in Acts 6:6, on the appointment of the Seven, and in the case of Barnabas and Saul, 13:3; also in 19:6; (*c*) in Heb. 6:2, the doctrine of the laying on of hands refers to the act enjoined upon an Israelite in connection, e.g., with the peace offerings, Lev. 3:2, 8, 13; 4:29, 33; upon the priests in connection with the sin offering, 4:4; 16:21; upon the elders, 4:15; upon a ruler, 4:24.¶

The principle underlying the act was that of identification on the part of him who did it with the animal or person upon whom the hands were
laid. In the Sept., 2 Chron. 25:27; Ezek. 23:11.¶ LAZY See
Note: For the laying of Christ's hands on the sick, see LAY, No. 10. GLUTTON, SLOTHFUL

LEAD, LED

1. AGŌ (ἄγω), to bear, bring, carry, lead, is translated by the verb to 71 AG:14B CB:1233C

lead, e.g., in Mark 13 : 11 ; Luke 4 : 1 ; 4 : 9, R.V. ; 4 : 29 ; 22 : 54 ; 23 : 1, A.V. only ; 23 : 32 ; John 18 : 28 (present tense, R.V.) ; Acts 8 : 32 ; metaphorically in Rom. 2 : 4, of the goodness of God ; 8 : 14 and Gal. 5 : 18, of the Spirit of God ; 1 Cor. 12 : 2, of the powers of darkness instigating to idolatry ; 2 Tim. 3 : 6, of divers lusts (in some mss., *aichmalōteuō*). In Luke 24 : 21 *agō* is used of the passing (or spending) of a day, and translated " it is (now the third day) ; " here the verb is probably to be taken impersonally, according to idiomatic usage, in the sense 'there is passing the third day.' See BRING, No. 10, KEEP, Note (2).

321
AG:53A 2. ANAGŌ (ἀνάγω), to lead up (*ana*, up), is used of Christ in being led
CB:— up by the Spirit into the wilderness, Matt. 4 : 1 ; Luke 4 : 5 (A.V., " taking up") ; by the elders of the people into their council, Luke 22 : 66, "led away." See BRING, No. 11.

520
AG:79C 3. APAGŌ (ἀπάγω), to lead away (*apo*, away), is used of a way leading
CB:— to destruction, Matt. 7 : 13 ; to life, ver. 14 ; of those who led Christ away from Gethsemane, Mark 14 : 44 ; in some mss., John 18 : 13, to Annas (the best mss. have No. 1 here) ; to Caiaphas, Matt. 26 : 57 ; Mark 14 : 53 ; to Pilate, Matt. 27 : 2 ; to the Prætorium, Mark 15 : 16 ; to crucifixion, Matt. 27 : 31 ; Luke 23 : 26 ; in some mss. John 19 : 16 ; of leading an animal away to watering, Luke 13 : 15 ; of being led away to idolatry, 1 Cor. 12 : 2, R.V., " led away " (A.V., " carried away "). Some mss. have it in Acts 24 : 7 (A.V., " took away "). It is translated " bring " in 23 : 17. In 12 : 19 it signifies to put to death. See BRING, No. 12, DEATH, C, No. 3.¶

4013
AG:645C 4. PERIAGŌ (περιάγω), used transitively, denotes to lead about,
5342 1 Cor. 9 : 5. For the intransitive use, see GO, No. 9.

AG:854D 5. PHERŌ (φέρω), to bear, carry, is used metaphorically of a gate,
CB:1264A as leading to a city, Acts 12 : 10. See BRING, No. 1.

3594
AG:553B 6. HODĒGEŌ (ὁδηγέω), to lead the way : see GUIDE, B, No. 1.

CB:1251A 7. EISAGŌ (εἰσάγω), to bring into, is translated " to be led into " in
1521
AG:232B Acts 21 : 37, A.V. (R.V., " to be brought into "). See BRING, A, No. 13.

4879
AG:784D 8. SUNAPAGŌ (συναπάγω), always in the Passive Voice, to be carried
CB:— or led away with, is translated " being led away with " in 2 Pet. 3 : 17, A.V. (R.V., " being carried away with "). See CARRY.

1806
AG:271C 9. EXAGŌ (ἐξάγω), to lead out, is rendered by the verb to lead, out or
CB:— forth, in Mark 15 : 20 (in some mss. in 8 : 23, the best have *ekpherō*, to bring out) ; Luke 24 : 50 ; John 10 : 3 ; Acts 7 : 36, 40 (A.V. " brought "), and 13 : 17, R.V. ; Acts 21 : 38 ; Heb. 8 : 9. See BRING, No. 14.

399
AG:63A 10. ANAPHERŌ (ἀναφέρω), to carry or lead up, is translated
CB:1235B " leadeth . . . up " in the A.V. of Mark 9 : 2 (R.V. " bringeth . . . up "). See BRING, No. 2.

1533
AG:233D 11. EISPHERŌ (εἰσφερω), to bring in, or into, is translated "lead
CB:1243B (us not) into," in Matt. 6 : 13 and Luke 11 : 4 (R.V., " bring . . . into "), of temptation. See BRING, No. 4.

12. PLANAŌ (πλανάω), to lead astray (akin to *planē*, a wandering), 4105
is translated "lead . . . astray," metaphorically, in Matt. 24:4, 5, 11 AG:665B CB:1265A
and Mark 13:5, 6 (A.V., "deceive").

13. APOPLANAŌ (ἀποπλανάω), to cause to go astray (*apo*, away 635
from, and No. 12), is used metaphorically of leading into error, Mark AG:97B CB:1237A
13:22, R.V., "lead astray" (A.V., "seduce"); Passive Voice in
1 Tim. 6:10 (A.V., "erred").¶

Notes: (1) In Rev. 13:10, some mss. have *sunagō*, to bring together, SUNAGŌ 4863
translated "leadeth (into captivity)," A.V. and R.V. marg. (R.V. text, AG:782A
"is for"). (2) For the verb *diagō*, to lead a life, 1 Tim. 2:2, see LIVE, CB:1270B
No. 7. (3) For *thriambeuō*, to "lead in triumph," 2 Cor. 2:14, R.V., DIAGŌ 1236
see TRIUMPH. (4) See also HAND (lead by the). AG:182C CB:—

THRIAMBEUŌ 2358 AG:363D CB:1272B

For LEADERS (Matt. 15:14) see GUIDE

LEAF

PHULLON (φύλλον), a leaf (originally *phulion*, Lat., *folium*; Eng., 5444
folio, foliaceous, foliage, foliate, folious, etc.), is found in Matt. 21:19; AG:869A CB:1264C
24:32; Mark 11:13 (twice); 13:28; Rev. 22:2.¶

LEAN

1. ANAKEIMAI (ἀνάκειμαι), to be laid up, to lie, is used of reclining 345
at table, and translated "leaning (on Jesus' bosom)" in the A.V. of AG:55D CB:1235A
John 13:23, R.V., "reclining" (for ver. 25 see No. 2). In ver. 28, it is
translated "at the table," lit., 'of (those) reclining.' See GUEST, RECLINE,
SIT, TABLE (at the).

2. ANAPIPTŌ (ἀναπίπτω), lit., to fall back (*ana*, back, *piptō*, to fall), 377
is used of reclining at a repast and translated "leaning back, (as he was, on AG:59C CB:1235B
Jesus' breast)" in John 13:25, R.V. (the A.V. follows the mss. which have
epipiptō, and renders it 'lying'); in 21:20, "leaned back," the Apostle's
reminder of the same event in his experience. See SIT.

LEAP

1. HALLOMAI (ἅλλομαι), to leap (akin to *halma*, a leap), is used 242
(*a*) metaphorically, of the springing up of water, John 4:14; (*b*) literally, AG:39D CB:1249A
of the leaping of healed cripples, Acts 3:8 (2nd part); 14:10.¶

2. SKIRTAŌ (σκιρτάω), to leap, is found in Luke 1:41, 44, and 4640
6:23, there translated "leap for joy;" in 1:44 the words "for joy" AG:755D CB:—
are expressed separately.¶

3. EXALLOMAI (ἐξάλλομαι), to leap up (lit., out, *ek*, and No. 1), is 1814
said in Acts 3:8 (1st part) of the cripple healed by Peter (cp. No. 1, AG:272C CB:—
above).¶ 2177

4. EPHALLOMAI (ἐφάλλομαι), to leap upon (*epi*, upon, and No. 1), AG:330A
is said of the demoniac in Acts 19:16.¶ CB:—

LEARN, LEARNED (be)

3129 1. MANTHANŌ (μανθάνω) denotes (*a*) to learn (akin to *mathētēs*, a
AG:490B disciple), to increase one's knowledge, or be increased in knowledge,
CB:1257C frequently to learn by enquiry, or observation, e.g., Matt. 9 : 13 ; 11 : 29 ; 24 : 32 ; Mark 13 : 28 ; John 7 : 15 ; Rom. 16 : 17 ; 1 Cor. 4 : 6 ; 14 : 35 ; Phil. 4 : 9 ; 2 Tim. 3 : 14 ; Rev. 14 : 3 ; said of learning Christ, Eph. 4 : 20, not simply the doctrine of Christ, but Christ Himself, a process not merely of getting to know the Person but of so applying the knowledge as to walk differently from the rest of the Gentiles ; (*b*) to ascertain, Acts 23 : 27, R.V., "learned" (A.V., "understood") ; Gal. 3 : 2, "This only would I learn from you," perhaps with a tinge of irony in the enquiry, the answer to which would settle the question of the validity of the new Judaistic gospel they were receiving ; (*c*) to learn by use and practice, to acquire the habit of, be accustomed to, e.g., Phil. 4 : 11 ; 1 Tim. 5 : 4, 13 ; Tit. 3 : 14 ; Heb. 5 : 8. See UNDERSTAND.

1097 2. GINŌSKŌ (γινώσκω), to know by observation and experience, is
AG:160D
CB:1248B translated to learn, in the R.V. of Mark 15 : 45 ; John 12 : 9. See ALLOW.

198
AG:33B 3. AKRIBOŌ (ἀκριβόω), to learn carefully, is so translated in Matt.
CB:— 2 : 7, 16, R.V. (A.V., "diligently enquired").¶

3453 4. MUEŌ (μυέω), to initiate into mysteries, is translated "I have
AG:529A
CB:1259B learned the secret" (Passive Voice, perfect tense) in Phil. 4 : 12, R.V. (A.V., "I am instructed"). See INSTRUCT.¶

3811 *Note : Paideuō*, to teach, instruct, train, is translated "instructed" in
AG:603D
CB:1261C Acts 7 : 22, R.V. (A.V., "learned") ; in 1 Tim. 1 : 20, "(that) they might be taught," A.V., "(that) they may learn."

LEARNING (Noun)

1121 1. GRAMMA (γράμμα), a letter, is used in the plural in Acts 26 : 24,
AG:165B
CB:1248C with the meaning "learning," "(thy much) learning (doth turn thee to madness)," R.V., possibly an allusion to the Jewish Scriptures, to which the Apostle had been appealing ; in John 7 : 15, "(How knoweth this Man) letters" (A.V. marg., "learning"), the succeeding phrase "not having learned" is illustrated in the papyri, where it indicates inability to write. See BILL.

1319 2. DIDASKALIA (διδασκαλία), teaching, instruction (akin to *didaskō*,
AG:191C
CB:1241B to teach), is translated "learning" in Rom. 15 : 4. See DOCTRINE.

LEAST

1646 1. ELACHISTOS (ἐλάχιστος), least, is a superlative degree formed
AG:248D
CB:1244A from the word *elachus*, little, the place of which was taken by *mikros* (the comparative degree being *elassōn*, less) ; it is used of (*a*) size, Jas. 3 : 4 ; (*b*) amount ; of the management of affairs, Luke 16 : 10 (twice) ; 19 : 17, "very little ;" (*c*) importance, 1 Cor. 6 : 2, "smallest (matters) ;" (*d*) authority : of commandments, Matt. 5 : 19 ; (*e*) estimation, as to

persons, Matt. 5 : 19 (2nd part) ; 25 : 40, 45 ; 1 Cor. 15 : 9 ; as to a town,
Matt. 2 : 6 ; as to activities or operations, Luke 12 : 26 ; 1 Cor. 4 : 3, " a
very small thing."¶ 1647

2. ELACHISTOTEROS (ἐλαχιστότερος), a comparative degree formed AG:248D (-ISTOS 2.b.)
from No. 1, is used in Eph. 3 : 8, " less than the least."¶ CB:1244A

3. MIKROS (μικρός), small, little, is translated " the least " in Acts 3398
8 : 10 and Heb. 8 : 11, with reference to rank or influence. See LITTLE, AG:521A CB:1258C
A, No. 1.

4. MIKROTEROS (μικρότερος), the comparative of No. 3, is used of 3398
(*a*) size, Matt. 13 : 32, A.V., " the least," R.V., " less ; " Mark 4 : 31 AG:521B (MIKROS 1.c.)
[cp. No. 1 (*a*)] ; (*b*) estimation, Matt. 11 : 11 and Luke 7 : 28, A.V., " least," CB:—
R.V., " but little," marg., " lesser " (in the Kingdom of Heaven), those
in the Kingdom itself being less than John the Baptist [cp. No. 1 (*e*)] ;
Luke 9 : 48. See LESS.¶ EXOUTHENEŌ

Notes : (1) In 1 Cor. 6 : 4, A.V., *exoutheneō*, in the Passive Voice, to 1848 AG:277C
be of no account, is translated " is least esteemed " (R.V., " are of no CB:1247C
account ") ; see ACCOUNT. (2) In Luke 19 : 42, the adverbial phrase KAIGE 2534
kai ge, " at least," is found in some mss. ; the R.V. follows those in which AG:152D
it is absent. (3) In 1 Cor. 9 : 2, A.V., the phrase *alla ge* is rendered (GE 3.c.) ALLA
" doubtless ; " R.V., " at least." (4) In Acts 5 : 15, the phrase *k'an* 235
(for *kai ean*, even if) denotes " at the least." AG:38A KAN

2579

LEATHERN

AG:402C

DERMATINOS (δερμάτινος) denotes of skin, leathern (from *derma*, 1193
skin, hide of beasts, akin to *derō*, to flay ; whence Eng., derm, dermal, AG:175C CB:—
dermatology) ; it is translated " leathern " in Matt. 3 : 4, of John the
Baptist's girdle ; in Mark 1 : 6, R.V. (A.V., " of a skin "). See SKIN.¶

LEAVE, LEFT

(*a*) *In the sense of leaving, abandoning, forsaking.*

1. APHIĒMI (ἀφίημι), *apo*, from, and *hiēmi*, to send, has three chief 863
meanings, (*a*) to send forth, let go, forgive ; (*b*) to let, suffer, permit ; AG:125C CB:1236B
(*c*) to leave, leave alone, forsake, neglect. It is translated by the verb
to leave (*c*), in Matt. 4 : 11 ; 4 : 20, 22, and parallel passages ; 5 : 24 ;
8 : 15, and parallel passages ; 8 : 22, R.V., " leave (the dead)," A.V., " let,"
and the parallel passage ; 13 : 36, R.V., " left (the multitude)," A.V.,
" sent . . . away ; " 18 : 12 ; 19 : 27, and parallel passages, R.V., " we
have left " (A.V., " we have forsaken ") ; so ver. 29 ; 22 : 22, 25 ; 23 : 23,
R.V., " have left undone " (A.V., " have omitted," in the 1st part, " leave
undone " in the second) ; 23 : 38, and the parallel passage ; 24 : 2, 40, 41,
and parallel passages ; 26 : 56, R.V., " left ; " Mark 1 : 18, " left ; "
1 : 31 ; 7 : 8, R.V., " ye leave ; " 8 : 13 ; 10 : 28, 29 ; 12 : 12, 19–22 ;
13 : 34 ; Luke 10 : 30 ; 11 : 42 (in some mss.) ; Luke 12 : 39, R.V. " have
left," A.V. " have suffered " (No. 9 in Matt. 24 : 43) ; John 4 : 3, 28, 52 ;
8 : 29 ; 10 : 12 ; 14 : 18, 27 ; 16 : 28, 32 ; Rom. 1 : 27 ; 1 Cor. 7 : 11, R.V.,

"leave" (A.V., "put away"); 7:13 (A.V. and R.V.); Heb. 2:8; 6:1; Rev. 2:4. See FORGIVE.

447 AG:69D CB:— 2. ANIĒMI (ἀνίημι), *ana*, back and *hiēmi*, to send, denotes to let go, loosen, forbear; it is translated "I will (never) leave (thee)" in Heb. 13:5. See FORBEAR.

2641 AG:413C CB:1254A 3. KATALEIPŌ (καταλείπω), to leave behind (*kata*, down, *leipō*, to leave), is everywhere rendered by the verb to leave except in the following: the A.V. of Rom. 11:4, "I have reserved" (R.V., "I have left"); Heb. 11:27, "he forsook;" 2 Pet. 2:15, A.V., "have forsaken," R.V., "forsaking." See FORSAKE, RESERVE.

620 AG:94D CB:— 4. APOLEIPŌ (ἀπολείπω), to leave behind (*apo*, from), is used (*a*) in the Active Voice, of leaving behind a cloak, 2 Tim. 4:13; a person, 2 Tim. 4:20; of abandoning a principality (by angels), Jude 6, R.V.; (*b*) in the Passive Voice, to be reserved, to remain, Heb. 4:6, 9; 10:26. See REMAIN, No. 3.¶ In the papyri it is used as a technical term in wills (Moulton and Milligan, Vocab.).

1459 AG:215D CB:— 5. ENKATALEIPŌ (ἐγκαταλείπω), lit., to leave behind in (*en*, in, and No. 3), signifies (*a*) to leave behind, Rom. 9:29, "a seed;" (*b*) to abandon, forsake, translated by the verb to leave in Acts 2:27, 31 (in some mss., No. 3) of the soul of Christ; in the following, by the verb to forsake, Matt. 27:46; Mark 15:34; 2 Cor. 4:9; 2 Tim. 4:10, 16; Heb. 10:25; 13:5 (see No. 2 in the same ver.). See FORSAKE.¶

5275 AG:845C CB:1252B 6. HUPOLEIPŌ (ὑπολείπω), to leave remaining, lit., to leave under (*hupo*), is used in the Passive Voice in Rom. 11:3, of a survivor.¶

4035 AG:648C (-OMAI) CB:1263B 7. PERILEIPŌ (περιλείπω), to leave over, is used in the Passive Vo ce in 1 Thess. 4:15, 17, R.V., "that are left" (A.V., "that remain"), lit., 'left over,' i.e., the living believers at the Lord's return. See REMAIN.¶

3973 AG:638A CB:— 8. PAUŌ (παύω), to make to cease, is used in the Middle Voice, signifying to cease, leave off, and is translated "had left" in Luke 5:4; "left" in Acts 21:32; elsewhere, to cease. See CEASE.

1439 AG:212C CB:— 9. EAŌ (ἐάω) signifies (*a*) to let, permit, suffer, e.g., Matt. 24:43; (*b*) to leave, Acts 23:32, of leaving horsemen; 27:40, of leaving anchors in the sea, R.V. [A.V., "committed (themselves)"]. See COMMIT, SUFFER.

5277 AG:845D CB:— 10. HUPOLIMPANŌ (ὑπολιμπάνω), *limpanō* being a late form for *leipō*, to leave, is used in 1 Pet. 2:21, "leaving (us an example)."¶

4052 AG:650C CB:1263C 11. PERISSEUŌ (περισσεύω), to be over and above (the number), hence, to be or remain over, is translated "was left," in Matt. 15:37, A.V. (R.V., "remained over," as in 14:20; Luke 9:17; John 6:12 and ver. 13, where the A.V. adds "and above"), of the broken fragments after the feeding of the multitudes. See ABOUND.

4051 AG:650C CB:1263C *Note*: The corresponding noun, *perisseuma*, that which is over and above, is used in the plural in Mark 8:8, R.V., "(of broken pieces) that remained over," A.V., "(of the broken meat) that was left," lit., 'of fragments of broken pieces.' See REMAIN.

12. EKBALLŌ (ἐκβάλλω), to cast out (*ek*, from, *ballō*, to cast), to drive 1544
out, is used in the sense of rejecting or leaving out, in Rev. 11 : 2, as to AG:237B CB:1243B
the measuring of the court of the Temple (marg., "cast without"). See
CAST, No. 5.

(*b*) *In the sense of giving leave.*

EPITREPŌ (ἐπιτρέπω) lit. denotes to turn to (*epi*, upon, to, *trepō*, to 2010
turn), and so (*a*) to commit, entrust (not in N.T.); (*b*) to permit, give AG:303C CB:—
leave, send, of Christ's permission to the unclean spirits to enter the swine, Mark 5 : 13; in Luke 8 : 32, R.V., "give . . . leave," "gave . . . leave" (A.V., "suffer" and "suffered"); in John 19 : 38, of Pilate's permission to Joseph to take away the body of the Lord; in Acts 21 : 39, of Paul's request to the chief captain to permit him to address the people, R.V., "give . . . leave" (for A.V., "suffer"); in 21 : 40, "he had given him leave" (A.V., ". . . licence"). See LET, LIBERTY, LICENCE, PERMIT, SUFFER.

(*c*) *In the sense of taking leave of, bidding farewell to.*

1. APOTASSŌ (ἀποτάσσω), used in the Middle Voice in the N.T., 657
lit. signifies to arrange oneself off (*apo*, from, *tassō*, to arrange); hence, AG:100D CB:—
to take leave of, Mark 6 : 46, R.V., "had taken leave of" (A.V., "had sent . . . away"); Acts 18 : 18; 18 : 21, R.V., "taking his leave of" (A.V., "bade . . . farewell"); 2 Cor. 2 : 13; in Luke 9 : 61, "to bid farewell;" in Luke 14 : 33 it has its other meaning "renouncing" (A.V.,
"forsaking"). See FAREWELL, FORSAKE, RENOUNCE.¶ —

2. APASPAZOMAI (ἀπασπάζομαι), to embrace, salute, take leave of AG:81D CB:—
(*apo*, from, *aspazomai*, to salute), is used in Acts 21 : 6, A.V., "when we ASPAZOMAI 782
had taken our leave" (R.V., "bade . . . farewell"). Some mss. have AG:116C
the simple verb *aspazomai*.¶ CB:1238A

LEAVEN (Noun and Verb)

A. Noun.

ZUMĒ (ζύμη), leaven, sour dough, in a high state of fermentation, was 2219
used in general in making bread. It required time to fulfil the process. AG:340A CB:1273C
Hence, when food was required at short notice, unleavened cakes were used, e.g., Gen. 18 : 6; 19 : 3; Ex. 12 : 8. The Israelites were forbidden to use leaven for seven days at the time of Passover, that they might be reminded that the Lord brought them out of Egypt "in haste," Deut. 16 : 3, with Ex. 12 : 11; the unleavened bread, insipid in taste, reminding them, too, of their afflictions, and of the need of self-judgment, is called "the bread of affliction." Leaven was forbidden in all offerings to the Lord by fire, Lev. 2 : 11; 6 : 17. Being bred of corruption and spreading through the mass of that in which it is mixed, and therefore symbolizing the pervasive character of evil, leaven was utterly inconsistent in offerings which typified the propitiatory sacrifice of Christ.

In the O.T. leaven is not used in a metaphorical sense. In the N.T. it is used (*a*) metaphorically (1) of corrupt doctrine, Matt. 13 : 33 and

Luke 13 : 21, of error as mixed with the truth (there is no valid reason for regarding the symbol here differently from its application elsewhere in the N.T.) ; Matt. 16 : 6, 11 ; Mark 8 : 15 (1st part) ; Luke 12 : 1 ; that the Kingdom of heaven is likened to leaven, does not mean that the Kingdom is leaven. The same statement, as made in other parables, shows that it is the whole parable which constitutes the similitude of the Kingdom ; the history of Christendom confirms the fact that the pure meal of the doctrine of Christ has been adulterated with error ; (2) of corrupt practices, Mark 8 : 15 (2nd part), the reference to the Herodians being especially applied to their irreligion ; 1 Cor. 5 : 7, 8 ; (*b*) literally, in Matt. 16 : 12, and in the general statements in 1 Cor. 5 : 6 and Gal. 5 : 9, where the implied applications are to corrupt practice and corrupt doctrine respectively.¶

B. Verb.

2220 AG:340A ZUMOŌ (ζυμόω) signifies to leaven, to act as leaven, Passive Voice
CB:1273C in Matt. 13 : 33 and Luke 13 : 21 ; Active Voice in 1 Cor. 5 : 6 and
Gal. 5 : 9.¶

For LED see LEAD

LEE

HUPOPLEŌ *Note :* This forms part of the R.V. rendering of two verbs, (1) ***hupopleō***,
5284 AG:846D to sail under (i.e., under the lee of), from ***hupo***, under, ***pleō***, to sail, Acts
CB:— 27 : 4, 7 (A.V., " sailed under ") ;¶ (2) ***hupotrechō***, to run in under (in
HUPOTRECHŌ navigation), to run under the lee of (***hupo***, and a form ***hupodramōn***, used
5295 AG:848B as an aorist participle of the verb), Acts 27 : 16, R.V., " running under
CB:— the lee of " (A.V., " running under "). See Run, Sail.¶

For LEFT (Verb) see LEAVE

LEFT (Adjective)

710 AG:106C 1. ARISTEROS (ἀριστερός), is used (*a*) of the left hand, in Matt. 6 : 3,
CB:1237C the word " hand " being understood ; in connection with the armour of righteousness, in 2 Cor. 6 : 7, " (on the right hand and) on the left," lit., ' (of the weapons . . . the right and) the left ; ' (*b*) in the phrase " on the left," formed by *ex* (for *ek*), from, and the genitive plural of this adjective, Mark 10 : 37 (some mss. have No. 2 here) ; Luke 23 : 33.¶

2176 AG:329D 2. EUŌNUMOS (εὐώνυμος), lit., of good name, or omen (*eu*, well,
CB:1247B *onoma*, a name), a word adopted to avoid the ill-omen attaching to the left (omens from the left being unlucky, but a good name being desired for them, cp. *aristeros*, lit., ' better of two,' euphemistic for the ill-omened *laios* and *skaios* ; cp., too, the Eng., sinister, from the Latin word meaning ' left '), is used euphemistically for No. 1, either (*a*) simply as an adjective in Rev. 10 : 2, of the left foot ; in Acts 21 : 3, " on the

left" (lit., 'left'); or (*b*) with the preposition *ex* (for *ek*), signifying on the left hand, Matt. 20 : 21, 23; 25 : 33, 41; 27 : 38; Mark 10 : 40 (for ver. 37, in some mss., see No. 1); 15 : 27.¶

LEG

SKELOS (σκέλος), the leg from the hip downwards, is used only 4628
of the breaking of the legs of the crucified malefactors, to hasten their AG:753C CB:—
death, John 19 : 31–33 (a customary act, not carried out in the case of Christ, in fulfilment of Ex. 12 : 46; Numb. 9 : 12). The practice was known as *skelokopia* (from *koptō*, to strike), or, in Latin, *crurifragium* (from *crus*, a leg, and *frango*, to break).¶

LEGION

LEGIŌN (λεγιών), otherwise spelt *legeōn*, a legion, occurs in Matt. 26 : 53, 3003
of angels; in Mark 5 : 9, 15, and Luke 8 : 30, of demons. Among the AG:467D CB:—
Romans a legion was primarily a chosen (*lego*, to choose) body of soldiers divided into ten cohorts, and numbering from 4,200 to 6,000 men (Gk. *speira*, see BAND). In the time of our Lord it formed a complete army of infantry and cavalry, of upwards of 5,000 men. The legions were not brought into Judæa till the outbreak of the Jewish war (A.D. 66), as they were previously employed in the frontier Provinces of the Empire. Accordingly in its N.T. use the word has its other and more general significance of a large number.¶

LEISURE (to have)

EUKAIREŌ (εὐκαιρέω), to have leisure or opportunity (*eu*, well, 2119
kairos, a time or season), is translated "they had . . . leisure" in AG:321B CB:1247B
Mark 6 : 31; in Acts 17 : 21, "spent their time" (R.V., marg., "had leisure for"); in 1 Cor. 16 : 12," he shall have opportunity," R.V. (A.V., ". . . convenient time"). See CONVENIENT, OPPORTUNITY, SPEND.¶
This verb differs from *scholazō*, to have leisure; it stresses the opportunity
of doing something, whereas *scholazō* stresses the leisure for engaging in it, SCHOLAZŌ
e.g., 1 Cor. 7 : 5, "(that) ye may give yourselves to." 4980 AG:797D CB:—

LEND, LENDER

A. Verbs.

1. DANEIZŌ (δανείζω) is translated to lend in Luke 6 : 34, 35 : see 1155 AG:170D
BORROW. CB:—

2. KICHRĒMI (κίχρημι), or CHRAŌ (χράω), to lend, is used in the After 2797
aorist (or 'point') tense, Active Voice, in Luke 11 : 5, in the request, AG:433A CB:—
"lend me three loaves." The radical sense of the verb is to furnish
what is needful (akin to *chreia*, which means both use and need, and to CHRAŌ(-OMAI) 5530
chrē, it is needful). Hence it is distinct from No. 1, the basic idea of which AG:884B
is to lend on security or return.¶ CB:1240A

B. Noun.

1157 AG:170D CB:1240B DANISTĒS or DANEISTĒS (δανειστής) denotes a money-lender (akin to A, No. 1), translated " lender " in Luke 7 : 41, R.V. (A.V., " creditor ").¶ In the Sept., 2 Kings 4 : 1 ; Ps. 109 : 11 ; Prov. 29 : 13.¶

LENGTH

3372 AG:518C CB:— MĒKOS (μῆκος), length, from the same root as *makros*, long (see FAR, LONG), occurs in Eph. 3 : 18 and Rev. 21 : 16 (twice).¶

LENGTH (at)

4218 AG:695A CB:1266B POTE (ποτέ) is translated " at length " in Rom. 1 : 10, where the whole phrase " if by any means now at length " suggests not only ardent desire but the existence of difficulties for a considerable time. See AFORETIME.

LEOPARD

3917 AG:623D CB:1262B PARDALIS (πάρδαλις) denotes a leopard or a panther, an animal characterized by swiftness of movement and sudden spring, in Dan. 7 : 6 symbolic of the activities of Alexander the Great, and the formation of the Grecian Kingdom, the third seen in the vision there recorded. In Rev. 13 : 2 the imperial power, described there also as a " beast," is seen to concentrate in himself the characteristics of those mentioned in Dan. 7.¶

LEPER

3015 AG:472A CB:1256C LEPROS (λεπρός), an adjective, primarily used of psoriasis, characterized by an eruption of rough, scaly patches ; later, leprous, but chiefly used as a noun, a leper, Matt. 8 : 2 ; 10 : 8 ; 11 : 5 ; Mark 1 : 40 ; Luke 4 : 27 ; 7 : 22 ; 17 : 12 ; especially of Simon, mentioned in Matt. 26 : 6 ; Mark 14 : 3.¶

LEPROSY

3014 AG:471D CB:1256C LEPRA (λέπρα), akin to *lepros* (above), is mentioned in Matt. 8 : 3 ; Mark 1 : 42 ; Luke 5 : 12, 13.¶ In the removal of other maladies the verb to heal (*iaomai*) is used, but in the removal of leprosy, the verb to cleanse (*katharizō*), save in the statement concerning the Samaritan, Luke 17 : 15, " when he saw that he was healed." Matt. 10 : 8 and Luke 4 : 27 indicate that the disease was common in the nation. Only twelve cases are recorded in the N.T., but these are especially selected. For the Lord's commands to the leper mentioned in Matthew 8 and to the ten in Luke 17, see Lev. 14 : 2–32.

LESS

1640 AG:248A CB:1244A 1. ELASSŌN (ἐλάσσων) serves as a comparative degree of *mikros*, little (see LEAST), and denotes ' less ' in (*a*) quality, as of wine, John 2 : 10, " worse ; " (*b*) age, Rom. 9 : 12, " younger ; " 1 Tim. 5 : 9, " under "

neuter, adverbially); (*c*) rank, Heb. 7:7. See UNDER, WORSE, YOUNG.¶
2. MIKROTEROS (μικρότερος), the comparative of *mikros*, is translated 3398 AG:521B
"less" in Matt. 13:32, R.V. (A.V., "least"), and Mark 4:31. See LEAST. (MIKROS l.c.) CB:—
3. HĒSSŌN (ἥσσων), inferior, is used in the neuter adverbially in 2276
2 Cor. 12:15, "the less." See WORSE. AG:349A CB:—

LEST

1. MĒ (μή), a negative particle, often used as a conjunction, is fre- 3361
quently translated "lest," e.g., Mark 13:36 (in ver. 5, R.V., "that no," AG:515D CB:1258A
for A.V., "lest"); Acts 13:40; 23:10.
2. HINA MĒ (ἵνα μή), in order that not, is rendered "lest," e.g., HINA
in Matt. 17:27; in some instances the R.V. renders the phrase "that . . . 2443 AG:376D
not," e.g., Luke 8:12, or "that . . . no," 1 Cor. 9:12 (A.V., "lest"). CB:1250C
3. MĒPOTE or MĒ POTE (μήποτε) denotes lest ever, lest perhaps, 3379
lest at any time, e.g., Matt. 4:6; "lest haply," Matt. 7:6, R.V. (A.V., AG:519B CB:1258B
"lest"), and in 13:15 (A.V., "lest at any time"); in 25:9, R.V.,
"peradventure" (A.V., "lest"). The R.V. does not translate this
simply by "lest," as in the A.V.; see further, e.g., in Matt. 27:64;
Mark 14:2; Luke 12:58; the addition of *pote* requires the fuller
rendering.
Note: In Luke 14:29, the conjunctive phrase *hina mēpote*, "lest
haply," is used.
4. MĒPŌS, or MĒ PŌS (μήπως), used as a conjunction, denotes lest 3381
somehow, lest haply, lest by any means, e.g., 2 Cor. 2:7, R.V., "lest by AG:519C CB:—
any means" (A.V., "lest perhaps"); so 12:20 (twice) and Gal. 4:11
(A.V., "lest"); in 1 Thess. 3:5 (A.V., "lest by some means"). —
5. MĒPOU, or MĒ POU (μήπου), lest perhaps, is used in Acts 27:29, AG:519C
R.V., "lest haply" (A.V., "lest"). CB:— EIS
Note: In 2 Cor. 4:4, A.V., the phrase *eis* (unto) *to* (the) *mē* (not), 1519
i.e., 'in order that . . . not,' is rendered "lest (the light) . . . should;" AG:228A CB:1243A
R.V., "that (the light) . . . should not." Mē 3361

AG:515D CB:1258A

LET (alone, go)

1. APHIĒMI (ἀφίημι), for the meanings of which see LEAVE, No. 1, 863
frequently denotes to let, suffer, permit, e.g., Matt. 5:40 (translated AG:125C CB:1236B
"let . . . have"); 7:4; 13:30; 15:14; 27:49 and Mark 15:36,
R.V., "let be," probably short for 'let us see' (Moulton and Milligan,
Vocab.); Mark 7:27; 11:6 ("let . . . go"); 14:6 ("let . . .
alone"); so Luke 13:8; John 11:48; in Acts 5:38 (where some mss.
have *eaō*, to permit, let, suffer); in John 11:44 and 18:8 ("let");
1 Cor. 7:11, 12, R.V., "let . . . leave," A.V., "let . . . put away;" 2010
7:13 ("let . . . leave"). AG:303C
2. EPITREPŌ (ἐπιτρέπω), for the meanings of which see LEAVE CB:—
(*b*), is translated "let (me)" in Luke 9:61, A.V., R.V., "suffer (me)." 630 AG:96C
3. APOLUŌ (ἀπολύω) signifies to set free, release, loose (*apo*, from, CB:1237A

luō, to loose), e.g., Luke 13 : 12; John 19 : 10; forgive, Luke 6 : 37; to release, dismiss, send away, translated to let go, e.g., in Luke 14 : 4; in some mss. 22 : 68; in Luke 23 : 22, John 19 : 12 and Acts 3 : 13, A.V., "let . . . go" (R.V., "release"); in Acts 4 : 21, "they let . . . go;" in ver. 23 (Passive Voice), "being let go;" 5 : 40; in 15 : 33, A.V., "let go" (R.V., "dismissed"); 16 : 35, 36; 17 : 9; in 23 : 22, R.V., "let . . . go" (A.V., "let . . . depart"); in 28 : 18, A.V., "let . . . go" (R.V., "set . . . at liberty"). See DISMISS.

1439 AG:212C CB:— 4. EAŌ (ἐάω), to let, occurs in Acts 27 : 32. See SUFFER.

1832 AG:275B CB:1247C *Note:* In Acts 2 : 29, the impersonal verb *exesti*, it is permitted, it is lawful, is rendered "let me," A.V. (R.V. and A.V., marg., "I may").

For LET (A.V. in Rom. 1 : 13 and 2 Thess. 2 : 7) see HINDER and RESTRAIN

LET DOWN

2524 AG:390B CB:— 1. KATHIĒMI (καθίημι), to send, or let down (*kata*, down, *hiēmi*, to send), is translated to let down, with reference to (*a*) the paralytic in Luke 5 : 19; (*b*) Saul of Tarsus, Acts 9 : 25; (*c*) the great sheet in Peter's vision, 10 : 11 and 11 : 5.¶

5465 AG:874B CB:— 2. CHALAŌ (χαλάω), to slacken, loosen, let loose, denotes in the N.T., to let down, to lower; it is used with reference to (*a*) the paralytic, in Mark 2 : 4, cp. No. 1 (*a*); (*b*) Saul of Tarsus, Acts 9 : 25, "lowering" [see also No. 1 (*b*)]; 2 Cor. 11 : 33, "was I let down" (Passive Voice); (*c*) nets, Luke 5 : 4, 5 (in the latter, R.V., "nets;" A.V., "net"); (*d*) the gear of a ship, Acts 27 : 17, R.V., "they lowered (the gear)," A.V., "they strake (sail);" (*e*) a ship's boat, ver. 30, R.V., "lowered" (A.V., "let down"). See LOWER, STRIKE.¶

LET OUT

1554 AG:238C CB:— EKDIDŌMI (ἐκδίδωμι), primarily, to give out, give up, surrender (*ek*, out, from, *didōmi*, to give), denotes to let out for hire; in the N.T. it is used, in the Middle Voice, with the meaning to let out to one's advantage, in the parable of the husbandman and his vineyard, Matt. 21 : 33, 41; Mark 12 : 1; Luke 20 : 9, A.V., "let . . . forth;" R.V., "let . . . out."¶

LETTER

1121 AG:165B CB:1248C 1. GRAMMA (γράμμα) primarily denotes that which is traced or drawn, a picture; then, that which is written, (*a*) a character, letter of the alphabet, 2 Cor. 3 : 7, "written," lit., '(in) letters'; Gal. 6 : 11; here the reference is not to the length of the Epistle (Paul never uses *gramma*, either in the singular or the plural, of his Epistles; of these he uses *epistolē*, No. 2), but to the size of the characters written by his own hand (probably from this verse to the end, as the use of the past tense, "I have written," is, according to Greek idiom, the equivalent of our 'I am writing'). Moreover, the word for "letters" is here in the dative case, ***grammasin***, 'with (how large) letters;' (*b*) a writing, a written document, a bond (A.V., "bill") Luke 16 : 6, 7; (*c*) a letter, by way of correspondence, Acts 28 : 21; (*d*) the Scriptures of the O.T., 2 Tim. 3 : 15; (*e*) learning, John 7 : 15, "letters;" Acts 26 : 24, "(much) learning" (lit., 'many letters'); in the papyri an illiterate person is often spoken of as one who does not know letters, "which never means anything else than inability to write" (Moulton and Milligan); (*f*) "the letter," the written commandments of the Word of God, in contrast to the inward operation of the Holy Spirit under the New Covenant, Rom. 2 : 27, 29; 7 : 6; 2 Cor. 3 : 6; (*g*) the books of Moses, John 5 : 47.¶

2. EPISTOLĒ (ἐπιστολή): see EPISTLE. 1992 AG:300D CB:1246A

For LEVEL see PLACE, *Note* (4)

For LEWD and LEWDNESS see VILE and VILLANY

LIAR

A. Nouns.

PSEUSTĒS (ψεύστης), a liar, occurs in John 8 : 44, 55; Rom. 3 : 4; 5583
1 Tim. 1 : 10; Tit. 1 : 12; 1 John 1 : 10; 2 : 4, 22; 4 : 20; 5 : 10.¶ AG:892C CB:1267C

B. Adjective.

PSEUDĒS (ψευδής), lying, false (Eng., pseudo-), rendered "false" 5571
in Acts 6 : 13 and in the R.V. of Rev. 2 : 2 (A.V., "liars"), is used as a AG:891C CB:1267C
noun, "liars," in Rev. 21 : 8. See FALSE.¶

Note: Many compound nouns are formed by the prefix *pseudo-*: see, e.g., APOSTLES, BRETHREN, CHRISTS, PROPHETS, TEACHERS, WITNESS.

LIBERAL, LIBERALITY, LIBERALLY

A. Noun.

1. HAPLOTĒS (ἁπλοτής) denotes (*a*) simplicity, sincerity, unaffected- 572
ness (from *haplous*, single, simple, in contrast to *diplous*, double), Rom. AG:85D CB:1249B
12 : 8, "simplicity;" 2 Cor. 11 : 3 (in some mss. in 1 : 12); Eph. 6 : 5 and Col. 3 : 22, "singleness;" (*b*) simplicity as manifested in generous giving, "liberality," 2 Cor. 8 : 2; 9 : 11 (A.V., "bountifulness," R.V. marg., "singleness"); 9 : 13 (A.V., "liberal"). See BOUNTY, No. 2.¶

2. CHARIS (χάρις) is rendered "liberality" in 1 Cor. 16 : 3, A.V. 5485
See BOUNTY, No. 3. AG:877B CB:1239C

B. Adverb.

HAPLŌS (ἁπλῶς), liberally, with singleness of heart, is used in Jas. 1 : 5 574
of God as the gracious and liberal Giver. The word may be taken either AG:86B CB:1249B
(*a*) in a logical sense, signifying unconditionally, simply, or (*b*) in a moral sense, generously; for the double meaning compare A, No. 1.¶ On this passage Hort writes as follows: "Later writers comprehend under the

one word the whole magnanimous and honourable type of character in which singleness of mind is the central feature."

LIBERTY

425 AG:65B
A. Nouns.

CB:— 1. ANESIS (ἄνεσις), a loosening, relaxation, is translated "liberty"
859 AG:125A in Acts 24 : 23, A.V. See INDULGENCE.
CB:1236B 2. APHESIS (ἄφεσις), dismissal, release, forgiveness, is rendered
1657 "liberty" in the A.V. of Luke 4 : 18, R.V., "release." See FORGIVENESS.
AG:250C CB:1244B 3. ELEUTHERIA (ἐλευθερία) : see FREEDOM.
1849 4. EXOUSIA (ἐξουσία), authority, right, is rendered "liberty" in
AG:277D CB:1247C 1 Cor. 8 : 9 (marg., "power"), "this liberty of yours," or 'this right which you assert.' See UTHORITY.

B. Adjective.

1658 AG:250D CB:1244B ELEUTHEROS (ἐλεύθερος) is rendered "at liberty" in 1 Cor. 7 : 39, A.V. (R.V. "free"). See FREE.

C. Verbs.

630 AG:96C CB:1237A 1. APOLUŌ (ἀπολύω), for the meanings of which see LET, No. 3, is translated "to set at liberty" in Acts 26 : 32 and Heb. 13 : 23. See DISMISS.
649 AG:98C CB:1237A 2. APOSTELLŌ (ἀποστέλλω), to send away, is translated "to set at liberty" in Luke 4 : 18. See SEND.
2010 AG:303C CB:— *Note :* In Acts 27 : 3, A.V., *epitrepō* is rendered "gave . . . liberty" (R.V. "gave . . . leave"). See LEAVE (*b*).

For LICENCE (in Acts 21 : 4 and 25 : 16, A.V.) see LEAVE (*b*) and OPPORTUNITY, A, No. 3

LICK

— AG:295D CB:— EPILEICHŌ (ἐπιλείχω), to lick over (*epi*, over, *leichō*, to lick), is said
APOLEICHŌ 621 AG:95A CB:— of the dogs in Luke 16 : 21. Some mss. have *apoleichō*, to lick off.¶

LIE (falsehood : Noun and Verb)

A. Nouns.

5579 AG:892B CB:1267C 1. PSEUDOS (ψεῦδος), a falsehood, lie (see also under LIAR), is translated "lie" in John 8 : 44 (lit., 'the lie'); Rom. 1 : 25, where it stands by metonymy for an idol, as, e.g., in Isa. 44 : 20 ; Jer. 10 : 14 ; 13 : 25 ; Amos 2 : 4 (plural) ; 2 Thess. 2 : 11, with special reference to the lie of ver. 4, that man is God (cp. Gen. 3 : 5) ; 1 John 2 : 21, 27 ; Rev. 21 : 27 ; 22 : 15 ; in Eph. 4 : 25, A.V. "lying," R.V., "falsehood," the practice ; in Rev. 14 : 5, R.V., "lie" (some mss. have *dolos*, "guile," A.V.) ; 2 Thess. 2 : 9, where "lying wonders" is, lit., 'wonders of falsehood,' i.e., wonders calculated to deceive (cp. Rev. 13 : 13–15), the purpose being to deceive people into the acknowledgement of the spurious claim to deity on the part of the Man of Sin.¶

Note : In Rom. 1 : 25 the lie or idol is the outcome of pagan religion ;

in 1 John 2 : 21, 22 the lie is the denial that Jesus is the Christ ; in 2 Thess. 2 : 11 the lie is the claim of the Man of Sin.

2. PSEUSMA (ψεῦσμα), a falsehood, or an acted lie, Rom. 3 : 7, where 5582
" my lie " is not idolatry, but either the universal false attitude of man AG:892C
toward God or that with which his detractors charged the Apostle ; the CB:—
former seems to be the meaning.¶

B. Adjectives.

1. PSEUDOLOGOS (ψευδολόγος) denotes speaking falsely (*pseudēs*, 5573
false, *logos*, a word) in 1 Tim. 4 : 2, where the adjective is translated AG:891D
" that speak lies," R.V. (A.V., " speaking lies ") and is applied to CB:1267C
" demons," the actual utterances being by their human agents.¶

2. APSEUDĒS (ἀψευδής) denotes free from falsehood (*a*, negative, 893
pseudēs, false), truthful, Tit. 1 : 2, of God, " who cannot lie."¶ AG:129C CB:1237B

C. Verb.

PSEUDŌ (ψεύδω), to deceive by lies (always in the Middle Voice in (-OMAI)
the N.T.), is used (*a*) absolutely, in Matt. 5 : 11, " falsely," lit., ' lying ' 5574 AG:891
(A.V., marg.) ; Rom. 9 : 1 ; 2 Cor. 11 : 31 ; Gal. 1 : 20 ; Col. 3 : 9 (where CB:1267C
the verb is followed by the preposition *eis*, to) ; 1 Tim. 2 : 7 ; Heb. 6 : 18 ; Jas. 3 : 14 (where it is followed by the preposition *kata*, against) ; 1 John 1 : 6 ; Rev. 3 : 9 ; (*b*) transitively, with a direct object (without a preposition following), Acts 5 : 3 (with the accusative case), " to lie to (the Holy Ghost)," R.V. marg., " deceive ; " ver. 4 (with the dative case) " thou hast (not) lied (unto men, but unto God)."¶

LIE (to lie down, on, upon)

1. KEIMAI (κεῖμαι), to be laid, to lie, used as the Passive Voice of 2749
tithēmi, to lay (see LAY, No. 14), is said (*a*) of the Child Jesus, Luke 2 : 12, AG:426C CB:1254C
16 ; (*b*) of the dead body of the Lord, Matt. 28 : 6 ; John 20 : 12 ; in Luke 23 : 53, " had . . . lain," R.V., A.V., " was laid " [see LAY, No. 14, *Note* (1)], in the tomb as hitherto empty ; (*c*) of the linen cloths, John 20 : 5, 6, 7 ; (*d*) figuratively of a veil as lying upon the hearts of the Jews, 2 Cor. 3 : 15, R.V., " lieth " (A.V., " is ") ; (*e*) metaphorically, of the world as lying in the evil one, 1 John 5 : 19, R.V. ; (*f*) of the Heavenly City, Rev. 21 : 16. For other instances in which the rendering is in the Passive Voice, see LAY, No. 14. See APPOINT.

2. KATAKEIMAI (κατάκειμαι), to lie down (*kata*, down, and No. 1), 2621
is used of the sick, Mark 1 : 30 ; 2 : 4 ; Luke 5 : 25 ; John 5 : 3, 6 ; Acts AG:411C CB:—
28 : 8 ; in Acts 9 : 33 it is rendered " had kept (his bed)," lit., ' lying (on a bed).' See SIT.

3. BALLŌ (βάλλω), to throw, cast, is used in the Passive Voice, with 906
reference to the sick, with the meaning to be laid, to lie, in Matt. 8 : 6, AG:130D CB:1238B
" (my servant) lieth (in the house)," lit., ' is laid ; ' 8 : 14, " lying," R.V. (A.V., " laid ") ; 9 : 2, " lying (on a bed)." See CAST.

4. EPIKEIMAI (ἐπίκειμαι), to lie upon, be laid upon, is translated 1945 AG:294C
with this meaning, intransitively in John 11 : 38 and Acts 27 : 20 ; tran- CB:—

ANAKEIMAI 345 sitively, in the Passive Voice, in John 21 : 9 and 1 Cor. 9 : 16. See
AG:55D IMPOSED.
CB:1235A *Notes :* (1) In Mark 5 : 40, some mss. have the verb ***anakeimai***, to be
BLEPō 991 laid up, translated " was lying," A.V. In the most authentic the word is
AG:143B absent. (2) In Acts 27 : 12, A.V., *blepō*, to look, is rendered " lieth,"
CB:1239A ECHō of the situation of the haven Phœnix (A.V., Phenice) ; R.V., " looketh."
2192 (3) In John 11 : 17, A.V., the verb *echō*, to have, to hold, used with ***en***, in,
AG:331D CB:1242C signifying to be in a certain condition, is translated " had *lain* " (R.V.,
ANAPIPTō " had been "). (4) In John 13 : 25, *anapiptō*, lit., to fall back (some mss.
377 AG:59C have ***epipiptō***, lit., to fall upon, hence the A.V., " lying "), is used of
CB:1235B EPIPIPTō John's position at the table, R.V., " leaning back (. . . on Jesus' breast)."

LIE IN WAIT

1968 AG:297C

A. Verb.

CB:—

1748 ENEDREUŌ (ἐνεδρεύω), to lie in wait for, to lay wait for (from ***en***, in,
AG:264C and ***hedra***, a seat, cp. B), occurs in Luke 11 : 54, " laying wait for ; " Acts
CB:— 23 : 21, " there lie in wait for."¶
1917 *Note :* In Acts 23 : 30, the word ***epiboulē***, a plot, necessitates the R.V.
AG:290C CB:— " (that there would be) a plot." For Eph. 4 : 14, A.V., see WILES.

B. Noun.

1747 (1749) AG:264C ENEDRA or ENEDRON (ἐνέδρα), akin to A, a lying in wait, an
CB:1245A ambush, occurs in Acts 23 : 16 (where some mss. have the form ***enedron***) ;
LIFEBOAT 25 : 3, " laying wait," lit., ' making an ambush.'¶ In the Sept., Josh.
See BOAT 8 : 7, 9 ; Ps. 10 : 8.¶

LIFE, LIVING, LIFETIME, LIFE-GIVING

A. Nouns.

2222 1. ZŌĒ (ζωή) (Eng., zoo, zoology) is used in the N.T. " of life as a
AG:340B CB:1273C principle, life in the absolute sense, life as God has it, that which the Father has in Himself, and which He gave to the Incarnate Son to have in Himself, John 5 : 26, and which the Son manifested in the world, 1 John 1 : 2. From this life man has become alienated in consequence of the Fall, Eph. 4 : 18, and of this life men become partakers through faith in the Lord Jesus Christ, John 3 : 15, who becomes its Author to all such as trust in Him, Acts 3 : 15, and who is therefore said to be ' the life ' of the believer, Col. 3 : 4, for the life that He gives He maintains, John 6 : 35, 63. Eternal life is the present actual possession of the believer because of his relationship with Christ, John 5 : 24 ; 1 John 3 : 14, and that it will one day extend its domain to the sphere of the body is assured by the Resurrection of Christ, 2 Cor. 5 : 4 ; 2 Tim. 1 : 10. This life is not merely a principle of power and mobility, however, for it has moral associations which are inseparable from it, as of holiness and righteousness. Death and sin, life and holiness, are frequently contrasted in the Scriptures.

" ZŌĒ is also used of that which is the common possession of all animals and men by nature, Acts 17 : 25 ; 1 John 5 : 16, and of the present sojourn of man upon the earth with reference to its duration, Luke 16 : 25 ;

1 Cor. 15 : 19 ; 1 Tim. 4 : 8 ; 1 Pet. 3 : 10. 'This life' is a term equivalent to 'the gospel,' 'the faith,' 'Christianity,' Acts 5 : 20."*

Death came through sin, Rom. 5 : 12, which is rebellion against God. Sin thus involved the forfeiting of the life. "The life of the flesh is in the blood," Lev. 17 : 11. Therefore the impartation of life to the sinner must be by a death caused by the shedding of that element which is the life of the flesh. "It is the blood that maketh atonement by reason of the life" (*id.*, R.V.). The separation from God caused by the forfeiting of the life could be removed only by a sacrifice in which the victim and the offerer became identified. This which was appointed in the typical offerings in Israel received its full accomplishment in the voluntary sacrifice of Christ. The shedding of the blood in the language of Scripture involves the taking or the giving of the life. Since Christ had no sins of his own to die for, His death was voluntary and vicarious, John 10 : 15 with Isa. 53 : 5, 10, 12 ; 2 Cor. 5 : 21. In His sacrifice He endured the Divine judgment due to man's sin. By this means the believer becomes identified with Him in His deathless life, through His resurrection, and enjoys conscious and eternal fellowship with God.

2. BIOS (*βίος*) (cp. Eng. words beginning with *bio-*), is used in three **979**
respects (*a*) of the period or duration of life, e.g., in the A.V. of 1 Pet. 4 : 3, **AG:141D CB:1239A**
"the time past of our life" (the R.V. follows the mss. which omit "of our life") ; Luke 8 : 14 ; 2 Tim. 2 : 4 ; (*b*) of the manner of life, life in regard to its moral conduct, 1 Tim. 2 : 2 ; 1 John 2 : 16 ; (*c*) of the means of life, livelihood, maintenance, living, Mark 12 : 44 ; Luke 8 : 43 ; 15 : 12, 30 ; 21 : 4 ; 1 John 3 : 17, "goods," R.V. (A.V., "good"). See GOODS.¶

Note : "While *zōē* is life intensive . . . *bios* is life extensive. . . . In *bios*, used as manner of life, there is an ethical sense often inhering which, in classical Greek at least, *zōē* does not possess." In Scripture *zōē* is "the nobler word, expressing as it continually does, all of highest and best which the saints possess in God" (Trench, Syn. §xxvii).

3. PSUCHĒ (*ψυχή*), besides its meanings, heart, mind, soul, denotes **5590**
life in two chief respects, (*a*) breath of life, the natural life, e.g., Matt. **AG:893B CB:1267C**
2 : 20 ; 6 : 25 ; Mark 10 : 45 ; Luke 12 : 22 ; Acts 20 : 10 ; Rev. 8 : 9 ; 12 : 11 (cp. Lev. 17 : 11 ; Esth. 8 : 11) ; (*b*) the seat of personality, e.g., Luke 9 : 24, explained in ver. 25 as "own self." See list under SOUL. See also HEART, MIND.

Notes : (1) "Speaking generally, *psuchē*, is the individual life, the living being, whereas *zōē*, is the life of that being, cp. Ps. 66 : 9, 'God . . . which holdeth our soul (*psuchē*) in life (*zōē*),' and John 10 : 10, 'I came that they may have life (*zōē*),' with ver. 11, 'The Good Shepherd layeth down
His life (*psuchē*) for the sheep.' "† (2) In Rev. 13 : 15, A.V., *pneuma*, **4151**
breath, is translated "life" (R.V., "breath"). (3) In 2 Cor. 1 : 8, **AG:674C CB:1265B**

* From Notes on Galatians by Hogg and Vine, pp. 324, 325.
† From Notes on Thessalonians by Hogg and Vine, p. 325.

2198 AG:336A "we despaired even of life," the verb *zaō*, to live, is used in the Infinitive
CB:1273B Mood, as a noun, and translated "life" (lit., 'living'). In Heb. 2 : 15
981 the Infinitive Mood of the same verb is translated "lifetime."
AG:142A CB:— 4. BIŌSIS (βίωσις), from *bioō*, to spend one's life, to live, denotes a
72 manner of life, Acts 26 : 4.¶
AG:14D CB:1233C 5. AGŌGĒ (ἀγωγή), a manner of life, 2 Tim. 3 : 10 ; see CONDUCT.
391 6. ANASTROPHĒ (ἀναστροφή), behaviour, conduct, is translated
AG:61C CB:1235B "manner of life" (A.V. "conversation") in the R.V. of Gal. 1 : 13 ;
1 Tim. 4 : 12 ; 1 Pet. 1 : 18 ; 3 : 16 ; "living," in 1 Pet. 1 : 15. See
BEHAVIOUR.

B. Adjectives.

982 1. BIŌTIKOS (βιωτικός), pertaining to life (*bios*), is translated "of
AG:142A CB:1239A this life," in Luke 21 : 34, with reference to cares ; in 1 Cor. 6 : 3," (things) that pertain to this life," and ver. 4, "(things) pertaining to this life," i.e., matters of this world, concerning which Christians at Corinth were engaged in public lawsuits one with another ; such matters were to be regarded as relatively unimportant in view of the great tribunals to come under the jurisdiction of saints hereafter. Moulton and Milligan (Vocab.) illustrate the word from phrases in the papyri, e.g., "business (documents) ;" "business concerning my livelihood ;" "(stories) of ordinary life."¶

895 AG:129C 2. APSUCHOS (ἄψυχος) denotes lifeless, inanimate (*a*, negative, and
CB:— *psuchē*, see A, No. 3), "without life," 1 Cor. 14 : 7.¶

C. Verb.

2227 AG:341D ZŌOPOIEŌ (ζωοποιέω), to make alive, cause to live, quicken (from
CB:1273C *zōē*, life, and *poieō*, to make), is used as follows :

"(*a*) of God as the Bestower of every kind of life in the universe, 1 Tim.
ZōOGONEō 6 : 13 (*zōogoneō*, to preserve alive, is the alternative reading adopted by
2225 most editors ; see LIVE, No. 6), and, particularly, of resurrection life,
AG:341C CB:1273C John 5 : 21 ; Rom. 4 : 17 ; (*b*) of Christ, who also is the Bestower of resurrection life, John 5 : 21 (2nd part) ; 1 Cor. 15 : 45 ; cp. ver. 22 ; (*c*) of the resurrection of Christ in "the body of His glory," 1 Pet. 3 : 18 ; (*d*) of the power of reproduction inherent in seed, which presents a certain analogy with resurrection, 1 Cor. 15 : 36 ; (*e*) of the 'changing,' or
SU(N)ZōOPOIEō 'fashioning anew,' of the bodies of the living, which corresponds with,
4806 and takes place at the same time as, the resurrection of the dead in Christ,
AG:776A CB:1271A Rom. 8 : 11 ; (*f*) of the impartation of spiritual life, and the communica-
DIAGō tion of spiritual sustenance generally, John 6 : 63 ; 2 Cor. 3 : 6 ; Gal.
1236 AG:182C 3 : 21."¶* See QUICKEN, and cp. *sunzōopoieō*, to quicken together with,
CB:— Eph. 2 : 5 and Col. 2 : 13.¶

POLITEUō (-OMAI) *Notes :* (1) For the verb *diagō*, to lead a life, see LIVE, No. 7. (2) For
4176 *politeuō*, in Phil. 1 : 27, R.V., "let your manner of life be," see LIVE,
AG:686C CB:1266A No. 8.

* From Notes on Galatians by Hogg and Vine, pp. 154, 155.

LIFT

1. EGEIRŌ (ἐγείρω), to awaken, raise up, is used in Matt. 12 : 11, 1453
of lifting a sheep out of a pit. In the following the R.V. has " raised " AG:214C
for A.V., " lifted : " Mark 1 : 31 ; 9 : 27 ; Acts 3 : 7. See ARISE, AWAKE, CB:1242C
RAISE.

2. AIRŌ (αἴρω) signifies (*a*) to raise, take up, lift, draw up, (*b*) to bear, 142
carry, (*c*) to take or carry away. It is used of lifting up the voice, Luke AG:24B
17 : 13 ; Acts 4 : 24 ; eyes, John 11 : 41 ; hand, Rev. 10 : 5. See AWAY, CB:1234A
BEAR, CARRY, DOUBT, A, No. 6, LOOSE, PUT, No. 17, REMOVE, TAKE.

3. EPAIRŌ (ἐπαίρω), to lift up, raise (*epi*, upon, and No. 2), is used 1869
of lifting up the eyes, Matt. 17 : 8 ; Luke 6 : 20 ; 16 : 23 ; 18 : 13 ; AG:281D
John 4 : 35 ; 6 : 5 ; 17 : 1 ; the head, Luke 21 : 28 ; the hands, Luke CB:—
24 : 50 ; 1 Tim. 2 : 8 ; the voice, Luke 11 : 27 ; Acts 2 : 14 ; 14 : 11 ; 22 : 22 ; a foresail, Acts 27 : 40 (" hoisting," R.V.) ; metaphorically, of the heel, John 13 : 18, as of one lifting up the foot before kicking ; the expression indicates contempt and violence ; in the Passive Voice, Acts 1 : 9, of Christ's Ascension, " was taken up ; " 2 Cor. 10 : 5, " is exalted " (with pride) ; 11 : 20, " exalteth himself." See EXALT, HOIST, TAKE.¶

4. HUPSOŌ (ὑψόω), to lift or raise up (akin to *hupsos*, height), is 5312
rendered by the verb to lift up in John 3 : 14, of the brazen serpent ; of AG:850
Christ in crucifixion (*id.*), and 8 : 28 ; 12 : 32, 34 ; metaphorically, to CB:1252B
exalt, lift up, e.g., Jas. 4 : 10, A.V., " shall lift . . . up," R.V., " shall exalt." See EXALT.

5. ANISTĒMI (ἀνίστημι), to raise up (*ana*, up, *histēmi*, to cause to 450
stand), is translated " lifted (her) up," in Acts 9 : 41, A.V. ; R.V., " raised AG:70A
(her) up." See ARISE, RAISE. CB:1235C

6. ANORTHOŌ (ἀνορθόω), to set upright (*ana*, up, *orthos*, straight), 461
is used of lifting up " hands that hang down," Heb. 12 : 12 ; of setting AG:72C
up a building, restoring ruins, Acts 15 : 16 (cp., e.g., 2 Sam. 7 : 13, 16 ; CB:—
1 Chron. 17 : 12 ; Jer. 10 : 12 ; often so used in the papyri) ; of the healing of the woman with a spirit of infirmity, Luke 13 : 13, " was made straight " (for ver. 11, see No. 7). See SET, STRAIGHT.¶

7. ANAKUPTŌ (ἀνακύπτω), to lift oneself up, is used (*a*) of the body, 352
Luke 13 : 11 ; John 8 : 7, 10 ; (*b*) metaphorically, of the mind, to look up, AG:56C
to be elated, Luke 21 : 28 (followed by No. 3, " lift up ") ; an instance CB:—
is found in the papyri in which a person speaks of the impossibility of ever looking up again in a certain place, for very shame (Moulton and Milligan, Vocab.).¶ In the Sept., Job 10 : 15.¶

LIGAMENT See JOINT

LIGHT, Noun, and Verb (bring to, give), LIGHTEN

A. Nouns.

1. PHŌS (φῶς), akin to *phaō*, to give light (from roots *pha*— and 5457 AG:871D
phan—, expressing light as seen by the eye, and, metaphorically, as CB:1264B

reaching the mind, whence *phainō*, to make to appear, *phaneros*, evident, etc.) ; cp. Eng., phosphorus (lit., light-bearing). " Primarily light is a luminous emanation, probably of force, from certain bodies, which enables the eye to discern form and colour. Light requires an organ adapted for its reception (Matt. 6 : 22). Where the eye is absent, or where it has become impaired from any cause, light is useless. Man, naturally, is incapable of receiving spiritual light inasmuch as he lacks the capacity for spiritual things, 1 Cor. 2 : 14. Hence believers are called ' sons of light,' Luke 16 : 8, not merely because they have received a revelation from God, but because in the New Birth they have received the spiritual capacity for it.

" Apart from natural phenomena, light is used in Scripture of (*a*) the glory of God's dwelling-place, 1 Tim. 6 : 16 ; (*b*) the nature of God, 1 John 1 : 5 ; (*c*) the impartiality of God, Jas. 1 : 17 ; (*d*) the favour of God, Ps. 4 : 6 ; of the King, Prov. 16 : 15 ; of an influential man, Job 29 : 24 ; (*e*) God, as the illuminator of His people, Isa. 60 : 19, 20 ; (*f*) the Lord Jesus as the illuminator of men, John 1 : 4, 5, 9 ; 3 : 19 ; 8 : 12 ; 9 : 5 ; 12 : 35, 36, 46 ; Acts 13 : 47 ; (*g*) the illuminating power of the Scriptures, Ps. 119 : 105 ; and of the judgments and commandments of God, Isa. 51 : 4 ; Prov. 6 : 23, cp. Ps. 43 : 3 ; (*h*) the guidance of God, Job 29 : 3 ; Ps. 112 : 4 ; Isa. 58 : 10 ; and, ironically, of the guidance of man, Rom. 2 : 19 ; (*i*) salvation, 1 Pet. 2 : 9 ; (*j*) righteousness, Rom. 13 : 12 ; 2 Cor. 11 : 14, 15 ; 1 John 2 : 9, 10 ; (*k*) witness for God, Matt. 5 : 14, 16 ; John 5 : 35 ; (*l*) prosperity and general well-being, Esth. 8 : 16 ; Job 18 : 18 ; Isa. 58 : 8–10."*

2. PHŌSTĒR (φωστήρ) denotes a luminary, light, or light-giver ; it is used figuratively of believers, as shining in the spiritual darkness of the world, Phil. 2 : 15 ; in Rev. 21 : 11 it is used of Christ as the Light reflected in and shining through the Heavenly City (cp. ver. 23).¶ In the Sept., Gen. 1 : 14, 16.¶

5462 AG:873C 3. PHŌTISMOS (φωτισμός), an illumination, light, is used meta-
CB:1264B phorically in 2 Cor. 4 : 4, of the light of the Gospel, and in ver. 6, of the
knowledge of the glory of God.¶ In the Sept., Job 3 : 9 ; Psa. 27 : 1 ;
44 : 3 ; 78 : 14 ; 90 : 8 ; 139 : 11.¶

5338 AG:854C 4. PHENGOS (φέγγος), brightness, lustre, is used of the light of the
CB:1264A moon, Matt. 24 : 29 ; Mark 13 : 24 ; of a lamp, Luke 11 : 33 (some mss.
3088 have *phōs*, here).¶

AG:483B CB:1257B 5. LUCHNOS (λύχνος), a hand-lamp : see LAMP.

2985 6. LAMPAS (λαμπάς), a torch : see LAMP.

AG:465C CB:1256C

B. Verbs.

5461 AG:872D 1. PHŌTIZŌ (φωτίζω), used (*a*) intransitively, signifies to shine,
CB:1264B give light, Rev. 22 : 5 ; (*b*) transitively, (1) to illumine, to light, enlighten,

* From Notes on Thessalonians by Hogg and Vine, pp. 159, 160.

to be lightened, Luke 11 : 36 ; Rev. 21 : 23 ; in the Passive Voice, Rev. 18 : 1 ; metaphorically, of spiritual enlightenment, John 1 : 9 ; Eph. 1 : 18 ; 3 : 9, "to make . . . see ;" Heb. 6 : 4 ; 10 : 32, "ye were enlightened," R.V. (A.V., ". . . illuminated") ; (2) to bring to light, 1 Cor. 4 : 5 (of God's act in the future) ; 2 Tim. 1 : 10 (of God's act in the past). See ENLIGHTEN, ILLUMINATE.¶

2. EPIPHAUSKŌ (ἐπιφαύσκω), or possibly *epiphauō*, to shine forth, 2017
is rendered "shall give . . . light," in Eph. 5 : 14, A.V. (R.V., "shall AG:304C CB:—
shine upon"), of the glory of Christ, illumining the believer who fulfils the conditions, so that being guided by His light he reflects His character. See SHINE.¶ Cp. *epiphōskō*, to dawn (really a variant form of *epiphauskō*).

3. LAMPŌ (λάμπω), to give the light of a torch, is rendered "giveth 2989
light" in Matt. 5 : 15, A.V. (R.V., "shineth"). See SHINE. AG:466A CB:1256C

4. EPIPHAINŌ (ἐπιφαίνω), transitively, to show forth (*epi*, upon, 2014
phainō, to cause to shine), is used intransitively and metaphorically in AG:304A CB:1246A
Luke 1 : 79, and rendered "to give light," A.V. (R.V., "to shine upon"). See APPEAR, SHINE.

5. HAPTŌ (ἅπτω), to kindle a fire and so give light : see KINDLE, 681 AG:102D
No. 1, Note. CB:1249B

6. KAIŌ (καίω), to burn, is translated "do (men) light" in Matt. 2545 AG:396B
5 : 15. See BURN. CB:1253A

7. ASTRAPTŌ (ἀστράπτω), to flash forth, lighten as lightning (akin 797
to *astrapē*, lightning), occurs in Luke 17 : 24 ; 24 : 4 (A.V. "shining ;" AG:118B CB:—
R.V., "dazzling"). See DAZZLING.

Note : In Luke 2 : 32, A.V., the noun *apokalupsis*, an unveiling, 602
revelation, preceded by *eis*, unto, with a view to, is rendered "to lighten" AG:92B CB:1236C
(R.V., "for revelation ;" marg., "(the) unveiling"). See REVELATION.

C. Adjective.

PHŌTEINOS (φωτεινός), from *phōs* (A, No. 1), bright, is rendered 5460
"full of light" in Matt. 6 : 22 ; Luke 11 : 34, 36 (twice), figuratively, of AG:872D CB:1264B
the single-mindedness of the eye, which acts as the lamp of the body ; in Matt. 17 : 5, "bright," of a cloud. See BRIGHT.¶

LIGHT (to light upon)

Notes : (1) In Matt. 3 : 16, A.V., *erchomai*, to come, is translated ERCHOMAI 2064
"lighting ;" R.V., "coming." (2) In Rev. 7 : 16, A.V., *piptō*, to fall, is AG:310B
translated "shall . . . light" (R.V., "shall . . . strike"). See STRIKE. CB:1246B PIPTō
(3) For Acts 27 : 41, R.V., see FALL, B, No. 8. 4098 AG:659B CB:1265A

LIGHT, LIGHTEN (as to weight)

A. Adjective.

ELAPHROS (ἐλαφρός), light in weight, easy to bear, is used of the 1645 AG:248C
burden imparted by Christ, Matt. 11 : 30 ; of affliction, 2 Cor. 4 : 17.¶ CB:—

B. Verb.

2893 AG:447B CB:— KOUPHIZŌ (κουφίζω), to make light, lighten (the adjective *kouphos*, not in N.T., denotes slight, light, empty), is used of lightening the ship, in Acts 27 : 38.

Note: For the phrase in ver. 18, A.V., " they lightened the ship," see FREIGHT.

C. Noun.

1644 AG:248C CB:— ELAPHRIA (ἐλαφρία), lightness, 2 Cor. 1 : 17, A.V. : see FICKLENESS.

LIGHT OF (make), LIGHTLY

272 AG:44D CB:— AMELEŌ (ἀμελέω) denotes (*a*) to be careless, not to care (*a*, negative, and *melei*, an impersonal verb, signifying it is a care : see CARE), Matt. 22 : 5, " they made light of (it)," lit., 'making light of (it),' aorist participle, indicating the definiteness of their decision. See NEGLECT, NEGLIGENT, REGARD.

5035 AG:807B (TACHUS 2.c.) CB:1271A *Note:* In Mark 9 : 39, A.V., the adverb *tachu*, quickly, is translated " lightly " (R.V., " quickly "). See QUICKLY.

LIGHTNING

796 AG:118A CB:1238A ASTRAPĒ (ἀστραπή) denotes (*a*) lightning (akin to LIGHT, B, No. 7), Matt. 24 : 27 ; 28 : 3 ; Luke 10 : 18 ; 17 : 24 ; in the plural, Rev. 4 : 5 ; 8 : 5 ; 11 : 19 ; 16 : 18 ; (*b*) " bright shining," or shining brightness, Luke 11 : 36. See SHINING.¶

LIKE, LIKE (as to, unto), (be) LIKE, (make) LIKE, LIKE (things), LIKEN

A. Adjectives.

3664 AG:566D CB:1251A 1. HOMOIOS (ὅμοιος), like, resembling, such as, the same as, is used (*a*) of appearance or form, John 9 : 9 ; Rev. 1 : 13, 15 ; 2 : 18 ; 4 : 3 (twice), 6, 7 ; 9 : 7 (twice), 10, 19 ; 11 : 1 ; 13 : 2, 11 ; 14 : 14 ; (*b*) of ability, condition, nature, Matt. 22 : 39 ; Acts 17 : 29 ; Gal. 5 : 21, " such like," lit., 'and the (things) similar to these ;' 1 John 3 : 2 ; Rev. 13 : 4 ; 18 : 18 ; 21 : 11, 18 ; (*c*) of comparison in parables, Matt. 13 : 31, 33, 44, 45, 47 ; 20 : 1 ; Luke 13 : 18, 19, 21 ; (*d*) of action, thought, etc., Matt. 11 : 16 ; 13 : 52 ; Luke 6 : 47, 48, 49 ; 7 : 31, 32 ; 12 : 36 ; John 8 : 55 ; Jude 7.¶

2470 AG:381A CB:1253A 2. ISOS (ἴσος), equal (the same in size, quality, etc.), is translated " like," of the gift of the Spirit, Acts 11 : 17. See EQUAL, MUCH (AS).

3946 AG:629B CB:1262C 3. PAROMOIOS (παρόμοιος), much like (*para*, beside, and No. 1), is used in Mark 7 : 13, in the neuter plural, " (many such) like things."¶

B. Verbs.

3666 AG:567B CB:1251A 1. HOMOIOŌ (ὁμοιόω), to make like (akin to A, No. 1), is used (*a*) especially in the parables, with the significance of comparing, likening, or, in the Passive Voice, 'being likened,' Matt. 7 : 24, 26 ; 11 : 16 ; 13 : 24 ; 18 : 23 ; 22 : 2 (R.V., " likened ") ; 25 : 1 ; Mark 4 : 30 ; Luke 7 : 31 ;

13 : 18, R.V., "liken" (A.V., "resemble"); ver. 20; in several of these instances the point of resemblance is not a specific detail, but the whole circumstances of the parable; (*b*) of making like, or, in the Passive Voice, of being made or becoming like, Matt. 6 : 8; Acts 14 : 11, "in the likeness of (men)," lit., 'being made like' (aorist participle, Passive); Rom. 9 : 29; Heb. 2 : 17, of Christ in being "made like" unto His brethren, i.e., in partaking of human nature, apart from sin (cp. ver. 14).¶

2. EOIKA (ἔοικα), a perfect tense with a present meaning (from an 1503
obsolete present, *eikō*), denotes to be like, to resemble, Jas. 1 : 6, 23.¶ In (EIKō) AG:280A
the Sept., Job 6 : 3, 25.¶ CB:1245B

3. PAROMOIAZŌ (παρομοιάζω), to be like (from *para*, by, and a 3945
verbal form from *homoios*, A, No. 1), is used in Matt. 23 : 27 (perhaps with AG:629B CB:1262C
intensive force), in the Lord's comparison of the scribes and Pharisees to
whitened sepulchres.¶

4. APHOMOIOŌ (ἀφομοιόω), to make like (*apo*, from, and No. 1), is 871
used in Heb. 7 : 3, of Melchizedek as "made like" the Son of God, i.e., AG:127B CB:1236C
in the facts related and withheld in the Genesis record.¶

Note: For the A.V. of Rom. 1 : 23, "made like," see LIKENESS, No. 1.

C. Adverbs.

1. HŌS (ὡς), used as a relative adverb of manner, means as, like as, 5613
etc. and is translated "like," e.g., in Matt. 6 : 29; Mark 4 : 31; Luke AG:897A CB:1251B
12 : 27; in Acts 3 : 22 and 7 : 37 (see R.V., marg.); in 8 : 32 (2nd part), R.V., "as" (A.V., "like"); Rev. 2 : 18, R.V. (the rendering should have been "as" here); 18 : 21, R.V., "as it were" (A.V., "like"); 21 : 11, 2nd part (ditto).

2. HŌSPER (ὥσπερ), just as, is rendered "like as" in Rom. 6 : 4. 5618 AG:899C

Notes: (1) In Heb. 4 : 15, the phrase *kath'homoiotēta* (*kata*, according CB:1251B
to, *homoiotēs*, a likeness, i.e., 'after the similitude'), is rendered "like as," HOMOIOTēS
in the statement that Christ has been tempted in all points "like as we 3665 AG:567A
are, yet without sin;" this may mean either 'according to the likeness CB:1251A
of our temptations,' or 'in accordance with His likeness to us.' (2) In the HōSEI
following the most authentic mss. have *hōs*, as, for *hōsei*, like, in the A.V.; 5616 AG:899B
Mark 1 : 10; Luke 3 : 22; John 1 : 32; Rev. 1 : 14. (3) In John 7 : 46, CB:—
A.V., the combination of the adverb *houtōs*, thus, with *hōs*, as, is translated HOUTō(-S) 3779
"like," R.V. "(never man) so (spake)." (4) For "in like manner" see AG:597C
MANNER. (5) In 1 Thess. 2 : 14, A.V., *ta auta*, the same (things), is trans- CB:— AUTOS
lated "like (things)," R.V., "the same (things)." 846 AG:122C CB:1238B

For (DID NOT) LIKE, Rom. 1 : 28, A.V., see REFUSE, No. 3

LIKEMINDED

1. ISOPSUCHOS (ἰσόψυχος), lit., of equal soul (*isos*, equal, *psuchē*, 2473
the soul), is rendered "like-minded" in Phil. 2 : 20.¶ In the Sept., AG:381B CB:1253A
Psa. 55 : 13.¶

3675 AG:569C 2. HOMOPHRŌN (ὁμόφρων), (*homos*, the same, *phrēn*, the mind),
CB:— occurs in 1 Pet. 3 : 8, R.V., "likeminded" (A.V., "of one mind").

PHRONEō 5426 *Note:* In Rom. 15 : 5; Phil. 2 : 2, *phroneō to auto*, to think the same thing,
AG:866A CB:1264C is translated, A.V., "be likeminded" (R.V., "be of the same mind").

LIKENESS, LIKENESS OF (in the)

3667 AG:567C 1. HOMOIŌMA (ὁμοίωμα) denotes that which is made like something,
CB:1251A a resemblance, (*a*) in the concrete sense, Rev. 9 : 7, "shapes" (R.V.,
marg., "likenesses"); (*b*) in the abstract sense, Rom. 1 : 23, R.V., "(for)
the likeness (of an image);" the A.V. translates it as a verb, "(into an
image) made like to;" the association here of the two words *homoiōma*
EIKōN 1504 and *eikōn* (see IMAGE) serves to enhance the contrast between the idol and
AG:222B "the glory of the incorruptible God," and is expressive of contempt;
CB:1243A in 5 : 14, "(the) likeness of Adam's transgression" (A.V., "similitude");
in 6 : 5, "(the) likeness (of His death); in 8 : 3, "(the) likeness (of sinful
flesh); in Phil. 2 : 7, "the likeness of men." "The expression 'likeness
of men' does not of itself imply, still less does it exclude or diminish, the
reality of the nature which Christ assumed. That . . . is declared in
the words 'form of a servant.' 'Paul justly says *in the likeness of men*,
because, in fact, Christ, although certainly perfect Man (Rom. 5 : 15;
1 Cor. 15 : 21; 1 Tim. 2 : 5), was, by reason of the Divine nature present
in Him, not simply and merely man . . . but the Incarnate Son of God'"
(Gifford, quoting Meyer). See SHAPE.¶ Ch. LIKE, B, (*b*).

3669 AG:568A 2. HOMOIŌSIS (ὁμοίωσις), a making like, is translated "likeness"
CB:1251A in Jas. 3 : 9, R.V. (A.V., "similitude").¶

3665 AG:567A 3. HOMOIOTĒS (ὁμοιοτής) is translated "likeness" in Heb. 7 : 15,
CB:1251A R.V. (A.V., "similitude").

499 AG:76A 4. ANTITUPON (ἀντίτυπον) is rendered "after a true likeness," in
CB:1236A 1 Pet. 3 : 21, R.V. (marg., "in the antitype"). See FIGURE, No. 2.

LIKEWISE

3668 AG:567D 1. HOMOIŌS (ὁμοίως), in like manner (from the adjective *homoios*,
CB:1251A see LIKE, A, No. 1), is rendered "likewise" in the A.V. of Matt. 22 : 26;
27 : 41, Luke 10 : 32; 16 : 25; John 5 : 19; Jas. 2 : 25; 1 Pet. 3 : 1,
7; Jude 8; Rev. 8 : 12 (in all these the R.V. has "in like manner");
in the following, A.V. and R.V. have "likewise;" Matt. 26 : 35; Luke
5 : 33; 6 : 31; 10 : 37; 17 : 28, 31; 22 : 36; John 6 : 11; 21 : 13;
Rom. 1 : 27; 1 Pet. 5 : 5.¶ See MANNER, So.

5615 AG:899B 2. HŌSAUTŌS (ὡσαύτως), a strengthened form of *hōs*, as, denotes in
CB:— like manner, just so, likewise; it is sometimes translated "likewise,"
e.g., Matt. 20 : 5; 21 : 30.

2532 3. KAI (καί), and, even, is translated "likewise" in the A.V. and
AG:391D CB:1253A R.V. of Matt. 20 : 10 (last *kai* in the verse), more lit., 'even they;' elsewhere the R.V. has "also," for the A.V., "likewise," Matt. 18 : 35;

24 : 33 ; Luke 3 : 14 ; 17 : 10 ; 19 : 19 ; 21 : 31 ; Acts 3 : 24 ; 1 Cor. 14 : 9 ; Col. 4 : 16 ; 1 Pet. 4 : 1 ; in Matt. 21 : 24, the A.V. has " in like wise " (R.V., " likewise ").

4. PARAPLĒSIŌS (παραπλησίως), from *para*, beside, and the adjective *plēsios*, near (akin to the adverb *pelas*, near, hard by), is used in Heb. 2 : 14, A.V., " likewise " (R.V., " in like manner "), expressing the true humanity of Christ in partaking of flesh and blood.¶ **3898 AG:621C CB:—**

Notes : (1) In Matt. 17 : 12 and Rom. 6 : 11, A.V., the adverb ***houtōs***, thus, so, is translated " likewise " (R.V., " so ") ; in Luke 15 : 7 and 10, A.V., " likewise," R.V., " even so ; " in Luke 14 : 33, A.V., followed by ***oun***, therefore, it is rendered " so likewise " (R.V., " so therefore "). **3779 AG:597C CB:—**

LILY

KRINON (κρίνον) occurs in Matt. 6 : 28 and Luke 12 : 27 ; in the former the Lord speaks of " the lilies of the field ; " the lily referred to was a flower of rich colour, probably including the Gladiolus and Iris species. The former " grow among the grain, often overtopping it and illuminating the broad fields with their various shades of pinkish purple to deep violet purple and blue. . . . Anyone who has stood among the wheat fields of Galilee . . . will see at once the appropriateness of our Saviour's allusion. They all have a reedy stem, which, when dry, would make such fuel as is used in the ovens. The beautiful Irises . . . have gorgeous flowers, and would suit our Saviour's comparison even better than the above. But they are plants of pasture grounds and swamps, and seldom found in grain fields. If, however, we understand by ' lilies of the field ' simply wild lilies, these would also be included in the expression. Our Saviour's comparison would then be like a ' composite photograph,' a reference to all the splendid colours and beautiful shapes of the numerous wild plants comprehended under the name ' lily ' " (G. E. Post, in Hastings' Bib. Dic.). **2918 AG:451A CB:—**

For LIMIT, in Heb. 4 : 7, A.V., see DEFINE

For LINE see PROVINCE, No. 2

For LINEAGE in Luke 2 : 4, A.V., see FAMILY

LINEN, LINEN CLOTH, FINE LINEN

1. SINDŌN (σινδών) was a fine linen cloth, an article of domestic manufacture (Prov. 31 : 24) used (*a*) as a garment or wrap, the " linen cloth " of Mark 14 : 51, 52 ; (*b*) as shrouds or winding sheets, Matt. 27 : 59 ; Mark 15 : 46, R.V., " linen cloth," for A.V., " linen ; " Luke 23 : 53 (ditto).¶ In the Sept., Judg. 14 : 12, " (thirty) sheets ; " Prov. 31 : 24 (see above).¶ The Mishna (the Great Collection of legal decisions by the **4616 AG:751C CB:1269A**

ancient Rabbis) records that the material was sometimes used for curtains.

3043 AG:475B CB:— 2. LINON (λίνον) denotes (*a*) flax, Matt. 12 : 20; (*b*) linen, in Rev. 15 : 6, A.V.; the best texts have *lithos*, "stone," R.V. See FLAX.

3608 AG:555C CB:— 3. OTHONION (ὀθόνιον), a piece of fine linen, is used in the plural, of the strips of cloth with which the body of the Lord was bound, after being wrapped in the *sindōn*, Luke 24 : 12; John 19 : 40; 20 : 5, 6, 7.¶ In the Sept., Judg. 14 : 13, "changes of raiment;" Hos. 2 : 5, 9.¶ The word is a diminutive of *othonē*, a sheet (see SHEET).

1040 AG:148D CB:— 4. BUSSOS (βύσσος), fine linen, made from a special species of flax, a word of Aramæan origin, used especially for the Syrian *byssus* (Arab. *bûs* is still used for native linen). Cp. Heb. *bûs*, in all O.T. passages quoted here, except Ezek. 27 : 7; Syriac *bûsâ* in Luke 16 : 19. It is the material mentioned in 1 Chron. 4 : 21, wrought by the house of Ashbea; 15 : 27, *bussinos*, No. 5 (David's robe); 2 Chron. 3 : 14, *bussos* (the veil of the Temple); 5 : 12, *bussinos* (the clothing of the Levite singers); Esth. 1 : 6 (the cords of the hangings in the king's garden); 8 : 15 (Mordecai's dress); Ezek. 27 : 7 (*bussos*, in Syrian trade with Tyre). In the N.T., Luke 16 : 19, the clothing of the "rich man."¶

1039 AG:148D CB:— 5. BUSSINOS (βύσσινος), an adjective formed from No. 4, denoting made of fine linen. This is used of the clothing of the mystic Babylon, Rev. 18 : 12, 16, and of the suitable attire of the Lamb's wife, 19 : 8, 14, figuratively describing "the righteous acts of the saints." The presumption of Babylon is conspicuous in that she arrays herself in that which alone befits the Bride of Christ.¶ For examples of the use in the Sept. see No. 4.

LINGER

691 AG:104C CB:— ARGEŌ (ἀργέω), to be idle, to linger (akin to *argos*, idle: see *katargeō*, under ABOLISH), is used negatively regarding the judgment of the persons mentioned in 2 Pet. 2 : 3.¶ In the Sept., Ezra 4 : 24; Eccles. 12 : 3.¶

LION

3023 AG:472D CB:1256C LEŌN (λέων) occurs in 2 Tim. 4 : 17, probably figurative of the imminent peril of death, the figure being represented by the whole phrase, not by the word "lion" alone; some suppose the reference to be to the lions of the amphitheatre; the Greek commentators regarded the lion as Nero; others understand it to be Satan. The language not improbably recalls that of Psa. 22 : 21 and Dan. 6 : 20. The word is used metaphorically, too, in Rev. 5 : 5, where Christ is called "the Lion of the tribe of Judah." Elsewhere it has the literal meaning, Heb. 11 : 33; 1 Pet. 5 : 8; Rev. 4 : 7; 9 : 8, 17; 10 : 3; 13 : 2.¶ Taking the O.T. and N.T. occurrences the allusions are to the three great features of the lion, (1) its majesty and strength, indicative of royalty, e.g., Prov. 30 : 30, (2) its courage, e.g., Prov. 28 : 1, (3) its cruelty, e.g., Psa. 22 : 13.

LIP

CHEILOS (χεῖλος) is used (*a*) of the organ of speech, Matt. 15 : 8 and 5491
Mark 7 : 6, where honouring with the lips, besides meaning empty words, AG:879C CB:1239C
may have reference to a Jewish custom of putting to the mouth the tassel of the tallith (the woollen scarf wound round the head and neck during prayer), as a sign of acceptance of the Law from the heart ; Rom. 3 : 13 ; 1 Cor. 14 : 21 (from Isa. 28 : 11, 12, speaking of the Assyrian foe as God's message to disobedient Israel) ; Heb. 13 : 15 ; 1 Pet. 3 : 10 ; (*b*) metaphorically, of the brink or edge of things, as of the sea shore, Heb. 11 : 12, lit., 'the shore (of the sea)'.¶

LIST (Verb)

2309 AG:354D

1. THELŌ (θέλω), to will, wish, is translated by the verb to list in CB:1271C
Matt. 17 : 12 ; Mark 9 : 13 ; John 3 : 8. See DESIRE, B, No. 6. 1014 AG:146A
2. BOULOMAI (βούλομαι), to will, be minded, is translated "listeth" CB:1239B
in Jas. 3 : 4 (R.V., "willeth"). See DESIRE, B, No. 7.

LISTEN See HEAR, LEARN

LITTLE

A. Adjectives.

1. MIKROS (μικρός), little, small (the opposite of *megas*, great), is used 3398
(*a*) of persons, with regard to (1) station, or age, in the singular, Mark AG:521A CB:1258C
15 : 40, of James "the less" (R.V. marg., "little"), possibly referring to age ; Luke 19 : 3 ; in the plural, little ones, Matt. 18 : 6, 10, 14 ; Mark 9 : 42 ; (2) rank or influence, e.g., Matt. 10 : 42 (see context) ; Acts 8 : 10 ; 26 : 22, "small," as in Rev. 11 : 18 ; 13 : 16 ; 19 : 5, 18 ; 20 : 12 ; (*b*) of things, with regard to (1) size, e.g., Jas. 3 : 5 (some mss. have No. 2 here) ; (2) quantity, Luke 12 : 32 ; 1 Cor. 5 : 6 ; Gal. 5 : 9 ; Rev. 3 : 8 ; (3) time, John 7 : 33 ; 12 : 35 ; Rev. 6 : 11 ; 20 : 3. See B, No. 1. See LEAST, SMALL.

2. OLIGOS (ὀλίγος), little, few (the opposite of *polus*, much), is 3641
translated "short" in Rev. 12 : 12 ; in the neut. sing., e.g., 2 Cor. 8 : 15. AG:563C CB:1260C
For Jas. 3 : 5, see No. 1. See FEW, SHORT, SMALL.

3. BRACHUS (βραχύς), short, is used to some extent adverbially of (*a*) 1024
time, with the preposition *meta*, after, Luke 22 : 58, "(after) a little AG:147B CB:1239B
while ;" in Acts 5 : 34, without a preposition, R.V., "a little while" (A.V., "a little space") ; in Heb. 2 : 7, 9, "a little" (A.V. marg. in ver. 7, and R.V. marg., in both, "a little while"), where the writer transfers to time what the Sept. in Psa. 8 : 5 says of rank ; (*b*) of quantity, John 6 : 7 ; in Heb. 13 : 22, preceded by the preposition *dia*, by means of, and with *logōn*, words (genitive plural) understood, "(in) few words ;" (*c*) of distance, Acts 27 : 28, R.V., "a little space" (A.V., "a little further"). See FEW, FURTHER, SPACE.¶

4. ELACHISTOS (ἐλάχιστος), which serves as the superlative of No. 1, 1646 AG:248D
is translated "a very little" in Luke 19 : 17. See LEAST. CB:1244A

3398
AG:521B
(MIKROS 1.c.)
CB:—
Note: For *mikroteros*, " but little," see LEAST, No. 4.

B. Adverbs.

3397
AG:521A
CB:1258C
1. MIKRON (μικρόν), the neuter of A, No. 1, is used adverbially (*a*) of distance, Matt. 26 : 39 ; Mark 14 : 35 ; (*b*) of quantity, 2 Cor. 11 : 1, 16 ; (*c*) of time, Matt. 26 : 73, " a while ; " Mark 14 : 70 ; John 13 : 33, " a little while ; " 14 : 19 ; 16 : 16–9 ; Heb. 10 : 37, with the repeated *hoson*, " how very," lit., ' a little while, how little, how little ! ' See WHILE.¶

3641
AG:563C
CB:1260C
2. OLIGON (ὀλίγον), the neuter of A, No. 2, is used adverbially of (*a*) time, Mark 6 : 31, " a while ; " 1 Pet. 1 : 6, R.V., " a little while (A.V., " a season") ; 5 : 10, R.V., " a little while " (A.V., " a while ") ; Rev. 17 : 10, R.V., " a little while " (A.V., " a short space ") ; (*b*) space, Mark 1 : 19 ; Luke 5 : 3 ; (*c*) extent, with the preposition *pros*, for, in 1 Tim. 4 : 8, R.V., " (for) a little " (A.V., and R.V. marg., " little "), where, while the phrase might refer to duration (as A.V. marg.), yet the antithesis " for all things " clearly indicates extent, i.e., ' physical training is profitable towards few objects in life.' See BRIEFLY, FEW, SEASON, C, *Note*.

3357
AG:515A
CB:—
3. METRIŌS (μετρίως), moderately, occurs in Acts 20 : 12, " a little."¶

For (NO) LITTLE see COMMON, B, *Note* (3)

LIVE

2198
AG:336A
CB:1273B
1. ZAŌ (ζάω), to live, be alive, is used in the N.T. of " (*a*) God, Matt. 16 : 16 ; John 6 : 57 ; Rom. 14 : 11 ; (*b*) the Son in Incarnation, John 6 : 57 ; (*c*) the Son in Resurrection, John 14 : 19 ; Acts 1 : 3 ; Rom. 6 : 10 ; 2 Cor. 13 : 4 ; Heb. 7 : 8 ; (*d*) spiritual life, John 6 : 57 ; Rom. 1 : 17 ; 8 : 13*b* ; Gal. 2 : 19, 20 ; Heb. 12 : 9 ; (*e*) the present state of departed saints, Luke 20 : 38 ; 1 Pet. 4 : 6 ; (*f*) the hope of resurrection, 1 Pet. 1 : 3 ; (*g*) the resurrection of believers, 1 Thess. 5 : 10 ; John 5 : 25 ; Rev. 20 : 4, and of unbelievers, ver. 5, cp. ver. 13 ; (*h*) the way of access to God through the Lord Jesus Christ, Heb. 10 : 20 ; (*i*) the manifestation of Divine power in support of Divine authority, 2 Cor. 13 : 4*b* ; cp. 12 : 10, and 1 Cor. 5 : 5 ; (*j*) bread, figurative of the Lord Jesus, John 6 : 51 ; (*k*) a stone, figurative of the Lord Jesus, 1 Pet. 2 : 4 ; (*l*) water, figurative

of the Holy Spirit, John 4 : 10 ; 7 : 38 ; (*m*) a sacrifice, figurative of the believer, Rom. 12 : 1 ; (*n*) stones, figurative of the believer, 1 Pet. 2 : 5 ; (*o*) the oracles, *logion*, Acts 7 : 38, and word, *logos*, Heb. 4 : 12 ; 1 Pet. 1 : 23, of God ; (*p*) the physical life of men, 1 Thess. 4 : 15 ; Matt. 27 : 63 ; Acts 25 : 24 ; Rom. 14 : 9 ; Phil. 1 : 21 (in the infinitive mood used as a noun, with the article, ' living '), 22 ; 1 Pet. 4 : 5 ; (*q*) the maintenance of physical life, Matt. 4 : 4 ; 1 Cor. 9 : 14 ; (*r*) the duration of physical life, Heb. 2 : 15 ; (*s*) the enjoyment of physical life, 1 Thess. 3 : 8 ; (*t*) the recovery of physical life from the power of disease, Mark 5 : 23 ; John 4 : 50 ; (*u*) the recovery of physical life from the power of death, Matt. 9 : 18 ; Acts 9 : 41 ; Rev. 20 : 5 ; (*v*) the course, conduct, and character of men, (1) good, Acts 26 : 5 ; 2 Tim. 3 : 12 ; Tit. 2 : 12 ; (2) evil, Luke 15 : 13 ; Rom. 6 : 2 ; 8 : 13*a* ; 2 Cor. 5 : 15*b* ; Col. 3 : 7 ; (3) undefined, Rom. 7 : 9 ; 14 : 7 ; Gal. 2 : 14 ; (*w*) restoration after alienation, Luke 15 : 32.

" *Note :* In 1 Thess. 5 : 10, to live means to experience that change, 1 Cor. 15 : 51, which is to be the portion of all in Christ who will be alive upon the earth at the Parousia of the Lord Jesus, cp. John 11 : 25, and which corresponds to the resurrection of those who had previously died in Christ, 1 Cor. 15 : 52–54.

" 2. SUNZAŌ (συνζάω), to live together with (*sun*, with, and *zaō*, to 4800
live), may be included with *zaō* in the above analysis as follows : (*g*) AG:775C CB:1271A
Rom. 6 : 8 ; 2 Tim. 2 : 11 ; (*s*), 2 Cor. 7 : 3.¶

" 3. ANAZAŌ (ἀναζάω) *ana*, again, and *zaō*, denotes ' to live again,' 326
' to revive,' Luke 15 : 24 ; cp. (*w*) in list above, and Rom. 7 : 9, to manifest AG:53D CB:1235B
activity again."¶*

Note : *Zaō* is translated " quick " (i.e., " living ") in Acts 10 : 42 ; 2 Tim. 4 : 1 ; 1 Pet. 4 : 5 ; in Heb. 4 : 12, A.V. (R.V., " living ").

4. BIOŌ (βιόω), to spend life, to pass one's life, is used in 1 Pet. 4 : 2.¶ 980 AG:142A CB:1239A

5. ANASTREPHŌ (ἀναστρέφω), used metaphorically, in the Middle 390
Voice, to conduct oneself, behave, live, is translated to live, in Heb. 13 : 18 AG:61B CB:1235B
(" honestly ") ; in 2 Pet. 2 : 18 (" in error "). See ABIDE, BEHAVE, etc.

6. ZŌOGONEŌ (ζωογονέω) denotes to preserve alive (from *zōos*, alive, 2225 AG:341C CB:1273C

* From Notes on Thessalonians by Hogg and Vine, pp. 173, 174.

and *ginomai*, to come to be, become, be made) ; in Luke 17 : 33, " shall preserve (it)," i.e., his life, R.V. marg., " save (it) alive ; " cp. the parallels *sōzō*, to save, in Matt. 16 : 25, and *phulassō*, to keep, in John 12 : 25 ; in Acts 7 : 19, " live," negatively of the efforts of Pharaoh to destroy the babes in Israel ; in 1 Tim. 6 : 13, according to the best mss. (some have *zōopoieō*, to cause to live), " quickeneth " (R.V., marg., " preserveth . . . alive," the preferable rendering). See PRESERVE, QUICKEN.¶

1236
AG:182C
CB:— 7. DIAGŌ (διάγω) is used of time in the sense of passing a life, 1 Tim. 2 : 2, " (that) we may lead (a tranquil and quiet, R.V.) life ; " Tit. 3 : 3, " living (in malice and envy)."¶

(-OMAI)
4176
AG:686C
CB:1266A 8. POLITEUŌ (πολιτεύω), to be a citizen (*politēs*), to live as a citizen, is used metaphorically of conduct as in accordance with the characteristics of the heavenly community ; in Acts 23 : 1, " I have lived ; " in Phil. 1 : 27, " let your manner of life (A.V., conversation) be." See CITIZENSHIP, No. 4, *Note*.¶

5225
AG:838A
CB:— 9. HUPARCHŌ (ὑπάρχω), to be in existence, to be, is translated " live (delicately) " in Luke 7 : 25. See BEING.

ESTHIŌ
2068
AG:312B
CB:1246C
SPATALAŌ
4684
AG:761A *Note :* In 1 Cor. 9 : 13, A.V., *esthiō*, to eat, is translated " live of." In Tim. 5 : 6 the A.V. renders *spatalaō* " liveth in pleasure."

LIVE LONG

3118
AG:488C
CB:— MAKROCHRONIOS (μακροχρόνιος), an adjective denoting of long duration, long-lived (*makros*, long, *chronos*, time), is used in Eph. 6 : 3, " (that thou mayest) live long," lit., ' (that thou mayest be) long-lived.'¶ In the Sept., Ex. 20 : 12 ; Deut. 4 : 40 ; 5 : 16 ; 17 : 20.¶

LIVELY

2198
AG:336A
CB:1273B *Note :* This is the A.V. translation of the present participle of the verb *zaō*, to live, in three passages, in each of which the R.V. has " living," Acts 7 : 38 ; 1 Pet. 1 : 3 ; 2 : 5.

For LIVING see BEHAVIOUR, B, No. 1, LIFE, Nos. 2, 6, and LIVE, No. 3, *Note*

For LIVING CREATURES see BEAST

LO !

1. IDE (ἴδε), an aorist or point tense, marking a definite point of time, of the imperative mood of *eidon*, to see (taken as part of *horaō*, to see), is used as an interjection, addressed either to one or many persons, e.g., Matt. 25 : 20, 22, 25 ; John 1 : 29, 36, 47 ; Gal. 5 : 2, the only occurrence outside Matthew, Mark and John. See BEHOLD, SEE. 2396 AG:369B CB:1252C

2. IDOU (ἰδού), a similar tense of No. 1, but in the Middle Voice, e.g., Matt. 1 : 20, 23 ; very frequent in the Synoptists and Acts and the Apocalypse. 2400 AG:370D CB:1252C

For LOAF see BREAD

LOCKED See SHUT

LOCUST

AKRIS (ἀκρίς) occurs in Matt. 3 : 4 and Mark 1 : 6, of the animals themselves, as forming part of the diet of John the Baptist ; they are used as food ; the Arabs stew them with butter, after removing the head, legs and wings. In Rev. 9 : 3, 7, they appear as monsters representing Satanic agencies, let loose by Divine judgments inflicted upon men for five months, the time of the natural life of the locust. For the character of the judgment see the whole passage.¶ 200 AG:33C CB:1234B

LODGE, LODGING

A. Verbs.

1. AULIZOMAI (αὐλίζομαι), properly, to lodge in a courtyard (*aulē*, see COURT, No. 2), then, to lodge in the open, denotes, in the N.T., to pass the night, to lodge anywhere, Matt. 21 : 17 ; Luke 21 : 37, R.V., " lodged " (A.V., " abode ").¶ See the metaphorical use in the Sept. and the Heb. of Psa. 30 : 5, ' (weeping) may come in to lodge (at even),' i.e., as a passing stranger. See ABIDE. 835 AG:121C CB:121C

2. KATASKĒNOŌ (κατασκηνόω), to pitch one's tent (*kata*, down, *skēnē*, a tent), is rendered to lodge, of birds, in Matt. 13 : 32 ; Mark 4 : 32 ; Luke 13 : 19. In Acts 2 : 26, it is used of the body of the Lord in the tomb, as dwelling in hope, R.V., " shall dwell " (marg., " tabernacle "), A.V., " shall rest." See DWELL, REST.¶ Cp. *kataskēnōsis*, a roosting place. 2681 AG:418C CB:1254B

3. KATALUŌ (καταλύω), in one of its meanings, signifies to unloose (*kata*, down, *luō*, to loose), unyoke, as of horses, etc., hence intransitively, 2647 AG:414B CB:1254A

In the following pages † indicates that the word referred to (preposition, conjunction, or particle) is not dealt with in this volume.

¶ indicates that all the N.T. occurrences of the Greek word under consideration are mentioned under the heading or sub-heading.

to take up one's quarters, to lodge, Luke 9 : 12 ; 19 : 7, R.V., " to lodge "
(A.V., " to be a guest "). See COME, Note (7) (come to nought), DESTROY,
DISSOLVE, OVERTHROW, THROW. Cp. *kataluma*, a guest chamber, inn.
3579 AG:547D 4. XENIZŌ (ξενίζω), to receive as a guest (*xenos*, a guest, stranger),
CB:1273B to entertain, lodge, is used in the Active Voice in Acts 10 : 23 ; 28 : 7, R.V.,
" entertained " (A.V., " lodged ") ; Heb. 13 : 2, " have entertained ; "
in the Passive Voice, Acts 10 : 6 (lit., ' he is entertained '), 18, 32 ;
21 : 16. Its other meaning, to think strange, is found in 1 Pet. 4 : 4, 12.
See ENTERTAIN, STRANGE.

B. Noun.

3578 AG:547B XENIA (ξενία), akin to A, No. 4, denotes (*a*) hospitality, entertain-
CB:1273B ment, Philm. 22 ; (*b*) by metonymy, a place of entertainment, a lodging-
place, Acts 28 : 23 (some put Philm. 22 under this section).¶

For LOFT, Acts 20 : 9, see STORY

LOINS

3751 AG:587D OSPHUS (ὀσφύς) is used (*a*) in the natural sense in Matt. 3 : 4 ;
CB:1261B Mark 1 : 6 ; (*b*) as the seat of generative power, Heb. 7 : 5, 10 ; metaphorically in Acts 2 : 30 ; (*c*) metaphorically, (1) of girding the loins in readiness for active service for the Lord, Luke 12 : 35 ; (2) the same, with truth, Eph. 6 : 14, i.e., bracing up oneself so as to maintain perfect sincerity and reality as the counteractive in Christian character against hypocrisy and falsehood ; (3) of girding the loins of the mind, 1 Pet. 1 : 13, R.V., " girding," suggestive of the alertness necessary for sobriety and for setting one's hope perfectly on " the grace to be brought . . . at the revelation of Jesus Christ " (the present participle, " girding," is introductory to the rest of the verse).¶

LONELY
See
DESERT

LONG (Adjective and Adverb)

A. Adjectives.

3117 AG:488C 1. MAKROS (μακρός) is used of long prayers (Matt. 23 : 14, in some
CB:— mss.), Mark 12 : 40 ; Luke 20 : 47. It denotes " far " in Luke 15 : 13 ;
19 : 12. See FAR.¶

2425 AG:374B 2. HIKANOS (ἱκανός), sufficient, much, long, is used with *chronos*,
CB:1250C time, in Luke 8 : 27 ; in 20 : 9 and 23 : 8 (A.V., " *season* ") the plural is
used, lit., ' long times ; ' Acts 8 : 11 ; 14 : 3. See ABLE (ABILITY), C,
No. 2, MANY, MUCH.

4183 AG:687C 3. POLUS (πολύς), much, is used with *chronos*, time, in Matt. 25 : 19 ;
CB:1266A John 5 : 6 ; in Acts 27 : 21, with *asitia*, A.V., " long abstinence," R.V.,
" long without food." See COMMON, Note (1).

5118 AG:823B 4. TOSOUTOS (τοσοῦτος), so long, is used with *chronos* in John 14 : 9
4214 and Heb. 4 : 7.

AG:694B 5. POSOS (πόσος), how much, is used with *chronos*, in Mark 9 : 21,
3745 AG:586B " how long time," R.V. (A.V., " how long ago ").

CB:1251B 6. HOSOS (ὅσος), how much, so much, is used after the preposition *epi* (*eph'*), and as an adjective qualifying *chronos*, signifying "for so long time," in Rom. 7 : 1 ; 1 Cor. 7 : 39 ; Gal. 4 : 1 ; see also B, No. 4.

Notes : (1) In Acts 14 : 28, A.V., the adjective *oligos*, little, with the
negative *ou*, not, and qualifying *chronos*, is rendered "long time ;" R.V., PLEIŌN
"no little (time)." (2) For the comparative adjective, *pleiōn*, see 4119 AG:687C
Longer, B. (POLUS II.)

B. Adverbs. CB:1265B

1. POLUS (πολύς), in one or other of its neuter forms, singular or 4183
plural, is used (*a*) of degree, greatly, much, many, e.g., Mark 1 : 45 ; AG:687C CB:1266A
(*b*) of time, e.g., Acts 27 : 14. Cp. A, No. 3. See Great, Much, Oft,
Sore, Straitly, While.

2. EPH' HIKANON (ἐφ' ἱκανόν), lit., 'unto much (time),' is rendered HIKANOS
"a long while" in Acts 20 : 11. Cp. A, No. 2. 2425 AG:374B

3. HEŌS POTE (ἕως πότε), lit., 'until when ?' signifies "how long ?" CB:1250C
Matt. 17 : 17 (twice) ; Mark 9 : 19 (twice) ; Luke 9 : 41 ; John 10 : 24 ; POTE 4219
Rev. 6 : 10. AG:695A

4. EPH' HOSON (ἐφ' ὅσον) signifies so long as, as long as (*epi*, upon, CB:1266B HOSOS
hosos, how much), Matt. 9 : 15 ; Mark 2 : 19 ; 2 Pet. 1 : 13. See Inasmuch, 3745
No. 2. AG:586B CB:1251B

Notes : (1) For the adverb Longer, see below. (2) In 2 Pet. 2 : 3, EKPALAI
A.V., the adverb *ekpalai*, "from of old," R.V. (*ek*, from, *palai*, of old, 1597 AG:243C
formerly), is translated "of a long time." CB:—

LONG (Verb), LONG (after, for), LONGING

A. Verb.

EPIPOTHEŌ (ἐπιποθέω), to long for greatly (a strengthened form of 1971
potheō, to long for, not found in the N.T.), is translated "I long," in AG:297D CB:1246A
Rom. 1 : 11 ; in 2 Cor. 5 : 2, R.V., "longing" (A.V., "earnestly desiring") ; in 1 Thess. 3 : 6 and 2 Tim. 1 : 4, R.V., "longing" (A.V., "desiring greatly") ; to long after, in 2 Cor. 9 : 14 ; Phil. 1 : 8 ; 2 : 26 ; to long for, in 1 Pet. 2 : 2, R.V. (A.V., "desire") ; Jas. 4 : 5, R.V., "long." See Desire.¶

B. Adjective.

EPIPOTHĒTOS (ἐπιπόθητος), akin to A, and an intensive form of 1973
pothētos, desired, greatly desired, "longed for," is used in Phil. 4 : 1.¶ AG:298A CB:—

C. Nouns.

1. EPIPOTHIA (ἐπιποθία), a longing (akin to A and B), is found in 1974 AG:298A
Rom. 15 : 23, R.V., "longing" (A.V., "great desire"). See Desire.¶ CB:1246A

2. EPIPOTHĒSIS (ἐπιπόθησις), a longing (perhaps stressing the 1972
process more than No. 1), is found in 2 Cor. 7 : 7, R.V., "longing" (A.V., AG:298A CB:1246A
"earnest desire") ; 7 : 11, R.V., "longing" (A.V., "vehement desire").¶

LONGER

A. Adverbs. 2089 AG:315C

1. ETI (ἔτι), yet, as yet, still, is translated "longer" in Luke 16 : 2 CB:1247A

(with separate negative); "any longer" in Rom. 6 : 2. See ALSO, EVEN, FURTHER, MORE, MOREOVER, STILL, THENCEFORTH, YET.

3765 AG:592C CB:— 2. OUKETI (οὐκέτι), no more, no longer (*ou*, not, *k*, euphonic, and No. 1), is rendered "no longer" in the R.V. of Mark 7 : 12 (A.V., "no more"); John 15 : 15, R.V. (A.V., "henceforth not"); Rom. 14 : 15, R.V. (A.V., "now . . . not"); Gal. 2 : 20, R.V. (A.V., "yet not"); Gal. 3 : 25; 4 : 7 (A.V., "no more"); Philm. 16 (A.V., "not now"). See HENCEFORTH, MORE, NOW, YET.

3371 AG:518C CB:— 3. MĒKETI (μηκέτι) also means no more, no longer, but generally suggests what is a matter of thought or supposition, whereas No. 1 refers to what is a matter of fact. It is rendered "any longer" in Acts 25 : 24; "no longer," in Mark 2 : 2, R.V., "no longer (room)," A.V., "no (room);" 2 Cor. 5 : 15, R.V. (A.V., "not henceforth"); Eph. 4 : 14, R.V. (A.V., "no more"); 4 : 17, R.V. (A.V., "henceforth . . . not"); 1 Thess. 3 : 1, 5; 1 Tim. 5 : 23; 1 Pet. 4 : 2. See (negatively) HENCEFORTH, HENCEFORWARD, HEREAFTER, NO MORE.

PLEIŌN (-ON) 4119 AG:687C (POLUS II.) 4. PLEION (πλεῖον), the neuter of *pleiōn*, more, the comparative degree of *polu*, much, is rendered "longer" in Acts 20 : 9, R.V. (A.V., "long").

B. Adjective.

CB:1265B PLEIŌN (πλείων), more, (cp. A, No. 4), is used with *chronos*, time, in Acts 18 : 20, "a longer time," R.V. (A.V., "longer").

LONGSUFFERING (Noun and Verb)

A. Noun.

3115 AG:488B CB:1257C MAKROTHUMIA (μακροθυμία), forbearance, patience, longsuffering (*makros*, long, *thumos*, temper), is usually rendered "longsuffering," Rom. 2 : 4; 9 : 22; 2 Cor. 6 : 6; Gal. 5 : 22; Eph. 4 : 2; Col. 1 : 11; 3 : 12; 1 Tim. 1 : 16; 2 Tim. 3 : 10; 4 : 2; 1 Pet. 3 : 20; 2 Pet. 3 : 15; "patience" in Heb. 6 : 12 and Jas. 5 : 10. See PATIENCE, and Note under FORBEAR.¶

B. Verb.

3114 AG:488A CB:1257C MAKROTHUMEŌ (μακροθυμέω), akin to A, to be patient, longsuffering, to bear with, lit., to be long-tempered, is rendered by the verb to be longsuffering in Luke 18 : 7, R.V. (A.V., "bear long"); in 1 Thess. 5 : 14, R.V. (A.V., "be patient"); so in Jas. 5 : 7, 8; in 2 Pet. 3 : 9, A.V. and R.V., "is longsuffering." See BEAR, No. 14, ENDURE, PATIENT, SUFFER.

Note : "Longsuffering is that quality of self-restraint in the face of provocation which does not hastily retaliate or promptly punish; it is the opposite of anger, and is associated with mercy, and is used of God, Ex. 34 : 6 (Sept.); Rom. 2 : 4; 1 Pet. 3 : 20. Patience is the quality that does not surrender to circumstances or succumb under trial; it is the opposite of despondency and is associated with hope, 1 Thess. 1 : 3; it is not used of God."*

---

* From Notes on Thessalonians by Hogg and Vine, pp. 183, 184.

LOOK

A. Verbs.

1. BLEPŌ (βλέπω), primarily, to have sight, to see, then, observe, 991
discern, perceive, frequently implying special contemplation (cp. No. 4), AG:143B CB:1239A
is rendered by the verb to look in Luke 9 : 62, "looking (back);" John 13 : 22 "(the disciples) looked (one on another)"; Acts 1 : 9, R.V., "were looking" (A.V., "beheld"); 3 : 4, "look (on us);" 27 : 12, R.V., looking," A.V., "that lieth (towards)," of the haven Phenix; Eph. 5 : 15, R.V., "look (therefore carefully how ye walk)," A.V., "see (that ye walk circumspectly);" Rev. 11 : 9 and 18 : 9, R.V., "look upon" (A.V., "shall see"). See BEHOLD.

2. ANABLEPŌ (ἀναβλέπω), denotes (*a*) to look up (*ana*, up, and No. 1), 308
e.g., Matt. 14 : 19; Mark 8 : 24 (in some mss. ver. 25); (*b*) to recover AG:50D CB:1235A
sight, e.g., Matt. 11 : 5; 20 : 34, R.V., "received their sight;" John 9 : 11. See SIGHT. Cp. *anablepsis*, recovering of sight, Luke 4 : 18.

3. PERIBLEPŌ (περιβλέπω), to look about, or round about, on 4017
(*peri*, around, and No. 1), is used in the Middle Voice, Mark 3 : 5, 34; AG:646B CB:—
5 : 32; 9 : 8; 10 : 23; 11 : 11; Luke 6 : 10.¶

4. APOBLEPŌ (ἀποβλέπω) signifies to look away from (*apo*) all else 578
at one object; hence, to look stedfastly, Heb. 11 : 26, R.V., "he looked" AG:89A CB:1236C
(A.V., "he had respect").¶ Cp. No. 8.

5. EMBLEPŌ (ἐμβλέπω), to look at (*en*, in, and No. 1), is translated 1689
to look upon in Mark 10 : 27; 14 : 67; Luke 22 : 61; John 1 : 36. AG:254C CB:1244B
This verb implies a close, penetrating look, as distinguished from Nos. 6 and 9. See BEHOLD, No. 3, GAZE, SEE, No. 6.

6. EPIBLEPŌ (ἐπιβλέπω), to look upon (*epi*, upon), is used in the 1914
N.T. of favourable regard, Luke 1 : 48, R.V., "he hath looked upon" AG:290B CB:—
(A.V., "hath regarded"), of the low estate of the Virgin Mary; in 9 : 38, in a request to the Lord to look upon an afflicted son; in Jas. 2 : 3, R.V., "ye have regard" (A.V., ". . . respect"), of having a partial regard for the well-to-do. See REGARD, RESPECT.¶

7. EIDON (εἶδον), used as the aorist tense of *horaō*, to see, in various (HORAō) 3708
senses, is translated to look, in the A.V. of John 7 : 52, R.V., "see;" AG:577D
Rev. 4 : 1 (R.V., "I saw"); so in 6 : 8; 14 : 1, 14 (as in A.V. of ver. 6), CB:1251A
and 15 : 5. See BEHOLD, CONSIDER, HEED, No. 2, PERCEIVE, SEE, SHEW.

8. APHORAŌ (ἀφοράω), to look away from one thing so as to see 872
another (*apo*, from, and No. 7), to concentrate the gaze upon, occurs in AG:127B CB:—
Phil. 2 : 23, "I shall see;" Heb. 12 : 2, "looking."¶

9. EPEIDON (ἐπεῖδον) denotes to look upon (*epi*, upon), (*a*) favour- 1896 AG:284B
ably, Luke 1 : 25; (*b*) unfavourably, in Acts 4 : 29.¶ CB:—

10. PARAKUPTŌ (παρακύπτω), lit. and primarily, to stoop sideways 3879
(*para*, aside, *kuptō*, to bend forward), denotes to stoop to look into, AG:619B CB:—
Luke 24 : 12, "stooping and looking in" (A.V., "stooping down"); John 20 : 5, 11; metaphorically in Jas. 1 : 25, of looking into the perfect

law of liberty; in 1 Pet. 1 : 12 of things which the angels desire "to look" into.¶

352 AG:56C CB:— 11. ANAKUPTŌ (ἀνακύπτω), to lift oneself up (*ana*, up), is translated "look up" in Luke 21 : 28, of being elated in joyous expectation (followed by *epairō*, to lift up). See LIFT.

4648 AG:756D CB:1269B 12. SKOPEŌ (σκοπέω), to look at, consider (Eng., scope), implying mental consideration, is rendered "while we look . . . at" in 2 Cor. 4 : 18; "looking to" (A.V., "on") in Phil. 2 : 4. See HEED, MARK.

1983 AG:298D CB:1246A 13. EPISKOPEŌ (ἐπισκοπέω), lit., to look upon (*epi*, and No. 12), is rendered "looking carefully" in Heb. 12 : 15, R.V. (A.V., "looking diligently"), *epi* being probably intensive here; in 1 Pet. 5 : 2, to exercise the oversight, to visit, care for. See OVERSIGHT.¶

1980 AG:298C CB:1246A 14. EPISKEPTOMAI (ἐπισκέπτομαι), a later form of No. 13, to visit, has the meaning of seeking out, and is rendered "look ye out" in Acts 6 : 3. See VISIT.

816 AG:119D CB:1238A 15. ATENIZŌ (ἀτενίζω), to look fixedly, gaze, is translated "looking stedfastly" in Luke 22 : 56, R.V. (A.V., ". . . earnestly"); in Acts 1 : 10, "looking stedfastly;" in 3 : 12, A.V., "look . . . earnestly" (R.V., "fasten ye your eyes," as in 3 : 4 and 11 : 6); so in the R.V. of 6 : 15; 10 : 4; 13 : 9; 14 : 9; in 7 : 55, "looked up stedfastly;" in 23 : 1, "looking stedfastly on" (A.V., "earnestly beholding"); in 2 Cor. 3 : 7, R.V., "look stedfastly" (A.V., "stedfastly behold"); in 3 : 13, R.V., ditto (A.V., "stedfastly look"). In Luke 4 : 20, "were fastened" (*ophthalmoi*, eyes, being used separately). See BEHOLD, No. 10.¶

2300 AG:353A CB:1271C 16. THEAOMAI (θεάομαι), to behold (of careful contemplation), is translated "look" in John 4 : 35, of looking on the fields; in 1 John 1 : 1, A.V. (R.V., "we beheld"), of the Apostles' personal experiences of Christ in the days of His flesh, and the facts of His Godhood and Manhood. See BEHOLD, No. 8.

2334 AG:360A CB:1272A 17. THEŌREŌ (θεωρέω), to look at, gaze at, behold, is translated "looking on" in Mark 15 : 40, A.V. (R.V., "beholding"). See BEHOLD, No. 6.

B. Noun.

3706 AG:577C CB:1251A HORASIS (ὅρασις), akin to A, No. 7, denotes (*a*) a vision (so the associated noun *horama*, e.g., Acts 7 : 31; *horasis* signifies especially the act of seeing, *horama* that which is seen), Acts 2 : 17; Rev. 9 : 17; (*b*) an appearance, Rev. 4 : 3, translated "to look upon" (twice in the R.V.; in the second instance the A.V. has "in sight").¶

LOOK (for), LOOKING (after, for)

A. Verbs.

4328 AG:712C CB:1267A 1. PROSDOKAŌ (προσδοκάω), to await, expect (*pros*, to or towards, *dokeō*, to think, be of opinion), is translated to look for, e.g., in Matt. 11 : 3; 2 Pet. 3 : 12, 13, 14; the R.V. renders it by the verb to expect, to be in expectation, in some instances, as does the A.V. in Luke 3 : 15 ; Acts 3 : 5. See EXPECT.

2. PROSDECHOMAI (προσδέχομαι), to receive favourably, also means 4327
to expect, and is rendered to look for, e.g., in Luke 2 : 38 ; 23 : 51 ; AG:712B CB:1267A
Acts 24 : 15, R.V. (A.V., " allow ") ; Tit. 2 : 13 ; Jude 21. See ACCEPT, A, No. 3, ALLOW, No. 4.

3. EKDECHOMAI (ἐκδέχομαι), primarily to receive from another, 1551
hence, to expect, to await, is translated " he looked for " in Heb. 11 : 10 ; AG:238B CB:1243C
in 1 Cor. 16 : 11, A.V., " I look for " (R.V., " I expect "). See EXPECT, No. 1.

Notes : (1) In Phil. 3 : 20 and Heb. 9 : 28, A.V., *apekdechomai* (the 553
verb in the preceding No. extended by *apo*, from), to await or expect AG:83C CB:1236B
eagerly, is translated " look for " (R.V., " wait for ; " so A.V. everywhere else). See WAIT. (2) In Acts 28 : 6, A.V., *prosdokaō*, to expect, is translated " they looked " (R.V., " they expected "), and " they had looked " (R.V., " they were long in expectation ").

B. Nouns.

1. PROSDOKIA (προσδοκία), akin to A, No. 1, is translated " a 4329
looking after " in Luke 21 : 26, A.V. (R.V., " expectation," as in Acts AG:712C CB:—
12 : 11, A.V. and R.V.). See EXPECTATION.¶

2. EKDOCHĒ (ἐκδοχή), akin to A, No. 3, is translated " looking 1561
for " in Heb. 10 : 27, A.V. See EXPECTATION.¶ AG:239A CB:1243C

LOOK (to)

1. BLEPŌ (βλέπω), to look (see LOOK, No. 1), has the meaning of 991 AG:143B
taking heed, looking to oneself, in 2 John 8. See HEED. CB:1239A

2. HORAŌ (ὁράω), to see (see LOOK, No. 7), has the meaning of seeing 3708
to or caring for a thing in Matt. 27 : 4, " see (thou to it) ; " in Acts 18 : 15, AG:577D CB:1251A
" look to it (yourselves) ; " the future (sing. *opsei*, plural, *opsesthe*), is used for the tense which is wanting in *horaō*, and stands for the imperative.

LOOSE

A. Verbs.

1. LUŌ (λύω) denotes (*a*) to loose, unbind, release, (1) of things, e.g., 3089
in Acts 7 : 33, R.V., " loose (the shoes)," A.V., " put off ; " Mark 1 : 7 ; AG:483C CB:1257B
(2) of animals, e.g., Matt. 21 : 2 ; (3) of persons, e.g., John 11 : 44 ; Acts 22 : 30 ; (4) of Satan, Rev. 20 : 3, 7, and angels, Rev. 9 : 14, 15 ; (5) metaphorically, of one diseased, Luke 13 : 16 ; of the marriage tie, 1 Cor. 7 : 27 ; of release from sins, Rev. 1 : 5 (in the most authentic mss.) ; (*b*) to loosen, break up, dismiss, dissolve, destroy ; in this sense it is translated to loose in Acts 2 : 24, of the pains of death ; in Rev. 5 : 2, of the seals of a roll. See BREAK, DESTROY, DISSOLVE, MELT, PUT (off), UNLOOSE.

2. APOLUŌ (ἀπολύω), *apo*, from, and No. 1, denotes (*a*) to set free, 630 AG:96C
release, translated " loosed " in Luke 13 : 12, of deliverance from an CB:1237A

infirmity; in Matt. 18:27, A.V., "loosed" (R.V., "released"), of a debtor; (*b*) to let go, dismiss, e.g., Matt. 14:15, 22. See DEPART, DISMISS, DIVORCE, FORGIVE, LET (go), LIBERTY, PUT (away), RELEASE, SEND (away).

447 AG:69D 3. ANIĒMI (ἀνίημι), to send back (*ana*, back, *hiēmi*, to send), to leave,
CB:— forbear, is translated to loose, in Acts 16:26, of the loosening of bonds;
27:40, rudder-bands. Elsewhere, Eph. 6:9; Heb. 13:5. See FORBEAR, LEAVE.¶

321 AG:53A— 4. ANAGŌ (ἀνάγω): see LAUNCH.

AIRō *Notes:* (1) In Acts 27:13, A.V., *airō*, to lift, is translated "loosing
142 AG:24B (thence)" (R.V., "they weighed anchor"). (2) For *katargeō*, translated
CB:1234A "she is loosed" in Rom. 7:2, A.V. (R.V. "discharged"), see ABOLISH.

KATARGEō

B. Noun.

2673 AG:417B LUSIS (λύσις), a loosening (akin to A, No. 1), 1 Cor. 7:27, of divorce,
CB:1254B is translated "to be loosed," lit., 'loosing.' In the second part of the
LUSIS 3080 verse the verb *luō* is used.¶ In the Sept., Eccles. 8:1, with the meaning
AG:482B CB:1257B "interpretation."¶

LORD, LORDSHIP

A. Nouns.

2962 1. KURIOS (κύριος), properly an adjective, signifying having power
AG:458D II. CB:1256B (*kuros*) or authority, is used as a noun, variously translated in the N.T.,
"'Lord,' 'master,' 'Master,' 'owner,' 'Sir,' a title of wide significance, occurring in each book of the N.T. save Tit. and the Epp. of John. It is used (*a*) of an owner, as in Luke 19:33, cp. Matt. 20:8; Acts 16:16; Gal. 4:1; or of one who has the disposal of anything, as the Sabbath, Matt. 12:8; (*b*) of a master, i.e., one to whom service is due on any ground, Matt. 6:24; 24:50; Eph. 6:5; (*c*) of an Emperor or King, Acts 25:26; Rev. 17:14; (*d*) of idols, ironically, 1 Cor. 8:5, cp. Isa. 26:13; (*e*) as a title of respect addressed to a father, Matt. 21:30, a husband, 1 Pet. 3:6, a master, Matt. 13:27; Luke 13:8, a ruler, Matt. 27:63, an angel, Acts 10:4; Rev. 7:14; (*f*) as a title of courtesy addressed to a stranger, John 12:21; 20:15; Acts 16:30; from the outset of His ministry this was a common form of address to the Lord Jesus, alike by the people, Matt. 8:2; John 4:11, and by His disciples, Matt. 8:25; Luke 5:8; John 6:68; (*g*) *kurios* is the Sept. and N.T. representative of Heb. Jehovah ('LORD' in Eng. versions), see Matt. 4:7; Jas. 5:11, e.g., of *adon*, Lord, Matt. 22:44, and of *Adonay*, Lord, 1:22; it also occurs for *Elohim*, God, 1 Pet. 1:25.

"Thus the usage of the word in the N.T. follows two main lines: one—*a*—*f*, customary and general, the other, *g*, peculiar to the Jews, and drawn from the Greek translation of the O.T.

"Christ Himself assumed the title, Matt. 7:21, 22; 9:38; 22:41-45; Mark 5:19 (cp. Ps. 66:16; the parallel passage, Luke 8:39, has 'God'); Luke 19:31; John 13:13, apparently intending it in the higher senses of its current use, and at the same time suggesting its O.T. associations.

" His purpose did not become clear to the disciples until after His resurrection, and the revelation of His Deity consequent thereon. Thomas, when he realised the significance of the presence of a mortal wound in the body of a living man, immediately joined with it the absolute title of Deity, saying, 'My Lord and my God,' John 20 : 28. Thereafter, except in Acts 10 : 4 and Rev. 7 : 14, there is no record that *kurios* was ever again used by believers in addressing any save God and the Lord Jesus ; cp. Acts 2 : 47 with 4 : 29, 30.

" How soon and how completely the lower meaning had been superseded is seen in Peter's declaration in his first sermon after the resurrection, 'God hath made Him—Lord,' Acts 2 : 36, and that in the house of Cornelius, 'He is Lord of all,' 10 : 36 ; cp. Deut. 10 : 14 ; Matt. 11 : 25 ; Acts 17 : 24. In his writings the implications of his early teaching are confirmed and developed. Thus Ps. 34 : 8, 'O taste and see that Jehovah is good,' is applied to the Lord Jesus, 1 Pet. 2 : 3, and 'Jehovah of Hosts, Him shall ye sanctify,' Isa. 8 : 13, becomes 'sanctify in your hearts Christ as Lord,' 3 : 15.

" So also James who uses *kurios* alike of God, 1 : 7 (cp. v. 5) ; 3 : 9 ; 4 : 15 ; 5 : 4, 10, 11, and of the Lord Jesus, 1 : 1 (where the possibility that *kai* is intended epexegetically, i.e.=even, cp. 1 Thess. 3 : 11, should not be overlooked) ; 2 : 1 (lit., 'our Lord Jesus Christ of glory,' cp. Ps. 24 : 7 ; 29 : 3 ; Acts 7 : 2 ; 1 Cor. 2 : 8) ; 5 : 7, 8, while the language of 4 : 10 ; 5 : 15, is equally applicable to either.

" Jude, v. 4, speaks of 'our only—Lord, Jesus Christ,' and immediately, v. 5, uses 'Lord' of God (see the remarkable marg. here), as he does later, vv. 9, 14.

" Paul ordinarily uses *kurios* of the Lord Jesus, 1 Cor. 1 : 3, e.g., but also on occasion, of God, in quotations from the O.T., 1 Cor. 3 : 20, e.g., and in his own words, 1 Cor. 3 : 5, cp. v. 10. It is equally appropriate to either in 1 Cor. 7 : 25 ; 2 Cor. 3 : 16 ; 8 : 21 ; 1 Thess. 4 : 6, and if 1 Cor. 11 : 32 is to be interpreted by 10 : 21, 22, the Lord Jesus is intended, but if by Heb. 12 : 5–9, then *kurios* here also=God. 1 Tim. 6 : 15, 16 is probably to be understood of the Lord Jesus, cp. Rev. 17 : 14.

" Though John does not use 'Lord' in his Epp., and though, like the other Evangelists, he ordinarily uses the personal Name in his narrative, yet he occasionally speaks of Him as 'the Lord,' John 4 : 1 ; 6 : 23 ; 11 : 2 ; 20 : 20 ; 21 : 12.

" The full significance of this association of Jesus with God under the one appellation, 'Lord,' is seen when it is remembered that these men belonged to the only monotheistic race in the world. To associate with the Creator one known to be a creature, however exalted, though possible to Pagan philosophers, was quite impossible to a Jew.

" It is not recorded that in the days of His flesh any of His disciples either addressed the Lord, or spoke of Him, by His personal Name. Where

Paul has occasion to refer to the facts of the gospel history he speaks of what the Lord Jesus said, Acts 20 : 35, and did, 1 Cor. 11 : 23, and suffered, 1 Thess. 2 : 15 ; 5 : 9, 10. It is our Lord Jesus who is coming, 1 Thess. 2 : 19, etc. In prayer also the title is given, 3 : 11 ; Eph. 1 : 3 ; the sinner is invited to believe on the Lord Jesus, Acts 16 : 31 ; 20 : 21, and the saint to look to the Lord Jesus for deliverance, Rom. 7 : 24, 25, and in the few exceptional cases in which the personal Name stands alone a reason is always discernible in the immediate context.

" The title ' Lord,' as given to the Saviour, in its full significance rests upon the resurrection, Acts 2 : 36 ; Rom. 10 : 9 ; 14 : 9, and is realised only in the Holy Spirit, 1 Cor. 12 : 3."*

1203 AG:176C 2. DESPOTĒS (δεσπότης), a master, lord, one who possesses supreme
CB:1240C authority, is used in personal address to God in Luke 2 : 29 ; Acts 4 : 24 ; Rev. 6 : 10 ; with reference to Christ, 2 Pet. 2 : 1 ; Jude 4 ; elsewhere it is translated " master," " masters," 1 Tim. 6 : 1, 2 ; 2 Tim. 2 : 21 (of Christ) ;
4462 Tit. 2 : 9 ; 1 Pet. 2 : 18. See MASTER.¶

AG:733A CB:1268A *Note :* For *rabboni*, rendered " Lord " in the A.V of Mark 10 : 51, see RABBONI.

3175 (-ES) AG:498C 3. MEGISTAN (μεγιστάν), akin to *megistos*, greatest, the superlative
CB:1258A degree of *megas*, great, denotes chief men, nobles ; it is rendered " lords "
(-ES) in Mark 6 : 21, of nobles in Herod's entourage ; " princes " in Rev. 6 : 15 and 18 : 23, R.V. (A.V., " great men ").¶

B. Verbs.

2961 AG:458D 1. KURIEUŌ (κυριεύω) denotes to be lord of, to exercise lordship
CB:1256B over, Luke 22 : 25 ; Rom. 6 : 9, 14 ; 7 : 1 ; 14 : 9 ; 2 Cor. 1 : 24 ; 1 Tim. 6 : 15 ; see DOMINION, B, No. 1.¶

2634 AG:412C 2. KATAKURIEUŌ (κατακυριεύω), a strengthened form of No. 1, is
CB:1254A rendered " lording it " in 1 Pet. 5 : 3, R.V. : see DOMINION, B, No. 2.

C. Adjective.

2960 AG:458C KURIAKOS (κυριακός), from *kurios* (A, No. 1), signifies pertaining
CB:1256B to a lord or master ; ' lordly ' is not a legitimate rendering for its use in the N.T., where it is used only of Christ ; in 1 Cor. 11 : 20, of the Lord's Supper, or the Supper of the Lord (see FEAST) ; in Rev. 1 : 10, of the Day of the Lord (see DAY, No. 1).¶

LOSE, (Suffer) LOSS, LOST

622 AG:95A 1. APOLLUMI (ἀπόλλυμι) signifies (I) In the Active Voice, (*a*) to
CB:1237A destroy, destroy utterly, kill, e.g., Matt. 10 : 28 ; Mark 1 : 24 ; 9 : 22 ; (*b*) to lose utterly, e.g., Matt. 10 : 42, of losing a reward ; Luke 15 : 4 (1st part), of losing a sheep ; Luke 9 : 25, of losing oneself (of the loss of well-being hereafter) ; metaphorically, John 6 : 39, of failing to save ; 18 : 9, of Christ's not losing His own ; (II) in the Middle Voice, (*a*) to perish, of things, e.g., John 6 : 12 " (that nothing) be lost " ; of persons, e.g., Matt. 8 : 25, " we perish ; " of the loss of eternal life, usually (always in the R.V.)

* From Notes on Thessalonians by Hogg and Vine, p. 25.

translated to perish, John 3 : 16 ; 17 : 12, A.V., "is lost," R.V., "perished ;" 2 Cor. 4 : 3, "are perishing," A.V., "are lost" (see PERISH) ; (*b*) to be lost, e.g., Luke 15 : 4 (2nd part), "which is lost ;" metaphorically, from the relation between shepherd and flock, of spiritual destitution and alienation from God, Matt. 10 : 6, "(the) lost (sheep)" of the house of Israel ; Luke 19 : 10 (the perfect tense translated "lost" is here intransitive). See DESTROY.

2. ZĒMIOŌ (ζημιόω), to damage (akin to *zēmia*, damage, e.g., Acts **2210**
27 : 10, 21), is used in the N.T., in the Passive Voice, signifying to suffer **AG:338C CB:1273C**
loss, forfeit, lose, Matt. 16 : 26 ; Mark 8 : 36, of losing one's soul or life ; **(-OMAI)**
Luke 9 : 25, R.V., "forfeit (his own self)," A.V., "be cast away" (for the preceding verb see No. 1) ; 1 Cor. 3 : 15, "he shall suffer loss," i.e., at the Judgment-Seat of Christ (see ver. 13 with 2 Cor. 5 : 10) ; 2 Cor. 7 : 9, "(that) ye might suffer loss," R.V. (A.V., "might receive damage") ; though the Apostle did regret the necessity of making them sorry by his letter, he rejoiced that they were made sorry after a godly sort, and that they thus suffered no spiritual loss, which they would have done had their sorrow been otherwise than after a godly manner ; in Phil. 3 : 8, "I suffered the loss (of all things)," R.V., i.e., of all things which he formerly counted gain (especially those in verses 5 and 6, to which the article before "all things" points). See CAST, FORFEIT.¶

LOSS

1. ZĒMIA (ζημία), akin to No. 2, above, is used in Acts 27 : 10, R.V., **2209**
"loss" (A.V., "damage") ; ver. 21, A.V. and R.V., "loss," of ship and **AG:338C CB:1273C**
cargo ; in Phil. 3 : 7, 8 of the Apostle's estimate of the things which he formerly valued, and of all things on account of "the excellency of the knowledge of Christ Jesus."¶

2. APOBOLĒ (ἀποβολή), lit., casting away (*apo*, away, *ballō*, to cast), **580**
is translated "loss" in Acts 27 : 22 ; in Rom. 11 : 15, "casting away," of **AG:89A CB:—**
the temporary exclusion of the nation of Israel from its position of Divine favour, involving the reconciling of the world (i.e., the provision made through the gospel, which brings the world within the scope of reconciliation).¶

3. HĒTTĒMA (ἥττημα) denotes a defect, loss, Rom. 11 : 12, R.V., **2275**
"loss," A.V., "diminishing" (for the meaning of which in regard to **AG:349C CB:1250B**
Israel see No. 2) ; 1 Cor. 6 : 7, R.V., "defect" (A.V., "fault"). See DEFECT.

Note : For "suffer loss" see LOSE, No. 2.

LOT, LOTS

A. Noun.

KLĒROS (κλῆρος) denotes (*a*) an object used in casting or drawing **2819**
lots, which consisted of bits, or small tablets, of wood or stone (the pro- **AG:435B CB:1255B**
bable derivation is from *klaō*, to break) ; these were sometimes inscribed

with the names of persons, and were put into a receptacle or a garment (a lap, Prov. 16 : 33), from which they were cast, after being shaken together; he whose lot first fell out was the one chosen. The method was employed in a variety of circumstances, e.g., of dividing or assigning property, Matt. 27 : 35; Mark 15 : 24; Luke 23 : 34; John 19 : 24 (cp., e.g., Numb. 26 : 55); of appointing to office, Acts 1 : 26 (cp., e.g., 1 Sam. 10 : 20); for other occurrences in the O.T., see, e.g., Josh. 7 : 14 (the earliest instance in Scripture); Lev. 16 : 7–10; Esth. 3 : 7; 9 : 24; (*b*) what is obtained by lot, an allotted portion, e.g., of the ministry allotted to the Apostles, Acts 1 : 17, R.V., "portion," marg., "lot" (A.V., "part"); in some mss. ver. 25, A.V., "part" (the R.V. follows those which have *topos*, "place"); Acts 8 : 21; it is also used like *klēronomia*, an inheritance, in Acts 26 : 18, of what God has in grace assigned to the sanctified; so Col. 1 : 12; in 1 Pet. 5 : 3 it is used of those the spiritual care of, and charge over, whom is assigned to elders, R.V., "the charge allotted to you" (plural, lit., 'the charges'), A.V., "(God's) heritage." From *klēros* the word "clergy" is derived (a transposition in the application of the term). See CHARGE, No. 4.¶

B. Verb.

2975 AG:462B CB:1256C LANCHANŌ (λαγχάνω) denotes (*a*) to draw lots, John 19 : 24; (*b*) to obtain by lot, to obtain, Luke 1 : 9, "his lot was," lit., 'he received by lot,' i.e., by Divine appointment; Acts 1 : 17, of the portion allotted by the Lord to His Apostles in their ministry (cp. A, above); 2 Pet. 1 : 1, "that have obtained (a like precious faith)," i.e., by its being allotted to them, not by acquiring it for themselves, but by Divine grace (an act independent of human control as in the casting of lots). See OBTAIN.¶

Note: For divide by lot see DIVIDE.

LOUD

3173 AG:497C CB:1258A MEGAS (μέγας), great, is used, besides other meanings, of intensity, as, e.g., of the force of a voice, e.g., Matt. 27 : 46, 50; in the following the R.V. has "great" for the A.V., "loud," Rev. 5 : 2, 12; 6 : 10; 7 : 2, 10; 8 : 13; 10 : 3; 12 : 10; 14 : 7, 9, 15, 18. See GREAT.

LOVE (Noun and Verb)

A. Verbs.

25 AG:4B CB:1233B 1. AGAPAŌ (ἀγαπάω) and the corresponding noun *agapē* (B, No. 1 below) present "the characteristic word of Christianity, and since the Spirit of revelation has used it to express ideas previously unknown, enquiry into its use, whether in Greek literature or in the Septuagint, throws but little light upon its distinctive meaning in the N.T. Cp., however, Lev. 19 : 18; Deut. 6 : 5.

"*Agapē* and *agapaō* are used in the N T. (*a*) to describe the attitude of God toward His Son, John 17 : 26; the human race, generally, John 3 : 16; Rom 5 : 8; and to such as believe on the Lord Jesus Christ,

particularly, John 14 : 21 ; (*b*) to convey His will to His children concerning their attitude one toward another, John 13 : 34, and toward all men, 1 Thess. 3 : 12 ; 1 Cor. 16 : 14 ; 2 Pet. 1 : 7 ; (*c*) to express the essential nature of God, 1 John 4 : 8.

" Love can be known only from the actions it prompts. God's love is seen in the gift of His Son, 1 John 4 : 9, 10. But obviously this is not the love of complacency, or affection, that is, it was not drawn out by any excellency in its objects, Rom. 5 : 8. It was an exercise of the Divine will in deliberate choice, made without assignable cause save that which lies in the nature of God Himself, cp. Deut. 7 : 7, 8.

" Love had its perfect expression among men in the Lord Jesus Christ, 2 Cor. 5 : 14; Eph. 2 : 4 ; 3 : 19 ; 5 : 2 ; Christian love is the fruit of His Spirit in the Christian, Gal. 5 : 22.

" Christian love has God for its primary object, and expresses itself first of all in implicit obedience to His commandments, John 14 : 15, 21, 23 ; 15 : 10 ; 1 John 2 : 5 ; 5 : 3 ; 2 John 6. Self-will, that is, self-pleasing, is the negation of love to God.

" Christian love, whether exercised toward the brethren, or toward men generally, is not an impulse from the feelings, it does not always run with the natural inclinations, nor does it spend itself only upon those for whom some affinity is discovered. Love seeks the welfare of all, Rom. 15 : 2, and works no ill to any, 13 : 8–10 ; love seeks opportunity to do good to ' all men, and especially toward them that are of the household of the faith,' Gal. 6 : 10. See further 1 Cor. 13 and Col. 3 : 12–14."*

In respect of *agapaō* as used of God, it expresses the deep and constant love and interest of a perfect Being towards entirely unworthy objects, producing and fostering a reverential love in them towards the Giver, and a practical love towards those who are partakers of the same, and a desire to help others to seek the Giver. See BELOVED.

2. PHILEŌ (φιλέω) is to be distinguished from *agapaō* in this, that *phileō* more nearly represents tender affection. The two words are used for the love of the Father for the Son, John 3 : 35 (No. 1), and 5 : 20 (No. 2) ; for the believer, 14 : 21 (No. 1) and 16 : 27 (No. 2) ; both, of Christ's love for a certain disciple, 13 : 23 (No. 1), and 20 : 2 (No. 2). Yet the distinction between the two verbs remains, and they are never used indiscriminately in the same passage ; if each is used with reference to the same objects, as just mentioned, each word retains its distinctive and essential character. 5368 AG:859B CB:1264A

Phileō is never used in a command to men to love God ; it is, however, used as a warning in 1 Cor. 16 : 22 ; *agapaō* is used instead, e.g., Matt. 22 : 37 ; Luke 10 : 27 ; Rom. 8 : 28 ; 1 Cor. 8 : 3 ; 1 Pet. 1 : 8 ; 1 John 4 : 21. The distinction between the two verbs finds a conspicuous instance in the narrative of John 21 : 15–17. The context itself indicates that

* From Notes on Thessalonians by Hogg and Vine, p. 105.

agapaō in the first two questions suggests the love that values and esteems (cp. Rev. 12 : 11). It is an unselfish love, ready to serve. The use of *phileō* in Peter's answers and the Lord's third question, conveys the thought of cherishing the Object above all else, of manifesting an affection characterised by constancy, from the motive of the highest veneration. See also Trench, Syn., §xii.

Again, to love (*phileō*) life, from an undue desire to preserve it, forgetful of the real object of living, meets with the Lord's reproof, John 12 : 25. On the contrary, to love life (*agapaō*) as used in 1 Pet. 3 : 10, is to consult the true interests of living. Here the word *phileō* would be quite inappropriate.

2309 *Note* : In Mark 12 : 38, A.V., *thelō*, to wish, is translated " love " (R.V.,
AG:354D
CB:1271C " desire ").

B. Nouns.

26 1. AGAPĒ (ἀγάπη), the significance of which has been pointed out in
AG:5B
CB:1233B connection with A, No. 1, is always rendered " love " in the R.V. where the A.V. has " charity," a rendering nowhere used in the R.V. ; in Rom. 14 : 15, where the A.V. has " charitably," the R.V., adhering to the translation of the noun, has " in love."

Note : In the two statements in 1 John 4 : 8 and 16, " God is love," both are used to enjoin the exercise of love on the part of believers. While the former introduces a declaration of the mode in which God's love has been manifested (vv. 9, 10), the second introduces a statement of the identification of believers with God in character, and the issue at the Judgment-Seat hereafter (ver. 17), an identification represented ideally in the sentence " as He is, so are we in this world."

5363 2. PHILANTHRŌPIA (φιλανθρωπία) denotes, lit., love for man
AG:858D
CB:1264A (*phileō* and *anthrōpos*, man) ; hence, kindness, Acts 28 : 2 ; in Tit. 3 : 4, " (His) love toward man."¶ Cp. the adverb *philanthrōpōs*, humanely, kindly, Acts 27 : 3.¶ See KINDNESS.

Note : For *philarguria*, love of money, 1 Tim. 6 : 10, see MONEY (love of). For *philadelphia*, see BROTHER, Note (1).

LOVE-FEASTS

26 AGAPĒ (ἀγάπη) is used in the plural in Jude 12, and in some mss. in
AG:5B
CB:1233B 2 Pet. 2 : 13 ; R.V. marg., " many ancient authorities read ' deceivings,' " (*apatais*) ; so the A.V. These love-feasts arose from the common meals of the early churches (cp. 1 Cor. 11 : 21). They may have had this origin in the private meals of Jewish households, with the addition of the observance of the Lord's Supper. There were, however, similar common meals among the pagan religious brotherhoods. The evil dealt with at Corinth (l.c.) became enhanced by the presence of immoral persons, who degraded the feasts into wanton banquets, as mentioned in 2 Pet. and Jude. In later times the *agapē* became detached from the Lord's Supper.

LOVELY

PROSPHILĒS (προσφιλής), pleasing, agreeable, lovely (*pros*, toward, **4375**
phileō, to love), occurs in Phil. 4 : 8.¶ In the Sept., Esth. 5 : 1 (3rd **AG:720B CB:—**
sentence).¶

LOVER

This is combined with other words, forming compound adjectives as
follows: **5377**
1. PHILOTHEOS (φιλόθεος), a lover of God, 2 Tim. 3 : 4.¶ **AG:860C CB:1264B**
2. PHILOXENOS (φιλόξενος), loving strangers (*xenia*, hospitality), **5382**
translated "a lover of hospitality" in Tit. 1 : 8, A.V. (R.V., "given to **AG:860D CB:1264B**
h."); elsewhere, in 1 Tim. 3 : 2; 1 Pet. 4 : 9. See HOSPITALITY.¶
3. PHILAGATHOS (φιλάγαθος), loving that which is good (*agathos*), **5358 AG:858B**
Tit. 1 : 8, "a lover of good," R.V.¶ **CB:1264A**

Note: The negative *aphilagathos* is found in 2 Tim. 3 : 3, "no lovers of **865**
good."¶ **AG:126C**

4. PHILARGUROS (φιλάργυρος), loving money (*arguros*, silver), **5366 AG:859A**
translated "lovers of money" in Luke 16 : 14; 2 Tim. 3 : 2, R.V. (A.V., **CB:1264A**
"covetous"). See COVETOUS.¶ **5367**
5. PHILAUTOS (φίλαυτος), loving oneself, 2 Tim. 3 : 2, "R.V.¶ **AG:859A CB:1264A**
6. PHILĒDONOS (φιλήδονος), loving pleasure (*hēdonē*, pleasure), **5369**
2 Tim. 3 : 4, "lovers of pleasure."¶ **AG:859C CB:1264A**

Note: For loving warmly, Rom. 12 : 10, see AFFECTION, B, No. 2.¶
For *aphilarguros*, no lover of money, 1 Tim. 3 : 3, R.V., and Heb. 13 : 5, **866**
R.V., see COVETOUS.¶ **AG:126C CB:—**

LOW (to bring, to make), LOW (estate, degree)

A. Verb.

TAPEINOŌ (ταπεινόω), to bring low, to humble, is translated "shall **5013**
be brought low" in Luke 3 : 5. See HUMBLE. **AG:804C CB:1271A**

B. Adjective.

TAPEINOS (ταπεινός) denotes of low degree or estate, Rom. 12 : 16, **5011**
"things that are lowly," R.V. (A.V., "men of low estate"). See BASE, **AG:804A CB:1271A**
DEGREE, ESTATE, HUMBLE, LOWLY.

C. Noun.

TAPEINŌSIS (ταπείνωσις), abasement, humiliation, low estate, is **5014**
translated "low estate" in Luke 1 : 48; in Jas. 1 : 10, "that he is made **AG:805A CB:1271A**
low," lit., 'in his abasement.' See HUMILIATION.

LOWER (Adjective, and Verb, to make), LOWEST

A. Adjectives.

1. KATŌTEROS (κατώτερος), the comparative degree of *katō*, beneath, **2737**
is used in Eph. 4 : 9, of Christ's descent into "the lower parts of the **AG:425A CB:1254C**
earth;" two of the various interpretations of this phrase are (1) that the
earth is in view in contrast to heaven, (2) that the region is that of Hades,

the Sheol of the O.T. Inasmuch as the passage is describing the effects not merely of the Inoarnation but of the Death and Resurrection of Christ, the second interpretation is to be accepted; cp., e.g., Ps. 16 : 10; 63 : 9; where the Sept. has the superlative; 139 : 15; Acts 2 : 31. Moreover, as Westcott says, it is most unlikely that the phrase would be used to describe the earth. The word *merē* (plural of *meros*), "parts," would have no force in such a meaning.¶

2078 AG:313D CB:1246C 2. ESCHATOS (*ἔσχατος*), last, utmost, lowest, is rendered "lowest" in Luke 14 : 9, 10, of the lowest place at a meal. See LAST.

B. Verb.

1642 AG:248B CB:— ELATTOŌ (*ἐλαττόω*) denotes to make less (*elattōn*, less), and is used in the Active Voice in Heb. 2 : 7, "Thou madest (Him) . . . lower," and in the Passive in ver. 9, "was made . . . lower," and John 3 : 30, "(I must) decrease," (lit., 'be made less').¶

For LOWER (Verb, to let down) see LET DOWN, No. 2 (*d*)

LOWLINESS, LOWLY

A. Noun.

5012 AG:804C CB:1271A TAPEINOPHROSUNĒ (*ταπεινοφροσύνη*), lowliness of mind, humbleness, is translated "lowliness" or "lowliness of mind" in Acts 20 : 19, R.V.; Eph. 4 : 2; Phil. 2 : 3. See HUMBLENESS OF MIND.

B. Adjective.

5011 AG:804A CB:1271A TAPEINOS (*ταπεινός*), low, lowly: see HUMBLE and LOW, B.

LOWRING (to be)

4768 AG:771D CB:— STUGNAZŌ (*στυγνάζω*), to have a gloomy, sombre appearance (akin to *stugnos*, sombre, gloomy, from a root *stug*—, to hate; cp. *stugētos*, hateful, Tit. 3 : 3), is said of the human countenance, Mark 10 : 22, R.V., "his countenance fell" (A.V., "he was sad"); of the sky, Matt. 16 : 3, "lowring." See COUNTENANCE, Note (3).¶ In the Sept., Ezek. 27 : 35; 28 : 19; 32 : 10.¶

LUCRE (filthy)

A. Noun.

2771 AG:429C CB:1255A KERDOS (*κέρδος*), gain (cp. *kerdainō*, to gain, get gain), is translated "gain" in Phil. 1 : 21 and 3 : 7; "lucre" in Tit. 1 : 11 (preceded by *aischros*, filthy). See GAIN.¶

B. Adjective.

146 AG:25A CB:1234A AISCHROKERDĒS (*αἰσχροκερδής*) denotes greedy of base gains (*aischros*, and A, as above), 1 Tim. 3 : 8, "greedy of filthy lucre;" so the R.V. in Tit. 1 : 7, A.V., "given to) filthy lucre." In some mss. 1 Tim 3 : 3.¶

147 AG:25B CB:— AISCHROKERDŌS (*αἰσχροκερδῶς*) denotes 'from eagerness for base gain,' 1 Pet. 5 : 2, "for filthy lucre."¶

LUKEWARM

CHLIAROS (χλιαρός), tepid, warm (akin to *chliō*, to become warm, 5513
not found in the N.T. or Sept.), is used metaphorically in Rev. 3 : 16, of AG:882C CB:1239C
the state of the Laodicean church, which afforded no refreshment to the
Lord, such as is ministered naturally by either cold or hot water.¶

LUMP

PHURAMA (φύραμα) denotes that which is mixed or kneaded (*phuraō*, 5445
to mix) ; hence, a lump, either of dough, Rom. 11 : 16 (cp. Numb. 15 : 21) ; AG:869A CB:1264C
1 Cor. 5 : 6, 7 ; Gal. 5 : 9 (see under LEAVEN) ; of potter's clay, Rom.
9 : 21.¶

For LUNATIC see EPILEPTIC

LUST (Noun and Verb)

A. Nouns.

1. EPITHUMIA (ἐπιθυμία) denotes strong desire of any kind, the 1939
various kinds being frequently specified by some adjective (see below). AG:293B CB:1246B
The word is used of a good desire in Luke 22 : 15 ; Phil. 1 : 23, and 1 Thess. 2 : 17 only. Everywhere else it has a bad sense. In Rom. 6 : 12 the injunction against letting sin reign in our mortal body to obey the lust thereof, refers to those evil desires which are ready to express themselves in bodily activity. They are equally the lusts of the flesh, Rom. 13 : 14; Gal. 5 : 16, 24 ; Eph. 2 : 3 ; 2 Pet. 2 : 18 ; 1 John 2 : 16, a phrase which describes the emotions of the soul, the natural tendency towards things evil. Such lusts are not necessarily base and immoral, they may be refined in character, but are evil if inconsistent with the will of God.

Other descriptions besides those already mentioned are :—" of the mind," Eph. 2 : 3 ; " evil (desire)," Col. 3 : 5 ; " the passion of," 1 Thess. 4 : 5, R.V. ; " foolish and hurtful," 1 Tim. 6 : 9 ; " youthful," 2 Tim. 2 : 22 ; " divers," 2 Tim. 3 : 6 and Tit. 3 : 3 ; " their own," 2 Tim. 4 : 3 ; 2 Pet. 3 : 3 ; Jude 16 ; " worldly," Tit. 2 : 12 ; " his own," Jas. 1 : 14 ; " your former," 1 Pet. 1 : 14, R.V. ; " fleshly," 2 : 11 ; " of men," 4 : 2 ; " of defilement," 2 Pet. 2 : 10 ; " of the eyes," 1 John 2 : 16 ; of the world (" thereof "), ver. 17 ; " their own ungodly," Jude 18. In Rev. 18 : 14 " (the fruits) which thy soul lusted after " is, lit., ' of thy soul's lust.' See DESIRE, A, No. 1 (where associated words are noted).

2. OREXIS (ὄρεξις), lit., a reaching or stretching after (akin to 3715
oregomai, to stretch oneself out, reach after), a general term for every kind AG:580A CB:1261A
of desire, is used in Rom. 1 : 27, " lust."¶

3. HĒDONĒ (ἡδονή), pleasure, is translated " lusts," in the A.V. of 2237 AG:344B
Jas. 4 : 1, 3 (R.V., " pleasures "). See PLEASURE. CB:1249C

Note : In 1 Thess. 4 : 5, A.V., *pathos*, passion (R.V., " passion "), is 3806 AG:602D
translated " lust," which is the better rendering of the next word CB:1262C

EPITHUMETES *epithumia*, rendered " concupiscence." *Pathos* is described by Trench as
1938 AG:293B " the diseased condition out of which *epithumia* springs." In 1 Cor. 10: 6
CB:— *epithumētēs*, a luster after, is rendered to lust.

B. Verb.

1937 AG:293A EPITHUMEŌ (ἐπιθυμέω), akin to A, No. 1, has the same twofold
CB:1246B meaning as the noun, namely (*a*) to desire, used of the Holy Spirit against the flesh, Gal. 5 : 17 (see below) ; of the Lord Jesus, Luke 22 : 15, " I have desired ; " of the holy angels, 1 Pet. 1 : 12 ; of good men, for good things, Matt. 13 : 17 ; 1 Tim. 3 : 1 ; Heb. 6 : 11 ; of men, for things without moral quality, Luke 15 : 16 ; 16 : 21 ; 17 : 22 ; Rev. 9 : 6 ; (*b*) of evil desires, in respect of which it is translated to lust in Matt. 5 : 28 ; 1 Cor. 10 : 6 ; Gal. 5 : 17 (1st part ; see below) ; Jas. 4 : 2 ; to covet, Acts 20 : 23 ; Rom. 7 : 7 ; 13 : 9. See COVET, DESIRE, B, No. 2.¶

Notes : (1) in Gal. 5 : 17, in the statement, " the flesh lusteth against the Spirit, and the Spirit against the flesh," the Holy Spirit is intended, as in the preceding verse. To walk by the Spirit involves the opposition here referred to. The verb " lusteth " is not repeated in the second part of the statement, but must in some way be supplied. Since in modern English the word " lust " is used exclusively in a bad sense, it is unsuitable as a translation of *epithumeō*, where the word is used in a good sense. As the rendering " desire " is used of the Lord Jesus (as mentioned above), it may be best so understood here in respect of the Holy Spirit.

1971 AG:297D (2) In James 4 : 5 the R.V. translates correctly in giving two questions,
CB:1246A each of a rhetorical character, asked by way of remonstrance. The first draws attention to the fact that it is impossible for the Scripture to speak in vain ; the second to the impossibility that the Holy Spirit, whom God has caused to dwell in the believer, should " long (unto envying)," *epipotheō* (A.V., " lust "). Here again, not the human spirit is in view, but the
LUXURY Spirit of God ; cp. 1 Cor. 6 : 19. See LONG.

See DELICATELY

For LYING (falsehood) see LIE, and for LYING (in wait) see LIE IN WAIT.

MAD, MADNESS

A. Verbs.

1. MAINOMAI (μαίνομαι), to rage, be mad, is translated by the verb 3105 AG:486B
to be mad in John 10 : 20 ; Acts 12 : 15 ; 26 : 24, 25 ; 1 Cor. 14 : 23 ; see CB:1257B
BESIDE ONESELF, No. 2.

2. EMMAINOMAI (ἐμμαίνομαι), an intensive form of No. 1, prefixed 1693 AG:255A
by *en*, in, implying fierce rage, to be furious against ; it is rendered " being CB:—
exceedingly mad " in Acts 26 : 11 (cp. 9 : 1).¶

B. Nouns.

1. MANIA (μανία), akin to A, and transliterated into English, denotes 3130 AG:490D
frenzy, madness, Acts 26 : 24 " (thy much learning doth turn thee to) CB:1257C
madness," R.V. ; A.V., " (doth make thee) mad."¶

2. ANOIA (ἄνοια), lit., without understanding (*a*, negative, *nous*, mind, 454 AG:70D
understanding), denotes folly, 2 Tim. 3 : 9, and this finding its expression CB:1235C
in violent rage, Luke 6 : 11. See FOLLY.¶

3. PARAPHRONIA (παραφρονία), madness (from *para*, contrary to, 3913 AG:623C
and *phrēn*, the mind), is used in 2 Pet. 2 : 16.¶ Cp. *paraphroneō*, 2 Cor. CB:—
11 : 23, 'I speak like one distraught.'¶

MADE (be)

A. Verbs.

1. GINOMAI (γίνομαι), to become, is sometimes translated by the 1096 AG:158A
Passive Voice of the verb to make, e.g., Matt. 9 : 16 ; John 1 : 3 (three CB:1248B
times), 10 ; 8 : 33 ; Rom. 11 : 9 ; 1 Cor. 1 : 30 ; 3 : 13 ; 4 : 9, 13 ; Eph. 2 : 13 ; 3 : 7 ; Phil. 2 : 7 (but R.V. marg., " becoming ") ; Col. 1 : 23, 25 ; Heb. 5 : 5 ; 6 : 4 ; 7 : 12, 16, 21, 26 ; 11 : 3 ; Jas. 3 : 9 ; 1 Pet. 2 : 7. In many places the R.V. translates otherwise, and chiefly by the verb to become, e.g., Matt. 25 : 6, " there is ; " 27 : 24, " was arising ; " John 1 : 14, " became ; " John 2 : 9, " become ; " Rom. 1 : 3, " born ; " 2 : 25, " is become ; " 10 : 20, " became ; " Gal. 3 : 13, " having become ; " 4 : 4, " born " (twice) ; Heb. 3 : 14, " are become ; " 7 : 22, " hath . . . become."

2. KEIMAI (κεῖμαι), to lie, is sometimes used as the Passive Voice of 2749 AG:426C
tithēmi, to put ; it is translated " is (not) made " in 1 Tim. 1 : 9, of the CB:1254C
Law, where a suitable rendering would be ' is (not) enacted.' 1080 AG:155B

Notes : (1) In 2 Pet. 2 : 12, A.V., the verb *gennaō*, to beget, in the CB:1248A

Passive Voice, to be born, is translated " made " (R.V., " born "). (2) In Luke 3 : 5, A.V. (3rd statement), the future tense of *eimi*, to be, is translated " shall be made " (R.V., " shall become ") ; in the next sentence there is nothing in the original representing " *shall be* made ". (3) In Acts 16 : 13, A.V., the infinitive mood of *eimi*, to be, is translated " to be made " (of prayer), R.V., " there was (a place of prayer)." (4) For the translation of words in which the Eng. " made " forms a part of another verb, see under those words, e.g., CONFESSION, KNOWN, LIKE, LOW, PAYMENT, RICH, SUBJECT.

B. Noun.

4161 AG:683B CB:1265C POIĒMA (ποίημα), whence Eng., poem, denotes that which is made (from *poieō*, to do, make), Rom. 1 : 20, " the things that are made ; " Eph. 2 : 10, " (His) workmanship."¶

MAGISTRATE

4755 AG:770C CB:1270A 1. STRATĒGOS (στρατηγός), besides its application to the captain of the Temple (see CAPTAIN), denotes a magistrate or governor, Acts 16 : 20, 22, 35, 36, 38. These were, in Latin terminology, the *duumviri* or *prætores*, so called in towns which were Roman colonies. They were attended by lictors or " serjeants," who executed their orders. In the circumstances of Acts 16 they exceeded their powers, in giving orders for Roman " citizens " to be scourged ; hence they became suppliants. See CAPTAIN.

758 AG:113D CB:1237B 2. ARCHŌN (ἄρχων), a ruler, denotes, in Luke 12 : 58, a local authority, a magistrate, acting in the capacity of one who received complaints, and possessing higher authority than the judge, to whom the magistrate remits the case. See CHIEF, PRINCE, RULER.

746 AG:111D CB:1237B *Notes :* (1) In Luke 12 : 11, A.V., *archē*, a beginning, rule, principality, is translated " magistrates ; " the word, however, denotes rulers in general : hence the R.V., " rulers." (2) For the A.V. of Tit. 3 : 1, " to obey magistrates," see OBEY, B, No. 3.

MAGNIFICENCE

3168 AG:496D CB:1258A MEGALEIOTĒS (μεγαλειότης) denotes splendour, magnificence (from *megaleios*, magnificent, " mighty," Acts 2 : 11, *megas*, great), translated " magnificence " in Acts 19 : 27, of the splendour of the goddess Diana. In Luke 9 : 43, R.V. (A.V., " mighty power ") ; in 2 Pet. 1 : 16, " majesty." In the papyri writings it is frequent as a ceremonial title.¶

MAGNIFY

3170 AG:497A CB:1258A MEGALUNŌ (μεγαλύνω), to make great (*megas*), is translated to magnify in Luke 1 : 46 ; in ver. 58, R.V., " had magnified (His mercy)," A.V., " had shewed great (mercy) ; " Acts 5 : 13 ; 10 : 46 ; 19 : 17 ; 2 Cor. 10 : 15, R.V. (A.V., " we shall be enlarged "), i.e., by their faith in its practical effect he will be so assisted as to enlarge the scope of his Gospel ministry and carry its message to regions beyond them ; in Phil. 1 : 20.

of the magnifying of Christ by him in his body, i.e., in all his activities and ways. In Matt. 23 : 5, it signifies to enlarge. See ENLARGE.¶

Note : In Rom. 11 : 13, A.V., the verb *doxazō*, to glorify, is translated **1392**
" I magnify (my office)," R.V., " I glorify (my ministry)." See GLORIFY. **AG:204C CB:1242B**

MAID, MAIDEN, MAIDSERVANT

1. PAIS (παῖς), a child, denotes a maid or maiden in Luke 8 : 51 and **3816**
54, R.V., " maiden " in both places. See CHILD, MANSERVANT, SERVANT, **AG:604C CB:1261C**
SON, YOUNG MAN.

2. PAIDISKĒ (παιδίσκη), a diminutive of No. 1, is translated " maid ", **3814**
" maids," in the A.V. and R.V. in Mark 14 : 66, 69 ; Luke 22 : 56 ; in **AG:604B CB:1261C**
the R.V. (A.V., " damsel "), in Matt. 26 : 69 ; John 18 : 17 ; Acts 12 : 13 ; 16 : 16 ; in Luke 12 : 45, " maidservants " (A.V. " maidens ") ; in Gal. 4 : 22, 23, 30, 31, R.V., " handmaid " (A.V., " bondmaid " or " bondwoman "). See BONDMAID, DAMSEL.¶

3. KORASION (κοράσιον), a colloquial, familiar term, is translated **2877**
" maid " in Matt. 9 : 24, 25, A.V. (R.V., " damsel "). See DAMSEL, No. 1. **AG:444B CB:1255C**

MAIMED

1. ANAPĒROS, or ANAPEIROS (ἀνάπηρος), crippled, maimed (from **376 AG:59C**
ana, up, and *pēros*, disabled in a limb), is found in Luke 14 : 13, 21.¶ **CB:—**

2. KULLOS (κυλλός) denotes crooked, crippled (akin to *kuliō*, to roll) : **2948**
in Matt. 15 : 30, 31, translated " maimed " ; so in 18 : 8, A.V. (R.V., **AG:457B CB:1256B**
" halt ") and Mark 9 : 43 (A.V. and R.V.). See HALT.¶

For MAINSAIL see FORESAIL

MAINTAIN

PROISTĒMI (προΐστημι), to preside, rule, also means to maintain, **4291 AG:707A**
Tit. 3 : 8 and 14, " to maintain (good works)," R.V. marg., " profess honest **CB:—**
occupations " (A.V., marg. . . " trades "). The usage of the phrase *kala erga* (good works) in the Pastoral Epistles is decisive for the rendering " good works," here. See OVER (to be), RULE.

MAJESTY

1. MEGALEIOTĒS (μεγαλειότης) : see MAGNIFICENCE. **3168 AG:496D**

2. MEGALŌSUNĒ (μεγαλωσύνη), from *megas*, great, denotes greatness, **CB:1258A**
majesty ; it is used of God the Father, signifying His greatness and **3172**
dignity, in Heb. 1 : 3, " the Majesty (on high)," and 8 : 1, " the Majesty **AG:497B CB:1258A**
(in the Heavens) ; " and in an ascription of praise acknowledging the attributes of God in Jude 25.¶

MAKE

1. POIEŌ (ποιέω), to do, to make, is used in the latter sense (*a*) of **4160 AG:680D**
constructing or producing anything, of the creative acts of God, e.g., **CB:1265C**

Matt. 19 : 4 (2nd part); Acts 17 : 24; of the acts of human beings, e.g., Matt. 17 : 4; Acts 9 : 39; (*b*) with nouns denoting a state or condition, to be the author of, to cause, e.g., peace, Eph. 2 : 15; Jas. 3 : 18; stumblingblocks, Rom. 16 : 17; (*c*) with nouns involving the idea of action (or of something accomplished by action), so as to express the idea of the verb more forcibly (the Middle Voice is commonly used in this respect, suggesting the action as being of special interest to the doer); for the Active Voice see, e.g., Mark 2 : 23, of making one's way, where the idea is not that the disciples made a path through the standing corn, but simply that they went, the phrase being equivalent to going, "(they began) as they went (to pluck the ears);" other instances of the Active are Rev. 13 : 13, 14; 16 : 14; 19 : 20; for the Middle Voice (the 'dynamic' or 'subjective' Middle), see, e.g., John 14 : 23, "will make Our abode;" in Acts 20 : 24, "none of these things move me," lit., 'I make account of none of these things;' 25 : 17, "I made no delay," R.V.; Rom. 15 : 26; Eph. 4 : 16; Heb. 1 : 2; 2 Pet. 1 : 10; (*d*) to make ready or prepare, e.g., a dinner, Luke 14 : 12; a supper, John 12 : 2; (*e*) to acquire, provide a thing for oneself, Matt. 25 : 16; Luke 19 : 18; (*f*) to render or make one or oneself anything, or cause a person or thing to become something, e.g., Matt. 4 : 19; 12 : 16, "make (Him known);" John 5 : 11, 15, to make whole; 16 : 2, lit., 'they shall make (you put out of the synagogue);' Eph. 2 : 14; Heb. 1 : 7; to change one thing into another, Matt. 21 : 13; John 2 : 16; 4 : 46; 1 Cor. 6 : 15; (*g*) to constitute one anything, e.g., Acts 2 : 36; (*h*) to declare one or oneself anything, John 5 : 18, "making (Himself equal with God);" 8 : 53; 10 : 33; 19 : 7, 12; 1 John 1 : 10; 5 : 10; (*i*) to make one do a thing, e.g., Luke 5 : 34; John 6 : 10; Rev. 3 : 9. See DO, No. 1, and other renderings there.

5087 AG:815D CB:1272C 2. TITHĒMI (τίθημι), to put, is used in the same way as No. 1 (*f*), Matt. 22 : 44; Mark 12 : 36; Luke 20 : 43; Acts 2 : 35; 1 Cor. 9 : 18 (of making the Gospel without charge); Heb. 1 : 13; 10 : 13; 2 Pet. 2 : 6; as No. 1 (*g*), Acts 20 : 28; Rom. 4 : 17. See APPOINT, No. 3.

1303 (-THEMAI) AG:189D CB:1241B 3. DIATITHĒMI (διατίθημι), to covenant, is rendered "I will make" (the noun *diathēkē*, a covenant, being expressed additionally), in the Middle Voice, in Acts 3 : 25; Heb. 8 : 10 and 10 : 16, lit., 'I will covenant' (see R.V., marg.). See APPOINT, No. 4.

2525 AG:390B CB:1254C 4. KATHISTĒMI (καθίστημι), to set down, set in order, appoint, is used in the same way as No. 1 (*g*) in Acts 7 : 10, 27, 35; Heb. 7 : 28, A.V. (R.V., "appointeth"); as No. 1 (*f*) in Rom. 5 : 19 (twice). See APPOINT, No. 2.

4921 AG:790C CB:1270C 5. SUNISTĒMI (συνίστημι), to commend, prove, establish, is used in Gal. 2 : 18, much as in No. 1 (*g*), "I make myself (a transgressor)," i.e., 'I constitute (or prove) myself etc.' See APPROVE, No. 2.

1325 AG:192C CB:1241C 6. DIDŌMI (δίδωμι), to give, is used in 2 Thess. 3 : 9 in much the same sense as No. 1 (*g*), "to make (ourselves an ensample);" in Rev. 3 : 9

(1st part), R.V., " I will give," the sense is virtually the same as *poieō* in
the 2nd part of the verse, see No. 1 (*i*). See GIVE.

7. EPITELEŌ (ἐπιτελέω), to complete, is translated " to make " in 2005 AG:302B
Heb. 8 : 5 (1st part), R.V. marg., " complete " [in the 2nd part No. 1 is CB:1246A
used in sense (*a*)]. See ACCOMPLISH. (-EISTHAI)

8. SUNTELEŌ (συντελέω), to end, fulfil, is translated " I will make " 4931 AG:792A
in Heb. 8 : 8 :, said of the new covenant. See END. CB:1271A

9. EIMI (εἰμί), to be, is translated " make " in Mark 12 : 42, lit., 'which 1510 AG:222D
is (a farthing).' CB:1243A

10. PROSPOIEŌ (προσποιέω), primarily, to claim, is used in the Middle 4364
Voice with the meaning to make as if, in Luke 24 : 28, of the Lord's action (-OMAI) AG:718B
regarding the two on the way to Emmaus.¶ In the Sept., 1 Sam. 21 : 13 ; CB:—
Job 19 : 14.¶

11. KATECHŌ (κατέχω), to hold fast (*kata*, down, intensive, *echō*, to 2722
hold), is used of making for a place, in Acts 27 : 40, R.V., " they made AG:422C CB:1254B
for " (A.V., " they made toward "). See HOLD.

12. PROKATARTIZŌ (προκαταρτίζω), to render fit (fitted ; *artos*, a 4294 AG:707C
joint) beforehand, is used in 2 Cor. 9 : 5, " to make up beforehand."¶ CB:1266C

Notes : (1) In Heb. 9 : 2, A.V., *kataskeuazō*, to prepare, is translated KATASKEUAZō 2680
" made " (R.V., " prepared "). (2) In Eph. 2 : 15, A.V., *ktizō*, to create, AG:418B
is translated " make " (R.V., " create "). (3) In Acts 26 : 16, A.V., CB:1254B
procheirizō, to determine, choose, is translated " make " (R.V., KTIZō 2936
" appoint "). (4) In Gal. 3 : 16, A.V., *erō*, to speak, is translated " were AG:455C
. . . made " (R.V., " were . . . spoken "). (5) In Luke 14 : 31, A.V., CB:1256B PROCHEIRIZō
sumballō, to meet with, in hostile sense, is rendered in combination with 4400 (-OMAI)
the phrase *eis polemon*, in war, " to make war ; " R.V., " to encounter AG:724C CB:1266C
(in war)." (6) In Rom. 14 : 19 " the things which make for peace " is, EIRō (ERō)
lit., ' the things of peace.' (7) In Acts 22 : 1 the verb " I make " repre- After 1518
sents no word in the original, lit., ' hear now my defence unto you.' AG:— CB:—
(8) The Eng. verb to make forms with many other verbs a rendering of SUMBALLō
single Greek verbs which are given under the respective headings. (9) 4820 AG:777B
For " made," Luke 19 : 16, R.V., see GAIN, *Note* (1). CB:—

MAKER

DĒMIOURGOS (δημιουργός), lit., one who works for the people (from 1217
dēmos, people, *ergon*, work ; an ancient inscription speaks of the magis- AG:178D CB:1240C
trates of Tarsus as *dēmiourgoi* : the word was formerly used thus regarding several towns in Greece ; it is also found used of an artist), came to denote, in general usage, a builder or maker, and is used of God as the Maker of the Heavenly City, Heb. 11 : 10. In that passage the first word of the two, *technitēs*, denotes an architect, designer, the second, *dēmiourgos*, is the actual Framer ; the city is the archetype of the earthly one which God chose for His earthly people.¶ Cp. *ktistēs*, creator.

For TENT-MAKER see Vol. IV, p. 1130

MALE

730 AG:109D CB:1237C ARSĒN or ARRĒN (ἄρσην) is translated " men " in Rom. 1 : 27 (three times) ; " man child " in Rev. 12 : 5 (ver. 13 in some mss.) ; " male " in Matt. 19 : 4 ; Mark 10 : 6 ; Luke 2 : 23 ; Gal. 3 : 28, " (there can be no) male (and female)," R.V., i.e., sex-distinction does not obtain in Christ ; sex is no barrier either to salvation or the development of Christian graces. See MAN.¶

MALEFACTOR

2557 AG:398B CB:1253B 1. KAKOURGOS (κακοῦργος), an adjective, lit., evil-working (*kakos*, evil, *ergon*, work), is used as a noun, translated " malefactor(–s) " in Luke 23 : 32, 33, 39, and in the R.V. in 2 Tim. 2 : 9 (A.V., " evil doer "). See EVIL, B, Note (1). In the Sept., Prov. 21 : 15.¶

2555 AG:397C CB:1253B 2. KAKOPOIOS (κακοποιός), an adjective, lit., doing evil, is used in 1 Pet. 2 : 12, 14 ; 3 : 16 (in some mss.) ; 4 : 15. See EVIL, B, No. 5.¶

MALICE, MALICIOUSNESS, MALICIOUS

2549 AG:397A CB:1253A KAKIA (κακία), badness in quality (the opposite of *aretē*, excellence), " the vicious character generally " (Lightfoot), is translated " malice " in 1 Cor. 5 : 8 ; 14 : 20 ; Eph. 4 : 31 ; Col. 3 : 8 ; Tit. 3 : 3 ; 1 Pet. 2 : 1, A.V. (R.V., " wickedness " ; marg., " malice ") ; " maliciousness " in Rom. 1 : 29 ; in 1 Pet. 2 : 16, A.V. (R.V., " wickedness ; " marg., " malice "). Elsewhere, Matt. 6 : 34 ; Acts 8 : 22 ; Jas. 1 : 21 (R.V. marg., " malice "). See EVIL, B, No. 1.¶

4190 AG:690D CB:1266A *Note :* In 2 John 10, A.V., *ponēros*, evil, wicked (see EVIL, A, No. 2), is translated " malicious " (R.V., " wicked ").

MALIGNITY

2550 AG:397B CB:— KAKOĒTHEIA (κακοήθεια), lit., bad manner or character (*kakos*, bad, *ēthos*, manner), hence, an evil disposition that tends to put the worst construction on everything, malice, malevolence, craftiness, occurs in Rom. 1 : 29, as the accompaniment of *dolos*, guile.¶

MAMMON

3126 AG:490A CB:1257C MAMŌNAS (μαμωνᾶς), a common Aramaic word for riches, akin to a Hebrew word signifying to be firm, stedfast (whence Amen), hence, that which is to be trusted ; Gesenius regards it as derived from a Heb. word signifying " treasure " (Gen. 43 : 23) ; it is personified in Matt. 6 : 24 ; Luke 16 : 9, 11, 13.¶

MAN (see also MEN)

444 AG:68B CB:1236A 1. ANTHRŌPOS (ἄνθρωπος) is used (*a*) generally, of a human being, male or female, without reference to sex or nationality, e.g., Matt. 4 : 4 ; 12 : 35 ; John 2 : 25 ; (*b*) in distinction from God, e.g., Matt. 19 : 6 ;

John 10 : 33 ; Gal. 1 : 11 ; Col. 3 : 23 ; (*c*) in distinction from animals etc., e.g., Luke 5 : 10 ; (*d*) sometimes, in the plural, of men and women, people, e.g., Matt. 5 : 13, 16 ; in Mark 11 : 2 and 1 Tim. 6 : 16, lit., 'no one of men ;' (*e*) in some instances with a suggestion of human frailty and imperfection, e.g., 1 Cor. 2 : 5 ; Acts 14 : 15 (2nd part) ; (*f*) in the phrase translated "after man," "after the manner of men," "as a man" (A.V.), lit. 'according to (*kata*) man,' is used only by the Apostle Paul, of "(1) the practices of fallen humanity, 1 Cor. 3 : 3 ; (2) anything of human origin, Gal. 1 : 11 ; (3) the laws that govern the administration of justice among men, Rom. 3 : 5 ; (4) the standard generally accepted among men, Gal. 3 : 15 ; (5) an illustration not drawn from Scripture, 1 Cor. 9 : 8 ; (6) probably='to use a figurative expression' (see A.V., marg.), i.e., to speak evil of men with whom he had contended at Ephesus as 'beasts' (cp. 1 Cor. 4 : 6), 1 Cor. 15 : 32 ; Lightfoot prefers 'from worldly motives ;' but the other interpretation, No. (4), seems to make better sense. See also Rom. 6 : 19, where, however, the Greek is slightly different, *anthrōpinos*, 'pertaining to mankind ;'" the meaning is as Nos. (5) and (6).*

(*g*) in the phrase "the inward man," the regenerate person's spiritual nature personified, the inner self of the believer, Rom. 7 : 22, as approving of the Law of God ; in Eph. 3 : 16, as the sphere of the renewing power of the Holy Spirit ; in 2 Cor. 4 : 16 (where *anthrōpos* is not repeated), in contrast to "the outward man," the physical frame, the man as cognizable by the senses ; the "inward" man is identical with "the hidden man of the heart," 1 Pet. 3 : 4.

(*h*) in the expressions "the old man," "the new man," which are confined to Paul's Epistles, the former standing for the unregenerate nature personified as the former self of a believer, which, having been crucified with Christ, Rom. 6 : 6, is to be apprehended practically as such, and to be "put off," Eph. 4 : 22 ; Col. 3 : 9, being the source and seat of sin ; the latter, "the new man," standing for the new nature personified as the believer's regenerate self, a nature "created in righteousness and holiness of truth," Eph. 4 : 24, and having been "put on" at regeneration, Col. 3 : 10 ; being "renewed after the image of Him that created him," it is to be "put on" in practical apprehension of these facts.

(*i*) often joined with another noun, e.g., Matt. 11 : 19, lit., 'a man, a glutton ;' 13 : 52, lit., 'a man, a householder ;' 18 : 23, "a certain king," lit., 'a man, a king.'

(*j*) as equivalent simply to 'a person,' or 'one,' whether man or woman, e.g., Acts 19 : 16 ; Rom. 3 : 28 ; Gal. 2 : 16 ; Jas. 1 : 19 ; 2 : 24 ; 3 : 8 (like the pronoun *tis*, someone ; *tis* is rendered "man" in Matt. 8 : 28) ; or, again (as *tis* sometimes signifies), "a man," e.g., Matt. 17 : 14 ; Luke 13 : 19.

* From Notes on Galatians by Hogg and Vine, p. 139.

(*k*) definitely, with the article, of some particular person, Matt. 12 : 13; Mark 3 : 3, 5; or with the demonstrative pronoun and the article, e.g., Matt. 12 : 45; Luke 14 : 30. For the phrase "the Son of man" see SON OF MAN. For "the man of sin," 2 Thess. 2 : 3, see INIQUITY, No. 1.

(*l*) in the phrase "the man of God," 2 Tim. 3 : 17, not used as an official designation, nor denoting a special class of believers, it specifies what every believer should be, namely, a person whose life and conduct represent the mind of God and fulfil His will; so in 1 Tim. 6 : 11, "O man of God." Some regard this in the O.T. sense as of a prophet acting in a distinctive character, possessed of Divine authority; but the context is of such a general character as to confirm the more extended designation here.

Notes: (1) In Gal. 3 : 28, the R.V. adds the italicised word "man" ("ye all are one *man* in Christ Jesus"), in accordance with Eph. 2 : 15, which speaks of Jew and Gentile as becoming "one new man" in Christ. The figure is closely analogous to that of "the body." In these two passages "one" is masculine, i.e., 'one person;' in John 10 : 30; 11 : 52; 17 : 21, 22, 23, "one" is neuter, 'one thing,' as in 1 Cor. 3 : 8; 11 : 5. The first two, in Gal. 3 and Eph. 2, express vital union, present and eternal; in John 17 the union is moral, a process in course of accomplishment. (2) For *philanthrōpia*, Tit. 3 : 4, "(His) love toward man," see KIND, C, No. 2.

(3) In Rev. 9 : 20, the R.V. translates the genitive plural of *anthrōpos* with the article, "mankind" (A.V., "the men"); it might have been rendered '(the rest) of men.'

435
AG:66C
CB:1235C
2. ANĒR (ἀνήρ) is never used of the female sex; it stands (*a*) in distinction from a woman, Acts 8 : 12; 1 Tim. 2 : 12; as a husband, Matt. 1 : 16; John 4 : 16; Rom. 7 : 2; Tit. 1 : 6; (*b*) as distinct from a boy or infant, 1 Cor. 13 : 11; metaphorically in Eph. 4 : 13; (*c*) in conjunction with an adjective or noun, e.g., Luke 5 : 8, lit., 'a man, a sinner;' 24 : 19, lit., 'a man, a prophet;' often in terms of address, e.g., Acts 1 : 16; 13 : 15, 26; 15 : 7, 13, lit., 'men, brethren;' with gentilic or local names (virtually a title of honour), e.g., Acts 2 : 14; 22 : 3, lit., 'Judæan men,' 'a Judæan man;' 3 : 12; 5 : 35, lit., 'Israelite men;' 17 : 22, 'Athenian men;' 19 : 35, lit., 'Ephesian men;' in Acts 14 : 15 it is used in addressing a company of men, without any descriptive term. In this verse, however, the distinction between *anēr* and *anthrōpos* (2nd part) is noticeable; the use of the latter comes under No. 1 (*e*); (*d*) in general, a man, a male person (used like the pronoun *tis*, No. 3), "a man" (i.e., a certain man), e.g., Luke 8 : 41; in the plural, Acts 6 : 11.

5100
AG:819D
CB:1272C
3. TIS (τις), some one, a certain one, is rendered "a man," a certain man, e.g., in Matt. 22 : 24; Mark 8 : 4, A.V. (R.V., "one"); 12 : 19; John 3 : 3, 5; 6 : 50; 14 : 23; 15 : 6, 13; Acts 13 : 41, A.V. (R.V., 'one');

1 Cor. 4 : 2 ; 1 Tim. 1 : 8 ; 2 Tim. 2 : 5, 21 ; Jas. 2 : 14, 18 ; 1 Pet. 2 : 19 ;
1 John 4 : 20. 730 AG:109D
4. ARRĒN and ARSĒN (ἄρσην) : see MALE. CB:1237C
5. TELEIOS (τέλειος), perfect, is translated " men " in 1 Cor. 14 : 20, 5046
R.V. marg., " of full age," A.V. marg., " perfect, or, of a ripe age." See AG:809A CB:1271B
PERFECT.

Note : In many cases the word " man " is combined with an adjective
to translate one word in the original. These will be found under various
other headings. MANAGER See STEWARD

For MAN-CHILD see MALE

MAN'S, OF MAN, MANKIND (see also MEN)

ANTHRŌPINOS (ἀνθρώπινος), human, belonging to man (from 442
anthrōpos, see MAN, No. 1), is used (*a*) of man's wisdom, in 1 Cor. 2 : 13 AG:67D CB:1236A
(some mss. have it in ver. 4, where indeed it is implied ; see, however,
the R.V.) ; (*b*) of " man's judgement," 1 Cor. 4 : 3 (marg., " day : " see
DAY) ; (*c*) of " mankind," Jas. 3 : 7, lit., " the human nature," R.V.
marg. (A.V. marg., " nature of man ") ; (*d*) of human ordinance, 1 Pet.
2 : 13 ; Moulton and Milligan show from the papyri how strongly antithetic to the Divine the use of the word is in this respect ; (*e*) of temptation, 1 Cor. 10 : 13, R.V., " such as man can bear " (A.V., " such as is
common to man "), i.e., such as must and does come to men ; (*f*) of
men's hands, Acts 17 : 25 ; (*g*) in the phrase " after the manner of men,"
Rom. 6 : 19.¶

Notes : (1) In Luke 16 : 12, A.V., *allotrios*, belonging to another 245
(*allos*, another), here used as a pronoun, is translated " another man's " AG:40C CB:1234C
(R.V., " another's ") ; so, as an adjective, in Rom. 14 : 4 ; 15 : 20 ;
2 Cor. 10 : 15, 16 (in this last the R.V. omits " man "). (2) In Acts
27 : 22 there is no word representing " *man's* ; " the R.V. has " of life."
(3) In Rom. 5 : 17, the R.V. rightly has " the trespass of the one," for A.V.,
" one man's offence."

MANGER

PHATNĒ (φάτνη), a manger, Luke 2 : 7, 12, 16, also denotes a stall, 5336
13 : 15.¶ So in the Sept., the word denoted not only a manger but, by AG:854B CB:—
metonymy, the stall or " crib " (Prov. 14 : 4) containing the manger.

MANIFEST (Adjective and Verb)

A. Adjectives.

1. EMPHANĒS (ἐμφανής), manifest (akin to *emphainō*, to show in, to 1717
exhibit ; *en*, in, *phainō*, to cause to shine), is used (*a*) literally in Acts AG:257C CB:1244B
10 : 40, R.V. " (gave Him to be made) manifest ; " (*b*) metaphorically in
Rom. 10 : 20, " (I was made) manifest ". See OPENLY.¶ Cp. B, No. 2. 5318 AG:852B
2. PHANEROS (φανερός), open to sight, visible, manifest (the root CB:1263C

phan—, signifying shining, exists also in No. 1), is translated " manifest " in Luke 8 : 17 ; Acts 4 : 16 ; 7 : 13, R.V. (A.V., " known ") ; Rom. 1 : 19 ; 1 Cor. 3 : 13 ; 11 : 19 ; 14 : 25 ; Gal. 5 : 19 ; Phil. 1 : 13 ; 1 Tim. 4 : 15 (A.V., " appear ") ; 1 John 3 : 10. See APPEAR, B, Note (2), KNOW, B, No. 2, OPENLY, OUTWARDLY.

852 AG:124C 3. APHANĒS (ἀφανής) denotes unseen, hidden, Heb. 4 : 13, " not
CB:— manifest " (*a*, negative, and *phainō*).¶ In the Sept., Neh. 4 : 8 ; Job
DēLOS 24 : 20.¶

1212 AG:178B *Notes :* (1) In 1 Cor. 15 : 27, A.V. *dēlos*, evident, is translated " mani-
CB:1240C fest " (R.V., " evident "). (2) So with *ekdēlos*, 2 Tim. 3 : 9, an intensive
EKDēLOS form of *dēlos*, signifying quite evident.¶ (3) In 1 Tim. 5 : 25, A.V., *prodēlos*,
1552 AG:238B evident beforehand, clearly evident, is translated " manifest beforehand "
PRODēLOS 4271 (R.V., " evident ") ; see EVIDENT. (4) For " manifest token," see TOKEN.

AG:704B

B. Verbs.

5319 AG:852D 1. PHANEROŌ (φανερόω), to make visible, clear, manifest, known
CB:1263C (akin to A, No. 2), is used especially in the writings of the Apostles John and Paul), occurring 9 times in the Gospel, 9 times in 1 John, 2 in Rev. ; in the Pauline Epistles (including Heb.) 24 times ; in the other Gospels, only in Mark, 3 times ; elsewhere in 1 Pet. 1 : 20 ; 5 : 4.

The true meaning is to uncover, lay bare, reveal. The following are variations in the rendering, which should be noted : Mark 16 : 12, 14 (R.V., " was manifested," A.V., " appeared ") ; John 21 : 1 (R.V., " manifested," A.V., " shewed ; " cp. ver. 14) ; Rom. 1 : 19 (R.V., " manifested," A.V., " hath shewed ") ; 2 Cor. 3 : 3 (R.V., " being made manifest," A.V., " are manifestly declared ") ; 2 Cor. 5 : 10 ; 7 : 12 and Rev. 3 : 18 (R.V., " be made manifest," A.V., " appear ") ; 2 Cor. 11 : 6 (R.V., " we have made it manifest," A.V., " we have been throughly made manifest ") ; Col. 1 : 26 (R.V., " hath it been manifested," A.V., " is made manifest ") ; 3 : 4 (R.V., " be manifested," A.V., " appear ; " so 1 Pet. 5 : 4) ; 1 Tim. 3 : 16 (R.V., " was manifested," A.V., " was manifest ") ; 2 Tim. 1 : 10 (R.V., " hath . . . been manifested," A.V., " is . . . made manifest ; " cp. Rom. 16 : 26 ; 2 Cor. 4 : 10, 11 ; 1 Pet. 1 : 20) ; Heb. 9 : 26 (R.V., " hath He been manifested," A.V., " hath He appeared ") ; 1 John 2 : 28 ; 3 : 2 (R.V., " is . . . made manifest," A.V., " doth appear "). See APPEAR, A, No. 4.

1718 AG:257D 2. EMPHANIZŌ (ἐμφανίζω), akin to A, No. 1, is translated to manifest,
CB:1244B make manifest, in John 14 : 21, 22 ; Heb. 11 : 14, R.V. ; see APPEAR, A, No. 5.

Note : For the adverb *phanerōs*, manifestly, see EVIDENTLY, OPENLY.

PHANERōSIS 5321 AG:853B CB:1263C

MANIFESTATION

APOKALUPSIS PHANERŌSIS (φανέρωσις), a manifestation (akin to *phaneros* and
602 AG:92B *phaneroō* ; see MANIFEST), occurs in 1 Cor. 12 : 7 and 2 Cor. 4 : 2.¶
CB:1236C *Note :* In Rom. 8 : 19, A.V., *apokalupsis*, an uncovering, laying bare,

revealing, revelation, is translated "manifestation" (R.V., "revealing"). See Revelation.

MANIFOLD

1. POIKILOS (ποικίλος), varied, is translated "manifold" in 4164
1 Pet. 1 : 6 ; 4 : 10 and in Jas. 1 : 2, R.V. (A.V., "divers"). See Divers, AG:683C CB:—
A, No. 2.

2. POLUPOIKILOS (πολυποίκιλος), much varied (*polus*, much, and 4182 AG:687B
No. 1), is said of the wisdom of God, in Eph. 3 : 10.¶ CB:—

3. POLLAPLASIŌN (πολλαπλασίων), many times more (from *polus*, 4179
much), occurs in Luke 18 : 30, "manifold more," and in many ancient AG:686D CB:—
authorities in Matt. 19 : 29 (R.V., marg. ; some editions in text) ; A.V. and R.V. text, "a hundredfold," translating *hekatontaplasiona.*¶ MANKIND See

---

For MANKIND see MAN, No. 1, Note (3), MAN'S (c), ABUSERS FLESH, MEN

MANNA

MANNA (μάννα), the supernaturally provided food for Israel during 3131
their wilderness journey (for details see Ex. 16 and Numb. 11). The AG:490D CB:1257C
Hebrew equivalent is given in Ex. 16 : 15, R.V. marg., "*man hu.*" The translations are, R.V., "what is it ?"; A.V. and R.V. marg., "it is manna." It is described in Ps. 78 : 24, 25 as "the corn of heaven" and "the bread of the mighty," R.V. text and A.V. marg. ("angels' food," A.V. text), and in 1 Cor. 10 : 3, as "spiritual meat." The vessel appointed to contain it as a perpetual memorial, was of gold, Heb. 9 : 4, with Ex. 16 : 33. The Lord speaks of it as being typical of Himself, the true Bread from Heaven, imparting eternal life and sustenance to those who by faith partake spiritually of Him, John 6 : 31–35. The "hidden manna" is promised as one of the rewards of the overcomer, Rev. 2 : 17 ; it is thus suggestive of the moral excellence of Christ in His life on earth, hid from the eyes of men, by whom He was "despised and rejected ;" the path of the overcomer is a reflex of His life.

None of the natural substances called manna is to be identified with that which God provided for Israel.¶

MANNER

A. Nouns.

1. ETHOS (ἔθος), a habit, custom (akin to the verb *ethō*, to be 1485
accustomed), is always translated "custom" in the R.V. ("manner" in AG:218D CB:1247A
the A.V. of John 19 : 40 ; Acts 15 : 1 ; 25 : 16 ; Heb. 10 : 25). See Custom, No. 1.

2239
2. ĒTHOS (ἦθος), primarily a haunt, abode, then, a custom, manner, AG:344C
occurs in the plural in 1 Cor. 15 : 33, i.e., ethical conduct, morals.¶ CB:1247A

3. TROPOS (τρόπος), a turning, fashion, manner, character, way of 5158 AG:827B
life, is translated "manner" in Acts 1 : 11, with reference to the Lord's CB:1273A

Ascension and Return ; in Jude 7, of the similarity of the evil of those mentioned in vv. 6 and 7. See CONVERSATION, MEANS, WAY.

Note : In Acts 15 : 11, the phrase *kath' hon tropon*, ' according to what manner,' is translated " in like manner as," R.V. (A.V., " even as ").

5179 AG:829D CB:1273B 4. TUPOS (τύπος), a mark or impress, is translated " manner " in Acts 23 : 25. See FORM, No. 3.

195 AG:33A CB:— 5. AKRIBEIA (ἀκρίβεια), exactness, precision (akin to *akribēs*, exact, careful ; see *akriboō*, to enquire carefully, and *akribōs*, carefully), occurs in Acts 22 : 3, R.V., " strict manner " (A.V., " perfect manner ").¶

ETHō 1486 AG:234A (EIōTHA) CB:— AGōGē 72 AG:14D CB:1233C ANASTROPHē 391 AG:61C CB:1235B *Notes :* (1) The verb *ethō*, to be accustomed, has a perfect tense *eiōtha*, with a present meaning, the neuter of the participle of which, *eiōthos*, used with the article, signifies " custom," Luke 4 : 16. In Acts 17 : 2 the A.V. translates it " manner " (R.V., " custom "). See CUSTOM, WONT. (2) For *agōgē*, in 2 Tim. 3 : 10, A.V., " manner of life " (R.V., " conduct "), see CONDUCT. (3) For *anastrophē*, " manner of life," see LIFE, A, No. 6 ; cp. LIVE, No. 5. *Agōge* suggests conduct according to one's leading ; *anastrophē*, conduct as one goes about and mingles with others.

B. Adjectives and Pronouns.

4217 AG:694D CB:— 1. POTAPOS (ποταπός), primarily, from what country, then, of what sort, is rendered " what manner of man," Matt. 8 : 27 ; so 2 Pet. 3 : 11 ; Mark 13 : 1 (twice) ; Luke 1 : 29 ; 7 : 39 ; 1 John 3 : 1.¶

4169 AG:684C CB:— 2. POIOS (ποῖος), of what sort, is translated " by what manner of (death) " in John 21 : 19, R.V., (A.V., " by what ") ; in Acts 7 : 49, " what manner of (house) ; " Rom. 3 : 27, " what manner of law ; " 1 Cor. 15 : 35, " what manner of body."

3634 AG:562C CB:1251A 3. HOIOS (οἷος), a relative pronoun, signifying what sort of or manner of, is translated by the latter phrase in 1 Thess. 1 : 5 ; some mss. have it in Luke 9 : 55, as in A.V. ; the R.V. follows those in which it is absent.

3697 AG:575D CB:— 4. HOPOIOS (ὁποῖος) is rendered " what manner of " in 1 Thess. 1 : 9 ; Jas. 1:24. See SORT, A.

C. Adverbs.

4187 AG:690A CB:— 1. POLUTROPŌS (πολυτρόπως), lit., ' much turning ' (*polus*, much, *tropos*, a turning), ' in many ways (or manners),' is rendered " in divers manners " in Heb. 1 : 1.¶

3779 AG:597C CB:— 2. HOUTŌS or HOUTŌ (οὕτως), thus, in this way, is rendered " after this manner " in Matt. 6 : 9 ; 1 Pet. 3 : 5 ; Rev. 11 : 5. See SO, THUS.

5615 AG:899B CB:— 3. HŌSAUTŌS (ὡσαύτως), a strengthened form of *hōs*, thus, signifies just so, likewise, in like manner e.g., 1 Tim. 2 : 9 ; in the following the R.V. has " in like manner," for A.V., " likewise ; " Mark 14 : 31 ; Luke 22 : 20 ; Rom. 8 : 26 ; 1 Tim. 3 : 8 ; 5 : 25 ; in Luke 20 : 31 the R.V. has " likewise," A.V., " in like manner." See LIKEWISE.

3668 AG:567D CB:1251A 4. HOMOIŌS (ὁμοίως), akin to the adjective *homoios*, like, signifies in like manner, equally ; in the following the R.V. has " in like manner " for A.V., " likewise ; " Matt. 27 : 41 ; Mark 4 : 16 ; 15 : 31 ; Luke 10 : 32 ; 13 : 3 ; 16 : 25 ; John 5 : 19 ; (Heb. 9 : 21 ;) Jas. 2 : 25 ; 1 Pet. 3 : 1, 7 ;

Rev. 8 : 12 ; in Rev. 2 : 15 the A.V. " which thing I hate " translates a
variant reading (*ho misō*). See LIKEWISE, So. 4459
5. PŌS (πῶς), how, is translated " after what manner " in Acts 20 : 18. AG:732D
See MEANS. CB:—

Note : For *paraplēsiōs*, Heb. 2 : 14, R.V., see LIKEWISE, No. 4. 3898 AG:621C

D. Preposition. CB:—

KATA (κατά), according to, is translated " after the manner " in 2596
John 2 : 6, i.e., ' in accordance with ; ' in Rom. 3 : 5 ; 1 Cor. 3 : 3 ; 9 : 8, AG:405C CB:1253C
R.V., " after the manner of " (A.V., " as ").

E. Verb.

TROPOPHOREŌ (τροποφορέω), to bear another's manners, is 5159
translated " suffered He (their) manners " in Acts 13 : 18. For this and AG:827C CB:—
the alternative reading see BEAR, No. 8.¶

Notes : (1) In the following the phrase *kata tauta*, or *kata ta auta*, lit., KAI
' according to the same things,' is translated " in (the) like (R.V., same) 2532 AG:391D
manner," Luke 6 : 23 ; ver. 26, R.V. (A.V., " so ") ; 17 : 30, R.V., " after CB:1253A
the same manner " (A.V., " even thus "). (2) In Phil. 2 : 18 the phrase HODE (TODE)
to . . . auto, lit., ' the same (thing),' used adverbially, is translated " in 3592
the same manner," R.V. (A.V., " for the same cause "). (3) In Mark AG:553A
13 : 29, A.V., *kai*, also (so R.V.), is translated " in like manner." (4) In CB:— ARA
Acts 15 : 23 some mss. have the demonstrative pronoun *tode* used 686 AG:103D
adverbially and rendered " after this manner " (A.V.). The R.V., CB:1237B
adhering to the mss. in which it is absent, inserts the word " *thus* " in TIS 5100
italics. (5) In Acts 25 : 20 a phrase lit. rendered ' (as to) the enquiry AG:819D
concerning these things ' (or according to some mss. ' this person,' whether CB:1272C ETHNIKōS
" Jesus " or " Paul," ver. 19), is translated " of such manner of questions," 1483
A.V. (R.V., " how to inquire concerning these things "). (6) In Luke AG:218B
1 : 66, A.V., *ara*, " then " (so R.V.), is rendered freely " (what) manner." CB:1246C PAS
(7) In Luke 24 : 17, A.V., the pronoun *tis*, who, what, in the plural (R.V., 3956
" what ") is translated " what manner of ; " similarly, in the singular in AG:631A CB:1262C
Mark 4 : 41 ; Luke 8 : 25 (R.V., " who ") ; John 7 : 36. (8) In Gal.
2 : 14, A.V., the adverb *ethnikōs*, in Gentile fashion (*ethnos*, a nation : in
the plural, Gentiles or nations), is translated " after the manner of
Gentiles " (R.V., " as do . : "). (9) In Matt. 12 : 31 ; Luke 11 : 42 ; Rev.
18 : 12, A.V., *pas*, " every " (so R.V.), is translated " all manner."

MANSERVANT

PAIS (παῖς), a child, boy, youth, also means a servant, attendant ; 3816
in Luke 12 : 45 it is used in the plural " menservants," in contrast to AG:604C CB:1261C
paidiskē, a maidservant. See CHILD, No. 4.

MANSIONS

MONĒ (μονή), primarily a staying, abiding (akin to *menō*, to abide), 3438
denotes an abode (Eng., manor, manse, etc.), translated " mansions " in AG:527A CB:1259B
John 14 : 2 ; " abode " in ver. 23. There is nothing in the word to

indicate separate compartments in Heaven; neither does it suggest temporary resting-places on the road.¶

MANSLAYERS

409 AG:64A CB:— ANDROPHONOS (ἀνδροφόνος), from *anēr*, a man, and *phoneus*, a murderer, occurs in the plural in 1 Tim. 1 : 9.¶

MANTLE

4018 AG:646C CB:1263B PERIBOLAION (περιβόλαιον), lit., that which is thrown around, is translated "mantle" in Heb. 1 : 12, R.V. (A.V., "vesture.") See COVERING, VEIL.

MANY

4183 AG:687C CB:1266A 1. POLUS (πολύς), much, many, great, is used especially of number when its significance is "many," e.g., Matt. 8 : 30; 9 : 10; 13 : 17; so the R.V. of Matt. 12 : 15, where some mss. follow the word by *ochloi*, multitudes; 1 Cor. 12 : 12; Rev. 1 : 15; it is more frequently used as a noun, "many (persons)," e.g., Matt. 3 : 7; 7 : 22; 22 : 14; with the article, "the many," e.g., Matt. 24 : 12, R.V.; Mark 9 : 26, R.V., "the more part" (A.V. "many"); Rom. 5 : 15, 19 (twice), R.V.; 12 : 5; 1 Cor. 10 : 17; ver. 33, R.V.; so 2 Cor. 2 : 17; in 1 Cor. 11 : 30, R.V., "not a few." In Luke 12 : 47 it is translated "many stripes," the noun being understood. See GREAT, MUCH.

Notes: (1) In Luke 23 : 8 some mss. have *polla*, "many things," though it is absent from the most authentic; see the R.V. (2) In Mark 6 : 20 the R.V., following the mss. which have *aporeō*, to be perplexed, translates *polla* by "much;" some mss. have *poieō*, to do; hence A.V., "did many things." (3) In Gal. 4 : 27 the plural of *polus*, with *mallon*, more, is translated "more" in the R.V. (A.V., "many more"), lit., 'many are the children of the desolate more than of her that etc.,' the phrase implying that both should have many children, but the desolate more than the other. (4) In John 7 : 40 there is no word in the original representing "*some*" or "many."

4119 AG:687C (POLUS II.) CB:1265B 2. PLEIŌN (πλείων), more, greater, the comparative of No. 1, is translated "many" in Acts 2 : 40; 13 : 31; 21 : 10; 24 : 17; 25 : 14; 27 : 20; 28 : 23 (A.V.; R.V., "in great number"); with the article, "most," R.V. (or rather, 'the more part'), Acts 19 : 32; 1 Cor. 10 : 5, and Phil. 1 : 14 (for A.V., "many," an important change); in 2 Cor. 2 : 6, R.V., "the many" (marg., "the more"); so 4 : 15; in 9 : 2, "very many" (marg., "the more part"); in Heb. 7 : 23, R.V., "many in number" (A.V., "many"). See GREATER, MORE.

2425 AG:374B CB:1250C 3. HIKANOS (ἱκανός), sufficient, when used of number sometimes signifies many, suggesting a sufficient number, (*a*) with nouns, Luke 8 : 32; 23 : 9; Acts 9 : 23, 43; 20 : 8; 27 : 7; (*b*) absolutely, some noun being understood, e.g., Acts 12 : 12 ; 14 : 21 ; 19 : 19 ; 1 Cor. 11 : 30. See ABLE, C, No. 2.

4. HOSOS (ὅσος), how much, how many, how great, as much as, as 3745
many as, is translated " as many as," e.g., in Matt. 14 : 36 ; Mark 3 : 10 ; AG:586B
Luke 9 : 5, R.V. (A.V., " whosoever ") ; Acts 2 : 39 ; in 9 : 16, R.V., CB:1251B
" how many things " (A.V., " how great things ") ; in Rom. 6 : 3 the R.V. renders it by " all we who " (A.V., " so many of us as "), a necessary alteration, not singling out some believers from others, as if some were not baptized, but implying what was recognized as true of all (see Acts 18 : 8) ; in 2 Cor. 1 : 20, R.V., " how many soever be " (A.V., " all "). See ALL, C.

5. POSOS (πόσος), how much, how great, how many, has the last 4214
meaning in Matt. 15 : 34 ; 16 : 9, 10 ; 27 : 13 (" how many things ") ; AG:694B
Mark 6 : 38 ; 8 : 5, 19, 20 ; 15 : 4 (" how many things ") ; Luke 15 : 17 ; CB:—
Acts 21 : 20. See GREAT.

6. TOSOUTOS (τοσοῦτος), so great, so much, so many, (*a*) qualifying 5118
a noun, is rendered " these many (years) " in Luke 15 : 29 ; " so many," AG:823B
John 12 : 37 ; 1 Cor. 14 : 10 ; (*b*) without a noun, John 6 : 9 ; 21 : 11 ; CB:—
Gal. 3 : 4, " so many things." See GREAT.

Note : In John 17 : 2, A.V., the neuter of *pas*, all, followed by the 3956
neuter of the relative pronoun 'what,' and then by the plural of the AG:631A
personal pronoun, is translated " to as many as " (R.V., " whatsoever . . . CB:1262C
to them ").

MARAN-ATHA

MARAN-ATHA (μαρὰν ἀθά), an expression used in 1 Cor. 16 : 22, is 3134
the Greek spelling for two Aramaic words, formerly supposed by some to AG:491B
be an imprecatory utterance or " a curse reinforced by a prayer," an idea CB:1257C
contrary to the intimations conveyed by its use in early Christian documents, e.g., " The Teaching of the Apostles," a document of the beginning of the 2nd cent., and in the " Apostolic Constitutions " (vii. 26), where it is used as follows : " Gather us all together into Thy Kingdom which Thou hast prepared. Maranatha, Hosanna to the Son of David ; blessed is He that cometh etc."

The first part, ending in 'n,' signifies 'Lord ;' as to the second part, the " Fathers " regarded it as a past tense, " has come." Modern expositors take it as equivalent to a present, " cometh," or future, " will come." Certain Aramaic scholars regard the last part as consisting of 'tha,' and regard the phrase as an ejaculation, 'Our Lord, come,' or 'O Lord, come.' The character of the context, however, indicates that the Apostle is making a statement rather than expressing a desire or uttering a prayer.

As to the reason why it was used, most probably it was a current ejaculation among early Christians, as embodying the consummation of their desires.

" At first the title *Marana* or *Maran,* used in speaking to and of

Christ was no more than the respectful designation of the Teacher on the part of the disciples." After His resurrection they used the title of or to Him as applied to God, "but it must here be remembered that the Aramaic-speaking Jews did not, save exceptionally, designate God as 'Lord;' so that in the 'Hebraist' section of the Jewish Christians the expression 'our Lord' (*Marana*) was used in reference to Christ only" (Dalman, *The Words of Jesus*).¶

MARBLE

3139 AG:492C CB:— MARMAROS (μάρμαρος) primarily denoted any glistering stone (from *marainō*, to glisten); hence, marble, Rev. 18:12.¶

MARINERS

3492 AG:534C CB:— NAUTĒS (ναύτης), a seaman, mariner, sailor (from *naus*, a ship, Eng., nautical), is translated "sailors" in Acts 27:27, 30, R.V. (A.V., "shipmen"); in Rev. 18:17, R.V., "mariners" (A.V., "sailors").¶

MARK (Noun)

5480 AG:876A CB:1239B 1. CHARAGMA (χάραγμα) denotes a stamp, impress, translated "mark" in Rev. 13:16, 17, etc. See GRAVEN.

4742 AG:768C CB:1270A 2. STIGMA (στίγμα) denotes a tattooed mark or a mark burnt in, a brand (akin to *stizō*, to prick), translated "marks" in Gal. 6:17.¶ "It is probable that the Apostle refers to the physical sufferings he had endured since he began to proclaim Jesus as Messiah and Lord [e.g., at Lystra and Philippi]. It is probable, too, that this reference to his scars was intended to set off the insistence of the Judaizers upon a body-mark which cost them nothing. Over against the circumcision they demanded as a proof of obedience to the law he set the indelible tokens, sustained in his own body, of his loyalty to the Lord Jesus. As to the origin of the figure, it was indeed customary for a master to brand his slaves, but this language does not suggest that the Apostle had been branded by His Master. Soldiers and criminals also were branded on occasion; but to neither of these is the case of Paul as here described analogous. The religious devotee branded himself with the peculiar mark of the god whose cult he affected; so was Paul branded with the marks of his devotion to the Lord Jesus. It is true such markings were forbidden by the law, Lev. 19:28, but then Paul had not inflicted these on himself.

"The marks of Jesus cannot be taken to be the marks which the Lord bears in His body in consequence of the Crucifixion; they were different in character."*

4649 AG:756D CB:1269B 3. SKOPOS (σκοπός), primarily a watcher, watchman (as in the Sept., e.g., Ezek. 3:17), then, a mark on which to fix the eye (akin to *skopeō*, to look at), is used metaphorically in Phil. 3:14, of an aim or object, R.V., "goal." See GOAL.¶

* From Notes on Galatians by Hogg and Vine, p. 344.

MARK (Verb)

1. EPECHŌ (ἐπέχω), lit., to hold upon (*epi*, upon, *echō*, to hold), 1907
signifies (like *parechō*) to hold out, Phil. 2 : 16, of the word of life ; then, to AG:285C
hold one's mind towards, to observe, translated "marked" in Luke CB:—
14 : 7, of the Lord's observance of those who chose the chief seats. See HEED, HOLD, STAY.

2. SKOPEŌ (σκοπέω), to look at, behold, watch, contemplate, 4648
(akin to *skopos*, a mark, see Noun above), is used metaphorically of looking AG:756D
to, and translated "mark" in Rom. 16 : 17, of a warning against those who CB:1269B
cause divisions, and in Phil. 3 : 17, of observing those who walked after the example of the Apostle and his fellow-workers, so as to follow their ways. See HEED, Note (1), LOOK.

MARKET, MARKET-PLACE

AGORA (ἀγορά), primarily an assembly, or, in general, an open space 58
in a town (akin to *ageirō*, to bring together), became applied, according AG:12C
to papyri evidences, to a variety of things, e.g., a judicial assembly, a CB:1233C
market, or even supplies, provisions (Moulton and Milligan, Vocab.). In the N.T. it denotes a place of assembly, a public-place or forum, a market-place. A variety of circumstances, connected with it as a public gathering-place, is mentioned, e.g., business dealings such as the hiring of labourers, Matt. 20 : 3; the buying and selling of goods, Mark 7 : 4 (involving risk of pollution) ; the games of children, Matt. 11 : 16 ; Luke 7 : 32 ; exchange of greetings, Matt. 23 : 7 ; Mark 12 : 38 ; Luke 11 : 43 ; 20 : 46 ; the holding of trials, Acts 16 : 19 ; public discussions, Acts 17 : 17. Mark 6 : 56 records the bringing of the sick there. The word always carries with it the idea of publicity, in contrast to private circumstances.

The R.V. always translates it "market-place" or in the plural. The A.V. sometimes changes the rendering to "markets" and translates it "streets" in Mark 6 : 56. See STREET.¶

MARRED

Note : In Mark 2 : 22, *apollumi*, to destroy, perish, is found in the most 622
authentic mss. as applying both to the wine and the wine skins, R.V., AG:95A
"perisheth ;" the A.V. follows the mss. which tell of the wine being CB:1237A
"spilled" (*ekcheō*, to pour out), and the skins (A.V., "bottles") being "marred." See DESTROY, No. 1.

MARRIAGE (give in), MARRY

A. Noun.

GAMOS (γάμος), a marriage, wedding, or wedding feast, is used to 1062
denote (*a*) the ceremony and its proceedings, including the marriage feast, AG:151B
John 2 : 1, 2 ; of the marriage ceremony only, figuratively, Rev. 19 : 7, CB:1248A
as distinct from the marriage feast (ver. 9) ; (*b*) the marriage feast, R.V.

in Matt. 22 : 2, 3, 4, 9 ; in ver. 8, 10, " wedding ; " in 25 : 10, R.V., " marriage feast ; " so Luke 12 : 36 ; 14 : 8 ; in Matt. 22 : 11, 12, the " wedding garment " is, lit., ' a garment of a wedding.' In Rev. 19, where, under the figure of a marriage, the union of Christ, as the Lamb of God, with His Heavenly Bride is so described, the marriage itself takes place in Heaven during the Parousia, ver. 7 (the aorist or point tense indicating an accomplished fact ; the Bride is called " His wife ") ; the marriage feast or supper is to take place on earth, after the Second Advent, ver. 9. That Christ is spoken of as the Lamb points to His atoning sacrifice as the ground upon which the spiritual union takes place. The background of the phraseology lies in the O.T. description of the relation of God to Israel, e.g., Is. 54 : 4, ff. ; Ezek. 16 : 7, ff. ; Hos. 2 : 19 ; (*c*) marriage in general, including the married state, which is to be " had in honour," Heb. 13 : 4, R.V.¶

Note : Among the Jews the marriage-supper took place in the husband's house and was the great social event in the family life. Large hospitality, and resentment at the refusal of an invitation, are indicated in Matt. 22 : 1–14. The marriage in Cana exhibits the way in which a marriage feast was conducted in humbler homes. Special honour attached to the male friends of the bridegroom, " the sons of the bride-chamber," Matt. 9 : 15, R.V. (see BRIDE-CHAMBER). At the close the parents conducted the bride to the nuptial chamber (cp. Judg. 15 : 1).

B. Verbs.

1060 AG:150D 1. GAMEŌ (γαμέω), to marry (akin to A), is used (*a*) of the man,
CB:1248A Matt. 5 : 32 ; 19 : 9, 10 ; 22 : 25 (R.V. ; A.V., " married a wife ") ; ver. 30 ; 24 : 38 ; Mark 6 : 17 ; 10 : 11 ; 12 : 25 ; Luke 14 : 20 ; 16 : 18 ; 17 : 27, R.V., " married " (A.V., " married wives ") ; 20 : 34, 35 ; 1 Cor. 7 : 28 (1st part) ; ver. 33 ; (*b*) of the woman, in the Active Voice, Mark 10 : 12 ; 1 Cor. 7 : 28 (last part) ; ver. 34 ; 1 Tim. 5 : 11, 14 ; in the Passive Voice, 1 Cor. 7 : 39 ; (*c*) of both sexes, 1 Cor. 7 : 9, 10, 36 ; 1 Tim. 4 : 3.¶

— AG:151A 2. GAMIZŌ (γαμίζω), to give in marriage, is used in the Passive Voice
CB:1248A in Matt. 22 : 30 (2nd clause), some mss. have No. 5 here ; Mark 12 : 25 (No. 3 in some mss.) ; Luke 17 : 27 (No. 5 in some mss.) ; 20 : 35 (last word), Passive (Nos. 3 and 4 in some mss.) ; in the Active Voice Matt. 24 : 38 (Nos. 3 and 5 in some mss.) ; further, of giving a daughter in marriage, 1 Cor. 7 : 38 (twice), R.V. (No. 5 in some mss.), which, on the whole, may be taken as the meaning. In this part of the Epistle, the Apostle was answering a number of questions on matters about which the church at Corinth had written to him, and in this particular matter the formal transition from marriage in general to the subject of giving a daughter in marriage, is simple. Eastern customs naturally would involve the inclusion of the latter in the enquiry and the reply.¶

1061 AG:151B 3. GAMISKŌ (γαμίσκω), an alternative for No. 2, Luke 20 : 34
CB:1248A (some mss. have No. 4) ; in some mss. in Mark 12 : 25; Luke 20 : 35.¶

4. EKGAMISKŌ (ἐκγαμίσκω), to give out in marriage (*ek*, out, and 1548 AG:—
No. 3): see Nos. 2 and 3.
5. EKGAMIZŌ (ἐκγαμίζω), an alternative for No. 4: see Nos. 2 and 3.¶ 1547 AG:238A
6. EPIGAMBREUŌ (ἐπιγαμβρεύω), to take to wife after (*epi*, upon, 1918 AG:290C CB:—
gambros, a connection by marriage), signifies to marry (of a deceased
husband's next of kin, Matt. 22 : 24).¶ Cp. Gen. 38 : 8.

Note: In Rom. 7 : 3 (twice) and ver. 4, A.V., *ginomai*, to become 1096 AG:158A CB:1248B
(here, to become another man's), is translated "be married" (R.V.,
"be joined").

MARROW

MUELOS (μυελός), marrow, occurs in Heb. 4 : 12, where, by a natural 3452 AG:528D CB:—
metaphor, the phraseology changes from the material to the spiritual.¶

For MARTYR see WITNESS

MARVEL (Noun and Verb), MARVELLOUS

A. Noun.

THAUMA (θαῦμα), a wonder (akin to *theaomai*, to gaze in wonder), 2295 AG:352A CB:1271C
is found in the most authentic mss. in 2 Cor. 11 : 14 (some mss. have the adjective *thaumastos:* see C, below), "(no) marvel;" in Rev. 17 : 6, R.V., "wonder" (A.V., "admiration"), said of John's astonishment at the vision of the woman described as Babylon the Great.¶ In the Sept., Job 17 : 8; 18 : 20; in some mss., 20 : 8 and 21 : 5.¶ Cp. *teras*, a wonder; *sēmeion*, a sign; *thambos*, wonder; *ekstasis*, amazement.

B. Verbs.

1. THAUMAZŌ (θαυμάζω) signifies to wonder at, marvel (akin to A); 2296 AG:352B CB:1271C
the following are R.V. differences from the A.V.: Luke 2 : 33, "were marvelling" for "marvelled;" Luke 8 : 25 and 11 : 14, "marvelled" for "wondered;" 9 : 43, "were marvelling" for "wondered;" 2 Thess. 1 : 10, "marvelled at" for "admired" (of the Person of Christ at the time of the shining forth of His Parousia, at the Second Advent). See WONDER.

Note: In Matt. 9 : 8, A.V. translates this verb; R.V., *phobeō*, "were 5399 AG:862B CB:1264B
afraid."

2. EKTHAUMAZŌ (ἐκθαυμάζω), a strengthened form of No. 1 (*ek*, — AG:240B CB:1244A
intensive), is found in the best mss. in Mark 12 : 17, R.V., "wondered greatly" (some mss. have No. 1).¶

C. Adjective.

THAUMASTOS (θαυμαστός), marvellous (akin to A and B), is said 2298 AG:352D CB:1271C
(*a*) of the Lord's doing in making the rejected Stone the Head of the corner, Matt. 21 : 42; Mark 12 : 11; (*b*) of the erstwhile blind man's astonishment that the Pharisees knew not from whence Christ had come, and yet He had given him sight, John 9 : 30, R.V., "the marvel," A.V., "a marvellous thing;" (*c*) of the spiritual light into which believers are
brought, 1 Pet. 2 : 9; (*d*) of the vision of the seven angels having the
seven last plagues, Rev. 15 : 1; (*e*) of the works of God, 15 : 3.¶

MASQUERADE See FASHION

MASTER (Noun and Verb)

A. Nouns.

1320 AG:191C CB:1241B 1. DIDASKALOS (διδάσκαλος), a teacher (from *didaskō*, to teach), is frequently rendered "Master" in the four Gospels, as a title of address to Christ, e.g., Matt. 8 : 19 ; Mark 4 : 38 (there are more instances in Luke than in the other Gospels) ; John 1 : 38, where it interprets "Rabbi ;" 20 : 16, where it interprets "Rabboni." It is used by Christ of Himself in Matt. 23 : 8 (see No. 6) and John 13 : 13, 14 ; by others concerning Him, Matt. 17 : 24 ; 26 : 18 ; Mark 5 : 35 ; 14 : 14 ; Luke 8 : 49 ; 22 : 11 ; John 11 : 28. In John 3 : 10, the Lord uses it in addressing Nicodemus, R.V., "the teacher" (A.V., "a master"), where the article does not specify a particular teacher, but designates the member of a class ; for the class see Luke 2 : 46, "the doctors" (R.V., marg., "teachers"). It is used of the relation of a disciple to his master, in Matt. 10 : 24, 25 ; Luke 6 : 40. It is not translated "masters" in the rest of the N.T., save in the A.V. of Jas. 3 : 1 "(be not many) masters," where obviously the R.V. "teachers" is the meaning. See TEACHER.

2962 AG:458D II. CB:1256B 2. KURIOS (κύριος), a lord, one who exercises power, is translated "masters" in Matt. 6 : 24 ; 15 : 27 ; Mark 13 : 35 ; Luke 16 : 13 ; Acts 16 : 16, 19 ; Rom. 14 : 4, A.V. (R.V., "lord") ; Eph. 6 : 5, 9 (twice), the 2nd time of Christ ; so in Col. 3 : 22 ; 4 : 1. See LORD.

1203 AG:176C CB:1240C 3. DESPOTĒS (δεσπότης), one who has "absolute ownership and uncontrolled power," is translated "masters" in 1 Tim. 6 : 1, 2 ; Tit. 2 : 9 ; 1 Pet. 2 : 18 ; of Christ, 2 Tim. 2 : 21 ; 2 Pet. 2 : 1, R.V. (for A.V., "Lord") ; in Jude 4, R.V., it is applied to Christ "(our only) Master (and Lord, Jesus Christ)," A.V. "(the only) Lord (God) ;" in Rev. 6 : 10, R.V., in an address to God, "O Master" (A.V., "O Lord"). It is rendered "Lord" in Luke 2 : 29 and Acts 4 : 24. See LORD.¶

Note : For "master of the house," see GOODMAN.

4461 AG:733A CB:1268A 4. RABBEI (ῥαββεί) was an Aramaic word signifying "my master," a title of respectful address to Jewish teachers.

"The Aramaic word *rabbei*, transliterated into Greek, is explicitly recognized as the common form of address to Christ, Matt. 26 : 25 (cp., however, ver. 22, *kurios*) ; 26 : 49 ; Mark 9 : 5, but Matt. 17 : 4, *kurios*" (Dalman, *The Words of Jesus*).

In the following the R.V. has "Rabbi" for A.V. "Master ;" Matt. 26 : 25, 49 ; Mark 9 : 5 ; 11 : 21 ; 14 : 45 ; John 4 : 31 ; 9 : 2 ; 11 : 8. In other passages the A.V. has "Rabbi," Matt. 23 : 7, 8 ; John 1 : 38, 49 ; 3 : 2, 26 ; 6 : 25.¶

4462 AG:733A CB:1268A *Note :* The form *Rabbounei* (*Rabboni*), in Mark 10 : 51, is retained in the R.V. (for A.V., "Lord") ; in John 20 : 16, in both A.V. and R.V. This title is said to be Galilean ; hence it would be natural in the lips of a woman of Magdala. It does not differ materially from Rabbi.¶

1988 AG:300B CB:1246A 5. EPISTATĒS (ἐπιστάτης) denotes a chief, a commander, overseer, master. It is used by the disciples in addressing the Lord, in recognition of His authority rather than His instruction (Nos. 1 and 6) ; it occurs only in Luke: 5 : 5 ; 8 : 24, 45 ; 9 : 33, 49 ; 17 : 13.¶ In the Sept., 2 Kings 25 : 19 ; 2 Chron. 31 : 12 ; Jer. 36 : 26 ; 52 : 25.¶

Note : " The form *epistata* . . . alongside of the commoner *didaskale* is . . . a Greek synonym for the latter, and both are to be traced back to the Aramaic *rabbei.*" Christ forbade His disciples to allow themselves to be called *rabbi,* " on the ground that He alone was their Master, Matt. 23 : 8. In reference to Himself the designation was expressive of the real relation between them. The form of address ' Good Master ' He, however, refused to allow, Mark 10 : 17, 18 . . . in the mouth of the speaker it was mere insolent flattery . . . the Lord was unwilling that anyone should thoughtlessly deal with such an epithet ; and here, as always, the honour due to the Father was the first consideration with Him. . . . The primitive community never ventured to call Jesus ' Our Teacher ' after He had been exalted to the Throne of God. The title *rabbi,* expressing the relation of the disciple to the teacher, vanished from use ; and there remained only the designation *maran,* the servant's appropriate acknowledgement of his Lord " (Dalman).

6. KATHĒGĒTĒS (καθηγητής), properly a guide (akin to *kathēgeomai,* 2519
to go before, guide ; *kata,* down, *hēgeomai,* to guide), denotes a master, AG:388D CB:—
a teacher, Matt. 23 : 10 (twice) ; some mss. have it in ver. 8, where the
most authentic have No. 1.¶

7. KUBERNĒTĒS (κυβερνήτης), the pilot or steersman of a ship, or, 2942
metaphorically, a guide or governor (akin to *kubernaō,* to guide : Eng., AG:456C CB:1256B
govern is connected ; cp. *kubernēsis,* a steering, pilotage, 1 Cor. 12 : 28,
" governments "), is translated " master " in Acts 27 : 11 ; " shipmaster "
in Rev. 18 : 17.¶ In the Sept., Prov. 23 : 34 ; Ezek. 27 : 8, 27, 28.¶

B. Verb.

KATAKURIEUŌ (κατακυριεύω), to exercise lordship (*kata,* down 2634
upon, *kurios,* a lord), is translated " mastered " in Acts 19 : 16, R.V., AG:412C CB:1254A
of the action of the evil spirit on the sons of Sceva (A.V., " overcame ").
In translating the word *amphoterōn* by its primary meaning, " both,"
the R.V. describes the incident as referring to two only. It has been
shown, however, that in the period of the *Koinē* (see Foreword to Vol. I)
amphoteroi, " both," was no longer restricted to two persons. Ramsay AMPHOTEROI 297 (-ROS)
ascribes the abruptness of the word here to the vivid narrative of an eye AG:47C
witness. See DOMINION, LORD, LORDSHIP. CB:1234C (-ROS)

MASTERBUILDER

ARCHITEKTŌN (ἀρχιτέκτων), from *archē,* rule, beginning, and 753
tektōn, an artificer (whence Eng., architect), a principal artificer, is used AG:113B CB:1237B
figuratively by the Apostle in 1 Cor. 3 : 10, of his work in laying the
foundation of the local church in Corinth, inasmuch as the inception of the
spiritual work there devolved upon him. The examples from the papyri
and from inscriptions, as illustrated by Moulton and Milligan, show that

the word had a wider application than our "architect," and confirm the
rendering "masterbuilder" in this passage, which is of course borne out
MAT by the context.¶
See BED

MATTER, MATTERS

3056 1. LOGOS (λόγος), a word, speech, discourse, account, hence also that
AG:477A CB:1257A which is spoken of, a matter, affair, thing, is translated "matter" in
Mark 1 : 45 ; Acts 8 : 21 ; 15 : 6 ; 19 : 38 ; in the R.V. of Phil. 4 : 15,
"in the matter of" (A.V., "concerning"). See ACCOUNT.
4229 AG:697A 2. PRAGMA (πρᾶγμα), akin to *prassō*, to do, denotes (*a*) that which
CB:1266B has been done, a deed, translated "matters" in Luke 1 : 1, R.V. (A.V.,
"things") ; "matter" in 2 Cor. 7 : 11 ; (*b*) that which is being done, an
affair, translated "matter" in Rom. 16 : 2, R.V. (A.V., "business") ;
1 Cor. 6 : 1, in a forensic sense, a law-suit (frequently found with this
meaning in the papyri) ; 1 Thess. 4 : 6, "in the matter," i.e., the matter
under consideration, which, as the preceding words show, is here the sin
of adultery. See BUSINESS, B, Note (1), THING.
1462 3. ENKLĒMA (ἔγκλημα), an accusation, charge, Acts 25 : 16, R.V.,
AG:216B CB:1245A "matter laid against him ;" elsewhere, Acts 23 : 29, "charge ;" see
ACCUSATION, A, No. 3.¶

Notes : (1) In Gal. 2 : 6, the statement "it maketh no matter" trans-
DIAPHERō 1308 lates the verb *diapherō*, to bear asunder, make a difference, with *ouden*,
AG:190B nothing, used adverbially, i.e., 'it makes no difference (to me) ;' his
CB:— commission from the Lord relieved him of responsibility to the authority
MEGAS 3173 of the Apostles. (2) In 1 Cor. 9 : 11, R.V., the neuter of the adjective
AG:497C *megas*, great, is translated "a great matter" (A.V., "a great thing").
CB:1258A HULē (3) In Jas. 3 : 5, A.V., *hulē*, a wood, forest, is translated "a matter"
5208 (R.V., and A.V. marg., "wood"). In older English the word "matter"
AG:836A CB:1251C actually meant "wood" (like its Latin original, *materia*). (4) In Acts
17 : 32, the A.V. adds "*matter*" to the pronoun "this," R.V., "(concerning) this." (5) In 2 Cor. 8 : 19, R.V., the phrase, lit., 'in this grace'
is translated "in *the matter of* (A.V., with) this grace." (6) In 2 Cor.
8 : 20, R.V., the phrase, lit., 'in this bounty' is translated "in *the matter
of* this bounty" (A.V., "in this abundance"). (7) In 2 Cor. 9 : 5, the
phrase, lit., 'as a bounty' is amplified to "as a matter of bounty."
MATURE (8) For 1 Pet. 4 : 15 see BUSYBODY. See also OTHER, THIS, THESE,
See WEIGHTIER, WRONG.
FULLGROWN, PERFECT

MAY, MAYEST, MIGHT

1410 AG:207A 1. DUNAMAI (δύναμαι), to be able, have power, whether by personal
CB:1242B ability, permission, or opportunity, is sometimes rendered "may" or
"might," e.g., Matt. 26 : 9 ; Mark 14 : 5 ; Acts 17 : 19 ; 1 Thess. 2 : 6.
In the following the R.V. substitutes "can," "canst," "couldst," for the
A.V., e.g., Matt. 26 : 42 ; Mark 4 : 32 ; 14 : 7 ; Luke 16 : 2 ; Acts 24 : 11 ;
25 : 11 ; 27 : 12 ; 1 Cor. 7 : 21 ; 14 : 31 (here the alteration is especially

important, as not permission for all to prophesy, but ability to do so, is the meaning) ; Eph. 3 : 4. In the following the R.V. substitutes the verb to be able, Acts 19 : 40 ; 24 : 8 ; Rev. 13 : 17. See ABLE, B, No. 1.

2. EXESTI (ἔξεστι), it is permitted, lawful (*eimi*, to be, prefixed by 1832
ek, from), is rendered " (I) may " in Acts 2 : 29, R.V. [A.V., " let (me) "]; AG:275B CB:1247C
in Acts 21 : 37, " may (I)," lit., 'is it permitted (me to speak) ?' Some
mss. have it in 8 : 37, " thou mayest " (A.V.). See LAWFUL.

3. ISŌS (ἴσως), equally (from the adjective *isos*, equal), is translated 2481 AG:384A
" it may be " in Luke 20 : 13 (i.e., 'perhaps ').¶ CB:—

4. TUNCHANŌ (τυγχάνω), to meet with, reach, obtain, denotes, 5177
intransitively, to happen, chance, befall ; used impersonally with the AG:829B CB:—
conjunction *ei*, if, it signifies ' it may be,' ' perhaps,' e.g., 1 Cor. 14 : 10 ;
15 : 37, " it may chance ; " 16 : 6.

Notes : (1) In Matt. 8 : 28, A.V., *ischuō*, to have strength, be strong, 2480
be well able, is translated " might " (R.V., " could "). (2) " May," AG:383D CB:1253A
" might," sometimes translate the prepositional phrase *eis*, unto, with the definite article, followed by the infinitive mood of some verb, expressing purpose, e.g., Acts 3 : 19, " may be blotted out," lit., ' unto the blotting out of ; ' Rom. 3 : 26, " that he might be," lit., ' unto his being ; ' so 8 : 29 ; 2 Cor. 1 : 4, " that we may be able," lit., ' unto our being able ; ' Eph. 1 : 18, " that ye may know," lit., ' unto your knowing ; ' Acts 7 : 19 ; Rom. 1 : 11 ; 4 : 16 ; 12 : 2 ; 15 : 13 ; Phil. 1 : 10 ; 1 Thess. 3 : 10, 13 ; 2 Thess. 1 : 5 ; 2 : 6, 10 ; Heb. 12 : 10. In Luke 20 : 20 the best mss. have *hōste*, " so as to," R.V., as, e.g., in 1 Pet. 1 : 21. Sometimes the article with the infinitive mood without a preceding preposition, expresses result, e.g., Luke 21 : 22 ; Acts 26 : 18 (twice), " that they may turn," R.V. ; cp. Rom. 6 : 6 ; 11 : 10 ; 1 Cor. 10 : 13 ; Phil. 3 : 10, " that I may know ; " Jas. 5 : 17.

(3) The phrases " may be," " might be," are frequently the rendering of the verb to be, in the subjunctive or optative moods, preceded by a conjunction introducing a condition, or expressing a wish or purpose, e.g., Matt. 6 : 4 ; John 14 : 3 ; 17 : 11. Sometimes the phrase translates simply the infinitive mood of the verb *eimi*, to be, e.g., Luke 8 : 38, lit., ' to be (with Him) ; ' so the R.V. in 2 Cor. 5 : 9 ; in 2 Cor. 9 : 5, " that (the same) might be," lit., ' (the same) to be.'

(4) In Heb. 7 : 9 the phrase *hōs* (' so ') *epos* (' a word ') *eipein* (' to say '), i.e., lit., ' so to say a word ' is an idiom, translated in the R.V., " so to say " (A.V., " if I may so say ") ; the Eng. equivalent is ' one might almost say.'

ME

EGō 1473 AG:217A CB:1242C
Notes : (1) The pronoun, whether alone or with some English preposition,
e.g., of, to, for, in, translates one or other of the oblique cases of *ego*, ' I.' EMAUTOU
(2) In Philm. 13 the reflexive pronoun *emauton*, myself, is translated " me," 1683 AG:253D
governed by the preposition *pros*, with, lit., ' with myself.' (3) In Tit. CB:—

1 : 3, for the A.V., "is committed unto me," the R.V. has "I was
EMOI intrusted." (4) In Phil. 2 : 23, "how it will go with me," is, lit., 'the
1698 AG:217 (things) concerning me.' (5) The phrase *en emoi*, 'in me,' is used
(EGo) (*a*) instrumentally (*en*, instrumental, by or through), e.g., 2 Cor. 13 : 3;
CB:— EMOS (*b*) subjectively, 'within me,' e.g., Gal. 2 : 20; (*c*) objectively, 'in my
1699 case,' e.g., 1 Cor. 9 : 15; 14 : 11; Gal. 1 : 16, 24; 1 Tim. 1 : 16. (6) In
AG:255C CB:1244B Luke 22 : 19 the possessive pronoun *emos*, my, is rendered "of Me," lit.,
'(into) My (remembrance).'

MEAL

224 AG:35D ALEURON (ἄλευρον), meal (akin to *aleuō*, to grind, and therefore,
CB:— lit., 'what is ground'), occurs in Matt. 13 : 33; Luke 13 : 21.¶

MEAL See MESS

MEAN (Adjective)

767 AG:115A ASĒMOS (ἄσημος), lit., without mark (*a*, negative, *sēma*, a mark),
CB:— i.e., undistinguished, obscure, was applied by the Apostle Paul negatively, to his native city, Tarsus, Acts 21 : 39.¶ Moulton and Milligan (Vocab.) have a note as follows: "This word occurs perpetually in the papyri to denote a man who is 'not distinguished' from his neighbours by the convenient scars on eyebrow or arm or right shin, which identify so many individuals in formal documents." Deissmann suggests that the word may have been the technical term for "uncircumcised," among the Greek Egyptians. In another papyrus document a pair of silver bracelets are described as of "unstamped" (*asēmos*) silver.

MEAN (Verb)

1510 1. EIMI (εἰμί), to be, in certain of its forms, has an explicative force,
AG:222D CB:1243A signifying to denote, to import, e.g., Matt. 9 : 13; 12 : 7, "(what this) meaneth," lit. '(what this) is;' Luke 18 : 36, "meant" (lit., 'might be'); Acts 10 : 17, "might mean," R.V. (lit., 'might be'); in Luke 15 : 26 the R.V. keeps to the verb to be, "(what these things) might be" (A.V., "meant"). In Acts 2 : 12 the verb to be is preceded by *thelō*, to will, and the phrase is translated "(what) meaneth (this)," lit., '(what) does (this) will to be?' in 17 : 20, lit., '(what do these things) will to be?'

3004 AG:468A 2. LEGŌ (λέγω), to say, sometimes has the significance of meaning
CB:1256C something; so the R.V. in 1 Cor. 1 : 12; A.V., "(this) I say."
MELLō 3195 *Notes:* (1) In Acts 27 : 2, A.V., *mellō*, to be about to, is translated
AG:500D "meaning" (R.V., "was about to"), with reference to the ship (according
CB:1258A POIEō to the best mss.). (2) In Acts 21 : 13, A.V., *poieō*, to do, is translated
4160 "(what) mean ye (to weep);" R.V., "(what) do ye, (weeping)." (3) The
AG:680D CB:1265C abbreviated original in 2 Cor. 8 : 13 is rendered by the italicised additions, A.V., "*I mean* (not)," R.V., "*I say* (not) *this*." Cp. the R.V. italics in Mark 6 : 2.

MEANING

DUNAMIS (δύναμις), power, force, is used of the significance or force 1411
of what is spoken, 1 Cor. 14 : 11. See MIGHT, POWER. AG:207B CB:1242B

MEANS (by all, by any, etc.)

1. PANTŌS (πάντως), an adverb from *pas*, all, denoting wholly, 3843
altogether, entirely, is used in 1 Cor. 9 : 22, " by all means." When the AG:609B CB:—
Apostle says, " I am become all things to all men, that I may by all means save some," he is simply speaking of his accommodating himself to various human conditions consistently with fidelity to the truth, with no unscriptural compliance with men, but in the exercise of self denial; " by all means " refers to the preceding context from ver. 18, and stresses his desire to be used in the salvation of some. It is found in Acts 21 : 22, R.V., " certainly." Some mss. have the word in this sense in Acts 18 : 21 (A.V.). See ALTOGETHER, B, No. 1.

2. PŌS (πως), at all, somehow, in any way, is used after the conjunction 4458
(*a*) *ei*, if, meaning ' if by any means,' e.g., Acts 27 : 12 ; Rom. 1 : 10 ; AG:732B CB:—
11 : 14 ; Phil. 3 : 11 ; (*b*) *mē*, lest, ' lest by any means,' e.g., 1 Cor. 8 : 9 ; 9 : 27 ; 2 Cor. 2 : 7, R.V. (A.V., " perhaps ") ; 9 : 4, R.V. (A.V., " haply ") ; 11 : 3 ; 12 : 20, R.V. ; Gal. 2 : 2 ; 4 : 11, R.V. (A.V., " lest ") ; 1 Thess. 3 : 5 (A.V., " lest by some means ").

3. EK (ἐκ), out of, from, by, suggesting the source from which some- 1537
thing is done, is sometimes rendered " by means of," e.g., Luke 16 : 9, AG:234A CB:1243B
R.V., " by means of (the mammon of unrighteousness) ; " A.V., " of ; " 2 Cor. 1 : 11, " by (the) means of (many)."

4. DIA (διά), by, by means of, when followed by the genitive case, is 1223
instrumental, e.g., 2 Pet. 3 : 6, R.V., " by which means " (A.V., " where- AG:179B CB:1241A
by ").

5. PŌS (πῶς), an interrogative adverb (different from No. 2), how, in 4459
what way, Luke 8 : 36, A.V., " by what means," R.V., " how ; " so John AG:732D CB:—
9 : 21 ; cp. Note (4) below.

Notes : (1) In Luke 5 : 18 the A.V. adds the word " *means* " in italics.
(2) The word *tropos*, a manner, way, is sometimes used in a prepositional TROPOS
phrase, e.g., 2 Thess. 2 : 3, A.V., " by any means," R.V., " in any wise," 5158 AG:827B
lit., ' in any manner ; ' 3 : 16, A.V., " by all means," R.V., " in all ways," CB:1273A
lit., ' in every manner.' (3) The double negative *ou mē*, i.e., ' no not,' OU (OUK) 3756
' not at all,' is translated " by no means," Matt. 5 : 26 ; in Luke 10 : 19, AG:590A
" by any means," A.V. (R.V., " in any wise ") ; Luke 12 : 59, R.V., " by CB:— MĒ
no means " (A.V., " not "). (4) In Acts 4 : 9, the phrase *en*, in or by, 3361
with *tini* (from *tis*, who), lit., " in whom " (R.V., marg.), is translated AG:515D
" by what means." (5) In Heb. 9 : 15, R.V., the verb *ginomai*, to come to CB:1258A GINOMAI
be, become, take place, used in its 2nd aorist participle, is rightly translated 1096
" (a death) having taken place ; " A.V., " by means of (death)." (6) In AG:158A CB:1248B
Rev. 13 : 14, R.V., *dia*, followed by the accusative case, is rightly translated

" by reason of," i.e., 'on account of' (A.V., wrongly, " by *the means of* ").

For MEANWHILE see WHILE

MEASURE (Noun and Verb)

A. Nouns.

3358 AG:515A CB:1258C 1. METRON (μέτρον) denotes (I) that which is used for measuring, a measure, (*a*) of a vessel, figuratively, Matt. 23 : 32 ; Luke 6 : 38 (twice) ; in John 3 : 34, with the preposition *ek*, " (He giveth not the Spirit) by measure," R.V. (which is a necessary correction ; the italicized words " *unto him*," A.V., detract from the meaning). Not only had Christ the Holy Spirit without measure, but God so gives the Spirit through Him to others. It is the Ascended Christ who gives the Spirit to those who receive His testimony and set their seal to this, that God is true. The Holy Spirit is imparted neither by degrees, nor in portions, as if He were merely an influence, He is bestowed Personally upon each believer, at the time of the new birth ; (*b*) of a graduated rod or rule for measuring, figuratively, Matt. 7 : 2 ; Mark 4 : 24 ; literally, Rev. 21 : 15 (in the best mss. ; see the R.V.) ; ver. 17 ; (II) that which is measured, a determined extent, a portion measured off, Rom. 12 : 3 ; 2 Cor. 10 : 13 (twice) ; Eph. 4 : 7, " (according to the) measure (of the gift of Christ) ; " the gift of grace is measured and given according to the will of Christ ; whatever the endowment, His is the bestowment and the adjustment ; ver. 13, " the measure (of the stature of the fulness of Christ)," the standard of spiritual stature being the fulness which is essentially Christ's ; ver. 16, " (according to the working in due) measure (of each several part)," i.e., according to the effectual working of the ministration rendered in due measure by every part.¶

3313 AG:505D CB:1258B 2. MEROS (μέρος), a part, portion, is used with the preposition *apo*, from, with the meaning " in some measure," Rom. 15 : 15, R.V. (A.V., " . . . sort"). See COAST, PART.

4568 AG:745B CB:— 3. SATON (σάτον) is a Hebrew dry measure (Heb., *seah*), about a peck and a half, Matt. 13 : 33 ; Luke 13 : 21 ; " three measures " would be the quantity for a baking (cp. Gen. 18 : 6 ; Judg. 6 : 19 ; 1 Sam. 1 : 24 ; the " ephah " of the last two passages was equal to three *sata*).¶

2884 AG:444D CB:1255C 4. KOROS (κόρος) denotes a *cor*, the largest Hebrew dry measure (ten *ephahs*), containing about 11 bushels, Luke 16 : 7 ; the hundred measures amounted to a very considerable quantity.¶

942 AG:137C CB:— 5. BATOS (βάτος) denotes a *bath*, a Jewish liquid measure (the equivalent of an *ephah*), containing between 8 and 9 gallons, Luke 16 : 6.¶

5518 AG:883B CB:— 6. CHOINIX (χοῖνιξ), a dry measure of rather less than a quart, about " as much as would support a person of moderate appetite for a day," occurs in Rev. 6 : 6 (twice). Usually eight *chœnixes* could be bought for a *denarius* (about 9½d.) ; this passage predicts circumstances in which the *denarius* is the price of one *chœnix*.¶ In the Sept., Ezek. 45 : 10, 11, where it represents the Heb. *ephah* and *bath*.¶

Notes : (1) In 2 Cor. 10 : 14, A.V., *huperekteinō*, to stretch out over- HUPEREKTEINŌ
much, is translated " we stretch (not ourselves) beyond measure," (R.V., 5239 AG:840D
" . . . overmuch) ". (2) In 2 Cor. 11 : 9, R.V., *prosanaplēroō*, to fill up CB:—
by adding to, to supply fully, is translated " supplied the measure " PROSANAPLĒROŌ 4322
(A.V., " supplied "). See SUPPLY. (3) For the phrases in the A.V., AG:711D
" beyond measure," Gal. 1 : 13 ; " out of measure," 2 Cor. 1 : 8, see CB:1267A PERISSOS
ABUNDANCE, A, No. 4, EXCEL, B. (4) In Mark 6 : 51, some mss. have 4053
the phrase *ek perissou*, " beyond measure " (A.V.). (5) For the phrase AG:651B CB:1263C
" be exalted above measure," 2 Cor. 12 : 7, A.V., see EXALT, A, No. 4.

B. Adverbs.

1. HUPERBALLONTŌS (ὑπερβαλλόντως), beyond measure (*huper*, 5234
over, beyond, *ballō*, to throw ; for the verb *huperballō*, see EXCEEDING), AG:840A CB:—
is rendered " above measure " in 2 Cor. 11 : 23.¶ 4057

2. PERISSŌS (περισσῶς), Mark 10 : 26 ; see EXCEED, B, No. 4. AG:651D CB:1263C

3. HUPERPERISSŌS (ὑπερπερισσῶς), Mark 7 : 37 : see ABUND- 5249
ANCE D, No. 3.¶ AG:842A CB:1252A

C. Adjective.

AMETROS (ἄμετρος), without measure (*a*, negative, and A, No. 1), 280
is used in the neuter plural in an adverbial phrase in 2 Cor. 10 : 13, 15, AG:45C CB:1234C
eis ta ametra, lit., ' unto the (things) without measure,' R.V., " (we will not glory) beyond our measure ; " A.V., "(we will not boast) of things without measure," referring to the sphere Divinely appointed for the Apostle as to his Gospel ministry ; this had reached to Corinth, and by the increase of the faith of the church there, would extend to regions beyond. His opponents had no scruples about intruding into the spheres of other men's work.¶

D. Verbs.

1. METREŌ (μετρέω), to measure (akin to A, No. 1), is used (*a*) of 3354
space, number, value, etc., Rev. 11 : 1, 2 ; 21 : 15, 16, 17 ; metaphorically, AG:514C CB:1258C
2 Cor. 10 : 12 ; (*b*) in the sense of measuring out, giving by measure, Matt. 7 : 2, " ye mete " (some mss. have No. 2) ; Mark 4 : 24 ; in some mss. in Luke 6 : 38 (see No. 2).¶

2. ANTIMETREŌ (ἀντιμετρέω), to measure in return (*anti*, back, in 488
return and No. 1), is used in the Passive Voice, and found in some mss. in AG:75B CB:—
Matt. 7 : 2 (the most authentic have No. 1) ; in Luke 6 : 38 the most authentic have this verb.¶ It is not found in the Sept.

MEAT

1. BRŌMA (βρῶμα), food (akin to *bibrōskō*, to eat, John 6 : 13¶), 1033
solid food in contrast to milk, is translated " food " in Matt. 14 : 15, AG:148A CB:1239B
R.V. (A.V., " victuals ") ; " meats," Mark 7 : 19 ; 1 Cor. 6 : 13 (twice) ; 1 Tim. 4 : 3 ; Heb. 9 : 10 ; 13 : 9 ; " meat," John 4 : 34 ; Rom. 14 : 15

(twice), 20 ; 1 Cor. 3 : 2 ; 8 : 8, 13 ; 10 : 3 ; " food," R.V., for A.V.,
" meat," Luke 3 : 11 ; 9 : 13.¶
1035 AG:148B 2. BRŌSIS (βρῶσις), akin to No. 1, denotes (*a*) the act of eating,
CB:1239B 1 Cor. 8 : 4 (see EAT) ; (*b*) food, translated " meat " in John 4 : 32 (for
ver. 34, see No. 1) ; 6 : 27 (twice, the second time metaphorically, of
spiritual food) ; 6 : 55, R.V., marg., " (true) meat ; " Rom. 14 : 17, A.V.,
" meat," R.V., " eating ; " Col. 2 : 16 ; in Heb. 12 : 16, R.V., " mess of
meat," A.V., " morsel of meat ; " in 2 Cor. 9 : 10, " food ; " in Matt.
6 : 19, 20, " rust." See EAT, EATING, B.¶
1034 AG:148B 3. BRŌSIMOS (βρώσιμος), eatable, Luke 24 : 41, A.V., " any meat "
CB:1239B (R.V., " anything to eat "). See EAT, C.¶
5160 AG:87D 4. TROPHĒ (τροφή), nourishment, food, is translated " meat " in the
5315 A.V. (R.V. " food ") except in two instances. See FOOD, No. 1.
AG:312B 5. PHAGŌ (φάγω), to eat, is used as a noun, in the infinitive mood, and
(ESTHIō) CB:1246C translated " meat " in Matt. 25 : 35, 42 (lit., ' to eat ') ; in Luke 8 : 55
(ESTHIō) the R.V. translates it literally, " to eat " (A.V., " meat "). See EAT, No. 2.
5132 AG:824B 6. TRAPEZA (τράπεζα), a table (Eng., trapeze), is used, by metonymy,
CB:1273A of the food on the table, in Acts 16 : 34 (R.V., marg., " a table "), and
translated " meat ; " cp. " table " in Rom. 11 : 9 ; 1 Cor. 10 : 21. See
TABLE.

PROSPHAGION 4371 *Notes :* (1) For *prosphagion*, John 21 : 5, A.V., " any meat," see EAT,
AG:719C B, No. 2. (2) In Luke 12 : 42, *sitometrion* denotes a measured portion of
SITOMETRION 4620 food (*sitos*, food, *metrios*, within measure). (3) In Matt. 15 : 37 and Mark
AG:752A 8 : 8, the A.V. translates the plural of *klasma*, a broken piece (from *klaō*,
KLASMA 2801 to break), " broken meat " (R.V., " broken pieces "). (4) In John 12 : 2,
AG:433B R.V., *anakeimai*, to recline at table, is translated " sat at meat " (A.V.,
CB:1255B " sat at the table ") ; in Mark 6 : 26, R.V., according to the best mss.,
ANAKEIMAI 345 " sat at meat," some have *sunanakeimai* (A.V., " sat with him ") ; in
AG:55D Mark 6 : 22, R.V., *sunanakeimai*, to recline at table together, is translated
CB:1235A SUNANAKEIMAI " that sat at meat with him." (5) In Acts 15 : 29, A.V., the neuter
4873 plural of *eidōlothutos*, sacrificed to idols, is translated " meats offered to
AG:784B EIDōLOTHUTON idols " (R.V., " things . . . ," as elsewhere in the A.V.). See IDOLS
1494 (offered to.) (6) For *kataklinō*, to sit down to (recline at) meat, see SIT,
AG:221B (-OS) No. 7.

CB:1243A KATAKLINō 2625

MEDIATOR

AG:411D MESITĒS (μεσίτης), lit., a go-between (from *mesos*, middle, and
MESITēS *eimi*, to go), is used in two ways in the N.T., (*a*) one who mediates between
3316 AG:506D two parties with a view to producing peace, as in 1 Tim. 2 : 5, though
CB:1258B more than mere mediatorship is in view, for the salvation of men necessitated that the Mediator should Himself possess the nature and attributes
of Him towards whom He acts, and should likewise participate in the
nature of those for whom He acts (sin apart) ; only by being possessed
both of Deity and humanity could He comprehend the claims of the one
and the needs of the other ; further, the claims and the needs could be
met only by One who, Himself being proved sinless, would offer Himself

an expiatory sacrifice on behalf of men ; (*b*) one who acts as a guarantee so as to secure something which otherwise would not be obtained. Thus in Heb. 8 : 6 ; 9 : 15 ; 12 : 24 Christ is the Surety of " the better covenant," " the new covenant," guaranteeing its terms for His people.

In Gal. 3 : 19 Moses is spoken of as a mediator, and the statement is made that " a mediator is not a mediator of one," ver. 20, that is, of one party. Here the contrast is between the promise given to Abraham and the giving of the Law. The Law was a covenant enacted between God and the Jewish people, requiring fulfilment by both parties. But with the promise to Abraham, all the obligations were assumed by God, which is implied in the statement, " but God is one."¶ In the Sept., Job 9 : 33, " daysman."¶

MEDITATE

1. MELETAŌ (μελετάω), primarily, to care for (akin to *meletē*, care ; 3191
cp. *melei*, it is a care), denotes (*a*) to attend to, practise, 1 Tim. 4 : 15, R.V., AG:500B
" be diligent in " (A.V., " meditate upon ") ; to practise is the prevalent CB:—
sense of the word, and the context is not against this significance in the R.V. rendering ; some mss. have it in Mark 13 : 11 ; (*b*) to ponder, imagine, Acts 4 : 25. See IMAGINE.¶

2. PROMELETAŌ (προμελετάω), to premeditate, is used in Luke 4304
21 : 14.¶ AG:708C CB:—

Note : In the corresponding passage in Mark 13 : 11, the most authentic
mss. have the verb *promerimnaō*, to be anxious beforehand (R.V.) ; see 4305
No. 1. AG:708C CB:1266C

For MEDDLER see BUSYBODY

MEEK, MEEKNESS

A. Adjective.

PRAŬS or PRAOS (πραΰς) denotes gentle, mild, meek ; for its 4239
significance see the corresponding noun, below, B. Christ uses it of His AG:698D CB:1266B
own disposition, Matt. 11 : 29 ; He gives it in the third of His Beatitudes, 5 : 5 ; it is said of Him as the King Messiah, 21 : 5, from Zech. 9 : 9 ; it is an adornment of the Christian profession, 1 Pet. 3 : 4.¶ Cp. *ēpios*, gentle, of a soothing disposition, 1 Thess. 2 : 7 ; 2 Tim. 2 : 24.¶

B. Nouns.

1. PRAŪTĒS, or PRAOTES, an earlier form, (πραΰτης) denotes meek- 4240
ness. In its use in Scripture, in which it has a fuller, deeper significance than AG:699A CB:1266B
in non-scriptural Greek writings, it consists not in a person's " outward behaviour only ; nor yet in his relations to his fellow-men ; as little in his mere natural disposition. Rather it is an inwrought grace of the soul ; and the exercises of it are first and chiefly towards God. It is that temper of spirit in which we accept His dealings with us as good, and therefore without disputing or resisting ; it is closely linked with the word

5012 AG:804C CB:1271A *tapeinophrosunē* [humility], and follows directly upon it, Eph. 4 : 2; Col. 3 : 12; cp. the adjectives in the Sept. of Zeph. 3 : 12, "meek and lowly;" . . . it is only the humble heart which is also the meek, and which, as such, does not fight against God and more or less struggle and contend with Him. This meekness, however, being first of all a meekness before God, is also such in the face of men, even of evil men, out of a sense that these, with the insults and injuries which they may inflict, are permitted and employed by Him for the chastening and purifying of His elect" (Trench, Syn. § xlii). In Gal. 5 : 23 it is associated with *enkrateia*, self-control.

The meaning of *praütēs* "is not readily expressed in English, for the terms meekness, mildness, commonly used, suggest weakness and pusillanimity to a greater or less extent, whereas *praütēs* does nothing of the kind. Nevertheless, it is difficult to find a rendering less open to objection than 'meekness;' 'gentleness' has been suggested, but as *praütēs* describes a condition of mind and heart, and as 'gentleness' is appropriate rather to actions, this word is no better than that used in both English Versions. It must be clearly understood, therefore, that the meekness manifested by the Lord and commended to the believer is the fruit of power. The common assumption is that when a man is meek it is because he cannot help himself; but the Lord was 'meek' because he had the infinite resources of God at His command. Described negatively, meekness is the opposite to self-assertiveness and self-interest; it is equanimity of spirit that is neither elated nor cast down, simply because it is not occupied with self at all.

"In 2 Cor. 10 : 1 the Apostle appeals to the 'meekness . . . of Christ.' Christians are charged to show 'all meekness toward all men,' Tit. 3 : 2, for meekness becomes 'God's elect,' Col. 3 : 12. To this virtue the 'man of God' is urged; he is to 'follow after meekness' for his own sake, 1 Tim. 6 : 11 (the best texts have No. 2 here, however), and in his service, and more especially in his dealings with the 'ignorant and erring,' he is to exhibit 'a spirit of meekness,' 1 Cor. 4 : 21, and Gal. 6 : 1; even 'they that oppose themselves' are to be corrected in meekness, 2 Tim. 2 : 25. James exhorts his 'beloved brethren' to 'receive with meekness the implanted word,' 1 : 21. Peter enjoins 'meekness' in setting forth the grounds of the Christian hope, 3 : 15."*¶

AG:698D CB:1266B 2. PRAÜPATHIA (πραϋπαθία), a meek disposition, meekness (*praus*, meek, *paschō*, to suffer), is found in the best texts in 1 Tim. 6 : 11.¶

MEET (Adjective and Verb)

A. Adjectives.

514 AG:78A CB:1238B 1. AXIOS (ἄξιος) has the meaning of being of weight, value, worth; also befitting, becoming, right on the ground of fitness, e.g., Matt. 3 : 8,

---

* From Notes on Galatians by Hogg and Vine, pp. 294, 295.

A.V., "meet" (R.V., "worthy"); so Acts 26:20; Luke 3:8 ("worthy");
23:41 ("due reward"). See REWARD, WORTHY.
2. HIKANOS (ἱκανός), sufficient, competent, fit, is translated "meet" 2425 AG:374B
in 1 Cor. 15:9. See ENOUGH, SUFFICIENT. CB:1250C
3. KALOS (καλός), good, is translated "meet" in Matt. 15:26 and 2570 AG:400B
Mark 7:27. See GOOD. CB:1253B
4. EUTHETOS (εὔθετος), well-placed, is translated "meet" in 2111
Heb. 6:7: see FIT. AG:320B CB:—
Note: In Phil. 1:7 and 2 Pet. 1:13, A.V., *dikaios*, just, is translated 1342
"meet" (R.V., "right"). For "meet . . . for use," 2 Tim. 2:21, see AG:195C
USE, *Note*. CB:1241C

B. Verbs.

1. DEI (δεῖ), an impersonal verb, it is necessary, one must, is translated 1163
"it was meet," in Luke 15:32; in Rom. 1:27, A.V., "was meet" (R.V., AG:172A CB:1240B
"was due"). See DUE, B, No. 2.
2. HIKANOŌ (ἱκανόω), to render fit, meet, to make sufficient, is 2427
translated "hath made . . . meet" in Col. 1:12; in 2 Cor. 3:6, R.V., AG:374D CB:1250C
"made . . . sufficient" (A.V., "hath made . . . able"). See ABLE.¶

MEET (Verb), MEET WITH, MET

A. Verbs.

1. APANTAŌ (ἀπαντάω), to go to meet, to meet (*apo*, from, *antaō*, 528
to meet with, come face to face with), is used in Mark 14:13 and Luke AG:80C CB:1236B
17:12. Some mss. have this verb for No. 3 in Matt. 28:9; Mark 5:2;
Luke 14:31; John 4:51; Acts 16:16.¶
2. SUNANTAŌ (συναντάω), to meet with, lit., to meet together with 4876
(*sun*, with, and *antaō*, see No. 1), is used in Luke 9:37 (in ver. 18, in some AG:784C CB:1270C
mss.); 22:10; Acts 10:25; Heb. 7:1, 10; metaphorically in Acts
20:22 ("shall befall"). See BEFALL.¶
3. HUPANTAŌ (ὑπαντάω), to go to meet, to meet, has the same 5221
meaning as No. 1, and is used in Matt. 8:28; Luke 8:27; John 11:20, AG:837D CB:1252A
30, and, in the most authentic mss., in Matt. 28:9; Mark 5:2; Luke
14:31 (of meeting in battle); John 4:51; 12:18 and Acts 16:16 (see
No. 1).¶
4. PARATUNCHANŌ (παρατυγχάνω), to happen to be near or present, 3909
to chance to be by (*para*, beside, near, *tunchanō*, to happen), occurs in AG:623A CB:—
Acts 17:17, "met with (him)."¶
5. SUMBALLŌ (συμβάλλω), to confer, to fall in with, meet with, is 4820
translated "met" in Acts 20:14, R.V. (A.V., "met with"), of the AG:777B CB:—
Apostle Paul's meeting his companions at Assos. See CONFER, No. 3.

B. Nouns.

1. HUPANTĒSIS (ὑπάντησις), a going to meet (akin to A, No. 3), 5222
preceded by the preposition *eis*, unto, lit., 'unto a meeting,' translated AG:837D CB:1252A
"to meet," is found in John 12:13, and in the most authentic mss. in
Matt. 8:34 (see No. 3) and 25:1 (see No. 2).¶ 529
2. APANTĒSIS (ἀπάντησις), a meeting (akin to A, No. 1), occurs in AG:80C CB:1236B

Matt. 25 : 6 (in some mss. in ver. 1, and in 27 : 32, in some mss.); Acts 28 : 15; 1 Thess. 4 : 17. It is used in the papyri of a newly arriving magistrate. "It seems that the special idea of the word was the official welcome of a newly arrived dignitary" (Moulton, Greek Test. Gram. Vol. I, p. 14).¶

4877 AG:784C CB:— 3. SUNANTĒSIS (συνάντησις), a coming to meet with (akin to A, No. 2), is found in some mss. in Matt. 8 : 34, of the coming out of all the people of a city to meet the Lord (see No. 1).¶

MELODY (Verb)

5567 AG:891A CB:1267B PSALLŌ (ψάλλω), primarily to twitch, twang, then, to play a stringed instrument with the fingers, and hence, in the Sept., to sing with a harp, sing psalms, denotes, in the N.T., to sing a hymn, sing praise; in Eph. 5 : 19, "making melody" (for the preceding word *ądō*, see SING). Elsewhere it is rendered "sing," Rom. 15 : 9; 1 Cor. 14 : 15; in Jas. 5 : 13, R.V., "let him sing praise" (A.V., "let him sing psalms"). See SING.¶

MELT

5080 AG:814B CB:1271B TĒKŌ (τήκω), to melt, melt down, is used in the Passive Voice in 2 Pet. 3 : 12, "shall melt" (lit., 'shall be melted'), of the elements (Eng., 'thaw' is etymologically connected).¶

3089 AG:483C CB:1257B *Note*: In verse 10, the A.V. "shall melt" represents the verb *luō*, to loosen, dissolve (R.V., "shall be dissolved," Passive Voice); so in vv. 11, 12.

MEMBER

3196 AG:501D CB:1258B MELOS (μέλος), a limb of the body, is used (*a*) literally, Matt. 5 : 29, 30; Rom. 6 : 13 (twice), 19 (twice); 7 : 5, 23 (twice); 12 : 4 (twice); 1 Cor. 12 : 12 (twice), 14, 18–20, 22, 25, 26 (twice); Jas. 3 : 5, 6; 4 : 1; in Col. 3 : 5, "mortify therefore your members which are upon the earth;" since our bodies and their members belong to the earth, and are the instruments of sin, they are referred to as such (cp. Matt. 5 : 29, 30; Rom. 7 : 5, 23, mentioned above); the putting to death is not physical, but ethical; as the physical members have distinct individualities, so those evils, of which the physical members are agents, are by analogy regarded as examples of the way in which the members work if not put to death; this is not precisely the same as "the old man," ver. 9, i.e., the old nature, though there is a connection; (*b*) metaphorically, of believers as members of Christ, 1 Cor. 6 : 15 (1st part); of one another, Rom. 12 : 5 (as with the natural illustration, so with the spiritual analogy, there is not only vital unity, and harmony in operation, but diversity, all being essential to effectivity; the unity is not due to external organization but to common and vital union in Christ); there is stress in ver. 5 upon "many" and "in Christ" and "members;" 1 Cor. 12 : 27 (of the members of a local church as a body); Eph. 4 : 25 (of the members of the whole Church as the mystical body of Christ); in 1 Cor. 6 : 15 (2nd part), of one who practises fornication.¶

MEMORIAL

MNĒMOSUNON (μνημόσυνον) denotes a memorial, that which keeps 3422
alive the memory of someone or something (from *mnēmōn*, mindful), AG:525B CB:1259A
Matt. 26 : 13; Mark 14 : 9; Acts 10 : 4.¶

For MEMORY (keep in) see KEEP, Note (8)

MEN

Notes: (1) For this plural see the nouns under MAN. (2) For ANTHRōPINOS 442
anthrōpinos, e.g., Rom. 6 : 19, "after the manner of men," see MAN'S, AG:67D
No. 1. (3) For the phrase *kat' anthrōpon*, "after the manner of men," CB:1236A ANDRIZō
see MAN, No. 1 (*f*). (4) The phrase "quit you like men," 1 Cor. 16 : 13, (-OMAI)
translates the verb *andrizō*, in the Middle Voice, to play the man (a verb 407
illustrated in the papyri). (5) See also ALL, GOOD, GREAT, LOW (estate), AG:64A CB:—
THESE, (of) WAR.

MEN-PLEASERS

ANTHRŌPARESKOS (ἀνθρωπάρεσκος), an adjective signifying study- 441
ing to please men (*anthrōpos*, man, *areskō*, to please), designates, "not AG:67D CB:1236A
simply one who is pleasing to men . . . , but one who endeavours to please men and not God" (Cremer). It is used in Eph. 6 : 6 and Col. 3 : 22.¶ In the Sept., Psa. 53 : 5.¶

MENSERVANTS

PAIS (παῖς), for the meanings of which see CHILD, No. 4, is translated 3816
"menservants" in Luke 12 : 45. AG:604C CB:1261C

MEN-STEALERS

ANDRAPODISTĒS (ἀνδραποδιστής), a slave-dealer, kidnapper, from 405
andrapodon, a slave captured in war, a word found in the plural in the AG:63D CB:1235B
papyri, e.g., in a catalogue of property and in combination with *tetrapoda*, four-footed things (*andrapodon*, *anēr*, a man, *pous*, a foot); *andrapodon* "was never an ordinary word for slave; it was too brutally obvious a reminder of the principle which made quadruped and human chattels differ only in the number of their legs" (Moulton and Milligan, Vocab.). The verb *andrapodizō* supplied the noun "with the like odious meaning," which appears in 1 Tim. 1 : 10.¶

MEND

KATARTIZŌ (καταρτίζω), from *kata*, down, intensive and *artios*, 2675
fit, has three meanings, (*a*) to mend, repair, Matt. 4 : 21; Mark 1 : 19, of AG:417D CB:1254B
nets; (*b*) to complete, furnish completely, equip, prepare, Luke 6 : 40; Rom. 9 : 22; Heb. 11 : 3 and in the Middle Voice, Matt. 21 : 16; Heb.

10 : 5 ; (*c*) ethically, to prepare, perfect, Gal. 6 : 1 ; 1 Thess. 3 : 10 ; 1 Pet. 5 : 10 ; Heb. 13 : 21 ; and in the Passive Voice, 1 Cor. 1 : 10 ; 2 Cor. 13 : 11. See FIT, FRAME, JOIN, PERFECT, PREPARE, RESTORE.¶

MENTION (Noun and Verb)

A. Noun.

3417 MNEIA (μνεία), remembrance, mention (akin to *mimnēskō*, to remind,
AG:524B remember), is always used in connection with prayer, and translated
CB:1259A "mention" in Rom. 1 : 9 ; Eph. 1 : 16 ; 1 Thess. 1 : 2 ; Philm. 4, in
each of which it is preceded by the verb to make ; "remembrance" in
Phil. 1 : 3 ; 1 Thess. 3 : 6 ; 2 Tim. 1 : 3. Some mss. have it in Rom.
12 : 13, instead of *chreiais*, necessities. See REMEMBRANCE.¶ Cp.
mnēmē, memory, remembrance, 2 Pet. 1 : 15.¶

B. Verb.

3421 MNĒMONEUŌ (μνημονεύω), which most usually means to call to mind,
AG:525A remember, signifies to make mention of, in Heb. 11 : 22. See REMEMBER.
CB:1259A

MERCHANDISE (Noun, and Verb, to make)

A. Nouns.

1711 1. EMPORIA (ἐμπορία) denotes commerce, business, trade [akin to
AG:256D No. 2, and to *emporos*, one on a journey (*en*, in, *poros*, a journey), a
CB:— merchant], occurs in Matt. 22 : 5.¶

1712 2. EMPORION (ἐμπόριον) denotes a trading-place, exchange
AG:257A (Eng., emporium), John 2 : 16, "(a house) of merchandise."¶
CB:—

1117 3. GOMOS (γόμος) is translated "merchandise" in Rev. 18 : 11, 12 :
AG:164D see BURDEN, A, No. 3.
CB:—

B. Verb.

1710 EMPOREUOMAI (ἐμπορεύομαι) primarily signifies to travel, especially
AG:256D for business ; then, to traffic, trade, Jas. 4 : 13 ; then, to make a gain of,
CB:1244B make merchandise of, 2 Pet. 2 : 3.¶

MERCHANT

1713 EMPOROS (ἔμπορος) denotes a person on a journey (*poros*, a journey),
AG:257A a passenger on shipboard ; then, a merchant, Matt. 13 : 45 ; Rev. 18 : 3,
CB:— 11, 15, 23.¶

MERCIFUL (Adjective, and Verb, to be), MERCY (Noun, and Verb, to have, etc.)

A. Nouns.

1656 1. ELEOS (ἔλεος) "is the outward manifestation of pity ; it assumes
AG:250A need on the part of him who receives it, and resources adequate to meet
CB:1244A the need on the part of him who shows it. It is used (*a*) of God, who is
rich in mercy, Eph. 2 : 4, and who has provided salvation for all men,
Tit. 3 : 5, for Jews, Luke 1 : 72, and Gentiles, Rom. 15 : 9. He is merciful
to those who fear him, Luke 1 : 50, for they also are compassed with

infirmity, and He alone can succour them. Hence they are to pray boldly for mercy, Heb. 4 : 16, and if for themselves, it is seemly that they should ask for mercy for one another, Gal. 6 : 16 ; 1 Tim. 1 : 2. When God brings His salvation to its issue at the Coming of Christ, His people will obtain His mercy, 2 Tim. 1 : 16 ; Jude 21 ; (*b*) of men ; for since God is merciful to them, He would have them show mercy to one another, Matt. 9 : 13 ; 12 : 7 ; 23 : 23 ; Luke 10 : 37 ; Jas. 2 : 13.

" Wherever the words mercy and peace are found together they occur in that order, except in Gal. 6 : 16. Mercy is the act of God, peace is the resulting experience in the heart of man. Grace describes God's attitude toward the law-breaker and the rebel ; mercy is His attitude toward those who are in distress."*

" In the order of the manifestation of God's purposes of salvation grace must go before mercy . . . only the forgiven may be blessed. . . . From this it follows that in each of the apostolic salutations where these words occur, grace precedes mercy, 1 Tim. 1 : 2 ; 2 Tim. 1 : 2 ; Tit. 1 : 4 (in some mss.) ; 2 John 3 " (Trench, Syn. § xlvii).

2. OIKTIRMOS (οἰκτιρμός), pity, compassion for the ills of others, is 3628
used (*a*) of God, Who is " the Father of mercies," 2 Cor. 1 : 3 ; His mercies AG:561D CB:1260C
are the ground upon which believers are to present their bodies a living sacrifice, holy, acceptable to God, as their reasonable service, Rom. 12 : 1 ; under the Law he who set it at nought died without compassion, Heb. 10 : 28 ; (*b*) of men ; believers are to feel and exhibit compassions one toward another, Phil. 2 : 1, R.V. " compassions," and Col. 3 : 12, R.V. "(a heart) of compassion ; " in these two places the word is preceded by No. 3, rendered " tender mercies " in the former, and " a heart " in the latter, R.V.¶

3. SPLANCHNON (σπλάγχνον), affections, the heart, always in the 4698
plural in the N.T., has reference to feelings of kindness, goodwill, pity, AG:763A CB:1269C
Phil. 2 : 1, R.V., " tender mercies ; " see AFFECTION, No. 2, and BOWELS.

Note : In Acts 13 : 34 the phrase, lit., ' the holy things, the faithful things (of David) ' is translated, " the holy and sure *blessings*," R.V. ; the A.V., following the mss. in which the words " holy and " are absent, has " the sure mercies," but notices the full phrase in the margin.

B. Verbs.

1. ELEEŌ (ἐλεέω), akin to A, No. 1, signifies, in general, to feel 1653
sympathy with the misery of another, and especially sympathy manifested AG:249C CB:1244A
in act, (*a*) in the Active Voice, to have pity or mercy on, to shew mercy to, e.g., Matt. 9 : 27 ; 15 : 22 ; 17 : 15 ; 18 : 33 ; 20 : 30, 31 (three times in Mark, four in Luke) ; Rom. 9 : 15, 16, 18 ; 11 : 32 ; 12 : 8 ; Phil. 2 : 27 ; Jude 22, 23 ; (*b*) in the Passive Voice, to have pity or mercy shown one, to obtain mercy, Matt. 5 : 7 ; Rom. 11 : 30, 31 ; 1 Cor. 7 : 25 ; 2 Cor. 4 : 1 ; 1 Tim. 1 : 13, 16 ; 1 Pet. 2 : 10.

* From Notes on Galatians by Hogg and Vine, pp. 340, 341.

3627 2. OIKTEIRŌ (οἰκτείρω), akin to A, No. 2, to have pity on (from
AG:561D *oiktos*, pity: *oi*, an exclamation,=oh!), occurs in Rom. 9 : 15 (twice),
CB:— where it follows No. 1 (twice); the point established there and in Ex. 33 : 19, from the Sept. of which it is quoted, is that the mercy and compassion shown by God are determined by nothing external to His attributes. Speaking generally *oikteirō* is a stronger term than *eleeō*.¶

2433 3. HILASKOMAI (ἱλάσκομαι) in profane Greek meant to conciliate,
AG:375C appease, propitiate, cause the gods to be reconciled; their goodwill was
CB:1250C not regarded as their natural condition, but as something to be earned. The heathen believed their gods to be naturally alienated in feeling from man. In the N.T. the word never means to conciliate God; it signifies (*a*) to be propitious, merciful, Luke 18 : 13, in the prayer of the publican; (*b*) to expiate, make propitiation for, Heb. 2 : 17, "make propitiation."

That God is not of Himself already alienated from man, see John 3 : 16. His attitude toward the sinner does not need to be changed by his efforts. With regard to his sin, an expiation is necessary, consistently with God's holiness and for His righteousness' sake, and that expiation His grace and love have provided in the atoning Sacrifice of His Son; man, himself a sinner, justly exposed to God's wrath (John 3 : 36), could never find an expiation. As Lightfoot says, "when the N.T. writers speak at length on the subject of Divine wrath, the hostility is represented, not as on the part of God, but of men." Through that which God has accomplished in Christ, by His death, man, on becoming regenerate, escapes the merited wrath of God. The making of this expiation [(*b*) above], with its effect in the mercy of God (*a*) is what is expressed in *hilaskomai*.¶ The Sept. uses the compound verb *exilaskomai*, e.g., Gen. 32 : 20; Ex. 30 : 10, 15, 16; 32 : 30, and frequently in Lev. and Numb. See PROPITIATION.

C. Adjectives.

1655 1. ELEĒMŌN (ἐλεήμων), merciful, akin to A, No. 1, not simply
AG:250A possessed of pity but actively compassionate, is used of Christ as a High
CB:1244A Priest, Heb. 2 : 17, and of those who are like God, Matt. 5 : 7 (cp. Luke 6 : 35, 36, where the R.V., "sons" is to be read, as representing characteristics resembling those of their Father).¶

3629 2. OIKTIRMŌN (οἰκτίρμων), pitiful, compassionate for the ills of
AG:561D others, a stronger term than No. 1 (akin to A, No. 2), is used twice in Luke
CB:1260C 6 : 36, "merciful" (of the character of God, to be expressed in His people); Jas. 5 : 11, R.V., "merciful," A.V., "of tender mercy."¶

2436 3. HILEŌS (ἵλεως), propitious, merciful (akin to B, No. 3), was used
AG:376A in profane Greek just as in the case of the verb (which see). There is
CB:1250C nothing of this in the use of the word in Scripture. The quality expressed by it there essentially appertains to God, though man is undeserving of it. It is used only of God, Heb. 8 : 12; in Matt. 16 : 22, "Be it far from Thee" (Peter's word to Christ) may have the meaning given in the R.V. marg., "(God) have mercy on Thee," lit., 'propitious to Thee' (A.V. marg., "Pity Thyself"). ¶ Cp. the Sept., 2 Sam. 20 : 20; 23 : 17.

4. ANELEOS or ANILEŌS (ἀνέλεος or ἀνίλεως), unmerciful, merciless 448 AG:64C
(*a*, negative, *n*, euphonic, and A, No. 1, or C, No. 3), occurs in Jas. 2 : 13, CB:1235C
said of judgment on him who shows no mercy.¶

MERCY-SEAT

HILASTĒRION (ἱλαστήριον), the lid or cover of the ark of the 2435 AG:375D
Covenant, signifies the Propitiatory, so called on account of the expiation CB:1250C
made once a year on the great day of atonement, Heb. 9 : 5. For the formation see Ex. 25 : 17–21. The Heb. word is *kapporeth*, the cover, a meaning connected with the covering or removal of sin (Psa. 32 : 1) by means of expiatory sacrifice. This mercy-seat, together with the ark, is spoken of as the footstool of God, 1 Chron. 28 : 2 ; cp. Ps. 99 : 5 ; 132 : 7. The Lord promised to be present upon it and to commune with Moses " from above the mercy-seat, from between the two cherubim," Ex. 25 : 22 (see CHERUBIM). In the Sept. the word *epithēma*, which itself means a cover, is added to *hilastērion; epithēma* was simply a translation of *kapporeth;* accordingly, *hilastērion*, not having this meaning, and being essentially connected with propitiation, was added. Eventually *hilastērion* stood for both. In 1 Chron. 28 : 11 the Holy of Holies is called " the House of the Kapporeth " (see R.V., marg.).

Through His voluntary expiatory sacrifice in the shedding of His blood, under Divine judgment upon sin, and through His Resurrection, Christ has become the Mercy-Seat for His people. See Rom. 3 : 25, and see PROPITIATION, B, No. 1.¶

MERRY (to be, to make)

1. EUPHRAINŌ (εὐφραίνω), in the Active Voice, to cheer, make 2165 AG:327C
glad, 2 Cor. 2 : 2, is used everywhere else in the Passive Voice, signifying, CB:1247B
to be happy, rejoice, make merry, and translated to be merry in Luke 12 : 19 ; 15 : 23, 24, 29, 32 ; in 16 : 19, " fared (sumptuously) ; " in Rev. 11 : 10, " make merry." See FARE, GLAD, REJOICE.

2. EUTHUMEŌ (εὐθυμέω), from *eu*, well, and *thumos*, the soul, as the 2114
principle of feeling, especially strong feeling, signifies to make cheerful ; AG:320D CB:—
it is used intransitively in the N.T., to be of good cheer, Acts 27 : 22, 25 ; in Jas. 5 : 13, R.V., " is (any) cheerful ? " (A.V., " . . . merry ? "). See CHEER.¶

MESS

BRŌSIS (βρῶσις), eating, food, is translated " mess of meat " in Heb. 1035 AG:148B
12 : 16, R.V. (A.V., " morsel of meat "). See FOOD, MEAT, No. 2. CB:1239B

MESSAGE

1. ANGELIA (ἀγγελία), akin to *angellō*, to bring a message, proclaim, 31 AG:7A
denotes a message, proclamation, news, 1 John 1 : 5 [some mss. have CB:1235C
epangelia : see Note (1)] ; 1 John 3 : 11, where the word is more precisely

EPANGELIA defined (by being followed by the conjunction " that," expressing the
1860 purpose that we should love one another) as being virtually equivalent to
AG:280C an order.¶
CB:1245B
PRESBEIA *Notes :* (1) *Epangelia* (*epi*, upon, and No. 1), a promise, is found in
4242 AG:699B some mss. in 1 John 1 : 5, " message " (see No. 1). See PROMISE. (2) In
CB:1266B Luke 19 : 14, A.V., *presbeia*, is translated " a message ; " R.V., " an
ambassage," as in 14 : 32. See AMBASSAGE.¶

189 2. AKOĒ (ἀκοή), hearing, also denotes the thing heard, a message ;
AG:30D
CB:1234B in 1 Thess. 2 : 13, it is associated with *logos*, a word, lit., ' the word of
hearing ' (R.V. marg.), R.V., " the word of the message," A.V., " the
word . . . which ye heard ; " so in Heb. 4 : 2, R.V., " the word of hearing "
(A.V., " the word preached "). See HEARING.

2782 AG:430D 3. KĒRUGMA (κήρυγμα), that which is proclaimed by a herald, a
CB:1255A proclamation, preaching, is translated " the message " in Tit. 1 : 3, R.V.
(A.V., " preaching "). See PREACHING.

MESSENGER

32
AG:7A 1. ANGELOS (ἄγγελος), a messenger, an angel, one sent, is translated
CB:1235C " messenger," of John the Baptist, Matt. 11 : 10 ; Mark 1 : 2 ; Luke
7 : 27 ; in the plural, of John's messengers, 7 : 24 ; of those whom Christ
sent before Him when on His journey to Jerusalem, 9 : 52 ; of Paul's
" thorn in the flesh," " a messenger of Satan," 2 Cor. 12 : 7 ; of the spies
as received by Rahab, Jas. 2 : 25. See ANGEL.

652
AG:99C 2. APOSTOLOS (ἀπόστολος), an apostle, is translated " messengers "
CB:1237A in 2 Cor. 8 : 23, regarding Titus and " the other brethren," whom Paul
describes to the Church at Corinth as " messengers of the churches," in
respect of offerings from those in Macedonia for the needy in Judæa ; in
Phil. 2 : 25, of Epaphroditus as the " messenger " of the church at Philippi
to the Apostle in ministering to his need ; R.V. marg. in each case,
" apostle." See APOSTLE.

For METE see MEASURE

For MID see MIDST

MIDDAY

MESOS *Note :* In Acts 26 : 13, " at midday " translates the adjective *mesos*,
3319 AG:507B middle, and the noun *hēmera*, a day, in a combined adverbial phrase.
CB:1258B See MIDST.
HēMERA
2250
AG:345D For MIDDLE see WALL
CB:1249C

3317
AG:507A
MIDNIGHT

CB:1258B MESONUKTION (μεσονύκτιον), an adjective denoting at, or of, midnight, is used as a noun in Mark 13 : 35 ; Luke 11 : 5 ; Acts 16 : 25 ; 20 : 7.¶

Note : In Matt. 25 : 6 " at midnight " translates the adjective ***mesos***, MESOS 3319
and noun ***nux***, night, in the combined adverbial phrase. In Acts 27 : 27 AG:507B
"about midnight" translates an adverbial phrase consisting of *kata*, CB:1258B
towards, followed by ***mesos***, middle and ***nux***, night, with the article, lit., NUX 3571
'towards (the) middle of the night.' See MIDST. AG:546B CB:1260B

MIDST

A. Adjective and Adverb.

MESOS (μέσος), an adjective denoting middle, in the middle or midst, 3319
is used in the following, in which the English requires a phrase, and the AG:507B CB:1258B
adjectival rendering must be avoided : Luke 22 : 55, " Peter sat in the midst of them," lit., 'a middle one of (them) ;' Luke 23 : 45, of the rending of the veil " in the midst ;" here the adjective idiomatically belongs to the verb " was rent," and is not to be taken literally, as if it meant 'the middle veil ;' John 1 : 26, " in the midst of you (standeth One)," R.V. (lit., 'a middle One') ; Acts 1 : 18, where the necessity of avoiding the lit. rendering is obvious. Cp. the phrases " at midday," " at midnight " (see MIDDAY, MIDNIGHT, above).

Notes : (1) *Mesos* is used adverbially, in prepositional phrases, (*a*) *ana m.*, e.g., 1 Cor. 6 : 5, " between ;" Matt. 13 : 25, " among ;" Rev. 7 : 17, " in the midst ;" (*b*) *dia m.*, e.g., Luke 4 : 30 ; 17 : 11, " through the midst ;" (*c*) *en m.*, Luke 10 : 3, R.V., " in the midst," A.V., " among ;" so 22 : 27 ; 1 Thess. 2 : 7 ; with the article after *en*, e.g., Matt. 14 : 6, R.V., " in the midst," A.V., " before ;" (*d*) *eis m.*, Mark 14 : 60, " in the midst ;" with the article, e.g., Mark 3 : 3, " forth " (lit., 'into the midst') ; (*e*) *ek m.*, " out of the way," lit., 'out of the midst,' Col. 2 : 14 ; 2 Thess. 2 : 7, where, however, removal is not necessarily in view ; there is no accompanying verb signifying removal, as in each of the other occurrences of the phrase ; with the article, e.g., 1 Cor. 5 : 2 ; 2 Cor. 6 : 17 ; see WAY ; (*f*) *kata m.*, Acts 27 : 27, " about mid(night)."

(2) The neuter, ***meson***, is used adverbially in Matt. 14 : 24, in some mss., " in the midst (of the waves) ;" in Phil. 2 : 15 in the best mss. (where some mss. have *en m.* . . .). (3) For Rev. 8 : 13, see HEAVEN, A, No. 2.

B. Verb.

MESOŌ (μεσόω), to be in the middle, is used of time in John 7 : 14, 3322
translated " when it was . . . the midst (of the feast)." lit., '(the feast) AG:508B CB:—
being in the middle.'¶

MIGHT (Noun), MIGHTY, MIGHTILY, MIGHTIER

A. Nouns.

1. DUNAMIS (δύναμις), power, (*a*) used relatively, denotes inherent 1411
ability, capability, ability to perform anything, e.g., Matt. 25 : 15, AG:207B CB:1242B

"ability;" Acts 3:12, "power"; 2 Thess. 1:7, R.V., "(angels) of His power" (A.V., "mighty"); Heb. 11:11, R.V., "power" (A.V., "strength"); see ABILITY; (*b*) used absolutely, denotes (1) power to work, to carry something into effect, e.g., Luke 24:49; (2) power in action, e.g., Rom. 1:16; 1 Cor. 1:18; it is translated "might" in the A.V. of Eph. 1:21 (R.V., "power"); so 3:16; Col. 1:11 (1st clause); 2 Pet. 2:11; in Rom. 15:19, A.V., this noun is rendered "mighty;" R.V., "(in the) power of signs." The R.V. consistently avoids the rendering "might" for *dunamis;* the usual rendering is "power." Under this heading comes the rendering "mighty works," e.g., Matt. 7:22, R.V. (A.V., "wonderful works"); 11:20–23; singular number in Mark 6:5; in Matt. 14:2 and Mark 6:14 the R.V. has "powers;" in 2 Cor. 12:12, R.V., "mighty works" (A.V., "mighty deeds"). See MIRACLE, especially POWER.

1849 AG:277D *Note: Dunamis,* power, is to be distinguished from *exousia,* the right
CB:1247C to exercise power. See DOMINION, Note.

2479 AG:383C 2. ISCHUS (ἰσχύς) denotes might, strength, power, (*a*) inherent and in
CB:1253A action as used of God, Eph. 1:19, R.V., "(the strength, *kratos,* of His) might," A.V., "(His mighty) power," i.e., power (over external things) exercised by strength; Eph. 6:10, "of His might;" 2 Thess. 1:9, R.V., "(from the glory) of His might" (A.V. "power"); Rev. 5:12, R.V., "might" (A.V., "strength"); 7:12, "might;" (*b*) as an endowment, said (1) of angels, 2 Pet. 2:11; here the order is No. 2 and No. 1, R.V., "might and power," which better expresses the distinction than the A.V., "power and might;" in some mss. in Rev. 18:2 it is said of the voice of an angel [see E, (*c*)]; the most authentic mss. have the adjective *ischuros,* "mighty;" (2) of men, Mark 12:30, 33; Luke 10:27 (R.V. and A.V., "strength," in all three verses); 1 Pet. 4:11, R.V., "strength" (A.V., "ability:" this belongs rather to No. 1). Either 'strength' or 'might' expresses the true significance of *ischus.* See ABILITY, POWER,
MEGALEIOTĒS 3168 STRENGTH.¶

AG:496D CB:1258A *Notes:* (1) In Luke 9:43, A.V., *megaleiotēs,* greatness, majesty, is
KRATOS translated "mighty power" (R.V., "majesty"). (2) Cp. *kratos* (see
2904 AG:449A POWER).

CB:1256A
B. Adjectives.

1415 AG:208C 1. DUNATOS (δυνατός), powerful, mighty (akin to A, No. 1), is used,
CB:1242B with that significance, (1) of God, Luke 1:49, "mighty;" Rom. 9:22, "power" (here the neuter of the adjective is used with the article, as a noun, equivalent to *dunamis*); frequently with the meaning "able" (see ABLE, C, No. 1); (2) of Christ, regarded as a prophet, Luke 24:19 ("in deed and word"); (3) of men: Moses, Acts 7:22 ("in his words and works"); Apollos, 18:24, "in the Scriptures;" of those possessed of natural power, 1 Cor. 1:26; of those possessed of spiritual power, 2 Cor. 10:4. For the shades of meaning in the translation "strong,"

see Rom. 15 : 1 ; 2 Cor. 12 : 10 ; 13 : 9. For Rev. 6 : 15, see No. 2,
below ; see STRONG. See also POSSIBLE.

2. ISCHUROS (ἰσχυρός), strong, mighty (akin to A, No. 2, and with 2478
corresponding adjectival significance), is usually translated "strong ;" AG:383A CB:1253A
"mighty" in Luke 15 : 14 (of a famine) ; Rev. 19 : 6 (of thunders) ;
19 : 18 (of men) : in the following, where the A.V. has "mighty," the R.V.
substitutes "strong," 1 Cor. 1 : 27 ; Rev. 6 : 15 (A.V., "mighty men") ;
18 : 10, 21 ; Heb. 11 : 34, R.V., "(waxed) mighty" (A.V., "valiant").
See BOISTEROUS, POWERFUL, STRONG (where the word is analysed).

3. ISCHUROTEROS (ἰσχυρότερος), stronger, mightier, the comparative 2478
degree of No. 2, is translated "mightier" in Matt. 3 : 11 ; Mark 1 : 7 ; (-UROS) AG:383A 1.a.
Luke 3 : 16 ; "stronger" in Luke 11 : 22 ; 1 Cor. 1 : 25 ; 10 : 22. See CB:1253A
STRONG.¶

4. BIAIOS (βίαιος), violent (from *bia*, force, violence, strength, found 972
in Acts 5 : 26 ; 21 : 35 ; 24 : 7 ; 27 : 41¶), occurs in Acts 2 : 2, of wind.¶ AG:141A CB:1239A

5. KRATAIOS (κραταιός), strong, mighty (akin to *kratos*, strength, 2900
relative and manifested power : see MIGHTILY, below), is found in 1 Pet. AG:448B CB:1256A
5 : 6, of the "mighty" hand of God.¶

6. MEGALEIOS (μεγαλεῖος) is rendered "mighty" in Acts 2 : 11, 3167
R.V. See WONDERFUL, Note (2). AG:496D CB:1258A

Notes : (1) In Luke 1 : 52, A.V., *dunastēs*, a potentate, prince, is DUNASTēS
translated "mighty" (R.V., "princes"). (2) In Rev. 6 : 13, A.V., 1413 AG:208C
megas, great, is translated "mighty" (R.V., "great"), of a wind. (3) In CB:1242B
Rev. 16 : 18, A.V., *tēlikoutos*, so great (when said of things), is translated MEGAS 3173
"so mighty" (R.V., "so great"), of an earthquake. AG:497C

C. Verb.
CB:1258A TēLIKOUTOS

DUNATEŌ (δυνατέω), to be powerful (akin to A, No. 1 and B, No. 1), 5082
is found in the most authentic mss. in Rom. 14 : 4 (some have *dunatos*, AG:814C CB:—
B, No. 1), R.V. "(the Lord) hath power," A.V., "(God) is able ;" simi- DUNATEō
larly, as regard mss., in 2 Cor. 9 : 8, where the R.V. and A.V. have "(God) 1414
is able ;" in 2 Cor. 13 : 3, A.V., "is mighty," R.V., "is powerful" AG:208C CB:1242B
(according to the general significance of *dunamis*).¶

Note : In Gal. 2 : 8, A.V., *energeō*, to work, work in (*en*, in, *ergon*, 1754
work), is first translated "wrought effectually," then "was mighty in" AG:265B CB:1245A
(R.V., "wrought for," in both places ; the probable meaning is 'in me').
See EFFECTUAL, WORK.

D. Adverb.

EUTONŌS (εὐτόνως), vigorously, vehemently (*eu*, well, *teinō*, to 2159
stretch), is translated "mightily" in Acts 18 : 28, A.V., of the power of AG:327B CB:—
Apollos in 'confuting' the Jews (R.V., "powerfully") ; in Luke 23 : 10
it is rendered "vehemently." See POWERFUL, VEHEMENTLY.¶ In the
Sept., Josh. 6 : 7, "(let them sound) loudly."¶

E. Phrases.

The following phrases signify "mightily :" (*a*) *en dunamei*, Col. 1 : 29,
of the inward power of God's working, lit., "in power," as R.V. marg.

(*en*, in, and A, No. 1); (*b*) *kata kratos*, Acts 19:20, of the increase of the word of the Lord in a place, lit., 'according to might;' (*c*) in Rev. 18:2 some mss. have *en ischui*, lit., 'in strength' (*en*, in, and A, No. 2), of the voice of an angel.

MILE

3400 AG:521D CB:— MILION (μίλιον), a Roman mile, a word of Latin origin (1680 yards), is used in Matt. 5:41.¶

MILK

1051 AG:149C CB:1248A GALA (γάλα) is used (*a*) literally, 1 Cor. 9:7; (*b*) metaphorically, of rudimentary spiritual teaching, 1 Cor. 3:2; Heb. 5:12, 13; 1 Pet. 2:2; here the meaning largely depends upon the significance of the word LOGIKOS 3050 AG:476C CB:1257A *logikos*, which the A.V. renders "of the word," R.V. "spiritual." While *logos* denotes a word, the adjective *logikos* is never used with the meaning assigned to it in the A.V., nor does the context in 1:23 compel this meaning. While it is true that the Word of God, like milk, nourishes the soul, and this is involved in the exhortation, the only other occurrence in the N.T. is Rom. 12:1, where it is translated "reasonable," i.e., rational, intelligent (service), in contrast to the offering of an irrational animal; so here the nourishment may be understood as of that spiritually rational nature which, acting through the regenerate mind, develops spiritual growth. God's Word is not given so that it is impossible to understand it, or that it requires a special class of men to interpret it; its character is such that the Holy Spirit who gave it can unfold its truths even to the young convert. Cp. 1 John 2:27.¶

MILL

3459 AG:529C CB:— MULŌN (μύλων) denotes a mill-house, where the millstone is, Matt. 24:41; some mss. have *mulos* (see next word).¶ In the Sept., Jer. 52:11, "grinding house" (lit., 'house of a mill').¶

MILLSTONE

A. Noun.

3458 AG:529B CB:1259B MULOS (μύλος) denotes a hand-mill, consisting of two circular stones, one above the other, the lower being fixed. From the centre of the lower a wooden pin passes through a hole in the upper, into which the grain is thrown, escaping as flour between the stones and falling on a prepared material below them. The handle is inserted into the upper stone near the circumference. Small stones could be turned by one woman (mill-grinding was a work deemed fit only for women and slaves; cp. Judg. ONIKOS 3684 AG:570C CB:1260C 16:21); larger ones were turned by two (cp. Matt. 24:41, under MILL), or more.

Still larger ones were turned by an ass (*onikos*), Matt. 18:6, R.V., "a great millstone" (marg., "a millstone turned by an ass"), indicating the immediate and overwhelming drowning of one who causes one young believer to stumble ; Mark 9 : 42 (where some mss. have *lithos mulikos*, a stone of a mill, as in Luke 17 : 2) ; Rev. 18 : 22 (some mss. have it in ver. 21, see below).¶

B. Adjectives. 3457

1. MULIKOS (μυλικός), ' of a mill,' occurs in Luke 17 : 2 (see above).¶ AG:529B CB:1259B

2. MULINOS (μύλινος), made of millstone, is used with *lithos*, a stone; —
and with the adjective *megas*, great, in the best mss. in Rev. 18 : 21 (some AG:529B CB:1259B
have the word *mulos* ; see A).¶

MIND (Noun and Verb)

A. Nouns.

1. NOUS (νοῦς), mind, denotes, speaking generally, the seat of reflec- 3563
tive consciousness, comprising the faculties of perception and under- AG:544C CB:1260A
standing, and those of feeling, judging and determining.

Its use in the N.T. may be analysed as follows : it denotes (*a*) the faculty of knowing, the seat of the understanding, Luke 24 : 45 ; Rom. 1 : 28 ; 14 : 5 ; 1 Cor. 14 : 15, 19 ; Eph. 4 : 17 ; Phil. 4 : 7 ; Col. 2 : 18 ; 1 Tim. 6 : 5 ; 2 Tim. 3 : 8 ; Tit. 1 : 15 ; Rev. 13 : 18 ; 17 : 9 ; (*b*) counsels, purpose, Rom. 11 : 34 (of the mind of God) ; 12 : 2 ; 1 Cor. 1 : 10 ; 2 : 16, twice (1) of the thoughts and counsels of God, (2) of Christ, a testimony to His Godhood ; Eph. 4 : 23 ; (*c*) the new nature, which belongs to the believer by reason of the new birth, Rom. 7 : 23, 25, where it is contrasted with " the flesh," the principle of evil which dominates fallen man. Under (*b*) may come 2 Thess. 2 : 2, where it stands for the determination to be stedfast amidst afflictions, through the confident expectation of the day of rest and recompense mentioned in the first chapter.¶

2. DIANOIA (διάνοια), lit. a thinking through, or over, a meditation, 1271
reflecting, signifies (*a*) like No. 1, the faculty of knowing, understanding, AG:187A CB:1241B
or moral reflection, (1) with an evil significance, a consciousness characterized by a perverted moral impulse, Eph. 2 : 3 (plural) ; 4 : 18 ; (2) with a good significance, the faculty renewed by the Holy Spirit, Matt. 22 : 37 ; Mark 12 : 30 ; Luke 10 : 27 ; Heb. 8 : 10 ; 10 : 16 ; 1 Pet. 1 : 13 ; 1 John 5 : 20 ; (*b*) sentiment, disposition (not as a function but as a product) ; (1) in an evil sense, Luke 1 : 51, " imagination ; " Col. 1 : 21 ; (2) in a good sense, 2 Pet. 3 : 1.¶

3. ENNOIA (ἔννοια), an idea, notion, intent, is rendered " mind " in 1771 AG:267A
1 Pet. 4 : 1 ; see INTENT. CB:1245B

4. NOĒMA (νόημα), thought, design, is rendered " minds " in 2 Cor. 3540 AG:540D
3 : 14 ; 4 : 4 ; 11 : 3 ; Phil. 4 : 7 ; see DEVICE, No. 2. CB:1259C

5. GNŌMĒ (γνώμη), a purpose, judgment, opinion, is translated 1106
" mind " in Philm. 14 and Rev. 17 : 13. See JUDGMENT, No. 4. AG:163A CB:1248B

6. PHRONĒMA (φρόνημα) denotes what one has in the mind, the 5427
thought (the content of the process expressed in *phroneō*, to have in mind, AG:866C CB:1264C
to think) ; or an object of thought ; in Rom. 8 : 6 (A.V., " to be carnally

minded" and "to be spiritually minded"), the R.V., adhering to the use of the noun, renders by "the mind of the flesh," in vv. 6 and 7, and "the mind of the spirit," in ver. 6. In ver. 27 the word is used of the mind of
PHRONēSIS the Holy Spirit.¶

5428 AG:866C *Notes:* (1) This word is to be distinguished from *phronēsis*, which
CB:1264C denotes an understanding, leading to right action, prudence, Luke 1 : 17;
PSUCHē Eph. 1 : 8.¶ (2) In three places, Acts 14 : 2; Phil. 1 : 27; Heb. 12 : 3,
5590 AG:893B the A.V. translates *psuchē*, the soul, by "mind" (R.V., "soul").

CB:1267C

B. Verbs.

5426 AG:866A 1. PHRONEŌ (φρονέω) signifies (*a*) to think, to be minded in a certain
CB:1264C way: (*b*) to think of, be mindful of. It implies moral interest or reflection, not mere unreasoning opinion. Under (*a*) it is rendered by the verb to mind in the following: Rom. 8 : 5, "(they that are after the flesh) do mind (the things of the flesh);" 12 : 16, "be of (the same) mind," lit., 'minding the same,' and "set (not) your mind on," R.V., A.V., "mind (not);" 15 : 5, "to be of (the same) mind," R.V., (A.V., "to be likeminded"); so the R.V. in 2 Cor. 13 : 11, A.V., "be of (one) mind;" Gal. 5 : 10, "ye will be (none otherwise) minded;" Phil. 1 : 7, R.V., "to be (thus) minded," A.V., "to think (this);" 2 : 2, R.V., "be of (the same) mind," A.V., "be likeminded," and "being . . . of (one) mind," lit., 'minding (the one thing);' 2 : 5, R.V., "have (this) mind," A.V., "let (this) mind be," lit., 'mind this;' 3 : 15, "let us . . . be (thus) minded," and "(if) . . . ye are (otherwise) minded" (some mss. have the verb in ver. 16); 3 : 19, "(who) mind (earthly things);" 4 : 2, "be of (the same) mind;" Col. 3 : 2, R.V. and A.V. marg., "set your mind," lit., 'mind (the things above),' A.V., "set your affection." See CAREFUL, B, No 6, REGARD, SAVOUR, THINK, UNDERSTAND.

363 AG:57D 2. ANAMIMNĒSKŌ (ἀναμιμνήσκω), to remind, call to remembrance
CB:1235A (*ana*, up, *mimnēskō*, to remind), is translated "called to mind," in Mark 14 : 72 (Passive Voice). See REMEMBRANCE.

1878 AG:282D *Note:* The lengthened form *epanamimnēskō* is used in Rom. 15 : 15,
CB:— A.V., "putting (you) in mind;" R.V., "putting (you) again (*epi*) in remembrance."¶

5279 AG:846A 3. HUPOMIMNĒSKŌ (ὑπομιμνήσκω), to cause one to remember, put
CB:1252B one in mind (*hupo*, under), is translated "put (them) in mind" in Tit. 3 : 1. See REMEMBER, REMEMBRANCE.

5294 AG:848B 4. HUPOTITHĒMI (ὑποτίθημι), lit., to place under (*hupo*, under,
CB:— *tithēmi*, to place), to lay down (of risking the life, Rom. 16 : 4), also denotes to suggest, put into one's mind, 1 Tim. 4 : 6, R.V., "put . . . in mind" (A.V., "put . . . in remembrance"). See LAY.¶

4993 AG:802A 5. SŌPHRONEŌ (σωφρονέω) signifies (*a*) to be of sound mind, or in
CB:1269B one's right mind, sober-minded (*sōzō*, to save, *phrēn*, the mind), Mark 5 : 15 and Luke 8 : 35, "in his right mind;" 2 Cor. 5 : 13, R.V., "we are of sober mind" (A.V., "we be sober"); (*b*) to be temperate, self-controlled, Tit. 2 : 6, to be sober-minded;" 1 Pet. 4 : 7, R.V., "be ye . . .

of sound mind" (A.V., "be ye sober"). See also Rom. 12 : 3. See SOBER.¶

Note: In Acts 20 : 13, A.V., *mellō*, to be about to, to intend, is trans- 3195 AG:500D
lated "minding" (R.V., "intending"). See INTEND. CB:1258A

C. Adjective.

HOMOPHRŌN (ὁμόφρων), agreeing, of one mind (*homos*, same, *phrēn*, 3675 AG:569C
the mind), is used in 1 Pet. 3 : 8.¶ CB:—

Notes: (1) For the noun *sōphronismos*, in 2 Tim. 1 : 7, see SŌPHRONISMOS 4995
DISCIPLINE.¶ (2) In Rom. 15 : 6, A.V., the adverb *homothumadon*, of AG:802B
one accord, is translated "with one mind" (R.V., "of one accord"). CB:—
See ACCORD. (3) See also CAST, CHANGE, DOUBTFUL, FERVENT, FOR- HOMOTHUMADON 3661
WARDNESS, HUMBLENESS, HUMILITY, LOWLINESS, READINESS, READY, AG:566C CB:1251A
WILLING.

MINDED

1. PHRONEŌ (φρονέω): see MIND, B, No. 1.

2. BOULOMAI (βούλομαι), to wish, will, desire, purpose (akin to 1014 AG:146A
boulē, counsel, purpose), is translated "was minded" in Matt. 1 : 19; CB:1239B
Acts 15 : 37, R.V. (A.V., "determined"); 18 : 27, R.V. (A.V., "was disposed"); 19 : 30, R.V. (A.V., "would have"); 5 : 33, R.V., "were minded" (A.V., "took counsel"); 18 : 15, R.V., "I am (not) minded (to be)," A.V., "I will (be no);" Heb. 6 : 17, "being minded," R.V. (A.V., "willing"), said of God. See COUNSEL.

3. BOULEUŌ (βουλεύω), to take counsel, is translated to be minded 1011 AG:145C
in Acts 27 : 39; 2 Cor. 1 : 17, Middle Voice in each case. See COUNSEL, CB:1239B (-OMAI)
B, No. 1.

Note: For the noun *phronēma* in Rom. 8 : 6, see MIND, A, No. 6.

MINDFUL OF (to be)

1. MIMNĒSKŌ (μιμνήσκω), the tenses of which are from the older 3403 AG:522B
verb *mnaomai*, signifies to remind; but in the Middle Voice, to remember, (-OMAI)
to be mindful of, in the sense of caring for, e.g., Heb. 2 : 6, "Thou art CB:1259A
mindful;" in 13 : 3, "remember;" in 2 Tim. 1 : 4, R.V., "remembering" (A.V., "being mindful of"); so in 2 Pet. 3 : 2. See REMEMBER.

2. MNĒMONEUŌ (μνημονεύω), to call to mind, remember, is rendered 3421 AG:525A
"they had been mindful" in Heb. 11 : 15. See MENTION, B, REMEMBER. CB:1259A

For MINE, MINE OWN (self), see MY

MINGLE

1. MIGNUMI (μίγνυμι), to mix, mingle (from a root *mik*; Eng., *mix* 3396 AG:499C
is akin), is always in the N.T. translated to mingle, Matt. 27 : 34; Luke (MEIG-)
13 : 1; Rev. 8 : 7; 15 : 2.¶ CB:—

2. KERANNUMI (κεράννυμι), to mix, to mingle, chiefly of the diluting 2767 AG:429A
of wine, implies "a mixing of two things, so that they are blended and CB:1255A

form a compound, as in wine and water, whereas *mignumi* (No. 1) implies a mixing without such composition, as in two sorts of grain" (Liddell and Scott, Lex.). It is used in Rev. 18 : 6 (twice) ; in 14 : 10, R.V., "prepared" (marg., "mingled;" A.V., "poured out"), lit., 'mingled,' followed by *akratos*, unmixed, pure (*a*, negative, and *kratos*, an adjective, from this verb *kerannumi*), the two together forming an oxymoron, the combination in one phrase of two terms that are ordinarily contradictory.¶

4669 AG:759A
Note: For the verb *smurnizō*, to mingle with myrrh, Mark 15 : 23, see
CB:1269B
MYRRH.¶

MINISTER (Noun and Verb)

A. Nouns.

1249 AG:184C CB:1241A
1. DIAKONOS (διάκονος), a servant, attendant, minister, deacon, is translated "minister" in Mark 10 : 43 ; Rom. 13 : 4 (twice) ; 15 : 8 ; 1 Cor. 3 : 5 ; 2 Cor. 3 : 6 ; 6 : 4 ; 11 : 15 (twice) ; Gal. 2 : 17 ; Eph. 6 : 21 ; Col. 1 : 7, 23, 25 ; 4 : 7 ; 1 Thess. 3 : 2 ; 1 Tim. 4 : 6. See DEACON.

3011 AG:471B CB:1256C
2. LEITOURGOS (λειτουργός) denoted among the Greeks, firstly, one who discharged a public office at his own expense, then, in general, a public servant, minister. In the N.T. it is used (*a*) of Christ, as a "Minister of the sanctuary" (in the Heavens), Heb. 8 : 2 ; (*b*) of angels, Heb. 1 : 7 (Psa. 104 : 4) ; (*c*) of the Apostle Paul, in his evangelical ministry, fulfilling it as a serving-priest, Rom. 15 : 16 ; that he used it figuratively and not in an ecclesiastical sense, is obvious from the context ; (*d*) of Epaphroditus, as ministering to Paul's needs on behalf of the church at Philippi, Phil. 2 : 25 ; here, representative service is in view ; (*e*) of earthly rulers, who though they do not all act consciously as servants of God, yet discharge functions which are the ordinance of God, Rom. 13 : 6.¶

5257 AG:842C CB:1252A
3. HUPĒRETĒS (ὑπηρέτης), properly an under rower (*hupo*, under, *eretēs*, a rower), as distinguished from *nautēs*, a seaman (a meaning which lapsed from the word), hence came to denote any subordinate acting under another's direction ; in Luke 4 : 20, R.V., "attendant," A.V., "minister," it signifies the attendant at the Synagogue service ; in Acts 13 : 5, it is said of John Mark, R.V., "attendant," A.V., "minister ;" in Acts 26 : 16, "a minister," it is said of Paul as a servant of Christ in the Gospel ; so in 1 Cor. 4 : 1, where the Apostle associates others with himself, as Apollos and Cephas, as "ministers of Christ." See ATTEND, C, OFFICER.

Note: Other synonymous nouns are *doulos*, a bondservant ; *oiketēs*, a household servant ; *misthios*, a hired servant ; *misthōtos* (ditto) ; *pais*, a boy, a household servant. For all these see SERVANT. Speaking broadly, *diakonos* views a servant in relation to his work ; *doulos*, in relation to his master ; *hupēretēs*, in relation to his superior ; *leitourgos*, in relation to public service.

B. Verbs.

1247 AG:184A CB:1241A
1. DIAKONEŌ (διακονέω), akin to A, No. 1, signifies to be a servant, attendant, to serve, wait upon, minister. In the following it is translated

to minister, except where to serve is mentioned: it is used (*a*) with a general significance, e.g., Matt. 4:11; 20:28; Mark 1:13; 10:45; John 12:26 (" serve," twice); Acts 19:22; Philm. 13; (*b*) of waiting at table, ministering to the guests, Matt. 8:15; Luke 4:39; 8:3; 12:37; 17:8, " serve;" 22:26, " serve," ver. 27, " serveth," twice; the 2nd instance, concerning the Lord, may come under (*a*); so of women preparing food, etc., Mark 1:31; Luke 10:40, " serve;" John 12:2, " served;" (*c*) of relieving one's necessities, supplying the necessaries of life, Matt. 25:44; 27:55; Mark 15:41; Acts 6:2, " serve;" Rom. 15:25; Heb. 6:10; more definitely in connection with such service in a local church, 1 Tim. 3:10, 13 [there is nothing in the original representing the word " office;" R.V., " let them serve as deacons," " they that have served (well) as deacons "]; (*d*) of attending, in a more general way, to anything that may serve another's interests, as of the work of an amanuensis, 2 Cor. 3:3 (metaphorical): of the conveyance of material gifts for assisting the needy, 2 Cor. 8:19, 20, R.V., " is ministered " (A.V., " is administered "); of a variety of forms of service, 2 Tim. 1:18; of the testimony of the O.T. prophets, 1 Pet. 1:12; of the ministry of believers one to another in various ways, 1 Pet. 4:10, 11 (not here of discharging ecclesiastical functions).¶

Note: In Heb. 1:14, A.V. (2nd part), the phrase *eis diakonian* is translated " to minister," R.V., " to do service," lit., 'for service;' for the noun " ministering " in the 1st part, see MINISTERING, B.

2. LEITOURGEŌ (λειτουργέω), (akin to A, No. 2), in classical Greek, **3008 AG:470C CB:1256C**
signified at Athens to supply public offices at one's own cost, to render public service to the State; hence, generally, to do service, said, e.g., of service to the gods. In the N.T. (see Note below) it is used (*a*) of the prophets and teachers in the church at Antioch, who " ministered to the Lord," Acts 13:2; (*b*) of the duty of churches of the Gentiles to minister in " carnal things " to the poor Jewish saints at Jerusalem, in view of the fact that the former had " been made partakers " of the " spiritual things " of the latter, Rom. 15:27; (*c*) of the official service of priests and Levites under the Law, Heb. 10:11 (in the Sept., e.g., Ex. 29:30; Numb. 16:9).¶

Note: The synonymous verb *latreuō* (properly, to serve for hire), which **3000 AG:467C CB:1256C**
is used in the Sept. of the service of both priests and people (e.g., Ex. 4:3; Deut. 10:12, and in the N.T., e.g., Heb. 8:5), and, in the N.T., of Christians in general, e.g., Rev. 22:3, is to be distinguished from *leitourgeō*, which has to do with the fulfilment of an office, the discharge of a function, something of a representative character (Eng., liturgy).

3. HUPĒRETEŌ (ὑπηρετέω), to do the service of a *hupēretēs* (see A, **5256 AG:842C CB:1252A**
No. 3), properly, to serve as a rower on a ship, is used (*a*) of David, as serving the counsel of God in his own generation, Acts 13:36, R.V., expressive of the lowly character of his service for God; (*b*) of Paul's toil in working with his hands, and his readiness to avoid any pose of ecclesias-

tical superiority, Acts 20 : 34 ; (*c*) of the service permitted to Paul's
friends to render to him, 24 : 23.¶
2418 AG:373C 4. HIEROURGEŌ (ἱερουργέω), to minister in priestly service (akin to
CB:1250C *hierourgos*, a sacrificing priest, a word not found in the Sept. or N.T. :
from *hieros*, sacred, and *ergon*, work), is used by Paul metaphorically of his
ministry of the Gospel, Rom. 15 : 16 ; the offering connected with his
priestly ministry is " the offering up of the Gentiles," i.e., the presentation
by Gentile converts of themselves to God.¶ The Apostle uses words
proper to the priestly and Levitical ritual, to explain metaphorically his
own priestly service. Cp. *prosphora*, " offering up," and *leitourgos*, in
the same verse.
3930 AG:626B 5. PARECHŌ (παρέχω), to furnish, provide, supply, is translated
CB:— " minister " in 1 Tim. 1 : 4, of the effect of " fables and endless genealogies."
See BRING, A, No. 21.
2038 AG:306D 6. ERGAZOMAI (ἐργάζομαι), to work, work out, perform, is translated
CB:1246C " minister " in 1 Cor. 9 : 13 ; the verb is frequently used of business, or
employment, and here the phrase means ' those employed in sacred things '
CHORēGEō or ' those who are assiduous in priestly functions.' See COMMIT, A, No. 1.
5524 *Notes :* (1) The verb *chorēgeō*, rendered " minister " in the A.V. of
AG:883D 2 Cor. 9 : 10, and the strengthened form *epichorēgeō*, rendered by the same
CB:— EPICHORēGEō verb in the A.V. of 2 Cor. 9 : 10 ; Gal. 3 : 5 ; Col. 2 : 19 ; 2 Pet. 1 : 11, in
2023 ver. 5, " add," are always translated to supply in the R.V. Both verbs
AG:305A suggest an abundant supply, and are used of material or of spiritual
CB:— DIDōMI provision. See SUPPLY. (2) In Eph. 4 : 29, A.V., *didōmi*, to give, is
1325 AG:192C translated " minister " (R.V., " give ").
CB:1241C

MINISTERING, MINISTRATION, MINISTRY

A. Nouns.

1248 AG:184B 1. DIAKONIA (διακονία), the office and work of a *diakonos* (see
CB:1241A MINISTER, A, No. 1), service, ministry, is used (*a*) of domestic duties,
Luke 10 : 40 ; (*b*) of religious and spiritual ministration, (1) of apostolic
ministry, e.g., Acts 1 : 17, 25 ; 6 : 4 ; 12 : 25 ; 21 : 19 ; Rom. 11 : 13,
R.V. (A.V., " office ") ; (2) of the service of believers, e.g., Acts 6 : 1 ;
Rom. 12 : 7 ; 1 Cor. 12 : 5, R.V., " ministrations " (A.V., " administrations ") ; 1 Cor. 16 : 15 ; 2 Cor. 8 : 4 ; 9 : 1 ; 9 : 12, R.V., " ministration ; "
ver. 13 ; Eph. 4 : 12, R.V., " ministering " (A.V., " the ministry," not in
the sense of an ecclesiastical function) ; 2 Tim. 4 : 11, R.V., " (for) ministering ; " collectively of a local church, Acts 11 : 29, " relief " (R.V. marg.,
" for ministry ") ; Rev. 2 : 19, R.V., " ministry " (A.V., " service ") ;
of Paul's service on behalf of poor saints, Rom. 15 : 31 ; (3) of the ministry
of the Holy Spirit in the Gospel, 2 Cor. 3 : 8 ; (4) of the ministry of angels,
Heb. 1 : 14, R.V., " to do service " (A.V., " to minister ") ; (5) of the work
of the Gospel, in general, e.g., 2 Cor. 3 : 9, " of righteousness ; " 5 : 18,
" of reconciliation ; " (6) of the general ministry of a servant of the Lord
in preaching and teaching, Acts 20 : 24 ; 2 Cor. 4 : 1 ; 6 : 3 ; 11 : 8 ;

1 Tim. 1 : 12, R.V., "(to His) service;" 2 Tim. 4 : 5; undefined in Col. 4 : 17; (7) of the Law, as a ministration of death, 2 Cor. 3 : 7; of condemnation, 3 : 9.¶

2. LEITOURGIA (λειτουργία), akin to *leitourgos* (see MINISTER, A, No. 2), to which the meanings of *leitourgia* correspond, is used in the N.T. of sacred ministrations, (*a*) priestly, Luke 1 : 23; Heb. 8 : 6; 9 : 21; (*b*) figuratively, of the practical faith of the members of the church at Philippi regarded as priestly sacrifice, upon which the Apostle's life-blood might be poured out as a libation, Phil. 2 : 17; (*c*) of the ministration of believers one to another, regarded as priestly service, 2 Cor. 9 : 12; Phil. 2 : 30. See SERVICE.¶ 3009 AG:471A CB:1256C

B. Adjective.

LEITOURGIKOS (λειτουργικός), of or pertaining to service, ministering, is used in Heb. 1 : 14, of angels as "ministering spirits" (for the word "do service" in the next clause, see A, No. 1).¶ In the Sept., Ex. 31 : 10; 39 : 13; Numb. 4 : 12, 26; 7 : 5; 2 Chron. 24 : 14.¶ 3010 AG:471B CB:1256C

MINSTREL

MOUSIKOS (μουσικός) is found in Rev. 18 : 22, R.V., "minstrels" (A.V., "musicians"); inasmuch as other instrumentalists are mentioned, some word like "minstrels" is necessary to make the distinction, hence the R.V.; Bengel and others translate it 'singers.' Primarily the word denoted 'devoted to the Muses' (the nine goddesses who presided over the principal departments of letters), and was used of anyone devoted to or skilled in arts and sciences, or 'learned.'¶ 3451 AG:528D CB:1259B

MINT

HĒDUOSMON (ἡδύοσμον), an adjective denoting sweet-smelling (*hēdus*, sweet, *osmē*, a smell), is used as a neuter noun signifying mint, Matt. 23 : 23; Luke 11 : 42.¶ 2238 AG:344B CB:1249C

MIRACLE

1. DUNAMIS (δύναμις), power, inherent ability, is used of works of a supernatural origin and character, such as could not be produced by natural agents and means. It is translated "miracles" in the R.V. and A.V. in Acts 8 : 13 (where variant readings give the words in different order); 19 : 11; 1 Cor. 12 : 10, 28, 29; Gal. 3 : 5; A.V. only, in Acts 2 : 22 (R.V., "mighty works"); Heb. 2 : 4 (R.V., "powers"). In Gal. 3 : 5, the word may be taken in its widest sense, to include miracles both physical and moral. See MIGHT, A, No. 1, POWER, WORK. 1411 AG:207B CB:1242B

2. SĒMEION (σημεῖον), a sign, mark, token (akin to *sēmainō*, to give a sign; *sēma*, a sign), is used of miracles and wonders as signs of Divine authority; it is translated "miracles" in the R.V. and A.V. of Luke 23 : 8; Acts 4 : 16, 22; most usually it is given its more appropriate meaning "sign," "signs," e.g., Matt. 12 : 38, 39, and in every occurrence 4592 AG:747D CB:1268C

in the Synoptists, except Luke 23 : 8 ; in the following passages in John's Gospel the R.V. substitutes " sign " or " signs " for the A.V., " miracle " or " miracles ; " 2 : 11, 23 ; 3 : 2 ; 4 : 54 ; 6 : 2, 14, 26 ; 7 : 31 ; 9 : 16 ; 10 : 41 ; 11 : 47 ; 12 : 18, 37 ; the A.V. also has " signs " elsewhere in this Gospel ; in Acts, R.V., " signs," A.V., " miracles," in 6 : 8 ; 8 : 6 ; 15 : 12 ; elsewhere only in Rev. 13 : 14 ; 16 : 14 ; 19 : 20. See SIGN, TOKEN, WONDER.

MIRE

1004 AG:145A CB:1239B BORBOROS (βόρβορος), mud, filth, occurs in 2 Pet. 2 : 22.¶ In the Sept., Jer. 38 : 6 (twice), of the mire in the dungeon into which Jeremiah was cast.¶

MIRROR

2072 AG:313B CB:1246C ESOPTRON (ἔσοπτρον), rendered " glass " in the A.V., is used of any surface sufficiently smooth and regular to reflect rays of light uniformly, and thus produce images of objects which actually in front of it appear to the eye as if they were behind it. Mirrors in Biblical times were, it seems, metallic ; hence the R.V. adopts the more general term " mirror ; " in 1 Cor. 13 : 12, spiritual knowledge in this life is represented metaphorically as an image dimly perceived in a mirror ; in Jas. 1 : 23, the " law of liberty " is figuratively compared to a mirror ; the hearer who obeys not is like a person who, having looked into the mirror, forgets the reflected image after turning away ; he who obeys is like one who gazes into the mirror and retains in his soul the image of what he should be.¶

2734 (-OMAI) AG:424D CB:— *Note :* For the verb *katoptrizō*, to reflect as a mirror (some regard it as meaning ' beholding in a mirror '), in 2 Cor. 3 : 18, see BEHOLD, No. 12.

For MISCHIEF, Acts 13 : 10, see VILLANY

MISERABLE, MISERABLY, MISERY

A. Adjectives.

1652 AG:249C CB:1244A 1. ELEEINOS (ἐλεεινός), pitiable, miserable (from *eleos*, mercy, pity ; see MERCY), is used in Rev. 3 : 17, in the Lord's description of the church at Laodicea ; here the idea is probably that of a combination of
(-NOS) misery and pitiableness.¶

1652 AG:249C CB:1244A *Note :* For the comparative degree *eleeinoteros*, rendered " most pitiable " in 1 Cor. 15 : 19, R.V. (A.V., " most miserable "), see PITIABLE.

2556 AG:397D CB:1253B 2. KAKOS (κακός), bad, evil, is translated " miserable " in Matt. 21 : 41, R.V. (A.V., " wicked "). See BAD.

B. Adverb.

2560 AG:398C CB:1253B KAKŌS (κακῶς), badly, ill, is translated " miserably " in Matt. 21 : 41 (see A, No. 2). Adhering to the meaning ' evil,' and giving the designed stress, the sentence may be rendered, ' evil (as they are) he will evilly destroy them.'

C. Noun.

TALAIPŌRIA (ταλαιπωρία), hardship, suffering, distress (akin to 5004
talaipōros, wretched, Rom. 7 : 24 ; Rev. 3 : 17,¶ and to *talaipōreō*, in the AG:803B CB:1271A
Middle Voice, to afflict oneself, in Jas. 4 : 9, " be afflicted "¶), is used as an TALAIPŌREŌ
abstract noun, " misery," in Rom. 3 : 16 ; as a concrete noun, " miseries," 5003 AG:803A
in Jas. 5 : 1.¶ CB:1271A

MIST

1. ACHLUS (ἀχλύς), a mist, especially a dimness of the eyes, is used in 887
Acts 13 : 11. " In the single place of its N.T. use it attests the accuracy AG:128B CB:—
in the selection of words, and not least of medical words, which ' the beloved physician ' so often displays. For him it expresses the mist of darkness . . . which fell on the sorcerer Elymas, being the outward and visible sign of the inward spiritual darkness which would be his portion for a while in punishment for his resistance to the truth " (Trench, Syn., § c).¶

2. HOMICHLĒ (ὁμίχλη), a mist (not so thick as *nephos* and *nephelē*, —
a cloud), occurs in 2 Pet. 2 : 17 (1st part), R.V., " mists ; " some mss. AG:565D CB:1251A
have *nephelai*, " clouds " (A.V.).¶

3. ZOPHOS (ζόφος) is rendered " mist " in the A.V. of 2 Pet. 2 : 17 2217
(2nd part), R.V., " blackness ; " ' murkiness ' would be a suitable AG:339D CB:—
rendering. For this and other synonymous terms see BLACKNESS, DARKNESS.

MITE

LEPTON (λεπτόν), the neuter of the adjective *leptos*, signifying, firstly, 3016
peeled, then, fine, thin, small, light, became used as a noun, denoting a AG:472A (-OS) CB:1256C
small copper coin, often mentioned in the Mishna as proverbially the
smallest Jewish coin. It was valued at $\frac{1}{8}$th of the Roman *as*, and the
$\frac{1}{128}$th part of the *denarius* : its legal value was about one third of an DENARION
English farthing ; Mark 12 : 42 lit. reads ' two *lepta*, which make a 1220 AG:179B
kodrantēs (a *quadrans*) ; ' in Luke 12 : 59 ' the last *lepton* ' corresponds in CB:—
effect to Matt. 5 : 26, ' the uttermost *kodrantēs*,' " farthing ; " elsewhere KODRANTĒS 2835
Luke 21 : 2 ; see FARTHING.¶ AG:437A CB:—

MIXED (with)

Note : In Heb. 4 : 2, A.V., *sunkerannumi*, lit., to mix with (*sun*, with, 4786
kerannumi, see MINGLE, No. 2), is so translated ; R.V., " were (not) united AG:773D CB:1270C
(by faith) with " [A.V., " (not) being mixed . . . in], as said of persons ;
in 1 Cor. 12 : 24 " hath tempered." See TEMPER TOGETHER.¶

MIXTURE

MIGMA 3395

MIGMA (μίγμα), a mixture (akin to *mignumi*, to mix, mingle : see AG:521A
MINGLE, No. 1), occurs in John 19 : 39 (some mss. have *heligma*, a roll).¶ AKRATOS 194
Note : In Rev. 14 : 10, A.V., *akratos* (*a*, negative, and *kerannumi*, to AG:33A

mingle) is translated " without mixture " (R.V., " unmixed ").¶ In the Sept., Psa. 75 : 8 ; Jer. 32 : 1.¶

MOCK, MOCKER, MOCKING

A. Verbs.

1702 AG:255D CB:1244B 1. EMPAIZŌ (ἐμπαίζω), a compound of *paizō*, to play like a child (*pais*), to sport, jest, prefixed by *en*, in or at, is used only in the Synoptists, and, in every instance, of the mockery of Christ, except in Matt. 2 : 16 (there in the sense of deluding, or deceiving, of Herod by the wise men) and in Luke 14 : 29, of ridicule cast upon the one who after laying a foundation of a tower is unable to finish it. The word is used (*a*) prophetically by the Lord, of His impending sufferings, Matt. 20 : 19 ; Mark 10 : 34 ; Luke 18 : 32 ; (*b*) of the actual insults inflicted upon Him by the men who had taken Him from Gethsemane, Luke 22 : 63 ; by Herod and his soldiers, Luke 23 : 11 ; by the soldiers of the governor, Matt. 27 : 29, 31 ; Mark 15 : 20 ; Luke 23 : 36 ; by the chief priests, Matt. 27 : 41 ; Mark 15 : 31.¶

3456 AG:529B CB:1259B 2. MUKTĒRIZŌ (μυκτηρίζω), from *muktēr*, the nose, hence, to turn up the nose at, sneer at, treat with contempt, is used in the Passive Voice in Gal. 6 : 7, where the statement " God is not mocked " does not mean that men do not mock Him (see Prov. 1 : 30, where the Sept. has the same verb) ; the Apostle vividly contrasts the essential difference between God and man. It is impossible to impose upon Him who discerns the thoughts and intents of the heart.¶

1592 (-TERIZŌ) AG:243B CB:1243C *Note : Ekmuktērizō*, a strengthened form of the above, to scoff at, is used in Luke 16 : 14 and 23 : 35 (R.V., " scoffed at ; " A.V., " derided "). See DERIDE, SCOFF.¶

5512 AG:882C CB:— 3. CHLEUAZŌ (χλευάζω), to jest, mock, jeer at (from *chleuē*, a jest), is said of the ridicule of some of the Athenian philosophers at the Apostle's testimony concerning the resurrection of the dead, Acts 17 : 32.¶

— AG:191A CB:— 4. DIACHLEUAZŌ (διαχλευάζω), an intensive form of No. 3, to scoff at, whether by gesture or word, is said of those who jeered at the testimony given on the day of Pentecost, Acts 2 : 13 (some mss. have No. 3).¶

B. Nouns.

1703 AG:255D CB:— 1. EMPAIKTĒS (ἐμπαίκτης), a mocker (akin to A, No. 1), is used in 2 Pet. 3 : 3, R.V., " mockers " (A.V., " scoffers ") ; Jude 18, R.V. and A.V., " mockers."¶ In the Sept., Is. 3 : 4.¶

1701 AG:255D CB:— 2. EMPAIGMOS (ἐμπαιγμός), the act of the *empaiktēs*, a mocking, is used in Heb. 11 : 36, " mockings."¶ In the Sept., Psa. 38 : 7 ; Ezek. 22 : 4.¶

— AG:255D CB:1244B 3. EMPAIGMONĒ (ἐμπαιγμονή), an abstract noun, mockery, is used in 2 Pet. 3 : 3 (some mss. omit it, as in A.V.) : (see also No. 1, above).¶

For MODERATION, Phil. 4 : 5, A.V., see FORBEARANCE, C, No. 2

MODEST

KOSMIOS (κόσμιος), orderly, well-arranged, decent, modest (akin to 2887
kosmos, in its primary sense as harmonious arrangement, adornment; AG:445C
cp. *kosmikos*, of the world, which is related to *kosmos* in its secondary sense CB:1255C
as the world), is used in 1 Tim. 2 : 9 of the apparel with which Christian women are to adorn themselves; in 3 : 2 (R.V., "orderly;" A.V., "of good behaviour"), of one of the qualifications essential for a bishop or overseer. "The well-ordering is not of dress and demeanour only, but of the inner life, uttering indeed and expressing itself in the outward conversation" (Trench, Syn., §xcii).¶ In the Sept., Eccl. 12 : 9.¶

MOISTURE

IKMAS (ἰκμάς), moisture (probably from an Indo-European root 2429 (HI-)
sik— indicating wet), is used in Luke 8 : 6.¶ In the Sept., Job 26 : 14; AG:375A
Jer. 17 : 8.¶ CB:—

MOMENT

A. Nouns.

1. ATOMOS (ἄτομος) lit. means indivisible (from *a*, negative, and 822
temnō, to cut; Eng., atom); hence it denotes a moment, 1 Cor. 15 : 52.¶ AG:120B CB:1238B
2. STIGMĒ (στιγμή), a prick, a point (akin to *stizō*, to prick), is 4743
used metaphorically in Luke 4 : 5, of a moment, with *chronos*, "a moment AG:768C CB:—
(of time)."¶

Note: It is to be distinguished from *stigma*, a mark or brand, Gal. 6 : 17, which is, however, also connected with *stizō*.

B. Adverb.

PARAUTIKA (παραυτίκα), the equivalent of *parauta*, immediately 3910
(not in the N.T.), i.e., *para auta*, with *ta pragmata* understood, 'at the AG:623B CB:—
same circumstances,' is used adjectivally in 2 Cor. 4 : 17 and translated "which is but for a moment;" the meaning is not, however, simply that of brief duration, but that which is present with us now or immediate (*para*, beside, with), in contrast to the future glory; the clause is, lit., 'for the present lightness (i.e., light burden, the adjective *elaphron*, light, being used as a noun) of (our) affliction.'¶ This meaning is confirmed by its use in the Sept. of Psa. 70 : 3, '(let them be turned back) immediately,' where the rendering could not be 'for a moment.'¶

MONEY

1. ARGURION (ἀργύριον), properly, a piece of silver, denotes (*a*) 694
silver, e.g., Acts 3 : 6; (*b*) a silver coin, often in the plural, "pieces of AG:104D CB:1237C
silver," e.g., Matt. 26 : 15; so 28 : 12, where the meaning is 'many, (*hikanos*) pieces of silver'; (*c*) money; it has this meaning in Matt. 25 : 18, 27; 28 : 15; Mark 14 : 11; Luke 9 : 3; 19 : 15, 23; 22 : 5; Acts 8 : 20 (here the R.V. has "silver").

Note: In Acts 7 : 16, for the A.V., "(a sum of) money," the R.V. has "(a price in) silver." See SILVER.

5536 AG:885C CB:1240A 2. CHRĒMA (χρῆμα), lit., a thing that one uses (akin to *chraomai*, to use), hence, (*a*) wealth, riches, Mark 10 : 23, 24 ; Luke 18 : 24 ; (*b*) money, Acts 4 : 37, singular number, a sum of money ; plural in 8 : 18, 20 ; 24 : 26.¶ See RICHES.

5475 AG:875A CB:1239B 3. CHALKOS (χαλκός), copper, is used, by metonymy, of copper coin, translated " money," in Mark 6 : 8 ; 12 : 41. See BRASS.

2772 AG:429D CB:— 4. KERMA (κέρμα), primarily a slice (akin to *keirō*, to cut short), hence, a small coin, change, is used in the plural in John 2 : 15, " the changers' money," probably considerable heaps of small coins.¶

3546 AG:541D CB:— 5. NOMISMA (νόμισμα), primarily that which is established by custom (*nomos*, a custom, law), hence, the current coin of a state, currency, is found in Matt. 22 : 19, " (tribute) money."¶ In the Sept., Neh. 7 : 71.¶

STATĒR 4715 AG:764C CB:1270A *Note :* In Matt. 17 : 27, A.V., *statēr* (a coin, estimated at a little over three shillings, equivalent to four *drachmæ*, the temple-tax for two persons), is translated " piece of money " (R.V., " shekel "). See SHEKEL.¶

DRACHMĒ 1406 AG:206C CB:— For MONEY-CHANGER, CHANGER OF MONEY, see CHANGER

MONEY (love of)

5365 AG:859A CB:1264A PHILARGURIA (φιλαργυρία), from *phileō*, to love, and *arguros*, silver, occurs in 1 Tim. 6 : 10 (cp. *philarguros*, covetous, avaricious). Trench contrasts this with *pleonexia*, covetousness. See under COVET, COVETOUSNESS.¶

MONTH, MONTHS

3376 AG:518D CB:1258B 1. MĒN (μήν), connected with *mēnē*, the moon, akin to a Sanskrit root *mā*—, to measure (the Sanskrit *māsa* denotes both moon and month, cp., e.g., Lat. *mensis*, Eng., moon and month, the moon being in early times the measure of the month). The interval between the 17th day of the second month (Gen. 7 : 11) and the 17th day of the seventh month, is said to be 150 days (8 : 3, 4), i.e., five months of 30 days each ; hence the year would be 360 days (cp. Dan. 7 : 25 ; 9 : 27 ; 12 : 7 with Rev. 11 : 2, 3 ; 12 : 6, 14 ; 13 : 5 ; whence we conclude that 3½ years or 42 months=1260 days, i.e., one year=360 days) ; this was the length of the old Egyptian year ; later, five days were added to correspond to the solar year. The Hebrew year was as nearly solar as was compatible with its commencement, coinciding with the new moon, or first day of the month. This was a regular feast day, Numb. 10 : 10 ; 28 : 11–14 ; the Passover coincided with the full moon (the 14th of the month Abib : see PASSOVER).

Except in Gal. 4 : 10 ; Jas. 5 : 17 ; Rev. 9 : 5, 10, 15 ; 11 : 2 ; 13 : 5 ; 22 : 2, the word is found only in Luke's writings, Luke 1 : 24, 26, 36, 56 ; 4 : 25 ; Acts 7 : 20 ; 18 : 11 ; 19 : 8 ; 20 : 3 ; 28 : 11, examples of Luke's care as to accuracy of detail.¶

5150 AG:826B CB:— 2. TRIMĒNOS (τρίμηνος), an adjective, denoting of three months (*tri*, for *treis*, three, and No. 1), is used as a noun, a space of three months, in Heb. 11 : 23.¶

3. TETRAMĒNOS (τετράμηνος), an adjective, denoting of four months 5072 (-ON) AG:813D
(*tetra*, for *tessares*, four, and No. 1), is used as a noun in John 4 : 35 (where CB:—
chronos, time, may be understood).¶

MOON

1. SELĒNĒ (σελήνη), from *selas*, brightness (the Heb. words are 4582
yarēach, wandering, and *lebānāh*, white), occurs in Matt. 24 : 29; Mark AG:746D CB:1268C
13 : 24; Luke 21 : 25; Acts 2 : 20; 1 Cor. 15 : 41; Rev. 6 : 12; 8 : 12; 12 : 1; 21 : 23. In Rev. 12 : 1, " the moon under her feet " is suggestive of derived authority, just as her being clothed with the sun is suggestive of supreme authority; everything in the symbolism of the passage centres in Israel. In 6 : 12 the similar symbolism of the sun and moon is suggestive of the supreme authority over the world, and of derived authority, at the time of the execution of Divine judgments upon nations at the close of the present age.¶

2. NEOMĒNIA (νεομηνία), or NOUMĒNIA, denoting a new moon 3561
(*neos*, new, *mēn*, a month : see MONTH), is used in Col. 2 : 16, of a Jewish AG:535D CB:1259C
festival.¶ Judaistic tradition added special features in the liturgy of the synagogue in connection with the observance of the first day of the month, the new moon time.

In the O.T. the R.V. has " new moon " for A.V., " month " in Numb. 29 : 6; 1 Sam. 20 : 27; Hos. 5 : 7. For the connection with feast days see Lev. 23 : 24; Numb. 10 : 10; 29 : 1; Psa. 81 : 3.

For MOOR see DRAW, B, *Note* (1)

MORE

A. Adverbs.

1. MALLON (μᾶλλον), the comparative degree of *mala*, very, very 3123
much, is used (*a*) of increase, " more," with qualifying words, with *pollǭ*, AG:489A CB:1257C
much, e.g., Mark 10 : 48, " the more (a great deal) ; " Rom. 5 : 15, 17, " (much) more ; " Phil. 2 : 12 (ditto) ; with *posǭ*, how much, e.g., Luke 12 : 24; Rom. 11 : 12; with *tosoutǭ*, by so much, Heb. 10 : 25; (*b*) without a qualifying word, by way of comparison, " the more," e.g., Luke 5 : 15, " so much the more ; " John 5 : 18, " the more ; " Acts 5 : 14 (ditto) ; Phil. 1 : 9; 1 Thess. 4 : 1, 10, " more and more ; " 2 Pet. 1 : 10, R.V., " the more " (A.V., " the rather ") ; in Acts 20 : 35, by a periphrasis, it is translated " more (blessed) ; " in Gal. 4 : 27, " more (than)," lit., ' rather (than) ; ' (*c*) with qualifying words, similarly to (*a*), e.g., Mark 7 : 36. See RATHER.

2. ETI (ἔτι), yet, as yet, still, used of degree is translated " more " 2089
in Matt. 18 : 16, " (one or two) more ; " Heb. 8 : 12 and 10 : 17, " (will I AG:315C CB:1247A
remember no) more ; " 10 : 2, " (no) more (conscience) ; " 11 : 32, " (what shall I) more (say) ? " Rev. 3 : 12, " (he shall go out thence no) more ; "

7 : 16, "(no) more" and "any more;" 9 : 12, A.V., "more" (R.V., "hereafter"); 18 : 21–23, "(no) more," "any more" (5 times); 20 : 3, "(no) more;" 21 : 1, 4 (twice); 22 : 3. See ALSO, No. 2.

3765 AG:592C CB:— 3. OUKETI (οὐκέτι), *ouk*, not, and No. 2, combined in one word, is translated "no more," e.g., in Matt. 19 : 6; Luke 15 : 19, 21; Acts 20 : 25, 38; Eph. 2 : 19. See HENCEFORTH, HEREAFTER, LONGER, NOW, Note (2).

4054 AG:651C CB:1263C 4. PERISSOTERON (περισσότερον), the neuter of the comparative degree of *perissos*, more abundant, is used as an adverb, "more," e.g., Luke 12 : 4; 2 Cor. 10 : 8, A.V. (R.V., "abundantly"); Heb. 7 : 15, R.V., "more abundantly" (A.V., "far more"). See ABUNDANTLY, C, No. 2.

Note: For the corresponding adverbs *perissōs* and *perissoterōs*, see ABUNDANTLY, EXCEEDINGLY.

3187 AG:497C (MEGAS) CB:1258A 5. MEIZON (μεῖζον), the neuter of *meizōn*, greater, the comparative degree of *megas*, great, is used as an adverb, and translated "the more" in Matt. 20 : 31. See GREATER.

5228 AG:838B CB:1252A 6. HUPER (ὑπέρ), a preposition, over, above, etc., is used as an adverb in 2 Cor. 11 : 23, "(I) more."

3745 AG:586B CB:1251B 7. HOSON (ὅσον), neuter of *hosos*, how much, is used adverbially in Mark 7 : 36 (1st part), "the more."

B. Adjectives (*some with adverbial uses*).

4119 AG:687C 1. PLEIŌN (πλείων), the comparative degree of *polus*, much, is used (*a*) as an adjective, e.g., John 15 : 2; Acts 24 : 11, R.V., "(not) more (than)" (A.V., "yet but"); Heb. 3 : 3; (*b*) as a noun, or with a noun understood, e.g., Matt. 20 : 10; Mark 12 : 43; Acts 19 : 32 and 27 : 12, "the more part;" 1 Cor. 9 : 19; (*c*) as an adverb, Matt. 5 : 20, "shall exceed," lit., '(shall abound) more (than);' 26 : 53; Luke 9 : 13. See ABOVE, No. 3, Note, GREATER.

2. PERISSOS (περισσός), more than sufficient, over and above, abundant (a popular substitute for No. 3), is translated "more," e.g., in Matt. 5 : 37, 47. In John 10 : 10 the neuter form is rendered "more abundantly," A.V., R.V., "abundantly" (marg., "abundance").

3. PERISSOTEROS (περισσότερος), the comparative degree of No. 2, is translated "much more (than a prophet)" in Matt. 11 : 9, R.V. (A.V., "more"); in Luke 7 : 26 both R.V. and A.V. have "much more." See ABUNDANT, C.

ALLOS 243 AG:39D CB:1234C PARA 3844 AG:609C CB:1261C *Notes:* (1) In Matt. 25 : 20 (2nd part), A.V., *allos*, "other" (so the R.V.), is translated "more." (2) In Jas. 4 : 6, A.V., the adjective *meizōn*, greater (see A, No. 5, above), is translated "more (grace)" (R.V. marg., "a greater grace"). See GRACE (at end). (3) Various uses of the word "more" occur in connection with other words, especially in the comparative degree. The phrase "more than" translates certain prepositions and particles: in Rom. 1 : 25, A.V., *para*, beside, compared with, is translated "more than" (R.V., "rather than"): cp. Rom. 12 : 3; *huper*, over,

above, "more than," in Matt. 10 : 37 (twice) ; in Philm. 21, A.V., "more EPANō 1883 AG:283B
than" (R.V., "beyond"). In Mark 14 : 5, A.V., *epanō*, above, is trans- e 2228
lated "more than" (R.V., "above"). In Luke 15 : 7 the particle *ē*, AG:342A 1.b.
than, is necessarily rendered "more than;" cp. Luke 17 : 2 and 1 Cor. EI 1487
14 : 19, "rather than." In Mark 8 : 14, the conjunction *ei*, if, with the AG:219A
negative *mē*, lit., 'if not,' signifying 'except,' is translated "more than CB:1242C
(one loaf)." Mē 3361 AG:515D

MOREOVER CB:1258A

1. ETI (ἔτι), yet, as yet, still, is translated "moreover" in Acts 2 : 26 ; 2089 AG:315C
in 21 : 28, R.V. (A.V., "further") ; Heb. 11 : 36. See More, A, No. 2. CB:1247A

2. KAI (καί), and, is translated "moreover" in Acts 24 : 6 ; in the 2532 AG:391D
A.V., where the R.V. has "and," Acts 19 : 26. CB:1253A

3. DE (δέ), a particle signifying 'and' or 'but,' is translated "more- 1161
over" in Matt. 18 : 15, A.V. (R.V., "and") ; Acts 11 : 12 (R.V., "and") ; AG:171C CB:—
Rom. 5 : 20, A.V. (R.V., "but") ; 8 : 30 ("and") ; 1 Cor. 15 : 1 (R.V., "now") ; 2 Cor. 1 : 23 (R.V., "but") ; 2 Pet. 1 : 15 (R.V., "yea").

4. ALLA KAI (ἀλλὰ καί), but also, yea even, is translated "moreover" ALLA 235
in Luke 24 : 22, R.V. (A.V., "yea, and") ; in 16 : 21, A.V., "moreover" AG:38A
(R.V., "yea, even"). CB:—

5. DE KAI (δὲ καί), but also, is translated "moreover" in 1 Tim. 3 : 7.

6. KAI . . . DE (καὶ . . . δέ) is translated "moreover" in Heb. 9 : 21.

7. LOIPON (λοιπόν), the neuter of the adjective *loipos*, the rest, used 3063
adverbially, most usually rendered "finally," is translated "moreover" AG:479D (LOIPOS 3.b.)
in 1 Cor. 4 : 2 (some mss. have *ho de loipon*, lit., 'but what is left,' A.V., CB:1257B
"moreover," for *hōde loipon*, "here, moreover," as in the R.V.). See Finally.

Note: In 1 Cor. 10 : 1, A.V., *gar*, 'for,' is translated "moreover" 1063
(R.V., "for") ; the R.V. is important here, as it introduces a reason for AG:151C CB:1248A
what has preceded in chap. 9, whereas "moreover" may indicate that a new subject is being introduced ; this incorrect rendering tends somewhat to dissociate the two passages, whereas *gar* connects them intimately.

MORNING (in the, early in the)

A. Adjectives.

1. PRŌÏOS (πρώϊος), early, at early morn (from *pro*, before), is used (-IA) 4405
as a noun in the feminine form *prōïa*, "morning" in Matt. 27 : 1 and AG:724D
John 21 : 4 (in some mss. in Matt. 21 : 18 and John 18 : 28, for B, No. 1, CB:—
which see). Its adjectival force is retained by regarding it as qualifying the noun *hōra*, an hour, i.e., 'at an early hour.'¶

2. PRŌÏNOS (πρωϊνός), a later form of No. 1, qualifies *astēr*, star, in 4407
Rev. 2 : 28 and 22 : 16 (where some mss. have No. 3). That Christ will AG:725A CB:1266C
give to the overcomer "the morning star" indicates a special interest for

such in Himself, as He thus describes Himself in the later passage. For Israel He will appear as "the sun of righteousness;" as the morning Star which precedes He will appear for the Rapture of the Church.¶

3720 AG:580C 3. ORTHRINOS or ORTHRIOS (ὀρθρινός), pertaining to dawn or
CB:— morning, in some mss. in Rev. 22 : 16 (see No. 2); see DAWN, B, Note.

B. Adverb.

4404 AG:724D PRŌÏ (πρωΐ), early, is translated "in the morning" in Matt. 16 : 3;
CB:1266C 20 : 1 (with *hama*, "early"); 21 : 18; Mark 1 : 35; 11 : 20; 13 : 35; 15 : 1; "early" in Mark 16 : 2 (with *lian*, very; A.V., "early in the morning"); 16 : 9; Matt. 21 : 18 and John 18 : 28 (in the best texts, for A, No. 1); 20 : 1; Acts 28 : 23 (with *apo*, from).¶

C. Noun.

3722 AG:580C ORTHROS (ὄρθρος) denotes daybreak, dawn, Luke 24 : 1; John 8 : 2;
CB:— Acts 5 : 21; see DAWN, B.¶

D. Verb.

3719 AG:580C ORTHRIZŌ (ὀρθρίζω), to do anything early in the morning, is trans-
CB:— lated "came early in the morning," in Luke 21 : 38.¶

MORROW

839 AG:122A 1. AURION (αὔριον), an adverb denoting to-morrow, is used (*a*) with
CB:— this meaning in Matt. 6 : 30; Luke 12 : 28; 13 : 32, 33; Acts 23 : 15
(in some mss.), 20; 25 : 22; 1 Cor. 15 : 32; Jas. 4 : 13; (*b*) with the
HeMERA word *hēmera*, day, understood (occurring thus in the papyri), translated as
2250 AG:345D a noun, "(the) morrow," Matt. 6 : 34 (twice); Luke 10 : 35; Acts 4 : 3
CB:1249C (A.V., "next day"); 4 : 5; Jas. 4 : 14.¶

1887 AG:283D 2. EPAURION (ἐπαύριον), *epi*, upon, and No. 1, is used as in (*b*) above;
CB:— the R.V. always translates it "on (the) morrow;" in the following the A.V. has "(the) next day," Matt. 27 : 62; John 1 : 29, 35 ("the next day after"); 12 : 12; Acts 14 : 20; 21 : 8; 25 : 6; "(the) day following," John 1 : 43; 6 : 22; "the morrow after," Acts 10 : 24.

1836 AG:276A *Note:* In Acts 25 : 17, A.V., the adverb *hexēs*, next, successively, in
CB:— order, is translated "on (the) morrow." See NEXT.

For MORSEL see MEAT, No. 2

MORTAL, MORTALITY

2349 AG:362D THNĒTOS (θνητός), subject or liable to death, mortal (akin to *thnēskō*,
CB:1272B to die), occurs in Rom. 6 : 12, of the body, where it is called "mortal," not simply because it is liable to death, but because it is the organ in and through which death carries on its death-producing activities; in 8 : 11, the stress is on the liability to death, and the quickening is not reinvigoration but the impartation of life at the time of the Rapture, as in 1 Cor. 15 : 53, 54 and 2 Cor. 5 : 4 (R.V., "what is mortal;" A.V., "mortality"); in 2 Cor. 4 : 11, it is applied to the flesh, which stands, not simply for the body, but the body as that which consists of the element of decay, and is

thereby death-doomed. Christ's followers are in this life delivered unto death, that His life may be manifested in that which naturally is the seat of decay and death. That which is subject to suffering is that in which the power of Him who suffered here is most manifested.¶

MORTIFY

1. THANATOŌ (θανατόω), to put to death (from *thanatos*, death, 2289
akin to *thnētos*, mortal, see above), is translated " mortify " in Rom. 8 : 13 AG:351C
(Amer. R.V., " put to death ") ; in 7 : 4, " ye were made dead " (Passive CB:1271C
Voice), betokens the act of God on the believer, through the Death of Christ ; here in 8 : 13 it is the act of the believer himself, as being responsible to answer to God's act, and to put to death " the deeds of the body." See DEATH, C, No. 1.

2. NEKROŌ (νεκρόω), to make dead (from *nekros*, see DEAD, A), is 3499
used figuratively in Col. 3 : 5 and translated " mortify " (Amer. R.V., AG:535C
" put to death "). See DEAD, B, No. 1. CB:1259C

MOST

1. PLEION (πλεῖον), the neuter of *pleiōn*, more, is used adverbially 4119
and translated " most " (of degree) in Luke 7 : 42 (without the article) ; AG:687C (POLUS II.)
in ver. 43 (with the article, ' the most ') ; 1 Cor. 10 : 5, R.V., " most " CB:1265B
(A.V., " many ") ; Phil. 1 : 14 (ditto). See MORE.

2. PLEISTOS (πλεῖστος), the superlative degree of *polus*, is used 4118
(*a*) as an adjective in Matt. 11 : 20 ; 21 : 8, R.V., " (the) most part of " AG:687C (POLUS III.)
(A.V., " a very great ") ; (*b*) in the neuter, with the article, adverbially, CB:—
" at the most," 1 Cor. 14 : 27 ; (*c*) as an elative (i.e., intensively) in Mark 4 : 1 (in the best mss. ; some have *polus*), " a very great (multitude)."

3. MALISTA (μάλιστα), an adverb, the superlative of *mala*, very, is 3122
translated " most of all " in Acts 20 : 38. See ESPECIALLY. AG:488D CB:—

Note : For combinations in the translation of other words, see BELIEVE, C, Note (4), EXCELLENT, GLADLY, HIGH, STRAITEST.

MOTE

KARPHOS (κάρφος), a small, dry stalk, a twig, a bit of dried stick 2595
(from *karphō*, to dry up), or a tiny straw or bit of wool, such as might fly AG:405C
into the eye, is used metaphorically of a minor fault, Matt. 7 : 3, 4, 5 ; CB:—
Luke 6 : 41, 42 (twice), in contrast with *dokos*, a beam supporting the roof of a building (see BEAM).¶ In the Sept., Gen. 8 : 11.¶

MOTH

SĒS (σής) denotes a clothes moth, Matt. 6 : 19, 20 ; Luke 12 : 33.¶ 4597
In Job 4 : 19 " crushed before the moth " alludes apparently to the fact AG:749B
that woollen materials, riddled by the larvæ of moths, become so fragile CB:1269A
that a touch demolishes them. In Job 27 : 18 " He buildeth his house as a moth " alludes to the frail covering which a larval moth constructs out

of the material which it consumes. The rendering " spider " (marg.) seems an attempt to explain a difficulty.

MOTH-EATEN

4598 AG:749C CB:— SĒTOBRŌTOS (σητόβρωτος), from *sēs*, a moth, and *bibrōskō*, to eat, is used in Jas. 5 : 2.¶ In the Sept. Job 13 : 28.¶

MOTHER

3384 AG:520A CB:1258C 1. MĒTĒR (μήτηρ) is used (*a*) of the natural relationship, e.g., Matt. 1 : 18 ; 2 Tim. 1 : 5 ; (*b*) figuratively, (1) of one who takes the place of a mother, Matt. 12 : 49, 50 ; Mark 3 : 34, 35 ; John 19 : 27 ; Rom. 16 : 13 ; 1 Tim. 5 : 2 ; (2) of the Heavenly and spiritual Jerusalem, Gal. 4 : 26, which is " free " (not bound by law imposed externally, as under the Law of Moses), " which is our mother " (R.V.), i.e., of Christians, the metropolis, mother-city, used allegorically, just as the capital of a country is " the seat of its government, the centre of its activities, and the place where the national characteristics are most fully expressed ; " (3) symbolically, of Babylon, Rev. 17 : 5, as the source from which has proceeded the religious harlotry of mingling pagan rites and doctrines with the Christian faith.

Note : In Mark 16 : 1 the article, followed by the genitive case of the name " James," the word " mother " being omitted, is an idiomatic mode of expressing the phrase " the mother of James."

3389 AG:520C CB:— 2. MĒTROLǬAS, or MĒTRALǬAS (μητραλῴας) denotes a matricide (No. 1, and *aloiaō*, to smite) ; 1 Tim. 1 : 9, " murderers of mothers ; " it probably has, however, the broader meaning of " smiters " (R.V., marg.), as in instances elsewhere than the N.T.¶

282 AG:46A CB:1234C 3. AMĒTŌR (ἀμήτωρ), without a mother (*a*, negative, and No. 1), is used in Heb. 7 : 3, of the Genesis record of Melchizedek, certain details concerning him being purposely omitted, in order to conform the description to facts about Christ as the Son of God. The word has been found in this sense in the writings of Euripides the dramatist and Herodotus the historian. See also under FATHER.¶

MOTHER-IN-LAW

3994 AG:642C CB:— PENTHERA (πενθερά), the feminine of *pentheros* (a father-in-law), occurs in Matt. 8 : 14 ; 10 : 35 ; Mark 1 : 30 ; Luke 4 : 38 ; 12 : 53 (twice).¶

MOTION See BECKON For MOTION, Rom. 7 : 5, A.V., see PASSION

MOUNT, MOUNTAIN

3735 AG:582B CB:1261B OROS (ὄρος) is used (*a*) without specification, e.g., Luke 3 : 5 (distinct from *bounos*, a hill, see HILL, No. 3) ; John 4 : 20 ; (*b*) of the mount of Transfiguration, Matt. 17 : 1, 9 ; Mark 9 : 2, 9 ; Luke 9 : 28, 37 (A.V., "hill"); 2 Pet. 1 : 18; (*c*) of Zion, Heb. 12 : 22; Rev. 14 : 1; (*d*) of Sinai, Acts 7 : 30, 38; Gal. 4 : 24, 25; Heb. 8 : 5; 12 : 20; (*e*) of the Mount of Olives, Matt. 21 : 1; 24 : 3; Mark 11 : 1; 13 : 3; Luke 19 : 29, 37; 22 : 39; John 8 : 1; Acts 1 : 12; (*f*) of the hill districts as distinct from the lowlands, especially of the hills above the Sea of Galilee, e.g., Matt. 5 : 1; 8 : 1; 18 : 12; Mark 5 : 5; (*g*) of the mountains on the east of Jordan and those in the land of Ammon and the region of Petra, etc., Matt. 24 : 16; Mark 13 : 14; Luke 21 : 21; (*h*) proverbially, of overcoming difficulties, or accomplishing great things, 1 Cor. 13 : 2; cp. Matt. 17 : 20; 21 : 21; Mark 11 : 23; (*i*) symbolically, of a series of the imperial potentates of the Roman Dominion, past and future, Rev. 17 : 9. See HILL.

MOURN, MOURNING

A. Verbs.

1. KOPTŌ (κόπτω), to cut or beat, used in the Middle Voice of beating **2875**
the breast or head in mourning (cp. Luke 23 : 27), is translated "shall **AG:444A CB:1255C**
mourn" in Matt. 24 : 30. See BEWAIL, No. 2, CUT, WAIL.

2. PENTHEŌ (πενθέω), to mourn for, lament, is used (*a*) of mourning **3996**
in general, Matt. 5 : 4; 9 : 15; Luke 6 : 25; (*b*) of sorrow for the death **AG:642C CB:1263A**
of a loved one, Mark 16 : 10; (*c*) of mourning for the overthrow of Babylon and the Babylonish system, Rev. 18 : 11, 15, R.V., "mourning" (A.V., "wailing"); ver. 19 (ditto); (*c*) of sorrow for sin or for condoning it, Jas. 4 : 9; 1 Cor. 5 : 2; (*d*) of grief for those in a local church who show no repentance for evil committed, 2 Cor. 12 : 21, R.V., "mourn" (A.V., "bewail"). See BEWAIL, No. 3.¶

3. THRĒNEŌ (θρηνέω), to lament, wail (akin to *thrēnos*, a lamentation, **2354**
a dirge), is used (*a*) in a general sense, of the disciples during the absence **AG:363B CB:1272B**
of the Lord, John 16 : 20, "lament;" (*b*) of those who sorrowed for the sufferings and the impending crucifixion of the Lord, Luke 23 : 27, "lamented;" the preceding word is *koptō* (No. 1); (*c*) of mourning as for the dead, Matt. 11 : 17, R.V., "wailed" (A.V., "have mourned"); Luke 7 : 32 (ditto). See BEWAIL, Note (1).¶

Notes: (1) Trench points out that *pentheō* is often joined with *klaiō*, to **KLAIō**
weep, 2 Sam. 19 : 1; Mark 16 : 10; Jas. 4 : 9; Rev. 18 : 15, indicating **2799 AG:433A**
that *pentheō* is used especially of external manifestation of grief (as with **CB:1255A**
koptō and *thrēneō*), in contrast to *lupeomai*, which may be used of inward **LUPEō**
grief (Syn. §xlv); though in Classical Greek *pentheō* was used of grief **3076 AG:481C**
without violent manifestations (Grimm-Thayer). (2) Among the well-to- **CB:1257B**
do it was common to hire professional mourners (men and women), who accompanied the dead body to the grave with formal music and the singing of dirges. At the death of Jairus' daughter male flute-players were present, Matt. 9 : 23 (see, however, Jer. 9 : 17).

B. Nouns.

3602 AG:555B
1. ODURMOS (ὀδυρμός), lamentation, mourning, is translated **CB:1260B**

"mourning" in Matt. 2 : 18 and 2 Cor. 7 : 7: see BEWAIL, Note (2).¶

3997 AG:642D CB:1263A 2. PENTHOS (πένθος), akin to A, No. 2, mourning, is used in Jas. 4 : 9; Rev. 18 : 7 (twice), R.V., "mourning" (A.V., "sorrow"); ver. 8, "mourning;" 21 : 4, R.V., "mourning" (A.V., "sorrow"). See SORROW.¶

MOUTH

A. Noun.

4750 AG:769D CB:1270A STOMA (στόμα), akin to *stomachos* (which originally meant a throat, gullet), is used (*a*) of the mouth of man, e.g., Matt. 15 : 11; of animals, e.g., Matt. 17 : 27; 2 Tim. 4 : 17 (figurative); Heb. 11 : 33; Jas. 3 : 3; Rev. 13 : 2 (2nd occurrence); (*b*) figuratively, of inanimate things, of the "edge" of a sword, Luke 21 : 24; Heb. 11 : 34; of the earth, Rev. 12 : 16; (*c*) figuratively, of the mouth, as the organ of speech, (1) of Christ's words, e.g., Matt. 13 : 35; Luke 11 : 54; Acts 8 : 32; 22 : 14; 1 Pet. 2 : 22; (2) of human, e.g., Matt. 18 : 16; 21 : 16; Luke 1 : 64; Rev. 14 : 5; as emanating from the heart, Matt. 12 : 34; Rom. 10 : 8, 9; of prophetic ministry through the Holy Spirit, Luke 1 : 70; Acts 1 : 16; 3 : 18; 4 : 25; of the destructive policy of two world potentates at the end of this age, Rev. 13 : 2, 5, 6; 16 : 13 (twice); of shameful speaking, Eph. 4 : 29 and Col. 3 : 8; (3) of the Devil speaking as a dragon or serpent, Rev. 12 : 15, 16; 16 : 13; (*d*) figuratively, in the phrase "face to face" (lit., 'mouth to mouth'), 2 John 12; 3 John 14; (*e*) metaphorically, of the utterances of the Lord, in judgment, 2 Thess. 2 : 8; Rev. 1 : 16; 2 : 16; 19 : 15, 21; of His judgment upon a local church for its lukewarmness, Rev. 3 : 16; (*f*) by metonymy, for speech, Matt. 18 : 16; Luke 19 : 22; 21 : 15; 2 Cor. 13 : 1.

3056 AG:477A CB:1257A *Note:* In Acts 15 : 27, *logos*, a word, is translated "word of mouth," R.V. (A.V., "mouth," marg., "word").

B. Verb.

1993 AG:301A CB:— EPISTOMIZŌ (ἐπιστομίζω), to bridle (*epi*, upon, and A), is used metaphorically of stopping the mouth, putting to silence, Tit. 1 : 11.¶ Cp. *phrassō*, to stop, close, said of stopping the mouths of men, in Rom. 3 : 19. See STOP.

MOVE, MOVED, MOVER, MOVING, UNMOVEABLE

A. Verbs.

2795 AG:432C CB:— 1. KINEŌ (κινέω), to set in motion, move (hence, e.g., Eng. kinematics, kinetics, cinema), is used (*a*) of wagging the head, Matt. 27 : 39; Mark 15 : 29; (*b*) of the general activity of the human being, Acts 17 : 28; (*c*) of the moving of mountains, Rev. 6 : 14, in the sense of removing, as in Rev. 2 : 5, of removing a lampstand (there figuratively of causing a local church to be discontinued); (*d*) figuratively, of exciting, stirring up feelings and passions, Acts 21 : 30 (Passive Voice); 24 : 5, "a mover;"

(*e*) of moving burdens, Matt. 23 : 4. See REMOVE, WAG.¶ Cp. *sunkineō*, to stir up, Acts 6 : 12.¶

2. METAKINEŌ (μετακινέω), in the Active Voice, to move something 3334
away (not in the N.T. ; in the Sept., e.g., Deut. 19 : 14 ; Is. 54 : 10) ; AG:511B
in the Middle Voice, to remove oneself, shift, translated in the Passive CB:—
in Col. 1 : 23, " be . . . not moved away (from the hope of the gospel)."¶

3. SEIŌ (σείω), to shake, move to and fro, usually of violent concussion 4579
(Eng., seismic, seismograph, seismology), is said (*a*) of the earth as destined AG:746C
to be shaken by God, Heb. 12 : 26 ; (*b*) of a local convulsion of the earth, CB:1268C
at the Death of Christ, Matt. 27 : 51, " did quake ; " (*c*) of a fig tree, Rev. 6 : 13 ; (*d*) metaphorically, to stir up with fear or some other emotion, Matt. 21 : 10, of the people of a city ; 28 : 4, of the keepers or watchers, at the Lord's tomb, R.V., " did quake " (A.V., " did shake ").¶

4. SALEUŌ (σαλεύω), to shake, properly of the action of stormy wind, 4531
then, to render insecure, stir up, is rendered " I should (not) be moved " AG:740C
in Acts 2 : 25, in the sense of being cast down or shaken from a sense of CB:1268B
security and happiness, said of Christ, in a quotation from Psa. 16 : 8. See SHAKE, STIR (up).

5. SAINŌ (σαίνω), properly, of dogs, to wag the tail, fawn ; hence, 4525
metaphorically of persons, to disturb, disquiet, 1 Thess. 3 : 3, Passive AG:740A
Voice, " (that no man) be moved (by these afflictions)." Some have CB:—
suggested the primary meaning, to be wheedled, befooled, by pleasing utterances ; but Greek interpreters regard it as synonymous with No. 3, or with *tarassō*, to disturb, and this is confirmed by the contrast with " establish " in ver. 2, and " stand fast " in ver. 8. A variant reading gives the verb *siainesthai*, to be disheartened, unnerved.¶

6. PHERŌ (φέρω), to bear, carry, is rendered " being moved " in 5342
2 Pet. 1 : 21, signifying that they were ' borne along,' or impelled, by the AG:854D
Holy Spirit's power, not acting according to their own wills, or simply CB:1264A
expressing their own thoughts, but expressing the mind of God in words provided and ministered by Him.

Notes : (1) In Mark 15 : 11, A.V., *anaseiō*, to shake to and fro, stir up, 383
is translated " moved " (R.V., " stirred up," as in Luke 23 : 5, A.V. and AG:60A
R.V.).¶ (2) In Acts 20 : 24 some mss. have a phrase translated " none CB:1235B
of these things move me." The text for which there is most support gives the rendering " but I hold not my life of any account, as dear unto myself." Field suggests a reading, the translation of which is, ' neither make I account of anything, nor think my life dear unto myself.' (3) In 1 Cor. 15 : 34, for the more literal A.V., " I speak this to your shame," the R.V. has " I speak this to move you to shame." (4) For " moved with godly fear " see FEAR, D, No. 2. (5) See also COMPASSION, ENVY, FEAR, INDIGNATION.

B. Adjectives.
761

1. ASALEUTOS (ἀσάλευτος), unmoved, immoveable (from *a*, nega- AG:114B
tive, and A, No. 4), is translated " unmoveable " in Acts 27 : 41 ; " which CB:1237C

cannot be moved" in Heb. 12 : 28, A.V. (R.V., "that cannot be shaken").¶ In the Sept., Ex. 13 : 16; Deut. 6 : 8; 11 : 18.¶

277 2. AMETAKINĒTOS (ἀμετακίνητος), firm, immoveable (*a*, negative,
AG:45C
CB:— and A, No. 2), is used in 1 Cor. 15 : 58.¶

C. Noun.

2796 KINĒSIS (κίνησις), a moving (akin to A, No. 1), is found in John 5 : 3
AG:432D
CB:— (in many ancient authorities, R.V., marg.), of the moving of the water at the pool of Bethesda.¶

MOW

270 AMAŌ (ἀμάω), to mow, is translated "mowed" in Jas. 5 : 4, R.V.
AG:44C
CB:— (A.V., "have reaped down"). "The cognate words seem to shew that the sense of cutting or mowing was original, and that of gathering-in secondary" (Liddell and Scott, Lex.).¶

MUCH

4183 1. POLUS (πολύς) is used (*a*) as an adjective of degree, e.g., Matt.
AG:687C
CB:1266A 13 : 5, "much (earth);" Acts 26 : 24, "much (learning);" in ver. 29, in the answer to Agrippa's "with but little persuasion," some texts have *pollō* (some *megalō*, 'with great'), R.V., "(whether with little or) with much;" of number, e.g., Mark 5 : 24, R.V., "a great (multitude)," A.V., "much (people);" so Luke 7 : 11; John 12 : 12; Rev. 19 : 1, etc.; (*b*) in the neuter singular form (*polu*), as a noun, e.g., Luke 16 : 10 (twice); in the plural (*polla*), e.g., Rom. 16 : 6, 12, "(laboured) much," lit., 'many things;' (*c*) adverbially, in the neuter singular, e.g., Acts 18 : 27; James 5 : 16; Matt. 26 : 9 (a genitive of price); in the plural, e.g., Mark 5 : 43, R.V., "much" (A.V., "straitly"); Mark 9 : 26, R.V., "much" (A.V., "sore"); John 14 : 30; and with the article, Acts 26 : 24; Rom. 15 : 22; 1 Cor. 16 : 19; Rev. 5 : 4. See GREAT.

2425 2. HIKANOS (ἱκανός), enough, much, many, is translated "much,"
AG:374B
CB:1250C e.g., in Luke 7 : 12 (in some mss. Acts 5 : 37; see the R.V.); Acts 11 : 24, 26; 19 : 26; 27 : 9. See ABLE, ENOUGH, A, No. 2, GREAT, LARGE, MANY, MEET, SECURITY, SORE, SUFFICIENT, WORTHY.

Notes: (1) For "much more," "so much the more," see MORE.
(2) In John 12 : 9, the R.V. has "the common people" for "much people."
TI(S)
5100 (3) In Acts 27 : 16, A.V., *ischuō*, to be able, with *molis*, scarcely, is trans-
AG:819D
CB:1272C lated "had much work" (R.V., "were able, with difficulty"). (4) in
TOSOUTOS Luke 19 : 15, A.V., the pronoun *ti*, "what" (R.V.), is translated "how
5118 much." (5) The adjective *tosoutos*, so great, so much, is translated "so
AG:823B
CB:— much (bread)," in Matt. 15 : 33, plural, R.V., "so many (loaves);" in the genitive case, of price, in Acts 5 : 8, "for so much;" in the dative case, of degree, in Heb. 1 : 4, R.V., "by so much" (A.V., "so much"); so in Heb. 10 : 25; in Heb. 7 : 22 "by so much" translates the phrase *kata tosouto;* in Rev. 18 : 7, "so much." (6) See DISPLEASED, EXHORTATION, PERPLEX, SPEAKING, WORK.

MUCH (AS) ISOS 2470

Notes: (1) In Luke 6 : 34 the phrase *ta isa*, lit., ' the equivalent (things),' AG:381A
is translated " as much " (of lending, to receive back the equivalent). CB:1253A
(2) In Rom. 1 : 15, the phrase *to kat' eme*, lit., ' the (thing) according to me,' KATA 2596
signifies " as much as in me is ; " cp. the A.V. marg. in 1 Pet. 5 : 2 [lit., AG:405C
' the (extent) in, or among, you ; ' the text takes the word ' flock ' as CB:1253C EAN
understood, the marg. regards the phrase as adverbially idiomatic] ; 1437
in Rom. 12 : 18 " as much as in you lieth " translates a similar phrase, lit., AG:211A CB:1242C
' the (extent) out of you.' (3) In Heb. 12 : 20, A.V., *kai ean* (contracted to OUDE
k'an), " if even " (R.V.), is translated " and if so much as." (4) The 3761 AG:591C
negatives *oude* and *mēde*, " not even " (R.V.) are translated " not so much MēDE
as " in the A.V. in Mark 2 : 2 ; Luke 6 : 3 and 1 Cor. 5 : 1 ; in the following 3366 AG:517D
the R.V. and A.V. translate them " not so much as," Mark 3 : 20 (some MēTE
mss. have *mēte*, with the same meaning) ; Acts 19 : 2 ; in Mark 6 : 31 3383 AG:519D
" no (leisure) so much as." (5) In Rom. 3 : 12, *heōs*, as far as, even unto, is HEōS
translated " so much as " in the R.V. ; the A.V. supplies nothing actually 2193 AG:334B
corresponding to it. (6) In John 6 : 11 *hosos* denotes " as much as." CB:1250A

MULTIPLY HOSOS 3745

1. PLĒTHUNŌ (πληθύνω), used (*a*) transitively, denotes to cause to AG:586B CB:1251B
increase, to multiply, 2 Cor. 9 : 10 ; Heb. 6 : 14 (twice) ; in the Passive PLēTHUNō
Voice, to be multiplied, Matt. 24 : 12, R.V., " (iniquity) shall be multi- 4129
plied " (A.V., " shall abound ") ; Acts 6 : 7 ; 7 : 17 ; 9 : 31 ; 12 : 24 ; AG:669A CB:1265B
1 Pet. 1 : 2 ; 2 Pet. 1 : 2 ; Jude 2 ; (*b*) intransitively it denotes to be
multiplying, Acts 6 : 1, R.V., " was multiplying " (A.V., " was multi- MUD See CLAY
plied "). See ABUNDANCE, B, No. 5.¶

2. PLEONAZŌ (πλεονάζω), used intransitively, to abound, is translated 4121
" being multiplied " in the R.V. of 2 Cor. 4 : 15 (A.V., " abundant ") ; AG:667B CB:1265B
the Active Voice, aorist tense, here would be more accurately rendered ' having superabounded ' or ' superabounding ' or ' multiplying.' See ABUNDANCE, B, No. 3.

MULTITUDE

1. OCHLOS (ὄχλος) is used frequently in the four Gospels and the 3793
Acts ; elsewhere only in Rev. 7 : 9 ; 17 : 15 ; 19 : 1, 6 ; it denotes (*a*) a AG:600C CB:1260B
crowd or multitude of persons, a throng, e.g., Matt. 14 : 14, 15 ; 15 : 33 ; often in the plural, e.g., Matt. 4 : 25 ; 5 : 1 ; with *polus*, much or great, it signifies " a great multitude," e.g., Matt. 20 : 29, or " the common people," Mark 12 : 37, perhaps preferably ' the mass of the people.' Field supports the meaning in the text, but either rendering is suitable. The mass of the people was attracted to Him (for the statement " heard Him gladly " cp. what is said in Mark 6 : 20 of Herod Antipas concerning John the Baptist) ; in John 12 : 9, " the common people," R.V., stands in contrast with their leaders (ver. 10) ; Acts 24 : 12, R.V., " crowd ; " (*b*) the populace, an unorganised multitude, in contrast to *dēmos*, the people as a body politic, e.g., Matt. 14 : 5 ; 21 : 26 ; John 7 : 12 (2nd part) ;

(*c*) in a more general sense, a multitude or company, e.g., Luke 6 : 17, R.V., "a (great) multitude (of His disciples)," A.V., "the company;" Acts 1 : 15, "a multitude (of persons)," R.V., A.V., "the number (of names);" Acts 24 : 18, R.V., "crowd" (A.V., "multitude"). See COMPANY, No. 1, NUMBER.

4128 AG:668B 2. PLĒTHOS (πλῆθος), lit., a fulness, hence, a large company, a
CB:1265B multitude, is used (*a*) of things: of fish, Luke 5 : 6; John 21 : 6; of sticks ("bundle"), Acts 28 : 3; of stars and of sand, Heb. 11 : 12; of sins, Jas. 5 : 20; 1 Pet. 4 : 8; (*b*) of persons, (1) a multitude: of people, e.g., Mark 3 : 7, 8; Luke 6 : 17; John 5 : 3; Acts 14 : 1; of angels, Luke 2 : 13; (2) with the article, the whole number, the multitude, the populace, e.g., Luke 1 : 10; 8 : 37; Acts 5 : 16; 19 : 9; 23 : 7; a particular company, e.g., of disciples, Luke 19 : 37; Acts 4 : 32; 6 : 2, 5; 15 : 30; of elders, priests, and scribes, 23 : 7; of the Apostles and the elders of the church in Jerusalem, Acts 15 : 12. See ASSEMBLY, No. 3, BUNDLE, No. 2, COMPANY, No. 5.

Note: In Luke 12 : 1, A.V., the phrase, lit., 'the myriads of the multitude' is translated "an innumerable multitude of people" (where "people" translates No. 1, above), R.V., "the many thousands of the multitude" (where "multitude" translates No. 1).

MURDER

5408 AG:864D PHONOS (φόνος) is used (*a*) of a special act, Mark 15 : 7; Luke 23 : 19,
CB:1264B 25; (*b*) in the plural, of murders in general, Matt. 15 : 19; Mark 7 : 21 (Gal. 5 : 21, in some inferior mss.); Rev. 9 : 21; in the singular, Rom. 1 : 29; (*c*) in the sense of slaughter, Heb. 11 : 37, "they were slain with the sword," lit., '(they died by) slaughter (of the sword);' in Acts 9 : 1, "slaughter." See SLAUGHTER.¶

5407 AG:864C *Note:* In Matt. 19 : 18, A.V., *phoneuō*, to kill (akin to *phoneus*, see
CB:— below), is translated "thou shalt do (no) murder" (R.V., "thou shalt (not) kill"). See KILL, SLAY.

MURDERER

5406 AG:864C 1. PHONEUS (φονεύς), akin to *phoneuō* and *phonos* (see above), is
CB:— used (*a*) in a general sense, in the singular, 1 Pet. 4 : 15; in the plural, Rev. 21 : 8; 22 : 15; (*b*) of those guilty of particular acts, Matt. 22 : 7; Acts 3 : 14, lit. 'a man (*anēr*), a murderer;' 7 : 52; 28 : 4.¶

443 AG:68A 2. ANTHROPOKTONOS (ἀνθρωποκτόνος), an adjective, lit., 'man-
CB:— slaying,' used as a noun, a manslayer, murderer (*anthrōpos*, a man, *kteinō*, to slay), is used of Satan, John 8 : 44; of one who hates his brother, and who, being a murderer, has not eternal life, 1 John 3 : 15 (twice).¶

3964 AG:636D 3. PATROLOAS (or PATRAL-) (πατρολῴας), a murderer of one's
CB:— father, occurs in 1 Tim. 1 : 9.¶

4607 AG:750B *Note:* For *sikarios*, in the plural, "murderers," in Acts 21 : 38, see
CB:— ASSASSIN.¶ See MOTHER, No. 2.

MURMUR, MURMURING

A. Verbs.

1. GONGUZŌ (γογγύζω), to mutter, murmur, grumble, say anything 1111
in a low tone (Eng., gong), an onomatopœic word, representing the AG:164B CB:—
significance by the sound of the word, as in the word "murmur" itself, is used of the labourers in the parable of the householder, Matt. 20 : 11 ; of the scribes and Pharisees, against Christ, Luke 5 : 30 ; of the Jews, John 6 : 41, 43 ; of the disciples, 6 : 61 ; of the people, 7 : 32 (of debating secretly) ; of the Israelites, 1 Cor. 10 : 10 (twice), where it is also used in a warning to believers.¶ In the papyri it is used of the murmuring of a gang of workmen ; also in a remark interposed, while the Emperor (late 2nd cent. A.D.) was interviewing a rebel, that the Romans were then murmuring (Moulton and Milligan, Vocab.).

2. DIAGONGUZŌ (διαγογγύζω), lit., to murmur through (*dia*, i.e., 1234
through a whole crowd, or among themselves), is always used of indignant AG:182C CB:—
complaining, Luke 15 : 2 ; 19 : 7.¶ 1690

3. EMBRIMAOMAI (ἐμβριμάομαι) is rendered "murmured against" AG:254D
in Mark 14 : 5 ; it expresses indignant displeasure : see CHARGE, C, No. 4. CB:1244B 4727

Note : For *stenazō*, Jas. 5 : 9, R.V., "murmur," see GRIEVE, No. 3. AG:766B

B. Noun. CB:1270A

GONGUSMOS (γογγυσμός), a murmuring, muttering (akin to A, No. 1), 1112
is used (*a*) in the sense of secret debate among people, John 7 : 12 (as with AG:164C CB:—
the verb in ver. 32) ; (*b*) of displeasure or complaining (more privately than in public), said of Grecian Jewish converts against Hebrews, Acts 6 : 1 ; in general admonitions, Phil. 2 : 14 ; 1 Pet. 4 : 9, R.V., "murmuring" (A.V., "grudging").¶

MURMURER

GONGUSTĒS (γογγυστής), a murmurer (akin to A, No. 1, and B, 1113
above), one who complains, is used in Jude 16, especially perhaps of AG:164C CB:—
utterances against God (see ver. 15).¶

For MUSING (*dialogizomai*, in Luke 3 : 15, A.V.) see REASON (Verb) 1260 AG:186A CB:1241B

MUSIC

SUMPHŌNIA (συμφωνία), lit., a sounding together (Eng., symphony), 4858
occurs in Luke 15 : 25.¶ In the Sept., Dan. 3 : 5, 7, 10, 15, for Aramaic AG:781A CB:1270B
sumpônyâ (not in ver. 7), itself a loan word from the Greek ; translated "dulcimer" (R.V., marg., "bagpipe").¶

For MUSICIAN, Rev. 18 : 22, A.V., see MINSTREL

MUST

1. DEI (δεῖ), an impersonal verb, signifying 'it is necessary' or 'one 1163 AG:172A
must,' 'one ought,' is found most frequently in the Gospels, Acts and the CB:1240B

Apocalypse, and is used (*a*) of a necessity lying in the nature of the case, e.g., John 3 : 30 ; 2 Tim. 2 : 6 ; (*b*) of necessity brought about by circumstances, e.g., Matt. 26 : 35, R.V., " must," A.V., " should ; " John 4 : 4 ; Acts 27 : 21, " should ; " 2 Cor. 11 : 30 ; in the case of Christ, by reason of the Father's will, e.g., Luke 2 : 49 ; 19 : 5 ; (*c*) of necessity as to what is required that something may be brought about, e.g., Luke 12 : 12, " ought ; " John 3 : 7 ; Acts 9 : 6 ; 1 Cor. 11 : 19 ; Heb. 9 : 26 ; (*d*) of a necessity of law, duty, equity, e.g., Matt. 18 : 33, " shouldest ; " 23 : 23, " ought ; " Luke 15 : 32, " it was meet ; " Acts 15 : 5, " it is needful " (R.V.) ; Rom. 1 : 27, R.V., " was due," A.V., " was meet " (of a recompense due by the law of God) ; frequently requiring the rendering " ought," e.g., Rom. 8 : 26 ; 12 : 3 ; 1 Cor. 8 : 2 ; (*e*) of necessity arising from the determinate will and counsel of God, e.g., Matt. 17 : 10 ; 24 : 6 ; 26 : 54 ; 1 Cor. 15 : 53, especially regarding the salvation of men through the Death, Resurrection and Ascension of Christ, e.g., John 3 : 14 ; Acts 3 : 21 ; 4 : 12. See BEHOVE, No. 2 (where see the differences in the meanings of synonymous words), MEET, NEED, NEEDFUL, OUGHT, SHOULD.

3784 AG:598D CB:1261A 2. OPHEILŌ (ὀφείλω), to owe, is rendered " must . . . needs " in 1 Cor. 5 : 10. See BEHOVE, No. 1.

2443 AG:376D CB:1250C *Notes :* (1) In Mark 14 : 49, A.V., the conjunction *hina* with the subjunctive mood, in order that, is represented by " must " (R.V., " that . . . might "). (2) In Heb. 13 : 17, A.V., the future participle of *apodidōmi*, to give, is translated " they that must give " (R.V., " they that shall give "). (3) In 2 Pet. 1 : 14, A.V., the verb to be, with *apothesis*, a putting off, is translated " I must put off," R.V., " (the) putting off . . . cometh," lit., ' is (swift).' (4) Sometimes the infinitive mood of a verb, with or without the article, is necessarily rendered by a phrase involving the word " must," e.g., 1 Pet. 4 : 17, A.V., " must (begin) ; " or " should," Heb. 4 : 6, R.V., " should " (A.V. " must "). (5) Sometimes the subjunctive mood of a verb, used as a deliberative, is rendered " must," etc., John 6 : 28, " (what) must (we do)," R.V. (A.V., " shall ").

MUSTARD

4615 AG:751C CB:1269A SINAPI (σίναπι), a word of Egyptian origin, is translated " mustard seed " in the N.T. " The conditions to be fulfilled by the mustard are that it should be a familiar plant, with a very small seed, Matt. 17 : 20 ; Luke 17 : 6, sown in the earth, growing larger than garden herbs, Matt. 13 : 31, having large branches, Mark 4 : 31, . . . attractive to birds, Luke 13 : 19 [R.V., ' (became) a tree ']. The cultivated mustard is *sinapis nigra*. The seed is well known for its minuteness. The mustards are annuals, reproduced with extraordinary rapidity . . . In fat soil they often attain a height of 10 or 12 feet, and have branches which attract passing birds " (A. E. Post, in Hastings' Bib. Dic.).¶

The correct R.V. translation in Matt. 13 : 32, " greater than the herbs," for the A.V., " greatest among herbs " (the mustard is not a herb), should be noted.

As the parable indicates, Christendom presents a sort of Christianity that has become conformed to the principles and ways of the world, and the world has favoured this debased Christianity. Contrast the testimony of the N.T., e.g., in John 17 : 14 ; Gal. 6 : 14 ; 1 Pet. 2 : 11 ; 1 John 3 : 1.

MUTUAL

Note : This is the A.V. rendering of the phrase *en allēlois* in Rom. 1 : 12, 240
translated in the R.V., " each of us by the other's (faith)." See OTHER, AG:39C CB:1234C
No. 5.

MUZZLE

PHIMOŌ (φιμόω), to close the mouth with a muzzle (*phimos*), is used 5392
(*a*) of muzzling the ox when it treads out the corn, 1 Cor. 9 : 9, A.V., AG:861D CB:—
" muzzle the mouth of," R.V., " muzzle," and 1 Tim. 5 : 18, with the lesson that those upon whom spiritual labour is bestowed should not refrain from ministering to the material needs of those who labour on their behalf ; (*b*) metaphorically, of putting to silence, or subduing to stillness, Matt. 22 : 12, 34 ; Mark 1 : 25 ; 4 : 39 ; Luke 4 : 35 ; 1 Pet. 2 : 15. See PEACE (hold), SILENCE.¶

MY (MINE)

EMOS (ἐμός), a possessive adjective of the first person, often used as a 1699
possessive pronoun with greater emphasis than the oblique forms of AG:255C CB:1244B
egō (see below), a measure of stress which should always be observed ; it denotes (I) subjectively, (*a*) what I possess, e.g., John 4 : 34 ; 7 : 16 (1st part) ; 13 : 35 ; 1 Cor. 16 : 21 ; Gal. 6 : 11 ; Col. 4 : 18 (1st clause) ; as a pronoun, absolutely (i.e., not as an adjective), e.g., Matt. 20 : 15 ; 25 : 27 ; Luke 15 : 31, R.V., " (all that is) mine," A.V., " (all that) I have " ; John 16 : 14, 15 ; 17 : 10 ; (*b*) ' proceeding from me,' e.g. Mark 8 : 38 ; John 7 : 16 (2nd part) ; 8 : 37 (here the repetition of the article with the pronoun, after the article with the noun, lends special stress to the pronoun ; more lit., ' the word, that which is mine ') ; so in John 15 : 12. Such instances are to be distinguished from the less emphatic order where the pronoun comes between the article and the noun, as in John 7 : 16, already mentioned ; (*c*) in the phrase ' it is mine ' (i.e., ' it rests with me '), e.g., Matt. 20 : 23 ; Mark 10 : 40 ; (II) objectively, pertaining or relating to me : (*a*) ' appointed for me,' e.g., John 7 : 6, " My time " (with the repeated article and special stress just referred to) ; (*b*) equivalent to an objective genitive (' of me ') e.g., Luke 22 : 19, " (in remembrance) of Me " (lit., ' in My remembrance ') ; so 1 Cor. 11 : 24.

Notes : (1) This pronoun frequently translates oblique forms of the 1473
first personal pronoun *egō*, I, e.g., of me, to me. These instances are AG:217A CB:1242C
usually unemphatic, always less so than those under *emos* (above).

(2) For " my affairs " and " my state " see AFFAIR, Notes. (3) In Matt. 26 : 12, " for My burial " translates a phrase consisting of the preposition *pros* (towards) governing the article with the infinitive mood, aorist tense, of *entaphiazō*, to bury, followed by the personal pronoun " Me," as the object, where the infinitive is virtually a noun, lit., ' towards the burying (of) Me.' (4) In 1 Tim. 1 : 11, " was committed to my trust " is, lit., ' (with) which I was entrusted ' (*pisteuō*, to entrust).

MYRRH

A. Noun.

4666
AG:758D
CB:1269B
SMURNA (σμύρνα), whence the name Smyrna, a word of Semitic origin, Heb., *mōr*, from a root meaning bitter, is a gum resin from a shrubby tree, which grows in Yemen and neighbouring regions of Africa ; the fruit is smooth and somewhat larger than a pea. The colour of myrrh varies from pale reddish-yellow to reddish-brown or red. The taste is bitter, and the substance astringent, acting as an antiseptic and a stimulant. It was used as a perfume, Ps. 45 : 8, where the language is symbolic of the graces of the Messiah ; Prov. 7 : 17 ; S. of Sol. 1 : 13 ; 5 : 5 ; it was one of the ingredients of the " holy anointing oil " for the priests, Ex. 30 : 23 (R.V., " flowing myrrh ") ; it was used also for the purification of women, Esth. 2 : 12 ; for embalming, John 19 : 39 ; as an anodyne (see B) ; it was one of the gifts of the Magi, Matt. 2 : 11.¶

B. Verb.

4669
AG:759A
CB:1269B
SMURNIZŌ (σμυρνίζω) is used transitively in the N.T., with the meaning to mingle or drug with myrrh, Mark 15 : 23 ; the mixture was doubtless offered to deaden the pain (Matthew's word " gall " suggests that myrrh was not the only ingredient). Christ refused to partake of any such means of alleviation ; He would retain all His mental power for the complete fulfilment of the Father's will.¶

MYSELF

1683
AG:253D
CB:—
1. EMAUTOU (ἐμαυτοῦ), a reflexive pronoun, of the first person, lit., of myself, is used (*a*) frequently after various prepositions, e.g., *hupo*, under, Matt. 8 : 9 ; Luke 7 : 8 ; R.V., " under myself ; " *peri*, concerning, John 5 : 31 ; 8 : 14, 18 ; Acts 24 : 10 ; *apo*, from, John 5 : 30 ; 7 : 17, R.V., " from " (A.V., " of," which is ambiguous) ; so ver. 28 ; 8 : 28, 42 ; 10 : 18 ; 14 : 10 (R.V., " from ") ; *pros*, unto, John 12 : 32, R.V., " unto Myself ; " 14 : 3 ; Philm. 13, " with me ; " *eis*, to, 1 Cor. 4 : 6 ; *huper*, on behalf of, 2 Cor. 12 : 5 ; *ek* (*ex*), out of, or from, John 12 : 49, R.V., " from Myself ; " (*b*) as the direct object of a verb, Luke 7 : 7 ; John 8 : 54 ; 14 : 21 ; 17 : 19 ; Acts 26 : 2 ; 1 Cor. 4 : 3 ; 9 : 19 ; 2 Cor. 11 : 7, 9 ; Gal. 2 : 18 ; Phil. 3 : 13 ; (*c*) in other oblique cases of the pronoun, without a preposition, e.g., Acts 20 : 24, " unto " (or to) ; 26 : 9, " with " (or ' to ') ; Rom. 11 : 4, R.V., " for " (A.V., " to ") ; 1 Cor. 4 : 4, R.V.,

" against myself " (A.V., inaccurately, " by ") ; in all these instances the pronoun is in the dative case ; in 1 Cor. 10 : 33, " mine own " (the genitive case) ; in 1 Cor. 7 : 7, " I myself " (the accusative case).¶

2. AUTOS (*αὐτός*), self (*a*) with *egō*, I, " I myself," Luke 24 : 39 ; 846
Acts 10 : 26 ; Rom. 7 : 25 ; 9 : 3 ; 2 Cor. 10 : 1 ; 12 : 13 ; (*b*) without AG:122C CB:1238B
the personal pronoun, Acts 24 : 16 (as the subject of a verb) ; in the nominative case, Acts 25 : 22 ; 1 Cor. 9 : 27 ; Phil. 2 : 24 ; in the genitive case, Rom. 16 : 2, R.V., " of mine own self."

MYSTERY

MUSTĒRION (*μυστήριον*), primarily that which is known to the 3466 AG:530A
mustēs, the initiated (from *mueō*, to initiate into the mysteries ; cp. Phil. CB:1259B
4 : 12, *mueomai*, " I have learned the secret," R.V.). In the N.T. it MUEō
denotes, not the mysterious (as with the Eng. word), but that which, 3453 AG:529A
being outside the range of unassisted natural apprehension, can be made CB:1259B
known only by Divine revelation, and is made known in a manner and at a time appointed by God, and to those only who are illumined by His Spirit. In the ordinary sense a mystery implies knowledge withheld ; its Scriptural significance is truth revealed. Hence the terms especially associated with the subject are " made known," " manifested," " revealed," " preached," " understand," " dispensation." The definition given above may be best illustrated by the following passage : " the mystery which hath been hid from all ages and generations : but now hath it been manifested to His saints " (Col. 1 : 26, R.V.). " It is used of :

" (*a*) spiritual truth generally, as revealed in the gospel, 1 Cor. 13 : 2 ; 14 : 2 [cp. 1 Tim. 3 : 9]. Among the ancient Greeks ' the mysteries ' were religious rites and ceremonies practised by secret societies into which any one who so desired might be received. Those who were initiated into these ' mysteries ' became possessors of certain knowledge, which was not imparted to the uninitiated, and were called ' the perfected,' cp. 1 Cor. 2 : 6–16 where the Apostle has these ' mysteries ' in mind and presents the gospel in contrast thereto ; here ' the perfected ' are, of course, the believers, who alone can perceive the things revealed ; (*b*) Christ, who is God Himself revealed under the conditions of human life, Col. 2 : 2 ; 4 : 3, and submitting even to death, 1 Cor. 2 : 1 [in some mss., for *marturion*, testimony], 7, but raised from among the dead, 1 Tim. 3 : 16, that the will of God to co-ordinate the universe in Him, and subject it to Him, might in due time be accomplished, Eph. 1 : 9 (cp. Rev. 10 : 7), as is declared in the gospel, Rom. 16 : 25 ; Eph. 6 : 19 ; (*c*) the Church, which is Christ's Body, i.e., the union of redeemed men with God in Christ, Eph. 5 : 32 [cp. Col. 1 : 27] ; (*d*) the rapture into the presence of Christ of those members of the Church which is His Body who shall be alive on the earth at His Parousia, 1 Cor. 15 : 51 ; (*e*) the operation of those hidden forces that either retard or accelerate the Kingdom of Heaven (i.e., of God), Matt. 13 : 11 ; Mark 4 : 11 ; (*f*) the cause of the present condition of

Israel, Rom. 11 : 25 ; (*g*) the spirit of disobedience to God, 2 Thess. 2 : 7 ; Rev. 17 : 5, 7 ; cp. Eph. 2 : 2."*

To these may be added (*h*) the seven local churches, and their angels, seen in symbolism, Rev. 1 : 20 ; (*i*) the ways of God in grace, Eph. 3 : 9. The word is used in a comprehensive way in 1 Cor. 4 : 1.†

* From Notes on Thessalonians by Hogg and Vine, pp. 256, 257.
† See The Twelve Mysteries of Scripture by Vine.

N

NAIL (Noun and Verb)

A. Noun.

HĒLOS (ἧλος) occurs in the remarks of Thomas regarding the print 2247 AG:345D
of the nails used in Christ's crucifixion, John 20 : 25.¶ CB:—

B. Verb.

PROSĒLOŌ (προσηλόω), to nail to (*pros*, to, and a verbal form of A), 4338
is used in Col. 2 : 14, in which the figure of a bond (ordinances of the Law) AG:714D CB:—
is first described as cancelled, and then removed; the idea in the verb itself is not that of the cancellation, to which the taking out of the way was subsequent, but of nailing up the removed thing in triumph to the Cross. The Death of Christ not only rendered the Law useless as a means of
salvation, but gave public demonstration that it was so.¶ NAIVE See INNOCENT

NAKED (Adjective and Verb), NAKEDNESS

A. Adjective.

GUMNOS (γυμνός) signifies (*a*) unclothed, Mark 14 : 52; in ver. 51 1131 AG:167D
it is used as a noun ("*his*" and "*body*" being italicised); (*b*) scantily CB:1248C
or poorly clad, Matt. 25 : 36, 38, 43, 44; Acts 19 : 16 (with torn garments); Jas. 2 : 15; (*c*) clad in the undergarment only (the outer being laid aside), John 21 : 7 (see CLOTHING); (*d*) metaphorically, (1) of a bare seed, 1 Cor. 15 : 37; (2) of the soul without the body, 2 Cor. 5 : 3; (3) of things exposed to the all-seeing eye of God, Heb. 4 : 13; (4) of the carnal condition of a local church, Rev. 3 : 17; (5) of the similar state of an individual, 16 : 15; (*b*) of the desolation of religious Babylon, 17 : 16.¶

B. Verb.

GUMNITEUŌ (γυμνιτεύω), to be naked or scantily clad (akin to A), 1130 (GUMNĒ-)
is used in 1 Cor. 4 : 11. In the *Koinē* writings (see Preface to Vol. 1) it AG:167D
is used of being light-armed.¶ CB:—

C. Noun.

GUMNOTĒS (γυμνότης), nakedness (akin to A), is used (*a*) of want of 1132 AG:168A
sufficient clothing, Rom. 8 : 35; 2 Cor. 11 : 27; (*b*) metaphorically, of CB:1248C
the nakedness of the body, said of the condition of a local church, Rev. 3 : 18.¶

NAME

A. Noun.

ONOMA (ὄνομα) is used (I) in general of the name by which a person 3686 AG:570D
or thing is called, e.g., Mark 3 : 16, 17, "(He) surnamed," lit., '(He added) CB:1260C

the name ;' 14 : 32, lit.,' (of which) the name (was) ;' Luke 1 : 63 ; John 18 : 10 ; sometimes translated "named," e.g., Luke 1 : 5, "named (Zacharias)," lit., 'by name ;' in the same verse, "named (Elizabeth)," lit., 'the name of her,' an elliptical phrase, with 'was' understood ; Acts 8 : 9, R.V., "by name," 10 : 1 ; the name is put for the reality in Rev. 3 : 1 ; in Phil. 2 : 9, the Name represents 'the title and dignity' of the Lord, as in Eph. 1 : 21 and Heb. 1 : 4 ;

(II) for all that a name implies, of authority, character, rank, majesty, power, excellence, etc., of everything that the name covers : (*a*) of the Name of God as expressing His attributes, etc., e.g., Matt. 6 : 9 ; Luke 1 : 49 ; John 12 : 28 ; 17 : 6, 26 ; Rom. 15 : 9 ; 1 Tim. 6 : 1 ; Heb. 13 : 15 ; Rev. 13 : 6 ; (*b*) of the Name of Christ, e.g., Matt. 10 : 22 ; 19 : 29 ; John 1 : 12 ; 2 : 23 ; 3 : 18 ; Acts 26 : 9 ; Rom. 1 : 5 ; Jas. 2 : 7 ; 1 John 3 : 23 ; 3 John 7 ; Rev. 2 : 13 ; 3 : 8 ; also the phrases rendered 'in the name ;' these may be analysed as follows : (1) representing the authority of Christ, e.g., Matt. 18 : 5 (with *epi*, 'on the ground of My authority') ; so Matt. 24 : 5 (falsely) and parallel passages ; as substantiated by the Father, John 14 : 26 ; 16 : 23 (last clause), R.V. ; (2) in the power of (with *en*, in), e.g., Mark 16 : 17 ; Luke 10 : 17 ; Acts 3 : 6 ; 4 : 10 ; 16 : 18 ; Jas. 5 : 14 ; (3) in acknowledgement or confession of, e.g., Acts 4 : 12 ; 8 : 16 ; 9 : 27, 28 ; (4) in recognition of the authority of (sometimes combined with the thought of relying or resting on), Matt. 18 : 20 ; cp. 28 : 19 ; Acts 8 : 16 ; 9 : 2 (*eis*, into) ; John 14 : 13 ; 15 : 16 ; Eph. 5 : 20 ; Col. 3 : 17 ; (5) owing to the fact that one is called by Christ's Name or is identified with Him, e.g. 1 Pet. 4 : 14 (with *en*, in) ; with *heneken*, for the sake of, e.g., Matt. 19 : 29 ; with *dia*, on account of, Matt. 10 : 22 ; 24 : 9 ; Mark 13 : 13 ; Luke 21 : 17 ; John 15 : 21 ; 1 John 2 : 12 ; Rev. 2 : 3 (for 1 Pet. 4 : 16, see Note below) ;

(III) as standing, by metonymy, for persons, Acts 1 : 15 ; Rev. 3 : 4 ; 11 : 13 (R.V., "persons").

Note : In Mark 9 : 41, the use of the phrase *en* with the dative case of *onoma* (as in the best mss.) suggests the idea of 'by reason of' or 'on the ground of' (i.e., 'because ye are My disciples') ; 1 Pet. 4 : 16, R.V., "in this Name" (A.V., "on this behalf"), may be taken in the same way.

B. Verbs.

3687 AG:573D CB:1261A 1. ONOMAZŌ (ὀνομάζω) denotes (*a*) to name, mention, or address by name, Acts 19 : 13, R.V., "to name" (A.V., "to call") ; in the Passive Voice, Rom. 15 : 20 ; Eph. 1 : 21 ; 5 : 3 ; to make mention of the Name of the Lord in praise and worship, 2 Tim. 2 : 19 ; (*b*) to name, call, give a name to, Luke 6 : 13, 14 ; Passive Voice, 1 Cor. 5 : 11, R.V., "is named" (A.V., "is called") ; Eph. 3 : 15 (some mss. have the verb in this sense in Mark 3 : 14 and 1 Cor. 5 : 1). See CALL, Note (1).¶

2028 AG:305C CB:1246B 2. EPONOMAZŌ (ἐπονομάζω), to call by a name, surname (*epi*, on, and No. 1), is used in Rom. 2 : 17, Passive Voice, R.V., "bearest the name of" (A.V., "art called"). See CALL, Note (1).¶

3. PROSAGOREUŌ (*προσαγορεύω*) primarily denotes to address, 4316
greet, salute ; hence, to call by name, Heb. 5 : 10, R.V., " named (of God AG:711B CB:—
a High Priest) " (A.V., " called "), expressing the formal ascription of the title to Him whose it is ; " called " does not adequately express the significance. Some suggest the meaning ' addressed,' but this is doubtful. The reference is to Ps. 110 : 4, a prophecy confirmed at the Ascension.¶ In the Sept., Deut. 23 : 6.¶

4. KALEŌ (*καλέω*), to call, is translated " named " in Acts 7 : 58, 2564
R.V. (A.V., " whose name was "). See CALL, No. 1 (*b*). AG:398D CB:1253B

Notes : (1) In Luke 19 : 2, A.V., *kaleō*, to call (with the dative case of *onoma*, ' by name '), is translated " named " (R.V., " called by name ") ; in Luke 2 : 21, A.V., the verb alone is rendered " named " (R.V., " called ").
(2) In Matt. 9 : 9 and Mark 15 : 7, A.V., the verb *legō*, to speak, to call by 3004
name, is rendered " named " (R.V., " called "). See CALL, No. 9. AG:468A CB:1256C

NAMELY

Notes : (1) In Rom. 13 : 9, the preposition *en*, in, with the article, 1722
lit., ' in the,' is translated " namely." (2) In 1 Cor. 7 : 26 the R.V., AG:258B CB:1244B
" *namely*," and A.V., " *I say*," do not translate anything in the original, but serve to reintroduce the phrase " that this is good."

NAPKIN

SOUDARION (*σουδάριον*), for which see HANDKERCHIEF, is translated 4676
" napkin " in Luke 19 : 20 ; John 11 : 44 ; 20 : 7. In Luke 19 : 20 the AG:759C CB:—
reference may be to a towel or any kind of linen cloth or even a sort of head-dress, any of which might be used for concealing money.

NARRATIVE

DIĒGĒSIS (*διήγησις*), translated " a declaration " in the A.V. of 1335
Luke 1 : 1, denotes a " narrative," R.V. (akin to *diēgeomai*, to set out in AG:195A CB:1241C
detail, recount, describe). See DECLARE, B, Note (1).¶ In the Sept., Judg. 7 : 15 ; Hab. 2 : 6.¶

NARROW

A. Adjective.

STENOS (*στενός*), from a root *sten-*, seen in *stenazō*, to groan, *stenagmos*, 4728
groaning (Eng., stenography, lit., narrow writing), is used figuratively AG:766B CB:1270A
in Matt. 7 : 13, 14, of the gate which provides the entrance to eternal life, narrow because it runs counter to natural inclinations, and " the way " is similarly characterized ; so in Luke 13 : 24 (where the more intensive word *agōnizomai*, " strive," is used) ; R.V., " narrow " (A.V., " strait ") in each place. Cp. *stenochōreō*, to be straitened, and *stenochōria*, narrowness, anguish, distress.¶

B. Verb.

THLIBŌ (*θλίβω*), to press, is translated " narrow " in Matt. 7 : 14, 2346 AG:362A CB:1272B

A.V., lit., 'narrowed' (R.V., "straitened;" the verb is in the perfect participle, Passive Voice), i.e., hemmed in, like a mountain gorge; the way is 'rendered narrow' by the Divine conditions, which make it impossible for any to enter who think the entrance depends upon self-merit, or who still incline towards sin, or desire to continue in evil. See AFFLICT, No. 4.

NATION

1484 AG:218B CB:1246C 1. ETHNOS (ἔθνος), originally a multitude, denotes (*a*) a nation or people, e.g., Matt. 24:7; Acts 10:35; the Jewish people, e.g., Luke 7:5; 23:2; John 11:48, 50–52; Acts 10:22; 24:2, 10, 17; in Matt. 21:43, the reference is to Israel in its restored condition; (*b*) in the plural, the nations as distinct from Israel. See GENTILES.

1085 AG:156A CB:1248B 2. GENOS (γένος), a race: see KIND (Noun).

246 AG:41A CB:1234C 3. ALLOPHULOS (ἀλλόφυλος), foreign, of another race (*allos*, another, *phulon*, a tribe), is used in Acts 10:28, "one of another nation."¶

1074 AG:153D CB:1248A *Note:* For Phil. 2:15, *genea* (A.V., "nation," R.V., "generation"), see AGE.

NATURAL, NATURALLY

A. Adjectives.

5446 AG:869B CB:1264C 1. PHUSIKOS (φυσικός) originally signifying produced by nature, inborn, from *phusis*, nature (see below), cp. Eng., physical, physics, etc., denotes (*a*) according to nature, Rom. 1:26, 27; (*b*) governed by mere natural instincts, 2 Pet. 2:12, R.V., "(born) mere animals", A.V. and R.V. marg., "natural (brute beasts)."¶

5591 AG:894B CB:1267C 2. PSUCHIKOS (ψυχικός), belonging to the *psuchē*, soul (as the lower part of the immaterial in man), natural, physical, describes the man in Adam and what pertains to him (set in contrast to *pneumatikos*, spiritual), 1 Cor. 2:14; 15:44 (twice), 46 (in the latter used as a noun); Jas. 3:15, "sensual" (R.V. marg., "natural" or "animal"), here relating perhaps more especially to the mind, a wisdom in accordance with, or springing from, the corrupt desires and affections; so in Jude 19.¶

B. Noun.

1078 AG:154D CB:1248A GENESIS (γένεσις), birth, is used in Jas. 1:23, of the "natural face," lit., 'the face of his birth,' "what God made him to be" (Hort). See GENERATION, NATURE, No. 2.

5449 AG:869B CB:1264C *Note:* In Rom. 11:21, 24 the preposition *kata*, according to, with the noun *phusis*, nature, is translated "natural," of branches, metaphorically describing members of the nation of Israel.

C. Adverb.

5447 AG:869B CB:1264C PHUSIKŌS (φυσικῶς), naturally, by nature (akin to A, No. 1), is used in Jude 10.¶

1104 AG:163A CB:— *Note:* In Phil. 2:20, A.V., *gnēsiōs*, sincerely, honourably, truly (from the adjective *gnēsios*, true, sincere, genuine; see, e.g., Phil. 4:3), is translated "naturally" (R.V., "truly;" marg., "genuinely").¶

NATURE

1. PHUSIS (φύσις), from *phuō*, to bring forth, produce, signifies (*a*) 5449
the nature (i.e., the natural powers or constitution) of a person or thing, AG:869B CB:1264C
Eph. 2 : 3 ; Jas. 3 : 7 (" kind ") ; 2 Pet. 1 : 4 ; (*b*) origin, birth, Rom. 2 : 27, one who by birth is a Gentile, uncircumcised, in contrast to one who, though circumcised, has become spiritually uncircumcised by his iniquity ; Gal. 2 : 15 ; (*c*) the regular law or order of nature, Rom. 1 : 26, against nature (*para*, against) ; 2 : 14, adverbially, " by nature " (for 11 : 21, 24, see NATURAL, Note) ; 1 Cor. 11 : 14 ; Gal. 4 : 8, " by nature (are no gods)," here " nature " is the emphatic word, and the phrase includes demons, men regarded as deified, and idols ; these are gods only in name (the negative, *mē*, denies not simply that they were gods, but the possibility that they could be).¶

2. GENESIS (γένεσις) is used in the phrase in Jas. 3 : 6, " the wheel 1078
of nature," R.V. (marg., " birth "). Some regard this as the course of AG:154D CB:1248A
birth or of creation, or the course of man's nature according to its original Divine purpose ; Mayor (on the Ep. of James) regards *trochos* here as a wheel, " which, catching fire from the glowing axle, is compared to the wide-spreading mischief done by the tongue," and shows that " the fully developed meaning " of *genesis* denotes " the incessant change of life . . . the sphere of this earthly life, meaning all that is contained in our life." The significance, then, would appear to be the whole round of human life and activity. Moulton and Milligan illustrate it in this sense from the papyri. See NATURAL, B.

For NAUGHTINESS, Jas. 1 : 21, A.V., see WICKEDNESS

NAY

1. OU (οὐ), no, not, expressing a negation absolutely, is rendered 3756
" nay," e.g., in Matt. 5 : 37 ; 13 : 29 ; John 7 : 12, A.V. (R.V., " not AG:590A CB:—
so ") ; Acts 16 : 37 ; 2 Cor. 1 : 17, 18, 19 ; Jas. 5 : 12.

2. OUCHI (οὐχί), a strengthened form of No. 1, is used, e.g., in Luke 3780
12 : 51 ; 13 : 3, 5 ; 16 : 30 ; Rom. 3 : 27. AG:598B CB:—

3. ALLA (ἀλλά), but, to mark contrast or opposition, is rendered 235
" nay " in Rom. 3 : 31, R.V., " nay " (A.V., " yea ") ; in 7 : 7, R.V., AG:38A CB:—
" howbeit " (A.V., " nay ") ; 8 : 37 ; 1 Cor. 3 : 2, R.V. ; 6 : 8 ; 12 : 22 ; in Heb. 3 : 16, R.V., " nay " (A.V., " howbeit ").

4. MENOUNGE (μενοῦνγε), (i.e., *men oun ge*), nay rather, is rendered 3304
" nay but " in Rom. 9 : 20 (in Rom. 10 : 18 and Phil. 3 : 8, " yea AG:503C CB:—
verily," A.V., " yea doubtless "). See YEA.¶

NEAR (Adverb), NEAR (come, draw), NEARER

A. Adverbs.

1. ENGUS (ἐγγύς), near, nigh, is used (*a*) of place, e.g., Luke 19 : 11, 1451 AG:214A
" nigh ; " John 3 : 23 ; 11 : 54, " near ; " 6 : 19, 23, " nigh ; " meta- CB:1245A

phorically in Rom. 10 : 8 ; Eph. 2 : 13, 17, " nigh ; " (*b*) of time, e.g., Matt. 24 : 32, 33, " nigh ; " so Luke 21 : 30, 31 ; as a preposition, Heb. 6 : 8, " nigh unto (a curse)," and 8 : 13, " nigh unto (vanishing away)." See HAND (at), NIGH, READY.

1452 AG:214A 2. ENGUTERON (ἐγγύτερον), the comparative degree of No. 1, and
(ENGUS) the neuter of the adjective *enguteros*, used adverbially, occurs in Rom.
CB:— 13 : 11.¶

4139 AG:672C 3. PLĒSION (πλησίον), near, close by, neighbouring (the neuter of the
CB:1265B adjective *plēsios*, used as an adverb), occurs in John 4 : 5. See NEIGHBOUR.

B. Adjective.

316 AG:52B ANANKAIOS (ἀναγκαῖος), necessary, is used, in a secondary sense, of
CB:1235B persons connected by bonds of nature or friendship, with the meaning 'intimate,' in Acts 10 : 24, " (his) near (friends) ; " it is found in this sense in the papyri. See NECESSARY, NEEDFUL.

C. Verbs.

1448 AG:213C 1. ENGIZŌ (ἐγγίζω), transitively, to bring near (not in N.T. ; in the
CB:1245A Sept., e.g., Gen. 48 : 10 ; Is. 5 : 8) ; intransitively, to draw near, e.g., Matt. 21 : 34 ; Luke 18 : 40 ; 19 : 41, R.V., " draw nigh ; " see APPROACH, A.

4334 AG:713A 2. PROSERCHOMAI (προσέρχομαι), to come to, go to, is translated
CB:1267A " drew near " in Acts 7 : 31 and Heb. 10 : 22. See COME, No. 10.

4317 3. PROSAGŌ (προσάγω) is used (*a*) transitively, to bring, Acts
AG:711B CB:— 16 : 20 ; 1 Pet. 3 : 18 ; (*b*) intransitively, to draw near, in the latter sense in Acts 27 : 27.¶

NECESSARY

316 AG:52B 1. ANANKAIOS (ἀναγκαῖος), necessary (from *anankē*, necessity ;
CB:1235B see below), is so rendered in Acts 13 : 46 ; 1 Cor. 12 : 22 ; 2 Cor. 9 : 5 ; Phil. 2 : 25 ; Tit. 3 : 14 ; Heb. 8 : 3, R.V. (A.V., " of necessity ") ; for Acts 10 : 24, " near friends," see NEAR, B.¶

318 AG:52B 2. ANANKĒ (ἀνάγκη), a necessity (see No. 1), is rendered " (it was)
CB:1235B necessary " in Heb. 9 : 23, lit., 'it was a necessity.' See DISTRESS, A, No. 1.

1876 AG:282D 3. EPANANKĒS (ἐπανάγκης), an adjective akin to the preceding,
CB:— with *epi*, used intensively, found only in the neuter form, is used as an adverb signifying 'of necessity' and translated as an adjective in Acts 15 : 28, " necessary," lit., '(things) of necessity.'¶

Note : For the A.V. of Acts 28 : 10 see NEED, A, No. 1.

NECESSITY (-TIES)

318 AG:52B 1. ANANKĒ (ἀνάγκη) signifies (*a*) a necessity, what must needs be
CB:1235B (see NEEDS), translated " necessity " (in some mss. in Luke 23 : 17) in 1 Cor. 7 : 37 ; 9 : 16 ; 2 Cor. 9 : 7 (with *ek*, out of) ; Philm. 14 (with *kata*, according to) ; Heb. 7 : 12 ; 9 : 16 ; (*b*) distress, pain, translated

"necessities" in 2 Cor. 6 : 4; 12 : 10. See DISTRESS, No. 1, and the synonymous words there, and NEEDS, NEEDFUL (also CONSTRAIN, Note).

2. CHREIA (χρεία), a need, and almost always so translated, is used in the plural in Acts 20 : 34, "necessities;" Rom. 12 : 13, R.V. (A.V., "necessity"); in Phil. 4 : 16, A.V., "necessity," R.V., "need". See NEED, NEEDFUL. 5532 AG:884D CB:1240A

NECK

TRACHĒLOS (τράχηλος) is used (*a*) literally, Matt. 18 : 6; Mark 9 : 42; Luke 17 : 2; of embracing, Luke 15 : 20; Acts 20 : 37; (*b*) metaphorically, in Acts 15 : 10, of putting a yoke upon; Rom. 16 : 4, singular in the original,' (laid down their) neck,' indicating the figurative use of the term rather than the literal. Prisca and Aquila in some way had risked their lives for the Apostle (the phrase is found with this significance in the papyri).¶ 5137 AG:825A CB:1273A

NEED, NEEDS, NEEDFUL

A. Nouns.

1. CHREIA (χρεία) denotes a need, in such expressions as 'there is a need;' or 'to have need of' something, e.g., Matt. 3 : 14; 6 : 8; 9 : 12, R.V., "(have no) need," A.V., "need (not)," the R.V. adheres to the noun form; so in 14 : 16; Mark 14 : 63; Luke 5 : 31; 22 : 71; Eph. 4 : 28; 1 Thess. 4 : 9; in the following, however, both R.V. and A.V. use the verb form, to need (whereas the original has the verb *echō*, to have, with the noun *chreia* as the object, as in the instances just mentioned): Luke 15 : 7; John 2 : 25; 13 : 10; 16 : 30; 1 Thess. 1 : 8; 1 John 2 : 27; Rev. 22 : 5; in all these the verb to have could well have been expressed in the translation. 5532 AG:884D CB:1240A

In Luke 10 : 42 it is translated "needful," where the "one thing" is surely not one dish, or one person, but is to be explained according to Matt. 6 : 33 and 16 : 26. In Eph. 4 : 29, for the A.V., "(to) the use (of edifying)," the R.V. more accurately has "(for edifying) as the need may be," marg., "the building up of the need," i.e., 'to supply that which needed in each case;' so Westcott, who adds "The need represents a gap in the life which the wise word 'builds up,' fills up solidly and surely." In Phil. 4 : 19 the R.V. has "every need of yours" (A.V., "all your need"); in 1 Thess. 4 : 12, R.V., "need" (A.V., "lack"); in Acts 28 : 10, R.V., "(such things) as we needed" (A.V., "as were necessary"), lit., 'the things for the needs (plural).' See BUSINESS, A, No. 1, LACK, NECESSITY, USE, WANT.

2. ANANKĒ (ἀνάγκη), a necessity, need, is translated "it must needs be" in Matt. 18 : 7, with the verb 'to be' understood (according to the best mss.); in Luke 14 : 18, "I must needs" translates the verb *echō*, to have, with this noun as the object, lit., 'I have need;' in Rom. 13 : 5 "(*ye*) must needs," lit., '(it is) necessary (to be subject).' See NECESSARY, No. 2, NECESSITY, No. 1. See also DISTRESS. 318 AG:52B CB:1235B

B. Verbs.

5535 AG:885B CB:1240A 1. CHRĒZŌ (χρήζω), to need, to have need of (akin to *chrē*, it is necessary, fitting), is used in Matt. 6 : 32 ; Luke 11 : 8 ; 12 : 30 ; Rom. 16 : 2, R.V., " may have need " (A.V., " hath need ") ; 2 Cor. 3 : 1.¶

1163 AG:172A CB:1240B 2. DEI (δεῖ), an impersonal verb, signifying ' it is necessary,' is rendered " must needs " in Mark 13 : 7 ; John 4 : 4 ; Acts 1 : 16, A.V. (R.V., " it was needful ") ; 17 : 3, A.V. (R.V., " it behoved ") ; (in some mss. in Acts 21 : 22) ; 2 Cor. 11 : 30 ; 12 : 1 ; in Acts 15 : 5, " it was needful."

1163 (DEI) AG:172A (DEI 6.) CB:1240C 3. DEON (δέον), the neuter of the present participle of No. 2, is used as a noun, signifying that which is needful, due, proper, in 1 Pet. 1 : 6, with the meaning ' need,' " (if) need (be)," with the verb to be understood. See OUGHT.

4326 AG:712A CB:1267A 4. PROSDEOMAI (προσδέομαι), to want besides, to need in addition (*pros*, besides, *deomai*, to want), is used in Acts 17 : 25, " (as though) He needed (anything) ; " the literal sense of *pros* is not to be stressed.¶ In the Sept., Prov. 12 : 9, " lacking (bread)."¶

3784 AG:598D CB:1261A 5. OPHEILŌ (ὀφείλω), to owe, be bound, obliged to do something, is translated " must ye needs," in 1 Cor. 5 : 10 ; in 7 : 36 it is used impersonally, signifying ' it is due,' and followed by the infinitive mood of *ginomai*, to become, to occur, come about, lit. ' it is due to become,' translated " (if) need (so) require." See BEHOVE, BOUND, DEBT, DUE, DUTY, GUILTY, INDEBTED, MUST, OUGHT, OWE.

5302 AG:849A CB:1252B *Note :* In Phil. 4 : 12, A.V., *hustereō*, to come short, fail, to be in want, is translated " to suffer need " (R.V., " to be in want "). See BEHIND.

C. Adjectives.

(-IOS) 316 AG:52B CB:1235B 1. ANANKAIOTEROS (ἀναγκαιότερος), the comparative degree of *anankaios*, necessary, is translated " more needful " in Phil. 1 : 24. See NECESSARY, No. 1.

2006 AG:302D CB:— 2. EPITĒDEIOS (ἐπιτήδειος), primarily, suitable, convenient, then, useful, necessary, is translated " needful " in Jas. 2 : 16, neuter plural, ' necessaries.' ¶ In the Sept., 1 Chron. 28 : 2, " suitable."¶

2121 AG:321C CB:1247B *Note :* In Heb. 4 : 16 *eukairos*, timely, seasonable, qualifying the noun *boētheia*, help, is translated " time of need," lit., ' for opportune help.' See CONVENIENT.

NEEDLE

4476 AG:734C CB:— 1. RHAPHIS (ῥαφίς), from *rhaptō*, to sew, occurs in Matt. 19 : 24 ; Mark 10 : 25.¶

— AG:139B CB:— 2. BELONĒ (βελόνη), akin to *belos*, a dart, denotes a sharp point, hence, a needle, Luke 18 : 25 (some mss. have No. 1).¶

Note : The idea of applying ' the needle's eye ' to small gates seems to be a modern one ; there is no ancient trace of it. The Lord's object in the statement is to express human impossibility and there is no need to endeavour to soften the difficulty by taking the needle to mean anything more than the ordinary instrument. Mackie points out (Hastings' Bib.

Dic.) that " an attempt is sometimes made to explain the words as a reference to the small door, a little over 2 feet square, in the large heavy gate of a walled city. This mars the figure without materially altering the meaning, and receives no justification from the language and traditions of Palestine."

NEGLECT, NEGLIGENT

1. AMELEŌ (ἀμελέω) denotes (*a*) to be careless, not to care (*a*, 272
negative, *melei*, it is a care ; from *melō*, to care, to be a care), Matt. 22 : 5, AG:44D CB:—
" made light of ; " (*b*) to be careless of, neglect, 1 Tim. 4 : 14 ; Heb. 2 : 3 ; 8 : 9, " I regarded (them) not." See LIGHT OF (make), REGARD.¶ (In the Sept., Jer. 4 : 17 ; 38 : 32.¶)

2. PARATHEŌREŌ (παραθεωρέω), primarily, to examine side by side, 3865
compare (*para*, beside, *theōreō*, to look at), hence, to overlook, to neglect, AG:616B CB:—
is used in Acts 6 : 1, of the neglect of widows in the daily ministration in Jerusalem.¶

Note : In 2 Pet. 1 : 12, some mss. have No. 1, hence the A.V., " I will not be negligent ; " the R.V. follows those which have the future tense of *mellō*, to be ready. See READY. For " neglect to hear " see HEAR, No. 7.

For NEGLECTING (Col. 2 : 23) see SEVERITY

NEIGHBOUR

1. GEITŌN (γείτων), lit., one living in the same land, denotes a 1069 AG:153C
neighbour, always plural in the N.T., Luke 14 : 12 ; 15 : 6, 9 ; John 9 : 8.¶ CB:—

2. PERIOIKOS (περίοικος), an adjective, lit., dwelling around (*peri*, 4040 AG:648D
around, *oikos*, a dwelling), is used as a noun in Luke 1 : 58, " neighbours."¶ CB:—

3. PLĒSION (πλησίον), the neuter of the adjective *plēsios* (from 4139
pelas, near), is used as an adverb accompanied by the article, lit., ' the AG:672C CB:1265B
(one) near ; ' hence, one's neighbour ; see refs. below.

This and Nos. 1 and 2 have a wider range of meaning than that of the Eng. word neighbour. There were no farmhouses scattered over the agricultural areas of Palestine ; the populations, gathered in villages, went to and fro to their toil. Hence domestic life was touched at every point by a wide circle of neighbourhood. The terms for neighbour were therefore of a very comprehensive scope. This may be seen from the chief characteristics of the privileges and duties of neighbourhood as set forth in Scripture, (*a*) its helpfulness, e.g., Prov. 27 : 10 ; Luke 10 : 36 ; (*b*) its intimacy, e.g., Luke 15 : 6, 9 (see No. 1) ; Heb. 8 : 11 ; (*c*) its sincerity and sanctity, e.g., Ex. 22 : 7, 10 ; Prov. 3 : 29 ; 14 : 21 ; Rom. 13 : 10 ; 15 : 2 ; Eph. 4 : 25 ; Jas. 4 : 12. The N.T. quotes and expands the command in Lev. 19 : 18, to love one's neighbour as oneself ; see, e.g., Matt. 5 : 43 ; 19 : 19 ; 22 : 39 ; Mark 12 : 31, 33 ; Luke 10 : 27 ; Gal.
5 : 14 ; Jas. 2 : 8. See also Acts 7 : 27. 2087 AG:315A
Note : In Rom. 13 : 8, for *heteron*, another, R.V. has " his neighbour." CB:1250A

NEIGHBOURHOOD

Note: This, in Acts 28 : 7, R.V., translates a phrase consisting of the
4012 AG:644B dative plural of the article followed by *peri*, around, governed by the
CB:1263B preposition *en*, in, " in the neighbourhood of (that place)," A.V., " in the
(same quarters)," lit., ' in the (parts) around (that place).'

NEITHER. See † p. 1.

For NEITHER AT ANY TIME, Luke 15 : 29, see NEVER

For NEPHEWS see GRANDCHILDREN

NEST

2682 AG:418C KATASKĒNŌSIS (κατασκήνωσις), properly an encamping, taking up
CB:1254B one's quarters, then, a lodging, abode (*kata*, down over, *skēnē*, a tent),
is used of birds' nests in Matt. 8 : 20 and Luke 9 : 58.¶ In the Sept.,
1 Chron. 28 : 2, " the building ; " Ezek. 37 : 27, " (My) tabernacle."¶
NOSSIA 3555 The word *nossia*, signifying a brood, Luke 13 : 34, used in the Sept.
AG:543D to denote a nest, e.g., in Deut. 22 : 6 ; 32 : 11, signifies the actual receptacle
CB:1260A built by birds in which to lay their eggs (having special reference to the
prospective brood) ; but the word *kataskēnōsis*, used by the Lord, denotes
a resting or roosting place. This lends force to His comparison. Not only
was He without a home, He had not even a lodging-place (cp. *kataskēnoō*,
to lodge, e.g., Matt. 13 : 32 ; Acts 2 : 26, R.V. marg., ' shall tabernacle ; '
see LODGE).

NET

293 AG:47B 1. AMPHIBLĒSTRON (ἀμφίβληστρον), lit., something thrown around
CB:— (*amphi*, around, *ballō*, to throw), denotes a casting-net, a somewhat small
net, cast over the shoulder, spreading out in a circle and made to sink
by weights, Matt. 4 : 18 (in some mss. in Mark 1 : 16 : the best have the
verb *amphiballō* alone).¶
1350 AG:198C 2. DIKTUON (δίκτυον), a general term for a net (from an old verb
CB:— *dikō*, to cast : akin to *diskos*, a quoit), occurs in Matt. 4 : 20, 21 ; Mark
1 : 18, 19 ; Luke 5 : 2, 4–6 ; John 21 : 6, 8, 11 (twice).¶ In the Sept. it
was used for a net for catching birds, Prov. 1 : 17, in other ways, e.g.,
figuratively of a snare, Job. 18 : 8 ; Prov. 29 : 5.
4522 AG:739C 3. SAGĒNĒ (σαγήνη) denotes a drag-net, a *seine ;* two modes were
CB:— employed with this, either by its being let down into the water and drawn
together in a narrowing circle, and then into the boat, or as a semicircle
drawn to the shore, Matt. 13 : 47, where Nos. 1 and 2 would not have
suited so well. The Greek historian Herodotus uses the corresponding
verb *sagēneuō* of a device by which the Persians are said to have cleared
a conquered island of its inhabitants.¶

NEVER

1. OUDEPOTE (οὐδέποτε), from *oude*, not even, and *pote*, at any time, 3763
is used in definite negative statements, e.g., Matt. 7 : 23 ; 1 Cor. 13 : 8 ; AG:592B CB:—
Heb. 10 : 1, 11, or questions, e.g., Matt. 21 : 16, 42 ; in Luke 15 : 29 (1st part), R.V., " never " (A.V., " neither . . . at any time ") ; A.V. and R.V., " never " (2nd part).

2. MĒDEPOTE (μηδέποτε), virtually the same as No. 1, the negative 3368 AG:518B
mē, however, conveying a less strong declarative negation, 2 Tim. 3 : 7.¶ CB:—

3. OUDEPŌ (οὐδέπω), not yet, is translated " never (man) yet " in 3764
John 19 : 41 (" man " representing the idiomatically used negative AG:592C CB:—
pronoun *oudeis*, ' no one ') ; some mss. have it in Luke 23 : 53, instead of *oupō*, not yet.

Notes : (1) In Mark 14 : 21, A.V., the negative particle *ouk*, not, is OU(K)
translated " never " (R.V., " not ") ; the negative particle *mē*, not (which 3756 AG:590A
suggests non-existence when the existence was after all possible, or even CB:—
probable, in contrast to *ou*, which implies non-existence absolutely), is Mē 3361
translated " never " in John 7 : 15, A.V. and R.V. (2) The phrase AG:515D
eis ton aiona, for ever (not to be rendered literally, ' unto the age,' see CB:1258A POTE
ETERNAL), preceded by the double negative *ou mē*, denotes ' never,' 4218
John 4 : 14 ; 8 : 51, 52 ; 10 : 28 ; 11 : 26 ; 13 : 8 ; so, preceded by *ouk*, AG:695A CB:1266B
not, in Mark 3 : 29. (3) In 2 Pet. 1 : 10, " never " is the translation of PōPOTE
ou mē pote, i.e., ' by no means ever ; ' so with the double negative followed 4455
by the extended word *pōpote*, i.e., ' by no means not even at any time,' AG:732A
John 6 : 35 (2nd part). (4) *Pōpote* follows *oudeis*, no one, in the dative CB:1266A OUDEIS
case (' to no man ') in John 8 : 33, R.V., " never yet " (A.V., " never ") ; 3762 AG:591D
so in Luke 19 : 30, where *oudeis* is in the nominative case, R.V., " no man CB:1261B
ever yet " (A.V., " yet never man ").

NEVERTHELESS : see † p. 1

NEW

1. KAINOS (καινός) denotes new, of that which is unaccustomed or 2537
unused, not new in time, recent, but new as to form or quality, of different AG:394A CB:1253A
nature from what is contrasted as old. " ' The new tongues,' *kainos*, of Mark 16 : 17 are the ' other tongues,' *heteros*, of Acts 2 : 4. These languages, however, were ' new ' and ' different,' not in the sense that they had never been heard before, or that they were new to the hearers, for it is plain from v. 8 that this is not the case ; they were new languages to the speakers, different from those in which they were accustomed to speak.

" The new things that the Gospel brings for present obedience and realization are : a new covenant, Matt. 26 : 28 in some texts ; a new commandment, John 13 : 34 ; a new creative act, Gal. 6 : 15 ; a new creation, 2 Cor. 5 : 17 ; a new man, i.e., a new character of manhood, spiritual and moral, after the pattern of Christ, Eph. 4 : 24 ; a new man, i.e., ' the Church which is His (Christ's) body,' Eph. 2 : 15.

" The new things that are to be received and enjoyed hereafter are: a new name, the believer's, Rev. 2 : 17; a new name, the Lord's, Rev. 3 : 12; a new song, Rev. 5 : 9; a new Heaven and a new Earth, Rev. 21 : 1; the new Jerusalem, Rev. 3 : 12; 21 : 2; 'And He that sitteth on the Throne said, Behold, I make all things new,' Rev. 21 : 5."*

Kainos is translated " fresh " in the R.V. of Matt. 9 : 17; Mark 2 : 22 (in the best texts) and Luke 5 : 38, of wineskins. Cp. *kainotēs*, newness (below).

3501 2. NEOS (νέος) signifies new in respect of time, that which is recent;
AG:535D it is used of the young, and so translated, especially the comparative
CB:1259C degree " younger; " accordingly what is *neos* may be a reproduction of the old in quality or character. *Neos* and *kainos* are sometimes used of the same thing, but there is a difference, as already indicated. Thus the " new man " in Eph. 2 : 15 (*kainos*) is new in differing in character; so in 4 : 24 (see No. 1); but the " new man " in Col. 3 : 10 (*neos*) stresses the fact of the believer's new experience, recently begun, and still proceeding. " The old man in him . . . dates as far back as Adam; a new man has been born, who therefore is fitly so called " [i.e., *neos*], Trench, Syn. §lx. The new Covenant in Heb. 12 : 24 is new (*neos*) compared with the Mosaic, nearly fifteen hundred years before; it is new (*kainos*) compared with the Mosaic, which is old in character, ineffective, 8 : 8, 13; 9 : 15.

The new wine of Matt. 9 : 17; Mark 2 : 22; Luke 5 : 37–39, is *neos*, as being of recent production; the new wine of the Kingdom, Matt. 26 : 29; Mark 14 : 25, is *kainos*, since it will be of a different character from that of this world. The rendering " new " (*neos*) is elsewhere used metaphorically in 1 Cor. 5 : 7, " a new lump." See YOUNG, YOUNGER.

4372
AG:719C 3. PROSPHATOS (πρόσφατος), originally signifying freshly slain,
CB:1267B acquired the general sense of new, as applied to flowers, oil, misfortune, etc. It is used in Heb. 10 : 20 of the " living way " which Christ " dedicated for us . . . through the veil . . . His flesh " (which stands for His expiatory death by the offering of His body, ver. 10).¶ In the Sept., Numb. 6 : 3; Deut. 32 : 17; Psa. 81 : 9; Eccl. 1 : 9.¶ Cp. the adverb *prosphatōs*, lately, recently, Acts 18 : 2.¶

46 *Note:* In Matt. 9 : 16 and Mark 2 : 21, A.V., *agnaphos* is translated
AG:10D " new " (R.V., " undressed "). Moulton and Milligan give an instance
CB:— in the papyri of its use in respect of a "new white shirt." See UNDRESSED.¶

For NEWBORN, 1 Pet. 2 : 2, see BEGET, C, No. 2

NEWNESS

2538
AG:394C KAINOTĒS (καινότης), akin to *kainos*, is used in the phrases (*a*)
CB:1253A " newness of life," Rom. 6 : 4, i.e., life of a new quality (see NEW, No. 1); the believer, being a new creation (2 Cor. 5 : 17), is to behave himself consistently with this in contrast to his former manner of life; (*b*) newness

* From Notes on Galatians by Hogg and Vine, pp. 337, 338.

of the spirit, R.V., Rom. 7 : 6, said of the believer's manner of serving the Lord. While the phrase stands for the new life of the quickened spirit of the believer, it is impossible to dissociate this (in an objective sense) from the operation of the Holy Spirit, by whose power the service is rendered.¶ (GOOD) NEWS See GOSPEL

NEXT

1. HEXĒS (ἑξῆς), an adverb (akin to *echō*, to have) denoting 'in order,' successively, next, is used adjectivally, qualifying the noun "day" in Luke 9 : 37 ; Acts 21 : 1, R.V., "next" (A.V., "following") ; 25 : 17, R.V., "next" (A.V., "on the morrow") ; in 27 : 18, with *hēmera*, day, understood ; in Luke 7 : 11, in the best mss., with the word *chronos*, time, understood, "soon afterwards" (marg., "on the next day," according to some ancient authorities). See AFTER, FOLLOW, *Note* (3), MORROW. 1836 AG:276A CB:—

2. METAXU (μεταξύ) signifies between, "next," in Acts 13 : 42. See BETWEEN, No. 2. 3342 AG:512D CB:—

3. ECHŌ (ἔχω), to have, in the Middle Voice, sometimes signifies to be next to, said of towns, in Mark 1 : 38 ; of a day, Acts 21 : 26 ; in 20 : 15 (2nd part), *hēmera*, day, is unexpressed. See HAVE. 2192 AG:331D CB:1242C

4. ERCHOMAI (ἔρχομαι), to come, is used in the present participle in Acts 13 : 44, "(the) next (sabbath)." See COME. 2064 AG:310B CB:1246B

Note : In Acts 7 : 26, A.V., *epeimi*, to come on or after, used with *hēmera*, day, is translated "next" (R.V., "following") ; so with *hēmera*, understood, Acts 16 : 11 ; 20 : 15 (1st part) ; in 21 : 18, R.V. and A.V., "following." EPEIMI 1966 (EPIOUSA) AG:284C CB:1245C HēMERA 2250 AG:345D CB:1249C

NEXT DAY

Notes : (1) For *aurion*, to-morrow, translated "next day" in Acts 4 : 3, and *epaurion*, on the morrow, Matt. 27 : 62 ; John 1 : 29, 35 ; 12 : 12 ; Acts 14 : 20 ; 25 : 6, see MORROW. (2) For *echō*, Acts 20 : 15, see NEXT, No. 3. (3) For *epeimi*, without the noun *hēmera*, "day," see NEXT (end of Note). (4) In Acts 20 : 15 (mid. of verse) *heteros*, other, signifies "next," with *hēmera*, understood. (5) In Acts 28 : 13 (end of ver.) the adjective *deuteraios*, second, is used in the masculine plural adverbially, signifying "the second (day)," R.V., A.V., "the next (day)." AURION 839 AG:122A CB:— EPAURION 1887 AG:283D CB:— HETEROS 2087 AG:315A CB:1250A DEUTERAIOS 1206 AG:177A CB:—

NIGH

A. Adverbs.

1. ENGUS (ἐγγύς), nigh or near, is translated in both ways in Matt. 24 : 32, 33 and Mark 13 : 28, 29, A.V. (R.V., "nigh" in both) ; in Acts 1 : 12, with *echon*, present participle neuter of *echō*, to have, R.V., "nigh unto . . .off" (A.V., "from"). See NEAR, No. 1. 1451 AG:214A CB:1245A

2. PARAPLĒSION (παραπλήσιον), the neuter of the adjective *paraplēsios*, *para*, beside, *plēsios*, near, nearly resembling, is translated "nigh unto," with reference to death, in Phil. 2 : 27.¶ 3897 AG:621C (-OS) CB:1262B

1448 **B. Verb.**

AG:213C CB:1245A ENGIZŌ (ἐγγίζω) : see APPROACH.

C. Preposition.

3844 AG:609C CB:1261C PARA (παρά), beside, alongside of, is translated " nigh unto " in Matt. 15 : 29 ; in Mark 5 : 21, R.V., " by " (A.V., " nigh unto ").

4314 AG:709C CB:1267A *Note :* In Mark 5 : 11, A.V., *pros*, towards, on the side of, is translated " nigh unto (the mountain)," R.V., " on (the mountain) side ; " the swine were not simply near the mountain.

NIGHT (by, in the)

3571 AG:546B CB:1260B NUX (νύξ) is used (I) literally, (*a*) of the alternating natural period to that of the day, e.g., Matt. 4 : 2 ; 12 : 40 ; 2 Tim. 1 : 3 ; Rev. 4 : 8 ; (*b*) of the period of the absence of light, the time in which something takes place, e.g., Matt. 2 : 14 (27 : 64, in some mss.) ; Luke 2 : 8 ; John 3 : 2 (7 : 50, in some mss.) ; Acts 5 : 19 ; 9 : 25 ; (*c*) of point of time, e.g., Matt. 14 : 27 (in some mss.), 30 ; Luke 12 : 20 ; Acts 27 : 23 ; (*d*) of duration of time, e.g., Luke 2 : 37 ; 5 : 5 ; Acts 20 : 31 ; 26 : 7 (note the difference in the phrase in Mark 4 : 27) ; (II) metaphorically, (*a*) of the period of man's alienation from God, Rom. 13 : 12 ; 1 Thess. 5 : 5, lit., 'not of night,' where " of " means 'belonging to ;' cp. " of the Way," Acts 9 : 2 ; " of shrinking back " and " of faith," Heb. 10 : 39, marg. ; (*b*) of death, as the time when work ceases, John 9 : 4.

NIGHT AND A DAY (A)

(-RON) 3574 AG:547A CB:— NUCHTHĒMEROS (νυχθήμερος), an adjective denoting lasting a night and a day (from *nux*, night, and *hēmera*, a day), is used in 2 Cor. 11 : 25, in the neuter gender, as a noun, the object of the verb *poieō*, to do, lit., ' I have done a night-and-a-day.'¶

NINE

1767 AG:267A CB:— ENNEA (ἐννέα) is found in Luke 17 : 17, and in connection with " ninety " (see below).¶

NINETY

1768 (KONTAENNEA) AG:265A CB:— ENENĒKONTA, or ENNĒN—(ἐνενήκοντα) is found in Matt. 18 : 12, 13 ; Luke 15 : 4, 7.¶

NINTH

1766 AG:267A (ENNEA) CB:— ENATOS, or ENN—(ἔνατος) is found in reference (*a*) to the ninth hour (3 o'clock, p.m.) in Matt. 20 : 5 ; 27 : 45, 46 ; Mark 15 : 33, 34 ; Luke 23 : 44 ; Acts 3 : 1 ; 10 : 3, 30 ; (*b*) to the topaz as the ninth foundation of the city wall in the symbolic vision in Rev. 21 (ver. 20).¶

NO : see † p. 1 .

NO LONGER, NO MORE

1. OUKETI (οὐκέτι), a negative adverb of time, signifies no longer, 3765
no more (*ou*, not, *k*, euphonic, *eti* longer), denying absolutely and directly, AG:592C CB:—
e.g., Matt. 19 : 6 ; John 4 : 42, " now . . . not ; " 6 : 66 ; Acts 20 : 25, 38 ;
2 Cor. 1 : 23, A.V., " not as yet ; " Eph. 2 : 19 ; with another negative, to
strengthen the negation, e.g., Matt. 22 : 46 ; Mark 14 : 25 ; 15 : 5, R.V.,
" no more (anything)," A.V., " yet . . . no (thing) ; " Acts 8 : 39 ;
Rev. 18 : 11, 14.

2. MĒKETI (μηκέτι), with the same meaning as No. 1, but generally 3371
expressing a prohibition, e.g., Matt. 21 : 19 ; John 5 : 14 ; Rom. 14 : 13 ; AG:518C CB:—
Eph. 4 : 28 ; 1 Tim. 5 : 23 ; 1 Pet. 4 : 2 ; indicating some condition
expressed or implied, e.g., 1 Thess. 3 : 5 ; or non-existence, when the
existence might have been possible under certain conditions, e.g., Mark
1 : 45 ; 2 : 2, R.V., " no longer " (A.V., " no "). See HENCEFORTH.

Notes : (1) The double negative *ou mē*, by no means, in no wise, OU
followed by *eti*, longer, still, yet, is rendered " no more " in Heb. 8 : 12 ; 3756 AG:590A
10 : 17 ; Rev. 3 : 12. (2) In John 15 : 4, A.V., *houtōs*, so, followed by *oude*, Mē
neither, is translated " no more " (R.V., " so neither "). 3361 AG:515D
CB:1258A ETI

NO MAN, NO ONE, NEITHER ANY MAN 2089 AG:315C

Note : *Oudeis* and *mēdeis*, no one, no man, are related to one another CB:1247A
in much the same way as indicated above under *ouketi* and *mēketi*. HOUTōS
Instances of *oudeis* are Matt. 6 : 24 ; 9 : 16 ; 24 : 36 (R.V., " no one ") ; 3779 AG:597C
John 1 : 18 ; 3 : 2, 13, 32 ; 14 : 6 and 16 : 22 (R.V., " no one ") ; 2 Cor.
7 : 2 (thrice) ; Heb. 12 : 14 ; 1 John 4 : 12 ; Rev. 2 : 17, R.V., " no one ; " OUDEIS
so 5 : 3, 4 ; 19 : 12 ; in 3 : 7, 8 and 15 : 8 (R.V., " none ") ; in 7 : 9 and 3762 AG:591D
14 : 3, " no man." In all these cases " man " stands for " person." CB:1261B MēDEIS
The spelling *outheis* occurs occasionally in the mss. ; Westcott and Hort 3367
adopt it in 2 Cor. 11 : 8, in the genitive case *outhenos*. AG:518A CB:1258A

Instances of *mēdeis* are Matt. 8 : 4 (almost all those in the Synoptists are cases of prohibition or admonition) ; Acts 9 : 7 ; Rom. 12 : 17 ; 1 Cor. 3 : 18, 21 ; Gal. 6 : 17 ; Eph. 5 : 6 ; Col. 2 : 18 ; 1 Thess. 3 : 3 ; 1 Tim. 4 : 12 ; Rev. 3 : 11, R.V., " no one."

Notes : (1) In some mss. the negative *mē* and the indefinite pronoun Mē
tis, some one, anyone, appear as one word, *mētis* (always separated in the 3361 AG:515D
best mss.), e.g., Matt. 8 : 28, " no man ; " so in 1 Cor. 16 : 11 ; 2 Cor. CB:1258A
11 : 16 ; 2 Thess. 2 : 3. The words are separated also in Matt. 24 : 4 ;
2 Cor. 8 : 20 (R.V., " any man," after " avoiding ") ; Rev. 13 : 17. These
instances represent either impossibility or prohibition (see under NO
LONGER, No. 2) ; contrast *ouch* (i.e., *ou*) . . . *tis* in Heb. 5 : 4, " no man
(taketh)," where a direct negative statement is made. (2) In 2 Cor. 11 : 10 OU (OUK)
the negative *ou*, " not," is translated " no man " (A.V. marg. " not ") ; 3756 AG:590A
in 1 Cor. 4 : 6, e.g., the negative *mē* is translated " no one ; " in Rom. CB:—
14 : 13, the negative *mē*, used in an admonition, is translated " no man."

NO WISE (in), ANYWISE (in)

OU 1. OU MĒ (οὐ μή), a double negative, strongly expressing a negation,
3756 AG:590A is translated "in no wise" in Matt. 5 : 18, 20, R.V. (A.V., "in no case");
CB:— 10 : 42; Luke 18 : 17; John 6 : 37; Acts 13 : 41; Rev. 21 : 27; in
Mē 3361 Matt. 13 : 14 (twice, R.V.; A.V., "not"); so in Mark 9 : 1; Luke 9 : 27;
AG:515D John 4 : 48; Acts 28 : 26 (twice); 1 Thess. 4 : 15; in Luke 10 : 19,
CB:1258A R.V. "(nothing) . . . in any wise" (A.V., "by any means").

Note: In 2 Thess. 2 : 3, R.V., "(no man) . . . in any wise" (A.V., "by any means"), the double negative is *mē . . . mēdena.*

3760 AG:591B 2. OUDAMŌS (οὐδαμῶς), akin to the adjective *oudamos*, not even one
CB:— (not in the N.T.), denotes by no means, in no wise, Matt. 2 : 6.¶

PANTōS 3. OU PANTŌS (οὐ πάντως), lit., 'not altogether,' i.e., 'wholly not'
3843 (from *pas*, all), is rendered "in no wise" in Rom. 3 : 9.
AG:609B CB:— *Note:* In Luke 13 : 11 the phrase *eis to panteles*, lit., unto the complete end (*pas*, all, *telos*, an end), i.e., completely, utterly, preceded by the negative *mē*, is translated "in no wise" ('who was utterly unable to lift herself up'). Cp. Heb. 7 : 25, where the same phrase is used without a negative, signifying "to the uttermost."

For ON THIS WISE see THUS (*b*)

NOBLE

2104 AG:319A 1. EUGENĒS (εὐγενής), an adjective, lit., well born (*eu*, well, and
CB:1247B *genos*, a family, race), (*a*) signifies noble, 1 Cor. 1 : 26; (*b*) is used with *anthrōpos*, a man, i.e., a nobleman, in Luke 19 : 12.¶ In the Sept., Job 1 : 3.¶

(-NēS) 2104 2. EUGENESTEROS (εὐγενέστερος), the comparative degree of No. 1,
AG:319A occurs in Acts 17 : 11, "more noble," i.e., more noble-minded.¶

2903 3. KRATISTOS (κράτιστος) is translated "most noble" in the A.V.
AG:449A CB:1256A of Acts 24 : 3 and 26 : 25 (R.V., "most excellent"). See EXCELLENT.

NOBLEMAN

937 AG:136D BASILIKOS (βασιλικός), an adjective, royal, belonging to a king
CB:1238C (*basileus*), is used of the command, 'thou shalt love thy neighbour as thyself,' "the royal law," Jas. 2 : 8; this may mean a law which covers or governs other laws and therefore has a specially regal character (as Hort suggests), or because it is made by a King (a meaning which Deissmann assigns) with whom there is no respect of persons; it is used with the pronoun *tis*, a certain one, in John 4 : 46, 49, of a courtier, one in the service of a king, "a nobleman" (some mss. have the noun *basiliskos*, a petty king, in these two verses). It is used of a country in Acts 12 : 20, "the king's (country)," and of royal apparel in ver. 21. See KING, ROYAL.¶

Note: For *eugenēs* in Luke 19 : 12, see NOBLE, No. 1.

NOISE

A. Adverb.

RHOIZĒDON (ῥοιζηδόν), from *rhoizos*, the whistling of an arrow, signifies 'with rushing sound,' as of roaring flames, and is used in 2 Pet. 3 : 10, of the future passing away of the heavens.¶ 4500 AG:737A CB:—

B. Verbs.

1. AKOUŌ (ἀκούω), to hear, is translated "it was noised" in Mark 2 : 1 (Passive Voice), of the rapid spread of the information that Christ was "in the house" in Capernaum. See HEAR. 191 AG:31D CB:1234B

2. DIALALEŌ (διαλαλέω), lit., to speak through, is rendered "were noised abroad" in Luke 1 : 65. See COMMUNE. 1255 AG:185C CB:—

Notes : (1) In Rev. 6 : 1, A.V., *phōnē*, a voice or sound, is translated "noise" (R.V., "voice"); it is used with *ginomai* in Acts 2 : 6, A.V., "(this) was noised abroad," R.V., "(this) sound was heard." (2) In Matt. 9 : 23, A.V., *thorubeō*, to make a tumult or uproar, in the Middle Voice, as in Mark 5 : 39 and Acts 20 : 10, is translated "making a noise" (R.V., "making a tumult"). See ADO, TROUBLE, TUMULT, UPROAR. PHōNē 5456 AG:870C CB:1264B THORUBEō 2350 AG:362D CB:1272B

NOISOME

KAKOS (κακός), evil, is translated "noisome" in Rev. 16 : 2. See BAD. 2556 AG:397D CB:1253B

For NONE see NO MAN

NOON

NOON See HOUR

MESĒMBRIA (μεσημβρία), lit., middle-day (*mesos*, middle, and *hēmera*, a day), signifies (*a*) noon, Acts 22 : 6; (*b*) the south, Acts 8 : 26.¶ 3314 AG:506D CB:—

NOR : see † p. 1

NORTH

BORRAS (βορρᾶς), primarily Boreas, the North Wind, came to denote the north (cp. Borealis), Luke 13 : 29; Rev. 21 : 13.¶ 1005 AG:145B CB:—

NORTH EAST, NORTH WEST

CHŌROS (χῶρος), Lat., *corus*, the Latin name for the north-west wind, hence, the north-west, occurs in Acts 27 : 12, A.V., R.V., "(north-east and) south-east," as the N.W. wind blows towards the S.E.¶ 5566 AG:891C II. CB:1240A

Note : In the same ver., *lips*, the south-west (lit., Libyan) wind, hence, the south-west (so A.V.), is rendered "north-east" in R.V., as the S.W. wind blows towards the N.E. The difficulty is that Lutro (commonly identified with Phœnix) faces E., not W. But there is a harbour opposite Lutro which does look S.W. and N.W., bearing the name Phineka (R.V. marg. renders the whole phrase literally). This seems the best solution. 3047 AG:475D CB:—

NOT : see † p. 1

NOTABLE, OF NOTE

1110 1. GNŌSTOS (γνωστός), an adjective, signifying 'known' (from
AG:164B
CB:1248B *ginōskō*, to know), is used (*a*) as an adjective, most usually translated "known," whether of facts, e.g., Acts 1 : 19; 2 : 14; 4 : 10; or persons, John 18 : 15, 16; it denotes "notable" in Acts 4 : 16, of a miracle; (*b*) as a noun, "acquaintance," Luke 2 : 44 and 23 : 49. See ACQUAINTANCE, KNOWN.

1978
AG:298B 2. EPISĒMOS (ἐπίσημος) primarily meant bearing a mark, e.g., of
CB:— money, 'stamped,' 'coined,' (from *epi*, upon, and *sēma*, a mark, a sign; cp. *sēmainō*, to give a sign, signify, indicate, and *sēmeioō*, to note; see below); it is used in the N.T., metaphorically, (*a*) in a good sense, Rom. 16 : 7, "of note," illustrious, said of Andronicus and Junias; (*b*) in a bad sense, Matt. 27 : 16, "notable," of the prisoner Barabbas.¶ In the Sept., Gen. 30 : 42; Esth. 5 : 4; 8 : 13, toward the end of the verse, "a distinct (day)".¶

2016 3. EPIPHANĒS (ἐπιφανής), illustrious, renowned, notable (akin to
AG:304B
CB:1246A *epiphainō*, to show forth, appear; Eng., epiphany), is translated "notable" in Acts 2 : 20, of the great Day of the Lord. The appropriateness of this word (compared with Nos. 1 and 2) to that future occasion is obvious.¶

NOTE (Verb)

4593 SĒMEIOŌ (σημειόω), from *sēmeion*, a sign, token, signifies to mark,
AG:748D
CB:— to note, in the Middle Voice, to note for oneself, and is so used in 2 Thess. 3 : 14, in an injunction to take cautionary note of one who refuses obedience to the Apostle's word by the Epistle.¶ In the Sept. Ps. 5 : 6.¶

NOTHING

3762
AG:591D 1. OUDEN (οὐδέν), the neuter of *oudeis*, no one, occurs, e.g., in Matt.
CB:1261B 5 : 13; 10 : 26; 23 : 16; adverbially, e.g., in Matt. 27 : 24; 2 Cor. 12 : 11 (1st part), "in nothing;" 1 Tim. 4 : 4; in the dative case, after *en*, "in," Phil. 1 : 20. Westcott and Hort adopt the spelling *outhen* in Luke 22 : 35; 23 : 14; Acts 15 : 9; 19 : 27; 26 : 26; 1 Cor. 13 : 2.

3367 2. MĒDEN (μηδέν), the neuter of *mēdeis*, no one, is related to No. 1,
AG:518A
CB:1258A in the same way as the masculine genders are; so with the negatives *ou* and *mē*, not, in all their usage and connections (see under NO MAN). Thus it is found, not in direct negative statements, as with No. 1, but in warnings, prohibitions, etc., e.g., Matt. 27 : 19; Acts 19 : 36; in expressions conveying certain impossibilities, e.g., Acts 4 : 21; comparisons, e.g., 2 Cor. 6 : 10; intimating a supposition to the contrary, 1 Tim. 6 : 4; adverbially, e.g., 2 Cor. 11 : 5, "not a whit." Westcott and Hort adopt
3756 the spelling *mēthen* in Acts 27 : 33.

AG:590A 3. OU (οὐ), not, is translated "nothing" in Luke 8 : 17; 11 : 6;
3361
AG:515D 1 Cor. 9 : 16; 2 Cor. 8 : 15 (in each case, an absolute and direct negative).
CB:1258A 4. MĒ (μή), not, is translated "nothing" in John 6 : 39 in a clause

expressing purpose ; in the A.V. of Luke 7 : 42 (R.V., “ not ”), in a temporal clause.

5. OU . . . TI (οὐ . . . τί), followed by the subjunctive mood, TI
“ (have) nothing (to eat),” lit., ‘ (they have) not what (they should eat),’ 5100
in Matt. 15 : 32 (in some mss. in Mark 6 : 36) ; Mark 8 : 2 ; the phrase AG:819D CB:1272C
conveys more stress than the simple negative (No. 3).

6. MĒ . . . TI (μὴ . . . τί), followed by the subjunctive mood, “ (they had) nothing (to eat),” R.V., “ (having) nothing (to eat),” A.V., lit., ‘ not (having) what (they should eat),’ in Mark 8 : 1 ; the negative is *mē* here because it is attached to a participle, ‘ having ; ’ whereas in No. 5 the negative *ou* is attached to the indicative mood, ‘ they have.’

7. MĒ TI (μή τι), lit., ‘ not anything,’ not used in simple, direct negations (see under NO MAN), occurs in John 6 : 12 in a clause of purpose ; in 1 Cor. 4 : 5, in a prohibition.

8. OUDE TI (οὐδέ τι), not even anything, is found in 1 Tim. 6 : 7 (2nd 3761
part); it is a more forceful expression than the simple *ouden* in the 1st AG:591C CB:—
part of the verse, as if to say, ‘ it is a fact that we brought nothing into the world, and most certainly we can carry out not even the slightest thing, whatever we may have possessed.’

Notes : (1) For “ nothing ” in Luke 1 : 37, A.V. see WORD, No. 2
(R.V.). (2) In John 11 : 49 the double negative *ouk* (not) . . . *ouden* OUDEPOTE 3763
(nothing) is translated “ nothing at all.” (3) In Acts 11 : 8 *pan*, every- AG:592B
thing, with *oudepote*, not even ever, is rendered “ nothing . . . ever,” CB:— ATHETEō
R.V., A.V., “ nothing . . . at any time.” (4) In 1 Cor. 1 : 19, A.V., 114
atheteō, to set aside, make void, reject, is translated “ I will bring to AG:21A CB:1238A
nothing ” (R.V., “ will I reject ”). NOTICE See

For NOTICE BEFORE, 2 Cor. 9 : 5, A.V., see AFOREPROMISED DECLARE, SUPERSCRIPTION

NOTWITHSTANDING NOTORIOUS See NOTABLE

Note : This is the A.V. rendering of (1) *alla*, but, in Rev. 2 : 20 (R.V., ALLA 235]
“ but ”) ; (2) *plēn*, howbeit, yet, except that, in Luke 10 : 11, 20, and AG:38A
Phil. 1 : 18 (R.V., “ only that ”) ; in 4 : 14, A.V., “ notwithstanding ” CB:— PLēN
(R.V., “ howbeit ”). 4133 AG:669B CB:1265B

NOUGHT (for, bring to, come to, set at)

A. Pronoun.

OUDEN (οὐδέν), nothing (the neuter of *oudeis*, no one), is translated 3762
“ nought ” in Acts 5 : 36. See NOTHING. AG:591D CB:1261B

B. Adverb.

DŌREAN (δωρεάν), freely, as a gift, is translated “ for nought ” in 1432
Gal. 2 : 21, R.V. (A.V., “ in vain ”) ; in 2 Thess. 3 : 8, in a denial by the AG:210C CB:1242A
Apostle that he lived on the hospitality of others at Thessalonica. See FREELY.

C. Verbs.

2673 AG:417B 1. KATARGEŌ (καταργέω) is used in 1 Cor. 1 : 28, "(that) He might
CB:1254B bring to nought;" 1 Cor. 2 : 6 (Passive Voice in the original); 1 Cor.
6 : 13, R.V., "will bring to nought" (A.V. "will destroy"); so 2 Thess.
2 : 8 and Heb. 2 : 14. See ABOLISH.

1848 AG:277C 2. EXOUTHENEŌ (ἐξουθενέω), to set at nought, treat with utter
CB:1247C contempt, despise, is translated "set at nought" in Luke 18 : 9, R.V.
(A.V., "despised"); in 23 : 11, "set (Him) at nought;" "was set at
nought" in Acts 4 : 11; in Rom. 14 : 3, R.V., "set at nought" (A.V.,
"despise"); ver. 10, "set at nought." See ACCOUNT, DESPISE.

1847 AG:277C 3. EXOUDENEŌ or EXOUDENOŌ (ἐξουδενέω) has the same
(-Eō) meaning as No. 2, and is virtually the same word (*outhen* being another
CB:1247C form of *ouden*, nothing), i.e., to treat as nothing (*ex*, intensive), and is
(-Eō) translated "be set at nought" in Mark 9 : 12.¶

1601 AG:243D 4. EKPIPTŌ (ἐκπίπτω), to fall out, is used in Rom. 9 : 6 in the sense
CB:1243C of falling from its place, failing, of the word of God, R.V., "hath come to
nought" (A.V., "hath taken none effect"). See FALL.

114 AG:21A 5. ATHETEŌ (ἀθετέω), to set aside, reject, is translated "set at
CB:1238A nought" in Heb. 10 : 28, R.V. (A.V., "despised"); so Jude 8. See
NOTHING, Note (4).

KATALUo 2647 *Notes:* (1) In Acts 5 : 38, A.V., *kataluō*, lit., to loosen down, hence,
AG:414B to overthrow, is translated "it will come to nought" (R.V., "it will be
CB:1254A ERēMOō overthrown"). See DESTROY. (2) In Rev. 18 : 17, A.V., *erēmoō*, to make
2049 desolate, is translated "is come to nought" (R.V., "is made desolate").
AG:309B CB:1246B See DESOLATE. (3) In Acts 19 : 27, A.V., the accusative case of
APELEGMOS *apelegmos*, confutation, disrepute, preceded by the verb *erchomai*, to come,
557 AG:83D and *eis*, unto or into, is translated "be set at nought" (R.V., "come into
CB:— disrepute"). See DISREPUTE.¶

NOURISH, NOURISHMENT

5142 AG:825C 1. TREPHŌ (τρέφω), to rear, feed, nourish, is translated by the verb
CB:— to nourish in Jas. 5 : 5 (of luxurious living); Rev. 12 : 14 (of God's care for
Israel against its enemies); so ver. 6, R.V. (A.V., "feed"); in Acts
12 : 20, R.V., "was fed" (A.V., "was nourished"). See FEED.

397 AG:62D 2. ANATREPHŌ (ἀνατρέφω), to nurse, bring up (*ana*, up, and No. 1),
CB:— is translated "nourished" in Acts 7 : 20 (A.V., "nourished up"); in
21, "nourished," A.V. and R.V. See BRING.

1625 AG:246C 3. EKTREPHŌ (ἐκτρέφω), *ek*, from, out of, and No. 1, primarily used
CB:1244A of children, to nurture, rear, is translated "nurture" of the care of one's
own flesh, Eph. 5 : 29, and in Eph. 6 : 4, R.V. (A.V., "bring . . . up").
See BRING.¶

1789 AG:269D 4. ENTREPHŌ (ἐντρέφω), to train up, nurture, is used metaphorically,
CB:— in the Passive Voice, in 1 Tim. 4 : 6, of being nourished in the faith.¶

For NOURISHMENT MINISTERED, Col. 2 : 19, see SUPPLY

NOVICE

NEOPHUTOS (νεόφυτος), an adjective, lit., newly-planted (from *neos*, 3504 AG:536C
new, and *phuō*, to bring forth, produce), denotes a new convert, neophyte, CB:1259C
novice, 1 Tim. 3 : 6, of one who by inexperience is unfitted to act as a bishop or overseer in a church.¶ In the Sept., Job 14 : 9 ; Psa. 128 : 3 ; 144 : 12 ; Is. 5 : 7.¶

NOW

A. Adverbs.

1. NUN (νῦν) is used (*a*) of time, the immediate present, whether in 3568 AG:545C
contrast to the past, e.g., John 4 : 18 ; Acts 7 : 52, or to the future, e.g., CB:1260A
John 12 : 27 ; Rom. 11 : 31 ; sometimes with the article, singular or plural, e.g., Acts 4 : 29 ; 5 : 38 ; (*b*) of logical sequence, often partaking also of the character of (*a*), now therefore, now however, as it is, e.g., Luke 11 : 39 ; John 8 : 40 ; 9 : 41 ; 15 : 22, 24 ; 1 Cor. 5 : 11, R.V. marg., " as it is."

Note : Under (*a*) comes the phrase in 2 Cor. 8 : 14, with *kairos*, a time, all governed by *en*, in, or at, A.V., " now at this time " (R.V., " at this present time ").

2. NUNI (νυνί), a strengthened form of No. 1, is used (*a*) of time, e.g., 3570
Acts 22 : 1 (in the best mss.) ; 24 : 13 ; Rom. 6 : 22 ; 15 : 23, 25 ; (*b*) with AG:546B CB:1260B
logical import, e.g., Rom. 7 : 17 ; 1 Cor. 13 : 13, which some regard as temporal (*a*) ; but if this is the significance, " the clause means, ' but faith, hope, love, are our abiding possession now in this present life.' The objection to this rendering is that the whole course of thought has been to contrast the things which last only for the present time with the things which survive. And the main contrast so far has been between love and the special [then] present activity of prophecy, tongues, knowledge. There is something of disappointment, and even of bathos, in putting as a climax to these contrasts the statement that in this present state faith, hope, love abide ; that is no more than can be said of [the then existing] prophecies, tongues and knowledge. If there is to be a true climax the ' abiding ' must cover the future as well as the present state. And that involves as a consequence that *nuni* must be taken in its logical meaning, i.e., ' as things are,' ' taking all into account ' . . . This logical sense of *nuni* . . . is enforced by the dominant note of the whole passage " (R. St. John Parry, in the Camb. Greek Test.).

It is certain that love will continue eternally ; and hope will not cease at the Parousia of Christ, for hope will ever look forward to the accomplishment of God's eternal purposes, a hope characterised by absolute assurance ; and where hope is in exercise faith is its concomitant. Faith will not be lost in sight.

3. ĒDĒ (ἤδη) denotes already, now already, " the subjective present, 2235 AG:344A
with a suggested reference to some other time, or to some expectation " CB:1242C

(Thayer), e.g., Matt. 3 : 10 ; 14 : 24 ; Luke 11 : 7 ; John 6 : 17 ; Rom. 1 : 10 ; 4 : 19 ; 13 : 11 ; Phil. 4 : 10.

737 4. ARTI (ἄρτι), expressing coincidence, and denoting strictly present
AG:110B CB:1237C time, signifies 'just now,' this moment, in contrast (*a*) to the past, e.g.,
Matt. 11 : 12 ; John 2 : 10 ; 9 : 19, 25 ; 13 : 33 ; Gal 1 : 9, 10 ; (*b*) to the future, e.g., John 13 : 37 ; 16 : 12, 31 ; 1 Cor. 13 : 12 (cp. No. 2 in ver. 13) ; 2 Thess. 2 : 7 ; 1 Pet. 1 : 6, 8 : (*c*) sometimes without necessary reference to either, e.g., Matt. 3 : 15 ; 9 : 18 ; 26 : 53 ; Gal. 4 : 20 ; Rev. 12 : 10.

534 5. APARTI (ἀπάρτι), sometimes written separately, *ap'arti*, i.e., *apo*,
AG:110B 3. CB:— from, and No. 4, denotes 'from now,' henceforth, John 13 : 19 ; 14 : 7 ;
Rev. 14 : 13. See HENCEFORTH.¶

3063 6. LOIPON (λοιπόν), the neuter of *loipos*, the rest, from now, is used
AG:479D (LOIPOS 3.b.) adverbially with the article and translated " now " in Mark 14 : 41.

CB:1257B

B. Conjunctions and Particles.

3767 1. OUN (οὖν), therefore, so then, is sometimes used in continuing a
AG:592D CB:— narrative, e.g., Acts 1 : 18 ; 1 Cor. 9 : 25 ; or resuming it after a digression,
usually rendered " therefore," e.g., Acts 11 : 19 ; 25 : 1, R.V. (A.V., " now "). In the following it is absent from the best mss., Mark 12 : 20 ; Luke 10 : 36 ; John 16 : 19 ; 18 : 24 ; 19 : 29.

Note : In 2 Cor. 5 : 20 *oun* is simply " therefore," as in R.V. (A.V., " now then ").

1161 2. DE (δέ), but, and, now, often implying an antithesis, is rendered
AG:171C CB:— " now " in John 19 : 23 ; 1 Cor. 10 : 11 ; 15 : 50 ; Gal. 1 : 20 ; Eph. 4 : 9 ;
in Acts 27 : 9 (1st part), R.V., " and " (A.V., " now ") ; in Gal. 4 : 1, R.V., " but " (A.V. " now ").

1211 3. DĒ (δή), a consecutive particle, giving stress to the word or words
AG:178B CB:— to which it is attached, sometimes with hardly any exact Eng. equivalent,
is translated " now " in Luke 2 : 15, in the words of the shepherds ; in Acts 15 : 36, R.V. (A.V., " and "). Some mss. have it in 2 Cor. 12 : 1 ; see R.V. marg.

Notes : (1) In 1 Cor. 4 : 7, A.V., B, No. 2, followed by *kai*, and, is translated " now " (R.V., " but "). (2) In Rom. 14 : 15 and Philm. 16, A.V., *ouketi*, no longer, is translated " now . . . not " and " not now " (R.V.,
OUKETI " no longer ") ; cp. John 4 : 42 and 21 : 6, " now . . . not." (3) The particle
3765 AG:592C *ara*, then, expressing a more informal inference than *oun* (B, No. 1 above),
CB:— is often in Paul's Epistles coupled with *oun*, the phrase meaning " so then,"
ARA 686 as A.V. and R.V. in Rom. 7 : 3, 25 ; 9 : 16 ; 14 : 12 ; in R.V. only (A.V.,
AG:103D " therefore "), Rom. 5 : 18 ; 8 : 12 ; 9 : 18 ; 14 : 19 ; Gal. 6 : 10 ; 1 Thess.
CB:1237B 5 : 6 ; 2 Thess. 2 : 15. In Eph. 2 : 19 the A.V. renders it " now therefore."
ENISTēMI 1764 (4) In 1 Tim. 1 : 4, the R.V. " *so do I now* " (A.V., " *so do* ") is added to
AG:266D CB:— complete the sentence. (5) In Heb. 9 : 9, R.V., the perfect participle of
NULLIFY *enistēmi*, to be present, is translated " (the time) *now* present " (A.V.,
See VOID, " then present," which misses the meaning). See COME, (AT) HAND,
DISANNUL PRESENT.

NUMBER

A. Nouns.

1. ARITHMOS (ἀριθμός), number, a number (Eng., arithmetic, etc.), 706
occurs in Luke 22 : 3 ; John 6 : 10 ; Rom. 9 : 27 ; elsewhere five times AG:106B CB:1237C
in Acts, ten times in the Apocalypse.

2. OCHLOS (ὄχλος), a multitude, is translated " number " in Luke 3793
6 : 17, R.V. (A.V., " multitude ") ; in Mark 10 : 46 and Acts 1 : 15 the AG:600C CB:1260B
renderings are reversed. See COMMON, COMPANY, CROWD, MULTITUDE,
PEOPLE.

B. Verbs.

1. ARITHMEŌ (ἀριθμέω), akin to A, is found in Matt. 10 : 30 ; Luke 705 AG:106B
12 : 7 ; Rev. 7 : 9.¶ CB:1237C

2. KATARITHMEŌ (καταριθμέω), to number or count among (*kata*, 2674 AG:417C
and No. 1), is used in Acts 1 : 17.¶ CB:—

3. ENKRINŌ (ἐγκρίνω), to reckon among (*en*, in, *krinō*, to judge or 1469
reckon), is translated " to number . . . (ourselves) with " in 2 Cor. 10 : 12 AG:216D CB:—
(R.V. marg., " to judge ourselves among or . . . with "), of the Apostle's
dissociation of himself and his fellow-missionaries from those who
commended themselves.¶

4. SUNKATAPSĒPHIZŌ (συγκαταψηφίζω), to vote or reckon (one) 4785
a place among (*sun*, with or among, *kata*, down, and *psēphizō*, to count or AG:773C (-OMAI)
vote, originally with pebbles, *psēphos*, a pebble), is used of the numbering CB:—
of Matthias with the eleven Apostles, Acts 1 : 26.¶

Notes : (1) Some mss. have verse 28 in Mark 15 (A.V.), where *logizomai*, LOGIZOMAI 3049
to reckon, is translated " He was numbered." (2) For *katalegō* 1 Tim. 5 : 9 AG:475D
(A.V., " let . . . be taken into the number "), see TAKE, *Note* (18). CB:1257A KATALEGŌ
(3) In Mark 5 : 13 see the italicised words in R.V. (4) In Heb. 7 : 23, 2639
R.V., the adjective *pleiōn*, more, many, is translated " many in number " AG:413B CB:—
(A.V., " many ") ; in Acts 28 : 23, R.V., " a great number " (A.V., PLEIŌN
" many "). 4119 AG:687C (POLUS II.) CB:1265B

NURSE

TROPHOS (τροφός), translated " nurse " in 1 Thess. 2 : 7, there denotes 5162
a nursing mother, as is clear from the statement " cherisheth her own AG:827D CB:1273A
children ; " this is also confirmed by the word *ēpios*, gentle (in the same
verse), which was commonly used of the kindness of parents towards
children. Cp. *trephō*, to bring up (see NOURISH).

For NURTURE (Eph. 6 : 4) see CHASTENING

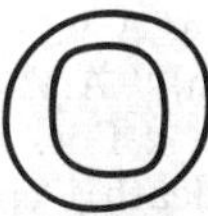

OATH

1. HORKOS (ὅρκος) is primarily equivalent to *herkos*, a fence, an enclosure, that which restrains a person; hence, an oath. The Lord's command in Matt. 5 : 33 was a condemnation of the minute and arbitrary restrictions imposed by the scribes and Pharisees in the matter of adjurations, by which God's Name was profaned. The injunction is repeated in Jas. 5 : 12. The language of the Apostle Paul, e.g., in Gal. 1 : 20 and 1 Thess. 5 : 27 was not inconsistent with Christ's prohibition, read in the light of its context. Contrast the oaths mentioned in Matt. 14 : 7, 9; 26 : 72; Mark 6 : 26. **3727 AG:581C CB:1251B**

Heb. 6 : 16 refers to the confirmation of a compact among men, guaranteeing the discharge of liabilities; in their disputes "the oath is final for confirmation." This is referred to in order to illustrate the greater subject of God's oath to Abraham, confirming His promise; cp. Luke 1 : 73; Acts 2 : 30.¶ Cp. the verbs *horkizō*, and *exorkizō*, under ADJURE.

2. HORKŌMOSIA (ὁρκωμοσία) denotes an affirmation on oath (from No. 1 and *omnumi*, to swear). This is used in Heb. 7 : 20, 21 (twice), 28, of the establishment of the Priesthood of Christ, the Son of God, appointed a Priest after the order of Melchizedek, and "perfected for evermore."¶ In the Sept., Ezek. 17 : 18, 19.¶ **3728 AG:581D CB:1251B**

Note: For *anathematizō* in Acts 23 : 21, A.V., "have bound (themselves) with an oath," see CURSE. **332 AG:54C CB:1235B**

OBEDIENCE, OBEDIENT, OBEY

A. Nouns.

1. HUPAKOĒ (ὑπακοή), obedience (*hupo*, under, *akouō*, to hear), is used (*a*) in general, Rom. 6 : 16 (1st part), R.V., "(unto) obedience," A.V., "(to) obey;" here obedience is not personified, as in the next part of the verse, "servants . . . of obedience" [see (*c*)], but is simply shown to be the effect of the presentation mentioned; (*b*) of the fulfilment of apostolic counsels, 2 Cor. 7 : 15; 10 : 6; Philm. 21; (*c*) of the fulfilment of God's claims or commands, Rom. 1 : 5 and 16 : 26, "obedience of faith," which grammatically might be objective, to the faith (marg.), or subjective, as in the text. Since faith is one of the main subjects of the Epistle, and is the initial act of obedience in the new life, as well as an essential characteristic thereof, the text rendering is to be preferred; Rom. 6 : 16 **5218 AG:837A CB:1251C**

(2nd part); 15:18, R.V. "(for) the obedience," A.V., "(to make) obedient;" 16:19; 1 Pet. 1:2, 14, R.V., "(children of) obedience," i.e., characterized by obedience, A.V., "obedient (children);" ver. 22, R.V., "obedience (to the truth)," A.V., "obeying (the truth);" (*d*) of obedience to Christ (objective), 2 Cor. 10:5; (*e*) of Christ's obedience, Rom. 5:19 (referring to His death; cp. Phil. 2:8); Heb. 5:8, which refers to His delighted experience in constant obedience to the Father's will (not to be understood in the sense that He learned to obey).¶

5292 AG:847D CB:1252B 2. HUPOTAGĒ (ὑποταγή), subjection (*hupo*, under, *tassō*, to order), is translated "obedience" in 2 Cor. 9:13, R.V. (A.V., "subjection"). See SUBJECTION.

B. Verbs.

5219 AG:837B CB:1251C 1. HUPAKOUŌ (ὑπακούω), to listen, attend (as in Acts 12:13), and so, to submit, to obey, is used of obedience (*a*) to God, Heb. 5:9; 11:8; (*b*) to Christ, by natural elements, Matt. 8:27; Mark 1:27; 4:41; Luke 8:25; (*c*) to disciples of Christ, Luke 17:6; (*d*) to the faith, Acts 6:7; the Gospel, Rom. 10:16; 2 Thess. 1:8; Christian doctrine, Rom. 6:17 (as to a form or mould of teaching); (*e*) to apostolic injunctions, Phil. 2:12; 2 Thess. 3:14; (*f*) to Abraham by Sarah, 1 Pet. 3:6; (*g*) to parents by children, Eph. 6:1; Col. 3:20; (*h*) to masters by servants, Eph. 6:5; Col. 3:22; (*i*) to sin, Rom. 6:12; (*j*) in general, Rom. 6:16.¶

3982 AG:639A CB:1263A 2. PEITHŌ (πείθω), to persuade, to win over, in the Passive and Middle Voices, to be persuaded, to listen to, to obey, is so used with this meaning, in the Middle Voice, e.g., in Acts 5:36, 37 (in ver. 40, Passive Voice, "they agreed"); Rom. 2:8; Gal. 5:7; Heb. 13:17; Jas. 3:3. The obedience suggested is not by submission to authority, but resulting from persuasion.

"*Peithō* and *pisteuō*, 'to trust,' are closely related etymologically; the difference in meaning is that the former implies the obedience that is produced by the latter, cp. Heb. 3:18, 19, where the disobedience of the Israelites is said to be the evidence of their unbelief. Faith is of the heart, invisible to men; obedience is of the conduct and may be observed. When a man obeys God he gives the only possible evidence that in his heart he believes God. Of course it is persuasion of the truth that results in faith (we believe because we are persuaded that the thing is true, a thing does not become true because it is believed), but *peithō*, in N.T. suggests an actual and outward result of the inward persuasion and consequent faith."* See ASSURANCE, B, No. 3.

3980 AG:638D CB:1263A 3. PEITHARCHEŌ (πειθαρχέω), to obey one in authority (No. 2, and *archē*, rule), is translated "obey" in Acts 5:29, 32; "to be obedient," Tit. 3:1, R.V. (A.V., "to obey magistrates"); in Acts 27:21, "hearkened." See HEARKEN.¶

* From Notes on Thessalonians by Hogg and Vine, pp. 254, 255.

4. APEITHEŌ (ἀπειθέω), to disobey, be disobedient (*a*, negative, and 544
No. 2), is translated " obey not " in Rom. 2 : 8 ; 1 Pet. 3 : 1 ; 4 : 17. See AG:82C CB:1236B
DISOBEDIENT.

Note: In 1 Cor. 14 : 34, A.V., *hupotassō*, to be in subjection (R.V.), 5293
is translated " to be under obedience ; " so Tit. 2 : 5, R.V., " being in AG:847D CB:1252B
subjection " (A.V., " obedient ") ; and ver. 9, R.V. (A.V., " to be (-OMAI)
obedient "). See SUBJECTION.

C. Adjective.

HUPĒKOOS (ὑπήκοος), obedient (akin to A, No. 1), giving ear, subject, 5255
occurs in Acts 7 : 39, R.V., " (would not be) obedient," A.V., " (would AG:842B CB:1252A
not) obey ; " 2 Cor. 2 : 9 ; Phil. 2 : 8, where the R.V. " *even* " is useful
as making clear that the obedience was not to death but to the Father.¶

For the verb OBJECT, Acts 24 : 19, see ACCUSATION, B, No. 4

For OBJECTS, R.V., in Acts 17 : 23, see WORSHIP OBLIGATED See DEBTOR

OBSERVATION, OBSERVE

A. Noun.

PARATĒRĒSIS (παρατήρησις), attentive watching (akin to *paratēreō*, 3907
to observe), is used in Luke 17 : 20, of the manner in which the Kingdom AG:622D CB:1262B
of God (i.e., the operation of the spiritual Kingdom in the hearts of men)
does not come, " in such a manner that it can be watched with the
eyes " (Grimm-Thayer), or, as A.V. marg., " with outward show."¶

B. Verbs.

1. ANATHEŌREŌ (ἀναθεωρέω), to observe carefully, consider well 333
(*ana*, up, intensive, and *theōreō*, to behold), is used in Acts 17 : 23, R.V., AG:54C CB:—
" observed " (of Paul's notice of the objects of Athenian worship), and 5083
Heb. 13 : 7, " considering." See BEHOLD.¶ AG:814D CB:1271B

2. TĒREŌ (τηρέω) : see KEEP, No. 1. 4933

3. SUNTĒREŌ (συντηρέω) : see KEEP, No. 3. AG:792C

4. PARATĒREŌ (παρατηρέω), to watch closely, observe narrowly 3906
(*para*, used intensively, and No. 2), is translated " ye observe " in Gal. AG:622C CB:1262B
4 : 10, where the Middle Voice suggests that their religious observance of
days etc. was not from disinterested motives, but with a view to their PHRONEō
own advantage. See WATCH. Cp. *phroneō* (to think), " regardeth " in 5426 AG:866A
Rom. 14 : 6, where the subject is connected with the above, though the CB:1264C
motive differs. 5442 AG:868B

5. PHULASSŌ (φυλάσσω) : see KEEP, No. 4. CB:1264C

6. POIEŌ (ποιέω), to do, is translated " to observe " in Acts 16 : 21. 4160 AG:680D
See DO. CB:1265C

OBTAIN, OBTAINING

A. Verbs.

1. TUNCHANŌ (τυγχάνω), to meet with, light upon, also signifies to 5177 AG:829B
obtain, attain to, reach, get (with regard to things), translated to obtain CB:—

in Acts 26 : 22, of " the help that is from God ; " 2 Tim. 2 : 10, of " the salvation which is in Christ Jesus with eternal glory ; " Heb. 8 : 6, of the ministry obtained by Christ ; 11 : 35, of " a better resurrection." See CHANCE.

2013 AG:303D 2. EPITUNCHANŌ (ἐπιτυγχάνω), primarily, to light upon (*epi*, upon,
CB:— and No. 1), denotes to obtain, Rom. 11 : 7 (twice) ; Heb. 6 : 15 ; 11 : 33 ;
Jas. 4 : 2.¶

2975 AG:462B 3. LANCHANŌ (λαγχάνω), to obtain by lot, is translated " that have
CB:1256C obtained " in 2 Pet. 1 : 1 ; in Acts 1 : 17, A.V., " had obtained " (R.V.,
" received "), with *klēros*, a lot or portion. See LOTS.

2932 AG:455A 4. KTAOMAI (κτάομαι), to procure for oneself, get, gain, acquire, is
CB:1256A translated " obtained " in Acts 1 : 18, R.V. (A.V., " purchased ") ;
8 : 20, R.V. (A.V., " may be purchased ") ; 22 : 28. See POSSESS, PROVIDE, PURCHASE.

2902 AG:448C 5. KRATEŌ (κρατέω), to be strong, also means to get possession of,
CB:1256A obtain, e.g., in Acts 27 : 13, " they had obtained (their purpose)." See HOLD.

2983 AG:464A 6. LAMBANŌ (λαμβάνω), to take, to receive, is translated by the verb
CB:1256C to obtain in 1 Cor. 9 : 25 ; Phil. 3 : 12, R.V.," (not that) I have (already) obtained " (contrast *katantaō*, to attain, ver. 11) ; Moule translates it 'not that I have already received,' i.e., the prize ; the verb does not signify to attain ; Heb. 4 : 16, A.V., " obtain." See ACCEPT, No. 4.

2147 AG:324D 7. HEURISKŌ (εὑρίσκω) denotes to find ; in the Middle Voice, to
CB:1250B find for oneself, to procure, get, obtain, with the suggestion of accomplishing the end which had been in view ; so in Heb. 9 : 12, " having obtained (eternal redemption)."

KATALAMBANŌ *Notes :* (1) In 1 Cor. 9 : 24, A.V., *katalambanō*, a strengthened form of
2638 No. 6 (*kata*, used intensively), is translated " obtain " (R.V., " attain ").
AG:412D (2) In Heb. 11 : 2, 4, 39, A.V., *martureō*, to bear witness, and in the
CB:1254A
(-OMAI) Passive Voice, to have witness borne to one, is translated to obtain a good
MARTUREŌ 3140 report, or to obtain witness (R.V., " had witness borne "). See WITNESS.
AG:492C (3) For the A.V. of Heb. 1 : 4, " He hath by inheritance obtained " (R.V.,
CB:1257C " He hath inherited "), and of Eph. 1 : 11, see INHERIT. (4) For the
ELEEŌ 1653 phrase to obtain mercy, the Passive Voice of *eleeō* in Matt. 5 : 7 ; Rom.
AG:249C CB:1244A 11 : 30, 31 ; 1 Cor. 7 : 25 ; 2 Cor. 4 : 1 (R.V.) ; 1 Tim. 1 : 13, 16 ; 1 Pet.
2 : 10 (twice), see MERCY.

B. Noun.

4047 AG:650A PERIPOIĒSIS (περιποίησις), lit., a making around (*peri*, around,
CB:1263B *poieō*, to do or make), denotes (*a*) the act of obtaining anything, as of salvation in its completeness, 1 Thess. 5 : 9 ; 2 Thess. 2 : 14 ; (*b*) a thing acquired, an acquisition, possession, Eph. 1 : 14, R.V., " (*God's* own) possession " [some would put this under (*a*)] ; so 1 Pet. 2 : 9, R.V., A.V., " a peculiar (people) ; " cp. Is. 43 : 21 ; (*c*) preservation ; this may be the meaning in Heb. 10 : 39, " saving " (R.V. marg., " gaining ") ; cp. the

corresponding verb in Luke 17 : 33 (in the best texts), "preserve."¶ In the Sept. the noun has the meaning (*b*) in Hag. 2 : 10 and Mal. 3 : 17, (*c*) in 2 Chron. 14 : 13.¶

OBVIOUS See **EVIDENT**

OCCASION

APHORMĒ (ἀφορμή), properly a starting point, was used to denote a 874
base of operations in war. In the N.T. it occurs as follows : "(*a*) the Law AG:127C CB:1236C
provided sin with a base of operations for its attack upon the soul, Rom. 7 : 8, 11 ; (*b*) the irreproachable conduct of the Apostle provided his friends with a base of operations against his detractors, 2 Cor. 5 : 12 ; (*c*) by refusing temporal support at Corinth he deprived these detractors of their base of operations against him, 2 Cor. 11 : 12 ; (*d*) Christian freedom is not to provide a base of operations for the flesh, Gal. 5 : 13 ; (*e*) unguarded behaviour on the part of young widows (and the same is true of all believers) would provide Satan with a base of operations against the faith, 1 Tim. 5 : 14."*¶

The word is found frequently in the papyri with meanings which illustrate those in the N.T. In the Sept., Prov. 9 : 9 ; Ezek. 5 : 7.¶

Notes : (1) For the R.V. renderings "occasion (or 'occasions') of stumbling," "occasion of falling," see FALLING, B, Note (3), OFFENCE. 1223
(2) In 2 Cor. 8 : 8, A.V., the phrase "by occasion of" translates the AG:179B
preposition *dia*, through, by means of (R.V., "through"). CB:1241A

For OCCUPATION, Acts 18 : 3, A.V., see TRADE

Notes : The phrase "of like occupation" in Acts 19 : 25 translates the phrase *peri* (about) *ta* (the) *toiauta* (such things), i.e., lit., '(occupied) about such things.'

OCCUPY

PERIPATEŌ (περιπατέω), to walk, is sometimes used of the state in 4043
which one is living, or of that to which a person is given, e.g., Heb. 13 : 9, AG:649A CB:1263B
"(meats, wherein they that) occupied themselves," R.V. (marg., "walked ;" A.V., "have been occupied"), i.e., exercising themselves about different kinds of food, regarding some as lawful, others as unlawful (referring especially to matters of the ceremonial details of the law).

Notes : (1) For "occupy," in the A.V. of Luke 19 : 13, see TRADE. (2) For "occupieth," in the A.V. of 1 Cor. 14 : 16, see FILL, No. 2.

ODOUR

OSMĒ (ὀσμή), a smell, an odour (akin to *ozō*, to smell), is translated 3744
"odour" in John 12 : 3 ; it is used metaphorically in Eph. 5 : 2, R.V., AG:586A CB:1261B
"an odour (of a sweet smell)," A.V., "(a sweet smelling) savour," of the effects Godward of the Sacrifice of Christ ; in Phil. 4 : 18 of the effect of

---

* From Notes on Galatians by Hogg and Vine, p. 269.

sacrifice, on the part of those in the church at Philippi, who sent material assistance to the Apostle in his imprisonment. The word is translated "savour" in 2 Cor. 2:14, 16 (twice).¶

THUMIAMA *Note:* For *thumiama*, incense, translated "odours" in the A.V. of
2368 AG:365A Rev. 5:8 (R.V., "incense"), see INCENSE. For *amōmon* (quoted in
CB:1272C AMōMON R.V. marg. in the Latinized form *amomum*) in Rev. 18:13, see SPICE.

OF

— *Note:* (1) In addition to the rendering of a number of prepositions,
AG:47D "of" translates the genitive case of nouns, with various shades of meaning.
CB:— Of these the subjective and objective are mentioned here, which need
careful distinction. Thus the phrase "the love of God," e.g., in 1 John
2:5 and 3:16, is subjective, signifying "God's love;" in 1 John 5:3,
it is objective, signifying our love to God. Again, "the witness of God,"
e.g., 1 John 5:9, is subjective, signifying the witness which God Himself
has given; in Rev. 1:2, 9, and 19:10, e.g., "the testimony of Jesus"
is objective, signifying the testimony borne to Him. In the A.V. "the
faith of" is sometimes ambiguous; with reference to Christ it is objective,
i.e., faith in Him, not His own faith, in the following passages in which
the R.V., "in" gives the correct meaning; Rom. 3:22; Gal. 2:16
(twice), 20, R.V., "I live in faith, the faith which is in the Son of
APO God;" 3:22; Eph. 3:12; Phil. 3:9 (cp. Col. 2:12, "faith in the
575 AG:86C working of God"). In Eph. 2:20, "the foundation of the apostles and
CB:1236C prophets" is subjective, i.e., the foundation laid by the apostles and
PARA prophets ("other foundation can no man lay than . . . Jesus Christ,"
3844 AG:609C 1 Cor. 3:11). (2) In the A.V. of John 16:13, "He shall not speak of
CB:1261C Himself," the preposition is *apo*, "from," as in the R.V.; the Spirit of
EK God often speaks of Himself in Scripture, the Lord's assurance was that
1537 AG:234A the Holy Spirit would not be the Source of His utterances. So with
CB:1243B regard to Christ's utterances, John 7:17, R.V., "I speak from (*apo*)
PERI Myself:" and 14:10. (3) In John 6:46; 15:15; 17:7; Acts 17:9,
4012 AG:644B the R.V., "from" is to be observed, as rightly translating *para* (A.V.,
CB:1263B "of"). (4) The following are instances in which "of" translates *ek*,
EPI or *ex*, out of, from, Matt. 21:25 (R.V., "from"); 1 Cor. 1:30; 15:6;
1909 AG:285D 2 Cor. 5:1 (R.V., "from"); Jas. 4:1. (5) In the following, *peri*,
CB:1245C concerning, is so translated in the R.V. (for A.V., "of"), e.g., Acts 5:24;
HUPER 1 Cor. 1:11; 1 John 1:1 (the R.V. is important); cp. John 16:8.
5228 AG:838B (6) *Epi*, over, is so translated in Matt. 18:13, R.V.; "concerning" in
CB:1252A Acts 4:9. (7) *Huper*, on behalf of, is so rendered in 2 Cor. 7:4, R.V.
HUPO (A.V., "of"); (8) For *hupo*, by, see the R.V. of Matt. 1:22; 2:16;
5259 AG:843A 11:27; Luke 9:7; Acts 15:4; 1 Cor. 14:24; 2 Cor. 8:19; Phil.
CB:1252A 3:12. (9) For other prepositions, etc., see † p. 1

OFF: see † p 1

OFFENCE

A. Nouns.

1. SKANDALON (σκάνδαλον) originally was " the name of the part of a trap to which the bait is attached, hence, the trap or snare itself, as in Rom. 11 : 9, R.V., ' stumblingblock,' quoted from Psa. 69 : 22, and in Rev. 2 : 14, for Balaam's device was rather a trap for Israel than a stumblingblock to them, and in Matt. 16 : 23, for in Peter's words the Lord perceived a snare laid for Him by Satan. 4625 AG:753A CB:1269A

" In N.T. *skandalon* is always used metaphorically, and ordinarily of anything that arouses prejudice, or becomes a hindrance to others, or causes them to fall by the way. Sometimes the hindrance is in itself good, and those stumbled by it are the wicked."*

Thus it is used (*a*) of Christ in Rom. 9 : 33, " (a rock) of offence ; " so 1 Pet. 2 : 8 ; 1 Cor. 1 : 23 (A.V. and R.V., " stumblingblock "), and of His Cross, Gal. 5 : 11 (R.V., ditto) ; of the " table " provided by God for Israel, Rom. 11 : 9 (see above) ; (*b*) of that which is evil, e.g., Matt. 13 : 41, R.V., " things that cause stumbling " (A.V., " things that offend "), lit., ' all stumblingblocks ; ' 18 : 7, R.V., " occasions of stumbling " and " occasion ; " Luke 17 : 1 (ditto) ; Rom. 14 : 13, R.V., " an occasion of falling " (A.V., " an occasion to fall "), said of such a use of Christian liberty as proves a hindrance to another ; 16 : 17, R.V., " occasions of stumbling," said of the teaching of things contrary to sound doctrine ; 1 John 2 : 10, " occasion of stumbling," of the absence of this in the case of one who loves his brother and thereby abides in the light. Love, then, is the best safeguard against the woes pronounced by the Lord upon those who cause others to stumble. See FALL, B, *Note* (3).¶ Cp. the Sept. in Hos. 4 : 17, " Ephraim partaking with idols hath laid stumblingblocks in his own path."

2. PROSKOMMA (πρόσκομμα), an obstacle against which one may dash his foot (akin to *proskoptō*, to stumble or cause to stumble ; *pros*, to or against, *koptō*, to strike), is translated " offence " in Rom. 14 : 20, in ver. 13, " a stumblingblock," of the spiritual hindrance to another by a selfish use of liberty (cp. No. 1 in the same verse) ; so in 1 Cor. 8 : 9. It is used of Christ, in Rom. 9 : 32, 33, R.V., " (a stone) of stumbling," and 1 Pet. 2 : 8, where the A.V. also has this rendering.¶ Cp. the Sept. in Ex. 23 : 33, " these (the gods of the Canaanites) will be an offence (stumblingblock) unto thee." 4348 AG:716B CB:1267A

3. PROSKOPĒ (προσκοπή), like No. 2, and formed from the same combination, occurs in 2 Cor. 6 : 3, R.V., " occasion of stumbling " (A.V., " offence "), something which leads others into error or sin.¶ Cp. the Sept. in Prov. 16 : 18, " a haughty spirit (becomes) a stumblingblock " (i.e., to oneself). 4349 AG:716B CB:1267B

Notes : (1) In the A.V. of Rom. 4 : 25 ; 5 : 15 (twice), 16, 17, 18, 20,

---

* From Notes on Galatians by Hogg and Vine, p. 262.

PARAPTōMA 3900 *paraptōma*, a trespass, is translated "offence." See TRESPASS. (2) In
AG:621D 2 Cor. 11 : 7, A.V., *hamartia*, a sin, is translated "an offence." See SIN.
CB:1262B **B. Adjective.**
HAMARTIA 266 APROSKOPOS (ἀπρόσκοπος), akin to A, No. 3, with *a*, negative,
AG:43A prefixed, is used (*a*) in the Active sense, not causing to stumble, in 1 Cor.
CB:1249B 10 : 32, metaphorically of refraining from doing anything to lead astray
APROSKOPOS 677 either Jews or Greeks or the church of God (i.e., the local church), R.V.,
AG:102C "no occasion of stumbling" (A.V., "none offence"); (*b*) in the Passive
CB:1237B sense, blameless, without stumbling, Acts 24 : 16, "(a conscience) void of
offence;" Phil. 1 : 10, "void of (A.V., without) offence." The adjective is found occasionally in the papyri writings.¶

OFFEND

4624 SKANDALIZŌ (σκανδαλίζω), from *skandalon* (OFFENCE, No. 1),
AG:752D signifies to put a snare or stumblingblock in the way, always metaphorically
CB:1269A in the N.T., in the same ways as the noun, which see. It is used 14 times in Matthew, 8 in Mark, twice in Luke, twice in John; elsewhere in 1 Cor. 8 : 13 (twice) and 2 Cor. 11 : 29. It is absent in the most authentic mss. in Rom. 14 : 21. The R.V. renders it by the verb to stumble, or cause to stumble, in every place save the following, where it uses the verb to
PTAIō offend, Matt. 13 : 57; 15 : 12; 26 : 31, 33; Mark 6 : 3; 14 : 27, 29.
4417 AG:727A *Notes:* (1) In Jas. 2 : 10; 3 : 2 (twice), A.V., *ptaiō*, to stumble, is
CB:1267C translated "offend;" see FALL, STUMBLE. (2) In Acts 25 : 8, A.V.,
HAMARTANō 264 *hamartanō*, to sin, is translated "have I offended;" see SIN.
AG:42B CB:1249A

OFFENDER

3781 AG:598B OPHEILETĒS (ὀφειλέτης), a debtor, is translated "offenders" in
CB:1261A Luke 13 : 4, R.V. (R.V. and A.V. marg., "debtors;" A.V., "sinners").
See DEBTOR.
91 AG:17C *Note:* In Acts 25 : 11, A.V., *adikeō*, to do wrong, is translated "be an
CB:1233A offender" (R.V., "am a wrong-doer").

OFFER, OFFERING

A. Verbs.

4374 AG:719C 1. PROSPHERŌ (προσφέρω), primarily, to bring to (*pros*, to, *pherō*,
CB:1267B to bring), also denotes to offer, (*a*) of the sacrifice of Christ Himself, Heb. 8 : 3; of Christ in virtue of his High Priesthood (R.V., "this *high priest;*" A. V., "this man"); 9 : 14, 25 (negative), 28; 10 : 12; (*b*) of offerings under, or according to, the Law, e.g., Matt. 8 : 4; Mark 1 : 44; Acts 7 : 42; 21 : 26; Heb. 5 : 1, 3; 8 : 3; 9 : 7, 9; 10 : 1, 2, 8, 11; (*c*) of offerings previous to the Law, Heb. 11 : 4, 17 (of Isaac by Abraham); (*d*) of gifts offered to Christ, Matt. 2 : 11, R.V., "offered" (A.V., "presented unto"); (*e*) of prayers offered by Christ, Heb. 5 : 7; (*f*) of the vinegar offered to Him in mockery by the soldiers at the Cross, Luke 23 : 36; (*g*) of the slaughter of disciples by persecutors, who think they

are 'offering' service to God, John 16 : 2, R.V. (A.V., " doeth ") ; (*h*) of money offered by Simon the sorcerer, Acts 8 : 18. See BRING, A, No. 8, DEAL WITH, No. 2.

2. ANAPHERŌ (ἀναφέρω), primarily, to lead or carry up (*ana*), also **399**
denotes to offer, (*a*) of Christ's sacrifice, Heb. 7 : 27 ; (*b*) of sacrifices under **AG:63A CB:1235B**
the Law, Heb. 7 : 27 ; (*c*) of such previous to the Law, Jas. 2 : 21 (of Isaac by Abraham) ; (*d*) of praise, Heb. 13 : 15 ; (*e*) of spiritual sacrifices in general, 1 Pet. 2 : 5. See BEAR, No. 3, BRING, A, No. 2.

3. DIDŌMI (δίδωμι), to give, is translated " to offer " in Luke 2 : 24 ; **1325 AG:192C**
in Rev. 8 : 3, A.V., " offer " (R.V., " add ; " marg., " give "). See GIVE. **CB:1241C**

4. PARECHŌ (παρέχω), to furnish, offer, present, supply, is used in **3930 AG:626B**
Luke 6 : 29, of offering the other cheek to be smitten after receiving a **CB:—**
similar insult ; for the A.V. marg., in Acts 17 : 31, see ASSURANCE, A, No. 1. See BRING, A, No. 21.

5. SPENDŌ (σπένδω), to pour out as a drink offering, make a libation, **4689 AG:761C**
is used figuratively in the Passive Voice in Phil. 2 : 17, " offered " (R.V. **CB:1269C**
marg., " poured out as a drink offering ; " A.V. marg., " poured forth "). In 2 Tim. 4 : 6, " I am already being offered," R.V. (marg., " poured out as a drink-offering "), the Apostle is referring to his approaching death, upon the sacrifice of his ministry.¶ This use of the word is exemplified in the papyri writings.

Notes : (1) In Luke 11 : 12, A.V, *epididōmi*, to give (*epi*, over, in the **EPIDIDoMI 1929**
sense of instead of, and No. 3), is translated " will he offer " (R.V., and **AG:292B**
A.V. marg., " will he give "). (2) In Acts 7 : 41, A.V., *anagō*, to lead up **ANAGō 321**
or bring up, is rendered " offered " (R.V., " brought "). (3) In Acts **AG:53A**
15 : 29 ; 21 : 25 and 1 Cor. 8 : 1, 4, 10 ; 10 : 19, A.V., *eidōlothutos*, sacrificed **EIDōLOTHUTON 1494**
to idols, is translated " offered to idols " (*thuō* denotes to sacrifice). See **AG:221B (-OS)**
SACRIFICE. **CB:1243A**

B. Nouns.

1. PROSPHORA (προσφορά), lit., a bringing to (akin to A, No. 1), **4376 AG:720B**
hence an offering, in the N.T. a sacrificial offering, (*a*) of Christ's sacrifice, **CB:1267B**
Eph. 5 : 2 ; Heb. 10 : 10 (of His body) ; 10 : 14 ; negatively, of there being no repetition, 10 : 18 ; (*b*) of offerings under, or according to, the Law, Acts 21 : 26 ; Heb. 10 : 5, 8 ; (*c*) of gifts in kind conveyed to needy Jews, Acts 24 : 17 ; (*d*) of the presentation of believers themselves (saved from among the Gentiles) to God, Rom. 15 : 16.¶ **3646 AG:564B**

2. HOLOKAUTŌMA (ὁλοκαύτωμα), a burnt offering : see BURNT. **CB:1251A**

3. ANATHĒMA (ἀνάθημα) denotes a gift set up in a temple, a votive **334 AG:54C**
offering (*ana*, up, *tithēmi*, to place), Luke 21 : 5, R.V. " offerings " (A.V., **CB:1235B**
" gifts ").¶ Cp. *anathema* (see CURSE).

Notes : (1) In Luke 21 : 4, A.V., the plural of *dōron*, a gift, is translated **1435 AG:210D**
" offerings " (R.V., " gifts "). (2) In Rom. 8 : 3 and Heb. 13 : 11, the **CB:1242A**
R.V., " *as an offering* " is added to complete the sacrificial meaning of *peri*.

OFFICE

A. Nouns.

4234 AG:697D CB:1266B 1. PRAXIS (πρᾶξις), a doing, deed (akin to *prassō*, to do or practise), also denotes an acting or function, translated "office" in Rom. 12 : 4. See DEED.

2405 AG:371D CB:1250B 2. HIERATEIA (ἱερατεία), or *hieratia*, denotes a priest's office, Luke 1 : 9; Heb. 7 : 5, R.V., "priest's office" (A.V., "office of the priesthood").¶

B. Verb.

2407 AG:371D CB:1250B HIERATEUŌ (ἱερατεύω), to officiate as a priest (akin to A, No. 2), is translated "he executed the priest's office" in Luke 1 : 8. The word is frequent in Inscriptions.¶

DIAKONIA 1248 AG:184B CB:1241A EPISKOPē 1984 AG:299A CB:1246A DIAKONEō 1247 AG:184A CB:1241A *Notes:* (1) In Rom. 11 : 13, A.V., *diakonia*, a ministry, is translated "office" (R.V., "ministry"). (2) In Acts 1 : 20, R.V., *episkopē*, an overseership, is translated "office" (marg., "overseership;" A.V., "bishoprick"). (3) In 1 Tim. 3 : 1, the word "office," in the phrase "the office of a bishop," has nothing to represent it in the original; the R.V. marg. gives "overseer" for "bishop," and the phrase lit. is 'overseership;' so in vv. 10, 13, where the A.V. has "use (and 'used') the office of a deacon," the R.V. rightly omits "office," and translates the verb *diakoneō*, to serve, "let them serve as deacons" and "(they that) have served (well) as deacons."

OFFICER

5257 AG:842C CB:1252A 1. HUPĒRETĒS (ὑπηρέτης), for the original of which see MINISTER, A, No. 3, is translated "officer," with the following applications, (*a*) to a magistrate's attendant, Matt. 5 : 25; (*b*) to officers of the Synagogue, or officers or bailiffs of the Sanhedrin, Matt. 26 : 58; Mark 14 : 54, 65; John 7 : 32, 45, 46; 18 : 3, 12, 18, 22; 19 : 6; Acts 5 : 22, 26. See MINISTER, SERVANT.

4233 AG:697D CB:1266B 2. PRAKTŌR (πράκτωρ), lit., one who does, or accomplishes (akin to *prassō*, to do), was used in Athens of one who exacts payment, a collector (the word is frequently used in the papyri of a public accountant); hence, in general, a court officer, an attendant in a court of justice (so Deissmann); the word is used in Luke 12 : 58 (twice).¶ In the Sept., Isa. 3 : 12.¶

OFFSCOURING

4067 (-SōMA) AG:653C CB:1263C PERIPSĒMA (περίψημα), that which is wiped off (akin to *peripsaō*, to wipe off all round; *peri*, around, *psaō*, to wipe), hence, offscouring, is used metaphorically in 1 Cor. 4 : 13. This and the synonymous word *perikatharma*, refuse, rubbish, "were used especially of condemned criminals of the lowest classes, who were sacrificed as expiatory offerings . . . because of their degraded life" (Lightfoot).¶

OFFSPRING

1. GENNĒMA (γέννημα), akin to *gennaō*, to beget, denotes the off- 1081
spring of men and animals, Matt. 3 : 7; 12 : 34; 23 : 33; Luke 3 : 7, AG:155D CB:1248A
R.V., "offspring" (A.V., "generation"). See FRUIT.¶

2. GENOS (γένος), a race, family (akin to *ginomai*, to become), denotes 1085
an offspring, Acts 17 : 28, 29; Rev. 22 : 16. See GENERATION, KIND. AG:156A CB:1248B

OFT, OFTEN, OFTENER, OFTENTIMES, OFT-TIMES

A. Adverbs.

1. POLLAKIS (πολλάκις), akin to *polus*, much, many, is variously 4178
translated, e.g., "oft-times," Matt. 17 : 15 (A.V., "oft," 2nd part); AG:686D CB:—
"many times," 2 Cor. 8 : 22, R.V. (A.V., "oftentimes"); "oft," 2 Cor.
11 : 23; "often" (ver. 26).

2. POLLA (πολλά), the neuter plural of *polus*, is translated "oft" in POLUS
Matt. 9 : 14; some ancient authorities omit it here (see R.V. marg.); 4183 AG:687C
in Rom. 15 : 22, with the article, R.V., "these many times" (A.V., CB:1266A
"much"). 4212

3. POSAKIS (ποσάκις), an interrogative numeral adverb, how many AG:694B
times, how oft (or often)? occurs in Matt. 18 : 21; 23 : 37; Luke 13 : 34.¶ CB:— 3740

4. HOSAKIS (ὁσάκις), a relative adverb, as often (or oft) as, 1 Cor. AG:585B
11 : 25, 26; Rev. 11 : 6.¶ CB:1251B

5. PUKNA (πυκνά), the neuter plural of *puknos* (see B), used 4437 AG:729A
adverbially, is translated "often" in Luke 5 : 33. CB:—

6. PUKNOTERON (πυκνότερον), the neuter singular of the com- (PUKNOS)
parative degree of *puknos* (cp. No. 5, and see B), very often, or so much the 4437 AG:729A
oftener, Acts 24 : 26, "the oftener."¶ CB:—

Notes: (1) In Luke 8 : 29, the phrase *pollois chronois*, lit., 'many times,' is translated "oftentimes" (R.V. marg., "of a long time"). (2) For the rendering "oft" in Mark 7 : 3, see DILIGENTLY, D, No. 2.

B. Adjective.

PUKNOS (πυκνός) primarily signifies close, compact, solid; hence, 4437 AG:729A
frequent, often, 1 Tim. 5 : 23. Cp. A, Nos. 5 and 6. CB:—

OIL

ELAION (ἔλαιον), olive-oil, is mentioned over 200 times in the Bible. 1637
Different kinds were known in Palestine. The "pure," R.V. (A.V., AG:247D CB:1244A
"beaten"), mentioned in Ex. 27 : 20; 29 : 40; Lev. 24 : 2; Numb. 28 : 5 (now known as virgin oil), extracted by pressure, without heat, is called "golden" in Zech. 4 : 12. There were also inferior kinds. In the N.T. the uses mentioned were (*a*) for lamps, in which the oil is a symbol of the Holy Spirit, Matt. 25 : 3, 4, 8; (*b*) as a medicinal agent, for healing, Luke 10 : 34; (*c*) for anointing at feasts, Luke 7 : 46; (*d*) on festive occasions, Heb. 1 : 9, where the reference is probably to the consecration of kings; (*e*) as an accompaniment of miraculous power, Mark 6 : 13, or

of the prayer of faith, Jas. 5 : 14. For its general use in commerce, see Luke 16 : 6 ; Rev. 6 : 6 ; 18 : 13.¶

OINTMENT

3464
AG:529D
CB:1259B
MURON (μύρον), a word derived by the ancients from *murō*, to flow, or from *murra*, myrrh-oil (it is probably of foreign origin ; see MYRRH). The ointment is mentioned in the N.T. in connection with the anointing of the Lord on the occasions recorded in Matt. 26 : 7, 9, 12 ; Mark 14 : 3, 4 ; Luke 7 : 37, 38, 46 ; John 11 : 2 ; 12 : 3 (twice), 5. The alabaster cruse mentioned in the passages in Matthew, Mark and Luke was the best of its kind, and the spikenard was one of the costliest of perfumes. Ointments were used in preparing a body for burial, Luke 23 : 56 (" ointments "). Of the act of the woman mentioned in Matt. 26 : 6–13, the Lord said, " she did it to prepare Me for burial ; " her devotion led her to antedate the customary ritual after death, by showing both her affection and her understanding of what was impending. For the use of the various kinds of ointments as articles of commerce, see Rev. 18 : 13.¶

OLD

A. Adjectives.

744
AG:111B
CB:1237B
1. ARCHAIOS (ἀρχαῖος), original, ancient (from *archē*, a beginning : Eng., archaic, archæology, etc.), is used (*a*) of persons belonging to a former age," (to) them of old time," Matt. 5 : 21, 33, R.V. ; in some mss. ver. 27 ; the R.V. rendering is right ; not ancient teachers are in view ; what was said to them of old time was " to be both recognized in its significance and estimated in its temporary limitations, Christ intending His words to be regarded not as an abrogation, but a deepening and fulfilling " (Cremer) ; of prophets, Luke 9 : 8, 19 ; (*b*) of time long gone by, Acts 15 : 21 ; (*c*) of days gone by in a person's experience, Acts 15 : 7, " a good while ago," lit., 'from old (days),' i.e., from the first days onward in the sense of originality, not age ; (*d*) of Mnason, " an early disciple," Acts 21 : 16, R.V., not referring to age, but to his being one of the first who had accepted the Gospel from the beginning of its proclamation ; (*e*) of things which are old in relation to the new, earlier things in contrast to things present, 2 Cor. 5 : 17, i.e., of what characterized and conditioned the time previous to conversion in a believer's experience, R.V., " they are become new," i.e., they have taken on a new complexion and are viewed in an entirely different way ; (*f*) of the world (i.e., the inhabitants of the world) just previous to the Flood, 2 Pet. 2 : 5 ; (*g*) of the Devil, as " that old serpent," Rev. 12 : 9 ; 20 : 2, old, not in age, but as characterized for a long period by the evils indicated.¶

Note : For the difference between this and No. 2, see below.

3820
AG:605D
CB:1261C
2. PALAIOS (παλαιός), akin to C, No. 1 (Eng., palæology, etc.), of what is of long duration, old in years, etc., a garment, wine (in contrast to *neos* ; see NEW), Matt. 9 : 16, 17 ; Mark 2 : 21, 22 (twice) ; Luke 5 : 36, 37,

39 (twice); of the treasures of Divine truth, Matt. 13 : 52 (compared with *kainos*: see NEW); of what belongs to the past, e.g., the believer's former self before his conversion, his " old man," old because it has been superseded by that which is new, Rom. 6 : 6; Eph. 4 : 22 (in contrast to *kainos*); Col. 3 : 9 (in contrast to *neos*); of the covenant in connection with the Law, 2 Cor. 3 : 14; of leaven, metaphorical of moral evil, 1 Cor. 5 : 7, 8 (in contrast to *neos*); of that which was given long ago and remains in force, an old commandment, 1 John 2 : 7 (twice), that which was familiar and well known in contrast to that which is fresh (*kainos*).¶

Note: *Palaios* denotes old, " without the reference to beginning and origin contained in *archaios* " (Abbott-Smith), a distinction observed in the papyri (Moulton and Milligan). While sometimes any difference seems almost indistinguishable, yet " it is evident that wherever an emphasis is desired to be laid on the reaching back to a beginning, whatever that beginning may be, *archaios* will be preferred (e.g., of Satan, Rev. 12 : 9; 20 : 2, see No. 1). That which . . . is old in the sense of more or less worn out . . . is always *palaios* " (Trench).

3. PRESBUTEROS (πρεσβύτερος), older, elder, is used in the plural, as a noun, in Acts 2 : 17, " old men." See ELDER. **4245 AG:699D CB:1266B**

B. Nouns.

1. GERŌN (γέρων) denotes an old man (from the same root comes Eng., grey), John 3 : 4.¶ **1088 AG:157A CB:1248B**

2. PRESBUTĒS (πρεσβύτης), " an old man," Luke 1 : 18, is translated " aged " in Tit. 2 : 2; Philm. 9 (for this, however, see the R.V. marg. See AGED. **4246 AG:700D CB:1266B**

3. GĒRAS (γῆρας), old age, occurs in Luke 1 : 36.¶ **1094 AG:157D CB:—**

Note: Augustine (quoted by Trench, §cvii, 2) speaks of the distinction observed among Greeks, that *presbutēs* conveys the suggestion of gravity.

C. Adverbs.

1. PALAI (πάλαι) denotes long ago, of old, Heb. 1 : 1, R.V., " of old time " (A.V., " in time past "); in Jude 4, " of old; " it is used as an adjective in 2 Pet. 1 : 9, " (his) old (sins)," lit., ' his sins of old.' See WHILE. **3819 AG:605C CB:1261C**

2. EKPALAI (ἔκπαλαι), from of old, for a long time (*ek*, from, and No. 1), occurs in 2 Pet. 2 : 3, R.V., " from of old " (A.V., " of a long time "); 3 : 5. See LONG, B, *Note* (2). **1597 AG:243C CB:—**

Note: In 1 Pet. 3 : 5, A.V., the particle *pote*, once, formerly, ever, sometime, is translated " in the old time " (R.V., " aforetime "); in 2 Pet. 1 : 21, " in old time " (R.V., " ever "), A.V. marg., " at any time." **4218 AG:695A CB:1266B**

D. Verbs.

1. PALAIOŌ (παλαιόω), akin to A, No. 2, denotes, in the Active Voice, to make or declare old, Heb. 8 : 13 (1st part); in the Passive Voice, to become old, of things worn out by time and use, Luke 12 : 33; Heb. 1 : 11, " shall wax old," lit., ' shall be made old,' i.e., worn out; in 8 : 13 (2nd part), R.V., " is becoming old " (A.V. " decayeth "); here and in the **3822 AG:606A CB:1261C**

1st part of the verse, the verb may have the meaning to abrogate; for the next verb in the verse, see No. 2.¶

1095 2. GĒRASKŌ (γηράσκω), from *gēras*, old age (akin to B, No. 1), to
AG:158A grow old, is translated "thou shalt be old," in John 21 : 18; "waxeth
CB:1248B aged," Heb. 8 : 13, R.V. (A.V., "waxeth old").¶

2192 *Notes:* (1) In John 8 : 57, *echō*, to have, is used with "fifty years" as
AG:331D the object, signifying, "Thou art (not yet fifty years) old," lit., 'Thou
CB:1242C hast not yet fifty years.' (2) In Mark 5 : 42, R.V., the verb *eimi*, to be, with the phrase 'of twelve years' is translated "was . . . old" (A.V., 'was *of the age* of').

OLDNESS

3821 PALAIOTĒS (παλαιότης), from *palaios* (see A, No. 2, above), occurs
AG:606A in Rom. 7 : 6, of "the letter," i.e., the law, with its rules of conduct, mere
CB:1261C outward conformity to which has yielded place in the believer's service to a response to the inward operation of the Holy Spirit. The word is contrasted with *kainotēs*, newness.¶

OLD WIVES'

1126 GRAŌDĒS (γραώδης), an adjective, signifying old-womanish (from
AG:167B *graus*, an old woman), is said of fables, in 1 Tim. 4 : 7.¶
CB:—

OLIVES (OLIVE BERRIES), OLIVE TREE

1636 1. ELAIA (ἐλαία) denotes (*a*) an olive tree, Rom. 11 : 17, 24; Rev.
AG:247D 11 : 4 (plural); the Mount of Olives was so called from the numerous
CB:1244A olive-trees there, and indicates the importance attached to such; the Mount is mentioned in the N.T. in connection only with the Lord's life on earth, Matt. 21 : 1; 24 : 3; 26 : 30; Mark 11 : 1; 13 : 3; 14 : 26; Luke 19 : 37; 22 : 39; John 8 : 1; (*b*) an olive, Jas. 3 : 12, R.V. (A.V., "olive berries").¶

1638 2. ELAIŌN (ἐλαιών), an olive-grove or olive-garden, the ending *—ōn*,
AG:248A as in this class of noun, here indicates "a place set with trees of the kind
CB:1244A designated by the primitive" (Thayer); hence it is applied to the Mount of Olives, Luke 19 : 29; 21 : 37; Acts 1 : 12 ("Olivet"): in the first two of these and in Mark 11 : 1, some mss. have the form of the noun as in No. 1.¶

2565 3. KALLIELAIOS (καλλιέλαιος), the garden olive (from *kallos*, beauty,
AG:400A and No. 1), occurs in Rom. 11 : 24, "a good olive tree."¶
CB:1253B

65 4. AGRIELAIOS (ἀγριέλαιος), an adjective (from *agrios*, growing in
AG:13D the fields, wild, and No. 1), denoting 'of the wild olive,' is used as a noun
CB:1233C in Rom. 11 : 17, 24, "a wild olive tree" (R.V., in the latter verse).¶

For OMITTED (Matt. 23 : 23, A.V.) see LEAVE (undone), No. 1

For OMNIPOTENT (Rev. 19 : 6) see ALMIGHTY

ON : see †, p. 1

ONCE (at ; for all)

1. HAPAX (ἅπαξ) denotes (*a*) once, one time, 2 Cor. 11 : 25 ; Heb. **530**
9 : 7, 26, 27 ; 12 : 26, 27 ; in the phrase " once and again," lit., ' once and **AG:80C CB:1249B**
twice,' Phil. 4 : 16 ; 1 Thess. 2 : 18 ; (*b*) once for all, of what is of perpetual validity, not requiring repetition, Heb. 6 : 4 ; 9 : 28 ; 10 : 2 ; 1 Pet. 3 : 18 ; Jude 3, R.V., " once for all " (A.V., " once ") ; ver. 5 (ditto) ; in some mss. 1 Pet. 3 : 20 (so the A.V.).¶

2. EPHAPAX (ἐφάπαξ), a strengthened form of No. 1 (*epi*, upon), **2178**
signifies (*a*) once for all, Rom. 6 : 10 ; Heb. 7 : 27, R.V. (A.V., " once ") ; **AG:330A CB:1245C**
9 : 12 (ditto) ; 10 : 10 ; (*b*) at once, 1 Cor. 15 : 6.¶

3. POTE (ποτέ) denotes once upon a time, formerly, sometime, e.g., **4218**
Rom. 7 : 9 ; Gal. 1 : 23, 1st part, R.V., " once " (A.V., " in times past ") ; **AG:695A CB:1266B**
2nd part, A.V. and R.V., " once ; " Gal. 2 : 6, R.V. marg., " what they once were " (to be preferred to the text, " whatsoever they were "), the reference probably being to the association of the twelve Apostles with the Lord during His ministry on earth ; upon this their partisans based their claim for the exclusive authority of these Apostles, which Paul vigorously repudiated ; in Eph. 5 : 8, R.V., " once " (A.V., " sometimes "). See AFORETIME, LAST, LENGTH (at), TIME (past).

Note : In Luke 23 : 18, A.V., *pamplēthei*, denoting with the whole **3826**
multitude (*pas*, all, *plēthos*, a multitude), is rendered " all at once," **AG:607B CB:—**
R.V., " all together ").¶

ONE

A. Numeral.

HEIS (εἷς), the first cardinal numeral, masculine (feminine and neuter **1520**
nominative forms are *mia* and *hen*, respectively), is used to signify (1) (*a*) one **AG:230D CB:1249C**
in contrast to many, e.g., Matt. 25 : 15 ; Rom. 5 : 18, R.V., " (through)
one (trespass)," i.e., Adam's transgression, in contrast to the " one act of **MIA**
righteousness," i.e., the Death of Christ (not as A.V., " the offence of one," **3391**
and " the righteousness of one ") ; (*b*) metaphorically, union and concord, **AG:230D (HEIS)**
e.g., John 10 : 30 ; 11 : 52 ; 17 : 11, 21, 22 ; Rom. 12 : 4, 5 ; Phil. 1 : 27 ; **CB:1258C**
(2) emphatically, (*a*) a single (one), to the exclusion of others, e.g., Matt. 21 : 24 ; Rom. 3 : 10 ; 1 Cor. 9 : 24 ; 1 Tim. 2 : 5 (twice) ; (*b*) one, alone, e.g., Mark 2 : 7, R.V. (A.V., " only ") ; 10 : 18 ; Luke 18 : 19 ; (*c*) one and the same, e.g., Rom. 3 : 30, R.V., " God is one," i.e., there is not one God for the Jew and one for the Gentile ; cp. Gal. 3 : 20, which means that in a promise there is no other party ; 1 Cor. 3 : 8 ; 11 : 5 ; 12 : 11 ; 1 John 5 : 8 (lit., ' and the three are into one,' i.e., united in one and the same witness) ; (3) a certain one, in the same sense as the indefinite pronoun *tis* (see B, No. 1), e.g., Matt. 8 : 19, R.V., " a (scribe)," marg., " one (scribe)," A.V., " a certain (scribe) ; " 19 : 16, " one ; " in Rev. 8 : 13, R.V. marg., " one (eagle) ; " ***heis tis*** are used together in Luke 22 : 50 ;

HEKASTOS John 11 : 49 ; this occurs frequently in the papyri (Moulton, Prol., p. 96) ;
1538 AG:236C (4) distributively, with *hekastos*, each, i.e., every one, e.g., Luke 4 : 40 ;
CB:1249C Acts 2 : 6, " every man " (lit., ' every one ') ; in the sense of ' one . . .
ALLOS and one,' e.g., John 20 : 12 ; or one . . . followed by *allos* or *heteros*, the
243 AG:39D other, e.g., Matt. 6 : 24 ; or by a second *heis*, e.g., Matt. 24 : 40, R.V.,
CB:1234C HETEROS " one ; " John 20 : 12 ; in Rom. 12 : 5 *heis* is preceded by *kata* (*kath'*)
2087 in the sense of " severally (members) one (of another)," R.V. (A.V., " every
AG:315A CB:1250A one . . . one ") ; cp. Mark 14 : 19 ; in 1 Thess. 5 : 11 the phrase in the
PRŌTOS 2nd part, " each other," R.V. (A.V., " one another "), is, lit., ' one the
4413 AG:725B one ; ' (5) as an ordinal number, equivalent to *prōtos*, first, in the phrase
CB:1267B " the first day of the week," lit. and idiomatically, ' one of sabbaths,' signifying ' the first day after the sabbath,' e.g., Matt. 28 : 1 ; Mark 16 : 2 ; Acts 20 : 7 ; 1 Cor. 16 : 2. Moulton remarks on the tendency for certain cardinal numerals to replace ordinals (Prol., p. 96).

B. Pronouns.

5100 AG:819D 1. TIS (τις), an indefinite pronoun signifying a certain one, some one,
CB:1272C any one, one (the neuter form *ti* denotes a certain thing), is used (*a*) like a noun, e.g., Acts 5 : 25 ; 19 : 32 ; 21 : 34 ; 1 Cor. 3 : 4 ; or with the meaning ' someone,' e.g., Acts 8 : 31, R.V., " some one " (A.V., " some man ") ; Rom. 5 : 7 ; (*b*) as an adjective ; see CERTAIN, Note (3), SOME.

3739 AG:583B 2. HOS (ὅς), as a relative pronoun, signifies " who ; " as a demonstra-
CB:— tive pronoun, " this," or " the one " in contrast with " the other," or " another," e.g., Rom. 14 : 2, A.V. (R.V., " one man ") ; 1 Cor. 12 : 8.

OUDEIS *Notes:* (1) The R.V. often substitutes " one " for " man," e.g., Matt.
3762 17 : 8 (*oudeis*, no one) ; 1 Cor. 3 : 21 (i.e., ' no person ') ; 1 Cor. 15 : 35 ;
AG:591D 1 Thess. 5 : 15 ; 2 Tim. 4 : 16 ; 1 John 2 : 27 ; 3 : 3. (2) The pronoun
CB:1261B HOUTOS *houtos* is sometimes translated " this one," e.g., Luke 7 : 8. (3) In 1 Pet.
3778 3 : 8, A.V., *homophrōn*, " likeminded " (R.V.), is translated " of one mind "
AG:596B CB:1251B (lit., ' of the same mind '). (4) In Acts 7 : 26, " at one," is, lit., ' unto
HOMOPHRŌN peace ' (see PEACE). (5) For " every one " in Acts 5 : 16 see EVERY,
3675 AG:569C No. 2. (6) In Mark 9 : 26 *nekros*, dead, is translated " one dead." (7) In
CB:— Acts 2 : 1 " in one place " translates *epi to auto*, lit., ' to the same,' which
HO 3588 may mean ' for the same (purpose) ; ' in 1 Cor. 11 : 20 and 14 : 23, the R.V.
AG:549B translates it " together." (8) In Mark 1 : 7, A.V., the article *ho*, the, is
CB:— PAS rendered " one " (R.V., " he that ") . (9) In Mark 7 : 14, A.V., the plural
3956 of *pas*, " all " (so R.V.), is translated " every one ; " in Matt. 5 : 28, A.V.,
AG:631A *pas*, with the article, is translated " whosoever " (R.V. " every one who ").
CB:1262C (10) In Acts 1 : 24, A.V., " whether " is, lit., and as the R.V., " the one whom." (11) In 2 Thess. 2 : 7, the article is rendered " one that," R.V. (A.V., " he who ").

See also ACCORD, CONSENT, B, No. 1, END, C, Note (6), EYE (with one), GREAT, HOLY, LITTLE, MIND, NATION, WICKED.

---

240 AG:39C ONE ANOTHER or ONE . . . ANOTHER, ONE . . . THE OTHER
CB:1234C *Notes:* (1) This translates a number of words and phrases, (*a*) *allēlōn*,

a reciprocal pronoun in the genitive plural, signifying of, or from, one another (akin to *allos*, another), e.g., Matt. 25 : 32 ; John 13 : 22 ; Acts 15 : 39 ; 19 : 38 ; 1 Cor. 7 : 5 ; Gal. 5 : 17 ; the accusative *allēlous* denotes " one another," e.g., Acts 7 : 26, lit., ' why do ye wrong one another ? ' ; 2 Thess. 1 : 3, R.V. ; in Eph. 4 : 32 and Col. 3 : 13, e.g., R.V., " each other ; " in 1 Thess. 5 : 15, " one (toward) another," R.V. ; the dative *allēlois* denotes " one to another," e.g., Luke 7 : 32 ; (*b*) different forms of
the plural of *heautou*, of himself, used as a reciprocal pronoun, e.g., **HEAUTOU**
Eph. 5 : 19, R.V., " one to another " (A.V., and R.V. marg., " to your- **1438 AG:211D**
selves ") ; see also Note (5) ; (*c*) *allos pros allon*, " one to another," **CB:1249B**
Acts 2 : 12 ; (*d*) *allos* . . . *heteros*, 1 Cor. 12 : 8 (for the difference between **(-OS) ALLOS**
allos and *heteros*, see ANOTHER) ; (*e*) *hos men* . . . *hos de* (in various forms **243**
of the pronoun), lit., ' this indeed . . . but that,' e.g., Luke 23 : 33 ; **AG:39D CB:1234C**
Rom. 9 : 21 ; 14 : 5 ; 1 Cor. 11 : 21 ; 2 Cor. 2 : 16 ; Phil. 1 : 16, 17 ; **HETEROS**
(*f*) *heteros* . . . *heteros*, one . . . another, 1 Cor. 15 : 40. (2) In Matt. **2087 AG:315A**
24 : 2 ; Mark 13 : 2 ; Luke 19 : 44, and 21 : 6, " one (stone upon) another " **CB:1250A**
is, lit., ' stone upon stone.' (3) In Heb. 10 : 25, " *one another* " is necessarily **HOS 3739**
added in English to complete the sense of *parakaleō*, to exhort. (4) In **AG:583B**
1 Pet. 3 : 8, A.V., " one of another " represents nothing in the original **CB:—**
(the R.V., " compassionate " sufficiently translates the adjective *sumpathēs* : see COMPASSION, C.). (5) In Mark 9 : 10, A.V., *pros heautous*, " among yourselves " (R.V.), is translated " one with another." (6) In 1 Tim. 5 : 21, A.V., the accusative case of *prosklisis*, partiality, preceded by *kata*, according to, is translated " preferring one before another " (R.V., " prejudice ; " marg., " preference," lit., ' according to partiality ').

ONLY

A. Adjectives.

1. MONOS (μόνος), alone, solitary, is translated " only," e.g., in Matt. **3441**
4 : 10 ; 12 : 4 ; 17 : 8 ; 1 Cor. 9 : 6 ; 14 : 36 ; Phil. 4 : 15 ; Col. 4 : 11 ; **AG:527C CB:1259B**
2 John 1 ; it is used as an attribute of God in John 5 : 44 ; 17 : 3 ; Rom. 16 : 27 ; 1 Tim. 1 : 17 ; 1 Tim. 6 : 15, 16 ; Jude 4, 25 ; Rev. 15 : 4. See ALONE, A.

2. MONOGENĒS (μονογενής), only begotten (No. 1 and *genos*, **3439**
offspring), has the meaning " only," of human offspring, in Luke 7 : 12 ; **AG:527B CB:1259B**
8 : 42 ; 9 : 38 ; the term is one of endearment, as well as of singleness. For Heb. 11 : 17 see ONLY BEGOTTEN.

B. Adverbs.

1. MONON (μόνον), the neuter of A, No. 1, only, exclusively, is **3440**
translated " only," e.g., in Matt. 5 : 47 ; 8 : 8 ; John 5 : 18 ; 11 : 52 ; **AG:527C CB:1259B**
12 : 9 ; 13 : 9 ; frequently in Acts, Romans and Galatians. See ALONE, B, No. 1.

2. PLĒN (πλήν), howbeit, except that, is translated " only that " in **4133**
the R.V. of Phil. 1 : 18 (A.V., " notwithstanding ") ; " only " in 3 : 16 **AG:669B CB:1265B**
(A.V., " nevertheless ").

1520 AG:230D CB:1249C *Notes:* (1) In Mark 2:7, A.V., *heis*, "one" (so R.V.), is translated "only;" in Jas. 4:12, R.V., "one only" (A.V., "one"). (2) For "only that" in Acts 21:25, A.V., see the R.V. (3) The conjunction *ei*, if, with the negative *mē*, not, is translated "but only" in Luke 4:26, R.V. (A.V., "save"); 4:27 (A.V., "saving") · "only" in 1 Cor. 7:17 (A.V., "but"); in some mss. in Acts 21:25 (A.V. "save only").

ONLY BEGOTTEN

3439 AG:527B CB:1259B MONOGENĒS (μονογενής) is used five times, all in the writings of the Apostle John, of Christ as the Son of God; it is translated "only begotten" in Heb. 11:17 of the relationship of Isaac to Abraham.

With reference to Christ, the phrase "the only begotten from the Father," John 1:14, R.V. (see also the marg.), indicates that as the Son of God He was the sole representative of the Being and character of the One who sent Him. In the original the definite article is omitted both before "only begotten" and before "Father," and its absence in each case serves to lay stress upon the characteristics referred to in the terms used. The Apostle's object is to demonstrate what sort of glory it was that he and his fellow-Apostles had seen. That he is not merely making a comparison with earthly relationships is indicated by *para*, "from." The glory was that of a unique relationship and the word "begotten" does not imply a beginning of His Sonship. It suggests relationship indeed, but must be distinguished from generation as applied to man.

We can only rightly understand the term "the only begotten" when used of the Son, in the sense of unoriginated relationship. "The begetting is not an event of time, however remote, but a fact irrespective of time. The Christ did not *become*, but necessarily and eternally *is* the Son. He, a Person, possesses every attribute of pure Godhood. This necessitates eternity, absolute being; in this respect He is not 'after' the Father" (Moule). The expression also suggests the thought of the deepest affection, as in the case of the O.T. word *yachid*, variously rendered, "only one," Gen. 22:2, 12; "only son," Jer. 6:26; Amos 8:10; Zech. 12:10; "only beloved," Prov. 4:3, and "darling," Psa. 22:20; 35:17.

In John 1:18 the clause "The Only Begotten Son, which is in the bosom of the Father," expresses both His eternal union with the Father in the Godhead and the ineffable intimacy and love between them, the Son sharing all the Father's counsels and enjoying all His affections. Another reading is *monogenēs Theos*, 'God only-begotten.' In John 3:16 the statement, "God so loved the world that He gave His Only Begotten Son," must not be taken to mean that Christ became the Only Begotten Son by Incarnation. The value and the greatness of the gift lay in the Sonship of Him who was given. His Sonship was not the effect of His being given. In John 3:18 the phrase "the Name of the Only Begotten Son of God" lays stress upon the full revelation of God's character and will, His love and grace, as conveyed in the Name of One who, being in a unique relationship to Him, was provided by Him as the Object of faith. In 1 John 4 : 9 the statement "God hath sent His Only Begotten Son into the world" does not mean that God sent out into the world one who at His birth in Bethlehem had become His Son. Cp. the parallel statement, "God sent forth the Spirit of His Son," Gal. 4 : 6, R.V., which could not mean that God sent forth One who became His Spirit when He sent Him.¶

For ONSET, Acts 14 : 5, R.V., see ASSAULT and IMPULSE

For ONWARD, 2 John 9, R.V., see GO, No. 10

OPEN, OPENING (for OPENLY, see below)

A. Verbs.

1. ANOIGŌ (ἀνοίγω) is used (1) transitively, (*a*) literally, of a door or 455
gate, e.g., Acts 5 : 19 ; graves, Matt. 27 : 52 ; a sepulchre, Rom. 3 : 13 ; AG:70D CB:1235C
a book, e.g., Luke 4 : 17 (some mss. have No. 4) ; Rev. 5 : 2–5 ; 10 : 8 ;
the seals of a roll, e.g., Rev. 5 : 9 ; 6 : 1 ; the eyes, Acts 9 : 40 ; the mouth of a fish, Matt. 17 : 27 ; "the pit of the abyss," Rev. 9 : 2, R.V. ; heaven and the heavens, Matt. 3 : 16 ; Luke 3 : 21 ; Acts 10 : 11 (for 7 : 56, see No. 2) ; Rev. 19 : 11 ; "the temple of the tabernacle of the testimony in heaven," Rev. 15 : 5 ; by metonymy, for that which contained treasures, Matt. 2 : 11 ; (*b*) metaphorically, e.g., Matt. 7 : 7, 8 ; 25 : 11 ; Rev. 3 : 7 ; Hebraistically, to open the mouth, of beginning to speak, e.g., Matt. 5 : 2 ; 13 : 35 ; Acts 8 : 32, 35 ; 10 : 34 ; 18 : 14 ; Rev. 13 : 6 (cp., e.g., Numb. 22 : 28 ; Job. 3 : 1 ; Isa. 50 : 5) ; and of recovering speech, Luke 1 : 64 ; of the earth opening, Rev. 12 : 16 ; of the opening of the eyes, Acts 26 : 18 ; the ears, Mark 7 : 35 (in the best mss. ; some have No. 2) ; (2) intransitively (perfect tense, active, in the Greek), (*a*) literally, of the heaven, John 1 : 51, R.V., "opened ;" (*b*) metaphorically, of speaking freely, 2 Cor. 6 : 11.

2. DIANOIGŌ (διανοίγω), to open up completely (*dia*, through, 1272
intensive, and No. 1), is used (*a*) literally, Luke 2 : 23 ; Acts 7 : 56, in AG:187B CB:1241B
the best mss. ; (*b*) metaphorically, of the eyes, Mark 7 : 34 ; Luke 24 : 31 ; of the Scriptures, ver. 32 and Acts 17 : 3 ; of the mind, Luke 24 : 45, R.V. (A.V., "understanding") ; of the heart, Acts 16 : 14.¶

3. AGŌ (ἄγω), to lead, or to keep or spend a day, is so used in Acts 71 AG:14B
19 : 38 : see KEEP, Note (2). CB:1233C

4. ANAPTUSSŌ (ἀναπτύσσω), to unroll (*ana*, back, *ptussō*, to roll), 380 AG:60A
is found in some mss. in Luke 4 : 17 (of the roll of Isaiah), and translated ANAKALUPTō
"He had opened" (A.V.) ; see No. 1.¶ 343

Notes : (1) For Heb. 4 : 13, "laid open," R.V. (A.V., "opened") see AG:55C CB:1235A
LAY, No. 18. (2) In 2 Cor. 3 : 18, A.V., *anakaluptō*, to unveil, is translated SCHIZō
"open" (R.V., "unveiled," which consistently continues the metaphor 4977 AG:797B
of the veil upon the heart of Israel). (3) In Mark 1 : 10, A.V., *schizō*, to CB:1268C

PRODēOS rend or split, is translated "opened," of the heavens, R.V., "rent
4271 AG:704B asunder," A.V. marg., "cloven, or, rent." (4) For *prodēlos*, in 1 Tim.
CB:— 5 : 24, A.V., "open beforehand," see EVIDENT, A, No. 3. (5) For "be
EPHPHATHA 2188 opened" see EPHPHATHA. (6) For "open (your hearts)," 2 Cor. 7 : 2,
AG:331B R.V., see RECEIVE, No. 18.

CB:1245C **B. Nouns.**

457 AG:71C 1. ANOIXIS (ἄνοιξις), an opening (akin to A, No. 1), is used in Eph.
CB:1235C 6 : 19, metaphorically of the opening of the mouth as in A, No. 1 (2), (*b*).¶
3692 2. OPE (ὀπή), an opening, a hole, is used in Jas. 3 : 11, of the orifice
AG:574D CB:— of a fountain: see CAVE, HOLE, PLACE.

OPENLY

3954 1. PARRHĒSIA (παρρησία), freedom of speech, boldness, is used
AG:630C CB:1262C adverbially in the dative case and translated "openly" in Mark 8 : 32,
of a saying of Christ; in John 7 : 13, of a public statement; in 11 : 54,
of Christ's public appearance; in 7 : 26 and 18 : 20, of His public
testimony; preceded by the preposition *en*, in, John 7 : 4, lit., 'in bold-
5320 ness' (cp. ver. 10, R.V., "publicly"). See BOLD, B.
AG:853A 2. PHANERŌS (φανερῶς), manifestly, openly: see EVIDENT, B.
CB:1263C *Notes:* (1) In Gal. 3 : 1, "openly set forth" translates the verb
PROGRAPHō 4270 *prographō*, lit., 'to write before,' as of the O.T., Rom. 15 : 4 (cp. Jude 4),
AG:704A and of a previous letter, Eph. 3 : 3. In Gal. 3 : 1, however, "it is probably
CB:1266C used in another sense, unexampled in the Scriptures but not uncommon
PHANEROS 5318 in the language of the day,='proclaimed,' 'placarded,' as a magistrate
AG:852B proclaimed the fact that an execution had been carried out, placarding
CB:1263C EMPHANēS his proclamation in a public place. The Apostle carries on his metaphor
1717 of the 'evil eye;' as a preventive of such mischief it was common to post
AG:257C CB:1244B up charms on the walls of houses, a glance at which was supposed to
DēMOSIOS counteract any evil influence to which a person may have been subjected.
1219 AG:179B 'Notwithstanding,' he says, in effect, 'that the fact that Christ had been
CB:1240C crucified was placarded before your very eyes in our preaching, you have
allowed yourselves to be . . . fascinated by the enemies of the Cross of
Christ, when you had only to look at Him to escape their malignant
influence;' cp. the interesting and instructive parallel in Num. 21 : 9."*
(2) In some mss. in Matt. 6 : 4, 6, 18, the phrase *en tō phanerō*, lit., 'in
the manifest,' is found (A.V., "openly"); see the R.V. (3) For *emphanēs*,
rendered "openly" in Acts 10 : 40, A.V., see MANIFEST. (4) In Acts
16 : 37, A.V., the dative case of the adjective *dēmosios*, belonging to the
people (*dēmos*, a people), "public" (so R.V.), used adverbially, is
translated "openly;" in 18 : 28 and 20 : 20, "publicly." For the
adjective itself, "public," see Acts 5 : 18. See PUBLIC.¶

OPINION See THINK

For OPERATION see WORKING

* From Notes on Galatians by Hogg and Vine, pp. 106, 107.

OPPORTUNITY (lack)

A. Nouns.

1. KAIROS (*καιρός*), primarily, a due measure, is used of a fixed and 2540
definite period, a time, season, and is translated "opportunity" in Gal. AG:394D CB:1253A
6:10 and Heb. 11:15. See SEASON, TIME, WHILE.

2. EUKAIRIA (*εὐκαιρία*), a fitting time, opportunity (*eu*, well, and 2120
No. 1), occurs in Matt. 26:16 and Luke 22:6.¶ Cp. *eukairos*, seasonable; AG:321B CB:1247B
see CONVENIENT.

3. TOPOS (*τόπος*), a place, is translated "opportunity" in Acts 5117
25:16, R.V. (A.V., "licence"). See PLACE, ROOM. AG:822B CB:1273A

B. Verbs.

1. EUKAIREŌ (*εὐκαιρέω*), to have time or leisure (akin to A, No. 2), 2119
is translated "he shall have opportunity" in 1 Cor. 16:12, R.V. (A.V., AG:321B CB:1247B
"convenient time"). See LEISURE.

2. AKAIREOMAI (*ἀκαιρέομαι*), to have no opportunity (*a*, negative, 170
and *kairos*, season), occurs in Phil. 4:10.¶ AG:29B CB:1234A

OPPOSE

480 AG:74B

1. ANTIKEIMAI (*ἀντίκειμαι*): see ADVERSARY, B. CB:—

2. ANTITASSŌ (*ἀντιτάσσω*) is used in the Middle Voice in the sense 498 (-OMAI)
of setting oneself against (*anti*, against, *tassō*, to order, set), opposing AG:76A
oneself to, Acts 18:6; elsewhere rendered by the verb to resist, Rom. CB:—
13:2; Jas. 4:6; 5:6; 1 Pet. 5:5. See RESIST.¶

3. ANTIDIATITHĒMI (*ἀντιδιατίθημι*) signifies to place oneself in 475
opposition, oppose (*anti*, against, *dia*, through, intensive, *tithēmi*, to place), (-EMAI) AG:74A
2 Tim. 2:25. The A.V. and R.V. translate this as a Middle Voice, CB:—
"them (A.V., those) that oppose themselves." Field (*Notes on the Trans. of the N.T.*) points out that in the only other known instance of the verb it is Passive. The sense is practically the same if it is rendered 'those who are opposed.'¶

OPPOSITIONS

ANTITHESIS (*ἀντίθεσις*), a contrary position (*anti*, against, *tithēmi*, 477
to place; Eng., antithesis), occurs in 1 Tim. 6:20.¶ AG:74B CB:—

OPPRESS

1. KATADUNASTEUŌ (*καταδυναστεύω*), to exercise power over 2616
(*kata*, down, *dunastēs*, a potentate: *dunamai*, to have power), to oppress, AG:410C CB:—
is used, in the Passive Voice, in Acts 10:38; in the Active, in Jas. 2:6.¶

2. KATAPONEŌ (*καταπονέω*): see DISTRESS, B, No. 4. 2669 AG:416D CB:—

OR: see † p. 1.

ORACLE

LOGION (*λόγιον*), a diminutive of *logos*, a word, narrative, statement, 3051
denotes a Divine response or utterance, an oracle; it is used of (*a*) the AG:476C CB:1257A

contents of the Mosaic Law, Acts 7 : 38 ; (*b*) all the written utterances of God through O.T. writers, Rom. 3 : 2 ; (*c*) the substance of Christian doctrine, Heb. 5 : 12 ; (*d*) the utterances of God through Christian teachers, 1 Pet. 4 : 11.¶

Note : Divine oracles were given by means of the breastplate of the High Priest, in connection with the service of the Tabernacle, and the Sept. uses the associated word *logeion* in Ex. 28 : 15, to describe the
DēMēGOREō 1215 breastplate.

AG:178D CB:— RHēTōR

ORATION

4489 AG:735D DĒMĒGOREŌ (δημηγορέω), from *dēmos*, the people and *agoreuō*,
CB:1268B to speak in the public assembly, to deliver an oration, occurs in Acts
TITHēMI 5087 12 : 21.¶

AG:815D CB:1272C KATHISTēMI

ORATOR

2525 RHĒTŌR (ῥήτωρ), from an obsolete present tense, *rheō*, to say (cp.
AG:390B Eng., rhetoric), denotes a public speaker, an orator, Acts 24 : 1, of
CB:1254C TASSō Tertullus. Such a person, distinct from the professional lawyer, was
5021 AG:805D hired, as a professional speaker, to make a skilful presentation of a case in
CB:1271A DIATASSō court. His training was not legal but rhetorical.¶

1299 AG:189C

ORDAIN

CB:1241B 1. TITHĒMI (τίθημι), to put : see APPOINT, No. 3.

HORIZō 3724 2. KATHISTĒMI (καθίστημι), from *kata*, down, or over against, and
AG:580D *histēmi*, to cause to stand, to set, is translated to ordain in the A.V. of
CB:1251B Tit. 1 : 5 ; Heb. 5 : 1 ; 8 : 3. See APPOINT, No. 2.

KRINō 2919 3. TASSŌ (τάσσω) is translated to ordain, in Acts 13 : 48 and Rom.
AG:451B 13 : 1. See APPOINT, No. 5.

CB:1256A PROORIZō 4. DIATASSŌ (διατάσσω) is translated to ordain in 1 Cor. 7 : 17 ;
4309 AG:709B 9 : 14 ; Gal. 3 : 19, the last in the sense of 'administered.' Cp. *diatagē*,
CB:— under DISPOSITION. See APPOINT, No. 6.

POIEō 4160 5. HORIZŌ (ὁρίζω) is twice used of Christ as Divinely " ordained " to
AG:680D be the Judge of men, Acts 10 : 42 ; 17 : 31. See DETERMINE, No. 2.

CB:1265C KATASKEUAZō 6. KRINŌ (κρίνω), to divide, separate, decide, judge, is translated
2680 " ordained " in Acts 16 : 4, of the decrees by the Apostles and elders in
AG:418B Jerusalem. See JUDGE.

CB:1254B CHEIROTONEō *Notes :* (1) In 1 Cor. 2 : 7, A.V., *proorizō*, to foreordain (see R.V.)
5500 is translated " ordained." See DETERMINE, No. 3. (2) In Mark 3 : 14,
AG:881A CB:1239C A.V., *poieō*, to make, is translated " ordained " (R.V., " appointed ").
PROETOIMAZō (3) In Heb. 9 : 6, A.V., *kataskeuazō*, to prepare (so R.V.), is translated
4282 AG:705D " were . . . ordained." See PREPARE. (4) In Acts 14 : 23, A.V.,
CB:1266C *cheirotoneō*, to appoint (R.V.), is translated " they had ordained." See
PROGRAPHō 4270 APPOINT, No. 11. (5) In Eph. 2 : 10, A.V., *proetoimazō*, to prepare before,
AG:704A is translated " hath before ordained " (R.V., " afore prepared ") ; see
CB:1266C PREPARE. (6) In Jude 4, A.V., *prographō*, lit., to write before, is

translated " were before . . . ordained " (R.V., " were . . . set forth ").
See SET (forth). (7) In Acts 1 : 22, A.V., *ginomai*, to become, is translated 1096
" be ordained " (R.V., " become "). (8) In Rom. 7 : 10, A.V., " *ordained* " AG:158A CB:1248B
represents no word in the original (see R.V.).

ORDER (Noun and Verb)

A. Nouns.

1. TAXIS (τάξις), an arranging, arrangement, order (akin to *tassō*, 5010
to arrange, draw up in order), is used in Luke 1 : 8 of the fixed succession AG:803D
of the course of the priests ; of due order, in contrast to confusion, in the CB:1271A
gatherings of a local church, 1 Cor. 14 : 40 ; of the general condition of such, Col. 2 : 5 (some give it a military significance here) ; of the Divinely appointed character or nature of a priesthood, of Melchizedek, as foreshadowing that of Christ, Heb. 5 : 6, 10 ; 6 : 20 ; 7 : 11 (where also the character of the Aaronic priesthood is set in contrast) ; 7 : 17 (in some mss., ver. 21).¶

2. TAGMA (τάγμα), a more concrete form of No. 1, signifying that 5001
which has been arranged in order, was especially a military term, denoting AG:802D
a company ; it is used metaphorically in 1 Cor. 15 : 23 of the various CB:—
classes of those who have part in the first resurrection.¶

B. Verbs.

1. ANATASSOMAI (ἀνατάσσομαι), to arrange in order (*ana*, up, and 392
the Middle Voice of *tassō*, to arrange), is used in Luke 1 : 1, A.V., " to set AG:61D
forth in order " (R.V., " to draw up ") ; the probable meaning is to CB:1235B
bring together and so arrange details in order.¶

2. DIATASSŌ (διατάσσω), to appoint, arrange, charge, give orders to, 1299
is used, in the Middle Voice, in Acts 24 : 23, " gave order " (R.V.) ; AG:189C
1 Cor. 11 : 34, " will I set in order ; " in the Active Voice, in 1 Cor. 16 : 1, CB:1241B
" I gave order " (R.V.). See COMMAND, No. 1.

3. EPIDIORTHOŌ (ἐπιδιορθόω), to set in order (*epi*, upon, *dia*, 1930
through, intensive, and *orthos*, straight), is used in Tit. 1 : 5, in the sense AG:292B
of setting right again what was defective, a commission to Titus, not to CB:—
add to what the Apostle himself had done, but to restore what had fallen into disorder since the Apostle had laboured in Crete ; this is suggested by the *epi*.¶

C. Adverb.

KATHEXĒS (καθεξῆς) is translated " in order " in Luke 1 : 3 ; Acts 2517
11 : 4, R.V. (A.V., " by order ") ; Acts 18 : 23. See AFTERWARD, No. 3. AG:388D
Note : In 2 Cor. 11 : 32, R.V., the phrase " in order to " (as with the CB:—
A.V., " desirous to ") represents nothing in the original : the infinitive mood of the verb *piazō* expresses the purpose, viz., " to take."

ORDERLY

KOSMIOS (κόσμιος), an adjective signifying decent, modest, orderly 2887 AG:445C
(akin to *kosmos*, order, adornment), is translated " modest " in 1 Tim. CB:1255C

2 : 9 ; "orderly" in 3 : 2, R.V. (A.V., "of good behaviour"). See MODEST.¶

4748 AG:769C CB:1270A *Note :* For *stoicheō*, in Acts 21 : 24, "thou walkest orderly," see WALK.

ORDINANCE

A. Nouns.

1345 AG:198A CB:1241C 1. DIKAIŌMA (δικαίωμα) : see JUSTIFICATION, No. 2.

1296 AG:189B 2. DIATAGĒ (διαταγή) is translated "ordinances," in Rom. 13 : 2. See DISPOSITION.

1378 AG:201C CB:1242A 3. DOGMA (δόγμα) is translated "ordinances" in Eph. 2 : 15 and Col. 2 : 14. See DECREE.

2937 AG:455D CB:1256A 4. KTISIS (κτίσις), a creation, creature, is translated "ordinance" in 1 Pet. 2 : 13. See CREATE, B, No. 1.

3862 AG:615D CB:1262A *Note :* In 1 Cor. 11 : 2, A.V., *paradosis*, a tradition (marg., and R.V., "traditions"), is translated "ordinances." See TRADITION.

B. Verb.

1379 AG:201B CB:1242A DOGMATIZŌ (δογματίζω), akin to A, No. 3, to decree, signifies, in the Middle Voice, to subject oneself to an ordinance, Col. 2 : 20.¶ In the Sept., Esth. 3 : 9 ; in some texts, Dan. 2 : 13, 15.¶

ORDINARY See MEAN, IGNORANT

OTHER

243 AG:39D CB:1234C 1. ALLOS (ἄλλος) indicates numeral distinction of objects of similar character, and is used (*a*) absolutely, e.g., Matt. 20 : 3 (plural) ; (*b*) attached to a noun, e.g., Matt. 21 : 36 ; (*c*) with the article, e.g. Matt. 5 : 39 ; 1 Cor. 14 : 29 (plural, R.V.) ; in Matt. 13 : 5 ; Luke 9 : 19 ; John 9 : 9, e.g., R.V., "others" (A.V., "some") ; in Matt. 25 : 20, R.V., "other" (A.V., "beside them . . . more"). See ANOTHER, MORE, B, Note (1), SOME.

2087 AG:315A CB:1250A 2. HETEROS (ἕτερος) indicates either numerical distinction, e.g., Luke 4 : 43 ; 5 : 7 ; or generic distinction, different in character, etc., e.g., Luke 9 : 29, "(the fashion of His countenance) was altered," lit., 'became other ;' 23 : 32, "two others, (malefactors)," R.V., where the plural serves to make the necessary distinction between them and Christ ; Acts 2 : 4 ; 19 : 39 ("other matters") ; 1 Cor. 14 : 21, A.V., "other" (R.V., "strange") ; 2 Cor. 11 : 4 (2nd and 3rd parts, R.V., "different ;" in the 1st clause, *allos*, "another"). For the distinction between this and No. 1, see under ANOTHER.

ORGIES See REVELLINGS

ORPHAN See FATHERLESS

3062 AG:479D CB:1257B 3. LOIPOS (λοιπός) signifies remaining, the rest. It is translated "other," or "others," e.g., in Matt. 25 : 11 ; Mark 4 : 19 ; Luke 18 : 9 ; 24 : 10 (in ver. 9, "the rest") ; but in Luke 8 : 10 ; Acts 28 : 9 ; Rom. 1 : 13 ; 1 Cor. 9 : 5 ; Eph. 2 : 3 ; 1 Thess. 4 : 13 ; 5 : 6 ; 1 Tim. 5 : 20, e.g., the R.V. renders this word "the rest" (A.V., "other" or "others") ; in Eph. 4 : 17, some mss. have *loipa*, neuter plural, A.V., "other (Gentiles) ;" see the R.V. See REMNANT, REST (the).

245 AG:40C CB:1234C 4. ALLOTRIOS (ἀλλότριος), belonging to another, not one's own, is translated "other men's" in 2 Cor. 10 : 15 ; 1 Tim. 5 : 22 ; in Heb.

9 : 25, R.V., " not his own " (A.V., " of others "). See ALIEN, MAN'S, Note (1), STRANGE, STRANGER.

5. ALLĒLŌN (ἀλλήλων), in Rom. 1 : 12, used in the dative case, is translated in the R.V. " (each of us by the) other's " (A.V., " mutual ") ; the accusative is translated " other " in Phil. 2 : 3. See MUTUAL and ONE ANOTHER. **240 AG:39C CB:1234C**

6. HEIS (εἷς), one, is sometimes translated " other " when expressing the second of a pair, e.g., Matt. 24 : 40, A.V. (R.V., " one "). See ONE, A (4). **1520 AG:230D CB:1249C**

7. EKEINOS (ἐκεῖνος), signifying that one, implying remoteness as compared with *houtos*, this, is translated " the other," e.g., in Matt. 23 : 23 ; Luke 11 : 42 ; 18 : 14. **1565 AG:239B CB:1243C**

Notes : (1) In Acts 26 : 22, A.V., *ouden ektos*, lit., ' nothing besides ' is translated " none other things " (R.V., " nothing but "). (2) The plural of the definite article is translated " others " in Acts 17 : 32 ; in Jude 23, A.V., " others " (R.V., " some "). (3) In Luke 24 : 1, the plural of *tis*, a certain one, is found in some mss., and translated " certain others " in the A.V. **EKTOS 1622 AG:246A CB:— TIS 5100 AG:819D CB:1272C**

For OTHER SIDE and OTHER WAY see SIDE and WAY

OTHERWISE

1. ALLOS (ἄλλος) is used, in its neuter form, *allo*, in Gal. 5 : 10, lit., ' another thing,' with the meaning " otherwise." See OTHER, No. 1. **243 AG:39D CB:1234C**

2. ALLŌS (ἄλλως), the adverb corresponding to No. 1, is translated " otherwise " in 1 Tim. 5 : 25 ; the contrast is not with works that are not good (No. 3 would signify that), but with good works which are not evident.¶ **247 AG:41A CB:1234C**

3. HETERŌS (ἑτέρως) is used in Phil. 3 : 15, " otherwise (minded)," i.e. differently minded.¶ Contrast No. 2, and for the corresponding difference between the adjectives *allos* and *heteros*, see ANOTHER. **2088 AG:315C CB:1250A**

4. EPEI (ἐπεί), when used of time, means since or when ; used of cause, it means since, because ; used elliptically it means otherwise or else ; " otherwise " in Rom. 11 : 6 (the 2nd part of the ver. is absent from the most authentic mss.) ; ver. 22 ; in Heb. 9 : 17, A.V., " otherwise (it is of no strength at all)," R.V., " for (doth it ever avail ?)." See ELSE. **1893 AG:284A CB:—**

Note : The phrase *ei*, if, *de*, but, *mēge*, not indeed, i.e., ' but if not indeed,' is translated " otherwise " in the A.V. of Matt. 6 : 1 ; Luke 5 : 36 (R.V., " else," in each place) ; in 2 Cor. 11 : 16, A.V., " if otherwise " (R.V., " but if *ye do* "). See also TEACH.

For the pronoun OUGHT (A.V.) see AUGHT

OUGHT (Verb)

1163 AG:172A CB:1240B

1. DEI (δεῖ) denotes ' it is necessary,' one must ; in Luke 24 : 26,

A.V., " ought " (R.V., " behoved it ") ; the neuter of the present participle, used as a noun, is translated " things which they ought (not) " in 1 Tim. 5 : 13 ; in Acts 19 : 36, " ye ought " (see NEED). See MUST, No. 1.

3784 AG:598D 2. OPHEILŌ (ὀφείλω), to owe, is translated " ought," with various
CB:1261A personal pronouns, in John 13 : 14 ; 19 : 7 ; Acts 17 : 29 ; Rom. 15 : 1 ;
Heb. 5 : 3, A.V. (R.V., " he is bound ") ; 5 : 12 ; 1 John 3 : 16 ; 4 : 11 ;
3 John 8 ; with other subjects in 1 Cor. 11 : 7, 10 ; 2 Cor. 12 : 14 ; Eph.
5 : 28 ; 1 John 2 : 6. See BEHOVE, OWE, etc.

5534 AG:885B 3. CHRĒ (χρή), an impersonal verb (akin to *chraomai*, to use), occurs in
CB:1240A Jas. 3 : 10, " (these things) ought (not so to be)," lit., ' it is not befitting,
these things so to be.'¶

OUR, OURS

HēMEIS 2249 *Notes :* (1) This usually translates *hēmōn*, the genitive of *hēmeis*, " we,"
AG:217A lit., ' of us,' e.g., Matt. 6 : 9, 11, 12. It is translated " ours," e.g., in
(EGo) Mark 12 : 7 ; Luke 20 : 14 ; 1 Cor. 1 : 2 ; 2 Cor. 1 : 14. (2) In 1 John
CB:— 4 : 17, the phrase *meta hēmōn*, rendered " our (love) " in the A.V., is
accurately translated in the R.V. " (herein is love made perfect) with
us," i.e., Divine love in Christ finds its expression in our manifestation
of it to others. (3) In Luke 17 : 5, " increase our faith " is, lit., ' add
faith to us.' (4) In Luke 24 : 22, " of our company " is, lit., ' from
HēMETEROS 2251 among us.' (5) *Hēmeteros*, a possessive pronoun, more emphatic than
AG:347D *hēmeis*, is used in Luke 16 : 12, in the best mss. (some have *humeteros*,
CB:1250A ' your own ') ; Acts 2 : 11 ; 24 : 6, in some mss. ; 26 : 5 ; 2 Tim. 4 : 15 ;
Tit. 3 : 14, " ours ; " 1 John 1 : 3 ; 2 : 2, " ours." (6) In Luke 23 : 41,
" of our deeds," is, lit., ' of what things we practised.' (7) In 1 Cor.
9 : 10, " for our sake," R.V. (twice), is, lit., ' on account of us.'

OUR OWN

1438 AG:211D 1. HEAUTŌN (ἑαυτῶν) is sometimes used as a reflexive pronoun of
CB:1249B the 1st person plural, signifying our own selves, translated " our own "
(-OS) in 1 Thess. 2 : 8, lit., ' (the souls) of ourselves.'

2398 AG:369C 2. IDIOS (ἴδιος), one's own, signifies " our own " in Acts 3 : 12 ;
CB:1252C 1 Cor. 4 : 12 ; in Acts 2 : 8, with *hēmōn*, forming a strong possessive,
lit., ' each in his own language of us.'

AUTOS 846

OURSELVES

AG:122C *Notes :* (1) This translates (*a*) *autoi*, the plural of *autos*, self, used
CB:1238B HēMEIS emphatically either alone, e.g., John 4 : 42 ; Rom. 8 : 23 (1st part) ;
2249 2 Cor. 1 : 4 (last part) ; 1 : 9, R.V., " we ourselves " (1st part) ; or joined
AG:217A with the plural pronouns, e.g., *hēmeis*, we, Rom. 8 : 23 (2nd part) ; (*b*) the
(EGo) HEAUTOU plural *hemeis* alone, e.g., Tit. 3 : 3 ; in 2 Cor. 4 : 7, R.V., *ex hēmōn*, is
1438 translated " from ourselves " (A.V., " of us ") ; (*c*) *heautōn*, governed by
AG:211D CB:1249B (-OS) the preposition *apo*, from, e.g., 2 Cor. 3 : 5 (1st part), lit., ' from ourselves '

(" of ourselves," in the text); (*d*) *heautois*, the dative case of (*c*), e.g., Rom. 15 : 1; governed by *en*, in, 2 Cor. 1 : 9 (1st part); by *epi*, on (2nd part). (*e*) *heautous*, the accusative case, e.g., Acts 23 : 14; 2 Cor. 3 : 1; 4 : 2, 5. (2) In Acts 6 : 4, A.V., *proskartereō*, to continue stedfastly (R.V.), is translated " give ourselves continually." (3) In 2 Cor. 10 : 12, A.V., *enkrinō*, to number (R.V.), is translated " to make ourselves of the number."

OUT, OUT OF

Notes : (1) The preposition *ek* (or *ex*), which frequently signifies " out **EK**
of " or " from the midst of," has a variety of meanings, among which **1537 AG:234A**
is " from," as virtually equivalent to *apo*, away from, e.g., 2 Cor. 1 : 10, **CB:1243B**
" who delivered us out of so great a death, and will deliver ; " since death **KATA**
was not actually experienced, but was impending, *ek* here does not signify **2596 AG:405C**
" out of the midst of." In Acts 12 : 7 it is used in the statement " his **CB:1253C**
chains fell off from his hands." In Matt. 17 : 9 it is used of descending **EKTOS 1622**
from a mountain, not ' out of ; ' " we are not to suppose that they had **AG:246A CB:—**
been in a cave " (Dr. A. T. Robertson, *Gram. of the Greek N.T.*). In 1 Thess. 1 : 10, " even Jesus, which delivereth us from the wrath to come," R.V., the question whether *ek* here means ' out of the midst of ' or ' away from,' is to be determined by some statement of Scripture where the subject is specifically mentioned ; this is provided, e.g., in 5 : 9, the context of which makes clear that believers are to be delivered from (not ' out of ') the Divine wrath to be executed on the nations at the end of the present age. (2) For the phrase *ek mesou*, " out of the way," see MIDST, Note (1), (*e*). (3) In Luke 8 : 4, A.V., the phrase *kata polin* is translated " out of every city " (R.V., " of every city," to be taken in connection with " they "). (4) *Ektos*, outside of, is translated " out of " in 2 Cor. 12 : 2 ; in 12 : 3 the best mss. have *chōris*, " apart from," R.V. (A.V., *ektos*, " out of "). (4) For other prepositions, and adverbs, see † **p. 1.**

OUTCOME See END

OUTER

EXŌTEROS (ἐξώτερος), the comparative degree of *exō*, without, is used of the outer darkness, Matt. 8 : 12 ; 22 : 13 ; 25 : 30.¶ **1857 AG:280A CB:—**

OUTGO

PROERCHOMAI (προέρχομαι), to go forward, go in advance, outgo, is used of time in Mark 6 : 33, " outwent," of the people who in their eagerness reached a spot earlier than Christ and His disciples. See GO, No. 17. **4281 AG:705B CB:1266C**

OUTRUN

PROTRECHŌ (προτρέχω), primarily, to run forward (*pro*, forward or before, *trechō*, to run), is used with *tachion*, more quickly, in John 20 : 4, " outran," R.V. (A.V., " did outrun "), lit., ' ran forward more quickly ; ' **4390 AG:722B CB:—**

in Luke 19 : 4, "he ran on before," R.V. (A.V., "ran before"). See RUN.¶ In the Sept., 1 Sam. 8 : 11; in some texts, Job 41 : 13, "destruction runneth before him," in the Eng. Versions, ver. 22.¶

OUTSIDE

1855 AG:279D 1. EXŌTHEN (ἔξωθεν), an adverb formed from *exō*, without, properly
CB:— signifies 'from without,' Mark 7 : 18 (in ver. 15 it is used as a preposition); with the article it is equivalent to a noun, "the outside," Matt. 23 : 25 (for ver. 27, see OUTWARD, No. 2); Luke 11 : 39; in ver. 40, R.V., "the outside" (A.V., "that which is without"). See OUTWARD, OUTWARDLY, WITHOUT.

1622 AG:246A 2. EKTOS (ἐκτός) is once used with the article, "the outside," Matt.
CB:— 23 : 26. See EXCEPT, No. 1.

OUTSIDER See WITHOUT

OUTWARD, OUTWARDLY

1854 AG:279B 1. EXŌ (ἔξω), without, is used metaphorically of the physical frame,
CB:1247C "the outward man," 2 Cor. 4 : 16. See WITHOUT.

1855 AG:279D 2. EXŌTHEN (ἔξωθεν) is translated "outward" in Matt. 23 : 27 (R.V., "outwardly"); it is used with the article, adjectivally, in 1 Pet.
CB:— 3 : 3, of outward adorning. See OUTSIDE, No. 1.

PHANEROS 5318 AG:852B CB:1263C *Notes:* (1) The phrase *en tǭ phanerǭ*, lit., 'in the open' (manifest), is rendered "outwardly" in Rom. 2 : 28. (2) For "with outward shew," A.V., marg., Luke 17 : 20, see OBSERVATION. (3) For the A.V., of 2 Cor. 10 : 7, "outward appearance," see FACE, No. 1.

OVEN

2823 AG:436B KLIBANOS (κλίβανος) is mentioned in Matt. 6 : 30 and Luke 12 : 28.
CB:— The form of oven commonly in use in the east indicates the kind in use as mentioned in Scripture. A hole is sunk in the ground about 3 feet deep and somewhat less in diameter. The walls are plastered with cement. A fire is kindled inside, the fuel being grass, or dry twigs, which heat the oven rapidly and blacken it with smoke and soot (see Lam. 5 : 10). When sufficiently heated the surface is wiped, and the dough is moulded into broad thin loaves, placed one at a time on the wall of the oven to fit its concave inner circle. The baking takes a few seconds. Such ovens are usually outside the house, and often the same oven serves for several families (Lev. 26 : 26). An oven of this sort is doubtless referred to in Ex. 8 : 3 (see Hastings, Bib. Dic.).¶

OVER, OVER AGAINST: see Note † p 1

OVER (to be, to have)

4291 AG:707A 1. PROISTĒMI (προΐστημι), lit., 'to stand before,' hence to lead, to
CB:— direct, attend to, is translated 'rule,' with reference to the family, in 1 Tim. 3 : 4, 5, 12; with reference to the church, in Rom. 12 : 8; 1 Thess.

5 : 12, " are over ; " 1 Tim. 5 : 17. In Tit. 3 : 8, 14, it signifies to maintain. See MAINTAIN.¶

2. PLEONAZŌ (πλεονάζω), used intransitively, signifies to abound, 4121
to superabound ; in 2 Cor. 8 : 15 it is used with the negative *ou*, " had AG:667B CB:1265B
nothing over," lit., 'had not more' (*pleon*, the comparative degree of *polus*, much).

For OVERBOARD, Acts 27 : 18, R.V., see FREIGHT, and, in 27 : 43, R.V., see CAST, No. 11.

BAREō 916

OVERCHARGE AG:133C

1. BAREŌ (βαρέω), or *barunō*, is rendered " overcharged " in Luke CB:1238C BARUNō
21 : 34. See BURDEN, B, No. 1. 925
2. EPIBAREŌ (ἐπιβαρέω) is rendered " overcharge " in 2 Cor. 2 : 5, AG:134B CB:1238C
A.V. See BURDEN, B, No. 2, and PRESS. EPIBAREō 1912 AG:290B

OVERCOME CB:1245C

1. NIKAŌ (νικάω) is used (*a*) of God, Rom. 3 : 4 (a law term), R.V., 3528
" mightest prevail ; " (*b*) of Christ, John 16 : 33 ; Rev. 3 : 21 ; 5 : 5 ; AG:539A CB:1259C
17 : 14 ; (*c*) of His followers, Rom. 12 : 21 (2nd part) ; 1 John 2 : 13, 14 ; 4 : 4 ; 5 : 4, 5 ; Rev. 2 : 7, 11, 17, 26 ; 3 : 5, 12, 21 ; 12 : 11 ; 15 : 2 ; 21 : 7 ; (*d*) of faith, 1 John 5 : 4 ; (*e*) of evil (Passive Voice), Rom. 12 : 21 ; (*f*) of predicted human potentates, Rev. 6 : 2 ; 11 : 7 ; 13 : 7.¶

2. HĒTTAOMAI (ἡττάομαι), to be made inferior, be enslaved, is 2274 (-Oō)
rendered " is (are) overcome," in 2 Pet. 2 : 19, 20. See INFERIOR. AG:349C CB:—

3. KATAKURIEUŌ (κατακυριεύω) is translated " overcome " in 2634
Acts 19 : 16 ; see MASTER, B. AG:412C CB:1254A

OVERFLOW, OVERFLOWING

A. Verbs.

1. HUPERPERISSEUŌ (ὑπερπερισσεύω), to abound more exceedingly, 5248
Rom. 5 : 20, is used in the Middle Voice in 2 Cor. 7 : 4, R.V., " I overflow AG:841D CB:1252A
(with joy)," A.V., " I am exceeding (joyful)." See ABUNDANCE, B, No. 2.

2. KATAKLUZŌ (κατακλύζω), to inundate, deluge (*kata*, down, 2626
kluzō, to wash or dash over, said, e.g., of the sea), is used in the Passive AG:411D CB:—
Voice in 2 Pet. 3 : 6, of the Flood.¶

B. Noun.

PERISSEIA (περισσεία) is translated " overflowing " in Jas. 1 : 21, 4050 AG:650C
R.V. See ABUNDANCE, A, No. 2. CB:1263C

OVERJOYED See REJOICE

OVERLAY

PERIKALUPTŌ (περικαλύπτω) denotes to cover around, cover up, 4028
or over ; it is translated " overlaid " in Heb. 9 : 4. See BLINDFOLD, AG:647D CB:—
COVER.

OVERLOOK

5237 AG:841D HUPEREIDON (ὑπερεῖδον), to overlook (an aorist form), is used in
(-RORAō) Acts 17 : 30, R.V. (A.V., "winked at"), i.e., God bore with them without
CB:— interposing by way of punishment, though the debasing tendencies of
idolatry necessarily developed themselves.¶

OVERMUCH

4054 AG:651C PERISSOTEROS (περισσότερος), the comparative degree of *perissos*,
CB:1263C abundant, is translated "overmuch" in 2 Cor. 2 : 7. See ABUNDANCE, C,
No. 2.

HPEREKTEINō *Notes:* (1) In 2 Cor. 10 : 14, R.V., the verb *huperekteinō*, to stretch
5239 AG:840D out over, is translated "we stretch (not ourselves) overmuch" (A.V.,
CB:— . . . beyond *our measure*"). See STRETCH.¶ (2) In 2 Cor. 12 : 7
HUPERAIRō 5229 (twice), R.V., *huperairō*, in the Middle Voice, to uplift oneself, is translated
(-OMAI) "I should (not) be exalted overmuch," A.V., ". . . above measure."
AG:839D CB:— See EXALT.

OVER-RIPE

3583 XĒRAINŌ (ξηραίνω) denotes to dry up, wither, translated in Rev.
AG:548C CB:1273B 14 : 15, "over-ripe," R.V. (A.V., "ripe"), said figuratively of the harvest
of the earth, symbolizing the condition of the world, political, especially
OVERPOWER See connected with Israel (Joel 3 : 9, 14), and religious, comprehensive of the
OVERCOME whole scene of Christendom (Matt. 13 : 38). See DRY.

For OVERSEER see BISHOP

OVERSHADOW

1982 1. EPISKIAZŌ (ἐπισκιάζω), to throw a shadow upon (*epi*, over,
AG:298D CB:1246A *skia*, a shadow), to overshadow, is used (*a*) of the bright cloud at the
Transfiguration, Matt. 17 : 5 ; Mark 9 : 7 ; Luke 9 : 34 ; (*b*) metaphorically
of the power of "the Most High" upon the Virgin Mary, Luke 1 : 35 ;
(*c*) of the Apostle Peter's shadow upon the sick, Acts 5 : 15.¶

2683 2. KATASKIAZŌ (κατασκιάζω), lit., to shadow down, is used of the
AG:418D CB:— "overshadowing" (R.V.) of the cherubim of glory above the mercy-seat,
Heb. 9 : 5 (A.V., "shadowing").¶

OVERSIGHT (exercise, take)

1983 EPISKOPEŌ (ἐπισκοπέω), lit., to look upon (*epi*, upon, *skopeō*, to look
AG:298D at, contemplate), is found in 1 Pet. 5 : 2 (some ancient authorities omit it),
CB:1246A "exercising the oversight," R.V. (A.V., "taking . . ."); "exercising"
is the right rendering ; the word does not imply the entrance upon such
responsibility, but the fulfilment of it. It is not a matter of assuming a
position, but of the discharge of the duties. The word is found elsewhere
in Heb. 12 : 15, "looking carefully," R.V. See LOOK.¶ Cp. *episkopē*
in 1 Tim. 3 : 1 (see BISHOP, No. 2).

OVERTAKE

1. KATALAMBANŌ (καταλαμβάνω), to lay hold of, has the significance 2638
of overtaking, metaphorically, in John 12 : 35 (R.V., " overtake," A.V., AG:412D CB:1254A
" come upon ") and 1 Thess. 5 : 4. See APPREHEND, No. 1. (-OMAI)

2. PROLAMBANŌ (προλαμβάνω), to anticipate (*pro*, before, *lambanō*, 4301
to take), is used of the act of Mary, in Mark 14 : 8 [see COME, Note (2)] ; AG:708B CB:1266C
of forestalling the less favoured at a social meal, 1 Cor. 11 : 21 ; of being overtaken in any trespass, Gal. 6 : 1, where the meaning is not that of detecting a person in the act, but of his being caught by the trespass, through his being off his guard (see 5 : 21 and contrast the premeditated practice of evil in 5 : 26). The modern Greek Version is ' even if a man, through lack of circumspection, should fall into any sin.' See TAKE.¶

OVERTHROW (Noun and Verb)

A. Noun.

KATASTROPHĒ (καταστροφή), lit., a turning down (*kata*, down, 2692
strophē, a turning ; Eng., catastrophe), is used (*a*) literally, 2 Pet. 2 : 6 ; AG:419B CB:—
(*b*) metaphorically, 2 Tim. 2 : 14, " subverting," i.e., the overthrowing of faith.¶ Cp. *kathairesis*, a pulling down, 2 Cor. 10 : 4, 8 ; 13 : 10.¶

B. Verbs.

1. KATASTREPHŌ (καταστρέφω), akin to A, lit. and primarily, 2690
to turn down or turn over, as, e.g., the soil, denotes to overturn, over- AG:419A CB:—
throw, Matt. 21 : 12 ; Mark 11 : 15 ; in Acts 15 : 16, Passive Voice,
" ruins," lit., ' the overthrown (things) of it ' (some mss. have *kataskaptō*, KATASKAPTŌ 2679
to dig down). See RUIN.¶ AG:418B

2. ANASTREPHŌ (ἀναστρέφω) is found in some mss. in John 2 : 15 390 AG:61B
(see No. 3). See ABIDE, No. 8. CB:1235B

3. ANATREPŌ (ἀνατρέπω), lit., to turn up or over (*ana*, up, *trepō*, to 396
turn), to upset, is used (*a*) literally, in the most authentic mss., in John AG:62C CB:—
2 : 15 (see No. 2) ; (*b*) metaphorically, in 2 Tim. 2 : 18, " overthrow (the faith of some) ; " in Tit. 1 : 11, R.V., " overthrow (whole houses)," A.V., " subvert . . . ," i.e., households. Moulton and Milligan (Vocab.) give an apt illustration from a 2nd cent. papyrus, of the complete upsetting of a family by the riotous conduct of a member.¶

4. KATALUŌ (καταλύω), lit., to loosen down, signifies to overthrow in 2647
Acts 5 : 38, R.V., "it will be overthrown" (A.V., "it will come to nought"); AG:414B CB:1254A
Rom. 14 : 20, R.V., " overthrow " (A.V., " destroy "). See DESTROY.

5. KATASTRŌNNUMI (καταστρώννυμι), primarily, to strew or spread 2693
over (*kata*, down, *strōnnumi*, or *strōnnuō*, to spread), then, to overthrow, AG:419B CB:—
has this meaning in 1 Cor. 10 : 5, " they were overthrown."¶ In the
Sept., Numb. 14 : 16 ; Job 12 : 23.¶ OVERTURN See OVERTHROW

OWE

A. Verbs.

1. OPHEILŌ (ὀφείλω), to owe, to be a debtor (in the Passive Voice, 3784 AG:598D CB:1261A

to be owed, to be due), is translated by the verb to owe in Matt. 18 : 28
(twice) ; Luke 7 : 41 ; 16 : 5, 7 ; Rom. 13 : 8 ; in 15 : 27, R.V., " they
(Gentile converts) owe it " (A.V., " it is their duty ") ; Philm. 18. See
BEHOVE, DEBT, DUE, DUTY, GUILTY, INDEBTED, MUST, NEED, OUGHT.
4359 AG:717D 2. PROSOPHEILŌ (προσοφείλω), to owe besides (*pros*, in addition,
CB:— and No. 1), is used in Philm. 19, " thou owest (to me even thine own self)
besides," i.e., ' thou owest me already as much as Onesimus' debt, and in
addition even thyself ' (not ' thou owest me much more ').

B. Noun.

3781 AG:598B OPHEILETĒS (ὀφειλέτης), a debtor (akin to A, No. 1), is translated
CB:1261A " which owed " in Matt. 18 : 24, lit., ' a debtor (of ten thousand talents).'
See DEBTOR.

GNēSIOS 1103 AG:162D

OWN (Adjective)

CB:1248B *Notes :* (1) *Gnēsios*, primarily, lawfully begotten, and hence ' true,'
MENō 3306 ' genuine,' is translated " own " in the A.V. of 1 Tim. 1 : 2 and Tit. 1 : 4
AG:503C (R.V., " true "). See SINCERITY, TRUE. (2) In Acts 5 : 4, " was it not
CB:1258B thine own ? " is, lit., ' did it not remain (*menō*) to thee ? ' (3) In Jude 6
HEAUTOU 1438 (1st part), A.V., *heautōn*, of themselves, " their own " (R.V.), is rendered
AG:211D " their ; " in the 2nd part, R.V., *idios*, one's own, is translated " their
CB:1249B (-OS) proper " (A.V., " their own "). (4) In Gal. 1 : 14, R.V., *sunēlikiōtēs*, is
IDIOS 2398 rendered " of mine own age " (A.V., " my equals ; " marg., " equals in
AG:369C years ").¶ (5) For " its own " in 1 Tim. 2 : 6, R.V., see DUE, A. (6) For
CB:1252C association with other words see ACCORD, BUSINESS, COMPANY, CONCEITS,
SUNēLIKIoTēS 4915 COUNTRY.
AG:789D CB:—

OWNER

2962 AG:458D II. 1. KURIOS (κύριος), one having power (*kuros*) or authority, a lord,
CB:1256B master, signifies an owner in Luke 19 : 33. See LORD, MASTER, SIR.
3490 AG:534B 2. NAUKLĒROS (ναύκληρος), a ship owner (*naus*, a ship, *klēros*, a lot),
CB:— a shipmaster, occurs in Acts 27 : 11, " (the) owner of the ship."¶

OWNETH

EIMI 1510 *Note :* In Acts 21 : 11, " that owneth this girdle," is lit., ' whose is
AG:222D (*esti*) this girdle.'
CB:1243A

OX

1016 AG:146C 1. BOUS (βοῦς) denotes an ox or a cow, Luke 13 : 15 ; 14 : 5, 19 ;
CB:1239B John 2 : 14, 15 ; 1 Cor. 9 : 9 (twice) ; 1 Tim. 5 : 18.¶
5022 AG:806B 2. TAUROS (ταῦρος), Latin *taurus*, is translated " oxen " in Matt.
CB:1271A 22 : 4 and Acts 14 : 13 ; " bulls " in Heb. 9 : 13 and 10 : 4.¶

P

PAGAN See GENTILE

PAIN (Noun and Verb)

A. Nouns.

1. PONOS (πόνος) is translated " pain " in Rev. 16 : 10 ; 21 : 4 ; " pains " in 16 : 11. See LABOUR. 4192 AG:691C CB:1266A

2. ŌDIN (ὠδίν), a birth pang, travail-pain, is rendered " travail," metaphorically, in Matt. 24 : 8 and Mark 13 : 8, R.V. (A.V., " sorrows ") ; by way of comparison, in 1 Thess. 5 : 3 ; translated " pains (of death)," Acts 2 : 24 (R.V., " pangs "). See SORROW, TRAVAIL.¶ Cp. *ōdinō*, to travail in birth. 5604 AG:895C CB:1260B

B. Verb.

BASANIZŌ (βασανίζω) primarily signifies to rub on the touchstone, to put to the test (from *basanos*, a touchstone, a dark stone used in testing metals) ; hence, to examine by torture, and, in general, to distress ; in Rev. 12 : 2, " in pain," R.V. (A.V., " pained "), in connection with parturition. See TORMENT. (In the Sept., 1 Sam. 5 : 3.¶). 928 AG:134C CB:1238C

Note : For Rom. 8 : 22, " travaileth in pain together," see TRAVAIL.

For PAINFULNESS (2 Cor. 11 : 27, A.V.) see TRAVAIL

PAIR

ZEUGOS (ζεῦγος), a yoke (akin to *zeugnumi*, to yoke), is used (*a*) of beasts, Luke 14 : 19 ; (*b*) of a pair of anything ; in Luke 2 : 24, of turtle-doves. See YOKE.¶ 2201 AG:337B CB:1273C

Note: In Rev. 6 : 5, A.V., *zugos*, a yoke (akin to *zeugos*), is translated " a pair of balances " (R.V., " a balance "). See BALANCE, YOKE. 2218 AG:339D CB:1273C

PALACE

1. AULĒ (αὐλή), a court, dwelling, palace : see COURT. 833 AG:121B CB:1238B

2. PRAITŌRION (πραιτώριον) signified originally a general's (prætor's) tent. Then it was applied to the council of army officers ; then to the official residence of the Governor of a Province ; finally, to the imperial bodyguard. In the A.V. the word appears only once, Mark 15 : 16, " the hall, called Prætorium " (R.V., " within the court which is the Prætorium," marg., " palace ") ; in the Greek of the N.T. it also occurs in Matt. 27 : 27, A.V., " the common hall," marg., " the governor's house ;" R.V., ' palace," see marg. ; John 18 : 28 (twice), A.V., " the hall of judgment ;" 4232 AG:697C CB:—

and "judgment hall," marg., "Pilate's house," R.V., "palace;" 18 : 33 and 19 : 9, A.V., "judgment hall," R.V., "palace," see marg.; so in Acts 23 : 35; in Phil. 1 : 13, A.V., "in all the palace," marg., "Cæsar's court," R.V., "throughout the whole prætorian guard," marg., "in the whole Prætorium."

"In the Gospels the term denotes the official residence in Jerusalem of the Roman governor, and the various translations of it in our versions arose from a desire either to indicate the special purpose for which that residence was used on the occasion in question, or to explain what particular building was intended. But whatever building the governor occupied was the Prætorium. It is most probable that in Jerusalem he resided in the well-known palace of Herod. . . . Pilate's residence has been identified with the castle of Antonia, which was occupied by the regular garrison. The probability is that it was the same as Herod's palace. Herod's palace in Cæsarea was used as the Prætorium there, and the expression in Acts 23 : 35, marg., 'Herod's prætorium,' is abbreviated from 'the prætorium of Herod's palace.'" (Hastings' Bib. Dic.).

In Phil. 1 : 13, marg., "the whole Prætorium" has been variously explained. It has been spoken of as 'the palace,' in connection with 4 : 22, where allusion is made to believers who belong to Cæsar's household. Others have understood it of the barracks of the prætorian guard, but Lightfoot shows that this use of the word cannot be established, neither can it be regarded as referring to the barracks of the palace guard. The phrase 'and to all the rest' in 1 : 13 indicates that persons are meant. Mommsen, followed by Ramsay (*St. Paul the Traveller*, p. 357) regards it as improbable that the Apostle was committed to the prætorian guard and holds the view that Julius the centurion, who brought Paul to Rome, belonged to a corps drafted from legions in the provinces, whose duty it was to supervise the corn supply and perform police service, and that Julius probably delivered his prisoners to the Commander of his corps. Eventually Paul's case came before the prætorian council, which is the prætorium alluded to by the Apostle, and the phrase "to all the rest" refers to the audience of the trial.¶

Note: Some scholars, believing that this Epistle was written during an Ephesian imprisonment, take the Prætorium here to be the residence in Ephesus of the Proconsul of the Province of Asia, and "Cæsar's household" to be the local Imperial Civil Service (Deissmann etc.).

PALLET
See BED

PALE

5515
AG:882D
CB:1240A

CHLŌROS (χλωρός), pale green, is translated "pale" (of a horse) in Rev. 6 : 8, symbolizing death. See GREEN.

PALM (of the hand)

4474
AG:734B
CB:1268A

Note: For *rhapizō*, to strike with a rod or with the palm of the hand, Matt. 26 : 67 (cp. 5 : 39), see SMITE.¶ For *rhapisma*, a blow, with *didōmi*, to give, translated " did strike (and, struck) . . . with the palm of his hand " (A.V., in Mark 14 : 65 ; John 18 : 22), see BLOW.

PALM (palm tree)

PHOINIX (φοῖνιξ) denotes the date palm ; it is used of palm trees in John 12 : 13, from which branches were taken ; of the branches themselves in Rev. 7 : 9.¶ The palm gave its name to Phœnicia and to Phœnix in Crete, Acts 27 : 12, R.V. Jericho was the city of palm trees, Deut. 34 : 3 ; Judg. 1 : 16 ; 3 : 13 ; 2 Chron. 28 : 15. They were plentiful there in the time of Christ. 5404 AG:864B I. CB:1264E

PALSY (sick of)

A. Adjective.

PARALUTIKOS (παραλυτικός), paralytic, sick of the palsy, is found in Matt. 4 : 24 (R.V., " palsied ") ; 8 : 6 ; 9 : 2 (twice), 6 ; Mark 2 : 3, 4, 5, 9, 10 ; in some mss. Luke 5 : 24 (see B).¶ 3885 AG:620B CB:1262A

B. Verb.

PARALUŌ (παραλύω), lit., to loose from the side, hence, to set free, is used in the Passive Voice of being enfeebled by a paralytic stroke, palsied, Luke 5 : 18, R.V., " palsied " (A.V., " taken with a palsy ") ; 5 : 24 (ditto), in the best mss. ; Acts 8 : 7 (ditto) ; 9 : 33, R.V., " he was palsied " (A.V., " was sick of the palsy ") ; Heb. 12 : 12, R.V., " palsied (knees)," A.V., " feeble." See FEEBLE.¶ 3886 AG:620B CB:1262A

For PANGS, Acts 2 : 24, R.V., see PAIN

For PAPS see BREAST

PAPER

CHARTĒS (χάρτης), a sheet of paper made of strips of papyrus (whence Eng., " paper "), Eng., chart, charter, etc. ; the word is used in 2 John 12.¶ The papyrus reed grew in ancient times in great profusion in the Nile and was used as a material for writing. From Egypt its use spread to other countries and it was the universal material for writing in general in Greece and Italy during the most flourishing periods of their literature. 5489 AG:879B CB:—

The pith of the stem of the plant was cut into thin strips, placed side by side to form a sheath. Another layer was laid upon this at right angles to it. The two layers were united by moisture and pressure and frequently with the addition of glue. The sheets, after being dried and polished, were ready for use. Normally, the writing is on that side of the papyrus on which the fibres lie horizontally, parallel to the length of the roll, but where the material was scarce the writer used the other side also (cp. Rev. 5 : 1). Papyrus continued to be used until the seventh cent., A.D., when the conquest of Egypt by the Arabs led to the disuse of the material for literary purposes and the use of vellum till the 12th century.

PARABLE

3850
AG:612B
CB:1262A
1. PARABOLĒ (παραβολή) lit. denotes a placing beside (akin to *paraballō*, to throw or lay beside, to compare). It signifies a placing of one thing beside another with a view to comparison (some consider that the thought of comparison is not necessarily contained in the word). In the N.T. it is found outside the Gospels, only in Heb. 9 : 9 and 11 : 19. It is generally used of a somewhat lengthy utterance or narrative drawn from nature or human circumstances, the object of which is to set forth a spiritual lesson, e.g., those in Matt. 13 and Synoptic parallels ; sometimes it is used of a short saying or proverb, e.g., Matt. 15 : 15 ; Mark 3 : 23 ; 7 : 17 ; Luke 4 : 23 ; 5 : 36 ; 6 : 39. It is the lesson that is of value ; the hearer must catch the analogy if he is to be instructed (this is true also of a proverb). Such a narrative or saying, dealing with earthly things with a spiritual meaning, is distinct from a fable, which attributes to things what does not belong to them in nature.

Christ's parables most frequently convey truths connected with the subject of the Kingdom of God. His withholding the meaning from His hearers as He did from the multitudes, Matt. 13 : 34, was a Divine judgment upon the unworthy.

Two dangers are to be avoided in seeking to interpret the parables in Scripture, that of ignoring the important features, and that of trying to make all the details mean something.

3942
AG:629B
CB:1262B
2. PAROIMIA (παροιμία) denotes a wayside saying (from *paroimos*, by the way), a byword, maxim, or problem, 2 Pet. 2 : 22. The word is sometimes spoken of as a parable, John 10 : 6, i.e., a figurative discourse (R.V. marg., " proverb ") ; see also 16 : 25, 29, where the word is rendered " proverbs " (marg. " parables ") and " proverb."¶

PARADISE

3857
AG:614A
CB:1262A
PARADEISOS (παράδεισος) is an Oriental word, first used by the historian Xenophon, denoting the parks of Persian kings and nobles. It is of Persian origin (Old Pers. *pairidæza*, akin to Gk. *peri*, around, and *teichos*, a wall) whence it passed into Greek. See the Sept., e.g., in Neh. 2 : 8 ; Eccl. 2 : 5 ; S. of Sol. 4 : 13. The Sept. translators used it of the garden of Eden, Gen. 2 : 8, and in other respects, e.g., Numb. 24 : 6 ; Is. 1 : 30 ; Jer. 29 : 5 ; Ezek. 31 : 8, 9.

In Luke 23 : 43, the promise of the Lord to the repentant robber was fulfilled the same day ; Christ, at His death, having committed His spirit to the Father, went in spirit immediately into Heaven itself, the dwelling place of God (the Lord's mention of the place as Paradise must have been a great comfort to the malefactor ; to the oriental mind it expressed the sum total of blessedness). Thither the Apostle Paul was caught up, 2 Cor. 12 : 4, spoken of as " the third heaven " (ver. 3 does not introduce a different vision), beyond the heavens of the natural creation (see Heb. 4 : 14, R.V., with reference to the Ascension). The same region is mentioned in Rev. 2 : 7, where the " tree of life," the figurative antitype of that in Eden, held out to the overcomer, is spoken of as being in " the Paradise of God " (R.V.), marg., " garden," as in Gen. 2 : 8.¶

PARALYTIC See PALSY

For PARCEL see GROUND, No. 4

PARCHMENT

MEMBRANA (μεμβράνα) is a Latin word, properly an adjective, from *membrum*, a limb, but denoting skin, parchment. The Eng. word 'parchment' is a form of *pergamena*, an adjective signifying 'of Pergamum,' the city in Asia Minor where parchment was either invented or brought into use. The word *membrana* is found in 2 Tim. 4 : 13, where Timothy is asked to bring to the Apostle " the books, especially the parchments." The writing material was prepared from the skin of the sheep or goat. The skins were first soaked in lime for the purpose of removing the hair, and then shaved, washed, dried, stretched and ground or smoothed with fine chalk or lime and pumice-stone. The finest kind is called vellum, and is made from the skins of calves or kids.¶ **3200 AG:502A CB:—**

PARENTS

1. GONEUS (γονεύς), a begetter, a father (akin to *ginomai*, to come into being, become), is used in the plural in the N.T., Matt. 10 : 21; Mark 13 : 12; six times in Luke (in Luke 2 : 43, R.V., " His parents," A.V., " Joseph and His mother "); six in John; elsewhere, Rom. 1 : 30; 2 Cor. 12 : 14 (twice); Eph. 6 : 1; Col. 3 : 20; 2 Tim. 3 : 2.¶ **1118 AG:165A CB:—**

2. PROGONOS (πρόγονος), an adjective signifying born before (*pro*, before, and *ginomai*, see No. 1), is used as a noun, in the plural, (*a*) of ancestors, " forefathers," 2 Tim. 1 : 3; (*b*) of living parents, 1 Tim. 5 : 4. See FOREFATHER.¶ **4269 AG:704A CB:—**

3. PATĒR (πατήρ), a father, is used in Heb. 11 : 23, in the plural, of both father and mother, the " parents " of Moses. See FATHER. **3962 AG:635A CB:1262C**

PART (Noun, a portion; Verb, to give or divide, partake)

A. Nouns.

1. MEROS (μέρος) denotes (*a*) a part, portion, of the whole, e.g., John 13 : 8; Rev. 20 : 6; 22 : 19; hence, a lot or destiny, e.g., Rev. 21 : 8; in Matt. 24 : 51 and Luke 12 : 46, " portion; " (*b*) a part as opposite to the whole, e.g., Luke 11 : 36; John 19 : 23; 21 : 6, " side; " Acts 5 : 2; 23 : 6; Eph. 4 : 16; Rev. 16 : 19; a party, Acts 23 : 9; the divisions of a province, e.g., Matt. 2 : 22; Acts 2 : 10; the regions belonging to a city, e.g., Matt. 15 : 21, R.V., " parts " (A.V., " coasts "); 16 : 13 (ditto); Mark 8 : 10, A.V. and R.V., " parts; " " the lower parts of the earth," Eph. 4 : 9; this phrase means the regions beneath the earth (see LOWER, A, No. 1); (*c*) a class, or category (with *en*, in, " in respect of "), Col. 2 : 16; " in this respect," 2 Cor. 3 : 10; 9 : 3, R.V. (A.V., **3313 AG:505D CB:1258B**

“ in this behalf ”). See BEHALF, COAST, CRAFT, PIECE, PORTION, RESPECT.

3310 AG:505A 2. MERIS (*μερίς*) denotes (*a*) a part or portion, Luke 10 : 42 ; Acts
CB:1258B 8 : 21 ; 2 Cor. 6 : 15 (R.V., “ portion ”) ; in Col. 1 : 12, “ partakers,”
lit., ‘ unto the part of ; ’ (*b*) a district or division, Acts 16 : 12, R.V.,
“ district ” (A.V., “ part ”). See DISTRICT, PARTAKER.¶

2824 AG:436B 3. KLIMA (*κλίμα*), primarily an incline, slope (Eng., clime, climate),
CB:— is used of a region, Rom. 15 : 23, A.V., “ parts ” (R.V., “ regions ”) ;
2 Cor. 11 : 10, A.V. and R.V., “ regions ; ” Gal. 1 : 21 (ditto). See
REGION.¶

2078 AG:313D 4. ESCHATOS (*ἔσχατος*), an adjective signifying last, utmost, extreme,
CB:1246C is often used as a noun ; in Acts 13 : 47, R.V., “ uttermost part ” (A.V.,
“ ends ”). See END, LAST, LOWEST, UTTERMOST.

5117 AG:822B 5. TOPOS (*τόπος*), a place, is translated “ parts ” in Acts 16 : 3, R.V.
CB:1273A (A.V., “ quarters ”). See PLACE, etc.

6. The plural of the article, followed first by the particle ***men***, indeed, and then by ***de***, but, is translated “ part . . . and part ” in Acts 14 : 4.

4009 7. PERAS (*πέρας*), an end, boundary, is translated “ utmost parts ”
AG:644A in the A.V. of Matt. 12 : 42 and Luke 11 : 31. See END, A, No. 3.
CB:1263B

Notes : (1) *Meros* is used with certain prepositions in adverbial phrases, (*a*) with *ana*, used distributively, 1 Cor. 14 : 27, “ in turn,” R.V., A.V., “ by course ” ; (*b*) with *kata*, according to, Heb. 9 : 5, R.V., “ severally ” (A.V., “ particularly ”) ; (*c*) with *apo*, from, “ in part,” Rom. 11 : 25 ; 2 Cor. 1 : 14 ; 2 : 5 (see also MEASURE) ; (*d*) with *ek*, from, 1 Cor. 13 : 9, 10, 12 ; in 1 Cor. 12 : 27, R.V., “ severally,” marg., “ each in his part ” (A.V., “ in particular ”). (2) In Mark 4 : 38 and Acts 27 : 41, A.V.,
prumna, a stern, is translated “ hinder part ” (R.V., “ stern ”). (3) In
KLeROS Acts 1 : 17, A.V., ***klēros***, a lot, is translated “ part ” (R.V., “ portion ; ”
2819 AG:435B marg., “ lot ”), of that portion allotted to Judas in the ministry of the
CB:1255B Twelve. See INHERITANCE, LOT. (4) In Acts 1 : 25, where the best mss.
HUPER 5228 have ***topos***, a place, R.V., “ (to take) the place (in this ministry),” some
AG:838B texts have ***klēros***, which the A.V. translates “ part.” (5) In Mark 9 : 40,
CB:1252A KATA A.V., the preposition ***huper***, on behalf of, is translated “ on (our) part,”
2596 R.V., “ for (us).” (6) In 1 Pet. 4 : 14, A.V., “ on (their) part,” “ on
AG:405C CB:1253C (your) part,” represents the preposition ***kata***, according to, followed by the
PAS personal pronouns ; the statements are not found in the most authentic
3956 AG:631A mss. (7) In Acts 9 : 32, A.V., the phrase ***dia pantōn***, lit., ‘ through all,’
CB:1262C is rendered “ throughout all ***quarters*** ” (R.V., “ throughout all parts ”).
(8) In 1 Cor. 12 : 23, the R.V. has “ ***parts*** ” for “ ***members ;*** ” A.V. and R.V. have “ ***parts*** ” in the end of the ver. ; see also ver. 24. (9) In 2 Cor. 10 : 16, the R.V. translates the neuter plural of the article “ the parts ” (A.V., “ the ***regions*** ”). (10) For “ inward part ” see INWARD.

B. Verbs.

3307 AG:504C 1. MERIZŌ (*μερίζω*), to divide, to distribute (akin to A, No. 1), is
CB:1258B translated “ divided (A.V., gave) a . . . part ” in Heb. 7 : 2, R.V. See
DEAL.

2. METECHŌ (μετέχω), to partake of, share in, Heb. 2 : 14 : see 3348 AG:514A
PARTAKE. CB:1258C

3. PARAGINOMAI (παραγίνομαι), to be beside, support (*para*, beside, 3854
ginomai, to become), is rendered " took (my) part " in 2 Tim. 4 : 16 (A.V., AG:613C CB:—
" stood with ") ; some mss. have *sunparaginomai*. See COME, No. 13, GO, PRESENT (to be).

Notes : (1) In Rev. 6 : 8, *tetartos*, a fourth, is rendered " the fourth 5067
part." (2) See GREATER, HINDER, INWARD, MORE, TENTH, THIRD, AG:813C CB:—
UTMOST, UTTERMOST.

PART (Verb, to separate)

1. DIAMERIZŌ (διαμερίζω), to part among, to distribute, is trans- 1266
lated by the verb to part (*a*) in the Middle Voice, with reference to the AG:186D CB:—
Lord's garments, Matt. 27 : 35, 1st part (in some mss., 2nd part) ; Mark 15 : 24 ; Luke 23 : 34 ; John 19 : 24 ; (*b*) in the Active Voice, of the proceeds of the sale of possessions and goods, Acts 2 : 45 ; (*c*) in the Passive Voice in Acts 2 : 3, of the " parting asunder " (R.V.) of tongues like fire (A.V., " cloven "). See CLOVEN, DIVIDE, No. 7.

2. DIISTĒMI (διίστημι), to set apart, separate (*dia*, apart, *histēmi*, to 1339
cause to stand), is used in the Active Voice in Luke 24 : 51, R.V., " He AG:195B CB:—
parted (from them)," A.V., " was parted." See GO, SPACE.

3. APOSPAŌ (ἀποσπάω), to draw off or tear away, is used in the 645
Passive Voice in Luke 22 : 41, R.V., " He was parted " (A.V., " was with- AG:98A CB:—
drawn "), lit. ' He was torn away,' indicating the reluctance with which Christ parted from the loving sympathy of the disciples. Moulton and Milligan suggest that the ordinary use of the verb does not encourage this stronger meaning, but since the simpler meaning is not found in the N.T., except in Acts 21 : 1, and since the idea of withdrawal is expressed in Matt. by *anachōreō*, Luke may have used *apospaō* here in the stronger sense. See DRAW, A, No. 6.

4. CHŌRIZŌ (χωρίζω), in Philm. 15, R.V., " parted : " see DEPART, 5563 AG:890A
No. 13. CB:1240A

5. APOCHŌRIZŌ (ἀποχωρίζω), to part from, Acts 15 : 39, R.V. : 673 AG:102B
see DEPART, No. 14. CB:—

PARTAKE, PARTAKER

A. Nouns.

1. KOINŌNOS (κοινωνός), an adjective, signifying having in common 2844
(*koinos*, common), is used as a noun, denoting a companion, partner, AG:439C CB:1255B
partaker, translated " partakers " in Matt. 23 : 30 ; 1 Cor. 10 : 18, A.V. (see COMMUNION, B) ; 2 Cor. 1 : 7 ; Heb. 10 : 33, R.V. (see COMPANION, No. 2) ; 2 Pet. 1 : 4 ; " partaker " in 1 Pet. 5 : 1. See PARTNER.

2. SUNKOINŌNOS (συγκοινωνός) denotes partaking jointly with 4791
(*sun*, and No. 1), Rom. 11 : 17, R.V., " (didst become) partaker with AG:774B CB:1270C
them " (A.V., " partakest ") ; 1 Cor. 9 : 23, R.V., " a joint partaker,"

i.e., with the Gospel, as co-operating in its activity; the A.V. misplaces the "with" by attaching it to the superfluous italicised pronoun "*you*"; Phil. 1 : 7, "partakers with (me of grace)," R.V., and A.V. marg.; not as A.V. text, "partakers (of my grace);" Rev. 1 : 9, "partaker with
3353 (you in the tribulation, etc.)," A.V., "companion." See COMPANION.¶

AG:514C 3. METOCHOS (μέτοχος): see FELLOW, No. 3, PARTNER.
CB:1258C

4830 4. SUMMETOCHOS (συμμέτοχος), partaking together with (*sun*,
AG:778C with, and No. 3), is used as a noun, a joint-partaker, Eph. 3 : 6, R.V.,
CB:— "fellow-partakers" (A.V., "partakers"); in 5 : 7, R.V. and A.V., "partakers."¶

482 *Notes:* (1) For *antilambanō*, to partake of, rendered "partakers"
AG:74C
CB:— in 1 Tim. 6 : 2, A.V., see B, No. 4. (2) For the phrase "to be partakers," Col. 1 : 12, see PART, A, No. 2.

B. Verbs.

2841
AG:438C 1. KOINŌNEŌ (κοινωνέω), to have a share of, to share with, take part
CB:1255B in (akin to A, No. 1), is translated to be partaker of in 1 Tim. 5 : 22; Heb. 2 : 14 (1st part), A.V., "are partakers of," R.V., "are sharers in" (for the 2nd part see No. 3); 1 Pet. 4 : 13; 2 John 11, R.V., "partaketh in" (A.V., "is partaker of"); in the Passive Voice in Rom. 15 : 27. See
4790
AG:774B COMMUNICATE, DISTRIBUTE.
CB:1270C 2. SUNKOINŌNEŌ (συγκοινωνέω): see FELLOWSHIP, B, No. 2.
3348
AG:514A 3. METECHŌ (μετέχω), to partake of, share in (*meta*, with, *echō*, to
CB:1258C have), akin to A, No. 3, is translated "of partaking" in 1 Cor. 9 : 10, R.V. (A.V., "be partaker of"); "partake of" in 9 : 12, R.V. (A.V., "be partakers of"); so in 10 : 17, 21; in ver. 30 "partake"; in Heb. 2 : 14, the A.V. "took part of" is awkward; Christ "partook of" flesh and blood, R.V.; cp. No. 1 in this verse; in Heb. 5 : 13, metaphorically, of receiving elementary spiritual teaching, R.V., "partaketh of (milk)," A.V., "useth;" in Heb. 7 : 13, it is said of Christ (the antitype of Melchizedek) as 'belonging to' (so R.V.) or 'partaking of' (R.V. marg.) another tribe than that of Levi (A.V., "pertaineth to"). See PERTAIN, USE.¶ See PARTNER, Note.

482
AG:74C 4. ANTILAMBANŌ (ἀντιλαμβάνω), to take hold of, to lay hold of
CB:— something before one, has the meaning to partake of in 1 Tim. 6 : 2, R.V., "partake of," marg., "lay hold of," A.V., "are . . . partakers of" (*anti*, in return for, *lambanō*, to take or receive); the benefit mentioned as partaken of by the masters would seem to be the improved quality of the service rendered; the benefit of redemption is not in view here. See HELP.

3335
AG:511B 5. METALAMBANŌ (μεταλαμβάνω), to have, or get, a share of, is
CB:1258B translated to be partaker (or partakers) of in 2 Tim. 2 : 6 and Heb. 12 : 10. See EAT, HAVE, RECEIVE, TAKE.

4829
(-OMAI) 6. SUMMERIZŌ (συμμερίζω), primarily, to distribute in shares (*sun*,
AG:778C with, *meros*, a part), in the Middle Voice, to have a share in, is used in
CB:— 1 Cor. 9 : 13, A.V., "are partakers with (the altar)," R.V., "have their

portion with," i.e., they feed with others on that which, having been sacrificed, has been placed upon an altar; so the believer feeds upon Christ (who is the altar in Heb. 13 : 10).¶

PARTIAL, PARTIALITY

A. Verb.

DIAKRINŌ (διακρίνω), to separate, distinguish, discern, judge, decide 1252
(*dia*, asunder, *krinō*, to judge), also came to mean to be divided in one's AG:185A CB:1241A
mind, to hesitate, doubt, and had this significance in Hellenistic Greek (though not so found in the Sept.). For the A.V., "are ye (not) partial" in Jas. 2 : 4, see DIVIDE, No. 4. "'This meaning seems to have had its beginning in near proximity to Christianity.' It arises very naturally out of the general sense of making distinctions" (Moulton and Milligan).

B. Noun.

PROSKLISIS (πρόσκλισις) denotes inclination (*pros*, towards, *klinō*, 4346
to lean); it is used with *kata* in 1 Tim. 5 : 21, lit., 'according to partiality.'¶ AG:716A CB:1267A

C. Adjective.

ADIAKRITOS (ἀδιάκριτος) primarily signifies not to be parted (*a*, 87
negative, and an adjectival form akin to A), hence, without uncertainty, AG:17A CB:1233A
or indecision, Jas. 3 : 17, A.V., "without partiality" (marg. "wrangling"), R.V., "without variance" (marg., "Or, doubtfulness Or, partiality"). See VARIANCE.¶ In the Sept., Prov. 25 : 1.¶

PARTICIPATE See COMMUNION, PARTAKE

For PARTICULAR and PARTICULARLY see EVERY, No. 3, SEVERALLY

Note: In Acts 21 : 19, for the A.V. "particularly" the R.V. has "one by one," translating the phrase. lit., 'according to each one.'

For PARTING see HIGHWAY

PARTITION

PHRAGMOS (φραγμός), primarily a fencing in (akin to *phrassō*, to 5418
fence in, stop, close), is used metaphorically in Eph. 2 : 14, of "the middle AG:865C CB:1264B
wall of partition;" "the partition" is epexegetic of "the middle wall," i.e., 'the middle wall, namely, the partition' between Jew and Gentile. J. A. Robinson suggests that Paul had in mind the barrier between the outer and inner courts of the Temple, notices fixed to which warned Gentiles not to proceed further on pain of death (see Josephus, *Antiq.* xv. 11. 5; *B. J.* v. 5. 2; vi. 2. 4; cp. Acts 21 : 29). See HEDGE.

PARTLY

Notes: (1) In the statement "I partly believe it," 1 Cor. 11 : 18, "partly" represents the phrase '*meros* (part) *ti* (some),' used adverbially, i.e., 'in some part,' 'in some measure.' (2) In Heb. 10 : 33, "partly . . . partly" is a translation of the antithetic phrases '*touto men*, this indeed,' and '*touto de*, but this,' i.e., 'on the one hand . . . and on the other hand.'

PARTNER

2844 AG:439C CB:1255B 1. KOINŌNOS (κοινωνός), an adjective, signifying having in common (*koinos*), is used as a noun, " partners " in Luke 5 : 10, " partner " in 2 Cor. 8 : 23 ; Philm. 17 (in spiritual life and business). See COMMUNION, B, COMPANION, No. 2, PARTAKER.

3353 AG:514C CB:1258C 2. METOCHOS (μέτοχος), an adjective, signifying having with, sharing, is used as a noun, " partners " in Luke 5 : 7. See FELLOW, PARTAKER.

Note : *Koinōnos* stresses the fact of having something in common, *metochos*, the fact of sharing ; the latter is less thorough in effect than the former.

PARTY See REVELLING

PASS, COME TO PASS (see Notes below)

3928 AG:625D CB:1262B 1. PARERCHOMAI (παρέρχομαι), from *para*, by, *erchomai*, to come or go, denotes (I), literally, to pass, pass by, (*a*) of persons, Matt. 8 : 28 ; Mark 6 : 48 ; Luke 18 : 37 ; Acts 16 : 8 ; (*b*) of things, Matt. 26 : 39, 42 ; of time, Matt. 14 : 15 ; Mark 14 : 35 ; Acts 27 : 9, A.V., " past " (R.V., " gone by ") ; 1 Pet. 4 : 3 ; (II), metaphorically, (*a*) to pass away, to perish, Matt. 5 : 18 ; 24 : 34, 35 ; Mark 13 : 30, 31 ; Luke 16 : 17 ; 21 : 32, 33 ; 2 Cor. 5 : 17 ; Jas. 1 : 10 ; 2 Pet. 3 : 10 ; (*b*) to pass by, disregard, neglect, pass over, Luke 11 : 42 ; 15 : 29, " transgressed." For the meaning to come forth or come, see Luke 12 : 37 ; 17 : 7, R.V. (Acts 24 : 7 in some mss.). See COME, No. 9.¶

1330 AG:194C CB:1241C 2. DIERCHOMAI (διέρχομαι) denotes to pass through or over, (*a*) of persons, e.g., Matt. 12 : 43, R.V., " passeth (A.V., walketh) through ; " Mark 4 : 35, A.V., " pass (R.V., go) over ; " Luke 19 : 1, 4 ; Heb. 4 : 14, R.V., " passed through " (A.V. " into ") ; Christ passed through the created heavens to the Throne of God ; (*b*) of things, e.g., Matt. 19 : 24, " to go through ; " Luke 2 : 35, " shall pierce through " (metaphorically of a sword). See COME, No. 5.

565 AG:84C CB:1236B 3. APERCHOMAI (ἀπέρχομαι), to go away, is rendered to pass in Rev. 9 : 12 ; 11 : 14 ; " passed away " in Rev. 21 : 4. See DEPART, No. 4.

4281 AG:705B CB:1266C 4. PROERCHOMAI (προέρχομαι), to go forward, is translated " passed on " in Acts 12 : 10. See GO.

492 AG:75C CB:— 5. ANTIPARERCHOMAI (ἀντιπαρέρχομαι) denotes to pass by opposite to (*anti*, over against, and No. 1), Luke 10 : 31, 32.¶

1224 AG:181C CB:— 6. DIABAINŌ (διαβαίνω), to step across, cross over, is translated " to pass " in Luke 16 : 26 (of passing across the fixed gulf : for the A.V. in the 2nd part of the ver., see No. 13) ; in Heb. 11 : 29, " passed through." See COME, No. 18.

3327 AG:510C CB:1258B 7. METABAINŌ (μεταβαίνω), to pass over from one place to another (*meta*, implying change), is translated " we have passed out of " (A.V.,

" from ") in 1 John 3 : 14, R.V., as to the change from death to life. See REMOVE, No. 1.

8. ANASTREPHŌ (ἀναστρέφω), lit., to turn back (*ana*, back, *strephō*, 390
to turn), in the Middle Voice, to conduct oneself, behave, live, is translated AG:61B
" pass (the time) " in 1 Pet. 1 : 17. See ABIDE, No. 8. CB:1235B

9. PARAGŌ (παράγω), to pass by, pass away, in Matt. 9 : 9, R.V., 3855
" passed by " (A.V., " forth "), is used in the Middle Voice in 1 John 2 : 8, AG:613D
R.V., " is passing away " (A.V., " is past "), of the passing of spiritual CB:—
darkness through the light of the Gospel, and in ver. 17 of the world. See DEPART, No. 2.

10. PARAPOREUOMAI (παραπορεύομαι), primarily, to go beside, 3899
accompany (*para*, beside, *poreuomai*, to proceed), denotes to go past, pass AG:621D
by, Matt. 27 : 39; Mark 9 : 30, " passed through " (some mss. have CB:—
poreuomai); 11 : 20; 15 : 29; in Mark 2 : 23, " going . . . through." See GO.¶

11. DIAPOREUOMAI (διαπορεύομαι), to pass across, journey through, 1279
is used in the Middle Voice, translated " pass by " in Luke 18 : 36, A.V., AG:187D
R.V., " going by." See GO. CB:—

12. HUPERBALLŌ (ὑπερβάλλω), in Eph. 3 : 19, " passeth : " see 5235
EXCEED, A, No. 1. AG:840B

13. HUPERECHŌ (ὑπερέχω), " passeth " in Phil. 4 : 7 : see BETTER 5242
(be), No. 4. AG:840D CB:1252A

14. DIAPERAŌ (διαπεράω), to pass over, cross over (used in Luke 1276
16 : 26, 2nd part : see No. 6) : see CROSS. AG:187C CB:—

15. DIODEUŌ (διοδεύω), to travel through, or along (*dia*, through, 1353
hodos a way), is translated " they had passed through " in Acts 17 : 1, AG:198D
lit., ' having passed through ; ' in Luke 8 : 1, " He went about," R.V. CB:—
(A.V., " throughout ").¶

16. CHŌREŌ (χωρέω), used intransitively, signifies to make room, 5562
retire, pass ; in Matt. 15 : 17, R.V., " passeth (into the belly)," A.V., AG:889C
" goeth." See COME, No. 24. CB:1240A

17. KATARGEŌ (καταργέω) is translated " was passing away " in 2673
2 Cor. 3 : 7 (A.V., " was to be done away ") ; " passeth away " in 3 : 11, AG:417B
R.V. (A.V., " is done away "). See ABOLISH. CB:1254B

18. PAROICHOMAI (παροίχομαι), to have passed by, to be gone by, is 3944
used in Acts 14 : 16, of past generations, A.V., " (in times) past," R.V., AG:629B
" (in the generations) gone by."¶ CB:—

Notes : (1) *Ginomai*, to become, take place, is often translated to come GINOMAI 1096
to pass ; frequently in the Synoptic Gospels and Acts (note the R.V. of AG:158A
Luke 24 : 21) ; elsewhere in John 13 : 19 ; 14 : 22, R.V., " (what) is come CB:1248B EIMI
to pass . . . ? " A.V., " (how) is it . . . ? " ; 14 : 29 (twice) ; 1 Thess. 1510
3 : 4 ; Rev. 1 : 1. (2) In Acts 2 : 17, 21 ; 3 : 23 and Rom. 9 : 26, the AG:222D CB:1243A
A.V. translates the future of *eimi*, to be, " it shall come to pass " (R.V., ERCHOMAI
" it shall be "). (3) In Acts 5 : 15, A.V., *erchomai*, to come, is translated 2064 AG:310B
" passing by " (R.V., " came by "). (4) For the A.V., " passing " in Acts CB:1246B

27 : 8, see Coasting, C. (5) In Mark 6 : 35, A.V., " the time is far passed " (R.V., " the day is . . far spent ") is, lit., ' the hour is much (*polus*).' (6)
HUPERAKMOS 5230 AG:839D CB:1252A For *huperakmos* in 1 Cor. 7 : 36, R.V., " past the flower of her age," see Flower.

PASSING OVER

PARESIS (πάρεσις), primarily a letting go, dismissal (akin to *pariēmi*, to let alone, loosen), denotes a passing by or prætermission (of sin), a suspension of judgment, or withholding of punishment, Rom. 3 : 25, R.V., " passing over " (A.V., " remission "), with reference to sins committed previously to the propitiatory sacrifice of Christ, the passing by not being a matter of Divine disregard but of forbearance.¶

PASSION

A. Nouns.

3804 AG:602B CB:1262C 1. PATHĒMA (πάθημα), a suffering or a passive emotion, is translated " passions " in Rom. 7 : 5, R.V., " (sinful) passions," A.V., " motions,' and Gal. 5 : 24, R.V. ; see Affection, A, No. 3, Afflict, B, No. 3.

3806 AG:602D CB:1262C 2. PATHOS (πάθος) : see Affection, A, No. 1.

B. Verb.

3958 AG:633D CB:1262C PASCHŌ (πάσχω), to suffer, is used as a noun, in the aorist infinitive with the article, and translated " passion " in Acts 1 : 3, of the suffering of Christ at Calvary. See Suffer.

C. Adjective.

3663 AG:566C CB:1251A HOMOIOPATHĒS (ὁμοιοπαθής), of like feelings or affections (*homoios*, like, and A, No. 2 ; Eng., homœopathy), is rendered " of like passions " in Acts 14 : 15 (R.V. marg., " nature ") ; in Jas. 5 : 17, R.V., ditto (A.V., " subject to like passions ").¶

PASSOVER

3957 AG:633B CB:1262C PASCHA (πάσχα), the Greek spelling of the Aramaic word for the Passover, from the Hebrew *pāsach*, to pass over, to spare, a feast instituted by God in commemoration of the deliverance of Israel from Egypt, and anticipatory of the expiatory sacrifice of Christ. The word signifies (I) the Passover Feast, e.g., Matt. 26 : 2 ; John 2 : 13, 23 ; 6 : 4 ; 11 : 55 ; 12 : 1 ; 13 : 1 ; 18 : 39 ; 19 : 14 ; Acts 12 : 4 ; Heb. 11 : 28 ; (II) by metonymy, (*a*) the Paschal Supper, Matt. 26 : 18, 19 ; Mark 14 : 16 ; Luke 22 : 8, 13 ; (*b*) the Paschal lamb, e.g., Mark 14 : 12 (cp. Ex. 12 : 21) ; Luke 22 : 7 ; (*c*) Christ Himself, 1 Cor. 5 : 7.

PAST

A. Verbs.

1096 AG:158A CB:1248B 1. GINOMAI (γίνομαι), to become, come to pass, is translated " was past " in Luke 9 : 36, A.V., and R.V. marg. (R.V., " came "), of the voice of God the Father at the Transfiguration ; " is past," 2 Tim. 2 : 18.

2. DIAGINOMAI (διαγίνομαι), *dia*, through, a stronger form than No. 1, 1230
used of time, denotes to intervene, elapse, pass, Mark 16 : 1, " was past ; " AG:182B CB:—
Acts 25 : 13, R.V., " were passed ; " 27 : 9, " was spent."¶

3. PROGINOMAI (προγίνομαι), to happen before (*pro*, before, and 4266
No. 1), is used in Rom. 3 : 25, A.V., " that are past " (R.V., " done afore- AG:703C CB:1266C
time "), of sins committed in times previous to the atoning sacrifice of Christ (see PASSING OVER).¶

Note: For the past tense of the verb to pass, see PASS, e.g., Nos. 1 and 17.

B. Particle.

POTE (ποτέ), once, formerly, sometime, is translated " in time (or 4218
times) past," in Rom. 11 : 30 ; Gal. 1 : 13 ; ver. 23, A.V. (R.V., " once ") ; AG:695A CB:1266B
Eph. 2 : 2, 11 (R.V., " aforetime ") ; ver. 3 (R.V., " once ") ; Philm. 11 (R.V., " aforetime ") ; 1 Pet. 2 : 10.

PASTOR

POIMĒN (ποιμήν), a shepherd, one who tends herds or flocks (not 4166
merely one who feeds them), is used metaphorically of Christian " pastors," AG:684A CB:1265C
Eph. 4 : 11. Pastors guide as well as feed the flock ; cp. Acts 20 : 28, which, with ver. 17, indicates that this was the service committed to elders (overseers or bishops) ; so also in 1 Pet. 5 : 1, 2, " tend the flock . . . exercising the oversight," R.V. ; this involves tender care and vigilant superintendence. See SHEPHERD.

PASTURE

NOMĒ (νομή) denotes (*a*) pasture, pasturage, figuratively in John 3542
10 : 9 ; (*b*) grazing, feeding, figuratively in 2 Tim. 2 : 17, of the doctrines AG:541A CB:1260A
of false teachers, lit., ' their word will have feeding as a gangrene.' See EAT.¶

PATCH See PIECE

PATH

1. TRIBOS (τρίβος), a beaten track (akin to *tribō*, to rub, wear down), 5147
a path, is used in Matt. 3 : 3 ; Mark 1 : 3 ; Luke 3 : 4.¶ AG:826B CB:—

2. TROCHIA (τροχία), the track of a wheel (*trochos*, a wheel ; *trechō*, 5163
to run), hence, a track, path, is used figuratively in Heb. 12 : 13.¶ In AG:828A CB:—
the Sept., Prov. 2 : 15 ; 4 : 11, 26, 27 ; 5 : 6, 21 ; in some texts, Ezek. 27 : 19.¶

PATIENCE, PATIENT, PATIENTLY

A. Nouns.

1. HUPOMONĒ (ὑπομονή), lit., an abiding under (*hupo*, under, 5281
menō, to abide), is almost invariably rendered " patience." " Patience, AG:846B CB:1252B
which grows only in trial, Jas. 1 : 3, may be passive, i.e., = endurance, as, (*a*) in trials, generally, Luke 21 : 19 (which is to be understood by Matt. 24 : 13) ; cp. Rom. 12 : 12 ; Jas. 1 : 12 ; (*b*) in trials incident to service in the gospel, 2 Cor. 6 : 4 ; 12 : 12 ; 2 Tim. 3 : 10 ; (*c*) under chastisement,

which is trial viewed as coming from the hand of God our Father, Heb. 12 : 7; (*d*) under undeserved affliction, 1 Pet. 2 : 20; or active, i.e.= persistence, perseverance, as (*e*) in well doing, Rom. 2 : 7 (A.V., 'patient continuance'); (*f*) in fruit bearing, Luke 8 : 15; (*g*) in running the appointed race, Heb. 12 : 1.

"Patience perfects Christian character, Jas. 1 : 4, and fellowship in the patience of Christ is therefore the condition upon which believers are to be admitted to reign with Him, 2 Tim. 2 : 12; Rev. 1 : 9. For this patience believers are 'strengthened with all power,' Col. 1 : 11, 'through His Spirit in the inward man,' Eph. 3 : 16.

"In 2 Thess. 3 : 5, the phrase 'the patience of Christ,' R.V., is possible of three interpretations, (*a*) the patient waiting for Christ, so A.V. paraphrases the words, (*b*) that they might be patient in their sufferings as Christ was in His, see Heb. 12 : 2, (*c*) that since Christ is 'expecting till His enemies be made the footstool of His feet,' Heb. 10 : 13, so they might be patient also in their hopes of His triumph and their deliverance. While a too rigid exegesis is to be avoided, it may, perhaps, be permissible to paraphrase: 'the Lord teach and enable you to love as God loves, and to be patient as Christ is patient.'"*

In Rev. 3 : 10, "the word of My patience" is the word which tells of Christ's patience, and its effects in producing patience on the part of those who are His (see above on 2 Thess. 3 : 5).

3115 AG:488B CB:1257C 2. MAKROTHUMIA (μακροθυμία), long-suffering (see B, No. 2), is rendered "patience" in Heb. 6 : 12; Jas. 5 : 10; see LONGSUFFERING.

B. Verbs.

5278 AG:845D CB:1252B 1. HUPOMENŌ (ὑπομένω), akin to A, No. 1, (*a*) used intransitively, means to tarry behind, still abide, Luke 2 : 43; Acts 17 : 14; (*b*) transitively, to wait for, Rom. 8 : 24 (in some mss.), to bear patiently, endure, translated "patient" (present participle) in Rom. 12 : 12; "ye take it patiently," 1 Pet. 2 : 20 (twice). See also under A, No. 1.

3114 AG:488A CB:1257C 2. MAKROTHUMEŌ (μακροθυμέω), akin to A, No. 2, to be long-tempered, is translated to have patience, or to be patient, in Matt. 18 : 26, 29; 1 Thess. 5 : 14, A.V. (R.V., "be longsuffering"); Jas. 5 : 7 (1st part, "be patient;" 2nd part, R.V., "being patient," A.V., "hath long patience"); in Heb. 6 : 15, R.V., "having (A.V., after he had) patiently endured." See LONGSUFFERING.

C. Adjectives.

EPIEIKēS 1933 AG:292C CB:1245C ANEXIKAKOS 420 AG:65A CB:— *Notes:* (1) For *epieikēs*, translated "patient" in 1 Tim. 3 : 3, A.V., see GENTLE. (2) For *anexikakos*, translated "patient" in 2 Tim. 2 : 24, A.V., see FORBEAR.¶

D. Adverb.

3116 AG:488C CB:1257C MAKROTHUMŌS (μακροθύμως), akin to A, No. 2, and B, No. 2, denotes "patiently," Acts 26 : 3.¶

* From Notes on Thessalonians by Hogg and Vine, pp. 222, 285.

PATRIARCH

PATRIARCHĒS (πατριάρχης), from *patria*, a family, and *archō*, to 3966
rule, is found in Acts 2 : 29 ; 7 : 8, 9 ; Heb. 7 : 4.¶ In the Sept., 1 Chron. AG:636D CB:—
24 : 31 ; 27 : 22 ; 2 Chron. 19 : 8 ; 23 : 20 ; 26 : 12.¶

PATTERN

A. Nouns.

1. TUPOS (τύπος) is translated "pattern" in Tit. 2 : 7, A.V. ; Heb. 5179 AG:829D
8 : 5 (A.V. and R.V.). See ENSAMPLE. CB:1273B

2. HUPOTUPŌSIS (ὑποτύπωσις) is translated "pattern" in 1 Tim. 5296 AG:848C
1 : 16, A.V. ; 2 Tim. 1 : 13, R.V. See ENSAMPLE, FORM.¶ CB:1252B

3. HUPODEIGMA (ὑπόδειγμα) is translated "patterns" in Heb. 5262 AG:844A
9 : 23, A.V. See COPY. CB:1252B

B. Adjective.

ANTITUPOS (ἀντίτυπος) is translated "like in pattern" in Heb. 499 AG:76A
9 : 24, R.V. See FIGURE, No. 2. CB:1236A

PAVEMENT

LITHOSTRŌTOS (λιθόστρωτος), an adjective, denoting paved with 3038
stones (*lithos*, a stone, and *strōnnuō*, to spread), especially of tessellated AG:474D CB:—
work, is used as a noun in John 19 : 13, of a place near the Prætorium in
Jerusalem, called Gabbatha, a Greek transliteration of an Aramaic word.¶
In the Sept., 2 Chron. 7 : 3 ; Esth. 1 : 6 ; S. of Sol. 3 : 10.¶ PAUPER See BEGGAR

PAY (Verb), PAYMENT

1. APODIDŌMI (ἀποδίδωμι), to give back, to render what is due, to 591
pay, used of various obligations in this respect, is translated to pay, to AG:90B CB:1236C
make payment, in Matt. 5 : 26 ; 18 : 25 (twice), 26, 28, 29, 30, 34 ; 20 : 8,
R.V. (A.V., "give"). See DELIVER.

2. TELEŌ (τελέω), to bring to an end, complete, fulfil, has the meaning 5055 AG:810D
to pay in Matt. 17 : 24 and Rom. 13 : 6. See ACCOMPLISH. CB:1271B

Notes : (1) In Matt. 23 : 23, A.V., *apodekatoō*, to tithe, is translated APODEKATOō
"ye pay tithe" (R.V., "ye tithe"). (2) In Heb. 7 : 9, *dekatoō* (Passive 586 AG:89D
Voice), to pay tithe, is translated "hath paid tithes," R.V. (perfect tense). CB:1236C
See TITHE. DEKATOō 1183 AG:174B CB:1240C

PEACE, PEACEABLE, PEACEABLY

A. Noun.

EIRĒNĒ (εἰρήνη) "occurs in each of the books of the N.T., save 1515
1 John and save in Acts 7 : 26 [' (at) one again '] it is translated "peace" AG:227B CB:1243A
in the R.V. It describes (*a*) harmonious relationships between men,
Matt. 10 : 34 ; Rom. 14 : 19 ; (*b*) between nations, Luke 14 : 32 ; Acts
12 : 20 ; Rev. 6 : 4 ; (*c*) friendliness, Acts 15 : 33 ; 1 Cor. 16 : 11 ; Heb.
11 : 31 ; (*d*) freedom from molestation, Luke 11 : 21 ; 19 : 42 ; Acts
9 : 31 (R.V., 'peace,' A.V., 'rest') ; 16 : 36 ; (*e*) order, in the State,

Acts 24 : 2 (R.V., 'peace,' A.V., 'quietness'); in the churches, 1 Cor. 14 : 33; (*f*) the harmonised relationships between God and man, accomplished through the gospel, Acts 10 : 36; Eph. 2 : 17; (*g*) the sense of rest and contentment consequent thereon, Matt. 10 : 13; Mark 5 : 34; Luke 1 : 79; 2 : 29; John 14 : 27; Rom. 1 : 7; 3 : 17; 8 : 6; in certain passages this idea is not distinguishable from the last, Rom. 5 : 1."*

"The God of peace" is a title used in Rom. 15 : 33; 16 : 20; Phil. 4 : 9; 1 Thess. 5 : 23; Heb. 13 : 20; cp. 1 Cor. 14 : 33; 2 Cor. 13 : 11. The corresponding Heb. word *shalom* primarily signifies wholeness: see its use in Josh. 8 : 31, "unhewn;" Ruth 2 : 12, "full;" Neh. 6 : 15, "finished;" Is. 42 : 19, marg., "made perfect." Hence there is a close
3929 AG:626B CB:1262B connection between the title in 1 Thess. 5 : 23 and the word *holoklēros*, "entire," in that verse. In the Sept. *shalom* is often rendered by *sōtēria*, salvation, e.g., Gen. 26 : 31; 41 : 16; hence the "peace-offering" is called the "salvation offering." Cp. Luke 7 : 50; 8 : 48. In 2 Thess. 3 : 16, the title "the Lord of peace" is best understood as referring to the Lord Jesus. In Acts 7 : 26, "would have set them at one" is, lit., 'was reconciling them (conative imperfect tense, expressing an earnest effort) into peace.'

B. Verbs.

1514 AG:227A CB:1243A 1. EIRĒNEUŌ (εἰρηνεύω), primarily, to bring to peace, reconcile, denotes in the N.T., to keep peace or to be at peace: in Mark 9 : 50, R.V., the Lord bids the disciples "be at peace" with one another, gently rebuking their ambitious desires; in Rom. 12 : 18 (R.V., "be at peace," A.V., "live peaceably") the limitation "if it be possible, as much as in you lieth," seems due to the phrase "with all men," but is not intended to excuse any evasion of the obligation imposed by the command; in 2 Cor. 13 : 11 it is rendered "live in peace," a general exhortation to believers; in 1 Thess. 5 : 13, "be at peace (among yourselves)."¶

1517 AG:228A CB:1243A 2. EIRĒNOPOIEŌ (εἰρηνοποιέω), to make peace (*eirēnē*, and *poieō*, to make), is used in Col. 1 : 20.¶ In the Sept., Prov. 10 : 10.¶

C. Adjective.

1516 AG:228A CB:1243A EIRĒNIKOS (εἰρηνικός), akin to A, denotes peaceful. It is used (*a*) of the fruit of righteousness, Heb. 12 : 11, "peaceable" (or 'peaceful') because it is produced in communion with God the Father, through His chastening; (*b*) of "the wisdom that is from above," Jas. 3 : 17.¶

2272 AG:349C CB:1250A *Note:* In 1 Tim. 2 : 2, A.V., *hēsuchios*, quiet, is translated "peaceable" (R.V., "quiet").

PEACE (hold one's)

4601 AG:749C CB:— 1. SIGAŌ (σιγάω) signifies (*a*), used intransitively, to be silent (from *sigē*, silence), translated to hold one's peace, in Luke 9 : 36; 18 : 39; 20 : 26; Acts 12 : 17; 15 : 13 (in ver. 12, "kept silence;" similarly

* **From Notes on Thessalonians by Hogg and Vine, p. 154.**

rendered in 1 Cor. 14 : 28, 30, A.V., " hold his peace," 34) ; (*b*) used transitively, to keep secret ; in the Passive Voice, to be kept secret, Rom. 16 : 25, R.V., " hath been kept in silence." See SECRET, SILENCE.

2. SIŌPAŌ (σιωπάω), to be silent or still, to keep silence (from *siōpē*, 4623
silence), is translated to hold one's peace, in Matt. 20 : 31 ; 26 : 63 ; Mark AG:752C CB:—
3 : 4 ; 9 : 34 ; 10 : 48 ; 14 : 61 ; Luke 19 : 40 ; Acts 18 : 9 ; in the Lord's command to the sea, in Mark 4 : 39, it is translated " peace " (for the next word " be still " see No. 4) ; in Luke 1 : 20, R.V., " thou shalt be silent " (A.V., " dumb "). See DUMB, B.¶

3. HĒSUCHAZŌ (ἡσυχάζω) signifies to be still ; it is used of holding 2270
one's peace, being silent, Luke 14 : 4 ; Acts 11 : 18 ; 21 : 14, " we ceased." AG:349A CB:1250A
See CEASE, A, No. 3, QUIET.

4. PHIMOŌ (φιμόω), to muzzle, is used metaphorically in the Passive 5392
Voice, in Mark 1 : 25 and Luke 4 : 35, " hold thy peace ; " in Mark AG:861D CB:—
4 : 39, " be still." See MUZZLE.

PEACEMAKER

EIRĒNOPOIOS (εἰρηνοποιός), an adjective signifying peace-making 1518
(*eirēnē*, and *poieō*, to make), is used in Matt. 5 : 9, " peacemakers." Cp. AG:228A CB:1243A
PEACE, B, No. 2.¶

PEAL See VOICE

PEARL

MARGARITĒS (μαργαρίτης), a pearl (Eng., Margaret), occurs in Matt. 3135
7 : 6 (proverbially and figuratively) ; 13 : 45, 46 ; 1 Tim. 2 : 9 ; Rev. AG:491C CB:1257C
17 : 4 ; 18 : 12, 16 ; 21 : 21 (twice).¶

For PECULIAR see POSSESSION, B, No. 3, and C

PEN

KALAMOS (κάλαμος), a reed, reed-pipe, flute, staff, measuring rod, 2563
is used of a writing-reed or pen in 3 John 13. This was used on papyrus. AG:398B CB:1253B
Different instruments were used on different materials ; the *kalamos* may have been used also on leather. " Metal pens in the form of a reed or quill have been found in the so-called Grave of Aristotle at Eretria." See REED.

PENCE, PENNY, PENNYWORTH

DĒNARION (δηνάριον), a Roman coin, a *denarius*, a little less than the 1220
value of the Greek *drachmē* (see PIECE), now estimated as amounting to AG:179B CB:—
about 9½d. in the time of our Lord, occurs in the singular, e.g., Matt. 20 : 2 ; 22 : 19 ; Mark 12 : 15 ; Rev. 6 : 6 ; in the plural, e.g., Matt. 18 : 28 ; Mark 14 : 5 ; Luke 7 : 41 ; 10 : 35 ; John 12 : 5 ; " pennyworth " in Mark 6 : 37 and John 6 : 7, lit., '(loaves of two hundred) pence.' Considering the actual value, " shilling " would have been a more accurate translation, as proposed by the American translators, retaining " penny " for the *as*, and " farthing " for the *quadrans*.

PENTECOST

(-Te) 4005 PENTĒKOSTOS (*πεντηκοστός*), an adjective denoting fiftieth, is used
AG:643A as a noun, with "day" understood, i.e., the fiftieth day after the Passover,
CB:1263A counting from the second day of the Feast, Acts 2 : 1; 20 : 16; 1 Cor.
16 : 8.¶ For the Divine instructions to Israel see Ex. 23 : 16; 34 : 22; Lev. 23 : 15–21; Num. 28 : 26–31; Deut. 16 : 9–11.

For PENURY (Luke 21 : 4, A.V., R.V., "want") see LACK

PEOPLE

2992 1. LAOS (*λαός*) is used of (*a*) the people at large, especially of people
AG:466C assembled, e.g., Matt. 27 : 25; Luke 1 : 21; 3 : 15; Acts 4 : 27; (*b*) a
CB:1256C people of the same race and language, e.g., Rev. 5 : 9; in the plural, e.g., Luke 2 : 31; Rom. 15 : 11; Rev. 7 : 9; 11 : 9; especially of Israel, e.g., Matt. 2 : 6; 4 : 23; John 11 : 50; Acts 4 : 8; Heb. 2 : 17; in distinction from their rulers and priests, e.g., Matt. 26 : 5; Luke 20 : 19; Heb. 5 : 3; in distinction from Gentiles, e.g., Acts 26 : 17, 23; Rom. 15 : 10; (*c*) of Christians as the people of God, e.g., Acts 15 : 14; Tit.
3793 2 : 14; Heb. 4 : 9; 1 Pet. 2 : 9.
AG:600C
CB:1260B 2. OCHLOS (*ὄχλος*), a crowd, throng: see CROWD, MULTITUDE.

1218 3. DĒMOS (*δῆμος*), the common people, the people generally (Eng.,
AG:179A demagogue, democracy, etc.), especially the mass of the people assembled
CB:1240C in a public place, Acts 12 : 22; 17 : 5; 19 : 30, 33.¶

1484 4. ETHNOS (*ἔθνος*) denotes (*a*) a nation, e.g., Matt. 24 : 7; Acts
AG:218B
CB:1246C 10 : 35; the Jewish people, e.g., Luke 7 : 5; Acts 10 : 22; 28 : 19; (*b*) in the plural, the rest of mankind in distinction from Israel or the Jews, e.g., Matt. 4 : 15; Acts 28 : 28; (*c*) the people of a city, Acts 8 : 9; (*d*) Gentile Christians, e.g., Rom. 10 : 19; 11 : 13; 15 : 27; Gal. 2 : 14. See GENTILES, NATION.

444 5. ANTHRŌPOS (*ἄνθρωπος*), man, without distinction of sex (cp.
AG:68B
CB:1236A *anēr*, a male), is translated "people" in John 6 : 10, R.V. (A.V., "men").

PERADVENTURE

A. Adverb.

5029 TACHA (*τάχα*), primarily quickly (from *tachus*, quick), signifies "perad-
AG:806C
CB:— venture" in Rom. 5 : 7; in Philm. 15, "perhaps." See PERHAPS.¶

B. Conjunction.

3379 MĒPOTE (*μήποτε*), often written as two words, usually signifies
AG:519B
CB:1258B lest ever, lest haply, haply; in indirect questions, 'if haply' or 'whether haply,' e.g., Luke 3 : 15, R.V.; in Matt. 25 : 9, R.V., "peradventure" (A.V., "lest"); "if peradventure," in 2 Tim. 2 : 25. See HAPLY.

PERCEIVE

1097
AG:160D 1. GINŌSKŌ (*γινώσκω*), to know by experience and observation, is
CB:1248B translated to perceive in Matt. 12 : 15, R.V. (A.V., "knew"); 16 : 8;

21 : 45 ; 22 : 18 ; 26 : 10, R.V., (A.V., " understood ") ; Mark 8 : 17 ;
12 : 12 and 15 : 10, R.V. (A.V., " knew ") ; so Luke 9 : 11 ; 18 : 34 ;
in Luke 7 : 39, R.V. (A.V., " known ") ; 20 : 19 (cp. No. 7 in ver. 23) ; **PERCH**
John 6 : 15 ; 8 : 27, R.V. (A.V., " understood ") ; 16 : 19, R.V. (A.V. **See**
" knew ") ; Acts 23 : 6 ; Gal. 2 : 9 ; in 1 John 3 : 16, A.V., " perceive ' **LODGE**
(R.V., " know," perfect tense, lit., 'we have perceived,' and therefore
know). See KNOW.

2. EPIGINŌSKŌ (ἐπιγινώσκω), a strengthened form of No. 1, to gain **1921**
a full knowledge of, to become fully acquainted with, is translated to **AG:291A CB:1245C**
perceive in Mark 5 : 30, R.V. (A.V., " knowing ") ; Luke 1 : 22 ; 5 : 22 ;
Acts 19 : 34, R.V. (A.V., " knew "). See ACKNOWLEDGE, KNOW.

3. EIDON (εἶδον) (akin to *oida*, to know), an aorist form used to supply **(HORAō)**
that tense of *horaō*, to see, is translated to perceive in Matt. 13 : 14 ; **3708 AG:577D**
Mark 4 : 12 ; Acts 28 : 26 ; in Luke 9 : 47, A.V. (R.V., " saw ") ; in Acts **CB:1251A**
14 : 9, A.V., " perceiving " (R.V., " seeing "). See BEHOLD, No. 1.

4. THEŌREŌ (θεωρέω), to be a spectator of, look at, discern, is trans- **2334**
lated to perceive in John 4 : 19 (indicating the woman's earnest contempla- **AG:360A CB:1272A**
tion of the Lord) ; so Acts 17 : 22 ; in John 12 : 19, R.V., " behold "
(A.V., " perceive ye "). See BEHOLD, No. 6.

5. AISTHANOMAI (αἰσθάνομαι), to perceive, to notice, understand, **143**
is used in Luke 9 : 45, R.V., " (that they should not) perceive," A.V., **AG:24D CB:1234A**
" (that) they perceived . . . (not)."¶

6. NOEŌ (νοέω), to perceive with the mind, to understand, is trans- **3539**
lated to perceive in Matt. 15 : 17, R.V. (A.V., " understand ") ; so 16 : 9, **(NOIEō) AG:540B**
11 ; John 12 : 40 ; Rom. 1 : 20 ; Eph. 3 : 4 ; in Mark 7 : 18 and 8 : 17, **CB:1259C**
A.V. and R.V., " perceive." See CONSIDER, No. 4.

7. KATANOEŌ (κατανοέω), a strengthened form of No. 6, to take note **2657**
of, consider carefully, is translated to perceive in Luke 6 : 41, A.V. (R.V., **AG:415A CB:1254A**
" considerest ") ; 20 : 23 ; Acts 27 : 39, R.V. (A.V., " discovered ").
See BEHOLD, No. 11.

8. KATALAMBANŌ (καταλαμβάνω), to lay hold of, apprehend, com- **2638**
prehend, is translated to perceive in Acts 4 : 13 ; 10 : 34. See APPRE- **AG:412D CB:1254A**
HEND, No. 1. **(-OMAI)**

Notes : (1) In Mark 12 : 28 the best mss. have *oida*, to know (so R.V.), **OIDA**
for *eidon*, to see, perceive (A.V.). (2) In Acts 8 : 23, A.V., *horaō*, to see, **1492 (EIDō)**
is translated " I perceive " (R.V., " I see "). (3) In 2 Cor. 7 : 8, A.V., *blepō*, **AG:555D**
to look at, consider, see, is translated " I perceive " (R.V., " I see "). **CB:1260B BLEPō**
(4) In Acts 23 : 29, A.V., *heuriskō*, to find, is translated " perceived " **991**
(R.V., " found "). **AG:143B CB:1239A**

HEURISKō

For PERDITION see DESTRUCTION, No. 1 **2147 AG:324D**

CB:1250B

PERFECT (Adjective and Verb), PERFECTLY

A. Adjectives.

5046 AG:809A

1. TELEIOS (τέλειος) signifies having reached its end (*telos*), finished, **CB:1271B**

complete, perfect. It is used (I) of persons, (*a*) primarily of physical development, then, with ethical import, fully grown, mature, 1 Cor. 2:6; 14:20 ("men;" marg., "of full age"); Eph. 4:13; Phil. 3:15; Col. 1:28; 4:12; in Heb. 5:14, R.V., "fullgrown" (marg., "perfect"), A.V., "of full age" (marg., "perfect"); (*b*) complete, conveying the idea of goodness without necessary reference to maturity or what is expressed under (*a*), Matt. 5:48; 19:21; Jas. 1:4 (2nd part); 3:2. It is used thus of God in Matt. 5:48; (II) of things, complete, perfect, Rom. 12:2; 1 Cor. 13:10 (referring to the complete revelation of God's will and ways, whether in the completed Scriptures or in the hereafter);
(-TēS) Jas. 1:4 (of the work of patience); ver. 25; 1 John 4:18.¶

5047 AG:809C CB:— 2. TELEIOTEROS (τελειότερος), the comparative degree of No. 1, is used in Heb. 9:11, of the very presence of God.¶

739 AG:110C CB:1237C 3. ARTIOS (ἄρτιος) is translated "perfect" in 2 Tim. 3:17: see COMPLETE, B.

B. Verbs.

5048 AG:809D CB:1271B 1. TELEIOŌ (τελειόω), to bring to an end by completing or perfecting, is used (I) of accomplishing (see FINISH, FULFIL); (II) of bringing to completeness, (*a*) of persons: of Christ's assured completion of His earthly course, in the accomplishment of the Father's will, the successive stages culminating in His Death, Luke 13:32; Heb. 2:10, to make Him perfect, legally and officially, for all that He would be to His people on the ground of His sacrifice; cp. 5:9; 7:28, R.V., "perfected" (A.V., "consecrated"); of His saints, John 17:23, R.V., "perfected" (A.V., "made perfect"); Phil. 3:12; Heb. 10:14; 11:40 (of resurrection glory); 12:23 (of the departed saints); 1 John 4:18; of former priests (negatively), Heb. 9:9; similarly of Israelites under the Aaronic priesthood, 10:1; (*b*) of things, Heb. 7:19 (of the ineffectiveness of the Law); Jas. 2:22 (of faith made perfect by works); 1 John 2:5, of the love of God operating through him who keeps His word; 4:12, of the love of God in the case of those who love one another; 4:17, of the love of God as "made perfect with" (R.V.) those who abide in God, giving them to be possessed of the very character of God, by reason of which 'as He is, even so are they in this world.'

2005 AG:302B CB:1246A (-EISTHAI) 2. EPITELEŌ (ἐπιτελέω), to bring through to the end (*epi*, intensive, in the sense of 'fully,' and *teleō*, to complete), is used in the Middle Voice in Gal. 3:3, "are ye (now) perfected," continuous present tense, indicating a process, lit., 'are ye now perfecting yourselves;' in 2 Cor. 7:1, "perfecting (holiness);" in Phil. 1:6, R.V., "will perfect (it)," A.V., "will perform." See ACCOMPLISH, No. 4.

2675 AG:417D CB:1254B 3. KATARTIZŌ (καταρτίζω), to render fit, complete (*artios*), "is used of mending nets, Matt. 4:21; Mark 1:19, and is translated 'restore' in Gal. 6:1. It does not necessarily imply, however, that that to which it is applied has been damaged, though it may do so, as in these passages; it signifies, rather, right ordering and arrangement,

Heb. 11 : 3, 'framed;' it points out the path of progress, as in Matt. 21 : 16; Luke 6 : 40; cp. 2 Cor. 13 : 9; Eph. 4 : 12, where corresponding nouns occur. It indicates the close relationship between character and destiny, Rom. 9 : 22, 'fitted.' It expresses the pastor's desire for the flock, in prayer, Heb. 13 : 21, and in exhortation, 1 Cor. 1 : 10, R.V., 'perfected' (A.V., 'perfectly joined'); 2 Cor. 13 : 11, as well as his conviction of God's purpose for them, 1 Pet. 5 : 10. It is used of the Incarnation of the Word in Heb. 10 : 5, 'prepare,' quoted from Ps. 40 : 6 (Sept.), where it is apparently intended to describe the unique creative act involved in the Virgin Birth, Luke 1 : 35. In 1 Thess. 3 : 10 it means to supply what is necessary, as the succeeding words show."* See FIT, B, No. 3.¶

Note: Cp. *exartizō*, rendered "furnished completely," in 2 Tim. 3 : 17, 1822
R.V.; see ACCOMPLISH, No. 1. AG:273C CB:1247C

C. Adverbs.

1. AKRIBŌS (ἀκριβῶς), accurately, is translated "perfectly" in 1 199
Thess. 5 : 2, where it suggests that Paul and his companions were careful AG:33B CB:—
ministers of the Word. See ACCURATELY, and see Note (2) below.

2. AKRIBESTERON (ἀκριβέστερον), the comparative degree of No. 197
1, Acts 18 : 26; 23 : 15 : see CAREFULLY, EXACTLY. AG:33B (-BŌS)

3. TELEIŌS (τελείως), perfectly, is so translated in 1 Pet. 1 : 13, 5049
R.V. (A.V., "to the end"), of setting one's hope on coming grace. See AG:810B CB:1271B
END.¶

Notes: (1) In Rev. 3 : 2, A.V., *plēroō*, to fulfil, is translated "perfect" 4137
(R.V., "fulfilled"). (2) For the adverb *akribōs* in Luke 1 : 3, A.V., see AG:670C CB:1265B
ACCURATELY; in Acts 24 : 22, A.V., see EXACT. (3) For the noun *akribeia* in Acts 22 : 3, see MANNER.

PERFECTION, PERFECTING (noun), PERFECTNESS

A. Nouns.

1. KATARTISIS (κατάρτισις), a making fit, is used figuratively in an 418A
ethical sense in 2 Cor. 13 : 9, R.V., "perfecting" (A.V., "perfection"), AG:418A CB:1254B
implying a process leading to consummation (akin to *katartizō*, see PERFECT, B, No. 3).¶

2. KATARTISMOS (καταρτισμός) denotes, in much the same way as 2677
No. 1, a fitting or preparing fully, Eph. 4 : 12.¶ AG:418A CB:1254B

3. TELEIŌSIS (τελείωσις) denotes a fulfilment, completion, per- 5050
fection, an end accomplished as the effect of a process, Heb. 7 : 11; in AG:810B CB:1271B
Luke 1 : 45, R.V., "fulfilment" (A.V., "performance").¶

4. TELEIOTĒS (τελειότης) denotes much the same as No. 3, but 5047
stressing perhaps the actual accomplishment of the end in view, Col. 3 : 14, AG:809C CB:1271B
"perfectness;" Heb. 6 : 1, "perfection."¶ In the Sept., Judg. 9 : 16, 19; Prov. 11 : 3; Jer. 2 : 2.¶

---

* From Notes on Thessalonians by Hogg and Vine, p. 101.

B. Verb.

5052 AG:810C CB:— TELESPHOREŌ (τελεσφορέω), to bring to a completion or an end in view (*telos*, an end, *pherō*, to bear), is said of plants, Luke 8 : 14.¶

PERFORM, PERFORMANCE

5055 AG:810D CB:1271B 1. TELEŌ (τελέω), to finish, is translated " performed " in Luke 2 : 39, A.V. : see ACCOMPLISH, No. 3.

658 AG:100D CB:— 2. APOTELEŌ (ἀποτελέω), to bring to an end, accomplish, is translated " I perform " in Luke 13 : 32, R.V. (A.V., " I do ") ; some mss. have No. 3 ; in Jas. 1 : 15, it is used of sin, " fullgrown " R.V. (A.V., " finished "). See FINISH, Note 2.¶

2005 AG:302B CB:1246A (-EISTHAI) 3. EPITELEŌ (ἐπιτελέω), Rom. 15 : 28, A.V., " performed " (R.V., " accomplished ") ; 2 Cor. 8 : 11, A.V., " perform " (R.V., " complete ") ; Phil. 1 : 6, A.V., " perform " (R.V., " perfect ") : see ACCOMPLISH, No. 4.

4160 AG:680D CB:1265C 4. POIEŌ (ποιέω), to do, is translated " to perform " in Rom. 4 : 21 ; in Luke 1 : 72, A.V. (R.V., " to shew "). See SHEW.

591 AG:90B CB:1236C 5. APODIDŌMI (ἀποδίδωμι), to give back, or in full, is translated " thou . . . shalt perform " in Matt. 5 : 33. See DELIVER. No. 3.

KATERGAZOMAI 2716 AG:421C GINOMAI 1096 AG:158A CB:1248B *Notes :* (1) In Rom. 7 : 18, A.V., *katergazomai*, to work, is translated " to perform " (R.V., " to do ; " marg., " work "). (2) In Luke 1 : 20, A.V., *ginomai*, to come to pass (R.V.), is translated " shall be performed." (3) For " performance " in Luke 1 : 45, see FULFILMENT.

PERHAPS

5029 AG:806C CB:— 1. TACHA (τάχα) is translated " perhaps " in Philm. 15. See PERADVENTURE.

686 AG:103D CB:1237B 2. ARA (ἄρα), a particle, 'then,' sometimes marking a result about which some uncertainty is felt, is translated " perhaps " in Acts 8 : 22.

4458 AG:732B CB:— *Note :* In 2 Cor. 2 : 7, A.V., *pōs*, anyhow, " by any means " (R.V.), is translated " perhaps."

PERFUME See OINTMENT

PERIL, see DANGER, Note : PERILOUS see GRIEVOUS

PERISH

622 AG:95A CB:1237A 1. APOLLUMI (ἀπόλλυμι), to destroy, signifies, in the Middle Voice, to perish, and is thus used (*a*) of things, e.g., Matt. 5 : 29, 30 ; Luke 5 : 37 ; Acts 27 : 34, R.V., " perish " (in some texts *piptō*, to fall, as A.V.) ; Heb. 1 : 11 ; 2 Pet. 3 : 6 ; Rev. 18 : 14 (2nd part), R.V., " perished " (in some texts *aperchomai*, to depart, as A.V.) ; (*b*) of persons, e.g., Matt. 8 : 25 ; John 3 : (15), 16 ; 10 : 28 ; 17 : 12, R.V., " perished " (A.V., " is lost ") ; Rom. 2 : 12 ; 1 Cor. 1 : 18, lit., ' the perishing,' where the perfective force of the verb implies the completion of the process of destruction (Moulton, *Proleg.*, p. 114) ; 8 : 11 ; 15 : 18 ; 2 Pet. 3 : 9 ; Jude 11. For the meaning of the word see DESTROY, No. 1.

2. SUNAPOLLUMI (συναπόλλυμι), in the Middle Voice, denotes to 4881 AG:785A
perish together (*sun*, with, and No. 1), Heb. 11 : 31.¶ CB:—
3. APOTHNĒSKŌ (ἀποθνήσκω), to die; in Matt. 8 : 32 "perished." 599 AG:91B
See DIE, No. 2. CB:1237B
4. APHANIZŌ (ἀφανίζω), to make unseen (*a*, negative, *phainō*, to 853
cause to appear), in the Passive Voice, is translated "perish" in Acts AG:124C CB:1236B
13 : 41 (R.V., marg., "vanish away"). See DISFIGURE.
5. DIAPHTHEIRŌ (διαφθείρω), to corrupt, is rendered "perish" 1311
in 2 Cor. 4 : 16, A.V. (R.V., "is decaying"). See CORRUPT, No. 3, DECAY. AG:190C CB:1241B
Notes: (1) In Acts 8 : 20, "(thy money) perish" is a translation of a
phrase, lit, 'be unto destruction,' *apōleia*; see DESTRUCTION, B, (II), APŌLEIA
No. 1. (2) In Col. 2 : 22, "to perish" is a translation of the phrase 684 AG:103B
eis pthoran, lit., 'unto corruption;' see CORRUPT, B, No. 1. (3) For CB:1237A
"shall utterly perish," in 2 Pet. 2 : 12, A.V., see CORRUPT, B, No. 1 (*b*). PHTHORA 5356
AG:858A

For PERJURED PERSON see FORSWEAR CB:1264C

PERMISSION

SUNGNŌMĒ (συγγνώμη), lit., a joint opinion, mind or understanding 4774
(*sun*, with, *gnōmē*, an opinion), a fellow-feeling, hence, a concession, allow- AG:773A CB:—
ance, is translated "permission," in contrast to "commandment," in
1 Cor. 7 : 6.¶ PERMISSIBLE See LAWFUL

PERMIT

EPITREPŌ (ἐπιτρέπω), lit., to turn to (*epi*, to, *trepō*, to turn), to en- 2010
trust, signifies to permit, Acts 26 : 1; 1 Cor. 14 : 34; 1 Cor. 16 : 7; AG:303 CB:—
1 Tim. 2 : 12, R.V. "permit" (A.V., "suffer"); Heb. 6 : 3. See LEAVE.

For PERNICIOUS, 2 Pet. 2 : 2, A.V., see LASCIVIOUS

PERPLEX, PERPLEXITY

A. Verbs.

1. APOREŌ (ἀπορέω) is rendered "perplexed" in 2 Cor. 4 : 8, and 639
in the most authentic mss. in Luke 24 : 4; see DOUBT, A, No. 1. AG:97C CB:—

2. DIAPOREŌ (διαπορέω), "was much perplexed" in Luke 9 : 7; 1280
see DOUBT, A, No. 2. AG:187D CB:—

B. Noun.

APORIA (ἀπορία), akin to A, No. 1, is translated "perplexity" in 640
Luke 21 : 25 (lit., 'at a loss for a way,' *a*, negative, *poros*, a way, resource), AG:97D CB:—
of the distress of nations, finding no solution to their embarrassments;
papyri illustrations are in the sense of being at one's wit's end, at a loss
how to proceed, without resources.¶

PERSECUTE, PERSECUTION

A. Verbs.

1. DIŌKŌ (διώκω) has the meanings (*a*) to put to flight, drive away, 1377 AG:201B CB:1242A

(*b*) to pursue, whence the meaning to persecute, Matt. 5 : 10–12, 44 ;
10 : 23 ; 23 : 34 ; Luke 11 : 49 (No. 2 in some mss.) ; 21 : 12 ; John
5 : 16 ; 15 : 20 (twice) ; Acts 7 : 52 ; 9 : 4, 5, and similar passages ;
Rom. 12 : 14 ; 1 Cor. 4 : 12 ; 15 : 9 ; 2 Cor. 4 : 9, A.V. (R.V., " pursued ") ;
Gal. 1 : 13, 23 ; 4 : 29 ; Gal. 5 : 11, R.V., " am . . . persecuted " (A.V.,
" suffer persecution ") ; so 6 : 12 ; Phil. 3 : 6 ; 2 Tim. 3 : 12, " shall
suffer persecution ; " Rev. 12 : 13. See FOLLOW, PURSUE.

1559 AG:239A 2. EKDIŌKŌ (ἐκδιώκω), *ek*, out, and No. 1, is used in 1 Thess. 2 : 15,
CB:1243C A.V., " persecuted " (R.V., " drave out "). See also No. 1. See DRIVE,
No. 2.¶

B. Noun.

1375 AG:201A DIŌGMOS (διωγμός), akin to A, No. 1, occurs in Matt. 13 : 21 ; Mark
CB:1242A 4 : 17 ; 10 : 30 ; Acts 8 : 1 ; 13 : 50 ; Rom. 8 : 35 ; 2 Cor. 12 : 10 ; 2 Thess.
1 : 4 ; 2 Tim. 3 : 11, twice (for ver. 12, see A, No. 1).¶ In the Sept.,
Prov. 11 : 19 ; Lam. 3 : 19.¶

2347 AG:362B *Note :* In Acts 11 : 19, A.V., *thlipsis*, " tribulation " (R.V.), is trans-
CB:1272B lated " persecution."

PERSECUTOR

1376 AG:201B DIŌKTĒS (διώκτης), akin to *diōkō* (see above), occurs in 1 Tim. 1 :
CB:1242A 13.¶

PERSEVERANCE

4343 AG:715D PROSKARTERĒSIS (προσκαρτέρησις) occurs in Eph. 6 : 18. Cp. the
CB:1267A verb (and the formation) under ATTEND, No. 2.¶

PERSON

4383 AG:720D 1. PROSŌPON (πρόσωπον), for the meaning of which see APPEAR-
CB:1267B ANCE, No. 2, is translated " person " or " persons " in Matt. 22 : 16 ;
Mark 12 : 14 ; Luke 20 : 21 ; 2 Cor. 1 : 11 ; 2 Cor. 2 : 10 ; Gal. 2 : 6 ;
Jude 16, lit., ' (admiring, or shewing respect of, R.V.) persons.'

444 AG:68B 2. ANTHRŌPOS (ἄνθρωπος), a generic name for man, is translated
CB:1236A " persons " in Rev. 11 : 13, R.V. (A.V., " men ").

HUPOSTASIS *Notes :* (1) In Heb. 1 : 3, A.V., *hupostasis*, substance, is translated
5287 AG:847A " person ; " see SUBSTANCE. (2) In Matt. 27 : 24, R.V., *toutou*, " of this . . .
CB:1252B (man)," is translated " of this . . . person " (A.V.). (3) In Philm. 12, the
AUTOS 846 pronoun *autos*, he, placed in a position of strong emphasis, is translated
AG:122C " in his own person," R.V., stressing the fact that in spite of the Apostle's
CB:1238B inclination to retain Onesimus, he has sent him, as being, so to speak,
PONēROS 4190 ' his very heart,' instead of adopting some other method. (4) In 1 Cor.
AG:690D 5 : 13, A.V., the adjective *ponēros*, wicked, used as a noun, is translated
CB:1266A " wicked person " (R.V., " . . . man "). (5) In 2 Pet. 2 : 5, A.V., *ogdoos*,
" eighth," is translated " the (lit., an) eighth *person* " (R.V., " with seven
others "). (6) Various adjectives are used with the word " persons,"
e.g., devout, perjured, profane.

PERSONS (respect of)

A. Nouns.

1. PROSŌPOLĒMPTĒS (προσωπολήμπτης) denotes a respecter of persons (*prosōpon*, a face or person, *lambanō*, to lay hold of), Acts 10 : 34.¶ 4381 AG:720D CB:1267B

2. PROSŌPOLĒMPSIA (in inferior texts without the letter m) (προσωποληψία) denotes respect of persons, partiality (akin to No. 1), the fault of one who, when responsible to give judgment, has respect to the position, rank, popularity, or circumstances of men, instead of their intrinsic conditions, preferring the rich and powerful to those who are not so, Rom. 2 : 11 ; Eph. 6 : 9 ; Col. 3 : 25 ; Jas. 2 : 1.¶ 4382 AG:720D CB:1267B

B. Verb.

PROSŌPOLĒMPTEŌ (προσωποληπτέω), to have respect of persons (see above), occurs in Jas. 2 : 9.¶ 4380 AG:720C CB:1267B

C. Adverb.

APROSŌPOLĒMPTŌS (ἀπροσωπολήμπτως), without respect of persons, impartially (*a*, negative), occurs in 1 Pet. 1 : 17.¶ 678 AG:102C CB:1237B (-TēS)

PERSUADE

1. PEITHŌ (πείθω) in the Active Voice, signifies to apply persuasion, to prevail upon or win over, to persuade, bringing about a change of mind by the influence of reason or moral considerations, e.g., in Matt. 27 : 20 ; 28 : 14 ; Acts 13 : 43 ; 19 : 8 ; in the Passive Voice, to be persuaded, believe (see BELIEVE, No. 2, and OBEY), e.g., Luke 16 : 31 ; 20 : 6 ; Acts 17 : 4, R.V. (A.V., "believed") ; 21 : 14 ; 26 : 26 ; Rom. 8 : 38 ; 14 : 14 ; 15 : 14 ; 2 Tim. 1 : 5, 12 ; Heb. 6 : 9 ; 11 : 13, in some mss. ; 13 : 18, R.V. (A.V., "trust"). See ASSURANCE, B, No. 3. 3982 AG:639A CB:1263A

Note : For Acts 26 : 28, A.V., "thou persuadest," see FAIN, Note.

2. ANAPEITHŌ (ἀναπείθω), to persuade, induce, in an evil sense (*ana*, back, and No. 1), is used in Acts 18 : 13.¶ In the Sept., Jer. 29 : 8.¶ 374 AG:59B CB:—

Note : For *plērophoreō*, rendered "being fully persuaded," in Rom. 4 : 21 and 14 : 5, A.V., see ASSURANCE, B, No. 2. 4135 AG:670B CB:1265B

PERSUASIVE, PERSUASIVENESS

A. Adjective.

PEITHOS (πειθός), an adjective (akin to *peithō*), not found elsewhere, is translated "persuasive" in 1 Cor. 2 : 4, R.V. (A.V., "enticing") ; see ENTICE, B.¶ 3981 AG:639A CB:1263A

B. Noun.

PITHANOLOGIA (πιθανολογία), persuasiveness of speech, is used in Col. 2 : 4, R.V. See ENTICE, B, Note.¶ 4086 AG:657B CB:1265A

PERSUASION

PEISMONĒ (πεισμονή), akin to *peithō*, is used in Gal. 5 : 8, where the meaning is ' this influence that has won you over, or that seems likely to 3988 AG:641B CB:1263A do so;' the use of *peithō*, in the sense of to obey, in ver. 7, suggests a play upon words here.¶

PERTAIN TO

3348 AG:514A METECHŌ (μετέχω), Heb. 7:13, A.V.; see BELONG, Note (*c*),
CB:1258C PARTAKE, B, No. 3.
PROS *Notes:* (1) In Rom. 15:17, the phrase *ta pros*, lit., 'the (things)
4314 AG:709C towards' is translated "things pertaining to," R.V. (A.V., "those things
CB:1267A which pertain to"); in Heb. 2:17 and 5:1, R.V. and A.V., "things
PERI 4012 pertaining to." (2) In Acts 1:3, A.V., the phrase *ta peri*, "the (things)
AG:644B concerning" (R.V.), is translated "the things pertaining to." (3) In
CB:1263B KATA Rom. 9:4, the R.V. rightly translates the relative pronoun *hōn*, lit., 'of
2596 whom' (from *hos*, who), by "whose is" (A.V., "to whom *pertaineth*").
AG:405C CB:1253C (4) In Rom. 4:1, A.V., *kata*, "according to" (R.V.), is translated
"as pertaining to." (5) For 1 Cor. 6:3, 4, see LIFE, B, No. 1.

PERVERSE, PERVERT

654 AG:100B 1. APOSTREPHŌ (ἀποστρέφω), to turn away (*apo*, from, *strephō*,
CB:1237A to turn), is used metaphorically in the sense of perverting in Luke 23:14
(cp. No. 2 in ver. 2). See BRING, No. 22.

1294 AG:189A 2. DIASTREPHŌ (διαστρέφω), to distort, twist (*dia*, through, and
CB:— *strephō*), is translated to pervert in Luke 23:2 (cp. No. 1 in ver. 14); Acts 13:10 [in ver. 8, "to turn aside" (A.V., "away")]; in the perfect participle, Passive Voice, it is translated "perverse," lit., 'turned aside,' 'corrupted,' in Matt. 17:17; Luke 9:41; Acts 20:30; Phil. 2:15.¶

3344 AG:513B 3. METASTREPHŌ (μεταστρέφω), to transform into something of
CB:— an opposite character (*meta*, signifying a change, and *strephō*,) as the Judaizers sought to "pervert the gospel of Christ," Gal. 1:7; cp. "the sun shall be turned into darkness," Acts 2:20; laughter into mourning and joy to heaviness, Jas. 4:9. See TURN.¶

1612 AG:245B 4. EKSTREPHŌ (ἐκστρέφω), to turn inside out (*ek*, out), to change
CB:— entirely, is used metaphorically in Tit. 3:11, R.V., "is perverted" (A.V., "is subverted"). See SUBVERT.¶

Note: For "perverse disputings," 1 Tim. 6:5, A.V., see DISPUTE, A, No. 3.

PESTILENCE, PESTILENT FELLOW

3061 AG:479D LOIMOS (λοιμός), a pestilence, any deadly infectious malady, is used
CB:— in the plural in Luke 21:11 (in some mss., Matt. 24:7); in Acts 24:5, metaphorically, "a pestilent fellow." See FELLOW.¶

PETITION

155 AG:26B AITĒMA (αἴτημα), from *aiteō*, to ask, is rendered "petitions" in 1 John
CB:1234A 5:15: see ASK, B, and cp. the distinction between A, Nos. 1 and 2.¶ Cp. *deēsis* (see PRAYER).

PHARISEES

PHARISAIOS (φαρισαῖος), from an Aramaic word *peras* (found in 5330
Dan. 5 : 28), signifying to separate, owing to a different manner of life AG:853C CB:1263C
from that of the general public. The Pharisees and Sadducees appear as distinct parties in the latter half of the 2nd cent. B.C., though they represent tendencies traceable much earlier in Jewish history, tendencies which became pronounced after the return from Babylon (537 B.C.). The immediate progenitors of the two parties were, respectively, the Hasidæans and the Hellenizers; the latter, the antedecents of the Sadducees, aimed at removing Judaism from its narrowness and sharing in the advantages of Greek life and culture. The Hasidæans, a transcription of the Hebrew *chasidim*, i.e., pious ones, were a society of men zealous for religion, who acted under the guidance of the scribes, in opposition to the godless Hellenizing party; they scrupled to oppose the legitimate High Priest even when he was on the Greek side. Thus the Hellenizers were a political sect, while the Hasidæans, whose fundamental principle was complete separation from non-Jewish elements, were the strictly legal party among the Jews, and were ultimately the more popular and influential party. In their zeal for the Law they almost deified it and their attitude became merely external, formal, and mechanical. They laid stress, not upon the righteousness of an action, but upon its formal correctness. Consequently their opposition to Christ was inevitable; His manner of life and teaching was essentially a condemnation of theirs; hence His denunciation of them, e.g., Matt. 6 : 2, 5, 16; 15 : 7 and chapter 23.

While the Jews continued to be divided into these two parties, the spread of the testimony of the Gospel must have produced what in the public eye seemed to be a new sect, and in the extensive development which took place at Antioch, Acts 11 : 19–26, the name "Christians" seems to have become a popular term applied to the disciples as a sect, the primary cause, however, being their witness to Christ (see CALL, A, No. 11). The opposition of both Pharisees and Sadducees (still mutually antagonistic, Acts 23 : 6–10) agains the new "sect" continued unabated during apostolic times.

PHILOSOPHER

PHILOSOPHOS (φιλόσοφος), lit., loving wisdom (*philos*, loving, *sophia*, 5386
wisdom), occurs in Acts 17 : 18.¶ AG:861B CB:1264B

PHILOSOPHY

PHILOSOPHIA (φιλοσοφία) denotes the love and pursuit of wisdom, 5385
hence, philosophy, the investigation of truth and nature; in Col. 2 : 8, AG:861B CB:1264A
the so-called philosophy of false teachers. "Though essentially Greek as a name and as an idea, it had found its way into Jewish circles . . . Josephus speaks of the three Jewish sects as three 'philosophies' . . .

It is worth observing that this word, which to the Greeks denoted the highest effort of the intellect, occurs here alone in Paul's writings . . . the Gospel had deposed the term as inadequate to the higher standard whether of knowledge or of practice, which it had introduced" (Lightfoot).¶

PHYLACTERY

5440 AG:868A CB:1264C PHULAKTĒRION (φυλακτήριον), primarily an outpost, or fortification (*phulax*, a guard), then, any kind of safeguard, became used especially to denote an amulet. In the N.T. it denotes a prayer-fillet, a phylactery, a small strip of parchment, with portions of the Law written on it; it was fastened by a leathern strap either to the forehead or to the left arm over against the heart, to remind the wearer of the duty of keeping the commandments of God in the head and in the heart; cp. Ex. 13 : 16; Deut. 6 : 8; 11 : 18. It was supposed to have potency as a charm against evils and demons. The Pharisees broadened their phylacteries to render conspicuous their superior eagerness to be mindful of God's Law, Matt. 23 : 5.¶

PHYSICAL See BODILY, FLESH

PHYSICIAN

2395 AG:368D CB:1252C IATROS (ἰατρός), akin to *iaomai*, to heal, a physician, occurs in Matt. 9 : 12; Mark 2 : 17; 5 : 26; Luke 4 : 23; 5 : 31 (in some mss., 8 : 43); Col. 4 : 14.¶

PICK See PLUCK, TAKE

PIECE

1915 AG:290C CB:— 1. EPIBLĒMA (ἐπίβλημα) primarily denotes that which is thrown over, a cover (*epi*, over, *ballō*, to throw); then, that which is put on, or sewed on, to cover a rent, a patch, Matt. 9 : 16; Mark 2 : 21; in the next sentence, R.V., "that which should fill" (A.V., "the new piece that filled"), there is no word representing "piece" (lit., 'the filling,' *plērōma*); see FILL, B; Luke 5 : 36.¶

1406 AG:206C CB:— 2. DRACHMĒ (δραχμή), a *drachma*, firstly, an Attic weight, as much as one can hold in the hand (connected with *drassomai*, to grasp with the hand, lay hold of, 1 Cor. 3 : 19), then, a coin, nearly equal to the Roman *denarius* (see PENNY), is translated "pieces of silver" in Luke 15 : 8, 1st part; "piece," 2nd part and ver. 9.¶

3313 AG:505D CB:1258B 3. MEROS (μέρος), a part, is translated "a piece (of a broiled fish)" in Luke 24 : 42. See BEHALF, PART.

2801 AG:433B CB:1255B 4. KLASMA (κλάσμα), a broken piece (from *klaō*, to break), is used of the broken pieces from the feeding of the multitudes, R.V., "broken pieces," A.V., "fragments," Matt. 14 : 20; Mark 6 : 43; 8 : 19, 20; Luke 9 : 17; John 6 : 12, 13; in Matt. 15 : 37 and Mark 8 : 8, R.V., "broken pieces" (A.V., "broken meat").¶

694 AG:104D CB:1237C 5. ARGURION (ἀργύριον), which frequently denotes "money," also represents a silver coin, of the value of a shekel or *tetradrachmon* (four

times the *drachmē*, see No. 2) ; it is used in the plural in Matt. 26 : 15 ; 27 : 3–9. In Acts 19 : 19, " fifty thousand pieces of silver," is, lit., ' fifty thousand of silver ' (probably drachmas). See MONEY, SILVER.

Notes : (1) In Acts 27 : 44, for A.V., " *broken pieces*," the R.V. translates *epi* (on) *tinōn* (certain things) *tōn* (the, i.e., those namely) by " on *other* things ; " there is no word in the original representing " pieces." (2) For the phrase to break to (in) pieces, Matt. 21 : 44, R.V., and Mark
5 : 4, see BREAK, A, Nos. 10 and 5 respectively. (3) In Luke 14 : 18, AGROS 68
A.V., *agros*, a field (R.V.), is translated " a piece of ground." (4) In AG:13D
Matt. 17 : 27, A.V., *statēr*, a shekel (R.V.), a *tetradrachmon* (see No. 5, CB:1233C
above), is translated " a piece of money." STATĒR 4715 AG:764C CB:1270A

PIERCE

1. DIIKNEOMAI (διϊκνέομαι), to go through, penetrate (*dia*, through, *ikneomai*, to go), is used of the power of the Word of God, in Heb. 4 : 12, " piercing."¶ In the Sept., Ex. 26 : 28.¶ 1338 AG:195B CB:—

2. DIERCHOMAI (διέρχομαι), to go through, is translated " shall pierce through " in Luke 2 : 35. See COME, No. 5. 1330 AG:194C CB:1241C

3. EKKENTEŌ (ἐκκεντέω), primarily, to prick out (*ek*, out, *kenteō*, to prick), signifies to pierce, John 19 : 37 ; Rev. 1 : 7.¶ 1574 AG:240C CB:—

4. NUSSŌ (νύσσω), to pierce or pierce through, often of inflicting severe or deadly wounds, is used of the piercing of the side of Christ, John 19 : 34 (in some mss., Matt. 27 : 49).¶ 3572 AG:547A CB:—

5. PERIPEIRŌ (περιπείρω), to put on a spit, hence, to pierce, is used metaphorically in 1 Tim. 6 : 10, of torturing one's soul with many sorrows, " have pierced (themselves) through."¶ 4044 AG:649D CB:—

PIETY (to shew)

EUSEBEŌ (εὐσεβέω), to reverence, to show piety towards any to whom dutiful regard is due (akin to *eusebēs*, pious, godly, devout), is used in 1 Tim. 5 : 4 of the obligation on the part of children and grandchildren (R.V.) to express in a practical way their dutifulness " towards their own family ; " in Acts 17 : 23 of worshipping God. See WORSHIP.¶ 2151 AG:326B CB:1247B

For PIGEON see DOVE, No. 1

PILGRIM

PAREPIDĒMOS (παρεπίδημος), an adjective signifying ' sojourning in a strange place, away from one's own people ' (*para*, from, expressing a contrary condition, and *epidēmeō*, to sojourn ; *dēmos*, a people), is used of O.T. saints, Heb. 11 : 13, " pilgrims " (coupled with *xenos*, a foreigner) ; of Christians, 1 Pet. 1 : 1, " sojourners (of the Dispersion)," R.V.; 2 : 11, " pilgrims " (coupled with *paroikos*, an alien, sojourner) ; the word is thus used metaphorically of those to whom Heaven is their own country, and who are sojourners on earth.¶ PAREPIDĒMOS 3927 AG:625D CB:1262B XENOS 3581 AG:548A CB:1273B PAROIKOS 3941 AG:629A CB:1262B

PILLAR

4769
AG:772A
CB:1270B
STULOS (στύλος), a column supporting the weight of a building, is used (*a*) metaphorically, of those who bear responsibility in the churches, as of the elders in the church at Jerusalem, Gal. 2 : 9 ; of a local church as to its responsibility, in a collective capacity, to maintain the doctrines of the faith by teaching and practice, 1 Tim. 3 : 15 ; some would attach this and the next words to the statement in ver. 16 ; the connection in the Eng. Versions seems preferable ; (*b*) figuratively in Rev. 3 : 12, indicating a firm and permanent position in the spiritual, heavenly and eternal Temple of God ; (*c*) illustratively, of the feet of the angel in the vision in Rev. 10 : 1, seen as flames rising like columns of fire, indicative of holiness and consuming power, and thus reflecting the glory of Christ as depicted in 1 : 15 ; cp. Ezek. 1 : 7.¶

PILLOW

4344
AG:715D
CB:—
PROSKEPHALAION (προσκεφάλαιον) denotes a pillow, a cushion for the head (*pros*, to, *kephalē*, a head), Mark 4 : 38 (R.V., "cushion").¶ In the Sept., Ezek. 13 : 18.¶

PINE AWAY

3583
AG:548C
CB:1273B
XĒRAINŌ (ξηραίνω), to dry up, wither, is rendered "pineth away" in Mark 9 : 18. See DRY.

PINNACLE

4419
AG:727B
CB:1267C
PTERUGION (πτερύγιον) denotes (*a*) a little wing (diminutive of *pterux*, a wing) ; (*b*) anything like a wing, a turret, battlement, of the temple in Jerusalem, Matt. 4 : 5 and Luke 4 : 9 (of the ***hieron***, the entire precincts, or parts of the main building, as distinct from the ***naos***, the sanctuary). This "wing" has been regarded (1) as the apex of the sanctuary, (2) the top of Solomon's porch, (3) the top of the Royal Portico, which Josephus describes as of tremendous height (*Antiq*. xv. 11.5).¶ It is used in the Sept. of the fins of fishes, e.g., Lev. 11 : 9–12 ; of the part of a dress, hanging down in the form of a wing, Ruth 3 : 9 ; 1 Sam. 24 : 5.

PIPE (Noun and Verb)

A. Noun.

836
AG:121C
CB:—
AULOS (αὐλός), a wind instrument, e.g., a flute (connected with *aēmi*, to blow), occurs in 1 Cor. 14 : 7.¶

B. Verb.

832
AG:121B
CB:1238B
AULEŌ (αὐλέω), to play on an *aulos*, is used in Matt. 11 : 17 ; Luke 7 : 32 ; 1 Cor. 14 : 7 (2nd part).¶

For PIPERS, Rev. 18 : 22, A.V., see FLUTE-PLAYERS

5421
AG:865D
CB:1264C

PIT

1. PHREAR (φρέαρ), a well, dug for water (distinct from ***pēgē***, a

fountain), denotes a pit in Rev. 9 : 1, 2, R.V., " the pit (of the abyss)," " the pit," i.e., the shaft leading down to the abyss, A.V., " (bottomless) pit ; " in Luke 14 : 5, R.V., " well " (A.V., " pit ") ; in John 4 : 11, 12, " well." See WELL.¶

2. BOTHUNOS (βόθυνος) is rendered " pit " in Matt. 12 : 11 : see 999 AG:144D
DITCH. CB:—

3. ABUSSOS (ἄβυσσος) : see BOTTOMLESS, B. 12 AG:2B

4. HUPOLĒNION (ὑπολήνιον) denotes a vessel or trough beneath a CB:1233A
winepress, to receive the juice, Mark 12 : 1, R.V., " a pit for the wine- 5276 AG:845C
press " (A.V., " *a place for* . . . the wine-fat ").¶ CB:—

Note : For " pits," 2 Pet. 2 : 4, R.V., see CHAIN *Note* (1).

PITCH (Verb)

PĒGNUMI (πήγνυμι), to make fast, to fix (cp. *prospēgnumi*, Acts 2 : 23, 4078
of crucifixion), is used of pitching a tent ; in Heb. 8 : 2, of the " true AG:656A CB:1263A
tabernacle," the Heavenly and spiritual, which " the Lord pitched."¶

PITCHER

KERAMION (κεράμιον), an earthen vessel (*keramos*, potter's clay), 2765
a jar or jug, occurs in Mark 14 : 13 ; Luke 22 : 10.¶ AG:428D CB:1255A

PITIABLE (most)

ELEEINOTEROS (ἐλεεινότερος), the comparative degree of *eleeinos*, 1652 (-NOS)
miserable, pitiable (*eleos*, pity), is used in 1 Cor. 15 : 19, " most pitiable " AG:249C (-NOS)
(R.V.), lit., ' more pitiable than all men.' See MISERABLE.¶ CB:1244A

PITIFUL, PITY

1. POLUSPLANCHNOS (πολύσπλαγχνος) denotes very pitiful or full 4184
of pity (*polus*, much, *splanchnon*, the heart ; in the plural, the affections), AG:689D CB:1266A
occurs in Jas. 5 : 11, R.V., " full of pity."¶

2. EUSPLANCHNOS (εὔσπλαγχνος), compassionate, tenderhearted, 2155
lit., ' of good heartedness ' (*eu*, well, and *splanchnon*), is translated AG:326C CB:1247B
" pitiful " in 1 Pet. 3 : 8, A.V., R.V., " tenderhearted," as in Eph. 4 : 32.¶

PLACE (Noun, Verb, Adverb)

A. Nouns.

1. TOPOS (τόπος), Eng., topic, topography etc., is used of a region or 5117
locality, frequently in the Gospels and Acts ; in Luke 2 : 7 and 14 : 22, AG:822B CB:1273A
" room ; " of a place which a person or thing occupies, a couch at table, e.g., Luke 14 : 9, 10, R.V., " place " (A.V., " room ") ; of the destiny of Judas Iscariot, Acts 1 : 25 ; of the condition of the " unlearned " or non-gifted in a church gathering, 1 Cor. 14 : 16, R.V., " place ; " the sheath of a sword, Matt. 26 : 52 ; a place in a book, Luke 4 : 17 ; see also Rev. 2 : 5 ; 6 : 14 ; 12 : 8 ; metaphorically, of condition, occasion, opportunity Acts 25 : 16, R.V., " opportunity " (A.V., " licence ") ; Rom. 12 : 19 ; Eph. 4 : 27. See OPPORTUNITY, ROOM.

5564 AG:890B 2. CHŌRION (χωρίον), a region (a diminutive of *chōra*, a land,
CB:1240A country), is used of Gethsemane, Matt. 26 : 36 ; Mark 14 : 32. See
FIELD.

5247 AG:841D 3. HUPEROCHĒ (ὑπεροχή), "high place," 1 Tim. 2 : 2 : see
CB:— AUTHORITY, No. 3.

4042 AG:648D 4. PERIOCHĒ (περιοχή), primarily a circumference, compass (*peri*,
CB:— around, *echō*, to have), hence denotes a portion circumscribed, that which
is contained, and in reference to a writing or book, a portion or passage of
its contents, Acts 8 : 32, "(the) place."¶

201 AG:33C 5. AKROATĒRION (ἀκροατήριον) denotes a place of audience
CB:— (*akroaomai*, to listen), Acts 25 : 23, "place of hearing."¶

4411 6. PRŌTOKLISIA (πρωτοκλισία) : see CHIEF, B, No. 7.

AG:725B CB:1267B *Notes :* (1) For *opē*, a hole, Jas. 3 : 11, A.V., "place," see OPENING :
OPē 3692 see also CAVE. (2) For "place of toll," Matt. 9 : 9 ; Mark 2 : 14, see
AG:574D CUSTOM (TOLL), No. 2. (3) In Heb. 4 : 5 "in this place" is, lit., 'in
CB:— this,' i.e., 'in this (passage).' (4) In Luke 6 : 17, R.V., *topos*, with *pedinos*,
PEDINOS 3977 level, is translated "level place" (A.V., "plain"). (5) For *amphodon*,
AG:638C rendered "a place where two ways met," Mark 11 : 4 (R.V., "the open
CB:1263A AMPHODON street"), see STREET.¶ (6) For *erēmia*, a desert place, see DESERT, A.
296 (7) In 1 Cor. 11 : 20 and 14 : 23, A.V., the phrase *epi to auto*, lit., 'to the
AG:47C CB:— same,' is translated "into one place," R.V., "together ;" perhaps = 'in
ERēMIA assembly.' (8) For "secret place," Luke 11 : 33, A.V., see CELLAR.
2047 AG:308D (9) For "place of prayer," Acts 16 : 13, R.V., see PRAYER. (10) For
CB:1246B Phil. 1 : 13 (A.V., "in all other places"), R.V., "to all the rest," see
PALACE. (11) For "rocky places," Mark 4 : 16, see ROCKY.

B. Verbs.

402 AG:63C 1. ANACHŌREŌ (ἀναχωρέω), to withdraw (*ana*, back, *chōreō*, to make
CB:1235A room, retire), is translated "give place" in Matt. 9 : 24. See DEPART,
No. 10.

1502 AG:222A 2. EIKŌ (εἴκω), to yield, give way, is rendered "gave place" in Gal.
CB:1243A 2 : 5.¶

1096 AG:158A 3. GINOMAI (γίνομαι), to become, take place, is translated "(a death)
CB:1248B having taken place" in Heb. 9 : 15, R.V., A.V., "by means of (death),"
referring, not to the circumstances of a testamentary disposition, but to
the sacrifice of Christ as the basis of the new covenant.

5562 AG:889C *Note :* For *chōreō* in John 8 : 37, A.V., "hath . . . place," see
CB:1240A COURSE, B.

C. Adverbs, etc.

5602 AG:895B 1. HŌDE (ὧδε), here, hither, is translated "to (unto, R.V.) this
CB:— place" in Luke 23 : 5. See HERE.

3837 AG:608B 2. PANTACHOU (πανταχοῦ), everywhere, is translated "in all places"
CB:— in Acts 24 : 3. See EVERYWHERE, No. 2.

Notes : (1) For "in divers places," Matt. 24 : 7, etc., see DIVERS,
1564 **B, Note.** (2) In the following the R.V. gives the correct meaning : in
AG:239B Mark 6 : 10, *ekeithen*, "thence" (A.V., "from that place") ; in Heb.

2 : 6 and 4 : 4, *pou*, "somewhere" (A.V., "in a certain place"); in POU
Matt. 12 : 6, *hōde*, "here" (A.V., "in this place"); in Mark 6 : 10, 4225 AG:696B
hopou ean, "wheresoever" (A.V., "in what place soever"). (3) The CB:1266B ENTOPIOS
adjective *entopios*, "of that place," occurs in Acts 21 : 12.¶ (4) In Jas. 1786
2 : 3 *kalōs*, well (A.V., marg.), is rendered "in a good place." See AG:269B CB:—
DWELLING, HEAVENLY, HOLY, MARKET, SKULL, STEEP, YONDER. KALōS 2573 AG:401B CB:1253B

PLAGUE

1. MASTIX (μάστιξ), a whip, scourge, Acts 22 : 24, "by scourging;" 3148
Heb. 11 : 36, "scourgings," is used metaphorically of disease or suffering, AG:495B CB:1257C
Mark 3 : 10; 5 : 29, 34; Luke 7 : 21. See SCOURGING.¶

2. PLĒGĒ (πληγή), a stripe, wound (akin to *plēssō*, to smite), is used 4127
metaphorically of a calamity, a plague, Rev. 9 : 20; 11 : 6; 15 : 1, 6, 8; AG:668A CB:1265A
16 : 9, 21 (twice); 18 : 4, 8; 21 : 9; 22 : 18. See STRIPE, WOUND.

For PLAIN (Noun) see PLACE, A, Note (4) PLAIN See MANIFEST

PLAIN (Adverb), PLAINLY, PLAINNESS

1. ORTHŌS (ὀρθῶς), rightly (from *orthos*, straight), is translated 3723 AG:580D
"plain," in Mark 7 : 35, of restored speech. See RIGHTLY. CB:1261B

2. PARRHĒSIA (παρρησία), boldness, is used adverbially in its dative 3954
case and rendered "plainly" in John 10 : 24; 11 : 14; 16 : 25; 16 : 29 AG:630C CB:1262C
(with *en*, lit., 'in plainness'). See BOLD, B, where see also "plainness of speech," 2 Cor. 3 : 12, R.V.

PLAIT

PLEKŌ (πλέκω), to weave, twist, plait, is used of the crown of thorns 4120 AG:667B
inflicted on Christ, Matt. 27 : 29; Mark 15 : 17; John 19 : 2.¶ CB:—

For PLAITING (of the hair) see BRAIDED, Note (1) PLAN See COUNSEL, MIND, PLOT, PURPOSE

For PLANK see BOARD PLANK See MOTE

PLANT (Noun, Verb, Adjective)

A. Noun.

PHUTEIA (φυτεία), firstly, a planting, then that which is planted, a 5451
plant (from *phuō*, to bring forth, spring up, grow, *phuton*, a plant), AG:870A CB:1264C
occurs in Matt. 15 : 13.¶ In the Sept., 2 Kings 19 : 29; Ezek. 17 : 7; Mic. 1 : 6.¶

B. Verb.

PHUTEUŌ (φυτεύω), to plant, is used (*a*) literally, Matt. 21 : 33; 5452
Mark 12 : 1; Luke 13 : 6; 17 : 6, 28; 20 : 9; 1 Cor. 9 : 7; (*b*) meta- AG:870A CB:1264C
phorically, Matt. 15 : 13; 1 Cor. 3 : 6, 7, 8.¶ 4854

C. Adjective.

AG:780D
SUMPHUTOS (σύμφυτος), firstly, congenital, innate (from *sumphuō*, to CB:1270B

make to grow together), then, planted or grown along with, united with, Rom. 6 : 5, A.V., " planted together," R.V., " united with *Him*," indicating the union of the believer with Christ in experiencing spiritually " the
EMPHUTOS 1721 likeness of His death." See UNITED.¶ Cp. *emphutos*, Jas. 1 : 21, R.V.,
AG:258A " implanted " (marg., " inborn "). See ENGRAFTED.
CB:1244B

PLATTER

3953
AG:630B 1. PAROPSIS (παροψίς), firstly, a side-dish of dainties (*para*, beside,
CB:— *opson*, cooked) ; then, the dish itself, Matt. 23 : 25 ; ver. 26, in some mss.¶
4094
AG:658C 2. PINAX (πίναξ) is translated platter in Luke 11 : 39 ; see CHARGER.
CB:—

PLAY

3815 PAIZŌ (παίζω), properly, to play as a child (*pais*), hence denotes to
AG:604C
CB:1261C play as in dancing and making merry, 1 Cor. 10 : 7.¶ Cp. *empaizō*, to mock.

PLEAD

1793 ENTUNCHANŌ (ἐντυγχάνω), to make petition, is used of the pleading
AG:270A
CB:1245B of Elijah against Israel, Rom. 11 : 2, R.V., " pleadeth with " (A.V., " maketh intercession to "). See DEAL WITH, INTERCESSIONS.

PLEASE, PLEASING (Noun), WELL-PLEASING, PLEASURE

A. Verbs.

700 1. ARESKŌ (ἀρέσκω) signifies (*a*) to be pleasing to, be acceptable to,
AG:105C
CB:1237C Matt. 14 : 6 ; Mark 6 : 22 ; Acts 6 : 5 ; Rom. 8 : 8 ; 15 : 2 ; 1 Cor. 7 : 32–34 ; Gal. 1 : 10 ; 1 Thess. 2 : 15 ; 4 : 1 (where the preceding *kai*, " and," is epexegetical, 'even,' explaining the 'walking,' i.e., Christian manner of life, as 'pleasing God ;' in Gen. 5 : 22, where the Hebrew has " Enoch walked with God," the Sept. has " Enoch pleased God ; " cp. Mic. 6 : 8 ; Heb. 11 : 5) ; 2 Tim. 2 : 4 ; (*b*) to endeavour to please, and so, to render service, doing so evilly in one's own interests, Rom. 15 : 1, which Christ did not, ver. 3 ; or unselfishly, 1 Cor. 10 : 33 ; 1 Thess. 2 : 4. This sense of the word is illustrated by Moulton and Milligan (Vocab.) from numerous Inscriptions, especially describing " those who have proved themselves of use to the commonwealth."¶

2100 2. EUARESTEŌ (εὐαρεστέω) signifies to be well-pleasing (*eu*, well,
AG:318C
CB:1247A and a form akin to No. 1) ; in the Active Voice, Heb. 11 : 5, R.V., " he had been well-pleasing (unto God)," A.V., " he pleased ; " so ver. 6 ; in the Passive Voice, Heb. 13 : 16.¶

2106 3. EUDOKEŌ (εὐδοκέω) signifies (*a*) to be well pleased, to think it
AG:319B
CB:1247A good [*eu*, well, and *dokeō*, see Note (1) below], not merely an understanding of what is right and good as in *dokeō*, but stressing the willingness and freedom of an intention or resolve regarding what is good, e.g., Luke 12 : 32, " it is (your Father's) good pleasure ; " so Rom. 15 : 26, 27, R.V. ; 1 Cor. 1 : 21 ; Gal. 1 : 15 ; Col. 1 : 19 ; 1 Thess. 2 : 8, R.V., " we

were well pleased " (A.V., " we were willing ") ; this meaning is frequently
found in the papyri in legal documents ; (*b*) to be well pleased with, or
take pleasure in, e.g., Matt. 3 : 17 ; 12 : 18 ; 17 : 5 ; 1 Cor. 10 : 5 ; 2 Cor.
12 : 10 ; 2 Thess. 2 : 12 ; Heb. 10 : 6, 8, 38 ; 2 Pet. 1 : 17.

4. THELŌ (θέλω), to will, wish, desire, is translated " it pleased 2309 AG:354D
(Him) " in 1 Cor. 12 : 18 ; 15 : 38, R.V. See DESIRE, B, No. 6. CB:1271C

5. SPATALAŌ (σπαταλάω), to live riotously, is translated " giveth 4684
herself to pleasure " in 1 Tim. 5 : 6, R.V. (A.V., " liveth in pleasure ") ; AG:761A CB:—
" taken your pleasure " in Jas. 5 : 5, A.V., " been wanton."¶

Notes : (1) In Acts 15 : 22, A.V., *dokeō*, to seem good to (R.V.), is DOKEō
translated " it pleased " (in some mss., ver. 34) ; in Heb. 12 : 10, A.V., 1380 AG:201D
" (after their own) pleasure," R.V.," (as) seemed good (to them)." (2) For CB:1242A
suneudokeō, rendered " have pleasure in " in Rom. 1 : 32, A.V., see SUNEUDOKEō 4909
CONSENT, No. 6. (3) For *truphaō*, rendered " lived in pleasure " in Jas. AG:788D
5 : 5, A.V., see DELICATELY. TRUPHAō 5171

B. Adjectives. AG:828C

1. ARESTOS (ἀρεστός) denotes pleasing, agreeable, John 8 : 29, 701
R.V., " (the things that are) pleasing," A.V., " (those things that) please ; " AG:105D CB:1237C
A.V. and R.V. in 1 John 3 : 22 ; in Acts 6 : 2, " fit " (R.V. marg., " pleas-
ing ") ; 12 : 3, " it pleased," lit., ' it was pleasing.' See FIT.¶

2. EUARESTOS (εὐάρεστος), *eu*, well, and No. 1, is translated " well- 2101
pleasing " in the R.V. except in Rom. 12 : 1, 2 (see marg., however). AG:318D CB:1247A
See ACCEPT, B, No. 4.

C. Noun.

ARESKEIA (or *-ia*) (ἀρεσκεία), a " pleasing," a giving pleasure, Col. 699
1 : 10, of the purpose Godward of a walk worthy of the Lord (cp. 1 Thess. AG:105C CB:1237C
4 : 1). It was used frequently in a bad sense in classical writers. Moulton
and Milligan illustrate from the papyri its use in a favourable sense, and
Deissmann (*Bible Studies*) from an inscription.¶ In the Sept., Prov.
31 : 30.¶

PLEASURE HēDONē

A. Nouns. 2237 AG:344B

1. HĒDONĒ (ἡδονή), pleasure, is used of the gratification of the natural CB:1249C
desire or sinful desires (akin to *hēdomai*, to be glad, and *hēdeōs*, gladly), EUDOKIA 2107
Luke 8 : 14 ; Tit. 3 : 3 ; Jas. 4 : 1, 3, R.V., " pleasures " (A.V., " lusts ") ; AG:319C
in the singular, 2 Pet. 2 : 13. See LUST.¶ CB:1247A APOLAUSIS

2. EUDOKIA (εὐδοκία), good pleasure (akin to *eudokeō*, PLEASE, 619
No. 3), Eph. 1 : 5, 9 ; Phil. 2 : 13 ; 2 Thess. 1 : 11. See DESIRE, A. No. 2. AG:94D

3. APOLAUSIS (ἀπόλαυσις), enjoyment, is used with *echō*, to have, CB:— THELēMA
and rendered " enjoy the pleasures " (lit., ' pleasure ') in Heb. 11 : 25. 2307 AG:354B
See ENJOY. CB:1271C

Notes : (1) In Rev. 4 : 11, A.V., *thelēma*, a will, is translated " (for CHARIS
Thy) pleasure," R.V., " (because of Thy) will." (2) For *charis*, trans- 5485 AG:877B
lated " pleasure " in the A.V. of Acts 24 : 27 and 25 : 9, see FAVOUR, A. CB:1239C

B. Adjective.

5369 AG:859C PHILĒDONOS (φιλήδονος), loving pleasure (*philos*, loving, and A,
CB:1264A No. 1), occurs in 2 Tim. 3 : 4, R.V., "lovers of pleasure" (A.V., ". . . pleasures"). See LOVER.¶

4684 AG:761A CB:— *Note :* In 1 Tim. 5 : 6 the R.V. renders *spatalaō* "giveth herself to pleasure."

PLEDGED See BETHROTH

PLENTEOUS

4183 AG:687C POLUS (πολύς), much, is rendered "plenteous" in Matt. 9 : 37, of
CB:1266A a harvest of souls, and Luke 10 : 2, R.V. (A.V., "great"). See GREAT.

PLENTIFULLY

2164 AG:327C *Note :* This translates the prefix *eu* (well) of the verb *euphoreō*, to pro-
CB:— duce well, in Luke 12 : 16, "brought forth plentifully."¶

PLOT

1917 AG:290C EPIBOULĒ (ἐπιβουλή), lit., a plan against (*epi*, against, *boulē*, a counsel,
CB:— plan), is translated "plot" in the R.V. (A.V., "laying await" and "lying in wait") in Acts 9 : 24 ; 20 : 3, 19 ; 23 : 30.¶

PLOUGH, PLOW

A. Noun.

723 AG:108B CB:— AROTRON (ἄροτρον), from *aroō*, to plough, occurs in Luke 9 : 62.¶

B. Verb.

722 AG:108B AROTRIAŌ (ἀροτριάω), akin to A, a later form of *aroō*, to plough,
CB:— occurs in Luke 17 : 7 and 1 Cor. 9 : 10.¶

PLUCK (out)

5089 AG:817A 1. TILLŌ (τίλλω) is used of plucking off ears of corn, Matt. 12 : 1 ;
CB:— Mark 2 : 23 ; Luke 6 : 1.¶ In the Sept., Isa. 18 : 7.¶

726 AG:109A 2. HARPAZŌ (ἁρπάζω), to seize, snatch, is rendered "pluck" in
CB:1249B John 10 : 28, 29, A.V., R.V., "snatch." For the meaning, see CATCH, No. 1.

1807 AG:271D 3. EXAIREŌ (ἐξαιρέω), to take out (*ex* for *ek*, out, *haireō*, to take),
CB:— is translated "pluck out," of the eye as the occasion of sin, in Matt. 5 : 29 ; 18 : 9, indicating that, with determination and promptitude, we are to strike at the root of unholy inclinations, ridding ourselves of whatever would stimulate them. Cp. Note (2) below. See DELIVER, No. 8.

1846 AG:277C 4. EXORUSSŌ (ἐξορύσσω), to dig out or up, is rendered "ye would
CB:— have plucked out (your eyes)" in Gal. 4 : 15, an indication of their feelings of gratitude to, and love for, the Apostle. The metaphor affords no real ground for the supposition of a reference to some weakness of his sight, and certainly not to the result of his temporary blindness at his conversion, the recovery from which must have been as complete as the infliction. There would be some reason for such an inference had the pronoun "ye" been stressed ; but the stress is on the word "eyes ;"

their devotion prompted a readiness to part with their most treasured possession on his behalf. For Mark 2 : 4 see BREAK, No. 14, DIG, No. 1, Note (2).¶ In the Sept., 1 Sam. 11 : 2 ; Prov. 29 : 22.¶

5. EKRIZOŌ (ἐκριζόω), to pluck up by the roots (*ek*, out, *rhiza*, a root), 1610
is so translated in Jude 12 (figuratively), and in the A.V. in Luke 17 : 6, AG:244D CB:1244A
R.V., "rooted up ;" "root up," Matt. 13 : 29 ; "shall be rooted up,"
15 : 13. See ROOT.¶

Notes : (1) In Mark 5 : 4, A.V., *diaspaō*, to rend asunder (R.V.), is DIASPAō
translated "plucked asunder," said of chains. (2) In Mark 9 : 47, A.V., 1288 AG:188C
ekballō, to cast out (R.V.), is translated "pluck . . . out." Cp. No. 3, CB:—
above. EKBALLō 1544 AG:237B CB:1243B

POET

POIĒTĒS (ποιητής), primarily a maker, later a doer (*poieō* to make, 4163
to do), was used, in classical Greek, of an author, especially a poet ; so AG:683B CB:1265C
Acts 17 : 28. See DOER.

POINT, POINTS

A. Phrases.

Notes : (1) In Heb. 4 : 15, "in all points" represents the phrase KATA
kata with the neuter plural of *pas*, all, lit., 'according to all (things).' 2596
(2) 'To be at the point of death' is a translation (*a*) of the verb *mellō*, AG:405C CB:1253C
to be about, with *teleutaō*, to end one's life, die, Luke 7 : 2 ; see DIE, MELLō
No. 4 ; (*b*) of *mellō* with *apothnēskō*, to die, John 4 : 47 ; (*c*) of the phrase 3195 AG:500D
mentioned under DEATH, C, Note. (3) In Jas. 2 : 10, *en heni* (the dative CB:1258A
case of *heis*, one), lit., 'in one,' is rendered "in one *point*."

B. Noun.

KEPHALAION (κεφάλαιον), the neuter of the adjective *kephalaios*, of 2774
the head, is used as a noun, signifying (*a*) a sum, amount, of money, Acts AG:429D CB:1255A
22 : 28 ; (*b*) a chief point, Heb. 8 : 1, not the summing up of the subject, as the A.V. suggests, for the subject was far from being finished in the Epistle ; on the contrary, in all that was being set forth by the writer "the chief point" consisted in the fact that believers have "a High Priest" of the character already described. See SUM.¶

C. Verb.

DĒLOŌ (δηλόω), to make plain (*dēlos*, evident), is translated "did 1213
point unto" in 1 Pet. 1 : 11, R.V. (A.V., "did signify"), of the operation AG:178C CB:1240C
of "the Spirit of Christ" in the prophets of the Old Testament in pointing on to the time and its characteristics, of the sufferings of Christ and subsequent glories. See SHEW, SIGNIFY.

POISON

IOS (ἰός) denotes something active as (*a*) rust, as acting on metals, 2447
affecting their nature, Jas. 5 : 3 ; (*b*) poison, as of asps, acting destructively AG:378D CB:1252C
on living tissues, figuratively of the evil use of the lips as the organs of speech, Rom. 3 : 13 ; so of the tongue, Jas. 3 : 8.¶

For POLLUTE see DEFILE, A, No. 1

POLLUTION

234 AG:37D CB:1234C (-MATA) ALISGĒMA (ἀλίσγημα), akin to a late verb *alisgeō*, to pollute, denotes a pollution, contamination, Acts 15 : 20, " pollutions of idols," i.e., all the contaminating associations connected with idolatry including meats from sacrifices offered to idols.¶

3393 AG:521A CB:1258C *Note :* For *miasma*, A.V., " pollutions," in 2 Pet. 2 : 20, see DEFILEMENT, B, No. 1.¶

POMP

5325 AG:853B CB:1263C PHANTASIA (φαντασία), as a philosophic term, denoted an imagination ; then, an appearance, like *phantasma*, an apparition ; later, a show, display, pomp (Eng., phantasy), Acts 25 : 23.¶ In the Sept., Hab. 2 : 18 ; 3 : 10 ; Zech. 10 : 1.¶

PONDER

4820 AG:777B CB:— SUMBALLŌ (συμβάλλω), to throw together, confer, etc., has the meaning to ponder, i.e., to put one thing with another in considering circumstances, in Luke 2 : 19. See CONFER.

POOL

2861 AG:442C CB:— KOLUMBĒTHRA (κολυμβήθρα) denotes a swimming pool (akin to *kolumbaō*, to swim, Acts 27 : 43), John 5 : 2 (ver. 4 in some mss.), 7 ; 9 : 7 (ver. 11 in some mss.).¶

POOR

A. Adjectives.

4434 AG:728B CB:1268A 1. PTŌCHOS (πτωχός), for which see BEG, B, has the broad sense of " poor," (*a*) literally, e.g., Matt. 11 : 5 ; 26 : 9, 11 ; Luke 21 : 3 (with stress on the word, ' a conspicuously poor widow ') ; John 12 : 5, 6, 8 ; 13 : 29 ; Jas. 2 : 2, 3, 6 ; the poor are constantly the subjects of injunctions to assist them, Matt. 19 : 21 ; Mark 10 : 21 ; Luke 14 : 13, 21 ; 18 : 22 ; Rom. 15 : 26 ; Gal. 2 : 10 ; (*b*) metaphorically, Matt. 5 : 3 ; Luke 6 : 20 ; Rev. 3 : 17.

3998 AG:642D CB:1263A 2. PENICHROS (πενιχρός), akin to B, needy, poor, is used of the widow in Luke 21 : 2 (cp. No. 1, of the same woman, in ver. 3) ; it is used frequently in the papyri.¶ In the Sept., Ex. 22 : 25 ; Prov. 28 : 15 ; 29 : 7.¶

B. Noun.

3993 AG:642C CB:1263A PENĒS (πένης), a labourer (akin to *penomai*, to work for one's daily bread), is translated " poor " in 2 Cor. 9 : 9.¶

C. Verb.

4433 AG:728A CB:1268A PTŌCHEUŌ (πτωχεύω), to be poor as a beggar (akin to A, No. 1), to be destitute, is said of Christ in 2 Cor. 8 : 9.¶

PORCH

1. STOA (στοά), a portico, is used (*a*) of the porches at the pool of 4745
Bethesda, John 5 : 2 ; (*b*) of the covered colonnade in the Temple, called AG:768D
Solomon's porch, John 10 : 23 ; Acts 3 : 11 ; 5 : 12, a portico on the CB:1270A
eastern side of the temple ; this and the other porches existent in the time of Christ were almost certainly due to Herod's restoration. Cp. *Stoics* (Acts 17 : 18), 'philosophers of the porch.'¶

2. PULŌN (πυλών), akin to *pulē*, a gate (Eng., pylon), is used of a 4440
doorway, porch or vestibule of a house or palace, Matt. 26 : 71. In the AG:729C
parallel passage Mark 14 : 68, No. 3 is used, and *pulōn* doubtless stands CB:1268A
in Matt. 26 for *proaulion*. See GATE, No. 2.

3. PROAULION (προαύλιον), the exterior court or vestibule, between 4259
the door and the street, in the houses of well-to-do folk, Mark 14 : 68, AG:702D
" porch " (R.V. marg., " forecourt ").¶ CB:—

PORTER

THURŌROS (θυρωρός), a door-keeper (*thura*, a door, *ouros*, a guardian), 2377
is translated " porter " in Mark 13 : 34 ; John 10 : 3 ; it is used of a female AG:366A
in John 18 : 16, 17, translated " (her) that kept the door."¶ In the CB:—
Sept., 2 Sam. 4 : 6 ; 2 Kings 7 : 11 ; Ezek. 44 : 11.¶

PORTION

A. Nouns.

1. MEROS (μέρος), a part, is translated " portion " in Matt. 24 : 51 ; 3313
Luke 12 : 46 ; 15 : 12. See PART. AG:505D CB:1258B

2. KLĒROS (κλῆρος), a lot, is translated " portion " in Acts 1 : 17, 2819
R.V. See CHARGE, INHERITANCE, LOT. AG:435B CB:1255B

3. MERIS (μερίς), a part, is translated " portion " in 2 Cor. 6 : 15, 3310
R.V. See PART. AG:505A CB:1258B

Note : For " portion of food," Luke 12 : 42, R.V., see FOOD, No. 4.

B. Verb.

SUMMERIZŌ (συμμερίζω), to have a part with (akin to A, No. 3), is 4829
translated " have their portion with " in 1 Cor. 9 : 13, R.V. See PAR- (-OMAI) AG:778C
TAKER.¶ CB:—

C. Adverb.

POLUMERŌS (πολυμερῶς) signifies 'in many parts' or portions 4181
(*polus*, many, and A, No. 1), Heb. 1 : 1, R.V. (A.V., "at sundry times ").¶ AG:687B CB:—

POSSESS, POSSESSION

A. Verbs.

1. KATECHŌ (κατέχω), to hold fast, hold back, signifies to possess, 2722
in 1 Cor. 7 : 30 and 2 Cor. 6 : 10. See HOLD. AG:422C CB:1254B

2. KTAOMAI (κτάομαι), to procure for oneself, acquire, obtain, hence, 2932
to possess (akin to B, No. 1), has this meaning in Luke 18 : 12 and 1 Thess. AG:455A CB:1256A
4 : 4 ; in Luke 21 : 19, R.V., " ye shall win " (A.V., " possess ye "), where

the probable meaning is 'ye shall gain the mastery over your souls,' i.e., instead of giving way to adverse circumstances. See OBTAIN.

5225 3. HUPARCHŌ (ὑπάρχω), to be in existence, and, in a secondary sense,
AG:838A CB:— to belong to, is used with this meaning in the neuter plural of the present participle with the article signifying one's possessions, "the things which he possesseth," Luke 12 : 15; Acts 4 : 32; in Heb. 10 : 34, R.V., "possessions" (A.V., "goods"); cp. B, No. 4. See GOODS.

1139 AG:169A 4. DAIMONIZOMAI (δαιμονίζομαι), to be possessed of a demon or
CB:1240B demons: see DEMON, B.

2192 AG:331D *Note:* In Acts 8 : 7 and 16 : 16, A.V., *echō*, have, is translated to be
CB:1242C possessed of, in the sense of No. 4, above, R.V., "had" and "having."

B. Nouns.

2933 AG:455B 1. KTĒMA (κτῆμα), akin to A, No. 2, denotes a possession, property,
CB:1256A Matt. 19 : 22; Mark 10 : 22; Acts 2 : 45; 5 : 1.¶

2697 AG:419C 2. KATASCHESIS (κατάσχεσις), primarily a holding back (akin to
CB:— A, No. 1), then, a holding fast, denotes a possession, Acts 7 : 5, or taking possession, ver. 45, with the article, lit., 'in the (i.e., their) taking possession.'¶

4047 AG:650A 3. PERIPOIĒSIS (περιποίησις), an obtaining, an acquisition, is trans-
CB:1263B lated "(*God's* own) possession" in Eph. 1 : 14, R.V., which may mean 'acquisition,' A.V., "purchased possession;" 1 Pet. 2 : 9, R.V., "*God's* own possession", A.V., "a peculiar (people)." See OBTAIN.

5223 AG:837D 4. HUPARXIS (ὕπαρξις), primarily subsistence (akin to A, No. 3),
CB:1252A later denoted substance, property, "possession" in Heb. 10 : 34, R.V. (A.V., "substance"). See GOODS, SUBSTANCE.

5564 AG:890B *Note:* In Acts 28 : 7, A.V., *chōria*, lands (R.V.), is translated
CB:1240A "possessions."

C. Adjective.

4041 AG:648D PERIOUSIOS (περιούσιος), of one's own possession, one's own, qualifies
CB:1263B the noun *laos*, people, in Tit. 2 : 14, A.V., "peculiar," see R.V.¶ In the Sept., Ex. 19 : 5; 23 . 22; Deut. 7 : 6; 14 : 2; 26 : 18.¶

POSSESSOR

2935 AG:455C KTĒTŌR (κτήτωρ), a possessor, an owner (akin to *ktaomai*, see
CB:— POSSESS, No. 2), occurs in Acts 4 : 34.¶

POSSIBLE

DUNATOS 1415

A. Adjective.

AG:208C CB:1242B DUNATOS (δυνατός), strong, mighty, powerful, able (to do), in its
DUNAMAI neuter form signifies "possible," Matt. 19 : 26; 24 : 24; 26 : 39; Mark
1410 9 : 23; 10 : 27; 13 : 22; 14 : 35, 36; Luke 18 : 27; Acts 2 : 24;
AG:207A CB:1242B 20 : 16 (27 : 39, in some mss.; *dunamai*, to be able, in the most authentic,
EIMI R.V., "they could"); Rom. 12 : 18; Gal. 4 : 15. See ABLE.

1510 AG:222D

B. Verb.

CB:1243A EIMI (εἰμί), to be, is used in the third person singular, impersonally, with the meaning " it is possible," negatively in 1 Cor. 11 : 20, R.V. (A.V., " it is not "), and Heb. 9 : 5, " we cannot," lit., ' it is not possible.'

Note: For Heb. 10 : 4, A.V., " it is not possible," see IMPOSSIBLE.

POT

1. XESTĒS (ξέστης) was a Sicilian corruption of the Latin liquid 3582 AG:548B
measure *sextarius*, about a pint ; in Mark 7 : 4 (ver. 8 also in some mss.) CB:—
it denotes a pitcher, of wood or stone.¶

2. STAMNOS (στάμνος), primarily an earthen jar for racking off 4713 AG:764B
wine, hence, any kind of jar, occurs in Heb. 9 : 4.¶ CB:1255A

For POTENTATE, used of God, 1 Tim. 6 : 15, see AUTHORITY, No. 4

POTTER

A. Noun.

KERAMEUS (κεραμεύς), a potter (from *kerannumi*, to mix, akin to 2763
keramos, potter's clay), is used (*a*) in connection with the " potter's AG:428D CB:1255A
field," Matt. 27 : 7, 10 ; (*b*) illustratively of the potter's right over the clay, Rom. 9 : 21, where the introductory " or " suggests the alternatives that either there must be a recognition of the absolute discretion and power of God, or a denial that the potter has power over the clay. There is no suggestion of the creation of sinful beings, or of the creation of any simply in order to punish them. What the passage sets forth is God's right to deal with sinful beings according to His own counsel.¶

B. Adjective.

KERAMIKOS (κεραμικός) denotes ' of (or made by) a potter ' (Eng., 2764 AG:428D
ceramic), earthen, Rev. 2 : 27.¶ CB:1255A

POUND

1. LITRA (λίτρα) was a Sicilian coin, the equivalent of a Latin *libra* 3046 AG:475D
or *as* (whence the metric unit, litre) ; in the N.T. it is used as a measure of CB:—
weight, a pound, John 12 : 3 ; 19 : 39.¶

2. MNA (μνᾶ), a Semitic word, both a weight and a sum of money, 3414 AG:524A
100 shekels (cp. 1 Kings 10 : 17, *maneh ;* Dan. 5 : 25, 26, *mene*), in Attic CB:—
Greek 100 *drachmai*, in weight about 15 oz., in value near about £4 1s. 3d. (see PIECE), occurs in Luke 19 : 13, 16 (twice), 18 (twice), 20, 24 (twice), 25.¶

POUR

1. BALLŌ (βάλλω), to throw, is used of pouring liquids, Matt. 26 : 12, 906 AG:130D
R.V., marg., " cast " (of ointment) ; John 13 : 5 (of water). See CAST, CB:1238B
No. 1.

2. KATACHEŌ (καταχέω), to pour down upon (*kata*, down, *cheō*, 2708 AG:420C
to pour), is used in Matt. 26 : 7 (cp. No. 1 in ver. 12) and Mark 14 : 3, of CB:—
ointment.¶

1632 AG:247B CB:1243B

3. EKCHEŌ (ἐκχέω), to pour out (*ek*, out), is used (*a*) of Christ's act as to the changers' money, John 2 : 15 ; (*b*) of the Holy Spirit, Acts 2 : 17, 18, 33, R.V., " He hath poured forth " (A.V., " . . . shed forth ") ; Tit. 3 : 6, R.V., " poured out " (A.V., " shed ") ; (*c*) of the emptying of the contents of the bowls (A.V., vials) of Divine wrath, Rev. 16 : 1–4, 8, 10, 12, 17 ; (*d*) of the shedding of the blood of saints by the foes of God, Rev. 16 : 6, R.V., " poured out " (A.V., " shed ") ; some mss. have it in Acts 22 : 20. See RUN, SHED, SPILL.

1632 AG:247B (EKCHEŌ) CB:1243B

4. EKCHUNŌ (ἐκχύνω) or *ekchunnō*, a Hellenistic form of No. 3, is used of the blood of Christ, Luke 22 : 20, R.V., " is poured out " (A.V., " is shed ") ; of the Holy Spirit, Acts 10 : 45. See GUSH OUT, RUN, SHED, SPILL.

2022 AG:305A CB:—

5. EPICHEŌ (ἐπιχέω), to pour upon (*epi*), is used in Luke 10 : 34, of the oil and wine used by the good Samaritan on the wounds of him who had fallen among robbers.¶

Note : For the A.V., " poured out " in Rev. 14 : 10 (R.V., " prepared"), see MINGLE, No. 2.

POVERTY

4432 AG:728A CB:1268A

PTŌCHEIA (πτωχεία), destitution (akin to *ptōcheuō*, see POOR), is used of the poverty which Christ voluntarily experienced on our behalf, 2 Cor. 8 : 9 ; of the destitute condition of saints in Judæa, ver. 2 ; of the condition of the church in Smyrna, Rev. 2 : 9, where the word is used in a general sense. Cp. synonymous words under POOR.¶

For POWDER see GRIND

POWER (Noun, and Verb, to have, bring under)

A. Nouns.

1411 AG:207B CB:1242B

1. DUNAMIS (δύναμις), for the different meanings of which see ABILITY, MIGHT, is sometimes used, by metonymy, of persons and things, e.g., (*a*) of God, Matt. 26 : 64 ; Mark 14 : 62 ; (*b*) of angels, e.g., perhaps in Eph. 1 : 21, R.V., " power," A.V., " might " (cp. Rom. 8 : 38 ; 1 Pet. 3 : 22) ; (*c*) of that which manifests God's power : Christ, 1 Cor. 1 : 24 ; the Gospel, Rom. 1 : 16 ; (*d*) of mighty works (R.V., marg., " power " or " powers "), e.g., Mark 6 : 5, " mighty work ; " so 9 : 39, R.V. (A.V., " miracle ") ; Acts 2 : 22 (ditto) ; 8 : 13, " miracles ; " 2 Cor. 12 : 12, R.V., " mighty works " (A.V., " mighty deeds ").

Note : For different meanings of synonymous terms, see Note under DOMINION, A, No. 1.

1849 AG:277D CB:1247C

2. EXOUSIA (ἐξουσία) denotes freedom of action, right to act ; used of God, it is absolute, unrestricted, e.g., Luke 12 : 5 (R.V. marg., " authority ") ; in Acts 1 : 7 ' right of disposal ' is what is indicated ; used of men, authority is delegated. Angelic beings are called " powers " in Eph. 3 : 10 (cp. 1 : 21) ; 6 : 12 ; Col. 1 : 16 ; 2 : 15 (cp. 2 : 10). See AUTHORITY, No. 1, see also PRINCIPALITY.

3. ISCHUS (ἰσχύς), ability, force, strength, is nowhere translated 2479 AG:383C
"power" in the R.V. (A.V. in 2 Thess. 1 : 9). See ABILITY, No. 2. CB:1253A
4. KRATOS (κράτος) is translated "power" in the R.V. and A.V. 2904
in 1 Tim. 6 : 16; Heb. 2 : 14; in Eph. 1 : 19 (last part); 6 : 10, A.V., AG:449A CB:1256A
"power" (R.V., "strength"): see DOMINION, A, No. 1, STRENGTH,
A, No. 3.
5 DUNATON (δυνατόν), the neuter of the adjective *dunatos*, powerful 1415
(akin to No. 1), is used as a noun with the article in Rom. 9 : 22, "(to make AG:208C CB:1242B
His) power (known)." See ABLE.
6. ARCHĒ (ἀρχή), a beginning, rule, is translated "power" in Luke 746
20 : 20, A.V. (R.V., "rule"). See BEGINNING, B. AG:111D CB:1237B

B. Verb.

EXOUSIAZŌ (ἐξουσιάζω), to exercise authority (akin to A, No. 2), 1850
is used (*a*) in the Active Voice, Luke 22 : 25, R.V., "have authority" AG:279A CB:1247C
(A.V., "exercise authority"), of the power of rulers; 1 Cor. 7 : 4 (twice), of marital relations and conditions; (*b*) in the Passive Voice, 1 Cor. 6 : 12, to be brought under the power of a thing; here, this verb and the preceding one connected with it, *exesti*, present a paronomasia, which Lightfoot brings out as follows: 'All are within my power; but I will not put myself under the power of any one of all things.' See AUTHORITY, B, No. 1.¶

Notes: (1) In Rev. 13 : 14, 15, A.V., *didōmi*, to give, is translated DIDōMI
"(he) had power;" R.V., "it was given (him)" and "it was given 1325 AG:192C
unto him;" the A.V. misses the force of the permissive will of God in the CB:1241C
actings of the Beast. (2) In Rom. 16 : 25, A.V., *dunamai*, to be able, is DUNAMAI 1410
translated "that is of power" (R.V., "that is able"). See ABLE. AG:207A
(3) The subject of power in Scripture may be viewed under the following CB:1242B
heads: (*a*) its original source, in the Persons in the Godhead; (*b*) its exercise by God in creation, its preservation and its government; (*c*) special manifestations of Divine power, past, present and future; (*d*) power existent in created beings, other than man, and in inanimate nature; (*e*) committed to man, and misused by him; (*f*) committed to those who, on becoming believers, were empowered by the Spirit of God, are indwelt by Him, and will exercise it hereafter for God's glory.

POWERFUL, POWERFULLY

A. Adjectives.

1. ENERGĒS (ἐνεργής): see ACTIVE. 1756 AG:265D CB:1245A
2. ISCHUROS (ἰσχυρός), strong, mighty, akin to *ischus* (see POWER, 2478
A, No. 3), is translated "powerful" in 2 Cor. 10 : 10, A.V. (R.V., AG:383A CB:1253A
"strong"). See STRONG.

B. Adverb.

EUTONŌS (εὐτόνως) signifies vigorously, vehemently (*eu*, well, *teinō*, 2159
to stretch), Luke 23 : 10, "vehemently," of the accusation of the chief AG:327B CB:—
priests and scribes against Christ; Acts 18 : 28, R.V., "powerfully"

(A.V., "mightily"), of Apollos in confuting Jews.¶ In the Sept., Josh. 6 : 8.¶

Note : For "is powerful," 2 Cor. 13 : 3, R.V., see MIGHTY, C.

For PRACTICES see COVETOUS, B, No. 3

PRACTISE

4238 AG:698B PRASSŌ (πράσσω) is translated by the verb to practise in the R.V.
CB:1266B in the following passages (the A.V. nowhere renders the verb thus) : John 3 : 20 (marg.) ; 5 : 29 (marg.) ; Acts 19 : 19 ; Rom. 1 : 32 (twice) ; 2 : 1, 2, 3 ; 7 : 15, 19 ; Gal. 5 : 21. See DO, No. 2.

For PRÆTORIUM and PRÆTORIAN GUARD see PALACE

PRAISE

A. Nouns.

136 AG:23D 1. AINOS (αἶνος), primarily a tale, narration, came to denote praise ;
CB:1234A in the N.T. only of praise to God, Matt. 21 : 16 ; Luke 18 : 43.¶

1868 AG:281C 2. EPAINOS (ἔπαινος), a strengthened form of No. 1 (*epi*, upon),
CB:1245B denotes approbation, commendation, praise ; it is used (*a*) of those on account of, and by reason of, whom as God's heritage, praise is to be ascribed to God, in respect of His glory (the exhibition of His character and operations), Eph. 1 : 12 ; in ver. 14, of the whole company, the Church, viewed as "*God's* own possession" (R.V.) ; in ver. 6, with particular reference to the glory of His grace towards them ; in Phil. 1 : 11, as the result of "the fruits of righteousness" manifested in them through the power of Christ ; (*b*) of praise bestowed by God, upon the Jew spiritually (Judah = praise), Rom. 2 : 29 ; bestowed upon believers hereafter at the Judgment-Seat of Christ, 1 Cor. 4 : 5 (where the definite article indicates that the praise will be exactly in accordance with each person's actions) ; as the issue of present trials, "at the revelation of Jesus Christ," 1 Pet. 1 : 7 ; (*c*) of whatsoever is praiseworthy, Phil. 4 : 8 ; (*d*) of the approbation by churches of those who labour faithfully in the ministry of the Gospel, 2 Cor. 8 : 18 ; (*e*) of the approbation of well-doers by human rulers, Rom. 13 : 3 ; 1 Pet. 2 : 14.¶

133 AG:23C 3. AINESIS (αἴνεσις), praise (akin to No. 1), is found in Heb. 13 : 15,
CB:1234A where it is metaphorically represented as a sacrificial offering.¶

ARETē *Notes :* (1) In 1 Pet. 2 : 9, A.V., *aretē*, virtue, excellence, is translated
703 AG:105D "praises" (R.V., "excellencies"). (2) In the following the A.V. trans-
CB:1237C lates *doxa*, glory, by "praise" (R.V., "glory") ; John 9 : 24, where
DOXA 1391 "give glory to God" signifies 'confess thy sins' (cp. Josh. 7 : 19, indicat-
AG:203C ing the genuine confession of facts in one's life which gives glory to God) ;
CB:1242B 12 : 43 (twice) ; 1 Pet. 4 : 11.

134 AG:23C

B. Verbs.

CB:1233C 1. AINEŌ (αἰνέω), to speak in praise of, to praise (akin to A, No. 1), is always used of praise to God, (*a*) by angels, Luke 2 : 13 ; (*b*) by men, Luke 2 : . ; 19 : 37 ; 24 : 53 ; Acts 2 : 20 47 ; 3 : 8, 9 ; Rom. 15 : 11 (No. 2 in some texts) ; Rev. 19 : 5.¶

2. EPAINEŌ (ἐπαινέω), akin to A, No. 2, is rendered " praise," 1 Cor. 1867 AG:281C
11 : 2, 17, 22 : see COMMEND, No. 1. CB:1245B

3. HUMNEŌ (ὑμνέω) denotes (*a*) transitively, to sing, to laud, sing to 5214 AG:836B
the praise of (Eng., hymn), Acts 16 : 25, A.V., " sang praises " (R.V., CB:1251C
" singing hymns ") ; Heb. 2 : 12, R.V., " will I sing (Thy) praise," A.V., " will I sing praise (unto Thee), " lit., ' I will hymn Thee ; ' (*b*) intransitively, to sing, Matt. 26 : 30 ; Mark 14 : 26, in both places of the singing of the paschal hymns (Psa. 113–118, and 136), called by Jews the Great Hallel.¶

4. PSALLŌ (ψάλλω), primarily, to twitch or twang (as a bowstring, 5567 AG:891A
etc.), then, to play (a stringed instrument with the fingers), in the Sept., CB:1267B
to sing psalms, denotes, in the N.T., to sing a hymn, sing praise ; in Jas. 5 : 13, R.V., " sing praise " (A.V., " sing psalms "). See MELODY, SING.

5. EXOMOLOGEŌ (ἐξομολογέω) in Rom. 15 : 9, R.V., " will I give 1843 AG:277A
praise " (A.V., and R.V. marg., " I will confess ") : see CONFESS, A, CB:1247C
No. 2 (*c*). (EXHO-)

Note : In Luke 1 : 64, A.V., *eulogeō*, to bless, is translated " praised " 2127 AG:322B
(R.V., " blessing "). CB:1247B

PRATE

PHLUAREŌ (φλυαρέω) signifies to talk nonsense (from *phluō*, to 5396 AG:862B
babble ; cp. the adjective *phluaros*, babbling, garrulous, " tattlers," CB:—
1 Tim. 5 : 13), to raise false accusations, 3 John 10.¶

PRAY, PRAYER

A. Verbs.

1. EUCHOMAI (εὔχομαι), to pray (to God), is used with this meaning 2172 AG:329B
in 2 Cor. 13 : 7 ; ver. 9, R.V., " pray " (A.V., " wish ") ; Jas. 5 : 16 ; CB:1247A
3 John 2, R.V., " pray " (A.V., wish). Even when the R.V. and A.V. translate by " I would," Acts 26 : 29, or " wished for," Acts 27 : 29 (R.V., marg., " prayed "), or " could wish," Rom. 9 : 3 (R.V., marg., " could pray "), the indication is that prayer is involved.¶

2. PROSEUCHOMAI (προσεύχομαι), to pray, is always used of prayer 4336 AG:713D
to God, and is the most frequent word in this respect, especially in the CB:1267A
Synoptists and Acts, once in Romans, 8 : 26 ; in Ephesians, 6 : 18 ; in Philippians, 1 : 9 ; in 1 Timothy, 2 : 8 ; in Hebrews, 13 : 18 ; in Jude, ver. 20. For the injunction in 1 Thess. 5 : 17, see CEASE, C.

3. ERŌTAŌ (ἐρωτάω), to ask, is translated by the verb to pray in 2065 AG:311D
Luke 14 : 18, 19 ; 16 : 27 ; John 4 : 31 ; 14 : 16 ; 16 : 26 ; 17 : 9, 15, 20 ; CB:1246C
in Acts 23 : 18, R.V., " asked " (A.V. " prayed "); in 1 John 5 : 16, R.V " should make request " (A.V. " shall pray "). See ASK, A, No. 2.

1189 AG:175A 4. DEOMAI (δέομαι), to desire, in 2 Cor. 5 : 20 ; 8 : 4, R.V., " beseech "
CB:1240C (A.V., " pray ") : see BESEECH, No. 3.

3870 AG:617A *Notes :* (1) *Parakaleō*, to call to one's aid, is rendered by the verb to
CB:1262A pray in the A.V. in the following : Matt. 26 : 53 (R.V., " beseech ") ; so Mark 5 : 17, 18 ; Acts 16 : 9 ; in 24 : 4, R.V., " intreat ; " in 27 : 34, R.V., " beseech." See BESEECH, No. 1. (2) In 1 Thess. 5 : 23 and 2 Tim. 4 : 16, there is no word in the original for " I pray," see the R.V.

B. Nouns.

2171 AG:329B 1. EUCHĒ (εὐχή), akin to A, No. 1, denotes a prayer, Jas. 5 : 15 ;
CB:1247A a vow, Acts 18 : 18 and 21 : 23. See VOW.¶

4335 AG:713B 2 PROSEUCHĒ (προσευχή), akin to A, No. 2, denotes (*a*) prayer (to
CB:1267A God), the most frequent term, e.g., Matt. 21 : 22 ; Luke 6 : 12, where the phrase is not to be taken literally as if it meant, 'the prayer of God' (subjective genitive), but objectively, " prayer to God." In Jas. 5 : 17, " He prayed fervently," R.V., is, lit., 'he prayed with prayer' (a Hebraistic form) ; in the following the word is used with No. 3 : Eph. 6 : 18 ; Phil. 4 : 6 ; 1 Tim. 2 : 1 ; 5 : 5 ; (*b*) " a place of prayer," Acts 16 : 13, 16, a place outside the city wall, R.V.

1162 AG:171D 3. DEĒSIS (δέησις), primarily a wanting, a need (akin to A, No.
CB:1240B 4), then, an asking, entreaty, supplication, in the N.T. is always addressed to God and always rendered " supplication " or " supplications " in the R.V. ; in the A.V. " prayer," or " prayers," in Luke 1 : 13 ; 2 : 37 ; 5 : 33 ; Rom. 10 : 1 ; 2 Cor. 1 : 11 ; 9 : 14 ; Phil. 1 : 4 (in the 2nd part, " request ") ; 1 : 19 ; 2 Tim. 1 : 3 ; Heb. 5 : 7 ; Jas. 5 : 16 ; 1 Pet. 3 : 12.

1783 AG:268D 4. ENTEUXIS (ἔντευξις) is translated " prayer " in 1 Tim. 4 : 5 ;
CB:1245B see INTERCESSION.

Notes : (1) *Proseuchē* is used of prayer in general ; *deēsis* stresses the sense of need ; it is used sometimes of request from man to man. (2) In the papyri *enteuxis* is the regular word for a petition to a superior. For the synonymous word *aitēma* see PETITION ; for *hiketēria*, Heb. 5 : 7, see SUPPLICATION.

(3) " Prayer is properly addressed to God the Father, Matt. 6 : 6 ; John 16 : 23 ; Eph. 1 : 17 ; 3 : 14, and the Son, Acts 7 : 59 ; 2 Cor. 12 : 8 ; but in no instance in the N.T. is prayer addressed to the Holy Spirit distinctively, for whereas the Father is in Heaven, Matt. 6 : 9, and the Son is at His right hand, Rom. 8 : 34, the Holy Spirit is in and with the believers, John 14 : 16, 17.

" Prayer is to be offered in the Name of the Lord Jesus, John 14 : 13, that is, the prayer must accord with His character, and must be presented in the same spirit of dependence and submission that marked Him, Matt. 11 : 26 ; Luke 22 : 42.

" The Holy Spirit, being the sole interpreter of the needs of the human heart, makes His intercession therein ; and inasmuch as prayer is impossible to man apart from His help, Rom. 8 : 26, believers are exhorted to pray at all seasons in the Spirit, Eph. 6 : 18 ; cp. Jude 20, and Jas.

5 : 16, the last clause of which should probably be read ' the inwrought [i.e., by the Holy Spirit] supplication of a righteous man availeth much ' (or ' greatly prevails,' *ischuō*, as in Acts 19 : 16, 20).

" None the less on this account is the understanding to be engaged in prayer, 1 Cor. 14 : 15, and the will, Col. 4 : 12 ; Acts 12 : 5 (where ' earnestly ' is, lit., ' stretched out ') and so in Luke 22 : 44.

" Faith is essential to prayer, Matt. 21 : 22 ; Mark 11 : 24 ; Jas. 1 : 5–8, for faith is the recognition of, and the committal of ourselves and our matters to, the faithfulness of God.

" Where the Jews were numerous, as at Thessalonica, they had usually a Synagogue, Acts 17 : 1 ; where they were few, as at Philippi, they had merely a *proseuchē*, or ' place of prayer,' of much smaller dimensions, and commonly built by a river for the sake of the water necessary to the preliminary ablutions prescribed by Rabbinic tradition, Acts 16 : 13, 16."*

PREACH, PREACHING

A. Verbs.

1. EUANGELIZŌ (*εὐαγγελίζω*) is almost always used of the good news 2097
concerning the Son of God as proclaimed in the Gospel [exceptions are, AG:317B CB:1247A
e.g., Luke 1 : 19 ; 1 Thess. 3 : 6, in which the phrase " to bring (or shew) good (or glad) tidings " does not refer to the Gospel] ; Gal. 1 : 8 (2nd part). With reference to the Gospel the phrase to bring, or declare, good, or glad, tidings is used in Acts 13 : 32 ; Rom. 10 : 15 ; Heb. 4 : 2.

In Luke 4 : 18 the R.V. " to preach good tidings " gives the correct quotation from Isaiah, rather than the A.V. " to preach the Gospel." In the Sept. the verb is used of any message intended to cheer the hearers, e.g., 1 Sam. 31 : 9 ; 2 Sam. 1 : 20. See GOSPEL, B, No. 1.

2. KĒRUSSŌ (*κηρύσσω*) signifies (*a*) to be a herald, or, in general, to 2784
proclaim, e.g., Matt. 3 : 1 ; Mark 1 : 45, " publish ; " in Luke 4 : 18, AG:431B CB:1255A
R.V., " to proclaim," A.V., " to preach ; " so verse 19 ; Luke 12 : 3 ; Acts 10 : 37 ; Rom. 2 : 21 ; Rev. 5 : 2. In 1 Pet. 3 : 19 the probable reference is, not to glad tidings (which there is no real evidence that Noah preached, nor is there evidence that the spirits of antediluvian people are actually " in prison "), but to the act of Christ after His resurrection in proclaiming His victory to fallen angelic spirits ; (*b*) to preach the Gospel as a herald, e.g., Matt. 24 : 14 ; Mark 13 : 10, R.V., " be preached " (A.V., " be published ") ; 14 : 9 ; 16 : 15, 20 ; Luke 8 : 1 ; 9 : 2 ; 24 : 47 ; Acts 8 : 5 ; 19 : 13 ; 28 : 31 ; Rom. 10 : 14, present participle, lit., ' (one) preaching,' " a preacher ; " 10 : 15 (1st part) ; 1 Cor. 1 : 23 ; 15 : 11, 12 ; 2 Cor. 1 : 19 ; 4 : 5 ; 11 : 4 ; Gal. 2 : 2 ; Phil. 1 : 15 ; Col. 1 : 23 ; 1 Thess. 2 : 9 ; 1 Tim. 3 : 16 ; (*c*) to preach the word, 2 Tim. 4 : 2 (of the ministry of the Scriptures, with special reference to the Gospel). See PROCLAIM, PUBLISH.

*** From Notes on Thessalonians by Hogg and Vine, pp. 189, 190.**

4283 AG:705D 3. PROEUANGELIZOMAI (προευαγγελίζομαι): see GOSPEL, B,
CB:1266C No. 2.

4296 4. PROKĒRUSSŌ (προκηρύσσω), lit., to proclaim as a herald (*pro*,
AG:707D CB:— before, and No. 2), is used in Acts 13:24, "had first preached." Some
mss. have the verb in Acts 3:20; for the best see APPOINT, No. 12.¶

3955 5. PARRHĒSIAZOMAI (παρρησιάζομαι), to be bold in speech, is
AG:631A CB:1262C translated to preach boldly in Acts 9:27 (2nd part); in ver. 29, R.V.
(A.V., "he spake boldly"). See BOLD, A, No. 2.

DIANGELLŌ *Notes:* (1) For *diangellō*, translated "preach" in Luke 9:60, see
1229 AG:182B DECLARE, A, No. 3. (2) *Katangellō*, to proclaim, is always so translated
CB:1241B in the R.V.; the A.V. renders it by to preach in Acts 4:2; 13:5, 38;
KATANGELLŌ 2605 15:36; 17:3, 13; 1 Cor. 9:14; Col. 1:28. (3) *Laleō*, to speak, is
AG:409B translated "preached," Mark 2:2, A.V., "preached" (R.V., "spake");
CB:1254A LALEŌ in Acts 8:25, 1st part, A.V. (R.V., "spoken"); so in 13:42 and 14:25;
2980 "preaching" in Acts 11:19, A.V., but what is indicated here is not a
AG:463A CB:1256B formal preaching by the believers scattered from Jerusalem, but a general
DIALEGOMAI testimony to all with whom they came into contact; in 16:6, R.V., "to
1256 AG:185C speak" (A.V., "to preach"). (4) For *dialegomai*, in A.V. of Acts 20:7,
CB:1241A 9, see DISCOURSE. (5) For A.V., "preached" in Heb. 4:2 (2nd part), see
PLĒROŌ 4137 HEARING. (6) In Rom. 15:19 *plēroō*, to fulfil (R.V., marg.), is rendered
AG:670C CB:1265B "I have fully preached."

B. Nouns.

2782 AG:430D KĒRUGMA (κήρυγμα), a proclamation by a herald (akin to A, No. 2),
CB:1255A denotes a message, a preaching (the substance of what is preached as distinct from the act of preaching), Matt. 12:41; Luke 11:32; Rom. 16:25; 1 Cor. 1:21; 2:4; 15:14; in 2 Tim. 4:17 and Tit. 1:3, R.V., "message," marg., "proclamation," A.V., "preaching." See MESSAGE.¶ In the Sept., 2 Chron. 30:5; Prov. 9:3; Jonah 3:2.¶

3056 AG:477A *Note:* In 1 Cor. 1:18, A.V., *logos*, a word, is translated "preaching,"
CB:1257A R.V., "the word (of the Cross)," i.e., not the act of preaching, but the substance of the testimony, all that God has made known concerning the subject. For Heb. 4:2, A.V., see HEAR, B, No. 1.

PREACHER

2783 AG:431A KĒRUX (κῆρυξ), a herald (akin to A, No. 2 and B, above), is used (*a*) of
CB:1255A the preacher of the Gospel, 1 Tim. 2:7; 2 Tim. 1:11; (*b*) of Noah, as a preacher of righteousness, 2 Pet. 2:5.¶

Notes: (1) For "a preacher," in Rom. 10:14, where the verb *kērussō* is used, see PREACH, A, No. 2. (2) *Kērux* indicates the preacher as giving a proclamation; *euangelistēs* points to his message as glad tidings; *apostolos* suggests his relationship to Him by whom he is sent.

PRECEDE

5348 AG:856D PHTHANŌ (φθάνω), to anticipate, to come sooner, is translated
CB:1264C "shall (in no wise) precede" in 1 Thess. 4:15, R.V. (A.V., "prevent"),

i.e., 'shall in no wise obtain any advantage over' (the verb does not convey the thought of a mere succession of one event after another); the Apostle, in reassuring the bereaved concerning their departed fellow-believers, declares that, as to any advantage, the dead in Christ will "rise first." See ATTAIN, No. 3, COME, No. 32.

PRECEPT

1. ENTOLĒ (ἐντολή), a commandment, is translated "precept" 1785
in Mark 10:5 (R.V., "commandment"); so Heb. 9:19. See COM- AG:269A CB:1245B
MANDMENT, No. 2.

2. ENTALMA (ἔνταλμα) is always translated "precepts" in the R.V.; 1778
see COMMANDMENT, No. 3. AG:268B CB:—

PRECIOUS, PRECIOUSNESS

1. TIMIOS (τίμιος), translated "precious," e.g., in Jas. 5:7; 1 Pet. 5093 AG:818A
1:19; 2 Pet. 1:4; in 1 Cor. 3:12, A.V. (R.V., "costly"): see COSTLY, CB:1272C
B, No. 1, DEAR, No. 1. 1784

2. ENTIMOS (ἔντιμος), "precious," 1 Pet. 2:4, 6: see DEAR, No. 2. AG:268D CB:1245B

3. POLUTELĒS (πολυτελής), very expensive, translated "very 4185
precious" in Mark 14:3, A.V. (R.V., "very costly"): see COSTLY, AG:690A CB:1266A
B, No. 2.

4. POLUTIMOS (πολύτιμος), of great value; comparative degree in 4186 AG:690A
1 Pet. 1:7; see COSTLY, B, No. 3, DEAR, No. 1 (for a less authentic reading). CB:—

5. BARUTIMOS (βαρύτιμος), of great value, exceeding precious 927 AG:134B
(*barus*, weighty, *timē*, value), is used in Matt. 26:7.¶ CB:1238C

6. ISOTIMOS (ἰσότιμος), of equal value, held in equal honour (*isos*, 2472
equal, and *timē*), is used in 2 Pet. 1:1, "a like precious (faith)," R.V. AG:381B CB:1253A
(marg., "an equally precious").¶

Note: In 1 Pet. 2:7, A.V., the noun *timē*, is translated "precious" 5092
(R.V., "preciousness"). See HONOUR, No. 1. AG:817B CB:1272C

PREDESTINATE

PROORIZŌ (προορίζω): see DETERMINE. 4309 AG:709B

Note: This verb is to be distinguished from *proginōskō*, to foreknow; CB:—
the latter has special reference to the persons foreknown by God; *proorizō* PROGINŌSKŌ
has special reference to that to which the subjects of His foreknowledge 4267 AG:703D
are predestinated. See FOREKNOW, A and B. CB:1266C

PRE-EMINENCE (to have the)

1. PRŌTEUŌ (πρωτεύω), to be first (*prōtos*), to be pre-eminent, is 4409 AG:725A
used of Christ in relation to the Church, Col. 1:18.¶ CB:—

2. PHILOPRŌTEUŌ (φιλοπρωτεύω), lit., to love to be pre-eminent 5383
(*philos*, loving), to strive to be first, is said of Diotrephes, 3 John 9.¶ AG:860D CB:1264A

PREFER, PREFERRING

4285 AG:706A

PROĒGEOMAI (προηγέομαι), to go before and lead, is used in Rom. CB:—

12 : 10, in the sense of taking the lead in showing deference one to another, " (in honour) preferring one another."¶

1096 AG:158A CB:1248B *Notes :* (1) In John 1 : 15, 30, A.V., *ginomai*, to become, is translated " is preferred " (R.V., " is become ") ; some mss. have it again in ver. 27. (2) For *prokrima*, 1 Tim. 5 : 21 (A.V., " preferring one before another "), see PREJUDICE.

PREGNANT See CHILD

PREJUDICE

4299 AG:708A CB:1266C PROKRIMA (πρόκριμα) denotes pre-judging (akin to *prokrinō*, to judge beforehand), 1 Tim. 5 : 21, R.V., " prejudice " (marg., " preference "), preferring one person, another being put aside, by unfavourable judgment due to partiality.¶

PREMEDITATE

3191 AG:500B CB:— *Note :* This is the A.V. rendering of *meletaō*, to care for, which occurs in some mss. in Mark 13 : 11, " (neither) do ye premeditate." It is absent from the best mss. See IMAGINE.

PREPARATION, PREPARE, PREPARED

A. Nouns.

2091 AG:316C CB:1250B 1. HETOIMASIA (ἑτοιμασία) denotes (*a*) readiness, (*b*) preparation ; it is found in Eph. 6 : 15, of having the feet shod with the preparation of the Gospel of peace ; it also has the meaning of firm footing (foundation), as in the Sept. of Ps. 89 : 14 (R.V., " foundation ") ; if that is the meaning in Eph. 6 : 15, the Gospel itself is to be the firm footing of the believer, his walk being worthy of it and therefore a testimony in regard to it. See READY.¶

3904 AG:622B CB:1262B 2. PARASKEUĒ (παρασκευή) denotes preparation, equipment. The day on which Christ died is called " the Preparation " in Mark 15 : 42 and John 19 : 31 ; in John 19 : 42 " the Jews' Preparation," R.V. ; in 19 : 14 it is described as " the Preparation of the Passover ; " in Luke 23 : 54, R.V., " the day of the Preparation (and the Sabbath drew on)." The same day is in view in Matt. 27 : 62, where the events recorded took place on " the day after the Preparation " (R.V.). The reference would be to the 6th day of the week. The title arose from the need of preparing food etc. for the Sabbath. Apparently it was first applied only to the afternoon of the 6th day ; later, to the whole day. In regard to the phraseology in John 19 : 14, many hold this to indicate the preparation for the paschal feast. It probably means ' the Preparation day,' and thus falls in line with the Synoptic Gospels. In modern Greek and ecclesiastical Latin, *Parascevē* = Friday.¶

B. Verbs.

2090 AG:316A CB:1250B 1. HETOIMAZŌ (ἑτοιμάζω), to prepare, make ready, is used (I) absolutely, e.g., Mark 14 : 15 ; Luke 9 : 52 ; (II) with an object, e.g., (*a*) of those things which are ordained (1) by God, such as future positions of authority, Matt. 20 : 23; the coming Kingdom, 25 : 34; salvation personified in Christ, Luke 2 : 31; future blessings, 1 Cor. 2 : 9; a city, Heb. 11 : 16; a place of refuge for the Jewish remnant, Rev. 12 : 6; Divine judgments on the world, Rev. 8 : 6; 9 : 7, 15; 16 : 12; eternal fire, for the Devil and his angels, Matt. 25 : 41; (2) by Christ: a place in Heaven for His followers, John 14 : 2, 3; (*b*) of human preparation for the Lord, e.g., Matt. 3 : 3; 26 : 17, 19; Luke 1 : 17 ("make ready"), 76; 3 : 4, A.V. (R.V., "make ye ready"); 9 : 52 ("to make ready"); 23 : 56; Rev. 19 : 7; 21 : 2; in 2 Tim. 2 : 21, of preparation of oneself for "every good work;" (*c*) of human preparations for human objects, e.g., Luke 12 : 20, R.V., "thou hast prepared" (A.V., "provided"); Acts 23 : 23; Philm. 22.

2. KATARTIZŌ (καταρτίζω), to furnish completely, prepare, is 2675
translated "didst Thou prepare" in Heb. 10 : 5 (A.V., "hast Thou AG:417D CB:1254B
prepared"), of the body of the Lord Jesus. See FIT, B, No. 3.

3. KATASKEUAZŌ (κατασκευάζω), to prepare, make ready (*kata*, 2680
used intensively, *skeuē*, equipment), is so translated in Matt. 11 : 10; AG:418B CB:1254B
Mark 1 : 2; Luke 1 : 17; 7 : 27; Heb. 9 : 2, R.V. (A.V., "made"); 9 : 6, R.V. (A.V., "were . . . ordained"); 11 : 7; 1 Pet. 3 : 20. See BUILD, No. 5.

4. PARASKEUAZŌ (παρασκευάζω), to prepare, make ready (*para*, 3903
beside), is used of making ready a meal, Acts 10 : 10: in the Middle AG:622A CB:1262B
Voice, of preparing oneself for war, 1 Cor. 14 : 8, R.V.; in the Passive Voice, of preparing an offering for the needy, 2 Cor. 9 : 2, "hath been prepared," R.V. (A.V., "was ready"); ver. 3, "ye may be prepared," R.V. (A.V., "ye may be ready"). See READY.¶

5. PROETOIMAZŌ (προετοιμάζω), to prepare beforehand (*pro*, before, 4282
and No. 1), is used of good works which God "afore prepared," for fulfil- AG:705D CB:1266C
ment by believers, Eph. 2 : 10, R.V. (A.V., "hath before ordained," marg., "prepared"); of "vessels of mercy," as "afore prepared" by God "unto glory," Rom. 9 : 23. See ORDAIN.¶

Notes: (1) Etymologically, the difference between *hetoimazō* and *paraskeuazō*, is that the former is connected with what is real (*etumos*) or ready, the latter with *skeuos*, an article ready to hand, an implement,
vessel. (2) In Mark 14 : 15, A.V., *hetoimos*, ready, is translated "pre- 2092
pared" (R.V., "ready"). It is absent in some mss. See READY. AG:316C CB:1250B

For PRESBYTERY see ELDER, A and B

PRESENCE

4383

A. Nouns. AG:720D

1. PROSŌPON (πρόσωπον): see FACE, No. 1 (also APPEARANCE, CB:1267B
No. 2). 3952
2. PAROUSIA (παρουσία): see COMING (Noun), No. 3. AG:629D CB:1262C

B. Adverbs and Prepositions.

1715 AG:257A CB:1244B 1. EMPROSTHEN (ἔμπροσθεν): see Before, A, No. 4.

1799 AG:270C CB:1245B 2. ENŌPION (ἐνώπιον) is translated "in the presence of" in Luke 1:19; 13:26; 14:10; 15:10; John 20:30; Rev. 14:10 (twice); in 1 Cor. 1:29, A.V., "in His presence" (R.V., "before God"): see Before, A, No. 9.

2714 AG:421B CB:1254B 3. KATENŌPION (κατενώπιον), *kata*, down, and No. 2, in the very presence of, is translated "before the presence of" in Jude 24. See Before, A, No. 10.

561 AG:84A CB:— 4. APENANTI (ἀπέναντι), over against, opposite to, is translated "in the presence of" in Acts 3:16. See Before, A, No. 7.

PRESENT (to be)

A. Verbs.

3918 AG:624A CB:1262B 1. PAREIMI (πάρειμι) signifies (*a*) to be by, at hand or present, of persons, e.g., Luke 13:1; Acts 10:33; 24:19; 1 Cor. 5:3; 2 Cor. 10:2, 11; Gal. 4:18, 20; of things, John 7:6, of a particular season in the Lord's life on earth, "is (not yet) come," or 'is not yet at hand;' Heb. 12:11, of chastening "(for the) present" (the neuter of the present participle, used as a noun); in 13:5 "such things as ye have" is, lit., 'the things that are present;' 2 Pet. 1:12, of the truth "(which) is with (you)" (not as A.V., "the present truth," as if of special doctrines applicable to a particular time); in ver. 9 "he that lacketh" is lit., 'to whom are not present;' (*b*) to have arrived or come, Matt. 26:50, "thou art come," R.V.; John 11:28; Acts 10:21; Col. 1:6.

1764 AG:266D CB:— 2. ENISTĒMI (ἐνίστημι), to set in, or, in the Middle Voice and perfect tense of the Active V., to stand in, be present, is used of the present in contrast with the past, Heb. 9:9, where the R.V. correctly has "(for the time) *now* present" (for the incorrect A.V., "then pr."); in contrast to the future, Rom. 8:38; 1 Cor. 3:22; Gal. 1:4, "present;" 1 Cor. 7:26, where "the present distress" is set in contrast to both the past and the future; 2 Thess. 2:2, where the R.V., "is *now* present" gives the correct meaning (A.V., incorrectly, "is at hand"); the saints at Thessalonica, owing to their heavy afflictions, were possessed of the idea that "the day of the Lord," R.V. (not as A.V., "the day of Christ"), had begun; this mistake the Apostle corrects; 2 Tim. 3:1, "shall come." See Come, No. 26.¶

2186 AG:330D CB:— 3. EPHISTĒMI (ἐφίστημι), to set over, stand over, is translated "present" in Acts 28:2. See Assault, A, Come, No. 27.

3854 AG:613C CB:— 4. PARAGINOMAI (παραγίνομαι), to be beside (*para*, by, *ginomai*, to become), is translated "were present" in Acts 21:18. See Come, No. 13.

3873 AG:617D CB:— 5. PARAKEIMAI (παράκειμαι), to lie beside (*para*, and *keimai*, to lie), to be near, is translated "is present" in Rom. 7:18, 21.¶

4840 AG:779A CB:— 6. SUMPAREIMI (συμπάρειμι), to be present with (*sun*, with, and No. 1), is used in Acts 25:24.¶

B. Adverbs.

1. ARTI (ἄρτι), just, just now, this moment, is rendered “ (this) 737
present (hour) ” in 1 Cor. 4 : 11 ; in 1 Cor. 15 : 6, R.V., “ now ” (A.V., AG:110B CB:1237C
“ this present ”). See Now.

2. NUN (νῦν), now, is translated “ present,” with reference to this 3568
age or period (“ world ”),in Rom. 8 : 18 ; 11 : 5 ; 2 Tim. 4 : 10 ; Tit. 2 : 12. AG:545C CB:1260A
See Henceforth, Now.

Notes : (1) *Endēmeō*, to be at home, is so rendered in 2 Cor. 5 : 6 (A.V. ENDēMEō
and R.V.) ; in vv. 8, 9, R.V., “ at home ” (A.V., “ present ”). See 1736 AG:263A
Home. (2) In John 14 : 25, A.V., *menō*, to abide, is translated “ being CB:1244C
present ” (R.V., “ abiding ”). (3) In Luke 5 : 17 the R.V. has “ with MENō 3306
Him,” for A.V., italicised, “ *present.*” AG:503C CB:1258B

PRESENT (Verb)

1. PARISTĒMI (παρίστημι) denotes, when used transitively, to place 3936
beside (*para*, by, *histēmi*, to set), to present, e.g., Luke 2 : 22 ; Acts 1 : 3, AG:627C CB:1262B
“ He shewed (Himself) ; ” 9 : 41 ; 23 : 33 ; Rom. 6 : 13 (2nd part), R.V.,
“ present,” A.V., “ yield ; ” so 6 : 19 (twice) ; 12 : 1 ; 2 Cor. 4 : 14 ;
11 : 2 ; Eph. 5 : 27 ; Col. 1 : 22, 28 ; 2 Tim. 2 : 15, R.V. (A.V., “ shew ”).
See Shew.

2. PARISTANŌ (παριστάνω), a late present form of No. 1, is used in 3936
Rom. 6 : 13 (1st part) and ver. 16, R.V., “ present ” (A.V., “ yield ”). AG:627C CB:1262B

Notes : (1) In Jude 24, A.V., *histēmi*, to cause to stand, to set, is trans- HISTēMI
lated “ to present ” (R.V., “ to set ”). (2) In Matt. 2 : 11, A.V., *prospherō*, 2476 AG:381D
to offer, is translated “ presented ” (R.V., “ offered ”). CB:1250C PROSPHERō 4374

For PRESENTLY see FORTHWITH, No. 1, and IMMEDIATELY, AG:719C CB:1267B
No. 1

PRESERVE

1. TĒREŌ (τηρέω) is translated to preserve in 1 Thess. 5 : 23, where 5083
the verb is in the singular number, as the threefold subject, “ spirit and AG:814D CB:1271B
soul and body,” is regarded as the unit, constituting the person. The
aorist or ‘ point ’ tense regards the continuous preservation of the believer
as a single, complete act, without reference to the time occupied in its 4933
accomplishment ; in Jude 1, A.V. (R.V., “ kept ”). See Keep, No. 1. AG:792C

2. SUNTĒREŌ (συντηρέω) : see Keep, No. 3. 2225 AG:341C

3. ZŌOGONEŌ (ζωογονέω), to preserve alive : see Live, No. 6. CB:1273C

4. PHULASSŌ (φυλάσσω), to guard, protect, preserve, is translated 5442
“ preserved ” in 2 Pet. 2 : 5, R.V. (A.V., “ saved ”). See Guard. AG:868B CB:1264C

Note : In 2 Tim. 4 : 18, A.V., *sōzō*, to save, is translated “ will preserve ” 4982
(R.V., “ will save ”). AG:798A CB:1269C

For PRESS (Noun) see CROWD, A

PRESS (Verb)

A. Verbs.

2346 AG:362A CB:1272B 1. THLIBŌ (θλίβω), to press, distress, trouble, is translated "pressed" in 2 Cor. 4 : 8, R.V. (A.V., "troubled"). See AFFLICT, No. 4.

598 AG:91B CB:— 2. APOTHLIBŌ (ἀποθλίβω), translated "press" in Luke 8 : 45 (end) : see CRUSH.

971 AG:140C CB:1239A 3. BIAZO (βιάζω), in the Middle Voice, to press violently or force one's way into, is translated "presseth" in Luke 16 : 16, A.V., R.V., "entereth violently," a meaning confirmed by the papyri. Moulton and Milligan also quote a passage from D. S. Sharp's *Epictetus and the N.T.*, speaking of "those who (try to) force their way in ;" the verb suggests forceful endeavour. See ENTER, Note (3), VIOLENCE, B, No. 2.

4912 AG:789A CB:1270C 4. SUNECHŌ (συνέχω) : for the significance of this in Acts 18 : 5, "was constrained by the word," R.V., i.e., Paul felt the urge of the word of his testimony to the Jews in Corinth, see CONSTRAIN, No. 3. It is used with No. 1 in Luke 8 : 45, R.V., "press" (A.V., "throng").

1758 AG:265D CB:1245A 5. ENECHŌ (ἐνέχω), lit., to hold in, also signifies to set oneself against, be urgent against, as the scribes and Pharisees were regarding Christ, Luke 11 : 53, R.V., "to press upon," marg., "set themselves vehemently against" (A.V., "to urge"). See ENTANGLE, No. 3.

1945 AG:294C CB:— 6. EPIKEIMAI (ἐπίκειμαι), to lie upon, press upon, is rendered "pressed upon" in Luke 5 : 1. See IMPOSED.

1968 AG:297C CB:— 7. EPIPIPTŌ (ἐπιπίπτω), to fall upon, is rendered "pressed upon" in Mark 3 : 10. See FALL, B, No. 5.

916 AG:133C CB:1238C 8. BAREŌ (βαρέω), to weigh down, burden, is rendered "we were pressed" in 2 Cor. 1 : 8, A.V. (R.V., "we were weighed down"). See BURDEN, B, No. 1.

1912 AG:290B CB:1245C 9. EPIBAREŌ (ἐπιβαρέω), 2 Cor. 2 : 5, R.V., "I press (not) too heavily" (A.V., "overcharge"). See BURDEN, B, No. 2, OVERCHARGE.

4085 AG:657B CB:— 10. PIEZŌ (πιέζω), to press down together, is used in Luke 6 : 38, "pressed down," of the character of the measure given in return for giving.¶ In the Sept., Mic. 6 : 15.¶

1377 AG:201B CB:1242A 11. DIŌKŌ (διώκω), to pursue, is used as a metaphor from the foot-race, in Phil. 3 : 12, 14, of speeding on earnestly, R.V., "I press on." See FOLLOW, No. 7.

5342 AG:854D CB:1264A 12. PHERŌ (φέρω), to bear, carry, is used in the Passive Voice in Heb. 6 : 1, "let us . . . press on," R.V., lit., 'let us be borne on' (A.V., "go on"). See GO, Note (2), (*h*).

B. Noun.

— AG:300B CB:— EPISTASIS (ἐπίστασις), primarily a stopping, halting (as of soldiers), then, an incursion, onset, rush, pressure (akin to *ephistēmi*, to set upon), is so used in 2 Cor. 11 : 28, "(that which) presseth upon (me)," A.V., "cometh upon," lit., '(the daily) pressure (upon me) ;' some have taken the word in its other meaning 'attention,' which perhaps is accounted for by the variant reading of the pronoun (*mou*, 'my', instead of *moi*, 'to

me,' 'upon me'), but that does not adequately describe the pressure or onset due to the constant call upon the Apostle for all kinds of help, advice, counsel, exhortation, decisions as to difficulties, disputes, etc. Cp. the other occurrence of the word in Acts 24 : 12, "stirring up," R.V. (A.V., "raising"), lit. 'making a stir' (in some mss., *episustasis*). **EPISUSTASIS**
See Come, Notes at end (9).¶ **1999 AG:301D CB:1246A**

For PRESUMPTUOUS see DARING, B

PRETENCE

PROPHASIS (πρόφασις): see Cloke (Pretence), No. 2

PREVAIL

1. ISCHUŌ (ἰσχύω), to be strong, powerful, is translated to prevail **2480 AG:383D**
in Acts 19 : 16, 20 ; Rev. 12 : 8. See Able, B, No. 4. **CB:1253A**

2. KATISCHUŌ (κατισχύω), to be strong against (*kata*, against, and **2729**
No. 1), is used in Matt. 16 : 18, negatively of the gates of Hades ; in Luke **AG:424A CB:1254C**
21 : 36 (in the most authentic mss. ; some have *kataxioō*, to count worthy ; see A.V.), of prevailing to escape judgments at the close of this age ; in Luke 23 : 23, of the voices of the chief priests, rulers and people against Pilate regarding the crucifixion of Christ.¶

3. ŌPHELEŌ (ὠφελέω), to benefit, do good, profit, is translated **5623**
"prevailed" in Matt. 27 : 24, R.V. (A.V., "could prevail"), of the **AG:900C CB:1261A**
conclusion formed by Pilate concerning the determination of the chief priests, elders and people. The meaning of the verb with the negative is better expressed by the phrase 'he would do no good;' so in John 12 : 19, "ye prevail (nothing)," lit., 'ye are doing no good.' See Advantage, Bettered, Profit.

4. NIKAŌ (νικάω), to conquer, prevail, is used as a law term in **3528**
Rom. 3 : 4, "(that) Thou . . . mightest prevail [A.V., 'overcome'] **AG:539A CB:1259C**
(when Thou comest into judgment);" that the righteousness of the judge's verdict compels an acknowledgement on the part of the accused, is inevitable where God is the Judge. God's promises to Israel provided no guarantee that an unrepentant Jew would escape doom. In Rev. 5 : 5, A.V., "hath prevailed" (R.V., "hath overcome"). See Conquer, No. 1.

For PREVENT, 1 Thess. 4 : 15, A.V., see PRECEDE : Matt. 17 : 25, A.V., see SPEAK No. 11

PRICE

A. Noun.

TIMĒ (τιμή) denotes a valuing, hence, objectively, (*a*) price paid or **5092**
received, Matt. 27 : 6, 9 ; Acts 4 : 34 (plural) ; 5 : 2, 3 ; 7 : 16, R.V., **AG:817B CB:1272C**
"price (in silver)," A.V., "sum (of money) ;" 19 : 19 (plural) ; 1 Cor.

6 : 20 ; 7 : 23 ; (*b*) value, honour, preciousness. See HONOUR, PRECIOUSNESS.

B. Verb.

5091 AG:817A TIMAŌ (*τιμάω*), to fix the value, to price, is translated "was priced"
CB:1272C and "did price" in the R.V. of Matt. 27 : 9 (A.V., "was valued" and
"did value"). See HONOUR.

C. Adjectives.

4185 AG:690A 1. POLUTELĒS (*πολυτελής*), "of great price," 1 Pet. 3 : 4 : see COST,
CB:1266A B, No. 2.

4186 AG:690A 2. POLUTIMOS (*πολύτιμος*), "of great price," Matt. 13 : 46 : see
CB:— COST, B, No. 3.

For PRICK (Noun) see GOAD

PRICK (Verb)

2660 AG:415C (-OMAI) KATANUSSŌ (*κατανύσσω*), primarily, to strike or prick violently, to
CB:— stun, is used of strong emotion, in Acts 2 : 37 (Passive Voice), "they
KATANUXIS 2659 were pricked (in their heart)."¶ Cp. *katanuxis*, stupor, torpor of mind,
AG:415C CB:— Rom. 11 : 8.¶

PRIDE

A. Nouns.

212 AG:34C 1. ALAZONIA (or —EIA) (*ἀλαζονία*) is translated "pride" in 1 John
CB:1234B 2 : 16, A.V. See BOAST, B, No. 2, VAINGLORY.

5243 AG:841A 2. HUPERĒPHANIA (*ὑπερηφανία*), pride, Mark 7 : 22 : see HAUGHTY.¶
CB:1252A

B. Verb.

5187 AG:831A TUPHOŌ (*τυφόω*), "lifted up with pride," 1 Tim. 3 : 6, A.V. (R.V.,
CB:— "puffed up"). See HIGH-MINDED.

PRIEST

2409 AG:372A 1. HIEREUS (*ἱερεύς*), one who offers sacrifice and has the charge of
CB:1250B things pertaining thereto, is used (*a*) of a priest of the pagan god Zeus, Acts 14 : 13 ; (*b*) of Jewish priests, e.g., Matt. 8 : 4 ; 12 : 4, 5 ; Luke 1 : 5, where allusion is made to the 24 courses of priests appointed for service in the Temple (cp. 1 Chron. 24 : 4ff.) ; John 1 : 19 ; Heb. 8 : 4 ; (*c*) of believers, Rev. 1 : 6 ; 5 : 10 ; 20 : 6. Israel was primarily designed as a nation to be a kingdom of priests, offering service to God, e.g., Ex. 19 : 6 ; the Israelites having renounced their obligations, Ex. 20 : 19, the Aaronic priesthood was selected for the purpose, till Christ came to fulfil His ministry in offering up Himself ; since then the Jewish priesthood has been abrogated, to be resumed nationally, on behalf of Gentiles, in the Millennial Kingdom, Is. 61 : 6 ; 66 : 21. Meanwhile all believers, from Jews and Gentiles, are constituted "a kingdom of priests," Rev. 1 : 6 (see above), "a holy priesthood," 1 Pet. 2 : 5, and "royal," ver. 9. The N.T. knows nothing of a sacerdotal class in contrast to the laity ; all

believers are commanded to offer the sacrifices mentioned in Rom. 12 : 1 ; Phil. 2 : 17 ; 4 : 18 ; Heb. 13 : 15, 16 ; 1 Pet. 2 : 5 ; (*d*) of Christ, Heb. 5 : 6 ; 7 : 11, 15, 17, 21 ; 8 : 4 (negatively) ; (*e*) of Melchizedek, as the foreshadower of Christ, Heb. 7 : 1, 3.

2. ARCHIEREUS (ἀρχιερεύς) designates (*a*) the high priests of the **749**
Levitical order, frequently called " chief priests " in the N.T., and **AG:112D**
including ex-high priests and members of high priestly families, e.g., **CB:1237B**
Matt. 2 : 4 ; 16 : 21 ; 20 : 18 ; 21 : 15 ; in the singular, a " high priest," e.g., Abiathar, Mark 2 : 26 ; Annas and Caiaphas, Luke 3 : 2, where the R.V. rightly has " in the high-priesthood of A. and C." (cp. Acts 4 : 6). As to the combination of the two in this respect, Annas was the high priest from A.D. 7–14, and, by the time referred to, had been deposed for some years ; his son-in-law, Caiaphas, the fourth high priest since his deposition, was appointed about A.D. 24. That Annas was still called the high priest is explained by the facts (1) that by the Mosaic law the high-priesthood was held for life, Numb. 35 : 25 ; his deposition was the capricious act of the Roman procurator, but he would still be regarded legally and religiously as high priest by the Jews ; (2) that he probably still held the office of deputy-president of the Sanhedrin (cp. 2 Kings 25 : 18) ; (3) that he was a man whose age, wealth and family connections gave him a preponderant influence, by which he held the real sacerdotal power ; indeed at this time the high-priesthood was in the hands of a clique of some half dozen families ; the language of the writers of the Gospels is in accordance with this, in attributing the high-priesthood rather to a caste than a person ; (4) the high priests were at that period mere puppets of Roman authorities who deposed them at will, with the result that the title was used more loosely than in former days.

The Divine institution of the priesthood culminated in the high priest, it being his duty to represent the whole people, e.g., Lev. 4 : 15, 16 ; ch. 16. The characteristics of the Aaronic high priests are enumerated in Heb. 5 : 1–4 ; 8 : 3 ; 9 : 7, 25 ; in some mss., 10 : 11 (R.V., marg.) ; 13 : 11.

(*b*) Christ is set forth in this respect in the Ep. to the Hebrews, where He is spoken of as " a high priest," 4 : 15 ; 5 : 5, 10 ; 6 : 20 ; 7 : 26 ; 8 : 1, 3 (R.V.) ; 9 : 11 ; " a great high priest," 4 : 14 ; " a great priest," 10 : 21 ; " a merciful and faithful high priest," 2 : 17 ; " the Apostle and high priest of our confession," 3 : 1, R.V. ; " a high priest after the order of Melchizedek," 5 : 10. One of the great objects of this Epistle is to set forth the superiority of Christ's High Priesthood as being of an order different from and higher than the Aaronic, in that He is the Son of God (see especially 7 : 28), with a priesthood of the Melchizedek order. Seven outstanding features of His priesthood are stressed, (1) its character, 5 : 6, 10 ; (2) His commission, 5 : 4, 5 ; (3) His preparation, 2 : 17 ; 10 : 5 ; (4) His sacrifice, 8 : 3 ; 9 : 12, 14, 27, 28 ; 10 : 4–12 ; (5) His sanctuary, 4 : 14 ; 8 : 2 ; 9 : 11, 12, 24 ; 10 : 12, 19 ; (6) His ministry, 2 : 18 ; 4 : 15 ;

7 : 25 ; 8 : 6 ; 9 : 15, 24 ; (7) its effects, 2 : 15 ; 4 : 16 ; 6 : 19, 20 ; 7 : 16, 25 ; 9 : 14, 28 ; 10 : 14–17, 22, 39 ; 12 : 1 ; 13 : 13–17.

748 *Note :* In Acts 4 : 6 the adjective *hieratikos*, high priestly, is trans-
(ARCHI-) AG:112D lated " of the high priest."

(ARCHI-) CB:1250B

PRIESTHOOD, PRIEST'S OFFICE

A. Nouns.

2406 AG:371D CB:1250B 1. HIERATEUMA (ἱεράτευμα) denotes a priesthood (akin to *hierateuō*, see below), a body of priests, consisting of all believers, the whole Church (not a special order from among them), called " a holy priesthood," 1 Pet. 2 : 5 ; " a royal priesthood," ver. 9 ; the former term is associated with offering spiritual sacrifices, the latter with the royal dignity of shewing forth the Lord's excellencies (R.V.)¶ In the Sept., Ex. 19 : 6 ; 23 : 22.¶

2420 AG:373C CB:1250C 2. HIERŌSUNĒ (ἱερωσύνη), a priesthood, signifies the office, quality, rank and ministry of a priest, Heb. 7 : 11, 12, 24, where the contrasts between the Levitical priesthood and that of Christ are set forth.¶ In the Sept., 1 Chron. 29 : 22.¶

2405 AG:371D CB:1250B 3. HIERATEIA (ἱερατεία), a priesthood, denotes the priest's office, Luke 1 : 9 ; Heb. 7 . 5, R.V., " priest's office."¶

B. Verb.

2407 AG:371D CB:1250B HIERATEUŌ (ἱερατεύω) signifies to officiate as a priest, Luke 1 : 8, " he executed the priest's office."¶

PRINCE

747 AG:112C CB:1237B 1. ARCHĒGOS (ἀρχηγός), primarily an adjective signifying originating, beginning, is used as a noun, denoting a founder, author, prince or leader, Acts 3 : 15, " Prince " (marg., " Author ") ; 5 : 31 ; see AUTHOR, No. 2.

758 AG:113D CB:1237B 2. ARCHŌN (ἄρχων), the present participle of the verb *archō*, to rule, denotes a ruler, a prince. It is used as follows (" p " denoting " prince," or " princes ; " " r," " ruler " or " rulers ") : (*a*) of Christ, as " the Ruler (A.V., Prince) of the kings of the earth," Rev. 1 : 5 ; (*b*) of rulers of nations, Matt. 20 : 25, R.V., " r," A.V., " p ; " Acts 4 : 26, " r ; " 7 : 27, " r ; " 7 : 35, " r " (twice) ; (*c*) of judges and magistrates, Acts 16 : 19, " r ; " Rom. 13 : 3, " r ; " (*d*) of members of the Sanhedrin, Luke 14 : 1, R.V., " r " (A.V., " chief ") ; 23 : 13, 35, " r ; " so 24 : 20 ; John 3 : 1 ; 7 : 26, 48 ; 12 : 42, R.V., " r " (A.V., " chief r.") ; " r " in Acts 3 : 17 ; 4 : 5, 8 ; 13 : 27 ; 14 : 5 ; (*e*) of rulers of synagogues, Matt. 9 : 18, 23, " r ; " so Luke 8 : 41 ; 18 : 18 ; (*f*) of the Devil, as " prince " of this world, John 12 : 31 ; 14 : 30 ; 16 : 11 ; of the power of the air, Eph. 2 : 2, " the air " being that sphere in which the inhabitants of the world live and which, through the rebellious and godless condition of humanity, constitutes the seat of his authority ; (*g*) of Beelzebub, the prince of the demons, Matt. 9 : 24 ; 12 : 24 ; Mark 3 : 22 ; Luke 11 : 15. See CHIEF, B, No. 10.¶

3. HĒGEMŌN (ἡγεμών), a leader, ruler, is translated "princes" 2232
(i.e., leaders) in Matt. 2 : 6 : see GOVERNOR, A, No. 1. AG:343B CB:1249C

Note: For *megistan*, Rev. 6 : 15 ; 18 : 23, R.V., "princes," see LORD, 3175 (-ES)
No. 3. AG:498C CB:1258A (-ES)

PRINCIPAL

PRŌTOS (πρῶτος), first, is translated "principal men" in the R.V. 4413
of Luke 19 : 47 and Acts 25 : 2. See CHIEF, A. AG:725B CB:1267B

Note: In Acts 25 : 23 the phrase *kat' exochēn*, lit., 'according to
eminence,' is translated "principal (men);" *exochē*, primarily a pro- 1851
jection (akin to *exechō*, to stand out), is used here metaphorically of AG:279A CB:—
eminence.¶ In the Sept., Job 39 : 28.¶

PRINCIPALITY

ARCHĒ (ἀρχή), beginning, government, rule, is used of supramundane 746
beings who exercise rule, called "principalities;" (*a*) of holy angels, AG:111D CB:1237B
Eph. 3 : 10, the Church in its formation being to them the great expression of "the manifold (or 'much-varied') wisdom of God;" Col. 1 : 16; (*b*) of evil angels, Rom. 8 : 38; Col. 2 : 15, some would put this under (*a*), but see SPOIL, B, No. 4; (*a*) and (*b*) are indicated in Col. 2 : 10. In Eph. 1 : 21, the R.V. renders it "rule" (A.V., "principality") and in Tit. 3 : 1, "rulers" (A.V., "principalities"). In Jude 6, R.V., it signifies, not the first estate of fallen angels (as A.V.), but their authoritative power, "their own" indicating that which had been assigned to them by God, which they left, aspiring to prohibited conditions. See BEGIN, B.

PRINCIPLES

1. ARCHĒ (ἀρχή), beginning, is used in Heb. 6 : 1, in its relative 746
significance, of the beginning of the thing spoken of; here "the first AG:111D CB:1237B
principles of Christ," lit., 'the account (or word) of the beginning of Christ,' denotes the teaching relating to the elementary facts concerning Christ. See BEGIN, B.

2. STOICHEION (στοιχεῖον) is translated "principles" in Heb. 5 : 12. 4747
See ELEMENTS. AG:768D CB:1270A

PRINT

TUPOS (τύπος), for which see ENSAMPLE, No. 1, is translated "print" 5179
in John 20 : 25 (twice), of the marks made by the nails in the hands of AG:829D CB:1273B
Christ.

PRISON, PRISON-HOUSE

1. DESMŌTĒRION (δεσμωτήριον), a place of bonds (from *desmos*, a 1201
bond, *deō*, to bind), a prison, occurs in Matt. 11 : 2; in Acts 5 : 21, 23 AG:176B CB:1240C
and 16 : 26, R.V., "prison-house" (A.V., "prison").¶

2. PHULAKĒ (φυλακή), for the various meanings of which see CAGE, 5438 AG:867D
denotes a prison, e.g., Matt. 14 : 10; Mark 6 : 17; Acts 5 : 19; 2 Cor. CB:1264C

11 : 23 ; in 2 Cor. 6 : 5 and Heb. 11 : 36 it stands for the condition of imprisonment ; in Rev. 2 : 10 ; 18 : 2, "hold" (twice, R.V., marg., "prison ;" in the 2nd case, A.V., "cage") ; 20 : 7.

5084 AG:815C 3. TĒRĒSIS (τήρησις), a watching, keeping, then, a place of keeping,
CB:1271B is translated "prison" in Acts 5 : 18, A.V. (R.V., "ward"). See
KEEPING, B.

OIKēMA 3612 *Notes:* (1) For *oikēma* in Acts 12 : 7, A.V., "prison," see CELL.
AG:557A (2) In Matt. 4 : 12, A.V., *paradidōmi*, to betray, deliver up, is translated
CB:— PARADIDōMI "was cast into prison" (R.V., "was delivered up") ; see BETRAY. In
3860 Mark 1 : 14, A.V., "was put in prison," R.V., as in Matt. 4 : 12 ; see
AG:614B CB:1262A PUT, No. 12.

For PRISON-KEEPER see JAILOR

PRISONER

1198 1. DESMIOS (δέσμιος), an adjective, primarily denotes binding,
AG:176A CB:1240C bound, then, as a noun, the person bound, a captive, prisoner (akin to
deō, to bind), Matt. 27 : 15, 16 ; Mark 15 : 6 ; Acts 16 : 25, 27 ; 23 : 18 ; 25 : 14, R.V. (A.V., "in bonds"), 27 ; 28 : 16, 17 ; Eph. 3 : 1 ; 4 : 1 ; 2 Tim. 1 : 8 ; Philm. 1, 9 ; in Heb. 10 : 34 and 13 : 3, "in bonds." See BOND, No. 2.¶

Note: The prison at Jerusalem (Acts 5) was controlled by the priests and probably attached to the high priest's palace, or the temple. Paul was imprisoned at Jerusalem in the fort Antonia, Acts 23 : 10 ; at Cæsarea, in Herod's Prætorium, 23 : 35 ; probably his final imprisonment
1202 in Rome was in the Tullianum dungeon.

AG:176B CB:1240C 2. DESMŌTĒS (δεσμώτης), akin to No. 1, occurs in Acts 27 : 1, 42.¶

4869 AG:783C 3. SUNAICHMALŌTOS (συναιχμάλωτος), a fellow-prisoner, primarily
CB:1270B one of fellow-captives in war (from *aichmē*, a spear, and *haliskomai*, to be
taken), is used by Paul of Andronicus and Junias, Rom. 16 : 7 ; of Epaphras, Philm. 23 ; of Aristarchus, Col. 4 : 10, on which Lightfoot remarks that probably his relations with the Apostle in Rome excited suspicion and led to a temporary confinement, or that he voluntarily shared his captivity by living with him.¶

PRIVATE, PRIVATELY

A. Adjective.

2398 AG:369C IDIOS (ἴδιος), one's own, is translated "private" in 2 Pet. 1 : 20 (see
CB:1252C under INTERPRETATION). See BUSINESS, B.

B. Adverbial Phrase.

KAT' IDIAN (κατ' ἰδίαν) is translated "privately" in Matt. 24 : 3 ; Mark 4 : 34, R.V. (A.V., "when they were alone") ; 6 : 32 (A.V. only) ; 7 : 33, R.V. ; 9 : 28 ; 13 : 3 ; Luke 10 : 23 ; Acts 23 : 19 ; Gal. 2 : 2. Contrast 2 : 14.

PRIVILY

LATHRĄ (λάθρᾳ), secretly, covertly (from a root *lath*— indicating 2977
unnoticed, unknown, seen in *lanthanō*, to escape notice, *lēthē*, forgetful- AG:462C CB:—
ness), is translated "privily" in Matt. 1 : 19; 2 : 7; Acts 16 : 37; "secretly" in John 11 : 28 (in some mss., Mark 5 : 33). See SECRETLY.¶

Note: In Gal. 2 : 4, *pareisaktos*, an adjective (akin to *pareisagō*, lit., PAREISAKTOS
to bring in beside, i.e., secretly, from *para*, by the side, *eis*, into, *agō*, to 3920 AG:624C
bring), is used, "privily brought in," R.V. (A.V., "unawares etc."), i.e., CB:—
as spies or traitors. Strabo, a Greek historian contemporary with Paul, PAREISERCHOMAI 3922
uses the word of enemies introduced secretly into a city by traitors within.¶ AG:624D
In the same verse the verb *pareiserchomai* (see COME, No. 8) is translated CB:1262B PAREISDU(N)O
"came in privily," of the same Judaizers, brought in by the circumcision 3921
party to fulfil the design of establishing the ceremonial law, and thus to AG:624D
accomplish the overthrow of the faith; cp. in Jude 4 the verb *pareisduō* CB:—
(or—*dunō*), to slip in secretly, steal in, R.V., "crept in privily" (A.V., ". . . unawares"). See CREEP, No. 2.

PRIVY

SUNOIDA (σύνοιδα): see KNOW, No. 6

PRIZE

1. BRABEION (βραβεῖον), a prize bestowed in connection with the 1017
games (akin to *brabeus*, an umpire, and *brabeuō*, to decide, arbitrate, AG:146D CB:1239B
"rule," Col. 3 : 15), 1 Cor. 9 : 24, is used metaphorically of the reward to be obtained hereafter by the faithful believer, Phil. 3 : 14; the preposition *eis*, "unto," indicates the position of the goal. The prize is not "the high calling," but will be bestowed in virtue of, and relation to, it, the heavenly calling, Heb. 3 : 1, which belongs to all believers and directs their minds and aspirations heavenward; for the prize see especially 2 Tim. 4 : 7, 8.¶

2. HARPAGMOS (ἁρπαγμός), akin to *harpazō*, to seize, carry off by 725
force, is found in Phil. 2 : 6, "(counted it not) a prize," R.V. (marg., AG:108C CB:1249B
"a thing to be grasped"), A.V., "(thought it not) robbery;" it may have two meanings, (*a*) in the Active sense, the act of seizing, robbery, a meaning in accordance with a rule connected with its formation; (*b*) in the Passive sense, a thing held as a prize. The subject is capably treated by Gifford in "*The Incarnation*," pp. 28, 36, from which the following is quoted:

"In order to express the meaning of the clause quite clearly, a slight alteration is required in the R.V., 'Counted it not a prize to be on an equality with God.' The form 'to be' is ambiguous and easily lends itself to the erroneous notion that to be on equality with God was something to be acquired in the future. The rendering 'counted it not a prize that He was on an equality with God,' is quite as accurate and more free from ambiguity. . . . Assuming, as we now may, that the equality was something which Christ possessed prior to His Incarnation, and then for a time resigned, we have . . . to choose between two meanings of the word *harpagmos:* (1) with the active sense 'robbery' or 'usurpation' we get the following meaning: 'Who *because* He was subsisting in the essential form of God, did not regard it as any usurpation that He was on an equality of glory and majesty with God, *but yet* emptied Himself of that co-equal glory. . . .' (2) The passive sense gives a different meaning to the passage: 'Who *though* He was subsisting in the essential form of God, *yet* did not regard His being on an equality of glory and majesty with God as a prize and a treasure to be held fast, *but* emptied himself thereof."

After reviewing the arguments *pro* and *con* Gifford takes the latter to be the right meaning, as conveying the purpose of the passage "to set forth Christ as the supreme example of humility and self-renunciation."

2603 AG:409B *Note:* For *katabrabeuō* (*kata*, down, and *brabeuō*, see No. 1), translated
CB:1254A "rob (you) of your prize," Col. 2:18, see Beguile, Note.

For PROBATION, R.V. in Rom. 5:4, see EXPERIENCE, No. 2

PROCEED

(-OMAI) 1. EKPOREUOMAI (ἐκπορεύομαι), to go forth, is translated to pro-
1607 AG:244B ceed out of in Matt. 4:4; 15:11, R.V.; 15:18; Mark 7:15, R.V.;
CB:1244A 7:20, R.V.; 7:21; 7:23, R.V.; Luke 4:22; John 15:26; Eph. 4:29; Rev. 1:16, R.V.; 4:5; 9:17, 18, R.V. (A.V., "issued"); 11:5; 19:15, R.V.; 19:21, A.V. (R.V., "came forth"); 22:1. See Come, No. 33, Go, Note (1).

1831 2. EXERCHOMAI (ἐξέρχομαι) is translated "proceed" in Matt. 15:
AG:274B
CB:1247C 19, A.V. (R.V., "come forth"); John 8:42, R.V., "came forth;" Jas. 3:10. The verb to proceed is not so suitable. See Come, No. 3.

4298 3. PROKOPTŌ (προκόπτω), lit., to cut forward (a way), is translated
AG:707D
CB:1266C "will proceed" in 2 Tim. 2:16, R.V. (A.V., "will increase") and "shall proceed" (both Versions) in 3:9. See Increase.

4369 4. PROSTITHĒMI (προστίθημι), to put to, to add, is translated
AG:718D
CB:1267B "proceeded" in Acts 12:3 (a Hebraism). See Add, No. 2.

PROCLAIM

2784 1. KĒRUSSŌ (κηρύσσω) is translated to proclaim in the R.V., for
AG:431B
CB:1255A A.V., to preach, in Matt. 10:27; Luke 4:19; Acts 8:5; 9:20. See Preach, No. 2.

2605 2. KATANGELLŌ (καταγγέλλω), to declare, proclaim, is translated
AG:409B
CB:1254A to proclaim in the R.V., for A.V., to shew, in Acts 16:17; 26:23; 1 Cor. 11:26, where the verb makes clear that the partaking of the elements at the Lord's Supper is a proclamation (an evangel) of the Lord's
4135 Death; in Rom. 1:8, for A.V., "spoken of;" in 1 Cor. 2:1, for A.V.,
AG:670B "declaring." See also Preach, Note (2), and Declare, A, No. 4.
CB:1265B 3. PLĒROPHOREŌ (πληροφορέω), to bring in full measure (*plērēs*,

full, *pherō*, to bring), hence, to fulfil, accomplish, is translated "might be fully proclaimed," in 2 Tim. 4 : 17, R.V., with *kērugma*, marg., "proclamation" (A.V. ". . . known"). See ASSURE, B, No. 2, BELIEVE, C, PRODUCE
Note (4), FULFIL, No. 6, KNOW, Note (2), PERSUADE, No. 2, Note, PROOF. See FRUIT, YIELD

PROCONSUL

ANTHUPATOS (ἀνθύπατος), from *anti*, instead of, and *hupatos*, 446
supreme, denotes a consul, one acting in place of a consul, a proconsul, the AG:69C CB:1236A
governor of a senatorial province (i.e., one which had no standing army). The proconsuls were of two classes, (*a*) ex-consuls, the rulers of the provinces of Asia and Africa, who were therefore proconsuls, (*b*) those who were ex-prætors or proconsuls of other senatorial provinces (a prætor being virtually the same as a consul). To the former belonged the proconsuls at Ephesus, Acts 19 : 38 (A.V., "deputies"); to the latter, Sergius Paulus in Cyprus, Acts 13 : 7, 8, 12, and Gallio at Corinth, 18 : 12. In the N.T. times Egypt was governed by a prefect. Provinces in which a standing army was kept were governed by an imperial legate (e.g., Quirinius in Syria, Luke 2 : 2): see GOVERNOR, A, No. 1.¶

Note: *Anthupateō*, to be proconsul, is in some texts in Acts 18 : 12. 445 AG:69C CB:—

PROFANE (Adjective and Verb)

A. Adjective.

BEBĒLOS (βέβηλος), primarily, permitted to be trodden, accessible 952
(from *bainō*, to go, whence *bēlos*, a threshold), hence, unhallowed, profane AG:138D CB:—
(opposite to *hieros*, sacred), is used of (*a*) persons, 1 Tim. 1 : 9; Heb. 12 : 16; (*b*) things, 1 Tim. 4 : 7; 6 : 20; 2 Tim. 2 : 16. "The natural antagonism between the profane and the holy or divine grew into a moral antagonism. . . . Accordingly *bebēlos* is that which lacks all relationship or affinity to God" (Cremer, who compares *koinos*, common, in the sense of ritual uncleanness).¶

B. Verb.

BEBĒLOŌ (βεβηλόω), primarily, to cross the threshold (akin to A, 953
which see), hence, to profane, pollute, occurs in Matt. 12 : 5 and Acts AG:138D CB:—
24 : 6 (the latter as in 21 : 28, 29: cp. DEFILE, A, No. 1, PARTITION).¶

PROFESS, PROFESSION

A. Verbs.

1. EPANGELLŌ (ἐπαγγέλλω), to announce, proclaim, profess, is 1861 AG:280D
rendered to profess in 1 Tim. 2 : 10, of godliness, and 6 : 21, of "the (-OMAI)
knowledge . . . falsely so called." See PROMISE. CB:1245B

2. HOMOLOGEŌ (ὁμολογέω) is translated to profess in Matt. 7 : 23 3670 AG:568A
and Tit. 1 : 16; in 1 Tim. 6 : 12, A.V. (R.V., "confess"). See CONFESS. CB:1251A

3. PHASKŌ (φάσκω), to affirm, assert: see AFFIRM, No. 3. 5335 AG:854B CB:—

B. Noun.

HOMOLOGIA (ὁμολογία), akin to A, No. 2, confession, is translated 3671 AG:568D
"profession" and "professed" in the A.V. only. See CONFESS. CB:1251A

PROFIT (Noun and Verb), PROFITABLE, PROFITING

A. Nouns.

5622 AG:900B 1. ŌPHELEIA (ὠφέλεια) primarily denotes assistance; then, advan-
CB:1261A tage, benefit, "profit," Rom. 3:1. See ADVANTAGE, No. 3.

3786 AG:599B 2. OPHELOS (ὄφελος), "profit" in Jas. 2:14, 16: see ADVANTAGE,
CB:— No. 2.

— AG:780C (-OS) CB:— 3. SUMPHERON (συμφέρον), the neuter form of the present participle of *sumpherō* (see B, No. 1), is used as a noun with the article in Heb. 12:10, "(for our) profit;" in some mss. in 1 Cor. 7:35 and 10:33 (see No. 4); in 1 Cor. 12:7, preceded by *pros*, with a view to, towards, translated "to profit withal," lit., 'towards the profiting.'¶

— AG:780C CB:— 4. SUMPHOROS (σύμφορος), akin to No. 3, an adjective, signifying profitable, useful, expedient, is used as a noun, and found in the best texts, with the article, in 1 Cor. 7:35 (see No. 3) and 10:33 (1st part), the word being understood in the 2nd part.¶

4297 AG:707D CB:1266C 5. PROKOPĒ (προκοπή), translated "profiting" in 1 Tim. 4:15, A.V. (R.V., "progress"); see FURTHERANCE.

B. Verbs.

4851 AG:780B CB:— 1. SUMPHERŌ (συμφέρω), to be "profitable," Matt. 5:29, 30; Acts 20:20: see EXPEDIENT.

5623 AG:900C CB:1261A 2. ŌPHELEŌ (ὠφελέω), akin to A, No. 1, is translated 'to profit' in Matt. 15:5; 16:26; Mark 7:11; 8:36; Luke 9:25, R.V.; John 6:63; Rom. 2:25; 1 Cor. 13:3; 14:6; Gal. 5:2; Heb. 4:2; 13:9. See ADVANTAGE, BETTERED, PREVAIL.

4298 AG:707D CB:1266C 3. PROKOPTŌ (προκόπτω) is translated "I profited" in Gal. 1:14, A.V. See ADVANCE.

C. Adjectives.

5539 AG:885D CB:— 1. CHRĒSIMOS (χρήσιμος), useful (akin to *chraomai*, to use), is translated as a noun in 2 Tim. 2:14, "to (no) profit," lit., 'to (nothing) profitable.'¶

2173 AG:329C CB:— 2. EUCHRĒSTOS (εὔχρηστος), useful, serviceable (*eu*, well, *chrēstos*, serviceable, akin to *chraomai*, see No. 1), is used in Philm. 11, "profitable," in contrast to *achrēstos*, "unprofitable" (*a*, negative), with a delightful play upon the name "Onesimus," signifying "profitable" (from *onēsis*, profit), a common name among slaves. Perhaps the prefix *eu* should have been brought out by some rendering like 'very profitable,' 'very serviceable,' the suggestion being that whereas the runaway slave had done great disservice to Philemon, now after his conversion, in devotedly serving the Apostle in his confinement, he had thereby already become particularly serviceable to Philemon himself, considering that the latter would have most willingly rendered service to Paul, had it been possible. Onesimus, who had belied his name, was now true to it on behalf of his erstwhile master, who also owed his conversion to the Apostle.

It is translated "meet for (the master's) use" in 2 Tim. 2:21;

"useful" in 4 : 11, R.V. (A.V., "profitable"). See USEFUL.¶ In the Sept., Prov. 31 : 13.¶

3. ŌPHELIMOS (ὠφέλιμος), useful, profitable (akin to B, No. 2), is translated "profitable" in 1 Tim. 4 : 8, both times in the R.V. (A.V., "profiteth" in the 1st part), of physical exercise, and of godliness; in 2 Tim. 3 : 16 of the God-breathed Scriptures; in Tit. 3 : 8, of maintaining good works.¶ 5624 AG:900D CB:—

PROGRESS

PROKOPĒ (προκοπή) is translated "progress" in Phil. 1 : 12, 25 and 1 Tim. 4 : 15: see FURTHERANCE.¶ 4297 AG:707D CB:1266C

PROLONG

PARATEINŌ (παρατείνω), to stretch out along (*para*, along, *teinō*, to stretch), is translated "prolonged" in Acts 20 : 7, R.V., of Paul's discourse: see CONTINUE, Note (1).¶ 3905 AG:622C CB:—

PROMINENT See CHIEF, HONOURABLE

PROMISE (Noun and Verb)

A. Nouns.

1. EPANGELIA (ἐπαγγελία), primarily a law term, denoting a summons (*epi*, upon, *angellō*, to proclaim, announce), also meant an undertaking to do or give something, a promise. Except in Acts 23 : 21 it is used only of the promises of God. It frequently stands for the thing promised, and so signifies a gift graciously bestowed, not a pledge secured by negotiation; thus, in Gal. 3 : 14, "the promise of the Spirit" denotes 'the promised Spirit:' cp. Luke 24 : 49; Acts 2 : 33 and Eph. 1 : 13; so in Heb. 9 : 15, "the promise of the eternal inheritance" is 'the promised eternal inheritance.' On the other hand, in Acts 1 : 4, "the promise of the Father," is the promise made by the Father. 1860 AG:280C CB:1245B

In Gal. 3 : 16, the plural "promises" is used because the one promise to Abraham was variously repeated (Gen. 12 : 1–3; 13 : 14–17; 15 : 18; 17 : 1–14; 22 : 15–18), and because it contained the germ of all subsequent promises; cp. Rom. 9 : 4; Heb. 6 : 12; 7 : 6; 8 : 6; 11 : 17. Gal. 3 is occupied with showing that the promise was conditional upon faith and not upon the fulfilment of the Law. The Law was later than, and inferior to, the promise, and did not annul it, ver. 21; cp. 4 : 23, 28. Again, in Eph. 2 : 12, "the covenants of the promise" does not indicate different covenants, but a covenant often renewed, all centring in Christ as the promised Messiah-Redeemer, and comprising the blessings to be bestowed through Him.

In 2 Cor. 1 : 20 the plural is used of every promise made by God: cp. Heb. 11 : 33; in 7 : 6, of special promises mentioned. For other applications of the word, see, e.g., Eph. 6 : 2; 1 Tim. 4 : 8; 2 Tim. 1 : 1; Heb. 4 : 1; 2 Pet. 3 : 4, 9; in 1 John 1 : 5 some mss. have this word, instead of *angelia*, "message."

The occurrences of the word in relation to Christ and what centres in Him, may be arranged under the headings (1) the contents of the promise, e.g., Acts 26 : 6 ; Rom. 4 : 20 ; 1 John 2 : 25 ; (2) the heirs, e.g., Rom. 9 : 8 ; 15 : 8 ; Gal. 3 : 29 ; Heb. 11 : 9 ; (3) the conditions, e.g., Rom. 4 : 13, 14 ; Gal. 3 : 14–22 ; Heb. 10 : 36.

1862 AG:281A CB:1245B 2. EPANGELMA (ἐπάγγελμα) denotes a promise made, 2 Pet. 1 : 4 ; 3 : 13.¶

B. Verbs.

1861 AG:280D (-OMAI) CB:1245B 1. EPANGELLŌ (ἐπαγγέλλω), to announce, proclaim, has in the N.T. the two meanings to profess and to promise, each used in the Middle Voice ; to promise (*a*) of promises of God, Acts 7 : 5 ; Rom. 4 : 21 ; in Gal. 3 : 19, Passive Voice ; Tit. 1 : 2 ; Heb. 6 : 13 ; 10 : 23 ; 11 : 11 ; 12 : 26 ; Jas. 1 : 12 ; 2 : 5 ; 1 John 2 : 25 ; (*b*) made by men, Mark 14 : 11 ; 2 Pet. 2 : 19. See PROFESS.

4279 AG:705B CB:1266C 2. PROEPANGELLŌ (προεπαγγέλλω), in the Middle Voice, to promise before (*pro*, and No. 1), occurs in Rom. 1 : 2 ; 2 Cor. 9 : 5. See AFORE-PROMISED.¶

3670 AG:568A CB:1251A 3. HOMOLOGEŌ (ὁμολογέω), to agree, confess, signifies to promise in Matt. 14 : 7. See CONFESS.

1843 AG:277A CB:1247C (EXHO-) *Note :* For *exomologeō* in Luke 22 : 6, see CONSENT, No. 1.

PRONOUNCE

3004 AG:468A CB:1256C LEGŌ (λέγω), to say, declare, is rendered " pronounceth (blessing) " in Rom. 4 : 6, R.V., which necessarily repeats the verb in ver. 9 (it is absent from the original), for A.V., " *cometh* " (italicised). See ASK, A, No. 6, DESCRIBE, No. 2, SAY.

PROOF

1382 AG:202D CB:1242A 1. DOKIMĒ (δοκιμή) : see EXPERIENCE, No. 2.

1383 AG:203A CB:1242A 2. DOKIMION (δοκίμιον), a test, a proof, is rendered " proof " in Jas. 1 : 3, R.V. (A.V., " trying ") ; it is regarded by some as equivalent to *dokimeion*, a crucible, a test ; it is the neuter form of the adjective *dokimios*, used as a noun, which has been taken to denote the means by which a man is tested and proved (Mayor), in the same sense as *dokimē* (No. 1) in 2 Cor. 8 : 2 ; the same phrase is used in 1 Pet. 1 : 7, R.V., " the proof (of your faith)," A.V., " the trial," where the meaning probably is 'that which is approved [i.e., as genuine] in your faith ;' this interpretation, which was suggested by Hort, and may hold good for Jas. 1 : 3, has been confirmed from the papyri by Deissmann (*Bible Studies*, p. 259, ff). Moulton and Milligan (Vocab.) give additional instances.¶

1732 AG:262D CB:1244C 3. ENDEIXIS (ἔνδειξις) : see DECLARE, B. Cp. the synonymous word *endeigma*, a token, 2 Thess. 1 : 5, which refers rather to the thing proved, while *endeixis* points to the act of proving.

5039 AG:808A CB:1271B 4. TEKMĒRION (τεκμήριον), a sure sign, a positive proof (from *tekmar*, a mark, sign), occurs in Acts 1 : 3, R.V., " proofs " (A.V., " infallible proofs;" a proof does not require to be described as infallible, the adjective is superfluous).¶

Note: For the A.V. in 2 Tim. 4:5, "make full proof," R.V., "fulfil" 4135 AG:670B
(*plērophoreō*), see FULFIL. CB:1265B

PROPER

1. ASTEIOS (ἀστεῖος) is translated "proper" in Heb. 11:23, R.V., 791 AG:117C
"goodly:" see BEAUTIFUL, No. 2. CB:—

2. IDIOS (ἴδιος), one's own, is found in some mss. in Acts 1:19, A.V., 2398
"proper;" in 1 Cor. 7:7, R.V., "own" (A.V., "proper"); in Jude 6, AG:369C CB:1252C
R.V., "their proper (habitation)," A.V., "their own."

PROPERTY See SUBSTANCE

PROPHECY, PROPHESY, PROPHESYING

A. Noun.

PROPHĒTEIA (προφητεία) signifies the speaking forth of the mind 4394 AG:722D
and counsel of God (*pro*, forth, *phēmi*, to speak: see PROPHET); in the CB:1267A
N.T. it is used (*a*) of the gift, e.g., Rom. 12:6; 1 Cor. 12:10; 13:2; (*b*) either of the exercise of the gift or of that which is prophesied, e.g., Matt. 13:14; 1 Cor. 13:8; 14:6, 22 and 1 Thess. 5:20, "prophesying (s);" 1 Tim. 1:18; 4:14; 2 Pet. 1:20, 21; Rev. 1:3; 11:6; 19:10; 22:7, 10, 18, 19.¶

"Though much of O.T. prophecy was purely predictive, see Micah 5:2, e.g., and cp. John 11:51, prophecy is not necessarily, nor even primarily, fore-telling. It is the declaration of that which cannot be known by natural means, Matt. 26:68, it is the forth-telling of the will of God, whether with reference to the past, the present, or the future, see Gen. 20:7; Deut. 18:18; Rev. 10:11; 11:3. . . .

"In such passages as 1 Cor. 12:28; Eph. 2:20, the 'prophets' are placed after the 'Apostles,' since not the prophets of Israel are intended, but the 'gifts' of the ascended Lord, Eph. 4:8, 11; cp. Acts 13:1; . . . . ; the purpose of their ministry was to edify, to comfort, and to encourage the believers, 1 Cor. 14:3, while its effect upon unbelievers was to show that the secrets of a man's heart are known to God, to convict of sin, and to constrain to worship, vv. 24, 25.

"With the completion of the canon of Scripture prophecy apparently passed away, 1 Cor. 13:8, 9. In his measure the teacher has taken the place of the prophet, cp. the significant change in 2 Pet. 2:1. The difference is that, whereas the message of the prophet was a direct revelation of the mind of God for the occasion, the message of the teacher is gathered from the completed revelation contained in the Scriptures."*

B. Adjective.

PROPHĒTIKOS (προφητικός), of or relating to prophecy, or proceeding 4397 AG:724B CB:1267A

---

* From Notes on Thessalonians by Hogg and Vine, pp. 196, 197.

from a prophet, prophetic, is used of the O.T. Scriptures, Rom. 16 : 26, "of the prophets," lit., '(by) prophetic (Scriptures);' 2 Pet. 1 : 19, "the word of prophecy (*made* more sure)", i.e., confirmed by the Person and work of Christ (A.V., "a more sure etc."), lit., 'the prophetic word.'¶

C. Verb.

4395
AG:723A PROPHĒTEUŌ (προφητεύω), to be a prophet, to prophesy, is used
CB:1267A (*a*) with the primary meaning of telling forth the Divine counsels, e.g., Matt. 7 : 22; 26 : 68; 1 Cor. 11 : 4, 5; 13 : 9; 14 : 1, 3–5, 24, 31, 39; Rev. 11 : 3; (*b*) of foretelling the future, e.g., Matt. 15 : 7; John 11 : 51; 1 Pet. 1 : 10; Jude 14.

PROPHET

4396
AG:723B 1. PROPHĒTĒS (προφήτης), one who speaks forth or openly (see
CB:1267A PROPHECY, A), a proclaimer of a divine message, denoted among the Greeks an interpreter of the oracles of the gods.

In the Sept. it is the translation of the word *rôeh*, a seer; 1 Sam. 9 : 9, indicating that the prophet was one who had immediate intercourse with God. It also translates the word *nābhî*, meaning either one in whom the message from God springs forth or one to whom anything is secretly communicated. Hence, in general, the prophet was one upon whom the Spirit of God rested, Numb. 11 : 17–29, one, to whom and through whom God speaks, Numb. 12 : 2; Amos 3 : 7, 8. In the case of the O.T. prophets their messages were very largely the proclamation of the Divine purposes of salvation and glory to be accomplished in the future; the prophesying of the N.T. prophets was both a preaching of the Divine counsels of grace already accomplished and the fore-telling of the purposes of God in the future.

In the N.T. the word is used (*a*) of the O.T. prophets, e.g., Matt. 5 : 12; Mark 6 : 15; Luke 4 : 27; John 8 : 52; Rom. 11 : 3; (*b*) of prophets in general, e.g., Matt. 10 : 41; 21 : 46; Mark 6 : 4; (*c*) of John the Baptist, Matt. 21 : 26; Luke 1 : 76; (*d*) of prophets in the churches, e.g., Acts 13 : 1; 15 : 32; 21 : 10; 1 Cor. 12 : 28, 29; 14 : 29, 32, 37; Eph. 2 : 20; 3 : 5; 4 : 11; (*e*) of Christ, as the afore-promised Prophet, e.g., John 1 : 21; 6 : 14; 7 : 40; Acts 3 : 22; 7 : 37, or, without the article, and, without reference to the Old Testament, Mark 6 : 15, Luke 7 : 16; in Luke 24 : 19 it is used with *anēr*, a man; John 4 : 19; 9 : 17; (*f*) of two witnesses yet to be raised up for special purposes, Rev. 11 : 10, 18; (*g*) of the Cretan poet Epimenides, Tit. 1 : 12; (*h*) by metonymy, of the writings of prophets, e.g., Luke 24 : 27; Acts 8 : 28.

5578
AG:892A 2. PSEUDOPROPHĒTĒS (ψευδοπροφήτης), a false prophet, is used of
CB:1267C such (*a*) in O.T. times, Luke 6 : 26; 2 Pet. 2 : 1; (*b*) in the present period since Pentecost, Matt. 7 : 15; 24 : 11, 24; Mark 13 : 22; Acts 13 : 6; 1 John 4 : 1; (*c*) with reference to a false prophet destined to arise as the supporter of the "beast" at the close of this age, Rev. 16 : 13; 19 : 20; 20 : 10 (himself described as "another beast," 13 : 11).¶

PROPHETESS

PROPHĒTIS (προφῆτις), the feminine of *prophētēs* (see above), is 4398
used of Anna, Luke 2 : 36; of the self-assumed title of " the woman AG:724B CB:1267C
Jezebel " in Rev. 2 : 20.¶

PROPITIATION

A. Verb.

HILASKOMAI (ἱλάσκομαι) was used amongst the Greeks with the 2433
significance to make the gods propitious, to appease, propitiate, inasmuch AG:375C CB:1250C
as their good will was not conceived as their natural attitude, but something to be earned first. This use of the word is foreign to the Greek Bible, with respect to God, whether in the Sept. or in the N.T. It is never used of any act whereby man brings God into a favourable attitude or gracious disposition. It is God who is propitiated by the vindication of His holy and righteous character, whereby, through the provision He has made in the vicarious and expiatory sacrifice of Christ, He has so dealt with sin that He can shew mercy to the believing sinner in the removal of his guilt and the remission of his sins.

Thus in Luke 18 : 13 it signifies to be propitious or merciful to (with the person as the object of the verb), and in Heb. 2 : 17 to expiate, to make propitiation for (the object of the verb being sins); here the R.V., " to make propitiation " is an important correction of the A.V., " to make reconciliation." Through the propitiatory sacrifice of Christ, he who believes upon Him is by God's own act delivered from justly deserved wrath, and comes under the covenant of grace. Never is God said to be reconciled, a fact itself indicative that the enmity exists on man's part alone, and that it is man who needs to be reconciled to God, and not God to man. God is always the same and, since He is Himself immutable, His relative attitude does change towards those who change. He can act differently towards those who come to Him by faith, and solely on the ground of the propitiatory sacrifice of Christ, not because He has changed, but because He ever acts according to His unchanging righteousness.

The expiatory work of the Cross is therefore the means whereby the barrier which sin interposes between God and man is broken down. By the giving up of His sinless life sacrificially, Christ annuls the power of sin to separate between God and the believer.

In the O.T. the Hebrew verb *kaphar* is connected with *kopher*, a covering (see MERCY-SEAT), and is used in connection with the burnt offering, e.g., Lev. 1 : 4; 14 : 20; 16 : 24, the guilt offering, e.g., Lev. 5 : 16, 18, the sin offering, e.g., Lev. 4 : 20, 26, 31, 35, the sin offering and burnt offering together, e.g., Lev. 5 : 10; 9 : 7, the meal offering and peace offering, e.g., Ezek. 45 : 15, 17, as well as in other respects. It is used of the ram offered at the consecration of the high priest, Ex. 29 : 33, and of the blood which God gave upon the altar to make propitiation for the souls of the people, and that because " the life of the flesh is in the blood," Lev. 17 : 11, and " it is the blood that maketh atonement by reason of the life " (R.V.). Man has forfeited his life on account of sin and God has provided the one and only way whereby eternal life could be bestowed, namely, by the voluntary laying down of His life by His Son, under Divine retribution. Of this the former sacrifices appointed by God were foreshadowings.

B. Nouns.

2435
AG:375D
CB:1250C
1. HILASTĒRION (ἱλαστήριον), akin to A, is regarded as the neuter of an adjective signifying propitiatory. In the Sept. it is used adjectivally in connection with *epithēma*, a cover, in Ex. 25 : 17 and 37 : 6, of the lid of the ark (see MERCY-SEAT), but it is used as a noun (without *epithēma*), of locality, in Ex. 25 : 18, 19, 20, 21, 22 ; 31 : 7 ; 35 : 12 ; 37 : 7, 8, 9 ; Lev. 16 : 2, 13, 14, 15 ; Numb. 7 : 89, and this is its use in Heb. 9 : 5.

Elsewhere in the N.T. it occurs in Rom. 3 : 25, where it is used of Christ Himself ; the R.V. text and punctuation in this verse are important : " whom God set forth *to be* a propitiation, through faith, by His blood." The phrase " by His blood " is to be taken in immediate connection with " propitiation." Christ, through His expiatory death, is the Personal means by whom God shows the mercy of His justifying grace to the sinner who believes. His " blood " stands for the voluntary giving up of His life, by the shedding of His blood in expiatory sacrifice, under Divine judgment righteously due to us as sinners, faith being the sole condition on man's part.

Note : " By metonymy, ' blood ' is sometimes put for ' death,' inasmuch as, blood being essential to life, Lev. 17 : 11, when the blood is shed life is given up, that is, death takes place. The fundamental principle on which God deals with sinners is expressed in the words ' apart from shedding of blood,' i.e., unless a death takes place, ' there is no remission ' of sins, Heb. 9 : 22.

" But whereas the essential of the type lay in the fact that blood was shed, the essential of the antitype lies in this, that the blood shed was that of Christ. Hence, in connection with Jewish sacrifices, ' the blood ' is mentioned without reference to the victim from which it flowed, but in connection with the great antitypical sacrifice of the N.T. the words ' the blood ' never stand alone ; the One Who shed the blood is invariably specified, for it is the Person that gives value to the work ; the saving efficacy of the Death depends entirely upon the fact that He Who died was the Son of God."*

2434
AG:375C
CB:1250C
2. HILASMOS (ἱλασμός), akin to *hileōs* (merciful, propitious), signifies an expiation, a means whereby sin is covered and remitted. It is used in the N.T. of Christ Himself as " the propitiation," in 1 John 2 : 2 and 4 : 10, signifying that He Himself, through the expiatory sacrifice of His Death, is the Personal means by whom God shows mercy to the sinner who believes

* From Notes on Thessalonians by Hogg and Vine, p. 168.

on Christ as the One thus provided. In the former passage He is described as " the propitiation for our sins ; and not for ours only, but also for the whole world." The italicised addition in the A.V., " *the sins of*," gives a wrong interpretation. What is indicated is that provision is made for the whole world, so that no one is, by Divine pre-determination, excluded from the scope of God's mercy ; the efficacy of the propitiation, however, is made actual for those who believe. In 4 : 10, the fact that God " sent His Son to be the propitiation for our sins," is shown to be the great expression of God's love toward man, and the reason why Christians should love one another.¶ In the Sept., Lev. 25 : 9 ; Numb. 5 : 8 ; 1 Chron. 28 : 20 ; Ps. 130 : 4 ; Ezek. 44 : 27 ; Amos 8 : 14.¶

PROPORTION

ANALOGIA (ἀναλογία), Eng., analogy, signified in classical Greek 356
" the right relation, the coincidence or agreement existing or demanded AG:57B CB:1235A
according to the standard of the several relations, not agreement as equality " (Cremer). It is used in Rom. 12 : 6, where " let us prophesy according to the proportion of our faith," R.V., recalls ver. 3. It is a warning against going beyond what God has given and faith receives. This meaning, rather than the other rendering, " according to the analogy of the faith," is in keeping with the context. The word *analogia* is not to be rendered literally. " Proportion " here represents its true meaning. The fact that there is a definite article before " faith " in the original does not necessarily afford an intimation that the faith, the body of Christian doctrine, is here in view. The presence of the definite article is due to the fact that faith is an abstract noun. The meaning " the faith" is not relevant to the context.¶

PROSELYTE

PROSĒLUTOS (προσήλυτος), akin to *proserchomai*, to come to, 4339
primarily signifies one who has arrived, a stranger ; in the N.T. it is used AG:715A CB:1267A
of converts to Judaism, or foreign converts to the Jewish religion, Matt. 23 : 15 ; Acts 2 : 10 ; 6 : 5 ; 13 : 43.¶ There seems to be no connexion necessarily with Palestine, for in Acts 2 : 10 and 13 : 43 it is used of those who lived abroad. Cp. the Sept., e.g., in Ex. 22 : 21 ; 23 : 9 ; Deut. 10 : 19, of the " stranger " living among the children of Israel.

PROSPER

EUODOŌ (εὐοδόω), to help on one's way (*eu*, well, *hodos*, a way or 2137
journey), is used in the Passive Voice signifying to have a prosperous AG:323D CB:—
journey, Rom. 1 : 10 ; metaphorically, to prosper, be prospered, 1 Cor. 16 : 2, R.V., " (as) he may prosper," A.V., " (as God) hath prospered (him)," lit., ' in whatever he may be prospered,' i.e., in material things ; the continuous tense suggests the successive circumstances of varying prosperity as week follows week ; in 3 John 2, of the prosperity of physical and spiritual health.¶

PROSTITUTE See HARLOT

PROTEST

3513 AG:537B CB:1259C *Note:* In 1 Cor. 15 : 31, "I protest by" is a rendering of *nē*, a particle of strong affirmation used in oaths.¶ In the Sept., Gen. 42 : 15, 16.¶

PROUD

5244 AG:841B CB:1252A HUPERĒPHANOS (ὑπερήφανος) signifies showing oneself above others, pre-eminent (*huper*, above, *phainomai*, to appear, be manifest); it is always used in Scripture in the bad sense of arrogant, disdainful, proud, Luke 1 : 51; Rom. 1 : 30; 2 Tim. 3 : 2; Jas. 4 : 6; 1 Pet. 5 : 5.¶

5187 AG:831A CB:— *Note:* For the A.V. renderings of the verb *tuphoō*, in 1 Tim. 3 : 6; 6 : 4; 2 Tim. 3 : 4, see HIGH-MINDED.

PROVE

A. Verbs.

1381 AG:202C CB:1242A 1. DOKIMAZŌ (δοκιμάζω), to test, prove, with the expectation of approving, is translated to prove in Luke 14 : 19; Rom. 12 : 2; 1 Cor. 3 : 13, R.V. (A.V., "shall try"); 11 : 28, R.V. (A.V., "examine"); 2 Cor. 8 : 8, 22; 13 : 5; Gal. 6 : 4; Eph. 5 : 10; 1 Thess. 2 : 4 (2nd part), R.V. (A.V., "trieth"); 5 : 21; 1 Tim. 3 : 10; in some mss., Heb. 3 : 9 (the most authentic have the noun *dokimasia*, a proving¶); 1 Pet. 1 : 7, R.V. (A.V., "tried"); 1 John 4 : 1, R.V. (A.V., "try"). See APPROVE.

584 AG:89C CB:1236C 2. APODEIKNUMI (ἀποδείκνυμι), to show forth, signifies to prove in Acts 25 : 7. See APPROVE, No. 3.

3936 AG:627C CB:1262B 3. PARISTĒMI (παρίστημι), to present, signifies to prove in Acts 24 : 13. See COMMEND, No. 4.

3985 AG:640B CB:1263A 4. PEIRAZŌ (πειράζω), to try, either in the sense of attempting, e.g., Acts 16 : 7, or of testing, is rendered "to prove" in John 6 : 6. See EXAMINE, TEMPT.

4822 AG:777D CB:— 5. SUMBIBAZŌ (συμβιβάζω), to join together, signifies to prove in Acts 9 : 22. See COMPACTED, No. 2.

4921 AG:790C CB:1270C 6. SUNISTĒMI or SUNISTANŌ (συνίστημι), to commend, to prove, is translated "I prove (myself a transgressor)" in Gal. 2 : 18 (A.V., "I make"). See COMMEND.

B. Noun.

3986 AG:640D CB:1263A PEIRASMOS (πειρασμός), (*a*) a trying, testing, (*b*) a temptation, is used in sense (*a*) in 1 Pet. 4 : 12, with the preposition *pros*, towards or with a view to, R.V., "to prove" (A.V., "to try"), lit., 'for a testing.' See TEMPTATION.

1096 AG:158A CB:1248B *Notes:* (1) In Luke 10 : 36, R.V., *ginomai*, to become, come to be, is translated "proved (neighbour)," A.V., "was . . . ;" so in Heb. 2 : 2.
4256 AG:702C CB:— (2) In Rom. 3 : 9, A.V., *proaitiaomai*, to accuse beforehand, is translated "we have before proved" (marg., "charged"); for the R.V., see CHARGE, C, No. 9.

For PROVERB see PARABLE, No. 2

PROVIDE, PROVIDENCE, PROVISION

A. Verbs.

2090
1. HETOIMAZŌ (ἑτοιμάζω), to prepare, is translated "hast provided" AG:316A
in Luke 12 : 20, A.V. See PREPARE. CB:1250B
2932
2. KTAOMAI (κτάομαι), to get, to gain, is rendered "provide" in AG:455A
Matt. 10 : 9. See OBTAIN, POSSESS. CB:1256A
3936
3. PARISTĒMI (παρίστημι), to present, signifies to provide in Acts AG:627C
23 : 24. See COMMEND, PROVE, No. 3. CB:1262B
4. PROBLEPŌ (προβλέπω), to foresee, is translated "having pro- 4265 AG:703C
vided" in Heb. 11 : 40. See FORESEE.¶ CB:—
5. PRONOEŌ (προνοέω), to take thought for, provide, is translated 4306 AG:708C
"provide . . . for" in 1 Tim. 5 : 8; in Rom. 12 : 17 and 2 Cor. 8 : 21, CB:1266C
R.V., to take thought for (A.V., to provide).¶

Note: In Luke 12 : 33, A.V., *poieō*, to make (R.V.), is translated 4160 AG:680D
"provide." CB:1265C

B. Noun.

PRONOIA (πρόνοια), forethought (*pro*, before, *noeō*, to think), is trans- 4307 AG:708D
lated "providence" in Acts 24 : 2; "provision" in Rom. 13 : 14.¶ CB:1266C

PROVINCE

1. EPARCHEIA, or -IA (ἐπαρχεία) was a technical term for the 1885 AG:283C
administrative divisions of the Roman Empire. The original meaning CB:—
was the district within which a magistrate, whether consul or prætor, exercised supreme authority. The word *provincia* acquired its later meaning when Sardinia and Sicily were added to the Roman territories, 227 B.C. On the establishment of the Empire the proconsular power over all provinces was vested in the Emperor. Two provinces, Asia and Africa, were consular, i.e., held by ex-consuls; the rest were prætorian. Certain small provinces, e.g. Judæa and Cappadocia, were governed by procurators. They were usually districts recently added to the Empire and not thoroughly Romanized. Judæa was so governed in the intervals between the rule of native kings; ultimately it was incorporated in the province of Syria. The province mentioned in Acts 23 : 34 and 25 : 1 was assigned to the jurisdiction of an *eparchos*, a prefect or governor (cp. GOVERNOR, PROCONSUL).¶ In the Sept., Esth. 4 : 11.¶

2. KANŌN (κανών) originally denoted a straight rod, used as a ruler 2583 AG:403A
or measuring instrument, or, in rare instances, the beam of a balance, the CB:1253B
secondary notion being either (*a*) of keeping anything straight, as of a rod used in weaving, or (*b*) of testing straightness, as a carpenter's rule; hence its metaphorical use to express what serves to measure or determine anything. By a common transition in the meaning of words, that which measures, was used for what was measured; thus a certain space at Olympia was called a *kanōn*. So in music, a canon is a composition in which a given melody is the model for the formation of all the parts. In general the word thus came to serve for anything regulating the actions

of men, as a standard or principle. In Gal. 6 : 16, those who "walk by this rule (*kanōn*)" are those who make what is stated in vv. 14 and 15 their guiding line in the matter of salvation through faith in Christ alone, apart from works, whether following the principle themselves or teaching it to others. In 2 Cor. 10 : 13, 15, 16, it is translated "province," R.V. (A.V., "rule" and "line of things"; marg., "line;" R.V. marg., "limit" or "measuring rod.") Here it signifies the limits of the responsibility in gospel service as measured and appointed by God.¶

For PROVING (*elenchos*) see REPROOF, A

PROVOCATION, PROVOKE

A. Nouns.

3894 AG:621B 1. PARAPIKRASMOS (παραπικρασμός), from *para*, amiss or from,
CB:1262B used intensively, and *pikrainō*, to make bitter (*pikros*, sharp, bitter), provocation, occurs in Heb. 3 : 8, 15.¶ In the Sept., Psa. 95 : 8.¶

3948 AG:629C 2. PAROXUSMOS (παροξυσμός) denotes a stimulation (Eng.,
CB:1262C paroxysm), (cp. B, No. 2): in Heb. 10 : 24, "to provoke," lit., 'unto a stimulation (of love).' See CONTENTION, No. 2.

B. Verbs.

3893 AG:621A 1. PARAPIKRAINŌ (παραπικραίνω), to embitter, provoke (akin to
CB:1262B A, No. 1), occurs in Heb. 3 : 16.¶

3947 AG:629C 2. PAROXUNŌ (παροξύνω), primarily, to sharpen (akin to A, No. 2),
CB:1262C is used metaphorically, signifying to rouse to anger, to provoke, in the Passive Voice, in Acts 17 : 16, R.V., "was provoked" (A.V., "was stirred"); in 1 Cor. 13 : 5, R.V., "is not provoked" (the word "easily" in A.V., represents no word in the original). See STIR.¶

2042 AG:308D 3. ERETHIZŌ (ἐρεθίζω), to excite, stir up, provoke, is used (*a*) in a
CB:— good sense in 2 Cor. 9 : 2, A.V., "hath provoked," R.V., "hath stirred
3949 up;" (*b*) in an evil sense in Col. 3 : 21, "provoke." See STIR.¶

AG:629D 4. PARORGIZŌ (παροργίζω), to provoke to wrath: see ANGER, B,
CB:1262C No. 2.

3863 AG:616A 5. PARAZĒLOŌ (παραζηλόω), to provoke to jealousy: see JEALOUSY.

653 AG:100B 6. APOSTOMATIZŌ (ἀποστοματίζω) in classical Greek meant to speak
CB:— from memory, to dictate to a pupil (*apo*, from, *stoma*, a mouth); in later Greek, to catechize; in Luke 11 : 53, "to provoke (Him) to speak."¶

4292 (-OMAI) 7. PROKALEŌ (προκαλέω), to call forth, as to a contest, hence to
AG:707B stir up what is evil in another, occurs in the Middle Voice in Gal. 5 : 26.¶
CB:—

PRUDENCE, PRUDENT

A. Nouns.

5428 AG:866C 1. PHRONĒSIS (φρόνησις), akin to *phroneō*, to have understanding
CB:1264C (*phrēn*, the mind), denotes practical wisdom, prudence in the management of affairs. It is translated "wisdom" in Luke 1 : 17; "prudence" in Eph. 1 : 8. See WISDOM.¶

2. SUNESIS (σύνεσις), understanding, is rendered " prudence " in 4907
1 Cor. 1 : 19, R.V. (A.V., " understanding ") ; it suggests quickness of AG:788C
apprehension, the penetrating consideration which precedes action. CB:1270C
Cp. B, in the same verse. See KNOWLEDGE, UNDERSTANDING.

B. Adjective.

SUNETOS (συνετός) signifies intelligent, sagacious, understanding 4908
(akin to *suniēmi*, to perceive), translated " prudent " in Matt. 11 : 25, AG:788D
A.V. (R.V., " understanding ") ; Luke 10 : 21 (ditto) ; Acts 13 : 7, R.V., CB:1270C
" (a man) of understanding ; " in 1 Cor. 1 : 19, " prudent," R.V. and A.V.¶
Cp. *asunetos*, " without understanding." ASUNETOS 801 AG:118C CB:1238A

PSALM

PSALMOS (ψαλμός) primarily denoted a striking or twitching with the 5568
fingers (on musical strings) ; then, a sacred song, sung to musical accom- AG:891B
paniment, a psalm. It is used (*a*) of the O.T. book of Psalms, Luke CB:1267C
20 : 42 ; 24 : 44 ; Acts 1 : 20 ; (*b*) of a particular psalm, Acts 13 : 33 (cp. ver. 35) ; (*c*) of psalms in general, 1 Cor. 14 : 26 ; Eph. 5 : 19 ; Col. 3 : 16.¶

Note : For *psallō*, rendered " let him sing psalms " in Jas. 5 : 13, see 5567 AG:891A
MELODY, SING. CB:1267B

PUBLIC, PUBLICLY

A. Adjective.

DĒMOSIOS (δημόσιος), belonging to the people (*dēmos*, the people), 1219
is translated " public " in Acts 5 : 18, R.V., " public (ward) ", A.V., AG:179B
" common (prison)." CB:1240C

B. Adverbs.

PHANERŌS (φανερῶς) : see OPENLY, No. 2. 5320

Note : For a form of *dēmosios* used as an adverb, " publicly," see AG:853A
OPENLY, Note (4). CB:1263C

PUBLICAN

TELŌNĒS (τελώνης) primarily denoted a farmer of the tax (from 5057
telos, toll, custom, tax), then, as in the N.T., a subsequent subordinate of AG:812B
such, who collected taxes in some district, a tax-gatherer ; such were CB:1271B
naturally hated intensely by the people ; they are classed with " sinners ", Matt. 9 : 10, 11 ; 11 : 9 ; Mark 2 : 15, 16 ; Luke 5 : 30 ; 7 : 34 ; 15 : 1 ; with harlots, Matt. 21 : 31, 32 ; with " the Gentile," Matt. 18 : 17 ; some mss. have it in Matt. 5 : 47, the best have *ethnikoi*, " Gentiles." See also Matt. 5 : 46 ; 10 : 3 ; Luke 3 : 12 ; 5 : 27, 29 ; 7 : 29 ; 18 : 10, 11, 13.¶

Note : For *architelōnēs*, a chief publican, see CHIEF, B, No. 4. 754 AG:113B CB:1237B

PUBLISH

1. KĒRUSSŌ (κηρύσσω), to be a herald, to proclaim, preach, is 2784
translated to publish in Mark 1 : 45 ; 5 : 20 ; 7 : 36 ; 13 : 10, A.V. (R.V., AG:431B
" preached ") ; Luke 8 : 39. See PREACH, PROCLAIM. CB:1255A

1308 AG:190B 2. DIAPHERŌ (διαφέρω), to bear through, is translated “ was pub-
CB:— lished ” in Acts 13 : 49, A.V. (R.V., “ was spread abroad ”). See BETTER (be), No. 1.

1096 AG:158A 3. GINOMAI (γίνομαι), to become, come to be, is translated “ was
CB:1248B published ” in Acts 10 : 37, lit., ‘ came to be.’

1229 AG:182B 4. DIANGELLŌ (διαγγέλλω), to publish abroad, is so translated in
CB:1241B Luke 9 : 60, R.V. (A.V., “ preach ”), and Rom. 9 : 17. See DECLARE, A, No. 3.

PUFF (up)

5448 AG:869B 1. PHUSIOŌ (φυσιόω), to puff up, blow up, inflate (from *phusa*,
CB:1264C bellows), is used metaphorically in the N.T., in the sense of being puffed up with pride, 1 Cor. 4 : 6, 18, 19 ; 5 : 2 ; 8 : 1 ; 13 : 4 ; Col. 2 : 18.¶

5187 AG:831A 2. TUPHOŌ (τυφόω) is always rendered to puff up in the R.V. See
CB:— HIGH-MINDED, PROUD.

PULL (down)

2507 AG:386C KATHAIREŌ (καθαιρέω), to take down, is translated “ I will pull
CB:— down ” in Luke 12 : 18. See DESTROY, No. 3.

HARPAZō *Notes :* (1) In Jude 23, A.V., *harpazō*, to seize, snatch away, is rendered
726 “ pulling . . . out.” See SNATCH. (2) In Acts 23 : 10, A.V., *diaspaō*, to
AG:109A CB:1249B rend or tear asunder, is translated “ should have been pulled in pieces ”
DIASPAō 1288 (R.V., “ should be torn in pieces ”). (3) *Ekballō*, to cast out, is translated
AG:188C to pull out in Matt. 7 : 4 and Luke 6 : 42 (twice), A.V. (R.V., “ cast out ”).
EKBALLō 1544 See CAST, No. 5. (4) For *anaspaō*, rendered “ pull out ” in Luke 14 : 5,
AG:237B A.V., see DRAW, No. 5. (5) For *kathairesis*, a casting down, 2 Cor.
CB:1243B 10 : 4, see CAST, A, No. 14, Note.

ANASPAō 385 AG:60B

PUNISH

KATHAIRESIS 1. KOLAZŌ (κολάζω) primarily denotes to curtail, prune, dock
2506 AG:386B (from *kolos*, docked) ; then, to check, restrain, punish ; it is used in the
KOLAZō Middle Voice in Acts 4 : 21 ; Passive Voice in 2 Pet. 2 : 9, A.V., to be
2849 AG:440C punished (R.V., “ under punishment,” lit., ‘ being punished ’), a futurative
CB:1255C present tense.¶

5097 2. TIMŌREŌ (τιμωρέω), primarily, to help, then, to avenge (from
AG:818C CB:— *timē*, value, honour, and *ouros*, a guardian), i.e., to help by redressing injuries, is used in the Active Voice in Acts 26 : 11, R.V., “ punishing ” (A.V., “ I punished ”) ; Passive V. in 22 : 5, lit., ‘ (that) they may be punished.’ Cp. No. 5, below.¶

Note : For 2 Thess. 1 : 9, “ shall suffer punishment,” R.V., see JUSTICE. See SUFFER, *Note* (10).

PUNISHMENT

1557 AG:238D 1. EKDIKĒSIS (ἐκδίκησις) : for 1 Pet. 2 : 14, A.V., “ punishment ”
CB:1243C (R.V., “ vengeance ”), see AVENGE, B, No. 2.

2. EPITIMIA (ἐπιτιμία) in the N.T. denotes penalty, punishment, 2009
2 Cor. 2 : 6.¶ Originally it signified the enjoyment of the rights and AG:303C CB:1246B
privileges of citizenship; then it became used of the estimate (*timē*)
fixed by a judge on the infringement of such rights, and hence, in general,
a penalty.

3. KOLASIS (κόλασις), akin to *kolazō* (PUNISH, No. 1), punishment, is 2851 AG:440D
used in Matt. 25 : 46, "(eternal) punishment," and 1 John 4 : 18, "(fear CB:1255B
hath) punishment," R.V. (A.V., "torment"), which there describes a
process, not merely an effect; this kind of fear is expelled by perfect love;
where God's love is being perfected in us, it gives no room for the fear of
meeting with His reprobation; the punishment referred to is the immediate consequence of the sense of sin, not a holy awe but a slavish fear,
the negation of the enjoyment of love.¶

4. DIKĒ (δίκη), justice, or the execution of a sentence, is translated 1349 AG:198C
"punishment" in Jude 7, R.V. (A.V., "vengeance"). See JUSTICE. CB:1242A

5. TIMŌRIA (τιμωρία), primarily help (see PUNISH, No. 2), denotes 5098 AG:818D
vengeance, punishment, Heb. 10 : 29.¶ CB:—

Note: The distinction, sometimes suggested, between No. 3 as being disciplinary, with special reference to the sufferer, and No. 5, as being penal, with reference to the satisfaction of him who inflicts it, cannot be maintained in the *Koinē* Greek of N.T. times.

KTAOMAI 2932

PURCHASE
AG:455A CB:1256A

1. KTAOMAI (κτάομαι): see OBTAIN, A, No. 4. PERIPOIEŌ

2. PERIPOIEŌ (περιποιέω) signifies to gain or get for oneself, 4046 (-OMAI)
purchase; Middle Voice in Acts 20 : 28 and 1 Tim. 3 : 13 (R.V., "gain"); AG:650A
see GAIN. CB:1263B

3. AGORAZŌ (ἀγοράζω) is rendered to purchase in the R.V. of Rev. (-OMAI) AGORAZŌ
5 : 9; 14 : 3, 4. See BUY, No. 1. 59

Note: For *peripoiēsis*, "purchased possession," Eph. 1 : 14, see AG:12D CB:1233C
POSSESSION. PERIPOIĒSIS

PURE, PURENESS, PURITY
4047 AG:650A

A. Adjectives.
CB:1263B

1. HAGNOS (ἁγνός), pure from defilement, not contaminated (from 53
the same root as *hagios*, holy), is rendered "pure" in Phil. 4 : 8; 1 Tim. AG:11D CB:1249A
5 : 22; Jas. 3 : 17; 1 John 3 : 3; see CHASTE.

2. KATHAROS (καθαρός), pure, as being cleansed, e.g., Matt. 5 : 8; 2513 AG:388A
1 Tim. 1 : 5; 3 : 9; 2 Tim. 1 : 3; 2 : 22; Tit. 1 : 15; Heb. 10 : 22; CB:1254B
Jas. 1 : 27; 1 Pet. 1 : 22; Rev. 15 : 6; 21 : 18; 22 : 1 (in some mss.).
See CHASTE, Note, CLEAN, A.

Note: In 1 Pet. 1 : 22 the A.V., "with a pure heart," follows those mss. which have this adjective (R.V., "from the heart").

3. EILIKRINĒS (εἰλικρινής) signifies unalloyed, pure; (*a*) it was used 1506
of unmixed substances; (*b*) in the N.T. it is used of moral and ethical AG:222D CB:—
purity, Phil. 1 : 10, "sincere;" so the R.V. in 2 Pet. 3 : 1 (A.V., "pure").

Some regard the etymological meaning as 'tested by the sunlight' (Cremer).¶ See CHASTE, Note, SINCERE.

Note : Wine mixed with water may be *hagnos*, not being contaminated ; it is not *katharos*, when there is the admixture of any element even though the latter is pure in itself.

B. Nouns.

54 AG:12A 1. HAGNOTĒS (ἁγνότης), the state of being *hagnos* (A, No. 1), occurs
CB:1249A in 2 Cor. 6 : 6, " pureness ; " 11 : 3, in the best mss., " (and the) purity," R.V.¶

47 AG:10D 2. HAGNEIA (ἁγνεία), synonymous with No. 1, " purity ", occurs
CB:1249A in 1 Tim. 4 : 12 ; 5 : 2, where it denotes the chastity which excludes all impurity of spirit, manner, or act.¶

PURGE

2508 AG:386D 1. KATHAIRŌ (καθαίρω), akin to *katharos* (see PURE, A, No. 2), to
CB:1254B cleanse, is used of pruning, John 15 : 2, A.V., " purgeth " (R.V., " cleanseth ").¶ In the Sept., 2 Sam. 4 : 6 ; Isa. 28 : 27 ; Jer. 38 : 28.¶

1571 AG:240B 2. EKKATHAIRŌ (ἐκκαθαίρω), to cleanse out, cleanse thoroughly, is
CB:1243C said of purging out leaven, 1 Cor. 5 : 7 ; in 2 Tim. 2 : 21, of purging oneself from those who utter " profane babblings," vv. 16–18.¶

1245 (-ARIZŌ) 3. DIAKATHAIRŌ (διακαθαίρω), to cleanse thoroughly, is translated
AG:183D " will throughly purge " in Luke 3 : 17, A.V. (R.V., " thoroughly to
CB:— cleanse ; " less authentic mss. have No. 5).¶

2511 AG:387B 4. KATHARIZŌ (καθαρίζω), to cleanse, make clean, is translated
CB:1254B " purging (all meats)," in Mark 7 : 19, A.V., R.V., " making (all meats) clean ; " Heb. 9 : 14, A.V., " purge " (R.V., " cleanse ") ; so 9 : 22 (for ver. 23, see PURIFY) and 10 : 2. See CLEAN, B, No. 1.

1245 AG:183D 5. DIAKATHARIZŌ (διακαθαρίζω), to cleanse thoroughly, is trans-
CB:— lated " will throughly purge " in Matt. 3 . 12, A.V. See CLEAN, B, No. 2. Cp. the synonymous verb No. 3.¶

2512 AG:387D *Notes :* (1) For Heb. 1 : 3, A.V., " had purged," see PURIFICATION.
CB:1254B (2) For the A.V. rendering of the noun *katharismos*, cleansing, " that he was purged," see CLEAN, C, No. 1.

PURIFICATION, PURIFY, PURIFYING

A. Nouns.

2512 AG:387D 1. KATHARISMOS (καθαρισμός) is rendered a cleansing (akin to
CB:1254B No. 4, above), Mark 1 : 44 ; Luke 5 : 14 ; in Heb. 1 : 3, R.V., " purification ".

2514 AG:388B 2. KATHAROTĒS (καθαρότης), cleansing, Heb. 9 : 13. See CLEAN,
CB:1254B C, No. 2.¶

49 AG:11A 3. HAGNISMOS (ἁγνισμός) denotes a ceremonial purification, Acts
CB:1249A 21 : 26, for the circumstances of which with reference to the vow of a Nazirite (R.V.), see Numb. 6 : 9–13.¶

B. Verbs.

1. HAGNIZŌ (ἁγνίζω), akin to *hagnos*, pure (see CHASTE), to purify, 48
cleanse from defilement, is used of purifying (*a*) ceremonially, John AG:11A CB:1249A
11 : 55 ; Acts 21 : 24, 26 (cp. No. 3 above) ; 24 : 18 ; (*b*) morally, the heart,
Jas. 4 : 8 ; the soul, 1 Pet. 1 : 22 ; oneself, 1 John 3 : 3.¶

2. KATHARIZŌ (καθαρίζω), to cleanse, make free from admixture, is 2511
translated to purify in Acts 15 : 9, A.V. (R.V., "cleansing") ; Tit. 2 : 14 ; AG:387B CB:1254B
Heb. 9 : 23, A.V. (R.V., "cleansed"). See CLEAN, B, No. 1.

PURLOIN

NOSPHIZŌ (νοσφίζω) is translated "purloining" in Tit. 2 : 10. See 3557 (-OMAI)
KEEP, A, No. 10. AG:543D CB:—

PURPLE

A. Noun.

PORPHURA (πορφύρα) originally denoted the purple-fish, then, 4209
purple dye (extracted from certain shell fish) : hence, a purple garment, AG:694A CB:1266A
Mark 15 : 17, 20 ; Luke 16 : 19 ; Rev. 18 : 12.¶

B. Adjective.

PORPHUREOS (πορφύρεος), purple, a reddish purple, is used of the (-OUS) 4210
robe put in mockery on Christ, John 19 : 2, 5 ; in Rev. 17 : 4 (in the best AG:694B
texts ; some have No. 1) ; 18 : 16, as a noun (with *himation*, a garment, CB:—
understood).¶

PURPLE (seller of)

PORPHUROPŌLIS (πορφυρόπωλις) denotes a seller of purple fabrics 4211 AG:694A
(from *porphura*, and *pōleō*, to sell), Acts 16 : 14.¶ CB:—

PURPOSE (Noun and Verb)

A. Nouns.

1. BOULĒMA (βούλημα), a purpose or will (akin to *boulomai*, to will, 1013 AG:145D
wish, purpose), a deliberate intention, occurs in Acts 27 : 43, "purpose ;" CB:1239B
Rom. 9 : 19, "will ;" 1 Pet. 4 : 3, in the best mss. (some have *thelēma*),
A.V., "will," R.V., "desire." See WILL.¶

2. PROTHESIS (πρόθεσις), a setting forth (used of the "shewbread"), 4286 AG:706A
a purpose (akin to B, No. 3), is used (*a*) of the purposes of God, Rom. 8 : 28 ; CB:1267B
9 : 11 ; Eph. 1 : 11 ; 3 : 11 ; 2 Tim. 1 : 9 ; (*b*) of human purposes, as to
things material, Acts 27 : 13 ; spiritual, Acts 11 : 23 ; 2 Tim. 3 : 10.
See SHEWBREAD.

3. GNŌMĒ (γνώμη), an opinion, purpose, judgment, is used in the 1106
genitive case with *ginomai*, to come to be, in Acts 20 : 3, "he purposed," AG:163A CB:1248B
A.V. (R.V., "he determined"), lit., 'he came to be of purpose.'

Notes : The following phrases are translated with the word "purpose :"
(*a*) *eis auto touto*, "for this same (or very) purpose," lit., 'unto this same EIS
(thing),' Rom. 9 : 17 ; Eph. 6 : 22 ; Col. 4 : 8 ; (*b*) *eis touto*, "for this 1519 AG:28A
purpose," Acts 26 : 16, A.V. (R.V., "to this end"), lit., 'unto this ;' so CB:1243A

1 John 3 : 8 ; (*c*) *eis ti,* "to what purpose," Matt. 26 : 8, lit., 'unto what ;' Mark 14 : 4, R.V., "to what purpose" (A.V., "why").

B. Verbs.

1011 1. BOULEUŌ (βουλεύω), to take counsel, resolve, always in the Middle
AG:145C CB:1239B Voice in the N.T., to take counsel with oneself, to determine with oneself,
(-OMAI) is translated "I purpose" in 2 Cor. 1 : 17 (twice). See COUNSEL, B, No. 1.

5087 AG:815D 2. TITHĒMI (τίθημι), to put, place, is used in the Middle Voice in
CB:1272C Acts 19 : 21, "purposed," in the sense of resolving.

4388 (-EMAI) 3. PROTITHĒMI (προτίθημι), to set before, set forth (*pro,* before,
AG:722B and No. 2, akin to A, No. 2), is used in Rom. 3 : 25, "set forth,"
CB:1267B R.V. marg., "purposed," A.V. marg., "foreordained," Middle Voice,
which lays stress upon the Personal interest which God had in so doing ; either meaning, to set forth or to purpose, would convey a Scriptural view, but the context bears out the former as being intended here ; in Rom. 1 : 13, "I purposed ;" Eph. 1 : 9, "He purposed (in Him)," R.V. See SET.¶

4160 AG:680D 4. POIEŌ (ποιέω), to make, is translated "He purposed" in Eph.
CB:1265C 3 : 11 (for the noun *prothesis,* in the same verse, see A, No. 2). See DO,
No. 1.

4255 (-OMAI) 5. PROAIREŌ (προαιρέω), to bring forth or forward, or, in the Middle
AG:702B Voice, to take by choice, prefer, purpose, is translated "He hath pur-
CB:— posed" in 2 Cor. 9 : 7, R.V. (A.V., "he purposed").¶

For PURSE see BAG, No. 2 and Note

PURSUE

1377 DIŌKŌ (διώκω), to put to flight, pursue, persecute, is rendered to
AG:201B pursue in 2 Cor. 4 : 9, R.V. (A.V., "persecute"), and is used metaphori-
CB:1242A cally of seeking eagerly after peace in 1 Pet. 3 : 11, R.V. (A.V., "ensue").
See FOLLOW.

PUT

5087 AG:815D 1. TITHĒMI (τίθημι), to place, lay, set, put, is translated to put in
CB:1272C Matt. 5 : 15 ; 12 : 18 ; in Matt. 22 : 44, R.V., "put (underneath Thy
feet) ;" Mark 4 : 21 (1st part), in the 2nd part, R.V., "put" (in some texts, No. 4, A.V., "set") ; 10 : 16, A.V. (R.V., "laying") ; Luke 8 : 16 (1st part) ; 2nd part, R.V. (A.V., "setteth") ; 11 : 33 ; John 19 : 19 ; Acts 1 : 7, A.V. (R.V., "set") ; 4 : 3 ; 5 : 18, 25 ; 12 : 4 ; Rom. 14 : 13 ; 1 Cor. 15 : 25 ; 2 Cor. 3 : 13 ; 1 Tim. 1 : 12, A.V. (R.V., "appointing") ; Rev. 11 : 9, A.V. (R.V., "laid"). See APPOINT, No. 3.

4060 AG:652C 2. PERITITHĒMI (περιτίθημι), to put around or on (*peri,* around,
CB:— and No. 1), is so used in Matt. 27 : 28 ; Mark 15 : 17, R.V., "put on"
(A.V., ". . . about") ; 15 : 36 ; John 19 : 29. See BESTOW, No. 5.

3. PARATITHĒMI (παρατίθημι), to set before (*para*, beside or before), 3908 AG:622D
is rendered to put forth (of a parable) in Matt. 13 : 24, 31, A.V. (R.V., CB:—
"set before"). See SET.

4. EPITITHĒMI (ἐπιτίθημι), to put on, upon, is so rendered in 2007 AG:302D
Matt. 19 : 13, A.V. (R.V., "lay"); so Mark 7 : 32; 8 : 25 (some mss. CB:1246B
have No. 1, here); Matt. 21 : 7; 27 : 29; John 9 : 15; 19 : 2 (1st part);
Acts 9 : 12 (R.V., "laying . . . on"); 15 : 10. See ADD, No. 1.

5. APOTITHĒMI (ἀποτίθημι), always in the Middle Voice in the N.T., 659 AG:101A
to put off (*apo*) from oneself, is rendered "to put away" in the R.V. in CB:1237B
the following: Eph. 4 : 22 (A.V., "put off"); Col. 3 : 8 (A.V., ditto);
Eph. 4 : 25; Jas. 1 : 21 (A.V., "laying apart"); 1 Pet. 2 : 1 (A.V.,
"laying aside"). See CAST, No. 16.

6. BALLŌ (βάλλω), to throw, cast, put, is translated to put, in Matt. 906 AG:130D
9 : 17 (twice); 25 : 27; 27 : 6; Mark 2 : 22; 7 : 33; Luke 5 : 37; CB:1238B
John 5 : 7; 12 : 6; 13 : 2 (of putting into the heart by the Devil); 18 : 11
(of putting up a sword); 20 : 25 (R.V. twice, A.V., "put" and "thrust");
ver. 27, R.V.; Jas. 3 : 3; Rev. 2 : 24 (R.V., "cast"). See CAST, No. 1.

Note: BLĒTEOS (a gerundive form from *ballō*), meaning '(that which) 992 AG:144A
one must put,' is found in Luke 5 : 38, and, in some mss., Mark 2 : 22.¶ CB:—

7. EKBALLŌ (ἐκβάλλω), to cast out, is translated to put forth or out 1544 AG:237B
in Matt. 9 : 25; Mark 5 : 40 (Luke 8 : 54 in some mss.); John 10 : 4; CB:1243B
Acts 9 : 40. See CAST, No. 5.

8. EPIBALLŌ (ἐπιβάλλω), to put to or unto, is so translated in Matt. 1911 AG:289D
9 : 16; Luke 5 : 36; 9 : 62; in Acts 12 : 1, R.V., "put forth (his CB:—
hands)," A.V., "stretched forth." See CAST, No. 7.

9. PERIBALLŌ (περιβάλλω), to put or throw around, is translated 4016 AG:646A
"put on" in John 19 : 2, A.V. (R.V., "arrayed . . . in"). See CAST, CB:—
No. 10, CLOTHE, No. 6.

10. PROBALLŌ (προβάλλω), to put forward, is so used in Acts 19 : 33. 4261 AG:702D
See SHOOT FORTH. CB:—

11. DIDŌMI (δίδωμι), to give, is rendered to put in Luke 15 : 22, of 1325 AG:192C
the ring on the returned prodigal's finger; 2 Cor. 8 : 16 and Rev. 17 : 17, CB:1241C
of putting into the heart by God; Heb. 8 : 10, of laws into the mind
(A.V., marg., "give"); 10 : 16, of laws on (R.V.: A.V., "into") the
heart. See GIVE.

12. PARADIDŌMI (παραδίδωμι), to give or hand over, is rendered 3860 AG:614B
"put in prison" in Mark 1 : 14, A.V. (R.V., "delivered up"). See CB:1262A
BETRAY.

13. POIEŌ (ποιέω), to do, make, is translated "to put" (with *exō*, 4160 AG:680D
"forth") in Acts 5 : 34, lit., 'do (them) outside.' CB:1265C

14. CHŌRIZŌ (χωρίζω), to separate, divide (cp. *chōris*, apart, separate 5563 AG:890A
from), is translated to put asunder in Matt. 19 : 6; Mark 10 : 9, of putting CB:1240A
away a wife.

1631 15. EKPHUŌ (ἐκφύω), to cause to grow out, put forth (*ek*, out,
AG:247A *phuō*, to bring forth, produce, beget), is used of the leaves of a tree, Matt.
CB:— 24 : 32 ; Mark 13 : 28, " putteth forth."¶

630 16. APOLUŌ (ἀπολύω), to set free, let go, is rendered to put away in
AG:96C reference to one who is betrothed, Matt. 1 : 19 ; a wife, 5 : 31, 32 (twice ;
CB:1237A in 2nd part, R.V. ; A.V., " is divorced ") ; 19 : 3, 7, 8, 9 (twice) ; Mark
10 : 2, 4, 11, 12 ; Luke 16 : 18 (twice). See DISMISS.

863 *Note :* In 1 Cor. 7 : 11, 12, A.V., *aphiēmi*, to send away, is translated
AG:125C to put away (R.V., " leave "), of the act of the husband toward the wife ;
CB:1236B in ver. 13, " leave," of the act of the wife toward the husband.

142 17. AIRŌ (αἴρω), to take up, remove, is rendered " put away," of
AG:24B bitterness, wrath, anger, clamour, railing and malice, Eph. 4 : 31 ; in
CB:1234A 1 Cor. 5 : 2 of the Divine effects of church discipline. See BEAR, No. 9.

1808 18. EXAIRŌ (ἐξαίρω), to put away from the midst of (*ek*, from, and
AG:272A No. 17), is used of church discipline, 1 Cor. 5 : 13.¶
CB:—

2673 19. KATARGEŌ (καταργέω) is rendered " I put away " in 1 Cor.
AG:417B 13 : 11 ; in 15 : 24, A.V., " shall have put down " (R.V., " abolished ").
CB:1254B See ABOLISH.

2507 20. KATHAIREŌ (καθαιρέω), to take down, put down, is rendered
AG:386C " He hath put down " in Luke 1 : 52. See CAST, A, No. 14.
CB:—

649 21. APOSTELLŌ (ἀποστέλλω), to send forth (*apo*, from or forth,
AG:98C *stellō*, to send), is said of using the sickle, Mark 4 : 29, R.V., " he putteth
CB:1237A forth," marg., " sendeth forth " (A.V., " putteth in "). See SEND, SET.

(-OMAI) 22. APEKDUŌ (ἀπεκδύω), to strip off clothes or arms, is used in the
554 Middle Voice in the N.T., Col. 2 : 15, R.V., " having put off from Himself,"
AG:83C (A.V., " having spoiled ") ; in 3 : 9, " ye have put off," of " the old man "
CB:1236B (see MAN). See SPOIL.¶

3179 23. METHISTĒMI or METHISTANŌ (μεθίστημι), to change, remove
AG:498D (*meta*, implying change, *histēmi*, to cause to stand), is used of putting
CB:— a man out of his stewardship, Luke 16 : 4 (Passive Voice). See REMOVE,
TRANSLATE, TURN (away).

321 24. ANAGŌ (ἀνάγω), to lead or bring up, is used nautically of ' putting
AG:53A out to sea,' Acts 27 : 2, 4, R.V. See LAUNCH.
CB:—

1877 25. EPANAGŌ (ἐπανάγω), to bring up or back, is used in the same
AG:282D sense as No. 24, in Luke 5 : 3, 4. See LAUNCH.
CB:—

1746 26. ENDUŌ (ἐνδύω), used in the Middle Voice, of putting on oneself,
AG:264A or on another, is translated to put on (*a*) literally, Matt. 6 : 25 ;
CB:1245A 27 : 31 ; Mark 6 : 9 ; 15 : 20 ; Luke 12 : 22 ; 15 : 22 ; (*b*) metaphorically,
of putting on the armour of light, Rom. 13 : 12 ; the Lord Jesus Christ,
13 : 14 ; Christ, Gal. 3 : 27 ; incorruption and immortality (said of the
body of the believer), 1 Cor. 15 : 53, 54 ; the new man, Eph. 4 : 24 ;
Col. 3 : 10 ; the whole armour of God, Eph. 6 : 11 ; the breastplate of

righteousness, 6 : 14, R.V. ; the breastplate of faith and love, 1 Thess. EMIBIBAZō 1688 AG:254C
5 : 8 ; various Christian qualities, Col. 3 : 12. See CLOTHE, No. 2. PROBIBAZō 4264

27. EMBIBAZŌ (ἐμβιβάζω), to put in (*en*, in, *bibazō*, not found in the AG:703C APOSTREPHō
N.T.), is used of putting persons on board ship, Acts 27 : 6.¶ In the
Sept., 2 Kings 9 : 28 ; Prov. 4 : 11.¶ 654 AG:100B

28. PROBIBAZŌ (προβιβάζω), to put forward, hence, to induce, incite, CB:1237A EKTEINō
is rendered "being put forward" in Matt. 14 : 8, R.V. (A.V., "being 1614
before instructed").¶ In the Sept., Ex. 35 : 34 ; Deut. 6 : 7.¶ AG:245B CB:1244A

29. APOSTREPHŌ (ἀποστρέφω), to turn away, remove, return, is LEGō
used of 'putting up again' a sword into its sheath, Matt. 26 : 52. See 3004 AG:468A
BRING, A, No. 22. CB:1256C

Notes : (1) *Ekteinō*, to stretch forth (always so translated in the APōTHEō 683 (-OMAI)
R.V., save in Acts 27 : 30, "lay out," of anchors), is rendered to put forth AG:103B LUō
in the A.V. of Matt. 8 : 3 ; Mark 1 : 41 ; Luke 5 : 13. (2) In Luke 14 : 7, 3089
A.V., *legō*, to speak (see R.V.), is translated "He put forth." (3) In Acts AG:483C CB:1257B
13 : 46, A.V., *apōtheō*, to thrust away (R.V.), is rendered "put . . . HUPOTASSō
from ;" in 1 Tim. 1 : 19, A.V., "having put away" (R.V., "having thrust 5293 AG:847D
from"), Middle Voice in each ; so in Acts 7 : 27, A.V. and R.V., "thrust CB:1252B (-OMAI)
away." See CAST, No. 13, THRUST. (4) For "to put away" in Heb. ANUPOTAKTOS 506
9 : 26, see PUTTING, *Note* (below). (5) In Acts 7 : 33, A.V., *luō*, to loose AG:76D
(R.V.), is translated "put off." See LOOSE. (6) For the A.V. of PROSPHERō 4374
hupotassō, "put under" in 1 Cor. 15 : 27, 28 ; Eph. 1 : 22 ; Heb. 2 : 8, see AG:719C
SUBJECT, and for the connected negative adjective *anupotaktos*, rendered CB:1267B
"not put under" in Heb. 2 : 8, A.V., see DISOBEDIENT, B, (Note). ANAMIMNēSKō 363
(7) In John 19 : 29, A.V., *prospherō*, to bring to, is translated "they put AG:57D
it to (His mouth)," R.V., "they brought it . . ." (8) For *anamimnēskō*, CB:1235A APOKTEINō
to put in remembrance, 1 Cor. 4 : 17, R.V., see REMEMBRANCE. (9) 615
For *apokteinō*, to kill, rendered "put to death" in Mark 14 : 1, etc., see AG:93D CB:1237A
DEATH, C, No. 4. (10) For 1 Thess. 2 : 4, A.V., "to be put in trust," DIAKRINō
see INTRUST. (11) For the phrase "put . . . to . . . account" in Philm. 18, 1252 AG:185A
see ACCOUNT, A, No. 2. (12) In Acts 15 : 9, A.V., *diakrinō*, to make a CB:1241A
distinction (R.V.), is translated "put (no) difference." (13) In Matt. PLēRōMA 4138
9 : 16, A.V., *plērōma*, the fulness or filling, is rendered "(that) which is AG:672A
put in to fill it up," R.V., "(that) which should fill it up." See FILL. CB:1265B PARADEIGMATIZō
(14) For *paradeigmatizō*, to put to an open shame, Heb. 6 : 6, see SHAME. 3856
(15) For *phimoō*, to put to silence, see SILENCE. (16) For "I will put My AG:614A CB:1262A
trust," Heb. 2 : 13, see TRUST. PHIMOō 5392 AG:861D

PUTTING

1. ENDUSIS (ἔνδυσις), a putting on (akin to *enduō*, PUT, No. 26), is ENDUSIS 1745
used of apparel, 1 Pet. 3 : 3.¶ In the Sept., Esth. 5 : 1 ; Job 41 : 4.¶ AG:263D EPITHESIS

2. EPITHESIS (ἐπίθεσις), a putting on (akin to *epitithēmi*, PUT, No. 4), 1936
is used of the putting or laying on of hands ; in 2 Tim. 1 : 6, R.V., "laying" AG:293A CB:1246B
(A.V., "putting"). See LAYING ON.

595 AG:91A 3. APOTHESIS (ἀπόθεσις), a putting off or away (akin to *apotithēmi*,
CB:1237B PUT, No. 5), is used metaphorically in 1 Pet. 3 : 21, of the " putting away " of the filth of the flesh ; in 2 Pet. 1 : 14, R.V., of " the putting off " of the body (as a tabernacle) at death (A.V., " I must put off ").¶

555 AG:83C 4. APEKDUSIS (ἀπέκδυσις), a putting off, stripping off (akin to
CB:1236B *apekduō*, PUT, No. 22), is used in Col. 2 : 11, of " the body of the flesh " (R.V., an important rendering).¶

115 AG:21B *Note :* For *athetēsis*, a putting away, translated " to put away " in
CB:1238A Heb. 9 : 26, lit., ' (unto) a setting aside,' see DISANNUL, B.¶

QUAKE

1. ENTROMOS (ἔντρομος), an adjective signifying trembling with 1790
fear (*en*, in, *tremō*, to tremble), is used with *eimi*, to be, in Heb. 12 : 21 AG:269D CB:—
(some mss. have *ektromos*, with the same meaning), "I quake," lit.,
'I am trembling.' It is used with *ginomai*, to become, in Acts 7 : 32,
"trembled," lit., 'became trembling,' and 16 : 29, R.V., "trembling for
fear" (A.V., "came trembling"). See TREMBLE.¶

2. SEIŌ (σείω), "did quake," Matt. 27 : 51, and 28 : 4, R.V. (A.V., 4579
"did shake"). See MOVE, No. 3, SHAKE, TREMBLE. AG:746C CB:1268C

For QUARREL see COMPLAINT, No. 2, and SET, No. 15, Mark 6 : 19, R.V.

QUARTER

3840

PANTOTHEN (πάντοθεν), from all sides, is translated "from every AG:608D
quarter" in Mark 1 : 45. See EVERY SIDE, ROUND ABOUT. CB:—

Notes : (1) In Rev. 20 : 8, A.V., *gōnia*, an angle, corner, is rendered GŌNIA 1137
"quarter" (R.V., "corner"). (2) In Acts 16 : 3, A.V., *topois*, "parts" AG:168D
(R.V.) is translated "quarters." (3) In Acts 9 : 32 the phrase *dia pantōn*, CB:1248C TOPOS
lit., 'throughout all,' is rendered "throughout all parts," R.V. (*meros*, a 5117
part, being understood), A.V., "throughout all *quarters*." (4) For AG:822B CB:1273A
"quarters" in Acts 28 : 7, A.V., see NEIGHBOURHOOD. PAS

3956

QUATERNION

AG:631A CB:1262C

TETRADION (τετράδιον), a group of four (*tetra*—, four), occurs in 5069
Acts 12 : 4. A quaternion was a set of four men occupied in the work of AG:813D CB:1271C
a guard, two soldiers being chained to the prisoner and two keeping watch ;
alternatively one of the four watched while the other three slept. The
night was divided into four watches of three hours each ; there would be
one quaternion for each watch by day and by night.¶ Cp. the "guard"
in Matt. 27 : 65 and 28 : 11.

QUEEN

BASILISSA (βασίλισσα), the feminine of *basileus*, a king, is used 938
(*a*) of the Queen of Sheba, Matt. 12 : 42 ; Luke 11 : 31 ; of Candace, AG:137A CB:1238C
Acts 8 : 27 ; (*b*) metaphorically, of Babylon, Rev. 18 : 7.¶

QUENCH, UNQUENCHABLE

A. Verb.

4570 AG:745B CB:1268C SBENNUMI (σβέννυμι) is used (*a*) of quenching fire or things on fire, Matt. 12 : 20, quoted from Is. 42 : 3, figurative of the condition of the feeble ; Heb. 11 : 34 ; in the Passive Voice, Matt. 25 : 8, of torches (see LAMP), R.V., " are going out," lit., 'are being quenched ;' of the retributive doom hereafter of sin unrepented of and unremitted in this life, Mark 9 : 48 (in some mss. in vv. 44, 46) ; (*b*) metaphorically, of quenching the fire-tipped darts of the evil one, Eph. 6 : 16 ; of quenching the Spirit, by hindering His operations in oral testimony in the church gatherings of believers, 1 Thess. 5 : 19. " The peace, order, and edification of the saints were evidence of the ministry of the Spirit among them, 1 Cor. 14 : 26, 32, 33, 40, but if, through ignorance of His ways, or through failure to recognise, or refusal to submit to, them, or through impatience with the ignorance or self-will of others, the Spirit were quenched, these happy results would be absent. For there was always the danger that the impulses of the flesh might usurp the place of the energy of the Spirit in the assembly, and the endeavour to restrain this evil by natural means would have the effect of hindering His ministry also. Apparently then, this injunction was intended to warn believers against the substitution of a mechanical order for the restraints of the Spirit."*¶ Cp. S. of Sol. 8 : 7.

B. Adjective.

762 AG:114B CB:1237C ASBESTOS (ἄσβεστος), not quenched (*a*, negative, and A), is used of the doom of persons described figuratively as " chaff," Matt. 3 : 12 and Luke 3 : 17, " unquenchable ; " of the fire of Gehenna (see HELL), Mark 9 : 43, R.V., " unquenchable fire " (in some mss. ver. 45).¶ In the Sept., Job 20 : 26.¶

QUESTION (Noun and Verb), QUESTIONING

A. Nouns.

2214 AG:339B CB:1273C 1. ZĒTĒSIS (ζήτησις), primarily a seeking, search (*zēteō*, to seek), for which see DISPUTATION, is used in John 3 : 25 ; Acts 25 : 20, R.V., " (being perplexed) how to inquire (concerning these things)," A.V. " (because I doubted of such manner) of questions," lit., 'being perplexed as to the enquiry (or discussion) concerning these things ;' in 1 Tim. 1 : 4 (in some mss.) ; 6 : 4 ; 2 Tim. 2 : 23 ; Tit. 3 : 9. See INQUIRY.

2213 AG:339B CB:— 2. ZĒTĒMA (ζήτημα), synonymous with No. 1, but, generally speaking, suggesting in a more concrete form the subject of an enquiry, occurs in Acts 15 : 2 ; 18 : 15 ; 23 : 29 ; 25 : 19 ; 26 : 3.¶

3056 AG:477A CB:1257A 3. LOGOS (λόγος), a word, is translated " question " in Matt. 21 : 24 (A.V., " thing ") ; in Mark 11 : 29 (R.V., marg., " word ") and Luke 20 : 3, A.V., " one thing : " there is no word in the original for " one," hence the R.V., " a question."

---

* From Notes on Thessalonians, by Hogg and Vine, p. 196.

4. EKZĒTĒSIS (ἐκζήτησις), a questioning, is found in the best texts — AG:240B
in 1 Tim. 1 : 4 (see R.V.) ; cp. No. 1.¶ CB:1244A
Notes : (1) In Matt. 22 : 41, there is no word in the original for SUZēTēSIS
" question." (2) For *suzētēsis* or *sunzētēsis*, a questioning together 4803 AG:775D
(*sun*, with), see DISPUTATION. (3) In Acts 19 : 40, A.V., *enkaleō*, to bring CB:—
a charge against, is translated " to be called in question " (R.V., " to ENKALEō 1458
be accused "). AG:215C

B. Verbs. CB:1245A

1. SUZĒTEŌ (συζητέω) or SUNZĒTEŌ, to search together (cp. Note, 4802
above), to discuss, dispute, is translated to question (or q. with or together) AG:775D CB:—
in Mark 1 : 27 ; 8 : 11 ; 9 : 10, 14, 16 ; 12 : 28, R.V. (A.V., " reasoning
together ") ; Luke 22 : 23, R.V. (A.V., " enquire ") ; 24 : 15, R.V. (A.V.,
" reasoned "). See DISPUTE, B, No. 3, INQUIRE, REASON.

2. EPERŌTAŌ (ἐπερωτάω), to ask, is translated " asked . . . a 1905
question," in Matt. 22 : 35, 41 ; in Luke 2 : 46, " asking . . . questions ;" AG:285B CB:1245C
" questioned " in Luke 23 : 9. See ASK, A, No. 3.

For QUICK, see DISCERN, C, LIVE, No. 3, Note

QUICKEN 2227

1. ZŌOPOIEŌ (ζωοποιέω), to make alive : see LIFE, C. AG:341D CB:1273C
2. ZŌOGONEŌ (ζωογονέω), to endue with life, produce alive, preserve 2225
alive : see LIVE, No. 6. AG:341C CB:1273C
3. SUZŌOPOIEŌ (συζωοποιέω) or SUNZŌOPOIEŌ, to quicken 4806
together with, make alive with (*sun*, with and No. 1), is used in Eph. AG:776A CB:1271A
2 : 5 ; Col. 2 : 13, of the spiritual life with Christ, imparted to believers
at their conversion.¶

QUICKLY

1. TACHU (ταχύ), the neuter of *tachus*, swift, quick, signifies quickly, 5035
Matt. 5 : 25 ; 28 : 7, 8 ; Mark 9 : 39, R.V. (A.V., " lightly ") ; Luke AG:807B CB:1271A
15 : 22 ; John 11 : 29 ; Rev. 2 : 16 (ver. 5 in some mss.) ; 3 : 11 ; 11 : 14 ;
22 : 7, 12, 20. See LIGHTLY.¶

2. TACHEION (τάχειον), the comparative degree of No. 1, is trans- 5032
lated " quickly " in John 13 : 27 ; " out(ran) " in 20 : 4, R.V., lit., ' (ran AG:806D (-EōS)
before) more quickly (than Peter) ; ' " shortly " in 1 Tim. 3 : 14 and CB:—
Heb. 13 : 23 ; in 13 : 19, " (the) sooner." See SHORTLY.¶

3. TACHEŌS (ταχέως), akin to No. 1, is translated " quickly " in 5030
Luke 14 : 21 ; 16 : 6 ; John 11 : 31, R.V. ; " shortly " in 1 Cor. 4 : 19 ; AG:806D CB:—
Phil. 2 : 19, 24 ; 2 Tim 4 : 9 ; with a suggestion of rashness in the following,
Gal. 1 : 6, R.V., " quickly " (A.V., " soon ") ; 2 Thess. 2 : 2 ; and 1 Tim.
5 : 22, " hastily," (A.V., " suddenly "). See HASTILY, C.¶ 5034

4. EN TACHEI (ἐν τάχει), lit., in, or with, swiftness, with speed (*en*, (TACHOS)
in, and the dative case of *tachos*, speed), is translated " quickly " in Acts AG:806D
12 : 7 ; 22 : 18 ; " speedily " in Luke 18 : 8 ; " shortly " in Acts 25 : 4 ; (-EōS) CB:—

Rom. 16 : 20; 1 Tim. 3 : 14 in some texts; Rev. 1 : 1; 22 : 6. In the last two places, "with speed" is probably the meaning. See SHORTLY, SPEEDILY.¶

QUICKSANDS

4950 AG:794C CB:— *Note:* This is the A.V. rendering in Acts 27 : 17 of *Surtis*, "Syrtis" (R.V.). The Syrtes, Major and Minor, lie on the North coast of Africa, between the headlands of Tunis and Barca. They have been regarded as dangerous to mariners from very early times, both from the character of the sands and from the cross currents of the adjoining waters. In the voyage described in this chapter the vessel had left the shelter of the island of Cauda and was drifting before the N.E. wind Euraquilo. The mariners might well fear that they would be driven on the Syrtes on the leeward of their course. The changing character of the tempest, however, drove them into the sea of Adria.¶

QUIET, QUIETNESS

A. Adjectives.

2263 AG:348B CB:— 1. ĒREMOS (ἤρεμος), quiet, tranquil, occurs in 1 Tim. 2 : 2, R.V., "tranquil" (A.V., "quiet"); it indicates tranquillity arising from without.¶

2272 AG:349C CB:1250A 2. HĒSUCHIOS (ἡσύχιος) has much the same meaning as No. 1, but indicates tranquillity arising from within, causing no disturbance to others. It is translated "quiet" in 1 Tim. 2 : 2, R.V. (A.V., "peaceable"); "quiet" in 1 Pet. 3 : 4, where it is associated with "meek," and is to characterize the spirit or disposition. See PEACEABLE.¶

B. Verbs.

2270 AG:349A CB:1250A 1. HĒSUCHAZŌ (ἡσυχάζω), akin to A, No. 2, to be still, to live quietly: see CEASE, A, No. 3.¶

2687 AG:419A CB:— 2. KATASTELLŌ (καταστέλλω) denotes to quiet: see APPEASE.

C. Nouns.

1515 AG:227B CB:1243A 1. EIRĒNĒ (εἰρήνη), peace, is translated "quietness" in Acts 24 : 2, A.V. (R.V., "peace"). See PEACE (*e*).

2271 AG:349B CB:1250A 2. HĒSUCHIA (ἡσυχία), akin to A, No. 2, and B. No. 1, denotes quietness, 2 Thess. 3 : 12; it is so translated in the R.V. of 1 Tim. 2 : 11, 12 (A.V., "silence"); in Acts 22 : 2, R.V., "(they were the more) quiet," A.V., "(they kept the more) silence," lit., 'they kept quietness the more.'¶

QUIT

525 AG:80A CB:1236B 1. APALLASSŌ (ἀπαλλάσσω), to free from, is used in the Passive Voice in Luke 12 : 58, R.V., "to be quit" (A.V., "to be delivered"). See DELIVER, A, No. 6.

(-OMAI) 407 AG:64A CB:— 2. ANDRIZŌ (ἀνδρίζω) signifies to make a man of (*anēr*, a man); in the Middle Voice, in 1 Cor. 16 : 13, to play the man, "quit you like men."¶

R

RABBI

RABBEI or RABBI (ῥαββεί), from a word *rab*, primarily denoting 4461
" master " in contrast to a slave ; this with the added pronominal suffix AG:733A
signified " my master " and was a title of respect by which teachers were CB:1268A
addressed. The suffix soon lost its specific force, and in the N.T. the word is used as courteous title of address. It is applied to Christ in Matt. 26 : 25, 49 ; Mark 9 : 5 ; 11 : 21 ; 14 : 45 ; John 1 : 38 (where it is interpreted as *didaskalos*, " master," marg., " teacher " (see also " Rabboni " in John 20 : 16) ; ver. 49 ; 3 : 2 ; 4 : 31 ; 6 : 25 ; 9 : 2 ; 11 : 8 ; to John the Baptist in John 3 : 26. In Matt. 23 : 7, 8 Christ forbids his disciples to covet or use it. In the latter verse it is again explained as *didaskalos*, " master " (some mss. have *kathēgētēs*, a guide).¶

RABBONI

RABBOUNEI or RABBŌNI (ῥαββουνεί), formed in a similar way 4462
to the above, was an Aramaic form of a title almost entirely applied to AG:733A
the president of the Sanhedrin, if such was a descendant of Hillel. It CB:1268A
was even more respectful than Rabbi, and signified ' My great master ; ' in its use in the N.T. the pronominal force of the suffix is apparently retained (contrast Rabbi above) ; it is found in Mark 10 : 51 in the best texts, R.V., " Rabboni " (A.V., " Lord "), addressed to Christ by blind Bartimæus, and in John 20 : 16 by Mary Magdalene, where it is interpreted by *didaskalos*, " Master " (marg., " Teacher ").¶

For RABBLE see COURT, No. 1

RACA

RAKA (ῥακά) is an Aramaic word akin to the Heb. *rêq*, empty, the 4469
first *a* being due to a Galilæan change. In the A.V. of 1611 it was spelt AG:733D
racha ; in the edition of 1638, *raca*. It was a word of utter contempt, CB:1268A
signifying empty, intellectually rather than morally, empty-headed, like Abimelech's hirelings, Judg. 9 : 4, and the " vain " man of Jas. 2 : 20. As condemned by Christ, Matt. 5 : 22, it was worse than being angry, inasmuch as an outrageous utterance is worse than a feeling unexpressed or somewhat controlled in expression ; it does not indicate such a loss of self-control as the word rendered " fool," a godless, moral reprobate.¶

For RACE (kindred) see KIND

RACE (contest)

73 AG:15A CB:1233C 1. AGŌN (ἀγών) is translated "race" in Heb. 12 : 1, one of the modes of athletic contest, this being the secondary meaning of the word. See CONFLICT.

4712 AG:764A CB:— 2. STADION (στάδιον), a stadium, denotes a racecourse, 1 Cor. 9 : 24. The stadium (about 600 Greek feet or ⅛ of a Roman mile) was the length of the Olympic course. See FURLONG.

Note : No. 1 signifies the race itself ; No. 2 the course.

RAGE, RAGING

A. Verb.

5433 AG:867B CB:— PHRUASSŌ (φρυάσσω) was primarily used of the snorting, neighing and prancing of horses ; hence, metaphorically, of the haughtiness and insolence of men, Acts 4 : 25.¶ In the Sept., Psa. 2 : 1.¶

B. Noun.

2830 AG:436D CB:— KLUDŌN (κλύδων), a billow, surge (akin to *kluzō*, "to wash over," said of the sea ; cp. *kludōnizomai*, to be tossed by the waves, Eph. 4 : 14), is translated "raging" in Luke 8 : 24 ; in Jas. 1 : 6, R.V., "surge" (A.V., "wave").¶

66 AG:13C CB:1233C *Note :* In Jude 13, A.V., the adjective *agrios*, wild, is translated "raging" (R.V., "wild"). See WILD.

RAIL, RAILER, RAILING

A. Verb.

987 AG:142C CB:1239A BLASPHĒMEŌ (βλασφημέω), to blaspheme, rail, revile (for the meanings of which see BLASPHEME), is translated to rail at, or on, in Matt. 27 : 39, R.V. (A.V., "reviled") ; Mark 15 : 29 ; Luke 23 : 39 ; 2 Pet. 2 : 10, R.V. (A.V., "to speak evil of") ; 2 : 12, R.V. (A.V., "speak evil of"). Cp. *loidoreō*, to revile (see REVILE), and B, No. 2 and C, No. 2.

B. Nouns.

988 AG:143A CB:1239A 1. BLASPHĒMIA (βλασφημία) is translated "railings" in Matt. 15 : 19, R.V. ; 1 Tim. 6 : 4, A.V. and R.V. ; "railing" in Mark 7 : 22, R.V. ; Col. 3 : 8, R.V. ; Jude 9, A.V. and R.V., lit., 'judgment of railing ;' in Eph. 4 : 31, R.V. (A.V., "evil speaking"). See BLASPHEMY.

3059 AG:479C CB:1257A 2. LOIDORIA (λοιδορία), abuse, railing, reviling, is rendered "reviling" in the R.V., 1 Pet. 3 : 9 (twice) ; in 1 Tim. 5 : 14, A.V. marg., "for their reviling." See REVILE, C.¶

C. Adjectives.

989 AG:143A CB:1239A 1. BLASPHĒMOS (βλάσφημος), akin to A, and B, No. 1 ; see BLASPHEME, C.

3060 AG:479C CB:1257B 2. LOIDOROS (λοίδορος), an adjective denoting reviling, railing (akin to B, No. 2), is used as a noun, "a railer," 1 Cor. 5 : 11. See REVILE.

RAIMENT HIMATION 2440

Notes: (1) For *himation*, rendered "raiment" in Matt. 17 : 2, A.V. AG:376B
(R.V., "garments"), so Matt. 27 : 31 ; Mark 9 : 3 ; Luke 23 : 34 ; John CB:1250C HIMATISMOS
19 : 24 ; Acts 22 : 20 ; Rev. 3 : 5, 18 ; 4 : 4 ; A.V. and R.V., Acts 18 : 6, 2441
see CLOTHING, No. 2 and ROBE. *Himatismos* is rendered "raiment" in AG:376D ENDUMA
Luke 9 : 29 ; *enduma* in Matt. 3 : 4 ; 6 : 25, 28 ; 28 : 3 and Luke 12 : 23. 1742
For *esthēs*, translated "raiment" in Jas. 2 : 2 (2nd part), A.V., see APPAREL. AG:263C CB:1245A
(2) For *skepasma*, a covering, rendered "raiment" in 1 Tim. 6 : 8, A.V., ESTHēS
see COVER, B, No. 2. 2066

AG:312B CB:1246C

RAIN (Noun and Verb) SKEPASMA

A. Nouns. 4629

AG:753D

1. HUETOS (ὑετός), from *huō*, to rain, is used especially, but not 5202
entirely, of showers, and is found in Acts 14 : 17 ; 28 : 2 ; Heb. 6 : 7 ; AG:833B
Jas. 5 : 7 (see EARLY AND LATTER) ; 5 : 18 ; Rev. 11 : 6 (see B).¶ CB:1251C

2. BROCHĒ (βροχή), akin to B, below, lit., a wetting, hence, rain, 1028
is used in Matt. 7 : 25, 27.¶ In the Sept., Ps. 68 : 9 ; 105 : 32.¶ It is AG:147D CB:1239B
found in the papyri in connection with irrigation in Egypt (Deissmann, *Light from the Ancient East*).

B. Verb.

BRECHŌ (βρέχω), akin to A, No. 2, signifies (*a*) to wet, Luke 7 : 38, 1026
44, R.V. (A.V., to wash) ; (*b*) to send rain, Matt. 5 : 45 ; to rain, Luke AG:147C CB:1239B
17 : 29 (of fire and brimstone) ; Jas. 5 : 17, used impersonally (twice) ; Rev. 11 : 6, where *huetos* (A, No. 1) is used as the subject, lit., '(that) rain rain (not).'¶

RAINBOW

IRIS (ἶρις), whence Eng., iris, the flower, describes the rainbow seen 2463
in the heavenly vision, "round about the throne, like an emerald to look AG:380C CB:1253A
upon," Rev. 4 : 3, emblematic of the fact that, in the exercise of God's absolute sovereignty and perfect counsels, He will remember His covenant concerning the earth (Gen. 9 : 9–17) ; in Rev. 10 : 1, "the rainbow," R.V., the definite article suggests a connection with the scene in 4 : 3 ; here it rests upon the head of an angel who declares that "there shall be delay no longer" (ver. 6, R.V. marg., the actual meaning) ; the mercy to be shown to the earth must be preceded by the execution of Divine judgments upon the nations who defy God and His Christ. Cp. Ezek. 1 : 28.¶

RAISE (up)

1. EGEIRŌ (ἐγείρω), for the various meanings of which see ARISE, 1453
No. 3, is used (*a*) of raising the dead, Active and Passive Voices, e.g. of the AG:214C CB:1242C
resurrection of Christ, Matt. 16 : 21 ; 17 : 23 ; 20 : 19, R.V. ; 26 : 32, R.V., "(after) I am raised up" (A.V., ". . . risen again") ; Luke 9 : 22 ; 20 : 37 ; John 2 : 19 ; Acts 3 : 15 ; 4 : 10 [not 5 : 30, see (*c*) below] ; 10 : 40 [not 13 : 23 in the best texts, see (*c*) below] ; 13 : 30, 37 ; Rom. 4 : 24, 25 ;

6 : 4, 9 ; 7 : 4 ; 8 : 11 (twice) ; 8 : 34, R.V. ; 10 : 9 ; 1 Cor. 6 : 14 (1st part) ; 15 : 13, 14, R.V. ; 15 : 15 (twice), 16, 17 ; 15 : 20, R.V. ; 2 Cor. 4 : 14 ; Gal. 1 : 1 ; Eph. 1 : 20 ; Col. 2 : 12 ; 1 Thess. 1 : 10 ; 1 Pet. 1 : 21 ; in 2 Tim. 2 : 8, R.V., " risen " ; (*b*) of the resurrection of human beings, Matt. 10 : 8 ; 11 : 5 ; Matt. 27 : 52, R.V. (A.V., " arose ") ; Mark 12 : 26, R.V. ; Luke 7 : 22 ; John 5 : 21 ; 12 : 1, 9, 17 ; Acts 26 : 8 ; 1 Cor. 15 : 29 and 32, R.V. ; 15 : 35, 42, 43 (twice), 44, 52 ; 2 Cor. 1 : 9 ; 4 : 14 ; Heb. 11 : 19 ; (*c*) of raising up a person to occupy a place in the midst of a people, said of Christ, Acts 5 : 30 ; in 13 : 23, A.V. only (the best texts have *agō*, to bring, R.V., " hath . . . brought ") ; of David, Acts 13 : 22 (for ver. 33 see No. 2) ; (*d*) metaphorically, of a horn of salvation, Luke 1 : 69 ; (*e*) of children, from stones, by creative power, Luke 3 : 8 ; (*f*) of the Temple, as the Jews thought, John 2 : 20, R.V., " wilt Thou raise (it) up " (A.V., " rear ") ; (*g*) of lifting up a person, from physical infirmity, Mark 1 : 31, R.V., " raised . . . up " (A.V., " lifted ") ; so 9 : 27 ; Acts 3 : 7 ; 10 : 26, R.V. (A.V., " took ") ; Jas. 5 : 15, " shall raise . . . up ; " (*h*) metaphorically, of raising up affliction, Phil. 1 : 17, R.V. (in the best texts ; the A.V., ver. 16, following those which have *epipherō*, has " to add "). See AWAKE, No. 1.

450 2. ANISTĒMI (ἀνίστημι), for the various applications of which see
AG:70A
CB:— ARISE, No. 1, is translated to raise or raise up, (*a*) of the resurrection of the dead by Christ, John 6 : 39, 40, 44, 54 ; (*b*) of the resurrection of Christ from the dead, Acts 2 : 24 (for ver. 30 see R.V., *kathizō*, to set, as in the best texts) ; 2 : 32 ; 13 : 34, see (*c*) below ; Acts 17 : 31 ; (*c*) of raising up a person to occupy a place in the midst of a nation, said of Christ, Acts 3 : 26 ; 7 : 37 ; 13 : 33, R.V., " raised up Jesus," not here by resurrection from the dead, as the superfluous " again " of the A.V. would suggest ; this is confirmed by the latter part of the verse, which explains the raising up as being by way of His Incarnation, and by the contrast in ver. 34, where stress is laid upon His being raised " from the dead," the same verb being used : (*d*) of raising up seed, Matt. 22 : 24 ; (*e*) of being raised from natural sleep, Matt. 1 : 24, A.V., " being raised " (R.V.,
DIEGEIRō " arose ") ; here some mss. have *diegeirō*, to arouse completely ; see
1326
AG:193D ARISE, No. 4.
CB:— *Note :* For the contrast between No. 1 and No. 2 see ARISE, No. 3 (parag. 2).

1825 3. EXEGEIRŌ (ἐξεγείρω), *ek*, out of, and No. 1, is used (*a*) of the
AG:273D
CB:— resurrection of believers, 1 Cor. 6 : 14 [2nd part ; see No. 1 (*a*) for the 1st part] ; (*b*) of raising a person to public position, Rom. 9 : 17, " did I raise thee up," R.V., said of Pharaoh.¶

1817 4. EXANISTĒMI (ἐξανίστημι), *ek*, out of, and No. 2, is used of raising
AG:272D
CB:1247C up seed, Mark 12 : 19 ; Luke 20 : 28 ; elsewhere, Acts 15 : 5, to rise up. See RISE.¶

4891
AG:785D 5. SUNEGEIRŌ (συνεγείρω), to raise together (*sun*, with, and No. 1),
CB:— is used of the believer's spiritual resurrection with Christ, Eph. 2 : 6 ;

Passive Voice in Col. 2 : 12, R.V., " ye were . . . raised (with Him)," A.V., " ye are risen ; " so 3 : 1. See RISE.

Notes : (1) In Acts 13 : 50, A.V., *epegeirō*, to rouse up, excite, is trans- EPEGEIRō 1892
lated " raised " (R.V., " stirred up," as in A.V. and R.V. in 14 : 2). (2) AG:284A
In Acts 24 : 12, *poieō*, to make, is used with *epistasis*, a collection of people, CB:— EPISTASIS
and translated " stirring up (a crowd)," R.V., lit., ' making a collection —
(of a crowd) ' ; some mss. have *episustasis*, a riotous throng, A.V., " raising AG:300B
up (the people)." (3) In Heb. 11 : 35, A.V., the noun *anastasis*, a resurrec- CB:— EPISUSTASIS
tion, preceded by *ex* (i.e., *ek*), out of, or by, instrumental, is translated 1999
" raised to life again " (a paraphrase), R.V., " by a resurrection." AG:301D CB:1246A

ANASTASIS 386 AG:60B CB:1235B

For RAN see RUN

RANKS

PRASIA (πρασιά), a garden-bed or plot (probably from *prason*, a leek), 4237
is used metaphorically in Mark 6 : 40 of ranks of persons arranged in orderly AG:698B CB:—
groups.¶

RANSOM

1. LUTRON (λύτρον), lit., a means of loosing (from *luō*, to loose), 3083
occurs frequently in the Sept., where it is always used to signify AG:482C CB:1257B
equivalence. Thus it is used of the ransom for a life, e.g., Ex. 21 : 30, of the redemption price of a slave, e.g., Lev. 19 : 20, of land, 25 : 24, of the price of a captive, Isa. 45 : 13. In the N.T. it occurs in Matt. 20 : 28 and Mark 10 : 45, where it is used of Christ's gift of Himself as " a ransom for many." Some interpreters have regarded the ransom price as being paid to Satan ; others, to an impersonal power such as death, or evil, or " that ultimate necessity which has made the whole course of things what it has been." Such ideas are largely conjectural, the result of an attempt to press the details of certain Old Testament illustrations beyond the actual statements of New Testament doctrines.

That Christ gave up His life in expiatory sacrifice under God's judgment upon sin and thus provided a ransom whereby those who receive Him on this ground obtain deliverance from the penalty due to sin, is what Scripture teaches. What the Lord states in the two passages mentioned involves this essential character of His death. In these passages the preposition is *anti*, which has a vicarious significance, indicating that the ransom holds good for those who, accepting it as such, no longer remain in death since Christ suffered death in their stead. The change of preposition in 1 Tim. 2 : 6, where the word *antilutron*, a substitutionary ransom, is used, is significant. There the preposition is *huper*, on behalf of, and the statement is made that He " gave Himself a ransom for all," indicating that the ransom was provisionally universal, while being of a vicarious character. Thus the three passages consistently show that while the provision was universal, for Christ died for all men, yet it is actual for those only who accept God's conditions, and who are described in the Gospel statements as "the many." The giving of His life was the giving of His entire Person, and while His death under Divine judgment was alone expiatory, it cannot be dissociated from the character of His life which, being sinless, gave virtue to His death and was a testimony to the fact that His death must be of a vicarious nature.¶

487 AG:75B CB:1236A 2. ANTILUTRON (ἀντίλυτρον), 1 Tim. 2:6. See under No. 1.¶

For RASH, RASHLY see HEADSTRONG

RATHER

A. Adverb.

3123 AG:489A CB:1257C MALLON (μᾶλλον), the comparative degree of *mala*, very, very much, is frequently translated "rather," e.g., Matt. 10:6, 28; 1 Cor. 14:1, 5; sometimes followed by "than," with a connecting particle, e.g., Matt. 18:13 ("more than"); or without, e.g., John 3:19; Acts 4:19, R.V. (A.V., "more"); in 1 Cor. 9:12, A.V., "rather" (R.V., "yet more"); 12:22, R.V., "rather" (A.V., "more"); 2 Cor. 3:9 (ditto); Philm. 16 (ditto); in 2 Pet. 1:10, A.V., "the rather" (R.V., "the more"). See MORE.

B. Verb.

2309 AG:354D CB:1271C THELŌ (θέλω), to will, wish, is translated "I had rather" in 1 Cor. 14:19. See DESIRE, B, No. 6.

C. Preposition.

3844 AG:609C CB:1261C PARA (παρά), beyond, in comparison with, is translated "rather than" in Rom. 1:25, R.V. (A.V., "more than;" marg., "rather").

D. Conjunction.

235 AG:38A CB:— ALLA (ἀλλά), but, on the contrary, is translated "and rather" in Luke 17:8.

PERISSOTERŌS 4056 AG:651D CB:1263C PLĒN 4133 AG:669B CB:1265B *Notes:* (1) In Heb. 13:19, A.V., *perissoterōs*, "the more exceedingly" (R.V.), is translated "the rather." (2) In Luke 11:41 and 12:31, A.V., *plēn*, an adverb signifying yet, howbeit, is translated "rather" (R.V., "howbeit"). (3) In Rom. 3:8, A.V., the negative particle *mē*, "not," is translated with "*rather*" in italics (R.V., "why not"). (4) In Luke 10:20, A.V., "rather rejoice," there is no word in the original for "rather" (see the R.V.).

RAVEN

2876 AG:444B CB:— KORAX (κόραξ), a raven (perhaps onomatopœic, representing the sound), occurs in the plural in Luke 12:24. The Heb. *oreb* and the Arabic *ghurab* are from roots meaning 'to be black;' the Arabic root also has the idea of leaving home. Hence the evil omen attached to the bird. It is the first bird mentioned in the Bible, Gen. 8:7. Christ used the ravens to illustrate and enforce the lesson of God's provision and care.¶

RAVENING

A. Adjective.

HARPAX (ἅρπαξ), an adjective signifying rapacious, is translated 727
" ravening " (of wolves) in Matt. 7 : 15 : see EXTORT, C. AG:109B CB:1249B

B. Noun.

HARPAGĒ (ἁρπαγή) is translated "ravening" in Luke 11 : 39, 724
A.V. : see EXTORT, B, No. 1. AG:108B CB:1249B

REACH

1. AKOLOUTHEŌ (ἀκολουθέω), to follow, is translated " have 190 AG:31A
reached," in Rev. 18 : 5, of the sins of Babylon. Some mss. have the CB:1234B
verb *kollaomai*, to cleave together, R.V., marg. ; see FOLLOW. 3713 (-OMAI)

2. OREGŌ (ὀρέγω), to reach or stretch out, is rendered " reached AG:579D CB:1261A
after " in 1 Tim. 6 : 10, R.V. ; see DESIRE, B, No. 5. (-OMAI)

3. PHERŌ (φέρω), to bear, carry, is used of reaching forth the hand 5342
in John 20 : 27 (twice). See BEAR, No. 2. AG:854D CB:1264A

4. EPHIKNEOMAI (ἐφικνέομαι), to come to, reach, is used in 2185
2 Cor. 10 : 13, 14.¶ AG:330C

5. KATANTAŌ (καταντάω), to come to a place, is translated " reach " 2658 AG:415B
in Acts 27 : 12, R.V. (A.V., " attain to "). See COME, No. 28. CB:1254A

Note : In Phil. 3 : 13, A.V., *epekteinō*, in the Middle Voice, to stretch (-OMAI) 1901
forward, is translated "reaching forth" (R.V., "stretching forward"). AG:284D CB:1245C

READ, READING

A. Verb.

ANAGINŌSKŌ (ἀναγινώσκω), primarily, to know certainly, to know 314
again, recognize (*ana*, again, *ginōskō*, to know), is used of reading written AG:51C CB:1235A
characters, e.g., Matt. 12 : 3, 5 ; 21 : 16 ; 24 : 15 ; of the private reading of Scripture, Acts 8 : 28, 30, 32 ; of the public reading of Scripture, Luke 4 : 16 ; Acts 13 : 27 ; 15 : 21 ; 2 Cor. 3 : 15 ; Col. 4 : 16 (thrice) ; 1 Thess. 5 : 27 ; Rev. 1 : 3. In 2 Cor. 1 : 13 there is a purposive play upon words ; firstly, " we write none other things unto you, than what ye read (*anaginōskō*) " signifies that there is no hidden or mysterious meaning in his Epistles ; whatever doubts may have arisen and been expressed in this respect, he means what he says ; then follows the similar verb *epiginōskō*, to acknowledge, " or even acknowledge, and I hope ye will acknowledge unto the end." The *paronomasia* can hardly be reproduced in English. Similarly, in 3 : 2 the verb *ginōskō*, to know, and *anaginōskō*, to read, are put in that order, and metaphorically applied to the church at Corinth as being an epistle, a message to the world, written by the Apostle and his fellow-missionaries, through their ministry of the gospel and the consequent change in the lives of the converts, an epistle " known and read of all men." For other instances of *paronomasia* see, e.g., Rom. 12 : 3, *phroneō*, *huperphroneō*, *sōphroneō ;* 1 Cor. 2 : 13, 14, *sunkrinō*, *anakrinō ;* 2 Thess. 3 : 11, *ergazomai*, and *periergazomai ;* 1 Cor.

7 : 31, *chraomai* and *katachraomai* ; 11 : 31, *diakrinō* and *krinō* ; 12 : 2, *agō* and *apagō* ; Phil. 3 : 2, 3, *katatomē* and *peritomē*.

B. Noun.

320 AG:52D CB:1235A ANAGNŌSIS (ἀνάγνωσις) in non-Biblical Greek denoted recognition or a survey (the latter found in the papyri) ; then, reading ; in the N.T. the public reading of Scripture, Acts 13 : 15 ; 2 Cor. 3 : 14 ; 1 Tim. 4 : 13, where the context makes clear that the reference is to the care required in reading the Scriptures to a company, a duty ever requiring the exhortation " take heed." Later, readers in churches were called *anagnōstai*.¶ In the Sept., Neh. 8 : 8.¶

READINESS

4288 AG:706C CB:1267B 1. PROTHUMIA (προθυμία), eagerness, willingness, readiness (*pro*, forward, *thumos*, mind, disposition, akin to *prothumos*, READY, A, No. 2), is translated " readiness of mind " in Acts 17 : 11, " readiness " in 2 Cor. 8 : 11 ; in ver. 12, R.V. (A.V., " a willing mind ") ; in ver. 19, R.V. " (our) readiness," A.V., " (your) ready mind ; " in 9 : 2, R.V., " readiness " (A.V., " forwardness of . . . mind ; " see FORWARDNESS, Note (4).¶

2092 AG:316C CB:1250B 2. HETOIMOS (ἕτοιμος), an adjective (see READY, A, No. 1), is used with *echō*, to have, and *en*, in, idiomatically, as a noun, in 2 Cor. 10 : 6, R.V., " being in readiness " (A.V., " having in readiness "), of the Apostle's aim for the church to be obedient to Christ. Cp. READY, C.

READY

A. Adjectives.

2092 AG:316C CB:1250B 1. HETOIMOS (ἕτοιμος), prepared, ready (akin to *hetoimasia*, preparation), is used (*a*) of persons, Matt. 24 : 44 ; 25 : 10 ; Luke 12 : 40 ; 22 : 33 ; Acts 23 : 15, 21 (for 2 Cor. 10 : 6, see above) ; Tit. 3 : 1 ; 1 Pet. 3 : 15 ; (*b*) of things, Matt. 22 : 4 (2nd part), 8 ; Mark 14 : 15, R.V., " ready " (A.V., " prepared ") ; Luke 14 : 17 ; John 7 : 6 ; 2 Cor. 9 : 5 ; 10 : 16, R.V., " things ready " (A.V., " things made ready ") ; 1 Pet. 1 : 5. See PREPARE, No. 5, Note (2).¶

4289 AG:706C CB:— 2. PROTHUMOS (πρόθυμος), predisposed, willing (akin to *prothumia*, see READINESS), is translated " ready " in Rom. 1 : 15, expressive of willingness, eagerness : in Mark 14 : 38, R.V., " willing " (A.V., " ready ") ; in Matt. 26 : 41, " willing." See WILLING.¶

B. Verbs.

3195 AG:500D CB:1258A 1. MELLŌ (μέλλω), to be about to, is translated to be ready in 2 Pet. 1 : 12, R.V., where the future indicates that the Apostle will be prepared, as in the past and the present, to remind his readers of the truths they know (some mss. have *ouk amelēsō*, " I will not be negligent," A.V. ; cp., however, ver. 15. Field, in *Notes on the Translation of the N.T.*, suggests that the true reading is *melēsō*, the future of *melō*, to be a care, or an object of care) ; in Rev. 3 : 2, R.V., " were ready " (some texts have the present tense, as in the A.V.). Elsewhere, where the A.V. has the

rendering to be ready, the R.V. gives renderings in accordance with the
usual significance as follows: Luke 7:2, "was . . . at the point of;"
Acts 20:7, "intending;" Rev. 12:4, "about (to)." 2090 AG:316A
2. HETOIMAZŌ (ἑτοιμάζω), make ready: see PREPARE, B, No. 1. CB:1250B
3. PARASKEUAZŌ (παρασκευάζω), to prepare, make ready: see 3903
PREPARE, B, No. 4. AG:622A CB:1262B
Note: On the difference between No. 2 and No. 3, see PREPARE,
Note (1) under No. 5.

C. Adverb.

HETOIMŌS (ἑτοίμως) readily (akin to A, No. 1), is used with *echō*, 2093
to have, lit., 'to have readily,' i.e., to be in readiness, to be ready, Acts AG:316D CB:—
21:13; 2 Cor. 12:14; 1 Pet. 4:5.¶ ENGUS
Notes: (1) In Heb. 8:13, A.V., *engus*, near, is translated "ready" 1451 AG:214A
(R.V., "nigh"). See NIGH. (2) For "ready to distribute," 1 Tim. 6:18, CB:1245A
see DISTRIBUTE, B. (3) In 2 Tim. 4:6, A.V., *spendomai*, "I am being ēDē 2235
offered," R.V., with *ēdē*, "already," is translated "I am now ready to AG:344A
be offered." See OFFER. (4) In 1 Pet. 5:2 *prothumōs*, willingly, with CB:1242C PROTHUMŌS
alacrity, is rendered "of a ready mind."¶ 4290

REAP AG:706D CB:—

THERIZŌ (θερίζω), to reap (akin to *theros*, summer, harvest), is used 2325
(*a*) literally, Matt. 6:26; 25:24, 26; Luke 12:24; 19:21, 22; Jas. 5:4 AG:359B
(2nd part), A.V., "have reaped"; (*b*) figuratively or in proverbial CB:1272B
expressions, John 4:36 (twice), 37, 38, with immediate reference to
bringing Samaritans into the Kingdom of God, in regard to which the REALIZE
disciples would enjoy the fruits of what Christ Himself had been doing See KNOW
in Samaria; the Lord's words are, however, of a general application in (HEAVENLY)
respect of such service; in 1 Cor. 9:11, with reference to the right of the REALMS See
Apostle and his fellow-missionaries to receive material assistance from the HEAVENLY
church, a right which he forbore to exercise; in 2 Cor. 9:6 (twice), with reference to rendering material help to the needy, either "sparingly" or "bountifully," the reaping being proportionate to the sowing; in Gal. 6:7, 8 (twice), of reaping "corruption," with special reference, according to the context, to that which is naturally shortlived transient (though the statement applies to every form of sowing to the flesh), and of reaping eternal life (characteristics and moral qualities being in view), as a result of sowing "to the Spirit," the reference probably being to the new nature of the believer, which is, however, under the controlling power of the Holy Spirit, ver. 9, the reaping (the effect of well doing) being accomplished, to a limited extent, in this life, but in complete fulfilment at and beyond the Judgment-Seat of Christ; diligence or laxity here will then produce proportionate results; in Rev. 14:15 (twice), 16, figurative of the discriminating judgment Divinely to be fulfilled at the close of this age, when the wheat will be separated from the tares (see Matt. 13:30).¶

For REAP DOWN, Jas. 5:4, see MOW

REAPER

2327 AG:359C THERISTĒS (θεριστής), a reaper (akin to *therizō*, see above), is used of
CB:1272B angels in Matt. 13 : 30, 39.¶

For REAR UP, John 2 : 20, see RAISE, No. 1 (f)

REASON (Noun)

3056 LOGOS (λόγος), a word, etc., has also the significance of the inward
AG:477A CB:1257A thought itself, a reckoning, a regard, a reason, translated "reason" in Acts 18 : 14, in the phrase "reason would," *kata logon*, lit., 'according to reason (I would bear with you);' in 1 Pet. 3 : 15, "a reason (concerning the hope that is in you)." See Word.

701 AG:105D *Note:* In Acts 6 : 2, A.V., the adjective *arestos*, pleasing, agreeable,
CB:1237C is translated "reason" (R.V., "fit," marg., "pleasing"). See Fit, No. 2.

For the prepositions rendered BY REASON OF see †p. 1

REASON (Verb)

1260 1. DIALOGIZOMAI (διαλογίζομαι), to bring together different
AG:186A CB:1241B reasons and reckon them up, to reason, is used in the N.T. (*a*) chiefly of thoughts and considerations which are more or less objectionable, e.g., of the disciples who reasoned together, through a mistaken view of Christ's teaching regarding leaven, Matt. 16 : 7, 8 and Mark 8 : 16, 17; of their reasoning as to who was the greatest among them, Mark 9 : 33, R.V., "were ye reasoning," A.V., "ye disputed" (for ver. 34, see Dispute); of the Scribes and Pharisees in criticising Christ's claim to forgive sins, Mark 2 : 6, 8 (twice) and Luke 5 : 21, 22; of the chief priests and elders in considering how to answer Christ's question regarding John's baptism, Matt. 21 : 25; Mark 11 : 31 (some mss. have *logizomai*, here, which is nowhere else rendered "to reason"); of the wicked husbandmen, and their purpose to murder the heir and seize his inheritance, Luke 20 : 14; of the rich man who "reasoned" within himself, R.V. (A.V., "thought"), as to where to bestow his fruits, Luke 12 : 17 (some mss. have it in
LOGIZOMAI John 11 : 50, the best have *logizomai*; see Account, No. 4); (*b*) of
3049 AG:475D considerations not objectionable, Luke 1 : 29, "cast in (her) mind;"
CB:1257A 3 : 15, R.V., and A.V., marg., "reasoned" (A.V., "mused"). See Cast, No. 15, Dispute, B, No. 2.¶

1256 AG:185C 2. DIALEGOMAI (διαλέγομαι), to think different things with oneself,
CB:1241A to ponder, then, to dispute with others, is translated to reason in Acts 17 : 2, A.V. and R.V.; 17 : 17, R.V.; 18 : 4, 19, A.V. and R.V.; 19 : 8, 9, R.V.; 24 : 25, A.V. and R.V.; Heb. 12 : 5, R.V., "reasoneth (with you)," A.V., "speaketh (unto you)." See Dispute, B, No. 1.

4817 3. SULLOGIZOMAI (συλλογίζομαι), to compute (*sun*, with, and
AG:777A CB— *logizomai*; cp. Eng., syllogism), also denotes to reason, and is so rendered in Luke 20 : 5.¶

4. SUZĒTEŌ (συζητέω), to seek or examine together (*sun*, with, 4802
zēteō, to seek), to discuss, is translated "reasoning" in Mark 12 : 28, A.V. AG:775D
(R.V., "questioning"); similarly in Luke 24 : 15. See DISPUTE, B, No. 3. CB:—

REASONABLE

LOGIKOS (λογικός), pertaining to the reasoning faculty, reasonable, 3050
rational, is used in Rom. 12 : 1, of the service (*latreia*) to be rendered by AG:476C CB:1257A
believers in presenting their bodies "a living sacrifice, holy, acceptable to God." The sacrifice is to be intelligent, in contrast to those offered by ritual and compulsion; the presentation is to be in accordance with the spiritual intelligence of those who are new creatures in Christ and are mindful of "the mercies of God." For the significance of the word in 1 Pet. 2 : 2, see under MILK.¶

REASONING

DIALOGISMOS (διαλογισμός), a thought, reasoning, inward question- 1261
ing [akin to *dialogizomai*, see REASON (Verb), No. 1], is translated AG:186A
"reasoning" or "reasonings" in Luke 5 : 22, R.V. (A.V., "thoughts"); CB:1241B
9 : 46; ver. 47, R.V. (A.V., "thoughts"); 24 : 38 (A.V., "thoughts"); Rom. 1 : 21 (A.V., "imaginations"); 1 Cor. 3 : 20 (A.V., "thoughts"). See DISPUTE, A, No. 1.

Note: In those mss. which contain Acts 28 : 29, occurs *suzētēsis*, 4803
a disputation, which is translated "reasoning" (A.V.).¶ AG:775D CB:—

REBELLION See ROBBER

REBUKE (Verb and Noun)

A. Verbs.

1. EPITIMAŌ (ἐπιτιμάω), primarily, to put honour upon, then, to 2008
adjudge, hence signifies to rebuke. Except for 2 Tim. 4 : 2 and Jude 9, AG:303B CB:1246B
it is confined in the N.T. to the Synoptic Gospels, where it is frequently used of the Lord's rebukes to (*a*) evil spirits, e.g., Matt. 17 : 18; Mark 1 : 25; 9 : 25; Luke 4 : 35, 41; 9 : 42; (*b*) winds, Matt. 8 : 26; Mark 4 : 39; Luke 8 : 24; (*c*) fever, Luke 4 : 39; (*d*) disciples, Mark 8 : 33; Luke 9 : 55; contrast Luke 19 : 39. For rebukes by others see Matt. 16 : 22; 19 : 13; 20 : 31; Mark 8 : 32; 10 : 13; 10 : 48, R.V., "rebuked" (A.V., "charged"); Luke 17 : 3; 18 : 15, 39; 23 : 40. See CHARGE, C, No. 7.

2. ELENCHŌ (ἐλέγχω), to convict, refute, reprove, is translated 1651
to rebuke in the A.V. of the following (the R.V. always has the verb to AG:249B CB:1244A
reprove): 1 Tim. 5 : 20; Tit. 1 : 13; 2 : 15; Heb. 12 : 5; Rev. 3 : 19. See CONVICT, No. 1.

Note: While *epitimaō* signifies simply a rebuke which may be either undeserved, Matt. 16 : 22, or ineffectual, Luke 23 : 40, *elenchō* implies a
rebuke which carries conviction. 1969 AG:297D

3. EPIPLĒSSŌ (ἐπιπλήσσω), to strike at (*epi*, upon or at, *plēssō*, to CB:—

strike, smite), hence, to rebuke, is used in the injunction against rebuking an elder, 1 Tim. 5 : 1,¶

AMōMOS 299 *Note:* In Phil. 2 : 15, the best texts have *amōmos*, without blemish
AG:47D (*a*, negative, *mōmos*, a blemish, a moral disgrace), R.V., " without
CB:1234C AMōMeTOS blemish ; " some mss. have *amōmētos* (*a*, negative, and *mōmaomai*, to
298 AG:47D blame), A.V., " without rebuke." Contrast *amemptos* in the same verse,
CB:1234C blameless on account of absence of inconsistency or ground of reproof,
AMEMPToS whereas *amōmos* indicates absence of stain or blemish. We may have
274 AG:45A blemish, with freedom from blame.

CB:1234C **B. Noun.**

1649 AG:249A ELENXIS (ἔλεγξις), akin to A, No. 2, denotes rebuke ; in 2 Pet. 2 : 16,
CB:1244A it is used with *echō*, to have, and translated " he was rebuked," lit., ' he had rebuke.'¶ In the Sept., Job 21 : 4, " reproof ; " 23 : 2, " pleading."¶

RECALL See REMEMBER

For RECEIPT see CUSTOM (Toll), No. 2

RECEIVE, RECEIVING

A. Verbs.

2983 AG:464A 1. LAMBANŌ (λαμβάνω) denotes either to take or to receive, (I)
CB:1256C literally, (*a*) without an object, in contrast to asking, e.g., Matt. 7 : 8 ; Mark 11 : 24, R.V., " have received " (the original has no object) ; (*b*) in contrast to giving, e.g., Matt. 10 : 8 ; Acts 20 : 35 ; (*c*) with objects, whether things, e.g., Mark 10 : 30 ; Luke 18 : 30, in the best mss. (some have No. 4) ; John 13 : 30 ; Acts 9 : 19, R.V., " took " (A.V., " received ") ; 1 Cor. 9 : 25, R.V., " receive " (A.V., " obtain ") ; or persons, e.g., John 6 : 21 ; 13 : 20 ; 16 : 14, R.V., " take ; " 2 John 10 ; in Mark 14 : 65, R.V., " received (Him with blows of their hands) ; " this has been styled a vulgarism ; (II) metaphorically, of the word of God, Matt. 13 : 20 ; Mark 4 : 16 ; the sayings of Christ, John 12 : 48 ; the witness of Christ, John 3 : 11 ; a hundredfold in this life, and eternal life in the world to come, Mark 10 : 30 ; mercy, Heb. 4 : 16, R.V., " may
-SIA receive " (A.V., " may obtain ") ; a person (*prosōpon*, see FACE), Luke
4382 20 : 21, " acceptest," and Gal. 2 : 6, " accepteth," an expression used in
AG:720D the O.T. either in the sense of being gracious or kind to a person, e.g.,
CB:1267B -TeS Gen. 19 : 21 ; 32 : 20, or (negatively) in the sense of being impartial,
4381 e.g., Lev. 19 : 15 ; Deut. 10 : 17 ; this latter is the meaning in the two
AG:720D CB:1267B N.T. passages just mentioned. See ACCEPT, A, No. 4, TAKE, etc.

-TEō *Lambanō* and *prosōpon* are combined in the nouns *prosōpolēmpsia*,
4380 AG:720C respect of persons, and *prosōpolēmptēs*, respecter of persons, and in the
CB:1267B verb *prosōpolēmptō*, to have respect of persons : see PERSON.

3880 2. PARALAMBANŌ (παραλαμβάνω), to receive from another (*para*,
AG:619B CB:1262A from beside), or to take, signifies to receive, e.g., in Mark 7 : 4 ; John 1 : 11 ; 14 : 3 ; 1 Cor. 11 : 23 ; 15 : 1, 3 ; Gal. 1 : 9, 12 ; Phil. 4 : 9 ; Col. 2 : 6 ; 4 : 17 ; 1 Thess. 2 : 13 (1st part) ; 4 : 1 ; 2 Thess. 3 : 6 ; Heb. 12 : 28. See TAKE.

3. ANALAMBANŌ (ἀναλαμβάνω), to take up (*ana*), to take to oneself, 353 AG:56D
receive, is rendered to receive in Mark 16 : 19 ; Acts 1 : 2, 11, 22, R.V., CB:1235A
" He was received up " (A.V., " taken ") ; 10 : 16 ; 1 Tim. 3 : 16. See
TAKE.

4. APOLAMBANŌ (ἀπολαμβάνω) signifies to receive from another, 618 AG:94B
(*a*) to receive as one's due (for Luke 18 : 30, see No. 1) ; Luke 23 : 41 ; CB:1237A
Rom. 1 : 27 ; Col. 3 : 24 ; 2 John 8 ; (*b*) without the indication of what
is due, Luke 16 : 25 ; Gal. 4 : 5 (in some mss. 3 John 8, for No. 7) ; (*c*) to
receive back, Luke 6 : 34 (twice) ; 15 : 27. For its other meaning, to take
apart, Mark 7 : 33, see TAKE.¶

5. PROSLAMBANŌ (προσλαμβάνω) denotes to take to oneself (*pros*, 4355 AG:717B
to) or to receive, always in the Middle Voice, signifying a special interest CB:1267B
on the part of the receiver, suggesting a welcome, Acts 28 : 2 ;
Rom. 14 : 1, 3 ; 15 : 7 ; Philm. 12 (in some mss. ; the best omit it) ;
ver. 17. See TAKE.

6. METALAMBANŌ (μεταλαμβάνω), to have or get a share of, partake 3335 AG:511B
of (*meta*, with), is rendered " receiveth " in Heb. 6 : 7. See EAT, HAVE, CB:1258B
PARTAKE, TAKE. In the Sept., Esth. 5 : 1.¶

7. HUPOLAMBANŌ (ὑπολαμβάνω), to take or bear up (*hupo*, under), 5274 AG:845B
to receive, is rendered " received " in Acts 1 : 9, of the cloud at the CB:1252B
Ascension ; in 3 John 8, R.V., " welcome " (A.V., " receive "). See
ANSWER, B, No. 3, SUPPOSE, WELCOME.

8. DECHOMAI (δέχομαι), to receive by deliberate and ready reception 1209 AG:177B
of what is offered, is used of (*a*) taking with the hand, taking hold, taking CB:1240B
hold of or up, e.g., Luke 2 : 28, R.V., " he received (Him)," A.V., " took he (Him) up ; " 16 : 6, 7 ; 22 : 17 ; Eph. 6 : 17 ; (*b*) receiving, said of a place receiving a person, of Christ into the Heavens, Acts 3 : 21 ; or of persons in giving access to someone as a visitor, e.g., John 4 : 45 ; 2 Cor. 7 : 15 ; Gal. 4 : 14 ; Col. 4 : 10 ; by way of giving hospitality, etc., e.g., Matt. 10 : 14, 40 (four times), 41 (twice) ; 18 : 5 ; Mark 6 : 11 ; 9 : 37 ; Luke 9 : 5, 48, 53 ; 10 : 8, 10 ; 16 : 4 ; ver. 9, of reception, " into the eternal tabernacles," said of followers of Christ who have used " the mammon of unrighteousness " to render assistance to (" make . . . friends of ") others ; of Rahab's reception of the spies, Heb. 11 : 31 ; of the reception, by the Lord, of the spirit of a departing believer, Acts 7 : 59 ; of receiving a gift, 2 Cor. 8 : 4 (in some mss. ; R.V. follows those which omit it) ; of the favourable reception of testimony and teaching, etc., Luke 8 : 13 ; Acts 8 : 14 ; 11 : 1 ; 17 : 11 ; 1 Cor. 2 : 14 ; 2 Cor. 8 : 17 ; 1 Thess. 1 : 6 ; 2 : 13, where *paralambanō* (No. 2) is used in the 1st part, " ye received," *dechomai* in the 2nd part, " ye accepted," R.V (A.V., " received "), the former refers to the ear, the latter, adding the idea of appropriation, to the heart ; Jas. 1 : 21 ; in 2 Thess. 2 : 10, " the love of the truth," i.e., love for the truth ; cp. Matt. 11 : 14, " if ye are willing to receive it," an elliptical construction frequent in Greek writings ; of receiving, by way of bearing with, enduring, 2 Cor. 11 : 16 ;

of receiving by way of getting, Acts 22 : 5 ; 28 : 21 ; of becoming partaker of benefits, Mark 10 : 15 ; Luke 18 : 17 ; Acts 7 : 38 ; 2 Cor. 6 : 1 ; 11 : 4 (last clause " did accept : " cp. *lambanō* in previous clauses) ; Phil. 4 : 18.¶

Note : There is a certain distinction between *lambanō* and *dechomai* (more pronounced in the earlier, classical use), in that in many instances *lambanō* suggests a self-prompted taking, whereas *dechomai* more frequently indicates " a welcoming or an appropriating reception " (Grimm-Thayer).

324 AG:53C CB:— 9. ANADECHOMAI (ἀναδέχομαι), to receive gladly, is used in Acts 28 : 7, of the reception by Publius of the shipwrecked company in Melita ; in Heb. 11 : 17, of Abraham's reception of God's promises, R.V., " gladly (*ana*, up, regarded as intensive) received." Moulton and Milligan point out the frequency of this verb in the papyri in the legal sense of taking the responsibility of something, becoming security for, undertaking, and say " The predominance of this meaning suggests its application in Heb. 11 : 17. The statement that Abraham had ' undertaken,' ' assumed the responsibility of,' the promises, would not perhaps be alien to the thought." The responsibility would surely be that of his faith in receiving the promises. In Classical Greek it had the meaning of receiving, and it is a little difficult to attach any other sense to the circumstances, save perhaps that Abraham's faith undertook to exercise the assurance of the fulfilment of the promises.¶

588 AG:90A CB:1236C 10. APODECHOMAI (ἀποδέχομαι), to welcome, to accept gladly (*apo*, from), to receive without reserve, is used (*a*) literally, Luke 8 : 40, R.V., " welcomed ; " 9 : 11 (in the best texts, some have No. 8) ; Acts 18 : 27 ; 21 : 17 ; 28 : 30 ; (*b*) metaphorically, Acts 2 : 41 ; 24 : 3, " we accept," in the sense of acknowledging, the term being used in a tone of respect. See ACCEPT, A No. 2.¶

1523 AG:232C CB:1243B 11. EISDECHOMAI (εἰσδέχομαι), to receive into (*eis*), is used only in 2 Cor. 6 : 17, where the verb does not signify to accept, but to admit (as antithetic to " come ye out," and combining Isa. 52 : 11 with Zeph. 3 : 20).¶

1926 AG:292A CB:— 12. EPIDECHOMAI (ἐπιδέχομαι), lit., to accept besides (*epi*, upon), to accept (found in the papyri, of accepting the terms of a lease), is used in the sense of accepting in 3 John 9 ; in ver. 10, in the sense of receiving with hospitality, in each verse said negatively concerning Diotrephes.¶

3858 AG:614B CB:— 13. PARADECHOMAI (παραδέχομαι), to receive or admit with approval (*para*, beside), is used (*a*) of persons, Acts 15 : 4 (in some texts, No. 10) ; Heb. 12 : 6 ; (*b*) of things, Mark 4 : 20, A.V., " receive " (R.V., " accept ") ; Acts 16 : 21 ; 22 : 18 ; 1 Tim. 5 : 9.¶ In the Sept., Ex. 23 : 1 ; Prov. 3 : 12.¶

4327 AG:712B CB:1267A 14. PROSDECHOMAI (προσδέχομαι), to receive to oneself, to receive favourably, also to look for, wait for, is used of receiving in Luke 15 : 2 ; Rom. 16 : 2 ; Phil. 2 : 29. See ACCEPT, A, No. 3, ALLOW, LOOK (for), TAKE, WAIT.

5264 AG:844B CB:— 15. HUPODECHOMAI (ὑποδέχομαι) denotes to receive under one's

roof (*hupo*, under), receive as a guest, entertain hospitably, Luke 10 : 38 ;
19 : 6 ; Acts 17 : 7 ; Jas. 2 : 25.¶
16. KOMIZŌ (κομίζω) denotes to bear, carry, e.g., Luke 7 : 37 ; in **2865**
the Middle Voice, to bear for oneself, hence (*a*) to receive, Heb. 10 : 36 ; **AG:442D CB:1255C**
11 : 13 (in the best texts ; some have *lambanō*, No. 1), 39 ; 1 Pet. 1 : 9 ; **(-OMAI)**
5 : 4 ; in some texts in 2 Pet. 2 : 13 (in the best mss. *adikeomai*, " suffering
wrong," R.V.) ; (*b*) to receive back, recover, Matt. 25 : 27 ; Heb. 11 : 19 ;
metaphorically, of requital, 2 Cor. 5 : 10 ; Col. 3 : 25, of ' receiving back
again ' by the believer at the Judgment-Seat of Christ hereafter, for wrong
done in this life ; Eph. 6 : 8, of receiving, on the same occasion, " whatsoever good thing each one doeth," R.V. ; see BRING, No. 20.¶
17. APECHŌ (ἀπέχω) denotes (*a*) transitively, to have in full, to have **568**
received ; so the R.V. in Matt. 6 : 2, 5, 16 (for A.V., " they have ") ; **AG:84D CB:1236B**
Luke 6 : 24, A.V., and R.V. ; in all these instances the present tense
(to which the A.V. incorrectly adheres in the Matt. 6 verses) has a perfective force, consequent upon the combination with the prefix *apo* (from),
not that it stands for the perfect tense, but that it views the action in
its accomplished result ; so in Phil. 4 : 18, where the A.V. and R.V.
translate it " I have ; " in Philm. 15, " (that) thou shouldest have (him
for ever)," A.V., " shouldest receive ; " see HAVE, No. 2, and the reference
to illustrations from the papyri of the use of the Verb in receipts ; (*b*) **CHōREō**
intransitively, to be away, distant, used with *porrō*, far, Matt. 15 : 8 ; **5562**
Mark 7 : 6 ; with *makran*, far off, afar, Luke 7 : 6 ; 15 : 20 ; without an **AG:889C CB:1240A**
accompanying adverb, Luke 24 : 13, " which was from." See ABSTAIN, **LANCHANō**
ENOUGH, HAVE. **2975 AG:462B**
18. CHŌREŌ (χωρέω), to give space, make room for (*chōra*, a place), **CB:1256C**
is used metaphorically, of receiving with the mind, Matt. 19 : 11, 12 ; **DIDōMI**
into the heart, 2 Cor. 7 : 2, R.V., " open your hearts," marg., " make **1325 AG:192C**
room " (A.V., " receive "). See COME, No. 24, CONTAIN, No. 1, COURSE, B. **CB:1241C**
19. LANCHANŌ (λαγχάνω), to obtain by lot, is translated " received " **ZēMIOō**
in Acts 1 : 17, R.V. (A.V., " had obtained "). See LOT. **2210 AG:338C**
Notes : (1) In Mark 2 : 2, A.V., *chōreō* is translated " there was (no) **CB:1273C (-OMAI)**
room to receive " [R.V., " there was (no longer) room (for)]." (2) In **ANABLEPō**
Rev. 13 : 16, A.V., *didōmi* is translated " to receive " (marg., " to give **308 AG:50D**
them "), R.V., " (that) there be given (them)." (3) In 2 Cor. 7 : 9, A.V., **CB:1235A**
zēmioō, to suffer loss (R.V.), is translated " ye might receive damage." **ELEEō**
(4) In Luke 7 : 22, R.V., *anablepō*, to recover sight, is translated " receive **1653 AG:249C**
their sight " (A.V., " see "). (5) For " received (R.V., hath taken) tithes," **CB:1244A**
Heb. 7 : 6, see TITHE. (6) For *eleeō*, in the Passive Voice, 2 Cor. 4 : 1, **PATROPARADOTOS 3970**
A.V., " having received mercy " (R.V., " obtained "), see MERCY. **AG:637A**
(7) For *patroparadotos*, in 1 Pet. 1 : 18, A.V., " *received* by tradition **SPEIRō 4687**
from your fathers," see HANDED DOWN. (8) In the A.V. of Matt. 13 : 19, **AG:761B**
20, 22, 23, *speirō*, to sow seed, is translated " received seed ; " see SOW. **CB:1269C**

B. Nouns. **3028 AG:473A**

1. LĒPSIS or LĒMPSIS (λῆμψις), a receiving (akin to *lambanō*, A. **CB:1256C**

No. 1), is used in Phil. 4 : 15.¶ In the Sept., Prov. 15 : 27, 29.¶

354 AG:57A CB:— 2. ANALĒ(M)PSIS (ἀνάλημψις), a taking up (*ana*, up, and No. 1), is used in Luke 9 : 51 with reference to Christ's Ascension ; "that He should be received up" is, lit., 'of the receiving up (of Him).' ¶ It has

3336 AG:511C CB:1258B (-ēMPSIS) 3. METALĒ(M)PSIS (μετάλημψις), a participation, taking, receiving, is used in 1 Tim. 4 : 3, in connection with food, "to be received," lit., 'with a view to (*eis*) reception.'¶

4356 AG:717C CB:1267B 4. PROSLĒ(M)PSIS (πρόσλημψις), *pros*, to, and No. 1, is used in Rom. 11 : 15, of the restoration of Israel.¶

RECKON, RECKONING

3049 AG:475D CB:1257A 1. LOGIZOMAI (λογίζομαι) is properly used (*a*) of numerical calculation, e.g., Luke 22 : 37 ; (*b*) metaphorically, by a reckoning of characteristics or reasons, to take into account, Rom. 2 : 26, "shall . . . be reckoned," R.V. (A.V., "counted"), of reckoning uncircumcision for circumcision by God's estimate in contrast to that of the Jew regarding his own condition (ver. 3) ; in 4 : 3, 5, 6, 9, 11, 22, 23, 24, of reckoning faith for righteousness, or reckoning righteousness to persons, in all of which the R.V. uses the verb to reckon instead of the A.V. to count or to impute ; in ver. 4 the subject is treated by way of contrast between grace and debt, which latter involves the reckoning of a reward for works ; what is owed as a debt cannot be reckoned as a favour, but the faith of Abraham and his spiritual children sets them outside the category of those who seek to be justified by self-effort, and, *vice versa*, the latter are excluded from the grace of righteousness bestowed on the sole condition of faith ; so in Gal. 3 : 6 (R.V., "was reckoned," A.V., "was accounted") ; since Abraham, like all the natural descendants of Adam, was a sinner, he was destitute of righteousness in the sight of God ; if, then, his relationship with God was to be rectified (i.e., if he was to be justified before God), the rectification could not be brought about by works of merit on his part ; in Jas. 2 : 23, R.V., "reckoned," the subject is viewed from a different standpoint (see under JUSTIFICATION, B, last four paragraphs) ; for other instances of reckoning in this respect see Rom. 9 : 8, R.V., "are reckoned" (A.V., "are counted") ; 2 Cor. 5 : 19, R.V., "(not) reckoning (trespasses)," A.V., "imputing ;" (*c*) to consider, calculate, translated to reckon in Rom. 6 : 11 ; 8 : 36 ; 2 Cor. 10 : 11, R.V., "let (such a one) reckon (this) ;" (*d*) to suppose, judge, deem, translated to reckon in Rom. 2 : 3, "reckonest thou (this)," R.V. (A.V., "thinkest") ; 3 : 28 (A.V., "we conclude") ; 8 : 18 ; 2 Cor. 11 : 5 (A.V., "I suppose") ; see ACCOUNT, A, No. 4, CONSIDER, No. 6, COUNT, No. 3, SUPPOSE ; (*e*) to purpose, decide, 2 Cor. 10 : 2, R.V., "count" (A.V., "think") ; see COUNT, No. 3.

3004 AG:468A CB:— 2. LEGŌ (λέγω), to say, speak, also has the meaning to gather, reckon, account, used in this sense in Heb. 7 : 11, R.V., "be reckoned" (A.V., "be called"). See ASK, A, No. 6.

3. SUNAIRŌ (συναίρω), to take up together (*sun*, with, *airō*, to take), 4868
is used with the noun *logos*, an account, signifying to settle accounts, AG:783C CB:—
Matt. 18 : 23, R.V., " make a reckoning " (A.V., " take account ") ; ver.
24, A.V. and R.V., " to reckon " (*logos* being understood) ; 25 : 19, R.V., LOGOS
" maketh a reckoning " (A.V., " reckoneth "). This phrase occurs not 3056 AG:477A
infrequently in the papyri in the sense of settling accounts (see Deissmann, CB:1257A
Light from the Ancient East, 118).¶ In the Sept. the verb occurs in its
literal sense in Ex. 23 : 5, " thou shalt help to raise " (lit., ' raise with ').¶

RECLINE

345
ANAKEIMAI (ἀνάκειμαι), lit., and in classical usage, to be laid up, AG:55D
laid, denotes, in the N.T., to recline at table ; it is translated " reclining " CB:1235A
in John 13 : 23, R.V. (A.V., " leaning ") ; cp. *anapiptō* in ver. 25, R.V., ANAPIPTŌ 377
" leaning back." See also ver. 12, marg. See LEAN, SIT, TABLE (at the) AG:59C
CB:1235B

For RECOMMEND, Acts 14 : 26 ; 15 : 40, A.V., see COMMEND, No. 2 RECOGNIZE See KNOW

RECOMPENCE, RECOMPENSE

A. Nouns.

1. ANTAPODOMA (ἀνταπόδομα), akin to *antapodidōmi*, to recompense 468
(see below), lit., a giving back in return (*anti*, in return, *apo*, back, *didōmi*, AG:73A CB:1236A
to give), a requital, recompence, is used (*a*) in a favourable sense, Luke
14 : 12 ; (*b*) in an unfavourable sense, Rom. 11 : 9, indicating that the
present condition of the Jewish nation is the retributive effect of their
transgressions, on account of which that which was designed as a blessing
(" their table ") has become a means of judgment.¶

2. ANTAPODOSIS (ἀνταπόδοσις), derived, like No. 1, from 469
antapodidōmi, is rendered " recompense " in Col. 3 : 24, R.V. (A.V., AG:73A CB:1236A
" reward ").¶

3. ANTIMISTHIA (ἀντιμισθία), a reward, requital (*anti*, in return, 489
misthos, wages, hire), is used (*a*) in a good sense, 2 Cor. 6 : 13 ; (*b*) in a bad AG:75B CB:1236A
sense, Rom. 1 : 27.¶

4. MISTHAPODOSIA (μισθαποδοσία), a payment of wages (from 3405
misthos, see No. 3, and *apodidōmi*, B, No. 2), a recompence, is used AG:523A CB:1259A
(*a*) of reward, Heb. 10 : 35 ; 11 : 26 ; (*b*) of punishment, Heb. 2 : 2.¶
Cp. *misthapodotēs*, a rewarder, Heb. 11 : 6.¶

B. Verbs.

1. ANTAPODIDŌMI (ἀνταποδίδωμι), akin to A, No. 1 and No. 2, 476
to give back as an equivalent, to requite, recompense (the *anti* expressing AG:73A CB:1236A
the idea of a complete return), is translated " render " in 1 Thess. 3 : 9,
here only in the N.T. of thanksgiving to God (cp. the Sept. of Ps. 116 : 12) ;
elsewhere it is used of recompense, " whether between men (but in that
case only of good, not of evil, see No. 2 in 1 Thess. 5 : 15), Luke 14 : 14
a, cp. the corresponding noun in v. 12 ; or between God and evil-doers,
Rom. 12 : 19, R.V. (A.V., " repay ") ; Heb. 10 : 30, cp. the noun in Rom.

11 : 9; or between God and those who do well, Luke 14 : 14 *b*; Rom. 11 : 35, cp. the noun in Col. 3 : 24; in 2 Thess. 1 : 6 both reward and retribution are in view."*¶

591 AG:90B CB:1236C 2. APODIDŌMI (ἀποδίδωμι), to give up or back, restore, return, is translated "shall recompense" in the R.V. of Matt. 6 : 4, 6, 18 (A.V., "shall reward"); in Rom. 12 : 17, A.V., "recompense" (R.V., "render"); in 1 Thess. 5 : 15, "render." See DELIVER, GIVE, PAY, PERFORM, RENDER, REPAY, REQUITE, RESTORE, REWARD, SELL, YIELD.

RECONCILE, RECONCILIATION

A. Verbs.

2644 AG:414A CB:1254A 1. KATALLASSŌ (καταλλάσσω) properly denotes to change, exchange (especially of money); hence, of persons, to change from enmity to friendship, to reconcile. With regard to the relationship between God and man, the use of this and connected words shows that primarily reconciliation is what God accomplishes, exercising His grace towards sinful man on the ground of the death of Christ in propitiatory sacrifice under the judgment due to sin, 2 Cor. 5 : 19, where both the verb and the noun are used (cp. No. 2, in Col. 1 : 21). By reason of this men in their sinful condition and alienation from God are invited to be reconciled to Him; that is to say, to change their attitude, and accept the provision God has made, whereby their sins can be remitted and they themselves be justified in His sight in Christ.

Rom. 5 : 10 expresses this in another way: "For if, while we were enemies, we were reconciled to God through the death of His Son . . .;" that we were "enemies" not only expresses man's hostile attitude to God but signifies that until this change of attitude takes place men are under condemnation, exposed to God's wrath. The death of His Son is the means of the removal of this, and thus we "receive the reconciliation," ver. 11, R.V. This stresses the attitude of God's favour toward us. The A.V. rendering "atonement" is incorrect. Atonement is the offering itself of Christ under Divine judgment upon sin. We do not receive atonement. What we do receive is the result, namely, "reconciliation."

The removal of God's wrath does not contravene His immutability. He always acts according to His unchanging righteousness and loving-kindness, and it is because He changes not that His relative attitude does change towards those who change. All His acts show that He is Light and Love. Anger, where there is no personal element, is a sign of moral health if, and if only, it is accompanied by grief. There can be truest love along with righteous indignation, Mark 3 : 5, but love and enmity cannot exist together. It is important to distinguish "wrath" and "hostility." The change in God's relative attitude toward those who

---

* From Notes on Thessalonians by Hogg and Vine, p. 226.

receive the reconciliation only proves His real unchangeableness. Not once is God said to be reconciled. The enmity is alone on our part. It was we who needed to be reconciled to God, not God to us, and it is propitiation, which His righteousness and mercy have provided, that makes the reconciliation possible to those who receive it.

When the writers of the N.T. speak upon the subject of the wrath of God, "the hostility is represented not as on the part of God, but of man. And this is the reason why the Apostle never uses *diallassō* [a word used only in Matt. 5 : 24, in the N.T.] in this connection, but always *katallassō*, because the former word denotes mutual concession after mutual hostility [frequently exemplified in the Sept.], an idea absent from *katallassō* " (Lightfoot, *Notes on the Epistles of Paul*, p. 288).

The subject finds its great unfolding in 2 Cor. 5 : 18–20, which states that God " reconciled us (believers) to Himself through Christ," and that " the ministry of reconciliation " consists in this, " that God was in Christ reconciling the world unto Himself." The insertion of a comma in the A.V. after the word " Christ " is misleading; the doctrine stated here is not that God was in Christ (the unity of the Godhead is not here in view), but that what God has done in the matter of reconciliation He has done in Christ, and this is based upon the fact that " Him who knew no sin He made to be sin on our behalf; that we might become the righteousness of God in Him." On this ground the command to men is " be ye reconciled to God."

The verb is used elsewhere in 1 Cor. 7 : 11, of a woman returning to her husband.¶

2. APOKATALLASSŌ (ἀποκαταλλάσσω), to reconcile completely (*apo*, from, and No. 1), a stronger form of No. 1, to change from one condition to another, so as to remove all enmity and leave no impediment to unity and peace, is used in Eph. 2 : 16, of the reconciliation of believing Jew and Gentile " in one body unto God through the Cross;" in Col. 1 : 21 not the union of Jew and Gentile is in view, but the change wrought in the individual believer from alienation and enmity, on account of evil works, to reconciliation with God; in ver. 20 the word is used of the Divine purpose to reconcile through Christ " all things unto Himself . . . whether things upon the earth, or things in the heavens," the basis of the change being the peace effected " through the blood of His Cross." It is the Divine purpose, on the ground of the work of Christ accomplished on the Cross, to bring the whole universe, except rebellious angels and unbelieving man, into full accord with the mind of God, Eph. 1 : 10. Things " under the earth," Phil. 2 : 10, are subdued, not reconciled.¶ **604 AG:92C CB:1237A**

3. DIALLASSŌ (διαλλάσσω), to effect an alteration, to exchange, and hence, to reconcile, in cases of mutual hostility yielding to mutual concession, and thus differing from No. 1 (under which see Lightfoot's remarks), is used in the Passive Voice in Matt. 5 : 24, which illustrates **1259 AG:186A (-OMAI) CB:1241A (-OMAI)**

the point. There is no such idea as "making it up" where God and man are concerned.¶

B. Noun.

2643 AG:414A CB:1254A KATALLAGĒ (καταλλαγή), akin to A, No. 1, primarily an exchange, denotes reconciliation, a change on the part of one party, induced by an action on the part of another; in the N.T., the reconciliation of men to God by His grace and love in Christ. The word is used in Rom. 5:11 and 11:15. The occasioning cause of the world-wide proclamation of reconciliation through the Gospel, was the casting away (partially and temporarily) of Israel. A new relationship Godward is offered to the Gentiles in the Gospel. The word also occurs in 2 Cor. 5:18, 19, where "the ministry of reconciliation" and "the word of reconciliation" are not the ministry of teaching the doctrine of expiation, but that of beseeching men to be reconciled to God on the ground of what God has wrought in Christ. See No. 1, above.¶

Note: In the O.T. in some passages the A.V. incorrectly has "reconciliation," the R.V. rightly changes the translation to "atonement," e.g., Lev. 8:15; Ezek. 45:20, R.V., "make atonement for" (A.V., "reconcile").

For RECONCILIATION (MAKE), Heb. 2:17, A.V., see PROPITIATION

For RECORD (A.V.) see TESTIFY, No. 3, TESTIMONY, No. 2

RECOVER

4982 AG:798A CB:1269C 1. SŌZŌ (σώζω), to save, is sometimes used of healing or restoration to health, the latter in John 11:12, R.V., "he will recover," marg., "be saved" (A.V., "he shall do well"). See HEAL, PRESERVE, SAVE, WHOLE.

366 AG:58B CB:1235B 2. ANANĒPHŌ (ἀνανήφω), to return to soberness, as from a state of delirium or drunkenness (*ana*, back, or again, *nēphō*, to be sober, to be wary), is used in 2 Tim. 2:26, "may recover themselves" (R.V. marg., "return to soberness," A.V. marg., "awake"), said of those who, opposing the truth through accepting perversions of it, fall into the snare of the Devil, becoming intoxicated with error; for these recovery is possible only by "repentance unto the knowledge of the truth." For a translation of the verse see CAPTIVE, B, No. 3.¶

Notes: (1) For "recovering of sight," Luke 4:18, see SIGHT. (2) In Mark 16:18, the phrase *echō kalōs*, lit., 'to have well,' i.e., "to be well," is rendered "they shall recover."

RED

A. Adjectives.

445 AG:731C CB:1268A 1. PURRHOS (πυρρός) denotes fire-coloured (*pur*, fire), hence, fiery red, Rev. 6:4; 12:3, in the latter passage said of the Dragon, indicative of the cruelty of the Devil.¶

2. ERUTHROS (ἐρυθρός) denotes red (the ordinary colour); the 2063
root *rudh*— is seen, e.g., in the Latin *rufus*, Eng., ruby, ruddy, rust, etc. AG:310B
It is applied to the Red Sea, Acts 7 : 36; Heb. 11 : 29.¶ The origin of CB:—
the name is uncertain; it has been regarded as due, e.g., to the colour of the corals which cover the Red Sea bed or line its shores, or to the tinge of the mountains which border it, or to the light of the sky upon its waters.

B. Verb.

PURRHAZŌ (πυρράζω), to be fiery red (akin to A, No. 1), is used of 4449
the sky, Matt. 16 : 2, 3.¶ In the Sept., *purrhizō*, Lev. 13 : 19, 42, 43, 49; AG:731B CB:1268A
14 : 37.¶

REDEEM, REDEMPTION

A. Verbs.

1. EXAGORAZŌ (ἐξαγοράζω), a strengthened form of *agorazō*, to 1805
buy (see BUY, No. 1), denotes to buy out (*ex* for *ek*), especially of purchasing AG:271B CB:1247B
a slave with a view to his freedom. It is used metaphorically (*a*) in Gal. 3 : 13 and 4 : 5, of the deliverance by Christ of Christian Jews from the Law and its curse; what is said of *lutron* (RANSOM, No. 1) is true of this verb and of *agorazō*, as to the Death of Christ, that Scripture does not say to whom the price was paid; the various suggestions made are purely speculative; (*b*) in the Middle Voice, to buy up for oneself, Eph. 5 : 16 and Col. 4 : 5, of "buying up the opportunity" (R.V. marg.; text, "redeeming the time," where "time" is *kairos*, a season, a time in which something is seasonable), i.e., making the most of every opportunity, turning each to the best advantage since none can be recalled if missed.¶

Note: In Rev. 5 : 9; 14 : 3, 4, A.V., *agorazō*, to purchase (R.V.) is 59 AG:12D
translated "redeemed." See PURCHASE. CB:1233C

2. LUTROŌ (λυτρόω), to release on receipt of ransom (akin to *lutron*, 3084
a ransom), is used in the Middle Voice, signifying to release by paying a AG:482D CB:1257B
ransom price, to redeem (*a*) in the natural sense of delivering, Luke 24 : 21, of setting Israel free from the Roman yoke; (*b*) in a spiritual sense, Tit. 2 : 14, of the work of Christ in redeeming men "from all iniquity" (*anomia*, lawlessness, the bondage of self-will which rejects the will of God); 1 Pet. 1 : 18 (Passive Voice), "ye were redeemed," from a vain manner of life, i.e., from bondage to tradition. In both instances the Death of Christ is stated as the means of redemption.¶

Note: While both No. 1 and No. 2 are translated to redeem, *exagorazō* does not signify the actual redemption, but the price paid with a view to it, *lutroō* signifies the actual deliverance, the setting at liberty.

B. Nouns.

1. LUTRŌSIS (λύτρωσις), a redemption (akin to A, No. 2), is used 3085
(*a*) in the general sense of deliverance, of the nation of Israel, Luke 1 : 68, AG:483A CB:1257B
R.V., "wrought redemption;" 2 : 38; (*b*) of the redemptive work of Christ, Heb. 9 : 12, bringing deliverance through His death, from the guilt

and power of sin.¶ In the Sept., Lev. 25 : 29, 48 ; Numb. 18 : 16 ; Judg. 1 : 15 ; Ps. 49 : 8 ; 111 : 9 ; 130 : 7 ; Isa. 63 : 4.¶

629 AG:96B 2. APOLUTRŌSIS (ἀπολύτρωσις), a strengthened form of No. 1, lit.,
CB:1237A a releasing, for (i.e., on payment of) a ransom. It is used of (*a*) " deliverance " from physical torture, Heb. 11 : 35, see DELIVER, B, No. 1 ; (*b*) the deliverance of the people of God at the Coming of Christ with His glorified saints, " in a cloud with power and great glory," Luke 21 : 28, a redemption to be accomplished at the 'outshining of His Parousia,' 2 Thess. 2 : 8, i.e., at His Second Advent ; (*c*) forgiveness and justification, redemption as the result of expiation, deliverance from the guilt of sins, Rom. 3 : 24, " through the redemption that is in Christ Jesus ; " Eph. 1 : 7, defined as " the forgiveness of our trespasses," R.V. ; so Col. 1 : 14, " the forgiveness of our sins," indicating both the liberation from the guilt and doom of sin and the introduction into a life of liberty, " newness of life " (Rom. 6 : 4) ; Heb. 9 : 15, " for the redemption of the transgressions that were under the first covenant," R.V., here " redemption of " is equivalent to 'redemption from,' the genitive case being used of the object from which the redemption is effected, not from the consequence of the transgressions, but from the transgressions themselves ; (*d*) the deliverance of the believer from the presence and power of sin, and of his body from bondage to corruption, at the Coming (the Parousia in its inception) of the Lord Jesus, Rom. 8 : 23 ; 1 Cor. 1 : 30 ; Eph. 1 : 14 ; 4 : 30.¶ See also PROPITIATION.

For REDOUND, 2 Cor. 4 : 15 (R.V., " abound "), see ABUNDANCE, B, No. 1 (*c*)

REED

2563 AG:398B KALAMOS (κάλαμος) denotes (*a*) the reed mentioned in Matt. 11 : 7 ;
CB:1253B 12 : 20 ; Luke 7 : 24, the same as the Heb., *qāneh* (among the various reeds in the O.T.), e.g., Isa. 42 : 3, from which Matt. 12 : 20 is quoted (cp. Job 40 : 21 ; Ezek. 29 : 6, a reed with jointed, hollow stalk) ; (*b*) a reed-staff, staff, Matt. 27 : 29, 30, 48 ; Mark 15 : 19, 36 (cp. *rhabdos*, a rod ; in 2 Kings 18 : 21, *rhabdos kalaminē*) ; (*c*) a measuring reed or rod, Rev. 11 : 1 ; 21 : 15, 16 ; (*d*) a writing reed, a pen, 3 John 13 ; see PEN.¶

REFINED

4448 AG:731A PUROOMAI (πυρόομαι), to burn, is translated " refined," as of metals,
CB:1268A in Rev. 1 : 15 and 3 : 18, R.V. (A.V., " burned," and " tried "). See BURN, No. 4.

For REFLECTING, 2 Cor. 3 : 18, R.V., see BEHOLD, No. 12

1357 AG:199A
REFORMATION

CB:1242A DIORTHŌSIS (διόρθωσις), properly, a making straight (*dia*, through,

orthos, straight ; cp. *diorthōma* in Acts 24 : 2 ; see CORRECTION, No. 1), DIORTHŌMA
denotes a "reformation" or reforming, Heb. 9 : 10 ; the word has the AG:199A
meaning either (*a*) of a right arrangement, right ordering, or, more usually, CB:—
(*b*) of restoration, amendment, bringing right again ; what is here indicated
is a time when the imperfect, the inadequate, would be superseded by a
better order of things, and hence the meaning (*a*) seems to be the right
one ; it is thus to be distinguished from that of Acts 24 : 2, mentioned
above.¶ The word is used in the papyri in the other sense of the
rectification of things, whether by payments or manner of life.

REFRAIN

1. PAUŌ (παύω), to stop, is used in the Active Voice, in the sense 3973 AG:638A
of making to cease, restraining in 1 Pet. 3 : 10, of causing the tongue to CB:—
refrain from evil ; elsewhere in the Middle Voice, see CEASE, No. 1.

2. APHISTĒMI (ἀφίστημι), to cause to depart, is used intransitively, 868
in the sense of departing from, refraining from, Acts 5 : 38. See DEPART, AG:126D CB:1236B
No. 20.

REFRESH, REFRESHING

A. Verbs.

1. ANAPAUŌ (ἀναπαύω), to give intermission from labour, to give 373
rest, refresh (*ana*, back, *pauō*, to cause to cease), is translated to refresh AG:58D CB:1235B
in 1 Cor. 16 : 18 ; 2 Cor. 7 : 13 ; Philm. 7, 20. See REST.

2. SUNANAPAUOMAI (συναναπαύομαι), to lie down, to rest with (*sun*, 4875
with, and No. 1 in the Middle Voice), is used metaphorically of being AG:784B CB:—
refreshed in spirit with others, in Rom. 15 : 32, A.V., "may with (you)
be refreshed" (R.V., ". . . find rest").¶ In the Sept., Isa. 11 : 6.¶

3. ANAPSUCHŌ (ἀναψύχω), to make cool, refresh (*ana*, back, 404
psuchō, to cool), is used in 2 Tim. 1 : 16 (cp. B).¶ In the papyri it is AG:63D CB:1235B
used of taking relaxation.

Note : In Acts 27 : 3, the verb *tunchanō*, to obtain or receive, with
the object *epimeleia*, care, is translated "to refresh himself" (R.V., marg., EPIMELEIA 1958
"to receive attention," i.e., to enjoy the kind attention of his friends). AG:296A CB:—

B. Noun.

ANAPSUXIS (ἀνάψυξις), a refreshing (akin to A, No. 3), occurs 403
in Acts 3 : 19.¶ In the Sept., Ex. 8 : 15.¶ In the papyri it is used of AG:63C CB:1235B
obtaining relief.

For REFUGE see FLEE, No. 3

REFUSE (Verb)

720

1. ARNEOMAI (ἀρνέομαι), to deny, renounce, reject, in late Greek AG:107D CB:1237C
came to signify to refuse to acknowledge, to disown, and is translated 3868
to refuse in Acts 7 : 35 ; Heb. 11 : 24. See DENY, No. 1. AG:616C

2. PARAITEOMAI (παραιτέομαι), for the various meanings of which CB:1262A

see Avoid, No. 3, denotes to refuse in Acts 25 : 11 ; 1 Tim. 4 : 7 ; 5 : 11 ; 2 Tim. 2 : 23, R.V. (A.V., " avoid ") ; Tit. 3 : 10, R.V. (marg., " avoid ; " A.V., " reject ") ; Heb. 12 : 25 (twice), perhaps in the sense of begging off. See Excuse, Intreat, Reject.

1381 AG:202C CB:1242A 3. DOKIMAZŌ (δοκιμάζω), to prove, to approve, used with a negative in Rom. 1 : 28, is translated " they refused," R.V. (A.V., " they did not like ") ; R.V. marg., " did not approve." See Approve, No. 1.

PARAKOUō 3878 AG:619A CB:1262A APOBLēTOS 579 AG:89A *Notes :* (1) For *parakouō*, to refuse to hear, R.V. in Matt. 18 : 17 (twice), see Hear, A, No. 7. (2) In 1 Tim. 4 : 4, A.V., *apoblētos*, " rejected " (R.V.), is translated " refused." See Reject.

REGARD

991 AG:143B CB:1239A 1. BLEPŌ (βλέπω), to behold, look, perceive, see, has the sense of regarding by way of partiality, in Matt. 22 : 16 and Mark 12 : 14. See Behold, No. 2.

1788 AG:269D CB:— 2. ENTREPŌ (ἐντρέπω), to turn about (*en*, in, *trepō*, to turn), is metaphorically used of putting to shame, e.g., 1 Cor. 4 : 14 ; in the Middle Voice, to reverence, regard, translated " regard " in Luke 18 : 2, 4. See Ashamed, Reverence, Shame.

5426 AG:866A CB:1264C 3. PHRONEŌ (φρονέω), to think, set the mind on, implying moral interest and reflection, is translated to regard in Rom. 14 : 6 (twice) ; the second part in the A.V. represents an interpolation and is not part of the original. The Scripture does not speak of not regarding a day. See Care, B, No. 6, Mind, Savour, Think, Understand.

1914 AG:290B CB:— 4. EPIBLEPŌ (ἐπιβλέπω), to look upon (*epi*, upon, and No. 1), in the N.T. to look on with favour, is used in Luke 1 : 48, A.V., " hath regarded " (R.V., " hath looked upon ") ; in Jas. 2 : 3, R.V., " ye have regard to " (A.V., " ye have respect to "). See Look, No. 6, Respect.

3643 AG:564A CB:1260C 5. OLIGŌREŌ (ὀλιγωρέω) denotes to think little of (*oligos*, little, *ōra*, care), to regard lightly, Heb. 12 : 5, R.V. (A.V., " despise "). See Despise, Note (3).¶ In the Sept., Prov. 3 : 11.¶

4337 AG:714B CB:1267A 6. PROSECHŌ (προσέχω), to take or give heed, is translated " they had regard " in Acts 8 : 11, A.V. (R.V., " they gave heed "). See Attend, No. 1.

272 AG:44D CB:— 7. AMELEŌ (ἀμελέω), not to care, is translated " I regarded . . . not " in Heb. 8 : 9. See Neglect.

EIS 1519 AG:228A CB:1243A *Notes :* (1) In Gal. 6 : 4, R.V., *eis*, into, is translated " in regard of (himself)," A.V., " in ; " so in 2 Cor. 10 : 16 ; Eph. 5 : 32. (2) In Rom. 6 : 20, the dative case of *dikaiosunē*, righteousness, signifies, not " from righteousness," A.V., but " in regard of righteousness," R.V., lit., ' free to righteousness ; ' i.e., righteousness laid no sort of bond upon them, they had no relation to it in any way. (3) In 2 Cor. 8 : 4 the accusative case of *charis* and *koinōnia* is, in the best texts, used absolutely, i.e., not as the objects of an expressed verb ; hence the R.V., " in regard to " (A.V., " that we would receive," where the verb is the result of a supplementary gloss). (4) For "not regarding" in Phil. 2 : 30, A.V. (R.V., "hazarding"), see HAZARD, No. 2.

REGENERATION

PALINGENESIA (παλιγγενεσία), new birth (*palin*, again, *genesis*, 3824 AG:606A
birth), is used of spiritual regeneration, Tit. 3 : 5, involving the com- CB:1261C
munication of a new life, the two operating powers to produce which are "the word of truth," Jas. 1 : 18 ; 1 Pet. 1 : 23, and the Holy Spirit, John 3 : 5, 6 ; the *loutron*, the laver, the washing, is explained in Eph.
5 : 26, "having cleansed it by the washing (*loutron*) of water with the LOUTRON 3067
word." AG:480C

The new birth and regeneration do not represent successive stages in CB:1257B
spiritual experience, they refer to the same event but view it in different aspects. The new birth stresses the communication of spiritual life in contrast to antecedent spiritual death ; regeneration stresses the inception of a new state of things in contrast with the old ; hence the connection of the use of the word with its application to Israel, in Matt. 19 : 28. Some regard the *kai* in Tit. 3 : 5 as epexegetic, 'even ;' but, as Scripture marks two distinct yet associated operating powers, there is not sufficient ground for this interpretation. See under EVEN.

In Matt. 19 : 28 the word is used, in the Lord's discourse, in the wider sense, of the "restoration of all things" (Acts 3 : 21, R.V.), when, as a result of the Second Advent of Christ, Jehovah 'sets His King upon His holy hill of Zion' (Ps. 2 : 6), and Israel, now in apostasy, is restored to its destined status, in the recognition and under the benign sovereignty of its Messiah. Thereby will be accomplished the deliverance of the world from the power and deception of Satan and from the despotic and antichristian rulers of the nations. This restitution will not in the coming Millennial age be universally a return to the pristine condition of Edenic innocence previous to the Fall, but it will fulfil the establishment of God's Covenant with Abraham concerning his descendants, a veritable re-birth of the nation, involving the peace and prosperity of the Gentiles. That the worldwide subjection to the authority of Christ will not mean the entire banishment of evil, is clear from Rev. 20 : 7, 8. Only in the new heavens and earth, "wherein dwelleth righteousness," will sin and evil be entirely absent.¶

REGION

1. CHŌRA (χώρα), a space lying between two limits, a country, land, 5561 AG:889B
is translated "region" in Matt. 4 : 16 ; Luke 3 : 1 ; Acts 8 : 1 ; 13 : 49 ; CB:1240A
16 : 6 ; 18 : 23, R.V. In the last three passages it has the technical sense of a subdivision of a Roman Province, Lat. *regio ;* as also No. 2 in Acts 14 : 6. See COUNTRY, No. 3.

2. PERICHŌROS (περίχωρος), a country or region round about (*peri*), 4066 AG:653C
is translated "region round about" in Matt. 3 : 5 ; 14 : 35, R.V. ; Mark CB:—

1 : 28 (in some mss. Mark 6 : 55) ; Luke 3 : 3, R.V. ; 4 : 14 ; 4 : 37, R.V. ; 7 : 17 ; Acts 14 : 6 (see No. 1). See COUNTRY, No. 4.

2824 AG:436B CB:— 3. KLIMA (κλίμα), an inclination, slope, is translated "regions" in Rom. 15 : 23, R.V. ; 2 Cor. 11 : 10 ; Gal. 1 : 21. See PART, A, No. 3.¶

Note : For "*regions* beyond," 2 Cor. 10 : 16, A.V., see PART, A, Note (9).

REGRET

A. Verb.

3338 (-MELL-) AG:511C CB:1258C METAMELOMAI (μεταμέλομαι), to regret, to repent one, is translated to regret in 2 Cor. 7 : 8, R.V. (twice), A.V., "repent." See REPENT.

B. Adjective.

278 AG:45C CB:1234C AMETAMELĒTOS (ἀμεταμέλητος), not repented of (*a*, negative, and A), is translated "which bringeth no regret" in 2 Cor. 7 : 10, R.V., said of repentance (A.V., "not to be repented of") ; elsewhere, in Rom. 11 : 29. See REPENT.¶

REGULATION See DECREE

For REGULAR, Acts 19 : 39, R.V., see LAW, C, No. 2

REHEARSE

312 AG:51B CB:1235B 1. ANANGELLŌ (ἀναγγέλλω), to bring back word (*ana*, back, *angellō*, to announce), is translated to rehearse in Acts 14 : 27 ; 15 : 4, R.V. See ANNOUNCE.

1834 AG:275D CB:1247C 2. EXĒGEOMAI (ἐξηγέομαι), primarily, to lead, show the way, is used metaphorically with the meaning to unfold, declare, narrate, and is translated to rehearse in the R.V. of Luke 24 : 35 ; Acts 10 : 8 ; 15 : 12, and 14, R.V. See DECLARE, No. 8.

756 (-OMAI) AG:113C CB:1237B *Note* : In Acts 11 : 4, the A.V. translates the middle Voice of *archō*, to begin, "rehearsed . . . from the beginning," R.V., "began, (and)."

REIGN (Verb and Noun)

936 AG:136C CB:1238C 1. BASILEUŌ (βασιλεύω), to reign, is used (I) literally, (*a*) of God, Rev. 11 : 17 ; 19 : 6, in each of which the aorist tense (in the latter, translated "reigneth") is "ingressive," stressing the point of entrance ; (*b*) of Christ, Luke 1 : 33 ; 1 Cor. 15 : 25 ; Rev. 11 : 15 ; as rejected by the Jews, Luke 19 : 14, 27 ; (*c*) of the saints, hereafter, 1 Cor. 4 : 8 (2nd part), where the Apostle, casting a reflection upon the untimely exercise of authority on the part of the church at Corinth, anticipates the due time for it in the future (see No. 2) ; Rev. 5 : 10 ; 20 : 4, where the aorist tense is not simply of a "point" character, but "constative," that is, regarding a whole action as having occurred, without distinguishing any steps in its progress (in this instance the aspect is future) ; ver. 6 ; 22 : 5 ; (*d*) of earthly potentates, Matt. 2 : 22 ; 1 Tim. 6 : 15, where "kings" is, lit., 'them that reign ;' (II) metaphorically, (*a*) of believers, Rom. 5 : 17,

where " shall reign in life " indicates the activity of life in fellowship with Christ in His sovereign power, reaching its fulness hereafter ; 1 Cor. 4 : 8 (1st part), of the carnal pride that laid claim to a power not to be exercised until hereafter ; (*b*) of Divine grace, Rom. 5 : 21 ; (*c*) of sin, Rom. 5 : 21 ; 6 : 12 ; (*d*) of death, Rom. 5 : 14, 17.¶

2. SUMBASILEUŌ (συμβασιλεύω), to reign together with (*sun*, with, 4821 AG:777C
and No. 1), is used of the future reign of believers together and with CB:1270B
Christ in the Kingdom of God in manifestation, 1 Cor. 4 : 8 (3rd part) ; ARCHō
of those who endure 2 Tim. 2 : 12, cp. Rev. 20 : 6.¶ 757

Notes : (1) In Rom. 15 : 12, A.V., *archō*, to rule (R.V., is translated AG:113C CB:1237B
" to reign." (2) In Rev. 17 : 18, *echō*, to have, with *basileia*, a kingdom, BASILEIA
is translated " reigneth," lit., ' hath a kingdom,' suggestive of a distinction 932 AG:134D
between the sovereignty of mystic Babylon and that of ordinary sovereigns. CB:1238C
(3) In Luke 3 : 1, *hēgemonia*, rule, is rendered " reign."¶ HēGEMONIA 2231 AG:343A

REINS CB:1249C

NEPHROS (νεφρός), a kidney (Eng., nephritis, etc.), usually in the 3510 AG:537A
plural, is used metaphorically of the will and the affections, Rev. 2 : 23, CB:1259C
" reins " (cp. Ps. 7 : 9 ; Jer. 11 : 20 ; 17 : 10 ; 20 : 12). The feelings and emotions were regarded as having their seat in the kidneys.¶

REJECT

A. Verbs.

1. APODOKIMAZŌ (ἀποδοκιμάζω), to reject as the result of 593 AG:90D
examination and disapproval (*apo*, away from, *dokimazō*, to approve), CB:1236C
is used (*a*) of the rejection of Christ by the elders and chief priests of the Jews, Matt. 21 : 42 ; Mark 8 : 31 ; 12 : 10 ; Luke 9 : 22 ; 20 : 17 ; 1 Pet. 2 : 4, 7 (A.V., " disallowed ") ; by the Jewish people, Luke 17 : 25 ; (*b*) of the rejection of Esau from inheriting " the blessing," Heb. 12 : 17. See DISALLOW.¶ Cp. and contrast *exoutheneō*, Acts 4 : 11. See DESPISE.

2. ATHETEŌ (ἀθετέω), properly, to do away with what has been laid 114 AG:21A
down, to make *atheton* (i.e., without place, *a*, negative, *tithēmi*, to place), CB:1238A
hence, besides its meanings to set aside, make void, nullify, disannul, signifies to reject ; in Mark 6 : 26, regarding Herod's pledge to Salome, it almost certainly has the meaning ' to break faith with ' (cp. the Sept. of Jer. 12 : 6, and Lam. 1 : 2, " dealt treacherously "). Moulton and Milligan illustrate this meaning from the papyri. Field suggests ' disappoint." In Mark 7 : 9 " ye reject (the commandment) " means ' ye set aside ; ' in Luke 7 : 30, " ye reject " may have the meaning of nullifying or making void the counsel of God ; in Luke 10 : 16 (four times), " rejecteth," R.V. (A.V., " despiseth ") ; " rejecteth " in John 12 : 48 ; " reject " in 1 Cor. 1 : 19 (A.V., " bring to nothing ") ; 1 Thess. 4 : 8, to despise, where the reference is to the charges in ver. 2 ; in 1 Tim. 5 : 12, R.V., " have rejected " (A.V., " have cast off "). See DESPISE, Notes (1), DISANNUL, No. 1.

1609 AG:244D CB:1244A 3. EKPTUŌ (ἐκπτύω), to spit out (*ek*, out, and *ptuō*, to spit), i.e., to abominate, loathe, is used in Gal. 4 : 14, " rejected " (marg., " spat out "), where the sentence is elliptical : ' although my disease repelled you, you did not refuse to hear my message.'¶

3868 AG:616C CB:1262A 4. PARAITEOMAI (παραιτέομαι), besides the meanings to beg from another, Mark 15 : 6 (in the best texts) ; to entreat that . . . not, Heb. 12 : 19 ; to beg off, ask to be excused, Luke 14 : 18, 19 ; 12 : 25 (see REFUSE, No. 2), is translated to reject in Tit. 3 : 10, A.V. See EXCUSE, INTREAT, REFUSE.

B. Adjectives.

96 AG:18C CB:1233A 1. ADOKIMOS (ἀδόκιμος), not standing the test (see CAST, C), is translated " rejected " in 1 Cor. 9 : 27, R.V. ; Heb. 6 : 8, A.V. and R.V. See REPROBATE.

579 AG:89A CB:— 2. APOBLĒTOS (ἀπόβλητος), lit., cast away (*apo*, from, *ballō*, to throw), occurs in 1 Tim. 4 : 4, R.V., " rejected " (A.V., " refused "). See REFUSE.¶

REJOICE

5463 AG:873B CB:1239B 1. CHAIRŌ (χαίρω), to rejoice, is most frequently so translated. As to this verb, the following are grounds and occasions for rejoicing, on the part of believers: in the Lord, Phil. 3 : 1 ; 4 : 4 ; His Incarnation, Luke 1 : 14 ; His power, Luke 13 : 17 ; His presence with the Father, John 14 : 28 ; His presence with them, John 16 : 22 ; 20 : 20 ; His ultimate triumph, 8 : 56 ; hearing the gospel, Acts 13 : 48 ; their salvation, Acts 8 : 39 ; receiving the Lord, Luke 19 : 6 ; their enrolment in Heaven, Luke 10 : 20 ; their liberty in Christ, Acts 15 : 31 ; their hope, Rom. 12 : 12 (cp. Rom. 5 : 2 ; Rev. 19 : 7) ; their prospect of reward, Matt. 5 : 12 ; the obedience and godly conduct of fellow-believers, Rom. 16 : 19, R.V., " I rejoice " (A.V., " I am glad ") ; 2 Cor. 7 : 7, 9 ; 13 : 9 ; Col. 2 : 5 ; 1 Thess. 3 : 9 ; 2 John 4 ; 3 John 3 ; the proclamation of Christ, Phil. 1 : 18 ; the gospel harvest, John 4 : 36 ; suffering with Christ, Acts 5 : 41 ; 1 Pet. 4 : 13 ; suffering in the cause of the gospel, 2 Cor. 13 : 9 (1st part) ; Phil. 2 : 17 (1st part) ; Col. 1 : 24 ; in persecutions, trials and afflictions, Matt. 5 : 12 ; Luke 6 : 23 ; 2 Cor. 6 : 10 ; the manifestation of grace, Acts 11 : 23 ; meeting with fellow-believers, 1 Cor. 16 : 17, R.V., " I rejoice ;" Phil. 2 : 28 ; receiving tokens of love and fellowship, Phil. 4 : 10 ; the rejoicing of others, Rom. 12 : 15 ; 2 Cor. 7 : 13 ; learning of the well-being of others, 2 Cor. 7 : 16. See FAREWELL, GLAD, GREETING, etc.

4796 AG:775A CB:1270C 2. SUNCHAIRŌ (συγχαίρω), to rejoice with (*sun*, and No. 1), is used of rejoicing together in the recovery of what was lost, Luke 15 : 6, 9 ; in suffering in the cause of the gospel, Phil. 2 : 17 (2nd part), 18 ; in the joy of another, Luke 1 : 58 ; in the honour of fellow-believers, 1 Cor. 12 : 26 ; in the triumph of the truth, 1 Cor. 13 · 6, R.V., " rejoiceth with."¶

21 AG:3D CB:1233B 3. AGALLIAŌ (ἀγαλλιάω), to rejoice greatly, to exult, is used, (I) in

the Active Voice, of rejoicing in God, Luke 1 : 47; in faith in Christ, 1 Pet. 1 : 8, R.V. (Middle V. in some mss.), " ye rejoice greatly;" in the event of the marriage of the Lamb, Rev. 19 : 7, " be exceeding glad," R.V.; (II) in the Middle Voice, (*a*) of rejoicing in persecutions, Matt. 5 : 12 (2nd part); in the light of testimony for God, John 5 : 35; in salvation received through the gospel, Acts 16 : 34, " he rejoiced greatly," R.V.; in salvation ready to be revealed, 1 Pet. 1 : 6; at the revelation of His glory, 1 Pet. 4 : 13, " with exceeding joy," lit., ' ye may rejoice (see No. 1) exulting;' (*b*) of Christ's rejoicing (greatly) " in the Holy Spirit," Luke 10 : 21, R.V.; said of His praise, as foretold in Ps. 16 : 9, quoted in Acts 2 : 26 (which follows the Sept., " My tongue "); (*c*) of Abraham's rejoicing, by faith, to see Christ's day, John 8 : 56.¶

4. EUPHRAINŌ (εὐφραίνω), in the Active Voice, to cheer, gladden **2165**
(*eu*, well, *phrēn*, the mind), signifies in the Passive Voice to rejoice, make **AG:327C**
merry; it is translated to rejoice in Acts 2 : 26, R.V., " was glad," A.V., **CB:1247B**
" did . . . rejoice," of the heart of Christ as foretold in Ps. 16 : 9 [cp. No. 3, II (*b*)]; in Acts 7 : 41, of Israel's idolatry; in Rom. 15 : 10 (quoted from the Sept. of Deut. 32 : 43, where it is a command to the Gentiles to rejoice with the Jews in their future deliverance by Christ from all their foes, at the establishment of the Messianic Kingdom) the Apostle applies it to the effects of the gospel; in Gal. 4 : 27 (touching the barrenness of Sarah as referred to in Is. 54 : 1, and there pointing to the ultimate restoration of Israel to God's favour, cp. 51 : 2), the word is applied to the effects of the gospel, in that the progeny of grace would greatly exceed the number of those who had acknowledged allegiance to the Law; grace and faith are fruitful, law and works are barren as a means of salvation; in Rev. 12 : 12, it is used in a call to the heavens to rejoice at the casting out of Satan and the inauguration of the Kingdom of God in manifestation and the authority of His Christ; in 18 : 20, of a call to heaven, saints, apostles, prophets, to rejoice in the destruction of Babylon. See GLAD, No. 3, MERRY, No. 1.

5. KAUCHAOMAI (καυχάομαι), to boast, to glory, is rendered to **2744**
rejoice, (*a*) Rom. 5 : 2, in hope of the glory of God; (*b*) 5 : 3, R.V. (A.V. **AG:425C**
" glory "), in tribulation; (*c*) 5 : 11, R.V. (A.V., " we joy "), in God; **CB:1254C**
(*d*) Phil. 3 : 3, R.V., " glory " (A.V., " rejoice ") in Christ Jesus;
(*e*) Jas. 1 : 9 (R.V., " glory," A.V., " rejoice "), the brother of low degree
in his high estate; the rich brother in being made low; (*f*) Jas. 4 : 16, **KATA-**
of evil glorying. See GLORY (to boast). **2620** **AG:411B**

Notes: (1) In Jas. 2 : 13, A.V., *katakauchaomai*, to glory, boast against, **CB:1254A**
is translated " rejoiceth against " (R.V., " glorieth against "). See **KAUCHēMA**
GLORY (to boast), A, No. 2. (2) The nouns *kauchēma*, *kauchēsis*, signifying **2745** **AG:426A**
glorying, boasting, are always so rendered in the R.V., where the A.V. has **CB:1254C**
" rejoicing," the former in 2 Cor. 1 : 14; Gal. 6 : 4; Phil. 1 : 26; 2 : 16; **KAUCHēSIS** **2746**
Heb. 3 : 6; the latter in 1 Cor. 15 : 31; 2 Cor. 1 : 12; 1 Thess. 2 : 19; **AG:426B**
Jas. 4 : 16. See GLORY, B, Nos. 1 and 2. **CB:1254C**

RELEASE

630 AG:96C CB:1237A APOLUŌ (ἀπολύω), to loose from, is translated to release in Matt. 18 : 27, R.V. (A.V., "loosed") ; 27 : 15, 17, 21, 26 ; Mark 15 : 6, 9, 11, 15 ; Luke 6 : 37 (twice), R.V. (A.V., "forgive" and "ye shall be forgiven") ; 23 : 16 (ver. 17, in some mss.), 18, 20, 25 ; 23 : 22, R.V. (A.V., "let . . . go") ; John 18 : 39 (twice) ; 19 : 10 ; in 19 : 12, in the 1st part, A.V. and R.V. ; in the 2nd part, R.V., "release" (A.V., "let . . . go") ; so in Acts 3 : 13. See DEPART, DISMISS.

RELATIVE See KIN

859 AG:125A CB:1236B *Note :* For ***aphesis***, "release," Luke 4 : 18, R.V., see DELIVERANCE.

RELIEF

1248 AG:184B CB:1241A 1. DIAKONIA (διακονία), ministry, is translated "relief" in Acts 11 : 29 [R.V., marg., "for (*eis*) ministry"].

425 AG:65B CB:— 2. ANESIS (ἄνεσις), a loosening, relaxation (akin to ***aniēmi***, to send away, let go, loosen), is translated "relief" in 2 Cor. 2 : 13 and 7 : 5 (A.V., "rest"). See REST.

RELIEVE

1884 AG:283C CB:— EPARKEŌ (ἐπαρκέω) signifies to be strong enough for, and so either to ward off, or to aid, to relieve (a strengthened form of ***arkeō***, which has the same three meanings, ***epi*** being intensive) ; it is used in 1 Tim. 5 : 10, 16 (twice).¶

RELIGION

2356 AG:363B CB:1272B 1. THRĒSKEIA (θρησκεία) signifies religion in its external aspect (akin to *thrēskos*, see below), religious worship, especially the ceremonial service of religion ; it is used of the religion of the Jews, Acts 26 : 5 ; of the "worshipping" of angels, Col. 2 : 18, which they themselves repudiate (Rev. 22 : 8, 9) ; "there was an officious parade of humility in selecting these lower beings as intercessors rather than appealing directly to the Throne of Grace" (Lightfoot) ; in Jas. 1 : 26, 27 the writer purposely uses the word to set in contrast that which is unreal and deceptive, and the "pure religion" which consists in visiting "the fatherless and widows in their affliction," and in keeping oneself "unspotted from the world." He is "not herein affirming . . . these offices to be the sum total, nor yet the great essentials, of true religion, but declares them to be the body, the *thrēskeia*, of which godliness, or the love of God, is the informing soul" (Trench).¶

1175 AG:173C CB:1240C 2. DEISIDAIMONIA (δεισιδαιμονία) primarily denotes fear of the gods (from *deidō*, to fear, *daimōn*, a pagan deity, Eng., demon), regarded whether as a religious attitude, or, in its usual meaning, with a condemnatory or contemptuous significance, superstition. That is how Festus regarded the Jews' religion, Acts 25 : 19, A.V. and R.V. marg., "superstition" (R.V., "religion"). See RELIGIOUS, Note (1), and under SUPERSTITIOUS.¶

Notes: (1) *Thrēskeia* is external, *theosebeia* is the reverential worship of God (see GODLINESS), *eusebeia* is piety (see GODLINESS), *eulabeia* the devotedness arising from godly fear (see FEAR). (2) For "the Jews' religion," Gal. 1 : 13, 14, see JEWS, B.

RELIGIOUS

THRĒSKOS (θρῆσκος), religious, careful of the externals of divine service, akin to *thrēskeia* (see above), is used in Jas. 1 : 26.¶ **2357 AG:363D CB:1272B**

Notes: (1) For *deisidaimōn*, Acts 17 : 22, R.V., marg., "religious," see SUPERSTITIOUS. (2) For "religious (proselytes)," A.V. in Acts 13 : 43, see DEVOUT, No. 3. **1174 (-MONESTEROS) AG:173D CB:1240C**

REMAIN

1. MENŌ (μένω), to stay, abide, is frequently rendered to remain, e.g., Matt. 11 : 23; Luke 10 : 7; John 1 : 33, A.V. (R.V., "abiding"); 9 : 41 (in 15 : 11, the best texts have the verb to be, see R.V.); 15 : 16, A.V. (R.V., "abide"); 19 : 31; Acts 5 : 4 (twice), R.V., "whiles it remained, did it (not) remain (thine own)?;" 27 : 41; 1 Cor. 7 : 11; 15 : 6; 2 Cor. 3 : 11, 14; 9 : 9, A.V. (R.V., "abideth"); Heb. 12 : 27; 1 John 3 : 9. See ABIDE. **3306 AG:503C CB:1258B**

2. DIAMENŌ (διαμένω), to remain throughout (*dia*, through, and No. 1), is translated to remain in Luke 1 : 22; Heb. 1 : 11, A.V. (R.V., "Thou continuest"). See CONTINUE, No. 4. **1265 AG:186C CB:—**

3. APOLEIPŌ (ἀπολείπω), in the Passive Voice, to be reserved, to remain, is translated "remaineth" in Heb. 4 : 6, 9; 10 : 26. See LEAVE, No. 4. **620 AG:94D CB:—**

4. PERILEIPŌ (περιλείπω), to leave over, used in the Middle Voice, is translated "remain" in 1 Thess. 4 : 15, 17, A.V. (R.V., "are left"), where it stands for the living believers at the coming (the beginning of the Parousia) of Christ.¶ **4035 AG:648C (-OMAI) CB:1263B**

5. PERISSEUŌ (περισσεύω), to abound, to be over and above, to remain over, is rendered "(that which) remained over" in Matt. 14 : 20, R.V.; and Luke 9 : 17, R.V. (A.V., "remained"); John 6 : 12, 13 (A.V., ". . . over and above"). See ABUNDANCE, B, No. 1. **4052 AG:650C CB:1263C**

Notes: (1) In Mark 8 : 8, *perisseuma*, an abundance, is used in the plural, R.V., "(of broken pieces) that remained over" (A.V. "that was left"). (2) In 1 Cor. 7 : 29, A.V., *to loipon*, lit., '(as to) what is left,' '(as for) the rest,' is translated "it remaineth" (R.V., "henceforth"); in Rev. 3 : 2, *ta loipa*, the plural, "the things that remain." **PERISSEUMA 4051 AG:650C CB:1263C LOIPOS 3062 AG:479D CB:1257B**

REMEMBER, REMEMBRANCE, REMINDED

A. Verbs.

1. MIMNĒSKŌ (μιμνήσκω), from the older form *mnaomai*, in the Active Voice signifies to remind; in the Middle Voice, to remind oneself of, hence, to remember, to be mindful of; the later form is found only **3403 AG:522B (-OMAI) CB:1259A**

in the present tense, in Heb. 2 : 6, "are mindful of," and 13 : 3, "remember;" the perfect tense in 1 Cor. 11 : 2 and in 2 Tim. 1 : 4 (R.V., "remembering," A.V., "being mindful of"), is used with a present meaning. R.V. variations from the A.V. are, in Luke 1 : 54, R.V., "that He might remember" (A.V., "in remembrance of"); 2 Pet. 3 : 2, "remember" (A.V., "be mindful of"); Rev. 16 : 19 (Passive Voice), "was remembered" (A.V., "came in remembrance"). The Passive Voice is used also in Acts 10 : 31, A.V. and R.V., "are had in remembrance." See MINDFUL OF (to be).

3421 AG:525A CB:1259A 2. MNĒMONEUŌ (μνημονεύω) signifies to call to mind, remember; it is used absolutely in Mark 8 : 18; everywhere else it has an object, (*a*) persons, Luke 17 : 32; Gal. 2 : 10; 2 Tim. 2 : 8, where the R.V. rightly has "remember Jesus Christ, risen from the dead;" Paul was not reminding Timothy (nor did he need to) that Christ was raised from the dead (A.V.), what was needful for him was to remember (to keep in mind) the One who rose, the Source and Supplier of all his requirements; (*b*) things, e.g., Matt. 16 : 9; John 15 : 20; 16 : 21; Acts 20 : 35; Col. 4 : 18; 1 Thess. 1 : 3; 2 : 9; Heb. 11 : 15, "had been mindful of;" 13 : 7; Rev. 18 : 5; (*c*) a clause, representing a circumstance etc., John 16 : 4; Acts 20 : 31; Eph. 2 : 11; 2 Thess. 2 : 5; Rev. 2 : 5; 3 : 3; in Heb. 11 : 22 it signifies to make mention of. See MENTION.¶

363 AG:57D CB:1235A 3. ANAMIMNĒSKŌ (ἀναμιμνήσκω), *ana*, back, and No. 1, signifies in the Active Voice to remind, call to one's mind, 1 Cor. 4 : 17, "put (A.V., bring) . . . into remembrance;" so 2 Tim. 1 : 6; in the Passive Voice, to remember, call to (one's own) mind, Mark 11 : 21, "calling to remembrance;" 14 : 72, "called to mind;" 2 Cor. 7 : 15, "remembereth;" Heb. 10 : 32, "call to remembrance."¶

5279 AG:846A CB:1252B 4. HUPOMIMNĒSKŌ (ὑπομιμνήσκω) signifies to cause one to remember, put one in mind of (*hupo*, under, often implying suggestion, and No. 1), John 14 : 26, "shall . . . bring . . . to (your) remembrance;" 2 Tim. 2 : 14, "put . . . in remembrance;" Tit. 3 : 1, "put . . . in mind;" 3 John 10, R.V., "I will bring to remembrance" (A.V., "I will remember"); Jude 5, "to put . . . in remembrance." In Luke 22 : 61 it is used in the Passive Voice, "(Peter) remembered," lit., 'was put in mind.'¶

1878 AG:282D CB:— 5. EPANAMIMNĒSKŌ (ἐπαναμιμνήσκω), to remind again (*epi*, upon, and No. 3), is used in Rom. 15 : 15, R.V., "putting (you) again in remembrance," A.V., "putting (you) in mind." See MIND.¶

5294 AG:848B CB:— *Note*: In 1 Tim. 4 : 6, A.V., *hupotithēmi*, to lay under, to suggest, is translated "put . . . in remembrance" (R.V., "put . . . in mind"). See MIND.

B. Nouns.

364 AG:58A CB:1235A 1. ANAMNĒSIS (ἀνάμνησις), a remembrance (*ana*, up, or again, and A, No. 1), is used (*a*) in Christ's command in the institution of the Lord's Supper, Luke 22 : 19; 1 Cor. 11 : 24, 25, not 'in memory of' but in an

affectionate calling of the Person Himself to mind; (*b*) of the remembrance of sins, Heb. 10:3, R.V., "a remembrance" (A.V., "a remembrance again;" but the prefix *ana* does not here signify again); what is indicated, in regard to the sacrifices under the law, is not simply an external bringing to remembrance, but an awakening of mind.¶ In the Sept., Lev. 24:7; Numb. 10:10; Pss. 38 and 70, Titles.¶

2. HUPOMNĒSIS (ὑπόμνησις) denotes a reminding, a reminder; in **5280 AG:846B CB:1252B**
2 Tim. 1:5 it is used with *lambanō*, to receive, lit., 'having received a reminder,' R.V., "having been reminded" (A.V., "when I call to remembrance"); in 2 Pet. 1:13 and 3:1, "remembrance."¶

Note: A distinction has been drawn between Nos. 1 and 2, in that *anamnēsis* indicates an unassisted recalling, *hupomnēsis*, a remembrance prompted by another.

3. MNEIA (μνεία) denotes a remembrance, or a mention. See **3417 AG:524B CB:1259A**
MENTION.

4. MNĒMĒ (μνήμη) denotes a memory (akin to *mnaomai*, A, No. 1), **3420 AG:524D CB:1259A**
remembrance, mention, 2 Pet. 1:15, "remembrance;" here, however, it is used with *poieō*, to make (Middle Voice), and some suggest that the meaning is 'to make mention.'¶

REMIND See REMEMBRANCE

REMISSION, REMIT

A. Nouns.

1. APHESIS (ἄφεσις), a dismissal, release (from *aphiēmi*, B), is used **859 AG:125A CB:1236B**
of the forgiveness of sins and translated "remission" in Matt. 26:28; Mark 1:4; Luke 1:77; 3:3; 24:47; Acts 2:38; 5:31 (A.V., "forgiveness"); 10:43; 13:38, R.V. (A.V., "forgiveness"); 26:18 (ditto); Heb. 9:22; 10:18. See FORGIVE, B, and A, No. 1.

2. PARESIS (πάρεσις), a passing by of debt or sin, Rom. 3:25, A.V., **3929 AG:626B CB:1262B**
"remission" (R.V. and A.V. marg., "passing over"). See PASSING OVER.¶

Note: No. 2 is a matter of forbearance, No. 1 a matter of grace.

B. Verb.

APHIĒMI (ἀφίημι), to send away (akin to A, No. 1), is translated to **863 AG:125C CB:1236B**
remit in John 20:23 (twice), A.V. (R.V., to forgive). Scripture makes clear that the Lord's words could not have been intended to bestow the exercise of absolution, which Scripture declares is the prerogative of God alone. There is no instance in the N.T. of this act on the part of the Apostles. The words are to be understood in a "declarative" sense; the statement has regard to the effects of their ministry of the gospel, with its twofold effects of remission or retention. They could not, nor could anyone subsequently, forgive sins, any more than that Joseph actually restored the butler to his office and hanged the baker (Gen. 41:13), or any more than that the prophets actually accomplished things when they declared that they were about to be done (Jer. 1:10; Ezek. 43:3). See FORGIVE, No. 1.

REMNANT

3062 1. LOIPOS (λοιπός), an adjective (akin to *leipō*, to leave) signifying
AG:479D remaining, is used as a noun and translated " the rest " in the R.V., where
CB:1257B the A.V. has " the remnant," Matt. 22 : 6 ; Rev. 11 : 13 ; 12 : 17 ; 19 : 21.
See Other, Residue, Rest (the).

3005 2. LEIMMA (λεῖμμα), that which is left (akin to *leipō*, to leave),
AG:470B
CB:1256C a remnant, is used in Rom. 11 : 5, " there is a remnant," more lit.,
' there has come to be a remnant,' i.e., there is a spiritual remnant saved by the gospel from the midst of apostate Israel. While in one sense there has been and is a considerable number, yet, compared with the whole nation, past and present, the remnant is small, and as such is an evidence of God's electing grace (see ver. 4).¶ In the Sept., 2 Kings 19 : 4.¶

— 3. HUPOLEIMMA (ὑπόλειμμα), *hupo*, under, signifying diminution,
AG:845C
CB:1252B and No. 2, is used in Rom. 9 : 27 : some mss. have *kataleimma*, which has
KATALEIMMA virtually the same meaning (*kata*, down, behind), a remnant, where the
2640 contrast is drawn between the number of Israel as a whole, and the small
AG:413C
CB:1254A number in it of those who are saved through the Gospel. The quotation
is chiefly from the Sept. of Isa. 10 : 22, 23, with a modification recalling Hosea 1 : 10, especially with regard to the word " number." The return of the remnant is indicated in the name " Shear-Jashub," see Isa. 7 : 3, marg. The primary reference was to the return of a remnant from captivity to their own land and to God Himself ; here the application is to
REMOTE the effects of the gospel. There is stress on the word " remnant." ¶

See DESERT

REMOVE, REMOVING

A. Verbs.

3327 1. METABAINŌ (μεταβαίνω), to pass over from one place to another
AG:510C
CB:1258B (*meta*, implying change, and *bainō*, to go), is translated to remove in
Matt. 17 : 20 (twice). See Pass, No. 7.

3179 2. METHISTĒMI (μεθίστημι) is used transitively in the sense of caus-
AG:498D
CB:— ing to remove, in Acts 13 : 22, of the removing of King Saul, by bringing
about his death ; in 1 Cor. 13 : 2, of removing mountains. See Put, No. 23, Translate, Turn.

3346 3. METATITHĒMI (μετατίθημι), to remove a person or thing from one
AG:513C
CB:1258C place to another (*meta*, implying change, *tithēmi*, to put), e.g., Acts 7 : 16,
" were carried over," signifies, in the Middle Voice, to change oneself, and is so used in Gal. 1 : 6 "(I marvel that) ye are . . . removing," R.V. (not as A.V., " removed ") ; the present tense suggests that the defection of the Galatians from the truth was not yet complete and would continue unless they changed their views. The Middle Voice indicates that they were themselves responsible for their declension, rather than the Judaizers who had influenced them. See Carry, No. 5.

3911
AG:623B 4. PARAPHERŌ (παραφέρω), lit., to bring to or before (*para*, beside,
CB:— *pherō*, to carry), to take or carry away, is translated " remove " in the

Lord's prayer in Gethsemane, Mark 14 : 36, R.V. (A.V., "take away"); Luke 22 : 42. See TAKE. In the Sept., 1 Sam. 21 : 13.¶

5. METOIKIZŌ (*μετοικίζω*), to remove to a new abode, cause to 3351
migrate (*meta*, implying change, *oikos*, a dwelling place), is translated AG:514B
"removed" in Acts 7 : 4; "I will carry . . . away" (ver. 43). See CB:—
CARRYING AWAY, B.

6. APOCHŌRIZŌ (*ἀποχωρίζω*), to separate, part asunder, is used in 673
the Passive Voice in Rev. 6 : 14, "(the heaven) was removed," R.V. AG:102B
(A.V., "departed"). See DEPART, No. 14. CB:—

Notes: (1) In Matt. 21 : 21 and Mark 11 : 23, *airō*, to lift, take up, is AIRō
translated "be thou removed" (R.V., "be thou taken up"). (2) In 142 AG:24B
Rev. 2 : 5, A.V., *kineō*, to move (R.V.), is translated "will remove." CB:1234A
See MOVE. KINEō 2795 AG:432C

B. Noun.

METATHESIS (*μετάθεσις*), change of position (transliterated in Eng., 3331
metathesis, a transposition of the letter of a word), from *meta*, implying AG:511A CB:1258C
change, and *tithēmi*, to place, is used only in Hebrews and translated "removing" in 12 : 27; "translation" in 11 : 5; "change" in 7 : 12. See CHANGE, A.¶

REND, RENT (Verb and Noun)

A. Verbs.

1. RHĒGNUMI (*ῥήγνυμι*), to tear, rend, is translated to rend in 4486 AG:735A
Matt. 7 : 6, of swine. See BREAK, A, No. 6. CB:—

2. DIARRHĒSSŌ, or DIARĒSSŌ (*διαρήσσω*), a late form of *diarr-* 1284
hēgnumi, to break asunder, rend (*dia*, through, and No. 1), is used of AG:188A CB:1241B
rending one's garments, Matt. 26 : 65; Mark 14 : 63; Acts 14 : 14. See BREAK, A, No. 7.

3. PERIRRHĒGNUMI, or PERIRĒGNUMI (*περιρήγνυμι*), to tear 4048 AG:650B
off all round (*peri*, around), is said of garments in Acts 16 : 22.¶ CB:—

4. SCHIZŌ (*σχίζω*), to split, rend open, translated to rend in Matt. 4977
27 : 51 (twice); Mark 1 : 10, R.V., "rent asunder" (A.V., "open"); AG:797B CB:1268C
15 : 38; Luke 5 : 36, R.V., "rendeth (from);" the A.V. follows the mss. which omit it in the 1st part of this verse; 23 : 45; John 19 : 24; 21 : 11, R.V., "rent" (A.V., "broken"), of a net. See BREAK, A, No. 12.

5. DIASPAŌ (*διασπάω*), to tear asunder, is translated "rent asunder" 1288
in Mark 5 : 4, R.V. (A.V., "plucked asunder"); for Acts 23 : 10, see AG:188C CB:—
TEAR.¶

Note: In Mark 9 : 26, A.V., *sparassō*, to tear (R.V.), is rendered 4682
"rent." See TEAR. AG:760D CB:—

B. Noun.

SCHISMA (*σχίσμα*), a rent, division (akin to A, No. 4), signifies a rent 4978
in wineskins in Matt. 9 : 16; Mark 2 : 21. See DIVISION, No. 3. AG:797C CB:1268C

RENDER

1. APODIDŌMI (*ἀποδίδωμι*), to give up or back, is translated to 591 AG:90B CB:1236C

render, (*a*) of righteous acts, (1) human, Matt. 21 : 41 ; 22 : 21 ; Mark 12 : 17 ; Luke 16 : 2, R.V. (A.V., " give ") ; Luke 20 : 25 ; Rom. 13 : 7 ; 1 Cor. 7 : 3 ; (2) Divine, Matt. 16 : 27, R.V., " shall render " (A.V., " shall reward "), an important R.V. change ; Rom. 2 : 6 ; 2 Tim. 4 : 14, R.V. (A.V., " reward ") ; Rev. 18 : 6 (ditto) ; 22 : 12, R.V. (A.V., " give ") ; (*b*) of unrighteous acts, Rom. 12 : 17, R.V. (A.V., " recompense ") ; 1 Thess. 5 : 15 ; 1 Pet. 3 : 9. See DELIVER, A, No. 3, RECOMPENSE, B, No. 2.

476 AG:73A CB:1236A 2. ANTAPODIDŌMI (ἀνταποδίδωμι), to give in return for, is translated " render " in 1 Thess. 3 : 9. See RECOMPENSE, REPAY.

3930 AG:626B CB:— 3. PARECHŌ (παρέχω), to furnish, provide, supply, is translated " render " in Col. 4 : 1, R.V. (A.V., " give "), of what is due from masters to servants. See GIVE, No. 8.

1325 AG:192C CB:1241C 4. DIDŌMI (δίδωμι), to give, is translated " rendering " in 2 Thess. 1 : 8, R.V. (A.V., " taking "), of the Divine execution of vengeance at the revelation of Christ from Heaven hereafter. See GIVE, No. 1.

RENEW, RENEWING (Verb and Noun)

A. Verbs.

341 AG:55C CB:1235A 1. ANAKAINOŌ (ἀνακαινόω), to make new (*ana*, back or again, *kainos*, new, not recent but different), to renew, is used in the Passive Voice in 2 Cor. 4 : 16, of the daily renewal of " the inward man " (in contrast to the physical frame), i.e., of the renewal of spiritual power ; in Col. 3 : 10, of " the new man " (in contrast to the old unregenerate nature), which " is being renewed unto knowledge," R.V. (cp. No. 3 in Eph. 4 : 23), i.e., the true knowledge in Christ, as opposed to heretical teachings.¶

Note : This word has not been found elsewhere in Greek writings as yet, though No. 2 is, which would prevent the supposition that the Apostle coined a new word.

340 AG:55B CB:1235A 2. ANAKAINIZŌ (ἀνακαινίζω) is a variant form of No. 1, used in Heb. 6 : 6, of the impossibility of renewing to repentance those Jews who professedly adhered to the Christian faith, if, after their experiences of it (not actual possession of its regenerating effects), they apostatized into their former Judaism.¶ In the Sept., 2 Chron. 15 : 8 ; Ps. 39 : 2 ; 103 : 5 ; 104 : 30 ; Lam. 5 : 21.¶

365 AG:58A CB:1235B 3. ANANEOŌ (ἀνανεόω), to renew, make young (*ana*, as in No. 1, and *neos*, recent, not different), is used in Eph. 4 : 23, " be renewed (in the spirit of your mind)." The renewal here mentioned is not that of the mind itself in its natural powers of memory, judgment and perception, but ' the spirit of the mind,' which, under the controlling power of the indwelling Holy Spirit, directs its bent and energies Godward in the enjoyment of " fellowship with the Father and with His Son, Jesus Christ," and of the fulfilment of the will of God.¶ The word is frequent in inscriptions and in the papyri.

B. Noun.

ANAKAINŌSIS (ἀνακαίνωσις), akin to A, No. 1, a renewal, is used in 342
Rom. 12 : 2, " the renewing (of your mind)," i.e., the adjustment of the AG:55C CB:1235A
moral and spiritual vision and thinking to the mind of God, which is designed to have a transforming effect upon the life ; in Tit. 3 : 5, where " the renewing of the Holy Spirit " is not a fresh bestowment of the Spirit, but a revival of His power, developing the Christian life ; this passage stresses the continual operation of the indwelling Spirit of God; the Romans passage stresses the willing response on the part of the believer.¶

RENOUNCE

1. APEIPON (ἀπεῖπον), lit., to tell from (*apo*, from, *eipon*, an aorist 550
form used to supply parts of *legō*, to say), signifies to renounce, 2 Cor. (-OMēN) AG:83B
4 : 2 (Middle Voice), of disowning "the hidden things of shame."¶ In CB:1237A
the Sept. of 1 Kings 11 : 2 it signifies to forbid, a meaning found in the (APOLEGō)
papyri. The meaning to renounce may therefore carry with it the thought of forbidding the approach of the things disowned.

2. APOTASSŌ (ἀποτάσσω), to set apart, to appoint, a meaning found 657
in the papyri (*apo*, from, *tassō*, to arrange), is used in the Middle Voice in AG:100D CB:—
the sense either of taking leave of, e.g., Acts 18 : 18, or forsaking, Luke 14 : 33, R.V., "renounceth" (A.V. "forsaketh"). See FORSAKE, LEAVE.

RENT See LET OUT

REPAY

1. APODIDŌMI (ἀποδίδωμι), to give back, is translated " I will repay " 591
in Luke 10 : 35. See DELIVER, A, No. 3, RECOMPENSE, B, No. 2, RENDER, AG:90B CB:1236C
No. 1.

2. ANTAPODIDŌMI (ἀνταποδίδωμι), to give in return for, is translated 476
" I will repay " in Rom. 12 : 19, A.V. (R.V., " I will recompense "). See AG:73A CB:1236A
RECOMPENSE, B, No. 1, RENDER, No. 2.

3. APOTINŌ or APOTIŌ (ἀποτίνω), signifying to pay off (*apo*, off, 661
tinō, to pay a fine), is used in Philm. 19, of Paul's promise to repay what- AG:101B CB:—
ever Onesimus owed Philemon, or to whatever extent the runaway slave had wronged his master.¶ The verb is very common in the papyri, e.g., in a contract of apprenticeship the father has to pay a forfeit for each day of the son's absence from work. Moulton and Milligan, who draw this and other illustrations in the way of repayment, point out that " this verb is stronger than *apodidōmi* (No. 1), and carries with it the idea of repayment by way of a fine or punishment, a fact which lends emphasis to its use in Philm. 19."

REPENT, REPENTANCE

A. Verbs.

1. METANOEŌ (μετανοέω), lit., to perceive afterwards (*meta*, after, 3340 AG:511D
implying change, *noeō*, to perceive ; *nous*, the mind, the seat of moral CB:1258C

reflection), in contrast to *pronoeō*, to perceive beforehand, hence signifies to change one's mind or purpose, always, in the N.T., involving a change for the better, an amendment, and always, except in Luke 17 : 3, 4, of repentance from sin. The word is found in the Synoptic Gospels (in Luke, nine times), in Acts five times, in the Apocalypse twelve times, eight in the messages to the churches, 2 : 5 (twice), 16, 21 (twice), R.V., " she willeth not to repent " (2nd part) ; 3 : 3, 19 (the only churches in those chapters which contain no exhortation in this respect are those at Smyrna and Philadelphia) ; elsewhere only in 2 Cor. 12 : 21. See also the general Note below.

3338 2. METAMELOMAI (μεταμέλομαι), *meta*, as in No. 1, and *melō*, to
(-MELL-)
AG:511C care for, is used in the Passive Voice with Middle Voice sense, signifying
CB:1258C to regret, to repent oneself, Matt. 21 : 29, R.V., " repented himself ; " ver. 32, R.V., " ye did (not) repent yourselves " (A.V., " ye repented not ") ; 27 : 3, " repented himself ; " 2 Cor. 7 : 8 (twice), R.V., " regret " in each case ; Heb. 7 : 21, where alone in the N.T. it is said (negatively) of God.¶

B. Adjective.

278 AMETAMELĒTOS (ἀμεταμέλητος), not repented of, unregretted (*a*,
AG:45C negative, and a verbal adjective of A, No. 2), signifies ' without change of
CB:1234C purpose ; ' it is said (*a*) of God in regard to his " gifts and calling," Rom. 11 : 29 ; (*b*) of man, 2 Cor. 7 : 10, R.V., "[repentance (*metanoia*, see C)] . . . which bringeth no regret " (A.V., " not to be repented of ") ; the difference between *metanoia* and *metamelomai*, illustrated here, is briefly expressed in the contrast between repentance and regret.¶

C. Noun.

3341 METANOIA (μετάνοια), after-thought, change of mind, repentance,
AG:512C
CB:1258C corresponds in meaning to A, No. 1, and is used of repentance from sin or evil, except in Heb. 12 : 17, where the word " repentance " seems to mean, not simply a change of Isaac's mind, but such a change as would reverse the effects of his own previous state of mind. Esau's birthright-bargain could not be recalled, it involved an irretrievable loss.

As regards repentance from sin, (*a*) the requirement by God on man's part is set forth, e.g., in Matt. 3 : 8 ; Luke 3 : 8 ; Acts 20 : 21 ; 26 : 20 ; (*b*) the mercy of God in giving repentance or leading men to it is set forth, e.g., in Acts 5 : 31 ; 11 : 18 ; Rom. 2 : 4 ; 2 Tim. 2 : 25. The most authentic mss. omit the word in Matt. 9 : 13 and Mark 2 : 17, as in the R.V.

Note : In the O.T., repentance with reference to sin is not so prominent as that change of mind or purpose, out of pity for those who have been affected by one's action, or in whom the results of the action have not fulfilled expectations, a repentance attributed both to God and to man, e.g., Gen. 6 : 6 ; Ex. 32 : 14 (that this does not imply anything contrary to God's immutability, but that the aspect of His mind is changed toward an object that has itself changed, see under RECONCILE).

In the N.T. the subject chiefly has reference to repentance from sin, and this change of mind involves both a turning from sin and a turning to God. The parable of the prodigal son is an outstanding illustration of this. Christ began His ministry with a call to repentance, Matt. 4 : 17, but the call is addressed, not as in the O.T. to the nation, but to the individual. In the Gospel of John, as distinct from the Synoptic Gospels, referred to above, repentance is not mentioned, even in connection with John the Baptist's preaching ; in John's Gospel and 1st Epistle the effects are stressed, e.g., in the new birth, and, generally, in the active turning from sin to God by the exercise of faith (John 3 : 3 ; 9 : 38 ; 1 John 1 : 9), as in the N.T. in general.

REPETITIONS (use vain)

BATTALOGEŌ or BATTOLOGEŌ (βατταλογέω), to repeat idly, is 945
used in Matt. 6 : 7, " use (not) vain repetitions ; " the meaning to stammer AG:137D CB:1239A
is scarcely to be associated with this word. The word is probably from an Aramaic phrase and onomatopoeic in character. The rendering of the Sinaitic Syriac is " Do not be saying *battalatha*, idle things," i.e., meaningless and mechanically repeated phrases, the reference being to pagan (not Jewish) modes of prayer. *Battalos*, " the Gabbler," was a nickname for Demosthenes, the great orator, assigned to him by his rivals.¶

REPLY

ANTAPOKRINOMAI (ἀνταποκρίνομαι) is translated " repliest against " 470
in Rom. 9 : 20 (*anti*, against, *apokrinomai*, to answer) ; in Luke 14 : 6, AG:73B CB:—
" answer again." See ANSWER, B, No. 2.¶

REPORT (Noun and Verb)

A. Nouns.

1. AKOĒ (ἀκοή), a hearing, is translated " report " in John 12 : 38 189
and Rom. 10 : 16, and in the R.V. of Matt. 4 : 24 ; 14 : 1 ; Mark 1 : 28. AG:30D CB:1234B
See HEARING, B, No. 1.

2. EUPHĒMIA (εὐφημία), a good report, good reputation (*eu*, well, 2162
phēmē, a saying or report), is used in 2 Cor. 6 : 8. Contrast No. 3.¶ AG:327C CB:—

3. DUSPHĒMIA (δυσφημία), evil-speaking, defamation (*dus-*, an 1426
inseparable prefix, the opposite to *eu*, well, see No. 2), is used in 2 Cor. AG:209D CB:—
6 : 8.¶

4. LOGOS (λόγος), a word, is translated " report," i.e., a story, narra- 3056
tive ; in Luke 5 : 15 (A.V., " fame ") ; 7 : 17 (A.V., " rumour ") ; Acts AG:477A CB:1257A
11 : 22 (A.V., " tidings "). See WORD.

Note : For *marturia*, rendered " report " in 1 Tim. 3 : 7, A.V., see 3141
TESTIMONY, WITNESS. AG:493C CB:1257C

B. Adjective.

EUPHĒMOS (εὔφημος), akin to A, No. 2, primarily, uttering words 2163
or sounds of good omen, then, avoiding ill-omened words, and hence AG:327C CB:—
fair-sounding, " of good report," is so rendered in Phil. 4 : 8.¶

C. Verbs.

3140 1. MARTUREŌ (μαρτυρέω), to be a witness, bear witness, testify,
AG:492C signifies, in the Passive Voice, to be well testified of, to have a good report,
CB:1257C Acts 6 : 3, " of good (A.V., honest) report," lit., ' being well testified of ; '
10 : 22 ; 16 : 2 ; 22 : 12 ; 1 Tim. 5 : 10 ; in Heb. 11 : 2, 39, A.V., " obtained a good report " (R.V., " had witness borne to them ") ; in 3 John 12, A.V., " hath good report " (R.V., " hath the witness "), lit., ' witness hath been borne.' See TESTIFY, WITNESS.

518 2. APANGELLŌ (ἀπαγγέλλω), to report (*apo*, from, *angellō*, to give a
AG:79B
CB:1236B message), announce, declare (by a messenger, speaker, or writer), is
translated " reported " in Acts 4 : 23 ; 16 : 36, R.V. (A.V., " told ") ; ver. 38 (some mss. have No. 3 ; A.V., " told ") ; " report " in 1 Cor. 14 : 25, A.V. (R.V., " declaring ") ; 1 Thess. 1 : 9, R.V., " report " (A.V., " shew ") ; so Acts 28 : 21. See DECLARE, No. 2.

312 3. ANANGELLŌ (ἀναγγέλλω), to bring back word, in later Greek came
AG:51B
CB:1235B to have the same meaning as No. 2, to announce, declare ; it is translated
" are reported " in 1 Pet. 1 : 12, A.V. (R.V., " have been announced "). See DECLARE, No. 1.

191 4. AKOUŌ (ἀκούω), to hear, is used in the Passive Voice, impersonally,
AG:31D
CB:1234B in 1 Cor. 5 : 1, lit., ' it is heard ' or ' there is heard,' translated " it is
reported." See HEAR.

987 5. BLASPHĒMEŌ (βλασφημέω), to speak slanderously, impiously,
AG:142C
CB:1239A profanely (*blaptō*, to injure, and *phēmē*, a saying), is translated " we be
slanderously reported " in Rom. 3 : 8 (Passive Voice). See BLASPHEME, B.

1310 *Note :* In Matt. 28 : 15, A.V., *diaphēmizō*, to spread abroad (*dia*,
AG:190C
CB:— throughout, *phēmē*, a saying, report), is translated " is commonly reported "
(R.V., " was spread abroad "). See BLAZE ABROAD.

REPROACH (Noun and Verb), REPROACHFULLY

A. Nouns.

3680 1. ONEIDISMOS (ὀνειδισμός), a reproach, defamation, is used in
AG:570B
CB:1260C Rom. 15 : 3 ; 1 Tim. 3 : 7 ; Heb. 10 : 33 ; 11 : 26 ; 13 : 13.¶

3681 2. ONEIDOS (ὄνειδος), akin to No. 1, is used in Luke 1 : 25 in the
AG:570B
CB:1260C concrete sense of a matter of reproach, a disgrace.¶ To have no children
was, in the Jewish mind, more than a misfortune, it might carry the implication that this was a Divine punishment for some secret sin. Cp. Gen. 30 : 1 ; 1 Sam. 1 : 6–10.

819
AG:120A 3. ATIMIA (ἀτιμία), dishonour, is translated " reproach " in 2 Cor.
CB:1238B 11 : 21, A.V. (R.V., " disparagement "). See DISHONOUR, SHAME, VILE.

5196
AG:832A *Note :* In 2 Cor. 12 : 10, A.V., *hubris*, insolence, injury, is translated
CB:1251B " reproaches " (R.V., " injuries "). See HARM.

B. Verbs.

3679 1. ONEIDIZŌ (ὀνειδίζω), akin to A, Nos. 1 and 2, signifies (*a*), in the
AG:570A
CB:1260C Active Voice, to reproach, upbraid, Matt. 5 : 11, R.V., " shall reproach "
(A.V., " shall revile ") ; 11 : 20, " to upbraid ; " 27 : 44, R.V., " cast

. . . reproach" [A.V., "cast . . . in (His) teeth"]; Mark 15 : 32, R.V., "reproached" (A.V., "reviled"); 16 : 14, "upbraided;" Luke 6 : 22, "shall reproach;" Rom. 15 : 3; Jas. 1 : 5, "upbraideth;" (*b*) in the Passive Voice, to suffer reproach, be reproached, 1 Tim. 4 : 10 (in some mss. in the 2nd part); 1 Pet. 4 : 14.¶

2. HUBRIZŌ (ὑβρίζω), akin to *hubris* (see A, Note), used transitively, **5195**
denotes to outrage, insult, treat insolently; it is translated "Thou **AG:831D** **CB:1251C**
reproachest" in Luke 11 : 45. The word is much stronger than to reproach; the significance is 'Thou insultest (even us),' i.e., who are superior to ordinary Pharisees. The lawyer's imputation was unjust; Christ's rebuke was not *hubris*, insult. What He actually said was by way of reproach (*oneidizō*). See DESPITEFULLY.

Notes: (1) For *anepilēptos*, "without reproach," R.V., in 1 Tim. **ANEPILĒPTOS**
3 : 2; 5 : 7; 6 : 14, see BLAMELESS, B, No. 5. (2) In 1 Tim. 5 : 14, **423** **AG:65B**
A.V., *loidoria*, reviling (R.V.), used in the genitive case with *charin*, in **(-ĒMPTOS)**
respect of, "for," is translated "reproachfully" (R.V., "for reviling"). **CB:1235C** **(-ĒMPTOS)**
Cp. *loidoreō*, to revile. See RAILING. **LOIDORIA** **3059** **AG:479C** **CB:1257A**

REPROBATE

ADOKIMOS (ἀδόκιμος), signifying 'not standing the test,' rejected **96**
(*a*, negative, *dokimos*, approved), was primarily applied to metals (cp. **AG:18C** **CB:1233A**
Is. 1 : 22); it is used always in the N.T. in a Passive sense, (*a*) of things, Heb. 6 : 8, "rejected," of land that bears thorns and thistles; (*b*) of persons, Rom. 1 : 28, of a "reprobate mind," a mind of which God cannot approve, and which must be rejected by Him, the effect of refusing "to have God in *their* knowledge;" in 1 Cor. 9 : 27 (for which see CAST, REJECTED); 2 Cor. 13 : 5, 6, 7, where the R.V. rightly translates the adjective "reprobate" (A.V., "reprobates"), here the reference is to the great test as to whether Christ is in a person; in 2 Tim. 3 : 8 of those "reprobate concerning the faith," i.e., men whose moral sense is perverted and whose minds are beclouded with their own speculations; in Tit. 1 : 16, of the defiled, who are "unto every good work reprobate," i.e., if they are put to the test in regard to any good work (in contrast to their profession), they can only be rejected.¶ In the Sept., Prov. 25 : 4; Isa. 1 : 22.¶

REPROOF, REPROVE

A. Noun.

—

ELEGMOS (ἐλεγμός), a reproof (akin to B), is found in the best texts **AG:249A** **CB:1244A**
in 2 Tim. 3 : 16 (some mss. have *elenchos*, which denotes a proof, proving, **ELENCHOS**
test, as in Heb. 11 : 1, "proving," R.V. marg., "test").¶ Cp. *elenxis*, **1650** **AG:249A**
rebuke, 2 Pet. 2 : 16 (lit., 'had rebuke').¶ **CB:1244A**

B. Verb.

ELENCHŌ (ἐλέγχω), to convict, rebuke, reprove, is translated to **1651** **AG:249B**
reprove in Luke 3 : 19; John 3 : 20, R.V. marg., "convicted;" the real **CB:1244A**

meaning here is "exposed" (A.V. marg., "discovered"); Eph. 5:11, 13, where to expose is again the significance; in John 16:8, A.V., "will reprove" (R.V., "will convict"); in 1 Cor. 14:24, R.V., "reproved" (A.V., "convinced"); in the following the R.V. has 'to reprove,' for
REPTILE A.V., 'to rebuke,' 1 Tim. 5:20; Tit. 2:15; Heb. 12:5; Rev. 3:19;
See for synonymous words see CONVICT and REBUKE.
CREEPING THING

REPUTATION, REPUTE

1380
AG:201D DOKEŌ (δοκέω) signifies (*a*) to be of opinion (akin to *doxa*, an opinion),
CB:1242A to suppose, e.g., Luke 12:51; 13:2 (see SUPPOSE); (*b*) to seem, to be reputed; in Gal. 2:2, R.V., "who were of repute" (A.V., "which were of reputation"); in 2:6 (twice), and 9, R.V., "were reputed" and "were of repute" (A.V., "seemed"); in each case the present participle of the verb with the article is used, lit., '(well) thought of' by them, persons held in consideration; in ver. 6, R.V., "(those) who were reputed to be somewhat" (A.V., "who seemed to be somewhat"); so ver. 9, where there is no irony [cp. the rendering "are accounted" in Mark 10:42 (i.e., not rulers nominally)], Paul recognized that James, Cephas, and John were, as they were reputed by the church at Jerusalem, its responsible guides; (*c*) impersonally, to think, to seem good. See SEEM and THINK.

The first meaning, to suppose, implies a subjective opinion based on thought; the second meaning, exemplified in the Galatians passages, expresses, from the standpoint of the observer, his own judgment about a
TIMIOS matter (Trench, Syn., § lxxx).
5093 *Notes:* (1) In Acts 5:34, A.V., *timios*, honoured, had in honour (R.V.),
AG:818A is translated "had in reputation." (2) In Phil. 2:29, A.V., *entimos*,
CB:1272C ENTIMOS honourable, with *echō*, to have, i.e., to hold in honour, is translated
1784 "hold . . . in reputation" (R.V., "hold . . . in honour"). (3) For
AG:268D CB:1245B *kenoō*, in Phil. 2:7, A.V., "made (Himself) of no reputation," see EMPTY.
KENOō 2758 AG:428A CB:1255A

REQUEST (Noun and Verb)

A. Nouns.

155 AG:26B 1. AITĒMA (αἴτημα) denotes that which has been asked for (akin
CB:1234A to *aiteō*, to ask); in Luke 23:24, R.V., "what they asked for" (A.V., "as they required"), lit., 'their request (should be done, *ginomai*);' in Phil. 4:6, "requests;" in 1 John 5:15, "petitions." See PETITION, REQUIRE.¶

1162 AG:171D 2. DEĒSIS (δέησις), an asking, entreaty, supplication, is translated
CB:1240B "request" in Phil. 1:4, A.V. (R.V., "supplication"). See PRAYER, SUPPLICATION.

1189
B. Verbs.

AG:175A 1. DEOMAI (δέομαι), akin to A, No. 2, to beseech, pray, request, is
CB:1240C translated to make request in Rom. 1:10. See BESEECH, No. 3.

2. AITEŌ (*αἰτέω*), to ask, is translated to make request in Col. 1 : 9, 154 AG:25D
R.V. (A.V., " to desire "). See ASK, No. 1. CB:1234A
3. ERŌTAŌ (*ἐρωτάω*), to ask, is translated to make request in 2065
1 John 5 : 16. See ASK, No. 2 and remarks on the difference between AG:311D CB:1246C
Nos. 1 and 2.

REQUIRE

1. ZĒTEŌ (*ζητέω*), to seek, seek after, also signifies to require, 2212 AG:338D
demand, " shall be required," Luke 12 : 48 ; in 1 Cor. 4 : 2, " it is required CB:1273C
(in stewards)." See DESIRE, Note (2), ENDEAVOUR, GO, Note (2) (*a*), SEEK.
2. EKZĒTEŌ (*ἐκζητέω*), to seek out (*ek*, out, and No. 1), also denotes 1567
to demand, require, Luke 11 : 50, 51, of executing vengeance for the AG:240A CB:1244A
slaughter of the prophets (cp. 2 Sam. 4 : 11 ; Ezek. 3 : 18). See SEEK.
3. APAITEŌ (*ἀπαιτέω*), to ask back, demand back (*apo*, from, or back, 523
aiteō, to ask), is translated " shall be required " in Luke 12 : 20, lit. ' do AG:80A CB:1236B
they require,' in the impersonal sense ; elsewhere, Luke 6 : 30, to ask
again.¶ It is used in the papyri frequently in the sense of demanding,
making demands.
4. PRASSŌ (*πράσσω*), to do, practise, perform, is used financially 4238
in the sense of exacting payment, in Luke 19 : 23. See EXTORT, A. AG:698B CB:1266B
Notes : (1) In Luke 23 : 23, A.V., *aiteō*, to ask (Middle Voice) is trans- AITEō
lated " requiring " (R.V., " asking ") ; so in 1 Cor. 1 : 22 (Active Voice), 154
A.V., " require " (R.V., " ask "). (2) In Luke 23 : 24, A.V., the noun AG:25D CB:1234A
aitēma (see REQUEST), that which is asked for, is translated " as they AITēMA
required " (R.V., " what they asked for "). (3) In 1 Cor. 7 : 36 the 155 AG:26B
rendering " need so requireth " (R.V.) represents the phrase *houtōs* CB:1234A
(thus) *opheilei* (it ought) *genesthai* (to become, i.e., to be done). OPHEILō 3784 AG:598D CB:1261A

REQUITE

AMOIBĒ (*ἀμοιβή*), a requital, recompence (akin to *ameibomai*, to repay, 287
not found in the N.T.), is used with the verb *apodidōmi*, to render, in 1 Tim. AG:46C CB:—
5 : 4, and translated " to requite."¶ This use is illustrated in the papyri
by way of making a return, conferring a benefaction in return for something (Moulton and Milligan).

RESCUE

EXAIREŌ (*ἐξαιρέω*), to take out (*ek*, from, *haireō*, to take), is used of 1807
delivering from persons and circumstances, and translated " rescued " AG:271D CB:—
in Acts 23 : 27. See DELIVER, No. 8, PLUCK.

For RESEMBLE, Luke 13 : 18, A.V., see LIKEN, B, No. 1

RESERVE

TĒREŌ (*τηρέω*), to guard, keep, preserve, give heed to, is translated 5083 AG:814D
to reserve, (*a*) with a happy issue, 1 Pet. 1 : 4 ; (*b*) with a retributive CB:1271B

issue, 2 Pet. 2 : 4 ; ver. 9, A.V. (R.V., "keep") ; 2 : 17 ; 3 : 7 ; Jude 6, A.V. (R.V., "hath kept") ; ver. 13 ; (*c*) with the possibility either of deliverance or execution, Acts 25 : 21, A.V. (R.V., "kept"). See KEEP.

2641 AG:413C CB:1254A *Note :* In Rom. 11 : 4, A.V., *kataleipō*, to leave behind, leave remaining, is translated "I have reserved" (R.V., "I have left"). See LEAVE.

RESIDUE

2645 AG:414B CB:1254A KATALOIPOS (κατάλοιπος), an adjective denoting 'left remaining' (*kata*, after, behind, *leipō*, to leave), akin to the verb in the Note above, is translated "residue" in Acts 15 : 17, from the Sept. of Amos 9 : 12.¶

3062 AG:479D CB:1257B *Note :* In Mark 16 : 13, A.V., the plural of *loipos*, left, is translated "residue" (R.V., "rest").

RESIST

436 AG:67B CB:— 1. ANTHISTĒMI (ἀνθίστημι), to set against (*anti*, against, *histēmi*, to cause to stand), used in the Middle (or Passive) Voice and in the intransitive 2nd aorist and perfect Active, signifying to withstand, oppose, resist, is translated to resist in Matt. 5 : 39 ; Acts 6 : 10, A.V. (R.V., "withstand") ; Rom. 9 : 19, A.V. (R.V., "withstandeth") ; 13 : 2 (2nd and 3rd parts ; for 1st part, see No. 3), A.V. (R.V., "withstandeth" and "withstand") ; Gal. 2 : 11, R.V. (A.V., "withstood") ; 2 Tim. 3 : 8 (2nd part), A.V. (R.V., "withstand") ; Jas. 4 : 7 ; 1 Pet. 5 : 9, A.V. (R.V., "withstand") ; to withstand in Acts 13 : 8 ; Eph. 6 : 13 ; 2 Tim. 3 : 8 (1st part) ; 4 : 15.¶

478 AG:74B CB:— 2. ANTIKATHISTĒMI (ἀντικαθίστημι), to stand firm against (*anti*, against, *kathistēmi*, to set down, *kata*), is translated "ye have (not) resisted" in Heb. 12 : 4.¶ In the Sept., Deut. 31 : 21 ; Josh. 5 : 7 ; Mic. 2 : 8.¶

498 (-OMAI) AG:76A CB:— 3. ANTITASSŌ (ἀντιτάσσω), *anti*, against, *tassō*, to arrange, originally a military term, to range in battle against, and frequently so found in the papyri, is used in the Middle Voice signifying to set oneself against, resist, (*a*) of men, Acts 18 : 6, "opposed themselves ;" elsewhere to resist, of resisting human potentates, Rom. 13 : 2 ; (*b*) of God, Jas. 4 : 6 ; 5 : 6, negatively, of leaving persistent evildoers to pursue their self-determined course, with eventual retribution ; 1 Pet. 5 : 5. See OPPOSE.¶

496 AG:75D CB:— 4. ANTIPIPTŌ (ἀντιπίπτω), lit., and primarily, to fall against or upon (*anti*, against, *piptō*, to fall), then, to strive against, resist, is used in Acts 7 : 51 of resisting the Holy Spirit.¶

RESOLVE

1097 AG:160D CB:1248B GINŌSKŌ (γινώσκω), to come to know, perceive, realize, is used in the 2nd aorist tense in Luke 16 : 4. "I am resolved," expressing the definiteness of the steward's realization, and his consequent determination of his course of action. See KNOW.

RESORT

1. ERCHOMAI (ἔρχομαι), to come, is translated "resorted" in 2064 AG:310B
Mark 2:13; in John 10:41 (R.V., "came"). See COME, No. 1. CB:1246B
2. EPIPOREUOMAI (ἐπιπορεύομαι), to travel or journey to a place 1975
(*epi*, to, *poreuomai*, to go), is translated "resorted" in Luke 8:4, R.V. AG:298A CB:—
(A.V., "were come").¶
3. SUNAGŌ (συνάγω), to gather or bring together (*sun*, with, *agō*, 4863 AG:782A
to bring), in the Passive Voice, to be gathered or come together, is trans- CB:1270B
lated "resorted" in John 18:2 (the aorist tense expressing repeated
action viewed cumulatively). See ASSEMBLE, GATHER, LEAD, Note (1).
Notes: (1) In the A.V. of John 18:20 and Acts 16:13, *sunerchomai*, SUNERCHOMAI 4905
to come together (R.V.), is translated to resort. (2) In Mark 10:1, A.V., AG:788A
sumporeuomai, to come together (R.V.), is translated "resort." CB:1270C SUMPOREUOMAI 4848

RESPECT (Noun and Verb) AG:780A CB:—

A. Noun.

MEROS (μέρος), a part, has occasionally the meaning of a class or 3313
category, and, used in the dative case with *en*, in, signifies 'in respect of,' AG:505D CB:1258B
2 Cor. 3:10, "in (this) respect;" 9:3, R.V., A.V., "in (this) behalf;"
Col. 2:16, "in respect of (a feast day)."

B. Verbs.

1. APOBLEPŌ (ἀποβλέπω), to look away from all else at one object 578
(*apo*, from), hence, to look stedfastly, is translated "he had respect" AG:89A CB:1236C
in Heb. 11:26, A.V. (R.V., "looked"). See LOOK. 1914
2. EPIBLEPŌ (ἐπιβλέπω), to look upon (*epi*), is translated "have AG:290B CB:—
respect" in Jas. 2:3 (R.V. "regard"); see LOOK, No. 6. PERI
Notes: (1) The following prepositions are translated "in respect 4012 AG:644B
of:" *peri*, concerning, in John 16:8, R.V.; *epi*, upon, over, in Heb. 11:4, CB:1263B
R.V.; marg., 'over (his gifts);' *kata*, in regard to, in Phil. 4:11. EPI 1909
(2) For "respect of persons" and "respecter of persons" see PERSON. AG:285D

CB:1245C KATA

REST (Noun and Verb) 2596 AG:405C

A. Nouns. CB:1253C

1. ANAPAUSIS (ἀνάπαυσις), cessation, refreshment, rest (*ana*, up, 372
pauō, to make to cease), the constant word in the Sept. for the Sabbath AG:58D CB:1235B
rest, is used in Matt. 11:29; here the contrast seems to be to the burdens imposed by the Pharisees. Christ's rest is not a rest from work, but in work, "not the rest of inactivity but of the harmonious working of all the faculties and affections—of will, heart, imagination, conscience—because each has found in God the ideal sphere for its satisfaction and development" (J. Patrick, in Hastings' Bib. Dic.); it occurs also in Matt. 12:43; Luke 11:24; Rev. 4:8, R.V., "(they have no) rest" [A.V., "(they) rest (not)"], where the noun is the object of the verb *echō*, to have; so in 14:11.¶

2663 AG:415D 2. KATAPAUSIS (κατάπαυσις), in classical Greek, denotes a causing
CB:1254A to cease or putting to rest; in the N.T., rest, repose; it is used (*a*) of God's
rest, Acts 7:49; Heb. 3:11, 18; 4:1, 3 (twice), R.V. (1st part),
"that rest" (the A.V., "rest," is ambiguous), 5, 11; (*b*) in a general
statement, applicable to God and man, 4:10.¶

425 AG:65B 3. ANESIS (ἄνεσις), for the significance of which see EASE, B, is trans-
CB:— lated "rest" in 2 Cor. 2:13, A.V. (R.V., "relief"); 7:5 (ditto); in
2 Thess. 1:7, the subject is not the rest to be granted to the saints, but the
Divine retribution on their persecutors; hence the phrase "and to you
that are afflicted rest with us," is an incidental extension of the idea of
recompense, and to be read parenthetically. The time is not that at
which the saints will be relieved of persecution, as in 1 Thess. 4:15–17,
when the Parousia of Christ begins, but that at which the persecutors
will be punished, namely, at the epiphany (or out-shining) of His Parousia
(2 Thess. 2:8). For similar parentheses characteristic of epistolary
writings see ver. 10; 1 Thess. 1:6; 2:15, 16.

4520 AG:739A 4. SABBATISMOS (σαββατισμός), a Sabbath-keeping, is used in Heb.
CB:1268B 4:9, R.V., "a sabbath rest," A.V. marg., "a keeping of a sabbath"
(akin to *sabbatizō*, to keep the sabbath, used, e.g., in Ex. 16:30, not in
the N.T.); here the sabbath-keeping is the perpetual sabbath rest to be
enjoyed uninterruptedly by believers in their fellowship with the Father
and the Son, in contrast to the weekly Sabbath under the Law. Because
this sabbath rest is the rest of God Himself, 4:10, its full fruition is yet
future, though believers now enter into it. In whatever way they enter
into Divine rest, that which they enjoy is involved in an indissoluble
relation with God.¶

2838 AG:437D 5. KOIMĒSIS (κοίμησις), a resting, reclining (akin to *keimai*, to lie),
CB:— is used in John 11:13, of natural sleep, translated "taking rest," R.V.¶

1515 AG:227B *Note:* In Acts 9:31, A.V., *eirēnē*, peace (R.V.), is translated "rest."

CB:1243A **B. Verbs.**

373 AG:58D 1. ANAPAUŌ (ἀναπαύω), akin to A, No. 1, in the Active Voice, signi-
CB:1235B fies to give intermission from labour, to give rest, to refresh, Matt. 11:28;
1 Cor. 16:18, "have refreshed;" Philm. 20, "refresh;" Passive Voice,
to be rested, refreshed, 2 Cor. 7:13, "was refreshed;" Philm. 7,
"are refreshed;" in the Middle Voice, to take or enjoy rest, Matt. 26:45;
Mark 6:31; 14:41; Luke 12:19, "take thine ease;" 1 Pet. 4:14;
Rev. 6:11; 14:13. See REFRESH.¶ In the papyri it is found as an
agricultural term, e.g., of giving land rest by sowing light crops upon it.
In inscriptions it is found on gravestones of Christians, followed by the
date of death (Moulton and Milligan).

2664 AG:415D 2. KATAPAUŌ (καταπαύω), akin to A, No. 2, used transitively,
CB:1254A signifies to cause to cease, restrain, Acts 14:18; to cause to rest,
Heb. 4:8; intransitively, to rest, Heb. 4:4, 10. See CEASE, A, No. 6,
1981 RESTRAIN.¶

AG:298D CB:1246A 3. EPISKĒNOŌ (ἐπισκηνόω), to spread a tabernacle over (*epi*, upon, *skēnē*, a tent), is used metaphorically in 2 Cor. 12 : 9, " may rest upon (me)," R.V., marg., " cover," " spread a tabernacle over."¶

4. KATASKĒNOŌ (κατασκηνόω), to pitch one's tent, lodge, is translated " shall rest," in Acts 2 : 26, A.V. (R.V., " shall dwell "). See LODGE. **2681 AG:418C CB:1254B**

5. HĒSUCHAZŌ (ἡσυχάζω), to be still, to rest from labour, is translated " they rested " in Luke 23 : 56. See PEACE hold one's), No. 3. **2270 AG:349A CB:1250A**

6. EPANAPAUŌ (ἐπαναπαύω), to cause to rest, is used in the Middle Voice, metaphorically, signifying to rest upon (*epi*, upon, and No. 1), in Luke 10 : 6 and Rom. 2 : 17.¶ **1879 (-OMAI) AG:282D (-OMAI) CB:1245B**

Note : For " find rest," Rom. 15 : 32, R.V., see REFRESH, No. 2.

REST (the)

1. LOIPOS (λοιπός), remaining (for which see REMNANT), is frequently used to mean " the rest," and is generally so translated in the R.V. (A.V., " others " in Luke 8 : 10 ; Acts 28 : 9 ; Eph. 2 : 3 ; 1 Thess. 4 : 13; 5 : 6 ; 1 Tim. 5 : 20 ; A.V., " other " in Luke 18 : 11 ; Acts 17 : 9 ; Rom. 1 : 13 ; 2 Cor. 12 : 13 ; 13 : 2 ; Gal. 2 : 13 ; Phil. 1 : 13 ; 4 : 3) ; the neut. plur., lit., ' remaining things,' is used in Luke 12 : 26 ; 1 Cor. 11 : 34. **3062 AG:479D CB:1257B**

2. EPILOIPOS (ἐπίλοιπος), signifying still left, left over (*epi*, over, and No. 1), is used in the neuter with the article in 1 Pet. 4 : 2, " the rest (of your time)."¶ **1954 AG:295D CB:—**

For RESTITUTION see RESTORATION

RESTLESS

AKATASTATOS (ἀκατάστατος), unsettled, unstable, disorderly (*a*, negative, *kathistēmi*, to set in order), is translated " unstable " in Jas. 1 : 8 ; " restless " in 3 : 8, R.V. [in the latter, the A.V. " unruly " represents the word *akataschetos*, signifying ' that cannot be restrained ' (*a*, negative, *katechō*, to hold down, restrain). In the Sept., Job 31 : 11¶]. See UNRULY, UNSTABLE.¶ In the Sept., Isa. 54 : 11.¶ **182 AG:30B CB:—**

RESTORATION

APOKATASTASIS (ἀποκατάστασις), from *apo*, back, again, *kathistēmi*, to set in order, is used in Acts 3 : 21, R.V., " restoration " (A.V., " restitution "). See under REGENERATION, concerning Israel in its regenerated state hereafter. In the papyri it is used of a temple cell of a goddess, a repair of a public way, the restoration of estates to rightful owners, a balancing of accounts. Apart from papyri illustrations the word is found in an Egyptian reference to a consummating agreement of the world's cyclical periods, an idea somewhat similar to that in the Acts passage (Moulton and Milligan).¶ **605 AG:92D CB:1237A**

RESTORE

1. APODIDŌMI (ἀποδίδωμι), to give back, is translated " I restore " in Luke 19 : 8. See DELIVER, A, No. 3. **591 AG:90B CB:1236C**

600 AG:91D CB:1237A 2. APOKATHISTĒMI or the alternative form APOKATHISTANŌ (ἀποκαθίστημι) is used (*a*) of restoration to a former condition of health, Matt. 12 : 13 ; Mark 3 : 5 ; 8 : 25 ; Luke 6 : 10 ; (*b*) of the Divine restoration of Israel and conditions affected by it, including the renewal of the Covenant broken by them, Matt. 17 : 11 ; Mark 9 : 12 ; Acts 1 : 6 ; (*c*) of giving or bringing a person back, Heb. 13 : 19.¶ In the papyri it is used of financial restitution, of making good the breaking of a stone by a workman by his substituting another, of the reclamation of land, etc. (Moulton and Milligan).

2675 AG:417D CB:1254B 3. KATARTIZŌ (καταρτίζω), to mend, to furnish completely, is translated "restore" in Gal. 6 : 1, metaphorically, of the restoration, by those who are spiritual, of one overtaken in a trespass, such a one being as a dislocated member of the spiritual body. The tense is the continuous present, suggesting the necessity for patience and perseverance in the process. See FIT, MEND, PERFECT.

RESTRAIN

2664 AG:415D CB:1254A 1. KATAPAUŌ (καταπαύω) ; see REST, B, No. 2.

2722 AG:422C CB:1254B 2. KATECHŌ (κατέχω), to hold fast or down, is translated "restraineth" in 2 Thess. 2 : 6 and 7. In ver. 6 lawlessness is spoken of as being restrained in its development : in ver. 7 "one that restraineth" is, lit., 'the restrainer' (the article with the present participle, 'the restraining one') ; this may refer to an individual, as in the similar construction in 1 Thess. 3 : 5, "the tempter" (cp. 1 : 10, lit., 'the Deliverer') ; or to a number of persons presenting the same characteristics, just as 'the believer' stands for all believers, e.g., Rom. 9 : 33 ; 1 John 5 : 10. Ver. 6 speaks of a principle, ver. 7 of the principle as embodied in a person or series of persons ; cp. what is said of "the power" in Rom. 13 : 3, 4, a phrase representing all such rulers. Probably such powers, i.e., 'constituted governments,' are the restraining influence here intimated (specifications being designedly withheld). For an extended exposition see Notes on Thessalonians, by Hogg and Vine, pp. 254–261.

RESULT See END, INSOMUCH, WHEREFORE

RESURRECTION

386 AG:60B CB:1235B 1. ANASTASIS (ἀνάστασις) denotes (I) a raising up, or rising (*ana*, up, and *histēmi*, to cause to stand), Luke 2 : 34, "the rising up ;" the A.V. "again" obscures the meaning ; the Child would be like a stone against which many in Israel would stumble while many others would find in its strength and firmness a means of their salvation and spiritual life ; (II) of resurrection from the dead, (*a*) of Christ, Acts 1 : 22 ; 2 : 31 ; 4 : 33 ; Rom. 1 : 4 ; 6 : 5 ; Phil. 3 : 10 ; 1 Pet. 1 : 3 ; 3 : 21 ; by metonymy, of Christ as the Author of resurrection, John 11 : 25 ; (*b*) of those who are Christ's at His Parousia (see COMING), Luke 14 : 14, "the resurrection of the just ;" Luke 20 : 33, 35, 36 ; John 5 : 29 (1st part), "the resurrection of life ;" 11 : 24 ; Acts 23 : 6 ; 24 : 15 (1st part) ;

1 Cor. 15 : 21, 42 ; 2 Tim. 2 : 18 ; Heb. 11 : 35 (2nd part), see RAISE, Note (3) ; Rev. 20 : 5, "the first resurrection ;" hence the insertion of "is" stands for the completion of this resurrection, of which Christ was "the firstfruits ;" 20 : 6 ; (*c*) of "the rest of the dead," after the Millennium (cp. Rev. 20 : 5) ; John 5 : 29 (2nd part), "the resurrection of judgment ;" Acts 24 : 15 (2nd part), "of the unjust ;" (*d*) of those who were raised in more immediate connection with Christ's resurrection, and thus had part already in the first resurrection, Acts 26 : 23 and Rom. 1 : 4 (in each of which "dead" is plural ; see Matt. 27 : 52) ; (*e*) of the resurrection spoken of in general terms, Matt. 22 : 23 ; Mark 12 : 18 ; Luke 20 : 27 ; Acts 4 : 2 ; 17 : 18 ; 23 : 8 ; 24 : 21 ; 1 Cor. 15 : 12, 13 ; Heb. 6 : 2 ; (*f*) of those who were raised in O.T. times, to die again, Heb. 11 : 35 (1st part), lit., 'out of resurrection.'¶

2. EXANASTASIS (ἐξανάστασις), *ek*, from or out of, and No. 1, **1815**
Phil. 3 : 11, followed by *ek*, lit., 'the out-resurrection from among the dead.' **AG:272D CB:1247C**
For the significance of this see ATTAIN, No. 1.¶

3. EGERSIS (ἔγερσις), a rousing (akin to *egeirō*, to arouse, to raise), **1454**
is used of the resurrection of Christ, in Matt. 27 : 53.¶ **AG:215B CB:1242C**

RETAIN

KRATEŌ (κρατέω), to be strong, obtain, hold, hold fast, is translated **2902**
to retain, of sins, John 20 : 23 (twice) ; see on REMIT. See HOLD, KEEP, **AG:448C CB:1256A**
OBTAIN, TAKE. **KATECHō**

Notes : (1) In Philm. 13, A.V., *katechō*, to hold fast, hold back, detain, **2722**
is translated to retain (R.V., to keep). (2) In Rom. 1 : 28, A.V., *echō*, **AG:422C CB:1254B**
"to have" (R.V.), is translated "to retain." **ECHō 2192**

RETURN **AG:331D CB:1242C**

1. ANALUŌ (ἀναλύω), to depart in Phil. 1 : 23, signifies to return **360**
in Luke 12 : 36, used in a simile of the return of a lord for his servants **AG:57C CB:1235A**
after a marriage feast (R.V.). See DEPART, No. 16.¶

2. ANASTREPHŌ (ἀναστρέφω), to turn back, is translated to return **390 AG:61B**
in Acts 5 : 22 and 15 : 16. See ABIDE, BEHAVE. **CB:1235B**

3. EPISTREPHŌ (ἐπιστρέφω), to turn about, or towards, is translated **1994**
to return in Matt. 12 : 44 ; 24 : 18 ; Mark 13 : 16, R.V. (A.V., "turn back **AG:301A CB:1246A**
again") ; Luke 2 : 39 ; 8 : 55, R.V. (A.V., "came again") ; 17 : 31 ; Acts 15 : 36, R.V. (A.V., "go again"). See CONVERT, A, No. 2, TURN.

4. HUPOSTREPHŌ (ὑποστρέφω), to turn behind, or back (*hupo*, **5290**
under), is translated to return (in some texts in Mark 14 : 40) in Luke **AG:847C CB:–**
1 : 56 ; 2 : 20, 43 ; ver. 45, R.V. (A.V., "turned back again") ; 4 : 1, 14 ; 7 : 10 ; 8 : 37 ; 10 : 17 ; 11 : 24, A.V. (R.V., "I will turn back") ; 17 : 18 ; 19 : 12 ; 23 : 48, 56 ; Acts 1 : 12 ; 12 : 25 ; 13 : 13 ; 13 : 34 ; 20 : 3 ; 21 : 6 ; 22 : 17, R.V. (A.V., "was come again") ; 23 : 32 ; Gal. 1 : 17 ; Heb. 7 : 1. See TURN (back).

5. ANAKAMPTŌ (ἀνακάμπτω), to turn or bend back, occurs in Matt. **344 AG:55C**
2 : 12 ; Luke 10 : 6 (i.e., as if it was unsaid) ; Acts 18 : 21 ; Heb. 11 : 15.¶ **CB:–**

1877 5. EPANAGŌ (ἐπανάγω), to bring up or back (primarily a nautical
AG:282D CB:— term for putting to sea ; see LAUNCH, PUT), is used intransitively, in Matt.
21 : 18, " He returned."

1880 *Note:* In Luke 19 : 15, A.V., *epanerchomai*, to come back again
AG:283A CB:— (R.V.) is translated " returned." See COME, No. 4.

REVEAL

601 AG:92A 1. APOKALUPTŌ (ἀποκαλύπτω) signifies to uncover, unveil (*apo*,
CB:1236C from, *kaluptō*, to cover) ; both verbs are used in Matt. 10 : 26 ; in Luke 12 : 2, *apokaluptō* is set in contrast to *sunkaluptō*, to cover up, cover completely. " The N.T. occurrences of this word fall under two heads, subjective and objective. The subjective use is that in which something is presented to the mind directly, as, (*a*) the meaning of the acts of God, Matt. 11 : 25 ; Luke 10 : 21 ; (*b*) the secret of the Person of the Lord Jesus, Matt. 16 : 17 ; John 12 : 38 ; (*c*) the character of God as Father, Matt. 11 : 27 ; Luke 10 : 22 ; (*d*) the will of God for the conduct of His children, Phil. 3 : 15 ; (*e*) the mind of God to the prophets of Israel, 1 Pet. 1 : 12, and of the Church, 1 Cor. 14 : 30 ; Eph. 3 : 5.

" The objective use is that in which something is presented to the senses, sight or hearing, as, referring to the past, (*f*) the truth declared to men in the gospel, Rom. 1 : 17 ; 1 Cor. 2 : 10 ; Gal. 3 : 23 ; (*g*) the Person of Christ to Paul on the way to Damascus, Gal. 1 : 16 ; (*h*) thoughts before hidden in the heart, Luke 2 : 35 ; referring to the future, (*i*) the coming in glory of the Lord Jesus, Luke 17 : 30 ; (*j*) the salvation and glory that await the believer, Rom. 8 : 18 ; 1 Pet. 1 : 5 ; 5 : 1 ; (*k*) the true value of service, 1 Cor. 3 : 13 ; (*l*) the wrath of God (at the Cross, against sin, and, at the revelation of the Lord Jesus, against the sinner), Rom. 1 : 18 ; (*m*) the Lawless One, 2 Thess. 2 : 3, 6, 8."* ¶

5537 AG:885C 2. CHRĒMATIZŌ (χρηματίζω), to give Divine admonition, instruction,
CB:1240A revelation, is translated " it had been revealed," in Luke 2 : 26. See ADMONITION, B, No. 3, CALL.

REVELATION

602 AG:92B APOKALUPSIS (ἀποκάλυψις), an uncovering (akin to *apokaluptō ;*
CB:1236C see above), " is used in the N.T. of (*a*) the drawing away by Christ of the veil of darkness covering the Gentiles, Luke 2 : 32 ; cp. Isa. 25 : 7 ; (*b*) ' the mystery,' the purpose of God in this age, Rom. 16 : 25 ; Eph. 3 : 3 ; (*c*) the communication of the knowledge of God to the soul, Eph. 1 : 17 ; (*d*) an expression of the mind of God for the instruction of the church, 1 Cor. 14 : 6, 26, for the instruction of the Apostle Paul, 2 Cor. 12 : 1, 7 ; Gal. 1 : 12, and for his guidance, Gal. 2 : 2 ; (*e*) the Lord Jesus Christ, to the saints at His Parousia, 1 Cor. 1 : 7, R.V. (A.V., ' coming ') ; 1 Pet. 1 : 7, R.V. (A.V., ' appearing '), 13 ; 4 : 13 ; (*f*) the

---

* From Notes on Galatians by Hogg and Vine, pp. 41, 42.

Lord Jesus Christ when He comes to dispense the judgments of God, 2 Thess. 1 : 7 ; cp. Rom. 2 : 5 ; (*g*) the saints, to the creation, in association with Christ in His glorious reign, Rom. 8 : 19, R.V., 'revealing' (A.V., 'manifestation') ; (*h*) the symbolic forecast of the final judgments of God, Rev. 1 : 1 (hence the Greek title of the book, transliterated 'Apocalypse' and translated 'Revelation')."* See APPEARING, COMING, LIGHTEN, B, Note, MANIFESTATION.¶

REVEL, REVELLING

1. TRUPHĒ (τρυφή), luxuriousness, daintiness, revelling, is translated 5172 AG:828D
freely by the verb "to revel" in 2 Pet. 2 : 13, R.V. (A.V., "to riot"), lit., CB:—
'counting revelling in the daytime a pleasure.' In Luke 7 : 25 it is used
with *en*, in, and translated "delicately." See DELICATELY, RIOT.¶

2. KŌMOS (κῶμος), a revel, carousal, the concomitant and conse- 2970
quence of drunkenness, is used in the plural, Rom. 13 : 13, translated by AG:461D CB:1255C
the singular, R.V., "revelling" (A.V., "rioting") ; Gal. 5 : 21 and 1
Pet. 4 : 3, "revellings." See RIOT.¶

Note : For *entruphaō*, 2 Pet. 2 : 13, R.V., "to revel," see SPORTING. 1792 AG:270A CB:—

For REVENGE and REVENGER see AVENGE and AVENGER

REVERENCE (Noun and Verb)

A. Verbs.

1. ENTREPŌ (ἐντρέπω), lit., to turn in (i.e., upon oneself), to put to 1788 AG:269D
shame, denotes, when used in the Passive Voice, to feel respect for, to show CB:—
deference to, to reverence, Matt. 21 : 37 ; Mark 12 : 6 ; Luke 20 : 13 ;
Heb. 12 : 9. See ASHAMED, A, No. 4, REGARD.

2. PHOBEŌ (φοβέω), to fear, is used in the Passive Voice in the 5399
N.T. ; in Eph. 5 : 33 of reverential fear on the part of a wife for a husband, AG:862B CB:1264B
A.V., "reverence" (R.V., "fear"). See FEAR, D, No. 1.

B. Noun.

2124 AG:321D
EULABEIA (εὐλάβεια), caution, reverence, is translated "reverence" CB:1247B
in Heb. 12 : 28 (1st part in the best mss ; some have *aidōs*). See FEAR. AIDōS 127 AG:22B CB:1233C

REVERENT

HIEROPREPĒS (ἱεροπρεπής), suited to a sacred character, reverend 2412
(*hieros*, sacred, *prepō*, to be fitting), is translated "reverent" in Tit. AG:372D CB:1250B
2 : 3, R.V. (A.V., "as becometh holiness"). See BECOME, B.¶

REVILE, REVILING, REVILER

A. Verbs.

1. LOIDOREŌ (λοιδορέω) denotes to abuse, revile, John 9 : 28 ; Acts 3058 AG:479C
23 : 4 ; 1 Cor. 4 : 12 ; 1 Pet. 2 : 23 (1st clause).¶ CB:1257A

---

* From Notes on Thessalonians by Hogg and Vine, pp. 228, 229.

3679 AG:570A CB:1260C 2. ONEIDIZŌ (ὀνειδίζω), to reproach, upbraid, is translated to revile in Matt. 5 : 11, A.V., and Mark 15 : 32 (R.V., "reproach"). See REPROACH.

987 AG:142C CB:1239A 3. BLASPHĒMEŌ (βλασφημέω), to speak profanely, rail at, is translated "reviled" in Matt. 27 : 39, A.V. (R.V., "railed on"); Luke 22 : 65, R.V., "reviling" (A.V., "blasphemously").

486 AG:75A CB:1236A 4. ANTILOIDOREŌ (ἀντιλοιδορέω), to revile back or again (*anti*, and No. 1), is found in 1 Pet. 2 : 23 (2nd clause).¶

1908 AG:285D CB:— *Note:* For *epēreazō*, 1 Pet. 3 : 16, R.V., "revile," see ACCUSE, B, No. 3.

B. Adjective.

3060 AG:479C CB:1257B LOIDOROS (λοίδορος), akin to A, No. 1, abusive, railing, reviling, is used as a noun, 1 Cor. 5 : 11, R.V., "a reviler" (A.V. "a railer"); 6 : 10, "revilers."¶ In the Sept., Prov. 25 : 24; 26 : 21; 27 : 15.¶

C. Noun.

3059 AG:479C CB:1257A LOIDORIA (λοιδορία), akin to A, No. 1, and B, abuse, railing, is used in 1 Tim. 5 : 14, R.V., "for (*charin*, for the sake of) reviling" (A.V., "to speak reproachfully"—a paraphrase); 1 Pet. 3 : 9 (twice), R.V., "reviling" (A.V., "railing"). See RAIL, B.¶

REVIVE

330 AG:54A CB:— 1. ANATHALLŌ (ἀναθάλλω), to flourish anew (*ana*, again, anew, *thallō*, to flourish or blossom), hence, to revive, is used metaphorically in Phil. 4 : 10, R.V., "ye have revived (your thought for me)," A.V., "(your care of me) hath flourished again."¶ In the Sept., Psa. 28 : 7; Ezek. 17 : 24; Hos. 8 : 9.¶

326 AG:53D CB:1235B 2. ANAZAŌ (ἀναζάω), to live again (*ana*, and *zaō*, to live), to regain life, is used of moral revival, Luke 15 : 24, "is alive again;" (*b*) of sin, Rom. 7 : 9, "revived," lit., 'lived again' i.e., it sprang into activity, manifesting the evil inherent in it; here sin is personified, by way of contrast to the man himself. Some mss. have it in Rom. 14 : 9, for *zaō*, as in the R.V., which italicises "*again*."¶

REWARD (Noun and Verb)

MISTHOS

A. Noun.

3408 AG:523B CB:1259A MISTHOS (μισθός), primarily wages, hire, and then, generally, reward, (*a*) received in this life, Matt. 5 : 46; 6 : 2, 5, 16; Rom. 4 : 4; 1 Cor. 9 : 17, 18; of evil rewards, Acts 1 : 18; see also HIRE; (*b*) to be received hereafter, Matt. 5 : 12; 10 : 41 (twice), 42; Mark 9 : 41; Luke 6 : 23, 35; 1 Cor. 3 : 8, 14; 2 John 8; Rev. 11 : 18; 22 : 12. See WAGES.

AXIOS 514 AG:78A CB:1238B ANTAPODOSIS 469 AG:73A CB:1236A KATABRABEUŌ 2603 AG:409B CB:1254A *Notes:* (1) In Luke 23 : 41, *axios*, worthy, befitting, used in the plur., is rendered "the due reward," lit., 'things worthy.' (2) For *antapodosis*, rendered "reward" in Col. 3 : 24, A.V., see RECOMPENSE. (3) For *katabrabeuō*, to rob of a reward, Col. 2 : 18, see BEGUILE, Note, and ROB.

B. Verb.

APODIDŌMI (ἀποδίδωμι), to give back, is nowhere translated to 591
reward in the R.V.; A.V., Matt. 6 : 4, 6, 18 (see RECOMPENSE, B, No. 2); AG:90B
Matt. 16 : 27; 2 Tim. 4 : 14; Rev. 18 : 6 (see RENDER). CB:1236C

REWARDER

MISTHAPODOTĒS (μισθαποδότης), one who pays wages (*misthos*, 3406
wages, *apo*, back, *didōmi*, to give), is used by metonymy in Heb. 11 : 6, AG:523A
of God, as the "Rewarder" of those who "seek after Him" (R.V.).¶ CB:1259A
Cp. *misthapodosia*, recompence.

RICH, RICHES, RICHLY, RICH MAN

A. Adjective.

PLOUSIOS (πλούσιος), akin to B, C, No. 1, rich, wealthy, is used 4145
(I) literally, (*a*) adjectivally (with a noun expressed separately) in Matt. AG:673C
27 : 57; Luke 12 : 16; 14 : 12; 16 : 1, 19; (without a noun), 18 : 23; 19 : 2; CB:1265B
(*b*) as a noun, singular, a rich man (the noun not being expressed), Matt. 19 : 23, 24; Mark 10 : 25; 12 : 41; Luke 16 : 21, 22; 18 : 25; Jas. 1 : 10, 11, "the rich," "the rich (man);" plural, Mark 12 : 41, lit., 'rich (ones);' Luke 6 : 24 (ditto); 21 : 1; 1 Tim. 6 : 17, "(them that are) rich," lit., '(the) rich;' Jas. 2 : 6, R.V., "the rich;" 5 : 1, R.V., "ye rich;" Rev. 6 : 15 and 13 : 16, R.V., "the rich;" (II) metaphorically, of God, Eph. 2 : 4 ("in mercy"); of Christ, 2 Cor. 8 : 9; of believers, Jas. 2 : 5, R.V., "(*to be*) rich (in faith);" Rev. 2 : 9, of spiritual enrichment generally; 3 : 17, of a false sense of enrichment.¶

B. Verbs.

1. PLOUTEŌ (πλουτέω), to be rich, in the aorist or point tense, to 4147
become rich, is used (*a*) literally, Luke 1 : 53, "the rich," present parti- AG:673D
ciple, lit., '(ones or those) being rich;' 1 Tim. 6 : 9, 18; Rev. 18 : 3, CB:1265B
15, 19 (all three in the aorist tense); (*b*) metaphorically, of Christ, Rom. 10 : 12 (the passage stresses the fact that Christ is Lord; see ver. 9, and the R.V.); of the enrichment of believers through His poverty, 2 Cor. 8 : 9 (the aorist tense expressing completeness, with permanent results); so in Rev. 3 : 18, where the spiritual enrichment is conditional upon righteousness of life and conduct (see GOLD, No. 2); of a false sense of enrichment, 1 Cor. 4 : 8 (aorist), R.V., "ye are become rich" (A.V., "ye are rich"); Rev. 3 : 17 (perfect tense, R.V., "I . . . have gotten riches," A.V., "I am . . . increased with goods"), see GOODS, Note (3); of not being rich toward God, Luke 12 : 21.¶

2. PLOUTIZŌ (πλουτίζω), to make rich, enrich, is rendered "making 4148
(many) rich" in 2 Cor. 6 : 10 (metaphorical of enriching spiritually). AG:674A
See ENRICH. CB:1265B

C. Nouns.

1. PLOUTOS (πλοῦτος) is used in the singular (I) of material riches, 4149
used evilly, Matt. 13 : 22; Mark 4 : 19; Luke 8 : 14; 1 Tim. 6 : 17; AG:674B
Jas. 5 : 2; Rev. 18 : 17; (II) of spiritual and moral riches, (*a*) possessed CB:1265B

by God and exercised towards men, Rom. 2 : 4, "of His goodness and forbearance and longsuffering ;" 9 : 23 and Eph. 3 : 16, "of His glory" (i.e., of its manifestation in grace towards believers) ; Rom. 11 : 33, of His wisdom and knowledge ; Eph. 1 : 7 and 2 : 7, "of His grace ;" 1 : 18, "of the glory of His inheritance in the saints ;" 3 : 8, "of Christ ;" Phil. 4 : 19, "in glory in Christ Jesus," R.V. ; Col. 1 : 27, "of the glory of this mystery . . . Christ in you, the hope of glory ;" (*b*) to be ascribed to Christ, Rev. 5 : 12 ; (*c*) of the effects of the gospel upon the Gentiles, Rom. 11 : 12 (twice) ; (*d*) of the full assurance of understanding in regard to the mystery of God, even Christ, Col. 2 : 2, R.V. ; (*e*) of the liberality of the churches of Macedonia, 2 Cor. 8 : 2 (where "the riches" stands for the spiritual and moral value of their liberality) ; (*f*) of "the reproach of Christ" in contrast to this world's treasures, Heb. 11 : 26.¶

5536 AG:885C CB:1240A 2. CHRĒMA (χρῆμα), what one uses or needs (*chraomai*, to use), a matter, business, hence denotes riches, Mark 10 : 23, 24 ; Luke 18 : 24 ; see MONEY, No. 2.

D. Adverb.

4146 AG:673D CB:1265B PLOUSIŌS (πλουσίως), richly, abundantly, akin to A, is used in Col. 3 : 16 ; 1 Tim. 6 : 17 ; Tit. 3 : 6, R.V., "richly" (A.V., "abundantly") ; 2 Pet. 1 : 11 (ditto).¶

RID See CAST OUT, PUT AWAY

For RID see CARE, A, No. 1, Note

RIDE

1910 AG:289D CB:— EPIBAINŌ (ἐπιβαίνω), to go upon (*epi*, upon, *bainō*, to go), is used of Christ's riding into Jerusalem, Matt. 21 : 5, R.V., "riding" (A.V., "sitting"). See COME, No. 16.

RIDICULE See MOCK

RIGHT (opp. to left), RIGHT HAND, RIGHT SIDE

1188 AG:174C CB:1241A DEXIOS (δεξιός), an adjective, used (*a*) of the right as opposite to the left, e.g., Matt. 5 : 29, 30 ; Rev. 10 : 5, R.V., "right hand ;" in connection with armour (figuratively), 2 Cor. 6 : 7 ; with *en*, followed by the dative plural, Mark 16 : 5 ; with *ek*, and the genitive plural, e.g., Matt. 25 : 33, 34 ; Luke 1 : 11 ; (*b*) of giving the right hand of fellowship, Gal. 2 : 9, betokening the public expression of approval by leaders at Jerusalem of the course pursued by Paul and Barnabas among the Gentiles ; the act was often the sign of a pledge, e.g., 2 Kings 10 : 15 ; 1 Chron. 29 : 24, marg. ; Ezra 10 : 19 ; Ezek. 17 : 18 ; figuratively Lam. 5 : 6 ; it is often so used in the papyri ; (*c*) metaphorically of power or authority, Acts 2 : 33 ; with *ek*, signifying "on," followed by the genitive plural, Matt. 26 : 64 ; Mark 14 : 62 ; Heb. 1 : 13 ; (*d*) similarly of a place of honour in the Messianic Kingdom, Matt. 20 : 21 ; Mark 10 : 37.

RIGHT (not wrong—Noun and Adjective), RIGHTLY

A. Noun.

1849 AG:277D CB:1247C EXOUSIA (ἐξουσία), authority power, is translated "right" in the

R.V., for A.V., "power," in John 1 : 12 ; Rom. 9 : 21 ; 1 Cor. 9 : 4, 5, 6, 12 (twice), 18 ; 2 Thess. 3 : 9, where the right is that of being maintained by those among whom the ministers of the gospel had laboured, a right possessed in virtue of the 'authority' given them by Christ, Heb. 13 : 10 ; Rev. 22 : 14.

Exousia first denotes freedom to act and then authority for the action. This is first true of God, Acts 1 : 7. It was exercised by the Son of God, as from, and in conjunction with, the Father when the Lord was upon earth, in the days of His flesh, Matt. 9 : 6 ; John 10 : 18, as well as in resurrection, Matt. 28 : 18 ; John 17 : 2. All others hold their freedom to act from God (though some of them have abused it), whether angels, Eph. 1 : 21, or human potentates, Rom. 13 : 1. Satan offered to delegate his authority over earthly kingdoms to Christ, Luke 4 : 6, who, though conscious of His right to it, refused, awaiting the Divinely appointed time. See AUTHORITY, No. 1, and for various synonyms see DOMINION, No. 1, Note.

B. Adjectives.

1. DIKAIOS (δίκαιος), just, righteous, that which is in accordance with **1342**
dikē, rule, right, justice, is translated "right" in Matt. 20 : 4 ; ver. 7, **AG:195C CB:1241C**
A.V. only (R.V. omits, according to the most authentic mss., the clause having been inserted from ver. 4, to the detriment of the narrative) ; Luke 12 : 57 ; Acts 4 : 19 ; Eph. 6 : 1 ; Phil. 1 : 7, R.V. (A.V., "meet") ; 2 Pet. 1 : 13 (A.V., "meet"). See JUST, RIGHTEOUS.

2. EUTHUS (εὐθύς), straight, hence, metaphorically, right, is so **2117**
rendered in Acts 8 : 21, of the heart ; 13 : 10, of the ways of the Lord ; **AG:321A CB:1247B**
2 Pet. 2 : 15. See STRAIGHT.

C. Adverb.

ORTHŌS (ὀρθῶς), rightly (akin to *orthos*, straight, direct), is translated **3723**
"plain" in Mark 7 : 35 ; in Luke 7 : 43 and 20 : 21, "rightly ;" in Luke **AG:580D CB:1261B**
10 : 28, "right."¶

Notes : (1) For "right mind" see MIND, B, No. 5. (2) For the A.V., "rightly" in 2 Tim. 2 : 15, see DIVIDE, A, No. 8.

RIGHTEOUS, RIGHTEOUSLY

A. Adjective.

DIKAIOS (δίκαιος) signifies 'just,' without prejudice or partiality, **1342**
e.g., of the judgment of God, 2 Thess. 1 : 5, 6 ; of His judgments, Rev. **AG:195C CB:1241C**
16 : 7 ; 19 : 2 ; of His character as Judge, 2 Tim. 4 : 8 ; Rev. 16 : 5 ; of His ways and doings, Rev. 15 : 3. See further under JUST, A, No. 1, RIGHT, B, No. 1.

In the following the R.V. substitutes "righteous" for the A.V. "just ;" Matt. 1 : 19 ; 13 : 49 ; 27 : 19, 24 ; Mark 6 : 20 ; Luke 2 : 25 ; 15 : 7 ; 20 : 20 ; 23 : 50 ; John 5 : 30 ; Acts 3 : 14 ; 7 : 52 ; 10 : 22 ; 22 : 14 ; Rom. 1 : 17 ; 7 : 12 ; Gal. 3 : 11 ; Heb. 10 : 38 ; Jas. 5 : 6 ; 1 Pet. 3 : 18 ; 2 Pet. 2 : 7 ; 1 John 1 : 9 ; Rev. 15 : 3.

B. Adverb.

1346 AG:198B CB:1241C DIKAIŌS (δικαίως) is translated "righteously" in 1 Cor. 15 : 34, R.V., "(awake up) righteously," A.V., "(awake to) righteousness;" 1 Thess. 2 : 10, R.V. (A.V., "justly"); Tit. 2 : 12; 1 Pet. 2 : 23. See JUSTLY.

DIKAIOō 1344 AG:197C CB:1241C DIKAIOKRISIA 1341 AG:195C CB:1241C *Notes:* (1) In Rev. 22 : 11 the best texts have *dikaiosunē*, righteousness, with *poieō*, to do, R.V., "let him do righteousness;" the A.V. follows those which have the Passive Voice of *dikaioō* and renders it "let him be righteous," lit., 'let him be made righteous.' (2) *Dikaiokrisia*, "righteous judgment" (*dikaios*, and *krisis*), occurs in Rom. 2 : 5.¶

RIGHTEOUSNESS

1343 AG:196B CB:1241C 1. DIKAIOSUNĒ (δικαιοσύνη) is the character or quality of being right or just; it was formerly spelled 'rightwiseness,' which clearly expresses the meaning. It is used to denote an attribute of God, e.g., Rom. 3 : 5, the context of which shews that "the righteousness of God" means essentially the same as His faithfulness, or truthfulness, that which is consistent with His own nature and promises; Rom. 3 : 25, 26 speaks of His righteousness as exhibited in the Death of Christ, which is sufficient to shew men that God is neither indifferent to sin nor regards it lightly. On the contrary, it demonstrates that quality of holiness in Him which must find expression in His condemnation of sin.

"*Dikaiosunē* is found in the sayings of the Lord Jesus, (*a*) of whatever is right or just in itself, whatever conforms to the revealed will of God, Matt. 5 : 6, 10, 20; John 16 : 8, 10; (*b*) whatever has been appointed by God to be acknowledged and obeyed by man, Matt. 3 : 15; 21 : 32; (*c*) the sum total of the requirements of God, Matt. 6 : 33; (*d*) religious duties, Matt. 6 : 1 (distinguished as almsgiving, man's duty to his neighbour, vv. 2–4, prayer, his duty to God, vv. 5–15, fasting, the duty of self-control, vv. 16–18).

"In the preaching of the Apostles recorded in Acts the word has the same general meaning. So also in Jas. 1 : 20; 3 : 18, in both Epp. of Peter, 1st John and the Revelation. In 2 Pet. 1 : 1, 'the righteousness of our God and Saviour Jesus Christ,' is the righteous dealing of God with sin and with sinners on the ground of the Death of Christ. 'Word of righteousness,' Heb. 5 : 13, is probably the gospel, and the Scriptures as containing the gospel, wherein is declared the righteousness of God in all its aspects.

"This meaning of *dikaiosunē*, right action, is frequent also in Paul's writings, as in all five of its occurrences in Rom. 6; Eph. 6 : 14, etc. But for the most part he uses it of that gracious gift of God to men whereby all who believe on the Lord Jesus Christ are brought into right relationship with God. This righteousness is unattainable by obedience to any law, or by any merit of man's own, or any other condition than that of faith in Christ. . . . The man who trusts in Christ becomes 'the righteousness of

God in Him,' 2 Cor. 5 : 21, i.e., becomes in Christ all that God requires a man to be, all that he could never be in himself. Because Abraham accepted the Word of God, making it his own by that act of the mind and spirit which is called faith, and, as the sequel showed, submitting himself to its control, therefore God accepted him as one who fulfilled the whole of His requirements, Rom. 4 : 3. . . .

" Righteousness is not said to be imputed to the believer save in the sense that faith is imputed (' reckoned ' is the better word) for righteousness. It is clear that in Rom. 4 : 6, 11, ' righteousness reckoned ' must be understood in the light of the context, ' faith reckoned for righteousness,' vv. 3, 5, 9, 22. ' For ' in these places is *eis*, which does not mean ' instead of,' but ' with a view to.' The faith thus exercised brings the soul into vital union with God in Christ, and inevitably produces righteousness of life, that is, conformity to the will of God."*

2. DIKAIŌMA (δικαίωμα) is the concrete expression of righteousness : 1345 AG:198A
see JUSTIFICATION, A, No. 2. CB:1241C

Note : In Heb. 1 : 8, A.V., *euthutēs*, straightness, uprightness (akin to 2118
euthus, straight, right), is translated " righteousness " (R.V., " upright- AG:321B CB:—
ness ; " A.V., marg., " rightness, or straightness ").

RING

1146 AG:170A
DAKTULIOS (δακτύλιος), a finger-ring, occurs in Luke 15 : 22.¶ CB:1240B

Note : Chrusodaktulios, an adjective signifying " with a gold ring," 5554
a gold-ringed (person), from *chrusos*, gold, and *daktulos*, a finger, occurs AG:888C CB:—
in Jas. 2 : 2.¶

RINGLEADER

PRŌTOSTATĒS (πρωτοστάτης), one who stands first (*prōtos*, first, 4414
histēmi, to cause to stand), was used of soldiers, one who stands in the AG:726C CB:1267B
front rank ; hence, metaphorically, a leader, Acts 24 : 5.¶

RIOT, RIOTING, RIOTOUS, RIOTOUSLY

A. Nouns.

1. ASŌTIA (ἀσωτία), prodigality, a wastefulness, profligacy (*a*, 810
negative, *sōzō*, to save), is rendered " riot " in Eph. 5 : 18, R.V. (A.V., AG:119C CB:—
" excess ") ; Tit. 1 : 6 and 1 Pet. 4 : 4 (A.V. and R.V., " riot "). The
corresponding verb is found in a papyrus writing, telling of ' riotous living ' ASELGEIA 766
(like the adverb *asōtōs*, see B).¶ In the Sept., Prov. 28 : 7.¶ Cp. the AG:114D
synonymous word *aselgeia* (under LASCIVIOUSNESS). CB:1238A

2. KŌMOS (κῶμος), a revel, is rendered " rioting " in Rom. 13 : 13, 2970 AG:461D
A.V. ; see REVEL. CB:1255C

3. TRUPHĒ (τρυφή), luxuriousness, is rendered " riot " in 2 Pet. 5172 AG:828D
2 : 13, A.V. ; see DELICATELY, REVEL. CB:—

4. STASIS (στάσις), primarily a standing (akin to *histēmi*, to cause to 4714 AG:764C CB:1270A

* From Notes on Galatians by Hogg and Vine, pp. 246, 247.

ASōTōS 811 stand), then an insurrection, is translated "riot" in Acts 19 : 40, R.V.
AG:119C CB:1238A (A.V., "uproar"). See DISSENSION, INSURRECTION, SEDITION, UPROAR.
EKCHUNō

B. Adverb.

1632 AG:247B ASŌTŌS (ἀσώτως), wastefully (akin to A, No. 1), is translated "with
(EKCHEō) riotous living" in Luke 15 : 13; though the word does not necessarily
CB:1243B AKMAZō signify 'dissolutely,' the parable narrative makes clear that this is the
187 meaning here.¶ In the Sept., Prov. 7 : 11.¶

AG:30D CB:1234B *Note:* The verb *ekchunō*, a Hellenistic form of *ekcheō* (though the form
XēRAINō actually used is the regular classical aorist passive of *ekcheō*), to pour out,
3583 AG:548C shed, is translated "ran riotously" in Jude 11, R.V. (A.V., "ran
CB:1273B greedily"); see POUR, SHED.

PARADIDōMI 3860 AG:614B

RIPE (to be fully)

CB:1262A 1. AKMAZŌ (ἀκμάζω), to be at the prime (akin to *akmē*, a point),
ANISTēMI 450 to be ripe, is translated "are fully ripe" in Rev. 14 : 18.¶
AG:70A 2. XĒRAINŌ (ξηραίνω), to dry up, wither, is used of ripened crops in
EXANISTēMI 1817 Rev. 14 : 15, R.V., "over-ripe," A.V., "ripe" (marg., "dried"). See
AG:272D DRY, B, OVER-RIPE, WITHER.
CB:1247C (-HIS-) 3. PARADIDŌMI (παραδίδωμι), to give over, commit, deliver, etc.,
EGEIRō also signifies to permit; in Mark 4 : 29, of the ripe condition of corn,
1453 AG:214C R.V., and A.V. marg., "is ripe;" R.V. marg., "alloweth" (the nearest
CB:1242C rendering); A.V., "is brought forth."

ANABAINō 305

RISE, RISING

AG:50A *Notes:* (1) For the various verbs *anistēmi*, *exanistēmi*, *egeirō*, *anabainō*,
CB:1235A ANATELLō *anatellō*, *sunephistēmi*, see under ARISE. (2) For the A.V., "should rise"
393 in Acts 26 : 23, see RESURRECTION. (3) *Exanistēmi*, transitively, to raise
AG:62A CB:1235B up (*ek*, out, from, out of), is used intransitively in Acts 15 : 5, "there rose
SUNEPHISTēMI up," i.e., from the midst of a gathered company. See RAISE. (4) For
4911 AG:789A the A.V. and R.V. of *sunegeirō*, to raise together with, and in the Passive
SUNEGEIRō Voice in Col. 2 : 12; 3 : 1, see RAISE. (5) For the word "rising," which
4891 AG:785D is used to translate the verbs *anatellō* in Mark 16 : 2, and *anistēmi*, in
KATEPHISTEMI Mark 9 : 10, see under ARISE, Nos. 9 and 1 respectively. (6) For *katephis-*
2721 AG:422C *tēmi*, Acts 18 : 12, R.V., see INSURRECTION, B. (7) *Epanistamai*, to rise
(-AMAI) up against, occurs in Matt. 10 : 21; Mark 13 : 12.¶ (8) *Anastasis*, is
EPANISTAMAI 1881 rendered "rising up" in Luke 2 : 34, R.V.

AG:283A (-TēMI)

RIVER

ANASTASIS 386 POTAMOS (ποταμός) denotes (*a*) a stream, Luke 6 : 48, 49; (*b*) a
AG:60B CB:1235B flood or floods, Matt. 7 : 25, 27; (*c*) a river, natural, Matt. 3 : 6, R.V.;
POTAMOS Mark 1 : 5; Acts 16 : 13; 2 Cor. 11 : 26, R.V. (A.V., "waters"); Rev.
4215 8 : 10; 9 : 14; 16 : 4, 12; symbolical, Rev. 12 : 15 (1st part), R.V.,
AG:694D "river" (A.V., "flood"); so ver. 16; 22 : 1, 2 (cp. Gen. 2 : 10; Ezek. 47);
CB:1266B figuratively, John 7 : 38, the effects of the operation of the Holy Spirit in
POTAMOPHORēTOS 4216 and through the believer. See FLOOD, WATER.¶
AG:694D CB:1266A *Note:* For *potamophorētos* in Rev. 12 : 15, see FLOOD, B.

ROAR, ROARING

A. Verbs.

1. MUKAOMAI (μυκάομαι), properly of oxen, an onomatopœic word, 3455 AG:529B
to low, bellow, is used of a lion, Rev. 10 : 3.¶ CB:—

2. ŌRUOMAI (ὠρύομαι), to howl or roar, onomatopœic, of animals 5612 AG:897A
or men, is used of a lion, 1 Pet. 5 : 8, as a simile of Satan.¶ CB:—

B. Noun.

2279
ĒCHOS (ἦχος), a noise or sound (Eng., echo), is used of the roaring of AG:349D
the sea in Luke 21 : 25, in the best mss., " for the roaring (of the sea and CB:1242C
the billows)," R.V.; some mss. have the present participle of *ēcheō*, to ēCHEō 2278
sound, A.V., " (the sea and the waves) roaring." See RUMOUR, SOUND. AG:349C
CB:1242C

ROB

1. SULAŌ (συλάω), to plunder, spoil, is translated " I robbed " in 4813 AG:776C
2 Cor. 11 : 8.¶ Cp. *sulagōgeō*, to make spoil of, Col. 2 : 8.¶ CB:1270B

2. KATABRABEUŌ (καταβραβεύω), to give judgment against, to 2603 AG:409B
condemn (*kata*, against, and *brabeus*, an umpire; cp. *brabeion*, a prize in CB:1254A
the games, 1 Cor. 9 : 24; Phil. 3 : 14, and *brabeuō*, to act as an umpire, arbitrate, Col. 3 : 15), occurs in Col. 2 : 18, R.V., " let (no man) rob (you) of your prize " (A.V., " . . . beguile . . . of your reward "), said of false teachers who would frustrate the faithful adherence of the believers to the truth, causing them to lose their reward. Another rendering, closer to the proper meaning of the word, as given above, is ' let no man decide for or against you ' (i.e., without any notion of a prize); this suitably follows the word " judge " in ver. 16, i.e., ' do not give yourselves up to the judgment and decision of any man ' (A.V., marg., " judge against ").¶

ROBBER

1. LĒSTĒS (λῃστής), a robber, brigand (akin to *leia*, booty), one 3027 AG:473A
who plunders openly and by violence (in contrast to *kleptēs*, a thief, see CB:1256C
below), is always translated " robber " or " robbers " in the R.V., as the
A.V. in John 10 : 1, 8; 18 : 40; 2 Cor. 11 : 26; the A.V. has " thief " or
" thieves " in Matt. 21 : 13, and parallel passages; 26 : 55, and parallel KLEPTēS 2812
passages; 27 : 38, 44 and Mark 15 : 27; Luke 10 : 30, 36; but " thief " AG:434B
is the meaning of *kleptēs*. See THIEF. CB:1255B

2. HIEROSULOS (ἱερόσυλος), an adjective signifying robbing temples 2417 AG:373C
(*hieron*, a temple, and *sulaō*, to rob), is found in Acts 19 : 37.¶ Cp. CB:1250C
hierosuleō, to rob a temple, Rom. 2 : 22, A.V., " commit sacrilege."¶

For ROBBERY see PRIZE

ROBE

1. STOLĒ (στολή), for which see CLOTHING, No. 8, is translated 4749 AG:769C
" robe " in Mark 16 : 5, R.V. (A.V., " garment "); " long robes " in CB:1270A
Luke 20 : 46.

5511 AG:882B CB:— 2. CHLAMUS (χλαμύς), a cloak, is translated " robe " in Matt. 27 : 28, 31. See CLOTHING, Note (4).¶

2440 AG:376B CB:1250C 3. HIMATION (ἱμάτιον) is translated " robe " in the A.V. of John 19 : 2, 5 (R.V., " garment "). See APPAREL, No. 2, CLOTHING, No. 2, GARMENT.

2066 AG:312B CB:1246C 4. ESTHĒS (ἐσθής), apparel, is translated " robe " in Luke 23 : 11 (R.V., " apparel "). See APPAREL, No. 1.

ROCK

4073 AG:654A CB:1263C 1. PETRA (πέτρα) denotes a mass of rock, as distinct from *petros*, a detached stone or boulder, or a stone that might be thrown or easily moved. For the nature of *petra*, see Matt. 7 : 24, 25 ; 27 : 51, 60 ; Mark 15 : 46 ; Luke 6 : 48 (twice), a type of a sure foundation (here the true reading is as in the R.V., " because it had been well builded ") ; Rev. 6 : 15, 16 (cp. Is. 2 : 19, ff. ; Hos. 10 : 8) ; Luke 8 : 6, 13, used illustratively ; 1 Cor. 10 : 4 (twice), figuratively, of Christ ; in Rom. 9 : 33 and 1 Pet. 2 : 8, metaphorically, of Christ ; in Matt. 16 : 18, metaphorically, of Christ and the testimony concerning Him ; here the distinction between *petra*, concerning the Lord Himself, and *Petros*, the Apostle, is clear (see above).¶

4694 AG:762C CB:— 2. SPILAS (σπιλάς), a rock or reef, over which the sea dashes, is used in Jude 12, " hidden rocks," R.V., metaphorical of men whose conduct is a danger to others.¶ A late meaning ascribed to it is that of " spots," (A.V.), but that rendering seems to have been influenced by the parallel passage in 2 Pet. 2 : 13, where *spiloi*, " spots," occurs.

ROCKY

4075 AG:655C CB:1263C PETRŌDĒS (πετρώδης), rock-like (*petra*, a rock, *eidos*, a form, appearance), is used of rock underlying shallow soil, Matt. 13 : 5, 20, R.V., " the rocky places " (A.V., " stony places ") ; Mark 4 : 5, R.V., " the rocky ground " (A.V., " stony ground ") ; ver. 16, R.V., " rocky places " (A.V., " stony ground ").¶

TRACHUS 5138 AG:825A CB:1273A TOPOS 5117 AG:822B CB:1273A *Note :* In Acts 27 : 29, A.V., the phrase *tracheis topoi*, lit., ' rough places,' is translated " rocks " (R.V., " rocky ground ").

ROD

A. Noun.

4464 AG:733B CB:1268A RHABDOS (ῥάβδος), a staff, rod, sceptre, is used (*a*) of Aaron's rod, Heb. 9 : 4 ; (*b*) a staff used on a journey, Matt. 10 : 10, R.V., " staff " (A.V., " staves ") ; so Luke 9 : 3 ; Mark 6 : 8, " staff ; " Heb. 11 : 21, " staff ; " (*c*) a ruler's staff, a " sceptre," Heb. 1 : 8 (twice) ; elsewhere a rod, Rev. 2 : 27 ; 12 : 5 ; 19 : 15 ; (*d*) a rod for chastisement (figuratively), 1 Cor. 4 : 21 ; (*e*) a measuring rod, Rev. 11 : 1. See STAFF.¶

B. Verb.

4463 AG:733B CB:1268A RHABDIZŌ (ῥαβδίζω), to beat with a rod, is used in Acts 16 : 22, R.V., " to beat . . . with rods ; " 2 Cor. 11 : 25. The rods were those of the Roman lictors or "serjeants" (*rhabdouchoi*, lit., rod-bearers); the Roman beating with rods is distinct from the Jewish infliction of stripes.¶ In the Sept., Judg., 6 : 11; Ruth 2 : 17.¶ Cp. Matt. 26 : 67, R.V. marg.; John 18 : 22 (A.V. marg., and R.V. marg.); 19 : 3, R.V. marg.; see SMITE.

ROLL (Noun and Verb)

A. Verbs.

1. APOKULIŌ or APOKULIZŌ (ἀποκυλίω), to roll away (*apo*, from, 617
kuliō, to roll; cp. Eng., cylinder, etc.), is used of the sepulchre-stone, AG:94B CB:—
Matt. 28 : 2; Mark 16 : 3 (ver. 4 in some mss.; see No. 2); Luke 24 : 2.¶
In the Sept., Gen. 29 : 3, 8, 10.¶

2. ANAKULIŌ (ἀνακυλίω), to roll up or back (*ana*), is found in the —
best texts, in Mark 16 : 4 (see No. 1).¶ AG:56C CB:—

3. PROSKULIŌ (προσκυλίω), to roll up or to (*pros*), is used in Matt. 4351
27 : 60; Mark 15 : 46, of the sepulchre-stone.¶ AG:716C CB:—

4. HEILISSŌ, or HELISSŌ (ἑλίσσω), to roll, or roll up, is used (*a*) of 1507
the rolling up of a mantle, illustratively of the heavens, Heb. 1 : 12, R.V.; (HEL1667) AG:251B
(*b*) of the rolling up of a scroll, Rev. 6 : 14, illustratively of the removing of CB:—
the heaven.¶

5. ENTULISSŌ (ἐντυλίσσω), to wrap up, roll round or about, is trans- 1794
lated "rolled up" in John 20 : 7, R.V., of the cloth or "napkin" that had AG:270B CB:—
been wrapped around the head of the Lord before burial. Both the R.V. and the A.V., "wrapped together," might suggest that this cloth had been rolled or wrapped up and put in a certain part of the tomb at the Lord's resurrection, whereas, as with the body wrappings, the head cloth was lying as it had been rolled round His head, an evidence, to those who looked into the tomb, of the fact of His resurrection without any disturbance of the wrappings either by friend or foe or when the change took place. It is followed by *en*, in, and translated "wrapped" in Matt. 27 : 59, a meaning and construction which Moulton and Milligan illustrate from the papyri; in Luke 23 : 53 it is followed by the dative of the noun *sindōn*, linen cloth, used instrumentally. See WRAP.¶

B. Noun.

KEPHALIS (κεφαλίς), lit., a little head (a diminutive of *kephalē*, a 2777
head; Lat., *capitulum*, a diminutive of *caput*), hence, a capital of a column, AG:430C CB:1255A
then, a roll (of a book), occurs in Heb. 10 : 7, R.V., "in the roll" (A.V., "in the volume"), lit., 'in the heading of the scroll' (from Ps. 40 : 7).¶

ROMAN

RHŌMAIOS (Ῥωμαῖος) occurs in John 11 : 48; Acts 2 : 10, R.V., 4514
"from Rome" (A.V., "of Rome"); 16 : 21, 37, 38; 22 : 25, 26, 27, AG:738C CB:—
29; 23 : 27; 25 : 16; 28 : 17.¶ For a note on Roman citizenship see CITIZEN, No. 3.

ROOF

4721 AG:765D CB:— STEGĒ (στέγη), a covering (*stegō*, to cover), denotes a roof, Mark 2 : 4 ; said of entering a house, Matt. 8 : 8 ; Luke 7 : 6.¶

ROOM

A. Nouns.

5117 AG:822B CB:1273A 1. TOPOS (τόπος), a place, is translated "room" in Luke 2 : 7 and 14 : 22, i.e., place ; in the A.V. in Luke 14 : 9, 10, R.V., "place" (of a couch at a feast) ; of a position or condition which a person occupies, 1 Cor. 14 : 16 (R.V., "place"). See OPPORTUNITY, PLACE.

4411 AG:725B CB:1267B 2. PRŌTOKLISIA (πρωτοκλισία), the chief reclining place at table, is rendered "uppermost rooms," in Matt. 23 : 6, A.V. (R.V., "chief place") ; in Mark 12 : 39, "uppermost rooms," A.V. (R.V., "chief places") ; in Luke 14 : 7, "chief rooms," A.V. (R.V., "chief seats") ; in ver. 8, A.V., "highest room" (R.V., "chief seat") ; in 20 : 46, A.V., "highest seats" (R.V., "chief seats"). See CHIEF, B, No. 7, PLACE, No. 5.¶

508 AG:51B (ANAGAION) CB:— 3. ANAGAION or ANŌGEON (ἀνάγαιον), an upper room (*ana*, above, *gē*, ground), occurs in Mark 14 : 15 ; Luke 22 : 12, a chamber, often over a porch, or connected with the roof, where meals were taken and privacy obtained.¶

5253 AG:842B CB:— 4. HUPERǬON (ὑπερῷον), the neuter of the adjective *huperǭos*, upper (from *huper*, above), used as a noun, denoted in classical Greek an upper storey or room where the women resided ; in the Sept. and the N.T., an upper chamber, a roof-chamber, built on the flat roof of the house, Acts 1 : 13, R.V., "upper chamber" (A.V. "upper room") ; see CHAMBER, No. 2.

B. Verb.

5562 AG:889C CB:1240A CHŌREŌ (χωρέω), to make room, is translated "there was . . . room" in Mark 2 : 2. See CONTAIN, No. 1.

C. Preposition.

473 AG:73C CB:1236A ANTI (ἀντί), in place of, instead of, is translated "in the room of" in Matt. 2 : 22.

POU 4225 AG:696B CB:1266B DIADOCHOS 1240 AG:182D CB:— Notes : (1) In Luke 12 : 17, A.V., *pou*, anywhere or where, with a negative, is translated "no room" (R.V., "not where"). (2) In Acts 24 : 27, A.V., *diadochos*, a successor, with *lambanō*, to receive, is translated "came into (Felix') room," R.V., "(Felix) was succeeded by." *Diadochos* often meant a deputy, a temporary successor.¶

ROOSTER See COCK

ROOT

A. Noun.

4491 AG:736A CB:1268B RHIZA (ῥίζα) is used (*a*) in the natural sense, Matt. 3 : 10 ; 13 : 6, 21 ; Mark 4 : 6, 17 ; 11 : 20 ; Luke 3 : 9 ; 8 : 13 ; (*b*) metaphorically (1) of cause, origin, source, said of persons, ancestors, Rom. 11 : 16, 17, 18 (twice) ; of things, evils, 1 Tim. 6 : 10, R.V., of the love of money as a root of all "kinds of evil" (marg., "evils;" A.V., "evil"); bitterness, Heb. 12 : 15; (2) of that which springs from a root, a shoot, said of offspring, Rom. 15 : 12; Rev. 5 : 5; 22 : 16.¶

B. Verbs.

1. RHIZOŌ (ῥιζόω), to cause to take root, is used metaphorically in 4492
the Passive Voice in Eph. 3 : 17, of being rooted in love; Col. 2 : 7, in AG:736B CB:1268B
Christ, i.e., in the sense of being firmly planted, or established.¶ In the (-OMAI)
Sept., Is. 40 : 24; Jer. 12 : 2.¶

2. EKRIZOŌ (ἐκριζόω), to root out or up (*ek*, out, and No. 1), is rendered 1610
to root up in Matt. 13 : 29; 15 : 13; see PLUCK. AG:244D CB:1244A

ROPE

SCHOINION (σχοινίον), a diminutive of *schoinos*, a rush, is used of 4979
the small cords of which Christ made a scourge, John 2 : 15; of the ropes AG:797D CB:—
of a boat, Acts 27 : 32. See CORD.¶

For ROSE see RISE

ROUGH

1. SKLĒROS (σκληρός), hard, is translated "rough" in Jas. 3 : 4, 4642 AG:756A
R.V., of winds (A.V., "fierce"). See AUSTERE, FIERCE, Note (1). CB:1269A

2. TRACHUS (τραχύς), rough, uneven, is used of paths, Luke 3 : 5; 5138
of rocky places, Acts 27 : 29. See ROCKY.¶ AG:825A CB:1273A

ROUND, ROUND ABOUT

1. KUKLOTHEN (κυκλόθεν), from *kuklos*, a circle, ring (Eng., cycle, 2943
etc.), occurs in Rev. 4 : 3, 4; in ver. 8, R.V., "round about," with AG:456D CB:—
reference to the eyes.¶

2. PANTOTHEN (πάντοθεν), on all sides (from *pas*, all), is translated 3840 AG:608D
"round about" in Heb. 9 : 4. See EVERYWHERE, No. 3. CB:—

3. PERIX (πέριξ), from the preposition *peri*, around, occurs in Acts 4038 AG:648D
5 : 16, "round about" (of cities).¶ CB:—

4. KUKLŌ (κύκλῳ), the dative case of the noun *kuklos*, a ring, is used 2944
as an adverb, and translated "round about" in Mark 3 : 34, A.V. (R.V., AG:456D CB:1256B
"round"); 6 : 6, 36; Luke 9 : 12; Rom. 15 : 19; Rev. 4 : 6; 7 : 11.¶ (-LOS)

Note: For combinations with other words see, e.g., COME, No. 38, COUNTRY, A, No. 6, A, No. 4, DWELL, No. 5, GO, No. 9, HEDGE, LOOK, A, No. 3, REGION, SHINE, STAND, B, No. 5.

ROUSE

EXUPNOS (ἔξυπνος), roused out of sleep (*ek*, out of, *hupnos*, sleep), 1853
occurs in Acts 16 : 27.¶ Cp. *exupnizō*, AWAKE, No. 4. AG:279B CB:—

ROW (Verb)

ELAUNŌ (ἐλαύνω), to drive, is used of rowing or sailing a boat, Mark 1643 AG:248C
6 : 48; John 6 : 19. See DRIVE. CB:—

ROYAL

934 AG:136A CB:1238C 1. BASILEIOS (βασίλειος), from *basileus*, a king, is used in 1 Pet. 2 : 9 of the priesthood consisting of all believers.¶ Cp. Luke 7 : 25, for which see COURT, No. 3. In the Sept., Ex. 19 : 6 ; 23 : 22 ; Deut. 3 : 10¶.

937 AG:136D CB:1238C 2. BASILIKOS (βασιλικός), belonging to a king, is translated " royal " in Acts 12 : 21 ; Jas. 2 : 8. See KING B, No. 2 NOBLEMAN.

RUB

5597 AG:894D CB:— PSŌCHŌ (ψώχω), to rub, to rub to pieces, is used in Luke 6 : 1.¶

RUDDER

4079 AG:656A CB:— PĒDALION (πηδάλιον), a rudder (akin to *pēdos*, the blade of an oar), occurs in Jas. 3 : 4, R.V., " rudder " (A.V., " helm "), and Acts 27 : 40, plural, R.V.," (the bands of) the rudders," A.V., " the rudder (bands)."¶

The *pēdalia* were actually steering-paddles, two of which were used as rudders in ancient ships.

RUDE

2399 AG:370C CB:1252C IDIŌTĒS (ἰδιώτης), for which see IGNORANT, No. 4, is translated " rude " in 2 Cor. 11 : 6.

RUDIMENTS

4747 AG:768D CB:1270A STOICHEION (στοιχεῖον), one of a row or series, is translated " rudiments " in the R.V. of Gal. 4 : 3, 9 ; Heb. 5 : 12, and the A.V. and R.V. of Col. 2 : 8, 20. See ELEMENTS.

RUE

4076 AG:655D CB:1263A PĒGANON (πήγανον), a shrubby plant with yellow flowers and a heavy smell, cultivated for medicinal purposes, is mentioned in Luke 11 : 42.¶

RUIN

4485 AG:735A CB:— 1. RHĒGMA (ῥῆγμα), akin to *rhēgnumi*, to break, denotes a cleavage, fracture (so in the Sept., e.g., 1 Kings 11 : 30, 31) ; by metonymy, that which is broken, a ruin, Luke 6 : 49.¶

(KATASTREPHō) 2690 AG:419A CB:— 2. KATESTRAMMENA (κατεστραμμένα), the neuter plural, perfect participle, Passive, of *katastrephō*, to overturn, is translated " ruins " in Acts 15 : 16 ; cp. DIG, No. 3. See OVERTHROW.

RULE (Noun and Verb)

A. Nouns.

746 AG:111D CB:1237B 1. ARCHĒ (ἀρχή), a beginning etc., denotes rule, Luke 20 : 20, R.V., " rule " (A.V., " power ") ; 1 Cor. 15 : 24 ; Eph. 1 : 21, R.V., " rule " (A.V., " principality "). See BEGINNING, B.

2583 AG:403A CB:1253B 2. KANŌN (κανών) is translated " rule " in the A.V. of 2 Cor. 10 : 13, 15 ; in Gal. 6 : 16, A.V. and R.V. ; in Phil. 3 : 16, A.V. (R.V., in italics) : see PROVINCE, No. 2.

B. Verbs.

1. ARCHŌ (ἄρχω), (akin to A, No. 1), in the Active Voice denotes 757
to rule, Mark 10 : 42 and Rom. 15 : 12, R.V., " to rule " (A.V., " to AG:113C CB:1237B
reign "). See BEGIN, A, No. 1.

2. OIKODESPOTEŌ (οἰκοδεσποτέω), from *oikos*, a house, and *despotēs*, 3616
a master, signifies to rule the household ; so the R.V. in 1 Tim. 5 : 14 AG:558A CB:1260B
(A.V., " guide the house "). See GUIDE, B, Note (1).¶ Cp. *oikodespotēs*,
a householder.

3. PROISTĒMI (προΐστημι), lit., ' to stand before,' hence, to lead, 4291
attend to (indicating care and diligence), is translated to rule (Middle AG:707A CB:—
Voice), with reference to a local church, in Rom. 12 : 8 ; perfect Active
in 1 Tim. 5 : 17 ; with reference to a family, 1 Tim. 3 : 4 and 12 (Middle
Voice) ; ver. 5 (2nd aorist, Active). See MAINTAIN.

4. HĒGEOMAI (ἡγέομαι), to lead, is translated to rule in Heb. 2233 AG:343C
13 : 7, 17, 24 (A.V. marg., in the first two, " are the guides " and " guide." CB:1249C

5. POIMAINO (ποιμαίνω), to act as a shepherd, tend flocks, is trans- 4165
lated to rule in Rev. 2 : 27 ; 12 : 5 ; 19 : 15, all indicating that the AG:683D CB:1265C
governing power exercised by the Shepherd is to be of a firm character ;
in Matt. 2 : 6, A.V., " shall rule " (R.V., " shall be shepherd of "). See
FEED.

6. BRABEUŌ (βραβεύω), properly, to act as an umpire (*brabeus*), 1018
hence, generally, to arbitrate, decide, Col. 3 : 15, " rule " (R.V., marg., AG:146D CB:1239B
" arbitrate "), representing " the peace of Christ " (R.V.) as deciding
all matters in the hearts of believers ; some regard the meaning as that of
simply directing, controlling, ruling.¶ Cp. *katabrabeuō* ; see ROB.

RULER

1. ARCHŌN (ἄρχων), a ruler, chief, prince, is translated " rulers," 758
e.g., in 1 Cor. 2 : 6, 8, R.V. (A.V., " princes ") ; " ruler," Rev. 1 : 5 (A.V., AG:113D CB:1237B
" prince "). See MAGISTRATE, PRINCE, No. 2.

2. ARCHĒ (ἀρχή), a rule, sovereignty, is rendered " rulers " in Luke 746 AG:111D
12 : 11, R.V. (A.V., " magistrates "). See BEGINNING. CB:1237B

3. KOSMOKRATŌR (κοσμοκράτωρ) denotes a ruler of this world 2888
(contrast *pantokratōr*, almighty). In Greek literature, in Orphic hymns, AG:445C CB:1255C
etc., and in Rabbinic writings, it signifies a ruler of the whole world,
a world-lord. In the N.T. it is used in Eph. 6 : 12, " the world-rulers
(of this darkness)," R.V., A.V., " the rulers (of the darkness) of this
world." The context (" not against flesh and blood ") shows that not
earthly potentates are indicated, but spirit powers, who, under the
permissive will of God, and in consequence of human sin, exercise Satanic
and therefore antagonistic authority over the world in its present condition of spiritual darkness and alienation from God. The suggested
rendering ' the rulers of this dark world ' is ambiguous and not phraseo-
logically requisite. Cp. John 12 : 31 ; 14 : 30 ; 16 : 11 ; 2 Cor. 4 : 4.¶ 4173 AG:686A

4. POLITARCHĒS (πολιτάρχης), a ruler of a city (*polis*, a city, *archō*, CB:1265C

to rule), a politarch, is used in Acts 17 : 6, 8, of the magistrates in Thessalonica, before whom the Jews, with a mob of market idlers, dragged Jason and other converts, under the charge of showing hospitality to Paul and Silas, and of treasonable designs against the Emperor. Thessalonica was a "free" city and the citizens could choose their own politarchs. The accuracy of Luke has been vindicated by the use of the term, for while classical authors use the terms *poliarchos* and *politarchos* of similar rulers, the form used by Luke is supported by inscriptions discovered at Thessalonica, one of which mentions Sosipater, Secundus, and Gaius among the politarchs, names occurring as those of Paul's companions. Prof. Burton of Chicago, in a paper on "The Politarchs," has recorded 17 inscriptions which attest their existence, thirteen of which belong to Macedonia and five presumably to Thessalonica itself, illustrating the influence of Rome in the municipal organization of the place.¶

755 5. ARCHITRIKLINOS (ἀρχιτρίκλινος) denotes the superintendent of
AG:113B CB:— a banquet, whose duty lay in arranging the tables and food (*archē*, ruler,
triklinos, lit., a room with three couches), John 2 : 8, 9.¶

HĒGEMŌN *Notes :* (1) In Mark 13 : 9 and Luke 21 : 12, A.V., *hēgemōn*, a leader,
2232 AG:343B a governor of a Province, is translated "ruler" (R.V., "governor").
CB:1249C See GOVERNOR, PRINCE, No. 3. (2) For ruler of the synagogue, see
KATHISTĒMI SYNAGOGUE. (3) In Matt. 24 : 45, A.V., *kathistēmi*, to appoint, is trans-
2525 AG:390B lated "hath made ruler" (R.V., "hath set"); so in ver. 47; 25 : 21, 23;
CB:1254C Luke 12 : 42, 44.

RUMOUR

189 1. AKOĒ (ἀκοή), a hearing, is translated "rumour" in Matt. 24 : 6;
AG:30D CB:1234B Mark 13 : 7. See HEARING, B, No. 1.
2279 2. ĒCHOS (ἦχος), a noise, sound, is translated "rumour" in Luke
AG:349D CB:1242C 4 : 37, R.V. (A.V., "fame"). See ROAR, SOUND.
3056 *Note :* In Luke 7 : 17, A.V., *logos*, a word, is translated "rumour"
AG:477A (R.V., "report").
CB:1257A

RUN, RAN

5143 1. TRECHŌ (τρέχω), to run, is used (*a*) literally, e.g., Matt. 27 : 48
AG:825D CB:1273A (*dramōn*, an aorist participle, from an obsolete verb *dramō*, but supplying
certain forms absent from *trechō*, lit., 'having run,' 'running,' expressive of the decisiveness of the act); the same form in the indicative mood is used, e.g., in Matt. 28 : 8; in the Gospels the literal meaning alone is used; elsewhere in 1 Cor. 9 : 24 (twice in 1st part); Rev. 9 : 9, A.V., "running" (R.V., "rushing"); (*b*) metaphorically, from the illustration of runners in a race, of either swiftness or effort to attain an end, Rom. 9 : 16, indicating that salvation is not due to human effort, but to God's sovereign right to exercise mercy; 1 Cor. 9 : 24 (2nd part), and ver. 26, of persevering activity in the Christian course with a view to obtaining the reward; so Heb. 12 : 1; in Gal. 2 : 2 (1st part), R.V., "(lest) I should be

running," continuous present tense, referring to the activity of the special service of his mission to Jerusalem; (2nd part), "had run," aorist tense, expressive of the continuous past, referring to the activity of his antagonism to the Judaizing teachers at Antioch, and his consent to submit the case to the judgment of the church in Jerusalem; in 5:7 of the erstwhile faithful course doctrinally of the Galatian believers; in Phil. 2:16, of the Apostle's manner of life among the Philippian believers; in 2 Thess. 3:1, of the free and rapid progress of "the word of the Lord."

2. PROSTRECHŌ (προστρέχω), to run to (*pros*, to, and No. 1), is 4370 AG:719B
used in Mark 9:15; 10:17; Acts 8:30.¶ CB:—

3. PERITRECHŌ (περιτρέχω), to run about (*peri*, around, and No. 1), 4063
is used in Mark 6:55, R.V., "ran round about" (A.V., "ran through").¶ AG:653A

4. SUNTRECHŌ (συντρέχω), to run together with (*sun*, with), is used 4936 AG:793A
(*a*) literally, Mark 6:33; Acts 3:11; (*b*) metaphorically, 1 Pet. 4:4, CB:1271A
of running a course of evil with others.¶ In the Sept., Psa. 50:18.¶ 4390 AG:722B

5. PROTRECHŌ (προτρέχω), to run before, Luke 19:4: see OUTRUN. 1532

6. EISTRECHŌ (εἰστρέχω), to run in (*eis*, in), occurs in Acts 12:14.¶ AG:233D

7. HUPOTRECHŌ (ὑποτρέχω), to run under (*hupo*, under), is used 5295
nautically in Acts 27:16.¶ AG:848B

8. EPISUNTRECHŌ (ἐπισυντρέχω), to run together again (*epi*, upon, 1998
or again, and No. 4), occurs in Mark 9:25.¶ AG:301D CB:—

9. EKCHUNNŌ or EKCHUNŌ (ἐκχύννω), to shed, is translated "ran 1632
riotously" in Jude 11, R.V. (A.V., "ran greedily"). See RIOTOUSLY, AG:247B (EKCHEŌ)
Note. See SHED, SPILL. CB:1243B

10. HUPEREKCHUNNŌ (ὑπερεκχύννω), a late form of *huperekcheō*, 5240
to overflow, is rendered "running over" in Luke 6:38.¶ AG:840D CB:—

11. EPIKELLŌ or EPOKELLŌ (ἐπικέλλω), to drive upon, is used in 2027
Acts 27:41 of running a ship ashore.¶ AG:294D

Notes: (1) *Hormaō*, to set in motion, urge on, but intransitively, HORMAŌ 3729
to hasten on, rush, is always translated to rush in the R.V.; A.V., "ran AG:581D
violently," Matt. 8:32; Mark 5:13; Luke 8:33; "ran," Acts 7:57; SUNDROMĒ 4890
"rushed", 19:29. See RUSH.¶ (2) In Acts 21:30, *sundromē*, a running AG:785D
together, with *ginomai*, to become, take place, is translated "ran together," EKCHEŌ 1632
lit., 'a running together took place.' (3) In Matt. 9:17, A.V., *ekcheō*, AG:247B
to pour out, used in the Passive Voice (R.V., "is spilled"), is translated CB:1243B EKPĒDAŌ
"runneth out." (4) In Acts 14:14, R.V., *ekpēdaō*, to spring forth, is —
translated "sprang forth" (this verb is found in the papyri); the A.V., AG:243D EISPĒDAŌ
"ran in" translates the mss. which have *eispēdaō*, to spring in. (5) 1530
Katatrechō, to run down, occurs in Acts 21:32.¶ AG:233C KATATRECHŌ 2701

RUSH, RUSHING

AG:419D

1. HORMAŌ (ὁρμάω), for which see RUN, Note (1), with refs., is 3729
akin to *hormē* (see ASSAULT) and *hormēma*, a rushing (see VIOLENCE). AG:581D

2. PHERŌ (φέρω), to bear, is used in the present participle, Passive 5342 AG:854D
Voice, in Acts 2:2, and translated "rushing," R.V., "the rushing (of CB:1264A

a mighty wind)," A.V., "a rushing (mighty wind)," lit., 'a violent wind borne (along).'

5143 AG:825D CB:1273A 3. TRECHŌ (τρέχω), to run, is translated "rushing (to war)" in Rev. 9:9, R.V., A.V., "running (to battle)."

RUST (Noun and Verb)

A. Nouns.

1035 AG:148B CB:1239B 1. BRŌSIS (βρῶσις), an eating (akin to *bibrōskō*, to eat), is used metaphorically to denote "rust" in Matt. 6:19, 20. See EAT, B, No. 1, FOOD, MEAT, MORSEL.

2447 AG:378D CB:1252C 2. IOS (ἰός), poison, denotes rust in Jas. 5:3. See POISON.

B. Verb.

2728 AG:424A CB:— KATIOŌ (κατιόω), an intensive form of *ioō*, to poison (akin to A, No. 2), strengthened by *kata*, down, to rust over, and in the Passive Voice, to become rusted over, occurs in Jas. 5:3, R.V., "are rusted" (A.V., "are cankered").¶ Cp. *gangraina*, a gangrene, 2 Tim. 2:17, R.V.¶

S

SABACHTHANI

SABACHTHANEI (σαβαχθανεί), an Aramaic word signifying 'Thou 4518
hast forsaken Me,' is recorded as part of the utterance of Christ on the AG:738B
Cross, Matt. 27 : 46 ; Mark 15 : 34, a quotation from Ps. 22 : 1. Recently CB:—
proposed renderings which differ from those of the A.V. and R.V. have not been sufficiently established to require acceptance.

SABAOTH

SABAŌTH (σαβαώθ) is the transliteration of a Hebrew word which 4519
denotes hosts or armies, Rom. 9 : 29 ; Jas. 5 : 4.¶ While the word AG:738B CB:1268B
"hosts" probably had special reference to angels, the title "the LORD of hosts" became used to designate Him as the One who is supreme over all the innumerable hosts of spiritual agencies, or of what are described as "the armies of heaven." Eventually it was used as equivalent to 'the LORD all-sovereign.' In the prophetical books of the O.T. the Sept. sometimes has *Kurios Sabaōth* as the equivalent of "the LORD of
hosts," sometimes *Kurios Pantokratōr ;* in Job, it uses *Pantokratōr* to PANTOKRATŌR
render the Hebrew Divine title *Shadday* (see ALMIGHTY). 3841 AG:608D CB:1261C

SABBATH

1. SABBATON (σάββατον) or SABBATA : the latter, the plural form, 4521
was transliterated from the Aramaic word, which was mistaken for a AG:739A CB:1268B
plural ; hence the singular, *sabbaton,* was formed from it. The root means to cease, desist (Heb., *shābath ;* cp. Arab., *sabata,* to intercept, interrupt) ; the doubled *b* has an intensive force, implying a complete cessation or a making to cease, probably the former. The idea is not that of relaxation or refreshment, but cessation from activity.

The observation of the seventh day of the week, enjoined upon Israel, was 'a sign' between God and His earthly people, based upon the fact that after the six days of creative operations He rested, Ex. 31 : 16, 17, with 20 : 8–11. The O.T. regulations were developed and systematized to such an extent that they became a burden upon the people (who otherwise rejoiced in the rest provided) and a byword for absurd extravagance. Two treatises of the Mishna (the *Shabbāth* and *'Ērūbin*) are entirely occupied with regulations for the observance ; so with the discussions in the Gemara, on Rabbinical opinions. The effect upon current opinion explains the antagonism roused by the Lord's cures wrought on the Sabbath, e.g., Matt. 12 : 9–13 ; John 5 : 5–16, and explains the fact that on a Sabbath the sick were brought to be healed after sunset, e.g., Mark 1 : 32. According to Rabbinical ideas, the disciples, by plucking ears of corn (Matt. 12 : 1 ; Mark 2 : 23), and rubbing them (Luke 6 : 1), broke the sabbath in two respects ; for to pluck was to reap, and to rub was to thresh. The Lord's attitude towards the sabbath was by way of freeing it from these vexatious traditional accretions by which it was made an end in itself, instead of a means to an end (Mark 2 : 27).

In the Epistles the only direct mentions are in Col. 2 : 16, " a sabbath day," R.V. (which rightly has the singular, see 1st parag., above), where it is listed among things that were " a shadow of the things to come " (i.e., of the age introduced at Pentecost), and in Heb. 4 : 4–11, where the
SABBATISMOS perpetual *sabbatismos* is appointed for believers (see REST) ; inferential
4520 AG:739A references are in Rom. 14 : 5 and Gal. 4 : 9–11. For the first three
CB:1268B centuries of the Christian era the first day of the week was never confounded with the sabbath ; the confusion of the Jewish and Christian institutions was due to declension from apostolic teaching.

Notes : (1) In Matt. 12 : 1 and 11, where the plural is used, the A.V. (as the R.V.) rightly has the singular, " the sabbath day ; " in ver. 5 the A.V. has the plural (see above). Where the singular is used the R.V. omits the word " day," ver. 2 ; 24 : 20 ; Mark 6 : 2 ; Luke 6 : 1 (" on a sabbath ") ; 14 : 3 ; John 9 : 14 (" it was the sabbath on the day when . . . "). As to the use or omission of the article the omission does not always require the rendering ' a sabbath ; ' it is absent, e.g., in Matt. 12 : 2. (2) In Acts 16 : 13, " on the sabbath day," is, lit., ' on the day of the sabbath ' (plural). (3) For Matt. 28 : 1, see LATE. (4) For " the first day of the week " see ONE, A, (5).

4315 AG:711A 2. PROSABBATON (προσάββατον) signifies " the day before the
CB:— sabbath " (*pro*, before, and No. 1), Mark 15 : 42 ; some mss. have *prin*, before, with *sabbaton* separately).¶

SACKCLOTH

4526 AG:740A SAKKOS (σάκκος), a warm material woven from goat's or camel's
CB:— hair, and hence of a dark colour, Rev. 6 : 12 ; Jerome renders it *saccus cilicinus* (being made from the hair of the black goat of Cilicia, the Romans called it *cilicium*) ; cp. Isa. 50 : 3 ; it was also used for saddle-cloths, Jos. 9 : 4 ; also for making sacks, e.g., Gen. 42 : 25, and for garments worn as expressing mourning or penitence, Matt. 11 : 21 ; Luke 10 : 13, or for purposes of prophetic testimony, Rev. 11 : 3.¶

SACRED

2413 AG:372D HIEROS (ἱερός) denotes consecrated to God, e.g., the Scriptures,
CB:1250B 2 Tim. 3 : 15, R.V., " sacred " (A.V. " holy ") ; it is used as a noun in the

neuter plural in 1 Cor. 9 : 13, R.V., "sacred things" (A.V., "holy things").¶ The neuter singular, *hieron*, denotes a temple. See TEMPLE. For a comparison of this and synonymous terms see HOLY, B, No. 1 (*b*) and Note (2).

SACRIFICE (Noun and Verb)

A. Noun.

THUSIA (θυσία) primarily denotes the act of offering; then, objec- **2378**
tively, that which is offered (*a*) of idolatrous sacrifice, Acts 7 : 41; (*b*) of **AG:366B CB:1272C**
animal or other sacrifices, as offered under the Law, Matt. 9 : 13; 12 : 7; Mark 9 : 49; 12 : 33; Luke 2 : 24; 13 : 1; Acts 7 : 42; 1 Cor. 10 : 18; Heb. 5 : 1; 7 : 27 (R.V., plural); 8 : 3; 9 : 9; 10 : 1, 5, 8 (R.V., plural), 11; 11 : 4; (*c*) of Christ, in His sacrifice on the Cross, Eph. 5 : 2; Heb. 9 : 23, where the plural antitypically comprehends the various forms of Levitical sacrifices in their typical character; 9 : 26; 10 : 12, 26; (*d*) metaphorically, (1) of the body of the believer, presented to God as a living sacrifice, Rom. 12 : 1; (2) of faith, Phil. 2 : 17; (3) of material assistance rendered to servants of God, Phil. 4 : 18; (4) of praise, Heb. 13 : 15; (5) of doing good to others and communicating with their needs, Heb. 13 : 16; (6) of spiritual sacrifices in general, offered by believers as a holy priesthood, 1 Pet. 2 : 5.¶

B. Verb.

THUŌ (θύω) is used of sacrificing by slaying a victim, (*a*) of the **2380**
sacrifice of Christ, 1 Cor. 5 : 7, R.V., "hath been sacrificed" (A.V., "is **AG:367A CB:1272C**
sacrificed"); (*b*) of the Passover sacrifice, Mark 14 : 12, R.V., "they sacrificed" (A.V., "they killed"); Luke 22 : 7, R.V., "(must) be sacrificed," A.V., "(must) be killed;" (*c*) of idolatrous sacrifices, Acts 14 : 13, 18; 1 Cor. 10 : 20 (twice). See KILL, No. 3.

Note: For *eidōlothutos*, sacrificed to idols, see IDOLS (offered to), **1494**
No. 1. **AG:221B (-OS) CB:1243A**

For SACRILEGE see ROBBER, No. 2, Rom. 2 : 22

For SAD see COUNTENANCE

For SADDUCEES see under PHARISEES

SAFE, SAFELY, SAFETY

A. Adjective.

ASPHALĒS (ἀσφαλής), certain, secure, safe (from *a*, negative, and **804**
sphallō, to trip up), is translated "safe" in Phil. 3 : 1. See CERTAIN, B. **AG:119A CB:1238A**

B. Nouns.

1. ASPHALEIA (ἀσφάλεια), certainty, safety (akin to A), is translated **803**
"safety" in Acts 5 : 23; 1 Thess. 5 : 3. See CERTAIN, A. **AG:118D CB:1238A**

2. SŌTĒRIA (σωτηρία), salvation, is translated "safety" in Acts **4991**
27 : 34, R.V. (A.V., "health"). See HEALTH, Note. **AG:801B CB:1269C**

C. Adverb.

806 AG:119A CB:1238A ASPHALŌS (ἀσφαλῶς), safely (akin to A, and B, No. 1), is so rendered in Mark 14 : 44 and Acts 16 : 23. See ASSURANCE, C. In the Sept., Gen. 34 : 25.¶

D. Verbs.

1295 AG:189A CB:1241B 1. DIASŌZŌ (διασώζω), to bring safely through danger, and, in the Passive Voice, to come safe through (*dia*, through, *sōzō*, to save), is translated "bring safe" in Acts 23 : 24; "escaped safe" in 27 : 44. See ESCAPE, HEAL, SAVE, WHOLE.

5198 AG:832B CB:1251C 2. HUGIAINŌ (ὑγιαίνω), to be sound, healthy (Eng., hygiene, etc.), is translated "safe and sound" in Luke 15 : 27, lit., 'being healthy.' See HEALTH, SOUND, WHOLE.

For SAIL (Noun, Acts 27 : 17, A.V.) see GEAR

SAIL (Verb)

4126 AG:668A CB:— 1. PLEŌ (πλέω), to sail, occurs in Luke 8 : 23; Acts 21 : 3; 27 : 2, 6, 24; Rev. 18 : 17, R.V., "saileth" (for the A.V. see COMPANY, A, No 7).¶

636 AG:97C CB:— 2. APOPLEŌ (ἀποπλέω), to sail away (*apo*, from, and No. 1), occurs in Acts 13 : 4; 14 : 26; 20 : 15; 27 : 1.¶

1602 AG:244A 3. EKPLEŌ (ἐκπλέω), to sail from, or thence (*ek*, from), occurs in Acts 15 : 39; 18 : 18; 20 : 6.¶

3896 AG:621B 4. PARAPLEŌ (παραπλέω), to sail by (*para*), occurs in Acts 20 : 16.¶

1277 AG:187C 5. DIAPLEŌ (διαπλέω), to sail across (*dia*, through), occurs in Acts 27 : 5.¶

5284 AG:846D CB:— 6. HUPOPLEŌ (ὑποπλέω), to sail under (*hupo*), i.e., under the lee of, occurs in Acts 27 : 4, 7.¶

321 AG:53A CB:— 7. ANAGŌ (ἀνάγω), to lead up, is used of putting to sea, Acts 13 : 13; 16 : 11; 18 : 21; 20 : 3, 13; 21 : 1; 27 : 21; 28 : 10, 11; see LAUNCH.

(-OMAI) 3881 AG:619D CB:— 8. PARALEGŌ (παραλέγω), to lay beside (*para*), is used in the Middle Voice, of sailing past in Acts 27 : 8, R.V., "coasting along" (A.V., "passing"); ver. 13, R.V., "sailed along" (A.V., "sailed").¶

1276 AG:187C CB:— 9. DIAPERAŌ (διαπεράω), to cross over, is translated "sailing over" in Acts 21 : 2, A.V. (R.V., "crossing over"). See PASS.

1020 AG:147A CB:— 10. BRADUPLOEŌ (βραδυπλοέω), to sail slowly (*bradus*, slow, *plous*, a voyage), occurs in Acts 27 : 7.¶

For SAILING see VOYAGE

For SAILORS see MARINERS

SAINT(S)

40 AG:9B CB:1249A HAGIOS (ἅγιος), for the meaning and use of which see HOLY, B, No. 1, is used as a noun in the singular in Phil. 4 : 21, where *pas*, "every,"

is used with it. In the plural, as used of believers, it designates all such and is not applied merely to persons of exceptional holiness, or to those who, having died, were characterized by exceptional acts of saintliness. See especially 2 Thess. 1 : 10, where " His saints " are also described as " them that believed," i.e., the whole number of the redeemed. They are called " holy ones " in Jude 14, R.V. For the term as applied to the Holy Spirit see HOLY SPIRIT. See also SANCTIFY.

Notes : (1) In Rev. 15 : 3 the R.V. follows those texts which have *aiōnōn*, " ages," and assigns the reading *ethnōn*, " nations," to the margin ; the A.V. translates those which have the inferior reading *hagiōn*, " saints," and puts " nations " and " ages " in the margin. (2) In Rev. 18 : 20, the best texts have *hagioi* and *apostoloi*, each with the article, each being preceeded by *kai*, " and," R.V., " and ye saints, and ye apostles ; " the A.V., " and ye holy apostles " follows those mss. from which the 2nd *kai* and the article are absent. (3) In Rev. 22 : 21, the R.V. follows those mss. which have *hagiōn*, with the article," (with) the saints ;" the A.V. those which simply have *pantōn*, all, but adds " you " (R.V., marg., " with all ").

SAKE (for the) : see † p. 1

SALT (Noun, Adjective and Verb), SALTNESS

A. Noun.

HALAS (ἅλας), a late form of *hals* (found in some mss. in Mark 9 : 49), 217
is used (*a*) literally in Matt. 5 : 13 (2nd part) ; Mark 9 : 50 (1st part, twice) ; AG:35A CB:1249A
Luke 14 : 34 (twice) ; (*b*) metaphorically, of believers, Matt. 5 : 13 (1st
part) ; of their character and condition, Mark 9 : 50 (2nd part) ; of HALS 251
wisdom exhibited in their speech, Col. 4 : 6.¶ AG:41B
Being possessed of purifying, perpetuating and antiseptic qualities, CB:1249A
salt became emblematic of fidelity and friendship among eastern nations. To eat of a person's salt and so to share his hospitality is still regarded thus among the Arabs. So in Scripture, it is an emblem of the covenant between God and His people, Num. 18 : 19 ; 2 Chron. 13 : 5 ; so again when the Lord says " Have salt in yourselves, and be at peace one with another " (Mark 9 : 50). In the Lord's teaching it is also symbolic of that spiritual health and vigour essential to Christian virtue and counteractive of the corruption that is in the world, e.g., Matt. 5 : 13, see (*b*) above. Food is seasoned with salt (see B) ; every meal offering was to contain it, and it was to be offered with all offerings presented by Israelites, as emblematic of the holiness of Christ, and as betokening the reconciliation provided for man by God on the ground of the Death of Christ, Lev. 2 : 13. To refuse God's provision in Christ and the efficacy of His expiatory sacrifice is to expose oneself to the doom of being " salted with fire," Mark 9 : 49.

While salt is used to fertilize soil, excess of it on the ground produces sterility (e.g., Deut. 29 : 23; Judg. 9 : 45; Jer. 17 : 6; Zeph. 2 : 9).

B. Verb.

233 AG:37D CB:1249A HALIZŌ (ἁλίζω), akin to A, signifies to sprinkle or to season with salt, Matt. 5 : 13; Mark 9 : 49 (see under A).¶ Cp. SAVOUR, B.

C. Adjectives.

252 AG:41B CB:1249A 1. HALUKOS (ἁλυκός) occurs in Jas. 3 : 12, " salt (water)."¶

358 AG:57B CB:1235A 2. ANALOS (ἄναλος) denotes saltless (*a*, negative, *n*, euphonic, and A), insipid, Mark 9 : 50, " have lost its saltness," lit., ' have become (*ginomai*) saltless (*analos*); " cp. *mōrainō* in Luke 14 : 34 (see SAVOUR, B).

For SALUTATION and SALUTE see GREET

SALVATION

A. Nouns.

4991 AG:801B CB:1269C 1. SŌTĒRIA (σωτηρία) denotes deliverance, preservation, salvation. Salvation is used in the N.T. (*a*) of material and temporal deliverance from danger and apprehension, (1) national, Luke 1 : 69, 71; Acts 7 : 25, R.V. marg., " salvation " (text, " deliverance "); (2) personal, as from the sea, Acts 27 : 34; R.V., " safety " (A.V., " health "); prison, Phil. 1 : 19; the flood, Heb. 11 : 7; (*b*) of the spiritual and eternal deliverance granted immediately by God to those who accept His conditions of repentance and faith in the Lord Jesus, in whom alone it is to be obtained, Acts 4 : 12, and upon confession of Him as Lord, Rom. 10 : 10; for this purpose the gospel is the saving instrument, Rom. 1 : 16; Eph. 1 : 13 (see further under SAVE); (*c*) of the present experience of God's power to deliver from the bondage of sin, e.g., Phil. 2 : 12, where the special, though not the entire, reference is to the maintenance of peace and harmony; 1 Pet. 1 : 9; this present experience on the part of believers is virtually equivalent to sanctification; for this purpose, God is able to make them wise, 2 Tim. 3 : 15; they are not to neglect it, Heb. 2 : 3; (*d*) of the future deliverance of believers at the Parousia of Christ for His saints, a salvation which is the object of their confident hope, e.g., Rom. 13 : 11; 1 Thess. 5 : 8, and ver. 9, where salvation is assured to them, as being deliverance from the wrath of God destined to be executed upon the ungodly at the end of this age (see 1 Thess. 1 : 10); 2 Thess. 2 : 13; Heb. 1 : 14; 9 : 28; 1 Pet. 1 : 5; 2 Pet. 3 : 15; (*e*) of the deliverance of the nation of Israel at the Second Advent of Christ at the time of ' the epiphany (or shining forth) of His Parousia ' (2 Thess. 2 : 8); Luke 1 : 71; Rev. 12 : 10; (*f*) inclusively, to sum up all the blessings bestowed by God on men in Christ through the Holy Spirit, e.g., 2 Cor. 6 : 2; Heb. 5 : 9; 1 Pet. 1 : 9, 10; Jude 3; (*g*) occasionally, as standing virtually for the Saviour, e.g., Luke 19 : 9; cp. John 4 : 22 (see SAVIOUR); (*h*) in ascriptions of praise to God, Rev. 7 : 10, and as that which it is His prerogative to bestow, 19 : 1 (R.V.).

2. SŌTĒRION (σωτήριον), the neuter of the adjective (see B), is used 4992
as a noun in Luke 2 : 30 ; 3 : 6, in each of which it virtually stands for the AG:801D (-OS 2.)
Saviour, as in No. 1 (*g*) ; in Acts 28 : 28, as in No. 1 (*b*) ; in Eph. 6 : 17, CB:1269C
where the hope of salvation [see No. 1 (*d*)] is metaphorically described as
a helmet.¶

B. Adjective.

SŌTĒRIOS (σωτήριος), saving, bringing salvation, describes the grace 4992 (-ON) AG:801D
of God, in Tit. 2 : 11.¶ CB:1269C

SAME

1. AUTOS (αὐτός) denotes 'the same' when preceded by the article, 846
and either with a noun following, e.g., Mark 14 : 39 ; Phil 1 : 30 ; 1 Cor. AG:122C CB:1238B
12 : 4, or without, e.g., Matt. 5 : 46, 47 ; Rom. 2 : 1 ; Phil. 2 : 2 ; 3 : 1 ;
Heb. 1 : 12 ; 13 : 8. It is thus to be distinguished from uses as a personal
and a reflexive pronoun.

2. HOUTOS (οὗτος), this (person or thing), or he (and the feminine and 3778
neuter forms), is sometimes translated "the same," e.g., John 3 : 2, 26 ; AG:596B CB:1251B
7 : 18 ; Jas. 3 : 2 ; sometimes the R.V. translates it by "this" or
"these," e.g., John 12 : 21, "these" (A.V., "the same") ; 2 Cor. 8 : 6,
"this" (A.V., "the same").

SANCTIFICATION, SANCTIFY

A. Noun.

HAGIASMOS (ἁγιασμός), sanctification, is used of (*a*) separation to 38 AG:9A
God, 1 Cor. 1 : 30 ; 2 Thess. 2 : 13 ; 1 Pet. 1 : 2 ; (*b*) the course of life CB:1249A
befitting those so separated, 1 Thess. 4 : 3, 4, 7 ; Rom. 6 : 19, 22 ; 1 Tim. 2 : 15 ; Heb. 12 : 14.¶ "Sanctification is that relationship with God into which men enter by faith in Christ, Acts 26 : 18 ; 1 Cor. 6 : 11, and to which their sole title is the death of Christ, Eph. 5 : 25, 26 ; Col. 1 : 22 ; Heb. 10 : 10, 29 ; 13 : 12.

"Sanctification is also used in N.T. of the separation of the believer from evil things and ways. This sanctification is God's will for the believer, 1 Thess. 4 : 3, and His purpose in calling him by the gospel, ver. 7 ; it must be learned from God, ver. 4, as He teaches it by His Word, John 17 : 17, 19 ; cp. Ps. 17 : 4 ; 119 : 9, and it must be pursued by the believer, earnestly and undeviatingly, 1 Tim. 2 : 15 ; Heb. 12 : 14. For
the holy character, *hagiōsunē*, 1 Thess. 3 : 13, is not vicarious, i.e., it cannot HAGIōSUNē
be transferred or imputed, it is an individual possession, built up, little by 42 AG:10B
little, as the result of obedience to the Word of God, and of following the CB:1249A
example of Christ, Matt. 11 : 29 ; John 13 : 15 ; Eph. 4 : 20 ; Phil. 2 : 5, in the power of the Holy Spirit, Rom. 8 : 13 ; Eph. 3 : 16.

"The Holy Spirit is the Agent in sanctification, Rom. 15 : 16 ; 2 Thess. 2 : 13 ; 1 Pet. 1 : 2 ; cp. 1 Cor. 6 : 11. . . . The sanctification of the Spirit is associated with the choice, or election, of God ; it is a Divine act preceding the acceptance of the Gospel by the individual."*

For synonymous words see HOLINESS.

B. Verb.

37 AG:8C HAGIAZŌ (ἁγιάζω), to sanctify, " is used of (*a*) the gold adorning the
CB:1249A Temple and of the gift laid on the altar, Matt. 23 : 17, 19; (*b*) food, 1 Tim. 4 : 5; (*c*) the unbelieving spouse of a believer, 1 Cor. 7 : 14; (*d*) the ceremonial cleansing of the Israelites, Heb. 9 : 13; (*e*) the Father's Name, Luke 11 : 2; (*f*) the consecration of the Son by the Father, John 10 : 36; (*g*) the Lord Jesus devoting Himself to the redemption of His people, John 17 : 19; (*h*) the setting apart of the believer for God, Acts 20 : 32; cp. Rom. 15 : 16; (*i*) the effect on the believer of the Death of Christ, Heb. 10 : 10, said of God, and 2 : 11; 13 : 12, said of the Lord Jesus; (*j*) the separation of the believer from the world in his behaviour—by the Father through the Word, John 17 : 17, 19; (*k*) the believer who turns away from such things as dishonour God and His gospel, 2 Tim. 2 : 21; (*l*) the acknowledgment of the Lordship of Christ, 1 Pet. 3 : 15.

" Since every believer is sanctified in Christ Jesus, 1 Cor. 1 : 2, cp. Heb. 10 : 10, a common N.T. designation of all believers is 'saints,' *hagioi*, i.e., 'sanctified' or 'holy ones.' Thus sainthood, or sanctification, is not an attainment, it is the state into which God, in grace, calls sinful men, and in which they begin their course as Christians, Col. 3 : 12; Heb. 3 : 1."†

SANCTUARY

39
AG:9B 1. HAGION (ἅγιον), the neuter of the adjective *hagios*, holy, is used
(HAGIOS 2a.) CB:— of those structures which are set apart to God, (*a*) of the Tabernacle in the
HAGIOS wilderness, Heb. 9 : 1, R.V., " its sanctuary, *a sanctuary* of this world "
40 AG:9B (A.V., " a worldly sanctuary "); in ver. 2 the outer part is called " the
CB:1249A Holy place," R.V. (A.V., " the sanctuary "); here the neuter plural *hagia* is used, as in verse 3.

Speaking of the absence of the article, Westcott says " The anarthrous form Ἅγια (literally *Holies*) in this sense appears to be unique, as also ἅγια ἁγίων below, if indeed the reading is correct. Perhaps it is chosen to fix attention on the character of the sanctuary as in other cases. The plural suggests the idea of the sanctuary with all its parts: cp. Moulton-Winer, p. 220." In their margin, Westcott and Hort prefix the article *ta* to *hagia* in vv. 2 and 3. In ver. 3 the inner part is called " the Holy of holies," R.V. (A.V., " the holiest of all "); in ver. 8, " the holy place " (A.V., " the holiest of all "), lit., '(the way) of the holiest;' in ver. 24 " a holy place," R.V. (A.V., " the holy places "), neuter plural; so in ver. 25, " the holy place " (A.V. and R.V.), and in 13 : 11, R.V., " the

---

* From Notes on Thessalonians by Hogg and Vine, pp. 115, 271.
† From Notes on Thessalonians by Hogg and Vine, pp. 113, 114.

holy place" (A.V., "the sanctuary"); in all these there is no separate word *topos*, place, as of the Temple in Matt. 24 : 15; (*b*) of "Heaven itself," i.e., the immediate presence of God and His Throne, Heb. 8 : 2, "the sanctuary" (R.V., marg., "holy things"); the neut. plur. with the article points to the text as being right, in view of 9 : 24, 25 and 13 : 11 (see above), exegetically designated "the true tabernacle;" neut. plur. in 9 : 12, "the holy place;" so 10 : 19, R.V. (A.V., "the holiest;" there are no separate compartments in the antitypical and Heavenly sanctuary), into which believers have "boldness to enter" by faith.¶

2. NAOS (ναός) is used of the inner part of the Temple in Jerusalem, in Matt. 23 : 35, R.V., "sanctuary." See TEMPLE. 3485 AG:533B CB:1259B

SAND

AMMOS (ἄμμος), sand or sandy ground, describes (*a*) an insecure foundation, Matt. 7 : 26; (*b*) numberlessness, vastness, Rom. 9 : 27; Heb. 11 : 12; Rev. 20 : 8; (*c*) symbolically in Rev. 13 : 1, R.V., the position taken up by the Dragon (not, as in the A.V., by John), in view of the rising of the Beast out of the sea (emblematic of the restless condition of nations; see SEA).¶ 285 AG:46B CB:—

SANDAL

SANDALION (σανδάλιον), a diminutive of *sandalon*, probably a Persian word, Mark 6 : 9; Acts 12 : 8. The sandal usually had a wooden sole bound on by straps round the instep and ankle.¶ 4547 AG:742A CB:—

SANHEDRIN See COUNCIL

SAPPHIRE

SAPPHEIROS (σάπφειρος) is mentioned in Rev. 21 : 19 (R.V., marg., "*lapis lazuli*") as the second of the foundations of the wall of the heavenly Jerusalem (cp. Is. 54 : 11).¶ It was one of the stones in the high priest's breastplate, Ex. 28 : 18; 39 : 11; as an intimation of its value see Job 28 : 16; Ezek. 28 : 13. See also Ex. 24 : 10; Ezek. 1 : 26; 10 : 1. The sapphire has various shades of blue, and ranks next in hardness to the diamond. 4552 AG:742C (-HIROS) CB:1268B

SARDIUS, SARDINE (A.V.)

SARDION or SARDINOS (σάρδιον) denotes the sardian stone. *Sardius* is the word in the best texts in Rev. 4 : 3 (R.V., "a sardius"), where it formed part of the symbolic appearance of the Lord on His Throne, setting forth His glory and majesty in view of the judgment to follow. There are two special varieties, one a yellowish brown, the other a transparent red (like a cornelian). The beauty of the stone, its transparent brilliance, the high polish of which it is susceptible, made it a favourite among the ancients. It forms the sixth foundation of the wall of the heavenly Jerusalem, Rev. 21 : 20.¶ 4556 AG:742D CB:1268B SARDINOS 4555 AG:742C CB:—

SARDONYX

4557 AG:742D SARDONUX (σαρδόνυξ), a name which indicates the formation of the
CB:1268B gem, a layer of sard, and a layer of onyx, marked by the red of the sard and the white of the onyx. It was used among the Romans both for cameos and for signets. It forms the fifth foundation of the wall of the heavenly Jerusalem, Rev. 21 : 20.¶

SATAN

4567 AG:744D SATANAS (Σατανᾶς), a Greek form derived from the Aramaic (Heb.,
(SATAN) *Sātān*), an adversary, is used (*a*) of an angel of Jehovah in Num. 22 : 22 (the
CB:1268C first occurrence of the word in the O.T.) ; (*b*) of men, e.g., 1 Sam. 29 : 4 ; Psa. 38 : 20 ; 71 : 13 ; four in Ps. 109 ; (*c*) of Satan, the Devil, some seventeen or eighteen times in the O.T. ; in Zech. 3 : 1, where the name receives its interpretation, "to be (his) adversary," R.V. (see marg. ; A.V., "to resist him").

In the N.T. the word is always used of Satan, the adversary (*a*) of God and Christ, e.g., Matt. 4 : 10 ; 12 : 26 ; Mark 1 : 13 ; 3 : 23, 26 ; 4 : 15 ; Luke 4 : 8 (in some mss.) ; 11 : 18 ; 22 : 3 ; John 13 : 27 ; (*b*) of His people, e.g., Luke 22 : 31 ; Acts 5 : 3 ; Rom. 16 : 20 ; 1 Cor. 5 : 5 ; 7 : 5 ; 2 Cor. 2 : 11 ; 11 : 14 ; 12 : 7 ; 1 Thess. 2 : 18 ; 1 Tim. 1 : 20 ; 5 : 15 ; Rev. 2 : 9, 13 (twice), 24 ; 3 : 9 ; (*c*) of mankind, Luke 13 : 16 ; Acts 26 : 18 ; 2 Thess. 2 : 9 ; Rev. 12 : 9 ; 20 : 7.

His doom, sealed at the Cross, is foretold in its stages in Luke 10 : 18 ; Rev. 20 : 2, 10. Believers are assured of victory over him, Rom. 16 : 20.

The appellation was given by the Lord to Peter, as a Satan-like man, on the occasion when he endeavoured to dissuade Him from death, Matt. 16 : 23 ; Mark 8 : 33.¶

Satan is not simply the personification of evil influences in the heart, for he tempted Christ, in whose heart no evil thought could ever have arisen (John 14 : 30 ; 2 Cor. 5 : 21 ; Heb. 4 : 15) ; moreover his personality is asserted in both the O.T. and the N.T., and especially in the latter, whereas if the O.T. language was intended to be figurative, the N.T. would have made this evident. See DEVIL.

SATISFY

5526
AG:883D 1. CHORTAZŌ (χορτάζω), to fill or satisfy with food, is translated
CB:1240A "satisfy" in Mark 8 : 4, A.V. (R.V., "to fill"). See FILL, No. 8.
1705
AG:256A 2. EMPIPLĒMI or EMPLĒTHŌ (ἐμπίπλημι), to fill up, fill full, satisfy
CB:1244B (*en*, in, *pimplēmi* or *plēthō*, to fill), is used metaphorically in Rom. 15 : 24, of taking one's fill of the company of others, R.V., "I shall have been satisfied" (A.V., "I be . . . filled"). See FILL, No. 6.

For SATISFYING, Col. 2 : 23, A.V., see INDULGENCE

For SAVE (Preposition) see † p. 1

SAVE, SAVING

A. Verbs.

1. SŌZŌ (σώζω), to save, is used (as with the noun *sōtēria*, salvation) 4982
(*a*) of material and temporal deliverance from danger, suffering, etc., AG:798A CB:1269C
e.g., Matt. 8 : 25; Mark 13 : 20; Luke 23 : 35; John 12 : 27; 1 Tim. 2 : 15; 2 Tim. 4 : 18 (A.V., "preserve"); Jude 5; from sickness, Matt. 9 : 22, "made . . . whole" (R.V., marg., "saved"); so Mark 5 : 34; Luke 8 : 48; Jas. 5 : 15; (*b*) of the spiritual and eternal salvation granted immediately by God to those who believe on the Lord Jesus Christ, e.g., Acts 2 : 47, R.V. "(those that) were being saved;" 16 : 31; Rom. 8 : 24, R.V., "were we saved;" Eph. 2 : 5, 8; 1 Tim. 2 : 4; 2 Tim. 1 : 9; Tit. 3 : 5; of human agency in this, Rom. 11 : 14; 1 Cor. 7 : 16; 9 : 22; (*c*) of the present experiences of God's power to deliver from the bondage of sin, e.g., Matt. 1 : 21; Rom. 5 : 10; 1 Cor. 15 : 2; Heb. 7 : 25; Jas. 1 : 21; 1 Pet. 3 : 21; of human agency in this, 1 Tim. 4 : 16; (*d*) of the future deliverance of believers at the Second Coming of Christ for His saints, being deliverance from the wrath of God to be executed upon the ungodly at the close of this age and from eternal doom, e.g., Rom. 5 : 9; (*e*) of the deliverance of the nation of Israel at the Second Advent of Christ, e.g., Rom. 11 : 26; (*f*) inclusively for all the blessings bestowed by God on men in Christ, e.g., Luke 19 : 10; John 10 : 9; 1 Cor. 10 : 33; 1 Tim. 1 : 15; (*g*) of those who endure to the end of the time of the great tribulation, Matt. 10 : 22; Mark 13 : 13; (*h*) of the individual believer, who, though losing his reward at the Judgment-Seat of Christ hereafter, will not lose his salvation, 1 Cor. 3 : 15; 5 : 5; (*i*) of the deliverance of the nations at the Millennium, Rev. 21 : 24 (in some mss.). See SALVATION.

2. DIASŌZŌ (διασώζω), to bring safely through (*dia*, through, and 1295
No. 1), is used (*a*) of the healing of the sick by the Lord, Matt. 14 : 36, AG:189A CB:1241B
R.V., "were made whole" (A.V. adds "perfectly"); Luke 7 : 3; (*b*) of bringing safe to a destination, Acts 23 : 24; (*c*) of keeping a person safe, 27 : 43; (*d*) of escaping through the perils of shipwreck, 27 : 44; 28 : 1, 4, Passive Voice; (*e*) through the Flood, 1 Pet. 3 : 20. See ESCAPE, WHOLE.¶

Note: In 2 Pet. 2 : 5, A.V., *phulassō*, to guard, keep, preserve, is 5442
translated "saved" (R.V., "preserved"). In Luke 17 : 33 some mss. AG:868B CB:1264C
have *sōzō* (A.V., "save"), for the R.V.: see GAIN, B, No. 3. For "save alive," Luke 17 : 33, R.V., see LIVE, No. 6.

B. Noun.

PERIPOIĒSIS (περιποίησις), (*a*) preservation, (*b*) acquiring or gaining 4047
something, is used in this latter sense in Heb. 10 : 39, translated "saving" AG:650A CB:1263B
(R.V. marg., "gaining"); the reference here is to salvation in its completeness. See OBTAIN, POSSESSION.

Note: In Heb. 11 : 7 *sōtēria* is rendered "saving." See SALVATION. 4991 AG:801B CB:1269C

SAVING (Preposition)

3924
AG:625A
CB:1262B PAREKTOS (παρεκτός), used as a preposition, denotes "saving," Matt. 5:32 (in some mss., 19:9). See EXCEPT.¶

Note: In Luke 4:27 and Rev. 2:17, A.V., *ei mē* (lit., 'if not'), is translated "saving" (R.V., "but only" and "but").

SAVIOUR

4990
AG:800D
CB:1269C SŌTĒR (σωτήρ), a saviour, deliverer, preserver, is used (*a*) of God, Luke 1:47; 1 Tim. 1:1; 2:3; 4:10 (in the sense of Preserver, since He gives "to all life and breath and all things"); Tit. 1:3; 2:10; 3:4; Jude 25; (*b*) of Christ, Luke 2:11; John 4:42; Acts 5:31; 13:23 (of Israel); Eph. 5:23 (the Sustainer and Preserver of the Church, His "body"); Phil. 3:20 (at His return to receive the Church to Himself); 2 Tim. 1:10 (with reference to His Incarnation, "the days of His flesh"); Tit. 1:4 (a title shared, in the context, with God the Father); 2:13, R.V., "our great God and Saviour Jesus Christ," the pronoun "our," at the beginning of the whole clause, includes all the titles; Tit. 3:6; 2 Pet. 1:1, "our God and Saviour Jesus Christ," R.V., where the pronoun "our," coming immediately in connection with "God," involves the inclusion of both titles as referring to Christ, just as in the parallel in ver. 11, "our Lord and Saviour Jesus Christ" (A.V. and R.V.); these passages are therefore a testimony to His Deity; 2 Pet. 2:20; 3:2, 18; 1 John 4:14.¶

SAVOUR (Noun and Verb)

A. Nouns.

2175
AG:329D
CB:1247B 1. EUŌDIA (εὐωδία), fragrance (*eu*, well, *ozō*, to smell), is used metaphorically (*a*) of those who in the testimony of the gospel are to God "a sweet savour of Christ," 2 Cor. 2:15; (*b*) of the giving up of His life by Christ for us, an offering and a sacrifice to God for an odour (*osmē*, see No. 2) of "a sweet smell," Eph. 5:2, R.V. [A.V., "a sweet smelling (savour)"]; (*c*) of material assistance sent to Paul from the church at Philippi "(an odour) of a sweet smell," Phil. 4:18. In all three instances the fragrance is that which ascends to God through the Person, and as a result of the Sacrifice, of Christ.¶

3744
AG:586A
CB:1261B 2. OSMĒ (ὀσμή), a smell, odour (from *ozō*, to smell; Eng., ozone), is translated "odour" in John 12:3; it is used elsewhere in connection with No. 1, in the three passages mentioned, as of an odour accompanying an acceptable sacrifice; in 2 Cor. 2:14, 16 (twice), of the "savour" of the knowledge of Christ through Gospel testimony, in the case of the perishing "a savour from death unto death," as of that which arises from what is dead (the spiritual condition of the unregenerate); in the case of the saved "a savour from life unto life," as from that which arises from what is instinct with life (the spiritual condition of the regenerate); in

Eph. 5 : 2, "a (sweetsmelling) savour;" in Phil. 4 : 18, "an odour (of a sweet smell);" cp. No. 1. See ODOUR.¶

B. Verb.

MŌRAINŌ (μωραίνω), primarily, to be foolish, is used of salt that has lost its savour, Matt. 5 : 13; Luke 14 : 34. See FOOLISH, B, No. 1. 3471 AG:531B CB:1259B

Note: In the A.V. of Matt. 16 : 23 and Mark 8 : 33, *phroneō*, to think, to mind, is translated "thou savourest" (R.V., "thou mindest"). 5426 AG:866A CB:1264C

SAW ASUNDER

PRIZŌ or PRIŌ (πρίζω), to saw asunder, occurs in Heb. 11 : 37. Some have seen here a reference to the tradition of Isaiah's martyrdom under Manasseh.¶ In the Sept., Amos 1 : 3.¶ Cp. *diapriō*, to cut to the heart, Acts 5 : 33; 7 : 54.¶ 4249 AG:701A CB:— DIAPRIŌ 1282 AG:187D CB:—

SAY

1. LEGŌ (λέγω), primarily, to pick out, gather, chiefly denotes to say, speak, affirm, whether of actual speech, e.g., Matt. 11 : 17, or of unspoken thought, e.g., Matt. 3 : 9, or of a message in writing, e.g., 2 Cor. 8 : 8. The 2nd aorist form *eipon* is used to supply that tense, which is lacking in *legō*. 3004 AG:468A CB:1256C

Concerning the phrase "he answered and said," it is a well known peculiarity of Hebrew narrative style that a speech is introduced, not simply by 'and he said,' but by prefixing "and he answered" (*apokrinomai*, with *eipon*). In Matt. 14 : 27, "saying," and Mark 6 : 50, "and saith," emphasis is perhaps laid on the fact that the Lord, hitherto silent as He moved over the lake, then addressed His disciples. That the phrase sometimes occurs where no explicit question has preceded (e.g., Matt. 11 : 25; 17 : 4; 28 : 5; Mark 11 : 14; 12 : 35; Luke 13 : 15; 14 : 3; John 5 : 17, 19), illustrates the use of the Hebrew idiom.

Note: A characteristic of *legō* is that it refers to the purport or sentiment of what is said as well as the connection of the words; this is illustrated in Heb. 8 : 1, R.V., "(in the things which) we are saying," A.V., "(which) we have spoken." In comparison with *laleō* (No. 2), *legō* refers especially to the substance of what is said, *laleō*, to the words conveying the utterance; see, e.g., John 12 : 49, "what I should say (*legō*, in the 2nd aorist subjunctive form *eipō*), and what I should speak (*laleō*);" ver. 50, "even as the Father hath said (*legō*, in the perfect form *eirēke*) unto Me, so I speak" (*laleō*); cp. 1 Cor. 14 : 34, "saith (*legō*) the law;" ver. 35, "to speak" (*laleō*). Sometimes *laleō* signifies the utterance, as opposed to silence, *legō* declares what is said; e.g., Rom. 3 : 19, "what things soever the law saith (*legō*), it speaketh (*laleō*) to them that are under the law;" see also Mark 6 : 50; Luke 24 : 6. In the N.T. *laleō* never has the meaning to chatter.

2. LALEŌ (λαλέω), to speak, is sometimes translated to say; in the following where the A.V. renders it thus, the R.V. alters it to the verb to 2980 AG:463A CB:1256B

speak, e.g., John 8 : 25 (3rd part), 26 ; 16 : 6 ; 18 : 20 (2nd part), 21 (1st part) ; Acts 3 : 22 (2nd part) ; 1 Cor. 9 : 8 (1st part) ; Heb. 5 : 5 ; in the following the R.V. uses the verb to say, John 16 : 18 ; Acts 23 : 18 (2nd part) ; 26 : 22 (2nd part) ; Heb. 11 : 18. See Note above, and SPEAK, TALK, TELL, UTTER.

5346 AG:856B 3. PHĒMI (φημί), to declare, say, (*a*) is frequently used in quoting
CB:1264A the words of another, e.g., Matt. 13 : 29 ; 26 : 61 ; (*b*) is interjected into the recorded words, e.g., Acts 23 : 35 ; (*c*) is used impersonally, 2 Cor. 10 : 10.

After 1518 AG:— 4. EIRŌ (εἴρω), an obsolete verb, has the future tense *ereō*, used, e.g.,
CB:— in Matt. 7 : 4 ; Luke 4 : 23 (2nd part) ; 13 : 25 (last part) ; Rom. 3 : 5 ; 4 : 1 ; 6 : 1 ; 7 : 7 (1st part) ; 8 : 31 ; 9 : 14, 19, 20, 30 ; 11 : 19 ; 1 Cor. 15 : 35 ; 2 Cor. 12 : 6 ; Jas. 2 : 18. The perfect is used, e.g., in John 12 : 50 ; see No. 1, Note. The 1st aorist passive, "it was said," is used in Rom. 9 : 12, 26 ; Rev. 6 : 11. See SPEAK, No. 13.

4302 AG:708B 5. PROEIPON (προεῖπον) and *proereō*, to say before, used as aorist
CB:1266C and future respectively of *prolegō* (*pro*, before, and No. 1), is used (*a*) of prophecy, e.g., Rom. 9 : 29 ; 'to tell before,' Matt. 24 : 25 ; Mark 13 : 23 ; "were spoken before," 2 Pet. 3 : 2 ; Jude 17 ; (*b*) of saying before, 2 Cor. 7 : 3 ; 13 : 2, R.V. (A.V., to tell before and foretell) ; Gal. 1 : 9 ; 5 : 21 ; in 1 Thess. 4 : 6, "we forewarned," R.V. See FORETELL,
471 FOREWARN, TELL.

(-EPō) AG:73B 6. ANTEIPON (ἀντεῖπον), to say against (*anti*, against, and No. 1),
CB:— is so rendered in Acts 4 : 14. See GAINSAY.

PHASKō *Notes :* (1) *Phaskō*, to affirm, assert, is translated "saying" in Acts
5335 AG:854B 24 : 9, A.V. (R.V., "affirming"), and Rev. 2 : 2 in some mss. (A.V.).
CB:— See AFFIRM, No. 3. (2) In Acts 2 : 14, A.V., *apophthengomai*, to speak
APOPHTHENGOMAI forth (R.V.), is rendered "said." (3) The phrase *tout 'esti* (i.e., *touto esti*),
669 AG:102A "that is," is so translated in Matt. 27 : 46, R.V. (A.V., "that is to say") ;
CB:1237A so Acts 1 : 19 ; in Heb. 9 : 11 and 10 : 20, A.V. and R.V., "that is to say ;"
(-GESTHAI) AUTOS in Mark 7 : 11 the phrase is *ho esti*, lit., 'which is ;' the phrase *ho legetai*,
846 AG:122C lit., 'which is said,' John 1 : 38 and 20 : 16, is rendered "which is to
CB:1238B say." (4) In Luke 7 : 40 and Acts 13 : 15, the imperative mood of *eipon*
EIPON and *legō*, respectively, is rendered "say on." (5) In Mark 6 : 22, A.V.,
3004 (LEGō) *autēs*, "herself," R.V., is rendered "the said." (6) In Heb. 5 : 11, "we
AG:226A have many things to say" is, lit., 'much (*polus*) is the word (or discourse,
CB:1243A *logos*) for us.'

SAYING

3056 AG:477A 1. LOGOS (λόγος), a word, as embodying a conception or idea, denotes
CB:1257A among its various meanings, a saying, statement or declaration, uttered (*a*) by God ; R.V., "word" or "words" (A.V., "saying"), e.g., in John 8 : 55 ; Rom. 3 : 4 ; Rev. 19 : 9 ; 22 : 6, 7, 9, 10 ; (*b*) by Christ, e.g., Mark 8 : 32 ; 9 : 10 ; 10 : 22 ; Luke 9 : 28 ; John 6 : 60 ; 21 : 23 ; the R.V. appropriately substitutes "word" or "words" for A.V.,

" saying " or " sayings," especially in John's Gospel, e.g., 7 : 36, 40 ; 8 : 51, 52 ; 10 : 19 ; 14 : 24 ; 15 : 20 ; 18 : 9, 32 ; 19 : 13 ; (*c*) by an angel, Luke 1 : 29 ; (*d*) by O.T. prophets, John 12 : 38 (R.V., " word ") ; Rom. 13 : 9 (ditto) ; 1 Cor. 15 : 54 ; (*e*) by the Apostle Paul in the Pastoral Epp., 1 Tim. 1 : 15 ; 3 : 1 ; 4 : 9 ; 2 Tim. 2 : 11 ; Tit. 3 : 8 ; (*f*) by other men, Mark 7 : 29 ; Acts 7 : 29 ; John 4 : 37 (in general). See ACCOUNT, and especially WORD.

2. RHĒMA (ῥῆμα), that which is said, a word, is rendered " saying " **4487**
or " sayings " in Mark 9 : 32 ; Luke 1 : 65 ; 2 : 17, 50, 51 ; 7 : 1 ; 9 : 45 **AG:735B CB:1268A**
(twice) ; 18 : 34. See WORD.

Note : In Acts 14 : 18, " with these sayings " is, lit., 'saying (*legō*)
these things.' For *lalia*, " saying," John 4 : 42, A.V., see SPEECH, No. 2. **2981 AG:464A CB:1256C**

SCALE

LEPIS (λεπίς), from *lepō*, to peel, occurs in Acts 9 : 18.¶ **3013 AG:471C CB:—**

For SCARCE, SCARCELY see DIFFICULTY

SCARLET

KOKKINOS (κόκκινος) is derived from *kokkos*, used of the ' berries ' **2847**
(clusters of the eggs of an insect) collected from the *ilex coccifera* ; the **AG:440B CB:1255B**
colour, however, is obtained from the cochineal insect, which attaches itself to the leaves and twigs of the coccifera oak ; another species is raised on the leaves of the *cactus ficus*. The Arabic name for this insect is *qirmiz*, whence the word crimson. It is used (*a*) of scarlet wool, Heb. 9 : 19 ; cp., in connection with the cleansing of a leper, Lev. 14 : 4, 6, " scarlet ; " with the offering of the red heifer, Numb. 19 : 6 ; (*b*) of the robe put on Christ by the soldiers, Matt. 27 : 28 ; (*c*) of the " beast " seen in symbolic vision in Rev. 17 : 3, " scarlet-coloured ; " (*d*) of the clothing of the " woman " as seen sitting on the " beast," 17 : 4 ; (*e*) of part of the merchandise of Babylon, 18 : 12 ; (*f*) figuratively, of the glory of the city itself, 18 : 16 ; the neuter is used in the last three instances.¶

SCATTER

A. Verbs.

1. SKORPIZŌ (σκορπίζω) is used in Matt. 12 : 30 ; Luke 11 : 23 ; **4650**
John 10 : 12 ; 16 : 32 ; 2 Cor. 9 : 9, R.V. See DISPERSE, No. 2.¶ **AG:757A CB:1269B**

2. DIASKORPIZŌ (διασκορπίζω), to scatter abroad, is rendered to **1287**
scatter in Matt. 25 : 24, 26, R.V. (A.V., " strawed ") ; 26 : 31 ; Mark **AG:188B CB:1241B**
14 : 27 ; Luke 1 : 51 ; John 11 : 52 ; Acts 5 : 37, R.V. See DISPERSE, No. 3.

3. DIASPEIRŌ (διασπείρω), to scatter abroad (*dia*, throughout, **1289**
speirō, to sow seed), is used in Acts 8 : 1, 4 ; 11 : 19, all of the church **AG:188C CB:1241B**
in Jerusalem scattered through persecution ; the word in general is

suggestive of the effects of the scattering in the sowing of the spiritual seed of the Word of life. See DISPERSE, No. 4.¶

4496 (-TEŌ 4495) AG:736C CB:— 4. RHIPTŌ (ῥίπτω), to throw, cast, hurl, to be cast down, prostrate, is used in Matt. 9 : 36 of people who were scattered as sheep without a shepherd. See CAST, No. 2, THROW.

3039 AG:474D CB:— 5. LIKMAŌ (λικμάω), to winnow (*likmos*, a winnowing-fan), is rendered "will scatter . . . as dust" in Matt. 21 : 44 and Luke 20 : 18, R.V. (A.V., "will grind . . . to powder"). See GRIND, Note.¶

1262 AG:186B CB:1241B 6. DIALUŌ (διαλύω), to dissolve, is translated "scattered" in Acts 5 : 36, A.V.; see DISPERSE, No. 1.¶

B. Noun.

1290 AG:188C CB:1241B DIASPORA (διασπορά), a dispersion, is rendered "scattered abroad" in Jas. 1 : 1, A.V.; "scattered" in 1 Pet. 1 : 1, A.V.; see DISPERSION, B.

For SCEPTRE see ROD

SCHISM

4978 AG:797C CB:1268C SCHISMA (σχίσμα), a rent, division, is translated "schism" in 1 Cor. 12 : 25, metaphorically of the contrary condition to that which God has designed for a local church in 'tempering the body together' (ver. 24), the members having "the same care one for another" ("the same" being emphatic). See DIVISION, No. 3, RENT.

SCHOOL

4981 AG:798A CB:— SCHOLĒ (σχολή) (whence Eng., school) primarily denotes leisure, then, that for which leisure was employed, a disputation, lecture; hence, by metonymy, the place where lectures are delivered, a school, Acts 19 : 9.¶

For SCHOOLMASTER, Gal. 3 : 24, 25, see INSTRUCTOR, B, No. 1

SCIENCE

108 AG:163D CB:1248B GNŌSIS (γνῶσις) is translated "science" in the A.V. of 1 Tim. 6 : 20; the word simply means "knowledge" (R.V.), where the reference is to the teaching of the Gnostics (lit., the knowers) 'falsely called knowledge.' Science in the modern sense of the word, viz., the investigation, discovery and classification of secondary laws, is unknown in Scripture. See KNOW, C, No. 1.

SCOFF

1592 (-TERIZŌ) AG:243B CB:1243C EKMUKTĒRIZŌ (ἐκμυκτηρίζω), to hold up the nose in derision at (*ek*, from, used intensively, *muktērizō*, to mock; from *muktēr*, the nose), is translated "scoffed at" in Luke 16 : 14, R.V. (A.V., "derided"), of the Pharisees in their derision of Christ on account of His teaching; in 23 : 35 (ditto), of the mockery of Christ on the Cross by the rulers of the people.¶ In the Sept., Ps. 2 : 4; 22 : 7; 35 : 16.¶

For SCOFFERS, 2 Pet. 3 : 3, A.V., see MOCKERS

SCORCH, SCORCHING

A. Verb.

KAUMATIZŌ (καυματίζω), to scorch (from *kauma*, heat), is used **2739 AG:425B CB:1254C**
(*a*) of seed that had not much earth, Matt. 13 : 6 ; Mark 4 : 6 ; (*b*) of men, stricken retributively by the sun's heat, Rev. 16 : 8, 9.¶

B. Noun.

KAUSŌN (καύσων), burning heat (akin to *kaiō*, to burn), is translated **2742 AG:425C CB:—**
" scorching heat " in Matt. 20 : 12 (A.V., " heat ") ; Luke 12 : 55 (ditto) ; in Jas. 1 : 11, R.V., " scorching wind " (A.V., " burning heat "), here the reference is to a hot wind from the east (cp. Job 1 : 19). See HEAT.¶ In the Sept., Job 27 : 21 ; Jer. 18 : 17 ; 51 : 1 ; Ezek. 17 : 10 ; 19 : 12 ; Hos. 12 : 1 ; 13 : 15 ; Jonah 4 : 8.¶

For SCORN see LAUGH

SCORPION

SKORPIOS (σκορπίος), akin to *skorpizō*, to scatter (which see), is a **4651 AG:757A CB:1269B**
small animal (the largest of the several species is 6 in. long) like a lobster, but with a long tail, at the end of which is its venomous sting ; the pain, the position of the sting and the effect are mentioned in Rev. 9 : 3, 5, 10. The Lord's rhetorical question as to the provision of a scorpion instead of an egg, Luke 11 : 12, is, firstly, an allusion to the egg-like shape of the creature when at rest ; secondly, an indication of the abhorrence with which it is regarded. In Luke 10 : 19, the Lord's assurance to the disciples of the authority given them by Him to tread upon serpents and scorpions conveys the thought of victory over spiritually antagonistic forces, the powers of darkness, as is shown by His reference to the " power of the enemy " and by the context in vv. 17, 20.¶

SCOURGE (Noun and Verb)

A. Noun.

PHRAGELLION (φραγέλλιον), a whip (from Latin, *flagellum*), is used **5416 AG:865B CB:1264B**
of the scourge of small cords which the Lord made and employed before cleansing the Temple, John 2 : 15. However He actually used it, the whip was in itself a sign of authority and judgment.¶

B. Verbs.

1. PHRAGELLOŌ (φραγελλόω) (akin to A : Latin, *flagello* ; Eng., **5417 AG:865B CB:1264B**
flagellate), is the word used in Matt. 27 : 26, and Mark 15 : 15, of the scourging endured by Christ and administered by the order of Pilate. Under the Roman method of scourging, the person was stripped and tied in a bending posture to a pillar, or stretched on a frame. The scourge was made of leathern thongs, weighted with sharp pieces of bone or lead, which tore the flesh of both the back and the breast (cp. Psa. 22 : 17).

Eusebius (*Chron.*) records his having witnessed the suffering of martyrs who died under this treatment.¶

Note: In John 19 : 1 the scourging of Christ is described by Verb No. 2, as also in His prophecy of His sufferings, Matt. 20 : 19; Mark 10 : 34; Luke 18 : 33. In Acts 22 : 25 the similar punishment about to be administered to Paul is described by Verb No. 3 (the scourging of Roman citizens was prohibited by the Porcian law of 197, B.C.).

3146 AG:495A CB:1257C 2. MASTIGOŌ (μαστιγόω), akin to ***mastix*** (see below), is used (*a*) as mentioned under No. 1; (*b*) of Jewish scourgings, Matt. 10 : 17 and 23 : 34; (*c*) metaphorically, in Heb. 12 : 6, of the chastening by the Lord administered in love to His spiritual sons.¶

Note: The Jewish method of scourging, as described in the Mishna, was by the use of three thongs of leather, the offender receiving thirteen stripes on the bare breast and thirteen on each shoulder, the "forty stripes save one," as administered to Paul five times (2 Cor. 11 : 24). See also SCOURGINGS (below).

3147 AG:495A CB:1257C 3. MASTIZŌ (μαστίζω), akin to No. 2, occurs in Acts 22 : 25 (see No. 1, above).¶ In the Sept., Numb. 22 : 25.¶

SCOURGING (-S)

3148 AG:495B CB:1257C MASTIX (μάστιξ), a whip, scourge, is used (*a*) with the meaning scourging, in Acts 22 : 24, of the Roman method (see above, B, No. 1, Note); (*b*) in Heb. 11 : 36, of the sufferings of saints in the O.T. times. Among the Hebrews the usual mode, legal and domestic, was that of beating with a rod (see 2 Cor. 11 : 25); (*c*) metaphorically, of disease or suffering: see PLAGUE, No. 1.

SCRIBE (-S)

1122 AG:165D CB:1248C GRAMMATEUS (γραμματεύς), from *gramma*, a writing, denotes a scribe, a man of letters, a teacher of the law; the scribes are mentioned frequently in the Synoptists, especially in connection with the Pharisees, with whom they virtually formed one party (see Luke 5 : 21), sometimes with the chief priests, e.g., Matt. 2 : 4; Mark 8 : 31; 10 : 33; 11 : 18, 27; Luke 9 : 22. They are mentioned only once in John's Gospel, 8 : 3, three times in the Acts, 4 : 5; 6 : 12; 23 : 9; elsewhere only in 1 Cor. 1 : 20, in the singular. They were considered naturally qualified to teach in the Synagogues, Mark 1 : 22. They were ambitious of honour, e.g., Matt. 23 : 5–11, which they demanded especially from their pupils, and which was readily granted them, as well as by the people generally. Like Ezra (Ezra 7 : 12), the scribes were found originally among the priests and Levites. The priests being the official interpreters of the Law, the scribes ere long became an independent company; though they never held political power, they became leaders of the people.

Their functions regarding the Law were to teach it, develop it, and use it in connection with the Sanhedrin and various local courts. They also occupied themselves with the sacred writings both historical and didactic. They attached the utmost importance to ascetic elements, by which the nation was especially separated from the Gentiles. In their régime piety was reduced to external formalism. Only that was of value which was governed by external precept. Life under them became a burden; they themselves sought to evade certain of their own precepts, Matt. 23:16, ff.; Luke 11:46; by their traditions the Law, instead of being a help in moral and spiritual life, became an instrument for preventing true access to God, Luke 11:52. Hence the Lord's stern denunciations of them and the Pharisees (see PHARISEES).

Note: The word *grammateus* is used of the town clerk in Ephesus, Acts 19:35.

For SCRIP see WALLET

SCRIPTURE

1. GRAPHĒ (γραφή), akin to *graphō*, to write (Eng., graph, graphic, etc.), primarily denotes a drawing, painting; then a writing, (*a*) of the O.T. Scriptures, (1) in the plural, the whole, e.g., Matt. 21:42; 22:29; John 5:39; Acts 17:11; 18:24; Rom. 1:2, where "the prophets" comprises the O.T. writers in general; 15:4; 16:26, lit., 'prophetic writings,' expressing the character of all the Scriptures; (2) in the singular in reference to a particular passage, e.g., Mark 12:10; Luke 4:21; John 2:22; 10:35 (though applicable to all); 19:24, 28, 36, 37; 20:9; Acts 1:16; 8:32, 35; Rom. 4:3; 9:17; 10:11; 11:2; Gal. 3:8, 22; 4:30; 1 Tim. 5:18, where the 2nd quotation is from Luke 10:7, from which it may be inferred that the Apostle included Luke's Gospel as "Scripture" alike with Deuteronomy, from which the first quotation is taken; in reference to the whole, e.g. Jas. 4:5 (see R.V., a separate rhetorical question from the one which follows); in 2 Pet. 1:20, "no prophecy of Scripture," a description of all, with special application to the O.T. in the next verse; (*b*) of the O.T. Scriptures (those accepted by the Jews as canonical) and all those of the N.T. which were to be accepted by Christians as authoritative, 2 Tim. 3:16; these latter were to be discriminated from the many forged epistles and other religious writings already produced and circulated in Timothy's time. Such discrimination would be directed by the fact that "every Scripture," characterized by inspiration of God, would be profitable for the purposes mentioned; so the R.V. The A.V. states truth concerning the completed Canon of Scripture, but that was not complete when the Apostle wrote to Timothy.

1124 AG:166A CB:1248C

The Scriptures are frequently personified by the N.T. writers (as by the Jews, John 7:42), (*a*) as speaking with Divine authority, e.g., John 19:37; Rom. 4:3; 9:17, where the Scripture is said to speak to Pharaoh, giving the message actually sent previously by God to him through Moses; Jas. 4:5 (see above); (*b*) as possessed of the sentient quality of foresight, and the active power of preaching, Gal. 3 : 8, where the Scripture mentioned was written more than four centuries after the words were spoken. The Scripture, in such a case, stands for its Divine Author with an intimation that it remains perpetually characterized as the living voice of God. This Divine agency is again illustrated in Gal. 3 : 22 (cp. ver. 10 and Matt. 11 : 13).

1121
AG:165B
CB:1248C
2. GRAMMA (γράμμα), a letter of the alphabet, etc. is used of the Holy Scriptures in 2 Tim. 3 : 15. For the various uses of this word see LETTER.

SCROLL

975
AG:141B
CB:1239A
BIBLION (βιβλίον), the diminutive of *biblos*, a book, is used in Rev. 6 : 14, of a scroll, the rolling up of which illustrates the removal of the heaven. See BOOK, No. 2.

SEA

A. Nouns.

2281
AG:350A
CB:1271C
1. THALASSA (θάλασσα) is used (*a*) chiefly literally, e.g., the Red Sea, Acts 7 : 36 ; 1 Cor. 10 : 1 ; Heb. 11 : 29 ; the sea of Galilee or Tiberias, Matt. 4 : 18 ; 15 : 29 ; Mark 6 : 48, 49, where the acts of Christ testified to His Deity ; John 6 : 1 ; 21 : 1 ; in general, e.g., Luke 17 : 2 ; Acts 4 : 24 ; Rom. 9 : 27 ; Rev. 16 : 3 ; 18 : 17 ; 20 : 8, 13 ; 21 : 1 ; in combination with No. 2, Matt. 18 : 6 ; (*b*) metaphorically, of the ungodly men described in Jude 13 (cp. Is. 57 : 20) ; (*c*) symbolically, in the apocalyptic vision of " a glassy sea like unto crystal," Rev. 4 : 6, emblematic of the fixed purity and holiness of all that appertains to the authority and judicial dealings of God ; in 15 : 2, the same, " mingled with fire," and, standing by it (R.V.) or on it (A.V. and R.V. marg.), those who had " come victorious from the beast " (chapt. 13) ; of the wild and restless condition of nations, Rev. 13 : 1 (see 17 : 1, 15), where " he stood " (R.V.) refers to the dragon, not John (A.V.) ; from the midst of this state arises the beast, symbolic of the final Gentile power dominating the federated nations of the Roman world (see Dan., chapts. 2, 7, etc.).

Note : For the change from " the sea " in Deut. 30 : 13, to " the abyss " in Rom. 10 : 7, see BOTTOM, B.

3989
AG:641B
CB:—
2. PELAGOS (πέλαγος), the deep sea, the deep, is translated " the depth " in Matt. 18 : 6, and is used of the Sea of Cilicia in Acts 27 : 5. See DEPTH, No. 2.¶ *Pelagos* signifies " the vast expanse of open water," *thalassa,* " the sea as contrasted with the land " (Trench, Syn., § xiii).

B. Adjectives.

ENALIOS
1724
AG:261D
1. ENALIOS (ἐνάλιος), " in the sea," lit., of, or belonging to, the salt water (from *hals*, salt), occurs in Jas. 3 : 7.¶

PARALIOS
3882
AG:620A
2. PARALIOS (παράλιος), by the sea, Luke 6 : 17 : see COAST.¶

PARATHALASSIOS
3864
AG:616A
3. PARATHALASSIOS (παραθαλάσσιος), by the sea, Matt. 4 : 13, see COAST, Note 2.¶

DITHALASSOS
1337
AG:195A
4. DITHALASSOS (διθάλασσος) primarily signifies divided into two

seas (*dis*, twice, and *thalassa*) ; then, dividing the sea, as of a reef or rocky projection running out into the sea, Acts 27 : 41.¶

SEAL (Noun and Verb)

A. Noun.

SPHRAGIS (σφραγίς) denotes (*a*) a seal or signet, Rev. 7 : 2, " the seal of the living God," an emblem of ownership and security, here combined with that of destination (as in Ezek. 9 : 4), the persons to be sealed being secured from destruction and marked for reward ; (*b*) the impression of a seal or signet, (1) literal, a seal on a book or roll, combining with the ideas of security and destination those of secrecy and postponement of disclosures, Rev. 5 : 1, 2, 5, 9 ; 6 : 1, 3, 5, 7, 9, 12 ; 8 : 1 ; (2) metaphorical, Rom. 4 : 11, said of circumcision, as an authentication of the righteousness of Abraham's faith, and an external attestation of the covenant made with him by God ; the Rabbis called circumcision " the seal of Abraham ; " in 1 Cor. 9 : 2, of converts as a seal or authentication of Paul's apostleship ; in 2 Tim. 2 : 19, " the firm foundation of God standeth, having this seal, The Lord knoweth them that are His," R.V., indicating ownership, authentication, security and destination, " and, Let every one that nameth the Name of the Lord depart from unrighteousness," indicating a ratification on the part of the believer of the determining counsel of God concerning him ; Rev. 9 : 4 distinguishes those who will be found without the seal of God on their foreheads [see (*a*) above and B, No. 1].¶ 4973 AG:796C CB:1269C

B. Verbs.

1. SPHRAGIZŌ (σφραγίζω), to seal (akin to A), is used to indicate (*a*) security and permanency (attempted but impossible), Matt. 27 : 66 ; on the contrary, of the doom of Satan, fixed and certain, Rev. 20 : 3, R.V., " sealed it over ; " (*b*) in Rom. 15 : 28, " when . . . I have . . . sealed to them this fruit," the formal ratification of the ministry of the churches of the Gentiles in Greece and Galatia to needy saints in Judæa, by Paul's faithful delivery of the gifts to them ; this material help was the fruit of his spiritual ministry to the Gentiles, who on their part were bringing forth the fruit of their having shared with them in spiritual things ; the metaphor stresses the sacred formalities of the transaction (Deissmann illustrates this from the papyri of Fayyum, in which the sealing of sacks guarantees the full complement of the contents) ; (*c*) secrecy and security and the postponement of disclosure, Rev. 10 : 4 ; in a negative command, 22 : 10 ; (*d*) ownership and security, together with destination, Rev. 7 : 3, 4, 5 (as with the noun in ver. 2 ; see A) ; the same three indications are conveyed in Eph. 1 : 13, in the metaphor of the sealing of believers by the gift of the Holy Spirit, upon believing (i.e., at the time of their regeneration, not after a lapse of time in their spiritual life, " having also believed "—not as A.V., " after that ye believed "— ; the aorist-participle marks the definiteness and completeness of the act of faith) ; the idea of destination is stressed by the phrase " the Holy Spirit of 4972 AG:796B CB:1269C

promise" (see also ver. 14); so 4 : 30, "ye were sealed unto the day of redemption;" so in 2 Cor. 1 : 22, where the Middle Voice intimates the special interest of the Sealer in His act; (*e*) authentication by the believer (by receiving the witness of the Son) of the fact that "God is true," John 3 : 33; authentication by God in sealing the Son as the Giver of eternal life (with perhaps a figurative allusion to the impress of a mark upon loaves), 6 : 27.¶

Note: In Rev. 7, after the 5th verse (first part) the original does not repeat the mention of the sealing except in ver. 8 (last part) (hence the
2696 omission in the R.V.).

AG:419C 2. KATASPHRAGIZŌ (κατασφραγίζω), No. 1, strengthened by *kata*,
CB:1254B intensive, is used of the book seen in the vision in Rev. 5 : 1, R.V., "close sealed (with seven seals)," the successive opening of which discloses the events destined to take place throughout the period covered by chapters 6 to 19.¶ In the Sept., Job 9 : 7; 37 : 7.¶

SEAM (without)

729
AG:104B ARAPHOS or ARRHAPHOS (ἄραφος) denotes "without seam"
CB:— (*a*, negative, and *rhaptō*, to sew), John 19 : 23.¶

SEARCH

2045
AG:306C 1. ERAUNAŌ or EREUNAŌ, an earlier form, (ἐραυνάω), to search,
CB:1246B examine, is used (*a*) of God, as searching the heart, Rom. 8 : 27; (*b*) of Christ, similarly, Rev. 2 : 23; (*c*) of the Holy Spirit, as searching all things, 1 Cor. 2 : 10, acting in the spirit of the believer; (*d*) of the O.T. prophets, as searching their own writings concerning matters foretold of Christ, testified by the Spirit of Christ in them, 1 Pet. 1 : 11 (cp. No. 2); (*e*) of the Jews, as commanded by the Lord to search the Scriptures, John 5 : 39, A.V., and R.V. marg., "search," R.V. text, "ye search," either is possible grammatically; (*f*) of Nicodemus as commanded
1830 similarly by the chief priests and Pharisees, John 7 : 52.¶

AG:274B 2. EXERAUNAŌ (ἐξεραυνάω), a strengthened form of No. 1 (*ek*, or
CB:1247C *ex*, out), to search out, is used in 1 Pet. 1 : 10, "searched diligently;"
(-Nō) cp. No. 1 (*d*).¶

1833
AG:275C 3. EXETAZŌ (ἐξετάζω), to examine closely, inquire carefully (from
CB:— *etazō*, to examine), occurs in Matt. 2 : 8, R.V., "search out;" so Matt. 10 : 11, R.V.: see INQUIRE, No. 4.

350
AG:56B *Note:* For *anakrinō*, rendered "searched" in Acts 17 : 11, A.V., see
CB:1235A EXAMINE.

For SEARED see BRANDED

SEASON (Noun)

A. Nouns.

2540
AG:394D 1. KAIROS (καιρός), primarily, due measure, fitness, proportion, is
CB:1253A used in the N.T. to signify a season, a time, a period possessed of certain

characteristics, frequently rendered " time " or " times ; " in the following the R.V. substitutes " season " for the A.V. " time," thus distinguishing the meaning from *chronos* (see No. 2) : Matt. 11 : 25 ; 12 : 1 ; 14 : 1 ; 21 : 34 ; Mark 11 : 13 ; Acts 3 : 19 ; 7 : 20 ; 17 : 26 ; Rom. 3 : 26 ; 5 : 6 ; 9 : 9 ; 13 : 11 ; 1 Cor. 7 : 5 ; Gal. 4 : 10 ; 1 Thess. 2 : 17, lit., 'for a season (of an hour) ;' 2 Thess. 2 : 6 ; in Eph. 6 : 18, " at all seasons " (A.V., " always ") ; in Tit. 1 : 3, " His own seasons " (marg., " its ; " A.V., " in due times ") ; in the preceding clause *chronos* is used.

The characteristics of a period are exemplified in the use of the term with regard, e.g., to harvest, Matt. 13 : 30 ; reaping, Gal. 6 : 9 ; punishment, Matt. 8 : 29 ; discharging duties, Luke 12 : 42 ; opportunity for doing anything, whether good, e.g., Matt. 26 : 18 ; Gal. 6 : 10 (" opportunity ") ; Eph. 5 : 16 ; or evil, e.g., Rev. 12 : 12 ; the fulfilment of prophecy, Luke 1 : 20 ; Acts 3 : 19 ; 1 Pet. 1 : 11 ; a time suitable for a purpose, Luke 4 : 13, lit., 'until a season ;' 2 Cor. 6 : 2 ; see further under No. 2. See ALWAYS, Note, OPPORTUNITY, TIME, WHILE.

2. CHRONOS (χρόνος), whence Eng. words beginning with chron—, 5550
denotes a space of time, whether long or short : (*a*) it implies duration, AG:887D CB:1240B
whether longer, e.g., Acts 1 : 21, " (all the) time ; " Acts 13 : 18 ; 20 : 18, R.V., " (all the) time " (A.V., " at all seasons ") ; or shorter, e.g., Luke 4 : 5 ; (*b*) it sometimes refers to the date of an occurrence, whether past, e.g., Matt. 2 : 7, or future, e.g., Acts 3 : 21 ; 7 : 17.

Broadly speaking, *chronos* expresses the duration of a period, *kairos* stresses it as marked by certain features ; thus in Acts 1 : 7, " the Father has set within His own authority " both the times (*chronos*), the lengths of the periods, and the seasons (*kairos*), epochs characterized by certain events ; in 1 Thess. 5 : 1, " times " refers to the length of the interval before the Parousia takes place (the presence of Christ with the saints when He comes to receive them to Himself at the Rapture), and to the length of time the Parousia will occupy ; " seasons " refers to the special features of the period before, during, and after the Parousia.

Chronos marks quantity, *kairos*, quality. Sometimes the distinction between the two words is not sharply defined as, e.g., in 2 Tim. 4 : 6, though even here the Apostle's " departure " signalizes the time (*kairos*). The words occur together in the Sept. only in Dan. 2 : 21 and Eccl. 3 : 1. *Chronos* is rendered " season " in Acts 19 : 22, A.V. (R.V., " a while ") ; 20 : 18 (R.V., "all the time," see above) ; Rev. 6 : 11, A.V. (R.V., " time ") ; so 20 : 3. In Luke 23 : 8 it is used with *hikanos* in the plural, R.V., " (of a long) time," more lit., '(for a sufficient number) of times.'

In Rev. 10 : 6 *chronos* has the meaning " delay " (R.V., marg.), an important rendering for the understanding of the passage (the word being akin to *chronizō*, to take time, to linger, delay, Matt. 24 : 48 ; Luke 12 : 45). See DELAY, B, Note, SPACE, TIME, WHILE.

3. HŌRA (ὥρα), an hour, is translated " season " in John 5 : 35 ; 5610 AG:896A
2 Cor. 7 : 8 ; Philm. 15 : see HOUR. CB:1251A

B. Adjective.

4340 AG:715B PROSKAIROS (πρόσκαιρος), temporary, transient, is rendered " for
CB:1267A a season " in Heb. 11 : 25. See TEMPORAL, TIME, WHILE.

C. Adverbs.

171 AG:29B 1. AKAIRŌS (ἀκαίρως) denotes " out of season," unseasonably
CB:1234A (akin to *akairos*, unseasonable, *a*, negative, and A, No. 1), 2 Tim. 4 : 2.¶

2122 AG:321C 2. EUKAIRŌS (εὐκαίρως), " in season " (*eu*, well), 2 Tim. 4 : 2 ;
CB:1247B it occurs also in Mark 14 : 11, " conveniently."¶

3641 AG:563C CB:1260C *Note :* For *oligon*, 1 Pet. 1 : 6, A.V., " for a season," see WHILE.

SEASON (Verb)

741 AG:111A ARTUŌ (ἀρτύω), to arrange, make ready (cp. *artios*, fitted), is used of
CB:1237C seasoning, Mark 9 : 50 ; Luke 14 : 34 ; Col. 4 : 6.¶

SEAT (Noun and Verb)

A. Nouns.

2515 AG:388B 1. KATHEDRA (καθέδρα), from *kata*, down, and *hedra*, a seat, denotes
CB:1254C a seat (Eng., cathedral), a chair, Matt. 21 : 12 ; Mark 11 : 15 ; of teachers,
Matt. 23 : 2.¶

4410 AG:725B 2. PRŌTOKATHEDRIA (πρωτοκαθεδρία), the first seat, Matt. 23 : 6 ;
CB:1267B Mark 12 : 39 ; Luke 11 : 43 ; 20 : 46 ; see CHIEF, No. 6. Cp. ROOM.¶

2362 AG:364B *Note :* For *thronos*, sometimes translated " seat " in the A.V., see
CB:1272B THRONE.

B. Verb.

2521 AG:389B KATHĒMAI (κάθημαι), to sit, be seated, is translated " shall . . .
CB:1254C be seated " in Luke 22 : 69, R.V. ; " is seated," Col. 3 : 1, R.V. (A.V.,
" shall . . . sit " and " sitteth "). See SIT.

SECOND, SECONDARILY, SECONDLY

1208 AG:177A 1. DEUTEROS (δεύτερος) denotes second in order with or without the
CB:1241A idea of time, e.g., Matt. 22 : 26, 39 ; 2 Cor. 1 : 15 ; Rev. 2 : 11 ; in
Rev. 14 : 8, R.V. only (" a second angel ") ; it is used in the neuter, *deuteron*, adverbially, signifying a second time, e.g., John 3 : 4 ; 21 : 16 ; Acts 7 : 13 ; Rev. 19 : 3, R.V. (A.V., " again ") ; Jude 5, " afterward " (R.V., marg., " the second time ") ; used with *ek* (of) idiomatically, the preposition signifying " for (the second time)," Mark 14 : 72 ; John 9 : 24 and Acts 11 : 9, R.V. (A.V., " again ") ; Heb. 9 : 28 ; in 1 Cor. 12 : 28, A.V., " secondarily," R.V., " secondly."

Note : In Acts 13 : 33 some mss. have *prōtos*, " (in the) first (psalm) ; " the 1st and 2nd Psalms were originally one, forming a prologue to the whole book ; hence the numbering in the Sept.

1206 AG:177A 2. DEUTERAIOS (δευτεραῖος), an adjective with an adverbial sense
CB:— (from No. 1), is used in Acts 28 : 13, R.V., " on the second day " (A.V.,
" the next day "), lit., ' second day (persons we came).'¶

1207 AG:177A *Note :* In Luke 6 : 1, the A.V. translates those mss. which have
CB:— *deuteroprōtos*, lit., ' second-first,' said of a sabbath (see R.V. marg.).¶

SECRET, SECRETLY

A. Adjectives.

1. KRUPTOS (κρυπτός), secret, hidden (akin to *kruptō*, to hide), 2927
Eng., crypt, cryptic etc., is used as an adjective and rendered " secret " in AG:454A
Luke 8 : 17, A.V. (R.V., " hid ") ; in the neuter, with *en*, in, as an adverbial CB:1256A
phrase, " in secret," with the article, Matt. 6 : 4, 6 (twice in each ver.) ; without the article, John 7 : 4, 10 ; 18 : 20 ; in the neuter plural, with the article, " the secrets (of men)," Rom. 2 : 16 ; of the heart, 1 Cor. 14 : 25 ; in Luke 11 : 33, A.V., " a secret place " (R.V., " cellar "). See CELLAR, HIDDEN, INWARDLY.

2. APOKRUPHOS (ἀπόκρυφος) (whence Apocrypha), hidden, is 614
translated " kept secret " in Mark 4 : 22, A.V. (R.V., " made secret ") ; AG:93D
" secret " in Luke 8 : 17, R.V. (A.V., " hid "). See HIDE, B, No. 2. CB:1237A

3. KRUPHAIOS (κρυφαῖος) occurs in the best mss. in Matt. 6 : 18 —
(twice ; some have No. 1).¶ AG:454D
CB:1256A

B. Adverbs.

1. KRUPHĒ (κρυφῇ), akin to A, No. 1, secretly, in secret, is used in 2931 AG:454D
Eph. 5 : 12.¶ CB:1256A

2. LATHRA (λάθρᾳ), akin to *lanthanō*, to escape notice, be hidden, is 2977
translated " secretly " in John 11 : 28. See PRIVILY. AG:462C
CB:—

C. Verb.

KRUPTŌ (κρύπτω), to hide, is translated " secretly " in John 19 : 38 2928
[perfect participle, Passive Voice, lit., ' (but) having been hidden '], AG:454B
referring to Nicodemus as having been a secret disciple of Christ ; in CB:1256A
Matt. 13 : 35, A.V., it is translated " kept secret " (R.V., " hidden ").

Notes : (1) For *tameion*, translated " secret chambers " in Matt. 24 : 26, TAMEION
see CHAMBER, No. 1. (2) For the A.V. rendering of *sigaō*, in Rom. 16 : 25, 5009 AG:803C
" kept secret," see PEACE (hold one's), No. 2, and SILENCE. (3) For CB:—
" I have learned the secret," see LEARN, No. 4. SIGAō 4601
AG:749C
CB:—

SECT

HAIRESIS (αἵρεσις), a choosing, is translated " sect " throughout the 139
Acts, except in 24 : 14, A.V., " heresy " (R.V., " sect ") ; it properly AG:23D
denotes a predilection either for a particular truth, or for a perversion of CB:1249A
one, generally with the expectation of personal advantage ; hence, a division and the formation of a party or sect in contrast to the uniting power of " the truth," held *in toto ;* a sect is a division developed and brought to an issue ; the order " divisions, heresies " (marg. " parties ") in " the works of the flesh " in Gal. 5 : 19–21 is suggestive of this. See HERESY.

SECURE (Verb)

PERIKRATĒS (περικρατής), an adjective, signifies 'having full 4031
command of' (*peri*, around, about, *krateō*, to be strong, to rule) ; it is AG:648B
used with *ginomai*, to become, in Acts 27 : 16, R.V., " to secure (the boat)," CB:—
A.V., " to come by."¶

275 *Note:* In Matt. 28 : 14, A.V., *amerimnos*, without anxiety, with
AG:45B CB:1234C *poieō*, to make, is translated " we will . . . secure (you)," R.V., " we
will . . . rid (you) of care." The Eng. " secure " is derived from the Latin *se*, free from, and *cura*, care. See CARE.

SECURITY

2425 HIKANOS (ἱκανός), sufficient, is used in its neuter form with the
AG:374B CB:1250C article, as a noun, in Acts 17 : 9, " (when they had taken) security,"
i.e., satisfaction, lit., ' the sufficient.' The use of ***hikanos*** in this construction is a Latinism in Greek. See Moulton, Proleg., p. 20. Probably the bond given to the authorities by Jason and his friends included an undertaking that Paul would not return to Thessalonica. Any efforts to have the bond cancelled were unsuccessful; hence the reference to the hindrance by Satan (1 Thess. 2 : 18). See ABLE, C, No. 2.

SEDITION

A. Nouns.

4714 1. STASIS (στάσις), a dissension, an insurrection, is translated
AG:764C CB:1270A " sedition " in Acts 24 : 5, A.V. (R.V., " insurrections "). See DISSENSION,
INSURRECTION.

1370 2. DICHOSTASIA (διχοστασία), lit., a standing apart (*dicha*, asunder,
AG:200B CB:1241B apart, *stasis*, a standing), hence a dissension, division, is translated
" seditions " in Gal. 5 : 20, A.V. See DIVISION, No. 2.

B. Verb.

387 ANASTATOŌ (ἀναστατόω), to excite, unsettle, ' to stir up to sedition,'
AG:61A CB:— is so translated in Acts 21 : 38, R.V. (A.V., " madest an uproar "); in
17 : 6, " have turned (the world) upside down," i.e., causing tumults; in Gal. 5 : 12, R.V., " unsettle " (A.V., " trouble "), i.e., by false teaching (here in the continuous present tense, lit., ' those who are unsettling you '). The word was supposed not to have been used in profane authors. It has been found, however, in several of the papyri writings. See TURN, UNSETTLE.¶

SEDUCE, SEDUCING

A. Verbs.

4105 1. PLANAŌ (πλανάω), to cause to wander, lead astray, is translated
AG:665B CB:1265A to seduce in 1 John 2 : 26, A.V. (R.V., " lead . . . astray "); in Rev.
2 : 20, to seduce. See DECEIT, C, No. 6.

635 2. APOPLANAŌ (ἀποπλανάω) is translated " seduce " in Mark 13 : 22
AG:97B CB:1237A (R.V., " lead astray "); see LEAD, No. 13.

B. Adjective.

4108 PLANOS (πλάνος), akin to A, lit., wandering, then, deceiving, is
AG:666A CB:1265A translated " seducing " in 1 Tim. 4 : 1. See DECEIVER, No. 1.

For SEDUCERS see IMPOSTORS

SEE, SEEING

A. Verbs.

1. BLEPŌ (βλέπω), to have sight, is used of bodily vision, e.g., Matt. **991**
11 : 4 ; and mental, e.g., Matt. 13 : 13, 14 ; it is said of God the Father in **AG:143B**
Matt. 6 : 4, 6, 18 ; of Christ as seeing what the Father doeth, John 5 : 19. **CB:1239A**
It especially stresses the thought of the person who sees. For the various uses see BEHOLD, No. 2 ; see Note below.

2. HORAŌ (ὁράω), with the form *eidon*, serving for its aorist tense, **3708**
and *opsomai*, for its future tense (Middle Voice), denotes to see, of bodily **AG:577D**
vision, e.g., John 6 : 36 ; and mental, e.g., Matt. 8 : 4 ; it is said of Christ **CB:1251A**
as seeing the Father, John 6 : 46, and of what He had seen with the Father, 8 : 38. It especially indicates the direction of the thought to the object seen. See BEHOLD, No. 1.

Note : " *Horaō* and *blepō* both denote the physical act : *horaō*, in general, *blepō*, the single look ; *horaō* gives prominence to the discerning mind, *blepō* to the particular mood or point. When the physical side recedes, *horaō* denotes perception in general (as resulting principally from vision) . . . *Blepō*, on the other hand, when its physical side recedes, gets a purely outward sense, look (open, incline) towards [as of a situation] " (Schmidt, Grimm-Thayer).

3. APHORAŌ (ἀφοράω), with *apeidon* serving as the aorist tense, to **872**
look away from one thing so as to see another (*apo*, from, and No. 2), as **AG:127B**
in Heb. 12 : 2, simply means to see in Phil. 2 : 23.¶ **CB:—**

4. KATHORAŌ (καθοράω), lit., to look down (*kata*, and No. 2), denotes **2529**
to discern clearly, Rom. 1 : 20, " are clearly seen."¶ In the Sept., Numb. **AG:391A**
24 : 2 ; Job 10 : 4 ; 39 : 26.¶ **CB:1254C**

5. DIABLEPŌ (διαβλέπω), to see clearly (*dia*, through, and No. 1), **1227**
is used in Matt. 7 : 5 ; Luke 6 : 42 ; in Mark 8 : 25, R.V., " he looked **AG:181D**
stedfastly " (No. 6 is used in the next clause ; No. 1 in ver. 24, and No. 2 **CB:—**
in the last part).¶

6. EMBLEPŌ (ἐμβλέπω), to look at (*en*, in, and No. 1), used of **1689**
earnestly looking, is translated " saw " in Mark 8 : 25 (last part) ; " could **AG:254C**
(not) see " in Acts 22 : 11. See BEHOLD, No. 3. **CB:1244B**

7. ANABLEPŌ (ἀναβλέπω), to look up, is translated " see," of the **308**
blind, in Luke 7 : 22, A.V. (R.V., " receive their sight "). See SIGHT. **AG:50D** **CB:1235A**

8. THEAOMAI (θεάομαι), to view attentively, to see with admiration, **2300**
desire, or regard, stresses more especially the action of the person beholding, **AG:353A**
as with No. 1, in contrast to No 2 ; it is used in Matt. 11 : 7 (R.V., " to **CB:1271C**
behold "), while *idein*, the infinitive of *eidon* (see under No. 2), is used in the questions in the next two verses ; in verse 7 the interest in the onlooker is stressed, in vv. 8, 9, the attention is especially directed to the object seen. The verb is translated to see in the A.V. and R.V. of Matt. 6 : 1 ; Mark 16 : 11, 14 ; John 6 : 5 ; Acts 8 : 18 (in some mss.) ; 21 : 27 ; Rom. 15 : 24 ; elsewhere, for the A.V., to see, the R.V. uses the verb to behold, bringing out its force more suitably. See BEHOLD, No. 8.

2334 9. THEŌREŌ (θεωρέω) denotes to be a spectator of, indicating the
AG:360A CB:1272A careful perusal of details in the object ; it points especially, as in No. 1,
to the action of the person beholding, e.g., Matt. 28 : 1 ; the R.V. frequently renders it by to behold, for the A.V., to see, e.g., John 14 : 17, 19 ; 16 : 10, 16, 17, 19. The difference between this verb and Nos. 1 and 2 is brought out in John 20 : 5, 6, 8 ; in ver. 5 *blepō* is used of John's sight of the linen cloths in the tomb, without his entering in ; he saw at a glance
MUōPAZō the Lord was not there ; in ver. 6 the closer contemplation by Peter is
3467 AG:531A expressed in the verb *theōreō*. But in ver. 8 the grasping by John of the
CB:— significance of the undisturbed cloths is denoted by *eidon* (see No. 2, and
PHAINō 5316 see WRAP).
AG:851B 10. MUŌPAZŌ (μυωπάζω), to be short-sighted (*muō*, to shut, *ōps*, the
CB:1263C IDE eye ; cp. Eng., myopy, myopic : the root *mu* signifies a sound made with
2396 closed lips, e.g., in the words mutter, mute), occurs in 2 Pet. 1 : 9, R.V.,
AG:369B CB:1252C " seeing only what is near " (A.V., " and cannot see afar off ") ; this does
IDOU not contradict the preceding word " blind," it qualifies it ; he of whom
2400 370D it is true is blind in that he cannot discern spiritual things, he is near-
CB:1252C sighted in that he is occupied in regarding worldly affairs.¶
OPTANō (-OMAI) 11. PHAINŌ (φαίνω), to cause to appear, and in the Passive Voice, to
3700 appear, be manifest, is rendered " (that) they may be seen " in Matt. 6 : 5 ;
AG:576C CB:1261A " it was (never so) seen," 9 : 33. See APPEAR.
HISTOREō *Notes :* (1) For *ide* and *idou*, regularly rendered " behold " in the
2477 R.V., see BEHOLD, No. 4. (2) For *optanō*, in Acts 1 : 3, A.V., " being
AG:383A CB:1251A seen," see APPEAR, A, No. 7. (3) For *historeō*, in Gal. 1 : 18, A.V., to see,
PROORAō see VISIT. (4) For *prooraō*, and *proeidon*, to see before, see FORESEE.
4308 AG:709A (5) For " make . . . see " see ENLIGHTEN.

CB:—

B. Noun.

990 BLEMMA (βλέμμα), primarily, a look, a glance (akin to A, No. 1),
AG:143B CB:— denotes sight, 2 Pet. 2 : 8, rendered " seeing ; " some interpret it as meaning " look ; " Moulton and Milligan illustrate it thus from the papyri ; it seems difficult, however to take the next word " hearing " (in the similar construction) in this way.¶

SEED

4690 AG:761D 1. SPERMA (σπέρμα), akin to *speirō*, to sow (Eng., sperm, spermatic
CB:1269C etc.), has the following usages, (*a*) agricultural and botanical, e.g., Matt. 13 : 24, 27, 32 (for the A.V. of vv. 19, 20, 22, 23, see SOW, as in the R.V.) ; 1 Cor. 15 : 38 ; 2 Cor. 9 : 10 ; (*b*) physiological, Heb. 11 : 11 ; (*c*) metaphorical and by metonymy for offspring, posterity, (1) of natural offspring, e.g., Matt. 22 : 24, 25, R.V., " seed " (A.V., " issue ") ; John 7 : 42 ; 8 : 33, 37 ; Acts 3 : 25 ; Rom. 1 : 3 ; 4 : 13, 16, 18 ; 9 : 7 (twice), 8, 29 ; 11 : 1 ; 2 Cor. 11 : 22 ; Heb. 2 : 16 ; 11 : 18 ; Rev. 12 : 17 ; Gal. 3 : 16, 19, 29 ; in the 16th ver., " He saith not, And to seeds, as of many ; but as of one, And to thy seed, which is Christ," quoted from the Sept. of Gen. 13 : 15 and 17 : 7, 8, there is especial stress on the word " seed," as

referring to an individual (here, Christ) in fulfilment of the promises to Abraham—a unique use of the singular. While the plural form " seeds," neither in Hebrew nor in Greek, would have been natural any more than in English (it is not so used in Scripture of human offspring; its plural occurrence is in 1 Sam. 8 : 15, of crops), yet if the Divine intention had been to refer to Abraham's natural descendants, another word could have been chosen in the plural, such as ' children ; ' all such words were, however, set aside, ' seed ' being selected as one that could be used in the singular, with the purpose of showing that the " seed " was Messiah. Some of the Rabbis had even regarded " seed," e.g., in Gen. 4 : 25 and Is. 53 : 10, as referring to the Coming One. Descendants were given to Abraham by other than natural means, so that through him Messiah might come, and the point of the Apostle's argument is that since the fulfilment of the promises of God is secured alone by Christ, they only who are " in Christ " can receive them ; (2) of spiritual offspring, Rom. 4 : 16, 18 ; 9 : 8 ; here " the children of the promise are reckoned for a seed " points, firstly, to Isaac's birth as being not according to the ordinary course of nature but by Divine promise, and, secondly, by analogy, to the fact that all believers are children of God by spiritual birth ; Gal. 3 : 29.

As to 1 John 3 : 9, " his seed abideth in him," it is possible to understand this as meaning that children of God (His seed) abide in Him, and do not go on doing (practising) sin (the verb to commit does not represent the original in this passage). Alternatively, the seed signifies the principle of spiritual life as imparted to the believer, which abides in him without possibility of removal or extinction ; the child of God remains eternally related to Christ, he who lives in sin has never become so related, he has not the principle of life in him. This meaning suits the context and the general tenor of the Epistle.

2. SPOROS (σπόρος), akin to No. 1, properly a sowing, denotes seed sown, (*a*) natural, Mark 4 : 26, 27 ; Luke 8 : 5, 11 (the natural being figuratively applied to the Word of God) ; 2 Cor. 9 : 10 (1st part) ; (*b*) metaphorically of material help to the needy, 2 Cor. 9 : 10 (2nd part), R.V., " (your) seed for sowing " (A.V., " seed sown ").¶ **4703 AG:763B CB:1269C**

3. SPORA (σπορά), akin to No. 1, and like No. 2, a sowing, seedtime, denotes seed sown, 1 Pet. 1 : 23, of human offspring.¶ In the Sept., 2 Kings 19 : 29.¶ **4701 AG:763B CB:1269C**

SEEING, SEEING THAT (conjunction), see † p. 1

SEEK

1. ZĒTEŌ (ζητέω) signifies (*a*) to seek, to seek for, e.g., Matt. 7 : 7, 8 ; 13 : 45 ; Luke 24 : 5 ; John 6 : 24 ; of plotting against a person's life, Matt. 2 : 20 ; Acts 21 : 31 ; Rom. 11 : 3 ; metaphorically, to seek by thinking, to seek how to do something, or what to obtain, e.g., Mark 11 : 18 ; Luke 12 : 29 ; to seek to ascertain a meaning, John 16 : 19, " do **2212 AG:338D CB:1273C**

ye inquire;" to seek God, Acts 17:27, R.V.; Rom. 10:20; (*b*) to seek or strive after, endeavour, to desire, e.g., Matt. 12:46, 47, R.V., "seeking" (A.V., "desiring"); Luke 9:9, R.V., "sought" (A.V., "desired"); John 7:19, R.V., "seek ye" (A.V., "go ye about"); so ver. 20; Rom. 10:3, R.V., "seeking" (A.V., "going about"); of seeking the kingdom of God and His righteousness, in the sense of coveting earnestly, striving after, Matt. 6:33; "the things that are above," Col. 3:1; peace, 1 Pet. 3:11; (*c*) to require or demand, e.g., Mark 8:12; Luke 11:29 (some mss. have No. 4); 1 Cor. 4:2, "it is required;" 2 Cor. 13:3, "ye seek." See About, B, Note, Desire, B, Note (2), Endeavour, Go, Note (2) (*a*), Inquire, Require.

327 2. ANAZĒTEŌ (ἀναζητέω), to seek carefully (*ana*, up, used intensively,
AG:53D CB:— and No. 1), is used of searching for human beings, difficulty in the effort being implied, Luke 2:44, 45 (some mss. have No. 1 in the latter ver.); Acts 11:25; numerous illustrations of this particular meaning in the papyri are given by Moulton and Milligan.¶ In the Sept., Job 3:4; 10:6.¶

1567 3. EKZĒTEŌ (ἐκζητέω) signifies (*a*) to seek out (*ek*) or after, to search
AG:240A CB:1244A for; e.g., God, Rom. 3:11; the Lord, Acts 15:17; in Heb. 11:6, R.V., "seek after" (A.V., "diligently seek"); 12:17, R.V., "sought diligently" (A.V., "sought carefully"); 1 Pet. 1:10, R.V., "sought" (A.V., "have inquired"), followed by *exeraunaō*, to search diligently; (*b*) to require or demand, Luke 11:50, 51. See Inquire, Note (3), Require.¶

1934 4. EPIZĒTEŌ (ἐπιζητέω), to seek after (directive, *epi*, towards), is
AG:292D CB:1246B always rendered in the R.V., by some form of the verb to seek, Acts 13:7, "sought" (A.V., "desired"); 19:39, "seek" (A.V., "inquire"); Phil. 4:17, "seek for" (A.V., "desire"), twice; elsewhere, Matt. 6:32; 12:39; 16:4; Mark 8:12 (in some texts); Luke 12:30; Acts 12:19; Rom. 11:7; Heb. 11:14; 13:14. See Desire, Inquire.¶

3713 (-OMAI) 5. OREGŌ (ὀρέγω), to reach out, or after, used in the Middle Voice
AG:579D CB:1261A (-OMAI) is translated "seeketh" in 1 Tim. 3:1, R.V., of 'seeking overseership' (A.V., "desireth"). See Desire, No. 5.

2206 *Note:* For the R.V. renderings of *zēloō*, in Gal. 4:17, 18, "they
AG:338A CB:1273B zealously seek," "ye may seek," "to be zealously sought," see Affect, Note, and Zealous.

SEEM

1380 DOKEŌ (δοκέω) denotes (*a*) to be of opinion (akin to *doxa*, opinion),
AG:201D CB:1242A e.g., Luke 8:18, R.V., "thinketh" (A.V., "seemeth"); so 1 Cor. 3:18; to think, suppose, Jas. 1:26, R.V., "thinketh himself" (A.V., "seem"); see Suppose, Think; (*b*) to seem, to be reputed, e.g., Acts 17:18; 1 Cor. 11:16; 12:22; 2 Cor. 10:9; Heb. 4:1; 12:11; for Gal. 2:2, 6, 9, see Repute; (*c*) impersonally (1) to think (see Think), (2) to seem good, Luke 1:3; Acts 15:22, R.V., "it seemed good" (A.V., "it pleased");

15 : 25, 28 (ver. 34 in some mss.) ; in Heb. 12 : 10, the neuter of the present participle is used with the article, lit., ' the (thing) seeming good,' R.V., " (as) seemed good," A.V., " after (their own) pleasure." See ACCOUNT No. 1.

Notes: In Matt. 11 : 26 and Luke 10 : 21, *eudokia*, good pleasure, satisfaction (*eu*, well, and *dokeō*), is used with *ginomai*, to become, and translated " it seemed good," A.V. (R.V., " it was well-pleasing "). (2) In Luke 24 : 11, A.V., *phainō*, to appear (Passive Voice), is translated " seemed " (R.V., " appeared "). EUDOKIA 2107 AG:319C CB:1247A PHAINō 5316 AG:851B CB:1263C

For SEEMLY, R.V., see COMELY, B, and Note (2)

Note: In 1 Pet. 2 : 12, R.V., *kalos*, good, fair, is rendered " seemly." 2570 AG:400B CB:1253B

SEIZE

1. SULLAMBANŌ (συλλαμβάνω), lit., to take together (*sun*, with, *lambanō*, to take or lay hold of), chiefly signifies to seize as a prisoner ; in the following the R.V. substitutes the more suitable and forceful verb, to seize, for A.V., to take : Matt. 26 : 55 ; Mark 14 : 48 ; Luke 22 : 54 ; John 18 : 12 ; Acts 12 : 3 ; 23 : 27 ; 26 : 21 ; in Acts 1 : 16, R.V. and A.V., " took." See CATCH, No. 8, CONCEIVE, HELP. SULLAMBANō 4815 AG:776D CB:1270B

2. SUNARPAZŌ (συναρπάζω) is translated " seized " in the R.V. of Luke 8 : 29 ; Acts 6 : 12 ; 19 : 29 ; see CATCH, No. 7. SUNARPAZō 4884 AG:785B CB:—

Note: In Matt. 21 : 38, the best texts have *echō*, to have (to take, R.V.) ; some have *katechō*, to lay hold of (A.V., " seize on "). ECHō 2192 AG:331D CB:1242C KATECHō 2722 AG:422C CB:1254B

SELF, SELVES

1. AUTOMATOS (αὐτόματος), of oneself (Eng., automatic, automaton, etc.), is used in Mark 4 : 28 ; Acts 12 : 10. See ACCORD, B, No. 2.¶ 844 AG:122C CB:1238B

2. AUTOS (αὐτός), he, also means self, in the reflexive pronouns myself, thyself, himself, etc. (see, e.g., HE), expressing distinction, exclusion, etc. ; it is usually emphatic in the nominative case, e.g., Luke 6 : 42 ; 11 : 4 ; John 18 : 28 ; Rom. 8 : 16, R.V., " Himself." 846 AG:122C CB:1238B

Note: In John 16 : 27, " the Father Himself (*autos*)," Field (*Notes on the Translation of the N.T.*) remarks that *autos* stands for *automatos*.

For SELF-CONDEMNED see CONDEMN, C, No. 1

SELF-CONTROL See SOBER

SELF-CONTROL (without)

AKRATĒS (ἀκρατής), powerless (*a*, negative, *kratos*, strength), is rendered " without self-control," in 2 Tim. 3 : 3, R.V. ; see INCONTINENT.¶ 193 AG:33A CB:1234B

SELFSAME

Notes : (1) In 2 Cor. 5 : 5, A.V., *auto touto*, this thing itself, " this very thing," R.V., is rendered " the selfsame ; " in 2 Cor. 7 : 11, R.V. and A.V., " this selfsame thing." (2) In Matt. 8 : 13, A.V., *ekeinos*, with AUTOS 846 AG:122C CB:1238B EKEINOS 1565 AG:239B CB:1243C the article, " that," R.V., is rendered " that selfsame." (3) In 1 Cor. 12 : 11, A.V., the article with *autos*, " the same," R.V., is rendered " the selfsame."

SELF-WILLED

829
AG:120D
CB:—
AUTHADĒS (αὐθάδης), self-pleasing (*autos*, self, *hēdomai*, to please), denotes one who, dominated by self-interest, and inconsiderate of others, arrogantly asserts his own will, " self-willed," Tit. 1 : 7; 2 Pet. 2 : 10 (the opposite of *epieikēs*, gentle, e.g., 1 Tim. 3 : 3), " one so far overvaluing any determination at which he has himself once arrived that he will not be removed from it " (Trench, who compares and contrasts *philautos*, loving self, selfish; Syn. §xciii).¶ In the Sept., Gen. 49 : 3, 7; Prov. 21 : 24.¶

SELL

4453
AG:731C
CB:1265C
1. PŌLEŌ (πωλέω), to exchange or barter, to sell, is used in the latter sense in the N.T., six times in Matthew, three in Mark, six in Luke; in John only in connection with the cleansing of the Temple by the Lord, 2 : 14, 16; in Acts only in connection with the disposing of property for distribution among the community of believers, 4 : 34, 37; 5 : 1; elsewhere, 1 Cor. 10 : 25; Rev. 13 : 17.

4097
AG:659A
CB:1265A
2. PIPRASKŌ (πιπράσκω), from an earlier form, *peraō*, to carry across the sea for the purpose of selling or to export, is used (*a*) literally, Matt. 13 : 46; 18 : 25; 26 : 9; Mark 14 : 5; John 12 : 5; Acts 2 : 45; 4 : 34; 5 : 4; (*b*) metaphorically, Rom. 7 : 14, " sold under sin," i.e., as fully under the domination of sin as a slave is under his master; the statement evinces an utter dissatisfaction with such a condition; it expresses, not the condemnation of the unregenerate state, but the evil of bondage to a corrupt nature, involving the futility of making use of the Law as a means of deliverance.¶

591
AG:90B
CB:1236C
3. APODIDŌMI (ἀποδίδωμι), to give up or back, also means in the Middle Voice, to give up of one's own will; hence, to sell; it is so used in Peter's question to Sapphira as to selling the land, Acts 5 : 8; of the act of Joseph's brothers, 7 : 9; of Esau's act in selling his birthright, Heb. 12 : 16.

1710
AG:256D
CB:1244B
Note: In Jas. 4 : 13, A.V., *emporeuomai*, to trade (R.V.), is rendered " buy and sell."

For SELLER see PURPLE

SENATE

1087
AG:156D
CB:1248B
GEROUSIA (γερουσία), a council of elders (from *gerōn*, an old man, a term which early assumed a political sense among the Greeks, the notion of age being merged in that of dignity), is used in Acts 5 : 21, apparently epexegetically of the preceding word *sunedrion*, " council," the Sanhedrin.¶

SEND

1. APOSTELLŌ (ἀποστέλλω), lit., to send forth (*apo*, from), akin to *apostolos*, an apostle, denotes (*a*) to send on service, or with a commission. (1) of persons; Christ, sent by the Father, Matt. 10:40; 15:24; 21:37; Mark 9:37; 12:6; Luke 4:18, 43; 9:48; 10:16; John 3:17; 5:36, 38; 6:29, 57; 7:29; 8:42; 10:36; 11:42; 17:3, 8, 18 (1st part), 21, 23, 25; 20:21; Acts 3:20 (future); 3:26; 1 John 4:9, 10, 14; the Holy Spirit, Luke 24:49 (in some texts; see No. 3); 1 Pet. 1:12; Rev. 5:6; Moses, Acts 7:35; John the Baptist, John 1:6; 3:28; disciples and apostles, e.g., Matt. 10:16; Mark 11:1; Luke 22:8; John 4:38; 17:18 (2nd part); Acts 26:17; servants, e.g., Matt. 21:34; Luke 20:10; officers and officials, Mark 6:27; John 7:32; Acts 16:35; messengers, e.g., Acts 10:8, 17, 20; 15:27; evangelists, Rom. 10:15; angels, e.g., Matt. 24:31; Mark 13:27; Luke 1:19, 26; Heb. 1:14; Rev. 1:1; 22:6; demons, Mark 5:10; (2) of things, e.g., Matt. 21:3; Mark 4:29, R.V., marg., "sendeth forth," text, "putteth forth" (A.V., ". . . in"); Acts 10:36; 11:30; 28:28; (*b*) to send away, dismiss, e.g., Mark 8:26; 12:3; Luke 4:18, "to set (at liberty)." See Note below, No. 2. **649 AG:98C CB:1237A**

2. PEMPŌ (πέμπω), to send, is used (*a*) of persons: Christ, by the Father, Luke 20:13; John 4:34; 5:23, 24, 30, 37; 6:38, 39, (40), 44; 7:16, 18, 28, 33; 8:16, 18, 26, 29; 9:4; 12:44, 45, 49; 13:20 (2nd part); 14:24; 15:21; 16:5; Rom. 8:3; the Holy Spirit, John 14:26; 15:26; 16:7; Elijah, Luke 4:26; John the Baptist, John 1:33; disciples and apostles, e.g., Matt. 11:2; John 20:21; servants, e.g., Luke 20:11, 12; officials, Matt. 14:10; messengers, e.g., Acts 10:5, 32, 33; 15:22, 25; 2 Cor. 9:3; Eph. 6:22; Phil. 2:19, 23, 25; 1 Thess. 3:2, 5; Tit. 3:12; a prisoner, Acts 25:25, 27; potentates, by God, 1 Pet. 2:14; an angel, Rev. 22:16; demons, Mark 5:12; (*b*) of things, Acts 11:29; Phil. 4:16; 2 Thess. 2:11; Rev. 1:11; 11:10; 14:15, 18, R.V., "send forth" (A.V., "thrust in"). **3992 AG:641D CB:1263A**

Notes: (1) *Pempō* is a more general term than *apostellō*; *apostellō* usually "suggests official or authoritative sending" (Thayer). A comparison of the usages mentioned above shows how nearly (in some cases practically quite) interchangeably they are used, and yet on close consideration the distinction just mentioned is discernible; in the Gospel of John, cp. *pempō* in 5. 23, 24, 30, 37, *apostellō* in 5:33, 36, 38; *pempō* in 6:38, 39, 44, *apostellō* in 6:29, 57; the two are not used simply for the sake of variety of expression. *Pempō* is not used in the Lord's prayer in chapt. 17, whereas *apostellō* is used six times.

(2) The sending of the Son by the Father was from the glory which He had with the Father into the world, by way of the Incarnation, not a sending out into the world after His birth, as if denoting His mission among and His manifestation to the people. "Hofmann, in support of his view that Jesus is called the Son of God only in virtue of His being

born of man, vainly urges that the simple accusative after *apostellō* also denotes what the Person is or becomes by being sent. What he states is true but only when the name of the object spoken of is chosen to correspond with the purposed mission, as e.g., in Mark 1 : 2 ; Luke 14 : 32 ; 19 : 14. We can no more say, 'God sent Jesus that He should be His Son' than we can render 'he sent his servants,' Matt. 21 : 34, in this manner. That the Sonship of Christ is anterior to His mission to the world . . . is clear from John 16 : 28 ; cp. especially also the double accusative in 1 John 4 : 14, 'the Father sent the Son the Saviour of the world.' The expression that Jesus is sent by God denotes the mission which He has to fulfil and the authority which backs Him" (Cremer, *Lexicon of N.T. Greek*).

1821 3. EXAPOSTELLŌ (ἐξαποστέλλω) denotes (*a*) to send forth : of the
AG:273A CB:1247C Son by God the Father, Gal. 4 : 4 ; of the Holy Spirit, 4 : 6 ; Luke 24 : 49
in the best texts (some have No. 1) ; an angel, Acts 12 : 11 ; the ancestors of Israel, Acts 7 : 12 ; Paul to the Gentiles, 22 : 21 ; of the word of salvation, 13 : 26 (some mss. have No. 1) ; (*b*) to send away, Luke 1 : 53 ; 20 : 10, 11 ; Acts 9 : 30 ; 11 : 22 ; 17 : 14.¶

375 AG:59B 4. ANAPEMPŌ (ἀναπέμπω) denotes (*a*) to send up (*ana*, up, and No. 2),
CB:— to a higher authority, Luke 23 : 7, 15 ; Acts 25 : 21 (in the best texts ; some have No. 2) ; this meaning is confirmed by examples from the papyri (Moulton and Milligan), by Deissmann (*Bible Studies*, p. 229) ; see also Field, *Notes on the Trans. of the N.T.* ; (*b*) to send back, Luke 23 : 11 ; Philm. 12.¶

1599 AG:243C 5. EKPEMPŌ (ἐκπέμπω) denotes to send forth (*ek*, out of), Acts 13 : 4,
CB:— "being sent forth" ; 17 : 10, "sent away."¶

906 AG:130D 6. BALLŌ (βάλλω), to cast, throw, is translated "to send (peace)"
CB:1238B in Matt. 10 : 34 (twice), (R.V., marg., "cast"). See CAST.

1544 AG:237B 7. EKBALLŌ (ἐκβάλλω), to cast out, or send out, is translated "sent
CB:1243B out" in Mark 1 : 43, R.V. (A.V., "sent away"), and in A.V. and R.V. in Jas. 2 : 25. See CAST, No. 5.

630 AG:96C 8. APOLUŌ (ἀπολύω), to set free, to let go, is translated to send
CB:1237A away in Matt. 14 : 15, 22, 23 ; Mark 6 : 36, 45 ; 8 : 3, 9 ; Luke 8 : 38 ; Acts 13 : 3, where the sending is not that of commissioning, but of letting go, intimating that they would gladly have retained them (contrast *ekpempō*, the act of commissioning by the Holy Spirit in ver. 4).

3343 AG:513B 9. METAPEMPŌ (μεταπέμπω), to send after or for, fetch (*meta*, after),
CB:— is used only in the Acts ; in the Middle Voice, translated to send for in 10 : 22, 29 (2nd part : Passive Voice in the 1st part) ; 20 : 1, R.V. only (some texts have *proskaleō*) ; 24 : 24, 26 ; 25 : 3 ; in 10 : 5 and 11 : 13, R.V., "fetch." See FETCH.¶

1032 AG:148A 10. BRUŌ (βρύω), to be full to bursting, was used of the earth in
CB:— producing vegetation, of plants in putting forth buds ; in Jas. 3 : 11 it is said of springs gushing with water, "(doth the fountain) send forth . . . ?"¶

11. SUNAPOSTELLŌ (*συναποστέλλω*), to send along with, is used in 4882 AG:785A
2 Cor. 12 : 18.¶ In the Sept., Ex. 33 : 2, 12.¶ CB:—

12. SUNPEMPŌ (*συνπέμπω*), to send along with, is used in 2 Cor. 4842 AG:779B
8 : 18, 22.¶ CB:—

Notes : (1) In Matt. 13 : 36, A.V., *aphiēmi*, to leave, is translated APHIēMI
" He sent . . . away " (R.V., " He left ") ; so in Mark 4 : 36, A.V., " they 863
had sent away," R.V., "leaving." (2) In Mark 6 : 46, *apotassomai*, to AG:125C CB:1236B
take leave of (R.V.) is translated " He had sent . . . away." (3) In APOTASSOMAI
John 13 : 16 *apostolos* is rendered " one (A.V., he) that is sent," R.V. 657 AG:100D
marg., " an apostle ". (4) *Paristēmi* is rendered " send " in Matt. 26 : 53, APOSTOLOS
R.V. 652 AG:99C CB:1237A PARISTēMI 3936 AG:627C CB:1262B

For SENSELESS see FOOLISH, No. 4

SENSES

AISTHĒTĒRION (*αἰσθητήριον*), sense, the faculty of perception, the
organ of sense (akin to *aisthanomai*, to perceive), is used in Heb. 5 : 14, 145 AG:25A
" senses," the capacities for spiritual apprehension.¶ In the Sept., CB:1234A
Jer. 4 : 19, ' (I am pained . . . in the) sensitive powers (of my heart).'¶

For SENSUAL see NATURAL, A, No. 2

SENTENCE

A. Nouns.

1. KRIMA (*κρίμα*), a judgment, a decision passed on the faults of 2917
others, is used especially of God's judgment upon men, and translated AG:450C CB:1256A
" sentence " in 2 Pet. 2 : 3, R.V. (A.V., " judgment "). See JUDGMENT,
No. 2.

2. KATADIKĒ (*καταδίκη*), a judicial sentence, condemnation, is —
translated " sentence " in Acts 25 : 15, R.V. (A.V., " judgment ") ; some AG:410B CB:1254A
mss. have *dikē*.¶ DIKē 1349

3. APOKRIMA (*ἀπόκριμα*) is translated " sentence " in 2 Cor. 1 : 9, AG:198C
A.V. (R.V., " answer "). See ANSWER, No. 2.¶ CB:1242A APOKRIMA 610

B. Verbs.

1. KRINŌ (*κρίνω*), to judge, to adjudge, is translated " (my) sentence AG:93B
is " in Acts 15 : 19, A.V., R.V., " (my) judgment is," lit., ' I (*egō*, KRINō 2919
emphatic) judge,' introducing the substance or draft of a resolution. AG:451B
See JUDGE, B, No. 1. CB:1256A EPIKRINō

2. EPIKRINŌ (*ἐπικρινω*), to give sentence, is used in Luke 23 : 24.¶ 1948 AG:295A CB:—

SEPARATE

A. Verbs.

1. APHORIZŌ (*ἀφορίζω*), to mark off by bounds (*apo*, from, *horizō*, 873
to determine ; *horos*, a limit), to separate, is used of " (*a*) the Divine AG:127B CB:1236C
action in setting men apart for the work of the gospel, Rom. 1 : 1 ; Gal.
1 : 15 ; (*b*) the Divine judgment upon men, Matt. 13 : 49 ; 25 : 32 ; (*c*) the

separation of Christians from unbelievers, Acts 19 : 9 ; 2 Cor. 6 : 17 ; (*d*) the separation of believers by unbelievers, Luke 6 : 22 ; (*e*) the withdrawal of Christians from their brethren, Gal. 2 : 12. In (*c*) is described what the Christian must do, in (*d*) what he must be prepared to suffer, and in (*e*) what he must avoid."¶*

5563 AG:890A CB:1240A
2. CHŌRIZŌ (χωρίζω), to put asunder, separate, is translated to separate in Rom. 8 : 35, 39 ; in the Middle Voice, to separate oneself, depart (see DEPART) ; in the Passive Voice in Heb. 7 : 26, R.V., "separated" (A.V., "separate"), the verb here relates to the resurrection of Christ, not, as A.V. indicates, to the fact of His holiness in the days of His flesh ; the list is progressive in this respect that the first three qualities apply to His sinlessness, the next to His Resurrection, the last to His Ascension. See PUT, No. 14.

592 AG:90D CB:—
3. APODIORIZŌ (ἀποδιορίζω), to mark off (*apo*, from, *dia*, asunder, *horizō*, to limit), hence denotes metaphorically to make separations, Jude 19, R.V. (A.V., "separate themselves"), of persons who make divisions (in contrast with ver. 20) ; there is no pronoun in the original representing "themselves."¶

B. Preposition.

5565 AG:890C CB:1240A
CHŌRIS (χωρίς), apart from, without (cp. *aneu*, without, a rarer word than this), is translated "separate from" in Eph. 2 : 12 (A.V., "without"). See APART, BESIDE, WITHOUT.

For SEPARATIONS see No. 3, above

SEPULCHRE

TAPHOS 5028 AG:806B CB:1271A
1. TAPHOS (τάφος), akin to *thaptō*, to bury, originally a burial, then, a place for burial, a tomb, occurs in Matt. 23 : 27 ; ver. 29, R.V. (A.V., "tombs") ; 27 : 61, 64, 66 ; 28 : 1 ; metaphorically, Rom. 3 : 13.¶

MNēMA 3418 AG:524C CB:1259A MNēMEION 3419 AG:524C CB:1259A
2 and 3. MNĒMA (μνῆμα) and MNĒMEION (μνημεῖον) : see GRAVE.

SERJEANT (-S)

4465 AG:733C CB:1268A
RHABDOUCHOS (ῥαβδοῦχος), a rod-bearer (*rhabdos*, a rod, *echō*, to hold), one who carries a staff of office, was, firstly, an umpire or judge, later, a Roman lictor, Acts 16 : 35, 38. The duty of these officials was to attend Roman magistrates to execute their orders, especially administering punishment by scourging or beheading ; they carried as their sign of office the fasces (whence "Fascist"), a bundle of rods with an axe inserted. At Philippi they acted under the *stratēgoi* or *prætors* (see MAGISTRATE, No. 1.)¶

SERPENT

3789 AG:600A CB:1261A
1. OPHIS (ὄφις) : the characteristics of the serpent as alluded to in

---

* From Notes on Galatians by Hogg and Vine, p. 83.

Scripture are mostly evil (though Matt. 10 : 16 refers to its caution in avoiding danger) ; its treachery, Gen. 49 : 17 ; 2 Cor. 11 : 3 ; its venom, Psa. 58 : 4 ; 1 Cor. 10 : 9 ; Rev. 9 : 19 ; its skulking, Job 26 : 13 ; its murderous proclivities, e.g., Psa. 58 : 4 ; Prov. 23 : 32 ; Eccl. 10 : 8, 11 ; Amos 5 : 19 ; Mark 16 : 18 ; Luke 10 : 19 ; the Lord used the word metaphorically of the Scribes and Pharisees, Matt. 23 : 33 (cp. *echidna*, viper, in Matt. 3 : 7 ; 12 : 34). The general aspects of its evil character are intimated in the Lord's rhetorical question in Matt. 7 : 10 and Luke 11 : 11. Its characteristics are concentrated in the arch-adversary of God and man, the Devil, metaphorically described as the serpent, 2 Cor. 11 : 3 ; Rev. 12 : 9, 14, 15 ; 20 : 2. The brazen serpent lifted up by Moses was symbolical of the means of salvation provided by God, in Christ and His vicarious death under the Divine judgment upon sin, John 3 : 14. While the living serpent symbolizes sin in its origin, hatefulness and deadly effect, the brazen serpent symbolized the bearing away of the curse and the judgment of sin ; the metal was itself figurative of the righteousness of God's judgment.¶

2. HERPETON (ἑρπετόν), a creeping thing (from *herpō*, to creep), a reptile, is rendered "serpents" in Jas. 3 : 7, A.V. (R.V., "creeping things," as elsewhere). See CREEP, B. 2062 AG:310B CB:—

SERVANT

A. Nouns.

1. DOULOS (δοῦλος), an adjective, signifying 'in bondage,' Rom. 6 : 19 (neuter plural, agreeing with *melē*, members), is used as a noun, and as the most common and general word for "servant", frequently indicating subjection without the idea of bondage ; it is used (*a*) of natural conditions, e.g., Matt. 8 : 9 ; 1 Cor. 7 : 21, 22 (1st part) ; Eph. 6 : 5 ; Col. 4 : 1 ; 1 Tim. 6 : 1 ; frequently in the four Gospels ; (*b*) metaphorically of spiritual, moral and ethical conditions : servants (1) of God, e.g., Acts 16 : 17 ; Tit. 1 : 1 ; 1 Pet. 2 : 16 ; Rev. 7 : 3 ; 15 : 3 ; the perfect example being Christ Himself, Phil. 2 : 7 ; (2) of Christ, e.g., Rom. 1 : 1 ; 1 Cor. 7 : 22 (2nd part) ; Gal. 1 : 10 ; Eph. 6 : 6 ; Phil. 1 : 1 ; Col. 4 : 12 ; Jas. 1 : 1 ; 2 Pet. 1 : 1 ; Jude 1 ; (3) of sin, John 8 : 34 (R.V., "bond-servants") ; Rom. 6 : 17, 20 ; (4) of corruption, 2 Pet. 2 : 19 (R.V., "bondservants") ; cp. the verb *douloō* (see B). See BONDMAN. 1401 AG:205C CB:1242B

2. DIAKONOS (διάκονος), for which see DEACON and Note there on synonymous words, is translated "servant" or "servants" in Matt. 22 : 13 (R.V. marg., "ministers") ; 23 : 11 (R.V. marg., ditto) ; Mark 9 : 35, A.V. (R.V., "minister") ; John 2 : 5, 9 ; 12 : 26 ; Rom. 16 : 1. 1249 AG:184C CB:1241A

3. PAIS (παῖς), for which see CHILD, No. 4, also denotes an attendant ; it is translated "servant" (*a*) of natural conditions, in Matt. 8 : 6, 8, 13 ; 14 : 2 ; Luke 7 : 7 ("menservants" in 12 : 45) ; 15 : 26 ; (*b*) of spiritual relation to God, (1) of Israel, Luke 1 : 54 ; (2) of David, Luke 1 : 69 ; Acts 4 : 25 ; (3) of Christ, so declared by God the Father, Matt. 3816 AG:604C CB:1261C

12 : 18; spoken of in prayer, Acts 4 : 27, 30, R.V. (A.V., "child"); the argument advanced by Dalman for the rendering "Child" in these passages, is not sufficiently valid as against the R.V., "Servant" in Acts 4, and the A.V. and R.V. in Matt. 12 (cp., e.g., the use of *pais* in the Sept. of Gen. 41 : 38; Jer. 36 : 24). The Matt. 12 passage by direct quotation, and the Acts 4 passages by implication, refer to the ideal "Servant of Jehovah" (Sept., *pais Kuriou*), of Is. 42 : 1 and following passages, thus identifying the Servant with the Lord Jesus; for the same identification, cp. Acts 8 : 35.

3610 4. OIKETĒS (οἰκέτης), a house-servant (*oikeō*, to dwell, *oikos*, a house),
AG:557A CB:1260B is translated "servant" in Luke 16 : 13 (R.V. marg., "household-
servant"); so Rom. 14 : 4 and 1 Pet. 2 : 18; in Acts 10 : 7, A.V. and
R.V., "household-servants."¶

5257 5. HUPĒRETĒS (ὑπηρέτης), for which see MINISTER, No. 3, and
AG:842C
CB:1252A OFFICER, is translated "servants" in the A.V. of Matt. 26 : 58; Mark
14 : 65 (R.V., "officers"); in John 18 : 36, A.V. and R.V. (R.V., marg.,
"officers").

2324 6. THERAPŌN (θεράπων), akin to *therapeuō*, to serve, to heal, an
AG:359B
CB:1272B attendant, servant, is a term of dignity and freedom, used of Moses in
Heb. 3 : 5.¶

4889
AG:785D 7. SUNDOULOS (σύνδουλος), a fellow-servant, is used (*a*) of natural
CB:1270C conditions, Matt. 18 : 28, 29, 31, 33; 24 : 49; (*b*) of servants of the same
Divine Lord, Col. 1 : 7; 4 : 7; Rev. 6 : 11; of angels, Rev. 19 : 10;
22 : 9.¶

Note: For *misthios* and *misthōtos*, see HIRED SERVANT.

B. Verb.

1402 DOULOŌ (δουλόω), to enslave, to bring into bondage (akin to A,
AG:206A
CB:— No. 1), e.g., 1 Cor. 9 : 19, R.V., "I brought (myself) under bondage (to
all)," A.V., "I made myself servant," denotes in the Passive Voice, to be
brought into bondage, to become a slave or servant, rendered "ye became
servants (of righteousness)" in Rom. 6 : 18; "being . . . become
servants (to God)," ver. 22. See BONDAGE, B, No. 2.

SERVE

1247 1. DIAKONEŌ (διακονέω), to minister (akin to *diakonos*, No. 2,
AG:184A
CB:1241A above), to render any kind of service, is translated to serve, e.g., in
Luke 10 : 40; 12 : 37; 17 : 8; 22 : 26, 27 (twice); see MINISTER, B,
No. 1.

1398 2. DOULEUŌ (δουλεύω), to serve as a *doulos* (No. 1, above), is used
AG:205A
CB:1242B (*a*) of serving God (and the impossibility of serving mammon also),
Matt. 6 : 24 and Luke 16 : 13; Rom. 7 : 6; in the gospel, Phil. 2 : 22;
(*b*) Christ, Acts 20 : 19; Rom. 12 : 11; 14 : 18; 16 : 18; Eph. 6 : 7;
Col. 3 : 24; (*c*) the Law of God, Rom. 7 : 25; (*d*) one another, Gal. 5 : 13,
R.V., "be servants to" (A.V., "serve"); (*e*) a father, Luke 15 : 29
(with a suggestion of acting as a slave); (*f*) earthly masters, Matt. 6 : 24;

Luke 16 : 13 ; 1 Tim. 6 : 2, R.V., " serve ; " (*g*) the younger by the elder, Rom. 9 : 12 ; (*h*) of being in bondage to a nation, Acts 7 : 7 ; Gal. 4 : 25, to the Romans, actually, though also spiritually to Judaizers ; (*i*) to idols, Gal. 4 : 8, R.V., " were in bondage " (A.V., " did service ") ; (*j*) to " the weak and beggarly rudiments," ver. 9 (R.V.), " to be in bondage " (aorist tense in the best texts, suggesting ' to enter into bondage '), i.e., to the religion of the Gentiles (" rudiments " being used in ver. 3 of the religion of the Jews) ; (*k*) sin, Rom. 6 : 6, R.V., " be in bondage " (A.V., " serve ") ; (*l*) " divers lusts and pleasures," Tit. 3 : 3 ; (*m*) negatively, to any man—a proud and thoughtless denial by the Jews, John 8 : 33.¶

3. LATREUŌ (λατρεύω), primarily to work for hire (akin to *latris*, a hired servant), signifies (1) to worship, (2) to serve ; in the latter sense it is used of service (*a*) to God, Matt. 4 : 10 ; Luke 1 : 74 (" without fear ") ; 4 : 8 ; Acts 7 : 7 ; 24 : 14, R.V., " serve " (A.V., " worship ") ; 26 : 7 ; 27 : 23 ; Rom. 1 : 9 (" with my spirit ") ; 2 Tim. 1 : 3 ; Heb. 9 : 14 ; 12 : 28, A.V., " we may serve," R.V., " we may offer service ; " Rev. 7 : 15 ; (*b*) to God and Christ (" the Lamb "), Rev. 22 : 3 ; (*c*) in the tabernacle, Heb. 8 : 5, R.V. ; 13 : 10 ; (*d*) to " the host of heaven," Acts 7 : 42, R.V., " to serve " (A.V., " to worship ") ; (*e*) to " the creature," instead of the Creator, Rom. 1 : 25, of idolatry : see WORSHIP. **3000 AG:467C CB:1256C**

Note : In Luke 2 : 37 the R.V. has " worshipping," for A.V., " served ; " in Heb. 9 : 9, " the worshipper," for A.V., " that did the service."

4. HUPĒRETEŌ (ὑπηρετέω), for which see MINISTER, B, No. 3, is translated to serve in Acts 13 : 36 ; there is a contrast intimated between the service of David, lasting for only a generation, and the eternal character of Christ's ministry as the One who not having seen corruption was raised from the dead. **5256 AG:842C CB:1252A**

SERVICE, SERVING

1. DIAKONIA (διακονία) is rendered " service " in Rom. 15 : 31, A.V. ; " serving " in Luke 10 : 40. See MINISTRY, A, No. 1. **1248 AG:184B CB:1241A**

2. LEITOURGIA (λειτουργία) is rendered " service " in 2 Cor. 9 : 12 ; Phil. 2 : 17, 30. See MINISTRY, A, No. 2. **3009 AG:471A CB:1256C**

3. LATREIA (λατρεία), akin to *latreuō* (see No. 3, above), primarily hired service, is used (*a*) of the service of God in connection with the Tabernacle, Rom. 9 : 4 ; Heb. 9 : 1, " Divine service ; " ver. 6, plural, R.V., " services " (A.V., " service ", and, in italics, " *of God* ") ; (*b*) of the intelligent service of believers in presenting their bodies to God, a living sacrifice, Rom. 12 : 1, R.V. marg., " worship ; " (*c*) of imagined service to God by persecutors of Christ's followers, John 16 : 2.¶ **2999 AG:467B CB:1256C**

Note : For " soldier on service," 2 Tim. 2 : 3, R.V., see SOLDIER, B.

SET
A. Verbs.

2476 AG:381D CB:1250C 1. HISTĒMI (ἵστημι), to cause to stand, is translated to set in Matt. 4 : 5 (aorist tense in the best texts; some have the present, as in A.V.); 18 : 2; 25 : 33; Mark 9 : 36; Luke 4 : 9; 9 : 47; John 8 : 3; Acts 4 : 7; 5 : 27; 6 : 6; ver. 13, "set up;" 22 : 30; in Jude 24, R.V., "to set" (A.V., "to present"). See ABIDE, No. 10.

2525 AG:390B CB:1254C 2. KATHISTĒMI (καθίστημι), lit., to set down (*kata*, down, and No. 1), to appoint, constitute, is translated to set in Matt. 24 : 45, 47; 25 : 21, 23, R.V. (A.V., "made"); so Luke 12 : 42, 44; it is found in some mss. in Heb. 2 : 7, and translated "set over" (A.V.). See APPOINT, No. 2.

5087 AG:815D CB:1272C 3. TITHĒMI (τίθημι), to put, to place, is translated to set in Acts 1 : 7, of times and seasons (A.V., "put"); Acts 13 : 47; Rev. 10 : 2; "setteth on" (of wine) in John 2 : 10, R.V. (A.V., "doth set forth"); in the A.V. of Mark 4 : 21 (2nd part) and in Luke 8 : 16 it is rendered "set" (R.V., "put"), of a lamp (some texts have No. 6 in both). In Mark 4 : 30 it is used of setting forth by parable the teaching concerning the Kingdom of God, R.V., "shall we set (it) forth" (A.V., "compare"). See APPOINT, No. 3.

3908 AG:622D CB:— 4. PARATITHĒMI (παρατίθημι), to place beside (*para*, beside, and No. 3), to set forth, of a parable, Matt. 13 : 24, R.V. (A.V., "put forth"); to set before, of food, Mark 6 : 41; 8 : 6 (twice), 7; Luke 9 : 16; 10 : 8; 11 : 6; Acts 16 : 34; 1 Cor. 10 : 27. See ALLEGE, No. 1, PUT, No. 3.

4060 AG:652C CB:— 5. PERITITHĒMI (περιτίθημι), to place or put around (*peri*, around, and No. 3), is translated to set about (of a hedge) in Mark 12 : 1. See BESTOW, No. 5, PUT.

2007 AG:302D CB:1246B 6. EPITITHĒMI (ἐπιτίθημι), to put, set or lay upon, is used of the placing over the head of Christ on the Cross "His accusation," Matt. 27 : 37, "set up;" of attacking a person, Acts 18 : 10, "shall set on." See ADD, No. 1.

4388 (-EMAI) AG:722B CB:1267B 7. PROTITHĒMI (προτίθημι), to set before (*pro*, before, and No. 3), is used in the Middle Voice, translated "set forth," of Christ, in Rom. 3 : 25 (R.V. marg., "purposed"). See PURPOSE, B, No. 3.

1325 AG:192C CB:1241C 8. DIDŌMI (δίδωμι), to give, is translated "I have set before" in Rev. 3 : 8 (R.V. marg., "given"). See GIVE.

In the following pages † indicates that the word referred to (preposition, conjunction, or particle) is not dealt with in this volume.

¶ indicates that all the N.T. occurrences of the Greek word under consideration are mentioned under the heading or sub-heading.

9. KATHIZŌ (καθίζω), used transitively, signifies to cause to sit down, 2523
set, appoint, translated to set in Acts 2 : 30, R.V. (A.V., incorrectly, " to AG:389D CB:1254C
sit ") ; in 1 Cor. 6 : 4, of appointing, i.e., obtaining the services of, judges
in lawcourts ; in Eph. 1 : 20, R.V., " made (Him) to sit " (A.V., " set ").
Note : In Heb. 8 : 1, *kathizō* is used intransitively, R.V., " sat down "
(A.V., " is set ") ; so in 12 : 2, R.V., " hath sat down " (A.V., " is set
down ") ; Rev. 3 : 21, R.V., " I . . . sat down " (A.V., " am set down ").
So *epikathizō* in Matt. 21 : 7 (last part), R.V., " He sat " [some mss. 1940
have the plural in a transitive sense, A.V., " they set (Him)]." See AG:293D CB:—
SIT, No. 8.

10. TASSŌ (τάσσω), to arrange, assign, order, is translated " set 5021
(under authority) " in Luke 7 : 8. In 1 Cor. 16 : 15, R.V., " have set AG:805D CB:1271A
(themselves)," A.V., " addicted." See APPOINT, No. 5.

11. ANATASSOMAI (ἀνατάσσομαι), to arrange in order, draw up in 392
order (*ana*, up, and the Middle Voice of No. 10), occurs in Luke 1 : 1, AG:61D CB:1235B
A.V., " to set forth in order," R.V., " to draw up." See DRAW, No. 9.¶

12. DUNŌ (δύνω), to sink into, is used of the setting of the sun, 1416
Mark 1 : 32, " did set ; " Luke 4 : 40, " was setting." The sun, moon AG:209A CB:1242B
and stars were conceived of as sinking into the sea when they set.¶

13. SUNALLASSŌ (συναλλάσσω), to reconcile (*sun*, together, *allassō*, — AG:784B
to change or exchange), is translated " he . . . would have set (them CB:—
at one, lit., ' into peace ') again " in Acts 7 : 26 (the imperfect tense being SUNELAUNŌ
conative, expressing an attempt) ; some mss. have *sunelaunō*, to drive 4900 AG:787B
together, force together.¶ CB:—

14. KATANGELLŌ (καταγγέλλω), to declare, proclaim, is translated 2605
" set forth " in Acts 16 : 21, R.V. (A.V., " teach ") ; " set I forth " AG:409B CB:1254A
in Acts 17 : 23, R.V. (A.V., " declare I "). See DECLARE, No. 4.

15. ENECHŌ (ἐνέχω), to hold in, has a secondary significance of 1758
setting oneself against a person, being urgent against, Mark 6 : 19 ; AG:265D CB:1245A
Luke 11 : 53 (R.V., marg.). See ENTANGLE, No. 3, QUARREL, URGE.

16. PROPEMPŌ (προπέμπω), lit., to send forward (*pro*, forward, 4311 AG:709B
pempō, to send), is translated " set forward " in Tit. 3 : 13, R.V. (A.V., CB:—
" bring ") and in 3 John 6, R.V. (A.V., " bring forward "), of practical
assistance to servants of God in their journeys. See ACCOMPANY, No. 4.

17. APODEIKNUMI (ἀποδείκνυμι), to show forth, declare, is 584
translated " set forth " in 1 Cor. 4 : 9, here, a technical term, used for AG:89C CB:1236C
exhibiting gladiators in an arena, " last of all " referring to the grand
finale, to make the most thrilling sport for the spectators (cp. 15 : 32) ;
prophets and others had preceded the apostles in the spectacle ; in
2 Thess. 2 : 4 it is used of the man of sin, who will " set (himself) forth (as
God)," A.V., " shewing." Elsewhere Acts 2 : 22 ; 25 : 7. See APPROVE,
PROVE.¶ The word is frequently used in the papyri of the proclamation
of the accession of a king or the appointment of an official. Cp. *apodeixis*, 1913
" demonstration," 1 Cor. 2 : 4.¶ AG:290B

18. EPIBIBAZŌ (ἐπιβιβάζω), to place upon, is used of causing persons CB:—

to mount animals for riding, Luke 10 : 34 ; 19 : 35 ; Acts 23 : 24.¶
4741 AG:768A 19. STĒRIZŌ (*στηρίζω*), to fix, establish, is rendered "He stedfastly
CB:1270A set (His face)" in Luke 9 : 51. See ESTABLISH, No. 1.
461 AG:72C 20. ANORTHOŌ (*ἀνορθόω*), to set straight, set up (*ana*, up, *orthos*,
CB:— straight), is used in Acts 15 : 16 in God's promise to set up the fallen
tabernacle (*skēnē*, tent) of David. The word is used in the papyri of
rearing buildings again. See LIFT, No. 6, STRAIGHT.
2749 AG:426C 21. KEIMAI (*κεῖμαι*), to lie, to be laid (used as the Passive Voice of
CB:1254C *tithēmi*, No. 3), is translated to be set, e.g., in Matt. 5 : 14 (of a city) ;
Luke 2 : 34 (of Christ) ; John 2 : 6 (of waterpots) ; 19 : 29 (of a vessel
of vinegar) ; Phil. 1 : 16, R.V. (ver. 17, A.V.) (of the Apostle Paul) ;
Rev. 4 : 2 (of the Throne in Heaven). See APPOINT, LAY, LIE.
345 AG:55D 22. ANAKEIMAI (*ἀνάκειμαι*), to be laid up (*ana*, up), to recline at
CB:1235A a meal, is so used in John 6 : 11, "(to them) that were set down." See
LEAN, LIE, Note (1) SIT, No. 3.
4295 AG:707C 23. PROKEIMAI (*πρόκειμαι*) signifies (*a*) to be set before (*pro*, before,
CB:1266C and No. 21), and is so rendered in Heb. 6 : 18 of the hope of the believer ;
12 : 1, of the Christian race ; ver. 2, of the joy set before Christ in the days
of His flesh and at His death ; (*b*) to be set forth, said of Sodom and
Gomorrah, in Jude 7. It is used elsewhere in 2 Cor. 8 : 12, for which
see FIRST, D, Note (2).¶
4270 AG:704A 24. PROGRAPHŌ (*προγράφω*), to write before, is translated "were
CB:1266C set forth (unto this condemnation)" in Jude 4, R.V. (A.V., "ordained") ;
the evil teachers were 'designated of old for this judgment' (cp. 2 Pet.
TAKTOS 2 : 3). For the meaning of this verb in Gal. 3 : 1, R.V., "openly set
5002 forth," see OPENLY, No. 2, Note. See WRITE.
AG:803A

B. Adjective.

APOLUŌ 630 TAKTOS (*τακτός*), an adjective (from *tassō*, A, No. 10), ordered, fixed,
AG:96C "set," is said of an appointed day, in Acts 12 : 21.¶ In the Sept., Job
CB:1237A APOSTELLŌ 12 : 5.¶
649 *Notes :* (1) For "to set at liberty" (*apoluō* and *apostellō*), see LIBERTY.
AG:98C CB:1237A (2) In Acts 21 : 2, A.V., *anagō*, to set sail (R.V.), is translated "set forth ;"
ANAGŌ 321 see LAUNCH. (3) In Luke 22 : 55, A.V., *sunkathizō*, to sit down together
AG:53A (R.V.), is translated "were set down together." See SIT, No. 10.
SUNKATHIZŌ (4) For Acts 7 : 5, "to set his foot on," see FOOT, A, No. 1, Note. (5) In
4776 AG:773B Acts 13 : 9, A.V., *atenizō*, to look fixedly, gaze, is rendered "set his eyes
ATENIZŌ on" (R.V., "fastened his eyes on"). See FASTEN, No. 1. (6) In Matt.
816 AG:119D 27 : 19, A.V., *kathēmai*, to sit, is rendered "he was set down" (R.V.,
CB:1238A "he was sitting"). See SIT, No. 1. (7) In John 13 : 12, A.V., *anapiptō*,
KATHĒMAI 2521 to recline at table, is translated "was set down" (R.V., "sat down ;"
AG:389B marg., "reclined"). See RECLINE. (8) In Matt. 27 : 66 there is no
CB:1254C word in the Greek representing the A.V. "setting ;" the R.V. has "the
ANAPIPTŌ 377 guard being with them," lit., 'with (*meta*) the guard.' (9) The verb is
AG:59C combined with other words, e.g., AFFECTION, FIRE, MIND, NOUGHT,
CB:1235B ORDER, SEAL, UPROAR, VARIANCE.

SETTER FORTH

KATANGELEUS (*καταγγελεύς*), a proclaimer, herald (akin to 2604
katangellō, to proclaim), is used in Acts 17 : 18, "a setter forth (of strange AG:409B CB:1254A
gods)." It is found in Inscriptions in connection with proclamations
made in public places.¶

SETTLE

TITHĒMI (*τίθημι*), to put, place, is translated "settle (it therefore 5087
in your hearts)" in Luke 21 : 14, Active Voice in the best texts (some AG:815D CB:1272C
have the Middle), the aorist tense signifying complete decision, i.e.,
'resolve' (not 'consider'); cp. Acts 5 : 4, to conceive in the heart, and
contrast Luke 1 : 66, 'to lay up' (both have aorist tense, Middle Voice). THEMELIOō 2311
See APPOINT, No. 3. AG:356A

Notes: (1) In 1 Pet. 5 : 10, some texts have *themelioō*, to lay a CB:1272A HEDRAIOS
foundation, used metaphorically, and translated "settle," A.V. (2) In 1476
Col. 1 : 23, A.V., *hedraios*, lit., seated (*hedra*, a seat), is translated AG:217D CB:1249C
"settled" (R.V., "stedfast"). (3) For *epiluō* see DETERMINE, No. 4. EPILUō 1956 AG:295D CB:1246A

SEVEN

HEPTA (*ἑπτά*), whence Eng. words beginning with hept—, corresponds 2033
to the Heb. *sheba'* (which is akin to *sāba'*, signifying to be full, abundant), AG:306B CB:1250A
sometimes used as an expression of fulness, e.g., Ruth 4 : 15 : it generally
expresses completeness, and is used most frequently in the Apocalypse;
it is not found in the Gospel of John, nor between the Acts and the
Apocalypse, except in Heb. 11 : 30 (in Rom. 11 : 4 the numeral is
heptakischilioi, seven thousand); in Matt. 22 : 26 it is translated HEPTAKIS-CHILIOI
"seventh" (marg., "seven"). 2035

Note: In 2 Pet. 2 : 5, R.V., "Noah with seven others" is a translation AG:306C
into idiomatic English of the Greek idiom "Noah the eighth *person*" CB:—
(so A.V., translating literally). See EIGHTH.

SEVENTH

HEBDOMOS (*ἕβδομος*) occurs in John 4 : 52; Heb. 4 : 4 (twice); 1442
Jude 14; Rev. 8 : 1; 10 : 7; 11 : 15; 16 : 17; 21 : 20.¶ AG:213A CB:—

SEVEN TIMES

HEPTAKIS (*ἑπτάκις*) occurs in Matt. 18 : 21, 22; Luke 17 : 4 2034
(twice).¶ AG:306B CB:1250A

SEVENTY

HEBDOMĒKONTA (*ἑβδομήκοντα*) occurs in Luke 10 : 1, 17; in Acts 1440
7 : 14 it precedes *pente*, five, lit., 'seventy-five,' rendered "threescore AG:212D CB:1249B
and fifteen;" for the details see FIFTEEN, Note (1); in 23 : 23 it is
translated "threescore and ten;" in 27 : 37 it precedes *hex*, six, lit.,
'seventy-six,' rendered "threescore and sixteen."¶

SEVENTY TIMES

1441 HEBDOMĒKONTAKIS (ἑβδομηκοντάκις) occurs in Matt. 18 : 22,
AG:213A
CB:— where it is followed by *hepta*, seven, "seventy times seven;" R.V. marg.
has "seventy times and seven," which many have regarded as the meaning; cp. Gen. 4 : 24 (Winer, in Winer-Moulton, Gram., p. 314, remarks that while this would be the strict meaning, it "would not suit the passage;" his translator, W. F. Moulton, in a footnote, expresses the opinion that it would. So also J. H. Moulton, Prol., p. 98, says: "A definite *allusion* to the Genesis story is highly probable: Jesus pointedly sets against the natural man's craving for seventy-sevenfold revenge the spiritual man's ambition to exercise the privilege of seventy-sevenfold forgiveness").

The Lord's reply "until seventy times seven" was indicative of completeness, the absence of any limit, and was designed to turn away Peter's mind from a merely numerical standard. God's forgiveness is limitless; so should man's be.¶

SEVER

2673 1. KATARGEŌ (καταργέω), lit., to reduce to inactivity (see ABOLISH,
AG:417B
CB:1254B where all the occurrences are given), is rendered "ye are severed (from
Christ)" in Gal. 5 : 4, R.V.; the aorist tense indicates that point of time at which there was an acceptance of the Judaistic doctrines; to those who accepted these Christ would be of no profit, they were as branches severed from the tree.

873 2. APHORIZŌ (ἀφορίζω), to separate from, is used of the work of the
AG:127B
CB:1236C angels at the end of this age, in severing the wicked from among the
righteous, Matt. 13 : 49, a pre-millennial act quite distinct from the Rapture of the Church as set forth in 1 Thess. 4. See DIVIDE, No. 1.

SEVERAL

IDIOS IDIOS (ἴδιος), one's own, is translated "several (ability)," in Matt.
2398 25 : 15.
AG:369C
CB:1252C *Note:* For Rev. 21 : 21, "the several gates," R.V., see EVERY, No. 3.
KATA
2596
AG:405C

SEVERALLY

CB:1253C
EK IDIĄ (ἰδίᾳ), the dative case, feminine, of *idios* (see above), is used
1537 adverbially, signifying "severally," in 1 Cor. 12 : 11.
AG:234A
CB:1243B *Notes:* (1) In Rom. 12 : 5, *kata* (*kath'*) followed by the numeral *heis*,
MEROS one, and preceded by the article, signifies "severally," R.V. (A.V., "every
3313
AG:505D one"). Cp. EVERY, Note (1). (2) In 1 Cor. 12 : 27, R.V., the phrase
CB:1258B *ek merous*, lit., out of a part (*meros*), is rendered "severally" (A.V., "in
SEVERE particular"). (3) In Heb. 9 : 5, R.V., the phrase *kata meros*, lit., according
See
GREAT to a part, is rendered "severally." (4) For Eph. 5 : 33, R.V., "severally,"
see EVERY, No. 3.

SEVERITY

1. APOTOMIA (ἀποτομία), steepness, sharpness (*apo*, off, *temnō*, to cut; *tomē*, a cutting), is used metaphorically in Rom. 11 : 22 (twice) of "the severity of God," which lies in His temporary retributive dealings with Israel.¶ In the papyri it is used of exacting to the full the provisions of a statute. Cp. the adverb *apotomōs*, sharply (which see). 663 AG:101C CB:—

2. APHEIDIA (ἀφειδία), primarily extravagance (*a*, negative, *pheidomai*, to spare), hence, unsparing treatment, severity, is used in Col. 2 : 23, R.V., "severity (to the body)," A.V., "neglecting of" (marg., "punishing, not sparing"); here it refers to ascetic discipline; it was often used among the Greeks of courageous exposure to hardship and danger.¶ 857 AG:124D CB:—

SEW

EPIRAPTŌ or EPIRRHAPTŌ (ἐπιράπτω) (*epi*, upon, *rhaptō*, to sew or stitch), is used in Mark 2 : 21.¶ 1976 AG:298A CB:—

SEXUAL IMMORALITY See FORNICATION

SHADOW (Noun)

1. SKIA (σκιά) is used (*a*) of a shadow, caused by the interception of light, Mark 4 : 32, Acts 5 : 15; metaphorically of the darkness and spiritual death of ignorance, Matt. 4 : 16; Luke 1 : 79; (*b*) of the image or outline cast by an object, Col. 2 : 17, of ceremonies under the Law; of the Tabernacle and its appurtenances and offerings, Heb. 8 : 5; of these as appointed under the Law, Heb. 10 : 1.¶ 4639 AG:755D CB:1269A

2. APOSKIASMA (ἀποσκίασμα), a shadow, is rendered "shadow that is cast" in Jas. 1 : 17, R.V.; the A.V. makes no distinction between this and No. 1. The probable significance of this word is overshadowing or shadowing-over (which *apo* may indicate), and this with the genitive case of *tropē*, "turning," yields the meaning 'shadowing-over of mutability' implying an alternation of shadow and light; of this there are two alternative explanations, namely, overshadowing (1) not caused by mutability in God, or (2) caused by change in others, i.e., "no changes in this lower world can cast a shadow on the unchanging Fount of light" [Mayor, who further remarks, "The meaning of the passage will then be, 'God is alike incapable of change (*parallagē*) and incapable of being changed by the action of others'"]. 644 AG:98A CB:1237A

For SHADOWING, Heb. 9 : 5, A.V., see OVERSHADOW

SHAKE

1. SALEUŌ (σαλεύω), to agitate, shake, primarily of the action of stormy winds, waves, etc., is used (*a*) literally, of a reed, Matt. 11 : 7; Luke 7 : 24; a vessel, shaken in filling, Luke 6 : 38; a building, Luke 6 : 48; Acts 4 : 31; 16 : 26; the natural forces of the heavens and heavenly bodies, Matt. 24 : 29; Mark 13 : 25; Luke 21 : 26; the 4531 AG:740C CB:1268B

earth, Heb. 12 : 26, "shook ;" (*b*) metaphorically, (1) of shaking so as to make insecure, Heb. 12 : 27 (twice) ; (2) of casting down from a sense of security, Acts 2 : 25, "I should (not) be moved ;" (3) to stir up (a crowd), Acts 17 : 13 ; (4) to unsettle, 2 Thess. 2 : 2, "(to the end that) ye be not (quickly) shaken (from your mind)," i.e., from their settled conviction and the purpose of heart begotten by it, as to the return of Christ before the Day of the Lord begins ; the metaphor may be taken from the loosening of a ship from its moorings by a storm. See MOVE, STIR.¶

4579 AG:746C CB:1268C 2. SEIŌ (σείω), to shake to and fro, is rendered to shake in Matt. 28 : 4, A.V. ; Heb. 12 : 26, A.V. ; Rev. 6 : 13, A.V. and R.V. ; see MOVE, No. 3.

660 AG:101B CB:1237B 3. APOTINASSŌ (ἀποτινάσσω), to shake off (*apo*, from, *tinassō*, to shake), is used in Luke 9 : 5, of dust from the feet ; Acts 28 : 5, of a viper from the hand.¶ In the Sept., Judg. 16 : 20 ; 1 Sam 10 : 2 ; Lam. 2 : 7.¶

1621 AG:245D CB:1244A 4. EKTINASSŌ (ἐκτινάσσω), to shake out, is used of shaking off the dust from the feet, Matt. 10 : 14 ; Mark 6 : 11 ; Acts 13 : 51 ; of shaking out one's raiment, Acts 18 : 6.¶

SHALL

3195 AG:500D CB:1258A MELLŌ (μέλλω), to be about (to be or do), is used of purpose, certainty, compulsion or necessity. It is rendered simply by "shall" or "should" (which frequently represent elsewhere part of the future tense of the verb) in the following (the R.V. sometimes translates differently, as noted): Matt. 16 : 27 (1st part), lit., 'is about to come ;' 17 : 12, 22 ; 20 : 22, R.V., "am about ;" 24 : 6 ; Mark 13 : 4 (2nd part), R.V., "are about ;" Luke 9 : 44 ; 21 : 7 (2nd part), R.V., "are about ;" ver. 36 ; Acts 23 : 3 ; 24 : 15 ; 26 : 2, R.V., "I am (to) ;" Rom. 4 : 24 ; 8 : 13 (1st part), R.V., "must ;" ver. 18 ; 2 Tim. 4 : 1 ; Heb. 1 : 14 ; 10 : 27 ; Jas. 2 : 12, R.V., "are to ;" 1 Pet. 5 : 1 ; Rev. 1 : 19 ; 2 : 10 (1st and 2nd parts), R.V., "art about," "is about ;" 3 : 10, R.V., "is (to) ;" 17 : 8 (1st part), R.V., "is about." See ABOUT, B.

Notes : (1) The use of shall, shalt, is frequently part of the rendering of a future tense of a verb. (2) The phrase "it shall come to pass" is the rendering of the future tense of *eimi*, to be, in Acts 2 : 17, 21 ; 3 : 23 ; Rom. 9 : 26.

SHAMBLES

3111 AG:487B CB:— MAKELLON (μάκελλον), a term of late Greek borrowed from the Latin *macellum*, denotes a meat-market, translated "shambles" in 1 Cor. 10 : 25. The word is found in the *koinē*, or vernacular Greek covering the time of the N.T., illustrating this passage (see Deissmann, *Light from the Ancient East*, 274). A plan, drawn by Lietzmann, of a forum in Pompeii, shows both the slaughter-house and the meat-shop next to the chapel of Cæsar. Some of the meat which had been used for sacrificial purposes was afterwards sold in the markets. The Apostle enjoins upon the believer to enter into no enquiry, so as to avoid the troubling of conscience (contrast ver. 28).¶

SHAME (Noun, and Verb)

A. Nouns.

1. ATIMIA (ἀτιμία) signifies (*a*) shame, disgrace, Rom 1 : 26, "vile (passions)," R.V., lit., '(passions) of shame;' 1 Cor. 11 : 14; (*b*) dishonour, e.g., 2 Tim. 2 : 20, where the idea of disgrace or shame does not attach to the use of the word; the meaning is that while in a great house some vessels are designed for purposes of honour, others have no particular honour (*timē*) attached to their use (the prefix *a* simply negatives the idea of honour). See DISHONOUR. 819 AG:120A CB:1238B

2. AISCHUNĒ (αἰσχύνη): see ASHAMED, B, No. 1. 152 AG:25B CB:1234A

3. ENTROPĒ (ἐντροπή), 1 Cor. 6 : 5 and 15 : 34. See ASHAMED, B, No. 2.¶ 1791 AG:269D CB:—

4. ASCHĒMOSUNĒ (ἀσχημοσύνη) denotes (*a*) "unseemliness," Rom. 1 : 27, R.V. (A.V., "that which is unseemly"); (*b*) shame, nakedness, Rev. 16 : 15, a euphemism for No. 2.¶ 808 AG:119B CB:—

B. Adjective.

AISCHROS (αἰσχρός), base, shameful (akin to *aischos*, shame), of that which is opposed to modesty or purity, is translated as a noun in 1 Cor. 11 : 6; 14 : 35, A.V. (R.V., "shameful"); Eph. 5 : 12; in Tit. 1 : 11, "filthy (lucre)," lit., 'shameful (gain).' See FILTHY. ¶ 150 AG:25B CB:1234A

C. Verbs.

1. ATIMAZŌ (ἀτιμάζω), to dishonour, put to shame (akin to A, No. 1): see DISHONOUR, C, No. 1. 818 AG:120A CB:1238A

2. ENTREPŌ (ἐντρέπω), lit., to turn in upon, to put to shame (akin to A, No. 3), is translated "to shame (you)" in 1 Cor. 4 : 14. See ASHAMED, A, No. 4. 1788 AG:269D CB:—

3. KATAISCHUNŌ (καταισχύνω), to put to shame (*kata*, perhaps signifying utterly), is translated "ye . . . shame (them)" in 1 Cor. 11 : 22, A.V., R.V., "ye . . . put (them) to shame." See ASHAMED, A, No. 3. 2617 AG:410D CB:1254A

4. PARADEIGMATIZŌ (παραδειγματίζω) signifies to set forth as an example (*para*, beside, *deiknumi*, to show), and is used in Heb. 6 : 6 of those Jews, who, though attracted to, and closely associated with, the Christian faith, without having experienced more than a tasting of the heavenly gift and partaking of the Holy Ghost (not actually receiving Him), were tempted to apostatize to Judaism, and, thereby crucifying the Son of God a second time, would "put Him to an open shame." So were criminals exposed.¶ In the Sept., Numb. 25 : 4; Jer. 13 : 22; Ezek. 28 : 17.¶ 3856 AG:614A CB:1262A

SHAMEFASTNESS (A.V., SHAMEFACEDNESS)

127 AG:22B CB:1233C AIDŌS (αἰδώς), a sense of shame, modesty, is used regarding the demeanour of women in the church, 1 Tim. 2 : 9 (some mss. have it in Heb. 12 : 28 for *deos*, "awe:" here only in N.T.). "Shamefastness is that modesty which is 'fast' or rooted in the character . . . The change to 'shamefacedness' is the more to be regretted because shamefacedness . . . has come rather to describe an awkward diffidence, such as we sometimes call sheepishness" (Davies; *Bible English*, p. 12).

As to *aidōs* and *aischunē* (see ASHAMED, B, No. 1), *aidōs* is more objective, having regard to others; it is the stronger word. "*Aidōs* would always restrain a good man from an unworthy act, *aischunē* would sometimes restrain a bad one" (Trench, Syn. § § xix, xx).

SHAMEFULLY (ENTREAT)

ATIMAZō 818 AG:120A CB:1238A HUBRIZō 5195 AG:831D CB:1251C *Note:* This forms part of the rendering of (*a*) *atimazō*, Mark 12 : 4, Luke 20 : 11, see DISHONOUR, C, No. 1, ENTREAT, Note, HANDLE, No. 4; (*b*) *hubrizō*, to insult, Acts 14 : 5, R.V.; 1 Thess. 2 : 2, "were (R.V., having been) shamefully entreated." See SPITEFULLY.

SHAPE

1491 AG:221B CB:1243A 1. EIDOS (εἶδος), rendered "shape" in the A.V. of Luke 3 : 22 and John 5 : 37: see FORM, No. 4.

3667 AG:567C CB:1251A 2. HOMOIŌMA (ὁμοίωμα), rendered "shapes" in Rev. 9 : 7: see LIKENESS, No. 1.

SHARE See PORTION

For SHARERS (Heb. 2 : 14) see PARTAKE, B, No. 1.

SHARP, SHARPER, SHARPLY, SHARPNESS

A. Adjectives.

3691 AG:574C CB:— 1. OXUS (ὀξύς) denotes (*a*) sharp (Eng., *oxy*—), said of a sword, Rev. 1 : 16; 2 : 12; 19 : 15; of a sickle, 14 : 14, 17, 18 (twice); (*b*) of motion, swift, Rom. 3 : 15. See SWIFT.¶

5114 (TOMōTEROS) AG:822A (TOMOS) CB:— 2. TOMOS (τομός), akin to *temnō*, to cut [Eng., (ana)tomy, etc.], is used metaphorically in the comparative degree, *tomōteros*, in Heb. 4 : 12, of the Word of God.¶

B. Adverb.

664 AG:101C CB:— APOTOMŌS (ἀποτόμως) signifies abruptly, curtly, lit., in a manner that cuts (*apo*, from, *temnō*, to cut), hence sharply, severely, 2 Cor. 13 : 10, R.V., "(that I may not . . . deal) sharply," A.V., "(use) sharpness;" the pronoun "you" is to be understood, i.e., 'that I may not use (or deal with) . . . sharply;' Tit. 1 : 13, of rebuking.¶ Cp. *apotomia*, severity.

SHAVE

3587 AG:549C CB:— XURAŌ (ξυράω), a late form of *xureō*, or *xurō*, from *xuron*, a razor, occurs in Acts 21 : 24 (Middle Voice), in connection with a vow (Numb.

6 : 2–18 ; cp. Acts 18 : 18 : see SHEAR) ; 1 Cor. 11 : 5, 6 (2nd part in each).¶

SHE

Note : The words under HE in their feminine forms are used for this pronoun.

SHEAR, SHEARER, SHORN

KEIRŌ (κείρω) is used (*a*) of shearing sheep, Acts 8 : 32, "shearer," lit., 'the (one) shearing ;' (*b*) in the Middle Voice, to have one's hair cut off, be shorn, Acts 18 : 18 ; 1 Cor. 11 : 6 (twice ; cp. *xuraō*, to shave ; see above).¶ **2751 AG:427A CB:—**

SHEATH

THĒKĒ (θήκη), a place to put something in (akin to *tithēmi*, to put), a receptacle, chest, case, is used of the sheath of a sword, John 18 : 11.¶ **2336 AG:360B CB:1271C**

SHED

1. EKCHEŌ (ἐκχέω), to pour out, is translated to shed or to shed forth in Acts 2 : 33 ; Tit. 3 : 6, A.V. ; of shedding blood in murder, Rom. 3 : 15. See POUR, No. 3. **1632 AG:247B CB:1243B**

2. EKCHUNŌ, or EKCHUNNŌ (ἐκχύνω), a later form of No. 1, is used of the voluntary giving up of His life by Christ through the shedding of His blood in crucifixion as an atoning sacrifice, Matt. 26 : 28 ; Mark 14 : 24 ; Luke 22 : 20, A.V., "is shed," R.V., "is poured out ;" these passages do not refer to the effect of the piercing of His side (which took place after His Death) ; of the murder of servants of God, Matt. 23 : 35 ; Luke 11 : 50 ; Acts 22 : 20 (in the best texts ; others have No. 1) ; of the love of God in the hearts of believers through the Holy Spirit, Rom. 5 : 5. For the 'pouring out' of the Holy Spirit, Acts 10 : 45, see POUR, No. 4. (The form in the last two passages might equally well come from No. 1, above.) See GUSH OUT, RUN, SPILL. **1632 AG:247B (EKCHEŌ) CB:1243B**

SHEEP

1. PROBATON (πρόβατον), from *probainō*, to go forward, i.e., of the movement of quadrupeds, was used among the Greeks of small cattle, sheep and goats ; in the N.T., of sheep only (*a*) naturally, e.g., Matt. 12 : 11, 12 ; (*b*) metaphorically, of those who belong to the Lord, the lost ones of the house of Israel, Matt. 10 : 6 ; of those who are under the care of the Good Shepherd, e.g., Matt. 26 : 31 ; John 10 : 1, lit., 'the fold of the sheep,' and vv. 2–27 ; 21 : 16, 17 in some texts ; Heb. 13 : 20 ; of those who in a future day, at the introduction of the Millennial Kingdom, have shewn kindness to His persecuted earthly people in their great tribulation, Matt. 25 : 33 ; of the clothing of false shepherds, Matt. 7 : 15 ; (*c*) figuratively, by way of simile, of Christ, Acts 8 : 32 ; of the disciples, e.g., Matt. 10 : 16 ; of true followers of Christ in general, Rom. 8 : 36 ; **4263 AG:703C CB:1266C**

of the former wayward condition of those who had come under His Shepherd care, 1 Pet. 2 : 25 ; of the multitudes who sought the help of Christ in the days of His flesh, Matt. 9 : 36 ; Mark 6 : 34.

AG:703A̅ CB:— 2. PROBATION (προβάτιον), a diminutive of No. 1, a little sheep, is found in the best texts in John 21 : 16, 17 (some have No. 1) ; distinct from *arnia*, lambs (ver. 15), but used as a term of endearment.¶

Note: For "keeping sheep," Luke 17 : 7, R.V., see CATTLE.

For SHEEPFOLD see FOLD

SHEEP *GATE*, SHEEP *MARKET*

4262 AG:703A CB:— PROBATIKOS (προβατικός), an adjective, used in the grammatically feminine form, in John 5 : 2, to agree with *pulē*, a gate, understood, R.V., "sheep *gate*" (not with *agora*, a market, A.V., "sheep *market*").¶ In the Sept., Neh. 3 : 1, 32 ; 12 : 39.¶ This sheep gate was near the Temple ; the sacrifices for the Temple probably entered by it.

SHEEPSKIN

3374 AG:518D CB:— MĒLŌTĒ (μηλωτή), from *mēlon*, a sheep or goat, occurs in Heb. 11 : 37.¶ In the Sept., 1 Kings 19 : 13, 19 ; 2 Kings 2 : 8, 13, 14.¶

SHEET

3607 AG:555C CB:— OTHONĒ (ὀθόνη) primarily denoted fine linen, later, a sheet, Acts 10 : 11 ; 11 : 5.¶ Cp. *othonion*, linen.

SHEKEL, HALF SHEKEL

4715 AG:764C CB:1270A 1. STATĒR (στατήρ), a *tetradrachmon* or four *drachmae*, originally 224 grains, in Tyrian currency, but reduced in weight somewhat by the time recorded in Matt. 17 : 24 ; the value was about three shillings, and would pay the Temple tax for two persons, Matt. 17 : 27, R.V., "shekel" (A.V., "a piece of money") ; in some mss., 26 : 16 ; see MONEY, Note.¶

1323 AG:192C CB:1241C 2. DIDRACHMON (δίδραχμον), a half-shekel (i.e., *dis*, twice, *drachmē*, a drachma, the coin mentioned in Luke 15 : 8, 9), was the amount of the tribute in the 1st cent., A.D., due from every adult Jew for the maintenance of the Temple services, Matt. 17 : 24 (twice).¶ This was based on Ex. 30 : 13, 24 (see also 38 : 24–26 ; Lev. 5 : 15 ; 27 : 3, 25 ; Numb. 3 : 47, 50 ; 7 : 13 ff. ; 18 : 16).

SHEPHERD

4166 AG:684A CB:1265C POIMĒN (ποιμήν) is used (*a*) in its natural significance, Matt. 9 : 36 ; 25 : 32 ; Mark 6 : 34 ; Luke 2 : 8, 15, 18, 20 ; John 10 : 2, 12 ; (*b*) metaphorically of Christ, Matt. 26 : 31 ; Mark 14 : 27 ; John 10 : 11, 14, 16 ; Heb. 13 : 20 ; 1 Pet. 2 : 25 ; (*c*) metaphorically of those who act as pastors in the churches, Eph. 4 : 11.¶ See PASTOR.

For CHIEF SHEPHERD see CHIEF, B, No. 3

SHEW (SHOW)

1. DEIKNUMI, or DEIKNUŌ, (δείκνυμι) denotes (*a*) to shew, exhibit, 1166
e.g., Matt. 4 : 8 ; 8 : 4 ; John 5 : 20 ; 20 : 20 ; 1 Tim. 6 : 15 ; (*b*) to AG:172D CB:1240C
shew by making known, Matt. 16 : 21 ; Luke 24 : 40 ; John 14 : 8, 9 ;
Acts 10 : 28 ; 1 Cor. 12 : 31 ; Rev. 1 : 1 ; 4 : 1 ; 22 : 6 ; (*c*) to shew by
way of proving, Jas. 2 : 18 ; 3 : 13.

2. ANADEIKNUMI (ἀναδείκνυμι) signifies (*a*) to lift up and shew, 322
shew forth, declare (*ana*, up, and No. 1), Acts 1 : 24 ; (*b*) to appoint, AG:53B CB:1235A
Luke 10 : 1. See Appoint, No. 14.¶

3. ENDEIKNUMI (ἐνδείκνυμι) signifies (1) to shew forth, prove (Middle 1731
Voice), said (*a*) of God as to His power, Rom. 9 : 17 ; His wrath, 9 : 22 ; AG:262C CB:—
the exceeding riches of His grace, Eph. 2 : 7 ; (*b*) of Christ, as to His
longsuffering, 1 Tim. 1 : 16 ; (*c*) of Gentiles, as to " the work of the Law
written in their hearts," Rom. 2 : 15 ; (*d*) of believers, as to the proof
of their love, 2 Cor. 8 : 24 ; all good fidelity, Tit. 2 : 10 ; meekness, 3 : 2 ;
love toward God's Name, Heb. 6 : 10 ; diligence in ministering to the
saints, ver. 11 ; (2) to manifest by evil acts, 2 Tim. 4 : 14, " did (me
much evil)," marg., " shewed."¶

4. EPIDEIKNUMI (ἐπιδείκνυμι), *epi*, upon, intensive, and No. 1, 1925
signifies (*a*) to exhibit, display, Matt. 16 : 1 ; 22 : 19 ; 24 : 1 ; Luke AG:291D CB:—
17 : 14 (in some mss. 24 : 40 ; No. 1 in the best texts) ; in the Middle
Voice, to display, with a special interest in one's own action, Acts 9 : 39 ;
(*b*) to point out, prove, demonstrate, Acts 18 : 28 ; Heb. 6 : 17.¶

5. HUPODEIKNUMI (ὑποδείκνυμι), primarily, to shew secretly 5263
(*hupo*, under), or by tracing out, hence, to make known, warn, is translated AG:844B CB:—
to shew in Luke 6 : 47 ; Acts 9 : 16 ; in 20 : 35, A.V. (R.V., " I gave . . .
an example "). See Example, Warn.

6. POIEŌ (ποιέω), to make, to do, is translated " He hath shewed " 4160
in Luke 1 : 51 ; " to shew (mercy)," ver. 72, R.V. (A.V., " perform ") ; AG:680D CB:1265C
" shewed (mercy)," 10 : 37 ; John 6 : 30, A.V., " shewest Thou," R.V.,
" doest Thou (for a sign) ; " Acts 7 : 36, A.V., " shewed," R.V.,
" wrought ; " Jas. 2 : 13, " shewed (no mercy) ; " in Mark 13 : 22 in the
best texts (some have *didōmi*), " shall shew (signs)." See Do, No. 1.

7. MĒNUŌ (μηνύω), to disclose, make known (what was secret), is 3377
rendered to shew in Luke 20 : 37 ; 1 Cor. 10 : 28 ; in a forensic sense, AG:519A CB:—
John 11 : 57 ; Acts 23 : 30, R.V. (A.V., " it was told "). See Tell.¶

8. PARISTĒMI (παρίστημι), to shew, in Acts 1 : 3 ; 2 Tim. 2 : 15 3936 AG:627C
(A.V.) : see Present, No. 1. CB:1262B

9. PARECHŌ (παρέχω), to afford, give, shew, etc., in the Active Voice, 3930
is translated " shewed " in Acts 28 : 2 ; in the Middle Voice, " shewing " AG:626B CB:—
in Tit. 2 : 7 (1st part). See Bring, No. 21.

10. EXANGELLŌ (ἐξαγγέλλω), to tell out, proclaim abroad, to 1804
publish completely (*ek*, or *ex*, out, *angellō*, to proclaim), is rendered " shew AG:271B CB:1247C
forth " in 1 Pet. 2 : 9 ; it indicates a complete proclamation (verbs
compounded with *ek* often suggest what is to be done fully).¶

1325 AG:192C 11. DIDŌMI (δίδωμι), to give, is rendered to shew in Matt. 24 : 24.
CB:1241C See also No. 6.
APODEIKNUMI 584 *Notes :* The A.V. translates the following words by the verb to shew
AG:89C in the passages indicated. The R.V. gives the better renderings : (1)
CB:1236C ANANGELLŌ *apodeiknumi* (to demonstrate), 2 Thess. 2 : 4, " setting (himself) forth,"
312 see SET, No. 17 ; (2) *anangellō* (to declare), Matt. 11 : 4, " tell ; " John
AG:51B CB:1235B 16 : 13–15, " declare ; " 16 : 25, " shall tell ; " Acts 19 : 18 and 20 : 20,
KATANGELLŌ " declaring ; " (3) *katangellō*, Acts 16 : 17 ; 26 : 23 ; 1 Cor. 11 : 26, " pro-
2605 AG:409B claim ; " in the last passage the partaking of the elements at the Lord's
CB:1254A Supper is not a showing forth of His death, but a proclamation of it ;
PHANEROŌ 5319 (4) *phaneroō*, John 7 : 4 ; 21 : 1 (twice), 14 ; Rom. 1 : 19, to manifest ;
AG:852D (5) *dēloō*, (to make plain), 2 Pet. 1 : 14, " signify ; " (6) *diēgeomai* (to
CB:1263C DĒLOŌ recount), Luke 8 : 39, " declare ; " (7) *emphanizō* (to manifest), Acts
1213 23 : 22, " hast signified ; " (8) *euangelizō*, Luke 1 : 19, " to bring glad
AG:178C CB:1240C tidings ; " (9) *katatithēmi* (to lay up), Acts 24 : 27, " to gain ; " (10) *legō*
DIĒGEOMAI (to tell), 1 Cor. 15 : 51, " I tell ; " (11) *energeō*, Matt. 14 : 2 and Mark 6 : 14,
1334 " work ; " (12) *ōphthē* (lit., ' was seen '), Acts 7 : 26, " He appeared ; "
AG:195A CB:1241C (13) *ginomai* (to become), Acts 4 : 22, " was wrought ; " (14) in Acts
EMPHANIZŌ 1718 10 : 40, *emphanēs*, manifest, with *didōmi* to give, and *ginomai*, to become,
AG:257D " gave . . . to be made manifest " (A.V. " shewed . . . openly ") ;
CB:1244B EUANGELIZŌ (15) *apangellō* (to announce), Matt. 11 : 4, " tell ; " 12 : 18, " declare ; "
2097 28 : 11, " told ; " Luke 14 : 21, " told ; " Acts 26 : 20, " declared ; "
AG:317B 28 : 21, " report ; " 1 Thess. 1 : 9, " report ; " 1 John 1 : 2, " declare ; "
CB:1247A KATATITHĒMI (16) In Luke 1 : 58, A.V., *megalunō*, to magnify (R.V.), is rendered
2698 " shewed great." (17) See also SHEWING.

AG:419C LEGŌ 3004

For SHEW BEFORE see FORESHEW

AG:468A CB:1256C ENERGEŌ

SHEWBREAD

1754 AG:265B *Note :* The phrase rendered " the shewbread " is formed by the
CB:1245A combination of the nouns *prothesis*, a setting forth (*pro*, before, *tithēmi*,
HORAŌ 3708 to place) and *artos*, a loaf (in the plural), each with the article, Matt. 12 : 4 ;
AG:577D Mark 2 : 26 and Luke 6 : 4, lit., ' the loaves of the setting forth ; ' in
CB:1251A Heb. 9 : 2, lit., ' the setting forth of the loaves.'¶ The corresponding
GINOMAI 1096 O.T. phrases are lit., ' bread of the face,' Ex. 25 : 30, i.e., the presence,
AG:158A referring to the Presence of God (cp. Isa. 63 : 9 with Ex. 33 : 14, 15) ;
CB:1248B EMPHANĒS ' the bread of ordering,' 1 Chron. 9 : 32, marg. In Numb. 4 : 7 it is
1717 called " the continual bread ; " in 1 Sam. 21 : 4, 6, " holy bread "
AG:257C CB:1244B (A.V., " hallowed "). In the Sept. of 1 Kings 7 : 48, it is called " the
APANGELLŌ bread of the offering " (*prosphora*, a bearing towards). The twelve loaves,
518 AG:79B representing the tribes of Israel, were set in order every Sabbath day
CB:1236B before the Lord, " on the behalf of the children," Lev. 24 : 8, R.V. (marg.,
MEGALUNŌ 3170 and A.V., " from "), " an everlasting covenant." The loaves symbolized
AG:497A the fact that on the basis of the sacrificial atonement of the Cross,
CB:1258A believers are accepted before God, and nourished by Him in the Person

of Christ. The shewbread was partaken of by the priests, as representatives of the nation. Priesthood now being co-extensive with all who belong to Christ, 1 Pet. 2 : 5, 9, He, the Living Bread, is the nourishment of all, and where He is, there, representatively, they are. **PROTHESIS 4286 AG:706A CB:1267B ARTOS 740 AG:110C CB:1237C**

SHEWING

ANADEIXIS (ἀνάδειξις), a shewing forth (*ana*, up or forth, and *deiknumi*, to show), is translated "shewing" in Luke 1 : 80.¶ **323 AG:53C CB:1235A**

Note : For "shewing," Rom. 3 : 25, 26, R.V., see DECLARE, B.

SHIELD

THUREOS (θυρεός) formerly meant a stone for closing the entrance of a cave; then, a shield, large and oblong, protecting every part of the soldier; the word is used metaphorically of faith, Eph. 6 : 16, which the believer is to take up 'in (*en* in the original) all' (all that has just been mentioned), i.e., as affecting the whole of his activities.¶ **2375 AG:366A CB:1272C**

SHINE, SHINING

A. Verbs.

1. PHAINŌ (φαίνω), to cause to appear, denotes, in the Active Voice, to give light, shine, John 1 : 5; 5 : 35; in Matt. 24 : 27, Passive Voice; so Phil. 2 : 15, R.V., "ye are seen" (for A.V., "ye shine"); 2 Pet. 1 : 19 (Active); so 1 John 2 : 8; Rev. 1 : 16; in 8 : 12 and 18 : 23 (Passive); 21 : 23 (Active). See APPEAR. **5316 AG:851B CB:1263C**

2. EPIPHAINŌ (ἐπιφαίνω), to shine upon (*epi*, upon, and No. 1), is so translated in Luke 1 : 79, R.V. (A.V., "to give light"). See APPEAR, No. 2. **2014 AG:304A CB:1246A**

3. LAMPŌ (λάμπω), to shine as a torch, occurs in Matt. 5 : 15, 16; 17 : 2; Luke 17 : 24; Acts 12 : 7; 2 Cor. 4 : 6 (twice).¶: see LIGHT, B, No. 3. **2989 AG:466A CB:1256C**

4. STILBŌ (στίλβω), to shine, glisten, is used in Mark 9 : 3 of the garments of Christ at His Transfiguration, R.V., "glistering," A.V., "shining."¶ Cp. *exastraptō*, "dazzling," in Luke 9 : 29, R.V. **4744 AG:768D CB:—**

5. EKLAMPŌ (ἐκλάμπω), to shine forth (*ek*, out, and No. 3), is used in Matt. 13 : 43, of the future shining forth of the righteous "in the Kingdom of their Father."¶ **1584 AG:242A CB:1243C**

6. PERILAMPŌ (περιλάμπω), to shine around (*peri*, around, and No. 3), is used in Luke 2 : 9, "shone round about," of the glory of the Lord; so in Acts 26 : 13, of the light from Heaven upon Saul of Tarsus.¶ **4034 AG:648C CB:1263B**

7. PERIASTRAPTŌ (περιαστράπτω), to flash around, shine round about (*peri*, and *astrapē*, shining brightness), is used in Acts 9 : 3 and 22 : 6 of the same circumstance as in 26 : 13 (No. 6).¶ **4015 AG:645D CB:—**

8. EPIPHAUSKŌ or EPIPHAUŌ (ἐπιφαύσκω), to shine forth, is used figuratively of Christ upon the slumbering believer who awakes and arises from among the dead, Eph. 5 : 14, R.V., "shall shine upon thee" (A.V., "shall give thee light").¶ **2017 AG:304C CB:—**

B. Noun.

796 AG:118A ASTRAPĒ (ἀστραπή) denotes (*a*) lightning, (*b*) bright shining, of a
CB:1238A lamp, Luke 11 : 36. See LIGHTNING. Cp. No. 7, above, and Note (1)
ASTRAPTō below.

797 AG:118B *Notes:* (1) In Luke 24 : 4, A.V., *astraptō*, to lighten, is translated
CB:— "shining" (R.V., "dazzling"). (2) In 2 Cor. 4 : 4, A.V., *augazō*, to
AUGAZō shine forth, is translated "shine" (R.V., "dawn").¶

826 AG:120C CB:1238B

SHIP, SHIPPING

4143 AG:673B 1. PLOION (πλοῖον), akin to *pleō*, to sail, a boat or a ship, always
CB:— rendered appropriately "boat" in the R.V. in the Gospels; "ship" in the Acts; elsewhere, Jas. 3 : 4; Rev. 8 : 9; 18 : 17 (in some mss.), 19. See BOAT, No. 2.

4142 AG:673B 2. PLOIARION (πλοιάριον), a diminutive form of No. 1, is translated
CB:— "ship" in the A.V. of Mark 3 : 9; 4 : 36 and John 21 : 8; "(took) shipping" in John 6 : 24, A.V., R.V. "(got into the) boats." See BOAT, No. 1.

3491 AG:534C 3. NAUS (ναῦς) denotes a ship (Lat. *navis*, Eng. nautical, naval, etc.),
CB:— Acts 27 : 41.¶ *Naus*, in classical Greek the ordinary word for a ship, survived in Hellenistic Greek only as a literary word, but disappeared from popular speech (Moulton, Proleg., p. 25). Blass (*Philology of the Gospels*, p. 186) thinks the solitary Lucan use of *naus* was due to a reminiscence of the Homeric phrase for beaching a ship.

1910 AG:289D *Note:* For *epibainō*, Acts 21 : 6, "we took ship," see TAKE, Note (16).
CB:—

For OWNER OF THE SHIP see OWNER, No. 2

For SHIPMEN see MARINERS

For SHIPMASTER see MASTER, A, No. 7

SHIPWRECK

3489 AG:534B NAUAGEŌ (ναυαγέω) signifies (*a*) literally, to suffer shipwreck (*naus*, a
CB:1259B ship, *agnumi*, to break), 2 Cor. 11 : 25; (*b*) metaphorically, to make shipwreck, 1 Tim. 1 : 19, "concerning the faith," as the result of thrusting away a good conscience (both verbs in this ver. are in the aorist tense, signifying the definiteness of the acts).¶

For SHIVERS (Rev. 2 : 27) see BREAK, A, No. 5

For SHOD see BIND, No. 3

SHOE

5266 AG:844C HUPODĒMA (ὑπόδημα) denotes a sole bound under the foot (*hupo*,
CB:— under, *deō*, to bind; cp. *hupodeō*, to bind under), a sandal, always translated "shoes," e.g., Matt. 3 : 11; 10 : 10; Mark 1 : 7.

SHOOT FORTH

PROBALLŌ (προβάλλω), lit., to throw before, is used of the putting 4261
forth of leaves, blossom, fruit, said of trees in general, Luke 21 : 30, AG:702D
" shoot forth." See PUT (forward), Acts 19 : 33.¶ CB:—

Note : In Mark 4 : 32, A.V., *poieō*, to do, make, is rendered " shooteth 4160
out," R.V., " putteth out." AG:680D CB:1265C

For SHORE see BEACH and LIP

For SHORT (Adjective and Adverb) see LITTLE, A, No 2 and B, No. 2

Note : In 1 Thess. 2 : 17, " a short season," is lit., ' a season of an hour ' 5610
(*hōra* ; see HOUR, SEASON, No. 1. AG:896A CB:1251A

SHORT (come, cut), SHORTEN

1. KOLOBOŌ (κολοβόω) denotes to cut off, amputate (*kolobos*, docked) ; 2856
hence, to curtail, shorten, said of the shortening by God of the time of the AG:442A
great tribulation, Matt. 24 : 22 (twice) ; Mark 13 : 20 (twice).¶ In the CB:1255C
Sept., 2 Sam. 4 : 12.¶

2. SUSTELLŌ (συστέλλω) denotes (*a*) to draw together (*sun*, together, 4958
stellō, to bring, gather), to contract, shorten, 1 Cor. 7 : 29, R.V., " (the AG:795A
time) is shortened " (A.V., " . . . is short ") ; the coming of the Lord CB:—
is always to be regarded as nigh for the believer, who is to be in constant expectation of His return, and thus is to keep himself from being the slave of earthly conditions and life's relationships ; (*b*) to wrap up, of enshrouding a body for burial, Acts 5 : 6, R.V., " they wrapped (A.V., wound) . . . . up."¶

3. SUNTEMNŌ (συντέμνω), primarily, to cut in pieces (*sun*, together, 4932
temnō, to cut), then, to cut down, cut short, is used metaphorically in AG:792B
Rom. 9 : 28 (twice in some texts), " the Lord will execute His word (*logos*, CB:—
not work, as A.V.) upon the earth, finishing it and cutting it short," HUSTEREŌ
i.e., in the fulfilment of His judgments pronounced upon Israel, a remnant 5302 AG:849A
only being saved ; the cutting short of His word is suggestive of the CB:1252B
summary and decisive character of the Divine act.¶ EUTHEŌS 2112

Note : For *hustereō*, to come short, fall short, see FALL, No. 10. AG:320B CB:1247B

SHORTLY

TACHEŌS 5030 AG:806D

1. EUTHEŌS (εὐθέως), straightway, directly, is translated " shortly " TACHEION
in 3 John 14. The general use of the word suggests something sooner than 5032
" shortly." See FORTHWITH, STRAIGHTWAY. AG:806D

TACHEI

2. TACHEŌS (ταχέως) : see QUICKLY, No. 3. 5034

3. TACHEION (τάχειον) : see QUICKLY, No. 2. (TACHOS) AG:806D

4. EN TACHEI (ἐν τάχει) : see QUICKLY, No. 4. (-EŌS)

Note : In 2 Pet. 1 : 14, A.V., *tachinos*, an adjective denoting swift TACHINOS 5031
(akin to the above), is translated " shortly " (R.V., " swiftly "), lit., ' the AG:807A
putting off of my tabernacle is swift ' (i.e., in its approach). Cp. 2 : 1. CB:1271A

SHOULD

Note : This is frequently part of the translation of the tense of a verb. Otherwise it translates the following :

3195 AG:500D CB:1258A 1. MELLŌ (μέλλω), to be about to (for the significance of which see SHALL), e.g., Mark 10 : 32, R.V., " were to ; " Luke 19 : 11, R.V., " was to ; " " should " in 22 : 23 ; 24 : 21 ; John 6 : 71 ; 7 : 39, R.V., " were to ; " 11 : 51 ; 12 : 4, 33 ; 18 : 32 ; Acts 11 : 28 ; 23 : 27, R.V., " was about (to be slain) ; " 1 Thess. 3 : 4, R.V., " are to ; " Rev. 6 : 11. See ABOUT, B.

1163 AG:172A CB:1240B 2. DEI (δεῖ), it needs, it should, e.g., Matt. 18 : 33 ; Acts 27 : 21 : see MUST.

3784 AG:598D CB:1261A *Note :* In 1 Cor. 9 : 10, A.V., *opheilō,* to owe, is rendered " should " (R.V., " ought to ").

SHOULDER

5606 AG:895D CB:— ŌMOS (ὦμος) occurs in Matt. 23 : 4 and Luke 15 : 5, and is suggestive (as in the latter passage) of strength and safety.¶

SHOUT (Noun and Verb)

A. Noun.

2752 (-UMA) AG:427B CB:1254C KELEUSMA (κέλευσμα), a call, summons, shout of command (akin to *keleuō,* to command), is used in 1 Thess. 4 : 16 of the shout with which (*en,* in, denoting the attendant circumstances) the Lord will descend from heaven at the time of the Rapture of the saints (those who have fallen asleep, and the living) to meet Him in the air. The shout is not here said to be His actual voice, though this indeed will be so (John 5 : 28).¶ In the Sept., Prov. 30 : 27, " (the locusts . . . at the) word of command (march in rank)."¶

B. Verb.

2019 AG:304D CB:1246A EPIPHŌNEŌ (ἐπιφωνέω), to call out (*epi,* upon, *phōneō,* to utter a sound), is translated " shouted " in Acts 12 : 22, R.V. (A.V., " gave a shout "). See CRY, B, No. 8.

SHOW See SHEW

SHOW (Noun)

3056 AG:477A CB:1257A LOGOS (λόγος), a word, is sometimes used of mere talk, the talk which one occasions ; hence, repute, reputation ; this seems to be the meaning in Col. 2 : 23, translated " a show (A.V. ' shew ') of wisdom," i.e., ' a reputation for wisdom,' rather than ' appearance,' ' reason ' etc. See WORD.

4392 AG:722C CB:— *Note :* In Luke 20 : 47, A.V., *prophasis,* a pretence (R.V.), is translated " shew." See CLOKE (Pretence), No. 2.

SHOW (make a)

1165 AG:172C CB:1240C 1. DEIGMATIZŌ (δειγματίζω), to make a show of, expose, is used in Col. 2 : 15 of Christ's act regarding the principalities and powers, displaying them " as a victor displays his captives or trophies in a triumphal procession" (Lightfoot). Some regard the meaning as being that He showed the angelic beings in their true inferiority (see under TRIUMPH). For its other occurrence, Matt. 1 : 19, see EXAMPLE, B, No. 1.¶

2. EUPROSŌPEŌ (εὐπροσωπέω) denotes to look well, make a fair show (*eu*, well, *prosōpon*, a face), and is used in Gal. 6 : 12, "to make a fair show (in the flesh)," i.e., to make a display of religious zeal. Deissmann illustrates the metaphorical use of this word from the papyri in ***Light from the Ancient East***, p. 96.¶ 2146 AG:324D CB:—

Note: For *paratērēsis*, A.V. marg. in Luke 17 : 20, "outward shew," see OBSERVATION.¶ 3907 AG:622D CB:1262B

SHOWER

OMBROS (ὄμβρος) denotes a heavy shower, a storm of rain, Luke 12 : 54.¶ 3655 AG:565B CB:1260C

For SHRANK and SHRINK see DRAW (*B*), No. 4

SHRINE

NAOS (ναός), the inmost part of a temple, a shrine, is used in the plural in Acts 19 : 24, of the silver models of the pagan shrine in which the image of Diana (Greek Artemis) was preserved. The models were large or small, and were signs of wealth and devotion on the part of purchasers. The variety of forms connected with the embellishment of the image provided "no little business" for the silversmiths. See TEMPLE. 3485 AG:533B CB:1259B

SHRIVELED See DRY

SHUDDER

PHRISSŌ (φρίσσω), primarily, to be rough, to bristle, then, to shiver, shudder, tremble, is said of demons, Jas. 2 : 19, R.V., "shudder" (A.V., "tremble").¶ Cp. Matt. 8 : 29, indicating a cognizance of their appointed doom. 5425 AG:866A CB:—

For SHUN see AVOID, No. 4, and DRAW, (*B*), No. 4

SHUT, SHUT UP

1. KLEIO (κλείω) is used (*a*) of things material, Matt. 6 : 6; 25 : 10; Luke 11 : 7; John 20 : 19, 26; Acts 5 : 23; 21 : 30; Rev. 20 : 3; figuratively, 21 : 25; (*b*) metaphorically, of the Kingdom of Heaven, Matt. 23 : 13; of heaven, with consequences of famine, Luke 4 : 25; Rev. 11 : 6; of compassion, 1 John 3 : 17, R.V. (A.V., "bowels *of compassion*"); of the blessings accruing from the promises of God regarding David, Rev. 3 : 7; of a door for testimony, 3 : 8.¶ 2808 AG:434A CB:1255B

2. APOKLEIŌ (ἀποκλείω), to shut fast (*apo*, away from, and No. 1), is used in Luke 13 : 25, expressing the impossibility of entrance after the closing.¶ 608 AG:93A CB:—

2623 AG:411C CB:— 3. KATAKLEIŌ (κατακλείω), lit., to shut down (the *kata* has, however, an intensive use), signifies to shut up in confinement, Luke 3 : 20 ; Acts 26 : 10.¶ In the Sept., Jer. 32 : 3.¶

4788 AG:774A CB:1270C 4. SUNKLEIŌ (συγκλείω) : see INCLOSE.

SICK, SICKLY, SICKNESS

A. Verbs.

770 AG:115B CB:1238A 1. ASTHENEŌ (ἀσθενέω), lit., to be weak, feeble (*a*, negative, *sthenos*, strength), is translated to be sick, e.g., in Matt. 10 : 8, " (the) sick ; " 25 : 36 ; ver. 39 in the best texts (some have B, No. 1) ; Mark 6 : 56 ; Luke 4 : 40 ; 7 : 10 (R.V. omits the word) ; 9 : 2 ; John 4 : 46 ; 5 : 3, R.V. (A.V., " impotent folk ") ; ver. 7 ; 6 : 2, R.V. (A.V., " were diseased ") ; 11 : 1–3, 6 ; Acts 9 : 37 ; 19 : 12 ; Phil. 2 : 26, 27 ; 2 Tim. 4 : 20 ; Jas. 5 : 14. See DISEASED, B, No. 1, IMPOTENT, and, especially, WEAK.

2577 AG:402A CB:— 2. KAMNŌ (κάμνω), primarily, to work, hence, from the effect of constant work, to be weary, Heb. 12 : 3, is rendered " (him) that is sick," in Jas. 5 : 15, R.V., A.V. " (the) sick." The choice of this verb instead of the repetition of No. 1 (ver. 14, see above), is suggestive of the common accompaniment of sickness, weariness of mind (which is the meaning of this verb), which not infrequently hinders physical recovery ; hence this special cause is here intimated in the general idea of sickness. In some mss. it occurs in Rev. 2 : 3.¶ In the Sept., Job 10 : 1 ; 17 : 2.¶

4912 AG:789A CB:1270C 3. SUNECHŌ (συνέχω), to hold in, hold fast, is used, in the Passive Voice, of being seized or afflicted by ills, Acts 28 : 8, " sick " (of the father of Publius, cp. Matt. 4 : 24 ; Luke 4 : 38, " taken with "). See CONSTRAIN, No. 3.

NOSEō 3552 AG:543C CB:1260A *Notes :* (1) *Noseō*, to be sick, is used metaphorically of mental ailment, in 1 Tim. 6 : 4, " doting " (marg., " sick "). (2) The adverb *kakōs*, evilly,
KAKōS 2560 AG:398C CB:1253B ill, with *echō*, to hold, to have, is rendered to be sick, in Matt. 4 : 24, R.V., " that were sick ; " 8 : 16 ; 9 : 12 ; 14 : 35 and Mark 1 : 32, R.V. (A.V., " diseased ") ; 1 : 34 ; 2 : 17 ; 6 : 55 ; Luke 5 : 31 ; 7 : 2. (3) For " sick of the palsy," Luke 5 : 24 ; Acts 9 : 33, see PALSY (sick of).

B. Adjectives.

772 AG:115C CB:1238A 1. ASTHENĒS (ἀσθενής), lit., without strength, hence, feeble, weak, is used of bodily debility, Matt. 25 : 43 (for ver. 39, see A, No. 1), 44 ; some texts have it in Luke 9 : 2 (the best omit it, the meaning being to heal in general) ; 10 : 9 ; Acts 5 : 15, 16 ; in 4 : 9 it is rendered " impotent." See FEEBLE, IMPOTENT, WEAK.

732 AG:109D CB:— 2. ARRHŌSTOS (ἄρρωστος), feeble, sickly (*a*, negative, *rhōnnumi*, to be strong), is translated " sick " in Matt. 14 : 14 ; Mark 16 : 18 ; " sick folk " in Mark 6 : 5 ; " that were sick " in 6 : 13 : " sickly " in 1 Cor. 11 : 30, here also of the physical state.¶ In the Sept., 1 Kings 14 : 5 ; Mal. 1 : 8.¶

C. Nouns.

1. ASTHENEIA (ἀσθένεια), weakness, sickness (akin to A, No. 1 and 769
B, No. 1), is translated "sickness" in John 11 : 4. See DISEASE, No. 1, AG:115A CB:1238A
INFIRMITY, WEAKNESS.

2. NOSOS (νόσος): see DISEASE, No. 3. 3554 AG:543C CB:1260A

SICKLE

DREPANON (δρέπανον), a pruning-hook, a sickle (akin to *drepō*, to 1407
pluck), occurs in Mark 4 : 29; Rev. 14 : 14, 15, 16, 17, 18 (twice), 19.¶ AG:206D CB:1242B

SIDE

A. Noun.

PLEURA (πλευρά), a side (cp. Eng., pleurisy), is used of the side of 4125
Christ, into which the spear was thrust, John 19 : 34; 20 : 20, 25, 27 AG:668A CB:—
(some mss. have it in Matt. 27 : 49; see R.V. marg.); elsewhere, in Acts
12 : 7.¶

B. Adverb.

PERAN (πέραν), an adverb, signifying beyond, on the other side, is 4008
used (*a*) as a preposition and translated "on the other side of," e.g., in AG:643D CB:—
Mark 5 : 1; Luke 8 : 22; John 6 : 1, R.V.; 6 : 22, 25; (*b*) as a noun
with the article, e.g., Matt. 8 : 18, 28; 14 : 22; 16 : 5. See BEYOND,
No. 2.

Notes: (1) In Luke 9 : 47, the preposition *para*, by the side of, with the 3844
dative case of the pronoun *heautou*, is rendered "by His side," R.V. AG:609C CB:1261C
(A.V., "by Him"). (2) See also EITHER, EVERYWHERE, No. 3, HIGHWAY, RIGHT.

SIFT

SINIAZŌ (σινιάζω), to winnow, sift (*sinion*, a sieve), is used figuratively 4617
in Luke 22 : 31.¶ AG:751D CB:1269A

SIGH

1. STENAZŌ (στενάζω), to groan, is translated "He sighed" in 4727
Mark 7 : 34. See GRIEF, GROAN. AG:766B CB:1270A

2. ANASTENAZŌ (ἀναστενάζω), to sigh deeply (*ana*, up, suggesting 389
'deep drawn,' and No. 1), occurs in Mark 8 : 12.¶ In the Sept., Lam. AG:61B CB:—
1 : 4.¶

SIGHT

A. Nouns.

1. EIDOS (εἶδος) is translated "sight" in 2 Cor. 5 : 7; see 1491 AG:221B
APPEARANCE, No. 1. CB:1243A

2. THEŌRIA (θεωρία) denotes a spectacle, a sight (akin to *theōreō*, to 2335 AG:360B
gaze, behold; see BEHOLD), in Luke 23 : 48.¶ CB:1272A

3. HORAMA (ὅραμα), that which is seen (akin to *horaō*, to see), 3705
besides its meaning, a vision, appearance, denotes a sight, in Acts 7 : 31. AG:577B CB:1251A
See VISION.

3788 AG:599B CB:1261A 4. OPHTHALMOS (ὀφθαλμός), an eye (Eng., ophthalmic, etc.), **in** Acts 1 : 9 is translated " sight " (plur., lit., ' eyes '). See EYE.

309 AG:51A CB:— 5. ANABLEPSIS (ἀνάβλεψις) denotes " recovering of sight " (*ana*, again, *blepō*, to see), Luke 4 : 18.¶ In the Sept., Isa. 61 : 1.¶

HORASIS 3706 AG:577C CB:1251A BLEPŌ 991 AG:143B CB:1239A PHANTAZŌ 5324 AG:853B CB:1263C PHOBĒTRON 5400 AG:863C CB:1264B *Notes :* (1) For *horasis* (akin to No. 3), translated " in sight " in Rev. 4 : 3, A.V. (R.V., " to look upon "), see LOOK, B. (2) In Luke 7 : 21, the infinitive mood of *blepō*, to see, is used as a noun, " (He bestowed, A.V., ' gave ') sight." In Acts 9 : 9 it is used in the present participle with *mē*, not, " without sight " (lit., ' not seeing '). (3) In Heb. 12 : 21 *phantazomai*, to make visible, is used in the present participle as a noun, with the article, " (the) sight."¶ (4) In Luke 21 : 11, A.V., *phobētron* (or *phobēthron*), plur., is translated " fearful sights " (R.V., " terrors ").¶

B. Verb.

ANABLEPŌ 308 AG:50D CB:1235A ANABLEPŌ (ἀναβλέπω), to look up, also denotes to receive or recover sight (akin to A, No. 5), e.g., Matt. 11 : 5 ; 20 : 34 ; Mark 10 : 51, 52 ; Luke 18 : 41–43 ; John 9 : 11, 15, 18 (twice) ; Acts 9 : 12, 17, 18 ; 22 : 13.

SIGHT OF (in the)

1799 AG:270C CB:1245B 1. ENŌPION (ἐνώπιον), for which see BEFORE, No. 9, is translated ' in the sight of ' in the R.V. (for A.V., " before ") in Luke 12 : 6 ; 15 : 18 ; 16 : 15 ; Acts 7 : 46 ; 10 : 33 ; 19 : 19 ; 1 Tim. 5 : 4, 21 ; 2 Tim. 2 : 14 ; 4 : 1 ; Rev. 13 : 12. The R.V. is more appropriate in most passages, as giving the real significance of the word.

2714 AG:421B CB:1254B 2. KATENŌPION (κατενώπιον), see BEFORE, No. 10, is translated " in the sight of " in 2 Cor. 2 : 17 (in some texts) ; Col. 1 : 22, A.V.

1715 AG:257A CB:1244B 3. EMPROSTHEN (ἔμπροσθεν), see BEFORE, No. 4, is translated " in the sight of " in Matt. 11 : 26 ; Luke 10 : 21 ; 1 Thess. 1 : 3, A.V.

1726 AG:261D CB:1244C 4. ENANTION (ἐναντίον), see BEFORE, No. 5, is translated " in the sight of " in Acts 7 : 10.

1725 AG:261D CB:1244C 5. ENANTI (ἔναντι), see BEFORE, No. 6, is translated " in the sight of " in Acts 8 : 21, A.V.

2713 AG:421B CB:— 6. KATENANTI (κατέναντι), see BEFORE, No. 8, is found in the best texts in 2 Cor. 12 : 19, " in the sight of," R.V., and in 2 : 17.

SIGN

4592 AG:747D CB:1268C 1. SĒMEION (σημεῖον), a sign, mark, indication, token, is used (*a*) of that which distinguished a person or thing from others, e.g., Matt. 26 : 48 ; Luke 2 : 12 ; Rom. 4 : 11 ; 2 Cor. 12 : 12 (1st part) ; 2 Thess. 3 : 17, " token," i.e., his autograph attesting the authenticity of his letters ; (*b*) of a sign as a warning or admonition, e.g., Matt. 12 : 39, " the sign of (i.e., consisting of) the prophet Jonas ; " 16 : 4 ; Luke 2 : 34 ; 11 : 29, 30 ; (*c*) of miraculous acts (1) as tokens of Divine authority and power, e.g., Matt. 12 : 38, 39 (1st part) ; John 2 : 11, R.V., " signs ; " 3 : 2 (ditto) ; 4 : 54, " (the second) sign," R.V. ; 10 : 41 (ditto) ; 20 : 30

in 1 Cor. 1 : 22, " the Jews ask for signs," R.V., indicates that the Apostles were met with the same demand from Jews as Christ had been : " signs were vouchsafed in plenty, signs of God's power and love, but these were not the signs which they sought. . . . They wanted signs of an outward Messianic Kingdom, of temporal triumph, of material greatness for the chosen people. . . . With such cravings the Gospel of a 'crucified Messiah' was to them a stumblingblock indeed" (Lightfoot) ; 1 Cor. 14 : 22 ; (2) by demons, Rev. 16 : 14 ; (3) by false teachers or prophets, indications of assumed authority, e.g., Matt. 24 : 24 ; Mark 13 : 22 ; (4) by Satan through his special agents, 2 Thess. 2 : 9 ; Rev. 13 : 13, 14 ; 19 : 20 ; (*d*) of tokens portending future events, e.g., Matt. 24 : 3, where " the sign of the Son of Man " signifies, subjectively, that the Son of Man is Himself the sign of what He is about to do ; Mark 13 : 4 ; Luke 21 : 7, 11, 25 ; Acts 2 : 19 ; Rev. 12 : 1, R.V. ; 12 : 3, R.V. ; 15 : 1.

Signs confirmatory of what God had accomplished in the atoning sacrifice of Christ, His resurrection and ascension, and of the sending of the Holy Spirit, were given to the Jews for their recognition, as at Pentecost, and supernatural acts by apostolic ministry, as well as by the supernatural operations in the churches, such as the gift of tongues and prophesyings ; there is no record of the continuance of these latter after the circumstances recorded in Acts 19 : 1–20.

SIGNAL **See SIGN**

2. PARASĒMOS (παράσημος), an adjective meaning 'marked at the side' (*para*, beside, *sēma*, a mark), is used in Acts 28 : 11 as a noun denoting the figure-head of a vessel.¶ **3902 AG:622A CB:—**

SIGNS (to make)

ENNEUŌ (ἐννεύω), to nod to (*en*, in, *neuō*, to nod), denotes to make a sign to in Luke 1 : 62.¶ In the Sept., Prov. 6 : 13 ; 10 : 10.¶ **1770 AG:267A CB:—**

Note : For *dianeuō*, Luke 1 : 22, R.V., see BECKON, No. 2. **1269 AG:187A CB:—**

For SIGNIFICATION, 1 Cor. 14 : 10, see DUMB, No. 2

SIGNIFY

1. SĒMAINŌ (σημαίνω), to give a sign, indicate (*sēma*, a sign : cp. SIGN, No. 1), to signify, is so translated in John 12 : 33 ; 18 : 32 ; 21 : 19 ; Acts 11 : 28 ; 25 : 27 ; Rev. 1 : 1, where perhaps the suggestion is that of expressing by signs.¶ **4591 AG:747C CB:1268C**

2. DĒLOŌ (δηλόω), to make plain (*dēlos*, evident), is translated to signify in 1 Cor. 1 : 11, R.V., " it hath been signified " (A.V., " declared ") ; Heb. 9 : 8 ; 12 : 27 ; 1 Pet. 1 : 11, A.V. (R.V., " point unto ") ; 2 Pet. 1 : 14, R.V., " signified " (A.V., " hath shewed "). See POINT (unto). **1213 AG:178C CB:1240C**

3. EMPHANIZŌ (ἐμφανίζω), to manifest, make known, is translated " signify " in Acts 23 : 15 ; ver. 22, R.V. (A.V., " hath shewed "). See APPEAR, No. 5. **1718 AG:257D CB:1244B**

Note : In Acts 21 : 26, A.V., *diangellō*, to announce, is rendered " to signify " (R.V., " declaring "). **1229 AG:182B CB:1241B**

SILENCE

A. Noun.

4602 AG:749D SIGĒ (σιγή) occurs in Acts 21 : 40 ; Rev. 8 : 1, where the silence is
CB:— introductory to the judgments following the opening of the seventh seal.¶
2271 AG:349B *Note :* For *hēsuchia*, A.V., " silence," in Acts 22 : 2 and 1 Tim. 2 : 11,
CB:1250A 12, see QUIETNESS.

B. Verbs.

5392 AG:861D 1. PHIMOŌ (φιμόω), to muzzle, is rendered " to put to silence " in
CB:— Matt. 22 : 34 ; 1 Pet. 2 : 15. See MUZZLE, PEACE (hold), SPEECHLESS, STILL.

4601 AG:749C 2. SIGAŌ (σιγάω), to be silent : see PEACE (hold), No. 1.
CB:—

For SILENT, Luke 1 : 20, R.V., see DUMB, B

SILK

4596 AG:751D SĒRIKOS or SIRIKOS (σιρικός), silken, an adjective derived from the
CB:— *Sēres*, a people of India, who seem to have produced silk originally as a marketable commodity, is used as a noun with the article, denoting silken fabric, Rev. 18 : 12.¶

For SILLY, 2 Tim. 3 : 6, see WOMAN, No. 2

SILVER

A. Nouns.

694 AG:104D 1. ARGURION (ἀργύριον) is rendered " silver " in Acts 3 : 6 ; 8 : 20,
CB:1237C R.V. (A.V., " money ") ; 20 : 33 ; 1 Cor. 3 : 12 (metaphorical) ; 1 Pet. 1 : 18. See MONEY, PIECE.

696 AG:105A 2. ARGUROS (ἄργυρος), akin to *argos*, shining, denotes silver. In
CB:1237C each occurrence in the N.T. it follows the mention of gold, Matt. 10 : 9 ;
1406 Acts 17 : 29 ; Jas. 5 : 3 ; Rev. 18 : 12.¶
AG:206C *Note :* For *drachmē*, Luke 15 : 8, see PIECE.

CB:— 693

B. Adjective.

AG:105A (-ROUS) ARGUREOS (ἀργύρεος) signifies made of silver, Acts 19 : 24 ; 2 Tim.
CB:1237C (-ROUS) 2 : 20 ; Rev. 9 : 20.¶

695

SILVERSMITH

AG:105A ARGUROKOPOS (ἀργυροκόπος), from *arguros* (see above) and *koptō*,
CB:— to beat, occurs in Acts 19 : 24.¶ In the Sept., Judg. 17 : 4 ; Jer. 6 : 29.¶

HOMOIŌMA 3667 AG:567C

SIMILITUDE

CB:1251A HOMOIOTĒS *Note :* For *homoiōma*, rendered " similitude " in Rom. 5 : 14, A.V.,
3665 AG:567A see LIKENESS, No. 1. For *homoiotēs*, " similitude " in Heb. 7 : 15. A.V.,
CB:1251A HOMOIŌSIS see LIKE, C, Note (1), and LIKENESS, No. 3. For *homoiōsis*, " similitude "
3669 AG:568A in Jas. 3 : 9, A.V., see LIKENESS, No. 2.

CB:1251A For SIMPLE see GUILELESS, No. 2, and HARMLESS

For SIMPLICITY see LIBERALITY

SIN (Noun and Verb)

A. Nouns.

1. HAMARTIA (ἁμαρτία) is, lit., a missing of the mark, but this 266
etymological meaning is largely lost sight of in the N.T. It is the most AG:43A CB:1249B
comprehensive term for moral obliquity. It is used of sin as (*a*) a principle or source of action, or an inward element producing acts, e.g., Rom. 3:9; 5:12, 13, 20; 6:1, 2; 7:7 (abstract for concrete); 7:8 (twice), 9, 11, 13, " sin, that it might be shewn to be sin," i.e., ' sin became death to me, that it might be exposed in its heinous character:' in the last clause, " sin might become exceeding sinful," i.e., through the holiness of the Law, the true nature of sin was designed to be manifested to the conscience;

(*b*) a governing principle or power, e.g., Rom. 6:6, " (the body) of sin ", here sin is spoken of as an organized power, acting through the members of the body, though the seat of sin is in the will (the body is the organic instrument); in the next clause, and in other passages, as follows, this governing principle is personified, e.g., Rom. 5:21; 6:12, 14, 17; 7:11, 14, 17, 20, 23, 25; 8:2; 1 Cor. 15:56; Heb. 3:13; 11:25; 12:4; Jas. 1:15 (2nd part);

(*c*) a generic term (distinct from specific terms such as No. 2, yet sometimes inclusive of concrete wrong doing, e.g., John 8:21, 34, 46; 9:41; 15:22, 24; 19:11); in Rom. 8:3, "God, sending His own Son in the likeness of sinful flesh," lit., ' flesh of sin,' the flesh stands for the body, the instrument of indwelling sin [Christ, pre-existently the Son of God, assumed human flesh, " of the substance of the Virgin Mary;" the reality of incarnation was His, without taint of sin (for *homoiōma*, likeness, see LIKENESS)], " and *as an offering* for sin," i.e., ' a sin-offering' (so the Sept., e.g., in Lev. 4:32; 5:6, 7, 8, 9), " condemned sin in the flesh," i.e., Christ, having taken human nature, sin apart (Heb. 4:15), and having lived a sinless life, died under the condemnation and judgment due to our sin; for the generic sense see further, e.g., Heb. 9:26; 10:6, 8, 18; 13:11; 1 John 1:7, 8; 3:4 (1st part; in the 2nd part, sin is defined as " lawlessness," R.V.), 8, 9; in these verses the A.V. use of the verb to commit is misleading; not the committal of an act is in view, but a continuous course of sin, as indicated by the R.V., " doeth." The Apostle's use of the present tense of *poieō*, to do, virtually expresses the meaning of *prassō*, to practise, which John does not use (it is not infrequent in this sense in Paul's Epp., e.g., Rom. 1:32, R.V.; 2:1; Gal. 5:21; Phil. 4:9); 1 Pet. 4:1 (singular in the best texts), lit., ' has been made to cease from sin,' i.e., as a result of suffering in the flesh, the mortifying of our members, and of obedience to a Saviour who suffered in flesh. Such no longer lives in the flesh, " to the lusts of men, but to the will of God;" sometimes the word is used as virtually equivalent to a condition of sin, e.g., John 1 : 29, "the sin (not sins) of the world;" 1 Cor. 15 : 17; or a course of sin, characterized by continuous acts, e.g., 1 Thess. 2 : 16; in 1 John 5 : 16 (2nd part) the R.V. marg., is probably to be preferred, "there is sin unto death," not a special act of sin, but the state or condition producing acts; in ver. 17, "all unrighteousness is sin" is not a definition of sin (as in 3 : 4), it gives a specification of the term in its generic sense;

(*d*) a sinful deed, an act of sin, e.g., Matt. 12 : 31; Acts 7 : 60; Jas. 1 : 15 (1st part); 2 : 9; 4 : 17; 5 : 15, 20; 1 John 5 : 16 (1st part).

Notes: (1) Christ is predicated as having been without sin in every respect, e.g., (*a*), (*b*), (*c*) above, 2 Cor. 5 : 21 (1st part); 1 John 3 : 5; John 14 : 30; (*d*) John 8 : 46; Heb. 4 : 15; 1 Pet. 2 : 22. (2) In Heb. 9 : 28 (2nd part) the reference is to a sin offering. (3) In 2 Cor. 5 : 21, "Him . . . He made to be sin" indicates that God dealt with Him as He must deal with sin, and that Christ fulfilled what was typified in the guilt offering. (4) For the phrase "man of sin" in 2 Thess. 2 : 3, see INIQUITY, No. 1.

265 AG:42D CB:1249B 2. HAMARTĒMA (ἁμάρτημα), akin to No. 1, denotes an act of disobedience to Divine law [as distinct from No. 1 (*a*), (*b*), (*c*)]; plural in Mark 3 : 28; Rom. 3 : 25; 2 Pet. 1 : 9, in some texts; sing. in Mark 3 : 29 (some mss. have *krisis*, A.V., "damnation"); 1 Cor. 6 : 18.¶

3900 AG:621D CB:1262B *Notes:* (1) For *paraptōma*, rendered "sins" in the A.V. in Eph. 1 : 7; 2 : 5; Col. 2 : 13 (R.V., "trespass"), see TRESPASS. In Jas. 5 : 16, the best texts have No. 1 (R.V., "sins"). (2) For synonymous terms see DISOBEDIENCE, ERROR, FAULT, INIQUITY, TRANSGRESSION, UNGODLINESS.

B. Adjective.

361 AG:57C CB:— ANAMARTĒTOS (ἀναμάρτητος), without sin (*a*, negative, *n*, euphonic, and C, No. 1), is found in John 8 : 7.¶ In the Sept., Deut. 29 : 19.¶

C. Verbs.

264 AG:42B CB:1249A 1. HAMARTANŌ (ἁμαρτάνω), lit., to miss the mark, is used in the N.T. (*a*) of sinning against God, (1) by angels, 2 Pet. 2 : 4; (2) by man, Matt. 27 : 4; Luke 15 : 18, 21 (Heaven standing, by metonymy, for God); John 5 : 14; 8 : 11; 9 : 2, 3; Rom. 2 : 12 (twice); 3 : 23; 5 : 12, 14, 16; 6 : 15; 1 Cor. 7 : 28 (twice), 36; 15 : 34; Eph. 4 : 26; 1 Tim. 5 : 20; Tit. 3 : 11; Heb. 3 : 17; 10 : 26; 1 John 1 : 10; in 2 : 1 (twice), the aorist tense in each place, referring to an act of sin; on the contrary, in 3 : 6 (twice), 8, 9, the present tense indicates, not the committal of an act, but the continuous practice of sin [see on A, No. 1 (*c*)]; in 5 : 16 (twice) the present tense indicates the condition resulting from an act, "unto death" signifying 'tending towards death;' (*b*) against Christ, 1 Cor. 8 : 12; (*c*) against man, (1) a brother, Matt. 18 : 15, R.V., "sin" (A.V., "trespass"); ver. 21; Luke 17 : 3, 4, R.V., "sin" (A.V., "trespass"); 1 Cor. 8 : 12; (2) in Luke 15 : 18, 21, against the father by the prodigal son, "in thy sight" being suggestive of befitting reverence; (*d*) against Jewish law, the Temple, and Cæsar, Acts 25 : 8, R.V., "sinned" (A.V., "offended"); (*e*) against one's own body, by fornication, 1 Cor. 6 : 18; (*f*) against earthly masters by servants, 1 Pet. 2 : 20, R.V., "(when) ye sin (and are buffeted for it)," A.V., "(when ye be buffeted) for your faults," lit., 'having sinned.'¶

2. PROAMARTANŌ (προαμαρτάνω), to sin previously (*pro*, before, 4258
and No. 1), occurs in 2 Cor. 12 : 21; 13 : 2, R.V. in each place, "have AG:702C CB:—
sinned heretofore" (so A.V. in the 2nd; in the 1st, "have sinned already").¶

SINCE: see † P. 1

SINCERE, SINCERELY, SINCERITY

A. Adjectives.

1. ADOLOS (ἄδολος), guileless, pure, is translated "sincere" in 97 AG:18D
1 Pet. 2 : 2, A.V., "without guile," R.V. See GUILELESS, No. 1. CB:1233A

2. GNĒSIOS (γνήσιος), true, genuine, sincere, is used in the neuter, 1103 AG:162D
as a noun, with the article, signifying "sincerity," 2 Cor. 8 : 8 (of love). CB:1248B
See OWN, TRUE.

3. EILIKRINĒS (εἰλικρινής): see PURE, A, No. 3. 1506 AG:222D CB:—

B. Adverb.

HAGNŌS (ἁγνῶς) denotes with pure motives, akin to words under 55
PURE, A, No. 1, and B, Nos. 1 and 2, and is rendered "sincerely" in AG:12A CB:1249A
Phil. 1 : 17, R.V. (ver. 16, A.V.).¶

C. Noun.

EILIKRINIA (or —EIA) (εἰλικρινία), akin to A, No. 3, denotes 1505
sincerity, purity; it is described metaphorically in 1 Cor. 5 : 8 as "un- AG:222D CB:—
leavened (bread);" in 2 Cor. 1 : 12, "sincerity (of God)," R.V., A.V., "(godly) sincerity," it describes a quality possessed by God, as that which is to characterize the conduct of believers; in 2 Cor. 2 : 17 it is used of the rightful ministry of the Scriptures.¶

Notes: (1) For 2 Cor. 8 : 8, see A, No. 2. (2) In Eph. 6 : 24, A.V., 861
aphtharsia, incorruption, is translated "sincerity" (R.V., "uncorrupt- AG:125B CB:1236C
ness," A.V. marg., "incorruption"); some inferior mss. have it in Tit. 2 : 7, A.V.; the R.V. follows those in which it is absent.

SINFUL

HAMARTŌLOS (ἁμαρτωλός), an adjective, akin to *hamartanō*, to sin, 268
is used as an adjective, "sinful" in Mark 8 : 38; Luke 5 : 8; 19 : 7 AG:44A CB:1249B
(lit., 'a sinful man'); 24 : 7; John 9 : 16, and 24 (lit., 'a man sinful'); Rom. 7 : 13, for which see SIN, A, No. 1 (*a*). Elsewhere it is used as a noun: see SINNER. The noun is frequently found in a common phrase in sepulchral epitaphs in the S.W. of Asia Minor, with the threat against any desecrator of the tomb, 'let him be as a sinner before the subterranean gods' (Moulton and Milligan).

Notes: (1) In Rom. 8 : 3, "sinful flesh" is, lit., 'flesh of sin' (R.V.

marg.): see SIN, No. 1 (*c*). (2) For the R.V. of Rom. 7:5, "sinful passions," see PASSION, No. 1.

103
SING, SINGING

AG:19B CB:1233A 1. ĄDŌ (ᾄδω) is used always of praise to God, (*a*) intransitively,
5567 Eph. 5:19; Col. 3:16; (*b*) transitively, Rev. 5:9; 14:3; 15:3.¶
AG:891A CB:1267B 2. PSALLŌ (ψάλλω): see MELODY.
5214 AG:836B CB:1251C 3. HUMNEŌ (ὑμνέω): see HYMN, B.

SINGLE

573 AG:86A HAPLOUS (ἁπλοῦς), simple, single, is used in a moral sense in Matt.
CB:1249B 6:22 and Luke 11:34, said of the eye; singleness of purpose keeps us
from the snare of having a double treasure and consequently a divided
heart.¶ The papyri provide instances of its use in other than the moral
sense, e.g., of a marriage dowry, to be repaid pure and simple by a husband
SINGLE See ONE (Moulton and Milligan). In the Sept., Prov. 11:25.¶

SINGLENESS

858 AG:124D 1. APHELOTĒS (ἀφελότης) denotes simplicity, Acts 2:46, "single-
CB:— ness," for which Moulton and Milligan, from papyri examples, suggest
"unworldly simplicity;" the idea here is that of an unalloyed benevolence expressed in act.¶
572 AG:85D CB:1249B 2. HAPLOTĒS (ἁπλότης): see BOUNTY, No. 2.

SINK

1036 AG:148C 1. BUTHIZŌ (βυθίζω) is used literally in Luke 5:7. See DROWN,
CB:— No. 1.
2670 AG:417A 2. KATAPONTIZŌ (καταποντίζω) is translated to sink in Matt.
CB:— 14:30 (Passive Voice). See DROWN, No. 3.
5087 AG:815D 3. TITHĒMI (τίθημι), to put, is rendered "let . . . sink" in Luke
CB:1272C 9:44, R.V. ("let . . . sink down," A.V.). See APPOINT, LAY.
2702 AG:419D *Note:* In Acts 20:9 (2nd part), A.V., *katapherō*, to bear down, is
CB:— translated "he sunk down" (R.V., "being borne down"); in the 1st
part it is rendered "being fallen," A.V., "borne down," R.V.

SINNER

268 AG:44A HAMARTŌLOS (ἁμαρτωλός), lit., one who misses the mark (a meaning
CB:1249B not to be pressed), is an adjective, most frequently used as a noun (see
SINFUL); it is the most usual term to describe the fallen condition of
men; it is applicable to all men, Rom. 5:8, 19. In the Synoptic Gospels
the word is used not infrequently, by the Pharisees, of publicans (tax-collectors) and women of ill repute, e.g., "a woman which was in the
city, a sinner," Luke 7:37; "a man that is a sinner," 19:7. In Gal.
2:15, in the clause "not sinners of the Gentiles," the Apostle is taking
the Judaizers on their own ground, ironically reminding them of their

claim to moral superiority over Gentiles ; he proceeds to show that the Jews are equally sinners with Gentiles.

Note : In Luke 13 : 4, A.V., *opheiletēs*, a debtor, is translated " sinners " 3781
(R.V., " offenders ; " R.V. and A.V. marg., " debtors "). AG:598B CB:1261A

SIR(-S)

2962
1. KURIOS (κύριος) : see LORD. AG:458D II.
2. ANĒR (ἀνήρ), a man, is translated " sirs " in Acts 7 : 26 ; 14 : 15 ; CB:1256B 435
19 : 25 ; 27 : 10, 21, 25. See MAN. AG:66C

Note : In John 21 : 5 the A.V. marg. has " sirs " for *paidia*, " children." 3816 AG:604C CB:1261C

SISTER

ADELPHĒ (ἀδελφή) is used (*a*) of natural relationship, e.g., Matt. 79
19 : 29 ; of the sisters of Christ, the children of Joseph and Mary after AG:15D CB:1233A
the Virgin Birth of Christ, e.g., Matt. 13 : 56 ; (*b*) of spiritual kinship with Christ, an affinity marked by the fulfilment of the will of the Father, Matt. 12 : 50 ; Mark 3 : 35 ; of spiritual relationship based upon faith in Christ, Rom. 16 : 1 ; 1 Cor. 7 : 15 ; 9 : 5, A.V. and R.V. marg. ; Jas. 2 : 15 ; Philm. 2, R.V.

Note : In Col. 4 : 10, A.V., *anepsios* (cp. Lat., *nepos*, whence Eng., 431
nephew), a cousin (so, R.V.), is translated " sister's son." See COUSIN.¶ AG:66A CB:—

SIT

1. KATHĒMAI (κάθημαι) is used (*a*) of the natural posture, e.g., 2521
Matt. 9 : 9, most frequently in the Apocalypse, some 32 times ; frequently AG:389B CB:1254C
in the Gospels and Acts ; elsewhere only in 1 Cor. 14 : 30 ; Jas. 2 : 3 (twice) ; and of Christ's position of authority on the throne of God, Col. 3 : 1, A.V., " sitteth " (R.V., " is, seated ") ; Heb. 1 : 13 (cp. Matt. 22 : 44 ; 26 : 64 and parallel passages in Mark and Luke, and Acts 2 : 34) ; often as antecedent or successive to, or accompanying, another act (in no case a superfluous expression), e.g., Matt. 15 : 29 ; 27 : 36 ; Mark 2 : 14 ; 4 : 1 ; (*b*) metaphorically in Matt. 4 : 16 (twice) ; Luke 1 : 79 ; of inhabiting a place (translated " dwell "), Luke 21 : 35 ; Rev. 14 : 6, R.V. marg., " sit " (in the best texts : some have *katoikeō*, to dwell). See DWELL.

2. SUNKATHĒMAI (συγκάθημαι), to sit with (*sun*, with, and No. 1), 4775
occurs in Mark 14 : 54 ; Acts 26 : 30.¶ In the Sept., Ps. 101 : 6, " dwell."¶ AG:773A CB:—

3. ANAKEIMAI (ἀνάκειμαι), to recline at table (*ana*, up, *keimai*, to 345
lie), is rendered to sit at meat in Matt. 9 : 10 (R.V., marg., " reclined ") ; AG:55D CB:1235A
26 : 7 ; 26 : 20, R.V., " He was sitting at meat " (A.V., " He sat down ") ; Mark 16 : 14 ; in some mss. Luke 7 : 37 (see No. 5) ; 22 : 27 (twice) ; in Mark 14 : 18, " sat ; " in John 6 : 11, " were set down ; " John 12 : 2 in the best texts (see No. 4). See GUEST, LEAN, LIE, Note (1), SET, No. 22,
TABLE (at the). 4873

4. SUNANAKEIMAI (συνανάκειμαι), to recline at table with or AG:784B CB:—

SITUATION See CALLING together (*sun,* and No. 3), to sit at meat or at table with, occurs in Matt. 9 : 10, " sat down ; " 14 : 9 ; Mark 2 : 15, R.V., " sat down with " (A.V., " sat . . . together with ") ; 6 : 22 ; Luke 7 : 49 ; 14 : 10, 15 ; John 12 : 2 (in some texts).¶

2621 AG:411C CB:— 5. KATAKEIMAI (κατάκειμαι), to lie down (*kata,* down, and *keimai,* cp. No. 3), is used of reclining at a meal, Mark 2 : 15 ; 14 : 3 ; Luke 5 : 29, R.V., " were sitting at meat " (A.V., " sat down ") ; 7 : 37 (in the best texts) ; 1 Cor. 8 : 10. See KEEP, LIE.

347 AG:56A CB:1235A (-OMAI) 6. ANAKLINŌ (ἀνακλίνω), to cause to recline, make to sit down, is used in the Active Voice, in Luke 12 : 37 (also in 2 : 7, of 'laying' the infant Christ in the manger) ; in the Passive, Matt. 8 : 11 ; 14 : 19 ; Mark 6 : 39 (in the best texts) ; in some texts, Luke 7 : 36 and 9 : 15 (see No. 7) ; 13 : 29. See LAY.¶

2625 AG:411D CB:— 7. KATAKLINŌ (κατακλίνω) is used only in connection with meals, (*a*) in the Active Voice, to make recline, Luke 9 : 14, 15 (in the best texts) ; in the Passive Voice, to recline, Luke 7 : 36 (in the best texts), " sat down to meat ; " 14 : 8 ; 24 : 30 (R.V., " had sat down . . . to meat ").¶

2523 AG:389D CB:1254C 8. KATHIZŌ (καθίζω) is used (*a*) transitively, to make sit down, Acts 2 : 30 (see also SET, No. 9) ; (*b*) intransitively, to sit down, e.g., Matt. 5 : 1, R.V., " when (He) had sat down " (A.V., " was set ") ; 19 : 28 ; 20 : 21, 23 ; 23 : 2 ; 25 : 31 ; 26 : 36 ; Mark 11 : 2, 7 ; 12 : 41 ; Luke 14 : 28, 31 ; 16 : 6 ; John 19 : 13 ; Acts 2 : 3 (of the tongues of fire) ; 8 : 31 ; 1 Cor. 10 : 7 ; 2 Thess. 2 : 4, " he sitteth," aorist tense, i.e., ' he takes his seat ' (as, e.g., in Mark 16 : 19) ; Rev. 3 : 21 (twice), R.V., " to sit down " and " sat down ; " 20 : 4.

3869 (-Zo) AG:616D 9. PARAKATHEZOMAI (παρακαθέζομαι), to sit down beside (*para*), **PARAKATHIZŌ 3869 AG:616D** in a Passive Voice form, occurs in the best mss. in Luke 10 : 39.¶ Some texts have the verb *parakathizō,* to set beside, Active form in Middle sense.

4776 AG:773B CB:— 10. SUNKATHIZŌ (συγκαθίζω) denotes (*a*) transitively, to make to sit together, Eph. 2 : 6 ; (*b*) intransitively, Luke 22 : 55, R.V., " had sat down together " (A.V., " were set down ").¶

339 AG:55B CB:— 11. ANAKATHIZŌ (ἀνακαθίζω), to set up, is used intransitively, to sit up, of two who were raised from the dead, Luke 7 : 15 ; Acts 9 : 40.¶

377 AG:59C CB:1235B 12. ANAPIPTŌ (ἀναπίπτω), to fall back (*ana,* back, *piptō,* to fall), denotes, in the N.T., to recline for a repast, Matt. 15 : 35 ; Mark 6 : 40 ; 8 : 6 ; Luke 11 : 37 ; 14 : 10 ; 17 : 7 ; 22 : 14 ; John 6 : 10 (twice) ; 13 : 12 ; in John 13 : 25 and 21 : 20 it is used of leaning on the bosom of Christ. See LEAN.¶ In the Sept., Gen. 49 : 9.¶

2516 AG:388C CB:1254C 13. KATHEZOMAI (καθέζομαι), to sit (down), is used in Matt. 26 : 55 ; Luke 2 : 46 ; John 4 : 6 ; 11 : 20 ; 20 : 12 ; Acts 6 : 15.¶

1910 AG:289D CB:— *Note :* For *epibainō,* " sitting upon," Matt. 21 : 5, A.V., see RIDE.

SIX

1803 AG:271B CB:1250B HEX (ἕξ), whence Eng. prefix, *hex-,* is used separately from other numerals in Matt. 17 : 1 ; Mark 9 : 2 ; Luke 4 : 25 ; 13 : 14 ; John 2 : 6 ;

12 : 1 ; Acts 11 : 12 ; 18 : 11 ; Jas. 5 : 17 ; Rev. 4 : 8. It sometimes suggests incompleteness, in comparison with the perfect number seven.

Notes : (1) In combination with *tessarakonta,* forty, it occurs in John 2 : 20 ; with *hebdomēkonta,* seventy, Acts 27 : 37, " (two hundred) threescore and sixteen." (2) It forms the first syllable of *hexēkonta,* sixty (see below), and *hexakosioi,* six hundred, Rev. 13 : 18 (see SIXTY, Note); 1812 AG:272B CB:—
14 : 20.

SIXTH

HEKTOS (ἕκτος) is used (*a*) of a month, Luke 1 : 26, 36 ; (*b*) an hour, 1623 AG:246A CB:—
Matt. 20 : 5 ; 27 : 45 and parallel passages ; John 4 : 6 ; (*c*) an angel, Rev. 9 : 13, 14 ; 16 : 12 ; (*d*) a seal of a roll, in vision, Rev. 6 : 12 ; (*e*) of the sixth precious stone, the sardius, in the foundations of the wall of the heavenly Jerusalem, Rev. 21 : 20.

SIXTY, SIXTYFOLD

HEXĒKONTA (ἑξήκοντα) occurs in Matt. 13 : 8, R.V. (A.V., " sixty- 1835 AG:276B CB:—
fold ") ; 13 : 23 ; Mark 4 : 8, where the R.V. and A.V. reverse the translation, as in Matt. 13 : 8, while in Mark 4 : 20 the R.V. has " sixtyfold ", A.V., " sixty " ; in Rev. 13 : 18, R.V., " sixty " (A.V., " threescore "). It is rendered " threescore " in Luke 24 : 13 ; 1 Tim. 5 : 9 ; Rev. 11 : 3 ; 12 : 6.¶

Note : In Rev. 13 : 18, the number of the " Beast," the human potentate destined to rule with Satanic power the ten-kingdom league at the end of this age, is given as " six hundred and sixty and six " (R.V.), and described as " the number of (a) man." The number is suggestive of the acme of the pride of fallen man, the fullest development of man under direct Satanic control, and standing in contrast to seven as the number of completeness and perfection.

SKIN

ASKOS (ἀσκός), a leather bottle, wineskin, occurs in Matt. 9 : 17 779 AG:116C CB:—
(four times) ; Mark 2 : 22 (four times) ; Luke 5 : 37 (three times), 38 ; in each place, R.V., " wineskins " or " skins," for A.V., " bottles." A whole goatskin, for example, would be used with the apertures bound up, and when filled, tied at the neck. They were tanned with acacia bark and left hairy on the outside. New wines, by fermenting, would rend old skins (cp. Josh. 9 : 13 ; Job 32 : 19). Hung in the smoke to dry, the skin-bottles become shrivelled (see Ps. 119 : 83).¶

Note : For " (a girdle) of a skin," Mark 1 : 6, see LEATHERN.

SKULL

KRANION (κρανίον), Lat., *cranium* (akin to *kara,* the head), is used of 2898 AG:448A CB:—
the scene of the Crucifixion, Matt. 27 : 33 ; Mark 15 : 22 ; John 19 : 17 ; in Luke 23 : 33, R.V., " (the place which is called) The skull," A.V.,

" Calvary " (from Latin *calvaria*, a skull : marg., " the place of a skull "). The locality has been identified by the traces of the resemblance of the hill to a skull.¶ In the Sept., Judg. 9 : 53 ; 2 Kings 9 : 35.¶

For SKY see HEAVEN

SLACK (Verb), SLACKNESS

A. Verb.

1019 AG:147A CB:— BRADUNŌ (βραδύνω), used intransitively signifies to be slow, to tarry (*bradus*, slow), said negatively of God, 2 Pet. 3 : 9, " is (not) slack ; " in 1 Tim. 3 : 15, translated " (if) I tarry." See TARRY.¶ In the Sept., Gen. 43 : 10 ; Deut. 7 : 10 ; Isa. 46 : 13.¶

B. Noun.

1022 AG:147A CB:— BRADUTĒS (βραδυτής), slowness (akin to A), is rendered " slackness " in 2 Pet. 3 : 9.¶

SLANDERER

1228 AG:182A CB:1241A DIABOLOS (διάβολος), an adjective, slanderous, accusing falsely, is used as a noun, translated " slanderers " in 1 Tim. 3 : 11, where the reference is to those who are given to finding fault with the demeanour and conduct of others, and spreading their innuendos and criticisms in the church ; in 2 Tim. 3 : 3, R.V. (A.V., " false accusers ") ; Tit. 2 : 3 (ditto) : see ACCUSER, DEVIL.

For SLANDEROUSLY see REPORT, C, No. 5

SLAUGHTER

4967 AG:795D CB:— 1. SPHAGĒ (σφαγή) is used in two quotations from the Sept., Acts 8 : 32 from Isa. 53 : 7, and Rom. 8 : 36 from Psa. 44 : 22 ; in the latter the quotation is set in a strain of triumph, the passage quoted being an utterance of sorrow. In Jas. 5 : 5 there is an allusion to Jer. 12 : 3, the luxurious rich, getting wealth by injustice, spending it on their pleasures, are " fattening themselves like sheep unconscious of their doom."¶

2871 AG:443C CB:— 2. KOPĒ (κοπή), a stroke (akin to *koptō*, to strike, to cut), signifies a smiting in battle, in Heb. 7 : 1.¶ In the Sept., Gen. 14 : 17 ; Deut. 28 : 25 ; Josh. 10 : 20.¶

5408 AG:864D CB:1264B 3. PHONOS (φόνος), a killing, murder, is rendered " slaughter " in Acts 9 : 1 ; see MURDER.

SLAVE

4983 AG:799A CB:1269B SŌMA (σῶμα), a body, is translated " slaves " in Rev. 18 : 13 (R.V. and A.V. marg., " bodies "), an intimation of the unrighteous control over the bodily activities of slaves ; the next word " souls " stands for the whole being. See BODY.

SLAY, SLAIN, SLEW

1. APOKTEINŌ (ἀποκτείνω), the usual word for to kill, is so trans- 615
lated in the R.V. wherever possible (e.g., for A.V., to slay, in Luke 11 : 49; AG:93D CB:1237A
Acts 7 : 52; Rev. 2 : 13; 9 : 15; 11 : 13; 19 : 21); in the following the
verb to kill would not be appropriate, Rom. 7 : 11, "slew," metaphorically
of sin, as using the commandment; Eph. 2 : 16, "having slain," said
metaphorically of the enmity between Jew and Gentile. See KILL, No. 1.

Note: Some mss. have it in John 5 : 16 (A.V., "to slay").

2. ANAIREŌ (ἀναιρέω), to take away, destroy, kill, is rendered to 337
slay in Matt. 2 : 16; Acts 2 : 23; 5 : 33, 36; 9 : 29, A.V. (R.V., to kill); AG:54D CB:—
10 : 39; 13 : 28; 22 : 20; 23 : 15, R.V.; in 2 Thess. 2 : 8 the best texts
have this verb (for *analiskō*, to consume, A.V. and R.V. marg.); hence the
R.V., "shall slay," of the destruction of the man of sin. See KILL, No. 2.

3. SPHAZŌ or SPHATTŌ (σφάττω), to slay, especially of victims for 4969
sacrifice (akin to *sphagē*: see SLAUGHTER), is used (*a*) of taking human AG:796A CB:1269C
life, 1 John 3 : 12 (twice); Rev. 6 : 4, R.V., "slay" (A.V., "kill");
in 13 : 3, probably of assassination, R.V., "smitten (unto death)," A.V.,
"wounded (to death)," R.V. marg., "slain;" 18 : 24; (*b*) of Christ, as
the Lamb of sacrifice, Rev. 5 : 6, 9, 12; 6 : 9; 13 : 8. See KILL, No. 7.¶ 2695 (-ATTō)

4. KATASPHAZŌ (κατασφάζω), to kill off (*kata*, used intensively, AG:419C
and No. 3), is used in Luke 19 : 27.¶. In the Sept., Ezek. 16 : 40; CB:—
Zech. 11 : 5.¶ 1315 (-OMAI)

5. DIACHEIRIZŌ (διαχειρίζω), to lay hands on, kill, is translated AG:191A
"slew" in Acts 5 : 30. See KILL, No. 6. CB:—

6. PHONEUŌ (φονεύω), to kill, to murder, is rendered "ye slew" 5407
in Matt. 23 : 35. See KILL, No. 4. AG:864C CB:—

Note: For *thuō*, Acts 11 : 7, A.V., "slay" (R.V., "kill"), see KILL, 2380
No. 3. AG:367A CB:1272C

For SLAIN BEASTS see BEAST, No. 5

For SLEEP see ASLEEP

SLEIGHT

KUBIA (or -EIA) (κυβία) denotes dice-playing (from *kubos*, a cube, 2940
a die as used in gaming); hence, metaphorically, trickery, sleight, AG:456C CB:—
Eph. 4 : 14. The Eng. word is connected with 'sly' (not with slight).¶

SLIP (AWAY) See CONVEY, CREEP, ESCAPE

For SLIP see DRIFT

SLOTHFUL

1. NŌTHROS (νωθρός), indolent, sluggish, is rendered "slothful" in 3576
Heb. 6 : 12, A.V. See DULL, and synonymous words there, and SLUGGISH. AG:547C CB:—

2. OKNĒROS (ὀκνηρός), shrinking, irksome, is translated "slothful" 3636
in Matt. 25 : 26, and Rom. 12 : 11, where "in diligence not slothful," AG:563A CB:—
R.V., might be rendered 'not flagging in zeal.' See GRIEVOUS, Note (2).

SLOW

1021 AG:147A CB:— BRADUS (βραδύς) is used twice in Jas. 1 : 19, in an exhortation to be slow to speak and slow to wrath ; in Luke 24 : 25, metaphorically of the understanding.¶

692 AG:104C CB:1237C *Note* : For "slow" (*argos*) in Tit. 1 : 12, see IDLE.

For SLOWLY (sailed) see SAIL, No. 10

SLUGGISH

3576 AG:547C CB:— NŌTHROS (νωθρός), for which see SLOTHFUL, is translated "sluggish" in Heb. 6 : 12, R.V. ; here it is set in contrast to confident and constant hope ; in 5 : 11 ("dull") to vigorous growth in knowledge. See DULL.¶

For SLUMBER (Noun) see STUPOR

SLUMBER (Verb)

3573 AG:547A CB:— NUSTAZŌ (νυστάζω) denotes to nod in sleep (akin to *neuō*, to nod), fall asleep, and is used (*a*) of natural slumber, Matt. 25 : 5 ; (*b*) metaphorically in 2 Pet. 2 : 3, negatively, of the destruction awaiting false teachers.¶

SMALL

3398 AG:521A CB:1258C 1. MIKROS (μικρός), little, small (of age, quantity, size, space), is translated "small" in Acts 26 : 22 ; Rev. 11 : 18 ; 13 : 16 ; 19 : 5, 18 ; 20 : 12. See LITTLE.

3641 AG:563C CB:1260C 2. OLIGOS (ὀλίγος), little, small (of amount, number, time), is translated "small" in Acts 12 : 18 ; 15 : 2 ; 19 : 23 ; ver. 24, A.V. (R.V., "little") ; 27 : 20.

Notes : (1) For "very small" and "smallest" see LEAST. (2) For combinations with other words, see CORD, FISH, ISLAND.

For SMELL see SAVOUR

SMELLING

3750 AG:587C CB:— OSPHRĒSIS (ὄσφρησις) denotes the sense of smell, 1 Cor. 12 : 17, "smelling."¶

SMITE

3960 AG:634D CB:1262C 1. PATASSŌ (πατάσσω), to strike, smite, is used (I) literally, of giving a blow with the hand, or fist or a weapon, Matt. 26 : 51, R.V., "smote" (A.V., "struck") ; Luke 22 : 49, 50 ; Acts 7 : 24 ; 12 : 7 ; (II) metaphorically, (*a*) of judgment meted out to Christ, Matt. 26 : 31 ; Mark 14 : 27 ; (*b*) of the infliction of disease, by an angel, Acts 12 : 23 ; of plagues to be inflicted upon men by two Divinely appointed witnesses, Rev. 11 : 6 ; (*c*) of judgment to be executed by Christ upon the nations,

Rev. 19 : 15, the instrument being His Word, described as a sword.¶
2. TUPTŌ (τύπτω), to strike, smite, beat, is rendered to smite in 5180
Matt. 24 : 49, A.V. (R.V., " beat ") ; 27 : 30 ; Mark 15 : 19 ; Luke 6 : 29 ; AG:830B
18 : 13 ; in some texts in 22 : 64 (1st part : R.V. omits ; for the 2nd part CB:1273B
see No. 3) ; 23 : 48 ; Acts 23 : 2, 3 (twice). See BEAT, No. 2.

3. PAIŌ (παίω) signifies to strike or smite (*a*) with the hand or fist, 3817
Matt. 26 : 68 ; Luke 22 : 64 (see No. 2) ; (*b*) with a sword, Mark 14 : 47 ; AG:605B
John 18 : 10, A.V. (R.V., " struck ") ; (*c*) with a sting, Rev. 9 : 5, CB:—
" striketh."¶

4. DERŌ (δέρω), to flay, to beat, akin to *derma*, skin, is translated to 1194
smite in Luke 22 : 63, A.V. (R.V., " beat ") ; John 18 : 23 ; 2 Cor. 11 : 20. AG:175D CB:1240C
See BEAT, No. 1.

5. PLĒSSŌ (πλήσσω), akin to *plēgē*, a plague, stripe, wound, is used 4141
figuratively of the effect upon sun, moon and stars, after the sounding AG:673A
of the trumpet by the fourth angel, in the series of Divine judgments CB:—
upon the world hereafter, Rev. 8 : 12.¶

6. RHAPIZŌ (ῥαπίζω), primarily to strike with a rod (*rhapis*, a rod), 4474
then, to strike the face with the palm of the hand or the clenched fist, AG:734B
is used in Matt. 5 : 39 ; 26 : 67, where the marg. of A.V. and R.V. has CB:1268A
" with rods." Cp. *rhapisma*, Note (2), below.¶ 2598

7. KATABALLŌ (καταβάλλω), to cast down, is translated " smitten AG:408D
down " in 2 Cor. 4 : 9, R.V. See CAST, No. 8. CB:1253C

8. PROSKOPTŌ (προσκόπτω), to beat upon, is translated " smote 4350 AG:716B
upon " in Matt. 7 : 27. See BEAT, No. 6. CB:1267B

9. SPHAZŌ (σφάζω), to slay, is translated " smitten unto death " 4969
in Rev. 13 : 3 ; see KILL, SLAY. AG:796A CB:1269C

Notes : (1) In Matt. 26 : 51, A.V., *aphaireō*, to take away, take off, APHAIREŌ
is translated " smote off " (R.V., " struck off "). (2) The noun *rhapisma*, 851
a blow, in the plural, as the object of *didōmi*, to give, in John 19 : 3 is AG:124B CB:1236B
translated " smote (Him) with their hands " (R.V., " struck etc."), lit., RHAPISMA
' gave . . . blows ' (R.V. marg., " with rods ") ; in 18 : 22 (where the 4475 AG:734C
phrase is used with the singular of the noun) the R.V. renders it " struck CB:1268A
. . . with his hand " (A.V., " struck . . . with the palm of his hand "), DIDŌMI 1325
marg. of both, " with a rod." AG:192C CB:1241C

The same word is used in Mark 14 : 65, " (received Him) with blows (of their hands) ", R.V. [A.V., " did strike Him with the palms (of their hands)," R.V. margin, " strokes of rods "]. See BLOW (Noun).¶ Cp. No. 6, above, re Matt. 26 : 67.

SMOKE (Noun and Verb)

A. Noun.

KAPNOS (καπνός), smoke, occurs in Acts 2 : 19 and 12 times in the 2586 AG:403B
Apocalypse.¶ CB:—

B. Verb.

5188 AG:831C
TUPHŌ (τύφω), to raise a smoke [akin to *tuphos*, smoke (not in the CB:—

TUPHOō 5187 N.T.), and *tuphoō*, to puff up with pride, see HIGH-MINDED], is used in
AG:831A the Passive Voice in Matt. 12 : 20, " smoking (flax)," lit., 'caused to
CB:— smoke,' of the wick of a lamp which has ceased to burn clearly, figurative
of mere nominal religiousness without the Spirit's power.¶ The Sept.
uses the verb *kapnizō* (akin to A).

SMOOTH

3006 AG:470B LEIOS (λεῖος), smooth, occurs in Luke 3 : 5, figurative of the change
CB:— in Israel from self-righteousness, pride and other forms of evil, to repentance, humility and submission.¶ In the Sept., Gen. 27 : 11 ; 1 Sam. 17 : 40 ; Prov. 2 : 20 ; 12 : 13 ; 26 : 23 ; Isa. 40 : 4.¶

5542 AG:886A *Note :* *Chrēstologia* (*chrēstos*, good, *legō*, to speak) is rendered
CB:1240A "smooth . . . (speech)," in Rom. 16 : 18, R.V. (A.V., "good words").¶

SNARE

3803 AG:602A 1. PAGIS (παγίς), a trap, a snare (akin to *pēgnumi*, to fix, and *pagideuō*,
CB:1261B to ensnare, which see), is used metaphorically of (*a*) the allurements to evil
by which the Devil ensnares one, 1 Tim. 3 : 7 ; 2 Tim. 2 : 26 ; (*b*) seductions to evil, which ensnare those who " desire to be rich," 1 Tim. 6 : 9 ;
SNAKE See SERPENT (*c*) the evil brought by Israel upon themselves by which the special
privileges Divinely granted them and centring in Christ, became a snare
SNEER See SCOFF to them, their rejection of Christ and the Gospel being the retributive
effect of their apostasy, Rom. 11 : 9 ; (*d*) of the sudden judgments of God
to come upon those whose hearts are " overcharged with surfeiting, and
drunkenness, and cares of this life," Luke 21 : 34 (ver. 35 in A.V.).¶

1029 AG:147D 2. BROCHOS (βρόχος), a noose, slip-knot, halter, is used meta-
CB:— phorically in 1 Cor. 7 : 35, "a snare" (R.V., marg., " constraint,"
HARPAZō 726 " noose").¶ In the Sept., Prov. 6 : 5 ; 7 : 21 ; 22 : 25.¶

AG:109A CB:1249B

SNATCH

CHIōN 5510 HARPAZŌ (ἁρπάζω), to snatch, is translated to snatch in the R.V.
AG:882B only, in Matt. 13 : 19, A.V., " catcheth away ;" John 10 : 12, A.V.,
CB:1239C HOUTō(-S) " catcheth ;" 10 : 28, 29, A.V., " pluck ;" Jude 23, A.V., " pulling."
3779 See CATCH, No. 1.

AG:597C HOUTOS 3778 AG:596B

SNOW

CB:1251B CHIŌN (χιών) occurs in Matt. 28 : 3 ; Rev. 1 : 14. Some mss. have
HOMOIōS it in Mark 9 : 3 (A.V.).¶

3668 AG:567D CB:1251A

SO

OUN 3767 *Notes :* (1) *Houtōs* or *houtō*, thus, is the usual word (see THUS).
AG:592D (2) Some form of *houtos*, this, is sometimes rendered " so," e.g., Acts
SUMBAINō 23 : 7 ; Rom. 12 : 20. (3) It translates *homoiōs*, likewise, e.g., in Luke
4819 AG:777B 5 : 10 ; *oun*, therefore, e.g., John 4 : 40, 53. (4) For " so many as," see
CB:— MANY ; for " so much as," see MUCH. (5) *Sumbainō*, when used of events,

signifies to come to pass, happen ; in Acts 21 : 35 it is rendered " so it EPOS
was." See BEFALL, HAPPEN. (6) In 1 Pet. 3 : 17, *thelō*, to will, is trans- 2031 AG:305D
lated " should so will," lit., ' willeth.' (7) In 2 Cor. 12 : 16, the imperative CB:1246B
mood, 3rd person singular, of *eimi*, to be, is used impersonally, and HōSAUTōS 5615
signifies " be it so." (8) In Heb. 7 : 9 *epos*, a word, is used in a phrase AG:899B
rendered " so to say ;" see WORD, Note (1). (9) In 1 Tim. 3 : 11, CB:899B HōS
hōsautōs, likewise, is translated " even so." (10) *Hōs*, as, is rendered 5613
" so " in Heb. 3 : 11 (R.V., " as "). For association with other words AG:897A CB:1251B
see † p. 1. SOB

See WEEP

SOBER, SOBERLY, SOBERMINDED

A. Adjective.

SŌPHRŌN (σώφρων) denotes of sound mind (*sōzō*, to save, *phrēn*, 4998 AG:802C
the mind) ; hence, self-controlled, soberminded, always rendered " sober- CB:1269B
minded " in the R.V. ; in 1 Tim. 3 : 2 and Tit. 1 : 8, A.V., " sober ;"
in Tit. 2 : 2, A.V., " temperate ;" in 2 : 5, A.V., " discreet."¶

Note : For *nēphalios* (akin to B, No. 1), translated " sober " in 1 Tim. 3524
3 : 11 ; Tit. 2 : 2, see TEMPERATE. AG:538D CB:1259C

B. Verbs.

1. NĒPHŌ (νήφω) signifies to be free from the influence of intoxicants ; 3525
in the N.T., metaphorically, it does not in itself imply watchfulness, but AG:538D CB:1259C
is used in association with it, 1 Thess. 5 : 6, 8 ; 2 Tim. 4 : 5 ; 1 Pet. 1 : 13 ;
4 : 7, R.V. (A.V., " watch ") ; 5 : 8.¶ Cp. *eknēphō* and *ananēphō*, under EKNēPHō
AWAKE, No. 3 and Note. 1594 AG:243B

2. SŌPHRONEŌ (σωφρονέω), akin to A, is rendered to think soberly, CB:1243C
Rom. 12 : 3 ; to be sober, 2 Cor. 5 : 13 ; to be soberminded, Tit. 2 : 6 ; ANANēPHō 366
in 1 Pet. 4 : 7, A.V. " be ye sober " (R.V., " of sound mind ") ; see AG:58B
MIND, B, No. 5. CB:1235B SōPHRONEō

3. SŌPHRONIZŌ (σωφρονίζω) denotes to cause to be of sound mind, 4993
to recall to one's senses ; in Tit. 2 : 4, R.V., it is rendered " they may AG:802A
train " (A.V., " they may teach . . . to be sober," marg., " wise ") ; CB:1269B SōPHRONIZō
" train " expresses the meaning more adequately ; the training would 4994
involve the cultivation of sound judgment and prudence.¶ AG:802A CB:—

C. Adverb.

SŌPHRONŌS (σωφρόνως), akin to A and B, Nos. 2 and 3, soberly, 4996
occurs in Tit. 2 : 12 ; it suggests the exercise of that self-restraint that AG:802C CB:1269B
governs all passions and desires, enabling the believer to be conformed to
the mind of Christ.¶

Note : For the phrase to think soberly, see B, No. 2.

SOBERNESS, SOBRIETY

SŌPHROSUNĒ (σωφροσύνη) denotes soundness of mind (see SOBER, 4997
A), Acts 26 : 25, " soberness ;" 1 Tim. 2 : 9, 15, " sobriety ;" ' sound AG:802C CB:1269B
judgment ' practically expresses the meaning ; " it is that habitual
inner self-government, with its constant rein on all the passions and

desires, which would hinder the temptation to these from arising, or at all events from arising in such strength as would overbear the checks and barriers which *aidōs* (shamefastness) opposed to it" (Trench Syn. § xx, end).¶

For SOFT see EFFEMINATE

SOIL See GROUND

For SOFTLY see BLOW (Verb), No. 2

SOJOURN, SOJOURNER, SOJOURNING

A. Verbs.

3939 AG:628D CB:1262B 1. PAROIKEŌ (παροικέω) denotes to dwell beside, among or by (*para*, beside, *oikeō*, to dwell); then, to dwell in a place as a *paroikos*, a stranger (see below), Luke 24:18, R.V., "Dost thou (alone) sojourn . . . ?" [marg.," Dost thou sojourn (alone)" is preferable], A.V., "art thou (only) a stranger?" (*monos*, alone, is an adjective, not an adverb); in Heb. 11:9, R.V., "he became a sojourner" (A.V., "he sojourned"), the R.V. gives the force of the aorist tense.¶

1927 AG:292A CB:— 2. EPIDĒMEŌ (ἐπιδημέω) is rendered to sojourn in Acts 17:21, R.V.

B. Adjectives.

3941 AG:629A CB:1262B 1. PAROIKOS (πάροικος), an adjective, akin to A, No. 1, lit., dwelling near (see above), then, foreign, alien (found with this meaning in Inscriptions), hence, as a noun, a sojourner, is used with *eimi*, to be, in Acts 7:6, "should sojourn," lit., 'should be a sojourner;' in 7:29, R.V., "sojourner" (A.V., "stranger"); in Eph. 2:19, R.V., "sojourners" (A.V., "foreigners"), the preceding word rendered "strangers" is *xenos*; in 1 Pet. 2:11, R.V., ditto (A.V., "strangers").¶

590 AG:90B CB:— 2. APODĒMOS (ἀπόδημος), gone abroad (*apo*, from, *dēmos*, people), signifies "sojourning in another country," Mark 13:34, R.V. (A.V., "taking a far journey").¶

3927 AG:625D CB:1262B 3. PAREPIDĒMOS (παρεπίδημος), sojourning in a strange place, is used as a noun, denoting a sojourner, an exile, 1 Pet. 1:1, R.V., "sojourners" (A.V., "strangers"). See PILGRIM.¶

C. Noun.

3940 AG:629A CB:1262B PAROIKIA (παροικία), a sojourning (akin to A and B, Nos. 1), occurs in Acts 13:17, rendered "they sojourned," R.V., A.V., "dwelt as strangers," lit., 'in the sojourning;' in 1 Pet. 1:17, "sojourning."¶

SOLDIER

A. Nouns.

4757 AG:770D CB:1270A 1. STRATIŌTĒS (στρατιώτης), a soldier, is used (*a*) in the natural sense, e.g., Matt. 8:9; 27:27; 28:12; Mark 15:16; Luke 7:8; 23:36; six times in John; thirteen times in Acts; not again in the N.T.; (*b*) metaphorically of one who endures hardship in the cause of Christ, 2 Tim. 2:3.

2. STRATEUMA (στράτευμα), an army, is used to denote a company 4753
of soldiers in Acts 23 : 10 ; in ver. 27, R.V., " the soldiers," A.V., " an AG:770B CB:1270A
army ; " in Luke 23 : 11 (plural), R.V., " soldiers," A.V., " men of war."
See ARMY.

3. SUSTRATIŌTĒS (συστρατιώτης), a fellow-soldier (*sun*, with, and 4961
No. 1), is used metaphorically in Phil. 2 : 25 and Philm. 2, of fellowship in AG:795B CB:—
Christian service.¶

B. Verb.

STRATEUŌ (στρατεύω), always in the Middle Voice in the N.T., is 4754
used (*a*) literally of serving as a soldier, Luke 3 : 14, " soldiers " (R.V., (-OMAI) AG:770B
marg., " soldiers on service," present participle) ; 1 Cor. 9 : 7, R.V., CB:1270A
" (what) soldier . . . serveth," A.V., " (who) goeth a warfare ; " 2 Tim.
2 : 4, R.V., " soldier on service," A.V., " man that warreth," lit., ' serving
as a soldier ; ' (*b*) metaphorically, of spiritual conflict : see WAR.

Notes : (1) For *spekoulatōr*, Mark 6 : 27, R.V., " soldier of his guard," SPEKOULATŌR 4688
see GUARD.¶ (2) In 2 Tim. 2 : 4 *stratologeō* is rendered " hath chosen AG:761C CB:—
(him) to be a soldier," A.V. (R.V., " enrolled (him) as a soldier ").¶ STRATOLOGEŌ 4758 AG:770D CB:1270A

SOLID

STEREOS (στερεός), for which see FIRM, No. 2, has the meaning 4731
" solid " in Heb. 5 : 12, 14, of food (A.V., " strong "). As solid food AG:766D CB:1270A
requires more powerful digestive organs than are possessed by a babe, so a fuller knowledge of Christ (especially here with reference to His Melchizedek priesthood) required that exercise of spiritual intelligence which is derived from the practical appropriation of what had already been received.

For SOLITARY, Mark 1 : 35, A.V., see DESERT, B

SOME, SOMEONE, SOMETHING, SOMEWHAT

Notes : (1) Various forms of the article and certain pronouns, followed
by the particles *men* and *de* denote " some." These are not enumerated MEN 3303
here. (2) The indefinite pronoun *tis* in its singular or plural forms, AG:502C
frequently means " some," " some one " (translated " some man," in CB:1258B
the A.V., e.g., of Acts 8 : 31 ; 1 Cor. 15 : 35), or " somebody," Luke 8 : 46 ; TIS 5100
the neuter plural denotes " some things " in 2 Pet. 3 : 16 ; the singular AG:819D
denotes " something," e.g., Luke 11 : 54 ; John 13 : 29 (2nd part) ; Acts CB:1272C MEROS
3 : 5 ; 23 : 18 ; Gal. 6 : 3, where the meaning is ' anything,' as in 2 : 6, 3313
" somewhat." It is translated " somewhat," in the more indefinite sense, AG:505D CB:1258B
in Luke 7 : 40 ; Acts 23 : 20 ; 25 : 26 ; 2 Cor. 10 : 8 ; Heb. 8 : 3. See ALLOS
also ONE, B, No. 1. (3) *Meros*, a part, a measure, preceded by the pre- 243 AG:39D
position *apo*, from, is translated " in some measure " in Rom. 15 : 15, CB:1234C
R.V. (A.V., " in some sort "), and ver. 24 (A.V., " somewhat "). (4) In
the following *alloi*, others (" some " in the A.V.), is translated " others "
in the R.V., Matt. 13 : 5, 7 ; Mark 4 : 7 (" other ") ; 8 : 28 ; Luke 9 : 19 ;

John 9 : 9. Followed by a correlative expression it denotes "some," e.g., Acts 19 : 32 ; 21 : 34 ; see OTHER, No. 1.

For SOMETIMES see TIME

SOMEWHERE

4225 AG:696B CB:1266B POU (πού), a particle, signifies "somewhere" in Heb. 2 : 6 and 4 : 4, R.V. (A.V., "in a certain place"); the writer avoids mentioning the place to add stress to his testimony. See HAPLY, No. 5, VERILY.

SON

5207 AG:833C CB:1251C HUIOS (υἱός) primarily signifies the relation of offspring to parent (see John 9 : 18–20 ; Gal. 4 : 30). It is often used metaphorically of prominent moral characteristics (see below). "It is used in the N.T. of (*a*) male offspring, Gal. 4 : 30 ; (*b*) legitimate, as opposed to illegitimate, offspring, Heb. 12 : 8 ; (*c*) descendants, without reference to sex, Rom. 9 : 27 ; (*d*) friends attending a wedding, Matt. 9 : 15 ; (*e*) those who enjoy certain privileges, Acts 3 : 25 ; (*f*) those who act in a certain way, whether evil, Matt. 23 : 31, or good, Gal. 3 : 7 ; (*g*) those who manifest a certain character, whether evil, Acts 13 : 10 ; Eph. 2 : 2, or good, Luke 6 : 35 ; Acts 4 : 36 ; Rom. 8 : 14 ; (*h*) the destiny that corresponds with the character, whether evil, Matt. 23 : 15 ; John 17 : 12 ; 2 Thess. 2 : 3, or good, Luke 20 : 36 ; (*i*) the dignity of the relationship with God whereinto men are brought by the Holy Spirit when they believe on the Lord Jesus Christ, Rom. 8 : 19 ; Gal. 3 : 26. . . .

"The Apostle John does not use *huios*, 'son,' of the believer, he reserves that title for the Lord ; but he does use *teknon*, 'child,' as in his Gospel, 1 : 12 ; 1 John 3 : 1, 2 : Rev. 21 : 7 (*huios*) is a quotation from 2 Sam. 7 : 14.

"The Lord Jesus used *huios* in a very significant way, as in Matt. 5 : 9, 'Blessed are the peacemakers, for they shall be called the sons of God,' and vv. 44, 45, 'Love your enemies, and pray for them that persecute you ; that ye may be (become) sons of your Father which is in heaven.' The disciples were to do these things, not in order that they might become children of God, but that, being children (note 'your Father' throughout), they might make the fact manifest in their character, might 'become sons.' See also 2 Cor. 6 : 17, 18.

"As to moral characteristics, the following phrases are used : (*a*) sons of God, Matt. 5 : 9, 45 ; Luke 6 : 35 ; (*b*) sons of the light, Luke 16 : 8 ; John 12 : 36 ; (*c*) sons of the day, 1 Thess. 5 : 5 ; (*d*) sons of peace, Luke 10 : 6 ; (*e*) sons of this world, Luke 16 : 8 ; (*f*) sons of disobedience, Eph. 2 : 2 ; (*g*) sons of the evil one, Matt. 13 : 38, cp. 'of the Devil,' Acts 13 : 10 ; (*h*) son of perdition, John 17 : 12 ; 2 Thess. 2 : 3. It is also used to describe characteristics other than moral, as : (*i*) sons of the resurrection, Luke 20 : 36 ; (*j*) sons of the Kingdom, Matt. 8 : 12 ; 13 : 38 ;

(*k*) sons of the bridechamber, Mark 2 : 19 ; (*l*) sons of exhortation, Acts 4 : 36 ; (*m*) sons of thunder, Boanerges, Mark 3 : 17."*

Notes : (1) For the synonyms *teknon* and *teknion* see under CHILD. TEKNON
The difference between believers as 'children of God' and as 'sons of 5043
God' is brought out in Rom. 8 : 14–21. The Spirit bears witness with AG:808B CB:1271B
their spirit that they are "children of God," and, as such, they are His PAIS
heirs and joint-heirs with Christ. This stresses the fact of their spiritual 3816 AG:604C
birth (vv. 16, 17). On the other hand, "as many as are led by the Spirit CB:1261C
of God, these are sons of God," i.e., 'these and no other.' Their conduct gives evidence of the dignity of their relationship and their likeness to His character. (2) *Pais* is rendered "son" in John 4 : 51. For Acts 13 : 13, 26 see below.

The Son of God

In this title the word Son is used sometimes (*a*) of relationship, sometimes (*b*) of the expression of character. "Thus, e.g., when the disciples so addressed Him, Matt. 14 : 33 ; 16 : 16 ; John 1 : 49, when the centurion so spoke of Him, Matt. 27 : 54, they probably meant that (*b*) He was a manifestation of God in human form. But in such passages as Luke 1 : 32, 35 ; Acts 13 : 33, which refer to the humanity of the Lord Jesus, . . . the word is used in sense (*a*).

"The Lord Jesus Himself used the full title on occasion, John 5 : 25 ; 9 : 35 [some mss. have 'the Son of man ;' see R.V. marg.]; 11 : 4, and on the more frequent occasions on which He spoke of Himself as 'the Son,' the words are to be understood as an abbreviation of 'the Son of God,' not of 'the Son of Man ;' this latter He always expressed in full ; see Luke 10 : 22 ; John 5 : 19, etc.

"John uses both the longer and shorter forms of the title in his Gospel, see 3 : 16–18 ; 20 : 31, e.g., and in his Epistles ; cp. Rev. 2 : 18. So does the writer of Hebrews, 1 : 2 ; 4 : 14 ; 6 : 6, etc. An eternal relation subsisting between the Son and the Father in the Godhead is to be understood. That is to say, the Son of God, in His eternal relationship with the Father, is not so entitled because He at any time began to derive His being from the Father (in which case He could not be co-eternal with the Father), but because He is and ever has been the expression of what the Father is ; cp. John 14 : 9, 'he that hath seen Me hath seen the Father.' The words of Heb. 1 : 3, 'Who being the effulgence of His (God's) glory, and the very image of His (God's) substance' are a definition of what is meant by 'Son of God.' Thus absolute Godhead, not Godhead in a secondary or derived sense, is intended in the title."†

Other titles of Christ as the Son of God are : "His Son," 1 Thess. 1 : 10 (in Acts 13 : 13, 26, R.V., *pais* is rendered "servant") ; "His own Son", Rom. 8 : 32 ; "My beloved Son," Matt. 3 : 17 ; "His Only Begotten Son," John 3 : 16 ; "the Son of His love," Col. 1 : 13.

* From Notes on Galatians, by Hogg and Vine, pp. 167–169, and on Thessalonians, pp. 158, 159. † From Notes on Galatians by Hogg and Vine, pp. 99, 100.

"The Son is the eternal object of the Father's love, John 17 : 24, and the sole Revealer of the Father's character, John 1 : 14; Heb. 1 : 3. The words, 'Father' and 'Son,' are never in the N.T. so used as to suggest that the Father existed before the Son; the Prologue to the Gospel according to John distinctly asserts that the Word existed 'in the beginning,' and that this Word is the Son, Who 'became flesh and dwelt among us.'"*

In addressing the Father in His prayer in John 17 He says, "Thou lovedst Me before the foundation of the world." Accordingly in the timeless past the Father and the Son existed in that relationship, a relationship of love, as well as of absolute Deity. In this passage the Son gives evidence that there was no more powerful plea in the Father's estimation than that co-eternal love existing between the Father and Himself.

The declaration "Thou art My Son, this day have I begotten Thee," Psa. 2 : 7, quoted in Acts 13 : 33; Heb. 1 : 5; 5 : 5, refers to the birth of Christ, not to His resurrection. In Acts 13 : 33 the verb "raise up" is used of the raising up of a person to occupy a special position in the nation, as of David in verse 22 (so of Christ as a Prophet in 3 : 22 and 7 : 37). The word "again" in the A.V. in ver. 33 represents nothing in the original. The R.V. rightly omits it. In ver. 34 the statement as to the resurrection of Christ receives the greater stress in this respect through the emphatic contrast to that in ver. 33 as to His being raised up in the nation, a stress imparted by the added words "from the dead." Accordingly ver. 33 speaks of His Incarnation, ver. 34 of His resurrection.

In Heb. 1 : 5, that the declaration refers to the Birth is confirmed by the contrast in verse 6. Here the word "again" is rightly placed in the R.V., "when He again bringeth in the Firstborn into the world." This points on to His Second Advent, which is set in contrast to His first Advent, when God brought His Firstborn into the world the first time (see FIRSTBORN).†

So again in Heb. 5 : 5, where the High Priesthood of Christ is shown to fulfil all that was foreshadowed in the Levitical priesthood, the passage stresses the facts of His humanity, the days of His flesh, His perfect obedience and His sufferings.

Son of Man

In the N.T. this is a designation of Christ, almost entirely confined to the Gospels. Elsewhere it is found in Acts 7 : 56, the only occasion where a disciple applied it to the Lord and in Rev. 1 : 13; 14 : 14 (see below).

---

* From Notes on Thessalonians by Hogg and Vine, pp. 46, 47.

† The Western text of Luke 3 : 22 reads "Thou art My Son, this day have I begotten Thee," instead of "Thou art My beloved Son, in Thee I am well pleased." There is probably some connection between this and those early heresies which taught that our Lord's Deity began at His Baptism.

"Son of Man" is the title Christ used of Himself; John 12 : 34 is not an exception, for the quotation by the multitude was from His own statement. The title is found especially in the Synoptic Gospels. The occurrences in John's Gospel, 1 : 51; 3 : 13, 14; 5 : 27; 6 : 27, 53, 62; 8 : 28 (9 : 35 in some texts); 12 : 23, 34 (twice); 13 : 31, are not parallel to those in the Synoptic Gospels. In the latter the use of the title falls into two groups, (*a*) those in which it refers to Christ's humanity, His earthly work, sufferings and death, e.g., Matt. 8 : 20; 11 : 19; 12 : 40; 26 : 2, 24; (*b*) those which refer to His glory in resurrection and to that of His future Advent, e.g., Matt. 10 : 23; 13 : 41; 16 : 27, 28; 17 : 9; 24 : 27, 30 (twice), 37, 39, 44.

While it is a Messianic title it is evident that the Lord applied it to Himself in a distinctive way, for it indicates more than Messiahship, even universal headship on the part of One who is Man. It therefore stresses His manhood, manhood of a unique order in comparison with all other men, for He is declared to be of heaven, 1 Cor. 15 : 47, and even while here below, was "the Son of Man, which is in Heaven," John 3 : 13. As the Son of Man He must be appropriated spiritually as a condition of possessing eternal life, John 6 : 53. In His death, as in His life, the glory of His Manhood was displayed in the absolute obedience and submission to the will of the Father (12 : 23; 13 : 31), and, in view of this, all judgment has been committed to Him, who will judge in full understanding experimentally of human conditions, sin apart, and will exercise the judgment as sharing the nature of those judged, John 5 : 22, 27. Not only is He man, but He is "Son of man," not by human generation but, according to the Semitic usage of the expression, partaking of the characteristics (sin apart) of manhood belonging to the category of mankind. Twice in the Apocalypse, 1 : 13 and 14 : 14, He is described as "One like unto a Son of man," R.V. (A.V., ". . . the Son of Man"), cp. Dan. 7 : 13. He who was thus seen was indeed the Son of Man, but the absence of the article in the original serves to stress what morally characterizes Him as such. Accordingly in these passages He is revealed, not as the Person known by the title, but as the One who is qualified to act as the Judge of all men. He is the same Person as in the days of His flesh, still continuing His humanity with His Deity. The phrase "like unto" serves to distinguish Him as there seen in His glory and majesty in contrast to the days of His humiliation.

SONG

ŌDĒ (ᾠδή), an ode, song, is always used in the N.T. (as in the Sept.), 5603
in praise of God or Christ; in Eph. 5 : 19 and Col. 3 : 16 the adjective AG:895C CB:1260B
"spiritual" is added, because the word in itself is generic and might be used of songs anything but spiritual; in Rev. 5 : 9 and 14 : 3 (1st part) the descriptive word is "new" (*kainos*, new in reference to character and form: see NEW), a song, the significance of which was confined to those

mentioned (ver. 3, and 2nd part); in 15 : 3 (twice), "the song of Moses . . . and the song of the Lamb," the former as celebrating the deliverance of God's people by His power, the latter as celebrating redemption by atoning sacrifice.¶

For SOON see IMMEDIATELY, No. 1 and QUICKLY, No. 3.

AS SOON AS: see † p. 1

For SOONER see QUICKLY, No. 2

SOOTHSAYING

3132 AG:491A CB:1257C MANTEUOMAI (μαντεύομαι), to divine, practise divination (from *mantis*, a seer, diviner), occurs in Acts 16 : 16.¶ The word is allied to *mainomai*, to rave, and *mania*, fury displayed by those who were possessed by the evil spirit (represented by the pagan god or goddess) while delivering their oracular messages. Trench (Syn. §vi) draws a distinction between this verb and *prophēteuō*, not only as to their meanings, but as to the fact of the single occurrence of *manteuomai* in the N.T., contrasted with the
PROPHēTEUō 4395 AG:723A CB:1267A frequency of *prophēteuō*, exemplifying the avoidance by N.T. writers of words the employment of which "would tend to break down the distinction between heathenism and revealed religion."

SOP

5596 AG:894D CB:— PSŌMION (ψωμίον), a diminutive of *psōmos*, a morsel, denotes a fragment, a sop (akin to *psōmizō*; see FEED), John 13 : 26 (twice), 27, 30. It had no connection with the modern meaning of sop, something given to pacify (as in the classical expression 'a sop to Cerberus').¶

SORCERER

3097 AG:484D CB:1257B 1. MAGOS (μάγος), (*a*) one of a Median caste, a magician: see WISE; (*b*) a wizard, sorcerer, a pretender to magic powers, a professor of the arts of witchcraft, Acts 13 : 6, 8, where Bar-Jesus was the Jewish name, Elymas, an Arabic word meaning "wise." Hence the name Magus, "the magician," originally applied to Persian priests. In the Sept., only in Dan. 2 : 2, 10, of the "enchanters," R.V. (A.V., "astrologers"), of Babylon. The superior Greek version of Daniel by Theodotion has it also at 1 : 20; 2 : 27; 4 : 7; 5 : 7, 11, 15.¶

5333 (-KEUS 5332) AG:854B CB:1263C 2. PHARMAKOS (φαρμακός), an adjective signifying 'devoted to magical arts,' is used as a noun, a sorcerer, especially one who uses drugs, potions, spells, enchantments, Rev. 21 : 8, in the best texts (some have *pharmakeus*), and 22 : 15.¶

SORCERY

A. Nouns.

5331 AG:854A CB:1263C 1. PHARMAKIA (or -EIA) (φαρμακία) (Eng., pharmacy etc.) primarily signified the use of medicine, drugs, spells; then, poisoning; then, sorcery, Gal. 5 : 20, R.V., "sorcery" (A.V., "witchcraft"), mentioned as one of "the works of the flesh." See also Rev. 9 : 21 ; 18 : 23.¶ In the Sept., Ex. 7 : 11, 22 ; 8 : 7, 18 ; Isa. 47 : 9, 12.¶ In sorcery, the use of drugs, whether simple or potent, was generally accompanied by incantations and appeals to occult powers, with the provision of various charms, amulets, etc., professedly designed to keep the applicant or patient from the attention and power of demons, but actually to impress the applicant with the mysterious resources and powers of the sorcerer.

2. MAGIA (or -EIA) (μαγία), the magic art, is used in the plural in 3095
Acts 8 : 11, "sorceries" (see Sorcerer, No. 1).¶ AG:484B CB:1257B

B. Verb.

MAGEUŌ (μαγεύω), akin to A, No. 2, to practise magic, Acts 8 : 9, 3096
"used sorcery," is used as in A, No. 2, of Simon Magnus.¶ AG:484D CB:1257B

SORE (Noun, Adjective, Adverb), SORER

A. Noun.

HELKOS (ἕλκος), a sore or ulcer (primarily a wound), occurs in 1668
Luke 16 : 21 ; Rev. 16 : 2, 11.¶ AG:251C CB:—

B. Verb.

HELKOŌ (ἑλκόω), to wound, to ulcerate, is used in the Passive Voice, 1669
signifying to suffer from sores, to be "full of sores," Luke 16 : 20 (perfect AG:251C CB:—
participle).¶

C. Adjectives.

1. HIKANOS (ἱκανός), used of things, occasionally denotes "much," 2425
translated "sore" in Acts 20 : 37, lit., 'there was much weeping of all.' AG:374B CB:1250C
See Able, C, No. 2.

2. CHEIRŌN (χείρων), worse (used as a comparative degree of *kakos*, 5501
evil), occurs in Heb. 10 : 29, "sorer." See Worse. AG:881B CB:—

D. Adverbs.

1. LIAN (λίαν), very, exceedingly, is translated "sore" in Mark 6 : 51 3029 AG:473B
(of amazement). See Exceed, B, No. 1. CB:1257A

2. SPHODRA (σφόδρα), very, very much, is translated "sore" in 4970
Matt. 17 : 6 (of fear). See Greatly, Note (1). AG:796A CB:1269C

Notes : (1) For the A.V., "sore vexed" in Matt. 17 : 15, see MEGAS
Grievously, B, No. 2, Note (2). (2) In Luke 2 : 9 *megas*, great, is used 3173 AG:497C
with *phobos*, fear, as the object of the verb to fear, "(they were) sore CB:1258A
(afraid)," lit., '(they feared) a great (fear).' (3) In Mark 9 : 26, A.V., POLUS
polla, much (R.V.), the neuter plur. of *polus*, used as an adverb, is trans- 4183 AG:687C
lated "sore." (4) In Matt. 21 : 15, *aganakteō*, to be moved with indig- CB:1266A
nation (R.V.), is translated "they were sore displeased." (5) For the AGANAKTEŌ 23
R.V., "sore troubled," Matt. 26 : 37 and Mark 14 : 33 (A.V., "very AG:4B
heavy"), see Trouble, B, No. 12. (6) For A.V., "were sore amazed" in SUNTRIBŌ 4937
Mark 14 : 33, see Amaze, B, No. 4. (7) In Luke 9 : 39, R.V., *suntribō*, to AG:793B
break, bruise, is rendered "bruiseth sorely." See Break, A, No. 5. EKPHOBOS 1630
(8) In Mark 9 : 6, *ekphobos* is rendered "sore afraid." AG:247A

SORROW (Noun and Verb), SORROWFUL

A. Nouns.

3077 1. LUPĒ (*λύπη*), grief, sorrow, is translated " sorrow " in Luke 22 : 45 ;
AG:482A CB:1257B John 16 : 6, 20–22 ; Rom. 9 : 2, R.V. (A.V., " heaviness ") ; 2 Cor. 2 : 1,
R.V. ; 2 : 3, 7 ; 7 : 10 (twice) ; Phil. 2 : 27 (twice). See GRIEF.

3601 AG:555B 2. ODUNĒ (*ὀδύνη*), pain, consuming grief, distress, whether of body
CB:1260B or mind, is used of the latter, Rom. 9 : 2, R.V., " pain ; " 1 Tim. 6 : 10.¶

5604 AG:895C 3. ŌDIN (*ὠδίν*), a birth-pang, travail, pain, " sorrows," Matt. 24 : 8 ;
CB:1260B Mark 13 : 8 ; see PAIN, A, No. 2.

3997 AG:642D 4. PENTHOS (*πένθος*), mourning, " sorrow," Rev. 18 : 7 (twice) ;
CB:1263A 21 : 4 : see MOURN.

B. Verbs.

3076 AG:481C 1. LUPEŌ (*λυπέω*), akin to A, No. 1 : see GRIEF, B, No. 1, SORRY,
CB:1257B A (below).

3600 AG:555A 2. ODUNAŌ (*ὀδυνάω*), to cause pain (akin to A, No. 2), is used in the
CB:— Middle Voice in Luke 2 : 48 ; Acts 20 : 38 : see ANGUISH, B, No. 3.

C. Adjectives.

4036 AG:648C 1. PERILUPOS (*περίλυπος*), very sad, deeply grieved (*peri*, intensive),
CB:— is used in Matt. 26 : 38 and Mark 14 : 34, " exceeding sorrowful ; "
Mark 6 : 26 ; Luke 18 : 23 (ver. 24 in some mss.).¶

253 AG:41C 2. ALUPOS (*ἄλυπος*) denotes free from grief (*a*, negative, *lupē*, grief),
CB:— comparative degree in Phil. 2 : 28, " less sorrowful," their joy would
mean the removal of a burden from his heart.¶

SORRY

A. Verb.

3076 LUPEŌ (*λυπέω*) is rendered to be sorry (Passive Voice) in Matt. 14 : 9,
AG:481C CB:1257B A.V. (R.V., " grieved ") ; 17 : 23 ; 18 : 31 ; 2 Cor. 2 : 2 [1st part, Active
V., " make sorry " (as in 7 : 8, twice) ; 2nd part, Passive] ; 2 : 4, R.V.,
" made sorry ; " 9 : 9 and 11, R.V., " ye were made sorry." See GRIEVE,
B, No. 1.

B. Adjective.

4036 AG:648C PERILUPOS (*περίλυπος*) is translated " exceeding sorry " in Mark
CB:— 6 : 26 : see SORROWFUL, C, No. 1.

SORT

A. Adjective.

3697 AG:575D HOPOIOS (*ὁποῖος*), of what sort, is so rendered in 1 Cor. 3 : 13. See
CB:— MANNER, SUCH AS. WHAT.

B. Noun.

3313 AG:505D MEROS (*μέρος*), a part, is used with *apo*, from, in Rom. 15 : 15 and
CB:1258B rendered " (in some) sort," A.V. (R.V., " . . . measure "). See BEHALF.

Note : See BASE, No. 3, GODLY, C, Notes (2) and (3).

For SOUGHT see SEEK

SOUL

PSUCHĒ (ψυχή) denotes the breath, the breath of life, then the soul, 5590
in its various meanings. The N.T. uses " may be analysed approximately AG:893B
as follows : CB:1267C

(*a*) the natural life of the body, Matt. 2 : 20 ; Luke 12 : 22 ; Acts 20 : 10 ; Rev. 8 : 9 ; 12 : 11 ; cp. Lev. 17 : 11 ; 2 Sam. 14 : 7 ; Esth. 8 : 11 ; (*b*) the immaterial, invisible part of man, Matt. 10 : 28 ; Acts 2 : 27 ; cp. 1 Kings 17 : 21 ; (*c*) the disembodied (or 'unclothed' or 'naked,' 2 Cor. 5 : 3, 4) man, Rev. 6 : 9 ; (*d*) the seat of personality, Luke 9 : 24, explained as = 'own self,' ver. 25 ; Heb. 6 : 19 ; 10 : 39 ; cp. Isa. 53 : 10 with 1 Tim. 2 : 6 ; (*e*) the seat of the sentient element in man, that by which he perceives, reflects, feels, desires, Matt. 11 : 29 ; Luke 1 : 46 ; 2 : 35 ; Acts 14 : 2, 22 ; cp. Ps. 84 : 2 ; 139 : 14 ; Isa. 26 : 9 ; (*f*) the seat of will and purpose, Matt. 22 : 37 ; Acts 4 : 32 ; Eph. 6 : 6 ; Phil. 1 : 27 ; Heb. 12 : 3 ; cp. Num. 21 : 4 ; Deut. 11 : 13 ; (*g*) the seat of appetite, Rev. 18 : 14 ; cp. Ps. 107 : 9 ; Prov. 6 : 30 ; Isa. 5 : 14 ('desire') ; 29 : 8 ; (*h*) persons, individuals, Acts 2 : 41, 43 ; Rom. 2 : 9 ; Jas. 5 : 20 ; 1 Pet. 3 : 20 ; 2 Pet. 2 : 14 ; cp. Gen. 12 : 5 ; 14 : 21 ('persons') ; Lev. 4 : 2 ('any one') ; Ezek. 27 : 13 ; of dead bodies, Num. 6 : 6, lit., 'dead soul ;' and of animals, Lev. 24 : 18, lit., 'soul for soul' ; (*i*) the equivalent of the personal pronoun, used for emphasis and effect :—1st person, John 10 : 24 ('us') ; Heb. 10 : 38 ; cp. Gen. 12 : 13 ; Num. 23 : 10 ; Jud. 16 : 30 ; Ps. 120 : 2 ('me') ; 2nd person, 2 Cor. 12 : 15 ; Heb. 13 : 17 ; Jas. 1 : 21 ; 1 Pet. 1 : 9 ; 2 : 25 ; cp. Lev. 17 : 11 ; 26 : 15 ; 1 Sam. 1 : 26 ; 3rd person, 1 Pet. 4 : 19 ; 2 Pet. 2 : 8 ; cp. Ex. 30 : 12 ; Job 32 : 2, Heb. 'soul,' Sept. 'self' ; (*j*) an animate creature, human or other, 1 Cor. 15 : 45 ; Rev. 16 : 3 ; cp. Gen. 1 : 24 ; 2 : 7, 19 ; (*k*) 'the inward man,' the seat of the new life, Luke 21 : 19 (cp. Matt. 10 : 39) ; 1 Pet. 2 : 11 ; 3 John 2.

" With (*j*) compare *a-psuchos*, soulless, inanimate, 1 Cor. 14 : 7.¶ APSUCHOS
" With (*f*) compare *di-psuchos*, two-souled, Jas. 1 : 8 ; 4 : 8 ;¶ *oligo-* 895 AG:129C
psuchos, feeble-souled, 1 Thess. 5 : 14 ;¶ *iso-psuchos*, like-souled, Phil. CB:—
2 : 20 ;¶ *sum-psuchos*, joint-souled ('with one accord'), Phil. 2 : 2.¶ DIPSUCHOS 1374
" The language of Heb. 4 : 12 suggests the extreme difficulty of dis- AG:201A
tinguishing between the soul and the spirit, alike in their nature and in CB:1242A OLIGOPSUCHOS
their activities. Generally speaking the spirit is the higher, the soul the 3642
lower element. The spirit may be recognised as the life principle bestowed AG:564A
on man by God, the soul as the resulting life constituted in the individual, CB:1260C ISOPSUCHOS
the body being the material organism animated by soul and spirit. . . . 72473 AG:381B
" Body and soul are the constituents of the man according to Matt. CB:1253A
6 : 25 ; 10 : 28 ; Luke 12 : 20 ; Acts 20 : 10 ; body and spirit according SUMPSUCHOS 4861
to Luke 8 : 55 ; 1 Cor. 5 : 3 ; 7 : 34 ; Jas. 2 : 26. In Matt. 26 : 38 the AG:781B
emotions are associated with the soul, in John 13 : 21 with the spirit ; CB:1270B
cp. also Ps. 42 : 11 with 1 Kings 21 : 5. In Ps. 35 : 9 the soul rejoices in God, in Luke 1 : 47 the spirit.

SōMA 4983 " Apparently, then, the relationships may be thus summed up,
AG:799A ' *Sōma*, body, and *pneuma*, spirit, may be separated, *pneuma* and *psuchē*,
CB:1269B PNEUMA 4151 soul, can only be distinguished ' (Cremer)."*

AG:674C SOUND (Noun and Verb)

CB:1265B **A. Nouns.**

5456 1. PHŌNĒ (φωνή), most frequently " a voice," is translated " sound "
AG:870C in Matt. 24 : 31 (A.V. marg., " voice ") ; John 3 : 8, A.V. (R.V., " voice ") ;
CB:1264B so 1 Cor. 14 : 7 (1st part), 8 ; Rev. 1 : 15 ; 18 : 22 (2nd part, R.V.,
" voice ") ; A.V. and R.V. in 9 : 9 (twice) ; in Acts 2 : 6, R.V., " (this)
sound (was heard)," A.V., " (this) was noised abroad."

2279 2. ĒCHOS (ἦχος), a noise, a sound of any sort (Eng., echo), is trans-
AG:349D lated " sound " in Acts 2 : 2 ; Heb. 12 : 19. See Roaring, B, Rumour.
CB:1242C 5353 3. PHTHONGOS (φθόγγος), akin to *phthengomai*, to utter a voice,
AG:857C occurs in Rom. 10 : 18 ; 1 Cor. 14 : 7.¶ In the Sept., Psa. 19 : 4.¶

CB:— **B. Verbs.**

2278 1. ĒCHEŌ (ἠχέω), akin to A, No. 2, occurs in 1 Cor. 13 : 1, " sounding
AG:349C CB:1242C (brass) ; " in some mss., Luke 21 : 25. See Roaring.¶
1837 2. EXĒCHEŌ (ἐξηχέω), to sound forth as a trumpet or thunder
(-OMAI) (*ex*, out, and No. 1), is used in 1 Thess. 1 : 8, " sounded forth," Passive
AG:276A CB:— Voice, lit., ' has been sounded out.'¶ In the Sept., Joel 3 : 14.¶
4537 3. SALPIZŌ (σαλπίζω), to sound a trumpet (*salpinx*), occurs in Matt.
AG:741A 6 : 2 ; 1 Cor. 15 : 52, " the trumpet shall sound ; " Rev. 8 : 6–8, 10, 12, 13 ;
CB:1268B 9 : 1, 13 ; 10 : 7 ; 11 : 15.¶
1001 4. BOLIZŌ (βολίζω), to heave the lead (*bolis*, that which is thrown
AG:144D or hurled, akin to *ballō*, to throw ; sounding-lead), to take soundings,
CB:— occurs in Acts 27 : 28 (twice).¶
1096 *Note :* In Luke 1 : 44, A.V., *ginomai*, to become, is rendered
AG:158A CB:1248B " sounded " (R.V., " came ").

SOUND (Adjective), BE SOUND

A. Adjective.

5199 HUGIĒS (ὑγιής), whole, healthy, is used metaphorically of " sound
AG:832C CB:1251C speech," Tit. 2 : 8. See Whole.

B. Verb.

5198 HUGIAINŌ (ὑγιαίνω), to be healthy, sound in health (Eng., hygiene
AG:832B CB:1251C etc.), translated " safe and sound " in Luke 15 : 27, is used metaphorically
of doctrine, 1 Tim. 1 : 10 ; 2 Tim. 4 : 3 ; Tit. 1 : 9 ; 2 : 1 ; of words,
1 Tim. 6 : 3, R.V. (A.V., " wholesome," R.V. marg., " healthful ") ;
2 Tim. 1 : 13 ; " in the faith," Tit. 1 : 13 (R.V. marg., " healthy ") ;
" in faith," Tit. 2 : 2 (R.V. marg., ditto).

Note : For " sound mind " in 2 Tim. 1 : 7, A.V., see Discipline ; in 1 Pet. 4 : 7 (A.V., " sober "), see Mind, B, No. 5.

---

* From Notes on Thessalonians by Hogg and Vine, pp. 205–207.

SOUNDNESS

HOLOKLĒRIA (ὁλοκληρία), completeness, soundness (akin to 3647
holoklēros, see ENTIRE), occurs in Acts 3 : 16.¶ In the Sept., Isa. 1 : 6.¶ AG:564C
CB:—

SOUTH, SOUTH WIND

NOTOS (νότος) denotes (*a*) the south wind, Luke 12 : 55 ; Acts 27 : 13 ; 3558
28 : 13 ; (*b*) south, as a direction, Luke 13 : 29 ; Rev. 21 : 13 ; (*c*) the AG:544A CB:1260A
South, as a region, Matt. 12 : 42 ; Luke 11 : 31.¶

Note : For *mesēmbria*, Acts 8 : 26, see NOON. 3314
AG:506D
CB:—

SOUTH WEST

LIPS (λίψ), lit., Libyan, denotes the S.W. wind, Acts 27 : 12, " (looking) 3047
north-east (and south-east)," R.V., lit., '(looking down) the south-west AG:475D
wind (and down the north-west wind) ;' to look down a wind was to look CB:—
in the direction in which it blows. A S.W. wind blows towards the N.E. ; SOUR
the aspect of the haven answers to this. See also under NORTH EAST, See BITTER
NORTH WEST.¶

SOVEREIGN See LORD, MASTER

SOW (Noun)

HUS (ὗς), swine (masc. or fem.), is used in the fem. in 2 Pet. 2 : 22.¶ 5300
AG:848D
CB:1252B

SOW (Verb), SOWER

SPEIRŌ (σπείρω), to sow seed, is used (1) literally, especially in the 4687
Synoptic Gospels ; elsewhere, 1 Cor. 15 : 36, 37 ; 2 Cor. 9 : 10, " the AG:761B
sower ;" (2) metaphorically, (*a*) in proverbial sayings, e.g., Matt. CB:1269C
13 : 3, 4 ; Luke 19 : 21, 22 ; John 4 : 37 ; 2 Cor. 9 : 6 ; (*b*) in the interpretation of parables, e.g., Matt. 13 : 19–23 (in these vv., R.V., " was sown," for A.V., " received seed ") ; (*c*) otherwise as follows : of sowing " spiritual things " in preaching and teaching, 1 Cor. 9 : 11 ; of the interment of the bodies of deceased believers, 1 Cor. 15 : 42–44 ; of ministering to the necessities of others in things temporal (the harvest being proportionate to the sowing), 2 Cor. 9 : 6, 10 (see above) ; of sowing to the flesh, Gal. 6 : 7, 8 (" that " in ver. 7 is emphatic, ' that and that only,' what was actually sown) ; in ver. 8, *eis*, " unto," signifies ' in the interests of ' ; of the " fruit of righteousness " by peacemakers, Jas. 3 : 18.

SPACE

A. Noun.

DIASTĒMA (διάστημα), an interval, space (akin to B), is used of 1292
time in Acts 5 : 7.¶ AG:188D
CB:—

B. Verb.

DIISTĒMI (διΐστημι), to set apart, separate (*dia*, apart, *histēmi*, to 1339
cause to stand), see A, is rendered " after the space of " in Luke 22 : 59 ; AG:195B CB:—
in Acts 27 : 28, with *brachu*, a little, R.V., " after a little space " (A.V., CHRONOS
" when they had gone a little further "). See PART. 5550 AG:887D

Notes : (1) In Acts 15 : 33 and Rev. 2 : 21, A.V., *chronos*, time (R.V.), CB:1240B

EPI is translated " space." (2) In Acts 19 : 8 and 10, *epi*, for or during (of
1909 AG:285D time), is translated " for the space of ; " in 19 : 34, " about the space of."
CB:1245C (3) In Acts 5 : 34, A.V., *brachu* (the neuter of *brachus*, short), used
BRACHUS 1024 adverbially, is translated " a little space " (R.V. " . . . while "). (4) In
AG:147B Gal. 2 : 1, *dia*, through, is rendered " after the space of," R.V., stressing
CB:1239B DIA the length of the period mentioned (A.V., " after," which would represent
1223 the preposition *meta*). (5) In Jas. 5 : 17 there is no word in the original
AG:179B CB:1241A representing the phrase " by the space of," A.V. (R.V., " for "). (6) In
APO Rev. 14 : 20, A.V., *apo*, away from, is translated " by the space of " (R.V.,
575 AG:86C " as far as "). (7) In Rev. 17 : 10, A.V., *oligon*, " a little while " (R.V.), is
CB:1236C rendered " a short space."

OLIGOS 3641 AG:563C CB:1260C

SPARE, SPARINGLY

A. Verbs.

5339 AG:854D CB:— PHEIDOMAI (φείδομαι), to spare, i.e., to forego the infliction of that evil or retribution which was designed, is used with a negative in Acts 20 : 29 ; Rom. 8 : 32 ; 11 : 21 (twice) ; 2 Cor. 13 : 2 ; 2 Pet. 2 : 4, 5 ; positively, in 1 Cor. 7 : 28 ; 2 Cor. 1 : 3 ; rendered " forbear " in 2 Cor. 12 : 6. See FORBEAR.¶

4052 AG:650C CB:1263C *Note :* In Luke 15 : 17, *perisseuō*, to abound, have abundance, is translated " have enough and to spare."

B. Adverb.

5340 AG:854D CB:1264A PHEIDOMENŌS (φειδομένως), akin to A, " sparingly," occurs in 2 Cor. 9 : 6 (twice), of sowing and reaping.¶

SPARROW

4765 AG:771C CB:1270B STROUTHION (στρουθίον), a diminutive of *strouthos*, a sparrow, occurs in Matt. 10 : 29, 31 ; Luke 12 : 6, 7.¶

3004 AG:468A

SPEAK

CB:1256C 1. LEGŌ (λέγω), to say, speak : see SAY, No. 1.

2980 AG:463A CB:1256B 2. LALEŌ (λαλέω), for which see SAY, No. 2, is used several times in 1 Cor. 14 ; the command prohibiting women from speaking in a church gathering, vv. 34, 35, is regarded by some as an injunction against chattering, a meaning which is absent from the use of the verb everywhere else in the N.T. ; it is to be understood in the same sense as in vv. 2, 3–6, 9, 11, 13, 18, 19, 21, 23, 27–29, 39.

4354 AG:717B CB:— 3. PROSLALEŌ (προσλαλέω), to speak to or with (*pros*, to, and No. 2), is used in Acts 13 : 43 and 28 : 20.¶

5350 AG:857A CB:— 4. PHTHENGOMAI (φθέγγομαι), to utter a sound or voice, is translated to speak in Acts 4 : 18 ; 2 Pet. 2 : 16 ; in 2 : 18, A.V., " speak " (R.V., " utter ").

669 AG:102A CB:1237A (-GESTHAI) 5. APOPHTHENGOMAI (ἀποφθέγγομαι), to speak forth (*apo*, forth, and No. 4), is so rendered in Acts 2 : 14, R.V. (A.V., " said "), and 26 : 25 ; in 2 : 2 it denotes to give utterance.¶

6. ANTILEGŌ (ἀντιλέγω), to speak against, is so rendered in Luke 483
2 : 34; John 19 : 12; Acts 13 : 45, A.V. (R.V., "contradicted"); AG:74D CB:—
28 : 19, 22. See CONTRADICT, GAINSAY.
7. KATALALEŌ (καταλαλέω), synonymous with No. 6 (*kata*, against, 2635 AG:412C
and No. 2), is always translated to speak against in the R.V. See CB:1254A
BACKBITER, Note. 2551
8. KAKOLOGEŌ (κακολογέω), to speak evil: see CURSE, B, No. 4. AG:397B CB:1253B
9. SULLALEŌ (συλλαλέω), to speak together (*sun*, with, and No. 2), 4814
is rendered "spake together" in Luke 4 : 36, R.V. See COMMUNE, AG:776C CB:—
No. 3, CONFER, No. 2, TALK.
10. PROEIPON (προεῖπον), to speak or say before (a 2nd aorist tense 4302
from an obsolete present), is rendered to speak before in Acts 1 : 16; 2 Pet. AG:708B CB:1266C
3 : 2; Jude 17. See FORETELL.
11. PROPHTHANŌ (προφθάνω), to anticipate (an extension, by 4399
pro, before, of *phthanō*, which has the same meaning), is rendered "spake AG:724B CB:—
first" in Matt. 17 : 25, R.V. (A.V., "prevented").¶
12. PROSPHŌNEŌ (προσφωνέω), to address, call to, is rendered 4377
"spake unto" (or "to") in Luke 23 : 20; Acts 21 : 40; 22 : 2; 'to call AG:720C CB:—
unto' (or 'to') in Matt. 11 : 16; Luke 6 : 13; 7 : 32; 13 : 12.¶ After 1518
13. EIRŌ (εἴρω), for which see SAY, No. 4, has a 1st aorist, passive AG:—
participle *rhēthen*, "spoken" or "spoken of," used in Matt. 1 : 22; CB:1246C DIALEGOMAI
2 : 15, 17, 23; 3 : 3; 4 : 14; 8 : 17; 12 : 17; 13 : 35; 21 : 4; 22 : 31; 1256
24 : 15; 27 : 9 (in some texts in 27 : 35 and Mark 13 : 14). AG:185C
Notes: (1) In Heb. 12 : 5, A.V., *dialegomai*, to discuss, to reason, is CB:1241A CHRĒMATIZŌ
translated "speaketh" (R.V., "reasoneth"). (2) In Heb. 12 : 25, A.V. 5537
chrēmatizō, to warn, instruct, is translated "spake" (R.V., "warned"): AG:885C CB:1240A
see ADMONISH. (3) In Eph. 4 : 31, A.V., *blasphēmia* is translated "evil BLASPHĒMIA
speaking:" see RAILING. (4) In Heb. 12 : 19, *prostithēmi*, to put to, add, 988 AG:143A
used with *logos*, a word, is rendered "(that no word) more should be CB:1239A
spoken," R.V. [A.V., "(that) the word should (not) be spoken (to them) PROSTITHĒMI 4369
any more"]. (5) In Acts 26 : 24, A.V., *apologeomai*, to make a defence AG:718D
(R.V.), is rendered "spake for himself." See ANSWER, B, No. 4. (6) In CB:1267B APOLOGEOMAI
Rom. 15 : 21, A.V., *anangellō*, to bring back word (R.V., "tidings . . . 626
came"), is translated "he was . . . spoken of." (7) For "is spoken AG:95D CB:1237A
of" in Rom. 1 : 8, A.V., see PROCLAIM, No. 2. (8) For "spake out" in ANANGELLŌ
Luke 1 : 42, A.V., see VOICE, *Note*. (9) In Gal. 4 : 15, there is no verb in 312
the original for the A.V., "ye spake of" (see R.V.). (10) For "spoken AG:51B CB:1235B
against" in Acts 19 : 36 see GAINSAY, C. (11) For "speak reproachfully," GINŌSKŌ 1097
1 Tim. 5 : 14, see REVILE, C. (12) In Acts 21 : 3, A.V., *ginōskō* is trans- AG:160D
lated "speak," R.V., "know." CB:1248B HĒGEOMAI

2233

SPEAKER (chief) AG:343C

Note: In Acts 14 : 12 the verb *hēgeomai*, to lead the way, be the chief, CB:1249C LOGOS
is used in the present participle with the article (together equivalent to a 3056
noun), followed by the genitive case of *logos*, speech, with the article, the AG:477A CB:1257A

phrase being rendered "the chief speaker," lit., 'the leader of the discourse.' See CHIEF, C.

SPEAKING (evil, much)

4180 AG:687B POLULOGIA (πολυλογία), loquacity, "much speaking" (*polus*, much,
CB:— *logos*, speech), is used in Matt. 6 : 7.¶ In the Sept., Prov. 10 : 19.¶

Note : For "evil speaking(s)," in Eph. 4 : 31, see RAILING ; in 1 Pet. 2 : 1, see BACKBITING. For "shameful speaking" see COMMUNICATION, B, Note.

SPEAR

3057 AG:479B LONCHĒ (λόγχη), primarily a spear-head, then, a lance or spear,
CB:— occurs in John 19 : 34 ; some texts have it in Matt. 27 : 49 ¶ As to John 19 : 29, there is an old conjecture, mentioned by Field (*Notes on the Trans. of the N.T.*), to the effect that the sponge was put on a spear (*hussos*, a javelin, the Roman *pilum*, instead of *hussōpos*, hyssop).

SPEARMAN

1187 AG:174C DEXIOLABOS (δεξιολάβος), from *dexios*, the right (hand), and
CB:— *lambanō*, to lay hold of, is used in the plural in Acts 23 : 23, "spearmen." Some texts have *dexiobolos*, one who throws with his right hand (*ballō*, to throw), 'right-handed slingers.'¶

SPECIAL

5177 AG:829B *Note : Tuchōn*, the 2nd aorist participle of *tunchanō*, to happen, meet
(TUCHANŌ) with, chance, is used with a negative signifying 'not common or ordinary,'
CB:— special, Acts 19 : 11 ; so in 28 : 2. See COMMON, B, Note (3).

SPECIAL See ABUNDANT, HIGH

For SPECIALLY see ESPECIALLY

SPECTACLE

2302 AG:353C THEATRON (θέατρον), akin to *theaomai*, to behold, denotes (*a*) a
CB:1271C theatre (used also as a place of assembly), Acts 19 : 29, 31 ; (*b*) a spectacle, a show, metaphorically in 1 Cor. 4 : 9. See THEATRE.¶

SPECK See MOTE

SPEECH

3056 AG:477A 1. LOGOS (λόγος), akin to *legō* (SPEAK, No. 1), most frequently rendered
CB:1257A 'word' (for an analysis see WORD), signifies speech, as follows : (*a*) discourse, e.g., Luke 20 : 20, R.V., "speech" (A.V., "words") ; Acts 14 : 12 (see SPEAKER) ; 20 : 7 ; 1 Cor. 2 : 1, 4 ; 4 : 19, A.V. (R.V., "word") ; 2 Cor. 10 : 10 ; (*b*) the faculty of speech, e.g., 2 Cor. 11 : 6 ; (*c*) the manner of speech, e.g., Matt. 5 : 37, R.V., "speech" (A.V., "communication") ; Col. 4 : 6 ; (*d*) manner of instruction, Tit. 2 : 8 ; 1 Cor. 14 : 9, R.V. (A.V., "words") ; Eph. 4 : 29, R.V. (A.V., "communication"). See SAYING.

2981 AG:464A CB:1256C 2. LALIA (λαλιά), akin to *laleō* (SPEAK, No. 2), denotes talk, speech, (*a*) of a dialect, Matt. 26 : 73 ; Mark 14 : 70 ; (*b*) utterances, John 4 : 42, R.V., " speaking " (A.V., " saying ") ; 8 : 43.¶

3. EULOGIA (εὐλογία) has the meaning fair speaking, flattering 2129
speech in Rom. 16 : 18, R.V., " fair speech " (A.V., " fair speeches "). AG:322D
See BLESSING, C, No. 1. CB:1247B

4. CHRĒSTOLOGIA (χρηστολογία), which has a similar meaning to 5542
No. 3, occurs with it in Rom. 16 : 18 [R.V., " smooth . . . (speech)"]. AG:886A
See SMOOTH, Note.¶ CB:1240A

Notes : (1) For " persuasiveness of speech," Col. 2 : 4, R.V., see PERSUASIVE, B. (2) In Acts 14 : 11 " the speech of Lycaonia " translates the adverb *Lukaonisti.* Lycaonia was a large country in the centre and south of the plateau of Asia Minor ; the villages retained the native language, but cities like Lystra probably had a Seleucid tone in their laws and customs (Ramsay on Galatians).

SPEECHLESS

1. ENEOS (or ENNEOS) (ἐνεός), dumb, speechless, occurs in Acts 1769
9 : 7.¶ In the Sept., Prov. 17 : 28 ; Isa. 56 : 10.¶ AG:265A CB:—

2. KŌPHOS (κωφός), which means either deaf or dumb (see DEAF), 2974
is translated " speechless " in Luke 1 : 22. AG:462A CB:1255C

Note : For *phimoō*, translated " he was speechless " in Matt. 22 : 12, 5392
see MUZZLE, SILENCE. AG:861D CB:—

SPEED, SPEEDILY

TACHISTA

Notes : (1) In Acts 17 : 15 " with all speed " is the rendering of the 5033
phrase *hōs*, as, *tachista*, most speedily (the superlative of *tachu*, speedily), AG:806D (TACHEŌS 3.)
i.e., as speedily as possible. (2) For " speedily," *en tachei*, in Luke TACHEI (-EN)
18 : 8, see QUICKLY, No. 4. (3) For " God speed " see GREETING, A, No. 2. 5034 (TACHOS) AG:806D (-EŌS)

SPEND, SPENT

1. DAPANAŌ (δαπανάω) denotes (*a*) to expend, spend, Mark 5 : 26 1159
[for Acts 21 : 24 see CHARGE, Note (5)] : 2 Cor. 12 : 15 (1st part : for AG:171A
" be spent," see No. 2) ; (*b*) to consume, squander, Luke 15 : 14 ; Jas. CB:—
4 : 3. See CONSUME, Note.¶

2. EKDAPANAŌ (ἐκδαπανάω), lit., to spend out (*ek*), an intensive 1550
form of No. 1, to spend entirely, is used in 2 Cor. 12 : 15, in the Passive AG:238B
Voice, with reflexive significance, to spend oneself out (for others), " will CB:—
. . . be spent," R.V. marg., " spent out " (see No. 1).¶

3. PROSDAPANAŌ (προσδαπανάω), to spend besides (*pros*, and 4325
No. 1), is used in Luke 10 : 35, " thou spendest more."¶ AG:712A CB:—

4. PROSANALISKŌ (προσαναλίσκω), to spend besides, a strengthened 4321
form of *analiskō*, to expend, consume (see CONSUME, No. 1), occurs in most AG:711C
texts in Luke 8 : 43.¶ CB:—

5. DIAGINOMAI (διαγίνομαι), used of time, to intervene, elapse, is 1230 AG:182B
rendered " was spent " in Acts 27 : 9. See PAST. CB:—

4298 AG:707D CB:1266C 6. PROKOPTŌ (*προκόπτω*), to cut forward a way, advance, is translated "is far spent," in Rom. 13 : 12, said metaphorically of "the night," the whole period of man's alienation from God. Though the tense is the aorist, it must not be rendered 'was far spent,' as if it referred, e.g., to Christ's first Advent. The aorist is here perfective. See ADVANCE.

2827 AG:436C CB:— 7. KLINŌ (*κλίνω*), to lean, decline, is said of the decline of day in Luke 24 : 29, "is (now) far spent," lit., 'has declined.' See Bow (Verb).

1096 AG:158A CB:1248B 8. GINOMAI (*γίνομαι*), to become, occur, is rendered "was far spent" in Mark 6 : 35, lit., 'much hour (i.e., many an hour) having taken place.'

4160 AG:680D CB:1265C 9. POIEŌ (*ποιέω*), to do, is translated "have spent (*but* one hour)," in Matt. 20 : 12, R.V. (A.V., "have wrought") lit., as in the Eng. idiom, 'have done one hour;' so in Acts 20 : 3, R.V., "when he had spent (lit., 'had done') three months" (A.V., "abode").

2119 AG:321B CB:1247B 10. EUKAIREŌ (*εὐκαιρέω*). to have leisure or devote one's leisure to, is translated "spent their time," in Acts 17 : 21. See LEISURE.

5551 AG:888C CB:1240B 11. CHRONOTRIBEŌ (*χρονοτριβέω*), to spend time (*chronos*, time, *tribō*, to rub, to wear out), occurs in Acts 20 : 16.¶

4183 AG:687C CB:1266A *Note: Polus*, much, is rendered "far spent" twice in Mark 6 : 35, R.V.

SPEW (A.V., SPUE)

1692 AG:254D CB:1244B EMEŌ (*ἐμέω*), to vomit (cp. Eng., emetic), is used in Rev. 3 : 16, figuratively of the Lord's utter abhorrence of the condition of the church at Laodicea.¶ In the Sept., Isa. 19 : 14.¶

SPICE(S)

759 AG:114B CB:1237C 1. ARŌMA (*ἄρωμα*), spice, occurs in Mark 16 : 1, R.V. "spices" (A.V., "sweet sp."); Luke 23 : 56; 24 : 1; John 19 : 40.¶ A papyrus document has it in a list of articles for a sacrifice.

— AG:47D CB:— 2. AMŌMON (*ἄμωμον*), *amomum*, probably a word of Semitic origin, a fragrant plant of India, is translated "spice" in Rev. 18 : 13, R.V. (A.V., "odours").¶

SPIKENARD

3487 AG:534A CB:— NARDOS (*νάρδος*) is derived, through the Semitic languages (Heb. *nērd*, Syriac *nardin*), from the Sanskrit *nalada*, a fragrant oil, procured from the stem of an Indian plant. The Arabs call it the Indian spike. The adjective *pistikos* is attached to it in the N.T., Mark 14 : 3; John
PISTIKOS 4101 AG:662B CB:— 12 : 3; *pistikos*, if taken as an ordinary Greek word, would signify 'genuine.' There is evidence, however, that it was regarded as a technical term. It has been suggested that the original reading was *pistakēs*, i.e., the *Pistacia Terebinthus*, which grows in Cyprus, Syria, Palestine, etc., and yields a resin of very fragrant odour, and in such inconsiderable quantities as to be very costly. "Nard was frequently mixed with aromatic ingredients . . . so when scented with the fragrant resin of the *pistakē* it would quite well be called *nardos pistakēs*" (E. N. Bennett,

in the *Classical Review* for 1890, Vol. iv, p. 319). The oil used for the anointing of the Lord's head was worth about £12, and must have been of the most valuable kind.¶ In the Sept., S. of Sol. 1 : 12 ; 4 : 13, 14.¶

SPILL

1632
EKCHUNNŌ (or EKCHUNŌ) (ἐκχύννω), to pour out, shed, is rendered AG:247B (EKCHEŌ)
"be spilled" in Luke 5 : 37. See POUR, SHED. CB:1243B

Note : Some texts have *ekcheō* in Mark 2 : 22 (so A.V.). The form in 1632
Luke 5 : 37 might also come from *ekcheō*. AG:247B CB:1243B

SPIN

NĒTHŌ (νήθω), to spin, is found in Matt. 6 : 28 and Luke 12 : 27, of 3514
the lilies of the field (see LILY).¶ AG:537C CB:—

SPIRIT

PNEUMA (πνεῦμα) primarily denotes the wind (akin to *pneō*, to 4151
breathe, blow) ; also breath ; then, especially the spirit, which, like the AG:674C CB:1265B
wind, is invisible, immaterial and powerful. The N.T. uses of the word may be analysed approximately as follows .

" (*a*) the wind, John 3 : 8 (where marg. is, perhaps, to be preferred) ; Heb. 1 : 7 ; cp. Amos 4 : 13, Sept. ; (*b*) the breath, 2 Thess. 2 : 8 ; Rev. 11 : 11 ; 13 : 15 ; cp. Job 12 : 10, Sept. ; (*c*) the immaterial, invisible part of man, Luke 8 : 55 ; Acts 7 : 59 ; 1 Cor. 5 : 5 ; Jas. 2 : 26 ; cp. Ecc. 12 : 7, Sept. ; (*d*) the disembodied (or 'unclothed,' or 'naked,' 2 Cor. 5 : 3, 4) man, Luke 24 : 37, 39 ; Heb. 12 : 23 ; 1 Pet. 4 : 6 ; (*e*) the resurrection body, 1 Cor. 15 : 45 ; 1 Tim. 3 : 16 ; 1 Pet. 3 : 18 ; (*f*) the sentient element in man, that by which he perceives, reflects, feels, desires, Matt. 5 : 3 ; 26 : 41 ; Mark 2 : 8 ; Luke 1 : 47, 80 ; Acts 17 : 16 ; 20 : 22 ; 1 Cor. 2 : 11 ; 5 : 3, 4 ; 14 : 4, 15 ; 2 Cor. 7 : 1 ; cp. Gen. 26 : 35 ; Isa. 26 : 9 ; Ezek. 13 : 3 ; Dan. 7 : 15 ; (*g*) purpose, aim, 2 Cor. 12 : 18 ; Phil. 1 : 27 ; Eph. 4 : 23 ; Rev. 19 : 10 ; cp. Ezra 1 : 5 ; Ps. 78 : 8 ; Dan. 5 : 12 ; (*h*) the equivalent of the personal pronoun, used for emphasis and effect : 1st person, 1 Cor. 16 : 18 ; cp. Gen. 6 : 3 ; 2nd person, 2 Tim. 4 : 22 ; Philm. 25 ; cp. Ps. 139 : 7 ; 3rd person, 2 Cor. 7 : 13 ; cp. Isa. 40 : 13 ; (*i*) character, Luke 1 : 17 ; Rom. 1 : 4 ; cp. Num. 14 : 24 ; (*j*) moral qualities and activities : bad, as of bondage, as of a slave, Rom. 8 : 15 ; cp. Isa. 61 : 3 ; stupor, Rom. 11 : 8 ; cp. Isa. 29 : 10 ; timidity, 2 Tim. 1 : 7 ; cp. Josh. 5 : 1 ; good, as of adoption, i.e., liberty as of a son, Rom. 8 : 15 ; cp. Ps. 51 : 12 ; meekness, 1 Cor. 4 : 21 ; cp. Prov. 16 : 19 ; faith, 2 Cor. 4 : 13 ; quietness, 1 Pet. 3 : 4 ; cp. Prov. 14 : 29 ; (*k*) the Holy Spirit, e.g., Matt. 4 : 1 (see below) ; Luke 4 : 18 ; (*l*) 'the inward man' (an expression used only of the believer, Rom. 7 : 22 ; 2 Cor. 4 : 16 ; Eph. 3 : 16) ; the new life, Rom. 8 : 4–6, 10, 16 ; Heb. 12 : 9 ; cp. Psa. 51 : 10 ; (*m*) unclean spirits, demons, Matt. 8 : 16 ; Luke 4 : 33 ; 1 Pet. 3 : 19 ; cp. 1 Sam. 18 : 10 ; (*n*) angels, Heb. 1 : 14 ;

cp. Acts 12 : 15 ; (*o*) divine gift for service, 1 Cor. 14 : 12, 32 ; (*p*) by metonymy, those who claim to be depositories of these gifts, 2 Thess. 2 : 2 ; 1 John 4 : 1–3 ; (*q*) the significance, as contrasted with the form, of words, or of a rite, John 6 : 63 ; Rom. 2 : 29 ; 7 : 6 ; 2 Cor. 3 : 6 ; (*r*) a vision, Rev. 1 : 10 ; 4 : 2 ; 17 : 3 ; 21 : 10."*

5326 AG:853C CB:1263C *Notes :* (1) For *phantasma*, rendered " spirit," Matt. 14 : 26 ; Mark 6 : 49, A.V., see APPARITION. (2) For the distinction between spirit and soul, see under SOUL, last three paragraphs.

The Holy Spirit

The Holy Spirit is spoken of under various titles in the N.T. (' Spirit ' and ' Ghost ' are renderings of the same word *pneuma ;* the advantage of the rendering ' Spirit ' is that it can always be used, whereas ' Ghost ' always requires the word ' Holy ' prefixed.) In the following list the omission of the definite article marks its omission in the original (concerning this see below) : " Spirit, Matt. 22 : 43 ; Eternal Spirit, Heb. 9 : 14 ; the Spirit, Matt. 4 : 1 ; Holy Spirit, Matt. 1 : 18 ; the Holy Spirit, Matt. 28 : 19 ; the Spirit, the Holy, Matt. 12 : 32 ; the Spirit of promise, the Holy, Eph. 1 : 13 ; Spirit of God, Rom. 8 : 9 ; Spirit of (the) living God, 2 Cor. 3 : 3 ; the Spirit of God, 1 Cor. 2 : 11 ; the Spirit of our God, 1 Cor. 6 : 11 ; the Spirit of God, the Holy, Eph. 4 : 30 ; the Spirit of glory and of God, 1 Pet. 4 : 14 ; the Spirit of Him that raised up Jesus from the dead (i.e., God), Rom. 8 : 11 ; the Spirit of your Father, Matt. 10 : 20 ; the Spirit of His Son, Gal. 4 : 6 ; Spirit of (the) Lord, Acts 8 : 39 ; the Spirit of (the) Lord, Acts 5 : 9 ; (the) Lord, (the) Spirit, 2 Cor. 3 : 18 ; the Spirit of Jesus, Acts 16 : 7 ; Spirit of Christ, Rom. 8 : 9 ; the Spirit of Jesus Christ, Phil. 1 : 19 ; Spirit of adoption, Rom. 8 : 15 ; the Spirit of truth, John 14 : 17 ; the Spirit of life, Rom. 8 : 2 ; the Spirit of grace, Heb. 10 : 29."†

The use or absence of the article in the original where the Holy Spirit is spoken of cannot always be decided by grammatical rules, nor can the presence or absence of the article alone determine whether the reference is to the Holy Spirit. Examples where the Person is meant when the article is absent are Matt. 22 : 43 (the article is used in Mark 12 : 36) ; Acts 4 : 25, R.V. (absent in some texts) ; 19 : 2, 6 ; Rom. 14 : 17 ; 1 Cor. 2 : 4 ; Gal. 5 : 25 (twice) ; 1 Pet. 1 : 2. Sometimes the absence is to be accounted for by the fact that *Pneuma* (like *Theos*) is substantially a proper name, e.g., in John 7 : 39. As a general rule the article is present where the subject of the teaching is the Personality of the Holy Spirit, e.g., John 14 : 26, where He is spoken of in distinction from the Father and the Son. See also 15 : 26 and cp. Luke 3 : 22.

In Gal. 3 : 3, in the phrase " having begun in the Spirit," it is difficult to say whether the reference is to the Holy Spirit or to the quickened spirit of the believer ; that it possibly refers to the latter is not to be

* From Notes on Thessalonians by Hogg and Vine, pp. 204, 205
† From Notes on Galatians by Hogg and Vine, p. 193.

determined by the absence of the article, but by the contrast with "the flesh;" on the other hand, the contrast may be between the Holy Spirit who in the believer sets His seal on the perfect work of Christ, and the flesh which seeks to better itself by works of its own. There is no preposition before either noun, and if the reference is to the quickened spirit it cannot be dissociated from the operation of the Holy Spirit. In Gal. 4:29 the phrase "after the Spirit" signifies 'by supernatural power,' in contrast to "after the flesh," i.e., 'by natural power,' and the reference must be to the Holy Spirit; so in 5:17.

The full title with the article before both *pneuma* and *hagios* (the "resumptive" use of the article), lit., 'the Spirit the Holy,' stresses the character of the Person, e.g., Matt. 12:32; Mark 3:29; 12:36; 13:11; Luke 2:26; 10:21 (R.V.); John 14:26; Acts 1:16; 5:3; 7:51; 10:44, 47; 13:2; 15:28; 19:6; 20:23, 28; 21:11; 28:25; Eph. 4:30; Heb. 3:7; 9:8; 10:15.

The Personality of the Spirit is emphasized at the expense of strict grammatical procedure in John 14:26; 15:26; 16:8, 13, 14, where the emphatic pronoun *ekeinos*, "He," is used of Him in the masculine, whereas the noun *pneuma* is neuter in Greek, while the corresponding word in Aramaic, the language in which our Lord probably spoke, is feminine (*rûchâ*, cf. Heb. *rûach*). The rendering "itself" in Rom. 8:16, 26, due to the Greek gender, is corrected to "Himself" in the R.V.

The subject of the Holy Spirit in the N.T. may be considered as to His Divine attributes; His distinct Personality in the Godhead; His operation in connection with the Lord Jesus in His Birth, His life, His baptism, His Death; His operations in the world; in the Church; His having been sent at Pentecost by the Father and by Christ; His operations in the individual believer; in local churches; His operations in the production of Holy Scripture; His work in the world, etc.

SPIRITUAL

A. Adjective

PNEUMATIKOS (πνευματικός) "always connotes the ideas of invisibility and of power. It does not occur in the Sept. nor in the Gospels; it is in fact an after-Pentecost word. In the N.T. it is used as follows: (*a*) the angelic hosts, lower than God but higher in the scale of being than man in his natural state, are 'spiritual hosts,' Eph. 6:12; (*b*) things that have their origin with God, and which, therefore, are in harmony with His character, as His law is, are 'spiritual,' Rom. 7:14; (*c*) 'spiritual' is prefixed to the material type in order to indicate that what the type sets forth, not the type itself, is intended, 1 Cor. 10:3, 4; (*d*) the purposes of God revealed in the gospel by the Holy Spirit, 1 Cor. 2:13a, and the words in which that revelation is expressed, are 'spiritual,' 13b, matching, or combining, spiritual things with spiritual words [or, alternatively, 'interpreting spiritual things to spiritual men,' see (*e*)

4152 AG:678D CB:1265C

below] ; 'spiritual songs' are songs of which the burden is the things revealed by the Spirit, Eph. 5 : 19 ; Col. 3 : 16 ; 'spiritual wisdom and understanding' is wisdom in, and understanding of, those things, Col. 1 : 9 ; (*e*) men in Christ who walk so as to please God are 'spiritual,' Gal. 6 : 1 ; 1 Cor. 2 : 13b [but see (*d*) above], 15 ; 3 : 1 ; 14 : 37 ; (*f*) the whole company of those who believe in Christ is a 'spiritual house,' 1 Pet. 2 : 5a ; (*g*) the blessings that accrue to regenerate men at this present time are called 'spiritualities,' Rom. 15 : 27 ; 1 Cor. 9 : 11 ; 'spiritual blessings,' Eph. 1 : 3 ; 'spiritual gifts,' Rom. 1 : 11 ; (*h*) the activities Godward of regenerate men are 'spiritual sacrifices,' 1 Pet. 2 : 5b ; their appointed activities in the churches are also called 'spiritual gifts,' lit., 'spiritualities,' 1 Cor. 12 : 1 ; 14 : 1 ; (*i*) the resurrection body of the dead in Christ is 'spiritual,' i.e., such as is suited to the heavenly environment, 1 Cor. 15 : 44 ; (*j*) all that is produced and maintained among men by the operations of the Spirit of God is 'spiritual,' 1 Cor. 15 : 46. . . .

"The spiritual man is one who walks by the Spirit both in the sense of Gal. 5 : 16 and in that of 5 : 25, and who himself manifests the fruit of the Spirit in his own ways. . . .

"According to the Scriptures, the 'spiritual' state of soul is normal for the believer, but to this state all believers do not attain, nor when it is attained is it always maintained. Thus the Apostle, in 1 Cor. 3 : 1–3, suggests a contrast between this spiritual state and that of the babe in Christ, i.e., of the man who because of immaturity and inexperience has not yet reached spirituality, and that of the man who by permitting jealousy, and the strife to which jealousy always leads, has lost it. The spiritual state is reached by diligence in the Word of God and in prayer ; it is maintained by obedience and self-judgment. Such as are led by the Spirit are spiritual, but, of course, spirituality is not a fixed or absolute condition, it admits of growth ; indeed growth in 'the grace and knowledge of our Lord and Saviour Jesus Christ,' 2 Pet. 3 : 18, is evidence of true spirituality."*

B. Adverb.

4153 PNEUMATIKŌS (πνευματικῶς), spiritually, occurs in 1 Cor. 2 : 14,
AG:679B CB:1265C with the meaning as (*j*) above, and Rev. 11 : 8, with the meaning as
in (*c*). Some mss. have it in 1 Cor. 2 : 13.¶
PNEUMA 4151 *Notes :* (1) In Rom. 8 : 6, the R.V. rightly renders the noun *pneuma*
AG:674C "(the mind) of the spirit," A.V., "spiritual (mind)." (2) In 1 Cor. 14 : 12
CB:1265B LOGIKOS the plural of *pneuma*, "spirits," R.V., marg., stands for "spiritual
3050 *gifts*" (text). (3) In 1 Pet. 2 : 2, the R.V. renders *iogikos* "spiritual."
AG:476C CB:1257A

SPIT

4429 1. PTUŌ (πτύω), to spit, occurs in Mark 7 : 33 ; 8 : 23 ; John 9 : 6.¶
AG:727D CB:— In the Sept., Numb. 12 : 14.¶

* From Notes on Galatians by Hogg and Vine, pp. 308–310.

2. EMPTUŌ (ἐμπτύω), to spit upon (*en*, in, and No. 1), occurs in 1716
Matt. 26 : 67 ; 27 : 30 ; Mark 10 : 34 ; 14 : 65 ; 15 : 19 ; Luke 18 : 32.¶ AG:257C
In the Sept., Numb. 12 : 14, in some texts ; Deut. 25 : 9.¶ CB:—

SPITEFULLY (ENTREAT)

HUBRIZŌ (ὑβρίζω), used transitively, denotes to outrage, treat 5195
insolently ; to entreat shamefully in Matt. 22 : 6, R.V. (A.V., "spite- AG:831D
fully") ; so in Luke 18 : 32, R.V. ; in Acts 14 : 5 (A.V., "use despite- CB:1251C
fully") ; in 1 Thess. 2 : 2, A.V. and R.V. ; in Luke 11 : 45, "reproachest."
See Despitefully, Entreat, Reproach, Shamefully.¶

SPLENDOR See GLORY

SPITTLE

PTUSMA (πτύσμα), akin to *ptuō*, to spit, occurs in John 9 : 6.¶ 4427 AG:727D CB:—

SPOIL (Noun and Verb), SPOILING

A. Nouns.

1. SKULON (σκῦλον), used in the plural, denotes arms stripped from 4661
a foe ; "spoils" in Luke 11 : 22.¶ AG:758B CB:—

2. AKROTHINION (ἀκροθίνιον), primarily the top of a heap (*akros*, 205
highest, top, and *this*, a heap), hence firstfruit offerings, and in war the AG:33D
choicest spoils, Heb. 7 : 4.¶ CB:—

3. HARPAGĒ (ἁρπαγή), pillage, is rendered "spoiling" in Heb. 724
10 : 34. See Extort, B, No. 1. AG:108B CB:1249B

B. Verbs.

1. DIARPAZŌ (διαρπάζω), to plunder, is found in Matt. 12 : 29, 1283
2nd part (the 1st has *harpazō*, in the best texts), lit., '(then) he will AG:188A
completely (*dia*, intensive) spoil (his house) ;' Mark 3 : 27 (twice).¶ CB:—

2. HARPAZŌ (ἁρπάζω), to seize, snatch away, is rendered "spoil" 726
in Matt. 12 : 29a (see No. 1). See Catch, No. 1. AG:109A CB:1249B

3. SULAGŌGEŌ (συλαγωγέω), to carry off as spoil, lead captive 4812
(*sulē*, spoil, *ago*, to lead), is rendered "maketh spoil of" in Col. 2 : 8, R.V. AG:776C
(A.V., "spoil"), rather 'carry you off as spoil.' The false teacher, CB:1270B
through his "philosophy and vain deceit," would carry them off as so much booty.¶

4. APEKDUŌ (ἀπεκδύω), in the Middle Voice is translated "having (-OMAI)
spoiled" in Col. 2 : 15, A.V., R.V., "having put off from Himself (the 554 AG:83C
principalities and the powers)." These are regarded by some as the CB:1236B
unsinning angels, because they are mentioned twice before in the Epistle (1 : 16 ; 2 : 10). It is also argued that the verb *apekduō*, rendered "having put off from Himself," in 2 : 15, is used in a somewhat different sense in 3 : 9. Such representations do not form a sufficiently cogent reason for regarding the principalities and the powers here mentioned as those of light, rather than those of darkness.

Others think that the reference is to the holy angels, which were in attendance at the giving of the Law (Acts 7 : 53 ; Gal. 3 : 19), and that

Christ wrought His work on the Cross, without any such attendance; or, again, that, even apart from the Law and its circumstances, the Lord stripped Himself of those who usually ministered to Him, as, e.g., in the wilderness and in the Garden of Gethsemane.

The exposition given by Lightfoot and others seems to be the right one. There is no doubt that Satan and his hosts gathered together to attack the soul of Christ, while He was enduring, in propitiatory sacrifice, the judgment due to our sins, and fulfilling the great work of redemption. There is an intimation of this in Psa. 22 : 21, " Save Me from the lion's mouth; yea, from the horns of the wild-oxen " (cp. vv. 12, 13). Doubtless the powers of darkness gathered against the Lord at that time, fiercely assaulting Him to the utmost of their power. He Himself had said, " This is your hour, and the power of darkness " (Luke 22 : 53). The metaphor of putting off from Himself these powers need not be pressed to the extent of regarding them as a garment clinging about Him. It seems to stand simply as a vivid description of His repulsion of their attack and of the power by which He completely overthrew them.

SPONGE

4699 AG:763B CB:— SPONGOS (σπόγγος) was the medium by which vinegar was carried to the mouth of Christ on the Cross, Matt. 27 : 48; Mark 15 : 36; John 19 : 29.¶

SPORTING

1792 AG:270A CB:— ENTRUPHAŌ (ἐντρυφάω) occurs in 2 Pet. 2 : 13 (R.V., " revel ").

SPOT (Noun and Verb)

A. Nouns.

4696 AG:762D CB:— 1. SPILOS (σπῖλος), a spot or stain, is used metaphorically (*a*) of moral blemish, Eph. 5 : 27; (*b*) of lascivious and riotous persons, 2 Pet. 2 : 13.¶

4694 AG:762C CB:— 2. SPILAS (σπιλάς) is rendered " spots " in Jude 12, A.V.: see ROCK, No. 2.

B. Verb.

4695 AG:762D CB:— SPILOŌ (σπιλόω), akin to A, No. 1, is used in Jude 23, in the clause " hating even the garment spotted by the flesh," the garment representing that which, being brought into contact with the polluting element of the flesh, becomes defiled: see CLOTHING, No. 3 (last par.). See DEFILE, No. 4.

C. Adjective.

784 AG:117A CB:1238A ASPILOS (ἄσπιλος), unspotted, unstained (*a*, negative, and A), is used of a lamb, 1 Pet. 1 : 19; metaphorically, of keeping a commandment without alteration and in the fulfilment of it, 1 Tim. 6 : 14; of the believer in regard to the world, Jas. 1 : 27, and free from all defilement in the sight of God, 2 Pet. 3 : 14.¶

299 AG:47D CB:1234C *Note*: For *amōmos*, in Heb. 9 : 14, A.V., see BLEMISH, B.

SPREAD

1. STRŌNNUŌ or STRŌNNUMI (στρωννύω), to spread, is so rendered 4766
in Matt. 21 : 8, R.V., twice ; Mark 11 : 8, R.V., once. See FURNISH. AG:771C CB:—

2. HUPOSTRŌNNUŌ (ὑποστρωννύω), to spread under (*hupo*), of 5291 (-UMI)
clothes, is used in Luke 19 : 36.¶ AG:847C CB:—

3. DIANEMŌ (διανέμω), to distribute, is used in the Passive Voice 1268
in Acts 4 : 17, "spread," lit., 'be spread about' (*dia*).¶ In the Sept., AG:186D CB:—
Deut. 29 : 26, to assign or divide (concerning the worship of other gods).¶

4. DIAPHERŌ (διαφέρω), to carry about, spread abroad: see 1308
PUBLISH, No. 2 ; for other meanings of the word see BETTER (be), No. 1. AG:190B CB:—

5. EKPETANNUMI (ἐκπετάννυμι), to spread out (as a sail), is rendered 1600
"did I spread out" in Rom. 10 : 21, R.V. (A.V., "I have stretched AG:243D CB:—
forth").¶

Notes: (1) In Mark 1 : 28 and 1 Thess. 1 : 8, A.V., *exerchomai*, to go EXERCHOMAI 1831
out or forth (R.V.), is rendered to spread abroad. (2) In Mark 6 : 14, AG:274B
A.V., *ginomai*, to become, with *phaneros*, manifest, is translated "had CB:1247C
spread abroad" (R.V., "had become known"). (3) In 2 Cor. 8 : 18, PHANEROS 5318
the R.V. "*is spread*" (A.V., "*is*") represents nothing in the original. AG:852B
(4) For R.V., "spread His tabernacle over," Rev. 7 : 15, see DWELL, CB:1263C
No. 9. (5) For Mark 1 : 45, see BLAZE ABROAD.

SPRING (Noun and Verb)

GINOMAI 1096 AG:158A CB:1248B

A. Verbs.

1. GINOMAI (γίνομαι), to become, is used in the best texts in GENNAō
Heb. 11 : 12, "sprang" (some have *gennaō*, in the Passive Voice, rendered 1080 AG:155B
in the same way). CB:1248A

2. ANATELLŌ (ἀνατέλλω), to arise, is rendered by the verb to spring, 393
or spring up, in Matt. 4 : 16 and Heb. 7 : 14. See ARISE, No. 9. AG:62A CB:1235B

3. EXANATELLŌ (ἐξανατέλλω), *ek* or *ex*, out, and No. 2, is used of 1816
the springing up of seeds, Matt. 13 : 5 ; Mark 4 : 5 (No. 7 in ver. 8).¶ AG:272D CB:—

4. PHUŌ (φύω), used transitively, to bring forth, produce, denotes, 5453
in the Passive Voice, to spring up, grow, of seed, Luke 8 : 6, 8, A.V., AG:870B
"was sprung up" and "sprang up" (R.V., "grew") ; in the Active CB:1264C
Voice, intransitively, in Heb. 12 : 15, of a root of bitterness. See GROW.¶

5. SUMPHUŌ (συμφύω), to cause to grow together (*sun*, with, and 4855
No. 4), occurs in Luke 8 : 7, R.V., "grew with," A.V., "sprang up AG:780D CB:—
with."¶

6. BLASTANŌ (βλαστάνω), to sprout, is rendered to spring up in 985
Matt. 13 : 26, of tare-blades, and Mark 4 : 27, of seed. See BRING, A, AG:142B CB:1239A
No. 26, BUD.

7. ANABAINŌ (ἀναβαίνω), to go up, is rendered "sprang up" in 305 AG:50A
Matt. 13 : 7, A.V., of thorns, and Mark 4 : 8, of seed (R.V., "grew up"). CB:1235A
See GROW, No. 4. 242 AG:39D

8. HALLOMAI (ἅλλομαι), to leap, spring, is rendered "springing CB:1249A

up," of well-water, in John 4 : 14, figurative of the Holy Spirit in the believer. See LEAP.

1530 AG:233C CB:— 9. EISPĒDAŌ (εἰσπηδάω), to spring or leap in, occurs in Acts 16 : 29, "sprang in."¶ In the Sept., Amos 5 : 19.¶

— AG:243D CB:— 10. EKPĒDAŌ (ἐκπηδάω), to spring forth, occurs in Acts 14 : 14, in the best texts. See RUN, Note (4).

B. Noun.

4077 AG:655D CB:1263A PĒGĒ (πηγή) is rendered "springs" in 2 Pet. 2 : 17, R.V.: see FOUNTAIN.

1920 AG:290D CB:— *Note:* For *epiginomai*, Acts 28 : 13, see BLOW (verb).

SPRINKLE, SPRINKLING

A. Verb.

4472 AG:734B CB:1268A RHANTIZŌ (ῥαντίζω), to sprinkle (a later form of *rhainō*), is used in the Active Voice in Heb. 9 : 13, of sprinkling with blood the unclean, a token of the efficacy of the expiatory sacrifice of Christ, His blood signifying the giving up of His life in the shedding of His blood (cp. 9 : 22) under Divine judgment upon sin (the voluntary act to be distinguished from that which took place after His death in the piercing of His side); so again in vv. 19, 21 (see B); in Heb. 10 : 22, Passive Voice, of the purging (on the ground of the same efficacy) of the hearts of believers from an evil conscience. This application of the blood of Christ is necessary for believers, in respect of their committal of sins, which on that ground receive forgiveness, 1 John 1 : 9. In Mark 7 : 4, the verb is found in the Middle Voice "in some ancient authorities" (R.V. marg.) instead of *baptizō*. In Rev. 19 : 13, the R.V., "sprinkled" follows those texts which have *rhantizō* (marg., "some anc. auth. read 'dipped in,'" *baptō*; so Nestle's text).¶ This requires mention as a variant text in Rev. 19 : 13 under DIP.

B. Nouns.

4473 AG:734B CB:1268A 1. RHANTISMOS (ῥαντισμός), sprinkling, akin to A, is used of the sprinkling of the blood of Christ, in Heb. 12 : 24 and 1 Pet. 1 : 2, an allusion to the use of the blood of sacrifices, appointed for Israel, typical of the sacrifice of Christ (see under A).¶

4378 AG:720C CB:1267A 2. PROSCHUSIS (πρόσχυσις), a pouring or sprinkling upon, occurs in Heb. 11 : 28, of the sprinkling of the blood of the Passover lamb.¶

For SPUE see SPEW

SPY (Noun and Verb)

A. Nouns.

1455 AG:215B CB:— 1. ENKATHETOS (ἐγκάθετος), an adjective denoting suborned to lie in wait (*en*, in, *kathiēmi*, to send down), is used as a noun in Luke 20 : 20, "spies."¶ In the Sept., Job. 19 : 12; 31 : 9.¶

2. KATASKOPOS (κατάσκοπος) denotes a spy (*kata*, down, signifying 2685
closely, and *skopeō*, to view), Heb. 11 : 31.¶ AG:418D CB:1254B

B. Verb.

KATASKOPEŌ (κατασκοπέω), to view closely (akin to A, No. 2), 2684
spy out, search out with a view to overthrowing, is used in Gal. 2 : 4.¶ AG:418D CB:—
In the Sept., 2 Sam. 10 : 3 ; 1 Chron. 19 : 3.¶

SQUALL See **STORM**

SQUANDER See **WASTE**

For STABLISH see ESTABLISH

STAFF, STAVES

1. RHABDOS (ῥάβδος), rendered " staff " or " staves " in Matt. 4464
10 : 10, parallel passages, and Heb. 11 : 21 : see ROD. AG:733B CB:1268A

2. XULON (ξύλον), wood, then, anything made of wood, e.g., a 3586
cudgel or staff, is rendered " staves " in Matt. 26 : 47, 55 and parallel AG:549A CB:1273B
passages. See STOCKS, TREE, WOOD.

For STAGGER see WAVER

STAIR

ANABATHMOS (ἀναβαθμός), an ascent (akin to *anabainō*, to go up), 304
denotes a flight of stairs, Acts 21 : 35, 40. These were probably the steps AG:50A CB:—
leading down from the castle of Antonia to the Temple. (See Josephus,
B.J., v., 5, 8.)¶ In the Sept., it is used, e.g., in the titles of the Songs
of Ascents, Psa. 120–134.

For STALL see MANGER

STANCH

HISTĒMI (ἵστημι), transitively, to cause to stand, is used intransitively 2476
(to stand still) in Luke 8 : 44, translated " stanched." See STAND. AG:381D CB:1250C

STAND (Noun and Verb), STANDING, STOOD

A. Noun.

LUCHNIA (λυχνία), a lampstand, is translated " stand " in Matt. 3087
5 : 15 and parallel passages (A.V., " candlestick "). See LAMPSTAND. AG:483A CB:1257B

B. Verbs.

1. HISTĒMI (ἵστημι), (*a*) transitively, denotes to cause to stand, 2476
to set ; in the Passive Voice, to be made to stand, e.g., Matt. 2 : 9, lit., AG:381D CB:1250C
' was made to stand ; ' so Luke 11 : 18 ; 19 : 8 (Col. 4 : 12 in some mss.) ; in Rev. 13 : 1 the R.V. follows the best texts, " he stood " (not as A.V., " I stood ") ; the reference is to the Dragon. In the Middle Voice, to take one's stand, place oneself, e.g., Rev. 18 : 15 ; (*b*) intransitively, in the 2nd aorist and perfect Active, to stand, stand by, stand still, e.g., Matt. 6 : 5 ; 20 : 32, " stood still ; " in Luke 6 : 8, " stand forth " and " stood forth ; " metaphorically, to stand firm, John 8 : 44 (negatively),

in the truth (see No. 7); Rom. 5 : 2, in grace; 1 Cor. 15 : 1, in the
gospel; Rom. 11 : 20, "by thy faith," R.V.; 2 Cor. 1 : 24, "by faith"
(marg., "by your faith"); of stedfastness, 1 Cor. 7 : 37; Eph. 6 : 11,
13, 14; Col. 4 : 12 [some mss. have the Passive, see (*a*)]. See APPOINT,
ESTABLISH, SET.

450 AG:70A 2. ANISTĒMI (ἀνίστημι), to raise, intransitively, to rise, is translated
CB:— to stand up in Matt. 12 : 41, R.V.; Mark 14 : 60; Luke 4 : 16; 10 : 25;
Acts 1 : 15; 5 : 34; 10 : 26; 11 : 28; 13 : 16; in 14 : 10, "stand
upright." See ARISE, No. 1.

2186 AG:330D 3. EPHISTĒMI (ἐφίστημι) (*epi*, upon, and No. 1), used intransitively,
CB:— denotes to stand upon or by, be present, Luke 2 : 9 and Acts 12 : 7, "stood
by," R.V. (A.V., "came upon"); Luke 4 : 39, "stood over;" 24 : 4 and
Acts 23 : 11, "stood by;" Acts 10 : 17, "stood;" 22 : 13, "standing
by (me)," R.V.; so ver. 20, A.V. and R.V. See ASSAULT, COME, No. 27,
HAND (AT), B, Note (2), INSTANT, PRESENT.

3936 AG:627C 4. PARISTĒMI (παρίστημι), intransitively, denotes to stand by or
CB:1262B beside (*para*, by, and No. 1), Mark 14 : 47, 69, 70; 15 : 35, 39 (R.V.,
"stood by"); Luke 19 : 24; John 18 : 22; 19 : 26; Acts 1 : 10; 9 : 39;
23 : 2, 4; 27 : 23; in 27 : 24, "stand before;" in 4 : 10, "doth . . .
stand here;" in Luke 1 : 19, "stand;" Rom. 14 : 10, "we shall . . .
stand before" (Middle Voice); 2 Tim. 4 : 17, R.V., "stood by" (A.V.,
". . . with"). See COMMEND, No. 4.

4026 AG:647C 5. PERIISTĒMI (περιίστημι), intransitively, to stand around (*peri*), is
CB:— so used in John 11 : 42; Acts 25 : 7. See AVOID, No. 4.

4921 AG:790C 6. SUNISTĒMI (συνίστημι), intransitively, denotes to stand with
CB:1270C (*sun*), Luke 9 : 32; for 2 Pet. 3 : 5, A.V., "standing," see COMPACTED,
No. 1: for other meanings see APPROVE, A, No. 2.

4739 AG:767D 7. STĒKŌ (στήκω), a late present tense from *hestēka*, the perfect of
CB:1270A *histēmi*, is used (*a*) literally, Mark 3 : 31; 11 : 25; John 1 : 26, in the
best texts (in some texts Rev. 12 : 4); (*b*) figuratively, Rom. 14 : 4,
where the context indicates the meaning 'standeth upright' rather than
that of acquittal; of standing fast, 1 Cor. 16 : 13, "in the faith," i.e., by
adherence to it; Gal. 5 : 1, in freedom from legal bondage; Phil. 1 : 27,
MENō "in one spirit;" Phil. 4 : 1 and 1 Thess. 3 : 8, "in the Lord," i.e., in
3306 AG:503C the willing subjection to His authority; 2 Thess. 2 : 15, in the Apostle's
CB:1258B teaching; some mss. have it in John 8 : 44, the most authentic have
KUKLOō 2944 *histēmi*, R.V., "stood" (A.V., "abode").¶

AG:456D 8. MENŌ (μένω), to abide, remain, is rendered "might stand," in Rom.
EGEIRō 1453 9 : 11, of the purpose of God, i.e., might abide for the permanent
AG:214C CB:1242C recognition of its true character. See ABIDE, No. 1.

PARAGINOMAI 3854 9. KUKLOŌ (κυκλόω), "stood round about," Acts 14 : 20: see
AG:613C COMPASS, No. 2.

SUMPARAGINOMAI *Notes*: (1) In Mark 3 : 3, *egeirō*, to raise, followed by the phrase
4836 *eis to meson*, 'into the midst,' is translated "stand forth." (2) In 2 Tim.
AG:779A 4 : 16, A.V., *paraginomai* (in some texts, *sumparaginomai*), to come up

to assist, is rendered " stood with (me)," R.V., " took (my) part." (3) In STASIS
Heb. 9 : 8, R.V., " is . . . standing " (A.V., " was . . . standing ") 4714 AG:764C
represents the phrase *echō*, to have, *stasis*, a standing, lit., ' has a standing.' CB:1270A
(4) For " stand . . . in jeopardy " see DANGER. (HUMAN) STANDARDS See FLESH

STAR

1. ASTĒR (ἀστήρ), a star, Matt. 2 : 2–10 ; 24 : 29 ; Mk. 13 : 25 ; 1 Cor. 792
15 : 41 ; Rev. 6 : 13 ; 8 : 10–12 ; 9 : 1 ; 12 : 1, 4, is used metaphorically, (*a*) of AG:117C CB:1238A
Christ, as " the morning star," figurative of the approach of the day when He will appear as the " sun of righteousness," to govern the earth in peace, an event to be preceded by the Rapture of the Church, Rev. 2 : 28 ; 22 : 16, the promise of the former to the overcomer being suggestive of some special personal interest in Himself and His authority ; (*b*) of the angels of the seven churches, Rev. 1 : 16, 20 ; 2 : 1 ; 3 : 1 ; (*c*) of certain false teachers, described as " wandering stars," Jude 13, as if the stars, intended for light and guidance, became the means of deceit by irregular movements.¶

2. ASTRON (ἄστρον), practically the same as No. 1, is used (*a*) in the 798
sing. in Acts 7 : 43, " the star of the god Rephan," R.V., the symbol or AG:118B CB:1238A
" figure," probably of Saturn, worshipped as a god, apparently the same as Chiun in Amos 5 : 26 (Rephan being the Egyptian deity corresponding
to Saturn, Chiun the Assyrian) ; (*b*) in the plur., Luke 21 : 25 ; Acts START See BEGIN, GO
27 : 20 ; Heb. 11 : 12.¶

For STATE see ESTATE, Notes STATEMENT See WORD

For STATURE see AGE, A, No. 3

For STAVES see STAFF

STAY

1. KATECHŌ (κατέχω), to hold fast, hold back, is used in the sense 2722
of detaining in Luke 4 : 42, " would have stayed (Him)," R.V. See AG:422C CB:1254B
HOLD.

2. EPECHŌ (ἐπέχω) has the meaning to wait in a place, to stay, in 1907 AG:285C
Acts 19 : 22. See HEED, HOLD, MARK. CB:—

3. KŌLUŌ (κωλύω), to hinder, is rendered " stayed " in Acts 27 : 43, 2967
R.V. (A.V., " kept ") ; so in 2 Pet. 2 : 16, R.V. (A.V., " forbad "). See AG:461B CB:1255C
HINDER.

For STEADFAST see STEDFAST

STEAL

KLEPTŌ (κλέπτω), to steal, akin to *kleptēs*, a thief (cp. Eng., klepto- 2813 AG:434C
mania), occurs in Matt. 6 : 19, 20 ; 19 : 18 ; 27 : 64 ; 28 : 13 ; Mark CB:1255B

10 : 19; Luke 18 : 20; John 10 : 10; Rom. 2 : 21 (twice); 13 : 9; Eph. 4 : 28 (twice).¶

STEDFAST, STEDFASTLY, STEDFASTNESS

A. Adjectives.

949 1. BEBAIOS (βέβαιος), firm, secure (akin to *bainō*, to go), is translated
AG:138B "stedfast" in 2 Cor. 1 : 7; Heb. 2 : 2; 3 : 14, A.V. (R.V., "firm");
CB:1239A 6 : 19. See FIRM, FORCE, SURE.

1476 2. HEDRAIOS (ἑδραῖος) primarily denotes seated (*hedra*, a seat);
AG:217D hence, stedfast, metaphorical of moral fixity, 1 Cor. 7 : 37; 15 : 58;
CB:1249C Col. 1 : 23, R.V. (A.V., "settled").¶

4731 3. STEREOS (στερεός), firm, is rendered "stedfast" in 1 Pet. 5 : 9.
AG:766D See FIRM, No. 2.
CB:1270A

B. Nouns.

4733 1. STEREŌMA (στερέωμα), primarily a support, foundation, denotes
AG:766D strength, stedfastness, Col. 2 : 5.¶ In the Sept., in Gen. 1 : 6, and
CB:— Ezek. 1 : 22, it is used of the firmament, which was believed to be a solid canopy. The corresponding Heb. word *rāqîa'* means 'expanse,' from *rāqa'*, to spread out.

4740 2. STĒRIGMOS (στηριγμός), a setting firmly, supporting, then
AG:768A fixedness, stedfastness (akin to *stērizō*, to establish), is used in 2 Pet.
CB:— 3 : 17.¶

Note: For STEDFASTLY see BEHOLD, No. 10, CONTINUE, No. 9, FASTEN, No. 1, LOOK, No. 15, SET, No. 19.

STEEP

2911
AG:450B KRĒMNOS (κρημνός), a steep bank (akin to *kremannumi*, to hang),
CB:— occurs in Matt. 8 : 32; Mark 5 : 13; Luke 8 : 33, R.V., "the steep"
KREMANNUMI
2910 (A.V., "a steep place").¶ In the Sept., 2 Chron. 25 : 12.¶
AG:450A
CB:1256A

For STEERSMAN see GOVERNOR, B, Note

STEP (Noun and Verb)

A. Noun.

2487 ICHNOS (ἴχνος), a footstep, a track, is used metaphorically of the
AG:384B steps (*a*) of Christ's conduct, 1 Pet. 2 : 21; (*b*) of Abraham's faith, Rom.
CB:— 4 : 12; (*c*) of identical conduct in carrying on the work of the Gospel, 2 Cor. 12 : 18.¶

B. Verb.

2597 KATABAINŌ (καταβαίνω), to go, or come, down, is translated
AG:408B
CB:1253C "steppeth down" in John 5 : 7. See COME, No. 19.

Note: Many ancient authorities have the passage in the A.V. in
1684
AG:254A John 5 : 4, which contains *embainō*, rendered "stepped in." See COME,
CB:— No. 21.

STERN

PRUMNA (πρύμνα), the feminine form of the adjective *prumnos*, 4403
hindmost, is rendered "stern" in Acts 27 : 29; and in the R.V. in AG:724D
ver. 41 and Mark 4 : 38. See PART, A, Note (2).¶ CB:—

STEWARD, STEWARDSHIP

A. Nouns.

1. OIKONOMOS (οἰκονόμος) primarily denoted the manager of a 3623
household or estate (*oikos*, a house, *nemō*, to arrange), a steward (such AG:560A
were usually slaves or freedmen), Luke 12 : 42; 16 : 1, 3, 8; 1 Cor. 4 : 2; CB:1260B
Gal. 4 : 2, R.V. (A.V., "governors"); in Rom. 16 : 23, the "treasurer" (R.V.) of a city (see CHAMBERLAIN, Note); it is used metaphorically, in the wider sense, of a steward in general, (*a*) of preachers of the Gospel and teachers of the Word of God, 1 Cor. 4 : 1; (*b*) of elders or bishops in churches, Tit. 1 : 7; (*c*) of believers generally, 1 Pet. 4 : 10.¶

2. EPITROPOS (ἐπίτροπος) is rendered "steward" in Matt. 20 : 8; 2012
Luke 8 : 3: see GUARDIAN. AG:303D
CB:1246B

3. OIKONOMIA (οἰκονομία) is rendered "stewardship" in Luke 3622
16 : 2, 3, 4, and in the R.V. in 1 Cor. 9 : 17: see DISPENSATION. AG:559C
CB:1260B

B. Verb.

OIKONOMEŌ (οἰκονομέω), akin to A, Nos. 1 and 3, signifies to be a 3621
house steward, Luke 16 : 2.¶ In the Sept., Psa. 112 : 5.¶ AG:559C
CB:1260B

STICK

PHRUGANON (φρύγανον) denotes a dry stick (from *phrugō*, to parch); 5434
in the plural, brushwood, Acts 28 : 3.¶ AG:867B
CB:—

STICK FAST

EREIDŌ (ἐρείδω), primarily to prop, fix firmly, is used intransitively 2043
in Acts 27 : 41 of a ship driving ashore, R.V., "struck."¶ AG:308D
CB:—

STIFFNECKED

SKLĒROTRACHĒLOS (σκληροτράχηλος), from *sklēros*, harsh, hard, 4644
trachēlos, a neck, is used metaphorically in Acts 7 : 51.¶ AG:756B
CB:1269A

STILL (Verb)

PHIMOŌ (φιμόω), in the Passive Voice, is rendered "be still" in 5392
Mark 4 : 39: see MUZZLE. AG:861D
CB:—

STILL (Adverb)

ETI (ἔτι), yet, as yet, still, is translated "still" in the R.V. in 1 Cor. 2089
12 : 31; 2 Cor. 1 : 10; Gal. 1 : 10 and 5 : 11; A.V. and R.V. in Rev. AG:315C CB:1247A
22 : 11 (four times), where the word indicates the permanent character, condition and destiny of the unrighteous and the filthy, the righteous

and the holy (for the verbs see the R.V.); in John 11 : 30, the best mss. have the word; so R.V. (A.V. omits).

Note: For combinations see ABIDE, IGNORANCE, B, No. 1, STAND.

For STING see GOAD

STINK

3605 AG:555C OZŌ (ὄζω), to emit a smell (cp. Eng., ozone), occurs in John 11 : 39.¶
CB:— In the Sept., Ex. 8 : 14.¶

STIR, STIR UP (Noun and Verb)

A. Noun.

5017 AG:805C TARACHOS (τάραχος), akin to *tarachē*, trouble, and *tarassō*, to trouble,
CB:1271A is rendered "stir" in Acts 12 : 18; 19 : 23.¶

B. Verbs.

329 AG:54A 1. ANAZŌPUREŌ (ἀναζωπυρέω) denotes to kindle afresh, or keep
CB:— in full flame (*ana*, up, or again, *zōos*, alive, *pur*, fire), and is used metaphorically in 2 Tim. 1 : 6, where "the gift of God" is regarded as a fire capable of dying out through neglect.¶ The verb was in common use in the vernacular of the time.

1892 AG:284A 2. EPEGEIRŌ (ἐπεγείρω), "stirred up" in Acts 14 : 2. See RAISE.

1326 3. DIEGEIRŌ (διεγείρω), "stir up" in 2 Pet. 1 : 13; 3 : 1: see
AG:193D ARISE, No. 4.

4579 AG:746C 4. SEIŌ (σείω), to move to and fro, is rendered "was stirred" in
CB:1268C Matt. 21 : 10, R.V. (A.V., "was moved"). See MOVE, QUAKE, SHAKE.

383 AG:60A 5. ANASEIŌ (ἀνασείω) primarily denotes to shake back or out, move
CB:1235B to and fro; then, to stir up, used metaphorically in Mark 15 : 11, R.V.,
4531 "stirred . . . up" (A.V., "moved"), and Luke 3 : 14; 23 : 5.¶

AG:740C CB:1268B 6. SALEUŌ (σαλεύω), "stirred up" in Acts 17 : 13: see SHAKE.

3951 7. PAROTRUNŌ (παροτρύνω), from *para*, used intensively, beyond
AG:629D CB:— measure, and *otrunō*, to urge on, rouse, occurs in Acts 13 : 50, "stirred
4787 up."¶

AG:773D 8. SUNKINEŌ (συγκινέω), to move together (*sun*, together, *kineō*, to
CB:— 4797 move), to stir up, excite, is used metaphorically in Acts 6 : 12.¶

AG:775A 9. SUNCHEŌ (συγχέω), to pour together, is used metaphorically
CB:— in Acts 21 : 27, "stirred up." See CONFOUND, B, No. 1.

3947 AG:629C 10. PAROXUNŌ (παροξύνω), "stirred" in Acts 17 : 16: see
CB:1262C PROVOKE, No. 2.

2042 AG:308D 11. ERETHIZŌ (ἐρεθίζω), "hath stirred" in 2 Cor. 9 : 2, R.V.
CB:— See PROVOKE, No. 3.

387 AG:61A 12. ANASTATOŌ (ἀναστατόω), to excite, unsettle (akin to *anistēmi*,
CB:— to raise up, and *anastasis*, a raising), is used (*a*) of stirring up to sedition, and tumult, Acts 17 : 6, "turned . . . upside down;" 21 : 38, R.V., "stirred up to sedition," A.V., "madest an uproar;" (*b*) to upset by false teaching, Gal. 5 : 12, R.V., "unsettle" (A.V., "trouble").¶

Note: In Acts 24 : 12, *poieō*, to make, with *epistasis*, a stopping (in some texts *episustasis*), signifies to collect (a crowd), A.V., " raising up (the people)," R.V., " stirring up (a crowd)." See Come, Note (9). EPISTASIS — AG:300B CB:— EPISUSTASIS 1999 AG:301D CB:1246A

For STOCK see KIND

STOCKS

XULON (ξύλον), wood, is used of stocks in Acts 16 : 24. See Staff, Tree, Wood. 3586 AG:549A CB:1273B

STOMACH

STOMACHOS (στόμαχος), properly a mouth, an opening, akin to *stoma*, a mouth, denotes the stomach in 1 Tim. 5 : 23.¶ 4751 AG:770B CB:—

STOMACH See BELLY

STONE (Noun, Verb, and Adjective)

A. Nouns.

1. LITHOS (λίθος) is used (I) literally, of (*a*) the stones of the ground, e.g., Matt. 4 : 3, 6 ; 7 : 9 ; (*b*) tombstones, e.g., Matt. 27 : 60, 66 ; (*c*) building stones, e.g., Matt. 21 : 42 ; (*d*) a millstone, Luke 17 : 2 ; cp. Rev. 18 : 21 (see Millstone) ; (*e*) the tables (or tablets) of the Law, 2 Cor. 3 : 7 ; (*f*) idol images, Acts 17 : 29 ; (*g*) the treasures of commercial Babylon, Rev. 18 : 12, 16 ; (II) metaphorically, of (*a*) Christ, Rom. 9 : 33 ; 1 Pet. 2 : 4, 6, 8 ; (*b*) believers, 1 Pet. 2 : 5 ; (*c*) spiritual edification by Scriptural teaching, 1 Cor. 3 : 12 ; (*d*) the adornment of the foundations of the wall of the spiritual and heavenly Jerusalem, Rev. 21 : 19 ; (*e*) the adornment of the seven angels in Rev. 15 : 6, R.V. (so the best texts ; some have *linon*, linen, A.V.) ; (*f*) the adornment of religious Babylon, Rev. 17 : 4 ; (III) figuratively, of Christ, Rev. 4 : 3 ; 21 : 11, where " light " stands for ' Light-giver ' (*phōstēr*). 3037 AG:474B CB:1257A

2. PSĒPHOS (ψῆφος), a smooth stone, a pebble, worn smooth as by water, or polished (akin to *psaō*, to rub), denotes (*a*) by metonymy, a vote (from the use of pebbles for this purpose ; cp. *psēphizō*, to count), Acts 26 : 10, R.V. (A.V., " voice ") ; (*b*) a (white) stone to be given to the overcomer in the church at Pergamum, Rev. 2 : 17 (twice) ; a white stone was often used in the social life and judicial customs of the ancients ; festal days were noted by a white stone, days of calamity by a black ; in the courts a white stone indicated acquittal, a black condemnation. A host's appreciation of a special guest was indicated by a white stone with the name or a message written on it ; this is probably the allusion here.¶ 5586 AG:892D CB:1267C

Note: In John 1 : 42 *petros* stands for the proper name, Peter, as the R.V. (A.V., " a stone " ; marg., " Peter ") ; *petros* denotes a piece of a rock, a detached stone or boulder, in contrast to *petra*, a mass of rock. See Rock. PETROS 4074 AG:654D CB:1263C PETRA 4073 AG:654A CB:1263C

B. Verbs.

3036 AG:474A CB:— 1. LITHOBOLEŌ (λιθοβολέω), to pelt with stones (A, No. 1, and *ballō*, to throw), to stone to death, occurs in Matt. 21 : 35 ; 23 : 37 ; Luke 13 : 34 (John 8 : 5 in some mss. : see No. 2) ; Acts 7 : 58, 59 ; 14 : 5 ; Heb. 12 : 20.¶

3034 AG:473D CB:— 2. LITHAZŌ (λιθάζω), to stone, virtually equivalent to No. 1, but not stressing the casting, occurs in John 8 : 5 (in the most authentic mss.) ; 10 : 31–33 ; 11 : 8 ; Acts 5 : 26 ; 14 : 19 ; 2 Cor. 11 : 25 ; Heb. 11 : 37.¶

2642 AG:413D CB:— 3. KATALITHAZŌ (καταλιθάζω), an intensive form of No. 2, to cast stones at, occurs in Luke 20 : 6.¶

C. Adjective.

3035 AG:474A CB:1257A LITHINOS (λίθινος), of stone (akin to A, No. 1), occurs in John 2 : 6 ; 2 Cor. 3 : 3 ; Rev. 9 : 20.¶

For STONY see ROCKY

STOOP

2955 AG:458A CB:— 1. KUPTŌ (κύπτω), to bow the head, stoop down, occurs in Mark 1 : 7 ; John 8 : 6, 8.¶

3879 AG:619B CB:— 2. PARAKUPTŌ (παρακύπτω) is rendered to stoop down in Luke 24 : 12 ; John 20 : 5, 11, R.V., " stooping and looking in " : see LOOK, No. 10.

STOP

5420 AG:865C CB:1264B 1. PHRASSŌ (φράσσω), to fence in (akin to *phragmos*, a fence), close, stop, is used (*a*) metaphorically, in Rom. 3 : 19, of preventing all excuse from Jew and Gentile, as sinners ; in 2 Cor. 11 : 10, lit., ' this boasting shall not be stopped to me ; ' Passive Voice in both ; (*b*) physically, of the mouths of lions, Heb. 11 : 33 (Active Voice).¶

4912 AG:789A CB:1270C 2. SUNECHŌ (συνέχω), to hold together, is rendered " stopped (their ears) " in Acts 7 : 57. See HOLD.

1993 AG:301A CB:— 3. EPISTOMIZŌ (ἐπιστομίζω), to stop the mouth, Tit. 1 : 11 : see MOUTH, B.¶

STORE (Verb)

2343 AG:361B CB:1272B 1. THĒSAURIZŌ (θησαυρίζω), to lay up, store up, is rendered " in store " (lit., ' storing '), with a view to help a special case of need, 1 Cor. 16 : 2 ; said of the heavens and earth in 2 Pet. 3 : 7, R.V., " have been stored up (for fire)," marg., " stored (with fire)," A.V., " kept in store (reserved unto fire)." See LAY, No. 17, TREASURE.

597 AG:91B CB:— 2. APOTHĒSAURIZŌ (ἀποθησαυρίζω), to treasure up, store away (*apo*), is used in 1 Tim. 6 : 19, of " laying up in store " a good foundation for the hereafter by being rich in good works.¶

For STORE-HOUSE, STORE-CHAMBER, see CHAMBER

STORM

LAILAPS (λαῖλαψ), a hurricane, whirlwind, is rendered " storm " in Mark 4 : 37 ; Luke 8 : 23 ; 2 Pet. 2 : 17, R.V. (A.V.. " tempest "). See TEMPEST.¶ 2978 AG:462D CB:1256B

STORY

TRISTEGOS (τρίστεγος), an adjective denoting of three stories (*treis*, three, *stegē*, a roof), occurs in Acts 20 : 9 (with *oikēma*, a dwelling, understood), R.V., " the third story " (A.V., " the third loft ").¶ 5152 (-ON) AG:826C CB:—

STRAIGHT

A. Adjectives.

1. EUTHUS (εὐθύς), direct, straight, right, is translated " straight," figuratively, of the paths of the Lord, Matt. 3 : 3 ; Mark 1 : 3 ; Luke 3 : 4 ; in ver. 5 of the rectification of the crooked, with reference to moral transformation ; in Acts 9 : 11, the name of a street in Damascus, still one of the principal thoroughfares. See RIGHT. 2117 AG:321A CB:1247B

2. ORTHOS (ὀρθός), used of height, denotes " upright," Acts 14 : 10 ; of line of direction, figuratively, said of paths of righteousness, Heb. 12 : 13.¶ 3717 AG:580B CB:1261B

B. Verbs.

1. EUTHUNŌ (εὐθύνω), akin to A, No. 1, is used of the directing of a ship by the steersman, Jas. 3 : 4 (see GOVERNOR, B, Note) ; metaphorically, of making straight the way of the Lord, John 1 : 23.¶ 2116 AG:320D CB:—

2. ANORTHOŌ (ἀνορθόω), to set up, make straight : see LIFT, No. 6. 461 AG:72C CB:—

For STRAIGHT COURSE, see COURSE, B, Note (1)

For STRAIGHTWAY see FORTHWITH, Nos. 1, 2, 3, and IMMEDIATELY, No. 1

STRAIN OUT

DIÜLIZŌ (διϋλίζω), primarily denotes to strain thoroughly (*dia*, through, intensive, *hulizō*, to strain), then, to strain out, as through a sieve or strainer, as in the case of wine, so as to remove the unclean midge, Matt. 23 : 24, R.V. (A.V., " strain at ").¶ In the Sept., Amos 6 : 6.¶ 1368 AG:200B CB:—

For the Adjective STRAIT see NARROW

STRAIT (be in a), STRAITENED

1. SUNECHŌ (συνέχω), to hold together, constrain, is translated " I am in a strait " in Phil. 1 : 23 (Passive Voice), i.e., being restricted on both sides, under a pressure which prevents a definite choice ; so in Luke 12 : 50, " (how) am I straitened," i.e., pressed in. See CONSTRAIN, A, No. 3. 4912 AG:789A CB:1270C

4729 AG:766C 2. STENOCHŌREŌ (στενοχωρέω), to be pressed for room (*stenos*,
CB:1270A narrow, *chōros*, a space), is rendered to be straitened in 2 Cor. 4:8, R.V.
(A.V., "distressed"); 6:12 (twice). See ANGUISH, B, No. 1.¶

2346 AG:362A 3. THLIBŌ (θλίβω), for which see AFFLICT, No. 4, is used in the perfect
CB:1272B participle Passive of a narrowed way, in Matt. 7:14, R.V., "straitened,"
A.V., "narrow," of the way "that leadeth unto life," i.e., hemmed in
like a narrow gorge between rocks.

STRAITEST

196 AG:33A AKRIBESTATOS (ἀκριβέστατος), the superlative degree of *akribēs*,
CB:— accurate, exact (cp. *akribōs*, see ACCURATELY and associated words there),
AKRIBēS occurs in Acts 26:5, "the straitest (sect)," R.V. (A.V., "most straitest").¶

---

196 AG:33B CB:—

STRAITLY

POLUS *Notes:* (1) For *polla*, A.V., "straitly" in Mark 3:12; 5:43, see
4183 AG:687C MUCH (R.V.). (2) In Acts 4:17 some mss. have *apeilē*, a threat, with
CB:1266A *apeileō* (Middle Voice), lit., 'let us threaten them with a threat,' A.V.,
APEILē 547 "let us straitly threaten;" the best texts omit the noun (so R.V.).
AG:83A Moulton and Milligan (Vocab.), arguing for the presence of the noun,
CB:— PARANGELIA consider that it "clearly reflects the literal rendering of a Semitic original
3852 reported to Luke from an eye-witness—was it Paul?" (3) A similar
AG:613A CB:1262B construction, *parangellō* with the noun *parangelia*, occurs in Acts 5:28,
EMBRIMAOMAI "we straitly charged you," lit., 'we charged you with a charge.' See
1690 AG:254D CHARGE, A, No. 6. (4) For *embrimaomai*, A.V., "charge straitly" (R.V.,
CB:1244B "strictly") in Matt. 9:30; Mark 1:43, see CHARGE, C, No. 4.

For STRAKE, Acts 27:17, A.V. (R.V., "lowered"), see LET DOWN, No. 2.

STRANGE

A. Adjectives.

3581 AG:548A 1. XENOS (ξένος) denotes (*a*) foreign, alien, Acts 17:18, of gods;
CB:1273B Heb. 13:9, of doctrines; (*b*) unusual, 1 Pet. 4:12, 2nd part, of the
fiery trial of persecution (for 1st part, see B). See STRANGER.

245 AG:40C 2. ALLOTRIOS (ἀλλότριος) denotes (*a*) belonging to another (*allos*), see
CB:1234C MAN'S, Note (1); (*b*) alien, foreign, strange, Acts 7:6; Heb. 11:9, A.V.,
R.V., "(a *land*) not his own." See ALIEN, STRANGER.

3861 AG:615D 3. PARADOXOS (παράδοξος), contrary to received opinion (*para*,
CB:— beside, *doxa*, opinion; Eng. paradox, – ical), is rendered "strange
things" in Luke 5:26.¶

1854 AG:279B 4. EXŌ (ἔξω), outside, is rendered "strange" in Acts 26:11, A.V.:
CB:1247C see FOREIGN.

2084 *Note:* In 1 Cor. 14:21 (1st part), R.V., *heteroglōssos*, signifying of a
AG:314D CB:1250A different tongue (*heteros*, another, *glōssa*, a tongue) is translated "of
strange (A.V., other) tongues."¶

B. Verb.

XENIZŌ (ξενίζω) denotes to think something strange, 1 Pet. 4 : 4, 3579
12, Passive Voice, i.e., 'they are surprised,' and 'be (not) surprised ;' AG:547D
in Acts 17 : 20, the present participle, Active, is rendered "strange," CB:1273B
i.e., 'surprising.' See ENTERTAIN, LODGE.

STRANGER

A. Adjectives (used as nouns).

1. XENOS (ξένος), strange (see No. 1 above), denotes a stranger, 3581
foreigner, Matt. 25 : 35, 38, 43, 44 ; 27 : 7 ; Acts 17 : 21 ; Eph. 2 : 12, AG:548A
19 ; Heb. 11 : 13 ; 3 John 5. CB:1273B

2. ALLOTRIOS (ἀλλότριος), "strangers," Matt. 17 : 25, 26 ; John 245
10 : 5 (twice) : see No. 2, above. AG:40C CB:1234C

3. ALLOGENĒS (ἀλλογενής) (*allos*, another, *genos*, a race) occurs in 241
Luke 17 : 18, of a Samaritan. Moulton and Milligan illustrate the use AG:39C CB:1234C
of the word by the inscription on the Temple barrier, "let no foreigner PAROIKOS
enter within the screen and enclosure surrounding the sanctuary ;" 3941
according to Mommsen this inscription was cut by the Romans : cp. AG:629A CB:1262B
PARTITION.¶ PAREPIDĒMOS

Notes : (1) For *paroikos*, in A.V., see SOJOURN, B, No. 1. For 3927
parepidēmos, in A.V., see PILGRIM. (2) The pronoun *heteros*, other, is AG:625D CB:1262B
translated "strangers" in 1 Cor. 14 : 21 (2nd part), R.V. (A.V., "other") ; HETEROS 2087
cp. STRANGE, A, Note. AG:315A

B. Verb. CB:1250A

XENODOCHEŌ (ξενοδοχέω), to receive strangers (*xenos*, No. 1, above, 3580 AG:548A
and *dechomai*, to receive), occurs in 1 Tim. 5 : 10, R.V., "(if) she hath CB:1273B
used hospitality to strangers," A.V., "(if) she have lodged strangers."¶ EPIDĒMEŌ 1927

Note : For *epidēmeō*, in A.V., see SOJOURNER, A, No. 2. For AG:292A
paroikeō, in A.V., see SOJOURN, A, No. 1. PAROIKEŌ 3939

C. Noun. AG:628D CB:1262B

PHILOXENIA (φιλοξενία), love of strangers, occurs in Rom. 12 : 13, 5381
"hospitality," and Heb. 13 : 2, R.V., "to shew love unto strangers," AG:860D
A.V., "to entertain strangers." See ENTERTAIN, Note.¶ CB:1264B

Note : For *paroikia* in Acts 13 : 17, see SOJOURN, C. 3940 AG:629A CB:1262B

STRANGLED

PNIKTOS (πνικτός), from *pnigō*, to choke, occurs in Acts 15 : 20, 29 ; 4156
21 : 25, of the flesh of animals killed by strangling, without shedding their AG:679D CB:1265C
blood (see, e.g., Lev. 17 : 13, 14).¶

For STRAWED see FURNISH and SCATTER, No. 2

For STREAM see RIVER

STREET

4113 AG:666D 1. PLATEIA (πλατεῖα), grammatically the feminine of *platus*, broad,
CB:1265A is used as a noun (*hodos*, a way, being understood, i.e., a broad way), a
street, Matt. 6 : 5 ; 12 : 19 (in some texts, Mark 6 : 56) ; Luke 10 : 10 ;
296 13 : 26 ; 14 : 21 ; Acts 5 : 15 ; Rev. 11 : 8 ; 21 : 21 ; 22 : 2.¶
AG:47C CB:— 2. AMPHODON (ἄμφοδον), properly a way around (*amphi*, around,
RHUMē *hodos*, a way), occurs in Mark 11 : 4, R.V., " the open street " (A.V.,
4505 " where two ways met ").¶
AG:737C CB:— AGORA *Note :* For *rhumē*, see LANE. For *agora*, see MARKET.

---

58 AG:12C STRENGTH, STRENGTHEN

CB:1233C 1411 A. Nouns.

AG:207B CB:1242B 1. DUNAMIS (δύναμις) is rendered " strength " in the R.V. and A.V. of Rev. 1 : 16 ; elsewhere the R.V. gives the word its more appropriate meaning " power," for A.V., " strength," 1 Cor. 15 : 56 ; 2 Cor. 1 : 8 ; 12 : 9 ; Heb. 11 : 11 ; Rev. 3 : 8 ; 12 : 10. See ABILITY, No. 1, POWER, No. 1.

2479 AG:383C 2. ISCHUS (ἰσχύς), ability, strength, is rendered " strength " in
CB:1253A Mark 12 : 30, 33 ; Luke 10 : 27 ; in Rev. 5 : 12, A.V. (R.V., " might "). See ABILITY, No. 2, MIGHT.

2904 AG:449A 3. KRATOS (κράτος), force, might, is rendered " strength " in Luke
CB:1256A 1 : 51, R.V. and A.V. ; R.V.," strength " (A.V.," power ") in Eph. 1 : 19
1849 AG:277D and 6 : 10. See DOMINION, No. 1, POWER, No. 4.

CB:1247C *Note :* In Rev. 17 : 13, A.V., *exousia*, freedom of action, is rendered
DUNAMOō 1412 " strength " (R.V., " authority ").

AG:208C B. Verbs.

CB:1242B 1. DUNAMOŌ (δυναμόω), to strengthen, occurs in Col. 1 : 11, and in
ENDUNAMOō 1743 the best texts in Heb. 11 : 34, " were made strong " (some have No. 2) ;
AG:263D some have it in Eph. 6 : 10 (the best have No. 2).¶ In the Sept., Psa.
CB:1245A ISCHUō 52 : 7 ; 68 : 28 ; Eccl. 10 : 10 ; Dan. 9 : 27.¶

2480 AG:383D 2. ENDUNAMOŌ (ἐνδυναμόω), to make strong, is rendered " increased
CB:1253A ENISCHUō . . . in strength " in Acts 9 : 22 ; to strengthen in Phil. 4 : 13 ; 2 Tim.
1765 2 : 1, R.V., " be strengthened ; " 4 : 17. See ENABLE, STRONG, B.

AG:266D CB:1245A 3. ISCHUŌ (ἰσχύω), akin to A, No. 2, to have strength, is so rendered
KRATAIOō 2901 in Mark 5 : 4, R.V. (A.V., " could ") ; in Luke 16 : 3, R.V., " I have not
AG:448B CB:1256A strength to " (A.V., " I cannot "). See AVAIL.

STHENOō 4. ENISCHUŌ (ἐνισχύω), akin to A, No. 2, a strengthened form of
4599 AG:749C No. 3, is used in Luke 22 : 43 and Acts 9 : 19.¶

STēRIZō 4741 5. KRATAIOŌ (κραταιόω), to strengthen, is rendered " to be
AG:768A CB:1270A strengthened " in Eph. 3 : 16. See STRONG, B.

STEREOō 6. STHENOŌ (σθενόω), from *sthenos*, strength, occurs in 1 Pet. 5 : 10,
4732 AG:766D in a series of future tenses, according to the best texts, thus constituting
Divine promises.¶

Notes : (1) For *ischuō*, Heb. 9 : 17, see AVAIL. (2) For *stērizō*, Luke 22 : 32, see ESTABLISH, No. 1. (3) For *stereoō*, Acts 3 : 7, see ESTABLISH,

No. 2. (4) *Epistērizō* is found in some texts in Acts 18 : 23, A.V., 1991
" strengthening." See CONFIRM, A, No. 2, ESTABLISH, No. 1. (5) For AG:300D CB:1246A
" without strength," Rom. 5 : 6, A.V., see WEAK.

STRETCH

1. EKTEINŌ (ἐκτείνω), to stretch out or forth, is so rendered in Matt. 1614
12 : 13 (twice), 49 ; 14 : 31 ; 26 : 51 ; Mark 3 : 5 (twice) ; Luke 6 : 10 ; AG:245B CB:—
in Matt. 8 : 3 ; Mark 1 : 41 and Luke 5 : 13, R.V. (A.V., " put forth ") ;
Luke 22 : 53 ; John 21 : 18 ; Acts 4 : 30 ; 26 : 1. For Acts 27 : 30 see
LAY, No. 13.¶

2. EPEKTEINŌ (ἐπεκτείνω), an intensive form of No. 1 (*epi*, forth), (-OMAI)
is used in Phil. 3 : 13, R.V., " stretching forward " (A.V., " reaching 1901 AG:284D
forth "), a metaphor probably from the foot race (rather than the chariot CB:1245C
race), so Lightfoot, who quotes Bengel's paraphrase, ' the eye goes before
and draws on the hand, the hand goes before and draws on the foot.'¶

3. HUPEREKTEINŌ (ὑπερεκτείνω), to stretch out beyond (*huper*, 5239
over, and No. 1), occurs in 2 Cor. 10 : 14, R.V., " we stretch (not) . . . AG:840D
overmuch " (A.V., " . . . beyond *our measure* ").¶ CB:—

Note : For *ekpetannumi*, Rom. 10 : 21, see SPREAD, No. 5. For EKPETANNUMI 1600
epiballō, Acts 12 : 1, see PUT, No. 8. AG:243D EPIBALLō 1911 AG:289D

STRICKEN (in years)

PROBAINŌ (προβαίνω), to go forward, is used metaphorically of age, 4260
in Luke 1 : 7, 18, with the phrases " in their (her) days," translated " well AG:702D CB:1266C
stricken in years " (see marg.) ; in 2 : 36, " of a great age " (marg.,
" advanced in many days "). See GO, No. 20.

For STRICT, R.V., see MANNER, A, No. 5. For STRICTLY,
R.V., see STRAITLY

STRIFE

1. ERIS (ἔρις), strife, contention, is the expression of enmity, Rom. 2054
1 : 29, R.V., " strife " (A.V., " debate ") ; 13 : 13 ; 1 Cor. 1 : 11, AG:309C CB:1246C
" contentions " (R.V. and A.V.) ; 3 : 3 ; 2 Cor. 12 : 20, R.V., " strife "
(A.V., " debates ") ; Gal. 5 : 20, R.V., " strife " (A.V., " variance ") ;
Phil. 1 : 15 ; 1 Tim. 6 : 4 ; Tit. 3 : 9, R.V., " strifes " (A.V., " conten- 2052
tions "). See CONTENTION, A, No. 1.¶ AG:309B

2. ERITHIA (or -EIA) (ἐριθία) : see FACTION. CB:1246C

3. ANTILOGIA (ἀντιλογία), "strife," Heb. 6 : 16, A.V. : see DISPUTE, 485 AG:75A
A, No. 4. 3163

4. MACHĒ (μάχη), " strifes," 2 Tim. 2 : 23 : see FIGHTING, A. AG:496C CB:1257B

5. PHILONEIKIA (φιλονεικία), " strife," Luke 22 : 24, A.V. : see 5379
CONTENTION, A, No. 3.¶ AG:860D CB:1264A

6. LOGOMACHIA (λογομαχία), " strife of words," 1 Tim. 6 : 4 : see 3055
DISPUTE, A, No. 2.¶ AG:477A CB:1257A

STRIKE

PIPTō *Notes:* (1) In Rev. 7 : 16, *piptō*, to fall, is rendered "strike" in the
4098 AG:659B R.V., A.V., "light (on)." (2) In Acts 27 : 41, *ereidō*, to fix firmly, is used
CB:1265A of a ship driving ashore, R.V., "struck" (A.V., "stuck fast").¶ (3) For
EREIDō 2043 *paiō*, to smite, Rev. 9 : 5, A.V., "striketh," see SMITE, No. 3. (4) For
AG:308D *patassō*, to smite, Matt. 26 : 51, A.V., "struck," see SMITE, No. 1. (5)
PAIō 3817 For *chalaō*, to let go, Acts 27 : 17, A.V., "strake," see LET DOWN, No. 2.
AG:605B (6) In Luke 22 : 64 some mss. have *tuptō*, to beat, imperfect tense, 'they
PATASSō 3960 were beating.' (7) For *rhapizō*, Matt. 26 : 67, and *rhapisma*, Mark 14 : 65,
AG:634D see BLOW, SMITE, No. 6 and Note (2). Some mss. have *ballō*, "struck."

CB:1262C CHALAō 5465

STRIKER

AG:874B TUPTō PLĒKTĒS (πλήκτης), a striker, a brawler (akin to *plēssō*, to strike,
5180 smite), occurs in 1 Tim. 3 : 3; Tit. 1 : 7.¶

AG:830B CB:1273B

RHAPIZō 4474 For STRING see BOND, No. 1

AG:734B

STRIP

CB:1268A RHAPISMA
4475 EKDUŌ (ἐκδύω), to take off, strip off, is used especially of clothes,
AG:734C and rendered to strip in Matt. 27 : 28 (some mss. have *enduō*, to clothe),
CB:1268A and Luke 10 : 30; to take off, Matt. 27 : 31; Mark 15 : 20; figuratively,
PLēKTēS 4131 2 Cor. 5 : 4, "unclothed" (Middle Voice), of putting off the body at
AG:669B death (the believer's state of being unclothed does not refer to the body
EKDUō 1562 in the grave but to the spirit, which awaits the "body of glory" at the
AG:239A resurrection).¶

CB:1243C

STRIPE

3468 AG:531A 1. MŌLŌPS (μώλωψ), a bruise, a wound from a stripe, is used in
CB:1259A 1 Pet. 2 : 24 (from the Sept. of Is. 53 : 5), lit., in the original, 'by whose
bruise,' not referring to Christ's scourging, but figurative of the stroke
of Divine judgment administered vicariously to Him on the Cross (a
comforting reminder to these Christian servants, who were not infrequently buffeted, ver. 20, by their masters).¶

4127 AG:668A 2. PLĒGĒ (πληγή), a blow, stripe, wound (akin to *plēssō*, to strike,
CB:1265A and *plēktēs*, a striker), is rendered "stripes" in Luke 12 : 48 (the noun
is omitted in the original in ver. 47 and the 2nd part of ver. 48); Acts
16 : 23, 33; 2 Cor. 6 : 5; 11 : 23. See PLAGUE, WOUND.

STRIVE

75 AG:15B 1. AGŌNIZOMAI (ἀγωνίζομαι), to contend (Eng., agonize), is rendered
CB:1233C to strive in Luke 13 : 24; 1 Cor. 9 : 25; Col. 1 : 29; 4 : 12, R.V. (A.V.,
"labouring fervently"). In 1 Tim. 4 : 10, the best texts have this verb
3164 (R.V., "strive") for *oneidizomai*, to suffer reproach, A.V.; see FIGHT,
AG:496C B, No. 1.
CB:1257B 2. MACHOMAI (μάχομαι), to fight, to quarrel, dispute, is rendered

to strive in John 6 : 52 ; Acts 7 : 26 ; 2 Tim. 2 : 24. See FIGHT, B, No. 3.

3. DIAMACHOMAI (διαμάχομαι), to struggle against (*dia*, intensive, 1264 AG:186C
and No. 2), is used of contending in an argument, Acts 23 : 9, " strove."¶ CB:—

4. ERIZŌ (ἐρίζω), to wrangle, strive (*eris*, strife), is used in Matt. 2051 AG:309B
12 : 19.¶ CB:—

5. LOGOMACHEŌ (λογομαχέω), to strive about words (*logos*, a word, 3054 AG:477A
and No. 2), is used in 2 Tim. 2 : 14.¶ CB:1257A

6. ANTAGŌNIZOMAI (ἀνταγωνίζομαι), to struggle against (*anti*), 464 AG:72D
is used in Heb. 12 : 4, " striving against."¶ CB:1236A

7. SUNAGŌNIZOMAI (συναγωνίζομαι), to strive together with (*sun*), 4865 AG:783B
is used in Rom. 15 : 30.¶ CB:1270B

8. SUNATHLEŌ (συναθλέω), to strive together, Phil. 1 : 27 : see 4866 AG:783B
LABOUR, B, No. 3. CB:1270C

Notes : (1) In 2 Tim. 2 : 5, A.V., *athleō*, to contend in games, wrestle ATHLEō
(*athlos*, a contest), is rendered " strive." See CONTEND. (2) For 118 AG:21B
philotimeomai, Rom. 15 : 20, see AIM. CB:1238A PHILOTIMEOMAI 5389 AG:861C CB:1264B

For STRIVINGS, Tit. 3 : 9, A.V., see FIGHTING

STROLLING

PERIERCHOMAI (περιέρχομαι), to go about, as an itinerant (*peri*, 4022 AG:646D
around, *erchomai*, to go), is used of certain Jews in Acts 19 : 13, R.V., CB:1263B
" strolling " (A.V., " vagabond "). See COMPASS, No. 6, WANDER.

STRONG, STRONGER

A. Adjectives.

1. DUNATOS (δυνατός), powerful, mighty, is translated " strong," 1415 AG:208C
in Rom. 15 : 1, where the " strong " are those referred to in ch. 14, in CB:1242B
contrast to " the weak in faith," those who have scruples in regard to eating meat and the observance of days ; 2 Cor. 12 : 10, where the strength lies in bearing sufferings in the realization that the endurance is for Christ's sake ; 2 Cor. 13 : 9, where " ye are strong " implies the good spiritual condition which the Apostle desires for the church at Corinth in having nothing requiring his exercise of discipline (contrast No. 2 in 1 Cor. 4 : 10). See ABLE, C, No. 1, MIGHTY, POSSIBLE, POWER.

2. ISCHUROS (ἰσχυρός), strong, mighty, is used of (*a*) persons : 2478 AG:383A
(1) God, Rev. 18 : 8 ; (2) angels, Rev. 5 : 2 ; 10 : 1 ; 18 : 21 ; (3) men, CB:1253A
Matt. 12 : 29 (twice) and parallel passages ; Heb. 11 : 34, A.V., " valiant " (R.V., " mighty ") ; Rev. 6 : 15 (in the best texts ; some have No. 1) ; 19 : 18, " mighty ; " metaphorically, (4) the church at Corinth, 1 Cor. 4 : 10, where the Apostle reproaches them ironically with their unspiritual and self-complacent condition ; (5) of young men in Christ spiritually strong, through the Word of God, to overcome the evil one, 1 John 2 : 14 ; of (*b*) things : (1) wind, Matt. 14 : 30 (in some mss.),

"boisterous;" (2) famine, Luke 15:14; (3) things in the mere human estimate, 1 Cor. 1:27; (4) Paul's letters, 2 Cor. 10:10; (5) the Lord's crying and tears, Heb. 5:7; (6) consolation, 6:18; (7) the voice of an
MEGAS angel, Rev. 18:2 (in the best texts; some have *megas*, "great");
3173 AG:497C (8) Babylon, Rev. 18:10; (9) thunderings, Rev. 19:6. See BOISTEROUS,
CB:1258A MIGHTY.

2478 (-UROS) 3. ISCHUROTEROS (*ἰσχυρότερος*), the comparative degree of No. 2,
AG:383A is used (*a*) of Christ, Matt. 3:11; Mark 1:7; Luke 3:16; (*b*) of "the
(-UROS 1.a.) CB:1253A weakness of God," as men without understanding regard it, 1 Cor. 1:25; (*c*) of a man of superior physical strength, Luke 11:22; (*d*) in 1 Cor. 10:22, in a rhetorical question, implying the impossibility of escaping the jealousy of God when it is kindled.¶

Notes: (1) For "strong delusion," 2 Thess. 2:11, A.V., see ERROR, No. 1. (2) For "strong (meat)," Heb. 5:12, 14, A.V., see SOLID.

B. Verbs.

1743 1. ENDUNAMOŌ (*ἐνδυναμόω*), to make strong (*en*, in, *dunamis*,
AG:263D CB:1245A power), to strengthen, is rendered "waxed strong" in Rom. 4:20, R.V. (A.V., "was strong"); "be strong," Eph. 6:10; "were made strong," Heb. 11:34. See ENABLE, STRENGTH, B, No. 2.

2901 2. KRATAIOŌ (*κραταιόω*), to strengthen (akin to *kratos*, strength),
AG:448B CB:1256A is rendered (a) to wax strong, Luke 1:80; 2:40; "be strong," 1 Cor. 16:13, lit., 'be strengthened;' "to be strengthened," Eph. 3:16 (Passive Voice in each place). See STRENGTHEN.¶

4732 3. STEREOŌ (*στερεόω*): see ESTABLISH, No. 2.
AG:766D CB:—

STRONGHOLDS

3794 OCHURŌMA (*ὀχύρωμα*), a stronghold, fortress (akin to *ochuroō*, to
AG:601A CB:1260B make firm), is used metaphorically in 2 Cor. 10:4, of those things in
STRUGGLE See STRIVE, WRESTLE which mere human confidence is imposed.¶

STUBBLE

2562 AG:398C KALAMĒ (*καλάμη*), a stalk of corn, denotes straw or stubble; in
CB:— 1 Cor. 3:12, metaphorically of the effect of the most worthless form of unprofitable doctrine, in the lives and conduct of those in a church who are the subjects of such teaching; the teachings received and the persons
STUBBORN See HARD who receive them are associated; the latter are "the doctrine exhibited
STUDENT See DISCIPLE in concrete form" (Lightfoot).¶

For STUCK see STICK

PHILOTIMEOMAI 5389 AG:861C

STUDY

CB:1264B *Notes:* For *philotimeomai*, "study," 1 Thess. 4:11, see AIM. For
SPOUDAZō 4704 *spoudazō*, 2 Tim. 2:15, A.V., see DILIGENCE, B, No. 1.

AG:763C CB:1269C For STUFF, Luke 17:31, A.V., see GOODS, No. 4

STUMBLE

1. PROSKOPTŌ (*προσκόπτω*), to strike against, is used of stumbling, 4350
(*a*) physically, John 11 : 9, 10 ; (*b*) metaphorically, (1) of Israel in regard AG:716B
to Christ, whose Person, teaching, and atoning Death, and the Gospel CB:1267B
relating thereto, were contrary to all their ideas as to the means of righteousness before God, Rom. 9 : 32 ; 1 Pet. 2 : 8 ; (2) of a brother in the Lord in acting against the dictates of his conscience, Rom. 14 : 21. See Beat, No. 6.

2. PTAIŌ (*πταίω*), to cause to stumble, signifies, intransitively, to 4417
stumble, used metaphorically in Rom. 11 : 11, in the sense (*b*) (1) in No. 1 ; AG:727A
with moral significance in Jas. 2 : 10 and 3 : 2 (twice), R.V., " stumble " CB:1267C
(A.V., " offend ") ; in 2 Pet. 1 : 10, R.V., " stumble " (A.V., " fall ").¶

Note : For *aptaistos*, " from stumbling," Jude 24, R.V., see Fall, 679
B, Note (6). AG:102C
CB:—

For STUMBLING, STUMBLING BLOCK, STUMBLING-STONE, see OFFENCE, A, Nos. 1, 2, 3 and B

STUPOR

KATANUXIS (*κατάνυξις*), a pricking (akin to *katanussō*, to strike or 2659
prick violently, Acts 2 : 37), is used in Rom. 11 : 8, R.V., " stupor " (A.V., AG:415C
" slumber "). It is suggested that this meaning arose from the influence CB:—
of the verb *katanustazō*, to nod or fall asleep (Field, *Notes on the Translation of the N.T.*). Evidently what is signified is the dulling of the spiritual sense.¶ In the Sept., Psa. 60 : 3 ; Isa. 29 : 10.¶

SUBDUE

KATAGŌNIZOMAI (*καταγωνίζομαι*), primarily, to struggle against 2610
(*kata*, against, *agōn*, a contest), came to signify to conquer, Heb. 11 : 33, AG:410A
" subdued."¶ CB:1254A

Note : For *hupotassō*, A.V., to subdue, in 1 Cor. 15 : 28 and Phil. 3 : 21, see Subject.

SUBJECT, SUBJECTION (Verb, Adjective, Noun)

A. Verb.

HUPOTASSŌ (*ὑποτάσσω*), primarily a military term, to rank under 5293
(*hupo*, under, *tassō*, to arrange), denotes (*a*) to put in subjection, to AG:847D
subject, Rom. 8 : 20 (twice) ; in the following, the R.V., has to subject CB:1252B (-OMAI)
for A.V., to put under, 1 Cor. 15 : 27 (thrice), 28 (3rd clause) ; Eph. 1 : 22 ; Heb. 2 : 8 (4th clause) ; in 1 Cor. 15 : 28 (1st clause), for A.V. " be subdued ; " in Phil. 3 : 21, for A.V., " subdue ; " in Heb. 2 : 5, A.V., " hath . . . put in subjection ; " (*b*) in the Middle or Passive Voice, to subject oneself, to obey, be subject to, Luke 2 : 51 ; 10 : 17, 20 ; Rom. 8 : 7 ; 10 : 3, R.V., " did (not) subject themselves " [A.V., " have (not) submitted themselves "] ; 13 : 1, 5 ; 1 Cor. 14 : 34, R.V., " be in

subjection " (A.V., " be under obedience ") ; 15 : 28 (2nd clause) ; 16 : 16, R.V., " be in subjection " (A.V., " submit, etc.") ; so Col. 3 : 18 ; Eph. 5 : 21, R.V., " subjecting yourselves " (A.V., " submitting, etc. ") ; ver. 22, R.V. in italics, according to the best texts ; ver. 24, " is subject ; " Tit. 2 : 5, 9, R.V., " be in subjection " (A.V., " be obedient ") ; 3 : 1, R.V., " to be in subjection " (A.V., " to be subject ") ; Heb. 12 : 9, " be in subjection ; " Jas. 4 : 7, R.V., " be subject " (A.V., " submit yourselves ") ; so 1 Pet. 2 : 13 ; ver. 18, R.V., " be in subjection ; " so 3 : 1,
DOULAGōGEō A.V. and R.V. ; ver. 5, similarly ; 3 : 22, " being made subject ; "
1396 AG:205A 5 : 5, R.V., " be subject " (A.V., " submit yourselves ") ; in some texts
CB:1242A in the 2nd part, as A.V. See OBEDIENT, SUBMIT.
(-ōGō) ANUPOTAKTOS *Note :* For *doulagōgeō,* 1 Cor. 9 : 27, A.V., " bring into subjection,"
506 see BONDAGE, B, No. 3. For *anupotaktos,* " not subject," Heb. 2 : 8,
AG:76D see DISOBEDIENT, B, Note.
CB:—

B. Adjective.

1777 AG:267D ENOCHOS (ἔνοχος), held in, bound by, in Heb. 2 : 15, " subject to : "
CB:1245B see DANGER, B, No. 1.

Note : For " subject to like passions," Jas. 5 : 17, A.V., see PASSION.

C. Noun.

5292 AG:847D HUPOTAGĒ (ὑποταγή), subjection, occurs in 2 Cor. 9 : 13 ; Gal. 2 : 5 ;
CB:1252B 1 Tim. 2 : 11 ; 3 : 4.¶

SUBMIT

5226 HUPEIKŌ (ὑπείκω), to retire, withdraw (*hupo,* under, *eikō,* to yield),
AG:838B
CB:— hence, to yield, submit, is used metaphorically in Heb. 13 : 17, of submitting to spiritual guides in the churches.¶

5293 *Note :* For *hupotassō,* see SUBJECT, A.
AG:847D
CB:1252B
(-OMAI)

SUBORN

5260 HUPOBALLŌ (ὑποβάλλω), to throw or put under, to subject, denoted
AG:843D
CB:— to suggest, whisper, prompt ; hence, to instigate, translated " suborned " in Acts 6 : 11. To suborn in the legal sense is to procure a person who will take a false oath. The idea of making suggestions is probably present in this use of the word.¶

SUBSTANCE

3776 1. OUSIA (οὐσία), derived from a present participial form of *eimi,*
AG:596A
CB:1261B to be, denotes substance, property, Luke 15 : 12, 13, R.V., " substance," A.V., " goods " and " substance."¶

5224 2. HUPARCHONTA (ὑπάρχοντα), the neuter plural of the present
AG:838A
(-CHō) participle of *huparchō,* to be in existence, is used as a noun with the
CB:1252A article, signifying one's goods, and translated " substance " in Luke 8 : 3. See GOODS, POSSESS, A, No. 3.

5223
AG:837D 3. HUPARXIS (ὕπαρξις), existence (akin to No. 2), possession : see
CB:1252A POSSESS, B, No. 4.

4. HUPOSTASIS (ὑπόστασις), for which see CONFIDENCE, A, No. 2, 5287
is translated "substance" (*a*) in Heb. 1:3, of Christ as "the very AG:847A
image" of God's "substance;" here the word has the meaning of the CB:1252B
real nature of that to which reference is made in contrast to the outward manifestation (see the preceding clause); it speaks of the Divine essence of God existent and expressed in the revelation of His Son. The A.V., "person" is an anachronism; the word was not so rendered till the 4th cent. Most of the earlier Eng. Versions have "substance;" (*b*) in Heb. 11:1 it has the meaning of confidence, "assurance" (R.V.), marg., "the giving substance to," A.V., "substance," something that could not equally be expressed by *elpis*, hope.

SUBTILLY

KATASOPHIZOMAI (κατασοφίζομαι), to deal subtilly (from *kata*, 2686
against, under, *sophos*, wise, subtle, used in the Sept. in 2 Sam. 13:3, of AG:418D
Jonadab), occurs in Acts 7:19.¶ In the Sept., Ex. 1:10.¶ CB:—

SUBTILTY

Note: For *dolos*, Matt. 26:4; Acts 13:10, see GUILE. For *panourgia*, DOLOS 1388
2 Cor. 11:3, see CRAFTINESS. AG:203B CB:— PANOURGIA 3834 AG:608A CB:1261C

SUBVERT, SUBVERTING

A. Verb.

ANASKEUAZŌ (ἀνασκευάζω), primarily, to pack up baggage (*ana*, 384
up, *skeuos*, a vessel), hence, from a military point of view, to dismantle AG:60A
a town, to plunder, is used metaphorically in Acts 15:24, of unsettling CB:—
or subverting the souls of believers. In the papyri it is used of going bankrupt.¶ ANATREPŌ 396

Note: For *anatrepō*, Tit. 1:11, see OVERTHROW, B, No. 3. For AG:62C
ekstrephō, Tit. 3:11, see PERVERT, No. 4. EKSTREPHŌ 1612 AG:245B

B. Noun.

KATASTROPHĒ (καταστροφή), an overthrow, 2 Pet. 2:6 (Eng., 2692
catastrophe), is rendered "subverting" in 2 Tim. 2:14. See OVER- AG:419B
THROW.¶ CB:—

For SUCCEED, Acts 24:27, R.V., see ROOM, Note (2)

For SUCCOUR see HELP, B, No. 4

SUCCOURER

PROSTATIS (προστάτις), a feminine form of *prostatēs*, denotes a 4368
protectress, patroness; it is used metaphorically of Phœbe in Rom. 16:2. AG:718D
It is a word of dignity, evidently chosen instead of others which might CB:—
have been used (see, e.g., under HELPER), and indicates the high esteem with which she was regarded, as one who had been a protectress of many.

Prostatēs was the title of a citizen in Athens, who had the responsibility of seeing to the welfare of resident aliens who were without civic rights. Among the Jews it signified a wealthy patron of the community.¶

For SUCH see † p. 1.

SUCH AS

Notes : (1) In Acts 2 : 47, A.V., the article with the present participle,
Passive, of *sōzō*, to save, lit., the (ones), i.e., those, being saved, is
translated " such as (should be saved) ; " the R.V., " those that (were
being saved)," gives the correct meaning, marking the kind of persons
HOIOS who were added to the company ; (2) " such as " is a rendering of certain
3634 AG:562C relative pronouns : *hoios*, what sort of, e.g., Matt. 24 : 21 ; 2 Cor. 12 : 20
CB:1251A (twice) ; Rev. 16 : 18 ; *hostis*, whoever, e.g., Mark 4 : 20 ; *hopoios*, of
HOSTIS 3748 what sort, preceded by *toioutos*, of such a sort, Acts 26 : 29 ; (3) *deina*,
AG:586D Matt. 26 : 18, denotes such a one (whom one cannot, or will not, name).¶
CB:— HOPOIOS (4) In Heb. 13 : 5, " such things as ye have " represents the phrase *ta*
3697 *paronta*, ' the (things) present ' (present participle of *pareimi*) ; (5) in
AG:575D Luke 11 : 41, *ta enonta*, A.V., " such things as ye have," lit., ' the (things)
CB:— TOIOUTOS within ' (*eneimi*, to be in), R.V., " those things which are within " (A.V.
5108 AG:821B marg., " as you are able," R.V., marg., " ye can "), perhaps signifying not
CB:1272C outward things such as lustrations, but ' what things ye have within
DEINA 1170 your cups and platters,' i.e., your possessions.
AG:173A
CB:—

SUCK (GIVE SUCK), SUCKLING

2337 AG:360C THĒLAZŌ (θηλάζω), from *thēlē*, a breast, is used (*a*) of the mother, to
CB:— suckle, Matt. 24 : 19 ; Mark 13 : 17 ; Luke 21 : 23 ; in some texts in
23 : 29 (the best have *trephō*) ; (*b*) of the young, to suck, Matt. 21 : 16,
" sucklings ; " Luke 11 : 27.¶

SUDDEN, SUDDENLY

A. Adjective.

160 AG:26D AIPHNIDIOS (αἰφνίδιος), sudden, occurs in 1 Thess. 5 : 3, where it
CB:— has the place of emphasis at the beginning of the sentence, as *olethros*,
destruction, which the adjective qualifies, has at the end ; in Luke 21 : 34,
it is used adverbially, R.V., " suddenly " (A.V., " unawares "). See
UNAWARES.¶

B. Adverbs.

869 AG:127A 1. APHNŌ (ἄφνω), suddenly, occurs in Acts 2 : 2 ; 16 : 26 ; 28 : 6.¶
1810 2. EXAIPHNĒS (ἐξαίφνης), a strengthened form, akin to No. 1, occurs
AG:272B in Mark 13 : 36 ; Luke 2 : 13 ; 9 : 39 ; Acts 9 : 3 ; 22 : 6.¶
1819 AG:273A 3. EXAPINA (ἐξάπινα), a later form of No. 2, occurs in Mark 9 : 8.¶
5030 AG:806D *Note :* For *tacheōs* in 1 Tim. 5 : 22, A.V., " suddenly," R.V., " hastily,"
see QUICKLY, No. 3.

For SUE see LAW, B, No. 2

SUFFER

A. Verbs.

(a) to permit

1. EAŌ (ἐάω), to let, permit, is translated to suffer in Matt. 24 : 43 ; 1439
Luke 4 : 41 ; 22 : 51 ; Acts 14 : 16 ; 16 : 7 ; 19 : 30 ; 28 : 4 ; 1 Cor. AG:212C
10 : 13. See LEAVE *(a)* No. 9, LET, No. 4. CB:—

2. PROSEAŌ (προσεάω), to permit further (*pros*, and No. 1), occurs 4330
in Acts 27 : 7.¶ AG:712D CB:—

3. EPITREPŌ (ἐπιτρέπω), for which see LEAVE, *(b)*, is rendered to 2010
suffer in A.V. and R.V. in Matt. 8 : 21 ; Mark 10 : 4 ; Luke 9 : 59 ; AG:303C
Acts 28 : 16 ; R.V. only, Luke 9 : 61 (A.V., "let") ; A.V. only, Acts CB:—
21 : 39 ; in some texts, Matt. 8 : 31, A.V. only. See LIBERTY, C, Note,
PERMIT.

4. APHIĒMI (ἀφίημι), to send away, signifies to permit, suffer, in 863
Matt. 3 : 15 (twice) ; Matt. 19 : 14 ; 23 : 13 ; Mark 1 : 34 ; 5 : 19, 37 ; AG:125C
10 : 14 ; 11 : 16 ; Luke 8 : 51 ; 12 : 39, A.V. (R.V., "left") ; 18 : 16 ; CB:1236B
John 12 : 7, R.V., A.V. and R.V. marg., "let (her) alone" ; Rev. 11 : 9. DIDōMI
See FORGIVE. 1325 AG:192C

Notes : (1) In Acts 2 : 27 and 13 : 35, A.V., *didōmi*, to give (R.V.), CB:1241C
is rendered to suffer. (2) In 1 Cor. 6 : 7, A.V., *apostereō*, in the Passive APOSTEREō 650
Voice, is rendered "*suffer yourselves to* be defrauded" (R.V., "be AG:99A
defrauded"). (3) For *kōluō* in Heb. 7 : 23, A.V., "were not suffered," CB:1237A KōLUō
see HINDER. 2967

(b) to endure suffering AG:461B CB:1255C

1. ANECHŌ (ἀνέχω), in the Middle Voice, to bear with, is rendered 430
to suffer in Matt. 17 : 17 and parallel passages ; A.V. only, 1 Cor. 4 : 12 AG:65D
(R.V., "endure") ; 2 Cor. 11 : 19, 20 and Heb. 13 : 22 (R.V., "bear CB:1235B
with"). See BEAR, ENDURE.

2. PASCHŌ (πάσχω), to suffer, is used (I) of the sufferings of Christ 3958
(a) at the hands of men, e.g., Matt. 16 : 21 ; 17 : 12 ; 1 Pet. 2 : 23 ; AG:633D
(b) in His expiatory and vicarious sacrifice for sin, Heb. 9 : 26 ; 13 : 12 ; CB:1262C
1 Pet. 2 : 21 ; 3 : 18 ; 4 : 1 ; *(c)* including both *(a)* and *(b)*, Luke 22 : 15 ; 24 : 26, 46 ; Acts 1 : 3, "passion ;" 3 : 18 ; 17 : 3 ; Heb. 5 : 8 ; *(d)* by the antagonism of the evil one, Heb. 2 : 18 ; (II) of human suffering, *(a)* of followers of Christ, Acts 9 : 16 ; 2 Cor. 1 : 6 ; Gal. 3 : 4 ; Phil. 1 : 29 ; 1 Thess. 2 : 14 ; 2 Thess. 1 : 5 ; 2 Tim. 1 : 12 ; 1 Pet. 3 : 14, 17 ; 5 : 10 ; Rev. 2 : 10 ; in identification with Christ in His crucifixion, as the spiritual ideal to be realized, 1 Pet. 4 : 1 ; in a wrong way, 4 : 15 ; *(b)* of others, physically, as the result of demoniacal power, Matt. 17 : 15, R.V., "suffereth (grievously)," A.V., "is (sore) vexed ;" cp. Mark 5 : 26 ; in a dream, Matt. 27 : 19 ; through maltreatment, Luke 13 : 2 ; 1 Pet. 2 : 19, 20 ; by a serpent (negatively), Acts 28 : 5, R.V., "took" (A.V., "felt :" see FEEL, Note) ; (c) of the effect upon the whole body through

the suffering of one member, 1 Cor. 12 : 26, with application to a church.

4310 AG:709B 3. PROPASCHŌ (προπάσχω), to suffer before (*pro*, and No. 2), occurs
CB:— in 1 Thess. 2 : 2.¶

4841 AG:779B 4. SUMPASCHŌ (συμπάσχω), to suffer with (*sun*, and No. 2), is used
CB:1270B in Rom. 8 : 17 of suffering with Christ ; in 1 Cor. 12 : 26 of joint suffering
in the members of the body.¶

5254 AG:842B 5. HUPECHŌ (ὑπέχω), to hold under (*hupo*, under, *echō*, to have or
CB:— hold), is used metaphorically in Jude 7 of suffering punishment.¶ In
the Sept., Ps. 89 : 50 ; Lam. 5 : 7.¶

2558 AG:398B 6. KAKOUCHEŌ (κακουχέω), to ill-treat (*kakos*, evil, and *echō*, to
CB:— have), is used in the Passive Voice in Heb. 11 : 37, R.V., " evil entreated "
(A.V., " tormented ") ; in 13 : 3, R.V., " are evil entreated " (A.V.,
" suffer adversity ").¶

4778 (-Eō) 7. SUNKAKOUCHEOMAI (συγκακουχέομαι), to endure adversity
AG:773B with, is used in Heb. 11 : 25 (*sun*, with, and No. 6), R.V., " to be evil
CB:— entreated with," A.V., " to suffer affliction with."¶

3114 AG:488A 8. MAKROTHUMEŌ (μακροθυμέω) is rendered " suffereth long "
CB:1257C in 1 Cor. 13 : 4. See PATIENCE.

91 AG:17C 9. ADIKEŌ (ἀδικέω), to do wrong, injustice (*a*, negative, *dikē*, right),
CB:1233A is used in the Passive Voice in 2 Pet. 2 : 13, R.V., " suffering wrong "
(some texts have *komizō*, to receive, A.V.) ; there is a play upon words
here which may be brought out thus, ' being defrauded (of the wages of
STEGō fraud),' a use of the verb illustrated in the papyri. See HURT.

4722 AG:765D *Notes :* (1) In 1 Cor. 9 : 12, A.V., *stegō*, to bear up under, is translated
CB:1270A " suffer " (R.V., " bear ") ; see BEAR, No. 11. (2) For *hupomenō*,
HUPOMENō 5278 rendered to suffer in 2 Tim. 2 : 12, see ENDURE, No. 2. (3) For suffer
AG:845D hardship, suffer trouble, see HARDSHIP, Nos. 1 and 2. (4) For suffer need,
CB:1252B Phil. 4 : 12, see WANT. (5) For suffer loss, 2 Cor. 7 : 9, R.V., see LOSE,
TROPOPHOREō 5159 No. 2. (6) For suffer persecution, see PERSECUTION. (7) For suffer
AG:827C shipwreck, see SHIPWRECK. (8) For *tropophoreō* in Acts 13 : 18, " suffered
BIAZō 971 . . . manners," see MANNER, E. (9) For " suffereth violence," *biazō*,
AG:140C CB:1239A see FORCE, B, No. 1, VIOLENCE, B, No. 2. (10) In 2 Thess. 1 : 9, R.V.,
TINō *tinō*, to pay a penalty, is rendered " shall suffer (punishment)."¶

5099 AG:818D

B. Adjective.

3805 PATHĒTOS (παθητός), akin to *paschō*, denotes one who has suffered,
AG:602D CB:1262C or subject to suffering, or destined to suffer ; it is used in the last sense of
the suffering of Christ, Acts 26 : 23.¶

SUFFERING

3804 AG:602B PATHĒMA (πάθημα) is rendered " sufferings " in the R.V. (A.V.,
CB:1262C " afflictions ") in 2 Tim. 3 : 11 ; Heb. 10 : 32 ; 1 Pet. 5 : 9 ; in Gal. 5 : 24,
" passions " (A.V., " affections "). See AFFLICTION, B, No. 3.

2552 AG:397B *Note :* For *kakopatheia*, Jas. 5 : 10, R.V., " suffering," see AFFLICTION,
CB:1253B B, No. 1.

SUFFICE, SUFFICIENT

A. Verbs.

1. ARKEŌ (ἀρκέω), to suffice, is rendered "is sufficient" in John 714
6:7; 2 Cor. 12:9; "it sufficeth" in John 14:8. See CONTENT, AG:107A CB:1237C
ENOUGH.

Note: For 1 Pet. 4:3, see B, No. 2.

2. HIKANOŌ (ἱκανόω), to make sufficient, render fit, is translated 2427
"made (us) sufficient" in 2 Cor. 3:6, R.V. (A.V., "hath made ... AG:374D CB:1250C
able"). See ABLE, B, No. 6, Note.

B. Adjectives.

1. HIKANOS (ἱκανός), akin to A, No. 2, enough, sufficient, fit, etc. is 2425 AG:374B
translated "sufficient" in 2 Cor. 2:6, 16; 3:5. See ABLE, C, No. 2. CB:1250C

2. ARKETOS (ἀρκετός), akin to A, No. 1, used with *eimi*, to be, is 713
translated "may suffice" in 1 Pet. 4:3. See ENOUGH, A, No. 1. AG:107A CB:1237C

SUFFICIENCY

1. AUTARKEIA (αὐτάρκεια) (*autos*, self, *arkeō*, see A, above; Eng., 841
autarchy), "contentment," 1 Tim. 6:6, is rendered "sufficiency" in AG:122B CB:1238B
2 Cor. 9:8.¶

2. HIKANOTĒS (ἱκανότης) is rendered "sufficiency" in 2 Cor. 3:5.¶ 2426 AG:374D CB:1250C

For SUIT (make), Acts 25:24, R.V., see DEAL WITH, Note (1)

SUM (Noun), SUM UP

KEPHALAION 2774 AG:429D CB:1255A

A. Noun.

Note: For *kephalaion*, Acts 22:28; Heb. 8:1, see POINT, B.¶ For TIMē 5092
timē, Acts 7:16, see PRICE, A. AG:817B CB:1272C

B. Verb.

ANAKEPHALAIOŌ (ἀνακεφαλαιόω), to sum up, gather up (*ana*, up, 346 (-IOMAI)
kephalē, a head), to present as a whole, is used in the Passive Voice in AG:55D
Rom. 13:9, R.V., "summed up" (A.V., "briefly comprehended"), CB:1235A (-IOMAI)
i.e., the one commandment expresses all that the Law enjoins, and to obey this one is to fulfil the Law (cp. Gal. 5:14); Middle Voice in Eph. 1:10, R.V., "sum up" (A.V., "gather together"), of God's purpose to sum up all things in the heavens and on the earth in Christ, a consummation extending beyond the limits of the Church, though the latter is to be a factor in its realization.¶

SULFUR See BRIMSTONE

SUMMER

THEROS (θέρος), akin to *therō*, to heat, occurs in Matt. 24:32; 2330
Mark 13:28; Luke 21:30.¶ AG:359D CB:1272B

SUMPTUOUS, SUMPTUOUSLY

A. Adjective.

LAMPROS (λαμπρός), bright, is rendered "sumptuous" in Rev. 2986 AG:465D
18:14, R.V. See BRIGHT, GOODLY, Note. CB:1256C

B. Adverb.

2988 AG:466A CB:1256C LAMPRŌS (λαμπρῶς), the corresponding adverb, is used in **Luke** 16 : 19, " sumptuously."¶

SUN

2246 AG:345C CB:1249C HĒLIOS (ἥλιος), whence Eng. prefix helio—, is used (*a*) as a means of the natural benefits of light and heat, e.g., Matt. 5 : 45, and power, Rev. 1 : 16 ; (*b*) of its qualities of brightness and glory, e.g., Matt. 13 : 43 ; 17 : 2 ; Acts 26 : 13 ; 1 Cor. 15 : 41 ; Rev. 10 : 1 ; 12 : 1 ; (*c*) as a means of destruction, e.g., Matt. 13 : 6 ; Jas. 1 : 11 ; of physical misery, Rev. 7 : 16 ; (*d*) as a means of judgment, e.g., Matt. 24 : 29 ; Mark 13 : 24 ; Luke 21 : 25 ; 23 : 45 ; Acts 2 : 20 ; Rev. 6 : 12 ; 8 : 12 ; 9 : 2 ; 16 : 8.

395 AG:62B CB:1235B *Note :* In Rev. 7 : 2 and 16 : 12, *anatolē*, rising, used with ***hēlios***, is translated " sunrising," R.V. (A.V., " east ").

For SUNDER (Asunder) see CUT, No. 6

For SUNDRY see PORTION, C

SUP

1172 AG:173B CB:1240C DEIPNEŌ (δειπνέω), to sup (said of taking the chief meal of the day), occurs in Luke 17 : 8 ; 22 : 20 (in the best texts), lit., ' (the) supping ; ' so 1 Cor. 11 : 25 ; metaphorically in Rev. 3 : 20, of spiritual communion between Christ and the faithful believer.¶

SUPERIOR See EXCELLENT

For SUPERFLUITY see ABUNDANCE, A, No. 2, B, No. 1

SUPERFLUOUS

4053 AG:651B CB:1263C PERISSOS (περισσός), abundant, more than sufficient, is translated " superfluous " in 2 Cor. 9 : 1. See ABUNDANT, C, No. 1, ADVANTAGE, MORE, B, No. 2.

SUPERSCRIPTION

1923 AG:291C CB:1245C EPIGRAPHĒ (ἐπιγραφή), lit., an over-writing (*epi*, over, ***graphō***, to write) (the meaning of the anglicized Latin word " superscription "), denotes an inscription, a title. On Roman coins the Emperor's name was inscribed, Matt. 22 : 20 ; Mark 12 : 16 ; Luke 20 : 24. In the Roman Empire, in the case of a criminal on his way to execution, a board on which was inscribed the cause of his condemnation, was carried before

TITLOS 5102 AG:820D CB:1272C him or hung round his neck ; the inscription was termed a title (*titlos*). The four Evangelists state that at the crucifixion of Christ the title was affixed to the cross, Mark (15 : 26) and Luke (23 : 38) call it a " superscription ; " Mark says it was " written over " (*epigraphō*, the corresponding verb). Matthew calls it " His accusation ; " John calls it " a title " (a technical term). The wording varies : the essential words are the same, and the variation serves to authenticate the narratives, shewing that there was no consultation leading to an agreement as to the details. See further under TITLE.¶

For SUPERSTITION see RELIGION

SUPERSTITIOUS

DEISIDAIMŌN (δεισιδαίμων), reverent to the deity (*deidō*, to fear; 1174
daimōn, a demon, or pagan god), occurs in Acts 17 : 22 in the comparative (-MONESTEROS) AG:173D
degree, rendered "somewhat superstitious," R.V. (A.V., "too s."), a CB:1240C
meaning which the word sometimes has; others, according to its comparative form, advocate the meaning 'more religious (than others),' 'quite religious' (cp. the noun in 25 : 19). This is supported by Ramsay, who renders it 'more than others respectful of what is divine;' so Deissmann in *Light from the Ancient East*, and others. It also agrees with the meaning found in Greek writers; the context too suggests that the adjective is used in a good sense; perhaps, after all, with kindly ambiguity (Grimm-Thayer). An ancient epitaph has it in the sense of 'reverent' (Moulton and Milligan).¶

SUPPER

DEIPNON (δεῖπνον) denotes a supper or feast (for an analysis of the 1173
uses see FEAST, No. 2). In John 13 : 2 the R.V., following certain texts, AG:173B CB:1240C
has "during supper" (A.V., "supper being ended").

Note: For "supper" in Luke 22 : 20 see SUP.

SUPPLICATION

1. DEĒSIS (δέησις) is always translated "supplication," or the plural, 1162
in the R.V. See PRAYER, B, No. 3. AG:171D CB:1240B

2. HIKETĒRIA (ἱκετηρία) is the feminine form of the adjective 2428
hiketērios, denoting 'of a suppliant,' and used as a noun, formerly an AG:375A CB:1250C
olive-branch carried by a suppliant (*hiketēs*), then later, a supplication, used with No. 1 in Heb. 5 : 7.¶ In the Sept., Job 40 : 22 (Eng. Vers. 41 : 3).¶

SUPPLY (Noun and Verb)

A. Verbs.

1. CHORĒGEŌ (χορηγέω) primarily, among the Greeks, signified to 5524
lead a stage chorus or dance (*choros*, and *hēgeomai*, to lead), then, to defray AG:883D CB:—
the expenses of a chorus; hence, later, metaphorically, to supply, 2 Cor. 9 : 10 (2nd part; see also No. 2), R.V., "supply" (A.V. "minister"); 1 Pet. 4 : 11, R.V., "supplieth" (A.V., "giveth"). See GIVE, Note (4), MINISTER, B, Note (1).¶

2. EPICHORĒGEŌ (ἐπιχορηγέω), to supply fully, abundantly (a 2023
strengthened form of No. 1), is rendered to supply in the R.V. of 2 Cor. AG:305A CB:—

9 : 10 (1st part) and Gal. 3 : 5 (for A.V., to minister), where the present continuous tense speaks of the work of the Holy Spirit in all His ministrations to believers individually and collectively; in Col. 2 : 19, R.V., "being supplied" (A.V., "having nourishment ministered"), of the work of Christ as the Head of the Church His body; in 2 Pet. 1 : 5, "supply" (A.V., "add"); in ver. 11, "shall be . . . . supplied" (A.V., "shall be ministered"), of the reward hereafter which those are to receive, in regard to positions in the Kingdom of God, for their fulfilment here of the conditions mentioned.¶

Note: In 2 Cor. 9 : 10 (see Nos. 1 and 2 above) the stronger verb No. 2 is used where the will and capacity to receive are in view.

378 AG:59C CB:1235B 3. ANAPLĒROŌ (ἀναπληρόω), to fill up, fulfil, is rendered to supply in 1 Cor. 16 : 17 and Phil. 2 : 30. See Fill, Fulfil, Occupy.

4322 AG:711D CB:1267A 4. PROSANAPLĒROŌ (προσαναπληρόω), to fill up by adding to, to supply fully (*pros*, to, and No. 3), is translated "supplieth" in 2 Cor. 9 : 12, A.V. (R.V., "filleth up the measure of"); in 11 : 9, R.V. and A.V., "supplied."¶

4137 AG:670C CB:1265B *Note:* In Phil. 4 : 19, A.V., *plēroō*, to fulfil (R.V.), is rendered "shall supply."

B. Noun.

2024 AG:305B CB:— EPICHORĒGIA (ἐπιχορηγία), a full supply, occurs in Eph. 4 : 16, "supplieth," lit., 'by the supply of every joint,' metaphorically of the members of the Church, the Body of which Christ is the Head, and Phil. 1 : 19, "the supply (of the Spirit of Jesus Christ)", i.e., 'the bountiful supply;' here "of the Spirit" may be taken either in the subjective sense, the Giver, or the objective, the Gift.¶

SUPPORT

ANTILAMBANOMAI 482 AG:74C CB:— ANTECHOMAI 472 AG:73B CB:— *Notes:* (1) In Acts 20 : 35, A.V., *antilambanomai*, to help (R.V.), is translated "support." See Help, B, No. 1. (2) In 1 Thess. 5 : 14, *antechomai* signifies to support: see Hold, No. 3.

SUPPOSE

3543 AG:541A CB:1260A 1. NOMIZŌ (νομίζω), to consider, suppose, think, is rendered to suppose in Matt. 20 : 10; Luke 2 : 34; 3 : 23; Acts 7 : 25; 14 : 19; 16 : 27; 21 : 29; 1 Tim. 6 : 5; in 1 Cor. 7 : 26, A.V. (R.V., "I think"); in Acts 16 : 13, the R.V. adheres to the meaning "to suppose," "(where) we supposed (there was a place of prayer);" this word also signifies 'to practise a custom' (*nomos*) and is commonly so used by Greek writers. Hence the A.V., "was wont (to be made);" it is rendered to think in Matt. 5 : 17; 10 : 34; Acts 8 : 20; 17 : 29; 1 Cor. 7 : 36. See Think.¶

1380 AG:201D CB:1242A 2. DOKEŌ (δοκέω), to be of opinion, is translated to suppose in Mark 6 : 49; Luke 24 : 37; John 20 : 15; Acts 27 : 13; in the following, A.V. "suppose," R.V., "think," Luke 12 : 51; 13 : 2; Heb. 10 : 29. It is most frequently rendered to think, always in Matthew; always in

John, except 11 : 31, " supposing," R.V. [where the best texts have this verb (for *legō*, A.V., " saying ")], and 20 : 15 (see above).

3. HUPOLAMBANŌ (ὑπολαμβάνω), when used of mental action, 5274
signifies to suppose, Luke 7 : 43, and Acts 2 : 15. See ANSWER, RECEIVE. AG:845B CB:1252B

4. HUPONOEŌ (ὑπονοέω), to suspect, to conjecture, is translated 5282
" suppose ye " in Acts 13 : 25, R.V. (A.V., " think ye ") ; " I supposed " AG:846D
in 25 : 18. See DEEM. CB:—

5. OIOMAI or OIMAI (οἴομαι) signifies to expect, imagine, suppose ; 3633
it is rendered to suppose in John 21 : 25 ; Phil. 1 : 17, R.V. (A.V., ver. AG:562C
16, " thinking ") ; " think " in Jas. 1 : 7. See THINK.¶ CB:—

Notes : (1) In 2 Cor. 11 : 5, A.V., *logizomai*, to reckon (R.V.), is LOGIZOMAI
rendered " I suppose ; " so in 1 Pet. 5 : 12, A.V., R.V., " (as) I account 3049
(him) ; " Silvanus was not supposed by Peter to be faithful, he was AG:475D CB:1257A
reckoned or regarded so. (2) In Phil. 2 : 25, A.V., *hēgeomai*, to reckon, HēGEOMAI
deem, is rendered " I supposed " (R.V., " I counted "). 2233 AG:343C CB:1249C

SUPREME

HUPERECHŌ (ὑπερέχω), to be superior, to excel, is translated 5242
" supreme " in 1 Pet. 2 : 13 : see EXCEL, No. 3. AG:840D CB:1252A

SURE

A. Adjectives.

1. ASPHALĒS (ἀσφαλής), safe, is translated " sure " in Heb. 6 : 19 804
See CERTAIN, B. AG:119A CB:1238A

2. BEBAIOS (βέβαιος), firm, stedfast, is used of (*a*) God's promise to 949
Abraham, Rom. 4 : 16 ; (*b*) the believer's hope, Heb. 6 : 19, " stedfast ; " AG:138B CB:1239A
(*c*) the hope of spiritual leaders regarding the welfare of converts, 2 Cor. 1 : 7, " stedfast ; " (*d*) the glorying of the hope, Heb. 3 : 6, " firm ; " (*e*) the beginning of our confidence, 3 : 14, R.V., " firm " (A.V., " stedfast ") ; (*f*) the Law given at Sinai, Heb. 2 : 2, " stedfast ; " (*g*) the testament (or covenant) fulfilled after a death, 9 : 17, " of force ; " (*h*) the calling and election of believers, 2 Pet. 1 : 10, to be made " sure " by the fulfilment of the injunctions in vv. 5–7 ; (*i*) the word of prophecy, " *made* more sure," 2 Pet. 1 : 19, R.V., A.V., " a more sure (word of prophecy) ; " what is meant is not a comparison between the prophecies of the O.T. and N.T., but that the former have been confirmed in the Person of Christ (vv. 16–18). See FIRM.¶

3. PISTOS (πιστός), faithful, is translated " sure " in Acts 13 : 34. 4103
See FAITHFUL. AG:664C CB:1265A

Note : In 2 Tim. 2 : 19, A.V., *stereos*, firm, is translated " sure," and 4731
connected with " standeth," R.V., " the firm (foundation of God AG:766D
standeth)," i.e., ' however much the faith may be misrepresented or CB:1270A
denied, the firm foundation of God's knowledge and truth, with its separating power, remains.'

B. Verb.

805 ASPHALIZŌ (ἀσφαλίζω), to make safe or sure (akin to A, No. 1), is
AG:119A CB:1238A rendered to make sure in Matt. 27 : 64, 65, 66, of the sepulchre of Christ ; elsewhere, Acts 16 : 24, of making feet fast in the stocks. See FAST.¶

Note : In the A.V. of John 16 : 30 ; Rom. 2 : 2 and 15 : 29, the verb *oida*, to know, is translated to be sure (R.V., in each place, to know). So with *ginōskō*, to know, in John 6 : 69. For the difference between the verbs see KNOW.

OIDA 1492

SURELY

(EIDō) AG:555D *Notes :* (1) In the A.V. of Matt. 26 : 73 ; Mark 14 : 70 ; John 17 : 8,
CB:1260B *alēthōs*, truly, is rendered " surely " (R.V., " of a truth ") ; so *pantōs*, at
GINōSKō 1097 all events, altogether, in Luke 4 : 23 (R.V., " doubtless "), and *nai*, yea,
AG:160D CB:1248B in Rev. 22 : 20 (R.V., " yea "). (2) In Heb. 6 : 14, " surely " represents
ALēTHōS the phrase *ei mēn* (so the best texts ; some have *ē mēn*). (3) For Luke
230 AG:37B 1 : 1, A.V., see BELIEVE, C, Note (4). (4) For " surely " in 2 Pet. 2 : 12,
CB:1234B PANTōS R.V., see CORRUPT, A, No. 2 (*b*).

3843 AG:609B

SURETY (Noun)

CB:— NAI ENGUOS (ἔγγυος) primarily signifies bail, the bail who personally
3483 answers for anyone, whether with his life or his property (to be dis-
AG:532D CB:— tinguished from *mesitēs*, a mediator) ; it is used in Heb. 7 : 22, " (by so
EI 1487 much also hath Jesus become) the Surety (of a better covenant)," referring
AG:219A to the abiding and unchanging character of His Melchizedek priesthood,
CB:1242C MēN by reason of which His suretyship is established by God's oath (vv. 20, 21).
3375 AG:518D As the Surety, He is the Personal guarantee of the terms of the new and
CB:1258B better covenant, secured on the ground of His perfect sacrifice
ENGUOS 1450 (ver. 27).¶

AG:214A CB:1245A For SURETY (of a), Acts 12 : 11, A.V., see TRUE, D, No. 1

2897 AG:448A CB:1255C

SURFEITING

METHē 3178 KRAIPALĒ (κραιπάλη) signifies the giddiness and headache resulting
AG:498D CB:1258C from excessive wine-bibbing, a drunken nausea, " surfeiting," Luke
OINOPHLUGIA 3632 21 : 34.¶ Trench (Syn. § lxi) distinguishes this and the synonymous
AG:562C CB:1260C words, *methē*, drunkenness, *oinophlugia*, wine-bibbing (A.V., " excess of
KōMOS 2970 wine," 1 Pet. 4 : 3), *kōmos*, revelling.

AG:461D CB:1255C For SURGE, Jas. 1 : 6, R V., see RAGE and WAVE

For SURMISE, SURMISINGS, see DEEM

SURNAME

1941 (-OMAI) AG:294A EPIKALEŌ (ἐπικαλέω), to put a name upon (*epi*, upon, *kaleō*, to call),
CB:1245C to surname, is used in this sense in the Passive Voice, in some texts in

Matt. 10 : 3 (it is absent in the best); in Luke 22 : 3, in some texts (the best have *kaleō*, to call); Acts 1 : 23; 4 : 36; 10 : 5, 18, 32; 11 : 13; 12 : 12, 25; in some texts, 15 : 22 (the best have *kaleō*).

Notes: (1) In Mark 3 : 16, 17, "He surnamed" is a translation of EPITITHēMI
epitithēmi, to put upon, to add to, with *onoma*, a name, as the object. 2007
(2) In Acts 15 : 37, A.V., *kaleō*, to call (R.V., "called"), is rendered AG:302D CB:1246B
"whose surname was." (3) The verb *eponomazō*, translated "bearest KALEō
the name" in Rom. 2 : 17, R.V., finds a literal correspondence in the 2564 AG:398D
word 'surname' (*epi*, upon, = *sur*), and had this significance in Classical CB:1253B
Greek.¶ EPONOMAZō 2028 AG:305C

CB:1246B

For SURPASS, 2 Cor. 3 : 10, see EXCEED, A, No. 1

SURPRISE See AMAZE, MARVEL

For SUSPENSE (hold in) see DOUBT, No. 6

SURROUNDING See ROUND

SUSTENANCE

CHORTASMA (χόρτασμα), fodder (akin to *chortazō*, to feed, fill, see 5527
FEED, No. 4), is used in the plural in Acts 7 : 11, "sustenance."¶ In AG:884A
the Sept., Gen. 24 : 25, 32; 42 : 27; 43 : 24; Deut. 11 : 15; Judg. CB:1240A
19 : 19.¶

SWADDLING-CLOTHES

SPARGANOŌ (σπαργανόω), to swathe (from *sparganon*, a swathing- 4683
band), signifies to wrap in swaddling-clothes in Luke 2 : 7, 12. The idea AG:760D
that the word means 'rags' is without foundation.¶ In the Sept., CB:—
Job 38 : 9; Ezek. 16 : 4.¶

SWALLOW (Verb)

KATAPINŌ (καταπίνω), to drink down (*kata*, and *pinō*, to drink), 2666
to swallow, is used with this meaning (*a*) physically, but figuratively, AG:416B
Matt. 23 : 24; Rev. 12 : 16; (*b*) metaphorically, in the Passive Voice, CB:1254B
of death (by victory), 1 Cor. 15 : 54; of being overwhelmed by sorrow,
2 Cor. 2 : 7; of the mortal body (by life), 5 : 4. See DEVOUR, No. 3,
DROWN, No. 2.

SWAY See REGARD, SHAKE

SWEAR, SWORN

OMNUMI (ὄμνυμι) or OMNUŌ (ὀμνύω) is used of affirming or denying 3660
by an oath, e.g., Matt. 26 : 74; Mark 6 : 23; Luke 1 : 73; Heb. 3 : 11, 18; AG:565D
4 : 3; 7 : 21; accompanied by that by which one swears, e.g., Matt. CB:1260C
5 : 34, 36; 23 : 16; Heb. 6 : 13, 16; Jas. 5 : 12; Rev. 10 : 6. Cp.
ADJURE.

Note: For "false swearers," 1 Tim. 1 : 10, see FORSWEAR.

SWEAT

2402

HIDRŌS (ἱδρώς) is used in Luke 22 : 44.¶ In the Sept., Gen. 3 : 19.¶ AG:371C CB:—

SWEEP

4563 SAROŌ (σαρόω) occurs in Matt. 12 : 44 ; Luke 11 : 25 ; 15 : 8.¶
AG:744D
CB:—

SWEET

1099 GLUKUS (γλυκύς) (cp. Eng., glycerine, glucose), occurs in Jas. 3 : 11,
AG:162A
CB:1248B 12 (A.V., " fresh " in this verse) ; Rev. 10 : 9, 10.¶

For SWEET SMELLING see SAVOUR, No. 1

SWELL, SWOLLEN

4092 PIMPRĒMI (πίμπρημι), primarily, to blow, to burn, later came to
AG:658B
CB:1265A denote to cause to swell, and, in the Middle Voice, to become swollen, Acts 28 : 6.¶ In the Sept., Numb. 5 : 21, 22, 27.¶

4248 *Note* : Some, connecting the word *prēnēs* in Acts 1 : 18 with *pimprēmi*,
AG:700D
CB:1266B give it the meaning ' swelling up : ' see HEADLONG.

SWELLING

5450 1. PHUSIŌSIS (φυσίωσις) denotes a puffing up, swelling with pride
AG:870A
CB:— (akin to *phusioō*, to puff up), 2 Cor. 12 : 20, " swellings."¶

5246 2. HUPERONKOS (ὑπέρογκος), an adjective denoting of excessive
AG:841C
CB:— weight or size, is used metaphorically in the sense of immoderate, especially of arrogant speech, in the neuter plural, virtually as a noun, 2 Pet. 2 : 18 ; Jude 16, " great swelling words," doubtless with reference to Gnostic phraseology.¶

SWERVE

795 ASTOCHEŌ (ἀστοχέω), to miss the mark, is translated " having
AG:118A
CB:1238A swerved " in 1 Tim. 1 : 6. See ERR, No. 3. Moulton and Milligan illustrate the use of the verb from the papyri, e.g., of a man in extravagant terms bewailing the loss of a pet fighting-cock, " (I am distraught, for my cock) has failed (me)."

SWIFT, SWIFTLY

3691
AG:574C
CB:— 1. OXUS (ὀξύς) denotes " swift " in Rom. 3 : 15. See SHARP.

5036 2. TACHUS (ταχύς), swift, speedy, is used in Jas. 1 : 19.¶ Cp.
AG:807B
CB:1271A *tacheōs*, *tachu* and *tacheion*, quickly, *tachos*, quickness, speed.

5031 3. TACHINOS (ταχινός), a poetical and late form of No. 2, of swift
AG:807A
CB:1271A approach, is used in 2 Pet. 1 : 14, R.V., " swiftly " (A.V., " shortly "), lit., ' (the putting off of my tabernacle is) swift,' i.e., imminent ; in 2 : 1, " swift (destruction)."¶ In the Sept., Prov. 1 : 16 ; Is. 59 : 7 ; Hab. 1 : 6.¶

SWIM

2860
AG:442C 1. KOLUMBAŌ (κολυμβάω), to dive, plunge, into the sea, hence, to
CB:— swim, occurs in Acts 27 : 43.¶ Cp. *kolumbēthra*, a pool.

2. EKKOLUMBAŌ (ἐκκολυμβάω), to swim out of (*ek*), occurs in 1579
Acts 27 : 42.¶ AG:241D
CB:—

SWINE

CHOIROS (χοῖρος), a swine, is used in the plural, in the Synoptic 5519
Gospels only, Matt. 7 : 6 ; 8 : 30, 31, 32 ; Mark 5 : 11–13, 16 ; Luke 8 : 32, AG:883B
33 ; Luke 15 : 15, 16. It does not occur in the O.T.¶ CB:1240A

SWORD

1. MACHAIRA (μάχαιρα), a short sword or dagger (distinct from No. 3162
2), e.g., Matt. 26 : 47, 51, 52 and parallel passages ; Luke 21 : 24 ; 22 : 38, AG:496B
possibly a knife (Field, *Notes on the Translation of the N.T.*) ; Heb. 4 : 12 CB:1257B
(see TWO-EDGED) ; metaphorically and by metonymy, (*a*) for ordinary violence, or dissensions, that destroy peace, Matt. 10 : 34 ; (*b*) as the instrument of a magistrate or judge, e.g., Rom. 13 : 4 ; (*c*) of the Word of God, "the sword of the Spirit," probing the conscience, subduing the impulses to sin, Eph. 6 : 17.

2. RHOMPHAIA (ῥομφαία), a word of somewhat doubtful origin, 4501
denoted a Thracian weapon of large size, whether a sword or spear is not AG:737A
certain, but usually longer than No. 1 ; it occurs (*a*) literally in Rev. 6 : 8 ; CB:1268B
(*b*) metaphorically, as the instrument of anguish, Luke 2 : 35 ; of judgment, Rev. 1 : 16 ; 2 : 12, 16 ; 19 : 15, 21, probably figurative of the Lord's judicial utterances.¶

SYCAMINE

SUKAMINOS (συκάμινος) occurs in Luke 17 : 6.¶ It is generally 4708
recognized as the Black Mulberry, with fruit like blackberries. The AG:776A
leaves are too tough for silkworms and thus are unlike the White Mulberry. CB:—
Neither kind is the same as the Mulberry of 2 Sam. 5 : 23, 24, etc. The town Haifa was called Sycaminopolis, from the name of the tree.

SYCAMORE

SUKOMOREA (συκομορέα) occurs in Luke 19 : 4.¶ This tree is 4809
of the fig species, with leaves like the mulberry and fruit like the fig. It (-RAIA)
is somewhat less in height than the sycamine and spreads to cover an AG:776B
area from 60 to 80 feet in diameter. It is often planted by the roadside, CB:—
and was suitable for the purpose of Zacchæus. Seated on the lowest branch he was easily within speaking distance of Christ.

SYNAGOGUE

SUNAGŌGĒ (συναγωγή), properly a bringing together (*sun*, together, 4864
agō, to bring), denoted (*a*) a gathering of things, a collection, then, of AG:782D
persons, an assembling, of Jewish religious gatherings, e.g., Acts 9 : 2 ; CB:1270B
an assembly of Christian Jews, Jas. 2 : 2, R.V., "synagogue" (A.V., marg. ; text, "assembly") ; a company dominated by the power and

activity of Satan, Rev. 2 : 9 ; 3 : 9 ; (*b*) by metonymy, the building in which the gathering is held, e.g. Matt. 6 : 2 ; Mark 1 : 21. The origin of the Jewish synagogue is probably to be assigned to the time of the Babylonish exile. Having no Temple, the Jews assembled on the sabbath to hear the Law read, and the practice continued in various buildings after the return. Cp. Ps. 74 : 8.

SYNAGOGUE (put out of the)

656
AG:100D
CB:1237B
APOSUNAGŌGOS (ἀποσυνάγωγος), an adjective denoting 'expelled from the congregation,' excommunicated, is used (*a*) with *ginomai*, to become, be made, John 9 : 22 ; 12 : 42 ; (*b*) with *poieō*, to make, John 16 : 2. This excommunication involved prohibition not only from attendance at the synagogue, but from all fellowship with Israelites.¶

SYNAGOGUE (ruler of the)

752
AG:113B
CB:—
ARCHISUNAGŌGOS (ἀρχισυνάγωγος) denotes the administrative official, with the duty of preserving order and inviting persons to read or speak in the assembly, Mark 5 : 22, 35, 36, 38 ; Luke 8 : 49 ; 13 : 14 ; Acts 13 : 15 ; "chief ruler" (A.V.) in Acts 18 : 8, 17.¶

Note : In Luke 8 : 41, "ruler of the synagogue" represents *archōn*, ruler, followed by the genitive case of the article and *sunagōgē*.

SYROPHŒNICIAN

4949
AG:794B
CB:—
SUROPHOINIKISSA or SUROPHUNISSA (Συροφοινίκισσα) occurs in Mark 7 : 26 as the national name of a woman called "a Canaanitish woman" in Matt. 15 : 22, i.e., not a Jewess but a descendant of the early inhabitants of the coast-land of Phœnicia. The word probably denoted a Syrian residing in Phœnicia proper.¶ There is a tradition that the woman's name was Justa and her daughter Bernice (*Clementine Homilies*, ii : 19 ; iii : 73). In Acts 21 : 2, 3, the two parts of the term are used interchangeably.

T

TABERNACLE

1. SKĒNĒ (σκηνή), a tent, booth, tabernacle, is used of (*a*) tents as 4633
dwellings, Matt. 17 : 4 ; Mark 9 : 5 ; Luke 9 : 33 ; Heb. 11 : 9, A.V., AG:754C
" tabernacles " (R.V., " tents ") ; (*b*) the Mosaic Tabernacle, Acts 7 : 44 ; CB:1269A
Heb. 8 : 5 ; 9 : 1 (in some mss.) ; 9 : 8, 21, termed " the tent of meeting," R.V. (i.e., where the people were called to meet God), a preferable description to " the tabernacle of the congregation," as in the A.V. in the O.T. ; the outer part, 9 : 2, 6 ; the inner sanctuary, 9 : 3 ; (*c*) the Heavenly prototype, Heb. 8 : 2 ; 9 : 11 ; Rev. 13 : 6 ; 15 : 5 ; 21 : 3 (of its future descent) ; (*d*) the eternal abodes of the saints, Luke 16 : 9, R.V., " tabernacles " (A.V., " habitations ") ; (*e*) the temple in Jerusalem, as continuing the service of the tabernacle, Heb. 13 : 10 ; (*f*) the house of David, i.e., metaphorically of his people, Acts 15 : 16 ; (*g*) the portable shrine of the god Moloch, Acts 7 : 43.¶

2. SKĒNOS (σκῆνος), the equivalent of No. 1, is used metaphorically 4636 AG:755B
of the body as the tabernacle of the soul, 2 Cor. 5 : 1, 4.¶ CB:1269A

3. SKĒNŌMA (σκήνωμα) occurs in Acts 7 : 46 ; 2 Pet. 1 : 13, 14 ; 4638 AG:755C
see HABITATION, No. 6.¶ CB:1269A

4. SKĒNOPĒGIA (σκηνοπηγία), properly the setting up of tents or 4634
dwellings (No. 1, and *pēgnumi*, to fix), represents the word " tabernacles " AG:754D CB:1269A
in " the feast of tabernacles," John 7 : 2.¶ This feast, one of the three Pilgrimage Feasts in Israel, is called " the feast of ingathering " in Ex. 23 : 16 ; 34 : 22 ; it took place at the end of the year, and all males were to attend at the tabernacle with their offerings. In Lev. 23 : 34 ; Deut. 16 : 13, 16 ; 31 : 10 ; 2 Chron. 8 : 13 , Ezra 3 : 4 (cp. Neh. 8 : 14–18), it is called " the feast of tabernacles " (or booths, *sukkôth*), and was appointed for seven days at Jerusalem from the 15th to the 22nd Tishri (approximately October), to remind the people that their fathers dwelt in these in the wilderness journeys. Cp. Num. 29 : 15–38, especially vers. 35–38, for the regulations of the eighth or " last day, the great day of the feast " (John 7 : 37).

Note : For *skēnoō*, to spread a tabernacle over, Rev. 7 : 15, R.V., 4637
see DWELL, No. 9. AG:755C CB:1269A

TABLE

1. TRAPEZA (τράπεζα) is used of (*a*) a dining-table, Matt. 15 : 27 ; 5132
Mark 7 : 28 ; Luke 16 : 21 ; 22 : 21, 30 ; (*b*) the table of shewbread, AG:824B CB:1273A
Heb. 9 : 2 ; (*c*) by metonymy, of what is provided on the table (the word

being used of that with which it is associated), Acts 16 : 34 ; Rom. 11 : 9 (figurative of the special privileges granted to Israel and centring in Christ) ; 1 Cor. 10 : 21 (twice), " the Lord's table," denoting all that is provided for believers in Christ on the ground of His Death (and thus expressing something more comprehensive than the Lord's Supper) ; " the table of demons," denoting all that is partaken of by idolaters as the result of the influence of demons in connection with their sacrifices ; (*d*) a money-changer's table, Matt. 21 : 12 ; Mark 11 : 15 ; John 2 : 15 ; (*e*) a bank, Luke 19 : 23 (cp. *trapezitēs* : see BANKERS) ; (*f*) by metonymy for the distribution of money, Acts 6 : 2. See BANK.¶

4109 AG:666A 2. PLAX (πλάξ) primarily denotes anything flat and broad, hence, a
CB:1265A flat stone, a tablet, 2 Cor. 3 : 3 (twice) ; Heb. 9 : 4.¶

2825 AG:436B *Note :* Some texts have the word *klinē*, a couch, in Mark 7 : 4 (A.V.,
CB:— " tables ").

TABLE (at the)

345 AG:55D ANAKEIMAI (ἀνάκειμαι), to recline at a meal table, is rendered
CB:1235A " sat at the table " in John 12 : 2, A.V., R.V., " sat at meat " (some
SUNANAKEIMAI texts have *sunanakeimai*) ; " sat," of course does not express the actual
4873 AG:784B attitude ; in John 13 : 23, R.V., " at the table reclining ; " A.V.,
CB:— " leaning ; " in 13 : 28, " at the table " (A.V. and R.V.), lit., ' of (those) reclining.'

For TABLET see WRITING TABLET

TACKLING

4631 AG:754A SKEUĒ (σκευή) denotes gear, equipment, tackling (of a ship), Acts
CB:— 27 : 19.¶

TAIL

3769 AG:593C OURA (οὐρά), the tail of an animal, occurs in Rev. 9 : 10 (twice),
CB:— 19 ; 12 : 4.¶

TAKE

2983 AG:464A 1. LAMBANŌ (λαμβάνω), to take, lay hold of, besides its literal sense,
CB:1256C e.g., Matt. 5 : 40 ; 26 : 26, 27, is used metaphorically, of fear, in taking hold of people, Luke 7 : 16, R.V. (A.V., " came . . . on ") ; of sin in " finding (occasion)," R.V. (A.V., " taking "), Rom. 7 : 8, 11, where sin is viewed as the corrupt source of action, an inward element using the commandment to produce evil effects ; of the power of temptation, 1 Cor. 10 : 13 ; of taking an example, Jas. 5 : 10 ; of taking peace from the earth, Rev. 6 : 4 ; of Christ in taking the form of a servant, Phil. 2 : 7 ; of taking rightful power (by the Lord, hereafter), Rev. 11 : 17. See
353 AG:56D ACCEPT, No. 4.
CB:1235A 2. ANALAMBANŌ (ἀναλαμβάνω) signifies (*a*) to take up (*ana*),

e.g., Acts 1 : 2, 11, 22 (R.V., "received") ; (*b*) to take to oneself, Acts
7 : 43 ; or to one's company, 20 : 13, 14 ; 23 : 31 ; 2 Tim. 4 : 11 ; of
taking up spiritual armour, Eph. 6 : 13, 16. See RECEIVE.

3. APOLAMBANŌ (ἀπολαμβάνω), besides its common meaning, to 618
receive, denotes to take apart or aside, Mark 7 : 33, Middle Voice. It AG:94B CB:1237A
is frequent in the papyri, and, in the sense of separation or drawing aside,
is illustrated in a message of sorrow, concerning the non-arrival of one
who with others had been 'shut up' as recluses in a temple (Moulton
and Milligan, Vocab.). See RECEIVE.

4. EPILAMBANŌ (ἐπιλαμβάνω), in the Middle Voice, to lay hold of, 1949 (-OMAI)
take hold of, is used literally, e.g., Mark 8 : 23 ; Luke 9 : 47 ; 14 : 4 ; AG:295A
metaphorically, e.g., Heb. 8 : 9, "(I) took them (by the hand) :" for (-OMAI) CB:1246A
other instances in each respect see HOLD, No. 7. 2638

5. KATALAMBANŌ (καταλαμβάνω), to lay hold of, is rendered to AG:412D
take, in Mark 9 : 18 ; John 8 : 3, 4. See APPREHEND. CB:1254A (-OMAI)

6. METALAMBANŌ (μεταλαμβάνω), to get, or have, a share of, is 3335
rendered "to take (food)" in Acts 2 : 46, R.V. (A.V., "did eat," see AG:511B CB:1258B
EAT, Note) ; 27 : 33, i.e., to share it together. See HAVE, PARTAKE,
RECEIVE.

7. PARALAMBANŌ (παραλαμβάνω), besides its meaning to receive, 3880
denotes to take to (or with) oneself, of taking a wife, e.g., Matt. 1 : 20, 24 ; AG:619B CB:1262A
of taking a person or persons with one, e.g., Matt. 2 : 13, 14, 20, 21 ;
4 : 5, 8 ; of demons, 12 : 45 ; of Christ and His disciples, 17 : 1 ; 20 : 17 ;
Mark 9 : 2 ; 10 : 32 ; 14 : 33 ; of witnesses, Matt. 18 : 16 ; of the removal of
persons from the earth in judgment, when "the Son of Man is revealed,"
Matt. 24 : 40, 41 ; Luke 17 : 34, 35 (cp. the means of the removal of
corruption, in ver. 37) ; of the taking of Christ by the soldiers for
scourging, Matt. 27 : 27, R.V., and to crucifixion, John 19 : 16 ; see
also Acts 15 : 39 ; 16 : 33 ; 21 : 24, 26, 32 ; 23 : 18. See RECEIVE.

8. SUMPARALAMBANŌ (συμπαραλαμβάνω), *sun*, with, and No. 7, 4838
denotes to take along with oneself, as a companion, Acts 12 : 25 ; 15 : 37, AG:779A CB:—
38 ; Gal. 2 : 1.¶

9. PROSLAMBANŌ (προσλαμβάνω), to take to oneself (*pros*), is used 4355
of food, Acts 27 : 33–36 ; of persons, of Peter's act toward Christ, AG:717B CB:1267B
Matt. 16 : 22 ; Mark 8 : 32 ; for evil purposes, Acts 17 : 5 ; for good
purposes, 18 : 26. See RECEIVE.

10. PROLAMBANŌ (προλαμβάνω) is rendered to take before in 1 Cor. 4301
11 : 21. See COME, Note (2) at end, OVERTAKE. AG:708B CB:1266C

11. SULLAMBANŌ (συλλαμβάνω), to seize, take, is rendered to take 4815
in Matt. 26 : 55 and Mark 14 : 48, A.V. (R.V., "seize") ; Luke 5 : 9 ; AG:776D CB:1270B
Acts 1 : 16 ; in 12 : 3 and 23 : 27, A.V. (R.V., "seize"). See CATCH,
CONCEIVE, HELP.

12. AIRŌ (αἴρω), to lift, carry, take up or away, occurs very frequently 142
with its literal meanings. In John 1 : 29 it is used of Christ as "the Lamb AG:24B CB:1234A
of God, which taketh away the sin of the world," not the sins, but sin,

that which has existed from the time of the Fall, and in regard to which God has had judicial dealings with the world; through the expiatory sacrifice of Christ the sin of the world will be replaced by everlasting righteousness; cp. the plural, "sins", in 1 John 3:5. Righteous judgment was "taken away" from Christ at human tribunals, and His life, while voluntarily given by Himself (John 10:17, 18), was "taken (from the earth)," Acts 8:33 (quoted from the Sept. of Isa. 53:8). In John 15:2 it is used in the Lord's statement "Every branch in Me that beareth not fruit, He taketh it away." This does not contemplate members of the "body" of Christ, but those who (just as a graft which being inserted, does not "abide" or "strike") are merely professed followers, giving only the appearance of being joined to the parent stem.

The Law described in Col. 2:14 as "the bond written in ordinances that was against us," Christ "took" out of the way at His Cross. In 1 Cor. 5:2, *airō* is used in the best texts (some have No. 14), of the Divine judgment which would have been exercised in 'taking away' from the church the incestuous delinquent, had they mourned before God. See AWAY, BEAR, No. 9, etc.

522 AG:79D
CB:— 13. APAIRŌ (ἀπαίρω), to lift off (*apo*, from, and No. 12), is used, in the Passive Voice, of Christ, metaphorically as the Bridegroom of His followers, Matt. 9:15; Mark 2:20; Luke 5:35.¶

1808 AG:272A
CB:— 14. EXAIRŌ (ἐξαίρω), to take away, is used of putting away a person in church discipline, 1 Cor. 5:13; for this verb as a variant reading in ver. 2, see No. 12.¶

1869 AG:281D
CB:— 15. EPAIRŌ (ἐπαίρω), to lift, raise, is used in the Passive Voice and rendered "He was taken up" in Acts 1:9. See EXALT, HOIST, LIFT.

337 AG:54D
CB:— 16. ANAIREŌ (ἀναιρέω), to take up (*ana*, up, and *haireō*, to take), is used of Pharaoh's daughter in taking up the infant Moses, Acts 7:21; of God's act in taking away the typical animal sacrifices under the Law, Heb. 10:9. See DEATH, C, No. 2, KILL, SLAY.

851 AG:124B
CB:1236B 17. APHAIREŌ (ἀφαιρέω), to take away (*apo*), is used with this meaning in Luke 1:25; 10:42; 16:3; Rom. 11:27, of the removal of the sins of Israel; Heb. 10:4, of the impossibility of the removal of sins by offerings under the Law; in Rev. 22:19 (twice). See CUT, No. 8.

2507 AG:386C
CB:— 18. KATHAIREŌ (καθαιρέω), to take down (*kata*), besides its meaning of putting down by force, was the technical term for the removal of the body after crucifixion, Mark 15:36, 46; Luke 23:53; Acts 13:29. See CAST, No. 14.

4014 AG:645D
CB:— 19. PERIAIREŌ (περιαιρέω), to take away that which surrounds (*peri*, around), is used (*a*) literally, of casting off anchors, Acts 27:40, R.V. (A.V., "having taken up"); 28:13 in some texts, for *perierchomai*, to make a circuit; (*b*) metaphorically, of taking away the veil off the hearts of Israel, 2 Cor. 3:16; of hope of rescue, Acts 27:20; of sins (negatively), Heb. 10:11.¶

20. DECHOMAI (δέχομαι), to receive, is rendered " take (thy bond, 1209
R.V., A.V., bill) " in Luke 16 : 6, 7 ; " take (the helmet of salvation)," AG:177B
Eph. 6 : 17, suggesting a heartiness in the taking. See ACCEPT, No. 1, CB:1240B
RECEIVE.

21. PROSDECHOMAI (προσδέχομαι), to receive favourably, is 4327
rendered " took " in Heb. 10 : 34. See ACCEPT, No. 3. AG:712B CB:1267A

22. KRATEŌ (κρατέω), to take hold of, get possession of, is translated 2902
to take in Matt. 9 : 25; 22 : 6; 26 : 4; Mark 1 : 31; 5 : 41; 9 : 27; AG:448C
14 : 1, 44, 46, 49 ; Luke 8 : 54 ; Acts 24 : 6. See HOLD, No. 6. CB:1256A

23. DRASSOMAI (δράσσομαι), to grasp with the hand, take hold of, 1405
is used metaphorically in 1 Cor. 3 : 19, " taketh (the wise in their AG:206C
craftiness)."¶ CB:—

24. DIDŌMI (δίδωμι), to give, found in the best texts in Mark 3 : 6, 1325
is rendered " took (counsel) ; " some have *poieō*, to make. AG:192C CB:1241C

25. KATECHŌ (κατέχω), to hold, is rendered " to take (the lowest 2722
place) " in Luke 14 : 9. See HOLD. AG:422C CB:1254B

26. PIAZŌ (πιάζω), to lay or take hold of forcefully, is always rendered 4084
to take in the R.V. See APPREHEND, No. 2. AG:657A CB:—

27. PARAPHERŌ (παραφέρω), to bear away (*para*, aside, *pherō*, to 3911
bear), remove, is rendered " take away " in Mark 14 : 36, A.V., R.V., AG:623B
" remove," as in Luke 22 : 42. See REMOVE.¶ CB:—

28. ECHŌ (ἔχω), to have, to hold, is used in Matt. 21 : 46 in the sense 2192
of regarding a person as something, " they took (Him) for (a prophet)." AG:331D
See HAVE. CB:1242C

29. SUNAGŌ (συνάγω), to bring together, is used of taking a person 4863
into one's house receiving hospitality, " took . . . . in," Matt. 25 : 35, AG:782A CB:1270B
38, 43 ; so in Acts 11 : 26, R.V., " were gathered together," A.V.,
" assembled ; " perhaps the meaning is ' they were entertained.' See
ASSEMBLE, BESTOW, GATHER.

30. EKDUŌ (ἐκδύω), to take off a garment from a person, is so rendered 1562
with reference to the soldiers' treatment of Christ, Matt. 27 : 31 ; AG:239A
Mark 15 : 20. See STRIP. CB:1243C

31. EKBALLŌ (ἐκβάλλω) has the meaning to bring or take out in 1544
Luke 10 : 35, " took out (two pence)," a word perhaps chosen to express AG:237B
the wholeheartedness of the act (lit., to throw out). See CAST, No. 5. CB:1243B

32. BASTAZŌ (βαστάζω), to bear, lift, is used of taking up stones, 941
John 10 : 31. As to Matt. 3 : 11, Moulton and Milligan supply evidences AG:137B CB:1238C
from the vernacular that the word signified to take off (the sandals), which
confirms Mark's word *luō*, to unloose (1 : 7). See BEAR, No. 1.

33. EPICHEIREŌ (ἐπιχειρέω), to take in hand (*epi*, upon, *cheir*, the 2021
hand), to attempt, take upon oneself, is rendered " have taken in hand," AG:304D
Luke 1 : 1 ; " took upon (them)," Acts 19 : 13. See GO, No. 30. CB:—

34. GINOMAI (γίνομαι), to become, to come to be, is rendered " he be 1096
taken " in 2 Thess. 2 : 7, lit., ' (until) he, or it, become ' (for a treatment AG:158A
of the whole passage see Notes on Thess. by Hogg and Vine). CB:1248B

SUNAIRŌ 4868 *Notes:* (1) For *sunairō* in Matt. 18 : 23, see RECKON. (2) Some
AG:783C texts have *apagō*, to take away, in Acts 24 : 7. (3) In John 6 : 24, A.V.,
APAGŌ 520 *embainō*, to enter, is rendered "took (shipping)," R.V., "got into (the
AG:79C boats)." (4) In 2 Thess. 1 : 8, A.V., *didōmi*, to give (R.V. "rendering"),
EMBAINŌ 1684 is translated "taking." (5) In Rom. 3 : 5, A.V., *epipherō*, to bring
AG:254A against, is rendered "taketh (vengeance)," R.V., "visiteth (with wrath)."
EPIPHERŌ 2018 (6) In Luke 4 : 5, A.V., *anagō*, to lead up (R.V., "led"), is rendered
AG:304C "took up." (7) In Acts 10 : 26, A.V., *egeirō*, to raise (R.V.), is rendered
CB:1246A ANAGŌ "took . . . up." (8) For taking up baggage, Acts 21 : 15, see BAGGAGE.
321 (9) For "taken from" in 1 Thess. 2 : 17, A.V., see BEREAVED, No. 1.
AG:53A (10) *Sunechō* is translated "taken with" in Matt. 4 : 24; Luke 4 : 38;
EGEIRŌ 1453 8 : 37. See HOLDEN. (11) In 2 Pet. 2 : 12 "to be taken" translates
AG:214C the phrase *eis halōsin*, lit., 'for capture' (*halōsis*, a taking). (12) In 1 Pet.
CB:1242C SUNECHŌ 2 : 20, *hupomenō*, to endure, is rendered "ye take . . . patiently."
4912 (13) In Matt. 11 : 12; John 6 : 15; Acts 23 : 10 *harpazō* (see CATCH)
AG:789A CB:1270C is rendered "take . . . by force." (14) For *apotassomai*, to take leave of,
HALŌSIS 259 see LEAVE, (*c*) No. 1. (15) For *apaspazomai*, rendered to take leave of
AG:42A in Acts 21 : 6, A.V., see LEAVE, (*c*) No. 2. (16) In Acts 21 : 6 some mss.
CB:1249A HUPOMENŌ have *epibainō*, A.V., "we took ship" (R.V., *embainō*, "we went on
5278 board"): cp. Note (3), above. (17) For "untaken" in 2 Cor. 3 : 14
AG:845D CB:1252B see UNLIFTED. (18) In 1 Tim. 5 : 9, A.V., *katalegō* is rendered to take
HARPAZŌ 726 into the number (R.V., "be enrolled").¶ (19) For "take . . . to
AG:109A CB:1249B record" see TESTIFY. See also CARE, HEED, JOURNEY, THOUGHT (to take).

APOTASSOMAI 657

TALENT

AG:100D APASPAZOMAI

A. Noun.

— TALANTON (τάλαντον), originally a balance, then, a talent in weight,
AG:81D was hence a sum of money in gold or silver equivalent to a talent. The
EPIBAINŌ 1910 Jewish talent contained 3,000 shekels of the sanctuary, e.g., Ex. 30 : 13
AG:289D (about 114 lbs.). In N.T. times the talent was not a weight of silver,
KATALEGŌ 2639 but the Roman-Attic talent, comprising 6,000 denarii or drachms, and
AG:413B equal to about £240. It is mentioned in Matthew only, 18 : 24; 25 : 15,
16, 20 (twice in the best texts), 22 (thrice), 24, 25, 28 (twice). In 18 : 24
5007 the vastness of the sum, 10,000 talents (£2,400,000), indicates the
AG:803C impossibility of man's clearing himself, by his own efforts, of the guilt
CB:— which lies upon him before God.¶

Note: That the talent denoted something weighed has provided the meaning of the Eng. word as a gift or ability, especially under the influence of the Parable of the Talents (Matt. 25 : 14–30).

B. Adjective

5006 TALANTIAIOS (ταλαντιαῖος) denotes 'of a talent's weight,' Rev.
AG:803B CB:— 16 : 21.¶

For TALES see TALK

TALITHA

TALEITHA or TALITHA (ταλειθά), an Aramaic feminine meaning 5008
'maiden,' Mark 5 : 41, has been variously transliterated in the N.T. AG:803C CB:1271A
Greek mss. *Koumi* or *Koum* (Heb. and Aram., *qûm*, arise), which follows, KOUM(I)
is interpreted by "I say unto thee, arise." *Koum* is the better attested 2891
word; so in the Talmud, where this imperative occurs "seven times AG:447B CB:—
in one page" (Edersheim, *Life and Times of Jesus*, i, p. 631).¶

TALK (Noun and Verb)

A. Nouns.

1. LOGOS (λόγος), a word, is translated "talk" in Matt. 22 : 15; 3056 AG:477A
Mark 12 : 13. See ACCOUNT, B. CB:1257A

2. LĒROS (λῆρος) denotes foolish talk, nonsense, Luke 24 : 11, R.V., 3026
"idle talk" (A.V., "idle tales").¶ AG:473A CB:—

B. Verbs.

1. LALEŌ (λαλέω), to speak, say, is always translated to speak in the 2980
R.V., where the A.V. renders it by to talk, Matt. 12 : 46; Mark 6 : 50; AG:463A CB:1256B
Luke 24 : 32; John 4 : 27 (twice); 9 : 37; 14 : 30; Acts 26 : 31; Rev.
4 : 1; 17 : 1; 21 : 9, 15. The R.V. rendering is preferable; the idea of chat
or chatter is entirely foreign to the N.T., and should never be regarded
as the meaning in 1 Cor. 14 : 34, 35. See COMMUNE, Note, SAY, No. 1,
Note, and No. 2, SPEAK.

2. SULLALEŌ (συλλαλέω), to speak with (*sun*), is translated to talk 4814 AG:776C
with, Matt. 17 : 3; Mark 9 : 4; Luke 9 : 30. See CONFER, No. 2. CB:—

3. HOMILEŌ (ὁμιλέω), to be in company with, consort with (*homilos*, 3656
a throng; *homilia*, company), hence, to converse with, is rendered to AG:565C CB:—
talk with, Acts 20 : 11. See COMMUNE, No. 2.

4. SUNOMILEŌ (συνομιλέω), to converse, talk with, occurs in Acts 4926
10 : 27.¶ AG:791C CB:—

TALKERS (vain)

MATAIOLOGOS (ματαιολόγος), an adjective denoting talking idly 3151
(*mataios*, vain, idle, *legō*, to speak), is used as a noun (plural) in Tit. 1 : 10.¶ AG:495C CB:1258A

TALKING (vain, foolish)

1. MATAIOLOGIA (ματαιολογία), a noun corresponding to the above, 3150 AG:495C
is used in 1 Tim. 1 : 6, R.V., "vain talking" (A.V., "vain jangling").¶ CB:1258A

2. MŌROLOGIA (μωρολογία), from *mōros*, foolish, dull, stupid, and 3473
legō, is used in Eph. 5 : 4; it denotes more than mere idle talk. Trench AG:531B CB:1259B
describes it as "that 'talk of fools' which is foolishness and sin together"
(Syn. § xxxiv).¶

TAME

DAMAZŌ (δαμάζω), to subdue, tame, is used (*a*) naturally in Mark 1150
5 : 4 and Jas. 3 : 7 (twice); (*b*) metaphorically, of the tongue, in Jas. AG:170B CB:—
3 : 8.¶ In the Sept., Dan. 2 : 40.¶

TANNER

1038
AG:148D
CB:—
BURSEUS (βυρσεύς), a tanner (from *bursa*, a hide), occurs in Acts 9 : 43 ; 10 : 6, 32.¶

For TARE (Verb) see TEAR

TARES

2215
AG:339C
CB:1273C
ZIZANION (ζιζάνιον) is a kind of darnel, the commonest of the four species, being the bearded, growing in the grain fields, as tall as wheat and barley, and resembling wheat in appearance. It was credited among the Jews with being degenerate wheat. The Rabbis called it "bastard." The seeds are poisonous to man and herbivorous animals, producing sleepiness, nausea, convulsions and even death (they are harmless to poultry). The plants can be separated out, but the custom, as in the parable, is to leave the cleaning out till near the time of harvest, Matt. 13 : 25–27, 29, 30, 36, 38, 40.¶ The Lord describes the tares as "the sons of the evil *one* ;" false teachings are indissociable from their propagandists. For the Lord's reference to the Kingdom see KINGDOM.

TARRY

3306
AG:503C
CB:1258B
1. MENŌ (μένω), to abide, is translated by the verb to abide, in the R.V., for A.V., to tarry, in Matt. 26 : 38 ; Mark 14 : 34 ; Luke 24 : 29 ; John 4 : 40 ; Acts 9 : 43 ; 18 : 20 ; the R.V. retains the verb to tarry in John 21 : 22, 23 ; in Acts 20 : 5, A.V., "tarried" (R.V., "were waiting"). Some mss. have it in Acts 20 : 15 (A.V., "tarried"). See ABIDE.

1961
AG:296B
CB:1246A
2. EPIMENŌ (ἐπιμένω), to abide, continue, a strengthened form of No. 1, is translated to tarry in Acts 10 : 48 ; 21 : 4, 10 ; 28 : 12, 14 ; 1 Cor. 16 : 7, 8 ; Gal. 1 : 18, R.V. (A.V., "abode"). See ABIDE, No. 2.

5278
AG:845D
CB:1252B
3. HUPOMENŌ (ὑπομένω), to endure, is rendered "tarried behind" in Luke 2 : 43. See ENDURE, No. 2.

4357
AG:717C
CB:1267B
4. PROSMENŌ (προσμένω), to abide still, continue, is translated "tarried" in Acts 18 : 18, suggesting patience and stedfastness in remaining after the circumstances which preceded ; in 1 Tim. 1 : 3, R.V., "to tarry" (A.V., "to abide still"). See ABIDE, No. 6.

1304
AG:190A
CB:—
5. DIATRIBŌ (διατρίβω), for which see ABIDE, No. 7, is invariably rendered to tarry, in the R.V. ; A.V., twice, John 3 : 22 ; Acts 25 : 6 ; "continued" in John 11 : 54 ; Acts 15 : 35 ; "abode," Acts 12 : 19 ; 14 : 3, 28 ; 20 : 6 ; "abiding," 16 : 12 ; "had been," 25 : 14.¶

5549
AG:887D
CB:1240B
6. CHRONIZŌ (χρονίζω), to spend or while away time ; to tarry, Matt. 25 : 5 ; Luke 1 : 21 ; Heb. 10 : 37. See DELAY, No. 2.

1019
AG:147A
CB:—
7. BRADUNŌ (βραδύνω), to be slow (*bradus*, slow), is rendered "I tarry long," 1 Tim. 3 : 15 ; "is . . . slack," 2 Pet. 3 : 9.¶

2523
AG:389D
CB:1254C
8. KATHIZŌ (καθίζω), to make to sit down, or, intransitively, to sit down, is translated "tarry ye" in Luke 24 : 49. See SIT.

9. MELLŌ (μέλλω), to be about to, is rendered " (why) tarriest 3195
thou ? " in Acts 22 : 16. See About, B. AG:500D CB:1258A

10. EKDECHOMAI (ἐκδέχομαι), to expect, await (*ek*, from, *dechomai*, 1551
to receive), is translated " tarry " in 1 Cor. 11 : 33, A.V. (R.V., " wait "). AG:238B
See Expect, Look, Wait. CB:1243C

Notes : (1) In Acts 27 : 33, A.V., *prosdokaō*, to wait, look for, is PROSDOKAŌ
translated " have tarried " (R.V., " wait "). (2) In Acts 15 : 33, *poieō*, 4328 AG:712C
to make or do, is used with *chronos*, time, A.V., " they had tarried a space," CB:1267A
R.V., " they had spent some time." POIEŌ 4160 AG:680D CB:1265C

TASTE

GEUŌ (γεύω), to make to taste, is used in the Middle Voice, signifying (-OMAI) 1089
to taste (*a*) naturally, Matt. 27 : 34 ; Luke 14 : 24 ; John 2 : 9 ; Col. AG:157A
2 : 21 ; (*b*) metaphorically, of Christ's tasting death, implying His Personal CB:1248B
experience in voluntarily undergoing death, Heb. 2 : 9 ; of believers (negatively) as to tasting of death, Matt. 16 : 28 ; Mark 9 : 1 ; Luke 9 : 27 ; John 8 : 52 ; of tasting the heavenly gift (different from receiving it), Heb. 6 : 4 ; " the good word of God, and the powers of the age to come," 6 : 5 ; " that the Lord is gracious," 1 Pet. 2 : 3. See Eat.

TASK See MINISTRY, WORK

TATTLER

PHLUAROS (φλύαρος), babbling, garrulous (from *phluō*, to babble : 5397
cp. *phluareō*, to prate against), is translated " tattlers " in 1 Tim. 5 : 13.¶ AG:862B CB:—

TAUGHT (Adjective)

1. DIDAKTOS (διδακτός), primarily what can be taught, then, taught, 1318
is used (*a*) of persons, John 6 : 45 ; (*b*) of things, 1 Cor. 2 : 13 (twice), AG:191B CB:1241B
" (not in words which man's wisdom) teacheth, (but which the Spirit) teacheth," lit., ' (not in words) taught (of man's wisdom, but) taught (of the Spirit).'¶

2. THEODIDAKTOS (θεοδίδακτος), God-taught (*Theos*, God, and No. 2312
1), occurs in 1 Thess. 4 : 9, lit., ' God-taught (persons) ;' while the AG:356B CB:—
missionaries had taught the converts to love one another, God had Himself been their Teacher. Cp. John 6 : 45 (see No. 1).¶

For TAXED, TAXING see ENROL, ENROLMENT

TEACH

A. Verbs.

1. DIDASKŌ (διδάσκω) is used (*a*) absolutely, to give instruction, 1321
e.g., Matt. 4 : 23 ; 9 : 35 ; Rom. 12 : 7 ; 1 Cor. 4 : 17 ; 1 Tim. 2 : 12 ; AG:192A CB:1241C
4 : 11 ; (*b*) transitively, with an object, whether persons, e.g., Matt. 5 : 2 ; 7 : 29, and frequently in the Gospels and Acts, or things taught, e.g., Matt. 15 : 9 ; 22 : 16 ; Acts 15 : 35 ; 18 : 11 ; both persons and things, e.g., John 14 : 26 ; Rev. 2 : 14, 20.

3811 AG:603D CB:1261C 2. PAIDEUŌ (παιδεύω), to instruct and train: see INSTRUCT, No. 2.
2727 3. KATĒCHEŌ (κατηχέω), for which see INFORM, No. 2, INSTRUCT,
AG:423D CB:1254B No. 1, is rendered to teach in 1 Cor. 14 : 19, A.V. (R.V., "instruct");
Gal. 6 : 6 (twice).
2085 4. HETERODIDASKALEŌ (ἑτεροδιδασκαλέω), to teach a different
AG:314D CB:1250A doctrine (*heteros*, "different," to be distinguished from *allos*, another of
the same kind: see ANOTHER), is used in 1 Tim. 1 : 3; 6 : 3, R.V., A.V.,
"teach (no) other d." and "teach otherwise," of what is contrary to the
MATHēTEUō faith.¶
3100 *Notes:* (1) For *mathēteuō*, to teach, in the A.V. of Matt. 28 : 19;
AG:485C CB:1258A Acts 14 : 21, see DISCIPLE, B. (2) In Acts 16 : 21, A.V., *katangellō*, to
KATANGELLō 2605 declare, preach, is rendered "teach" (R.V., "set forth"). (3) For
AG:409B "teacheth" in 1 Cor. 2 : 13, see TAUGHT, No. 1 (*b*).
CB:1254A

B. Adjective.

1317 AG:191B DIDAKTIKOS (διδακτικός), skilled in teaching (akin to No. 1 above:
CB:1241B Eng., didactic), is translated "apt to teach" in 1 Tim. 3 : 2; 2 Tim.
2 : 24.¶

TEACHER, FALSE TEACHERS

1320 AG:191C 1. DIDASKALOS (διδάσκαλος) is rendered "teacher" or "teachers"
CB:1241B in Matt. 23 : 8, by Christ, of Himself; in John 3 : 2 of Christ; of
Nicodemus in Israel, 3 : 10, R.V.; of teachers of the truth in the churches,
Acts 13 : 1; 1 Cor. 12 : 28, 29; Eph. 4 : 11; Heb. 5 : 12; Jas. 3 : 1,
R.V.; by Paul of his work among the churches, 1 Tim. 2 : 7; 2 Tim.
1 : 11; of teachers, wrongfully chosen by those who have "itching ears,"
2 Tim. 4 : 3. See MASTER, RABBI.
2567 AG:400A 2. KALODIDASKALOS (καλοδιδάσκαλος) denotes a teacher of what
CB:1253B is good (*kalos*), Tit. 2 : 3.¶
5572 AG:891C 3. PSEUDODIDASKALOS (ψευδοδιδάσκαλος), a false teacher, occurs
CB:1267C in the plural in 2 Pet. 2 : 1.¶

For TEACHING (Noun) see DOCTRINE, Nos. 1 and 2

TEARS

1144 AG:170A DAKRUON or DAKRU (δάκρυον), akin to *dakruō*, to weep, is used
CB:— in the plural, Mark 9 : 24; Luke 7 : 38, 44 (with the sense of washing
therewith the Lord's feet); Acts 20 : 19, 31; 2 Cor. 2 : 4; 2 Tim. 1 : 4;
Heb. 5 : 7; 12 : 17; Rev. 7 : 17; 21 : 4.¶

TEAR, TORN

4682 1. SPARASSŌ (σπαράσσω), denotes to tear, rend, convulse, Mark
AG:760D CB:— 1 : 26; 9 : 20 (in some mss.), 26, R.V., "having . . . torn" (A.V.,
4952 "rent"); Luke 9 : 39.¶ In the Sept., 2 Sam. 22 : 8, of the foundations
AG:794C of heaven; Jer. 4 : 18, of the heart.¶
CB:— 2. SUSPARASSŌ (συσπαράσσω), to tear violently (*sun*, with, intensive),

convulse completely, a strengthened form of No. 1, is used in Mark 9 : 20, in the best texts (some have No. 1) ; Luke 9 : 42.¶

3. DIASPAŌ (διασπάω), to break or tear asunder, is translated "should be torn in pieces" in Acts 23 : 10, R.V. (A.V., ". . . pulled . . ."). See REND, No. 5. 1288 AG:188C CB:—

4. RHĒGNUMI (ῥήγνυμι), to break, is rendered "teareth" in Mark 9 : 18, A.V. (R.V., "dasheth . . . down"). See HINDER, No. 1. 4486 AG:735A CB:—

TEDIOUS (to be)

ENKOPTŌ (ἐνκόπτω), to hinder, is rendered to be tedious in Acts 24 : 4, of detaining a person unnecessarily. See HINDER, No. 1. 1465 AG:216C CB:1245A

For TEETH see TOOTH

TELL

LEGō 3004 AG:468A CB:1256C

1. LEGŌ (λέγω) and the 2nd aorist form *eipon*, used to supply this tense in *legō*, are frequently translated to tell, e.g., Matt. 2 : 13, R.V., "I tell," A.V., "I bring (thee) word" ; 10 : 27. See SAY, No. 1. EIPON 3004 (LEGō) AG:226A CB:1243A

2. LALEŌ (λαλέω), for which see SAY, No. 2, is usually rendered to speak, in the R.V. (for A.V., to tell), e.g., Matt. 26 : 13 ; Luke 1 : 45 ; 2 : 17, 18, 20 ; Acts 11 : 14 ; 27 : 25 ; but R.V. and A.V., to tell in John 8 : 40 ; Acts 9 : 6 ; 22 : 10. 2980 AG:463A CB:1256B

3. EKLALEŌ (ἐκλαλέω), to speak out (*ek*), is translated "tell" in Acts 23 : 22.¶ 1583 AG:242A

4. EIRŌ (εἴρω), for which see SAY, No. 4, is rendered to tell in Matt. 21 : 24 ; Mark 11 : 29 ; John 14 : 29 ; Rev. 17 : 7. After 1518 AG:—

5. APANGELLŌ (ἀπαγγέλλω), to announce, declare, report (usually as a messenger), is frequently rendered to tell, e.g., Matt. 8 : 33 ; 14 : 12. See BRING, No. 36. 518 AG:79B CB:1236B

6. ANANGELLŌ (ἀναγγέλλω), to bring back word, announce, is sometimes rendered to tell, e.g., John 5 : 15 ; 2 Cor. 7 : 7. See DECLARE, No. 1. 312 AG:51B CB:1235B

7. DIĒGEOMAI (διηγέομαι), for which see DECLARE, No. 6, is rendered to tell, in the A.V. and R.V., in Mark 9 : 9 ; Heb. 11 : 32. 1334 AG:195A CB:1241C

8. EXĒGEOMAI (ἐξηγέομαι), for which see DECLARE, No. 8, is translated "told" in Luke 24 : 35, A.V. (R.V., "rehearsed"). 1834 AG:275D CB:1247C

9. DIASAPHEŌ (διασαφέω), to make clear (*dia*, throughout, *saphēs*, clear), explain fully, is translated "told" in Matt. 18 : 31. See EXPLAIN. 1285 AG:188B

10. MĒNUŌ (μηνύω) is rendered "told" in Acts 23 : 30, A.V. : see SHEW, No. 7. 3377 AG:519A

11. PROEIRŌ (PROLEGŌ) (προείρω), to tell before, is so rendered in Matt. 24 : 25 : see FORETELL, FOREWARN. 4280 (-EREō) AG:704D (-EIPON)

Note : In the following, *oida*, to know, is translated "tell" in the A.V. (R.V., "know"), Matt. 21 : 27 ; Mark 11 : 33 ; Luke 20 : 7 ; John 3 : 8 ; 8 : 14 ; 16 : 18 ; 2 Cor. 12 : 2. 1492 (EIDō) AG:555D CB:1260B

TEMPER TOGETHER

4786 AG:773D CB:1270C SUNKERANNUMI (συγκεράννυμι), to mix or blend together, is used in 1 Cor. 12 : 24, of the combining of the members of the human body into an organic structure, as illustrative of the members of a local church (see ver. 27, where there is no definite article in the original). See MIXED (with).

TEMPERANCE, TEMPERATE

A. Noun.

1466 AG:216C CB:1245A ENKRATEIA (ἐγκράτεια), from *kratos*, strength, occurs in Acts 24 : 25 ; Gal. 5 : 23 ; 2 Pet. 1 : 6 (twice), in all of which it is rendered "temperance ;" the R.V. marg., "self-control" is the preferable rendering, as temperance is now limited to one form of self-control ; the various powers bestowed by God upon man are capable of abuse ; the right use demands the controlling power of the will under the operation of the Spirit of God ; in Acts 24 : 25 the word follows "righteousness," which represents God's claims, self-control being man's response thereto ; in 2 Pet. 1 : 6, it follows "knowledge," suggesting that what is learnt requires to be put into practice.¶

B. Adjectives.

1468 AG:216D CB:1245A 1. ENKRATĒS (ἐγκρατής), akin to A, denotes exercising self-control, rendered "temperate" in Tit. 1 : 8.¶

3524 AG:538D CB:1259C 2. NĒPHALIOS (νηφάλιος), for which see SOBER, is translated "temperate" in 1 Tim. 3 : 2, R.V. (A.V., "vigilant") ; in 3 : 11 and Tit. 2 : 2, R.V. (A.V., "sober").¶

4998 AG:802C CB:1269B *Note :* In Tit. 2 : 2, A.V., *sōphrōn*, sober, is rendered "temperate" (R.V., "soberminded").

C. Verb.

1467 AG:216C CB:1245A ENKRATEUOMAI (ἐγκρατεύομαι), akin to A and B, No. 1, rendered "is temperate" in 1 Cor. 9 : 25, is used figuratively of the rigid self-control practised by athletes with a view to gaining the prize. See CONTINENCY.

TEMPEST

2366 AG:365A CB:— 1. THUELLA (θύελλα), a hurricane, cyclone, whirlwind (akin to *thuō*, to slay, and *thumos*, wrath), is used in Heb. 12 : 18.¶ In the Sept., Ex. 10 : 22 ; Deut. 4 : 11 ; 5 : 22.¶

4578 AG:746B CB:1268C 2. SEISMOS (σεισμός), a shaking (Eng., seismic, etc.), is used of a tempest in Matt. 8 : 24. See EARTHQUAKE.

5494 AG:879D CB:— 3. CHEIMŌN (χειμών), winter, a winter storm, hence, in general, a tempest, is so rendered in Acts 27 : 20. See WEATHER, WINTER.

2978 AG:462D CB:1256B 4. LAILAPS (λαῖλαψ), "a tempest," 2 Pet. 2 : 17, A.V. : see STORM.

Note : For "tossed with a tempest," Acts 27 : 18, A.V., see LABOUR, B, No. 2.

TEMPESTUOUS

TUPHŌNIKOS (τυφωνικός), from *tuphōn*, a hurricane, typhoon, is 5189
translated " tempestuous " in Acts 27 : 14.¶ AG:831C
CB:—

TEMPLE

1. HIERON (ἱερόν), the neuter of the adjective *hieros*, sacred, is used 2411
as a noun denoting a sacred place, a temple, that of Artemis (Diana), AG:372B
Acts 19 : 27 ; that in Jerusalem, Mark 11 : 11, signifying the entire building CB:1250B
with its precincts, or some part thereof, as distinct from the *naos*, the inner sanctuary (see No. 2) ; apart from the Gospels and Acts, it is mentioned only in 1 Cor. 9 : 13. Christ taught in one of the courts, to which all the people had access. *Hieron* is never used figuratively. The Temple mentioned in the Gospels and Acts was begun by Herod in B.C. 20, and destroyed by the Romans in A.D. 70.

2. NAOS (ναός), a shrine or sanctuary, was used (*a*) among the heathen, 3485
to denote the shrine containing the idol, Acts 17 : 24 ; 19 : 24 (in the AG:533B
latter, miniatures) ; (*b*) among the Jews, the sanctuary in the Temple, CB:1259B
into which only the priests could lawfully enter, e.g., Luke 1 : 9, 21, 22 ; Christ, as being of the tribe of Judah, and thus not being a priest while upon the earth (Heb. 7 : 13, 14 ; 8 : 4), did not enter the *naos* ; for 2 Thess. 2 : 4 see Note (below) ; (*c*) by Christ metaphorically, of His own physical body, John 2 : 19, 21 ; (*d*) in apostolic teaching, metaphorically, (1) of the Church, the mystical Body of Christ, Eph. 2 : 21 ; (2) of a local church, 1 Cor. 3 : 16, 17 ; 2 Cor. 6 : 16 ; (3) of the present body of the individual believer, 1 Cor. 6 : 19 ; (4) of the Temple seen in visions in the Apocalypse, 3 : 12 ; 7 : 15 ; 11 : 19 ; 14 : 15, 17 ; 15 : 5, 6, 8 ; 16 : 1, 17 ; (5) of the Lord God Almighty and the Lamb, as the Temple of the New and Heavenly Jerusalem, Rev. 21 : 22. See SANCTUARY and HOLY, B (*b*), par. 4.

Notes : (1) The temple mentioned in 2 Thess. 2 : 4 (*naos*), as the seat of the Man of Sin, has been regarded in different ways. The weight of Scripture evidence is in favour of the view that it refers to a literal temple in Jerusalem, to be reconstructed in the future (cp. Dan. 11 : 31 and 12 : 11, with Matt. 24 : 15). For a fuller examination of the passage, see
Notes on Thessalonians by Hogg and Vine, pp. 250–252. (2) For *oikos*, 3624
rendered " temple," Luke 11 : 51, A.V., see HOUSE, No. 1. AG:560B
CB:1260B

TEMPLE-KEEPER

NEŌKOROS (νεωκόρος), Acts 19 : 35, R.V., and A.V. marg., " temple- 3511
keeper " (A.V., " worshipper "), is used in profane Greek of one who has AG:537B
charge of a temple. Coin inscriptions show that it was an honorary title CB:1259C
given to certain cities, especially in Asia Minor, where the cult of some god or of a deified human potentate had been established, here to Ephesus in respect of the goddess Artemis. Apparently the Imperial cult also

existed at Ephesus. Josephus applies the word to Jews as worshippers, but this is not the meaning in Acts 19.¶

TEMPORAL

4340 AG:715B CB:1267A PROSKAIROS (πρόσκαιρος), for a season (*pros*, for, *kairos*, a season), is rendered "temporal" in 2 Cor. 4 : 18. See SEASON, WHILE.

TEMPT

A. Verbs.

3985 AG:640B CB:1263A 1. PEIRAZŌ (πειράζω) signifies (1) to try, attempt, assay (see TRY); (2) to test, try, prove, in a good sense, said of Christ and of believers, Heb. 2 : 18, where the context shows that the temptation was the cause of suffering to Him, and only suffering, not a drawing away to sin, so that believers have the sympathy of Christ as their High Priest in the suffering which sin occasions to those who are in the enjoyment of communion with God; so in the similar passage in 4 : 15; in all the temptations which Christ endured, there was nothing within Him that answered to sin. There was no sinful infirmity in Him. While He was truly man, and His Divine nature was not in any way inconsistent with His Manhood, there was nothing in Him such as is produced in us by the sinful nature which belongs to us; in Heb. 11 : 37, of the testing of O.T. saints; in 1 Cor. 10 : 13, where the meaning has a wide scope, the verb is used of testing as permitted by God, and of the believer as one who should be in the realization of his own helplessness and his dependence upon God (see PROVE, TRY); in a bad sense, to tempt (*a*) of attempts to ensnare Christ in His speech, e.g., Matt. 16 : 1; 19 : 3; 22 : 18, 35, and parallel passages; John 8 : 6; (*b*) of temptations to sin, e.g., Gal. 6 : 1, where one who would restore an erring brother is not to act as his judge, but as being one with him in liability to sin, with the possibility of finding himself in similar circumstances, Jas. 1 : 13, 14 (see note below); of temptations mentioned as coming from the Devil, Matt. 4 : 1, and parallel passages; 1 Cor. 7 : 5; 1 Thess. 3 : 5 (see TEMPTER); (*c*) of trying or challenging God, Acts 15 : 10; 1 Cor. 10 : 9 (2nd part); Heb. 3 : 9; the Holy Spirit, Acts 5 : 9 : cp. No. 2.

Note: *" James 1 : 13–15 seems to contradict other statements of Scripture in two respects, saying (*a*) that 'God cannot be tempted with evil,' and (*b*) that 'He Himself tempteth no man.' But God tempted, or tried, Abraham, Heb. 11 : 17, and the Israelites tempted, or tried, God, 1 Cor. 10 : 9. Ver. 14, however, makes it plain that, whereas in these cases the temptation or trial, came from without, James refers to temptation, or trial, arising within, from uncontrolled appetites and from evil passions, cp. Mark 7 : 20–23. But though such temptation does not proceed from God, yet does God regard His people while they endure it, and by it tests and approves them."

* From Notes on Thessalonians by Hogg and Vine, p. 97.

2. EKPEIRAZŌ (ἐκπειράζω), an intensive form of the foregoing, is 1598
used in much the same way as No. 1 (2) (*c*), in Christ's quotation from AG:243C
Deut. 6 : 16, in reply to the Devil, Matt. 4 : 7; Luke 4 : 12; so in CB:1243C
1 Cor. 10 : 9, R.V., " the Lord " (A.V., " Christ ") ; of the lawyer who tempted Christ, Luke 10 : 25.¶ In the Sept., Deut. 6 : 16; 8 : 2, 16; Ps. 78 : 18.¶ Cp. *dokimazō* (see PROVE).

B. Adjective.

APEIRASTOS (ἀπείραστος), untempted, untried (*a*, negative, and A, 551
No. 1), occurs in Jas. 1 : 13, with *eimi*, to be, " cannot be tempted," AG:83B
' untemptable ' (Mayor).¶ CB:1236B

TEMPTATION

PEIRASMOS (πειρασμός), akin to A, above, is used of (1) trials with 3986
a beneficial purpose and effect, (*a*) of trials or temptations, Divinely AG:640D
permitted or sent, Luke 22 : 28; Acts 20 : 19; Jas. 1 : 2; 1 Pet. 1 : 6; CB:1263A
4 : 12, R.V., " to prove," A.V., " to try ; " 2 Pet. 2 : 9 (singular) ; Rev. 3 : 10, R.V., " trial " (A.V., " temptation ") ; in Jas. 1 : 12, " temptation" apparently has meanings (1) and (2) combined (see below), and is used in the widest sense ; (*b*) with a good or neutral significance, Gal. 4 : 14, of Paul's physical infirmity, " a temptation " to the Galatian converts, of such a kind as to arouse feelings of natural repugnance ; (*c*) of trials of a varied character, Matt. 6 : 13 and Luke 11 : 4, where believers are commanded to pray not to be led into such by forces beyond their own control ; Matt. 26 : 41 ; Mark 14 : 38 ; Luke 22 : 40, 46, where they are commanded to watch and pray against entering into temptations by their own carelessness or disobedience ; in all such cases God provides " the way of escape," 1 Cor. 10 : 13 (where *peirasmos* occurs twice). (2) Of trial definitely designed to lead to wrong doing, temptation, Luke 4 : 13 ; 8 : 13 ; 1 Tim. 6 : 9 ; (3) of trying or challenging God, by men, Heb. 3 : 8.¶

TEMPTER

Note : The present participle of *peirazō*, to tempt, preceded by the 3985
article, lit., ' the (one) tempting,' is used as a noun, describing the Devil AG:640B
in this character, Matt. 4 : 3 ; 1 Thess. 3 : 5.¶ CB:1263A

TENANT See HUSBANDMAN

TEN

DEKA (δέκα), whence the Eng. prefix *deca-*, is regarded by some as 1176
the measure of human responsibility, e.g., Luke 19 : 13, 17 ; Rev. 2 : 10 ; AG:173D
it is used in a figurative setting in Rev. 12 : 3 ; 13 : 1 ; 17 : 3, 7, 12, 16. CB:1240C

Notes : (1) In Acts 23 : 23, *hebdomēkonta*, seventy, is translated 1440
" threescore and ten." (2) For " ten thousand " see THOUSAND. AG:212D
CB:1249B

For TEND, John 21 : 16 ; 1 Pet. 5 : 2, R.V., see FEED, No. 2

TENDER

527 HAPALOS (ἁπαλός), soft, tender, is used of the branch of a tree,
AG:80B CB:— Matt. 24 : 32 ; Mark 13 : 28.¶

Note : For Luke 1 : 78, " tender mercy ; " Phil. 1 : 8 ; 2 : 1, " tender mercies," see BOWELS.

For TENDER-HEARTED see PITIFUL, No. 2

TENTH

1182 1. DEKATOS (δέκατος), an adjective from *deka*, ten, occurs in John
AG:174A CB:1240C 1 : 39 ; Rev. 11 : 13 ; 21 : 20.¶

1181 2. DEKATĒ (δεκάτη), grammatically the feminine form of No. 1,
AG:174A with *meris*, a part, understood, is used as a noun, translated " a tenth
(-TOS) CB:1240C part " in Heb. 7 : 2, " a tenth," ver. 4 ; " tithes " in vv. 8, 9.¶

For TENTS see TABERNACLE, No. 1

TENT-MAKERS

4635 SKĒNOPOIOS (σκηνοποιός), an adjective, ' tent-making ' (*skēnē*,
AG:755A CB:1269A a tent, *poieō*, to make), is used as a noun in Acts 18 : 3.¶

TERM (appointed)

4287 PROTHESMIOS (προθέσμιος), an adjective denoting appointed
AG:706B (-MIA) beforehand (*pro*, before, *tithēmi*, to put, appoint : see APPOINT, No. 3,
CB:— Note), is used as a noun, *prothesmia* (grammatically feminine, with *hēmera*, a day, understood), as in Greek law, a day appointed before, Gal. 4 : 2, R.V., " the term appointed," i.e., ' a stipulated date ' (A.V., " the time appointed ").¶

TERRESTRIAL

1919 EPIGEIOS (ἐπίγειος), on earth, earthly (*epi*, on, *gē*, the earth), is
AG:290C CB:1245C rendered " terrestrial " in 1 Cor. 15 : 40 (twice), in contrast to *epouranios*, heavenly. See EARTHLY, No. 2.

TERRIBLE See GRIEVOUS

For TERRIBLE, Heb. 12 : 21, see FEARFUL, B, No. 1

TERRIFY

A. Verbs.

4422 AG:727C 1. PTOEŌ (πτοέω), to terrify, is used in the Passive Voice, Luke
CB:— 21 : 9 ; 24 : 37.¶

1629 AG:247A 2. EKPHOBEŌ (ἐκφοβέω), to frighten away (*ek*, out, *phobos*, fear),
CB:— occurs in 2 Cor. 10 : 9.¶

4426 AG:727D 3. PTURŌ (πτύρω), to scare, Phil. 1 : 28 : see AFFRIGHTED, B,
CB:— No. 1.¶

B. Adjective.

EMPHOBOS (ἔμφοβος), terrified. is so rendered in the R.V. of Acts 1719
24 : 25. See TREMBLE. AG:257D CB:—

TERROR

1. PHOBOS (φόβος), fear, is rendered "terror" in Rom. 13 : 3; 5401 AG:863C
in 2 Cor. 5 : 11 and 1 Pet. 3 : 14, A.V. (R.V., "fear"). See FEAR, No. 1. CB:1264B

2. PHOBĒTRON (φόβητρον), that which causes fright, a terror, is 5400 AG:863C
translated "terrors" in Luke 21 : 11, R.V. (A.V., "fearful sights").¶ CB:1264B
See FEAR, A, Note. For *ptoēsis*, see AMAZEMENT. PTOēSIS 4423 AG:727C

For TESTAMENT see COVENANT CB:—

TESTATOR

DIATITHĒMI (διατίθημι), to arrange, dispose, is used only in the 1303
Middle Voice in the N.T.; in Heb. 9 : 16, 17, the present participle (-THEMAI) AG:189D
with the article, lit., 'the (one) making a testament (or covenant),' CB:1241B
virtually a noun, "the testator" (the covenanting one); it is used of making a covenant in 8 : 10 and 10 : 16 and Acts 3 : 25. In covenant-making, the sacrifice of a victim was customary (Gen. 15 : 10; Jer.
34 : 18, 19). He who made a covenant did so at the cost of a life. While TEST
the terminology in Heb. 9 : 16, 17 has the appearance of being appropriate See TRY, PROVE
to the circumstances of making a will, there is excellent reason for adhering to the meaning 'covenant-making.' The rendering "the death of the testator" would make Christ a Testator, which He was not. He did not die simply that the terms of a testamentary disposition might be fulfilled for the heirs. Here He who is "the Mediator of a new covenant" (ver. 15) is Himself the Victim whose death was necessary. The idea of making a will destroys the argument of ver. 18. In spite of various advocacies of the idea of a will, the weight of evidence is confirmatory of what Hatch, in *Essays in Biblical Greek*, p. 48, says: "There can be little doubt that the word (*diathēkē*) must be invariably taken in this sense of 'covenant' in the N.T., and especially in a book . . . so impregnated with the language of the Sept. as the Epistle to the Hebrews" (see also Westcott, and W. F. Moulton). We may render somewhat literally thus: 'For where a covenant (is), a death (is) necessary to be brought in of the one covenanting; for a covenant over dead ones (victims) is sure, since never has it force when the one covenanting lives' [Christ being especially in view]. The writer is speaking from a Jewish point of view, not from that of the Greeks. "To adduce the fact that in the case of wills the death of the testator is the condition of validity, is, of course, no proof at all that a death is necessary to make a covenant valid. . . To support his argument, proving the necessity of Christ's death, the writer adduces the general law that he who makes a covenant does so at the expense of life" (Marcus Dods). See APPOINT, MAKE.

TESTIFY

3140 AG:492C 1. MARTUREŌ (μαρτυρέω), for which see WITNESS, is frequently
CB:1257C rendered to bear witness, to witness, in the R.V., where A.V. renders
it to testify, John 2 : 25 ; 3 : 11, 32 ; 5 : 39 ; 15 : 26 ; 21 : 24 ; 1 Cor.
15 : 15 ; Heb. 7 : 17 ; 11 : 4 ; 1 John 4 : 14 ; 5 : 9 ; 3 John 3. In the
following, however, the R.V., like the A.V., has the rendering to testify,
John 4 : 39, 44 ; 7 : 7 ; 13 : 21 ; Acts 26 : 5 ; Rev. 22 : 16, 18, 20.

1957 AG:296A 2. EPIMARTUREŌ (ἐπιμαρτυρέω), to bear witness to (a strengthened
CB:1246A form of No. 1), is rendered "testifying" in 1 Pet. 5 : 12.¶

3143 AG:494A 3. MARTUROMAI (μαρτύρομαι), primarily, to summon as witness,
CB:1257C then, to bear witness (sometimes with the suggestion of solemn protestation), is rendered to testify in Acts 20 : 26, R.V. (A.V., "I take . . . to record") ; 26 : 22, in the best texts (some have No. 1), R.V. ; Gal. 5 : 3 ; Eph. 4 : 17 ; 1 Thess. 2 : 11, in the best texts (some have No. 1), R.V., "testifying" (A.V., "charged").¶

1263 AG:186C 4. DIAMARTUROMAI (διαμαρτύρομαι), to testify or protest solemnly,
CB:1241B an intensive form of No. 3, is translated to testify in Luke 16 : 28 ; Acts 2 : 40 ; 8 : 25 ; 10 : 42 ; 18 : 5 ; 20 : 21, 23, 24 ; 23 : 11 ; 28 : 23 ; 1 Thess. 4 : 6 ; Heb. 2 : 6 ; to charge in 1 Tim. 5 : 21 ; 2 Tim. 2 : 14 ; 4 : 1.¶

4303 AG:708C 5. PROMARTUROMAI (προμαρτύρομαι), to testify beforehand, occurs
CB:— in 1 Pet. 1 : 11, where the pronoun "it" should be "He" (the "it" being due to the grammatically neuter form of *pneuma* ; the Personality of the Holy Spirit requires the masculine pronoun).¶

4828 AG:778B *Note :* In Rev. 22 : 18 some texts have *summartureō*, to bear witness
CB:1270B with. See WITNESS.

TESTIMONY

3142 AG:493D 1. MARTURION (μαρτύριον), a testimony, witness, is almost entirely
CB:1257C translated "testimony" in both A.V. and R.V. The only place where both have "witness" is Acts 4 : 33. In Acts 7 : 44 and Jas. 5 : 3, the R.V. has "testimony" (A.V., "witness").

In 2 Thess. 1 : 10, "our testimony unto you," R.V., refers to the fact that the missionaries, besides proclaiming the truths of the gospel, had
KĒRUGMA borne witness to the power of these truths. *Kērugma*, the thing preached,
2782 AG:430D the message, is objective, having especially to do with the effect on the
CB:1255A hearers ; *marturion* is mainly subjective, having to do especially with the preacher's personal experience. In 1 Tim. 2 : 6 the R.V. is important, "the testimony (i.e., of the gospel) *to be borne* in its own times," i.e., in the times Divinely appointed for it, namely, the present age, from Pentecost till the Church is complete. In Rev. 15 : 5, in the phrase, "the temple of the tabernacle of the testimony in Heaven," the testimony is the witness to the rights of God, denied and refused on earth, but about to be vindicated by the exercise of the judgments under the pouring forth of the seven bowls or vials of Divine retribution. See WITNESS.

2. MARTURIA (μαρτυρία), witness, evidence, testimony, is almost 3141
always rendered "witness" in the R.V. (for A.V., "testimony" in John AG:493C
3 : 32, 33 ; 5 : 34 ; 8 : 17 ; 21 : 24, and always for A.V., "record," e.g., CB:1257C
1 John 5 : 10, 11), except in Acts 22 : 18 and in the Apocalypse, where both, with one exception, have "testimony," 1 : 2, 9 ; 6 : 9 ; 11 : 7 ; 12 : 11, 17 ; 19 : 10 (twice) ; 20 : 4 (A.V., "witness"). In 19 : 10, "the testimony of Jesus" is objective, the testimony or witness given to Him (cp. 1 : 2, 9 ; as to those who will bear it, see Rev. 12 : 17, R.V.). The statement "the testimony of Jesus is the spirit of prophecy," is to be understood in the light, e.g., of the testimony concerning Christ and Israel in the Psalms, which will be used by the godly Jewish remnant in the coming time of "Jacob's Trouble." All such testimony centres in and points to Christ. See WITNESS.

TETRARCH

A. Noun.

TETRAARCHĒS or TETRARCHĒS (τετραάρχης) denotes one of four 5076
rulers (*tetra*, four, *archē*, rule), properly, the governor of the fourth part AG:814A
of a region ; hence, a dependent princeling, or any petty ruler subordinate CB:—
to kings or ethnarchs ; in the N.T., Herod Antipas, Matt. 14 : 1 ; Luke 3 : 19 ; 9 : 7 ; Acts 13 : 1.¶

B. Verb.

TETRAARCHEŌ or TETRARCHEŌ (τετρααρχέω), to be a tetrarch, 5075
occurs in Luke 3 : 1 (thrice), of Herod Antipas, his brother Philip and AG:814A
Lysanias. Antipas and Philip each inherited a fourth part of his father's CB:—
dominions. Inscriptions bear witness to the accuracy of Luke's details.¶

THAN : see † p. 1

THANK, THANKS (Noun and Verb), THANKFUL, THANKFULNESS, THANKSGIVING, THANKWORTHY

A. Nouns.

1. CHARIS (χάρις), for the meanings of which see GRACE, No. 1, is 5485
rendered "thank" in Luke 6 : 32, 33, 34 ; in 17 : 9, "doth he thank" AG:877B
is lit., 'hath he thanks to ;' it is rendered "thanks (be to God)" in Rom. CB:1239C
6 : 17, R.V. (A.V., "God be thanked") ; "thanks" in 1 Cor. 15 : 57 ; in 1 Tim. 1 : 12 and 2 Tim. 1 : 3, "I thank" is, lit., 'I have thanks ;' "thankworthy," 1 Pet. 2 : 19, A.V. (R.V., "acceptable"). See ACCEPT, D, No. 2.

2. EUCHARISTIA (εὐχαριστία), *eu*, well, *charizomai*, to give freely 2169
(Eng., eucharist), denotes (*a*) gratitude, "thankfulness," Acts 24 : 3 ; AG:328C
(*b*) giving of thanks, thanksgiving, 1 Cor. 14 : 16 ; 2 Cor. 4 : 15 ; 9 : 11, 12 CB:1247A
(plur.) ; Eph. 5 : 4 ; Phil. 4 : 6 ; Col. 2 : 7 ; 4 : 2 ; 1 Thess. 3 : 9 ("thanks") ; 1 Tim. 2 : 1 (plur.) ; 4 : 3, 4 ; Rev. 4 : 9, "thanks ;" 7 : 12.¶

B. Verbs.

2168 AG:328A CB:1247A 1. EUCHARISTEŌ (εὐχαριστέω), akin to A, No. 2, to give thanks, (*a*) is said of Christ, Matt. 15 : 36 ; 26 : 27 ; Mark 8 : 6 ; 14 : 23 ; Luke 22 : 17, 19; John 6 : 11, 23 ; 11 : 41 ; 1 Cor. 11 : 24; (*b*) of the Pharisee in Luke 18 : 11 in his self-complacent prayer ; (*c*) is used by Paul at the beginning of all his Epistles, except 2 Cor. (see, however, *eulogētos* in 1 : 3), Gal., 1 Tim., 2 Tim. (see, however, *charin echō*, 1 : 3), and Tit., (1) for his readers, Rom. 1 : 8 ; Eph. 1 : 16 ; Col. 1 : 3 ; 1 Thess. 1 : 2 ; 2 Thess. 1 : 3 (cp. 2 : 13) ; virtually so in Philm. 4 ; (2) for fellowship shown, Phil. 1 : 3 ; (3) for God's gifts to them, 1 Cor. 1 : 4 ; (*d*) is recorded (1) of Paul elsewhere, Acts 27 : 35 ; 28 : 15 ; Rom. 7 : 25 ; 1 Cor. 1 : 14 ; 14 : 18 ; (2) of Paul and others, Rom. 16 : 4 ; 1 Thess. 2 : 13 ; of himself, representatively, as a practice, 1 Cor. 10 : 30 ; (3) of others, Luke 17 : 16 ; Rom. 14 : 6 (twice) ; 1 Cor. 14 : 17 ; Rev. 11 : 17 ; (*e*) is used in admonitions to the saints, the Name of the Lord Jesus suggesting His character and example, Eph. 5 : 20 ; Col. 1 : 12 ; 3 : 17 ; 1 Thess. 5 : 18 ; (*f*) as the expression of a purpose, 2 Cor. 1 : 11, R.V. ; (*g*) negatively of the ungodly, Rom. 1 : 21.¶ Thanksgiving is the expression of joy Godward, and is therefore the fruit of the Spirit (Gal. 5 : 22) ; believers are encouraged to abound in it (e.g., Col. 2 : 7, and see C, below).

1843 AG:277A CB:1247C (EXHO-) 2. EXOMOLOGEŌ (ἐξομολογέω), in the Middle Voice, signifies to make acknowledgment, whether of sins (to confess), or in the honour of a person, as in Rom. 14 : 11 ; 15 : 9 (in some mss. in Rev. 3 : 5) ; this is the significance in the Lord's address to the Father, " I thank (Thee)," in Matt. 11 : 25 and Luke 10 : 21, the meaning being 'I make thankful confession' or 'I make acknowledgment with praise.' See CONFESS, No. 2, CONSENT, PROMISE.

437 AG:67B CB:— 3. ANTHOMOLOGEOMAI (ἀνθομολογέομαι), to acknowledge fully, to celebrate fully (*anti*) in praise with thanksgiving, is used of Anna in Luke 2 : 38.¶

3670 AG:568A CB:1251A *Note :* For *homologeō*, rendered " giving thanks " in Heb. 13 : 15 (R.V., " make confession "), see CONFESS, A, No. 1 (*d*).

C. Adjective.

2170 AG:329A CB:1247A EUCHARISTOS (εὐχάριστος), primarily, gracious, agreeable (as in the Sept., Prov. 11 : 16, of a wife, who brings glory to her husband¶), then grateful, thankful, is so used in Col. 3 : 15.¶

THAT (Conjunction, etc.) : see † **p. 1**

For THAT (Demonstrative Pronoun), see THIS

THEATRE

2302 AG:353C CB:1271C THEATRON (θέατρον), a theatre, was used also as a place of assembly, Acts 19 : 29, 31 ; in 1 Cor. 4 : 9 it is used of a show or spectacle. See SPECTACLE.¶

THEE

Note: This translates the oblique forms of the pronoun *su*, thou. SU 4771
In 2 Tim. 4 : 11, it translates the reflexive pronoun *seautou*, thyself. AG:772A SEAUTOU 4572 AG:745C

THEFT

1. KLOPĒ (κλοπή), akin to *kleptō*, to steal, is used in the plural in 2829 AG:436D
Matt. 15 : 19; Mark 7 : 22.¶ CB:—

2. KLEMMA (κλέμμα), a thing stolen, and so, a theft, is used in the 2809
plural in Rev. 9 : 21.¶ In the Sept., Gen. 31 : 39; Ex. 22 : 3, 4.¶ AG:434B CB:—

THEIR, THEIRS

Note: These pronouns are the rendering of (1) *autōn*, the genitive plur. AUTOS 846
of *autos*, he, e.g., Matt. 2 : 12; (2) *heautōn*, of themselves, the genitive AG:122C
plur. of *heautou*, of himself, e.g., Matt. 8: 22; Rom. 16 : 4, 18, "their CB:1238B
own;" or the accusative plur. *heautous*, e.g., 2 Cor. 8 : 5, "their own HEAUTOU 1438
selves" (for John 20 : 10, see HOME, A, No. 3); (3) *idious*, the accusative AG:211D
plur. of *idios*, one's own, e.g., 1 Cor. 14 : 35, "their own;" (4) *toutōn*, CB:1249B (-OS)
lit., 'of these,' the gen. plur. of *houtos*, this, Rom. 11 : 30, "their (dis- IDIOS 2398
obedience);" (5) *ekeinōn*, the gen. plur. of *ekeinos*, that one (emphatic), AG:369C
e.g., 2 Cor. 8 : 14 (twice), "their," lit., 'of those;' 2 Tim. 3 : 9, "theirs." CB:1252C HOUTOS 3778

THEM, THEMSELVES

AG:596B CB:1251B

Note: These translate the plural, in various forms, of (1) *autos* [see EKEINOS
(1) above], e.g., Matt. 3 : 7; (2) *heatou* [see (2) above], e.g., Matt. 15 : 30; 1565
(3) *houtos* (*toutous*) [see (4) above], e.g., Acts 21 : 24; (4) *ekeinos* [see (5) AG:239B
above], e.g., Matt. 13 : 11. Regarding *allēlōn*, of one another, and its CB:1243C 240
other forms, the R.V. substitutes "one another" for the A.V. "them- AG:39C
selves" in Mark 8 : 16; 9 : 34; Luke 4 : 36; John 6 : 52; 11 : 56; 16 : 17; CB:1234C
19 : 24; Acts 26 : 31; 28 : 4; Rom. 2 : 15, but adheres to the rendering
"themselves" in Mark 15 : 31; Acts 4 : 15; 28 : 25.

THEN

1. TOTE (τότε), a demonstrative adverb of time, denoting at that time, 5119
is used (*a*) of concurrent events, e.g., Matt. 2 : 17; Gal. 4 : 8, "at that AG:823D
time;" ver. 29, "then;" 2 Pet. 3 : 6, "(the world) that then was," lit., CB:1273A
'(the) then (world);' (*b*) of consequent events, then, thereupon, e.g.,
Matt. 2 : 7; Luke 11 : 26; 16 : 16, "[from (A.V., since)] that time;"
John 11 : 14; Acts 17 : 14; (*c*) of things future, e.g., Matt. 7 : 23;
24 : 30 (twice), 40; eight times in ch. 25; 1 Cor. 4 : 5; Gal. 6 : 4;
1 Thess. 5 : 3; 2 Thess. 2 : 8. It occurs 90 times in Matthew, more than
in all the rest of the N.T. together.

2. EITA (εἶτα) denotes sequence (*a*) of time, then, next, Mark 4 : 17, 1534
R.V., "then;" 4 : 28, in some texts; 8 : 25, R.V., "then" (A.V., "after AG:233D
that"); Luke 8 : 12; John 13 : 5; 19 : 27; 20 : 27; in some texts CB:1243B

in 1 Cor. 12 : 28 ; 1 Cor. 15 : 5, 7, 24 ; 1 Tim. 2 : 13 ; 3 : 10 ; Jas. 1 : 15 ;
(*b*) in argument, Heb. 12 : 9, " furthermore."¶

1899 AG:284C 3. EPEITA (ἔπειτα) is used only of sequence, thereupon, thereafter,
CB:— then (in some texts, Mark 7 : 5 ; *kai*, " and," in the best) ; Luke 16 : 7 ;
John 11 : 7 ; 1 Cor. 12 : 28, R.V., " then " (A.V., " after that ") ; 15 : 6
and 7 (ditto) ; ver. 23, R.V., A.V., " afterward " (No. 2 in ver. 24) ;
ver. 46 (ditto) ; Gal. 1 : 18 ; ver. 21, R.V. (A.V., " afterwards ") ; 2 : 1 ;
1 Thess. 4 : 17 ; Heb. 7 : 2, R.V. (A.V., " after that ") ; ver. 27,
3063 Jas. 3 : 17 ; 4 : 14. See AFTER.¶

AG:479D 4. LOIPON (λοιπόν), finally, for the rest, the neuter of *loipos*, (the) rest,
(LOIPOS 3.b.) CB:1257B used adverbially, is rendered " then " in Acts 27 : 20, A.V. (R.V., " now.").

3767 AG:592D 5. OUN (οὖν), a particle expressing sequence or consequence, is
rendered " then," e.g., Matt. 22 : 43 ; 27 : 22 ; Luke 11 : 13.

3766 AG:592D 6. OUKOUN (οὐκοῦν), an adverb formed from *ouk*, not, *oun*, therefore,
with the negative element dropped, meaning 'so then,' is used in John
18 : 37.¶

Notes : (1) In James 2 : 24, where in some texts the inferential particle
5106 *toinun*, therefore, occurs, the A.V. renders it by " then " (R.V. follows the
AG:821A CB:— superior mss. which omit it). (2) For conjunctions (*ara*, so ; *de*, but ;
gar, for ; *kai*, and ; *te*, and), sometimes translated " then," see † p. 9.

THENCE (from)

1564 AG:239B EKEITHEN (ἐκεῖθεν) is used (*a*) of place, e.g., Matt. 4 : 21, " from
CB:— thence ; " 5 : 26 ; in Acts 20 : 13, " there ; " often preceded by *kai*,
written *kakeithen*, e.g., Mark 9 : 30 and Luke 11 : 53 (in the best texts) ;
Acts 7 : 4 ; 14 : 26 ; (*b*) of time, Acts 13 : 21, " and afterward." See
AFTER.

3606 AG:555C *Note :* In Acts 28 : 13, *hothen*, from whence, is translated " from
CB:— thence."

THENCEFORTH

2089 AG:315C CB:1247A ETI (ἔτι), yet, still, further, is rendered " thenceforth " in Matt. 5 : 13.
MELLō *Notes :* (1) In Luke 13 : 9, R.V., the phrase *eis to mellon*, lit., ' unto
3195 AG:500D the about to be ' (*mellō*, to be about to), is translated " thenceforth "
CB:1258A (A.V., " after that "). (2) In John 19 : 12, A.V., *ek toutou*, from this, is
HOUTOS translated " from thenceforth " (R.V., " upon this ").

3778 AG:596B CB:1251B

THERE, THITHER

1563 AG:239A 1. EKEI (ἐκεῖ) signifies (*a*) there, e.g., Matt. 2 : 13, frequently in the
CB:1243C Gospels ; (*b*) thither, e.g., Luke 17 : 37 ; in Rom. 15 : 24, " thitherward."

1566 AG:240A 2. EKEISE (ἐκεῖσε), properly, ' thither,' signifies " there " in Acts
21 : 3 ; 22 : 5.¶ In the Sept., Job 39 : 29.¶

1564 AG:239B 3. EKEITHEN (ἐκεῖθεν), thence, is rendered " there " in Acts 20 : 13.
See THENCE.

1759 AG:266A 4. ENTHADE (ἐνθάδε), here, hither, is rendered " there " in Acts
10 : 18. See HERE, HITHER.

5. AUTOU (αὐτοῦ), the genitive case, neuter, of *autos*, he, lit., 'of it,' 847
is used as an adverb, "there," in Acts 18 : 19 ; 21 : 4 (in some texts in AG:124A AUTOS
15 : 34). See HERE. 846

Notes: (1) In Luke 24 : 18 and Acts 9 : 38, "there" translates the AG:122C CB:1238B
phrase *en autē*, 'in it.' (2) In John 21 : 9, "there" is used to translate KEIMAI
the verb *keimai*. (3) In Matt. 24 : 23 (2nd part), A.V., *hōde*, "here" 2749
(R.V.), is translated "there." (4) In Acts 17 : 21, "there" forms part AG:426C CB:1254C
of the translation of *epidēmeō*, to sojourn, "sojourning there," R.V. HōDE
("which were there," A.V.). 5602 AG:895B

EPIDēMEō

THEREABOUT 1927 AG:292A

Note: The phrase *peri toutou*, 'concerning this,' is rendered "there- PERI
about" in Luke 24 : 4. 4012 AG:644B

CB:1263B

THEREAT

Note: The phrase *di'autēs*, lit., 'by (*dia*) it,' is rendered "thereat" DIA
in Matt. 7 : 13, A.V. (R.V., "thereby"). 1223 AG:179B

CB:1241A

THEREBY

Notes: (1) *Di'autēs* (see above) occurs in Matt. 7 : 13 ; John 11 : 4 ; DIA
Heb. 12 : 11. (2) *Dia tautēs*, by means of this, "thereby," occurs in 1223 AG:179B
Heb. 12 : 15 ; 13 : 2. (3) *En autē*, in, or by, it, is rendered "thereby" CB:1241A
in Rom. 10 : 5 ; *en autō* in Eph. 2 : 16 (some texts have *en heautō*, EN
'in Himself') ; 1 Pet. 2 : 2. 1722 AG:258B

CB:1244B

THEREFORE, † p. 1

THEREIN, THEREINTO, THEREOF, THEREON, THEREOUT, THERETO, THEREUNTO, THEREUPON, THEREWITH

Note: These translate various phrases consisting of a preposition
with forms of either the personal pronoun *autos*, he, or the demonstrative AUTOS
houtos, this. 846 AG:122C

CB:1238B HOUTOS

For THESE see THIS

THEY, THEY THEMSELVES 3778 AG:596B CB:1251B

Note: When not forming part of the translation of the 3rd pers., EKEINOS
plur. of a verb, (1) these translate the plural of the pronouns under HE, 1565 AG:239B
in their various forms, *autos*, *houtos*, *ekeinos*, *heautou*. (2) In Acts 5 : 16, CB:1243C
hoitines, the plural of *hostis*, anyone who, is translated "they ;" so in HEAUTOU 1438
23 : 14, translated "and they ;" in 17 : 11, "in that they" (some texts AG:211D
have it in Matt. 25 : 3). (3) Sometimes the plural of the article is rendered CB:1249B (-OS)
"they," e.g., Phil. 4 : 22 ; Heb. 13 : 24 ; in 1 Cor. 11 : 19, "they which HOSTIS
are (approved)" is, lit., 'the approved ;' in Gal. 2 : 6, "they . . . 3748 AG:586D
(who were of repute)," R.V. CB:—

For THICK see GATHER, A, No. 8

THIEF, THIEVES

2812 AG:434B 1. KLEPTĒS (κλέπτης) is used (*a*) literally, Matt. 6 : 19, 20 ; 24 : 43 ;
CB:1255B Luke 12 : 33, 39 ; John 10 : 1, 10 ; 12 : 6 ; 1 Cor. 6 : 10 ; 1 Pet. 4 : 15 ; (*b*) metaphorically of false teachers, John 10 : 8 ; (*c*) figuratively, (1) of the Personal coming of Christ, in a warning to a local church, with most of its members possessed of mere outward profession and defiled by the world, Rev. 3 : 3 ; in retributive intervention to overthrow the foes of God, 16 : 15 ; (2) of the Day of the Lord, in Divine judgment upon the world, 2 Pet. 3 : 10 and 1 Thess. 5 : 2, 4 ; in ver. 2, according to the order in the original "the word 'night' is not to be read with 'the day of the Lord,' but with 'thief,' i.e., there is no reference to the time of the coming, only to the manner of it. To avoid ambiguity the phrase may be paraphrased, 'so comes as a thief in the night comes.' The use of the present tense instead of the future emphasises the certainty of the coming. . . . The unexpectedness of the coming of the thief, and the unpreparedness of those to whom he comes, are the essential elements in the figure ; cp. the entirely different figure used in Matt. 25 : 1–13."¶*

3027 AG:473A 2. LĒSTĒS (λῃστής) is frequently rendered "thieves" in the A.V.,
CB:1256C e.g., Matt. 21 : 13. See ROBBER.

THIGH

3382 AG:519D MĒROS (μηρός) occurs in Rev. 19 : 16 ; Christ appears there in the
CB:— manifestation of His judicial capacity and action hereafter as the Executor of Divine vengeance upon the foes of God ; His Name is spoken of figuratively as being upon His thigh (where the sword would be worn ; cp. Ps. 45 : 3), emblematic of His strength to tread down His foes, His action being the exhibition of His Divine attributes of righteousness and power.¶

For THINE see THY

THING(S)

3056 AG:477A 1. LOGOS (λόγος), a word, an account, etc., is translated "thing"
CB:1257A in Matt. 21 : 24, A.V. (1st part), and Luke 20 : 3, A.V., R.V., "question" (in Matt. 21 : 24, 2nd part, "these things" translates *tauta,* the neut. plur. of *houtos*, this) ; Luke 1 : 4 ; Acts 5 : 24, A.V. (R.V., "words") See ACCOUNT.

4229 AG:697A 2. PRAGMA (πρᾶγμα), for which see MATTER, No. 2, is translated
CB:1266B "thing" in Matt. 18 : 19, as part of the word "anything," lit., 'every thing ;' Luke 1 : 1, A.V. only ; Acts 5 : 4 ; in Heb. 6 : 18 ; 10 : 1, and 11 : 1, "things." See BUSINESS, MATTER, WORK.

4487 AG:735B 3. RHĒMA (ῥῆμα), a saying, word, is translated "thing" in Luke

CB:1268A * From Notes on Thessalonians by Hogg and Vine, pp. 153, 154.

2 : 15 ; ver. 19, A.V. (R.V., " saying ") ; in Acts 5 : 32, " things." See SAYING.

Notes : (1) The neuter sing. and plur. of the article are frequently rendered " the thing " and " the things ; " so with *tauta*, " these things,"
the neut. plur. of *houtos*, this. (2) So in the case of the neut. plur. of 3778
certain pronouns and adjectives without nouns, e.g., all, base, heavenly, AG:596B CB:1251B
which. (3) When " thing " represents a separate word in the original, it is a translation of one or other of Nos. 1, 2, 3, above. (4) In Phil. 2 : 10, " *things* " is added in italics to express the meaning of the three adjectives.

THINK

1. DOKEŌ (δοκέω), to suppose, to think, to form an opinion, which 1380
may be either right or wrong, is sometimes rendered to think, e.g., AG:201D
Matt. 3 : 9 ; 6 : 7 ; see ACCOUNT, No. 1, SUPPOSE, No. 2. CB:1242A

2. HĒGEOMAI (ἡγέομαι), for which see ACCOUNT, No. 3, is rendered 2233
to think in Acts 26 : 2 ; 2 Cor. 9 : 5, " I thought ; " Phil. 2 : 6, A.V. AG:343C
(R.V., " counted ") ; 2 Pet. 1 : 13. CB:1249C

3. NOEŌ (νοέω), to perceive, understand, apprehend, is rendered 3539 (NOIEō)
" think " in Eph. 3 : 20. See PERCEIVE, UNDERSTAND. AG:540B CB:1259C

4. HUPONOEŌ (ὑπονοέω), to suppose, surmise (*hupo*, under, and No. 5282
3), is rendered to think in Acts 13 : 25, A.V. (R.V., " suppose "). See AG:846D
DEEM. CB:—

5. LOGIZOMAI (λογίζομαι), to reckon, is rendered to think, in 3049
Rom. 2 : 3, A.V. (R.V., " reckonest "); 1 Cor. 13 : 5, A.V., R.V., AG:475D
" taketh (not) account of," i.e., love does not reckon up or calculatingly CB:1257A
consider the evil done to it (something more than refraining from imputing motives) ; 13 : 11, " I thought ; " in the following, for the A.V., to think, in 2 Cor. 3 : 5, R.V., " to account ; " 10 : 2 (twice), " count ; " 10 : 7, " consider ; " 10 : 11, " reckon ; " 12 : 6, " account." In Phil. 4 : 8, " think on (these things)," it signifies ' make those things the subjects of your thoughtful consideration,' or ' carefully reflect on them ' (R.V. marg., " take account of "). See ACCOUNT, A, No. 4.

6. NOMIZŌ (νομίζω), to suppose, is sometimes rendered to think, 3543
e.g., Matt. 5 : 17. See SUPPOSE, No. 1. AG:541A CB:1260A

7. PHRONEŌ (φρονέω), to be minded in a certain way (*phrēn*, the 5426
mind), is rendered to think, in Rom. 12 : 3 (2nd and 3rd occurrences), AG:866A
R.V., " not to think of himself more highly (*huperphroneō*, see No. 13) CB:1264C
than he ought to think (*phroneō*) ; but so to think (*phroneō*) as to think soberly [*sōphroneō*, see Note (3)] ; " the play on words may be expressed by a literal rendering somewhat as follows : ' not to over-think beyond what it behoves him to think, but to think unto sober-thinking ; ' in 1 Cor. 4 : 6, some inferior texts have this verb, hence the A.V. " to think ; " in the best texts, it is absent, hence the R.V., puts " *go* " in italics ; lit., the sentence is ' that ye might learn the (i.e., the rule) not beyond what

things have been written.' The saying appears to be proverbial, perhaps a Rabbinical adage. Since, however, *graphō*, to write, was a current term for framing a law or an agreement (so Deissmann, *Bible Studies*, and Moulton and Milligan, *Vocab.*), it is quite possible that the Apostle's meaning is 'not to go beyond the terms of a teacher's commission, thinking more of himself than the character of his commission allows;' this accords with the context and the whole passage, 3:1–4:5. In Phil. 1:7, A.V., "to think" (R.V., "to be . . . minded"). See AFFECTION, B, Note (1) and list there.

3633 AG:562C 8. OIOMAI or OIMAI (οἴομαι), to imagine, is rendered "I suppose"
CB:— in John 21:25; "thinking" in Phil. 1:17, R.V. (ver. 16, A.V., "supposing"); "let (not that man) think," Jas. 1:7. See SUPPOSE.¶

5316 AG:851B 9. PHAINŌ (φαίνω), in the Passive Voice, to appear, is rendered
CB:1263C "(what) think (ye)" in Mark 14:64, lit., 'what does it appear to you?' See APPEAR, No. 1.

2106 AG:319B 10. EUDOKEŌ (εὐδοκέω), to be well-pleasing, is rendered "we thought
CB:1247A it good" in 1 Thess. 3:1. See PLEASE.

515 AG:78C 11. AXIOŌ (ἀξιόω), to regard as worthy (*axios*), to deem it suitable,
CB:1238B is rendered "thought (not) good" in Acts 15:38. See WORTHY, B.

1760 AG:266A 12. ENTHUMEOMAI (ἐνθυμέομαι), to reflect on, ponder, is used in
CB:1245B Matt. 1:20; 9:4: see No. 14. Cp. *enthumēsis*, consideration (see THOUGHT).¶

5252 AG:842A 13. HUPERPHRONEŌ (ὑπερφρονέω), to be overproud, high-minded,
CB:1252A occurs in Rom. 12:3, rendered "to think of himself more highly." See No. 7.¶

— AG:194A 14. DIENTHUMEOMAI (διενθυμέομαι), to consider deeply (*dia*,
CB:— through, and No. 12), is used of Peter in Acts 10:19, in the best texts (some have No. 12).¶

1911 AG:289D 15. EPIBALLŌ (ἐπιβάλλω), to throw oneself upon, is used meta-
CB:— phorically in Mark 14:72, "when he thought thereon (he wept)," lit., 'thinking thereon,' but to think is an exceptional sense of the word (see BEAT, CAST, LAY, PUT); hence various suggestions have been made. Field, following others, adopts the meaning 'putting (his garment) over (his head),' as an expression of grief. Others regard it as having here the same meaning as *archomai*, to begin (at an early period, indeed, *archomai* was substituted in the text for the authentic *epiballō*); Moulton
KRINŌ 2919 confirms this from a papyrus writing. Another suggestion is to under-
AG:451B stand it as with *dianoian*, mind, i.e., 'casting his mind thereon.'

CB:1256A DIALOGIZOMAI *Notes:* (1) In Acts 26:8, A.V., *krinō*, to judge, reckon, is translated
1260 "should it be thought" (R.V., "is it judged"). (2) In Luke 12:17,
AG:186A CB:1241B A.V., *dialogizomai*, to reason (R.V., "reasoned"), is translated "thought."
SŌPHRONEŌ (3) In Rom. 12:3, *sōphroneō*, "to think soberly," R.V., is, lit., 'unto
4993 AG:802A sober-thinking,' the infinitive mood of the verb being used as a noun
CB:1269B (A.V. marg., "to sobriety"): cp. No. 7. See SOBER, B, No. 2.

THIRD, THIRDLY

TRITOS (τρίτος) is used (*a*) as a noun, e.g., Luke 20 : 12, 31 ; in 5154
Rev. 8 : 7–12 and 9 : 15, 18, " the third part," lit., ' the third ; ' (*b*) as an AG:826C
adverb, with the article, " the third time," e.g., Mark 14 : 41 ; John CB:1273A
21 : 17 (twice) ; without the article, lit., ' a third time,' e.g., John 21 : 14 ; 2 Cor. 12 : 14 ; 13 : 1 ; in enumerations, in Matt. 26 : 44, with *ek*, from, lit., ' from the third time ' (the *ek* indicates the point of departure, especially in a succession of events, cp. John 9 : 24 ; 2 .Pet. 2 : 8) ; absolutely, in the accusative neuter, in 1 Cor. 12 : 28, " thirdly ; " (*c*) as an adjective (its primary use), e.g., in the phrase " the third heaven," 2 Cor. 12 : 2 [cp. HEAVEN, A, No. 1 (*c*), PARADISE] ; in the phrase " the third hour," Matt. 20 : 3 ; Mark 15 : 25 ; Acts 2 : 15 (" . . . of the day ") ; 23 : 23 (" . . . of the night ") ; in a phrase with *hēmera*, a day, " on the third day " (i.e., ' the next day but one '), e.g., Matt. 16 : 21 ; Luke 24 : 46 ; Acts 10 : 40 ; in this connection the idiom " three days and three nights," Matt. 12 : 40, is explained by ref. to 1 Sam. 30 : 12, 13, and Esth. 4 : 16 with 5 : 1 ; in Mark 9 : 31 and 10 : 34, the R.V., " after three days," follows the texts which have this phrase, the A.V., " the third day," those which have the same phrase as in Matt. 16 : 21, etc.

Note : For " third story," Acts 20 : 9, R.V., see STORY.

THIRST (Noun and Verb), THIRSTY (to be), ATHIRST

A. Noun.

DIPSOS (δίψος), thirst (cp. Eng., dipsomania), occurs in 2 Cor. 11 : 27.¶ 1373

B. Verb. AG:200D CB:1242A

DIPSAŌ (διψάω) is used (*a*) in the natural sense, e.g., Matt. 25 : 35, 1372
37, 42 ; in ver. 44, " athirst " (lit., ' thirsting ') ; John 4 : 13, 15 ; 19 : 28 ; AG:200C
Rom. 12 : 20 ; 1 Cor. 4 : 11 ; Rev. 7 : 16 ; (*b*) figuratively, of spiritual CB:1242A
thirst, Matt. 5 : 6 ; John 4 : 14 ; 6 : 35 ; 7 : 37 ; in Rev. 21 : 6 and 22 : 17, " that is athirst."

THIRTY, THIRTYFOLD

TRIAKONTA (τριάκοντα) is usually rendered " thirty," e.g., Matt. 5144
13 : 23 ; " thirtyfold," in Matt. 13 : 8, A.V. only ; in Mark 4 : 8, R.V. AG:826A
only ; in Mark 4 : 20, A.V. and R.V. CB:—

THIS, THESE

Note : The singular and plural translate various forms of the following :
(1) *houtos*, which is used (*a*) as a noun, this one, followed by no noun, 3778
e.g., Matt. 3: 17 ; translated in Luke 2 : 34, " this *child* ; " in 1 Cor. 5 : 3, AG:596B
R.V., " this thing " (A.V., " this deed ") ; for " this fellow " see FELLOW, CB:1251B
Note (3) ; in Acts 17 : 32 the R.V. rightly omits " *matter* ; " in Heb. 4 : 5 " *place* " is italicized ; it is frequently rendered " this man," e.g., Matt. 9 : 3 ; John 6 : 52 ; " of this sort," 2 Tim. 3 : 6, A.V. (R.V., " of these ") ; (*b*) as an adjective with a noun, either with the article and before it, e.g.,

EKEINOS Matt. 12 : 32, or after the noun (which is preceded by the article), e.g.,
1565 AG:239B Matt. 3 : 9 and 4 : 3, " these stones ; " or without the article often forming
CB:1243C a predicate, e.g., John 2 : 11 ; 2 Cor. 13 : 1 ; (2) *ekeinos*, that one, rendered
AUTOS " this " in Matt. 24 : 43 ; (3) ***autos***, he, rendered " this " in Matt. 11 : 14,
846 AG:122C lit., ' he ; ' in John 12 : 7, A.V. (R.V., " it ") ; in the feminine, Luke
CB:1238B 13 : 16 ; (4) the article *ho*, Matt. 21 : 21 (*to*, the neuter), A.V. (R.V.,
HO 3588 " what ") ; in Rom. 13 : 9 (1st part) ; Gal. 5 : 14 ; Heb. 12 : 27, the
AG:549B article *to* is virtually equivalent to ' the following.'
CB:— The demonstrative pronouns THAT and the plural THOSE translate the same pronouns (1), (2), (3) mentioned above. In Heb. 7 : 21, A.V., " those " translates the article, which requires the R.V., " they."

THISTLE

5146 AG:826A CB:1273A TRIBOLOS (τρίβολος) occurs in Matt. 7 : 16 and Heb. 6 : 8 (A.V., " briers ").¶ In the Sept., Gen. 3 : 18 ; 2 Sam. 12 : 31 ; Prov. 22 : 5 ; Hos. 10 : 8.¶ Cp. THORNS.

For THITHER, THITHERWARD see THERE

3699 AG:576A CB:— *Note :* In John 7 : 34, 36, A.V., *hopou*, " where " (R.V.), is amplified by the italicized word " *thither*."

For THONG see LATCHET

THORN, THORNS (of)

A. Nouns.

173 AG:29C CB:1234A 1. AKANTHA (ἄκανθα), a brier, a thorn (from *akē*, a point), is always used in the plural in the N.T., Matt. 7 : 16 and parallel passage in Luke 6 : 44 ; Matt. 13 : 7 (twice), 22 and parallels in Mark and Luke ; in Matt. 27 : 29 and John 19 : 2, of the crown of thorns placed on Christ's head (see also B) in mock imitation of the garlands worn by emperors. They were the effects of the Divine curse on the ground (Gen. 3 : 18 ; contrast Is. 55 : 13). The thorns of the crown plaited by the soldiers, are usually identified with those of the *Zizyphus spina Christi*, some 20 feet high or more, fringing the Jordan and abundant in Palestine ; its twigs are flexible. Another species, however, the Arabian *qundaul*, crowns of which are plaited and sold in Jerusalem as representatives of Christ's crown, seems likely to be the one referred to. The branches are easily woven and adapted to the torture intended. The word *akantha* occurs also in Heb. 6 : 8.¶

4647 AG:756C CB:1269B 2. SKOLOPS (σκόλοψ) originally denoted anything pointed, e.g., a stake ; in Hellenistic vernacular, a thorn (so the Sept., in Numb. 33 : 55 ; Ezek. 28 : 24 ; Hos. 2 : 6¶), 2 Cor. 12 : 7, of the Apostle's " thorn in the flesh ; " his language indicates that it was physical, painful, humiliating ; it was also the effect of Divinely permitted Satanic antagonism ; the verbs rendered " that I should (not) be exalted overmuch " (R.V.) and " to buffet" are in the present tense, signifying recurrent action, indicating a constantly repeated attack. Lightfoot interprets it as "a stake driven through the flesh," and Ramsay agrees with this. Most commentators adhere to the rendering "thorn." Field says "there is no doubt that the Alexandrine use of *skolops* for thorn is here intended, and that the ordinary meaning of 'stake' must be rejected." What is stressed is not the metaphorical size, but the acuteness of the suffering and its effects. Attempts to connect this with the circumstances of Acts 14:19 and Gal. 4:13 are speculative.¶

B. Adjective.

AKANTHINOS (ἀκάνθινος), of thorns (from A, No. 1), is used in 174
Mark 15:17 and John 19:5.¶ In the Sept., Isa. 34:13.¶ AG:29C CB:1234A

THOROUGHLY (THROUGHLY)

Note: This is usually part of the translation of a verb, e.g., CLEANSE, 3956
FURNISH, PURGE. In 2 Cor. 11:6, the phrase *en panti*, "in everything," AG:631A
R.V., is translated "throughly" in the A.V. CB:1262C

For THOSE see THIS (last part of Note)

THOU

Note: Frequently this forms part of the translation of a verb in the
2nd person, singular. Otherwise it translates (*a*) the pronoun *su*, used SU
for emphasis or contrast, e.g., John 1:19, 21 (twice), 25, 42 (twice); 4771
8:5, 13, 25, 33, 48, 52, 53; Acts 9:5; in addressing a person or place, AG:772A CB:—
e.g., Matt. 2:6; Luke 1:76; John 17:5; perhaps also in the phrase AUTOS
su eipas, "thou hast said," e.g., Matt. 26:64 (sometimes without 846 AG:122C
emphasis, e.g., Acts 13:33); (*b*) in the oblique cases, e.g., the dative *soi*, CB:1238B
lit., to thee, e.g., Matt. 17:25, "what thinkest thou?" (lit., 'what does SEAUTOU 4572
it seem to thee?'); (*c*) *autos*, self, e.g., Luke 6:42; Acts 21:24, "thou AG:745C
thyself;" (*d*) the reflexive pronoun, *seauton*, Rom. 2:19, "thou thyself." CB:—

THOUGH: see † p. 1

For THOUGHT (Verb) see THINK

THOUGHT (Noun)

1. EPINOIA (ἐπίνοια), a thought by way of a design (akin to *epinoeō*, 1963
to contrive, *epi*, intensive, *noeō*, to consider), is used in Acts 8:22.¶ In AG:296C
the Sept., Jer. 20:10.¶ CB:1246A

2. NOĒMA (νόημα), a purpose, device of the mind (akin to *noeō*, see 3540
No. 1), is rendered "thought" in 2 Cor. 10:5, "thoughts" in Phil. AG:540D
4:7, R.V.: see DEVICE, No. 2. CB:1259C

3. DIANOĒMA (διανόημα), a thought, occurs in Luke 11:17, where 1270 AG:187A
the sense is that of machinations.¶ CB:1241B

ENTHUMĒSIS 1761 4. ENTHUMĒSIS (ἐνθύμησις), is translated "thoughts" in Matt. 9 : 4;
AG:266B CB:1245B 12 : 25; Heb. 4 : 12: see DEVICE, No. 1.
LOGISMOS 3053 5. LOGISMOS (λογισμός) is translated "thoughts" in Rom. 2 : 15:
AG:476D see IMAGINATION, No. 1.
CB:1257A 6. DIALOGISMOS (διαλογισμός), reasoning, is translated "thoughts"
DIALOGISMOS 1261 in Matt. 15 : 19; Mark 7 : 21; Luke 2 : 35; 6 : 8; in 5 : 22, A.V., R.V.,
AG:186A "reasonings;" in 9 : 47, A.V., R.V., "reasoning," and 24 : 38, A.V., R.V.,
CB:1241B "reasonings;" so 1 Cor. 3 : 20; in Luke 9 : 46, A.V. and R.V.,
MERIMNAŌ 3309 "reasoning;" "thoughts" in Jas. 2 : 4, A.V. and R.V. See DISPUTE,
AG:505A CB:1258B IMAGINATION, REASONING.

PROMERIMNAŌ 4305

THOUGHT (to take)

AG:708C CB:1266C 1. MERIMNAŌ (μεριμνάω) denotes to be anxious, careful. For the
PHRONEŌ 5426 A.V., to take thought, the R.V. substitutes to be anxious in Matt.
AG:866A 6 : 25, 27, 28, 31, 34; 10 : 19; Luke 12 : 11, 22, 25, 26. See CARE,
CB:1264C B, No. 1.
PRONOEŌ 4306 2. PROMERIMNAŌ (προμεριμνάω), to be anxious beforehand, occurs
AG:708C CB:1266C in Mark 13 : 11.¶
CHILIOI 5507 3. PHRONEŌ (φρονέω): for Phil. 4 : 10, R.V., "ye did take thought,"
see CARE, B, No. 6.
AG:882A CB:1239C 4. PRONOEŌ (προνοέω), to provide, is rendered to take thought in
CHILIAS 5505 Rom. 12 : 17 and 2 Cor. 8 : 21. See PROVIDE.

AG:882A CB:1239C

THOUSAND (-S)

DIS- 1367 1. CHILIOI (χίλιοι), a thousand, occurs in 2 Pet. 3 : 8; Rev. 11 : 3;
AG:200A 12 : 6; 14 : 20; 20 : 2–7.¶
CB:1242A TRIS- 5153 2. CHILIAS (χιλιάς), one thousand, is always used in the plural,
AG:826C *chiliades*, but translated in the sing. everywhere, except in the phrase
CB:1273A "thousands of thousands," Rev. 5 : 11.
TETRAKIS- 5070 *Notes*: (1) The following compounds of No. 1 represent different
AG:813D multiples of a thousand: *dischilioi*, 2,000, Mark 5 : 13;¶ *trischilioi*,
CB:1271C 3,000, Acts 2 : 41;¶ *tetrakischilioi*, 4,000, Matt. 15 : 38; 16 : 10;
PENTAKIS- 4000 Mark 8 : 9, 20; Acts 21 : 38;¶ *pentakischilioi*, 5,000, Matt. 14 : 21;
AG:643A 16 : 9; Mark 6 : 44; 8 : 19; Luke 9 : 14; John 6 : 10;¶ *heptakischilioi*,
CB:1263A HEPTAKIS- 7,000, Rom. 11 : 4.¶ (2) *Murias*, a myriad, a vast number, "many
2035 thousands," Luke 12 : 1, R.V.; Acts 21 : 20; it also denotes 10,000, Acts
AG:306C MURIAS 19 : 19, lit., 'five ten-thousands;' Jude 14, "ten thousands;" in Rev.
3461 5 : 11 "ten thousand times ten thousand" is, lit., 'myriads of myriads;'
AG:529C in Rev. 9 : 16 in the best texts, *dismuriades muriadōn*, "twice ten thousand
DISMURIADES 3461 times ten thousand" R.V. (A.V., "two hundred thousand thousand"):
(MURIAS) AG:199D see INNUMERABLE. (3) *Murioi* (the plur. of *murios*), an adjective
(-IAS) signifying numberless, is used in this indefinite sense in 1 Cor. 4 : 15 and
MURIOI 3463 14 : 19; it also denotes the definite number "ten thousand," Matt.
AG:529D 18 : 24.¶

THREATEN

1. APEILEŌ (*ἀπειλέω*) is used of Christ, negatively, in 1 Pet. 2 : 23 ; 546
in the Middle Voice, Acts 4 : 17, where some texts have the noun *apeilē* in AG:82D
addition, hence the A.V., " let us straitly threaten," lit., ' let us threaten CB:—
. . . with threatening ' (see THREATENING).¶ (See also STRAITLY.)

2. PROSAPEILEŌ (*προσαπειλέω*), to threaten further (*pros*, and No. 4324
1), occurs in the Middle Voice in Acts 4 : 21.¶ AG:711D
CB:—

THREATENING

APEILĒ (*ἀπειλή*), akin to *apeileō* (see above), occurs in Acts 4 : 29 547
(in some mss. ver. 17) ; 9 : 1 ; Eph. 6 : 9.¶ AG:83A
CB:—

THREE

TREIS (*τρεῖς*) is regarded by many as a number sometimes symbolically 5140
indicating fulness of testimony or manifestation, as in the Three Persons AG:825B
in the Godhead, cp. 1 Tim. 5 : 19 ; Heb. 10 : 28 ; the mention in 1 John CB:1273A
5 : 7 is in a verse which forms no part of the original ; no Greek ms. earlier than the 14th century contained it ; no version earlier than the 5th cent. in any other language contains it, nor is it quoted by any of the Greek or Latin " Fathers " in their writings on the Trinity. That there are those who bear witness in Heaven is not borne out by any other Scripture. It must be regarded as the interpolation of a copyist.

In Mark 9 : 31 and 10 : 34 the best texts have *meta treis hemeras*, " after three days," which idiomatically expresses the same thing as *tȩ̄ tritȩ̄ hēmerą*, " on the third day," which some texts have here, as, e.g., the phrase " the third day " in Matt. 17 : 23 ; 20 : 19 ; Luke 9 : 22 ; 18 : 33, where the repetition of the article lends stress to the number, lit., ' the day the third ; ' 24 : 7, 46 ; Acts 10 : 40. For THREE TIMES see THRICE.

THREE HUNDRED

TRIAKOSIOI (*τριακόσιοι*) occurs in Mark 14 : 5 and John 12 : 5.¶ 5145
AG:826A
CB:—

For THREESCORE see SIXTY and SEVENTY

For THREE THOUSAND see THOUSAND

THRESH

ALOAŌ (*ἀλοάω*), to thresh, is so rendered in 1 Cor. 9 : 10 ; in ver. 9 248
and 1 Tim. 5 : 18, " that treadeth out the corn."¶ AG:41A
CB:—

THRESHING-FLOOR

HALŌN (*ἅλων*), a threshing-floor, is so translated in Matt. 3 : 12, and 257
Luke 3 : 17, R.V. (A.V., " floor "), perhaps by metonymy for the grain.¶ AG:41D
CB:1249A

For THREW see THROW

THRICE

5151 AG:826B TRIS (τρίς) occurs in Matt. 26 : 34, 75 and parallel passages ; in Acts
CB:1273A 10 : 16 and 11 : 10, preceded by *epi*, up to ; 2 Cor. 11 : 25 (twice) ; 12 : 8.

THROAT (Noun), to take by the (Verb)

A. Noun.

2995 AG:467B LARUNX (λάρυγξ), a throat (Eng., larynx), is used metaphorically
CB:— of speech in Rom. 3 : 13.¶

B. Verb.

4155 AG:679D PNIGŌ (πνίγω), to choke, is rendered "took . . . by the throat" in
CB:1265C Matt. 18 : 28. See CHOKE, No. 1.

THRONE

2362 AG:364B 1. THRONOS (θρόνος), a throne, a seat of authority, is used of the
CB:1272B throne (*a*) of God, e.g., Heb. 4 : 16, "the throne of grace," i.e., from which grace proceeds ; 8 : 1 ; 12 : 2 ; Rev. 1 : 4 ; 3 : 21 (2nd part) ; 4 : 2 (twice) ; 5 : 1 ; frequently in Rev. ; in 20 : 12, in the best texts, "the throne" (some have *Theos*, "God," A.V.) ; cp. 21 : 3 ; Matt. 5 : 34; 23 : 22 ; Acts 7 : 49 ; (*b*) of Christ, e.g., Heb. 1 : 8 ; Rev. 3 : 21 (1st part) ; 22 : 3 ; His seat of authority in the Millennium, Matt. 19 : 28 (1st part) ; (*c*) by metonymy for angelic powers, Col. 1 : 16 ; (*d*) of the Apostles in Millennial authority, Matt. 19 : 28 (2nd part) ; Luke 22 : 30 ; (*e*) of the elders in the Heavenly vision, Rev. 4 : 4 (2nd and 3rd parts), R.V., "thrones" (A.V., "seats") ; so 11 : 16 ; (*f*) of David, Luke 1 : 32 ; Acts 2 : 30 ; (*g*) of Satan, Rev. 2 : 13, R.V., "throne" (A.V., "seat") ; (*h*) of "the beast," the final and federal head of the revived Roman Empire, Rev. 13 : 2 ; 16 : 10.

968 AG:140B 2. BĒMA (βῆμα), for which see JUDGMENT-SEAT, is used of the throne
CB:1239A or tribunal of Herod, Acts 12 : 21.

THRONG (Verb)

2346 AG:362A 1. THLIBŌ (θλίβω), to press, is rendered "throng," Mark 3 : 9. See
CB:1272B AFFLICT, No. 4.

4918 AG:790A 2. SUNTHLIBŌ (συνθλίβω), to press together, on all sides (*sun*,
CB:— together, and No. 1), a strengthened form, is used in Mark 5 : 24, 31.¶

4846 AG:779D 3. SUMPNIGŌ (συμπνίγω), to choke, is used of thronging by a crowd,
CB:1270B Luke 8 : 42. See CHOKE, No. 3.

4912 AG:789A *Note :* For *sunechō*, to hold together, press together, Luke 8 : 45
CB:1270C (A.V., "throng"), see PRESS.

THROUGH and THROUGHOUT : see † **p. 1**

For THROUGHLY see THOROUGHLY

THROW

1. BALLŌ (βάλλω), to cast, to throw, is rendered to throw in Mark 906
12:42, A.V. (R.V., "cast"); so Acts 22:23 (2nd part); to throw AG:130D
down, Rev. 18:21 (2nd part), A.V. (R.V., "cast down"). See CAST, CB:1238B
No. 1.

2. RHIPTŌ (ῥίπτω), to hurl, throw, throw off, is rendered "had 4496
thrown . . . down" in Luke 4:35, R.V. (A.V., "had thrown"). See AG:736C
CAST, No. 2. CB:—

3. KATAKRĒMNIZŌ (κατακρημνίζω), to throw over a precipice 2630
(*krēmnos*), cast down headlong, is rendered "throw . . . down" in AG:412A
Luke 4:29 (A.V., "cast . . . down headlong").¶ CB:—

4. KATALUŌ (καταλύω), lit., to loosen down, is rendered to throw 2647
down (of the stones of the Temple) in Matt. 24:2 and parallel passages. AG:414B
See DESTROY, No. 5. CB:1254A

THRUST

1. BALLŌ (βάλλω), for which cp. THROW, No. 1, is rendered to thrust 906
in John 20:25, 27, A.V. (R.V., "put"); Acts 16:24, A.V. (R.V., AG:130D
"cast"); so Rev. 14:16, 19. See CAST, No. 1. CB:1238B

2. EKBALLŌ (ἐκβάλλω), to cast out, is rendered "thrust . . . 1544
out" in Luke 4:29, A.V. (R.V., "cast . . . forth"); so 13:28 and AG:237B
Acts 16:37. See CAST, No. 5. CB:1243B

3. APŌTHEŌ (ἀπωθέω), to thrust away, is used in the Middle Voice, 683
to thrust away from oneself, and translated "thrust away" in Acts (-OMAI)
7:27, 39; "thrust . . . from," 13:46, R.V. (A.V., "put . . . from"); AG:103B CB:—
"having thrust from them," 1 Tim. 1:19, R.V. (A.V., "having put
away"). See CAST, No. 13.

4. KATATOXEUŌ (κατατοξεύω), to strike down with an arrow, 2700
shoot dead, occurs in Heb. 12:20 in some mss. (in a quotation from AG:419D
Ex. 19:13, Sept.).¶ CB:— KATABAINŌ

Notes: (1) In Matt. 11:23 and Luke 10:15 the best texts have 2597
katabainō, to go down (R.V.), instead of *katabibazō*, in the Passive Voice, AG:408B CB:1253C
to be thrust down or brought down (A.V.). (2) In Acts 27:39, A.V., KATABIBAZŌ
exōtheō, to drive out, is rendered "to thrust in," R.V., "drive (the ship) 2601
upon (it [i.e., the beach])." (3) In Rev. 14:15, 18, A.V., *pempō*, to AG:409A
send (R.V., "send forth"), is translated "thrust in." (4) For Luke EXŌTHEŌ 1856
5:3, A.V., see LAUNCH, No. 2. AG:280A PEMPŌ 3992 AG:641D CB:1263A

THUNDER, THUNDERING

BRONTĒ (βροντή): in Mark 3:17 "sons of thunder" is the 1027
interpretation of Boanērges, the name applied by the Lord to James AG:147D
and John; their fiery disposition is seen in 9:38 and Luke 9:54; CB:1239B
perhaps in the case of James it led to his execution. The name and its interpretation have caused much difficulty; some suggest the meaning 'the twins.' It is however most probably the equivalent of the Aramaic

benê regesh, 'sons of tumult;' the latter of the two words was no doubt
used of thunder in Palestinian Aramaic; hence the meaning "the sons
of thunder;" the cognate Hebrew word *ragash,* to rage, is used in Ps. 2:1
and there only. In John 12:29 *brontē* is used with *ginomai,* to take place,
and rendered "it had thundered;" lit., 'there was thunder;' elsewhere,
Rev. 4:5; 6:1; 8:5; 10:3, 4; 11:19; 14:2; 16:18; 19:6.¶

THUS

3779 AG:597C HOUTŌS or HOUTŌ (οὕτως), in this way, so, thus, is used (*a*) with
CB:— reference to what precedes, e.g., Luke 1:25; 2:48; (*b*) with reference
to what follows, e.g., Luke 19:31, rendered "on this wise," in Matt.
1:18; John 21:1, and before quotations, Acts 7:6; 13:34; Rom.
10:6, A.V. (R.V., "thus"); Heb. 4:4; (*c*) marking intensity, rendered
"so," e.g., Gal. 1:6; Heb. 12:21; Rev. 16:18; (*d*) in comparisons,
rendered "so," e.g., Luke 11:30; Rom. 5:15. See FASHION, B,
LIKEWISE, Note (1), MANNER, C, No. 2, SO, Note (1).

HOUTOS *Notes:* (1) *Touto,* the neuter of *houtos,* this, is translated "thus" in
3778 AG:596B 2 Cor. 1:17; 5:14; Phil. 3:15; the neuter plural, *tauta,* these things,
CB:1251B HODE e.g., in Luke 18:11; 19:28; John 9:6; 11:43; 13:21; 20:14;
3592 Acts 19:41. (2) *Tade,* these things (the neuter plural of *hode,* this), is
AG:553A translated "thus" in Acts 21:11. (3) In Luke 17:30, A.V., *kata tauta,*
CB:— KATA lit., 'according to these things,' is rendered "thus" (R.V., "after the
2596 AG:405C same manner," follows the reading *kata ta auta,* lit., 'according to the
CB:1253C same things').

THY, THINE, THINE OWN, THYSELF

SOS 4674 *Note:* These are translations of (1) the possessive pronoun *sos,* and
AG:759B its inflections, e.g., Matt. 7:3 (1st part); it is used as a noun with the
CB:— SU article, in the phrases *to son,* "that which is thine," Matt. 20:14; 25:25,
4771 "thine own;" *hoi soi,* "thy friends," Mark 5:19; *ta sa,* "thy goods,"
AG:772A Luke 6:30, lit., 'the thine;' (2) one of the oblique cases of *su,* thou; *sou,*
CB:— SEAUTOU of thee, e.g., Matt. 1:20; 7:3 (2nd part), "thine own;" *soi,* to thee,
4572 e.g., Mark 5:9; with *menō,* to remain, Acts 5:4 (1st part), "thine own,"
AG:745C CB:— lit., 'remain to thee;' in Matt. 26:18, *pros se,* "at thy house," lit.,
HEAUTOU 'with thee;' (3) *seauton,* "(as) thyself," Rom. 13:9; *seautou,* of thyself,
1438 AG:211D e.g., Matt. 4:6; *seautǭ,* to thyself, Acts 16:28; (4) *heautou* (with *apo,*
CB:1249B from), John 18:34, "of thyself," lit., 'from thyself;' (5) *autos,* self, is
(-OS) AUTOS sometimes used for "thyself," e.g., Luke 6:42.
846 AG:122C CB:1238B

THYINE (WOOD)

2367 AG:365A THUĪNOS (θύϊνος) is akin to *thuia,* or *thua,* an African aromatic and
CB:— coniferous tree; in Rev. 18:12 it describes a wood which formed part
of the merchandise of Babylon; it was valued by Greeks and Romans
for tables, being hard, durable and fragrant (A.V. marg., "sweet").¶

TIDINGS

A. Noun.

PHASIS (φάσις), akin to *phēmi*, to speak, denotes information, 5334
especially against fraud or other delinquency, and is rendered "tidings" AG:854B CB:—
in Acts 21 : 31.¶

Note: In Acts 11 : 22, A.V., *logos*, a word, a "report" (R.V.), is 3056
rendered "tidings." AG:477A CB:1257A

B. Verbs.

1. EUANGELIZŌ (εὐαγγελίζω) is used of any message designed to 2097
cheer those who receive it; it is rendered to bring, declare, preach, or AG:317B CB:1247A
show good or glad tidings, e.g., Luke 1 : 19; 2 : 10; 3 : 18, R.V.; 4 : 43, R.V.; 7 : 22, R.V.; 8 : 1; Acts 8 : 12 and 10 : 36, R.V.; 14 : 15, R.V.; in 1 Thess. 3 : 6, "brought us glad (A.V., good) tidings;" in Heb. 4 : 2, R.V., "we have had good tidings preached;" similarly, 4 : 6; in 1 Pet. 1 : 25 *rhēma*, a word, is coupled with this verb, "the word of good tidings which was preached," R.V. (A.V., "the word which by the gospel is preached"). See PREACH, A, No. 1.

2. ANANGELLŌ (ἀναγγέλλω), to announce, declare, is rendered 312
"(no) tidings . . . . came," in Rom. 15 : 21, R.V., A.V., "was (not) AG:51B CB:1235B
spoken of." See TELL.

TIE

1. DEŌ (δέω), to bind, is rendered to tie in Matt. 21 : 2; Mark 11 : 2, 1210
4; Luke 19 : 30. See BIND. AG:177D CB:1240C

2. PROTEINŌ (προτείνω), to stretch out or forth, is used of prepara- 4385
tions for scourging, Acts 22 : 25, R.V., "had tied (him) up" (A.V., AG:721D CB:—
"bound").¶

TILES, TILING

KERAMOS (κέραμος), potter's clay, or an earthen vessel, denotes 2766
in the plural "tiles" in Luke 5 : 19, R.V., A.V., "tiling."¶ In the AG:429A CB:1255A
Sept., 2 Sam. 17 : 28.¶

For TILL (Conjunction) see † p. 1

TILL (Verb)

GEŌRGEŌ (γεωργέω), to till the ground, is used in the Passive Voice 1090
in Heb. 6 : 7, R.V., "it is tilled" (A.V., ". . . dressed").¶ Moulton AG:157B CB:—
and Milligan point out that, agriculture being the principal industry in Egypt, this word and its cognates (*geōrgion*, see HUSBANDRY, and *geōrgos*, see HUSBANDMAN) are very common in the papyri with reference to the cultivation of private allotments and the crown lands.

TIME

A. Nouns. 5550

1. CHRONOS (χρόνος) denotes a space of time, whether short, e.g., AG:887D CB:1240B

Matt. 2 : 7; Luke 4 : 5, or long, e.g., Luke 8 : 27; 20 : 9; or a succession of times, shorter, e.g., Acts 20 : 18, or longer, e.g., Rom. 16 : 25, R.V., " times eternal;" or duration of time, e.g., Mark 2 : 19, 2nd part, R.V., " while" (A.V., " as long as"), lit., ' for whatever time.' For a fuller treatment see SEASON, A, No. 2.

2540 AG:394D 2. KAIROS (καιρός), primarily due measure, due proportion, when
CB:1253A used of time, signified a fixed or definite period, a season, sometimes an
opportune or seasonable time, e.g., Rom. 5 : 6, R.V., " season"; Gal. 6 : 10, " opportunity." In Mark 10 : 30 and Luke 18 : 30, " this time" (*kairos*), i.e., in this lifetime, is contrasted with ' the coming age.' In 1 Thess. 5 : 1, " the times and the seasons," " times" (*chronos*) refers to the duration of the interval previous to the Parousia of Christ and the length of time it will occupy (see COMING, No. 3, Vol. I, top of p. 209), as well as other periods; " seasons" refers to the characteristics of these periods. See SEASON, A, No. 1, and the contrasts between *chronos* and *kairos* under SEASON, A, No. 2.

5610 AG:896A 3. HŌRA (ὥρα), primarily, any time or period fixed by nature, is
CB:1251A translated " time" in Matt. 14 : 15; Luke 14 : 17; Rom. 13 : 11, " high
time;" in the following the R.V. renders it " hour," for A.V., " time," Matt. 18 : 1; Luke 1 : 10; John 16 : 2, 4, 25; 1 John 2 : 18 (twice); Rev. 14 : 15; in Mark 6 : 35, R.V., " day;" in 1 Thess. 2 : 17, R.V.,
PōPOTE 4455 " a short (season)," lit., ' (the season, A.V., time) of an hour.' See HOUR.

AG:732A

B. Adverbs.

CB:1266A ēDē 1. PŌPOTE (πώποτε), ever yet, is rendered " at any time" in John
2235 1 : 18; 5 : 37; 1 John 4 : 12. For Luke 15 : 29 see Note (14) below.
AG:344A CB:1242C See NEVER.

PALAI 3819 2. ĒDĒ (ἤδη), already, now, is translated " by this time" in John
AG:605C 11 : 39. See ALREADY.

CB:1261C 3. PALAI (πάλαι), long ago, of old, is rendered " of old time" in
HēMERA 2250 Heb. 1 : 1 (A.V., " in time past"). See OLD.

AG:345D *Notes:* (1) In Luke 9 : 51 and Acts 8 : 1, A.V., *hēmera*, a day, is
CB:1249C MELLō translated " time," in the former, plural, R.V., " the days;" in Luke
3195 23 : 7 (plural), R.V. " (in these) days," A.V., " (at that) time." (2) In
AG:500D 1 Tim. 6 : 19 the phrase *eis to mellon*, lit., ' unto the about-to-be,' i.e.,
CB:1258A NUN ' for the impending (time),' is rendered " against the time to come."
3568 (3) In 1 Cor. 16 : 12, A.V., *nun*, " now" (R.V.), is rendered " at this time;"
AG:545C CB:1260A in Acts 24 : 25, the phrase *to nun echon*, lit., ' the now having,' is rendered
POLUMERōS 4181 " at this time" (the verb is adjectival); the phrase is more expressive
AG:687B than the simple " now." Cp. *heōs tou nun*, " until now," Matt. 24 : 21
PROSKAIROS and Mark 13 : 19, R.V., A.V., " unto (this time)." (4) For *polumerōs*,
4340 strangely rendered " at sundry times," in Heb. 1 : 1, A.V., see PORTION, C.
AG:715B CB:1267A (5) For " long time," see LONG. (6) For " nothing . . . at any time," see
TOTE 5119 NOTHING, Note (3). (7) For *proskairos*, rendered " for a time" in
AG:823D Mark 4 : 17, A.V., see SEASON, WHILE. (8) In Matt., *apo tote*, " from that
CB:1273A time," lit., ' from then,' occurs thrice, 4 : 17; 16 : 21; 26 : 16; in Luke

16 : 16, R.V. (A.V., " since that time ") ; in John 6 : 66, A.V., " from EPI 1909
that time " translates *ek toutou*, lit., ' from, or out of, this,' R.V., " upon AG:285D
this." (9) In Luke 4 : 27, the preposition *epi* signifies " in the time of." CB:1245C GENEA
(10) For *genea*, rendered " times " in Acts 14 : 16, " time " in 15 : 21, 1074
see AGE, No. 2 (R.V., " generations "). (11) For " at every time," AG:153D CB:1248A
2 Pet. 1 : 15, R.V., see ALWAYS, No. 2. (12) For " in time of need," POTE
Heb. 4 : 16, see CONVENIENT, and NEED, C, Note. (13) In Heb. 2 : 1, 4218 AG:695A
pote signifies " at any time ; " in 1 Pet. 3 : 5, " in the old time ; " in CB:1266B
2 Pet. 1 : 21, " in old time." See PAST. In the following where OUDEPOTE 3763
the A.V. has " sometimes " the R.V. has " once " in Eph. 2 : 13 AG:592B
and 5 : 8 ; " aforetime " in Tit. 3 : 3. (14) In Luke 15 : 29, A.V., EUKAIREŌ
" *oudepote* ," never, is rendered " neither . . . at any time " (R.V., 2119 AG:321B
" never "). (15) For *eukaireō*, to spend time, Acts 17 : 21, see SPEND, CB:1247B
No. 10. (16) For *chronotribeō*, to spend time, see SPEND, No. 11. CHRONOTRIBEŌ 5551
(17) For *prolegō*, rendered " told . . . in time past," in Gal. 5 : 21, A.V., AG:888C
see FOREWARN. (18) In Luke 12 : 1, " in the mean time " is a rendering CB:1240B PROTHESMIOS
of the phrase *en hois*, lit., ' in which (things or circumstances).' (19) In 4287
Rev. 5 : 11 there is no word representing " times : " see THOUSAND, AG:706B (-MIA)
Note (2). (20) In Gal. 4 : 2 *prothesmios* (in its feminine form, with HEKASTOTE
hēmera, day, understood) is rendered " time appointed " (see APPOINT, 1539 AG:236D
No. 3 and Note, TERM).

For TINKLING see CLANGING

TIP

AKRON (ἄκρον), the top, an extremity, is translated " tip " in Luke 206
16 : 24. See END, C, Note (6), TOP. AG:34A CB:—

For TITHES (Noun) see TENTH, No. 2

TITHE (Verb)

1. DEKATOŌ (δεκατόω), from *dekatos*, tenth, in the Active Voice 1183
denotes to take tithes of, Heb. 7 : 6, R.V., " hath taken (A.V., received) AG:174B CB:1240C
tithes ; " in the Passive, to pay tithes, 7 : 9, R.V., " hath paid (A.V., payed) tithes."¶ In the Sept., Neh. 10 : 37.¶

2. APODEKATOŌ (ἀποδεκατόω) denotes (*a*) to tithe (*apo*, from, 586
dekatos, tenth), Matt. 23 : 23 (A.V., " pay tithe of "); Luke 11 : 42 ; in AG:89D CB:1236C
Luke 18 : 12 (where the best texts have the alternative form *apodekateuō*), " I give tithes ; " (*b*) to exact tithes from, Heb. 7 : 5.¶

3. APODEKATEUŌ (ἀποδεκατεύω), to give tithes, in Luke 18 : 12 —
(some texts have No. 2).¶ AG:89D CB:1236C

Note : Heb. 7 : 4–9 shows the superiority of the Melchizedek priesthood to the Levitical, in that (1) Abraham, the ancestor of the Levites, paid tithes to Melchizedek (Gen. 14 : 20) ; (2) Melchizedek, whose genealogy is outside that of the Levites, took tithes of Abraham, the recipient himself of the Divine promises ; (3) whereas death is the natural lot of those who receive tithes, the death of Melchizedek is not recorded ; (4) the Levites who received tithes virtually paid them through Abraham to Melchizedek.

TITLE

5102 AG:820D CB:1272C TITLOS (τίτλος), from Latin *titulus*, is used of the inscription above the Cross of Christ, John 19 : 19, 20. See SUPERSCRIPTION.¶

TITTLE

2762 AG:428D CB:1255A KERAIA or KEREA (κεραία), a little horn (*keras*, a horn), was used to denote the small stroke distinguishing one Hebrew letter from another. The Rabbis attached great importance to these ; hence the significance of the Lord's statements in Matt. 5 : 18 and Luke 16 : 17, charging the Pharisees with hypocrisy, because, while professing the most scrupulous reverence to the Law, they violated its spirit.

Grammarians used the word to denote the accents in Greek words.¶

For TO see † p. 1

TO-DAY, THIS DAY

4594 AG:749A CB:1268A SĒMERON (σήμερον), an adverb (the Attic form is *tēmeron*), akin to *hēmera*, a day, with the prefix *t* originally representing a pronoun. It is used frequently in Matthew, Luke and Acts ; in the last it is always rendered " this day ; " also in Heb. 1 : 5, and the R.V. of 5 : 5 (A.V., " to day ") in the same quotation ; " to-day " in 3 : 7, 13, 15 ; 4 : 7 (twice) ; 13 : 8 ; also Jas. 4 : 13.

The clause containing *sēmeron* is sometimes introduced by the conjunction *hoti*, ' that,' e.g., Mark 14 : 30 ; Luke 4 : 21 ; 19 : 9 ; sometimes without the conjunction, e.g., Luke 22 : 34 ; 23 : 43, where " to-day " is to be attached to the next statement, " shalt thou be with Me ; " there are no grammatical reasons for the insistence that the connection must be with the statement " Verily I say unto thee," nor is such an idea necessitated by examples from either the Sept. or the N.T. ; the connection given in the A.V. and R.V. is right.

In Rom. 11 : 8 and 2 Cor. 3 : 14, 15, the lit. rendering is ' unto the to-day day,' the emphasis being brought out by the R.V., " unto (until) this very day."

In Heb. 4 : 7, the " to-day " of Ps. 95 : 7 is evidently designed to extend to the present period of the Christian faith.

TOGETHER

3674 AG:569B CB:— 1. HOMOU (ὁμοῦ), used in connection with place, in John 21 : 2 ; Acts 2 : 1 (in the best texts), R.V., " together " (A.V., " with one accord," translating the inferior reading *homothumadon* : see ACCORD, A), is used without the idea of place in John 4 : 36 ; 20 : 4.¶

260 AG:42A CB:1249A 2. HAMA (ἅμα), at once, is translated " together " in Rom. 3 : 12 ; 1 Thess. 4 : 17 ; 5 : 10. See EARLY, Note, WITHAL.

3826 AG:607B CB:— *Notes :* (1) For *pamplēthei*, Luke 23 : 18, R.V., see ONCE, Note. (2) In 1 Thess. 5 : 11, A.V., *allēlous*, " one another " (R.V.), is rendered

“ yourselves together ; ” in Luke 23 : 12, A.V., *meta allēlōn*, lit., with ALLēLōN
one another, is rendered “ together ” (R.V., “ with each other ”) ; so 240 AG:39C
in Luke 24 : 14, A.V., *pros allēlous*, R.V., “ with each other.” (3) In CB:1234C
the following, “ together ” translates the phrase *epi to auto*, lit., ‘ to (upon, AUTOS
or for) the same,’ Matt. 22 : 34 ; Luke 17 : 35 ; Acts 1 : 15 ; 2 : 44 (3 : 1, 846 AG:122C
in some texts) ; 4 : 26 ; 1 Cor. 7 : 5 ; 14 : 23, R.V. : see PLACE, A, Note (7). CB:1238B
(4) In Acts 14 : 1, it translates *kata to auto*, ‘ at the same ; ’ it may mean ‘ in the same way ’ (i.e., as they had entered the synagogue at Pisidian Antioch). (5) In many cases “ together ” forms part of another word.

TOIL (Verb and Noun)

A. Verbs.

1. KOPIAŌ (κοπιάω), to be weary, to labour, is rendered to toil in 2872
Matt. 6 : 28 ; Luke 5 : 5 (12 : 27, in some mss.) ; in 1 Cor. 4 : 12, R.V. AG:443C
(A.V., “ we labour ”). See LABOUR. CB:1255C

2. BASANIZŌ (βασανίζω), primarily, to rub on the touchstone, to 928
put to the test, then, to examine by torture (*basanos*, touchstone, AG:134C
torment), hence denotes to torture, torment, distress ; in the Passive CB:1238C
Voice it is rendered “ toiling ” in Mark 6 : 48, A.V. (R.V., “ distressed ”). See PAIN, TORMENT, VEX.

B. Noun.

KOPOS (κόπος), labour, trouble, is rendered “ toil ” in Rev. 2 : 2, 2873
R.V. (A.V., “ labour ”). See LABOUR. AG:443C CB:1255C

TOKEN

1. SĒMEION (σημεῖον), a sign, token or indication, is translated 4592
“ token ” in 2 Thess. 3 : 17, of writing of the closing salutations, the Apostle AG:747D
using the pen himself instead of his amanuensis, his autograph attesting CB:1268C
the authenticity of his Epistles. See MIRACLE, SIGN.

2. SUSSĒMON (σύσσημον), a fixed sign or signal, agreed upon with 4953
others (*sun*, with), is used in Mark 14 : 44, “ a token.”¶ In the Sept., AG:794D
Judg. 20 : 38, 40 ; Is. 5 : 26 ; 49 : 22 ; 62 : 10.¶ CB:—

3. ENDEIGMA (ἔνδειγμα), a plain token, a proof (akin to *endeiknumi*, 1730
to point out, prove), is used in 2 Thess. 1 : 5, “a manifest token,” said AG:262C
of the patient endurance and faith of the persecuted saints at Thessalonica, CB:—
affording proof to themselves of their new life, and a guarantee of the vindication by God of both Himself and them (see No. 4, Note).¶ 1732

4. ENDEIXIS (ἔνδειξις), a pointing out, showing forth, is rendered AG:262D CB:1244C
“ evident token ” in Phil. 1 : 28. See DECLARE, B, PROOF. Cp. *apodeixis*, APODEIXIS
1 Cor. 2 : 4. 585 AG:89D

Note : No. 4 refers to the act or process of proving, No. 3 to the thing CB:1236C
proved. While the two passages, Phil. 1 : 28 and 2 Thess. 1 : 5, contain similar ideas, *endeigma* indicates the token as acknowledged by those referred to ; *endeixis* points more especially to the inherent veracity of the token.

TOLERABLE

414 ANEKTOS (ἀνεκτός) (akin to *anechō*, in the Middle Voice, to endure,
AG:64C CB:1235C see ENDURE, No. 5) is used in its comparative form, *anektoteros*, in Matt.
10 : 15; 11 : 22, 24; Luke 10 : 12, 14; some texts have it in Mark
6 : 11.¶

For TOLL see CUSTOM (Toll)

TOMB

3419 1. MNĒMEION (μνημεῖον) is almost invariably rendered "tomb" or
AG:524C CB:1259A "tombs" in the R.V., never "grave," sometimes "sepulchre;" in the
A.V., "tomb" in Matt. 8 : 28; 27 : 60; Mark 5 : 2; 6 : 29. See
GRAVE, No. 1, SEPULCHRE.

3418 2. MNĒMA (μνῆμα), rendered "tombs" in Mark 5 : 3, 5; Luke 8 : 27:
AG:524C CB:1259A see GRAVE, No. 2, SEPULCHRE.

5028 3. TAPHOS (τάφος), akin to *thaptō*, to bury, is translated "tombs"
AG:806B CB:1271A in Matt. 23 : 29; elsewhere "sepulchre." See SEPULCHRE.

TO-MORROW

839 AURION (αὔριον) is used either without the article, e.g., Matt. 6 : 30;
AG:122A CB:— 1 Cor. 15 : 32; Jas. 4 : 13; or with the article in the feminine form, to
agree with *hēmera*, day, e.g., Matt. 6 : 34; Acts 4 : 3, R.V., "the
morrow" (A.V., "next day"); Jas. 4 : 14; preceded by *epi*, on, e.g.,
Luke 10 : 35; Acts 4 : 5.

TONGUE (-S)

A. Nouns.

1100 1. GLŌSSA (γλῶσσα) is used of (1) the "tongues . . . like as of
AG:162B CB:1248B fire" which appeared at Pentecost; (2) the tongue, as an organ of speech,
e.g., Mark 7 : 33; Rom. 3 : 13; 14 : 11; 1 Cor. 14 : 9; Phil. 2 : 11;
Jas. 1 : 26; 3 : 5, 6, 8; 1 Pet. 3 : 10; 1 John 3 : 18; Rev. 16 : 10;
(3) (*a*) a language, coupled with *phulē*, a tribe, *laos*, a people, *ethnos*, a
nation, seven times in the Apocalypse, 5 : 9; 7 : 9; 10 : 11; 11 : 9;
13 : 7; 14 : 6; 17 : 15; (*b*) the supernatural gift of speaking in another
language without its having been learnt; in Acts 2 : 4–13 the circumstances are recorded from the view-point of the hearers; to those in whose language the utterances were made it appeared as a supernatural phenomenon; to others, the stammering of drunkards; what was uttered was not addressed primarily to the audience but consisted in recounting "the mighty works of God;" cp. 2 : 46; in 1 Cor., chapters 12 and 14, the use of the gift of tongues is mentioned as exercised in the gatherings of local churches; 12 : 10 speaks of the gift in general terms, and couples with it that of "the interpretation of tongues;" chapt. 14 gives instruction concerning the use of the gift, the paramount object being the edification

of the church; unless the tongue was interpreted the speaker would speak "not unto men, but unto God," ver. 2; he would edify himself alone, ver. 4, unless he interpreted, ver. 5, in which case his interpretation would be of the same value as the superior gift of prophesying, as he would edify the church, vv. 4–6; he must pray that he may interpret, ver. 13; if there were no interpreter, he must keep silence, ver. 28, for all things were to be done "unto edifying," ver. 26. "If I come . . . speaking with tongues, what shall I profit you," says the Apostle (expressing the great object in all oral ministry), "unless I speak to you either by way of revelation, or of knowledge, or of prophesying, or of teaching?" (ver. 6). Tongues were for a sign, not to believers, but to unbelievers, ver. 22, and especially to unbelieving Jews (see ver. 21): cp. the passages in the Acts.

There is no evidence of the continuance of this gift after Apostolic times nor indeed in the later times of the Apostles themselves; this provides confirmation of the fulfilment in this way of 1 Cor. 13:8, that this gift would cease in the churches, just as would "prophecies" and "knowledge" in the sense of knowledge received by immediate supernatural power (cp. 14:6). The completion of the Holy Scriptures has provided the churches with all that is necessary for individual and collective guidance, instruction, and edification.

2. DIALEKTOS (διάλεκτος), language (Eng., dialect), is rendered 1258
"tongue" in the A.V. of Acts 1:19; 2:6, 8; 21:40; 22:2; 26:14. AG:185D
See LANGUAGE.¶ CB:1241A

B. Adjective.

HETEROGLŌSSOS (ἑτερόγλωσσος) is rendered "strange tongues" 2084
in 1 Cor. 14:21, R.V. (*heteros*, another of a different sort—see ANOTHER— AG:314D
and A, No. 1), A.V., "other tongues."¶ CB:1250A

C. Adverb.

HEBRAISTI (or EBRAISTI, Westcott and Hort) (Ἑβραϊστί) 1447
denotes (*a*) "in Hebrew," Rev. 9:11, R.V. (A.V., "in the Hebrew tongue"); AG:213C
so 16:16; (*b*) in the Aramaic vernacular of Palestine, John 5:2, A.V., CB:1249C
"in the Hebrew tongue" (R.V., "in Hebrew"); in 19:13, 17, A.V.,
"in the Hebrew" (R.V., "in Hebrew"); in ver. 20, A.V. and R.V.,
"in Hebrew;" in 20:16, R.V. only, "in Hebrew (Rabboni)."¶ HELLĒNISTI 1676
Note: Cp. *Hellēnisti*, "in Greek," John 19:20, R.V.; Acts 21:37, AG:252B CB:1249C
"Greek."¶ See also *Rhōmaisti*, under LATIN. RHŌMAISTI 4515 AG:738C CB:—

TOOTH, TEETH

ODOUS (ὀδούς) is used in the sing. in Matt. 5:38 (twice); elsewhere 3599
in the plural, of the gnashing of teeth, the gnashing being expressive of AG:555A
anguish and indignation, Matt. 8:12; 13:42, 50; 22:13; 24:51; CB:1260B
25:30; Mark 9:18; Luke 13:28; Acts 7:54; in Rev. 9:8, of the beings seen in a vision and described as locusts.¶

TOP

A. Noun.

206 AKRON (ἄκρον), for which see TIP, is used of Jacob's staff, Heb. 11 : 21.
AG:34A
CB:—

B. Phrases.

509 *Note :* In Matt. 27 : 51 and Mark 15 : 38, *apo anōthen,* " from the top "
AG:77A (lit., ' from above '), is used of the upper part of the Temple veil. In
CB:1236A John 19 : 23, the different phrase *ek tōn anōthen* is used of the weaving
of the Lord's garment (the *chitōn* : see CLOTHING), lit., ' from the parts
above.'

TOPAZ

5116 TOPAZION (τοπάζιον) is mentioned in Rev. 21 : 20, as the ninth of
AG:822B the foundation stones of the wall of the Heavenly Jerusalem ; the stone
CB:1273A is of a yellow colour (though there are topazes of other colours) and is
almost as hard as the diamond. It has the power of double refraction,
and when heated or rubbed becomes electric.¶ In the Sept., Ex. 28 : 17 ;
39 : 10 ; Job 28 : 19 ; Ps. 119 : 127," (gold and) topaz " ; Ezek. 28 : 13.¶

TORCH

2985 LAMPAS (λαμπάς), a torch, is used in the plur. and translated
AG:465C "torches" in John 18 : 3 ; in Rev. 8 : 10, R.V., " torch " (A.V., " lamp ").
CB:1256C See LAMP.

TORMENT (Noun and Verb)

A. Nouns.

929 1. BASANISMOS (βασανισμός), akin to *basanizō* (see TOIL, No. 2),
AG:134C is used of Divine judgments in Rev. 9 : 5 ; 14 : 11 ; 18 : 7, 10, 15.¶
CB:1238C
931 2. BASANOS (βάσανος), primarily a touchstone, employed in testing
AG:134D metals, hence, torment, is used (*a*) of physical diseases, Matt. 4 : 24 ;
CB:1238C (*b*) of a condition of retribution in Hades, Luke 16 : 23, 28.¶
2851 *Note :* In 1 John 4 : 18, A.V., *kolasis,* " punishment " (R.V.), is
AG:440D rendered " torment." See PUNISHMENT, No. 3.
CB:1255B

B. Verbs.

928 1. BASANIZŌ (βασανίζω), for which see TOIL, No. 2, is translated
AG:134C to torment, (*a*) of sickness, Matt. 8 : 6 ; (*b*) of the doom of evil spirits,
CB:1238C Mark 5 : 7 ; Luke 8 : 28 ; (*c*) of retributive judgments upon impenitent
mankind at the close of this age, Rev. 9 : 5 ; 11 : 10 ; (*d*) upon those who
worship the Beast and his image and receive the mark of his name,
14 : 10 ; (*e*) of the doom of Satan and his agents, 20 : 10.
2558 2. KAKOUCHEŌ (κακουχέω), to treat evilly, in the Passive Voice is
AG:398B translated " tormented " in Heb. 11 : 37, A.V. (R.V., " evil entreated ").
CB:— See SUFFER, No. 6.
3600
AG:555A 3. ODUNAŌ (ὀδυνάω), for which see ANGUISH, B, No. 3, in the Passive
CB:— Voice is rendered " I am (thou art) tormented " in Luke 16 : 24, 25, A.V.

TORMENTOR

BASANISTĒS (βασανιστής), properly, a torturer (akin to *basanizō*, see 930
Torment, B), one who elicits information by torture, is used of jailors, AG:134D CB:1238C
Matt. 18 : 34.¶

TORTURE See TORMENT

TORTURE (Verb)

TUMPANIZŌ (τυμπανίζω) primarily denotes to beat a drum (*tumpanon*, 5178
a kettle-drum, Eng., tympanal, tympanitis, tympanum), hence, to AG:829D CB:—
torture by beating, to beat to death, Heb. 11 : 35.¶ In the Sept., 1 Sam. 21 : 13, "(David) drummed (upon the doors of the city)."¶ The tympanum as an instrument of torture seems to have been a wheel-shaped frame upon which criminals were stretched and beaten with clubs or thongs.

TOSS

1. RHIPIZŌ (ῥιπίζω), primarily to fan a fire (*rhipis*, a fan, cp. *rhipē*, 4494
twinkling), then, to make a breeze, is used in the Passive Voice in Jas. AG:736B CB:1268B
1 : 6, "tossed," of the raising of waves by the wind.¶

2. KLUDŌNIZOMAI (κλυδωνίζομαι) signifies to be tossed by billows 2831
(*kludōn*, a billow); metaphorically, in Eph. 4 : 14, of an unsettled condition AG:436D CB:—
of mind influenced and agitated by one false teaching and another, and characterized by that immaturity which lacks the firm conviction begotten by the truth.¶ In the Sept., Isa. 57 : 20.¶

Note: For "being . . . tossed," Acts 27 : 18, see Labour, B, No. 2.

TOUCH (Verb)

1. HAPTŌ (ἅπτω), primarily, to fasten to, hence, of fire, to kindle, 681
denotes, in the Middle Voice (*a*) to touch, e.g., Matt. 8 : 3, 15; 9 : 20, 21, AG:102D CB:1249B
29; (*b*) to cling to, lay hold of, John 20 : 17; here the Lord's prohibition as to clinging to Him was indicative of the fact that communion with Him would, after His ascension, be by faith, through the Spirit; (*c*) to have carnal intercourse with a woman, 1 Cor. 7 : 1; (*d*) to have fellowship and association with unbelievers, 2 Cor. 6 : 17; (*e*) (negatively) to adhere to certain Levitical and ceremonial ordinances, in order to avoid contracting external defilement, or to practise rigorous asceticism, all such abstentions being of "no value against the indulgence of the flesh," Col. 2 : 21, A.V. (R.V., "handle"); (*f*) to assault, in order to sever the vital union between Christ and the believer, said of the attack of the Evil One, 1 John 5 : 18. See Handle, No. 2, Kindle, Light.

2. THINGANŌ (θιγγάνω), to touch, a lighter term than No. 1, though 2345
Heb. 11 : 28 approximates to it, in expressing the action of the Destroyer AG:361D CB:—
of the Egyptian firstborn; in Heb. 12 : 20 it signifies to touch, and is not to be interpreted by Ps. 104 : 32, "He toucheth (No. 1 in the Sept.) the hills and they smoke;" in Col. 2 : 21, R.V. (A.V., "handle"). See Handle, No. 2.¶

4379 AG:720C CB:— 3. PROSPSAUŌ (προσψαύω), to touch upon, to touch slightly, occurs in Luke 11 : 46.¶

5584 AG:892C CB:— 4. PSĒLAPHAŌ (ψηλαφάω), to feel, to handle, is rendered "that might be touched" in Heb. 12 : 18. See FEEL, No. 3, HANDLE, No. 1.

2609 AG:410A CB:— 5 KATAGŌ (κατάγω), to bring down, is used of bringing a ship to land in Acts 27 3. See BRING No. 16.

4834 AG:778D CB:1270B 6. SUMPATHEŌ συμπαθέω), for which see COMPASSION, A, No. 3, is rendered be touched with" in Heb. 4 : 15.

3846 AG:611D CB:1262A 7. PARABALLŌ (παραβάλλω), for which see ARRIVE, No. 4, COMPARE, No. 2, is rendered "touched at" in Acts 20 : 15, R.V.

For TOUCHING (Preposition) see † **p. 1**

For TOWARD (Preposition), see † **p. 1**

TOWEL

3012 AG:471C CB:— LENTION (λέντιον) denotes a linen cloth or towel (Lat., *linteum*), as used by the Lord, John 13 : 4, 5; it was commonly used by servants in a household.¶

TOWER

4444 AG:730D CB:— PURGOS (πύργος) is used of a watch-tower in a vineyard, Matt. 21 : 33; Mark 12 : 1; probably, too, in Luke 14 : 28 (cp. Is. 5 : 2); in Luke 13 : 4, of the tower in Siloam, the modern Silwan, which is built on a steep escarpment of rock.¶

TOWN

2969 AG:461D CB:— 1. KŌMOPOLIS (κωμόπολις) denotes a country town, Mark 1 : 38, a large village usually without walls.¶

2968 AG:461D CB:1255C 2. KŌMĒ (κώμη), a village, or country town without walls. The R.V. always renders this "village" or "villages," A.V., "town" or "towns," Matt. 10 : 11; Mark 8 : 23, 26 (twice), 27; Luke 5 : 17; 9 : 6, 12; John 7 : 42; 11 : 1, 30. See VILLAGE.

TOWNCLERK

1122 AG:165D CB:1248C GRAMMATEUS (γραμματεύς), a writer, scribe, is used in Acts 19 : 35 of a state clerk, an important official, variously designated, according to inscriptions found in Græco-Asiatic cities. He was responsible for the form of decrees first approved by the Senate, then sent for approval in the popular assembly, in which he often presided. The decrees having been passed, he sealed them with the public seal in the presence of witnesses. Such an assembly frequently met in the theatre. The Roman administration viewed any irregular or unruly assembly as a grave and even capital offence, as tending to strengthen among the people the consciousness of their power and the desire to exercise it. In the circumstances at Ephesus the townclerk feared that he might himself be held responsible for the irregular gathering. See SCRIBE.

TRACE

A. Verb.

PARAKOLOUTHEŌ (παρακολουθέω), to follow up, is used of **3877**
investigating or tracing a course of events, Luke 1 : 3, where the writer, **AG:618D**
humbly differentiating himself from those who possessed an essential **CB:1262A**
apostolic qualification, declares that he "traced the course of all things" (R.V.) about which he was writing (A.V., "having had . . . understanding, etc."). See FOLLOW, No. 5.

B. Adjective.

ANEXICHNIASTOS (ἀνεξιχνίαστος) signifies 'that cannot be traced **421**
out' (*a*, negative, *ex*, for *ek*, out, *ichnos*, a track), is rendered "past **AG:65A**
tracing out" in Rom. 11 : 33, R.V. (A.V., "past finding out"); in Eph. **CB:—**
3 : 8, "unsearchable." See FIND, Note (3), UNSEARCHABLE.¶ In the Sept., Job 5 : 9; 9 : 10; 34 : 24.¶

TRADE (Noun and Verb)

A. Verbs.

1. ERGAZOMAI (ἐργάζομαι), to work, is rendered "traded" in Matt. **2038**
25 : 16; in Rev. 18 : 17, A.V., "trade," R.V., "gain their living." See **AG:306D** **CB:1246C**
COMMIT, DO, LABOUR, B, Note (1), MINISTER, WORK.

2. PRAGMATEUOMAI (πραγματεύομαι) is rendered "trade ye" **4231** **AG:697B**
in Luke 19 : 13, R.V., which adds "*herewith*:" see OCCUPY.¶ **CB:1266B**

3. DIAPRAGMATEUOMAI (διαπραγματεύομαι), to accomplish by **1281** **AG:187D**
traffic, to gain by trading, occurs in Luke 19 : 15.¶ **CB:1241B**

4. EMPOREUOMAI (ἐμπορεύομαι) is rendered "trade" in Jas. 4 : 13, **1710**
R.V.: see BUY, Note, MERCHANDISE, B. **AG:256D** **CB:1244B**

B. Nouns.

1. TECHNĒ (τέχνη), an art (Eng., technique, technical), is used in **5078**
Acts 18 : 3 (2nd part) of a "trade," R.V. (A.V., "occupation"). For **AG:814B** **CB:1271A**
the 1st part see Note below. See ART.

2. MEROS (μέρος), a portion, is used of a trade in Acts 19 : 27. See **3313**
CRAFT, No. 5. **AG:505D** **CB:1258B**

Note: For the adjective *homotechnos*, "of the same trade," Acts **3673**
18 : 3, 1st part, R.V., see CRAFT, No. 4.¶ **AG:569B** **CB:—**

TRADITION

PARADOSIS (παράδοσις), a handing down or on (akin to *paradidōmi*, **3862**
to hand over, deliver), denotes a tradition, and hence, by metonymy, **AG:615D** **CB:1262A**
(*a*) the teachings of the Rabbis, interpretations of the Law, which was thereby made void in practice, Matt. 15 : 2, 3, 6; Mark 7 : 3, 5, 8, 9, 13; Gal. 1 : 14; Col. 2 : 8; (*b*) of apostolic teaching, 1 Cor. 11 : 2, R.V., "traditions" (A.V., "ordinances"), of instructions concerning the

gatherings of believers (instructions of wider scope than ordinances in the limited sense); in 2 Thess. 2:15, of Christian doctrine in general, where the Apostle's use of the word constitutes a denial that what he preached originated with himself, and a claim for its Divine authority (cp. *paralambanō*, to receive, 1 Cor. 11:23; 15:3); in 2 Thess. 3:6, it is used of instructions concerning everyday conduct.¶

TRAIN See EXERCISE, INSTRUCT

For TRAIN, Tit. 2:4, R.V., see SOBER, B, No. 3

TRAITOR

4273 AG:704C CB:—

PRODOTĒS (προδότης) denotes a betrayer, traitor; the latter term is assigned to Judas, virtually as a title, in Luke 6:16; in 2 Tim. 3:4 it occurs in a list of evil characters, foretold as abounding in the last days. See BETRAY, B.

TRAMPLE

2662 AG:415D CB:1254A

KATAPATEŌ (καταπατέω), to tread down, trample under foot, is rendered "trample" in Matt. 7:6. See TREAD, No. 2.

TRANCE

1611 AG:245A CB:1244A

EKSTASIS (ἔκστασις), for which see AMAZE, A, No. 1, denotes a trance in Acts 10:10; 11:5; 22:17, a condition in which ordinary consciousness and the perception of natural circumstances were withheld, and the soul was susceptible only to the vision imparted by God.

For TRANQUIL, 1 Tim. 2:2, R.V., see QUIET, No. 1

For TRANSFER (in a figure) see FASHION, C, No. 1, and FIGURE, Note (2).

TRANSFIGURE

3339 AG:511D CB:1258C

METAMORPHOŌ (μεταμορφόω), to change into another form (*meta*, implying change, and *morphē*, form: see FORM, No. 1), is used in the Passive Voice (*a*) of Christ's transfiguration, Matt. 17:2; Mark 9:2; Luke (in 9:29) avoids this term, which might have suggested to Gentile readers the metamorphoses of heathen gods, and uses the phrase *egeneto heteron*, "was altered", lit., 'became (*ginomai*) different (*heteros*);' (*b*) of believers, Rom. 12:2, "be ye transformed," the obligation being to undergo a complete change which, under the power of God, will find expression in character and conduct; *morphē* lays stress on the inward change, *schēma* (see the preceding verb in that verse, *suschēmatizō*) lays stress on the outward (see FASHION, No. 3, FORM, No. 2); the present continuous tenses indicate a process; 2 Cor. 3:18 describes believers as being "transformed (R.V.) into the same image" (i.e., of Christ in all His moral excellencies), the change being effected by the Holy Spirit.¶

TRANSFORM

1. METAMORPHOŌ (μεταμορφόω) is rendered "transformed" in 3339 AG:511D
Rom. 12 : 2 : see TRANSFIGURE. CB:1258C

2. METASCHĒMATIZŌ (μετασχηματίζω) in the Passive Voice is 3345
rendered to be transformed in the A.V. of 2 Cor. 11 : 13, 14, 15 : see AG:513B CB:1258C
FASHION, C, No. 1.

TRANSGRESS, TRANSGRESSION

A. Verbs.

1. PARABAINŌ (παραβαίνω), lit., to go aside (*para*), hence to go 3845
beyond, is chiefly used metaphorically of transgressing the tradition of AG:611C CB:1262A
the elders, Matt. 15 : 2 ; the commandment of God, 15 : 3 ; in Acts 1 : 25, of Judas, A.V., "by transgression fell" (R.V., "fell away") ; in 2 John 9 some texts have this verb (A.V., "transgresseth"), the best have *proagō* (see GO, No. 10).¶

2. HUPERBAINŌ (ὑπερβαίνω), lit., to go over (*huper*), used meta- 5233
phorically and rendered "transgress" in 1 Thess. 4 : 6 (A.V., "go AG:840A CB:1252A
beyond"), i.e., of overstepping the limits separating chastity from licentiousness, sanctification from sin.¶.

3. PARERCHOMAI (παρέρχομαι), to come by (*para*, by, *erchomai*, 3928
to come), pass over, and hence, metaphorically, to transgress, is so used AG:625D CB:1262B
in Luke 15 : 29. See COME, No. 9, PASS.

B. Nouns.

1. PARABASIS (παράβασις), akin to A, No. 1, primarily a going 3847
aside, then, an overstepping, is used metaphorically to denote trans- AG:611D CB:1262A
gression (always of a breach of law) : (*a*) of Adam, Rom. 5 : 14 ; (*b*) of Eve, 1 Tim. 2 : 14 ; (*c*) negatively, where there is no law, since transgression implies the violation of law, none having been enacted between Adam's transgression and those under the Law, Rom. 4 : 15 ; (*d*) of transgressions of the Law, Gal. 3 : 19, where the statement "it was added because of transgressions" is best understood according to Rom. 4 : 15 ; 5 : 13 and 5 : 20 ; the Law does not make men sinners, but makes them transgressors ; hence sin becomes "exceeding sinful," Rom. 7 : 7, 13. Conscience thus had a standard external to itself ; by the Law men are taught their inability to yield complete obedience to God, that thereby they may become convinced of their need of a Saviour ; in Rom. 2 : 23, R.V., "transgression (of the Law)," A.V., "breaking (the Law) ;" Heb. 2 : 2 ; 9 : 15.¶

2. PARANOMIA (παρανομία), law-breaking (*para*, contrary to, 3892
nomos, law), is rendered "transgression" in 2 Pet. 2 : 16, R.V. (A.V., AG:621A CB:—
"iniquity").¶

Note : In 1 John 3 : 4 (1st part), A.V., *poieō*, to do, with *anomia*,
lawlessness, is rendered "transgresseth . . . the law" (R.V., "doeth . . . ANOMIA 458
lawlessness") ; in the 2nd part *anomia* alone is rendered "transgression AG:71D
of the law," A.V. (R.V., "lawlessness"). CB:1235C

TRANSGRESSOR

3848
AG:612A 1. PARABATĒS (παραβάτης), lit. and primarily, one who stands
CB:1262A beside, then, one who oversteps the prescribed limit, a transgressor (akin to *parabainō*, to transgress, see above); so Rom. 2:25, R.V. (A.V., "a breaker"); ver. 27, R.V., "a transgressor" (A.V., "dost transgress"); Gal. 2:18; Jas. 2:9, 11.¶

268 *Note: Hamartōlos*, a sinner, one who misses the mark, is applicable
AG:44A
CB:1249B to all men without distinction; *parabatēs* stresses the positive side of sin, and is applicable to those who received the Law.

459 2. ANOMOS (ἄνομος), without law (*a* –, negative), is translated
AG:72A
CB:1235C "transgressors" in Luke 22:37 (in some texts, Mark 15:28), in a quotation from Isa. 53:12. See LAW, C, No. 3, LAWLESS, A.

TRANSLATE, TRANSLATION

A. Verbs.

3179 1. METHISTĒMI or METHISTANŌ (μεθίστημι), to change, remove
AG:498D
CB:— (*meta*, implying change, *histēmi*, to cause to stand), is rendered "hath translated" in Col. 1:13. See PUT, REMOVE, TURN (away).

3346 2. METATITHĒMI (μετατίθημι), to transfer to another place (*meta*,
AG:513C see above, *tithēmi*, to put), is rendered to translate in Heb. 11.5 (twice).
CB:1258C See CARRY, CHANGE, REMOVE, TURN.

B. Noun.

3331 METATHESIS (μετάθεσις), a change of position (akin to A, No. 2),
AG:511A
CB:1258C is rendered "translation" in Heb. 11:5. See CHANGE, REMOVING.

For TRANSPARENT, Rev. 21:21, see DAWN, A, No. 2, Note

TRAP
See
SNARE

TRAP

2339 THĒRA (θήρα) denotes a hunting, chase, then, a prey; hence,
AG:360D
CB:— figuratively, of preparing destruction by a net or "trap," Rom. 11:9.¶

TRAVAIL (Noun and Verb)

A. Nouns.

3449 1. MOCHTHOS (μόχθος), labour, involving painful effort, is rendered
AG:528D
CB:1259A "travail" in 2 Cor. 11:27, R.V. (A.V., "painfulness"); in 1 Thess. 2:9 and 2 Thess. 3:8 it stresses the toil involved in the work.¶

5604 2. ŌDIN (ὠδίν), a birth pang, travail pain, is used illustratively in
AG:895C
CB:1260B 1 Thess. 5:3 of the calamities which are to come upon men at the beginning of the Day of the Lord; the figure used suggests the inevitableness of the catastrophe. See PAIN, No. 2, SORROW.

B. Verbs.

5605 1. ŌDINŌ (ὠδίνω), akin to A, No. 2, is used negatively in Gal. 4:27,
AG:895D
CB:1260B "(thou) that travailest (not)," quoted from Isa. 54:1; the Apostle applies the circumstances of Sarah and Hagar (which doubtless Isaiah was recalling) to show that, whereas the promise by grace had temporarily

been replaced by the works of the Law (see Gal. 3 : 17), this was now reversed, and, in the fulfilment of the promise to Abraham, the number of those saved by the Gospel would far exceed those who owned allegiance to the Law. Isa. 54 has primary reference to the future prosperity of Israel restored to God's favour, but frequently the principles underlying events recorded in the O.T. extend beyond their immediate application.

In 4 : 19 the Apostle uses it metaphorically of a second travailing on his part regarding the churches of Galatia; his first was for their deliverance from idolatry (ver. 8), now it was for their deliverance from bondage to Judaism. There is no suggestion here of a second regeneration necessitated by defection. There is a hint of reproach, as if he was enquiring whether they had ever heard of a mother experiencing second birthpangs for her children.

In Rev. 12 : 2 the woman is figurative of Israel; the circumstances of her birth-pangs are mentioned in Isa. 66 : 7 (see also Micah 5 : 2, 3). Historically the natural order is reversed. The Man-child, Christ, was brought forth at His first Advent; the travail is destined to take place in "the time of Jacob's trouble," the "great tribulation," Matt. 24 : 21; Rev. 7 : 14. The object in 12 : 2 in referring to the Birth of Christ is to connect Him with His earthly people Israel in their future time of trouble, from which the godly remnant, the nucleus of the restored nation, is to be delivered (Jer. 30 : 7).¶

2. SUNŌDINŌ (συνωδίνω), to be in travail together, is used metaphorically in Rom. 8 : 22, of the whole creation.¶ **4944 AG:793D CB:—**

3. TIKTO (τίκτω), to beget, is rendered "travail" in John 16 : 21. **5088 AG:816D CB:1272C**

For TRAVEL (companions in), Acts 19 : 29, and TRAVEL WITH, 2 Cor. 8 : 19, see COMPANION, No. 1.

TRAVEL

DIERCHOMAI (διέρχομαι), to go or pass through, is translated "travelled" in Acts 11 : 19. See COME, No. 5. **1330 AG:194C CB:1241C**

Note: For *apodēmeō*, rendered "travelling" in Matt. 25 : 14, A.V., see GO, No. 27. **589 AG:90A CB:1236C**

TREAD, TRODE, TRODDEN

1. PATEŌ (πατέω) is used (*a*) intransitively and figuratively, of treading upon serpents, Luke 10 : 19; (*b*) transitively, of treading on, down or under, of the desecration of Jerusalem by its foes, Luke 21 : 24; Rev. 11 : 2; of the avenging, by the Lord in Person hereafter, of this desecration and of the persecution of the Jews, in Divine retribution, metaphorically spoken of as the treading of the winepress of God's wrath, Rev. 14 : 20; 19 : 15 (cp. Isa. 63 : 2, 3).¶ **3961 AG:634D CB:1262C**

2. KATAPATEŌ (καταπατέω), to tread down, trample under foot, is used (*a*) literally, Matt. 5 : 13; 7 : 6; Luke 8 : 5; 12 : 1; (*b*) meta- **2662 AG:415D CB:1254A**

phorically, of 'treading under foot' the Son of God, Heb. 10:29, i.e., turning away from Him, to indulge in wilful sin.¶

For TREADING out the corn, see THRESH

TREASURE (Noun and Verb)

A. Nouns.

2344 1. THĒSAUROS (θησαυρός) denotes (1) a place of safe keeping
AG:361C (possibly akin to *tithēmi*, to put), (*a*) a casket, Matt. 2:11; (*b*) a store-
CB:1272B house, Matt. 13:52; used metaphorically of the heart, Matt. 12:35, twice (R.V., "out of his treasure"); Luke 6:45; (2) a treasure, Matt. 6:19, 20, 21; 13:44; Luke 12:33, 34; Heb. 11:26; treasure (in heaven or the heavens), Matt. 19:21; Mark 10:21; Luke 18:22; in these expressions (which are virtually equivalent to that in Matt. 6:1, "with your Father which is in Heaven") the promise does not simply refer to the present life, but looks likewise to the hereafter; in 2 Cor. 4:7 it is used of "the light of the knowledge of the glory of God in the face of Jesus Christ," descriptive of the Gospel, as deposited in the earthen vessels of the persons who proclaim it (cp. ver. 4); in Col. 2:3, of the wisdom and knowledge hidden in Christ.¶

1047 2. GAZA (γάζα), a Persian word, signifying royal treasure, occurs in
AG:149B
CB:— Acts 8:27.¶

B. Verb.

2343
AG:361B THĒSAURIZŌ (θησαυρίζω), akin to A, No. 1, is used metaphorically
CB:1272B in Rom. 2:5 of treasuring up wrath. See LAY, No. 17.

For TREASURER see CHAMBERLAIN, Note

TREASURY

1049 1. GAZOPHULAKION (γαζοφυλάκιον), from *gaza*, a treasure, *phulakē*,
AG:149B
(-EION) a guard, is used by Josephus for a special room in the women's court in
CB:1248A the Temple in which gold and silver bullion was kept. This seems to be referred to in John 8:20; in Mark 12:41 (twice), 43 and Luke 21:1 it is used of the trumpet-shaped or ram's-horn-shaped chests, into which the temple-offerings of the people were cast. There were 13 chests, six for such gifts in general, seven for distinct purposes.¶

2878 2. KORBANAS (κορβανᾶς), signifying the place of gifts, denoted the
AG:444C
CB:1255C Temple treasury, Matt. 27:6. See CORBAN.¶

TREAT
See DO,
DEAL WITH For TREATED, Acts 27:3, R.V., see ENTREAT (to deal with)

TREATISE

3056
AG:477A LOGOS (λόγος), a word, denotes a treatise or written narrative in
CB:1257A Acts 1:1. See WORD.

TREE

1. DENDRON (δένδρον), a living, growing tree (cp. Eng., rhodo- 1186
dendron, lit., rose-tree), known by the fruit it produces, Matt. 12 : 33 ; AG:174C
Luke 6 : 44 ; certain qualities are mentioned in the N.T. ; "a good tree," CB:1240C
Matt. 7 : 17, 18 ; 12 : 33 ; Luke 6 : 43 ; "a corrupt tree" (ditto) ; in Jude 12, metaphorically, of evil teachers, "autumn trees (A.V., trees whose fruit withereth) without fruit, twice dead, plucked up by the roots," R.V. ; in Luke 13 : 19 in some texts, "a great tree," A.V. (R.V., "a tree") ; for this and Matt. 13 : 32 see MUSTARD ; in Luke 21 : 29 the fig tree is illustrative of Israel, "all the trees" indicating Gentile nations.

2. XULON (ξύλον) wood, a piece of wood, anything made of wood 3586
(see STAFF, STOCKS), is used, with the rendering "tree," (*a*) in Luke AG:549A
23 : 31, where "the green tree" refers either to Christ, figuratively of all CB:1273B
His living power and excellencies, or to the life of the Jewish people while still inhabiting their land, in contrast to "the dry," a figure fulfilled in the horrors of the Roman massacre and devastation in A.D. 70 (cp. the Lord's parable in Luke 13 : 6–9 ; see Ezek. 20 : 47, and cp. 21 : 3) ; (*b*) of the Cross, the tree being the *stauros*, the upright pale or stake to which Romans nailed those who were thus to be executed, Acts 5 : 30 ; 10 : 39 ; 13 : 29 ; Gal. 3 : 13 ; 1 Pet. 2 : 24 ; (*c*) of the tree of life, Rev. 2 : 7 ; 22 : 2 (twice), 14, 19, R.V., A.V., "book." See WOOD.

TREMBLE, TREMBLING

A. Verbs.

1. TREMŌ (τρέμω), to tremble, especially with fear, is used in Mark 5141
5 : 33 ; Luke 8 : 47 (Acts 9 : 6, in some mss.) ; 2 Pet. 2 : 10, R.V., "they AG:825B
tremble (not)," A.V., "they are (not) afraid."¶ CB:—

2. SEIŌ (σείω), to move to and fro, shake, is rendered "will I make 4579 AG:746C
to tremble" in Heb. 12 : 26, R.V. (A.V., "I shake"). See QUAKE, SHAKE. CB:1268C

Notes : (1) For *phrissō* in Jas. 2 : 19, A.V., "tremble," see SHUDDER. PHRISSō
(2) For the adjective *entromos*, trembling, Acts 7 : 32 ; 16 : 29, R.V., 5425 AG:866A
"trembling for fear," see QUAKE, No. 1. (3) The adjective *emphobos*, ENTROMOS
used with *ginomai*, to become, is rendered "trembled" in Acts 24 : 25 1790 AG:269D
(R.V., "was terrified") ; in Luke 24 : 5, R.V., "they were affrighted," EMPHOBOS
A.V., "they were afraid." See AFFRIGHTED, A. 1719 AG:257D

B. Noun.

TROMOS (τρόμος), a trembling (akin to A, No. 1), occurs in Mark 5156
16 : 8, R.V., "trembling (. . . had come upon them) ;" 1 Cor. 2 : 3 ; AG:827A
2 Cor. 7 : 15 ; Eph. 6 : 5 ; Phil. 2 : 12.¶ CB:1273A

TRENCH

CHARAX (χάραξ), primarily a pointed stake, hence, a palisade or 5482
rampart, is rendered "trench" in Luke 19 : 43, A.V. (R.V., "bank," AG:876B
marg., "palisade"). In A.D. 70, Titus, the Roman general, surrounded CB:1239C
Jerusalem with a palisaded mound (Tyndale, *l.c.*, renders it "mound").

The Jews in one of their sorties destroyed this *charax*, after which Titus surrounded the city with a wall of masonry.¶

TRESPASS (Noun and Verb)

A. Noun.

3900 AG:621D CB:1262B PARAPTŌMA (παράπτωμα), primarily a false step, a blunder (akin to *parapiptō*, to fall away, Heb. 6:6), lit., 'a fall beside,' used ethically, denotes a trespass, a deviation, from uprightness and truth, Matt. 6 : 14, 15 (twice) ; 18:35, in some mss. ; Mark 11:25, 26 ; in Romans the R.V. substitutes "trespass" and "trespasses" for A.V., "offence" and "offences," 4 : 25, "for (i.e., because of) our trespasses ;" 5 : 15 (twice), where the trespass is that of Adam (in contrast to the free gift of righteousness, ver. 17, a contrast in the nature and the effects) ; 5 : 16, where "of many trespasses" expresses a contrast of quantity ; the condemnation resulted from one trespass, the free gift is "of (*ek*, expressing the origin, and throwing stress upon God's justifying grace in Christ) many trespasses ;" ver. 17, introducing a contrast between legal effects and those of Divine grace ; ver. 18, where the R.V., "through one trespass," is contrasted with "one act of righteousness ;" this is important, the difference is not between one man's trespass and Christ's righteousness (as A.V.), but between two acts, that of Adam's trespass and the vicarious Death of Christ ; ver. 20 [cp. TRANSGRESSION, B, No. 1 (*d*)] ; in 2 Cor. 5 : 19, A.V. and R.V., "trespasses ;" in Eph. 1 : 7, R.V., "trespasses" (A.V., "sins") ; in 2 : 1, R.V., "(dead through your) trespasses," A.V., "(dead in) trespasses ;" 2 : 5, R.V., "(dead through our) trespasses," A.V., "(dead in) sins ;" so Col 2 : 13 (1st part) ; in the 2nd part, A.V. and R.V., "trespasses."

In Gal. 6 : 1, R.V., "(in any) trespass" (A.V., "fault"), the reference is to "the works of the flesh" (5 : 19), and the thought is that of the believer's being found off his guard, the trespass taking advantage of him ; in Jas. 5 : 16, A.V., "faults" (R.V., "sins" translates the word *hamartias*, which is found in the best texts), auricular confession to a priest is not in view here or anywhere else in Scripture ; the command is comprehensive, and speaks either of the acknowledgment of sin where one has wronged another, or of the unburdening of a troubled conscience to a godly brother whose prayers will be efficacious, or of open confession before the church.

In Rom. 11 : 11, 12, the word is used of Israel's "fall," i.e., their deviation from obedience to God and from the fulfilment of His will (to be distinguished from the verb *ptaiō*, "fall," in the 1st part of ver. 11, which indicates the impossibility of recovery). See FALL, A, No. 2.¶

B. Verb.

264 AG:42B CB:1249A HAMARTANŌ (ἁμαρτάνω) to sin, is translated to trespass, in the A.V. of Matt. 18 : 15, and Luke 17 : 3, 4 (R.V., to sin).

Note : For the different meanings of words describing sin, see SIN.

Paraptōma, and *hamartēma* (a sinful deed) are closely associated, with
regard to their primary meanings : *parabasis* seems to be a stronger term, PARABASIS 3847
as the breach of a known law (see TRANSGRESSION). AG:611D CB:1262A

TRIAL

1. DOKIMĒ (δοκιμή), for which see EXPERIENCE, No. 2, is rendered 1382
" trial " in 2 Cor. 8 : 2, A.V. (R.V., " proof "). AG:202D CB:1242A

2. PEIRA (πεῖρα), a making trial, an experiment, is used with 3984
lambanō, to receive or take, in Heb. 11 : 29, rendered " assaying," and AG:640A CB:1263A
ver. 36, in the sense of ' having experience of ' (akin to *peiraō*, to assay,
to try), " had trial."¶ In the Sept., Deut. 28 : 56.¶

3. PEIRASMOS (πειρασμός), akin to No. 2, is rendered " trials " in 3986
Acts 20 : 19, R.V. See TEMPTATION. AG:640D CB:1263A

4. PURŌSIS (πύρωσις), akin to *puroō*, to set on fire, signifies (*a*) a 4451
burning ; (*b*) a refining, metaphorically in 1 Pet. 4 : 12, " fiery trial," or AG:731C CB:1268A
rather ' trial by fire,' referring to the refining of gold (1 : 7). See
BURNING.

Note : For *dokimion*, rendered " trial " in 1 Pet. 1 : 7, A.V., see 1383
PROOF, No. 2. AG:203A CB:1242A

TRIBE (–S)

1. PHULĒ (φυλή), a company of people united by kinship or 5443
habitation, a clan, tribe, is used (*a*) of the peoples of the earth, Matt. AG:868D CB:1264C
24 : 30 ; in the following the R.V. has " tribe(–s) " for A.V., " kindred(–s),"
Rev. 1 : 7 ; 5 : 9 ; 7 : 9 ; 11 : 9 ; 13 : 7 ; 14 : 6 ; (*b*) of the tribes of Israel,
Matt. 19 : 28 ; Luke 2 : 36 ; 22 : 30 ; Acts 13 : 21 ; Rom. 11 : 1 ; Phil.
3 : 5 ; Heb. 7 : 13, 14 ; Jas. 1 : 1 ; Rev. 5 : 5 ; 7 : 4–8 ; 21 : 12.¶

2. DŌDEKAPHULOS (δωδεκάφυλος), an adjective signifying ' of 1429
twelve tribes ' (*dōdeka*, twelve, and No. 1), used as a noun in the neuter, AG:210B (-ON)
occurs in Acts 26 : 7.¶ CB:1242 (-ON)

TRIBULATION

THLIPSIS (θλῖψις), for which see AFFLICTION, B, No. 4, is translated 2347
" tribulation " in the R.V. (for A.V., " affliction ") in Mark 4 : 17 ; AG:362B CB:1272B
13 : 19 ; plural in 2 Thess. 1 : 4, A.V., " tribulations," R.V., " afflictions " ;
in Acts 14 : 22 " many tribulations " (A.V., " much tribulation ") ; in
Matt. 24 : 9, " unto tribulation " (A.V., " to be afflicted ") ; in 2 Cor.
1 : 4 ; 7 : 4 ; 2 Thess. 1 : 6, A.V., " tribulation " for R.V., " affliction ; "
R.V. and A.V., " tribulation(–s)," e.g., in Rom. 2 : 9 ; 5 : 3 (twice) ;
8 : 35 ; 12 : 12 ; Eph. 3 : 13 ; Rev. 1 : 9 ; 2 : 9, 10, 22.

In Rev. 7 : 14, " the great tribulation," R.V., lit., ' the tribulation, the great one ' (not as A.V., without the article), is not that in which all saints share ; it indicates a definite period spoken of by the Lord in Matt. 24 : 21, 29 ; Mark 13 : 19, 24, where the time is mentioned as preceding His Second Advent, and as a period in which the Jewish nation, restored to Palestine in unbelief by Gentile instrumentality, will suffer an unprecedented outburst of fury on the part of the antichristian powers confederate under the Man of Sin (2 Thess. 2 : 10–12 ; cp. Rev. 12 : 13–17) ; in this tribulation Gentile witnesses for God will share (Rev. 7 : 9), but it will be distinctly " the time of Jacob's trouble " (Jer. 30 : 7) ; its beginning is signalized by the setting up of the " abomination of desolation " (Matt. 24 : 15 ; Mark 13 : 14, with Dan. 11 : 31 ; 12 : 11).

2346 AG:362A CB:1272B *Note :* For the verb *thlibō*, in the Passive Voice rendered " suffer tribulation " in 1 Thess. 3 : 4, A.V. (R.V., " suffer affliction "), see AFFLICT, No. 4.

TRIBUTE

5411 AG:865A CB:1264B 1. PHOROS (φόρος), akin to *pherō*, to bring, denotes tribute paid by a subjugated nation, Luke 20 : 22 ; 23 : 2 ; Rom. 13 : 6, 7.¶

2778 AG:430D CB:1255A 2. KĒNSOS (κῆνσος), Lat. and Eng., census, denote poll tax, Matt. 17 : 25 ; 22 : 17, 19 ; Mark. 12 : 14.¶

1323 AG:192C CB:1241C 3. DIDRACHMON (δίδραχμον), the half-shekel, is rendered " tribute " in Matt. 17 : 24 (twice) : see SHEKEL, No. 2.¶

TRIM

2885 AG:445A CB:1255C KOSMEŌ (κοσμέω), to arrange, adorn, is used of trimming lamps, Matt. 25 : 7. See ADORN, GARNISH.

TRIUMPH

2358 AG:363D CB:1272B THRIAMBEUŌ (θριαμβεύω) denotes (*a*) to lead in triumph, used of a conqueror with reference to the vanquished, 2 Cor. 2 : 14. Theodoret paraphrases it 'He leads us about here and there and displays us to all the world.' This is in agreement with evidences from various sources. Those who are led are not captives exposed to humiliation, but are displayed as the glory and devoted subjects of Him who leads (see the context). This is so even if there is a reference to a Roman " triumph." On such occasions the general's sons, with various officers, rode behind his chariot (Livy, xlv. 40). But there is no necessary reference here to a Roman " triumph " (Field, in *Notes on the Trans. of the N.T.*). The main thought is that of the display, " in Christ " being the sphere ; its evidences are the effects of gospel testimony.

In Col. 2 : 15 the circumstances and subjects are quite different, and relate to Christ's victory over spiritual foes at the time of His Death ; accordingly the reference may be to the triumphant display of the defeated.¶

For TRODE see TREAD

TROUBLE (Noun and Verb)

A. Noun.

THLIPSIS (θλῖψις), for which see AFFLICTION, No. 4, and TRIBULATION, 2347
is rendered "trouble" in the A.V. of 1 Cor. 7 : 28 (R.V., "tribulation"); AG:362B
2 Cor. 1 : 4 (2nd clause), 8 (R.V., "affliction"). CB:1272B

Note: In some mss. *tarachē*, an agitation, disturbance, trouble, is 5016
found in Mark 13 : 8 (plur.) and John 5 : 4 (R.V. omits).¶ AG:805C CB:1271A

B. Verbs.

1. TARASSŌ (ταράσσω), akin to *tarachē* (A, Note), is used (1) in a 5015
physical sense, John 5 : 7 (in some mss. ver. 4), (2) metaphorically, (*a*) of AG:805B
the soul and spirit of the Lord, John 11 : 33, where the true rendering is CB:1271A
'He troubled Himself;' (*b*) of the hearts of disciples, 14 : 1, 27; (*c*) of the minds of those in fear or perplexity, Matt. 2 : 3; 14 : 26; Mark 6 : 50; Luke 1 : 12; 24 : 38; 1 Pet. 3 : 14; (*d*) of subverting the souls of believers, by evil doctrine, Acts 15 : 24; Gal. 1 : 7; 5 : 10; (*e*) of stirring up a crowd, Acts 17 : 8; ver. 13 in the best texts, "troubling (the multitudes)," R.V.¶

2. DIATARASSŌ (διαταράσσω), to agitate greatly (*dia*, throughout, 1298
and No. 1), is used of the Virgin Mary, Luke 1 : 29.¶ AG:189B CB:—

3. EKTARASSŌ (ἐκταράσσω), to throw into great trouble, agitate, is 1613
used in Acts 16 : 20, "do exceedingly trouble (our city)."¶ In the Sept., AG:245B
Psa. 18 : 4; 88 : 16.¶ CB:—

4. THLIBŌ (θλίβω), to afflict, is rendered to trouble in the A.V., e.g., 2346
2 Cor. 4 : 8 (R.V., "pressed"); 7 : 5, but never in the R.V.: see AFFLICT, AG:362A
No. 4, PRESS, STRAITENED, TRIBULATION. CB:1272B

5. ENOCHLEŌ (ἐνοχλέω), from *en*, in, *ochlos*, a throng, crowd, is 1776
used in Heb. 12 : 15 of a root of bitterness; in Luke 6 : 18 (in the best AG:267D
texts; some have *ochleō*), R.V., "were troubled" (A.V., "were vexed").¶ CB:1245B

6. PARENOCHLEŌ (παρενοχλέω), to annoy concerning anything 3926
(*para*, and No. 5), occurs in Acts 15 : 19, "we trouble (not them)."¶ AG:625C CB:—

7. SKULLŌ (σκύλλω), primarily to flay, hence, to vex, annoy ("there 4660
was a time when the Greek, in thus speaking, compared his trouble to the AG:758B
pains of flaying alive," Moulton, *Proleg.*, p. 89), is used in the Active Voice CB:—
in Mark 5 : 35; Luke 8 : 49; in the Passive Voice, Matt. 9 : 36, in the best texts, R.V., "they were distressed" (some have *ekluō*, A.V., "they fainted"); in the Middle Voice, Luke 7 : 6, "trouble (not thyself)."¶ The word is frequent in the papyri.

8. ANASTATOŌ (ἀναστατόω) is rendered "trouble" in Gal. 5 : 12, 387
A.V.: see STIR, No. 12, TURN, No. 15, UPROAR. AG:61A CB:—

9. THORUBEŌ (θορυβέω), akin to *thorubos*, a tumult, in the Middle 2350
Voice, to make an uproar, is rendered "trouble not yourselves" in Acts AG:362D
20 : 10, A.V. See ADO, TUMULT. CB:1272B

10. THROEŌ (θροέω), to make an outcry (*throos*, a tumult), is used 2360
in the Passive Voice, Matt. 24 : 6; Mark 13 : 7; Luke 24 : 37; 2 Thess. AG:364A
2 : 2.¶ In the Sept., S. of Sol. 5 : 4.¶ CB:—

— AG:362D 11. THORUBAZŌ (θορυβάζω), to disturb, to trouble (akin to No. 9),
CB:1272B is used in Luke 10 : 41, in the best texts (in some, *turbazō*, with the same
TURBAZŌ meaning).¶
5182 AG:830D 12. ADĒMONEŌ (ἀδημονέω), to be much troubled, distressed (perhaps
CB:— from *a*, negative, and *dēmōn*, knowing, the compound therefore originally
ADĒMONEŌ suggesting bewilderment), is translated "sore troubled" in Matt. 26 : 37
85 AG:16D and Mark 14 : 33, R.V. (A.V., "very heavy"); so the R.V. in Phil.
CB:— 2 : 26 (A.V., "full of heaviness"); Lightfoot renders it "distressed,"
a meaning borne out in the papyri. See HEAVY.¶
1278 AG:187C 13. DIAPONEŌ (διαπονέω) denotes to work out with toil, hence, to
(-OMAI) be "sore troubled;" so the R.V. in Acts 4 : 2 and 16 : 18 (A.V.,
CB:— "grieved"); Mark 14 : 4 in some texts.¶
KOPOS *Notes:* (1) The noun *kopos*, a striking, beating, then, laborious toil,
2873 AG:443C trouble, used with *parechō*, to furnish, to supply, is rendered to trouble
CB:1255C (lit., to give trouble to), in Matt. 26 : 10; Mark 14 : 6; Luke 11 : 7;
PARECHŌ 3930 18 : 5; Gal. 6 : 17; the meaning is to embarrass a person by distracting
AG:626B his attention, or to give occasion for anxiety. In the last passage the
CB:— Apostle expresses his determination not to allow the Judaizing teachers to
distract him any further. See LABOUR, A, No. 1. (2) For "suffer
trouble" in 2 Tim. 2 : 9, see HARDSHIP.

TROW

1380 AG:201D *Note:* Some mss. have *dokeō*, to think, in Luke 17 : 9, A.V., "I trow
CB:1242A (not)."

For TRUCE-BREAKERS see IMPLACABLE

TRUE, TRULY, TRUTH

A. Adjectives.

227 AG:36D 1. ALĒTHĒS (ἀληθής), primarily, unconcealed, manifest (*a*, negative,
CB:1234B *lēthō*, to forget, = *lanthanō*, to escape notice), hence, actual, true to fact,
is used (*a*) of persons, truthful, Matt. 22 : 16; Mark 12 : 14; John 3 : 33;
7 : 18; 8 : 26; Rom. 3 : 4; 2 Cor. 6 : 8; (*b*) of things, true, conforming
to reality, John 4 : 18, "truly," lit., 'true;' 5 : 31, 32; in the best texts,
6 : 55 (twice), "indeed;" 8 : 13, 14 (ver. 16 in some texts: see No. 2),
17; 10 : 41; 19 : 35; 21 : 24; Acts 12 : 9; Phil. 4 : 8; Tit. 1 : 13;
1 Pet. 5 : 12; 2 Pet. 2 : 22; 1 John 2 : 8, 27; 3 John 12.¶
228 AG:37A 2. ALĒTHINOS (ἀληθινός), akin to No. 1, denotes true in the sense
CB:1234B of real, ideal, genuine; it is used (*a*) of God, John 7 : 28 (cp. No. 1 in
7 : 18, above); 17 : 3; 1 Thess. 1 : 9; Rev. 6 : 10; these declare that
God fulfils the meaning of His Name, He is "very God," in distinction
from all other gods, false gods (*alēthēs*, see John 3 : 33 in No. 1, signifies
that He is veracious, true to His utterances, He cannot lie); (*b*) of Christ,
John 1 : 9; 6 : 32; 15 : 1; 1 John 2 : 8; 5 : 20 (thrice); Rev. 3 : 7, 14;
19 : 11; His judgment, John 8 : 16 (in the best texts, instead of No. 1);
(*c*) God's words, John 4 : 37; Rev. 19 : 9; 21 : 5; 22 : 6; the last three

are equivalent to No. 1; (*d*) His ways, Rev. 15 : 3; (*e*) His judgments, Rev. 16 : 7; 19 : 2; (*f*) His riches, Luke 16 : 11; (*g*) His worshippers, John 4 : 23; (*h*) their hearts, Heb. 10 : 22; (*i*) the witness of the Apostle John, John 19 : 35; (*j*) the spiritual, antitypical Tabernacle, Heb. 8 : 2; 9 : 24, not that the wilderness Tabernacle was false, but that it was a weak and earthly copy of the Heavenly.¶

Note: " *Alēthinos* is related to *alēthēs* as form to contents or substances; *alēthēs* denotes the reality of the thing, *alēthinos* defines the relation of the conception to the thing to which it corresponds=genuine" (Cremer).

3. GNĒSIOS (γνήσιος), primarily lawfully begotten (akin to *ginomai*, **1103**
to become), hence, true, genuine, sincere, is used in the Apostle's exhorta- **AG:162D**
tion to his " true yoke-fellow" in Phil. 4 : 3. See OWN, SINCERITY. **CB:1248B**

Note: In the A.V. of 2 Cor. 1 : 18 and 1 Tim. 3 : 1, *pistos*, " faithful" **4103**
(R.V.), is translated " true." **AG:664C**
CB:1265A

B. Verb.

ALĒTHEUŌ (ἀληθεύω) signifies to deal faithfully or truly with **226**
anyone (cp. Gen. 42 : 16, Sept., " whether ye deal truly or no"), Eph. **AG:36C**
4 : 15, " speaking the truth;" Gal. 3 : 16, " I tell (you) the truth," where **CB:1234B**
probably the Apostle is referring to the contents of his Epistle.¶

C. Noun.

ALĒTHEIA (ἀλήθεια), truth, is used (*a*) objectively, signifying " the **225**
reality lying at the basis of an appearance; the manifested, veritable **AG:35**
essence of a matter" (Cremer), e.g., Rom. 9 : 1; 2 Cor. 11 : 10; **CB:1234B**
especially of Christian doctrine, e.g., Gal. 2 : 5, where " the truth of the Gospel" denotes the true teaching of the Gospel, in contrast to perversions of it; Rom. 1 : 25, where " the truth of God" may be 'the truth concerning God' or 'God whose existence is a verity;' but in Rom 15 : 8 " the truth of God" is indicative of His faithfulness in the fulfilment of His promises as exhibited in Christ; the word has an absolute force in John 14 : 6; 17 : 17; 18 : 37, 38; in Eph. 4 : 21, where the R.V., " even as truth is in Jesus," gives the correct rendering, the meaning is not merely ethical truth, but truth in all its fulness and scope, as embodied in Him; He was the perfect expression of the truth; this is virtually equivalent to His statement in John 14 : 6; (*b*) subjectively, truthfulness, truth, not merely verbal, but sincerity and integrity of character, John 8 : 44; 3 John 3, R.V.; (*c*) in phrases, e.g., " in truth" (*epi*, on the basis of), Mark 12 : 14; Luke 20 : 21; with *en*, in, 2 Cor. 6 : 7; Col. 1 : 6; 1 Tim. 2 : 7, R.V. (A.V., " in .... verity"); 1 John 3 : 18; 2 John 1, 3, 4.

Note: In Matt. 15 : 27, A.V., *nai*, " yea" (R.V.), is translated **3483**
" truth." **AG:532D**
CB:—

D. Adverbs.

1. ALĒTHŌS (ἀληθῶς), truly, surely, is rendered " of a truth" in **230**
AG:37B
Matt. 14 : 33; 26 : 73 and Mark 14 : 70, R.V. (A.V., " surely"); Luke **CB:1234B**

9 : 27 ; 12 : 44 ; 21 : 3 ; John 6 : 14 ; 7 : 40 ; 17 : 8, R.V., " of a truth" (A.V., " surely ") ; Acts 12 : 11, R.V. (A.V., " of a surety ") ; " in truth," 1 Thess. 2 : 13 ; " truly," Matt. 27 : 54 ; Mark 15 : 39. See INDEED, No. 3.

1104 AG:163A CB:— 2. GNĒSIŌS (γνησίως), sincerely, honourably (akin to A, No. 3), is rendered " truly " (marg., " genuinely ") in Phil. 2 : 20 (A.V., " naturally ").¶

ARA *Notes :* (1) The particles *ara, men,* and *de* are sometimes rendered
686 AG:103D " truly " in the A.V., but are differently rendered in the R.V. (2) In 1
CB:1237B Cor. 14 : 25, A.V., *ontōs* (R.V., " indeed ") is rendered " of a truth."
MEN See CERTAIN, C, No. 1, INDEED, No. 4. (3) In John 20 : 30, A.V., the
3303 AG:502C particle *oun,* therefore (R.V.), is rendered " truly."

CB:1258B DE 1161 AG:171C

TRUMP, TRUMPET

A. Noun.

CB:— ONTōS SALPINX (σάλπιγξ) is used (1) of the natural instrument, 1 Cor.
3689 AG:574A 14 : 8 ; (2) of the supernatural accompaniment of Divine interpositions, (*a*) at Sinai, Heb. 12 : 19 ; (*b*) of the acts of angels at the Second Advent
CB:— of Christ, Matt. 24 : 31 ; (*c*) of their acts in the period of Divine judgments
SALPINX 4536 preceding this, Rev. 8 : 2, 6, 13 ; 9 : 14 ; (*d*) of a summons to John to
AG:741A CB:1268B the presence of God, Rev. 1 : 10 ; 4 : 1 ; (*e*) of the act of the Lord in raising from the dead the saints who have fallen asleep and changing the bodies of those who are living, at the Rapture of all to meet Him in the air, 1 Cor. 15 : 52, where " the last trump " is a military allusion, familiar to Greek readers, and has no connection with the series in Rev. 8 : 6 to 11 : 15 ; there is a possible allusion to Num. 10 : 2–6, with reference to the same event, 1 Thess. 4 : 16, " the (lit., a) trump of God " (the absence of the article suggests the meaning 'a trumpet such as is used in God's service ').¶

B. Verb.

4537 AG:741A CB:1268B SALPIZŌ (σαλπίζω), to sound a trumpet, Matt. 6 : 2 ; as in (2) (*c*) above, Rev. 8 : 6, 7, 8, 10, 12, 13 ; 9 : 1, 13 ; 10 : 7 ; 11 : 15 ; as in (2) (*e*), 1 Cor. 15 : 52.¶

TRUMPETER

4538 AG:741B CB:1268B SALPISTĒS (σαλπιστής) occurs in Rev. 18 : 22.¶

TRUST (Noun and Verb)

A. Noun.

4006 AG:643B CB:1263B PEPOITHĒSIS (πεποίθησις) is rendered " trust " in 2 Cor. 3 : 4, A.V. ; see CONFIDENCE, No. 1.

B. Verbs.

3982 AG:639A CB:1263A 1. PEITHŌ (πείθω), intransitively, in the perfect and pluperfect Active, to have confidence, trust, is rendered to trust in Matt. 27 : 43 ; Mark 10 : 24 ; Luke 11 : 22 ; 18 : 9 ; 2 Cor. 1 : 9 ; 10 : 7 ; Phil. 2 : 24 ; 3 : 4, A.V. (R.V., " to have confidence ") ; Heb. 2 : 13 ; in the present

Middle, Heb. 13 : 18, A.V. (R.V., " are persuaded "). See AGREE, No. 5, TRUSTWORTHY See
PERSUADE. FAITHFUL

2. PISTEUŌ (πιστεύω), to entrust, or, in the Passive Voice, to be 4100
entrusted with, is rendered to commit to one's trust, in Luke 16 : 11 ; AG:660B
1 Tim. 1 : 11 ; to be put in trust with, 1 Thess. 2 : 4, A.V. (R.V., " to be CB:1265A
intrusted "). 1679

Note : Wherever *elpizō*, to hope, is translated to trust in the A.V., AG:252C CB:1244B
the R.V. substitutes to hope. So *proelpizō*, to hope before. See HOPE. 4276

For TRUTH see TRUE AG:705A CB:1266C

TRY, TRIED

1. DOKIMAZŌ (δοκιμάζω) is rendered to try in the A.V. in 1 Cor. 3 : 13 ; 1381
1 Thess. 2 : 4 ; 1 Pet. 1 : 7 ; 1 John 4 : 1 : see PROVE, No. 1. AG:202C CB:1242A

2. PEIRAZŌ (πειράζω) is rendered to try in Heb. 11 : 17 ; Rev. 2 : 2, 3985
10 ; 3 : 10. In Acts 16 : 7 it is rendered " assayed ; " in 24 : 6, R.V., AG:640B
" assayed " (A.V., " hath gone about ") : see GO, Note (2) (*b*). See CB:1263A
EXAMINE, PROVE, TEMPT. Cp. *peiraō* in Acts 26 : 21, R.V., " assayed " PEIRAō
(A.V., " went about ") ; see GO, Note (2) (*c*). 3987 AG:641A

Notes : (1) In Rev. 3 : 18, A.V., *puroō*, in the Passive Voice, to be CB:1263A
purified by fire (R.V., " refined "), is rendered " tried." (2) For PUROOMAI 4448
dokimion, Jas. 1 : 3, A.V., " trying," see PROOF. (3) For *dokimos*, Jas. AG:731A
1 : 12, A.V., " tried," see APPROVED. (4) In 1 Pet. 4 : 12, A.V., the CB:1268A DOKIMION
phrase *pros peirasmon*, lit., ' for trial,' i.e., for testing, is rendered " to 1383
try (you) ", R.V., " to prove (you)." AG:203A CB:1242A

TUMULT

DOKIMOS 1384

1. AKATASTASIA (ἀκαταστασία) is rendered " tumults " in Luke AG:203A CB:1242A
21 : 9, R.V. ; 2 Cor. 6 : 5 ; 12 : 20. See CONFOUND, A, No. 1. PEIRASMOS

2. THORUBOS (θόρυβος), a noise, uproar, tumult, is rendered 3986 AG:640D
" tumult " in Matt. 27 : 24 and Mark 5 : 38 ; in Matt. 26 : 5, R.V. (A.V., CB:1263A
" uproar "), so in Mark 14 : 2 ; in Acts 20 : 1, " uproar," A.V. and R.V. ; AKATASTASIA
in 24 : 18, " tumult ; " in 21 : 34, A.V., " tumult " (R.V., " uproar "). ¶ 181 AG:30A

Note : For *thorubeō*, R.V., to make a tumult, see NOISE, *Note* (2). CB:1234B THORUBOS

TURN

2351 AG:363A

1. STREPHŌ (στρέφω) denotes (1) in the Active Voice, (*a*) to turn CB:1272B
(something), Matt. 5 : 39 ; (*b*) to bring back, Matt. 27 : 3 (in the best THORUBEō 2350
texts ; some have No. 2) ; (*c*) reflexively, to turn oneself, to turn the AG:362D
back to people, said of God, Acts 7 : 42 ; (*d*) to turn one thing into another, CB:1272B
Rev. 11 : 6 (the only place where this word occurs after the Acts) ; (2) STREPHō 4762
in the Passive Voice, (*a*) used reflexively, to turn oneself, e.g. Matt. 7 : 6 ; AG:771A
John 20 : 14, 16 ; (*b*) metaphorically, Matt. 18 : 3, R.V., " (except) ye CB:1270B APOSTREPHō
turn " (A.V., " . . . be converted ") ; John 12 : 40 (in the best texts ; some 654
have No. 4). See CONVERT, A, No. 1. AG:100B CB:1237A

2. APOSTREPHŌ (ἀποστρέφω) denotes (*a*) to cause to turn away

(*apo*), to remove, Rom. 11 : 26 ; 2 Tim. 4 : 4 (1st clause) ; metaphorically, to turn away from allegiance, pervert, Luke 23 : 14 ; (*b*) to make to return, put back, Matt. 26 : 52 ; (*c*) in the Passive Voice, used reflexively, to turn oneself away from, Matt. 5 : 42 ; 2 Tim. 1 : 15 ; Tit. 1 : 14 ; Heb. 12 : 25 ; in the Active Voice, Acts 3 : 26. See PERVERT, PUT.¶

1294 3. DIASTREPHŌ (διαστρέφω), to distort (*dia*, asunder), is rendered
AG:189A " to turn aside," R.V. (A.V., " . . . away "), in Acts 13 : 8. See PERVERT,
CB:— No. 2.

1994 4. EPISTREPHŌ (ἐπιστρέφω) is used (*a*) transitively, to make to turn
AG:301A towards (*epi*), Luke 1 : 16, 17 ; Jas 5 : 19, 20 (to convert) ; (*b*) intran-
CB:1246A sitively, to turn oneself round, e.g , in the Passive Voice, Mark 5 : 30 (see RETURN) ; in the Active Voice, Matt. 13 : 15, R.V., " turn again " (A.V., " be converted ") ; Acts 11 : 21 ; 14 : 15 ; 15 : 19 ; 1 Thess. 1 : 9, " ye turned," the aorist tense indicating an immediate and decisive change, consequent upon a deliberate choice ; conversion is a voluntary act in response to the presentation of truth. See CONVERT.

3344 5. METASTREPHŌ (μεταστρέφω) signifies, in the Passive Voice,
AG:513B to be turned (of a change into something different, *meta*) in Acts 2 : 20
CB:— and Jas. 4 : 9 : see PERVERT, No. 3.

5290 6. HUPOSTREPHŌ (ὑποστρέφω) is used intransitively of turning
AG:847C back, behind (*hupo*), e.g., Luke 17 : 15, " turned back ; " in 2 : 45, R.V.,
CB:— " returned : " see RETURN.

576 7. APOBAINŌ (ἀποβαίνω), to go from, is used metaphorically of
AG:88C events, to issue, turn out, Luke 21 : 13 ; Phil. 1 : 19. See GO, No. 21.

3329 8. METAGŌ (μετάγω), to move from one side to another, is rendered
AG:510D to turn about in Jas. 3 : 3, 4.¶

3346 9. METATITHĒMI (μετατίθημι), to change, is translated " turning
AG:513C (the grace of God) " in Jude 4. See CARRY, CHANGE, REMOVE, TRANSLATE.
CB:1258C

344 10. ANAKAMPTŌ (ἀνακάμπτω), *ana*, back, *kamptō*, to bend, is
AG:55C rendered " shall turn . . . again," in Luke 10 : 6. See RETURN.

1624 11. EKTREPŌ (ἐκτρέπω), to cause to turn aside (*ek*, from, *trepō*,
AG:246B to turn), is used in the Passive Voice, with Middle sense, in 1 Tim. 1 : 6 ;
CB:1244A 5 : 15 ; 6 : 20, R.V., " turning away " (A.V., " avoiding ") ; 2 Tim. 4 : 4 (2nd clause) ; Heb. 12 : 13, " be (not) turned out of the way " (R.V., marg., " put out of joint ") ; some adhere to the meaning to turn aside, go astray ; the interpretation depends on the antithesis which follows, " but rather be healed " (R.V.), which is not the antithesis to turning aside or being turned out of the way ; accordingly the marg. is to be preferred (the verb is often used medically).¶ In the Sept., Amos 5 : 8.¶

665 12. APOTREPŌ (ἀποτρέπω), to cause to turn away (*apo*), is used in
AG:101C the Middle Voice in 2 Tim. 3 : 5.¶
CB:1237B

4062 13. PERITREPŌ (περιτρέπω), to turn about (*peri*), is rendered " doth
AG:653A turn (thee to madness) " in Acts 26 : 24, R.V., A.V., " doth make (thee mad)."¶

3179
AG:498D 14. METHISTĒMI (μεθίστημι) is used metaphorically in Acts 19 : 26,

"turned away (much people)." See Put, Remove, Translate.

15. ANASTATOŌ (ἀναστατόω), to stir up, excite, unsettle (*ana*, up, 387
histēmi, to cause to stand), is rendered "have turned (the world) upside AG:61A
down" in Acts 17:6. See Trouble, Uproar. CB:—

16. GINOMAI (γίνομαι), to become, is rendered "shall be turned" 1096
in John 16:20 (of sorrow into joy). AG:158A CB:1248B

17. EKKLINŌ (ἐκκλίνω), to turn aside (*ek*, from, *klinō*, to lean), 1578
is rendered "have . . . turned aside" in Rom. 3:12 (A.V., "are . . . AG:241C
gone out of the way"); 16:17, R.V., "turn away" (A.V., "avoid"); CB:—
1 Pet. 3:11, R.V., ditto (A.V., "eschew").¶

18. DIADECHOMAI (διαδέχομαι), to receive through another, to 1237
receive in turn (*dia*, through, *dechomai*, to receive), occurs in Acts 7:45, AG:182C
R.V., "in their turn . . . when they entered" (A.V., "that came CB:—
after"); the meaning here is 'having received (it) after,' i.e., as from Moses under Joshua's leadership. In the papyri the word is used similarly of visiting as deputy (see also Field, *Notes on the Trans. of the N.T.*, 116).¶

Notes: (1) In Matt. 2:22, A.V., *anachōreō*, to retire, withdraw, is ANACHŌREŌ
rendered "turned aside" (R.V., "withdrew"). (2) For "turned to 402
flight," ***klinō***, Heb. 11:34, see Flight, B. (3) For the phrase "by turn" AG:63C CB:1235A
in 1 Cor. 14:27 see Course, B, Note (3). KLINŌ
2827 AG:436C CB:—

TURNING

TROPĒ (τροπή), used especially of the revolution of the heavenly 5157
orbs (akin to ***trepō***, to turn), occurs in Jas. 1:17, "(neither shadow) AG:827A CB:—
that is cast by turning," R.V. (A.V., "of turning"). For a more detailed treatment of the passage, see Shadow, No. 2.¶

For TURTLE-DOVE see DOVE

For TUTOR see GUARDIAN and INSTRUCTOR, No. 1.

TWAIN, TWO

DUO (δύο) is rendered "twain" in Matt. 5:41; 19:5, 6; 21:31; 1417
27:21, 51; Mark 10:8 (twice); 15:38; in 1 Cor. 6:16 and Eph. 5:31, AG:209A CB:1242B
R.V. (A.V., "two"); Eph. 2:15; in Rev. 19:20, R.V. (A.V., "both").

Notes: (1) In the following phrases the numeral is used distributively: (*a*) *ana duo*, "two apiece," John 2:6 (in some mss., Luke 9:3); in Luke 10:1, "two and two" ('by twos'); (*b*) *kata duo*, "by two," 1 Cor. 14:27; (*c*) *duo duo*, "by two and two," lit., 'two (and) two,' Mark 6:7 (not a Hebraism; the form of expression is used in the papyri); (*d*) *eis duo*, 'into two,' "in twain," Matt. 27:51 and Mark 15:38 (see above). (2) In Luke 17:34 *duo* stands for "two men;" in ver. 35 for "two women."

TWELFTH 1428

DŌDEKATOS (δωδέκατος) occurs in Rev. 21:20.¶ AG:210B CB:—

TWELVE

1427 DŌDEKA (δώδεκα) is used frequently in the Gospels for the twelve
AG:210A Apostles, and in Acts 6 : 2 ; 1 Cor. 15 : 5 ; Rev. 21 : 14b ; of the tribes
CB:1242A of Israel, Matt. 19 : 28 ; Luke 22 : 30 ; Jas. 1 : 1 ; Rev. 21 : 12c (cp. 7 : 5–8 ; 12 : 1) ; in various details relating to the Heavenly Jerusalem, Rev. 21 : 12–21 ; 22 : 2. The number in general is regarded as suggestive of Divine administration.

TWENTY

1501 EIKOSI (εἴκοσι) occurs in Luke 14 : 31 ; John 6 : 19 ; Acts 1 : 15 ;
AG:222A 27 : 28 ; 1 Cor. 10 : 8 ; of the four and twenty elders, in Rev. 4 : 4 (twice),
CB:1243A 10 ; 5 : 8 ; 11 : 16 ; 19 : 4 (combined in one numeral with *tessares*, four, in some mss.).¶

TWICE

1364 DIS (δίς) occurs in Mark 14 : 30, 72 ; Luke 18 : 12 ; Jude 12 ; combined
AG:199D with *muriades*, ten thousand, in Rev. 9 : 16 ; rendered "again" in
CB:— Phil. 4 : 16 and 1 Thess. 2 : 18. See Again.¶

TWINKLING

4493 RHIPĒ (ῥιπή), akin to *rhiptō*, to hurl, was used of any rapid move-
AG:736B ment, e.g., the throw of a javelin, the rush of wind or flame ; in 1 Cor.
CB:1268B 15 : 52 of the twinkling of an eye.¶

For TWO see TWAIN

TWO-EDGED

1366 DISTOMOS (δίστομος), lit., 'two-mouthed' (*dis*, and *stoma*, a mouth),
AG:200A was used of rivers and branching roads ; in the N.T. of swords, Heb.
CB:1242A 4 : 12 ; Rev. 1 : 16 ; 2 : 12, R.V., "two-edged" (A.V., "with two edges").¶ In the Sept., Judg. 3 : 16 ; Psa. 149 : 6 ; Prov. 5 : 4.¶

For TWOFOLD MORE see DOUBLE

TWO HUNDRED

1250 DIAKOSIOI (διακόσιοι) occurs in Mark 6 : 37 ; John 6 : 7 ; 21 : 8 ;
AG:185A Acts 23 : 23 (twice) ; 27 : 37, "two hundred (threescore and sixteen) ;"
CB:— Rev. 11 : 3, "(a thousand) two hundred (and threescore) ;" so 12 : 6.¶

Note : In Acts 27 : 37, some ancient authorities read "about threescore and sixteen souls" (R.V., margin). The confusion was quite natural when the word *diakosioi* was not written in full but represented by one Greek letter. The larger number is by no means improbable : Josephus sailed for Rome in A.D. 63 in a ship which had 600 on board (*Life*, ch. 3).

For TWO THOUSAND see THOUSAND, Note (1)

For UNAPPROACHABLE, 1 Tim. 6 : 16, R.V., see APPROACH, B

UNAWARES LANTHANŌ

Notes: (1) In Heb. 13 : 2, *lanthanō*, to escape notice, is used with the aorist participle of *xenizō*, to entertain, signifying "entertained . . . unawares" (an idiomatic usage common in classical Greek). (2) For *aiphnidios*, "unawares," in Luke 21 : 34, A.V., see SUDDENLY. (3) In Gal. 2 : 4, A.V., *pareisaktos*, brought in secretly, is rendered "unawares brought in." See PRIVILY, *Note*: cp. BRING, No. 17.¶ (4) In Jude 4, A.V., *pareisdunō*, to slip in secretly, is rendered "crept in unawares." See CREEP, A, No. 2.¶

2990 AG:466B CB:1256C AIPHNIDIOS 160 AG:26D CB:— PAREISAKTOS 3920 AG:624C CB:— PAREISDUNŌ 3921 AG:624D CB:—

UNBELIEF

1. APISTIA (ἀπιστία), "unbelief" 12 times, but see BELIEF, C, Note (2) for references. 570 AG:85C CB:1236C

2. APEITHEIA (ἀπείθεια) is always rendered "disobedience" in the R.V.; in Rom. 11 : 30, 32 and Heb. 4 : 6, 11, A.V., "unbelief." See DISOBEDIENCE, A, No. 1. 543 AG:82C CB:1236B

UNBELIEVER

APISTOS (ἄπιστος), an adjective, is used as a noun, rendered "unbeliever" in 2 Cor. 6 : 15 and 1 Tim. 5 : 8, R.V.; plural in 1 Cor. 6 : 6 and 2 Cor. 6 : 14; A.V. only, Luke 12 : 46 (R.V., "unfaithful"). See BELIEF, C, Note (3), FAITHLESS, INCREDIBLE. 571 AG:85D CB:1236C

UNBELIEVING

A. Adjective.

APISTOS (ἄπιστος): see BELIEF, C, Note (3). 571 AG:85D CB:1236C

B. Verb.

APEITHEŌ (ἀπειθέω): see DISBELIEVE, DISOBEDIENT, C. 544 AG:82C CB:1236B

UNBLAMEABLE, UNBLAMEABLY

A. Adjectives.

1. AMEMPTOS (ἄμεμπτος), "unblameable" (from *a*, negative, and *memphomai*, to find fault), is so rendered in 1 Thess. 3 : 13, i.e., free from all valid charge. See BLAME, B, No. 3. 273 AG:45A CB:1234C

2. AMŌMOS (ἄμωμος): see BLEMISH, B. 299 AG:47D CB:1234C

B. Adverb.

274 AMEMPTŌS (ἀμέμπτως) is used in 1 Thess. 2 : 10, " unblameably,"
AG:45A CB:1234C signifying that no charge could be maintained, whatever charges might be made. See BLAME, C.

For UNCEASING see CEASE, B. For UNCEASINGLY, R.V., in Rom. 1 : 9, see CEASE, C

UNCERTAIN, UNCERTAINLY, UNCERTAINTY

A. Adjective.

82 ADĒLOS (ἄδηλος) denotes (*a*) unseen ; with the article, translated
AG:16C CB:— " which appear not " (*a*, negative, *dēlos*, evident), Luke 11 : 44 ; (*b*) " uncertain," indistinct, 1 Cor. 14 : 8.¶ In the Sept., Ps. 51 : 6.¶

B. Adverb.

84 AG:16D ADĒLŌS (ἀδήλως), uncertainly (akin to A), occurs in 1 Cor. 9 : 26.¶

CB:1233A

C. Noun.

83 AG:16D ADĒLOTĒS (ἀδηλότης), uncertainty (akin to A and B), occurs in 1
CB:— Tim. 6 : 17, " (the) uncertainty (of riches)," R.V. (the A.V. translates it as an adjective, " uncertain "), i.e., riches the special character of which is their uncertainty ; the Greek phrase is a rhetorical way of stressing the noun " riches ; " when a genitive (here " of riches ") precedes the governing noun (here " uncertainty ") the genitive receives emphasis.¶

UNCHANGEABLE

531 AG:80D APARABATOS (ἀπαράβατος) is used of the priesthood of Christ, in
CB:1236B Heb. 7 : 24, " unchangeable," unalterable, inviolable, R.V., marg. (a meaning found in the papyri) ; the more literal meaning in A.V. and R.V. margins, " that doth not pass from one to another," is not to be preferred. This active meaning is not only untenable, and contrary to the constant usage of the word, but does not adequately fit with either the preceding or the succeeding context.¶

For UNCIRCUMCISED and UNCIRCUMCISION see CIRCUMCISION

UNCLEAN

A. Adjectives.

169 1. AKATHARTOS (ἀκάθαρτος), unclean, impure (*a*, negative, *kathairō*,
AG:29A CB:1234B to purify), is used (*a*) of unclean spirits, frequently in the Synoptists, not in John's Gospel ; in Acts 5 : 16 ; 8 : 7 ; Rev. 16 : 13 ; 18 : 2a (in the 2nd clause the birds are apparently figurative of destructive Satanic agencies) ; (*b*) ceremonially, Acts 10 : 14, 28 ; 11 : 8 ; 1 Cor. 7 : 14 ; (*c*)
-TēS 168 morally, 2 Cor. 6 : 17, including (*b*), R.V.; " no unclean thing ; " Eph.
AG:29A 5 : 5 ; Rev. 17 : 4, R.V., " the unclean things " (A.V. follows the texts
CB:— which have the noun *akathartēs*, " the filthiness ").
2839 AG:438A 2. KOINOS (κοινός), common, is translated " unclean " in Rom. 14 : 14
CB:1255B (thrice) ; in Rev. 21 : 27, R.V. (A.V., " that defileth," follows the inferior

texts which have the verb *koinoō:* see B). See COMMON, DEFILE, C, UNHOLY, No. 2.

B. Verb.

KOINOŌ (*κοινόω*), to make *koinos*, to defile, is translated " unclean " 2840
in Heb. 9 : 13, A.V., where the perfect participle, Passive, is used with AG:438B
the article, hence the R.V., " them that have been defiled." See DEFILE, CB:1255B
A, No. 1.

C. Noun.

AKATHARSIA (*ἀκαθαρσία*), akin to A, No. 1, denotes uncleanness, 167
(*a*) physical, Matt. 23 : 27 (instances in the papyri speak of tenants keeping AG:28D
houses in good condition) ; (*b*) moral, Rom. 1 : 24 ; 6 : 19 ; 2 Cor. 12 : 21 ; CB:1234B
Gal. 5 : 19 ; Eph. 4 : 19 ; 5 : 3 ; Col. 3 : 5 ; 1 Thess. 2 : 3 (suggestive of the fact that sensuality and evil doctrine are frequently associated) ; 4 : 7.¶

Note : In 2 Pet. 2 : 10, A.V., *miasmos*, a defilement, is rendered " un- 3394
cleanness ; " see DEFILEMENT, B, No. 2.¶ AG:521A
CB:1258C

For UNCLOTHED see STRIP

UNCOMELY

ASCHĒMŌN (*ἀσχήμων*), shapeless (*a*, negative, *schēma*, a form), 809
the opposite of *euschēmōn*, comely, is used in 1 Cor. 12 : 23.¶ In the AG:119B
Sept., Gen. 34 : 7 ; Deut. 24 : 3.¶ CB:1238A

Note : For the verb *aschēmoneō*, rendered to behave oneself uncomely 807
in 1 Cor. 7 : 36, A.V., see BEHAVE, No. 4. AG:119B
CB:—

UNCONDEMNED

AKATAKRITOS (*ἀκατάκριτος*), rendered " uncondemned " in Acts 178
16 : 37 ; 22 : 25 (*a*, negative, *katakrinō*, to condemn), properly means AG:29D
' without trial,' not yet tried. Sir W. M. Ramsay points out that the CB:—
Apostle, in claiming his rights, would probably use the Roman phrase *re incognita*, i.e., ' without investigating our case ' (*The Cities of St. Paul*, p. 225).¶

For UNCORRUPTIBLE see CORRUPT, C, No. 2. For UNCORRUPTNESS, see CORRUPT, B, No. 4

UNCOVER

APOSTEGAZŌ (*ἀποστεγάζω*) signifies to unroof (*apo*, from, *stegē*, 648
a roof), Mark 2 : 4.¶ AG:98C
CB:—

For UNCOVERED, 1 Cor. 11 : 5, 13, see UNVEILED

For UNCTION see ANOINT, B

UNDEFILED

283 AG:46B AMIANTOS (ἀμίαντος), undefiled, free from contamination (*a*, negative,
CB:1234C *miainō*, to defile), is used (*a*) of Christ, Heb. 7 : 26 ; (*b*) of pure religion,
Jas. 1 : 27 ; (*c*) of the eternal inheritance of believers, 1 Pet. 1 : 4 ; (*d*)
of the marriage bed as requiring to be free from unlawful sexual intercourse, Heb. 13 : 4.¶

UNDER, UNDERNEATH

5270 AG:844D 1. HUPOKATŌ (ὑποκάτω), an adverb signifying under, is used as a
CB:— preposition and rendered " under " in Mark 6 : 11 ; 7 : 28 ; Luke 8 : 16 ;
Heb. 2 : 8 ; Rev. 5 : 3, 13 ; 6 : 9 ; 12 : 1 ; " underneath " in Matt. 22 : 44,
2736 R.V. (Mark 12 : 36 in some mss.) ; John 1 : 50, R.V. (A.V., " under ").¶
AG:425B 2. KATŌTERŌ (κατωτέρω), the comparative degree of *katō*, below,
CB:— 1640 beneath, occurs in Matt. 2 : 16, " under."
AG:248A 3. ELASSON (ἐλάσσον), the neuter of the adjective *elassōn*, less, is
CB:1244A EPI used adverbially in 1 Tim. 5 : 9, " under " (or ' less than '). See LESS.
1909 *Notes :* (1) The preposition *epi*, upon, is rendered " under " in Heb.
AG:285D CB:1245C 7 : 11 ; 9 : 15 ; 10 : 28, A.V. (R.V., " on *the word of* "). (2) The pre-
EN position *en*, in, is rendered " under " in Matt. 7 : 6 ; Rom. 3 : 19 (1st part).
1722 AG:258B (3) The usual preposition is *hupo*.
CB:1244B HUPO 5259

UNDERGIRD

AG:843A HUPOZŌNNUMI (ὑποζώννυμι), *hupo*, under, *zōnnumi*, to gird, is used
CB:1252A HUPOZŌNNUMI of frapping a ship, Acts 27 : 17, bracing the timbers of a vessel by means
5269 of strong ropes.¶
AG:844D CB:—

UNDERSTAND, UNDERSTOOD

A. Verbs.

4920 AG:790A 1. SUNIĒMI (συνίημι), primarily, to bring or set together, is used
CB:1270C metaphorically of perceiving, understanding, uniting (*sun*), so to speak,
the perception with what is perceived, e.g., Matt. 13 : 13–15, 19, 23, 51 ;
15 : 10 ; 16 : 12 ; 17 : 13, and similar passages in Mark and Luke ;
Acts 7 : 25 (twice) ; 28 : 26, 27 ; in Rom. 3 : 11, the present participle,
with the article, is used as a noun, lit., ' there is not the understanding
(one),' in a moral and spiritual sense ; Rom. 15 : 21 ; 2 Cor. 10 : 12, R.V.,
" are (without) understanding," A.V., " are (not) wise ; " Eph. 5 : 17,
R.V., " understand." See CONSIDER, Note (2).

3539 (NOIEō) 2. NOEŌ (νοέω), to perceive with the mind, as distinct from per-
AG:540B ception by feeling, is so used in Matt. 15 : 17, A.V., " understand," R.V.,
CB:1259C " perceive ; " 16 : 9, 11 ; 24 : 15 (here rather perhaps in the sense of
considering) and parallels in Mark (not in Luke) ; John 12 : 40 ; Rom.
1 : 20 ; 1 Tim. 1 : 7 ; Heb. 11 : 3 ; in Eph. 3 : 4, A.V., " may under-
1097 stand " (R.V., " can perceive ") ; 3 : 20, " think ; " 2 Tim. 2 : 7, " con-
AG:160D sider." See CONSIDER, No. 4.¶
CB:1248B 3. GINŌSKŌ (γινώσκω), to know, to come to know, is translated to

understand in the A.V. in Matt. 26 : 10 and John 8 : 27 (R.V., to perceive);
A.V. and R.V. in John 8 : 43; 10 : 6; in 10 : 38, R.V. (in some texts
pisteuō, A.V., " believe "); A.V. and R.V. in 12 : 16; 13 : 7, R.V., A.V.,
" know " (see Note under KNOW, No. 2); Acts 8 : 30; in Phil. 1 : 12,
A.V., R.V., " know " (in some texts, Acts 24 : 11, A.V.). See KNOW,
No. 1.

4. EPISTAMAI (ἐπίσταμαι), to know well, is rendered to understand 1987
in Mark 14 : 68; Jude 10, R.V., 2nd clause (A.V., " know "). See AG:300A
KNOW, No. 5. CB:1246A

5. PUNTHANOMAI (πυνθάνομαι), to inquire, is rendered to under- 4441
stand in Acts 23 : 34. See INQUIRE. AG:729C CB:—

6. GNŌRIZŌ (γνωρίζω), to make known, is rendered " I give . . . to 1107
understand " in 1 Cor. 12 : 3. See KNOW, No. 8. AG:163B CB:1248B

7. AGNOEŌ (ἀγνοέω), to be ignorant, is rendered " they understood 50
not " in Mark 9 : 32; Luke 9 : 45; in 2 Pet. 2 : 12, A.V., R.V., " they AG:11B
are ignorant of." See IGNORANT, B, No. 1. CB:1233B

Notes: (1) In 1 Cor. 13 : 2, A.V., *oida*, to know, to perceive, is rendered OIDA
" understand " (R.V., " know "); so in 14 : 16. (2) For *manthanō*, 1492 (EIDō) AG:555D
rendered " understand " in Acts 23 : 27, A.V., see LEARN, No. 1. (3) CB:1260B
In 1 Cor. 13 : 11, A.V., *phroneō*, to be minded, is rendered "I understood " MANTHANō 3129
(R.V., " I felt "). (4) For *parakoloutheō*, Luke 1 : 3, A.V., " have perfect AG:490B
understanding of," see TRACE. CB:1257C PHRONEō

B. Adjectives. 5426

1 EUSĒMOS (εὔσημος) primarily denotes conspicuous or glorious (as AG:866A CB:1264C
in Ps. 81 : 3, Sept.; E.V., " solemn "¶), then, distinct, clear to under- PARAKOLOUTHEō
standing, 1 Cor. 14 : 9, " easy to be understood " (A.V., marg., " signifi- 3877
cant ").¶ AG:618D CB:1262A

2. DUSNOĒTOS (δυσνόητος), hard to be understood (*dus*, a prefix EUSēMOS
like Eng., *mis-* or *un-*, and A, No. 2), occurs in 2 Pet. 3 : 16.¶ 2154 AG:326C

DUSNOēTOS

UNDERSTANDING 1425 AG:209D

A. Nouns. CB:1242C

1. NOUS (νοῦς), for which see MIND, No. 1, is translated " under- 3563
standing " in Luke 24 : 45, A.V. (R.V., " mind "); 1 Cor. 14 : 14, 15 AG:544C CB:1260A
(twice), 19; Phil. 4 : 7; Rev. 13 : 18.

2. SUNESIS (σύνεσις), akin to *suniēmi*, to set together, to understand, 4907
denotes (*a*) the understanding, the mind or intelligence, Mark 12 : 33; AG:788C CB:1270C
(*b*) understanding, reflective thought, Luke 2 : 47; 1 Cor. 1 : 19, R.V.,
" prudence;" Eph. 3 : 4, R.V. (A.V., " knowledge "); Col. 1 : 9; 2 : 2;
2 Tim. 2 : 7 ¶ See PRUDENCE, No. 2.

3. DIANOIA (διάνοια), for which see MIND, No. 2, is rendered " under- 1271
standing " in Eph. 4 : 18; 1 John 5 : 20 (in some texts, Eph. 1 : 18, A.V., AG:187A CB:1241B
for *kardia*, " heart," R.V.).

B. Adjective. 801

ASUNETOS (ἀσύνετος), without understanding or discernment (*a*, AG:118C CB:1238A

SUNETOS negative, *sunetos*, intelligent, understanding), is translated "without
4908 AG:788D understanding" in Matt. 15 : 16; Mark 7 : 18; Rom. 1 : 31; 10 : 19,
CB:1270C R.V., "void of understanding" (A.V., "foolish"); in Rom. 1 : 21, R.V.,
"senseless" (A.V., "foolish").¶

5424 AG:865D *Note:* In 1 Cor. 14 : 20, A.V., *phrēn*, the mind, is translated "under-
CB:1264C standing" (twice), R.V., "mind."

For UNDONE (leave) see LEAVE, No. 1

UNDRESSED

46 AG:10D AGNAPHOS (ἄγναφος), uncarded (*a*, negative, *knaptō*, to card wool),
CB:— is rendered "undressed," of cloth, in Matt. 9 : 16 and Mark 2 : 21, R.V.
(A.V., "new").¶

For UNEQUALLY see YOKED

UNFAITHFUL

571 AG:85D APISTOS (ἄπιστος), unbelieving, faithless, is translated "unfaithful"
CB:1236C in Luke 12 : 46, R.V. (A.V., "unbelievers"). See Belief, C, Note (3),
Faithless, Incredible.

For UNFEIGNED see DISSIMULATION, C

For UNFRUITFUL see FRUIT, B, No. 2

UNGODLINESS, UNGODLY

A. Noun.

763 AG:114C ASEBEIA (ἀσέβεια), impiety, ungodliness, is used of (*a*) general
CB:1238A impiety, Rom. 1 : 18; 11 : 26; 2 Tim. 2 : 16; Tit. 2 : 12; (*b*) ungodly
deeds, Jude 15, R.V., "works of ungodliness"; (*c*) of lusts or desires
after evil things, Jude 18. It is the opposite of *eusebeia*, godliness.¶

458 AG:71D *Note:* *Anomia* is disregard for, or defiance of, God's laws; *asebeia*
CB:1235C is the same attitude towards God's Person.

B. Adjective.

765 AG:114C ASEBĒS (ἀσεβής), impious, ungodly (akin to A), without reverence
CB:1238A for God, not merely irreligious, but acting in contravention of God's
demands, Rom. 4 : 5; 5 : 6; 1 Tim. 1 : 9; 1 Pet. 4 : 18; 2 Pet. 2 : 5
(v. 6 in some mss.); 3 : 7; Jude 4, 15 (twice).¶

C. Verb.

764 AG:114C ASEBEŌ (ἀσεβέω), akin to A and B, signifies (*a*) to be or live ungodly,
CB:1238A 2 Pet. 2 : 6; (*b*) to commit ungodly deeds, Jude 15.¶

UNHOLY

462 AG:72C 1. ANOSIOS (ἀνόσιος) (*a*, negative, *n*, euphonic, *hosios*, holy), unholy,
CB:1235C profane, occurs in 1 Tim. 1 : 9; 2 Tim. 3 : 2.¶ Cp. Holy. In the Sept.,
Ezek. 22 : 9.¶

2. KOINON (κοινόν), the neut. of *koinos*, common, is translated " an 2839
unholy thing " in Heb. 10 : 29. See COMMON, DEFILE, C, UNCLEAN, A, AG:438A CB:1255B
No. 2.

For UNITED, Rom. 6 : 5, R.V., see PLANT, C; in Heb. 4 : 2, see UNITED See CLEAVE
MIXED (with), Note UNIVERSE See WORLD

UNITY

HENOTĒS (ἑνότης), from *hen*, the neuter of *heis*, one, is used in 1775
Eph. 4 : 3, 13.¶ AG:267C CB:1250A

UNJUST

ADIKOS (ἄδικος), not in conformity with *dikē*, right, is rendered 94
" unjust " in the A.V. and R.V. in Matt. 5 : 45; Luke 18 : 11; Acts AG:18B CB:1233A
24 : 15; elsewhere for the A.V. " unjust " the R.V. has " unrighteous."
See UNRIGHTEOUS.

Note: For *adikeō*, to be unrighteous, or do unrighteousness, Rev. ADIKEō 91
22 : 11, R.V., and *adikia*, " unrighteous," Luke 16 : 8 and 18 : 6, R.V., AG:17C
see UNRIGHTEOUSNESS. CB:1233A ADIKIA 93 AG:17D CB:1233A

For UNKNOWN see IGNORANCE, B, No. 1, and KNOW, B, No. 4

UNLADE

APOPHORTIZŌ (ἀποφορτίζω), to discharge a cargo (*apo*, from, *phortizō*, (-OMAI) 670
to load), is used in Acts 21 : 3.¶ AG:102 CB:—

UNLAWFUL

ATHEMITOS (ἀθέμιτος), a late form for *athemistos* (*themis*, custom, 111
right; in classical Greek, divine law), contrary to what is right, is rendered AG:20D CB:—
" an unlawful thing " (neuter) in Acts 10 : 28; in 1 Pet. 4 : 3, " abominable."¶

Note: For 2 Pet. 2 : 8, A.V., see LAWLESS.

UNLEARNED

1. AGRAMMATOS (ἀγράμματος), lit., unlettered (*grammata*, letters: 62
graphō, to write), Acts 4 : 13, is explained by Grimm-Thayer as meaning AG:13B CB:1233C
" unversed in the learning of the Jewish schools; " in the papyri, however, it occurs very frequently in a formula used by one who signs for another who cannot write, which suggests that the rulers, elders and scribes regarded the Apostles as " unlettered " (Moulton and Milligan).¶ 261

2. AMATHĒS (ἀμαθής), unlearned (*manthanō*, to learn), is translated AG:42B CB:—
" unlearned " in 2 Pet. 3 : 16, A.V. (R.V., " ignorant ").¶ 521

3. APAIDEUTOS (ἀπαίδευτος), uninstructed (*paideuō*, to train, teach), AG:79D
is translated " unlearned " in 2 Tim. 2 : 23, A.V. (R.V., " ignorant ").¶ CB:1236A 2399

Note: For *idiōtēs*, rendered " unlearned " in 1 Cor. 14 : 16, 23, 24, AG:370C
see IGNORANT, No. 4. CB:1252C

For UNLEAVENED see BREAD, No. 2

For UNLESS see EXCEPT

UNLIFTED

343 ANAKALUPTŌ (ἀνακαλύπτω), to uncover, unveil, used in 2 Cor. 3 : 14
AG:55C
CB:1235A with the negative *mē*, not, is rendered " unlifted," R.V., A.V., " untaken away " (a paraphrase rather than translation); the R.V. marg., " remaineth, it not being revealed that it is done away," is not to be preferred. The best rendering seems to be, ' the veil remains unlifted (for it is in Christ that it is done away).' Judaism does not recognise the vanishing of the glory of the Law as a means of life, under God's grace in Christ. In 3 : 18 the R.V., " unveiled (face) " (A.V., " open ") continues the metaphor of the veil (vv. 13–17), referring to hindrances to the perception of spiritual realities, hindrances removed in the unveiling.¶

UNLOOSE

3089 LUŌ (λύω), to loose, is rendered to unloose in Mark 1 : 7; Luke 3 : 16;
AG:483C
CB:1257B John 1 : 27; in Acts 13 : 25, R.V.: see LOOSE.

UNMARRIED

22 AGAMOS (ἄγαμος), *a*, negative, *gameō*, to marry, occurs in 1 Cor.
AG:4B
CB:1233B 7 : 8, 11, 32, 34.¶

UNMERCIFUL

415 ANELEĒMŌN (ἀνελεήμων), without mercy (*a*, negative, *n*, euphonic,
AG:64C
CB:— *eleēmōn*, merciful), occurs in Rom. 1 : 21.¶

For UNMIXED, Rev. 14 : 10, R.V., see MIXTURE, Note

For UNMOVEABLE, Acts 27 : 41, see MOVE, B, No. 1; in 1 Cor. 15 : 58, MOVE, B, No. 2

UNPREPARED

532 APARASKEUASTOS (ἀπαρασκεύαστος), from *a*, negative, and
AG:80D
CB:1236B *paraskeuazō* (see PREPARE, B, No. 4), occurs in 2 Cor. 9 : 4.¶

UNPROFITABLE, UNPROFITABLENESS

A. Adjectives.

888 1. ACHREIOS (ἀχρεῖος), useless (*chreia*, use), unprofitable, occurs
AG:128C
CB:— in Matt. 25 : 30 and Luke 17 : 10.¶ In the Sept., 2 Sam. 6 : 22.¶

890 2. ACHRĒSTOS (ἄχρηστος), unprofitable, unserviceable (*chrēstos*,
AG:128C
CB:1233A serviceable), is said of Onesimus, Philm. 11, antithetically to *euchrēstos*,
(-ON) profitable, with a play on the name of the converted slave (from *onēsis*, profit).¶

Note: *Achreios* is more distinctly negative than *achrēstos*, which suggests positively hurtful.

3. ALUSITELĒS (ἀλυσιτελής), not advantageous, not making good 255
the expense involved (*lusitelēs*, useful), occurs in Heb. 13 : 17.¶ AG:41C
CB:—

4. ANŌPHELĒS (ἀνωφελής), not beneficial or serviceable (*a*, negative, 512 (-LES)
n, euphonic, *ōpheleō*, to do good, to benefit), is rendered "unprofitable" AG:77C
in Tit. 3 : 9; in the neuter, used as a noun, "unprofitableness," Heb. CB:—
7 : 18, said of the Law as not accomplishing that which the "better hope" could alone bring.¶ In the Sept., Prov. 28 : 3; Isa. 44 : 10; Jer. 2 : 8.¶

B. Verb.

ACHREOŌ, or ACHREIOŌ (ἀχρεόω), akin to A, No. 1, to make use- 889
less, occurs in Rom. 3 : 12, in the Passive Voice, rendered "they have . . . AG:128C
become unprofitable."¶ CB:—

For UNQUENCHABLE see QUENCH

UNREASONABLE

1. ALOGOS (ἄλογος), without reason, irrational, is rendered "un- 249
reasonable" in Acts 25 : 27. See BRUTE. AG:41A
CB:1234C

2. ATOPOS (ἄτοπος), lit., 'out of place' (*topos*, a place), is translated 824
"unreasonable" in 2 Thess. 3 : 2, where the meaning intended seems to AG:120C
be 'perverse,' 'truculent.' See AMISS. CB:—

For UNREBUKEABLE see BLAME, B, No. 5

UNRIGHTEOUS

ADIKOS (ἄδικος), not conforming to *dikē*, right, is translated "un- 94
righteous" in Luke 16 : 10 (twice), R.V., 11; Rom. 3 : 5; 1 Cor. 6 : 1, AG:18B
R.V.; 6 : 9; Heb. 6 : 10; 1 Pet. 3 : 18, R.V.; 2 Pet. 2 : 9, R.V.: see CB:1233A
UNJUST.

UNRIGHTEOUSNESS

A. Noun.

ADIKIA (ἀδικία) denotes (*a*) injustice, Luke 18 : 6, lit., 'the judge of 93
injustice;' Rom. 9 : 14; (*b*) unrighteousness, iniquity, e.g., Luke 16 : 8, AG:17D
lit., "the steward of unrighteousness," R.V. marg., i.e., characterized by CB:1233A
unrighteousness; Rom. 1 : 18, 29; 2 : 8; 3 : 5; 6 : 13; 1 Cor. 13 : 6, R.V., "unrighteousness;" 2 Thess. 2 : 10, "[with all (lit., in every) deceit] of unrighteousness," i.e., deceit such as unrighteousness uses, and that in every variety; Antichrist and his ministers will not be restrained by any scruple from words or deeds calculated to deceive; 2 Thess. 2 : 12, of those who have pleasure in it, not an intellectual but a moral evil; distaste for truth is the precursor of the rejection of it; 2 Tim. 2 : 19, R.V.; 1 John 1 : 9, which includes (*c*); (*c*) a deed or deeds violating law and justice (virtually the same as *adikēma*, an unrighteous act), e.g., Luke 13 : 27, "iniquity;" 2 Cor. 12 : 13, "wrong," the wrong of depriving

another of what is his own, here ironically of a favour ; Heb. 8 : 12, 1st clause, " iniquities," lit., ' unrighteousnesses ' (plural, not as A.V.) ; 2 Pet. 2 : 13, 15, R.V., " wrong doing," A.V., " unrighteousness ; " 1 John 5 : 17. See INIQUITY.

458 AG:71D *Notes :* (1) In 2 Cor. 6 : 14, A.V., ***anomia***, lawlessness, is translated
CB:1235C " unrighteousness " (R.V., " iniquity "). (2) ***Adikia*** is the comprehensive term for wrong, or wrong-doing, as between persons ; ***anomia***, lawlessness, is the rejection of Divine law, or wrong committed against it.

B. Verb.

91 AG:17C ADIKEŌ (ἀδικέω), to do wrong, is rendered in Rev. 22 : 11, R.V.,
CB:1233A firstly, " he that is unrighteous," lit., ' the doer of unrighteousness ' (present participle of the verb, with the article), secondly, " let him do unrighteousness (still)," the retributive and permanent effect of a persistent course of unrighteous-doing (A.V., " he that is unjust, let him be unjust "). See HURT, OFFENDER, Note, WRONG.

For UNRIPE, UNTIMELY, see FIG, No. 2

UNRULY

506 AG:76D 1. ANUPOTAKTOS (ἀνυπότακτος), not subject to rule (*a*, negative,
CB:— ***n***, euphonic, ***hupotassō***, to put in subjection), is used (*a*) of things, Heb. 2 : 8, R.V., " not subject " (A.V., " not put under ") ; (*b*) of persons, " unruly," 1 Tim. 1 : 9, R.V. (A.V., " disobedient ") ; Tit. 1 : 6, 10. See DISOBEDIENT, B, Note.¶

813 AG:119C 2. ATAKTOS (ἄτακτος) is rendered " unruly " in 1 Thess. 5 : 14, A.V.
CB:— (marg. and R.V., " disorderly "). See DISORDERLY, A.¶

183 AG:30B *Note :* In Jas. 3 : 8, some texts have ***akataschetos***, ' that cannot be
CB:— restrained,' A.V., " unruly : " see RESTLESS.¶

UNSEARCHABLE

419 AG:65A 1. ANEXERAUNĒTOS, or ANEXEREUNĒTOS (ἀνεξεραύνητος),
CB:1235C ***a***, negative, ***n***, euphonic, ***ex*** (***ek***), out, ***eraunaō***, to search, examine, is used in Rom. 11 : 33, of the judgments of God.¶

421 AG:65A 2. ANEXICHNIASTOS (ἀνεξιχνίαστος), with the same prefixes as in
CB:— No. 1, and an adjectival form akin to *ichneuō*, to trace out (*ichnos*, a footprint, a track), is translated " unsearchable " in Eph. 3 : 8, of the riches of Christ ; in Rom. 11 : 33, " past tracing out," of the ways of the Lord (cp. No. 1, in the same verse). The ways of God are the outworkings of His judgment. Of the two questions in ver. 34, the first seems to have reference to No. 1, the second to No. 2. See FIND, Note (3), TRACE.¶

UNSEEMLINESS, UNSEEMLY

808 AG:119B ASCHĒMOSUNĒ (ἀσχημοσύνη), from ***aschēmōn***, unseemly, is rendered
CB:— " unseemliness " in Rom. 1 : 27, R.V. : see SHAME, No. 4.

Note : For " behave . . . unseemly " see BEHAVE, No. 4.

For UNSETTLE, Gal. 5 : 12, R.V., see STIR, No. 12

For UNSKILFUL, Heb. 5 : 13, see EXPERIENCE, No. 1

UNSPEAKABLE

1. ANEKDIĒGĒTOS (ἀνεκδιήγητος) denotes inexpressible (*a*, negative, 411
n, euphonic, *ekdiēgeomai*, to declare, relate), 2 Cor. 9 : 15, "unspeakable" AG:64B
(of the gift of God) ; regarding the various explanations of the gift, it CB:—
seems most suitable to view it as the gift of His Son.¶

2. ANEKLALĒTOS (ἀνεκλάλητος) denotes unable to be told out 412
(*eklaleō*, to speak out), 1 Pet. 1 : 8, of the believer's joy.¶ AG:64B CB:—

3. ARRHĒTOS (ἄρρητος), primarily, unspoken (*a*, negative, *rhētos*, 731
spoken), denotes unspeakable, 2 Cor. 12 : 4, of the words heard by Paul AG:109C
when caught up into Paradise.¶ The word is common in sacred CB:1237C
inscriptions especially in connection with the Greek Mysteries ; hence Moulton and Milligan suggest the meaning 'words too sacred to be uttered.'

UNSPIRITUAL See CARNAL

For UNSPOTTED see SPOT, C

UNSTABLE, UNSTEDFAST

1. ASTĒRIKTOS (ἀστήρικτος), *a*, negative, *stērizō*, to fix, is used in 793
2 Pet. 2 : 14 ; 3 : 16, A.V., "unstable," R.V., "unstedfast."¶ AG:118A CB:—

2. AKATASTATOS (ἀκατάστατος), from *kathistēmi*, to set in order, 182
is rendered "unstable" in Jas. 1 : 8 : see RESTLESS. AG:30B CB:—

For UNTAKEN AWAY, 2 Cor. 3 : 14, A.V., see UNLIFTED

UNTHANKFUL

ACHARISTOS (ἀχάριστος) denotes ungrateful, thankless (*charis*, 884
thanks), Luke 6 : 35 ; 2 Tim. 3 : 2.¶ AG:128B CB:—

UNTIE See LOOSE

UNTIL and UNTO : see † p. 1

For UNTIMELY see FIG, No. 2

For UNTOWARD see CROOKED

UNVEILED

AKATAKALUPTOS (ἀκατακάλυπτος), uncovered (*a*, negative, 177
katakaluptō, to cover), is used in 1 Cor. 11 : 5, 13, R.V., "unveiled," AG:29D
with reference to the injunction forbidding women to be unveiled in a CB:1234A
church gathering.¶ Whatever the character of the covering, it is to be on her head as "a sign of authority" (ver. 10), R.V., the meaning of which is indicated in ver. 3 in the matter of headships, and the reasons for

which are given in vv. 7–9, and in the phrase "because of the angels," intimating their witness of, and interest in, that which betokens the headship of Christ. The injunctions were neither Jewish, which required men to be veiled in prayer, nor Greek, by which men and women were alike unveiled. The Apostle's instructions were "the commandment of the Lord" (14 : 37) and were for all the churches (vv. 33, 34).

343 AG:55C *Note:* For the verb *anakaluptō*, rendered "unveiled" in 2 Cor. 3 : 18,
CB:1235A R.V., see UNLIFTED (2nd ref.).

UNWASHEN

449 AG:69D ANIPTOS (ἄνιπτος), unwashed (*a*, negative, *niptō*, to wash), occurs
CB:1235C in Matt. 15 : 20; Mark 7 : 2 (ver. 5 in some mss.).¶

UNWILLING

2309 AG:354D *Note:* "I am unwilling" is the R.V. rendering of *thelō*, to will, with
CB:1271C the negative *ou*, in 3 John 13 (A.V., "I will not").

UNWISE

453 AG:70D 1. ANOĒTOS (ἀνόητος) is translated "unwise" in Rom. 1 : 14, A.V.;
CB:1235C see FOOLISH, No. 2.

878 AG:127D 2. APHRŌN (ἄφρων) is translated "unwise" in Eph. 5 : 17, A.V.;
CB:1236C see FOOLISH, No. 1.

781 AG:116C 3. ASOPHOS (ἄσοφος), *a*, negative, is rendered "unwise" in Eph.
CB:1238A 5 : 15, R.V. (A.V., "fools").¶

UNWORTHILY, UNWORTHY

A. Adverb.

371 AG:58D ANAXIŌS (ἀναξίως) is used in 1 Cor. 11 : 27, of partaking of the
CB:1235B Lord's Supper unworthily, i.e., treating it as a common meal, the bread and cup as common things, not apprehending their solemn symbolic import. In the best texts the word is not found in ver. 29 (see R.V.).¶

B. Adjective.

370 AG:58C ANAXIOS (ἀνάξιος), *a*, negative, *n*, euphonic, *axios*, worthy, is used
CB:1235B in 1 Cor. 6 : 2. In modern Greek it signifies "incapable."¶

514 AG:78A *Note:* In Acts 13 : 46, "unworthy" represents the adjective *axios*,
CB:1238B preceded by the negative *ouk*.

UP

ANATELLŌ 393 *Notes:* (1) In Matt. 13 : 6 and Mark 4 : 6, A.V., *anatellō*, to rise
AG:62A (of the sun), is rendered "was up." See RISE. (2) The adverb is
CB:1235B ANŌ used with numerous Eng. verbs to translate single Greek verbs. In
507 John 11 : 41 and Heb. 12 : 15, however, the adverb *anō*, up, is used
AG:76D CB:1235B separately: see ABOVE, BRIM, HIGH.

For UPBRAID see REPROACH, B, No. 1

UPHOLD

PHERŌ (φέρω), to bear, carry, uphold, is rendered "upholding" 5342
in Heb. 1 : 3. See Bear. AG:854D CB:1264A

UPON : see † p. 1

For UPPER see CHAMBER, COUNTRY, B, No. 1, ROOM

UPPERMOST

PROTO-KATHEDRIA
Note : In Luke 11 : 43 *prōtokathedria*, a chief seat, is translated 4410
"uppermost seats," A.V. (R.V., "chief seats"). In Matt. 23 : 6 and AG:725B CB:1267B
Mark 12 : 39, A.V., *prōtoklisia*, a chief place, is translated "uppermost PRŌTO-KLISIA
rooms" (R.V., "chief place" and "chief places"). See Chief, B, Nos. 4411
6 and 7. AG:725B CB:1267B

UPRIGHT : see STRAIGHT, No. 2 ; UPRIGHTLY : see WALK, No. 6 UPRIGHT See JUST, RIGHTEOUS

UPRIGHTNESS

EUTHUTĒS (εὐθύτης), from *euthus*, straight, is rendered "upright- EUTHUTĒS 2118
ness" in Heb. 1 : 8, R.V., A.V., "righteousness," marg., "rightness," AG:321B
or, "straightness."¶ THORUBOS 2351

For UPROAR (Noun), *thorubos*, see TUMULT, and for *stasis* see RIOT AG:363A CB:1272B STASIS 4714

UPROAR (Verbs)

AG:764C
THORUBEŌ (θορυβέω), used in the Middle Voice, denotes to make CB:1270A
a noise or uproar, or, transitively, in the Active Voice, to trouble, throw THORUBEŌ 2350
into confusion, Acts 17 : 5. See Ado, Noise, Trouble. AG:362D

Note : For *suncheō*, to confuse, Acts 21 : 31 (A.V., "was in an up- CB:1272B SUNCHEŌ
roar"), see Confusion ; for *anastatoō*, Acts 21 : 38 (A.V., "madest an 4797
uproar"), see Stir Up. AG:775A ANASTATOŌ 387

For UPSIDE DOWN see TURN, No. 15 AG:61A

URGE

PAROTRUNŌ 3951 AG:629D
Notes : (1) In Acts 13 : 50, A.V., *parotrunō*, to urge on (R.V.), is PEITHŌ
rendered "stirred up".¶ (2) In Acts 13 : 43, *peithō*, to persuade, is 3982
rendered "urged," R.V. (A.V., "persuaded"). (3) For *enechō*, rendered AG:639A CB:1263A
"to urge" in Luke 11 : 53, A.V., see Entangle, No. 3. ENECHŌ 1758

US

AG:265D CB:1245A
The oblique cases of *hēmeis*, we, are the genitive *hēmōn*, of us, the dative URGE See BESEECH
hēmin, to us, the accusative *hēmas*, us. When the nominative *hēmeis*
is used, it is always emphatic, e.g., John 11 : 16, "(let) us (go);" lit., 'we, 2249
let us go ;' 1 Thess. 5 : 8, "let us . . . be sober," lit., 'we . . . let us AG:217A
be sober.' Sometimes the oblique cases are governed by prepositions. (EGŌ)

USE (Noun), USEFUL

1838 AG:276B 1. HEXIS (ἕξις), akin to *echō*, to have, denotes habit, experience,
CB:1250B “ use,” Heb. 5 : 14.¶
5532 2. CHREIA (χρεία), need, is translated “ uses ” in Tit. 3 : 14 ; in Eph.
AG:884D CB:1240A 4 : 29, A.V., “ (for the) use (of edifying),” R.V., “ (as the) need (may be).”
See Necessity, Need.

5540 3. CHRĒSIS (χρῆσις), use (akin to *chraomai*, to use), occurs in
AG:885D CB:— Rom. 1 : 26, 27.¶
EUCHRēSTOS *Notes :* (1) In 2 Tim. 2 : 21, the adjective *euchrēstos*, useful, serviceable
2173 (*eu*, well, *chraomai*, to use), is translated “ meet for . . . use ; ” in 4 : 11,
AG:329C SUNēTHEIA “ useful,” R.V. (A.V., “ profitable ”) ; in Philm. 11, “ profitable.” See
4914 Profitable, B, No. 2.¶ (2) In 1 Cor. 8 : 7 the best texts have the noun
AG:789C CHRēSTOS *sunētheia*, R.V., “ being used,” lit., ‘ by the custom (of the idol) ’, i.e., by
890 being associated. See Custom. In the Sept., Prov. 31 : 13.¶ Contrast
AG:128C CB:1233A (-ON) *achrēstos*, unprofitable, Philm. 11.¶

USE (Verb)

5530 1. CHRAOMAI (χράομαι), from *chrē*, it is necessary, denotes (*a*)
AG:884B CB:1240A to use, Acts 27 : 17 ; 1 Cor. 7 : 21, where “ use it rather ” means ‘ use your bondservice rather ; ’ 7 : 31, where “ they that use (this world) ” is followed by the strengthened form *katachraomai*, rendered “ abusing,” or “ using to the full ” (R.V., marg.) ; 9 : 12, 15 ; 2 Cor. 1 : 17 ; 3 : 12 ; 13 : 10 ; 1 Tim. 1 : 8, of using the Law lawfully, i.e., agreeably to its designs ; 1 Tim. 5 : 23 ; (*b*) deal with, Acts 27 : 3. See Entreat (to treat). Cp. the Active *chraō* (or *kichrēmi*), to lend, Luke 11 : 5. See Lend.¶
2192 2. ECHŌ (ἔχω), to have, is rendered “ using ” in 1 Pet. 2 : 16 (marg.,
AG:331D CB:1242C “ having ”) ; see Have.
390 3. ANASTREPHŌ (ἀναστρέφω) chiefly denotes to behave, to live in a
AG:61B CB:1235B certain manner, rendered “ (were so) used ” in Heb. 10 : 33 (Passive Voice) ; the verb, however, does not mean to treat or use ; here it has the significance of living amidst sufferings, reproaches etc. See Abide, Behave, Live, Overthrow, Pass, Return.

PRASSō 4238 *Notes :* (1) In Acts 19 : 19, A.V., *prassō*, to practise (R.V.), is rendered
AG:698B “ used.” (2) For Heb. 5 : 13, A.V., “ useth (milk),” see Partake,
CB:1266B GINOMAI B, No. 3. (3) In 1 Thess. 2 : 5, “ were we found using ” is the rendering
1096 AG:158A of the verb *ginomai*, to become, with the preposition *en*, in, governing the
CB:1248B noun, “ words (or speech) [of flattery] ; ” this idiomatic phrase signifies to be engaged in, to resort to. A rendering close to the meaning of the Greek is ‘ for neither at any time did we fall into the use of flattering speech ; ’ cp. 1 Tim. 2 : 14, “ fallen into transgression.” (4) To use is
USELESS combined in Eng. with other words, e.g., Deceit, Despitefully, Hos-
See VAIN pitality, Repetitions.

---

671 AG:102A
USING

CB:— APOCHRĒSIS (ἀπόχρησις), a strengthened form of *chrēsis*, a using, and signifying a misuse (akin to *apochraomai*, to use to the full, abuse), is translated "using" in Col. 2 : 22; the clause may be rendered 'by their using up.' "The unusual word was chosen for its expressiveness; the *chrēsis* here was an *apochrēsis*; the things could not be used without rendering them unfit for further use" (Lightfoot).¶

For USURP see AUTHORITY, B, No. 3

USURY

Note: The R.V., "interest," Matt. 25 : 27; Luke 19 : 23, is the
preferable rendering of *tokos* here. See INTEREST.¶ 5110 AG:821D CB:1272C

For UTMOST PART see END, A, No. 3

UTTER

1. LALEŌ (λαλέω), to speak, is rendered to utter in 2 Cor. 12 : 4 2980
and Rev. 10 : 3, 4 (twice). See PREACH, SAY, SPEAK, TALK, TELL. AG:463A CB:1256B

2. EREUGOMAI (ἐρεύγομαι), primarily, to spit or spue out, or, of 2044
oxen, to bellow, roar, hence, to speak aloud, utter, occurs in Matt. AG:308D CB:—
13 : 35.¶ This affords an example of the tendency for certain words to become softened in force in late Greek.

3. APHIĒMI (ἀφίημι), to send forth, is used of uttering a cry, Mark 863
15 : 37, of Christ's final utterance on the Cross, R.V., "uttered" (A.V., AG:125C CB:1236B
"cried"). See FORGIVE, LAY, Note (2), LEAVE, LET, OMITTED, PUT, REMIT, SUFFER, YIELD.

4. DIDŌMI (δίδωμι), to give, is translated "utter" in 1 Cor. 14 : 9. 1325 AG:192C
See GIVE. CB:1241C

5. PHTHENGOMAI (φθέγγομαι), to utter a sound or voice, is trans- 5350 AG:857A
lated "uttering" in 2 Pet. 2 : 18, R.V.: see SPEAK, No. 4. CB:—

Notes: (1) In Rom. 8 : 26, *alalētos*, inexpressible (*a*, negative, *laleō*, ALALĒTOS 215
to speak), is rendered "which cannot be uttered."¶ (2) In Heb. 5 : 11, AG:34D
A.V., *dusermēneutos*, followed by *legō*, to speak, [translated "hard of CB:1234B
interpretation" (R.V.), *dus* (whence *dys-* in Eng., dyspeptic, etc.), a prefix DUSERMĒNEUTOS 1421
like Eng., un-, or mis-, and *hermēneuō*, to interpret], is rendered "hard to AG:209C
be uttered."¶ LEGŌ 3004 AG:468A CB:1256C

UTTERANCE

LOGOS (λόγος), a word, is translated "utterance" in 1 Cor. 1 : 5; 3056
2 Cor. 8 : 7; Eph. 6 : 19. See WORD. AG:477A CB:1257A

Notes: (1) In Col. 4 : 3, A.V., *logos* is rendered "(a door) of utterance."
(2) For *apophthengomai*, rendered "utterance" in Acts 2 : 4, see SPEAK, 669
No. 5. AG:102A CB:1237A (-GESTHAI)

For UTTERLY, 1 Cor. 6 : 7, see ACTUALLY; 2 Pet. 2 : 12, see CORRUPT, A, No. 2 (*b*)

UTTERMOST

3838 AG:608C CB:1261C 1. PANTELES (παντελές), the neuter of the adjective *pantelēs*, complete, perfect, used with *eis to* ('unto the'), is translated "to the uttermost" in Heb. 7 : 25, where the meaning may be 'finally;' in Luke 13 : 11 (negatively), "in no wise."¶

5056 AG:811B CB:1271B 2. TELOS (τέλος), an end, is rendered "the uttermost" in 1 Thess. 2 : 16, said of Divine wrath upon the Jews, referring to the prophecy of Deut. 28 : 15–68; the nation as such, will yet, however, be delivered (Rom. 11 : 26; cp. Jer. 30 : 4–11). The full phrase is *eis telos*, to the uttermost, which is probably the meaning in John 13 : 1, "to the end."

Notes: (1) For "uttermost (farthing)," Matt. 5 : 26, A.V., see LAST. For "uttermost" in Acts 24 : 22, see DETERMINE, No. 5. (2) For "uttermost part (-s)", see END, A, No. 3 (*a*) and C (*b*).

For VAGABOND see STROLLING

For VAIL see VEIL

VAIN, IN VAIN, VAINLY

A. Adjectives.

1. KENOS (κενός), empty, with special reference to quality, is translated "vain" (as an adjective) in Acts 4 : 25 ; 1 Cor. 15 : 10, 14 (twice) ; Eph. 5 : 6 ; Col. 2 : 8 ; Jas. 2 : 20 ; in the following the neuter, *kenon*, follows the preposition *eis*, in, and denotes "in vain," 2 Cor. 6 : 1 ; Gal. 2 : 2 ; Phil. 2 : 16 (twice) ; 1 Thess. 3 : 5. See EMPTY, B, where the applications are enumerated. **2756 AG:427D CB:1255A**

2. MATAIOS (μάταιος), void of result, is used of (*a*) idolatrous practices, Acts 14 : 15, R.V., "vain things" (A.V., "vanities") ; (*b*) the thoughts of the wise, 1 Cor. 3 : 20 ; (*c*) faith, if Christ is not risen, 1 Cor. 15 : 17 ; (*d*) questionings, strifes, etc., Tit. 3 : 9 ; (*e*) religion, with an unbridled tongue, Jas. 1 : 26 ; (*f*) manner of life, 1 Pet. 1 : 18.¶ For the contrast between No. 1 and No. 2 see EMPTY. **3152 AG:495C CB:1258A**

Note : For *mataiologoi*, Tit. 1 : 10, see TALKERS (vain).¶ **3151 AG:495C CB:1258A**

B. Verbs.

1. MATAIOŌ (ματαιόω), to make vain, or foolish, corresponding in meaning to A, No. 2, occurs in Rom. 1 : 21, "became vain."¶ **3154 AG:495D CB:1258A**

2. KENOŌ (κενόω), to empty, corresponding to A, No. 1, is translated "should be in vain" in 2 Cor. 9 : 3, A.V. See EFFECT, EMPTY, VOID. **2758 AG:428A CB:1255A**

C. Adverbs.

1. MATĒN (μάτην), properly the accusative case of *matē*, a fault, a folly, signifies in vain, to no purpose, Matt. 15 : 9 ; Mark 7 : 7.¶ **3155 AG:495D CB:1258A**

2. DŌREAN (δωρεάν), the accusative of *dōrea*, a gift, is used adverbially, denoting (*a*) freely (see FREE, D) ; (*b*) uselessly, "in vain," Gal. 2 : 21, A.V. (R.V., "for nought"). See CAUSE, A, under "*without a cause.*" **1432 AG:210C CB:1242A**

3. EIKĒ (εἰκῇ) denotes (*a*) without cause, "vainly," Col. 2 : 18 ; (*b*) to no purpose, "in vain," Rom. 13 : 4 ; Gal. 3 : 4 (twice) ; 4 : 11. See CAUSE, A, Note (1), under "*without a cause.*" **1500 AG:221D CB:—**

VAINGLORY, VAINGLORIOUS

A. Nouns.

2754 AG:427C CB:1255A 1. KENODOXIA (κενοδοξία), from *kenos*, vain, empty, *doxa*, glory, is used in Phil. 2 : 3.¶

212 AG:34C CB:1234B 2. ALAZONEIA, or –IA (ἀλαζονεία) denotes boastfulness, vaunting, translated "vainglory" in 1 John 2 : 16, R.V. (A.V., "pride"); in Jas. 4 : 16, R.V., "vauntings" (A.V., "boastings"). Cp. *alazōn*, a boaster.¶

B. Adjective.

2755 AG:427D CB:1255A KENODOXOS (κενόδοξος), akin to A, No. 1, is rendered "vainglorious" in Gal. 5 : 26, R.V. (A.V., "desirous of vain glory").¶

For VALIANT see MIGHTY, B, No. 2, STRONG, No. 2 (*a*) (3)

VALLEY

5327 AG:853C CB:— PHARANX (φάραγξ) denotes a ravine or valley, sometimes figurative of a condition of loneliness and danger (cp. Psa. 23 : 4); the word occurs in Luke 3 : 5 (from the Sept. of Isa. 40 : 4).¶

VALUE

A. Verb.

1308 AG:190B CB:— DIAPHERŌ (διαφέρω), used intransitively, means to differ, to excel, hence to be of more value, Matt. 6 : 26, R.V., "are (not) ye of (much) more value" (A.V., "better"); 12 : 12 and Luke 12 : 24, ditto; Matt. 10 : 31; Luke 12 : 7. See BETTER (be), CARRY, No. 4, DIFFER, DRIVE, No. 7, EXCELLENT, MATTER, Note (1), PUBLISH, No. 2.

5091 AG:817A CB:1272C *Note:* For *timaō*, rendered to value in Matt. 27 : 9 (twice), A.V., see PRICE.

B. Noun.

5092 AG:817B CB:1272C TIMĒ (τιμή) denotes a valuing, a price, honour; in Col. 2 : 23, R.V., "(not of any) value (against the indulgence of the flesh)" [A.V., "(not in any) honour . . ."], i.e., the ordinances enjoined by human tradition are not of any value to prevent (*pros*, against; cp. Acts 26 : 14) indulgence of the flesh. See HONOUR, PRECIOUS, PRICE, SUM.

VANISH, VANISHING

A. Verb.

853 AG:124C CB:1236B APHANIZŌ (ἀφανίζω), to render unseen, is translated "vanisheth away" in Jas. 4 : 14 (Passive Voice, lit., 'is made to disappear'). See CONSUME, DISFIGURE, PERISH.

2673 AG:417B CB:1254B *Note:* In 1 Cor. 13 : 8, A.V., *katargeō*, to abolish, is rendered "it shall vanish away" (R.V., ". . . be done away"). See ABOLISH.

B. Noun.

854 AG:124D CB:— APHANISMOS (ἀφανισμός), *a*, negative, *phainō*, to cause to appear

(akin to A), occurs in Heb. 8 : 13, R.V., " (nigh unto) vanishing away ; " the word is suggestive of abolition.¶

Note : In Luke 24 : 31, the adjective *aphantos* (akin to A and B), 855
invisible, used with *ginomai*, to become, and followed by *apo*, from, AG:124D
with the plural personal pronoun, is rendered " He vanished out of their CB:—
sight " (A.V., marg., " He ceased to be seen of them "), lit., ' He became invisible from them.'¶

VANITY

MATAIOTĒS (ματαιότης), emptiness as to results, akin to *mataios* 3153
(see EMPTY, VAIN), is used (*a*) of the creation, Rom. 8 : 20, as failing AG:495D
of the results designed, owing to sin ; (*b*) of the mind which governs the CB:1258A
manner of life of the Gentiles, Eph. 4 : 17 ; (*c*) of the " great swelling *words* " of false teachers, 2 Pet. 2 : 18.¶

Note : For *mataios*, in the neut. plur. in Acts 14 : 15, " vanities," 3152
see VAIN, A, No. 2 (*a*). AG:495C CB:1258A

VAPOUR

ATMIS (ἀτμίς) is used of smoke, Acts 2 : 19 ; figuratively of human 822
life, Jas. 4 : 14.¶ AG:120B CB:—

VARIABLENESS, VARIATION

PARALLAGĒ (παραλλαγή) denotes, in general, a change (Eng., 3883
parallax, the difference between the directions of a body as seen from AG:620A CB:—
two different points), a transmission from one condition to another ; it occurs in Jas. 1 : 17, R.V., " variation " (A.V., " variableness ") ; the reference may be to the sun, which varies its position in the sky.¶ In the Sept., 2 Kings 9 : 20.¶

VARIANCE

DICHAZŌ (διχάζω), to cut apart, divide in two, is used metaphorically 1369
in Matt. 10 : 35, " to set at variance."¶ AG:200B CB:—

Notes : (1) In Gal. 5 : 20, A.V., *eris*, strife (R.V.), is rendered ERIS
" variance." (2) For *adiakritos*, Jas. 3 : 17, R.V., " without variance " 2054
(marg., " doubtfulness, or partiality "), A.V., " without partiality " AG:309C
(marg., " without wrangling "), see PARTIAL.¶ CB:1246C ADIAKRITOS 87 AG:17A CB:1233A

VAUNT (ONESELF)

PERPEREUOMAI (περπερεύομαι), to boast or vaunt oneself (from 4068
perperos, vainglorious, braggart, not in the N.T.), is used in 1 Cor. 13 : 4, AG:653D
negatively of love.¶ CB:—

For VAUNTINGS see VAINGLORY

For VEHEMENT see DESIRE, A, No. 3

VEHEMENTLY

1171 AG:173B 1. DEINŌS (δεινῶς), for which see GRIEVOUS, B, No. 1, is rendered
CB:— "vehemently" in Luke 11 : 53.

2159 AG:327B 2. EUTONŌS (εὐτόνως), vigorously, is translated "vehemently" in
CB:— Luke 23 : 10, of accusations against Christ. See MIGHTY, D.

After 1599 AG:243C 3. EKPERISSŌS (ἐκπερισσῶς), formed from *ek*, out of, and the
CB:— adverb *perissōs*, exceedingly, the more, is found in Mark 14 : 31, in the best texts (some have *ek perissou*, the genitive case of the adjective *perissos*, more), R.V., "exceeding vehemently" (A.V., "the more vehemently"), of Peter's protestation of loyalty; the R.V. gives the better rendering.¶

Note: For "brake (A.V., beat) vehemently," Luke 6 : 48, 49, see BEAT, No. 8.

VEIL

2665 AG:416A 1. KATAPETASMA (καταπέτασμα), lit., that which is spread out
CB:1254A (*petannumi*) before (*kata*), hence, a veil, is used (*a*) of the inner veil of the Tabernacle, Heb. 6 : 19; 9 : 3; (*b*) of the corresponding veil in the Temple, Matt. 27 : 51; Mark 15 : 38; Luke 23 : 45; (*c*) metaphorically of the "flesh" of Christ, Heb. 10 : 20, i.e., His body which He gave up to be crucified, thus by His expiatory Death providing a means of the spiritual access of believers, the "new and living way," into the presence of God.¶

2571 (-UMA) 2. KALUMMA (κάλυμμα), a covering, is used (*a*) of the veil which Moses
AG:400D put over his face when descending Mount Sinai, thus preventing Israel
CB:1253B from beholding the glory, 2 Cor. 3 : 13; (*b*) metaphorically of the spiritually darkened vision suffered retributively by Israel, until the conversion of the nation to their Messiah takes place, vv. 14, 15, 16. See under UNLIFTED.¶

4018 AG:646C 3. PERIBOLAION (περιβόλαιον), rendered "a veil" in the A.V.
CB:1263B marg. of 1 Cor. 11 : 15: see COVER, B, No. 1, VESTURE.¶

VENGEANCE

1557 AG:238D EKDIKĒSIS (ἐκδίκησις), lit., '(that which proceeds) out of justice,'
CB:1243C not, as often with human vengeance, out of a sense of injury or merely out of a feeling of indignation. The word is most frequently used of Divine vengeance, e.g., Rom. 12 : 19; Heb. 10 : 30. For a complete list see AVENGE, B, No. 2. The judgments of God are holy and right (Rev. 16 : 7), and free from any element of self-gratification or vindictiveness.

DIKē 1349 *Notes:* (1) *Dikē*, justice, is translated "vengeance" in the A.V. of
AG:198C CB:1242A Acts 28 : 4 and Jude 7: see JUSTICE. (2) In Rom. 3 : 5, A.V., *orgē*, wrath
ORGē 3709 (R.V.), is rendered "vengeance": see ANGER, WRATH
AG:578D CB:1261A

For VENOMOUS see BEAST, No. 2

VERILY

1. ALĒTHŌS (ἀληθῶς), truly (akin to *alētheia*, truth), is translated 230
" verily " in 1 John 2 : 5. See INDEED, No. 3, SURELY, TRULY. AG:37B CB:1234B
2. AMĒN (ἀμήν), the transliteration of a Heb. word = ' truth,' is 281
usually translated " verily " in the four Gospels ; in John's Gospel the AG:45C
Lord introduces a solemn pronouncement by the repeated word " verily, CB:1234C
verily " twenty-five times. See AMEN.
3. ONTŌS (ὄντως), really (connected with *eimi*, to be), is rendered 3689
" verily " in Mark 11 : 32, R.V., and Gal. 3 : 21. See INDEED, No. 4. AG:574A CB:—
Notes : (1) In Acts 16 : 37, *gar*, for, is translated " verily." (2) In Heb. GAR
2 : 16, *dēpou* (in some texts *dē pou*), a particle meaning of course, we know, 1063
is rendered " verily."¶ (3) In Luke 11 : 51, A.V., *nai*, yea (R.V.), is trans- AG:151C CB:1248A
lated " verily." (4) The particle *men* (see INDEED, No. 1) is rendered DēPOU 1222
" verily," e.g., in 1 Cor. 5 : 3 ; 14 : 17 ; Heb. 12 : 10 ; in the A.V., AG:179B
Heb. 3 : 5 ; 7 : 5, 18 ; 1 Pet. 1 : 20 ; in Acts 26 : 9 it is combined with NAI 3483
oun (therefore) : see YEA, No. 4. AG:532D MEN

For VERITY, 1 Tim. 2 : 7, A.V., see TRUTH 3303 AG:502C CB:1258B

VERY

OUN 3767
Notes : (1) When " very " forms part of the translation of numerous AG:592D
other words (e.g., act, bold, many, precious, sorrowful, well), there is no SPHODRA 4970
separate word in the original. (2) For *sphodra*, exceedingly, sometimes AG:796A
rendered " very " in the A.V., see EXCEEDING, B, No. 2. (3) Occasionally CB:1269C
one of the forms of the pronoun *autos*, self, same, is translated " very ;" AUTOS 846
the R.V. rendering is sometimes " himself " etc., e.g., 1 Thess. 5 : 23, AG:122C
" (The God of peace) Himself ; " see, however, John 14 : 11, CB:1238B KAI
" (the) very (works) ; " Rom. 13 : 6 and Phil. 1 : 6, " (this) very (thing) ;" 2532
Heb. 10 : 1, " (the) very (image) ; " and the R.V., " very " (A.V., " same ") AG:391D
in Luke 12 : 12 ; 20 : 19 ; 24 : 13, 33 ; Acts 16 : 18 ; Rom. 9 : 17 ; CB:1253A EMOS
Eph. 6 : 22. (4) Sometimes it translates the conjunction *kai*, in the 1699 AG:255C
sense of " even," e.g., Matt. 10 : 30 ; in 24 : 24, A.V., " very " (R.V., CB:1244B
" even ") ; Luke 12 : 59. (5) In Philm. 12, R.V., " my very " translates PAMPOLUS 3827
the possessive pronoun *emos* (in the neuter plural, *ema*) used with emphasis. AG:607B
(6) In Mark 8 : 1 some texts have *pampollou*, " very great," A.V. (from LIAN 3029
pas, all, *polus*, much), R.V., "a great (*pollou*) multitude " (after *palin*, AG:473B
again). (7) For " very great " in Matt. 21 : 8 see GREAT, Note (6). CB:1257A
(8) The adverb *lian* is translated " very " in Mark 16 : 2 ; 2 Cor. 11 : 5 ;
12 : 11. See EXCEEDING, B, No. 1.

VESSEL

1. SKEUOS (σκεῦος) is used (*a*) of a vessel or implement of various 4632
kinds, Mark 11 : 16 ; Luke 8 : 16 ; John 19 : 29 ; Acts 10 : 11, 16 ; 11 : 5 ; AG:754A CB:1269A
27 : 17 (a sail) ; Rom. 9 : 21 ; 2 Tim. 2 : 20 ; Heb. 9 : 21 ; Rev. 2 : 27 ;
18 : 12 ; (*b*) of goods or household stuff, Matt. 12 : 29 and Mark 3 : 27,

"goods;" Luke 17 : 31, R.V., "goods" (A.V., "stuff"); (*c*) of persons, (1) for the service of God, Acts 9 : 15, "a (chosen) vessel;" 2 Tim. 2 : 21, "a vessel (unto honour);" (2) the subjects of Divine wrath, Rom. 9 : 22; (3) the subjects of Divine mercy, Rom. 9 : 23; (4) the human frame, 2 Cor. 4 : 7; perhaps 1 Thess. 4 : 4; (5) a husband and wife, 1 Pet. 3 : 7; of the wife, probably, 1 Thess. 4 : 4; while the exhortation to each one "to possess himself of his own vessel in sanctification and honour" is regarded by some as referring to the believer's body [cp. Rom. 6 : 13; 1 Cor. 9 : 27; see No. (4)], the view that the "vessel" signifies the wife, and that the reference is to the sanctified maintenance of the married state, is supported by the facts that in 1 Pet. 3 : 7 the same word *timē*, honour, is used with regard to the wife; again in Heb.
VICINITY 13 : 4, *timios*, honourable (R.V., "in honour") is used in regard to
See marriage; further, the preceding command in 1 Thess. 4 is against fornica-
BORDER tion, and the succeeding one (ver. 6) is against adultery.¶ In Ruth 4 : 10, Sept., *ktaomai*, to possess, is used of a wife.

See 30 AG:8B 2. ANGOS (ἄγγος) denotes a jar or pail, Matt. 13 : 48, in the best
CB:— 30 texts (some have No. 3). It is used, in an inscription, of a cinerary urn.¶

AG:6D 3. ANGEION (ἀγγεῖον) denotes a small vessel (a diminutive of No. 2),
CB:— 5337 e.g., for carrying oil, Matt. 25 : 4.¶

AG:854C CB:1264A *Note:* For *phaulos*, Jas. 3 : 16, R.V., see EVIL, A, No. 3.

VESTURE

2440 AG:376B 1. HIMATION (ἱμάτιον), an outer garment, is rendered "vesture"
CB:1250C 2441 in Rev. 19 : 13, 16, A.V. (R.V., "garment"). See APPAREL, No. 2.

AG:376D 2. HIMATISMOS (ἱματισμός), used of clothing in general, is translated
CB:— "vesture" in Matt. 27 : 35, A.V., in a quotation from Ps. 22 : 18 (R.V., following the better texts, omits the quotation); in John 19 : 24, A.V. and R.V.; see CLOTHING, No. 4.

4018 AG:646C 3. PERIBOLAION (περιβόλαιον) is translated "vesture" in Heb.
CB:1263B 1 : 12, A.V. (R.V., "mantle"). See COVER, B, No. 1.

VEX

3791 AG:600C 1. OCHLEŌ (ὀχλέω), to disturb, trouble, is used in the Passive Voice,
CB:— 928 of being troubled by evil spirits, Acts 5 : 16.¶

AG:134C 2. BASANIZŌ (βασανίζω), to torment, is translated "vexed" in
CB:1238C 2 Pet. 2 : 8. See TORMENT.

ENOCHLEŌ 1776 AG:267D *Notes:* (1) In Luke 6 : 18, the best texts have *enochleō*, R.V.,
CB:1245B "troubled." See TROUBLE, B, No. 5. (2) In 2 Pet. 2 : 7, A.V., *kataponeō*.
KATAPONEŌ 2669 to wear down with toil, is translated "vexed." See DISTRESS, B, No. 4.
AG:416D (3) In Acts 12 : 1, A.V., *kakoō*, to afflict (R.V.), is translated "to vex."
KAKOŌ 2559 See AFFLICT, No. 1. (4) For Matt. 17 : 15, A.V., "vexed," see GRIEV-
AG:398B CB:1253B OUSLY, B, Note (2).

For VIAL see BOWL

VICTORY, VICTORIOUS

A. Nouns. 3529

1. NIKĒ (*νίκη*), victory, is used in 1 John 5 : 4.¶ AG:539C CB:1259C

2. NIKOS (*νῖκος*), a later form of No. 1, is used in Matt. 12 : 20; 3534
1 Cor. 15 : 54, 55, 57.¶ AG:539D CB:1259C

B. Verb.

NIKAŌ (*νικάω*), to conquer, overcome, is translated "(them) that 3528
come victorious (from)" in Rev. 15 : 2, R.V. (A.V., "that had gotten the AG:539A CB:1259C
victory"). See CONQUER, OVERCOME, PREVAIL.

VICTUALS

EPISITISMOS (*ἐπισιτισμός*), provisions, food (*epi*, upon, *sitizō*, to 1979
feed, nourish; *sitos*, food), is translated "victuals" in Luke 9 : 12.¶ AG:298C CB:—

Note: In Matt. 14 : 15, A.V., *brōma*, food, meat, is translated 1033
"victuals" (R.V., "food"). See MEAT. AG:148A CB:1239B

For VIGILANT, 1 Tim. 3 : 2, see TEMPERATE; 1 Pet. 5 : 8, see WATCHFUL

VILE

A. Noun.

ATIMIA (*ἀτιμία*), dishonour, is translated "vile" in Rom. 1 : 26, 819
R.V., marg., "(passions) of dishonour." See DISHONOUR. AG:120A CB:1238B

B. Adjectives.

1. RHUPAROS (*ῥυπαρός*), filthy, dirty, is used (*a*) literally, of old 4508
shabby clothing, Jas. 2 : 2, "vile;" (*b*) metaphorically, of moral defile- AG:738A CB:1268B
ment, Rev. 22 : 11 (in the best texts).¶ In the Sept., Zech. 3 : 3, 4.¶

2. PONĒROS (*πονηρός*), evil, is translated "vile" in Acts 17 : 5, 4190
R.V. (A.V., "lewd"). See BAD, EVIL. AG:690D CB:1266A

Note: For "vile" in the A.V. of Phil. 3 : 21, see HUMILIATION.

VILLAGE

KŌMĒ (*κώμη*), a village, or country town, primarily as distinct 2968
from a walled town, occurs in the Gospels; elsewhere only in Acts 8 : 25. AG:461D CB:1255C
The difference between *polis*, a city, and *kōmē*, is maintained in the N.T., as in Josephus. Among the Greeks the point of the distinction was not that of size or fortification, but of constitution and land. In the O.T. the city and the village are regularly distinguished. The Mishna makes the three distinctions, a large city, a city and a village.

The R.V. always substitutes "village(-s)" for A.V., "town(-s)," Matt. 10 : 11; Mark 8 : 23, 26, 27; Luke 5 : 17; 9 : 6, 12; John 7 : 42; 11 : 1, 30. See TOWN.

VILLANY

1. RHᾼDIOURGIA (*ῥᾳδιουργία*) lit. and primarily denotes ease in 4468 AG:733C
working (*rhᾳdios*, easy, *ergon*, work), easiness, laziness; hence recklessness, CB:—

wickedness, Acts 13 : 10, R.V., " villany," A.V., " mischief."¶ In the papyri it is used of theft.

4467 2. RHĄDIOURGĒMA (ῥᾳδιούργημα), a reckless act (akin to No. 1),
AG:733C CB:— occurs in Acts 18 : 14, R.V., " villany " (A.V., " lewdness ").¶

VINE, VINTAGE

288 AMPELOS (ἄμπελος) is used (*a*) lit., e.g., Matt. 26 : 29 and parallel
AG:46D CB:1234C passages ; Jas. 3 : 12 ; (*b*) figuratively, (1) of Christ, John 15 : 1, 4, 5 ;
(2) of His enemies, Rev. 14 : 18, 19, " the vine of the earth " (R.V., " vintage " in v. 19), probably figurative of the remaining mass of apostate Christendom.¶

VINEDRESSER

289 AMPELOURGOS (ἀμπελουργός), a worker in a vineyard (from
AG:47A *ampelos*, a vine, and *ergon*), is rendered " vine-dresser " in Luke 13 : 7,
CB:1234C R.V. (A.V., " dresser of the vineyard ").¶

VINEGAR

3690 OXOS (ὄξος), akin to *oxus*, sharp, denotes sour wine, the ordinary
AG:574B drink of labourers and common soldiers ; it is used in the four Gospels
CB:1261B of the vinegar offered to the Lord at His crucifixion. In Matt. 27 : 34 the best texts have *oinos*, " wine " (R.V.). Some have *oxos* (A.V., vinegar), but Mark 15 : 23 (A.V. and R.V.) confirms the R.V. in the passage in Matthew. This, which the soldiers offered before crucifying, was refused by Him, as it was designed to alleviate His sufferings ; the vinegar is mentioned in Mark 15 : 36 ; so Luke 23 : 36, and John 19 : 29, 30.¶ In the Sept., Numb. 6 : 3 ; Ruth 2 : 14 ; Ps. 69 : 21 ; Prov. 25 : 20.¶

VINEYARD

290 AMPELŌN (ἀμπελών) is used 22 times in the Synoptic Gospels ;
AG:47A CB:1234C elsewhere in 1 Cor. 9 : 7.

VIOLENCE, VIOLENT, VIOLENTLY

A. Nouns.

970 AG:140C 1. BIA (βία) denotes force, violence, said of men, Acts 5 : 26 ; 21 : 35 ;
CB:1239A 24 : 7 ; of waves, 27 : 41.¶

3731 2. HORMĒMA (ὅρμημα), a rush (akin to *hormaō*, to urge on, to rush),
AG:581D CB:— is used of the fall of Babylon, Rev. 18 : 21, A.V., " violence," R.V., " mighty fall."¶

973 3. BIASTĒS (βιαστής), a forceful or violent man, is used in Matt.
AG:141A CB:1239A 11 : 12. See FORCE, B, No. 1, Note.¶

1411 *Note :* In Heb. 11 : 34, A.V., *dunamis*, power (R.V.), is rendered
AG:207B CB:1242B " violence."

B. Verbs.

1286 1. DIASEIŌ (διασείω), to shake violently, is used in Luke 3 : 14,
AG:188B CB:1241B " do violence," including intimidation.¶ In the Sept., Job 4 : 14.¶

2. BIAZŌ (βιάζω), in the Passive Voice, is rendered "suffereth 971
violence" in Matt. 11 : 12; see FORCE, B, Nos. 1 and 2. Some, e.g., AG:140C
Cremer (Lexicon) and Dalman (*Words of Jesus*, pp. 139, ff.), hold that the CB:1239A
reference is to the antagonism of the enemies of the Kingdom, but Luke 16 : 16 (Middle Voice : R.V., "entereth violently") indicates the meaning as referring to those who make an effort to enter the Kingdom in spite of violent opposition : see PRESS, A, No. 3.¶

Note : For *hormaō*, rendered "ran violently," in Matt. 8 : 32 and 3729
parallels, see RUN, RUSH. AG:581D
CB:—

VIPER

ECHIDNA (ἔχιδνα) is probably a generic term for poisonous snakes. 2191
It is rendered "viper" in the N.T., (*a*) of the actual creature, Acts 28 : 3; AG:331D
(*b*) metaphorically in Matt. 3 : 7; 12 : 34; 23 : 33; Luke 3 : 7.¶ CB:—

VIRGIN

PARTHENOS (παρθένος) is used (*a*) of the Virgin Mary, Matt. 1 : 23; 3933
Luke 1 : 27; (*b*) of the ten virgins in the parable, Matt. 25 : 1, 7, 11; AG:627A
(*c*) of the daughters of Philip the evangelist, Acts 21 : 9; (*d*) those CB:1262C
concerning whom the Apostle Paul gives instructions regarding marriage, 1 Cor. 7 : 25, 28, 34; in vv. 36, 37, 38, the subject passes to that of 'virgin *daughters*' (R.V.), which almost certainly formed one of the subjects upon which the church at Corinth sent for instructions from the Apostle; one difficulty was relative to the discredit which might be brought upon a father (or guardian), if he allowed his daughter or ward to grow old unmarried. The interpretation that this passage refers to a man and woman already in some kind of relation by way of a spiritual marriage and living together in a vow of virginity and celibacy, is untenable if only in view of the phraseology of the passage; (*e*) figuratively, of a local church in its relation to Christ, 2 Cor. 11 : 2; (*f*) metaphorically, of chaste persons, Rev. 14 : 4.¶

VIRGINITY

PARTHENIA (παρθενία), akin to the above, occurs in Luke 2 : 36.¶ 3932
In the Sept., Jer. 3 : 4.¶ AG:626D
CB:1262C

VIRTUE

ARETĒ (ἀρετή) properly denotes whatever procures pre-eminent 703
estimation for a person or thing; hence, intrinsic eminence, moral good- AG:105D
ness, virtue, (*a*) of God, 1 Pet. 2 : 9, "excellencies" (A.V., "praises"); CB:1237C
here the original and general sense seems to be blended with the impression made on others, i.e., renown, excellence or praise (Hort); in 2 Pet. 1 : 3, "(by His own glory and) virtue," R.V. (instrumental dative), i.e., the manifestation of His divine power; this significance is frequently illustrated in the papyri and was evidently common in current Greek

speech; (*b*) of any particular moral excellence, Phil. 4 : 8; 2 Pet. 1 : 5 (twice), where virtue is enjoined as an essential quality in the exercise of faith, R.V., " (in your faith supply) virtue."¶

1411 AG:207B CB:1242B *Note:* In the A.V. of Mark 5 : 30; Luke 6 : 19; 8 : 46, ***dunamis***, " power " (R.V.), is rendered " virtue."

VISIBLE See MANIFEST

VISIBLE

3707 AG:577C CB:1251A HORATOS (ὁρατός), from *horaō*, to see, occurs in Col. 1 : 16.¶

VISION

3705 AG:577B CB:1251A 1. HORAMA (ὅραμα), that which is seen (*horaō*), denotes (*a*) a spectacle, sight, Matt. 17 : 9; Acts 7 : 31 (" sight "); (*b*) an appearance, vision, Acts 9 : 10 (ver. 12 in some mss.); 10 : 3, 17, 19; 11 : 5; 12 : 9; 16 : 9, 10; 18 : 9.¶

3706 AG:577C CB:1251A 2. HORASIS (ὅρασις), sense of sight, is rendered " visions " in Acts 2 : 17; Rev. 9 : 17. See LOOK, B.

3701 AG:576C CB:1261A 3. OPTASIA (ὀπτασία) (a late form of ***opsis***, the act of seeing), from *optanō*, to see, a coming into view, denotes a vision in Luke 1 : 22; 24 : 23; Acts 26 : 19; 2 Cor. 12 : 1.¶

VISIT

1980 AG:298C CB:1246A 1. EPISKEPTOMAI (ἐπισκέπτομαι), primarily, to inspect (a late form of *episkopeō*, to look upon, care for, exercise oversight), signifies (*a*) to visit with help, of the act of God, Luke 1 : 68, 78; 7 : 16; Acts 15 : 14; Heb. 2 : 6; (*b*) to visit the sick and afflicted, Matt. 25 : 36, 43; Jas. 1 : 27; (*c*) to go and see, pay a visit to, Acts 7 : 23; 15 : 36; (*d*) to look out certain men for a purpose, Acts 6 : 3. See LOOK.¶

Note: In the Sept., to visit with punishment, e.g., Psa. 89 : 32; Jer. 9 : 25.

2477 AG:383A CB:1251A 2. HISTOREŌ (ἱστορέω), from *histōr*, one learned in anything, denotes to visit in order to become acquainted with, Gal. 1 : 18, R.V., " visit " (A.V., " see "), R.V. marg., " become acquainted with."¶

2018 AG:304C CB:1246A 3. EPIPHERŌ (ἐπιφέρω), for which see BRING, No. 6, is rendered " visiteth (with wrath) " in Rom. 3 : 5, R.V., A.V., " taketh (vengeance)."

VISITATION

1984 AG:299A CB:1246A EPISKOPĒ (ἐπισκοπή), for which see BISHOP, No. 2, denotes a visitation, whether in mercy, Luke 19 : 44, or in judgment, 1 Pet. 2 : 12.

For VOCATION, Eph. 4 : 1, see CALL, B

VOICE

5456 AG:870C CB:1264B PHŌNĒ (φωνή), a sound, is used of the voice (*a*) of God, Matt. 3 : 17; John 5 : 37; 12 : 28, 30; Acts 7 : 31; 10 : 13, 15; 11 : 7, 9; Heb. 3 : 7, 15; 4 : 7; 12 : 19, 26; 2 Pet. 1 : 17, 18; Rev. 18 : 4; 21 : 3; (*b*) of Christ,

(1) in the days of His flesh, Matt. 12 : 19 (negatively) ; John 3 : 29 ; 5 : 25 ; 10 : 3, 4, 16, 27 ; 11 : 43 ; 18 : 37 ; (2) on the Cross, Matt. 27 : 46, and parallel passages ; (3) from heaven, Acts 9 : 4, 7 ; 22 : 7, 9, 14 ; 26 : 14 ; Rev. 1 : 10, 12 (here, by metonymy, of the speaker), 15 ; 3 : 20 ; (4) at the resurrection "to life", John 5 : 28 ; 1 Thess. 4 : 16, where "the voice of the archangel" is, lit., 'a voice of an archangel,' and probably refers to the Lord's voice as being of an archangelic character ; (5) at the resurrection to judgment, John 5 : 28 [not the same event as (4)] ; (*c*) of human beings on earth, e.g., Matt. 2 : 18 ; 3 : 3 ; Luke 1 : 42, in some texts, A.V., "voice", and frequently in the Synoptists ; (*d*) of angels, Rev. 5 : 11, and frequently in the Apocalypse ; (*e*) of the redeemed in heaven, e.g., Rev. 6 : 10 ; 18 : 22 ; 19 : 1, 5 ; (*f*) of a pagan god, Acts 12 : 22 ; (*g*) of things, e.g., wind, John 3 : 8, R.V., "voice" (A.V., "sound"). See SOUND.

Notes : (1) In Luke 1 : 42 (1st part), A.V., *anaphōneō*, to lift up one's 400
voice, is rendered "spake out," R.V., "lifted up (her) voice." (2) AG:63B
In Acts 26 : 10, A.V., "I gave my voice" (R.V., ". . . vote") : see CB:—
STONE, No. 2.

VOID

1. KENOŌ (κενόω), to empty, make of no effect, is rendered to make 2758
void, in Rom. 4 : 14 ; 1 Cor. 1 : 17, R.V. ; 9 : 15 ; 2 Cor. 9 : 3, R.V. AG:428A
See EFFECT (of none), No. 3, EMPTY, VAIN, B, No. 2. CB:1255A

2. ATHETEŌ (ἀθετέω), for which see DISANNUL, No. 1, is rendered 114
to make void in Gal. 2 : 21, R.V. (A.V., "frustrate"); 3 : 15, R.V. AG:21A
CB:1238A

3. AKUROŌ (ἀκυρόω), for which see DISANNUL, No. 2, is rendered 208
to make void in Matt. 15 : 6 ; Mark 7 : 13, R.V. AG:34B
CB:—

Notes : (1) In Rom. 3 : 31, A.V., *katargeō* is translated to make void. 2673
See ABOLISH, EFFECT (of none), No. 2. (2) See also IMPOSSIBLE, B, AG:417B
OFFENCE, UNDERSTANDING. CB:1254B

For VOLUME see ROLL, B

VOLUNTARY

Note : In Col. 2 : 18, *thelō* (for which see DESIRE, B, No. 6) is rendered 2309
"(in a) voluntary (humility)," present participle, i.e., "being a voluntary AG:354D
(in humility)," A.V. marg., R.V. marg., "of his own mere will (by CB:1271C
humility)," *en*, in, being rendered as instrumental; what was of one's own mere will, with the speciousness of humility, would mean his being robbed of his prize.

VOMIT

EXERAMA (ἐξέραμα), a vomit (from *exeraō*, to disgorge), occurs 1829 AG:274B
in 2 Pet. 2 : 22.¶ CB:—

For VOTE, Acts 26 : 10, R.V., see STONE, No. 2

VOUCHSAFE

3670
AG:568A
CB:1251A
HOMOLOGEŌ (ὁμολογέω), to agree, is found in the best texts in Acts 7 : 17, and rendered "vouchsafed," R.V., with reference to God's promise to Abraham; some mss. have *ōmosen*, "swore" (***omnumi***, to swear), as in A.V. See CONFESS, PROFESS, PROMISE, THANKS, B, *Note*.

VOW

2171
AG:329B
CB:1247A
EUCHĒ (εὐχή) denotes also a vow, Acts 18 : 18; 21 : 23, with reference to the vow of the Nazirite (wrongly spelt Nazarite), see Numb. 6, R.V.; in Jas. 5 : 15, "prayer." See PRAYER.¶

VOYAGE

4144
AG:673C
CB:—
PLOOS or PLOUS (πλόος) is rendered a voyage (***pleō***, to sail) in Acts 27 : 10 (A.V. and R.V.); in 21 : 7, R.V. (A.V., "course"); in 27 : 9, R.V. (A.V., "sailing"). See COURSE, B, Note (4).¶

WAG

KINEŌ (κινέω), **to move,** is used of those who mocked the Lord at 2795
His crucifixion, nodding their heads in the direction of the Cross as if sneer- AG:432C
ing at this supposed ending of His career, Matt. 27 : 39 ; Mark 15 : 29. CB:—
Cp. 2 Kings 19 : 21 ; Job 16 : 4 ; Psa. 22 : 7 ; 109 : 25 ; Is. 37 : 22.
See MOVE, No. 1. WAIST See LOINS

WAGES

1. OPSŌNION (ὀψώνιον), for which see CHARGE, A, No. 5, denotes OPSōNION
(*a*) soldiers' pay, Luke 3 : 14 ; 1 Cor. 9 : 7 (" charges ") ; (*b*) in general, 3800 AG:602A
hire, wages of any sort, used metaphorically, Rom. 6 : 23, of sin ; 2 Cor. CB:1261
11 : 8, of material support which Paul received from some of the churches MISTHOS
which he had established and to which he ministered in spiritual things ; 3408 AG:523B
their support partly maintained him at Corinth, where he forebore to CB:1259A
receive such assistance (vv. 9, 10).¶ ALALAZō 214

2. MISTHOS (μισθός), hire, is rendered " wages " in John 4 : 36 ; AG:34D KOPTō
in 2 Pet. 2 : 15, A.V. (R.V., " hire "). See HIRE, A. 2875 AG:444A

WAIL, WAILING

CB:1255C PENTHEō

Notes : (1) For *alalazō*, rendered to wail in Mark 5 : 38, see CLANGING. 3996
(2) For *koptō*, rendered to wail in Rev. 1 : 7, A.V. (R.V., " shall mourn ") AG:642C CB:1263A
and 18 : 9, R.V., " wail " (A.V., " lament "), see BEWAIL. (3) For *pentheō*, KLAUTHMOS
rendered to wail in Rev. 18 : 15, 19, A.V., see MOURN. (4) For *klauthmos*, 2805 AG:433C
rendered " wailing " in Matt. 13 : 42, 50, A.V., see WEEP. (5) In Matt. CB:1255B
11 : 17 and Luke 7 : 32, A.V., *thrēneō*, to wail (R.V.), is rendered to mourn. THRēNEō 2354
See BEWAIL, Note (1), MOURN. AG:363B CB:1272B

WAIT

1. EKDECHOMAI (ἐκδέχομαι), for which see EXPECT, No. 1, is 1551
rendered to wait in John 5 : 3, A.V. ; Acts 17 : 16 ; 1 Cor. 11 : 33, R.V. AG:238B CB:1243C

2. APEKDECHOMAI (ἀπεκδέχομαι), to await or expect eagerly, is 553
rendered to wait for in Rom. 8 : 19, 23, 25 ; 1 Cor. 1 : 7 ; Gal. 5 : 5 ; AG:83C
Phil. 3 : 20, R.V. (A.V., " look for ") ; Heb. 9 : 28, R.V. (A.V., " look for "), CB:1236B
here " them that wait " represents believers in general, not a section of
them ; 1 Pet. 3 : 20 (in the best texts ; some have No. 1). See LOOK
(for), Note (1).¶ 4327 AG:712B

3. PROSDECHOMAI (προσδέχομαι), to look for with a view to CB:1267A

favourable reception, is rendered to wait for in Mark 15 : 43 ; Luke 2 : 25 ; 12 : 36 ; 23 : 51. See Look (for), No. 2.

4328 4. PROSDOKAŌ (προσδοκάω), to await, is rendered to wait for in
AG:712C CB:1267A Luke 1 : 21 ; 8 : 40 ; Acts 10 : 24 ; in 27 : 33, R.V., " ye wait " (A.V.,
" have tarried "). See Look (for), No. 1.

362 5. ANAMENŌ (ἀναμένω), to wait for (*ana*, up, used intensively, and
AG:57D CB:1235A *menō*, to abide), is used in 1 Thess. 1 : 10, of waiting for the Son of God
from Heaven ; the word carries with it the suggestion of waiting with patience and confident expectancy.¶

4037 6. PERIMENŌ (περιμένω), to await an event, is used in Acts 1 : 4,
AG:648C CB:1263B of waiting for the Holy Spirit, " the promise of the Father."¶ In the
Sept., Gen. 49 : 18.¶

4342 7. PROSKARTEREŌ (προσκαρτερέω), to continue stedfastly, is
AG:715C CB:1267A rendered to wait on, in Mark 3 : 9 and Acts 10 : 7. See Continue, No. 9
(in the Sept., Numb. 13 : 21¶).

— 8. PAREDREUŌ (παρεδρεύω), to sit constantly beside (*para*, beside,
AG:624A CB:— *hedra*, a seat), is used in the best texts in 1 Cor. 9 : 13, R.V., " wait upon
(A.V., at) (the altar)."¶ In the Sept., Prov. 1 : 21 ; 8 : 3.¶

5281 *Notes :* (1) In 2 Thess. 3 : 5, A.V., *hupomonē*, patience (so R.V.), is
AG:846B CB:1252B rendered " patient waiting " (marg., " patience "). See Patience.
(2) For " lie in wait " in Eph. 4 : 14, A.V., see Wiles. (3) For " lying in wait," Acts 20 : 19, A.V., and " laid wait," 20 : 3 ; 23 : 30, see Plot.

WAKE

1127 GRĒGOREŌ (γρηγορέω), translated " wake " in 1 Thess. 5 : 10, is
AG:167B CB:1248C rendered " watch " in the R.V. marg., as in the text in ver. 6, and the
R.V. in the twenty-one other places in which it occurs in the N.T. (save 1 Pet. 5 : 8, " be watchful "). It is not used in the metaphorical sense of ' to be alive ; ' here it is set in contrast with *katheudō*, ' to sleep,' which is never used by the Apostle with the meaning ' to be dead ' (it has this meaning only in the case of Jairus' daughter). Accordingly the meaning here is that of vigilance and expectancy as contrasted with laxity and indifference. All believers will live together with Christ from the time of the Rapture described in chap. 4 ; for all have spiritual life now, though their spiritual condition and attainment vary considerably. Those who are lax and fail to be watchful will suffer loss (1 Cor. 3 : 15 ; 9 : 27 ; 2 Cor. 5 : 10, e.g.), but the Apostle is not here dealing with that aspect of the subject. What he does make clear is that the Rapture of believers at the Second Coming of Christ will depend solely on the Death of Christ for them, and not upon their spiritual condition. The Rapture is not a matter of reward, but of salvation. See Watch.

WALK

4043 1. PERIPATEŌ (περιπατέω) is used (*a*) physically, in the Synoptic
AG:649A CB:1263B Gospels (except Mark 7 : 5) ; always in the Acts except in 21 : 21 ; never in

the Pauline Epistles, nor in those of John; (*b*) figuratively, "signifying the whole round of the activities of the individual life, whether of the unregenerate, Eph. 4 : 17, or of the believer, 1 Cor. 7 : 17; Col. 2 : 6. It is applied to the observance of religious ordinances, Acts 21 : 21; Heb. 13 : 9, marg., as well as to moral conduct. The Christian is to walk in newness of life, Rom. 6 : 4, after the spirit, 8 : 4, in honesty, 13 : 13, by faith, 2 Cor. 5 : 7, in good works, Eph. 2 : 10, in love, 5 : 2, in wisdom, Col. 4 : 5, in truth, 2 John 4, after the commandments of the Lord, v. 6. And, negatively, not after the flesh, Rom. 8 : 4; not after the manner of men, 1 Cor. 3 : 3; not in craftiness, 2 Cor. 4 : 2; not by sight, 5 : 7; not in the vanity of the mind, Eph. 4 : 17; not disorderly, 2 Thess. 3 : 6."* See Go, Note (2) (*r*).

2. POREUŌ (πορεύω), for which see DEPART, No. 8, and GO, No. 1, 4198
is used in the Middle Voice and rendered to walk in Luke 1 : 6, of the AG:692B
general activities of life; so in Luke 13 : 33, A.V., "walk" (R.V., "go on CB:1266A
My way"); Acts 9 : 31; 14 : 16; 1 Pet. 4 : 3; 2 Pet. 2 : 10; Jude, 16, 18.

3. EMPERIPATEŌ (ἐμπεριπατέω), to walk about in, or among (*en*, 1704
in, and No. 1), is used in 2 Cor. 6 : 16, of the activities of God in the lives AG:256A
of believers.¶ CB:1244B

4. STOICHEŌ (στοιχέω), from *stoichos*, a row, signifies to walk in line, 4748
and is used metaphorically of walking in relation to others (No. 1 is used AG:769C
more especially of the individual walk); in Acts 21 : 24, it is translated CB:1270A
"walkest orderly;" in Rom. 4 : 12, "walk (in . . . steps);" in Gal. 5 : 25 it is used of walking "by the Spirit," R.V., in an exhortation to keep step with one another in submission of heart to the Holy Spirit, and therefore of keeping step with Christ, the great means of unity and harmony in a church (contrast No. 1 in ver. 16; ver. 25 begins a new section which extends to 6 : 10); in 6 : 16 it is used of walking by the rule expressed in vv. 14, 15; in Phil. 3 : 16 the reference is to the course pursued by the believer who makes "the prize of the high calling" the object of his ambition.¶ In the Sept., Eccl. 11 : 6.¶

5. DIERCHOMAI (διέρχομαι), to go through (*dia*), is rendered to walk 1330
through in the A.V. of Matt. 12 : 43 and Luke 11 : 24 (R.V., "passeth AG:194C
through"). See COME, No. 5, PASS, No. 2. CB:1241C

6. ORTHOPODEŌ (ὀρθοποδέω), to walk in a straight path (*orthos*, 3716
straight, *pous*, a foot), is used metaphorically in Gal. 2 : 14, signifying a AG:580A
course of conduct by which one leaves a straight track for others to CB:1261B
follow ("walked . . . uprightly").¶

Note: In Mark 1 : 16, A.V., *paragō*, to pass along (R.V., "passing 3855
along"), is translated "walked." AG:613D
CB:—

WALL

1. TEICHOS (τεῖχος), a wall, especially one around a town, is used 5038
AG:808A
CB:1271B

* From Notes on Thessalonians by Hogg and Vine, p. 67.

(*a*) literally, Acts 9 : 25 ; 2 Cor. 11 : 33 ; Heb. 11 : 30 ; (*b*) figuratively, of the wall of the Heavenly city, Rev. 21 : 12, 14, 15, 17, 18, 19.¶

5109 AG:821C CB:1272C 2. TOICHOS (τοῖχος), a wall, especially of a house, is used figuratively in Acts 23 : 3, " (thou whited) wall."¶

3320 AG:508A CB:1258B 3. MESOTOICHON (μεσότοιχον), a partition wall (*mesos*, middle, and No. 2), occurs in Eph. 2 : 14, figuratively of the separation of Gentile from Jew in their unregenerate state, a partition demolished by the Cross for both on acceptance of the Gospel. Cp. PARTITION.¶

WALLET

4082 AG:656C CB:1263B PĒRA (πήρα), a traveller's leathern bag or pouch for holding provisions, is translated " wallet " in the R.V. (A.V., " scrip "), Matt. 10 : 10 ; Mark 6 : 8 ; Luke 9 : 3 ; 10 : 4 ; 22 : 35, 36.¶ Deissmann (*Light from the Ancient East*) regards it as an alms-bag.

WALLOW (Verb and Noun)

A. Verb.

2947 (-IOō) AG:457B CB:— KULIŌ (κυλίω) in the Active Voice denotes to roll, roll along ; in the Middle Voice in Mark 9 : 20, rendered " wallowed."¶

B. Noun.

2946 (-MA) AG:457B CB:— KULISMOS (κυλισμός), a rolling, wallowing, akin to A (some texts have *kulisma*), is used in 2 Pet. 2 : 22, of the proverbial sow that had been washed.¶

WANDER

A. Verb.

4105 AG:665B CB:1265A PLANAŌ (πλανάω), for which see DECEIT, C, No. 6, is translated to wander in Heb. 11 : 38, Passive Voice, lit., ' were made to wander.'

4022 AG:646D CB:1263B *Note :* In the A.V. of 1 Tim. 5 : 13 and Heb. 11 : 37, *perierchomai*, to go about or around, is translated to wander about. See GO, No. 29.

B. Noun.

4107 AG:666A CB:1265A PLANĒTĒS (πλανήτης), a wanderer (Eng., planet), is used metaphorically in Jude 13, of the evil teachers there mentioned as " wandering (stars)."¶ In the Sept., Hos. 9 : 17.¶

WANT (Noun and Verb)

A. Nouns.

5304 AG:849C CB:1252B 1. HUSTERĒSIS (ὑστέρησις), akin to B, No. 1 (below), occurs in Mark 12 : 14 and Phil. 4 : 11.¶

5303 AG:849B CB:1252B 2. HUSTERĒMA (ὑστέρημα) denotes (more concretely than No. 1) (*a*) that which is lacking (see LACK) ; (*b*) need, poverty, want, rendered " want " in Luke 21 : 4 (A.V., " penury ") ; 2 Cor. 8 : 14 (twice) ; 9 : 12 ; 11 : 9 (2nd occurrence), R.V., " want " (A.V., " that which was lacking ").

5532 AG:884D CB:1240A 3. CHREIA (χρεία) is rendered " want " in Phil. 2 : 25, A.V. (R.V., " need "). See BUSINESS.

B. Verbs.

1. HUSTEREŌ (ὑστερέω) signifies to be in want, Luke 15 : 14 ; 2 Cor. 5302
11 : 9 (1st occurrence) ; Phil. 4 : 12, R.V. (A.V. " to suffer need ") ; AG:849A
in John 2 : 3, A.V., " wanted " (R.V., " failed "). See BEHIND, B, No. 1. CB:1252B

2. LEIPŌ (λείπω), to leave, is rendered ' to be wanting ' in Tit. 1 : 5 3007
and 3 : 13, and in the A.V. in Jas. 1 : 4. See LACK, C, No. 3. AG:470B
CB:1256C

WANT
See WILL,
WOULD

WANTONNESS, WANTON, WANTONLY

A. Nouns.

1. ASELGEIA (ἀσέλγεια), lasciviousness, licentiousness, is rendered 766
" wantonness " in 2 Pet. 2 : 18, A.V. ; see LASCIVIOUSNESS. AG:114D
CB:1238A

2. STRĒNOS (στρῆνος), insolent luxury, is rendered " wantonness " 4764
in Rev. 18 : 3, R.V. (marg., " luxury ; " A.V., " delicacies," not a AG:771C
sufficiently strong rendering).¶ CB:—

B. Verbs.

1. STRĒNIAŌ (στρηνιάω), akin to A, No. 2, to run riot, is rendered 4763
" waxed wanton " in Rev. 18 : 7, R.V., and " lived wantonly " in ver. 8. AG:771C
See DELICATELY, Note (1). The root of the verb is seen in the Latin CB:—
strenuus.¶

2. KATASTRĒNIAŌ (καταστρηνιάω), an intensive form of No. 1, to wax 2691
wanton against, occurs in 1 Tim. 5 : 11.¶ AG:419B
CB:—

WAR (Verb and Noun)

A. Verbs.

1. POLEMEŌ (πολεμέω) (Eng., polemics), to fight, to make war, is 4170
used (*a*) literally, Rev. 12 : 7 (twice), R.V. ; 13 : 4 ; 17 : 14 ; 19 : 11 ; AG:685A
(*b*) metaphorically, Rev. 2 : 16, R.V. ; (*c*) hyperbolically, Jas. 4 : 2. See CB:1265C
FIGHT, B, Note (1).¶

2. STRATEUŌ (στρατεύω), used in the Middle Voice, to make war 4754
(from *stratos*, an encamped army), is translated to war in 2 Cor. 10 : 3 ; (-OMAI)
metaphorically, of spiritual conflict, 1 Tim. 1 : 18 ; 2 Tim. 2 : 3, A.V. ; AG:770B
Jas. 4 : 1 ; 1 Pet. 2 : 11. See SOLDIER, B. CB:1270A

3. ANTISTRATEUOMAI (ἀντιστρατεύομαι), not found in the Active 497
Voice *antistrateuō*, to make war against (*anti*), occurs in Rom. 7 : 23.¶ AG:75D
CB:—

Note : For " men of war," Luke 23 : 11, A.V., see SOLDIER, No. 2.

B. Noun.

POLEMOS (πόλεμος), war (akin to A, No. 1), is so translated in the 4171
R.V., for A.V., " battle," 1 Cor. 14 : 8 ; Rev. 9 : 7, 9 ; 16 : 14 ; 20 : 8 ; AG:685A
for A.V., " fight," Heb. 11 : 34 ; A.V. and R.V. in Jas. 4 : 1, hyperbolically CB:1265C
of private quarrels ; elsewhere, literally, e.g., Matt. 24 : 6 ; Rev. 11 : 7.
See BATTLE.

WARD

1. PHULAKĒ (φυλακή), a guard, is used of the place where persons 5438
are kept under guard (akin to *phulax*, a keeper), and translated " ward " AG:867D
CB:1264C

in Acts 12 : 10. See CAGE, HOLD (Noun), IMPRISONMENT, PRISON, WATCH.

5084 AG:815C 2. TĒRĒSIS (τήρησις) primarily denotes a watching (*tēreō*, to watch);
CB:1271B hence imprisonment, ward, Acts 4 : 3 (A.V., "hold"); 5 : 18, R.V., "(public) ward" [A.V., "(common) prison"]. See HOLD (Noun), KEEPING, B, PRISON.

Note: For "were kept in ward," Gal. 3 : 23, see GUARD, B, No. 3, KEEP, No. 6.

WARE OF

5442 AG:868B PHULASSŌ (φυλάσσω) denotes to guard, watch; in 2 Tim. 4 : 15,
CB:1264C "of (whom) be thou ware" (Middle Voice): see BEWARE, No. 3.

4894 (SUNEIDŌ) *Note:* For *sunoida*, translated "were ware" in Acts 14 : 6, A.V.
AG:791B CB:1270C (R.V., "became aware of it"), see KNOW, A, No. 6.

WARFARE

4752 STRATEIA, or -TIA (στρατεία), primarily a host or army, came to
AG:770B CB:1270A denote a warfare, and is used of spiritual conflict in 2 Cor. 10 : 4; 1 Tim. 1 : 18.¶

STRATIA 4756 *Note:* For the verb to go a warfare, 1 Cor. 9 : 7, A.V., see SOLDIER,
AG:770D CB:1270A B, No. 1.

WARM (Verb)

2328 AG:359C THERMAINŌ (θερμαίνω), to warm, heat (Eng. thermal etc.), when
CB:1272B used in the Middle Voice, signifies to warm oneself, Mark 14 : 54, 67;
NOUTHETEŌ 3560 John 18 : 18 (twice), 25; Jas. 2 : 16.¶

AG:544B CB:1260A

WARN

HUPODEIKNUMI 5263 1. NOUTHETEŌ (νουθετέω), to put in mind, warn, is translated to
AG:844B warn in the A.V., in the passages mentioned under ADMONISH, B, No. 1
CHRĒMATIZŌ 5537 (which see); the R.V. always translates this word by the verb to admonish.

AG:885C 2. HUPODEIKNUMI (ὑποδείκνυμι), primarily, to show secretly (*hupo*,
CB:1240A under, *deiknumi*, to show), hence, generally, to teach, make known, is
EIMI 1510 translated to warn in Matt. 3 : 7; Luke 3 : 7; 12 : 5, R.V. (A.V., "fore-
AG:222D warn"). See FOREWARN, Note, SHEW.

CB:1243A GINOMAI 3. CHRĒMATIZŌ (χρηματίζω), for which see ADMONISH, B, No. 3,
1096 is translated to warn in Matt. 2 : 12, 22; Acts 10 : 22; Heb. 8 : 5, R.V.
AG:158A CB:1248B (A.V., "admonished"); 11 : 7; 12 : 25, R.V. (A.V., "spake").

HUPARCHŌ 5225

WAS, WAST, WERE, WERT

AG:838A ECHŌ *Note:* When not part of another verb, or phrase, these translate *eimi*,
2192 AG:331D to be, e.g., Matt. 1 : 18, or the following: (*a*) *ginomai*, to become, e.g.,
CB:1242C Matt. 8 : 26; (*b*) *huparchō*, to exist, especially when referring to an already
APECHŌ 568 existing condition, e.g., Luke 8 : 41; Acts 5 : 4 (2nd part); 16 : 3;
AG:84D 27 : 12; Rom. 4 : 19, A.V., "when he was" (R.V., "he being"); (*c*)
CB:1236B *echō*, to have, e.g., Acts 12 : 15; (*d*) *apechō*, to be away, to be distant, e.g.,

Luke 7 : 6 ; 24 : 13 ; (*e*) *mellō*, to be about to, e.g., Luke 19 : 4 ; Acts MELLō
21 : 27, 37, A.V. (R.V., " was about to ") ; (*f*) *sumbainō*, to come to pass, 3195 AG:500D
happen, e.g., Acts 21 : 35 ; (*g*) in Gal. 4 : 28, the preposition *kata*, according CB:1258A
to, is rendered " was," in the phrase " as Isaac was," lit., ' like Isaac ; ' SUMBAINō 4819
as Isaac's birth came by Divine interposition, so does the spiritual birth AG:777B
of every believer. KATA 2596 AG:405C CB:1253C

WASH

1. NIPTŌ (νίπτω) is chiefly used of washing part of the body, John 3538
13 : 5, 6, 8 (twice, figuratively in 2nd clause), 12, 14 (twice) ; in 1 Tim. AG:540B CB:1259C
5 : 10, including the figurative sense ; in the Middle Voice, to wash oneself, Matt. 6 : 17 ; 15 : 2 ; Mark 7 : 3 ; John 9 : 7, 11, 15 ; 13 : 10.¶ For the corresponding noun see BASON.

2. APONIPTŌ (ἀπονίπτω), to wash off, is used in the Middle Voice, 633 AG:97A
in Matt. 27 : 24.¶ (-IZō) CB:—

3. LOUŌ (λούω) signifies to bathe, to wash the body, (*a*) Active Voice, 3068
Acts 9 : 37 ; 16 : 33 ; (*b*) Passive Voice, John 13 : 10, R.V., " bathed " AG:480D CB:1257B
(A.V., " washed ") ; Heb. 10 : 22, lit., ' having been washed as to the body,' metaphorical of the effect of the Word of God upon the activities of the believer ; (*c*) Middle Voice, 2 Pet. 2 : 22. Some inferior mss. have it instead of *luō*, to loose, in Rev. 1 : 5 (see R.V.).¶

4. APOLOUŌ (ἀπολούω), to wash off or away, is used in the Middle 628
Voice, metaphorically, to wash oneself, in Acts 22 : 16, where the com- AG:96A CB:1237A
mand to Saul of Tarsus to wash away his sins indicates that by his public confession, he would testify to the removal of his sins, and to the complete change from his past life ; this ' washing away ' was not in itself the actual remission of his sins, which had taken place at his conversion ; the Middle Voice implies his own particular interest in the act (as with the preceding verb " baptize," lit., ' baptize thyself,' i.e., ' get thyself baptized ') ; the aorist tenses mark the decisiveness of the acts ; in 1 Cor. 6 : 11, lit., ' ye washed yourselves clean ; ' here the Middle Voice (rendered in the Passive in A.V. and R.V., which do not distinguish between this and the next two Passives ; see R.V. marg.) again indicates that the converts at Corinth, by their obedience to the faith, voluntarily gave testimony to the complete spiritual change Divinely wrought in them.¶ In the Sept., Job 9 : 30.¶

5. PLUNŌ (πλύνω) is used of washing inanimate objects, e.g., nets, 4150 AG:674C
Luke 5 : 2 (some texts have *apoplunō*) ; of garments, figuratively, Rev. CB:1265B
7 : 14 ; 22 : 14 (in the best texts ; the A.V. translates those which have APOPLUNō
the verb *poieō*, to do, followed by *tas entolas autou*, " His command- 637 AG:97C
ments ").¶ CB:—

6. RHANTIZŌ (ῥαντίζω), to sprinkle, is used in the Middle Voice in 4472
Mark 7 : 4, in some ancient texts, of the acts of the Pharisees in their AG:734B CB:1268A
assiduous attention to the cleansing of themselves after coming from the market place (some texts have *baptizō* here). See SPRINKLE.

1026 7. BRECHŌ (βρέχω), to wet, is translated to wash in Luke 7 : 38,
AG:147C 44, A.V. ; the R.V., " to wet " and " hath wetted," gives the correct
CB:1239B rendering. See RAIN, B.

907 8. BAPTIZŌ (βαπτίζω) is rendered " washed " in Luke 11 : 38. See
AG:131C BAPTIZE.
CB:1238C

Note : With regard to Nos. 1, 3, 5, the Sept. of Lev. 15 : 11 contains all three with their distinguishing characteristics, No. 1 being used of the hands, No. 3 of the whole body, No. 5 of the garments.

WASHING

909 1. BAPTISMOS (βαπτισμός) denotes the act of washing, ablution,
AG:132D with special reference to purification, Mark 7 : 4 (in some texts, ver. 8) ;
CB:1238C Heb. 6 : 2, " baptisms ; " 9 : 10, " washings." See BAPTISM.¶

3067 2. LOUTRON (λουτρόν), a bath, a laver (akin to *louō*, see above),
AG:480C is used metaphorically of the Word of God, as the instrument of spiritual
CB:1257B cleansing, Eph. 5 : 26 ; in Tit. 3 : 5, of " the washing of regeneration "
(see REGENERATION).¶ In the Sept., S. of Sol. 4 : 2 ; 6 : 6.¶

WASTE (Noun and Verb)

A. Noun.

684 APŌLEIA (ἀπώλεια), destruction, is translated " waste " in Matt.
AG:103B
CB:1237A 26 : 8 ; Mark 14 : 4. See DESTRUCTION, B, II, No. 1.

B. Verbs.

1287 1. DIASKORPIZŌ (διασκορπίζω), to scatter abroad, is used meta-
AG:188B phorically of squandering property, Luke 15 : 13 ; 16 : 1. See DISPERSE,
CB:1241B SCATTER.

4199 2. PORTHEŌ (πορθέω), to ravage, is rendered " wasted " in Gal.
AG:693A 1 : 13, A.V. ; see DESTROY, Note, HAVOCK.
CB:—

3075 3. LUMAINŌ (λυμαίνω), to outrage, maltreat, is used in the Middle
AG:481C Voice in Acts 8 : 3, of Saul's treatment of the church, R.V., " laid waste "
CB:— (A.V., " made havock of ").¶

WATCH (Noun and Verb), WATCHERS, WATCHFUL, WATCHINGS

A. Nouns.

5438 1. PHULAKĒ (φυλακή) is used (*a*) with the meaning ' a watch,'
AG:867D actively, a guarding, Luke 2 : 8, lit., ' (keeping, *phulassō*) watches ; '
CB:1264C (*b*) of the time during which guard was kept by night, a watch of the
night, Matt. 14 : 25 ; 24 : 43 ; Mark 6 : 48 ; Luke 12 : 38. See CAGE, HOLD, IMPRISONMENT, PRISON.

Note : Among the Jews the night was divided into three watches (see, e.g., Ex. 14 : 24 ; Judg. 7 : 19), and this continued on through Roman times. The Romans divided the night into four watches ; this was recognized among the Jews (see Mark 13 : 35).

2892
AG:447B 2. KOUSTŌDIA (κουστωδία), from Lat., *custodia* (cp. Eng., custody),
CB:— is rendered " watch " in Matt. 27 : 65, 66 and 28 : 11, A.V. : see GUARD.¶

3. AGRUPNIA (ἀγρυπνία), sleeplessness (akin to B, No. 4), is rendered 70
"watchings" in 2 Cor. 6:5; 11:27.¶ AG:14A

B. Verbs. CB:1233C

1. GRĒGOREŌ (γρηγορέω), to watch, is used (*a*) of keeping awake, 1127
e.g., Matt. 24:43; 26:38, 40, 41; (*b*) of spiritual alertness, e.g., Acts AG:167B
20:31; 1 Cor. 16:13; Col. 4:2; 1 Thess. 5:6, 10 (for which see CB:1248C
WAKE); 1 Pet. 5:8, R.V., "be watchful" (A.V., "be vigilant");
Rev. 3:2, 3; 16:15.

2. TĒREŌ (τηρέω), to keep, is rendered to watch, of those who kept 5083
guard at the Cross, Matt. 27:36, 54; 28:4, R.V., "watchers" (A.V., AG:814D
"keepers"), lit., 'the watching ones.' See HOLD, No. 8, KEEP, OBSERVE, CB:1271B
PRESERVE, RESERVE.

3. PARATĒREŌ (παρατηρέω), to observe, especially with sinister 3906
intent (*para*, near, and No. 2), is rendered to watch in Mark 3:2; Luke AG:622C
6:7; 14:1; 20:20; Acts 9:24. See OBSERVE. CB:1262B

4. AGRUPNEŌ (ἀγρυπνέω), to be sleepless (from *agreuō*, to chase, 69
and *hupnos*, sleep), is used metaphorically, to be watchful, in Mark 13:33; AG:14A
Luke 21:36; Eph. 6:18; Heb. 13:17. The word expresses not mere CB:1233C
wakefulness, but the watchfulness of those who are intent upon a thing.¶

5. NĒPHŌ (νήφω), to abstain from wine, is used metaphorically of 3525
moral alertness, and translated to watch, in the A.V. of 2 Tim. 4:5. AG:538D
See SOBER. CB:1259C

WATER (Noun and Verb), WATERING, WATERLESS

A. Noun.

HUDŌR (ὕδωρ), whence Eng. prefix, *hydro–*, is used (*a*) of the natural 5204
element, frequently in the Gospels; in the plural especially in the AG:832D
Apocalypse; elsewhere, e.g., Heb. 9:19; Jas. 3:12; in 1 John 5:6, CB:1251C
that Christ "came by water and blood," may refer either (1) to the elements that flowed from His side on the Cross after His Death, or, in view of the order of the words and the prepositions here used, (2) to His baptism in Jordan and His Death on the Cross. As to (1), the water would symbolize the moral and practical cleansing effected by the removal of defilement by our taking heed to the Word of God in heart, life and habit; cp. Lev. 14, as to the cleansing of the leper. As to (2), Jesus the Son of God came on His mission by, or through, water and blood, namely, at His baptism, when He publicly entered upon His mission and was declared to be the Son of God by the witness of the Father, and at the Cross, when He publicly closed His witness; the Apostle's statement thus counteracts the doctrine of the Gnostics that the Divine *Logos* united Himself with the Man Jesus at His baptism, and left him at Gethsemane. On the contrary, He who was baptized and He who was crucified was the Son of God throughout in His combined Deity and humanity.

The word water is used symbolically in John 3:5, either (1) of the Word of God, as in 1 Pet. 1:23 (cp. the symbolic use in Eph. 5:26), or, in view of the preposition *ek*, out of, (2) of the truth conveyed by baptism, this being the expression, not the medium, the symbol, not the cause, of the believer's identification with Christ in His Death, Burial and Resurrection. So the new birth is, in one sense, the setting aside of all that the believer was according to the flesh, for it is evident that there must be an entirely new beginning. Some regard the *kai*, " and," in John 3 : 5, as epexegetic, = ' even,' in which case the water would be emblematic of the Spirit, as in John 7 : 38 (cp. 4 : 10, 14), but not in 1 John 5 : 8, where the Spirit and the water are distinguished. " The water of life," Rev. 21 : 6 and 22 : 1, 17, is emblematic of the maintenance of spiritual life in perpetuity. In Rev. 17 : 1 the waters are symbolic of nations, peoples, etc.

4215 AG:694D *Note :* For *potamos*, rendered " waters " in 2 Cor. 11 : 26, see RIVER.

CB:1266B

B. Verb.

4222 AG:695D CB:1266B POTIZŌ (ποτίζω), to give to drink, is used (*a*) naturally in Luke 13 : 15, " watering," with reference to animals ; (*b*) figuratively, with reference to spiritual ministry to converts, 1 Cor. 3 : 6–8. See DRINK, B, No. 3.

HUDROPOTEŌ 5202 AG:832D ANUDROS 504 AG:76C *Notes :* (1) For *hudropoteō*, to drink water, 1 Tim. 5 : 23, see DRINK, B, No. 5. (2) For the adjective *anudros*, waterless (R.V.), without water, see DRY, No. 2.

WATERPOT

5201 AG:832C CB:— HUDRIA (ὑδρία) occurs in John 2 : 6, 7 ; 4 : 28.¶

WAVE

2949 AG:457C CB:— 1. KUMA (κῦμα), from *kuō*, to be pregnant, to swell, is used (*a*) literally in the plural, Matt. 8 : 24 ; 14 : 24 ; Mark 4 : 37 (Acts 27 : 41, in some mss.) ; (*b*) figuratively, Jude 13.¶

4535 AG:741A CB:1268B 2. SALOS (σάλος) denotes a tossing, especially the rolling swell of the sea, Luke 21 : 25, A.V., " waves " (R.V., " billows ").¶

2830 AG:436D CB:— 3. KLUDŌN (κλύδων), a billow, is translated " wave " in Jas. 1 : 6, A.V. (R.V., " surge ") ; in Luke 8 : 24 it is translated " raging (of the water)." See RAGE, B.¶

WAVER, WAVERING

A. Adjective.

186 AG:30C CB:— AKLINĒS (ἀκλινής), without bending (*a*, negative, *klinō*, to bend), occurs in Heb. 10 : 23, A.V., " without wavering," R.V., " that it waver not."¶

B. Verb.

1252 AG:185A CB:1241A DIAKRINŌ (διακρίνω) is rendered to waver in Rom. 4 : 20, R.V. (A.V., " staggered ") ; in Jas. 1 : 6 (twice). See DOUBT, No. 3.

WAX

4298 AG:707D CB:1266C 1. PROKOPTŌ (προκόπτω), for which see ADVANCE, is rendered to wax in 2 Tim. 3 : 13.

2. GINOMAI (γίνομαι), to become, is translated "waxed" in Luke 1096
13:19, A.V. (R.V., "became"); in Heb. 11:34, A.V. and R.V., AG:158A CB:1248B
"waxed:" see COME, No. 12, etc.

Note: This verb forms part of the translation of certain tenses of other verbs; see, e.g., BOLD, A, No. 2, COLD, C, CONFIDENT, B, No. 1, CORRUPT, A, No. 2, GROSS, OLD, D, No. 2, STRONG, B, No. 2, WANTON, B, Nos. 1 and 2, WEARY, No. 2, WROTH, No. 1.

WAY

1. HODOS (ὁδός) denotes (*a*) a natural path, road, way, frequent in the 3598
Synoptic Gospels; elsewhere, e.g., Acts 8:26; 1 Thess. 3:11; Jas. AG:553D CB:1251A
2:25; Rev. 16:12; (*b*) a traveller's way (see JOURNEY); (*c*) metaphorically, of a course of conduct, or way of thinking, e.g., of righteousness,
Matt. 21:32; 2 Pet. 2:21; of God, Matt. 22:16, and parallels, i.e.,
the way instructed and approved by God; so Acts 18:26 and Heb. PARODOS 3938
3:10, "My ways" (cp. Rev. 15:3); of the Lord, Acts 18:25; "that AG:628D
leadeth to destruction," Matt. 7:13; ". . . unto life," 7:14; of peace, CB:—
Luke 1:79; Rom. 3:17; of Paul's ways in Christ, 1 Cor. 4:17 (plural); TROPOS 5158
"more excellent" (of love), 1 Cor. 12:31; of truth, 2 Pet. 2:2; of the AG:827B
right way, 2:15; of Balaam (*id.*); of Cain, Jude 11; of a way consisting CB:1273A
in what is from God, e.g., of life, Acts 2:28 (plural); of salvation, Acts POREIA 4197
16:17; personified, of Christ as the means of access to the Father, AG:692A
John 14:6; of the course followed and characterized by the followers TOPOS 5117
of Christ, Acts 9:2; 19:9, 23; 24:22. See HIGHWAY. AG:822B

Note: In Luke 5:19 and 19:4 the noun is not expressed in the CB:1273A MAKRAN
original, but is understood. 3112

2. PARODOS (πάροδος), a passing or passage, is used with *en*, in, 1 AG:487C CB:1257C
Cor. 16:7, "by the way" (lit, 'in passing').¶ PORRō

3. TROPOS (τρόπος), a turning, a manner, is translated "way" 4206
in Rom. 3:2, "(every) way;" Phil. 1:18, "(in every) way." See AG:693D CB:1266A
CONVERSATION, MANNER, MEANS. PLANAō 4105

Notes: (1) In Jas. 1:11, A.V., *poreia*, a journey, a going, is rendered AG:665B
"ways" (R.V., "goings"). (2) In Heb. 12:17, *topos*, a place, is rendered CB:1265A MESOS
in A.V. marg., "way (to change his mind)." (3) For the A.V. rendering of 3319
makran, a good (or great) way off, Matt. 8:30; Luke 15:20, see FAR, B, AG:507B
No. 1. (4) In Luke 14:32, *porrō* is rendered "a great way off." (5) In Heb. CB:1258B ALLACHOTHEN
5:2, A.V., *planaō*, Middle Voice, to wander, is rendered "(them) that are 237
out of the way," R.V., "(the) erring." (6) In Col. 2:14 and 2 Thess. AG:39B EN
2:7, *ek mesou*, is translated "out of the way;" see MIDST, Note (1) (*e*). 1722
(7) For "two ways" in Mark 11:4, A.V., see STREET. (8) In John 10:1, AG:258B
the adverb *allachothen*, from some other place (from *allos*, another), CB:1244B HUPOTAGē
is translated "some other way". (9) In 2 Pet. 3:1, the A.V. translates 5292
en "by way of" ("by", R.V.). (10) In Gal. 2:5, the renderings "by," AG:847D
A.V., "in the way of," R.V., serve to express the dative case of *hupotagē*, CB:1252B PROPEMPō
subjection. (11) For *propempō*, to bring on one's way, Acts 15:3; 21:5, 4311 AG:709B

and the A.V. of 2 Cor. 1 : 16 (R.V., "to be set forward on my journey"),
APERCHOMAI 565 see BRING, No. 25. (12) *Aperchomai*, to go away, is rendered to go one's
AG:84C way, e.g., Matt. 13 : 25; 20 : 4; Mark 11 : 4; 12 : 12; Luke 19 : 32;
CB:1236B John 11 : 46; Acts 9 : 17; Jas. 1 : 24: see GO, No. 14. (13) In Luke
POREUOMAI 4198 8 : 14, A.V., *poreuomai*, to go on one's way (R.V.), is rendered "go forth;"
AG:692B in 13 : 33, A.V., "walk" (R.V., "go on my way"); in Matt. 24 : 1, A.V.,
CB:1266A it is rendered "departed" (R.V., "was going on his way"): see DEPART,
PANTĒ 3839 No. 8. (14) In Acts 24 : 3, *pantē* is rendered "in all ways" (A.V.,
AG:608D CB:— "always").¶ (15) In Rom. 3 : 12, A.V., *ekklinō*, to turn aside (R.V.),
EKKLINŌ 1578 is rendered "are gone out of the way." (16) See also ESCAPE, B,
AG:241C CB:— LASCIVIOUS.

WE

2249 *Note:* When this is not part of the translation of a verb or phrase, it
AG:217A stands for some case of *hēmeis*, the plural of *egō*, I; this separate use of
(EGŌ) CB:— the pronoun is always emphatic. For "we ourselves," see OURSELVES.

WEAK, WEAKENED, WEAKER, WEAKNESS

A. Adjectives.

772 1. ASTHENĒS (ἀσθενής), lit., strengthless (see IMPOTENT), is translated
AG:115C CB:1238A "weak," (*a*) of physical weakness, Matt. 26 : 41; Mark 14 : 38; 1 Cor. 1 : 27; 4 : 10; 11 : 30 (a judgment upon spiritual laxity in a church); 2 Cor. 10 : 10; 1 Pet. 3 : 7 (comparative degree); (*b*) in the spiritual sense, said of the rudiments of Jewish religion, in their inability to justify anyone, Gal. 4 : 9; of the Law, Heb. 7 : 18; in Rom. 5 : 6, R.V., "weak" (A.V., "without strength"), of the inability of man to accomplish his salvation; (*c*) morally or ethically, 1 Cor. 8 : 7, 10; 9 : 22; (*d*) rhetorically, of God's actions according to the human estimate, 1 Cor. 1 : 25, "weakness," lit., 'the weak things of God.' See FEEBLE, SICK.

102 2. ADUNATOS (ἀδύνατος), lit., not powerful, is translated "weak"
AG:19A CB:1233A in Rom. 15 : 1, of the infirmities of those whose scruples arise through lack of faith (see 14 : 22, 23), in the same sense as No. 1 (*c*); the change in the adjective (cp. 14 : 1) is due to the contrast with *dunatoi*, the "strong," who have not been specifically mentioned as such in chap. 14. See IMPOSSIBLE.

B. Verb.

770 ASTHENEŌ (ἀσθενέω), to lack strength, is used in much the same way
AG:115B CB:1238A as A, No. 1, and translated "being . . . weak" in Rom. 4 : 19, A.V. (R.V., "being weakened"); 8 : 3; 14 : 1, 2 (in some texts, 1 Cor. 8 : 9); 2 Cor. 11 : 21, 29 (twice); 12 : 10; 13 : 3, 4, 9. See DISEASED, IMPOTENT, SICK.

C. Noun.

769 ASTHENEIA (ἀσθένεια), for which see INFIRMITY, is rendered "weak-
AG:115A CB:1238A ness," of the body, 1 Cor. 2 : 3; 15 : 43; 2 Cor. 11 : 30, R.V.; 12 : 5 (plural, R.V.), 9, 10, R.V.; Heb. 11 : 34; in 2 Cor. 13 : 4, "He was

crucified through weakness" is said in respect of the physical sufferings to which Christ voluntarily submitted in giving Himself up to the death of the Cross.

WEALTH

EUPORIA (εὐπορία), primarily facility (*eu*, well, *poros*, a passage), 2142
hence plenty, wealth, occurs in Acts 19 : 25.¶ Cp. *euporeō*, to be well AG:324B
provided for, to prosper, Acts 11 : 29.¶ CB:—

Note: In 1 Cor. 10 : 24, the A.V., "*wealth*," R.V., "*good*," is, lit., 'the (thing) of the other.'

WEAPONS

HOPLON (ὅπλον), always in the plur., is translated "weapons" 3696
in John 18 : 3 and 2 Cor. 10 : 4, the latter metaphorically of those used in AG:575C
spiritual warfare. See ARMOUR, INSTRUMENTS. CB:1251A

WEAR, WEARING

A. Verbs.

1. PHOREŌ (φορέω), a frequentative form of *pherō*, to bear, and de- 5409
noting repeated or habitual action, is chiefly used of clothing, weapons, etc., AG:864D
of soft raiment, Matt. 11 : 8; fine clothing, Jas. 2 : 3; the crown of CB:—
thorns, John 19 : 5. See BEAR, No. 7.

2. ENDIDUSKŌ (ἐνδιδύσκω), to put on, is used in the Active Voice 1737
in Mark 15 : 17 (in good mss.; some have No. 3); in Luke 8 : 27 (Middle AG:263A
Voice), in some texts; the best have No. 3. For Luke 16 : 19, see CB:—
CLOTHE, No. 3.¶

3. ENDUŌ (ἐνδύω) is rendered to wear in Luke 8 : 27 (Middle Voice; 1746
see No. 2). See CLOTHE, No. 2, PUT, No. 26. AG:264A CB:1245A

4. KLINŌ (κλίνω), to bend, decline, is used of a day, wearing away, 2827
Luke 9 : 12 (in 24 : 29, "is far spent"). See BOW, No. 4, FLIGHT, B, AG:436C
LAY, No. 6, SPEND. CB:—

5. HUPŌPIAZŌ (ὑπωπιάζω) is translated "wear (me) out" in Luke 5299
18 : 5, R.V. (A.V., "weary"). For this and the somewhat different AG:848D
application in 1 Cor. 9 : 27, see BUFFET, No. 2.¶ CB:1252B

B. Noun.

PERITHESIS (περίθεσις), a putting around or on (*peri*, around, 4025
tithēmi, to put), is used in 1 Pet. 3 : 3 of wearing jewels of gold (R.V.).¶ AG:647C CB:—

For WEARINESS, 2 Cor. 11 : 27, R.V., see LABOUR, No. 1

WEARY

1. KOPIAŌ (κοπιάω), to grow weary, be beaten out (*kopos*, a beating, 2872 AG:443C
toil), is used of the Lord in John 4 : 6 (used in His own word "labour" in CB:1255C
Matt. 11 : 28), in Rev. 2 : 3, R.V. See, LABOUR, TOIL. 2577

2. KAMNŌ (κάμνω), to be weary, is rendered to wax weary in Heb. AG:402A CB:—

1573 12 : 3, R.V. See FAINT, No. 3, SICK.
(EKK-) AG:215C 3. EKKAKEŌ or ENKAKEŌ (ἐκκακέω), for which see FAINT, No. 2,
CB:1245A is rendered to be weary in Gal. 6 : 9 ; 2 Thess. 3 : 13.
5299 *Note :* For *hupōpiazō*, rendered to weary in Luke 18 : 5, A.V., see
AG:848D CB:1252B WEAR, A, No. 5.

WEATHER

2105 AG:319A 1. EUDIA (εὐδία), akin to *eudios*, calm, denotes "fair weather,"
CB:1247A Matt. 16 : 2.¶
5494 AG:879D 2. CHEIMŌN (χειμών), winter, also a winter storm, is translated
CB:— "foul weather" in Matt. 16 : 3. See TEMPEST, WINTER.

WEEDS See TARES

For WEDDING see MARRIAGE

WEEK

4521 AG:739A SABBATON (σάββατον) is used (*a*) in the plural in the phrase "the
CB:1268B first day of the week," Matt. 28 : 1 ; Mark 16 : 2, 9 ; Luke 24 : 1 ; John
20 : 1, 19 ; Acts 20 : 7 ; 1 Cor. 16 : 2. For this idiomatic use of the word
see ONE, A, (5) ; (*b*) in the singular, Luke 18 : 12, "twice in the week,"
lit., 'twice of the sabbath,' i.e., twice in the days after the sabbath. See
SABBATH.

WEEP, WEEPING

A. Verbs.

KLAIŌ 2799 1. KLAIŌ (κλαίω) is used of any loud expression of grief, especially
AG:433A in mourning for the dead, Matt. 2 : 18 ; Mark 5 : 38, 39 ; 16 : 10 ; Luke
CB:1255A 7 : 13 ; 8 : 52 (twice) ; John 11 : 31, 33 (twice) ; 20 : 11 (twice), 13, 15 ;
DAKRUŌ 1145 Acts 9 : 39 ; otherwise, e.g., in exhortations, Luke 23 : 28 ; Rom. 12 : 15 ;
AG:170A Jas. 4 : 9 ; 5 : 1 ; negatively, "weep not," Luke 7 : 13 ; 8 : 52 ; 23 : 28 ;
CB:— THRĒNEŌ Rev. 5 : 5 (cp. Acts 21 : 13) ; in 18 : 9, R.V., "shall weep" (A.V., "be-
2354 wail"). See BEWAIL.
AG:363B CB:1272B 2. DAKRUŌ (δακρύω), to shed tears (*dakruon*, a tear), is used only
ALALAZŌ of the Lord Jesus, John 11 : 35.¶
214 AG:34D *Note :* Other synonymous verbs are *thrēneō*, to mourn, of formal
CB:— lamentation : see BEWAIL, Note (1) ; *alalazō*, to wail ; *stenazō*, to groan
STENAZŌ 4727 (*oduromai*, to lament audibly, is not used in N.T. ; see the noun *odurmos*,
AG:766B mourning).

CB:1270A

B. Noun.

2805 AG:433C KLAUTHMOS (κλαυθμός), akin to A, No. 1, denotes weeping, crying,
CB:1255B Matt. 2 : 18 ; 8 : 12 ; 13 : 42, 50, R.V. (A.V., "wailing") ; 22 : 13 ;
24 : 51 ; 25 : 30 ; Luke 13 : 28 ; Acts 20 : 37.¶

WEIGH, WEIGHT, WEIGHTY, WEIGHTIER

A. Verbs.

916 AG:133C 1. BAREŌ (βαρέω), to weigh down, is so rendered in 2 Cor. 1 : 8, R.V. ;
CB:1238C see BURDEN, B, No. 1.

2. HISTĒMI (ἵστημι), to cause to stand, is used in Matt. 26 : 15, 2476
R.V., " they weighed (unto) " (of pieces of silver), A.V., metaphorically, AG:381D
" covenanted (with)." CB:1250C

B. Nouns.

1. BAROS (βάρος), akin to A, is rendered " weight " in 2 Cor. 4 : 17. 922
See Burden, A, No. 1. AG:133D CB:1238C
2. ONKOS (ὄγκος) denotes a bulk or mass ; hence, metaphorically, 3591
an encumbrance, weight, Heb. 12 : 1.¶ AG:553A CB:1260C

C. Adjective.

BARUS (βαρύς), heavy (akin to A and B, No. 1), is rendered " weighty " 926
in 2 Cor. 10 : 10, of Paul's letters. The comparative degree is used in the AG:134B CB:1238C
neuter plural in Matt. 23 : 23, " (the) weightier matters (of the Law)."
See Grievous, Heavy.

WELCOME

1. APODECHOMAI (ἀποδέχομαι), to receive gladly, is rendered to 588
welcome in the R.V. of Luke 8 : 40 ; 9 : 11. See Receive. AG:90A CB:1236C
2. HUPOLAMBANŌ (ὑπολαμβάνω), to take up, to entertain, is 5274
rendered " to welcome " in 3 John 8, R.V., of a hearty welcome to servants AG:845B CB:1252B
of God. See Receive.

WELL (Noun) 5421

PHREAR (φρέαρ), a pit, is translated a " well " in John 4 : 11, 12. AG:865D
See Pit. CB:1264C 4077
Note : For *pēgē*, translated " well " in John 4 : 6 (twice), 14 ; 2 Pet. AG:655D
2 : 17, see Fountain. CB:1263A

--- KALoS 2573

WELL (Adverb) AG:401B

1. KALŌS (καλῶς), finely (akin to *kalos*, good, fair), is usually trans- CB:1253B KALLION
lated " well," indicating what is done rightly ; in the Epistles it is most 2566
frequent in 1 Tim. (3 : 4, 12, 13 ; 5 : 17) ; twice it is used as an exclamation AG:401B (KALōS 7.)
of approval, Mark 12 : 32 ; Rom. 11 : 20 ; the comparative degree KALOS
kallion, " very well," occurs in Acts 25 : 10. See Good, C, No. 1. 2570
Note : The neuter form of the adjective *kalos*, with the article and the AG:400B CB:1253B
present participle of *poieō*, to do, is translated " well-doing " in Gal. 6 : 9. EU
2. EU (εὖ), primarily the neuter of an old word, *eus*, noble, good, is used 2095 AG:317B
(*a*) with verbs, e.g., Mark 14 : 7, " do (*poieō*) . . . good ; " Acts 15 : 29 CB:1247A BELTION
(*prassō*) ; Eph. 6 : 3 (*ginomai*, to be) ; (*b*) in replies, good, " well done," 957
Matt. 25 : 21, 23 ; in Luke 19 : 17, *eu ge* (in the best texts). The word AG:139B
is the opposite of *kakōs*, evilly. See Good, C, No. 2.¶ (-IōN) HoS
Notes : (1) In 2 Tim. 1 : 18, *beltion*, the neuter form of what is used 5613
as the comparative degree of *agathos*, good, is used adverbially and trans- AG:897A CB:1251B
lated " very well."¶ (2) For John 2 : 10, " have well drunk " (R.V., KATHōS
" freely "), see Drink, B, No. 2. (3) *Hōs*, as, with *kai*, also (and), is 2531 AG:391B
rendered " as well as " in Acts 10 : 47 (*kathōs* in some mss.) and 1 Cor. CB:1254C

2509 AG:387A 9 : 5. (4) In Heb 4 : 2 *kathaper*, even as, with *kai*, is translated "as well
CB:— as :" see EVEN, No. 8.

WELL (do), WELL-DOING

A. Verbs.

15 AG:2C 1. AGATHOPOIEŌ (ἀγαθοποιέω), to do good (*agathos*, good, *poieō*,
CB:1233B to do), is used (*a*) of such activity in general, 1 Pet. 2 : 15, "well-doing ;" ver. 20, "do well ;" 3 : 6, 17 ; 3 John 11, "doeth good ;" (*b*) of acting for another's benefit, Mark 3 : 4 ; Luke 6 : 9, 33, 35.¶

2569 AG:400B 2. KALOPOIEŌ (καλοποιέω), to do well, excellently, act honourably
CB:1253B (*kalos*, good, *poieō*, to do), occurs in 2 Thess. 3 : 13.¶ The two parts of the word occur separately in Rom. 7 : 21 ; 2 Cor. 13 : 7 ; Gal. 6 : 9 ; Jas. 4 : 17.

Notes : (1) The distinction between Nos. 1 and 2 follows that between *agathos* and *kalos* (see GOOD). (2) In John 11 : 12, A.V., *sōzō* (Passive Voice, to be saved), is rendered "he shall do well" (R.V., "he will recover").

B. Noun.

16 AG:2C AGATHOPOIIA (ἀγαθοποιΐα), well-doing (akin to A, No. 1), occurs
CB:1233B in 1 Pet. 4 : 19.¶

C. Adjective.

17 AG:2C AGATHOPOIOS (ἀγαθοποιός), doing good, beneficent, is translated
CB:1233B "them that do well" in 1 Pet. 2 : 14, lit., 'well-doing (ones).'¶

For WELL-BELOVED see BELOVED

WELL-NIGH

SUMPLēROō 4845 *Note :* This forms part of the translation of *sumplēroō*, to fulfil, in Luke
AG:779C 9 : 51, "were well-nigh" come (see COME, No. 36), and *plēroō*, to fulfil,
CB:1270B PLēROō in Acts 7 : 23, "was well-nigh . . .," lit., 'a time (of forty years) was
4137 fulfilled (to him)' (see FULFIL, A, No. 1).
AG:670C
CB:1265B

WELL PLEASED

A. Noun.

2107 EUDOKIA (εὐδοκία), good pleasure, occurs in the genitive case in
AG:319C Luke 2 : 14, lit., "(men) of good pleasure" (so R.V. marg.), R.V., "(men)
CB:1247A in whom He is well pleased" (the genitive is objective) ; the A.V., "good will (toward men)," follows the inferior texts which have the nominative. See DESIRE, PLEASURE, SEEM, WELL-PLEASING, WILL.

B. Verb.

2106 AG:319B EUDOKEŌ (εὐδοκέω), to be well pleased : see PLEASE, A, No. 3,
CB:1247A WILLING, B, No. 3.

WELL-PLEASING

2101 AG:318D
A. Adjective.

CB:1247A EUARESTOS (εὐάρεστος) is used in Rom. 12 : 1, 2, translated

" acceptable " (R.V. marg., " well-pleasing ") ; in the following the R.V. has " well-pleasing," Rom. 14 : 18 ; 2 Cor. 5 : 9 ; Eph. 5 : 10 ; in Phil. 4 : 18 and Col. 3 : 20 (R.V. and A.V.) ; in Tit. 2 : 9, R.V., " well-pleasing " (A.V., " please . . . well ") ; in Heb. 13 : 21, R.V. and A.V. See ACCEPTABLE.¶

B. Verb.

EUARESTEŌ (εὐαρεστέω), akin to A, is rendered to be well-pleasing 2100
in Heb. 11 : 5, 6, R.V. (A.V., " please ") ; in Heb. 13 : 16, " is well AG:318C
pleased."¶ CB:1247A

C. Noun.

EUDOKIA (εὐδοκία), lit., 'good pleasure,' is rendered " well-pleasing " 2107
in Matt. 11 : 26 and Luke 10 : 21. See DESIRE, PLEASURE, SEEM, WELL AG:319C CB:1247A
PLEASED, WILL.

For WENT see GO

WEST

DUSMĒ (δυσμή), the quarter of the sun-setting (*dusis*, a sinking, 1424
setting ; *dunō*, to sink), hence, the west, occurs in Matt. 8 : 11 ; 24 : 27 ; AG:209D
Luke 12 : 54 (some regard this as the sunset) ; 13 : 29 ; Rev. 21 : 13.¶ CB:—

For WET, Luke 7 : 38, 44, R.V., see WASH, No. 7 KeTOS 2785

WHALE AG:431D CB:1255A

KĒTOS (κῆτος) denotes a huge fish, a sea-monster, Matt. 12 : 40.¶ HOS
In the Sept., Gen. 1 : 21 ; Job 3 : 8 ; 9 : 13 ; 26 : 12 ; Jonah 1 : 17 3739
(twice) ; 2 : 1, 10.¶ AG:583B TIS 5101 AG:818D

WHAT CB:1272C

Notes : (1) Most frequently this is a translation of some form of the HOIOS
relative pronoun *hos* or the interrogative *tis*. (2) Other words are (*a*) 3634 AG:562C
hoios, of what kind, e.g., 2 Cor. 10 : 11, R.V. (A.V., " such as ") ; 1 Thess. CB:1251A
1 : 5, " what manner of men ; " 2 Tim. 3 : 11 (twice), lit., ' what sorts of POIOS
things,' ' what sorts of persecutions ; ' (*b*) *poios*, what sort of, e.g., Matt. 4169 AG:684C
21 : 23, 24, 27 ; 24 : 42, 43 ; Luke 5 : 19 ; 6 : 32–34 ; 20 : 2, 8 ; 24 : 19 ; HOPOIOS
John 12 : 33, " what manner of ; " so in 18 : 32 ; 21 : 19 ; Rom. 3 : 27 ; 3697 AG:575D
1 Cor. 15 : 35 ; in Jas. 4 : 14, " what ; " 1 Pet. 2 : 20 and Rev. 3 : 3 HOSOS
(ditto) ; 1 Pet. 1 : 11, " what manner of ; " (*c*) *hopoios*, " what sort of," 3745 AG:586B
1 Cor. 3 : 13 ; " what manner of," 1 Thess. 1 : 9 ; (*d*) *hosos*, how great, CB:1251B
Mark 6 : 30 (twice), R.V., " whatsoever ; " Acts 15 : 12 ; Rom. 3 : 19, POSOS
" what things soever ; " Jude 10 (1st part), " what soever things," R.V. ; 4214 AG:694B
(2nd part) " what ; " (*e*) *posos*, how great, how much, 2 Cor. 7 : 11, " what HOSTIS 3748
(earnest care)," R.V. (*posos* here stands for the repeated words in the AG:586D
Eng. Versions, the adjective not being repeated in the original) ; (*f*) HOUTōS 3779
hostis, " what (things)," Phil. 3 : 7 ; (*g*) in Matt. 26 : 40, *houtōs*, thus, AG:597C

POTAPOS so, is used as an exclamatory expression, translated " What " (in a word
4217 immediately addressed by the Lord to Peter), lit., ' So ; ' (*h*) for *potapos*,
AG:694D rendered " what " in Mark 13 : 1 (2nd part), A.V., see MANNER ; (*i*) in
CB:— ē 1 Cor. 6 : 16, 19, A.V., the particle *ē*, " or " (R.V.), is rendered " What ? " ;
2228 AG:342A in 1 Cor. 14 : 36, A.V. and R.V., " what ? " (*j*) in 1 Cor. 11 : 22, *gar*, in
CB:— truth, indeed, has its exclamatory use " What ? ". (3) In John 5 : 19
GAR " but what " translates a phrase, lit., ' if not anything.' (4) In Matt.
1063 AG:151C 8 : 33 " what " is, lit., ' the things ' (neuter plural of the article).
CB:1248A

WHATSOEVER

AN *Note :* For this see Notes on words under WHAT. Frequently by
302 AG:48B the addition of the particle *an*, or the conjunction *ean*, if, the phrase has
CB:— the more general idea of " whatsoever," e.g., with *hos*, Matt. 10 : 11 ;
EAN 1437 with *hosos*, Matt. 17 : 12 ; with *hostis*, neuter form, Luke 10 : 35.

AG:211A CB:1242C For WHEAT see CORN

For WHEEL, Jas. 3 : 6, R.V., see COURSE, A, No. 4

DIA 1223 AG:179B For WHEN, WHENCE, WHENSOEVER, WHERE, etc., see † p. 1

CB:1241A DIATI

WHEREFORE

1302 AG:179B *Note :* This represents (1) some phrases introduced by the preposition
(DIA B.II.2.) DIO *dia*, on account of, *dia touto*, on account of this, e.g., Matt. 12 : 31 ; Rom.
1352 5 : 12 ; Eph. 1 : 15 ; 3 John 10 ; *dia hēn* (the accusative feminine of *hos*,
AG:198D CB:1242A who), on account of which (*aitia*, a cause, being understood), e.g., Acts
DIOPER 10 : 21 (with *aitia*, expressed, Tit. 1 : 13 ; Heb. 2 : 11) ; *dia ti* on account
1355 AG:199A of what ? (sometimes as one word, *diati*), e.g., Luke 19 : 23 ; Rom. 9 : 32 ;
HOTHEN 2 Cor. 11 : 11 ; Rev. 17 : 7 ; (2) *dio* = *dia ho* (the neuter of the relative
3606 AG:555C pronoun *hos*), on account of which (thing), e.g., Matt. 27 : 8 ; Acts 15 : 19 ;
TI 20 : 31 ; 24 : 26 ; 25 : 26 ; 27 : 25, 34 ; Rom. 1 : 24 ; 15 : 7 ; 1 Cor.
5101 AG:818D 12 : 3 ; 2 Cor. 2 : 8 ; 5 : 9 ; 6 : 17 ; Eph. 2 : 11 ; 3 : 13 ; 4 : 8, 25 ; 5 : 14 ;
CB:1272C Phil. 2 : 9 ; 1 Thess. 5 : 11 ; Philm. 8 ; Heb. 3 : 7, 10 ; 10 : 5 ; 11 : 16 ;
HENEKA 12 : 12, 28 ; 13 : 12 ; Jas. 1 : 21 ; 4 : 6 ; 1 Pet. 1 : 13 ; 2 Pet. 1 : 10,
1752 AG:264D 12 ; 3 : 14 ; (3) *dioper*, for which very reason (a strengthened form of the
CB:1250A preceding), 1 Cor. 8 : 13 ; 10 : 14 (14 : 13 in some mss.) ;¶ (4) *hothen*
CHARIN 5484 (which denotes ' whence ', when used of direction or source, e.g., Matt.
AG:877A 12 : 44), used of cause and denoting ' wherefore ' in Heb. 2 : 17 ; 3 : 1 ;
CB:1239C (-IS) 7 : 25 ; 8 : 3 ; (5) *ti*, what, why, John 9 : 27 ; Acts 22 : 30 ; Gal. 3 : 19, A.V.
EIS (R.V., " what ") ; (6) *heneka* with *tinos* (the genitive case of *ti*), because
1519 AG:228A of what, Acts 19 : 32 ; (7) *charin* with *hou*, the genitive case, neuter of
CB:1243A *hos*, for the sake of what, Luke 7 : 47 ; (8) *eis*, unto, with *ti*, what, Matt.
ARA 686 14 : 31 ; with *ho*, which (the accusative neuter of *hos*), 2 Thess. 1 : 11,
AG:103D A.V. (R.V., " to which end ") ; (9) *ara*, so, 2 Cor. 7 : 12, A.V. (R.V.,
CB:1237B " so ") ; with *ge*, at least, Matt. 7 : 20, A.V. (R.V., " therefore ") ; (10)

hina, in order that, with *ti*, what, Matt. 9 : 4 ; (11) *toigaroun*, therefore, HINA 2443
rendered " wherefore " in Heb. 12 : 1, A.V. ; (12) in Matt. 26 : 50, *epi*, AG:376D
unto, with *ho*, as in No. (8) above, A.V., " wherefore (art thou come) ? " CB:1250C
R.V., " (*do* that) for which (thou art come) ; " (13) *oun*, a particle TOIGAROUN 5105
expressing sequence or consequence, e.g., Matt. 24 : 26 ; Acts 6 : 3 ; AG:821A
(14) *hōste*, so that, " wherefore," e.g., Rom. 7 : 12, 13 ; 1 Cor. 10 : 12 ; EPI 1909
11 : 27, 33 ; 14 : 22, 39 ; 2 Cor. 5 : 16 ; Gal. 3 : 24 ; 4 : 7 ; Phil. 4 : 1 ; AG:285D
1 Thess. 4 : 18 ; 1 Pet. 4 : 19. CB:1245C OUN

WHETHER : see † p 1 3767 AG:592D HōSTE

WHICH 5620 AG:899D

Notes : (1) This is the translation of (*a*) the article with nouns, HO
adjectives, numerals, participles, etc., e.g., " that which " etc. ; (*b*) the 3588 AG:549B
relative pronoun *hos*, " who," in one of its forms (a frequent use) ; (*c*) CB:—
hostis, whoever, differing from *hos* by referring to a subject in general, HOS 3739
as one of a class, e.g., Rom. 2 : 15 ; Gal. 4 : 24 (twice) ; 5 : 19 ; Rev. AG:583B
2 : 24 ; 20 : 4 ; (*d*) the interrogative pronoun *tis*, who ? which ?, e.g., CB:— HOSTIS
Matt. 6 : 27 ; John 8 : 46 ; (*e*) *hoios*, of what kind, e.g., Phil. 1 : 30 ; 3748
(*f*) *poios*, the interrogative of (*e*), e.g., John 10 : 32 ; (*g*) *hosos*, whatsoever, AG:586D CB:—
etc. ; plural, how many, translated " which " in Acts 9 : 39. (2) In TIS
Acts 8 : 26, A.V., *hautē* (the feminine of *houtos*, this), " the same " (R.V.), 5101
is translated " which." (3) In the triple title of God in Rev. 1 : 4, 8 ; AG:818D CB:1272C
4 : 8, " which " is the translation, firstly, of the article with the present HOIOS
participle of *eimi*, to be, lit., ' the (One) being,' secondly, of the article 3634 AG:562C
with the imperfect tense of *eimi* (impossible of lit. translation, the title CB:1251A
not being subject to grammatical change), thirdly, of the article with the POIOS 4169
present participle of *erchomai*, to come, lit., ' the coming (One) ; ' in 11 : 17 AG:684C
and 16 : 5 the wording of the A.V. and R.V. differs ; in 11 : 17 the A.V. CB:— HOSOS
follows the inferior mss. by adding " and art to come " (R.V. omits) ; 3745
in 16 : 5, the A.V., " and shalt be," represents *kai* (and) followed by the AG:586B CB:1251B
article and the future participle of *eimi*, to be, lit., ' and the (One) about HOUTOS
to be ; ' the R.V. substitutes the superior reading " Thou Holy One," 3778 AG:596B
lit., ' the holy (One) : ' see HOLY, B, No. 2. (4) In Phil. 2 : 21, A.V., " the CB:1251B
things of Jesus Christ " (R.V.), is rendered " the things which are Jesus
Christ's.

WHILE, WHILES, WHILST PROSKAIROS 4340

Notes : (1) See LITTLE, B, No. 1. (2) In Matt. 13 : 21, *proskairos* AG:715B
estin, lit., ' is for a season,' is rendered " dureth (R.V., endureth) for a CB:1267A CHRONOS
while." (3) *Chronos*, time, is rendered " while " in Luke 18 : 4 ; John 5550
7 : 33 ; 12 : 35 (1st part) ; 1 Cor. 16 : 7 ; *kairos*, a season, " a while," AG:887D CB:1240B
Luke 8 : 13 ; in Acts 19 : 22, R.V., " while " (A.V., " season ") ; for KAIROS
the different meanings of these words see SEASON. (4) In Acts 18 : 18, 2540 AG:394D
A.V., " a good while," is, lit., ' sufficient days,' R.V., " many days." CB:1253A

PALAI 3819 (5) In Acts 28 : 6, A.V., *epi polu,* lit., ' upon much,' is rendered " a great
AG:605C CB:1261C while " (R.V., " long "). (6) For Mark 1 : 35 see DAY, B. (7) In Mark
ACHRI(S) 15 : 44 *palai,* long ago, is rendered " any while." (8) In Acts 27 : 33
891 AG:128D and Heb. 3 : 13 *achri* (or *achris*) followed by *hou,* the genitive case of the
CB:1233A relative pronoun *hos,* lit., ' until which,' is rendered " while ; " cp. *en*
EN 1722 *hō̧,* in Mark 2 : 19 ; Luke 5 : 34 ; John 5 : 7 ; *en tō̧,* in Luke 1 : 21, R.V.,
AG:258B " while ; " in Heb. 3 : 15, " while it is said," is, lit., ' in the being said '
CB:1244B (*en,* with the article and the pres. infin., Passive of *legō*) ; so, e.g., in Matt.
HEōS 2193 13 : 25 (9) In Heb. 10 : 33, AV., " whilst ye were made," partly translating
AG:334B the present participle of *theatrizomai,* to become a gazing-stock, R.V.,
CB:1250A HIKANOS " being made ; " in the 2nd part, *ginomai,* to become, is translated " whilst
2425 ye became," A.V. (R.V., " becoming ").¶ (10) The conjunction *heōs,*
AG:374B CB:1250C until, etc., has the meaning " while " in Matt. 14 : 22 ; Mark 6 : 45 ;
HōS 14 : 32 ; in some texts, John 9 : 4 ; 12 : 35, 36 ; with *hotou,* whatever (an
5613 AG:897A oblique case, neuter, of *hostis,* whoever), " whiles," Matt. 5 : 25. (11) In
CB:1251B Acts 20 : 11 *hikanos,* sufficient, is rendered " a long while." (12) *Hōs,*
HOTAN 3752 as, " while " in Luke 24 : 32 (twice) ; John 12 : 35, 36 ; Acts 1 : 10 ;
AG:587D 10 : 17. (13) *Hotan,* when, is rendered " while " in 1 Cor. 3 : 4, A.V.
BRACHUS 1024 (R.V., " when "). (14) *Hote,* when, is rendered " while " in John 17 : 12 ;
AG:147B Heb. 9 : 17. (15) In John 4 : 31 *metaxu,* between, used with *en tō̧,* ' in the,'
CB:1239B is rendered " meanwhile ; " in Rom. 2 : 15 *metaxu* is itself rendered " the
HOTE 3753 mean while " (R.V., " between "). (16) In Acts 18 : 18, R.V., *hikanos* is
AG:588B rendered " many " (A.V., " good "). (17) In 1 Pet. 1 : 6, R.V., *oligon,* a
CB:1251B little, is rendered " for a little while " (A.V., " for a season ").
METAXU 3342 AG:512D

WHISPERER, WHISPERING

OLIGOS 3641 1. PSITHURISTĒS (ψιθυριστής), a whisperer, occurs in an evil sense
AG:563C in Rom. 1 : 29.¶
CB:1260C PSITHURISTēS 2. PSITHURISMOS (ψιθυρισμός), a whispering, is used of secret slander
5588 in 2 Cor. 12 : 20.¶ In the Sept., Eccl. 10 : 11, of a murmured enchant-
AG:893A CB:1267C ment.¶
PSITHURISMOS 5587 *Note :* Synonymous with No. 1 is *katalalos,* a backbiter (Rom. 1 : 30¶),
AG:892D CB:1267C KATALALOS the distinction being that this denotes one guilty of open calumny,
2637 *psithuristēs,* one who does it clandestinely.
AG:412D CB:1254A

For WHIT see EVERY WHIT and NOTHING, No. 2

WHITE (Adjective and Verb)

A. Adjective.

3022 AG:472B LEUKOS (λευκός) is used of (*a*) clothing (sometimes in the sense of
CB:1257A bright), Matt. 17 : 2 ; 28 : 3 ; Mark 9 : 3 ; 16 : 5 ; Luke 9 : 29 ; John
20 : 12 ; Acts 1 : 10 ; symbolically, Rev. 3 : 4, 5, 18 ; 4 : 4 ; 6 : 11 ; 7 : 9,
13 ; 19 : 14 (2nd part) ; (*b*) hair, Matt. 5 : 36 ; Christ's head and hair
(in a vision ; cp. Dan. 7 : 9), Rev. 1 : 14 (twice) ; ripened grain, John
4 : 35 ; a stone, Rev. 2 : 17, an expression of the Lord's special delight

in the overcomer, the new name on it being indicative of a secret communication of love and joy ; a horse (in a vision), 6 : 2 ; 19 : 11, 14 (1st part) ; a cloud, 14 : 14 ; the throne of God, 20 : 11.¶

Note : Lampros, bright, clear, is rendered " white " in Rev. 15 : 6, 2986
A.V., of " white (linen) " (R.V., " bright," following those mss. which AG:465D
have *lithon*, stone) ; in 19 : 8 (R.V., " bright "). See Bright, Clear, CB:1256C
Goodly, Note, Gorgeous.

B. Verbs.

1. LEUKAINŌ (λευκαίνω), to whiten, make white (akin to A), is used 3021
in Mark 9 : 3 ; figuratively in Rev. 7 : 14.¶ AG:472B CB:—

2. KONIAŌ (κονιάω), from *konia*, dust, lime, denotes to whiten, 2867
whitewash, of tombs, Matt. 23 : 27 ; figuratively of a hypocrite, Acts AG:443A
23 : 3.¶ In the Sept., Deut. 27 : 2, 4 ; Prov. 21 : 9.¶ CB:1255C

WHITHER, WHITHERSOEVER, see † p. 1

WHO, WHOM, WHOSE HOS

Notes : These are usually the translations of forms of the relative 3739
pronoun *hos*, or of the interrogative pronoun *tis* ; otherwise of *hostis*, AG:583B TIS
whoever, usually of a more general subject than *hos*, e.g., Mark 15 : 7 ; 5101
Luke 23 : 19 ; Gal. 2 : 4 ; *hosos*, as many as, Heb. 2 : 15 ; in Acts 13 : 7, AG:818D
A.V., *houtos*, this (man), is translated " who," R.V., " the same." CB:1272C HOSTIS

3748 AG:586D

WHOLE (made), WHOLLY, WHOLESOME HOSOS 3745

A. Adjectives. AG:586B

1. HOLOS (ὅλος), for which see All, A, No. 3, and Altogether, CB:1251B
signifies " whole," (*a*) with a noun, e.g., Matt. 5 : 29, 30 ; Mark 8 : 36 ; HOUTOS 3778
15 : 1, 16, 33 ; Luke 11 : 36 (1st part), though *holon* may here be used AG:596B
adverbially with *phōteinon*, ' wholly light ' [as in the 2nd part, R.V., CB:1251B
" wholly (full of light) "] ; John 11 : 50 ; 1 Cor. 12 : 17 (1st part) ; 1 John HOLOS 3650
2 : 2 ; 5 : 19 ; (*b*) absolutely, as a noun, e.g., Matt. 13 : 33 ; 1 Cor. 12 : 17 AG:564D
(2nd part). CB:1251A

2. PAS (πᾶς), for which see All, A, No. 1, is sometimes translated 3956
" the whole " when used with the article, e.g., Matt. 8 : 32, 34 ; Rom. AG:631A CB:1262C
8 : 22.

3. HAPAS (ἅπας), for which see All, A, No. 2, is rendered " the whole," 537
e.g., in Luke 19 : 37 ; 23 : 1. AG:81D CB:1249B

4. HOLOKLĒROS (ὁλόκληρος), from No. 1 and *klēros*, a lot, is 3648
rendered " whole " in 1 Thess. 5 : 23 : see Entire. AG:564C CB:—

5 HUGIĒS (ὑγιής) (cp. Eng., hygiene) is used especially in the
Gospels of making sick folk " whole," Matt. 12 : 13 ; 15 : 31 ; Mark 3 : 5 ; 5199 AG:832C
5 : 34 ; Luke 6 : 10 ; John 5 : 4, 6, 9, 11, 14, 15 ; 7 : 23 ; also Acts 4 : 10 ; CB:1251C
of " sound (speech)," Tit. 2 : 8. See Sound.¶

6. HOLOTELĒS (ὁλοτελής), " wholly," 1 Thess. 5 : 23, is lit., ' whole- 3651 AG:565A
complete ' (A, No. 1, and *telos*, an end), i.e., ' through and through ; ' CB:—

the Apostle's desire is that the sanctification of the believer may extend to every part of his being. The word is similar in meaning to No. 4; *holoklēros* draws attention to the person as a whole, *holotelēs* to the several parts which constitute him.¶

Note: In 1 Tim. 4 : 15, the sentence freely rendered "give thyself wholly to them" is, lit., 'be in these (things)'.

B. Verbs.

5198 1. HUGIAINŌ (ὑγιαίνω), to be in good health, akin to A, No. 5,
AG:832B CB:1251C is rendered "they that are whole" in Luke 5 : 31; "whole" in 7 : 10
(present participle); "wholesome" in 1 Tim. 6 : 3, A.V. (R.V., "sound;"
marg., "healthful"). See HEALTH, SOUND.

4982 2. SŌZŌ (σώζω), to save, is sometimes rendered to make whole, and,
AG:798A CB:1269C in the Passive Voice, to be made whole, or to be whole, e.g., Matt. 9 : 21, 22
(twice), and parallel passages; Acts 4 : 9. See HEAL, SAVE.

2390 AG:368B 3. IAOMAI (ἰάομαι), to heal, is rendered to make whole, Matt. 15 : 28;
CB:1252C Acts 9 : 34, A.V. (R.V., "healeth"). See HEAL.

2480 AG:383D 4. ISCHUŌ (ἰσχύω), to be strong, is rendered "they that are whole"
CB:1253A in Matt. 9 : 12 and Mark 2 : 17. See ABLE, B, No. 4.

1295 AG:189A 5. DIASŌZŌ (διασώζω), to save thoroughly (*dia*), is used in the Passive
CB:1241B Voice and rendered "were made whole" in Matt. 14 : 36, R.V. (A.V.,
"were made perfectly whole"). See ESCAPE, HEAL, SAVE.

For WHORE, WHOREMONGER see FORNICATION, HARLOT

AN 302 WHOSO, WHOSOEVER

AG:48B HOSPER *Note:* The same pronouns as those under WHO are used for the above,
3746 often with the addition of the particle *an* and a change of construction
AG:583B when a generalisation is expressed. Some texts in Mark 15 : 6 have
I.10ē. EI *hosper*, a strengthened form of *hos*, A.V., "whomsoever." For sentences
1487 introduced by the conjunction *ei* or *ean*, if, see † p. 1.

AG:219A CB:1242C

EAN 1437 WHY: see † p. 1

AG:211A CB:1242C

WICKED

4190 AG:690D 1. PONĒROS (πονηρός), for which see BAD, No. 2, EVIL, A and B,
CB:1266A No. 2, is translated "wicked" in the A.V. and R.V. in Matt. 13 : 49;
18 : 32; 25 : 26; Luke 19 : 22; Acts 18 : 14; 1 Cor. 5 : 13; in the following the R.V. substitutes "evil" for A.V., "wicked:" Matt. 12 : 45 (twice); 13 : 19; 16 : 4; Luke 11 : 26; Col. 1 : 21; 2 Thess. 3 : 2; and in the following, where Satan is mentioned as "the (or that) evil one:" Matt. 13 : 38; Eph. 6 : 16; 1 John 2 : 13, 14; 3 : 12 (1st part); 5 : 18; in ver. 19 for A.V., "wickedness;" he is so called also in A.V. and R.V. in John 17 : 15; 2 Thess. 3 : 3; A.V. only in Luke 11 : 4; in 3 John 10, A.V., the word is translated "malicious," R.V., "wicked."

2. ATHESMOS (ἄθεσμος), lawless (*a*, negative, *thesmos*, law, custom), 113
“ wicked,” occurs in 2 Pet. 2 : 7 ; 3 : 17.¶ An instance of the use of the AG:21A
word is found in the papyri, where a father breaks off his daughter's engage- CB:—
ment because he learnt that her fiancé was giving himself over to lawless
deeds (Moulton and Milligan, Vocab.).

Notes : (1) In Matt. 21 : 41, A.V., *kakos* (for which see BAD, No. 1, KAKOS
EVIL, A, No. 1), is translated “ wicked ” (R.V., “ miserable ”). (2) In 2556 AG:397D
Acts 2 : 23 and 2 Thess. 2 : 8, A.V., *anomos*, “ lawless ” (R.V.), is translated CB:1253B
“ wicked.” ANOMOS 459 AG:72A CB:1235C

WICKEDNESS

1. PONĒRIA (πονηρία), akin to *ponēros* (see above, No. 1), is always 4189
rendered “ wickedness ” save in Acts 3 : 26 : see INIQUITY, No. 4. AG:690C CB:1266A

2. KAKIA (κακία), evil, is rendered “ wickedness ” in Acts 8 : 22 ; 2549
R.V. in Jas. 1 : 21, A.V., “ naughtiness.” See EVIL, B, No. 1, MALICE. AG:397A CB:1253A

Notes : (1) For the A.V. of 1 John 5 : 19 see WICKED, No. 1. (2)
In Acts 25 : 5, A.V., the word *atopos* (R.V., “ amiss ”) is incorrectly 824 AG:120C
rendered “ wickedness.” CB:—

For WIDE see BROAD

WIDOW

CHĒRA (χήρα), Matt. 28 : 13 (in some texts) ; Mark 12 : 40, 42, 43 ; 5503
Luke 2 : 37 ; 4 : 25, 26, lit., ‘ a woman a widow ; ’ 7 : 12 ; 18 : 3, 5 ; AG:881C CB:1239C
20 : 47 ; 21 : 2, 3 ; Acts 6 : 1 ; 9 : 39, 41 ; 1 Tim. 5 : 3 (twice), 4, 5, 11, 16 (twice) ; Jas. 1 : 27 ; 1 Tim. 5 : 9 refers to elderly widows (not an ecclesiastical “ order ”), recognized, for relief or maintenance by the church (cp. vv. 3, 16), as those who had fulfilled the conditions mentioned ; where relief could be ministered by those who had relatives that were widows (a likely circumstance in large families), the church was not to be responsible ; there is an intimation of the tendency to shelve individual responsibility at the expense of church funds. In Rev. 18 : 7, it is used figuratively of a city forsaken.¶

WIFE, WIVES

1. GUNĒ (γυνή) denotes (1) a woman, married or unmarried (see 1135
WOMAN) ; (2) a wife, e.g., Matt. 1 : 20 ; 1 Cor. 7 : 3, 4 ; in 1 Tim. 3 : 11, AG:168B CB:1248C
R.V., “ women,” the reference may be to the wives of deacons, as the A.V. takes it.

2. GUNAIKEIOS (γυναικεῖος), an adjective denoting womanly, **female**, 1134
is used as a noun in 1 Pet. 3 : 7, A.V., “ wife,” R.V., “ woman.”¶ AG:168B CB:1248C

Note : In John 19 : 25 the article stands idiomatically for “ **the *wife*** (of) ;” in Matt. 1 : 6, the article is rendered “ her ***that had been the wife*** (of).’

WIFE'S MOTHER

3994 AG:642C PENTHERA (πενθερά) denotes a mother-in-law, Matt. 8 : 14;
CB:— 10 : 35; Mark 1 : 30; Luke 4 : 38; 12 : 53 (twice).¶

WILD

66 AG:13C AGRIOS (ἄγριος) denotes (*a*) of or in fields (*agros*, a field), hence, not
CB:1233C domestic, said of honey, Matt. 3 : 4; Mark 1 : 6; (*b*) savage, fierce, Jude
13, R.V., metaphorically, "wild (waves)," A.V., "raging."¶ It is used
in the papyri of a malignant wound.

2342 AG:361A *Note:* In Rev. 6 : 8 the R.V. renders *thērion* (plural) "wild beasts"
CB:1272B (A.V., "beasts").

WILDERNESS

2047 AG:308D 1. ERĒMIA (ἐρημία), an uninhabited place, is translated "wilder-
CB:1246B ness" in the A.V. of Matt. 15 : 33 and Mark 8 : 4 (R.V., "a desert place");
R.V. and A.V., "wilderness" in 2 Cor. 11 : 26. See DESERT, A. (In
the Sept., Is. 60 : 20; Ezek. 35 : 4, 9.¶)

2048 AG:309A 2. ERĒMOS (ἔρημος), an adjective signifying desolate, deserted,
CB:1246B lonely, is used as a noun, and rendered "wilderness" 32 times in the
A.V.; in Matt. 24 : 26 and John 6 : 31, R.V., "wilderness" (A.V.,
"desert"). For the R.V., "deserts" in Luke 5 : 16 and 8 : 29 see DESERT, B.

WILES

3180 AG:499A METHODIA, or –EIA (μεθοδία) denotes craft, deceit (*meta*, after,
CB:1258C *hodos*, a way), a cunning device, a wile, and is translated "wiles (of
error)" in Eph. 4 : 14, R.V. [A.V. paraphrases it, "they lie in wait (to
deceive)"], lit., '(with a view to) the craft (singular) of deceit;' in 6 : 11,
"the wiles (plural) (of the Devil.)"¶

WILFULLY

A. Adverb.

1596 AG:243C HEKOUSIŌS (ἑκουσίως) denotes voluntarily, willingly, Heb. 10 : 26,
CB:— (of sinning) "wilfully;" in 1 Pet. 5 : 2, "willingly" (of exercising oversight over the flock of God).¶

B. Verb.

2309 AG:354D THELŌ (θέλω), to will, used in the present participle in 2 Pet. 3 : 5,
CB:1271C is rendered "wilfully (forget)" in the R.V., A.V., "willingly (are ignorant
of)," lit., 'this escapes them (i.e., their notice) willing (i.e. of their own
will).' See WILL, C, No. 1, WILLING, B, No. 1.

WILL, WOULD

A. Nouns.

2307 AG:354B 1. THELĒMA (θέλημα) signifies (*a*) objectively, that which is willed,
CB:1271C of the will of God, e.g., Matt. 18 : 14; Mark 3 : 35, the fulfilling being a
sign of spiritual relationship to the Lord; John 4 : 34; 5 : 30; 6 : 39, 40;
Acts 13 : 22, plural, 'my desires;' Rom. 2 : 18; 12 : 2, lit., 'the will

of God, the good and perfect and acceptable ;' here the repeated article is probably resumptive, the adjectives describing the will, as in the Eng. Versions ; Gal. 1 : 4 ; Eph. 1 : 9 ; 5 : 17, " of the Lord ; " Col. 1 : 9 ; 4 : 12 ; 1 Thess. 4 : 3 ; 5 : 18, where it means ' the gracious design,' rather than ' the determined resolve ; ' 2 Tim. 2 : 26, which should read ' which have been taken captive by him [(*autou*), i.e., by the Devil ; the R.V., " by the Lord's servant " is an interpretation, it does not correspond to the Greek] unto His (*ekeinou*) will ' (i.e., God's will ; the different pronoun refers back to the subject of the sentence, viz., God) ; Heb. 10 : 10 ; Rev. 4 : 11, R.V., " because of Thy will ; " of human will, e.g., 1 Cor. 7 : 37 ; (*b*) subjectively, the will being spoken of as the emotion of being desirous, rather than as the thing willed ; of the will of God, e.g., Rom. 1 : 10 ; 1 Cor. 1 : 1 ; 2 Cor. 1 : 1 ; 8 : 5 ; Eph. 1 : 1, 5, 11 ; Col. 1 : 1 ; 2 Tim. 1 : 1 ; Heb. 10 : 7, 9, 36 ; 1 John 2 : 17 ; 5 : 14 ; of human will, e.g., John 1 : 13 ; Eph. 2 : 3, " the desires of the flesh ; " 1 Pet. 4 : 3 (in some texts) ; 2 Pet. 1 : 21. See DESIRE, A, No. 5, PLEASURE, Note (1).

2. THELĒSIS (θέλησις) denotes a willing, a wishing [similar to No. 1 2308 AG:354C
(*b*)], Heb. 2 : 4.¶ CB:1271C

3. BOULĒMA (βούλημα), a deliberate design, that which is purposed, 1013 AG:145D
Rom. 9 : 19 ; 1 Pet. 4 : 3 (in the best texts). See PURPOSE, A, No. 1. CB:1239B

4. EUDOKIA (εὐδοκία) (*eu*, well, *dokeō*, to think) is rendered " good 2107
will " in Luke 2 : 14, A.V. (see WELL PLEASED) ; Phil. 1 : 15 : see DESIRE, AG:319C CB:1247A
PLEASURE, SEEM, WELL-PLEASING.

5. EUNOIA (εὔνοια), good will (*eu*, well, *nous*, the mind), occurs in 2133 AG:323B
Eph. 6 : 7 (in some texts, 1 Cor. 7 : 3).¶ BOULē

Notes : (1) In Acts 13 : 36, A.V., *boulē*, " counsel " (R.V.), is translated 1012
" will." (2) In Rev. 17 : 17, A.V., *gnōmē*, an opinion, R.V., " mind," AG:145D CB:1239B
is translated " will." (3) For " will-worship," Col. 2 : 23, see WORSHIP, GNōMē 1106
B, No. 2. AG:163A CB:1248B

B. Adjectives.

1. HEKŌN (ἑκών), of free will, willingly, occurs in Rom. 8 : 20, R.V., 1635
" of its own will " (A.V., " willingly ") ; 1 Cor. 9 : 17, R.V., " of my own AG:247D
will " (A.V., " willingly ").¶ In the Sept., Ex. 21 : 13 ; Job 36 : 19.¶ CB:—

2. AKŌN (ἄκων), *a*, negative, and No. 1, unwillingly, occurs in 1 Cor. 210
9 : 17, R.V., " not of mine own will " (A.V., " against my will ").¶ In AG:34B CB:—
the Sept., Job 14 : 17.¶

C. Verbs.

When " will " is not part of the translation of the future tense of verbs, it represents one of the following :

1. THELŌ (θέλω), for the force of which see DESIRE, B, No. 6, usually 2309
expresses desire or design ; it is most frequently translated by " will " AG:354D CB:1271C
or " would ; " see especially Rom. 7 : 15, 16, 18–21. In 1 Tim. 2 : 4, R.V., " willeth " signifies the gracious desire of God for all men to be saved ; not all are willing to accept His condition, depriving themselves either by the self-established criterion of their perverted reason, or

because of their self-indulgent preference for sin. In John 6 : 21, the A.V. renders the verb " willingly " (R.V., " they were willing ") ; in 2 Pet. 3 : 5, A.V., the present participle is translated " willingly " (R.V., " wilfully ").

The following are R.V. renderings for the A.V., ' will : ' Matt. 16 : 24, 25, " would ; " " wouldest," 19 : 21 and 20 : 21 ; " would," 20 : 26, 27 ; Mark 8 : 34, 35 ; 10 : 43, 44 ; " would fain," Luke 13 : 31 ; " would," John 6 : 67 ; " willeth," 7 : 17 ; in 8 : 44, " it is your will (to do) ; " " wouldest," Rom. 13 : 3 ; " would," 1 Cor. 14 : 35 and 1 Pet. 3 : 10.

1014 AG:146A CB:1239B
2. BOULOMAI (βούλομαι), for the force of which see DESIRE, B, No. 7, usually expresses the deliberate exercise of volition more strongly than No. 1, and is rendered as follows in the R.V., where the A.V. has " will : " Matt. 11 : 27 and Luke 10 : 22, " willeth ; " Jas. 4 : 4, " would ; " in Jas. 3 : 4, R.V., " willeth " (A.V., " listeth "). In Jas. 1 : 18 the perfect participle is translated " of His own will," lit. ' having willed.'

3195 AG:500D CB:1258A
3. MELLŌ (μέλλω), to be about to, is translated " will " in Matt. 2 : 13 and John 7 : 35 (twice) ; " wilt," John 14 : 22 ; " will," Acts 17 : 31 ; " wouldest," 23 : 20 ; " will," 27 : 10 and Rev. 3 : 16. See ABOUT, B.

WILLING (Adjective and Verb)

A. Adjectives.

4289 AG:706C CB:—
1. PROTHUMOS (πρόθυμος) is rendered " willing " in Matt. 26 : 41 ; Mark 14 : 38, R.V. See READY, No. 2.

1595 (-ON) AG:243B CB:—
2. HEKOUSIOS (ἑκούσιος), willing, is used with *kata* in Philm. 14, lit., ' according to willing,' R.V., " of free will " (A.V., " willingly ").¶

B. Verbs.

2309 AG:354D CB:1271C
1. THELŌ (θέλω) is rendered " ye were willing " in John 5 : 35. See WILL, C, No. 1.

1014 AG:146A CB:1239B
2. BOULOMAI (βούλομαι) is rendered " (if) Thou be willing " in Luke 22 : 42 ; in 2 Pet. 3 : 9, A.V. (R.V., " wishing "). See WILL, C, No. 2.

2106 AG:319B CB:1247A
3. EUDOKEŌ (εὐδοκέω), to be well pleased, to think it good, is rendered " we are willing " in 2 Cor. 5 : 8 ; in 1 Thess. 2 : 8, A.V., " we were willing " (R.V., " we were well pleased "). See PLEASE, PLEASURE.

830 AG:121A CB:—
Notes : (1) In 2 Cor. 8 : 3, A.V., *authairetos*, of one's own accord (R.V.), is rendered " willing of themselves ; " in ver. 17, " of his own accord." See ACCORD.¶ (2) For " willing to communicate," 1 Tim. 6 : 18, see COMMUNICATE, C.

For WILLING MIND see READINESS

HEKŌN 1635 AG:247D CB:— HEKOUSIŌS 1596 AG:243C CB:—

WILLINGLY

Notes : (1) For *hekōn* see WILL, B, No. 1. (2) For *hekousiōs*, see WILFULLY. (3) For Philm. 14 see WILLING, A, No. 2. (4) For 2 Pet. 3 : 5 see WILL, C, No. 1.

For WIN see POSSESS, A, No. 2

WIND (Noun)

1. ANEMOS (ἄνεμος), besides its literal meaning, is used metaphorically 417
in Eph. 4 : 14, of variable teaching. In Matt. 24 : 31 and Mark 13 : 27 AG:64D CB:1235C
the four winds stand for the four cardinal points of the compass ; so in
Rev. 7 : 1, " the four winds of the earth " (cp. Jer. 49 : 36 ; Dan. 7 : 2) ;
the contexts indicate that these are connected with the execution of
Divine judgments. Deissmann (*Bible Studies*) and Moulton and Milligan
(Vocab.) illustrate the phrase from the papyri.

2. PNOĒ (πνοή), a blowing, blast (akin to *pneō*, to blow), is used of the 4157 AG:680B
rushing wind at Pentecost, Acts 2 : 2. See BREATH. CB:1265C

3. PNEUMA (πνεῦμα) is translated " wind " in John 3 : 8 (R.V., marg., 4151
" the Spirit breatheth," the probable meaning) ; in Heb. 1 : 7 the R.V. AG:674C CB:1265B
has " winds " for A.V., " spirits." See SPIRIT. PNEō

Notes : (1) For *pneō*, to blow (" wind " in Acts 27 : 40), see BLOW, 4154
No. 1. (2) For ***anemizō***, Jas. 1 : 6, " driven by the wind," see DRIVE, AG:679C CB:1265B
No. 8.¶ ANEMIZō 416 AG:64C CB:—

WIND (Verb)

1. DEŌ (δέω), to bind, is translated " wound (it in linen clothes)," 1210
John 19 : 40, A.V., of the body of Christ (R.V., " bound "). See BIND, AG:177D CB:1240C
No. 1, TIE.

2. SUSTELLŌ (συστέλλω) is translated " wound . . . up " in Acts 4958
5 : 6 (R.V., " wrapped . . . round "). See SHORTEN, No. 2, WRAP. AG:795A CB:—

3. ENEILEŌ (ἐνειλέω), to roll in, wind in, is used in Mark 15 : 46, 1750
of winding the cloth around the Lord's body, R.V., " wound " (A.V., AG:264C CB:—
" wrapped ").¶

WINDOW

THURIS (θυρίς), a diminutive of ***thura***, a door, occurs in Acts 20 : 9 ; 2376
2 Cor. 11 : 33.¶ AG:366A CB:—

WINE

1. OINOS (οἶνος) is the general word for wine. The mention of the 3631
bursting of the wineskins, Matt. 9 : 17 ; Mark 2 : 22 ; Luke 5 : 37, implies AG:562A CB:1260C
fermentation. See also Eph. 5 : 18 (cp. John 2 : 10 ; 1 Tim. 3 : 8 ; Tit.
2 : 3). In Matt. 27 : 34, the R.V. has " wine " (A.V., " vinegar," translating the inferior reading *oxos*).

The drinking of wine could be a stumbling-block and the Apostle enjoins abstinence in this respect, as in others, so as to avoid giving an occasion of stumbling to a brother, Rom. 14 : 21. Contrast 1 Tim. 5 : 23, which has an entirely different connection. The word is used metaphorically (*a*) of the evils ministered to the nations by religious Babylon, 14 : 8 ; 17 : 2 ; 18 : 3 ; (*b*) of the contents of the cup of Divine wrath
upon the nations and Babylon, Rev. 14 : 10 ; 16 : 19 ; 19 : 15. 1098 AG:162A
2. GLEUKOS (γλεῦκος) denotes sweet " new wine," or must, Acts CB:1248B

2 : 13, where the accusation shows that it was intoxicant and must have been undergoing fermentation some time.¶ In the Sept., Job 32 : 19.¶

Note: In instituting the Lord's Supper He speaks of the contents of the cup as the "fruit of the vine." So Mark 14 : 25.

For GIVEN TO WINE see BRAWLER, No. 1

WINE-BIBBER

3630 AG:562A OINOPOTĒS (*οἰνοπότης*), a wine-drinker (*oinos*, and *potēs*, a drinker),
CB:1260C is used in Matt. 11 : 19 ; Luke 7 : 34.¶ In the Sept., Prov. 23 : 20.¶

For WINEBIBBINGS see EXCESS, Note (2)

WINEPRESS, WINE-FAT

3025 1. LĒNOS (*ληνός*) denotes a trough or vat, used especially for the
AG:473A treading of grapes, Matt. 21 : 33. Not infrequently they were dug out in
CB:— the soil or excavated in a rock, as in the rock-vats in Palestine to-day. In Rev. 14 : 19, 20 (twice) and 19 : 15 (where *oinos* is added, lit., 'the winepress of the wine') the word is used metaphorically with reference to the execution of Divine judgment upon the gathered foes of the Jews at the close of this age preliminary to the establishment of the Millennial kingdom.¶

5276 2. HUPOLĒNION (*ὑπολήνιον*) was a vessel or trough beneath the press
AG:845C itself (*hupo*, beneath, and No. 1), for receiving the juice, Mark 12 : 1,
CB:— R.V., "a pit for the winepress."¶ In the Sept., Isa. 16 : 10 ; Joel 3 : 13 ; Hag. 2 : 16 ; Zech. 14 : 10.¶

For WINE-SKINS see SKIN

WING

4420 PTERUX (*πτέρυξ*) is used of birds, Matt. 23 : 37 ; Luke 13 : 34 ;
AG:727B
CB:1267C symbolically in Rev. 12 : 14, R.V., "the two wings of the great eagle" (A.V., "two wings of a great eagle"), suggesting the definiteness of the action, the wings indicating rapidity and protection, an allusion, perhaps, to Ex. 19 : 4 and Deut. 32 : 11, 12 ; of the "living creatures" in a vision, Rev. 4 : 8 ; 9 : 9.¶ Cp. *pterugion*, a pinnacle.

For WINK AT see OVERLOOK

WINTER (Noun and Verb)

A. Noun.

5494 AG:879D CHEIMŌN (*χειμών*) denotes winter, in Matt. 24 : 20 ; Mark 13 : 18 ;
CB:— John 10 : 22 ; 2 Tim. 4 : 21. See TEMPEST.

3914 AG:623D

B. Verb.

CB:— PARACHEIMAZŌ (*παραχειμάζω*) denotes to winter at a place (*para*,

at, and A), Acts 27 : 12 (2nd part) ; 28 : 11 ; 1 Cor. 16 : 6 ; Tit. 3 : 12.¶
Note : In Acts 27 : 12 (1st part) *paracheimasia,* a wintering, is 3915
rendered " (to) winter in."¶ AG:623D
CB:—

WIPE

1. APOMASSŌ (ἀπομάσσω), to wipe off, wipe clean (*apo,* from, 631
massō, to touch, handle), is used in the Middle Voice, of wiping dust from (-OMAI)
the feet, Luke 10 : 11.¶ AG:96D
CB:—
2. EKMASSŌ (ἐκμάσσω), to wipe out (*ek*), wipe dry, is used of wiping 1591
tears from Christ's feet, Luke 7 : 38, 44 ; John 11 : 2 ; 12 : 3 ; of Christ's AG:243B
wiping the disciples' feet, John 13 : 5.¶ CB:—
3. EXALEIPHŌ (ἐξαλείφω), to wipe out or away (*ek,* or *ex,* out, 1813
aleiphō, to anoint), is used metaphorically of wiping away tears from AG:272C
the eyes, Rev. 7 : 17 ; 21 : 4. See BLOT OUT. CB:1247B

WISDOM

1. SOPHIA (σοφία) is used with reference to (*a*) God, Rom. 11 : 33 ; 4678
1 Cor. 1 : 21, 24 ; 2 : 7 ; Eph. 3 : 10 ; Rev. 7 : 12 ; (*b*) Christ, Matt. 13 : 54 ; AG:759C
Mark 6 : 2 ; Luke 2 : 40, 52 ; 1 Cor. 1 : 30 ; Col. 2 : 3 ; Rev. 5 : 12 ; CB:1269B
(*c*) wisdom personified, Matt. 11 : 19 ; Luke 7 : 35 ; 11 : 49 ; (*d*) human
wisdom (1) in spiritual things, Luke 21 : 15 ; Acts 6 : 3, 10 ; 7 : 10 ; 1 Cor.
2 : 6 (1st part) ; 12 : 8 ; Eph. 1 : 8, 17 ; Col. 1 : 9, R.V., " (spiritual)
wisdom," 28 ; 3 : 16 ; 4 : 5 ; Jas. 1 : 5 ; 3 : 13, 17 ; 2 Pet. 3 : 15 ; Rev.
13 : 18 ; 17 : 9 ; (2) in the natural sphere, Matt. 12 : 42 ; Luke 11 : 31 ;
Acts 7 : 22 ; 1 Cor. 1 : 17, 19, 20, 21 (twice), 22 ; 2 : 1, 4, 5, 6 (2nd part),
13 ; 3 : 19 ; 2 Cor. 1 : 12 ; Col. 2 : 23 ; (3) in its most debased form, Jas.
3 : 15, " earthly, sensual, devilish " (marg., " demoniacal ").¶
2. PHRONĒSIS (φρόνησις), understanding, prudence, i.e., a right use 5428
of *phrēn,* the mind, is translated " wisdom " in Luke 1 : 17. See PRUDENCE. AG:866C
Note : " While *sophia* is the insight into the true nature of things, CB:1264C
phronēsis is the ability to discern modes of action with a view to their
results ; while *sophia* is theoretical, *phronēsis* is practical " (Lightfoot). SUNESIS
Sunesis, understanding, intelligence, is the critical faculty ; this and 4907 AG:788C
phronēsis are particular applications of *sophia.* CB:1270C

WISE, WISER, WISELY

A. Adjectives.

1. SOPHOS (σοφός) is used of (*a*) God, Rom. 16 : 27 ; in 1 Tim. 1 : 17 4680
and Jude 25 *sophos* is absent, in the best mss. (see the R.V.), the com- AG:760B
parative degree, *sophōteros,* occurs in 1 Cor. 1 : 25, where " foolishness " CB:1269B
is simply in the human estimate ; (*b*) spiritual teachers in Israel, Matt.
23 : 34 ; (*c*) believers endowed with spiritual and practical wisdom,
Rom. 16 : 19 ; 1 Cor. 3 : 10 ; 6 : 5 ; Eph. 5 : 15 ; Jas. 3 : 13 ; (*d*) Jewish
teachers in the time of Christ, Matt. 11 : 25 ; Luke 10 : 21 ; (*e*) the

naturally learned, Rom. 1 : 14, 22 ; 1 Cor. 1 : 19, 20, 26, 27 ; 3 : 18, 20.¶

5429 AG:866D 2. PHRONIMOS (φρόνιμος), prudent, sensible, practically wise, Matt.
CB:1264C 7 : 24 ; 10 : 16 ; 24 : 45 ; 25 : 2, 4, 8, 9 ; Luke 12 : 42 ; 16 : 8 (comparative degree, *phronimōteros*) ; 1 Cor. 10 : 15 ; in an evil sense, " wise (in your own conceits)," lit., ' wise (in yourselves),' i.e., ' judged by the standard of your self-complacency,' Rom. 11 : 25 ; 12 : 16 ; ironically, 1 Cor. 4 : 10 ; 2 Cor. 11 : 19.¶

B. Noun.

3097 AG:484D MAGOS (μάγος) denotes a Magian, one of a sacred caste, originally
CB:1257B Median, who apparently conformed to the Persian religion while retaining their old beliefs ; it is used in the plural, Matt. 2 : 1, 7, 16 (twice), " wise men." See also SORCERER.

C. Verbs.

4679 AG:760B 1. SOPHIZŌ (σοφίζω) is rendered to make wise in 2 Tim. 3 : 15 :
CB:1269B see DEVISED.

4920 AG:790A 2. SUNIĒMI or SUNIŌ (συνίημι), to perceive, understand, is used
CB:1270C negatively in 2 Cor. 10 : 12, A.V., " are not wise " (R.V., " are without understanding "). See UNDERSTAND.

D. Adverbs.

5430 AG:866D PHRONIMŌS (φρονίμως), wisely (akin to A, No. 2), occurs in Luke
CB:1264C 16 : 8.¶

WISE (IN NO)

OU 3756 1. OU MĒ (οὐ μή), a double negative, expressing an emphatic negation,
AG:590A ' by no means,' is rendered " in no wise " in Matt. 10 : 42 ; Luke 18 : 17 ;
CB:— John 6 : 37 ; Acts 13 : 41 ; Rev. 21 : 27.
Mē 3361 2. PANTŌS (πάντως), altogether, by all means, is used with the
AG:515D negative *ou* (not) in Rom. 3 : 9, stating a complete denial, rendered
CB:1258A " No, in no wise." See ALL, B, 3, ALTOGETHER, B, 1.
PANTōS 3843 AG:609B 3. PANTELES (παντελές), the neuter of *pantelēs*, is used with the
CB:— negative *mē*, and with *eis to*, ' unto the,' in Luke 13 : 11, and translated
PANTELēS " in no wise," lit., ' not to the uttermost : ' see UTTERMOST, No. 1.
3838
AG:608C
CB:1261C

For WISE (ON THIS) see THUS

WISH

2172 AG:329B 1. EUCHOMAI (εὔχομαι) is rendered to wish in Acts 27 : 29 (R.V.
CB:1247A marg., " prayed ") ; so Rom. 9 : 3 ; in 2 Cor. 13 : 9 and 3 John 2, R.V., " pray : " see PRAY.

1014 AG:146A 2. BOULOMAI (βούλομαι), in Mark 15 : 15, R.V., is translated " wish-
CB:1239B ing " (A.V., " willing ") ; so 2 Pet. 3 : 9 ; in Acts 25 : 22, R.V., " could wish " (A.V., " would "). See WILL, C, No. 2.

2309 AG:354D 3. THELŌ (θέλω), in 1 Cor. 16 : 7, R.V., is translated " wish " (A.V.,
CB:1271C " will ") ; Gal. 4 : 20, " I could wish " (A.V. " I desire "). See WILL, C, No. 1.

WIST

OIDA (οἶδα), to know, in the pluperfect tense (with imperfect meaning) 1492
is rendered " wist " (the past tense of the verb to wit : cp. WOT) in Mark (EIDō)
9 : 6 ; 14 : 40 ; Luke 2 : 49 ; John 5 : 13 ; Acts 12 : 9 ; 23 : 5. See AG:555D CB:1260B
KNOW, No. 2.

WIT (TO)

A. Adverb.

HŌS (ὡς), a relative adverb signifying ' as,' or ' how,' is used in 2 Cor. 5613
5 : 19 to introduce the statement " that God was . . .," and rendered AG:897A
" to wit," lit., ' how.' CB:1251B

B. Verb.

GNŌRIZŌ (γνωρίζω), to know, to make known, is rendered " we do 1107
(you) to wit " in 2 Cor. 8 : 1, A.V., R.V., " we make known (to you)." AG:163B CB:1248B
See KNOW, No. 8.

Note : In Rom. 8 : 23 the italicized words *" to wit "* are added to specify the particular meaning of " adoption " there mentioned.

For WITCHCRAFT see SORCERY

WITH : see † p. 1

WITHAL

HAMA (ἅμα), at the same time, is rendered " withal " in Acts 24 : 26, 260
R.V. (A.V., " also ") ; 1 Tim. 5 : 13 (with *kai*, ' also ') ; Philm. 22. AG:42A CB:1249A

Notes : (1) In Eph. 6 : 16, R.V., the phrase *en pasin* (*en*, in, and the
dative plural of *pas*, all) is rightly rendered " withal " (A.V., " above PAS 3956
all ") ; the shield of faith is to accompany the use of all the other parts AG:631A
of the spiritual equipment. (2) In 1 Cor. 12 : 7 *sumpherō* is rendered CB:1262C
" profit withal." See EXPEDIENT, PROFIT, B, No. 1. (3) In Acts 25 : 27,
kai, also, is rendered " withal."

WITHDRAW

1. HUPOSTELLŌ (ὑποστέλλω) is translated " withdraw " in Gal. 5288
2 : 12 : see DRAW (*B*), No. 4. AG:847B CB:—

2. APOSPAŌ (ἀποσπάω), in the Passive Voice, is translated " was 645
withdrawn " in Luke 22 : 41, A.V. : see PART (Verb), No. 3. AG:98A CB:—

3. ANACHŌREŌ (ἀναχωρέω) is translated to withdraw in the R.V. 402
of Matt. 2 : 22 and John 6 : 15 ; R.V. and A.V. in Matt. 12 : 15 and AG:63C
Mark 3 : 7. See DEPART, No. 10. CB:1235A

4. HUPOCHŌREŌ (ὑποχωρέω), to retire, is translated " withdrew 5298
Himself " in Luke 5 : 16 ; elsewhere in 9 : 10, R.V., " withdrew apart " AG:848C
(A.V., " went aside "). See GO, No. 16.¶ CB:—

5. STELLŌ (στέλλω), to bring together, gather up (used of furling 4724 AG:766A
sails), hence, in the Middle Voice, signifies to shrink from a person or CB:1270A

thing, 2 Thess. 3 : 6, " withdraw ; " elsewhere, 2 Cor. 8 : 20, " avoiding."
868 See AVOID.¶ Cp. No. 1.
AG:126D *Note :* In 1 Tim. 6 : 5, some texts have ***aphistēmi***, rendered **" withdraw**
CB:1236B **thyself,"** A.V.

WITHER (away)

3583 AG:548C XĒRAINŌ (ξηραίνω), to dry up, parch, wither, is translated to
CB:1273B wither, (*a*) of plants, Matt. 13 : 6 ; 21 : 19, 20 ; Mark 4 : 6 ; 11 : 20,
R.V. (A.V., " dried up "), 21 ; Luke 8 : 6 ; John 15 : 6 ; Jas. 1 : 11 ;
1 Pet. 1 : 24 ; (*b*) of members of the body, Mark 3 : 1, and, in some
texts, 3. See DRY, B, OVER-RIPE, PINE AWAY, RIPE.
3584 *Notes :* (1) For the adjective *xēros*, dry, withered, see DRY, A, No. 1.
AG:548C CB:1273B (2) For " whose fruit withereth," Jude 12, A.V., see AUTUMN.

2967

WITHHOLD

AG:461B CB:1255C KŌLUŌ (κωλύω), to hinder, restrain, is translated " withhold (not) "
ENTOS 1787 in Luke 6 : 29, R.V., A.V., " forbid (not) to take." See FORBID, HINDER,
AG:269B KEEP, Note (7), SUFFER, WITHSTAND.
CB:1245B *Note :* For " withholdeth " in 2 Thess. 2 : 6 see RESTRAIN.

EN 1722 AG:258B CB:1244B

WITHIN

ESŌTHEN *Note :* This is a translation of (*a*) *entos* : see INSIDE, No. 1 ; in Luke
2081 AG:314B 17 : 21 the R.V. marg., " in the midst of," is to be preferred ; the Kingdom
ESŌ of God was not in the hearts of the Pharisees ; (*b*) *en*, of thinking or saying
2080 within oneself, e.g., Luke 7 : 39, 49 (marg., " among ") ; locally, e.g.,
AG:214B CB:1246C Luke 19 : 44 ; (*c*) *esōthen*, 2 Cor. 7 : 5 ; Rev. 4 : 8 ; 5 : 1 ; " from within,"
PROS Mark 7 : 21, 23 ; Luke 11 : 7 ; " within ", Matt. 23 : 25 ; Luke 11 : 40,
4314 AG:709C R.V., " inside ; " in Matt. 23 : 27, 28, R.V., " inwardly ; " (*d*) *esō*, John
CB:1267A 20 : 26 ; Acts 5 : 23 ; 1 Cor. 5 : 12 (i.e., within the church) ; (*e*) *pros*,
DIA to, or with, in Mark 14 : 4, A.V., " within " (R.V., " among ") ; (*f*)
1223 AG:179B *dia*, through, rendered " within (three days) " in Mark 14 : 58, A.V. (R.V.,
CB:1241A " in," looking through the time to the event, and in keeping with the
ESŌTEROS 2082 metaphor of building) ; (*g*) *esōteros*, Heb. 6 : 19, the comparative degree
AG:314C CB:1246C of *esō*, used with the article translated " that within," lit., ' the inner
ENEIMI (part of the veil) ', i.e., inside : see INNER, No. 2 ; (*h*) in Luke 11 : 41,
1751 AG:264C R.V., *eneimi*, to be in, is rendered " are within " (A.V., " ye have ").

EXŌ 1854 AG:279B

WITHOUT

CB:1247C *Notes :* (1) This is a translation of (*a*) *exō*, outside, e.g., Matt. 12 : 46,
EXŌTHEN 1855 47 ; " (them that are) without," 1 Cor. 5 : 12, 13 ; Col. 4 : 5 ; 1 Thess.
AG:279D 4 : 12 (the unregenerate) ; Heb. 13 : 11–13 ; (*b*) *exōthen*, from without,
CHŌRIS or without, e.g., Mark 7 : 15, 18 ; Luke 11 : 40 ; 2 Cor. 7 : 5 ; 1 Tim. 3 : 7 ;
5565 AG:890C as a preposition, Rev. 11 : 2 ; (*c*) *chōris*, apart from, frequently used as a
CB:1240A preposition, especially in Hebrews [4 : 15 ; 7 : 7, 20, 21 ; 9 : 7, 18, 22,
ANEU 427 28 ; 11 : 6 ; in 11 : 40, R.V., " apart from " (A.V., " without ") ; 12 : 8,
AG:65C 14] ; (*d*) *aneu*, like *chōris*, but rarer, Matt. 10 : 29 ; Mark 13 : 2 ;

1 Pet. 3 : 1 ; 4 : 9 ;¶ (*e*) *ater*, Luke 22 : 6, marg., "without (tumult) ;" **ATER 817**
ver. 35 ;¶ (*f*) *ektos*, out of, outside, 1 Cor. 6 : 18 : see OTHER, OUT, OUT- **AG:120A**
SIDE ; (*g*) *parektos*, besides, in addition, 2 Cor. 11 : 28, " (those things that **EKTOS 1622**
are) without," R.V., marg., " (the things which) I omit," or " (the things **AG:246A**
that come) out of course." (2) In Acts 5 : 26, *ou*, not, *meta*, with, is rendered **PAREKTOS 3924**
" without (violence)." (3) In Acts 25 : 17, A.V., " without (any delay) " **AG:625A**
represents *poieō*, to make, and *mēdemian*, no, R.V., " I made no (delay)." **CB:1262B OU**
(4) For "without ceasing," Acts 12 : 5, A.V., see EARNESTLY, C, No. 1. **3756**
(5) In many nouns the negative prefix *a* forms part of the word and is **AG:590A MēDEIS**
translated " without." **3367 AG:518A CB:1258A**

WITHSTAND

1. KŌLUŌ (κωλύω), to hinder, is rendered " withstand " in Acts **2967**
11 : 17. See FORBID, HINDER. **AG:461B CB:1255C**

2. ANTHISTĒMI (ἀνθίστημι), to set against, is translated to with- **436**
stand in Acts 13 : 8 (Middle Voice) ; in the intransitive 2nd aorist, Active **AG:67B CB:—**
Voice, Eph. 6 : 13 ; 2 Tim. 3 : 8 (1st part ; Middle Voice in 2nd part) ;
4 : 15. See RESIST.

WITNESS (Noun and Verb)

A. Nouns.

1. MARTUS or MARTUR (μάρτυς) (whence Eng., martyr, one who **3144**
bears witness by his death) denotes one who can or does aver what he has **AG:494B**
seen or heard or knows ; it is used (*a*) of God, Rom. 1 : 9 ; 2 Cor. 1 : 23 ; **CB:1257C**
Phil. 1 : 8 ; 1 Thess. 2 : 5, 10 (2nd part) ; (*b*) of Christ, Rev. 1 : 5 ; 3 : 14 ;
(*c*) of those who witness for Christ by their death, Acts 22 : 20 ; Rev. 2 : 13 ;
Rev. 17 : 6 ; (*d*) of the interpreters of God's counsels, yet to witness in
Jerusalem in the times of the Antichrist, Rev. 11 : 3 ; (*e*) in a forensic
sense, Matt. 18 : 16 ; 26 : 65 ; Mark 14 : 63 ; Acts 6 : 13 ; 7 : 58 ; 2 Cor.
13 : 1 ; 1 Tim. 5 : 19 ; Heb. 10 : 28 ; (*f*) in a historical sense, Luke 11 : 48 ;
24 : 48 ; Acts 1 : 8, 22 ; 2 : 32 ; 3 : 15 ; 5 : 32 ; 10 : 39, 41 ; 13 : 31 ; 22 : 15 ;
26 : 16 ; 1 Thess. 2 : 10 (1st part) ; 1 Tim. 6 : 12 ; 2 Tim. 2 : 2 ; Heb.
12 : 1, " (a cloud) of witnesses," here of those mentioned in chapt. 11,
those whose lives and actions testified to the worth and effect of faith,
and whose faith received witness in Scripture ; 1 Pet. 5 : 1.¶

2. MARTURIA (μαρτυρία), testimony, a bearing witness, is translated **3141**
" witness " in Mark 14 : 55, 56, 59 ; Luke 22 : 71 ; John 1 : 7, 19 (R.V.) ; **AG:493C**
3 : 11, 32 and 33 (R.V.) ; 5 : 31, 32, 34 (R.V.), 36 ; R.V. in 8 : 13, 14, 17 ; **CB:1257C**
19 : 35 ; 21 : 24 ; A.V. in Tit. 1 : 13 ; A.V. and R.V. in 1 John 5 : 9
(thrice), 10a ; R.V. in 10b, 11 ; 3 John 12 : see TESTIMONY, No. 2.

3. MARTURION (μαρτύριον), testimony or witness as borne, a declara- **3142**
tion of facts, is translated " witness " in Matt. 24 : 14, A.V. ; Acts 4 : 33 ; **AG:493D**
7 : 44 (A.V.) ; Jas. 5 : 3 (A.V.) : see TESTIMONY, No. 1. **CB:1257C**

4. PSEUDOMARTUS or –TUR (ψευδομάρτυς) denotes a false witness, **5575 AG:892A**
Matt. 26 : 60 ; 1 Cor. 15 : 15.¶ **CB:1267C**

5577 AG:892A CB:1267C 5. PSEUDOMARTURIA (ψευδομαρτυρία), false witness, occurs in Matt. 15 : 19 ; 26 : 59.¶

B. Verbs.

3140 AG:492C CB:1257C 1. MARTUREŌ (μαρτυρέω) denotes (I) to be a *martus* (see A, No. 1), or to bear witness to, sometimes rendered to testify (see TESTIFY, No. 1) ; it is used of the witness (*a*) of God the Father to Christ, John 5 : 32, 37 ; 8 : 18 (2nd part) ; 1 John 5 : 9, 10 ; to others, Acts 13 : 22 ; 15 : 8 ; Heb. 11 : 2, 4 (twice), 5, 39 ; (*b*) of Christ, John 3 : 11, 32 ; 4 : 44 ; 5 : 31 ; 7 : 7 ; 8 : 13, 14, 18 (1st part) ; 13 : 21 ; 18 : 37 ; Acts 14 : 3 ; 1 Tim. 6 : 13 ; Rev. 22 : 18, 20 ; of the Holy Spirit, to Christ, John 15 : 26 ; Heb. 10 : 15 ; 1 John 5 : 7, 8, R.V., which rightly omits the latter part of ver. 7 (it was a marginal gloss which crept into the original text : see THREE) ; it finds no support in Scripture ; (*c*) of the Scriptures, to Christ, John 5 : 39 ; Heb. 7 : 8, 17 ; (*d*) of the works of Christ, to Himself, and of the circumstances connected with His Death, John 5 : 36 ; 10 : 25 ; 1 John 5 : 8 ; (*e*) of prophets and apostles, to the righteousness of God, Rom. 3 : 21 ; to Christ, John 1 : 7, 8, 15, 32, 34 ; 3 : 26 ; 5 : 33, R.V. ; 15 : 27 ; 19 : 35 ; 21 : 24 ; Acts 10 : 43 ; 23 : 11 ; 1 Cor. 15 : 15 ; 1 John 1 : 2 ; 4 : 14 ; Rev. 1 : 2 ; to doctrine, Acts 26 : 22 (in some texts, so A.V. ; see No. 2) ; to the Word of God, Rev. 1 : 2 ; (*f*) of others, concerning Christ, Luke 4 : 22 ; John 4 : 39 ; 12 : 17 ; (*g*) of believers to one another, John 3 : 28 ; 2 Cor. 8 : 3 ; Gal. 4 : 15 ; Col. 4 : 13 ; 1 Thess. 2 : 11 (in some texts : see No. 2) ; 3 John 3, 6, 12 (2nd part) ; (*h*) of the Apostle Paul concerning Israel, Rom. 10 : 2 ; (*i*) of an angel, to the churches, Rev. 22 : 16 ; (*j*) of unbelievers, concerning themselves, Matt. 23 : 31 ; concerning Christ, John 18 : 23 ; concerning others, John 2 : 25 ; Acts 22 : 5 ; 26 : 5 ; (II) to give a good report, to approve of, Acts 6 : 3 ; 10 : 22 ; 16 : 2 ; 22 : 12 ; 1 Tim. 5 : 10 ; 3 John 12 (1st part) ; some would put Luke 4 : 22 here.¶

3143 AG:494A CB:1257C 2. MARTUROMAI (μαρτύρομαι), strictly meaning to summon as a witness, signifies to affirm solemnly, adjure, and is used in the Middle Voice only, rendered to testify in Acts 20 : 26, R.V. (A.V., " I take . . . to record ") ; 26 : 22, R.V., in the best texts [see No. 1 (*e*)] ; Gal. 5 : 3 ; Eph. 4 : 17 ; 1 Thess. 2 : 11, in the best texts [see No. 1 (*g*)].¶

4828 AG:778B CB:1270B 3. SUMMARTUREŌ (συμμαρτυρέω) denotes to bear witness with (*sun*), Rom. 2 : 15 ; 8 : 16 ; 9 : 1.¶

4901 AG:787B 4. SUNEPIMARTUREŌ (συνεπιμαρτυρέω) denotes to join in bearing witness with others, Heb. 2 : 4.¶

2649 AG:414D CB:1254A KATĒGOREŌ 2723 AG:423A 5. KATAMARTUREŌ (καταμαρτυρέω) denotes to witness against (*kata*), Matt. 26 : 62 ; 27 : 13 ; Mark 14 : 60 (in some mss., 15 : 4, for *katēgoreō*, to accuse, R.V.).¶

CB:1254B 5576 AG:891D CB:1267C 6. PSEUDOMARTUREŌ (ψευδομαρτυρέω), to bear false witness (*pseudēs*, false), occurs in Matt. 19 : 18 ; Mark 10 : 19 ; 14 : 56, 57 ; Luke 18 : 20 ; in some texts, Rom. 13 : 9.¶

C. Adjectives.

AMARTURОS (ἀμάρτυρος) denotes without witness (*a*, negative, and 267
martus), Acts 14 : 17.¶ AG:44A
CB:—

WOE

OUAI (οὐαί), an interjection, is used (*a*) in denunciation, Matt. 11 : 21 ; 3759
18 : 7 (twice) ; eight times in ch. 23 ; 24 : 19 ; 26 : 24 ; Mark 13 : 17 ; AG:591A
14 : 21 ; Luke 6 : 24, 25 (twice), 26 ; 10 : 13 ; six times in ch. 11 ; 17 : 1 ; CB:1261B
21 : 23 ; 22 : 22 ; 1 Cor. 9 : 16 ; Jude 11 ; Rev. 8 : 13 (thrice) ; 12 : 12 ; as a noun, Rev. 9 : 12 (twice) ; 11 : 14 (twice) ; (*b*) in grief, " alas," Rev. 18 : 10, 16, 19 (twice in each).¶

WOLF

LUKOS (λύκος) occurs in Matt. 10 : 16 ; Luke 10 : 3 ; John 10 : 12 3074
(twice) ; metaphorically, Matt. 7 : 15 ; Acts 20 : 29.¶ AG:481B
CB:1257B

WOMAN

1. GUNĒ (γυνή), for which see also WIFE, is used of a woman unmarried 1135
or married, e.g., Matt. 11 : 11 ; 14 : 21 ; Luke 4 : 26, of a widow ; Rom. AG:168B
7 : 2 ; in the vocative case, used in addressing a woman, it is a term not of CB:1248C
reproof or severity, but of endearment or respect, Matt. 15 : 28 ; John 2 : 4, where the Lord's words to His mother at the wedding in Cana, are neither rebuff nor rebuke. The question is, lit., ' What to Me and to thee ? ' and the word " woman," the term of endearment, follows this. The meaning is ' There is no obligation on Me or you, but love will supply the need.' She confides in Him, He responds to her faith. There was lovingkindness in both hearts. His next words about ' His hour ' suit this ; they were not unfamiliar to her. Cana is in the path to Calvary ; Calvary was not yet, but it made the beginning of signs possible. See also 4 : 21 ; 19 : 26.

In Gal. 4 : 4 the phrase " born of a woman " is in accordance with the subject there, viz., the real humanity of the Lord Jesus ; this the words attest. They declare the method of His Incarnation and " suggest the means whereby that humanity was made free from the taint of sin consequent upon the Fall, viz., that He was not born through the natural process of ordinary generation, but was conceived by the power of the Holy Spirit . . . To have written ' born of a virgin ' would have carried the argument in a wrong direction . . . Since that man is born of woman is a universal fact, the statement would be superfluous if the Lord Jesus were no more than man " (Notes on Galatians, by Hogg and Vine, pp. 184 f.). 1133

2. GUNAIKARION (γυναικάριον), a diminutive of No. 1, a little AG:168B
woman, is used contemptuously in 2 Tim. 3 : 6, a silly woman.¶ CB:1248C

3. PRESBUTEROS (πρεσβύτερος), elder, older, in the feminine plural, 4245 AG:699D
denotes " elder women " in 1 Tim. 5 : 2. See ELDER, A, No. 1. CB:1266B

4247 AG:700D 4. PRESBUTIS (πρεσβῦτις), the feminine of *presbutēs*, aged, is used
CB:1266B in the plural and translated "aged women" in Tit. 2:3.¶
(THĒLUS) 5. THĒLEIA (θήλεια), the feminine of the adjective *thēlus*, denotes
2338 AG:360C female, and is used as a noun, Rom. 1:26, 27. See FEMALE.
CB:1271C

WOMB

2836 AG:437B 1. KOILIA (κοιλία) denotes the womb, Matt. 19:**12**; Luke 1:15,
CB:1255B 41, 42, 44; 2:21; 11:27; 23:29; John 3:4; Acts 3:2; 14:8;
Gal. 1:15. See BELLY, No. 1.
1064 AG:152C 2. GASTĒR (γαστήρ), is rendered "womb" in Luke 1:31. See
CB:— BELLY, No. 2.
3388 AG:520B 3. MĒTRA (μήτρα), the matrix (akin to *mētēr*, a mother), occurs in
CB:1258C Luke 2:23; Rom. 4:19.¶

WONDER (Noun and Verb)

5059 AG:812C
A. Nouns.

CB:1271B THAMBOS 1. TERAS (τέρας), something strange, causing the beholder to marvel,
2285 is always used in the plural, always rendered "wonders," and generally
AG:350C CB:1271C follows *sēmeia*, "signs;" the opposite order occurs in Acts 2:22, 43;
THAUMA 6:8, R.V.; 7:36; in Acts 2:19 "wonders" occurs alone. A sign is
2295 intended to appeal to the understanding, a wonder appeals to the imagina-
AG:352A CB:1271C tion, a power (*dunamis*) indicates its source as supernatural. "Wonders"
SĒMEION are manifested as Divine operations in thirteen occurrences (9 times in
4592 AG:747D Acts); three times they are ascribed to the work of Satan through human
CB:1268C agents, Matt. 24:24; Mark 13:22 and 2 Thess. 2:9.
EKTHAMBOS 2. THAMBOS (θάμβος), amazement, is rendered "wonder" in
1569 AG:240B Acts 3:10. See AMAZE, A, No. 2.
CB:1244A PSEUDOS *Notes:* (1) For *thauma*, a wonder (rendered "admiration" in Rev.
5579 17:6, A.V.), see MARVEL. (2) In Rev. 12:1, 3 and 13:13 *sēmeion*, a
AG:892B sign, is translated in the A.V., "wonder(s)," R.V., "sign(s)." (3) In
CB:1267C THAUMAZŌ Acts 3:11 *ekthambos* (*ek*, intensive, and No. 2) is translated "greatly
2296 wondering."¶ (4) For *pseudos*, 2 Thess. 2:9, "lying wonders," see
AG:352B CB:1271C FALSE, B. Cp. AMAZE, B, Nos. 3 and 4.

EXISTĒMI
B. Verbs.

1839 AG:276B *Note:* For *thaumazō*, see MARVEL; for *existēmi*, Acts 8:13, A.V.,
CB:1247C see AMAZE, B, No. 1.
(EXHI-) DUNAMIS

1411
WONDERFUL (THING, WORK)

AG:207B *Notes:* (1) In Matt. 7:22, A.V., *dunamis* (in the plural) is rendered
CB:1242B MEGALEIOS "wonderful works" (R.V., "mighty works," marg., "powers"). See
3167 POWER. (2) In Acts 2:11, A.V., the adjective *megaleios*, magnificent, in
AG:496D CB:1258A the neuter plural with the article, is rendered "the wonderful works"
THAUMASIOS (R.V., "the mighty works").¶ (3) In Matt. 21:15, the neuter plural
2297 AG:352D of the adjective *thaumasios*, wonderful, is used as a noun, "wonderful
CB:1271C things," lit., 'wonders.'

WONT

ETHŌ (ἔθω), to be accustomed, is used in the pluperfect tense (with 1486
imperfect meaning), *eiōtha*, rendered "was wont" in Matt. 27 : 15 ; Mark AG:234A
10 : 1. See CUSTOM, B, No. 2, MANNER, A, Note (1). (EIŌTHA) CB:—

Notes : (1) In Mark 15 : 8, "he was wont to do," R.V., represents the
imperfect tense of *poieō*, to do (A.V., "he had ever done"). (2) In Luke
22 : 39, A.V., *ethos*, a custom, preceded by ***kata*** and the article, lit., ETHOS
'according to the (i.e., His) custom', is translated "as He was wont" 1485
(R.V., "as His custom was") : see CUSTOM, A, No. 1. (3) In Acts 16 : 13 AG:218D CB:1247A
the A.V., "was wont", translates the texts which have the Passive Voice NOMIZŌ
of ***nomizō*** with its meaning to hold by custom ; the R.V., "we supposed," 3543 AG:541A
translates the texts which have the imperfect tense, Active, with the CB:1260A
meaning to consider, suppose.

WOOD

1. XULON (ξύλον) denotes timber, wood for any use, 1 Cor. 3 : 12 ; 3586
Rev. 18 : 12 (twice). See STAFF, STOCKS, TREE. AG:549A CB:1273B

2. HULĒ (ὕλη) denotes a wood, a forest, Jas. 3 : 5 (A.V., "matter", 5208
marg., "wood").¶ See MATTER, Note (3). AG:836A CB:1251C

WOOL

ERION (ἔριον) occurs in Heb. 9 : 19 ; Rev. 1 : 14.¶ 2053 AG:309C CB:—

WORD

1. LOGOS (λόγος) denotes (I) the expression of thought—not the 3056
mere name of an object—(*a*) as embodying a conception or idea, e.g., AG:477A
Luke 7 : 7 ; 1 Cor. 14 : 9, 19 ; (*b*) a saying or statement, (1) by God, e.g., CB:1257A
John 15 : 25 ; Rom. 9 : 9 ; 9 : 28, R.V., "word" (A.V., "work") ; Gal. 5 : 14 ; Heb. 4 : 12 ; (2) by Christ, e.g., Matt. 24 : 35 (plur.) ; John 2 : 22 ; 4 : 41 ; 14 : 23 (plur.) ; 15 : 20. In connection with (1) and (2) the phrase "the word of the Lord," i.e., the revealed will of God (very frequent in the O.T.), is used of a direct revelation given by Christ, 1 Thess. 4 : 15 ; of the gospel, Acts 8 : 25 ; 13 : 49 ; 15 : 35, 36 ; 16 : 32 ; 19 : 10 ; 1 Thess. 1 : 8 ; 2 Thess. 3 : 1 ; in this respect it is the message from the Lord, delivered with His authority and made effective by His power (cp. Acts 10 : 36) ; for other instances relating to the gospel see Acts 13 : 26 ; 14 : 3 ; 15 : 7 ; 1 Cor. 1 : 18, R.V. ; 2 Cor. 2 : 17 ; 4 : 2 ; 5 : 19 ; 6 : 7 ; Gal. 6 : 6 ; Eph. 1 : 13 ; Phil. 2 : 16 ; Col. 1 : 5 ; Heb. 5 : 13 ; sometimes it is used as the sum of God's utterances, e.g., Mark 7 : 13 ; John 10 : 35 ; Rev. 1 : 2, 9 ; (*c*) discourse, speech, of instruction etc., e.g., Acts 2 : 40 ; 1 Cor. 2 : 13 ; 12 : 8 ; 2 Cor. 1 : 18 ; 1 Thess. 1 : 5 ; 2 Thess. 2 : 15 ; Heb. 6 : 1, R.V., marg. ; doctrine, e.g., Matt. 13 : 20 ; Col. 3 : 16 ; 1 Tim. 4 : 6 ; 2 Tim. 1 : 13 ; Tit. 1 : 9 ; 1 John 2 : 7 ;

(II) The Personal Word, a title of the Son of God ; this identification is substantiated by the statements of doctrine in John 1 : 1–18, declaring in verses 1 and 2 (1) His distinct and superfinite Personality, (2) His relation in the Godhead (*pros*, with, not mere company, but the most intimate communion), (3) His Deity; in ver. 3 His creative power; in ver. 14 His Incarnation (" became flesh," expressing His voluntary act; not as A.V., " was made "), the reality and totality of His human nature, and His glory " as of the only begotten from the Father," R.V. (marg., " an only begotten from a father "), the absence of the article in each place lending stress to the nature and character of the relationship; His was the Shekinah glory in open manifestation; ver. 18 consummates the identification: " the only-begotten Son (R.V. marg., many ancient authorities read ' God only begotten,'), which is in the bosom of the Father, He hath declared Him," thus fulfilling the significance of the title " *Logos*," the Word, the personal manifestation, not of a part of the Divine nature, but of the whole Deity (see IMAGE).

The title is used also in 1 John 1, " the Word of life " combining the two declarations in John 1 : 1 and 4 and Rev. 19 : 13 (for 1 John 5 : 7 see THREE).

4487 2. RHĒMA (ῥῆμα) denotes that which is spoken, what is uttered in
AG:735B speech or writing; in the singular, a word, e.g., Matt. 12 : 36; 27 : 14;
CB:1268A 2 Cor. 12 : 4; 13 : 1; Heb. 12 : 19; in the plural, speech, discourse, e.g., John 3 : 34; 8 : 20; Acts 2 : 14; 6 : 11, 13; 11 : 14; 13 : 42; 26 : 25; Rom. 10 : 18; 2 Pet. 3 : 2; Jude 17; it is used of the gospel in Rom. 10 : 8 (twice), 17, R.V., " the word of Christ " (i.e., the word which preaches Christ); 10 : 18; 1 Pet. 1 : 25 (twice); of a statement, command, instruction, e.g., Matt. 26 : 75; Luke 1 : 37, R.V., " (no) word (from God shall be void of power); " ver. 38; Acts 11 : 16; Heb. 11 : 3.

The significance of *rhēma* (as distinct from *logos*) is exemplified in the
EPOS injunction to take " the sword of the Spirit, which is the word of God,"
2031 Eph. 6 : 17; here the reference is not to the whole Bible as such, but to
AG:305D the individual scripture which the Spirit brings to our remembrance for use
CB:1246B CHRĒSTOLOGIA in time of need, a prerequisite being the regular storing of the mind with
5542 AG:886A Scripture.

CB:1240A LOGIKOS *Notes:* (1) *Epos*, a word, is used in a phrase in Heb. 7 : 9, lit., ' (as to
3050 say) a word,' R.V., " (so to) say," A.V., " (as I may so) say; " *logos* is
AG:476C CB:1257A reasoned speech, *rhēma*, an utterance, *epos*, " the articulated expression
APANGELLŌ 518 of a thought " (Abbott-Smith). (2) In Rom. 16 : 18, A.V., *chrēstologia*,
AG:79B useful discourse (*chrēstos*, beneficial), is rendered " good words " [R.V.,
CB:1236B EIPON " smooth . . . (speech) "].¶ (3) For *logikos*, 1 Pet. 2 : 2 (R.V., "spiritual "),
3004 (LEGŌ) rendered " of the word," A.V., see MILK. (4) For the verb *apangellō*,
AG:226A CB:1243A rendered to bring word, see BRING, No. 36. (5) In Matt. 2 : 13, A.V.,
SUNTOMŌS *eipon*, to tell (R.V.), is rendered " bring . . . word." (6) For " enticing
4935 AG:793A words," Col. 2 : 4, see ENTICE and PERSUASIVENESS. (7) For " strifes
CB:— of words," 1 Tim. 6 : 4, A.V., and " strive . . . about words," 2 Tim. 2 : 14, see STRIFE, STRIVE. (8) For *suntomōs*, Acts 24 : 4, " a few words," see FEW, B.¶ For the same phrase see FEW, A, Nos. 1 and 2.

WORK (Noun and Verb), WROUGHT

A. Nouns.

1. ERGON (ἔργον) denotes (I) work, employment, task, e.g., Mark 2041
13 : 34 ; John 4 : 34 ; 17 : 4 ; Acts 13 : 2 ; Phil. 2 : 30 ; 1 Thess. 5 : 13 ; AG:307D
in Acts 5 : 38 with the idea of enterprise ; (II) a deed, act, (*a*) of God, CB:1246C
e.g., John 6 : 28, 29 ; 9 : 3 ; 10 : 37 ; 14 : 10 ; Acts 13 : 41 ; Rom. 14 : 20 ; Heb. 1 : 10 ; 2 : 7 ; 3 : 9 ; 4 : 3, 4, 10 ; Rev. 15 : 3 ; (*b*) of Christ, e.g., Matt. 11 : 2 ; especially in John, 5 : 36 ; 7 : 3, 21 ; 10 : 25, 32, 33, 38 ; 14 : 11, 12 ; 15 : 24 ; Rev. 2 : 26 ; (*c*) of believers, e.g., Matt. 5 : 16 ; Mark 14 : 6 ; Acts 9 : 36 ; Rom. 13 : 3 ; Col. 1 : 10 ; 1 Thess. 1 : 3, " work of faith," here the initial act of faith at conversion (turning to God, ver. 9) ; in 2 Thess. 1 : 11, " *every* work of faith," R.V., denotes every activity undertaken for Christ's sake ; 2 : 17 ; 1 Tim. 2 : 10 ; 5 : 10 ; 6 : 18 ; 2 Tim. 2 : 21 ; 3 : 17 ; Tit. 2 : 7, 14 ; 3 : 1, 8, 14 ; Heb. 10 : 24 ; 13 : 21 ; frequent in James, as the effect of faith [in 1 : 25, A.V., " (a doer) of the work," R.V., " (a doer) that worketh "] ; 1 Pet. 2 : 12 ; Rev. 2 : 2 and in several other places in chapts. 2 and 3 ; 14 : 13 ; (*d*) of unbelievers, e.g., Matt. 23 : 3, 5 ; John 7 : 7 ; Acts 7 : 41 (for idols) ; Rom. 13 : 12 ; Eph. 5 : 11 ; Col. 1 : 21 ; Tit. 1 : 16 (1st part) ; 1 John 3 : 12 ; Jude 15, R.V. ; Rev. 2 : 6, R.V. ; of those who seek justification by works, e.g., Rom. 9 : 32 ; Gal. 3 : 10 ; Eph. 2 : 9 ; described as the works of the law, e.g., Gal. 2 : 16 ; 3 : 2, 5 ; dead works, Heb. 6 : 1 ; 9 : 14 ; (*e*) of Babylon, Rev. 18 : 6 ; (*f*) of the Devil, John 8 : 41 ; 1 John 3 : 8. See DEED.

2. ERGASIA (ἐργασία) denotes a work or business, also a working, 2039 AG:307C
performance, Eph. 4 : 19, where preceded by *eis*, to, it is rendered " to CB:1246B
work " (marg., " to make a trade of "). See DILIGENCE, GAIN. LOGOS
Notes : (1) In Rom. 9 : 28, A.V., *logos*, a word (R.V.), is rendered 3056 AG:477A
" work." (2) For *pragma*, Jas. 3 : 16, rendered " work " in A.V., the CB:1257A
R.V. has " deed." (3) For *praxis*, a doing, Matt. 16 : 27, R.V. marg., PRAGMA 4229
A.V., " works," see DEED. (4) For the A.V., " much work," Acts 27 : 16, AG:697A
see DIFFICULTY. (5) For " workfellow," Rom. 16 : 21, A.V., see WORKER, CB:1266B PRAXIS
No. 2. (6) In Matt. 14 : 2 and Mark 6 : 14, A.V., *dunameis*, " powers," 4234
R.V., is translated " mighty works ;" in Acts 2 : 22, R.V., " mighty AG:697D CB:1266B
works," A.V., " miracles." (7) For " wonderful works " see WONDERFUL, DUNAMIS
Note (2). 1411 AG:207B

B. Verbs. CB:1242B

1. ERGAZOMAI (ἐργάζομαι) is used (I) intransitively, e.g., Matt. 2038
21 : 28 ; John 5 : 17 ; 9 : 4 (2nd part) ; Rom. 4 : 4, 5 ; 1 Cor. 4 : 12 ; AG:306D
9 : 6 ; 1 Thess. 2 : 9 ; 4 : 11 ; 2 Thess. 3 : 8, 10–12 (for the play upon words in ver. 11 see BUSYBODY, A) ; (II) transitively, (*a*) to work something, produce, perform, e.g., Matt. 26 : 10, " she hath wrought ; " John 6 : 28, 30 ; 9 : 4 (1st part) ; Acts 10 : 35 ; 13 : 41 ; Rom. 2 : 10 ; 13 : 10 ; 1 Cor. 16 : 10 ; 2 Cor. 7 : 10a, in the best texts, some have No. 2 ; Gal. 6 : 10, R.V., " let us work ; " Eph. 4 : 28 ; Heb. 11 : 33 ; 2 John 8 ; (*b*) to earn CB:1246C

by working, work for, John 6 : 27, R.V., "work" (A.V., "labour"). See COMMIT, DO, LABOUR, MINISTER, TRADE.

2716 2. KATERGAZOMAI (κατεργάζομαι), an emphatic form of No. 1,
AG:421C signifies to work out, achieve, effect by toil, rendered to work (past tense,
CB:— wrought) in Rom. 1 : 27 ; 2 : 9, R.V. ; 4 : 15 (the Law brings men under condemnation and so renders them subject to Divine wrath) ; 5 : 3 ; 7 : 8, 13 ; 15 : 18 ; 2 Cor. 4 : 17 ; 5 : 5 ; 7 : 10 (see No. 1), 11 ; 12 : 12 ; Phil. 2 : 12, where "your own salvation" refers especially to freedom from strife and vainglory ; Jas. 1 : 3, 20 ; 1 Pet. 4 : 3. See DO, No. 5.

1754 3. ENERGEŌ (ἐνεργέω), lit., to work in (*en*, and A, No. 1), to be
AG:265B active, operative, is used of "(*a*) God, 1 Cor. 12 : 6 ; Gal. 2 : 8 ; 3 : 5 ;
CB:1245A Eph. 1 : 11, 20 ; 3 : 20 ; Phil. 2 : 13a ; Col. 1 : 29 ; (*b*) the Holy Spirit, 1 Cor. 12 : 11 ; (*c*) the Word of God, 1 Thess. 2 : 13 (Middle Voice ; A.V., 'effectually worketh') ; (*d*) supernatural power, undefined, Matt. 14 : 2 ; Mark 6 : 14 ; (*e*) faith, as the energizer of love, Gal. 5 : 6 ; (*f*) the example of patience in suffering, 2 Cor. 1 : 6 ; (*g*) death (physical) and life (spiritual), 2 Cor. 4 : 12 ; (*h*) sinful passions, Rom. 7 : 5 ; (*i*) the spirit of the Evil One, Eph. 2 : 2 ; (*j*) the mystery of iniquity, 2 Thess. 2 : 7."*

To these may be added (*k*) the active response of believers to the inworking of God, Phil. 2 : 13b, R.V., "to work (for)," A.V., "to do (of) ;" (*l*) the supplication of the righteous, Jas. 5 : 16, R.V., "in its working" (A.V., "effectual fervent").

4160 4. POIEŌ (ποιέω), to do, is rendered to work in Matt. 20 : 12, A.V.
AG:680D (R.V., "spent") ; Acts 15 : 12, "had wrought ;" 19 : 11 ; 21 : 19 ;
CB:1265C Heb. 13 : 21 ; Rev. 16 : 14 ; 19 : 20 ; 21 : 27, A.V. (R.V., "maketh ;" marg., "doeth"). See DO.

4903 5. SUNERGEŌ (συνεργέω), to work with or together (*sun*), occurs
AG:787C in Mark 16 : 20 ; Rom. 8 : 28, "work together ;" 1 Cor. 16 : 16, "helpeth
CB:1270C with ;" 2 Cor. 6 : 1, "workers together," present participle, 'working together ;' the "***with Him***" represents nothing in the Greek ; Jas. 2 : 22, "wrought with." See HELP.¶

1096 6. GINOMAI (γίνομαι), to become, take place, is rendered "wrought"
AG:158A in Mark 6 : 2 ; Acts 5 : 12, "were . . . wrought."
CB:1248B

WORKER, WORKFELLOW, FELLOW-WORKERS, WORKMAN

2040 1. ERGATĒS (ἐργάτης) is translated "workers" in Luke 13 : 27
AG:307C ("of iniquity") ; 2 Cor. 11 : 13 ("deceitful") ; Phil. 3 : 2 ("evil") ;
CB:1246B "workman," Matt. 10 : 10, A.V. (R.V., "labourer") ; "workman," 2 Tim. 2 : 15 ; "workmen," Acts 19 : 25. See LABOURER.

4904 2. SUNERGOS (συνεργός) denotes a worker with, and is rendered
AG:787D "workfellow" in Rom. 16 : 21, A.V., R.V., "fellow-worker ;" in Col.
CB:1270C 4 : 11, "fellow-workers" (see R.V.). See the R.V., "God's fellow-workers," in 1 Cor. 3 : 9. See COMPANION, HELPER, LABOURER, Note.

Note : For "workers at home," Tit. 2 : 5, see HOME, B.

* From Notes on Galatians by Hogg and Vine, pp. 114, 115.

WORKING

1. ENERGEIA (ἐνέργεια) (Eng., energy) is used (1) of the power of 1753
God, (*a*) in the resurrection of Christ, Eph. 1 : 19 ; Col. 2 : 12, R.V., AG:265A
" working " (A.V., " operation ") ; (*b*) in the call and enduement of Paul, CB:1245A
Eph. 3 : 7 ; Col. 1 : 29 ; (*c*) in His retributive dealings in sending " a working of error " (A.V., " strong delusion ") upon those under the rule of the Man of Sin who receive not the love of the truth, but have pleasure in unrighteousness, 2 Thess. 2 : 11 ; (2) of the power of Christ (*a*) generally, Phil. 3 : 21 ; (*b*) in the Church, individually, Eph. 4 : 16 ; (3) of the power of Satan in energising the Man of Sin in his ' parousia,' 2 Thess. 2 : 9, " coming."¶

2. ENERGĒMA (ἐνέργημα), what is wrought, the effect produced by 1755
No. 1, occurs in 1 Cor. 12 : 6, R.V., " workings " (A.V., " operations ") ; AG:265A CB:1245A
ver. 10.¶

For WORKMANSHIP see MADE, B

WORLD

1. KOSMOS (κόσμος), primarily order, arrangement, ornament, adorn- 2889
ment (1 Pet. 3 : 3, see ADORN, B), is used to denote (*a*) the earth, e.g., AG:445D
Matt. 13 : 35 ; John 21 : 25 ; Acts 17 : 24 ; Rom. 1 : 20 (probably here CB:1255C
the universe : it had this meaning among the Greeks, owing to the order observable in it) ; 1 Tim. 6 : 7 ; Heb. 4 : 3 ; 9 : 26 ; (*b*) the earth in contrast with Heaven, 1 John 3 : 17 (perhaps also Rom. 4 : 13) ; (*c*) by metonymy, the human race, mankind, e.g., Matt. 5 : 14 ; John 1 : 9 [here " that cometh (R.V., coming) into the world " is said of Christ, not of " every man ; " by His coming into the world He was the light for all men] ; ver. 10 ; 3 : 16, 17 (thrice), 19 ; 4 : 42, and frequently in Rom., 1 Cor. and 1 John ; (*d*) Gentiles as distinguished from Jews, e.g., Rom. 11 : 12, 15, where the meaning is that all who will may be reconciled (cp. 2 Cor. 5 : 19) ; (*e*) the present condition of human affairs, in alienation from and opposition to God, e.g., John 7 : 7 ; 8 : 23 ; 14 : 30 ; 1 Cor. 2 : 12 ; Gal. 4 : 3 ; 6 : 14 ; Col. 2 : 8 ; Jas. 1 : 27 ; 1 John 4 : 5 (thrice) ; 5 : 19 ; (*f*) the sum of temporal possessions, Matt. 16 : 26 ; 1 Cor. 7 : 31 (1st part) ; (*g*) metaphorically, of the tongue as " a world (of iniquity)," Jas. 3 : 6, expressive of magnitude and variety.

2. AIŌN (αἰών), an age, a period of time, marked in the N.T. usage 165
by spiritual or moral characteristics, is sometimes translated " world ; " AG:27B
the R.V. marg. always has " age." The following are details concerning CB:1234A
the world in this respect ; its cares, Matt. 13 : 22 ; its sons, Luke 16 : 8 ; 20 : 34 ; its rulers, 1 Cor. 2 : 6, 8 ; its wisdom, 1 Cor. 1 : 20 ; 2 : 6 ; 3 : 18 ; its fashion, Rom. 12 : 2 ; its character, Gal. 1 : 4 ; its god, 2 Cor. 4 : 4. The phrase " the end of the world " should be rendered " the end of the age," in most places (see END, A, No. 2) ; in 1 Cor. 10 : 11, A.V., " the ends (*telē*) of the world," R.V., " the ends of the ages," probably signifies

the fulfilment of the Divine purposes concerning the ages, in regard to the Church [this would come under END, A, No. 1, (*c*)]. In Heb. 11 : 3 [lit., 'the ages (have been prepared)'] the word indicates all that the successive periods contain; cp. 1 : 2.

Aiōn is always to be distinguished from *kosmos*, even where the two seem to express the same idea, e.g., 1 Cor. 3 : 18, *aiōn*, ver. 19, ***kosmos***; the two are used together in Eph. 2 : 2, lit., 'the age of this world.' For a list of phrases containing *aiōn*, with their respective meanings, see EVER, B.

3625 3. OIKOUMENĒ (οἰκουμένη), the inhabited earth (see EARTH, No. 2),
AG:561B is used (*a*) of the whole inhabited world, Matt. 24 : 14; Luke 4 : 5; 21 : 26;
CB:1260C Rom. 10 : 18; Heb. 1 : 6; Rev. 3 : 10; 16 : 14; by metonymy, of its
inhabitants, Acts 17 : 31; Rev. 12 : 9; (*b*) of the Roman Empire, the
world as viewed by the writer or speaker, Luke 2 : 1; Acts 11 : 28;
24 : 5; by metonymy, of its inhabitants, Acts 17 : 6; 19 : 27; (*c*) the
Gē inhabited world in a coming age, Heb. 2 : 5.¶

1093 *Notes:* (1) In Rev. 13 : 3, A.V., *gē*, the earth (R.V.), is translated
AG:157C **CB:1248A** "world." (2) For phrases containing *aiōnios*, e.g., Rom. 16 : 25; 2 Tim.
AIōNIOS 1 : 9; Tit. 1 : 2, see ETERNAL, No. 2.

166
AG:28B
CB:1234A

WORLDLY

2886 KOSMIKOS (κοσμικός), pertaining to this world, is used (*a*) in Heb.
AG:445B 9 : 1, of the tabernacle, A.V., "worldly," R.V., "of this world" (i.e.,
CB:1255C made of mundane materials, adapted to this visible world, local and
transitory); (*b*) in Tit. 2 : 12, ethically, of "worldly lusts," or desires.¶

For WORLD-RULERS, Eph. 6 : 12, R.V., see RULER, No. 3

WORM

4663 1. SKŌLĒX (σκώληξ), a worm which preys upon dead bodies, is used
AG:758C metaphorically by the Lord in Mark 9 : 48; in some mss. vv. 44, 46,
CB:— cp. Is. 66 : 24. The statement signifies the exclusion of the hope of
restoration, the punishment being eternal.¶

4662 2. SKŌLĒKOBRŌTOS (σκωληκόβρωτος) denotes devoured by worms
AG:758C (*skōlēx*, and *bibrōskō*, to eat), Acts 12 : 23.¶
CB:—

WORMWOOD

894 APSINTHOS (ἄψινθος) (Eng., absinth), a plant both bitter and
AG:129C deleterious, and growing in desolate places, figuratively suggestive of
(-THION) **CB:1237B** calamity (Lam. 3 : 15) and injustice (Amos 5 : 7), is used in Rev. 8 : 11
(twice; in the 1st part as a proper name).¶

WORRY
See CARE

WORSE

5501
A. Adjectives.

AG:881B 1. CHEIRŌN (χείρων), used as the comparative degree of ***kakos***,
CB:—

evil, describes (*a*) the condition of certain men, Matt. 12 : 45 ; Luke 11 : 26 ; 2 Pet. 2 : 20 ; (*b*) evil men themselves and seducers, 2 Tim. 3 : 13 ; (*c*) indolent men who refuse to provide for their own households, and are worse than unbelievers, 1 Tim. 5 : 8, R.V. ; (*d*) a rent in a garment, Matt. 9 : 16 ; Mark 2 : 21 ; (*e*) an error, Matt. 27 : 64 ; (*f*) a person suffering from a malady, Mark 5 : 26 ; (*g*) a possible physical affliction, John 5 : 14 ; (*h*) a punishment, Heb. 10 : 29, " sorer." See SORE.¶

2. ELASSŌN or ELATTŌN (ἐλάσσων) is said of wine in John 2 : 10. **1640 AG:248A**
See LESS. **CB:1244A**

3. HĒSSŌN or HĒTTŌN (ἥσσων), less, inferior, used in the neuter, **2276**
after *epi*, for, is translated " worse " in 1 Cor. 11 : 17 ; in 2 Cor. 12 : 15 **AG:349A (HēSSōN)**
the neuter, used adverbially, is translated " the less."¶ **CB:—**

B. Verbs.

1. HUSTEREŌ (ὑστερέω) is rendered " are we the worse " in 1 Cor. **5302**
8 : 8. See BEHIND, B, No. 1, COME, No. 39, DESTITUTE, FAIL, Note (2), **AG:849A CB:1252B**
LACK, WANT.

2. PROECHŌ (προέχω), to hold before, promote, is rendered " are we **4284**
better " in Rom. 3 : 9, A.V. (Passive Voice) ; R.V., " are we in worse **(-OMAI) AG:705D**
case." See BETTER (be), Note (1).¶ **CB:—**

WORSHIP (Verb and Noun), WORSHIPPING

A. Verbs.

1. PROSKUNEŌ (προσκυνέω), to make obeisance, do reverence to **4352**
(from *pros*, towards, and *kuneō*, to kiss), is the most frequent word **AG:716C CB:1267B**
rendered to worship. It is used of an act of homage or reverence (*a*) to God, e.g., Matt. 4 : 10 ; John 4 : 21–24 ; 1 Cor. 14 : 25 ; Rev. 4 : 10 ; 5 : 14 ; 7 : 11 ; 11 : 16 ; 19 : 10 (2nd part) and 22 : 9 ; (*b*) to Christ, e.g., Matt. 2 : 2, 8, 11 ; 8 : 2 ; 9 : 18 ; 14 : 33 ; 15 : 25 ; 20 : 20 ; 28 : 9, 17 ; John 9 : 38 ; Heb. 1 : 6, in a quotation from the Sept. of Deut. 32 : 43, referring to Christ's Second Advent ; (*c*) to a man, Matt. 18 : 26 ; (*d*) to the Dragon, by men, Rev. 13 : 4 ; (*e*) to the Beast, his human instrument, Rev. 13 : 4, 8, 12 ; 14 : 9, 11 ; (*f*) the image of the Beast, 13 : 15 ; 14 : 11 ; 16 : 2 ; (*g*) to demons, Rev. 9 : 20 ; (*h*) to idols, Acts 7 : 43.

Note : As to Matt. 18 : 26, this is mentioned as follows, in the " List of readings and renderings preferred by the American Committee " (see R.V. *Classes of Passages*, IV) : " At the word ' worship ' in Matt. 2 : 2, etc., add the marginal note ' The Greek word denotes an act of reverence, whether paid to man (see chap. 18 : 26) or to God (see chap. 4 : 10) '." The Note to John 9 : 38 in the American Standard Version in this connection is most unsound ; it implies that Christ was a creature. J. N. Darby renders the verb ' do homage ' [see the Revised
Preface to the Second Edition (1871) of his *New Translation*]. **4576**

2. SEBOMAI (σέβομαι), to revere, stressing the feeling of awe or **AG:746A CB:1268C**

devotion, is used of worship (*a*) to God, Matt. 15 : 9; Mark 7 : 7; Acts 16 : 14; 18 : 7, 13; (*b*) to a goddess, Acts 19 : 27. See DEVOUT, No. 3.

4573 AG:745C 3. SEBAZOMAI (σεβάζομαι), akin to No. 2, to honour religiously,
CB:1268C is used in Rom. 1 : 25.¶

3000 AG:467C 4. LATREUŌ (λατρεύω), to serve, to render religious service or homage,
CB:1256C is translated to worship in Phil. 3 : 3, "(who) worship (by the Spirit of God)," R.V., A.V., "(which) worship (God in the spirit)"; the R.V. renders it to serve (for A.V., to worship) in Acts 7 : 42; 24 : 14; A.V. and R.V., "(the) worshippers" in Heb. 10 : 2, present participle, lit., '(the ones) worshipping.' See SERVE.

2151 AG:326B 5. EUSEBEŌ (εὐσεβέω), to act piously towards, is translated "ye
CB:1247B worship" in Acts 17 : 23. See PIETY (to shew).

Notes: (1) The worship of God is nowhere defined in Scripture. A consideration of the above verbs shows that it is not confined to praise; broadly it may be regarded as the direct acknowledgement to God, of His nature, attributes, ways and claims, whether by the outgoing of the heart in praise and thanksgiving or by deed done in such acknowledg-
2323 AG:359A ment. (2) In Acts 17 : 25 *therapeuō*, to serve, do service to (so R.V.),
CB:1272B is rendered "is worshipped." See CURE, HEAL.

B. Nouns.

4574 AG:745D 1. SEBASMA (σέβασμα) denotes an object of worship (akin to A,
CB:1268C No. 3); Acts 17 : 23 (see DEVOTION); in 2 Thess. 2 : 4, "that is worshipped;" every object of worship, whether the true God or pagan idols, will come under the ban of the Man of Sin.¶

1479 AG:218A 2. ETHELOTHRĒSKEIA (or -IA) (ἐθελοθρησκεία), will-worship
CB:— (*ethelō*, to will, *thrēskeia*, worship), occurs in Col. 2 : 23, voluntarily adopted worship, whether unbidden or forbidden, not that which is imposed by others, but which one affects.¶

2356 AG:363B 3. THRĒSKEIA (θρησκεία), for which see RELIGION, is translated
CB:1272B "worshipping" in Col. 2 : 18.

1391 AG:203C *Note:* In Luke 14 : 10, A.V., *doxa*, "glory" (R.V.), is translated
CB:1242B 'worship.'

WORSHIPPER

4353 AG:717B CB:1267B 1. PROSKUNĒTĒS (προσκυνητής), akin to *proskuneō* (see WORSHIP,
3511 A, No. 1), occurs in John 4 : 23.¶

AG:537B CB:1259C 2. NEŌKOROS (νεωκόρος) is translated "worshipper" in Acts 19 : 35,
2318 A.V.: see TEMPLE-KEEPER.¶

AG:358B CB:1272B 3. THEOSEBĒS (θεοσεβής) denotes 'reverencing God' (*theos*, God,
THEOSEBEIA *sebomai*, see WORSHIP, A, No. 2), and is rendered "a worshipper of God"
2317 AG:358B in John 9 : 31.¶ Cp. *theosebeia*, godliness, 1 Tim. 2 : 10.¶

CB:1272A *Note:* For Heb. 10 : 2, see WORSHIP, A, No. 4.

WORTH See VALUE

WORTHY, WORTHILY

A. Adjectives.

1. AXIOS (ἄξιος), of weight, worth, worthy, is said of persons and 514
their deeds: (*a*) in a good sense, e.g., Matt. 10:10, 11, 13 (twice), 37 AG:78A
(twice), 38; 22:8; Luke 7:4; 10:7; 15:19, 21; John 1:27; Acts CB:1238B
13:25; 1 Tim. 5:18; 6:1; Heb. 11:38; Rev. 3:4; 4:11; 5:2,
4, 9, 12; (*b*) in a bad sense, Luke 12:48; 23:15; Acts 23:29; 25:11,
25; 26:31; Rom. 1:32; Rev. 16:6. See MEET, REWARD.

2. HIKANOS (ἱκανός), sufficient, is translated "worthy" in this 2425
sense in Matt. 3:11 (marg., "sufficient"); so 8:8; Mark 1:7; Luke AG:374B
3:16; 7:6. See ABILITY, C, No. 2, etc. CB:1250C

3. ENOCHOS (ἔνοχος), held in, bound by, is translated "worthy 1777
(of death)" in Matt. 26:66 and Mark 14:64, R.V. (marg., "liable to;" AG:267D
A.V., "guilty"). See DANGER. CB:1245B

Notes: (1) In Jas. 2:7, A.V., *kalos*, good, fair, is translated "worthy" 2570
(R.V., "honourable"). (2) For the A.V. of Eph. 4:1; Col. 1:10; AG:400B
1 Thess. 2:12, see C, below. CB:1253B

B. Verbs.

1. AXIOŌ (ἀξιόω), to think or count worthy, is used (1) of the 515
estimation formed by God (*a*) favourably, 2 Thess. 1:11, "may count (you) AG:78C
worthy (of your calling)," suggestive of grace (it does not say 'may make CB:1238B
you worthy'); Heb. 3:3, "of more glory," of Christ in comparison with Moses; (*b*) unfavourably, 10:29, "of how much sorer punishment;" (2) by a centurion (negatively) concerning himself, Luke 7:7; (3) by a church, regarding its elders, 1 Tim. 5:17, where "honour" stands probably for 'honorarium,' i.e., material support. See also DESIRE, B, No. 1 (Acts 28:22), THINK (Acts 15:38).¶

2. KATAXIOŌ (καταξιόω), a strengthened form of No. 1, occurs in 2661
Luke 20:35; 21:36, in some texts; Acts 5:41; 2 Thess. 1:5.¶ See AG:415C
ACCOUNT, A, No. 5. CB:1254B

C. Adverb.

AXIŌS (ἀξίως), worthily, so translated in the R.V. [with one exception, 516
see (*c*)], for A.V., "worthy" and other renderings, (*a*) "worthily of AG:78D
God," 1 Thess. 2:12, of the Christian walk as it should be; 3 John 6, CB:1238B
R.V., of assisting servants of God in a way which reflects God's character and thoughts; (*b*) "worthily of the Lord," Col. 1:10; of the calling of believers, Eph. 4:1, in regard to their "walk" or manner of life; (*c*) "worthy of the gospel of Christ," Phil. 1:27, of a manner of life in accordance with what the gospel declares; (*d*) "worthily of the saints," R.V., of receiving a fellow-believer, Rom. 16:2, in such a manner as befits those who bear the name of "saints."¶ Deissmann (*Bible Studies*, pp. 248 ff.) shows from various inscriptions that the phrase "worthily of the god" was very popular at Pergamum.

For WORTHY DEEDS, Acts 24:2, A.V., see CORRECTION

WOT

OIDA 1492 *Note :* This form, the 1st person singular and the plural of the present
(EIDō) tense of an Anglo-Saxon verb *witan,* to see or to know (for the past
AG:555D tense cp. WIST), is a rendering of (1) *oida,* to know, in Acts 3 : 17 ; 7 : 40 ;
CB:1260B GNōRIZō Rom. 11 : 2 (see KNOW, No. 2) ; (2) *gnōrizō,* to come to know, in Phil.
1107 1 : 22 (see KNOW, No. 8).
AG:163B CB:1248B

WOULD

Notes : (1) This is often a translation of various inflections of a Greek verb. When it represents a separate word, it is always emphatic, and is a translation of one or other of the verbs mentioned under WILL. (2)
OPHELON *Ophelon* (the 2nd aorist tense of *opheilō,* to owe) expresses a wish, " I
3785 AG:599A would that," either impracticable, 1 Cor. 4 : 8, R.V. (A.V., " would to
CB:1261A God ") ; or possible, 2 Cor. 11 : 1 ; Gal. 5 : 12 ; Rev. 3 : 15. (3) *Euchomai,*
EUCHOMAI 2172 to pray, with the particle *an,* expressing a strong desire with a remote
AG:329B possibility of fulfilment, is used in Acts 26 : 29, " I would (to God, that)."
CB:1247A

WOUND (Noun and Verb)

A. Nouns.

5134 AG:824D TRAUMA (τραῦμα), a wound, occurs in Luke 10 : 34.¶
CB:— 4127 *Note :* *Plēgē,* a blow, a stroke, is used in Luke 10 : 30 with
AG:668A *epitithēmi,* to lay on, lit., 'laid on blows,' R.V., " beat " (A.V.,
CB:1265A " wounded "). In Rev. 13 : 3, 12, *plēgē* is used with the genitive case of *thanatos,* death, lit., 'stroke of death,' R.V., " death-stroke " (A.V., " deadly wound ") ; the rendering " wound " does not accurately give the meaning ; in ver. 14, with the genitive of *machaira,* a sword, A.V., " wound " (R.V., " stroke ").

B. Verbs.

5135 AG:824D TRAUMATIZŌ (τραυματίζω), to wound (from A), occurs in Luke
CB:— 20 : 12 and Acts 19 : 16.¶

4969 *Note :* In Rev. 13 : 3, A.V., *sphazō,* to slay, is translated " wounded,"
AG:796A CB:1269C R.V., " smitten " (A.V. and R.V. marg., " slain ").

For WOUND (wrapped) see WIND (Verb)

WOVEN

5307 HUPHANTOS (ὑφαντός), from *huphainō,* to weave (found in good
AG:849D CB:— mss. in Luke 12 : 27), is used of Christ's garment, John 19 : 23.¶

WRANGLINGS

— DIAPARATRIBĒ (διαπαρατριβή), found in 1 Tim. 6 : 5, denotes
AG:187C CB:— constant strife, 'obstinate contests' (Ellicott), 'mutual irritations'
(Field), A.V., " perverse disputings " (marg., " gallings one of another "),

R.V. "wranglings."* Some texts have *paradiatribē*. The preposition 3859
dia- is used intensively, indicating thoroughness, completeness.¶ The AG:614B
simple word *paratribē* (not found in the N.T.), denotes hostility, enmity. CB:—
See DISPUTE, No. 3.

WRAP

1. ENEILEŌ (ἐνειλέω), to roll in, wind in, occurs in Mark 15 : 46; 1750
see WIND (Verb), No. 3.¶ AG:264C CB:—
2. ENTULISSŌ (ἐντυλίσσω), to roll in, occurs in Matt. 27 : 59; Luke 1794
23 : 53; John 20 : 7: see ROLL, No. 5.¶ AG:270B CB:—
3. SUSTELLŌ (συστέλλω), to wrap or wind up, Acts 5 : 6; see WIND, 4958
No. 2; 1 Cor. 7 : 29, see SHORTEN, No. 2.¶ AG:795A CB:—

WRATH 3709

1. ORGĒ (ὀργή): see ANGER and Notes (1) and (2). AG:578D CB:1261A
2. THUMOS (θυμός), hot anger, passion, for which see ANGER, Notes 2372
(1) and (2), is translated "wrath" in Luke 4 : 28; Acts 19 : 28; Rom. AG:365B
2 : 8, R.V.; Gal. 5 : 20; Eph. 4 : 31; Col. 3 : 8; Heb. 11 : 27; Rev. CB:1272C
12 : 12; 14 : 8, 10, 19; 15 : 1, 7; 16 : 1; 18 : 3; "wraths" in 2 Cor.
12 : 20; "fierceness" in Rev. 16 : 19; 19 : 15 (followed by No. 1).¶
3. PARORGISMOS (παροργισμός) occurs in Eph. 4 : 26: see ANGER, 3950
A, Note (2).¶ AG:629D CB:1262C
Note: For the verb *parorgizō*, to provoke to wrath, Eph. 6 : 4, A.V., 3949
see ANGER, B, No. 2. AG:629D CB:1262C

WREST

STREBLOŌ (στρεβλόω), to twist, to torture (from *streblē*, a winch or 4761
instrument of torture, and akin to *strephō*, to turn), is used metaphorically AG:771A CB:—
in 2 Pet. 3 : 16, of wresting the Scriptures on the part of the ignorant
and unstedfast.¶ In the Sept., 2 Sam. 22 : 27.¶

WRESTLE, WRESTLING

PALĒ (πάλη), a wrestling (akin to *pallō*, to sway, vibrate), is used 3823
figuratively in Eph. 6 : 12, of the spiritual conflict engaged in by believers, AG:606A CB:—
R.V., "(our) wrestling," A.V., "(we) wrestle."¶

WRETCHED

TALAIPŌROS (ταλαίπωρος), distressed, miserable, wretched, is used 5005
in Rom. 7 : 24 and Rev. 3 : 17.¶ Cp. *talaipōria*, misery, and *talaipōreō* AG:803B CB:1271A
(see AFFLICT).

WRINKLE 4512

RHUTIS (ῥυτίς), from an obsolete verb *rhuō*, signifying to draw AG:738B CB:—

together, occurs in Eph. 5 : 27, describing the flawlessness of the complete Church, as the result of the love of Christ in giving Himself up for it, with the purpose of presenting it to Himself hereafter.¶

WRITE, WROTE, WRITTEN

A. Verbs.

1125 1. GRAPHŌ (γράφω) is used (*a*) of forming letters on a surface or
AG:166C writing material, John 8 : 6 ; Gal. 6 : 11, where the Apostle speaks of his
CB:1248C having written with large letters in his own hand, which not improbably means that at this point he took the pen from his amanuensis and finished the Epistle himself ; this is not negatived by the fact that the verb is in the aorist or past definite tense, lit., 'I wrote,' for in Greek idiom the writer of a letter put himself beside the reader and spoke of it as having been written in the past ; in Eng. we should say 'I am writing,' taking our point of view from the time at which we are doing it ; cp. Philm. 19 (this Ep. is undoubtedly a holograph), where again the equivalent English translation is in the present tense (see also Acts 15 : 23 ; Rom. 15 : 15) ; possibly the Apostle, in Galatians, was referring to his having written the body of the Epistle but the former alternative seems the more likely ; in 2 Thess. 3 : 17 he says that the closing salutation is written by his own hand and speaks of it as "the token in every Epistle" which some understand as a purpose for the future rather than a custom ; see, however, 1 Cor. 16 : 21 and Col. 4 : 18. The absence of the token from the other Epistles of Paul can be explained differently, their authenticity not being dependent upon this ; (*b*) to commit to writing, to record, e.g., Luke 1 : 63 ; John 19 : 21, 22 ; it is used of Scripture as a standing authority, "it is written," e.g., Mark 1 : 2 ; Rom. 1 : 17 (cp. 2 Cor. 4 : 13) ; (*c*) of writing directions or giving information, e.g., Rom. 10 : 5, "(Moses) writeth," R.V. (A.V., "describeth") ; 15 : 15 ; 2 Cor. 7 : 12 ; (*d*) of that which contained a record or message, e.g., Mark 10 : 4, 5 ; John 19 : 19 ; 21 : 25 ; Acts 23 : 25.

1989 2. EPISTELLŌ (ἐπιστέλλω) denotes to send a message by letter, to
AG:300C
CB:1246A write word (*stellō*, to send ; Eng., epistle), Acts 15 : 20 ; 21 : 25 (some mss. have *apostellō*, to send) ; Heb. 13 : 22.¶

4270 3. PROGRAPHŌ (προγράφω) denotes to write before, Rom. 15 : 4
AG:704A
CB:1266C (in the best texts ; some have *graphō*) ; Eph. 3 : 3. See SET (forth).

1449 4. ENGRAPHŌ (ἐγγράφω) denotes to write in, Luke 10 : 20 ; 2 Cor.
AG:213D
CB:1245A 3 : 2, 3.¶

1924 5. EPIGRAPHŌ (ἐπιγράφω) is rendered to write over or upon (*epi*)
AG:291C
CB:1245C in Mark 15 : 26 ; figuratively, on the heart, Heb. 8 : 10 ; 10 : 16 ; on the gates of the Heavenly Jerusalem, Rev. 21 : 12. See INSCRIPTION.

APOGRAPHŌ
583 *Notes :* (1) For *apographō*, Heb. 12 : 23, A.V., "written," see ENROL.
AG:89B (2) In 2 Cor. 3 : 7 "written" is a translation of *en*, in, with the dative
CB:1236C plural of *gramma*, a letter, lit., 'in letters.'

B. Adjective.

GRAPTOS (γραπτός), from A, No. 1, written, occurs in Rom. 2 : 15.¶ 1123
AG:166A
CB:1248C

WRITING

GRAMMA (γράμμα), from *graphō*, to write, is rendered " writings " 1121
in John 5 : 47. See LETTER, No. 1. AG:165B
CB:1248C

Notes : (1) For *biblion*, " writing," A.V. in Matt. 19 : 7, see BILL, BIBLION
No. 1. (2) In John 19 : 19, A.V., " the writing (was) " is a translation 975
AG:141B
of the perfect participle, Passive Voice, of *graphō*, R.V., " (there was) CB:1239A
written." GRAPHō
1125
AG:166C
CB:1248C

WRITING TABLET (A.V., WRITING TABLE)

PINAKIDION (πινακίδιον) occurs in Luke 1 : 63, a diminutive of 4093
pinakis, a tablet, which is a variant reading here.¶ AG:658B
CB:—

WRONG (Noun and Verb), WRONG-DOER, WRONG-DOING

A. Nouns.

1. ADIKIA (ἀδικία), *a*, negative, *dikē*, right, is translated " wrong " 93
in 2 Pet. 2 : 13 (2nd part), 15, R.V., " wrong-doing " (A.V., unrighteous- AG:17D
CB:1233A
ness) ; in 2 Cor. 12 : 13, it is used ironically. See INIQUITY, UNJUST, UNRIGHTEOUSNESS.

2. ADIKĒMA (ἀδίκημα) denotes a misdeed, injury, in the concrete 92
sense (in contrast to No. 1), Acts 18 : 14, " a matter of wrong ; " 24 : 20, AG:17D
CB:1233A
R.V., " wrong-doing " (A.V., " evil doing "). See INIQUITY.

B. Verb.

ADIKEŌ (ἀδικέω), to do wrong, is used (*a*) intransitively, to act un- 91
righteously, Acts 25 : 11, R.V., " I am a wrong-doer " (A.V., " . . . an AG:17C
offender ") ; 1 Cor. 6 : 8 ; 2 Cor. 7 : 12 (1st part) ; Col. 3 : 25 (1st part) ; CB:1233A
cp. Rev. 22 : 11 (see UNRIGHTEOUSNESS, B) ; (*b*) transitively, to wrong, Matt. 20 : 13 ; Acts 7 : 24 (Passive Voice), 26, 27 ; 25 : 10 ; 2 Cor. 7 : 2, ver. 12 (2nd part ; Passive Voice) ; Gal. 4 : 12, " ye did (me no) wrong," anticipating a possible suggestion that his vigorous language was due to some personal grievance ; the occasion referred to was that of his first visit ; Col. 3 : 25 (2nd part), lit., ' what he did wrong,' which brings consequences both in this life and at the Judgment-Seat of Christ ; Philm. 18 ; 2 Pet. 2 : 13 (1st part) ; in the Middle or Passive Voice, to take or suffer wrong, to suffer (oneself) to be wronged, 1 Cor. 6 : 7. See HURT, OFFENDER, UNJUST.

WRONGFULLY

ADIKŌS (ἀδίκως), akin to the above, occurs in 1 Pet. 2 : 19.¶ 95
AG:18B
Note : For "exact wrongfully," Luke 3 : 14, R.V., see ACCUSE, B, No. 5. CB:1233A

WROTH (be) 3710
AG:579C

1. ORGIZŌ (ὀργίζω), always in the Middle or Passive Voice in the CB:1261A

N.T., is rendered "was (were) wroth" in Matt. 18 : 34; 22 : 7; Rev. 11 : 18, R.V., (A.V., "were angry"); 12 : 17, R.V., "waxed wroth." See Anger, B, No. 1.

2373 2. THUMOŌ (θυμόω) signifies to be very angry (from *thumos*, wrath,
AG:365C
CB:1272C hot anger), to be stirred into passion, Matt. 2 : 16, of Herod (Passive
Voice).¶

5520 3. CHOLAŌ (χολάω), primarily, to be melancholy (*cholē*, gall),
AG:883B
CB:— signifies to be angry, John 7 : 23, R.V., "are ye wroth" (A.V.,
". . . angry").¶

For WROUGHT see WORK

YE, YOU, YOURSELVES, YOUR OWN SELVES

Notes: (1) These are most frequently the translations of various HUMEIS
inflections of a verb; sometimes of the article before a nominative used 5210 AG:772A
as a vocative, e.g., Rev. 18 : 20, "ye saints, and ye apostles, and ye (SU) CB:—
prophets" (lit., 'the saints, etc.'). When the 2nd person plural pronouns SU
are used separately from a verb, they are usually one or other of the 4771
forms of *humeis*, the plural of *su*, "thou," and are frequently emphatic, AG:772A CB:—
especially when they are subjects of the verb, an emphasis always to AUTOS
be noticed, e.g., Matt. 5 : 13, 14, 48; 6 : 9, 19, 20; Mark 6 : 31, 37; 846
John 15 : 27a; Rom. 1 : 6; 1 Cor. 3 : 17, 23; Gal. 3 : 28, 29a; Eph. AG:122C CB:1238B
1 : 13a; 2 : 8; 2 : 11, 13; Phil. 2 : 18; Col. 3 : 4, 7a; 4 : 1; 1 Thess. HEAUTOU)
1 : 6; 2 : 10, 19, 20; 3 : 8; 2 Thess. 3 : 13; Jas. 5 : 8; 1 Pet. 2 : 9a; 1438 AG:211D
1 John 2 : 20, 24 (1st and 3rd occurrences), 27a; 4 : 4; Jude 17, 20. CB:1249B
(2) The addition of *autoi*, yourselves, to the pronoun marks especial (-OS)
emphasis, e.g., Mark 6 : 31; John 3 : 28; 1 Cor. 11 : 13; 1 Thess. 4 : 9.
Sometimes *autoi* is used without the pronoun, e.g., Luke 11 : 46, 52;
Acts 2 : 22; 20 : 34; 1 Thess. 2 : 1; 3 : 3; 5 : 2; 2 Thess. 3 : 7; Heb.
13 : 3. (3) The reflexive pronoun "yourselves" represents the various
plural forms of the reflexive pronoun *heautou* (frequently governed by
some preposition), e.g., Matt. 3 : 9; 16 : 8; 23 : 31; 25 : 9; Mark 9 : 50;
Luke 3 : 8; 12 : 33, 57; 16 : 9; 21 : 30, "of your own selves;" 21 : 34;
Acts 5 : 35; in Rom. 11 : 25, "in your own (conceits)," lit., 'in (*en*;
some texts have *para*, among) yourselves;' so 12 : 16 (with *para*);
1 Pet. 4 : 8; Jude 20, 21; in Eph. 5 : 19, R.V., "one to another"
(A.V., and R.V. marg., "to yourselves").

Note: In 1 Thess. 5 : 11, A.V., *allēlous*, "one another" (R.V.), is 240 AG:39C
rendered "yourselves together." CB:1234C

YEA, YES

1. NAI (*ναί*), a particle of affirmation, is used (*a*) in answer to a 3483
question, Matt. 9 : 28; 11 : 9; 13 : 51; 17 : 25; 21 : 16; Luke 7 : 26; AG:532D CB:—
John 11 : 27; 21 : 15, 16; Acts 5 : 8; 22 : 27; Rom. 3 : 29; (*b*) in
assent to an assertion, Matt. 15 : 27, R.V. (A.V., "truth"); Mark 7 : 28;
Rev. 14 : 13; 16 : 7, R.V. (A.V., "even so"); (*c*) in confirmation of an
assertion, Matt. 11 : 26 and Luke 10 : 21, R.V. (A.V., "even so"); Luke
11 : 51, R.V. (A.V., "verily"); 12 : 5; Phil. 4 : 3 (in the best texts);
Philm. 20; (*d*) in solemn asseveration, Rev. 1 : 7 (A.V. and R.V., "even

so"); 22 : 20, R.V. (A.V., "surely"); (*e*) in repetition for emphasis,
Matt. 5 : 37; 2 Cor. 1 : 17; Jas. 5 : 12; (*f*) singly in contrast to *ou*, "nay,"
2 Cor. 1 : 18, 19 (twice), 20, "(the) yea," R.V.¶

235 2. ALLA (ἀλλά), but, is translated "yea" in John 16 : 2; Rom.
AG:38A CB:— 3 : 31, A.V. (R.V., "nay"); 1 Cor. 4 : 3; 2 Cor. 7 : 11 (six times);
Gal. 4 : 17, A.V. (R.V., "nay"); Phil. 1 : 18; 2 : 17; 3 : 8; Jas. 2 : 18.

2532 AG:391D 3. KAI (καί), and, even, is rendered "yea," e.g., Luke 2 : 35; John
CB:1253A 16 : 32; 1 Cor. 2 : 10; 2 Cor. 8 : 3; in Acts 7 : 43, A.V. (R.V., "and").

3304 AG:503C 4. MEN OUN (μὲν οὖν), in some texts *menounge*, i.e., *men-oun-ge*,
CB:— "yea rather," occurs, e.g., in Luke 11 : 28; in Rom. 10 : 18, "yea (A.V.,
yes) verily;" in Phil. 3 : 8, R.V., "yea verily" (A.V., "yea doubtless").

Ē *Notes:* (1) In 1 Cor. 15 : 15 the R.V. translates *kai* by "and" (A.V.,
2228 AG:342A "yea"). (2) In Luke 24 : 22 the R.V. translates *alla kai* "moreover"
EI (A.V., "yea . . . and"). (3) In 1 Cor. 16 : 6, A.V., *ē kai*, "or even"
1487 AG:219A (R.V.), is translated "yea, and." (4) In 2 Cor. 5 : 16, A.V., the phrase
CB:1242C *ei kai* (some texts have *ei de kai*) is translated "yea, though" (R.V.,
DE "even though"). (5) In Phil. 2 : 8, R.V., the particle *de*, but, is trans-
1161 AG:171C lated "yea" (A.V., "even").

ETOS 2094

YEAR

AG:316D

A. Nouns.

CB:— 1. ETOS (ἔτος) is used (*a*) to mark a point of time at or from which
ENIAUTOS 1763 events take place, e.g., Luke 3 : 1 (dates were frequently reckoned from the
AG:266B time when a monarch began to reign); in Gal. 3 : 17 the time of the giving
CB:1245A of the Law is stated as 430 years after the covenant of promise given to
From p. 1257 Abraham; there is no real discrepancy between this and Ex. 12 : 40;
DIETIA 1333 the Apostle is not concerned with the exact duration of the interval;
AG:194D it certainly was not less than 430 years; the point of the argument is that
CB:— TRIETIA the period was very considerable; Gal. 1 : 18 and 2 : 1 mark events in
5148 Paul's life; as to the former the point is that three years elapsed before
AG:826B he saw any of the Apostles; in 2 : 1 the 14 years may date either from his
CB:— HĒMERA conversion or from his visit to Peter mentioned in 1 : 18; the latter
2250 seems the more natural (for a full discussion of the subject see Notes on
AG:345D CB:1249C Galatians by Hogg and Vine, pp. 55 ff.); (*b*) to mark a space of time, e.g.,
DIETĒS Matt. 9 : 20; Luke 12 : 19; 13 : 11; John 2 : 20; Acts 7 : 6, where the
1332 AG:194D 400 years mark not merely the time that Israel was in bondage in Egypt,
CB:— but the time that they sojourned or were strangers there (the R.V. puts
HEKATONTAETĒS a comma after the word "evil"); the Genevan Version renders Gen.
1541 AG:236D 15 : 13 "thy posterity shall inhabit a strange land for 400 years;"
CB:— PERUSI Heb. 3 : 17; Rev. 20 : 2–7; (*c*) to date an event from one's birth, e.g.,
4070 Mark 5 : 42; Luke 2 : 42; 3 : 23; John 8 : 57; Acts 4 : 22; 1 Tim.
AG:653D CB:1263C 5 : 9; (*d*) to mark recurring events, Luke 2 : 41 (with *kata*, used dis-
MEGAS tributively); 13 : 7; (*e*) of an unlimited number, Heb. 1 : 12.

3173 AG:497C 2. ENIAUTOS (ἐνιαυτός), originally a cycle of time, is used (*a*) of a
CB:1258A particular time marked by an event, e.g., Luke 4 : 19; John 11 : 49, 51;

18 : 13 ; Gal. 4 : 10 ; Rev. 9 : 15 ; (*b*) to mark a space of time, Acts 11 : 26 ; 18 : 11 ; Jas. 4 : 13 ; 5 : 17 ; (*c*) of that which takes place every year, Heb. 9 : 7 ; with *kata* [cp. (*d*) above], Heb. 9 : 25 ; 10 : 1, 3.¶

3. DIETIA (διετία) denotes a space of two years (*dis*, twice, and No. 1), Acts 24 : 27 ; 28 : 30.¶

4. TRIETIA (τριετία) denotes a space of three years (*treis*, three, and No. 1), Acts 20 : 31.¶

Note : In Luke 1 : 7, 18, *hēmera*, a day, is rendered "years."

B. Adjectives.

1. DIETĒS (διετής), akin to A, No. 3, denotes lasting two years, two years old, Matt. 2 : 16.¶

2. HEKATONTAETĒS (ἑκατονταετής) denotes a hundred years old, Rom. 4 : 19.¶

C. Adverb.

PERUSI (πέρυσι), last year, a year ago (from *pera*, beyond), is used with *apo*, from 2 Cor. 8 : 10 ; 9 : 2.¶

Note : In Heb. 11 : 24, A.V., *ginomai*, to become, with *megas*, great, is rendered "when he was come to years" (R.V., "when he was grown up").

For YES, see YEA

YESTERDAY

ECHTHES or CHTHES (ἐχθές) occurs in John 4 : 52 ; Acts 7 : 28 ; Heb. 13 : 8.¶

YET

Notes : This represents (1) the adverb *eti*, implying addition or duration, e.g., Matt. 12 : 40 ; Rom. 3 : 7 ; 5 : 6, 8 ; 9 : 19 ; in Heb. 12 : 26, 27, "yet . . . more ;" (2) *alla*, but, marking antithesis or transition, e.g., Mark 14 : 29 ; 1 Cor. 4 : 4, 15 ; 9 : 2 ; (3) *mentoi*, nevertheless, John 4 : 27 ; 20 : 5 ; (4) *akmēn*, even to this point of time (the accusative case of *akmē*, a point), Matt. 15 : 16 ; ¶ (5) *ouketi*, no longer, Mark 15 : 5, A.V., "yet . . . nothing" (R.V., "no more . . . anything") ; 2 Cor. 1 : 23, A.V., "not as yet ;" "yet not," e.g. Gal. 2 : 20, A.V. ; (6) *oupō*, "not yet," John 7 : 39 and 1 Cor. 8 : 2 (*oudepō*, in some mss., A.V., "nothing yet") ; *oudepō*, John 19 : 41, "never yet ;" 20 : 9, "as yet . . . not ;" (7) *mēpō*, not yet, Rom. 9 : 11 ; Heb. 9 : 8 ; ¶ (8) *kai*, and, even, also, "yet" in Luke 3 : 20 ; in Gal. 3 : 4, *ei ge kai*, A.V., "if . . . yet" (R.V., "if . . . indeed") ; (9) *ge*, a particle meaning 'indeed,' "yet," Luke 11 : 8 ; (10) *oudeis pōpote*, 19 : 30, R.V., "no man ever yet," A.V., "yet never man," lit., 'no one at any time (yet) ;' (11) the following, in which the R.V. gives the correct meaning for the A.V., "yet :" *ēdē*, "now," Mark 13 : 28 ; *pote*, "ever," Eph. 5 : 29 (A.V., "ever yet") ; *kai . . . de*, John 8 : 16, "yea and" (A.V., "and yet") ; *ou pleious*, Acts 24 : 11,

For DIETIA to MEGAS See p. 1256

YEAST See LEAVEN

ECHTHES — AG:331B CB:1242 (THOS) CHTHES 5504 AG:881D ETI 2089 AG:315C CB:1247A ALLA 235 AG:38A MENTOI 3305 AG:503C AKMēN 188 AG:30D CB:1234B OUKETI 3765 AG:592C OUPō 3768 AG:593C CB:1261B OUDEPō 3764 AG:592C MēPō 3380 AG:518B KAI 2532 AG:391D CB:1253A GE 1065 AG:152D PōPOTE 4455 AG:732A CB:1266A ēDē 2235 AG:344A CB:1242C POTE 4218 AG:695A CB:1266B PLEIōN 4119 AG:687C (POLUS II.) CB:1265B

3195 AG:500D CB:1258A "not more;" (12) *mellō*, to be about to, "are yet," Rev. 8 : 13; (13) other combinations with AND, AS, NOR, NOT.

YIELD

1325 AG:192C CB:1241C 1. DIDŌMI (δίδωμι), to give, is translated to yield, i.e., to produce, in Matt. 13 : 8, R.V. (A.V., "brought forth"); Mark 4 : 7, 8. See GIVE.

591 AG:90B CB:1236C 2. APODIDŌMI (ἀποδίδωμι), to give up or back, is translated to yield in Heb. 12 : 11; Rev. 22 : 2 (in each case, of bearing fruit). See DELIVER, A, No. 3, etc.

3936 AG:627C CB:1262B 3. PARISTĒMI or PARISTANŌ (παρίστημι), to present, is translated to yield in Rom. 6 : 13 (twice), 16, 19 (twice), R.V., to present, in each place. See COMMEND, etc.

4160 AG:680D CB:1265C 4. POIEŌ (ποιέω), to make, to do, is translated "yield" in Jas. 3 : 12. See DO.

863 AG:125C CB:1236B 5. APHIĒMI (ἀφίημι), to send away, is translated "yielded up (His spirit)" in Matt. 27 : 50 (cp. *paratithēmi*, "I commend," Luke 23 : 46, and *paradidōmi*, "He gave up," John 19 : 30). See FORGIVE, etc.

3982 AG:639A CB:1263A 6. PEITHŌ (πείθω), to persuade, in the Passive Voice, to be persuaded, is translated "do (not) thou yield," Acts 23 : 21. See PERSUADE.

1634 AG:247C CB:— *Note:* In Acts 5 : 10, A.V., *ekpsuchō*, to breathe one's last, expire (*ek*, out, *psuchē*, the life), is translated "yielded up (R.V., gave up) the ghost." See GHOST (give up the), No. 2.

YOKE, YOKED

A. Noun.

2218 AG:339D CB:1273C 1. ZUGOS (ζυγός), a yoke, serving to couple two things together, is used (1) metaphorically, (*a*) of submission to authority, Matt. 11 : 29, 30, of Christ's yoke, not simply imparted by Him but shared with Him; (*b*) of bondage, Acts 15 : 10 and Gal. 5 : 1, of bondage to the Law as a supposed means of salvation; (*c*) of bondservice to masters, 1 Tim. 6 : 1; (2) to denote a balance, Rev. 6 : 5. See BALANCE.¶

2201 AG:337B CB:1273C 2. ZEUGOS (ζεῦγος), a pair of animals, Luke 14 : 19. See PAIR.

B. Verb.

2086 AG:314D CB:1250A HETEROZUGEŌ (ἑτεροζυγέω), to be unequally yoked (*heteros*, another of a different sort, and A, No. 1), is used metaphorically in 2 Cor. 6 : 14.¶

YOKE-FELLOW

4805 AG:775D CB:1271A SUNZUGOS or SUZUGOS (σύνζυγος), an adjective denoting yoked together, is used as a noun in Phil. 4 : 3, a yoke-fellow, fellow-labourer; probably here it is a proper name, Synzygus, addressed as "true," or genuine (*gnēsios*), i.e., properly so-called.¶

YONDER

1563 AG:239A CB:1243C EKEI (ἐκεῖ), there, is rendered "yonder" in Matt. 26 : 36; "to yonder place," 17 : 20. See THERE, THITHER.

For YOU see YE

YOUNG, YOUNG (children, daughter, man, men, woman, women)

1. **NEŌTEROS** (*νεώτερος*), the comparative degree of *neos*, new, (NEOS)
youthful, is translated "young" in John 21 : 18; in the plural, Acts 5 : 6, 3501
"young men" (marg., "younger"); Tit. 2 : 6, A.V., R.V., "younger AG:535D CB:1259C
men." See YOUNGER.

2. **NEOS** (*νέος*), in the feminine plural, denotes "young women," 3501
Tit. 2 : 4. See NEW, No. 2. AG:535D CB:1259C

3. **NEANIAS** (*νεανίας*), a young man, occurs in Acts 7 : 58; 20 : 9; 3494
23 : 17, 18 (in some texts).¶ AG:534C CB:—

4. **NEANISKOS** (*νεανίσκος*), a diminutive of No. 3, a youth, a young 3495
man, occurs in Matt. 19 : 20, 22; Mark 14 : 51 (1st part; R.V. omits AG:534C
in 2nd part); 16 : 5; Luke 7 : 14; Acts 2 : 17; 5 : 10 (i.e., attendants); CB:1259C
23 : 18 (in the best texts), 22; 1 John 2 : 13, 14, of the second branch
of the spiritual family.¶

5. **NOSSOS** or **NEOSSOS** (*νοσσός*), a young bird (akin to No. 2), is 3502
translated "young" in Luke 2 : 24.¶ Cp. *nossia*, a brood, Luke 13 : 34, AG:543
and the noun *nossion*, used in the neuter plural, *nossia*, in Matt. 23 : 37,
"chickens;" *nossion* is the diminutive of *nossos*.¶ PAIS

Notes: (1) In Acts 20 : 12, A.V., *pais*, a "lad" (R.V.), is translated 3816 AG:604C
"young man." (2) In Mark 7 : 25, A.V., *thugatrion*, a diminutive of CB:1261C
thugatēr, a daughter, is rendered "young (R.V., little) daughter." (3) THUGATRION 2365
In Mark 10 : 13, A.V., *paidion*, in the neuter plural, is rendered "young AG:365A
(R.V., little) children." (4) In Acts 7 : 19, A.V., *brephos*, in the neuter PAIDION 3813
plural, is rendered "young children," R.V., "babes." See BABE, No. 1. AG:604A CB:1261C BREPHOS

YOUNGER

1025
1. **NEŌTEROS** (*νεώτερος*), for which see No. 1, above, occurs in AG:147B CB:1239B
Luke 15 : 12, 13; 22 : 26; 1 Tim. 5 : 1 ("younger men"); 5 : 2, feminine; NEŌTEROS
ver. 11, "younger (widows);" ver. 14, "younger (*widows*)," R.V., marg. 3501
and A.V., "younger (women)" (see WIDOW); 1 Pet. 5 : 5. For Tit. 2 : 6 AG:535D (NEOS)
see YOUNG, No. 1.¶ CB:1259C

2. **ELASSŌN** (*ἐλάσσων*) is rendered "younger" in Rom. 9 : 12: 1640
see LESS. AG:248A CB:1244A

YOUR, YOURS

Notes: (1) "Your" is most frequently the translation of *humōn*,
lit., of you, the genitive plural of *su*, thou, you; it is translated "yours"
in 1 Cor. 3 : 21, 22; in 8 : 9, "of yours;" 16 : 18; 2 Cor. 12 : 14. In HUMEIS 5210
the following the dative plural, *humin*, lit., 'to you,' is translated "your;" AG:772A
Luke 16 : 11, lit., '(who will entrust) to you;' in 21 : 15 "your adver- (SU) CB:—
saries" is, lit., '(those opposed) to you;' in 1 Cor. 6 : 5 and 15 : 34, A.V., SU
"(I speak to) your (shame)," R.V., "(I say *this* to move) you (to shame)," 4771 AG:772A
is, lit., '(I speak unto a shame) to you.' The accusative plural, *humas*, CB:—

preceded by *kata*, according to, is rendered in Acts 18 : 15 " your own (law)," R.V., A.V., " your (law)," lit., ' (of the law) according to you,' with emphasis and scorn ; in Eph. 1 : 15 the same construction is used of faith, but *kata* here means " among," as in the R.V., " (the faith . . . which is) among you," A.V., " your (faith) ; " in John 14 : 26 " He shall . . . bring to your remembrance " is, lit., ' He shall . . . put you in mind of.'
HUMETEROS 5212 AG:836A CB:— (2) The possessive pronoun, *humeteros*, your, is used in Luke 6 : 20 ; John 7 : 6 ; 8 : 17 ; 15 : 20 ; Acts 27 : 34 ; Rom. 11 : 31 ; 1 Cor. 15 : 31 ; 16 : 17 ; 2 Cor. 8 : 8 ; Gal. 6 : 13 ; in Luke 16 : 12, " your own."¶ (3) In Rom. 16 : 19, A.V., the phrase *to epi humin*, lit., ' the (matter) over you,' is rendered " on your behalf " (R.V., " over you," following the mss. which omit the neuter article *to*).

YOUTH

3503 AG:536C CB:1259C NEOTĒS (νεότης), from *neos*, new, occurs in Mark 10 : 20 ; Luke 18 : 21 ; Acts 26 : 4 ; 1 Tim. 4 : 12 (in some mss., Matt. 19 : 20).¶

YOUTHFUL

3512 AG:537B CB:— NEŌTERIKOS (νεωτερικός), from *neōteros*, the comparative degree of *neos*, new, is used especially of qualities, of lusts, 2 Tim. 2 : 22.¶

Z

ZEAL

ZĒLOS (ζῆλος) denotes zeal in the following passages: John 2 : 17, 2205
with objective genitive, i.e., 'zeal for Thine house;' so in Rom. 10 : 2, AG:337D
"a zeal for God;" in 2 Cor. 7 : 7, R.V., "(your) zeal (for me)," A.V., CB:1273B
"(your) fervent mind (toward me);" used absolutely in 7 : 11; 9 : 2; Phil. 3 : 6 (in Col. 4 : 13 in some texts; the best have *ponos*, "labour," R.V.). See ENVY, Note, FERVENT, C, Note (2), INDIGNATION, A, Note (3), JEALOUSY.

ZEALOUS

A. Noun.

ZĒLŌTĒS (ζηλωτής) is used adjectivally, of being zealous (*a*) "of the 2207
Law," Acts 21 : 20; (*b*) "toward God," lit., 'of God,' 22 : 3, R.V., "for AG:338A
God;" (*c*) "of spiritual gifts," 1 Cor. 14 : 12, i.e., for exercise of spiritual CB:1273B
gifts (lit., 'of spirits,' but not to be interpreted literally); (*d*) "for (A.V., of) the traditions of my fathers," Gal. 1 : 14, of Paul's loyalty to Judaism before his conversion; (*e*) "of good works," Tit. 2 : 14.

The word is, lit., 'a zealot,' i.e., an uncompromising partisan. The "Zealots" was a name applied to an extreme section of the Pharisees, bitterly antagonistic to the Romans. Josephus (*Antiq*. xviii. 1. 1, 6; *B.J.* ii. 8. 1) refers to them as the "fourth sect of Jewish philosophy" (i.e., in addition to the Pharisees, Sadducees, and Essenes), founded by Judas of Galilee (cp. Acts 5 : 37). After his rebellion in A.D. 6, the Zealots nursed the fires of revolt, which, bursting out afresh in A.D. 66, led to the destruction of Jerusalem in 70. To this sect Simon, one of the Apostles, had belonged, Luke 6 : 15; Acts 1 : 13. The equivalent Hebrew and Aramaic term was "Cananæan" (Matt. 10 : 4); this is not connected with Canaan, as the A.V. "Canaanite" would suggest, but is derived from Heb. *qannâ*, jealous.¶

B. Verbs.

1. ZĒLOŌ (ζηλόω), to be jealous, also signifies to seek or desire eagerly; 2206
in Gal. 4 : 17, R.V., "they zealously seek (you)," in the sense of taking AG:338A
a very warm interest in; so in ver. 18, Passive Voice, "to be zealously CB:1273B
sought" (A.V., "to be zealously affected"), i.e., to be the object of warm interest on the part of others; some texts have this verb in Rev. 3 : 19 —
(see No. 2). See AFFECT, Note, COVET, DESIRE, ENVY, JEALOUS. AG:337C

2. ZĒLEUŌ (ζηλεύω), a late and rare form of No. 1, is found in the CB:1273B
best texts in Rev. 3 : 19, "be zealous."¶ 4704 AG:763C

Note: For *spoudazō*, Gal. 2 : 10, R.V., see DILIGENT, B, No. 1. CB:1269C

ADDITIONAL NOTES.

(1) On the Particle KAI (καί).

(*a*) The particle *kai*, "and," chiefly used for connecting words, KAI
clauses and sentences (the copulative or connective use), not infrequently 2532 AG:391D
signifies "also." This is the *adjunctive*, or *amplificatory*, use, and it is CB:1253A
to be distinguished from the purely copulative significance "and." A good illustration is provided in Matt. 8 : 9, in the words of the centurion, "I also am a man under authority." Other instances are Matt. 5 : 39, 40 ; 8 : 9 ; 10 : 18 ; 18 : 33 ; 20 : 4 ; Luke 11 : 49 ; 12 : 41, 54, 57 ; 20 : 3 ; John 5 : 26, "the Son also," R.V. ; 7 : 3 ; 12 : 10 ; 14 : 1, 3, 7, 19 ; 15 : 9, 27 ; 17 : 24 ; Acts 11 : 17 ; Rom. 1 : 13 ; 6 : 11 ; 1 Cor. 7 : 3 ; 11 : 25 ; 15 : 30 ; Gal. 6 : 1 ; Phil. 4 : 12, "I know also," R.V. ; 1 Thess. 3 : 12. In 1 Cor. 2 : 13 the *kai* phrase signifies 'which are the very things we speak, with the like power of the Holy Spirit.'

This use includes the meanings "so," or "just so," by way of comparison, as in Matt. 6 : 10, and "so also," e.g., John 13 : 33 ; cp. Rom. 11 : 16. In Heb. 7 : 26 the most authentic mss. have *kai* in the first sentence, which may be rendered 'for such a High Priest also became us.' Here it virtually has the meaning "precisely."

(*b*) Occasionally *kai* tends towards an *adversative* meaning, expressing
a contrast, "yet," almost the equivalent of *alla*, "but ;" see, e.g., Mark ALLA
12 : 12, 'yet they feared ;' Luke 20 : 19 ; John 18 : 28, 'yet they them- 235 AG:38A
selves entered not.' Some take it in this sense in Rom. 1 : 13, where, CB:—
however, it may be simply parenthetic. Sometimes in the English Versions the "yet" has been added in italics, as in 2 Cor. 6 : 8, 9, 10.

(*c*) In some passages *kai* has the meaning "and yet," e.g., Matt. 3 : 14, 'and yet comest Thou to me ? ;' 6 : 26, 'and yet' (R.V. "and," A.V., "yet") your Heavenly Father feedeth them ;' Luke 18 : 7, 'and yet He is longsuffering ;' John 3 : 19, 'and yet men loved the darkness ;' 4 : 20, 'and yet we say ;' 6 : 49, 'and yet they died ;' 1 Cor. 5 : 2, 'and yet ye are puffed up ;' 1 John 2 : 9, 'and yet hateth his brother.' The same is probably the case in John 7 : 30, 'and yet no man laid hands on Him ;' some rule this and similar cases out because of the negative in the sentence following the *kai*, but that seems hardly tenable.

(*d*) In some passages it has a *temporal* significance, "then." In Luke 7 : 12 the *kai*, which is untranslated in the English Versions, provides the meaning 'then, behold, there was carried out ;' so Acts 1 : 10, 'then, behold, two men stood.' This use is perhaps due to the influence of the Septuagint, reflecting the Hebrew idiom, especially when *idou*, "behold" follows the *kai*.

(*e*) There is also the *inferential* use before a question, e.g., Mark 10 : 26, " then who can be saved ? " R.V. This is commonly expressed by the English " and," as in Luke 10 : 29 ; John 9 : 36.

HOTI 3754 AG:588C CB:1251B (*f*) Occasionally it has almost the sense of *hoti*, " that," e.g., Matt. 26 : 15 (first part) ; Mark 14 : 40 (last part) ; Luke 5 : 12, 17, where, if the *kai* had been translated, the clause might be rendered ' that, behold, a man . . . ,' lit., ' and behold . . . ;' so ver. 17 ; see also 9 : 51, where *kai*, ' that,' comes before " He stedfastly set ; " in 12 : 15, ' take heed that ye keep.' What is said under (*d*), regarding the influence of the Septuagint, is applicable also to this significance.

(*g*) Sometimes it has the consecutive meaning of " and so : " e.g., Matt. 5 : 15, ' and so it shineth ; ' Phil. 4 : 7, ' and so the peace . . . ; ' Heb. 3 : 19, ' and so we see.'

(*h*) The *epexegetic* or *explanatory* use. This may be represented by the expressions ' namely, ' ' again ,' ' and indeed,' ' that is to say ; ' it is usually translated by ' and. ' In such cases not merely an addition is in view. In Matt. 21 : 5, ' and upon a colt ' means ' that is to say, upon a colt.' In John 1 : 16 the clause " and grace for grace " is explanatory of the " fulness." In John 12 : 48, " and receiveth not My sayings," is not simply an addition to " that rejecteth Me," it explains what the rejection involves, as the preceding verse shows. In Mark 14 : 1, " and the unleavened bread " is perhaps an instance, since the Passover feast is so defined in Luke 22 : 1. In Acts 23 : 6 the meaning is ' the hope, namely, the resurrection of the dead.' In Rom. 1 : 5 " grace and apostleship " may signify ' grace expressed in apostleship.' In Eph. 1 : 1 " and the faithful " does not mark a distinct class of believers, it defines " the saints ; " but in this case it goes a little further than what is merely epexegetical, it adds a more distinctive epithet than the preceding and may be taken as meaning ' yes indeed.'

For the suggestion as to the epexegetic use of *kai* in John 3 : 5, ' water, even the Spirit,' see Vol. IV, p. 202, ll. 6–9.

In regard to Titus 3 : 5, " the renewing of the Holy Ghost " is coordinate with " the washing of regeneration," and some would regard it as precisely explanatory of that phrase, taking the *kai* as signifying ' namely. ' Certainly the " renewing " is not an additional and separate impartation of the Holy Spirit ; but the scope of the renewal is surely not limited to regeneration ; the second clause goes further than what is merely epexegetic of the first. Just so in Rom. 12 : 2, " the renewing of your mind " is not a single act, accomplished once and for all, as in regeneration. See under RENEW, B. The Holy Ghost, as having been ' shed on us,' continues to act in renewing us, in order to maintain by His power the enjoyment of the relationship into which He has brought us. " The man is cleansed in connection with the new order of things ; but the Holy Ghost is a source of an entirely new life, entirely new thoughts ; not only of a new moral being, but of the communication of all that in which this new being develops itself . . . He ever communicates more and more of the things of this new world into which He has brought us . . . 'the renewing of the Holy Ghost' embraces all this . . . so that it is not only that we are born of Him, but that He works in us, communicating to us all that is ours in Christ" (J. N. Darby). Both the washing and the renewing are His work.

(i) The *ascensive* use. This is somewhat similar to the epexegetic significance. It represents, however, an advance in thought upon what precedes and has the meaning "even." The context alone can determine the occurrences of this use. The following are some instances. In Matt. 5 : 46, 47, the phrases "even the publicans" and "even the Gentiles" represent an extension of thought in regard to the manner of reciprocity exhibited by those referred to, in comparison with those who, like the Pharisees, were considered superior to them. In Mark 1 : 27, "even the unclean spirits" represents an advance in the minds of the people concerning Christ's miraculous power, in comparison with the authority exercised by the Lord in less remarkable ways. So in Luke 10 : 17. In Acts 10 : 45, the *kai*, rendered "also," in the phrase "on the Gentiles also," seems necessary to be regarded in the same way, in view of the amazement manifested by those of the circumcision, and thus the rendering will be 'even on the Gentiles was poured out the gift;' cp. 11 : 1.

In Rom. 13 : 5, the clause "but also for conscience sake" should probably be taken in this sense. In Gal. 2 : 13, the phrase "even Barnabas" represents an advance of thought in comparison with the waywardness of others; as much as to say, 'the Apostle's closest associate, from whom something different might be expected, was surprisingly carried away.' In Phil. 4 : 16 there are three occurrences of *kai*, the first ascensive, "even"; the second (untranslated) meaning "both," before the word "once;" the third meaning "and." In 1 Thess. 1 : 5, in the cause "and in the Holy Ghost," the *kai* rendered "and," is ascensive, conveying an extension of thought beyond "power;" that is to say, 'power indeed, but the power of the Holy Spirit.' In 1 Pet. 4 : 14 "the Spirit of God" is "the Spirit of glory." Here there is an advance in idea from the abstract to the Personal. The phrase "the Spirit of God" does more than define "the Spirit of glory;" it is explanatory but ascensive also.

When preceded or followed by the conjunction *ei*, "if," the phrase EI
signifies "even if," or "if even," e.g., Mark 14 : 29; Phil. 2 : 17; 1 Pet. 1487
3 : 1. AG:219A
CB:1242C

ON THE PARTICLE DE (δέ)

DE The particle *de* has two chief uses, (*a*) *continuative* or *copulative*,
1161 signifying 'and,' or 'in the next place,' (*b*) *adversative*, signifying 'but,'
AG:171C CB:— or 'on the other hand.' The first of these, (*a*), is well illustrated in the
genealogy in Matt. 1 : 2–16, the line being simply reckoned from Abraham to Christ. So in 2 Cor. 6 : 15, 16, where the *de* anticipates a negative more precisely than would be the case if *kai* had been used. In 1 Cor. 15 : 35 ; Heb. 12 : 6, e.g., the *de* " and (scourgeth) " is purely copulative.

(*b*) The adversative use distinguishes a word or clause from that which precedes. This is exemplified, for instance, in Matt. 5 : 22, 28, 32, 34, 39, 44, in each of which the *egō*, " I," stands out with pronounced stress by way of contrast. This use is very common. In Matt. 23 : 4 the first *de* is copulative, " Yea, they bind heavy burdens " (R.V.), the second is adversative, " but they themselves will not . . . "

In John 3 : 1, R.V., it may not at first sight seem clear whether the *de*, " Now," is copulative, introducing an illustration of Christ's absolute knowledge, or adversative, signifying 'But.' In the former case the significance would be that, however fair the exterior might be, as exemplified in Nicodemus, he needs to be born again. In the latter case it introduces a contrast, in regard to Nicodemus, to what has just been stated, that " Jesus did not trust Himself " (2 : 24) to those mentioned in v. 23. And, inasmuch as He certainly did afford to Nicodemus the opportunity of learning the truths of the new birth and the Kingdom of God, as a result of which he became a disciple (" secret " though he was), he may be introduced in the Apostle's narrative as an exception to those who believed simply through seeing the signs accomplished by the Lord (2 : 23).

In Rom. 3 : 22, in the clause " even the righteousness," the *de* serves to annexe not only an explanation, defining " a righteousness of God " (v. 21, R.V.), but an extension of the thought ; so in 9 : 30, " even the righteousness which is of faith."

In 1 Cor. 2 : 6, in the clause " yet a wisdom," an exception (not an addition) is made to what precedes ; some would regard this as belonging to (*a*) ; it seems, however, clearly adversative. In 4 : 7 the first *de* is copulative, " and what hast thou . . . ? ; " the second is adversative, " but if thou didst receive . . . "

In 1 Thess. 5 : 21 " many ancient authorities insert 'but' " (see R.V. marg.), so translating *de*, between the two injunctions " despise not prophesyings " and " prove all things," and this is almost certainly the correct reading. In any case the injunctions are probably thus contrastingly to be connected.

In 2 Pet. 1 : 5–7, after the first *de*, which has the meaning " yea," the six which follow, in the phrases giving virtues to be supplied, suggest the thought 'but there is something further to be done.' These are not merely connective, as expressed by the English " and," but adversative, as indicating a contrast to the possible idea that to add virtue to our faith is sufficient for the moral purpose in view.

De, in combination with the negatives *ou* and *mē* (*oude* and *mēde,* usually " but not," " and not," " neither ", " nor,"), sometimes has the force of " even," e.g., *oude* in Matt. 6 : 29, " even Solomon . . . was not arrayed . . . ;" Mark 6 : 31, lit., ' (they had) not even leisure to eat ; ' Luke 7 : 9, lit., ' not even in Israel have I found such faith ; ' John 7 : 5, " For even His brethren did not believe on Him ; " Acts 4 : 32, lit., ' not even one of them ; ' 1 Cor. 5 : 1, " not even among the Gentiles ;" *mēde,* in Mark 2 : 2, " not even about the door ;" 1 Cor 5 : 11, lit., ' with such a one not even to eat.'

OU 3756 AG:590A CB:— OUDE 3761 AG:591C CB:— Mē 3361 AG:515D CB:1258A MēDE 3366 AG:517D CB:—

ON THE PREPOSITIONS ANTI (ἀντί) AND HUPER (ὑπέρ).

ANTI 473 AG:73C CB:1236A The basic idea of *anti* is " facing." This may be a matter of opposition, unfriendliness or antagonism, or of agreement. These meanings are exemplified in compounds of the preposition with verbs, and in nouns. The following are instances: *antiparerchomai* in Luke 10 : 31, 32, where the verb is rendered " passed by on the other side," i.e., of the road, but facing the wounded man; *antiballō* in Luke 24 : 17, where the *anti* suggests that the two disciples, in exchanging words (see R.V. marg.), turned to face one another, indicating the earnest nature of their conversation. The idea of antagonism is seen in *antidikos*, an adversary, Matt. 5 : 25, *antichristos*, antichrist, 1 John 4 : 3, etc.

There is no instance of the uncompounded preposition signifying " against." Arising from the basic significance, however, there are several other meanings attaching to the separate use of the preposition. In the majority of the occurrences in the N.T., the idea is that of " in the place of," " instead of," or of exchange; e.g., Matt. 5 : 38, " an eye for (*anti*) an eye ; " Rom. 12 : 17, " evil for evil ; " so 1 Thess, 5 : 15 ; 1 Pet. 3 : 9, and, in the same verse, " reviling for reviling." The ideas of substitution and exchange are combined, e.g., in Luke 11 : 11, " for a fish . . . a serpent ; " Heb. 12 : 16, " for one mess of meat . . his own birthright." So in Matt. 17 : 27, " a shekel (*statēr*) . . . for thee and Me," where the phrase is condensed ; that is to say, the exchange is that of the coin for the tax demanded from Christ and Peter, rather than for the persons themselves. So in 1 Cor. 11 : 15, where the hair is a substitute for the covering.

Of special doctrinal importance are Matt. 20 : 28 ; Mark 10 : 45, " to give His life a ransom (*lutron*) for (*anti*) many." Here the substitutionary significance, " instead of," is clear, as also with the compound *antilutron* in 1 Tim. 2 : 6, " who gave Himself a ransom (*antilutron*) for (*huper*) all ; " here the use of *huper*, " on behalf of," is noticeable. Christ gave Himself as a ransom (of a substitutionary character), not instead of all men, but on behalf of *all*. The actual substitution, as in the passages in Matthew and Mark, is expressed by the *anti*, instead of, " *many*." The unrepentant man should not be told that Christ was his substitute, for in that case the exchange would hold good for him and though unregenerate he would not be in the place of death, a condition in which, however, he exists while unconverted. Accordingly the " many " are those who, through faith, are delivered from that condition. The substitutionary meaning is exemplified in Jas. 4 : 15, where the A.V. and R.V. render the *anti* " for that " (R.V., marg., " instead of ").

In Heb. 12 : 2, " for (*anti*) the joy that was set before Him endured the cross," neither the thought of exchange nor that of substitution is conveyed ; here the basic idea of facing is present. The cross and the joy faced each other in the mind of Christ and He chose the one with the other in view.

In John 1 : 16 the phrase "grace for grace" is used. The idea of 'following upon' has been suggested, as wave follows wave. Is not the meaning that the grace we receive corresponds to the grace inherent in Christ, out of whose fulness we receive it ?

The primary meaning of *huper* is "over," "above." Hence, metaphorically, with the accusative case, it is used of superiority, e.g., Matt. 10 : 24, "above his master" (or teacher) ; or of measure in excess, in the sense of beyond, e.g., 1 Cor. 4 : 6, "beyond the things that are written ;" or "than", after a comparative, e.g., Luke 16 : 8 ; Heb. 4 : 12 ; or "more than," after a verb, e.g., Matt. 10 : 37. With the genitive it means (1) on behalf of, in the interests of, e.g., of prayer, Matt. 5 : 44 ; of giving up one's life, and especially of Christ's so doing for man's redemption, e.g., John 10 : 15 ; 1 Tim. 2 : 6, 'on behalf of all' (see under *Anti*) ; 2 Thess. 2 : 1, 'in the interest of (i.e., 'with a view to correcting your thoughts about') the Coming.' The difficult passage, 1 Cor. 15 : 29, possibly comes here. With an alteration of the punctuation (feasible from the ms. point of view), the reference may be to baptism as taught elsewhere in the N.T., and the verse may read thus : 'Else what shall they do which are being baptized ? (i.e., what purpose can they serve ?) ; (it is) in the interest of the dead, if the dead are not raised at all. Why then are they baptized in the interest of them ? ' That is to say, they fulfil the ordinance in the interest of a Christ who is dead and in joint witness with (and therefore, in the interest of) believers who never will be raised, whereas an essential element in baptism is its testimony to the resurrection of Christ and of the believer.

HUPER
5228
AG:838B
CB:1252A

In some passages *huper* may be used in the substitutionary sense, e.g., John 10 : 11, 15 ; Rom. 8 : 32 ; but it cannot be so taken in the majority of instances. Cp. 2 Cor. 5 : 15, in regard to which, while it might be said that Christ died in place of us, it cannot be said that Christ rose again in the place of us.

ON THE PREPOSITIONS APO (ἀπό) AND EK (ἐκ).

APO 575 AG:86C CB:1236C The primary meaning of *apo* is "off;" this is illustrated in such compounds as *apokaluptō*, to take the veil off, to reveal; *apokoptō*, to cut off; hence there are different shades of meaning, the chief of which is "from" or "away from," e.g., Matt. 5:29, 30; 9:22; Luke 24:31, lit., 'He became invisible from them;' Rom. 9:3.

EK 1537 AG:234A CB:1243B The primary meaning of *ek* is "out of," e.g., Matt. 3:17, "a voice out of the heavens" (R.V.); 2 Cor. 9:7, lit., 'out of necessity.' Omitting such significances of *ek* as origin, source, cause, occasion, etc., our consideration will here be confined to a certain similarity between *apo* and *ek*. Since *apo* and *ek* are both frequently to be translated by "from" they often approximate closely in meaning. The distinction is largely seen in this, that *apo* suggests a starting point from without, *ek* from within; this meaning is often involved in *apo*, but *apo* does not give prominence to the "within-ness," as *ek* usually does. For instance, *apo* is used in Matt. 3:16, where the R.V. rightly reads "Jesus . . . went up straightway from the water;" in Mark 1:10 *ek* is used, "coming up out of the water;" *ek* (which stands in contrast to *eis* in v. 9) stresses more emphatically than *apo* the fact of His having been baptized in the water. In all instances where these prepositions appear to be used alternately this distinction is to be observed.

The literal meaning "out of" cannot be attached to *ek* in a considerable number of passages. In several instances *ek* obviously has the significance of 'away from;' and where either meaning seems possible, the context, or some other passage, affords guidance. The following are examples in which *ek* does not mean 'out of the midst of' or 'out from within,' but has much the same significance as *apo*: John 17:15, "that Thou shouldest keep them from the evil one;" 1 Cor. 9:19, "though I was free from all men;" 2 Cor. 1:10, "who delivered us from so great a death" (A.V.); 2 Pet. 2:21, "to turn back from the holy commandment;" Rev. 15:2, "them that had come victorious from the beast, and from his image, and from the number of his name" (*ek* in each case).

Concerning the use of *ek*, in 1 Thess. 1:10, "Jesus, which delivereth (the present tense, as in the R.V., is important) us from the wrath to come" [or, more closely to the original, 'our Deliverer (cp. the same phrase in Rom. 11:26) from the coming wrath'], the passage makes clear that the wrath signifies the calamities to be visited by God upon men when the present period of grace is closed. As to whether the *ek* here denotes 'out of the midst of' or 'preservation from,' this is determined by the statement in 5:9, that "God appointed us not unto wrath, but unto the obtaining of salvation;" the context there shows that the salvation is from the wrath just referred to. Accordingly the *ek* signifies 'preservation from' in the same sense as *apo*, and not 'out from the midst of.'

ON THE PREPOSITION EN (ἐν).

En, " in," is the most common preposition. It has several meanings, **EN**
e.g., of place (e.g., Heb. 1 : 3, lit., ' on the right hand,' i.e., in that posi- **1722**
tion), and time, e.g., in 1 Thess. 2 : 19; 3 : 13; 1 John 2 : 28, in each **AG:258B**
of which the phrase " at His coming " (inadequately so rendered, and **CB:1244B**
lit., ' in His Parousia ') combines place and time; the noun, while denoting a period, also signifies a presence involving accompanying circumstances, e.g., 1 Thess. 4 : 15.

Further consideration must here be confined to the instrumental use,
often rendered " with " (though *en* in itself does not mean " with "),
e.g., Matt. 5 : 13, " wherewith " (lit., ' in what,' i.e., by what means) shall
it be salted ; " 7 : 2, " with what measure ye mete." Sometimes the
instrumental is associated with the locative significance (which indeed
attaches to most of its uses), e.g., Luke 22 : 49, " shall we smite with
the sword ? " the smiting being viewed as located in the sword ; so in
Matt. 26 : 52, " shall perish with the sword ; " cp. Rev. 2 : 16 ; 6 : 8 ;
13 : 10. In Matt. 12 : 24, " by (marg., ' in ') Beelzebub," indicates that
the casting out is located in Beelzebub. Cp. Luke 1 : 51, " with His arm."
In Heb. 11 : 37, the statement " they were slain with the sword " is,
lit., ' they died by (*en*) slaughter of the sword.' There is a noticeable
change in Rom. 12 : 21, from *hupo*, by, to *en*, with, in this instrumental
and locative sense ; the lit. rendering is ' be not overcome by (*hupo*) **HUPO**
evil, but overcome evil with (*en*) good,' *en* expressing both means and **5259**
circumstances. A very important instance of the instrumental *en* is in **AG:843A**
Rom. 3 : 25, where the R.V., " faith, by His blood," corrects the A.V., **CB:1252A**
" faith in His blood," and the commas which the R.V. inserts are necessary. Thus the statement reads " whom God set forth to be a propitiation,
through faith, by His blood." Christ is a propitiation, by means of His
blood, i.e., His expiatory death. Faith is exercised in the living God,
not in the blood, which provides the basis of faith.

GREEK-ENGLISH INDEX

Note: The English words in this Index are not necessarily the meanings of the Greek words under which they are found. Rather, they are the articles in which these Greek words are discussed. For the system of transliteration of Greek letters into English, see the Introduction, page x.

Key to the Symbols

1. **Numbers:**

a. The number following the Greek word refers to the system of Strong's *Exhaustive Concordance to the Bible.*

b. "**AG:**" refers to the Arndt and Gingrich (and Danker) edition of Bauer's *Greek-English Lexicon*, page and "quadrant":

A	C
B	D

c. "**CB:**" refers to the third volume (the master index) of Colin Brown's *New International Dictionary of NT Theology*, page and column: | A| B| C|

d. Page 1349 contains a Table to convert references to the third volume of Colin Brown's *Dictionary* to the pagination of the index volume of the four-volume set first published in 1986.

2. **Symbols:**

a. "*" An asterisk after a Greek word indicates that it is not discussed under that English heading (though the English word is a rendering of the RV or KJV).

b. "***Note***" following an English word indicates that word is discussed in a Note rather than in a numbered article.

c. "**Cf.**" following "CB:" refers to a word closely related to the word indexed, which will shed light on its root definition. Many other such references (though not as cautiously chosen) appear in the articles themselves.

d. "( )" Parentheses in Greek words are used to indicate alternate spellings:

1) ACHRE(I)Oō is spelled both ACHREOō and ACHREIOō.

2) AMUNō (-OMAI) is spelled both AMUNō and AMUNOMAI.

3) When an alternate spelling follows the Greek word itself, the spelling varies between many resources (see above); when it follows one of the index numbers, only that resource is affected (see AITION).

e. "-" A dash is used with English and Greek words to indicate letters common to both spellings:

1) See above for Greek examples.

2) "strange, -er" indicates the word ALLOTRIOS is translated by both "strange" and "stranger."

f. "," A comma separates two English translations which have been set on one line to save space (see above).

GREEK-ENGLISH INDEX

A

ABARēS 4
AG:1B CB:—
burdensome

ABBA 5
AG:1B CB:1233A
abba

ABUSSOS 12
AG:2B CB:1233A
abyss*
bottom
deep *Note*
pit

ACHARISTOS 884
AG:128B CB:—
unthankful

ACHEIROPOIēTOS 886
AG:128B CB:1233A
hands (not made with)

ACHLUS 887
AG:128B CB:—
mist

ACHRE(I)Oō 889
AG:128C CB:—
unprofitable

ACHREIOS 888
AG:128C CB:—
unprofitable

ACHRēSTOS 890
AG:128C CB:1233A (-ON)
unprofitable
use *Note*

ACHRI(S) 891
AG:128D CB:1233A
hitherto
until*
while *Note*

ACHURON 892
AG:129A CB:—
chaff

ADAPANOS 77
AG:15C CB:—
charge

ADēLOS 82
AG:16C CB:—
appear (not) *Note*
uncertain

ADēLōS 84
AG:16D CB:1233A
uncertainly

ADēLOTēS 83
AG:16D CB:—
uncertain
uncertainly

ADELPHē 79
AG:15D CB:1233A
believer *Note*
sister

ADELPHOS 80
AG:15D CB:1233A
brother
disciple *Note*

ADELPHOTēS 81
AG:16C CB:1233A
brotherhood *Note*

ADēMONEō 85
AG:16D CB:—
heaviness
heavy
trouble

ADIAKRITOS 87
AG:17A CB:1233A
partiality
variance *Note*

ADIALEIPTOS 88
AG:17B CB:1233A
cease
continual
unceasing*

ADIALEIPTōS 89
AG:17B CB:1233A
cease
unceasingly*

ADIAPHTHORIA 90
AG:17B CB:—
uncorruptness*

ADIKēMA 92
AG:17D CB:1233A
evil *Note*
iniquity
wrong

ADIKEō 91
AG:17C CB:1233A
hurt
injure
offender *Note*
suffer
unjust *Note*
unrighteousness
wrong
wrong-doer

ADIKIA 93
AG:17D CB:1233A
iniquity
unjust *Note*
unrighteousness
wrong

ADIKOS 94
AG:18B CB:1233A
unjust
unrighteous

ADIKōS 95
AG:18B CB:1233A
wrongfully

ADō 103
AG:19B CB:1233A
sing

ADOKIMOS 96
AG:18C CB:1233A
cast
reject
reprobate

ADOLOS 97
AG:18D CB:1233A
guileless
sincere

ADUNATEō 101
AG:19A CB:—
impossible

ADUNATOS 102
AG:19A CB:1233A
impossible
impotent
weak

AEI 104
AG:19C CB:1233A
always
ever

AēR 109
AG:20B CB:1233A
air

AETOS 105
AG:19D CB:1233B
eagle

AGALLIAō 21
AG:3D CB:1233B
glad
joy
rejoice

AGALLIASIS 20
AG:3D CB:1233B
gladness
joy

AGAMOS 22
AG:4B CB:1233B
unmarried

AGANAKTEō 23
AG:4B CB:—
anger *Note*
displeased
indignation
sore *Note*

AGANAKTēSIS 24
AG:4B CB:—
anger *Note*
indignation

AGAPAō 25
AG:4B CB:1233B
beloved
love

AGAPē 26
AG:5B CB:1233B
charity*
dear *Note*
deceit *Note*
feast
love, love-feast

AGAPēTOS 27
AG:6B CB:1233B
beloved
dear

AGATHOPOIEō 15
AG:2C CB:1233B
good (to do)
well
well-doing

AGATHOPOIIA 16
AG:2C CB:1233B
well-doing

AGATHOPOIOS 17
AG:2C CB:1233B
well (do)

AGATHOS 18
AG:2D CB:1233B
benefit
good, goods
kind

AGATHōSUNē 19
AG:3D CB:1233B
goodness

AGATHOURGEō (-OER-)
14 AG:2B CB:1233B
good (to do)

AGELē 34
AG:8B CB:—
herd

AGENEALOGēTOS 35
AG:8C CB:1233B
genealogy

AGENēS 36
AG:8C CB:—
base

AGNAPHOS 46
AG:10D CB:—
new *Note*
undressed

AGNOēMA 51
AG:11C CB:1233B
error
ignorance

AGNOEō 50
AG:11B CB:1233B
ignorant, -ly
know
understand

AGNOIA 52
AG:11D CB:1233B
ignorance

AGNōSIA 56
AG:12B CB:1233C
ignorance
knowledge

AGNōSTOS 57
AG:12B CB:1233C
known
unknown*

AGō 71
AG:14B CB:1233C
bring
carry *Note*
go
keep *Note*
lead
open
AGōGē 72
AG:14D CB:1233C
conduct
life
manner *Note*
AGōN 73
AG:15A CB:1233C
conflict
contention *Note*
fight
race
AGōNIA 74
AG:15A CB:1233C
agony
AGōNIZOMAI 75
AG:15B CB:1233C
contend *Note*
fervently *Note*
fight
labour *Note*
strive
AGORA 58
AG:12C CB:1233C
market
market-place
street *Note*
AGORAIOS 60
AG:13A CB:1233C
baser
court
AGORAZō 59
AG:12D CB:1233C
buy
purchase
redeem *Note*
AGRA 61
AG:13A CB:—
draught
AGRAMMATOS 62
AG:13B CB:1233C
ignorant
unlearned
ARAULEō 63
AG:13B CB:—
abide
AGREUō 64
AG:13B CB:—
catch
AGRIELAIOS 65
AG:13D CB:1233C
olive tree (wild)
AGRIOS 66
AG:13C CB:1233C
raging *Note*
wild
AGROS 68
AG:13D CB:1233C
country
farm
AGROS (continued)
field
ground *Note*
land
piece *Note*
AGRUPNEō 69
AG:14A CB:1233C
watch
AGRUPNIA 70
AG:14A CB:1233C
watching
AICHMALōSIA 161
AG:26D CB:1233C
captivity
AICHMALōTEUō 162
AG:26D CB:1233C
captive
AICHMALōTIZō 163
AG:27A CB:1233C
captive
captivity
AICHMALōTOS 164
AG:27A CB:1233C
captive
AIDIOS 126
AG:22ā CB:1233C
eternal
everlasting
AIDōS 127
AG:22B CB:1233C
ashamed *Note*
reverence
shamefastness
AIGEIOS 122
AG:21D CB:—
goat (skin)
AIGIALOS 123
AG:21D CB:—
beach
shore*
AINEō 134
AG:23C CB:1233C
praise
AINESIS 133
AG:23C CB:1234A
praise
AINIGMA 135
AG:23C CB:1234A
darkly *Note*
AINOS 136
AG:23D CB:1234A
praise
AIōN 165
AG:27B CB:1234A
age
course
eternal
ever
evermore
world
AIōNIOS 166
AG:28B CB:1234A
age *Note*
eternal
everlasting
world *Note*
AIPHNIDIOS 160
AG:26D CB:—
sudden
unawares *Note*
AIRō 142
AG:24B CB:1234A
away *Note*
bear
carry *Note*
doubt (make to)
hoise, hoist up
lift
loose *Note*
put
remove *Note*
suspense*
take
AISCHROKERDēS 146
AG:25A CB:1234A
filthy
lucre
AISCHROKERDōS 147
AG:25B CB:—
filthy
lucre
AISCHROLOGIA 148
AG:25B CB:1234A
communication *Note*
AISHROLOGIA 148
AG:25B CB:1234A
filthy *Note*
AISCHROS 150
AG:25B CB:1234A
ashamed
filthy
shame
AISCHROTēS 151
AG:25B CB:1234A
filthiness
AISCHUNē 152
AG:25B CB:1234A
ashamed
dishonesty
shame
AISCHUNō (-OMAI) 153
AG:25C CB:1234A
ashamed
AISTHANOMAI 143
AG:24D CB:1234A
perceive
AISTHēSIS 144
AG:25A CB:1234A
judgment *Note*
AISTHēTēRION 145
AG:25A CB:1234A
sense
AITēMA 155
AG:26B CB:1234A
ask
petition
request
require *Note*
AITEō 154
AG:25D CB:1234A
ask
beg *Note*
call
AITEō (continued)
crave
desire
request
require *Note*
AITIA 156
AG:26B CB:1234A
accusation
case
cause
charge
crime*
fault *Note*
AITIōMA 157 (-AMA)
AG:26D CB:1234A
accusation
charge
complaint
AITION 158
AG:26D (-OS) CB:1234A
cause
fault
AITIOS 159
AG:26D CB:1234A
author
AKAIREOMAI 170
AG:29B CB:1234A
opportunity (lack)
AKAIRōS 171
AG:29B CB:1234A
season
AKAKOS 172
AG:29B CB:1234A
guileless
harmless
innocent
simple*
AKANTHA 173
AG:29C CB:1234A
thorns (of)
AKANTHINOS 174
AG:29C CB:1234A
thorns (of)
AKARPOS 175
AG:29D CB:1234A
fruit
unfruitful*
AKATAGNōSTOS 176
AG:29D CB:—
condemn
AKATAKALUPTOS 177
AG:29D CB:1234A
uncovered*
unveiled
AKATAKRITOS 178
AG:29D CB:—
uncondemned
AKATALUTOS 179
AG:30A CB:1234A
endless
AKATAPAUSTOS 180
AG:30A CB:—
cease *Note*
AKATASCHETOS 183
AG:30B CB:—
unruly *Note*

AKATASTASIA 181
AG:30A CB:1234B
commotion*
confusion
tumult

AKATASTATOS 182
AG:30B CB:—
restless
unstable

AKATHARSIA 167
AG:28D CB:1234B
uncleanness

AKATHARTeS 168
AG:29A CB:—
foul
unclean

AKATHARTOS 169
AG:29A CB:1234B
filthy *Note*
foul
unclean

AKERAIOS 185
AG:30B CB:—
harmless
simple*

AKLINeS 186
AG:30C CB:—
waver

AKMAZō 187
AG:30D CB:1234B
ripe (to be fully)

AKMeN 188
AG:30D CB:1234B (AKMe)
yet *Note*

AKOe 189
AG:30D CB:1234B
ear
fame *Note*
hear
hearing
message
report
rumour

AKOLOUTHEō 190
AG:31A CB:1234B
follow
reach

AKōLUTōS 209
AG:34B CB:—
forbid

AKōN 210
AG:34B CB:—
will

AKOUō 191
AG:31D CB:1234B
audience
ear *Note*
hear
hearer *Note*
hearing
hearken
noise
report

AKRASIA 192
AG:33A CB:1234B
excess
incontinency

AKRATeS 193
AG:33A CB:1234B
incontinent
self-control (without)

AKRATOS 194
AG:33A CB:—
mixture *Note*
unmixed*

AKRIBEIA 195
AG:33A CB:—
exact
manner
strict*

AKRIBeS 196
AG:33B CB:—
straitest

AKRIBESTERON 197
AG:33B (-BōS) CB:—
carefully *Note*
exact, exactly
perfectly

AKRIBESTATOS 196
AG:33A CB:—
straitest

AKRIBOō 198
AG:33B CB:—
exact
inquire *Note*
learn

AKRIBōS 199
AG:33B CB:—
accurately
carefully
circumspectly*
diligently
perfectly

AKRIS 200
AG:33C CB:1234B
locust

AKROATeRION 201
AG:33C CB:—
hearing
place

AKROATeS 202
AG:33C CB:1234B
hearer

AKROBUSTIA 203
AG:33D CB:1234B
circumcision
uncircumcision*

AKROGōNIAIOS 204
AG:33D CB:1234B
chief
corner *Note*

AKRON 206
AG:34A CB:—
end *Note*
tip, top
uttermost part*

AKROTHINION 205
AG:33D CB:—
spoil

AKUROō 208
AG:34B CB:—
disannul
effect
void

ALABASTRON 211
AG:34C CB:—
box
cruse

ALALAZō 214
AG:34D CB:—
clanging
tinkle*
wail *Note*
weep *Note*

ALALeTOS 215
AG:34D CB:1234B
utter *Note*

ALALOS 216
AG:34D CB:1234B
dumb

ALAZōN 213
AG:34D CB:1234B
boast
boastful
glory (boast) *Note*

ALAZON(E)IA 212
AG:34C CB:1234B
boast
glory (boast) *Note*
pride
vainglory
vaunt*

ALEIPHō 218
AG:35B CB:1234B
anoint

ALEKTōR 220
AG:35C CB:—
cock

ALEKTOROPHōNIA 219
AG:35B CB:1234B
cock-crowing

ALeTHEIA 225
AG:35 CB:1234B
fable
true, truth
verity*

ALeTHeS 227
AG:36D CB:1234B
indeed
true, truly
truth

ALeTHEUō 226
AG:36C CB:1234B
truth

ALeTHINOS 228
AG:37A CB:1234B
true

ALeTHō 229
AG:37B CB:—
grind

ALeTHōS 230
AG:37B CB:1234B
indeed
surely *Note*
true, truly
truth
verily

ALEURON 224
AG:35D CB:—
meal

ALISGeMA 234
AG:37D CB:1234C (-MATA)
pollution

ALLA 235
AG:38A CB:—
indeed
(at) least *Note*
moreover
nay
notwithstanding
rather
yea
yet *Note*
Notes p. 1263

ALLACHOTHEN 237
AG:39B CB:—
way *Note*

ALLACHOU —
AG:39B CB:—
elsewhere

ALLASSō 236
AG:39A CB:1234C
change

ALLeGOREō 238
AG:39B CB:1234C
allegory
contain *Note*

ALLeLōN 240
AG:39C CB:1234C
each other
mutual
one another *Note*
other
themselves *Note*
together *Note*
ye *Note*
yourselves *Note*

ALLOGENeS 241
AG:39C CB:1234C
stranger

ALLOPHULOS 246
AG:41A CB:1234C
foreigner *Note*
nation

ALLOS 243
AG:39D CB:1234C
another
more *Note*
one *Note*
one another *Note*
other
otherwise
some *Note*

ALLōS 247
AG:41A CB:1234C
otherwise

ALLOTRIOEPISKOPOS 244
AG:40C CB:1234C
busybody
meddler*

ALLOTRIOS 245
AG:40C CB:1234C
alien
foreigner *Note*
man's (another) *Note*
other
strange, -er

ALOAō 248
AG:41A CB:—
corn *Note*
thresh
tread*

ALOē 250
AG:41B CB:—
aloes

ALOGOS 249
AG:41A CB:1234C
brute
unreasonable

ALōPēX 258
AG:41D CB:1234C
fox

ALUPOS (-OTEROS) 253
AG:41C CB:—
sorrowful (less)

ALUSITELēS 255
AG:41C CB:—
unprofitable

AMACHOS 269
AG:44C CB:1234C
brawler
contentious

AMAō 270
AG:44C CB:—
mow
reap down*

AMARANTINOS 262
AG:42B CB:—
corruptible *Note*
fade

AMARANTOS 263
AG:42C CB:—
corruptible *Note*
fade

AMARTUROS 267
AG:44A CB:—
witness

AMATHēS 261
AG:42B CB:—
unlearned

AMELEō 272
AG:44D CB:—
light of (make)
neglect
negligent
regard

AMEMPTOS 273
AG:45A CB:1234C
blameless
faultless
unblameable

AMEMPTōS 274
AG:45A CB:1234C
blame (without)
blameless
rebuke *Note*
unblameably

AMēN 281
AG:45C CB:1234C
amen
verily

AMERIMNOS 275
AG:45B CB:1234C
care *Note*
carefulness *Note*
rid*
secure *Note*

AMETAKINēTOS 277
AG:45C CB:—
move
unmoveable*

AMETAMELēTOS 278
AG:45C CB:1234C
regret
repent
repentance

AMETANOēTOS 279
AG:45C CB:1234C
impenitent

AMETATHETOS 276
AG:45B CB:1234C (-TON)
immutable
immutability

AMETHUSTOS 271
AG:44C CB:1234C
amethyst

AMēTōR 282
AG:46A CB:1234C
mother

AMETROS 280
AG:45C CB:1234C
measure

AMIANTOS 283
AG:46B CB:1234C
undefiled

AMMOS 285
AG:46B CB:—
sand

AMNOS 286
AG:46C CB:1234C
lamb

AMOIBē 287
AG:46C CB:—
requite

AMōMēTOS 298
AG:47D CB:1234C
blameless
rebuke *Note*

AMōMON —
AG:47D CB:—
odour *Note*
spice

AMōMOS 299
AG:47D CB:1234C
blame (without)
blemish
faultless *Note*
rebuke *Note*
spot *Note*
unblameable

AMPELōN 290
AG:47A CB:1234C
vineyard

AMPELOS 288
AG:46D CB:1234C
vine

AMPELOURGOS 289
AG:47A CB:1234C
dresser
vinedresser

AMPHIBALLō 906 (BALLō)
AG:47B CB:1234C
cast

AMPHIBLēSTRON 293
AG:47B CB:—
net

AMPHIENNUMI 294
AG:47C CB:—
clothe

AMPHODON 296
AG:47C CB:—
place *Note*
street

AMPHOTEROI (-ROS) 297
AG:47C CB:1234C
master *Note*

AMUNō (-OMAI) 292
AG:47A CB:—
defend

AN 302
AG:48B CB:—
whatsoever *Note*
whosoever *Note*

ANA 303
AG:49D CB:1235A
apiece
each
every *Note*

ANABAINō 305
AG:50A CB:1235A
arise, ascend*
climb up
come
enter
go *Note*
grow
rise *Note*
spring

ANABALLō 306 (-OMAI)
AG:50C CB:—
defer

ANABATHMOS 304
AG:50A CB:—
stair

ANABIBAZō 307
AG:50D CB:—
draw

ANABLEPō 308
AG:50D CB:1235A
look
receive *Note*
see, sight

ANABLEPSIS 309
AG:51A CB:—
sight

ANABOAō 310
AG:51A CB:1235A
cry

ANABOLē 311
AG:51A CB:—
defer *Note*
delay

ANACHōREō 402
AG:63C CB:1235A
depart, go
place
turn *Note*
withdraw

ANACHUSIS 401
AG:63C CB:—
excess

ANADECHOMAI 324
AG:53C CB:—
receive

ANADEIKNUMI 322
AG:53B CB:1235A
appoint
shew

ANADEIXIS 323
AG:53C CB:1235A
shewing

ANADIDōMI 325
AG:53C CB:—
deliver

ANAGAION (See ANōGEON)

ANAGENNAō 313
AG:51C CB:1235A
beget, born*

ANAGINōSKō 314
AG:51C CB:1235A
read

ANAGNōRIZō 319 (-OMAI)
AG:52D CB:—
known *Note*

ANAGNōSIS 320
AG:52D CB:1235A
reading

ANAGō 321
AG:53A CB:Cf. AGō (1233C)
bring
depart
launch
lead
loose
offer *Note*
put
sail
set *Note*
take *Note*

ANAID(E)IA 335
AG:54C CB:—
importunity

ANAIREō 337
AG:54D CB:—
death
kill
slay
take

ANAIRESIS 336
AG:54D CB:—
death

ANAITIOS 338
AG:55B CB:1235A
blameless
guiltless

ANAKAINIZō 340
AG:55B CB:1235A
renew

ANAKAINOō 341
AG:55C CB:1235A
renew

ANAKAINōSIS 342
AG:55C CB:1235A
renewing

ANAKALUPTō 343
AG:55C CB:1235A
open *Note*
unlifted
untaken*
unveiled *Note*

ANAKAMPTō 344
AG:55C CB:—
return, turn

ANAKATHIZō 339
AG:55B CB:—
sit

ANAKEIMAI 345
AG:55D CB:1235A
guest
lean
lie *Note*
meat *Note*
recline
set, sit
table (at the)

ANAKEPHALAIOō (-IOMAI) 346
AG:55D CB:1235A
comprehend*
gather *Note*
sum up

ANAKLINō 347
AG:56A CB:1235A (-OMAI)
lay
sit

ANAKOPTō 348
AG:56B CB:—
hinder

ANAKRAZō 249
AG:56B CB:—
cry

ANAKRINō 350
AG:56B CB:1235A
ask
discern
examine
judge
search *Note*

ANAKRISIS 351
AG:56C CB:—
examination

ANAKULIō —
AG:56C CB:—
roll

ANAKUPTō 352
AG:56C CB:—
lift
look

ANALAMBANō 353
AG:56D CB:1235A
receive
take

ANALēPSIS 354
AG:57A CB:—
receive

ANALISKō 355
AG:57A CB:—
consume

ANALOGIA 356
AG:57B CB:1235A
proportion

ANALOGIZOMAI 357
AG:57B CB:Cf. LOG-(1257A)
consider

ANALOS 358
AG:57B CB:1235A
saltness

ANALUō 360
AG:57C CB:1235A
depart
return

ANALUSIS 359
AG:57B CB:—
departure

ANAMARTēTOS 361
AG:57C CB:—
sin

ANAMENō 362
AG:57D CB:1235A
wait

ANAMIMNēSKo 363
AG:57D CB:1235A
mind
put *Note*
remember
remembrance

ANAMNēSIS 364
AG:58A CB:1235A
remembrance

ANANEOō 365
AG:58A CB:1235B
renew

ANANēPHō 366
AG:58B CB:1235B
recover
sober *Note*

ANANGELLō 312
AG:51B CB:1235B
announce
declare
rehearse
report
shew *Note*
speak *Note*
tell
tidings

ANANKAIOS 316
AG:52B CB:1235B
near
necessary

ANANKAIOTEROS (-IOS) 316
AG:52B CB:1235B
needful

ANANKASTōS 317
AG:52B CB:1235B
constraint

ANANKAZō 315
AG:52A CB:1235B
compel
constrain

ANANKē 318
AG:52B CB:1235B
anguish *Note*
constrain *Note*
distress
necessary
necessity
needs

ANANTIRRHēTOS 368
AG:58C CB:—
gainsay
speak*

ANANTIRRHēTōS 369
AG:58C CB:—
gainsay

ANAPAUō 373
AG:58D CB:1235B
ease
refresh, rest

ANAPAUSIS 372
AG:58D CB:1235B
rest

ANAPEITHō 374
AG:59B CB:—
persuade

ANAPEMPō 375
AG:59B CB:—
send

ANAPē(I)ROS 376
AG:59C CB:—
maimed

ANAPHAINō 398
AG:63A CB:Cf. PHAINō (1263C)
appear
discover

ANAPHERō 399
AG:63A CB:1235B
bear
bring
carry *Note*
lead
offer

ANAPHōNEō 400
AG:63B CB:—
voice *Note*

ANAPIPTō 377
AG:59C CB:1235B
lean
lie *Note*
recline
set *Note*
sit

ANAPLēROō 378
AG:59C CB:1235B
fill, fulfil
supply

ANAPOLOGēTOS 379
AG:60A CB:1235B
excuse
inexcusable*

ANAPSUCHō 404
AG:63D CB:1235B
refresh

ANAPSUXIS 403
AG:63C CB:1235B
refreshing

ANAPTō 381
AG:60A CB:—
kindle

ANAPTUSSō 380
AG:60A CB:—
close
open

ANARITHMēTOS 382
AG:60A CB:—
innumerable

ANASEIō 383
AG:60A CB:1235B
move *Note*
stir

ANASKEUAZō 384
AG:60A CB:—
subvert

ANASPAō 385
AG:60B CB:—
draw
pull *Note*

ANASTASIS 386
AG:60B CB:1235B
raise *Note*
resurrection
rising *Note*

ANASTATOō 387
AG:61A CB:—
sedition
stir
trouble
turn
uproar *Note*

ANASTAUROō 388
AG:61A CB:1235B
crucify

ANASTENAZō 389
AG:61B CB:—
deeply *Note*
sigh

ANASTREPHō 390
AG:61B CB:1235B
abide
behave
conversation
live
overthrow
pass
return, use

ANASTROPHē 391
AG:61C CB:1235B
behaviour
conversation
life, living
manner *Note*

ANATASSOMAI 392
AG:61D CB:1235B
draw
order
set (forth)

ANATELLō 393
AG:62A CB:1235B
arise
rise *Note*
rising *Note*
spring
up *Note*

ANATHALLō 330
AG:54A CB:—
flourish*
revive
ANATHEMA 331
AG:54A CB:1235B
anathema*
curse
ANATHēMA 334
AG:54C CB:1235B
gift *Note*
offering
ANATHEMATIZō 332
AG:54C CB:1235B
curse, oath
ANATHEōREō 333
AG:54C CB:Cf. THE-(1272A)
behold
consider
observe
ANATITHēMI 394 (-EMAI)
AG:62B CB:—
communicate *Note*
declare *Note*
lay
ANATOLē 395
AG:62B CB:1235B
arise *Note*
dayspring
east
sun *Note*
ANATREPHō 397
AG:62D CB:—
bring
nourish
ANATREPō 396
AG:62C CB:—
overthrow
subvert *Note*
ANAXIOS 370
AG:58C CB:1235B
unworthy
ANAXIōS 371
AG:58D CB:1235B
unworthily
ANAZAō 326
AG:53D CB:1235B
alive*
live
revive
ANAZēTEō 327
AG:53D CB:—
seek
ANAZōNNUMI 328
AG:53D CB:Cf. ZōN-(1273C)
gird
ANAZōPUREō 329
AG:54A CB:—
stir
ANDRAPODISTēS 405
AG:63D CB:1235B
men-stealers
ANDRIZō (-OMAI) 407
AG:64A CB:1235B
men *Note*
quit

ANDROPHONOS 409
AG:64A CB:—
manslayer
ANECHOMAI (-CHō) 430
AG:65D CB:1235B
bear
endure
forbear
suffer
ANEKDIēGēTOS 411
AG:64B CB:—
unspeakable
ANEKLALēTOS 412
AG:64B CB:—
unspeakable
ANEKLEIPTOS 413
AG:64B CB:—
fail
ANēKō 433
AG:66B CB:1235C
befit
convenient
fit
ANEKTOS (-TEROS) 414
AG:64C CB:1235C
tolerable
ANELEēMōN 415
AG:64C CB:1235C
unmerciful
ANELEOS (ANIL-) 448
AG:64C CB:1235C
mercy
ANēMEROS 434
AG:66C CB:—
fierce
ANEMIZō 416
AG:64C CB:—
drive
wind *Note*
ANEMOS 417
AG:64D CB:1235C
wind
ANENDEKTOS 418
AG:65A CB:—
impossible
ANENKLēTOS 410
AG:64B CB:1235C
blameless
unreprovable*
ANEPAISCHUNTOS 422
AG:65A CB:—
ashamed
ANEPILē(M)PTOS 423
AG:65B CB:1235C
blameless
reproach *Note*
unrebukeable*
ANEPSIOS 431
AG:66A CB:—
cousin
sister *Note*
ANēR 435
AG:66C CB:1235C
fellow
husband
man, sir

ANERCHOMAI 424
AG:65B CB:—
go
ANESIS 425
AG:65B CB:—
eased
indulgence
liberty
relief, rest
ANETAZō 426
AG:65C CB:—
examine
ANēTHON 432
AG:66A CB:1235C
anise
ANEU 427
AG:65C CB:—
apart *Note*
without *Note*
ANEURISKō 429
AG:65D CB:—
find
ANEUTHETOS 428
AG:65C CB:—
commodious (not)
ANEXERAUNēTOS (-REU-) 419
AG:65A CB:1235C
unsearchable
ANEXICHNIASTOS 421
AG:65A CB:—
find *Note*
trace
unsearchable
ANEXIKAKOS 420
AG:65A CB:—
forbearing
patient *Note*
ANGAREUō 29
AG:6D CB:—
compel
ANGEION 30
AG:6D CB:—
vessel
ANGELIA 31
AG:7A CB:1235C
message
ANGELOS 32
AG:7A CB:1235C
angel
messenger
ANGOS See 30
AG:8B CB:—
vessel
ANIēMI 447
AG:69D CB:—
forbear
leave, loose
ANIPTOS 449
AG:69D CB:1235C
unwashen
ANISTēMI 450
AG:70A CB:1235C (ANHI-)
arise, lift
raise (up)
rise *Note*
stand

ANKALē 43
AG:10C CB:1235C
arm
ANKISTRON 44
AG:10C CB:—
hook
ANKURA 45
AG:10C CB:—
anchor
ANō 507
AG:76D CB:1235C
above
brim
high
up *Note*
ANOCHē 463
AG:72C CB:1235C
forbearance
ANOēTOS 453
AG:70D CB:1235C
fool
foolish
unwise
ANōGEON 508
AG:51B (ANAGAION) CB:—
room
ANOIA 454
AG:70D CB:1235C
folly
madness
ANOIGō 455
AG:70D CB:1235C
open
ANOIKODOMEō 456
AG:71C CB:Cf. OIK-(1260B)
build
ANOIXIS 457
AG:71C CB:1235C
open
opening
ANOMIA 458
AG:71D CB:1235C
iniquity
lawlessness
transgression *Note*
ungodliness *Note*
unrighteousness *Note*
ANOMOS 459
AG:72A CB:1235C
law, lawless
transgressor
unlawful*
wicked *Note*
ANOMōS 460
AG:72B CB:1235C
law
ANōPHELēS 512 (-LES)
AG:77C CB:—
unprofitable
ANORTHOō 461
AG:72C CB:—
lift, set
straight
ANOSIOS 462
AG:72C CB:1235C
unholy

ANōTERIKOS 510
AG:77C CB:—
country
upper*
ANōTERON (-OS) 511
AG:77C CB:—
above
higher
ANōTHEN 509
AG:77A CB:1236A
above
again *Note*
anew
first
top *Note*
ANTAGōNIZOMAI 464
AG:72D CB:1236A
strive
ANTALLAGMA 465
AG:72D CB:1236A
exchange
ANTANAPLēROō 466
AG:72D CB:1236A
fill
ANTAPODIDōMI 476
AG:73A CB:1236A
recompense
render
repay
ANTAPODOMA 468
AG:73A CB:1236A
recompense
ANTAPODOSIS 469
AG:73A CB:1236A
recompense
reward *Note*
ANTAPOKRINOMAI 470
AG:73B CB:—
answer
reply
ANTECHō (-OMAI) 472
AG:73B CB:—
hold
support *Note*
ANTEIPON 471 (-EPo)
AG:73B CB:—
gainsay
say
ANTHISTēMI 436
AG:67B CB:—
resist
withstand
ANTHOMOLOGEOMAI 437
AG:67B CB:—
thanks
ANTHOS 438
AG:67C CB:1236A
flower
ANTHRAKIA 439
AG:67C CB:Cf. -RAX (1236A)
coals
ANTHRAX 440
AG:67C CB:1236A
coal
ANTHRōPARESKOS 441
AG:67D CB:1236A
men-pleasers

ANTHRōPINOS 442
AG:67D CB:1236A
man's
men *Note*
ANTHRōPOKTONOS 443
AG:68A CB:—
murderer
ANTHRōPOS 444
AG:68B CB:1236A
man
people
person
ANTHUPATEUō 445
AG:69C CB:—
proconsul *Note*
ANTHUPATOS 446
AG:69C CB:1236A
deputy*
proconsul
ANTI 473
AG:73C CB:1236A
cause
room
Notes p. 1268
ANTIBALLō 474
AG:74A CB:—
exchange *Note*
have
ANTICHRISTOS 500
AG:76B CB:1236A
Antichrist
ANTIDIATITHēMI 475 (-EMAI)
AG:74A CB:—
oppose
ANTIDIKOS 476
AG:74A CB:1236A
adversary
ANTIKALEō 479
AG:74B CB:Cf. KALEō (1253B)
bid
ANTIKATHISTēMI 478
AG:74B CB:—
resist
ANTIKEIMAI 480
AG:74B CB:—
adversary
contrary
oppose
ANTILAMBANō (-OMAI) 482
AG:74C CB:—
help
partake *Note*
partaker
support *Note*
ANTILEGō 483
AG:74D CB:—
answer
contradict
deny
gainsay
gainsayer
speak
ANTILē(M)PSIS 484
AG:75A CB:—
help

ANTILOGIA 485
AG:75A CB:—
contradiction
dispute
gainsaying
strife
ANTILOIDOREō 486
AG:75A CB:1236A
revile
ANTILUTRON 487
AG:75B CB:1236A
ransom
ANTIMETREō 488
AG:75B CB:—
measure
ANTIMISTHIA 489
AG:75B CB:1236A
recompense
ANTIPARERCHOMAI 492
AG:75C CB:—
pass
ANTIPIPTō 496
AG:75D CB:—
resist
ANTISTRATEUOMAI 497
AG:75D CB:—
war
ANTITASSō 498 (-OMAI)
AG:76A CB:—
oppose, resist
ANTITHESIS 477
AG:74B CB:—
opposition
ANTITUPOS (-ON) 499
AG:76A CB:1236A
figure
likeness
pattern
ANTLēMA 502
AG:76C CB:—
draw *Note*
ANTLEō 501
AG:76C CB:—
draw
ANTOPHTHALMEō 503
AG:76C CB:—
bear
face *Note*
ANUDROS 504
AG:76C CB:—
dry
water *Note*
ANUPOKRITOS 505
AG:76D CB:—
dissimulation
hypocrisy
unfeigned*
ANUPOTAKTOS 506
AG:76D CB:—
disobedient *Note*
put *Note*
subject *Note*
unruly
AORATOS 517
AG:79A CB:1236A
invisible

79C CB:Cf. AGō (1233C)
bring
carry
death
lead
take *Note*
APAIDEUTOS 521
AG:79D CB:1236A
unlearned
APAIRō 522
AG:79D CB:—
take
APAITEō 523
AG:80A CB:1236B
require
APALGEō 524
AG:80A CB:—
feel
APALLASSō 525
AG:80A CB:1236B
deliver
depart
quit
APALLOTRIOō 526
AG:80B CB:1236B
alien
alienated
APANCHō 519 (-OMAI)
AG:79C CB:—
hang
APANGELLō 518
AG:79C CB:1236B
bring
declare
go *Note*
report
shew *Note*
tell
word *Note*
APANTAō 528
AG:80C CB:1236B
meet
APANTēSIS 529
AG:80C CB:1236B
meet
APARABATOS 531
AG:80D CB:1236B
unchangeable
APARASKEUASTOS 532
AG:80D CB:1236B
unprepared
APARCHē 536
AG:81B CB:1236B
firstfruit(s)
APARNEOMAI 533
AG:81A CB:1236B
deny
APARTI 534
AG:110B 3. CB:—
henceforth
now (from)
APARTISMOS 535
AG:81B CB:—
complete
finish *Note*

APOBAINō 576
AG:88C CB:—
come *Note*
get, go
turn

APOBALLō 577
AG:88D CB:—
cast

APOBLEPō 578
AG:89A CB:1236C
look
respect

APOBLēTOS 579
AG:89A CB:—
refuse *Note*
reject

APOBOLE 580
AG:89A CB:—
cast *Note*
lost

APOCHōREō 672
AG:102A CB:—
depart

APOCHōRIZō 673
AG:102B CB:—
depart, part
remove

APOCHRēSIS 671
AG:102A CB:—
using

APODECHOMAI 588
AG:90A CB:1236C
accept
receive
welcome

APODEIKNUMI 584
AG:89C CB:1236C
approve
prove, set
shew *Note*

APODEIXIS 585
AG:89D CB:1236C
demonstration
token

APODEKATEUō —
AG:89D CB:1236C
tithe

APODEKATOō 586
AG:89D CB:1236C
pay *Note*
tithe

APODEKTOS 587
AG:90A CB:1236C
acceptable

APODēMEō 589
AG:90A CB:1236C
country
far *Note*
go, journey
travel *Note*

APODēMOS 590
AG:90B CB:—
country
far *Note*
journey *Note*
sojourn

APODIDōMI 591
AG:90B CB:1236C
deliver
give, pay
perform
recompense
render, repay
restore
reward
sell
yield

APODIORIZō 592
AG:90D CB:—
separate

APODOCHē 594
AG:91A CB:1236C
acceptation

APODOKIMAZō 593
AG:90D CB:1236C
disallow
reject

APOGINOMAI 581 (-MENOS)
AG:89B CB:1236C
die

APOGRAPHē 582
AG:89B CB:—
enrolment
taxing (Note)

APOGRAPHō 583
AG:89B CB:1236C
enrol
tax (Note)
write (Note)

APOKALUPSIS 602
AG:92B CB:1236C
appearing
coming (Note)
lighten (Note)
manifestation (Note)
revelation

APOKALUPTō 601
AG:92A CB:1236C
reveal

APOKARADOKIA 603
AG:92C CB:1236C
expectation

APOKATALLASSō 604
AG:92C CB:1237A
reconcile

APOKATASTASIS 605
AG:92D CB:1237A
restitution*
restoration

APOKATHISTēMI (-STANō) 600
AG:91D CB:1237A
restore

APOKEIMAI 606
AG:92D CB:—
appoint
lay

APOKEPHALIZō 607
AG:93A CB:—
behead

APOKLEIō 608
AG:93A CB:—
shut

APOKOPTō 609
AG:93A CB:1237A
cut

APOKRIMA 610
AG:93B CB:—
answer
sentence

APOKRINOMAI 611
AG:93B CB:—
answer

APOKRISIS 612
AG:93D CB:—
answer

APOKRUPHOS 614
AG:93D CB:1237A
hid
hidden
secret

APOKRUPTō 613
AG:93D CB:1237A
hide

APOKTEINō 615
AG:93D CB:1237A
death
kill
put *Note*
slay

APOKUEō 616
AG:94A CB:1237A
beget
bring

APOKULIō (-IZō) 617
AG:94B CB:—
roll

APOLAMBANō 618
AG:94B CB:1237A
receive
take

APOLAUSIS 619
AG:94D CB:—
enjoy
pleasure

APōLEIA 684
AG:103B CB:1237A
destruction
perdition*
perish *Note*
pernicious*
waste

APOLEICHō 621
AG:95A CB:—
lick

APOLEIPō 620
AG:94D CB:Cf. KATAL-(1254A)
leave
remain

APOLLUMI 622
AG:95A CB:1237A
destroy
destroyer *Note*
die *Note*
fall *Note*
lose
marred
perish

APOLOGEOMAI 626
AG:95D CB:1237A
answer
defense
excuse
speak *Note*

APOLOGIA 627
AG:96A CB:1237A
answer
clearing *Note*
defence

APOLOUō 628
AG:96A CB:1237A
wash

APOLUō 630
AG:96C CB:1237A
depart
dismiss
divorce
forgive *Note*
go *Note*
let
liberty
loose, put
release, send
set *Note*

APOLUTRōSIS 629
AG:96B CB:1237A
deliverance
redemption

APOMASSō 631 (-OMAI)
AG:96D CB:—
wipe

APONEMō 632
AG:97A CB:—
give

APONIPTō 633
AG:97A (-IZō) CB:—
wash

APOPHERō 667
AG:101D CB:Cf. PHERō (1264A)
bring
carry *Note*

APOPHEUGō 668
AG:101D CB:1237A
escape

APOPHORTIZō (-OMAI) 670
AG:102 CB:—
unlade

APOPHTHENGOMAI 669
AG:102A CB:1237A (-GESTHAI)
say *Note*
speak
utterance *Note*

APOPIPTō 634
AG:97B CB:—
fall

APOPLANAō 635
AG:97B CB:1237A
err, lead
seduce

APOPLEō 636
AG:97C CB:—
sail

APOPLUNō 637
AG:97C CB:—
wash

APONIGō 638
AG:97C CB:1237A
choke
APOPSUCHō 674
AG:102B CB:—
fail *Note*
APOREō 639
AG:97C CB:—
doubt
perplex
APORIA 640
AG:97D CB:—
perplexity
APORPHANIZOMAI (-Zō) 642
AG:98A CB:Cf. ORP-(1261B)
bereave
APORIPTō 641 (-RR-)
AG:97D CB:—
cast
APOSKEUAZō 643
AG:98A CB:—
baggage *Note*
carriage*
APOSKIASMA 644
AG:98A CB:1237A
cast
shadow
APOSPAō 645
AG:98A CB:—
draw
get *Note*
part
withdraw
APOSTASIA 646
AG:98B CB:1237A
falling
forsake
APOSTASION 647
AG:98B CB:1237A
divorcement
APOSTEGAZō 648
AG:98C CB:—
uncover
APOSTELLō 649
AG:98C CB:1237A
liberty
put, send
set *Note*
APOSTEREō 650
AG:99A CB:1237A
bereft
defraud
destitute
fraud
suffer *Note*
APOSTOLē 651
AG:99B CB:1237A
apostleship
APOSTOLOS 652
AG:99C CB:1237A
apostle
messenger
send *Note*
APOSTOMATIZō 653
AG:100B CB:—
provoke

APOSTREPHō 654
AG:100B CB:1237A
bring
pervert
put
turn
APOSTUGEō 655
AG:100C CB:—
abhor
APOSUNAGōGOS 656
AG:100D CB:1237B
synagogue (put out of the)
APOTASSō (-OMAI) 657
AG:100D CB:—
bid farewell
farewell
forsake
leave
renounce
send *Note*
take *Note*
APOTELEō 658
AG:100D CB:—
do *Note*
finish *Note*
perform
APOTHēKē 596
AG:91A CB:—
barn
garner
APōTHEō 683 (-OMAI)
AG:103B CB:—
cast
put *Note*
thrust
APOTHēSAURIZō 597
AG:91B CB:—
store
APOTHESIS 595
AG:91A CB:1237B
putting
APOTHLIBō 598
AG:91B CB:—
crush
press
APOTHNēSKō 599
AG:91B CB:1237B
die
perish
APOTINASSō 660
AG:101B CB:1237B
shake
APOTINō (-TIō) 661
AG:101B CB:—
repay
APOTITHēMI 659
AG:101A CB:1237B
cast
lay
put
APOTOLMAō 662
AG:101B CB:—
bold
APOTOMIA 663
AG:101C CB:—
severity

APOTOMōS 664
AG:101C CB:—
sharply, -ness
APOTREPō 665
AG:101C CB:1237B
turn
APOUSIA 666
AG:101D CB:—
absense
APROSITOS 676
AG:102C CB:—
approach
APROSKOPOS 677
AG:102C CB:1237B
offence
stumbling*
APROSōPOLēMPTōS 678
AG:102C CB:1237B (-TēS)
persons (respect of)
APSEUDēS 893
AG:129C CB:1237B
lie
APSINTHOS 894
AG:129C (-THION) CB:1237B
wormwood
APSUCHOS 895
AG:129C CB:—
life
soul *Note*
APTAISTOS 679
AG:102C CB:—
falling *Note*
stumbling *Note*
ARA (I.) 685
AG:103D CB:1237B
curse
ARA (II.) 686
AG:103D CB:1237B
doubt (no) *Note*
haply
manner *Note*
now *Note*
perhaps
then *Note*
truly *Note*
whatsoever *Note*
ARAGE 686 (ARA)
AG:104A (ARA) CB:—
haply
ARCHANGELOS 743
AG:111A CB:1237B
archangel
ARCHAIOS 744
AG:111B CB:1237B
old
ARCHē 746
AG:111D CB:1237B
beginning
corner
estate *Note*
first
magistrate *Note*
power
principality
principles
rule, ruler

ARCHēGOS 747
AG:112C CB:1237B
author
captain
prince
ARCHIERATIKOS 748
AG:112D CB:1237B
priest*
ARCHIEREUS 749
AG:112D CB:1237B
chief
priest
ARCHIPOIMēN 750
AG:113A CB:1237B
chief
shepherd*
ARCHISUNAGōGOS 752
AG:113B CB:—
chief
synagogue (ruler of the)
ARCHITEKTōN 753
AG:113B CB:1237B
masterbuilder
ARCHITELōNēS 754
AG:113B CB:1237B
chief
publican *Note*
ARCHITRIKLINOS 755
AG:113B CB:—
governor
ruler
ARCHō (-OMAI) 757 (756)
AG:113C CB:1237B
begin
beginning
rehearse *Note*
reign *Note*
rule
ARCHōN 758
AG:113D CB:1237B
chief
magistrate
prince
ruler
ARēN 704
AG:106A CB:1237C
lamb
ARESKEIA 699
AG:105C CB:1237C
pleasing
ARESKō 700
AG:105C CB:1237C
please
ARESTOS 701
AG:105D CB:1237C
fit
please
reason *Note*
ARETē 703
AG:105D CB:1237C
excellence *Note*
praise *Note*
virtue
ARGEō 691
AG:104C CB:—
linger

ARGOS 692
AG:104C CB:1237C
barren
idle
slow *Note*
ARGURION 694
AG:104D CB:1237C
money, piece
silver
ARGUROKOPOS 695
AG:105A CB:—
silversmith
ARGUREOS (-ROUS) 693
AG:105A CB:1237C
silver
ARGUROS 696
AG:105A CB:1237C
silver
ARISTAō 709
AG:106C CB:—
dine
ARISTEROS 710
AG:106C CB:1237C
left
ARISTON 712
AG:106D CB:—
dinner
ARITHMEō 705
AG:106B CB:1237C
number
ARITHMOS 706
AG:106B CB:1237C
number
ARKEō 714
AG:107A CB:1237C
content
enough
suffice
sufficient
ARKETOS 713
AG:107A CB:1237C
enough
suffice
sufficient
ARK(T)OS 715
AG:107B CB:—
bear
ARNEOMAI 720
AG:107D CB:1237C
deny
refuse
ARNION 721
AG:108B CB:1237C
lamb
ARōMA 759
AG:114B CB:1237C
spice(s)
AROTRIAō 722
AG:108B CB:—
plough (plow)
AROTRON 723
AG:108B CB:—
plough (plow)
ARRABōN 728
AG:109B CB:1237C
earnest

AR(RH)APHOS 729
AG:104B CB:—
seam (without)
ARRēN (ARSēN) 730
AG:109D CB:1237C
male, man
ARRHēTOS 731
AG:109C CB:1237C
unspeakable
ARRHōSTOS 732
AG:109D CB:—
sick
ARSENOKOITēS 733
AG:109D CB:1237C
abuser
ARTEMōN 736
AG:110A CB:—
foresail
mainsail*
ARTI 737
AG:110B CB:1237C
henceforth
hitherto
now, present
ARTIGENNēTOS 738
AG:110C CB:—
beget
newborn*
ARTIOS 739
AG:110C CB:1237C
complete
perfect
ARTOS 740
AG:110C CB:1237C
bread, loaf
shewbread *Note*
ARTUō 741
AG:111A CB:1237C
season
ASALEUTOS 761
AG:114B CB:1237C
move
unmoveable*
ASBESTOS 762
AG:114B CB:1237C
quench
unquenchable*
ASCHēMōN 809
AG:119B CB:1238A
uncomely
ASCHēMONEō 807
AG:119B CB:—
behave
uncomely *Note*
ASCHēMOSUNē 808
AG:119B CB:—
shame
unseemliness
unseemly
ASEBEIA 763
AG:114C CB:1238A
ungodliness
ungodly
ASEBEō 764
AG:114C CB:1238A
ungodly

:1238A
ungodly
ASELGEIA 766
AG:114D CB:1238A
filthy
lasciviousness
riot
wantonness
ASēMOS 767
AG:115A CB:—
mean
ASIARCHēS 775
AG:116A CB:—
chief
ASITIA 776
AG:116B CB:—
abstinence *Note*
fast *Note*
food *Note*
ASITOS 777
AG:116B CB:—
fasting
ASKEō 778
AG:116B CB:1238A
exercise
ASKOS 779
AG:116C CB:—
bottle*
skin
ASMENōS 780
AG:116C CB:—
gladly
ASOPHOS 781
AG:116C CB:1238A
unwise
ASōTIA 810
AG:119C CB:—
excess *Note*
riot
ASōTōS 811
AG:119C CB:1238A
riotous
ASPASMOS 783
AG:117A CB:1238A
greeting
salutation*
ASPAZOMAI 782
AG:116C CB:1238A
embrace
farewell *Note*
greet
leave
salute*
ASPHALEIA 803
AG:118D CB:1238A
certainty
safety
ASPHALēS 804
AG:119A CB:1238A
certain, -ty
safe, sure
ASPHALIZō 805
AG:119A CB:1238A
fast (to make)
sure

ASPHALōS 806
AG:119A CB:1238A
assuredly
safely
ASPILOS 784
AG:117A CB:1238A
spot
unspotted*
ASPIS 785
AG:117B CB:1238A
asp
ASPONDOS 786
AG:117B CB:—
covenant-breaker *Note*
implacable
truce-breaker*
ASSARION 787
AG:117B CB:—
farthing
ASSON 788
AG:117B CB:—
close (Adverb)
ASTATEō 790
AG:117B CB:—
certain *Note*
dwelling (place)
ASTEIOS 791
AG:117C CB:—
beautiful
exceedingly *Note*
fair
goodly *Note*
proper
ASTēR 792
AG:117C CB:1238A
star
ASTēRIKTOS 793
AG:118A CB:—
unstable
ASTHENEIA 769
AG:115A CB:1238A
disease
infirmity
sickness
weakness
ASTHENēMA 771
AG:115C CB:—
infirmity
ASTHENEō 770
AG:115B CB:1238A
diseased
impotent
sick, weak
ASTHENēS 772
AG:115C CB:1238A
feeble
impotent
sick
weak
ASTOCHEō 795
AG:118A CB:1238A
err
swerve
ASTORGOS 794
AG:118A CB:1238A
affection

ARGOS 692
ASTRAPē 796
AG:118A CB:1238A
lightning
shining
ASTRAPTō 797
AG:118B CB:—
dazzling
lighten
shine *Note*
ASTRON 798
AG:118B CB:1238A
star
ASUMPHōNOS 800
AG:118C CB:—
agree
ASUNETOS 801
AG:118C CB:1238A
foolish
prudent *Note*
senseless*
understanding
ASUNTHETOS 802
AG:118D CB:—
covenant-breakers
ATAKTEō 812
AG:119C CB:—
behave
disorderly
ATAKTOS 813
AG:119C CB:—
disorderly
unruly
ATAKTōS 814
AG:119D CB:—
disorderly
ATEKNOS 815
AG:119D CB:Cf. TEK-(1271B)
childless
ATENIZō 816
AG:119D CB:1238A
behold
earnestly *Note*
fasten, look
set *Note*
ATER 817
AG:120A CB:—
absence
without *Note*
ATHANASIA 110
AG:20C CB:1238A
immortality
ATHEMITOS 111
AG:20D CB:—
abominable
unlawful
ATHEOS 112
AG:20D CB:1238A
God (without)
ATHESMOS 113
AG:21A CB:—
wicked
ATHETEō 114
AG:21A CB:1238A
bring *Note*
cast *Note*
despise *Note*

ATHETEō (Continued)
disannul
frustrate *Note*
nothing *Note*
nought
reject, void
ATHETēSIS 115
AG:21B CB:1238A
disannuling
put *Note*
ATHLEō 118
AG:21B CB:1238A
contend
strive *Note*
ATHLēSIS 119
AG:21C CB:1238A
conflict
fight
ATHōOS 121
AG:21D CB:—
innocent
ATHROIZō —
AG:21C CB:1238B
gather
ATHUMEō 120
AG:21C CB:—
discourage
ATIMAō 821 (-MOo)
AG:120A CB:—
handle
ATIMAZō 818
AG:120A CB:1238A
despise *Note*
dishonour
entreat *Note*
handle
shame
shamefully *Note*
ATIMIA 819
AG:120A CB:1238B
dishonour
disparagement
reproach
shame, vile
ATIMOS 820
AG:120B CB:1238B
despised
dishonour
honour (without)
ATIMOTEROS (-MOS) 820
AG:120B CB:1238B
honourable
ATMIS 822
AG:120B CB:—
vapour
ATOMOS 822
AG:120B CB:1238B
moment
ATOPOS 824
AG:120C CB:—
amiss, harm
unreasonable
wickedness *Note*
AUCHMēROS 850
AG:124B CB:—
dark

AUGAZō 826
AG:120C CB:1238B
dawn
shine *Note*
AUGē 827
AG:120D CB:1238B
day
AULē 833
AG:121B CB:1238B
court
fold, hall
palace
praetorium*
AULEō 832
AG:121B CB:1238B
pipe
AULēTēS 834
AG:121B CB:—
flute-players
piper*
AULIZOMAI 835
AG:121C CB:—
abide
lodge
AULOS 836
AG:121C CB:—
pipe
AURION 839
AG:122A CB:—
morrow
next day *Note*
to-morrow
AUSTēROS 840
AG:122B CB:—
austere
AUTARKEIA 841
AG:122B CB:1238B
contentment
sufficiency
AUTARKēS 842
AG:122B CB:1238B
content
AUTHADēS 829
AG:120D CB:—
self-willed
AUTHAIRETOS 830
AG:121A CB:—
accord
willing *Note*
AUTHENTEō 831
AG:121A CB:1238B (-TEIN)
authority
dominion *Note*
AUTOCHEIR 849
AG:124A CB:—
hand (with one's own)
AUTOKATAKRITOS 843
AG:122C CB:1238B
condemn
AUTOMATOS 844
AG:122C CB:1238B
accord
self
AUTOPTēS 845
AG:122C CB:—
eye-witness

AUTOS 846
AG:122C CB:1238B
cause
company (Note)
halt, here
he, his
like (Note)
myself
ourselves (Note)
person (Note)
same
say (Note)
self
selfsame (Note)
their (Note)
them (Note)
themselves (Note)
there
therein (Note)
they (Note)
this (Note)
thou (Note)
thyself (Note)
together (Note)
very (Note)
ye (Note)
AUTOU 847
AG:124A CB:—
here, there
AUXANō 837
AG:121C CB:1238B
grow
increase
AUXēSIS 838
AG:122A CB:1238B
grow (Note)
increase*
AXINē 513
AG:77D CB:—
axe
AXIOō 515
AG:78C CB:1238B
desire
think
worthy, -ily
AXIOS 514
AG:78A CB:1238B
due (Note)
meet
reward (Note)
unworthy (Note)
worthy
AXIōS 516
AG:78D CB:1238B
become (Note)
godly (Note)
worthy
AZUMOS 106
AG:19D CB:1238B
bread

B

BAION 902
AG:130C CB:—
branch
BALLANTION 905
AG:130D CB:1238B
bag

BALLō 906
AG:130D CB:1238B
arise *Note*
beat, cast
dung
lay, lie
pour
put, send
throw, thrust

BAPTISMA 908
AG:132C CB:1238B
baptism

BAPTISMOS 909
AG:132D CB:1238C
baptism
washing

BAPTISTēS 910
AG:132D CB:1238C
Baptist

BAPTIZō 907
AG:131C CB:1238C
baptize

BAPTō 911
AG:132D CB:1238C
dip

BARBAROS 915
AG:133B CB:1238C
barbarian
barbarous

BAREō 916
AG:133C CB:1238C
burden
charge *Note*
heavy
overcharge
press, weigh

BAREōS 917
AG:133C CB:1238C
dull

BAROS 922
AG:133D CB:1238C
burden
weight

BARUNō 925
AG:134B CB:1238C
overcharge

BARUS 926
AG:134B CB:1238C
grievous
heavy
weighty

BARUTIMOS 927
AG:134B CB:1238C
exceeding *Note*
precious

BASANISMOS 929
AG:134C CB:1238C
torment

BASANISTēS 930
AG:134D CB:1238C
tormentor

BASANIZō 928
AG:134C CB:1238C
distress
pain, toil
torment, vex

BASANOS 931
AG:134D CB:1238C
torment

BASILEIA 932
AG:134D CB:1238C
kingdom

BASILEION 933
AG:136A (-IOS) CB:1238C
court

BASILEIOS 934
AG:136A CB:1238C
king
royal

BASILEUō 936
AG:136C CB:1238C
king *Note*
reign

BASILEUS 935
AG:136A CB:1238C
king

BASILIKOS 937
AG:136D CB:1238C
king
nobleman
royal

BASILISSA 938
AG:137A CB:1238C
queen

BASIS 939
AG:137A CB:1238C
foot

BASKAINō 940
AG:137A CB:1238C
bewitch

BASTAZō 941
AG:137B CB:1238C
bear
carry *Note*
take

BATHEōS (BATHUS) 901
AG:130 CB:1238
deeply *Note*
early

BATHMOS 898
AG:130A CB:—
degree

BATHOS 899
AG:130A CB:1238C
deep, deepness
depth

BATHUNō 900
AG:130B CB:—
deep

BATHUS 901
AG:130B CB:1238C
deep

BATOS 942
AG:137C CB:—
bramble*
bush, measure

BATRACHOS 944
AG:137D CB:—
frog

BATTOLOGEō 945
AG:137D CB:1239A
repetitions

BDELUGMA 946
AG:137D CB:1239A
abomination

BDELUKTOS 947
AG:138A CB:—
abominable

BDELUSSō 948
AG:138A (-OMAI) CB:—
abhor
abominable

BEBAIOō 950
AG:138C CB:1239A
confirm
establish
stablish

BEBAIOS 949
AG:138B CB:1239A
firm, force
stedfast, sure

BEBAIōSIS 951
AG:138D CB:1239A
confirmation

BEBēLOō 953
AG:138D CB:—
profane

BEBēLOS 952
AG:138D CB:—
profane

BELIAL (-AR) 955
AG:139A CB:1239A
Belial

BELONē —
AG:139B CB:—
needle

BELOS 956
AG:139B CB:1239A
dart

BELTION 957
AG:139B (-IōN) CB:—
well (Adverb)

BēMA 968
AG:140B CB:1239A
judgment-seat
throne

BēRULLOS 969
AG:140B CB:1239A
beryl

BIA 970
AG:140C CB:1239A
dominion *Note*
violence

BIAIOS 972
AG:141A CB:1239A
mighty

BIASTēS 973
AG:141A CB:1239A
force *Note*
violence
violent

BIAZō 971
AG:140C CB:1239A
enter *Note*
force *Note*
press
suffer
violence

BIBLARIDION 974
AG:141A CB:Cf. BIBLOS (1239A)
book

BIBLION 975
AG:141B CB:1239A
bill
book, scroll
writing

BIBLOS 976
AG:141C CB:1239A
book

BIBRōSKō 977
AG:141C CB:—
eat

BIOō 980
AG:142A CB:1239A
live

BIOS 979
AG:141D CB:1239A
good(s)
life, living

BIōSIS 981
AG:142A CB:—
life

BIōTIKOS 982
AG:142A CB:1239A
life

BLABEROS 983
AG:142B CB:—
hurtful

BLAPTō 984
AG:142B CB:1239A
hurt

BLASPHēMEō 987
AG:142C CB:1239A
blaspheme
defame, rail
report
revile

BLASPHēMIA 988
AG:143A CB:1239A
blasphemy
evil speaking
railing
speak

BLASPHēMOS 989
AG:143A CB:1239A
blasphemous
railing, -ers

BLASTANō 985
AG:142B CB:1239A
bring
bud, spring

BLEMMA 990
AG:143B CB:—
seeing

BLEPō 991
AG:143B CB:1239A
behold
beware
heed (take)
lie *Note*
look
perceive
regard
see, sight

BLēTEOS 992
AG:144A CB:—
put
BOAō 994
AG:144B CB:1239B
cry
BOē 995
AG:144C CB:1239B
cry
BOēTHEIA 996
AG:144C CB:—
help
BOēTHEō 997
AG:144C CB:—
help
succour
BOēTHOS 998
AG:144B CB:1239B
helper
BOLē 1000
AG:144D CB:—
cast
dart
BOLIS 1002
AG:144D CB:—
dart *Note*
BOLIZō 1001
AG:144D CB:—
dart
sound
BōMOS 1041
AG:148D CB:1239B
altar
BORBOROS 1004
AG:145A CB:1239B
mire
BORRAS 1005
AG:145B CB:—
north
BOSKō 1006
AG:145B CB:1239B
feed
keep *Note*
BOTANē 1008
AG:145B CB:1239B
herb
BOTHUNOS 999
AG:144D CB:—
ditch
pit
BOTRUS 1009
AG:145C CB:—
cluster
BOULē 1012
AG:145D CB:1239B
advise
counsel
will
BOULēMA 1013
AG:145D CB:1239B
desire *Note*
purpose
will
BOULEUTēS 1010
AG:145C CB:—
counsellor

BOULEUō 1011
AG:145C CB:1239B (-OMAI)
consult
counsel
minded
purpose
BOULOMAI 1014
AG:146A CB:1239B
desire
determine *Note*
disposed
fain, intend
list
minded
will, willing
wish
BOUNOS 1015
AG:146C CB:—
hill
BOUS 1016
AG:146C CB:1239B
ox
BRABEION 1017
AG:146D CB:1239B
prize
BRABEUō 1018
AG:146D CB:1239B
rule
BRACHIōN 1023
AG:147B CB:—
arm
BRACHUS 1024
AG:147B CB:1239B
few
further *Note*
little
space, while
words
BRADUNō 1019
AG:147A CB:—
slack, tarry
BRADUPLOEō 1020
AG:147A CB:—
sail
BRADUS 1021
AG:147A CB:—
dull *Note*
slow
BRADUTēS 1022
AG:147A CB:—
slackness
BRECHō 1026
AG:147C CB:1239B
rain, wash
BREPHOS 1025
AG:147B CB:1239B
babe
child *Note*
infant*
young
BROCHē 1028
AG:147D CB:1239B
rain
BROCHOS 1029
AG:147D CB:—
snare

BRōMA 1033
AG:148A CB:1239B
food, meat
victuals
BRONTē 1027
AG:147D CB:1239B
thunder
BRōSIMOS 1034
AG:148B CB:1239B
eat, meat
BRōSIS 1035
AG:148B CB:1239B
eating
food
meat
rust
BRUCHō 1031
AG:148A CB:1239B
gnash
BRUGMOS 1030
AG:147D CB:1239B
gnashing
BRUō 1032
AG:148A CB:—
send
BURSEUS 1038
AG:148DCB:—
tanner
BUSSINOS 1039
AG:148D CB:—
linen (fine)
BUSSOS 1040
AG:148D CB:—
linen (fine)
BUTHIZō 1036
AG:148C CB:—
deep *Note*
drown
sink
BUTHOS 1037
AG:148C CB:—
deep

C

CHAIRō 5463
AG:873B CB:1239B
farewell
glad
God-speed
greeting
hail
joy
rejoice
CHALAō 5465
AG:874B CB:—
let down
lower
strake
strike
CHALAZA 5464
AG:874B CB:1239B
hail
CHALEPOS 5467
AG:874C CB:1239B
fierce
grievous
perilous

CHALINAGōGEō 5468
AG:874C CB:—
bridle
CHALINOS 5469
AG:874C CB:—
bit*
bridle
CHALKēDōN 5472
AG:874D CB:1239B
chalcedony
CHALKEOS 5470
AG:875B (-KOUS) CB:—
brass
CHALKEUS 5471
AG:874D CB:1239B
brass
coppersmith*
CHALKION 5473
AG:874D CB:1239B
brazen
CHALKOLIBANON 5474
AG:875A CB:1239B
brass
CHALKOS 5475
AG:875A CB:1239B
brass
money
CHAMAI 5476
AG:875B CB:—
ground
CHARA 5479
AG:875C CB:1239B
gladness
greatly
joy
joyfulness
CHARAGMA 5480
AG:876A CB:1239B
graven
image *Note*
mark
CHARAKTēR 5481
AG:876B CB:1239C
image
CHARAX 5482
AG:876B CB:1239C
trench
CHARIN 5484
AG:877A CB:1239C (-IS)
cause
CHARIS 5485
AG:877B CB:1239C
acceptable
benefit
bounty
favour
gift *Note*
grace, gracious
liberality
pleasure
thank(s)
thankworthy
CHARISMA 5486
AG:878D CB:1239C
free *Note*
gift

CHARITOō 5487
AG:879A CB:1239C
accepted *Note*
favour
freely *Note*
grace *Note*
CHARIZOMAI 5483
AG:876C CB:1239C
bestow
deliver
forgive
frankly
freely *Note*
give, grant
CHARTēS 5489
AG:879B CB:—
paper
CHASMA 5490
AG:879B CB:—
gulf
CHEILOS 5491
AG:879C CB:1239C
lip
shore
CHEIMARRHOS 5493
AG:879C CB:—
brook
CHEIMAZō 5492
AG:879C CB:—
labour
CHEIMōN 5494
AG:879D CB:—
tempest
weather
winter
CHEIR 5495
AG:879D CB:1239C
hand
CHEIRAGōGEō 5496
AG:880D CB:—
hand (lead by the)
CHEIRAGōGOS 5497
AG:880D CB:—
hand (lead by the)
CHEIROGRAPHOS (-ON) 5498
AG:880C CB:1239C
bond
handwriting*
CHEIRōN 5501
AG:881B CB:—
sorer
worse
CHEIROPOIēTOS 5499
AG:880D CB:1239C
hands (made by)
CHEIROTONEō 5500
AG:881A CB:1239C
appoint
choose
ordain
CHEROUBIM 5502
AG:881B (CHEROUB) CB:1239C
cherubim
CHēRA 5503
AG:881C CB:1239C
widow

CHILIARCHOS 5506
AG:881D CB:1239C
captain
CHILIAS 5505
AG:882A CB:1239C
thousand
CHILIOI 5507
AG:882A CB:1239C
thousands
CHIōN 5510
AG:882B CB:1239C
snow
CHITōN 5509
AG:882B CB:—
clothes
coat*
garment
CHLAMUS 5511
AG:882B CB:—
clothing *Note*
robe
CHLEUAZō 5512
AG:882C CB:—
mock
CHLIAROS 5513
AG:882C CB:1239C
lukewarm
CHLōROS 5515
AG:882D CB:1240A
green
pale
CHOIKOS 5517
AG:883A CB:1240A
earthy
CHOINIX 5518
AG:883B CB:—
measure
CHOIROS 5519
AG:883B CB:1240A
swine
CHOLAō 5520
AG:883B CB:—
angry
wroth (be)
CHOLē 5521
AG:883B CB:1240A
gall
CHōLOS 5560
AG:889A CB:1240A
cripple*
halt, lame*
CHOOS (CHOUS) 5522
AG:884B CB:1240A
dust
CHōRA 5561
AG:889B CB:1240A
coast *Note*
country
farm *Note*
field
ground, land
CHORēGEō 5524
AG:883D CB:—
give *Note*
minister
supply

CHōREō 5562
AG:889C CB:1240A
come
contain
course
go *Note*
heart
pass, place
receive
room
CHōRION 5564
AG:890B CB:1240A
field
ground
land
parcel
pass, place
possession
CHōRIS 5565
AG:890C CB:1240A
apart
beside
separate
without
CHōRIZō 5563
AG:890A CB:1240A
depart
put
separate
CHOROS 5525
AG:883D CB:—
dancing
CHōROS 5566
AG:891C II. CB:1240A
north-west
CHORTASMA 5527
AG:884A CB:1240A
sustenance
CHORTAZō 5526
AG:883D CB:1240A
feed
fill
satisfy
CHORTOS 5528
AG:884A CB:1240A
blade*
grass
hay*
CHRAō (-OMAI) 5530
AG:884B CB:1240A
deal with *Note*
entreat
lend
treat
use
CHRē 5534
AG:885B CB:1240A
ought
CHREIA 5532
AG:884D CB:1240A
business
lack *Note*
necessary
necessity
need, -ful
use
want

CHRēMA 5536
AG:885C CB:1240A
money
riches
CHRēMATISMOS 5538
AG:885D CB:1240A
answer
CHRēMATIZō 5537
AG:885C CB:1240A
admonish
call
reveal
speak, warn
CHREōPHEILETēS 5533
AG:885B CB:—
debtor
CHRēSIMOS 5539
AG:885D CB:—
profit
CHRēSIS 5540
AG:885D CB:—
use
CHRēSTEUOMAI 5541
AG:886A CB:1240A
kind (be)
CHRēSTOLOGIA 5542
AG:886A CB:1240A
word
CHRēSTOS 5543
AG:886A CB:1240A
better *Note*
easy
good, -ness
gracious
kind
CHRēSTOTēS 5544
AG:886B CB:1240A
gentleness *Note*
good, -ness
kindness
CHRēZō 5535
AG:885B CB:1240A
need
CHRIō 5548
AG:887C CB:1240A
anoint
CHRISMA 5545
AG:886C CB:1240A
anointing
unction
CHRISTOS 5547
AG:886D CB:1240A
Christ
CHRISTIANOS 5546
AG:886C CB:1240A
Christian
CHRONIZō 5549
AG:887D CB:1240B
delay
tarry
CHRONOS 5550
AG:887D CB:1240B
delay *Note*
season
space
time, while

CHRONOTRIBEō 5551
AG:888C CB:1240B
spend
time
CHRōS 5559
AG:889A CB:—
body
CHRUSEOS (-OUS) 5552
AG:888D CB:1240B
gold
golden
CHRUSION 5553
AG:888C CB:1240B
gold
jewels
CHRUSODAKTULIOS 5554
AG:888C CB:—
gold ring
ring
CHRUSOLITHOS 5555
AG:888C CB:1240B
chrysolite
CHRUSOō 5558
AG:889A CB:1240B
deck
CHRUSOPRASOS 5556
AG:888D CB:1240B
chrysoprasus
CHRUSOS 5557
AG:888D CB:1240B
gold
CHTHES (ECH-) 5504
AG:881D CB:—
yesterday

D

DAIMōN 1142
AG:169D CB:1240B
demon
devil
DAIMONIōDēS 1141
AG:169D CB:—
demoniacal
devilish*
DAIMONION 1140
AG:169A CB:1240B
demon
DAIMONIZOMAI 1139
AG:169A CB:1240B
demon
possess
DAKNō 1143
AG:169D CB:—
bite
DAKRU (-UON) 1144
AG:170A CB:—
tears
DAKRUō 1145
AG:170A CB:—
weep
DAKTULIOS 1146
AG:170A CB:1240B
ring
DAKTULOS 1147
AG:170A CB:1240B
finger

DAMALIS 1151
AG:170D CB:1240B
heifer
DAMAZō 1150
AG:170B CB:—
tame
DANEION 1156
AG:170D CB:—
debt
DAN(E)ISTēS 1157
AG:170D CB:1240B
creditor*
lender
DANEIZō 1155
AG:170D CB:—
borrow
lend
DAPANAō 1159
AG:171A CB:—
charges *Note*
consume *Note*
spend
DAPANē 1160
AG:171A CB:—
cost
DE 1161
AG:171C CB:—
even
moreover
now
truly *Note*
yea *Note*
Notes p. 1266
Dē 1211
AG:178B CB:—
now
DECHOMAI 1209
AG:177B CB:1240B
accept
receive
take
DEēSIS 1162
AG:171D CB:1240B
prayer
request
supplication
DEI 1163
AG:172A CB:1240B
behove
bound *Note*
due
meet
must
needful
needs
ought
should
DEIGMA 1164
AG:172C CB:1240B
example
DEIGMATIZō 1165
AG:172C CB:1240C
example
show (make a)
DEIKNUMI (-NUō) 1166
AG:172D CB:1240C
shew

DEILIA 1167
AG:173A CB:1240C
fear
fearfulness
DEILIAō 1168
AG:173A CB:1240C
afraid*
fearful
DEILOS 1169
AG:173A CB:—
fearful
DEINA 1170
AG:173A CB:—
such as *Note*
DEINōS 1171
AG:173B CB:—
grievously
vehemently
DEIPNEō 1172
AG:173B CB:1240C
sup
DEIPNON 1173
AG:173B CB:1240C
feast
supper
DEISIDAIMōN
1174 (-MONESTEROS)
AG:173D CB:1240C
religious *Note*
superstitious
DEISIDAIMONIA 1175
AG:173C CB:1240C
religion
superstition*
DEKA 1176
AG:173D CB:1240C
ten
DEKADUO 1177
AG:173D (DEKA) CB:—
twelve*
DEKAPENTE 1178
AG:173D (DEKA) CB:—
fifteen
DEKATē 1181
AG:174A (-TOS) CB:1240C
tenth, tithe*
DEKATESSARES 1180
AG:173D (DEKA) CB:—
fourteen
DEKATOō 1183
AG:174B CB:1240C
pay *Note*
tithe
DEKATOS 1182
AG:174A CB:1240C
tenth
DEKTOS 1184
AG:174B CB:1240C
acceptable
DēLAUGōS —
AG:178B CB:—
clearly
DELEAZō 1185
AG:174B CB:—
beguile
entice

DēLOō 1213
AG:178C CB:1240C
declare
point
shew *Note*
signify
DēLOS 1212
AG:178B CB:1240C
bewray
certain *Note*
evident
manifest *Note*
DēMēGOREō 1215
AG:178D CB:—
oration
DēMIOURGOS 1217
AG:178D CB:1240C
craftsman *Note*
maker
DēMOS 1218
AG:179A CB:1240C
people
DēMOSIOS 1219
AG:179B CB:1240C
common *Note*
openly *Note*
public, -ly
DēNARION 1220
AG:179B CB:—
mite
pence, penny
pennyworth
DENDRON 1186
AG:174C CB:1240C
tree
DEō 1210
AG:177D CB:1240C
bind, knit
tie, wind
DEOMAI 1189
AG:175A CB:1240C
beseech
pray
request
DEOS 127 (AIDoS)
AG:175B CB:—
awe
DEON 1163 (DEI)
AG:172A (DEI 6.) CB:1240C
need
DēPOU 1222
AG:179B CB:—
verily *Note*
DERMA 1192
AG:175C CB:1240C
goatskin
DERMATINOS 1193
AG:175C CB:—
leathern
DERō 1194
AG:175D CB:1240C
beat
smite
DESMē 1197
AG:176A CB:1240C
bundle

DESMEō (-EUō) 1195
AG:175D CB:1240C
bind
DESMIOS 1198
AG:176A CB:1240C
bind *Note*
bond
prisoner
DESMOPHULAX 1200
AG:176B CB:1240C
jailor
prison-keeper*
DESMOS 1199
AG:176A CB:1240C
band
bind *Note*
bond
chain *Note*
string*
DESMōTēRION 1201
AG:176B CB:1240C
prison
prison-house
DESMōTēS 1202
AG:176B CB:1240C
prisoner
DESPOTēS 1203
AG:176C CB:1240C
lord
master
DEURO 1204
AG:176C CB:1241A
come *Note*
hither *Note*
hitherto
DEUTE 1205
AG:176D CB:1241A
come *Note*
follow *Note*
DEUTERAIOS 1206
AG:177A CB:—
next day *Note*
second
DEUTEROPRōTOS 1207
AG:177A CB:—
second *Note*
DEUTEROS 1208
AG:177A CB:1241A
again *Note*
second, -arily
DEXIOLABOS 1187
AG:174C CB:—
spearman
DEXIOS 1188
AG:174C CB:1241A
right, -hand
right side
DIA 1223
AG:179B CB:1241A
cause
hereof
means (by)
occasion *Note*
space *Note*
thereat, thereby
wherefore *Note*
within *Note*

DIABAINō 1224
AG:181C CB:—
come, pass
DIABALLō 1225
AG:181D CB:1241A
accuse
DIABEBAIOOMAI 1226
AG:181D CB:Cf. BEBIOō (1239A)
affirm
confidence *Note*
DIABLEPō 1227
AG:181D CB:Cf. BLEPō (1239A)
clearly *Note*
see
DIABOLOS 1228
AG:182A CB:1241A
accuser
devil
slanderer
DIACHEIRIZō 1315 (-OMAI)
AG:191A CB:—
kill, slay
DIACHōRIZō 1316 (-OMAI)
AG:191A CB:1241A (-ESTHAI)
depart
DIACHLEUAZō —
AG:191A CB:—
mock
DIADECHOMAI 1237
AG:182C CB:—
come *Note*
turn
DIADēMA 1238
AG:182D CB:1241A
crown
diadem
DIADIDōMI 1239
AG:182D CB:—
distribute
divide
give
DIADOCHOS 1240
AG:182D CB:—
room *Note*
DIAGINOMAI 1230
AG:182B CB:—
past
spent
DIAGINōSKō 1231
AG:182B CB:—
decide *Note*
determine
inquire *Note*
know *Note*
DIAGNōRIZō 1232
AG:182B CB:—
known *Note*
DIAGNōSIS 1233
AG:182C CB:—
decision
hearing
DIAGō 1236
AG:182C CB:—
lead *Note*
life *Note*
live

DIAGONGUZō 1234
AG:182C CB:—
murmur
DIAGRēGOREō 1235
AG:182C CB:—
awake
DIAIREō 1244
AG:183D CB:—
divide
DIAIRESIS 1243
AG:183C CB:1241A
difference
diversity
DIAKATELENCHOMAI 1246
AG:184A CB:—
confute
convince
DIAKATHAIRō 1245 (-ARIZō)
AG:183D CB:—
purge
DIAKATHARIZō 1245
AG:183D CB:Cf. KATH-(1254B)
cleanse
purge
DIAKōLUō 1254
AG:185C CB:—
forbid *Note*
hinder
DIAKONEō 1247
AG:184A CB:1241A
administer*
minister
office *Note*
serve
DIAKONIA 1248
AG:184B CB:1241A
administration*
minister, -ing
ministration
ministry
office *Note*
relief
service
serving
DIAKONOS 1249
AG:184C CB:1241A
deacon
minister
servant
DIAKOSIOI 1250
AG:185A CB:—
two hundred
DIAKOUō 1251 (-OMAI)
AG:185A CB:—
hear
DIAKRINō 1252
AG:185A CB:1241A
contend
decide
difference
discern
divide
doubt, judge
partial
put *Note*
stagger*
waver

DIAKRISIS 1253
AG:185B CB:1241A
decision
discern
DIALALEō 1255
AG:185C CB:—
commune
noise
DIALEGOMAI 1256
AG:185C CB:1241A
discourse
dispute
preach *Note*
reason
speak *Note*
DIALEIPō 1257
AG:185D CB:1241A
cease
DIALEKTOS 1258
AG:185D CB:1241A
language
tongue
DIALLASSō (-OMAI) 1259
AG:186A CB:1241A
reconcile
DIALOGISMOS 1261
AG:186A CB:1241B
disputation, -ing
doubting
imagination
reasoning
thought
DIALOGIZOMAI 1260
AG:186A CB:1241B
cast
consider *Note*
dispute, musing
reason
think *Note*
DIALUō 1262
AG:186B CB:1241B
disperse
scatter
DIAMACHOMAI 1264
AG:186C CB:—
strive
DIAMARTUROMAI 1263
AG:186C CB:1241B
charge
testify, witness
DIAMENō 1265
AG:186C CB:Cf. MENō (1258B)
continue
remain
DIAMERISMOS 1267
AG:186D CB:1241B
division
DIAMERIZō 1266
AG:186D CB:—
cloven
divide, part
DIANGELLō 1229
AG:182B CB:1241B
declare
preach *Note*
publish
signify

DIANEMō 1268
AG:186D CB:—
spread
DIANEUō 1269
AG:187A CB:—
beckon
signs (to make) *Note*
DIANOēMA 1270
AG:187A CB:1241B
thought
DIANOIA 1271
AG:187A CB:1241B
heart *Note*
imagination
mind
understanding
DIANOIGō 1272
AG:187B CB:1241B
open
DIANUKTEREUō 1273
AG:187B CB:1241B
continue
DIANUō 1274
AG:187B CB:—
finish
DIA PANTOS (PAS) 1275
AG:179B (A.II.1a.) CB:1262C
always
continually
DIAPARATRIBē 3859 (PARADIA-)
AG:187C CB:—
disputing
wrangling
DIAPERAō 1276
AG:187C CB:—
cross
go *Note*
pass, sail
DIAPHANēS 1307
AG:190B CB:—
dawn *Note*
transparent*
DIAPHeMIZō 1310
AG:190C CB:—
blaze abroad
commonly *Note*
fame
report *Note*
DIAPHERō 1308
AG:190B CB:Cf. PHERō (1264A)
better (be)
carry
differ
drive
excellent
matter *Note*
publish
spread
value
DIAPHEUGō 1309
AG:190C CB:—
escape
DIAPHOROS 1313
AG:190D CB:—
differing
divers
excellent

DIAPHORōTEROS (-OROS) 1313
AG:190D CB:—
excellent
DIAPHTHEIRō 1311
AG:190C CB:1241B
corrupt
decay
destroy
perish
DIAPHTHORA 1312
AG:190D CB:1241B
corruption
DIAPHULASSō 1314
AG:191A CB:—
guard
keep
DIAPLEō 1277
AG:187C CB:—
sail
DIAPONEō 1278
AG:187C (-OMAI) CB:—
grieve *Note*
trouble
DIAPOREō 1280
AG:187D CB:—
doubt
perplex
DIAPOREUō (-OMAI) 1279
AG:187D CB:—
go
journey
pass
DIAPRAGMATEUOMAI 1281
AG:187D CB:1241B
gain
trade
DIAPRIō 1282
AG:187D CB:—
cut
saw asunder
DIARPAZō 1283
AG:188A CB:—
spoil
DIARRHēGNUMI (-ēSSō) 1284
AG:188A CB:1241B
break, rend
DIASAPHEō 1285
AG:188B CB:—
explain
tell
DIASEIō 1286
AG:188B CB:1241B
fear *Note*
violence
DIASKORPIZō 1287
AG:188B CB:1241B
disperse
scatter
strawed*
waste
DIASōZō 1295
AG:189A CB:1241B
escape
heal
safe, save
whole

DIASPAō 1288
AG:188C CB:—
pluck *Note*
pull *Note*
rend, tear
DIASPEIRō 1289
AG:188C CB:1241B
disperse
scatter
DIASPORA 1290
AG:188C CB:1241B
disperse
scatter
DIASTELLō (-OMAI) 1291
AG:188D CB:1241B
charge
command *Note*
DIASTēMA 1292
AG:188D CB:—
space
DIASTOLē 1293
AG:188D CB:—
difference
distinction*
DIASTREPHō 1294
AG:189A CB:—
perverse
pervert, turn
DIATAGē 1296
AG:189B CB:—
disposition
ordinance
DIATAGMA 1297
AG:189B CB:1241B
commandment
DIATARASSō 1298
AG:189B CB:—
trouble
DIATASSō 1299
AG:189C CB:1241B
appoint
command
ordain, order
DIATELEō 1300
AG:189C CB:Cf. TELEo (1271B)
continue
DIATēREō 1301
AG:189D CB:1241B
keep
DIATHēKē 1242
AG:183A CB:1241B
covenant
testament*
DIATI 1302
AG:179B (DIA B.II.2.) CB:—
wherefore *Note*
DIATITHēMI 1303 (-EMAI)
AG:189D CB:1241B
appoint
make
testator
DIATRIBō 1304
AG:190A CB:—
abide
continue *Note*
tarry

AG:190A CB:—
food
DIAUGAZō 1306
AG:190A CB:1241B
dawn
DIAUGeS —
AG:190B CB:—
dawn *Note*
DIAZōNNUMI 1241
AG:182D CB:1241B
gird
DICHAZō 1369
AG:200B CB:—
variance
DICHOSTASIA 1370
AG:200B CB:1241B
division
sedition
DICHOTOMEō 1371
AG:200C CB:—
cut
DIDACHē 1322
AG:192B CB:1241B
doctrine
teaching*
DIDAKTIKOS 1317
AG:191B CB:1241B
teach
DIDAKTOS 1318
AG:191B CB:1241B
taught
teach*
DIDASKALIA 1319
AG:191C CB:1241B
doctrine
learning
teaching*
DIDASKALOS 1320
AG:191C CB:1241B
doctor
master
teacher
DIDASKō 1321
AG:192A CB:1241C
teach
DIDōMI 1325
AG:192C CB:1241C
add
adventure
bestow
cause
commit
deliver
give, grant
make
minister *Note*
offer
power *Note*
put
receive *Note*
render
set, shew
smite *Note*
suffer *Note*
take
utter, yield

DIDRACHMON 1323
AG:192C CB:1241C
half-shekel*
shekel
tribute
DIEGEIRō 1326
AG:193D CB:Cf. EGEIRō (1242C)
arise, awake
raise
stir up
DIēGEOMAI 1334
AG:195A CB:1241C
declare
shew *Note*
tell
DIēGēSIS 1335
AG:195A CB:1241C
declaration *Note*
narrative
DIēNEKēS 1336 (-KES)
AG:195A CB:—
continually
ever *Note*
DIENTHUMEOMAI —
AG:194A CB:—
think
DIERCHOMAI 1330
AG:194C CB:1241C
come
depart
go *Note*
pass
pierce
travel, walk
DIERMēNEUō 1329
AG:194B CB:1241C
expound
interpret
interpretation
DIERMēNEUTēS 1328
AG:194B CB:1241C
interpreter
DIERōTAō 1331
AG:194D CB:—
inquiry
DIETēS 1332
AG:194D CB:—
year
DIETIA 1333
AG:194D CB:—
year
DIEXODOS 1327
AG:194A CB:1241C
highway
DIIKNEOMAI 1338
AG:195B CB:—
pierce
DIISCHURIZOMAI 1340
AG:195B CB:—
affirm
confidence *Note*
DIISTēMI 1339
AG:195B CB:—
go *Note*
part
space

DIKAIOKRISIA 1341
AG:195C CB:1241C
judgment *Note*
righteous *Note*
DIKAIōMA 1345
AG:198A CB:1241C
act
judgment *Note*
justification
ordinance
righteousness
DIKAIOō 1344
AG:197C CB:1241C
free *Note*
justify
justifier
righteous *Note*
DIKAIOS 1342
AG:195C CB:1241C
just
meet
right
righteous
DIKAIōS 1346
AG:198B CB:1241C
justly
righteously
righteousness
DIKAIōSIS 1347
AG:198B CB:1241C
justification
DIKAIOSUNē 1343
AG:196B CB:1241C
justification *Note*
righteousness
DIKASTēS 1348
AG:198B CB:—
judge
DIKē 1349
AG:198C CB:1242A
judgment *Note*
justice
punishment
sentence
vengeance *Note*
DIKTUON 1350
AG:198C CB:—
net
DILOGOS 1351
AG:198D CB:—
double-tongued
DIO 1352
AG:198D CB:1242A
wherefore *Note*
DIODEUō 1353
AG:198D CB:—
go, pass
DIōGMOS 1375
AG:201A CB:1242A
persecution
DIōKō 1377
AG:201B CB:1242A
ensue*
follow
give
persecute, -tion
press, pursue

DIōKTēS 1376
AG:201B CB:1242A
persecutor
DIOPER 1355
AG:199A CB:—
wherefore *Note*
DIOPETēS 1356
AG:199A CB:—
fall *Note*
DIORTHōMA —
AG:199A CB:—
correction
deed *Note*
reformation
DIORTHōSIS 1357
AG:199A CB:1242A
reformation
DIORUSSō 1358
AG:199B CB:1242A
break
dig *Note*
DIPLOō 1363
AG:199D CB:—
double
DIPLOUS 1362
AG:199C CB:1242A
double
twofold*
DIPSAō 1372
AG:200C CB:1242A
thirst
DIPSOS 1373
AG:200D CB:1242A
thirst
DIPSUCHOS 1374
AG:201A CB:1242A
double-minded
soul *Note*
DIS 1364
AG:199D CB:—
again, twice
DISCHILIOI 1367
AG:200A CB:1242A
thousand *Note*
DISMURIADES 3461 (MURIAS)
AG:199D (-IAS) CB:—
thousand *Note*
DISTAZō 1365
AG:200A CB:1242A
doubt
DISTOMOS 1366
AG:200A CB:1242A
edge
two-edged
DITHALASSOS 1337
AG:195A CB:—
sea
DIūLIZō 1368
AG:200B CB:—
strain out
DOCHē 1403
AG:206B CB:1242A
feast
DōDEKA 1427
AG:210A CB:1242A
twelve

DōDEKAPHULOS (-ON) 1429
AG:210B CB:1242
tribes
DōDEKATOS 1428
AG:210B CB:—
twelfth
DOGMA 1378
AG:201C CB:1242A
decree
ordinance
DOGMATIZō 1379
AG:201B CB:1242A
ordinance
DOKEō 1380
AG:201D CB:1242A
account
please *Note*
pleasure
reputation
repute
seem, suppose
think, trow
DOKIMAZō 1381
AG:202C CB:1242A
allow
approve
discern
examine
prove
refuse, try
DOKIMē 1382
AG:202D CB:1242A
experience
experiment
probation*
proof, trial
DOKIMION 1383
AG:203A CB:1242A
proof
trial *Note*
try *Note*
DOKIMOS 1384
AG:203A CB:1242A
approved
tried *Note*
DOKOS 1385
AG:203A CB:—
beam
DOLIOō 1387
AG:203B CB:—
deceit
DOLIOS 1386
AG:203B CB:—
deceitful
DOLOō 1389
AG:203B CB:1242A
deceitfully
handle
DOLOS 1388
AG:203B CB:—
craft
deceit
guile
subtilty *Note*
DOMA 1390
AG:203C CB:—
gift

DōMA 1430
AG:210B CB:1242A
housetop
DōREA 1431
AG:210B CB:1242A
gift
DōREAN 1432
AG:210C CB:1242A
cause
freely
nought, vain
DōRēMA 1434
AG:210D CB:1242A
boon
gift
DōREō (-OMAI) 1433
AG:210C CB:1242A
give, grant
DōRON 1435
AG:210D CB:1242A
gift
offering *Note*
DOSIS 1394
AG:204D CB:1242A
gift
DOTēS 1395
AG:205A CB:1242A
giver
DOULAGōGEō 1396
AG:205A CB:1242A (-oGo)
bondage
subjection *Note*
DOULē 1399
AG:205C CB:—
handmaid*
DOULEIA 1397
AG:205A CB:1242B
bondage
DOULEUō 1398
AG:205A CB:1242B
bondage
serve
DOULOō 1402
AG:206A CB:—
bondage
enslaved
give *Note*
servant
DOULOS 1401
AG:205C CB:1242B
bondman
bondservant
deacon *Note*
servant
DOXA 1391
AG:203C CB:1242B
dignity
glory
honour
praise *Note*
worship *Note*
DOXAZō 1392
AG:204C CB:1242B
glorify
honour
magnify *Note*

DRACHMē 1406
AG:206C CB:—
money *Note*
piece
silver *Note*
DRAKōN 1404
AG:206B CB:1242B
dragon
DRASSOMAI 1405
AG:206C CB:—
take
DREPANON 1407
AG:206D CB:1242B
sickle
DROMOS 1408
AG:206D CB:1242B
course
DUNAMAI 1410
AG:207A CB:1242B
able, can
may, possible
power *Note*
DUNAMIS 1411
AG:207B CB:1242B
ability
abundance *Note*
deed *Note*
dominion *Note*
meaning
might, miracle
power, strength
violence *Note*
virtue *Note*
wonderful (work) *Note*
work
DUNAMOō 1412
AG:208C CB:1242B
able
strengthen
DUNASTēS 1413
AG:208C CB:1242B
authority
mighty *Note*
potentate*
DUNATEō 1414
AG:208C CB:1242B
able, mighty
DUNATOS (-ON) 1415
AG:208C CB:1242B
able, mighty
possible
power, strong
DUNō 1416
AG:209A CB:1242B
set
DUO 1417
AG:209A CB:1242B
twain, two*
DUSBASTAKTOS 1419
AG:209B CB:—
grievous
DUSENTERION 1420 (-RIA)
AG:209C CB:—
dysentery
DUSERMēNEUTOS 1421
AG:209C CB:—
utter

DUSKOLOS 1422
AG:209C CB:—
hard
DUSKOLōS 1423
AG:209D CB:—
hardly
DUSMē 1424
AG:209D CB:—
west
DUSNOēTOS 1425
AG:209D CB:1242C
understood
DUSPHēMEō —
AG:209D CB:—
defame
DUSPHēMIA 1426
AG:209D CB:—
report

E

ē 2228
AG:342A CB:—
either
more (than) *Note*
what *Note*
yea *Note*
EA 1436
AG:211A CB:—
ah!
alone*
EAN 1437
AG:211A CB:1242C
(at) least *Note*
much (as) *Note*
whatsoever *Note*
whosoever *Note*
EAō 1439
AG:212C CB:—
commit *Note*
leave, let
suffer
ēCHEō 2278
AG:349C CB:1242C
roar
sound
ECHIDNA 2191
AG:331D CB:—
viper
ECHō 2192
AG:331D CB:1242C
ability, able
accompany
can, case
could, count
do *Note*
fare
follow *Note*
have, hold
keep
lie *Note*
next
old *Note*
possess *Note*
seize *Note*
retain *Note*
take, use
was (etc.) *Note*

ēCHOS 2279
AG:349D CB:1242C
fame *Note*
roar
rumour
sound
ECHTHES —
AG:331B CB:1242 (-THOS)
yesterday
ECHTHRA 2189
AG:331B CB:1242C
enmity
hatred
ECHTHROS 2190
AG:331B CB:1242C
enemy
foe
EDAPHIZo 1474
AG:217C CB:—
dash
level *Note*
ground
EDAPHOS 1475
AG:217D CB:—
ground
ēDē 2235
AG:344A CB:1242C
already
now
ready *Note*
time
yet *Note*
EGEIRō 1453
AG:214C CB:1242C
arise, awake
lift
raise (up)
rear*
rise *Note*
stand *Note*
take *Note*
EGERSIS 1454
AG:215B CB:1242C
resurrection
EGō 1473
AG:217A CB:1242C
I
me *Note*
myself *Note*
EI 1487
AG:219A CB:1242C
indeed
more (than) *Note*
surely *Note*
whosoever *Note*
yea *Note*
Notes p. 1265
EIDEA (IDEA) 2397
AG:369C CB:—
appearance
countenance
EIDōL(E)ION 1493
AG:221B CB:1243A
idol's temple
EIDōLOLATREIA 1495
AG:221C CB:1243A
idolatry

EIDōLOLATRēS 1496
AG:221C CB:1243A
idolater
EIDōLON 1497
AG:221C CB:1243A
idol
EIDōLOTHUTON 1494
AG:221B (-OS) CB:1243A
idols (offered to)
meat *Note*
offer *Note*
sacrifice *Note*
EIDON (See HORAō)
EIDOS 1491
AG:221B CB:1243A
appearance
fashion
form, image
shape
sight
EIKē 1500
AG:221D CB:—
cause *Note*
vain, vainly
EIKō 1502
AG:222A CB:1243A
place
EIKōN 1504
AG:222B CB:1243A
image
likeness
EIKOSI 1501
AG:222A CB:1243A
twenty
EILIKRIN(E)IA 1505
AG:222D CB:—
sincerity
EILIKRINēS 1506
AG:222D CB:—
pure
sincere
EIMI (to be) 1510
AG:222D CB:1243A
being
belong *Note*
can, come
consist
give *Note*
have, hold
make, mean
might*
owneth
pass *Note*
possible
was (etc.) *Note*
EIPON 3004 (LEGō)
AG:226A CB:1243A
bid, call
command
say *Note*
speak*, tell
word *Note*
EIRēNē 1515
AG:227B CB:1243A
peace
quietness
rest *Note*

EIRēNEUō 1514
AG:227A CB:1243A
peace
peaceably
EIRēNIKOS 1516
AG:228A CB:1243A
peaceable
EIRēNOPOIEō 1517
AG:228A CB:1243A
peace
EIRēNOPOIOS 1518
AG:228A CB:1243A
peacemaker
EIRō (ERō) After 1518
AG:— CB:1246C
make *Note*
say
speak
tell
EIS 1519
AG:228A CB:1243A
cause *Note*
end *Note*
hereunto
insomuch as
intent *Note*
lest *Note*
purpose *Note*
regard (in ... to) *Note*
wherefore *Note*
EISAGō 1521
AG:232B CB:Cf. AGo (1233C)
bring
lead
EISAKOUō 1522
AG:232B CB:1243B
hear
EISDECHOMAI 1523
AG:232C CB:1243B
receive
EISEIMI 1524
AG:232C CB:—
enter
go
EISERCHOMAI 1525
AG:232C CB:1243B
arise
come
enter
go *Note*
EISKALEō 1528
AG:233B (-OMAI) CB:1243B
call
EISODOS 1529
AG:233B CB:1243B
coming
enter
entering
entrance
EISPēDAō 1530
AG:233C CB:—
run *Note*
spring
EISPHERō 1533
AG:233D CB:1243B
bring
lead

EISPOREUOMAI 1531
AG:233C CB:Cf. POR-(1266A)
come *Note*
enter
go
EISTRECHō 1532
AG:233D CB:—
run
EITA 1534
AG:233D CB:1243B
afterward *Note*
furthermore
then
EK 1537
AG:234A CB:1243B
hereby
means (by)
of *Note*
out *Note*
out of *Note*
severally *Note*
Notes p. 1270
EKBAINō —
AG:237B CB:—
come
go *Note*
EKBALLō 1544
AG:237B CB:1243B
bring
cast
drive
expel*
leave
pluck (out) *Note*
pull *Note*
put
send
take
thrust
EKBASIS 1545
AG:237D CB:—
end
escape
issue
EKBOLē 1546
AG:238A CB:—
freight
EKCHEō 1632
AG:247B CB:1243B
pour
run *Note*
shed
spill *Note*
EKCHōREo 1633
AG:247C CB:—
depart
EKCHUN(N)ō 1632
AG:247B (EKCHEō) CB:1243B
gush out
pour
riotously *Note*
run
shed
spill
EKDAPANAOMAI (-Aō) 1550
AG:238B CB:—
spend

EKDECHOMAI 1551
AG:238B CB:1243C
expect
look
tarry
wait
EKDēLOS 1552
AG:238B CB:—
manifest *Note*
EKDēMEō 1553
AG:238B CB:1243C
absent
EKDIDōMI 1554
AG:238C CB:—
let out
EKDIēGEOMAI 1555
AG:238C CB:1243C
declare
EKDIKEō 1556
AG:238C CB:1243C
avenge
revenge*
EKDIKēSIS 1557
AG:238D CB:1243C
avenge
punishment
revenge*
vengeance
EKDIKOS 1558
AG:238D CB:1243C
avenger
revenger*
EKDIōKō 1559
AG:239A CB:1243C
drive
persecute
EKDOCHē 1561
AG:239A CB:1243C
expectation
looking
EKDOTOS 1560
AG:239A CB:1243C
deliver
EKDUō 1562
AG:239A CB:1243C
strip
take
unclothed*
EKEI 1563
AG:239A CB:1243C
there
thither*
yonder
EKEINOS 1565
AG:239B CB:1243C
he, it*
other
selfsame *Note*
she*
that*
their *Note*
them *Note*
they *Note*
this *Note*
EKEISE 1566
AG:240A CB:—
there

EKEITHEN 1564
AG:239B CB:—
afterward
place *Note*
thence (from)
there
EKGAMISKo 1548
AG:See -IZo CB:—
marriage (give in)
EKGAMIZo 1547
AG:238A CB:—
marriage (give in)
EKGONOS 1549 (-NON)
AG:238A CB:—
grandchildren
nephews*
EKKAIo 1572
AG:240C CB:—
burn
EKKAKEo (See ENKAKEo)
EKKATHAIRo 1571
AG:240B CB:1243C
purge
EKKENTEo 1574
AG:240C CB:—
pierce
EKKLAo 1575
AG:240C CB:1243C
break
EKKLEIo 1576
AG:240C CB:—
exclude
EKKLeSIA 1577
AG:240D CB:1243C
assembly
church*
congregation
EKKLINo 1578
AG:241C CB:—
avoid, eschew
go *Note*
turn
way *Note*
EKKOLUMBAo 1579
AG:241D CB:—
swim
EKKOMIZo 1580
AG:241D CB:—
carry (out)
EKKOPTo 1581
AG:241D CB:1243C
cut, hew
hinder
EKKREMANNUMI 1582 (-MAMAI)
AG:242A CB:—
attentive
hang
EKLALEo 1583
AG:242A CB:—
tell
EKLAMPo 1584
AG:242A CB:1243C
shine
EKLANTHANOMAI 1585
AG:242B CB:—
forget

EKLEGo (-OMAI) 1586
AG:242B CB:1243C
choice
choose
EKLEIPo 1587
AG:242C CB:1243C
fail
EKLEKTOS 1588
AG:242D CB:1243C
chosen
elect
EKLOGe 1589
AG:243A CB:1243C
chosen
election
EKLUo 1590
AG:243A CB:1243C
faint
EKMASSo 1591
AG:243B CB:—
wipe
EKMUKTeRIZo 1592 (-TER-)
AG:243B CB:1243C
deride
laugh
mock *Note*
scoff
EKNePHo 1594
AG:243B CB:1243C
awake
sober *Note*
EKNEUo 1593
AG:243B CB:—
convey
EKPALAI 1597
AG:243C CB:—
long *Note*
old
EKPeDAo —
AG:243D CB:—
run *Note*
spring
EKPEIRAZo 1598
AG:243C CB:1243C
tempt
EKPEMPo 1599
AG:243C CB:—
send
EKPERISSoS After 1599
AG:243C CB:—
vehemently
EKPETANNUMI 1600
AG:243D CB:—
spread
stretch *Note*
EKPHERo 1627
AG:246D CB:Cf. PHERo (1264A)
bear, bring
carry *Note*
EKPHEUGo 1628
AG:246D CB:1243C
escape
flee
EKPHOBEo 1629
AG:247A CB:—
terrify

EKPHOBOS 1630
AG:247A CB:—
fear
sore *Note*
EKPHUo 1631
AG:247A CB:—
put
EKPIPTo 1601
AG:243D CB:1243C
cast
effect *Note*
fail, fall
nought
EKPLEo 1602
AG:244A CB:—
sail
EKPLeROo 1603
AG:244A CB:1243C
accomplish *Note*
fulfil
EKPLeRoSIS 1604
AG:244B CB:—
accomplishment
EKPLeSSo 1605
AG:244B CB:1243C
amaze
astonish*
EKPNEo 1606
AG:244B CB:1243C
ghost (give up the)
EKPOREUo (-OMAI) 1607
AG:244B CB:1244A
come, depart
go *Note*
issue
proceed
EKPORNEUo 1608
AG:244D CB:—
fornication
EKPSUCHo 1634
AG:247C CB:—
ghost (give up the)
yield *Note*
EKPTUo 1609
AG:244D CB:1244A
reject
EKRIZOo 1610
AG:244D CB:1244A
pluck, root
EKSTASIS 1611
AG:245A CB:1244A
amazement
astonishment*
trance
EKSTREPHo 1612
AG:245B CB:—
pervert
subvert *Note*
EKTARASSo 1613
AG:245B CB:—
trouble
EKTEINo 1614
AG:245B CB:1244A
cast *Note*
lay, put *Note*
stretch

EKTELEo 1615
AG:245C CB:—
finish
EKTENEIA 1616
AG:245C CB:—
earnestly
instantly *Note*
EKTENeS 1618
AG:245C CB:—
cease *Note*
fervent
EKTENESTERON 1617
AG:245 (EKTENeS) CB:—
earnestly
EKTENoS 1619
AG:245D CB:1244A
earnestly
fervently
EKTHAMBEo 1568
AG:240B CB:1244A
affright
amaze
EKTHAMBOS 1569
AG:240B CB:1244A
amaze
wonder *Note*
EKTHAUMAZo —
AG:240B CB:1244A
marvel, wonder*
EKTHETOS 1570
AG:240B CB:—
cast
EKTINASSo 1621
AG:245D CB:1244A
shake
EKTITHeMI 1620
AG:245D CB:—
cast
expound
EKTOS 1622
AG:246A CB:—
except
other *Note*
out of *Note*
outside
unless*
without *Note*
EKTREPHo 1625
AG:246C CB:1244A
bring
nourish
EKTREPo 1624
AG:246B CB:1244A
avoid
turn
EKTRoMA 1626
AG:246C CB:1244A
beget
EKTROMOS —
AG:246C CB:—
fear
EKZeTEo 1567
AG:240A CB:1244A
inquire *Note*
require
seek

EKZēTēSIS
AG:240B CB:1244A
questioning
ELACHISTOS 1646
AG:248D CB:1244A
least
little, small
ELACHISTOTEROS 1647
AG:248D (-TOS 2.b.) CB:1244A
least
ELAIA 1636
AG:247D CB:1244A
olive (berry)
olive tree
ELAION 1637
AG:247D CB:1244A
anoint *Note*
oil
ELAIōN 1638
AG:248A CB:1244A
Olives
Olivet
ELAPHRIA 1644
AG:248C CB:—
fickleness
lightness
ELAPHROS 1645
AG:248C CB:—
light
ELASSōN 1640
AG:248A CB:1244A
less, under
worse
younger
ELATTONEō 1641
AG:248B CB:—
lack
ELATTOō 1642
AG:248B CB:—
decrease
inferior
lower
ELAUNō 1643
AG:248C CB:—
carry *Note*
drive, row
ELEEINOS 1652
AG:249C CB:1244A
miserable
ELEEINOTEROS (-NOS) 1652
AG:249C CB:1244A
miserable
pitiable (most)
ELEēMōN 1655
AG:250A CB:1244A
merciful
ELEēMOSUNē 1654
AG:249D CB:1244A
alms
almsdeeds
ELEEō 1653
AG:249C CB:1244A
compassion
mercy
obtain *Note*
receive *Note*

ELEGMOS
AG:249A CB:1244A
reproof
ELENCHō 1651
AG:249B CB:1244A
convict
fault
rebuke
reprove
ELENCHOS 1650
AG:249A CB:1244A
reproof
ELENXIS 1649
AG:249A CB:1244A
rebuke
ELEOS 1656
AG:250A CB:1244A
mercy
ELEPHANTINOS 1661
AG:251A CB:—
ivory
ELEUSIS 1660
AG:251A CB:1244B
coming
ELEUTHERIA 1657
AG:250C CB:1244B
freedom
liberty
ELEUTHEROō 1659
AG:250D CB:1244B
deliver
free
ELEUTHEROS 1658
AG:250D CB:1244B
free, freeman
freewoman
liberty
ELLOGEō (-Aō) 1677
AG:252B CB:1244B
account
impute
ELPIS 1680
AG:252D CB:1244B
faith *Note*
hope
ELPIZō 1679
AG:252C CB:1244B
hope
trust *Note*
EMAUTOU 1683
AG:253D CB:—
me *Note*
myself
EMBAINō 1684
AG:254A CB:—
come, enter
get
go *Note*
step *Note*
take *Note*
EMBALLō 1685
AG:254A CB:1244B
cast
EMBAPTō 1686
AG:254B CB:Cf. BAPTō (1238C)
dip

EMBATEUō 1687
AG:254B CB:—
dwell
EMIBIBAZō 1688
AG:254C CB:—
put
EMBLEPō 1689
AG:254C CB:1244B
behold, gaze*
look, see
EMBRIMAOMAI 1690
AG:254D CB:1244B
charge
groan
murmur
straitly *Note*
EME 1691
AG:217 (EGō) CB:—
me*
EMEō 1692
AG:254D CB:1244B
spew
EMMAINOMAI 1693
AG:255A CB:—
mad
EMMENō 1696
AG:255B CB:1244B
continue
EMOI 1698
AG:217 (EGō) CB:—
me *Note*
EMOS 1699
AG:255C CB:1244B
me *Note*
my, mine
very *Note*
EMPAIGMONē —
AG:255D CB:1244B
mockery
EMPAIGMOS 1701
AG:255D CB:—
mocking
EMPAIKTēS 1703
AG:255D CB:—
mocker
scoffer*
EMPAIZō 1702
AG:255D CB:1244B
mock
EMPERIPATEō 1704
AG:256A CB:1244B
walk
EMPHANēS 1717
AG:257C CB:1244B
appear *Note*
manifest
openly *Note*
shew *Note*
EMPHANIZō 1718
AG:257D CB:1244B
appear
declare *Note*
inform
manifest
shew *Note*
signify

EMPHOBOS 1719
AG:257D CB:—
affrighted
terrify
tremble *Note*
EMPHUSAō 1720
AG:258A CB:1244B
breathe
EMPHUTOS 1721
AG:258A CB:1244B
engrafted
implanted
plant
EMPIPLAō (-PLēMI) 1705
AG:256A CB:1244B
fill
EMPIPLēMI 1705
AG:256A CB:1244B
fill
satisfy
EMPIPRēMI (EMPRēTHō) 1714
AG:256B CB:—
burn
EMPIPTō 1706
AG:256B CB:—
fall
EMPLEKō 1707
AG:256C CB:—
entangle
EMPLOKē 1708
AG:256C CB:—
braided *Note*
plaiting*
EMPNEō 1709
AG:256C CB:1244B
breathe
EMPOREUOMAI 1710
AG:256D CB:1244B
buy *Note*
merchandise
sell *Note*
trade
EMPORIA 1711
AG:256D CB:—
merchandise
EMPORION 1712
AG:257A CB:—
merchandise
EMPOROS 1713
AG:257A CB:—
merchant
EMPROSTHEN 1715
AG:257A CB:1244B
before
presence
sight of (in the)
EMPTUō 1716
AG:257C CB:—
spit
EN 1722
AG:258B CB:1244B
case (in ...)
hereby, herein
namely
thereby *Note*
under *Note*

EN (Continued)
way (by ... of) *Note*
while *Note*
within *Note*
Notes p. 1271
ENALIOS 1724
AG:261D CB:—
sea
ENANKALIZOMAI 1723
AG:261D CB:1244C
arm (physical) *Note*
ENANTI 1725
AG:261D CB:1244C
before
sight of (in the)
ENANTION 1726
AG:261D CB:1244C
before
contrariwise
sight of (in the)
ENANTIOS 1727
AG:262A CB:1244C (-ON)
contrary
ENARCHOMAI 1728
AG:262B CB:Cf. ARCHō (1237B)
begin
ENCHRIō (EGCH-) 1472
AG:217A CB:Cf. CHRIō (1240A)
anoint
ENDECHOMAI 1735 (-ETAI)
AG:262D CB:—
can
ENDEeS 1729
AG:262C CB:—
lack
ENDEIGMA 1730
AG:262C CB:—
token
ENDEIKNUMI 1731
AG:262C CB:—
shew
ENDEIXIS 1732
AG:262D CB:1244C
declare, proof
shew*, token
ENDeMEō 1736
AG:263A CB:1244C
home
present *Note*
ENDIDUSKō 1737
AG:263A CB:—
clothe, wear
ENDIKOS 1738
AG:263B CB:—
just
ENDOMeSIS 1739
AG:264B CB:—
building
ENDOXAZō 1740
AG:263 (-OMAI) CB:1245A
glorify
ENDOXOS 1741
AG:263B CB:1245A
glorious, glory
gorgeously*
honourable

ENDUMA 1742
AG:263C CB:1245A
clothing
garment
raiment *Note*
ENDUNAMOō 1743
AG:263D CB:1245A
enable
strength, -then
strong
ENDUNō 1744
AG:263D CB:—
creep
ENDUō 1746
AG:264A CB:1245A
clothe
endue
have
put
wear
ENDUSIS 1745
AG:263D CB:—
clothing *Note*
putting
ENECHō 1758
AG:265D CB:1245A
entangle
press
quarrel*
set
urge *Note*
ENEDRA (-DRON) 1747 (1749)
AG:264C CB:1245A
lie in wait
ENEDREUō 1748
AG:264C CB:—
lie in wait
ENEILEō 1750
AG:264C CB:—
wind
wrap
ENEIMI 1751
AG:264C CB:—
have *Note*
within *Note*
ENENeKONTA 1768 (KONTAENNEA)
AG:265A CB:—
ninety
ENEOS (See ENNEOS)
ENERGEIA 1753
AG:265A CB:1245A
dominion *Note*
effectual *Note*
operation*
strong*
working
ENERGeMA 1755
AG:265A CB:1245A
operation*
working
ENERGEō 1754
AG:265B CB:1245A
do *Note*
effectual
mighty *Note*
shew *Note*
work

ENERGeS 1756
AG:265D CB:1245A
active
effectual
powerful
ENEULOGEOMAI (-Eō) 1757
AG:265D CB:1245A
bless
ENGIZō 1448
AG:213C CB:1245A
approach
come *Note*
draw
hand (at)
near, near
ENGRAPHō 1449
AG:213D CB:1245A
write in
ENGUOS 1450
AG:214A CB:1245A
surety
ENGUS 1451
AG:214A CB:1245A
hand (at)
near
nigh
ready *Note*
ENGUTERON 1452
AG:214A (ENGUS) CB:—
nearer
ENIAUTOS 1763
AG:266B CB:1245A
year
ENISCHUō 1765
AG:266D CB:1245A
strengthen
ENISTeMI 1764
AG:266D CB:—
come
hand (at) *Note*
now *Note*
present
ENKAINIA 1456
AG:215B CB:—
dedication
ENKAINIZō 1457
AG:215B CB:1245A
consecrate
dedicate
ENKAKEō (EKK-) 1573
AG:215C CB:1245A
faint
ENKAKEō —
AG:215C CB:1245A
weary
ENKALEō 1458
AG:215C CB:1245A
accuse
call *Note*
charge
implead*
question *Note*
ENKATALEIPō 1459
AG:215D CB:—
forsake
leave

ENKATHETOS 1455
AG:215B CB:—
spy
ENKATOIKEō 1460
AG:216A CB:—
dwell
ENKAUCHAOMAI —
AG:216A CB:1245A
glory
ENKENTRIZō 1461
AG:216A CB:1245A
graff, graft
ENKLeMA 1462
AG:216B CB:1245A
accusation
charge
crime*
matter
ENKOMBOOMAI 1463
AG:216B CB:—
clothe *Note*
ENKOPe 1464
AG:216B CB:1245A
hinder
hindrance
ENKOPTō 1465
AG:216C CB:1245A
cut *Note*
hinder
tedious (to be)
ENKRATEIA 1466
AG:216C CB:1245A
temperance
ENKRATeS 1468
AG:216D CB:1245A
temperate
ENKRATEUOMAI 1467
AG:216C CB:1245A
contain*
continency
temperate
ENKRINō 1469
AG:216D CB:—
number
ENKRUPTō 1470
AG:216D CB:1245B
hide
ENKUOS 1471
AG:216D CB:—
child
ENNATOS 1766
AG:267A (ENNEA) CB:—
ninth
ENNEA 1767
AG:267A CB:—
nine
ENNEOS 1769
AG:265A (ENEOS) CB:—
speechless
ENNEUō 1770
AG:267A CB:—
signs (to make)
ENNOIA 1771
AG:267A CB:1245B
intent
mind

ENNOMOS 1772
AG:267B CB:1245B
law
lawful *Note*
regular*
ENNUCHA 1773 (-ON)
AG:267B (-OS) CB:—
day
ENOCHLEō 1776
AG:267D CB:1245B
trouble
vex *Note*
ENOCHOS 1777
AG:267D CB:1245B
danger
guilty
subject
worthy
ENOIKEō 1774
AG:267B CB:1245B
dwell
ENōPION 1799
AG:270C CB:1245B
before
presence
sight of (in the)
ENORKIZō Cf. 3726
AG:267C CB:—
adjure
charge *Note*
ENōTIZOMAI 1801
AG:271A CB:1245B
hearken
ENTALMA 1778
AG:268B CB:—
commandment
precept
ENTAPHIASMOS 1780
AG:268B CB:1245B
burying
ENTAPHIAZō 1779
AG:268B CB:1245B
bury, burial
ENTELLō (-OMAI) 1781
AG:268B CB:1245B
charge
command
enjoined
ENTEUTHEN 1782
AG:268C CB:—
either *Note*
hence
ENTEUXIS 1783
AG:268D CB:1245B
intercessions
prayer
ENTHADE 1759
AG:266A CB:—
here, hither
there
ENTHEN —
AG:266A CB:—
hence
ENTHUMEOMAI 1760
AG:266A CB:1245B
think

ENTHUMēSIS 1761
AG:266B CB:1245B
device
thought
ENTIMOS 1784
AG:268D CB:1245B
dear
honour *Note*
honourable
precious
reputation *Note*
ENTIMOTEROS (-MOS) 1784
AG:268D CB:1245B
honourable
ENTOLē 1785
AG:269A CB:1245B
commandment
precept
ENTOPIOS 1786
AG:269B CB:—
place *Note*
ENTOS 1787
AG:269B CB:1245B
inside
within *Note*
ENTREPHō 1789
AG:269D CB:—
nourish
ENTREPō 1788
AG:269D CB:—
ashamed
regard
reverence
shame
ENTROMOS 1790
AG:269D CB:—
fear
quake
trembling *Note*
ENTROPē 1791
AG:269D CB:—
ashamed
shame
ENTRUPHAō 1792
AG:270A CB:—
delicately *Note*
revel *Note*
sport
ENTULISSō 1794
AG:270B CB:—
roll, wrap
ENTUNCHANō 1793
AG:270A CB:1245B
deal with *Note*
intercessions
plead
suit *Note*
ENTUPOō 1795
AG:270B CB:—
engrave
ENUBRIZō 1796
AG:270B CB:—
despite
ENUPNIAZō (-OMAI) 1797
AG:270B CB:1245B
dream, dreamer

ENUPNION 1798
AG:270C CB:1245B
dream
EOIKA 1503 (EIKō)
AG:280A CB:1245B
like
EPAGō 1863
AG:281B CB:Cf. AGō (1233C)
bring
EPAGōNIZOMAI 1864
AG:281B CB:1245B
contend
earnestly *Note*
EPAINEō 1867
AG:281C CB:1245B
commend
praise
EPAINOS 1868
AG:281C CB:1245B
praise
EPAIRō 1869
AG:281D CB:—
exalt
hoist up
lift
take
EPAISCHUNOMAI 1870
AG:282A CB:1245B
ashamed
EPAITEō 1871
AG:282B CB:Cf. AITEō (1234A)
beg
EPAKOLOUTHEō 1872
AG:282B CB:1245B
follow
EPAKOUō 1873
AG:282C CB:1245B
hear
hearken
EPAKROAOMAI 1874
AG:282C CB:1245B
hear
EPANAGō 1877
AG:282D CB:—
launch
put
return
thrust*
EPANAMIMNēSKō 1878
AG:282D CB:—
mind *Note*
remembrance
EPANANKēS 1876
AG:282D CB:—
necessary
EPANAPAUō (-OMAI) 1879
AG:282D CB:1245B
rest
EPANERCHOMAI 1880
AG:283A CB:Cf. ERC-(1246B)
come
return *Note*
EPANGELIA 1860
AG:280C CB:1245B
message *Note*
promise

EPANGELLō 1861
AG:280D (-OMAI) CB:1245B
profess
promise
EPANGELMA 1862
AG:281A CB:1245B
promise
EPANISTAMAI 1881
AG:283A (-TēMI) CB:—
rise *Note*
EPANō 1883
AG:283B CB:—
above
more *Note*
EPANORTHōSIS 1882
AG:283A CB:1245C
correction
EPAPHRIZō 1890
AG:283D CB:—
foam
EPARATOS —
AG:283C CB:1245C
accursed*
cursed
EPARCH(E)IA 1885
AG:283C CB:—
province
EPARKEō 1884
AG:283C CB:—
relieve
EPATHROIZō 1865
AG:281B CB:Cf. SUNA-(1270C)
gather
EPAULIS 1886
AG:283D CB:—
habitation
EPAURION 1887
AG:283D CB:—
follow *Note*
morrow
next day *Note*
EPAUTOPHōRō 1888
AG:125A (AUTOPHōROS) CB:—
act
EPECHō 1907
AG:285C CB:—
heed
hold
mark
stay
EPEGEIRō 1892
AG:284A CB:—
raise *Note*
stir
EPEI 1893
AG:284A CB:—
else
otherwise
EPEIDON 1896
AG:284B CB:—
look
EPEIMI 1966 (EPIOUSA)
AG:284C CB:1245C
follow
next *Note*
next day *Note*

EPEISAGōGē 1898
AG:284C CB:—
bringing
EPEITA 1899
AG:284C CB:—
afterward(s) *Note*
then
EPEKEINA 1900
AG:284D CB:—
beyond
EPEKTEINō (-OMAI) 1901
AG:284D CB:1245C
reach *Note*
stretch
EPENDUō (-OMAI) 1902
AG:284D CB:1245C
clothe
EPENDUTēS 1903
AG:285A CB:—
clothing
EPERCHOMAI 1904
AG:285A CB:1245C
come
EPēREAZō 1908
AG:285D CB:—
accuse
despitefully
revile *Note*
EPERōTAō 1905
AG:285B CB:1245C
ask
demand
desire *Note*
question
EPERōTēMA 1906
AG:285C CB:1245C
answer *Note*
interrogation
EPHALLOMAI 2177
AG:330A CB:—
leap
EPHAPAX 2178
AG:330A CB:1245C
once
EPHēMERIA 2183
AG:330C CB:—
course
EPHēMEROS 2184
AG:330C CB:—
course
daily
EPHEURETēS 2182
AG:330B CB:—
inventor
EPHIKNEOMAI 2185
AG:330C CB:—
reach
EPHISTēMI 2186
AG:330D CB:—
assault
come
hand (at) *Note*
instant
present
stand

EPHPHATHA 2188
AG:331B CB:1245C
ephphatha
open *Note*
EPI 1909
AG:285D CB:1245C
inasmuch as
of *Note*
respect *Note*
space *Note*
time *Note*
under *Note*
wherefore *Note*
EPIBAINō 1910
AG:289D CB:—
aboard
come, embark*
enter
foot *Note*
go *Note*
ride
ship *Note*
sit *Note*
take *Note*
EPIBALLō 1911
AG:289D CB:—
beat
cast, fall
lay, put
stretch *Note*
think
EPIBAREō 1912
AG:290B CB:1245C
burden
chargeable *Note*
overcharge
press
EPIBIBAZō 1913
AG:290B CB:—
set
EPIBLēMA 1915
AG:290C CB:—
piece
EPIBLEPo 1914
AG:290B CB:Cf. BLEPō (1239A)
look, regard
respect
EPIBOAō 1916
AG:290C CB:—
cry
EPIBOULē 1917
AG:290C CB:—
lie *Note*
plot
EPICHEIREō 2021
AG:304D CB:—
go
hand (take in)
take
EPICHEō 2022
AG:305A CB:—
pour
EPICHORēGEō 2023
AG:305A CB:—
add
minister *Note*
supply

EPICHORēGIA 2024
AG:305B CB:—
supply
EPICHRIō 2025
AG:305B CB:Cf. CHRIō (1240A)
anoint
EPIDE (EPEIDON) 1896
AG:284C CB:Cf. IDOU (1252C)
behold
EPIDECHOMAI 1926
AG:292A CB:—
receive
EPIDEIKNUMI 1925
AG:291D CB:—
shew
EPIDēMEō 1927
AG:292A CB:—
sojourn
stranger *Note*
there *Note*
EPIDIATASSō (-OMAI) 1928
AG:292B CB:—
add
EPIDIDōMI 1929
AG:292B CB:—
deliver
give
offer *Note*
EPIDIORTHOō 1930
AG:292B CB:—
order
EPIDUō 1931
AG:292C CB:—
go
EPIEIKEIA 1932
AG:292C CB:1245C
clemency
gentleness
EPIEIKēS 1933
AG:292C CB:1245C
forbearance
gentle
moderation*
patient *Note*
EPIGAMBREUō 1918
AG:290C CB:—
marry
EPIGEIOS 1919
AG:290C CB:1245C
earth, earthly
terrestrial
EPIGINOMAI 1920
AG:290D CB:—
blow *Note*
spring *Note*
EPIGINōSKō 1921
AG:291A CB:1245C
acknowledge
know
knowledge
perceive
EPIGNōSIS 1922
AG:291B CB:1245C
acknowledgement
know
knowledge

EPIGRAPHē 1923
AG:291C CB:1245C
superscription
EPIGRAPHō 1924
AG:291C CB:1245C
inscription
write
EPIKALEō (-OMAI) 1941
AG:294A CB:1245C
appeal
call
surname
EPIKALUMMA 1942
AG:294B CB:—
cloke (pretence)
EPIKALUPTō 1943
AG:294C CB:Cf. KAL-(1253B)
cover
forgive
EPIKATARATOS 1944
AG:294C CB:1245C
cursed
EPIKATHIZō 1940
AG:293D CB:—
set *Note*
EPIKEIMAI 1945
AG:294C CB:Cf. KEI-(1254C)
imposed
instant
lay, lie
press
EPIKELLō (EPOK-) 2027
AG:294D CB:—
run
EPIKOURIA 1947
AG:294D CB:—
help
EPIKRINō 1948
AG:295A CB:—
give *Note*
sentence
EPILAMBANō (-OMAI) 1949
AG:295A CB:1246A
catch
hold
lay *Note*
take
EPILANTHANOMAI 1950
AG:295B CB:—
forget, -ful
EPILEGō 1951 (-OMAI)
AG:295C CB:1246A
call
choose
EPILEICHō —
AG:295D CB:—
lick
EPILEIPō 1952
AG:295C CB:—
fail
EPILēSMONē 1953
AG:295D CB:—
forget, -ful
EPILOIPOS 1954
AG:295D CB:—
rest (the)

EPEPILUō 1956
AG:295D CB:1246A
determine
expound
settle *Note*
EPILUSIS 1955
AG:295D CB:1246A
interpretation
EPIMARTUREō 1957
AG:296A CB:1246A
testify
EPIMELEIA 1958
AG:296A CB:—
refresh *Note*
EPIMELEOMAI 1959
AG:296A CB:—
care
EPIMELōS 1960
AG:296A CB:—
diligently
EPIMENō 1961
AG:296B CB:1246A
abide
continue
tarry
EPINEUō 1962
AG:296C CB:—
consent
EPINOIA 1963
AG:296C CB:1246A
thought
EPIORKEō 1964
AG:296D CB:—
forswear
EPIORKOS 1965
AG:296D CB:—
forswear
perjured person*
ēPIOS 2261
AG:348B CB:1246A
gentle
EPIOUSIOS 1967
AG:296D CB:1246A
daily
EPIPHAINō 2014
AG:304A CB:1246A
appear
light, shine
EPIPHANEIA 2015
AG:304A CB:1246A
appearing
brightness *Note*
EPIPHANēS 2016
AG:304B CB:1246A
notable
EPIPHAUō (-USKō) 2017
AG:304C CB:—
light, shine
EPIPHERō 2018
AG:304C CB:1246A
bring
take *Note*
visit
EPIPHōNEō 2019
AG:304D CB:1246A
cry, shout

EPIPHōSKō 2020
AG:304D CB:—
dawn, draw
EPIPIPTō 1968
AG:297C CB:—
fall
lie *Note*
press
EPIPLēSSō 1969
AG:297D CB:—
rebuke
EPIPOREUOMAI 1975
AG:298A CB:Cf. POR-(1266A)
come*
resort
EPIPOTHEō 1971
AG:297D CB:1246A
desire *Note*
long
lust *Note*
EPIPOTHeSIS 1972
AG:298A CB:1246A
desire
longing
EPIPOTHeTOS 1973
AG:298A CB:—
long (verb)
EPIPOTHIA 1974
AG:298A CB:1246A
desire
longing
EPIRRHAPTō 1976
AG:298A CB:—
sew
EPIRIPTō 1977
AG:298B CB:—
cast
EPISCHUō 2001
AG:302A CB:—
fierce *Note*
EPISēMOS 1978
AG:298B CB:—
notable, note
EPISITISMOS 1979
AG:298C CB:—
victuals
EPISKēNOō 1981
AG:298D CB:1246A
rest
EPISKEPTOMAI 1980
AG:298C CB:1246A
look
visit
EPISKEUAZō —
AG:298C (-OMAI) CB:—
baggage
carriage*
EPISKIAZō 1982
AG:298D CB:1246A
overshadow
EPISKOPē 1984
AG:299A CB:1246A
bishop
bishoprick
office *Note*
visitation

EPISKOPEō 1983
AG:298D CB:1246A
bishop *Note*
carefully *Note*
exercise *Note*
look
oversight
EPISKOPOS 1985
AG:299B CB:1246A
bishop
overseer*
EPISōREUō 2002
AG:302A CB:—
heap
EPISPAOMAI 1986
AG:299D CB:—
circumcised
uncircumcised*
EPISPHALēS 2000
AG:302A CB:—
dangerous
EPISTAMAI 1987
AG:300A CB:1246A
know
understand
EPISTASIS —
AG:300B CB:—
come *Note*
press
raise *Note*
stir *Note*
EPISTATēS 1988
AG:300B CB:1246A
master
EPISTELLō 1989
AG:300C CB:1246A
write
EPISTēMōN 1990
AG:300C CB:—
endue *Note*
knowledge
understanding*
EPISTēRIZō 1991
AG:300D CB:1246A
confirm
strengthen *Note*
EPISTOLē 1992
AG:300D CB:1246A
epistle
letter
EPISTOMIZō 1993
AG:301A CB:—
mouth, stop
EPISTREPHō 1994
AG:301A CB:1246A
come *Note*
convert
go *Note*
return, turn
EPISTROPHē 1995
AG:301C CB:1246A
conversion
EPISUNAGō 1996
AG:301D CB:1246A
assemble *Note*
gather

EPISUNAGōGē 1997
AG:301D CB:1246A
assembling
gathering
EPISUNTRECHō 1998
AG:301D CB:—
come *Note*
run
EPISUSTASIS 1999
AG:301D CB:1246A
come *Note*
press
raise *Note*
stir *Note*
EPITAGē 2003
AG:302A CB:—
authority
commandment
EPITASSō 2004
AG:302B CB:1246A
charge *Note*
command
enjoin
EPITēDEIOS 2006
AG:302D CB:—
needful
EPITELEō 2005
AG:302B CB:1246A (-EISTHAI)
accomplish
complete
do *Note*
finish
make
perfect
perform
EPITHANATIOS 1935
AG:292D CB:—
appointed
death
doomed*
EPITHESIS 1936
AG:293A CB:1246B
laying on
putting
EPITHUMEō 1937
AG:293A CB:1246B
covet
desire
fain
lust
EPITHUMēTēS 1938
AG:293B CB:—
covet
lust *Note*
EPITHUMIA 1939
AG:293B CB:1246B
concupiscence*
coveting
desire
lust
EPITIMAō 2008
AG:303B CB:1246B
charge
rebuke
EPITIMIA 2009
AG:303C CB:1246B
punishment

EPITITHēMI 2007
AG:302D CB:1246B
add
lade *Note*
lay, put
set
surname *Note*
EPITREPō 2010
AG:303C CB:—
leave
let
liberty *Note*
licence*
permit
suffer
EPITROPē 2011
AG:303D CB:—
commission
EPITROPOS 2012
AG:303D CB:1246B
guardian
instructor
steward
tutor*
EPITUNCHANō 2013
AG:303D CB:—
obtain
EPIZēTEō 1934
AG:292D CB:1246B
desire *Note*
inquire *Note*
seek
EPOIKODOMEō 2026
AG:305B CB:1246B
build
EPONOMAZō 2028
AG:305C CB:1246B
call *Note*
name
surname *Note*
EPOPTēS 2030
AG:305D CB:1246B
behold *Note*
eye-witness
EPOPTEUō 2029
AG:305C CB:1246B
behold
EPOS 2031
AG:305D CB:1246B
so *Note*
word *Note*
EPOURANIOS 2032
AG:305D CB:1246B
celestial*
heavenly
ERCHOMAI 2064
AG:310B CB:1246B
bring *Note*
come
enter *Note*
fall
go *Note*
grow
light (to ... upon) *Note*
next
pass *Note*
resort

ERAUNAō (EREU-) 2045
AG:306C CB:1246B
search
EREIDō 2043
AG:308D CB:—
stick fast
strike *Note*
ERēMIA 2047
AG:308D CB:1246B
desert
place *Note*
wilderness
ERēMOō 2049
AG:309B CB:1246B
desolation
desolate
nought *Note*
ERēMOS 2048
AG:309A CB:1246B
desert
desolate
solitary*
wilderness
ēREMOS 2263
AG:348B CB:—
quiet
tranquil*
ERēMōSIS 2050
AG:309B CB:1246B
desolation
ERETHIZō 2042
AG:308D CB:—
anger *Note*
provoke
stir
EREUGOMAI 2044
AG:308D CB:—
utter
ERGASIA 2039
AG:307C CB:1246B
business
craft
diligence
gain, work
ERGATēS 2040
AG:307C CB:1246B
labourer
worker, -man
ERGAZOMAI 2038
AG:306D CB:1246C
commit
do
faithful *Note*
forbear *Note*
gain *Note*
labour *Note*
minister
trade
work, working
ERGON 2041
AG:307D CB:1246C
deed
labour *Note*
work
ERION 2053
AG:309C CB:—
wool

ERIPHION 2055
AG:309D CB:1246C
goat
ERIPHOS 2056
AG:309D CB:1246C
goat, kid*
ERIS 2054
AG:309C CB:1246C
contention
debate*
strife
variance *Note*
ERITH(E)IA 2052
AG:309B CB:1246C
contention *Note*
contentious *Note*
faction
strife
ERIZō 2051
AG:309B CB:—
strive
ERō (See EIRō)
ERōTAō 2065
AG:311D CB:1246C
ask
beseech
desire
intreat
pray
request
ERUTHROS 2063
AG:310B CB:—
red
ESCHATOS 2078
AG:313D CB:1246C
end
last
lowest
part
uttermost*
ESCHATōS 2079
AG:314B CB:1246C
death *Note*
ESō 2080
AG:214B CB:1246C
inner
inward
within *Note*
ESOPTRON 2072
AG:313B CB:1246C
glass
mirror
ESōTEROS 2082
AG:314C CB:1246C
inner
within *Note*
ESōTHEN 2081
AG:314B CB:—
inside
inward, -dly
within *Note*
ESTHēS 2066
AG:312B CB:1246C
apparel
clothing
raiment *Note*
robe

ESTHēSIS 2067
AG:312B (ESTHēS) CB:—
apparel
garment
ESTHIō 2068
AG:312B CB:1246C
devour
eat
live *Note*
ETHELOTHRēSK(E)IA 1479
AG:218A CB:—
worship
ETHIZō 1480
AG:218B CB:—
custom
ETHNARCHēS 1481
AG:218B CB:—
governor
ETHNIKOS 1482
AG:218B CB:1246C
Gentile(s)
heathen*
ETHNIKōS 1483
AG:218B CB:1246C
Gentiles
manner *Note*
ETHNOS 1484
AG:218B CB:1246C
Gentiles
heathen*
nation
people
ETHō 1486
AG:234A (EIōTHA) CB:1243A (EIōTHOS)
custom
manner *Note*
wont
ETHOS 1485
AG:218D CB:1247A
custom
law
manner
wont *Note*
ēTHOS 2239
AG:344C CB:1247A
manner
ETI 2089
AG:315C CB:1247A
also, even
further
longer
more, moreover
no more *Note*
still
thenceforth
yet *Note*
ETOS 2094
AG:316D CB:—
year
EU 2095
AG:317B CB:1247A
good
well
EUANGELION 2098
AG:317D CB:1247A
evangelist *Note*
gospel

EUANGELISTēS 2099
AG:318C CB:1247A
evangelist

EUANGELIZō 2097
AG:317B CB:1247A
evangelist *Note*
gospel
preach
shew *Note*
tidings

EUARESTEō 2100
AG:318C CB:1247A
please
well-pleasing

EUARESTOS 2101
AG:318D CB:1247A
acceptable
please
well-pleasing

EUARESTōS 2102
AG:318D CB:—
acceptably

EUCHARISTEō 2168
AG:328A CB:1247A
thank, -ful

EUCHARISTIA 2169
AG:328C CB:1247A
thanks
thankfulness
thanksgiving

EUCHARISTOS 2170
AG:329A CB:1247A
thankful

EUCHē 2171
AG:329B CB:1247A
prayer
vow

EUCHOMAI 2172
AG:329B CB:1247A
pray, wish
would *Note*

EUCHRēSTOS 2173
AG:329C CB:—
profitable
use *Note*

EUDIA 2105
AG:319A CB:1247A
fair
weather

EUDOKEō 2106
AG:319B CB:1247A
please
pleasure
think
well-pleasing
willing*

EUDOKIA 2107
AG:319C CB:1247A
desire
pleasure
seem *Note*
well-pleasing
will, willing

EUERGESIA 2108
AG:319D CB:1247A
benefit
deed

EUERGETEō 2109
AG:320A CB:1247A
good (to do)

EUERGETēS 2110
AG:320A CB:1247A
benefactor

EUGENēS 2104
AG:319A CB:1247B
noble
nobleman *Note*

EUGENESTEROS (-NēS) 2104
AG:319A 2. CB:—
noble

EUKAIREō 2119
AG:321B CB:1247B
convenient
leisure
opportunity
spend
time *Note*

EUKAIRIA 2120
AG:321B CB:1247B
convenient
opportunity

EUKAIROS 2121
AG:321C CB:1247B
convenient
need *Note*

EUKAIRōS 2122
AG:321C CB:1247B
conveniently
season

EUKOPōTEROS 2123
AG:321D (-POS) CB:—
easier

EULABEIA 2124
AG:321D CB:1247B
devout *Note*
fear
godly *Note*
reverence

EULABEOMAI 2125
AG:321D CB:1247B
devout *Note*
fear
godly *Note*
moved*

EULABēS 2126
AG:322A CB:1247B
devout

EULOGEō 2127
AG:322B CB:1247B
bless
praise *Note*

EULOGēTOS 2128
AG:322C CB:1247B
blessed

EULOGIA 2129
AG:322D CB:1247B
blessing
bounty
fair *Note*
speech

EUMETADOTOS 2130
AG:323A CB:—
distribute

EUNOEō 2132
AG:323B CB:—
agree

EUNOIA 2133
AG:323B CB:—
benevolence
will

EUNOUCHIZō 2134
AG:323C CB:1247B
eunuch

EUNOUCHOS 2135
AG:323C CB:1247B
eunuch

EUōDIA 2175
AG:329D CB:1247B
savour
smell*

EUODOō 2137
AG:323D CB:—
journey
prosper

EUōNUMOS 2176
AG:329D CB:1247B
left

EUPAREDROS —
AG:324A CB:—
attend

EUPEITHēS 2138
AG:324A CB:—
intreat

EUPERISTATOS 2139
AG:324A CB:—
beset
easily *Note*

EUPHēMIA 2162
AG:327C CB:—
report

EUPHēMOS 2163
AG:327C CB:—
gracious *Note*
report

EUPHOREō 2164
AG:327C CB:—
bring
plentifully

EUPHRAINō 2165
AG:327C CB:1247B
fare
glad, merry
rejoice

EUPHROSUNē 2167
AG:328A CB:1247B
gladness
joy

EUPOIEō (See EU and POIEō) –
AG:— CB:—
good (to do) *Note*

EUPOIIA 2140
AG:324A CB:—
good

EUPOREō 2141
AG:324B CB:—
ability

EUPORIA 2142
AG:324B CB:—
wealth

EUPREPEIA 2143
AG:324B CB:—
grace

EUPROSDEKTOS 2144
AG:324C CB:1247B
acceptable, -ted

EUPROSEDROS 2145
AG:324D CB:—
attend

EUPROSōPEō 2146
AG:324D CB:—
fair *Note*
show (make a)

EUPSUCHEō 2174
AG:329D CB:—
comfort

EURUCHōROS 2149
AG:326A CB:—
broad

EUSCHēMōN 2158
AG:327A CB:Cf. -MOSUNē (1247B)
comely
estate
honourable

EUSCHēMONōS 2156
AG:327A CB:—
decently
honestly

EUSCHēMOSUNē 2157
AG:327A CB:1247B
comeliness

EUSEBEIA 2150
AG:326A CB:1247B
godliness
holiness *Note*

EUSEBEō 2151
AG:326B CB:1247B
godly *Note*
piety (to shew)
worship

EUSEBēS 2152
AG:326B CB:1247B
devout
godly

EUSEBōS 2153
AG:326C CB:1247B
godly

EUSēMOS 2154
AG:326C CB:—
understood

EUSPLANCHNOS 2155
AG:326C CB:1247B
pitiful
tenderhearted*

EUTHEōS 2112
AG:320B CB:1247B
forthwith
immediately
shortly
straightway *Note*

EUTHETOS 2111
AG:320B CB:—
fit, meet

EUTHUDROMEō 2113
AG:320D CB:—
course *Note*

EUTHUMEō 2114
AG:320D CB:—
cheer, -ful
merry
EUTHUMOS 2115
AG:320D CB:—
cheer
EUTHUMōS 2115 (-MOS)
AG:320D CB:—
cheerfully
EUTHUMōTERON 2115 (-MOS)
AG:320D (-MōS) CB:—
cheerfully
EUTHUNō 2116
AG:320D CB:—
governor *Note*
straight
steersman*
EUTHUS (adj) 2117
AG:321A CB:1247B
right
straight
EUTHUS (adv) 2117
AG:321A CB:1247B
anon
forthwith
immediately
straightway *Note*
EUTHUTēS 2118
AG:321B CB:—
righteousness *Note*
uprightness
EUTONōS 2159
AG:327B CB:—
mightily
powerfully
vehemently
EUTRAPELIA 2160
AG:327C CB:—
jesting
EXAGō 1806
AG:271C CB:Cf. AGō (1233C)
bring
fetch *Note*
lead
EXAGORAZō 1805
AG:271B CB:1247B
redeem
EXAIPHNēS 1810
AG:272B CB:—
suddenly
EXAIREō 1807
AG:271D CB:—
deliver
pluck
rescue
EXAIRō 1808
AG:272A CB:—
put, take
EXAITEō (-OMAI) 1809
AG:272A CB:1247B
ask *Note*
desire *Note*
EXAKOLOUTHEō 1811
AG:272B CB:1247B
follow

EXALEIPHō 1813
AG:272C CB:1247B
blot, wipe
EXALLOMAI 1814
AG:272C CB:—
leap
EXANASTASIS 1815
AG:272D CB:1247C
resurrection
EXANATELLō 1816
AG:272D CB:—
spring
EXANGELLō 1804
AG:271B CB:1247C
shew
EXANISTēMI 1817
AG:272D CB:1247C (-HIS-)
arise, raise
rise *Note*
EXAPATAō 1818
AG:273A CB:1247C
beguile
deceive
EXAPINA 1819
AG:273A CB:—
suddenly
EXAPOREō 1820 (-OMAI)
AG:273A CB:—
despair
EXAPOSTELLō 1821
AG:273A CB:1247C
send
EXARTIZō 1822
AG:273C CB:1247C
accomplish
complete
furnish
perfect *Note*
EXASTRAPTō 1823
AG:273D CB:—
dazzling
glister*
EXAUTēS 1824
AG:273D CB:—
forthwith
immediately
presently*
straightway *Note*
EXēCHEō 1837 (-OMAI)
AG:276A CB:—
sound
EXEGEIRō 1825
AG:273D CB:—
raise (up)
EXēGEOMAI 1834
AG:275D CB:1247C
declare
rehearse
tell
EXEIMI 1826
AG:275B (EXESTI) CB:1247C
depart
get, go
EXELENCHō 1827
AG:274A CB:Cf. ELE-(1244A)
convict

EXELKō 1828
AG:274A CB:—
draw
EXERAMA 1829
AG:274B CB:—
vomit
EXERAUNAō 1830
AG:274B CB:1247C (-No)
search
EXERCHOMAI 1831
AG:274B CB:1247C
come
depart
escape *Note*
get
go *Note*
proceed
spread *Note*
EXESTI 1832
AG:275B CB:1247C
lawful
let *Note*
may
EXETAZō 1833
AG:275C CB:—
ask
inquire
search
EXISCHUō 1840
AG:276C CB:—
able *Note*
EXISTēMI 1839
AG:276B CB:1247C (EXHI-)
amaze
beside oneself
bewitch
wonder *Note*
EXō 1854
AG:279B CB:1247C
foreign
forth
outward
strange
without *Note*
EXOCHē 1851
AG:279A CB:—
principal *Note*
EXODOS 1841
AG:276D CB:1247C
decease
departure
EXOLOTHREUō (-OLE-) 1842
AG:276D CB:1247C
destroy
EXOMOLOGEō 1843
AG:277A CB:1247C (EXHO-)
confess
consent
praise
promise *Note*
thank
EXORKISTēS 1845
AG:277B CB:1247C (EXHO-)
exorcist
EXORKIZō 1844
AG:277B CB:1247C (EXHO-)
adjure

EXORUSSō 1846
AG:277C CB:—
break
dig *Note*
pluck
EXōTEROS 1857
AG:280A CB:—
outer
EXōTHEN 1855
AG:279D CB:—
outside
outward
outwardly
without *Note*
EXōTHEō 1856
AG:280A CB:—
drive
thrust *Note*
EXOUDENOō (-Eō) 1847
AG:277C CB:1247C
nought
EXOUSIA 1849
AG:277D CB:1247C
authority
dominion
jurisdiction
liberty
might *Note*
power
right
strength *Note*
EXOUSIAZō 1850
AG:279A CB:1247C
authority
exercise *Note*
power
EXOUTHENEō 1848
AG:277C CB:1247C
account
contemptible*
despise
esteem *Note*
least *Note*
nought
EXUPNIZō 1852
AG:279B CB:—
asleep*
awake
EXUPNOS 1853
AG:279B CB:—
asleep
rouse
sleep*

G

GALA 1051
AG:149C CB:1248A
milk
GALēNē 1055
AG:150B CB:1248A
calm
GAMEō 1060
AG:150D CB:1248A
marry
GAMISKō 1061
AG:151B CB:1248A
marriage (give in)

GAMIZō —
AG:151A CB:1248A
marriage (give in)

GAMOS 1062
AG:151B CB:1248A
feast
marriage
marriage feast
wedding*

GANGRAINA 1044
AG:149A CB:—
canker*
gangrene

GAR 1063
AG:151C CB:1248A
doubt (no) *Note*
indeed
moreover *Note*
verily *Note*
what *Note*, why*
yea*, yet*

GASTēR 1064
AG:152C CB:—
belly
glutton
womb

GAZA 1047
AG:149B CB:—
treasure

GAZOPHULAKION 1049
AG:149B (-EION) CB:1248A
treasury

GE 1065
AG:152D CB:—
yet *Note*

Gē 1093
AG:157C CB:1248A
country *Note*
earth
ground, land
world

GEENNA 1067
AG:153B CB:1248A (GEH-)
hell

GEITōN 1069
AG:153C CB:—
neighbour

GELAō 1070
AG:153C CB:1248A
laugh

GELōS 1071
AG:153C CB:1248A
laughter

GEMIZō 1072
AG:153C CB:1248A
fill
full *Note*

GEMō 1073
AG:153D CB:1248A
full, laden

GENEA 1074
AG:153D CB:1248A
age
generation
nation *Note*
time *Note*

GENEALOGEō 1075
AG:154B CB:1248A
descent*
genealogy

GENEALOGIA 1076
AG:154B CB:1248A
genealogy

GENēMA —
AG:155A CB:—
fruit

GENESIA 1077
AG:154C CB:—
birthday

GENESIS 1078
AG:154D CB:1248A
generation
nature
natural

GENETē 1079
AG:155A CB:—
birth

GENNAō 1080
AG:155B CB:1248A
bear, beget
bring forth
conceive
deliver *Note*
gender*
made (be) *Note*
spring

GENNēMA 1081
AG:155D CB:1248A
fruit *Note*
generation *Note*
offspring

GENNēSIS 1083
AG:156A CB:—
birth

GENNēTOS 1084
AG:156A CB:—
beget

GENOS 1085
AG:156A CB:1248B
beget
country *Note*
countrymen
diversity *Note*
generation *Note*
kind
kindred
nation
offspring
stock*

GEōRGEō 1090
AG:157B CB:—
dress
till

GEōRGION 1091
AG:157B CB:—
husbandry

GEōRGOS 1092
AG:157B CB:—
husbandman

GēRAS 1094
AG:157D CB:1248B (GēRōN)
aged
old

GēRASKō 1095
AG:158A CB:1248B
aged
old

GERōN 1088
AG:157A CB:1248B
old

GEROUSIA 1087
AG:156D CB:1248B
senate

GEUō (-OMAI) 1089
AG:157A CB:1248B
eat
taste

GINOMAI 1096
AG:158A CB:1248B
arise
assemble *Note*
become *Note*
befall, behave
being
bring *Note*
come
continue
divide
do, draw
end *Note*
fall
far *Note*
finish
follow
forbid *Note*
fulfill *Note*
grow, have
keep *Note*
made (be) *Note*
marry *Note*
means (by ... of) *Note*
ordain *Note*
pass *Note*
past
perform *Note*
place (take)
prefer *Note*
prove *Note*
publish
shew *Note*
sound, spent
spring
take, turn
use *Note*
was (etc.) *Note*
wax, work

GINōSKō 1097
AG:160D CB:1248B
allow, can
feel
know
knowledge
learn
perceive
resolve
speak *Note*
sure *Note*
understand

GLEUKOS 1098
AG:162A CB:1248B
wine

GLōSSA 1100
AG:162B CB:1248B
tongue

GLōSSOKOMON 1101
AG:162D CB:1248B
bag

GLUKUS 1099
AG:162A CB:1248B
fresh *Note*
sweet

GNAPHEUS 1102
AG:162D CB:—
fuller

GNēSIOS 1103
AG:162D CB:1248B
own *Note*
sincerity
true

GNēSIōS 1104
AG:163A CB:—
naturally *Note*
truly

GNōMē 1106
AG:163A CB:1248B
advice, agree
judgment
mind
purpose
will *Note*

GNOPHOS 1105
AG:163A CB:—
blackness

GNōRIZō 1107
AG:163B CB:1248B
certify *Note*
declare *Note*
know
understand
wit, wot *Note*

GNōSIS 1108
AG:163D CB:1248B
knowledge
science

GNōSTēS 1109
AG:164A CB:—
expert

GNōSTOS 1110
AG:164B CB:1248B
acquaitance
known
notable

GOēS 1114
AG:164D CB:1248C
impostor
seducer *Note*

GOMOS 1117
AG:164D CB:—
burden
merchandise

GONEUS 1118
AG:165A CB:—
parents

GONGUSMOS 1112
AG:164C CB:—
grudging
murmuring

GONGUSTēS 1113
AG:164C CB:—
murmurer
GONGUZō 1111
AG:164B CB:—
murmur
GōNIA 1137
AG:168D CB:1248C
corner
quarter *Note*
GONU 1119
AG:165A CB:1248C
knee
kneel
GONUPETEō 1120
AG:165B CB:1248C
bow
kneel
GRAMMA 1121
AG:165B CB:1248C
bill
bond
learning
letter
scripture
writing
GRAMMATEUS 1122
AG:165D CB:1248C
lawyer
scribe
townclerk
GRAōDēS 1126
AG:167B CB:—
old wives
GRAPHē 1124
AG:166A CB:1248C
scripture
GRAPHō 1125
AG:166C CB:1248C
describe
write
writing
GRAPTOS 1123
AG:166A CB:1248C
written
GRēGOREō 1127
AG:167B CB:1248C
vigilant*
wake
watch, -ful
GUMNASIA 1129
AG:167D CB:1248C
exercise
GUMNAZō 1128
AG:167C CB:1248C
exercise
GUMNITEUō 1130 (GUMNē-)
AG:167D CB:—
naked
GUMNOS 1131
AG:167D CB:1248C
bare
naked
GUMNOTēS 1132
AG:168A CB:1248C
nakedness

GUNAIKARION 1133
AG:168B CB:1248C
woman
GUNAIKEIOS 1134
AG:168B CB:1248C
wife
GUNē 1135
AG:168B CB:1248C
wife
woman

H

HADēS 86
AG:16D CB:1248C
Hades
hell *Note*
HADROTēS 100
AG:18D CB:—
abundance
bounty
HAGIASMOS 38
AG:9A CB:1249A
holiness
sanctification
HAGIAZO 37
AG:8C CB:1249A
beloved *Note*
hallow
holy
sanctify
HAGION 39
AG:9B (-OS 2a.) CB:—
sanctuary
HAGIOS 40
AG:9B CB:1249A
holy
saint
sanctuary
HAGIōSUNē 42
AG:10B CB:1249A
holiness
sanctification
HAGIOTēS 41
AG:10B CB:1249A
holiness
HAGNEIA 47
AG:10D CB:1249A
purity
HAGNISMOS 49
AG:11A CB:1249A
purification
HAGNIZō 48
AG:11A CB:1249A
purify
HAGNOS 53
AG:11D CB:1249A
chaste
clear *Note*
pure
HAGNōS 55
AG:12A CB:1249A
sincerely
HAGNOTēS 54
AG:12A CB:1249A
pureness
purity

HAIMA 129
AG:22C CB:1249A
blood
HAIMATEKCHUSIA 130
AG:23B CB:1249A
blood
HAIMORRHOEō 131
AG:23C CB:—
blood
HAIREō 138 (-OMAI)
AG:24A CB:1249A
choose
HAIRESIS 139
AG:23D CB:1249A
heresy
sect
HAIRETIKOS 141
AG:24A CB:1249A
faction
heretical
HAIRETIZō 140
AG:24A CB:1249A
choose
HALIEUō 232
AG:37D CB:—
fish
HALIEUS 231
AG:37C CB:—
fisher
fisherman
HALIZō 233
AG:37D CB:1249A
salt
HALLēLOUIA 239
AG:39C CB:1249A
Hallelujah
HALLOMAI 242
AG:39D CB:1249A
leap
spring
HALōN 257
AG:41D CB:1249A
threshing-floor
HALōSIS 259
AG:42A CB:1249A
take *Note*
HALAS 217
AG:35A CB:1249A
salt
HALS 251
AG:41B CB:1249A
salt
HALUKOS 252
AG:41B CB:1249A
salt
HALUSIS 254
AG:41C CB:—
bond
chain
HAMA 260
AG:42A CB:1249A
early *Note*
together
withal

HAMARTANō 264
AG:42B CB:1249A
fault *Note*
offend *Note*
sin
trespass
HAMARTēMA 265
AG:42D CB:1249B
sin
HAMARTIA 266
AG:43A CB:1249B
offence *Note*
sin, sinful*
HAMARTōLOS 268
AG:44A CB:1249B
sinful
sinner
transgressor *Note*
HAPALOS 527
AG:80B CB:—
tender
HAPAS 537
AG:81D CB:1249B
all, every
whole
HAPAX 530
AG:80C CB:1249B
once
HAPHē 860
AG:125A CB:1249B
joint
HAPLOUS 573
AG:86A CB:1249B
single
HAPLōS 574
AG:86B CB:1249B
liberally
HAPLOTēS 572
AG:85D CB:1249B
bountifulness
liberal, -ity
simplicity*
singleness
HAPTō 681
AG:102D CB:1249B
handle
kindle, light
touch
HARMA 716
AG:107B CB:1249B
chariot
HARMOS 719
AG:107D CB:1249B
joint
HARMOZō 718
AG:107C CB:1249B
espouse
HARPAGē 724
AG:108B CB:1249B
extortion
ravening
spoiling
HARPAGMOS 725
AG:108C CB:1249B
prize
robbery*

HARPAX 727
AG:109B CB:1249B
extortioner
ravening
HARPAZō 726
AG:109A CB:1249B
catch
force
pluck
pull *Note*
snatch
spoil
take *Note*
HEAUTOU (etc.) 1438
AG:211D CB:1249B (-OS)
alone *Note*
conceits
herself*
he himself
his, his own
itself*
one ... another *Note*
our own
ourselves *Note*
own *Note*
their *Note*
them *Note*
themselves *Note*
they *Note*
thyself
ye *Note*
yourselves*
HEBDOMēKONTA 1440
AG:212D CB:1249B
seventy
ten *Note*
HEBDOMēKONTAKIS 1441
AG:213A CB:Cf. -TA (1249B)
seventy times
HEBDOMOS 1442
AG:213A CB:—
seventh
HEBRAISTI (EBR-) 1447
AG:213C CB:1249C
tongue
(in Hebrew)
(in the Hebrew)
HēDEōS 2234
AG:343D CB:1249C
gladly
HēDISTA 2236
AG:343D (HēDEōS) CB:—
gladly
HēDONē 2237
AG:344B CB:1249C
lust
pleasure
HEDRAIōMA 1477
AG:218A CB:1249C
ground
HEDRAIOS 1476
AG:217D CB:1249C
settled *Note*
stedfast
HēDUOSMON 2238
AG:344B CB:1249C
mint

HēGEMōN 2232
AG:343B CB:1249C
governor
prince
ruler *Note*
HēGEMONEUō 2230
AG:343A CB:—
governor
HēGEMONIA 2231
AG:343A CB:1249C
reign *Note*
HēGEOMAI 2233
AG:343C CB:1249C
account
chief
count
esteem
governor
guide *Note*
judge *Note*
rule
speaker (chief) *Note*
suppose *Note*
think
HEILISSō (HEL-) 1507 (1667)
AG:251B CB:—
fold*
roll
HEIS 1520
AG:230D CB:1249C
each
first
one
only *Note*
other
HEKASTOS 1538
AG:236C CB:1249C
each
every
one *Note*
HEKASTOTE 1539
AG:236D CB:—
always
time*
HEKATON 1540
AG:236D CB:—
hundred
hundredfold
HEKATONTAETēS 1541
AG:236D CB:—
year
HEKATONTAPLASIōN 1542
AG:237A CB:—
hundredfold
HEKATONTARCHēS 1543
AG:237A CB:1249C
centurion
HEKATONTARCHOS 1543
AG:237A CB:1249C
centurion
HēKō 2240
AG:344C CB:1249C
come
HEKōN 1635
AG:247D CB:—
will
willingly *Note*

HEKOUSIOS 1595 (-ON)
AG:243B CB:—
will
willingly
HEKOUSIōS 1596
AG:243C CB:—
wilfully
willingly *Note*
HEKTOS 1623
AG:246A CB:—
sixth
HēLIKIA 2244
AG:345A CB:1249C
age
stature *Note*
HēLIKOS 2245
AG:345C CB:—
great
HēLIOS 2246
AG:345C CB:1249C
sun
HELKō (-KUō) 1670
AG:251C CB:—
drag, draw
HELKOō 1669
AG:251C CB:—
sore
HELKOS 1668
AG:251C CB:—
sore
HELLēN 1672
AG:251D CB:1249C
Gentiles
HELLēNISTI 1676
AG:252B CB:1249C
tongue *Note*
HēLOS 2247
AG:345D CB:—
nail
HēMEIS (etc.) 2249
AG:217A (EGo) CB:—
company *Note*
our *Note*
ourselves *Note*
us, we
HēMERA 2250
AG:345D CB:1249C
age
always *Note*
daily *Note*
day
ever
judgment
midday
next *Note*
next day
tomorrow
time *Note*
year *Note*
HēMETEROS 2251
AG:347D CB:1250A
our *Note*
ours *Note*
HēMIōRON 2256
AG:348A CB:—
hour *Note*

HēMISUS 2255 (-SU)
AG:348A CB:—
half
HēMITHANēS 2253
AG:348A CB:—
(half) dead
HENDEKA 1733
AG:262D CB:—
eleven
HENDEKATOS 1734
AG:262D CB:—
eleventh
HENEKA 1752
AG:264D CB:1250A
cause
wherefore *Note*
HENOTēS 1775
AG:267C CB:1250A
unity
HEORTAZō 1858
AG:280A CB:1250A
feast
HEORTē 1859
AG:280B CB:1250A
feast
holy day
HEōS 2193
AG:334B CB:1250A
far *Note*
hitherto
much (as) *Note*
while *Note*
HEPTA 2033
AG:306B CB:1250A
seven, seventh
HEPTAKIS 2034
AG:306B CB:1250A
seven times
HEPTAKISCHILIOI 2035
AG:306C CB:—
seven
thousand *Note*
HERMēNEIA 2058
AG:310A CB:1250A
interpretation
HERMēNEUō 2059
AG:310A CB:1250A
interpret
interpretation
HERPETON 2062
AG:310B CB:—
creeping
serpent
HESPERA 2073
AG:313C CB:—
evening
eventide
HESPERINOS —
AG:313C CB:—
evening *Note*
HeSSoN (See HeTTōN)
HēSUCHAZō 2270
AG:349A CB:1250A
cease
peace (hold one's)
quiet, rest

HēSUCHIA 2271
AG:349B CB:1250A
quietness
silence *Note*
HēSUCHIOS 2272
AG:349C CB:1250A
peaceable *Note*
quiet
HETAIROS 2083
AG:314C CB:1250A
fellow
friend
HETERODIDASKALEō 2085
AG:314D CB:1250A
teach
HETEROGLōSSOS 2084
AG:314D CB:1250A
strange *Note*
tongue
HETEROS 2087
AG:315A CB:1250A
another
different
neighbour *Note*
next day *Note*
one *Note*
one another *Note*
other
strange *Note*
stranger *Note*
HETERōS 2088
AG:315C CB:1250A
otherwise
HETEROZUGEō 2086
AG:314D CB:1250A
another
yoke
HETOIMASIA 2091
AG:316C CB:1250B
preparation
HETOIMAZō 2090
AG:316A CB:1250B
hold *Note*
prepare
provide
ready
HETOIMOS 2092
AG:316C CB:1250B
prepared *Note*
readiness
ready
HETOIMōS 2093
AG:316D CB:—
ready
HēTTAOMAI 2274 (-Oō)
AG:349C CB:—
defect *Note*
inferior
overcome
HēTTēMA 2275
AG:349C CB:1250B
defect
diminishing
fault *Note*
inferior
loss

HēTTōN 2276
AG:349A (HēSSōN) CB:—
defect *Note*
inferior
less, worse
HEURISKō 2147
AG:324D CB:1250B
find, get
obtain
perceive *Note*
HEX 1803
AG:271B CB:1250B
six
HEXAKOSIOI 1812
AG:272B CB:—
six hundred *Note*
HEXēKONTA 1835
AG:276B CB:—
sixty, sixtyfold
HEXēS 1836
AG:276A CB:—
afterwards
follow *Note*
morrow *Note*
next
HEXIS 1838
AG:276B CB:1250B
use
HIDRōS 2402
AG:371C CB:—
sweat
HIERATEIA 2405
AG:371D CB:1250B
office
priesthood
priest's office
HIERATEUMA 2406
AG:371D CB:1250B
priesthood
HIERATEUō 2407
AG:371D CB:1250B
execute
office
priest's office
HIERATIKOS (ARCHI-) 748
AG:112D CB:1250B
priest *Note*
HIEREUS 2409
AG:372A CB:1250B
priest
HIERON 2411
AG:372B CB:1250B
temple
HIEROPREPēS 2412
AG:372D CB:1250B
become
holiness *Note*
reverent
HIEROS 2413
AG:372D CB:1250B
holy *Note*
sacred
HIEROSULEō 2416
AG:373C CB:1250B
commit *Note*
sacrilege*

HIEROSULOS 2417
AG:373C CB:1250C
robber
HIERōSUNē 2420
AG:373C CB:1250C
priesthood
HIEROTHUTOS —
AG:372B CB:1250C
idols (sacrificed to)
HIEROURGEō 2418
AG:373C CB:1250C
minister
HIKANOō 2427
AG:374D CB:1250C
able *Note*
meet
sufficient
HIKANOS 2425
AG:374B CB:1250C
able
content
enough
good *Note*
great
large
long
many
meet
much
security
sore
sufficient
while *Note*
worthy
HIKANOTēS 2426
AG:374D CB:1250C
sufficiency
HIKETēRIA 2428
AG:375A CB:1250C
supplication
HILAROS 2431
AG:375B CB:1250C
cheerful
HILAROTēS 2432
AG:375B CB:—
cheerfulness
HILASKOMAI 2433
AG:375C CB:1250C
merciful
propitiation
reconciliation*
HILASMOS 2434
AG:375C CB:1250C
propitiation
HILASTēRION 2435
AG:375D CB:1250C
mercy-seat
propitiation
HILEōS 2436
AG:376A CB:1250C
far *Note*
merciful
HIMAS 2438
AG:376B CB:—
latchet
thong*

HIMATION 2440
AG:376B CB:1250C
apparel
clothes
garment
raiment *Note*
robe
vesture
HIMATISMOS 2441
AG:376D CB:—
apparel
array*
clothing
raiment *Note*
vesture
HIMATIZō 2439
AG:376B CB:Cf. -ION (1250C)
clothe
HIMEIROMAI 2442
AG:565B (HOM-) CB:—
affection *Note*
desire
HINA 2443
AG:376D CB:1250C
albeit
end *Note*
intent, lest
must *Note*
wherefore *Note*
HIPPEUS 2460
AG:380C CB:—
horsemen
HIPPIKOS 2461 (-ON)
AG:380C CB:1250C
horsemen
HIPPOS 2462
AG:380C CB:1250C
horse
HISTēMI 2476
AG:381D CB:1250C
abide
appoint
bring *Note*
charge *Note*
continue *Note*
covenant *Note*
establish
holden *Note*
present *Note*
set, stand
stanch
weigh
HISTOREō 2477
AG:383A CB:1251A
see *Note*
visit
HO 3588
AG:549B CB:—
concern (-eth)
one (the) *Note*
this *Note*
which *Note*
HODE (TODE) 3592
AG:553A CB:—
manner *Note*
these*
thus *Note*

HōDE 5602
AG:895B CB:—
here
hither
place
there *Note*
HODēGEō 3594
AG:553B CB:1251A
guide
lead
HODēGOS 3595
AG:553C CB:1251A
guide
leader*
HODEUō 3593
AG:553B CB:—
journey
HODOIPOREō 3596
AG:553D CB:1251A
go *Note*
journey
HODOIPORIA 3597
AG:553D CB:—
journey
journeyings
HODOS 3598
AG:553D CB:1251A
highway
highwayside
journey
way
HOIOS 3634
AG:562C CB:1251A
manner
such as *Note*
what *Note*
which *Note*
HOLOKAUTōMA 3646
AG:564B CB:1251A
burnt (offering)
offering
HOLOKLēRIA 3647
AG:564C CB:—
entire *Note*
soundness
HOLOKLēROS 3648
AG:564C CB:—
all *Note*
entire
whole
HOLOS 3650
AG:564D CB:1251A
all
altogether
every whit
whole
HOLōS 3654
AG:565B CB:1251A
actually
all
altogether
commonly *Note*
utterly*
HOLOTELēS 3651
AG:565A CB:—
all *Note*
wholly

HOMEIROMAI (see HIMEIROMAI)
HOMICHLē —
AG:565D CB:1251A
mist
HOMILEō 3656
AG:565C CB:—
commune
talk
HOMILIA 3657
AG:565C CB:—
communication *Note*
company
HOMILOS 3658
AG:565D CB:—
company
HOMOIAZō 3662
AG:566C CB:—
agree *Note*
HOMOIōMA 3667
AG:567C CB:1251A
like (made)*
image
likeness
shape
similitude *Note*
HOMOIOō 3666
AG:567B CB:1251A
like (make)
liken
resemble*
HOMOIOPATHēS 3663
AG:566C CB:1251A
passions
HOMOIOS 3664
AG:566D CB:1251A
like
HOMOIōS 3668
AG:567D CB:1251A
likewise
manner
so *Note*
HOMOIōSIS 3669
AG:568A CB:1251A
likeness
similtude *Note*
HOMOIOTēS 3665
AG:567A CB:1251A
like as *Note*
likeness
similtude *Note*
HOMOLOGEō 3670
AG:568A CB:1251A
acknowledge *Note*
confess
profess
promise
thanks
vouchsafe
HOMOLOGIA 3671
AG:568D CB:1251A
confession
profession
professed
HOMOLOGOUMENōS 3672
AG:569A CB:—
controversy (without)

HOMOPHRōN 3675
AG:569C CB:—
likeminded
mind
one *Note*
HOMōS 3676
AG:569C CB:—
even, yet*
HOMOTECHNOS 3673
AG:569B CB:—
craft
trade *Note*
HOMOTHUMADON 3661
AG:566C CB:1251A
accord
mind *Note*
HOMOU 3674
AG:569B CB:1251A (-OIOS)
accord *Note*
together
HOPLIZō 3695
AG:575C CB:1251A
arm
HOPLON 3696
AG:575C CB:1251A
armour
instruments
weapons
HOPOIOS 3697
AG:575D CB:—
manner, sort
such as *Note*
what *Note*
HOPOU 3699
AG:576A CB:—
thither
HōRA 5610
AG:896A CB:1251A
day*
hour
instant *Note*
season
short *Note*
time
HōRAIOS 5611
AG:896D CB:1251A
beautiful
HORAMA 3705
AG:577B CB:1251A
sight
vision
HORAō 3708
(with EIDON and OPTOMAI)
AG:577D CB:1251A
appear
behold
consider
heed (take)
look, look to
perceive
see
shew *Note*
HORASIS 3706
AG:577C CB:1251A
look
sight *Note*
vision

HORATOS 3707
AG:577C CB:1251A
visible
HORION 3725
AG:581B CB:1251B
border
coast
HORIZō 3724
AG:580D CB:1251B
appoint
declare
define
determine
determinate
limit*
ordain
HORKIZō 3726
AG:581B CB:1251B
adjure
charge *Note*
HORKōMOSIA 3728
AG:581D CB:1251B
oath
HORKOS 3727
AG:581C CB:1251B
oath
HORMAō 3729
AG:581D CB:—
run *Note*
rush
violently *Note*
HORMē 3730
AG:581D CB:1251B
assault
impulse
HORMēMA 3731
AG:581D CB:—
violence
HOROTHESIA 3734
AG:582A CB:—
bound
HOS 3739
AG:583B CB:—
he that
one
one ... another *Note*
what *Note*
whatsoever *Note*
which *Note*
who *Note*
whosoever*
HōS 5613
AG:897A CB:1251B
about
according as
even as
like
so *Note*
well (as) *Note*
wit (to)
while *Note*
HOSAKIS 3740
AG:585B CB:1251B
oft, often
HōSANNA 5614
AG:899A CB:1251B
Hosanna

HōSAUTōS 5615
AG:899B CB:—
even so *Note*
likewise
manner
so *Note*
HōSEI 5616
AG:899B CB:—
about
like *Note*
HOSGE —
AG:583B I.10b. CB:—
he that
HOSIOS 3741
AG:585C CB:1251B
blessing *Note*
holy
mercy*
HOSIōS 3743
AG:585D CB:—
holily
HOSIOTēS 3742
AG:585D CB:1251B
holiness
HOSOS 3745
AG:586B CB:1251B
all
great
inasmuch as
long
many, more
much (as) *Note*
what *Note*
whatsoever *Note*
which *Note*
who *Note*
whosoever*
HOSPER 3746
AG:583B I.10e. CB:—
whosoever *Note*
HōSPER 5618
AG:899C CB:1251B
even as
like as
HōSTE 5620
AG:899D CB:—
as*
insomuch that
wherefore *Note*
HOSTIS 3748
AG:586D CB:—
he that *Note*
such as *Note*
they *Note*
what *Note*
which *Note*
who *Note*
whosoever*
HOTAN 3752
AG:587D CB:—
while *Note*
HOTE 3753
AG:588B CB:1251B
while *Note*
HOTI 3754
AG:588C CB:1251B
Notes p. 1264

HOTHEN 3606
AG:555C CB:—
thence (from) *Note*
wherefore *Note*
HOUTOS 3778
AG:596B CB:1251B
fellow *Note*
he, hereby
herein, hereof
hereunto
one *Note*
same, she*
so *Note*
that*
their *Note*
them *Note*
thenceforth *Note*
therein *Note*
they *Note*
thing *Note*
this *Note*
thus *Note*
which *Note*
who *Note*
HOUTō(-S) 3779
AG:597C CB:—
even so
fashion
like *Note*
likewise *Note*
manner
no more *Note*
so *Note*
thus
what *Note*
HUAKINTHINOS 5191
AG:831B CB:—
jacinth
HUAKINTHOS 5192
AG:831B CB:1251B
jacinth
HUALINOS 5193
AG:831D CB:1251B
glass
HUALOS 5194
AG:831D CB:—
glass
HUBRIS 5196
AG:832A CB:1251B
harm, hurt
injury
reproach *Note*
HUBRISTēS 5197
AG:832A CB:1251C
despiteful *Note*
injurious
insolent
HUBRIZō 5195
AG:831D CB:1251C
despitefully *Note*
entreat*
reproach
shamefully *Note*
spitefully
HUDōR 5204
AG:832D CB:1251C
water

HUDRIA 5201
AG:832C CB:—
waterpot
HUDRōPIKOS 5203
AG:832D CB:—
dropsy
HUDROPOTEō 5202
AG:832D CB:—
drink
water *Note*
HUETOS 5202
AG:833B CB:1251C
rain
HUGIAINō 5198
AG:832B CB:1251C
health
safe, sound
sound (be)
whole
wholesome
HUGIēS 5199
AG:832C CB:1251C
sound
whole
HUGROS 5200
AG:832C CB:1251C
green
HUIOS 5207
AG:833C CB:1251C
child
foal
son
HUIOTHESIA 5206
AG:833B CB:1251C
adoption
children *Note*
HULē 5208
AG:836A CB:1251C
matter *Note*
wood
HUMEIS 5210
AG:772A (SU) CB:—
ye *Note*
you*
your *Note*
HUMETEROS 5212
AG:836A CB:—
your *Note*
yours *Note*
HUMNEō 5214
AG:836B CB:1251C
hymn
praise
sing
HUMNOS 5215
AG:836B CB:1251C
hymn
HUPAGō 5217
AG:836C CB:—
depart
get, go
HUPAKOē 5218
AG:837A CB:1251C
obedience
obedient
obey

HUPAKOUō 5219
AG:837B CB:1251C
answer *Note*
hearken *Note*
obedient
obey
HUPANDROS 5220
AG:837C CB:—
husband
HUPANTAō 5221
AG:837D CB:1252A
meet
HUPANTēSIS 5222
AG:837D CB:1252A
meet
HUPARCHō 5225
AG:838A CB:—
being
exist
goods *Note*
have
live
possess
was (etc.) *Note*
HUPARCHONTA 5224
AG:838A (-CHō) CB:1252A
substance
HUPARXIS 5223
AG:837D CB:1252A
goods
possession
substance
HUPECHō 5254
AG:842B CB:—
suffer
HUPEIKō 5226
AG:838B CB:—
submit
HUPēKOOS 5255
AG:842B CB:1252A
obedient
HUPENANTIOS 5227
AG:838B CB:1252A (-ION)
adversary
contrary
HUPER 5228
AG:838B CB:1252A
behalf
beyond
more
of *Note*
part *Note*
Notes p. 1269
HUPERAIRō 5229 (-OMAI)
AG:839D CB:—
exalt
overmuch *Note*
HUPERAKMOS 5230
AG:839D CB:1252A
age
flower
pass *Note*
HUPERAUXANō 5232
AG:840A CB:1252A
grow

HUPERBAINō 5233
AG:840A CB:1252A
go *Note*
transgress

HUPERBALLō 5235
AG:840B CB:—
abundance *Note*
exceed
excel
pass
surpass*

HUPERBALLONTōS 5234
AG:840A CB:—
abundantly *Note*
measure

HUPERBOLē 5236
AG:840B CB:—
abundance
exceeding
excel
excellency
excellent
far *Note*
greatness
measure*

HUPERECHō 5242
AG:840D CB:1252A
better (be)
excellency
higher
pass
supreme

HUPEREIDON 5237
AG:841D (-RORAō) CB:—
overlook
wink*

HUPEREKCHU(N)Nō 5240
AG:840D CB:—
run

HUPEREKEINA 5238
AG:840C CB:—
beyond *Note*

HUPEREKPERISSOU After 5240
AG:840C CB:1252A
abundantly
exceeding
exceedingly

HUPEREKTEINō 5239
AG:840D CB:—
beyond *Note*
measure *Note*
overmuch *Note*
stretch

HUPERENTUNCHANō 5241
AG:840D CB:1252A
intercession

HUPERēPHANIA 5243
AG:841A CB:1252A
pride

HUPERēPHANOS 5244
AG:841B CB:1252A
haughty
proud

HUPēRETEō 5256
AG:842C CB:1252A
minister
serve

HUPēRETēS 5257
AG:842C CB:1252A
attendant
deacon *Note*
minister
officer
servant

HUPERLIAN After 5244
AG:841B CB:—
chiefest

HUPERNIKAō 5245
AG:841C CB:1252A
conquer

HUPEROCHē 5247
AG:841D CB:—
authority
excellency
place

HUPERONKOS 5246
AG:841C CB:—
swelling

HUPERōON 5253
AG:842B CB:—
chamber
room *Note*

HUPERPERISSEUō 5248
AG:841D CB:1252A
abound
joyful *Note*
overflow

HUPERPERISSōS 5249
AG:842A CB:1252A
abundantly *Note*
measure

HUPERPHRONEō 5252
AG:842A CB:1252A
think

HUPERPLEONAZō 5250
AG:842A CB:1252A
abundant

HUPERUPSOō 5251
AG:842A CB:1252A
exalt

HUPHANTOS 5307
AG:849D CB:—
woven

HUPNOS 5258
AG:843A CB:1252A
asleep
sleep*

HUPO 5259
AG:843A CB:1252A
of *Note*
under *Note*
Notes p. 1271

HUPOBALLō 5260
AG:843D CB:—
suborn

HUPOCHōREō 5298
AG:848C CB:—
go
withdraw

HUPODECHOMAI 5264
AG:844B CB:—
receive

HUPODEIGMA 5262
AG:844A CB:1252B
copy
ensample
example
pattern

HUPODEIKNUMI 5263
AG:844B CB:—
example
forewarn *Note*
shew, warn

HUPODēMA 5266
AG:844C CB:—
shoe

HUPODEō 5265
AG:844B CB:Cf. DEō (1240C)
bind, shod*

HUPODIKOS 5267
AG:844C CB:—
guilty *Note*
judgment

HUPOGRAMMOS 5261
AG:843D CB:1252B
copy
example

HUPOKATō 5270
AG:844D CB:—
under, -neath

HUPOKRINOMAI 5271
AG:845A CB:1252B
feign

HUPOKRISIS 5272
AG:845A CB:1252B
dissimulation
hypocrisy

HUPOKRITēS 5273
AG:845B CB:1252B
hypocrite

HUPOLAMBANō 5274
AG:845B CB:1252B
answer
receive
suppose
welcome

HUPOLEIMMA —
AG:845C CB:1252B
remnant

HUPOLEIPō 5275
AG:845C CB:1252B
leave

HUPOLēNION 5276
AG:845C CB:—
wine-fat
pit

HUPOLIMPANō 5277
AG:845D CB:—
leave

HUPOMENō 5278
AG:845D CB:1252B
abide
behind
endure
patient, -ly
suffer *Note*
take *Note*
tarry

HUPOMIMNēSKō 5279
AG:846A CB:1252B
mind
remember
remembrance

HUPOMNēSIS 5280
AG:846B CB:1252B
remembrance

HUPOMONē 5281
AG:846B CB:1252B
continuance*
enduring
forbearance *Note*
patience
patient
wait *Note*

HUPONOEō 5282
AG:846D CB:—
deem
suppose
surmise*
think

HUPONOIA 5283
AG:846D CB:—
surmising*

HUPOPHERō 5297
AG:848C CB:Cf. PHERō (1264A)
bear
endure

HUPōPIAZō 5299
AG:848D CB:1252B
buffet
wear
weary *Note*

HUPOPLEō 5284
AG:846D CB:—
lee, sail

HUPOPNEō 5285
AG:846D CB:—
blow

HUPOPODION 5286
AG:846D CB:—
footstool

HUPOSTASIS 5287
AG:847A CB:1252B
assurance
boast *Note*
confidence
person *Note*
substance

HUPOSTELLō 5288
AG:847B CB:—
draw (back)
keep *Note*
shrink*, shun*
withdraw

HUPOSTOLē 5289
AG:847C CB:1252B
draw (back)

HUPOSTREPHō 5290
AG:847C CB:—
come*
return
turn

HUPOSTRōNNUō 5291 (-UMI)
AG:847C CB:—
spread

HUPOTAGē 5292
AG:847D CB:1252B
obedience
subjection
way *Note*
HUPOTASSō 5293
AG:847D CB:1252B (-OMAI)
obedience *Note*
obedient *Note*
put *Note*
subdue *Note*
subject
submit *Note*
HUPOTITHēMI 5294
AG:848B CB:—
lay, mind
remembrance *Note*
HUPOTRECHō 5295
AG:848B CB:—
lee
run
HUPOTUPōSIS 5296
AG:848C CB:1252B
ensample
figure *Note*
form
pattern
HUPOZōNNUMI 5269
AG:844D CB:—
undergird
HUPOZUGION 5268
AG:844C CB:—
ass
HUPSēLOPHRONEō 5309
AG:850A CB:1252B
high-minded
HUPSēLOS 5308
AG:849B CB:1252B
exalt
high, highly
HUPSISTOS 5310
AG:850B CB:1252B
high, highest
HUPSōMA 5313
AG:851C CB:1252B
height, high
HUPSOō 5312
AG:850 CB:1252B
exalt
lift
HUPSOS 5311
AG:850C CB:1252B
estate
height, high
HUS 5300
AG:848D CB:1252B
sow
HUSSōPOS 5301
AG:849A CB:—
hyssop
HUSTERēMA 5303
AG:849B CB:1252B
behind
lacking
penury*
want
HUSTEREō 5302
AG:849A CB:1252B
behind, come
destitute
fail *Note*
fall, lack
need *Note*
short (come) *Note*
want, worse
HUSTERēSIS 5304
AG:849C CB:1252B
want
HUSTERON 5305
AG:849C CB:1252B
afterward(-s)
last
HUSTEROS 5306
AG:849C CB:1252B
later
latter *Note*

I

IAMA 2386
AG:368A CB:1252C
healing
IAOMAI 2390
AG:368B CB:1252C
heal, whole
IASIS 2392
AG:368C CB:1252C
cure
heal, -ing
IASPIS 2393
AG:368D CB:1252C
jasper
IATROS 2395
AG:368D CB:1252C
physician
ICHNOS 2487
AG:384B CB:—
step
ICHTHUDION 2485
AG:384B CB:1252C
fish
ICHTHUS 2486
AG:384B CB:1252C
fish
IDE 2396
AG:369B CB:1252C
behold
lo, see *Note*
IDEA (See EIDEA)
IDIOS 2398
AG:369C CB:1252C
acquaintance
alone *Note*
apart *Note*
business
company, due
his, his own
home *Note*
our own
own *Note*
private, -ly
proper
several, -ly
their *Note*
IDIōTēS 2399
AG:370C CB:1252C
ignorant
rude
unlearned *Note*
IDOU 2400
AG:370D CB:1252C
behold
lo, see *Note*
IēSOUS 2424
AG:373D CB:1252C
Jesus
IKMAS 2429 (HI-)
AG:375A CB:—
moisture
IOS 2447
AG:378D CB:1252C
poison
rust
IōTA 2503
AG:386A CB:1252C
jot
IOUDAIKOS 2451
AG:379B CB:1252C
Jewish
IOUDAIKōS 2452
AG:379B CB:1252C
Jew (as do the)
IOUDAIOS 2453
AG:379B CB:1252C
Jew(s)
Jewess
Jewish
Jewry
IOUDAISMOS 2454
AG:379D CB:1252C
Jews' religion
IOUDAIZō 2450
AG:379B CB:1252C
Jews (live as do the)
IRIS 2463
AG:380C CB:1253A
rainbow
ISANGELOS 2465
AG:380D CB:1253A
angel *Note*
ISCHUō 2480
AG:383D CB:1253A
able
avail
can, could
do
good *Note*
may *Note*
might*
prevail
strength
whole
work *Note*
ISCHUROS 2478
AG:383A CB:1253A
able *Note*
boisterous
mighty
powerful
strong
valiant*
ISCHUROTEROS (-UROS) 2478
AG:383A 1.a. CB:1253A
mightier
stronger
ISCHUS 2479
AG:383C CB:1253A
ability
dominion *Note*
might
power
strength
ISOPSUCHOS 2473
AG:381B CB:1253A
equal *Note*
likeminded
soul *Note*
ISOS 2470
AG:381A CB:1253A
agree
equal, like
much (as) *Note*
ISōS 2481
AG:384A CB:—
may
ISOTēS 2471
AG:381B CB:1253A
equal, -ity
ISOTIMOS 2472
AG:381B CB:1253A
equal *Note*
precious

K

KAI 2532
AG:391D CB:1253A
also, even
indeed
(at) least *Note*
likewise
manner *Note*
moreover
very *Note*
yea, yet *Note*
Notes p. 1263
KAIGE 2534
AG:152D (GE 3.c.) CB:—
(at) least *Note*
KAINOS 2537
AG:394A CB:1253A
new
KAINOTēS 2538
AG:394C CB:1253A
newness
KAIō 2545
AG:396B CB:1253A
burn
light
KAIPER 2539
AG:394C CB:—
yet*
KAIROS 2540
AG:394D CB:1253A
always *Note*
opportunity
season
time
while *Note*

KAKIA 2549
AG:397A CB:1253A
evil
malice
maliciousness
naughtiness*
wickedness

KAKOēTHEIA 2550
AG:397B CB:—
malignity

KAKOLOGEō 2551
AG:397B CB:1253B
curse
evil
speak

KAKOō 2559
AG:398B CB:1253B
affect
afflict
entreat*
evil
harm, hurt
vex *Note*

KAKOPATHEIA 2552
AG:397B CB:1253B
affliction
suffering *Note*

KAKOPATHEō 2553
AG:397C CB:1253B
afflict
endure *Note*
hardship
suffer*

KAKOPOIEō 2554
AG:397C CB:1253B
evil
harm

KAKOPOIOS 2555
AG:397C CB:1253B
evil-doer
malefactor

KAKOS 2556
AG:397D CB:1253B
bad, evil
harm, ill
miserable
noisome
wicked *Note*

KAKōS 2560
AG:398C CB:1253B
amiss
diseased
evil
grievously
miserably
sick *Note*
sore*

KAKōSIS 2561
AG:398C CB:1253B
affliction

KAKOUCHEō 2558
AG:398B CB:—
afflict
entreat
evil
suffer
torment

KAKOURGO 2557
AG:398B CB:1253B
doer *Note*
evil-doer *Note*
malefactor

KALAMē 2562
AG:398C CB:—
stubble

KALAMOS 2563
AG:398B CB:1253B
pen
reed

KALEō 2564
AG:398D CB:1253B
bid
call
name
surname *Note*

KALLIELAIOS 2565
AG:400A CB:1253B
olive tree

KALLION 2566
AG:401B (KALōS 7.) CB:—
well

KALODIDASKALOS 2567
AG:400A CB:1253B
teacher

KALOPOIEō 2569
AG:400B CB:1253B
well-doing

KALOS 2570
AG:400B CB:1253B
beautiful *Note*
better
fair
good
goodly
honest
honourable
meet
seemly
well *Note*
worthy *Note*

KALōS 2573
AG:401B CB:1253B
good
honestly
place *Note*
well

KALUMMA 2571 (-UMA)
AG:400D CB:1253B
veil

KALUPTō 2572
AG:401A CB:1253B
cover
forgive
hide

KAMēLOS 2574
AG:401C CB:1253B
camel

KAMINOS 2575
AG:401D CB:—
furnace

KAMMUō 2576
AG:402A CB:—
close

KAMNō 2577
AG:402A CB:—
faint
sick
weary

KAMPTō 2578
AG:402B CB:1253B
bow

KAN 2579
AG:402C CB:—
(at) least *Note*

KANōN 2583
AG:403A CB:1253B
line*
province
rule

KAPēLEUō 2585
AG:403A CB:1253B
corrupt

KAPNOS 2586
AG:403B CB:—
smoke

KARDIA 2588
AG:403B CB:1253B
heart

KARDIOGNōSTēS 2589
AG:404C CB:1253B
heart (knowing the)
knowing *Note*

KARPHOS 2595
AG:405C CB:—
mote

KARPOPHOROS 2593
AG:405B CB:—
fruitful

KARPOPHOREō 2592
AG:405A CB:1253B
bear *Note*
fruit, -ful

KARPOS 2590
AG:404C CB:1253B
fruit

KARTEREō 2594
AG:405B CB:1253C
endure

KATA 2596
AG:405C CB:1253C
affair *Note*
coast *Note*
divers *Note*
every *Note*
happen *Note*
inasmuch as
manner
much (as) *Note*
out of *Note*
part *Note*
pertain to *Note*
points *Note*
respect *Note*
severally *Note*
thus *Note*
was (etc.) *Note*

KATABAINō 2597
AG:408B CB:1253C
come
descend

KATABAINō (Continued)
fall
get
go *Note*
step
thrust *Note*

KATABALLō 2598
AG:408D CB:1253C
cast
lay
smite

KATABAREō 2599
AG:408D CB:1254A
burden

KATABASIS 2600
AG:409A CB:—
descent

KATABIBAZō 2601
AG:409A CB:—
bring
thrust *Note*

KATABOLē 2602
AG:409A CB:1254A
conceive *Note*
foundation

KATABRABEUō 2603
AG:409B CB:1254A
beguile *Note*
prize *Note*
reward *Note*
rob

KATACHEō 2708
AG:420C CB:—
pour

KATACHRAOMAI 2710
AG:420D CB:—
abuse

KATACHTHONIOS 2709
AG:420D CB:1254A
earth

KATADēLOS 2612
AG:410B CB:—
evident

KATADEō 2611
AG:410B CB:Cf. DEō (1240C)
bind

KATADIKAZō 2613
AG:410B CB:1254A
condemn

KATADIKē —
AG:410B CB:1254A
judgment *Note*
sentence

KATADIōKō 2614
AG:410C CB:1254A
follow

KATADOULOō 2615
AG:410C CB:—
bondage

KATADUNASTEUō 2616
AG:410C CB:—
oppress

KATAGELAō 2606
AG:409C CB:1254A
laugh to scorn

KATAGINōSKō 2607
AG:409D CB:1254A
blame *Note*
condemn
KATAGNUMI 2608
AG:409D CB:—
break
KATAGō 2609
AG:410A CB:Cf. AGō (1233C)
bring
land *Note*
touch
KATAGōNIZOMAI 2610
AG:410A CB:1254A
subdue
KATAISCHUNō 2617
AG:410D CB:1254A
ashamed
confound
dishonour
shame
KATAKAIō 2618
AG:411A CB:—
burn
KATAKALUPTō 2619
AG:411A CB:1254A (-OMAI)
cover
KATAKAUCHAOMAI 2620
AG:411B CB:1254A
boast
glory
rejoice *Note*
KATAKEIMAI 2621
AG:411C CB:Cf. KEIMAI (1254C)
keep *Note*
lie, sit
KATAKLAō 2622
AG:411C CB:Cf. KLAō (1255A)
break
KATAKLEIō 2623
AG:411C CB:—
shut
KATAKLēRODOTEō 2624
AG:411D CB:—
divide *Note*
KATAKLINō 2625
AG:411D CB:—
meat *Note*
sit
KATAKLUSMOS 2627
AG:411D CB:1254A
flood
KATAKLUZō 2626
AG:411D CB:—
overflow
KATAKOLOUTHEō 2628
AG:412A CB:Cf. AKO-(1234B)
follow
KATAKOPTō 2629
AG:412A CB:Cf. APOK(1237A)
cut
KATAKRēMNIZō 2630
AG:412A CB:—
cast *Note*
headlong
throw

KATAKRIMA 2631
AG:412A CB:1254A
condemnation
KATAKRINō 2632
AG:412A CB:1254A
condemn
KATAKRISIS 2633
AG:412B CB:1254A
condemn
condemnation
KATAKURIEUō 2634
AG:412C CB:1254A
dominion
exercise *Note*
lord
master
overcome
KATALALEō 2635
AG:412C CB:1254A
backbiting *Note*
speak
KATALALIA 2636
AG:412D CB:1254A
backbiting
evil speaking
KATALALOS 2637
AG:412D CB:1254A
backbiter
whisperer *Note*
KATALAMBANō 2638
AG:412D CB:1254A (-OMAI)
apprehend
attain
come *Note*
find
obtain *Note*
overtake
perceive
take
KATALEGō 2639
AG:413B CB:—
enrol *Note*
number *Note*
take *Note*
KATALEIMMA 2640
AG:413C CB:1254A
remnant
KATALEIPō 2641
AG:413C CB:1254A
behind *Note*
forsake
leave
reserve *Note*
KATALITHAZō 2642
AG:413D CB:—
stone
KATALLAGē 2643
AG:414A CB:1254A
atonement
reconciliation
KATALLASSō 2644
AG:414A CB:1254A
reconcile
KATALOIPOS 2645
AG:414B CB:1254A
residue

KATALUMA 2646
AG:414B CB:1254A
guest-chamber
inn
KATALUō 2647
AG:414B CB:1254A
come *Note*
destroy
dissolve
guest *Note*
lodge
nought *Note*
overthrow
throw
KATAMANTHANō 2648
AG:414C CB:—
consider
KATAMARTUREō 2649
AG:414D CB:1254A
witness
KATAMENō 2650
AG:414D CB:—
abide
KATA MONAS 2651
AG:527C (MONOS 3.) CB:1253C
alone
KATANALISKō 2654
AG:414D CB:—
consume
KATANARKAō 2655
AG:414D CB:—
burdensome
chargeable *Note*
KAT(AN)ATHEMA 2652
AG:414D CB:1254B
curse
KATANATHEMATIZō 2653
AG:414D CB:1254B
curse
KATANEUō 2656
AG:415A CB:—
beckon
KATANGELEUS 2604
AG:409B CB:1254A
setter forth
KATANGELLō 2605
AG:409B CB:1254A
declare
foretell *Note*
preach *Note*
proclaim
set
shew *Note*
teach *Note*
KATANOEō 2657
AG:415A CB:1254A
behold
consider
discover
perceive
KATANTAō 2658
AG:415B CB:1254A
arrive
attain
come
reach

KATANUSSō 2660
AG:415C (-OMAI) CB:—
prick
KATANUXIS 2659
AG:415C CB:—
prick *Note*
stupor
KATAPATEō 2662
AG:415D CB:1254A
foot *Note*
trample, tread
KATAPAUō 2664
AG:415D CB:1254A
cease
rest
restrain
KATAPAUSIS 2663
AG:415D CB:1254A
rest
KATAPETASMA 2665
AG:416A CB:1254A
veil
KATAPHAGō (KATESTHIō) 2719
AG:422A CB:—
devour, eat
KATAPHERō 2702
AG:419D CB:—
bear down *Note*
fall *Note*
give
sink *Note*
KATAPHEUGō 2703
AG:420A CB:1254B
flee
KATAPHILEō 2705
AG:420B CB:1254B
kiss
KATAPHRONEō 2706
AG:420B CB:1254B
despise
KATAPHRONēTēS 2707 (-NTēS)
AG:420C CB:1254B
despiser
KATAPHTHEIRō 2704
AG:420A CB:Cf. PHT-(1264C)
corrupt
KATAPINō 2666
AG:416B CB:1254B
devour
drown
swallow
KATAPIPTō 2667
AG:416C CB:1254B
fall
KATAPLEō 2668
AG:416D CB:—
arrive
KATAPONEō 2669
AG:416D CB:—
distress
oppress
vex *Note*
KATAPONTIZō 2670
AG:417A CB:—
drown
sink

KATAPSUCHō 2711
AG:421A CB:—
cool

KATARA 2671
AG:417A CB:1254B
curse, cursing

KATARAOMAI 2672
AG:417A CB:1254B
curse

KATARGEō 2673
AG:417B CB:1254B
abolish
cease *Note*
cumber
destroy
discharged
do *Note*
effect
fail *Note*
idle *Note*
loose *Note*
nought, pass
put, sever
vanish *Note*
void *Note*

KATARITHMEō 2674
AG:417C CB:—
number

KATARTISIS 418A
AG:418A CB:1254B
perfection

KATARTISMOS 2677
AG:418A CB:1254B
perfecting

KATARTIZō 2675
AG:417D CB:1254B
fit, frame
join *Note*
mend
perfect
prepare
restore

KATASCHESIS 2697
AG:419C CB:—
possession

KATASEIō 2678
AG:418A CB:1254B
beckon

KATASKAPTō 2679
AG:418B CB:—
dig
overthrow
ruin*

KATASKēNOō 2681
AG:418C CB:1254B
dwell
lodge
rest

KATASKēNōSIS 2682
AG:418C CB:1254B
nest

KATASKEUAZō 2680
AG:418B CB:1254B
build
make *Note*
ordain *Note*
prepare

KATASKIAZō 2683
AG:418D CB:—
overshadow

KATASKOPEō 2684
AG:418D CB:—
spy

KATASKOPOS 2685
AG:418D CB:1254B
spy

KATASOPHIZOMAI 2686
AG:418D CB:—
deal with *Note*
devised *Note*
subtilly

KATASPHAZō 2695 (-ATTō)
AG:419C CB:—
kill
slay

KATASPHRAGIZō 2696
AG:419C CB:1254B
seal

KATASTELLō 2687
AG:419A CB:—
appease
quiet

KATASTēMA 2688
AG:419A CB:—
behaviour
demeanour

KATASTOLē 2689
AG:419A CB:—
apparel
clothing *Note*

KATASTREPHō 2690
AG:419A CB:—
dig
overthrow
ruin

KATASTRēNIAō 2691
AG:419B CB:—
delicately *Note*
wanton

KATASTRōNNUMI 2693
AG:419B CB:—
overthrow

KATASTROPHē 2692
AG:419B CB:—
overthrow
subverting

KATASURō 2694
AG:419B CB:—
drag *Note*
hale

KATATITHēMI 2698
AG:419C CB:—
do *Note*
gain *Note*
lay
shew *Note*

KATATOMē 2699
AG:419D CB:1254B
concision

KATATOXEUō 2700
AG:419D CB:—
thrust

KATATRECHō 2701
AG:419D CB:—
run *Note*

KATAXIOō 2661
AG:415C CB:1254B
account
count *Note*
worthy

KATēCHEō 2727
AG:423D CB:1254B
inform
instruct
teach

KATECHō 2722
AG:422C CB:1254B
have *Note*
hold
keep *Note*
make, possess
restrain
retain *Note*
seize *Note*
stay, take
withhold*

KATēGOREō 2723
AG:423A CB:1254B
accuse
witness

KATēGORIA 2724
AG:423C CB:1254B
accusation

KATēGOROS 2725
AG:423C CB:1254B
accuser

KATEIDōLOS 2712
AG:421A CB:1254B
idols (full of)

KATENANTI 2713
AG:421B CB:—
before
contrary *Note*
sight of (in the)

KATENōPION 2714
AG:421B CB:1254B
before
presence
sight of (in the)

KATēPHEIA 2726
AG:423C CB:—
heaviness

KATEPHISTEMI 2721
AG:422C (-AMAI) CB:—
insurrection
rise *Note*

KATERCHOMAI 2718
AG:422A CB:Cf. ERC-(1246B)
come, depart
descend
go *Note*
land

KATERGAZOMAI 2716
AG:421C CB:—
cause
deed *Note*
do
perform *Note*
work

KATESTHIō 2719
AG:422A CB:—
devour
eat

KATESTRAMMENA (KATASTREPHō) 2690
AG:419A CB:—
ruin

KATEUTHUNō 2720
AG:422B CB:—
direct
guide

KATEXOUSIAZō 2715
AG:421C CB:1254B
authority
exercise *Note*

KATHAIREō 2507
AG:386C CB:—
cast
depose
destroy
pull (down)
put
take

KATHAIRESIS 2506
AG:386B CB:—
cast *Note*
destruction
pull *Note*

KATHAIRō 2508
AG:386D CB:1254B
clean *Note*
purge

KATHAPER 2509
AG:387A CB:—
even as
well as *Note*

KATHAPTō 2510
AG:387A CB:—
fasten

KATHARISMOS 2512
AG:387D CB:1254B
cleansing
purge *Note*
purification
purifying

KATHARIZō 2511
AG:387B CB:1254B
clean
cleanse
purge
purify

KATHAROS 2513
AG:388A CB:1254B
clean
clear *Note*
pure

KATHAROTēS 2514
AG:388B CB:1254B
cleanness
purifying

KATHEDRA 2515
AG:388B CB:1254C
seat

KATHēGēTēS 2519
AG:388D CB:—
master

KATHēKō 2520
AG:389A CB:1254C
convenient
fit
fitting
KATHēMAI 2521
AG:389B CB:1254C
dwell
seat
set *Note*
sit
KATHēMERINOS 2522
AG:389D CB:—
daily
KATHEUDō 2518
AG:388D CB:1254C
asleep
KATHEXēS 2517
AG:388D CB:—
afterward
follow *Note*
order
KATHEZOMAI 2516
AG:388C CB:1254C
sit
KATHIēMI 2524
AG:390B CB:—
let down
KATHISTēMI 2525
AG:390B CB:1254C
appoint
conduct
make
ordain
ruler *Note*
set
KATHIZō 2523
AG:389D CB:1254C
continue *Note*
dwell
set
sit
tarry
KATHO 2526
AG:390D CB:—
according as
inasmuch as
insomuch as
KATHOLOU 2527
AG:391A CB:—
all *Note*
KATHOPLIZō 2528
AG:391A CB:Cf. HOP-(1251A)
arm
KATHORAō 2529
AG:391A CB:1254C
clearly *Note*
see
KATHōS 2531
AG:391B CB:1254C
according as
even as
well as *Note*
KATHOTI 2530
AG:391B CB:—
according as
inasmuch as

KAUSōN 2742
AG:425C CB:—
burning
heat
scorching
KAUSOō 2741
AG:425B CB:—
heat
KAUSTēRIAZō (KAUT-) 2743
AG:425C CB:1254C
branded
KEIMAI 2749
AG:426C CB:1254C
appoint
lay
lie
made (be)
set
there *Note*
KEIRIA 2750
AG:427A CB:—
grave-clothes
KEIRō 2751
AG:427A CB:—
shear
shearer
KELEUō 2753
AG:427B CB:1254C
bid
command
KELEUSMA 2752 (-UMA)
AG:427B CB:1254C
shout
KENODOXIA 2754
AG:427C CB:1255A
vainglory
KENODOXOS 2755
AG:427D CB:1255A
vainglory
KENOō 2758
AG:428A CB:1255A
effect (of none)
empty
reputation *Note*
vain
void
KENOPHōNIA 2757
AG:428A CB:—
babblings
KENOS 2756
AG:427D CB:1255A
empty
vain
KENōS 2761
AG:428C CB:—
vain (in)*
KēNSOS 2778
AG:430D CB:1255A
tribute
KENTRON 2759
AG:428B CB:1255A
goad
KENTURIōN 2760
AG:428C CB:1255A
centurion

KATIOō 2728
AG:424A CB:—
rust
KATISCHUō 2729
AG:424A CB:1254C
able *Note*
prevail
KATō 2736
AG:425A CB:1254C
beneath
bottom
KATOIKEō 2730
AG:424A CB:1254C
dwell
dweller
KATOIKēSIS 2731
AG:424C CB:—
dwelling
KATOIKēTēRION 2732
AG:424C CB:1254C
habitation
KATOIKIA 2733
AG:424C CB:—
habitation
KATOIKIZō —
AG:424C CB:1254C
dwell
KATOPTRIZō 2734 (-OMAI)
AG:424D CB:—
behold
mirror *Note*
KATORTHōMA 2735
AG:424D CB:—
correction
deed *Note*
KATōTERō 2736
AG:425B CB:—
under
KATōTEROS 2737
AG:425A CB:1254C
lower
KAUCHAOMAI 2744
AG:425C CB:1254C
boast
glory
joy
rejoice
KAUCHēMA 2745
AG:426A CB:1254C
boasting
glory, -ing
rejoice *Note*
KAUCHēSIS 2746
AG:426B CB:1254C
boasting
glory, -ing
rejoice *Note*
KAUMA 2738
AG:425B CB:1254C
heat
KAUMATIZō 2739
AG:425B CB:1254C
scorch
KAUSIS 2740
AG:425B CB:—
burning

KEPHALAION 2774
AG:429D CB:1255A
chief
point
sum *Note*
KEPHAL(A)IOō 2775
AG:430A CB:1255A
head (to wound in the)
KEPHALē 2776
AG:430A CB:1255A
head
KEPHALIS 2777
AG:430C CB:1255A
roll
KēPOS 2779
AG:430D CB:—
garden
KēPOUROS 2780
AG:430D CB:—
gardener
KERAIA (KEREA) 2762
AG:428D CB:1255A
tittle
KERAMEUS 2763
AG:428D CB:1255A
potter
KERAMIKOS 2764
AG:428D CB:1255A
potter
KERAMION 2765
AG:428D CB:1255A
pitcher
KERAMOS 2766
AG:429A CB:1255A
tiling
KERANNUMI 2767
AG:429A CB:1255A
fill *Note*
mingle
KERAS 2768
AG:429B CB:1255A
horn
KERATION 2769
AG:429B CB:—
husks
KERDAINō 2770
AG:429C CB:1255A
gain, get
KERDOS 2771
AG:429C CB:1255A
gain
lucre
KēRION 2781
AG:430D CB:—
honey-comb
KERMA 2772
AG:429D CB:—
money
KERMATISTēS 2773
AG:429D CB:—
changer
KēRUGMA 2782
AG:430D CB:1255A
message
preaching
testimony

KēRUSSō 2784
AG:431B CB:1255A
preach
preacher, -ing
proclaim
publish

KēRUX 2783
AG:431A CB:1255A
preacher

KēTOS 2785
AG:431D CB:1255A
whale

KIBōTOS 2787
AG:431D CB:1255A
ark

KICHRēMI After 2797
(CHRAō) (5531)
AG:433A CB:—
lend

KINDUNEUō 2793
AG:432B CB:1255A
danger

KINDUNOS 2794
AG:432B CB:1255A
danger *Note*
peril*

KINEō 2795
AG:432C CB:—
move
mover
remove *Note*
wag

KINēSIS 2796
AG:432D CB:—
moving

KINNAMōMON 2792
AG:432D CB:—
cinnamon

KITHARA 2788
AG:432A CB:—
harp

KITHARIZō 2789
AG:432A CB:—
harp

KITHARōDOS 2790
AG:432A CB:—
harper

KLADOS 2798
AG:433A CB:1255A
branch

KLAIō 2799
AG:433A CB:1255A
bewail
mourn *Note*
weep

KLAō (KLAZō) 2806
AG:433D CB:1255A
break

KLASIS 2800
AG:433B CB:1255A
breaking

KLASMA 2801
AG:433B CB:1255B
break
meat *Note*
piece

KLAUTHMOS 2805
AG:433C CB:1255B
wailing *Note*
weeping

KLEIō 2808
AG:434A CB:1255B
shut

KLEIS 2807
AG:433D CB:1255B
key

KLēMA 2814
AG:434C CB:1255B
branch

KLEMMA 2809
AG:434B CB:—
theft

KLEOS 2811
AG:434B CB:1255B
glory

KLEPTēS 2812
AG:434B CB:1255B
robber
thief

KLEPTō 2813
AG:434C CB:1255B
steal

KLēRONOMEō 2816
AG:434D CB:1255B
heir
inherit

KLēRONOMIA 2817
AG:435A CB:1255B
inheritance

KLēRONOMOS 2818
AG:435B CB:1255B
heir

KLēROō 2820
AG:435D CB:1255B
heritage
inheritance

KLēROS 2819
AG:435B CB:1255B
charge
inheritance
lot, part *Note*
portion

KLēSIS 2821
AG:435D CB:1255B
call, -ing

KLēTOS 2822
AG:436A CB:1255B
called

KLIBANOS 2823
AG:436B CB:—
oven

KLIMA 2824
AG:436B CB:—
part
region

KLINARION Cf. 2825 (-Nē)
AG:436B CB:—
bed

KLINē 2825
AG:436B CB:—
bed
table *Note*

KLINIDION 2826
AG:436C CB:—
couch

KLINō 2827
AG:436C CB:—
bow
flight
lay
spent
turn *Note*
wear

KLISIA 2828
AG:436D CB:—
company

KLOPē 2829
AG:436D CB:—
theft

KLUDōN 2830
AG:436D CB:—
raging
wave

KLUDōNIZOMAI 2831
AG:436D CB:—
toss

KNēTHō 2833
AG:437A CB:—
itching

KODRANTēS 2835
AG:437A CB:—
farthing
mite

KOILIA 2836
AG:437B CB:1255B
belly
womb

KOIMAō (-OMAI) 2837
AG:437C CB:1255B
asleep
dead (to be)*
die
fall *Note*

KOIMēSIS 2838
AG:437D CB:—
rest

KOINōNEō 2841
AG:438C CB:1255B
communicate
distribute *Note*
fellowship
partake, -er

KOINōNIA 2842
AG:438D CB:1255B
communication
communion
contribution
distribution *Note*
fellowship

KOINōNIKOS 2843
AG:439C CB:1255B
communicate

KOINōNOS 2844
AG:439C CB:1255B
communion
companion
fellowship
partaker
partner

KOINOō 2840
AG:438B CB:1255B
call *Note*
common
defile
unclean

KOINOS 2839
AG:438A CB:1255B
common
defiled
unclean
unholy

KOITē 2845
AG:440A CB:1255B
bed
chambering
conceive *Note*

KOITōN 2846
AG:440B CB:—
chamberlain

KOKKINOS 2847
AG:440B CB:1255B
scarlet

KOKKOS 2848
AG:440C CB:—
corn *Note*
grain

KOLAK(E)IA 2850
AG:440D CB:—
flattery
flattering

KOLAPHIZō 2852
AG:441A CB:1255B
buffet

KOLASIS 2851
AG:440D CB:1255B
punishment
torment *Note*

KOLAZō 2849
AG:440C CB:1255C
punish

KOLLAō 2853
AG:441C CB:1255C
cleave
company
join

KOLLOURION 2854
AG:441D CB:1255C
eye-salve

KOLLUBISTēS 2855
AG:442A CB:—
changer

KOLOBOō 2856
AG:442A CB:1255C
shorten

KōLON 2966
AG:461B CB:—
carcase

KOLōNIA 2862
AG:442C CB:—
colony

KOLPOS 2859
AG:442B CB:1255C
bay
bosom

KOLUMBAō 2860
AG:442C CB:—
swim
KOLUMBēTHRA 2861
AG:442C CB:—
pool
KōLUō 2967
AG:461B CB:1255C
forbid
hinder
keep *Note*
stay
suffer *Note*
withhold
withstand
KOMAō 2863
AG:442D CB:—
hair
KOMē 2864
AG:442D CB:—
hair
KōMē 2968
AG:461D CB:1255C
town
village
KOMIZō 2865
AG:442D CB:1255C (-OMAI)
bring
receive
KōMOPOLIS 2969
AG:461D CB:—
town
KōMOS 2970
AG:461D CB:1255C
revelling
rioting
surfeiting *Note*
KOMPSOTERON 2866
AG:443A CB:—
amend
KONIAō 2867
AG:443A CB:1255C
white
KONIORTOS 2868
AG:443B CB:—
dust
KOPAZō 2869
AG:443B CB:—
cease
KōNōPS 2971
AG:462A CB:1255C
gnat
KOPē 2871
AG:443C CB:—
slaughter
KOPETOS 2870
AG:443B CB:1255C
bewail
KOPHINOS 2894
AG:447C CB:—
basket, -ful
KōPHOS 2974
AG:462A CB:1255C
deaf
dumb
speechless

KOPIAō 2872
AG:443C CB:1255C
bestow
labour
toil
weary
KOPOS 2873
AG:443C CB:1255C
labour
toil
trouble *Note*
weariness*
KOPRIA 2874
AG:443D CB:1255C
dung
dunghill
KOPRION —
AG:443D CB:1255C
dung
KOPTō 2875
AG:444A CB:1255C
bewail
cut
mourn
wail *Note*
KORASION 2877
AG:444B CB:1255C
damsel
maid
KORAX 2876
AG:444B CB:—
raven
KORBAN 2878
AG:444B CB:1255C
Corban
KORBANAS 2878
AG:444C CB:1255C
treasury
KORENNUMI 2880
AG:444C CB:—
eat
enough *Note*
fill
KOROS 2884
AG:444D CB:1255C
measure
KOSMEō 2885
AG:445A CB:1255C
adorn
garnish
trim
KOSMIKOS 2886
AG:445B CB:1255C
worldly
KOSMIOS 2887
AG:445C CB:1255C
behaviour
modest
orderly
KOSMOKRATōR 2888
AG:445C CB:1255C
ruler
KOSMOS 2889
AG:445D CB:1255C
adorning
world

KOUM(I) 2891
AG:447B CB:—
talitha
KOUPHIZō 2893
AG:447B CB:—
lighten
KOUSTōDIA 2892
AG:447B CB:—
guard
watch
KRABBATOS 2895
AG:447C CB:—
bed
couch
KRAIPALē 2897
AG:448A CB:1255C
surfeiting
KRANION 2898
AG:448A CB:—
Calvary
skull
KRASPEDON 2899
AG:448B CB:—
border
KRATAIOō 2901
AG:448B CB:1256A
strengthen
strong
KRATAIOS 2900
AG:448B CB:1256A
mighty
KRATEō 2902
AG:448C CB:1256A
hands on (lay)
hold, -en
keep
obtain
retain
take
KRATISTOS 2903
AG:449A CB:1256A
excellent
noble
KRATOS 2904
AG:449A CB:1256A
dominion
might *Note*
power
strength
KRAUGAZō 2905
AG:449B CB:1256A
cry
KRAUGē 2906
AG:449C CB:—
clamour
cry, -ing
KRAZō 2896
AG:447C CB:1256A
cry
KREAS 2907
AG:449C CB:1256A
flesh
KREISSōN 2908
(KREITTōN) (2909)
AG:449D CB:1256A
better

KREMANNUMI 2910
AG:450A CB:1256A
hang
steep
KRēMNOS 2911
AG:450B CB:—
steep
KRIMA 2917
AG:450C CB:1256A
condemnation
judgment
sentence
KRINō 2919
AG:451B CB:1256A
call
conclude *Note*
condemn
decree *Note*
determine
esteem
judge *Note*
judgment, law
ordain
sentence
think *Note*
KRINON 2918
AG:451A CB:—
lily
KRISIS 2920
AG:452C CB:1256A
accusation *Note*
condemnation
judgment
KRITēRION 2922
AG:453B CB:—
judge *Note*
judgment *Note*
judgment-seat
KRITēS 2923
AG:453C CB:1256A
judge
KRITHē 2915
AG:450C CB:—
barley
KRITHINOS 2916
AG:450C CB:—
barley
KRITIKOS 2924
AG:453D CB:1256A
discerner
KROUō 2925
AG:453D CB:1256A
knock
KRUPHAIOS —
AG:454D CB:1256A
secret
KRUPHē 2931
AG:454D CB:1256A
secret
KRUPTē 2926
AG:454A CB:1256A
cellar
KRUPTō 2928
AG:454B CB:1256A
hide
secretly

KRUPTOS 2927
AG:454A CB:1256A
hid
hidden
inwardly *Note*
secret

KRUSTALLIZō 2929
AG:454D CB:1256A
clear
crystal

KRUSTALLOS 2930
AG:454D CB:1256A
crystal

KTAOMAI 2932
AG:455A CB:1256A
get
obtain
possess
provide
purchase
win*

KTēMA 2933
AG:455B CB:1256A
possession

KTēNOS 2934
AG:455B CB:1256A
beast
cattle

KTēTōR 2935
AG:455C CB:—
possessor

KTISIS 2937
AG:455D CB:1256A
building
creation
creature
ordinance

KTISMA 2938
AG:456B CB:1256A
creature

KTISTēS 2939
AG:456B CB:1256B
Creator

KTIZō 2936
AG:455C CB:1256B
create
Creator
make *Note*

KUBEIA (-BIA) 2940
AG:456C CB:—
sleight

KUBERNēSIS 2941
AG:456C CB:1256B
government

KUBERNēTēS 2942
AG:456C CB:1256B
government *Note*
master

KUKLEUō —
AG:456D CB:—
compass

KUKLOō 2944
AG:456D CB:—
come
compass
stand

KUKLō 2944
AG:456D CB:1256B (-LOS)
about
round about

KUKLOTHEN 2943
AG:456D CB:—
about
round about

KULIō 2947 (-IOo)
AG:457B CB:—
wallow

KULISMOS 2946 (-MA)
AG:457B CB:—
wallowing

KULLOS 2948
AG:457B CB:1256B
halt *Note*
maimed

KUMA 2949
AG:457C CB:—
wave

KUMBALON 2950
AG:457C CB:—
cymbal

KUMINON 2951
AG:457C CB:1256B
cummin

KUNARION 2952
AG:457D CB:1256B
dog

KUōN 2965
AG:461B CB:1256B
dog

KUPTō 2955
AG:458A CB:—
stoop

KURIA 2959
AG:458B CB:1256B
lady

KURIAKOS 2960
AG:458C CB:1256B
Lord

KURIEUō 2961
AG:458D CB:1256B
dominion
exercise *Note*
lord
lordship

KURIOS 2962
AG:458D II. CB:1256B
lord
master
owner
sir

KURIOTēS 2963
AG:460D CB:1256B
dominion
government *Note*

KUROō 2964
AG:461A CB:1256B
confirm

L

LACHANON 3001
AG:467D CB:1256B
herb

LAILAPS 2978
AG:462D CB:1256B
storm
tempest

LAKEō (LASKō) 2997
AG:463A CB:1256C
burst

LAKTIZō 2979
AG:463A CB:—
kick

LALEō 2980
AG:463A CB:1256B
commune *Note*
preach *Note*
say
speak
talk
tell, utter

LALIA 2981
AG:464A CB:1256C
saying *Note*
speech

LAMA 2982
AG:464A CB:1224B
lama

LAMBANō 2983
AG:464A CB:1256C
accept
attain *Note*
bring *Note*
call *Note*
catch, find
have *Note*
hold *Note*
obtain
receive
take

LAMPAS 2985
AG:465C CB:1256C
lamp, light
torch

LAMPō 2989
AG:466A CB:1256C
light
shine

LAMPROS 2986
AG:465D CB:1256C
bright
clear
fine*, gay*
goodly *Note*
gorgeous
sumptuous
white

LAMPRōS 2988
AG:466A CB:1256C
bright *Note*
clear *Note*
sumptuously

LAMPROTēS 2987
AG:466A CB:1256C
brightness

LANCHANō 2975
AG:462B CB:1256C
lot
obtain
receive

LANTHANō 2990
AG:466B CB:1256C
forget
hide
ignorant
unawares *Note*

LAOS 2992
AG:466C CB:1256C
Gentile *Note*
people

LARUNX 2995
AG:467B CB:—
throat

LATHRA 2977
AG:462C CB:—
privily
secretly

LATOMEō 2998
AG:467B CB:—
hew

LATREIA 2999
AG:467B CB:1256C
divine
service

LATREUō 3000
AG:467C CB:1256C
minister *Note*
serve
service
worship

LAXEUTOS 2991
AG:466C CB:—
hewn

LEGEōN (LEGIōN) 3003
AG:467D CB:—
legion

LEGō 3004
AG:468A CB:1256C
allege *Note*
ask
bid *Note*
boast
call
describe
give, mean
name *Note*
pronounce
put *Note*
reckon
say
shew *Note*
speak
tell
utter *Note*

LEIMMA 3005
AG:470B CB:1256C
remnant

LEIOS 3006
AG:470B CB:—
smooth

LEIPō 3007
AG:470B CB:1256C
destitute
lack, want

LEITOURGEō 3008
AG:470C CB:1256C
minister

LEITOURGIA 3009
AG:471A CB:1256C
ministration
ministry
service
LEITOURGIKOS 3010
AG:471B CB:1256C
ministering
LEITOURGOS 3011
AG:471B CB:1256C
deacon *Note*
minister
Lē(M)PSIS 3028
AG:473A CB:1256C
receiving
LēNOS 3025
AG:473A CB:—
wine-press
LENTION 3012
AG:471C CB:—
towel
LEōN 3023
AG:472D CB:1256C
lion
LEPIS 3013
AG:471C CB:—
scale
LEPRA 3014
AG:471D CB:1256C
leprosy
LEPROS 3015
AG:472A CB:1256C
leper
LEPTON 3016
AG:472A (-OS) CB:1256C
mite
LēROS 3026
AG:473A CB:—
talk
LēSTēS 3027
AG:473A CB:1256C
robber
thief
LēTHē 3024
AG:472D CB:1256C
forget
LEUKAINō 3021
AG:472B CB:—
white
LEUKOS 3022
AG:472B CB:1257A
white, very*
LIAN 3029
AG:473B CB:1257A
exceeding
great *Note*
greatly
sore
very *Note*
while*
LIBANOS 3030
AG:473C CB:1257A
frankincense
LIBANōTOS 3031
AG:473D CB:1257A
censer

LIKMAō 3039
AG:474D CB:—
dust
grind *Note*
scatter
LIMēN 3040
AG:475A CB:—
haven
LIMNē 3041
AG:475A CB:1257A
lake
LIMOS 3042
AG:475A CB:1257A
famine
hunger
LINON 3043
AG:475B CB:—
flax
linen
LIPAROS 3045
AG:475C CB:—
dainty
LIPS 3047
AG:475D CB:—
north-east *Note*
south-west
LITHAZō 3034
AG:473D CB:—
stone
LITHINOS 3035
AG:474A CB:1257A
stone
LITHOBOLEō 3036
AG:474A CB:—
stone
LITHOS 3037
AG:474B CB:1257A
stone
LITHOSTRōTOS 3038
AG:474D CB:—
pavement
LITRA 3046
AG:475D CB:—
pound
LOG(E)IA 3048
AG:475D CB:1257A
collection
gathering *Note*
LOGIKOS 3050
AG:476C CB:1257A
milk *Note*
reasonable
spiritual *Note*
word *Note*
LOGION 3051
AG:476C CB:1257A
oracle
LOGIOS 3052
AG:476D CB:1257A
eloquent
LOGISMOS 3053
AG:476D CB:1257A
imagination
thought

LOGIZOMAI 3049
AG:475D CB:1257A
account
charge *Note*
conclude *Note*
consider *Note*
count
despise *Note*
esteem
impute
number *Note*
reason
reckon
suppose *Note*
think
LOGOMACHEō 3054
AG:477A CB:1257A
strive
LOGOMACHIA 3055
AG:477A CB:1257A
dispute
strife
LOGOS 3056
AG:477A CB:1257A
account
cause
communication
do *Note*
doctrine *Note*
fable
fame *Note*
intent
matter
mouth *Note*
preaching *Note*
question
reason
reckon
report
rumour *Note*
saying
show
speech
speaker (chief) *Note*
talk
thing
tidings *Note*
treatise
utterance
word
work
LOIDOREō 3058
AG:479C CB:1257A
revile
LOIDORIA 3059
AG:479C CB:1257A
railing
reproachfully *Note*
reviling
LOIDOROS 3060
AG:479C CB:1257B
railer
reviler
LOIMOS 3061
AG:479D CB:—
fellow *Note*
pestilence
pestilent fellow

LOIPON 3063
AG:479D (LOIPOS 3.b.) CB:1257B
besides
finally
furthermore *Note*
henceforth
kind *Note*
moreover
now, then
LOIPOS 3062
AG:479D CB:1257B
other
remain *Note*
remnant
residue *Note*
rest (the)
LONCHē 3057
AG:479B CB:—
spear
LOUō 3068
AG:480D CB:1257B
bathed
wash
LOUTRON 3067
AG:480C CB:1257B
regeneration
washing
LUCHNIA 3087
AG:483A CB:1257B
lampstand
stand
LUCHNOS 3088
AG:483B CB:1257B
lamp
light
LUKOS 3074
AG:481B CB:1257B
wolf
LUMAINō (-OMAI) 3075
AG:481C CB:—
havock
lay waste
waste
LUō 3089
AG:483C CB:1257B
break
destroy
dissolve
loose
melt *Note*
put *Note*
unloose
LUPē 3077
AG:482A CB:1257B
grief
grievous *Note*
grudgingly
heaviness
sorrow
LUPEō 3076
AG:481C CB:1257B
grief
grieve
heaviness
mourn *Note*
sorrow, -ful
sorry

LUSIS 3080
AG:482B CB:1257B
loose
LUSITELEō 3081 (-LEI)
AG:482B CB:—
better (be)
LUTRON 3083
AG:482C CB:1257B
ransom
LUTROō 3084
AG:482D CB:1257B
redeem
LUTRōSIS 3085
AG:483A CB:1257B
redeem
redemption
LUTRōTēS 3086
AG:483A CB:1257B
deliverer

M

MACHAIRA 3162
AG:496B CB:1257B
sword
MACHē 3163
AG:496C CB:1257B
fighting
strife
MACHOMAI 3164
AG:496C CB:1257B
fight, strive
MAG(E)IA 3095
AG:484B CB:1257B
sorcery
MAGEUō 3096
AG:484D CB:1257B
sorcery
MAGOS 3097
AG:484D CB:1257B
sorcerer
wise
MAINOMAI 3105
AG:486B CB:1257B
beside oneself
mad
MAKARIOS 3107
AG:486C CB:1257C
blessed
happy
MAKARISMOS 3108
AG:487A CB:1257C
blessedness
blessing
gratulation
MAKARIZō 3106
AG:486C CB:1257C
bless
count *Note*
happy
MAKELLON 3111
AG:487B CB:—
shambles
MAKRAN 3112
AG:487C CB:1257C
afar, far
hence *Note*
way *Note*

MAKROCHRONIOS 3118
AG:488C CB:—
live long
MAKROS 3117
AG:488C CB:Cf. -RAN (1257C)
far
long
MAKROTHEN 3113
AG:487D CB:1257C
afar
far
MAKROTHUMEō 3114
AG:488A CB:1257C
bear
endure
longsuffering
patient
patience
suffer
MAKROTHUMIA 3115
AG:488B CB:1257C
forbearance *Note*
longsuffering
patience
MAKROTHUMōS 3116
AG:488C CB:1257C
patiently
MALAKIA 3119
AG:488C CB:1257C
disease
MALAKOS 3120
AG:488D CB:Cf. -KIA (1257C)
effeminate
MALISTA 3122
AG:488D CB:—
chiefly
especially
most
MALLON 3123
AG:489A CB:1257C
more
rather
MAMMē 3125
AG:490A CB:—
grandmother
MAMōNAS (MAMMōN) 3126
AG:490A CB:1257C
mammon
MANIA 3130
AG:490D CB:1257C
mad
madness
MANNA 3131
AG:490D CB:1257C
manna
MANTEUOMAI 3132
AG:491A CB:1257C
soothsaying
MANTHANō 3129
AG:490B CB:1257C
learn
learned (be)
understand *Note*
MARAINō 3133
AG:491B CB:—
fade

MARAN-ATHA 3134
AG:491B CB:1257C
Maran-atha
MARGARITēS 3135
AG:491C CB:1257C
pearl
MARMAROS 3139
AG:492C CB:—
marble
MARTUREō 3140
AG:492C CB:1257C
charge *Note*
give *Note*
honest *Note*
obtain *Note*
report
testify *Note*
testimony
witness
MARTURIA 3141
AG:493C CB:1257C
report *Note*
testimony
witness
MARTURION 3142
AG:493D CB:1257C
testimony
witness
MARTUROMAI 3143
AG:494A CB:1257C
testify
witness
MARTUS (-UR) 3144
AG:494B CB:1257C
witness
MAS(S)AOMAI 3145
AG:495A CB:—
gnaw
MASTIGOō 3146
AG:495A CB:1257C
scourge
MASTIX 3148
AG:495B CB:1257C
plague
scourging
MASTIZō 3147
AG:495A CB:1257C
scourge
MASTOS 3149
AG:495B CB:1258A
breast
MATAIOLOGIA 3150
AG:495C CB:1258A
talking (vain)
MATAIOLOGOS 3151
AG:495C CB:1258A
talkers (vain)
vain *Note*
MATAIOō 3154
AG:495D CB:1258A
vain
MATAIOS 3152
AG:495C CB:1258A
empty
vain
vanity *Note*

MATAIOTēS 3153
AG:495D CB:1258A
vanity
MATēN 3155
AG:495D CB:1258A
vain
MATHēTēS 3101
AG:485C CB:1258A
disciple
MATHēTEUō 3100
AG:485C CB:1258A
disciple
instruct
teach *Note*
MATHēTRIA 3102
AG:486A CB:Cf. -TēS (1258A)
disciple
Mē 3361
AG:515D CB:1258A
lest
means (by no) *Note*
more (no) *Note*
never *Note*
no more *Note*
no one *Note*
no wise (in)
wise (in no)
nothing
Notes p. 1267
MēDE 3366
AG:517D CB:—
much (as) *Note*
Notes p. 1267
MēDEIS (-DEN) 3367
AG:518A CB:1258A
no man *Note*
no one *Note*
nothing
without *Note*
MēDEPOTE 3368
AG:518B CB:—
never
MEGALAUCHEō 3166
AG:496D CB:—
boast
MEGALEIOS 3167
AG:496D CB:1258A
great *Note*
mighty
wonderful (work) *Note*
MEGALEIOTēS 3168
AG:496D CB:1258A
magnificence
majesty
mighty *Note*
MEGALOPREPES 3169
AG:497A CB:—
excellent
MEGALōS 3171
AG:497B CB:—
greatly
MEGALōSUNē 3172
AG:497B CB:1258A
majesty

MEGALUNō 3170
AG:497A CB:1258A
enlarge
great *Note*
magnify
shew *Note*

MEGAS 3173
AG:497C CB:1258A
great
greatest
high
large
loud
matter *Note*
mighty *Note*
sore *Note*
strong
years *Note*

MEGETHOS 3174
AG:498C CB:—
greatness

MEGISTAN(-ES) 3175
AG:498C CB:1258A
great *Note*
lord
prince *Note*

MEGISTOS 3176
AG:497C (MEGAS 2b.) CB:1258A
great *Note*

MEIZōN 3187
AG:497C (MEGAS) CB:1258A
best
elder
greater
greatest
more

MEIZOTEROS 3186
AG:497C (MEGAS) CB:Cf. -ZoN (1258A)
greater

MēKETI 3371
AG:518C CB:—
henceforth
henceforward
longer
no longer
no more

MēKOS 3372
AG:518C CB:—
length

MēKUNOMAI 3373 (-Nō)
AG:518D CB:—
grow

MELAN 3188
AG:499D CB:1258A
ink

MELAS 3189
AG:499D CB:1258A
black

MELEI 3190
AG:500A CB:Cf. MELō (1258B)
care

MELETAō 3191
AG:500B CB:—
diligent
imagine
meditate
premeditate

MELI 3192
AG:500C CB:—
honey

MELISSIOS 3193
AG:500D CB:—
honey-comb

MELLō 3195
AG:500D CB:1258A
about, almost
begin
come
hereafter
intend
mean *Note*
mind *Note*
point *Note*
ready
shall, should
tarry
thenceforth *Note*
time *Note*
was (etc.) *Note*
will
yet *Note*

MELō 3199
AG:500A CB:1258B
care

MELOS 3196
AG:501D CB:1258B
member

MēLoTē 3374
AG:518D CB:—
sheepskin

MEMBRANA 3200
AG:502A CB:—
parchment

MEMPHOMAI 3201
AG:502B CB:1258B
blame *Note*
fault

MEMPSIMOIROS 3202
AG:502C CB:1258B
complainer

MEN 3303
AG:502C CB:1258B
even *Note*
indeed
some *Note*
truly *Note*
verily *Note*

MēN (I) 3375
AG:518D CB:1258B
indeed
surely *Note*

MēN (II) 3376
AG:518D CB:1258B
month

MENō 3306
AG:503C CB:1258B
abide
continue
dwell
endure
own *Note*
present *Note*
remain, stand
tarry

MENOUN (MENOUNGE) 3304
AG:503C CB:—
nay
yea

MENTOI 3305
AG:503C CB:—
yet *Note*

MēNUō 3377
AG:519A CB:—
shew
tell

MēPō 3380
AG:518B CB:—
yet *Note*

MēPōS 3381
AG:519C CB:—
haply
lest

MēPOTE 3379
AG:519B CB:1258B
haply
lest
peradventure

MēPOU —
AG:519C CB:—
haply
lest

MERIMNA 3308
AG:504D CB:1258B
care

MERIMNAō 3309
AG:505A CB:1258B
care
careful
thought (to take)

MERIS 3310
AG:505A CB:1258B
district
part
portion

MERISMOS 3311
AG:505C CB:—
dividing
gift

MERISTēS 3312
AG:505D CB:—
divider

MERIZō 3307
AG:504C CB:1258B
deal
difference
distribute
divide
give *Note*
part

MēROS 3382
AG:519D CB:—
thigh

MEROS 3313
AG:505D CB:1258B
behalf
coast *Note*
country *Note*
course
craft
measure
part
piece
portion
respect
severally *Note*
somewhat *Note*
sort
trade

MESēMBRIA 3314
AG:506D CB:—
noon
south *Note*

MESITēS 3316
AG:506D CB:1258B
mediator

MESITEUō 3315
AG:506D CB:1258B
confirm
interposed

MESONUKTION 3317
AG:507A CB:1258B
midnight

MESOō 3322
AG:508B CB:—
midst

MESOS 3319
AG:507B CB:1258B
between
midday
midnight
midst
way *Note*

MESOTOICHON 3320
AG:508A CB:1258B
wall

MESOURANēMA 3321
AG:508A CB:—
heaven

MESTOō 3325
AG:508C CB:—
fill

MESTOS 3324
AG:508B CB:1258B
full

META 3326
AG:508C CB:1258B
hence *Note*
hereafter *Note*

METABAINō 3327
AG:510C CB:1258B
depart
go, pass
remove

METABALLō 3328
AG:510D CB:—
change

METADIDōMI 3330
AG:510D CB:1258B
give
impart

METAGō 3329
AG:510D CB:—
turn

METAIRō 3332
AG:511A CB:—
depart

METAKALEō 3333
AG:511A CB:1258B (-OMAI)
call
METAKINEō 3334
AG:511B CB:—
move
METALAMBANō 3335
AG:511B CB:1258B
eat *Note*
have
partake
receive
take
METALēPSIS 3336
AG:511C CB:1258B (-ēMP-)
receive
METALLASSō 3337
AG:511C CB:1258C
change
exchange
METAMELOMAI 3338 (-MELL-)
AG:511C CB:1258C
regret
repent
METAMORPHOō 3339
AG:511D CB:1258C
change *Note*
transfigure
transform
METANOEō 3340
AG:511D CB:1258C
repent
METANOIA 3341
AG:512C CB:1258C
repentance
METAPEMPō 3343
AG:513B CB:—
call *Note*
fetch, send
METASCHēMATIZō 3345
AG:513B CB:1258C
anew *Note*
change *Note*
fashion
figure *Note*
transform
METASTREPHō 3344
AG:513B CB:—
pervert
turn
METATHESIS 3331
AG:511A CB:1258C
change
removing
translation
METATITHēMI 3346
AG:513C CB:1258C
carry
change
remove
translate
turn
METAXU 3342
AG:512D CB:—
between
next
while *Note*

MēTE 3383
AG:519D CB:—
much (as) *Note*
METECHō 3348
AG:514A CB:1258C
belong *Note*
part
partake, -er
pertain
METEōRIZō 3349
AG:514A (-OMAI) CB:—
doubtful
METEPEITA 3347
AG:514A CB:—
afterward
MeTeR 3384
AG:520A CB:1258C
mother
METHē 3178
AG:498D CB:1258C
drunkenness
surfeiting *Note*
METHERMēNEUō 3177
AG:498D CB:1258C
interpret
interpretation
METHISTēMI (-TANō) 3179
AG:498D CB:—
put
remove
translate
turn
METHOD(E)IA 3180
AG:499A CB:1258C
wiles
METHORION 3181 (-OS)
AG:499B CB:—
border
coast *Note*
METHUō 3184
AG:499C CB:1258C
drink
drunk
drunken
METHUSKō 3182
AG:499B CB:1258C
drunk
drunken
METHUSOS 3183
AG:499B CB:1258C
drunkard
MēTI 3385
AG:520B CB:—
indeed
METOCHē 3352
AG:514C CB:1258C
fellowship
METOCHOS 3353
AG:514C CB:1258C
fellow
partaker
partner
METOIKESIA 3350
AG:514B CB:1258C
bring *Note*
carrying away

METOIKIZō 3351
AG:514B CB:—
carry away
remove
METōPON 3359
AG:515B CB:—
forehead
MēTRA 3388
AG:520B CB:1258C
womb
MēTRALōAS (METRO-) 3389
AG:520C CB:—
mother
METREō 3354
AG:514C CB:1258C
measure, mete*
METRēTēS 3355
AG:514D CB:1258C
firkin
METRIOPATHEō 3356
AG:514D CB:—
bear
compassion
gently *Note*
METRIōS 3357
AG:515A CB:—
little
METRON 3358
AG:515A CB:1258C
measure
MIA 3391
AG:230D (HEIS) CB:1258C
first
one
MIAINō 3392
AG:520D CB:1258C
defile
MIASMA 3393
AG:521A CB:1258C
defilement
pollution *Note*
MIASMOS 3394
AG:521A CB:1258C
defilement
uncleanness *Note*
MIGMA 3395
AG:521A CB:—
mixture
MIGNUMI 3396
AG:499C (MEIG-) CB:—
mingle
MIKROS (-ON) 3398 (3397)
AG:521A CB:1258C
least
less
little
small
while*
MIKROTEROS 3398
AG:521B (MIKROS l.c.) CB:—
least
less
little *Note*
MILION 3400
AG:521D CB:—
mile

MIMEOMAI 3401
AG:521D CB:1259A
follow
imitate *Note*
MIMēTēS 3402
AG:522A CB:1259A
follower *Note*
imitator
MIMNēSKō 3403
AG:522B (-OMAI) CB:1259A
mindful
remember, -rance
MISEō 3404
AG:522C CB:1259A
hate
MISTHAPODOSIA 3405
AG:523A CB:1259A
recompence
MISTHAPODOTēS 3406
AG:523A CB:1259A
rewarder
MISTHIOS 3407
AG:523A CB:1259A
deacon *Note*
hired servant
MISTHōMA 3410
AG:523D CB:1259A
dwelling
hired house
MISTHOō 3409
AG:523D CB:1259A
hire
MISTHOS 3408
AG:523B CB:1259A
hire, reward
wages
MISTHōTOS 3411
AG:523D CB:1259A
deacon *Note*
hired servant
hireling
MNA 3414
AG:524A CB:—
pound
MNEIA 3417
AG:524B CB:1259A
mention
remembrance
MNēMA 3418
AG:524C CB:1259A
grave
sepulchre
tomb
MNēMē 3420
AG:524D CB:1259A
remembrance
MNēMEION 3419
AG:524C CB:1259A
grave
sepulchre
tomb
MNēMONEUō 3421
AG:525A CB:1259A
mention
mindful
remember

MNēMOSUNON 3422
AG:525B CB:1259A
memorial
MNēSTEUō 3423
AG:525C CB:—
betroth
espoused
MOCHTHOS 3449
AG:528D CB:1259A
labour *Note*
travail
MODIOS 3426
AG:525D CB:—
bushel
MOGILALOS 3424
AG:525D CB:1259A
impediment
MOGIS 3425
AG:525D CB:—
hardly
MOICHALIS 3428
AG:526A CB:1259A
adulteress, -ous
MOICHAō 3429
AG:526A CB:1259A
adultery
MOICHEIA 3430
AG:526B CB:1259A
adultery
MOICHEUō 3431
AG:526B CB:1259A
adultery
MOICHOS 3432
AG:526C CB:1259A
adulterer
MOLIS 3433
AG:526D CB:—
difficulty
hardly
MōLōPS 3468
AG:531A CB:1259A
stripe
MOLUNō 3435
AG:526D CB:1259A
defile
MOLUSMOS 3436
AG:527A CB:1259A
defilement
filthiness
MōMAOMAI 3469
AG:531A CB:—
blame
MōMOS 3470
AG:531A CB:—
blemish
MOMPHē 3437
AG:527A CB:—
complaint
MONē 3438
AG:527A CB:1259B
abode
mansion
MONOGENēS 3439
AG:527B CB:1259B
child, only
only begotten

MONOō 3443
AG:528B CB:—
desolate
MONOPHTHALMOS 3442
AG:528B CB:Cf. OPH-(1261A)
eye (with one)
MONOS (-ON) 3441 (3340)
AG:527C CB:1259B
alone
only
MōRAINō 3471
AG:531B CB:1259B
foolish
savour
MōRIA 3472
AG:531B CB:1259B
foolishness
MōROLOGIA 3473
AG:531B CB:1259B
foolish *Note*
talking (foolish)
MōROS 3474
AG:531C CB:1259B
fool
foolish
foolishness
MORPHē 3444
AG:528B CB:1259B
form
image
MORPHOō 3445
AG:528C CB:1259B
formed
MORPHōSIS 3446
AG:528C CB:1259B
form
MOSCHOPOIEō 3447
AG:528C CB:—
calf
MOSCHOS 3448
AG:528C CB:1259B
calf
MOUSIKOS 3451
AG:528D CB:1259B
minstrel
MUELOS 3452
AG:528D CB:—
marrow
MUEō 3453
AG:529A CB:1259B
instruct
learn
mystery
MUKAOMAI 3455
AG:529B CB:—
roar
MUKTēRIZō 3456
AG:529B CB:1259B
mock
MULIKOS 3457
AG:529B CB:1259B
millstone
MULINOS —
AG:529B CB:1259B
millstone

MULōN 3459
AG:529C CB:—
mill
MULOS 3458
AG:529B CB:1259B
millstone
MUōPAZō 3467
AG:531A CB:—
afar *Note*
see
MURIAS 3461
AG:529C CB:—
company *Note*
innumerable
thousand(s) *Note*
MURIOI 3463
AG:529D CB:—
innumerable
ten thousand*
thousand *Note*
MURIZō 3462
AG:529D CB:—
anoint
MURON 3464
AG:529D CB:1259B
anoint *Note*
ointment
MUSTēRION 3466
AG:530A CB:1259B
mystery
MUTHOS 3454
AG:529A CB:1259B
fable

N

NAI 3483
AG:532D CB:—
even so
surely *Note*
truth *Note*
verily *Note*, yea
NAOS 3485
AG:533B CB:1259B
sanctuary
shrine
temple
NARDOS 3487
AG:534A CB:—
spikenard
NAUAGEō 3489
AG:534B CB:1259B
shipwreck
NAUKLēROS 3490
AG:534B CB:—
owner
NAUS 3491
AG:534C CB:—
ship
NAUTēS 3492
AG:534C CB:—
mariners
Nē 3513
AG:537B CB:1259C
protest
NEANIAS 3494
AG:534C CB:—
young (man)

NEANISKOS 3495
AG:534C CB:1259C
young (man)
NEKROō 3499
AG:535C CB:1259C
dead
mortify
NEKROS 3498
AG:534D CB:1259C
dead
NEKRōSIS 3500
AG:535C CB:1259C
deadness
NEōKOROS 3511
AG:537B CB:1259C
temple-keeper
worshipper
NEOMēNIA (NOUM-) 3561
AG:535D CB:1259C
moon
NEOPHUTOS 3504
AG:536C CB:1259C
novice
NEOS 3501
AG:535D CB:1259C
fresh
new
young
N(E)OSSOS 3502
AG:543 CB:—
young
NEōTERIKOS 3512
AG:537B CB:—
youthful
NEōTEROS 3501
AG:535D (NEOS) CB:1259C
young, -er
young (man)
NEOTēS 3503
AG:536C CB:1259C
youth
NēPHALIOS 3524
AG:538D CB:1259C
sober *Note*
temperate
NEPHELē 3507
AG:536D CB:1259C
cloud
NēPHō 3525
AG:538D CB:1259C
sober
watch
NEPHOS 3509
AG:537A CB:1259C
cloud
NEPHROS 3510
AG:537A CB:1259C
reins
NēPIAZō 3515
AG:537C CB:Cf. -IOS (1259C)
babe *Note*
child
NēPIOS 3516
AG:357C CB:1259C
babe
child

NēSION 3519
AG:538A CB:—
island
NēSOS 3520
AG:538A CB:—
island, isle
NēSTEIA 3521
AG:538A CB:1259C
fast, -ing
NēSTEUō 3522
AG:538B CB:1259C
fast
NēSTIS 3523
AG:538C CB:1259C
fasting
NēTHō 3514
AG:537C CB:—
spin
NEUō 3506
AG:536D CB:—
beckon
NIKAō 3528
AG:539A CB:1259C
conquer
get *Note*
overcome
prevail
victorious
victory
NIKE 3529
AG:539C CB:1259C
victory
NIKOS 3534
AG:539D CB:1259C
victory
NIPTēR 3537
AG:540A CB:—
bason
NIPTō 3538
AG:540B CB:1259C
wash
NOēMA 3540
AG:540D CB:1259C
device
mind
thought
NOEō 3539 (NOIEō)
AG:540B CB:1259C
consider
perceive
think
understand
NOMē 3542
AG:541A CB:1260A
eat
pasture
NOMIKOS 3544
AG:541B CB:1260A
law
lawyer
NOMIMōS 3545
AG:541C CB:1260A
lawfully
NOMISMA 3546
AG:541D CB:—
money

NOMIZō 3543
AG:541A CB:1260A
suppose
think
wont *Note*
NOMODIDASKALOS 3547
AG:541D CB:1260A
doctor
lawyer
teacher*
NOMOS 3551
AG:542A CB:1260A
law
NOMOTHESIA 3548
AG:541D CB:1260A
law
NOMOTHETEō 3549
AG:541D CB:1260A
enact
establish
law
NOMOTHETēS 3550
AG:542A CB:1260A
lawgiver
NOSēMA 3553
AG:543C CB:1260A
disease
NOSEō 3552
AG:543C CB:1260A
dote
sick *Note*
NOSOS 3554
AG:543C CB:1260A
disease
infirmity *Note*
sickness
NOSPHIZō 3557 (-OMAI)
AG:543D CB:—
keep
purloin
NOSSIA 3555
AG:543D CB:1260A
brood
nest
NOSSION 3556
AG:543D CB:—
brood
NOTHOS 3541
AG:540D CB:1260A
bastard
NōTHROS 3576
AG:547C CB:—
dull
slothful
sluggish
NOTOS 3558
AG:544A CB:1260A
south
south wind
NōTOS 3577
AG:547C CB:—
back
NOUNECHōS 3562
AG:544B CB:—
discreetly

NOUS 3563
AG:544C CB:1260A
mind
understanding
NOUTHESIA 3559
AG:544A CB:1260A
admonition
NOUTHETEō 3560
AG:544B CB:1260A
admonish
warn
NUCHTHēMEROS (-ON) 3574
AG:547A CB:—
night and a day (a)
NUMPHē 3565
AG:545B CB:1260A
bride
daughter-in-law
NUMPHIOS 3566
AG:545B CB:1260A
bridegroom
NUMPHōN 3567
AG:545B CB:1260A
bride-chamber
wedding*
NUN 3568
AG:545C CB:1260A
henceforth
late *Note*
now
present
time *Note*
NUNI 3570
AG:546B CB:1260B
now
NUSSō 3572
AG:547A CB:—
pierce
NUSTAZō 3573
AG:547A CB:—
slumber
NUX 3571
AG:546B CB:1260B
midnight *Note*
night

O

OCHLEō 3791
AG:600C CB:—
vex
OCHLOPOIEō 3792
AG:600C CB:—
company
crowd
OCHLOS 3793
AG:600C CB:1260B
common *Note*
company
crowd
multitude
number
people
OCHURōMA 3794
AG:601A CB:1260B
strongholds

ōDe 5603
AG:895C CB:1260B
hymn *Note*
song
ōDIN 5604
AG:895C CB:1260B
pain
sorrow
travail
ōDINō 5605
AG:895D CB:1260B
birth
travail
ODOUS 3599
AG:555A CB:1260B
tooth
ODUNAō 3600
AG:555A CB:—
anguish
sorrow
torment
ODUNē 3601
AG:555B CB:1260B
sorrow
ODURMOS 3602
AG:555B CB:1260B
bewail *Note*
mourning
OGDOēKONTA 3589
AG:552D CB:—
fourscore
OGDOOS 3590
AG:552D CB:1260B
eighth
OIDA 1492 (EIDo)
AG:555D CB:1260B
can
know
perceive *Note*
sure *Note*
tell *Note*
understand *Note*
wist, wot *Note*
OIKEIOS 3609
AG:556D CB:1260B
house
household
OIKēMA 3612
AG:557A CB:—
cell
prison *Note*
OIKEō 3611
AG:557A CB:1260B
dwell
OIKETEIA —
AG:556D CB:—
household
OIKēTēRION 3613
AG:557B CB:1260B
habitation
house *Note*
OIKETēS 3610
AG:557A CB:1260B
deacon *Note*
household-servant
servant

OIKIA 3614
AG:557B CB:1260B
home *Note*
house
household

OIKIAKOS 3615
AG:557D CB:—
household

OIKODESPOTEō 3616
AG:558A CB:1260B
guide *Note*
householder
rule

OIKODESPOTēS 3617
AG:558A CB:1260B
goodman
householder
master*

OIKODOMē 3619
AG:558D CB:1260B
building
edification
edify

OIKODOMEō 3618
AG:558A CB:1260B
build
builder
edify
embolden

OIKODOMIA 3620
AG:559C CB:—
dispensation

OIKONOMEō 3621
AG:559C CB:1260B
steward

OIKONOMIA 3622
AG:559C CB:1260B
dispensation
stewardship

OIKONOMOS 3623
AG:560A CB:1260B
chamberlain *Note*
governor
steward

OIKOS 3624
AG:560B CB:1260B
family
home
house
household
temple *Note*

OIKOUMENē 3625
AG:561B CB:1260C
earth
world

OIKOUR(G)OS 3626
AG:561C CB:—
home

OIKTEIRō 3627
AG:561D CB:—
compassion
mercy

OIKTIRMōN 3629
AG:561D CB:1260C
merciful
mercy

OIKTIRMOS 3628
AG:561D CB:1260C
compassion
mercy

OINOPHLUGIA 3632
AG:562C CB:1260C
excess *Note*
surfeiting *Note*
wine*
winebibbings*

OINOPOTēS 3630
AG:562A CB:1260C
wine-bibber

OINOS 3631
AG:562A CB:1260C
wine

OIOMAI (OIMAI) 3633
AG:562C CB:—
suppose
think

OKNEō 3635
AG:563A CB:—
delay

OKNēROS 3636
AG:563A CB:—
grievous *Note*
irksome
slothful

OKTAēMEROS 3637
AG:563A CB:—
eighth

OKTō 3638
AG:563A CB:1260C
eight

OLETHROS 3639
AG:563B CB:1260C
destruction

OLIGOPISTOS 3640
AG:563B CB:Cf. PISTIS (1265A)
faith (of little)

OLIGOPSUCHOS 3642
AG:564A CB:1260C
fainthearted
soul *Note*

OLIGōREō 3643
AG:564A CB:1260C
despise *Note*
regard

OLIGOS (-ON) 3641
AG:563C CB:1260C
briefly
few
little
season *Note*
small
space *Note*
while *Note*

OLOLUZō 3649
AG:564C CB:—
howl

OLOTHREUō 3645
AG:564B CB:1260C
destroy

OLOTHREUTēS 3644
AG:564B CB:1260C
destroyer

OLUNTHOS 3653
AG:565A CB:—
fig

OMBROS 3655
AG:565B CB:1260C
shower

OMMA 3659
AG:565D CB:1260C
eye

OMNUMI (OMNUō) 3660
AG:565D CB:1260C
adjure
swear

ōMOS 5606
AG:895D CB:—
shoulder

ONAR 3677
AG:569D CB:1260C
dream

ONARION 3678
AG:570A CB:1260C
ass

ONEIDISMOS 3680
AG:570B CB:1260C
reproach

ONEIDIZō 3679
AG:570A CB:1260C
cast *Note*
reproach
revile

ONEIDOS 3681
AG:570B CB:1260C
reproach

ōNEOMAI 5608
AG:895D CB:1260C
buy

ONIKOS 3684
AG:570C CB:1260C
millstone *Note*

ONINēMI 3685
AG:570D CB:1260C
joy

ONKOS 3591
AG:553A CB:1260C
weight

ONOMA 3686
AG:570D CB:1260C
call *Note*
name

ONOMAZō 3687
AG:573D CB:1261A
call *Note*
name

ONOS 3688
AG:574A CB:1261A
ass

ONTōS 3689
AG:574A CB:—
certainly
clean *Note*
indeed
truth *Note*
verily

ōON 5609
AG:896A CB:—
egg

OPē 3692
AG:574D CB:—
cave
hole
opening
place *Note*

OPHEILē 3782
AG:598C CB:1261A
debt, due

OPHEILēMA 3783
AG:598C CB:1261A
debt

OPHEILETēS 3781
AG:598B CB:1261A
debtor
offender
owe
sinner *Note*

OPHEILō 3784
AG:598D CB:1261A
behove
bound (to be)
debt *Note*
debtor *Note*
due, duty
guilty *Note*
indebted
must
needs
ought
owe
require *Note*
should *Note*

ōPHELEIA 5622
AG:900B CB:1261A
advantage
profit

ōPHELEō 5623
AG:900C CB:1261A
advantage
bettered
prevail
profit

ōPHELIMOS 5624
AG:900D CB:—
advantage *Note*
profit, -able

OPHELON 3785
AG:599A CB:1261A
would *Note*

OPHELOS 3786
AG:599B CB:—
advantage
profit

OPHIS 3789
AG:600A CB:1261A
serpent

OPHRUS 3790
AG:600B CB:—
brow

OPHTHALMODOULIA 3787
AG:599B CB:—
eye-service

OPHTHALMOS 3788
AG:599B CB:1261A
eye
sight

OPISō 3694
AG:575A CB:1261A
back, backward
behind
OPISTHEN 3693
AG:574D CB:1261A
backside
behind
OPōRA 3703
AG:576D CB:—
fruits
OPSARION 3795
AG:601B CB:1261A
fish
OPSE 3796
AG:601B CB:1261A
end *Note*
evening
late
OPSIA 3798 (-IOS)
AG:601C CB:—
even, evening
OPSIMOS 3797
AG:601C CB:1261A
latter
OPSIS 3799
AG:601D CB:1261A
appearance
countenance
face
OPSōNION 3800
AG:602A CB:1261A
charges
wages
OPTANō (-OMAI) 3700
AG:576C CB:1261A
appearing
see *Note*
OPTASIA 3701
AG:576C CB:1261A
vision
OPTOMAI (See HORAō)
OPTOS 3702
AG:576C CB:—
broiled
ORCHEō (-OMAI) 3738
AG:583B CB:1261A
dance
OREGō (-OMAI) 3713
AG:579D CB:1261A
covet
desire
reach, seek
OREINOS 3714
AG:580A CB:1261A
country
hill
OREXIS 3715
AG:580A CB:1261A
lust
ORGē 3709
AG:578D CB:1261A
anger
indignation *Note*
vengeance *Note*
wrath

ORGILOS 3711
AG:579D CB:1261A
angry
ORGIZō 3710
AG:579C CB:1261A
angry
wroth (be)
ORGUIA 3712
AG:579D CB:—
fathom
ORNEON 3732
AG:581D CB:—
bird
ORNIS 3733
AG:582A CB:1261B
hen
OROS 3735
AG:582B CB:1261B
hill
mount
mountain
ORPHANOS 3737
AG:583A CB:1261B
bereaved *Note*
comfortless *Note*
desolate
fatherless
ORTHOPODEō 3716
AG:580A CB:1261B
walk
ORTHOS 3717
AG:580B CB:1261B
even *Note*
straight
ORTHōS 3723
AG:580D CB:1261B
plain
right, -ly
ORTHOTOMEō 3718
AG:580B CB:1261B
divide
handle
ORTHRINOS 3720
AG:580C CB:—
dawn *Note*
early
morning
ORTHRIOS 3721
AG:580C CB:—
dawn *Note*
early
ORTHRIZō 3719
AG:580C CB:—
dawn *Note*
morning
ORTHROS 3722
AG:580C CB:—
dawn
early
morning
ōRUOMAI 5612
AG:897A CB:—
roar
ORUSSō 3736
AG:582D CB:—
dig

OSMē 3744
AG:586A CB:1261B
odour
savour
OSPHRēSIS 3750
AG:587C CB:—
smelling
OSPHUS 3751
AG:587D CB:1261B
loins
OSTEON 3747
AG:586C CB:1261B
bone
OSTRAKINOS 3749
AG:587C CB:1261B
earthen
ōTARION 5621 (ōTION)
AG:900B CB:—
ear *Note*
OTHONē 3607
AG:555C CB:—
sheet
OTHONION 3608
AG:555C CB:—
linen
ōTION 5621
AG:900B CB:—
ear
OU (OUK) 3756
AG:590A CB:—
means (by no) *Note*
nay
never *Note*
no man *Note*
no more *Note*
no wise (in)
nothing
wise (in no)
without *Note*
Notes p. 1267
OUA 3758
AG:591A CB:—
ah
OUAI 3759
AG:591A CB:1261B
woe
OUCHI 3780
AG:598B CB:—
nay
OUDAMōS 3760
AG:591B CB:—
no wise (in)
OUDE 3761
AG:591C CB:—
indeed
much (as) *Note*
nothing
Notes p. 1267
OUDEIS (-DEN) 3762
AG:591D CB:1261B
never *Note*
no man *Note*
no one *Note*
one *Note*
nothing
nought

OUDEPō 3764
AG:592C CB:—
never
yet *Note*
OUDEPOTE 3763
AG:592B CB:—
never
nothing *Note*
time *Note*
OUKETI 3765
AG:592C CB:—
henceforth
hereafter
longer (no)
more (no)
no longer
now *Note*
yet *Note*
OUKOUN 3766
AG:592D CB:—
then
OUN 3767
AG:592D CB:—
now
so *Note*
then
verily *Note*
wherefore *Note*
OUPō 3768
AG:593C CB:1261B
hitherto
yet *Note*
OURA 3769
AG:593C CB:—
tail
OURANIOS 3770
AG:593C CB:1261B
heavenly
OURANOS 3772
AG:593D CB:1261B
air
heaven(s)
OURANOTHEN 3771
AG:593D CB:1261B
heaven
OUS 3775
AG:595C CB:1261B
ear
OUSIA 3776
AG:596A CB:1261B
substance
OUTHEN (OUDEIS) 3762
AG:591D CB:1261B
nothing
OXOS 3690
AG:574B CB:1261B
vinegar
OXUS 3691
AG:574C CB:—
sharp
swift
OZō 3605
AG:555C CB:—
stink

P

PACHUNō 3975
AG:638B CB:1261B
gross (to wax)
PAGIDEUō 3802
AG:602A CB:—
ensnare
entangle
PAGIS 3803
AG:602A CB:1261B
snare
PAGOS 697
AG:105B CB:1261B
hill *Note*
PAIDAGōGOS 3807
AG:603A CB:1261B
instructor
tutor*
PAIDARION 3808
AG:603B CB:1261B
child
PAIDEIA 3809
AG:603B CB:1261B
chastening
chastisement
instruction
PAIDEUō 3811
AG:603D CB:1261C
chasten
chastise
correcting
instruct
learn *Note*
learned *Note*
teach
PAIDEUTēS 3810
AG:603D CB:1261C
correct
instructor
PAIDION 3813
AG:604A CB:1261C
child
damsel
young *Note*
PAIDIOTHEN 3812
AG:604A CB:Cf. -ON (1261C)
child *Note*
PAIDISKē 3814
AG:604B CB:1261C
bondmaid
damsel
maid, maiden
PAIō 3817
AG:605B CB:—
smite
strike *Note*
PAIS 3816
AG:604C CB:1261C
boy, child
maid, maiden
manservant
menservants
servant
sir *Note*
son *Note*
young man *Note*
PAIZō 3815
AG:604C CB:1261C
play
PALAI 3819
AG:605C CB:1261C
great *Note*
long *Note*
old
time
while *Note*
PALAIOō 3822
AG:606A CB:1261C
decay
old
PALAIOS 3820
AG:605D CB:1261C
old
PALAIOTēS 3821
AG:606A CB:1261C
oldness
PALē 3823
AG:606A CB:—
wrestle
wrestling
PALIN 3825
AG:606C CB:1261C
again
PALINGENESIA 3824
AG:606A CB:1261C
regeneration
PAMPLēTHEI 3826
AG:607B CB:—
once *Note*
together *Note*
PAMPOLUS 3827
AG:607B CB:—
very *Note*
PANDOCHEION 3829
AG:607C CB:—
inn
PANDOCHEUS 3830
AG:607D CB:—
host
PANēGURIS 3831
AG:607D CB:1261C
assembly
PANOIKEI 3832
AG:607D CB:—
house
PANOPLIA 3833
AG:607D CB:1261C
armour
PANOURGIA 3834
AG:608A CB:1261C
craftiness
subtilty *Note*
PANOURGOS 3835
AG:608A CB:1261C
crafty
PANTACHē —
AG:608B CB:—
everywhere
PANTACHOTHEN 3836
AG:608B CB:—
every quarter *Note*
PANTACHOU 3837
AG:608B CB:—
everywhere
place
PANTē 3839
AG:608D CB:—
always
way *Note*
PANTELēS 3838
AG:608C CB:1261C
uttermost
wise (in no)
PANTOKRATōR 3841
AG:608D CB:1261C
almighty
sabaoth
PANTōS 3843
AG:609B CB:—
all
altogether
certainly
doubt (no)
means (by all)
no wise (in)
surely *Note*
wise (in no)
PANTOTE 3842
AG:609B CB:1261C
always
ever
evermore
PANTOTHEN 3840
AG:608D CB:—
every side
quarter
round about
PARA 3844
AG:609C CB:1261C
contrary
more *Note*
nigh
of *Note*
rather
side *Note*
PARABAINō 3845
AG:611C CB:1262A
fall
transgress
transgression
PARABALLō 3846
AG:611D CB:1262A
arrive
compare
touch
PARABASIS 3847
AG:611D CB:1262A
breaking
transgression
trespass *Note*
PARABATēS 3848
AG:612A CB:1262A
breaker
transgressor
PARABIAZOMAI 3849
AG:612B CB:—
constrain
PARABOLē 3850
AG:612B CB:1262A
comparison
figure
parable
PARABO(U)LEUOMAI 3851
AG:612B CB:—
hazard
PARACHEIMASIA 3915
AG:623D CB:—
winter *Note*
PARACHEIMAZō 3914
AG:623D CB:—
winter
PARACHRēMA 3916
AG:623D CB:—
forthwith *Note*
immediately
PARADECHOMAI 3858
AG:614B CB:—
receive
PARADEIGMATIZō 3856
AG:614A CB:1262A
example
put *Note*
shame
PARADEISOS 3857
AG:614A CB:1262A
paradise
PARADIATRIBē 3859
AG:614B CB:—
disputing
wrangling
PARADIDōMI 3860
AG:614B CB:1262A
betray
bring *Note*
cast *Note*
commend
commit
deliver
give
hazard
prison *Note*
put
ripe
PARADOSIS 3862
AG:615D CB:1262A
ordinance *Note*
tradition
PARADOXOS 3861
AG:615D CB:—
strange
PARAGINOMAI 3854
AG:613C CB:—
arrive
come
go *Note*
part
present
stand *Note*
PARAGō 3855
AG:613D CB:—
depart
pass
walk *Note*

PARAINEō 3867
AG:616B CB:1262A
admonish
exhort
PARAITEOMAI 3868
AG:616C CB:1262A
avoid
excuse
intreat
refuse, reject
PARAKALEō 3870
AG:617A CB:1262A
beseech
call *Note*
comfort
desire *Note*
exhort
intreat
pray *Note*
PARAKALUPTō 3871
AG:617D CB:Cf. KAL-(1253B)
conceal
hide
PARAKATATHēKē 3872
AG:617D CB:Cf. PARATHēKē (1262B)
commit *Note*
PARAKATHEZOMAI 3869 (-Zō)
AG:616D CB:—
sit
PARAKATHIZō 3869
AG:616D CB:—
sit
PARAKEIMAI 3873
AG:617D CB:—
present (to be)
PARAKLēSIS 3874
AG:618A CB:1262A
comfort
consolation
encouragement
exhortation
intreaty
PARAKLēTOS 3875
AG:618B CB:1262A
Comforter
PARAKOē 3876
AG:618D CB:1262A
disobedience
PARAKOLOUTHEō 3877
AG:618D CB:1262A
attain *Note*
follow
know *Note*
trace
understand *Note*
PARAKOUō 3878
AG:619A CB:1262A
hear
refuse *Note*
PARAKUPTō 3879
AG:619B CB:—
look
stoop
PARALAMBANō 3880
AG:619B CB:1262A
receive
take

PARALEGō (-OMAI) 3881
AG:619D CB:—
coasting
sail
PARALIOS 3882
AG:620A CB:—
coast
sea
PARALLAGē 3883
AG:620A CB:—
variableness
PARALOGIZOMAI 3884
AG:620B CB:1262A
beguile
deceive
delude
PARALUō 3886
AG:620B CB:1262A
feeble *Note*
palsy (sick of)
PARALUTIKOS 3885
AG:620B CB:1262A
palsy (sick of)
PARAMENō 3887
AG:620C CB:1262A
abide
continue
PARAMUTHEOMAI 3888
AG:620D CB:1262B
comfort
console
encourage
PARAMUTHIA 3889
AG:620D CB:1262B
comfort
consolation
PARAMUTHION 3890
AG:620D CB:1262B
comfort
consolation
PARANGELIA 3852
AG:613A CB:1262B
charge
commandment
straitly *Note*
PARANGELLō 3853
AG:613B CB:1262B
charge
command
declare
PARANOMEō 3891
AG:621A CB:1262B
law
PARANOMIA 3892
AG:621A CB:—
iniquity
transgression
PARAPHERō 3911
AG:623B CB:—
remove
take
PARAPHRONEō 3912
AG:623C CB:—
fool
beside oneself (to be)

PARAPHRONIA 3913
AG:623C CB:—
madness
PARAPIKRAINō 3893
AG:621A CB:1262B
provoke
PARAPIKRASMOS 3894
AG:621B CB:1262B
provocation
PARAPIPTō 3895
AG:621B CB:1262B
fall
PARAPLEō 3896
AG:621B CB:—
sail
PARAPLēSION 3897
AG:621C (-OS) CB:1262B
nigh
PARAPLēSIōS 3898
AG:621C CB:—
likewise
manner *Note*
PARAPOREUOMAI 3899
AG:621D CB:—
go
pass
PARAPTōMA 3900
AG:621D CB:1262B
fall
fault *Note*
offence *Note*
sin *Note*
trespass
PARARHEō 3901 (-RRHUEō)
AG:621D CB:1262B
drift
PARASēMOS 3902
AG:622A CB:—
sign
PARASKEUAZō 3903
AG:622A CB:1262B
prepare
ready
PARASKEUē 3904
AG:622B CB:1262B
preparation
PARATEINō 3905
AG:622C CB:—
continue *Note*
prolong
PARATēREō 3906
AG:622C CB:1262B
observe
watch
PARATēRēSIS 3907
AG:622D CB:1262B
observation
show *Note*
PARATHALASSIOS 3864
AG:616A CB:—
coast *Note*
sea
PARATHēKē 3866
AG:616B CB:1262B
commit

PARATHEōREō 3865
AG:616B CB:—
neglect
PARATITHēMI 3908
AG:622D CB:—
allege
commend
commit
keeping *Note*
put
set
PARATUNCHANō 3909
AG:623A CB:—
meet (verb)
PARAUTIKA 3910
AG:623B CB:—
moment
PARAZēLOō 3863
AG:616A CB:—
jealousy
provoke
PARDALIS 3917
AG:623D CB:1262B
leopard
PARECHō 3930
AG:626B CB:Cf. ECHō (1242C)
bring *Note*
do
give
keep *Note*
minister
offer
render
shew
trouble *Note*
PAREDREUō —
AG:624A CB:—
wait
PARēGORIA 3931
AG:626D CB:—
comfort
PAREIMI 3918
AG:624A CB:1262B
come *Note*
have*
here (to be)
lack *Note*
present (to be)
PAREISAGō 3919
AG:624C CB:Cf. AGō (1233C)
bring
PAREISAKTOS 3920
AG:624C CB:—
privily *Note*
unawares *Note*
PAREISDU(N)ō 3921
AG:624D CB:—
creep
privily *Note*
unawares *Note*
PAREISERCHOMAI 3922
AG:624D CB:1262B
beside *Note*
come
enter
privily *Note*

PAREISPHERō 3923
AG:625A CB:—
add
give *Note*
PAREKTOS 3924
AG:625A CB:1262B
except
saving
without *Note*
PAREMBOLē 3925
AG:625B CB:1262B
army
PARENOCHLEō 3926
AG:625C CB:—
trouble
PAREPIDēMOS 3927
AG:625D CB:1262B
pilgrim
sojourner
stranger *Note*
PARERCHOMAI 3928
AG:625D CB:1262B
come
go *Note*
pass
transgress
PARESIS 3929
AG:626B CB:1262B
passing over
remission
PARIēMI 3935
AG:627C CB:1262B
hang
PARISTANō 3936
AG:627C CB:1262B
present (verb)
yield
PARISTēMI 3936
AG:627C CB:1262B
bring *Note*
come
commend
give *Note*
help *Note*
present (verb)
prove
provide
send *Note*
shew
stand
yield
PARODOS 3938
AG:628D CB:—
way
PAROICHOMAI 3944
AG:629B CB:—
pass
PAROIKEō 3939
AG:628D CB:1262B
sojourn
stranger *Note*
PAROIKIA 3940
AG:629A CB:1262B
dwell
strangers *Note*
sojourning

PAROIKOS 3941
AG:629A CB:1262B
foreigner *Note*
pilgrim *Note*
sojourner
stranger *Note*
PAROIMIA 3942
AG:629B CB:1262B
parable
PAROINOS 3943
AG:629B CB:1262C
brawler
wine *Note*
PAROMOIAZō 3945
AG:629B CB:1262C
like
PAROMOIOS 3946
AG:629B CB:1262C
like
PAROPSIS 3953
AG:630B CB:—
platter
PARORGISMOS 3950
AG:629D CB:1262C
anger *Note*
wrath
PARORGIZō 3949
AG:629D CB:1262C
anger
provoke
wrath *Note*
PAROTRUNō 3951
AG:629D CB:—
stir
urge *Note*
PAROUSIA 3952
AG:629D CB:1262C
coming
presence
PAROXUNō 3947
AG:629C CB:1262C
provoke
stir
PAROXUSMOS 3948
AG:629C CB:1262C
contention
provoke
PARRHēSIA 3954
AG:630C CB:1262C
boldness
confidence
freely *Note*
openly
plainly, -nness
PARRHēSIAZOMAI 3955
AG:631A CB:1262C
bold
freely *Note*
preach
PARTHENIA 3932
AG:626D CB:1262C
virginity
PARTHENOS 3933
AG:627A CB:1262C
daughter
virgin

PAS 3956
AG:631A CB:1262C
all
every
everywhere *Note*
manner *Note*
many *Note*
one *Note*
part *Note*
quarter *Note*
thoroughly *Note*
whatsoever*
whole
whosoever*
withal *Note*
PASCHA 3957
AG:633B CB:1262C
Easter
passover
PASCHō 3958
AG:633D CB:1262C
feel *Note*
passion
suffer
PATASSō 3960
AG:634D CB:1262C
smite
strike *Note*
PATEō 3961
AG:634D CB:1262C
tread
PATēR 3962
AG:635A CB:1262C
father
parent
PATHēMA 3804
AG:602B CB:1262C
affection
affliction
passion
suffering
PATHēTOS 3805
AG:602D CB:1262C
afflicted *Note*
suffer
PATHOS 3806
AG:602D CB:1262C
affection
lust *Note*
passion
PATROLōAS (PATRA-) 3964
AG:636D CB:—
murderer
PATRIA 3965
AG:636D CB:1263A
family
kindred *Note*
PATRIARCHēS 3966
AG:636D CB:—
patriarch
PATRIKOS 3967
AG:636D CB:1263A
father
PATRIS 3968
AG:636D CB:1263A
country

PATRōOS 3971
AG:637B CB:—
father
PATROPARADOTOS 3970
AG:637A CB:—
father
handed down
receive *Note*
PAUō 3973
AG:638A CB:—
cease
leave
refrain
PēCHUS 4083
AG:656D CB:—
cubit
PēDALION 4079
AG:656A CB:—
rudder
PEDē 3976
AG:638C CB:—
fetter
PEDINOS 3977
AG:638C CB:1263A
place *Note*
PēGANON 4076
AG:655D CB:1263A
rue
PēGē 4077
AG:655D CB:1263A
fountain
spring
well *Note*
PēGNUMI 4078
AG:656A CB:1263A
pitch
PEINAō 3983
AG:640A CB:1263A
hunger, hungry
PEIRA 3984
AG:640A CB:1263A
trial
PEIRAō 3987
AG:641A CB:1263A
go *Note*
try
PEIRASMOS 3986
AG:640D CB:1263A
prove
temptation
trial
try *Note*
PEIRAZō 3985
AG:640B CB:1263A
examine
go *Note*
prove
tempt, -er *Note*
try
PEISMONē 3988
AG:641B CB:1263A
persuasion
PEITHARCHEō 3980
AG:638D CB:1263A
hearken
obey

PEITHō 3982
AG:639A CB:1263A
agree
assure
believe
confident
friend
obey
persuade
trust
urge *Note*
yield

PEITHOS 3981
AG:639A CB:1263A
enticing
persuasive

PELAGOS 3989
AG:641B CB:—
depth
sea

PELEKIZō 3990
AG:641C CB:—
behead

PēLIKOS 4080
AG:656B CB:—
great
large

PēLOS 4081
AG:656B CB:1263A
clay

PEMPō 3992
AG:641D CB:1263A
send
thrust *Note*

PEMPTOS 3991
AG:641C CB:—
fifth

PENēS 3993
AG:642C CB:1263A
poor

PENICHROS 3998
AG:642D CB:1263A
poor

PENTAKIS 3999
AG:643A CB:—
five times

PENTAKISCHILIOI 4000
AG:643A CB:1263A
five
thousand *Note*

PENTAKOSIOI 4001
AG:643A CB:—
five (hundred)

PENTE 4002
AG:643A CB:1263A
five

PENTEKAIDEKATOS 4003
AG:643A CB:—
fifteenth *Note*

PENTēKONTA 4004
AG:643A CB:—
fifty

PENTēKOSTOS (-Tē) 4005
AG:643A CB:1263A
Pentecost

PENTHEō 3996
AG:642C CB:1263A
bewail
mourn
wail *Note*

PENTHERA 3994
AG:642C CB:—
mother-in-law
wife's mother

PENTHEROS 3995
AG:642C CB:—
father-in-law

PENTHOS 3997
AG:642D CB:1263A
mourning
sorrow

PEPOITHēSIS 4006
AG:643B CB:1263B
confidence
trust

PēRA 4082
AG:656C CB:1263B
wallet

PERAN 4008
AG:643D CB:—
beyond
side

PERAS 4009
AG:644A CB:1263B
end, final
part

PERI 4012
AG:644B CB:1263B
affairs *Note*
concern (-eth)
neighbourhood
of *Note*
pertain to *Note*
respect *Note*
thereabout

PERIAGō 4013
AG:645C CB:—
compass
go, lead

PERIAIREō 4014
AG:645D CB:—
cast, take

PERIAPTō —
AG:645D CB:—
kindle

PERIATRAPTō 4015
AG:645D CB:—
shine

PERIBALLō 4016
AG:646A CB:—
cast
clothe, put

PERIBLEPō 4017
AG:646B CB:Cf. BLEPō (1239A)
look

PERIBOLAION 4018
AG:646C CB:1263B
clothing *Note*
covering
mantle
veil
vesture

PERICHōROS 4066
AG:653C CB:—
country
region

PERIDEō 4019
AG:646C CB:Cf. DEō (1240C)
bind

PERIECHō 4023
AG:647A CB:1263B
contain

PERIERCHOMAI 4022
AG:646D CB:1263B
circuit
compass
go
strolling
wander *Note*

PERIERGAZOMAI 4020
AG:646D CB:1263B
busybody

PERIERGOS 4021
AG:646D CB:1263B
arts
busybody
curious

PERIISTēMI 4026
AG:647C CB:—
avoid
stand

PERIKALUPTō 4028
AG:647D CB:Cf. KAL-(1253B)
blindfold
cover
overlay

PERIKATHARMA 4027
AG:647D CB:1263B
filth

PERIKEIMAI 4029
AG:647D CB:—
bound (to be)
compass
hang

PERIKEPHALAIA 4030
AG:648A CB:1263B
helmet

PERIKRATēS 4031
AG:648B CB:—
secure

PERIKRUPTō 4032
AG:648B (-UBo) CB:—
hide

PERIKUKLOō 4033
AG:648B CB:—
compass

PERILAMPō 4034
AG:648C CB:1263B
shine

PERILEIPō 4035
AG:648C (-OMAI) CB:1263B
leave
remain

PERILUPOS 4036
AG:648C CB:—
sorrowful
sorry

PERIMENō 4037
AG:648C CB:1263B
wait

PERIOCHē 4042
AG:648D CB:—
place

PERIOIKEō 4039
AG:648D CB:—
dwell

PERIOIKOS 4040
AG:648D CB:—
neighbour

PERIOUSIOS 4041
AG:648D CB:1263B
possession

PERIPATEō 4043
AG:649A CB:1263B
go
occupy
walk

PERIPEIRō 4044
AG:649D CB:—
pierce

PERIPHERō 4064
AG:653B CB:1263B
bear
carry *Note*

PERIPHRONEō 4065
AG:653B CB:1263B
despise

PERIPIPTō 4045
AG:649D CB:1263B
fall

PERIPOIEō (-OMAI) 4046
AG:650A CB:1263B
gain
purchase

PERIPOIēSIS 4047
AG:650A CB:1263B
obtaining
possession
purchase *Note*
saving

PERIPSēMA 4067 (-SōMA)
AG:653C CB:1263C
offscouring

PERIRRHēGNUMI 4048
AG:650B CB:—
rend

PERISPAō 4049
AG:650B CB:—
cumber

PERISSEIA 4050
AG:650C CB:1263C
abundance
overflowing

PERISSEUMA 4051
AG:650C CB:1263C
abundance
leave *Note*
remain *Note*

PERISSEUō 4052
AG:650C CB:1263C
abound
abundance
better (be)

PERISSEUō (Continued)
enough *Note*
exceed
excel
increase
leave
remain
spare *Note*

PERISSOS 4053
AG:651B CB:1263C
abundant
advantage
measure *Note*
more
superfluous

PERISSōS 4057
AG:651D CB:1263C
abundantly
exceedingly
measure
more *Note*

PERISSOTEROS (-ON) 4054
AG:651C CB:1263C
abundant
far *Note*
greater
more
overmuch

PERISSOTERōS 4056
AG:651D CB:1263C
abundantly
earnest *Note*
exceedingly
more *Note*
rather *Note*

PERISTERA 4058
AG:651D CB:1263C
dove

PERITEMNō 4059
AG:652B CB:1263C
circumcise

PERITHESIS 4025
AG:647C CB:—
wearing

PERITITHēMI 4060
AG:652C CB:Cf. TITHēMI (1272C)
bestow
put, set

PERITOMē 4061
AG:652D CB:1263C
circumcision

PERITRECHō 4063
AG:653A CB:—
run

PERITREPō 4062
AG:653A CB:—
turn

PERIX 4038
AG:648D CB:—
round about

PERIZōNNUMI 4024
AG:647B CB:1263C
gird

PERPEREUOMAI 4068
AG:653D CB:—
glory (boast) *Note*
vaunt

PERUSI 4070
AG:653D CB:1263C
year

PETAOMAI 4072
AG:654A (PETOMAI) CB:—
fly

PETEINON 4071
AG:654A CB:1263C
bird

PETOMAI 4072
AG:654A CB:—
fly

PETRA 4073
AG:654A CB:1263C
rock
stone *Note*

PETRōDēS 4075
AG:655C CB:1263C
ground *Note*
rocky

PETROS 4074
AG:654D CB:1263C
stone *Note*

PEZEUō 3978
AG:638D CB:—
foot
land *Note*

PEZOS 3979 (PEZē)
AG:638D CB:—
foot

PHAGō (ESTHIō) 5315
AG:312B CB:1246C
eat, meat

PHAGOS 5314
AG:851A CB:—
gluttonous

PHAILONēS 5341 (PHEL-)
AG:851A CB:—
clothing

PHAINō 5316
AG:851B CB:1263C
appear
see
seem *Note*
shine
think

PHANEROō 5319
AG:852D CB:1263C
appear
declare *Note*
manifest
shew *Note*

PHANEROS 5318
AG:852B CB:1263C
appear *Note*
evident *Note*
known
manifest
openly *Note*
outwardly *Note*
spread *Note*

PHANERōS 5320
AG:853A CB:1263C
evidently
openly
publicly

PHANERōSIS 5321
AG:853B CB:1263C
appearance *Note*
manifestation

PHANOS 5322
AG:853B CB:—
lantern

PHANTASIA 5325
AG:853B CB:1263C
pomp

PHANTASMA 5326
AG:853C CB:1263C
apparition
spirit *Note*

PHANTAZō 5324
AG:853B CB:1263C
appearance
sight *Note*

PHARANX 5327
AG:853C CB:—
valley

PHARISAIOS 5330
AG:853C CB:1263C
Pharisees

PHARMAK(E)IA 5331
AG:854A CB:1263C
sorcery
witchcraft*

PHARMAKOS 5333
(PHARMAKEUS 5332)
AG:854B CB:1263C
sorcerer

PHASIS 5334
AG:854B CB:—
tidings

PHASKō 5335
AG:854B CB:—
affirm
profess
say *Note*

PHATNē 5336
AG:854B CB:—
manger

PHAULOS 5337
AG:854C CB:1264A
evil
ill
vessel *Note*

PHEIDOMAI 5339
AG:854D CB:—
forbear
spare

PHEIDOMENōS 5340
AG:854D CB:1264A
sparingly

PHELONēS 5341
AG:851A (PHAIL-) CB:—
clothing

PHēMē 5345
AG:856B CB:—
fame

PHēMI 5346
AG:856B CB:1264A
affirm
say

PHENGOS 5338
AG:854C CB:1264A
light

PHERō 5342
AG:854D CB:1264A
bear
bring
carry
come
drive
endure
go *Note*
lay *Note*
lead
move, press
reach
rushing
uphold

PHEUGō 5343
AG:855D CB:1264A
escape
flee

PHIALē 5357
AG:858B CB:—
bowl

PHILADELPHIA 5360
AG:858C CB:1264A
brother *Note*

PHILADELPHOS 5361
AG:858C CB:1264A
brother *Note*

PHILAGATHOS 5358
AG:858B CB:1264A
lover

PHILANDROS 5362
AG:858C CB:1264A
husband

PHILANTHRōPIA 5363
AG:858D CB:1264A
kindness
love

PHILANTHRōPōS 5364
AG:858D CB:1264A
courteously
kindly

PHILARGURIA 5365
AG:859A CB:1264A
money (love of)

PHILARGUROS 5366
AG:859A CB:1264A
covetous
lover

PHILAUTOS 5367
AG:859A CB:1264A
lover

PHILēDONOS 5369
AG:859C CB:1264A
lover
pleasure

PHILēMA 5370
AG:859C CB:1264A
kiss

PHILEō 5368
AG:859B CB:1264A
kiss
love

PHILIA 5373
AG:859D CB:1264A
friendship
PHILONEIKIA 5379
AG:860D CB:1264A
contention
strife
PHILONEIKOS 5380
AG:860D CB:1264A
contentious
PHILOPHRōN 5391
AG:861D CB:1264A
courteous *Note*
PHILOPHRONōS 5390
AG:861D CB:1264A
courteously
PHILOPRōTEUō 5383
AG:860D CB:1264A
pre-eminence
PHILOS (PHILē) 5384
AG:861A CB:1264A
friend
PHILOSOPHIA 5385
AG:861B CB:1264A
philosophy
PHILOSOPHOS 5386
AG:861B CB:1264B
philosopher
PHILOSTORGOS 5387
AG:861C CB:1264B
affection
PHILOTEKNOS 5388
AG:861C CB:1264B
children
PHILOTHEOS 5377
AG:860C CB:1264B
lover
PHILOTIMEOMAI 5389
AG:861C CB:1264B
aim
labour *Note*
strive *Note*
study *Note*
PHILOXENIA 5381
AG:860D CB:1264B
entertain *Note*
hospitality
stranger
PHILOXENOS 5382
AG:860D CB:1264B
hospitality
lover
PHIMOō 5392
AG:861D CB:—
muzzle
peace (hold one's)
put *Note*
silence
speechless *Note*
still
PHLOGIZō 5394
AG:862A CB:—
fire
PHLOX 5395
AG:862A CB:—
flame, -ing

PHLUAREō 5396
AG:862B CB:—
prate
PHLUAROS 5397
AG:862B CB:—
tattler
PHOBEō 5399
AG:862B CB:1264B
fear
marvel *Note*
reverence
PHOBEROS 5398
AG:862B CB:1264B
fearful
PHOBēTRON 5400
AG:863C CB:1264B
fearful *Note*
sight *Note*
terror
PHOBOS 5401
AG:863C CB:1264B
fear
terror
PHOINIX 5404
AG:864B I. CB:1264B
palm (tree)
PHōLEOS 5454
AG:870B CB:—
hole
PHōNē 5456
AG:870C CB:1264B
noise *Note*
sound
voice
PHōNEō 5455
AG:870B CB:1264B
call, cry
PHONEUō 5407
AG:864C CB:—
kill
murder *Note*
slay
PHONEUS 5406
AG:864C CB:—
murderer
PHONOS 5408
AG:864D CB:1264B
murder
slaughter
PHOREō 5409
AG:864D CB:—
bear
wear
PHOROS 5411
AG:865A CB:1264B
tribute
PHORTION 5413
AG:865A CB:1264B
burden
lading
PHORTIZō 5412
AG:865A CB:1264B
lade
PHORTOS 5414
AG:865B CB:1264B
lading

PHōS 5457
AG:871D CB:1264B
lamp
light
PHōSPHOROS 5459
AG:872D CB:1264B
day-star
PHōSTēR 5458
AG:872C CB:1264B
light
PHōTEINOS 5460
AG:872D CB:1264B
bright
light
PHōTISMOS 5462
AG:873C CB:1264B
light
PHōTIZō 5461
AG:872D CB:1264B
enlighten
light, -en
PHRAGELLION 5416
AG:865B CB:1264B
scourge
PHRAGELLOō 5417
AG:865B CB:1264B
scourge
PHRAGMOS 5418
AG:865C CB:1264B
hedge
partition
PHRASSō 5420
AG:865C CB:1264B
stop
PHRAZō 5419
AG:865C CB:—
declare
explain
PHREAR 5421
AG:865D CB:1264C
pit
well
PHRēN 5424
AG:865D CB:1264C
understanding *Note*
PHRENAPATAō 5422
AG:865D CB:—
deceive
PHRENAPATēS 5423
AG:865D CB:—
deceiver
PHRISSō 5425
AG:866A CB:—
shudder
tremble *Note*
PHRONēMA 5427
AG:866C CB:1264C
mind
minded *Note*
PHRONEō 5426
AG:866A CB:1264C
affection *Note*
careful
feel
likeminded *Note*
mind, minded

PHRONEō (Continued)
minded
observe
regard
savour *Note*
think
thought (to take)
understand *Note*
PHRONēSIS 5428
AG:866C CB:1264C
mind *Note*
prudence
wisdom
PHRONIMOS 5429
AG:866D CB:1264C
wise
PHONIMōS 5430
AG:866D CB:1264C
wisely
PHRONTIZō 5431
AG:866D CB:1264C
careful
PHROUREō 5432
AG:867B CB:1264C
guard, keep
PHRUASSō 5433
AG:867B CB:—
rage
PHRUGANON 5434
AG:867B CB:—
stick
PHTHANō 5348
AG:856D CB:1264C
already *Note*
arrive
attain
come
precede
PHTHARTOS 5349
AG:857A CB:1264C
corruptible
PHTHENGOMAI 5350
AG:857A CB:—
speak, utter
PHTHEIRō 5351
AG:857B CB:1264C
corrupt
defile
destroy
PHTHINOPōRINOS 5352
AG:857C CB:—
autumn
fruit *Note*
PHTHONEō 5354
AG:857C CB:1264C
envy
PHTHONGOS 5353
AG:857C CB:—
sound
PHTHONOS 5355
AG:857D CB:1264C
envy, -ing
PHTHORA 5356
AG:858A CB:1264C
corruption
destroy
perish *Note*

PHUGē 5437
AG:867C CB:1264C
flight
PHULAKē 5438
AG:867D CB:1264C
cage
hold (Noun)
imprisonment
prison
ward, watch
PHULAKIZō 5439
AG:868A CB:1264C
imprison
PHULAKTēRION 5440
AG:868A CB:1264C
phylactery
PHULASSō 5442
AG:868B CB:1264C
beware
guard
keep
observe
preserve
save *Note*
ware of
PHULAX 5441
AG:868B CB:1264C
guard
keeper
PHULē 5443
AG:868D CB:1264C
kindred *Note*
tribe
PHULLON 5444
AG:869A CB:1264C
leaf
PHUō 5453
AG:870B CB:1264C
grow
spring
PHURAMA 5445
AG:869A CB:1264C
lump
PHUSIKOS 5446
AG:869B CB:1264C
natural
PHUSIKōS 5447
AG:869B CB:1264C
naturally
PHUSIOō 5448
AG:869B CB:1264C
puff (up)
PHUSIōSIS 5450
AG:870A CB:—
swelling
PHUSIS 5449
AG:869B CB:1264C
kind (noun)
nature
natural *Note*
PHUTEIA 5451
AG:870A CB:1264C
plant
PHUTEUō 5452
AG:870A CB:1264C
plant

PIAZō 4084
AG:657A CB:—
apprenhend
catch
hands (lay ... on)
take
PIEZō 4085
AG:657B CB:—
press
PIKRAINō 4087
AG:657B CB:1265A
bitter
PIKRIA 4088
AG:657C CB:1265A
bitterness
PIKROS 4089
AG:657C CB:1265A
bitter
PIKRōS 4090
AG:657D CB:1265A
bitterly
PIMPLēMI (PLēTHō) 4130
AG:658A CB:1265A
accomplish
fill
furnish
PIMPRēMI 4092
AG:658B CB:1265A
swell
PINAKIDION 4093
AG:658B CB:—
writing-table
PINAX 4094
AG:658C CB:—
charger
platter
PINō 4095
AG:658C CB:1265A
drink
PIOTēS 4096
AG:659A CB:1265A
fatness
PIPRASKō 4097
AG:659A CB:1265A
sell
PIPTō 4098
AG:659B CB:1265A
fail, fall
light (to ... upon) *Note*
strike *Note*
PISTEUō 4100
AG:660B CB:1265A
believe, -er
commit
intrust
trust
PISTIKOS 4101
AG:662B CB:—
spikenard
PISTIS 4102
AG:662B CB:1265A
assurance
belief
faith
faithfulness
fidelity

PISTOō 4104
AG:665B CB:1265A
assured
PISTOS 4103
AG:664C CB:1265A
believer, -ing
faithful, -ly
sure
true *Note*
PITHANOLOGIA 4086
AG:657B CB:1265A
enticing *Note*
persuasiveness
PLANAō 4105
AG:665B CB:1265A
deceive
err
lead
seduce
wander
way *Note*
PLANē 4106
AG:665D CB:1265A
deceit *Note*
delusion
error
PLANēTēS 4107
AG:666A CB:1265A
wandering
PLANOS 4108
AG:666A CB:1265A
deceiver
seducing
PLASMA 4110
AG:666B CB:—
formed
PLASSō 4111
AG:666C CB:1265A
formed
PLASTOS 4112
AG:666C CB:—
feigned
PLATEIA 4113
AG:666D CB:1265A
street
PLATOS 4114
AG:666D CB:1265A
broad
PLATUNō 4115
AG:667A CB:1265A
broad
enlarge
PLATUS 4116
AG:667A CB:1265A
wide*
PLAX 4109
AG:666A CB:1265A
table
PLēGē 4127
AG:668A CB:1265A
plague
stripe
wound *Note*
PLEGMA 4117
AG:667A CB:—
braided

PLEIōN (-ON) 4119
AG:687C (POLUS II.) CB:1265B
above *Note*
excellent
greater
long *Note*
longer
many
more
most
number *Note*
yet
PLEISTOS 4118
AG:687C (POLUS III.) CB:—
great *Note*
most
PLEKō 4120
AG:667B CB:—
plait
PLēKTēS 4131
AG:669B CB:—
striker
PLēMMURA 4132
AG:669B CB:—
flood
PLēN 4133
AG:669B CB:1265B
except
notwithstanding
only
rather *Note*
PLEō 4126
AG:668A CB:—
sail
PLEONAZō 4121
AG:667B CB:1265B
abundant
increase
multiply
over
PLEONEKTEō 4122
AG:667C CB:1265B
advantage
defraud
gain *Note*
get *Note*
wrong*
PLEONEKTēS 4123
AG:667C CB:1265B
covetous
PLEONEXIA 4124
AG:667D CB:1265B
covetousness
extortion
PLēRēS 4134
AG:669D CB:1265B
full
PLēRōMA 4138
AG:672A CB:1265B
fill up
fulfilling
fulness
put *Note*
PLēROō 4137
AG:670C CB:1265B
accomplish
complete

PLēROō (Continued)
end
expire
fill
fulfil
perfect *Note*
preach *Note*
supply *Note*
well-nigh *Note*

PLēROPHOREō 4135
AG:670B CB:1265B
assure
believe *Note*
complete
fulfil
know *Note*
persuade *Note*
proclaim
proof *Note*

PLēROPHORIA 4136
AG:670C CB:1265B
assurance
fulness *Note*

PLēSION 4139
AG:672C CB:1265B
near
neighbour

PLēSMONē 4140
AG:673A CB:—
indulgence

PLēSSō 4141
AG:673A CB:—
smite

PLēTHo (See PIMPLēMI)

PLēTHOS 4128
AG:668B CB:1265B
assembly
bundle
company
multitude

PLēTHUNō 4129
AG:669A CB:1265B
abound
multiply

PLEURA 4125
AG:668A CB:—
side

PLOIARION 4142
AG:673B CB:—
boat
ship

PLOION 4143
AG:673B CB:—
boat
ship, -ping

PLOOS 4144
AG:673C CB:—
course *Note*
voyage

PLOUSIOS 4145
AG:673C CB:1265B
rich
rich man

PLOUSIōS 4146
AG:673D CB:1265B
abundantly
richly

PLOUTEō 4147
AG:673D CB:1265B
get *Note*
goods *Note*
rich

PLOUTIZō 4148
AG:674A CB:1265B
enrich
rich

PLOUTOS 4149
AG:674B CB:1265B
riches

PLUNō 4150
AG:674C CB:1265B
wash

PNEō 4154
AG:679C CB:1265B
blow
wind *Note*

PNEUMA 4151
AG:674C CB:1265B
breath
life *Note*
soul *Note*
spirit
Spirit
spiritual *Note*
wind

PNEUMATIKOS 4152
AG:678D CB:1265C
spiritual

PNEUMATIKōS 4153
AG:679B CB:1265C
spiritually

PNIGō 4155
AG:679D CB:1265C
choke
throat (take by the)

PNIKTOS 4156
AG:679D CB:1265C
strangled

PNOē 4157
AG:680B CB:1265C
breath
wind

PODēRēS 4158
AG:680B CB:—
clothing *Note*
foot

POIēMA 4161
AG:683B CB:1265C
deed *Note*
made (be)
workmanship*

POIEō 4160
AG:680D CB:1265C
abide
appoint
bear
bring
cause
commit
continue *Note*
deal with
do
execute
exercise

POIEō (Continued)
fulfil *Note*
gain *Note*
give
hold *Note*
keep
make
mean *Note*
observe
ordain *Note*
perform
provide *Note*
purpose
put, shew
shoot forth *Note*
spend
take
tarry *Note*
work, yield

POIēSIS 4162
AG:683B CB:1265C
deed

POIēTēS 4163
AG:683B CB:1265C
doer, poet

POIKILOS 4164
AG:683C CB:—
divers
manifold

POIMAINō 4165
AG:683D CB:1265C
cattle *Note*
feed, rule

POIMēN 4166
AG:684A CB:1265C
pastor
shepherd

POIMNē 4167
AG:684C CB:1265C
flock
fold *Note*

POIMNION 4168
AG:684C CB:1265C
flock

POIOS 4169
AG:684C CB:—
manner
what *Note*
which *Note*

POLEMEō 4170
AG:685A CB:1265C
fight *Note*
war

POLEMOS 4171
AG:685A CB:1265C
battle
fight *Note*
war

PōLEō 4453
AG:731C CB:1265C
sell

POLIS 4172
AG:685B CB:1265C
city

POLITARCHēS 4173
AG:686A CB:1265C
ruler

POLITEIA 4174
AG:686A CB:1265C
citizenship
commonwealth*
freedom *Note*

POLITēS 4177
AG:686D CB:1265C
citizen

POLITEUMA 4175
AG:686B CB:1265C
citizenship
commonwealth*
conversation

POLITEUō (-OMAI) 4176
AG:686C CB:1266A
citizen *Note*
conversation
life *Note*
live

POLLAKIS 4178
AG:686D CB:—
oft, often
oftentimes
oft-times

POLLAPLASIōN 4179
AG:686D CB:—
manifold

PōLOS 4454
AG:731D CB:1266A
colt

POLULOGIA 4180
AG:687B CB:—
speaking (much)

POLUMERōS 4181
AG:687B CB:—
portion
time *Note*

POLUPOIKILOS 4182
AG:687B CB:—
divers *Note*
manifold

POLUS 4183
AG:687C CB:1266A
abundant
common *Note*
great, -ly
long
many
much, oft
plenteous
sore *Note*
spent *Note*
straitly *Note*

POLUSPLANCHNOS 4184
AG:689D CB:1266A
pitiful

POLUTELēS 4185
AG:690A CB:1266A
costly
precious
price

POLUTIMOS 4186
AG:690A CB:—
costly
dear *Note*
precious
price

POLUTROPōS 4187
AG:690A CB:—
divers
manners
POMA 4188
AG:690B CB:1266A
drink
PONēRIA 4189
AG:690C CB:1266A
iniquity
wickedness
PONēROS 4190
AG:690D CB:1266A
bad
evil
grievous
harm
malicious *Note*
person *Note*
vile
wicked
PONOS 4192
AG:691C CB:1266A
labour
pain
PōPOTE 4455
AG:732A CB:1266A
never *Note*
time
yet *Note*
POREIA 4197
AG:692A CB:—
journey *Note*
way *Note*
POREUō (-OMAI) 4198
AG:692B CB:1266A
depart
go
journey
walk
way *Note*
PORISMOS 4200
AG:693A CB:—
gain
PORNē 4204
AG:693C CB:1266A
harlot
whore*
PORNEIA 4202
AG:693B CB:1266A
fornication
PORNEUō 4203
AG:693C CB:1266A
fornication
PORNOS 4205
AG:693D CB:1266A
fornicator
whoremonger*
PōROō 4456
AG:732A CB:1266A
blind
harden
PōRōSIS 4457
AG:732A CB:1266A
blindness
hardening
hardness

PORPHURA 4209
AG:694A CB:1266A
purple
PORPHUREOS (-OUS) 4210
AG:694B CB:—
purple
PORPHUROPōLIS 4211
AG:694A CB:—
purple (seller of)
PORRō 4206
AG:693D CB:1266A
far
way *Note*
PORRōTERON (PORRō) 4206
AG:693D CB:Cf. PORRō (1266A)
further
PORRōTHEN 4207
AG:693D CB:Cf. PORRō (1266A)
afar
PORTHEō 4199
AG:693A CB:—
destroy *Note*
havock
waste
PōS (1) 4458
AG:732B CB:—
haply
means (by any etc.)
perhaps *Note*
PōS (2) 4459
AG:732D CB:—
manner
means
POSAKIS 4212
AG:694B CB:—
oft, often
POSIS 4213
AG:694B CB:1266A
drink
POSOS 4214
AG:694B CB:—
great
long
many
what *Note*
POTAMOPHORēTOS 4216
AG:694D CB:1266A
flood
river *Note*
POTAMOS 4215
AG:694D CB:1266B
flood
river
water *Note*
POTAPOS 4217
AG:694D CB:—
manner
what *Note*
POTE (1) 4218
AG:695A CB:1266B
aforetime
haply
last *Note*
length (at)
never *Note*
old *Note*

POTE (Continued)
once
past
sometimes*
time *Note*
time (some) *Note*
(ever) yet
POTE (2) 4219
AG:695A CB:1266B
long
POTēRION 4221
AG:695B CB:1266B
cup
POTIZō 4222
AG:695D CB:1266B
drink
feed
water
POTOS 4224
AG:696A CB:1266B
carousings
POU 4225
AG:696B CB:1266B
about
haply
place *Note*
room *Note*
somewhere
POUS 4228
AG:696C CB:1266B
foot
PRAGMA 4229
AG:697A CB:1266B
business *Note*
deed *Note*
matter
thing
work
PRAGMATEIA 4230
AG:697B CB:1266B
affair
PRAGMATEUOMAI 4231
AG:697B CB:1266B
trade
PRAITōRION 4232
AG:697C CB:—
guard *Note*
hall
palace
PRAKTōR 4233
AG:697D CB:1266B
officer
PRASIA 4237
AG:698B CB:—
ranks
PRASSō 4238
AG:698B CB:1266B
act
commit *Note*
deed
do
exact
extort
keep *Note*
practise
require
use *Note*

PRAUPATHIA —
AG:698D CB:1266B
meekness
PRAUS (-OS) 4239
AG:698D CB:1266B
meek
PRAUTēS (-OTēS) 420
AG:699A CB:1266B
gentleness *Note*
meekness
PRAXIS 4234
AG:697D CB:1266B
deed
office
work
PRēNēS 4248
AG:700D CB:1266B
fall *Note*
headlong
swell *Note*
PREPō 4241
AG:699B CB:1266B
become
befit
comely *Note*
PRESBEIA 4242
AG:699B CB:1266B
ambassage
message *Note*
PRESBEUō 4243
AG:699C CB:1266B
ambassador
PRESBUTERION 4244
AG:699C CB:1266B
elder
estate *Note*
PRESBUTEROS 4245
AG:699D CB:1266B
bishop *Note*
elder
eldest
old
woman (elder)
PRESBUTēS 4246
AG:700D CB:1266B
aged
old
PRESBUTIS 4247
AG:700D CB:1266B
aged
woman (aged)
PRIN 4250
AG:701A CB:—
before
PRIZō (PRIō) 4249
AG:701A CB:—
saw asunder
PROAGō 4254
AG:702A CB:Cf. AGō (1233C)
bring
foregoing
go
PROAIREō 4255 (-OMAI)
AG:702B CB:—
purpose

PROAITIAOMAI 4256
AG:702C CB:—
accuse *Note*
charge
prove *Note*
PROAKOUō 4257
AG:702C CB:—
hear
PROAMARTANō 4258
AG:702C CB:—
already *Note*
sin
PROAULION 4259
AG:702D CB:—
porch
PROBAINō 4260
AG:702D CB:1266C
go
stricken (in years)
PROBALLō 4261
AG:702D CB:—
put
shoot forth
PROBATIKOS 4262
AG:703A CB:—
gate *Note*
sheep gate
sheep market
PROBATION —
AG:703A CB:—
sheep
PROBATON 4263
AG:703C CB:1266C
sheep
PROBIBAZō 4264
AG:703C CB:—
draw *Note*
instruct
put
PROBLEPō 4265
AG:703C CB:—
foresee
provide
PROCHEIRIZō 4400 (-OMAI)
AG:724C CB:1266C
appoint
choose *Note*
make *Note*
PROCHEIROTONEō 4401
AG:724C CB:1266C
choose
PRODēLOS 4271
AG:704B CB:—
evident
manifest *Note*
open *Note*
PRODIDōMI 4272
AG:704C CB:—
give
PRODOTēS 4273
AG:704C CB:—
betrayer
traitor
PRODROMOS 4274
AG:704C CB:1266C
forerunner

PROECHō 4284 (-OMAI)
AG:705D CB:Cf. ECHō (1242C)
better (be) *Note*
case
worse
PROēGEOMAI 4285
AG:706A CB:—
prefer
PROEIDON (PROORAō) 4308
AG:709A CB:—
foresee
see *Note*
PROEIPON (PROLEGō) 4302
AG:708B CB:1266C
foretell
forewarn
say
speak
PROEIRō 4280 (-EREō)
AG:704D (-EIPON) CB:—
tell
PROELPIZō 4276
AG:705A CB:1266C
hope
trust *Note*
PROENARCHOMAI 4278
AG:705A CB:Cf. ARCHō (1237B)
begin
PROEPANGELLō (-OMAI) 4279
AG:705B CB:1266C
aforepromised
promise
PROERCHOMAI 4281
AG:705B CB:1266C
go, outgo
pass
PROETOIMAZō 4282
AG:705D CB:1266C
ordain *Note*
prepare
PROEUANGELIZOMAI 4283
AG:705D CB:1266C
gospel
preach
PROGINOMAI 4266
AG:703C CB:1266C
past
PROGINōSKō 4267
AG:703D CB:1266C
foreknow
foreordain*
know
predestinate *Note*
PROGNōSIS 4268
AG:703D CB:1266C
foreknowledge
PROGONOS 4269
AG:704A CB:—
forefather
parents
PROGRAPHō 4270
AG:704A CB:1266C
openly *Note*
ordain *Note*
set
write

PRōI 4404
AG:724D CB:1266C
early
morning
PRōIMOS 4406
AG:706D CB:1266C
early
PRōINOS 4407
AG:725A CB:1266C
morning
PRōIOS (-IA) 4405
AG:724D CB:—
day *Note*
early
morning
PROISTēMI 4291
AG:707A CB:—
maintain
over (to be)
rule
PROKALEō 4292 (-OMAI)
AG:707B CB:—
provoke
PROKATANGELLō 4293
AG:707B CB:1266C
foreshew
foretell *Note*
shew*
PROKATARTIZō 4294
AG:707C CB:1266C
make
PROKEIMAI 4295
AG:707C CB:1266C
first *Note*
set
PROKēRUSSō 4296
AG:707D CB:—
preach
PROKOPē 4297
AG:707D CB:1266C
advance *Note*
furtherance
profiting
progress
PROKOPTō 4298
AG:707D CB:1266C
advance
increase
proceed
profit
spent, wax
PROKRIMA 4299
AG:708A CB:1266C
prefer *Note*
prejudice
PROKUROō 4300
AG:708B CB:1266C
confirm
PROLAMBANō 4301
AG:708B CB:1266C
come *Note*
overtake, take
PROLEGō (See PROEIPON)
PROMARTUROMAI 4303
AG:708C CB:—
testify

PROMELETAō 4304
AG:708C CB:—
meditate
PROMERIMNAō 4305
AG:708C CB:1266C
thought (to take)
meditate *Note*
PRONOEō 4306
AG:708C CB:1266C
provide
thought (to take)
PRONOIA 4307
AG:708D CB:1266C
providence
provision
PROORAō 4308
AG:709A CB:—
foresee
see *Note*
PROORIZō 4309
AG:709B CB:—
determine
ordain *Note*
predestinate
PROORMIZō (PROS-) 4358
AG:717D CB:—
draw
PROPASCHō 4310
AG:709B CB:—
suffer
PROPATōR See 3962 (PATēR)
AG:709B CB:1266C
forefather
PROPEMPō 4311
AG:709B CB:—
accompany
bring
conduct
journey
set, way *Note*
PROPETēS 4312
AG:709C CB:—
heady
headstrong
PROPHASIS 4392
AG:722C CB:—
cloke (pretence)
excuse, pretence*
show (Noun) *Note*
PROPHERō 4393
AG:722D CB:Cf. PHERō (1264A)
bring
PROPHēTEIA 4394
AG:722D CB:1267A
prophecy
prophesying
PROPHēTēS 4396
AG:723B CB:1267A
prophet
PROPHēTEUō 4395
AG:723A CB:1267A
prophesy
soothsaying *Note*
PROPHēTIKOS 4397
AG:724B CB:1267A
prophecy

PROPHeTIS 4398
AG:724B CB:1267C
prophetess
PROPHTHANo 4399
AG:724B CB:—
speak
PROPOREUOMAI 4313
AG:709C CB:—
go
PRoRA 4408
AG:725A CB:—
foreship
PROS 4314
AG:709C CB:1267A
belong *Note*
compare
conditions
end *Note*
intent *Note*
nigh *Note*
pertain to *Note*
within *Note*
PROSABBATON 4315
AG:711A CB:—
sabbath
PROSAGo 4317
AG:711B CB:Cf. AGo (1233C)
bring
draw
near (draw)
PROSAGoGe 4318
AG:711C CB:1267A
access
PROSAGOREUo 4316
AG:711B CB:—
call *Note*
name
PROSAITEo 4319
AG:711C CB:—
beg
PROSANABAINo 4320
AG:711C CB:—
go
PROSANALISKo 4321
AG:711C CB:—
spend
PROSANAPLeROo 4322
AG:711D CB:1267A
measure *Note*
supply
PROSANATITHeMI 4323
AG:711D CB:—
add
confer
impart
PROSAPEILEo 4324
AG:711D CB:—
threaten
PROSCHUSIS 4378
AG:720C CB:1267A
sprinkling
PROSDAPANAo 4325
AG:712A CB:—
spend

PROSDECHOMAI 4327
AG:712B CB:1267A
accept
allow
look (for)
receive
take
wait
PROSDEOMAI 4326
AG:712A CB:1267A
need
PROSDOKAo 4328
AG:712C CB:1267A
expect, -tation
look (for)
tarry *Note*
wait
PROSDOKIA 4329
AG:712C CB:—
expectation
looking (after)
PROSEAo 4330
AG:712D CB:—
suffer
PROSECHo 4337
AG:714B CB:1267A
attend
attendance
beware
give, heed
regard
PROSEDREUo 4332
AG:712D CB:—
wait*
PROSENGIZo 4331
AG:712D CB:Cf. ENG-(1245A)
come
PROSeLOo 4338
AG:714D CB:—
nail
PROSeLUTOS 4339
AG:715A CB:1267A
proselyte
PROSERCHOMAI 4334
AG:713A CB:1267A
come
consent
draw
go *Note*
near (come)
PROSERGAZOMAI 4333
AG:713A CB:—
gain *Note*
PROSEUCHe 4335
AG:713B CB:1267A
earnestly *Note*
fervently *Note*
prayer
PROSEUCHOMAI 4336
AG:713D CB:1267A
pray, prayer
PROSKAIROS 4340
AG:715B CB:1267A
season
temporal
time *Note*
while *Note*

PROSKALEo 4341 (-OMAI)
AG:715C CB:1267A
call
PROSKARTEREo 4342
AG:715C CB:1267A
attend
continue
give *Note*
instant *Note*
wait
PROSKARTEReSIS 4343
AG:715D CB:1267A
perseverance
PROSKEPHALAION 4344
AG:715D CB:—
pillow
PROSKLeROo 4345
AG:716A CB:1267A
consort
PROSKLISIS 4346
AG:716A CB:1267A
partiality
PROSKOLLAo 4347
AG:716A CB:1267A
cleave
join
PROSKOMMA 4348
AG:716B CB:1267A
offence
PROSKOPe 4349
AG:716B CB:1267B
offence
PROSKOPTo 4350
AG:716B CB:1267B
beat, dash
smite
stumble
PROSKULIo 4351
AG:716C CB:—
roll
PROSKUNEo 4352
AG:716C CB:1267B
beseech *Note*
worship
PROSKUNeTeS 4353
AG:717B CB:1267B
worshipper
PROSLALEo 4354
AG:717B CB:—
speak
PROSLAMBANo 4355
AG:717B CB:1267B
receive
take
PROSLe(M)PSIS 4356
AG:717C CB:1267B
receiving
PROSMENo 4357
AG:717C CB:1267B
abide, cleave
continue
tarry
PROSOCHTHIZo 4360
AG:717D CB:—
displease
grieve *Note*

PROSOPHEILo 4359
AG:717D CB:Cf. OPH-(1261A)
besides *Note*
PROSoPOLe(M)PSIA 4382
AG:720D CB:1267B
persons (respect of)
receive
PROSoPOLe(M)PTEo 4380
AG:720C CB:1267B
persons (respect of)
receive
PROSoPOLe(M)PTeS 4381
AG:720D CB:1267B
persons (respect of)
receive
PROSoPON 4383
AG:720D CB:1267B
appearance
countenance
face, fashion
person
presence
PROSORMIZo 4358
AG:717D CB:—
draw *Note*
moor*
PROSOPHEILo 4359
AG:717D CB:—
owe
PROSPeGNUMI 4362
AG:718A CB:—
crucify
PROSPEINOS 4316
AG:718A CB:—
hungry
PROSPHAGION 4371
AG:719C CB:—
eat
meat *Note*
PROSPHATOS 4372
AG:719C CB:1267B
new
PROSPHAToS 4373
AG:719C CB:—
lately
PROSPHERo 4374
AG:719C CB:1267B
bring
deal with
do *Note*
offer
present (Verb) *Note*
put *Note*
PROSPHILeS 4375
AG:720B CB:—
lovely
PROSPHoNEo 4377
AG:720C CB:—
call *Note*
speak
PROSPHORA 4376
AG:720B CB:1267B
offering
PROSPIPTo 4363
AG:718A CB:—
beat, fall

PROSPOIEō 4364
AG:718B CB:—
make
PROSPOREUOMAI 4365
AG:718B CB:Cf. POR-(1266A)
come
PROSPSAUō 4379
AG:720C CB:—
touch
PROSRēGNUMI 4366
AG:718B (-ēSSō) CB:—
beat
break
PROSTASSo 4367
AG:718C CB:1267B
bid *Note*
command
PROSTATIS 4368
AG:718D CB:—
succourer
PROSTITHēMI 4369
AG:718D CB:1267B
add
give
increase
lay
proceed
speak *Note*
PROSTRECHō 4370
AG:719B CB:—
run
PROTASSō 4384
AG:721D CB:1267B
appoint
PROTEINō 4385
AG:721D CB:—
bind
tie
PROTEROS (-ON) 4386
AG:721D CB:1267B
aforetime
before
first
former
PRōTEUō 4409
AG:725A CB:—
pre-eminence
PROTHESIS 4286
AG:706A CB:1267B
purpose
shewbread*
PROTHESMIOS 4287
AG:706B (-MIA) CB:—
appoint *Note*
term
time *Note*
PROTHUMIA 4288
AG:706C CB:1267B
forwardness
readiness
willing*
PROTHUMOS 4289
AG:706C CB:—
ready
willing

PROTHUMōS 4290
AG:706D CB:—
ready *Note*
PROTITHēMI 4388 (-EMAI)
AG:722B CB:1267B
purpose
set
PRōTOKATHEDRIA 4410
AG:725B CB:1267B
chief
seat
uppermost *Note*
PRōTOKLISIA 4411
AG:725B CB:1267B
chief
place
room
uppermost *Note*
PRōTON 4412
AG:725 (-OS) CB:1267B
before
beginning
chiefly *Note*
first
PRōTOS 4413
AG:725B CB:1267B
best
chief, chiefest
estate *Note*
first
former
one *Note*
principal
PRōTōS —
AG:727A CB:—
first
PRōTOSTATēS 4414
AG:726C CB:1267B
ringleader
PRōTOTOKIA 4415
AG:726C CB:Cf. -KOS (1267B)
birthright
PRōTOTOKOS 4416
AG:726C CB:1267B
first-begotten
firstborn
PROTRECHō 4390
AG:722B CB:—
outrun
run
PROTREPō 4389
AG:722B CB:—
encourage
exhort
PROūPARCHō 4391
AG:722C CB:—
before
beforetime
PRUMNA 4403
AG:724D CB:—
stern
PSALLō 5567
AG:891A CB:1267B
melody
praise
psalm *Note*
sing

PSALMOS 5568
AG:891B CB:1267C
hymn *Note*
psalm
PSēLAPHAō 5584
AG:892C CB:—
feel
handle
touch
PSēPHIZō 5585
AG:892D CB:—
count
PSēPHOS 5586
AG:892D CB:1267C
stone
PSEUDADELPHOS 5569
AG:891B CB:1267C
brother *Note*
PSEUDAPOSTOLOS 5570
AG:891B CB:1267C
apostle *Note*
PSEUDēS 5571
AG:891C CB:1267C
false
liar
PSEUDOCHRISTOS 5580
AG:892B CB:1267C
Antichrist *Note*
(false) Christ
PSEUDODIDASKALOS 5572
AG:891C CB:1267C
(false) teacher
PSEUDOLOGOS 5573
AG:891D CB:1267C
lie
PSEUDō (-OMAI) 5574
AG:891 CB:1267C
falsely
lie
PSEUDOMARTUREō 5576
AG:891D CB:1267C
witness
PSEUDOMARTURIA 5577
AG:892A CB:1267C
witness
PSEUDOMARTUS (-UR) 5575
AG:892A CB:1267C
witness
PSEUDōNUMOS 5581
AG:892C CB:1267C
falsely
PSEUDOPROPHēTēS 5578
AG:892A CB:1267C
prophet
PSEUDOS 5579
AG:892B CB:1267C
falsehood
guile *Note*
lie, lying*
wonder (lying) *Note*
PSEUSMA 5582
AG:892C CB:—
lie
PSEUSTēS 5583
AG:892C CB:1267C
liar

PSICHION 5589
AG:893A CB:—
crumb
PSITHURISMOS 5587
AG:892D CB:1267C
whispering
PSITHURISTēS 5588
AG:893A CB:1267C
whisperer
PSōCHō 5597
AG:894D CB:—
rub
PSōMION 5596
AG:894D CB:—
sop
PSōMIZō 5595
AG:894D CB:—
bestow
feed
PSUCHē 5590
AG:893B CB:1267C
doubt
heart
heartily
life
mind *Note*
soul
PSUCHIKOS 5591
AG:894B CB:1267C
natural
PSUCHō 5594
AG:894D CB:1267C
cold
PSUCHOS 5593
AG:894C CB:1267C
cold
PSUCHROS 5592
AG:894C CB:1267C
cold
PTAIō 4417
AG:727A CB:1267C
fall *Note*
offend *Note*
stumble
PTēNON 4421
AG:727C (-OS) CB:—
bird
PTERNA 4418
AG:727B CB:1267C
heel
PTERUGION 4419
AG:727B CB:1267C
pinnacle
PTERUX 4420
AG:727B CB:1267C
wing
PTōCHEIA 4432
AG:728A CB:1268A
poverty
PTōCHEUō 4433
AG:728A CB:1268A
poor
PTōCHOS 4434
AG:728B CB:1268A
beggar, -ly
poor

PTOEō 4422
AG:727C CB:—
terrify
PTOēSIS 4423
AG:727C CB:—
amazement *Note*
terror
PTōMA 4430
AG:727D CB:1268A
body
carcase
corpse
PTōSIS 4431
AG:728A CB:1268A
fall
PTUō 4429
AG:727D CB:—
spit
PTUON 4425
AG:727C CB:1268A
fan
PTURō 4426
AG:727D CB:—
affrighted
terrify
PTUSMA 4427
AG:727D CB:—
spittle
PTUSSō 4428
AG:727D CB:—
close (verb)
PUGMē 4435
AG:728C CB:1268A
diligently
PUKNOS (-NA) 4437
AG:729A CB:—
often
PUKNOTERON (-NOS) 4437
AG:729A CB:—
oftener
PUKTEUō 4438 (PUKTEō)
AG:729A CB:—
fight
PULē 4439
AG:729B CB:1268A
city *Note*
gate
PULōN 4440
AG:729C CB:1268A
gate
porch
PUNTHANOMAI 4441
AG:729C CB:—
ask
inquire
understand
PUR 4442
AG:729D CB:1268A
fire
PURA 4443
AG:730C CB:1268A
fire
PURESSō 4445
AG:730D CB:1268A
fever (be sick of)
PURETOS 4446
AG:730D CB:1268A
fever
PURGOS 4444
AG:730D CB:—
tower
PURINOS 4447
AG:731A CB:1268A
fire
PUROOMAI (-Oō) 4448
AG:731A CB:1268A
burn
fiery
fire
refined
try *Note*
PURōSIS 4451
AG:731C CB:1268A
burning
fiery *Note*
trial
PURRHAZō 4449
AG:731B CB:1268A
red
PURRHOS 445
AG:731C CB:1268A
red
PUTHōN 4436
AG:728D CB:1268A
divination

R

RABBI (-BEI) 4461
AG:733A CB:1268A
master
Rabbi
RABBōNI (-BOUNEI) 4462
AG:733A CB:1268A
lord *Note*
master *Note*
Rabboni
RHABDIZō 4463
AG:733B CB:1268A
beat
rod
RHABDOS 4464
AG:733B CB:1268A
rod
staff
RHABDOUCHOS 4465
AG:733C CB:1268A
serjeant
RHADIOURGēMA 4467
AG:733C CB:—
villany
RHADIOURGIA 4468
AG:733C CB:—
villany
RHAKA 4469
AG:733D CB:1268A
raca
RHAKOS 4470
AG:734A CB:—
cloth
RHANTISMOS 4473
AG:734B CB:1268A
sprinkling
RHANTIZō 4472
AG:734B CB:1268A
sprinkle
wash
RHAPHIS 4476
AG:734C CB:—
needle
RHAPISMA 4475
AG:734C CB:1268A
blow (Noun)
smite *Note*
strike *Note*
RHAPIZō 4474
AG:734B CB:1268A
palm (of the hand)
smite
strike *Note*
RHEDē 4480 (-DA)
AG:734D CB:—
chariot
RHēGMA 4485
AG:735A CB:—
ruin
RHēGNUMI 4486
AG:735A CB:—
break
burst
dash
rend, tear
RHēMA 4487
AG:735B CB:1268A
saying
thing
word
RHEō 4482
AG:735A CB:1268A
flow
RHEō (See EIRō) 4483
AG:226A (EIPON 3.c.) CB:1268A
command *Note*
RHēTōR 4489
AG:735D CB:1268B
orator
RHēTōS 4490
AG:736A CB:—
expressly
RHIPē 4493
AG:736B CB:1268B
twinkling
RHIPIZō 4494
AG:736B CB:1268B
toss
RHIPTō (-TEō) 4496 (4495)
AG:736C CB:—
cast
scatter
throw
RHIZA 4491
AG:736A CB:1268B
root
RHIZOō 4492
AG:736B CB:1268B (-OMAI)
root
RHOIZēDON 4500
AG:737A CB:—
noise
RHōMAIOS 4514
AG:738C CB:—
Roman
RHōMAISTI 4515
AG:738C CB:—
Latin
tongue *Note*
RHōMAIKOS 4513
AG:738C CB:—
Latin
RHOMPHAIA 4501
AG:737A CB:1268B
sword
RHōNNUMI 4517
AG:738D CB:—
farewell
RHUMē 4505
AG:737C CB:—
lane
street *Note*
RHUOMAI 4506
AG:737C CB:1268B
deliver
deliverer
RHUPAINō —
AG:737D CB:1268B
filthy (to make)
RHUPARIA 4507
AG:738A CB:1268B
filthiness
RHUPAROS 4508
AG:738A CB:1268B
filthy
vile
RHUPAREUOMAI (-EUō) —
AG:738A CB:1268B
filthy
RHUPOō 4510
AG:738B CB:1268B (-Eo)
filthy
RHUPOS 4509
AG:738A CB:1268B
filth
RHUSIS 4511
AG:738B CB:1268B
issue
RHUTIS 4512
AG:738B CB:—
wrinkle

S

SABACHTHANEI 4518
AG:738B CB:—
sabachthani
SABAōTH 4519
AG:738B CB:1268B
sabaoth
SABBATISMOS 4520
AG:739A CB:1268B
rest
sabbath
SABBATON 4521
AG:739A CB:1268B
sabbath
week

SAGēNē 4522
AG:739C CB:—
net
SAINō 4525
AG:740A CB:—
move
SAKKOS 4526
AG:740A CB:—
sackcloth
SALEUō 4531
AG:740C CB:1268B
move
shake
stir
SALOS 4535
AG:741A CB:1268B
wave
SALPINX 4536
AG:741A CB:1268B
trump
trumpet
SALPISTēS 4538
AG:741B CB:1268B
trumpeter
SALPIZō 4537
AG:741A CB:1268B
sound
trumpet
SANDALION 4547
AG:742A CB:—
sandal
SANIS 4548
AG:742A CB:—
board
SAPPHEIROS 4552
AG:742C (-HIROS) CB:1268B
sapphire
SAPROS 4550
AG:742B CB:1268B
bad
corrupt
SARDINOS 4555
AG:742C CB:—
sardine
SARDIOS (-ON) 4556
AG:742D CB:1268B
sardius
SARDONUX 4557
AG:742D CB:1268B
sardonyx
SARGANē 4553
AG:742C CB:—
basket
SARKIKOS 4559
AG:742D CB:1268B
carnal
flesh
fleshly
SARKINOS 4560
AG:743A CB:1268C
carnal
flesh
fleshly
SAROō 4563
AG:744D CB:—
sweep

SARX 4561
AG:743B CB:1268C
flesh
SATANAS 4567
AG:744D (SATAN) CB:1268C
Satan
SATON 4568
AG:745B CB:—
measure
SBENNUMI 4570
AG:745B CB:1268C
go
quench
SCHEDON 4975
AG:797A CB:—
almost
SCHēMA 4976
AG:797B CB:1268C
fashion
SCHISMA 4978
AG:797C CB:1268C
division
rent
schism
SCHIZō 4977
AG:797B CB:1268C
break
divide *Note*
open *Note*
rend, rent
SCHOINION 4979
AG:797D CB:—
cord, rope
SCHOLAZō 4980
AG:797D CB:—
empty
give
leisure
SCHOLē 4981
AG:798A CB:—
school
SEAUTOU 4572
AG:745C CB:—
thee *Note*
thou *Note*
thyself
SEBASMA 4574
AG:745D CB:1268C
devotion
worship
SEBASTOS 4575
AG:745D CB:1268C
emperor
SEBAZOMAI 4573
AG:745C CB:1268C
worship
SEBō (-OMAI) 4576
AG:746A CB:1268C
devout
worship
SEIō 4579
AG:746C CB:1268C
move
quake
shake, stir
tremble

SEIRA 4577
AG:746B CB:—
chain *Note*
SEIROS 4577 (-RA)
AG:751 (SIROS) CB:—
pits*
SEISMOS 4578
AG:746B CB:1268C
earthquake
tempest
SELēNē 4582
AG:746D CB:1268C
moon
SELēNIAZō (-OMAI) 4583
AG:746D CB:1268C
epileptic
SēMAINō 4591
AG:747C CB:1268C
signify
SēMEION 4592
AG:747D CB:1268C
miracle
sign
token
wonder *Note*
SEMEIOō (Sē-) 4593
AG:748D CB:—
note (verb)
SēMERON 4594
AG:749A CB:1268A
daily *Note*
to-day
this day*
SEMIDALIS 4585
AG:746D CB:—
flour
SEMNOS 4586
AG:746D CB:1269A
grave (Adjective)
honest
honourable
SEMNOTēS 4587
AG:747A CB:1269A
gravity
honesty
SēPō 4595
AG:749B CB:—
corrupt
SēRIKOS (SIR-) 4596
AG:751D CB:—
silk
SēS 4597
AG:749B CB:1269A
moth
SēTOBRōTOS 4598
AG:749C CB:—
moth-eaten
SIAGōN 4600
AG:749C CB:—
cheek
SIDēREOS (-ROUS) 4603
AG:750A CB:1269A
iron
SIDēROS 4604
AG:750A CB:1269A
iron

SIGAō 4601
AG:749C CB:—
close (Verb) *Note*
peace (hold one's)
secret *Note*
silence
SIGē 4602
AG:749D CB:—
silence
SIKARIOS 4607
AG:750B CB:—
assassin
murderer *Note*
SIKERA 4608
AG:750B CB:—
drink
SIMIKINTHION 4612
AG:751A CB:—
apron
SINAPI 4615
AG:751C CB:1269A
mustard
SINDōN 4616
AG:751C CB:1269A
linen
SINIAZō 4617
AG:751D CB:1269A
sift
SIōPAō 4623
AG:752C CB:—
dumb
peace (hold one's)
SITEUTOS 4618
AG:752A CB:1269A
fatted
SITION (-TOS) 4621
AG:752A CB:1269A
corn
SITISTOS 4619
AG:752A CB:—
fatling
SITOMETRION 4620
AG:752A CB:—
food
meat *Note*
SITOS 4621
AG:752B CB:1269A
corn
wheat*
SKANDALIZō 4624
AG:752D CB:1269A
offend
SKANDALON 4625
AG:753A CB:1269A
fall *Note*
falling
offence
SKAPHē 4627
AG:753C CB:—
boat
SKAPTō 4626
AG:753B CB:—
dig
SKELOS 4628
AG:753C CB:—
leg

SKēNē 4633
AG:754C CB:1269A
habitation
tabernacle
SKēNōMA 4638
AG:755C CB:1269A
habitation
tabernacle
SKēNOō 4637
AG:755C CB:1269A
dwell
tabernacle *Note*
SKēNOPēGIA 4634
AG:754D CB:1269A
tabernacle
SKēNOPOIOS 4635
AG:755A CB:1269A
tent-maker
SKēNOS 4636
AG:755B CB:1269A
tabernacle
SKEPASMA 4629
AG:753D CB:—
covering
raiment *Note*
SKEUē 4631
AG:754A CB:—
tackling
SKEUOS 4632
AG:754A CB:1269A
gear
goods
vessel
SKIA 4639
AG:755D CB:1269A
image
shadow
SKIRTAō 4640
AG:755D CB:—
leap
SKLēROKARDIA 4641
AG:756A CB:1269A
heart (hardness of)
SKLēROS 4642
AG:756A CB:1269A
austere *Note*
fierce *Note*
hard, rough
SKLēROTēS 4643
AG:756B CB:1269A
hardness
SKLēROTRACHēLOS 4644
AG:756B CB:1269A
stiffnecked
SKLēRUNō 4645
AG:756B CB:1269A
harden
SKōLēKOBRōTOS 4662
AG:758C CB:—
worm
SKōLēX 4663
AG:758C CB:—
worm
SKOLIOS 4646
AG:756B CB:—
crooked
SKOLOPS 4647
AG:756C CB:1269B
thorn
SKOPEō 4648
AG:756D CB:1269B
consider *Note*
heed (to take) *Note*
look
mark
SKOPOS 4649
AG:756D CB:1269B
goal
mark
SKORPIOS 4651
AG:757A CB:1269B
scorpion
SKORPIZō 4650
AG:757A CB:1269B
disperse
scatter
SKOTEINOS 4652
AG:757B CB:1269B
dark
darkness
SKOTIA 4653
AG:757B CB:1269B
dark
darkness
SKOTIZō 4654
AG:757C CB:1269B
darken
SKOTOō 4656
AG:758A CB:1269B
darken
darkness
SKOTOS 4655
AG:757C CB:1269B
darkness
SKUBALON 4657
AG:758A CB:1269B
dung
SKULLō 4660
AG:758B CB:—
distress
trouble
SKULON 4661
AG:758B CB:—
spoil
SKUTHRōPOS 4659
AG:758B CB:—
countenance *Note*
SMARAGDINOS 4664
AG:758C CB:1269B
emerald
SMARAGDOS 4665
AG:758C CB:1269B
emerald
SMURNA 4666
AG:758D CB:1269B
myrrh
SMURNIZō 4669
AG:759A CB:1269B
mingle
myrrh
SōMA 4983
AG:799A CB:1269B
body
slave
soul *Note*
SōMATIKOS 4984
AG:800B CB:1269B
bodily
SōMATIKōS 4985
AG:800B CB:1269B
bodily
SOPHIA 4678
AG:759C CB:1269B
wisdom
SOPHIZō 4679
AG:760B CB:1269B
devised (cunningly)
wise
SOPHOS 4680
AG:760B CB:1269B
wise
SōPHRōN 4998
AG:802C CB:1269B
discreet
sober, -minded
temperate *Note*
SōPHRONEō 4993
AG:802A CB:1269B
mind
sober, -minded
think *Note*
watch*
SōPHRONISMOS 4995
AG:802B CB:—
discipline
mind *Note*
SōPHRONIZō 4994
AG:802A CB:—
soberminded
SōPHRONōS 4996
AG:802C CB:1269B
soberly
SōPHROSUNē 4997
AG:802C CB:1269B
soberness
sobriety
SōREUō 4987
AG:800C CB:—
heap
lade
SOROS 4673
AG:759B CB:—
bier
SOS 4674
AG:759B CB:—
thine *Note*
thy
SōTēR 4990
AG:800D CB:1269C
saviour
SōTēRIA 4991
AG:801B CB:1269C
health *Note*
safety
salvation
saving *Note*
SōTēRION 4992
AG:801D (-OS 2.) CB:1269C
salvation
SōTēRIOS 4992 (-ON)
AG:801D CB:1269C
salvation
SOUDARION 4676
AG:759C CB:—
handkerchief
napkin
SōZō 4982
AG:798A CB:1269C
heal
preserve *Note*
recover
save
whole
SPAō 4685
AG:761A CB:—
draw
SPARASSō 4682
AG:760D CB:—
rend *Note*
tear
SPARGANOō 4683
AG:760D CB:—
swaddling-clothes
SPATALAō 4684
AG:761A CB:—
delicately *Note*
live *Note*
please
pleasure *Note*
wanton*
SPEIRA 4686
AG:761A CB:—
band
SPEIRō 4687
AG:761B CB:1269C
receive *Note*
sow
sower
SPEKOULATōR 4688
AG:761C CB:—
guard
soldier *Note*
SPēLAION 4693
AG:762C CB:1269C
cave
den
SPENDō 4689
AG:761C CB:1269C
offer
SPERMA 4690
AG:761D CB:1269C
issue *Note*
seed
SPERMOLOGOS 4691
AG:762B CB:1269C
babbler
SPEUDō 4692
AG:762B CB:1269C
desire
earnestly *Note*
haste

SPHAGē 4967
AG:795D CB:—
kill
slaughter
SPHAGION 4968
AG:796A CB:—
kill
beast
SPHAZō (-ATTō) 4969
AG:796A CB:1269C
kill
slay
smite
wound *Note*
SPHODRA 4970
AG:796A CB:1269C
exceeding, -ly
greatly *Note*
sore
very *Note*
SPHODRōS 4971
AG:796B CB:—
exceedingly
SPHRAGIS 4973
AG:796C CB:1269C
seal
SPHRAGIZō 4972
AG:796B CB:1269C
seal
SPHURON 4974
AG:797A CB:—
ankle-bones
SPILAS 4694
AG:762C CB:—
rock
spot
SPILOō 4695
AG:762D CB:—
defile
spot
SPILOS 4696
AG:762D CB:—
spot
SPLANCHNON (-NA) 4698
AG:763A CB:1269C
affection
bowels
compassion
mercy
SPLANCHNIZOMAI 4697
AG:762D CB:1269C
compassion
SPODOS 4700
AG:763B CB:—
ashes
SPONGOS 4699
AG:763B CB:—
sponge
SPORA 4701
AG:763B CB:1269C
seed
SPORIMOS 4702
AG:763B CB:Cf. -ROS (1269C)
corn
cornfield
field

SPOROS 4703
AG:763B CB:1269C
seed
SPOUDAIOS 4705
AG:763C CB:1269C
careful
diligent
earnest
forward
SPOUDAIōS 4709
AG:763D CB:1269C
carefully
diligently
earnestly
instantly
SPOUDAIOTEROS (-IOS) 4706
AG:763D CB:1269C
diligent
earnest
SPOUDAIOTERōS (-IōS) 4708
AG:763D CB:1269C
carefully
diligently
SPOUDAZō 4704
AG:763C CB:1269C
diligence, -gent
endeavour
forward
labour *Note*
study *Note*
zealous
SPOUDē 4710
AG:763D CB:1269C
business *Note*
care, carefulness
diligence
earnestness
forwardness
haste
SPURIS 4711
AG:764A CB:—
basket
STACHUS 4719
AG:765D CB:1269C
corn
ear (of corn)
STADION 4712
AG:764A CB:—
furlong
race
STAMNOS 4713
AG:764B CB:—
pot
STAPHULē 4718
AG:765C CB:—
cluster *Note*
grape
STASIASTēS —
AG:764B CB:—
insurrection
STASIS 4714
AG:764C CB:1270A
dissension
insurrection
riot, sedition
standing *Note*
uproar

STATēR 4715
AG:764C CB:1270A
money *Note*
piece *Note*
shekel
STAUROō 4717
AG:765B CB:1270A
crucify
STAUROS 4716
AG:764D CB:1270A
cross
STEGē 4721
AG:765D CB:—
roof
STEGō 4722
AG:765D CB:1270A
bear, forbear
suffer *Note*
STEIROS 4723
AG:766A (-RA) CB:—
barren
STēKō 4739
AG:767D CB:1270A
stand
STELLō 4724
AG:766A CB:1270A
avoid
withdraw
STEMMA 4725
AG:766A CB:1270A
garland
STENAGMOS 4726
AG:766B CB:1270A
groaning
STENAZō 4727
AG:766B CB:1270A
grief
groan
murmur *Note*
sigh, weep *Note*
STENOCHōREO 4729
AG:766C CB:1270A
anguish
distress
straitened
STENOCHōRIA 4730
AG:766C CB:1270A
anguish
distress
STENOS 4728
AG:766B CB:1270A
narrow
STEPHANOō 4737
AG:767C CB:1270A
crown
STEPHANOS 4735
AG:767A CB:1270A
crown
STEREōMA 4733
AG:766D CB:—
stedfastness
STEREOō 4732
AG:766D CB:—
establish
strength, -en *Notes*
strong

STEREOS 4731
AG:766D CB:1270A
firm
solid
stedfast
strong*
sure *Note*
STēRIGMOS 4740
AG:768A CB:—
steadfastness
STēRIZō 4741
AG:768A CB:1270A
establish
fix, set
strengthen *Note*
STēTHOS 4738
AG:767D CB:—
breast
STHENOō 4599
AG:749C CB:—
strengthen
STIGMA 4742
AG:768C CB:1270A
branded *Note*
mark
STIGMē 4743
AG:768C CB:—
moment
STILBō 4744
AG:768D CB:—
shine
STOA 4745
AG:768D CB:1270A
porch
STOIBAS 4746
AG:768B (-BOS) CB:—
branch
STOICHEION 4747
AG:768D CB:1270A
elements
principles
rudiments
STOICHEō 4748
AG:769C CB:1270A
orderly *Note*
walk
STOLē 4749
AG:769C CB:1270A
clothing
garment
robe
STOMA 4750
AG:769D CB:1270A
edge
face *Note*
mouth
STOMACHOS 4751
AG:770B CB:—
stomach
STRATēGOS 4755
AG:770C CB:1270A
captain
magistrate
STRATEIA 4752
AG:770B CB:1270A
warfare

STRATEUMA 4753
AG:770B CB:1270A
army
soldier
STRATEUō 4754 (-OMAI)
AG:770B CB:1270A
go *Note*
soldier
war, warfare*
STRATIA 4756
AG:770D CB:1270A
host (of angels etc)
warfare
STRATIōTeS 4757
AG:770D CB:1270A
soldier
STRATOLOGEō 4758
AG:770D CB:1270A
choose *Note*
enrol *Note*
soldier *Note*
STRATOPEDARCHeS 4759
AG:771A CB:1270B
captain *Note*
guard *Note*
STRATOPEDON 4760
AG:771A CB:1270B
army
STREBLOō 4761
AG:771A CB:—
wrest
STReNIAō 4763
AG:771C CB:—
delicately *Note*
wanton
STReNOS 4764
AG:771C CB:—
delicacies
wantonness
STREPHō 4762
AG:771A CB:1270B
convert
turn
STRōNNUMI (-Uō) 4766
AG:771C CB:—
bed *Note*
furnish
spread
STROUTHION 4765
AG:771C CB:1270B
sparrow
STUGeTOS 4767
AG:771D CB:—
hateful
STUGNAZō 4768
AG:771D CB:—
countenance *Note*
lowring (to be)
STULOS 4769
AG:772A CB:1270B
pillar
SU 4771
AG:772A CB:—
thee, thou *Notes*
thine, thy *Notes*
ye, your *Notes*

SUKAMINOS 4708
AG:776A CB:—
sycamine
SUKe (SUKEA) 4808
AG:776B CB:1270B
fig tree
SUKOMōREA 4809 (-RAIA)
AG:776B CB:—
sycamore
SUKON 4810
AG:776B CB:—
fig
SUKOPHANTEō 4811
AG:776C CB:—
accuse
exact (Verb)
SULAGōGEō 4812
AG:776C CB:1270B
spoil
SULAō 4813
AG:776C CB:1270B
rob
SULLALEō 4814
AG:776C CB:—
commune
confer
speak
talk
SULLAMBANō 4815
AG:776D CB:1270B
catch
conceive
help
seize, take
SULLEGō 4816
AG:777A CB:1270B
gather
SULLOGIZOMAI 4817
AG:777A CB:—
reason
SULLUPEō (See SUNLUPEō)
SUMBAINō 4819
AG:777B CB:—
befall
happen
so *Note*
was (etc.) *Note*
SUMBALLō 4820
AG:777B CB:—
confer
encounter
help
make *Note*
meet
ponder
SUMBASILEUō 4821
AG:777C CB:1270B
reign
SUMBIBAZō 4822
AG:777D CB:—
assuredly *Note*
bring
compacted
conclude
instruct
knit together
prove

SUMBOULEUō 4823
AG:777D CB:1270B
consult
counsel
SUMBOULION 4824
AG:778A CB:1270B
consultation
council
SUMBOULOS 4825
AG:778B CB:1270B
counsellor
SUMMARTUREō 4828
AG:778B CB:1270B
testify *Note*
witness
SUMMATHeTeS 4827
AG:778B CB:Cf. MATH-(1258A)
disciple
SUMMERIZō 4829 (-OMAI)
AG:778C CB:—
partaker
portion
SUMMETOCHOS 4830
AG:778C CB:—
partaker
SUMMIMeTeS 4831
AG:778C CB:1270B
follower *Note*
imitator
SUMMORPHIZō —
AG:778D CB:1270B (-OMAI)
conformed
SUMMORPHOō 4833
AG:778D CB:1270B (-OMAI)
conformable
SUMMORPHOS 4832
AG:778D CB:1270B
conformed
fashion
SUMPARAGINOMAI 4836
AG:779A CB:—
come
stand *Note*
SUMPARAKALEō 4837
AG:779A CB:Cf. PAR-(1262A)
comfort
SUMPARALAMBANō 4838
AG:779A CB:—
take
SUMPARAMENō 4839
AG:779A CB:Cf. MENō (1258B)
continue
SUMPAREIMI 4840
AG:779A CB:—
present (to be)
SUMPASCHō 4841
AG:779B CB:1270B
suffer
SUMPATHEō 4834
AG:778D CB:1270B
compassion
feeling
touch
SUMPATHeS 4835
AG:779A CB:Cf. -THEō (1270B)
compassion, -ate

SUMPEMPō (SUNP-) 4842
AG:779B CB:—
send
SUMPERILAMBANō 4843
AG:779C CB:—
embrace
SUMPHeMI 4852
AG:780C CB:—
consent
SUMPHERō 4851
AG:780B CB:Cf. PHERō (1264A)
better (be) *Note*
bring
expedient
good (to be) *Note*
profitable
SUMPHERON —
AG:780C (-OS) CB:—
profit
SUMPHōNEō 4856
AG:780D CB:—
agree
SUMPHōNeSIS 4857
AG:781A CB:—
concord
SUMPHōNIA 4858
AG:781A CB:1270B
music
SUMPHōNOS 4859
AG:781B CB:—
agree *Note*
consent
SUMPHOROS —
AG:780C CB:—
profitable
SUMPHULETeS 4853
AG:780C CB:—
countryman
SUMPHUō 4855
AG:780D CB:—
grow, spring
SUMPHUTOS 4854
AG:780D CB:1270B
plant
SUMPINō 4844
AG:779C CB:—
drink
SUMPLeROō 4845
AG:779C CB:1270B
come
fill
well-nigh *Note*
SUMPNIGō 4846
AG:779D CB:1270B
choke
throng
SUMPOLITeS 4847
AG:780A CB:1270B
citizen
SUMPOREUOMAI 4848
AG:780A CB:—
go
resort *Note*
SUMPOSION 4849
AG:780A CB:—
company

SUMPRESBUTEROS 4850
AG:780A CB:—
elder

SUMPSēPHIZō 4860
AG:781B CB:—
count

SUMPSUCHOS 4861
AG:781B CB:1270B
accord
soul *Note*

SUNAGō 4863
AG:782A CB:1270B
assemble
bestow
come *Note*
gather
lead *Note*
resort
take

SUNAGōGē 4864
AG:782D CB:1270B
assemble
congregation
synagogue

SUNAGōNIZOMAI 4865
AG:783B CB:1270B
strive

SUNAICHMALōTOS 4869
AG:783C CB:1270B
prisoner

SUNAIRō 4868
AG:783C CB:—
reckon
take *Note*

SUNAKOLOUTHEō 4870
AG:783D CB:1270B
follow

SUNALIZō 4871
AG:783D CB:1270B
assemble

SUNALLASSō —
AG:784B CB:—
set

SUNANABAINō 4872
AG:784B CB:Cf. ANAB-(1235A)
come

SUNANAKEIMAI 4873
AG:784B CB:—
meat *Note*
sit
table (at the)

SUNANAMIGNUMI 4874
AG:784B CB:—
company

SUNANPAUOMAI 4875
AG:784B CB:—
find *Note*
refresh

SUNANTAō 4876
AG:784C CB:1270C
befall
meet

SUNANTēSIS 4877
AG:784C CB:—
meet

SUNANTILAMBANō(-OMAI) 4878
AG:784C CB:—
help

SUNAPAGō 4879
AG:784D CB:—
carry
condescend*
lead

SUNAPOLLUMI 4881
AG:785A CB:—
perish

SUNAPOSTELLō 4882
AG:785A CB:—
send

SUNAPOTHNēSKō 4880
AG:784D CB:1270C
die

SUNARMOLOGEō 4883
AG:785B CB:—
fitly
frame
join *Note*

SUNARPAZō 4884
AG:785B CB:—
catch
seize

SUNATHLEō 4866
AG:783B CB:1270C
labour
strive

SUNATHROIZō 4867
AG:783B CB:1270C
call *Note*
gather

SUNAUXANō 4885
AG:785B CB:—
grow

SUNCHAIRō 4796
AG:775A CB:1270C
rejoice

SUNCHEō(SUNCHUN[N]ō) 4797
AG:775A CB:—
confound
confuse
stir
uproar *Note*

SUNCHRAOMAI 4798
AG:775B CB:—
dealings with

SUNCHUSIS 4799
AG:775C CB:—
confusion

SUNDEō 4887
AG:785C CB:Cf. DEō (1240C)
bind

SUNDESMOS 4886
AG:785B CB:1270C
band
bind *Note*
bond

SUNDOULOS 4889
AG:785D CB:1270C
servant

SUNDOXAZō 4888
AG:785D CB:1270C
glorify

SUNDROMē 4890
AG:785D CB:—
run *Note*

SUNECHō 4912
AG:789A CB:1270C
anguish
constrain
hold
keep
press
sick
stop
strait
straiten
take *Note*
throng *Note*

SUNēDOMAI 4913
AG:789C CB:—
delight in

SUNEDRION 4892
AG:786A CB:1270C
council

SUNEGEIRō 4891
AG:785D CB:—
raise
rise *Note*

SUNEIDēSIS 4893
AG:786C CB:1270C
conscience

SUNEIDON (SUNOIDA) 4894 (-Dō)
AG:791B CB:1270C
consider
know
privy
ware*

SUNEIMI 4895
AG:787A CB:—
gather *Note*

SUNEISERCHOMAI 4897
AG:787A CB:1270C
enter
go *Note*

SUNEKDēMOS 4898
AG:787A CB:—
companion

SUNEKLEKTOS 4899
AG:787B CB:—
elect

SUNELAUNō 4900
AG:787B CB:—
set

SUNēLIKIōTēS 4915
AG:789D CB:—
equal
own *Note*

SUNEPHISTēMI 4911
AG:789A CB:—
arise
rise *Note*

SUNEPIMARTUREō 4901
AG:787B CB:—
witness

SUNEPOMAI 4902
AG:787C CB:—
accompany

SUNERCHOMAI 4905
AG:788A CB:1270C
accompany
appear *Note*
assemble
come
company
go *Note*
resort *Note*

SUNERGEō 4903
AG:787C CB:1270C
help
work
worker

SUNERGOS 4904
AG:787D CB:1270C
companion
helper
labourer *Note*
worker
work-fellow

SUNESIS 4907
AG:788C CB:1270C
knowledge *Note*
prudence
understanding
wisdom *Note*

SUNESTHIō 4906
AG:788B CB:—
eat

SUNēTHEIA 4914
AG:789C CB:—
custom
use *Note*

SUNETOS 4908
AG:788D CB:1270C
prudent
understanding

SUNEUDOKEō 4909
AG:788D CB:—
allow
consent
content
please *Note*

SUNEUōCHEō 4910
AG:789A (-OMAI) CB:—
feast

SUNGENEIA 4772
AG:772C CB:1270C
kindred

SUNGENēS 4773
AG:772C CB:1270C
cousins
kin
kinsfolk*, -man*

SUNGENEUS (-NēS) 4773
AG:772C CB:1270C
kin
kinsfolk*

SUNGENIS —
AG:772D CB:—
cousin
kin
kinswoman*

SUNGNōMē 4774
AG:773A CB:—
permission

SUNIēMI (SUNIō) 4920
AG:790A CB:1270C
consider *Note*
understand
wise
SUNISTēMI 4921
AG:790C CB:1270C
approve
commend
compacted
consist
make
prove
stand
SUNKAKOPATHEō 4777
AG:773B CB:1270C
hardship
SUNKAKOUCHEOMAI 4778 (-Eō)
AG:773B CB:—
affliction *Note*
entreat
suffer
SUNKALEō 4779
AG:773B CB:Cf. KALEō (1253B)
call
SUNKALUPTō 4780
AG:773B CB:1270C
cover
SUNKAMPTō 4781
AG:773B CB:—
bow
SUNKATABAINō 4782
AG:773C CB:—
go
SUNKATAPSēPHIZō 4785
AG:773C (-OMAI) CB:—
number
SUNKATATHESIS 4783
AG:773C CB:—
agreement
SUNKATATITHēMI 4784 (-EMAI)
AG:773C CB:—
agree *Note*
consent
SUNKATHēMAI 4775
AG:773A CB:—
sit
SUNKATHIZō 4776
AG:773B CB:—
set *Note*
sit
SUNKERANNUMI 4786
AG:773D CB:1270C
mixed (with)
temper together
SUNKINEō 4787
AG:773D CB:—
stir
SUNKLEIō 4788
AG:774A CB:1270C
conclude *Note*
inclose
shut
SUNKLēRONOMOS 4789
AG:774A CB:1270C
heir

SUNKOINōNEō 4790
AG:774B CB:1270C
communicate
fellowship
partake, -er
SUNKOINōNOS 4791
AG:774B CB:1270C
companion
partake
partaker
SUNKOMIZō 4792
AG:774C CB:—
carry
SUNKRINō 4793
AG:774D CB:1270C
compare
SUNKUPTō 4794
AG:775A CB:—
bow
SUNKURIA 4795
AG:775A CB:—
chance
SUNLUPEō (SULL-) 4818
AG:777A CB:—
grieve
SUNOCHē 4928
AG:791D CB:Cf. SUNECHō (1270C)
anguish
distress
SUNODEUō 4922
AG:791A CB:—
journey
SUNODIA 4923
AG:791A CB:—
company
SUNōDINō 4944
AG:793D CB:—
travail
SUNOIDA 4894 (SUNEIDō)
AG:791B CB:1270C
consider
know
privy
ware *Note*
SUNOIKEō 4924
AG:791C CB:—
dwell
SUNOIKODOMEō 4925
AG:791C CB:1270C
build
SUNOMILEō 4926
AG:791C CB:—
talk
SUNOMOREō 4927
AG:791C CB:—
join
SUNōMOSIA 4945
AG:793D CB:—
conspiracy
SUNTASSō 4929
AG:791D CB:—
appoint
command *Note*
SUNTELEIA 4930
AG:792A CB:1271A
end

SUNTELEō 4931
AG:792A CB:1271A
complete
end
finish
fulfil
make
SUNTEMNō 4932
AG:792B CB:—
cut
short
SUNTēREō 4933
AG:792C CB:—
keep
observe
preserve
SUNTHAPTō 4916
AG:789D CB:1271A
bury
SUNTHLAō 4917
AG:790A CB:—
break
SUNTHLIBō 4918
AG:790A CB:—
throng
SUNTHRUPTō 4919
AG:790A CB:—
break
SUNTITHēMI 4934 (-EMAI)
AG:790C CB:—
agree
covenant
SUNTOMōS 4935
AG:793A CB:—
few
word *Note*
SUNTRECHō 4936
AG:793A CB:1271A
run
SUNTRIBō 4937
AG:793B CB:—
break
bruise
sore *Note*
SUNTRIMMA 4938
AG:793C CB:—
destruction
SUNTROPHOS 4939
AG:793C CB:—
bring *Note*
foster-brother
SUNTUNCHANō 4940
AG:793C CB:—
come
SUNUPOKRINOMAI 4942
AG:793D CB:—
dissemble
SUNUPOURGEō 4943
AG:793D CB:—
help
SURō 4951
AG:794C CB:—
drag
draw
hale

SUROPHOINIKISSA (-PHUNISSA) 4949
AG:794B CB:—
Syrophoenician
SURTIS 4950
AG:794C CB:—
quicksands
SUSCHēMATIZō 4964
AG:795C CB:1271A
conform
fashion
SUSPARASSō 4952
AG:794C CB:—
grievously *Note*
tear
SUSSēMON 4953
AG:794D CB:—
token
SUSSōMOS 4954
AG:794D CB:—
body
SUSTASIASTēS 4955
AG:794D CB:—
insurrection
SUSTATIKOS 4956
AG:795A CB:—
commendation
SUSTAUROō 4957
AG:795A CB:1271A
crucify
SUSTELLō 4958
AG:795A CB:—
short
wind, wrap
SUSTENAZō 4959
AG:795B CB:Cf. STEN-(1270A)
groan
SUSTOICHEō 4960
AG:795B CB:1271A
answer
SUSTRATIōTēS 4961
AG:795B CB:—
soldier
SUSTREPHō 4962
AG:795C CB:1271A
gather
SUSTROPHē (SUN-) 4963
AG:795C CB:—
banded
concourse
SU(N)ZAō 4800
AG:775C CB:1271A
live
SU(N)ZēTEō 4802
AG:775D CB:—
dispute
inquire *Note*
question
reason
SUZēTēSIS 4803
AG:775D CB:—
disputation
question *Note*
reasoning *Note*
SUZēTēTēS 4804
AG:775D CB:—
disputer

SU(N)ZEUGNUMI —
AG:775C CB:1271A
join
SU(N)ZōOPOIEō 4806
AG:776A CB:1271A
life *Note*
quicken
SU(N)ZUGOS 4805
AG:775D CB:1271A
yoke-fellow

T

TACHA 5029
AG:806C CB:—
peradventure
perhaps
TACHEI (-EN) 5034 (TACHOS)
AG:806D (-EōS) CB:—
quickly
shortly
speedily *Note*
TACHEION 5032
AG:806D (-EōS) CB:—
quickly
shortly
TACHEōS 5030
AG:806D CB:—
hastily
quickly
shortly
suddenly *Note*
TACHINOS 5031
AG:807A CB:1271A
shortly *Note*
swift
swiftly
TACHISTA 5033
AG:806D (TACHEōS 3.) CB:—
speed *Note*
TACHU 5035
AG:807B (TACHUS 2.c.) CB:1271A
lightly *Note*
quickly
TACHUS 5036
AG:807B CB:1271A
swift
TAGMA 5001
AG:802D CB:—
order
TAKTOS 5002
AG:803A CB:—
set
TALAIPōREō 5003
AG:803A CB:1271A
afflict
misery *Note*
TALAIPōRIA 5004
AG:803B CB:1271A
affliction *Note*
misery
TALAIPōROS 5005
AG:803B CB:1271A
afflicted *Note*
wretched
TALANTIAIOS 5006
AG:803B CB:—
talent
TALANTON 5007
AG:803C CB:—
talent
TAL(E)ITHA 5008
AG:803C CB:1271A
talitha
TAMEION 5009
AG:803C CB:—
barn *Note*
chamber
secret *Note*
TAPEINOō 5013
AG:804C CB:1271A
abase
humble
low
TAPEINOPHRōN —
AG:804C CB:1271A
courteous
humble-minded
TAPEINOPHROSUNē 5012
AG:804C CB:1271A
humbleness
humility
lowliness
meekness
TAPEINOS 5011
AG:804A CB:1271A
base
cast *Note*
degree *Note*
estate *Note*
humble
low, lowly
TAPEINōSIS 5014
AG:805A CB:1271A
estate
humiliation
low (estate)
TAPHē 5027
AG:806B CB:1271A
burial
TAPHOS 5028
AG:806B CB:1271A
sepulchre
tomb
TARACHē 5016
AG:805C CB:1271A
trouble
TARACHOS 5017
AG:805C CB:1271A
stir
TARASSō 5015
AG:805B CB:1271A
trouble
TARTAROō 5020
AG:805D CB:—
hell *Note*
TASSō 5021
AG:805D CB:1271A
appoint
determine
ordain, set
TAUROS 5022
AG:806B CB:1271A
ox
TAXIS 5010
AG:803D CB:1271A
order
TE 5037
AG:807B CB:—
also *Note*
even *Note*
TECHNē 5078
AG:814B CB:1271A
art
craft
trade
TECHNITēS 5079
AG:814B CB:1271B
builder
craftsman
TEICHOS 5038
AG:808A CB:1271B
wall
TEKMēRION 5039
AG:808A CB:1271B
proof
TEKNION 5040
AG:808A CB:1271B
child
TEKNOGONEō 5041
AG:808A CB:1271B
children
TEKNOGONIA 5042
AG:808B CB:1271B
child-bearing
TEKNON 5043
AG:808B CB:1271B
child
daughter *Note*
son *Note*
TEKNOTROPHEō 5044
AG:808D CB:1271B
children
TēKō 5080
AG:814B CB:1271B
melt
TEKTōN 5045
AG:809A CB:1271B
carpenter
TēLAUGōS 5081
AG:814C CB:—
clearly
TELEIOō 5048
AG:809D CB:1271B
accomplish
consecrate
do
finish
fulfil
perfect
TELEIOS 5046
AG:809A CB:1271B
age
entire *Note*
man
perfect
TELEIōS 5049
AG:810B CB:1271B
end *Note*
perfectly
TELEIōSIS 5050
AG:810B CB:1271B
fulfilment
perfection
TELEIOTEROS (-TēS) 5047
AG:809C CB:—
perfect
TELEIOTēS 5047
AG:809C CB:1271B
perfection
perfectness
TELEIoTēS 5051
AG:810C CB:1271B
finisher *Note*
TELEō 5055
AG:810D CB:1271B
accomplish
end
expire
fill *Note*
finish
fulfil
go
pay
perform
TELESPHOREō 5052
AG:810C CB:—
perfection
TELEUTAō 5053
AG:810C CB:1271B
decease
die
TELEUTē 5054
AG:810C CB:1271B
death
TēLIKOUTOS 5082
AG:814C CB:—
great
mighty *Note*
TELōNēS 5057
AG:812B CB:1271B
publican
TELōNION 5058
AG:812C CB:1271B
custom (toll)
TELOS 5056
AG:811B CB:1271B
continual
custom (toll)
end, ending
finally
uttermost
TEPHROō 5077
AG:814B CB:—
ashes
TERAS 5059
AG:812C CB:1271B
wonder
TēREō 5083
AG:814D CB:1271B
charge
hold
keep, keeper
observe
preserve
reserve
watch

TēRēSIS 5084
AG:815C CB:1271B
hold
keeping
prison
ward
TESSARAKONTA 5062
AG:813A CB:1271B
forty
TESSARAKONTAETēS 5063
AG:813B CB:—
forty (years) *Note*
TESSARES 5064
AG:813B CB:1271B
four
TESSARESKAIDEKATOS 5065
AG:813B CB:—
fourteenth
TETARTAIOS 5066
AG:813C CB:—
four
TETARTOS 5067
AG:813C CB:—
four, fourth
part *Note*
TETRA(A)RCHEō 5075
AG:814A CB:—
tetrarch
TETRA(A)RCHēS 5076
AG:814A CB:—
tetrarch
TETRADION 5069
AG:813D CB:1271C
quaternion
TETRAGōNOS 5068
AG:813C CB:—
foursquare
TETRAKISCHILIOI 5070
AG:813D CB:1271C
thousand *Note*
TETRAKOSIA 5071
AG:813D (-SIOI) CB:—
four hundred
TETRAMēNOS 5072 (-ON)
AG:813D CB:—
months
TETRAPLOOS 5073
AG:813D (-OUS) CB:—
fourfold
TETRAPOUS 5074
AG:814A CB:—
beast
fourfooted
THALASSA 2281
AG:350A CB:1271C
sea
THALPō 2282
AG:350B CB:—
cherish
THAMBEō 2284
AG:350C CB:1271C
amaze
THAMBOS 2285
AG:350C CB:1271C
amazement
wonder

THANASIMOS 2286
AG:350D CB:—
deadly
THANATēPHOROS 2287
AG:350D CB:—
deadly
THANATOō 2289
AG:351C CB:1271C
dead
death
kill
mortify
THANATOS 2288
AG:350D CB:1271C
death
grave *Note*
Hades *Note*
THAPTō 2290
AG:351D CB:1271C
bury
THARREō 2292
AG:352A CB:1271C
bold, boldly
confident
confidence
courage
THARSEō 2293
AG:352A CB:1271C
cheer
comfort *Note*
THARSOS 2294
AG:352A CB:—
courage
THAUMA 2295
AG:352A CB:1271C
marvel
wonder *Note*
THAUMASIOS 2297
AG:352D CB:1271C
wonderful (thing) *Note*
THAUMASTOS 2298
AG:352D CB:1271C
marvel
marvellous
THAUMAZō 2296
AG:352B CB:1271C
marvel
wonder *Note*
THEA 2299
AG:353A CB:1271C
goddess
THEAOMAI 2300
AG:353A CB:1271C
behold
look
see
THEATRIZō 2301
AG:353C CB:1271C (-OMAI)
gazingstock
THEATRON 2302
AG:353C CB:1271C
spectacle
theatre
THEIōDeS 2306
AG:354A CB:—
brimstone

THEION 2303
AG:353D CB:1271C
brimstone
THEIOS 2304
AG:353D CB:1271C
divine
THEIOTēS 2305
AG:354A CB:1271C
Divinity
THēKē 2336
AG:360B CB:1271C
sheath
THēLAZō 2337
AG:360C CB:—
suck
suckling
THēLEIA (-LUS) 2338
AG:360C CB:1271C
woman
THELēMA 2307
AG:354B CB:1271C
desire
pleasure *Note*
will
THELēSIS 2308
AG:354C CB:1271C
will
THELō 2309
AG:354D CB:1271C
desire
disposed
fain
forward (be)
intend
list
love *Note*
pleased
rather
unwilling
voluntary
wilfully
will
willing
wish
would*
THēLUS 2338
AG:360C CB:1271C
female
woman
THEMELIOō 2311
AG:356A CB:1272A
found
grounded
settle *Note*
THEMELIOS (-ON) 2310
AG:355D CB:1272A
foundation
THEODIDAKTOS 2312
AG:356B CB:—
taught
THEOMACHEō 2313
AG:356C CB:—
fight *Note*
THEOMACHOS 2314
AG:356C CB:1272A
fighting

THEOPNEUSTOS 2315
AG:356C CB:1272A
inspiration
THEōREō 2334
AG:360A CB:1272A
behold
consider
look
perceive
see
THEōRIA 2335
AG:360B CB:1272A
sight
THEOS 2316
AG:356D CB:1272A
God
godly *Note*
THEOSEBEIA 2317
AG:358B CB:1272A
devout *Note*
godliness
worshipper *Note*
THEOSEBēS 2318
AG:358B CB:1272B
devout *Note*
worshipper
THEOSTUGēS 2319
AG:358C CB:1272B
hateful
hater
THEOTēS 2320
AG:358C CB:1272B
Divinity
THēRA 2339
AG:360D CB:—
trap
THERAPEIA 2322
AG:358D CB:1272B
healing
household
THERAPEUō 2323
AG:359A CB:1272B
cure
heal
worship *Note*
THERAPōN 2324
AG:359B CB:1272B
deacon *Note*
servant
THēREUō 2340
AG:360D CB:—
catch
THēRIOMACHEō 2341
AG:360D CB:—
fight
THēRION 2342
AG:361A CB:1272B
beast
wild *Note*
THERISMOS 2326
AG:359C CB:1272B
harvest
THERISTēS 2327
AG:359C CB:1272B
reaper

THERIZō 2325
AG:359B CB:1272B
reap
THERMAINō 2328
AG:359C CB:1272B
warm
THERMē 2329
AG:359C CB:1272B
heat
THEROS 2330
AG:359D CB:1272B
summer
THēSAURIZō 2343
AG:361B CB:1272B
lay
store
treasure
THēSAUROS 2344
AG:361C CB:1272B
treasure
THINGANō 2345
AG:361D CB:—
handle
touch
THLIBō 2346
AG:362A CB:1272B
afflict
narrow
press
straitened
throng
tribulation *Note*
trouble
THLIPSIS 2347
AG:362B CB:1272B
afflict
affliction
anguish
burdened *Note*
distress
persecution *Note*
tribulation
trouble
THNēSKō 2348
AG:362C CB:1272B
die
THNēTOS 2349
AG:362D CB:1272B
mortal
mortality
THōRAX 2382
AG:367C CB:1272B
breastplate
THORUBAZō —
AG:362D CB:1272B
trouble
THORUBEō 2350
AG:362D CB:1272B
ado
noise *Note*
trouble
tumult *Note*
uproar
THORUBOS 2351
AG:363A CB:1272B
tumult
uproar

THRAUō 2352
AG:363B CB:—
bruise
THREMMA 2353
AG:363B CB:1272B
cattle
THRēNEō 2354
AG:363B CB:1272B
bewail *Note*
mourn
wail *Note*
weep *Note*
THRēNOS 2355
AG:363B CB:1272B
lamentation*
THRēSKEIA 2356
AG:363B CB:1272B
religion
worship
THRēSKOS 2357
AG:363D CB:1272B
religious
THRIAMBEUō 2358
AG:363D CB:1272B
cause
lead *Note*
triumph
THRIX 2359
AG:363D CB:1272B
hair
THROEō 2360
AG:364A CB:—
trouble
THROMBOS 2361
AG:364B CB:—
drop
THRONOS 2362
AG:364B CB:1272B
seat *Note*
throne
THUELLA 2366
AG:365A CB:—
tempest
THUGATēR 2364
AG:364D CB:1272C
daughter
THUGATRION 2365
AG:365A CB:—
daughter
young *Note*
THUINOS 2367
AG:365A CB:—
thyine (wood)
THUMIAMA 2368
AG:365A CB:1272C
incense
odour *Note*
THUMIAō 2370
AG:365B CB:1272C
incense
THUMIATēRION 2369
AG:365B CB:1272C
censer

THUMOMACHEō 2371
AG:365B CB:—
anger *Note*
displease
THUMOō 2373
AG:365C CB:1272C
anger *Note*
wroth (be)
THUMOS 2372
AG:365B CB:1272C
anger
fierceness
indignation *Note*
wrath
THUō 2380
AG:367A CB:1272C
kill
sacrifice
slay *Note*
THURA 2374
AG:365D CB:1272C
door, gate *Note*
THUREOS 2375
AG:366A CB:1272C
shield
THURIS 2376
AG:366A CB:—
window
THURōROS 2377
AG:366A CB:—
door *Note*
porter
THUSIA 2378
AG:366B CB:1272C
sacrifice
THUSIASTēRION 2379
AG:366D CB:1272C
altar
TIKTō 5088
AG:816D CB:1272C
beget, bear
bring
deliver *Note*
travail, usury*
TILLō 5089
AG:817A CB:—
pluck
TIMAō 5091
AG:817A CB:1272C
esteem *Note*
honour
price
value *Note*
TIMē 5092
AG:817B CB:1272C
honour
precious *Note*
price
sum *Note*
value
TIMIOS 5093
AG:818A CB:1272C
costly
dear
honourable
precious
reputation *Note*

TIMIOTēS 5094
AG:818B CB:—
costliness
TIMōREō 5097
AG:818C CB:—
punish
TIMōRIA 5098
AG:818D CB:—
punishment
TINō 5099
AG:818D CB:—
punish*
suffer *Note*
TIS; TI (1) 5100
AG:819D CB:1272C
certain *Note*
divers *Note*
every *Note*
he *Note*
he that *Note*
kind *Note*
man
manner *Note*
much *Note*
nothing
one
some *Note*
somebody *Note*
someone *Note*
something *Note*
somewhat *Note*
TIS; TI (2) 5101
AG:818D CB:1272C
what *Note*
wherefore *Note*
which *Note*
who *Note*
whom *Note*
TITHēMI 5087
AG:815D CB:1272C
appoint
bow (Verb)
commit
conceive
give *Note*
kneel
lay
make
ordain
purpose
put
set, settle
sink
TITLOS 5102
AG:820D CB:1272C
superscription
title
TODE (See HODE)
TOICHOS 5109
AG:821C CB:1272C
wall
TOIGAROUN 5105
AG:821A CB:—
wherefore *Note*
TOINUN 5106
AG:821A CB:—
then *Note*

TOIOUTOS 5108
AG:821B CB:1272C
fellow *Note*
such as *Note*
TOKOS 5110
AG:821D CB:1272C
interest
usury
TOLMAō 5111
AG:821D CB:1272C
bold
dare
TOLMēROTERōS (-RON) 5112
AG:822A (-MēROS) CB:1272C (-TORON)
boldly
TOLMēTēS 5113
AG:822A CB:1272C
daring
TOMOS 5114 (TOMōTEROS)
AG:822A CB:—
sharp
TOMōTEROS 5114
AG:822A (TOMOS) CB:—
sharper
TOPAZION 5116
AG:822B CB:1273A
topaz
TOPOS 5117
AG:822B CB:1273A
everywhere *Note*
opportunity
part
place
quarter *Note*
rocky *Note*
room
way *Note*
TOSOUTOS 5118
AG:823B CB:—
great
long
many
much *Note*
TOTE 5119
AG:823D CB:1273A
then
time *Note*
TOUNANTION 5121
AG:261D (ENANTION) CB:—
contrariwise
TOXON 5115
AG:822B CB:1273A
bow (Noun)
TRACHēLIZō 5136
AG:824D CB:—
lay
TRACHēLOS 5137
AG:825A CB:1273A
neck
TRACHUS 5138
AG:825A CB:1273A
rocky *Note*
rough
TRAGOS 5131
AG:824B CB:1273A
goat

TRAPEZA 5132
AG:824B CB:1273A
bank
meat
table
TRAPEZITēS 5133
AG:824D CB:—
banker
TRAUMA 5134
AG:824D CB:—
wound
TRAUMATIZō 5135
AG:824D CB:—
wound
TRECHō 5143
AG:825D CB:1273A
course *Note*
run
rush
TREIS 5140
AG:825B CB:1273A
three
TRēMA —
AG:826A CB:—
eye *Note*
TREMō 5141
AG:825B CB:—
tremble
TREPHō 5142
AG:825C CB:—
bring
feed
nourish
TRIAKONTA 5144
AG:826A CB:—
thirty
thirtyfold
TRIAKOSIOI 5145
AG:826A CB:—
three hundred
TRIBOLOS 5146
AG:826A CB:1273A
thistle
TRIBOS 5147
AG:826B CB:—
path
TRICHINOS 5155
AG:827A CB:—
hair
TRIETIA 5148
AG:826B CB:—
year
TRIMēNOS 5150
AG:826B CB:—
months
TRIS 5151
AG:826B CB:1273A
thrice
TRISCHILIOI 5153
AG:826C CB:1273A
thousand *Note*
TRISTEGOS 5152 (-ON)
AG:826C CB:—
story

TRITOS 5154
AG:826C CB:1273A
third
thirdly
TRIZō 5149
AG:826B CB:—
gnash
grind
TROCHIA 5163
AG:828A CB:—
path
TROCHOS 5164
AG:828A CB:1273A
course, wheel*
TRōGō 5176
AG:829B CB:1273A
eat
TROMOS 5156
AG:827A CB:1273A
trembling
TROPē 5157
AG:827A CB:—
turning
TROPHē 5160
AG:87D CB:—
food
meat
TROPHOS 5162
AG:827D CB:1273A
nurse
TROPOPHOREō 5159
AG:827C CB:—
bear
manner
suffer *Note*
TROPOS 5158
AG:827B CB:1273A
conversation
even as *Note*
manner
means *Note*
way *Note*
TRUBLION 5165
AG:828B CB:—
dish
TRUGAō 5166
AG:828B CB:1273A
gather
TRUGōN 5167
AG:828B CB:—
dove
TRUMALIA 5168
AG:828B CB:—
eye *Note*
TRUPēMA 5169
AG:828C CB:—
eye
TRUPHAō 5171
AG:828C CB:—
delicately (live)
pleasure
TRUPHē 5172
AG:828D CB:—
delicately
revel
riot

TUCHōN 5177
AG:829B (TUCHANō) CB:—
special
TUMPANIZō 5178
AG:829D CB:—
torture
TUNCHANō 5177
AG:829B CB:—
attain
chance
common *Note*
enjoy
may
obtain
TUPHLOō 5186
AG:831A CB:Cf. -OS (1273A)
blind
TUPHLOS 5185
AG:830D CB:1273A
blind
TUPHō 5188
AG:831C CB:—
smoke
TUPHōNIKOS 5189
AG:831C CB:—
tempestuous
TUPHOō 5187
AG:831A CB:—
high minded
pride
proud *Note*
puff (up)
smoke
TUPOS 5179
AG:829D CB:1273B
ensample
example
fashion
figure
form
manner
pattern
print
TUPTō 5180
AG:830B CB:1273B
beat
smite
strike *Note*
wound*
TURBAZō 5182
AG:830D CB:—
trouble

X

XENIA 3578
AG:547B CB:1273B
lodging
XENIZō 3579
AG:547D CB:1273B
entertain
lodge
strange
XENODOCHEō 3580
AG:548A CB:1273B
hospitality *Note*
stranger

XENOS 3581
AG:548A CB:1273B
foreigner *Note*
host (of guests)
pilgrim *Note*
strange, -er

XēRAINō 3583
AG:548C CB:1273B
dry
over-ripe
pine away
ripe
wither

XēROS 3584
AG:548C CB:1273B
dry
land
withered *Note*

XESTēS 3582
AG:548B CB:—
pot

XULINOS 3585
AG:549A CB:—
wood*

XULON 3586
AG:549A CB:1273B
staff
stocks
tree
wood

XURAō 3587
AG:549C CB:—
shave

Z

ZAō 2198
AG:336A CB:1273B
lifetime *Note*
live, lively
living

ZēLEUō —
AG:337C CB:1273B
zealous

ZēLOō 2206
AG:338A CB:1273B
affect *Note*
covet
desire
earnestly *Note*
envy
jealous
seek *Note*
zealously

ZēLOS 2205
AG:337D CB:1273B
envy
fervent *Note*
fierceness
indignation *Note*
jealousy
zeal

ZēLōTēS 2207
AG:338A CB:1273B
zealous

ZēMIA 2209
AG:338C CB:1273C
loss

ZēMIOō 2210
AG:338C CB:1273C (-OMAI)
cast *Note*
forfeit
lose
loss*
receive *Note*

ZEō 2204
AG:337C CB:1273C
fervent

ZESTOS 2200
AG:337B CB:1273C
hot

ZēTēMA 2213
AG:339B CB:—
question

ZēTEō 2212
AG:338D CB:1273C
about *Note*
desire *Note*
endeavour
go *Note*
inquire
require
seek

ZēTēSIS 2214
AG:339B CB:1273C
disputation
inquire
question

ZEUGOS 2201
AG:337B CB:1273C
pair
yoke

ZEUKTēRIA 2202
AG:337B CB:—
band

ZIZANION 2215
AG:339C CB:1273C
tares

Zōē 2222
AG:340B CB:1273C
life

ZōGREō 2221
AG:340A CB:—
captive
catch

ZōNē 2223
AG:341B CB:1273C
bag
girdle

ZōNNUMI 2224
AG:341C CB:1273C
gird

ZōOGONEō 2225
AG:341C CB:1273C
life
live
preserve
quicken

ZōON 2226
AG:341C CB:1273C
beast
creature

ZōOPOIEō 2227
AG:341D CB:1273C
life
quicken

ZOPHOS 2217
AG:339D CB:—
blackness
darkness
mist

ZUGOS 2218
AG:339D CB:1273C
balance
pair *Note*
yoke

ZUMē 2219
AG:340A CB:1273C
leaven

ZUMOō 2220
AG:340A CB:1273C
leaven

CONVERSION TABLE:

Pagination of Two Editions of Colin Brown's *Dictionary* Compared

CB3 = Index (third) volume of the three-volume set (1978)
CB4 = Index (fourth) volume of the three-volume set (1986)

CB3 Page		CB4 Page	CB3 Page		CB4 Page	CB3 Page		CB4 Page	CB3 Page		CB4 Page
1233	=	339	1244	=	350	1255	=	361	1266	=	372
1234	=	340	1245	=	351	1256	=	362	1267	=	373
1235	=	341	1246	=	352	1257	=	363	1268	=	374
1236	=	342	1247	=	353	1258	=	364	1269	=	375
1237	=	343	1248	=	354	1259	=	365	1270	=	376
1238	=	344	1249	=	355	1260	=	366	1271	=	377
1239	=	345	1250	=	356	1261	=	367	1272	=	378
1240	=	346	1251	=	357	1262	=	368	1273	=	379
1241	=	347	1252	=	358	1263	=	369			
1242	=	348	1253	=	359	1264	=	370			
1243	=	349	1254	=	360	1265	=	371			

The column designations (A, B, C) are identical between the two editions and require no conversion.